NEW BOOKS FOR YOUR SHELVES

Discover inspiring books from Bloomsbury Education
to enhance your teaching and support your students.

TRANSFORM YOUR TEACHING

9781801990011 | £16.99

APRIL 2022

9781472989345 | £12.99

JUNE 2022

9781472992468 | £19.99

MAY 2022

PROMOTE DIVERSITY AND INCLUSION IN YOUR SCHOOL

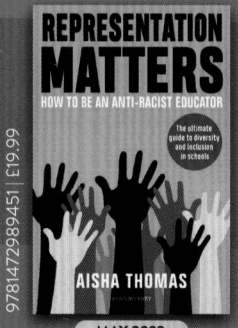

9781472989451 | £19.99

MAY 2022

9781472977922 | £16.99

9781472986948 | £14.99

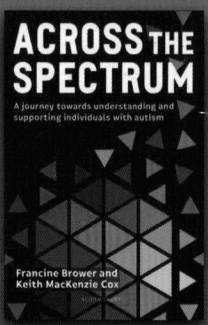

9781472984524 | £24.99

ENHANCE STUDENT AND TEACHER WELLBEING

9781472974655 | £19.99

9781801990318 | £14.99

JULY 2022

9781472986412 | £19.99

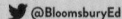
🐦 @BloomsburyEd   **BLOOMSBURY EDUCATION**   🌐 Bloomsbury.com/Education

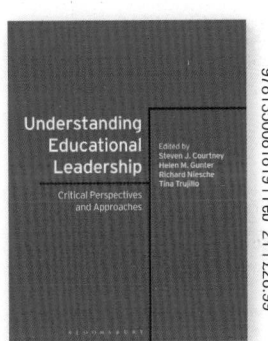

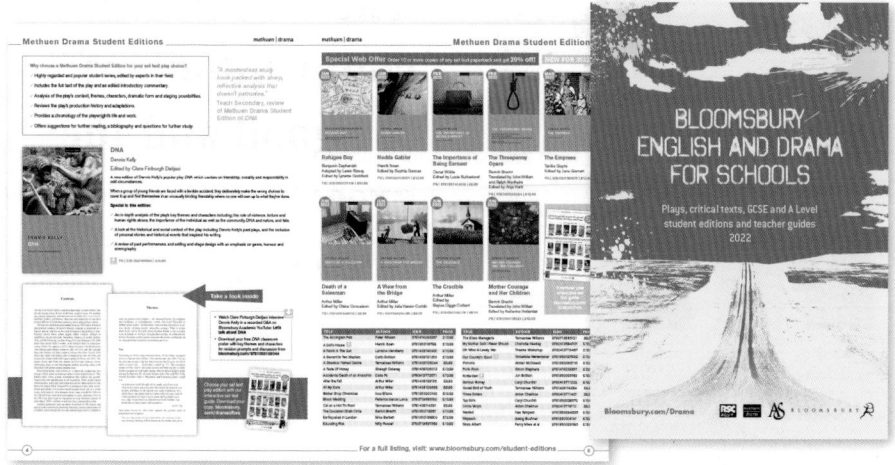

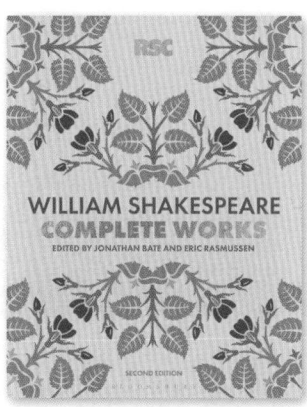
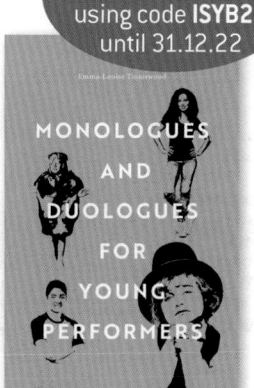

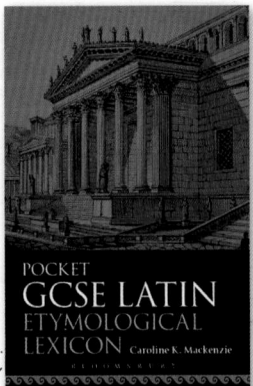

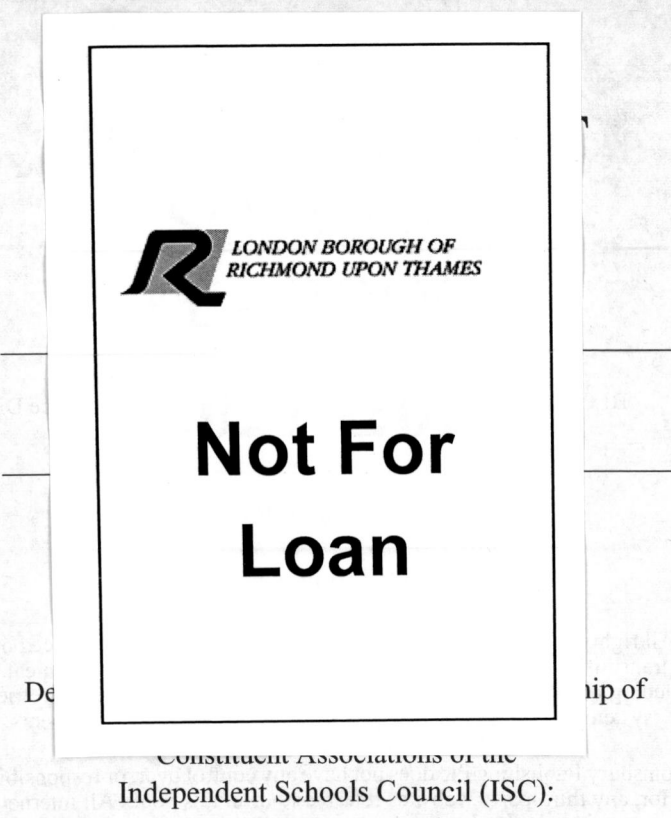

De... ...ip of

Constituent Associations of the
Independent Schools Council (ISC):

Headmasters' and Headmistresses' Conference (HMC)
Girls' Schools Association (GSA)
The Society of Heads
Independent Association of Prep Schools (IAPS)
Independent Schools Association (ISA)

Edited by
RUTH NORTHEY

Tel: 020 3745 9354; email: isyb@acblack.com
website: www.independentschoolsyearbook.co.uk

BLOOMSBURY YEARBOOKS
LONDON · OXFORD · NEW YORK · NEW DELHI · SYDNEY

BLOOMSBURY YEARBOOKS
Bloomsbury Publishing Plc
50 Bedford Square, London, WC1B 3DP, UK
29 Earlsfort Terrace, Dublin 2, Ireland

BLOOMSBURY, BLOOMSBURY YEARBOOKS and the Diana
logo are trademarks of Bloomsbury Publishing Plc

First published in Great Britain 1889
This edition published 2022

A catalogue record for this book is available from the British Library.

ISBN: PB 978-1-4729-9104-1

2 4 6 8 10 9 7 5 3 1

Printed and bound in Great Britain by CPI Group (UK) Ltd,
Croydon CR0 4YY

To find out more about our authors and books visit www.bloomsbury.com
and sign up for our newsletters.

INDEPENDENT SCHOOLS YEARBOOK 2021–2022

CONTENTS

PART I: HEADMASTERS' AND HEADMISTRESSES' CONFERENCE

287 schools for pupils from age 11 to 18, whose Heads are members of HMC; 49 of these are international members. They are all-boys schools (some admitting girls to the Sixth Form), co-educational schools, "Diamond" schools (girls and boys taught separately in the 11–16 age range), and some are all-girls schools. Many of the schools also have a Preparatory/Junior school or department.

PART II: GIRLS' SCHOOLS ASSOCIATION

97 schools for pupils from age 11 to 16/18, whose Heads are members of GSA. They are all-girls schools in the 11–16 age range, some admit boys to the Sixth Form and some are "Diamond" schools (girls and boys taught separately in the 11–16 age range). Some of the schools also have a Preparatory/Junior school or department.

. . ./continued

PART III: THE SOCIETY OF HEADS
             77 schools for pupils from age 11 to 18 whose Heads are members
             of The Society of Heads. The majority are co-educational schools,
             but Membership is open to boys and girls schools. Many of the
             schools also have a Preparatory/Junior school or department.

PART IV: INDEPENDENT ASSOCIATION OF PREP SCHOOLS
             495 schools whose Heads are members of IAPS; 19 of these are
             overseas members. Most of the schools are co-educational; some
             cater for boys only or girls only. The preparatory school age range is
             7 to 11/13, but many of the schools have a pre-preparatory
             department for children up to age 7.

PART V: INDEPENDENT SCHOOLS ASSOCIATION
             204 schools in membership of ISA. Schools in this Association are
             not confined to one age range and can cater for any age range of
             pupils up to 18/19 years.

ISC
INDEPENDENT SCHOOLS COUNCIL
www.isc.co.uk

The ISC is established:
- to support the aims and objectives of its seven member associations;
- to provide authoritative research and intelligence about the sector;
- to promote public affairs and parliamentary engagement on behalf of the sector;
- to provide online access and support informing parental decisions;
- to promote the sector through agreed national messaging and communications.

The Constituent Associations of the ISC are:

Association of Governing Bodies of Independent Schools (AGBIS)
Girls' Schools Association (GSA)
Headmasters' and Headmistresses' Conference (HMC)
Independent Association of Prep Schools (IAPS)
Independent Schools Association (ISA)
Independent Schools' Bursars Association (ISBA)
The Society of Heads

Secretariat

Chairman
Barnaby Lenon

Chief Executive
Julie Robinson

Independent Schools Council
First Floor, 27 Queen Anne's Gate, London SW1H 9BU

Tel: 020 7766 7070
Website: www.isc.co.uk

HMC

HEADMASTERS' AND HEADMISTRESSES' CONFERENCE

www.hmc.org.uk

The HMC dates from 1869, when the celebrated Edward Thring of Uppingham asked thirty-seven of his fellow headmasters to meet at his house to consider the formation of a 'School Society and Annual Conference'. Twelve headmasters accepted the invitation. From that date there have been annual meetings. Thring's intention was to provide an opportunity for discussion at regular intervals, both on practical issues in the life of a school and on general principles in education. He believed that his guests would discharge their practical business more effectively at a residential meeting where they could also enjoy being in the company of like-minded men. Annual Meetings of the HMC still combine formal debate on current educational questions with the second element of conversational exchanges in an agreeable environment. These gatherings, which up to 1939 were usually at individual schools, then took place at a University. Nowadays they are held in major hotels and conference centres in the Autumn term. In addition to these annual conferences attended by all members, there are local meetings each term arranged by the ten branches or Divisions into which the country is divided.

Present full membership of the HMC is a total of two hundred and ninety-seven, which now includes headmasters and headmistresses of boys', girls' and co-educational schools. In considering applications for election to membership, the Committee has regard to the degree of independence enjoyed by the Head and his/her school. Eligibility also depends on the academic standards obtaining in the school, as reflected by the proportion of pupils in the Sixth Form pursuing a course of study beyond GCSE and by the school's public examination results, including A Levels, the International Baccalaureate and the Cambridge Pre-U.

The Constitution provides that the full membership shall consist only of heads of independent schools in the UK and Ireland. At the same time, it is held to be a strength that the Conference includes heads of schools from the maintained sector as well as other influential figures from the world of education. There is provision therefore for the election of a small number of HMC Associates. In addition the HMC has a number of International members, who are heads of high-quality schools from around the world. The International division meets regularly and the Chair is a member of the HMC Committee. There is also a small number of Honorary Associates who have been elected to life membership on retirement.

The HMC is closely associated with the other independent sector associations that also belong to the Independent Schools Council (ISC), and with the Association of School and College Leaders (ASCL), which represents the Heads and senior staff of secondary schools and colleges in both the maintained and independent sectors.

The HMC Committee 2021–2022

Elected Members

Chair	Richard Backhouse	Berkhamsted School
Vice-Chair	Sally-Anne Huang	St Paul's School
Chair-Elect	Melvyn Roffe	George Watson's College
Treasurer	Brendan Wignall	Ellesmere College

Divisional Members

Chair – East	Chris Townsend	Felsted School
Secretary – East	Jonathan Reddin	Ratcliffe College
Chair – Irish	Robert Robinson	Campbell College
Secretary – Irish	David Burnett	Royal School Dungannon
Chair – London	Alastair Land	Harrow School
Secretary – London	Ceri Jones	Caterham School
Chair – North East	Simon Hinchliffe	Bradford Grammar School
Secretary – North East	James Lockwood	Woodhouse Grove School
Chair – North West	Craig Mairs	Oldham Hulme Grammar School
Secretary – North West	John Browne	Stonyhurst College
Chair – Scottish	Lisa Kerr	Gordonstoun
Secretary – Scottish	Barry Welsh	The Edinburgh Academy
Chair – South Central	Matthew Judd	Leighton Park School
Secretary – South Central	William le Fleming	The Abbey School
Chair – South East	Ben Charles	King's Rochester
Secretary – South East	Dominic Oliver	Lancing College
Chair – South West	Jaideep Barot	Bristol Grammar School
Secretary – South West	Chris Wheeler	Monkton Senior School
Chair – West	Gareth Doodes	The King's School, Worcester
Secretary – West	Rob Jones	Rendcomb College
Chair – International	Mark Steed	Kellett School, Hong Kong
Secretary – International	Matthew Taylor	King's College, Madrid

Co-opted Members

Chair of Academic Policy	Martin Collier	Haileybury
Chair of Professional Development	Ben Vessey	Canford School
Chair of Universities	Nick Weaver	Ipswich School
Chair of Inspection	Jason Slack	The King's School in Macclesfield
Chair of Communications	Philip Britton	Bolton School
Chair of Membership	George Hartley	King's School, Chester
Chair of Sports	Kevin Knibbs	Hampton School
Chair of Pastoral & Safeguarding	Sarah Kerr-Dineen	Oundle School

General Secretary & CEO: Simon Hyde
Director of Finance & Operations: Chris Silver

Headmasters' and Headmistresses' Conference
12 The Point, Rockingham Road, Market Harborough, Leicestershire LE16 7QU
Tel: 01858 465260 · email: office@hmc.org.uk

GSA
GIRLS' SCHOOLS ASSOCIATION
gsa.uk.com

The Girls' Schools Association represents the Heads of a diverse range of girls' schools among which are some of the top-performing schools in the UK. Members are united by their commitment to educating girls in a girls-only environment which provides freedom from gender stereotypes, enabling girls to grow into themselves without pressure to conform to gender-weighted expectations.

The GSA helps girls and their teachers to flourish and is a powerful, well-respected voice within the educational establishment, highlighting the benefits of girls' schools, helping to inform and influence the national and international education debate, undertaking and collating pertinent research, and enabling continual professional development through a wide range of collaborative conferences and courses.

GSA schools are internationally respected and have an impressive global reputation for excellence in and out of the classroom, attracting pupils from around the world. They encourage the highest standards of education, pastoral care and co-curricular activity, with a wealth of extra-curricular opportunity in art, music, drama, sport and more. They share experience, specialisms, events and facilities in a variety of independent-state school partnerships, and some schools offer means-tested bursaries for families of limited financial means.

New research* has shown that girls in girls' schools are more confident and emotionally in control. Further, girls in GSA schools are significantly more likely to study STEM (science, technology, engineering & maths) subjects and take up sport. GSA schools are widely recognised for their exceptional academic provision and performance with the majority of pupils progressing to top universities. (*Soft Skills Development & Gender, AQR International – see https://gsa.uk.com/research/soft-skills-2021/)

Twenty-first century girls' schools come in many different shapes and sizes. Whether they are day, boarding, junior, senior, large, small, urban or rural, the education they provide ensures girls have numerous opportunities to realise their potential as active, equal, confident and competent leaders, participants and contributors. Former GSA school students are among the most noteworthy high achievers of the UK and indeed the world. Often thriving in traditionally male-dominated professions, they include world leading scientists, international campaigners and activists, artists and actresses, foreign correspondents, Olympic medallists and businesswomen at the highest levels.

The GSA works closely with the Association of School and College Leaders, is a member of the Independent Schools Council, and joins hands with organisations in the UK and internationally – such as the Association of State Girls' Schools (UK), the National Coalition of Girls' Schools (US) and the Alliance of Girls' Schools Australasia – in the interests of girls' education worldwide.

Officers 2021–2022

President:	Samantha Price	Benenden School
Vice-President:	Jane Prescott	Portsmouth High School GDST
President Elect 2022:	Heather Hanbury	Lady Eleanor Holles School
Treasurer:	Antonia Beary	Mayfield Girls

Committee Chairs

Boarding:	Liz Hewer	St George's School, Ascot
Education:	Alex Hutchinson	James Allen's Girls' School
Inclusion:	Heather Hanbury	Lady Eleanor Holles School
Membership & Accreditation:	Wendy Kempster	Palmers Green High School
Sport and Wellness:	Sarah Wilson	Heathfield School
Universities:	Millan Sachania	Streatham & Clapham High School GDST

Regional Representatives

East:	Bronwen Goulding	St Francis' College
London:	Millan Sachania	Streatham & Clapham High School GDST
Midlands:	Richard Nicholson	Warwick Independent Schools Foundation
North East:	Nina Gunson	Sheffield High School GDST
North West:	Sarah Haslam	Withington Girls' School
Scotland:	Alex Hems	St George's School for Girls, Edinburgh
South Central:	Jane Gandee	St Swithun's School
South East:	Anna King	Notre Dame School
South West & Wales:	Jessica Miles	Monmouth School for Girls

Secretariat

Chief Executive:	Donna Stevens
Membership Director:	Jane Carroll
Executive Assistant to the Chief Executive:	Jeven Sharma
Membership Manager:	Jannette Davison
Conference & Events Manager:	Jennifer Purser
Digital Manager:	Imogen Vanderpump
Communications Manager:	Rachel Kerr
Finance Officer:	Rehana Alimahomed

Girls' Schools Association
Suite 105, 108 New Walk, Leicester, LE1 7EA
Tel: 0116 254 1619 · email: office@gsa.uk.com

THE SOCIETY OF HEADS

www.thesocietyofheads.org.uk

The Society is an Association of Heads of just under 130 well-established independent schools. It was founded in 1961 when a group of Heads decided they needed a forum in which to share ideas and experience. Since then the Society has grown substantially in size, reputation and effectiveness and represents a vibrant community of independent schools throughout England and Wales with some additional overseas members.

The Society's policy is to maintain high standards in member schools, to promote independent education, to provide an opportunity for the sharing of ideas and common concerns, to foster links with the wider sphere of higher education and to strengthen relations with the maintained sector by promoting partnerships

Within the membership there is a wide variety of educational experience. Some schools are young, some have evolved from older foundations, some have behind them a long tradition of pioneer and specialist education; a number are at the leading edge of education in music, dance and the arts; and several are well known for their effective support for those with specific learning difficulties. The great majority are co-educational but we also have some all-boys and all-girls schools. Many have a strong boarding element; others are day only. All offer a stimulating sixth-form experience and give a sound and balanced education to pupils of widely varying abilities and interests.

The Society is one of the constituent Associations of the Independent Schools Council. Every Full Member school has been accredited through inspection by the Independent Schools Inspectorate (or Estyn in Wales and HMIE in Scotland) and is subject to regular visits to monitor standards and ensure that good practice and sound academic results are maintained. The Society is also represented on many other educational bodies.

All members are in membership of the Association of School and College Leaders (ASCL) or other union for school leaders and Full Member schools belong to AGBIS or an equivalent professional body supporting governance.

There are also categories of Alliance and Alliance Overseas Membership to which Heads are elected whose schools do not fulfil all the criteria for Full Membership but whose personal contribution to the Society is judged to be invaluable.

The Society hosts the autumn meeting, summer meeting and the annual conference for members. The Society also provides an extensive professional development programme.

Officers 2021–2022

Chair: Sarah Raffray, St Augustine's Priory
Vice-Chair: Adrian Meadows, The Peterborough School
Chair Designate: Sue Hannam, Lichfield Cathedral School
Hon. Treasurer: Christine Cunniffe, LVS Ascot

Committee 2021–2022

Sarah Raffray, St Augustine's Priory
Adrian Meadows, The Peterborough School
Sue Hannam, Lichfield Cathedral School
Christine Cunniffe, LVS Ascot
Guy Ayling, Mount Kelly
Gareth Doodes, The King's School
Damian Ettinger, Cokethorpe School
David Gajadharsingh, The Royal Ballet School
Emma-Kate Henry, St Christopher School
David Holland, Hill House School
Rob Jones, Rendcomb College
Julian Noad, Queen's College, Taunton
Richard Notman, Stover School
David Tickner, Newcastle School for Boys
Jessica Ward, Elmhurst Ballet School

Secretariat

CEO: Clive Rickart

The Society of Heads
12 The Point, Rockingham Road, Market Harborough, Leicestershire LE16 7QU
Tel: 01858 433760 · email: info@thesocietyofheads.org.uk

IAPS

INDEPENDENT ASSOCIATION OF PREP SCHOOLS

iaps.uk

IAPS is the voice of independent prep and linked junior school education. We work with and lobby governments on an international stage to ensure the needs of our members, and the independent sector as a whole, are met.

Schools can only join IAPS if they have been accredited through a satisfactory inspection and the head is suitably qualified. In addition, they must demonstrate the highest standards of education and care. Our member schools offer an all-round, values-led, broad education which produces confident, adaptable, motivated children with a lifelong passion for learning.

While the values may be the same, each of our schools is independent and distinct: we have single-sex and co-educational, boarding, day and mixed, urban and rural. Sizes vary from more than 800 pupils to around 100.

We have one of the independent sector's top training programmes which includes a broad range of professional development courses. New members are offered a highly qualified IAPS coach as support and members are divided into district groups by geographical location, giving them the chance to meet with fellow heads on a regular basis. We organise sporting tournaments for pupils to a national standard in a wide range of sports. Our annual conference brings together members and leaders in educational thinking, politics and business.

With 616 member schools in the UK and 47 abroad, IAPS offers excellent opportunities to members for fellowship and networking.

The Council and Officers for 2021–2022

Chairman of IAPS: Andrew Nott
Vice-Chairman: Charlotte Johnston

Members of Council:

Martin Barker	Luke Harrison
Mark Brearey	Karen McNerney
Matthew Bryan	Sean Price
Richard Chapman	Elaine Rawlings
Amanda Childs	Rebecca Smith
Christine Cook	Clive Smith-Langridge
John Gilmour	Finola Stack
David Goulbourn	William Toleman
Philip Hardy	Mark Turner

Officers:

Chief Executive: Christopher King
Director of Education: Mark Brotherton
Director of Membership Services: Emilie Darwin
Head of Finance: Jackie Moore
Membership Secretary: Petra Hancock
Association Administrator: Christine McCrudden

Independent Association of Prep Schools
Bishop's House, Artemis Drive, Tachbrook Park, Warwick, CV34 6UD
Tel: 01926 887833 · email: iaps@iaps.uk

ISA
INDEPENDENT SCHOOLS ASSOCIATION
www.isaschools.org.uk

The Independent Schools Association is a registered charity with a service-led approach to supporting its Members and the wider educational community. The Association's dedication to its Members, including the delivery of instant 24/7 expert advice, has resulted in significant growth over the last ten years and ISA is now regarded as the most representative of any organisation within the sector. Its growth is simply unprecedented within the sector.

Membership is open to independent school Heads and Proprietors provided they meet the necessary criteria, which include accreditation by any government-approved inspectorate. ISA makes no requirements upon Members for other memberships or affiliations, or for schools to operate in any specific way, beyond the requirements of the appropriate regulations. A strong regional network of fellow Heads supports each Member, and all Members receive a free high-level compliance check in the run-up to their next scheduled inspection, as well as an annual pastoral visit from a dedicated regional representative. An extensive programme of training events and conferences helps Members and their staff to keep up-to-date with the latest thinking on teaching and learning.

ISA celebrates a wide-ranging membership, not confined to any one type of school, but including all: nursery, pre-preparatory, junior, preparatory and senior, all-through schools, specialist sixth-forms, co-educational, single-sex, boarding, day, faith schools and performing arts and special schools.

Promoting best practice and fellowship for Members remains at the core of the Association, just as it did when it began over 140 years ago. The 560 Members and their schools enjoy high quality national conferences and courses that foster excellence in independent education. The Association's Annual ISA Awards ceremony celebrates the best of good practice across Members' schools. The ISA central office also supports Members and provides expert advice in areas such as HR, curriculum, finance, leadership and governance, and represents the views of its membership at national and governmental levels. Pupils in ISA schools enjoy a wide variety of competitions, including a wealth of sporting, artistic and academic activities at Area and National level, often at world-class venues.

Council and Officers for 2021–2022

President: Lord Lexden OBE

Vice-Presidents:
Angela Culley
Barry Huggett OBE
Sarah Lockyer
Neil Roskilly
Richard Walden

Honorary Officers:
John Southworth (*Chair*)
Jeff Shaw (*Vice-Chair*)
Phil Soutar (*Vice-Chair*)

Elective Councillors:

Matthew Burke	Stephen McKernan
Elizabeth Brown	Dominic Price
Helen Chalmers	Claudette Salmon
Lawrence Collins	Craig Wardle
Natasha Dangerfield	James Wilding
Penny Ford	Tracey Wilson
Sue Knox	

Area Coordinators:

East Anglia: Pauline Wilson	*Midlands*: David Preston
London North: Dan Sayers	*North*: Jeremy Duke
London South: Phil Soutar	*South West*: Dionne Seagrove
London West: Jonathan Hetherington	

Officials
Chief Executive Officer: Rudolf Eliott Lockhart
Deputy Chief Executive Officer: Peter Woodroffe
Director of Education and Inclusion: Helen Stanton-Tonner
Professional Development Officer: Alice Thompson
Office Manager and PA to the CEO: Karen Goddard

Independent Schools Association
ISA House, 5–7 Great Chesterford Court, Great Chesterford, Essex CB10 1PF
Tel: 01799 523619 · email: isa@isaschools.org.uk

AGBIS
ASSOCIATION OF GOVERNING BODIES OF INDEPENDENT SCHOOLS
REGISTERED CHARITY NO. 1108756

www.agbis.org.uk

The Association of Governing Bodies of Independent Schools (AGBIS) supports and advises governing bodies of schools in the independent sector on all aspects of governance.

The charitable objects of AGBIS are the advancement of education and the promotion of good governance in independent schools.

AGBIS offers a number of services* to their members including:

- Training seminars for new and experienced governors, webinars on a variety of topics and free eLearning courses on safeguarding and for new governors.
- An advisory service on all aspects of governing schools via telephone, email and the website.
- 'Guidelines for Governors' (Published March 2019) a manual of good practice.
- Annual survey of salaries and benefits of heads and bursars.
- eNewsletters to keep governors informed on current topics of interest and/or concern.
- On-site and virtual training for governing bodies, leading governors' strategy days and reviews of governance for schools.
- Annual conference and AGM for representatives of member schools.
- Maintaining a list of potential new governors.

*Some of the AGBIS services are offered for a fee.

Board

AGBIS is a registered charity (No 1108756) and company (No 0521716) limited by guarantee governed by a Board which meets at least once every school term. Board members are nominated by school governing bodies and serve initially for a three year period. The Board is advised by three committees: Training and Membership, Nominations and Governance and Finance.

The AGBIS Board includes three honorary officers:

Chair: Mark Taylor (Tring Park School for the Performing Arts)
Deputy Chair: Mike Gregson (The Edinburgh Academy)
Treasurer: Sarah Phillips (King Alfred School)

Chief Executive: Richard Harman
Director of Training: Cheryl Connelly

Association of Governing Bodies of Independent Schools
The Grange, 3 Codicote Road, Welwyn, Hertfordshire AL6 9LY
Tel: 01438 840730 · email: enquiries@agbis.org.uk

ISBA

INDEPENDENT SCHOOLS' BURSARS ASSOCIATION

www.theisba.org.uk

The Independent Schools' Bursars Association (ISBA) is the only national association to represent school bursars and business managers of independent schools, providing them with the professional support they need to manage their schools successfully and provide a world class education to their pupils.

The association can trace its history back to the founding of the Public Schools Bursars' Association which held its first general meeting on 26 April 1932 at the offices of Epsom College. Its name then changed to the Independent Schools' Bursars Association in 1983.

The ISBA now has more than 1,100 independent school members, including international associate members, from smaller preparatory schools to larger and well-renowned senior schools, including both boarding and day schools. Although it is the school and not the bursar who becomes a member of the association, it is usually the bursar or equivalent who is the school's nominated representative.

The association is one of the constituent members of the Independent Schools Council (ISC) and also works closely with the other seven constituent associations of the ISC. It is represented on the ISC Governing Council and a number of ISC committees and is also often called on to represent the ISC at meetings with the Department for Education, Health & Safety Executive and Teachers' Pensions providing advice on bursarial matters.

Full membership of the ISBA is open to schools who are members of one of the constituent associations in membership of the ISC. Associate membership is open to certain other schools/organisations which are recognised as educational charities.

Day-to-day the ISBA advises many different staff within a school's senior management team including the bursar, finance director, chief operations officer, business manager, deputy or assistant with areas of responsibility encompassing accounting, financial management and reporting, risk management, regulatory compliance, facilities management, HR, technology, environmental sustainability, auxiliary services and more. As part of its range of support services the association offers schools:

- guidance and legislative briefings, and model policies to download from its online reference library;
- a comprehensive professional development programme covering finance, legal, HR, inspections and other key operational issues and tailored to suit staff at all levels;
- information, advice and networking opportunities at the ISBA Annual Conference (the 2022 conference will take place from Monday 16th to Wednesday 18th May 2022);
- a 'Bursar's Guide' – providing the latest information on legislation affecting schools;
- termly copies of the ISBA's magazine – The Bursar's Review – and monthly e-bulletins covering the latest legal, financial and HR news and more;
- an online job vacancies page where schools can advertise any of their vacant bursary management roles for free.

The ISBA Board consists of the Chair of the Association, Eleanor Sharman, Bursar at Rendcomb College, and the bursars of between eight and 12 other leading independent schools.

The Independent Schools' Bursars Association is a Registered Charity, number 1121757, and a Company Limited by Guarantee, registered in England and Wales, number 6410037.

Chief Executive: Mr David Woodgate

Independent Schools' Bursars Association
Bluett House, Unit 11–12, Manor Farm, Cliddesden, Basingstoke, Hampshire RG25 2JB
Tel: 01256 330369 · email: office@theisba.org.uk

BSA
BOARDING SCHOOLS' ASSOCIATION
www.boarding.org.uk

Since its foundation in 1966, the Boarding Schools' Association (BSA) has had the twin objectives of promoting boarding education and the development of quality boarding through high standards of pastoral care and boarding accommodation. Parents and prospective pupils choosing a boarding school can, therefore, be assured that more than 600 schools in nearly 40 countries worldwide that make up the membership of the BSA are committed to providing the best possible boarding environment for their pupils.

A UK boarding school can only be a full member of the BSA if it is also a member of one of the Independent Schools Council (ISC) constituent associations, or in membership of the State Boarding Forum (SBF). These two bodies require member schools to be regularly inspected by the Independent Schools' Inspectorate (ISI) or Ofsted. Other boarding schools who are not members of these organisations can apply to be affiliate members. Similar arrangements are in place for overseas members. Boarding inspection of ISC accredited independent schools has been conducted by ISI since September 2012. Ofsted retains responsibility for the inspection of boarding in state schools and non-association independent schools.

Boarding inspections must be conducted every three years. Boarding is judged against the National Minimum Standards for Boarding Schools which are due to be updated in the next few months.

Relationship with government

The BSA is in regular communication with the Department for Education (DfE) on all boarding matters. The Children Act (1989) and the Care Standards Act (2001) require boarding schools to conform to national legislation and the promotion of this legislation and the training required to carry it out are matters on which the DfE and BSA work together. BSA has worked especially closely with the DfE and other government departments during the coronavirus pandemic over the past 18 months, supporting the safety and continuity of education for its member schools' pupils and staff, both domestically and internationally.

Boarding training

BSA delivers the world's largest professional development programme for boarding staff. It offers:

- Two-year courses for graduate and non-graduate boarding staff – these involve eight study days and two assignments, each about 4,000 words long. This is the flagship training opportunity for staff seriously interested in boarding excellence
- A Diploma course for senior experienced boarding staff, involving three study days and two assignments spread between March and October
- A broad range of day seminars on topics of particular interest to boarding/pastoral staff – e.g. Essentials of Boarding, Leading the Boarding Team, Meeting the Needs of Overseas Boarders
- Specialist one or two-day conferences for Boarding Staff, Heads, Health & Wellbeing staff**, Marketing and Admissions staff* and State Boarding Schools staff and Safeguarding Leads**
- Basic training online, for those very new to boarding.

* With Sacpa (Safeguarding and Child Protection Association), part of the BSA Group
** With Hieda (Heath in Education Association), part of the BSA Group
** With BAISIS (British Association of Independent Schools with International Students), part of the BSA Group

State Boarding Forum (SBF)

BSA issues information regarding its state boarding school members and BSA should be contacted for details of these schools. In these schools, parents pay for boarding but not for education, so fees are substantially lower than in an independent boarding school.

BSA Group Leadership Team

Chief Executive: Robin Fletcher

Chief Operating Officer and Director, Sacpa: Aileen Kane

Director of Safeguarding, Professional Development and Accreditation: Dale Wilkins

International Director and Director, BAISIS: Caroline Nixon

Director of Guardianship and Inclusion: Ammy Davies-Potter

Director of Health and Wellbeing and Director, Hieda: Jane Graham

The Boarding Schools' Association
First Floor, 27 Queen Anne's Gate, London SW1H 9BU
Tel: +44 (0)20 7798 1580 · email: bsa@boarding.org.uk

ISEB

INDEPENDENT SCHOOLS EXAMINATIONS BOARD

www.iseb.co.uk

COMMON ENTRANCE

COMMON PRE-TESTS

COMMON ACADEMIC SCHOLARSHIP

ISEB PROJECT QUALIFICATION

Executive Chairman:
Durell Barnes, BA (Hons), PGCE

Chief Executive:
Julia Martin, MA, BA (Hons), PGCE

COMMON ENTRANCE

The Common Entrance Examinations are used for transfer to senior schools at the ages of 11+ and 13+. The syllabuses are devised and regularly monitored by the Independent Schools Examinations Board which comprises members of the Headmasters' and Headmistresses' Conference (HMC), the Girls' Schools Association (GSA) and the Independent Association of Prep Schools (IAPS).

The papers are set by examiners appointed by the Board, but the answers are marked by the senior school for which a candidate is entered. Common Entrance is not a public examination as, for example, GCSE, and candidates may normally be entered only if they have been offered a place at a senior school, subject to their passing the examination.

Candidates normally take the examination in their own junior or preparatory schools, either in the UK or overseas.

Common Entrance at 11+ consists of papers in English, Mathematics and Science. At 13+, in addition to these core subjects, a wide range of additional papers is available in modern and classical languages, and the humanities subjects. Tiered papers are available for many subjects.

Mandarin Chinese is offered as an online examination which can be taken at any age.

Dates

The 11+ examination is held in early November or mid-January.

The 13+ examination commences either on the first Monday in November, the last Monday in January or on the first Tuesday in after the half-term break in June.

Entries

In cases where candidates are at schools in membership of the Independent Association of Prep Schools, it is usual for heads of these schools to make arrangements for entering candidates for the appropriate examination after consultation with parents and senior school heads. In the case of candidates at schools which do not normally enter candidates, it is the responsibility of parents to arrange for candidates to be entered for the appropriate examination in accordance with the requirements of senior schools.

Conduct of the Examination

Regulations for the conduct of the examination are laid down by the Independent Schools Examinations Board.

Past Papers and Other Resources

Copies of past Common Entrance papers can be purchased from Galore Park:

website: www.galorepark.co.uk

email: customer.services@galorepark.co.uk

Tel: 01235 400555

ISEB-endorsed Common Entrance textbooks, revision guides and practice exercises are available from a number of publishers, listed on the ISEB website.

.../cont.

COMMON PRE-TESTS

The Common Pre-Tests are age-standardised tests used to assess pupils' attainment and potential when they are in Year 6 or Year 7, prior to entry to their senior schools. Pupils who sit the tests may also be required to sit the Common Entrance examinations.

ISEB commissions the tests from GL Assessment which has long been associated with providing high-quality and reliable assessments in education. The tests are taken online, usually in the pupil's current school, and include multiple-choice tests in Mathematics, English, verbal and non-verbal reasoning. Senior schools will inform parents if their son or daughter needs to be entered for the tests.

No special preparation is needed for the tests and no past papers are available, although a short familiarisation test is provided for candidates. Examples and practice questions are provided during the test itself so that candidates understand what they have to do.

Further details are available for schools in the Schools section of the ISEB website and for parents in the Parents section of the ISEB website.

COMMON ACADEMIC SCHOLARSHIP

ISEB sets Scholarship examination papers at 13+ which a number of independent senior schools use to assess potential scholars. Papers are set in English, Mathematics, Science, History, Geography, TPR (Theology, Philosophy and Religion), French and Latin. Questions are based on the Common Entrance syllabuses and past papers are available from Galore Park.

Candidates are entered by the senior schools for which they are registered and the papers are marked by the senior schools themselves.

ISEB PROJECT QUALIFICATION (iPQ)

Developed with reference to project qualifications higher up in the curriculum, Prep schools can now offer pupils a framework to teach and assess independent project learning through the iPQ in a way that harnesses pupils' individuality, diversity, strengths and interests to create a project that is truly their own and, contributes to a portfolio of qualifications and skills to equip them for life beyond Prep. Pupils are marked on the process of devising a project, undertaking research and evaluating their findings as well as the outcome. It offers the freedom for pupils to explore their own interests beyond the classroom, their extra curricular talents or for schools to use the framework to explore a cross-curricular project.

The iPQ is available for Years 5 & 6 and a further iPQ qualification for Years 7 & 8. Candidates are entered by their Prep schools and the projects are marked by iPQ moderators.

Fees

The Independent Schools Examinations Board decides the fees to be charged for each candidate. Schools are notified annually of fees payable for the next academic year. Parents seeking information about current fees should look on the ISEB website or contact the ISEB office.

Correspondence

Correspondence about academic matters relating to the Examinations and requests for further information about the administration of the Examinations should be addressed to the Chief Executive.

Independent Schools Examinations Board
Suite 3, Endeavour House, Crow Arch Lane, Ringwood, Hampshire BH24 1HP
Tel: 01425 470555 · email: enquiries@iseb.co.uk

COBIS
COUNCIL OF BRITISH INTERNATIONAL SCHOOLS
www.cobis.org.uk
twitter: @COBISorg · @COBIS_CEO

Representing over 400 members and supporting associates, COBIS is the global association for international British schools overseas. The organisation has developed markedly since its foundation, changing to meet the needs and aspirations of its growing global school membership base.

COBIS exists to serve, support and represent its member schools – their leaders, governors, staff and students by:

- Providing Quality Assurance in member schools via The Patron's Accreditation and Compliance scheme
- Representing member schools with the British Government, educational bodies and the corporate sector
- Providing effective professional development for senior leaders, governors, teachers and support staff
- Facilitating, coordinating and supporting professional networking opportunities for British International schools
- Promoting child protection and safer recruitment and employment practices
- Engaging, challenging and inspiring students of all ages and abilities by delivering excellent interschool student competitions and events
- Providing access to information about trends and developments in UK education
- Facilitating high impact 'Member to Member' professional networking
- Promoting career opportunities within the global COBIS network
- Connecting suppliers and companies operating in the education sector with international British schools overseas in its role as Trade Challenge Partner of the Department for International Trade (DIT)
- Brokering a cost-effective consultancy service between schools and approved educational support service providers

COBIS Executive 2021–2022

Honorary President
The Rt. Hon. Lord Knight of Weymouth

Honorary Vice Presidents
The Rt. Hon. Lord Andrew Adonis
Michael Cooper OBE
Priya Lakhani OBE
Lord Lexden OBE
Dame Judith Mayhew Jonas DBE
Dr Andreas Schleicher
Jean Scott

COBIS Head Office
CEO: Colin Bell

COBIS Board
Elected:
Chairman: Trevor Rowell, Governor, GEMS International School Metropark, Kuala Lumpur
Vice Chairman: Dr Steffen Sommer, Principal, Doha College, Qatar
Fiona Cottam, Principal, Hartland International School, Dubai
Craig Heaton, Headteacher, St Saviour's School Ikoyi, Nigeria
Paul Morgan, Principal, The British School of Amsterdam
Simon O'Connor, Director, Deira International School, Dubai
David Tongue, Principal and CEO, St George's British International School, Rome, Italy
Kai Vacher, Principal, British School Muscat, Oman

Co-opted:
Dr Martin Coles, Former COBIS Principal, and Former Assistant Director,
The National College for School Leadership (*Treasurer*)
Jennifer Bray MBE, Former COBIS Head and Governor
Vivienne Stern, Director of Universities UK International
Abra Stoakley, Head of School, Grange School, Nigeria

Council of British International Schools
55-56 Russell Square, Bloomsbury, London WC1B 4HP
Tel: +44 (0)20 3826 7190 · email: pa@cobis.org.uk

INDEPENDENT SCHOOLS INSPECTORATE

www.isi.net

ISI provides assurance on the standards and quality of school life for children and young people in association independent schools in England. The inspectorate reports to the Department for Education on the extent to which these schools meet the statutory Independent School Standards. This process recognises strong practice and drives improvement across the 1,200 schools ISI inspects.

Safeguarding is a focus of all inspections. Inspectors review evidence relating to a school's safeguarding arrangements and report to the Department for Education on the extent to which schools meet their responsibilities. Listening to pupils is central to this process, and every inspection uses anonymous pupil, parent and staff questionnaires as a crucial part of the inspection evidence. Inspectors also speak to pupils in groups on inspection.

For schools providing pupil accommodation, ISI also inspects against additional requirements set out in the National Minimum Standards (NMS) for Boarding Schools. All inspection reports are published on the ISI website.

Schools undergo a scheduled inspection, on average, every three years. ISI currently undertakes two types of routine inspection: Regulatory Compliance (RCI), which checks that a school's policies and practices are compliant with the regulations set by the Department for Education; and Educational Quality (EQI), which considers the quality of education a school provides and checks a targeted section of policies and practices. There are also three types of non-routine inspection, including 'additional inspections' where the Department for Education have reason for a school to be inspected urgently. This could be due to concerns raised by parents, staff or pupils with either ISI or the Department for Education.

Quality assurance is embedded at every stage of ISI's inspection process. This includes a high-quality training and development programme for their 900-strong inspector workforce. Every year ISI delivers, on average, over 300 hours of qualification, induction and annual training.

ISI's independence is essential to delivering reliable and valid judgements on the schools they inspect. Their governance structure and policies ensure they operate as a fully independent inspectorate. They have an independent Board of Directors, which holds the senior management team to account for the delivery and quality of inspections.

In November 2020, Vanessa Ward was appointed as Chief Executive-Chief Inspector at ISI, following endorsement by the Secretary of State for Education. Ward previously led inspections in the state and independent sectors as one of Her Majesty's Inspectors (HMI) for Ofsted.

ISI will shortly begin a wide-ranging consultation around its next inspection framework, which will come into effect from September 2023.

Independent Schools Inspectorate
CAP House, 9-12 Long Lane, London EC1A 9HA
Tel: 020 7600 0100 · email: info@isi.net

GDST

THE GIRLS' DAY SCHOOL TRUST

www.gdst.net

Chair:	Juliet Humphries
Deputy Chairs:	Kathryn Davis, Vicky Tuck
Chief Executive:	Cheryl Giovannoni

The Girls' Day School Trust (GDST) is the UK's leading family of independent girls' schools. We also have two academies. In all of our schools, academic excellence is a given, but GDST girls also learn to be confident, happy and fearless, prepared for the opportunities of the future.

We tailor our approach to how girls learn best, providing them with the attributes they need to excel. We focus not only on what is learned but *how* it is learned.

We concentrate on creating an environment where all can thrive and learn from one another. Physical and emotional wellbeing is paramount, which is why every GDST school provides an incredible array of extra-curricular activities and wellbeing programmes.

Nothing holds our girls back – they're encouraged to embrace every role and subject. As a result, they trust their own abilities and are alive to every opportunity. At GDST schools, girls learn without limits.

GDST schools

Blackheath High School
Brighton Girls
Bromley High School
Croydon High School
Howell's School Llandaff, Cardiff
Kensington Prep School
Newcastle High School for Girls
Northampton High School
Northwood College for Girls
Norwich High School for Girls
Notting Hill & Ealing High School
Nottingham Girls' High School

Oxford High School
Portsmouth High School
Putney High School
The Royal High School, Bath
Sheffield High School for Girls
Shrewsbury High School
South Hampstead High School
Streatham & Clapham High School
Sutton High School
Sydenham High School
Wimbledon High School

GDST academies

The Belvedere Academy, Liverpool
Birkenhead High School Academy

Information on the schools can be found in the Yearbook or on the GDST website: www.gdst.net

The Girls' Day School Trust is a Registered Charity, number 306983.

The Girls' Day School Trust
10 Bressenden Place, London SW1E 5DH
Tel: 020 7393 6666 · email: info@wes.gdst.net

CISC
CATHOLIC INDEPENDENT SCHOOLS' CONFERENCE
www.catholicindependentschools.com

The Catholic Independent Schools' Conference is a dynamic and forward-thinking family of schools with members in England, Scotland, Ireland, France, Spain, Gibraltar and Italy. There are 124 schools in CISC, educating more than 38,000 pupils from nursery age through to eighteen.

There is a wide variety of types of school in CISC, with co-educational, single-sex, day, boarding, junior, prep, senior and all-through. We also have in our family of schools ten special schools (two independent and eight non-maintained special schools) serving a wide range of complex needs from profound physical disability to visual impairment and autism.

Most of our schools have their foundation in a Religious Order or Congregation. These orders, many from the Continent, set up Catholic schools in Britain when there was little educational provision for the Catholic population. Despite the great variety of these religious foundations there is a strong common goal to serve the mission of the Church by educating young men and women to take their place in society as young disciples, or for those who are not of the Catholic faith, principled citizens with values based on the Gospel who will work for the common good.

CISC is very much part of this living tradition and is committed to playing its part in the mission of the Church in education. A priority for us is to support the formation of our members, the heads of our Catholic independent schools. We are also committed to developing the next generation of leaders and and collaborate with EducareM on a personalised journey of formation at each stage of career progression, including recently qualified teachers, those leading and those aspiring to leadership of a Catholic school.

CISC sees itself as a distinctive, traditional, yet forward thinking part of the Catholic educational landscape, which enriches and is enriched by collaborations across all elements of Catholic education, namely the maintained sector, dioceses and the Catholic Education Service (CES). As such, CISC works closely with the CES across a range of policy areas and supports and contributes to their Formatio programme, developed specifically for those in executive leadership.

CISC is a charitable organisation and the main beneficiaries are our members and their colleagues. CISC is governed by a committee of serving heads who are trustees of the charity. It employs a Secretariat who is responsible for delivering on the strategic aims of the organisation.

For more information, please visit our website or contact Dr Maureen Glackin: info@catholicindependentschools.com.

CHOIR SCHOOLS' ASSOCIATION

www.choirschools.org.uk

Patron: The Duchess of Kent

Committee:

Chairman: Clive Marriott, Salisbury Cathedral School

Vice-Chairs:

Neil Chippington, St John's College School, Cambridge

Yvette Day, King's College School, Cambridge

Andrew de Silva, St Edmund's School, Canterbury
William Goldsmith, St George's School Windsor
Simon Larter-Evans, St Paul's Choir School, London

David Morton, The King's School, Gloucester
Richard Murray, Christ Church Cathedral School, Oxford

CSA Full and Associate Members

Blackburn Cathedral
Bristol Cathedral Choir School
The Cathedral School, Llandaff
Chetham's School of Music, Manchester
Christ Church Cathedral School, Oxford
City of London School
Croydon Minster
Dean Close Preparatory School, Cheltenham
Durham Cathedral Schools Foundation
Exeter Cathedral School
Frideswide Voices, Oxford
Hereford Cathedral School
King's College School, Cambridge
King's Ely Junior, Ely
King's Rochester Preparatory School
The King's School, Gloucester
The King's School, Peterborough
The King's School, Worcester

Lanesborough School, Guildford
Leicester Cathedral
Lichfield Cathedral School
Lincoln Cathedral
Lincoln Minster School
The London Oratory School
Magdalen College School, Oxford
Merton College, Oxford
The Minster School, Southwell
New College School, Oxford
Norwich School
Old Palace School, Croydon
The Pilgrims' School, Winchester
The Portsmouth Grammar School
The Prebendal School, Chichester
Queen Elizabeth Grammar School, Wakefield
Reigate St Mary's Preparatory and Choir School
Ripon Cathedral
Runnymede St Edward's School, Liverpool

Salisbury Cathedral School
St Cedd's School, Essex
St Edmund's Junior School, Canterbury
St Edward's College, Liverpool
St George's School, Windsor
St John's College School, Cambridge
St John's College, Cardiff
St Mary's Music School, Edinburgh
St Nicholas Cathedral, Newcastle-upon-Tyne
St Paul's Cathedral School, London
St Peter's Collegiate Church, Wolverhampton
St Peter's School, York
Truro School
Wells Cathedral School
Westminster Abbey Choir School, London
Westminster Cathedral Choir School, London
Whitgift School, Croydon

St Thomas Choir School, New York, USA

The Choir Schools' Association celebrated its Centenary in 2018.

45 schools in the UK educate some or all of the choristers at cathedrals, churches or college chapels all over the country. Between them they educate more than 25,000 pupils, including some 1,200 choristers. Westminster Abbey Choir School is the only school to educate choristers and probationers only. The Association's associate membership includes cathedrals and churches without choir schools.

Choir schools offer a very special opportunity for children who enjoy singing. They receive a first-class academic and all-round education combined with excellent music training. The experience and self-discipline choristers acquire remain with them for life. There is a wide range of schools: some cater for children aged 7–13, others are junior schools with senior schools to 18; most are Church of England but the Roman Catholic, Scottish and Welsh churches are all represented.

Most CSA members are fee-paying schools and Deans and Chapters provide fee assistance while Government support comes in the shape of the Choir Schools' Scholarship Scheme. Under the umbrella of the Music and Dance Scheme, funds are available to help those who cannot afford even the reduced school fees. Government funding through the Music and Dance Scheme (MDS), along with other monies in its Bursary Trust Fund, is administered by the CSA. Applications are means-tested and an award made once a child has secured a place at a choir school.

Each CSA member school has its own admissions procedure for choristers. However, every child will be assessed both musically and academically. A growing number of children are given informal voice tests which enable the organist or director of music to judge whether they have the potential to become choristers. Some are offered places immediately or will be urged to enter the more formal voice trial organised by the school. In some cases a family may be advised not to proceed. Alternatively, the child's voice may be more suitable for one of the other choir schools.

A number of special ingredients help make a good chorister: potential, a keen musical ear and an eagerness to sing. A clutch of music examination certificates is not vital – alertness and enthusiasm are! At the same time, school staff must be satisfied that a new recruit can cope with school work and the many other activities on offer as well as the demanding choir workload.

To find out more about choir schools please visit the CSA website: **www.choirschools.org.uk**

CSA members can be contacted direct or you can write, email or telephone
for further information about choir schools to:

Ian Jones, General Secretary
Email: ian.jones@choirschools.org.uk
Telephone: 07903 850597
Address: 39 Bournside Road, Cheltenham, Gloucestershire GL51 3AL

CIFE
COUNCIL FOR INDEPENDENT EDUCATION
www.cife.org.uk

President:
Lord Lexden OBE

Vice President:
Hugh Monro, MA

Chairman:
Mark Shingleton, BA, MA, PGCE

Vice-Chairman:
Tom Caston, BA, MSc

Independent sixth-form colleges are extremely well placed to offer what is needed for students preparing for university and beyond. The best such colleges are generally members of CIFE, the Council for Independent Education, an organisation which was founded more than 40 years ago. There are 23 CIFE colleges, geographically spread across the country, each one offering individual features but all subject to high standards of accreditation. For example, there are some colleges that specialise in students wishing to retake in order to improve exam grades, some offering GCSE and pre-GCSE programmes as well as full A Level courses, which may be residential, homestay, day, or a mix of all three. Several colleges offer foundation programmes and are twinned with universities. In short, CIFE colleges offer a wide range of educational environments in which students can succeed.

Teaching in CIFE colleges really helps and supports students since teaching groups are small and teachers highly experienced and specialists in their subject. The 'tutorial' system derives directly from Oxbridge where it continues to be world famous. A student in a small group receives a greater degree of individual attention. Regular testing ensures that she/he maintains good progress, and the emphasis on study skills provides essential support for the AS/A Level subjects.

It is not surprising that a student gains confidence and self-belief within such an environment. Colleges engender a strong work ethic in their student communities. Many of the minor rules and regulations essential for schools are not necessary at CIFE colleges. Good manners and an enthusiastic attitude are every bit as important, but uniform, strict times for eating or homework, assemblies or games participation are not part of the picture. It can be seen from the large numbers of students going on to higher education from CIFE colleges that universities regard our students highly.

Increasing numbers of young people are deciding to move school at the age of 16, not because they are unhappy with their school, but because they see the need for a change at this stage. It may be that they wish to study a subject which their school does not offer, such as Accounting, Law, Psychology or Photography. Perhaps they are looking for a more adult environment or one where they can focus on their academic subjects to the exclusion of other things. However, it would be misleading to suggest that CIFE colleges are lacking in extracurricular activities, as every CIFE college recognises the need for enrichment of all sorts, sporting, social and creative. The difference is that activities are at the choice of the student.

As with schools, choosing a college calls for careful research. CIFE colleges undergo regular inspection either by the Independent Schools Inspectorate, Ofsted and/or the British Accreditation Council, recognised bodies which regulate the provision and standards of teaching, safety and pastoral care. While each college has its own individual character, all share the desire to provide each individual student with a superb preparation for higher education.

Members of CIFE

Ashbourne Independent Sixth-form College, London
Bales College, London
Bath Academy, Bath
Bosworth Independent College, Northampton
Brooke House College, Market Harborough
Cambridge Tutors College, London
Carfax College, Oxford
CATS College, Cambridge
CATS College, Canterbury
CATS College, London
Cherwell College, Oxford
Collingham, London

David Game College, London
LSI Independent Sixth Form College, London
Mander Portman Woodward, Birmingham
Mander Portman Woodward, Cambridge
Mander Portman Woodward, London
Oxford International College, Oxford
Oxford Sixth Form College, Oxford
Padworth College, Reading
Regent College, London
Rochester Independent College
Westminster Tutors, London

Further information can be obtained from:

CIFE
Tel: 020 8767 8666 · email: enquiries@cife.org.uk

High quality education in an actively Christian environment for all

AMCIS

ASSOCIATION FOR ADMISSIONS, MARKETING AND COMMUNICATIONS IN INDEPENDENT SCHOOLS

FOUNDED 1993

www.amcis.co.uk

Objectives:
- To promote and develop good marketing practice in admissions, marketing and communications in independent education
- To help increase the effectiveness of the admissions, marketing and communications representatives of member schools
- To encourage personal development within the schools' admissions, marketing and communications professionals

Achieved through:
- Seminars, webinars and workshops on a variety of admissions, marketing and communications-led subjects held throughout the year
- Annual residential conference
- Online networking meetings
- Training – Diploma in Schools' Marketing & Diploma in Admissions Management
- Helpline
- Website with member-only resource section
- LinkedIn Group Forum
- Twitter feed
- Facebook Group
- On-line News bulletins throughout the year
- Speakers provided for conferences, inset days and similar

Membership:
- School Membership, renewable annually by subscription
- Corporate Membership, renewable annually by subscription

The Association is directed by a Chair, Vice Chair and Treasurer together with a Board of Directors.

CEO: Tory Gillingham

AMCIS
57A Market Place, Malton, North Yorkshire YO17 7LX
Tel: 01653 699800 · email: enquiries@amcis.co.uk

AROPS – THE SCHOOLS' ALUMNI ASSOCIATION

FOUNDED 1971

arops.org.uk

President:

Bill Gillen (Old Arnoldians and Belfast Old Instonians' Association)

Vice-Presidents:

Margaret Carter-Pegg (Old Crohamian), Guy Cliff (Old Silcoatian),
John Kidd, Tim Neale (Radleian Society), Anthony Phillips (The Lancing Club),
Q D Seymour-Smith (Old Decanian and Old Millfiledian), Trish Woodhouse

Committee

Co-Chairman: Peter Jakobek (Old Bristolians)
Co-Chairman: Alan Cooper (Old Waynfletes)
Secretary: Caitlin Spencer (Bristol Grammar School)
Treasurer: Vijay Khullar (Old Roffensian)
Registrar: Keith Balkham (KGS Friends)
and 10 committee members

AROPS was founded in 1971 by Mike Comer of the Old Johnians, St John's School, Leatherhead.

Aim: To provide a friendly forum for the exchange of views and experiences between representatives of school alumni societies.

Membership: Open to representatives of any school alumni society. New members are always welcome. Details are available on the website – arops.org.uk – where you can also find information on events and member societies' news, regularly updated. Please contact us by email: arops@arops.org.uk.

Meetings: Our annual Conference, usually held in May, is our main event and an ideal opportunity to meet with other representatives and to share thoughts on current topics.

Our 2022 Conference will be held at Bristol Grammar School on Saturday 14 May.

Apart from the Conference and the AGM, AROPS also organises a series of online *Video Network Meetings* which allow members to discuss items concerning alumni engagement on an informal basis.

Subscription: £50 per annum (with discounts for smaller societies). Please email the Administrator, at arops@arops.org.uk, including a name and telephone contact number along with your enquiry.

MOSA
MEDICAL OFFICERS OF SCHOOLS ASSOCIATION

FOUNDED 1884

www.mosa.org.uk

Objects

It is the objective of the Association to offer guidance and support and to encourage the application of the highest of medical standards in the educational environment. MOSA offers its members mutual assistance in promoting school health and the holding of meetings for consideration of all subjects connected with the special work of medical officers and health professionals of schools.

Membership

Medical officers of schools and medical and dental practitioners, nurses and health professionals, especially concerned with the health of the schoolchild are eligible for membership, and members of the teaching profession, and those related to independent school management, for associate membership. The membership currently stands at 290.

The work of the Association

The Council meets three times a year and is chaired by the current President, Dr Stephen Haynes, MO to Bloxham School. MOSA council members are available for advice to members and non-members. Members have access to a secure online discussion forum where questions and topics are discussed giving access to up-to-date resources and peer support.

Two clinical meetings are arranged each year at a member school. Research projects are carried out individually and collectively. The Association strongly recommends that all independent schools appoint medical officers to carry out preventative medicine duties which are undertaken in maintained schools by the School Health Service.

MOSA Consultancy Service

MOSA offers a consultancy service for any school which will offer a review of the medical care provided within the school environment.

This can be tailored to the school's needs but tends to be one of two types:

- A general review of the overall medical/nursing provision in the school
- A review of a specific area of concern.

Initially there will be discussion between the MOSA team leader and the school representative so that the Terms of Reference can be drawn up. MOSA will then provide the necessary team to perform the investigation with the most suitably qualified professionals, being able to draw from a pool of highly experienced school doctors and nurses. The team will then visit the appropriate areas of the school and carry out any necessary interviews.

If you are interested in this service, please contact the Executive Secretary, email: mosa.execsec@gmail.com.

Publications

The Association publishes administrative and clinical guidelines for its Medical Officers and members; these are updated regularly and can be found on the Association's website.

For further information about the Association and other related business, enquiries should in the first instance be directed to *The Executive Officer*, email: mosa.execofficer@gmail.com

For administrative information and background please contact:
The Executive Secretary
Tel: 07928 562605 • email: mosa.execsec@gmail.com

THE ENGLISH-SPEAKING UNION

UK REGISTERED CHARITY NO. 273136

www.esu.org/sse

Secondary School Exchange Scholarships to the USA

A gap year with a difference – since 1928 the English-Speaking Union has offered young people the opportunity to spend a life-changing year at a private American high school.

The ESU offers three-term Secondary School Exchange (SSE) Scholarships:
- The closing date for applications is in February (in your final year of A Levels or equivalent)
- Interviews are in March
- Leave for the US in September (after completion of your A Levels or equivalent)

About the Scholarship

Each scholarship covers the cost of tuition, board and lodging, worth $40,000-$65,000. Scholars are fully fledged students at their host school, with access to world class facilities and a range of extra-curricular activities. Alumni of the programme include singer KT Tunstall, Sir Ian Blair, former Metropolitan Police Commissioner, Sir Richard Dearlove KCMG OBE, former head of MI6, 'City Superwoman' Nicola Horlick, the actress and comedienne Dawn French, and former HSBC chairman, Sir John Bond.

SSE is both an academic and cultural gap year programme. Scholars study a range of subjects at their host schools including some they dropped at GCSE, subjects they will study at university, and even subjects that don't feature in UK schools. The skills that can be gained from the exchange have proven to be beneficial at University: American teaching emphasises independence of thought, and discussions play a large part in the classroom. Scholars also enjoy American rites of passage such as spring break, prom, and graduation.

Scholars are responsible for additional costs including travel, insurance, and expenses. The ESU offers means-tested assistance to help towards these additional costs to successful applicants who would otherwise be unable to take up a scholarship. It also offers one full award, designed to cover all the additional costs related to the scholarship. Grants may be awarded. Many scholars use the summer holidays or the six-month gap between finishing school and leaving for the US to save money for their time abroad.

For further information please visit www.esu.org/programmes/secondary-school-exchange.

Eligibility
- You must have completed your A Levels (or equivalent) and be intending to study at a UK university on your return
  Your place does not need to be confirmed or deferred, and some scholars reapply during their scholarship year
- Applications from students intending to study at a US university at undergraduate level will not be accepted
- You must have a minimum of 3 Grade Cs at A Level or equivalent
- You should be under 19 years and 6 months old when you take up the scholarship
- Scholars are expected to commit to the full term of their scholarship (three-term: 9 months)
- You must be a British or Irish Citizen and have studied/be studying A Levels (or equivalent) at a school in the UK

About the English-Speaking Union

Founded in 1918, the ESU is an international educational charity and membership organisation that promotes oracy skills, mutual understanding, and fosters friendship and exchange throughout the world.

The English-Speaking Union
37 Charles Street, London W1J 5ED
Tel: 020 7529 1550 · email: rachel.fernandes@esu.org

PART I
Schools whose Heads are members of the Headmasters' and Headmistresses' Conference

ALPHABETICAL LIST OF SCHOOLS

The following schools, whose Heads are members of both HMC and GSA, can be found in the GSA section:

Badminton School
Edgbaston High School
Howell's School Llandaff
Lady Eleanor Holles
Notting Hill and Ealing High School
Redmaids High School
St Paul's Girls' School
St Swithun's School
South Hampstead High School
Wimbledon High School

HMC
GEOGRAPHICAL LIST OF SCHOOLS

Individual School Entries

Abingdon School

Park Road, Abingdon, Oxfordshire OX14 1DE

Tel:	01235 521563 School
	01235 849041 Admissions
	01235 849022 Finance and Operations
email:	heads.pa@abingdon.org.uk
	admissions@abingdon.org.uk
	bursars.sec@abingdon.org.uk
website:	www.abingdon.org.uk
Twitter:	@abingdonschool
Facebook:	@abingdonschool
Instagram:	@abingdon_school
LinkedIn:	/school/abingdonschool

The foundation of the School appears to date from the twelfth century; the first clear documentary reference occurs in 1256. After the dissolution of Abingdon Abbey, the School was re-endowed in 1563 by John Roysse, of the Mercers' Company in London. It was rebuilt in 1870 on its present site, and many further buildings have been added including extensive facilities for the arts, sport and a new science centre. A new sixth form centre, library and art department were added in 2018 and a further 3-storey building housing new facilities for the Business and Economics and Computer Science Departments opened in autumn 2020. Abingdon Preparatory School is situated close by at Frilford (*see entry in IAPS section*).

The total establishment numbers about 1,300 boys. In the Senior School there are about 1,060 boys aged 11–18, of whom approximately 137 are boarders. Boarding starts from age 13.

Boarding is organised in three houses: School House (Mr Mike Litchfield), Austin House (Mr James Golding) and Crescent House (Mr Matthew Kendry). The School values its boarding element very highly and weekly boarding features strongly as part of a policy aimed at asserting a distinctive regional identity for the School.

Pastoral Care. The Lower School has a self-contained system of pastoral care, led by the Lower School Housemaster. All boys join a senior house on entering the Middle School. Within the house system there are distinct tutoring arrangements for Middle School and Upper School boys, which are coordinated by the Middle Master and Upper Master respectively. Special emphasis is placed on the value of parental involvement and also on the provision of careers guidance at appropriate points in a boy's development. Great importance is attached to pastoral care and the School's teaching philosophy is based on a tutorial approach.

Land and Buildings. The School is surrounded by 35 acres of its own grounds, yet is within a few hundred yards of the historic centre of Abingdon, which lies 6 miles down the Thames from Oxford. A further 30 acres of playing fields are located at the Preparatory School, three miles from Abingdon. The School has additional extensive sports facilities at the Tilsley Park Sports Centre in Abingdon.

The last quarter-century has seen a considerable expansion in the School's stock of buildings with a new Sports Centre and impressive Science Centre which transformed the science facilities and enabled redevelopment of the existing science block for other subjects. In 2018 the sixth form facilities were given a tremendous boost with the opening of a new sixth form centre in Beech Court which also houses a new library and art department. Further facilities for Computing and Business and Economics opened in autumn 2020 along with additional houserooms.

Sports facilities have been greatly enhanced by the sports centre with a superb 8-lane swimming pool, fitness suites, classroom space, squash courts, climbing wall and a martial arts and fencing studio. This follows the opening of a beautiful timber-framed boathouse situated on the River Thames a short distance from the School. The School took over the lease for Tilsley Park Sports Centre which enhances the School's facilities still further with all-weather surfaces for rugby, hockey, football and athletics.

Courses of Study. The School is essentially academic in character and intention and levels of both expectation and achievement are high. Subjects taught include English, D&T, History, French, German, Spanish, Mandarin Chinese, Latin, Greek, Ancient History, Economics, Business Studies, Geography, Mathematics, Physics, Chemistry, Biology, Art, Religious Studies, Music and Theatre Studies. Over the last few years there has been increasing collaboration with the School of St Helen and St Katharine with joint tuition particularly in Theatre Studies, D&T, Economics and Government and Politics. The School is well equipped with computing facilities and audio-visual teaching aids.

All boys spend three years in the Middle School (13 to 16 year olds), in which many different subject combinations are possible, and there is no specialisation before the Sixth Form. In the Sixth Form many boys combine courses in arts and sciences; four subjects are normally taken in the first term of the Lower Sixth, followed by three or four in the Upper Sixth. Classroom teaching at all levels is supplemented by a programme of specialist lectures and outside visits. In general terms, the curriculum aims to combine academic discipline and excellence with the fullest encouragement of a wide range of interests and pursuits.

Games and Activities. The School enjoys some 80 acres of playing fields and has its own sports centre, swimming pool, fitness suites, climbing wall, squash and tennis courts and a boathouse on the River Thames. The major sports are rowing, rugby, cricket, hockey, football, tennis, athletics and cross-country. Particular success has been achieved recently in rugby, rowing, fencing, badminton, swimming and shooting. Other sports include sailing, golf and canoe polo.

Importance is attached to the development of a sense of social responsibility, through voluntary membership of Community Service and the Duke of Edinburgh's Award schemes. There is a contingent of the Combined Cadet Force based on voluntary recruitment.

There are numerous societies catering for all kinds of interests and enthusiasms. Music is particularly strong, with around half the boys taking instrumental or vocal lessons in school and 30 chamber ensemble groups including Chapel Choir, Choral Society and two orchestras.

Religion. Boys of all denominations are welcome, and normally attend, by year group, a short non-denominational service approximately once a week.

Health. The School has its own doctor and counselling service and there is a well-equipped health centre in the school grounds. In cases of emergency boys are admitted to one of the local hospitals.

Admission. The normal ages of entry to the Senior School are 11, 13 and 16; there are occasionally vacancies at other ages. About half of each year's intake enter the School at age 11 and most of the rest at age 13. Registration by the October of the year prior to joining is recommended. Abingdon Preparatory School has its own entrance arrangements (*see entry in IAPS section*).

Details of the entrance examination procedures for all age groups are available on the School's website. Entry to the Sixth Form, at 16, generally depends on promising GCSE grades and written tests where it is appropriate, as well as on interviews and a report from the previous school.

Term of Entry. September is the usual date of entry and is preferred by the School. Boys may be accepted in any of the three terms, if vacancies occur in their age group.

Fees per term (2021–2022). The tuition fee, for dayboys, is £7,200. This includes the cost of lunches and textbooks.

For boarders, the total fee (including tuition and all extras except for instrumental music lessons and some disbursements directly incurred by individual boys) is £11,990 (weekly) and £14,690 (full).

Scholarships and Bursaries. The School offers a number of scholarships and means-tested bursaries at ages 11, 13 and 16; Scholarships and awards categories include: Academic, All-Rounder, Music, Art and Design, Sport and Drama.

Full details are available, on application, from the Registry or from our website: www.abingdon.org.uk

The majority of awards are made at 13+ entry and are open to external and internal candidates. Some additional awards are available on entry to Sixth Form and to the Lower School. Scholarships carry an entitlement to a nominal fee remission of £300 per year plus remission of up to 100% of the tuition fee on a means-tested bursary basis. Music scholarships also carry an entitlement to remission on instrument tuition fees.

Honours. Numerous places are won each year at Oxford and Cambridge and on other highly selective university courses.

Old Abingdonian Club. Administrator: c/o Abingdon School.

Charitable status. Abingdon School Limited is a Registered Charity, number 1071298. It exists to provide educational opportunities which are open to talented boys without regard to their families' economic standing. Its curriculum is designed to promote intellectual rigour, personal versatility and social responsibility.

Governing Body:
Professor Michael Stevens (*Chairman*)
Mr Damian Tracey (*Vice Chairman*)

Mr Tom Ayling
Mr Robbie Barr
Mrs Glynne Butt

Mr Jonathan Carroll
Miss Penny Chapman
Mr Mike Farwell
Mr Mark Lascelles
Mr Matthew Tate
Mr Ken Welby
Ms Harriet Woollard

Clerk to the Governors: Mr Justin Hodges

Head: **Mr Michael Windsor**, BA Hons, MA, PGCE

Second Master: Mr David Dawswell, BSc
Deputy Head, Academic: Mr Graeme May, MA
Deputy Head, Pastoral: Mr Mark Hindley, LLB, UCL, MA
Director of Teaching & Learning: Mrs Ronnie Reading, BA
Chaplain: Revd Dr Simon Steer, BA, MDiv, PhD
Upper Master: Mr Nick O'Doherty, BSc
Middle Master: Mr Andrew Crisp, BA
Lower School Housemaster: Mr Adam Jenkins, BA
Director of eLearning: Mr Adam Treadaway, MA
Curriculum Director: Mr Oliver Lomax, MA
Master of Scholars: Dr Chris Burnand, MA, DPhil
Master i/c the Other Half: Mr Henry Morgan, MMath
Director of Partnerships: Mr Rob Southwell-Sander, BA, PGCE
Head of Wellbeing: Revd P D B Gooding, MA

Housemasters:

Boarders:
Head of Boarding and Crescent House: Mr Matthew Kendry, MA, MEng
School House: Mr Mike Litchfield, BSc
Austin House: Mr James Golding, BSc

Dayboys:
Mr David Border, BSc
Mr Tom Donnelly, BSc
Mr David Franklin, MA
Mr Simon James, MA
Mr Adam Jenkins, MA (*Lower School*)
Mrs Emily O'Doherty, MA
Mr Richard Pygott, MA, MSc, PGCE

Teaching Staff:
* *Head of Department*

Art and Design:
*Mr Paul Williamson, BA, PGCE
Mrs Sarah Brown, MFA, PGCE
Ms Elizabeth Hancock, BA
Mrs Emily O'Doherty, MA

Classics:
*Mr Hugh Price, BA
Dr Chris Burnand, MA, DPhil
Mr David Franklin, MA
Mr Oscar Hird, MA
Mr Adam Jenkins, MA
Mrs AJ McKend, BA, MA

Computer Science:
Dr A P Willis, BSc, PhD

Design and Technology:
*Mr Dan Hughes, BA
Mr David James, BEng, PGCE
Mr Mark Johnson, MEng
Mr Mike Webb, BSc

Drama:
*Mr Ben Phillips, BA
Mr Graeme May, MA
Mr Joe McDonnell, MA
Mr Jeremy Taylor, MA

Economics and Business Studies:
*Mr Tony Gray, BA
Mr Dean Evans, BA
Mr Simon Grills, BSc, MSc, MPhil
Dr Laura Haar, BSc, MA, PhD
Mr Adam Hepworth, BSc, PGCE
Mr Callum Richardson, BA

English:
*Mr Matthew Coolin, BA, MA, PGCE
Mrs Jo Bridgeworth, BA
Mrs Katherine Burrows, BA, MA
Mr Stuart Evans, BA
Mr Mark Hindley, LLB, MA
Miss K Isle, BA
Mr Andrew Jamison, BA, MLitt, PGCE
Mrs Mary-Rose Phillips-Grey, MA, PGCE
Miss Emma Williamson, BA, MA

Geography:
*Miss Amy Atkinson, BA
Mr Alex Axon, BA, PGCE
The Reverend Paul Gooding, MA, Dip Theo, Dip Min
Mr Peter Moore, BSc
Mr Nick O'Doherty, BSc
Mr Richard Pygott, MA, MSc, PGCE
Mr Robin Southwell-Sander, BA
Mr William Stockdale, MA
Mrs Kathy Yarker, BSc, PGCE

History:
*Mr Nicholas Knowland, BA, MA, PGCE
Mr Tom Allen, BA, PGCE
Mr Timothy Chase, BA
Mr Mark Earnshaw, BA, MA
Mr Richard Jackson, MA
Mr David McGill, BA
Mrs Lucy Moonen, MA, MSc, PGCE

Mathematics:
*Mrs Samantha Coull, BA, MA
Mr Nick Ball, BSc, PGCE
Mr Graham Cook, MMath
Mr David Dawswell, BSc, ACGI
Mr Julian Easterbrook, BA
Mrs Maris Elmore, MMath, PGCE
Mrs Eleanor Kaye, BSc
Mr Matthew Kendry, MA, MEng
Mr Henry Morgan, MMath
Mrs Catherine Muller, BSc
Mr Ben Murphy, MEng
Mr David Panter, MEng, PGCE
Mr Martin Poon, MMath
Mrs Behnoosh Sabah, BSc, PGCE
Mr Jason Taylor, DPhil

Modern Languages:
Mr James Ambrose, BA, MSt, DPhil
Mr Nathan Brittain, BA (*French*)
Mrs Maud Cottrell, PGCE
Mr Andrew Crisp, BA
Mrs Regina Engel-Hart, MA (*Spanish*)
Ms Raquel Fraile, MA

Mrs Victoria Middleton, MA
Mrs Sophie Payne, MA (*Spanish*)
Mrs Esther Peternek, MA, PGCE
Miss Sarah-Jane Poole, BSc (*German*)
Mrs Victoria Pradas Muñoz, BA
Mrs Ronnie Reading, BA, PGCE
Ms Alexandra von Widdern, BA
Ms Gao Zhang, MSc

Music:
*Mr Michael Stinton, MA, LRAM, ARCM
Mr Christopher Fletcher-Campbell, MA
Mr Jason Preece, BMus, MSt
Mrs Lynette Stulting
Mr Andrew Treadaway, BA, MA
Mr Andrew Yeats

Physical Education:
*Mr Pete Bignell, BEd
Mr Andrew Broadbent, BEd
Mr Elliot Birkbeck, BSc
Mr Mike Davies, BSc, MSc
Mr Tom Donnelly, BSc
Mr Matthew Gold, BA
Mr James Golding, BSc
Mr Steven Richards, MSc, PGCE

Philosophy and Theology:
*Mr Tom Eames-Jones, BA, PGCE
Mr Henry Barnes, BA
Miss Natalie Spurling-Holt, BA
The Reverend Dr Simon Steer, BA, MDiv, PhD
Miss Lucinda Whiteman, BA, PGCE

Psychology:
Mrs Elizabeth Guinney, BA, PGCE

Science:

Biology:
*Mr Ben Whitworth, BA
Mrs Rebecca Binnington, BSc, PGCE
Mr Simon Bliss, BSc
Mr Mathew Dempsey, BSc
Mrs Sarah Gibbard, BSc
Mr Richard Taylor, BA

Chemistry:
*Mr Michael Frampton, MA, DPhil
Mr David Border, BSc
Mr Richard Fisher, BSc
Mr Timothy Goodman, MBiochem, PGCE
Dr Rebecca Howe, MSc, DPhil
Mrs Kate Ley, BSc
Mr Mike Litchfield, BSc
Mr Ian Middleton, MA
Dr Mark Simpson, BA, MA, DPhil

Physics:
*Mr Ben Simmons, BSc
Mr Lawrence Barber, BSc
Mr John Brooks, BSc
Mr Chris Hack, MSci
Mr Simon James, MPhys
Mr Robert Jenkins, BSc
Mr Oliver Lomax, MA
Mr Kevin Magee, MSc
Mr Dan Mason, BSc
Miss Alice Perry, BSc
Miss Sarah Stringer, MSci
Mr Jeremy Thomas, BSc, MSc

Dr AP Willis, BSc, PhD

Librarians:
Dr Graham Gardner, BA, PhD
Mrs Wendy Hole, BSc
Mrs Lynn Mills

EFL:
*Miss Katy Lee, BSocSc, MEd
Ms Vanessa Clark, BSc
Mrs Amanda Streatfield, BEd

Learning Support:
*Mrs Sarah Beynon, MA, MSc
Mrs Celia Collins, MA
Mrs Hettie Preiss-Chapman, BA

Director of Finance and Operations: Mr Justin Hodges, MSc

Director of Admissions and Marketing: Mrs Jane Jørgensen, MA

AKS Lytham
United Learning

Clifton Drive South, Lytham St Annes, Lancashire FY8 1DT

Tel: 01253 784100
email: headmaster@akslytham.com
          info@akslytham.com
website: www.akslytham.com
Twitter: @aksschool
Facebook: @AKSSchoolLytham
Instagram: @aks_lytham

In September 2012, Arnold (Blackpool) and KEQMS (Lytham) merged as ArnoldKEQMS (AKS), part of the United Learning group of independent schools and academies. With over 300 years of history and tradition, the school has a reputation for high standards and excellence in achievement, both academic and non-academic, as well as encouraging participation within an inclusive and caring community environment. Hockey has triumphed at national level, while rugby and drama also hold prestigious awards, and music has an international reputation. Sports teams tour in the UK, Europe and the Southern Hemisphere, and a large number of pupils participate in the Duke of Edinburgh's Award scheme at bronze, silver and gold level. The school also has a popular CCF and a thriving House structure, and charity features prominently in school actions, both in support of local needs as well as international needs. AKS is also a full global member of Round Square International.

Our Location. AKS dominates an impressive position in Lytham, overlooking the sand dunes and the Fylde coast. Preston, the Ribble Valley, the Lake District and Manchester are all within easy reach by direct motorway.

Our Opportunities. Through our membership of United Learning all teaching staff benefit from a high standard of professional training. All schools within the United Learning group communicate frequently and mutual support is always available, at all levels. International exchange opportunities are available through Round Square.

Our Co-curricular. Whilst the pursuit of high academic standards is undoubtedly important, all our pupils take advantage of the broad range of experience which our school offers, to nurture creativity and to encourage a spirit of voluntary contribution to the school and the wider community. Our main games are rugby, football, hockey, cricket and athletics, with strong fixture lists and several national and regional titles. This extensive programme provides competition and challenge for all pupils and touring sides have travelled as far afield as Argentina, Chile, the Caribbean, Canada, Australia and South Africa. As well as sport we also offer a Combined Cadet Force, Duke of Edinburgh's Award, Tycoon in Schools, World Challenge, debating, dance, chess and much more. Drama and music also feature prominently and inspire countless pupils each year to take part in top-quality productions, concerts and recitals.

Admission. Prospectus and Admissions forms can be obtained from the Admissions Secretary.

All entries to the Senior School are made through the Headmaster. Pupils are admitted to the Senior School on the basis of the School's own examinations in English, Mathematics and Non-Verbal Reasoning. The main intake to the Senior School is at 11, though entry at other times is possible depending on availability of places.

For entry at Sixth Form level, respectable GCSE grades in at least five subjects are normally expected in addition to a satisfactory report from the pupil's current Head.

Entry into the Nursery and Preparatory School (2–11 years) is normally at the ages of 2, 4 and 7. Enquiries should be made to the Admissions Secretary (01253 784104).

Fees per term (2021–2022). Tuition (including books and stationery): Seniors £4,336; Preparatory £3,265. Extras are minimal.

Entrance Scholarships. Several scholarships (including those for Music, Drama and Sport) are available for entry at 11+ and in the Sixth Form. Bursaries and Assisted Places are also available. Further particulars from the Admissions Secretary (01253 784104).

Registration. Pupils may be registered at any time although this should be as early as possible if entry is requested at ages other than 2, 4, 7 or 11 years. Candidates will be called for examination in the year of entry, although those who live at a distance may have the papers sent to their schools.

Charitable status. AKS is part of United Learning which comprises: UCST (a Company Limited by Guarantee, Registered in England, number 2780748, and a Registered Charity, number 1016538) and ULT (a Company Limited by Guarantee, Registered in England, number 4439859, and an Exempt Charity).

Mrs C Dineley, BA Hons
Mr S McNicholas
Mr G Melling, BSc Hons, MRICS, MFPWS
Mrs Z Fleming, LLB, TEP
Mr D Littler

Bursar and Clerk to the Governors: Mrs A Sanderson

Senior School Management:

Headmaster: Mr D A Harrow, MA

Deputy Head: Mr A McKeown, BSc
Head of Nursery and Preparatory School: Mrs A Ilhan, BEd
Director of External Relations: Mrs A Brown, BSc, MSc, CPsychol, CIPD, eMBA
Admissions Secretary: Mrs E Wyatt
Head of Sixth Form: Mr K Maund, BA
Head of Middle School: Mr P Rudd, BSc
Head of Lower School: Mrs H House, BA
Assistant Head (Pastoral): Mr P Hayden, BA
Assistant Head (Teaching & Learning): Dr C Jessop, BSc, PhD
Assistant Head (Curriculum & Organisation): Mr D Culpan, BSc
Assistant Head (Staff & Student Development): Mrs F Marland, BA
Examinations Officer: Mr P Klenk, BA

Head of Art: Mrs J Wild, BA
Head of Biology: Mr S Downey, BSc
Head of Business Education: Mr G McIntyre, BA
Head of Careers: Mr K Maund, BA
Head of Chemistry: Dr C Jessop, BSc, PhD
Head of Computing: Mr D Culpan, BSc
Head of DT: Ms S Burke, BA Hons
Head of English: Mr J Bridges, BA
Head of Geography: Mr N O'Loughlin, MA
Head of History: Mr I Cowlishaw, BA
Head of Learning Support: Mrs E Luke, BEd
Head of Mathematics: Mr L Sobey, BSc
Head of MFL: Mrs F Burnett, BA
Director of Performing Arts: Mr M Waterhouse, BMus
Head of Physics: Mr J Riding, BEng
Head of PSHE: Mrs H House, BA
Head of Psychology: Mr S Collings, BA, MSc
Head of RS: Mr L Donovan, BA Hons
Head of Science: Mr S Downey, BSc
Director of Sport: Mr M Walmsley, BSc

Alleyn's School

Townley Road, Dulwich, London SE22 8SU

Tel: 020 8557 1500
email: enquiries@alleyns.org.uk
website: www.alleyns.org.uk
Twitter: @Alleyns_School
Facebook: @Alleynsschool
Instagram: @alleyns_school

Motto: *God's Gift*

Alleyn's is one of London's leading co-educational day schools for girls and boys aged 11–18, where academic excellence goes hand-in-hand with an extensive co-curriculum and the strongest possible pastoral care. Celebrating the School's 400th anniversary in 2019, we are a progressive community, built on a long and proud heritage in the heart of London.

Our holistic approach to education aims to nurture every pupil to fulfil their potential while making lasting friendships and enjoying life to the full.

Entrance. A registration fee of £150 is charged for applications. This fee is waived for applicants who qualify for the Pupil Premium. Candidates should be registered for the School before mid-October for 16+ and late October for 11+ entry for admission the following September.

Prospective entrants to Year 7 will complete the ISEB Common Pre-test in November, either at their own school or at Alleyn's. Candidates who reach a satisfactory standard in this test will be invited to complete Alleyn's own entrance examination in January. The examination consists of English and Mathematics papers. Children whose assessment results and school report demonstrate that they will flourish both inside and outside the classroom at Alleyn's will then be invited for interview.

For entry at 16+, the examination is in early November and all candidates sit three general papers that test their skills in Critical Writing, and Qualitative and Quantitative Reasoning, regardless of their A Level choices. Candidates reaching a satisfactory standard in the assessments will be invited for interviews consisting of a general interview plus three interviews in three of their A level subject choices. All candidates are considered for an academic scholarship.

Fees per term (2021–2022). £7,125 (£21,375 per annum).

Scholarships, Exhibitions and Bursaries.

Academic Scholarships, worth up to £5,000 p.a., are available at 11+ and 16+ and are awarded based on the results of the entrance examination and interview. They are not means-tested and can also be awarded in conjunction with bursaries.

Music Scholarships, worth up to £5,000 p.a. plus free tuition on principal instrument, are available at both entry points, and *Music Exhibitions* (free tuition on principal instrument) are available at 11+.

Art and DT Scholarships, worth up to £2,000 p.a. respectively, are available at 11+.

Sports Scholarships, worth up to £5,000 p.a., and *Sports Exhibitions* (£250 p.a.) are available at 11+.

Bursaries: Means-tested bursary places (up to 100% of the School fees) are available at 11+ and 16+ for academically able candidates whose families might not otherwise be able to afford the fees. In addition, the W. J. Smith Trust offers means-tested bursary assistance (up to 100% of the School fees) to candidates who demonstrate exceptional music promise at the musical scholarship audition.

Curriculum. All pupils follow a broad and balanced curriculum in the first three years, including English, Mathematics, Modern Languages, Latin, Biology, Chemistry, Physics, Geography, History, Religious Studies, Art, Computing, Music, Design Technology, Food & Nutrition, Drama, Dance, and the Alleyn's Learners' Programme. In Years 10 and 11, pupils take nine, ten or 11 GCSE subjects including English, English Literature, Mathematics, Biology, Chemistry, Physics and one Modern Foreign Language. In addition, they choose three further subjects from a broad range of options.

In Year 12, students take four subjects and in Year 13 they study three or four A Levels. In addition to those subjects listed above, Classical Civilisation, Economics, Further Mathematics, Classical Greek, Latin, History of Art, Film Studies, Philosophy, Politics, Psychology, Physical Education and Drama and Theatre Studies are also available.

Almost all our students go on to top UK universities, including Oxford and Cambridge, and to study Medicine, but every year students will also successfully gain places on prestigious music and drama courses, Foundation Art programmes or choose to study overseas (in Canada and the USA). Our hope and aim is that every student is encouraged to apply for the path that best suits them.

Organisation. The Lower School (Years 7 and 8) has its own building and its own Head. The Middle School (Years 9 to 11) and Upper School (Years 12 and 13) each has its own Head, and pupils from Year 9 up belong to one of eight Houses. Each Head of House is responsible, under the leadership of the Head of School section, for the welfare of each of their pupils during their time in the School. This care is supplemented by a system of form tutors for supervision of academic progress and pastoral support. Parents are invited to Consultation Evenings during the year, at which pupils' work and progress are discussed with the teaching staff. From Year 10 upwards, the children also attend these evenings.

PE and Games. Innovative strategies in teaching and learning, coupled with a forward-thinking performance programme that takes a holistic and values-driven approach, enables high-end performers to excel on and off the pitch, providing numerous opportunities for all to engage in a wide and varied range of activities. That Alleyn's can compete at the very highest level in numerous sports and has claimed several national championships in recent years is – apart from benefiting from excellent sports facilities – the happy coincidence of a committed, dedicated and skilled department supported unreservedly by senior leaders.

Religious Education. Alleyn's is a Church of England Foundation and warmly welcomes girls and boys from all backgrounds, whatever their faith position. Religious Education of a non-denominational nature is given throughout the School, and pupils attend worship in assembly and once each term in the Foundation Chapel or in St Barnabas Church. The Chaplain holds voluntary Holy Communion Services during term time. Pupils, if they wish, are prepared for Confirmation in an annual service. The Chaplain is assisted by an Assistant Chaplain and the Chaplaincy area is a place of relaxation and reflection.

Facilities. The original building dates from 1887. In addition, there is a RIBA London award-winning Lower School, accommodating Years 7 and 8, a fully-equipped sports hall, with cutting-edge weights and fitness suite, a refurbished deck-level swimming pool (with a tiered viewing gallery and Olympic timing system), an art department with kiln and multimedia art provision, a technology centre, a music school, two digital language laboratories, a large library, a refurbished science block with rooftop observatory, a brand new multi-use games area, a second all-weather playing surface, seven netball courts, eight football pitches, a sports hall and pavilion, a gym, computer rooms and a RIBA award-winning learning and performing arts centre (the Edward Alleyn Building), containing a 350-seat theatre, a Sixth Form study centre, lecture theatre, film classroom, and a studio for the National Youth Theatre.

Music, Drama, Art and Dance feature very strongly in the life of the School. There are various major concerts each year, including an annual concert at St John's Smith Square and a Jazz Night at the Hideaway club. There are multiple orchestras, bands, and choirs, including over 30 Chamber groups. A number of dramatic productions are staged each year, from the Lower, Middle and Upper School plays to our student-led Bear Pit productions, including shows that Middle and Upper School pupils have regularly taken to the Edinburgh Fringe. Dance is strong; there are currently five different Dance Companies and the standard of choreography is very high. The annual Dance Show regularly features over 120 boys and girls from across the year groups. Art plays a prominent role in life at Alleyn's. There is the exciting annual summer art exhibition that showcases ambitious GCSE and A Level works that range from impressive paintings and sculpture to installation and film exploring a range of concepts and contemporary issues. In addition, there are other exhibitions and art events throughout the year. Pupils' work forms part of a permanent display around School and large billboards with their work adorn the playgrounds.

Co-curricular Activities. Pupils are offered a wide range of co-curricular activities each term. There are 60 weekly sports clubs (not counting matches and fixtures which involve over 150 teams playing more than 1,200 competitive games across the year), including mixed Cricket and Football, Water Polo, Gymnastics, Lacrosse and Fives, in addition to Hockey, Basketball, Netball, Athletics, Tennis and Swimming. There are plenty of opportunities for Music, Drama and Dance, including the Technical and Creative Team, individual music lessons and LAMDA. There are more than 180 exciting and diverse co-curricular options to choose from outside the classroom, including Cookery, Molecular Gastronomy, Art, Design, Film and Photography, Classics, Debating, Alleyn's Radio, Podcast Club, Gardening, Model United Nations and Science.

Pupils can choose an optional year of **Combined Cadet Force (CCF)** in Year 9 and then choose between **CCF, The Duke of Edinburgh's Award** and **Volunteering** in the community in Year 10. Many students continue and develop these options further throughout their Sixth Form years. A dynamic and evolving careers programme is available for Alleyn's pupils throughout their time at School. Co-created with pupils, parents and staff and led by a qualified careers guidance professional, this includes work experience, guidance interviews and aptitude tests, interaction with employers, employability programmes, exploration of how careers link to the academic curriculum, a programme of careers lessons, talks and more.

A School Council and Learning Council, with members from each section of the School, represent pupils' views to the Headmaster. There are other pupils' committees discussing life at School, lunches and co-curricular activities.

Relations with Parents. The Alleyn's Parents' Association is a dynamic and enthusiastic parent organisation which nurtures close links between parents and the School and raises considerable funds for the benefit of the whole School community.

The Edward Alleyn Club. The official foundation meeting of the Edward Alleyn Club was held on 18 April 1884. All past pupils are given membership to the Edward

Alleyn Club. This enables them to take part in sporting and social activities and receive regular updates from the School, including a biannual newsletter and invitations to year group reunions, bespoke networking events and important fundraising activities.

Charitable status. Alleyn's School is a Registered Charity, number 1161864, and a Charitable Company Limited by Guarantee, registered in England and Wales, number 09401357. Registered office: Townley Road, SE22 8SU.

Chair of Governors: Mr I Barbour, BSc Econ Hons, ACIB

Head: **Mrs Jane Lunnon**, BA Bristol

Senior Deputy Head: Mr Andy Skinnard, MA Oxon
   (*Designated Lead for Safeguarding*)
Deputy Head (*Personnel & Administration*): Ms S P
   Chandler, BSc, PG Dip
Deputy Head (*Academic*): Mrs A McAuliffe, BA

Assistant Heads:
Head of Upper School: Dr R C J Atkinson, PhD, MSci, MA
   Cantab
Co-Curricular & Partnerships: Mr N J G Green, BEd
Teaching & Learning: Mrs C L Heindl, BA
Head of Middle School: Mrs M A Joel, BA
Director of Studies: Mr A J Sproat-Clements, MA Cantab
Head of Lower School: Ms L Thornton, BA

Bursar: Mr S R Born, BA
Director of Finance: Mrs C Morgan, BSc, FCA
Registrar: Ms L Mawer, LLB

Ardingly College
A Woodard School

Haywards Heath, West Sussex RH17 6SQ

Tel: 01444 893000
email: head@ardingly.com
website: www.ardingly.com
Twitter: @ArdinglyCollege
Facebook: @ArdinglyCollegeUK
LinkedIn: /school/ardingly-college

Motto: *Beati Mundo Corde*

History and Development of the College. Ardingly College, the third of Nathaniel Woodard's schools, was founded in Shoreham in 1858 and moved to its present, beautiful 230-acre site in Mid Sussex, about halfway between Gatwick and Brighton, in 1870. The College now consists of a Nursery, Pre-Prep day School, a weekly boarding and day Prep School for boys and girls between the ages of 2 and 13 and a boarding and day Senior School for boys and girls aged between 13 and 18.

There are over 1,000 pupils at Ardingly College split between the Prep School, Senior School and Sixth Form. There is a relatively even balance between boys and girls and boarders and day pupils.

Academic. Ardingly has an excellent academic record. Both the International Baccalaureate and A Levels are offered.

Results for 2021. 82% A*–A in A Levels. Our IB Diploma mean grade was an outstanding 41.3. 100% of university applicants gained entry to their first or second choice university, 83% to Russell Group.

Top 50 A Level ranking among UK independent schools.

Curriculum. In Year 9 a broad curriculum is offered with a wide range of subject options at GCSE, including Triple, Dual and Single science.

Sixth Form Curriculum: IB, A level and BTEC are all offered. Electives are also taken for the joy of learning, including Criminology, Anthropology and Astronomy.

Pastoral. As of 2022 Senior School starts at Year 7. Year 7 & 8 are knows as the Lower School and have 4 Co-ed houses. Year 9 – Lower VI Boys and Girls join one of 9 single sex, day or boarding houses. In the Upper Sixth all boys and girls transfer to a separate, integrated co-educational House, Godwin Hall, in which they are able to concentrate more fully on their studies and where they are given greater responsibility and independence to better prepare them for life at University and the outside world. Each House has its own Housemaster or Housemistress. From Year 9 they have Academic House Tutors, including day houses. Every boy and girl has a Tutor who has responsibility for their work, progress, choices and many other aspects of the pupil's life. Tutorials are regular: weekly group tutorials and regular individual tutorials. PHSE is also taught and includes social media use plus general life skills.

There is an efficient Health and Wellness Centre located in the heart of the campus with qualified medical staff.

Expressive Arts.

Music: Choir, Chamber Choir, *Schola Cantorum*, Jazz Choir, Orchestras, Concert Band and Chamber Music. Instrumental lessons are taken by over half of the pupils.

Art: Painting, drawing, printing, ceramics, sculpture, fashion & textiles, photography and etching.

Design Technology: Real design problems solved in a variety of materials and forms.

Photography: Offered at A Level.

Drama: Four productions in the course of the year for all ages. Large flexible theatre space and drama teaching studios including a new Dance studio.

Dance

The expressive arts are studied throughout Year 9, are offered as options for GCSE and A Level and scholarships for talented candidates are available at 11+, 13+ and 16+.

Sport. Boys play Football, Hockey, Cricket, Tennis, Athletics; Girls play Hockey, Netball, Tennis, Athletics, with Football and Cricket also available. Hockey and Football are particularly strong at Ardingly College with many country and regional competitions won, including historically the 1XI ISFA National Boodles Cup, the most prestigious title in independent schools football. Ardingly prides itself on developing its teams in extra coaching sessions, without compromising studies.

There is also Cross Country, Swimming, Golf, Volleyball, Basketball, Badminton, Sailing, rowing etc. Over 130 clubs and societies are on offer.

The indoor pool is open to both Prep and Senior School pupils. There is a high-achieving competitive swim team and Olympian Karen Pickering heads up the Swim provision.

Activities. Extensive Enrichment Programme, The Duke of Edinburgh's Award, Astronomy, Debating and Charity Focus, which includes overseas trips to Kenya and India.

Admission to the Senior School can take place at 11+, 13+ and 16+.

ISEB Common Pre-Test is taken in the Michaelmas Term of Year 6, with offers made in the March of Year 6 for Year 9 entry. Common Entrance is used for setting purposes, but not for admission. We also require a report and reference from the pupil's previous school. The Head of College or the Head of Senior School will interview prospective pupils and there is a full assessment day.

The selection of candidates for direct entry to the Sixth Form takes place in November of the year prior to entry. All candidates sit a pre-screener CAT test, if selected, they go forward to an assessment day to include testing and an interview. A report and reference is also required. Places will then be offered subject to GCSE results and specific subject entry requirements.

The Prep School has entry at any time between the ages of 7 and 9.

Scholarships. A number of Scholarships are offered for annual competition at 11+, 13+ and 16+. They include Academic, Art, Drama, Music and Sports Awards. The Prep School offers Academic, Art, Music and Sports Awards at 11+. All can be supplemented by a means-tested bursary if required.

Please address all enquiries about admissions, scholarships and bursaries to the Admissions department via email at registrar@ardingly.com.

Term of Entry. Main entry intake is September. Intake at other ages and other times on an individual basis.

Registration. The School Prospectus is on our website: www.ardingly.com

Registration can be made at any age, subject to the availability of places. No separate registration is required for children transferring from the Prep to the Senior School.

Fees per term (2021–2022). Boarding Year 9–Sixth £12,111–£12,552, Flexi Boarding Year 9–11 £10,335, Day Pupils Year 9–Sixth £8,395. Day Pupils Year 3–8 £4,727–£5,874.

Fees are inclusive.

Further Particulars. For further information, please contact: registration@ardingly.com

Charitable status. Ardingly College Limited is a Registered Charity, number 1076456. It exists to provide high-quality education for boys and girls aged 2½ to 18.

School Council:

Mr Robert Haynes Brown, BSc, MSc (*Chairman and Chair of Education and Nominations Committees*)

Mrs Jane Armstrong, BA Hons (*Governor with Responsibility for Development*)

Mrs Sophie V Bradshaw, BA Hons

Mrs Siân L Champkin, LLB

Mr Guy W Dixon, BA Hons, DipTP, MRTPI (*Chair of Estates, Governor with Responsibility for Health & Safety*)

Mr Mark Dixon, BSc Hons, PGCE

Ms Veera Johnson, MBA

Mr Douglas H T Johnson-Poensgen, BEng Hons (*Chair of Finance & General Purposes, Governor with responsibility for ICT*)

Dr Simon Kay, PhD (*Governor with Responsibility for Compliance*)

Mrs Louise E Lindsay, FCIPD, LLM, BA Hons (*Chair of the Education Committee, Governor with Responsibility for Safeguarding*)

Mrs Emily Martin, MSc Hons

Mrs Jenny Martin, MA

Mr Richard Martin

Ms Kate E C Sweeney, MA

Provost: Rt Revd Jonathan Meyrick

Head of College: Mr Ben Figgis, MA, MEd

Head of Senior School: Mr James Johnson, BA, MPhil
Deputy Head Academic: Mrs Georgina A Stafford, MA
Deputy Head Pastoral & Co-Curricular: Mrs Joanna M Hayter, BSC
Deputy Head Staff & Operations: Mrs Nicola Burns, BSc
Assistant Head Pupil Welfare: Miss Leonie Gurd, BSc
Head of Middle School: Mr Chris Quayle, BA, MEd
Head of Staff Development – Teaching: Mr Daniel Davies, BSC
Head of Academic Systems: Mr Marco Couch, MSci
Director of Admissions, Marketing & Communications: Mrs Pamela Bower-Nye, BA, DipM, MCIM, FIDM
Head of the Prep School: Harry Hastings, BA Hons, MEd Oxon

Ashford School
United Learning

East Hill, Ashford, Kent TN24 8PB

Tel:	01233 625171
email:	registrar@ashfordschool.co.uk
website:	www.ashfordschool.co.uk
Twitter:	@AshfordSchool
Facebook:	@AshfordSchool
Instagram:	@AshfordSchool
LinkedIn:	/ashford-school

Ashford School, founded in 1898, is a dynamic environment in which our students are inspired by our adventurous approach to learning.

Ashford School is an independent co-educational day and boarding school for children from 3 months to 18 years old, situated in the heart of Kent and just 37 minutes from London. We offer an exceptional and inspiring education in which all pupils can be happy and successful. Based on two sites, the School includes: Bridge Nursery (3 months to 3 years) and Ashford Senior School (Years 7–13) on East Hill in Ashford, and 2½ miles away we have The Stables Nursery (3 months to 3 years) and Ashford Prep School (3 to 11 years) in the village of Great Chart. We have a broad, vibrant, outward-looking educational approach which has become Ashford School's hallmark.

Our learning is underpinned by four key factors, namely *Celebrating Individuality, Optimising Potential, Academic Rigour* and *Adventurous Learning*. We believe that learning should be challenging, motivating and lead to a sense of fulfilment, which is why we strive to provide an inspiring environment that encourages growth and adventure so that our students can develop into all they are capable of being.

Our School is made up of a diverse community of staff and children from all over the world. We embrace individual talent and consider our School to be a place where students and staff are inspired and in turn inspire others. There are over 500 students in the Senior School (11–18) and a similar number in the Prep School and nurseries (0–11). At full capacity there are 170 boarders in the Senior School, mostly from overseas, cared for by several resident teachers and support staff; 24 nationalities are represented.

Ashford School is growing on the back of a reputation for innovation and quality – we were voted *Independent School of the Year* in 2010/11 and have been shortlisted for the same award twice since. Several of our staff have won national awards for excellence. Most recently, this year we have been shortlisted for the *TES Student Initiative of the Year* award and the *Independent School Parent Community Initiative of the Year* award. Our staff have a diverse range of experiences and many teachers and support staff have enjoyed successful first careers in other walks of life. From journalists, to barristers, to naval architects and to economists; Ashford is a School which values different life experiences and actively seeks out those who can share different passions.

Academic Success. Ashford takes pride in its emphasis on academic rigour, and are students are taught by passionate subject specialists throughout the Senior School. Ashford also has a strong tradition of academic success. In recent years, over 20% of students have consistently secured places at one of the UK's top ten universities and over 50% at Russell Group institutions. Typically about 85% have achieved places at their firm-choice university, with 95 securing their firm or insurance choice. Over the last three years, approximately 80% of A Levels taken were graded A/B, over 50% were graded A*/A.

At GCSE, students typically study nine GCSEs including a modern foreign language and separate sciences (Biology, Chemistry and Physics) at either dual or triple-award level.

At A Level, students have a choice of over 20 subjects; incorporating the courses most valued by the leading universities; students normally study three or four A levels and may add other qualifications such as the EPQ and BTEC. Underpinning our academic philosophy is a commitment to stretch and challenge all students, reflected best by our four learning habits, which are woven throughout academic life at the school. The School consistently achieves high valued added scores at both levels.

Co-Curricular. The School prides itself on the extensive range of co-curricular activities – over 80 are offered in total. The dominant areas of the programme are sport, music, drama and outdoor activities. The School has received national and regional recognition in many areas of sport and other activities.

Campus and Facilities. The School is located on two sites – a few miles apart. The Senior School occupies a 25+ acre site in a prominent position close to the centre of Ashford and near to the International Station. It is a green and secure haven in a busy and growing commuter town. There are good rail, road and bus links to Ashford and London (37 minutes) and the School operates its own bus services to outlying villages.

The Senior School has playing fields on-site, together with a newly opened Sports Centre, gym, fitness suite, an indoor swimming pool, floodlit AstroTurf, tennis and netball courts, boarding houses, and dining hall. The School enjoys all the specialist teaching facilities you would expect of an independent school and we have embarked on a programme to refurbish and extend our facilities as we grow. Over the last ten years, this has included the partial refurbishment of boarding, the creation of new maths classrooms, atrium café, language laboratory and classrooms, learning centre and fitness suite.

The Bridge Nursery is also located on this site and benefits from the proximity to the Senior School, as well as having its own dedicated and well-resourced accommodation and staff.

The Prep School and Stables Nursery sits in a stunning location on the edge of the village of Great Chart, with modern and specialist facilities. The Stables Nursery was opened in 2020 and is an inspiring, state-of-the-art Early Years facility. The Prep School itself is a very modern, well-resourced environment which presents a stimulating, purpose-built learning space for the pupils. The Prep School comprises: two Halls, specialist music, science, art, DT and food rooms in addition to a wonderful library and extensive outdoor play areas. The vast outdoor sports facilities extend over the beautiful 35-acre site, enhanced by a recently completed pavilion and changing facility. There is also a floodlight AstroTurf, swimming pool and Sports Hall.

Entry Requirements. Please visit the Admissions section of our website for all details about entrance requirements and the process you will need to follow to apply for a place at Ashford School.

Scholarships. Academic, Art, Sport, Music and Drama scholarships are available for Years 7, 9 and 12. Please visit our website for further information.

Fees per term (2021–2022). Reception, Years 1 & 2: £3,605; Years 3 to 6: £5,200; Years 7 to 13: £6,098. Full boarding (Years 7 to 13 only): £12,926

Our fees are all-inclusive. There are no compulsory extras to pay for at the end of the term, allowing you to budget with confidence. Where relevant, fees include lunches for day pupils/children and all meals for boarders, as well as most books, equipment and compulsory visits. Public examinations, such as GCSEs, A Levels and music exams, are charged as extras in arrears. All fees are payable in advance of the start of each term in September, January and April.

Charitable Status. Ashford School is part of United Learning which comprises: UCST (a Company Limited by Guarantee, Registered in England, number 2780748, and a Registered Charity, number 1016538) and ULT (a Company Limited by Guarantee, Registered in England, number 4439859, and an Exempt Charity).

Governing Body:
Chair: Mrs D Geering
Professor P Freemont
Mr A Richards
Mr J B Rimmer
Mrs E Rose
Mr M Sutton
The Ven S Taylor
Ms S Morris
Ms N Ratchford

Head: Mr Michael Hall, BA Liverpool, MA

Head of the Senior School: Mr Michael Hall, BA Liverpool, MA
Senior Deputy Head: Ms N Timms, BEng Loughborough

Deputy Head, Academic: Mrs J Russell, BA Leeds
Deputy Head, Co-Curricular and Community Partnerships:
    Mr T Wilde, MA Warwick, BSc Brighton

Head of Ashford Prep School: Mr Nick Tiley-Nunn
Deputy Head, Teaching and Learning: Mrs R Clifford, BSc
Deputy Head, Pastoral: Mr C Neesham, BA

Bablake and King Henry VIII School

Part of the Coventry School Foundation

BKHS Bablake Senior
Coundon Road, Coventry CV1 4AU

Tel: 024 7627 1200
email: info.bablake@bkhs.org.uk
Twitter: @BKHSBablake
Facebook: @BKHSBablake

BKHS King Henry VIII Senior
Warwick Road, Coventry CV3 6AQ

Tel: 024 7627 1111
email: info.khviii@bkhs.org.uk
Twitter: @BKHSKHVIII
Facebook: @BKHSKingHenryVIII

website: www.bkhs.org.uk

BKHS brings together the rich heritages of Bablake and King Henry VIII schools. The School continues the tradition of an exceptional education within the city, built upon outstanding opportunities, superb teaching and learning, and strong pastoral care.

The School is represented on the Headmasters' Conference and on the Association of Governing Bodies of Independent Schools. The governing body is the Coventry School Foundation, on which are represented Sir Thomas White's Charity, the Coventry Church Charities, Coventry General Charities and Birmingham, Coventry, Oxford and Warwick Universities. There are also several co-opted Governors.

BKHS Bablake was originally part of the College of the same name founded by Queen Isabella in 1344. After the dissolution of the monasteries, it was refounded in 1560 by the city; it is chiefly associated with the name of Thomas Wheatley, whose indentures of 1563 put its finances on a firm foundation.

Number in School. There are approximately 746 Day Pupils (including 198 in the Sixth Form) and 360 in the Preparatory School and Pre Prep.

BKHS Bablake Facilities. On the 11-acre site stands the main buildings, which have been considerably extended to include a Sports Centre, heated indoor swimming pool and a purpose-built Modern Languages Block and a purpose-built English, Music and Drama Block. For further details of the Prep and Pre Prep, also on this site, *see* BKHS Prep and Pre Prep entry in IAPS section. There are 27 acres of playing fields, a large pavilion, and two all-weather hockey pitches located a mile from the School.

BKHS King Henry VIII was founded in 1545 by John Hales, Clerk of the Hanaper to the King, under Letters Patent of King Henry VIII.

Number in School. There are approximately 611 Day Pupils (including 202 in the Sixth Form) and 380 in the Preparatory School.

BKHS King Henry VIII Facilities. The School moved to its present site in Coventry in 1885. The Governors have continually improved, extended and restored the buildings which are well equipped to cope with the demands of an up-to-date, relevant and challenging curriculum. The School has extensive playing fields, some of which are located on the main site, other fields are ten minutes away by minibus.

The School has an Art facility, a Sixth Form Centre, a Sports Hall, a six-lane, 25m swimming pool, and fitness suite. There is also a dedicated Archive room containing a timeline from 1545 to 2014 and original Tudor artefacts.

BKHS Curriculum. The curriculum is broad and balanced, integrating National Curriculum principles and practices where appropriate. The Senior School curriculum provides courses leading to the GCSE examinations and A levels. Subjects available currently are Art, Biology, Business Studies, Chemistry, Classical Civilisation, Computer Science, Drama and Theatre Studies, Economics, English, French, Food and Nutrition, Geography, German, History, Latin, Law, Mathematics (and Further Mathematics), Music, Philosophy, Religion and Ethics, Photography, Psychology, Physics, and Spanish. All pupils follow a structured PSHE course. Separate sciences are taught up to IGCSE. Most pupils study 10 subjects at GCSE, the majority progressing into the Sixth Form where the A level curriculum is followed, with three subjects being examined at the end of the two years. All students study an academic enrichment programme, leading to an additional qualification, for example an Extended Project Qualification (EPQ). Physical Education and Sport are also considered to be a vital part of the curriculum and are available as an A level option.

Courses in Key Skills/Complementary Studies and Critical Thinking are offered in the Sixth Form. There is a wide range of Enrichment Studies options including Art, Astronomy, Chinese, Computing, Cookery, Design, Drama, Music, Photography and many others.

Examination results at all levels are excellent.

BKHS Games. Rugby, Hockey, Netball, Basketball, Cross-Country, Athletics, Rounders, Tennis, Cricket, Swimming, and Orienteering. The School has an extensive artificial turf games area, used mainly for hockey, but providing an additional 24 tennis courts (in the summer).

BKHS Co-Curricular Activities. The School is noted for the excellence of its sport, music, drama, debating, public speaking and outdoor pursuits. All pupils are encouraged to contribute to the extracurricular life of the School. The School has close connections with many universities including Oxford and Cambridge. All pupils are involved in the charity work of the School and there is a large Community Service programme for the Senior pupils in Year 11 and the Sixth Form.

BKHS Admission. Entry is via the School's own Entrance Examination held annually in October for entrance the following September. The normal age of entry is 11 but there are smaller intakes at 12, 13 and 14.

Entry to the Sixth Form is based on gaining at least five GCSE passes at grade 6 or above (with a grade 7 preferred in the subjects chosen to study at A level, and required in some cases) and an interview with the Headmaster and Head of Sixth Form.

Enquiries about admissions should be addressed to the Admissions Office: admissions@bkhs.org.uk.

BKHS Scholarships. Academic, Art and Music scholarships are available for entry into Year 7.

Academic, Sport and Music scholarships are available for Sixth Form entry.

The Governors also annually award a number of bursaries for those entering at Year 7 and Sixth Form; these are dependent on academic ability and parental means.

BKHS Fees per term (2021–2022). Senior School £4,220; Prep School £3,265; Pre Prep £2,810.

Charitable status. Coventry School Foundation is a Registered Charity, number 528961. It exists to provide quality education for boys and girls.

Chair of Governors: Mr I Dunn

BKHS Bablake Headmaster: **Dr D Smith**, MA, PhD

Pastoral Deputy Head: Mrs G Press, BEd

BKHS King Henry VIII Headmaster: **Mr P Dearden**, MEd, BA

Pastoral Deputy Head: Dr M Cuthbert, BSc, MEd, HDipEd, WITS

Deputy Head: Mr R Sewell, BA
Deputy Head, Head of Sixth Form: Mrs C Dowding, BSc

Bancroft's School

High Road, Woodford Green, Essex IG8 0RF

Tel: 020 8505 4821
email: office@bancrofts.org
website: www.bancrofts.org
Twitter: @BancroftsSchool
Facebook: @bancroftsschool
Instagram: @bancrofts_social_media

Motto: *Unto God only be honour and glory*

By the Will of Francis Bancroft (1727) all his personal estate was bequeathed on trust to the Worshipful Company of Drapers of the City of London to build and endow almshouses for 24 old men, with a chapel and schoolroom for 100 poor boys and 2 dwelling-houses for masters. The Foundation was originally situated at Mile End, but by a scheme established by the Charity Commissioners in 1884 the almshouses were abolished and the School transferred to Woodford Green, Essex. In 1976 the School reverted to independence, and became a fully co-educational day school, with a Preparatory School being added in 1990.

Bancroft's School is a co-educational day school of about 1,100 pupils across the Senior and Prep Schools. It stands in its own grounds with about five acres of playing fields and it has a further 16 acres of playing fields near Woodford Station. Its buildings have successfully combined the spacious style of the original architecture with the constant additions demanded by developing needs. These include a swimming pool, enhanced science facilities, music resources and art rooms. In 2006 a new building, housing

kitchens, additional teaching space and a new Sixth Form Centre, was opened; a new sports centre and performing arts studio were opened in 2007. A digital language lab and a new ICT suite were added in 2009. 2011 saw the addition of an enhanced Sixth Form study area, new Arts and Ceramics Workshops and additional science laboratories. In 2015 and 2017 the workshop and classroom facilities for Design Technology were increased and enhanced.

Meals are taken in a well-equipped central dining room, and there is a good variety of menu with self-service on the cafeteria principle.

Pupils are grouped in four Houses – North, East, West and School. Each of the Houses has its own Housemaster or Housemistress and a tutorial system.

The School offers a wide range of subjects at GCSE and A Level and has a strong record of academic success. Virtually all Bancroftians progress to university, with about 12 each year to Oxford or Cambridge. On average 75% of pupils will go on to study at Russell Group institutions. Bancroft's has a very strong record of pupils studying medicine and dentistry.

The major sports for girls are hockey, netball, tennis and athletics; the main curricular games for boys are rugby, hockey, cricket and athletics. Swimming, soccer, badminton and basketball are also provided. The Physical Education programme includes gymnastics, trampolining, basketball and badminton.

The School has a Contingent of the CCF (both Army and RAF sections), a Sea Scout Unit, and a branch of the Duke of Edinburgh's Award Scheme. The wide programme of concerts and plays throughout the school year offers opportunities for pupils of all age groups.

Preparatory School. The Prep School opened in September 1990 occupying purpose-built accommodation on a separate site within the school grounds. There are 12 classrooms, a hall, a library, a performing arts studio and specialist rooms for art and science. Although self-contained, the Prep School makes extensive use of the Senior School's sports, music and drama facilities.

(*For further details, see Preparatory School entry in IAPS section.*)

Admission. 66 places are available each year for boys and girls wishing to enter the Preparatory Department at 7+; entry tests take place in the January. Transfer to the Senior School is guaranteed. At 11+ there are another 60 places available for children entering Bancroft's who sit an examination in Mathematics, English and a computer based reasoning test in January. For candidates of other ages individual arrangements are made. Applications for 7+ and 11+ entry must be made before 1 December in the year prior to entry. There is a direct entry for boys and girls into the Sixth Form dependent upon GCSE results and performance in the School's 16+ entrance examination which is sat in the November of Year 11.

Scholarships. Academic Awards are awarded on an honorary two-year basis at 11+ and 16+. They carry no fee remission, but Scholars are rewarded with a prize. Music Awards are awarded at both 11+ and 16+, again for a two year period; Music Awards include tuition fees on one or two instruments. Drama, Art, Sports and Community Awards are awarded to pupils already at Bancrofts from year 8 onwards. Pupils maybe given awards at other points in their school careers.

Assisted Places, are available at age 11, which can cover the full fees. These are awarded based on disclosure of family finances and performance in the Entrance Examination. Two means-tested Assisted Place are available for entrants to the Prep School at age 7; these only cover Prep School fees. Assisted Places may also be available for entrants into the Sixth Form.

Fees per term (2021–2022). Senior School £6,587, Prep School £5,413 Fees include lunch and books.

Old Bancroftians' Association. Hon Secretary: Mrs C Lavender, obasecretary@bancroftians.net. School contact: sxd@bancrofts.org.

There is a strong Old Bancroftians' Association, organising a variety of social, sporting and networking event throughout the year including an annual dinner at the School and OBs Day in the summer term.

Charitable status. Bancroft's School is a Registered Charity, number 1068532. It exists to provide an academic education to able children.

The Worshipful Company of Drapers

President: The Master of the Drapers' Company

Trustees and Governors:

Appointed by the Drapers' Company:
B S Laden, MBE, FRSA, FBII
R van Maanen, BSc, FRICS, ACIArb, ACIOB [OB]
J Rose, BA
R Williamson, BA, FRGS
Ms L Wingham, MA
Co-opted:
Mrs B Conroy, MA [OB]
H H J B Mensah
E Sautter, MA [OB] (*Acting Chair*)

[OB] Old Bancroftian

Head: S R J Marshall, MA, MA, MPhil

Senior Deputy Head: Ms D Picton, MA
Deputy Head (*Academic*): Dr M Lim, MEd, MBA
Deputy Head (*Pastoral*): Mrs E F de Renzy Channer, MA

Senior Tutor: R B de Renzy Channer, MA

Assistant Heads:
Academic: A Gocoldas, BSC
Pastoral: J Barr, MEng
Co-Curriculum & Activities; Ms E Burnside, MA

Head of Sixth Form: P J Harrison, MA
Head of Section, Middle School: Miss S Hancock, MA
Head of Section, Lower School: J P Dickinson, MEng
Director of Teaching & Learning Mrs V Talbot, BA
Deputy Heads of Sixth Form: Mrs S C Hampson, BSc, Miss H Korcz, BSc
Assistant Head of Middle School: Mr J Foley, BSc
Assistant Heads of Lower School: Miss M Stone, MA; Mr J Smith, BSc

Head of Careers, Innovation and Entrepreneurship: Mrs M Dean
†*Director of Learning Strategy*: Mrs A Fryer-Green, BSc

Head, Preparatory School: J P Layburn, MA, QTS

Assistant Staff:
* *Head of Department/Subject*
† *Housemaster/mistress*

Art:
*A D Ford, MA
Mrs S O'Sullivan, MA
Mrs N Vetta, BA
Ms I Ward, MA

Biology:
Mrs A C Carter, BSc
†Miss A Grimwood, BSc
*Mrs S C Hampson, BSc
J Smith, BSc

Chemistry:
Dr A Ahmed, MScI
J Choy, MSci (*Head of Medics*)
*N Goalby, MEng
Dr G M Ismail, BSc (*Junior Science)
Miss H Korcz, BSc, MEd
†Miss H J Prescott-Morrin, BSc

Classics:
*Mrs M J Baker, BA
†Mrs L J Coyne, BA
Ms D Picton, MA
A J Smethurst, MA
†Miss H E Stewart, BA

Computer Science & ICT:
Dr C Ivascu, MA
*Mr A D Shaw, BSc

Drama:
Ms G Entwhistle, BA
*Miss E M Middleton, BA
Mrs J Whitbread, MA

Economics & Business Studies:
*Mrs L R Anthony, BSc
Mr J S Chapman, BA
Mrs K J Dean, BA, ACA
Ms M Dean, BCom, MBA
Mr A Gocoldas, BSc

English:
*Ms E Burnside, MA (*Acting Head of Dept*)
Miss C G Edwards, BA
Miss N Evans, MEd (*Junior English)
K P Gallagher, BA
Mrs S Khere Kye, MA
Dr A J Mill, MA
Miss O Oni, BA
R E Young, BA

Geography:
*Miss R S Burridge, BSc
J S Foley, BSc
P J Harrison, MA
†R M Hitching, BA
Miss G E McIlfatrick, MA
Miss A J Reed, BA
Mrs V Talbot, BA

Politics:
J S Chapman, BA
Mrs K J Dean, BA, ACA
†R M Hitching, BA
*Dr S A Hunn, BA, MSt

History:
*L J Brennand, BA
R B de Renzy Channer, MA
Mrs K J Dean, MA, ACA

Dr S A Hunn, BA, MSt
Mrs M Sparkes, MA
Miss M Stone, MA
†Miss A M H Wainwright, BA
A Whibley, BA

Learning Support:
†Mrs A Fryer-Green, BSc
*Mrs J Collins
Mrs A Hubbard
Mrs R Sheikh, BSc

Mathematics:
C J Atkinson, MA (*Junior Mathematics*)
P A Caira, BSc
Mr J Ceeraz, BSc
Miss G K Chana, BSc
A M Conington, BSc
J P Dickinson, MEng
M J Flaherty, MA
Dr J D Larwood, BSc
J E Osborne, BSc
L Pollock, BSc
M H Salamut, BA
*S P Taylor, BEng (*Sixth Form Mathematics*)
R Tse, MSc
Mrs E J Tynan, MEng (*KS4 Mathematics*)
Ms L Waters-Rudge, BA

Modern Languages:
Mrs A Abbott-Imboden, BA (*Modern Languages,
    German)
M Bequignon, MA (*French*)
Mrs E F de Renzy Channer, MA
Mrs S Cooper-James, MA
B Dawlatly, MA
Miss M Fleet, MA
Miss J Grossman, Staatsexamen (*French*)
Ms S Hancock, MA
Ms M Marota Beuno, MA
Miss J K Robbins, BA
Mrs P R Tindall, BA
Mr I Urreaga Gorostidi, BA (*Spanish*)
Mrs L Whalley, BA (*Russian*)

Music:
R Aitken, BSc
Mrs C J Foinette, BA
*Mrs J Whitbread, MA (*Director of Music*)

Physical Education:
D J Argyle, BEd
Mrs S Cheshire (*Swimming Coach*)
Ms J Cresswell, BSc
A Eghoyan, BSc (*Strength & Conditioning Coach*)
R Faiers, BA (*Head of Department, Games Coordinator
    Boys*)
Mrs J Fryer-Green, BA (*Head of Department, Games
    Coordinator Girls*)
C Greenidge (*Cricket*)
Mrs H E Marchant (*Netball*)
Mrs K Osman (*Netball Coach*)
J C Pollard, BEd (*PE*)
Miss L Poulter, BSc
†Miss A M H Wainwright, MA (*Tennis*)
Mr M W Wardkey (*Football*)
D Webster (*Hockey*)

Physics:
J Barr, MEng
A N Busch, MSci
J Ceeraz, BSc
N A Jaques, MA (*Science*)
L Pollock, BSc
*J Prole, BSc

Politics:
J S Chapman, BA
Mrs K J Dean, BA, ACA
†R M Hitching, BA
*Dr S A Hunn, BA, MSt

Religious Studies:
*Miss L Jones, MA
Revd I Moore, MA, BTh (*School Chaplain*)
†Miss H C Nadasan-Mead, BA
M Willingham, MA

Technology:
T Peddle, BEng
*M J Rogers, BA
A Whitbread, DipEd
S P Woolley, BSc

Preparatory School:

Mrs C Ablitt (*Swimming Coach*)
Mrs A Adams, BA
D Archer, BA
A D Baum, BA
Mrs S K Bhangal, BEd
Mrs C Biston, BA
N Bleasdale, BSc
T Carson, BA
Miss C Dack, BSc (*Graduate Sports Assistant*)
Mrs L Dalton, BA
Mrs N Doctors, BA
Miss L Ellery, MSc
C P Hall, BSc
R Harrison, BSc (*Sports Coach*)
Mrs J M Hitching, BA
Mrs S M Jones, BA
Mrs T Jones (*Learning Support Assistant*)
Mrs A Kanolik, BA
J P Layburn, MA (*Head*)
Mrs L Life, BA (*Deputy Head*)
Mrs K McNelis, BSc
T Paramour, BA
C Pearson, BA
Mrs B Rathod, BA
Mrs S Strong, MA
Miss H Sylvester, BA
Mrs K Yelverton, BA
Mrs L Ware, BA

Bursar: L Green

Matron: Mrs A Hancock

Barnard Castle School

Newgate, Barnard Castle, County Durham DL12 8UN

Tel: 01833 690222
email: genoffice@barneyschool.org.uk
website: www.barnardcastleschool.org.uk
Twitter: @barney_school
Facebook: @BarnardCastleSchool
Instagram: @barnardcastleschool
LinkedIn: /company/barnard-castle-school

Motto: *Parvis imbutus tentabis grandia tutus*

The St John's Hospital in Barnard Castle was founded in the 13th century by John Baliol, whose widow founded the Oxford College. By a Scheme of the Charity

Commissioners, bequests under the will of Benjamin Flounders of Yarm were combined with the funds of the St John's Hospital and public subscriptions to build and endow the present foundation in 1883. Originally known as the North Eastern County School, the name was changed to Barnard Castle School in 1924.

'Barney', as it is affectionately known, is a day and boarding school for boys and girls between the ages of 4 and 18.

Organisation and Numbers. There are 512 pupils aged 11–18 in the Senior School, of whom 110 are boarders. The Preparatory School comprises a Pre-Prep Department of 48 pupils between the ages of 4 and 7, and 132 pupils between the ages of 7 and 11, of whom 13 are boarders. (*See also Preparatory School entry in IAPS section.*) The Senior and Preparatory Schools are located on adjacent sites and operate separately on a day-to-day basis whilst enjoying the mutual benefits of being able to share a number of resources and facilities. Girls were first admitted in 1981 and the School has been fully co-educational since 1993.

Location. The School is situated on its own extensive grounds on the outskirts of an historic market town in an area of outstanding natural beauty. The area is well served by Teesside International and Newcastle airports as well as Darlington railway station. The School also operates its own bus service for pupils from a wide area.

Curriculum. This is designed to provide a broad, balanced and flexible programme, avoiding undue specialisation at too early a stage. In the Prep School emphasis is given to literacy and numeracy skills, as well as Science, History, Geography, French (from age 8), Religious Education, Technology, Art, Music, Information Technology, Physical Education (including swimming) and Games. These subjects are developed further in the Senior School, with the addition of Latin or Classical Civilisation, Personal, Social and Health Education, and three separate sciences. German or Spanish is added at age 12, whilst Business Studies and Engineering increase the list of GCSE options at age 14. There are some twenty A, AS or Pre-U Level subjects, which give a wide choice in the Sixth Form. Almost all Sixth Form leavers go on to University or College courses. A Learning Support Department provides specialist help for those who need it in both the Preparatory and Senior Schools, and tuition is offered in English as a Second Language.

Religious Education. The School is a Christian foundation and the Chapel stands at the heart of the School in more than just a geographical sense. The School Chaplain, who plays an important role in the pastoral structure of the School as well as being responsible for Religious Studies and Chapel worship, is an ordained member of the Church of England, but the School is a multi-denominational one which welcomes and supports pupils of all faiths and none. Pupils attend weekday morning assemblies in Chapel, and there is a Sunday service for boarders.

Boarding and Day Houses. There are eight single-sex Houses within the Senior School – three boarding and five day – each small enough for pupils to know each other well, but large enough to allow a mixture of interests, backgrounds and abilities, as well as opportunities for leadership. Housemasters and Housemistresses, each supported by a team of Tutors and Assistants, are responsible for the welfare and progress of each pupil in their charge.

Junior Boarders (boys and girls aged 7–11) and Senior Girl Boarders live in their own modern Houses in the School grounds, alongside their Houseparents, Boarding Tutors and Matrons. The two Senior Boys' Boarding Houses have recently undergone a major programme of restructuring and refurbishment, and offer comfortable accommodation within the main building of the School. The resident Housemasters are supported by resident boarding tutors and matrons, and by the School Sister in the School's Medical Centre. The School Doctor visits daily.

Cultural and other activities. The School has a flourishing music department in which the Chapel Choir, Orchestras, Wind and Jazz Bands and smaller ensembles perform regularly.

Drama is also prominent, with a regular programme of productions taking place throughout the year. There is a strong tradition of after-school activities; both day and boarding pupils take part in a wide range of clubs and societies, selecting from over 100 weekly activities.

Games. Rugby, Hockey, Netball, Cricket, Athletics, Squash, Cross-Country Running, Tennis and Swimming are the main sports, and other options such as soccer, badminton, basketball and golf are available. The School has extensive playing fields, a modern Sports Hall, and Fitness Centre, squash and tennis courts, and a heated indoor swimming pool. A full-size, floodlit AstroTurf-style pitch is available for all to use. Regular inter-school matches are arranged at all levels.

Outdoor Activities. There is a strong emphasis on providing instruction, opportunity and challenge in a wide range of outdoor activities. Much of this takes place under the auspices of a flourishing Cadet Force (Army and RAF sections) or The Duke of Edinburgh's Gold and Silver Award schemes.

Careers. There is a well-equipped Careers Room, and a team of careers staff work together with the Higher Education Coordinator to provide pupils at all stages of the School with expert advice and help in decision-making and application procedures.

Admission. Pupils are admitted at all stages either via the School's own Entrance Assessments. There is also direct entry into the Sixth Form subject to satisfactory performance at GCSE level. Details of the application procedure are obtainable from the Registrar (admissions@ barneyschool.org.uk).

Scholarships and Assisted Places. Academic Scholarships and Exhibitions are awarded to entrants to the Senior School at Year 7, Year 9 and the Sixth Form, on the basis of the School's own entrance examinations held in February.

Music Scholarships and Exhibitions: There are two Music Exhibitions available in Year 7, a further two Scholarships in Year 9 and in the Sixth Form.

Sport Exhibitions based on potential are available at Year 7 and Scholarships are available at Year 9 and in the Sixth Form. Four Exhibitions may be awarded in Year 7, followed by up to four Scholarships in Year 9 and a further two Scholarships in the Sixth Form.

Art Scholarships and Exhibitions are available from Year 9 and in the Sixth Form.

Drama Scholarships and Exhibitions are available to candidates entering the Sixth Form.

Awards may be supplemented by means-tested Bursaries.

The School is also able to offer a small number of means-tested assisted places. Details are available from the Admissions Secretary.

Fees per term (2021–2022). Senior School (Years 7–13): Day £4,876; Junior Boarder (Years 7–8) £8,231; Junior International Boarder (Years 7–8) £9,384; Senior Boarder (Years 9–13) £8,808; International Boarder £9,961. Fees are inclusive and subject to annual review.

Charitable status. Barnard Castle School is a Registered Charity, number 1125375, whose aim is the education of boys and girls.

The Governing Body:
Chairman: Mrs C J Sunley
Vice-Chair: Dr J Elphick
Chair of Finance & Estates Sub-Committee: Mrs C J Sunley
Chair of Education, Welfare and Staff Development Sub-Committee: Mr P Kelsall
Chair of Strategy, Marketing & Development Sub-Committee: Mr J Hunter
Chair of Governance Sub-Committee: Dr J Elphick

Mr M Allison
Mr N Bliss
Mr P Hodges
Mr I Moffatt
Mr P Mothersill
Ms C Newnam
Mr D C Osborne

Mr D Penny
Mr E Rendall
Councillor G Richardson
Mr D F Starr
Dr N Thorpe
Mrs D Vinsome

Clerk to the Governors: Mrs S Metcalf, BA, FCCA

Headmaster: **Tony C Jackson**, BA

Second Master: Martin Pepper, BA
Deputy Head (i/c of Sixth Form): Fiona Beadnell, MA
Deputy Head (Pastoral): Peter Lavery, BA Hons
Deputy Head (Academic): Matthew Corke, BA Hons

Registrar: Bronwyn Huddleston
International Registrar: Nicola Slater

Housemasters/mistresses:
Bowes: Caroline J Riley, MA
Dale: Christopher D M McTurk, BA Hons
Durham: David Riley, BA Hons
Marwood: Olivia J Isaac, BA Hons
Longfield: Lesley J Burgess, BEd
Northumberland: Luke D Monument, BSc
Tees: Henry W Fairwood, BSc
York: Matt S Gooch

Heads of Departments:
Art: Kate Baptist, BA
Biology: Rebecca K B Gibson, MSc, BSc
Chemistry: Janine Wilson, MA
Classics: John D N Gedye, BA
Design & Technology: Alan M Beaty, BSc
Drama: Scott Edwards, BA
English: Amanda Gorman, BA Hons
Geography: David W Dalton, MA
History: Martin P Ince, BA
ICT: Judith Brown, MSc
Maths: Mark D Robson, BSc, MEd
MFL: Helen D Kent, MPhil, BA
Music: Richard J Dawson
Physics: Christopher Butler, MSc, MA
Politics: Andrea J Campbell, BA

Psychology: Michelle Abela, BA, LLCM, ALCM
Religious Studies: Caroline J Snaith, MA, LLB
SEN: Judith A Gibbons
Sport: Rachael S Masterman, MA, BSc

Teaching Staff:

Charles H Alderson, BSc
Erin E Beaty, BA
Melissa L Benbow, MPhys
Tanya C Broadbent, BA
Caroline Connor, BSc
Nick J Connor, BA
Kevin B Cosstick, JP, PhD, BSc
Ciaran Davis, MA
Mick Donnelly, FLCM, Cert Ed
Andy M Dunn, MSc, MPhil
Sam S Forsyth, BSc
Peter Foster, MSc
Daniel S Gorman, BA Hons
Elizabeth Gorman, MA
Carla Lavery
Alan J Maude, BSc
Chris Misiak, BA Hons
Sebastian T Nichols, PhD
Mike H Nicholson, BSc, BA
Fiona Norrie, BEd
David Riley
Rachel A Romano
Sarah Rothwell, MA
Hannah Shairp, MA
Neil Toyne, BSc
Ben C Usher, BSc

Combined Cadet Force:
Commanding Officer: Major Caroline E Hall, BSc
SSI: Tony Wardman

Preparatory School

Headmistress: Laura E R Turner, MA

Deputy Head: Claire L Bale, BA
Deputy Head (Academic): Simon Ayres, BA
Deputy Head (Pastoral): Rebecca A Robertson, BEd

Teaching Staff:
Martin A Burgess, BA
Martine Chapman
Hannah V Crosbie
Nathan J Joy, BA
Fiona M Killeen, BA
Louise E Rowlandson, BA
Katie J Shearn, BA
Emma J Small, BA
Jennifer D Strachan, BA
Nina F Summerson-Brown, BA
Alexandra A White, BSc Hons

Medical Centre:
School Nurse: Mrs Tanya A Farren, RGN
School Nurse: Mrs Alex A Robson, RGN
School Counsellor: Mrs Donna J Thirling, BA, SAC Dip

Bedales School

Church Road, Steep, Petersfield, Hampshire GU32 2DG

Tel:	Telephone: 01730 300100
	Admissions: 01730 711733
email:	admissions@bedales.org.uk
website:	www.bedales.org.uk
Twitter:	@BedalesSchool
Facebook:	@BedalesSchool
Instagram:	@BedalesSchool
LinkedIn:	/bedales-school

Number in school. 472 pupils: 224 boys, 248 girls; 327 boarders

Fees per term (2021–2022). Boarders £12,710; Day £9,990

Bedales stands in an estate of 120 acres in the heart of the Hampshire countryside in the South Downs National Park. Although only one hour from London by train, this is one of the most beautiful corners of rural England. Founded in 1893 to be different from the schools of its time, Bedales is one of the oldest co-educational boarding schools. True to its founding principles, the school remains innovative – recent examples include a project-based curriculum in Block 3 (Year 9), Bedales Assessed Courses to replace many GCSEs and a Living with the Land Sixth form course. The community is a stimulating and happy one, in which tolerance and supportive relationships thrive at all levels.

The school has strong traditions in both the Humanities and the Sciences, in Art, Design, Drama and Music. The school estate supports a thriving 'Outdoor Work' programme, including the management of livestock and a variety of traditional crafts.

The school is known for its liberal values, the individualism and creativity of its students, and a sense that the students are generally at ease with who they are. The atmosphere is relaxed (first-name terms for staff and students; no uniform), and it is underpinned by a firm structure of values, rules, guidance and support. Bedales has recently joined the Round Square network of international schools that share a commitment to character education and experiential learning.

Admission. Entry to the school is from 3+, 7+ (Bedales Pre-prep, Dunannie), 8+, 11+ (Bedales Prep, Dunhurst), 13+ and 16+ (Bedales Senior). Once in the school, pupils are assessed before proceeding to the next stage.

Entry tests. Entry for newcomers at 10+, 11+ and 13+ takes the form of residential tests in the January approximately 20 months before entry. Entry at 16+ is by a series of interviews on a single day. Contact the Admissions team in the first instance.

Senior School (13 to 18). Our Block 3 (Year 9) curriculum is a rich, experiential project-based year. In September, at the beginning of the year, there is a challenging week of outdoor pursuits and team-building at an outdoor activities centre. Here, students will work with tutors alongside the dedicated and professional staff at the centre. On their return, they are introduced to the curriculum so they can make informed subject choices. They also get a taste of the co-curricular life of the school, with plenty of opportunities for Sport, Music, and Drama.

Students are also encouraged to give something back to the community. This includes weekly outdoor work culminating in a celebration at the end of the year using the produce they have grown and prepared, and where they showcase the fruits of their humanities projects to real audiences. During the course of Block 3 it is expected that each student will establish effective working habits and an appropriate balance between academic work and other pursuits.

Bedales has a long tradition of leading the way in educational change. Its determination to do what is right for its students led to the creation of a unique curriculum, Bedales Assessed Courses (BACs) for Blocks 4 and 5 with a range of innovative courses designed to complement a core of I/GCSEs. The curriculum is built around a compulsory group of five core IGCSE subjects and two non-examined courses, plus a choice of BACs and other GCSEs. Well regarded by universities, the content of BACs is broad and stimulating, offering significant cross-curricular and independent-learning opportunities.

Since its aim is to develop a broad range of skills through the delivery of BACs, internal assessment includes a mixture of written assignments, presentations, projects and performances, together with terminal examinations as appropriate. Each course is externally moderated.

In class, and particularly in the BACs, students are encouraged to question, to challenge, to think for themselves – visitors comment on a 'no fear' classroom atmosphere.

The Sixth Form at Bedales offers an unusually broad and stimulating environment in which to spend the final years at school and to prepare for life beyond. Serious academic responsibility and opportunities for leadership combine to create a challenging and rewarding experience. New qualification options in addition to A Levels have been added in recent years including Pre-U Global Perspectives and Research, BTEC Sport Science and a sustainability course in Living with the Land.

In particular, inspired by the success of the BAC courses, Bedales has developed an additional strand of the curriculum to replace a fourth A Level. The Bedales Enrichment Programme consists of a series of one-term courses chosen from a broad range of offerings developed by enthusiastic staff and shaped by student requests. Courses are grouped under the Bedalian banner of 'head, hand and heart', and students are expected to pursue at least one course in each area.

Each student's programme will also include a combination of academic study, sport, Outdoor Work, cultural and current affairs, service to the community, and global awareness. Sixth Form students are also expected to take on positions of responsibility in the school, such as contributing to one of the many student committees or acting as role model and mentor to younger students.

Bedales Prep School, Dunhurst (8 to 13). (*See Dunhurst entry in IAPS section*).

Bedales Pre-prep School, Dunannie (3 to 8). Currently 89 pupils. Entrance at 3+ is by date of registration; after this acceptances are made following informal assessments, should vacancies arise. Dunannie has six classes including a nursery. Its aim is for children to develop a lifetime's love of learning in a stimulating environment.

Dunannie aims to inspire children by learning through doing in a community based on mutual respect. Children help to form the rules of caring behaviour towards one another and are on first name terms with teachers. The children are encouraged to have confidence to make their own decisions and to formulate their own ideas in class, supported by their teachers.

The children at Dunannie benefit from an indoor swimming pool, tennis courts, sports hall, pitches, farm and theatre which are all close by on the Bedales estate. The outdoor play areas include a stunning orchard with a climbing frame, Sound Garden of outdoor instruments and a hill fort.

The children have many opportunities to thrive and flourish. Dunannie offers a rich and varied curriculum that allows for rigour in basic skills, and also embraces creativity. Children are encouraged to think and be independent in their response to cross-curricular activities. First-hand experiences are an integral part of learning. All children from Nursery to Year 3 go on inspiring visits that enrich their classroom experiences. There are close links between Dunannie, Dunhurst and Bedales. Children in Year 3 can automatically transfer from Dunannie to Dunhurst unless there are exceptional circumstances. Sport is a strength with a comprehensive programme of activities including swimming, gymnastics, tennis, netball, football and orienteering. Year 3 children have sport with Dunhurst Group 1 (Year 4) children and have the opportunity to play inter-school matches. Dunannie is a very friendly school with happy, confident children who relish being at school.

Scholarships. Personal development is central to the Bedales concept of scholarship. It aims to align scholarship beneficiaries closely with the school's aim "to develop inquisitive thinkers with a love of learning who cherish independent thought".

The school has introduced a scheme for pupils with particular talents in Art, Design, Music, Drama, Sport and other academic subjects to encourage their appetite for research, enquiry and development. Depending on their specialist subject, most scholarship holders have access to a research fund to support their individual scholarly projects. There is no reduction in school fees – research grants are non-means tested and hence have a relatively small financial value (up to £500 per year for 2021/22). The award of a scholarship is reviewed annually based on student performance.

Bursaries. Ranging from part-fee contributions up to full 100% bursaries (with further support for additional costs), these awards enable pupils (generally from 11+ upwards) with an appetite for learning to attend Bedales Prep, Dunhurst and Bedales Senior who otherwise would have been unable to pay the fees. Awards are based on an assessment of the family's financial means. The school's John Badley Foundation supports 100% bursaries.

Pupils can benefit from the award of either a scholarship or a bursary, or both. Although bursary financial assistance is not dependent on a scholarship award, the school aims to enable pupils with particularly strong talents to attend the school, therefore a number of bursary beneficiaries also benefit from scholarship awards. Please contact the Head of Admissions (email: admissions@bedales.org.uk; tel: 01730 711733) if you would like to discuss suitability for a scholarship or bursary to Bedales Prep, Dunhurst or Bedales Senior.

Fees per term (2021–2022). Bedales: Boarders £12,710, Day £9,990. Bedales Prep, Dunhurst: Boarders £8,735, Half-boarding (3 nights) £7,780, Day £5,930–£6,575. Bedales Pre-prep, Dunannie: £3,495–£4,610.

Charitable status. Bedales School is a Registered Charity, number 307332. Its aims and objectives are to educate children as broadly as possible in a creative and caring environment.

Governors:
Claudia Arney, MBA
Clare Bradbury, BSc, PGCE
Felix Grey, MChem, MPhil
Mark Hanson
Michele Johnson, BA
Owen Jonathan, LLB Hons
Dr Anna Keay, PhD
Matthew Rice, BA
Stephen Nokes (*Chairman*)
Edward Rees BA Ed Hons
Timothy Wise

Acting Head: **Will Goldsmith**, MA Edinburgh, Graduate Teacher Programme with QTS Brunel, PGCAEP Oxford Brookes

Head, Bedales Prep, Dunhurst: Colin Baty, NPQH, BEd, Dip Teach Waikato University NZ, BPP Roehampton

Head, Bedales Pre-prep, Dunannie: Fiona Read, BEd Hons Kingston, PGDip Open University

Bursar and Clerk to the Governors: Richard Lushington, BA, MCIPD Thames Polytechnic London

Director of External Relations: Rob Reynolds, BSc Royal Holloway London, MBA Strathclyde, MCIM

Bede's Senior School

Upper Dicker, East Sussex BN27 3QH

Tel:	01323 843252
email:	school.office@bedes.org
website:	www.bedes.org
Twitter:	@bedesnews
Facebook:	@bedesseniorschool

Founded in 1978 Bede's discovers the talents of each student through breadth of academic curriculum and co-curricular. It is academically ambitious for all and the pastoral care, delivered through the House and Tutor systems, is inspiring and nurturing and ensures Bede's sends its young people into the outside world self-aware, happy and confident in what they can achieve and looking forward to the challenges they will meet.

The Senior School owes its existence in part to the success and vitality of Bede's Preparatory School in Eastbourne, one of the first boys' Preparatory Schools to become fully co-educational and now one of the largest co-educational Preparatory Schools in the country. The Senior School has 819 students. Of these 325 are boarders (full and weekly), 494 are day students, 325 are Sixth Formers, 60 per cent are boys and 40 per cent are girls. Bede's enjoys an enviable reputation internationally. Currently 20% of our students are from over 40 countries.

The School takes great pride in the variety of its students and the outstanding range of opportunities available to them.

The breadth of choice means every student can find what they naturally excel at. Students at Bede's pick from a wide array of over 100 clubs and activities, guided by personal tutors.

Aims. Bede's aims include the provision of an outstanding education, in an inclusive co-educational environment. That education is predicated on flexibility for the student; a broad and varied curriculum; personalisation of study programmes and respect for students' choices and aptitudes. Coupled with this is the provision of an extensive and exceptional variety of co-curricular activities that allows students to find, nurture and develop their interests and talents. The programme caters for everyone, from elite performers to hobbyists, and no activity is considered more important than another.

Bede's provides pastoral care that aims to support and safeguard each student, and in so doing, develops values of respect and humanity within a framework of friendly, non-confrontational relationships between all people, adults and students alike.

Facilities. Bede's buildings are friendly, in enviable settings and a far cry from the overbearing, institutional character of much school architecture. In 2007 the School opened two innovative and award-winning boarding houses and two more were opened in February 2012. Bede's is currently adding to its portfolio of boarding accommodation with a new £8million boarding house development in the heart of the Senior School site with stunning atrium and additional breakout and learning spaces, due to open in the summer 2022. The multi-purpose Hall, also opened in 2007, is used for School Assemblies, examinations and many sports, including basketball, badminton, cricket, football, netball and tennis. The Performing Arts Centre, in a beautiful setting next to the lake, provides studio space for both drama and dance and 2008 saw the opening of a new Music Centre. A new multi-purpose games area, water-based astro and cricket pavilion were all opened in 2015. The zoo – which originally opened in 2011 – currently hosts over 70 species of mammals, birds, amphibians, reptiles, fish and invertebrates. In 2018 it was extended with six brand-new enclosures, housing African birds, Madagascan lemurs, and South American squirrel monkeys.

Curriculum. A new first year curriculum launched in September 2015 offering a range of new, fresh courses. The programme has an emphasis on the core skills of literacy, numeracy and scientific discovery and also includes "21st Century Studies", encompassing "soft skills" such as team work and time management as well as "hard skills" including cooking and first aid. All children also study a carousel of subjects as part of a course entitled "The World", which will cover global politics, history and geography. There is also an emphasis on creative subjects with children given the opportunity to experience art in many forms.

In the Fifth Form (Year 10) most students begin two-year courses leading to the GCSE (Key Stage 4) examinations. Students usually follow nine subjects of a possible 40 at GCSE; Mathematics, Science and English are compulsory subjects. Potential optional courses include: Art and Design, Business Studies, Dance, Design & Technology, Drama, Geography, History, Home Economics, Information Technology, Latin and Greek, Media Studies, Modern Languages (French, Spanish, German), Music, Performing Arts (Dance), Physical Education, Religious Studies, Science (Triple Award), Science (Double Award), Science (Single Award). Some IGCSEs are also offered along with

some short-course GCSEs. A Pre-Sixth course is offered for those who need a year of intensive English before embarking on an A Level course.

During the first three years those with particular needs, such as those with any form of Dyslexia and those who are non-native speakers of English, can follow organised programmes within the timetable taught by suitably qualified teachers.

In the Sixth Form students can follow the traditional three or four A Level courses and some Pre-U courses, which can provide a broader education. Most GCSE subjects are offered at A Level plus Economics, Media Studies, Government & Politics, Philosophy and Ethics and Theatre Studies. Bede's also offers Cambridge Pre-U in a number of subjects. Sixth Form students can also take the Extended Project Qualification, Level 2 Award in Sports Leadership, Level 2 Certificate in Financial Education or Arts Award Gold.

Vocational provision: BTEC National Certificate in Sport, Music Performance, Animal Management and Business Management.

Bede's also runs the Legat Professional Dance Course which is fully integrated with the academic programme.

Current class sizes average 16 up to GCSE level and 12 at A Level.

Co-Curricular Programme including Games. The extensive programme includes the many sporting and games playing opportunities open to students, The Duke of Edinburgh's Award scheme, numerous outdoor pursuits and a daily programme of activities within the fields of Art, Drama, Music, Journalism, Science, Technology, Engineering and Social Service. There are currently over 14 Club Activities running each week and an average daily choice from 40 options. Games and Sports include Aerobics, Archery, Athletics, Badminton, Basketball, Canoeing, Climbing, Cricket, Cross-Country, Fishing, Football, Golf (the School has its own practice course), Hockey, Dance, Netball, Orienteering, Photography, Riding, Rounders, Rugby, Squash, Swimming, Target Rifle Shooting, Tennis and Volleyball. Bede's has a fine sporting reputation with students past and present representing their country at cricket, football, rugby, hockey, athletics and showjumping. The Emerging Talent Programme brings together pupils across different sports who have potential to become professional sports people and provides training in areas such as nutrition, sports psychology and media handling.

Pastoral Care. There are three boys' boarding houses and two girls' houses, the numbers in each house averaging 60, with three resident staff in each. An appropriately selected tutor provides a mentor for each student during their time at the School. These tutors are responsible for ensuring that each student's academic and social well-being is carefully looked after. Tutors act in liaison with Housemasters and Housemistresses and are readily available for discussions with parents. All parents have several formal opportunities each year to meet those who teach or otherwise look after their sons or daughters. In 2015 a Day Boarding concept was launched allowing day pupils to be part of a boarding house, complete prep in house and return home on the late bus service.

Religion. The School maintains the Village Church for the local community. Confirmation classes are available, if requested. All students attend weekly meetings in the church which are appropriate to boys and girls of all religions and are of outstanding variety. Bede's does not impose any singular religious observance on its students but would rather either that their existing faith is further strengthened by their being full members of the congregation of local churches or that they grow to appreciate and value the importance of a strong spiritual life through the thoughtful and varied programme of 'School Meetings'. There is a choice of four types of observance on Sundays: the Multi-Religious School Meeting, Church of England, Roman Catholic and Free Church.

Admission. The usual points of entry are at Year 9 and Year 12, although a small number of places are usually available for entry into Year 10. Pupils entering Year 9 will be invited to attend a Bede's Experience Day in Year 7 when pupils will take part in group activities, take a cognitive test, be interviewed and participate in an activity of choice. School reports and references are also taken into account. Entry into the Sixth Form will be conditional on GCSE results, reports and references.

Scholarships and Bursaries. Bede's invests in excess of ten per cent of its annual income in means-tested fee remission and academic, art, dance, drama, music and sports scholarships. Prospective students who wish to join outside of the scholarship process are able to apply for means-tested fee remission.

Further details regarding scholarships and bursaries are available from the Admissions Office, email: admissions @bedes.org.

Fees per term (2021–2022). Full Boarders £12,450, Weekly Boarders £11,700, Day Pupils £7,800, Day Boarding £7,960.

Charitable status. St Bede's School Trust Sussex is a Registered Charity, number 278950. It exists to provide quality education.

Governors:
Mrs Geraldine Watkins (*Chair*)
Mr John Burbidge, BA Hons, ACA
Mr C Heinrich, BA, PGCE
Mrs Sarah Jelly
Mr Dermot Keegan
Dr C Lemaigre, MA Hons, DClinPsychol
Professor Andrew Lloyd, MA Cantab, PhD
Mr Mark MacFadden, MRICS, ACIArb
Mr Nicholas Mercer, BA Hons
Mrs Katherine Nash, BEd
Mr Edward Plumley, BA Hons, MSc, MBA, MRIC
Ms A Sharma
Mr S Smith, FRSA
Mrs Jenifer Woodhouse, Cert Ed London

Senior Management:

Headmaster: Mr P Goodyer, BSc, MBA, FRSA

Senior Management:
Deputy Head: Mr J Tuson, MA, GTP (*English*)
Deputy Head, Operations: Mr P Wise, BSc Hons, MA, PGCE
School Chaplain: Mr J Taylor, BTh, TEEC South Africa
Assistant Head (Pupil Welfare): Ms A Lowe, BA Hons, PGCE, MTeach
Assistant Head (*Teaching & Learning*), Mr N Abrams, BSc Hons, PGCE
Assistant Head (*Innovation & Development*), Mr S Choithramani
Senior Registrar: Mr R Mills, BA Hons, PGCE

Director of Summer School: Mr R Edwards, BSc, Msc
Assistant Head (Day): Mr N Driver, BCom, PGCE
Assistant Head (Boarding): Mr P Juniper, BSc Hons, PGCE, CBiol, MSB
Director of Marketing and Admissions: Mrs R Nairne, BA Hons
Director of Safeguarding: Ms A Hodge
Director of People: Emma Maynard, MCIPD
Bursar: Dr J Northway, MB, FRCS

Housemasters and Housemistresses:
Bloomsbury: Mrs L Devereux
Camberlot: Mr F McKeefry, BA Hons, PGCE
Crossways: Ms K Chinn, BA Hons, PGCE
Charleston: Mr T Mpandawana, BSc, DipEd
Deis: Mr L Pianet, BA Hons
Dicker: Mr C Abraham, BSc Hons, Dip Law, PGCE
Dorms: Mr R Hickman BA Hons, GTP
Dorter: Dr S Lewis BSc Hons, DPhil, PGCE
Knights: Mr A Waterhouse, HDE Secondary
Stud: Mr P Jones, BSc Hons, MSc, PGCE

Heads of Departments/Subjects:
Mr J Turner, BA Hons, PGCE (*Creative Arts Faculty & Photography*)
Mr A Hammond, BA Hons, MA, GTP (*Ceramics & Head of Teacher Development*)
Mr B Jackson (*Business Studies & Economics*)
Mr N Potter, BSc Hons, PGCE (*Design & Technology*)
Mr S Choithramani (*Assistant Head (Innovation & Development), Drama,Theatre Studies*)
Mr J Cook, RSA, TEFLA (*EAL*)
Mr M Oliver, BA Hons, PGCE (*Languages Faculty*)
Miss P Saoulidou, BA, MSc (*Classics*)
Mr J Slinger, BA, MA, PGCE (*Geography*)
Mr P Gibbs, BA Hons, PGCE (*Director of Higher Education*)
Mr J Whittaker, BA Hons, PGCE (*Humanities Faculty*)
Mr C Betts, BSc Hons (*Computing and Information Technology*)
Mrs C MacGregor, BSc, QTS, PGCE (*Director of Learning Enhancement*)
Mr N Abrams, BSc Hons, PGCE (*Assistant Head (Teaching & Learning), Further Mathematics*)
Mr R Williams, BA Hons, GTP, Dip Media Ed (*Film & Media Studies*)
Ms V Ganivet (*MFL*)
Mr R Scamardella, MMus, MMP, FRSM, FRCO (*Director of Music*)
Mrs K Lewis, BA, PGCE (*Director of Performing Arts*)
Mr W Rennison, BA Hons, PGCE (*Academic Drama*)
Miss S Pennington, AISTD (*Legat School of Dance*)
Mrs M Newbery, BA Hons (*Physical Education*)
Mr D Byrne, BA Hons (*Director of Sport*)
Mr S Costi, BA Hons, PGCE (*Religion & Philosophy*)
Ms L Finat-Duclos (*Chemistry*)
Mrs N Morton-Freeman, BSc Hons, PGCE (*Biology*)
Mr S Manos, BSc Hons, PGCE (*Maths*)
Ms J French, BSc, PGCE (*STEM Faculty*)
Mr O Froom, MPhys Hons, PGCE (*Physics*)
Mrs Y Stainsby, MSc, PGCE (*Psychology*)
Mr P Juniper, BSc Hons, PGCE CBiol, MSB (*Assistant Head (Boarding), Animal Management*)
Ms G Wainwright, MAES, BA Hons, PGCE (*Inquiry Learning*)
Mrs P Nikiteas, BA Hons, TEFL, Cert in SEN, CICTL (*PSHE*)

Mr D Caryer, BA Hons, UEFA B Licence (*Director of Football*)

Mr T Dowse, BA Hons EH Level 2 Coach (*Director of Hockey*)

Ms F Scollo, LTA Level 4 performance coach, MSc (*Senior School Tennis*)

Mr A Wells, ECB Level 4 & PGDip (*Director of Cricket*)

Year Heads:

Mr L Backler, BA Hons, PGCE, MA Ed (*First Year*)

Mr D Cheshire, BA Hons, MA, GTP (*Deputy Head of Sixth Form*)

Mr J Henham, BSc Hons, PGCE (*Sixth Form (Academic Progress)*)

Dr E Onofeghara, LLB, LLM, PGCE (*Assistant Director of Studies (GCSE)*)

Mr J Sealey, MA, BA Hons, PGCE (*Pre-Sixth and Blended Learning, Acting Head of Sixth Form (Engagement)*)

Mrs C Sutton, BA Hons, MSc, PGCE (*Sixth Form (Engagement)*)

Mrs M Waterhouse, H Dip, FDE (*Director of Studies (GCSE)*)

Mr A Hayes, MA, BSc Hons, PGCE (*Director of Curriculum Management*)

Bedford Modern School

Manton Lane, Bedford, Bedfordshire MK41 7NT

Tel: 01234 332500
email: info@bedmod.co.uk
website: www.bedmod.co.uk
Twitter: @BedfordModern
Facebook: @BedfordModernSchool
LinkedIn: /bedford-modern-school

Bedford Modern School is one of the Harpur Trust Schools in Bedford, sharing equally in the educational endowment bequeathed for the establishment of a school in Bedford by Sir William Harpur in 1566. Bedford Modern School was a Direct Grant Grammar School which became independent in 1976. It became co-educational in September 2003.

Number of Students. There are 249 students in the Junior School (aged 7–11) and 1,039 students in the Senior School (aged 11–18).

(*See also Bedford Modern Junior School entry in IAPS section.*)

Facilities. The School occupies an attractive forty-acre wooded site to the north of Bedford. The main buildings date from 1974 and there have been substantial additions since that time, most notably a new assembly hall, performance arena and classrooms to the Junior School (2002); a Sixth Form Study Centre and Refectory (The Rutherford Building – 2006) and new Library Resource Centre (2007). There are extensive facilities for Science, Technology and Information Technology. There have been recent extensions to the Music School and Performing Arts Centre. Each year group has its own common room.

A state-of-the-art Science Centre opened in September 2017. The exciting design provides current and future generations of BMS students with an inspirational learning environment.

The playing fields are all on the School site with extensive facilities for Rugby, Football, Cricket and Athletics. There is also a large swimming pool, a fitness suite, gym and sports hall. Recent additions include two large all-weather training areas and netball courts. The School shares a large and well-stocked Boathouse with the other Harpur Trust Schools on the River Ouse.

Admissions. Pupils are admitted between the ages of 7 and 16. The School conducts its own entrance assessments which are held in January of the year prior to September entry.

Registration fee is £100.

Fees per annum (2021–2022). Tuition: Junior School £10,528, Senior School and Sixth Form £14,443.

Assistance with Fees. The School offers bursaries which are available to pupils joining the School from Year 7 (11+) upwards and have been designed to provide opportunities for children with potential academically, in sport, performance arts, music and art/design and information technology. All bursaries are means-tested and are also dependent on a pupil's academic success in the entrance assessments. Further details may be obtained from the School.

Curriculum. The Junior School (ages 7–11) curriculum covers Mathematics, English, Humanities (History, Geography and RE), Science, Information and Communication Technology (ICT), Modern Foreign Languages, PE, Art, Drama, PSHE and Games. Pupils benefit both from a purpose-built practical skills centre containing art and science rooms as well as specialist computer and technology rooms, and from the Senior School, music, PE and games facilities including the swimming pool.

In the Senior School, the curriculum includes all the core subjects, as well as Technology, IT, RE, PE, Music, Art and Drama. All pupils experience French, German, and Spanish in Year 7 and Latin in Year 8 before making choices. Pupils opt for ten GCSE subjects. For the Sixth Form, pupils select four from a wide range of 2 subjects. In addition to all the traditional options, the choice of subjects also includes Computer Science, Government and Politics, Economics, Business, Religious Studies, Philosophy, DT Systems and Control, DT Product Design, Classical Civilisation, Theatre Studies, PE, Psychology and Film Studies. The majority will continue three subjects to A Level.

ICT Facilities. The School boasts a range of ICT facilities offering both staff and pupils an individual network account and email address so that they are able to access over 400 networked PCs across the School in addition to high-speed broadband Internet access, wireless classroom laptop sets, networked printing, and an extensive subject software library including a range of training courseware material.

All standard classrooms are equipped with a computer linked to ceiling mounted data projector and speakers. There are a number of interactive whiteboards and additional presentation equipment is also available for use. The School's website can be viewed at www.bedmod.co.uk.

Religious and Moral Education. The School is multi-faith and multicultural, and religious and moral education is given throughout. Personal, social and health education is a fundamental and well-established part of the timetable.

Individual Care. Every pupil has a personal tutor, who supervises and takes an interest in his or her academic progress, co-curricular activities and sporting interests. Tutors meet with their tutees on a daily basis and there is at least one longer pastoral session each week. Each Year Group has its own common room for use at break and lunchtimes and other non-taught times with a study area and recreational facilities.

We believe that common sense and courtesy lie at the heart of pastoral care. We stress self-discipline and high standards of personal conduct. The tutorial system and the academic organisation are discrete, working in parallel to complement each other. Teaching class sizes are a maximum of twenty-four and often many fewer. We aim to provide a relaxed but purposeful environment; a culture in which all feel at ease and are ambitious to achieve their best.

Drama. There are several large-scale productions each year, a Drama Festival hosted for local schools, and several smaller events. There are separate drama and dance studios and a 300-seat theatre. Speech and Drama is offered throughout the School, leading to LAMDA examinations. Ballet, tap and modern dance lessons follow the ISTD syllabus.

Music. Pupils can learn all the orchestral and band instruments as well as piano, keyboard, guitar, electric guitar and singing. The School has a large variety of choirs, orchestra, bands and ensembles. Pupils can follow courses for GCSE and A Level Music. Music accommodation includes a music technology suite with ten Apple computers and state-of-the-art recording facilities.

Activities. There are many school societies and clubs catering for a variety of tastes and interests. The voluntary Combined Cadet Force is strong with Army, Navy and RAF and Marine sections. There is a structured programme of outdoor education which includes residential trips from Years 6, 7 and 8 with international expeditions available for older students. Outreach including community service and the Duke of Edinburgh's Award scheme are very popular.

Sport. Rugby, football, cricket and rowing are major sports for boys; hockey, cricket, netball and rowing for girls. Additional activities include: table tennis, water polo, badminton, hockey (boys), equestrian, snowsports, cycling, cross-country, weights and fitness, fencing, fives, sevens, swimming, dance, athletics, rounders, tennis, climbing, and gymnastics. There is regular representation at national, divisional and regional levels.

Higher Education. The great majority of sixth form leavers go on to a degree course at their chosen university. More than 30% take courses in STEM (Science, Technology, Engineering and Mathematics) subjects.

Old Bedford Modernians' Club. For further details see the OBM section of the School website or please contact externalrelations@bedmod.co.uk.

Charitable status. Bedford Modern School is part of the Harpur Trust which is a Registered Charity, number 1066861. It includes in its aims the provision of high quality education for boys and girls.

Governors and Staff:
Chairman of School Governors: Shirley Jackson

Leadership Team:
Headmaster: Mr A N J Tate, MA
Senior Deputy Head: Mr A Whomsley, BA, QTS
Deputy Head Academic: Mr M R Price, MA Cantab, PGCE
Deputy Head Pastoral: Mrs J Goodacre, BA Hons, PGCE, MBA

Head of Junior School: Mrs J C Rex, BA Hons, PGCE
Director of Sixth Form: Mr J P White, BEd Hons
Director of External Relations: Ms J Ridge, BA Hons
Director of Operations: Mr R Pooley, BA Hons

Bedford School

De Parys Avenue, Bedford MK40 2TU

Tel:	01234 362216
email:	admissions@bedfordschool.org.uk
website:	www.bedfordschool.org.uk
Twitter:	@bedfordschool
Facebook:	@Bedford-School
Instagram:	@bedfordschool_uk
LinkedIn:	/school/bedfordschool

Bedford School is a leading boarding and day school for boys aged 13–18. The school, which was established in 1552, is situated in an extensive 50-acre estate in the heart of Bedford and is just 40 minutes from London by train.

'That they be good men'. Bedford School recognises that every single boy is different, and, indeed is proud to observe that there is no one 'Bedford boy'. Instead, with both inspiration and support, they seek to nurture each boy's individual interests and encourage him to develop them as far as he can take them. They aim for balanced, outward-looking, forward-thinking, kind and sociable young men who are comfortable in their own skins. When it is time to take the next step, each boy leaves as a good man, secure in his values, happy and ready to take his place in the world.

Number in School. 704 boys aged between 13–18 years: 199 weekly and full boarders, 505 day boys.

Boarders and Day Boys. There is a balanced mix of day boys, weekly boarders and full boarders, who combine in lessons, games and all other school activities. There are six Senior Boarding Houses, each containing up to 51 boys.

Academic. Academic excellence is central to life at Bedford School. Consistent high exam results at GCSE, A Level and the IB set the standard for academic achievement throughout the school. The curriculum extends learning well beyond the national requirements and is structured to provide a balanced and varied choice of subjects, which will challenge each boy's strengths.

Boys are encouraged to achieve through a balance of different teaching techniques, small class sizes and (where appropriate) setting, well-resourced and subject-specific classrooms, specialist teachers, prep setting, regular lecture series and visiting speakers, lunchtime and after school academic clinics. Technology is used extensively to support and enhance learning.

University and Careers. A strong Careers and UCAS provision enables all boys, throughout their school years, to access tailored, professional experience and advice. In addition to an annual careers fair, regular information evenings, lectures and seminars are also held. The school is a member of the Independent Schools Careers Organisation and holds E2E Gold status and the Career Mark.

Almost all leavers go on to higher education. In 2021, 80% of boys went on to Russell Group and/or Times Top 30 Universities.

Extracurricular. The school offers a diverse programme of extracurricular activities every evening between 4.15pm and 6.00pm for boarders and day boys alike, many of which involve girls from Harpur Trust sister school, Bedford Girls' School. Activities include the Combined Cadet Force (CCF), Duke of Edinburgh's Award scheme, community partnership work, fundraising groups, and more than 60 other clubs and societies from Astronomy to Young Enterprise. Concerts, plays, lectures and film performances are given in the Great Hall, the Recital Hall, the Erskine May Hall and the Quarry Theatre.

Service. In 2019, the school launched a new community partnership programme to create true partnerships that are valued and respected equally by the boys, the school and those that are supported. By the end of 2021, every boy leaving the school in the Upper Sixth has contributed to his local community through a long-term and meaningful partnership. The boys' community partnership work sits alongside a wide range of charity work that pupils throughout the school already undertake, including ongoing support for the men's health charity: Movember, House charity fundraising events, Duke of Edinburgh and IB CAS.

Sport. The school aims to inspire a lifelong interest in sport for all, promoting teamwork, well-being, fitness and fun. A team of dedicated, passionate specialist teachers and coaches are on hand to provide high-quality guidance and help each boy to develop his skills. Many boys go on to excel at sport, and the majority of major sport first teams are of county standard or beyond.

The school's major sports are rugby, hockey, rowing and cricket but the range of sports on offer extends to athletics, badminton, basketball, cross country, fencing, fives, golf, sailing, soccer, squash, swimming, tennis, water polo and weight training/conditioning.

First-class facilities include a twin AstroTurf complex with floodlights, an indoor 25m swimming pool, 28 tennis courts, four squash courts, a golf development centre with golf simulator, a climbing wall and acres of immaculate grass pitches.

Music. All boys have the opportunity to explore and perform, with a wide range of musical instruments and groups from which to choose. As well as the two Senior Symphony Orchestras, a Chamber Orchestra, a Concert Band and a large Choral Society, there is a Chapel Choir trained in the English Cathedral tradition, two Junior Orchestras, a Dance Band, Jazz Band, Rock Band, a large number of chamber music groups, and a Music Society. There is a full music programme throughout the year, with at least one concert a week.

The Music department is situated in a £3 million, state-of-the-art, purpose-built development, which includes a superb recital hall, music technology suite, multi-track recording studio and the school's radio station.

Drama. All boys can get involved in Bedford School's vibrant drama scene, whether on stage or behind the scenes. Each year a range of formal and informal dramatic productions are performed by all age groups.

The drama department is housed in the school's Quarry Theatre. The 286-seat theatre and 60-seat studio-theatre provide a superb venue for school productions and the extensive programme performed by visiting touring companies.

Art and Design. The art department works to develop each boy's individual artistic talents and encourages pupils to engage with and appreciate the world around them. Boys are encouraged to develop a lifelong appreciation of the creative arts with visits to museums and galleries, annual study tours abroad, weekly life drawing classes and a series of art lectures.

The Art School, located in a characterful mid-1750s Georgian building, has three specialist studios for painting, printmaking and sculpture. All three Art staff are practising artists.

Admissions. The majority of boys enter Bedford Prep School from the age of seven and the Upper School at 13 or 16 years of age. The Prep School has its own Headmaster and specialist staff. (*See Bedford Preparatory School entry in IAPS section.*)

Parents wishing to send their sons to Bedford School should apply to the Director of Admissions. All applicants are expected to provide evidence of good character and suitability from their previous school. Year 9 applicants from Preparatory Schools wishing to enter the Upper School are assessed in Year 6 or Year 7 by an initial Pre-test and interview. In Year 8 all applicants undertake a computer-based test (designed to measure raw academic potential) at the school, along with written English and Mathematics papers.

Boys looking to join the Sixth Form are invited for an assessment day in the January before entry. Applicants sit a Verbal Reasoning paper and have an interview with a senior member of staff. The school also takes up a reference with the boy's current school and considers his application along with his predicted grades at GCSE.

Additional information is available on the website: www.bedfordschool.org.uk/admissions.

Scholarships and Bursaries. The school offers a range of generous scholarships and bursaries to boys who excel academically or show outstanding talent in art, drama, music or sport (including golf).

Awards are available for boys joining the school at 13+ and 16+ entry points. For more information, please visit www.bedfordschool.org.uk/scholarships.

Fees per term (2021–2022). Day Boys £6,983; Full Boarders £11,810; Weekly Boarders £11,419.

Old Bedfordians Club. For further details, visit www.bedfordschool.org.uk/association/ob-club.

Charitable status. Bedford School is part of the Harpur Trust which is a Registered Charity, number 1066861.

Chairman of Governors: Sir Clive Loader, KCB, OBE, ADC, FRAeS

Head Master: Mr J S Hodgson, BA

Vice Master: Dr D Koch, BA, DPhil

Deputy Head (Academic): Mr S Baldock, MA, FRSB

Assistant Head (Teaching & Learning): Mr W Montgomery, BSc

Assistant Head (Pastoral): Mr M Gracie, BSc, MEd

Director of Finance and Operations and Clerk to the Governors: Mr A Macfarlane, BSc, MSc

Director of Marketing and Communications: Mrs J Dickson, BSc

Director of Bedford School Association: Mr H Maltby, BA

Director of Admissions: Mr R Midgley, BA Ed

Benenden School

Cranbrook, Kent TN17 4AA

Tel: 01580 240592
email: registry@benenden.school
website: www.benenden.school
Twitter: @benendenschool
Facebook: @benendenschool
Instagram: @benendenschool

Benenden aims to give each girl a complete education in which she achieves her academic potential and grows as an individual. We want her to relish all that school life has to offer so that she leaves us as a confident, positive young woman truly prepared for her future.

We expect each girl to be a responsible and considerate citizen who is outward looking, courageous and compassionate. We support her in being aspirational and in developing her interests and talents whilst learning to achieve balance in her life.

By emphasising the importance of spiritual growth, we hope that each girl will enjoy making a contribution to our supportive school and to be inspired to make a difference throughout her life in her future communities.

General Information. The School is an independent boarding school for 550 girls between the ages of 11 and 18, standing in its own parkland of 250 acres an hour from London.

All girls are boarders and the School is introduced day boarders from September 2021. On any given weekend, around two-thirds of girls are in School – perhaps no surprise considering Benenden offers the country's finest programme of Weekend activities. There is also a breathtaking array of co-curricular opportunities and numerous curriculum trips, with more than 150 activities on offer every week.

Headmistress. Mrs Samantha Price began as Headmistress in January 2014. Educated at Malvern Girls' College and Edinburgh University, after graduating Mrs Price joined the Tate Britain and started her teaching career in 1999 as a History of Art and History teacher at Reading Blue Coat School, where she stayed for a number of years. She then joined King's Canterbury as a Housemistress, History and History of Art teacher. Her next post was to be Deputy Head at Hereford Cathedral School and from there she became Head of Godolphin in 2010.

Samantha is married with a daughter and a son. Her husband is an Army Chaplain.

Curriculum. The curriculum is innovative and imaginative, and highly bespoke for each student.

Benenden uses five themes to frame the hundreds of enrichment, co-curricular, weekend and boarding opportunities: Physical Health and Wellbeing, Mind and Spirit, Life Skills, Global Awareness and Creativity and Culture. Students are encouraged to undertake activities from all five areas and move beyond their comfort zone, and their participation is accredited in a record of achievement.

The Professional Skills Programme teaches Sixth Formers practical skills that are vital for the workplace.

The Benenden Diploma is our bespoke curriculum for the Fourths and Upper Fourths (the two youngest year groups).

Facilities. Our new School Hall and Music School will open in 2022.

Other notable facilities include the All-Weather Pitch, state-of-the-art Science Centre, beautiful eco-classroom and impressive Theatre and Drama teaching complex.

Sport. Lacrosse, netball, tennis, hockey, swimming, rounders, badminton, athletics and cross country, squash, gym, dance, fencing, rugby, judo, karate, trampolining, exercise and fitness, equestrian, scuba diving and cricket.

Opportunities in Music. Tuition is available in all orchestral and keyboard instruments as well as singing. Numerous opportunities exist for instrumental and choral performance and hosts recitals by musicians of international calibre.

Opportunities in Speech and Drama. Students are able to pursue drama as an extracurricular activity throughout their School career by participating in drama workshops, House and Lower and Upper School plays. Speech and drama lessons are available and students are prepared for both Trinity and LAMDA examinations.

Optional Extras. We offer more than 150 co-curricular activities, including the Duke of Edinburgh's Award, Combined Cadet Force, karate, journalism, ballet, modern dance and many others.

Fees per term (2021–2022). £13,616 payable before the start of term. The fees include the country's finest programme of Weekend Activities at no extra charge, as well as a breathtaking array of co-curricular opportunities and numerous curriculum trips.

Admission. Entrance to the School is after internal assessment at Preview Weekend, (11+ a year ahead, 13+ two years ahead), but dependent upon candidates meeting the School's standard at 11+ Common Entrance or in entrance papers. 13+ firm offers may be made following Preview Weekend. There is also a small intake at Sixth Form level, with competitive entry by the School's own examination.

Scholarships and Bursaries. Benenden is proud to offer bursary support to ensure that all those worthy of a place at the School have the same opportunities regardless of their financial circumstances. There are five main types of bursary award available and these are listed in full on our website,

We offer scholarships recognising girls' performance in Academic, Music, Art and Design, Design and Technology, Sport, and All-Round performance.

For further information, please contact the Director of Admissions.

Charitable status. Benenden School (Kent) Limited is a Registered Charity, number 307854. It is a charitable foundation for the education of girls.

Governors:
Chairman of the Governing Council: The Hon Mrs A Birkett, MA, MBA
Vice Chairman of the Governing Council: Mrs A McNab, BA, FCA
Mrs W M Carey, BA
Dr F Cornish, MA, FRCGP
Mrs D Coslett, BA Hons, MBA, PGCE, NPQH
Mrs F Blakemore, MEng EEM Oxford, ACA
Dr R Evenett, MA, MSc, PhD, FCA
Mr P Marshall, BComm
Mrs M McDonald-Kelly, Dip Grafton Academy Hons, CERT Management Science

Mrs A J Mogridge, BA, FCIPR, FPRCA
Mr C G Nicolle, MA Oxon
Mr J Pearce, MA Oxford
Mr G Pugh, MA, ACMA, MBA
Mr P Simpkin, MA Hons
Prof L Taub, BA, MA, PhD

Senior Staff:

Headmistress: Samantha Price

Director of Strategic Projects: Matt Commander
*Executive Director – Curriculum and Professional
    Excellence:* Lesley Tyler
First Deputy: Steve Miller
Deputy Head – Academic: Helen Semple
Deputy Head – Boarding and Pastoral Care: Anne
    Wakefield
Development Director: Kyle Johnson
Director of Finance and Operations: Julie Lerbech
Assistant Head – Head of Co-Curricular: Neal George
Director of Marketing and Communications: Ian Read
*Assistant Head – Teaching, Learning and Academic
    Extension:* Farah Dawood

Berkhamsted Schools Group

Overton House
131 High Street, Berkhamsted, Hertfordshire HP4 2DJ

Tel: 01442 358000 (General enquiries)
        01442 358001 (Admissions)
email: enquiries@berkhamsted.com
        admissions@berkhamsted.com
        boys@berkhamsted.com
        girls@berkhamsted.com
        sixth@berkhamsted.com
website: www.berkhamsted.com
Twitter: @berkhamstedsch
Facebook: @berkhamstedschool
LinkedIn: /Berkhamsted-School

Our family of six schools offers a 'Diamond model' with co-educational and single-sex tuition for boys and girls, providing the best of both worlds in one family of Schools. At the Pre-Prep and Prep, boys and girls are taught together until the age of 11, separately from 11–16 (Berkhamsted Boys and Berkhamsted Girls), enabling them to flourish academically, with numerous co-educational activities, trips and events, before coming back together again in a joint Sixth. Heatherton provides a co-educational nursery class (3–4) and single-sex education for girls from age 4 to 11. *Please also refer to separate entries for Berkhamsted Prep, Berkhamsted Pre-Prep and Heatherton.*

We are a family of Schools with a long history and proud traditions, yet we have a firm eye on current best educational practice and use of leading-edge teaching technologies. We are proud of our excellent academic standards without being academic hothouses. The Berkhamsted family of Schools have all the advantages of access to large-school resources with a small school sense of community and individual care. Our House system places academic progress and pastoral care at the centre of your child's education. There is a range of options to make life easier for time-pressured families: a day nursery that

operates 50 weeks a year from 07.30 to 18.00, wrap-around care and extended hours, the choice of flexible, weekly or full boarding, coach routes and a multi-activity holiday camp and other courses on offer during the main school holidays through Camp Beaumont: Berkhamsted.

There are 406 pupils in the flourishing co-educational Sixth. Between the ages of 11 and 16, 495 boys at the Boys School (Castle) and 395 girls at the Girls School (Kings), are taught in single-sex groups.

The Principal is a member of both HMC and GSA.

Aims. At Berkhamsted we believe that excellent academic results do not have to be won at the expense of the wider attributes of a good education. All pupils are supported and encouraged to reach their full potential, with appropriate teaching environments for each age group and a structure that offers the best of both co-educational and single-sex tuition. In addition to the development of the intellect, social, sporting and cultural activities play an important part within the framework of a disciplined and creative community based on Christian values. It is important that pupils come to value both the individual and the Community through school life. The School seeks to encourage spiritual and moral values and a sense of responsibility as an essential part of the pursuit of excellence.

Location. The School stands in the heart of Berkhamsted, a historic and thriving town only 30 miles from London. It enjoys excellent communications to London, the airports, to the Midlands and the communities of Buckinghamshire, Bedfordshire and Hertfordshire.

Facilities. The original site has at its heart a magnificent Tudor Hall used as a schoolroom for over 300 years. Other buildings are from late Victorian to modern periods and of architectural interest (especially the Chapel modelled on the Church of St Maria dei Miracoli in Venice). With separate Pre-Prep and Prep sites, and two Senior School campuses, the School is well equipped with a range of facilities. There are new Science laboratories, Library and Learning Resources Centres, Information Technology suites, Sixth Form centres located on the two Senior School campuses, Careers libraries, Dining halls, Medical centre, House rooms, Deans' Hall (an Assembly Hall) and Centenary Theatre (a modern 500-seat theatre also used for concerts and theatre productions). Recreational and sports facilities include extensive playing fields, Eton Fives courts, Squash courts, Tennis courts, Gymnasium, Drama studio, Music school and Art studios. Additional facilities include a Sports Hall and 25m indoor swimming pool and a state-of-the-art Design Centre as well as the Nash-Harris Building at Kings comprising a new dining facility, classrooms and Chapel. More recent additions include a new sports pavilion and changing rooms at the School's Chesham Road Playing Fields and upgrades to the Football and Rugby pitches, as well as a high ropes course at the Haresfoot site and a brand new, floodlit 4G AstroTurf sports pitch at Kings.

Curriculum. The Senior School curriculum includes: English, English Literature, Mathematics, Biology, Chemistry, Physics, History, Geography, Religious Studies, French/Spanish, Latin/Classics, Mandarin, Music, Art, Physical Education and Design and Technology. Up to eleven subjects may be taken for GCSE. In the Sixth Form, courses are offered in 28 subjects and all students benefit from an Enrichment Programme with the option to complete an Extended Project Qualification. Pupils are prepared for university entrance, including Oxbridge. Careers guidance and personal tutoring are offered throughout.

Day and Boarding. Pupils may be full boarders, weekly boarders, flexible boarders or day pupils. The two Boarding houses, accommodating boys and girls separately, are well-equipped and within a few minutes' walk of the main campus. There are up to 60 boarding places. Day pupils come from both Berkhamsted and the surrounding areas of Hertfordshire, Buckinghamshire and Bedfordshire.

Pastoral Care and Discipline. The School Houses are the main social and pastoral unit; the Head of House and House Tutors. They provide continuity of support and advice and monitor each individual pupil's progress. The aim is to encourage self-discipline so that pupils work with a sense of responsibility and trust. Pupils are expected to be considerate, courteous, honest, and industrious.

Pupil wellbeing is of vital importance at Berkhamsted. The Deputy Heads, alongside the Pupil Wellbeing and Personal Development team, support teaching staff across the whole school in implementing a proactive strategy that focuses primarily on keeping pupils well and looking for early signs of potential issues. There is a Medical Centre with qualified staff. The School Medical Officer has special responsibility for boarders. Qualified Counsellors are available to all pupils for confidential counselling. The School also has a full-time Chaplain.

Sport and Leisure Activities. Major sports for Girls are Lacrosse, Netball and Tennis and for Boys, Rugby, Football and Cricket. A number of other sports are also pursued including Athletics, Badminton, Cross-Country, Equestrian, Eton Fives, Golf, Hockey, Judo, Rowing, Shooting, Squash and Swimming. Team games are encouraged and pupils are selected for regional and national squads.

There is a flourishing Duke of Edinburgh's Award at all levels. The CCF, community service, work experience and Young Enterprise are offered. The format of the school day allows pupils in the Senior School to choose from a wide range of clubs, societies or courses, which are attended during school hours. Regular school theatre productions, orchestral and choral concerts achieve high standards of performance.

Enrichment. At Berkhamsted, we recognise that intelligence takes many forms and we encourage all our pupils to pursue their talents and interests through the many enrichment opportunities on offer for each age group. These opportunities are available for academic subjects and co-curricular topics. For the more academically adventurous, there are a number of avenues through which to fulfil their potential at each school.

Careers. A team of advisors, internal and external, is directed by the Head of Careers who also arranges Careers Lunches, Applying to Higher Education training sessions, Medicine and Law Careers Taster Days and an annual Higher Education, Careers, Apprenticeships and GAP Year Fair. Heads of House oversee pupils' applications for higher education, together with parents and Careers advisors. The great majority of leavers proceeds to university and higher education.

Entry. Entry to the Pre-Prep School is from the age of 3, entry to the Prep School from 7, and entry to the Senior Boys & Girls from 11. Children are assessed for entry to the Nursery year group during a meeting with the Headteacher and attend an informal assessment day for Year 2 entry. The School's Entrance Assessments and an interview are required for entry to the Prep and Senior Boys and Girls.

In order to gain admission to Berkhamsted Sixth, students require 43 points across their best 8 GCSE subjects with a minimum requirement of a Grade 6 in the subjects they wish to study. There are also specific admission requirements relating to certain courses, although competition amongst external candidates means that it is the norm that top grades are required.

Scholarships and Bursaries. It is the Governors' policy to award Scholarships and Exhibitions on merit to pupils whom the Governors wish to attract to Berkhamsted because of the contribution that they are able to make to School life, be that academic, musical, sporting, creative or as potential leaders.

Academic Scholarships are awarded on the basis of academic merit alone on entrance to the School.

Who can apply? Applications are welcome from pupils who qualify from their performance in the Entrance Examination and sit Scholarship Examinations in English, Mathematics and other appropriate subjects. These are usually only at 11+, 13+ and 16+.

Incent Awards are made to talented pupils from financially or socially disadvantaged backgrounds.

They are awarded to enable pupils who would not otherwise be able to attend Berkhamsted, to afford to do so.

Candidates must demonstrate academic potential or have a particular talent(s) or skill(s) so that they will make a significant contribution to some other area of School life.

The Award shall be up to 100% of the school fees, and, where appropriate, will also include financial assistance for School uniform and sports kit, travel to and from school, school trips and expeditions, extra lessons e.g. Music, Drama etc if applicable.

Whilst most applications for Incent Awards will be received from candidates who are presently in maintained sector schools, Berkhamsted does work with a number of feeder schools in the independent sector who offer awards on a similar basis and thus will entertain applications from pupils who are presently in receipt of means-tested awards of this nature.

Music, Drama, Art and Sports Scholarships are also offered.

Where there is a demonstrated need, additional means-tested funding may be available to those awarded Scholarships.

More information about Scholarships and Bursaries may be obtained from the Admissions Manager or on the School website.

Fees per term (2021–2022). Day Pupils £3,610–£7,390; Boarding Pupils £11,870 (full), £9,950 (weekly 4 nights).

Further information about the School's aims, its academic curriculum, facilities, activities, admissions, scholarships and awards is published in the School's prospectus and is available on the School website. Admissions enquiries should be made in the first instance to the Admissions Manager, who will be pleased to arrange for parents to visit the School.

Old Berkhamstedians. There is a vibrant and growing community of Old Berkhamstedians: www.theold berkhamstedians.org. President: Mrs Emma Jeffrey.

Charitable status. Berkhamsted Schools Group is a Registered Charity, number 310630.

Principal: **Mr R P Backhouse**, MA Cantab

Vice Principal: Mr A Ford, BA
Chief Operating Officer: Mr J Anthony, BSc, FCA
Chief People Officer: Mrs T L Evans, CIPD, FlnstLM
Assistant Vice-Principal (*External Relations*): Mr R
    Thompson, BA
Headteacher, Berkhamsted Sixth: Mr M Walker, BA
Headteacher, Berkhamsted Boys (*Boys 11–16*): Mrs M-C
    Startin, BA, MA
Headteacher, Berkhamsted Girls (*Girls 11–16*): Mrs E A
    Richardson, BA
Deputy Head, Berkhamsted Sixth: Ms E Watson, BEng
Deputy Head, Berkhamsted Boys (*Boys 11–16*): Mr R
    Mackay
Deputy Head, Berkhamsted Girls (*Girls 11–16*): Mrs L
    Simson, BA Cantab
Deputy Head, Curriculum: Mr W R C Gunary, BSc
Deputy Head, Teaching & Innovation: Mrs H Butland, MA
Deputy Head, Academic Performance: Mr N Cale
Deputy Head, Pupil Wellbeing and Personal Development,
    Mr G Anker, BA, MA
Deputy Head, Leadership, Mr D Hardy
Director of IT: Mr P Samtani
Finance Director: Mr S Elliff

Birkdale School

Oakholme Road, Sheffield S10 3DH

Tel: 0114 266 8408
            Admissions: 0114 266 8409
email: headmaster@birkdaleschool.org.uk
            admissions@birkdaleschool.org.uk
            enquiries@birkdaleschool.org.uk
website: www.birkdaleschool.org.uk
Twitter: @BirkdaleSchool
Facebook: @BirkdaleSchool

Motto: *Res non verba*

Birkdale School is an HMC day school for 850 pupils,
boys from age 4 to 18 with a co-educational Sixth Form of
over 200 pupils. The age 4–11 Prep School is on a separate
campus nearby. (*For further details see IAPS section.*)
Birkdale has begun the process of becoming fully co-
educational by admitting girls in Reception to Year 4 and
will continue until the school is fully co-educational. The
Governing Body is in membership of the Association of
Governing Bodies of Independent Schools.

Set in a pleasant residential area near the University 1.5
miles from the city centre, and 5 miles from the Peak
District National Park, the school has expanded in recent
years to provide for Sheffield and South Yorkshire the only
independent secondary school for boys, with a co-
educational Sixth Form. Birkdale Prep School for 250 pupils
is on a separate campus half a mile from the Senior School.
School coaches bring pupils from Worksop, Chesterfield,
North Derbyshire, Rotherham and Barnsley.

Birkdale is a Christian school, reflecting its foundation in
the evangelical tradition. There is nothing exclusive about
this: entrance is open to all, and there is no denominational
emphasis. We seek to develop the full potential of each
individual: body, mind and spirit. Within a framework of
high academic standards, pastoral care is given a high
priority, balanced by an emphasis on sport and outdoor

pursuits, music and drama with a wide range of
extracurricular activities available.

At 18, over 95% of pupils go on to university, with a good
proportion each year gaining places at prestigious
universities including Oxford and Cambridge.

Admission. The main ages of admission are at 4, 7, 11
and 16, although it is possible to admit pupils at other ages if
a place is available. Entrance examinations for candidates at
11 are held annually towards the end of January. Entrance to
the co-educational Sixth Form is subject to interview and a
satisfactory performance in GCSE examinations. In the first
instance, enquiries should be addressed to the Registrar.

Academic Curriculum. Over 20 subjects are offered at
A Level. A full range of academic subjects are offered to
GCSE. All pupils study English Language and Literature,
Mathematics, Double Award Science, at least one Modern
Foreign Language (French, German, Spanish) and at least
one of the Humanities subjects (Classical Studies,
Geography, History, RE). Optional subjects include Art,
Design & Technology, Latin, Drama and Music. The wider
curriculum includes ICT, Religious Education, Health
Education, Careers and Economic Awareness. Latin,
German and Spanish are compulsory subjects in the Lower
School (11–13) in addition to the usual range of National
Curriculum subjects.

Games and Outdoor Pursuits. The major games are
Rugby, Soccer, Cricket and Athletics, with Cross Country,
Hockey, Netball, Tennis, Squash, Basketball, Volleyball,
Swimming and Golf also available. The playing fields are a
short bus ride away from the school. A 10-lane cricket net
facility, constructed to full English Cricket Board standards
was opened in 2012. The netting system is retractable and so
the area can also be fully utilised for football and hockey
outside of the cricket season. All members of the school
play games weekly. Additional team practices take place on
Saturdays or at other times, and there is a full fixture list in
the major sports. The school enjoys regular use of the
university swimming pool nearby. Additionally, we use two
local international venues, Ponds Forge and the English
Institute of Sport for basketball, netball, dance and athletics.
Birkdale's Sports Hall is at the centre of the Senior School
campus.

Outdoor Pursuits play an important part in the overall
leadership training programme. All members of the school
participate in regular training sessions leading in each age
group to a major expedition. This programme culminates in
the 4th Form camp held annually in Snowdonia. Virtually all
members of the Third Form undertake the Bronze Award of
the Duke of Edinburgh's Award scheme, and an increasing
number progress to Silver and Gold awards.

Music and the Arts. Music, Art and Drama flourish both
within and outside the formal curriculum. A full annual
programme of dramatic and musical productions is
arranged. Over 120 pupils receive weekly instrumental
music lessons at school, and a wide range of orchestras and
choirs provide opportunities for pupils to experience group
musical activities at an appropriate level.

Extracurricular Activities. In addition to the activities
above there is a broad range of clubs and societies which
meet at lunchtime and outside the formal school day,
providing opportunities for members of the school to
explore and excel in activities such as Chess, Debating and
Design as well as in the usual activities such as Sport,
Drama, Outdoor Pursuits, Art and Music. Awards are often
won in local and national competitions.

Careers. The school is a member of the Inspiring Futures careers guidance service and there is a well equipped Careers Centre on site. A biennial Careers Convention is held in the school and regular visits are made by services liaison officers and others to give advice and help to pupils under the guidance of the school's careers staff.

Fees per term (2021–2022). Sixth Form £4,740; Senior School: £4,685 (Years 9–11), £4,610 (Years 7 and 8); Prep School £3,850; Pre-Prep Department £3,140 including lunches, textbooks and stationery (with the exception of Sixth Form textbooks).

Scholarships and Bursaries. Academic and Music Scholarships are normally available at 11 and 16. Bursaries are available to increase awards up to 100% of fees in cases of proven financial need. In addition we offer the Arkwright Scholarship at 16+.

Charitable status. Birkdale School is a Registered Charity, number 1018973, and a Company Limited by Guarantee, registered in England, number 2792166. It exists to develop the full potential of its members within a Christian community.

Chairman of Governors: P Houghton, FCA

Bursar and Clerk to the Governors: D H Taylor, BSc

Head Master: **P Harris**, MSc

Deputy Head (*Pastoral*): P R King, BA

Deputy Head (*Academic*): R D Becks, BSc

Heads of Departments:
Art: A Armitage, BA, Dip Ed Management
Biology: Mrs B Holder, MA, BSc
Careers: C J Cook, BSc
Classics: Ms M Fforde, MA, BA
Design & Technology: P S Offer, BA
Drama: A G Low, BA
Economics & Business Studies: S B Stoddard, BA
English: Mrs S J Burt, BA
Geography: H Parker, BSc
History: M S Clarke, MA
ICT: G Morton, BSc
Mathematics: M E Roach, BSc
Modern Languages: Mrs K M Higham, BA, MEd
Music: A M Jordan, BMus
Outdoor Pursuits: S Watchman, BA
Physical Education: S C Depledge, BSc
Science & Physics: Dr P C Jukes, PhD, MA
Religious Education: T J Pearson, BA
Chemistry: Dr P D Myatt, BSc, DPhil
SENCO: Mrs L E Marsh, BA
Counsellor: Miss B C McPeake, MA

Prep School:
Head of Prep School: C J Burch, BA, PGCE
Deputy Head: J R Leighton, BEd
Director of Studies: A J Oakey, MScEd, BA
Senior Mistress: Mrs E J Arcari, BA / Mrs J Kitchen, MEd, BEd

Birkenhead School

58 Beresford Road, Oxton, Birkenhead, Merseyside CH43 2JD

Tel: 0151 652 4014
email: enquire@birkenheadschool.co.uk
website: www.birkenheadschool.co.uk
Twitter: @BirkenheadSchl
Facebook: @birkenheadschool

Motto: *Beati mundo corde*

Birkenhead School is a leading co-educational independent school situated in Oxton, Wirral. The School offers outstanding educational opportunities for girls and boys from three months to eighteen years and attracts students from Wirral, Cheshire, Liverpool and North Wales.

The School was established in 1860 and at the heart of the School is a strong and welcoming student and parent community.

The *Good Schools Guide* comments 'A happy school consistently producing confident and considerate individuals as well as top results. Birkenhead may appear traditional from the outside but there is a strong streak of innovation running through all areas that shows it does not rest on past successes.'

School buildings are grouped around a spacious campus with a beautiful 'village green' at the centre. The different parts of the School have their own distinct areas and the School offers an educational journey from Nursery to Sixth Form and children move seamlessly from one year to the next.

Exam results position the School as one of the leading independent schools within the North-West. The aim is academic excellence for all through inspirational teaching that looks to embed a lifelong love of learning. By knowing each individual, the School aims to recognise and celebrate each student's unique skills and passions, adding value at every stage of the educational journey. Details of the curriculum at each key stage are available on the school website.

The education goes beyond the confines of the National Curriculum and students enjoy an extensive co-curricular programme of clubs and activities alongside programmes such as 'Enrich and Explore', 'Future Skills' and 'Beyond the Curriculum'.

Music plays an important role at the School, with students encouraged to learn a musical instrument from a young age. There is a wide range of musical bands to join including both Prep and Seniors Orchestras, Concert Band, Big Band and various ensembles. The School hosts an annual Festival of Music that includes a wide range of concerts, lunchtime recitals and musical workshops which are open to both the School and wider community.

The School has its own Chapel and School Chaplain. The School has a reputation for Choral music and offers a Chapel Choir that sings at weekday services and the weekly Sunday Evensong service.

Sports offered at the School include rugby, hockey, netball and lacrosse during the winter terms and cricket, athletics, tennis and rounders during the summer. There are representative teams at all levels and the playing fields cover approximately 40 acres on three different sites. Facilities include a floodlit AstroTurf surface, strength and conditioning gym, cardio gym, squash court, fitness suites and a climbing wall. The School has its own Duke of Edinburgh's Award scheme.

There is a strong tradition of drama, with regular Prep and Senior productions, alongside annual House Drama and House Music competitions.

The School's 'Inspiring Talks Series' encompasses the Nicholls Lecture Series for sixth form students, the Boumphrey Lecture Programme for younger pupils in Prep and a Parent Seminar Programme. Since 2017, the School has also welcomed high-profile public figures to the School for events that are open to members of the public and recently launched a 'No Limits' Workshop programme for female students.

The School works closely within its community and has links with a number of business organisations, the Chamber of Commerce and many local charities. The School offers a range of events for children across Wirral including author talks, science events for local Brownies and Cub groups and sports festivals.

The legacy of an education at the School is about confidence, social awareness, and a breadth of skills and knowledge that will stay with students for a lifetime and set them apart from their peers. The majority of students continue their learning at Russell Group universities including Oxbridge and the School has a long tradition of producing Medical students. Upon leaving the School, The Old Birkonian Society offers young people membership of an established and extensive community and a range of alumni events provide valuable networking opportunities.

Fees per term (2021–2022). Seniors £4,055–£4,370; Prep £2,900–£3,295.

Admissions. Both the Headmaster and Head of Prep meet personally with prospective parents to discuss individual children's passions and abilities and admissions are managed by their respective PAs. Prospective families are welcomed and encouraged to visit the School for a personalised visit at any time during the year and early application is encouraged. The School hosts Open Events during the Michaelmas, Lent and Summer terms. Entrance into the Prep is through individual assessments and interviews. Entry into Seniors at age 11 is by progression from the Prep and, for external applicants, through Assessment and Taster Days hosted by the School in Years 5 and 6. Entry into the Sixth Form is based on GCSE grades and interview.

Charitable status. Birkenhead School is a Registered Charity, number 1093419. The charitable status means the School not only accepts fee-paying pupils but can offer places to able children from less advantaged backgrounds.

Visitor: The Rt Revd Dr Peter Forster, The Lord Bishop of Chester

President: Sir Andreas Whittam Smith, CBE

Chair of Governors: Mr A Cross, LLB Hons

Company Secretary and Clerk to the Governors: Mr M J Turner, MA Oxon, MInstLM (*Bursar*)

Headmaster: Mr P R Vicars, MA

Deputy Head (Pastoral): Mrs K Pankhurst, BA
Deputy Head (Academic): Mr T Whitworth, BA

Head of Prep: Mr H R FitzHerbert, BA
Deputy Head of Prep: Mr R A Halpin, BSc

Bishop's Stortford College

School House, Maze Green Road, Bishop's Stortford, Hertfordshire CM23 2PQ

Tel: 01279 838575
email: admissions@bishopsstortfordcollege.org
website: www.bishopsstortfordcollege.org
Twitter: @BSCollege
Facebook: @bishopsstortfordcollege
Instagram: @thebishopsstortfordcollege

Motto: *Soli Deo Gloria*

Bishop's Stortford College is a friendly, co-educational, day and boarding community providing high academic standards, good discipline and an excellent all-round education. We aim to equip our pupils with the vital qualifications, skills, adaptability and, above all, confidence to thrive as adults in a rapidly changing world. A flourishing Prep School and Pre-Prep, sharing many facilities with the Senior School, give all the advantages of educational continuity whilst retaining their own distinctive characters.

The College welcomes children of all denominations and faiths, and, while the majority of current pupils' homes are in the Home Counties and East Anglia, a substantial number of parents work and live overseas.

There are typically 600 pupils in the Senior School (boarders and day), 510 pupils in the Prep School and 130 in the Pre-Prep.

Location. Bishop's Stortford is midway between London and Cambridge and can be reached quickly via Liverpool Street Station, M25 and M11. Stansted Airport is a ten-minute drive. The College is situated on the edge of the town adjacent to open countryside. The gardens and grounds cover about 130 acres.

Facilities. Purpose-built Pre-Prep accommodation, Prep and Senior School libraries, extensive ICT facilities and campus-wide Wi-Fi, outstanding sports facilities, well-resourced centres for Design and Technology, the Sciences, Languages, Music and Drama and a superb Art Centre. The main school Library and state-of-the-art indoor swimming pool are notable features. All school Houses offer a welcoming, family-like environment.

At the centre of the campus stands the Memorial Hall, used daily for Assembly. Originally built in 1921, it stands in memory of Old Stortfordians who served and fell during the Wars.

Academic Organisation. The Curriculum is designed to give as broad a course of study as possible up to the specialisation at A Level and Oxbridge entry.

In addition to the three Sciences, English, Maths, Geography and History, all new pupils joining the Fourth Form (Year 9) take Design and Technology, ICT, Art, Ethics Philosophy and Theology and PE/Swimming. Pupils take two modern foreign languages chosen from French, German and Spanish. Pupils additionally choose 2 subjects from DT, Drama, Music and Latin.

All Lower and Upper Fifth Forms (Years 10 and 11), take 'core' subjects; English Language, English Literature, Maths and the three Sciences. Four other subjects, one of which must be a modern foreign language, are chosen from History, Geography, Design and Technology, Latin, French, Spanish, German, Art and Design, Music, Drama and Ethics Philosophy and Theology. Pupils also have one period each of non-GCSE courses in PE, Swimming and Personal, Social and Health Education.

At all stages, progress is carefully monitored by Housemasters, Housemistresses and Tutors, Heads of Department, and in Staff Meetings. Throughout the Senior School, grades for Effort and Attainment are given twice termly, and full written reports are sent home twice a year for each year group.

Careers. A purpose-built Higher Education and Careers Centre is open daily with three specialist staff. The College has close ties with Inspiring Futures, local commerce and industry and the Hertfordshire Careers Service. Links with local businesses are strong and there is an extensive programme of Work Experience organised for pupils in the Upper Fifth and Lower Sixth Forms.

The Sixth Form. Pupils choose between three and four subjects in the Lower Sixth, before specialising in the Upper Sixth. Sixth Formers select from the following subjects: Art, Biology, Business, Chemistry, Classical Civilisation, Design and Technology: Product Design, Drama and Theatre Studies, Economics, English Language, English Literature, Ethics Philosophy and Theology, Film Studies, French, Geography, German, History, Maths, Further Maths, Latin, Music, Physical Education, Physics, Politics, Psychology and Spanish.

Pupils can take an Extended Project Qualification (EPQ) which requires independent study into an area of individual interest, perhaps an extension of a particular aspect of the syllabus or something outside the curriculum. The structure of EPQ works to prepare pupils for Higher Education and employment while inspiring and motivating them.

An extensive PSHEE programme operates throughout the school and there is a weekly Sixth Form lecture.

Each department organises visits and invites guest speakers to meetings of Societies, which are held in lunch hours or evenings. These, together with small group teaching, seminars and excellent resources, encourages pupils to develop their self-reliance, analytical skills and their spirit of academic enquiry to equip them for Higher Education and beyond.

Progress is closely monitored, as in Senior School, with the addition of overall supervision from the Head of Sixth Form. Parents are closely involved and regular Parents' Meetings are held.

Worship. The Religious Instruction, Sunday Worship and occasional weekday services are interdenominational. The opportunity of exploring faith and being prepared for adult membership of particular churches (including Confirmation) is offered each year through the Chaplain.

Personal Development Programme (PDP). The College promotes an environment of wholehearted participation and thus the Personal Development Programme enables pupils to enjoy a range of extra-curricular opportunities to support their inter-personal development. The initiatives offered come under three broad categories: creative, active and service. Creative opportunities may include, amongst many others, Computer Coding and Programming, Film Making or Cake Decorating. Active opportunities can include: Dance, Squash, Beekeeping or Hockey Academy. Service opportunities include Police Cadets and various forms of Community Service and Duke of Edinburgh's Awards. The programme also allows pupils to build on their academic progress and passion, transferring their academic learning to more practical scenarios. PDP is compulsory for Fourth and Lower Fifth Form pupils and is actively encouraged for all those in the upper reaches of the College.

Music and Drama. An interest in and appreciation for all kinds of music is encouraged throughout the school. In Form One and Form Two (Years 3 and 4), all Prep School pupils are taught an instrument in class and those who show promise are encouraged to continue individually in the Senior School.

There are numerous ensembles including Orchestra, Wind Band, guitar and string quartets, brass group, a Choral Society, and Choirs. Pupils are also encouraged to make music in small groups from the earliest stages. The College has a fully equipped Recording Studio. The Music Staff includes 27 visiting teachers of singing and all the main instruments, together with the Director of Music, an Assistant Director and a Musician in Residence. The House Music Competition is a major event in the school year and involves all pupils. There are regular opportunities to perform in public at Pupils' Concerts and in school assemblies.

Drama is an area of strength with significant developments in recent years to the theatre facilities, curriculum and performing opportunities in which all pupils can participate. A Level Theatre Studies is offered, as is GCSE Drama.

Sport. The College has an excellent reputation in all areas of sporting achievement. Physical Education is taught in the Fourth and Fifth Forms and facilities include a Sports Hall, an impressive indoor swimming pool, all-weather surface courts for netball and tennis, two floodlit AstroTurf pitches for hockey and tennis, a multi-use games area and 100 acres of playing fields.

Health. The Medical Centre is staffed by a resident full-time Nurse, part-time Nurse and full-time Health Care Assistant. Regular surgeries are held by the School's Medical Officer.

Varied and wholesome meals, included in the fees, are provided for all pupils in the College Dining Hall.

Prep School. The organisation of the Prep School (for pupils up to age 13+) is largely separate from that of the Senior School, but the curricula of the two schools are carefully integrated. Pupils are able to share resources in Sport, Design and Technology and Music.

(*For further details see entry in IAPS section.*)

Admission. The main ages of admission are 4, 7, 11, 13 and 16, but entry at intermediate stages is possible. Entry to the Senior School at 13+ is based on school reference, interview and entry test results. Sixth Form Entry Interviews and Examinations are held in the November before year of entry.

Scholarships. The following annual awards are available:

10+ (Year 6): Academic, Music

11+ (Year 7): Academic, Music, Art, Sport

13+ (Year 9): Academic, Music, Art, Sport

Sixth Form: Academic, Music, Art, Sport

Financial Assistance. Means-tested bursaries are awarded based on individual need. Awards range from partial assistance of 5% up to (in exceptional circumstances) 100% of the full fees.

Fees per term (2021–2022). Senior School: Full Boarders £11,495; Overseas Boarders £11,946; Weekly Boarders £10,932; 2 Day Part-Time Boarding £8,838–£8,900; 3 Day Part-Time Boarding £9,455–£9,507; Day £6,783–£6,844.

Prep School: Full Boarders £8,566; Overseas Boarders £8,746; Weekly Boarders £8,314; Day £5,126–£5,576.

Pre-Prep: £3,320–£3,385.

Fees are inclusive except for individual music tuition.

Charitable status. The Incorporated Bishop's Stortford College Association is a Registered Charity, number 311057. Its aims and objectives are to provide high quality Independent Day and Boarding education for boys and girls from age 4 to 18.

Governing Council:

Mr G E Baker, BSc, MRICS (*Chairman*)
Mrs I M Pearman, MA, MRICS (*Vice Chairman*)
Mr D Alexander
Dr P J Hargrave, BSc, PhD, FREng
Mr S R Lehec
Mrs P Mullender, MA
Mr D F Thomson, BAcc, CA

Representative Governors Appointed by the Council:
Mr A J W Conti, BEng, FCA (*Parent Representative*)
Mr R C V Harrison, BCom, ACA (*United Reformed Church Representative*)
Mr C P Solway, BSc, MRICS (*Baptist Union Representative*)
Dr S Nurbhai, MB ChB, MRCP UK
Mr P Dodd, BSc
Professor G Barker, CBW, FBA, FSA, FRGS

Head: Mrs Kathy Crewe-Read

Deputy Head (*Boarding*): Mr Graham Brooks, BA
Deputy Head (*Pastoral*) *& Senior Designated Safeguarding Lead*: Mrs Jane Pawulska, BA
Head of Sixth Form: Mrs Katie Banks, MA
Examinations Officer: Mr Tim Herbert, MA
Head of Operations and Logistics: Mr Matt Drury
Policy Coordinator: Mrs Beth Wheeler, BSc
Educational Data: Mr Mark McGrath
Director of Teaching and Learning: Mr Peter O'Connor

Housemasters/Housemistresses:
Alliott House: Mrs Sarah Wilson, BA
Benson House: Miss Kate Gregory, BA
Collett House: Mr Alex Swart-Wilson, MA
Hayward House: Mr Simon Lipscombe, BA
Robert Pearce House: Mr Richard Honey, MA
Rowe House: Mr Peter Griffin, BSc
Sutton House: Mr Christopher Sutherland
Tee House: Mrs Sasha Gunes
Trotman House: Mrs Pippa Bell
Young House: Mrs Tina Hood, BSc, BEd

Heads of Department:
Art: Ms Charlotte Munck
Biology: Mrs Beth Wheeler, BSc
Chemistry: Mr Charlie Bannister, MA

Classics: Dr Lucy Cresswell, PhD
Design & Technology: Mr John Trant, BA
Director of Drama: Mr Richard Norman, BA
Economics & Business Studies: Mr John Birchall, MA
English for Speakers of Other Languages: Mrs Caroline Edmunds
English: Mrs Claire Bond, MA
Ethics, Philosophy and Theology: Mr Patrick Winter, MEd
French: Mrs Marie-Lorraine Cunin
Geography: Mr Nicholas Tether
German: Miss Kate Gregory, BA
Higher Education and Careers: Mrs Deborah Hearne
History: Mr Tom Stuart, MA
Director of IT: Mr Andrew Pawlowicz
Mathematics: Mr Mark McGrath
Film and Media Studies: Mr Steven Baxter
Music: Mr Paul West
Physics: Mr Adrian Baker, BSc
Politics: Mrs Alison Self, BA
PSHE: Mrs Jane Pawulska, BA
Psychology: Ms Jenny Taylor, BSc
Science: Dr Stuart McPeake, PhD
Spanish: Mrs Ruth Bravo
Swimming: Mrs Deborah Huggett
Director of College Sport: Mr Nick Prowse

Senior School Librarian: Mrs Sara Bloomfield

Prep School:
Head of Prep School: W J Toleman, BA
Deputy Head: Mr Graham Millard, BA
Head of Shell & Deputy Designated Safeguarding Lead: Mrs Kirsty Brooks, BA
Senior Teacher (*Pastoral*) *& Designated Safeguarding Lead*: Mr Richard Clough, BA
Senior Teacher (*Operations*): Mr Adrian Hathaway, BEd
Director of Studies: Mrs Wendy Sharman, MSc

Heads of Department:
Art: Miss Alice Beckley
Drama: Lucinda Neville
English: Miss Jane Mitchell
French: Miss Emmanuelle Carme, MA
Geography: Mr Richard Clough, BA
German: Mrs Imogen Cowan, BA
History: Mr Rupert Snow
ICT: Mrs Frances Sharpsmith, BSc
Mathematics: Mr Andre Beukes
Director of Music: Mr Paul West
PSHEE: Mr Rupert Snow
RE: Mrs Livia Fraser
Science: Mrs Julia Krosny-Reed
Spanish: Mrs Fiona Jones, BA
Swimming: Mrs Deborah Huggett

Prep School Librarian: Mrs Elizabeth Hall

Learning Support:
Head of Learning Support: Mrs Anne Grass MA Ed, BEd, PGCE SpLD with AMBDA
Mrs Fatima Pabani, PGCE, BSc
Mrs Louise Vandenburg, SEN TA

Pre-Prep:
Head of Pre-Prep: Miss Belinda Callow, BEd
Miss C Cuthbert
Mrs K Howes
Mrs E Hathaway
Mrs R Smith, BA

Mrs N Rossington
Mrs C Martin

Learning Support:
Mrs Anita Foy

College Chaplain: Mr Ian Morris
Bursar: Mr Paul Stanley
Senior School Admissions Officer: Mrs Christine Stanley
Prep School Admissions Officer: Mrs Fiona Brett
Pre-Prep Admissions Officer: Mrs Sally McGuiness
Director of Marketing and Engagement: Mrs Eleanor
    Blatherwick

Blundell's School

Tiverton, Devon EX16 4DN

Tel: 01884 252543
email: info@blundells.org
website: www.blundells.org
Twitter: @BlundellsSchool
Facebook: @blundellsschool

Blundell's is a thriving co-educational day and boarding
School combining strong academic achievement and
excellent co-curricular activities in a secure and happy
environment. The deep friendships that are formed at
Blundell's fostered by the great community, together with
the intellectual, physical and cultural interests, provide
pupils with skills for life. The School was built and endowed
in 1604 at the sole charge of the estate of Mr Peter Blundell,
Clothier, of Tiverton, by his executor the Lord Chief Justice,
Sir John Popham. In 1882 the School was moved to its
present site on the outskirts of Tiverton.

Admission. Entry is at 11, 13 and 16 for most pupils.
This is via the Blundell's Entrance Test or the Common
Entrance Examination. Most join the School in September,
though a January entry is welcome.

Numbers. There are 614 pupils of whom 254 are girls;
360 board (full, weekly, flexi). There are three boys' Houses
and two girls' Houses for Years 9–12 and a separate Upper
Sixth House. Years 7 and 8 have a separate House with
separate pastoral and academic leadership.

Fees per term (2021–2022). Full Boarding £8,885–
£12,995; Weekly Boarding £7,700–£10,945; Day £5,045–
£8,005. Flexi boarding is also available.

Scholarships and Bursaries. Open Scholarships and
Exhibitions: Up to half of the chosen designation fee (i.e.
boarding, weekly, flexi, day) are offered on the basis of our
own examinations held in January (13+) and November
(Sixth Form). Awards for Art, Music, Drama, Sport and All-
round ability are also made. At 11+ Junior Exhibitions only
are awarded for academic and musical ability (January
examination) and are deducted from the basic tuition fees.

Services Package available to the children of serving
members of the Armed Forces and Diplomatic Corps.

Awards may occasionally be supplemented by means-
tested bursaries at the discretion of the Head.

Full details of all scholarships and bursaries are available
from the Registrars' Office.

School Work. There are four forms at age 11 and five at
age 13. During the first three years most pupils will study

Art, Biology, Chemistry, Design and Technology, Divinity,
Drama, English, French, Geography, History, Information
Technology, Mathematics, Music (Class), Personal and
Social Development, Physical Education and Physics. Latin,
Greek, German and Spanish are also available.

During the GCSE years the range of subjects remains
broad. Extensive advice is provided by the School to assist
both GCSE and A Level choices.

Sixth Form options enable a wide combination of
subjects to be taken. Four of the following are taken to AS
Level and three to A Level: Art, Biology, Business Studies,
Chemistry, Classical Civilisations, Design Technology,
Drama, Economics, English, Film Studies, French,
Geography, German, History (Modern & Early Modern
options), ICT, Latin, Mathematics and Further Mathematics,
Music, Photography, Physical Education, Physics,
Psychology, Religious Studies (Ethics) and Spanish.

Mark Orders, Tutorial System and Reports. Good
communication is a central concept. Frequent Mark Orders
and Staff Meetings are held to monitor each pupil's work.
All pupils have academic tutors. Parents receive termly
formal written feedback in addition to receiving Mark Order
summaries every few weeks. There are regular parents'
meetings and information forums.

Music and Drama. Blundell's music is excellent. Based
in our own music school there are several choirs, an
orchestra and varying musical ensembles. These range from
a jazz band through a chamber choir to brass, woodwind and
string groups. The Department has state-of-the-art recording
equipment. In addition to School concerts there are visits
from professional musicians. The Choir recently performed
in Carnegie Hall in New York.

Similarly, Drama plays a key role in the School. There are
three major School Plays each year, as well as House plays.
The magnificent, purpose-built Ondaatje Hall offers the
combined facilities of a theatre, a concert hall and an art
studio. Frequent visits are made by theatre companies and
Blundell's is a cultural venue for Mid-Devon.

Games and Physical Training. Boys play rugby in the
Autumn Term whilst girls play hockey. Spring Term sports
include cross-country, squash, rugby, fives, hockey, soccer,
fencing, basketball, netball and rugby sevens. In the
Summer Term cricket, tennis, swimming, athletics and golf
take place. The Sports Hall gives further scope to the range
of sport, as does the all-weather floodlit pitch; there is also a
Fitness Suite. Elite sportsmen and women are supported
with specialised fitness programmes. A variety of other
sports, such as clay pigeon shooting, fly fishing, canoeing
and miniature range shooting, are available through the
extensive activity programme.

Computing and Technology. All pupils have access to
the school IT network and will develop a range of skills
during their time at school to support their studies.

Recent New Facilities. There have been extensive
developments at Blundell's over the past two decades which
include upgrading the Science Departments, provision of
advanced technological and careers arrangements as part of
the resources included in the redesigned Library, a new
Modern Languages block, ongoing refurbishment of all
boarding houses, a Fitness Suite, a Music School, IT suites
and extension to Westlake (Y13 Boarding House) to
incorporate new study areas and a library. With Blundell's
Preparatory School on site, the whole campus provides
education from the age of 3 to 18 years.

Community Service. The School is involved in a wide variety of activities, both local and national, and pupils regularly raise around £20,000 per annum for a variety of charities, as well as taking part in practical tasks locally.

Adventure Training. Blundell's is well placed to make full use of Dartmoor and Exmoor, the coast and rivers of the area, for academic fieldwork or adventure training. For many years the School has entered teams for the Ten Tors Expedition on Dartmoor, canoes the Devizes–Westminster race and takes part in The Duke of Edinburgh's Award scheme up to Gold level.

CCF. Everyone in Year 10 serves for a year in the CCF. Thereafter it is voluntary and comprises senior pupils who provide the NCO Instructors. There are links with the 18 Cadet Training Team, Derriford, and the Rifle Volunteers.

Boarding. Blundell's is built around the ethos of boarding and all pupils (full boarding, weekly, flexi boarding and day) are accommodated in one of seven houses on the campus. A full range of weekend activities is offered including a Leadership Programme, Ten Tors, sport and a range of local trips and activities.

Religion. The School maintains a Christian tradition, while welcoming members of other faiths. All pupils are expected to attend weekday morning Chapel and boarders go to the School Service on Sundays. The Chaplain prepares pupils who wish to be confirmed; the Confirmation Service takes place annually in the Spring Term.

Accessibility. Blundell's is close to the M5, and is served by Tiverton Parkway Station, under two hours from Paddington, London. Airports at Bristol and Exeter are close at hand.

Prospectus. Fuller details of School life are given in the prospectus, available from the Registrars. Prospective parents are invited to visit the School, when they will meet the Head and a Housemaster or Housemistress and have a full tour of the School with a current pupil. The Blundell's website (www.blundells.org) is regularly updated throughout the academic year.

Preparatory School. Blundell's Preparatory School for children aged 3 to 11 years is part of the site at Blundell's. For further information apply to the Headmaster, Mr A D Southgate. (*See also entry in IAPS section*).

Charitable status. Blundell's School is a Registered Charity, number 1081249. It exists to provide education for children.

Board of Governors:
Mr N P Hall
Dr S B Ansell
Mr N Arnold
Mr N J Cryer
Mr G L Howe
Mr M J Lovett
Mrs J M A Mannix
Fr R Maudsley
Rt Revd N McKinnel
Mr I R G Thomas
Mrs J S Thomson
Dr M E Wood

Mr R W Thane (*Representative Governor*)
Sir Christopher Ondaatje, OC, CBE (*Honorary Governor Emeritus*)

Bursar and Clerk to the Governors: Mrs Annika Hedrich-Wiggans

Head: **Mr Bart Wielenga**

Second Master: Mr Matt Radley
Deputy Head (Academic): Mr Charles List
Deputy Head (Co-curricular): Mr Ed Saunders
Designated Safeguarding Lead: Mrs Nicky Klinkenberg

Heads of Department:
Art: Gil Armstrong Williams
Biology: Jonathan Ratcliffe
Careers Education & Advice: Pippa Bucknell
Chemistry: Andy Mead
Classics: Becky Milne
Design & Technology: Bruce Wheatley
Drama: Tammy Winsley
Economics & Business Studies: Tom Candler
English: Rebecca Isdell-Carpenter
Examinations: Katie List
Film Studies: Charlotte Mercer
French: Kate Wheatley
Geography: Guy Bucknall
German: Isobel Scott
History & Politics: Richard Moore
IT: Martin Dyer
Learning Support: Sara-Jane Soutar
Mathematics: Henry Roffe-Silvester
Modern Languages: Nick Lecharpentier
Music: Oliver Leaman
PHSE: Belinda Jones
Physical Education: Rebecca Manley
Physics: Adam Lambert
Psychology: Emma Weaver
Religious Studies: Andrew Berrow
Science: Georgina Batting
Sport: Ed Saunders

Director of Development: Mr Ben Boswell
Director of Marketing: Mr Dylan Smart

Head's PA: Mrs Heather Vincent

Registrars:
Mr Peter Klinkenberg
Mrs Charlotte Botting

Preparatory School

Headmaster: Mr Andy Southgate

Julie Aldridge (*Art & DT*)
Joshua Allen
Susie Allen (*Mathematics & Music*)
Lisa Baily (*Girls' Games*)
Bronte Barber
Tracey Barfoot (*Teaching Assistant*)
Michelle Bennett (*Teaching Assistant*)
Jo Carter
Tiggy Charlesworth (*Drama, SENCO*)
Sue Clark
Laura Clifford (*Head of Pre-Prep*)
Bethan Cracknell (*Music*)
Edward Frances
Claire FitzHerbert (*French*)
Tim Genders (*English*)
Simon Howkins (*Deputy Head, PSHEE*)
Jessica Lampard (*Food Technology*)
Jane Lawrence (*Geography*)
Hannah Mahon (*Science*)
Lee Moore (*Academic Leader, RE*)
Charlotte Morris (*Drama, Outdoor Learning*)

Daniel Morris (*Assistant Head Curriculum, Mathematics, ICT*)
Tracy Nash (*English & Librarian*)
Joanne Read
Joanna Richardson
Jane Roberts
Jessica Roberts
Alison Spencer
Alexandra Steel (*RE*)
Simon Swain (*Boys' Games*)
Deborah Taylor
Jo Thomas (*Teaching Assistant*)
Emma Thornton (*Geography & History*)
Clare Whitten

Miss Gloria Butt (*Administration*)
Miss Beverley Stone (*Headmaster's PA*)

Bolton School Boys' Division

Chorley New Road, Bolton BL1 4PA

Tel: 01204 840201
email: seniorboys@boltonschool.org
website: www.boltonschool.org/seniorboys
Twitter: @BoltonSchool
          @Philip_Britton
          @nfordteacher
Facebook: @boltonschool.org
Instagram: @bolton_school_foundation
LinkedIn: /bolton-school

Motto: *Mutare vel timere sperno*

Bolton School Boys' Division, founded ante 1516 as Bolton Grammar School for Boys, was rebuilt and endowed by Robert Lever in 1644. In 1913 the first Viscount Leverhulme gave a generous endowment to the Bolton Grammar School for Boys and the High School for Girls on condition that the two schools should be equal partners known as Bolton School (Boys' and Girls' Divisions).

Bolton School today – the TES' Independent School of the Year in 2019 – is a family of schools, where children enjoy an all-through education, joining our co-educational Nursery or Pre-School Class for 3 and 4 year olds or Infant School before moving up to our single-sex Junior and Senior Schools with Sixth Forms. We are strong believers that girls and boys from 7+ perform best in a single-sex environment, but one where there are co-educational activities – the best of both worlds.

Situated in imposing sandstone buildings on a thirty-two acre site, Bolton School Boys' Division, which comprises a Senior School and Sixth Form, educates over 900 day pupils. The Senior School is fed by our Junior Boys' School (200+ boys aged 7–11 years), which is part of Bolton School's Primary Division.

Bolton School seeks to realise the potential of each pupil. We provide challenge, encourage initiative, promote teamwork and develop leadership capabilities. It is our aim that students leave the School as self-confident young people equipped with the knowledge, skills and attributes that will allow them to lead happy and fulfilled lives and to make a difference for good in the wider community.

We do this through offering a rich and stimulating educational experience which encompasses academic, extra-curricular and social activities. We provide a supportive and industrious learning environment for pupils selected on academic potential, irrespective of means and background.

Curriculum. The GCSE programme comprises a core curriculum of English Language, English Literature, Mathematics, Biology, Chemistry, Physics and Sport. In addition, pupils select a further 4 options chosen from Art, Drama, French, Geography, German, Greek, History, Latin, Music, Philosophy and Ethics, RE, Russian, Science Enrichment, Spanish and Technology. One of these choices must be a foreign language. At A Level approximately 30 different subjects are currently on offer. Boys generally begin by studying four subjects, with the majority reducing to three A Levels in Year 13. A small number of subjects offer the AS level qualification. While many boys elect to take standard combinations of either Arts or Science subjects in the Sixth Form, a high degree of flexibility ensures that any desired combination of subjects can be offered. Our enrichment programme allows students to pursue other qualifications. Examples include the Extended Project Qualification, Artsmark, Science Crest Award and a Youth Leadership Award amongst others. All students participate in sports lessons and in community service work. In 2017 the School won the Queen's Award for Voluntary Service, the MBE for organisations.

Facilities and Organisation. The Boys' and Girls' Divisions of Bolton School are housed in separate buildings on the same site and, though the organisation of the two Divisions provides single-sex schools, there are many opportunities for boys and girls to meet and to cooperate in the life of the school community. This is particularly so in the Riley Sixth Form Centre, where boys and girls share a Common Room, cafe and learning areas equipped with the very latest technology. Single-sex teaching remains the norm in the Sixth Form, although in a very few subjects co-educational arrangements are in operation. The buildings of the Boys' Division include the Great Hall, two libraries, gymnasium, sports hall, swimming pool, laboratories, art rooms, sixth form common room and ICT learning centre, design technology centre, performing arts centre, MFL laboratory, classrooms and dining hall. The Junior School building has recently been extended and refurbished and contains eight form rooms and specialist rooms for ICT, art & design and science & technology together with a gymnasium, library and its own dining accommodation. Use of the new £1m all-weather sports surface, the sports hall, the adjacent 25-metre swimming pool and the arts centre is shared by all sections of the school.

Games and PE. The extensive playing fields which adjoin the School contain thirteen pitches. Principal games are football, rugby and cricket. Tennis, hockey, swimming, water polo, badminton, athletics, golf and orienteering are also all played at representative school level. All boys also undertake a gymnastics programme and play volleyball and basketball. The School is divided into four Houses for the purpose of internal competitions.

Art, Drama, Design, Music. In addition to timetabled sessions in each discipline there are many opportunities for extra-curricular activities in all these pursuits. Facilities in the art department include a pottery room with kiln; within the very active musical life of the School there are choral groups, orchestras and ensembles catering for all ages and abilities. In addition arrangements can be made for individual lessons on all orchestral instruments, piano, organ and in singing. Drama is an important part of the work of the English department and boys are encouraged to develop their talents in the drama studio and arts centre. The annual major school play, musical or opera is produced in cooperation with the Girls' Division. Design and technology features strongly in the curriculum in both Junior and Senior Schools with considerable success each year in the A Level technology courses, many boys gaining industrial sponsorships as a result. In addition, a wide variety of extracurricular opportunities exists in both the design technology base and the computer rooms. All boys are encouraged to take part in the extensive lunchtime programme when over 120 clubs, societies and practices are offered to different groups. The School has Platinum Artsmark status.

Outdoor Pursuits. All junior school pupils and all students up to and including Year 12 in the senior school undertake an annual period of outdoor education within curriculum time. In addition, camps, trips, exchanges and expeditions ordinarily go to 63 destinations over two years, 17 of them abroad. The School has its own 60-bed Outdoor Pursuits Centre, Patterdale Hall in Cumbria, used by parties of boys regularly for curriculum, weekend, holiday and fieldwork expeditions. In Year 8, boys have the opportunity to undertake sail training lessons on Tenacity of Bolton, the boat built by boys at the School. There is a large and active Scout Group with its own modern headquarters on school premises.

Religion. The School is non-denominational; all boys have periods devoted to religious education. In assemblies the basic approach is Christian although a great variety of readings and methods of presentation are adopted.

Careers and Higher Education. Careers education and guidance, and life-long learning are key elements of the curriculum. In Year 8 pupils take part in a Work Sampling Day. As an aid to Sixth Form choices, the Morrisby Test with follow-up interviews and extensive feedback is undertaken in Years 10 and 11. All pupils take part in Work Experience placements at the end of Year 11 and throughout the Sixth Form.

In Year 12, all pupils attend a 3-day residential business training course at Patterdale Hall and take part in an e-business competition. Mock interviews are conducted on Interview Skills Evenings. Year 13 pupils are guided through UCAS procedures and careers advice is always available from the Head of Careers.

Transport. The School provides an extensive coach service covering 20 routes which offers secure and easy access for pupils from a wide surrounding catchment area.

Admission. An entrance examination is held in January annually for boys over 7 and under 8 on August 31st of the year of admission. Fifty places are available at 7+ and a few additional places thereafter. Admission to the first year of the Senior School (140 places) is by entrance examination held annually in mid-January. Boys who are over 10 and under 12 on August 31st of the year of entry are eligible. Entry to the Sixth Form is available to boys who have taken GCSE examinations elsewhere on the basis of interview and agreed levels of performance in these public examinations. Boys are also admitted at other ages when vacancies occur; in these cases admission is gained through satisfactory interview and test performances. There is a co-educational pre-preparatory section – Beech House Infants' School –

which has recently moved to new purpose-built, state-of-the-art premises. Admission is from the age of 4 and enquiries should be made to infants@boltonschool.org. There is also a nursery providing facilities for children from 3 months to 4 years old.

Fees per term (2021–2022). Senior School and Sixth Form £4,237; Infant and Junior Schools £3,389. Fees include lunches.

Fee Assistance. Means-tested Foundation Grants are available and one in five Senior School pupils receives assistance with fees. Scholarships are also available and are offered regardless of parental income, to those pupils whose achievement in the Entrance Examination and the Interviews places them at the top of the cohort.

Prospectus and Open Day. The School holds an annual Open Morning in mid-October for the benefit of prospective candidates and their parents. Individual tours can be arranged on working days throughout the year. Further information concerning all aspects of the School is contained in the School Prospectus, copies of which may be obtained from the Admissions Registrar. More detail can be found on the School website. Enquiries concerning admission are welcome at any time of the School year.

Charitable status. The Bolton School is a Registered Charity, number 1110703.

Chairman of Governors: Mr I Riley, MEng, MBA

Head of Foundation: P J Britton, MBE, MEd

Head of Boys' Division: N L Ford, BSc

Deputy Head (Pastoral): Mrs H M Brandon, MA
Deputy Head (Admissions & Achievement): Dr F H
  Mullins, BSc, PhD
Assistant Head: K M Hiepko, MA
Assistant Head (Operations): D L Stevens, BSc
Senior Teacher: Miss H Tunstall, BSc, MSc

Heads of Department:
Art and Design: Mrs M A Ryder, BA & Mrs L Turner, BA
Biology: Dr N Morgan, BSc, PhD
Business Studies: D W Kettle, BA
Chemistry: Dr M Yates, BSc, PhD
Classics: Mr D V B Lamb, MA
Economics: D W Kettle, BA
English: Ms H Thomson, BA, MA
French: A C Robson, BA
Geography: P Newbold, BA
German: R A Catterall, MA
History: Miss S V Burgess, MA
ICT: P J Humphrey, BSc
Mathematics: D N Palmer, BSc
Music (Curriculum): Miss H Sherry, BMus
Physical Education:
P Fernside, BA (*Head of Games*)
M Johnson, BSc (*Head of PE*)
Physics: M R Ormerod, BSc
Religious Studies: Mrs C E Fox, BA
Russian: P G Davidson, BA
Spanish: Mrs J L Cotton, BA, MA
Technology: C J Walker, BA

Instrumental Music Staff:
Brass, Cello, Clarinet, Guitar, Oboe, Organ, Percussion,
  Piano, Saxophone, Singing, Viola, Violin

Junior School (Age 7–11):
Head: Mr F Morris, BA

Deputy Head: Mrs Winstanley, BCom

Head of Boys' Division's Personal Assistant: Mrs J
   Higham

Head of Boys' Division's Secretary & Admissions
   Registrar: Miss A Fenton

Bootham School

Bootham, York YO30 7BU

Tel: 01904 623261 (School)
          01904 623261 (Headmaster)

email: office@boothamschool.com

website: www.boothamschool.com

Twitter: @BoothamSchool

Facebook: @BoothamSchool

Instagram: @boothamschool

LinkedIn: /school/bootham-school

Bootham offers Full, Weekly and Flexi Boarding and
Day Education to students from ages 11–18, together with
day education from the age of 3 at Bootham Junior School.
There are now over 470 pupils in the Senior School and 130
day pupils in the Junior School (*see entry in IAPS section*).

The School was founded in 1823 by Quakers, but pupils
of all denominations or none are welcomed. All pupils
attend Meetings for Worship and arrangements are made for
pupils to be prepared for confirmation or membership of
their own churches.

Curriculum. In Years 7–9 all pupils pursue a course of
study which includes English, History, Religious Studies,
Geography, Classics, Latin, French, German, Spanish,
Mathematics, the three separate Sciences, Music, Drama,
Art and Craft, Physical Education, Design & Technology,
Computer Science, Careers, Health and the Environment
and Thinking Skills.

In Years 10 and 11 pupils follow a curriculum leading to
10 subjects at GCSE.

The College Classes (Sixth Form) are preparatory to
university entrance. The majority of pupils remain at school
until the age of 18 and each year there is a strong Oxbridge
entry. A wide choice of subjects is offered. It is usual to
study 3 or 4 examination subjects and to study subjects of
wider interest.

Students are able to choose from a wide variety of
subjects. These are: Mathematics, Further Mathematics,
Computer Science, Physics, Chemistry, Psychology,
Biology, English, French, German, Spanish, History,
Classics, Latin, Geography, Economics, Business Studies,
Music, Art, Design Technology, Religious Studies, Drama
and Theatre Studies, and Sports Studies and Physical
Education.

Site and Buildings. The School is situated close to York
Minster. From the road it appears as an impressive line of
Georgian houses but behind this is the spacious main school
campus. There is a steady programme of development, and
the buildings now include 8 well-equipped Laboratories, an
impressive Arts Centre (open 2014) with Auditorium and
Darkroom (photography), 2 ICT Suites, 2 DT workshops, an
Astronomical Observatory, an up-to-date Physical
Education Department with Sports Hall, Indoor Swimming

Pool, Fitness Suite and Squash Courts, and a modern
Assembly Hall, which received a national RIBA award. The
buildings are complemented by formal gardens and playing
fields, overlooked by York Minster. Further playing fields
are situated nearby, in Clifton, which also houses Bootham
Junior School in a new purpose-built complex.

Pastoral Care. As a Quaker School, Bootham places
great emphasis on caring relationships within a friendly
community. There are three boarding houses, under the
special care of House staff. Each House has its own
recreational facilities. Throughout the School, both boarding
and day pupils are supervised and guided by form tutors. In
College, pupils have Personal Tutors who are responsible
for both academic and pastoral matters, and guidance
towards Higher Education or other alternatives.

Admission. Pupils usually enter Bootham at the age of
11. Entry is also usually possible at 12, 13 and 14. The main
entrance assessment is held annually in January and this
forms the basis of Scholarship and Bursary selection. Sixth
form entry is welcomed and selection is on the bases of
school report and GCSE performance. In special
circumstances late entrants can be considered.

Leisure Time Activities. The School has long been
recognised as a pioneer in the provision of enrichment
activities. The Natural History Society, founded in 1832, is
the oldest society of its kind in this country. Other clubs and
societies include Social Action, Debate, Drama, Bridge,
Chess, Cookery and Jazz. There are around 100 activities
offered each week. Pupils follow the Duke of Edinburgh's
Award scheme and are involved in Community Services.

Music. The Director of Music is supported by visiting
teachers. Tuition is arranged in a wide variety of instruments
and a strong tradition of music in the School is maintained.
Recent leavers have secured places at the Royal College of
Music and there is a strong tradition of students gaining
places and scholarships at music colleges.

Games. Football, Hockey, Tennis, Fencing, Cricket,
Swimming, Athletics, Netball, Basketball, Badminton,
Squash, Rounders. There is no cadet force.

Fees per term (2021–2022). Full Boarding: £6,750–
£10,670. Day: £5,785–£6,300.

Fees for instrumental music lessons are extra. Enquiries
for up-to-date information are welcome.

Scholarships and Bursaries. *Academic* Scholarships
(honorary and without fee reduction) are awarded on an
annual basis at the end of each academic year and are based
on performance throughout the year. Academic Scholarships
are subject to annual reviews.

Sixth Form: We offer a means-tested scholarship/bursary
to candidates from state-maintained schools who perform
well at GCSE.

Music Scholarships of up to 50% fee remission are
available for candidates of good all-round musical and
academic ability or potential. These are available for entry at
11+ and 13+ (Years 7 and 9) and are awarded on the basis of
performance in the entrance assessment, and in tests and an
audition with the Director of Music.

Means-tested Bursaries (supported by the Bootham
Trust) are available:

- to assist Friend (Quaker) children, or the children of
  Friend (Quaker) parents, to attend the School;
- to assist children, whose families would not be able to
  afford an independent school education, to attend the
  School.

Applicants will be assessed by academic performance in the entrance assessment at 11+ and 13+ and in addition, for Music Scholars, their performance at the Music Scholarship tests and audition. Applications for bursaries need to be made in the Autumn term prior to entry to the school.

Bootham Old Scholars' Association. There is an annual Reunion in York during the second weekend in May. The Bootham Old Scholars' Association has branches in all parts of the country and Eire.

Charitable status. Bootham School is a Registered Charity, number 513645.

Head: Christopher Jeffery, BA, FRSA

Deputy Head: Martyn Beer, BA, PGCE, NPQH

Head of Junior School: Helen Todd, BA, MA Ed, QTS

Assistant Heads:
William Lewis, MA
James Ratcliffe, BSc

Bursar: Gavin Blackstone, CPFA, BA

Admissions Registrar: Fiona Ward, MA, PGCE

Bradford Grammar School

Keighley Road, Bradford, West Yorkshire BD9 4JP

Tel: 01274 542492
email: admissions@bradfordgrammar.com
website: www.bradfordgrammar.com
Twitter: @BradfordGrammar
Facebook: @bradfordgrammarschool
LinkedIn: /bradfordgrammar

Motto: *Hoc Age*

With a heritage dating back to 1548, Bradford Grammar School (BGS) is one of the oldest and most respected institutions in Yorkshire. Our illustrious past spans hundreds of years. In 1662, Charles II granted BGS's Charter, a document that the school proudly displays. Having occupied three locations since our establishment, the iconic building that BGS inhabits today was opened in 1949. A long history of excellence inspires BGS pupils to fulfil their potential and make their own mark upon the future of BGS.

With a 'first-class, academic and outward-looking approach' (*Good Schools Guide*), BGS is one of the UK's leading independent schools, providing an outstanding education for 1,016 girls and boys aged six to 18. The school is fully co-educational: girls have been admitted to the Sixth Form since 1984 and in all intakes from 1999.

BGS provides every opportunity for its Junior, Senior and Sixth Form pupils to embrace academic, sporting and creative excellence within an aspirational, caring environment in which happiness is the key to an individual's success. With its impressive 'value added' provision, academic excellence is available to all.

Pupil Numbers. 1,016 day pupils (559 boys, 457 girls). Junior School (6–11): 143 pupils (79 boys, 64 girls). Senior School (11–18): 873 pupils (480 boys, 393 girls).

Location and Facilities. The school, comprising six main buildings and a separate junior school building, stands in extensive grounds situated just a mile from Bradford city centre. The School thrives upon the opportunities created by this dynamic hub of enterprise and innovation.

The majority of our pupils travel by bus or train from areas such as Ilkley, Skipton, Leeds, Halifax and Huddersfield. We provide dedicated buses from a number of locations, including Oakwood, Headingley, Adel, Oxenhope, Huddersfield, Batley, Luddendenfoot, Halifax, Brighouse and Ilkley. Frizinghall train station is within a five-minute walk of the school and we provide a daily patrol team who ensure that pupils walk between the station and the school safely and sensibly. There are direct rail connections from Frizinghall train station to Leeds, Airedale and Wharfedale, Skipton, Ilkley and Apperley Bridge.

Nestling on the edge of the Yorkshire Dales, and within striking distance of the Lake District, opportunities abound for outdoor visits and residential trips.

Facilities include a dedicated Sixth Form centre with full Wi-Fi, the Hockney Theatre, Design Technology workshops, Computer Aided Design (CAD) suites, fitness suite with rowing machines, cycling machines, treadmills and weights, a music auditorium, recording studio, debating chamber, dedicated Science building, a state-of-the-art library, a 25m competition swimming pool, sports pavilion, and squash courts, and our new outstanding £4m sport facilities – comprising cricket lanes, netball and tennis courts and astro-turfed hockey pitches, as well as our all-weather sports barn. The Price Hall is the centrepiece of the main school building and provides a magnificent setting for assemblies, concerts and other major events.

Bradford Grammar Junior School occupies Clock House, a seventeenth century Manor House within the wooded and tranquil school grounds, where it enjoys its own assembly hall, Computing and Design Technology facilities and teaching accommodation. *For further details, please see separate entry in IAPS section.*

Senior School Curriculum.

In *Years Seven and Eight* all pupils study English, Mathematics, French, German, Latin, Biology, Physics, Chemistry, Geography, History, Art, Music, Design and Technology (DT), Religious Studies (RS), Personal Development, Drama, Computing and PE/Games.

In *Year Nine* pupils follow a common core of English, Mathematics, Geography, History, Physics, Chemistry, Biology, RS, Personal Development and PE/Games, choose one core Modern Foreign Language from a choice of French, German or Spanish and choose three optional subjects from a choice of German, Spanish, Latin, Greek, Art, Music, DT and Computer Science.

In *Years Ten and Eleven* pupils follow ten GCSE courses. All pupils follow a common core of English Language, English Literature, Mathematics, Biology, Chemistry, Physics, and PE/Games, choose a core Modern Foreign Language from French, German or Spanish, and choose three optional subjects from Geography, History, French, German, Spanish, Computer Science, Drama, Physical Education, Latin, Greek, Art, Music, DT and RS.

Year 12 (Lower Sixth Form). Pupils choose *either* three subjects and complete the EPQ *or* choose four subjects from Art, Biology, Business Studies, Chemistry, Classical Civilisation, Computer Science, Drama & Theatre, DT, Economics, English Literature, English Language, Extended Project Qualification (EPQ), French, Further Mathematics, Geography, German, Greek, History, Latin, Mathematics, Music, Music Technology, Physical

Education, Physics, Politics, Psychology, RS and Spanish. The AS Level exam is available in some subjects. In addition, they also take one or two Enrichment courses from a wide range of certificated or non-examined options.

Year 13 (Upper Sixth Form). Pupils usually take three of their Year 12 courses through to A Level. Some pupils take a fourth A Level or complete the EPQ.

For further details please see the booklets *A Guide to GCSE Courses* and *A Guide to Sixth Form Courses*, both of which can be downloaded from our website at www.bradfordgrammar.com.

Results.

A Level: Terrifically successful at A and AS Levels, BGS has been recognised as having the highest average university admission points per student of any school in West Yorkshire. In 2020, 125 A Level students celebrated outstanding success with 26% of all exams awarded A* and 63% A*/A grades. The comparable figures for 2021 are even better, 25% and 69% respectively.

GCSEs: At GCSE, our results far exceed the national average. A record-breaking 79% of all exams taken in 2020 were awarded A/A* or 9–7 grades, well over three times higher than the national average of recent years. The comparable figure for 2021 was an impressive 77%. (Pupils at BGS take a mixture of IGCSEs and GCSEs, graded either 9–1 or A*–G.)

Co-curricular Activities. We actively encourage pupils to engage in co-curricular activities. Pupils in the Senior School normally have a choice of over 50 clubs and societies covering a wide range of sports, drama, music, academic subjects and other areas of interest – from rowing, orienteering, war games, debating, Biomedical and Classics Societies to Micro:bit, Games, volunteering, fundraising and Handmade Clubs, there is something for everyone. Pupils can take part in The Duke of Edinburgh's Award scheme, the Combined Cadet Force (both RAF and Army) and World Challenge expeditions. There are many exciting and enriching school trips and tours, domestic and overseas.

Pastoral Care. Outstanding pastoral support contributes to the happiness of Bradford Grammar School pupils, creating a positive, friendly atmosphere for all. The School works closely with parents to ensure each child receives the best possible pastoral care during their time at BGS. The team of form tutors, Heads of Year, school nurses, school counsellor, Learning Support Department and pastoral prefects work together to promote pupils' happiness and progress and ensure that every child receives the attention they deserve. Pupils who need extra support are quickly identified by our pastoral team and given the help they need as they make their way up the school. The BGS Personal Development (PSHE) programme includes modules on wellbeing and mental health as well as RSHE for every year group.

The School encourages pupils to participate in physical exercise and a wide range of co-curricular opportunities, so that they are further developed beyond the classroom too.

Admission. Boys and girls can join the school at the ages of 6, 7, 8, 9, 10 in the Junior School or 11, 12, 13 or 16 in the Senior School. Pupils are admitted into the Sixth Form on the basis of their GCSE results (at least 20 points, grade B, preferably A, in sixth form subjects), an interview and a satisfactory reference from the candidate's current school. Candidates for entry into Year 2 (6+), Year 3 (7+) and Year 4 (8+) will be invited to spend an informal day in the Junior School. Admission for all other ages is by examination in Mathematics and English in January each year.

Assisted places. Places are awarded on a means-tested basis, each case being reviewed annually. The award depends on parental circumstances, the amount of capital available at the time of the examination and the academic ability of the candidate.

Scholarships. Needs-blind academic scholarships up to 25% of the fee are available for Year 7 entry.

Fees per term (2021–2022). Junior School £3,530, Senior School £4,511, Sixth Form £4,511.

Former Pupils include trail-blazing artist David Hockney, Chancellor of the Exchequer Denis Healey, Olympic champions Alistair and Jonny Brownlee and Team GB Performance Analyst Dr Deborah Sides.

Old Bradfordians Association. President: Mr I Holland, c/o Bradford Grammar School.

The Parents' Association (previously BGS Society). Chairman: Mr W Shirt, c/o Bradford Grammar School.

Charitable status. Bradford Grammar School (The Free Grammar School of King Charles II at Bradford) is a Registered Charity, number 529113. It exists to provide education for children.

Governors:

Chairman: Lady Morrison, LLB
Vice-Chairman: Professor C Mellors, OBE, BA, MA, PhD, FAcSS, FHEA, FRSA
President: A H Jerome, MBE, MA [OB]

Ex-officio:
vacant

Co-optative:
C Beck, FCCA
P Cogan, BA, FCA
V L Davey, LLB
D J Davies, MBE, BEng, MA
S R Davies, BA, FRSA
J E Disley, BA
Professor A Francis, BSc, ACGI, FBAM, CCMI, AcSS
C Hamilton Stewart, MBE
His Honour J A Lewis
I McAleese, FCIPD
District Judge A Pema [OB]
C M Wontner-Smith, BA, FCA [OB]
Sir David Wootton, MA [OB]

Representing the University of Bradford:
vacant

Representing the University of Leeds:
Professor Sir Alexander F Markham, BSc, PhD, MBBS, DSc, FRCP, FRCPath

Representing Chamber of Commerce:
S R Watson, MCIPR

Governors Emeriti:
J E Barker, MA [OB]
P J M Bell ,JP, FCIS, CText, FTI, FRSA [OB]
R G Bowers, DL, BSc, CEng, FRSA [OB]
A Craig, DL, DCR
I Crawford, FCA
J D Fenton, MCSP, SRP
J G Ridings, FCA

[OB]: Old Bradfordian

Bursar and Clerk to the Governors: H Najib

Headmaster: **Dr S Hinchliffe**, BA, MEd, PhD, FRSA

Deputy Headmaster: J Boardman
Assistant Head, Pastoral: M J Chapman, MA
Assistant Head, Curriculum: G P Woods, MA
Assistant Head, Development: P Merckx, BSc
HR Manager: C Macdonald
Headmaster, Junior School: R Ribeiro

Brentwood School

Middleton Hall Lane, Brentwood, Essex CM15 8EE

Tel: 01277 243243
email: headmaster@brentwood.essex.sch.uk
website: www.brentwoodschool.co.uk
Twitter: @Brentwood_Sch
Facebook: @BrentwoodSchoolUK
Instagram: @brentwood_sch
LinkedIn: /school/brentwood-school-uk

Motto: *Virtue, Learning and Manners*

Brentwood School was founded in 1557 and received its charter as the Grammar School of Antony Browne, Serjeant at Law, on 5th July, 1558. The Founder became Chief Justice of Common Pleas shortly before the death of Queen Mary, and was knighted a few months before his death in 1567. The Foundation Stone over the door of Old Big School was laid on 10th April, 1568, by Edmund Huddleston and his wife Dorothy, who was the step-daughter of the Founder. The Elizabethan silver seal of the School Corporation is still in the possession of the Governors. In 1622 Statutes were drawn up for the School by Sir Antony Browne, kinsman of the Founder, George Monteigne, Bishop of London, and John Donne, Dean of St Paul's.

Brentwood School is a co-educational school with a total of 1,918 pupils including 589 in the Preparatory School. The Preparatory School is fully co-educational as is the Sixth Form (of 371 pupils), but boys and girls are taught separately between the ages of 11 and 16. Boarding is available for boys and girls from age 13.

Buildings and Grounds. The School occupies a 75-acre site on high ground at the northern end of the town some 20 miles north-east of London. Old Big School, the original School room, is still in regular use, thus maintaining a direct link with the School's founder. Over recent years a major building programme has seen extensions to the Science and Modern Languages buildings and Dining Halls; Boarding Houses and Sixth Form accommodation; the building of the magnificent Brentwood School Sports Centre; a Performing Arts Centre, an all-weather pitch, an Art and Design Centre and an indoor heated swimming pool. In November 2011, HRH Prince Edward The Earl of Wessex formally opened the School's new Sixth Form Centre and Wessex Auditorium. The Sixth Form Centre, which has become the intellectual powerhouse of the School, provides an exemplary educational environment for the International Baccalaureate programme. Facilities include common rooms and private study areas, 16 additional classrooms, a dedicated computer suite and multi-purpose 400-seat auditorium. The award-winning Bean Academic Centre was opened to pupils at the end of March 2016. With large classroom spaces, a lecture theatre & café, it provides a state-of-the-art environment within which pupils can develop independent learning. A multi-million pound development has been completed at the Preparatory School.

Organisation. The School is one community within which, for good educational reasons, girls and boys are taught separately from age 11 to 16. They are encouraged to participate together in all co-curricular activities. The Senior School is divided into Year Groups. Each Year Group has a Head of Year and Deputy who oversee it. The vast majority of pupils join the School at 11 after successfully completing the Entrance Examination. A broad curriculum is followed through the first three years and this continues through careful choice of GCSE and IGCSE subjects to the end of the Fifth Year. Entry to the Sixth Form is conditional upon success in the GCSE examinations. There is a wide choice of subjects, whether students want to follow the International Baccalaureate Diploma Programme (IBDP), BTEC Extended Diploma (Sport and Business) or A Levels. Most go on to University. Pass rates at A Level reach 100% and many pupils gain places at Oxford and Cambridge each year.

Religion. Although Brentwood is a Christian School, pupils and staff from all faiths, or none, are welcome. There is a resident Chaplain and pupils attend Chapel weekly. Regular Communion Services are held.

Boarding. There are two Boarding Houses, both of which have been thoroughly modernised. The boys reside in Hough House which can accommodate up to 42 students; the girls reside in Mill Hill House where 27 can be accommodated. The public rooms are spacious and both Houses are generously staffed. Full and weekly boarding are available. A qualified Matron runs an efficient Sanatorium.

Pastoral Care. Brentwood School has an outstanding level of pastoral care which is provided by Heads of Year, Tutors and our Pastoral Team, ably supported by the delegated senior Deputy Head, Mrs Jenkin, and by all colleagues, who together create the enabling, supportive ethos. Tutors combine pastoral care with detailed academic monitoring, thus treating the whole person. Their encouragement to their pupils to participate in a wide range of activities successfully engenders greater self-confidence and self-awareness. In addition to Mrs Jenkin, Senior Deputy Head (Pastoral), Heads of Year and Tutors, there are three pastoral managers in the Senior School.

Music, Drama and Art. We are proud to be a Steinway School, enabling our pupils to learn on the very best-made pianos in the world, as well as some rare instruments otherwise unavailable to them. Brentwood is also a partnership school with the Guildhall School of Music and Drama, one of the finest musical institutions in the world. Music plays an important part in the life of the School, as do Drama and Art. There are four orchestras and several ensembles and jazz groups. The Big Band is internationally acclaimed. There are at least three dramatic productions each year, together with regular Art Exhibitions.

Careers. There is an excellent University Entrance and Careers Department where students receive advice and can obtain information about courses and/or careers. Aptitude Tests; Work Experience; visits to colleges, universities and places of work; visiting speakers are all part of the provision. A careers convention is held in March each year.

CCF, VSA & DofE. All pupils either join the Combined Cadet Force or, through the Voluntary Service Activity, engage in a wide-ranging series of activities which bring them into contact with the Community. The Duke of Edinburgh's Award scheme runs alongside these activities.

School Societies. There are many flourishing societies covering a wide range of interests, catering for all ages. The ACES programme in the Prep School encompasses the areas of Arts, Community, Enrichment and Sports, and the Sir Antony Browne Society (SABS) is a society for Sixth Form students, which provides them with an opportunity for intellectual discussion and cultural interest.

Sports Facilities. Brentwood School was one of the official training venues for the London 2012 Games. The playing fields are part of the School complex and provide ample space for soccer, cricket, hockey, rugby and tennis. There is a world-class all-weather athletics track. The Brentwood School Sports Centre includes an indoor soccer/ hockey pitch, six badminton courts, indoor cricket nets, basketball courts and a fencing salle, as well as squash courts and a fitness suite. There is a heated indoor swimming pool and an all-weather pitch. Provision is made for golf, sailing and table tennis. The two AstroTurfs and netball courts are floodlit for use in winter.

Preparatory School. *See entry in IAPS section for details.*

Entry. Entrance Examinations for both boys and girls aged 11 are held at the School in January each year. Entries are also accepted at 13 plus, following the Common Entrance Examination, vacancies permitting. Transfers at other ages are also possible. Sixth Form entry is through GCSE success, and interview.

Scholarships and Bursaries. In addition to Academic scholarships the School offers Chess, Dance, Drama, Music (including singing) and Sport scholarships at 11+. These may be supplemented by means-tested Bursaries. Art, Dance, Drama, Music and Sport scholarships are offered for Sixth Form. There are also academic scholarships available for entry into the Sixth Form.

The School offers a considerable number of Bursaries in addition to the awards described above. Over a fifth of pupils receive such assistance.

Fees per term (2021–2022). Day £6,866, Boarding £13,455.

Old Brentwoods Society. There is a flourishing Society for pupils to stay in touch once they have left the School; email: oldbrentwoods@brentwood.essex.sch.uk.

Charitable status. Brentwood School (part of Sir Antony Browne's School Trust, Brentwood) is a Registered Charity, number 1153605. It is a Charitable Trust for the purpose of educating children.

Governors:
Sir Michael Snyder, DSc, FCA, FRSA [OB] (*Chairman*)
R I McLintock, MSc, DMS, DipEd (*Vice-Chairman*)
P C Beresford, FNAEA, MARLA
Lord Black of Brentwood, MA, MCIPR, FRSA [OB]
Mrs J Bryan, CTA, LLB
Mrs S Dalgarno, MA, PGCE, JP
D J Elms, MA, FCA, FCSI
Professor B J W Evans, BSc Hons, PhD [OB]
J Fergus
Lord Flight of Worcester, MA, MBA [OB]
J Griffith-Jones, MA, ACA, TD
M Hampson, BEng Hons, FBCS
Mrs A Hardy, QC, LLB Hons, LLM Tax, AKC
S Jeevan, BA Hons, MA, MBA, MST

Mrs J M Jones, BA Hons, ARCM
The Venerable D Lowman, BD, AKC
Ms R Martin, MEd, NPQH
S Norris, BSc Hons [OB]
Dr C Tout, MA, PhD [OB]
J Tumbridge, CC, MCIArb, LLB Hons

[OB] *Old Brentwood*

Bursar and Clerk to the Governors: J Blunden, CBE, LVO, BSc Hons

Headmaster: **M Bond**, BA

Senior Deputy Head (*Pastoral*): Mrs N Jenkin, BA, MA
Deputy Head (*Academic*): J Barfield Moore, MA
Deputy Head (*Staffing, Co-Curricular & Operations*): Miss A Miller, BA, MA, MA

Heads of Year:
Director of Sixth Form: Miss L Austen, BA, MA
Academic Director (*Director of IB*): Mrs H Carter, BSc
Academic Director (*Innovative Curriculum*): G Justham, BSc
Academic Director (*Director of Studies*): D Endlar, MChem
Director of Pedagogy & Staff Development: Mrs H Barfield Moore, BA, AKC
Head of Research & Development: Dr I Ross, MA, PhD
Heads of Academic Enrichment: Mrs C Bowley, BA, MA; J G Bowley, MA, Maîtrise, MIL, FCIEA, FRSA
Director of Pupil Wellbeing: Mrs M Carabache, BA, MA
Calendar & Visits Co-ordinator: Mrs S Davis, BSc [OB]
Director of Co-Curricular Activities: Mrs J McLeod, BSc
Head of KS2/3 Transition: Mrs K Semple, BA [OB]
Sixth Form, Head of Upper Sixth: T Sellers, BA
Sixth Form, Head of Lower Sixth: Mrs A Roberts, BA
Year 11: Mrs Z Hill, BA, MA, GTP
Year 10: A Linton, MA, BA
Year 9: Mrs J Khush, MSc
Year 8: Miss R Bishop, BA
Year 7: A Clarke, BA, MA

Houses & Housemasters/mistresses:
East: J McCann, BEng
Hough: S Taylor, LLB
Mill Hill: T Cope, MEng
North: Miss M Swettenham BA [OB]
South: Miss C Hanly, BA
Weald: D Wright, BSc, QTS
West: Mrs A Wall, BA

* *Head of Department*

Art:
*C Lonsdale, MA, BA
Miss V Cooper, BA
Miss K Lerman, BA
Miss E Stimpson, BA

O Prinn, BSc
Mrs G Robertson, BSc [OB]

Business Studies:
*Mrs K Giles, BA
A Giles, BA
Miss J Haron, BSc
Mrs K Lee BA, PGDL
Miss L McCrory BEd
Miss M Parmar, LLB, LPC
N Turnbull, BA

Biology:
*Dr E Parades, BA Mod, PG Dip, PDE, PhD
Miss J P Byrne, MSc, BSc
Dr J Crocker, BSc, PhD
Dr K Dingwell, BSc
Mrs P Ebden, BSc, MSc
Miss E Faulkner, BScEd
K Gray, BSc
Miss V Kerslake, BSc
Mrs C Meiring, BSc, BSc

Chemistry:
*Dr N Law, MA, PhD
D Endlar, MChem
Miss E Faulkner, BScEd
Mrs V Harrison, BSc

Mrs C James
Mrs J Khush, MSc
Revd Dr A McConnaughie, BA, MA, PhD, BA
Mrs C Meiring, BSc, BSc
Dr A North, MChem
Miss R Pettingill, BSc
Dr I Ross, MA, PhD
L Schramm

Classics:
*S Hitchings, BA, MA
Mrs C Hardy, BA [OB]
Mrs Z Hill, BA, MA, GTP
Mrs J Gray, BA
Dr C Prouatt, BA, MPhil
Mrs K L Semple, BA [OB]
Miss M Swettenham, BA

Computing & ICT:
*G Kiff, BSc
C Chambrier
G Justham, BSc
J McCann, BEng
Miss J Scotland, BSc Hons

Dance:
*Mrs M Carabache, BA, MA, AMTLA
Miss K Herterich, ISTD (*Director of Dance Academy*)
Miss E Preston, BSc

_
Design & Technology:
*Miss L Hall, BA, MA
Ms J Hardy, BA
Miss K Lerman, BA
B LoBue, BSc
Mrs J Shufflebotham, BA
Miss A Tipler, BA

Drama:
*M Bulmer, BA, MA (*Director of Performing Arts*)
Mrs M Carabache, BA, MA, AMTLA
Mrs R Clark, MA, BA
Mrs A Ellis, BA
Mrs S Hermosa, BA
Mrs D Veares, BA

Economics:
*Ms A Cash, LLB, BEcon, GradDipEd
A Giles, BA
Miss J Haron, BSc
Mrs C Micallef
P Rees, BA

English:
*Miss A Cooper, BA, MA
Mrs L Austen, BA, MA
Mrs M Callender, MA
Miss R Coates, BA
Miss R Dawick, BA, BA, MDev.Studies MA
Mrs A Ellis, BA

Miss M Gilroy, BA
Miss C Hanly, BA
R Irvine, BA
Miss A Kwolek, BA, MA, UG Dip
S Levien, MA
Miss H L Nicholls, BA
Mrs T Oldland, BA
Mrs A Roberts, BA
Miss B Selfridge, BA [OB]
Miss F Spriggs, MA
S Taylor, LLB, PGD

EAL:
*M Bauer, MA
B Clements, BA, MPhil, Dip RSA
Mrs A Hall, BA

Food & Nutrition:
*Miss M O'Rourke, BA
Mrs D Asher, BEd ORD

Geography:
*Miss J Collins, BA
Mrs H Carter, BSc, MA
Miss L Coverson, BSc
Mrs S Davis, BSc
A Linton, MA, BA
C M Long, BA
Mrs C Priddle
D Wright, BSc, QTS

History:
*Ms B Fuller, BA
Dr C Bryan, EdD, BA, MSc
M Clark, BA
A Clarke, BA, MA
Mrs R Coppell, MA
Dr C Harvey, BA, PhD
M Howard, BA, MA
Miss E Keegan, BA
D Rogers
T Sellers, BA
Miss M Smith, BA

Learning Support:
*Miss R Coates, BA
Mrs F Appleton
Miss I Dissanayake, BA
Mrs G Robertson, BSc [OB]

Mathematics:
*Miss E Warnes, BSc, MEd
Mrs K Bowes, BSc
Mrs L Chapman, BSc
M Chan, MSc, BSc
M Childs, BA
T Conlan
T Cope, MEng
Miss G Cutbill, BA
Mrs R Dryden, BSc
R Ewin, BSc
Mrs S Ewin, BSc
Miss G Furnell, BSc
Dr F Gergely, PaedDr

B Paredes, BA, MA
Miss E Preston, BSc
Ms E Scholz, MEd
J Stevens, BSc
Miss L Williams, BSc
D Wood, BSc, MSc [OB]

Modern Languages:
*Dr B Priest, BA Hons, MPhil (*Head of Languages*, *Italian*)
Mrs N Piejko, BTS, BEd (*French*)
Mrs J Rodgers, BA, MSc (*Chinese*)
Mrs M Morris, BA, MA Maîtrise (*German*)
G Smith, BA, MA (*Spanish*)
Miss P Appiah, BA
M Bauer, MA
Mrs C Bowley, BA, MA
J Bowley, MA, Maîtrise, MIL, FCIEA, FRSA
Miss R Campbell, BA
Mrs L G M Dearmer-Decup, BA
Mrs A Hall, BA
Mrs N Jenkin, BA, MA
Miss C Lacotte, DEUG, BA
Mrs J Milne, MA Cantab
Mrs I Penalver-Edwards, BA
K Richter MSc
Mrs S J Roast, BEd
Miss B Selfridge, BA [OB]
Mrs A Wall, BA
Mrs M Watts-Jimenez, BA

Music:
*F Cooper, BA [OB] (*Director of Music*)
D Revels, MA Oxon, MMus, LRSM (*Assistant Director of Music*)
S Barber
G Cuciuc
T Heard, MA, BMus
O El-Holiby, BA

Physics:
*C Beadling, BSc
Mx C Astolfi, MA
Miss Y Calo
Dr S Gascoyne
D Goldberg, MEng
L C Jenkins, MSc, FRAS
Ms J Law, BEd
B LoBue, BSc
N Sexton, BSc

Physical Education & Games:
*Mrs J McLeod, BSc (*Director of Co-Curricular Activities*)

*N Gamester (*Director of Sport*)
*J Baird (*Director of Sport – Prep Lead*)
W Castleman (*Master i/c Rugby*)
B Crickmay, BSc Hons
C Galesloot, FIE (*Master i/c Fencing*)
Miss A Helsby, BSc (*Head of Girls' Games – Prep*)
Mrs W L Juniper, BEd
D Jupp (*Head of Football*)
Miss P Lake
Miss J Lazenby, BSc
C M Long, BA (*Head of Golf*)
J Mickelburgh (*Cricket Professional*)
Miss L Morrell, BA (*Head of Girls' Games/Head of Hockey*)
A Nolan, BSc (*Head of Cricket*)
O Prior, BSc
Miss L Reeder, BA
Mrs A Simpson-Crick, BSc Hons [OB] (*Head of Tennis & Netball*)
M Simpson-Crick (*Head of Tennis Academy – Prep*)
C Smith, BSc (*Head of Boys' Games*)
C Warburton, BSc Hons (*Head of Academic PE/ Head of Athletics*)
Mrs N Watson, HND (*Head of Swimming & Water Polo*)
D Wood, BSc, MSc [OB] (*Head of Squash*)

Politics:
*Ms B Fuller, BA
Dr C Bryan, EdD, MSc, BA
Mrs R Coppell, MA
Dr C Harvey, BA, PhD
Miss E Keegan, BA

Psychology:
*Ms S Afsar, BA, BSc, LLM
Miss J Atkinson, BSc
Dr C Bryan, EdD, MSc, BA
Miss J Campbell-May
Mrs J O'Connell, BSc

Theology & Philosophy:
*R Gale, BA, MA
Mrs H Barfield Moore, BA, AKC
J Barfield Moore, MA
Miss R Bishop, BA
B Clements, BA, MPhil, Dip RSA
R Jenkins, BA

Miss A Miller, BA, MA,
  MA
M Monro, BA, AKA

Admissions Registrar: Mrs D Cook
Headmaster's PA: Mrs J Beazley
School Medical Officer: Dr Nasif

Brighton College

Eastern Road, Brighton BN2 0AL

Tel: 01273 704200
           01273 704339 Head Master
           01273 704260 Bursar
           01273 704210 Prep School
           01273 704259 Pre-Prep School
email: admissions@brightoncollege.net
website: www.brightoncollege.org.uk
Twitter: @BrightonCollege
Facebook: @BrightonCollegeUK

Motto: TO Δ'EY NIKATΩ ~ *Let the right prevail*

Thoroughly progressive, academic, inclusive and, above all, focused on the importance of kindness, Brighton College has become a powerhouse in independent education. Founded in 1845 in the heart of Brighton's Kemptown area, its historic quad and listed buildings speak of a rich educational heritage. Its dynamic head teacher Richard Cairns, however, is far more interested in the future and has become known nationally for his ground-breaking approach both educationally and pastorally.

Mr Cairns has overseen an ambitious capital project during his tenure which includes the new 20-classroom Yeoh Building, including a Creative Learning Centre, and the School of Science and Sport, including 18 university-standard laboratories, 25-metre swimming pool and double height sports hall.

The College regularly achieves the best GCSE and A Level results in Sussex and some of the highest in the country. In the most recent exam results, the school's Sixth Formers achieved 99% A*–B in their A Level, while the most common grade at GCSE was the top grade of 9, with 96% of exam grades being 9–7/A*–A. The school had 34 Oxbridge offers in 2021, and 117 pupils have attended Cambridge in the last six years.

The school has been the recipient of many awards: named 'United Kingdom Independent School of the Decade' and 'United Kingdom Independent School of the Year' 2019 and 2013 by *The Sunday Times*, Mr Cairns was named 'Public School Headmaster of the Year 2012–13' by *Tatler* magazine. *The Week* called Brighton College the 'Most Forward-thinking School in Britain' for two years running in 2017–19.

There is a wealth of extracurricular activities on offer, in particular sport, music and the performing arts. There are now some 1090 pupils, of whom a third are boarders. In its most recent inspection in 2015, the Independent Schools Inspectorate gave Brighton College and its Prep & Pre-Prep School the highest possible grade across every single inspection category, with a rare 'Exceptional' for Achievement and Learning.

Buildings. An extensive programme of development has taken place which has seen many of the new builds win architectural awards. In 2020 The School of Science and Sport opened, containing 18 university-standard labs, plus a 25-metre pool and rooftop running track; in 2015 the Music School opened, home to state-of-the-art recording facilities and a 150-seat recital hall. In September 2017, the tenth new building in ten years opened, the Hopkins-designed Yeoh Building, with its innovative top-floor double-height Creative Learning Centre.

Admission. Pupils are admitted to the Lower Third at the age of 11 via assessments held at the College in January; to the Fourth Form between the ages of 13 and 14 via the Common Entrance examination, the Academic Scholarship examination or by special assessment and interview; and into the Sixth Form for A Levels between the ages of 16 and 17. In all cases pupils must also produce evidence of good character and conduct from their previous school. The College prospectus and registration form can be obtained from the Director of Admissions.

Houses. An extensive refurbishment programme is nearing completion across the day and boarding houses. A third of the pupils are boarders in the school and weekly boarding is increasingly popular, giving pupils the opportunity to go home on Friday afternoon and return either on Sunday evening or Monday morning.

Health. There is a Central Health Centre with a team of qualified nurses, and the Medical Officer visits regularly.

Catering. There is self-service dining room, managed by a qualified Catering Manager.

Holidays. School holidays are around three weeks each at Christmas and Easter, and eight weeks in the Summer. There is a half-term holiday of one week in all three terms.

Religion. A short morning service is held in Chapel on two days a week, with one service aimed to embrace all faiths.

Curriculum. The School is divided into seven forms: Lower Third, Upper Third, Fourth, Lower Fifth, Upper Fifth, Lower Sixth and Upper Sixth. In the Sixth Form almost 30 subjects are available at A Level. For GCSE, pupils select their subjects – usually 10 – at the end of the Fourth Form. 99% of pupils proceed to university. Preparation for the UCAS process begins in the second term of the Lower Sixth, and pupils are guided towards appropriate choices by the Head of Sixth Form in conjunction with the individual pupil's tutor.

Sport. The College enjoys a strong record of excellence at sports. The main playing field (the Home Ground) is part of the College campus and the Jubilee Ground is a mile away at East Brighton Park. All pupils take part in the College's extensive games programme. The main sports for boys are rugby and cricket and for girls, netball, hockey and cricket. In addition, a host of other options are available including football, squash, tennis, golf, beach volleyball, aerobics, rounders, yoga, athletics and cross country.

Service. All pupils from the Lower Fifth onwards are expected to participate in a service activity on one afternoon a week. Pupils may participate in charity work or, in the Sixth Form, Community Service; alternatively they may join The Duke of Edinburgh's Award scheme or enter one of the three sections of the CCF.

Music. There is a strong musical tradition and pupils reach a very high level of performance. The Choir, Chamber Orchestra, Symphony Orchestra, Concert Band and Swing

Band perform regularly both inside and outside the College. There are several Chamber groups, and the Choral Society and Orchestra usually perform major works at the annual Brighton Festival.

Drama. The College has a strong tradition of excellence in drama, and there are opportunities for anyone to be involved. In addition to the regular calendar of a musical, Sixth Form studio production, Sixth Form play, Fourth Form play, Lower School play and House Drama festival, there are also many productions mounted entirely by pupils.

Activities. Creative activities are encouraged both in and out of school time, and the College has its own Art School and Gallery. Dance is a very popular activity with many pupils performing in regional and national productions.

Careers. The Head of Careers with a team of tutors advise pupils on careers. The College is a member of the Independent Schools Careers Organisation.

Scholarships. The following Scholarships are available:

11+ Entry: Academic, All-Rounder (Art, Dance, Drama, Music and Sport), Chess and Choral.

13+ Entry: Academic, All-Rounder, Art & Photography, Chess, Choral, Dance, Drama, DT, Music and Sport.

Sixth Form Entry: Academic, Sport and Expressive Arts (Art, Dance, Drama, Music) and Opening Doors.

For further details about scholarships, please contact the Admissions Office.

Fees per term (2021–2022). Weekly Boarding: £12,220 (Fourth Form) to £12,590 (Upper 6th). Full Boarding: £13,770 (Fourth Form EU) to £17,640 (Upper 6th Non-EU). Day: £6,120 (Lower Third) to £8,900 (Upper Sixth).

Old Brightonians, the College's alumni network, has annual dinners and a number of flourishing sports clubs.

Preparatory School. The College has its own co-educational Nursery, Pre-Prep & Prep School. (*For details see entry in IAPS section.*)

Charitable status. Brighton College is a Registered Charity, number 307061.

Chair of Governors: The Lord Mogg, KCMG

Senior Management Team:

Head Master: **Mr R J Cairns**, MA, FRSA

Group Chief Operating Officer: Mr P Westbrook, BA, FCA
Second Master: Mr S Marshall-Taylor, BA
Executive Head of Prep Schools: Mr G R Owton, BA

Deputy Heads:
Mr N J Fraser, MA
Miss L Hamblett, MA
Mr A T Patton, MA
Mrs J A Riley, MA
Mr M C Sloan, BA

Bursar: Ms E Dobson, MA CIMA

Assistant Head (Sixth Form): Ms O Upchurch, MEd
Assistant Head (Middle School): Mr C Fowler, BA
Assistant Head (Co-Curriculum): Dr A Baragwanath, PhD
Assistant Head (Outreach and Partnerships): Miss Rachel Hughes, MA
Assistant Head (Director of Boarding): Mrs J Hamblett-Jahn, LLB
Assistant Head (Director of Studies): Mr G Brocklesby, BA
Assistant Head (London Academy of Excellence): Mr J Carr-Hill, MSc

Director of Admissions/Registrar: Mr A Merrett, BSc
Chaplain: Revd R Amess, BA

Bristol Grammar School

University Road, Bristol BS8 1SR

Tel: 0117 973 6006
email: headmaster@bgs.bristol.sch.uk
website: www.bristolgrammarschool.co.uk
Twitter: @bgsbristol
Facebook: @bgsbristol

Motto: Ex Spinis Uvas

'The Grammar School in Bristowe' existed under a lay master in 1532 in which year, under a charter of Henry VIII, it was endowed with the estates of St Bartholomew's Hospital by the merchant and geographer Robert Thorne and others. The trust was placed in the care of the Corporation of Bristol and then the Trustees of the Bristol Municipal Charities. In September 2004 the School incorporated as a company limited by guarantee with registered charitable status and is now governed under Memorandum and Articles of Association approved by the Charity Commission in 2004.

Co-educational since 1980, Bristol Grammar School is a day school providing a wide-ranging and challenging education for c. 1,000 boys and girls aged between 11–18, while BGS Infants and Juniors, based on the same site, caters for those in the 4–11 age range.

Pupils learn in an atmosphere that motivates them to enjoy their education and as a result BGS has a deserved reputation as one of the leading academic schools in the South West. The School has a friendly and lively environment and pupils are encouraged to make the most of the wide-ranging opportunities available to them. When pupils join the School at 11+, they are based in the same building in their House form groups, which helps ease their transition to senior school, as well as providing an important opportunity for the year-group to bond socially. In Years 8–11, each House group has its own base, although teaching is spread throughout the School's specialist facilities.

Close to the city centre and adjacent to the University, Bristol Grammar School is well placed to take advantage of the city's many amenities. It is also committed to a continuing programme of investment to ensure its own facilities continue to offer the best possible opportunities to its pupils.

The Houses. The School is divided into six Houses, each organised by a Head of House with the assistance of a Deputy Head of House and House Form Tutors. Form Tutors will typically remain with pupils throughout their time in the Senior School from Years 7–11. Older pupils become leaders within their House, while social, theatrical, musical, sporting and other opportunities allow those from all year-groups to work together in a friendly and cooperative atmosphere. As well as providing continuity of pastoral care and enhancing school/home links, the Houses operate as families within the School community, encouraging a real sense of belonging among pupils.

Curriculum. The School takes note of the National Curriculum but – in keeping with its academic ethos and focus on every learner being enabled to make the most of their individual ability – a far wider range of subjects and opportunities is offered. Setting is used in Maths, the Sciences and some Modern and Classical languages to ensure optimal individual progress, but there is no streaming. In Year 7 all pupils follow a curriculum which includes English, Mathematics, Science, French, Spanish, History, Geography, Design & Technology, Food & Nutrition, ICT, Latin, PRE (Philosophy, Religion and Ethics), Art, Music, Drama, Dance, and Physical Education. In Year 8 the core curriculum is continued but pupils are offered a further choice of languages to include German and Russian. In Year 9 pupils personalise their curriculum, making choices from all subjects studied thus far and other areas such as Classical Civilisation, Greek, Business Studies and Computer Science, and pupils then choose their GCSE options from this broad base. Most pupils take ten GCSEs at the end of Year 11 in the core subjects of English, Mathematics, Biology, Chemistry, Physics, a humanities subject and a modern language, together with a selection of other subjects, chosen from a carefully balanced range of options.

BGS currently offers IGCSEs in Mathematics; the Sciences; Geography; History; French; German; Spanish; Business Studies; Food & Nutrition; and Philosophy, Religion & Ethics (PRE). The Sixth Form provides the opportunity to study either A levels or the International Baccalaureate (IB) Diploma Programme. There are a wide range of subjects on offer in the Sixth Form: English Language (A level only), English Literature, Mathematics and Further Mathematics, Biology, Chemistry, Physics, Design & Technology (A level only), French, German, Russian, Spanish, Latin, Greek, Classical Civilisation (A level only), History, Global Politics (IB only), Geography, Economics, Business Studies (A level only), Computer Science, Psychology, Philosophy, Drama & Theatre Studies, Dance, Physical Education, Art, Music, and Music Technology (A level only). In addition, many pupils take an elective course; their options include the Extended Project Qualification, a Sports Leadership award, Creative Writing, Further Mathematics, and Mathematical Studies. Many also choose to complete their Gold Duke of Edinburgh's Award. All Sixth-form pupils follow enrichment courses and attend a richly diverse programme of weekly lectures by visiting speakers. Many also attend enrichment lessons to support university preparation for Russell Group and Oxbridge Universities, including for Medicine, Veterinary Science and Law. Two experienced Higher Education and Careers Advisors guide pupils to proceed on a pathway that is best suited to their ambitions, whether that be an apprenticeship, the world of work or attending one of the wide range of universities in the UK and abroad, with the majority securing places at their first-choice universities.

There are frequent opportunities for parents to consult Form Tutors and Heads of Houses and regular meetings are held for parents to meet the teaching staff. The School also has three teachers to support pupils with SEN (including dyslexia and EAL).

Games. The Games options – which vary for different age-groups – include rugby, hockey, netball, football, cross-country, cricket, athletics, tennis, and weight training. Facilities for orienteering, aerobics, climbing, dance, judo, fencing, badminton and squash are also available. There is a Pavilion and extensive playing fields at Failand, which includes an all-weather 3G pitch, two AstroTurf hockey pitches and netball and tennis areas. Below the Sixth Form,

all pupils participate in School games sessions; the full range of sports is available to Sixth-form pupils. Major sports tours are run on a three-year cycle: recent destinations have included New Zealand, South America, South Africa, and Sri Lanka and Malaysia.

Activities and Societies. Pupils take part in a wide-ranging programme of activities (this forms part of the compulsory curriculum for some year-groups), and there are many clubs and societies at lunchtimes and after school, including Astronomy Club, Model United Nations (MUN), Beekeeping, and Architecture Club. There are flourishing choirs and orchestras; individual tuition can also be arranged on a large number of instruments. Drama and Dance productions are regularly staged by different age levels and by the Houses. Pupils may join the Duke of Edinburgh's Award scheme in Year 10 and there is an active Community Service unit.

Admission. Entry to the School is normally in September at age 11+ following a satisfactory performance in the entrance examination held in the previous spring and a creditable school report or reference. All Year 7 applicants are also invited to meet with a member of staff to discuss their school work, interests and hobbies. A small number of places become available each year at age 13+, with a further thirty–forty places at 16+. Pupils may also be accepted into the School during the year at other points, subject to the availability of places.

Applications should be made to the Admissions Office at the School. Prospective entrants and their families are always welcome to visit; please see the website for information about open days, tours and taster days.

Bursaries. The School's Bursary Scheme is able to offer substantial financial assistance towards the fees of able pupils whose parents have limited means. The scheme is kept under regular review by the Governors who constantly seek to extend it.

Scholarships. Scholarships are available for entry at 11+ and 16+ and are awarded for academic ability; all applicants who take the entrance assessments in January are automatically considered for these, there is no separate assessment. Scholarships are also available at 11+ for Sport and Creative & Performing Arts.

The School runs a Scholars' Programme designed to meet the educational needs of its most gifted pupils. This programme offers extended individual learning opportunities, group activities and mentoring in and out of School by the Director of Scholars. At 16+ pupils may apply to become specific Subject Scholars and work more closely with Heads of Subject.

Fees per term (2021–2022). Senior School £5,159. Juniors: Years 3–6 £3,517. Infants: Years 1 & 2 £3,268, Reception £2,992. Fees include the cost of most textbooks and stationery and lunch for Reception to Year 11 pupils.

BGS Infants and Juniors. The Junior School extended its provision to include Infants, with its first Reception class in September 2010. The School admits children from 4–11 and is housed in its own buildings on the same site as the Senior School. (*For further details see entry in IAPS section.*)

Old Bristolians Society. Close contact is maintained with former pupils through the Old Bristolians Society whose Honorary Secretary can be contacted at the School.

Charitable status. Bristol Grammar School is a Registered Charity, number 1104425. It has existed since 1532 to provide an education for Bristol children.

Governors:
Mrs A J Arlidge, BA
A Barr, LLB
Mrs S Boccaccini, MEd
Ms M Crayton, BA, MCIM
Miss H Drake, MA
Dr M Gainsborough
Mrs C Gil, BSc, ACA
J May, MA
P Meehan, BEd Hons, FPFS
Dr J O'Gallagher, MBChB, MRCP, FRCPCH, FHEA
N Pickersgill, BSc, FCA
Dr M Ransome, BA, PhD
Ms K Redshaw, BA Hons Oxon
D Shelton, FCIM
Mrs M Simmons-Bird
J Sisman, BSc Hons, MRICS
Dr D Thompson, MBChB, MRCGP Dist
R Vaitilingam, BA Hons Oxon, MBE (*Chairman*)
M Wilson, BSc Hons, MRICS

Senior Leadership Team:

Headmaster: J M Barot, MA, MSc

Head of BGS Infants and Juniors: Miss H Hughes, BSc, MEd
Deputy Head: P R Roberts, BSc, MSc
Deputy Head: Ms R L Davies, BA, MSc
Deputy Head: Miss F A Ripley, BSc
Deputy Head: D J Stone, BSc
Bursar: G Mitchell, BA

Assistant Head: G S Clark, BSc
Assistant Head: B Schober, BSc, MA
Assistant Head: J S Harford, BSc
Assistant Head: O L Chambers, BSc
Assistant Head: A N Gunawardana, BA

Bromley High School
GDST

Blackbrook Lane, Bickley, Bromley, Kent BR1 2TW

Tel: 020 8781 7000
email: bhs@bro.gdst.net
website: www.bromleyhigh.gdst.net
Twitter: @bromleyhs
Facebook: @bromleyhighschoolGDST
Instagram: @bromleyhighschoolgdst
LinkedIn: @bromleyhighschoolGDST

Bromley High School is a selective school offering an exceptional education to girls aged 4–18 years. Set in leafy parkland and benefitting from first rate facilities, both Junior and Senior Schools provide a beautiful and buzzy environment where bright girls flourish.

The school is part of the GDST (Girls' Day School Trust), the leading network of independent girls' schools in the UK. Founded in 1883, Bromley High School was originally situated in the centre of Bromley. In 1981 it moved to Bickley to occupy modern purpose-built buildings set in 24 acres of leafy parkland.

In the classroom, each girl's intellectual potential is challenged and developed by inspirational teachers whose concern for your daughter ranges infinitely beyond her performance in examinations; teachers who have a capacity to develop a love of learning, a spirit of enquiry and an independence of mind. Girls learn to collaborate and to compete; to be creative and intellectually curious and their learning is underpinned by the school's ethos of achievement for all and by the subject passion, enthusiasm and expertise of their teachers.

Results are consistently superb. In 2021, 80% of new GCSE Grades were 8–9. Achievement at A Level was 43% A*, 80% A*/A and 92% A*–B. The school is most proud of its consistently impressive Value Added results at GCSE and A Level which demonstrate the care taken to bring out the best in every girl. In the 2016 ISI Inspection Report, Learning and Achievement were graded as Exceptional.

However, outstanding success at Bromley High School is not purely academic. Bromley High girls are resilient and well-rounded young women participating with enthusiasm and commitment in Music, Drama, Sport, Duke of Edinburgh's Award and an overabundant range of activities – and where they have interest or talent or enthusiasm, it is nurtured so that they learn to excel. Sport is exceptional with recent leavers gaining sports scholarships to Princeton and Yale.

Pastoral care is thoughtful and developmental, actively encouraging girls to develop key attributes: Confidence, Courage, Composure, and Commitment. Every house takes on the responsibility of supporting its own charity and the school has a highly valued tradition of volunteering and charitable activity.

Bromley High School pupils are confident, cheerful, considerate and enthusiastic about the myriad of opportunities their school has to offer.

Pupil Numbers. Senior School (ages 11–18): 571 (including the Sixth Form). Junior School (ages 4–11): 303.

The Junior School. Our two-form entry Junior School provides a stimulating and happy environment in which our pupils are encouraged to strive for excellence in all they do and to derive satisfaction from their achievements both great and small. From the earliest years we offer a broad curriculum which encourages, challenges and excites the young mind. Our aim is to foster a love of learning, develop independent thinking and promote a spirit of enquiry that leads to a depth of understanding. In our approach to teaching and learning we blend the traditional with progressive insights into learning styles and the particular needs of young girls as learners in a modern world. We teach the full range of the National Curriculum, including French, Spanish, German and also Latin and accord sports and the creative arts a significant place in the timetable, whilst ensuring that the foundations of the core subjects are well established. Class lessons are differentiated and we offer extension and support where appropriate and specialist teaching, sometimes from Senior School staff, in a number of subjects.

Bromley High believes in preparing girls for the challenges beyond school and values the importance of a holistic approach. The school provides many varied opportunities within a vibrant co-curricular programme including sporting, musical, dramatic and other creative activities. We make the most of our beautiful school grounds to provide opportunities for outdoor learning, in which our Forest School is a vital part.

Forest School is a planned programme that takes place in a woodland environment with the aim of developing opportunities for the learner to encounter the beauty, joy, awe and wonder of the natural environment. The approach is 'hands on' and seeks to promote the holistic development of the unique child, including physical, spatial, linguistic, emotional and spiritual aspects. Self-confidence and independence are increased through freedom, time and space to learn. A safe and secure environment allows the girls to extend their learning beyond their comfort zone; to challenge their existing boundaries and ideas and to tackle investigations and tasks which in the classroom may not be possible. Collaboration and cooperation between the learners, their peers and the forest school leader is at the core of the Forest School programme. Social skills develop through risk-taking and an understanding of the consequences of your own actions, whilst self-awareness, self-regulation and empathy for others are also developed. Forest School enables children to be active participants in their own education and development.

In the delivery of our curriculum we are well served by outstanding facilities which, in addition to comprehensively equipped classrooms, include a music wing, a library, ICT suite, a science room, an art and technology room, a sensory garden and outdoor 'classrooms'. Our new multi-million pound extension and refurbishment of the Junior School offers specialist teaching spaces which reflect the importance we place on providing the best possible learning environment, alongside our exceptional teaching. The girls are all enjoying our new Science Lab, Digital Hub and light-filled Art Studio and Design and Food Technology room, which look onto fields and woodland. We share many other facilities with the Senior School including a swimming pool, gymnasium, sports hall, tennis courts and an all-weather pitch.

The Senior School. Bromley High combines a tradition of scholarship with an innovative curriculum and expansive co-curricular provision. In the classroom, an emphasis on independent learning and growth mindset is designed to inculcate a spirit of enquiry, an independence of mind and a love of learning. Girls participate with enthusiasm and commitment in Music, Drama, Sport and an overabundant range of activities – and where they have interest or talent or enthusiasm, it is nurtured so that they learn to excel. In 2018, the school was awarded the EBA (Education Business Awards) for Outstanding Progress in an Independent School and the award for Best STEM (Science, Technology, Engineering and Mathematics) Provision in the UK.

Consistent investment has developed new science facilities, library, sixth form centre, drama studio, and specialist teaching rooms for the creative arts enabling departments to have their own dedicated spaces for teaching and extracurricular activities. Visual and creative arts are highly valued with Photography, Drama and Dance offered to A level and students regularly progressing to study at Central St Martin's and other prestigious Arts Foundation courses and to Ballet Schools.

Academic. Languages, both ancient and modern, are a particular strength, with French, German and Spanish offered from Year 7. Latin and Classics are both popular A Level choices, with Ancient Greek offered as an optional extra GCSE. As a girls' school, Bromley High lays great emphasis on STEM subjects – Science, Technology, Engineering and Mathematics. Teaching rooms are equipped with Smart Boards and all have Wi-Fi and digital projector facilities which allow pupils to use iPads, Chrome Books, or their own mobile computer devices. Teachers are encouraged to enrich the curriculum and teach lively, challenging lessons. Myriad trips and activities, including music tours abroad from Year 7, and Lower School trips to Florence, Venice and Iceland. The modern foreign languages department has links with France, Germany and Spain and arranges exchanges, visits and work experience placements.

Girls study 10 GCSE subjects including Mathematics, Biology, Chemistry, Physics, English and English Literature and a Modern Language. Three further options are chosen from French, Spanish and German, Latin and Classical Civilisation; Computer Science, Music, Art, Photography, Drama, Dance, Design Technology, Economics, Geography, History, Physical Education.

Sport. Sports facilities on the school's 25-acre site are superb, including a large, well-equipped Sports Hall, a new fitness suite, a gymnasium, a 400-metre athletics track, two grass hockey pitches, a fine indoor heated swimming pool, and floodlit AstroTurf pitches and courts. Sport is both integral to the curriculum and an important part of the extracurricular life of the school. The school is proud of its tradition of producing national level athletes and swimmers and the number of girls who play county level hockey, netball, swimming, tennis and athletics. In 2018, the U16 Hockey Team reached the U16 National Indoor Hockey Finals as East of England Champions.

Sixth Form. The Sixth Form Centre provides a bright, modern setting for traditional scholarship. Students select from a broad range of A Levels supplemented by Extended Project, AS Thinking Skills and electives such as Young Enterprise, Magazine Editing, Fashion, etc. Careers education is supported by the extensive GDST network of more than 70,000 alumnae. Sixth Formers benefit from GDST-wide initiatives, such as leadership and Oxbridge conferences and residential course on topics such as Engineering and Environmental Sustainability.

Extracurricular Activities. A great emphasis is put on an enthusiastic involvement in music, art, sport and drama. The annual Dance production is a significant event in the school calendar, and in recent years the school has staged concerts in major London venues such as the Royal Albert Hall, Southwark Cathedral and The Swiss Church.

Girls contribute to local, national and international charities and to community service. Almost all girls participate in the Duke of Edinburgh's Award scheme in Year 10, with some continuing to completion of Gold Award in Sixth Form. The Eco Society promotes a keen interest in environmental issues. There are regular exchanges to France, Germany and Spain as well as Geography and Biology field trips as far as Iceland. Annual World Challenge expeditions have recently visited Madagascar, Mongolia and Costa Rica. The Year 6 and 7 Music Tours have recently visited Paris, Brussels, Normandy and Bruges with the Senior Music Tour performing in Berlin, Prague, New York and Los Angeles. It is first only all-girls senior school in the world to have all Steinway status and musicians benefit from a Musician-in-Residence.

Fees per term (2021–2022). Senior School £5,897, Junior School £4,755.

Fees cover tuition, stationery, textbooks and scientific and games materials as well as entry fees for GCSE and

GCE Advanced Level examinations. Extra tuition in Music and Speech and Drama is available at recognised rates.

Bursaries. Bursaries are means-tested and provide, for successful applicants, assistance with fees to enable bright girls to benefit from a GDST education. For those receiving full remission of fees, the award may include uniform and trips allowances.

Scholarships. There are Academic, Art, Music and Sport scholarships for the most successful candidates in the assessments at 11+ and for entry into the Sixth Form.

Admission and Entrance Examination. Admission into the school is at 4+ (Reception) and 7+ (Year 3) by assessment and testing. Pupils from the Junior School progress automatically to the Senior School but external applicants, or those wishing to be considered for scholarship or bursary are assessed at 11+. The examination tests verbal and non-verbal skills, as well as creative writing. Entry to the Sixth Form is dependent on interview and school reference, including predicted grades and is contingent on results at GCSE.

Charitable status. Bromley High School is part of The Girls' Day School Trust, which is a Registered Charity, number 306983.

Chair of the Local Governors: Mr Dominic Broom, LLB

Headmistress: Mrs A Drew, BA Hons, MBA Dunelm

Deputy Head (Pastoral): Mrs H Elkins, BA King's College London

Deputy Head (Academic): Dr S Lindfield, BSc Oxon, PhD Liverpool

Assistant Head (Head of Sixth Form): Mrs C Bird, BA Manchester

Assistant Head (Organisation): Mr P Isted, BA Bristol

Director of Finance & Operations: Mr R Taylor, MA

Head of Junior School: Mrs C Dickerson, BA Anglia

Deputy Head of Junior School: Mrs K Powell, BEd Primary Ed Greenwich

Director of Marketing and Communications: Ms N Messih, BA Leeds

Admissions Registrar: Mrs L Clarke

Bromsgrove School

Worcester Road, Bromsgrove, Worcestershire B61 7DU

Tel: 01527 579679
email: admissions@bromsgrove-school.co.uk
website: www.bromsgrove-school.co.uk
Twitter: @bromsschool
Facebook: @bromsgroveschool
Instagram: @bromsgroveschool
LinkedIn: /school/bromsgrove-school

Motto: *Deo Regi Vicino*

The date of the School's Foundation is unknown but it was reorganised by Edward VI in 1553 and was granted a Royal Charter 6 years later. It was refounded in 1693 by Sir Thomas Cookes, Bt, at the same time as Worcester College,

Oxford (formerly Gloucester Hall). The link between School and College has been maintained ever since.

Location. This co-educational boarding and day school is situated some 13 miles north of the Cathedral City of Worcester and an equal distance south of Birmingham. Birmingham International Airport and Station are a 20-minute drive by motorway. The M5, M6, M42 and M40 motorways provide easy access to the School.

The School stands in 100 acres of grounds on the south side and within walking distance of the market town of Bromsgrove.

Facilities. The School has outstanding academic facilities including an award-winning Art, Design and Technology building, a twenty-classroom Humanities building and eighteen recently built or refurbished Science laboratories. Latest developments include a new Performing Arts complex, which was formally opened in November 2017. The complex includes two 300-seat venues: historic Routh Hall on the Senior campus and Cobham Theatre based within the Preparatory campus.

Sports facilities are extensive with a major sports complex houses an arena large enough for eight badminton courts, and bleacher seating for 500. Dance studios, gym, teaching rooms and hospitality suite/sports viewing room enhances the existing all-weather, floodlit sports facilities which sit comfortably alongside the extensive grass pitches.

Boarding. The boarding environment at Bromsgrove is happy, stable, disciplined and nurturing. Bromsgrove Senior School's boarding community is made up of boarders from over 50 nationalities accommodated between six Houses, one of which is Housman Hall a Sixth Form co-ed house, formerly home of OB and poet A E Housman, which has been sympathetically refurbished and is situated just off the School campus. All accommodation is finished to a very high standard. The stability and continuity that enable boarders to thrive are provided by resident houseparents (all academic members of staff) and their families, assistant houseparents, housemothers and a team of house-based tutors. All meals are taken centrally in the School, with the exception of the evening meal at Housman Hall.

Day pupils also benefit from the House system and all belong to one of six day houses, there are three boys houses and three houses for girls including the newly opened Ottilie Hild House. Houseparents and tutors work in each day house and give pupils the pastoral and academic support they need. Pupils are very loyal to their House and competitions between day and boarding Houses, including sport, music, drama and debating, are keenly contested.

Numbers. There are 990 pupils in the Senior School, of whom over 480 are boarders. The Preparatory, Pre-Preparatory and Pre-School has a further 720 pupils aged 3 to 13, including 85 boarders aged 7+. (*See also Preparatory & Pre-Preparatory School entry in IAPS section.*)

Curriculum. In the Preparatory School, a broadly based curriculum is followed. In addition to the usual academic subjects, time is given to Art, Music, ICT, Drama, Design Technology and to a full programme of Physical Education. Languages on offer include French, German, Spanish and Latin.

As pupils move up the School, GCSE choices are made for the start of Year 9. Eleven subjects is the norm at GCSE, with a broad core including the three separate sciences, a modern language and three further optional subjects. The minimum qualification for automatic entry into the Sixth

Form is a six point average at GCSE with areas of strength also evident. Pupils may study the IB Diploma or take the A Level route whilst BTECs are also available in Sports Science and Business Studies. Flexibility in timetabling aims to ensure that all pupils' subject choices are catered for whatever the combination. Many A Level subjects are available including, Art, Biology, Business, Chemistry, Classics, Design and Technology, Drama and Theatre Studies, Design, Economics, Engineering, English, French, Geography, German, Latin, Mathematics and Further Mathematics, Music, Physical Education, Physics, Politics, Religious Studies, Spanish and Textiles. Under the IB umbrella, Italian, Environmental Systems, Mandarin, Global Politics and Psychology are also on offer. With two-thirds of students achieving A*/A at both GCSE and A Level and an IB average of 40.2 points, virtually all pupils proceed to degree courses usually at Russell Group universities. The most popular university destinations in recent years have been University and King's Colleges in London followed by Exeter, Bath and Bristol with an increasing number continuing to a QS World Top 100 university.

Performing Arts. The performing arts are well supported at Bromsgrove School and rightly thrive. The School boasts a fantastic Performing Arts Centre which includes a state-of-the-art concert hall, full-sized theatre, a large drama studio and a suite of music classrooms and practice areas. Historic Routh Hall has been transformed into a concert hall, tuned exclusively for musical performances and making use of its exceptional acoustic qualities. Adjacent, a new Music School houses a suite of specialist classrooms, recording studios and 12 instrumental practice rooms, as well as a reception foyer and box office. The Performing Arts Avenue leads to an equivalent home for Drama. Cobham Theatre has flexible seating (with a capacity of 300), the hydraulic thrust stage allows for a wide range of dramatic and dance performances. The facility also boasts a 90-seat performance studio, with large scenic workshops, props stores and modern dressing rooms available for both lessons and productions.

Music and Drama flourish both within and outside the formal curriculum. House Music Competitions, Jazz Gigs and a variety of informal concerts happen throughout the year. There is plenty of scope for involvement in the School Orchestra and String, Wind and Brass Ensembles, Chamber Groups, Jazz Bands, a 50-strong Chapel Choir and large Choral Society. The timetable is sufficiently flexible to allow special arrangements to be made for outstanding musicians. Each year, the Chamber Choir takes the opportunity to sing in some spectacular cathedrals and chapels, including singing Evensong at Worcester College Oxford, Hereford Cathedral and St Paul's Cathedral. Major musical productions such as *Grease* and *Hairspray* are also highlights of the school year with extensive casts and backstage crew made up of pupils. School musicians take part in festivals, which have included the Upton Jazz Festival and Cheltenham Festival of Arts and there is a strong Choral Society which performs in venues including Birmingham Town Hall.

Discrete Drama forms part of the curriculum for every student from Year 5 to Year 8. The option is available for students to take the subject to GCSE level and at A Level the school offers Theatre Studies. Senior, Fourth Form and Prep School productions, alongside a number of House Drama Competitions at all levels, form the main spine of co-curricular Drama at Bromsgrove which has a reputation for

very high production standards. A high level of training for aspiring theatre technicians and designers ensures a vibrant dramatic life within the School for both performers and those wishing to work backstage.

Drama Scholarships are awarded to students joining at 13+ and 16+ whilst Music Scholarships are available at 11+, 13+ and 16+.

Careers. The School employs a fully qualified, full-time Careers Advisor and a comprehensive careers counselling programme, called Bromsgrove Futures is available to pupils of all ages. Many former pupils return to talk to and advise current pupils about university courses and careers possibilities.

Co-curricular activities. A wide range of sports and activities is offered, giving opportunities to participate at a competitive level in Rugby, Hockey, Netball, Athletics, Badminton, Basketball, Clay Pigeon Shooting, Cricket, Cross Country, Debating, Fencing, Golf, Horse Riding, Rounders, Soccer, Squash, Swimming, Table Tennis, Tennis and Young Enterprise.

The Saturday timetable, in conjunction with the weekday programme, allows the activities programme more flexibility to offer both recreational and academic choices. Pupils may select from a diverse range of recreational activities including Academic extension and support, Revision for GCSE, A Levels, IB, SATs and Oxbridge, Biology, Chemistry and Physics Olympiad, Aerobics, Art, Badminton, Board Game Design, Body Balance, Chess, Coding, Cookery, Corps of Drums, Design Technology, Drama, EPP (Economics, Politics and Philosophy), Engineering, Forest Schools, Golf driving range, Handicrafts, History Society, Horse Riding, ICT, Literary Society, MedVet Society, Military skills, Music, Outdoor pursuits (including climbing, high ropes, kayaking, orienteering, raft building, sailing), Mahjong, Park Run, Photography, Plaster Modelling, School Magazine, Table tennis, Website design, Weight training and Ultimate Frisbee. There are opportunities to gain qualifications in Life saving, First Aid, LAMDA, Sports/Dance Leader Awards and Martial Arts. In addition to the activities programme, Year 9 pupils participate in Bromsgrove Badge, comprising a selection of activities that help to prepare them for the Bronze Duke of Edinburgh's Award and culminating in a four-day camp at the end of the year. There is a thriving Combined Cadet Force (Army and RAF), and many pupils are involved in The Duke of Edinburgh's Award scheme. The School's Bromsgrove Service programme caters for large numbers of pupils and provides a wide range of activities; examples include working in local schools and charity shops, visiting residential homes, acting as Learning Mentors and Student Listeners, helping in animal sanctuaries, supporting conservation projects and fundraising for charities.

Admission. Entrance at 13 is by Bromsgrove School Entrance Examinations. Boys and Girls may be admitted to the Preparatory School at any age from 7 to 12 inclusive. 11+ and 13+ Entrance Tests take place in November and mid-January for entry into other years. Places are available in the Sixth Form for boys and girls who have had their GCSE education elsewhere.

Scholarships and Bursaries. Awards are made on the results of scholarship examinations held at the School in January. A significant number of scholarships, means-tested bursaries and Foundation bursaries for pupils of academic ability are awarded at 11+, 13+ and 16+. A number of Music scholarships and exhibitions are awarded each year at ages 11, 13 and 16, offering free tuition on up to two instruments. Scholarships for pupils talented in Arts/Textiles, Sport or Drama are awarded at 13+ and 16+. Means-tested bursaries may be used to supplement any scholarship. Full details are available from the Admissions Department.

Fees per term (2021–2022). Senior School (age 13+): £13,385 full boarding, £8,870 weekly boarding, £5,980 day inc lunch. Preparatory School (age 7–13): £8,700–£10,730 full boarding, £6,345–£7,680 weekly boarding, £4,175–£5,415 day inc lunch. Pre-Preparatory (age 4–7): £2,865–£3,155 day. Nursery (age 2–4): £53.75 per full day session.

Charitable status. Bromsgrove School is a Registered Charity, number 1098740. It exists to provide education for boys and girls.

Patron: A Denham-Cookes

President: S Towe

A Vice-President: V S Anthony
A Vice-President: N J Birch
A Vice-President: R D Brookes
A Vice-President: J A Hall
A Vice-President: T M Horton
A Vice-President: R Lane

Governing Body:
P West (*Chairman*)
Lt Col M Ballard

Dr C Barnett	M Luckman
C Cameron	J W Roden
A Cleary	I Stringer
Dr D Cunningham	D Walters
Dr C Lidbury	D Waltier
J Loynton	

Company Secretary: J Sommerville

Headmaster: P Clague, BA, MBA

Bursar: Mrs L Brookes, ACMA
Assistant Head: Miss R M Scannell, BA, PGCE
Deputy Head (*Academic*): P S Ruben, BSc, MPhil, MBA
Deputy Head (*Co-Curricular*): P S T Mullan, BA, PGCE
Deputy Head (*Pastoral*): A McClure, BA, PGCE
Deputy Head (*Teaching*): Mrs J Holden, MA Oxon, PGCE
Senior Mistress: Miss Z Leech, BA (*Bromsgrove Futures*)
Senior Master: S Matthews, BA, PGCE
School Medical Officer: Dr D Law, MA, MBChB Oxon, MRCGP, DRCOG, DFFP

Staff:
* *Head of Department*
† *Houseparent*

S J Kingston, BEd
Mrs C E Turner, BA, PGCE
Mrs S Shinn, BSc, PGCE (*Timetabler*)
Dr A R Johns, BSc, PhD, PGCE (**Biology*)
Ms S J Cronin, BA, DMS, PGCE
Mrs F K Bateman, BSc, PGCE
Mrs S E Ascough, BSc, PGCE (*Director of Operations*)
†D G Wilkins, BA, SCITT
M A C Beet, MA Cantab, PGCE (**German*)
Miss F E Diver, BA, PGCE
N C J Riley, BSc, PGCE (**Mathematics*)
Mrs E L E Buckingham, BA (**Girls' PE & Games*)
Miss S A Franks, BSc, PGCE
Miss M M Smith, BA, PGCE (**Spanish*)

†Mrs T L Helmore, BA, PGCE
O A Matthews, BEng, PGCE (**Design and Technology*)
Dr M Thompson, BSc, PhD, MInstP, PGCE (*IB Coordinator*)
Revd P Hedworth, BEd, BA (*Chaplain*)
Dr M K Ruben, BA, PhD, PGCE (**Gifted and Talented*)
G N Delahunty, BA, PGCE (**Politics*)
Ms E L Densem, BA, PGCE (**Sixth Form Enrichment*)
†H Bell, MA, PGCE
Miss J Zafar, BA, PGCE (**History*)
S Broadbent, BA, QTS
D Tamplin, BSc, PGCE
Mrs K Hands, BA, PGCE (**Religious Studies*)
D Fallows (*Director of Cricket*)
Ms G Tyrrell, BA, PGCE (**French*)
D Williams, BA, PGCE
A Carrington-Windo (*Director of Rugby*)
Miss L Davenport, BSc, PGCE
†S Noble, BSc, PGCE
Miss A Baker, BSc, MMath, MEd
J Baldrey, BA, PGCE
Mrs L Newton, BEng, PGCE
Mrs E Gill, BA, PGCE
A Helmore, BA, MA, PGCE
†J Holdsworth, BSC, PGCE
S Matthews, BA, PGCE (*Senior Master*)
Mrs D Sutherland, BA, HDipMaths, QTS
Mrs J Holdsworth, BA, PGCE
J McKelvey, BA, PGCE (*Director of Music*)
†Mrs K Hannah, BA, PGCE
†T Clinton, BSc, PGCE
Mrs J Boonnak, BA, MA, PGCE (**International Education*)
L Mullan, BSc, PGCE (**Boys' PE & Games*)
Miss L Hunter, BA, PGCE
†M Giles, BSc, PGCE
Miss S Hankinson, BSc, PGCE
Miss R Green, BSc, PGCE (*Director of GCSE*)
†Ms G Hanson, BA, PGCE
S Higgins, BEd (**PE*)
Miss N Langford, BA, GTTP
Miss F McCanlis, BMus, PGCE
H Pothecary, BSc, PGCE (**TOK*)
†Dr R Whitbread, MA, PhD (*i/c Extended Project Qualification*)
Mrs G Wright, BSc, PGCE
†Mrs V Adams, BA,MA, PGCE
D Atkinson, BSc, MSc, PGCE
Mrs A Eaton, MA, GTP
†G Evans, BSc, PGCE
T Hinde, BA, MA
A Kelly, BSc, MDip Ed (*Examinations Officer*)
Ms A Linehan, BSC, MEd, PG Dip Ed
Mrs N Reid, BA, PGCE
Dr D Rimmer, PhD, MA (*Master of Scholars*)
Dr R Short, MChem, PhD, PGCE (*i/c DofE Silver*)
Miss C O'Connell, BA
Miss P Woolley, MChem, PGCE (*i/c Bromsgrove Service*)
Mrs J Bradford, BA (**Drama*)
O Spencer-Burton, BA, PGCE
P Dinnen, MA (**English*)
S Kettle, BSc, PGCE (**Science*, **Physics*)
Mrs J Talbot, MA, PGCE
T Norton, BA (*Director of Performing Arts*)
R Vernon, BA, GTP
A Gooderham (*Director of Hockey*)

S Coleman, BSc, PGCE
D Corns, MPhil (*Classics*)
Dr A Davies, PhD, PGCE
Miss E Hill, BSc, PGCE (*Business*)
T Holdsworth, BSc, PGCE
A Summerfield, MSc, QTS, PGCE
G Tasker, BSc, PGCE
R Unterhalter, BA, PGCE (*President of the Common Room*)
B Vice, MChem (*Chemistry*)
Mrs A Webb, BA, PGCE
Miss G Aust, BA, PGCE
J Huckle, BA, PGCE
Dr M Jewkes, BA, MA, PhD
I Jones, BSc, MSc, PGCE
Dr D West, BSc, PhD, MA, PGCE (*CAS*)
J Wingfield, BA, PGCE (*Director of A Level*)
Miss G Farrel BA, MA, PGCE (*Life Skills*)
Dr K Morris BSc, PGCE, PhD (*Extended Essay*)
G Patel MSc, BSc, PGCE
Mr D Pover, BA, PGCE
G Young, BSc, PGCE
Mrs J Barnes, MA, MSc
Miss C Cunningham, BSc, PGDipEd
Dr A Alcoholado Feltstrom, BA, MA, PGCE, PhD
Dr E Fraser, BSc, PhD
R Higgins, MA, PGCE
Mrs F Linfield, BA (*Economics*)
Mrs J McCarthy (*Curriculum Support*)
P Prouse, MSc, PGCE, DipNLP, FRAS, MIstP
J Snelling, BSc, PGCE, CGeog, FFCCT
Mrs J Tidmarsh, BA, PGCE
Dr E Jones, BA, PhD, PGCE
Mrs J Williams, BA, PGCE
Miss L Blakely, BA, MA, PGCE (*Art*)
T Barfield, BA, PGCE
W Colson, BSc, PGCE
C Harrison, BSc, PGCE
C McDonald, BA, MEd, PGCE
Ms S Palitti, BA, PGCE
Ms G Scutt, BScTech, PGCE
Ms E Shaw, BSc, PGCE
E Smith, BA, PGCE
Ms R Williams, BA, PGCE
R Watkins, BA, PGCE
Ms M Anglada Escude, BA, MA, PGCE, PhD

Houses and Houseparents:
Boarding:
Elmshurst (*Boys*): M Giles
Housman Hall (*Sixth Form*): S Noble
Mary Windsor (*Girls*): Mrs T Helmore
Oakley (*Girls*): Mrs V Adams
Webber (*Sixth Form*): Mrs J Courtney
Wendron-Gordon (*Boys*): D Wilkins

Day:
Hazeldene (*Girls*): Dr R Whitbread
Lupton (*Boys*): G Evans
Lyttelton (*Boys*): J Holdsworth
Ottile HIld (*Girls*): Ms G Hanson
School (*Boys*): T Clinton
Thomas Cookes (*Girls*): Mrs K Hannah
Walters (*Boys*): H Bell

Music Staff:
J McKelvey, BA, PGCE (*Director of Music*)
Mrs M Corrie (*Music, Preparatory School*)

Ms F McCanlis, BMus, PGCE
T Martin, BA, Dip ABRSM (*Head of Jazz*)
Mrs J Russell, BA, PGCE
Miss H Bool, GBSM, ABSM, BTech Nat (*Head of Percussion*)
J Dunlop, BA, GBSM, ABSM (*Head off Wind and Brass*)
Ms F Swadling, BA, ABSM, GBSM (*Head of Strings*)
MIss S Vango, BMus, PG Cert, Cons (*Head of Vocal Studies*)
S Cowperthwaite (*Organist*)
J Macdowell Scott, (*Organist in Residence*)
Mrs M Cullen, BA (*Music Administrator*)
Mrs C Hinde, MA (*Performing Arts Administrator*)

Visiting Music Staff:
N Barry, GGSM, LTCL (*Piano*)
Miss V Brawn BMus, DipVirtuosite (*Oboe*)
M Broadhead LTCL, DipTCL (*Cello*)
Mrs R Brown, BMus (*Singing*)
R Bull (*Guitar*)
P Campbell-Kelly, GMus, RNCM, PG Dip RNCM, PPRNCM (*Violin*)
Ms J Chaddock (*Double Bass*)
Mrs S Chatt, GBSM (*Percussion*)
Miss S Clarke, GBSM (*Violin*)
Mrs K Fawcett, BA, MA, PG Dip (*Viola, Violin*)
A Gittens, BTec, HND (*Electric Guitar*)
Mrs J A Hattersley, CT ABRSM, LRSM (*Brass*)
Mrs J Hiles, GBSM, ABSM (*Flute, Piano*)
Mrs J Porter, BMus (*Piano*)
E Rooney, BA, DipABRSM (*Piano*)
Miss K Stevens, MMus, BMus (*Clarinet*)
R Tattam (*Bassoon*)
A D C Thayer, MA, BMus, PG Dip (*Piano*)
W Theunissen (*Singing*)
Mrs K Thompson, PG Dip RNCM, PPRNCM, ARCM, LRSM, RNCM (*Piano*)
J Topp, Bmus, LGSMD (*French Horn*)

Preparatory & Pre-Preparatory School

Headmaster: M Marie, BA, PGCE

Deputy Head (*Pastoral*): C Lee, BSc, PGCE
Deputy Head (*Academic*): Mrs T Hill, BA, PGCE
Deputy Head (*Operations*): Mrs K Ison, BEd
Head of Junior Department: Mrs K Ivison, BA, PGCE (*Year 3*)

Mrs C S Abraham, BA, MA, QTS
Mr J Amphlett, BA, PGCE
Miss J Balkham, BA, PGCE
Mr R Barnett, BSc, GTP
Dr V Barron, BA, MA, PGCE, PhD (*Art, *Year 8*)
Mrs G Billig, BSc, PGCE
Mrs R Boardman, BA, PGCE (*Spanish/German*)
Mrs L Browning, BA, PGCE
Miss S Cadwallader, BA, PGCE (*Year 6*)
Mr G Clark, BEd (*Year 7*)
Mrs M Corrie, GTCL, LTCL (*Music*)
Mrs S Dakin, BA (*Forest School*)
Mrs J Danks, BMus, PGCE (*Girls' PE*)
Mrs A Davis, BA, PGCE, CCET (*Curriculum Support*)
Mrs T Faulkner-Petrova, BA, BSc, MSc, PGCE (*EAL*)
Mrs K Finnegan, BA, PCGE (*French*)
Mrs C Goodall, BA, PGCE
Mrs S Grove, BEd
Mr J P Grumball, BSc, PGCE (*IT*)
Mrs D Hepburn, BSc, MA, PGCE

Mrs S James, BSc, MA, QTS
Mr G Jones, BA, PGCE (*Boys' PE*)
Mrs G Judson, BSc, PGCE (*President of the Common Room*)
Mrs S Keynes, BA, OTS (*Year 5*)
Mrs J Kingston BMus, PGCE
Mr C D Kippax, BA, PGCE (*MFL*)
Mrs E Lally, BA, PGCE (*English*)
Mrs R Laurenson, BA, PGCE (*Year 4*)
Mrs C Leather, BSc, PGCE (*PSHEE*)
J Liqurish, BA, PGCE
Rev. Dr S J P Loone, Mphi, MEd, BA, BTheol, PhD. PGCE, CTC, NPQH
Miss M Mimberg, BA, PGCE
Miss A Read, BTec, BA, PGCE
Miss C Roskell, BEng, PGCE
Mrs J Russell, BA, PGCE
Mrs A Scheppel, BA, PGCE (*History*)
Mr R Shone, BA, PGCE
Mrs L Singh, BDes, PGCE (*RE*)
Mrs V Sitlu, BA, PGCE
Mr P Sutherland, HD Ed (*Design & Technology*)
Miss C Troughton, BA, PGCE
J Thornley, BSc, PGCE
Mr M Turner, BSc, PGCE (*Mathematics*)
Mrs S Webley, BSc, PGCE, MEd (*Year 8, Acting *Girls PE*)
Mr M Wilkinson, BSc, PGCE
Mrs H Worton, BA, PGCE

Boarding House and Houseparents:
Page : Mr & Mrs R Lawton
Senior Page: Mr S Jenkins & Ms T Salt

Pre-Preparatory Staff:
Deputy Head Pastoral, Head of Pre-Preparatory Department: B Etty-Leal, BSc, PGCE
Deputy Head Academic: Mrs K Western, BEd

Mrs J Townsend, BA, PGCE (*Early Years*)
Mrs C Cattell, BA, PGCE (*Key Stage 1*)
Miss E Lewis, BA Ed
Mrs J Lockhart, BEd
Mrs N. Marie, BA, PGCE
Mrs M Martin, BA, GTP
Mrs N St John, BA, PGCE
Mrs S Symonds, BA

Bryanston School

Blandford, Dorset DT11 0PX

Tel: 01258 484632
email: headmaster@bryanston.co.uk
website: www.bryanston.co.uk
Twitter: @BryanstonSchool
Facebook: @bryanstonschool

Motto: *Et nova et vetera*

Bryanston School is different from other independent schools. Inspired by 90 years of innovative practice, our approach to education and our distinctive culture nurtures purposeful, curious and well-rounded individuals. At the heart of our approach is our method of education, the Bryanston Method. It has been the keystone of the School's

philosophy since our foundation, tailored to the needs and interests of each pupil. There is no Bryanston 'type' – we want our pupils to think for themselves. Alongside high academic standards and expectations, we provide an emotionally and intellectually supportive environment, allowing pupils to develop independent, creative, and unbounded thinking.

The Pastoral and the Academic integrate through our one-to-one tutorial system. Each pupil is carefully matched to their tutor and the relationship lasts for the duration of the pupil's years at Bryanston. The tutor guides each tutorial pupil in becoming responsible for their own learning and discusses their wellbeing and progress at the weekly one-to-one tutorial. At all times, they act as each pupil's champion and advocate.

Situation. The school is located in beautiful Dorset countryside near the market town of Blandford. There are 400 acres of grounds, which include a stretch of river used for rowing and canoeing, playing fields, woodland and parkland.

Numbers. There are approximately 380 boys and 320 girls in the school.

Admission. Boys and girls are normally admitted between 13 and 14 years of age. Prospective pupils will be required to sit the ISEB pre-test during the autumn term of year 7. The results of the test will allow the school to make an offer of a place on either the Main Entry List or on the Development List. The ISEB pre-test is not considered a pass or fail assessment, as the school recognises that children develop at different stages.

Sixth form entrants are admitted after testing and interview, conditional upon securing at least 40 points at GCSE.

Scholarships. Academic, Art, D&T, Music, Performing Arts, Sport and the Richard Hunter All-Rounder Scholarships are available annually for entry at 13+.

Academic, Art, Drama and Music Scholarships, plus Udall Awards for Sport are available annually for entry to the sixth form.

Scholarships range in value and may be supplemented by means-tested bursaries. Music Scholarships carry free musical tuition, optional Alexander Technique lessons and a weekly accompaniment lesson.

Further details may be obtained from the Director of Admissions.

Organisation. The school is organised on a house basis with five senior boys' houses, five girls' houses, and two junior boys' houses, although the house system is less rigid and formal at Bryanston than in many senior schools. All pupils have a personal tutor throughout their time in the school, with whom they meet on a one-to-one basis at least once a week. All sixth-form pupils in their final year have individual study-bedrooms, while lower-sixth formers usually share study-bedrooms. All meals are served centrally in the Dining Hall, providing additional opportunities for friendships to be formed across house and year groups.

Religion. Christian inspiration and Christian ideals are fundamental to the Bryanston philosophy, but the school recognises that pupils may come from homes which follow other faiths or have no strong religious affiliation. There is, therefore, no attempt to impose worship on pupils, rather the intention is to provide an atmosphere in which spiritual values can be discovered and developed.

School Work. The school aims to lead pupils, over a period of five years, from the comparative dependence on class teaching when they join the school, to a position where they are capable of working on their own, for a university degree or professional qualification, or in business. In addition to traditional class teaching, there is, therefore, increasing time given to private work as a pupil moves up the school in the form of assignments to be completed within a week or a fortnight. Teachers are available to give individual help when required, and tutors supervise pupils' work and activities in general on a one-to-one basis.

Every pupil is encouraged to explore a range of opportunities. All pupils follow the same broad and challenging curriculum in D (Year 9), if at all possible. This curriculum includes Latin, Modern Languages, three separate Sciences, Creative Arts, Technology and Music as well as English and Mathematics. GCSEs are taken after three years when a pupil is in B (Year 11). There is a highly flexible choice of subjects at this level and subjects are setted independently. In the sixth form pupils can choose between A Levels and either the International Baccalaureate Diploma or the International Baccalaureate Career-Related Programme. All lower-sixth formers follow a compulsory Personal and Social Education course and the academic enrichment programme provides supplementary sessions to develop key skills and approaches to learning.

Music. Bryanston has an exceptional musical tradition, and music is at the heart of school life. Inclusion and participation, as well as excellence, are core values and to achieve these every pupil in D (year 9) learns an instrument for the entire year. An extraordinary range of concerts, recitals and musical groups take place, with over 600 individual music lessons taught each week.

Drama. A well-equipped, modern theatre provides the venue for the many school productions which take place during the year as well as for touring professional companies. In addition to acting, pupils are involved in stage management, stage lighting and sound, and front-of-house work. There is also a large Greek Theatre in the grounds.

Sport and Leisure. A wide variety of sports is on offer at the school, including athletics, archery, badminton, canoeing, climbing, cricket, cross country, fencing, fives, hockey, indoor hockey, kayaking, lacrosse, netball, riding, rowing, rugby, rugby 7s, sailing, squash, swimming and tennis. Extensive playing fields between the school and the River Stour provide 42 tennis courts, two AstroTurf pitches, nine netball courts, a grass athletics track and grass pitches for all major sports, an all-weather riding manège and cross-country course. A sports complex provides an indoor heated 25m, six-lane swimming pool, Performance Sports gym with dual axis force platforms and 360-degree motion cameras, 40m indoor sprint track, two large indoor sports halls, four squash courts, three indoor fives courts, spinning studio, 200 sqm fitness suite, bouldering wall, multi-purpose studios, analysis room, physio room, and an outdoor and adventure hall and storage. Sailing takes place at Poole Harbour; this is in addition to a huge number of clubs and societies, catering for a wide range of interests, meeting in the evenings and at weekends.

Additional Activities. To encourage pupils to contribute to their community, use their time proactively and develop a growing self-reliance, all pupils take part in all or some of the following:

- Community and Social Service

- Extracurricular activities chosen from a wide range of options
- The Duke of Edinburgh's Award
- Adventure Training

Dress. There is no school uniform but there is a dress code.

Careers. The Sixth Form and Careers Department include four members of staff who work closely with tutors, houses and departmental heads to provide guidance for pupils at every academic age and stage of development, at a pace that is right for each individual. Our goal is to empower pupils to develop confidence and self-awareness, to reflect on their abilities and aspirations, and to gain insights into their future career options and higher education pathways. Work-related learning is actively included as part of curriculum development, with psychometric profiling offered in year 11. Higher Education and 'next steps' events are organised annually, providing the chance to meet with employers, academic subject specialists and overseas universities. Ongoing support is provided one-to-one, in small groups, via PSRE and guidance events. Bespoke support is available for those who are applying to university overseas.

Further Education. The vast majority of pupils in the sixth form gain admission to universities or other academies of further education.

Fees per term (2021–2022). £13,630.

Charitable status. Bryanston School Incorporated is a Registered Charity, number 306210. It is a charitable trust for the purpose of educating children.

Governors:
J R Greenhill, MA, QC (*Chair*)
N Bickford, BA
S F Bowes
B P Broad, BA
S O Conran
J A F Fortescue, BA
S Foulser, BA
M A S Laurence
C G Martin, ACA, MA
V M McDonaugh, MA, DL
M E McKeown, BA, MSc
Dr H Pharaoh, MBBS, DRCOG, MRCGP, DFSRH
L M V Soden, BA, MA
R Swallow
D M Trick

Acting Head: **R G Jones**, BA, MEd

Deputy Head, Academic: S B Green, BA, MA (*Maths*)
Director of Academic Administration: M S Deketelaere, BA, MSc & DIC, PGCE

Staff:
* *Head of Department*
† *Housemaster/Housemistress*

Art:
*D G Knight, BA, PGCE
G J Cedeira, BA
A Connolly, BA, PGCE
†H E Dean, BA, PGCE
†J A K Dickson, BA, PCGE
J E Jehu, BA, PGCE
M Hilde, BA

S M Macpherson, MA
M L Sinclair-Smith, BA, PGCE

Classics:
*C T Holland, MA
†Dr H L Fearnley, BA, PhD
D Fowler-Watt, MA (*Director of Performing Arts*)
L M Jones, BA, MA
A J Sanghrajka, BA (*IB ToK Coordinator*)

Drama, Theatre Studies and Film:
*J F Quan, BA, MA (*Director of Drama*)
S N Wheeler, BA, PGCE (*Head of Film*)
G A Martin, BA Videographer

Economics and Business Studies:
*B E Leigh, LLB, MSc
Dr P S Bachra, MA, EdD (*Head of Pastoral*)
†J J A Beales, BA, PGCE
A N R Bray, BA (*Head of Work-Related Learning*)
†M S Christie, MA, PGCE
G E S Drake, BSc, PGCE
R H Ings, BSc, PGCE
N L Payne, BA, PGCE

English:
*H E J Weatherby, MA
C R Bentinck, BA, PGCE (*Admissions Tutor*)
L R Boothman, BA, PGCE (*D Coordinator*)
A R Croot, BA, PGCE
†S H Davies, MA
N M Kelly, BA, PGCE
O Nicholson, BA, MA, PGCE
S Page, BA, PGCE

Geography:
*K E Andrews, BA, PGCE
R J Boulton, BA, PGCE
V L Chappell, BA, MEd
M S Deketelaere, BA, MSc & DIC, PGCE (*Head of Curriculum Planning*)
L C Kearney, BEd (*International Coordinator*)
J E G Ralphs, BA, PGCE (*Head of Sixth Form*)

History and Politics:
*A L Smith, BA, MSc, PGCE
W J Bridges, BSc, PGCE
P Quarrell, BA, PGCE (*Senior Tutor*)
A B L de Steiger Khandwala, MA, MA, MPhil, PGCE
J G Strange, MA, PGCE
T Strongman, BA, PGCE
S M Vincent, BA, PGCE (*Admissions Tutor*)

History of Art:
*S A Wilson, BA, MA
S A E Stacpoole, BA
M Wilson, BA

Mathematics:
*T Bourne, PGCE
†C B Craig, BSc (*B/C Coordinator*)
S B Green, BSc, PGCE
P A Griffin, BSc, PGCE
C L Lorek, BSc, PGCE
K M Lewin, BSc, MSc, PGCE
D J Melbourne, BSc, PGCE
C E Murray, BSc, PGCE
V R M Peck, BSc
A K Tarafder, BSc, PGCE

Modern Foreign Languages:
*L C Johnson, MA (*Head of Modern Languages, Senior Tutor*)
C Dechirot, BA, MA (*Head of French*)
E Flitters, BA, MA (*Head of German*)
M Sanger, BA (*Head of Spanish*)
L C Blanco, BA
A J Gilbert, BA, PGCE
L R Haynes, BA, PGCE
R A Pakenham-Walsh, BA, PGCE
†J M I Velasco, BA, PGCE

Music:
*X Illes, BA, PGCE (*Director of Music*)
G M Scott, BA, PGCE, Premier Prix, ARCO, LTCL (*Assistant Director of Music*)
W P Ings, MA, PGCE, ARCO (*Head of Teaching and Learning*)
C S Scott, BMus, PGCE, FTCL, ARCM, LTCL (*Head of Strings*)
D Andrews (*Head of Jazz*)
A Dickinson (*Head of Singing*)
R B K Rowntree, BMus (*Singing Coordinator*)

Philosophy and Religious Studies:
*L J D Pollard, BA
Revd J Davis (*Chaplain*)
S Carter

PE and Sport Studies:
*A Fermor-Dunman, BSc, MA (*Director of Sport*)
B C Rodford, BSc, PGCE (*Assistant Director of Sport*)
M Boote, BSc, PGCE
†C L Bray, BSc, PGCE
C L Miller, BA Ed (*Head of Boarding*)
J E Morris
*S E Morris, BSc, PGCE
A Murfin

Psychology:
*Dr H A Hogarth, BSc, MSc, PhD (*IB Extended Essay Coordinator*)
R Talfourd-Cook

Science:
†N G Welford, BSc, PGCE
C A Çava, MPhys (*Head of Physics*)
A J Elliot, BSc, PGCE (*Head of Chemistry*)
E L Silcock, BSc, PGCE (*Head of Biology*)
C G Bloomfield, BSc, PGCE
R J Collcott, MEng, MSc, PGCE
G S Elliot, BA, PGCE
S J Fazakerley, BA, PGCE
R M Hallam, MPhys, PGCE
A M Harwood, BSc, PGCE
P L Haywood, BSc, PGCE
†R J Johnson, BSc, PGCE
S H Jones, BSc, PGCE
Dr M T Kearney, MA, PhD, CEng, MRAeS, CPhys, MInstP
A J Pattison, BSc, MSc, PGCE
R J Perkins, HND
J D Pritchard, MSc, PGCE

Technology:
*A J Barnes, BA, CertEd (*Director of Technology*)
M J Davis, BSc, PGCE (*Head of Computer Science*)
*C J Mills, BA, PGCE (*Head of Design and Technology*)
M T Bolton, BA

N J Davies, BEd
R H Ings, BSc, PGCE
J Ladd-Gibbon, BA, MA
P A Sillett-Scoggins, BEd
H L Southby, BSc

Careers:
A N R Bray, BA (*Head of Work-Related Learning*)
L C Kearney, BEd (*International Coordinator*)

Academic Support:
*A Hicks
J S Bell, MA
A J Casely, BA, PGCE, Dip SpLD
K E Heminsley
C Steven-Fountain, BA, PGCE, Cert SpLD

Library:
E C Minter, BA, PG Dip ISM, MCLIP

Outdoor Education:
D P T Curry, BSc

Director of Admissions: A Megdiche

Bury Grammar Schools

Tenterden Street, Bury, Lancs BL9 0HN

Tel: 0161 696 8600
email: communications@burygrammar.com
website: www.burygrammar.com
Twitter: @BuryGrammar
Facebook: @BuryGrammarSchools
LinkedIn: /burygrammarschools

Motto: *Sanctas clavis fores aperit*

The School, formerly housed in the precincts of the Parish Church of St Mary the Virgin, was first endowed by Henry Bury in 1634, but there is evidence that it existed before that date. It was re-endowed in 1726 by the Revd Roger Kay and moved to its current site in 1966. The school is a selective grammar school which aims to provide a first-class academic and extracurricular education; to nurture the whole person in a safe, stimulating, challenging and friendly community in which each individual is encouraged to fulfil his potential; and to prepare each pupil for an adulthood of fulfilling work, creative leisure and responsible citizenship.

Numbers of Pupils. Infants: 111; Juniors: 198; Seniors: 754; Sixth Form: 173.

Admission, Scholarships and Bursaries. Admission is by examination and interview. Most pupils join the school at either 7 or 11, although, subject to places being available, admission is possible at other ages. A number of means-tested bursaries, based on academic performance and financial need, are awarded each year.

Fees per term (2021–2022). Senior School £3,847; Junior School £2,868.

Facilities and Development. Bury Grammar School has a distinguished history of excellence dating back to the 1570s. Proud of its historic links with the town of Bury and the surrounding area, Bury Grammar School possesses a full range of modern facilities. These facilities enable the School to offer a broad and rich academic curriculum and extra-curricular programme. Since 1993 the Junior School has

occupied its own site opposite the Senior School. Junior School pupils are able to take advantage of the additional specialist facilities and resources in the Senior School. A new Learning Resource Centre, consisting of a Library, extensive ICT provision and private study facilities, was opened in 2002, and a new Art Centre in 2004. State-of-the-art Science laboratories were completed in 2010 and a new university-style Sixth Form Centre opened in 2014. In 2016 brand new sports facilities were opened to include a 3G artificial pitch and a multi-use games area so that sports can continue in inclement weather. Bury Grammar School is constantly striving to improve its facilities and to provide the best possible educational experience for all its pupils.

Pastoral Care. Bury Grammar School prides itself on excellent pastoral care and its ability to work as a family to nurture and care for every individual. It cares for and respects its students and, in turn, expects them to care for and respect others. The BGS philosophy for pastoral care is simple: BGS students should be happy, secure and ready for all that life has to offer. BGS offers individualised pastoral support for every student and is always keenly aware that it is a privilege to work alongside young people. BGS is fortunate to have on site a highly dedicated and skilled School Health Team who work closely with pupils, parents and staff to ensure that the medical, health and wellbeing needs are met. BGS also offers the services of a qualified counsellor who is on site on a weekly basis to provide confidential support and advice to those students who need it. Each pupil has a Form Tutor who has primary responsibility for their pastoral care and for oversight of their academic progress and their extra-curricular programme. Form Tutors are led by Heads of Year who also oversee a pupil's academic progress. There is also a strong House system for a wide range of sporting, musical and cultural inter-house competitions.

Curriculum. Bury Grammar School is immensely proud of its traditions and happy to be a modern school, continually embracing new technologies and innovative teaching methods. BGS is the leading school in the area where pupils continually reach outstanding academic standards, achieving exceptional examination results at GCSE and A Level and gaining places on competitive courses at elite universities. In response to the increasing demands of newly-reformed GCSE and A Level qualifications, BGS introduced a new enhanced curriculum model throughout the School to strengthen further the quality of education it offers – ensuring breadth alongside academic challenge – to enable pupils to obtain the very best examination results of which they are capable and to open doors to even greater opportunities in the future. It also delivers an enhanced extra-curricular and co-curricular offering, to maintain the School's strong tradition of nurturing fully-rounded individuals.

Art. Well-equipped facilities allow all pupils to develop skills in print making, ceramics, sculpture, painting, drawing, textiles, new media and animation. There are frequent visits to galleries, both locally and further afield. Pupils' artwork is proudly displayed throughout the school and BGS hosts regular exhibitions which are opened to the School community.

Music and Drama. Music is an important part of school life. As an academic subject it is offered at GCSE and A Level. At least three major musical events take place each year. Visiting peripatetic teachers teach over 170 pupils. Students have the opportunity to involve themselves in musical groups such as orchestra, concert band, dance orchestra and BGS Beatz and festival choir. As well as this, pupils can take part in show-stopping musical productions, which showcase the incredible musical talents of the girls and boys across both Senior Schools and Sixth Form.

Physical Education and Sport. Sport at Bury Grammar School embodies the core aims of participation, performance, enjoyment, health and partnerships. The School has a longstanding reputation for sporting endeavour and prowess and strives to provide excellent sporting opportunities for all pupils. We offer a diverse and inclusive programme of activities in which every pupil participates, through our curriculum and extensive enrichment programme. All our pupils are encouraged to try their hand at a range of sports and physical activities, whatever their level of ability. We believe that physical health and wellbeing play a crucial role in the educational journey of young people, developing leadership, teamwork, communication skills and self-discipline.

BGS pupils have been successful at local, regional and national level in netball, basketball, rugby, football, swimming and athletics and many of our pupils attain representative honours, including international selection. Other sports on offer include table tennis, badminton, rounders, tennis, handball and yoga.

Essentially we strive for all our pupils to be physically active whilst at the same time, aspiring to the highest level of elite performance.

Our sports facilities:
- 3G All Weather Pitch
- Spring & Jump Track
- Multi Use Games Area (MUGA)
- Sports Hall (Tenterden Street)
- Cricket & Athletics Field
- Cricket Nets
- Swimming Pool
- Hockey & Athletics Field
- Buckley Wells Playing Fields
- Tennis & Netball Courts
- Sports Hall (Bridge Road)
- Gymnasium
- Climbing Wall
- Fitness & Dance Studio
- Infant School Sports Hall

Outdoor Education. In the senior school a residential course is offered to Year 7 pupils at an outdoor centre to participate in water and land-based activities. We are delighted to offer participation in the Duke of Edinburgh's Award Scheme at Bronze, Silver and Gold level and also long and short haul expeditions with World Challenge.

CCF. The Bury Grammar School CCF was established in 1892 and is one of the oldest CCFs in the country. BGS is immensely proud of its CCF, the largest voluntary CCF in the country. It brings together an Army section (Royal Regiment of Fusiliers) and an RAF section. The current strength of the Contingent is 300+ cadets. The CCF helps the students develop qualities such as self-discipline, resourcefulness and perseverance, a sense of responsibility and skills of management and leadership.

Careers. The Careers Department aims to provide all pupils with access to the information and advice they need to make informed and sensible decisions about their futures.

Guidance is provided by individual interviews and regular careers conventions and mock interview mornings. All pupils are also required to complete a period of work experience during Year 10 and Year 12.

Bury Grammar School Alumni Associations. The BGS journey carries through to our Alumni Associations; friendships formed at Bury Grammar School really do last a lifetime.

BGS Old Boys' Association Secretary: Matt Cooke, email: mjcooke01@aol.com

BGS Old Girls' Association Secretary: Suzanne Gauge, email: suzanne.gauge@btinternet.com

Charitable status. Bury Grammar Schools Charity is a Registered Charity, number 526622. The aim of the charity is to promote educational opportunities for boys and girls living in or near Bury.

Governing Body:

Chair of Governors: Mrs G Winter
Vice Chair of Governors: Mr M Edge

Mr M J Entwistle	Mr P Lee
Mrs S Gauge	Ms N Waring
Mr A H Spencer	Mr T McDougall
Mr S Wild	Dr S Hyde
Mr D Long	Ms N Smith

Director of Finance: Mrs J Stevens, BFocFC, ACA
Clerk to the Governors: Miss E McDonnell

Principal of The Bury Grammar Schools, Headmistress of Bury Grammar School Girls: Mrs J Anderson, BA, PGCE, MEd

Vice Principal, Headmaster of Bury Grammar School Boys: Mr D P Cassidy, BSc, PGCE, FRSC, FCCT

Assistant Principal, Director of Academic & IT Provision, Director of Operations: Mrs V Leaver, BSc (*Geography*)

Head of Sixth Form: Mrs H Hammond, BA (*Drama*)
Deputy Head, Enrichment: Mr A Dennis, BSc (*Mathematics, Head of Outdoor Activities*)
Deputy Head, Pastoral (Boys): Mr R Lees, BA (*MFL*)
Deputy Head, Pastoral (Girls): Mrs R Newbold, BSc (*Physical Education & Geography*)
Director of Studies: Mrs K Lewis, MSc (*Physics*)
Director of Communications & School Information: Mrs C Lynskey
Director of Arts & Culture: Miss K Gore, BA, MA, FRSA (*Art*)

Principal of The Bury Grammar Primary Schools: Mrs C Howard, CIPS

PA to Principal: Mrs A Cloke
Headmaster's PA: Mrs Z Royle

Campbell College

Belmont Road, Belfast, Co Antrim BT4 2ND, Northern Ireland

Tel: +44 (0)28 9076 3076
email: hmoffice@campbellcollege.co.uk
website: www.campbellcollege.co.uk
Twitter: @CampbellCollege
Facebook: @CampbellCollege1894
Instagram: @campbellcollege
LinkedIn: /school/campbell-college-belfast

Motto: *Ne Obliviscaris*

Campbell College, which was opened in 1894, was founded and endowed in accordance with the will of Henry James Campbell, Esq (Linen Merchant) of Craigavad, Co Down. It has a reputation as one of the leading educational environments in the country. Our commitment is to welcome, challenge and inspire each and every pupil to be the very best they can be, to push themselves and to stand tall as contributors to a global society.

Ethos. Our commitment is to welcome, challenge and inspire each and every pupil to be the very best they can be, to push themselves and to stand tall as contributors to a global society.

Confidence, commitment and achievement are at the heart of everything we do. From the classroom to the extracurricular activities, we are dedicated to ensuring that boys make the most of their talents within Campbell and beyond.

We nurture the individual and prepare them for the world. Academic achievements are important and we expect our pupils to strive for high grades; it is also our duty to harness the potential in every pupil whether it is academic, creative, physical or otherwise.

We want boys to leave the school with an assured set of values; we want them to believe they can truly make a difference in society. We want our boys to leave the school with things that are going to matter to them for the rest of their lives.

Pastoral Care. We believe that pupils learn best when they are happy, safe and secure and the purpose of our pastoral care is to provide such an environment. The strong, caring ethos of the College is demonstrated by its commitment to the welfare of the pupils and staff.

In Senior School all boys are allocated a Personal Tutor as the first point of contact for parents and our comprehensive Child Protection Policy is issued to all parents before their child commences school. Above and beyond this level of care we have a dedicated medical centre on campus led by the College Matron and a School Doctor who visits our boarders three times a week.

Boarding. We have a successful boarding department which brings an international dimension and unique character to the College; this will enable our pupils to thrive in the increasingly global world in which we all must live and work. We have approximately 150 boarders.

The Curriculum. This is focused upon giving our boys the maximum opportunity to produce the best possible examination results from a varied choice of subjects which meet the needs of the 21st century.

Class sizes are capped at 26 throughout Key Stage 3 to allow boys to grow in confidence and security in their learning as they make the transition from Primary School to Senior School. The teacher to pupil ratio is a generous 1:14, and the curriculum followed at Year 8 comprises English, Maths, Science, Geography, History, Religious Education, French, Art, Drama, Music, Technology, ICT, PE and Learning for Life and Work.

The Campus. Campbell College stands in a secure and impressive 100-acre wooded estate where the academic, boarding, artistic and sporting pursuits are all catered for on site. The College has its own indoor swimming pool, AstroTurf pitches, squash courts, shooting range, running track and numerous rugby and cricket pitches. It has a variety of sports and assembly halls, drama studio, computer suites and technology areas.

Other Activities. Campbell College is able to provide boys with a host of activities which naturally complement the culture of learning promoted within the school. Whilst the College is widely acknowledged for its sporting excellence, especially in rugby, hockey and cricket, there are many other opportunities available. Alongside a diverse range of sports there are opportunities to participate in The Combined Cadet Force, Duke of Edinburgh's Award scheme, Drama and Music productions and the Charity Action Group.

A competitive House system allows all boys to compete, with camaraderie and collegiality, in numerous inter-House competitions so all have an opportunity to represent their House as well as their school.

Holidays. There are three annual holidays: two weeks at Christmas and Easter, and eight in the summer. In the Christmas and Easter terms there is a half-term break of one week, during which parents of boarders are required to make provision for their sons to be away from school.

Admissions. Campbell College welcomes students at a variety of entry levels. Day boys can begin in Kindergarten and stay through to Sixth Form; boarders may start at Year 8. The school structure is designed to offer our students easy transitions as they grow and mature; they begin in Junior School, then move aged 11 to Middle School, before progressing to Senior School to prepare for their public examinations (GCSE, AS and A2 Level).

There are approximately 1,000 students in the Senior School of whom 150 are boarders, and 267 students in the Junior School.

Fees per annum (2021–2022) Boarding (Years 8–14): £15,960 (UK & Irish Citizens), £17,995 (EU citizens), £22,140 (Rest of the World). Day: £2,965 (UK & Irish Citizens), £5,000 (EU Citizens), £9,145 (Rest of World).

As a Voluntary B Grammar School, Campbell College charges an annual fee to all pupils for development and maintenance. The Board of Governors seeks to support applications to the College by offering scholarships and bursaries, the details of which may be found in the Prospectus.

Prospectus. Further information is included in our prospectus which can be obtained from the College Office or you may download a copy from the College website.

Old Campbellian Society. There is a link from the College website.

Charitable status. Campbell College is registered with the Inland Revenue as a charity, number XN45154/1. It exists to provide education for boys.

Governors:
His Honour Judge A F W Devlin (*Chair*)
Mr I D Jordan, FCA, MA Cantab
Mr J Andrews, BSc Hons, FCA
Mr G C Browne, BEng Hons, CEng, FIStructE, MICE,
    MaPS, MConsE
Mr M G B Campbell, BA Hons (*Parent Governor*)
Mr M E J Graham, BSc, MSc, FCIOB, FICE
Mr J R Hassard, MA, BEd, DASE, AdvCertEd, PQH
Mr J Andrews, BSc Hons Chem, FCA
Mr A Colmer, LLB Barrister at Law
Mr G Elliott, BSc Hons, MRIC
Mrs J Kelly, BA Hons, FCA
Mr A Wilson, BA Hons, MSc, ACMA
Mr H J McKinney, BSc, CertEd (*Teachers' Governor*)

Headmaster: Mr R M Robinson, MBE, BSc, PGCE,
    MEd, PQH NI

Vice-Principals:
Mr W E Keown, MA, PGCE
Mr C G Oswald, BSc, PGCE, AdvCertEd, MEd

Senior Teachers:
Mr H J McKinney, BSc, CertEd
Mr H H Robinson, BSc, PGCE
Mrs K E Sheppard, MSc, BSc, PGCE (*Learning Support*)
Mrs S L Coetzee, BMus, PCGE, PGCE Careers
Mr C McIvor, MA, PGCE

Assistant Teachers:
Mr A Doherty, BMus Hons, PGCE
Mr C G A Farr, BA, DASE, AdvCertEd, MEd, CertPD
Mr D M McKee, BA, PGCE, DipModLit
Ms B M Coughlin, BEd, PGCertComp
Mrs G E Wilson, BMus, MTD
Mr D Styles, BA, PGCE, Dip IndStudies
Mr B F Robinson, BA, PGCE, MSc
Mr A W Templeton, BSc, PGCE
Mr N R Ashfield, BSc, PGCE
Mr S P Collier, BA, PGCE
Mrs R McNaught, MA, PGCE
Mr G Fry, BA, PGCE
Mr D Walker, BEd
Mr J McCurdy, BD, MA, PGCE
Mr M Cousins, BSc, PGCE
Mrs L Haughian, BA, PGCE
Mr M G Chalkley, BA, PGCE, MEd, PQH
Mr N McGarry, BA, PGCE
Mrs M Debbadi, BA, PGCE, MSc
Dr J A Breen, BSc, PGCE, PhD
Mr R D Hall, BSc, PGCE
Mrs E McIlvenny, BA, PGCE
Mrs K Magreehan, BA, PGCE
Ms L Anderson, BA, QTS
Mrs J Bailie, BA, PGCE
Mrs C A M Irwin, BSc, PGCE
Mr P D A Campbell, BEd
Mr T R Thompson, BSc, PGCE
Mr A McCrea, BEng, PGCE
Mrs W Pearson, BEd
Mr J H Rea, BSc, PGCE
Mrs K Murphy, BSc, PGCE
Mrs V Spottiswoode, BA, PGCE
Mr F N Mukula, BSc, AssDipTh, PGCE
Miss G Lamont, BEd, MSSc
Mr G P Young, BEd
Mr J P Cupitt, BSc, PGCE

Mrs W Shannon, BA, PGCE
Ms K M Marshall, MA, QTS
Mrs K McGarvey, MSci, PGCE
Mr J McNerlin, BSc, PGCE
Mr J Smyth, BSc, PGCE
Mrs J L Hempstead, MA, PGCE
Ms S Kirsch, BA, PGCE
Dr A Dunne, MA, PhD, PGCE
Mrs E McInerney, BSC, MEd
Mr M Brown, MA, PGCE
Ms L Donly, MA, PGCE
Ms D Chada, MA, PGCE
Ms P McCaul, MA, PGCE
Mrs E Reynolds, BSc, PGCE
Mr R McMaster, BSc. PGCE
Miss A Beckett, BSc, PGCE
Mr D Ledwich, BSc, PGCE
Ms E Anderson, BA, PGCE
Mr M Snodden, BA, PGCE
Miss V Wightman, BSc, PGCE

Visiting Music Teachers:
Mrs M Fenn (*Woodwind*)
Mrs J Leslie (*Brass and Piano*)
Mrs K Lowry (*Lower Strings*)
Mrs H Neale (*Upper Strings and Piano*)
Mr M Wilson (*Brass*)
Mrs L Lynch (*Percussion*)
Mr R Nellis (*Guitar*)

Bursar: K J Wilson, FCA
Headmaster's Secretary: Mrs L Crawford
Medical Officers:
Dr G Millar, BMSc, MBChB, MRCGP
Matron: Mrs E M Hoey, SRN

Junior School:
Head: Miss A Brown, BA, PGCE, MEd, PQH
Mrs E M Gwynne, BEd
Mrs H M Jennings, BEd Hons, Dip PD
Mrs S Lismore, MEd, BEd Hons
Mr A Russell, BA Hons, PGCE
Mr M Boyd, BEd Hons
Mr A P Jemphrey, BEd, DASE
Mr S Bolingbroke, BA Hons, PGCE
Mr C Irvine, LLB, QTS
Mrs S Nickels, BSc, PGCE
Miss K Courtney, MA, PGCE
Mrs P McGarry, BEd
Mrs L M Leyland, MEd, BEd
Miss K Courtney, MA, PGCE
Miss L Reid, LLB, PGCE
Ms C Martin, BA, PGCE
Mrs S Smith, BSc, PGCE
Mr P Martin, MEd, BA Hons, PGCE

The Cathedral School Llandaff

A Woodard School

Llandaff, Cardiff CF5 2YH

Tel: 029 2056 3179
email: registrar@cathedral-school.co.uk
website: www.cathedral-school.co.uk
Twitter: @cslcardiff
Facebook: @cslcardiff
Instagram: @cslcardiff

Set in 15 acres of parkland and playing fields within minutes of Cardiff city centre, the Cathedral School was founded in 1880. Acknowledged by Estyn as "excellent" in all five inspection areas (2018), there are currently 800 pupils at the co-educational school between the ages of 3 and 18 years. The Cathedral School is a member of the Woodard Corporation and adheres to a firmly Christian ethos. Pupils of all denominations and faiths are welcomed.

Track record for excellence. At the Cathedral School, our excellent academic results and exceptional co-curricular programme foster the growth of intellectual curiosity, offering enormous breadth of opportunity. High-quality pastoral care and the School's Christian ethos give our students the opportunity to reach their full potential in a vibrant, fun and supportive environment.

Our beautiful campus and our links with Llandaff Cathedral inspire a sense of heritage, whilst our first-class curriculum enables our young people to look confidently to the future.

Nursery, Infants & Juniors. A positive experience of learning in our earliest years at school sets the foundations for being an engaged and successful learner later in life. The classroom is a place of energy and creativity, a place of high expectations within an atmosphere of nurture and encouragement.

Beyond the classroom walls there are extensive opportunities to enjoy competitive sport, especially team games which have busy and challenging fixture lists; opportunities to perform music at an excellent standard including opportunities for boys and girls to join choirs and to sing in Llandaff Cathedral, along with drama, dance and elocution; opportunities to enjoy the outdoors, wildlife, outward bound activities; opportunities to get involved in action for good causes, including environmental awareness and charity work. There are also plenty of inter-house activities to get involved with which create a vibrant atmosphere.

Nearly all pupils transfer into the Senior Section to continue their educational journey through to 18.

The Seniors. We pride ourselves upon being a strong learning community. It is important that everyone feels valued and that they have a meaningful part to play. From the initial Year 7 bonding weekend creating new friendships, to the competitive house system, a mutually supportive environment means that every pupil's skill, interest, talent and potential are nurtured.

Regularly recognised, whether by the education inspectorate Estyn, or in newspaper league tables, as one of the highest achieving schools in Wales academically, a great emphasis is also placed upon the co-curricular. For Years 10–13 the Duke of Edinburgh's Award (DofE) is hugely popular and delivered by our own dedicated staff. For Years 7–9, the Head's Award, underpins what we do, recognising character and breadth of achievement and celebrating our pupils' sense of motivation, organisation and willingness to be involved.

The quality of music at the Cathedral School is outstanding. It is our boys and girls who sing Llandaff Cathedral's choral services day by day, and the same excellence of musicianship rubs off in school within a wide range of genres, from the classical to rock and pop, chamber music to jazz. On the sports field a similar appetite for excellence pervades all we do. With a very high coach to player ratio and a busy, competitive fixture list, rugby, football, sevens, cricket, hockey, netball, rounders, cross-country and tennis all thrive here. Equally, participation in public speaking and debating competitions, challenging drama productions and various genres of fine art all add to the opportunities for all pupils to achieve standards which help them grow in confidence.

Sixth Form. We were incredibly proud of the outstanding results achieved by our A Level cohort this year, in what has been the most difficult of years. Our students progress to the most selective and sought after universities, including Oxford, Imperial College London, Bristol, Cardiff, Bath, Leeds and Nottingham.

With a full range of academic subjects available, very small classes, highly-experienced staff with close university links, our sixth form culture is ambitious and supportive in equal measure.

Sixth formers are encouraged to engage in the professional mentoring programme, which pairs them with leading professional figures for advice and guidance. Practitioners from a range of professions are regularly invited to address the students and they have the opportunity to network at Cardiff Business Club.

A Level Subjects: Art, Biology, Business, Chemistry, Computer Science, Design & Technology, Drama & Theatre, Economics, English Literature, French, Geography, German, Politics, History, Latin, Mathematics, Further Mathematics, Music, Physical Education, Physics, Psychology, Religious Studies, Spanish, and the Extended Project Qualification (EPQ).

Scholarships & Bursaries. Financial support via means-tested bursaries is available at Year 7 and 12 entry, with scholarships in a range of disciplines from academic to sport and music.

School Transport. School transport is available with bus routes from Castleton, Cowbridge, Caerphilly, Colwinston, Llantrisant and Lisvane. Working parents are helped by wraparound care from 8.00am to 6.00pm and a holiday club for our pupils and their siblings.

Fees per term (2021–2022). Years 12 & 13 £4,671, Years 7–11 £4,605, Years 5 & 6 £4,220, Years 3 & 4 £3,746, Reception, Years 1 & 2 £3,284, Nursery £2,820.

Charitable status. The Cathedral School Llandaff Limited is a Registered Charity, number 1103522. It exists to provide a high standard of education for girls and boys underpinned by a caring Christian ethos.

Chairman of the Council: M R Havard

Senior Management Team:

Head: **Mrs Clare Sherwood**, MA

Deputy Head Pastoral: Mr Lawrence Moon, BA, MA

Deputy Head Academic: Dr Nathan Horleston, PhD, MSci

Head of Sixth Form: Mrs Catrin Ellis-Owen, BA

Head of Primary: Mrs Sally Walsh, BEd, NPQH

Assistant Head (KS2): Mr Chris Morgan, BA

Assistant Head (EYFS & KS1): Mrs Karen Price, BA, MA

Assistant Head (Safeguarding): Dr Stuart Bailey, PhD, MEng

Bursar: Mr Robert Leek

Charterhouse

Godalming, Surrey GU7 2DX

Tel: Admissions: 01483 291501
         General Enquiries: 01483 291500
email: admissions@charterhouse.org.uk
         reception@charterhouse.org.uk
website: www.charterhouse.org.uk
Twitter: @CharterhouseSch
Facebook: @charterhousesch
LinkedIn: /charterhouse

Motto: *Deo Dante Dedi*

Founded in 1611, Charterhouse is one of the UK's leading independent schools.

With around 900 pupils, the School welcomes girls and boys at 13+ entry and 16+ entry, either as boarders or day pupils.

Campus. The School is set within an inspiring 250 acre campus, conveniently located close to London and within 50 minutes of Heathrow and Gatwick airports.

With 17 grass sports pitches, 3 full sized Astroturf pitches, an athletics track, a sports centre, 24 tennis courts and a 9 hole golf course, not to mention beautiful lawns and gardens, the campus is one of the best, if not the best, in the country. Combined with a 235-seat theatre and separate music performance and art display spaces, the School's setting encourages pupils to contribute, and provides a safe community in which to explore and grow.

Academic. A Charterhouse education is all about choice for the individual, with the breadth of options available to each pupil at every stage helping it to stand out from the rest.

The curriculum is firmly rooted in academic rigour. Alongside the traditional curriculum of sciences, languages, humanities, a new programme in Year 9 provides a stimulating foundation in the creative arts before GCSE choices are made. The School runs a course in informatics (computing) for all its youngest pupils, alongside the innovative Enquiry Series that encourages pupils to develop their independent thinking by studying rhetoric and understanding the origins of fake news. Intellectual curiosity is piqued by the academic clubs and societies that proliferate during the afternoons and evenings.

Once GCSEs have been completed, pupils can choose between A Levels or the IB Diploma Programme in the Sixth Form. The internationally-renowned IB Diploma Programme focuses on cross-curricular collaborative learning and the acquisition of intellectual independence.

Alternatively, students may follow A Level courses complemented by the Extended Project Qualification (EPQ), plus a wonderful range of non-examined electives (Creative Writing, History of Art, *ab initio* languages, the Ivy House Leadership Award and a Diploma in Entrepreneurship are all available). The university destinations of leavers reflect both their abilities and the quality of the education provided at the School: Oxbridge, Ivy League, Russell Group and the top European institutions all feature in abundance this year.

Co-curricular activities are an essential element of a Charterhouse education. They combine opportunities for leadership development, creativity, exercise and teamwork. They are also great fun. With more than 80 different sports and activities, including music, drama and other creative subjects, all pupils are encouraged to develop existing interests to exciting levels and to take up new ones. The timetable enables all pupils to enjoy themselves across a wide range of sports and creative arts activities, making use of the School's impressive facilities. A great many clubs and societies are pupil led and, alongside our sport and outdoor education programmes, offer real leadership opportunities and few limits to what can be pursued.

Houses. Inclusivity sits at the heart of life at Charterhouse and whether you are a boarder or a day pupil, the House is a welcoming home from home.

All pupils are under the care of their resident Head of House, who is their day-to-day mentor and is responsible for looking after them throughout their time at Charterhouse.

The Heads of Houses and their families live in the Houses, and are supported by a team of pastoral staff and tutors. Every pupil is allocated a tutor who takes a particular interest in their academic progress, co-curricular commitments and who guides them through the Reach Out (PHSE) programme. The tutor takes responsibility for one year group within their House and is therefore able to maintain good oversight of key pressure points within their year. Tutors meet with their tutees formally three times a week as well as meeting informally on the tutor's weekly duty evening in House. One of the House tutors is appointed the Deputy Head of House; they also play an integral role in running the House.

The House Teams are supported by a 24-hour Health Centre and pupils also have access to support through the welling centre, counsellors and chaplaincy.

Admissions. Charterhouse is an academically selective school and admission is by competitive assessment, interview and subject to a reference from a child's current school.

Prospective parents and their children are warmly invited to visit Charterhouse and experience the School for themselves.

13+ entry. Children need to be registered by 1 October, when they are in their Year 6, prior to taking the ISEB pre-test. A quarter of the places are reserved for children to take the entrance assessments when they are in their Year 7.

Sixth Form. Charterhouse welcomes over 110 new pupils into the Sixth Form each year. Applications for the Sixth Form can be submitted from the start of the Summer Term of Year 10, up until the beginning October of Year 11 (the year before entry).

Full details on the Admissions processes are available on the School website: www.charterhouse.org.uk/admissions.

Fees per term (2021–2022). Boarders £13,802, Day Boarders £11,406. The Governing Body reserves the right to alter the School fee at its discretion. At least one term's notice is required before the removal of a pupil from the School.

Scholarships and Bursaries.

Scholarships, Exhibitions and Awards are available for entry at Year 9 and Year 12. They are offered in Academic, Art or Design Technology, Music and Sport. There is also an All-Rounder Award (for entry at Year 9) which can be offered to those candidates who are yet to excel in their chosen area, but show talent, potential and skills in Art, Music, Drama or Sport.

Charterhouse is able to offer a number of bursaries each year for pupils entering either Year 9 or Year 12, with preference given to those who gain a Scholarship or an Award (not including Exhibitions), who would benefit from a boarding education, but whose parents are unable to afford the fees.

All bursaries are means-tested and are subject to funds being available. The award is reviewed annually for changes in parents' financial circumstances and may be adjusted as a result. Awards may cover up to 100% of the school fee.

Charitable status. Charterhouse School is a Registered Charity, number 312054. Its aims and objectives are the provision of education through the medium of a secondary boarding school for boys and girls.

Governing Body:
Mrs Vicky Tuck, BA, MA (*Chair*)
Mr Kwaku Awuku-Asabre, BSc, Dip. Law
Mrs Camilla Baldwin, MA
Mr Durell Barnes, BA
Mrs Caroline Brown, MA, PgoL, LPC
Professor Vince Emery, PhD, FSB
Mr James Goldsmith, BSc, MRICS
The Very Revd Dianna Gwilliams, BA, MA
Dr Nihara Krause, BSc, MSc, PsychD, C.Psychol, C.Sci
Mr David Macey, FCA
Mr Pete Malcolm
Mr Jeremy McIlroy, FCA, ATII
Mr John Olsen, BA
Mr Charles Oulton, MA
Mr Andrew Reid, MA, MBA, FCA
Mr David Royds, BSc
Mr Michael Walton, MA, MBA, FRICS

Clerk to the Governing Body: Mrs Alex Warburton, BA

Senior Leadership Team:

Head: Dr Alex Peterken, BA, MA, EdD

Director of Finance and Strategy: Mr David Armitage, MBE, BSc, MSc
Senior Deputy Head: Mr Andrew Turner, BA, LLM
Director of Business Development and External Relations: Mr James Davey, MEng
Deputy Head (Academic): Mr Duncan Byrne, BA, MA, MEd
Deputy Head (Pastoral): Ms Karen Davies, MA, MBA
Deputy Head (Pupils & Community): Mrs Louise Wilson, BA, MA
Assistant Head (Academic): Mr Simon Allen, MA, MEd
Assistant Head (Pastoral): Mr Edward Poynter, BA, MEd
Assistant Head (Pupil Welfare): Mr John Richardson, BA
Director of Admissions: Mrs Iona Hutchinson, BA
Director of Wellbeing: Mrs M Jolly, BA, MA

Heads of Houses:
Bodeites: Mr David McCombes, MA
Chetwynd: Mrs Michelle Creer, BA
Daviesites: Mr Sam James, MA
Fletcherites: Mrs Catherine McDonald, MA
Girdlestoneites: Mr James Hazeldine, BA
Gownboys: Mr Andrew Marshall-Taylor, MA
Hodgsonites: Mr Ian Richards, MA
Lockites: Mr Andrew Hunt, MA
Northbrook: Mrs Rebecca Pugh, BA
Pageites: Mr Paul Martin, BSc, MA
Robinites: Mr Andrew Brinkley, BA
Saunderites: Mrs Suzanne Allen, MA
Sutton: Mrs Janicen Lambeth, BSc
Verites: Mr Edward Reid, MMath
Weekites: Mr Edward Poynter, BA, MEd

Cheltenham College

Bath Road, Cheltenham, Gloucestershire GL53 7LD

Tel: 01242 265600
email: admissions@cheltenhamcollege.org
website: www.cheltenhamcollege.org
Twitter: @cheltcollege
Facebook: @cheltcollege
Instagram: @cheltcollege

Motto: *Labor Omnia Vincit* "Work Conquers All"

Situated in 72 acres of beautiful grounds in the heart of Regency Cheltenham Spa, Cheltenham College is one of the country's leading co-educational independent schools for boarding and day pupils aged 13–18. Combining a strong academic record with a considerable reputation for sport, drama, music and outward-bound activities, Cheltenham College offers an outstanding all-round education. Founded in 1841, it was the first of the great Victorian public schools.

Location. Stunning buildings and first-class playing fields provide a magnificent setting near the heart of the beautiful Cotswolds. There are excellent road and rail connections with London and the major airports, and Cheltenham College offers all the advantages of life in a thriving town community, whilst maintaining a separate campus life.

Numbers. Boys: 318 Boarders; 77 Day Boys. Girls: 270 Boarders; 69 Day Girls.

Admission. Entry to College is into Third Form at 13+ or Lower Sixth at 16+. A small number of pupils may also be admitted into the Fourth Form at 14+. Entry at 13+ can be secured in three ways: Common Entrance, College Entrance papers or College Academic Scholarship papers. Entry at 16+ can be secured by scholarship and entry tests in November or March, good GCSE predictions and a testimonial from the previous school. Full details, prospectuses and application forms can be obtained from the Admissions Office. There is a registration fee of £200 and a final acceptance fee of £1,000 (for pupils aged 13–16) or £1,350 (for Sixth Form entrants) which is deducted from the final term's account.

Scholarships and Bursaries. Scholarships and exhibitions are available for entry at both 13+ and 16+. They are offered in Academic, Art, Drama, Music (including 16+

Organ and Choral awards) and Sport. Generous discounts for Armed Forces families and bursaries are also available.

Fees per term (2021–2022). Boarders £13,165, Day Pupils £9,875. Sixth Form: Boarders £13,520, Day Pupils £10,230.

Chapel. Each day, all year, groups gather together for a short service in the Chapel; the main service takes place each Sunday. There is a Confirmation service every year.

Houses. The 11 Houses, nine Boarding and two Day, are at the heart of College life and are all located around the Cheltenham College campus. Girls are in five Houses and boys are in six Houses. Accommodation and pastoral care are outstanding for both boys and girls.

Planned Developments. There has been a significant £25 million investment in Cheltenham College over the past decade, with refurbishment of the library 'Big Modern', the theatre 'Big Classical', the Science Centre, a new girls' House, and new catering facilities already completed. Looking forward, a rolling programme of Boarding House refurbishment will continue whilst at the same time completing many exciting new development projects including the creation of a new Business and Economics learning centre.

Curriculum. On entry at 13+, pupils follow a broad course for one year, before embarking upon GCSEs in the Fourth Form. The core of the curriculum comprises English Language and English Literature, Mathematics, and at least two Sciences. All pupils then choose at least one Modern Language (French, German, Spanish); and four options from Art, Classical Civilisation, Design Technology (Resistant Materials, Textiles), Drama, Geography, Greek, History, Latin, Music, PE and Theology, Philosophy and Ethics. In the Sixth Form, over 25 A Level subjects are offered and all students complete an EPQ to enhance their opportunities. Students are given extensive preparation for entrance to MDV, Oxbridge, universities, Apprenticeships and careers after College.

Cultural Activities. The arts are central to the life of College, with at least six plays being staged each year. Pupils are encouraged to attend concerts, plays, films and lectures not only in Cheltenham but in nearby Oxford, Stratford, Bristol and London. Cheltenham College is fortunate to have the renowned Cheltenham Jazz, Science, Literature and Music Festivals on its doorstep, which pupils can take advantage of. Art is housed in an elegant early 19th-century mansion, with a dedicated gallery that exhibits current art and also serves as an excellent chamber music concert hall, housing the superb Steinway concert grand piano. The beautiful Chapel holds a magnificent 3-manual Harrison & Harrison organ. Music plays a vital part in College life, with pupils able to learn just about every orchestral instrument imaginable, even bagpipes. The Chapel Choir, Chamber Choir and numerous other groups enable singers to reach very high standards and many achieve university Choral Scholarships. The numerous instrumental groups and ensembles, from the Orchestra, Chamber Orchestra and Wind Band to the Jazz Bands and String Quartets, perform in Cheltenham's Town Hall and Pump Rooms, as well as in the College Chapel and other venues.

Sports. Cheltenham College is one of the strongest schools nationally in a wide cross-section of sports and benefits from top-level sports professionals and coaches. Every week, over 1,100 pupils actively participate in over 20 different sports. In recent years the school has been named Rugby School of the Year, had multiple teams experience unbeaten seasons and won national titles in sports ranging from polo to rackets. In addition to the two AstroTurf pitches, the sports hall and swimming pool, there are excellent facilities for other sports available, which include rackets, squash, equestrian, golf, athletics, cross country, badminton, polo, and shooting. All pupils, whether simply participating or looking to progress to the highest levels, benefit from coaching by sports professionals; a range of coaches across all sports that have competed at the highest level. In recent years, Cheltenham College staff has been joined by Ben Marsden (GB Hockey Olympian) as Director of Sport and Sam Cook (England Netball player) as Director of Netball, joining existing coaches including Olly Morgan (England Rugby player) and Gwyn Williams (Wales Mens Hockey Coach), to provide the best support for athletes.

Activities. On entry to College, a structured programme of outdoor pursuits, team building exercises and leadership initiatives are provided for one year. Options such as CCF, the Duke of Edinburgh's Award at Bronze and Gold level, and a wide range of expeditions are available. Up to 30 clubs operate weekly, including shooting, dance, pottery, film-making and drama.

Service. Giving is a large part of life at Cheltenham College. All staff and pupils give back to the community around them through Charitable Fundraising, Community Action and Partnerships with other schools and organisations. Their involvement in these activities assists our pupils to make a difference in the community and develops the virtue of voluntary service and an awareness of communities of disadvantage. Every Wednesday over 100 pupils volunteer for a cause that they are passionate about.

University Entry and Careers. Students benefit from a dedicated Higher Education and Careers department during their time at College. College has a dedicated and informative Careers Library, which is committed to offering information and guidance on: gap years; degree courses; universities, apprenticeships and institutes, both in the UK and abroad. Each Sixth Former has a tutor who works with them to ensure that he or she is fully aware of the opportunities and challenges available.

Cheltonian Society. Tel: 01242 265694.

Cheltenham College Preparatory School. *For details see entry in IAPS section.*

Charitable status. Cheltenham College is a Registered Charity, number 311720. As a charity, it is established for the purpose of providing an efficient course of education for boys and girls.

The Council:
President: Mr W J Straker-Nesbit
Deputy President: Mr H Monro
Secretary to Council: Mr J Champion

Mr B Beardmore-Gray	Mr L Humphreys-Davies
Mr A Barr	Mr N Roskilly
Mr P Brettell	Mr T Smith
Dr A Butland	Mr D Stewart
Mr M Chicken	Reverend Canon K
Mr C Cooper	Wilkinson
Ms G Elwood	Dr P Wingfield
Miss C Fisher	Mr M Wynne
Mrs E Goldsmith	

Head: **Mrs Nicola Huggett**, MA Oxford

Deputy Head (Academic): Mr Tim Brewis, BA Exeter, MEd Buckingham, MSc Oxford
Deputy Head (Co-curricular): Mr Stephen McQuitty, BSc Nottingham
Deputy Head (Learning and Wellbeing): Dr Mary Plint, BEd Johannesburg, MEd, PhD Gloucestershire
Deputy Head (Pastoral): Mrs Anna Cutts, BEd Middlesex

Bursar: Mr Phil Attwell, BA Sussex, MSc Sheffield
Senior Housemaster: Mr Richard Penny
Registrar: Mr Simon Conner, BSc Durham

Cheltenham Ladies' College

Bayshill Road, Cheltenham, Gloucestershire GL50 3EP

Tel: 01242 520691
email: enquiries@cheltladiescollege.org
website: www.cheltladiescollege.org
Twitter: @cheltladiescoll
Facebook: @CheltLadiesColl
Instagram: @cheltladiescoll
LinkedIn: /school/the-cheltenham-ladies-college

A College education gives pupils the best possible opportunities to achieve their potential in both the academic and personal spheres.

Academic excellence forms the basis of College life, but just as important is the formation of character. We recognise that a 21st-century education needs to inspire, prepare and equip young people to sustain a lifetime of independently sought learning, and to give them the flexibility and resourcefulness to flourish in our rapidly changing world.

We believe that the wellbeing of our students is as important as their academic outcomes; it has a direct bearing on the quality of the engagement and interactions, including their receptiveness as learners. Pupils are encouraged to be self-determining and caring towards others, building the foundations of character and self-sufficiency for success and fulfilment in the years beyond school.

Students are encouraged to embrace a broad range of co-curricular activities to suit their interests, from the sporting to the intellectual and cultural. A global outlook encourages them to play a part in the wider world, creating young women who value and contribute to their communities. Life at College promotes mutual respect, integrity and courage, while nurturing intellectual curiosity, creativity, confidence and an enduring love of learning.

Our pupils are at the heart of all College does; we are ambitious for their futures, collectively and individually.

Numbers. Approximately 191 day and 688 boarding.

Fees per term (2021–2022). Day £8,900, Boarding £13,260. New Entrants to Sixth Form: Day £10,130, Boarding £14,930. Some extras are charged, e.g. music, riding.

Admission. Entry at 11+, 13+ and 16+ via College's own examinations. An interview is also required for some entry points.

Academic. Our curriculum aims to instil in each student a curiosity about the world in which she lives and equip her with tools to question, reason and communicate articulately. Our Lower College curriculum provides exceptional breadth, building foundations for the GSCE years. Pupils study separate sciences, computing, humanities and a language acquisition course, as well as music, drama, art and design, and engineering, enterprise and technology. As a large school, College is able to offer extraordinary advantages in resources and choices. Pupils have a free choice of options for GCSE but are encouraged to maintain a broad curriculum, tailored to their individual strengths and interests. In Sixth Form, they have the option of taking A Levels or the International Baccalaureate (IB) Diploma Programme. Our exam results for GCSE, A Level and IB are consistently excellent, leading to College winning a number of awards for academic excellence over the last five years, including being named *South West Independent Secondary School of the Decade* by Parent Power, The Sunday Times Schools Guide 2021.

Pastoral Care and Wellbeing. As a large school, College is able to offer extraordinary advantages in resources and choices, but we are also divided into small groups too, through the three academic Divisions (LC, UC & SFC), Tutor groups and Houses. These create interlocking layers of pastoral care, which work alongside our whole-school Wellbeing Programme, to enable every pupil, the reserved as well as the extrovert, to find opportunities to lead a confident, fulfilled and enjoyable life at College. This network is backed up by an experienced and well-resourced Medical Centre based in College, an informed and skilled Catering Department and the support of the College Chaplain. Pastoral care isn't something that happens when things go wrong; it's a constant support network for every student throughout her time in College.

Buildings and Grounds. College is set in a 36-acre dispersed estate in the centre of Cheltenham. The single teaching site is built in a Gothic revival style, complete with the stunning Princess Hall. It is complemented by the more recent Art and Technology block, housing College's Engineering, Enterprise and Technology Department, the Parabola Arts Centre, with a 325-seat theatre, and College's Health and Fitness Centre, which opened in 2018. This sports complex and the Day and Boarding Houses are located in nearby residential areas within a short walking distance of the main site.

Houses. There are six Junior Boarding Houses and three Junior Day Houses. All students then move into one of six Houses in Sixth Form, which is an excellent stepping stone to university life. Each House is run by a Housemistress, Deputy Housemistress and a team of staff, as well as a dedicated Chef. All Houses have dining rooms, common rooms, prep rooms, computer rooms, space for music practice and laundry facilities. Day girls are fully integrated into all College activities, regularly joining boarders on weekend trips and expeditions.

Music, Drama and Dance. More than 1,000 individual music lessons take place each week, which are scheduled around the curriculum to ensure girls do not miss academic lessons. There are also many choirs, orchestras and concerts throughout the year and at least five drama productions, with Sixth Form girls performing an open-air Shakespeare play in the Summer Term. Dance and gymnastics are also available and very popular.

Sport and Co-curricular. At College, we are deeply committed to promoting the health, fitness and wellbeing of all pupils and to developing talent and a lifelong enthusiasm for sport and exercise, regardless of ability or expertise. The main sports are hockey, lacrosse, netball, swimming, athletics and tennis, but College aims to provide activities pupils enjoy and more than 30 different sports are offered. Alongside the existing 25 m swimming pool, tennis and netball facilities, and AstroTurf pitches, the new Health and Fitness Centre includes a second sports hall, multi-purpose studios, a dance studio, and a gym and fitness suite. More than 140 co-curricular opportunities are on offer, including astronomy, life drawing, hip hop dance, beginner's Russian, fencing, debating, journalism, yoga, ethical hacking, martial arts, Model UN, philosophy, engineering, Young Enterprise, medical and ethical club and international society.

Scholarships and Bursaries. A number of Academic, Art, Music and Sport Scholarships and other awards are made annually for pupils of all ages.

Applications for bursaries are welcome from girls whose parents require financial assistance in order to help their daughter join College.

Beyond College. Our dedicated Professional Guidance Centre provides specialist careers and higher education advice to pupils throughout their time at College. Sixth Form tutors also provide significant support in this area. The majority of our girls gain places at Russell Group universities, including Oxbridge, or at top US universities to study a diverse range of subjects.

Former Pupils (Guild). There are over 8,000 Guild members in more than 70 different countries across the world, and many are actively involved in helping current girls prepare for the future, including supporting networking dinners, interview preparation, hosting careers and networking events, and arranging speakers from universities and the professions.

Charitable status. Cheltenham Ladies' College is a Registered Charity, number 311722. It exists to provide a high standard of education for girls.

Chair of Council: Mr Nick Baird, MA, CMG, CVO

Principal: **Ms Eve Jardine-Young**, MA

Vice-Principal: Mr Richard Dodds, BSc
Vice-Principal (*Academic*): Miss Jackie Adams, BSc

Chief Operating Officer: Mr Nigel Richards, BSc
Director of Admissions: Mrs Charlotte Coull, BA
Director of External Relations: Mrs Dragana Hartley, BSc, FCIM, FRSA
Co-Curricular Director: Mr James Pothecary, MSci
Head of Pastoral Care: Miss Caroline Ralph, BEd
Head of Sixth Form College: Mr Josh Sumner, BA, MA
Head of Upper College and Assistant Head Academic: Dr David Gamblin, MChem, MRSC
Head of Lower College: Ms Charlotte Woodhead, BEd Hons

Chetham's School of Music

Long Millgate, Manchester M3 1SB

Tel: 0161 834 9644
email: chets@chethams.com
website: www.chethams.com

Chetham's School of Music is a co-educational school for boarding and day students aged eight to eighteen. The

School teaches a broad curriculum set within a framework of music. At the centre of every child's course is a 'musical core' of experiences rooted in a determination to educate the whole person. There are two Principals, one focusing on Academic and Pastoral Care, the other on Music. Originally founded in 1653, through the Will of Humphrey Chetham, as a Bluecoat orphanage, the School was reconstituted in 1969 as a specialist music school.

The School numbers 329 students, there are 219 boarders. Admission is by musical audition, and any orchestral instrument, keyboard, guitar, voice, Jazz or composition, may be studied. Each student studies two instrumental studies, or voice and one instrument, as well as following academic courses which lead to GCSE and A Levels and to university entrance and conservatoire. The School stands on the site of Manchester's original 12th century Manor House adjacent to the Cathedral and is housed partly in the fine 15th century College Buildings, and partly in the New School Building which houses all the instrumental, musical and academic teaching. The building also includes an Outreach Centre and two Concert Halls: the Carole Nash Hall and The Stoller Hall.

Music. Instrumental tuition is guided and monitored by Heads of Department in each specialism, they survey students' work, conduct internal examinations and arrange for external professionals to give masterclasses. Internationally renowned musicians hold residences at the School and there are three Music Courses throughout the year. The Joint Principal (Director of Music) has responsibility for the full-time Music Staff and for about 130 visiting tutors. All students receive three sessions of individual instrumental tuition each week. Practice is rigorously set and supervised. Academic Music is studied at GCSE and A Level.

Boarding. There are two boarding houses for girls and boys aged 13 to 18 and one for Juniors aged 8 to 13. Each House is run by Heads of House in residence, with resident assistants. All full-time teachers act as Tutors and are involved with pastoral care. In addition, there is a well-staffed Medical Centre with Nurses, School Doctor, Counselling, Psychotherapy, Hearing Nurse and Physiotherapy.

Recreation. Chetham's School of Music offers students a pioneering 'Fit to Perform' programme – a bespoke programme, for each individual student, which is closely aligned with their motivations and requirements, not only in terms of conditioning and general fitness, but also in respect of injury prevention as young musicians.

Chetham's as a specialist music school has student well-being at its heart. Our holistic approach to student well-being is delivered by personal trainers and specialist activity leaders throughout the day and evenings following individual, initial information-gathering and needs analysis. The School's medical staff, physiotherapist and caterers also contribute to the programme.

Applications, Visits. Entry is by audition only. Preliminary assessment auditions are held throughout the year, with final auditions in the Christmas and Spring terms.

The Prospectus and application forms are sent on request and are available on the School's website. Parents and prospective students are welcome to visit the School by arrangement with the Auditions Administrator.

Fees, Grants. All entrants from the United Kingdom are eligible for grants under the Department for Education's Music and Dance Scheme. Parental contributions are calculated according to means and parents on low incomes qualify automatically for full fee remission. The Bursar will be glad to advise about the scales.

Choristers. The School is a member of the Choir Schools' Association and Choristerships at Manchester Cathedral for day boys and girls are available under a separate scheme. Choristers' Fee: £9,954 pa (subject to Cathedral Bursaries).

Charitable status. Chetham's School of Music is a Registered Charity, number 526702. It exists to educate exceptionally gifted young musicians.

Governors:

M Edge (*Chairman*)

Mrs S Barnes	L Pratt
Ms C Baxendale	H Ross
Prof B Brennan	Ms K Russell
Councillor J Davies	N Shepherd
Mrs E Halstead	L Stephens
K Jaquiss	Canon M Wall
S McKendrick	Dr S Zhi
Prof L Merrick	

Staff:

Joint Principal: Miss N Smith, BA, NPQH
Joint Principal: T Redmond, BA

Bursar: Mrs S C Newman, BSc Hons, FCA
Assistant Principal and Head of Sixth Form: Mrs J Harrison, MA
Head of Middle School: A Henderson, BA
Head of Lower School: Mrs S Hales, BA

Music:
Joint Principal, Director of Music and Artistic Director: Mr Tom Redmond
PA to the Joint Principal (*TR*): Mrs J Scott
Music Department Manager: Mr I Mayer
Concert Manager: Mrs N Pierce
Concerts Administrator: Miss A Mallon
Music Department Timetabler: Ms J Severyn
Music Department Assistant: Mr D Curtis
Auditions Administrator: Mrs A Herbert
Music Department Secretary: Miss J Taylor

Brass and Percussion:
Head of Department (*and Assistant Principal*): David Chatterton
Euphonium Tutors: Bill Millar, David Thornton
Horn Tutors: Julian Plummer, Richard Bourn, Tom Redmond, Lindsey Stoker, Tim Jackson, Helen Varley
Percussion Tutors: Sophie Hastings (*Latin percussion and Kit*), David Hext, Paul Patrick, Andrea Vogler, Le Yu
Trombone Tutors: Robert Burtenshaw, Philip Goodwin, Katy Jones, Les Storey
Trumpet Staff: David Chatterton
Tutors: John Dickinson, Neil Fulton, Tom Osborne, Tracey Redfern, Gareth Small
Tuba Tutors: Brian Kingsley

Keyboard:
Head of Department: Dr Murray McLachlan
Tutors: Gemma Beeson, Simon Bottomley, Sam Brook, Hazel Fanning, Jill Fogden, Benjamin Frith, Duncan Glenday, Alison Havard, Marta Karbownicka, Helen Krizos, BingBing Li, Jonathan Middleton, Dr Sarah Murphy, Kathryn Page, Dina Parakhina, Ben Powell,

Marie-Louise Taylor, Charlotte Turner, Lulu Yang, Jeremy Young
Harpsichord Tutor: Charlotte Turner
Jazz Piano Tutor: Les Chisnall
Organ Tutors: Simon Passmore, Geoffrey Woollatt, Christopher Stokes
Chamber Tutors: Benjamin Frith, Jeremy Young

Strings:
Head of Department: Nicholas Jones
Assistant Head of Department: Dr Owen Cox
Senior Chamber Music Tutor: Graham Oppenheimer
Chamber Music Tutor: Pavel Fischer
Violin Staff: Owen Cox
Violin Tutors: Jiafeng Chen, Connie del Vecchio, Krystoffer Dolatko, Ruth Hahn, Benedict Holland, Daniella Meagher, Jan Repko, Yumi Sasaki, Katie Stillman, Deirdre Ward, Qian Wu
Viola Tutors: Sebastian Mueller, Graham Oppenheimer
Viola da Gamba: Roberto Carrillo-Garcia
Cello Staff: Nicholas Jones
Cello Tutors: Barbara Grunthal, Jennifer Langridge, Li Lu, David Smith, Gillian Thoday
Double Bass Tutors: Yi Xin Salvage, Steve Berry (*Jazz*), Rachel Meerloo, Gemma Ashcroft
Harp Tutors: Eleanor Hudson, Marie Leenhardt
Guitar Tutors: Jim Faulkner (*Jazz*), Wendy Jackson

Woodwind:
Head of Department: Belinda Gough
Recorder/Baroque Ensembles Tutor: Chris Orton
Baroque Flute and Historical Performance: Dr Martyn Shaw
Oboe Tutors: Rachael Clegg, Matthew Jones, Stephane Rancourt
Flute Tutors: Katherine Bryan, Rachel Forgreive, Fiona Fulton, Belinda Gough
Clarinet Tutors: Rosa Campos-Fernandez, Sergio Castello-Lopez, Jim Muirhead, Marianne Rawles, Andrew Wilson
Saxophone Tutors: Iain Dixon (*Jazz/improvisation*), Jim Muirhead, Carl Raven (*Jazz/improvisation*), Andrew Wilson
Bassoon Tutors: Ben Hudson, Graham Salvage, Elena Comelli, Adam Mackenzie
Contra-Bassoon Tutor: Simon Davies

Vocal Department:
Head of Department: Marcus Farnsworth
Tutors: Helen Francis, Margaret McDonald, Stuart Overington, Diana Palmerston

Staff Accompanists:
Head of Department: Nicholas Oliver
Staff: Elena Namilova, Martyn Parkes, Simon Passmore, Gemma Webster

Composition:
Dr Jeremy Pike, MA, MPhil, PhD, LRAM, Hon ARAM, D Mason, BA, Ian Stephens

Music Technology:
Adrian Horn, BMus, Dr Jeremy Pike, MA, MPhil, PhD, LRAM, Hon ARAM

Practice Team Leaders:
Kristine Healy, Daniella Meagher

Big Band:
Directors: Richard Iles, Jim Muirhead

Improvisation:
Steve Berry, Les Chisnall (*Keyboard*), Iain Dixon

Alexander Technique:
Patrick Grundy-White, Anne Whitehead

Academic Music:
S King, BA, MA, MPhil, PhD
Ms R Aldred, BMus
Miss C Campbell Smith, MA
D Mason, BA
Dr S Murphy, PhD, BA
Mrs S Oliver, BA
Mrs A Price, MA

Art:
Miss A Boothroyd, BA

Compensatory Education/Special Needs:
Mrs B L Owen, BEd, RSA Dip SpLD
Miss S Coward, BA
Miss L Fogg, MA

Drama & Theatre Studies:
Mrs J Sherlock, MA

English:
Miss C Raffo, MA
Mrs J Harrison, MA
Miss L Jones, BA
J Runswick-Cole, MEd
Mrs A Sanderson-Leigh, BA
Mrs J Sherlock, MA

Humanities & PSHE:
A Kyle, BA
Mrs S Cox, BA
C Newman, MA
Miss J Southern, BA

Information Technology:
Miss C Whittaker, BA

Junior Department:
Miss C Tomlinson, PGCE
M Wong, MA

Languages:
Ms N Greschwendt, PGCE
P Chillingworth, BA
Mrs S Hales, BA
Mrs R Jordan, BA
Dr C Law, PhD, MA

Mathematics:
E Leeson, BEng
Dr A Clow, PhD
Ms C Dackombe, MSc
Mrs K Kyle, BSc

Recreation:
A Spagnolo, BSc
Miss M Whitehead, BSc
Miss C Whittaker, BA

Sciences:
A Henderson, BA
J Blundell, BSc
C Davidson, PGCE
Mrs C Shiells, BSc
Ms E Storey, BSc

Librarian: Miss K Morgan, MSc

Careers:
Dr S Murphy, PhD, MMus, BA (*Music Colleges*)
Mrs J Harrison, MA (*Universities*)

Houses:
Mr D Ledson (*Millgate*)
Mrs A Martinez Navarrate (*New College*)
Miss S Clarke & Miss L Cody (*Victoria*)

School Doctor: Dr D Hedwat
Nurse: Mrs K Scott, RGN

PA to the Joint Principal (NS): Mrs L Haslam

Christ College
Brecon

Brecon, Powys LD3 8AF

Tel: 01874 615440
email: enquiries@christcollegebrecon.com
website: www.christcollegebrecon.com

Motto: *Possunt quia posse videntur*

Founded by Henry VIII, 1541. Reconstituted by Act of Parliament, 1853.

Christ College, Brecon lies in a setting of outstanding natural beauty at the foot of the Brecon Beacons on the edge of the small market town of Brecon, two minutes' walk away on the opposite side of the river. The River Usk flows alongside the playing fields providing good canoeing and fishing while the nearby Llangorse Lake is available for sailing and windsurfing.

The school was founded by King Henry VIII in 1541 when he dissolved the Dominican Friary of St Nicholas. The 13th Century Chapel and Dining Hall are at the centre of school life and the school's mix of important, historic buildings and modern architecture represents the continuity of education at the school.

Estyn, Her Majesty's Inspectorate for Education & Training in Wales, inspected the school in 2017 and rated the school's current performance as 'Excellent'.

Organisation. Christ College was a boys only school until 1987 when girls were admitted to the Sixth Form. In 1995 the school became fully co-educational. There are 383 pupils in the school of whom 221 are boys and 162 girls. Approximately 60% of pupils board and there are two senior boys' houses, School House and Orchard House, two senior girls' houses, Donaldsons House and de Winton House, one co-educational house St Davids, and a lower school house, Alway House, for 11–13 year old boys and girls. Alway House also offers weekly boarding for our younger boarders in St Nicholas House. St Nicholas House is a junior day and boarding section for boys and girls aged 7–11 years.

Chapel. Chapel services are conducted in accordance with the liturgy of the Anglican church, but entrance to Christ College is open to boys and girls of all faiths. The ownership of Chapel by the boys and girls, demonstrated through their participation in services and their singing, is a feature of the school. Pupils are prepared for Confirmation by the School's Chaplain who lives on site.

Curriculum. Year 11 pupils follow a balanced curriculum leading to GCSE at which most pupils take 10 subjects. Options are chosen at the end of Year 9.

The Sixth Form follow the linear A Level syllabus. The Extended Project Qualification (EPQ) is also available for pupils.

Alongside their A Levels, pupils follow our second curriculum – Curriculum for Life. The curriculum offers a varied programme to enable them to thrive in their chosen career and personal life. The core timetable provides a series of sessions and guest lectures covering a range of life skill topics including financial literacy, preparing for university/ work and health and wellbeing, politics and society. Pupils are exposed to a wide variety of influential external speakers who have been handpicked to complement the course to demonstrate how pupils may achieve their goals and work towards the next stage of their lives. The second section of the programme provides pupils with time to further develop life skills, such as participating in outdoor pursuits, Duke of Edinburgh's Award, community involvement, independent academic study, creative and music practice and physical strength and conditioning.

Class sizes rarely exceed 20 up to GCSE and average fewer than 10 at A Level.

Games. The main school games are Rugby Football, Cricket, Hockey, Soccer, Netball, Cross-Country and Athletics. Tennis, Badminton, Squash, Volleyball, Basketball, Golf, Fishing, Swimming, Shooting, Mountain Biking, Canoeing, Fencing, Indoor Cricket, Climbing, Triathlon and Aerobics are also available. The playing fields are extensive and lie adjacent to the school. Christ College has entered into a corporate partnership with Cradoc Golf Club, two miles outside of Brecon, to encourage pupils of all ages and experience in the fundamentals of the game of golf. The opportunity to play at Cradoc Golf Club and receive professional instruction is also extended to all parents of pupils attending Christ College.

Thursday Afternoons. On Thursday afternoons the CCF Contingent meets. There is a choice between Army and Royal Air Force sections and the CCF has its own Headquarters, Armoury and covered 30m Range in the school grounds. Pupils take their proficiency certificate after two years and may then choose to continue as Instructors, undergo training for the Duke of Edinburgh's Award scheme or leave the CCF and may become involved in community service.

Music. The Chapel Choir is large and enjoys an excellent reputation with radio and television broadcasts as well as overseas tours to its credit. As befits a school in Wales singing on all school occasions is committed, energetic and frequently with natural harmony. The school has a Chamber Choir, plus multiple wind, brass and string ensembles and its pupils play a prominent role in the South Powys Youth Orchestra and works in partnership with the Welsh Sinfonia to provide opportunities for pupils to play alongside professional musicians. There are many other opportunities to play in ensemble groups throughout the school. Individual instrumental and singing lessons are delivered by visiting musicians.

Activities. In addition to sporting pastimes a wide range of activities are available to pupils including Sixth Form Film Society, Advanced Chemistry, Art, Badminton, Basketball, Brass Group, Canoeing, Chamber Choir, Chess, Choir, Climbing, Community Service, Disability Sport, Drama, Fencing, Fitness, Golf, Indoor Cricket, IT Projects,

Mandarin Chinese, Modern Dance/Jazz, Modern Language Film Society, Music Practice, Music Theory, Percussion Group, Project Science, Railway Modelling, Shooting, Stage Management, String Group, String Quartet, Technology, Wado Kai Karate, Wind Sinfonia, and Young Enterprise. The Duke of Edinburgh's Award scheme has been popular for many years and the majority of pupils gain at least a Bronze award, and a significant number go on to achieve the Gold award.

Overseas Travel is frequent and extensive. In recent years tours, expeditions and exchanges have taken place to Beijing, Canada, China, Japan, New York and South Africa as well as a number of European destinations.

Careers. Two members of staff also serve in the Careers department which also enlists the help of the Independent Schools Careers Organisation as well as the local Careers organisations. Former pupils return annually for Careers evenings and in this the Old Breconian Association is very helpful.

Entrance. Pupils are admitted at the age of 7+, 11+, 13+ and 16+ following the school's own entrance papers in English and Mathematics plus an IQ test, school report and interview. These tests are usually held in Jan/Feb, but individual arrangements can be made. The majority of 11 year old entrants come from local State Primary Schools, those at 13 from Preparatory schools when, instead of the Common Entrance examination, pupils face the same entrance procedures as at 11. Boys and girls also enter the Sixth Form on the basis of GCSE grade estimates, an IQ test and an interview. Although these are standard entry points, pupils will be considered for entry in Years 4, 5, 6, 8 and Year 10.

Term of Entry. Pupils are accepted in the Michaelmas, Lent and Summer terms.

Scholarships. Scholarships are available for entry at age 11, 13 and 16.

Competitive Scholarships – 11+, 13+, 6th Form Award

All Rounder – Up to 20%

Academic – Up to 20%

Art – Up to 20%

Drama – Up to 20%

Music – Up to 20%

Science – Up to 20%

Sport – Up to 20%

Process: Interview and Assessment.

Bursaries are available at all ages and are subject to a means test.

10% bursaries are available each year for the children of serving members of the Armed Forces in receipt of CEA.

Fees per term (2021–2022). Years 3–6: Day from £3,194, Boarding from £5,426; Years 7–11: Day from £5,463, Boarding from £7,855; Years 12–13: Day £6,528, Boarding £11,473

Charitable status. Christ College, Brecon is a Registered Charity, number 525744. Its aims and objectives are to provide a fully rounded education for boys and girls between the ages of 7 and 18.

Visitor: Her Majesty The Queen

Chair of Governors: Prof M C R Davies

***Head*: Mr Gareth Pearson**, BEng

Deputy Head (*Academic*): Mr J D Bush, MA Cantab
Deputy Head (*Welfare*): Mr S Hill, BA Hons
Bursar: Mr M Allen
Marketing and Admissions: Mrs L Griffin
Admissions Registrar: Mrs M L Stephens
Development Director: Mr M Thomas

Christ's Hospital

Horsham, West Sussex RH13 0LJ

Tel:	01403 211293
email:	hmsec@christs-hospital.org.uk
website:	www.christs-hospital.org.uk
Twitter:	@CHSchoolHorsham
Facebook:	@christshospitalschool

Christ's Hospital (CH) is one of the famous Royal Hospitals of London, whose foundation marked the beginning of the social services in Tudor England. Inspired by a sermon by Nicholas Ridley, Bishop of London, the young King Edward VI instructed the Lord Mayor, Sir Richard Dobbs, to appoint a committee of leading citizens to consider remedies and relief for the City's homeless poor. Their work, and subsequently their philanthropy, led to the founding of the five great Hospitals all supporting different needs. CH, established in the monastery of the Grey Friars in Newgate Street, embraced the task of educating and nourishing the destitute children of the City and took children of all social backgrounds and ages.

In November 1552, CH opened its doors to 380 pupils and, within a year, the number had increased to over 500. Many children, including 100 of the first 380, were infants who were sent away to CH Hertford to be looked after. When they reached 10 they returned to CH London.

Today Christ's Hospital is an independent co-educational boarding and day school of 900 pupils with an equal mix of boys and girls aged 11–18. The School is located in West Sussex in the south east of England. It is situated in stunning countryside between London and Brighton.

Christ's Hospital is unique for a UK independent boarding school in that it offers more bursary places than other schools. This stems from our founding charter as a charitable school. School fees are paid on a means-tested basis, with substantial subsidies paid by the School, so that pupils from all corners of society are able to have a high-quality, independent boarding school education that would otherwise be beyond their means.

Facilities. The Christ's Hospital campus is nothing short of majestic. From the moment you arrive you'll see that it is a very special place. Sweeping sports fields, beautiful buildings and our spectacular Quad are immediately visible.

We also have 16 boarding houses, two Upper Sixth Form residences, our own purpose-built theatre, modern sports centre, music school and art school. The School has in place an ongoing programme of renovation and rebuilding.

The majority of pupils and teachers live on site, creating a community where pupils are happy and secure, with a wide range of activities on their doorstep. The seven-day week boarding school environment provides the time and space for pupils to develop their interests and talents, and to live and work successfully with others from a diverse range of backgrounds.

Christ's Hospital welcomes day pupils who are within a commutable distance from the School. Day pupils enjoy all the advantages of a top boarding school with access to an exceptional co-curricular programme.

Admission. Normally entry to Christ's Hospital is at Year 7, Year 9 or Sixth Form. Occasionally, we can admit children at Year 8 or 10. The Admissions Office will be able to advise you if places are available.

We encourage you to visit CH on one of our termly Open Mornings to enable you to see the school in action.

Our selection process is designed to determine whether a child will flourish in a busy boarding school environment with a strong academic ethos, enjoying the wide range of opportunities on offer, and feel at home at Christ's Hospital.

Parents are advised to start the Admissions process as early as possible and ideally at least eighteen months before their child would be due to enter the school.

Places at the school are academically selective and are offered on the basis of Christ's Hospital's own assessments.

Year 7 Entry. We are looking for candidates working at the higher end of the ability range: those currently working above the expected level in English, Maths and Science.

Year 9 Entry. Candidates should be targeted to achieve an average of 60% at Common Entrance or a current working grade of 6 or above in English, Maths and Science.

Sixth Form Entry. Applicants should be predicted to achieve an 8 or 9 grade at GCSE in the subjects that they wish to continue on to A Level or Higher Level for International Baccalaureate. Students need to achieve a minimum of four grade 6 and four grade 7 at GCSE, including a grade 4 or above in Mathematics and English.

Additional Entry Information. In all cases reports will be requested from a candidate's current school and it is recommended that parents contact their child's current school early in the admissions process to ask about their child's predicted SATs/Common Entrance/GCSE results.

Scholarships and Bursaries. Scholarships are awarded for academic excellence and for outstanding ability in music, art, drama and sport. The awards are offered to pupils entering the school at 13+ and Sixth Form with a value between 5% and 20%. The Christ's Hospital scholarships include the Joe Launchbury Scholarship for a promising and talented young rugby player, The Sir Colin Davis Music Scholarship for a young musician and the Queen Victoria Scholarship, for a bright pupil from the Isle of Wight with academic potential.

The School uses its own tests and assessments in order to determine scholarship awards.

Uniquely, Christ's Hospital is able to offer substantial, means-tested bursaries to over 75% of its pupils and scholarships may be linked to this bursarial assistance.

Fees per term (2021–2022). Boarding £12,200; Day: £6,300 (Years 7–8), £7,930 (Years 9–13).

Charitable status. Christ's Hospital School is a Registered Charity, number 1120090, supported by the Christ's Hospital Foundation, Registered Charity number 306975.

Head Teacher: **Simon Reid**, BA (*English*)

Deputy Heads:
R M J Brading, BA, MA, PhD (*English*)

L W G Walters, BA, MA (*English*)

Assistant Heads:
Assistant Head (*Academic*): M I Medley, MSc, PhD (*Chemistry*)
Assistant Head (*Admissions*): A R Wines, MA, PhD (*History*)
Assistant Head (*Curriculum Development*): S J O'Boyle, BSc, ARCS (*Mathematics*)
Assistant Head (*Pastoral*): S C Young, MSc, MEd (*Chemistry*)

Chaplain:
Revd C Huxley-Jones, BA (*Theology & Philosophy*)

Assistant Staff:
* Head of Department

R A Ahmed-Geere, BA (*English*)
N Albrecht, MPhil (*History*)
R I Allcorn, MSc (*Biology*)
R A K Ashley, BA (*Mathematics*)
J M Azancot, BA (*Design & Technology*)
J Ball (*Theology & Philisophy*)
L F Bamford (*Graduate Assistant*)
F J Bardsley, BA (**Drama & Theatre Studies*)
E L Blackett, BA (*English*)
F M Blair, BSc, MDes (*Designer in Residence*)
E L Blackett, BA (*English*),
F M Blair, BSc, MDes (*Designer in Residence*)
S V M Bramson, BA, MA, PGDip (*Music & *Singing*)
C Bridgman, BA (*English*)
N R Brown (*Graduate Assistant Chaplain*)
P J Bryant, BA (**Economics*)
H C Burt, BTh (*Theology & Philosophy*)
D A Calder, BA, MSc, PhD (*Theology & Philosophy*)
B J Callaghan, BA (*Classics*)
J B Callas, BSc (**Biology*)
T M Carter, BMus, LRSM, AMusTCL (*Band Director & *Woodwind*)
A Cassidy, MA (**French*)
J M Cave, MA (*French*)
C M Chanin-Cowley, BA (*English ESL*)
P L Corker-Marin, BA, MA (*Artist in Residence*)
S A Cowley, BA (**History of Art, Art*)
D R Dai (*Mandarin Language Assistant*)
I E Davies, MSc (*Chemistry, Sport*)
P A Deller, BA (**Art*)
A K Dewhurst, BSc (*Geography*)
C W Donoghue, BSc (**Phyics*)
N Dotor Cespedes, BSc (*Biology*)
G L Douch, BSc (*Food & Nutrition*)
P R Drummond, MA (*English*)
J D Duffield, BSc (*Mathematics*)
J R E Dyer, BSc, MSc, PhD (*Physics*)
D J Farnfield, BA (*Geography*)
W Feng (*Mandarin*)
D A Field, BA (*English ESL*)
S E Freestone, BSc (*Chemistry*)
S Fritsch (**German*)
J E Gall, BEd (*Biology, Sports Science & PE*)
B Gillespie, BEng, MSc (*Mathematics*)
J I Green, BSc (*Chemistry*)
J A Grindrod, BA (**Sports Science & PE*)
D C B Hallett (*Graduate Sports Assistant*)
P D Hall-Palmer, BA (**Design & Technology*)
J O Hand, BSc (*Mathematics*)
K H Hannavy, BSc, DPhil (*Chemistry*)

E W G Hatton, MA, Dip Law, MCCT (*Classics*)
C G Hawkins, MA (*English*)
O B Hawkins, BA (*Mathematics*)
A E Henocq, BSc (*Chemistry*)
H Hillier, BSc (*Teaching & Learning Skills Support*)
C Y Hitchcock, BA (*Economics*)
P A Hodgkinson, MA (**Music*)
S T Hudson, BA (*Drama & Theatre Studies*)
A W Horn (*German Language Assistant*)
E K Jaxon, BSc (*Physics*)
E Jones, MA (**Music*)
J P Keet, MA (*History*)
K Kendall, BSc (*Geography*)
J P Kimber (*Graduate Sports Assistant*)
R J Krebs, BA (**PSHE, Geography*)
M K Lacewing, BA, BPhil, PhD (*Theology & Philosophy*)
P J Laughton, BA (**Food & Nutrition*)
T R Leonard, MSci, PhD (**Chemistry*)
L M Lepage (*French Language Assistant*)
E J Marsden, BMus, MA (**Head of Strings*)
J M Marshall, BSc (*Food & Nutrition*)
N W Martin, BA, MSt, MCCT (**History*)
K McArtney, BA, MA, MBCS (**Computer Studies*)
N McGovern, BA (*Teaching & Learning Support Skills*)
F McKenna, BTech (*Computer Studies, Design & Technology*)
J D McNaught, BA (*Geography*)
D M McQue, BA (*Drama & Theatre Studies*)
D H Messenger, BA (**Director of Sport*)
A K Mester, MSc (*German*)
M L Moore, MA (*Librarian*)
D J Mulae, BSc (*Biology, General Science*)
Z M Munday, BA (*Drama & Theatre Studies*) [maternity leave]
S Murton, BA (*Theology & Philosophy*)
A J Naylor, BA (*Art*)
H N Nwandu, BSc (*Sports Science & Physical Education*)
C K O'Callaghan (*Graduate Sports Assistant*)
J O'Connor, MA (*Biology*)
P I O'Regan, BSc (*Physics*)
C E P Page, BSc (*PE & Sport*)
S R Patel, BA (*Classics*)
C Payne, MA (*Classics*)
D L Petford, BSc (**Geography*)
E M Purvis, BA (*English*)
P Radley, BSc (*Mathematics*)
L V Ransley, BA (*French*)
F H Reckless, BSc (*Mathematics*)
M Reid, BA (*French*)
W A Richards, BSc (*Physics*)
C N Rivas, LLBV (*Spanish Language Assistant*)
L B Russell, MA (*Biology*)
A Saha, MA, BA (*English*)
J P Salisbury, BSc (*Chemistry*)
T D Scrivener, MSc (*Economics*)
G R Seddon, BSc (*Sports Science & PE*)
R L Seddon, BA (*Geography*)
A E Self, BSc, MSc (*Mathematics*)
R D Sharkey, BSc (*Economics*)
D J Stamp, BEd (*Mathematics*)
I N Stannard, BD, AKC (**Theology & Philosophy*)
M S Stephens, BSc (*Mathematics*)
J Y Sterlini, BSc (*Director of Hockey*)
S E Stuart, MA (*History*)
R F Sutherland, BMus (*Music, Organist*)
E V Sword (*Graduate Sports Assistant*)

A G Taylor, BA (*Theology & Philosophy*)
R J Thompson, MM, BMus (*Music*)
L E A Thornton, MA (*History*)
S M Titchener, BA, MMus (*Music*)
C Villalba Garrido, MA (*Spanish*)
O M Walsh (*French*)
S W Walsh, MA (**English*)
C Ward, MA (*Teaching & Learning Skills Support*)
R L Watson, BSc (*Design & Technology*)
L Wegg, BSc (**Mathematics*)
G P Whitely, BA (*Art*)
L S Williams, BSc (**Teaching & Learning Support Skills*)
M P Wright, BN, MA (**Spanish*)
D Yan, MSc (**Mandarin*)

Clerk and Chief Operating Officer: N J Tesseyman
Head Teacher's P.A: K J Bernaldo de Quirós

Churcher's College

Ramshill, Petersfield, Hampshire GU31 4AS

Tel: 01730 263033
email: admissions@churcherscollege.com
website: www.churcherscollege.com
Twitter: @churchers1722
Facebook: @churchers1722
Instagram: @Churchers1722
LinkedIn: /churcher's-college

Motto: Limitless Potential

Churcher's College is an independent day school for girls and boys offering Nursery, Junior, Senior and Sixth Form education. With 950 pupils at the Senior School and 250 pupils at the Junior School (excluding the Nursery) of approximately equal numbers of boys and girls aged 3 to 18 years old, Churcher's College enjoys recognition as one of the most accomplished independent, co-educational day schools in the country.

The school is hosted on two campus sites in Hampshire enabling the Junior School and Nursery pupils to flourish in their own beautiful grounds in Liphook, whilst maintaining close links with the Senior School and Sixth Form located in nearby Petersfield. Both sites offer on-site playing fields and unrivalled facilities, providing the comfort and opportunities of an open, healthy environment.

Senior School Admissions. We welcome girls and boys at 11+ (Year 7) and 16+ (Sixth Form) at the Senior School. Entry at other points may be possible, depending on availability of places.

Our Admissions Team are always happy to help, so for any enquiries please contact admissions@churcherscollege .com.

Years 1–5: From the 11+ entry, pupils follow an academic programme comprising of Mathematics, English, Physics, Chemistry, Biology, Latin, Classical Civilisation, Geography, Religion & Philosophy, Music, Art & Design, Design & Technology, Computing, Drama and PE. In the First Year pupils study Spanish alongside their personal choice between French and German. In Year 2 an additional Modern European language (German or Spanish) is added to the programme. All pupils follow a broad curriculum and are not asked to specialise until they reach GCSE.

All pupils follow GCSE courses in Mathematics, English Language and Literature, a Modern Language, a Humanity and at least two additional optional subjects. All pupils begin the AQA GCSE 'Trilogy' course in the third year, which leads to two GCSE grades, but at the end of the Third Year, some pupils are offered the opportunity to transfer onto the Separate Sciences course, based on aptitude and ability.

Pupils are tested and examined regularly with formal assessment procedures each half term and each end of term.

The Sixth Form. The Sixth Form offers a wide variety of strong, widely-recognised A Level courses. The Churcher's Sixth Form curriculum allows you to build a portfolio of excellence, demonstrating to university admissions tutors and employers a depth and breadth of understanding in a wide range of fields.

Although precise programmes of study vary, based on the individual, most students will study three A Level qualifications, with Further Maths being taken as an additional fourth. In addition to this, a number of the most academically-inquisitive pupils will complete the Extended Project Qualification.

A Level course subjects include: Ancient History, Art, Biology, Business, Chemistry, Computing, Design & Technology, Drama, Economics, English Literature, French, Geography, German, History, Latin, Mathematics, Further Mathematics, Music, including the Advanced Musicians Course, Physics, Politics, Psychology, Religion & Philosophy, Spanish, Sports Science.

There is a fully equipped Sixth Form Centre, for both study and recreation, a floor of the Library dedicated to Sixth Form private study, an excellent Careers Library and full-time Careers Officer and specialist Sixth Form teaching rooms and ICT facilities.

Facilities. Churcher's academic facilities include impressive purpose-built teaching accommodation, a Music School, extensive D&T workshops, ICT suites, drama studios, art and design studios and a science block. Sports facilities include a swimming pool, sports halls and tennis courts, netball courts, rugby pitches, all-weather hockey pitches and cricket squares. Churcher's has the facilities and resources to support an extensive range of extracurricular activities.

Games and Other Activities. The major sports played are Rugby, Hockey, Netball and Cricket. There are also facilities for Swimming, Badminton, Basketball, Volleyball, Tennis, Athletics, Aerobics and Cross-country, to name but a few. The School has a strong CCF unit with Army, Air Force and Naval Sections, and a flourishing Duke of Edinburgh's Award programme. Other activities include Mountain Biking, Canoeing, Gliding, Climbing, Adventurous Training, Tycoon Enterprise Competitions, Dance, Karate, Fencing, Football, Sailing, Table Tennis, Basketball, Chess, Debating, Drama and Photography.

Music and drama are very strong in the school with highly acclaimed school productions and music performances plus opportunity to work on lighting and sound backstage. The school also has a significant range of orchestras, wind bands and choirs and ensembles.

Careers. Planning for a successful future is an essential part of education and Churcher's College strives to deliver an excellent Careers and Higher Education service for its students. The Head of Careers and Higher Education is available to students for advice and information at any stage of their school career. CEIAG is provided through the Head of Careers and HE, PSHE programme, annual Careers Convention, specialised careers testing and careers visits. HE information is delivered through interviews, talks, tutorials and opportunities to attend various external conventions and exhibitions. In addition, the Head of Careers attends parents' evenings at appropriate times in the academic year but is available throughout the year to pupils and parents.

Parents' Association. The Parents' Association's main purpose is to promote a positive school community, build an effective partnership between home and school and raise funds for various initiatives, events or needed school items. They meet once a term at school.

Fees per term (2021–2022). Senior School £5,480, Junior School £3,610–£3,855. Fees include charges for examination fees and textbooks, but exclude lunches and individual music lessons.

Charitable status. Churcher's College is a Registered Charity, number 1173833, and is a Charitable Company Limited by Guarantee, registered in England and Wales, company number 10813349.

Governing Body:
M J Gallagher, DipArch Hons, RIBA, MIOD, FIMgt (*Chairman*)
Mrs J Bloomer, LLB (*Vice-Chairman*)
S Barrett
S Beecham
Dr C J D Bush, MBSS, BSc, DFFP, MRCGP
J Franklin, BA, MA
Mrs C Herraman-Stowers
Mrs E Hynes-Laitt
W A Jones, MA
P Lawrence
M Leigh
R May, MIOD
Mrs D Moses, FCA
A Robinson, BSc, PGCE, MCGI
C Strick
R Oates, BA Hons, CFA

Clerk to the Governors: N Medley, MPhys Oxford

Headmaster: S H L Williams, BSc, MA

Deputy Heads:
Mrs S M J Dixon, BSc (*Staff and Co-curricular*)
C D P Jones, MA (*Pastoral*)
I G Knowles, BSc (*Academic*)

Head of Sixth Form: W Baker, BA, MSc, FRSA
Senior Teacher: Mrs J E Jamouneau, BEd, MSc (*Pastoral*)
Director of Studies: Mrs S L Cockerill, BSc
Academic Registrar: I M Crossman, BA

* *Head of Faculty*

Creative Arts Faculty:
*T. Strange MA, BA Goldsmiths
Miss R Humpries BA
Miss E Ecneilage BA
D Robertson, BA
Mrs G K Roff, BA

English Faculty:
*Ms C Unsworth-Hughes, MA, BA York, MEd Birmingham
Mrs P Daniel, BA (*Assistant Head of Nelson House*)

Mrs S Herrington, BA (*Assistant Senior Teacher, Head of Drake House*)
Mrs A P Jones, BA
Mrs P Priestley MA, BA Southampton
Mrs S-J Naym, BA
S Reeves, BA, MA
Mrs L Wade, BA

Humanities Faculty:
*J E Hegan, BA (*Head of Classics*)
Head of Business: R A West, BSc, PGDSM (*Deputy Head of Sixth Form – Co-curricular*)
Head of Economics: M J Hill, BA (*Assistant Senior Teacher, Deputy Head of Sixth Form, Politics, EPQ Coordinator, i/c Enterprise Education*)
Head of Geography: D J Nighy, BSc, FRGS
Head of History: Mrs H L Jolliffe, MA
Head of Politics: P Cheshire, MA, BA (*Assistant Head of Sixth Form*)
Head of Psychology: Dr G M Glasspool, BSc, MEd, EdD (*Assistant Senior Teacher, Head of Teaching & Learning*)
Head of Religion & Philosophy: T Ostersen, BA (*i/c CAS*)
W Baker, BA, MSc, FRSA (*Head of Sixth Form, Religion & Philosophy*)
Mrs A Clark, BSc (*Psychology*)
Ms A Bridger, MSc, BSc (*Psychology*)
Mrs S M J Dixon, BSc (*Deputy Head – Staff and Co-curricular, Geography*)
Miss P Elson-Cooper, BA (*Latin*)
S Gibbins, BA (*Classics*)
Mrs C Hadley, BSc (*Psychology*)
J S Harris, BSc (*Head of Nelson House, Geography*)
Mrs C L Hill, MA, BA (*History*)
Mrs L E Jenkinson-Brown, BA (*Classics*) [Maternity Leave]
C D P Jones, MA (*Deputy Head – Pastoral, History*)
J Lofthouse, BA, MMus, PGDip (*Assistant Head of Pupil Well-Being, Religion & Philosophy*)
J N McLearie, MA (*History*)
Mrs N L M Plewes, BSc (*Deputy Head of Sixth Form, Geography*)
B R Seal, BA, MBA (*Head of Collingwood House, Economics, History*)
Mrs H Butler, BA (*History*)
Mrs H Trent, BSc, MA (*Geography, Religion & Philosophy*)
Ms L K Yardley, BSc, MA (*Geography*)

Mathematics Faculty:
*Mrs T L Greenaway, BSc
J Daniel, BSc (*Physical Education, Assistant Head of Drake House, i/c First Challenge*)
Miss A Dickson, BSc
Mrs L A Holmes, BSc, ACA
Dr N A Jackson, BSc, MSc, DPhil
Miss N Phillips, BSc
S Pyle, BSc
J Seaton, BA (*Head of Grenville House*)
Mrs L J Selby, BSc
G T Wilson, BSc
Mrs A Thomas, BSc
Miss R Blewett, BSc

Modern Languages Faculty:
*Mrs K A Shaw, BA (*French, German*)
Head of French: Mrs N Sparks, BA (*German*)

Head of German: Dr A S Broomfield, BA, MA, PhD (*French*)
Head of Spanish: Mrs A-M Giffin, BA (*French*)
I M Crossman, BA (*Academic Registrar, French, German*)
V J Leysen, BA, MA (*French, Spanish*)
Mrs C H Mann, BA (*French, Spanish*)
Mrs M L Robertson, BEng (*Spanish*)
H A Sutherland, BA (*French, Spanish*)

Performing Arts Faculty:
*Mrs H J Purchase, BA, LTCL (*Director of Music*)
Head of Drama: Miss S Carty, BA, MA
P L Cree, BA (*Assistant Director of Music – Academic*)
J James, BA (*Assistant Director of Music – Contemporary*)
Miss E Magennis, BA (*Drama*)
Mrs R Northey, BA (*Drama*)
F Wickham, BA (*Music*)

Science Faculty:
Head of Faculty/Biology: Ms M J Westwood, BSc
Head of Chemistry: D J Dunster, MA
Head of Physics: M C Kelly, BSc
Mrs L Barton, BSc (*Chemistry*)
J Chen, BSc (*Chemistry*)
Mrs S L Cockerill, BSc (*Director of Studies, Chemistry*)
Dr J Harris, BSc (*Biology*)
R M Hoe, BSc (*Assistant Senior Teacher – Well-being, Physics*)
Mrs J E Jamouneau, BEd, MSc (*Senior Teacher – Pastoral, Biology*)
I G Knowles, BSc (*Deputy Head – Academic, Biology*)
J M Lucraft, MA, MEng (*Physics*)
Mrs J B Millard, BSc, MSc, ARCS (*Senior Teacher – Staff, Biology*)
Dr F H Perry, MSc, PhD (*Biology*)
Mrs N M Rivett, BSc, (*Biology, Chemistry*)
Mrs E C Smith, BSc (*Springboard Coordinator, Chemistry*)
W J Statham, BSc (*Biology, Chemistry, PSHE Coordinator*)
R Calverd, MA Cambridge, BSc Durham (*Physics*)
Miss L Davison, BSc
Dr R G Whittle, MEng (*Physics, Chemistry, i/c STEAM*)
J G Yugin-Power, BSc (*Head of Rodney House, Chemistry*)
O Longcroft-Wheaton, BSc, PHD

Sports Faculty:
Director of Sport: Mrs L J A Taylor, BSc (*Coordinator of Community Partnerships and Outreach*)
T Blong, BA (*Head of Hockey*)
Mr B Skirving, BA (*Head of Rugby*)
Miss H Dart, BA
J Daniel, BSc (*Maths, Assistant Head of Drake House, i/c First Challenge*)
Mrs K Higgins, BA (*Assistant Head of Rodney, Head of Swimming*)
Mrs T A Jenkins (*Head of Tennis*)
K A Maguire, BA (*i/c Strength and Conditioning, ICT*)
R Maier (*Assistant Head of Grenville House, Head of Cricket*)
Miss A Sexton, BSc
Mrs L K Snowball, BSc (*Head of Sports Science, Fifth Year Pastoral Coordinator*)

Technology Faculty:
Head of Faculty/Computing & ICT: Mrs K D McCathie, BSc
Head of Design & Technology: S J Edington, BEd

Miss C A Evans, BA (*Design & Technology, Assistant Head of Collingwood House*)
K A Maguire, BA (*Computing & ICT*)
Miss S J Murrell, BA (*Design & Technology*)
A H Sangster, BSc (*Computing & ICT*)

Adventure Faculty:
*A P N Rowley, BSc (*Head of Adventurous Activities, CCF Contingent Commander*)
Mrs A Harris, MBA , BA (*Assistant Head of Adventurous Activities and CCF School Staff Instructor*)

Curriculum Support:
*Mrs R Saunders, BSc
Ms K Jarman, BSc
Mrs C Reyes, BSc

Head of Careers & Higher Education: Dr K Verney, BSc, BDS (*Assistant Head of Sixth Form*)

Librarians:
Mrs T D Greenall, BA (*Publications Officer*)
Mrs C Hewett, BA

Bursar: N Medley, MPhys Oxford

City of London Freemen's School

Ashtead Park, Ashtead, Surrey KT21 1ET

Tel: 01372 822400
email: admissions@freemens.org
website: www.freemens.org
Twitter: @HelloFreemens
Facebook: @HelloFreemens

Motto: *Domine dirige nos*

City of London Freemen's School is an independent co-educational day and boarding school which provides continuity of education for children aged 7 to 18. The School was founded in Brixton in 1854 by the Corporation of the City of London to provide 'a religious and virtuous education' for the orphaned children of Freemen of the City of London; Christian principles remain at the heart of its ethos, although the School is non-denominational. It is one of three schools governed and maintained by the City of London Corporation.

In 1926 the School moved to Ashtead Park, its present site and now educates approximately 900 girls and boys. Most of these pupils are day pupils, but the School remains firmly committed to the provision of boarding for a number of its pupils.

Alongside excellent academic results, our innovative enrichment programme is at the heart of our commitment to developing the whole person. We have the facilities, staff and grounds to ensure our students are happy, secure and fulfilled. We place particular emphasis on the individual and their needs, and in providing the opportunities to identify and develop their skills to flourish throughout their time at Freemen's, and beyond.

There are 900 pupils in the School, approximately equal numbers of boys and girls, including up to 30 female and 30 male boarders. The student population is split equally across the Junior and Senior sections of the School.

The School stands in 57 acres of playing fields and parkland between Epsom and Leatherhead with easy access to Heathrow and Gatwick – both of which are only 22 miles away – via the M25. Buildings include a central Georgian Mansion, a floodlit all-weather pitch and a Sports Hall complex. A multimillion-pound building programme in the 1990s saw the addition of an Art and Design Centre and a Science and Technology Centre. New teaching facilities for all subject Departments including Library and IT facilities were completed with the opening of the Haywood Centre in September 2000. A Studio Theatre was opened in October 2001, providing an auditorium for all productions, recitals, concerts and lecture facilities. The all-weather pitch has been replaced, bringing both up to modern national representative standards. A state-of-the-art music school, including a Steinway-D concert grand piano, and a co-educational boarding house for 60 pupils were completed and opened in 2014. An award-winning swimming pool was opened in 2017 and an ambitious refurbishment project on the Main House building, which houses a state-of-the-art Sixth Form Centre, was completed in 2021.

Junior School. Since September 1988 the Junior School has been accommodated in a new complex in Ashtead Park. This provides 20 classrooms for up to 400 pupils. The Junior School is fully integrated within the framework and policies of the whole school and other facilities include specialist rooms for Art and Design, Science, Music and ICT as well as an Assembly Hall and extended Library. *See Junior School entry in IAPS section.*

Organisation and Entry. The School is divided into two sections but is administered as a single unit. The Junior School has its own specially trained staff and its own self-contained building, but otherwise all staff teach throughout the School. Pupils seeking entry to the Junior School sit the School's own entrance examination at 7+ or 11+ (normally in November).

Pupils seeking entry to the Senior School take Common Entrance or the School's own entrance examination at 13+. Pupils may pre-test for entry in Year 6 or Year 7. Freemen's Junior School pupils may expect to transfer directly to the Senior School at 13+ without sitting further examinations.

Pupils seeking entry to the Sixth Form will be expected to be taking at least eight GCSEs and must meet the minimum academic entry requirements: an average GCSE point score of 5.5, with at least grade 5 in English and Mathematics and subject-specific grade requirements for the subjects they wish to study at A Level.

Curriculum. The first four years (Years 3 to 6) are largely taught by class teachers up to Key Stage 2 following the broad outlines of the National Curriculum. Up to the age of about 14, all pupils have substantially the same curriculum which comprises English, French/German/Spanish, Mathematics, Physics, Chemistry, Biology, History, Geography, Religious Education, Latin, Design Technology, Computing, Food Technology, Art, Music, PE and Games.

Thereafter, apart from a common core of English, French or German or Spanish, Mathematics and the three separate Sciences, GSCEs can be selected from subjects including Art and Design, Business Studies, Computer Science, Design Technology, Drama, Food Preparation and Nutrition, French, Geography, German, History, Latin, Music, Philosophy, Ethics and Religion and Spanish, so that most pupils will take 10 subjects. Physical Education and Personal, Social and Health Education are included in the curriculum at all levels and all age groups have an Enrichment afternoon.

Sixth Form courses include the following: Art, Biology, Business, Chemistry, Classical Civilisation, Computer Science, Design and Technology, Drama, Economics, English Literature, French, Further Mathematics, Geography, German, Politics, History, Mathematics, Music, Philosophy, Ethics and Religion, Physics, Psychology, Spanish and Sport Studies.

The Sixth Form curriculum is designed to ensure that Freemen's students are well prepared for university entry and future employment. The range of subjects available aims to allow all potential Sixth Formers to follow a programme that meets their interests, abilities and career aspirations. For each Sixth Form student, 3 pathways are offered through the Curriculum (from 2021):

- 4 A Levels to include Mathematics and Further Mathematics
- 3 A Levels + Extended Project Qualification + Free Minds
- 3 A Levels + Free Minds

This is complemented by enrichment mornings, a varied programme of games on Wednesday afternoons and a course of careers guidance and personal, social and health education.

The School has an excellent academic record. Recent GCSE results have been excellent, with 45% of students achieving the highest grade (9) and 89% of examinations awarded grades A*/A or equivalent (7–9). A Level results have been equally impressive with 49% of grades at the highest level (A*) and 95% of examinations awarded A*–B grades. Nearly all leavers go on to degree courses at universities or other higher education institutes. 2021 saw 67% of students receive an offer at a Russell Group university and 89% of students achieving their first choice or chosen insurance offer.

Each pupil is allocated to a House comprising a cross-section of boys and girls, both day and boarding, throughout the School. House teams compete in all forms of sport as well as music, drama and debating.

Games. Each pupil is treated as an individual and we give them the opportunity to forge their own path of physical activity to suit them. To do this we ensure our programme is broad, to enable pupils to try numerous sports, and give our pupils a choice of activity in Games for their latter years at the School, making our programme more relevant to each of our pupils.

Freemen's sports programme for Junior pupils includes swimming, football, rugby, hockey, netball, cricket, tennis and athletics. Pupils in Year 11 to Year 13 are given the option of selecting from fourteen different activities in Games each term. There are competitive fixtures in fencing, football, hockey, netball, rugby, swimming and squash as well as tennis, athletics and cricket in the summer term. We also compete in fixtures for cross country, fencing, indoor hockey, rugby sevens, squash, and swimming throughout the School.

There is a very wide choice of Co-curricular activities throughout the School. The Duke of Edinburgh's Award scheme is a very popular option in the Senior School. Students may also participate in the Army or RAF Sections of the Combined Cadet Force (CCF).

Fees per term (2021–2022). Junior School: £5,067–£5,629 (day); Senior School: £6,965 (day), £10,945 (weekly boarding), £12,121 (full boarding); Sixth Form: £7,175 (day), £11,155 (weekly boarding), £12,331 (full boarding).

Instrumental Music lessons: £257 per term. School lunches: £246–£274 per term

Scholarships and Bursaries. Freemen's Scholarships are awarded in recognition of excellence, achievement and potential in academic study or music. They carry considerable prestige for the award holder but are of limited financial value (up to 5% discount of the fees). The following Scholarships are available to both internal and external applicants:

- *11+ Academic Scholarships* Available to pupils seeking entry to Year 7. Following the 11+ entrance examinations and interviews (external candidates) or by invitation (internal candidates), a small selection of candidates will be invited to take the Freemen's Scholarship examinations.

- *13+ Academic Scholarships* Available to pupils seeking entry to Year 9. Following the 13+ entrance examinations and interviews (external candidates) or by invitation (internal candidates), a small selection of candidates will be invited to take the Freemen's Scholarship examinations.

- *16+ Academic Scholarships* Available to pupils seeking entry to the Sixth Form. Candidates must meet our Sixth Form entry requirements and will, in addition, sit examination papers in Critical Thinking and General Knowledge and an extended writing task. Subject to satisfactory performance in the Scholarship examinations, selected candidates will be invited to attend an interview with the Headmaster.

- *11+ Music Scholarships* Applicants who wish to audition for a Music Scholarship should be playing at Grade 3 standard. It is desirable for a candidate to offer a second instrument/voice. Candidates must meet the academic requirements for entry to the School and will be invited to an audition and interview with the Director of Music.

- *13+ Music Scholarships* Applicants who wish to audition for a Music Scholarship should be playing at Grade 5 standard. It is desirable for a candidate to offer a second instrument/voice. Candidates must meet the academic requirements for entry to the School and will be invited to an audition and interview with the Director of Music.

- *16+ (Sixth Form) Music Scholarships* Applicants who wish to audition for a Music Scholarship should be playing at Grade 7 standard. It is desirable for a candidate to offer a second instrument/voice. Candidates must meet the academic requirements for entry to the School and will be invited to an audition and interview with the Director of Music.

Freemen's is committed to support academically able students, whose parents many not otherwise be able to afford the full cost of fees. Bursaries of up to 100% of the fees are available to pupils entering the School at 7+, 11+, 13+ and 16+. Bursaries are awarded based on performance in the entrance examinations and are subject to financial means-testing and annual review.

The Bhargava Award, a means-tested 'Women in STEM' initiative award is available to girls applying for entry into the Sixth Form to study Mathematics at A Level and seeking to study STEM subjects at university. The award, made possible by a generous legacy, is open to girls living within 15 miles of the School who are currently attending a maintained sector school or academy. The Bhargava Award provides financial support to cover tuition fees and extras such as transport, uniform and school trips.

Board of Governors:
Philip Woodhouse, Deputy (*Chairman*)
Michael Hudson (*Deputy Chairman*)
Roger Chadwick, OBE, Deputy
John Bennett
Kevin Everett, Deputy
Nicholas Goddard
Michael Hudson
Bronek Masojada (*Alderman*)
Andrew McMillan
Tracy Graham
Graham Packham
Elizabeth Rogula, Deputy
Councillor Chris Townsend
Gillian Yarrow
Nicholas Bensted-Smith (*ex-officio member*)
Tim Levene (*ex-officio member*)
Robert Howard (*Alderman*)

Clerk to the Governors: Polly Dunn

Headmaster: Mr Roland Martin

Deputy Head: Mr Stuart Bachelor
Academic Deputy Head: Mr Paul Bridges
Head of Sixth Form: Mrs Sarah Stewart
Head of Upper School & Co-Curricular: Mrs Jemima Edney
Head of Junior School: Mr Matthew Robinson
Bursar: Mrs Joanne Moore
Director of External Relations: Mr Jason Harrison-Miles
Director of Teaching, Learning and Innovation: Mr James Felgate
Head of Boarding: Mr Alan Auld
Deputy Head of Boarding: Miss Georgina Farrington
Assistant Head (Junior School): Mrs Louise Jowitt
Assistant Head (Sixth Form): Mr Adrian Parkin
Head of Year 9: Mr Andrew McEwan
Head of Year 10: Mr Peter McKee
Head of Year 11: Mrs Georgia Middlehurst
Head of Year 12: Mr Daniel Moran
Head of Year 13: Mrs Justine Marvin

* Head of Department

English:
*Mr Markus Klinge
Mr Christopher Bloomer
Mrs Sarah Stewart
Miss Emma Newton
Mr Paul Carabine
Mrs Kathryn de Villiers
Ms Fiona Moncur (*KS2 Coordinator*)
Miss Ashleigh Callow (*EAL Teacher*)
Mr Andrew McEwan

Mathematics:
*Mr Ewan Bramhall
Mrs Marie Cast
Mrs Zara Field
Mrs Stella Hippolyte
Mrs Louise Sharpe
Mrs Cecilia Inns
Mrs Louise Jowitt (*KS2 Coordinator*)

Mr Tom Marsden
Mr Adrian Parkin
Mr Kenneth Rose
Mrs Elizabeth Rowlands
Mr David Murray

Modern Languages:
*Mrs Sarah Hankin

French and German:
*Mrs Sarah Hankin
Mrs Linda Headon
Mrs Julia Rosin (*KS2 Coordinator*)
Miss Lorna Vickers
Miss Rebecca Willis

Spanish:
*Mrs Christina Salisbury
Miss Rebecca Willis
Mrs Maria Willis-Jones
Ms Carol Creevey

Classics:
*Mr Alan Chadwick
Mrs Ida Ashworth
Mr William Ash
Mrs Rosemary Holmes

Science:
Mrs Michelle Restall (*KS2 Coordinator*)

Biology:
*Mr John Graham
Mrs Judith Vatcher
Mrs Raylene Fox
Mrs Susan Meek

Chemistry:
*Dr Sarah Pinniger
Mrs Torna Burton
Mr Jonathan Davies
Ms Alex Mistry
Mr Daniel Moran

Physics:
*Mr James Hallam
Mrs Helen Irwin
Mr Mark Newcome
Mr Brandon O'Donnell
Mrs Penni Thornton

Technology, Electronics and Design:
*Mr Steve Sarsfield
Mr James Fish (*KS2 Coordinator*)
Mr Max Hicks

Food Technology:
*Mrs Tina Judge

Art & Design:
*Mrs Elizabeth Bowey
Mrs Rebecca Houseman
Ms Ginny Humphreys
Mrs Vanessa Symonds (*KS2 Coordinator*)
Mrs Katie Moilliet

Economics and Business:
*Mrs Justine Marvin
Mr Stuart Davis
Mrs Kate Jepson-Taylor

Computer Science and Information Technology:
*Mr Oliver James

Drama:
*Mrs Joanne McCullagh
Miss Sarah Marr
Mr Jeremy Colton

Enrichment:
*Mr Andrew Weston
Miss Harriet Pennington (*EPQ Coordinator*)

PSHE:
*Mrs Philippa Whiteley

Careers:
Head of Sixth Form Careers: Miss Rebecca Willis
Assistant Careers Advisor: Miss Lorna Vickers

Mrs Janet Wilby-King (*KS2 Coordinator*)

Geography:
*Mrs Ofelia Bueno-Lopez
Mrs Georgia Middlehurst
Mrs Harriet Pennington
Mrs Emma Smith (*KS2 Coordinator*)

History and Politics:
*Mr Andrew Weston
Mrs Rosemary Holmes
Mrs Elizabeth Joss (*KS2 Coordinator*)
Miss Georgina Farrington
Miss Claire Robinson

Music:
*Mrs Natalka Eaglestone
Mrs Ida Ashworth
Mrs Sarah Gillespie (*KS2 Coordinator*)

Philosophy and Religion:
*Mr Tim Wright
Miss Nicola Bax
Mr Andrew Illingworth
Mrs Louise Jowitt
Mrs Catherine Williams (*KS2 Coordinator*)

Psychology:
*Miss Joanna Vinall
Mrs Joanna Wright

PE and Games:
*Mr Tim Deakin
Miss Hannah McLaughlin
Mrs Rachel Keightley
Mrs Louise Shaill
Mr Jamie Shore-Nye
Mr Peter McKee
Mr Jon Moore
Miss Amy Edwards

Physical Education GCSE/A Level:
Mr James Felgate
Mr Jon Moore
Mrs Louise Shaill

Coaches:
Cricket: Mr Neil Stewart
Netball: Mrs Alison Bennett
Netball: Mrs Natalie Marchant
Tennis: Mr John Thistlethwaite
Rugby: Mr Mike Cudmore
Rugby: Mr Nick Harris
Squash: Mr Paul Steward

Learning Support:
Learning Support Manager: Mr Andrew Illingworth
Learning Support Coordinator (*Junior School*): Ms Fiona Moncur
Mr Mark Newcome

Junior School

Year 3 (Form 1):
Head of Year: Mrs Janet Wilby-King
Mrs Catherine Williams
Mrs Michelle Restall
Mrs Venssa Ielpi
Miss Megan Warwick

Year 4 (L2):
Head of Year: Mrs Sarah Gillespie
Mrs Jenny Cooper
Mr Richard Metcalfe
Mrs Anna Jansen
Miss Anna Golitzin

Year 5 (U2):
Head of Year: Mrs Vanessa Symonds
Mrs Fiona Ford
Mr Simon Davies

Year 6 (L3):
Head of Year: Mrs Emma Smith

Duke of Edinburgh's Award:
DofE Senior Coordinator: Revd Jon Prior

Boarding House:
Head of Boarding: Mr Alan Auld
Deputy Head of Boarding: Miss Georgina Farrington
Boarding House Tutors:
Mr Andrew McEwan; Mr Tom Marsden; Mrs Jemima Edney

Combined Cadet Force:
CCF School Staff Instructor: Mr Alexander Truelove
Mr Daniel Moran

Medical Centre:
School Nurse Managers: Mrs Kate Barron; Mrs Elizabeth Holmden
School Nurses: Mrs Diana Carter; Mrs Priscilla Mills

Non-Teaching Staff:
Bursar: Mrs Joanne Moore
Executive Assistant to the Headmaster: Mrs Kathy Hurst
HR Manager: Mrs Anna Atkins
HR Officer: Miss Helen Lambert
Finance Manager: Mrs Kathleen Sparrowhawk
Finance Officers: Mrs Debbie Widmer (*Fees*); Mrs Jane Arnett (*Creditors*); Mrs Suzanne Wilding (*Lettings Administrator/Bursary Assistant*)
Director of External Relations: Mr Jason Harrison-Miles
Head of Admissions: Ms Debbie Bellenger
Head of Communications: Mrs Sarah Sergeant
Marketing and Communications Officer: Miss Gemma Roberts
Admissions Officers: Mrs Cheryl Turnbull; Mrs Winggee Lau (*International*)
Community and Partnerships Officer: Mrs Catherine Bennett

Mr Martin Valkenburg
Miss Rosalie Broccardo

Year 7 (U3):
Head of Year: Mr Haydon Jones
Mr Tom Marsden
Mrs Philippa Whiteley
Mr Max Hicks
Mrs Louise Sharpe
Mr James Fish
Mrs Louise Shaill
Miss Sarah Marr

Year 8 (L4):
Head of Year: Mrs Fiona Moncur
Mr Oliver James
Mrs Zara Field
Mr Paul Carabine
Mr Jeremy Colton
Mr Jamie Shore-Nye
Mrs Emily Johnson
Mr Teddy Brooks

Senior Management Secretariat Team Leader: Mrs Amanda Moss

Senior School Secretary: Mrs Lucy Ryckaert

Senior School Receptionist/Administrator: Mrs Karen Shelton

PA to Head of Junior School: Mrs Gillian Anklesaria

Music Administrator: Mrs Samantha Grover

Sports Administrator: Mrs Tracey Clarke

Examinations Officer: Mrs Nicketa Williams

Senior Librarian: Mrs Sue Dawes

Assistant Librarians: Mrs Ashley Bate; Ms Charlotte Bellsham-Revell

Technicians:

Mrs Joanna Wojcik (*Senior Technician Physics*)

Mrs Mary Marrett (*Senior Technician Chemistry*)

Mrs Jane Dallyn (*Science, Junior School*)

Mr Lewis Grover (*Biology & Physics*)

Mrs Emma Eshelby (*Chemistry*)

Ms Emma Hughes-Phillips (*Art & Design*)

Miss Zoe Halliday (*Art & Design*)

Mrs Sarah Baxter (*Food Technology*)

Mr Chris Ruby (*Facilities, Theatre Facilities*)

Mr David Holloway (*Technologies*)

Director of Digital Services: Mr Paul Hykin

Manager Infrastructure and Projects: Mr Adam Cohen

Data Manager: Mr Anthony Richmond

Data Officer: Mrs Julia Donovan

Media Services Co-ordinator: Mr Matthew Skilton

IT Support Technician: Mr Jonah Williams

ICT Apprentice: Mr George Cowdry

ICT Support Co-ordinator: Mr Giles Tilley

Head of Operations: Mr Edward Kennedy

Head of Grounds & Gardens: Mr Gary Marshall

Gardeners/Groundspersons: Mr Craig Morgan; Mr Matthew Lunn

Facilities Manager: Mr Gyorgy Simon

Facilities Supervisor: Mr Simon Phelan

Maintenance Assistants: Mr Ian Foster; Mr Carl Gallagher

Chaplain: Revd Jonathan Prior

Visiting Music Teachers:

Ms Nicola Berg (*Singing*)

Mrs Alice Bishop (*Singing*)

Mrs Victoria Brockless (*Violin, Viola*)

Miss Ruth Chappell (*Flute*)

Mrs Hilary Dilnot (*Piano*)

Mr David Eaglestone (*Trombone, Tuba, French Horn*)

Ms Jennifer Janse (*Cello, Double Bass*)

Ms Catherine McKay-Upcott (*Singing*)

Ms Elenlucia Pappalardo (*Piano*)

Mr Tim Peake (*Piano*)

Mr Tim Peters (*Music Production and DJ*)

Miss Holly Redshaw (*Bassoon*)

Mr Richard Russell (*Clarinet*)

Mr Paul Smith (*Saxophone, Clarinet, Oboe, Piano*)

Miss Ruth Stockdale (*Flute*)

Mr Simon Sturgeon-Clegg (*Trumpet, Trombone, Euphonium*)

Mr Joseph Sweeney (*Percussion*)

Mr John Wallace (*Guitar*)

City of London School

Queen Victoria Street, London EC4V 3AL

Tel:	020 3680 6300
email:	admissions@cityoflondonschool.org.uk
	reception@cityoflondonschool.org.uk
website:	www.cityoflondonschool.org.uk
Twitter:	@CityofLdnSchool
Facebook:	@CityofLondonSchool

City of London School understands that for pupils to thrive, they must be happy. It is why we cherish individuality, shun stereotypes, and encourage every pupil to be the very best version of themselves. With a vibrant, diverse, multicultural city on our doorstep, we draw strength from difference, recognising that diverse perspectives can help answer big questions.

We aspire to be a school that fully prepares respectful, optimistic and inquisitive boys for the rapidly changing demands of the twenty-first century. We aim always to provide an education in the broadest sense, combining academic excellence with exceptional pastoral care, framed by an outward-looking and forward-thinking approach. We also strive to make that education available to as many talented boys as possible, including through transformational bursaries for those who may not otherwise be able to afford the fees.

We occupy a unique river side location in the heart of the capital. We trace our origins to a bequest left by John Carpenter (Town Clerk of the City of London) in 1442 for the education of 'four poor boys'. The City of London Corporation was authorised by an Act of Parliament in 1834 to use this and other endowments to establish and maintain a School for boys. The current School lies in the heart of the City next to the Millennium Bridge, with St Paul's Cathedral to the north and the Globe Theatre and Tate Modern across the Thames to the south. A new Library was added in 2016 and a new on-site fitness centre will be built in 2022. Our sister school, the City of London School for Girls (CLSG) is located a short walk away.

Admissions. Pupils are admitted aged 10, 11 and 13 (as on 1 September of year of entry), on the results of the School's own entrance examinations held each year. Note that pupils applying for entry at age 13 are examined when they are in Year 6. Those admitted at 16 into the Sixth Form are selected by test and interview in the previous November. Applicants must register for examinations using the School's online system.

Fees per term (2021–2022). £6,665.

Scholarships. Academic, Music and Sports Scholarships are awarded annually.

Bursaries. We offer transformational bursaries, up to the value of full fees, to assist families of academically very bright pupils, who otherwise could not access private education. Candidates for entry to the School may also apply to be a chorister in the Choir of Her Majesty's Chapel Royal, St James's Palace for which they will receive a Choral Bursary. Potential choristers may also take voice auditions and academic tests in Year 4; the School also has a number of choristers who sing in the Temple Church Choir.

Curriculum. All pupils follow the same broad and engaging curriculum up to and including the Third Form

(Year 9). In the Third Form pupils spend eight afternoons throughout the year exploring the world around them on educational visits to institutions and places of interest in and around the City. Latin, French and Mandarin are started by all in the First Form. Choices are made from Latin, Latin/ Greek, Classical Civilisation, Spanish, German or Mandarin, along with at least one from Music, Drama, Art or an exciting new bespoke course on Design, Computing & Robotics. Fourth and Fifth Form pupils take a core of English, Mathematics, three Sciences, at least one Modern Foreign Language (which can include Russian), at least one humanity (History, Geography, R&P, Classical Civilisation) and choose two other subjects from a wide range of subjects available for study to GCSE/IGCSE. In the Sixth Form, pupils study either four A level subjects, or three and an EPQ (Extended Project Qualification). Virtually all pupils leaving the Sixth Form proceed to their first or second choice of Russell Group University, with a large number applying successfully overseas.

Games. Our 20 acres of playing fields, at Grove Park in south-east London, offer excellent facilities for football, cricket, athletics, and tennis. Sporting facilities on the School site include an astroturf pitch, sports hall, a gymnasium with conditioning room and a 25-metre swimming pool. A newly expanded and refurbished fitness area will open by September 2022.

School Societies. There is a large number of School clubs and societies, catering for a very wide range of interests, and a Freshers' Fair is held early each year to allow societies to promote themselves. Every opportunity is taken to benefit from the School's central position by participation in the cultural and educational life of London, and of the City in particular. We have a strong musical tradition; tuition is available in a large range of instruments (all First Form (Year 7) pupils are given the opportunity to be taught a musical instrument as part of the normal curriculum), and membership of the School choirs and orchestras is encouraged. The School also has a fully-equipped Theatre and a Drama Studio. There is a large CCF Contingent run jointly with CLSG which pupils may join from the age of 13, with Army, Navy and RAF Sections. There is also a successful Community Service programme. Many pupils also take part in the Duke of Edinburgh's Award scheme.

Alumni, known as Old Citizens, enjoy a programme of year reunions careers and networking events throughout the year and receive regular e-news and an annual alumni magazine. Members of this vibrant alumni community also deliver varied talks to pupils throughout the year and mentoring support to Sixth Formers contemplating university and career choices.

Chairman of Governors: Mr T Levene

Head: A R Bird, MA, MSc

Senior Deputy Head: M Wardrop, M Chem
Deputy Head (*Pastoral*): Mrs A K Martineau, MA
Deputy Head (*Co-Curricular & Operations*): A J V McBroom, BA
Deputy Head (*Teaching & Innovation*): A Zivanic, BA, MA
Director of Studies & Senior Mistress: Miss N H Murphy, BA
Director of Admissions & Communications: P S Marshall, MA
Director of Development: Ms K Ostermann, BA
Head of Sixth Form: C R Webb, BSc

Head of Middle School: B S Savage, BA
Head of Lower School: P P Sanders, MA, MEd
Bursar: A Flanaghan

Head of Senior Sixth Form: M N Everard-Pennell, MChem, PhD
Head of Junior Sixth Form: Ms T R Tooze, BA
Assistant Head of Sixth Form: T L Robinson, BSc
Head of Fifth Form: Ms K A Saunt, BA
Head of Fourth Form: T H White, BA, MA
Head of Third Form: J E McArdle, BA
Assistant Head of Third Form: F J Isaac, BA
Head of Second Form: Miss F G Eason, BA
Head of First Form: B A Medlock, BA
Head of Old Grammar: Miss E L Pollock, MSc, MEd

* *Head of Department*

Art & Design:
*S Beresford-Zahra, BA
Miss A E Gill, BA
Miss B Easton, BA
S R Lewington, Master Craftsman LCGI
P P Sanders, MA, MEd

Classics:
*S A Swann, BA, MPhil
Miss C L Rose, BA
Miss Z L Connolly, MA
J E Pile, BA
J E McArdle, MA
Ms V Herrenschmidt, BA
Mrs C Knight, BSc (*Junior Humanities*)

Drama:
*Miss S H Dobson, BA
Mr M C Biltcliffe, BA
Miss J R Martin, BA

Economics:
*D P Rey, BSc, MA
M Wacey, BSc
C R Webb, BSc

English:
*R J Bryant, BA
J Norman, MA
Miss E J Green, BA
Mrs H Sebban, BA
Ms T Tooze, BA
Ms L E Hines, BA
F J Isaac, BA
Ms I L Taylor, MA

Geography:
*J D Innes, MA,
P S Marshall, MA
O J Ignotus, BA
Ms A D Edkins, BA
Mrs C Knight, BSc (*Junior Humanities*)

History and Politics:
*A J Bracken, BA, MA
Miss N H Murphy, BA
A J V McBroom, BA
Ms K A Saunt, BA
S J Brown, BA, MA
P J Wright, BA

Ms D C Patel, MA, PhD
Ms S H Badr, BA
Mrs C Knight, BSc (*Junior Humanities*)

Information Technology:
*Mrs S L Ralph, BA
M Wells-Gray, BA, MA

Mathematics:
*B P Broadhurst, MSc
Miss C A Hudson, BSc
S S Fernandes, BSc, MA
Mrs C S Musgrove, MA
Miss J C L Mesure, MA
Miss E L McCallan, MA
S J Dugdale, BSc, PhD
T G Betchley, BSc, MA
Miss S Golleck, PhD, MPhil
Miss Y Feng, BSc, MPhil
Ms E C Russell, BA
S Mozakka, BA
Mrs E M Betchley, BSc, MSc, MA

Modern Languages:
*R Edmundson, MA
Miss V Vincent, MA
P R Eteson, BA (*French)
Ms M J Ciechanowicz, MA
B Pollard, MA (*German)
Miss F G Easton, BA
T H White, BA, MA
Mrs E Bunnage, BA, MA (*Mandarin)
A M Thomson, BA
Miss B L Manion, MA
Ms A Waugh, BA
T A Pandolfino, BA, MA
B S Savage, BA

Music:
*R Quesnel, MA
Miss J E Jones, BA
A J Crockatt, BA, BMus
J McHardy, BMus (**Director of Music*, *Chapel Royal*)

Physical Education:
*N F Cornwell, BEd
B J Silcock, BPE

J P Santry, BEng
S E Robinson, BA
B A Medlock, BSc
S Dorrington, BSc

Religion & Philosophy
*J M Fenton, MA
Mrs A Giannorou, BSc,
  BA, MPhil
Ms A K Martineau, MA
J Findlay, MSc
Ms K E Weare, MA, MA
Mrs C Knight, BSc (*Junior
  Humanities*)

Science:
Mrs P C McCarthy, BSc
  (*Chemistry, *Science*)
A A Wood, MSci
  (*Physics*)
A Zivanic, BA, MA
  (*Biology*)

R Mackrell, BSc
G W Dawson, BSc
K P Rogers, MChem
Mrs K L Pattison, BSc,
  PhD
G H Browne, BA, BSc
M N Everard-Pennell,
  MChem, PhD
R J Dharamshi, BA
T L Robinson, BSc
Miss H Stanley, BSc
Miss E L Pollock, BSc,
  MEd
S L Clifford, BSc
S A Hall, BSc
Ms O R Babb, BSc (*Junior
  Science*)
N A Boney, BSc
N J Lowe, MEng
M Wardrop, MChem

There are Visiting Music Teachers for Bassoon, Cello, Double Bass, French Horn, Flute, Guitar, Jazz, Oboe, Organ, Percussion, Piano, Saxophone, Singing, Trombone, Trumpet, Tuba, Viola, Violin.

Learning Support:
*Ms A C DiStefano, BAH, BEd
Mrs A J Fountaine, MSci, MA, Dip RSA
M C Biltcliffe, BA
Mrs K J Ireland, BA
Ms M Bousiopoulou, BA

Library:
*D A Rose, BA, Dip Lib, ALA
Ms J Grantham, MA
Miss R Stocks, BA
M Evans
Mrs R Howley
Ms K Symonds (*Archivist*)
Mr T J Osborne (*Bookshop Manager*)

Admissions Registrar: Mrs V J Haley, LLB

Director of Partnerships: Ms L E Hines, BA

City of London School for Girls

St Giles' Terrace, Barbican, London EC2Y 8BB

Tel: 020 7847 5500
email: info@clsg.org.uk
website: www.clsg.org.uk
Twitter: @clsggirls
Facebook: @clsggirls
Instagram: @cityoflondonschoolforgirls
LinkedIn: /company/city-of-london-school-for-girls

Motto: *Domine Dirige Nos*

City of London School for Girls is an academically selective, non-denominational, independent day school for girls aged 7–18. There is an infectious vibrancy and energy at "City". Its distinctive location in the Barbican Centre provides immediate access to the wealth of London's educational and cultural opportunities, while the teaching

staff and girls imbue the place with a sense of happiness, purpose, enthusiasm and fulfilment.

The School Course includes English language and literature, history, geography, religion, philosophy and ethics, Latin, Greek, French, German, Spanish, mathematics, biology, chemistry, physics, economics and politics, art, music, physical education, design and technology, theatre studies and Chinese.

Pupils are prepared for GCSE and A Level Examinations offered by Edexcel, OCR, CIE, AQA and WJEC. They are also prepared for entrance to Oxford, Cambridge and other Universities. Sixth form courses are designed to meet the needs of students wishing to proceed to other forms of specialised training.

Facilities are provided for outdoor and indoor games and the school has its own indoor swimming pool and an all-weather sports pitch. Co-curricular activities before school, in the lunch hour or at the end of afternoon school include debating, football, drama, science, technology, fencing, netball, gymnastics, swimming, tennis, climbing and classes in Chinese, as well as many more. Guest speakers are frequently invited to the school, especially in the sixth form. There are also junior and senior choirs, a madrigal group, barbershop group, junior and senior orchestras, wind ensemble, chamber orchestra and a swing band. Lunch hour music recitals, with visiting professional players, are encouraged. Many pupils take the Duke of Edinburgh's Award scheme at bronze, silver and gold level.

Admission. Main entry points to the school are at 7, 11 and 16 years of age. For other entry points, vacancies are only occasional. The initial entrance assessments for 7+, 11+ and 16+ entry are held in the autumn term.

Applications for all applicable entry points open in spring the year before entry. Specific deadlines can be found on the website.

Scholarships and Bursaries. The school offers art, music, sport and drama scholarships, and means-tested bursaries, for entry at 11+ and 16+.

Fees per term (2021–2022). £6,888. Optional extras: individual music lessons: £307 (ten lessons) per term

School Governors:
Chairman: Nicholas Bensted-Smith, JP
Deputy Chairman: Peter Bennett

Headmistress: **Mrs Jenny Brown**, MA Oxon

Senior Deputy Head (Staff and Special Projects): Justine
  Venditti, BEng Swansea

Deputy Head (Academic): Neil Codd, BA Hons Oxon
Deputy Head (Pastoral): Susannah Gilham, BA Oxon
Deputy Head (Partnerships and Co-Curricular): Rosie
  Lockyear, BA Hons Cantab

Bursar: John Hall, MA Cantab, MInstRE, MBPsS

*Assistant Head Teaching, Learning and Research &
  Development*: Ben Chappell, BA Loughborough, MA
  London
Assistant Head of Diversity & Inclusion: Soumia Arif, BA
  London

Head of Sixth Form: Georgie Hankinson, BSc Staffordshire
Head of Senior School: Madeleine Davis, MA Sheffield
Head of Lower School: Elly Nicoll, MA Oxon, MA London
  [Maternity Leave]

Acting Head of Lower School: Sophie Colbourne, BA,
  PGCE London
Head of Prep School: Rachel Thompson, BA Dunelm
Assistant Head of Prep School: Caroline Wright, BA
  Manchester, PGCE Institute of Education London

An up-to-date list of staff can be found on the school website. www.clsg.org.uk/about-us/our-staff

Clifton College

Guthrie Road, Clifton, Bristol BS8 3EZ

Tel: 0117 315 7110
email: admissions@cliftoncollege.com
           prepadmissions@cliftoncollege.com
website: www.cliftoncollege.com
Twitter: @Clifton_College
Facebook: @CliftonCollegeUK
Instagram: @CliftonCollegeUK
LinkedIn: /Clifton-College

Motto: *Spiritus intus alit*

Clifton College is a top co-educational boarding and day
school for 0–18, founded in 1862 and incorporated by Royal
Charter in 1877. The school is nestled in the heart of Clifton,
and takes advantage of the many cultural and educational
activities on offer in the modern and vibrant city of Bristol,
with plenty of countryside nearby.

Admission. Pupils are normally admitted in September,
between the ages of 13 and 14. Most are required to pass the
Common Entrance examination, which can be taken at their
Preparatory Schools. Each pupil is assessed by considering
their academic potential, along with their educational
background and profile, including conduct and attitude.
Their current school's recommendation is an important part
of this process. For an applicant resident overseas, the entry
requirements will be appropriate to previous educational
experience. Such pupils for entry into Years 9, 10 and 11
will normally be asked to sit UKISET entry tests, focusing
on aptitude.

Interested families should get in touch with the College's
admissions team on 0117 3157 110 or admissions
@cliftoncollege.com who will then provide an application
form to complete. Once the non-refundable registration fee
has been paid, the arrangement of interviews and
appropriate entry tests will begin.

Houses. Pupils are assigned a House when they join the
College, where they will meet their Tutors, spend time with
their peers and benefit from a supervised environment in
which they can meet, work or relax, providing a true home
away from home. Each House is led by a Housemaster/
Housemistress and their spouse, along with Tutors, Matrons
and the occasional House dog.

Day Pupils and Day Boarders. There are four boarding
Houses for boys; Moberly's, Wiseman's, School House and
Watson's House and three Houses for girls; Hallward's,
Oakley's and Worcester. There are a further three day
Houses for boys, and two for day girls, these have the same
status as Boarding Houses and day pupils are encouraged to
take part in the abundant activities available as an active
member of their House.

Catering. In-house catering is managed by our own
experienced caterers, with pupils and staff enjoying a wide
variety of food at lunchtime. Meals are eaten in the main
dining hall, this includes supper for Boarders, and day pupils
if prearranged.

Fees per term (2021–2022). Years 9–13: Boarders
£12,875–£13,270; Flexi Boarders (4 nights) £11,605–
£11,930; Day Pupils £8,635–£8,775. Sixth Form Joiners
(from other schools): Boarders £14,065; Day Boarders (4
nights) £12,210; Day Pupils £9,095.

Academic structure. While the College strongly
believes a first-rate education is not something which can be
measured in league tables alone, a strong emphasis is placed
on academic standards. It is these rigorous standards that
enable Clifton pupils to go on to pursue the future they
choose, whether that is attending Oxbridge or a Russell
Group university, or diving straight into the world of
industry or commerce.

Pupils enter the Upper school in Year 9 and follow a
general course for their first year, with GCSEs chosen at the
end of Year 9.

The majority of pupils then move up to the Sixth Form
and typically choose four A Level subjects in the Lower
Sixth, before narrowing this to three in the Upper Sixth. A
great many combinations of subjects are available, including
a number of BTEC Level 3 qualifications.

Service. The Outdoor Education Department at Clifton
College facilitates and develops teamwork, leadership,
confidence and self-esteem. A programme of various
outdoor activities are available that include; geocaching,
archery, low ropes, initiative tasks, bouldering, indoor
climbing, first aid and mountain biking. As well as the
weekly programme, pupils also participate in 2 field days
where they get to work as a team in height based and water
based activities. Kayaking and Canoeing, the Duke of
Edinburgh Award, Overseas Expeditions, Winter
Mountaineering and Wilderness and Survival Skills are also
encouraged.

Combined Cadet Force (CCF) is offered at the College,
and provides a disciplined youth organisation, enabling
pupils to develop powers of leadership. Girls and boys may
join any of the three sections: Army, Royal Navy and Royal
Air Force. The Army concentrates on the self-discipline of
field tactics; the Navy provides the opportunity to engage in
a wide range of maritime activities, using the College's own
boats located in the nearby docks; whilst the RAF takes full
advantage of the availability of local air experience flights.

There is a certain amount of military training, including
shooting, which is designed to give young people a chance
to exercise responsibility and leadership, to provide them
with some knowledge of our defence forces, and to
encourage those who might be interested in becoming
members of the Armed Services.

Societies. The College provides a varied programme of
events for day and boarding pupils, ensuring each child is
given the opportunity to develop and nurture lifelong
interests. More than just add-on 'extras', the societies and
clubs form a central part of the well-rounded education that
is the Clifton College Experience. Mid-week activities take
place in the Art, Technology and Music departments. These
are complemented by physical activities such as dance,
basketball, real tennis, fencing, volleyball, swimming, horse
riding and fitness. At the weekend, pupils can take part in
organised voluntary activities, theatre or cinema trips, cycle
rides, horse riding or dry-slope skiing.

Music and Art. The musical activities of the school are wide and varied, and are designed for musicians of all standards. They include the Chapel Choir, Choral Society and Chamber Choir, a full orchestra, two string orchestras, two wind bands, a jazz band, as well as numerous chamber music activities. Visiting concert artists regularly run masterclasses, and there are numerous opportunities to perform. Music lessons are available for virtually all instruments, across many styles. Annual instrumental and vocal competitions are held both at House level and individually. The well-equipped and recently refurbished Music School includes practice facilities, computers, a dedicated recording studio, an extensive sheet music library and a large Vinyl record and CD library.

Drawing, Painting, Sculpture, Pottery, Textiles and various Crafts are taught under the supervision of the Director of Art in the Art School. There is an annual House Art Competition and various exhibitions throughout the year, with many pupils also choosing Photography.

Theatre. Drama and Dance play an important part in the life of the school with an increasing number of pupils achieving success in LAMDA, PCERT LAM and RAD examinations. The Redgrave Theatre is used for school plays, the House Drama Festival, and for plays prepared and performed by individual Houses, the staff or the Modern Languages Society. It is also used for teaching purposes, and in addition for concerts, lectures and meetings.

Physical Education. Clifton College offers a proven pathway to excellence in Sport and has produced many international and current professional players. High Performance Sports Programmes and player-specific conditioning is offered by professional coaches such as a GB Hockey Olympian, former Superleague Netball player, former Welsh Cricketer and former players for England, Bristol and Ireland Rugby.

In the Michaelmas Term, boys play Rugby and girls play Hockey, with an extensive multi-sport option for seniors who are not in team squads. In the Lent Term, Hockey and Football are the main options for boys whilst girls mostly play Netball. Rowing, Running, Squash, Swimming, Shooting, Climbing and Rackets are among the alternative options.

In the Summer Term, Cricket is the main sport for boys and Tennis for girls, with Athletics, Rowing, Swimming and Shooting as alternatives for seniors. The College's 90 acre Beggar's Bush site includes three floodlit all-weather Hockey and Football pitches, six floodlit Tennis courts, a 3G artificial pitch for Football and Rugby, a water-based Hockey pitch with training D, and a Real Tennis court. An indoor facility for Tennis and Netball is one of the best in the region.

Careers. Careers advice is led by a dedicated staff member in charge of Careers, with Housemasters/mistresses overseeing individual applications. Tutors, Heads of Departments and the Head of Sixth Form also offer a wealth of support. The College hosts an excellent Careers Fair in the Summer Term, alongside careers seminars and events throughout the year. The Old Cliftonian community offers a host of advice and work experience opportunities which pupils are encouraged to explore. The school is a subscribing member of the Independent Schools Careers Organisation and of the Careers Research and Advisory Centre at Cambridge.

Clifton College Preparatory School.
Headmaster: J Walton, BA

There is no 'one size fits all' approach at Clifton College Preparatory School, a friendly and inspiring co-educational boarding and day school for boys and girls aged 8–13. Each child is considered and treated as an individual with a unique profile of skills, passions, talents and undiscovered potential. Clifton College offers a stimulating and challenging curriculum, which combines traditional methods with programmes of study relevant to the needs of the next century.

For further details see entry for Clifton College Preparatory School in IAPS section.

The Cliftonian Society. Secretary: J Greenbury, 32 College Road, Clifton, Bristol BS8 3JH (Tel: 0117 3157 155).

Charitable status. Clifton College is a Registered Charity, number 311735. It is a charitable trust providing boarding and day education for boys and girls aged 0–18.

Chairman of College Council: Mr Nick Tolchard

Council:
President: Mr Stephen Zimmerman
Chair: Mr N Tolchard, BSc
Vice-Chair: Mrs Teresa Fisk
Treasurer: Mr S Smith, BSc, DPhil, FCA

Head Master: Dr T M Greene, MA, DPhil

Deputy Head (Academic): Mr G E Simmons, BSc
Deputy Head (Co-curricular & Planning): Mr J Mather, MSc
Deputy Head (Pastoral): Mrs R Coomber, BSc

Head of Sixth Form: Mr N Mills, MA
Director of Admissions: Mr J Hills, MA
Chaplain: Revd Simon Chapman, BA

Clongowes Wood College

Clane, Co Kildare W91 DN40, Ireland

Tel: 00 353 45 868202
email: reception@clongowes.net
website: www.clongowes.net

Motto: *Aeterna non Caduca*

Clongowes Wood College was founded in 1814 in a rebuilt Pale castle – Castle Brown in North Kildare, about 25 miles from Dublin. A boarding school for boys from 12–18, the school has developed steadily ever since and now has circa 500 pupils on the rolls, all of whom are seven-day boarders.

The College is situated on 150 acres of land, mostly comprising sports fields and a 9-hole golf course. It is surrounded by about 300 acres of farmland. Clongowes is listed as an historic building.

Admission. Application for admission should be made to the Headmaster. There is a registration fee of €50. An assessment day is held in May prior to the year of entry and entry is determined by a variety of factors including: suitability of the student to boarding life, family association, geographical spread including Northern Ireland and abroad, date of registration, and an understanding of the values that animate the College. Normal entry is at the age of 12; entry in later years is possible if a place becomes available.

Curriculum. A wide choice of subjects is available throughout the school and pupils are prepared for the Irish Junior Certificate and the Irish Leaving Certificate. This latter is the qualifying examination for entry to Irish Universities and other third-level institutions. It is acceptable for entry to almost all Universities in the United Kingdom, provided the requisite grades are obtained. All pupils take a Transition Year programme following the Junior Certificate. This programme is recommended by the Department of Education in Ireland. Work experience modules, social outreach programmes, exchanges with other countries and opportunities to explore different areas of study are all included in this programme.

Religious Teaching. Clongowes is a Jesuit school in the Roman Catholic tradition and there are regular formal and informal liturgies. Boys are given a good grounding in Catholic theology and are encouraged to participate in retreats, prayer groups and pilgrimages (Taize, Lourdes). Social Outreach is part of the curriculum in Transition Year and is encouraged throughout the school. A small number of boys of other faiths are pupils in the school.

Sport. All boys play rugby in their first year in school. They then have the choice to continue in that game or to play other games. There are several rugby pitches, a golf course, tennis courts, soccer pitches, squash courts, a cross-country track, an athletics and cricket oval, a gymnasium and a new swimming pool; these facilities provide plenty of opportunity for a variety of activities. Athletics, Gaelic football and cricket are popular activities in the third term. Clongowes has a strong rugby tradition and has won the Leinster Championship twice in the last decade.

Other activities. Following the Jesuit tradition, the school has a fine reputation for debating and has won competitions in three different languages (English, Irish, French) in the last decade. A large school orchestra and school choir gives a formal concert at Christmas and another before the summer holidays. Drama productions take place at every level within the school. A large-scale summer project for charity has been undertaken each year. A residential holiday project for children with disabilities takes place in the school each summer and is animated by teachers and pupils. The College has recently created link programmes with schools in Hungary and Romania.

Pastoral Care. The school is organised horizontally into Lines. Two 'prefects', or housemasters look after each year within a Line, composed of two years, with a Line Prefect in charge of the Line itself. In addition, an Academic Year Head oversees the academic work of each of the 70 pupils within each year. A Spiritual Father or Chaplain is attached to each line. There is a strong and positive relationship with parents and a good community spirit throughout the school. The school seeks to foster competence, conscience and compassionate commitment in each of the boys in its care.

Fees per annum (2021–2022). €20,800. Parents are also asked to support the continuing development of the College through various fundraising activities.

Clongowes Union. This association of past pupils of the school can be contacted through: The Secretary, The Clongowes Union, Clongowes Wood College, Clane, Co Kildare; email: development@clongowes.net.

Cokethorpe School

Witney, Oxfordshire OX29 7PU

Tel: 01993 703921
email: hma@cokethorpe.org
         admissions@cokethorpe.org
website: www.cokethorpe.org
Twitter: @CokethorpeSch
Facebook: @CokethorpeSch
Instagram: @CokethorpeSch
LinkedIn: /company/cokethorpe-school

Motto: *Inopiam Ingenio Pensant*

Founded in 1957, Cokethorpe School provides a liberal education to roughly 630 boys and girls aged four to eighteen in a dynamic and vigorous day school environment. Set in 150 acres of parkland, the School sits two miles from Witney and just ten from Oxford.

Aims. The School creates a community of rounded, considerate and confident young people with high personal expectations. The pupils are provided with an exceptional breadth of opportunities to further their learning and expand horizons, whilst the individual focus afforded to pupils ensures that they are supported in making the right choices for their development.

These qualities are formulated in the School's leadership traits: integrity, courage, empathy, judgement, ambition, and responsibility. These are characteristics the School instils in every pupil. In the Prep School, these take the form of the Cokethorpe Characters, with attributions reflecting attitudes to learning.

Curriculum. Whilst the National Curriculum is broadly followed throughout the Prep School and on to GCSE, there is plenty of space afforded to push beyond, providing plentiful scope for intellectual challenge and curiosity to flourish. An exceptional breadth of subjects is offered at age groups across the Prep and Senior Schools.

At GCSE, all pupils study core subjects of English, Maths and Science and have a wide choice of subject options in addition. Sixth Formers typically choose to either study three subjects at A Level and complete the EPQ or select four A Level subjects. A further group opt to follow the Extended Diploma in Business programme. The small size of teaching groups is particularly conducive to rigorous individual attention and encouragement. Students can select from 24 subjects for Sixth Form, including, to name but a few: Philosophy, Politics, Economics, Latin, Further Mathematics, Psychology and Sociology.

Admissions. The main entry points are: Reception (4+), Year 3 (7+), First Form (11+), Third Form (13+) and Sixth Form (16+). Places in other year groups are considered if a place becomes available during the academic year. For the specific requirements of each entry point, please refer to the School's website.

Bursaries. Financial assistance is available, through the award of means-tested bursaries, to those families entering the School from ages 11 through to 18 (and occasionally into the Prep School). The value of the bursary can be up to 100% of fees. Scholarships are assessed separately and awarded annually.

Setting. The elegant Queen Anne Mansion House is both home to the Prep School and entrance to myriad facilities beyond. A range of modern buildings host the Senior School's academic endeavours around a series of quads, and beyond, a 200-seat black-box theatre is the perfect setting for the Performing Arts and visiting speakers. The core sports are complimented by the Outdoor Education programme, which includes clay pigeon shooting, climbing, sailing, and a popular and hugely successful kayaking programme. The extensive extra-curricular programme (known as 'AOBs') plays a prominent part in a pupil's timetable and includes over 160 weekly activities to select and savour.

Fees per term (2021–2022). Prep School: Reception–Year 2 £4,560, Years 3–4 £4,890, Years 5–6 £5,100.

Senior School: £6,950.

Fees include lunch. Extras are kept to a minimum.

The Cokethorpe Society. Director of Development: Gareth Simpson, Cokethorpe School, email: development@cokethorpe.org.

Charitable Status. Cokethorpe Educational Trust Limited is a Registered Charity, number 309650.

Governing Body:
Chairman: Mr J Bennett, BSc

Mr A Bark, ACIB
Mr M Booty
Dr C Easmon, MBBS, MRCP, MSc Public Health, DTM&H, DOccMed
The Right Revd C Fletcher
Mrs R Gunn, MA
Mrs W E Hart, CFQ, MA, ICAEW
Dr W W Lau, PhD, MSc, BSc
Mr R Palmer, FRSA MCCT
Mr P Tolley, BSc, FRICS
Governor Emeritus: Mr M St John Parker, MA

Headmaster: Mr D J Ettinger, BA, MA, PGCE, FRSA

Deputy Headmaster: Mr J C Stevens, BEng, FRSA
Bursar: Mrs H J Stapleton, FCCA
Head of Prep School: Mrs N A Black, BA
Director of Studies: Mr A E Uglow, BA, PGCE
Director of Co-Curricular: Mr G J Sheer, BA, PGCE
Head of Sixth Form: Mr E J Tolputt, BA, MA, MEng
Deputy Head of Sixth Form: Mrs M H D Cooper, BA PGCE
Deputy Head of Sixth Form: Mr A P Gale, BSc, PGCE

Housemasters and Housemistresses:
Feilden: Mr J E Hughes, BA, BMus
Gascoigne: Mrs E Semenzato, DLit, PGCE
Harcourt: Miss A M Woodcock, BSc
Queen Anne: Mrs S A Orton, BA, PGCE
Swift: M Joiner, BSc, MA, PGCE
Vanbrugh: Ms L A Mountain, MA, PGCE
Lower House: M J P O'Connor, BEd

Heads of Departments:
Art: Ms E F Williams, BA, PGCE
Business Studies and Economics: Mrs N Silversides, BEd, CELTA
Classics: Mrs J H Speight, BA, PGCE
Design Technology: Mrs H V Brown, BA, PGCE
Drama: Mrs C L Hooper, Dip Act, DCL
English: Mrs E Oram, BA, MA, PGCE
Geography: Mr J A W Capel, MA, PGCE
History: Mr S G Carter, MA, PGCE
Learning Development: Mrs S J Arbuckle, BA, PGCE, NASENCO
Mathematics: Mr A G M Ladell-Stuart, MMath, PGCE
Modern Foreign Languages: Miss M Bertholle, BA, PGCE
Music: Miss R Mitchell, BMus
Philosophy: Mr A D Waldron, BA
Physical Education: Mr R W L Cook, BSc
Psychology: Miss K J Rogers, BSc, PGCE
Religious Studies: Mr D J Ettinger, BA, PGCE
Science: Mr O L Richards, BA, MA

Colfe's School

Horn Park Lane, London SE12 8AW

Tel: 020 8852 2283
email: head@colfes.com
website: www.colfes.com
Twitter: @ColfesSchool
Facebook: @ColfesSchool

Colfe's is an independent day school for girls and boys from age 3–18. It is one of London's oldest schools and was nearly 100 years old when Abraham Colfe, Vicar of Lewisham, re-established it in 1652. In his will, he entrusted the care of Colfe's to the Leathersellers' City Livery Company, which governs the school to this day.

Entrance is selective and academic standards are high. Over the last three years, 89% of A Level results have been A*–B, with over 63% of grades either A* or A. In 2021, over 80% of students went to their first choice university, with ten students securing offers at Oxford or Cambridge. At GCSE in 2021, 71% of grades were 9–7 and over 90% were 9–6*. We have an exceptional and popular programme of activities outside the classroom.

Colfe's has a strong reputation for all-round quality and innovation – in December 2016 the school was rated as 'Excellent' by the Independent Schools Council following an ISI inspection. We have also been awarded two TES Awards for Education Initiative of the Year (2014 and 2016) for our outstanding pastoral programmes.

We offer a number of fully funded means-tested scholarships in the Sixth Form. In so doing we draw on strong working relationships with a number of local comprehensive schools in two of London's most deprived boroughs.

We are proud of our 360-year history but we are not burdened or defined by it. Colfe's doesn't promote a single mould. It is very much a school of the present day.

Admissions. There are approximately 800 pupils in the Senior School, including 220 in the Sixth Form. The Junior School caters for a further 460 pupils. All sectors of the school are fully co-educational. The main points of entry to the Junior School are 3+ and 4+ (EYFS). The majority of the Junior School pupils transfer to the Senior School at 11. Approximately 60 to 70 pupils from a range of local state primary and prep schools enter the Senior School directly at 11 and there are a limited number of places available to pupils wishing to join in the Sixth Form at Year 12.

Buildings. All the teaching accommodation is modern and purpose built. Specialist on-site facilities include the Sports and Leisure Centre, comprising sports hall, swimming pool, and fitness suite. The Leathersellers' Sports Ground, located less than a mile from the main school campus, provides extensive playing fields and related facilities. There is also a dedicated forest school nearby for younger pupils. The school also holds the freehold of the Old Colfeians ground at Horn Park. The opening of the Stewart Building in 2015, comprising a purpose-built Sixth Form suite and eight hi-tech classrooms, marked the end of a £10 million phase of site improvement.

Curriculum. The curriculum follows the spirit of the National Curriculum in both Junior and Senior Schools. Pupils are entered for the separate Sciences at GCSE and follow the IGCSE Mathematics course. A wide range of subjects is available at A Level, 27 in total, including Drama, Politics, Media Studies, Psychology and Philosophy.

Physical Education and Games. Physical Education and Games are compulsory for all pupils up to and including Year 11. Full use is made of the wide range of facilities available on site, including a fully-equipped Sports Centre, swimming pool and all-weather surface.

Both boys and girls play rugby, cricket, football and athletics. Other sports available include swimming, gymnastics, basketball, health-related fitness and tennis.

Music and Drama. Music and Drama thrive alongside each other in the purpose-built Performing Arts Centre. The music department is home to a wide range of performance groups ranging from beginners to advanced ensembles in both classical and contemporary genres. There are regular performance opportunities given throughout the year, some held in the purpose-built recital hall and others in external venues. A team of visiting instrumental teachers provide further opportunities for pupils to enjoy making music. Drama is a popular subject at both GCSE and A Level, with large numbers of pupils also involved outside the classroom.

Careers. The Careers and Higher Education Department is staffed on a full-time basis. Regular events include University Information Evenings and Careers Fairs.

Fees per term (2021–2022). Senior School £6,100 (excluding lunch); Junior School (KS2) £5,045 (excluding lunch); KS1 £4,770 (including lunch); EYFS £4,570 (including lunch).

Devices. From September 2022 Colfe's will begin the rollout of a 'Pupil Device' initiative. On entry to the school, parents will be asked to purchase a device for their children to use in lessons and for homework. The initiative will begin with Years 7 and 12 in September 2022, rolling out the programme to all pupils from September 2023.

Scholarships. Scholarships are awarded mainly on the basis of outstanding performance in the Entrance Examination. The exam is designed to identify and reward academic potential, as well as achievement.

Means-tested scholarships are also available at 11+ and 16+. These may, in exceptional circumstances, cover the total cost of tuition fees. Applications can be made online via the Colfe's School website.

A limited number of Art, Drama, Music and Sports awards are also available at 11+ and 16+. In the case of Music scholars, free instrumental tuition may accompany the award. Details of Music and Sports awards can be obtained from the website.

The Colfeian Society. Enquiries to the Alumni Relations Officer, Colfe's School, London SE12 8AW; email: development@colfes.com.

Charitable status. Colfe's School is a Registered Charity, number 1109650. It exists to provide education for boys and girls.

Important note: All public examination results (GCSE and A Level), in all schools in 2020 and 2021, were awarded entirely on the basis of school assessments. Comparisons between schools and with previous cohorts are therefore potentially misleading. Parents in search of a more meaningful indicator of schools' outcomes are encouraged to consider the university and other destinations of recent cohorts.

Visitor: HRH Prince Michael of Kent

The current Governors provide between them a broad range of relevant experience and qualifications. A majority are Members or appointees of the Leathersellers' Company to which Abraham Colfe entrusted the School in his will when he died in 1657.

The activities of the Leathersellers are many and varied but the School and its fortunes continue to feature prominently on the Company's agenda. The Master of the Company is, *ex officio*, a member of the Board of Governors.

Board of Governors:
Mr Gavin Bacon (*Master of the Leathersellers' Company*)
Mr Matthew Pellereau, BSc, FRICS (*Chairman*)
Mr Sean Williams, MA Oxon, MPA Harvard
Mr Mark Williams
Mr James Russell, BA
Mr Timothy Lister, FCA
Mr Daniel Coulson, BSc Hons, MA, MRICS
Prof Angela Brueggemann, DPhil
Mr John Guyatt, MA Oxon
Mrs Belinda Canham, BA Hons
Mr David Sheppard, MA Oxon, FRSA
Mrs J Bradley, LLB
Mr Christopher Ramsey, MA Cantab
Mr Joseph Mafe, BSc

Headmaster: **Mr R Russell**, MA Cantab

Deputy Head: Mrs D Graham, GRSM, LRAM
Bursar and Clerk to the Governors: Mr M Adamson, MA Cantab, FCA
Director of Studies: Mr L Rogers, MA Cantab
Director of Pastoral Care: Mrs J German, BA Hons
Director of Sixth Form: Mr S Drury, BA Hons, MA
Director of Teaching and Learning: Mrs J Sansome, BSc Hons, MSc
Head, Junior School: Miss C Macleod, BA Hons, MSc
Director of Admissions and Communications: Mrs K Bridgman, BA Hons

Heads of Departments:
Art: Mrs N Gudge, BA Hons
Classics: Ms H Batten, BA Hons
Design & Technology: Mrs C Cox, BA Hons

Drama: Mrs N Maher, BA Hons, Acting Dip
Economics & Business: Mr S Drury, BA Hons, MA
English: Mrs K Guy, BA Hons
Geography: Mrs H Nissinen, BSc Hons, MA
History: Ms O Crummay, MSc
Learning Support: Miss A Coode, BA Hons, DTLLS
    Literacy
Maths: Mr A Guy, MEng Hons
Media Studies: Mr C Foxall, BA Hons
Modern Languages: Mr M Koutsakis, MA
French: Mrs C Davies, BA Hons
German: Mr M Koutsakis, MA
Spanish: Miss L Chapman, BA Hons
Music: Mr B Holmes, BA Hons, MA Cantab
Outdoor Education: Major C Cherry, BSc Hons
Physical Education: Mrs N Rayes, BEd Hons, EMBA
Politics: Mr M Poolton, BA Hons, MSc
Religion & Philosophy: Miss Z Kendrick, BA Hons, MEd
Biology: Dr G Zimmermann, BSc, PhD
Chemistry: Mr T Armstrong, BSc
Physics: Mr J Fishwick, BSc Hons
Psychology: Dr J Lea, PhD, BSc Hons

Colston's

Bell Hill, Stapleton, Bristol BS16 1BJ

Tel: 0117 965 5207
email: admissions@colstons.org
website: www.colstons.org
Twitter: @colstonsschool
Facebook: @Colstons-School
Instagram: @colstonsschool

Motto: *Go and do thou likewise*

Colston's is a thriving co-educational day school for pupils aged 3 to 18 located on a spacious 30-acre site in Stapleton village in north Bristol. Our traditional pastoral structures and house system promote a sense of community and belonging amongst pupils.

A Colston's education extends far beyond the classroom with opportunities for sport, music, service and co-curricular activities all playing their part in creating the unique experience on offer at the school.

Organisation. There are approximately 800 pupils at Colston's. The Lower School, which caters for the 3–11 age range, includes a nursery and is adjacent to the main site which accommodates the Upper School, which pupils attend from 11–18 (Years 7 to Sixth Form).

For details of the Lower School, see entry in IAPS section.

Admission. Pupils are admitted at 11+ through the school's own examinations. Pupils also join the school for the Sixth Form. Academic scholarships are available as well as scholarships for pupils excelling in art, drama, music and sport. Bursaries are also available which are means tested.

Work. Colston's offers a wide ranging and engaging curriculum in line with the provisions of the National Curriculum. Art, Business Studies, Computing, Drama, Design Technology, French, Geography, History, Music, Physical Education, Religious Studies and Spanish are optional subjects. There is a wide choice of A Level subjects and some BTECs and CTECs available in the Sixth Form.

Religious Denomination. Colston's is a Church of England Foundation, and use is made of neighbouring Stapleton Parish Church for morning assemblies and other services. Pupils of other denominations are also warmly welcomed.

Sport and Games. Colston's has a shining sporting legacy, perhaps unsurprisingly given the impressive on-site facilities that are unique in Bristol. Sport plays a huge part in the life of pupils and while excellence is pursued for those with talent, everyone is encouraged, regardless of ability, to get involved. Opportunities to represent the school are abundant and an impressive number of teams are fielded each week. The main sports for boys are rugby, hockey, cricket and tennis and for girls it is hockey, netball, cricket and tennis.

Music and Drama. The drama department is one of the most successful in the country. It is based in the Harry Crook Theatre which offers an exceptionally well-equipped 200-seat auditorium. Music is vibrant and inclusive, with one-third of pupils taking individual instrumental lessons. Performances are given regularly in the dedicated concert hall.

Careers. Colston's is proud of its careers provision which is available to all pupils. The school is a member of the Independent Schools Careers Organisation. Through a highly successful programme of careers guidance, pupils are helped to make the right decisions to ensure success. The careers library and interactive resources help pupils think about career options and the Head of Careers and Employability meets with each pupil regularly throughout their time at Colston's.

Service and Community. Pupils are given many opportunities to contribute to the wider community. Colston's Combined Cadet Force, one of the most successful in the South West, allows cadets to regularly take part in expeditions and activities. Pupils also undertake The Duke of Edinburgh's Award which seeks to develop lifelong skills. Pupils relish the opportunity to get involved in a diverse range of volunteering projects across the city.

Fees per term (2021–2022). £5,065 (Catering Fee £245).

Modernisation. In the Autumn Term of 2021 an extensive refurbishment project was completed on the Sports Halls, creating a state-of-the-art facility for all to enjoy. Over the past few years significant investment has also been made to provide new teaching classrooms, a 210-seat concert hall and purpose-built CCF headquarters. Additionally the library, laboratories and Sixth Form facilities have been completely refurbished to create a 21st-century learning environment.

Situation. Colston's is located in Stapleton village which is within the city of Bristol, and enjoys the advantage of having all its playing fields and facilities on site. The 30-acre campus provides a wonderful environment for pupils to explore, learn and excel.

The school is large enough to sustain a wide range of activities at a high level and yet small enough for each pupil to contribute actively and be known as an individual. Every effort is made to provide for and develop pupils' abilities in academic, cultural and other co-curricular activities. The school aims to encourage a strong sense of community and service, and to fully develop and extend the talents of every boy and girl.

Charitable status. Colston's School is a Registered Charity, number 1079552. Its aims and objectives are the provision of education.

Governors:
Chair of Governors: Mr N Baker
Mrs B Allpress
Mr M Burchfield
Mrs A Burrell
Mrs G Cross
Mrs C Duckworth
Mr C Green CBE
Mr M Hughes
Mr C Lucas
Dr A Seddon
Mrs J Worthington
Mr J Wright

Headmaster: **Mr J McCullough**, MA Oxon

Deputy Headmaster: Dr P Hill, BSc, PhD
Assistant Head, Co-Curricular: Mr E Beavington, MA
Assistant Head, Curriculum: Dr Z Bell, PhD
Head of Sixth Form: Ms S Matthews, MA Oxon
Assistant Head, Academic: Dr J Tovey, BA, PhD
Assistant Head, Pastoral: Miss A Willis, BA
Director of Finance: Mrs E Jennings, FCA, BSc

Cranleigh School

Horseshoe Lane, Cranleigh, Surrey GU6 8QQ

Tel: 01483 276377
email: admissions@cranleigh.org
website: www.cranleigh.org
Twitter: @cranleighschool
Facebook: @cranleigh-school
LinkedIn: /cranleigh-school

Motto: *Ex cultu robur*

Cranleigh is a leading co-educational weekly boarding and day school set in a stunning rural location in more than 280 acres on the edge of the Surrey Hills. Cranleigh's beautiful campus is exceptionally well equipped, with outstanding classrooms, studio, performance and sports facilities, including three theatres, twelve rehearsal and performance spaces, competition pitches, stables, sports centres, golf course, outdoor education centre and swimming pool.

There are strong links between the School and nearby Cranleigh Preparatory School and pupils also join from a wide variety of other prep schools across London and the home counties, creating a lively, House-based community of young people who are drawn together by their inherent love of life and getting involved in everything Cranleigh has to offer.

Cranleigh School's principal aim is to provide an environment in which pupils can flourish, enabling them to capitalise on the diverse range of opportunities offered by the School and to achieve to the best of their ability within a framework of shared values and standards. The School's 280-acre site, situated eight miles from Guildford on the Surrey/West Sussex border, lies on the outskirts of Cranleigh Village and within 45 minutes of London. The

School is fully co-educational, with some 284 girls and 406 boys between the ages of 13 and 18, including a Sixth Form of about 250. It is a predominantly boarding community, attracting boarders from both the local area and further afield; it also, however, welcomes day pupils, who are fully integrated into the Cranleigh community, playing their part in the activities of their respective houses and benefiting from the advantages thereby offered.

Each house (separate for boys and girls) has a resident Housemaster or Housemistress, a resident Deputy, Matrons and a team of Tutors for both the Lower School and Sixth Form. There is also a strong and active partnership between parents and the School.

Cranleighans are encouraged to relish a challenge, to feel they are known as individuals, and to become talented and wise adults with the ability to adapt to a fast-changing world. Both the Prep and the Senior Schools are proud of their excellent academic track records, culminating in outstanding performances at Common Entrance, GCSE and A Level. 99% of pupils go onto Higher Education and Cranleigh also has a consistently strong Oxbridge contingent.

Academic Patterns. Cranleigh enjoys an academic life that is both exciting and demanding. We have high expectations of our pupils, our academic results are strong and teachers are committed to ensure Cranleighans appreciate that acquiring a love of learning is crucial in leading a personally fulfilled and professionally successful life. Indeed, education finds its purpose in the value of the well-lived lives it makes possible, a value which goes far beyond economic prosperity. Our aim is to act within the spirit of the National Curriculum, but to offer more, taking full advantage of our independence and the extra time available to a boarding school. We, therefore, retain a very broad curriculum in the Fourth Form and have an options system in the Lower and Upper Fifth Forms which enables a pupil to take between nine and eleven GCSE subjects before moving on to A Levels in the Sixth Form. In the Sixth Form, pupils can select from a wide choice of subjects.

Lessons are focused, pacey and engaging, with the focus being on how the pupils learn, as opposed to how the teachers teach. Traditional teaching methods absolutely have their place, but we strongly advocate lessons in which pupils are actively involved in a dynamic process of thinking. Learning, it is said, is 'supervised trying' and we insist that working hard and working intelligently must always be the root of our success. We also know that learning is most rewarding in a community that is lively, co-operative, critical and, fundamentally, engaged with the joy of discovery.

Independent learning is a hugely important aim for us. With this in mind, all year 10 pupils have taken the Higher Project qualification since September 2017 and from September 2016 onwards, the majority of our Sixth Formers have taken the Extended Project Qualification. These qualifications will encourage pupils to think for themselves and come to answers through discussion and reflection.

We believe that education is richer and deeper when students approach their learning philosophically, asking themselves questions that lead to deeper thinking, and engaging with problems to which there may be no agreed answers. Education in this rich sense is more than a preparation for future work: it is a preparation for life in the complex and uncertain world that our students will enter.

Of course, examination success is important too and whilst pupils are encouraged to learn independently, they are also taught the knowledge and skills required for excellent performance in examinations. Independent learning is excellent preparation for examination success, but there will always be a place for precise instruction in the requirements of different assessment types, the essentials of examination technique, and the analysis of past examination performance.

Creative and Performing Arts. Cranleigh has maintained an enviable reputation for Music over many years, and the Merriman Music School offers pupils some of the finest facilities available. We send Choral Scholars to Oxford, Cambridge and major Music Departments and Colleges elsewhere; boys and girls of all ages successfully take part in national competitions and well over a third of the School learns a musical instrument. Keyboard players have access to our Mander two-manual tracker organ, purposefully designed for versatility and teaching, and to two Steinway concert grand pianos. Our exciting Cranleigh Music initiative is now well established, bringing together the Music Departments of Cranleigh School and Cranleigh Preparatory School under a single performing, management and administrative structure. Whilst facilities remain on separate sites (both sides of Horseshoe Lane), the ethos is that of a single Music Faculty encompassing the full 7–18 age range, whose cohesive structure will help to nurture and progress talent from a very young age, so ensuring that all pupils are able to perform in an environment commensurate with their individual ability.

Cranleigh also boasts a strong Drama department. Regular large-scale productions take place in the Speech Hall, to which is linked a studio theatre, the Vivian Cox Theatre, while a flourishing Technical Theatre department encourages the development of 'backstage' skills. The School's proximity to London allows for regular attendance at professional theatre, music and opera productions.

Art and Design Engineering. Both subject areas house a talented mix of practising artists, teachers and designers. The Woodyer Art Studios provide some of the best school art facilities in the country and is spread over several buildings, with a mix of dedicated airy studios. Six large art studios provide specialist provision for painting, printmaking, photography, sculpture and ceramics. A Sixth Form studio enables each student to have their own working space; two suites of computers provide digital facilities while photography is also equipped with a traditional darkroom. The printmaking studio is equipped for relief printing, acid-based etching, and screen-printing. A large project studio provides for a weekly Sixth Form life class and for exhibitions of student work.

The Design Engineering department boasts three fully equipped design studios and workshops. Each design studio features a suite of both PCs and Macs running the latest 2D and 3D CAD software, alongside ample space for the delivery of theoretical content and sketching. Each studio is equipped with a 3D Printer allowing for the rapid prototyping of 3D models created on Autodesk Fusion 360. The department also features a CAM mezzanine which is an excellent space for building 3D printers, housing the large format printer and vinyl plotter. The main Design Engineering workshop is housed within the school's original sports hall which allows for a considerably sized, open-plan workshop kitted out with the required tools and machinery. Branching from the main workshop space is an electronics lab for soldering and electronic circuit development, a CAM area consisting of a large format CNC Router and a Laser Cutter, and a heat treatment bay for welding and brazing.

The studios are open every day and appropriate use is made of the Faculty library, ICT and digital video and photo facilities. External visits are encouraged (both nationally and internationally) and all students exhibit throughout the year.

Sport. Cranleigh has an extensive range of extremely high-standard sporting facilities. During their time at Cranleigh, pupils will have the chance to try a variety of sports. Due to our Sport for All philosophy, all pupils will have the opportunity to train and compete regularly as part of a team throughout the year.

The School possesses an impressive array of sports facilities, including 3 full-size Astroturf pitches (one of which is floodlit), a 9-hole golf course, Cricket Pavilion and 5 outdoor Cricket Squares, with one all-weather match pitch, an Equestrian Centre with two sand schools, one 30m x 60m, one 20m x 40m, both with floodlights, cross-country jumping field and on-site hacking, 6 fives courts, 12 hard tennis courts, 9 astro tennis courts, 8 netball courts, an indoor swimming pool and eco-friendly, purpose-built fitness gym with a range of cardiovascular and weighted equipment as well as a physiotherapy room. For Rugby, Football and Cricket, Cranleigh also has 10 grass pitches on site, including an International standard 1st XV pitch. The large Sports Hall complex, the Trevor Abbott Sports Centre, provides a popular venue for netball, tennis, badminton and basketball, and also includes a separate dance studio. There is also a separate Indoor Cricket Bubble for year-round development.

High standards are set for the numerous competitive teams, with an extensive programme of fixtures at all levels and for all ages. 'Sport for All' is a key philosophy at the School, supported by an experienced and talented team of coaches, many of whom have competed themselves at county, national and Olympic level. The School has witnessed some outstanding team and individual successes in recent years, including National representation in hockey, rugby, riding and cricket; taking National titles in horse riding (show jumping and dressage), kayaking, cricket, rugby 7s, swimming and hockey and also seeing several recent Old Cranleighans continue to compete in the international arena and as Olympic hopefuls.

In the Michaelmas term the majority sports are hockey for girls and rugby for boys; in the Lent term, the majority sports are netball for girls and hockey for boys. During the winter terms, pupils can also compete in lacrosse, cross country, golf, water polo, football, fives, and riding, plus badminton and canoeing for the Sixth Form. All pupils in the Fourth and Lower Fifth Forms take part in the majority sport, while an element of choice is gradually introduced for the older pupils. All pupils in the School take part in sport, even in the Sixth Form. In the Summer term, the main team sport for boys is cricket, whilst some boys compete in tennis, swimming, athletics and golf. For girls, the main sport is tennis, with competitive swimming, athletics, rounders and cricket popular additional offerings.

Service Activities. There are opportunities for pupils to take part in a range of 'service' activities. Boys and girls may join the CCF or get involved with Voluntary Action or the Cranleigh School Environmental Action Group. Cranleighans help local people in community settings and also have links with local schools for children with learning difficulties and with a home for adults with similar difficulties. All houses and the Fundraising Group raise money for various charities.

Wider initiatives also include the School's 'Beyond Cranleigh' partnership – a key partnership between Cranleigh School and Beyond Ourselves, a London-based charity that works to improve the lives of disadvantaged young people in both London and in Zambia. This partnership has led to Cranleigh's sponsorship of a primary school in Kawama, to which Sixth Form pupils regularly make visits to help with building and teaching initiatives. Cranleigh has also pledged to support social enterprise projects in Kawama to provide jobs and skills training for locals post-education. Such initiatives are designed to focus pupils' thoughts on life beyond the School.

Outdoor Education. Cranleigh operates a large Duke of Edinburgh's Award scheme, with many pupils completing the Gold Award before leaving school. By way of introduction, all Fifth Form pupils undergo an Outdoor Education programme in order to improve their self-awareness and confidence. There are many other opportunities for Outdoor Education through the CCF, and there is a well-attended climbing club (which has its own bouldering wall).

Religion. The striking, neo-Gothic Chapel was built as a central point of the School, and Cranleigh maintains its concern to present the Christian way of life. It welcomes pupils of all faiths and none.

Developments. The Cranleigh School Development Plan of 2015 initiated the production of a master plan. The results of this master plan were to take a phased approach to campus development with the first phase commencing in 2016 and taking broadly four years. The overall theme of the Development Plan was to enhance pastoral support, and teaching and learning. It was considered that the girls' boarding houses, at around 110 pupils, were too large and that two new boarding houses for girls should be developed, leading to four girls' houses, each for around 75 pupils, in addition to the four boys' houses, each of around 100 pupils.

The teaching facilities in the Connaught Block (to the right of Speech Hall) were considered to be past their best and so a decision was made to build a new teaching facility for English, the Humanities, Economics and Business Studies as well as Learning Support and Careers; the latter being broadened to Cranleigh Futures. A need was also identified at the Senior School for new squash courts and a modern café for pupils. At the Prep School, a number of the older buildings in the middle of the campus were outdated and it was decided to build new teaching facilities for Science, Design Technology and Art.

Girls' Boarding Houses. The first major project was the creation of a third girls' boarding house, Rhodes. This project was completed in October 2017 and after one year it has bedded into the Cranleigh landscape seamlessly. The opening of the van Hasselt Centre allowed existing classrooms in the Connaught Block to be converted back to their original use as boarding accommodation. We were delighted to open a fourth girls' house in September 2019, named Martlet (after the birds on the School's shield).

New Teaching Buildings. The building of the two new teaching buildings, one at each school, started in early 2017. The Prep School building progressed on schedule and their exciting new facility, including a flexible area for staff known as the Hub, was opened in early July by the former Chair of the Governing Body, Anthony Townsend, whose name the building takes. The new van Hasselt Centre at the Senior School, which includes both new classrooms and social spaces in the old squash courts, was completed in November 2018 and is now in full use. The centre is named after Marc van Hasselt, Cranleigh's Headmaster from 1970–84. These two new facilities are both spectacular and evidence of the School's strong commitment to core academic subjects.

Squash Courts. The final element of the master plan will be to build new squash courts to replace the old courts which have been subsumed into the van Hasselt Centre. These will be built onto the side of the Trevor Abbott Sports Centre and a new gym will be included.

These new facilities add to the already impressive campus and will take Cranleigh School forward as a leading co-educational dedicated boarding community. It is an exciting time to be at Cranleigh.

Planning for our Pupils' Future. Cranleigh takes the future of its pupils very seriously. It maintains good contacts with various professions, industry and commerce, through links developed as part of the careers advice structure. All pupils are regularly assessed during their time at the School, and this process includes a period of Work Experience at the end of the Upper Fifth year. Closely linked with the Old Cranleighan Society and the School, the Cranleigh Network oversees skills training, CV advice, postgraduate work experience and mentoring.

Admission and Registration. If you do not already know Cranleigh, we strongly recommend an initial visit during one of our small group visits or open mornings, dependent on age of entry. These will enable you and your child to have a tour of the school, ground and facilities and meet a few key members of staff to answer any initial questions. Our visits and open mornings are very popular and so advance booking via the Admissions office is essential to avoid disappointment. Please call the Admissions Office for more information on 01483 276377.

Awards. The Master of Scholars has a specific responsibility for all Scholars. They are members of their houses and attend normal lessons, but also have an additional programme throughout their time at the School that covers a wide variety of academic, cultural, social and commercial areas beyond the syllabus and which encourages independent thinking and research.

At age 13, Cranleigh School offers a variety of awards and scholarships. In certain circumstances, additional consideration may be given to sons or daughters of public servants, members of the armed forces and the clergy of the Church of England.

Fees per annum (2021–2022): Boarding: £40,710. Day: £33,510. It is the policy of the School to keep extras down to an absolute minimum, and limited to such charges as individual music tuition. Textbooks are supplied until the Sixth Form, at which point pupils are encouraged to buy their own so that they may take them on to university. A scheme is available for the payment of fees in advance.

Preparatory School. Cranleigh is closely linked with Cranleigh Preparatory School, where boys and girls are normally admitted at seven or eight, but also at other ages. For further information, apply to the Headmaster of the Preparatory School (*see entry in IAPS section*).

Charitable status. Cranleigh School is a Registered Charity, number 1070856. It exists to provide education for children aged 13–18 and the Preparatory School for those aged 7–13.

Governing Body:
Chairman: Mr A J Lajtha, MA, FCIB
Deputy Chairman: Mrs M M S Fisher, MA
S E Bayliss, MA
Colonel J W Boyd, OBE, MA
J A Brown, MA Oxon
Dr R M Chesser, MA, MB BChir, MRCP
M Foster, MA
P S P Going, BSC, MRICS
S Gunapala, BEng, MEng, FCA
K J S Kerr
J Kurshid, QC
J A M Knight, BA Hons
A J Lye, BA
C H Severs, LLB Hons
E Stanton, BSc, ACA
J J D C Tate, BA Hons, DipArch, MArch, ARB, RIBA
S J Watkinson, BSc, ACA
O A R Weiss, MA
P M Wells, BEd
D G Westcott, BA, BCL, QC
S J Whitehouse, BA Cantab
R J Wilkins, MA, DPHIL
D A E Williams, BA, FCA
M J Williamson

Clerk to the Governors: Mr P T Roberts, MBE, DChA

Headmaster: Mr Martin Reader, MA Oxon, MPhil, MBA

Deputy Head: Mr S D Bird, BA, MEd, QTS
Deputy Head (Pastoral): Dr A Saxel, BSc, PhD
Deputy Head (Academic): Mr D R Boggitt, BEng, PGCE
Assistant Head (Co-Curricular): Mr C H D Boddington, BA, PGCE
Assistant Head (Director of IT): Mr D J Futcher, BSc, MBCS, QTS
Assistant Head (Learning, Teaching and Innovation): Dr J L Taylor, BA, BPhil, PhD, PGCE
Assistant Head (Liaison): Mr S J Batchelor
Director of Operations: Mr P A Dunn, MA
Director of Finance: Miss J A Underdown
Director of External Relations: Mrs J R Cooksley, MA, BA Hons, NCJT Prof Cert
Strategic Development Director: Mr J Dale-Adcock
Chair of Common Room: Miss S L Greenwood, BA

Members of Common Room:
† *Housemaster/mistress*

Miss M Baffou, BA
Mr A K Barker, BSc, PGCE
Mrs R L Barker, BSc, PGCE (†*South*)
Mr J Bartlett, BA
Miss A M L Bartlett, BA
Mrs S E Baumann, BA, PGCE
Mr R R B Bellak, BA, PGCE
Mrs P M Bigg
Miss A M Billson, MTheo, MDiv
Mr S D Bird, BA, MA
Mr C H D Boddington, BA, PGCE
Mr D R Boggitt, BEng, PGCE, MEd
Mr E J P Bradnock, BA, PGCE (†*East*)
Mr S R Broad, BA, PGCE
Mr B W Browne, BSc, PGCE
Mr S Brown, BA, PGCE

Mrs C C E Bruns, BSc
Mrs G L Bukowska, MSc, PGCE (†*Rhodes*)
Mrs O Burt, BA, MA
Mr E J Carson, BSc
Mrs H K Carson, BSc, PGCE
Mr W E Chadwick, BA, PGCE
Miss D F Chapman, BA, MA
Mrs C L Constable, MA, PGCE
Mr S T Cooke, BA (†*Cubitt*)
Mrs C E Cooper, BA
Mr R P Cootes
Miss K G Cummins, MA, PGCE
Mrs N J R Davison, BA, IPGCE
Mrs E G M Dellière, BA
Mr N Drake, BA, PG Dip, PGCE
Mrs V C Dutton
Mr D M Eaglestone, BA, MSc, PGCE
Mr M P D Emley, BA, QTS, MA
Mr T R Fearn, BSc, PGCE
Mrs K J Flack, BA, HND
Mr A P Forsdike, MA, PGCE (†*North*)
Miss C E Frude, BA
Mr D J Futcher, BSc, QTS
Mrs C Gangemi, BSc, PGCE
Mrs E H Glass, BSc
Miss R S Gibson, BTh, MA
Miss S L Greenwood, BA
Mr A J Guppy, BA
MR S J W Haddock, MA, PGCE
Miss C R Hall, BA, PGCE
Mr R M Hardy, BSc, PGCE
Revd J A N Harrison, BA
Ms L A Hellberg, BA, PGCE
Miss P E Henderson, BA, PGCE
Mr A G C Hillen, BA, MA, PGCE
Dr D A W Hogg, MA, MSt, DPhil, PGCE
Mr B P Hopcroft, MA
Miss S J Houghton, BA, BSc
Mr A R Houston, BSc, GTP
Mr R Humes, BSc, PGCE
Miss A E Johnson, MA, PGCE
Miss C M Johnson
Mr R C E K Kefford, BSc, PGCE
Dr S L Kemp, BSc, PhD, PGCE
Mr C W Kinnersly, BA, MA, GTP
Mr J H W L Ladd Gibbon
Mr R G Lane, MEng, PGCE (†*Loveday*)
Mr F P A Laughton, BSc, PGCE
Mr P M Leamon, BA, PGAS, PGCE
Mr T G Leeke, BSc
Mrs C J Lock, BSc, PGCE, PGDIPP
Miss O R McConnell-Wood, BA
Mrs E R McGhee, BA, PGCE
Mrs G L McMillan, BSc, PGCE
Mr N G A Miller, BA, GTP, QTS
Mr J B Nairne, BFA, PGCE
Mr G J N Neill, BA, MA, PGCE
Miss C Nicholls, MA, PGCE
Mr E J E Peerless, BSc, PGCE
Mr R J Organ
Mr E J E Peerless, BSc, PGCE
Mr G V Pritchard, BSc, PGCE
Mr S G Quinn, BSc, PD, PGCE
Mr S P Rayer, BSc, QTS
Mrs A E Reader, BA, PGCE
Mr D C Reed, BA, MSc

Mr A D Robinson, MA, PGCE
Mrs A L J Robinson, BA, MFA
Mr A S J Rothwell, MPhil, PGCE, MA
Mr G C Royall, BSc
Dr A P Saxel, BSc, PhD
Mr R J Saxel, BA, DipRam, LRAM, ARAM
Mr A J Scarisbrick, BSc
Mr J H Schofield-Newton, BA, MA
Mr J Scott, BA, PGCE, MBA
Mrs R J C Scott, BA, QTS (†*Martlet*)
Mr P N Scriven, BA, MA, LRAM, MM (*Organist in Residence*)
Mrs A C Smuts, BSc, GTP
Miss M Summers, BSc, MSc, PGCE
Dr J L Taylor, BA, BPhil, PGCE, DPhil
Mr J J Taylor, BA, QTS
Dr A L J Thomas, BMus, MPhil, PhD
Dr B R Tyrrell, MChem, DPhil
Mr D N Vaiani, BA
Mr R J O Venables, MA, PGCE
Mr R Verdon, BA, MBA, PGCE
Dr M Ward, BA, PhD, LGSM, MMus, Dip RCM, ARCM
Mr K W Weaver, BA Music, PG Dip
Mr M J Weighton, BA, PGCE
Mr S Welch
Miss M K C Williams, BA
Mrs R A C Williams, BSc, PGCE
Mrs A W Worsley, BSc, PGCE (†*West*)
Mr M A Worsley, LLB
Mrs U C Yardley, BA, PGCE
Dr S A H Young, BSc, MSc, PhD, PGCE

Culford School

Bury St Edmunds, Suffolk IP28 6TX

Tel: 01284 728615
email: admissions@culford.co.uk
website: www.culford.co.uk
Twitter: @CulfordSchool
Facebook: @officialculfordscool
Instagram: @culfordschool

Motto: *Viriliter Agite Estote Fortes*

Culford School was founded in 1881 in Bury St Edmunds and moved to its present site on the Culford estate in 1935. The School is one of eight owned by the Methodist Independent Schools Trust and is administered by a Board of Governors, to whom local control is devolved.

About Culford School. Culford is a co-educational boarding and day school for 800 pupils aged between 1 and 18 across three schools: the Pre-Prep & Nursery, Prep and Senior Schools, all of which are situated within 480 acres of beautiful Suffolk parkland.

Where is Culford School? Culford is conveniently located four miles north of Bury St Edmunds and is within easy reach of Cambridge and Norwich (to which the school runs a daily bus shuttle service), Ipswich and Stansted Airport, and Heathrow and Gatwick airports are within two hours of Culford.

Teaching & Learning. We believe education should be challenging, enriching and fun and are committed to helping our pupils achieve excellence in all areas of school life. Hard work in the classroom is complemented by full sporting and extracurricular programmes.

Curriculum. We aim to give a broad and balanced education that enables every pupil to fulfil their academic potential. Core subjects at GCSE are English language and literature, mathematics, the three sciences and a foreign language. Pupils can choose additional subjects from a wide range of options and receive guidance from the Deputy Head, their teachers and personal tutor, who, along with their Housemaster or Housemistress, has responsibility for their academic and social progress.

Culford Sixth Formers usually study three or four subjects at A Level. The majority of students go on to university, including Oxbridge and the prestigious Russell Group universities. Sixth Formers may also study for a Culford Independent Research Project which enables students to study beyond the confines of A Level specifications; it can be an essay, a film, a composition or even something created in Design and Technology.

Facilities. Culford is centred on the magnificent Culford Hall, an 18th century mansion formerly the seat of Marquis Cornwallis and Earl Cadogan. The Hall houses Culford's music department and purpose-built Studio Theatre. Further facilities include a new £2.2m landmark library at the academic heart of the school. In September 2019, we opened a brand new art centre, a modern, dynamic space that can be used for lessons, exhibitions and events. More recent developments include: a state-of-the-art, 24-track recording studio; the installation of two dance studios which both include a high sprung Harlequin floor, the same used by professional dancers. There will also be a state-of-the-art Creative Technology Centre, due for completion in January 2022.

Teaching Facilities. Teachers are specialists in their fields and are united by a passion to help the children in their care achieve their goals, whatever they may be. Classrooms are modern and well equipped, and in the case of specialist subjects, such as languages and sciences, have the latest technologies installed.

Sports Facilities. Culford's fantastic Sports and Tennis Centre is a state-of-the-art facility which comprises a four-court, championship-standard Indoor Tennis Centre, a 25m indoor pool, gym, strength and conditioning suite, golf swing studio and a large sports hall with a climbing wall and indoor cricket nets. Outside there are further tennis courts, two of which are seasonally covered, two artificial turf pitches (one in partnership with Bury Hockey Club) and numerous rugby and hockey pitches. In September 2021, we opened a renovated Strength & Conditioning suite alongside a new fitness gym.

Pupils can also pursue athletics, horse riding, archery, CCF and the Duke of Edinburgh's Award. Culford launched a new Football Academy programme in 2018 to sit alongside its already well-established tennis, golf and swimming programmes.

Boarding. Culford accepts boarders aged 7 to 18 and for a whole host of reasons, including an 'Excellent' ISI rating, boarding is extremely popular with over half of Senior pupils boarding. Boarders enjoy an amazing range of weekend activities and have full access to Culford's impressive Sports and Tennis Centre.

Culford's boarding Houses offer children a comfortable, secure and fun place to live during term time. Culford offers flexible arrangements for other boarders where possible:

part and occasional boarding is available providing space is free. We do not have an enforced exeat at the weekends; children may stay at school throughout the term, going home at the weekend or to stay with friends when they or their parents wish them to.

All pupils have access to our fully-equipped Medical Centre, supervised by a resident nurse, and this includes provision for residential care when necessary.

Culford Pre-Prep & Nursery School. Our purpose-designed Nursery accepts children from age 1 to 3 and perfectly prepares them for School life. Culford's Nursery opened in 2017 and is available for 50 weeks per year.

Culford Pre-Prep occupies a combination of new and entirely refurbished buildings and provides teaching for 80 children from Nursery at age three through age seven in a delightful setting within the grounds.

Both Pre-Prep and Nursery schools take part in Forest School activities, a way of learning outdoors that helps children to develop personal, social and technical skills in a woodland setting.

Music & Drama. Music plays an important part in the life of the School. There are numerous choirs, orchestras and bands and regular concerts are held to give pupils the chance to perform in public. Individual music tuition is offered in voice, piano, organ and all orchestral instruments. Drama is also very popular and there are regular House plays and concerts as well as major productions: these include musicals and plays for different sections of the School.

Activities. There is a huge array of clubs and societies on offer – from academic and creative to sporting and community. Pupils are encouraged to take part in Community Service Activities and many participate in the Duke of Edinburgh's Award Scheme or choose to join the Combined Cadet Force (CCF).

Culford's popular Dance Programme features a professional high-sprung floor and classes in all types of dance, including ballet, contemporary, jazz and choreography.

Staff regularly take pupils out on visits and expeditions too, and every summer a group of Sixth Formers and teachers spend 3 weeks in Malawi helping with various development projects; a trip that is universally viewed as a life-changing experience. Other recent trips have included tours to New York, skiing in France and scuba diving in Tobago as well as sports tours worldwide.

Entry. The majority of pupils join in September at ages 1–7 (Pre-Prep), 7+, 8+ and 11+ (Preparatory School); and at 13+ and 16+ (Senior School). Entry to the Sixth Form is on the basis of GCSE performance or its equivalent for overseas candidates.

Entry to Culford Pre-Preparatory School is by informal assessment just prior to enrolment.

Applications are welcome from individuals throughout the year, subject to places being available.

Visiting Culford School. If you would like to visit Culford, the Headmaster will be delighted to welcome you. Please contact the Admissions Office to arrange an appointment and a tour on 01284 385308 or to request a copy of the School prospectus. We also hold regular Open Mornings each term, please visit www.culford.co.uk to find out more.

Scholarships and Exhibitions. Culford holds its Scholarship examinations between November (Sixth Form) and January/February for entry in the following September.

Scholarships and Exhibitions are awarded according to merit in the following categories:

11+: Academic, Music, Swimming, Tennis, Cricket and Golf

13+: Headmaster's Foundation Scholarship, Academic, Art, Design & Technology, Drama, Music, Hockey, Rugby, Swimming, Tennis and Sport

16+: Headmaster's Foundation Scholarship, Professor Watson Scholarship, Academic, Art, Drama, Music, Design & Technology, Hockey, Rugby, Swimming, Tennis, Golf and Sport

11+, 13+ and 16+: Jubilee Scholarships for all-rounders who board are worth up to 25% of boarding fees.

16+: The William Miller Scholarship for a pupil studying sciences is worth up to 25% of tuition fees. The Arkwright Scholarship for a pupil studying Design & Technology allows an amount over two years to be shared between the pupil and the School.

Swimming and Tennis Scholarships and Exhibitions may be available at any age from 10+.

The Headmaster's Foundation Scholarship is worth up to 50% of tuition fees; the Professor Watson Scholarship (restricted to pupils coming from state schools) is worth 25% of day or boarding fees; all other scholarships are worth up to 25% of tuition fees, and Exhibitions are worth up to 10%.

Bursaries are available to those in genuine financial need.

A generous Forces Allowance is available to parents who are serving members of the Armed Forces and are in receipt of the MOD CEA.

For further details please apply to The Registrar, Tel: 01284 385308 or email: admissions@culford.co.uk.

Senior School Fees per term (2021–2022). Day £6,895, Full Boarding £10,760.

Charitable status. Culford School is part of the Methodist Independent Schools Trust, which is a Registered Charity, number 1142794.

Chairman of Governors: Air Vice Marshall S Abbott, CBE, MPhil, BA

Headmaster: **J F Johnson-Munday**, MA, MBA

Prep School Head: C Bentley, MEd

Deputy Head: Dr J Guntrip, BSc, PhD

Assistant Head: D V Watkin, BEd

Dauntsey's

West Lavington, Devizes, Wiltshire SN10 4HE

Tel:	01380 814500
email:	info@dauntseys.org
website:	www.dauntseys.org
Twitter:	@DauntseysSchool
Facebook:	@DauntseysSchool
Instagram:	@dauntseysschool
LinkedIn:	/dauntsey's-school

Founded in 1542, Dauntsey's is a leading co-educational boarding and day school for 11–18 year olds, set in a 150-

acre estate on the edge of Salisbury Plain in Wiltshire. We offer our 865 pupils challenge and inspiration both inside and outside the classroom.

Academic endeavour is at the heart of all that we do, and we expect pupils to leave with strong exam results and a love of learning. But our ethos is about much more than exam grades. Drama, music, art and sport all flourish here and the rural surroundings provide an ideal setting for many outdoor activities. Our extensive adventure education programme encourages our pupils to develop important life skills, such as resilience, communication, creativity and teamwork.

The school's uniquely lively and friendly atmosphere encourages pupils "to have a go", try new things and so develop their self-confidence and self-belief. Our school community thrives on a culture of kindness and mutual respect which leads to a real sense of belonging.

For more information please visit our regularly updated and informative website www.dauntseys.org which provides a real flavour of life at Dauntsey's.

"Our ultimate priority is the happiness and fulfilment of every person in our community. In our experience, if our pupils are happy, then success will follow." Mark Lascelles, Head Master, Dauntsey's

The Community. Our house system is the cornerstone of our community, giving pupils a secure source of support and guidance on every aspect of life, as well as the chance to get together and have fun. Every pupil joins either a boarding or day house, which are co-educational in the Lower School (ages 11 to 13) and single sex in the Upper School (ages 14 to 18). Each house is run by a housemaster or housemistress and a team of tutors who take a close and active interest in pupils' academic and social development, as well as encouraging them to make the most of the activities on offer. Above all, they really do make sure that the house is a home from home.

Curriculum. Throughout the School, the curriculum is broad and balanced, offering the opportunity to study an extensive range of subjects. The academic curriculum is well balanced, wide-ranging and offers a good amount of choice. The timetable offers a great deal of flexibility, with well-structured weekly lessons and extensive options that cater for the different interests and aptitudes of all our pupils. Dauntsey's promotes independent learning, enabling pupils to fulfil their potential and develop the key skills they will need in later life. Gifted and talented pupils have access to work and experiences at the higher cognitive levels, to stimulate interest and develop advanced thinking skills, while pupils with mild learning difficulties get expert help and support from a dedicated team of specialist teachers.

Games. The major sports are Rugby, Football, Hockey, Cricket and Netball. Other games options include Tennis, Squash, Athletics, Swimming, Soccer, Water Polo, Fencing, Badminton and Basketball. In the Sixth Form further options include Triathlon training, Canoeing, Basketball, Rifle-shooting, Yoga, Cross-Country, Ballet and Dance. Sixth Formers can also choose to do volunteer work within the community.

Extra-Curricular Activities. Our adventure education and extra-curricular programmes set us apart, encouraging pupils to try new experiences. From drama, dance, music, sport and a huge range of clubs and societies, to our lecture series, adventure programmes and volunteering initiatives – there are opportunities to suit everyone. We aim to push our pupils out of their comfort zone, inside and outside the classroom, and we bring that spirit of adventure to everything we do.

Fees per term (2021–2022). Boarders £11,200; Day Pupils £6,765. There are no compulsory extras.

Admission. Boys and girls are admitted at 11 and 13 (boarding only) by examination, school report and interview; to the Sixth Form by I/GCSE grade predictions or equivalent and interview.

Scholarships and Bursaries. Scholarships and awards are available for boarding and day places at 11+, 13+ and 16+ and carry a maximum fee remission of 10%. Scholarship supplements are available to those who have been awarded a scholarship and provide financial help with the school fees. For further details please contact the Registrar.

Charitable status. Dauntsey's School is a Registered Charity, number 1115638. It is dedicated to the education of boys and girls.

Chairman of Governors: Mrs L F Walsh Waring, BA

***Head Master*: Mark Lascelles**, BA

Deputy Head (Pastoral): Mrs A L Jackson, BA

Second Master: Mr A Collins, BA, MSc Oxon

Deputy Head (Academic): Mr D Noble, MA Oxon, MA, MBA

Head of Lower School: Miss E S Conidaris, BSc

Bursar: Mr Will Ethelston, BA, MA, FCA
Registrar: Mrs J H Sagers, BA
Head Master's Secretary: Mrs C Holgate

Dean Close School

Shelburne Road, Cheltenham, Gloucestershire
GL51 6HE

Tel: 01242 258000
email: registrar@deanclose.org.uk
website: www.deanclose.org.uk
Twitter: @DeanCloseSchool
Facebook: @DeanCloseSchool

Motto: *Verbum Dei Lucerna*

Sitting on a beautifully landscaped 50-acre site in the Regency town of Cheltenham, Dean Close School is an attractive mixture of old, traditional buildings and modern, hi-tech facilities. The School was opened in 1886 in memory of Francis Close, Rector of Cheltenham 1826–55 and later Dean of Carlisle, and has been co-educational since 1967. Dean Close is a Christian school which believes that education is as much about building character and relationships as it is about gaining knowledge. Dean Close Preparatory School was established in 1949.

Admission and Withdrawal. Admission to the Senior School at 13 is through Common Entrance or direct entrance tests in English, Maths and Verbal Reasoning. Sixth Form: examination and interview, 6 grade 6s minimum at GCSE. We advise pupils to have at least an A in the subjects they wish to study at A Level. Prospectus and application forms are available from the Registrar who is also happy to arrange a visit at a time to suit. There is a non-returnable registration fee of £100 and a deposit is payable one year before entry. One term's notice is required before a pupil is withdrawn from the School.

Fees per term (2021–2022). Boarding £12,625–£13,150, International Boarding £13,500–£13,900, Flexi Boarding £9,800–£12,400, Day £8,470–£8,980.

Term of Entry. We prefer to accept pupils in September but will make exceptions at any time of year, even in the middle of a term, if a good reason exists.

Scholarships and Bursaries. The School offers scholarships, exhibitions and bursaries at age 13 and for entry into the Sixth Form. The six areas of talent which are recognised are academic, music, sport, drama, art and design technology. The size of award is set according to performance. Dean Close Preparatory School also offers scholarships at ages 7 and 11.

Academic: The 13+ ISEB Common Scholarship Examination, for which specimen papers are available from the ISEB, is held annually at the school in February. Candidates for academic scholarships from state schools should contact the Admissions team. The Sixth Form Scholarship examination takes place in November.

Music (including Choral and Organ) and Drama Scholarships are based on audition, interviews and exam (Drama). Individual specialist tuition is free to all scholars and exhibitioners.

Art and Design Technology Scholarships may be awarded, based on portfolio, drawing / technical test and interview.

Sports Scholarships are awarded to reflect all-round sporting ability and commitment. Assessment by conditioning tests, skills tests in two or more sports and interviews.

Means-tested bursaries for sons and daughters of clergy and missionaries. Automatic discounts, known as Thierry Awards, are offered to parents serving in HM Armed Forces on a scale according to rank. Foundation Bursaries for families in the locality unable otherwise to benefit from a Dean Close education.

Number and Organisation. There are 490 in the Senior School (13–18). The Sixth Form comprises approximately 40% of the School. There are ten Houses: three for boy boarders (one Sixth Form only), three for girl boarders (one Sixth Form only) two day houses for boys and two day houses for girls. Houseparents take immediate responsibility for pupils' work, careers, applications for universities and further education. A tutorial system ensures that all pupils have a member of the teaching staff who takes a particular interest in them, both academically and pastorally. There is a Futures department giving advice on careers, university programmes and choices on leaving school. The Preparatory School (2–13) has approximately 453 pupils of whom 222 are girls.

Work. In the lower part of the School, pupils are set rather than streamed; included in the timetable is a Creative Studies course introducing pupils to a wide range of artistic and creative subjects, embracing Art, Drama, Music, PDT and Physical Education. The language centre, music school, art school, sports hall, modern laboratories, IT Suite, electronics and creative workshops combine excellent teaching and leisure facilities which are available both in timetabled and extra-curricular time. Much of the

accommodation has been built in the last twenty years and is modern and purpose-built. A professional 550-seat theatre houses an ambitious programme of productions. There is also an open-air theatre. As well as several orchestras, wind band, many ensembles and the Chapel Choir, the School has a Choral Society which performs a major work at least once a year. The Strings Department is headed up by the internationally renowned Carducci Quartet. Tuition in any number of musical instruments is available as an extra. Free tuition is provided for music award holders and high-grade musicians. The theatre also affords first-class concert facilities.

Religious Education. The teaching and Chapel services are in accordance with the Church of England and the School's strong Evangelical tradition is maintained. The Chaplain prepares members of the School for confirmation each year. Most services are in the School Chapel.

Games. The School has a 25m indoor swimming pool and a £3m sports hall, both used year round. There are two international standard AstroTurf pitches, a large number of tennis courts and grass pitches for rugby, cricket and athletics. Hockey, rugby, cricket, netball, athletics, tennis, and cross-country are the main sports.

Health. The School has three qualified Sisters with Assistants and visiting Doctors. There is a surgery and a medical centre.

Outside Activities. There is a huge range of clubs, activities and societies, from climbing to creative writing, salsa dancing to Warhammer, theatre tech to horse riding. A very active Combined Cadet Force with RN and Army sections trains every Wednesday afternoon and some pursue Bronze and Gold Duke of Edinburgh's Award. There is an active outward bound club and a large Community Action group gets involved with projects on a local, national and international level, particularly with a link school in Uganda.

Charitable status. Dean Close School is a Registered Charity, number 1086829. It exists to provide education for children.

Deputy Head Pastoral: Mrs J A Davis, MA, PGCE
Deputy Head Academic: J A Hole, MA
Director of International Pupils: Mrs R J Vest, BA, PGCE, MAELT

Bursar: A P Bowcher, MBA, FCIB, DipFS
Chaplain: Revd J C Ash, BA

Preparatory School:
(see entry in IAPS section)
Headmaster: P Moss, BA
Deputy Head Operations: J Harris, BA, PGCE
Academic Director: J Gould

Pre-Preparatory School:
(see entry in IAPS section)
Headmistress: Dr C A Shelley, BEd, PhD
Deputy Head: J E Cowling, BA, PGCE
Early Years Foundation Stage Coordinator: Miss A Moorhouse, BEd

Director of Admissions: Mrs R Chaplain, BSc
Registrar, Pre-Preparatory: Lesley Miller
Head of Admissions, Preparatory: Mrs K Fergusson
Head of Admissions, Senior: Mrs K Serjeant, BA

Downe House

Cold Ash, Thatcham, Berkshire RG18 9JJ

Tel:	01635 200286
email:	registrar@downehouse.net
website:	www.downehouse.net
Twitter:	@DowneHouse
Facebook:	@downehouse
Instagram:	@downe_house
LinkedIn:	/downe-house-school

What makes a Downe House girl? The answer is in the Downe House DNA: Collaboration – Resilience – Creativity – Aspiration – Compassion – Communication – Outward looking – Digital Ready.

In the classroom, on the pitch, on stage and everywhere in between, these values are the hope, aim and aspiration for every girl in the school. However, there is no 'typical Downe House girl'. Upon stepping through the school gates, every student is treated and celebrated as an individual. Whether she is an artist with an aptitude for mathematics, a scientist with a love of music, or an athlete with an interest in politics, Downe House will introduce, nurture and encourage every student's passion.

The dynasty of Down House women who preceded, and the sheer variety of the career paths and achievements of our alumnae is testimony to our ethos. They all carry with them the imprint of the Downe House DNA.

At a glance. Established in 1907, Downe House is a traditional boarding and day school with a modern approach for girls aged 11–18. Situated in a beautiful Berkshire 110-acre woodland estate, Downe House offers family-friendly boarding, balanced with an exceptional range of opportunities. Downe House has been a Microsoft Showcase School since 2018.

Global outlook. Downe House honours an exceptional programme to nurture global citizens and expands the girls' cultural horizons. Every girl in the Lower Fourth (Year 8) spends a term at our school in France, the Downe House Sauveterre, a beautiful chateau that allows the students to experience French life, language and culture. Older girls have the opportunity to take part in the Global Schools' Exchange Programme, studying abroad in one of 15 partner schools across 6 continents. There is also a Global Internship Programme as well as DH LINKS, the School's comprehensive networking and careers initiative, along with our World Ready Programme, which is layered into every aspect of School life, tailored for every stage of development, as girls progress up through the year groups, to prepare them for the wider world.

Academic. Academically, Downe House encourages ambition and ignites a love of learning through a supportive community. The curriculum includes the study of English, History, Geography, Religious Studies, French, German, Spanish, Italian, Mandarin Chinese, Latin, Greek, Mathematics, Physics, Chemistry, Biology, Design and Technology, Information & Communication Technology, Music, Art, Drama and Theatre Studies, Food Technology and Textiles. In addition, Classical Civilisation, Business Studies, Sports Science, Politics, Economics, Photography and History of Art are offered at A Level. Leiths Food & Wine Certificate is also offered to girls in the Sixth Form.

Although personal triumphs and individual achievements are the most celebrated within School, the foundation of academic success is evident from the GCSE and A Level statistics. In 2021, at I/GCSE 89% of grades were 9–7 and remarkably 71% achieved grades 9–8 (A*–A**). Most pleasing of all was the number of grade 9s across all subjects, which once again stands at 46%. At A Level 98% of girls achieved A* to B grades with the A*/D1/D2 percentage remaining consistently high, at 51%. These outstanding results ranked Downe House as the fourth best Girls Boarding School in the UK, and achieved places at some of the world's top universities for our graduates.

Pastoral Care. "Downe House was everything we hoped for in the next step for our daughter's education. You have evidently done a wonderful job of creating the right environment to foster achievement and happiness." (New parent, 2021)

Downe House was founded as 'a school where every individual within the community matters', and this has not changed. We work in partnership with parents to ensure that every Downe House girl leaves school with a lifelong intellectual curiosity, the confidence that she can face life's challenges, and a steadfast place in a lively school community.

Boarding. Downe House offers idyllic accommodation onsite, with a wealth of activities as part of our boarding model. So well-suited to the needs of a busy modern family, that over 90% of girls are boarding students. Offering both boarding and day places, Downe House provides every girl with the gift of time and space for extra-curricular activities balanced with important family time.

Fees per term (2021–2022). £14,030 for boarders, £10,435 for day girls.

Admissions. Girls may enter the school at 11+, 12+ or 13+ upon successful assessment, interview and Common Entrance. Girls can also join the Sixth Form after completing our interview and entrance test. Application for entry should be made well in advance. Prospective parents are asked to make an appointment to visit the School and meet the Headmistress prior to their daughter's start date.

Scholarships. The School offers a number of Academic Scholarships at 11+, 12+, 13+ and for entry into the Sixth Form. Scholarships are also awarded in Music, Art and Sport (11+ and 13+) and Drama (13+ and 16+) and there are Headmistress's Awards for outstanding all-round performers. As a Scholar or Exhibitioner, girls have access to our specialist Scholarship programme which offers a range of specialist enrichment activities to inspire her and extend her knowledge. A mentor is provided to guide and encourage her on her journey as well as important leadership opportunities, designed to stretch and challenge her. For more information on Scholarships please visit the website: www.downehouse.net/admissions/scholarships.

Bursaries. Downe House is committed to extending access to the education and welcoming girls who would otherwise be denied the opportunity of a boarding experience of the highest calibre and quality. For more information on Bursaries please visit our website: www.downehouse.net/admissions/bursaries.

Location. An easy drive from London takes you to our beautiful, secure school campus in the heart of rural West Berkshire. Our stunning 110-acre woodland estate overlooks the historic Berkshire Downs. Girls enjoy the close proximity to other schools for match fixtures and enrichment events, as well as hosting and attending socials with local prep schools and independent schools such as Eton College, Radley College, Bradfield College and Harrow School.

Be a Downe House girl. As one Sixth Former summed up the experience, 'I left Downe House with the feeling there was nothing I couldn't achieve.'

Charitable status. Downe House School is a Registered Charity, number 1015059. Our aim is the provision of a sound and broadly based education for girls, which will equip them for university entrance and beyond.

Governors:
Ms Fru Hazlitt, BA (*Chair of Governors*)
Mr Timothy Boucher, BA, FCA (*Chairman of Finance and General Purposes Committee*)
Ms Elizabeth Clarke, BA, CPE
Ms Veryan Exelby, MA
Mrs Fiona Holmes, BComm
Mr Nicholas Hornby, BSc
Dr Christopher O'Kane, MA, MB BChir, MSc, DPhil
Dr Clare Ratnage, BSc MBChB, MRCP, MRCGP
Mr Mark Ridley, BA, MA, MRICS
Mr Joe Smith, BA MEd PGCE (*Chairman of Education Committee*)
Mr Mark Wippell, MA, LLM

The Finance and Administration Bursar, Mr Colin Cockburn, FCCA acts as Clerk to the Governors.

Leadership Team:

Headmistress: Mrs Emma McKendrick, BA, PGCE, FRSA

Deputy Head: Mr Matthew Godfrey, BA, MA Ed, PGCE
Deputy Head (*Academic*): Mr Mark Hill, BA, MA, MEd, PGCE
Deputy Head (*Pastoral*): Mrs Genevieve Ford, BA, PGCE

Assistant Head (*Sixth Form*): Ms Melissa Stimson, MA, PGCE
Assistant Head (*Upper School*): Mrs Anna Dourountakis, BA, HDE Post Graduate

Assistant Head (*Lower School*): Mrs Judith Gilpin Jones, LWCMD
Assistant Head (*Operations*): Mrs Philippa Toogood, BA, MSt, PGCE

Finance Bursar: Mr Colin Cockburn, FCCA
Director of IS: Mr David McClymont, PG Dip, MCITP EA
Director of HR: Ms Kate Tuttle, MCIPD
Director of Estates, Property and Services: Mr Alasdair Heath
Director of Business Development: Mr Huw Morgan, LLB
PA to the Headmistress: Ms Judy Davies

Admissions:
Registrar: Miss Angela Nutt
Registrar@downehouse.net

Downside School

Stratton-on-the-Fosse, Radstock, Bath, Somerset BA3 4RJ

Tel: 01761 235100
email: reception@downside.co.uk
website: www.downside.co.uk
Twitter: @downsideschool
Facebook: @DownsideSchool
Instagram: @downside_school
LinkedIn: /school/11123663

At Downside, we are committed to working in partnership with families and to providing an environment which nurtures young people of integrity who can think for themselves, stand up for their beliefs, and act to make a positive difference in the world.

Founded in c.1614 and based just 25 minutes from the famous World Heritage City of Bath, we are one of England's oldest and most distinguished Catholic schools. We are a forward-thinking school, home to 340 pupils where boarders and day pupils share six Houses; four for boys and two for girls. We welcome pupils from overseas and currently have 34 different nationalities represented.

Our School is set in 500 acres of beautiful English countryside with extensive facilities including an indoor swimming pool, a Mac Suite dedicated to music, a 24/7 Health Centre, and a Performing Arts Centre housing a 400-seat Theatre and a Recording Studio.

All pupils benefit from our boarding ethos whether they are boarders, as 76% are, or day pupils, with all that means in terms of friendships, independence and life skills. Whilst Catholic, we welcome pupils and parents of all faiths who set store by emphasising the importance of moral courage, integrity and service to others.

We are uncompromising in the pursuit of academic excellence. We aim for the highest standards in our extensive and exciting co-curricular programme with over 100 activities, and we provide plentiful and varied opportunities for service and leadership. We celebrate the achievements and successes of our pupils, but do not allow these to define them.

Pupils achieve impressively in the Sciences, Maths and the Arts, and the vast majority of our pupils gain entry to their first choice of university, and a gratifying number of them achieve First Class Honours at their chosen place of study. Typical destinations include Oxford, Cambridge, Exeter, Durham, Warwick and Edinburgh.

Weekends are busy and purposeful, where pupils are engaged in a wide variety of activity options: clubs, games, sporting fixtures, socials, trips out and Sunday Mass. With all this on offer, there is never 'nothing to do'! Quite the opposite.

Academic. Strong intellectual traditions focusing on academic subjects, with a range of additional options to encourage independent learning and an enquiring mind. In 2020, at A Level, the proportion of A* grades rose to 27% (15% in 2019) and A*/A grades to 58% (36% in 2019).

Boarding. 75% of Downside pupils are 7-day-a-week boarders and approximately 40% are international; from all over Europe and worldwide. 27 different nationalities are represented at the school. Weekends for boarders are busy with Saturday morning lessons, sports fixtures in the afternoon and a full programme of activities; film nights, theatre trips, cookery and quiz competitions to name but a few. Pupils are all invited to celebrate Mass in the Abbey Church on Sunday morning.

Downside has six boarding houses: Powell, Isabella, Caverel, Barlow, Roberts and Smythe, with boarders and day pupils integrated together in all the houses. Junior boys join Powell House at 11, 12 & 13, before moving up to one of three senior boys' houses: Barlow, Roberts or Smythe, whilst girls join Isabella House at 11 and can move to Caverel House from the Third Form. Day pupils are integrated across the Houses and and benefit tremendously from being at a school that is primarily boarding.

Each House has its own spirit, character and traditions. Pupils have friends across the Houses but avidly compete in inter-house games, drama, music and other activities.

Downside School is proud to provide 24/7 professional nursing care, with access to three GP surgeries on site each week.

Sport. Pupils compete in a range of high-quality fixtures throughout the year in Rugby, Hockey, Netball, Cricket, Tennis, Cross-Country, Athletics and Football. Additional disciplines are offered as activities, ranging from Fencing to Squash, and Paddle Boarding to Polo.

Downside School believes that physical activity plays an important role in every pupil's life. Sport for All is a central part of the school's philosophy as is the desire for every pupil to enjoy sport and achieve their own personal best. With all our facilities on campus pupils can also swim, use the gym and play tennis in their own time and for budding athletes a cross country run need never leave the estate.

Arts. You'll discover that Art, Drama, Music, and Design & Technology are very popular amongst Downside pupils, both at GCSE and A level, and via the wide range of co-curricular options on offer.

Concerts are held in the magnificent Abbey Church throughout the year, while plays and other arts events are held in our Performing Arts Centre, which houses a 400-seat Theatre and recording Studio. We have an Artist-in-Residence who continually inspires the children, and the very latest equipment in our Design workshops from 3D printers to an iMac suite.

Founded over a century ago, Downside's Schola Cantorum is the oldest Roman Catholic school choir in the UK. Formed of boys and girls, it gives concerts of large-scale sacred works throughout the year and has topped the charts with its CDs, The Abbey and Gregorian Moods. There are three Chamber Choirs at Downside, plus opportunities in orchestral, band (rock, jazz, pipe) and chamber music, with frequent concerts and recitals as well as a new recording studio for budding professionals.

Alumni.

Tom Bethell (Journalist)

Rocco Forte (Hotelier)

Brion Gysin (Artist)

Jared Harris (Actor)

Christopher Jamison (Monk)

Emmanuel de Merode (Conservationist)

David Mlinaric (Designer)

William Nicholson (Writer)

Anthony Palliser (Artist)

John Pope-Hennessy (Art Historian)

Auberon Waugh (Journalist)

Adam Zamoyski (Historian)

Fees per term (2021–2022). Boarding £8,968–£12,032; Day £5,827–£6,908. Day Plus (2 nights accommodation) £6,841–£8,555; Day Plus (3 nights accommodation) £7,349–£9,379.

Scholarships are available for gifted and talented pupils in a range of areas. Please contact our Admissions Department for the latest assessment deadlines.

Charitable status. Downside School is a Registered Charity, number 1184700.

Chairman of School Governors: Dr G Mercer

Head: **A R Hobbs**, MA

Deputy Head: M Randall, BSc

Senior Leadership:
Director of Pastoral Care: Mrs C Murphy, BSc

House Mistress of Caverel: Ms A McGarry, BA
House Mistress of Isabella: Mrs K Westlake, BA
House Master of Barlow: S J Potter, BA
House Master of Roberts: J Freeman, BA, PGCE
House Master of Smythe: J Storey, BA
House Master of Powell: J Dolman, BSc

School Chaplains: Dom James Hood, Dom Boniface Hill, Mr Paul Andrewartha (*Lay Chaplain*)

Director of Music: J McNamara, MA
Director of Sport: R Jones, BA

Heads of Faculty:
Art & Design: N J Barrett, BEd
English: Mrs J Rainey, MA
Humanities: O G Simper, BA
Languages: R C Rawlins, MA
Mathematics: Dr J Tapia Amador, PhD
Science: P Rigby, BSc
Theology & RS: H F Walters, MA

Learning Support: Mrs C Storey

Head of Nursing: Miss M Pye

Director of Admissions & Marketing: Mrs I Hartnell

Marketing Manager: Mrs B Ward Murphy, BA

Development Manager: Mrs J Newman

Dulwich College

Dulwich Common, London SE21 7LD

Tel: 020 8693 3601
email: info@dulwich.org.uk
website: www.dulwich.org.uk
Twitter: @DulwichCollege
Facebook: @DulwichCollege

Motto: *Detur gloria soli Deo ~ Let Glory be given to God alone*

Dulwich College was founded in 1619 by Edward Alleyn, the Elizabethan actor, and marked its 400th anniversary in 2019 with a programme of events and activities.

The College is an academically selective, independent day and boarding school for boys aged 7–18; full and weekly boarding is available for boys aged 11–18. Situated in over 70 acres of grounds and playing fields, the campus is just 10 minutes by train from London Victoria. A Dulwich education ensures each pupil fulfils their academic potential whilst taking advantage of the wide range of sporting, cultural and adventurous activities on offer.

Boys move on to universities, medical and dental schools, music and art colleges. Almost all enter higher education, but an increasing number of boys are following vocational paths. Pupils are prepared for entry to the most competitive universities such as Oxford, Cambridge and Imperial, where a very good record of places is maintained each year.

The College's principal aims for all its boys are:

- to offer an appropriate academic challenge which enables each pupil to realise his potential;
- to create an environment which promotes an independent work ethic and encourages all boys to acquire a love of learning;
- to provide a wide range of sporting, cultural and adventurous activities for pupils to enjoy and through which they can learn to work cooperatively and to take a lead;
- to nurture a supportive community that encourages a sense of social responsibility and spiritual and personal development;
- to ensure that pupils from a broad variety of backgrounds can feel equally secure and valued;
- to offer boys and staff opportunities to benefit from and contribute to the College's international and UK educational partnerships.

Organisation. The College, comprising some 1,600 boys, has four specific schools: Junior School, Lower School, Middle School and Upper School. Each of these has its own Head who is responsible to The Master for that part of the College. Within each School there are Heads of Year and Form Tutors who have daily contact with boys in their care. These teams are responsible for overseeing the pastoral and academic welfare of the boys and they ensure that close links are fostered between parents and the College.

DUCKS. Dulwich College's Kindergarten and Infants' School is the only coeducational element of the College providing a secure foundation for future learning and development for children from 6 months to Year 2. Most children from DUCKS enter leading independent schools in south London, and many boys will pass the entrance examination for the College.

Day House system. A thriving Day House system offers boys the opportunity to take part in a wide range of competitive activities including art, chess, poetry, general knowledge, debating, drama and music. They can also compete in a number of sports throughout the academic year, including rugby, soccer, hockey, cricket and athletics.

Curriculum. In Years 7 and 8 all boys follow a broad and balanced curriculum, including all standard core subjects and French or Spanish, Chinese, Latin, Wellbeing, PE, Computing, Drama, DT, Art and Music. In Year 8, boys make a choice between Latin, Chinese or German; this reduces the number of languages studied to two, allowing boys the time to engage rigorously in their chosen languages and make significant progress. In Year 9 boys continue with the core subjects, Wellbeing and PE together with French or Spanish, and they choose a second language from German, Chinese, French, Spanish, Latin or Italian. This second language may be a continuation of languages they have previously studied, or they may start them from scratch. In Years 10 and 11 boys take between nine and 10 GCSE subjects, comprising English, English Literature, Mathematics, Biology, Chemistry, Physics and French or Spanish plus three optional subjects; they all continue with Wellbeing and PE. In the Upper School (Years 12 and 13), there is a free choice of three A Level subjects (four if they are studying Further Mathematics) and since 2017 every pupil has opted for an A Level 'Plus' option which is an in-house qualification that aims to provide enrichment, cross-curricular links and programmes that reflect the likely courses boys choose at university. Boys will also choose a 'Link' course in conjunction with James Allen's Girls' School that will provide breadth to their educational profile, including a regular lecture series and community service options. The concept of Free Learning (supra-curricular and other learning beyond the curriculum) is now fully embedded in the life of the College across all year groups.

Facilities. Over the years the College has developed its complex of buildings to meet the needs of boys' education in the twenty-first century, and this development continues. In the summer of 2022, work will begin on the complete refurbishment of the Lower School for Years 7 and 8.

One of these developments is The Laboratory, a new state-of-the-art building that brings together the twin cultures of Science and Art. There are 21 laboratories, three preparation rooms and the James Caird Hall, which houses the rescue boat of one of the College's most famous Old Alleynians, Sir Ernest Shackleton. There are five adaptable 'Informatics' suites with free-thinking spaces for creative learning and cross-curricular collaboration and a seminar room with full videoconferencing facilities. In addition there is a versatile 240-seat auditorium which is available to the whole Dulwich community for events and exhibitions and an outdoor piazza for recreation and performance.

Extensive IT facilities are available to all pupils. The IT network gives pupils and staff access to a wide range of centrally stored learning resources through the College's own virtual learning environment, 'MyDulwich'. Three separate libraries, all staffed by professional librarians, cater to the specific needs of different age groups. Exhibitions, drawn from the College archive, are regularly mounted in the Wodehouse Library.

The College has two separate dining areas which provide a wide choice of food, including a vegetarian option, on a cafeteria basis for both pupils and staff. The College also has its own shop, the Commissariat, where uniform, equipment and stationery can be purchased. The Medical Centre provides professional nursing care on a round-the-clock basis for boarders and day boys. The College Counsellor, based in the Medical Centre, provides confidential consultation for pupils and parents.

Sport is integral to life at Dulwich College both within the curriculum and as part of the wider co-curricular programme. There are over 70 acres of playing fields. The Sports Centre includes a substantial sports hall and a modern indoor 25-metre swimming pool. The College owns a boathouse on the Thames, accommodating the thriving Boat Club, and an Outdoor Centre in the Brecon Beacons which is used for a variety of activities and residential courses. The sports programme provides a continuity and breadth of experience across the age range, with 24 different sports on offer, giving all boys the opportunity to reach their sporting potential.

Music and Drama. A professionally equipped, purpose-built Music School provides all pupils with the opportunity to study a musical instrument. More than 500 pupils receive individual tuition every week from 35 experienced specialist musicians, led by the Heads of Strings, Wind, Brass, Keyboard and Singing. The College Chapel Choir, an ancient foundation, leads regular services in the Foundation Chapel (Christ's Chapel) and also at other venues throughout the country. The Edward Alleyn Theatre is a fully rigged auditorium with a capacity of 250; over 50 events are staged annually and the facility includes rehearsal and teaching spaces, as well as dressing rooms. In 2019 Dulwich College was awarded 'Independent School of the Year for the Performing Arts', acknowledging the work and talent of the Drama and Music departments. The award was conferred by *Independent School Parent* magazine.

Clubs and Societies. A wide variety of clubs and societies, many run by the pupils themselves, take place during the lunch break and after school. These range from Lego for the younger boys to the Political Society which is responsible for inviting prominent public figures to speak. The College is particularly renowned for its Debating success that in 2016 culminated in a Year 12 pupil captaining Team England to victory in the World Schools Debating Championships. The College encourages boys to take part in expeditions as well as many community-based activities which can include membership of the Combined Cadet Force, Scouts, the Duke of Edinburgh's Award scheme and Community Action. Academic, cultural and sporting excursions take place at various points throughout the school year.

Careers. Specialist careers staff, professional external advisors, dedicated IT facilities and an accredited library provide an up-to-date service assisting boys in planning higher education and careers. Boys and their parents attend the annual Courses and Careers Convention to consult with representatives from key employers, professional institutes and around 25 universities. Upper School boys receive guidance on how degree course choices might influence their future careers.

Boarding. There are three boarding houses in Dulwich College, all situated within or close to the campus. Each house has a Housemaster who is resident with his family. Boys in Years 7–13 live in Old Blew and The Orchard and boys in the Upper School live in Blew House and Ivyholme, where each boy has his own room with en-suite facilities. At present, there are around 140 boarders. Boarding at Dulwich is truly international with boys coming from all over the world and this adds to an atmosphere of cultural tolerance and intellectual curiosity.

ISI Inspection November 2014. ISI Inspectors awarded Dulwich College, Dulwich College Junior School and DUCKS 'Excellent' in every category, 'Exceptional' for 'the quality of pupils' achievements and learning' for the senior school – the only category for which this grading can be given – and 'Outstanding' for the EYFS (Kindergarten, Nursery and Reception).

Entry. Pupils are admitted to the College as day pupils, boarders, weekly boarders or occasional boarders. Places are available at age 7, 11, 13 and 16. Casual vacancies occur from time to time at ages 8, 9, 10 and 12. At age 7 places are awarded on the basis of interview, report and practical assessment during the Lent Term. At age 11 places are awarded on the results of the Combined Entrance and Scholarship Examination held in the Lent Term. Candidates take papers in English and Mathematics and also a Verbal/Non-Verbal Reasoning test. At age 13 boys may take the College's own Entrance Examinations held in the Lent Term. Entrance is by examination and interview. At 16+ places are offered on the results from subject specific tests, interview and GCSE grades. Application should generally be in the year before desired date of entry. For further information please see the Admissions section on the College website. A non-refundable registration fee of £150 is charged for all applications and £300 for overseas applications.

Fees per term (2021–2022). Day £7,224 (includes lunch for Junior and Lower School pupils up to Year 8); Full Boarding £15,078; Weekly Boarding £14,136.

Scholarships and Bursaries. Over 35% of boys at Dulwich College are supported with financial awards. A significant number of academic scholarships are awarded each year up to one-third of the tuition fee. There are also scholarships for Music, Art and Sports. Scholarships can be enhanced by Bursaries in cases of financial need. A substantial number of Bursaries are awarded annually to new boys entering Year 3, Year 7 or Year 9 where parents are unable to pay the full tuition fee. Bursaries are means-tested and reviewed annually. All applicants will be considered on the basis of their performance in the entrance examination and interview. A Bursary and a Scholarship might be awarded together up to a maximum value of 100% of the school fees. In addition to school fees, means-tested support may be available for trips and other enrichment activities.

Old Alleynians. Founded in 1873, The Alleyn Club is a flourishing former pupils' association with over 10,000 Old Alleynian (OA) members living in more than 90 countries. The club's name acknowledges the founder, Edward Alleyn, actor, theatre manager and contemporary of William Shakespeare.

Charitable status. Dulwich College is a Registered Charity, number 1150064.

The Governing Body:
Chair: Adrian JS Carr, PhD [OA]
Fred Binka [OA]
Dr Irene Bishop, CBE, BEd, MA, LLD
Keri Elborn, BA, FCA

Karen Fowler, MA
Randa Hanna, BA, AA Dip RIBA
Howard Kerr, MA, MBA
David Parfitt
Catherine Polli, LLB
Tim Pethybridge
Malik Ramadhan, OBE [OA]
Kirsty Rutter, BSc, ACMA

Honorary International Advisor to the Governors:
His Excellency Khun Anand Panyarachun, Hon KBE, MA
    [OA]

Special Advisor to the Governors: Sir John H Riblat,
    FRICS, Hon FRIBA [OA]

[OA] *Old Alleynian*

Clerk to the Governors: Ms K Jones, LLB

Master of the College: Dr J A F Spence, BA Hons, PhD

Deputy Masters:
Mrs F M Angel, BA (*Senior Deputy*)
Mr D A P King, MA (*Academic*)
Dr C S B Pyke, MA, MMus, PhD (*External*)
Mr I L H Scarisbrick, BSc (*Co-curricular*)
Mr E Read, MA (*Pastoral and Co-curricular*)

Chief Operating Officer: Mr S J Yiend, MA
Chief Financial Officer: Mr B Hoo, ACA

Director of Communications: Ms J M Scott, MA, MBA
Director of Development: Mr M Jarrett, BA
Director of Admissions, Libraries & Archives: Dr N D
    Black, BA, PhD

Head of Upper School: Mr A J Threadgould, BSc
Head of Middle School: Mr S Tanna, BA
Head of Lower School: Ms F Cooke, BA
Head of Junior School: Dr T G A Griffiths, PGCE, MA,
    MSc, DPhil
Head of DUCKS (*Kindergarten and Infants' School*): Mrs
    M Norris, BEd, ILMP, MEd

Registrar: Mrs S Betts
Archivist: Mrs C M Lucy, BA, MCLIP
Head of Academic Administration: Dr J Kinch, BA, BPhil,
    DPhil
Head of Outings & Expeditions: Mr S Croucher
Examinations Officer: Mr M Grantham-Hill, BSc
Staff Tutor: Mr P J Whibley, BA

Heads of Departments:

Art: Mrs S Mulholland, BA (*Director of Art & DT*)
Classics: Dr J-M Hulls, MPhil, PhD

Drama:
Mr P V Jolly, BA, Dip RSA (*Director of Drama*)
Mrs K Norton-Smith, BA (*Head of Academic Drama*)

EAL: Miss S E Horsfield, BA
Economics: Dr J Wisson
English: Mr R Fisher, BA
Geography: Dr C Nayeri

Higher Education & Careers:
Mr R F Sutton (*Director of Higher Education*)
Ms N Stoney (*Head of Careers*)

Politics: Mr I Hollingshead
History: Mr C O Siochru

ICT:
Mr J D Cartwright, MA (*Head of Computer Science*)
Dr A C Storey, BA, MSc, PhD (*Director of ICT*)

Learning Support: Miss E Walters
Libraries: Mr P J Fletcher, BA, DipLib, MCLIP (*Head of
    Libraries*)
Lower & Junior School Science: Mrs J Ratnasabapathy
Mathematics: Mr A England

Modern Languages:
Mr R S Baylis, MA, MA (*Head of Modern Languages*)
Chinese: Mr A M Stark, BA, DMS, MA
German: Mr W Dugdale, BA
Spanish: Mr A Iltchev, BA

Music:
Mr R G Mayo, MA, MusB, FRCO (*Director of Music*)
Ms C Cousens, MA, FRCO (*Head of Academic Music*)

Physical Education:
Mr P C Greenaway, BSc (*Director of Sport*)
Mr M Burdekin, BA (*Assistant Director of Sport*)

Religion and Theology: Mr S Dungate-Jones, BA
Scholars: Dr N T Croally, MA, PhD [OA]

Science:
Dr R E McIlwaine, MChem, PGCE, PhD (*Director of
    Studies*)
Biology: Mr N Gardner, MSc, BSc
Chemistry: Dr J Flanagan, PhD, MSci
Physics: Miss L Kelly, BA
Psychology: Dr P Cue, BSc, PhD

DUCKS (*Dulwich College Kindergarten and Infants'
    School*):
Mrs M Norris, BEd, ILMP, MEd (*Head of DUCKS*)
Mrs S Donaldson, NNEB, MA (*Head of Kindergarten*)

Medical Centre Charge Nurse: Mrs C Baxter-Wilks, RN,
    BSc, MSc
College Counsellor: Ms J Ray, IATE
Medical Officer: Dr R A Leonard, MBE, MA, MB, BChir,
    MRCGP, DRCOG

PA to the Master: Mrs M Wood
PA Governance & Finance: Ms S White

The High School of Dundee

Euclid Crescent, Dundee, Tayside DD1 1HU

Tel: 01382 202921
email: enquiries@highschoolofdundee.org.uk
website: www.highschoolofdundee.org.uk
Twitter: @HSofDundee
Facebook: @highschoolofdundee
LinkedIn: /high-school-of-dundee

Motto: *Prestante Domino*

The present School traces its origins directly back to a
13th century foundation by the Abbot and Monks of
Lindores. It received a Royal Charter in 1859. Various Acts
of Parliament in the 19th Century were finally consolidated
in an Order in Council constituting the High School of
Dundee Scheme 1965, which was revised in 1987.

Admission. The School comprises three sections:

The Nursery – 41 pupils (age 3–5; pre-school and ante pre-school).

The Junior Years – 292 pupils (Primary 1 to Primary 7).

The Senior Years – 637 pupils (S1 to S6).

The normal stages of entry are Nursery, Primary 1 and S1. Entry to Primary 1 (age 4½ to 5½ years) is by interview held in January and to S1 (age 11 to 12 years) by an Entrance Assessment held in January. Where vacancies exist entrance is usually available at all other stages subject to satisfactory performance in an entrance assessment.

Bursaries. A number of means-tested bursaries are provided for entry to P6/7 and from S1 in the Senior Years, to help those who otherwise could not afford the fees.

Fees per term (2021–2022). Primary: £3,206 (P1 to P3), £3,359 (P4 to P5), £3,816 (P6 to P7); Secondary £4,550. Nursery varies according to the number of sessions selected.

Buildings. The six main school buildings are in the centre of the city and form an architectural feature of the area. Two excellent, extensive playing fields – Dalnacraig and Mayfield – are situated some 1½ miles to the east of the school. As well as grass pitches, the facilities include an international standard synthetic water-based hockey surface and a sand-dressed synthetic hockey pitch which is up to national standard. The school's Mayfield Sports Centre, comprising a state-of-the-art games hall, dance studio, gymnasium and fitness suite, is adjacent to the playing fields. The Nursery is also located at Mayfield. In 2013 the School acquired the former Head Post Office Building, located just yards from the city centre campus, and is currently in the midst of an ambitious project to transform this landmark building into a flagship centre of excellence for performing and visual arts, both for the school and for the wider community.

Curriculum. The Junior Years follow a wide-ranging primary curriculum. Subject specialists are employed in PE, ICT, Music, Science, Modern Languages, Art, Drama and Health and Food Technology.

In the Senior Years, after two years of a general curriculum, some specialisation takes place with pupils currently being prepared for the Scottish Qualifications Authority examinations at National 5, Higher and Advanced Higher which lead directly to university entrance. Results in public examinations are amongst the best in Scotland, with pupils regularly achieving the top marks nationally in individual subjects, and 90–95% of leavers enrolling at universities in the UK or abroad.

Co-Curricular Activities. Almost 100 co-curricular activities are offered. Sports teams compete at the highest levels and each year a number of pupils represent their country in a wide range of sports. Music plays an important part in the life of the school, with a large number of orchestras, bands, choirs and musical ensembles to choose from. Special tuition is provided in a wide variety of instruments.

There is a flourishing contingent of the Combined Cadet Force including a pipe band. Drama, Public Speaking and Debating, Chess and The Duke of Edinburgh's Award scheme are examples of the wide variety of activities available.

Charitable status. The Corporation of the High School of Dundee is a Registered Charity, number SC011522. The school is a charity to provide quality education for boys and girls.

The Board of Directors comprises: Chairman, 2 ex officiis Directors, viz, The Lord Dean of Guild and The Parish Minister of Dundee. The Guildry of Dundee, the Nine Trades of Dundee, the Old Boys' Club and the Old Girls' Club and the Parents' Association each elect one Director. Six Directors are elected by Friends of the High School and up to 6 co-opted by the Board.

School Staff:

Rector: Mrs L A M Hudson, MA

Deputy Rector (*Senior Years*): Mrs S J Watson, MA

Deputy Rector (*Junior Years*): Mrs J Rose, BEd

Bursar: Miss C MacDonald, LLB CA

Deputy Heads – Senior School:
Mr D A Brett, BSc
Mr N R Clarke, BSc, MSc
Mr D G Smith, BSc

Deputy Heads – Junior Years:
Mr R Petrie, BA
Mrs C E Proudfoot, MA, DELL

Director of ICT: Mrs W Wilson, BSc

Junior Years:

Miss M Cardno, MA, CEEd	Mr N W Joss, MA
Mrs A Davie, MEd	Mrs C E Rankin, BA
Mrs L Coupar, MA	Mrs E Morenikeji, BEd
Mrs S Fish, BEd	Mrs A J Steven, BA
Miss K A Reith, MEd, DELL	Mrs C E Proudfoot, MA, DELL
Miss L Carrie, MA, MPhil	Mr R Petrie, BA
Mrs M R Leburn, MA	Miss E Innes, BSc
Miss J Wallace, BEd	Miss C Devlin, MA
Mrs D Sager, MA	Miss H Burleigh, BA Hons
Mrs F A Trotter, BSc	Miss I McFarlane, MA, MSc
Mrs G Johnson, BEd	

Nursery:
Manager: Mrs S C Tosh, MA, PGCE

Mrs L C Yule, BA	Miss A Mackie
Mrs D M Irving, BA	Miss R McFadden
Miss A A Balfour	Miss J Wakeford
Miss N V Whyte	Mrs J McGahie
Mrs K Roberts	Miss C Hutton
Mrs S Crotti	

Senior School:
* *Head of Department*

English:
*Mrs A Tevendale, BA Hons, MEd
Mr C Anderson, MA
Ms J Fulton, MA
Mr M A Stewart, MA, MPhil
Mr D M Finlay, MA
Mr D P Campbell, MA

Drama and Media Studies:
*Mrs L M Drummond, Dip Drama
Mr M R Readman, BA
Mrs L E Sangster, BA

History and Modern Studies:
*Mr G Fyall, BA, Dip Ed
Mrs L Jack, MA
Mrs L A Hudson, MA
Mr R W Welsh, MA
Miss K H E Douglas, MA
Mr G J Rennet, MA

Geography:
*Miss J L Stewart, BSc
Mr C R McAdam, MA
Mrs R Lloyd, MA, MSc
Mrs S J Watson, MA

Philosophy and Religion:
*A W Cummins, BD, Dip Min

Business Education:
*Mr N S Higgins, BSc
Miss A Campbell, MA Hons
Mr N Duncan, BA Hons

Classics:
*Mr E Faulkes, BA
Dr A Lazani, BA, MA

Modern Languages:
*Mr N A MacKinnon, MA
Mrs I M McGrath, MA
Mrs J Brown, BA
Ms A Aguero, BA
Mr F M McAvinue, MA, MSc
Mr J P Nolan, MA
Mrs D M Wedderburn, MA
Mrs Y Murdoch, MSc
Mrs L C Smith, MA

Mathematics:
*Mrs L A Craig, BSc
Mr N R Clarke, BSc, MSc
Mr R C Middleton, BSc
Miss D Macdonald, BSc
Dr P A Smith, BA, MEng, MA, PhD
Dr F Spiezia, MSc, PhD
Dr N McReynolds, MPhys, PhD
Dr A K Pepper, MChem, PhD, FRSC

Chemistry:
*Dr N Kiernan, MChem, PhD
Mrs R J Broom, BSc
Mr D A Brett, BSc
Mr A S Downie, BSc
Dr E R T Robinson, MChem, PhD
Dr A K Pepper, MChem, PhD, FRSC

Biology:
*Dr E Duncanson, BSc, PhD
Dr M W Fotheringham, MA, PhD
Mr G M S Rodger, BSc
Mr R H Bunting, BSc

Physics:
*Mr J Darby, BSc
Dr D G Brown, BSc, PhD
Dr G MacKay, BSc, MSc, PhD

Technologies:
*Mr S McBride, BSc
Mr D G Smith, BSc
Mr A N Wilson, BA
Mr S Hill

Art and Design:
*Mr A Kerr, BA
Mrs M Angus, BA
Mrs A Douglas, BDes
Mrs J Cura, MDes

Music:
*Dr L S Steuart Fothringham, MA, PhD, FRCO
Mr D G Love, Dip RSAMD
Ms G Simpson, Dip Mus, ALCM
Mr S Armstrong, Dip RSAMD
Mrs S Sneddon, LTCL, ALCM
Miss A Evans, BA, LTCL
Ms S Morgan, BMus
Mrs J Petrie, BA, CPGS
Mrs E M J Stevenson, MA
Mrs S Colgan, BEd, PG Dip, LRAM
Mr D W S Wilton, BA
Mr E J Tonner, BMus

Learning Skills:
*Mrs J M Downie, MA, Dip ASL
Mrs K L Whiting, BSc
Mrs L Duff, MA
Mrs C McDonald, BEd
Mrs K Goldie, BEd

Physical Education:
*Mr E D Jack, BEd
Mr G R E Merry, BSc
Miss L A Allan, Dip Ed
Miss P Geatons, BEd
Mr I Strachan
Mr C K Allan, BSc
Mrs L S L Baxter, BEd
Mrs L Anderson, BEd (*Head of Hockey*)
Mr P J Godman (*Head of Rugby*)
Mr C D O'Donnell, BSc
Miss A A Robinson, MA
Mr R A Aitken, BSc

Home Economics:
*Mrs L J Ross, MA
Mrs O Anderson, BSc

Library:
*Ms S M I A Lloyd-Wiggins, BA
Mrs J S Hutton, MA

Guidance:
Mr N R Clarke, BSc, MSc (*Deputy Head with responsibility for Guidance*)

Principal Teachers:
Mr R W Welsh, MA
Mrs L S L Baxter, BEd
Mrs J Brown, BA

Assistant Principal Teachers:
Mr C K Allan, BSc
Mr G R E Merry, BSc
Mr A S Downie, BSc

Ms J Fulton, MA
Mrs L Jack, MA

Head of Careers:
Mr G M S Rodger, BSc

Outdoor Activities Coordinator:
Mr G M Ross, BA

Head of Academic Administration:
Mrs I M McGrath, MA

Eastbourne College

Old Wish Road, Eastbourne, East Sussex BN21 4JX

Tel: Admissions: 01323 452323
              Headmaster: 01323 452300
              Bursar: 01323 452300
email: reception@eastbourne-college.co.uk
website: www.eastbourne-college.co.uk
Twitter: @EBCollegeLife
Facebook: @EastbourneCollege
Instagram: @eastbournecollege
LinkedIn: /eastbourne-college

Founded 1867; Incorporated 1911.

Endless horizons endless opportunities

Few top senior independent schools in Britain offer a six-minute stroll to the doorstep of a national park, an international tennis venue, a county cricket ground, two challenging golf courses, award-winning beaches, theatres, a modern art gallery, a brand new shopping centre with state-of-the-art cinema, and a mainline station to London (85 minutes), London Gatwick Airport (55 minutes), and Ashford International (direct trains to Europe).

Independently minded since 1867

Founded over 150 years ago, today Eastbourne College reaches out like never before, connecting its boarding and day pupils with a raft of opportunities that abound within a few hundred metres of the school. The College's learning environment is second to none thanks to a recently completed £33 million development, an outstanding, supportive house system, and a timetable which optimises educational contact time, provides guided optional Saturday morning enrichment sessions, and promotes a busy calendar of competitive sport and time to socialise.

A traditional heart. A modern mind.

We've always done things differently at Eastbourne College. We're proud of our heritage, but always looking forward. Progressive and innovative. Empowering our pupils to question the answers and find their own path in life. Set in idyllic coastal surroundings, this is a place that truly makes a lasting impression. We encourage children to be confident and also teach them to be kind, courteous and considerate of others, put simply, good people that others want to be around.

Why Eastbourne College?

- Holistic approach to learning, nurturing success in and out of the classroom
- Over 91% A*–C at GCSE and over 94% A*–C at A Level
- We sit in the top 4% of schools nationally for academic 'value added' which means on average our pupils achieve one grade above their predicted grade

- Diverse and exciting co-curriculum, offering everything from Art to Zumba
- Strong support network where pupils feel at home from day one
- Flexible, family-friendly for both boarders and day pupils, and those that need a combination of the two

World-class campus

In 2019, Dame Katherine Grainger DBE officially opened Eastbourne College's Project 150. The £33 million P150 development places the College at the forefront of learning environments in the UK.

Facilities include:

- 32 state-of-the-art classrooms
- two technology suites
- cricket pavilion with live-stream match video analysis
- dance studio with sprung floor and ceiling recess for ballet lifts and throws
- large Sport England compliant sports hall (5 badminton courts long); year-round multi-sport training
- Sport England compliant six lane 25m indoor swimming pool
- fitness suite for elite and inclusive participation
- two glass-backed squash courts
- alfresco-feel dining hall
- Tim's café
- stunning entertainment and exhibition spaces.

Admissions

Year 9 entry. Early registration for a place is recommended in Year 5/6. The College runs an Early Offer system which uses underlying ability score data and a detailed headmaster/mistress reference about a Year 6 or 7 pupil who is registered with us and whom we have been able to meet during a personal visit in order to make a firm offer of a place. Please contact the Admissions Department for more information.

Sixth form entry. Applicants for the sixth form should be predicted a GCSE grade average of 6.5 or above and receive a very positive reference from their current school. We normally expect sixth form applicants to complete a minimum of 8 GCSEs. If you would like to be considered for entry to the sixth form at the College in August 2022, please contact us to arrange a visit. This should be done as early as possible and certainly no later than by the end of the first term of Year 11.

Scholarships and Bursaries. Academic, creative arts and sports awards are offered. In line with most top independent schools, the great majority of awards given at the College are valued at between 5% and 20% of the day or boarding fees, but more may be offered in exceptional circumstances and awards may be supplemented by a means-tested bursary.

Bursaries are means tested according to the Charity Commission criteria.

Entry forms for scholarships can be obtained from the Admissions Department.

Fees per term (2021–2022). Boarding: £12,565 (Years 9–11), £12,760 (Sixth Form); Day: £8,245 (Years 9–11), £8,410 (Sixth Form). An additional supplement for overseas pupils applies. Fees include meals and most extras.

Preparatory School. The charitable bodies governing Eastbourne College and the independent prep school, St Andrew's Prep, amalgamated in February 2010 to become one charity. Collaboration between the two schools had always been extremely close but, until then, there had been no formal financial or governance links between them. This was a change of governance and not of the school. The schools continue to operate independently and St Andrew's prepares boys and girls for a variety of schools including the College.

The **Eastbournian Society** brings together all those with a College connection: parents of current and former pupils, current and former staff, Old Eastbournians, friends, neighbours and local businesses. In particular, strong links are maintained with former pupils who offer careers assistance to current pupils (there is a convention every year to support the careers and higher education programme). The Society provides a series of social events and career and business networking opportunities. It comprises also the College's fundraising activity, providing funds for bursaries and new developments.

The **Devonshire Society** (legacy club) meets annually.

Charitable status. Eastbourne College Incorporated is a Registered Charity, number 307071. It exists for the purpose of educating children.

Board of Governors:

President: His Grace The Duke of Devonshire, KCVO, CBE, DL

Vice-Presidents:
The Earl of Burlington
His Excellency Nasser Judeh, BSc
General The Lord Richards of Herstmonceux, GCB, CBE, DSO, DL

Chairman: Mr P A J Broadley, MA Oxon, MSc, FCA
Vice-Chairman: Mr J P Watmough, LLB

College Chaplaincy:
Chaplain: Revd D J Merceron, BA Institute of Archaeology

Chief Operating Officer and Clerk to the Board of Governors: Abbey Gough, BA, FCA

Senior Management Team:

***Headmaster*: The Hon T N M Lawson**, MA Christ Church Oxford

Second Master: Mr C W Symes, BSc, MEd, MCGI Edinburgh
Deputy Head (Academic): Mr J M Gilbert, BSc Cardiff, MBA, MRSC
Deputy Head (Co-curricular): Mr A T Lamb, MBE, BA University of New England NSW Australia, Dip Ed, DL
Deputy Head (Pastoral): Mrs G E Taylor-Hall, BA Liverpool
Development Director, Eastbournian Society: Mrs E C B Garrett, BA Warwick
Director of Marketing and Admissions to the Eastbourne College Charity: Mrs G L Crowhurst, BA Oxford Brookes

The Edinburgh Academy

42 Henderson Row, Edinburgh EH3 5BL

Tel: 0131 556 4603
           0131 624 4987 (Admissions)
email: office@edinburghacademy.org.uk
           admissions@edinburghacademy.org.uk
website: www.edinburghacademy.org.uk
Twitter: @edinburghacad
Facebook: @TheEdinburghAcademy
Instagram: @edinburghacad

The Edinburgh Academy is a co-educational day school for pupils aged 2 to 18 with a proud history and outward vision. Founded in 1824 with the aspiration to create a school where excellence could always be achieved, the School motto translates as 'Always Excel'. The Edinburgh Academy is built on strong traditions but is always seeking to innovate.

The Edinburgh Academy consists of a Nursery of 100 children, a Junior School of 404 children and a Senior School of 662. The School's size allows it to cater for the individual needs and ambitions of each child whilst high staff ratios means that at each stage it can tailor the teaching and pastoral care to the needs of each pupil, giving them the best possible chance to develop their unique talents. Through a rounded education Academy pupils enhance their social, emotional and spiritual capacities; equipping them for citizenship in a challenging and changing world. The attributes of an Academy Learner are that they are curious, creative, independent, collaborative and resilient.

Campus. A strength of the Academy is the split campus. This allows for purpose-built facilities and high-quality teaching at each age and stage through which all children can flourish.

Situated in Edinburgh's New Town since 1824, the Senior School is a stunning architectural blend of traditional and modern buildings. The most recent additions have been the splendid Science Centre (inspired by an alumnus of the school, mathematical physicist James Clerk Maxwell) and the Salvesan Performing Arts Centre.

The Junior School, Nursery and Playing Fields are on Arboretum Road: next to the world-renowned Royal Botanic Gardens. The recently opened McTavish Wing at the Junior School has created a new library, learning resource centre and four additional classrooms whilst the purpose-built Nursery provides a bright, functional and fun environment ensuring the best of opportunities for learning through play and experience both inside and out.

Academic. The Academy supports each child on their preferred education path and gets to know each individual extremely well in helping them to reach their personal goals and achieve to the best of their ability. The pre-14 curriculum offers flexibility; giving a very good grounding in basic skills whilst allowing pupils to progress through developing the critical higher order skills inherent in the best parts of 'A Curriculum for Excellence'. Older Senior School pupils present for exams in a wide range of subjects at National 5, Higher and Advanced Higher.

In keeping with the stated vision of producing children who are 'Grounded in Scotland, Ready for the World', the school takes pride in the fact that there are Academicals (alumni) around the globe who look back on their Academy education as their first crucial step on the ladder to success.

Class Sizes. Class sizes are kept relatively small to allow teachers to identify and nurture each child's strengths. In the Junior School the aim is to keep class sizes of around 22 children. In the Senior School, no teaching group is larger than 20 pupils, and most are substantially smaller.

Courses of Study. A very wide general curriculum is taught at the Edinburgh Academy between the ages of 2 and 14. Away from the valuable lessons taught by their class teacher, Nursery pupils receive specialist teaching in Science, PE, Modern European Languages and Music. In Junior School this is further complimented by Art and Mandarin (from Primary 5) whilst in Senior School specialist Latin, Drama and Design Technology are introduced. Maths is set from Primary 3 and all subjects are taught by Secondary School specialist teachers from Primary 7 (Geits).

Eight subjects are taken for National 5 (GCSE equivalent): English, Maths, a foreign language and a science must be taken and it is recommended that pupils complete the balance by adding either History or Geography, and one of Art, Music, Drama, PE or a technical subject.

In the final years of the Senior School the emphasis increasingly moves towards preparing young people for higher education and beyond. The penultimate year sees the breadth inherent in Scottish Highers followed by the greater depth of Advanced Highers. In Art and Music a two-year A Level course is offered in the belief that this is better suited to the needs of pupils looking to progress in those specialisms.

Physical Education. All Academy pupils are encouraged to stay active and healthy. Over 25 acres of sports pitches, including four all-weather surfaces, squash, tennis and fives courts and a sports centre, are coupled with top-class coaching to help them enjoy their chosen sports. Pupils can choose from a full range of winter and summer sports and teams represent the School in rugby, hockey, football, cricket, tennis, squash, badminton, fives, athletics, skiing, shooting, golf, shooting, sailing, swimming, cross country running, basketball, netball and dance.

In March of 2015 the Academy opened a brand new state-of-the-art Climbing and Bouldering Facility that is without doubt the best school arena of this type in the country.

Outdoor Education. The Edinburgh Academy has invested significantly in its recently established 'Spirit of Adventure Fund'. As well as the Climbing Wall this has allowed for the recruitment of both a Head of Outdoor Education and an Early Years Outdoor Learning specialist. This example of 'EA Innovation' means that all Academy children from the youngest in the Nursery to those completing their Gold Duke of Edinburgh's Award benefit from the resilience and character most easily developed in the outdoors.

Music, Drama, Art. The Creative Arts are an important part of Edinburgh Academy life and pupils are encouraged to take part from Junior School and beyond. Most pupils learn a musical instrument and are members of the various choirs, orchestras, bands and ensembles. All Junior School pupils take part in an annual drama production whilst the Senior School produces extremely high-quality performances at regular intervals throughout the year.

In Art, a large number of pupils take the A Level and the success rate for being accepted into Art College is very high. A number of students join the Academy each year with their primary objective being to study Fine Art. This is complemented in Design and Technology where there is a fully furnished Jewellery Studio. At the end of each year there is a major exhibition in these subjects where pupils' work is displayed and sold.

Extra-Curricular. The Academy recognises that significant learning takes place outside the formal classroom and believes in a balance between academic and co-curricular activities; offering a wide range of opportunities to participate and represent the Academy in sport, music and a variety of expressive and creative arts.

There is an extremely broad range of co-curricular activities available including Debating, Photography, Computing, Model United Nations, Modern Languages, Jazz, Politics, Scripture Union, Film Club, Bridge, Chess, Eco Group, Sailing, Cross Country, Climbing, Football and many, many more.

Combined Cadet Force and The Duke of Edinburgh's Award. All pupils over the age of 14 must participate in either the CCF (Army, RAF or Pipe Band sections) or The Duke of Edinburgh's Award scheme for a period of three terms after which further participation is voluntary. The CCF sections offer training in field craft, weapons handling, orienteering, drill and first aid and affords young people the opportunity to develop their leadership potential.

Fees per annum (2021–2022). Nursery £2,927–£12,693. Junior School (P1–P6) £9,165–£11,400, Senior School (P7–7ths/S6): £12,360–£15,342. When 3 or more siblings are in attendance at the School (excluding Nursery) at the same time, a reduction of one-third of the tuition fees is made for each sibling after the first two. For further details about the financial package available please contact Accounts on 0131 624 4916.

Scholarships and Bursaries. Means-tested Bursaries of up to 100% of fees are offered to pupils who are most able to benefit from an Edinburgh Academy education; irrespective of financial means. These are generally available to Senior School pupils.

A number of Scholarships (age 11+) are offered to candidates of very high ability either academically or in Art, Music or Sport. Examinations and assessments are held in January.

Admissions. The majority of new pupils join at the beginning of the Autumn Term in late August though some also join during the session. Other than for Nursery, all candidates for admission to the Edinburgh Academy must be assessed by the School and assessment days are held in November (Junior School P2–6) and January (P1 and Senior School). The Academy is always delighted to welcome families outwith this time. Initial enquiries should be made to the Admissions Registrar: Tel: 0131 624 4987; email: admissions@edinburghacademy.org.uk.

Edinburgh Academical Club. There is a strong former pupil community and the Club works hard to remain in contact with former pupils all over the world. They host events each year, both from a social and career perspective, and have established a career mentoring and internship service to help former pupils. Contact: Tel: 0131 624 4958, email: accies@edinburghacademy.org.uk.

Charitable Status. The Edinburgh Academy is a Registered Charity, number SC016999. It exists for the advancement of education and the contribution to the educational life of Scotland in its widest sense.

Court of Directors:
Chair: R Bogie, BA

Bursar and Clerk to the Court: G G Cartwright, MA CA

Rector: Mr Barry Welsh

Junior School Staff:
Head of the Junior School: Mr G A Calder, MA Hons, PGCE, Dip Ed Leadership
Deputy Head of the Junior School: Mrs L Htet Khin, LLB Hons

Senior School Staff:
Deputy Rector (*Director of Studies*): Mr T J Halsall, BA, MEd, PGCE
Deputy Rector (*Pastoral and Personnel*): Mr M Bryce, BSc
Deputy Rector (*Learning and Teaching*): Mrs C E Hancox, MA, PGCE

Elizabeth College

The Grange, St Peter Port, Guernsey, Channel Islands GY1 2PY

Tel: 01481 726544
email: office@elizabethcollege.gg
website: www.elizabethcollege.gg
Twitter: @Eliz_Coll
Facebook: @ElizabethCollegeGuernsey

Motto: *Semper Eadem*

Elizabeth College was founded in 1563 by Queen Elizabeth I in order to provide education for boys seeking ordination in the Church of England. It is one of the original members of HMC and has Direct Grant status. It provides a broad education while maintaining the Christian aspirations of its Foundress. There are approximately 860 pupils in the College, of whom about 260 are in the Junior School. The Junior School is co-educational and the College will be co-educational throughout eventually. Girls joined the Upper School in Year 7 and Year 12 from September 2021 and will continue phasing in over the next four years. Our well established Sixth Form partnership with nearby Ladies' College continues.

Buildings and Grounds. The Upper School (for pupils over 11 years) with its imposing main building (1829) overlooks the town and harbour of St Peter Port. The classrooms and laboratories, all of which are equipped with appropriate modern teaching facilities, the Hall, Sports Hall and Swimming Pool are accommodated on this site. Improvements in recent years have included a new Refectory, six fully refurbished Science Laboratories, the creation of the Science Quad and outdoor learning spaces at both the Upper and Junior School sites. There are two large games fields, one of which includes an artificial pitch for hockey. Elizabeth College Junior School (ECJS) comprises ECJS Queen's Road, the Junior School (years 3–6) and ECJS Kings Road, our infant school and pre-school. The Junior School has its own site ten minutes' walk from Elizabeth College. It takes boys and girls from 4 to 11 years old and also has a pre-school facility for younger children.

Perrot Court. There have been a number of landmark moments in the lifetime of the College; self-evidently the most important is its foundation in 1563 with the grant of the original site. 459 years on, we are at another landmark in the life of the College. The purchase of the adjacent building, Perrot Court, allows us to enhance the facilities at the College to ensure that we are able to fully support the educational demands of current and future pupils. The new building will give a 40% increase in floor space and, most importantly, the opportunity to create new, flexible spaces for learning and being, something which has become more challenging in the constrained environs of an historic College main building and site originally intended for 150 pupils.

Academic Curriculum. At Key Stage 3, pupils follow a broad curriculum which is common to all, covering arts, sciences, creative and practical subjects. Information Technology is timetabled in all three years to develop the skills needed for the demands of GCSE and A Level courses. Opportunity is also afforded to pupils to sample both Latin and a second Modern Foreign Language in addition to French. PSHE & Life Skills, RS, PE, Games and Drama are timetabled throughout. In Years 10 and 11 the aim is to produce a high level of achievement and choice at GCSE by offering flexibility wherever possible. Three separate sciences or Core and Additional Science are studied. At least one modern language should be taken, although more are available as options. English Literature is studied within the English teaching groups, but is not compulsory for all. Other GCSE options combine the traditional with the contemporary: Art, Business Studies, Ancient History, Computing, Drama, Graphics or Resistant Materials, History, Latin, Music and PE are currently offered. Alongside the GCSE courses PSHE & Life Skills and PE/Games continue to be taught. The Sixth Form is run in partnership with The Ladies' College, with interchange of pupils between schools and shared teaching of many groups. The Sixth Form offers a very broad array of subjects across the two schools enabling a wide variety of choices, with subjects ranging from the traditional to the new, including Computing, Psychology, Film Studies and Economics. Tutorial periods ensure that vocational, careers and pastoral guidance are available.

Music. There is a lively extra-curricular music programme which includes the College Orchestra, Wind Ensemble and Pop and Jazz Bands, with numerous small ensembles running alongside these larger groups. There is a variety of choral groups ranging from the fun and inclusive College Choir to the more selective College Chapel Choir and the senior Close Harmony Group. The latter two groups appear regularly in events around the island and usually take part in visits to France to sing in Cathedrals and at concerts. Individual instruction is available in instrumental and vocal studies, catering for a wide range of interests including piano, organ and traditional orchestral studies as well as contemporary and jazz styles. The Junior School has its own choirs, orchestra, recorder group and steel pan band.

Games. The sports fields cover some 20 acres. The Junior School has its own small playing field, and also has access to the facilities of the Upper School. The major College games are Association Football, Hockey and Cricket. Athletics, Badminton, Basketball, Cross-country Running, Fencing, Golf, Rugby Football, Sailing, Shooting, Squash and Swimming also flourish. Physical Education forms a regular part of the curriculum for all pupils up to the end of Year 11. Some seniors specialise in Outdoor Pursuits

as their Games option under the guidance of a fully qualified expert. Despite the size of the Island, plentiful opposition for sports fixtures is available. The College competes against other Island schools, has a traditional rivalry with Victoria College in Jersey, makes regular tours to the UK mainland and hosts return visits from UK schools.

Combined Cadet Force. This is voluntary and optional from Year 10 and is Tri-Service. Cadets commit for two years with the option to extend their service for a further two years in Sixth Form. Cadets travel regularly to the UK and beyond for proficiency training, camps, courses, qualifications and competitions, as well as adventurous training. Competition shooting forms a major part of the CCF and there is a long and distinguished record at Bisley. The CCF has an important role in providing Guards of Honour for Island ceremonial occasions.

Duke of Edinburgh's Award. Pupils are encouraged to participate in this scheme. Both Bronze and Gold Awards are offered as extra-curricular activities. Bronze expedition work takes place locally in the Channel Islands whilst the expedition work necessary for the Gold Award takes place on the UK mainland during the Easter and Summer holidays.

Community Service. We encourage pupils in all year groups to support our regular charity days that are led and run by a Sixth form team. All pupils in Year 9 will take a five-week activity on conservation and eco awareness; including a visit to the school allotment. From Year 10 onwards pupils can opt to serve in the CCF, where they will be involved in numerous island parades and ceremonies; Sports Leadership, whereby pupils are encouraged to coach and take charge of sports fixtures and games for younger teams on the island; and conservation, in which pupils are involved in growing crops that can be used by themselves, the College kitchen and others; or working with a local charity such as Health Connections. The College also runs an annual trip to Kenya where Sixth form pupils spend some time teaching in local Primary schools, working with a local charity for children; there is also an educational bursary linked to this charity, that has been set up and organised by pupils from the College.

Scouts. There is an active Elizabeth College Scout and Explorer Group, which meets on Friday evenings at the College Field. There is a Cub Scout Group for ECJS pupils, also based at College Field.

Clubs and Societies. The College stresses the importance of extra-curricular activity. Among over thirty currently active clubs are those which foster Bell Ringing, Chess, Climbing, Debating, Design Technology, Fencing, Life Saving, Model Railways, Sailing, Shooting, Squash and War Gaming.

Pastoral Care. In the Upper School each year has a Head of Year assisted by four Tutors. Acorn and Beechwood have Form Tutors. All these staff provide pastoral care and academic guidance for their own sections of the College. They are supported by a Chaplain who conducts services in all three schools as well as preparing pupils for Confirmation.

Parental Involvement. Parents are strongly encouraged to take an active part in their child's education. There are regular assessments and reports, parents' evenings, pastoral information evenings and parent workshops. Heads of Year keep in regular contact with parents through newsletters and email. The Heads of Year and pupils' tutors are always available to meet with parents to discuss any concerns.

Admission. The principal ages for admission into the school are 4, 7, 11 and 16, but there are sometimes vacancies for entry at other ages. Entry is by means of assessment and/or interview which are adapted to the age of the applicant. There is a £110 non-refundable registration fee. Applications for entry should be addressed to the Registrar.

Scholarships to the College. The Gibson Fleming Trust provides Awards on a means-tested basis for current pupils to support them in their involvement with extra-curricular activities.

Foundation Bursary Scheme. Our first Foundation Bursary pupils started at the College in Years 7 and 12 in September 2021. This is a means tested bursary which supports pupils who would not be able to access a College education without additional financial support. We currently offer the equivalent of 5 full bursaries for entry into Year 7 and 2 full bursaries for entry into Year 12. We welcome applications from children with enquiring minds who would benefit from our broad curriculum, outstanding extra-curricular and enrichment activities, diverse community and inspirational environment.

Choral and Instrumental Scholarships. The Gibson Fleming Trust provides Choral and Instrumental Scholarships to current pupils with some financial assistance available alongside the awards. Details of the scholarships may be obtained from the Director of Music.

Scholarships to the Universities. The College Exhibitions, Scholarships and Prizes include the Queen's Exhibition, the Lord de Sausmarez Exhibition, the Mainguy Scholarship, the Mansell Exhibition, the University of Winchester prize.

Travel. There are several flights each day from Southampton, Gatwick and Stansted. There are also regular flights to the West Country and to Midlands and northern airports. There are frequent sailings to and from Portsmouth and Poole, which offer vehicle transportation.

Alumni. The Honorary Secretary of the Old Elizabethan Association is Kin Tang who may be contacted via www.oea.org.gg.

Fees per term (2021–2022). Acorn House (Pre-Prep): £3,814; Beechwood (Prep): £4,122; Upper School (11–18): £4,324

Directors:
The Very Revd T Barker, Dean of Guernsey (*Chairman*)

R Bowyer	J Roche
K Bray	S Sharman
M Ferbrache	A Tautscher
M Galpin	M R Thompson
K Lord	L Trott

Principal: **Mrs J M Palmer**, BA

Vice-Principal: R J W James, BA
Assistant Principal (*Teaching & Learning*): T I Addenbrooke, BEng, MSc, PhD
Assistant Principal (*Sixth Form*): C R W Cottam, MA, CT ABRSM
Assistant Principal (*Training, Development and Engagement*): Mrs J F Roberts, MA, MA, PGDip
Assistant Principal (*Pastoral & Wellbeing*): C D Eyton-Jones, BA Ed
Head of the Junior School: R I Fyfe, BA
Foundation & Marketing Director: Mrs D A Carruthers, BSc

Bursar & Clerk to the Directors: J G Couchman, BA

Members of Teaching Staff:

E C Adams, BA	Mrs M E Gordon, MA
Ms M L Adkins, BA	S J Huxtable, MA
B E H Aplin, BSc	D R L Inderwick, BA, MA
Mrs E F Blazina, BA	M Johnson, BA
Mrs M D M Bolt, BA, MA	C Johnston
Mrs C S Buchanan, BA	Mrs R Lee
M A M Buchanan, BA	Mrs S Lee, Mgr
R G Campbell, BSc, MSc	R G Le Sauvage, BSc
J J Conner, BSc	Ms E A Loveridge, BA
Mrs P S Copeland, BA	D R Loweth, MA, MEd
D J Costen, BA	Mrs H M Mauger, BA
C R W Cottam, MA, CT ABRSM	Mrs E C S Meijer, BA
G S Cousens, BA	R A Morris, BA
Mrs G Dallin, BSc	A R Mulholland, BSc, MA
P G Davis, BSc	Miss C B Newall, BA
R M Davis, BSc	Mrs K A Norman, BA
Ms F De Garis	Ms J M Pendleton, BA
J A Depnering, MA, DPhil	Mrs P J Read, MSci, MA
T R de Putron, BSc	J R D Rowson, BA
Miss A C M Demongeot, BA, MA	Miss M Schofield, BA
	Miss R L Seymour, BSc
T P Edge, BA, MA	T C Slann, Dip NEBSS
J Edwards	Ms T L Smith, BA, MA
L R G Garland, BSc, MA	M A G Stephens, BA
M Garnett, BA	A G Stewart, BSc
B M Geoghegan	Ms S L A Tribe, BA
A J Good, BSc	M I Walters, BA, MEd

Chaplain: The Revd P A Graysmith, BSc
Director of Music: Miss E D Willcocks, BMus, MA
Games and Physical Education: T P Eisenhuth, BPhysEd

Prep:
Deputy Head Pastoral: Mrs E Bott, BEd
Deputy Head Academic: Mrs E J Spiller, BSc

Mrs M Brady, BA	Mrs K Reed, BA
Mrs D Dowding, BA	Mrs J Ricketts, BA
Mrs S Ellis	Mrs B Santi, BSc, MA
Mrs C Hervé, BA	P Sargent, BA
Mrs C Martel, BA Ed	Mrs N Stevens, BEd
Mrs E Parkes, BEd	M Stokes, BA
Mrs A M Pollard, BEd	R Sutton, BA
Miss E Randall	Mrs C Wray, BSc

Pre-Prep:
Deputy Head: Mrs J Atkinson, BEd

Mrs C Bowden, BEd	Mrs L Du Port, BA
Miss R Curtis, BA Ed	Mrs J Hamilton, BA
Miss S Dorey, BEd	Mrs E Jones, BA Ed

Ellesmere College
A Woodard School

Ellesmere, Shropshire SY12 9AB

Tel: 01691 622321
email: hmsecretary@ellesmere.com
website: www.ellesmere.com
Twitter: @ellesmerecoll
Facebook: @Ellesmere-College
Instagram: @ellesmere_college
LinkedIn: /school/ellesmere-college

Motto: *Pro Patria Dimicans*

Ellesmere College is a fully co-educational school set in the beautiful Shropshire countryside in North West England. As one of the leading independent schools in the region, it offers students between the ages of 7 to 18 the chance to achieve both personal and academic success in their studies and a wide range of activities, including music, art, sport and drama, in a happy, friendly atmosphere. **In 2021 Ellesmere College was accredited as a High Performance Learning World Class School – one of only 39 schools worldwide to hold the distinction.** We prepare students for their i/GCSEs, A Levels, BTEC and the International Baccalaureate (IB) as well as giving them the opportunity to enjoy a full and varied sports and co-curricular programme. Founded in 1884 and standing in its own stunning grounds covering more than 50 hectares, the school is conveniently located near the small, historic town of Ellesmere, with easy access to Manchester, Birmingham, Liverpool and London.

The House Systems. The Lower School (ages 7–13) has a competitive system based on 3 houses – Brownlow, Phillips and Heywood.

The Senior School (Yr 9–13) has a competitive 'house point' system – academic and sporting – based on 4 houses, all of which are co-educational and combine boarding and day pupils:

• Meynell House

• Talbot House

• Wakeman-Lambart House

• Woodard House

Separate from the competitive Houses is the residential House system for day and boarding arrangements:

There are 3 girls' boarding houses:

• St. Aidan's – Middle School (13–16 years)

• St. Oswald's & St. Hilda's – Sixth Form

There are 4 boys' boarding houses:

• St. Patrick's & St. Cuthbert's – Middle School (13–16 years)

• St. Bede's & St. Luke's – Sixth Form

Curriculum. In the first year in the Senior School a full range of subjects is studied, designed to give all pupils a comprehensive introduction before focusing on their core elective subjects for i/GCSE. At i/GCSE all pupils take English, Mathematics, and either Dual Award Science or the three Sciences studied separately. Other subjects depend on individual aptitude and choice.

In the Sixth Form over 24 academic subjects are available for study to A Level, BTEC Diploma or International Baccalaureate (IB) Diploma to prepare for university entrance, the Services and the Professions, or to the USA degree system via our SATs pathway.

Ellesmere College will be launching its International Foundation Programme (IFP) for entry into university as a one-year foundation programme course soon.

Music. The College has very strong musical traditions and has been awarded Artsmark Platinum in recognition of the award-winning arts provision at the College. It possesses two of the finest organs in the country, including the internationally renowned St Mary Tyne Dock Schulze Organ. The Chapel Choir has a wide repertoire of Church Music and a number of other ensembles, all of which give regular concerts. There are House Music Competitions every year, Celebrity concerts, and the community Sinfonia Orchestra.

The Music School is part of the College Arts Centre which provides first-class facilities, including a 220-seat theatre, 8 Practice Rooms, a Recording Studio and Teaching Rooms.

Arts Centre. This purpose-built complex hosts Drama, Dance, Film, Music and Art Exhibitions. A programme is organised in which international artists in all these fields visit the Centre, which shares its facilities with the local community.

Careers. At all levels pupils are encouraged to seek advice from the College careers Masters and Mistresses as well as representatives from the Independent Schools Careers Organisation. A Careers Convention is held each year for pupils in Year 11. Students also take ESB (English Speaking Board), ILM (Institute of Leadership & Management Level 3), SATs and mentoring programmes.

Games and Physical Education. Ellesmere has a long tradition of sporting excellence and has a total of 7 Sporting Academies: rugby, football, tennis, swimming, golf, cricket, and shooting. The sporting excellence is supported by the Rugby Academy programme, the Tennis Academy, and the Ellesmere College Titans Swimming Team. The Cricket Academy was launched in 2009, the Shooting Academy in 2010, Golf Academy in 2015 and the Football Academy in 2016. The LTA approved indoor Tennis Centre was completed in 2017 and there is also a High Performance Hockey Programme with a pathway to international progression.

All members of the School are required to participate in a regular programme of games, though particular inclinations and aptitudes are taken fully into consideration. Facilities include two sports halls, floodlit multi-sports AstroTurf pitches, a fitness centre, squash courts, a heated indoor swimming pool, indoor and outdoor shooting ranges, two high-tech gymnasia, a purpose-built LTA-accredited indoor 4-court tennis centre, 6 floodlit all-weather tennis courts, a golf course, indoor golf Sky-Trak, rugby pitches, all-weather hockey pitches, cricket squares and an athletics track. The school also has access to nearby lakes, rivers and hills providing opportunities to develop other skills including sailing, canoeing, and horse riding.

All pupils are expected to join one of the following: D of E (Duke of Edinburgh's Award – Bronze, Silver & Gold), Outdoor Training Unit, Combined Cadet Force (CCF – Army, Navy, RAF), Social Service. These activities occur on one full afternoon a week, but, in order to extend their activities, twice a year 3 days are set aside when all members of the College participate in 48-hour expeditions. In the Lent Term a single day is devoted to expeditions.

Admission. Students are admitted at all points of entry into the school. Entrance examinations are held in February for Lower School entry. Scholarships for Prep School candidates are held in May, while others take the Common Entrance Examination in June.

Scholarships and Bursaries. A wide range of Awards recognising a range of talents are available:

- *Academic:* a maximum of 50% fee remission.
- *All-Rounder:* a maximum of 25% fee remission.
- *Art:* a maximum of 25% fee remission. Applications welcome for the The Adlard Scholarship.
- *Drama:* a maximum of 25% fee remission.
- *Music:* a maximum of 50% fee reduction and free tuition in two instruments. Exhibitions are worth up to a maximum of 25% fee reduction and free tuition in one instrument.
- The *Schulze Organ Award* is for Sixth Form candidates only – valued at 50% of fees.
- *Sports:* a maximum of 50% fee remission.

In cases of need, all awards may be supplemented by means-tested bursaries.

There are reduced fees for children of the Clergy and Service personnel.

Foundation and Regional awards are also available for local children.

Fees per term (2021–2022). Upper School: Boarders £11,855, Weekly Boarders £8,465, Day £6,520.

Lower School: Boarders £9,505, Weekly Boarders £8,030, Day £3,995–£4,595.

Fees are inclusive of general College charges.

For more information visit: www.ellesmere.com/the-schools/all/admissions/fees

'Old Ellesmerians' Former pupils of the school become members of The Ellesmerian Club, which in turn enables them to take part in a number of societies and activities. For further information, contact: Olivia Beckett, External Relations Officer – olivia.beckett@ellesmere.com

Charitable status. Registered Charity, number 1103049. It exists to provide education for children.

Founder: The Revd Nathaniel Woodard, DCL, then Dean of Manchester
Visitor: The Rt Revd The Lord Bishop of Lichfield

College Council:

D C Brewitt	C E Lillis
Mrs F M Christie	J A Mathias, FCA
The Reverend Canon B C	A L Morris
Clover	Mrs C S Newbold, BA
Mrs S Connor	Mrs R E Paterson
J S Hopkins	The Reverend M J Rylands
R A K Hoppins	M D T Sampson

Headmaster: **B J Wignall**, BA, MA, MCMI, FRSA

Deputy Head (*Pastoral*): Dr R Chatterjee, BSc, MSc, PhD, Cert SpLD
Deputy Head (*Academic*): Mrs S V Pritt-Roberts, BEd, MEd, NPQH
Deputy Head (*External Relations*): S B Mullock, BA
Head of Sixth Form: Dr T Gareh, BSc, MSc, PhD, CSci, CChem, MRSC
Head of Middle School: Mrs S Phillips, MA
Head of Lower School: Mrs S Owen, BEd
Director of Activities: C Davies, BA

Chaplain: The Revd Phillip Gration
Director of Operations: M McCarthy, BSc, DMS
Registrar: Ms K Randall, BSc

Eltham College

Grove Park Road, Mottingham, London SE9 4QF

Tel:	020 8857 1455
email:	mail@eltham-college.org.uk
website:	www.elthamcollege.london
Twitter:	@ElthamCollegeUK
Facebook:	@ElthamCollegeOfficial
Instagram:	@ElthamCollegeLondon
LinkedIn:	/Old-Elthamians

Eltham College is a thriving co-educational independent day school for students aged 7 to 18.

It is a highly successful school which aims to provide a broad and balanced education to both girls and boys that will prepare them for the modern world. The College is one of the leading academic schools in the country, and boasts many county and national players in a range of sports. The co-curricular programme is broad and varied. The school is a Top 30 school in the Sunday Times Parent Power Good Schools Guide and a Microsoft-accredited Showcase School, one of only 50 across the UK.

Eltham College has a distinct character, born out of its Christian heritage, and it continues to focus on the care of the individual. Strong pastoral care and a relaxed and unpretentious atmosphere make the school a happy and vibrant place.

There is an ambitious programme of development and expansion as well as a strong emphasis on staff development. Many staff choose to stay; but equally others are prepared and trained for future promotion in leading HMC schools.

History. The College was founded in 1842 as the 'School for the Sons of Missionaries' and it began life as a small boarding school catering for the children of missionaries whose parents were serving overseas, and famously GB Olympic athlete Eric Liddell. The College moved to its present extensive site in Mottingham, south-east London in 1912 that includes around 70 acres of playing fields surrounding an elegant 18th century mansion, itself a former naval college. The College has since developed into a day school for boys with girls accepted into the Sixth Form since 1980. However, the school is turning fully co-educational and, since September 2020, has accepted girls as well as boys into its Junior and Senior Schools. The school has grown considerably over the past few years and there are now around 1,050 pupils, with 780 pupils in the Senior School and approximately 270 in the Junior School.

Location. The College is located on a spacious 70 acre site with extensive playing fields in the London Borough of Bromley, adjacent to the boroughs of Royal Greenwich and Lewisham. It lies within easy reach of both central London and the Kent countryside. There are regular and fast train services to London Bridge, Charing Cross and Victoria stations (15–20 minutes) while the nearby A20 main road links to the M25 in less than 10 minutes. Students come from a wide local area that includes Blackheath, Bexley,

Bromley, Chislehurst, Bexley, Dartford, Dulwich, Greenwich, and London Docklands.

Facilities. The College enjoys superb facilities which have been improved considerably in recent years. These include the Gerald Moore Gallery, new/refurbished Science laboratories, two floodlit all-weather AstroTurf pitches, and an extended Dining Hall. The award-winning Turberville Centre opened in 2019 with new Languages and Maths classrooms, a seminar room, and a Sixth Form cafe and study area. Nearby, a new £3 million Medical and Wellbeing Centre has also opened and is now home to the school nurses, counsellors and Chaplain. The Eric Liiddell Sports Centre comprises sports hall, dance studio and fitness suite and the school's 25 metre swimming pool.

Curriculum. The curriculum is broad and balanced, incorporating both traditional and modern elements. For example, all students in Year 7 study French, Latin, German and Spanish and all students go on to study at least one Modern Language to GCSE, and separate Sciences are available to all. Most students take ten GCSEs and three A Levels, chosen from a wide range of subjects, plus the EPQ. Recent examination results place Eltham amongst the top schools in the country: in 2021, 85% of all grades were 9/8 and more than 95% of the year group achieved eight or more grades at 9/8/7.

A Level results are consistently high. In 2021, 72% of A Level grades were A* and 92% were A*/A. More than half of Eltham College students achieved at least three A*s at A Level and 94% achieved their first choice university that include Oxbridge, leading Russell Group universities in the UK, as well as specialist colleges and conservatoires in the UK and overseas universities.

Co-Curricular. The co-curricular activities provide an impressively wide range of opportunities while ensuring that academic potential is fulfilled. The College has an enviable reputation in Sport, Music and Drama. There are a number of international and Olympic standard sports coaches; the quality and range of Music participation and performance is strong; and audiences are frequently treated to spectacular school productions in the purpose-built school theatre.

The majority of students participate in the vast amount of clubs and societies available, including (to name but a few), Duke of Edinburgh's Award, Debating Society, Chess, Japanese Club, Eco-Eltham, Rocket Club and Water Polo. Students are encouraged to help those less fortunate than them by participating in charity fundraising events and the Lower Sixth take part in a Community Service scheme helping local charities.

Trips and expeditions are a major feature of life at Eltham College. These range from the traditional UK visits to more ambitious overseas trips which in recent years have included: Uganda, China, Iceland and Switzerland. Language trips and exchanges are encouraged and these have included visits to Bordeaux, Spain, Beijing and Berlin. Sport, Drama and Music tours are frequent occurrences, both in the UK and overseas and these have included the USA, South Africa, Sri Lanka and The Netherlands.

Admission. Students are admitted at 11+ (Year 7) and 16+ (Sixth Form) via an entrance examination and interview. Occasional vacancies do sometimes occur outside of the traditional entrance points. The College is academically highly selective, with nearly 10 applicants for every place. Approximately half of students come from local primary schools and half from the independent sector.

The College has a wide social mix, thanks, in part, to our generous Bursary scheme, which provides financial assistance for those unable to afford the full fees.

Scholarships. The College offers a number of scholarships and bursaries to attract the brightest and most talented students to the College. Scholarships and Bursaries (financial assistance) are available to all students applying to the Senior School and Sixth Form.

Scholarships offering fee remission are awarded on Academic performance at 11+ and 16+. There are also scholarships in Music, Drama, Art and Sport.

Bursaries. As befits a school founded for the sons of missionaries and a former Direct Grant School, a significant number of students receive financial support to attend the College. Bursaries are available up to 100% of fees subject to ISBA confidential means-tested basis.

Term of Entry. The College normally accepts students only for the beginning of the academic year in September but, if gaps in particular year groups occur, it is willing to interview and test at any point in the year with a view to immediate or subsequent entry. However, the school is usually over-subscribed.

Junior School. The Junior School is based on the main school campus in a separate building sometimes known as The Grange. This is a large house on the College estate that was converted and extended and which accommodates about 260 day pupils in classes of around 22 children. In addition to classrooms are an Assembly and Games Hall, Science Room, Music Room, and an Art, Design and Technology Room. With an emphasis on English and Mathematics, the curriculum (which includes Mandarin, French and German), provides an excellent foundation for the academic journey on through the Senior School.

Excellence is also pursued outside the classroom whether on the sports field, stage or concert hall. In recent years, rugby teams have had 100% season wins, trebles have sung at world famous venues, and actors have earned a host of awards at local festivals. The Junior School is managed by its own Head, who is responsible to the Headmaster.

Admission is at 7+ (into Year 3), though there are occasional places at 8+. There is no entrance test for students from Eltham College Junior School wishing to enter into the Senior School. Recommendation for continuing to the Senior School is made on the basis of a student's performance during their time in the Junior School and on their potential to flourish in the Senior School. Almost all students therefore progress seamlessly through to Eltham College Senior School.

Junior School applications should be made to the Head of Admissions

Fees per term (2021–2022). Senior School/Sixth Form £6,557; Junior School £5,699. Lunch £311.

Charitable status. Eltham College is a Registered Charity, number 1058438. It exists to provide education for boys and girls.

Governors:

The Governing Body comprises the Chairman and Vice Chair, ten Trust Governors and eight Nominated Governors representing the Baptist Missionary Society, the Council for World Mission, the United Reformed Church, the London Boroughs of Bexley and Bromley, the Parents (two representatives elected by the parental body) and the Staff

Common Room (one representative elected by the Teaching Staff).

Chairman of the Board: Mr P Doyle

Headmaster: Mr G Sanderson, MA Oxon, FRSA

Bursar: Mr A Butterworth
Deputy Head: Mr J Martin
Deputy Head (*Curriculum*): Mr E Wright
Deputy Head (*Pastoral*): Mrs A Massey

Senior School Teaching Staff:

Art:
Miss S Heraghty, BA (*Director of Art*)
Mrs K Duke
Mrs M Franklin, MA
Mrs A C E Richards, BA [part-time]

Biology:
Mr H Sleath, BSc
Mrs N Colwell, BSc
Mr S Marlow, BSc
Mr A Merrett
Mrs J C Perry, BSc

Chemistry:
Mr J Copley, MSci
Ms S Baig
Ms E Lucas, BSc, MA
Dr J N Hill, BSc
Mrs J C Perry, BSc
Mrs K Pender

Classics:
Dr E Michalopoulou, BA, MA, PhD
Ms M Cogni

Computing and Computer Science:
Mr T Collins, MSc, BEng
Miss J Muirhead

Design and Technology:
Mr M E L Gennari, BSc (*Head of Universities and Enrichment*)
Mr N Dale
Miss M Johnson
Mr P Wren
Mr C Quinton
Mr E Wright

Drama:
Mrs K Robinson, BA, MA
Mr C Devellerez, BA, MA

Economics:
Miss D Ellis
Mr J Boggan
Mr S G Milne, MA (*Head of Sixth Form*)
Mrs S Potter

English:
Mr C Cook
Mr T C Mitchell, BA (*Head of Creative Writing*)
Miss V Barsby, BA
Miss E Bush
Mr P Hopwood
Mr J Smith
Mrs N Whittaker

Geography:
Mr P Angel, MA, BSc, NPQSL
Mr A D Beattie, MA

Mr J P Chesterton, BSc
Mrs L Clough
Miss K Richard, BSc
Mr J Willatt, BSc (*Assistant Head – Co-curricular*)
Miss M Calwell

Geology:
Mr P Angel, MA, BSc, NPQSL
Mrs L Clough
Miss K Richard, BSc

History:
Dr A Davies, BA, MA, PhD
Mr M E R Chesterton, BA
Mr D R Grinstead, BA
Mr J Martin

Mathematics:
Mr T Brook
Mr J L Baldwin, BSc
Mrs R E Bevington, BSc
Mrs N Bilsby, BSc, MA (*Head of Wellbeing*)
Mr V Broncz, BSc
Dr M Cianciaruso
Mr J P Crowley, BEng
Ms R Gordon, BSc (*Assistant Head – Teaching and Learning*)
Mr A Hon (*Deputy Head of Sixth Form*)
Ms A Tysba
Mr L Watts, BSc (*Assistant Head – Head of Middle School*)
Mrs S Wood, BSc [part-time]
Mr P Rodrigo

Modern Languages:
Miss L Scarantino, BA (*Head of Modern Foreign Languages*)
Ma C Franz, MA (*Head of German*)
Ms E Paull (*Head of Spanish*)
Ms M Su BA, MA (*Head of Mandarin Chinese*)
Mrs E Brooke
Ms S Hill
Mr J Houghton, MA (*Chaplain*)
Mr F Meier, MA (*Assistant Head – Head of Lower School*)
Mr F Nieto Almada, MA
Mrs S Chevrier-Clarke

Music:
Ms L Swadkin, BMus (*Acting Head of Music*)
Mr H Bryans
Mr Sach Keen
Mr S Thompson
Ms Brits
Mr T Bullard
Miss O'Leary
Mrs D Bailey

Physics:
Mr A Hindocha, BSc
Mr A Chan, MEng
Dr M Cianciaruso, PhD
Mr J Crowley, BEng
Mrs E Goakes
Mr G Hammond
Mr S Whittaker, MSc (*Head of Science*)
Mr E B Wright, MA

Politics:
Mrs S Powis-Holt (*Head of Politics*)
Mrs A Massey
Mr M Chesterton

Psychology:
Ms M M Pokorny, BSc
Mr A Higginson

Religious Studies:
Ms E G Haste, BA
Mr E Cavendish
Mr J Skipworth

Sport:
Mr E T Thorogood, BSc (*Head of School Sports*)
Miss P Caudle (*Head of Girls Sport*)
Miss K Harding
Miss B Holmes
Mr J Kelly
Mr B King, BSc (*Director of Rugby*)

Learning Support:
Mrs C Georgulas
Mrs N MacAulay

Library:
Mrs C M Roche, MiL

Development Director: Mr S O'Donovan
Head of Admissions: Mrs C St Clair-Charles
Head of Communications: Mr E Funnell

Junior School:

Head of the Junior School: Mrs V Meier, MA

Deputy Head of the Junior School (*Academic*): Mrs N
  Devon
Deputy Head of the Junior School (*Pastoral*): Mr A Taylor

Junior School Teaching Staff:
Mrs N J Chamberlain, BEd (*Head of Years 3 and 4*)
Mr I Wearmouth (*Head of Years 5 and 6*)
Mr M Alexander, BA (*Head of Junior School Music*)
Mrs A Carey, BA (*Head of English*)
Mrs N Chamberlain (*Head of Years 3 and 4*)
Mr N Dale, BA (*Head of History*)
Mrs E Goakes (*Head of Science*)
Miss M S Johnson, BA (*Head of Design and Technology*)
Mr T Laubach, (*Head of Transition and RS*)
Mrs B Martin (*Head of Modern Foreign Languages*)
Mr H Mitchell-Morgan
Mr M O'Dwyer, BEd (*Head of Co-curricular*)
Mr S Oliver, BSc (*Head of Mathematics*)
Mrs H Pan, (*Head of Junior School Mandarin*)
Mrs H L Sargeant, BSc (*Head of Computing*)
Mr W Schaper, BEd (*Head of Geography*)
Miss N L Tutchings, BEd (*Subject Leader PSHE, Form
  Tutor Year 4*)

Emanuel School

Battersea Rise, London SW11 1HS

Tel: 020 8870 4171
email: enquiries@emanuel.org.uk
website: www.emanuel.org.uk
Twitter: @Emanuel_School
Instagram: @Emanuel.school

Motto: *Pour bien désirer* (the noble aim)

Emanuel School was founded in Westminster by Lady Anne Dacre in 1594 and moved to its present site on the north side of Wandsworth Common in 1883 as one of the five schools of The United Westminster and Grey Coat Foundation.

Emanuel is a fully co-educational day school for ages 10–18. We have approximately 1,050 pupils across the school.

Admission. Each September, 48 pupils are admitted into Year 6 (10+), 96 pupils into Year 7 (11+) and 20–30 into the Sixth Form.

Applicants will be required to submit their last full year school report. We will also request a reference from their current headteacher (or equivalent) and they will sit an entrance exam and have an interview with a member of staff.

Registration for all entry points closes in mid-October the year before entry.

Prospective parents are warmly encouraged to visit the school and there are many opportunities to do so. Please see our website for details.

Fees per term (2021–2022). £6,715 covering tuition, books and lunch. Extras charged are for individual instrumental tuition and some external visits and trips.

Site and buildings. Emanuel School is located on a beautiful, leafy 12-acre site in Battersea, on the north edge of Wandsworth Common, only 10 minutes' walk from Clapham Junction rail station. The original Victorian building is the core of the school, with teaching and learning space, a large and well-stocked library, theatre and a beautiful chapel. The Dacre building opened in 2017, with outstanding art and design facilities and a film studio. The school has begun work on a masterplan to improve and further develop teaching and learning facilities over the coming years.

The school's playing fields adjoin the school buildings together with a sports hall, full-sized indoor swimming pool and fives courts. The school has a boathouse on the Thames by Barnes Bridge and further pitches at 'Blagdons' near Raynes Park.

Scholarships and assistance with fees (bursaries). Academic and co-curricular scholarships are available and pupils may hold more than one type of scholarship.

All applicants are considered for academic scholarships, which are awarded on the basis of outstanding performance in the school entrance examinations.

Applicants applying for Music, Art, Drama and Sports scholarships must pass the entrance exams before a scholarship can be awarded. Thereafter, each department has specific criteria for their scholarship requirements.

As well as awarding academic and co-curricular scholarships, Emanuel School is committed to widening access by offering fee assistance. Fee-assisted places (bursaries) are available dependent on financial need and can hold the value of up to 100% of the school fees, including covering the costs of uniform and school trips.

Please see our website for more details about scholarships and fee assistance.

Organisation. There are two forms for pupils who join at Year 6 (10+). Pupils joining at Year 7 (11+) are placed into six forms. Primary responsibility for their care rests with the form tutor and the head of year, under the overall supervision of the Head of Lower School, who deals with Years 6, 7 and 8. As all pupils move from Year 9 into Year 10 there is a regrouping along the lines of the subjects chosen for GCSE examinations. The tutor system continues throughout the school.

Pupils are placed in houses when they join the school and they stay in these houses throughout their school career. Although originally intended as a means of fostering competition in games, these houses have developed a strong community spirit over many years. Pupils join a house-led peer mentoring group which meets fortnightly and is led by at least two students from the Upper Sixth. Specially trained, the Sixth Form mentors, with the support of the heads of house, organise discussions and short activities designed to help pupils with day-to-day school life, make friends across the years, and informally share advice on future academic plans.

Times. The normal school day runs from 8.25am to 3.45pm, but many activities take place after school. Some school activities, especially sports fixtures, but also music and drama rehearsals, take place at the weekend.

Curriculum. Pupils in the Lower and Middle School study a wide range of subjects, including English, Mathematics, Biology, Chemistry and Physics (as separate sciences), Geography, History, Religious Studies, Computing, Design and Robotics (CDR), Music, Art and Design, Drama and Modern Languages. In Year 6, pupils have taster courses in French, German and Spanish. In Year 7, pupils choose two languages from a choice of Spanish/French and Latin/German. There is a double period PE lesson, a Games afternoon and a Life Education lesson each week. Pupils also have a weekly lesson called 'Ethos'; this is an introduction to critical thinking, informed discussion and debating, aiming to develop independence and resilience in our younger pupils.

In the Sixth Form, pupils choose three A Level subjects from 25 on offer (including additional options such as Psychology, Economics and Photography) and also complete the Extended Project Qualification (EPQ). Sixth Form leavers go on to a variety of institutions, including Oxbridge and Russell Group universities, art college, music and drama conservatoires or universities overseas.

Art, Music & Drama. Emanuel has a long-standing tradition of excellence in Art, Music and Drama and all pupils are encouraged to participate in the breadth of opportunities available.

The music department caters to a wide range of musical interests, from choral and orchestral to contemporary music. Pupils take part in concerts, workshops and ensembles including rock and pop concerts, house music competitions and DJing workshops. The music department collaborates with the drama department to produce an annual whole-school musical.

Drama is taught throughout the school with many pupils continuing through GCSE and A Level. There are many opportunities for co-curricular participation through year-group productions and trips. Every other year, the Emanuel Theatre Company takes over 20 students to the Edinburgh Fringe Festival to perform two shows.

Art facilities include specialist paint and print studios, a dark room for photography, a ceramics room with dedicated kiln and glazing rooms and a sculpture studio. Pupils follow a broad syllabus where they can develop a range of creative skills. There are plenty of extra-curricular opportunities for budding artists to enjoy, including trips, drawing masterclasses and exhibitions. Emanuel students gain places to study at some of the best art colleges in the country.

Sport & Activities. Rugby, cricket, rowing and football are the main school games for boys. For girls, the main activities are netball, cricket, hockey and rowing. Many other activities become available as a pupil moves up the school. Each pupil will have one games afternoon each week and other opportunities for physical education and swimming. The school has its own playing fields, sports hall, mini astro, swimming pool, fives, netball and tennis courts and boathouse on the Thames.

There are over 50 weekly clubs and activities taking place over lunchtime and after school as well as over 40 subject clinics. The most popular clubs include Film and Media Club, Bouldering Club (on our climbing wall), Costume Making Club, Junior Equality Club and Dr Who Club, as well as a number of sports and performing arts clubs.

The Duke of Edinburgh's Award scheme is offered to pupils from Year 9 upwards. Community outreach is arranged for senior pupils and can involve hospital visiting or voluntary work in local primary schools, charity shops or our local hospice.

Partnerships and Outreach. A central point of our ethos is the cultivation of an altruistic, caring and outward-looking community. All Lower Sixth students are involved in our award-winning outreach initiative, Primary Ambitions. Each Friday, our students spend one hour teaching a variety of subjects to Year 6 children from our local partner schools. Students gain confidence as well as developing their leadership and organisational skills. In turn, we hope that the programme will inspire and challenge young people within our community to develop some new skills, relish newfound opportunities and explore new friendships – and most importantly, have fun!

Careers. Careers and higher education advice is readily available from an experienced team. There is an annual careers convention for senior pupils where many representatives from a wide variety of industries and professional areas visit the school to talk about career options.

More formal work experience is offered as part of an extensive careers and further education advice programme from Year 9 upwards. There is a very strong Young Enterprise programme in the Lower Sixth; Emanuel has a good record and has been within one round of the national finals for the last two years.

Old Emanuel Association. *Membership Secretary*: OEAMember@gmail.com.

Charitable status. Emanuel School (administered by The United Westminster and Grey Coat Foundation) is a Registered Charity, number 1181012.

Chairman of the Governors: Mr M Jaigirder, MA

Headmaster: Mr Robert Milne, MA King's College
  London

Senior Management Team:

Deputy Head (*Pastoral*): Mr R Kothakota, MEd
  Buckingham
Deputy Head (*Academic & Staff*): Mrs J L Peters, MA
  Oxon
Deputy Head (*Co-curricular, Partnerships & Admissions*:
  Mr S W Turner, MEd Birmingham
Assistant Head (*Academic*): Mrs R Brown, DPhil Oxon
Director of Studies: Mr R M Evans, DPhil, Oxon
Director of Teaching and Learning: Ms J A Johnson, MA
  Oxon
Head of Sixth Form: Mr W Quayle, BSc Dunelm
Head of Middle School: Mrs J McIsaac, MA Lond
Acting Head of Lower School: Ms R C Chetwood, BA
  Cardiff
Bursar: Mr M Russell, ACMA
Senior Tutor: Mr S P Andrews, BA Swansea

Epsom College

College Road, Epsom, Surrey KT17 4JQ

Tel: 01372 821004 (Headmaster)
          01372 821234 (Director of Admissions)
          01372 821133 (Bursar)
email: admissions@epsomcollege.org.uk
website: www.epsomcollege.org.uk
Twitter: @EpsomCollegeUK
Facebook: /Epsom-College

  Motto: *Deo non Fortuna*

Founded in 1855, Epsom College is a boarding and day
school for girls and boys aged 11–18, situated in 72 acres of
parkland estate close to Epsom Downs and is only 15 miles
from central London. In the last year that A Levels were
externally-moderated (2019), Epsom was the most
successful co-ed school in Surrey, (*The Times* and *The
Telegraph* league tables). 90% of A-levels were A*–B. 67%
were A*–A.

Almost all leavers go on to degree courses, especially at
research-led universities. The Russell Group universities are
particularly popular, with Bristol, Durham, and Oxford and
Cambridge strongly represented each year. Increasingly our
pupils study overseas, with places at US universities on the
rise.

Boarding is central to the College with many of our
boarders – both weekly and full boarders – living within 25
miles. The House system ensures a strong sense of
community and support. All pupils, whether day, weekly or
full boarders, are placed within one of our 13 Houses. Year
groups mix, and a strong sense of pride in the House, and
care for fellow pupils of all ages is encouraged.

Numbers and Houses. There are 1,070 pupils in the
School, around 60% are day pupils. There are 368 in the
Sixth Form and 180 in the Lower School (Years 7 and 8).

Around 16% of pupils are from overseas and there is a
spread of 38 nationalities.

The school is fully co-ed, with a 50/50 split in Years 7
and 8, and a 60/50 male to female split in the senior years.
There are 6 separate houses for girls: two boarding houses,
Crawfurd and Wilson; three day houses, Murrell, Raven and
Rosebery; and White House, for both boarding and day
girls.

The boys' boarding houses are: Fayrer, Forest, Granville
and Holman. All boarding Sixth and Fifth Formers and
Upper Fourth Formers have study-bedrooms in the
modernised Houses.

In the Michaelmas Term there are two weekend exeats
roughly halfway through each half term, in addition to a
two-week half-term holiday. In each of the other two terms
there is one exeat in the first half followed by a one-week
half-term holiday. Weekly boarders can go home every
weekend.

The day boy Houses are: Carr, Propert and Robinson.
Day boys and girls are full members of the School
community and have lunch and tea in College. All members
of the School, boarders and day, eat centrally in the Dining
Room which makes for efficiency and strengthens the sense
of community.

Pupils who are ill are looked after in the School Medical
Centre which has a qualified sister always on duty.

Academic Work. In the Lower School the design of the
curriculum follows a number of key principles: Skills for the
future, learning to learn, well-being and 21st century
education. Outside of the normal curriculum, all pupils have
timetabled wellbeing and mindfulness, service in the
community, and are able to select from a carousel of 150 co-
curricular activities, encompassing everything from
gardening to STEM.

Middle Fourth (Year 9) pupils take English, Mathematics,
Physics, Chemistry, Biology, Religious Studies, Drama,
Geography, History, Art, Music, a Modern Language
(French, German, Spanish or Mandarin), Computer Science
and Design Technology. Pupils can then choose to study a
second modern language, Latin or Classical Civilisation, or
an additional Creative Arts subject (Design & Technology,
Art or Music). With the exception of Maths and Languages,
setting continues to be mixed ability.

Pupils will choose their GCSEs at the end of Year 9 to
commence study in Year 10. They take 10 subjects, seven
are compulsory, three can be chosen. The compulsory
subjects are English Language, English Literature,
Mathematics, Biology, Chemistry, Physics and a Modern or
Classical Language (from French, German, Spanish,
Mandarin, Latin or Classical Civilisation). The optional
three subjects are taken from Art, Computer Science,
Design & Technology, Drama, French, Geography, History,
Latin, Music, Photography, PE, Religious Studies or
Spanish.

Almost everyone then enters the Sixth Form. Students
will choose 3 principal subjects to study at A Level. These
will then be enhanced by choices from the core curriculum
where they can choose from: Core Maths, US College Board
Advanced Placement in English Language and
Composition, Extended Project Qualification or Young
Enterprise. They will also benefit from a varied lecture
programme and Epsom's award-winning service
programme. A wide range of A Level subjects are offered.
Options in Business, Politics and Government, Photography
and Economics are introduced to complement the broad
range of subjects already available at GCSE. The courses

are linear meaning all examinations are taken at the end of Upper Sixth.

There are excellent facilities for work in one's own study, in the main Library or one of the specialist Departmental Libraries.

Higher Education. Almost all students go on to university, with the occasional student choosing to follow another path, such as Art Foundation. In recent years, Medicine, Law, Engineering, Economics and Business degrees have proved particularly popular degree options, but Epsom students have been successful in gaining places on a broad variety of competitive courses. 82% of all pupils go to Russell Group universities each year. Overseas universities – particularly in the US – are increasingly popular, with 11% of 2021's leavers choosing this route. Epsom has a dedicated programme to support overseas applications.

Careers. Careers education is offered from the first term at Epsom and is particularly well developed in the Sixth Form. Epsom has an experienced team of careers tutors with specialists in Medicine, Oxbridge Entrance, Engineering and American University Entrance. Much care is taken to assess a pupil's potential and aptitude and to provide proper guidance on careers. All pupils belong to Inspiring Futures and all Fifth Form pupils take careers aptitude tests through their Futurewise programme. There is a well-established work experience programme and a Careers Convention is organised each year for the Fifth Form and Lower Sixth. The College also hosts a GAP Year Fair.

The **Religious Teaching** and the Chapel Services follow the doctrines of the Church of England, but there are always pupils of other denominations and faiths. Multi-faith services take place regularly. There is a Senior Chaplain who works together with a visiting Rabbi and a Hindu priest to ensure a multi-faith approach. Muslim pupils attend prayers at the College.

Games and other Activities. Games contribute much to the general physical development of girls and boys at Epsom and the College has a strong tradition of high standards in many sports. The very large number of teams means that almost all pupils are able to represent the School each year. A wide range of sports is available: Rugby, Hockey, Netball, Cricket, Tennis, Athletics and Swimming, Squash (6 courts), Target Rifle Shooting (with an indoor range), Football, Cross-Country, Golf, Badminton, Rounders, and Basketball. The Indoor Sports Centre, housing two sports halls, squash courts, a fitness centre and gym, and climbing wall, was opened in 1989 by the Patron of Epsom College, Her Majesty The Queen.

The Target Rifle Team has a long history of excellence at Target Rifle Shooting, both small-bore and full-bore, and over the last 20 years has consistently been the premier rifle shooting school in the UK. The College Rifle team has won the National Championships – the Ashburton Shield – 14 times in the past 26 years and 15 times overall. The College holds the record for the highest number of Ashburton wins by a single school.

The CCF has Naval, Army and RAF Sections and pupils over the age of 14 are expected to join for 2 years when much time is spent on camping and expeditions. Older boys and girls may join instead The Duke of Edinburgh's Award scheme, while others are involved with the service programme in Epsom where they contribute to the community and take a leadership role in service projects.

The College ensures that all pupils take advantage of an extensive range of activities from Dance to Design Textiles.

Over 150 clubs and societies are accessible each week, and the co-curricular programme at the College has been ranked as the 'best of the best in UK independent education' by *The Week* magazine.

Music, Art and Drama. There are three full-time Music teachers and a large staff of visiting music teachers. Over one-third of the pupils learn musical instruments and virtually any instrument can be taught, and many take singing lessons. There are four Choirs, a School Orchestra and seven major instrumental ensembles, including Big Band, Clarinet, Saxophone and Classical Guitar. Visits are arranged each term to concerts in London and elsewhere. The Music School has a Concert Hall and 18 practice rooms. Recent productions have included *Footloose, Spamalot, The Sound of Music, Les Misérables, Jesus Christ Superstar* and *Cabaret*.

Art, which includes pottery, printing and sculpture as well as painting and drawing, is housed in a spacious building with 8 studios, a Library, an Exhibition Room and an Exhibition Hall. There are two full-time Art teachers and one part-time, and Art is studied up to GCSE and A Level.

There are several major Drama productions each year, from classical theatre to the modern musical, produced by a range of staff and pupils. These give boys and girls an opportunity to develop their talents and interests in Drama.

Admission. Almost all pupils enter Epsom College in September. There are 3 entry levels: 11+, 13+ and 16+.

For those entering at 11+ candidates will be assessed for entry in January of Year 6. They will sit papers in English, Mathematics non-verbal and verbal reasoning, and these tests will be supported by a short interview and a report from their current school.

Pupils wishing to enter at 13+ sit our entrance exam in their Year 6 and are offered a deferred place, conditional upon maintaining the same standards at the present school. Some enter the school later than this and there is always a direct entry into the Sixth Form, both for girls and boys.

A boy or girl may be registered at any age by sending in the registration form and fee. All enquiries should be sent to the Director of Admissions from whom a prospectus may be obtained.

Fees per term (2021–2022). Boarders £13,493; Weekly Boarders £12,257; Day Pupils £9,150. Lower School: Day pupils £6,861.

The fees are inclusive and cover the normal cost of a pupil's education. The main extras are for examination fees, private tuition and a pupil's personal expenses. Fees for day pupils include lunch and tea.

There is a College Store for the provision of uniform, clothing and other requirements.

Entrance Scholarships. Scholarships are available at 11+, 13+ and 16+ entry for excellence in academic study, performing arts (drama or music) and sport.

Girls and boys holding awards invariably go on to contribute much to school life throughout their time at Epsom. The College community holds them in high regard.

Candidates may apply for more than one award. Scholarships and Exhibitions will only be awarded if candidates of sufficient merit present themselves.

If a Scholarship or Exhibition is not awarded on entry to the College in Year 7 or 9, there is a further opportunity to be promoted to the status of an award holder in Year 12 (Lower Sixth).

Bursaries. Over the past six years, Epsom has reduced the value of non means-tested Scholarships and Awards, which can be worth up to 10% a year. This has enabled us to double the bursary fund which is allocated to families with demonstrable financial need.

In turn this has helped us, with Educational Trust support, to widen our access to disadvantaged families. This is one of the College's declared aims in line with both Government and HMC guidance. Potential scholarship applicants are encouraged to seek extra financial support, if appropriate, by way of a means-tested Bursary. Application forms are available on request from the Bursar or Admissions Registrar.

Old Epsomians. The Old Epsomian Club promotes sporting activities, social gatherings and networking events among its former pupils, with eight international chapters and an online database. On leaving the College, all pupils automatically become lifelong members of the OE Club and they are invited back regularly for reunions, the OE Dinner and Founder's Day. They also receive several publications each year, including the OE magazine. Bursaries are available for the sons and daughters of OEs who wish to attend the College.

Charitable status. Epsom College is a Registered Charity, number 312046. It exists for the advancement of education.

Patron: Her Most Gracious Majesty The Queen

Chairman: Dr A J Wells, MB BS, DRCOG, MRCGP
Vice-Chair: Mrs Karen Thomas, BM Soton, FRCS Orth
Treasurer: Mr A J Pianca, FCA
Mrs T Botting, MEd
Mrs F Boulton, BSc, MA
Mr E Chandler, MA Cantab
Mrs B Dolbear, LLB
The Very Revd D Gwilliams, BA, MA
Mr J A Hay
Mr D Mahoney, MA Cantab
Mr G B Pincus, MBE, MIPA
Mr A Russell, MA Hons, NPQH
Mr P Stanford, BA
Mr Clive Watson, MA, ACA

Bursar and Clerk to the Governing Body: Mrs S Teasdale, BSc UCL, FCA

Headmaster: Mr J A Piggot, BA Cardiff, MA Liverpool

Second Master: Mr P J Williams, BSc Dunelm
Deputy Head Academic: Mr R J Alton, MA Cantab, MPhys
Director of Academic Operations: Mrs T Muller, MA Oxon
Assistant Head, Total Curriculum: Mr A J Bustard, BA Swansea
Assistant Head, Teaching Staff and Examinations: Mr W L S Keat, BSc UCL, MA King's College London
Assistant Head, Sixth Form: Mr N J Russell, MA Liverpool
Assistant Head, Pupil Welfare: Mrs H E Keevil, BA Exeter
Assistant Head, DSL & Academic Advancement: Ms M Bosa, BA Trent Canada, BEd Queen's Canada
Head of Lower School: Mr E G Lance, BSc Dunelm

Heads of Year:
Head of Sixth Form: Mr N J Russell, MA Liverpool
Head of Lower Sixth: Mr L C Fisher, BA Cantab, MA King's College London
Head of Fifth Form: Mr J Stephens, BSc Liverpool

Head of Upper Fourth: Mr S J Head, BSc Univeristy of the West of England
Head of Lower Fourth: Miss K Allen, BA Oxon, MA Birkbeck
Head of Third Form: Miss B Thomas, BA Exeter
Director of Transition and Integration: Mrs F C Drinkall, BSc Loughborough

Chaplaincy:
Senior Chaplain: Revd Canon A M J Haviland, BEd Leeds, PGDipCMM Surrey, FCCT, FRSA, CF(v)
Assistant Chaplain: Mrs R Catterall
Hindu Chaplain: Ms M Joshi
Muslim Chaplain: Dr H Hammuda

Headmaster's Office:
Headmaster's PA: Mrs S Lawrence
Deputy Heads' Secretary: Mrs E Bauchop

Admissions and Marketing Office:
Director of Admissions: Mrs C Kent
Director of Marketing: Mr M Tobin
Admissions Registrar: Mrs L Watkins

Bursars Office:
Bursar's PA: Ms K Everett

Epsom College Education Trust and OE Club:
Development Director: Ms H Tranter
OE Club Coordinator: Mrs S Croucher

Epsom Library:
Librarian: Mrs S Perry

College Archive:
College Archivist: Ms R Jallot

Eton College

Windsor, Berkshire SL4 6DW

Tel: 01753 370611 (Admissions)
01753 370100 (Head Master)
01753 370540 (Bursar)
email: admissions@etoncollege.org.uk
website: www.etoncollege.com
Twitter: @Eton_College
Facebook: @Eton-College-117613119649208
Instagram: @eton.college

Eton College is a full boarding school for boys with 1,344 pupils, situated next to the historic town of Windsor, Berkshire. It was founded in 1440 by King Henry VI. The school's ethos is to take talented pupils with character and give them the skills to progress through life as happy, successful and socially responsible adults. Academic results are important but so too are the skills gained from co-curricular activities including music, drama, art, sports, Combined Cadet Force, outdoor education, the many different societies and our community engagement programme. At Eton, the emphasis is on finding, nurturing and giving value to each pupil's unique talents.

Approximately one fifth of the boys at the school currently receive financial aid. See our website www.etoncollege.com for further details.

The Tony Little Centre for Innovation and Research in Learning. The world of teaching and the way young people learn is being transformed through the advent of new technologies and a better understanding of neuroscience. Our Centre for Innovation and Research in Learning puts Eton into the forefront of global teaching and learning development.

The Centre works alongside schools and universities around the world to exchange ideas and share best practice, carry out research and analyse new developments – with the aim of continually improving our outstanding teaching and learning experience for our pupils, as well as society more widely.

Academic Achievement. Academic excellence is central to Eton life, with the vast majority of our pupils going on to attend leading universities; an increasing number are also attending top universities in the United States. Our pupils go on to study a range of subjects as undergraduates, for instance the sciences (including medicine), humanities/English, modern languages and economics/business. Eton has its own dedicated Learning Support Centre for boys with special educational needs, or specific learning challenges, such as dyslexia or dyspraxia.

Sport plays a central role in school life. There are nearly 30 different activities on offer, ranging from the more familiar football, rugby, cricket and rowing to Eton's own unique sports – the Wall and Field Games.

We have a range of highly skilled professional coaches and masters leading our extensive games programme. Success on the field is important, and we have provision for elite athletes, but at Eton we consider the central ethos of sport – encouraging teamwork as well as leadership, dedication, respect, physical fitness and well-being, to be the real goal for our pupils.

The Arts. Over 1,250 music lessons are taught each week at The Music Schools. The majority of our 78 teachers balance their work at Eton with successful performing careers in the music industry, with many holding positions at leading music colleges. Our facilities include two concert halls, a recording studio, three music technology suites, drum suites, a music library, and a large number of teaching and practice rooms. There are two Chapel choirs, a concert choir, a choral society, three orchestras, two concert bands, two big bands and a large number of smaller ensembles. Senior boys regularly put on their own concerts – a tradition initiated by Hubert Parry during his time as a boy at Eton. A number of music scholarships are available.

Eton's Director of Drama is Rebecca Farley MA. More than 20 theatrical productions are staged at the school each year, affording boys the opportunity to take part both onstage and behind the scenes; these opportunities have seen a number of former pupils forging very successful careers in the industry. Facilities include the 400-seat Farrer Theatre, a flexible auditorium with state-of-the-art lighting and sound, a scenic workshop, wardrobe, make-up studio and dressing rooms. The smaller Caccia Studio and Empty Space Theatre seat 100 and 60 people respectively. There is also a film unit and radio drama opportunities.

The Drawing Schools have opportunities for printmaking, computer graphics and digital photography, painting and drawing. There are 3D studios with facilities for sculpture (in wood, metal, plaster) and ceramics. Regular professional art exhibitions are staged and there is also an ambitious Artist-in-Residence programme. Art and design features in the curriculum and consistently achieves high examination standards. Students are also encouraged to use the Drawing Schools as a leisure and hobby area in their free time.

Additional activities. Eton societies are extremely popular and there are a large number available (over 70), covering a broad range of topics – from the Mountaineering Society to the Political Society, the Culinary Society to the Medical Society and the recently formed Tech Club and Journalism Society.

Eton also has a very successful Combined Cadet Force and outdoor education programme, alongside a growing department for community engagement allowing boys to balance their co-curricular programme with volunteering valued as much as individual endeavour. Pupils are encouraged to develop a sense of social responsibility and give back in a number of ways, including volunteering with school children or the elderly and taking part in charity fundraising events, such as the annual Eton Community Fair.

Pastoral Care. The welfare of boys at Eton College is taken extremely seriously and a robust system is in place, specifically designed to enable staff to spot problems as early as possible. The house structure, tutor groups, our own health centre (the Stephenson Centre for Wellbeing, which houses an adolescent psychiatrist, two clinical psychologists and a counsellor) and the chaplaincy teams (with representatives of multiple faiths) all play a role within this system. Our pastoral care procedures are reviewed regularly by the Head Master, Lower Master, Deputy Head (Pastoral) and Director of Safeguarding.

Admissions. The majority of pupils are admitted to the school aged 13. For entry up to and including 2025, registration is required by 30th June in UK School Year 5 (the academic year in which a boy reaches the age of 10); please note these are strict deadlines. There are scholarships for entry aged 13 – the academic King's Scholarship and various Music Awards. When a boy is awarded a scholarship it is still possible to apply for a means-tested bursary for the remainder of the fees but the awarding of a scholarship does not guarantee that a bursary application will be successful. There are also a small number of places available in the Sixth Form, namely Orwell Awards (funded places for students for whom studying at Eton would be a transformative experience).

The Admissions process for entry up to and including 2025 consists of two stages. The first consists of the ISEB Common Pre-Tests and a report from the boy's current school, and the second stage, held at Eton, consists of a specially designed computer test and an interview.

A visit to the school either before registration or before assessment is recommended. Please contact the Admissions Team via www.etoncollege.com for further details.

Fees per term (2021–2022). £14,698.

Charitable status. Eton College is a Registered Charity, number 1139086.

Provost: The Lord Waldegrave of North Hill, PC, MA
Vice-Provost: Peter McKee, MA

Executive Leadership Team:

Head Master: **Simon Henderson**, MA

Lower Master: Susan Wijeratna, BA

Bursar: Janet Walker, MA, FCA

Deputy Head (*Academic*): Tom Hawkins, MA

Deputy Head (Co-Curricular): Jonathan Newton, MA
Deputy Head (Partnerships): Tom Arbuthnott, MA, MPhil
Deputy Head (Pastoral): David Gregg, BSc

Clerk & Legal Advisor to Provost & Fellows: Karen Neale, BA
Buildings & Facilities Director: Christopher Reeve, BSc, MRICS
Director of Development: Justin Nolan, MA
Director of Admissions: Paul Smith, MA, MSt
Director of Safeguarding: Alice Vicary-Stott, BA

Exeter School

Victoria Park Road, Exeter, Devon EX2 4NS

Tel: 01392 273679 (Head/Director of Admissions & Marketing)
           01392 258712 (Bursar/Office)
email: admissions@exeterschool.org.uk
website: www.exeterschool.org.uk
Twitter: @ExeterSchoolUK
Facebook: @ExeterSchoolUK
Instagram: @exeterschooluk

Motto: ΧΡΥΣΟΣ ΑΡΕΤΗΣ ΟΥΚ ΑΝΤΑΞΙΟΣ

Founded in 1633, Exeter School occupies a 25-acre site, located within a mile of the city centre, having moved from its original location in the High Street in 1880. Some of its well-designed buildings date from that time but many new buildings have been added over the past twenty years and the school now enjoys first-rate facilities on a very attractive open site.

The school is fully co-educational and offers education to boys and girls from 7 to 18. It has its own junior school of around 200 pupils, nearly all of whom transfer to the senior school at the age of 11. The senior school has around 720 pupils, including a sixth form of 220. (*For further information about Exeter Junior School, see entry in IAPS section.*)

The New School joined the Exeter School family in March 2021; a co-educational pre-prep for girls and boys from nursery to Year 2.

Exeter School is a well-run school with high all-round standards and very good academic results. It prides itself on strong cultural, sporting and extra curricular achievement. Its music is outstanding and there is a strong tradition of performance drawn from all age groups in the school. It offers a very wide range of sports and maintains consistently high standards especially in hockey, rugby and cricket. It is well placed for outdoor pursuits (e.g. Duke of Edinburgh's Award scheme and Ten Tors on Dartmoor) and has its own very large voluntary CCF unit. The School is closely involved with the life of the City of Exeter and its university and it has a substantial commitment to support the local community.

Buildings, Grounds and General Facilities. The senior school block includes a large multi-purpose assembly hall, a library, a private study area, dining hall and Sixth Form Centre as well as many well-appointed classrooms. A major refurbishment of the former boarding accommodation to include a new Library and Study Centre was completed for September 2006. There are separate buildings on the site

housing the Chapel, the Music School, the Science Centre, Art Studios, Drama Studio, Design and Technology Centre and Exonian Centre. The Science Centre provides 14 laboratories and there are four fully-equipped computer rooms. All departments have access to their own computers and the School has a wide, controlled access to the internet. In 2005 the school opened a new dance studio and a fitness suite to add to the existing sports facilities of a large modern well-equipped Sports Hall with its own squash courts and access to on-site floodlit all-weather sports arena, top-grade all-weather tennis/netball courts and a 25m indoor swimming pool, built in 2017. The playing fields, which are immediately adjacent to the School buildings are well kept and provide, in season, rugby, cricket, hockey, football, rounders and athletics areas. The junior school, which was extended in 2017 to provide additional changing room facilities and a STEAM room for DT, science and cookery, has access to all the senior school facilities but is self-contained on the estate. The playground benefitted from a substantial refurbishment over the summer of 2021 including bespoke wooden playground equipment and an outdoor classroom.

Admission. The majority of pupils enter the junior school at 7 or 9 and the senior school at 11 or 13. Admission is also possible at other ages where space allows and a significant number of pupils join at the age of 16 for sixth form studies.

Entrance to the junior school is by assessment in January. This includes a report from the child's previous school, classroom sessions in the company of other prospective pupils, and literacy and numeracy tasks.

Entrance examinations for the senior school are held in January.

Assessment for entry to the sixth form at 16 is by interview and a report from the applicant's previous school. Dedicated interview days are held monthly from December to March each year and the entry requirement is a minimum of 3 passes at grade 7 and 3 passes at grade 6 at GCSE, including English and mathematics, with normally a grade 7–9 in the subjects chosen for study.

Registration Fee £100.

Fees per term (2021–2022). Junior School: Years 3 & 4 £4,040, Years 5 & 6 £4,120 (Overseas £16,765 per annum). Senior School: £4,900 (Overseas £20,220 per annum).

Sibling discount of 5% for the second child and 10% for the third or subsequent child attending concurrently. Fees are collected termly.

Scholarships and Financial Awards.

Academic scholarships for 7+ pupils new to Exeter Junior School are awarded based on the results of the entrance assessments sat in January of the year of entry. Exeter School offers a range of scholarship opportunities to pupils who are talented in their chosen discipline. Scholarships are available at 11+, 13+ and 16+ for pupils who show excellence in art, drama, music, and sport. Academic scholarships for pupils new to Exeter School are awarded based on the results of the entrance assessments sat in January of the year of entry. All registered candidates for the 11+, 13+ and 16+ examinations are automatically considered for an academic scholarship or exhibition based on their performance in the examinations and interviews.

Bursaries are means-tested awards based on parental circumstances and are awarded on an annual basis. They are available to external candidates who meet the school's academic entry requirement and whose parents could not afford to send their child to Exeter School without financial assistance.

Free places – As part of its bursary programme, Exeter School is able to offer up to nine free places in the senior school and sixth form as a result of donations and legacies from former pupils and grants from a local charity.

Curriculum. In the first three years in the senior school all pupils take English, history, geography, two modern foreign languages (French, German or Spanish), classical studies, mathematics, IT, physics, chemistry, biology, art, design technology, drama, music and religious and physical education. After this there is a wide choice of subjects at GCSE level, including English, one compulsory modern foreign language, mathematics, dual or triple award science and three of the following: Latin, French, German, Spanish, classical civilisation, religious studies, history, geography, music, drama, art, design and technology, and computer science.

Pupils enter the sixth form choosing over 20 different subjects for A Level study and are prepared for university scholarships, university entrance and admission to other forms of further education or vocational training. Over 95% go on annually to Degree Courses.

Houses. There are ten pupil houses. Each is under the personal care of a Head of House and his/her deputy, with whom parents are invited to keep in touch on any matter affecting their child's general development and progress throughout the school.

Religion. All pupils attend religious education classes, which include sixth form discussion groups.

Games. Rugby, hockey, cricket, swimming, athletics, dance, cross country, tennis, badminton, squash, shooting, basketball, netball and golf. Further activities are available for the sixth form, including football and multi-gym sessions.

Community and other Service. All pupils learn to serve the community. Many choose to take part in social service, helping old people and the handicapped young. There is a voluntary CCF Contingent with thriving RN, Army and RAF Sections. The CCF offers a large variety of outdoor activities, including adventure training camps, Ten Tors Expedition training as well as specialist courses. Pupils are encouraged to participate in the Duke of Edinburgh's Award scheme.

Music. Pupils are taught singing and musical appreciation and are encouraged to learn to play musical instruments. More than one third of all pupils have individual lessons on at least one instrument. There are four orchestras, a Choral Society which annually performs a major work in Exeter Cathedral and four choirs, three jazz bands, and numerous smaller groups from string quartets to rock bands. There are over 30 visiting instrumental teachers. Over 20 public concerts are given each year. Recent summer music trips have included Salzburg and New York.

Drama. Drama is developed both within and outside the curriculum. The School Hall with its large and well-equipped stage provides for the dual purpose of studio workshop and the regular production of plays and musicals. The recently refurbished Drama Studio is used for smaller productions.

There are three productions every year: the senior school play operates on a three-year rotation (Shakespeare, straight play, musical), embracing a variety of styles, genres and challenges; the lower school play (Years 7–11) is performed in the summer term in the main school hall and offers a very exciting opportunity for pupils to get on stage and show their talents and the Middle Fifth play, which is performed in February in the drama studio, is open to Year 10 only, meaning actors don't miss out in the transition between the seniors and the juniors. The drama department hosts National Youth Theatre auditions every year and has introduced LAMDA as an extracurricular option.

Art and Design. Art lessons are given to junior and senior forms. Apart from the formal disciplines of GCSE and A Level, which can be taken by those who choose, all pupils have opportunity for artistic expression in painting, print-making, photography and construction in many materials. All younger pupils learn to develop craft skills in wood, metal and plastic and to use them creatively in design work. Some then follow GCSE or A Level courses in design and technology. There is an annual art exhibition in July.

Expeditions. Throughout the school a large number of residential field trips and expeditions take place each year including a Third Form residential camping on the school field, various departmental excursions, several foreign exchanges and Duke of Edinburgh's Award expeditions. In recent summers, the school has run its own adventure trips to Namibia, Peru, Vietnam, the Himalayas, Cuba and Borneo. There is a programme of major and minor sports tours.

Societies and Clubs. Pupils are encouraged to pursue their interests by joining one of the school societies. Groups of enthusiasts can form new societies or clubs, but the following are at present available: art, badminton, basketball, chess, Choral Society, computing, dance, drama, electronics, model railway, MUN, music, politics, shooting and squash.

Social. Close contact is maintained with the city and the university. Association between members of the school and the wider society outside is fostered wherever opportunity offers.

The staff believe strongly in the value of association with parents, who are invited to meetings annually throughout their sons' or daughters' time at the school. A termly lecture by a visiting speaker is provided for parents.

Careers. Careers education begins at the age of 7 and continues on a progressive programme until pupils leave the school. Careers evenings are held annually when pupils and their parents have the opportunity to consult representatives of the professions, industry and commerce. A work experience programme is organised for Year 11 pupils each summer, and a scheme of mock interviews with career professionals for pupils in the sixth form. A major Careers Convention is held at the school each Autumn for pupils from Years 9 to 13.

Honours. Pupils regularly gain admission to Oxford and Cambridge. The school encourages application to the leading universities, including the Russell and 1994 Groups.

Leading musicians have gained places at the Royal College of Music and the Royal Academy of Music.

Charitable status. Exeter School is a Registered Charity, number 1093080, and a Company Limited by Guarantee, registered in England, number 04470478. Registered Office: Victoria Park Road, Exeter, Devon EX2 4NS.

Patrons:
The Lord Lieutenant of the County of Devon
The Right Reverend the Lord Bishop of Exeter
The Right Worshipful the Lord Mayor of Exeter

Governors:
James Gaisford, BSc, ACA (*Chair*)
Gillian Hodgetts MSc, MCIPR, BA Hons, DMS, DN, RGN
   (*Vice-Chair*)
Ruth Vigers (*Vice-Chair, Nominated Safeguarding
   Governor*)
Rowan Edbrooke, BEd Hons (*Vice-Chair*)
Adrian Burbanks, BA
Helen Clark
Paul Fisher, MA Oxon
Catherine Gibaud, QC, BBus Sc Hons, MA
Martin Grossel, MA, PhD
Stephen Hodder, BSc
Richard May, BA, MRICS
David McGahey, MA, PGCE

Head: Ms L A Simpson, BSc

Senior Deputy Headmaster: M J Hughes, MA
Deputy Head: Miss A Dunning, BA
Deputy Head: G S Bone, BSc
Deputy Head: Dr J L Wilson, MPhys, DPhil

Assistant Staff:
* *Head of Department*
[OE] *Old Exonian*

Art & Design:
*Mrs A J Escott, BA [maternity leave]
Mrs J H Rafferty-White, BA
Ms S Tucker, BA (*Acting Head of Department*) [maternity
   cover]
Mr I A Wilkins, MA

Biology:
*Mrs J H Metcalf, MA (*Director of Science*)
Mr P J C Boddington, BSc
Mrs J M Seaton-Burn, MSc (*Chair of Teaching and
   Learning Committee*)
Mrs K A Coe, BSc
Mrs A C Johnson, BSc

Chemistry:
*Mr R F J Tear, BSc
Mr P I O'Connor, BSc
Dr S P Smale, PhD (*CCF Contingent Commander and
   Head of RAF section, CCF*)
Mrs F J Tamblyn, BSc
Ms D H Wilson, MBA

Classical Subjects:
*Mrs E K J Dunlop
Dr E L Keane, DPhil
Mrs S T Shrubb, MA

Computer Science:
*Ms A O Pinches, BEng
Mr G J McGrath, BSc
Design Technology
*Mr M J Rose, BSc
Mr R A Collard, BSc

Drama:
*Mr J S Brough, BSc, LAMDA
Mr C C Harknett, BA

Electronics:
*Mr M E Schramm (*see Physics*)
English:
*Mr A S Dobson, MA
Mrs J H Daybell, BA, MA
Mrs E K J Dunlop, BA, MA, MPhil
Mr R O Evans, BA
Mr C C Harknett (*see Drama*)
Mr S S Healey, BA
Mrs K L Ridler-Murray, BA, MA
Mr E J Seaton-Burn, BA

Geography:
*Mr P M Hyde, BSc
Mr J W J Bird, BSc, MA, MSc
Mrs A Roff, BSc, MSc
Mrs H M Sail, MA
Careers and Higher Education
Mrs R Cheesman, MSc

History:
*Mr G N Trelawny, BEd, MA
Mr R J Baker (*see Social Studies*)
Mr M J G Connolly (*see Social Studies*)
Mrs A-J Culley, BA, BSc
Ms J R Hodgetts, BA, MA
Mrs M F Sheehan (*see Social Studies*)

Languages:
*Ms L Trotman, BA
Mr R A Charters, BA
Mrs N H R Cushion, BA
Miss A Dunning (*see Deputy Heads*)
Mrs A M Francis, MA
Mr M F Latimer, MA, MSt
Mrs D D S Masters, BA
Mrs S C Wilson, BA

Learning Support:
Mrs A L Reeves, BSc (*Head of RN Section, CCF*)
Mrs H E Coogan, BEd

Mathematics:
*Mrs E V Cartwright, BSc
Dr G J D Chapman, BSc, PhD, MSc
Mr M F C Glanville, BSc
Mr B M Hall, BA
Mr M J Hughes (*see Senior Deputy Head*)
Ms M McCluskey, BA, MSc
Mr S J Parry, BA
Mr A J Reynolds, BSc (*Examinations Officer*)
Mr G R Willson, BSc

Music:
*Mr P Tamblyn, MA, MMus (*Director of Music*)
Mr G M Davies, MA (*Assistant Director of Music*)
Mr P J Adcock, MA
Mrs R Allnatt, Dip RCM, Cert Adv Study
Mr D Bowen, BEd
Mr M R Cann, BA
Mr S J Crossen
Mr A Daldorph, BA
Mr A Gillett, ARCM
Mr M F Greenwood, LRAM
Mrs T M Guthrie, BA
Mr B R Moore, BA, MA
Mr P K Painter, Dip Mus Ed
Mrs R L Willson, BA

Physical Education:
*Mr D J Gibson, BSc (*Director of Sport*)
Miss R A Carter, BSc
Miss B G Johnson
Mr E P M Jones, BSc (*Head of Raleigh House*)
Miss D S Lunn, BSc
Mrs A Marsh, BEd (*Head of Sixth Form*)
Mr A C F Mason, BA
Mrs H L Hayden, BSc
Mr T N Ross, BSc
Mr G Skinner, BEd [OE]

Physics:
*Mr D L N Tuohey, BSc, MA
Mr G S Bone (*see Deputy Heads*)
Dr M J Commin, MA, PhD
Dr G B N Robb, MA, PhD (*Master i/c Aquatics*)
Mr M E Schramm, BSc
Mr D I Trim, BSc (*Head of Army Section, CCF*)
Dr J L Wilson (*see Deputy Heads*)

Psychology:
*Mrs C Gooddy, MSc
Mrs A M Godfroy, BA
Religious Studies:
*Mr J F M Gooddy, MA
Mrs A J Marsh (*see Physical Education*)
Mrs J M K Murrin, BA

Social Studies:
Mr S K Mackintosh, BA (*Economics*)
Mr R J Baker, BA (*Politics*)
Mr P Bell, MA, BA
Mr M J G Connolly, BA
Mrs M F Sheehan, BA (*Politics*)

Junior School

Headmistress: Mrs Saskia van Schalkwyk, BA Hons, QTS

Deputy Head: Mr J S Wood, BA

Assistant Staff:
Ms J A Barnes, BA
Mrs H E Coogan, BEd
Miss E C Cox, BA
Mr A P Cunningham, BA
Mr R W I Evans, MA
Mrs C H Handley, BEd
Mrs L L Hardy, MA
Mrs K L Jones, BSc
Mrs S S Morgan, BA
Mrs R E Pettet, BA
Mr R J Pidwell, BA
Mrs H D Russell, BA
Miss K E Wright, BA

Bursar and Clerk to the Governors: M C M MacEacharn, FCA, BSc
Deputy Bursar and Company Secretary: Mrs G M Robins, BA, FCCA
Operations Manager: C A Stewart
Director of Development and Alumni: Miss A S A Holohan, BA
Director of Admissions and Marketing: Mrs E S Williams
Communications Manager: Mrs K Brookes-Ferrari, BA
Headmaster's PA: Mrs K Leach
Bursar's PA: Mrs L M Stewart
Information Manager: A D R Carter, BEng
Network Manager: P D Sprake, MCSA

Librarian: Mrs B J Jackson, MSc
School Nurse: Mrs L J Barlass, BSc

Felsted School

Felsted, Dunmow, Essex CM6 3LL

Tel: 01371 822606 (Headmaster)
       01371 822608 (Admissions Registrar)
email: reception@felsted.org
website: www.felsted.org
Twitter: @felstedschool
Facebook: @felstedschool
Instagram: @felsted-school
LinkedIn: /felsted-school

Founded in 1564 by Lord Richard Riche, Felsted educates boys and girls aged 4 to 18. Felsted is ideally situated in a safe, picturesque North Essex village, close to both London and Cambridge, and within easy reach of Stansted and other international airports. Felsted is a Church of England foundation but welcomes pupils from all religious traditions and none. The Senior School, for 13 to 18 year olds, has around 570 pupils; the majority are boarders and weekend arrangements are flexible. The Preparatory School is also home to approximately 500 pupils, with a buoyant boarding house, home to full, weekly and flexible boarders.

Felsted seeks to develop the character of every student, to help prepare them for life beyond school. This is done through a broad and holistic education with strength in Music, Drama, Sport, The Arts, Leadership and Service. Felsted seeks to develop and stretch students academically, to be lifelong learners, well-rounded, aspirational and globally minded, with the skills to flourish beyond school, applying the principles of a growth mindset, to be the best they can be.

Felsted celebrated its 450th anniversary in 2014, and was honoured by a visit from HM The Queen and HRH Prince Phillip.

The School is a Global Member of the Round Square Organisation offering international exchanges and collaboration, and offers both A Levels and the International Baccalaureate Diploma in the Sixth Form, plus the Extended Project Qualification (EPQ). The website hosts much information about the school plus many videos, including one called 'Boarding at Felsted'. A Boarding Schools' Association (BSA) member school, Felsted had an Ofsted boarding and welfare inspection in 2011 and was rated 'outstanding' in every aspect, and also received an 'excellent' rating in all aspects in the Independent Schools Inspectorate inspection in 2019. The school also passed with flying colours in a full compliance inspection across both the Preparatory and Senior Schools in 2019. Details are available on our website, and directly on the ISI website. Felsted was shortlisted for five TES Independent School Awards in 2018, including Boarding School of the Year. In 2019, Felsted was shortlisted for three TES Awards, including Prep School of the Year and Sports School of the Year. And in 2020 Felsted was once again shortlisted for Boarding School of the Year. In 2021, Felsted won the TES Marketing Award.

The Houses. There are ten Houses at Felsted, a day house for boys, a day house for girls, three boarding houses for boys, three boarding houses for girls, an Upper Sixth House for boys and an Upper Sixth House for girls. Each House is under the direction of a resident Housemaster or Housemistress.

Each Boarding House is supported by a pastoral team comprising a resident Assistant House Parent, a matron responsible for overseeing the domestic arrangements, and several House tutors, a number of whom are resident.

The Curriculum. All pupils study English Language, English Literature, Mathematics and Sciences (Double or Triple Award) to GCSE and choose a further four subjects from the following: History, Geography, TEP (Theology, Ethics and Philosophy), French, German, Spanish, Latin, Classical Civilisation, Art and Design, Music, Drama, Triple Science, Design & Technology (Resistant Materials), Physical Education and Computer Science.

One of the options is expected to be a Modern Foreign Language and one is expected to be a Humanities subject. Pupils also complete the Felsted Diploma Project (FDP).

In the Sixth Form pupils have a choice between A Levels and the International Baccalaureate Diploma.

Those studying A Levels normally choose three subjects to study along with an Extended Project Qualification (EPQ). The following subjects are offered: Art and Design, Business, Classical Civilisation, Computer Science, Design Technology, Drama and Theatre, Economics, English Literature, Geography, History, Latin, Mathematics, Further Mathematics, Media Studies, Modern Foreign Languages (French, German, Spanish), Music, Physical Education, Politics, Psychology, Sciences (Biology, Chemistry, Physics) and TEP (Theology, Ethics and Philosophy).

IB pupils study six subjects, one from each of the following categories: Language and Literature (English, German, Italian, Self-Study Language, Spanish and French), Language A (English, German, Italian, Self-Taught), Language (Other) (French, German, English, Spanish, Latin and Italian 'ab initio'), Humanities (Economics, Geography, History, Philosophy, Psychology), Sciences (Biology, Chemistry, Design Technology, Physics, Sports Exercise and Health Science), Mathematics (Maths Analysis and Approaches or Maths Applications and Interpretation), The Arts/Elective (Music, Visual Arts, Biology, Economics, French B, Spanish ab initio). They also follow a course on the Theory of Knowledge, write an extended essay and are fully involved in the Creativity, Action and Service Programme.

Scholarships, Awards and Bursaries. Academic, Music, Drama, Art, Design/Technology/Engineering and Sports Scholarships are awarded annually for entry into Year 7, 9, 10 and 12, up to the value of 20% of the fees.

The assessments for Year 7 entry take place in November and the following January. For Year 9, 10 and 12 in November and February (Academic only) in the year preceding entry.

Awards recognising all-round ability or a specific ability in one area, are also available.

Means-tested Bursaries may be available to increase an award.

At least two Open Bursaries (100%) each year may be available to those who might otherwise not be able to consider Felsted, due to financial circumstances, as well as a Royal Docks Scholarship (100%) and the school has recently developed a link with the Royal Springboard Foundation to support a further two pupils a year.

Talented students in Design are also entered at 16+ for Arkwright Foundation Scholarships.

Fee reductions are available for children of those serving in the Armed Services, or the Foreign Office.

Full details are available at www.felsted.org and from the Admissions Office.

Registration and entry. Boys' and girls' names can be registered at any time. Registration fee £125.

Before admission to Felsted, prospective pupils must pass the Felsted Entrance assessment, or the ISEB online pre-test (Year 9 entry), provide a Head Teacher's report and have an interview with the Headmaster. For Sixth Form entry, a minimum of 32 points must be gained across their best six subjects at GCSE, with at least a 6 in the subjects to be studied at A Level or at Higher Level in the IB Diploma.

Fees per term (2021–2022). Senior School: Full Boarding (7 nights) £13,055, Weekly Boarding (5 nights) £12,095, Contemporary Boarding (3 nights) £10,445, Day £8,530. Preparatory School: Day £3,290–£6,445, Weekly Boarding £8,355, Full Boarding £8,875.

Felsted Preparatory School, whose Head is a member of IAPS (The Independent Association of Prep Schools), shares the same governing body with Felsted School. It has its own campus, with approximately 500 pupils aged 4 to 13. There is a dedicated teaching centre for 11–13 year-olds and a state-of-the-art Pre-Preparatory Department, which opened in 2011. (For further information, see entry in IAPS section.)

The Old Felstedian Society organises both social and sporting activities, plus networking opportunities across a variety of industries. The Old Felstedian Liaison Manager, Miss Selina Joslin, would be pleased to answer queries about the Alumni (ofs@felsted.org) and further information can be found via the school's website.

Charitable status. Felsted School is a Registered Charity, number 310870. The charity is based upon the Foundation established by Richard Lord Riche in 1564 with the objective of teaching and instructing children across a broad curriculum as ordained from time to time by its Trustees.

Governing Body:
Chair of Governors: Robert Brown

John Davies, OBE	Ann Carrington
Philip Hutley	Geoffrey Boult
Bobbi Davy	Julia Abel Smith
Dr James Nicholson	Mike Beale
Oliver Stocken, CBE	Stephen Wolfe
James Tibbitts	Patricia Wardell
Jane Crouch	Alison Sefton
William Sunnucks	Lucilla Poston
Revd Nic Stuchfield	

Bursar and Clerk to the Governors: Andrew Clayton MA

Headmaster: **Christopher Townsend**, BA

Bursar: Andrew Clayton, MA
Senior Deputy Head: George Masters, BA
Deputy Head (*Academic*): Sarah Capewell, MA
Designated Safeguarding Lead: Nicola O'Brien
Director of Global Education: Daniel Emmerson, MA
Prep School Headmaster: Simon James, BA

† *Housemaster/mistress*

Art:
E A M Jackson, BA University College for the Creative Arts
J N Buniak
A V Warner, BA Maidstone College of Art

Classics:
E M McLaren, MA Cambridge (*Roberts Society Coordinator*)
S R Capewell, MA Edinburgh (*Deputy Head Academic*)
E Clark
A J Quinlan, BA Oxford

Computer Science:
G Dean, BA (*Director of Digital Strategy*)
E Abegglen, BSc (*Head of Computer Science*)
M W J Redding (*Head of ICT Services*)

Design and Technology:
M A Pitts, BEng Loughborough
H K Pheloung, BA Northumbria
W Bayliss-Brown, BA Oxford Brookes

Drama:
M C Donaldson, BA Derby (*Director of Performing Arts*)
K Charters
L Macey, BA Roehampton
L J Mann, BA Essex
A Moore

Economics and Business Studies:
F M Barrett, BA Calway. PGD University of Waikato
M L McIlvenna, BA Brighton, MEd Cambridge
A T Mohindru, LLB Brunel
†S D Wilson, BA Humberside
E Grant, BSc Loughborough
J K Peddy, BSc Bradford

English:
E L Predebon, MA Anglia Ruskin
G J Catchpole
M Crossley, BA Reading
C M James, BA Leeds (*Head of Project Qualifications*)
R J Purdy, BA Essex (*PSHE, Director Co-Curriculum, MUN Coordinator*)
N M Sunshine-Harris, BA East London
H Sunshine, BA Nottingham
L Fell, BA Goldsmiths
Z Ball, MA London

Geography:
T P C Galvin, BSc St Andrews
K Moir-Smith, BA London
G R Stringer, BSc Durham
A McCaughern, BSc Queen's

History & Politics:
R Pathak, BA Oxford
B R Maude-Barker, MA Cambridge
L M Scofield, BA Reading (*Director of Professional Guidance*)
Dr T Strange, PhD Manchester

Mathematics:
M J Campbell, MSc St Andrews
J C Andrews, MA Exeter
C Donaldson, BSc Reading
R L Feldman, MSc London (*Director of Reports and Reviews*)
J M Jevons, BA Nottingham

A Munns, MA Nottingham
H Lavin, BSc Northumbria
J Adams, BA, PhD Cambridge
N Pritchard, BSc Southampton

Modern Languages:
L Robertson, MA London (*French and German*)
A N Fazekas, MA Dresden (*German*)
R Grant, BA Leeds (*Spanish, Round Square Coordinator*)
N F S O'Brien, MA Glasgow (*Spanish, EAL DSL*)
F Sanchez del Rio, Licenciatura Cadiz (*Spanish, Editor of 'The Felstedian'*)
G Scholz (*German*)
M Trucco, MA Turin (*Italian and French*)
T Catmur, BA Anglia Ruskin
J White, BA Cambridge
R Perez Cabrera, MA Salamanca

Music:
W J Warns, MA Cambridge, Dip ABRSM, FNCM, FGMS, FNFCM, MISM (*Director of Music*)
R A Thear, BA Leeds
C McGlone, BA Oxford

Physical Education and Sport:
L Willis, BSc Durham (*Director of Girls' Sport & Head of Girls' Hockey*)
M Anthony (*GRA Sport*)
†S Barrett, BSc Sheffield Hallam
†B J Bury, BA Exeter
J E R Gallian (*Director of Cricket*)
C S Knightley, BA UWIC (*Director of Sport*)
†A Le Chevalier, PGCE (*Director of Rugby*)
N J Lockhart, ECB3, EH2 (*Head of Grounds & Cricket Professional*)
R Marriott-Cox (*Director of Tennis*)
N J Phillips, BA Durham (*Head of Boys' Hockey*)
C E Rudd, BSc Cardiff

Project Qualifications:
C M James, BA Leeds

PSHE:
R J Purdy, BA Essex (*English, Director of Diploma & Co-Curricular*)
L Page (*Head of Wellbeing*)

Psychology and TEP:
V L Smith, BSc OU
M Cacace, BA Exeter (*Head of IB Core*)
TEP (Theology, Ethics & Philosophy):
B S Roberts Jones, BSc Kent, MEd Cambridge
Revd N J Little, BA Middlesex (*Chaplain, i/c Charities*)
L M Keable, BA Bath Spa
G W S Masters, BA Durham (*Senior Deputy Head*)
L K Stefanini, BSc London School Economics, MA London (*Assistant Head Academic*)
St John Lambert, PhD University of Southampton

Science:
H J Mollison, BSc Hertfordshire (*Head of Science, Chemistry*)
L E Barden, BSc Bath (*Chemistry*)
J Entwistle, BSc UAE (*Biology*)
K Farr, MSc Surrey (*Biology*)
†C H Palmer, MA Cambridge (*Physics, Mathematics*)
A J A Pask, BSc York (*Chemistry*)
A L F Simpson, BSc London (*Director of Assessment and Tracking*)
R Sloman, MSc Exeter

D T Smith, BSc Newcastle Upon Tyne (*Physics*)
K L Woodhouse, BSc Birmingham (*Physics*, *Director of International Baccalaureate*)
R Williams, BSc Bristol

Support for Learning:
J W Hipkin, BA Manchester QTS, MEd
S J Beale, BA Bristol
N J Johnson, CDip
E L Masters, MA Aberdeen
Dr P H Milner, BSc, PhD, CChem, MRSC Nottingham
†C M Phillips, MCILIP W London
†A L Salmon, BA Leicester, MEd Middlesex
J C Turner Jones, BA Birmingham

EAL:
D K Guerrero, BA Middlesex, Dip TEFLA

CCF:
†C H Palmer, MA Cambridge (*CCF Contingent Commander*)
L W Jay

Duke of Edinburgh's Award & Educational Visits:
D L Whittock

Library:
N S Howorth, BA Edge Hill, Dip Lib, MCLIP

Houses and Housemasters/mistresses:

Boys' Houses:
Deacon's: Barny Bury
Elwyn's: Thomas Galvin
Gepp's: Luke McIlvenna
Montgomery's: Andrew Le Chevalier
Windsor's: Clifford Palmer

Girls' Houses:
Follyfield: Sonia Wilson
Garnetts: Sarah Barrett
Manor: Carolyn Phillips
Stocks': Anna Salmon
Thorne: Connie Donaldson

Director of Marketing: Mr Jack Dougherty
Head of Admissions: Miss Gemma Kilby
School Chaplain: Reverend Nigel Little
Medical Officer: Mrs Sally Staines

Fettes College

Carrington Road, Edinburgh EH4 1QX

Tel: +44 (0)131 311 6744
email: admissions@fettes.com
website: www.fettes.com
Twitter: @Fettes_College
Facebook: @FettesCollegeFettesPrep
Instagram: @fettes.college

Motto: *Industria*

Fettes is uniquely situated in 100 acres of private, extensive grounds close to the heart of Edinburgh and enjoys the reputation as one of the UK's pre-eminent boarding schools for boys and girls aged 7–18.

Learning. Fettes is renowned for the quality of education it provides, which naturally includes superb academic results across GCSE, A Level and the IB. A Fettes education means so much more than academic success and the skills and talents of each of our students are recognised and rewarded, whether that be in the classroom, on the sports field, in the concert hall, on the stage or in the gallery. We strongly believe that with expert tuition and encouragement, every student can realise their ambitions.

Life. Boarding Houses are a vital part of boarding life, a caring community of students living together. A wealth of house activities cements the strong bond between housemates, younger students learn from older students and older students take responsibility to care for others. We are a full-boarding school (meaning we do not offer flexi- or weekly boarding) and each boarding house (2 in the Prep School and 9 in The College) is a caring community of students and staff designed to be a real home-from-home.

Sport. Sport is an integral part of a healthy and active lifestyle, developing key life skills such as teamwork and communication. We expect students to show commitment, determination and drive, whatever team they are in. We offer over 20 sporting options, both competitively and recreationally, so that students can find a sport they love. Specialist coaches, access to a wealth of on-site facilities and a busy calendar of sporting fixtures are key elements of our sporting provision.

The Arts. We allocate generous time to the arts because it encourages creativity and builds confidence helping our students to explore and understand the world around them, gain confidence and think creatively. Fettes offers a true all-round education and the provision of the arts is central to that philosophy. All students have the opportunities and support to develop confidence in their creative ability and to perform in front of others.

Co-Curricular. We encourage all of our students to try new activities, push themselves and embrace all of the opportunities Fettes has on offer. Whether choosing from 40 plus activities, supporting local charities or utilising the cultural highlights of Edinburgh, our self-motivated students emerge with new-found skills and experiences. The benefits of these opportunities are immense, fostering independence whilst creating life-long memories.

Proudly Scottish. Fettes College is situated in the heart of Edinburgh, one of the most beautiful capital cities in the world. Edinburgh is a thriving city renowned as culturally vibrant with world-class galleries, theatres, music venues and sporting arenas, but only a short drive away lies the magnificent Scottish countryside, or the stunning Scottish coastline giving our students the freedom to sail, climb, walk, ski and cycle.

Fees per term (2021–2022). Boarders £12,400, Day Pupils £10,290 (3 terms per academic year). Please note that fees include the cost of all meals taken.

Chairman of Governors: I M Osborne

Head: Mrs Helen Harrison

Forest School

Snaresbrook, London E17 3PY

Tel: 020 8520 1744
email: admissions@forest.org.uk
website: www.forest.org.uk
Twitter: @ForestSchoolE17
Facebook: @ForestSchoolE17
LinkedIn: /company/forest-school

Motto: *In Pectore Robur*

Established in 1834, Forest School is a large, outstanding all-round school, offering a breadth and depth of opportunity in which pupils' all-round personal development is outstanding and academic attainment very high. It is, above all, a happy school which understands the rich inter-relationship between curricular, the co-curricular and the pastoral. The school is located on an attractive large site at the edge of the capital's largest open space, Epping Forest.

There are currently 1,490 pupils in the School – 759 boys and 731 girls. All pupils share the main school campus and facilities such as the Chapel, Dining Hall, Sports Hall, playing fields, Deaton Theatre and the Martin Centre for Innovation. Sixth Form pupils enjoy use of a dedicated Sixth Form Centre, including collaborative IT work-spaces, group study areas and a careers room. The School site and playing fields cover 50 acres.

Curriculum. The Forest School curriculum parallels the National Curriculum, although the School exercises its independence to enable teachers to exploit the high academic ability of the pupils. In Y7–Y9 a broad range of core subjects is taught, including Modern and Classical Languages, incorporating Mandarin Chinese, and the three Sciences. Options in Y9 include Computer Science, Ancient Greek and Food & Nutrition, as well as more traditional subjects. At GCSE, all pupils follow a core curriculum of English Language & Literature, a Modern Foreign Language, Maths and Science (separate or Double Award, according to preference) as well as a choice from around 15 optional subjects. A distinctive feature of the curriculum is that all pupils also submit work for the Higher Project Qualification (HPQ) – a research-based dissertation on a subject of the pupil's own choosing, following a taught course of critical thinking and project skills, and then assessed at GCSE level.

In the Sixth Form, pupils take the Forest Diploma. A Levels provide the core academic element and Sixth Formers can choose from 27 different A Level subjects, with most choosing three main subjects, examined at the end of the two-year course, and taught in small teaching groups of typically around ten to fifteen pupils. All Diploma pupils begin a course in Project Skills in Year 12 and will produce an Extended Project Qualification (EPQ), which may take the form of a dissertation-style essay, or 'creative artefact', such as a film, composition or even a computer program.

The School places considerable emphasis on teaching the effective use of Information and Communications Technology. Every pupil in the Senior School is required to have with them a keyboard-enabled device in school, and all pupils are trained in the use of mobile devices as an appropriate tool for some learning tasks. All teachers incorporate digital materials and applications within their teaching, when the learning task requires it. Computer Science, with an emphasis on programming, is available from Y9 as an academic subject.

The curriculum is augmented by a wide range of popular academic super-curricular activities which supplement timetabled subjects. Lessons in Italian and Russian are offered, as well as opportunities to develop skills through Science and Maths competitions, societies and online courses.

Co-Curriculum. The School has a large Music Department with more than 50 visiting staff, teaching a wide range of instruments and voice. Regular concerts take place in School venues and outside including House Music and national competitions. Drama offers three major productions per year alongside House Drama competitions, and regular showings for curricular Drama. Art presents exhibitions and cross-curricular projects with English and other departments. Our PE department boasts a heritage of sporting excellence for both girls and boys in a wide range of both mainstream and less conventional sports with pupils regularly selected at district, county and national level. Other activities include Forest's Combined Cadet Force, which is linked to the Royal Green Jackets, and The Duke of Edinburgh's Award scheme which offers Bronze, Silver and Gold levels with high completion rates at all stages. Pupils can choose anything from horse riding to chess, technology to debating, drama and a wide range of musical activities, to some of the best sporting offerings. Pupils participate in a diverse programme of activities that encourage the learning of physical, cultural and leadership skills throughout their time at Forest. The co-curricular programme at Forest builds and develops five core principles – Creativity, Challenge, Culture, Community and Careers.

Games. The main games for boys are association football, hockey, cricket, athletics, and swimming. The main games for girls are hockey, netball, cricket, football, athletics, tennis and rounders. The sporting facilities are extensive and include an all-weather AstroTurf facility, tennis and netball courts, indoor and outdoor cricket nets, gym, sports hall, two swimming pools, strength and conditioning suite, 5-a-side 3G and acres of sporting fields. Additional sports such as fencing, rowing, golf, squash, mountain biking, table tennis, badminton and water polo are also available to boys and girls.

Fees per term (2021–2022). Reception to Year 2: £4,916, Year 3: £5,231 Year 4 to 6: £5,629, Year 7 to 13: £6,980. Fee reductions are available for children of the Clergy.

Careers. Many of the pupils go on to take up places at Oxford, Cambridge and Russell Group universities, however, Forest is successful at placing pupils in professional apprenticeships with companies including PricewaterhouseCoopers and Morgan Stanley.

Admission – Preparatory School. The only entry point to the Prep School is 4+. In principle, pupils are assessed on the basis of:

4+ entry

• A series of low-key activities which include: picture recognition, some letter recognition, following a pattern, knowing colours, counting, drawing, naming simple shapes, sequencing, listening to a story, playing and responding sensibly to the adults who are present

Admissions – Senior School. In principle, pupils are assessed based on:

11+ entry and 13+ entry

- Performance in English and Mathematics examinations
- An interview with a senior member of staff
- A written confidential report from the present school

16+ entry

- The entrance examination consists of a compulsory critical thinking paper
- An interview with a senior member of staff
- Entry into the Forest Sixth Form requires at least three grade 7s or above; and at least three grade 6s or above; and at least grade 4 in English and Maths; and the required grade at I/GCSE in the qualifying subject/s required for their chosen courses.

Full GCSE grade requirements can be found on the School website: www.forest.org.uk. A written confidential report from the present school will also be requested.

Scholarships and Bursaries are available at 11+, 13+ and 16+ entry. The maximum non-means-tested fee remission awarded in respect of any one pupil is 20% of full fees, whether in one area of excellence or in a combination of one or more areas of excellence.

Bursaries are means-tested and are awarded in addition to Scholarships, up to and including the total remission of fees; in other words, a free place. Bursaries are only given in conjunction with a Scholarship.

In addition, seven 11+ Assisted Places may be awarded annually to pupils who pass the entrance exam and have the greatest financial need.

11+ entry:

Up to the equivalent of 6 places may be given annually to pupils at 11+ following Scholarship assessment in January of the year of entry. This figure includes both Scholarships and Bursaries.

- Academic Scholarships
- Music Scholarships
- Sport Scholarships

13+ entry:

Up to the equivalent of 2 places may be given annually to internal and external applicants at 13+ following Scholarship assessment.

13+ entry will be phased out in 2024.

- Academic Scholarships
- Music Scholarships
- Sport Scholarships

16+ entry:

Scholarships are awarded for outstanding academic ability and exceptional attainment in Art, Drama, Music and Sport.

Up to the equivalent of six places may be given annually to both internal and new entrants to the Sixth Form.

For full details visit www.forest.org.uk.

Charitable status. Forest School, Essex is a Registered Charity, number 312677. The objective of the School is Education.

Governing Council:

Chairman of Governors: David Wilson, LLB Hons, FRSA, FRGS

Geraldine Atlee

The Venerable Elwin Cockett
Jane Davies
William Fuller
Dr Saniya Hadi, BSc Hons, MBBS, MRCOG
Glynis Jenkinson, AGSM, Dip Ed
William Kennedy
Penny Oates
Simon Perry

Leadership Team:

Warden: Mr M Cliff Hodges, BA University College Cardiff, MA University College London

Bursar and Clerk to the Governors: Mrs D E Coombs, BSc Cape Town, Hons B&A, MBA Stellenbosch

Deputy Warden: Mr G du Toit, MA King's College London

Head of Preparatory School: Mr J E R Sanderson, BMus Perf Hons Elder Conservatorium, BMus Adelaide, FRSA, FCCT

Deputy Head Academic: Mr M E Key, BA Birmingham, MA Warwick, MSt Harris Manchester College, Oxford

Deputy Head Pastoral: Mrs N Milton, BA Roehampton, NPQH

Director of Pupil Welfare and Designated Safeguarding Lead: Mr J H Kayne, BSc Nottingham Trent, NPQH

Deputy Head Co-Curricular: Miss G Van Praagh, BA American Academy of Dramatic Arts

Head of Sixth Form: Ms K Spencer Ellis, MA Christ Church Oxford

Head of Middle School: Miss H Dyke, BA Nottingham

Head of Lower School: Mrs L E Lechmere-Smith, BA Sheffield

Heads of Subject Departments:

Art: Mr J W Stevenson
Biology: Ms A Plumb
Chemistry: Miss C Averre
Classics: Mrs A G Gould
Computer Science: Mr A Lindsey
Design and Technology: Mr L D Barker
Drama: Mrs S Moon
Economics and Business: Mr M A Egan
English: Mrs C L Nightingale
Food & Nutrition: Miss L J Harris
French: Dr A Gray
Geography: Mr E W Morris
German: Mrs H P R Miller
Politics: Mr L Flynn
History: Mr J Pendred
Learning Support: Mrs M Wright
Mandarin: Mrs L Chen
Mathematics: Mr M J Taylor
Music: Mr I A McGregor
Physical Education: Mr B D Adams
Physics: Mr P T S Aspery
Projects: Mrs E Bellieu
Religious Studies & Philosophy: Miss R Mackie
Science: Miss J White
Spanish: Mrs K C Adams
Wellbeing: Mrs L Parrales

Houses:

Boys' Houses:
Bishop's: Mr O E Ling
Copeland's: Mrs H P R Miller
Doctor's: Mr E J G Stockwell
Guy's: Mr L Bouzguenda
Johnians: Mr J Miller
Miller's: Ms E L Arthur
Poole's: Mr B J D P Lumley

Girls' Houses:
Astell: Miss C A Heath
Baylis: Mrs J E Hayes
Eliot: Ms H Edwards
Franklin: Mrs H Cole
Hepworth: Mr H Clough
Kingsley: Ms L Baber
School: Mr J T Sloan

Support Staff:

Admissions:
Registrar: Ms D Cleveland-Hurley
Assistant Registrar: Miss R Begum
Admissions Administrator: Mr C Cheung

External Relations Strategic Co-Ordinator: Mrs S Gautama
(*Alumni, Marketing and Outreach*)

Bursar's Office:
Chief Accountant: Mr N Asghar, BA East London
Assistant Accountant: Ms T Jones
Accounts Clerk: Mrs E Kearney
Assistant Accounts Clerk: Ms S Morl

Careers:
Careers Manager: Mrs S Coates, LLB Exeter

Clerk to the Governors: Ms A Crawley

Francis Holland School, Regent's Park

Ivor Place, London NW1 6XR

Tel: +44 (0)20 7723 0176
email: admin@fhs-nw1.org.uk
website: www.fhs-nw1.org.uk
Twitter: @FHSRegentsPark
Facebook: @FHSRegentsPark
Instagram: @fhsregentspark
LinkedIn: /company/francis-holland-school-regent's-park

Founded 1878.

There are 534 day girls and entry by examination and interview is normally at 11+, with a number joining at 16+ for the Sixth Form. The school was founded in 1878 and is affiliated to the Church of England, but girls of all Christian denominations and other faiths are accepted.

Curriculum. Girls are prepared for GCSE, A Levels, and for admission to Universities, and Colleges of Art and Music. Sport takes place in Regent's Park and full use is made of the museums, theatres and galleries in central London. Extra lessons are available including fencing, music, Speech and Drama, kickboxing, Mandarin Chinese,

cookery, street dance, yoga and cheerleading. For the first five years, to GCSE, girls follow a broad curriculum and normally take between 9 and 11 GCSE subjects. Careers advice is given from the third year, and all pupils receive individual guidance through to the Sixth Form. Sixth Formers can study four subjects over the two years or they can opt to take three main subjects and an additional course, an elective. Some of these additional courses lead to a qualification and all of them are designed both to extend and to enrich learning.

Scholarships and Bursaries. Francis Holland is committed to providing a service to the local and wider community.

Bursary awards are typically offered at Year 7 and on entry to the Sixth Form and are reviewed annually. Our decisions about the award of bursaries take account of a number of factors, including:

• The ability of the girl and her fit with the school
• The overall financial circumstances of the fee payers, both income and assets
• The family circumstances of the applicant
• The financial position of the Trust

Remission of a third of the fees is available to places offered to daughters of the clergy.

Fees per term (2021–2022). £7,150

Situation. The school is situated just outside Regent's Park and is three minutes from Baker Street and Marylebone stations. Victoria and Hampstead buses pass the school.

Charitable status. The Francis Holland (Church of England) Schools Trust Limited is a Registered Charity, number 312745. It exists to provide high quality education for girls.

Patron: The Right Revd and Right Hon The Lord Bishop of London

Council of Governors:

Chairman: Patrick Sherrington LLB, LLM, FCI, Arb

Dr F Baawuah, MB, ChB, MRCGP, MRCP
Mr R Backhouse, MA
Dr C Barker, MA, BM, BCh, MRCPCH, PhD
Mr G Bennett, MA, ACA
Mr M Cuthbert, FRICS, BSc, MBA, DipProjMan
Mr A Fincham, MA
Prof C Gwenlan, MSci, PhD
Mrs S Nedas
Ms E Regina, MSc Arch, ARB, RIBA
Mr I Ramsay, BSc, FCA
Ms N de Renzo, MSc, Bocconi
Dr Mary Short, BA, PGCE, PhD
Dr H Spoudeas, MBBS, DRCOG, FRCPCH, FRCP, MD
Revd A Walker
Ms J Woodham-Smith, MA

Bursar: Mr G Wilmot, BA, ACA
Clerk to the Governors: Mrs R Abel

Senior Leadership Team:

Headmaster: **Mr C B Fillingham**, MA King's College London, MSc Jesus College Oxford

Senior Deputy Head: Ms A Slocombe, MA Magdalene College Cambridge
Academic Deputy Head: Miss J Zugg, BSc Cape Town, South Africa

Pastoral Deputy Head: Miss C Mahieu, BEd Sydney, Australia

Assistant Head (Operations): Ms S Hack, BA Portsmouth, FRGS

Assistant Head (Teaching & Learning): Ms K Lewis, BA Murray Edwards Cambridge, MA University College London

Assistant Head (Sixth Form): Mr N Gridelli, BA Bologna, Italy

Director of External Relations: Mrs V McKinley, BA Business School Greenwich

Director of Information Services: Mr D Nanton, FInstLM, MBCS, AAPM, MCSE

Francis Holland School, Sloane Square

39 Graham Terrace, London SW1W 8JF

Tel: 020 7730 2971
email: office@fhs-sw1.org.uk
website: www.fhs-sw1.org.uk
Twitter: @FHSSloaneSquare
Facebook: @FHSSloaneSquare
Instagram: @fhssloanesquare
LinkedIn: /company/francis-holland-school-sloane-square

Founded 1881.

Numbers and age of entry. There are 715 Day Girls in the School and entry is at 4+ for the Junior School (ages 4–11), 11+ for the Senior School (ages 11–18) (member of The London 11+ Consortium) and 16+ for Sixth Form.

Curriculum and Aims. Excellent academic standards are achieved through the provision of a challenging academic curriculum and talented staff who encourage an enthusiasm for learning, intellectual curiosity and creativity. This allows our girls to thrive in a relaxed and happy environment where they are respected as individuals and able to fulfil their unique potential.

Junior School. There is a Junior Department attached to the school.

Religious Education. The school's foundation is Anglican but girls of other faiths are welcomed.

Physical Education. Netball, Hockey, Football and Cricket are our main sports. Girls also have the opportunity to partake in Gymnastics, Athletics, Tennis and Swimming. New activities such as fencing, table tennis, dance and ultimate frisbee has been added to the curriculum. Senior girls have a choice of additional activities including spinning, Judo, pilates, strength and conditioning and use of the fitness suite.

Fees per term (2021–2022). £6,700–£7,380

Scholarships and Bursaries. There are the following competitive awards each year:

11+ Academic, Music, Drama, Art, Sport and Ballet scholarships are available to the value of 5% of fees.

Sixth Form: Academic scholarships (internal and external) up to the value of 25% of fees, Music scholarships up to the value of 25% of fees, Drama scholarships up to the value of 25% of fees.

We will consider awarding a bursary to girls who demonstrate the ability to succeed at Francis Holland, but whose parents might not have sufficient financial resources. The level of assistance provided will depend on individual circumstances, which will be reviewed annually. The number of bursaries awarded each year is at the discretion of the Governors and may vary.

Remission of a third of the fees is available for places offered to daughters of the clergy.

Charitable status. The Francis Holland (Church of England) Schools Trust Limited is a Registered Charity, number 312745. It exists to provide high quality education for girls.

Patron: The Right Revd and Right Hon The Lord Bishop of London

Council of Governors:

Chairman: Patrick Sherrington, LLB, LLM, FCI, ARB
Deputy Chairman: Mr A Fincham, MA
Dr F Baawuah, MB, ChB, MRCGP, MRCP
Mr R Backhouse, MA
Dr C Barker, MA, BM, BCh, MRCPCH, PhD
Mr G Bennett, MA, ACA
Mr M Cuthbert, FRICS, BSc, MBA, DipProjMan
Prof C Gwenlan, MSci, PhD
Mrs S Nedas
Ms E Regina, MSc Arch, ARB, RIBA
Mr I Ramsay, BSc, FCA
Ms N de Renzo, MSc, Bocconi
Dr Mary Short, BA, PGCE, PhD
Dr H Spoudeas, MBBS, DRCOG, FRCPCH, FRCP, MD
Revd A Walker
Ms J Woodham-Smith, MA

Bursar: Mr G Wilmot, BA, ACA
Clerk to the Governors: Mrs R Abel

Senior Leadership Team:

Headmistress: **Mrs L Elphinstone**, MA Cantab, FRSA (*English*)

Senior Deputy Head: Mr P Jeanes, BMus London, FRSA (*Music*)

Deputy Head Academic: Mr R Cawley, MA, BA Lancaster (*Theology & Philosophy*)

Joint Head of Sixth Form: Mrs R Sawyer, MA Cantab (*History*)

Joint Head of Sixth Form: Mrs J Banks, MA London, BA Durham (*English/Debating*)

Director of Creative Enterprise: Mr N Dyson, BA Southampton (*Geography*)

Head of Junior School: Mrs S Dixon, MA King's, BA Leeds

Director of External Relations: Mrs V McKinley, BA London

Director of Information Systems: Mr D Nanton, FInstLM

Development Director: Mr T Robertson, MA Edinburgh

Frensham Heights

Rowledge, Farnham, Surrey GU10 4EA

Tel: 01252 792561
email: hello@frensham.org
website: www.frensham.org
Twitter: @FrenshamHeights
Facebook: @frensham

Frensham Heights is a highly distinctive day and boarding school in the beautiful Surrey Hills.

Founded in 1925, we welcome students from the age of 3 to 18. Located close to the beautiful Georgian market town of Farnham and 15 miles from the historic city of Guildford, we are about an hour from London, Heathrow and Gatwick airports.

Ours is a culture that says come and be you; the beauty of Frensham lies in diversity.

Musicians learn with scientists, authors with future engineers. They discover creative and academic subjects and each finds his or her own passions, strengths and self-belief. We achieve exceptional academic standards, providing a robust academic environment alongside a much richer experience. Our students are confident in themselves; those who value themselves are more likely to be successful.

We're looking to the future. We encourage young people to be open-minded; not afraid to ask the difficult questions.

Our young people leave Frensham with the skill set to succeed in the workplace of tomorrow. We encourage our students to think, understand and ask questions and our teachers to be open-minded and creative in their teaching. Our students pursue a huge range of careers from dance to dentistry with the self-belief that helps them succeed; they learn the skills to build a life, not just a living.

With real adventure, the unexpected will happen and it is then that students discover their true strengths and exceed their personal limits.

Outdoor Education includes Forest Classes for the youngest children to Duke of Edinburgh's Award, mountaineering and overseas ventures for older students. Year 9 students spend two weeks in the furthest reaches of Scotland; no phones, no social pressures, just children remembering how to be children. Whatever the adventure, our students enjoy the freedom to explore, investigate, experience and take small but significant risks that help them grow into curious and self-aware adults.

We welcome boarders from Year 7 upwards.

We offer flexi boarding to our Year 7 & 8 students and full/weekly boarding for those in years 9–13. Alongside our many and varied extracurricular activities, boarders are offered additional activities and trips. Students bond with dedicated staff and parents feel confident that we know and look after their children. Our co-educational boarding houses are relaxed, warm, lively and supportive with boys and girls accommodated in separate areas, but sharing comfortable common rooms where they can study and socialise.

Student numbers. 540 boys and girls aged 3 to 18 years. Average class size: 18.

Admissions. Children entering Nursery to Year 6 are informally assessed by the Head of the Junior School and teachers. Children entering the school at the age of 11+ and 13+ sit the Frensham Heights entrance tests in January. Entrance to the Sixth Form is by examination and interview with a minimum of six GCSE passes at Level 9–4 (minimum Level 6 in A Level subjects).

Curriculum. Most students take nine or ten GCSE subjects of which the compulsory elements are English Language and Literature, Mathematics, a modern foreign language and triple or double award Science. Students also choose from Geography, History, Business Studies, a second modern language, Art, 3D Design, Dance, Design Technology, Photography, Drama, Music, or PE. There is a choice of 24 subjects at A Level. The AQA Extended Project Qualification is offered for suitable candidates. PSME is taught throughout the school.

Extracurricular Activities. An extensive and varied selection of activities includes sports of all sorts, outdoor education, art, music, dance, drama, hobbies and clubs.

Religion. Frensham Heights is non-denominational and there are no religious services.

Dress. No uniform. Dress code is based on respect for others and suitability for purpose.

Welfare and Discipline. Discipline is founded on good staff-student relationships reflecting school values: respect, tolerance, self-discipline, cooperation and creativity. Every student has a personal tutor. There is a school nurse and a counsellor.

Learning Support. We can support children with mild learning difficulties.

Overseas Students. We admit boarders from overseas and provide tuition in English as a Second Language as part of their curriculum. All boarders must have a UK based guardian.

Fees per term (2021–2022). Nursery fees: EYFE session (free from 0830–1130) plus £20 (morning session, including lunch), £37 (afternoon session, including lunch), £40 (full day); Reception £2,455; Years 1–2 £3,000; Year 3 £3,590; Year 4 £3,675; Years 5–6 £4,545; Years 7–8: £6,520 (day), £9,470 (boarding); Years 9–11: £6,840 (day), £10,650 (boarding); New Sixth Form Entrants: £7,265 (day), £11,065 (boarding).

Scholarships and Bursaries. Honorary scholarships are awarded for academic distinction or exceptional promise in Music, Art, Dance, Drama and Sport and scholars access dedicated enrichment activities. A small number of means-tested bursaries are available.

Charitable status. Frensham Heights Educational Trust is a Registered Charity, number 312052. It exists to provide a high quality, progressive education for boys and girls.

Governors:
Chair: Bill Bird, BA, MA, MBA, MBCS, FRAeS, MBE
Vice Chair: Gerry Holden, MA, PGCE, CAPSE, FRSA
Treasurer: Angus Carlill, MA Oxon
Clerk to the Governors: Susie Birdsall, BA Hons
Martin Lupton, MRCOG, MBBS, MA, Cert MEd, Dip MEd, MEd
Kate Love, MA Oxon
Katy Poulsom
Jackie Sullivan, MRICS
Phil Ward, BEd
Richard Fry, MA, MEng Cambs

Peter Molyneux
Will Marriott
Sally Marriott

Head: Rick Clarke, BA Hons, PGCE

Chief Operations Officer: Ann Marie Dalton-Pillay, FCIS, MSc
Deputy Head: Becks Scullion, BSc, PGCE
Deputy Head (Academic): Laura Griffiths, BA, MA
Head of Junior School: Katherine Bluck, MA, PGCE, QTS

George Heriot's School

Lauriston Place, Edinburgh EH3 9EQ

Tel: 0131 229 7263
email: enquiries@george-heriots.com
website: www.george-heriots.com

Motto: *I distribute chearfullie*

Heriot's Hospital was founded in 1628 to care for the fatherless children of Edinburgh. Today it is a fully co-educational day school.

The School is attractively situated in its own grounds close to the city centre and within easy walking distance of bus and rail terminals. A number of bus routes also service the School. Edinburgh Castle forms a magnificent backdrop, and Edinburgh's flourishing financial centre, the University of Edinburgh, the College of Art, the National Library and the Royal Scottish Museum are located close by.

The original building, described as a 'bijou of Scottish Renaissance Architecture', has been carefully preserved and, as a historic monument, is open at certain times to the public during school holidays. The Chapel, Council Room and Quadrangle are particularly notable.

Over the years a succession of new buildings has provided the full complement of educational facilities. A state-of-the-art sports centre was opened in 2012 and new Refectory and Wraparound Care facility in 2018. The School has excellent sports fields and facilities at Goldenacre.

Our aim is to introduce all our pupils to the broadest possible spectrum of academic, cultural and sporting interests and experiences, which will enable them to develop into articulate, self-reliant, hard-working and kind adults who play their full part in an ever-changing society. The School had a highly successful QUIPE inspection by HMISS in September 2016.

Heriot's has long enjoyed a reputation for academic excellence, with outstanding examination results and we value scholarship and effort. In the same spirit, every pupil is encouraged to participate in an extensive array of co-curricular activities. We encourage participation and success in an unusually wide range of sports including basketball, football, cross-country running, hockey, rowing, rugby, athletics and tennis, but we also strongly encourage more minority sports.

We have an outstanding record in music, both choral and instrumental, and in drama. Both Junior and Senior schools boast a huge range of clubs, with particular strength in our Debating Society, our Pipe Band, our Drama productions, the Duke of Edinburgh's Award and our Combined Cadet Force. The School proudly holds Gold level in UNICEF's Rights-Respecting Schools Award. There is a heavy emphasis throughout the School on charitable fundraising and community service including our award-winning S6 Voluntary Service programme.

The Nursery (32 children). The Nursery accommodates children in their pre-school year. It is part of the Early Years Department. Admission to the Nursery is open to all.

The Junior School (594 pupils). The Junior School follows a bespoke curriculum with a focus on academic rigour and solid subject content, particularly with regard to literacy, numeracy and science. Art, drama, modern languages, music, computing and all areas of physical education are taught by specialists. Philosophy is a key strength in the Junior School.

The Senior School (1,044 pupils). For the first two years, a broad curriculum is followed. An unrivalled choice of subjects is available from S3 to S6 in preparation for Scottish Qualifications Authority examinations at every level. Most pupils stay on for our carefully designed Sixth Year and proceed to university or other forms of tertiary education.

Heriot's enjoys a reputation as a caring community. The greatest importance is given to pastoral care and a sophisticated careers advisory programme is in place. The Support for Learning Department provides invaluable help to many Junior School and Senior School pupils.

Admission: Admission (other than for Nursery) is by assessment or examination. Application for occasional places is welcome at any time, but for the main stages should normally be submitted by the 1st of December.

Fees per annum (2021–2022). Junior School: £9,315 (Nursery, P1 & P2), £11,309 (P3 to P7); Senior School: £13,970

A limited number of Bursaries is available from Primary Six and there are Scholarships for entry at S1. Fatherless and motherless children may qualify for free education and other benefits through the Foundation. Full information is available from the Finance Office on request.

Charitable status. George Heriot's Trust is a Registered Charity, number SC011463. It exists to provide education for children.

Governors of George Heriot's Trust:
Chairman: Mrs J Cullen
Vice-Chairman: Prof M Strachan
Finance & Resources Convener: Mr A Simm
Education Convener: Dr P Sangster
Mr H Bruce-Gardyne
Mrs K Cherry
Mr I Herok
Mr V Lal
Mr A McGeough
Mr C Stott
Mr J Thomson
Mr A Urquhart

***Principal*: Mr G Warren**

School Management Team:
Mr A Murray (*Bursar*)
Miss S Donnelly (*HR Manager*)
Mrs M Henderson (*Director of External Relations*)
Mr P Fairclough (*Head of Senior School*)
Mr A Morrison (*Head of Junior School*)
Mr A MacLachlan (*Estates Manager*)

Mrs K O'Hagan (*Deputy Head of Junior School*)
Mr A Semmler (*Director of IT*)

Deputes, Senior School:
Mrs A Henderson
Mrs J Arnott
Mr M Mallinson
Dr A Neilson
Mr R Simpson

Deputes, Junior School:
Mr C McCloghry
Mrs K Stevens
Mrs L Reid

Giggleswick School

Giggleswick, Settle, North Yorkshire BD24 0DE

Tel: 01729 893000 Headmaster's Office
         01729 893012 Bursar's Office
email: admissions@giggleswick.org.uk
website: www.giggleswick.org.uk
Twitter: @giggschool
Facebook: @GiggleswickSchool
Instagram: @giggschool
LinkedIn: /company/giggleswick-school

Giggleswick School is based on the edge of the Yorkshire Dales National Park, offering affordable independent education and academic excellence for girls and boys aged 2 to 18. The school was awarded 'excellent' in an impressive six aspects of provision by the Independent Schools Inspectorate (ISI).

Located on the edge of the beautiful Yorkshire Dales National Park, the school sits within a 200-acre campus of stunning countryside, where you'll find 500 years of heritage, exceptional modern facilities and a happy, welcoming community.

334 boys and girls attend Giggleswick, either as full-time or flexi boarders or day pupils. It is a traditional British boarding school with 65% of pupils boarding (increasing to 80% in Sixth Form), 17% of whom are from military families and 17% from the international community. The approach to education combines excellent academic achievement, ambition and strong self-belief, with a strong focus on personal development. The school's core values are participation, ambition and respect.

In 2021, 83% achieved A*–B grades at A level. BTEC options continue to deliver excellent results for our students and this year 93% of our pupils achieved the D*D or D*D* (A*/A or A*/A* equivalent) grade. At GCSE, 51% achieved 7–9 grades. Our dramatists were among the top performers with 80% achieving the higher grades 7–9. Classified as the hardest subjects by the CEM Centre, Physics and German have been an area of strength with 50% achieving grades 7–9 in Physics and 71% in German.

However, life is about more than great grades at Giggleswick. The extended day and boarding ethos gives all pupils the chance to participate in any of over 70 co-curricular activities that encourage pupils to explore new horizons, challenge themselves and often achieve beyond their expectations. 50% of pupils take part in music lessons

at Grade 6 or above with 120 pupils in drama productions. Average class sizes are 13.5 in Key Stage 3 and 4 and 6.5 in Sixth Form.

All boarders live in one of seven boarding houses with a dedicated co-ed house for young boarders in Years 6 to 8. The first phase of a multimillion pound investment in boarding facilities was completed in September 2018, which is shaping a new family-friendly model of boarding to create a modern home away from home with a real focus on community and wellbeing.

There are excellent sports coaches at all levels, superb facilities and regular programmed training sessions. Each year a number of pupils gain representative honours in a range of sports and a place on the Elite Sports Programme. This includes specialist coaching, mentoring, professional sports visits and strength and conditioning training.

Facilities include a floodlit AstroTurf, a state-of-the-art fitness centre, two indoor sports halls and an indoor swimming pool. The Outdoor Pursuits Department is staffed by a Mountaineering and Climbing instructor and eleven Mountain, Hill and Moorland Leaders and climbing Instructors. Staff also hold Paddlesports, Mountain Biking and Caving qualifications. The school has its own indoor climbing wall, crag, 10km mountain bike trail and a shooting range on campus. There are a number of local, nationally recognised, crags and caves and the hills of the Yorkshire Dales.

Giggleswick's Art Department provides a lively and stimulating environment where pupils can explore and develop their creative skills. The department includes a resident ceramic artist, who works and teaches in the Department. There is a well-equipped ceramics studio, a vacuum silkscreen printing bed, plus facilities to make photo silkscreens, and a large etching press.

Drama takes place in the state-of-the-art Richard Whiteley Theatre, a 250-seat professional venue. There are opportunities to develop skills in stage management, sound and lighting as well as acting in productions such as *Much Ado About Nothing*.

In the music department there is a Head of Instrumental Music as well as a Head of Department and four full-time musicians. They are assisted by a team of 13 visiting teachers, and ensembles include the School Orchestra, Concert Band, Chapel Choir, Concert Choir, a Brass Ensemble and a String Quartet as well as a number of rock bands. Numerous performance opportunities are offered including trips abroad.

Giggleswick is not a selective school. The school has an equal opportunities policy and is happy to consider applications from any child so long as other entrance criteria are met. Various scholarships and bursaries are also available.

The school is an hour's drive from Leeds, Manchester and The Lakes. It can be reached from the M6 or M1 motorways or by rail via Settle or Giggleswick stations. Overseas students fly to Leeds/Bradford or Manchester Airports.

Fees per term (2021–2022). Reception–Year 2: Day £2,950; Years 3 & 4 Day £4,650; Years 5 & 6 Boarders £7,700, Day £4,650; Years 7 & 8: Boarders £8,800, Day £5,700; Years 9–11: Boarders £11,500, Day £7,100; L6–U6: Boarders £11,900, Day £7,700. 5-night and 3-night flexi boarding also available.

Charitable status. Giggleswick School is a Registered Charity, number 1109826.

The Governing Body:

Chair: A V Thursby, BBA

Vice-Chair: R R Waldie, BA

Bursar & Clerk to the Governors: M Z Hodge, BA, CPFA

Headmaster: **S Hart**, BEng

Deputy Head: C A San José, MA

Senior Master: N A Gemmell, BA

Deputy Head (Academic): Miss A L Wood, MA

PA to the Headmaster: Mrs C A Jowett

The Glasgow Academy

Colebrooke Street, Glasgow G12 8HE

Tel:	0141 342 5494
email:	admissions@tga.org.uk
website:	www.theglasgowacademy.org.uk
Twitter:	@glasgowacademy
Facebook:	@glasgowacademy
Instagram:	@glasgowacademy
LinkedIn:	/school/the-glasgow-academy

Motto: *Serva Fidem*

Founded in May 1845, The Glasgow Academy is the oldest continuously independent school in the west of Scotland. It has been co-educational since 1991, when it merged with Westbourne School for Girls. Mergers with Atholl Preparatory School in Milngavie (1999) and Dairsie House School in Newlands (2005) have given parents a choice of three locations for their children in the Nursery to Prep 4 age group, contributing to the school's enduring success as a school covering the whole of west central Scotland. Children from The Glasgow Academy Milngavie and Newlands transition to our west end campus at Kelvinbridge in Prep 5. The school's affairs are managed by The Glasgow Academicals' War Memorial Trust, formed to commemorate the 327 former pupils killed in the war of 1914–18.

Organisation. The Preparatory School roll is 808 pupils (416 boys, 392 girls) between the ages of 3 and 11 and educates pupils from the earliest stages for the work of the Senior School. The Senior School roll is 777 pupils (400 boys, 377 girls). They are prepared for the National Qualifications at National 5 level at the end of S4, Higher at the end of S5 and Advanced Higher or Higher at the end of S6. The Sixth Form provides courses in most subjects leading to presentation at Advanced Higher. Pupils are prepared for entrance to Oxford and Cambridge. The Academy has a history of successes at Oxford, Cambridge and the Scottish Universities. It aims to offer a unique combination of academic, musical, dramatic, sporting, co-curricular, social and outdoor education opportunities, backed up by high levels of pastoral care. There are numerous opportunities for children to develop leadership skills and take on responsibilities.

Buildings. The magnificent main building (1878) contains the Senior School library as its centrepiece and classrooms. Recent purpose-built facilities include a Music School (1994), Art and Design School (1998), Preparatory School (2008) and multiple award-winning science centre, auditorium and hospitality/social area (2015). Two drama studios, a dance studio, rowing studio, medical centre and fitness area were also created in 2015. There are extensive sports facilities, including new astros, rugby/cricket pitches and a water-based hockey pitch.

Health and Wellbeing. The school places great importance on supporting pupils' health and wellbeing. Pupils are at the heart of this with an influential School Council meeting each week, with a HWB sub-committee working in partnership with staff to lead improvement in safeguarding, a regularly reviewed and evolving PSE curriculum, and provision of assemblies and guest speakers on a range of topics relevant to young people's lives. S6 pupils lead a school buddy system, including the delivery of digital awareness and online safety workshops to younger pupils and parents. The school website features information for parents on how to support their child's wellbeing.

Music and Drama. Music tuition is offered in a wide range of instruments by 21 tutors. There are Senior, Junior and Theatre Choirs, a Concert Band, Pipe Band, Brass Group, Percussion Ensemble, Orchestra and various Prep School groups. Concerts and large-scale drama productions take place regularly and are supplemented by plays mounted by smaller groups. There are music tours to places such as New York, Rome and Barcelona.

Societies and Activities. These range from Basketball, Chess, Debating and Public Speaking to Engineering, Fairtrade and Research clubs. Very large numbers of pupils undertake each section of the Duke of Edinburgh's Award and there is a thriving Young Enterprise group. Residential education is an integral part of the curriculum at various stages of both the Prep and Senior schools. These experiences augment the PSE programme by promoting team building and personal and social development through outdoor challenges.

Games. Teams represent the school in Hockey, Rugby, Cricket, Swimming, Golf, Tennis, Athletics, Rowing, Football, Shooting and Squash. Options include Badminton, Cross-Country running, Dance and Outdoor education.

Combined Cadet Force. The Academy has a strong voluntary contingent with Royal Navy, Army and RAF sections.

Childcare outside school hours. The Academy provides care before and after school for its younger pupils. There is also provision for children between the ages of 3 and 12 through the holidays.

Entrance. Pupils may be registered at any age. The main entry points are (a) in the Preparatory School: age 3, 4 and 10; (b) in the Senior School: age 11 or 12 or for Sixth Form. Bursaries are available for P7–S6.

Fees per term (2021–2022). Preparatory School: P1 £2,971–£3,233, P2 £3,059–£3,329, P3–P4 £3,382–£3,632, P5 £3,632, P6–P7 £4,255. Senior School: S1–S2 £4,062, S3–S5 £4,408, S6 £4,408, (Autumn & Spring Terms), £3,596 (Summer Term).

Charitable status. The Glasgow Academy is a Registered Charity, number SC015638. It exists to provide education for girls and boys.

Chairman of Governors: Duncan Mackison

Deputy Chair of Governors: Mrs J Gotts, MA Hons

Nominated and Elected Governors:
Peter Brown, MA, CA
Chris Cockburn, B Arch Hons, RIBA, RIAS
Paul Frame, LLB Hons, Chartered FSCI
Gavin Halliday, FCBI
Margaret Khnichich, BAcc, CA, CTA
John Mason, BAcc, CA
Kristeen Percival, MB ChB, MRCGP
Anita Salwan, LLB Hons, Dip LP, Ce MAP
Andrew Sime, BA
Richard I C Smith, LLB, DipLP, NP
Matthew Walters, MBE, MBChB, MSc, FRCP, MD

Secretary: T W Gemmill, LLB, NP

Rector: M K Pearce, BA Dunelm

Deputy Rector and Head of Senior School: M Gibson, BSc
Edinburgh, PhD Edinburgh

Deputy Heads:
K R Graham, BSc Newcastle-upon-Tyne, MEd Aberdeen
A N MacRae, BSc Strathclyde
G Spreng, MA Glasgow

Heads of Department:
English: A F Watters, MA St Andrews
Mathematics: K.M Russell, BSc, Heriot-Watt, PG
Advanced Dip Mathematics, Hull
Modern Languages: Mrs E B Holland, MA Glasgow
Biology: J Laycock, BSc Edinburgh
Chemistry: C A Main, MSci Glasgow, PhD Glasgow
Physics: H McMillan, BSc Strathclyde
Art/Craft & Design: J M McNaught, BA Glasgow
Classics: S A A McKellar, MA Glasgow
Computing Science: Mrs J E McDonald, MA Glasgow
Drama: G E Waltham, MA Glasgow
Economics & Business Studies: A Taylor, BA Glasgow
Food Technology: C Dolan, BSc Manchester Metropolitan
University
Geography: V Magowan, MA Glasgow
History & Modern Studies: S M Wood, MA St Andrews
Music: T E Mills, BMus Bangor

Physical Education/Sport:
Director of Sport: R Toft, BEd Heriot-Watt
Head of PE: M A Manson, BA Strathclyde
Head of Rugby: J Gordon, BSc Edinburgh Napier
Head of Hockey: A Meikle, BA, Strathclyde

Outdoor Education: R Goolden, Mountain Instructor
Certificate, Outdoor Education Diploma & National
Governing Body Awards, Newbury College

Learning Support: A A Harvie, BA Strathclyde, PG Dip
Ind Admin Glasgow Caledonian

Careers: A J McCaskey, MA Glasgow

Counsellor: A F Young, MA Glasgow, MRes Strathclyde,
PG Dip Psychodynamic Counselling Garnethill Centre
University of the West of Scotland, BACP

Preparatory School:
Head: A Mathewson, BEd Strathclyde
Deputy Head: S Fairlie-Clarke, BSc Glasgow, PG Dip
Napier
Deputy Head: L Smith, MA Glasgow

The Glasgow Academy Milngavie:
Head: J McMorran, DCE, PG Dip, DipTEFL

The Glasgow Academy Newlands:
Head: H J Logie, BEd Oxon

After-school Care:
After-school Care Manager: C Bremridge, BA Childhood
Practice Glasgow

Administration/Finance:
Bursar: J Galloway, BA Strathclyde, MCIPD

Admissions/Development:
Director of External Relations: S A Dignall, BA
Strathclyde

Rector's PA: L Fletcher

Administration Manager: A Clarke, BA Strathclyde

Combined Cadet Force:
Contingent Commander: Captain L Smith
SSI: Major C J Duff

Chaplains:
Revd D J M Carmichael, MA, BD
Revd A Frater, BA, BD
Revd R S M Fulton, BA Sheffield, BD Glasgow
Revd G Kirkwood, BSc, BD, PGCE
Revd S Matthews BD, MA

The High School of Glasgow

637 Crow Road, Glasgow G13 1PL

Tel: 0141 954 9628
email: admin@hsog.co.uk
website: www.highschoolofglasgow.co.uk
Twitter: @HSofG

Motto: *Sursum semper*

The High School of Glasgow is a vibrant, caring and high-achieving co-educational day school, which has been part of Glasgow's story since the 12th century and is the oldest continuous school in Scotland. Its present incarnation came into being in 1976 following a merger involving the Former Pupil Club of the High School, then a selective state grammar school, and Drewsteignton School in Bearsden.

Buildings. The Senior School occupies modern purpose-built buildings at Anniesland on the western outskirts of the city immediately adjacent to twenty-three acres of playing fields. The Junior School is in the extended and modernised former Drewsteignton School buildings in Bearsden about three miles away. New facilities opened during the last few years include a purpose-built Science extension, a water-based artificial pitch and 3G multi-sports area, a Junior School extension, a Drama Studio, a Refectory, a Fitness Centre, a Grandstand and an Information and Communications Technology building, and in 2017 a Health and Wellbeing Centre.

Organisation. The School is a day school with 966 boys and girls. The Junior School, which includes a pre-school Kindergarten, has 280 pupils (aged 3–10). Primary 7 pupils are included in the Senior School which has 686 pupils (aged 11–18). A general curriculum is followed until the Third Year of the Senior School when, with the Scottish Qualifications Authority examinations in view, a measure of choice is introduced. In Fifth Year Higher examinations are taken and in Sixth Year courses for Advanced Highers are offered. Whilst the majority of pupils are aiming for the Scottish universities, places are regularly gained at Oxford, Cambridge and other English universities.

Throughout the School, time is allocated to Art, Music, Personal, Social and Health Education, Physical Education and Religion and Philosophy. All pupils will also take courses in Computing Studies, Drama and Health and Food Technology at various stages in their school careers.

Games. The main sports are hockey, rugby, athletics, cricket, tennis and swimming. Pupils participate in a wide variety of other sports, including badminton, basketball, netball, football, volleyball, golf, cross-country running and skiing.

Activities. Pupils are encouraged to participate in extra-curricular activities. Clubs and societies include debating, Scripture Union groups, computer, table tennis, chess, art, bridge, chemistry, electronics, drama and film clubs. Pupils take part in the Duke of Edinburgh's Award Scheme and the Young Enterprise Scheme, and parties regularly go on tour. There are choirs, orchestras, jazz and concert bands and a pipe band and tuition in Instrumental Music is arranged as requested. Each year there are several concerts and dramatic productions. The Chamber Choir was BBC Songs of Praise Senior School Choir of the Year 2013.

Admission. Entrance tests and interviews are held in January. The principal points of entry are at Kindergarten (age 3–4), Junior 1 (age 5), Transitus (age 11) and First Year (age 12) but pupils are taken in at other stages as vacancies occur.

Fees per term (2021–2022). Junior School: £3,485–£4,070; Senior School: £4,122–£4,237.

Bursaries. The School operates a Bursary Fund to give assistance with fees in the Senior School in cases of need.

Former Pupils' Club. The Glasgow High School Club Limited is the former pupils' association of the old and new High Schools. Former pupils all over the world maintain an interest in the life and work of the School. *Secretary*: Murdoch C Beaton, LLB

Charitable status. The High School of Glasgow Limited is a Registered Charity, number SC014768. It is a recognised educational charity.

Governing Body:
Honorary President: Lord Macfarlane of Bearsden, KT
Chair: S J MacAulay
Vice Chair: Mrs P Galloway, FCA
P B Gray
Dr M N Gupta, BSc Hons, MBChB, MD FRCP
A Horn, MA Hons, LLB
E W Hugh, CA
Dr M McColl
C M Mackie, BSc Hons
S C Miller, WS, LLB Hons, Dip L
Dr N Crick, BA Hons, MA, DPhil
J K Panesar, B.Sc
Mr S Pengelley, BA
K M Revie, LLB Hons
Dr C M Stephen, MBChB, DGM
Mrs M A Stewart, LLB Hons, Dip LP, DFM
N Watson
J G Williamson

Adviser to the Board: Professor Sir V A Muscatelli, MA Hons, PhD, FRSE, FRSA

Rector: **J O'Neill**, MA Hons

Head of Senior School: K J A Robertson, BSc Hons

Deputy Heads:
Ms S Gibson, BEd Hons
P Graham, BSc Hons
I S Leighton, BSc Hons

Staff:
* *Head of Department*
† *House Staff*

English:
*P A Toner, MA Hons
†P D C Ford, MA Hons
Mrs R A Baynham, MA Hons
Mrs S de Groot, MA Hons
Mrs N Lawther, MA Hons, MPhil
T Lyons, MA Hons
Mrs J Muir, MA Hons
Mrs M Noonan, BA Hons (*Drama*)
Mrs A Viswanathan, MA Hons (*Drama*)

Mathematics:
*Mrs C V M Anderson, BSc Hons
†J G MacCorquodale, BSc Hons
†Miss N Park, BSc Hons
Mrs J B Armstrong, BSc Hons
Mrs E Clark, BSc Hons
D K Hamilton, BSc Hons, PhD
T A Lockyer, LLB
D R MacGregor, BSc Hons
Mrs H S Mills, MEng

Computer Studies:
*Mrs S E Sterkenburg, BSc Hons, PgC MLE
D D Muir, BSc Hons
I R Purdie, BSc Hons

Science:
N M E Dougall, BSc Hons, MSc, (*Biology*)
Mrs K S M O'Neil, BSc Hons (*Chemistry*)
Dr D R Went, MSc, PhD (*Physics*)
†Mrs M R Peek, MSc
J Campion, BSc Hons
Miss G B Gardiner, BSc Hons, PCert LAM
Dr M McKie, BSc Hons, PhD
Mrs A E McNeil, BSc Hons, MSc
Dr N J Penman, BSc Hons, PhD
K J A Robertson, BSc Hons
I J Smith, BSc Hons

Modern Languages:
*N F Campbell, MA Hons, LLB

Mrs K J Bhatia, BA Hons
†Mrs J M Horne, MA Hons
Miss M B Cranie, BA Hons
Mrs K Evans, MA Hons (*Careers)
Mrs K McCartney, MA Hons
Mrs A M T Drapeau-Magee, L-ès-L, M-ès-L
Mrs V MacCorquodale, MA Hons

Classics:
*J Bullen, BA Hons
Mrs C Bell, MA Hons
Mrs J Deeks-Nisbet, BA Hons

Economics and Business Studies:
*T J Jensen, MEd, BComm
P Graham, BSc Hons
C Hutcheson, BA Hons

Geography and Modern Studies:
*Miss N L Cowan, MA Hons
I S Leighton, BSc Hons
Mrs C McKeown, BA Hons
Miss K Macpherson, MA Hons
Dr H Ross, MA Hons
C Totten, BSc Hons

History:
*C MacKay, BA Hons
†Miss N Sutherland, MA Hons
Mrs G A C Lindsay, MA Hons
Dr H Ross, MA Hons

Art:
*Mrs C J Bell, BA Hons
Miss N J Henderson, BDes
Mrs J Stewart, BA Hons

Health and Food Technology:
*Miss K D Moore, BA Hons
†Mrs C Elsby, BA Hons

Learning Support:
*Mrs J Dougall, MA Hons
†Miss N Park, BSc Hons
Mrs R Owen, BEd Hons

Music:
*Mrs S C Stuart, MA Hons/
  Mus Oxon, MSt Oxon,
  PG Adv Dip RCM
L D Birch, BA Hons,
  LRAM, DRSAMD
B Docherty, DRSAM
R McKeown, DRSAMD
Mrs C N Mitchell, MMus,
  BMus
Mrs J Tierney, BMus
F Walker, BA Hons,
  ARCO

Religion & Philosophy:
*Mrs G A C Lindsay, MA
  Hons

*Sport and Physical
  Education:*
*P J Smith, BEd Hons

Junior School Staff:
Head Teacher: Miss H Fuller, BEd Hons
Mrs G Morrans, BEd Hons (*Deputy Head*)
Mrs M Pollock, BA Hons, PG Dip Mus, MMus (*Deputy
  Head*)
Miss N Barrett, BEd Hons
Ms L Boothroyd, BA Hons
Miss C E Carnall, BMus, MA Hons (*Music*)
Mrs L Cowan, BEd Hons
Ms N Crawford, MA, LLB, PGCE
B Docherty, DRSAM
Mrs A Dougherty, BA Hons
Miss A Downie, MA Hons
Mrs A M T Drapeau-Magee, L-ès-L, M-ès-L (*French*)
Mrs M Duncan, SVQ3 Social Services
Mrs H M Eustace, BEd Hons
Mrs S A Foster, MA Hons
J Gask, MBiol, PGCE
Mrs S Gibson, SVQ3 Childcare Learning & Development
Miss K Hallam, BEd Hons
Mrs L A Lambie, BEd Hons
Ms D Lamont, MA Hons (*Principal Teacher*)
Mrs K McCartney, MA Hons
Mrs E J McConechy, BEd Hons
R McKeown, DRSAMD
Mrs J MacLaren, BEd Hons, MA Hons Cert (*Principal
  Teacher*)
Mrs C Mitchell, BLE Hons
Mrs M I Moreland, DCE, AEE
Ms D Mutch, SVQ3 Social Services
C Nicol, MEd, PGDE
Miss I Rashid, BA Hons
Mrs G Reid, MA Hons (*Principal Teacher*)
Mrs P Rooney, MA Hons, Dip SfL (*Principal Teacher*)
Miss R Saunders, BEd Hons
Mrs J Steel, BSc Hons
Miss A Taylor, MA Hons
Mrs S Ure, BEd Hons, CEPE
Mrs R Young, BA Hons, SVQ4 Social Services

Bursar: Mrs J M Simpson, BAcc, CA

Rector's PA: Miss P McConnell

Mrs A Cox, BEd Hons
  (*Girls' PE*)
†S Leggat, BEd Hons
K F FitzGerald, BSc Hons
Ms S Gibson, BEd Hons
F J Gillies, BSc Hons
G Hunter BSc Hons
J McCarthy, BEd Hons
Miss S McGilverary
Miss R Ward, BSc Hons
Mrs R Owen, BEd Hons
Mrs H Cannon, BEd Hons
Mrs S Dougan, BEd Hons
Ms J Hood, BEd Hons
Mrs D McCluskey, BSc
  Hons
Mrs S Mitchell, BEd Hons

Glenalmond College

Glenalmond, Perth, Perthshire PH1 3RY

Tel: 01738 842000
        Admissions Office: 01738 842144
email: registrar@glenalmondcollege.co.uk
website: www.glenalmondcollege.co.uk
Twitter: @GlenalmondColl
Facebook: @GlenalmondCollege
LinkedIn: /GlenalmondCollege

Motto: *Floreat Glenalmond*

Religion. The College has an Episcopalian foundation and has a splendid Chapel. However pupils from a wide range of ethnic, religious and cultural backgrounds are welcomed.

Admission. Glenalmond offers both day and boarding. There is Second Form entry for pupils in Primary 7, based on tests in English, Maths and Verbal reasoning. Pupils from Prep Schools sit Common Entrance Exams. Glenalmond College is becoming increasingly popular as a Sixth Form option and admission is welcome at any year.

Curriculum. In the Second and Third Form (Years 8 and 9, S1 and S2) all pupils take a wide range of subjects including English, Mathematics, History, Geography, French, Spanish or German, Latin or Ancient Civilisation, Biology, Chemistry, Physics, Technology, Music, PSHCE, Drama, Art and ICT. In the Fourth and Fifth Forms pupils may choose three options from a wide range of subjects (including Latin and Greek), along with the core subjects of Mathematics, English Language and Literature, French and the three Sciences. Each pupil is guided by an academic tutor who meets regularly with their tutor group.

The Sixth Form curriculum is designed to allow pupils as wide a choice as possible with 22 A Level subjects being offered and 10 Higher subjects. There are weekly lectures from outside speakers on social, economic and cultural subjects which foster academic excellence across the age ranges and the William Bright Society promotes cross year group discussion on relevant academic and moral issues.

Careers. Over 98% of pupils continue to university and around half of pupils go to Russell Group universities, with a good number gaining places at Oxbridge each year.

Art, Drama and Music. Music plays a central part in the life of the school: there is an Orchestra as well as smaller String, Woodwind and Brass Groups, the pipe band and choirs. The Drama and Art departments flourish, in conjunction with the well-established Design and Technology Centre.

Sport and Recreation. There is a wide variety of sporting activities to choose from including Rugby, Hockey, Lacrosse, Cross-Country, Cricket, Athletics, Basketball, Shooting, Sailing, Tennis and Golf. There is a large indoor heated Swimming Pool and Squash Courts, Tennis Courts, a nine-hole (James Braid designed) Golf Course and a world-class, water-based astroturf pitch for Hockey. The school has recently built a new indoor golf hub, complete with simulation screens. The ski slopes of Glenshee are just over an hour away.

Combined Cadet Force. There is a contingent of the Combined Cadet Force with strong links with the Armed Forces.

Fees per term (2021–2022). Boarding fees range from £8,200 to £12,700 with full details available at: www.glenalmondcollege.co.uk/admissions/fees. Our school fees are as inclusive as possible and cover all of the teaching, accommodation and living costs.

Scholarships. Pupils with exceptional potential, who intend to join Glenalmond in our Third Form, can apply for Scholarships in their area of excellence. As well as the kudos of being a Glenalmond Scholar, successful applicants also benefit from a fee remission of up to 10%. The Scholarships come in two forms: named Academic Scholarships; and College Scholarships in Art, Drama, Music, Piping or Sport. Sixth Form Scholarships are also available.

Remissions. A sibling discount policy recognises the burden of fees for more than one child at a time and is applied with a 5% remission for a second child, 20% remission for a third child, and 50% remission for a fourth (or more) child. Financial assistance is provided for serving members of the Armed Forces and members of the Clergy, both attracting an automatic 10% remission on fees.

Council:

**President of Council*: The Primus of the Episcopal Church in Scotland, The Most Reverend Mark Strange, Bishop of Moray, Ross and Caithness

**Chairman of Council*: N S K Booker, MA Hons [OG]

* *Committee of Council*
[OG] *Old Glenalmond*

Warden: **Dr M P Alderson**, BA, MA, PhD

Sub-Warden, Academic (*Joint*):
G O'Neill, BSc Belfast, PGCE
Mrs J Davey, MA Edinburgh, PGCE

Sub-Warden, Pastoral: Mrs S Sinclair, BSc Edinburgh, PGCE

Bursar & Clerk to the Council: D Lish, BSc Newcastle, MSc Cranfield, CMgr MCMI
Director of Admissions: Eileen Cathrae
Chaplain: Reverend S A Graham SSC, BA MA Belfast, PGDip, PGCE

Godolphin and Latymer School

Iffley Road, Hammersmith, London W6 0PG

Tel: 020 8741 1936; 020 8735 9595 (Bursar)
email: office@godolphinandlatymer.com
website: www.godolphinandlatymer.com
Twitter: @GandLSchool
Facebook: @GandLSchool

Motto: *Francha Leale Toge*

Foundation. Godolphin and Latymer, originally a boys' school, became a girls' day school in 1905. It was aided by the London County Council from 1920 onwards and by the Inner London Education Authority when it received Voluntary Aided status after the 1944 Education Act. Rather than become part of a split-site Comprehensive school it reverted to Independent status in 1977.

Godolphin and Latymer is an independent day school for approx. 800 girls, aged 11 to 18. The school stands in a six-acre site in Hammersmith, near Hammersmith Broadway and excellent public transport. Historic buildings – including a converted church – sit side-by-side with modern facilities interconnected by tranquil gardens and courtyards. Facilities include a pottery room, computing classes, science and technology laboratories, art studios, a dark room and an ecology garden. The girls benefit from a recently renewed all-weather surface for hockey and tennis, as well as netball courts and a Sixth Form Centre. The Rudland Music School opened in the Autumn Term 2008 and the renovated church, The Bishop Centre for the performing arts, was completed in early Spring 2009. These state-of-the-art developments provide a range of teaching and performance spaces, recording studios and a music technology suite. The Bishop Centre provides an auditorium to seat over 800. In September 2015 a new Sports Complex, the Hampton Centre, was opened.

Godolphin and Latymer aims to provide a stimulating, enjoyable environment and to foster intellectual curiosity and independence. We strive for a love of learning and academic excellence, emphasising the development of the individual, within a happy, supportive community.

While girls are expected to show a strong commitment to their studies they are encouraged to participate in a range of extracurricular activities. We aim to develop the girls' self-respect, self-confidence and resilience, together with consideration and care for others so that they feel a sense of responsibility and are able to take on leadership roles within the school and the wider community.

Pastoral Care. The school has a close relationship with parents, and every member of the staff takes an interest in the girls' academic and social welfare. Each girl has a co-form teacher and a deputy form teacher and there is a Head of Lower School, Head of Middle School and a Head of Sixth Form, each with at least two deputies.

Curriculum. We offer a broad, balanced curriculum including appropriate education concerning personal, health, ethical economics and social issues. During the first three years, girls study the following subjects: Philosophy and Religion; English; French, Spanish or German; Mandarin; Latin; History; Geography; Mathematics; Physics; Chemistry; Biology; Food Preparation and Nutrition; Design Technology; Art; Music; Drama; and Physical Education are studied. In Year 9, students may study Gratin or Classical Civilisation. In Year 10 Greek become available. Computing is studied in Years 7 and 8, and Computer Science is now available at GCSE and A Level. Girls take ten subjects to GCSE.

In the Sixth Form, there is a choice of curriculum between the A Level and the International Baccalaureate Diploma. All subjects (except PE, Food Preparation and Nutrition and Design Technology) offered to GCSE can be continued into the Sixth Form with the addition of Ancient History, Economics, Politics and History of Art. Sixth Formers also undertake the Extended Project Qualification (AL) or Extended Essay and Theory of Knowledge (IB) and attend lectures given by outside speakers.

The Sixth Form. The Sixth Form facilities include a Common Room, Work Room and Terrace. The 210 girls in the Sixth Form play a leading role in the school, taking responsibility for many extracurricular activities, producing form plays and organising clubs. They undertake voluntary work and lead our Social Impact Committee.

Higher Education and Careers Advice. A strong careers team offers advice to girls and parents. Our specialist room is well stocked with up-to-date literature and course information, and lectures and work shadowing are arranged. Almost all girls proceed to Higher Education degree courses (including an average of 18 a year to Oxford and Cambridge and around 15 to US universities and colleges).

The Creative Arts. Music and Drama flourish throughout the school. The Rudland Music School has outstanding facilities for music: 20 soundproofed rooms for individual or group work, a recording studio, ICT suite and two classrooms which open out into a very large rehearsal space for choirs and orchestras. There are four choirs, two orchestras and several small ensembles, and a joint orchestra. Individual music lessons are offered in many different instruments. Each year there is a pantomime, Year 10 and Sixth Form plays as well as the school productions. The refurbished church, known as The Bishop Centre, offers a superb performing arts space for music, drama and dance.

Physical Education is a vital part of a girl's development as an individual and as a team member. Younger girls play netball, hockey, tennis and rounders and have gymnastic and dance lessons. In the senior years there is a wider range of activities offered, including rowing and squash off site. A state-of-the-art Sport and Fitness Centre opened in September 2015 providing a Sports Hall, climbing wall, dance studio and fitness suite. Tennis/netball courts and an astroturf hockey pitch are also on site.

Extracurricular Activities. The many opportunities for extracurricular activities include Dissection Club, Wild Aspirations, Computing, Chess, Model United Nations, Debating, Creative Writing, Classics Club and the Duke of Edinburgh's Award scheme, as well as a wide range of sporting activities such as karate, fencing, rowing and trampolining.

Activities outside the School. In normal times we organise language exchanges to Germany and France and a musical exchange to Hamburg and Sixth Form work experience in Versailles and Berlin. Each year, Year 9 girls ski in the USA and there are study visits to Spain, Italy and France and History of Art visits to Paris, Bruges, Venice and Florence.

We take advantage of our London location by arranging visits to conferences, theatres, exhibitions and galleries. Field courses are an integral part of study in Biology and Geography.

Admission. Girls are normally admitted into Year 7 (First Year Entrance) or into our Sixth Form. Examinations and held in November. There are occasional vacancies in other years. Entry is on a competitive basis.

Fees per term (from January 2022). £7,918. Fees are liable to change each January. Private tuition in music and speech and drama is extra. Most girls have school lunch.

Scholarships. Music scholarships are available on entry to Year 7 and in the Sixth Form and include free tuition in one instrument.

An Art scholarship is available in the Sixth Form.

All scholarships are worth up to 30% of fees and may be topped up by means-tested bursaries in cases of need. For all awards, candidates must satisfy the academic requirements of the school.

Bursaries. A number of school bursaries are available annually.

Uniform. Uniform is worn by girls up to and including Year 11.

Charitable status. The Godolphin and Latymer School is a Registered Charity, number 312699. It exists to provide education to girls aged 11 to 18.

Governors:
Chair: Mrs A J S Paines, MA Cantab
Mr S Davies, BA Oxon
Ms S Davies, BA Wimbledon College of Art, MA London
Mr M Esiri, LLB London, MBA Greenwich
Mr G Fendley, BSc Birmingham
Mr T Howe QC, MA Oxon, GDL City
Mrs S Kinross, BA Exeter
Mr K Knibbs, MA Oxon
Dr L Magrill, BSc Edinburgh, MCom Birmingham, PhD Bradford
Mr N McLaughlan, BA Durham
Ms T Meller, BA Glasgow School of Art, Dip Arch Oxford Brookes, RIBA
Mrs D Rose, MA Cantab
Mrs K Slesinger, MA Cantab
Mr O Waring, BA Oxon, LLB London
Mrs E Watson, BA Exeter

Clerk to the Governors: Mrs D Lynch, BSc Kingston, FCCA

Staff:

Head Mistress: Dr F Ramsey, MA DPhil Oxon

Senior Deputy Head (Pastoral), Deputy Designated Safeguarding Lead: Mrs A Paul, BA Durham
Deputy Head (Academic): Dr S Harnett, MA DPhil Oxon

Senior Teachers:
Learning and Teaching and New Technologies: Dr C Badger, MSci PhD Cantab, FCCT, MA UCL
School Organisation and Co-Curricular: Mr J Carroll, BSc Durham
Director of Sixth Form: Dr J Carter, BA Oxon, MA Chicago, MSt DPhil Oxon
Staff Professional Development, Designated Safeguarding Lead: Ms A Triccas, BA MA London, FCCT

Heads of Departments:
Art and Design: Miss L Cooper, BA Staffordshire, MA Wimbledon School of Art
Classics: Mrs L Duffett, BA Oxon, MA London
Computing: Mrs G Oliver, MA Cantab
Design and Technology: Ms M Martins, BA Leeds
Drama: Ms S Adams, BEd Melbourne
Economics: Mr A Shah, BA City of London Polytechnic, MEd Sheffield
English: Mr C Griffin, BA Exeter
Geography: Mr M Golland, BA London, MEd Cantab, FCCT
History and Politics: Mrs A Armstrong, BA York
Dr B Snook, BA MPhil, PhD Cantab
History of Art: Dr G Williams, BA Leeds, MA UCL, PhD York
Individual Learning Needs: Ms A Clark, BA Oxon, BSc Open
International Baccalaureate Coordinator: Ms A Dubois, BA MA Le Littoral
Mathematics: Mr J Ramsden, BSc Durham
Modern Foreign Languages: Mrs C Corcoran, MA Orléans, MA Southampton

French: Mrs C Corcoran, MA Orléans, MA Southampton
German: Mrs U Fenton, MA Freiburg
Italian: Miss L Padalino, BA Bologna
Mandarin: Mrs S Whittaker, BA Durham
Spanish: Miss H Matthews, BA Cantab
Music: Miss L McAdam, MA Cantab
Philosophy and Religion: Mr L Higgins, BA Nottingham, MEd Cantab
Physical Education: Miss E Elfick, BEd Exeter
Science: Ms G Andrade, BSc London, MA East London
Biology: Miss T Dean, BSc Edinburgh, FCCT
Chemistry: Mrs A Swann, MChem Oxon
Physics: Mr J McGrath, BSc Wales, MSc Cranfield

Bursar: Mrs D Lynch, BSc Kingston, FCCA
Registrar: Mrs F Lundberg, CIPD
Higher Education and Careers: Mrs A Armstrong, BA York
PA to the Head Mistress: Miss V Stearns

School Nurses:
Mrs T Vardigans, RN, SpCPHN-SN Brunel (*Senior School Nurse*)
Ms E Jewitt, BSc KCL, BMus Trinity Laban

Godolphin School

Milford Hill, Salisbury SP1 2RA

Tel: 01722 430500
email: admissions@godolphin.org
website: www.godolphin.org
Twitter: @GodolphinSchool
Facebook: @godolphinschool
Instagram: @godolphinschool
LinkedIn: /company/godolphinschool

Motto: *Franc Ha Leal Eto Ge* (Frank and Loyal art though)

Inspiring Girls from 11–18 years, Godolphin is an independent boarding and day school offering flexi, weekly and full boarding. Founded by Elizabeth Godolphin in 1726, the school continues to honour its traditional values, whilst educating girls for the 21st Century. The school has 290 girls in the senior school, 100 in the Sixth Form. Godolphin Prep educates girls from 3–11 years. The school stands in 16 acres of landscaped grounds on the edge of the historic cathedral city of Salisbury, overlooking open countryside.

Curriculum. A strong academic life combines with thriving art, drama, music and sport. A five-studio art centre provides excellent art and design facilities, while the Blackledge Theatre provides a professional environment for drama and music performance. Sciences are taught within the well-equipped laboratories.

High academic standards are combined with a wide range of clubs, societies and weekend activities; also an outstanding programme of trips and expeditions. Activities include: Duke of Edinburgh's Award, Combined Cadet Force, community service, debating, creative writing, academic societies and wide ranging opportunities in art, drama, music and sport. 24 subjects are available at A Level, and virtually all students continue to higher education, most to universities, including Oxbridge; around 95% of students gain a place at their first-choice university and around 50%

at a Russell Group University. There is considerable emphasis on Careers guidance known as 'Bright Futures', including an excellent work shadowing scheme.

Religious Instruction. Godolphin has strong affiliation with the Church of England, but religious instruction covers all major world faith.

Physical Education. Strong sporting record with pupils regularly selected for county and regional teams; also at national level. 22 sporting options include lacrosse, hockey, netball, tennis, athletics, swimming, gymnastics, dance, rounders and cross-country. Each girl is encouraged to get involved with PE at some level.

Entrance Examination. Godolphin's own assessment and interview at 11+ and Common Entrance Examination at 13+. Examination and interview at all other levels, including Sixth Form.

Scholarships and Bursaries. 11+ and 13+ for outstanding merit or promise in academic work, music, sport or art. Candidates for music awards should have attained at least Grade 4 at 11+ (Grade 6 at 13+) on one instrument. They are also expected to reach an acceptable academic standard.

Sixth Form Academic, Art, Drama, Music and Sports scholarships are also available.

Foundation Bursaries are available and the Old Godolphin Bursary is awarded by the Old Godolphin Association to the daughter of an Old Godolphin.

Fees per term (2021–2022). Senior School: Boarding £12,650–£13,055 (International), £9,640–£11,310 (Full); £6,700–£7,445 (Day)

Extra Subjects. Individual tuition in music, speech and drama, tennis, fencing, judo, EFL and learning support.

Old Godolphin Association. *Secretary*: Mrs Nikki Hutchins email: oga@godolphin.org.

Charitable status. The Godolphin School is a Registered Charity, number 309488. Its object is to provide and conduct in or near Salisbury a boarding and day school for girls.

Governing Body:
Lt General Sir N Pope (*Chairman*)

Mr J Booker	Dr C Mannion-Watson
Sir T Boughton	Mrs S Nolan
Mrs A Burchmore	Dr Lady Joanne Pope
Mr R Franks	Dr E Shaw
Mr G W Green	Mr P Smith
Mrs M Guillebaud	Mrs R Tear
Mrs R Hawley	Mr C Thompson

***Headmistress*: Mrs E Hattersley**, BA Dunelm, Postgrad RAM

Senior Deputy Head: Mr R Dain, MA Oxon, PGCE London
Deputy Head Academic: Dr C Hillman, MPhys, PhD Southampton
Deputy Head Pastoral: Mrs J Price, BA Dunelm, PGCE Cambridge

Head of Admissions: Mrs C Florence

For a full Staff List please visit www.godolphin.org

Gordonstoun

Elgin, Moray IV30 5RF

Tel: +44 (0)1343 837837
email: admissions@gordonstoun.org.uk
             principalpa@gordonstoun.org.uk
website: www.gordonstoun.org.uk
Twitter: @gordonstoun
Facebook: @GordonstounSchool
LinkedIn: /company/gordonstoun-school

"Gordonstoun doesn't have to try to be different – it just is. It's the original holistic education, using outdoor challenges and service to others to build confidence and improve academic performance…if you want an escape from the academic sausage factory and the chance to think out of the box, sign up now." *Good Schools Guide 2020*

As well as preparing students for exams, Gordonstoun prepares them for life. The school motto is 'Plus est en vous' – There is more in you. At Gordonstoun, this sense of possibility is presented to its students, every single day.

'It wasn't until we saw the curriculum and the schedule of what they would be doing each day that we truly understood the difference between Gordonstoun and other schools.' *Current parent*.

Gordonstoun's location on a 200-acre woodland estate in the North of Scotland provides the background for its world-beating outdoor education programme which was the inspiration for the Duke of Edinburgh Awards, named after one of its most famous alumni. Expeditions to the Scottish Highlands or sail training on the School's 80ft boat are an integral part of school life.

Active engagement in service to the local community comprises a core part of Gordonstoun's 'working week', further expanding the students' sense of personal and social responsibility and building self-esteem. Students volunteer for one of nine services and it is the only school in the UK to have its own Fire Engine, staffed by senior students who respond to genuine emergencies.

Gordonstoun understands that the broader the experience, the broader the mind.

"The extensive range of opportunities for personal achievements in the senior school, as part of the Gordonstoun broader curriculum, is outstanding." *HM Inspectors, 2019*.

The School. Gordonstoun is a co-educational boarding and day school for children aged 4–18. There are approximately 113 pupils in the Junior school and a further 429 in the Senior School. Gordonstoun prides itself on the balanced make-up of the student body with approximately one third from overseas, one third from Scotland and one third from the rest of the UK. Gordonstoun is a founding member of The Round Square Organisation and in Year 10 approximately 20 students each year participate in a term's exchange with other Round Square schools in countries such as New Zealand, Australia, Canada, South Africa, Germany, Denmark and the USA. A corresponding number of students from the recipient schools arrive at Gordonstoun each Spring Term.

Boarding. Gordonstoun is one of the few remaining full-boarding schools in the UK and nearly 90% of students in the Senior School are full boarders. A full programme of activities is offered throughout weekends and day pupils join in with weekend activities.

Pastoral Care.

"The positive, caring, family ethos of Gordonstoun School promotes a sense of trust, respect and kindness for all." *HM Inspectors, 2019*

Our systems are built around our pastoral aims, which closely reflect the Gordonstoun ethos and our aim of developing the whole person. As well as house parents, tutors and every member of staff are trained to look after the children. There is a secure online system to keep track of every child and share necessary information.

"The pastoral set up is the best I've seen. Well planned, supportive and built around the child." *Good Schools Guide, 2020*

Curriculum. Gordonstoun follows the English National Curriculum of GCSE and A Level examinations. There are a wide range of subjects available at both levels.

In Year 12 most students choose three A Level subjects and an optional EPQ. BTEC's are also offered. Most non-English speaking students take their native language at A Level.

Gordonstoun has a wide support network for those students requiring Learning Support and there is the opportunity to receive one-to-one or small-group teaching.

"My son came from a school down south. He's a different boy without the pressure. In fact, his work is improving simply because he's happy." *Current parent*.

Academic Results. In 2021 37% of A level results were A*-A and 41% of GCSE results were the top grades of 7–9. We are a non-selective school which means we cannot be compared with schools who select only the most academic students. 87% of our final-year students secured their first choice of university.

Destination of Leavers. Students go on to Universities, Colleges and Art Schools all over the world, including Oxbridge.

The wide range of activities students undertake during their school years, including training with the Coastguard Service, Fire Service and as Lifeguards, help them to stand out at interview and ensure they have the right skills for rewarding careers.

Sport and Activities.

"Outdoor pursuits are huge and every single student gets involved. Sailing, skiing, hillwalking, climbing. The school owns a 80ft sail-training-vessel, *Ocean Spirit*, which makes annual trips to destinations such as the Arctic. Sailing is taught in the same kind of cutters as those used by Prince Philip when he was at Gordonstoun. Why? Because they have a crew of eight and teamwork is integral. All pupils are trained in expedition skills and try everything from backpacking and canoeing to exploration. And of course the school offers a full DofE programme – they did invent it after all, naming it after their most famous alumnus." *Good Schools Guide 2020*

In addition to sailing and expeditions, which form an integral part of the curriculum, the School has competitive teams in rugby, football, hockey, basketball, cricket, tennis, athletics and squash for the boys; hockey, netball, tennis, athletics and squash for the girls; and mixed teams in golf and tennis. These teams participate in national competitions and players are regularly chosen to represent district and regional teams. There are also opportunities to compete in swimming galas, cross-country running, skiing, sailing and adventure races. There is a wide range of recreational sports available including: riding, target shooting, badminton, golf, aerobics, yoga, mountain biking, cycling, climbing, kayaking, orienteering and table tennis.

Gordonstoun prides itself on the strength of its Performing Arts. Dance, Drama and Music are available to all students and there are regular collaborations between the three departments to produce major theatrical productions. A weekly Dance activity is available to all students and there is also an annual Dance Show, regular Shakespeare productions and an annual Theatre Festival. The School also routinely takes shows to the Edinburgh Fringe Festival. Music students are encouraged to become accustomed to performing in front of audiences large and small via a weekly series of relaxed lunchtime concerts as well as full-scale, formal musical events. Nearly half of the student body receives individual musical tuition in a wide range of instruments. The art department has a teacher from virtually every discipline: fine art to photography.

Wednesday afternoons are also dedicated to service projects. Service to others develops a sense of responsibility and requires each student giving up his or her time and effort to benefit others without expecting return or reward. It fosters links with the local community and includes training which leads to nationally recognised qualifications which prove useful beyond School life.

Admissions. Gordonstoun will be different from any other school you have looked at or visited. We run regular Virtual Taster Days as well as hosting personal visits to our campus.

We do not hold Open Days as we like to tailor-make your visit. We are happy to assist you with your travel plans and pick you up from Inverness or Aberdeen airports.

Please contact admissions@gordonstoun.org.uk

Fees per term (2021–2022). Senior School: Day £9,460 (Years 9–12), £10,360 (Year 12 direct entry); Boarding £13,350 (Years 9–12), £14,250 (Year 12 direct entry). Junior School: Day £5,595; Boarding £9,050. Weekly boarding (£9,050) is available in the Junior School only.

Scholarships and Bursaries Awards are generally for 10% of the annual fee. Additional awards may be available based on means-testing.

Charitable status. Gordonstoun Schools Limited is a Registered Charity, number SC037867.

Chair of Governors: David White

***Principal*: Lisa Kerr**

Head of Senior School: Richard Devey

Head of Junior School: Cath Lyall

Deputy Head (Pastoral Care): Philip Schonken

Deputy Head (Curriculum): Danielle Cowan

Key Stage 5 Leader: Mel James

Key Stage 4 Leader: Kim Barton

Key Stage 3 Leader: Chrystelle Main

Director of Admissions: Sabine Richards

Financial Director: Pamela Muir

Director of Gordonstoun International Summer School: Claire McGillivray

The Grange School

Bradburns Lane, Hartford, Northwich, Cheshire CW8 1LU

Tel: 01606 539039
email: office@grange.org.uk
website: www.grange.org.uk
Twitter: @Grange_Cheshire
Facebook: @GrangeCheshire
LinkedIn: /the-grange-school

Motto: E Glande Robur/Live Your Education

The Grange School is a co-educational independent school for 4–18 year olds. We are located in the heart of Cheshire, in the semi-rural village of Hartford, just south of Northwich.

At The Grange we ensure that our young people live their education by creating a learning environment where they are fully immersed in their school experience. Our hard-working, learner-focused teachers, outstanding facilities and broad enrichment opportunities ensure that every child receives an education that prepares them for life after school. They leave equipped with the tools to become ambitious, respectful and confident adults.

Junior School. The Grange Junior School provides an outstanding start to any child's educational journey. We understand the importance of these formative years in the development of each young person and want every child to develop a love for school and for learning.

Our first priority is to provide a caring atmosphere in which the children can thrive and learn. This requires staff that welcome and understand each and every child, giving them – and their parents – the attention that they deserve. This allows us to help them successfully navigate their way through the inevitable difficulties of growing up and life in general. Happy children will learn.

We offer a learning programme from Reception to Year 6 that is designed to be both broad and flexible, creating a full, balanced education. Children develop particular academic interests and passions; ensuring they attain at the highest level of which they are capable. With a focus on staff development, an average class size of 21, a teaching staff: child ratio of 1:12 and modern, well-equipped facilities, it is no surprise our children consistently attain beyond expectation.

We enable our children to flourish as individuals; encouraging children to pursue their own interests and strengths. As well as sports and creative arts we offer leadership opportunities, the chance to engage in charitable events and hear from guest speakers. We also arrange numerous day trips and offer residential stays both in the UK and overseas.

Senior School. A Grange Senior School Education is all about unleashing our students' creative minds and developing their passions and skills to aid them in their futures through a curriculum that inspires.

Before students select their GCSE options, we make sure they have the opportunity to try every subject, from Maths to Food & Nutrition. We understand the value of educating students through a wide and varied curriculum. It is this that lets young people discover an unknown talent they can pursue and thrive in.

Students participate in the many Enrichment opportunities we provide and they understand the importance of this as a part of their education. We also have a dedicated Student Welfare and Support Team who are here for students to help them through any challenges they face.

We believe in educating the whole child. When students leave us, they are fully prepared for the adult world as open-minded, confident individuals because they were given the chance to live their education at The Grange.

Sixth Form. The Grange Sixth Form is transformational. Through developing their leadership and academic skills, our students leave us as young, motivated individuals ready for adult life. We have an enviable academic record in helping our students achieve outstanding results and the majority go on to secure university places at the country's top institutions. With a dedicated Careers Department, advice is always available. Whilst students are offered unrivalled support for their academic studies, they also enjoy greater freedom and independence, to prepare them for life after The Grange. The modern Sixth Form Centre provides a stimulating atmosphere where students can study, meet and socialise; further developing a deeper experience and community spirit based on the principles of self-management as well as collective responsibility.

Beyond the academic arena, there is a broad range of enrichment and leadership experiences for students. These include the Duke of Edinburgh scheme, a Peer Support scheme, our Extended Project Qualification as well as drama, music and sporting opportunities. Tolerance and mutual respect of others, in line with our values, are promoted and students are encouraged to support the wider community through volunteering and charitable activities. Above all, the Sixth Form is a happy place where students can explore academic curiosity in a motivating environment.

Results

GCSE results 2019:

- 44% of all entries graded 8–9
- Over three times the national average of all entries achieving Grades 7–9
- Three out of 837 students in the country to achieve seven or more Grade 9s were from The Grange
- 75% of all Science entries at Grades 7–9
- 20% of Humanities' entries at Grade 9

A Level results 2019:

- 64% of all entries A*–A
- 87% of all entries A*–B
- 80% of students went on to their first choice university
- Over 60% of students went on to Russell Group universities

Fees per term (2021–2022). Junior School: £2,995 (Reception & Year 1), £3,250 (Years 2–6); Senior School & Sixth Form £4,010.

Scholarships. Several scholarships are offered for entry to the Senior School for exceptional academic ability and music. A number of Sixth Form Scholarships are awarded for outstanding academic potential after an examination held at the end of spring term preceding Sixth Form entry.

Bursaries worth up to full fees and assessed according to means are available to new entrants to the Senior School.

Charitable status. The Grange School is a Registered Charity, number 525918. It exists to provide high quality education for boys and girls.

Chair: Nigel Parkinson

Head: Dr L Earps

Senior School:
Deputy Head Pastoral: Mr R Oakes
Deputy Head Academic: Mr J Gribben
Assistant Head (Co-Curricular): Mrs H Eaton
Assistant Head (Sixth Form): Mr J Walker
Director of Finance and Operations: Mrs D Torjussen

PA to the Head: Mrs J Ward
Bursar: Mrs L Foxley
Estates Manager: Mr C Lupton
Marketing Manager: Ms Emma Corkish
Admissions Registrar: Miss L Hough

Junior School:
Head of Junior School: Mr G Rands
Deputy Head Pastoral Care: Miss A Evans
Deputy Head Academic Development: Mrs A Stubbs

PA to the Headmaster/Admissions Coordinator: Mrs N Pratt

Guildford High School – Senior School
United Learning

London Road, Guildford, Surrey GU1 1SJ

Tel: 01483 561440
email: guildford-admissions@guildfordhigh.co.uk
website: www.guildfordhigh.co.uk
Twitter: @guildfordhigh
Facebook: @GuildfordHigh
Instagram: @GuildfordHigh

Age Range. Girls 11–18.

Number of pupils. 700.

Fees per term (2021–2022). £6,100. Fees exclude lunches. Textbooks and stationery are provided.

Guildford High School consistently boasts some of the best academic results in the country and was awarded the *Sunday Times Independent School of the Decade* in 2020, but we are proud to be a local school serving the local community since 1888. Located next to London Road train station our pupils travel in from the surrounding towns and villages each morning and a successful train buddy scheme ensures our younger pupils do not travel alone.

Awarded the leading Independent school in the country for pastoral care by The Week Magazine 2018, we believe that young people learn best when they are happy and with that in mind we have carefully created an environment in which pupils feel safe to push their boundaries and challenge themselves. Our annual 'Well-being Week' is an established highlight of the school calendar and in previous years has featured yoga, circus skills, a silent disco and mindfulness. Our pastoral staff, led by our vibrant Deputy Head Pastoral, are second to none.

Creating an environment in which pupils feel safe and valued allows them to throw themselves into their learning. Joining the Senior School in Year 7, pupils will find themselves studying Current Affairs, Philosophy and Latin in addition to the more traditional subjects you would expect to find on the timetable. As they go through the school, subject options increase again and new subjects such as Greek are offered at GCSE and Psychology, Politics and Economics at A Level.

Homework is kept to a minimum at Guildford High School. In Years 7–9, our pupils spend no more than one hour per evening on homework and no homework needs to be handed in the next day. This allows time for extracurricular activities to be enjoyed and new skills developed. Similarly, no homework is set for holidays – this is time for family visits, relaxing and enjoying hobbies.

Pupils joining us in Year 7 or for Sixth Form come from a huge number of schools throughout the local area and there is no one type of 'GHS pupil'. We are a community of actors, musicians, artists, scientists, bookworms and sports women. In an environment that buzzes with creativity and rings with laughter, pupils are unlimited in their belief in each other and themselves. Our former pupils go on to achieve great things in all walks of life.

Facilities. Facilities include libraries, 11 well-equipped laboratories, whiteboards in every classroom, an Information Technology Centre, a Design Technology Centre, Art and Design Studios, a Food Technology Room, Music Rooms, Music Technology Studio, a Careers Room and Dining Hall. The school also opened a £5 million Sports Hall and indoor swimming pool in 2006, and a new Music Recital Hall in 2016.

Charitable status. Guildford High School Senior School is part of United Learning which comprises: UCST (a Company Limited by Guarantee, Registered in England, number 2780748, and a Registered Charity, number 1016538) and ULT (a Company Limited by Guarantee, Registered in England, number 4439859, and an Exempt Charity).

Governing Body: The Council of United Learning

Patron: The Most Revd and Rt Hon Justin Welby, Archbishop of Canterbury

Local Governing Body:
Ms Kate Richards (*Chair*)
Ms Zip Jila (*EYFS Representative*)
Rev Canon Robert Cotton
Mrs Anna Lise Gordon (*Child Protection Representative*)
Mr Robert Turnbull
Mr Nigel Wickham (*Health and Safety Representative*)
Ms Karen Braganza
Mrs Elizabeth Burrows
Dr Sian Jones (*Health and Safety Representative*)
Mr Richard Webb (*E-safety Representative*)

Headmistress: Mrs Fiona J Boulton, BSc Hons Cardiff, MA London

Deputy Heads:
Pastoral: Mrs Karen Laurie, BA Hons Leeds
Academic: Mr Duncan Peel, BA Hons Bristol, MA London
Co-curricular: Mr William Saunders, BA Hons Bristol, MA St Mary's Twickenham

Haberdashers' Boys' School

Butterfly Lane, Elstree, Hertfordshire WD6 3AF

Tel: 020 8266 1700
email: office@habsboys.org.uk
website: www.habsboys.org.uk
Twitter: @habsboys
Facebook: @habsboys
Instagram: @habsboysschool
LinkedIn: /school/habsboys

The School was founded in 1690, endowed by an estate left in trust to the Haberdashers' Company by Robert Aske, Citizen of London and Liveryman of the Haberdashers' Company. In 1898 it was transferred from Hoxton to Hampstead and in 1961 to Aldenham Park, Elstree, Hertfordshire.

The aim of the School is the fullest possible development of the varied talents of every boy within it, and to this end a broad curriculum is provided, together with extensive facilities for the development of each boy's cultural, physical, personal and intellectual gifts. The School sets out to achieve high academic standards and sets equally high standards in cultural and other fields. In matters of behaviour a large degree of self-discipline is expected, and of mutual tolerance between members of the School community.

Organisation. The School, which is a day school, has 73 boys in the Pre-Prep (ages 5–7) and over 200 boys in the Preparatory School (ages 7–11), 300 in the Junior School (ages 11–13), over 500 in the Senior School (ages 13–16) and over 300 in the Sixth Form (over 16). There are 6 Houses. The School regards pastoral care as important; all the Heads of House, Deputy Heads of House and Heads of Section have a large responsibility in this field but so also do House Tutors and the Chaplain, as well as other members of the staff.

Forms. In the Pre-Prep School there are two forms in Years 1 and 2 with approximately 19 boys in each form. In the Preparatory School there are three forms in Years 3, 4, 5 and 6 each with about 18 boys. In the Senior School there are six forms in Years 7 and 8 with approximately 25 boys in each form. There are twelve forms in Year 9 each with about 15 boys. Years 10 and 11 are divided amongst eighteen forms each with 14–16 boys. The usual size of teaching groups in the Sixth Form is about 10–15. We will launching our first ever reception class in September 2022.

Facilities. The School and its sister School, Haberdashers' Girls' School, enjoy the use of a campus of over 140 acres with extensive woodlands. The playing fields surround the buildings, which in the Boys' School include the following: Assembly Hall, Dining Hall, Sixth Form Common Room, Music Auditorium, special accommodation for Classics, English (including a Drama Room), History, Geography, Mathematics, Information Technology, Modern Languages including 2 Languages Laboratories, Music School, Science and Geography Centre with 19 laboratories and 8 classrooms, a Design Centre for Art, Craft and Technology, state-of-the-art Sports Centre, Gymnasium, Indoor Swimming Pool, Climbing Wall, Squash Courts, two Artificial Grass Pitches and much more.

The Prep School is situated on the same campus in a new building of its own. (*For further details, see Prep School entry in IAPS section.*) The Pre-Prep is situated on its own nearby campus.

The Curriculum up to the age of 13 is common for all, with no streaming or setting except in Mathematics in Year 8. From the age of 11 in addition to the usual subjects it includes three separate Sciences and two foreign languages which are taught as a carousel to ensure all boys have sampled all languages before making informed choices. From the age of 13, subjects are taught in sets of mixed abilities. GCSE courses start in Year 10, when boys take ten subjects. In the Sixth Form students study four subjects to AS in the Lower Sixth, narrowing to three A2 subjects in the Upper Sixth. The School takes seriously its commitment to Enrichment and Enhancement; this non-examined part of the curriculum occupies 10% of the week in both Upper and Lower Sixth. Boys are entered for the GCE examination at A Level at the age of 18 and are prepared for entry to degree courses at Universities. The wide scope of the School's curriculum gives ample opportunity for all its boys whether preparing for University (overwhelmingly their primary interest), for a profession, for the services, or for commerce or industry. The University Applications and Careers Departments have their own modern facilities, and careers advice is readily available to parents and to boys.

Religious Education. The School is by tradition a Church of England school, but there are no religious barriers to entry and no quotas. It is part of the ethos of the School that all its members respect the deeply-held beliefs and faith of other members. The School Chaplain is available to, and holds responsibility for, all boys in the School of whatever faith. He prepares for Confirmation those who wish it, and there are weekly celebrations of Holy Communion and an annual Carol Service in St Albans Abbey. The morning assembly and class teaching, however, are non-denominational in character. Faith assemblies are held on Thursday mornings, and comprise separate meetings for Christians, Jews, Muslims, Hindus, Jains, Sikhs, Buddhists and Humanists.

Physical Education. A wide variety of sports is available, including Athletics, Badminton, Basketball, Cricket, Cross-Country Running, Fencing, Golf, Gymnastics, Hockey, Rugby, Football, Sailing, Squash, Shooting, Swimming, Tennis, Table Tennis and Water Polo. All boys are expected to take part in physical education unless exempt on medical grounds.

Out of School Activities. The extensive range includes a period of two hours on Friday afternoon when boys can choose one of a large variety of activities of a service nature. This includes Community Service, both on the School campus and among those who need help in the surrounding district. It also includes the Combined Cadet Force, which has Royal Navy, Army and Royal Air Force sections, and Adventure Training.

Music and Drama. Both have a prominent place in the School. The Music School has a Recital Hall and some twelve other rooms; 20 visiting instrumental teachers between them teach 500 instrumental pupils each week covering all the normal orchestral instruments together with Piano and Organ. There is a Choir of 250, and several orchestras. For Drama the facilities include a generously equipped stage and a separate Drama Room with its own lighting and stage equipment.

School Societies. School Societies and expeditionary activities in term time and holidays include Amnesty, Archery, Art, Badminton, Bridge, Canoeing, Chess, Choral, Classical, Crosstalk, Debating, Duke of Edinburgh's Award, Dramatics, English, Football, History, Jazz, Jewish Society, Life-saving, Life Drawing, Modern Languages, Mountaineering, Philosophical, Photography, Politics, Puzzles and Games, Rifle, Sailing, Science, Squash, Stamp Club, Windsurfing and many more.

Transport. There is a joint schools coach service providing an extensive network of routes and some 110 pick-up points, to enable boys and girls to attend the School from a wide area, and to remain for after-school activities.

Admission. Boys are admitted only at the beginning of the school year in September. They may be admitted at the age of 4 and may remain in the School until the end of the academic year in which the age of 19 is attained, subject to satisfactory progress at each stage of the course and to compliance with the School Rules currently in force. Each year approximately 36 boys are admitted at age 4, a further 18 boys at age 7, approximately 100 at age 11 and approximately 25 at age 13. There are competitive examinations including written and oral tests of intelligence, literacy and numeracy at the ages of 7 and 11, held in December for admission in the following September. Applicants aged 13 also take examinations at the beginning of January and are interviewed later in the month for entry in September. Registration Fee: £100.

An Open Day for prospective parents is held each year early in October.

Scholarships and Bursaries. A number of Academic Scholarships are awarded annually to pupils entering the Senior School. A smaller number of Creative Art Scholarships (Drama, Art and Music) are awarded each year to students who show additional special promise in these specific areas.

A significant number of means-tested Governors' Bursaries are awarded at age 11+, valued from a few hundred pounds to full fees, depending upon financial need. Open equally to boys progressing from the Prep School and to those applying from other Schools.

Full details of all these awards are included in the prospectus available from the School Registrar who is happy to answer enquiries. Alternatively you can request a prospectus via the school's website: www.habsboys.org.uk.

Fees per term (2021–2022). Main School £7,159 exc lunch; Prep School (Years 3–6) £7,053 exc lunch; Pre-Prep (Years 1 & 2) £5,397 inc lunch.

Instrumental lessons (individual tuition) £245 per instrument; Group classes £150; Aural & Theory classes £75; Instrument hire £35.

Honours. In 2021, 15 boys secured a place at Oxford or Cambridge.

Charitable status. The Haberdashers' Aske's Charity is a Registered Charity, number 313996. It exists to promote education.

The Governors:
The Revd J Power (*Master of The Haberdashers' Company*)
S Cartmell, OBE (*Chairman of the Aske Board*)

Headmaster: **A R Lock**, MA

Head of the Prep and Pre-Prep Schools: M E Rossetti, MA

Senior Deputy Head: N Hamshaw, MA
Deputy Head Pastoral: C E Shooter, BA
Acting Deputy Head Academic: R D Sykes, BA
Director of Finance and Operations: D S Thompson, BA
Director of Admissions: K R Pollock, MA
Director of Co-curricular: A J Simm, BA
Director of Teaching: J S Bown, BA

Head of the Sixth Form: G Noble, MEd
Head of the Middle School: A M Lawrence, MA
Head of the Lower School: T B Hardman, BEd
Joint Schools Director of Development: W Friar, MS
Director of Foundation: R de H Llewellyn, MA
*Joint Schools Director of Marketing, Communications &
   Culture*: A Tooley, BA
Director of Outreach & Partnership: J Plotkin, MA
Director of Operations: M Lewis MBE, BEng Hons
Director of Finance & Resources: N Leon, BSc

Heads of Department:

Academic Support: F McEwan-Cox, MEd
Art: K R Weber, BA Hons
Careers: K Nash, BA
Classics: C Joyce, PhD
Computing & ICT: C Ovia, MA
Design & Technology: S Vincent, MA
Economics: J Wolfson, BSc Econ Hons
English & Drama: I D Wheeler, BA Hons
Examinations: A Thakar, BSc Hons
Geography: S C Edwards, BSc Hons
History: S P Clark, BA Hons
Libraries & Archives: D Beazleigh
Mathematics: A M Ward, BSc Hons
Modern Languages: R J Thompson, BA Hons
Music: R T Osmond, MA
Performance Music: T Taylor, MMus
Physical Education & Games:
Director of Sport: R J McIntosh, MEd
Head of PE: D H Kerry, BSc
Politics: S P Clark, BA Hons
PSHEE: C R Bass, BA
Science: G R Hobbs, PhD
Theology & Philosophy: R Davis, MA

Heads of House:
Calverts: P H Bartlett, MA
Hendersons: T Jones, BSc
Joblings: G Chapmen, PhD
Meadows: D C Taberner, MSc
Russells: M Broadwith, MSc
Strouts: A F Metcalfe, BSc

Chaplain: The Revd M Brandon, MA, MTh

Prep School:
Head: M A Rossetti, MA
Deputy Head (Academic): P Swindell, BA
Deputy Head (Pastoral): G Thomas, BA
Senior Teacher: H M R Pullen, BEd

Pre-Prep School:
Head: V Huggett, BSc

Halliford School

Russell Road, Shepperton, Middlesex TW17 9HX

Tel: 01932 223593
email: registrar@hallifordschool.co.uk
website: www.hallifordschool.co.uk
Twitter: @hallifordhead
Facebook: @hallifordschool
Instagram: @hallifordschoolshepperton
LinkedIn: /halliford-school-limited

Halliford School was founded in 1921 and moved to its
present site in 1929. The Headmaster is a member of both
HMC and the Society of Heads.

Facilities. Halliford School is situated on the Halliford
bend of the River Thames. The old house, a graceful
eighteenth-century building, which stands in six acres of
grounds, is the administrative centre of the School. There
are six additional acres of sports fields some 500 yards from
the school gates. Over the years, there has been a steady
development programme, including the 320-seat theatre, a
refurbished kitchen and dining room, new classrooms and a
new Science laboratory. There is an impressive Sports Hall
with a climbing wall and changing facilities. Most recently,
the Philip Cottam building was further developed. This
incorporates the Sixth Form Centre and Café, the Art
Studios, and Music Centre, including the Recital Hall. There
is also a wonderful design studio and workshop for the
Design & Technology students.

Admission. There are approximately 445 pupils on roll
with a three-form entry at Year 7 (approximately 60 pupils).
There is a further entry at Year 9, and admission is possible
into other year groups dependent on the availability of
places. Entrance is by examination (English, Mathematics
and Reasoning) and interview. Siblings are given priority as
long as they can benefit from a sound academic education.
This policy creates a strong feeling of a family community
and helps reinforce the close partnership that exists with
parents. Girls and Boys are admitted into the Sixth Form
based on their GCSE predictions, a report from their current
school and an interview.

Curriculum. In Years 7 to 9 pupils study the following
subjects: English, Mathematics, two languages (French,
German or Spanish), Latin/Classical Civilisation, Biology,
Chemistry, Physics, History, Geography, Art, Drama,
Music, Design and Technology, Computing, Religious
Studies and Physical Education. In Years 10 and 11 (GCSE),
there is a compulsory core of English Language and
Literature, Mathematics (some also take Further
Mathematics), a Modern Foreign Language (French,
German or Spanish), and the three separate Sciences. Pupils
choose a further three subjects: a second Modern Foreign
Language, Latin, Classical Civilisation, History, Geography,
Religious Studies, Art, Drama, Music, PE, Business Studies,
Design Technology (either Resistant Materials or Graphic
Products) or Computing Science.

In the Sixth Form, some 22 subjects are available at A
Level, and all teaching is co-educational. Many pupils also
complete an extended project.

Games. Rugby, Football, Cricket are the main games
played at Halliford. Athletics, Basketball, Badminton,

Volleyball and Golf are available, plus a number of other activities.

Pastoral Organisation. The health and wellbeing of our students are paramount to everything we do at Halliford. Our students are designated a House that will act as both pastoral support, and a community throughout their time at the School. Houses have a tutor in each year group and a Head of House. In addition, we have a Head of Year for Year 7 to ensure our students have a positive transition into the School. Likewise, we have a Head of Sixth Form to support the students who choose Halliford for the final two years of their school career. Tutors are always willing to see parents, and the Headmaster can usually be seen at very short notice. We have two part-time Matrons covering the full week who look after our students, alongside staff who are all first aid trained. We have a school counsellor available to our students, plus our Sixth Formers act as mentors to the younger students.

Out of School Activities. These include very successful Drama, Music and Art Departments.

There is a long list of clubs including Chess, Design, Computing, Film, Creative Writing, Modern Languages, Science and Art. In addition, there are Senior and Junior Debating and Academic Societies and Inter-House Public Speaking and Unison Singing Competitions. The Duke of Edinburgh's Award is available as an additional activity.

School Council. Each Tutor group elects a representative to the School Council. This is not a cosmetic exercise, and in recent times the School Council has effected real changes. Halliford believes that pupils have good ideas which can be implemented for the wellbeing of the School as a whole.

Prospective Parents. The main School Open Mornings are held on the last Saturday in February and the first Saturday in October. Further Visitor Mornings are held in November, March and May during the school week. Also, the School holds a Sixth Form Open Evening in May and October. Prospective parents are welcome at other times by appointment.

Fees per term (2021–2022). £5,995

Scholarships and Bursaries. The School offers scholarships up to the value of 10% per annum of the annual tuition fees for entry at Year 7, Year 9 and in the Sixth Form. The scholarships awarded are Academic, Art, Drama, Music and Sport.

The School is also keen to help those who could not otherwise afford the fees, and means-tested Bursaries are available on application.

Old Hallifordians. *Chairman:* Sam Lawrence.

Charitable status. Halliford School is a Registered Charity, number 312090. It exists to provide high-quality education.

Governors:

Chairman: Mr K Woodward	Mr B Harris
	Mr A Hirst
Deputy Chairman: Mr C Squire	Mrs P Horner
	Mr A Lenoel
Mrs N Cook	Mr P Roberts
Mr M Crosby	Dr M Sachania
Mr R Davison	

Headmaster: Mr James Davies

Bursar: Elspeth Sanders
Senior Deputy Head: Mr James Bown

Deputy Head (*Academic*): Mr Richard Fulford
Assistant Head Co-Curricular: Mr Sean Slocock
Head of Sixth Form: Mr John MacLean

Hampton School

Hanworth Road, Hampton, Middlesex TW12 3HD

Tel:	020 8979 5526
email:	headmaster@hamptonschool.org.uk
	admissions@hamptonschool.org.uk
website:	hamptonschool.org.uk

Motto: *Praestat opes sapientia*

Founded in the academic year of 1556/57 by Robert Hammond, a Hampton merchant, and re-established in 1612. From 1910 the School was administered by the local authority, latterly as a voluntary aided school, but in 1975 reverted to independent status.

Hampton is a lively, friendly and caring day school where innovative teaching is underpinned by strong shared values and complemented by outstanding pastoral care. Currently around 1,300 boys aged 11 to 18, including a Sixth Form of about 400. The School achieves all-round excellence, encouraging academic ambition, personal responsibility and independent thinking in an energetic, happy and well-disciplined community. It aims to provide a challenging and stimulating education for boys of high academic promise from the widest possible variety of social backgrounds.

Consistently in the top academic echelon nationally, Hampton is distinctive in being concurrently one of the country's most successful sporting schools and among the leading educational settings for music, drama and community partnerships. The School places paramount importance upon striking the right balance between academic and cultural, sporting and artistic endeavours, allowing boys to be happy and to fulfil their potential wherever their interests may lie. No pupil is funnelled down a particular route; boys are allowed to follow their own path in a nurturing, inspiring and aspirational environment. Standards are extremely high and result naturally and organically from the fun boys have at Hampton and their enthusiastic, well-balanced involvement in the huge range of opportunities on offer. The School places fundamental emphasis upon the importance of boys being personally ambitious while supporting those around them (in the School community and beyond) with kindness and compassion.

In the most recent ISI integrated inspection (March 2016) Hampton was awarded the highest judgement possible in each individual category. The quality of pupils' achievements in academic and co-curricular areas is exceptional and the contribution of arrangements for pastoral care excellent. The School achieves excellence in the spiritual, moral, social and cultural development of pupils and meets its aim to provide a friendly and supportive environment. The teaching at the School is described as excellent and teachers display expert subject knowledge which is used to inspire and guide pupils. Many lessons have a real sense of scholarly collaboration between teachers and pupils, based on mutual respect and a shared love of learning. It was also noted that the curriculum is enriched by an extensive, varied range of co-curricular activities and strong links with the community. The inspection report confirmed the School's success in meeting its aim of producing mature, confident yet grounded young people who aim for personal success while supporting those around them with kindness.

Hampton is academically selective and virtually all boys go on to leading Russell Group or equivalent universities, with increasing numbers to American Ivy League Universities. Examination results in 2021 at A Level (92.2% A*–A grades, 66.5% at A*) and GCSE (97.8% 9–7/ A*–A grades) were extremely strong. Over 95% of boys gained places at Russell Group Universities or equivalent. The Sixth Form has a strong emphasis on deep academic enquiry, breadth of study, critical thinking and independent learning.

An annual exchange programme offers boys the chance to visit Spain, Germany, France, Italy and Russia as well as Asia, Africa and the Far East. Boys visit many countries through academic and sporting initiatives and there is an extraordinary range of trips available.

The extensive co-curricular programme forms an essential part of the balanced education which Hampton provides and includes a diverse range of clubs from beekeeping and archaeology to radio, Lego robotics and drone club. Music and drama are central to the character of the School and concerts, musicals and plays involve all age groups throughout the year. Over half the boys learn musical instruments and there are frequent music and choir tours abroad. A notable number of Organ and Choral Scholarships to Oxbridge colleges have been won over recent years.

Drama is included in the curriculum, in addition to regular School and year group productions. There are major joint music and drama productions regularly with neighbouring LEH. Recent highlights include *Guys and Dolls, Return to the Forbidden Planet, Crazy for You, Anything Goes, West Side Story, Mack & Mabel, Jekyll & Hyde*, Shakespeare's *The Tempest*, Joseph Kesselring's *Arsenic and Old Lace*, Jez Butterworth's *Jerusalem* and *Oliver Twist* and *The Wizard of Oz*, both the latter being joint productions with one of the School's partnership schools, Waldegrave School for Girls.

Hampton has an outstanding reputation for sport and standards are very high indeed; many boys play at county and national level in a wide range of sports. Particular strengths are cricket, football, rowing, rugby, tennis and chess. Inspired by the First XI's national title win in the 2019 U18 English Schools FA (ESFA) Cup Final, the Second XI, Under 16As and Under 16Bs were crowned 2020 English Schools FA (ESFA) champions while the First XV rugby squad reached the semi-final in the prestigious RFU Champions Trophy. Boys benefit from superb facilities and specialist coaching. Hampton has produced many schoolboy internationals in a wide range of sports and also Olympic rowers; the School shares a nearby boathouse on the River Thames with LEH.

Integrity and social conscience are encouraged implicitly through the daily interaction of boys and teachers, as well as explicitly through School assemblies, PSHE lessons, extensive Charity, Environment and Community Service programmes, and long-standing links with the Hampton Safe Haven, now a government approved primary school in Malawi. The School was one of the two founding schools of the 'Mindfulness in Schools Project' promoting pupil well-being and emotional resilience.

Hampton School and LEH are served by 23 coach routes across south-west London, Surrey and Berkshire.

Buildings and Grounds. The School has been situated on its present site since 1939.

Set within grounds of some 28 acres, all facilities (with the exception of the Boat House) are on site including four rugby pitches, seven football pitches, six cricket squares, six hard tennis courts and a rock climbing wall. Buildings include an Assembly Hall, Dining Hall, large multi-purpose Sports Hall, fully-equipped Library and specialist facilities for Art, Science, Technology, Computing and Coding and Languages. A rigorous development programme ensures that all boys continue to benefit from first-class facilities. More recent additions include; a three-storey Atrium extension providing further classrooms and a large display area; a state-of-the-art all-weather 3G sports ground for football, rugby and recreational use and a bespoke Sixth Form Study & Careers Centre opened in 2019.

The magnificent Hammond Theatre provides exceptional facilities for the performing arts, doubling as a theatre and concert hall.

The Millennium Boat House, located on the nearby River Thames and shared with LEH, was opened in 2000 by Sir Steve and Lady Redgrave and provides the focal point for the popular and highly successful Boat Club.

Community. Community is integral to life at Hampton and the School's aim is for boys to leave as happy, educated and well-rounded young men with a sense of social responsibility and the desire to make the world a better place.

The School enjoys a wide range of thriving partnerships with local schools, charities and other organisations. In 2020, over 2,200 pupils from 49 different schools took part in a range of different partnership activities, including GCSE and A level revision classes for local secondary school pupils; Music and Drama workshops university preparation assistance; Hampton senior pupils also visit Hampton High and Twickenham Academy to provide peer mentoring for Maths.

Strong links are also maintained with the numerous local state primary schools which provide around 50% of the First Year intake. Year 5 and Year 6 pupils from a number of local state primary schools attend teaching sessions in a range of subjects on Saturday mornings as part of the School's Lion Learning Programme and regular Maths, English and Science competitions and workshops are held. Hampton teachers also undertake outreach work in local schools offering support in the Sciences, English and Maths.

Hampton Sixth formers undertake placements in local primary schools as part of their Curriculum Enrichment Programme, working with young children on literacy, numeracy, computing and sport. Many boys in the Fourth Year and above volunteer their assistance in primary schools, residential homes for the elderly and local charities. Various joint activities are run with LEH, including an annual autumn tea party and a Christmas Party for local senior citizens, together with trips for children with special needs to LEGOLAND and the Discovery Centre.

The School enjoys particularly strong links with their immediate neighbouring schools, Hampton High and LEH. These two schools participate in a wide range of activities with Hampton pupils including Drama and Music and the very popular visiting speakers 'Talk!' programme.

Hampton is one of the foundation partners, in collaboration with LEH and Reach Academy, of a new sixth form college opening in September 2022. Feltham College is an exciting new model of post-16 education, which brings together a powerful partnership of education, business and health service providers to broaden choice for local young people and offer them transformative opportunities. The College will be a centre of academic and vocational excellence at the heart of the town, playing a key role in rejuvenating a historically deprived area that has experienced significant pandemic-related job losses.

Curriculum. Boys in the Lower School follow a wide curriculum, including Design Engineering, Computing and Coding, Physics, Chemistry, Biology, a Modern Language (French, German or Spanish), Latin, Art, Drama and Religious Studies. Mandarin, Greek and Russian are optional subjects available from the Third Year. In the Fourth and Fifth Years all boys continue to study, in addition to PE, Sport and Mindfulness, the following: English Language, English Literature, a Modern Language, Mathematics and the three sciences for either GCSE or IGCSE. They choose three subjects from the following: Art, Ancient History, Computer Science, Design Engineering, Drama, French, Geography, German, Greek, History, Latin, Mandarin, Music, Religious Studies, Russian and Spanish. Most of these GCSEs/IGCSEs are taken at the end of the Fifth Year. The most able mathematicians also take Additional Mathematics GCSE.

The Sixth Form offers a free choice of A level subjects, in addition to a wide range of courses delivered through the Curriculum Enrichment Programme, including Critical Thinking and Oracy. Pupils in the Lower Sixth study at least three A levels, which continue to be studied in the Upper Sixth and a further course, which may lead to an internal or external qualification. Additional teaching and preparation is provided for boys seeking entrance to highly-selective universities, including Oxford and Cambridge, to which around twenty-five to thirty boys are admitted each year. About fifty boys a year also opt for the Hampton Extended Project, a substantial piece of independent research of around 5,000 words.

Sport. Sport and Physical Education are part of every boy's School week and the sporting programme combines strength, depth and breadth. All Hamptonians have a free choice of sport and pupils can choose between football and rugby in the autumn and spring terms; cricket, athletics and tennis are offered in the summer term. From the Third Year upwards, a large number of pupils chose to join the Boat Club. A broad programme of specialist sports provides opportunities for boys to involve themselves in basketball, cross-country, swimming, badminton, volleyball, golf, table tennis, squash, sailing and skiing. A large number of boys take part in voluntary sport on Saturdays; fixtures, at a range of ability levels, are arranged for each age group.

Careers. Each boy receives advice from the Careers and UCAS department at those points when subject choices should be made. The School is a member of Inspiring Futures, who provide Morrisby testing and interviews as part of the Fifth Year currriculum. A Higher Education Fair is held annually and there are advice evenings for parents and pupils on Sixth Form choices and on university decision-making.

Pastoral Care. This is one of the strongest features of the School. A boy's Form Tutor is responsible in the first instance for his academic and pastoral welfare and progress.

The work of Form Tutors is supported and coordinated by Assistant Heads of Year and Heads of Year under the direction of the Deputy Head (Pastoral). The School works in partnership with parents who are always welcome to discuss their son's development with any of his teachers; Parents' Evenings provide an opportunity to meet subject teachers. Year group Pastoral Forums provide parents with an opportunity to meet staff responsible for pupil welfare and to discuss a variety of pastoral issues.

Mindfulness and Wellbeing education is a compulsory and timetabled part of the curriculum for boys in the Fourth Year; Lower Sixth pupils study it in PSHE and a further course is offered to Sixth Form boys in the School's Curriculum Enrichment programme. In recent years, consideration of adolescent mental health has increased as a core element of the PSHE programme across the School. To support pupils' wellbeing, boys have access to a team of on-site Counsellors, which includes three visiting School counsellors, all of whom have wide experience of working with young people. The School also runs a LGBTQ+ group and pupils hear from a range of speakers on a wider variety of topics including digital safety, drug awareness, mental health, gambling awareness and personal safety.

Societies. The very active Adventure Society provides opportunities for kayaking, climbing, orienteering, camping and expeditions both in the UK and abroad. An exceptionally large number of boys undertake The Duke of Edinburgh's Award – Gold and Silver.

The musical programme is extremely rich and varied and includes a New Boys' Concert, two Christmas Concerts in addition to a Carol Service, Jazz in the Park, a Summer Concert and two Rock Concerts. The School's 45-strong male-voice choir Voices of Lions perform annually at the Edinburgh Fringe, regularly attracting audiences of over 100 per day. 30% of pupils take lessons in School on at least one instrument, with a significant number of these learning more than one; in addition there are over 30 ensembles and choirs that perform regularly. The Joint Choral Society, with the neighbouring LEH, gives a performance of a major choral work annually. There are numerous drama productions, with at least one dramatic production each term, and also an annual musical. In all these activities, as in the Community Service work, the School enjoys close cooperation with LEH. Hampton is also an *All-Steinway* school.

A programme of visiting outside speakers, 'Talk!', is open to pupils and members of the local community. Recent contributors include Olivier Evans (leading civil servant), Biologist and wildlife photographer David Fettes, Diplomat and Former Ambassador to Germany and France, Sir Christopher Mallaby, British climber Neil Gresham and BBC Foreign Correspondent Nick Bryant. During the national lockdowns we hosted virtual events with celebrity and author Gyles Brandreth and ITV News at Ten anchor Julie Etchingham.

There is an extensive range of 50+ co-curricular clubs and societies, among which Chess, Beekeeping, Debating, Lego Robotics, Drone Club and The Writers' Room are particularly strong.

The pupil-led campaign group, Genocide80Twenty, aims to raise awareness of recent genocides among younger people and attracts national and international plaudits from politicians, journalists and public figures.

Admission. Boys are usually admitted to the School into the First Year (Year 7), Third Year (Year 9) and the Sixth Form. Approximately 150 boys join the First Year at 11+

each September and a further 40–45 join the Third Year at 13+. A small number join the Sixth Form each year.

Candidates for entry at 11+ and 13+ sit the School's own entrance examination when they are in Year 6. Approximately half of those who sit the assessments are invited for interview and a confidential reference is sought from the current Head. A 10+ Advance Place exam is open to boys in Year 5 for deferred entry to the First Year (Year 7) and a further Pre-test is held in Year 7 for those who sat the Year 6 Pre-test for 13+ entry without gaining an offer, as well as to those who have not sat before. Full details regarding admissions procedures are provided on the School's website.

Boys may also be admitted to fill occasional vacancies at other ages at the discretion of The Headmaster. Further details may be obtained from the Head of Admissions (Tel: 020 8979 9273).

Fees per term (2021–2022). £7,300 inclusive of books and stationery.

Scholarships and Bursaries. Hampton welcomes applications from boys whose parents cannot afford fees (in full or in part) and the School awards a significant number of bursaries each year. The Hampton School Trust is fully committed to continuing to increase the number of transformative bursaries (i.e. free places) at the School for boys whose parents cannot pay any fees. The value of the award, which may be up to 110% of the tuition fees, is related to a family's financial circumstances. In addition, a growing number of transformative Fitzwygram Foundation free place Scholarships are awarded each year. The Fitzwygram Foundation, established as a separate linked charity in 2016, is specifically aimed at helping children from disadvantaged backgrounds (i.e. those for whom pupil premium funding would apply in a maintained school setting) to access a Hampton education. All Fitzwygram Foundation Scholars receive full fee remission and additional financial assistance with other costs (e.g. coach travel, lunches, uniform, School trips).

Scholarships (remitting between 5% and 25% of tuition fees) are awarded for academic merit and to boys demonstrating exceptional ability in art, chess, drama, music and sport at 11+ and 13+. Choral Scholarships, awarded in conjunction with the Chapel Royal, Hampton Court Palace, are also available at 11+ entry.

Further details on all Awards may be obtained from the Admissions Office.

Hampton School Alumni. Hamptonians join a successful global alumni network of 11,500+. The lifelong relationship with the School provides opportunities for mentoring and a programme of alumni events. The Alumni Office is located in the heart of the School and regularly welcomes Hamptonians back to their School.

Charitable status. Hampton School is a Registered Charity, number 1120005.

Governors:
Chairman: A J Roberts, OH (1962), CBE, BA, FRSA, FColl
Vice-Chairman: A H Munday, LLB, QC
Vice-Chairman: N J Spooner, BA
S A Bull, BSc, ACA
R G Alexander, MA Oxon, OH (1989)
O J C Boardman, OH (1996)
M L Ellis, Cert Ed
J A Gore-Randall, MA Cantab

Revd B R Lovell, BEng Hons, BA Hons, MA
R Mercer, BA Hons, PGCE
D N Rey, BA Hons, OH (1988)
F A Steadman, MEd
C P Walsh, BSc, FCA, CFA, OH (1996)
L H Welch, BArch Hons, RIBA, RIAS
M A Woolhouse, FCMA, CGMA, OH (1989)
A Yandle, MA Oxon

Clerk to the Governors: M A King, BSc (*Bursar*)

OH – *Old Hamptonian*

Senior Leadership Team:

Headmaster: **Kevin Knibbs**, MA Oxon

Deputy Heads:
Dr Sarah A Hendry, PhD
Pippa Z S Message, BSc
J Owen Morris, MA Cantab

Assistant Heads:
Mark A J Nicholson, BA
S Andrew Wilkinson, MA Oxon
N D Woods, MA, MEng Cantab

Bursar: Mike A King, BSc
Director of Studies: Alasdair N R McBay, MSc

Departmental Staff:
* *Head of Department*

Art:
*Karen A Williams, BA
Joel Baker, BA
Adrian J Bannister, MA
Stephanie Kirby, BA
Joanna G Moore, MA Cantab
Jerry Blighton (*Technician*)

Biology:
*Phil H Langton, BSc, Dip EnvSci (*Head of Tennis*)
Guy K Baker, MBiochem Oxon (*Head of Fifth Year*)
Joseph B Cumberbatch, BSc
Richard J Davieson, BSc
Victoria Halford, MSc (*Asst Head of First Year*)
Sarah Hendry, PhD (*Deputy Head*)
Polly A Holmes, BSc (*Head of Upper Sixth*)
Katya L Martin, MA Oxon
Pippa Z S Message, BSc (*Deputy Head, Designated Safeguarding Officer*)
Katie Mimnagh, BMedSci
Harry Moore, BSc (*Asst Head of Third Year*)
Janice Green (*Senior Technician*)
Milagrosa Estavillo (*Technician*)

Chemistry:
*David Schofield, MA Oxon (*Asst Head of Careers & UCAS*)
Rosanna Sophie Boone, BA Oxon
Neil J I Double, BSc (*Asst Head of Upper Sixth*)
Aidan Doyle, BSc (*Asst Head of Careers & UCAS*)
Anthony F Ellison, BSc
Polly A Holmes, BSc (*Head of Upper Sixth*)
Vonn Jimenez, MSci
J Francesca Knibbs, BSc
Jonathan Neville, MChem (*Asst Head of Third Year*)
Lelja Puljic, DPhil
Natty Thevananth, BSc
Delith Wainer (*Technician*)
Gillian Winskell (*Technician*)

Andrew Deevey (*Assistant Technician*)
Matthew King (*Assistant Technician*)

Classics:
*J Wesley Barber, MA Oxon
Gemma J Busby, BA Oxon
Henry McTernan, BA Cantab
Christoper W Saunders, MA
Amy Winstock, BA
Alex Ziegler, MPhil Cantab (*Asst Head of First Year*)

Computer Science:
*Gordon Clark, BSc
Chris Arnold, MPhys (*Asst Head of Fifth Year*)
Tanya Scorer, BSc
Matt Stockdale, MEng
Vincent Ting, MSc

Design & Engineering:
*Jason Holdaway, BEng
Mark Preston, BSc
Michael Richards, BSc
Joseph O Sarpong, BSc
Diane C Woodward, BSc
A [Tony] Barun (*Technician*)
Oliver Keattch (*Technician*)

Drama:
*Joanne James, MA
Nikki Plowman, BA
Elizabeth Tiller, BA

Economics:
*Ski Paraskos, MA Oxon
Alexandra M Hopton, MA
Cem Kandemir, BSc
Eileen Mullan, BSc
Tom F Rigby, BA (*Head of Third Year*)

English:
*Catherine E Rigby, BA
Esther Louise Arnott, BA
Michael M Baker, MA
Tessa Bartholomew, BA (*Asst Head of Lower Sixth*)
Martha B Bedford, BA (*Asst Head of Fourth Year*)
Caroline Ruth Bellingan, BA
Helen V Booker, BA
Oliver Ellsworth, BA (*Asst Head of Fourth Year*)
Toby Green, BA
Joanne P James, MA Cantab (*Director of Drama*)
Markus Klinge, PhD
Will S Leafe
Alexandra C McLusky, BA
Carli Minchin, BA
Rachel L Morse
David Sharkey, BA
Victoria Whitwam, BA Cantab (*Arts' Award Coordinator*)

Geography:
*Barney S Bett, MA
Charlotte Brown, BA
Frances Highton, MA
Thomas E Hill, BA (*Joint Head of First Year*)
Rachael Kugele, MSc (*Asst Head of Second Year*)
Ladea Michelsen, BSc
Dominic Saul, BSc

History:
*Holly E Partridge, BA (*acting*)
Esther Arnott, BA
Caroline R Bellingan

David R Clarke, BHum (*Senior Tutor*)
Martin P Cross, BA
Shelley Ann Havord, MA
Kevin Knibbs, MA Oxon (*Headmaster*)
Andy J Lawrence, BA Oxon
J Owen Morris, MA Cantab (*Deputy Head, Designated Safeguarding Lead*)
Jim Parrish, BA (*Head of Lower Sixth*)
Jennifer L Peattie, BA (*Joint Head of First Year*)
Victoria M Smith, BA (*Joint Head of Third Year*)
Sarah Willcox, MA

Learning Support:
*Caroline Conway (*Head of Learning Support*)
Nicola Day, BEd
Sylvia Garrido-Soriano, BA (*Academic Extension & Think! Coordinator KS3*)
Caroline King (*Cover Supervisor*)
Sian Reeve, BA (*Cover Supervisor*)
J Moffitt, ACIS (*Learning Support & SEN Administrator*)

Library:
*Karl Hemsley, MA
Emma Rommer (*Charities Coordinator*)

Mathematics:
*Joanna R Condon, MMath Oxon
Christopher G Aubrey, MA Oxon
Gareth Bailey, BSc
Ami Banerjee, MBA (*Head of Cricket*)
Jon Barnes, BSc
Rosamund Bradbury, MA Cantab
Adrienne S Burke
Hannah Clarke, BSc
Mark Curtis, DPhil Oxon
Anna Czumaj, BSc
Bernadette K Frith, BSc
Daniel Griller, BA Cantab (*Oxbridge and Olympiad Coordinator*)
George R Haynes, BSc
Aidan Kershaw, BSc
Thomas A Lees
Alasdair N R McBay, MSc (*Director of Studies*)
Hannah M Mason, MA
Caroline H Reyner, MSc Oxon
Christopher M Schurch, BSc
Verity Short, MA Cantab
Nick Stebbings, BEng (*Asst Head of Lower Sixth*)
Rohit R Trivedi, MA Cantab (*KS4 Coordinator*)
Geert Van Mook, BSc
Nivetha Vasanthakumar, BSc
Marta Watson-Evans, MA (*KS5 Coordinator*)

Modern Languages:
*Frederic Chaveneau, BA
Marc Boardman, BA (*Head of French*)
Isabell Jacobson, BA (*Head of Spanish*)
Katya White, BA (*Head of Russian*)
Katherine Willett-Pecnik, BA Oxon (*Head of German*)
Yi Hong Zhang, MA (*Head of Mandarin*)
Haig Agulian, MA
Christopher J Blachford, BA
Shirley A Buckley, BA
Margaret Chandler, MA
Maria Doncel-Cervantes, BA
Silvia Garrido-Soriano, BA (*Academic Extension & Think! Coordinator KS3*)
Sam Gordon, MA

Charles Malston, BA (*Asst Head of Second Year*)
Sophie E May, BA Oxon
Natalie Noble, BA (*Asst Head of Fourth Year*)
Jill C Owen, BA (*Head of Second Year*)
Philipp Studt, MA (*Asst Head of Fourth Year*)
Paddy G Turner, BA
Sophie C Yoxon, MA
Joan Herrero Burguillos (*Spanish Assistant*)
Yulia Isaeva (*Russian Conversation*)
Maria Parra Lopez (*Spanish Assistant*)
Lydia van Odijk (*German Assistant*)
Lina Vincent (*French Assistant*)

Music:
*Daniel E Roland, MusB
Elizabeth Esser, BA (*Head of Academic Music*)
James C Ferrier, BA
Sarah Mattinson, BA
Ewan J Zuckert, BMus (*Acting Head of Academic Music*)

Personal, Health & Social Education:
*Victoria Halford, MSc
Rebecca J Nicholson, MPhys Oxon (*Asst Head of PHSE*)

Physical Education and Games:
*Carlos Mills, BSc (*Director of Sport*)
Andrew Beattie (*Director of Rugby*)
David Burke (*Director of Football*)
Colin Greenaway (*Director of Rowing*)
Matthew K Sims, BSc (*Head of PE Sports Rehabilitation*)
David R Clarke, BHum (*Senior Tutor*)
Nick Rowett (*Asst Director of Rowing*)
C William Saunders, MA (*Head of Tennis*)
Scott Cowie (*Rowing Coach*)
Geoffrey Jones (*Boatman*)
Jamie Lashley (*Cover Supervisor, Sports Assistant*)
Harry Perry (*Rowing Intern*)

Physics:
*Mark G Yates, PhD
Christopher P Arnold, MPhys (*Asst Head of Fifth Year*)
Gordon H Clark, BSc
Dan J Fendley, BEng (*Senior Tutor, Induction Tutor*)
Daan Fuldner, MSc
Stephen Gray, BSc
Rebecca J Nicholson, MPhys Oxon (*Asst Head of PHSE*)
Christine Reilly, MSc
Rebecca Singleton, BEng
Amy White, MA
Tim E Wilson, MPhys
Nicholas D Woods, MA, MEng Cantab (*Assistant Head*)
Ollie M Worrall, MSc (*Cantab*)
David A Hughes, HNC (*Senior Technician*)
Rebecca Galan (*Technician*)

Politics:
*Jenny A Field, MA Cantab
Robin Hardman, MA
Will S Leafe, BA
Tom F Rigby, BA (*Joint Head of Third Year*)

Psychology:
*Alice Goodman, BSc
Lorcan P Dow, BSc
Rachael O'Connor, MA
Holly Peck, MSc
Raeisa S Perreira, BSc

Religious Studies & Philosophy:
*Ben Clark, MSt

Carlo Lori, BA Cantab
Mark A J Nicholson, BA (*Assistant Head*)
Mark Scott, BA
Rupert Vann-Alexander, BA
S Andrew Wilkinson, MA Oxon (*Assistant Head*)

Administrative Staff:
Examinations Officer: Michelle Barnes
Headmaster's PA: Clare Espley, BA
Head of Admissions & Marketing: Dorothy Jones, BA, Dip Mar
Deputy Admissions Manager: Caroline Elia
Admissions Assistants: Karen Saul; Chanel Morris
School Nurses: S Rivers; Elizabeth Searle

Harrow School

Harrow on the Hill, Middlesex HA1 3HP

Tel:	+44 (0)20 8872 8000 (Enquiries)
	+44 (0)20 8872 8003 (Head Master)
	+44 (0)20 8872 8007 (Admissions)
	+44 (0)20 8872 8320 (Bursar)
email:	harrow@harrowschool.org.uk
website:	www.harrowschool.org.uk

Mottos: *Stet Fortuna Domus* (May the fortune of the house stand); *Donorum dei dispensatio fidelis* (The faithful stewardship of the gifts of God).

Harrow School is a full-boarding school for boys aged 13 to 18. It was founded in 1572, under a royal charter from Queen Elizabeth I, by a local landowning farmer, John Lyon, whose original intention was to provide 30 boys of the parish with a classical education. Today, the School's purpose is to prepare boys with diverse backgrounds and abilities for a life of learning, leadership, service and personal fulfilment; distinguished Old Harrovians include seven British prime ministers and the first prime minister of India, Pandit Nehru, as well as poets and writers as diverse as Byron, Sheridan and Richard Curtis. This statement of purpose is borne out through our various areas of activity: teaching that helps boys achieve their best academically, pastoral care that matures them both emotionally and spiritually, and an extra-curricular programme that develops their characters and interests. The School's 324 acres have a collegiate feel, its historical architecture complemented by modern buildings that meet its pupils' developing needs. Approximately 830 boys attend Harrow, from across the UK and further afield.

Academic. Harrovians routinely progress into higher education that ranks among the best the world has to offer. The vast majority of boys who go to university attend either Oxbridge, Russell Group or well-known international institutions, particularly in the USA. These include Stanford, Harvard, Yale, Princeton and Cornell. Following 2020 A Level results, Harrovians will be attending seven of the world's top ten universities, including Harvard, Oxford, Cambridge and Stanford, and over a hundred Harrovians are taking up places at Russell Group universities. However, no two Harrovians are the same: some live in London, others much further afield in the UK or overseas; a number come from established Harrow families, others have no experience of public schooling; many excel in sport or the arts, others are very strong academically. What Harrovians experience through their extra-curricular activities, and by leading and serving others, are just as important as their lessons.

The Super-Curriculum. Beyond the examination syllabus, our Super-Curriculum focuses on the aspects of scholarship that are not formally assessed: habitual reading, independent research, reflection and debate. Central to this is the electives system, in which boys select a challenging off-syllabus course that is taught in small groups. These courses promote lateral thinking, problem-solving and the articulation of profound thought, while also allowing boys to lead their own learning. On virtually every night of the week, there are seminars and society meetings, and we are able to attract eminent speakers from all walks of life to enrich and broaden the boys' experience of academic and cultural life.

Boarding. Our leafy 300-acre estate contains 12 Boarding Houses. The buildings are quite individual, with their own gardens and facilities, helping to set each one apart. The Houses inspire fierce loyalty from the boys and old boys, who take pride in their own part of Harrow. House Masters and their families live in the Houses, and are assisted by an Assistant House Master, Matron, Year Group Tutors and Health Education Tutors. In addition, the chaplaincy, full-time psychologist and pastoral support committee provide further layers of nurturing and support. Approximately 70 boys live in each House. There are no dormitories: a boy shares his room with a boy of the same age for the first year or so, and thereafter has a room to himself. Every boy has a computer in his room and each House has common rooms and shared kitchens. All teachers live in the School. Typically, for the first two weekends of a term, all pupils are in the School. If they are able to, parents come and visit. On the third weekend – an exeat – all pupils go home or to friends; the weekend starts around noon on Friday and ends at 9.00pm on Sunday. The next two weekends are followed by a nine-day half term.

Sport. With afternoon games available in around 30 sports, five times a week, sporting fixtures against other schools and the chance to compete regularly in House matches, boys are kept healthy and active. Under the expert guidance of some of the country's leading coaches, boys develop their skills, character and confidence. Through games such as rugby, soccer, cricket and Harrow football, they learn how to be team players. Equal emphasis is placed on the many individual sports offered here that cultivate resilience, self-discipline and enjoyment. Surrounded by acres of sports fields, AstroTurf pitches, a golf course, swimming pool, sports centre, tennis, rackets and fives courts, Harrow has a breadth of sporting opportunities. Our elite sportsmen have an impressive record of achieving excellent standards and some go on to enjoy successful, professional sporting careers. Unique occasions like the annual cricket match versus Eton at Lord's provide memorable highlights in the School year.

The Arts. The arts are an extremely important part of Harrow's packed calendar of activities. Whether it's learning a musical instrument, playing in orchestras and ensembles, singing in choirs or in houses, performing in plays or discovering beauty in fine art, sculpture and ceramics, the opportunity for creative expression at Harrow not only sets our boys on a lifetime of personal enrichment and enjoyment, but also teaches them to be more self-disciplined, attentive and better at planning and organising their busy lives. Boys who participate in the vast spectrum of Harrow's creative and performing arts also find that this involvement has a broader, more beneficial effect on their overall academic performance. By encouraging boys to perform in the highest-quality School and house concerts, plays and competitions, we see them finding their own voice and the confidence to express their individual creativity, regardless of innate talent.

After Harrow. Virtually all of our boys take up places at selective universities. Boys who are heading towards Oxbridge, Ivy League and other competitive institutions are given specific guidance and preparation from their House Masters and our dedicated Universities Team.

The Harrow Association, Harrow's Old Boys' Society, has a thriving membership of over 10,000. Tel: 020 8872 8200, email: ha@harrowschool.org.uk.

Admission. Boys are typically admitted for entry at 13 and a smaller number at 16. Visit www.harrowschool .org.uk/admissions/admissions-home for more information.

Fees per term (2021–2022). £14,555, including board, tuition, textbooks, a stationery allowance and laundry. For any subject requiring additional tuition, there is an extra charge.

Scholarships and Bursaries. A large number of scholarships are awarded every year. Scholarships have a value of 5% of the fee and are held throughout a boy's time at Harrow, subject to satisfactory performance. Boys may apply for more than one of the different types of scholarship, which include Academic, Music, Art, Sport and Outstanding Talent. Boys do not necessarily need to be awarded a scholarship to be considered for a bursary. In this case, bursary support is considered for strong candidates upon application to the School. Sometimes, candidates will be asked to achieve a scholarship to be eligible for a bursary. More than 10% of boys in the School receive support with their fees.

Charitable status. The School is constituted as a Royal Charter Corporation known as The Keepers and Governors of the Possessions Revenues and Goods of the Free Grammar School of John Lyon, which is a Registered Charity, number 310033.

Senior Management Team:

Head Master: **W M A Land**, MA

Deputy Head Master: N Page, BA, MCIL

Director of Studies: C E G Bailey, BA, FCCT

Director of Pastoral Care: Dr S A Harrison, BSc, PhD, CMath, MIMA

Director of Safeguarding: P J Evans, BA, LTCL

Academic and Universities Director: Ms H R Fox, MA

Director of Shaftesbury Enterprise: T M Dalton, BSc

Registrar: Dr E R Sie, BSc, PhD, CChem

Bursar: N A Shryane, MBE, BA, MPhil

Chief Executive of the Harrow Development Trust: D L Collins

Director of Operations: R G Arundell

Highgate School

North Road, London N6 4AY

Tel: 020 8340 1524 (Office)
            020 8347 3564 (Admissions)
email: office@highgateschool.org.uk
            admissions@highgateschool.org.uk
            communications@highgateschool.org.uk
website: www.highgateschool.org.uk
Twitter: @highgate1565
Facebook: @HighgateSchoolLondon
LinkedIn: /school/highgate-school

Motto: *Altiora in votis*

Founded over 450 years ago, Highgate is one of the UK's leading co-educational independent schools. Based within Highgate Village, the School is a short distance from central London and adjacent to Hampstead Heath.

Our Pre-Preparatory School is for pupils aged 4–7, and is located on Bishopswood Road in Highgate, overlooking our sports grounds. The Junior School is based in a new building that opened in September 2016, for pupils aged 7–11. Our Senior School is for pupils aged 11–18, and most teaching takes place on our North Road site, in the heart of Highgate Village. Pupils also have lessons in art, design, engineering and technology in our Mills Centre on Bishopswood Road.

Highgate School is a place for learning and scholarship where we:

- Develop learning as an end in itself and as a way of living
- Are ambitious about what and how our pupils learn
- Cultivate confidence, creativity and risk-taking in our pupils as they study, in preparation for higher education and the world of work
- Value and promote different intelligences

We promote high levels of achievement and effort, however we push the boundaries beyond mere acquisition of knowledge; we want our pupils to develop the confidence to investigate and enquire, to solve problems, and to take responsibility for their learning. We aim to enrich the learning experience of our pupils, broadening their social horizons and cultural interests.

Pupil wellbeing is at the heart of all our thinking. We understand that developing the whole person, a child who feels happy, healthy and confident in themselves, with skills to manage ups and downs, is of utmost importance not only during their time here at Highgate, but when they leave and move into the adult world. We nurture confidence and strength of character, supporting pupils to grow and thrive in their emotional, mental and physical health.

Sport. Highgate pupils are taught sports and exercise by specialist coaches and teachers to ensure a high-quality experience. Our extensive playing fields are complemented by facilities at the Mallinson Sports Centre, by courts for squash, tennis and Eton Fives, by our all-weather pitch, by our cricket nets, and by our location next to Hampstead Heath.

Co-curricular and Community. Beyond the classroom, there is an extensive selection of co-curricular activities available to our pupils, providing countless opportunities to have fun, make new friends and learn beyond the classroom. Our offering of activities continues to evolve and develop in response to the changing needs of our pupils and the world around us.

We encourage our pupils to play an active role in their community – at School and beyond. Within the Senior School, there are several pupil working groups to help steer and drive initiatives across the School, along with a wide-reaching programme of community service. Together with our co-curricular offering, pupils are encouraged to develop interests and hobbies, forge lasting friendships, belong to teams, ensembles and casts, and learn the value of community.

Facilities. The School combines Victorian buildings (our Chapel, Central hall classrooms and Sir Martin Gilbert Library) with modern facilities like our 200-seat auditorium and dedicated recital spaces, science laboratories, modern language classrooms, and high-tech ICT suites. There is a newly refurbished 25m indoor pool and extensive sports facilities.

Our Mills Centre for Art and Design provides studio and gallery space, with facilities for print-making, sculpture, pottery and film-making, plus an IT suite for graphics and computer aided design, and a photographic darkroom. In addition, we have well-equipped design and engineering workshops (which host a suite of 3D printers and laser cutters), an electro-pneumatic lap and an automotive workshop.

Highgate Junior School opened in a new building in September 2016, which is built to the highest specification with specialists facilities for computing, science, art, DTE, drama and music, plus a retractable-seat hall, outside play spaces and a small amphitheatre.

Our Pre-Prep is based on Bishopswood Road in Highgate, in a light, airy and colourful building. We overlook the open spaces of our sports grounds and have our own playground, which was enlarged in 2016. At that time, four of our classrooms were refurbished and enlarged, creating a separate music room and learning support room.

Transport links to Highgate Village and our School include bus routes and the Northern line of the London Underground, meaning central London is just twenty minutes away. We also offer a School bus service for Junior and Senior School pupils.

Pupil Numbers. 1,881 (955 boys, 926 girls)

Fees per term (2021–2022). Senior School: £7,200; Junior School: £6,600; Pre-Preparatory School: £6,235 (Reception–Year 2), £3,110 (Nursery).

Bursaries. Our Admissions Officer (Widening Access), email: admissions@highgateschool.org.uk, can provide information about the process for bursary applications at 7+, 11+ and 16+.

Charitable status. Highgate School is a Registered Charity, number 312765

Chairman of Governors: Bob Rothenberg, MBE, BA, FCA, CTA

Head: **A S Pettitt**, MA

Hurstpierpoint College
A Woodard School

College Lane, Hurstpierpoint, West Sussex BN6 9JS

Tel: 01273 833636
email: registrar@hppc.co.uk
website: www.hppc.co.uk
Twitter: @Hurst_College
Facebook: @HurstCollege

Motto: *Beati mundo corde*

Founded 1849 by Nathaniel Woodard, Canon of Manchester.

Hurstpierpoint College is a co-educational day and boarding school for boys and girls aged between 4 and 18 years. Pre-Prep, Prep and Senior Schools are linked by common values and a common academic and administrative framework, to provide a complete education. There are currently 487 boys and 426 girls. 50% of the pupils are boarders. The Preparatory and Pre Prep School has a further 366 pupils (178 boys and 188 girls).

The school is truly co-educational throughout and offers boarding for boys and girls in the Senior School. Boarding is a particularly popular option at the school with many day pupils and flexi boarders later opting to become weekly boarders. In their Upper Sixth year at Hurst, pupils join St John's House, a co-educational day and boarding house where, appropriately supervised, they enjoy greater freedom and are encouraged to further develop their independent learning skills in preparation for university.

Buildings and Facilities. At the heart of the school's large country campus lie the core school buildings and Chapel arranged around three attractive quadrangles built of traditional Sussex knapped flint. Key facilities nearby include three floodlit AstroTurfs, art school, sports hall, music school, dance and drama studios, 320-seat theatre, indoor swimming pool and Medical Centre. Other facilities include a new Library and fully-equipped IT Centre. The new performing arts building opened in November 2018. The extensive grounds are laid mainly to playing fields and include one of the largest and most attractive school cricket pitches in the country.

Chapel. As a Woodard School, Hurstpierpoint is a Christian foundation and underpinned by Christian values, although pupils of other faiths or of no faith are warmly welcomed. Pupils attend up to three assemblies during the week. The main Eucharist, which parents and friends are most welcome to attend, takes place early on Friday evenings, although there are also occasional Sunday services in addition to voluntary celebrations of the Holy Communion. Pupils who wish to do so are prepared in small classes for the annual Confirmation taken by one of the Bishops of the diocese.

Curriculum. The five-day academic week is structured to allow boys and girls to study a variety of subject options that can be adapted to suit their natural ability. The entry year (Shell) gives pupils the chance to experience most of our GCSE subjects before they choose their options. It involves the study of English, History, Geography, French, Spanish, Latin, Classical Greek, Mathematics, Physics, Chemistry, Biology, Religious Studies, Art, Design & Technology, Music, Dance, Drama, Physical Education and Computer Science. In the second (Remove) and in the third (Fifth) years the curriculum is split into two parts: core subjects (English, maths, three sciences) and optional subjects such as Art & Design, Classical Greek, Computer Science, Dance, Drama, Humanities, Modern Foreign Languages, Design Technology, Latin.

Students entering the sixth form study A Levels with the majority selecting 3 subjects and some selecting 4 and all sixth form pupils take the EPQ as an extension of one of their A Level subjects. The subject choice is wide from: Art & Design, Business, Classical Civilisation, Classical Greek, Computer Science, Dance, Design & Technology, Drama & Theatre, Economics, English Literature, Geography, History, Latin, Maths and Further Maths, Modern Languages, Music, Music Technology, Physical Education, Politics, Psychology, Religious Studies, Sciences (Physics, Chemistry, Biology) and Sociology.

All pupils' work is overseen by academic tutors and we take particular care to ensure that university applications are properly targeted to suit the students' aspirations and talents.

Games. The School operates a "Sport for All" policy that seeks to place pupils in games most suited to their tastes and abilities. During the first two years they are expected to take part in at least some of the major sports but thereafter a greater element of choice occurs. The major sports are Rugby, Hockey, Cricket and Athletics for boys; Hockey, Netball, Athletics and Cricket for girls. Recent tours for major sports include Rugby (Italy), Netball (Barbados), Dubai (Cricket), South Africa (Hockey). In addition there are teams in Basketball, Cross Country, Football, Golf, Polo, Swimming, Triathlon and Tennis. The Sports Hall and indoor Swimming Pool provide opportunities for many other pursuits such as Aerobics, Badminton, Equestrian, Fencing, Gymnastics, Power Walking, Weight Training and Water Polo, while the Outdoor Pursuits enable pupils to enjoy challenges such as Rock Climbing, Mountain Biking, Sailing, Kayaking and Canoeing.

Service Afternoons. On Wednesdays all pupils other than the Shell (Year 9) are expected to take part in The Duke of Edinburgh's Award activities alongside the Combined Cadet Force (Army, RN or RAF sections), Community Service or Environmental Conservation.

Music. There has always been a strong musical tradition at Hurstpierpoint with an orchestra and other more specialised ensembles. A large proportion of the pupils, currently 160, take individual instrumental lessons and give frequent recitals. The Chapel Choir plays a major part in regular worship and there are several other choral groups.

Drama. The Shakespeare Society is the oldest such school society in the country and organises an annual production and an annual musical. Drama covers a wide range and varies from major musicals to more modest House plays and pupil-directed productions. The new (opened in November 2018) 320-seat Bury Theatre also gives the more technically minded ample opportunity to develop stage management, lighting and sound skills.

Other Activities. The Thursday afternoon activity programme is for Shell and Remove pupils (Years 9 & 10) and includes Art, Climbing, Dance, Self-Defence, Car Maintenance, Girls' Football, Hurst Farm, Robotics, Japanese, LAMDA, Ninjitsu, Shooting, Horse Riding, Polo, Karate, Golf Range, Squash, Clay Pigeon Shooting, Dinghy Sailing and Surfing alongside a variety of music clubs and literary clubs. Other activities also take place during the school week.

Hurst Johnian Club. In addition to providing facilities and events for Old Pupils, the Club also assists with careers and supports the current pupils in various ways, e.g. Gap Year travel fund and tour sponsorship contributions.

Fees per term (2021–2022). Senior School: Weekly Boarding £10,540–£10,665; Flexi Boarding £9,890–£10,015; Day £8,370–£8,495.

Scholarships and Bursaries. Awards available at 13+: Academic, 'Hurst' All-Rounder, Art, Dance, Drama, Music and 'Downs' Sports. Please note that candidates entering for awards other than Academic are not eligible to apply for All-Rounder awards. Such candidates will be considered for All-Rounder awards as part of their other applications. Awards available at 16+: Academic, Art, Drama, Music and 'Downs' Sports.

Academic Award examinations are held annually in May for 13+ candidates. Assessments for All-Rounder, Art, Drama and Sports Awards are held in February.

Music Award assessments are held in December of the year prior to entry for entrants to the Prep School and in February of the year of entry for entrants to the Senior School. Awards are offered with free musical tuition in up to two instruments. Informal auditions are encouraged and may be held at any time by arrangement with the Director of Music. The Awards are given subject to satisfactory Scholarship or Common Entrance results or the College's own entry tests.

Art Scholarships: A folio of work is presented and there is an observation test as well as an interview.

Assessment for Sixth Form awards takes place in November of the year prior to entry.

Means-tested bursaries may be available to supplement awards.

Admission. For 13+ entry, pupils must be registered on the School's list and will sit the Common ISEB Pre-Test in Year 6. Candidates are then invited to attend an assessment and experience day and offers are made following this in March of Year 6.

To matriculate into the sixth form at Hurst pupils require at least 4 level 7 GCSEs. They should achieve a level 7 or above in the subjects they intend to study and, where a pupils wishes to start a new subject which they have not studied before, they need to have achieved a level 7 or above in a GCSE subject closely related to it (i.e. for Economics, ideally a pupil should have a level 7 in Maths GCSE). Students should also have a minimum of a level 5 at GCSE in Mathematics and English.

Please contact the Senior School Admissions Office for further information.

Preparatory School. *See entry in IAPS section.*

Charitable status. Hurstpierpoint College is a Registered Charity, number 1076498. It aims to provide a Christian education to boys and girls between the ages of four and eighteen in the three schools on the campus.

Governors:

Chairman: Mr A Jarvis, BEd, MA, FRSA

Dr S Brydie, MBBS, MD, MRCGP
Dr J A Chocqueel-Mangan, BEng, MSc, DBA, CEng, MIMechE, FRSA
Mrs L J Corbett, OBE
R J Ebdon, BSc Hons, MAPM, ICIOB, FRSA
Dr I S Francis

Mrs F M Hampton
Revd W Kemp
Mrs K M Mack, BA Hons, ACA
Mr K S Powell, FCA
Mr G A Rushton

Headmaster: **Mr Tim J Manly**, BA Oriel College Oxon, MSc LSE

Head of Senior School: Mr Dominic W Mott, MA Queens' College Cantab
Deputy Head Academic: Mr Lloyd P Dannatt, MEng Imperial College, London
Deputy Head Pastoral: Mrs Caty E Jacques, BSc Surrey
Deputy Head Co-Curricular: Mr Nick Creed, BA Wales, MEd Buckingham
Head of Prep School: Mr Ian D Pattison, BSc Southampton
Bursar: Mr Darren J Carpenter, BA Brighton
Chief Operating Officer: Mr Dan M Higgins, BA, Cert Ed Loughborough
Director of Staff and Pupil Wellbeing: Mr Mike Lamb, BSc Nottingham, MA Edge Hill
Director of Professional Development and Performance: Mrs Michelle Zeidler, BEd Homerton College Cantab, MEd OU
Prep School Deputy Head: Mr Nick J Oakden, BA Wales, MEd Buckingham, NPQH

Directors:
Mr Liam J Agate, BA Sidney Sussex College Cantab (*Academic Development*)
Mrs Sue M Atkinson, BA, FCIPD (*Human Resources*)
Mrs Keramy J Austin, BSc Edinburgh, CChem FRSC CSci (*Academic Administration*)
Mr Richard A Cuerden, BA Winchester School of Art, MA Royal College of Art (*Art & Photography*)
Mrs Jami A Edwards-Clarke, BA Cardiff (*Diversity and Inclusion*)
Mr Luke A Gasper, BA Hatfield College Dunelm (*Drama*)
Mr Oliver J J Gospel, BEng Liverpool (*Activities and Service*)
Mr Simon A Hilliard, CEP(YJ) OU (*Safeguarding*)
Mrs Caty E Jacques, BSc Surrey (*PSHCEE*)
Mr Rob M Kift, BEd Madeley College of PE (*Sport*)
Mr Mike Lamb, BSc Nottingham, MA Edge Hill (*Staff and Pupil Wellbeing*)
Mrs Jan Leeper, BA University College London (*Senior Mistress, i/c Careers*)
Mr Tim F Q Leeper, BSc Edinburgh, CBiol, MIBiol (*Senior Master*)
Mr Neil Matthews, BA St John's College Durham (*Music*)
Mr Fred Simkins, GCGI, CVQO Surrey (*Outdoor Education*)
Mrs Debbie K Stoneley, BEd London (*Safeguarding*)
Mrs Michelle Zeidler, BEd Homerton College Cantab, MEd OU (*Professional Development and Performance*)

Housemasters/Housemistresses:
Mr Rob J Ashley, BA Manchester, MA Melbourne (*Woodard*)
Mr Richard A Cuerden, BA Winchester School of Art, MA Royal College of Art (*Wolf*)
Mr Andrew G Daville, MA Lady Margaret Hall Oxon (*Crescent*)
Mrs Jami A Edwards-Clarke, BA Cardiff (*Martlet*)
Miss Tania C Fielden, BA Brighton (*Pelican*)
Mrs Helena E Higgins, BA, Cert Ed Loughborough (*Phoenix*)

Mr Adam J Hopcroft, MEng Bath (*Eagle*)
Miss Rebecca M Hughes, BA Brighton (*Fleur*)
Mrs Carey Jones (*Shield*)
Mr Owain J Jones, MA St Edmund Hall Oxon (*Star*)
Mr Mike Lamb, BSc Nottingham, MA Edge Hill (*St John's*)
Mr Duffy E Parry, MA Edinburgh (*Chevron*)
Mrs Alice S Paterson, BSc Edinburgh (*St John's*)
Mr Richard R J Taylor-West, AKC King's College London, MA Sussex (*Red Cross*)

Heads of Years:
Years 3–6: Mrs Alexandra E A Oakden, MA St Andrews
Year 7&8: Mr Ian D Pattison, BSc Southampton
Shell: Miss Georgina L Cave, BA Bristol; Mr Simon D Lilley, BSc Loughborough
Remove: Mr Will J S Poole, BSc Oxford Brookes
Fifth Form: Mr Nick E F Chadwell, BSc Oxford Brookes
Head of Upper Sixth Form: Mr Brian T Schofield, BA Pembroke College, Oxon
Heads of Lower Sixth Form: Mr William G D Bradley, BA Essex; Miss Deanna M L Cappella, BA Sussex

Heads of Department:

Art:
Mr Richard A Cuerden, MA Royal College of Art (*Director of Art & Photography*)
Mrs Lucy A Lane, BA West Surrey College (*Years 3–8*)

Business & Economics:
Mr Liam J Agate, BA Sidney Sussex College Cantab

Classics:
Miss Clemmie Faulkner, BA Warwick, MA King's College (*Years 3–13*)

Computer Science:
Mr Steve J Crook, BSc East Anglia

Dance:
Miss Nicola C Dominy, BA Surrey (*Years 7–13*)

Design and Technology:
Mr Kaeran D K MacDonald, BA Brunel (*Years 7–13*)

Drama:
Mr Luke A Gasper, BA Dunelm (*Director of Drama*)
Mr Liam Harris, BA Royal Central School of Speech and Drama London (*Academic Drama*)
Miss Rose E Hall–Smith, BEd Edinburgh, MA London (*Years 3–8*)

English:
Mr Nick Fanthorpe, BA Trinity College Oxon
Miss Carole A Saville, BA Trevelyan College Dunelm, MSt St Peter's College Oxon (*Years 7&8*)
Mrs Sarah L Deelman, BSc Surrey (*Years 3–6*)

ESL:
Mrs Kay L B Goddard, MA The Queen's College Oxon

Geography:
Miss Rebecca L Bownas, BSc East Anglia
Mr Tom B B Williams, BSc Manchester (*Years 3–8*)

History:
Miss Joanna C Clarke, BA Edinburgh
Mrs Alexandra E A Oakden, MA St Andrews (*Years 3–8*)

Learning Support:
Mrs Jill C Silvey, BA Newcastle NSW
Mrs Kate J Parker, BA Liverpool, MA London (*Reception–Year 8*)

Modern Foreign Languages:

French:
Dr Edqard J Still, MSt, DPhil St Catherine's College Oxon (*Years 12&13*)
Mrs Grace I Butler, BA Birmingham (*Years 9–11*)
Mrs Alison Filkins, BA Roehampton (*Years 3–8*)

Spanish
Miss Madeleine K Hyman, BA St John's College Dunelm (*Years 12&13, Years 9–11*)
Mrs Amy V Flint, BA Cardiff, MSc Green Templeton College Oxon (*Years 9–11*) [maternity leave]
Mrs Lucy Boucke, BA Newcastle (*Years 7&8*)

Mathematics:
Dr Graham Moir, BA, PhD Trinity College Dublin (*Head of Faculty*)
Mrs Leah J Mackinder, BSc Nottingham (*Years 12&13*)
Mr Adam M Swinton, BA Girton College Cantab, MSc Warwick (*Further Maths Years 12&13*)
Mr Jack Denning, BSc Trinity College Dublin, MA Sussex (*Year 10*)
Miss Saffron E Usher, BA Selwyn College Cantab (*Years 7&8*)
Miss Hattie C Thompson, BSc Bristol (*Years 3–6*)
Mrs Lauren S Johnson, BA Brighton (*Numeracy Reception–Year 2*)

Music:
Mr Neil Matthews, BA St John's College, Dunelm (*Director of Music*)
Mr Will Carroll, BSc Montreal (*Music Technology*)
Mr Cyrus L Dean, BMus Royal Holloway London, MMus Southampton (*Academic Music Years 7–13*)
Mrs Claudette C Hastilow, BMus Trinity College of Music, MEd Homerton College Cantab (*Academic Music Reception–Year 6*)

PE & Sports Science:
Mr Steve J May, BSc Chichester
Mr James Baldwin, BSc Exeter (*Academic PE Years 3–8*)

Politics:
Mr Brian T Schofield, BA Pembroke College Oxon

Psychology:
Ms Phoebe S Lewis, BSc Southampton

Religion, Ethics and Philosophy:
Mr Richard R J Taylor-West, AKC King's College London, MA Sussex
Mr Martin Clay, MBA OU (*Years 3–8*)

Science:
Mr Peter A Browne, BSc Leeds & Sussex
Mrs Alice M Edwards-Clarke, BSc Sussex (*Reception–Year 6*)

Biology:
Miss Emily L Grapes, BA Selwyn College Cantab
Dr Kathryn T Hutchinson, BSc Cardiff, MSc St Edmund Hall Oxon, PhD Leeds (*Years 7&8*)

Chemistry:
Mr Peter A Browne, BSc Leeds & Sussex
Miss Ankita Sengupta, BSc Sussex (*Years 7&8*)

Physics:
Mrs Naomi C Smith, MPhys Leeds

Sociology:
Miss Rebecca L Bownas, BSc East Anglia

Enrichment:
Mr Liam J Agate, BA Sidney Sussex College Cantab
(*Director of Academic Development*)

The Library:
Ms Dominique B Collins, MA UCL (*Head of Library & EPQ*)
Mrs Trisha A Barrett, BA Birmingham, MA Chichester
(*Prep School Librarian*)

Outdoor Education:
Mr Fred Simkins, GCGI, CVQO Surrey (*Director of Outdoor Education*)
Mrs Sarah K Peach, BA Northumbria (*Assistant Director of Outdoor Education*)

Combined Cadet Force:
Maj. Sam Amos (*Contingent Commander*)

Sport:
Mr Rob M Kift, BEd Madeley College of PE (*Director of Sport*)
Mr Ben M Dewey, BSc Northampton (*Head of Boys' Sport Years 3–8*)
Mrs Rebecca J Jutson (*Assistant Director of Sport, Girls*)
Mr Steve J May, BSc Chichester (*Assistant Director of Sport, Boys*)
Mis Kristina Money, BSc Birmingham (*Head of Girls' Sport Years 3–8*)

Head of Admissions and Marketing: Mrs Dianne S Allison

Hymers College

Hymers Avenue, Hull, East Yorkshire HU3 1LW

Tel: 01482 343555
email: enquiries@hymers.org
website: www.hymerscollege.co.uk
Twitter: @Hymers_College
Facebook: @HymersCollege
Instagram: @hymers_college

Hymers College is a co-educational day school offering the very best for young people aged 8–18 through its supportive pastoral care, outstanding academic teaching, wide-ranging co-curricular offer and first-rate facilities.

Hymers College was originally opened as a school for boys in 1893 when the Reverend John Hymers, Fellow of St John's College Cambridge and Rector of Brandesburton, left money in his will for a school to be built 'for the training of intelligence in whatever social rank of life it may be found among the vast and varied population of the town and port of Hull'. Although the school has remained true to its Founder's intentions through a generous fee remission scheme, the catchment area now stretches across the city of Hull, East Yorkshire and North Lincolnshire, and the School became fully co-educational in 1989.

Number of Pupils. 979.

The Junior School has 198 pupils aged 8–11. There is a full range of academic, sporting, music and co-curricular activities.

The Senior School has 573 pupils in Years 7–11 and the Sixth Form has 208 pupils.

Admission is by assessment at ages 8, 9, and 11, together with an interview with the Headteacher. The two exceptions to this are pupils at Hessle Mount Preparatory School (a Hymers College Associate School) who do not sit an assessment for entry to Year 4 of the Junior School. In addition, pupils in Hymers College Junior School do not sit an assessment for entry to the Senior School.

Almost all pupils qualify for the Sixth Form through GCSE results. Pupils from other schools are admitted to the Sixth Form on the basis of good GCSE results, an interview with the Headmaster and a computer-based assessment.

Pupils are prepared for the GCSE in a broad curriculum including music, business-related subjects, computer studies, technology and the arts.

There is a full range of courses leading to A Level examinations, and special preparation is given for Oxford and Cambridge entrance.

Facilities. Set in 45 acres of grounds the buildings consist of 35 classrooms, 11 specialist laboratories, a computerised language laboratory, extensive ICT facilities, audio-visual room, 200-seater theatre, Art/Design Technology Centre, a gymnasium and a large sports hall. There is a specialist music block providing a full range of music facilities including a recital hall, rehearsal and music technology rooms and a recording studio. The award-winning Learning Resources Centre, the most recent building addition to the School, houses a café, library and study area and break out rooms. In recent years the school has refurbished many science laboratories as well as the Sixth Form Common Room and Reception areas. The Junior School building contains 9 classrooms and specialist rooms for music, DT, art, ICT and science, along with a library, sports hall and changing rooms. The grounds include a recently upgraded all-weather astro pitch, upgraded tennis and netball courts, rugby and cricket pitches and a swimming pool and sports centre including a fitness suite.

Co-curricular Activities. All pupils are strongly encouraged to participate in the very wide range of co-curricular activities and a longer lunch break allows adequate time for pupils to do this. The main school games are rugby, cricket, hockey, netball, tennis and athletics. The school regularly competes at national level and provides members of county and national teams. Many pupils take part in The Duke of Edinburgh's Award scheme and Hymers is the only Independent school to host the National Citizen Service at the School. Over 80 clubs and activities are offered throughout the School including British Sign Language, water polo, chess, Law Society, debating and Time Capsule Club. Drama is particularly strong, with several productions a year. Music is a major school activity; from full orchestras to choir and chamber groups in each part of the school. Individual tuition is available in most instruments.

Fees per term (2021–2022). Senior School £4,139; Junior School £3,443–£3,639; Sixth Form £4,139. Hymers Bursaries are typically awarded at ages 8, 9, 11 and 16.

The Old Hymerians Association, c/o Development Manager, Hymers College, Hull HU3 1LW.

Charitable status. Hymers College is a Registered Charity, number 529820-R. Its aims and objectives are education.

Governors:
Mr J M V Redman, BSc, FIDM, MIOD (*Chair of Governors*)

Mr M P Astell, BEng, MBA, FIMechE, CEng (*Vice Chair*)
Mrs S Anwar West, LLB, LLM
Mr P A B Beecroft, BSc, MA, MBA, FInstP
Professor P G Burgess, BA, MA, PhD Cantab, FRHistS
Mr A H Chicken, BA Hons, MEd
Mr J F Connolly, BSc
Mr D A Gibbons, BSc, MRICS
Mrs G A Greendale
Mr M C S Hall, BSc
Mr J G Leafe
Mrs E A Maliakal, LLB
Mr C M Read, MA Oxon, MRICS
Mr D U Rosinke, BSc, ACA
Mrs N Shipley, FCA
Mrs G V Vickerman, BSc, MSc, MRICS
Mr J R Wheldon, LLB Hons, MRICS, ACI Arb
Mrs E A Wilson, BEd, AGSM

Headmaster: **Mr J P Stanley**, MA, MBA

Deputy Head (*Management*): Mr R Wright
Deputy Head (*Pastoral*): Mrs H Jackson
Directors of Teaching & Learning: Dr M Pickles and Mr R
  Simpson
Director of Co-Curricular: Mr D Thompson
Director of Finance: Mrs K F Walker
Head of Junior School: Mr P C Doyle, BSc

Ibstock Place School

Clarence Lane, London SW15 5PY

Tel: General Enquiries: 020 8876 9991
         Head's PA: 020 8392 5802
         Bursar's Office: 020 8392 5804
         Registrar: 020 8392 5803
email: office@ibstockplaceschool.co.uk
website: www.ibstockplaceschool.co.uk
Twitter: @IBSTOCKPLACE

Age Range. 4–18 Co-educational.

Number in School. 981: 512 Boys, 469 Girls.

Ibstock Place School is located in spacious grounds of some eight acres adjacent to Richmond Park and with easy access to Putney, Barnes, Richmond and Hammersmith. The school offers a balanced education combining a traditional academic curriculum with an extensive range of co-curricular opportunities. Succeeding his predecessor's 20 years' service, Mr Christopher Wolsey took over the Headship in January 2021 having been Deputy Head and Head of Sixth Form.

This co-educational school has grown and prospered with significant building development. A Sports Hall opened in 2008. New School, occupying Clarence Lane and Priory wings and comprising twenty-one classrooms, six laboratories and two computer suites, opened in 2011. Additional facilities include: a stunning purpose-built Library accommodated over two floors, a Music Technology studio, Innovation Centre, all-weather and sports pitches on the adjacent Cooper's Campus site, and a swimming pool. A Theatre, including flexible, state-of-the-art stage, fully-equipped Drama Studio and backstage facilities comprising Dressing Rooms, Green Room and Workshop opened in 2015. A new Refectory opened in

January 2020, also providing dedicated Sixth Form study facilities on a mezzanine floor.

The Preparatory Department and the Senior School remain distinctive and are housed separately, so that each child benefits from a small-school ambience and the younger pupils gain from many of the facilities enjoyed by the Senior School. The Prep School, which incorporates Pre-Prep, provides a rich and stimulating environment, with a wide range of curricular activity carefully planned to realise each child's abilities and talents.

The Senior School, age 11–18, offers a full range of Arts, Humanities, Languages, Science and Technology subjects. All pupils follow a core curriculum which includes a requirement to study two languages at GCSE/IGCSE, along with many opportunities for enrichment. Co-curricular emphasis is placed on Art, Drama, Music and Sport, as well as engaging pupils in an extensive Outreach and Partnership programme in the local community. Language, Debating and Choral visits take place to a host of international destinations. There is an outstanding programme of outdoor education, a wide range of after-school clubs, including The Duke of Edinburgh's Award scheme. All pupils are supported by a strong and effective pastoral system which operates through four houses. House Groups are vertically organised to engender companionship and aspiration.

Following A Level/Pre-U results in 2021, 88% of pupils proceeded to their first choice university, including five to Oxbridge. In 2020, 91% of entries were awarded A*–B grades and 68% were awarded A*–A. *The Sunday Times* 2019 'Parent Power' rated Ibstock Place School 73rd best independent School in the UK (up from 121st in 2018) and 28th best in London.

Over recent years our leavers have proceeded to an impressive range of world-class institutions including Cambridge, Oxford, St Andrews, Imperial College, Durham, Lancaster, UCL, Warwick, Leeds, LSE, Bath and Exeter, and there is now barely a single Top 50 university in the UK which does not boast at least one Ibstonian undergraduate.

In PVI (Year 11) pupil results of 2020, 83.4% of entries were graded at 9–7.

Entry to the Pre-Prep is by age-appropriate assessment. There is now assured 11+ progression from the Prep School to the Senior School for candidates admitted at 7+ and above. Prospective pupils and parents are advised to consult the school's website for the latest information on admissions arrangements.

The school offers Open Mornings and Evenings in September and May each year. Occasional places may arise from time to time (e.g. at 13+). Further information is available from the Registrar.

Fees per term (2021–2022). £5,870–£7,450 (including lunches).

Charitable status. Ibstock Place School is a Registered Charity, number 1145565.

Chairman of Governors: Gabby Covill

Headmaster: **Christopher Wolsey**, MA Nottingham, MEd
  Buckingham

School Executive:
Deputy Head (*Academic*): Zoe Jarvis, MA King's
Deputy Head (*Pastoral*): J-D Price, BSc Exeter
Senior Master: Christopher Banfield, MA Leeds, MSc
  Open

Bursar: John Hutchison, MIB Southern Cross, MBA Dallas

The Senior Management Team:
Director of Operations/Head of PVI: Russell Collins, BSc Hons Cape Town
Advisor: Lee Faith, BSc London Metropolitan
Deputy Head of Sixth Form and PVI, Sutherland Tutor: Sophie Gillen, MA Oxon
Director of Digital Strategy: Rob Gorrie, MA Oxon
Head of Sixth Form: Rachel Palmer, BSc Exeter
Director of Teaching and Learning: Ed Swift, BA Exeter, MA London

Head of Pre-Prep and Preparatory School: Lee Faith, BSc London Metropolitan

Immanuel College

Elstree Road, Bushey, Hertfordshire WD23 4EB

Tel: 020 8950 0604
email: enquiries@immanuelcollege.co.uk
website: www.immanuelcollege.co.uk
Twitter: @ICBushey
Facebook: @ImmanuelCollegeUK

Motto: *Torah im Derech Eretz ~ Jewish learning leading to secular success*

Immanuel College is a selective, co-educational day school founded in 1990 by the late Chief Rabbi, Lord Jakobovits to fulfil his vision of a school affirming modern orthodox Jewish values and practice in the context of rigorous secular studies. The College aims at giving its pupils a first-class education that encourages them to connect Jewish and secular wisdom, to think independently and to exercise responsibility. Its ethos is characterised by attentiveness to individual pupils' progress, high academic achievement and the integration of Jewish and secular learning. There are both Jewish and non-Jewish teachers at the school, the common element being enthusiasm for their work and concern for their pupils. Its results at GCSE and A Level have been increasingly impressive in recent years. In 2019 70% of all GCSE entries were graded A or A* (7, 8, 9) and 68% of A Levels were graded A or A*. In 2020 the respective percentages were 74% and 78%.

Age Range. 4–11 and 11–18. The Preparatory School opened in September 2011 and now includes Reception to Year 6 classes.

School Roll. There are 685 pupils on roll, of whom 320 are girls and 365 are boys. There are 129 pupils in the Sixth Form.

Buildings and Grounds. The College is situated in a tranquil 11-acre site dominated by Caldecote Towers, a Grade II-listed 19th-century mansion. Facilities include the Joyce King Theatre, two suites of science laboratories, a fitness suite, a large all-weather surface for tennis and netball, cricket and football pitches, and grounds for field events and athletics. Professor Lord Winston opened a new multi-functional 8-classroom building in September 2010, and a further building for an enhanced Jewish Learning facility (Atar-Zwillenberg Beit K'nesset), additional classrooms and state-of-the-art laboratories was opened in November 2014 by Chief Rabbi Ephram Mervis. Dining room facilities were upgraded in 2017, along with a new 6th Form Art Studio and an expanded library. In 2019 a completely refurbished computing suite was installed, along with a new Music Technology facility, and there have been further improvements to playgrounds and security features.

Admissions (Senior School). Most boys and girls enter in September, though pupils are accepted in all three terms. Admission into the Senior School is on the basis of performance in the College's entrance examination and interview. The principal entry is at 11+, but the School considers pupils for admission at any point. A growing number of boys and girls join the College in the Sixth Form; offers of places are gained by entrance examinations and interview and are conditional upon GCSE results and suitability for A Level courses.

Admissions (Preparatory School). Admission into Reception and Year 1 is on the basis of informal assessment consisting of a play session and a focus activity. For Year 2 there is a short Mathematics activity and a reading/writing task.

Fees per annum (2021–2022). Senior School: £19,845; Lunch £310 per term. Preparatory School: £11,025; Lunch £210 per term.

Scholarships and Bursaries. Immanuel Jakobovits Academic and Jewish Studies Scholarships are awarded on a competitive basis to outstanding 11+ entrants. Exhibitions to the value of £2,000 per annum are awarded to pupils who show exceptional promise in Art and Music. Means-tested bursaries are awarded to a number of boys and girls from less affluent families who are academically and personally suited to the education the College provides.

Curriculum. The articles of the College's faith are that Jewish and secular learning shed light on one another, that the appreciation of each is deepened by study of the other, and that the life of the mind and spirit should not be compartmentalised but holistic. As such, the school offers a wide range of secular subjects, including English, Mathematics, Further Mathematics, Computing, Electronics and the Sciences, as well as Art and Design, Photography, Drama, Geography, History, French, Spanish, Modern Hebrew, Music, Personal, Social and Health Education and Physical Education. At A Level, additional subjects include Economics, Government & Politics, Media Studies, Sociology, Business and Psychology. Throughout a pupil's time at Immanuel, Jewish Studies forms part of the core curriculum. Jewish ethics, philosophy, history and religion and Israel Education are studied by way of close textual learning and through guest speakers and seminars, developing *Chochma* (wisdom) and well-founded Jewish identities. All members of the College have informal and formal opportunities to deepen their understanding of Jewish faith and practice with team members from the School's Jewish Study Centre, the Beit.

Pastoral Care. The College prides itself on attentiveness to the needs of individual pupils. The Pastoral Team includes Form Tutors and Heads of Section, who in Years 7 to 11 work under the direction of the Deputy Head for Pastoral Care. The Director of Sixth Form is in charge of a team of Sixth Form Tutors. Parental consultation evenings take place regularly, most recently online. The Pastoral Hub, staffed by people outside the Teaching faculty, provides important individual support. The Student Council, which meets frequently, gives pupils the opportunity to express their views and make suggestions about further improving school life.

Religious Life. The College commemorates and celebrates landmarks in the Jewish and Israel calendar such as Purim, Chanukah, Succot and Yom Ha'atzmaut. Each January, on Holocaust Memorial Day, Lower Sixth Form students share the knowledge and insights that they have gained on their trip to Poland with pupils in the first five years of the Senior School, but it has not been possible to visit Poland at the the time of the Pandemic. The College also commemorates Yom Hazikaron. Pupils attend morning and afternoon prayers on a daily basis.

The Inclusion and Learning Support Department supports teachers to help pupils become independent and successful learners. In addition to the programme followed by all pupils, the Department provides a range of tailored programmes to pupils whose learning needs are more specific. Pupils with a variety of learning profiles are thereby helped to develop confidence and to exceed their predictions and reach their potential.

Art, Music and Drama. The College enjoys a tradition of excellence in the visual arts (the annual Gottlieb Art Show being the highlight of the artistic year) and drama (recent school productions have included *Macbeth, An Inspector Calls, The Happiest Days of Your Life, Pygmalion, The Trojan Women, Twelfth Night, Three Sisters, The Crucible, Rumours, Mary Poppins, My Fair Lady, Annie Jr* and *Fiddler On The Roof*). There is a yearly Music Festival and the calendar includes a number of concerts and recitals involving soloists, ensembles and orchestra.

Games. The PE and Games staff involve pupils in activities that range from aerobics, golf, and trampolining to athletics, cricket, football, hockey, table tennis, netball, badminton and tennis. Over twenty sports clubs meet weekly. Physical Education may be studied for GCSE and A Level. Sports facilities include an all-weather surface and a fitness suite. The College has won trophies in many sporting competitions in recent years and were recently crowned District Cricket Champions at Years 7, 8 & 10.

Enrichment Activities. The many co-curricular activities on offer include opportunities for pupils to participate in leadership programmes, volunteering schemes, Charity fundraising (Shevet Achim), The Duke of Edinburgh's Award, public speaking, debating competitions and The Alan Sennit Programme. There are also clubs in areas such as philosophy, medicine, law, chess, art, STEM, military history, Jewish life and learning, world affairs and modern European languages.

Educational Trips. In Year 7 pupils visit Amsterdam; in Year 8 they visit an outward bound centre in France; in Year 9 they spend three weeks in Israel; in Year 10 they visit Strasbourg and Madrid; and in the Lower Sixth they spend eight days in Poland, although the Covid Pandemic has interrupted these visits in the last two years. These experiences encourage pupils to understand themselves, bond with one another and comprehend the forces that have shaped contemporary Jewry. Photography students benefit from trips to foreign locations of great natural beauty.

Careers. The guidance provided by the College supports pupils in their research about choices beyond Immanuel. Through assemblies, the lower years are encouraged to start thinking about their own strengths and weaknesses and likes and dislikes which lead to discussions about future pathways. Even at this stage, any experience in the labour market is encouraged and supported. By the time GCSE subject choices need to be made, pupils are aware of the wider world around them and are closely monitored throughout the process. During Year 10 and Year 11, pupils make use of the weekly Careers Clinic, where they may collect information about relevant courses, one-day events and other opportunities to engage directly with people from specific areas of work. Year 11 pupils may also undertake testing by My Future Choice (formerly known as Cambridge Occupational Analysts) and this, along with a personal interview after mock examinations, helps pupils and their parents to feel confident about making the right A Level choices. Pupils continue to enrol in career-specific courses and events throughout the Sixth Form, and all are welcomed to our Careers Fair.

Charitable status. Immanuel College is a Registered Charity, number 803179. It exists to combine academic excellence and Jewish tradition in a contemporary society.

The Board of Governors:

Professor Anthony Warrens, DM Oxon, PhD, FRCP, FRCPath, FEBS, FHEA (*Chairman*)

Mrs Annette Koslover, LLB Hons (*Designated Child Protection Governor, Co–Vice Chair*)

Mrs Hannah Boyden, BA Hons (*Health & Safety Governor, Kodesh Governor, Co–Vice Chair*)

Mrs Valerie Eppel, BA Hons, FCA (*Treasurer*)

Mr Daniel Levy

Rabbi Eliezer Zobin, MA (*Principal*)

Dr Daphna Atar–Zwillenberg, PhD

Mrs Lynda Dullop, BA Hons

Mrs Mandy Berkman, BA Prim Ed SA, NPQH (*Early Years Foundation Stage*)

Mr Neal Menashe, CA SA

Mrs Lisa Zimmerman

Rabbinic Advisor: Dayan Ivan Binstock, BSc

Clerk to the Governors: Mr David Laird, CMgr, MSc, LLM

Head Master: Mr Gary Griffin, BA Hons

Senior Leadership Team:

Principal Rabbi: Eliezer Zobin, MA

Deputy Heads:
Pastoral: Mrs Anne Pattinson, BA Hons (*Designated Safeguarding Leader – Safeguarding and Child Protection*)
Academic: Mr Barnaby Nemko, MSc, MA
Logistics: Mr Paul Abrahams, BA Hons

Assistant Heads:
Mr Richard Felsenstein, BA Hons (*Community & Communication*)
Mrs Jo Fleet, BA Hons (*Director of Studies*)
Mr Lee Rich, BA Hons (*Teaching Quality and Pupil Learning*)
Mrs Sharron Shackell, BA Hons (*Director of Sixth Form, Deputy Designated Safeguarding Leader – Safeguarding and Child Protection*)
Rabbi Danny Baigel, BA Hons (*Director of Jewish Education*)
Mr Antony Berkin, BA Hons, FCA (*Bursar*)
Mrs Alexis Gaffin, BEd Hons Cantab (*Head of Immanuel College Preparatory School*)
Ms Rachelle Hackenbroch, BA Hons (*Director of Human Resources*)
Mr Aryeh Richman, BA Hons (*Head of Inclusion and Learning Support, Deputy Designated Safeguarding Leader – Safeguarding and Child Protection*)

* Head of Department

Art and Photography:
*Mrs Alison Ardeman, BA Hons (*Art*)
Miss Susan Ribeiro, BA Hons (*Deputy Head of Art*)
Mrs Dawn Goulde, BA Hons, MA (**Photography*)
Mrs Bettina Jacobs, BA Hons
Mrs Ana Sklabinska (*Art Technician*)
Mr Michael Callinicos, BA Hons (*Photography Technician*)
Ms Sharon Moss, BA Hons (*Art*)

Business and Economics:
*Mrs Charlotte Lichman, BSc Hons
Mr Ben Freedman, BSc Hons (*Assistant Director of Studies (IT Applications for Teaching)*)
Ms Julia Stock, MA (*Business, Economics*)

Computing:
*Mr Aizaz Niazi, BSc Hons

Electronics:
*Ms Kirsti Cullen, BSc Hons

English:
*Mr Gordon Spitz, BA Hons, MA
Ms Naomi Amdurer, BA Hons (*Head of Middle School/ Charity & Social Action*)
Mrs Anne Pattinson, BA Hons (*Assistant Head of English, Deputy Head (Pastoral)*)
Mrs Danielle Kestenbaum, BA Hons (*Second in English*)
Mr Greg Broad, MA Hons, RSA Dip. TEFLA
Mrs Sarah Minde, BA Hons (**PSHE*)
Miss Alessandra Rivalta , BA Hons, MA
Mr Ben Wolfin, BA Hons (*KS3 Coordinator English*)
Ms Celia Newman, BA Hons, MA

Geography:
*Mr Lee Raby, BA Hons
Ms Staycie Domzalski, MSc, BSc Hons
Miss Karen Porter, BSc

History, Government and Politics:
*Mr Geordie Raine, MA, BA Hons, BEd
Ms Jyoti Atwal, Msc, LLB (*Head of Upper School, Politics*)
Mr Barnaby Nemko, MSc, MA (*Deputy Head (Academic)*)
Mr Richard Felsenstein, BA Hons (*Assistant Head (Community & Communication)*)
Mr Lee Rich, BA Hons (*Assistant Head (Teaching Quality and Pupil Learning)*)
Mrs Sharron Shackell, BA Hons (*Assistant Head (Director of Sixth Form)*)
Mr Liam Suter, BA Hons (*Coordinator of Enrichment, Oxbridge and Partnership, HE Coordinator*)
Mrs Laura Hill, BA Hons (*History*)

Jewish Education:
*Rabbi Danny Baigel, BA Hons (*Director of Jewish Education*)
Mr Richard Felsenstein, BA Hons (*Assistant Head (Community & Communication)*)
Mr Aryeh Richman, BA Hons (*Head of Inclusion and Learning Support, NQT Coordinator, Assistant Head of Middle School, Deputy Designated Safeguarding Leader – Safeguarding and Child Protection for Senior School*)
Mrs Deborah Unsdorfer, BSc Hons (*JS Enrichment Coordinator*)
Mr Jonathan Atkins, BA Hons (*Professional Development Lead (Senior School)*)

Mr Michael Lewis, MA, BA Hons (*Assistant Head of Department (Jewish Studies)*)
Mr Bradley Conway, BA Hons (*KS3 Coordinator Jewish Studies*)
Mrs Abi Korc, BSc Hons
Rabbi Yitzy Hill, BTL (*Duke of Edinburgh Coordinator*)
Ms Chava Nussbaum, BSc, MA
Rabbi Eliezer Zobin, MA (*Principal*)
Mrs Daniella Neifeld, BA, MA (*Head of Informal Education*)
Mr Gavriel Cohn (*Informal Jewish Educator*)
Rabbi Ephraim Levine (*Head of Informal Education*)
Miss Rivka Gould (*Informal Jewish Educator*)

Learning Support Department:
*Mr Aryeh Richman, BA Hons (*Head of Inclusion and Learning Support, Deputy Designated Safeguarding Leader – Safeguarding and Child Protection for Senior School*)
Mrs Vicky Arnold, BA Hons (*Assistant SENCO (Preparatory School), Joint Head of Year 7 (Girls)*)
Ms Debby Benjamin
Mr Greg Broad, MA Hons, RSA Dip. TEFLA
Miss Amreen Rajulawalla, BA Hons (*Learning Support Assistant (Music)*)
Mrs Sonal Solanki, MSc, BSc Hons (*Learning Support Assistant*)
Mrs Michelle Solomon (*Learning Support Assistant*)
Mrs Sheila Tunwell (*Learning Support Assistant*)
Mrs Shelley Cowen (*Learning Support Assistant*)
Miss Emma Willis, BA Hons, MA (*Learning Support Assistant, Library and Independent Learning*)
Mr Alex Coope, MA (*Independent Learning Coordinator*)
Mrs Laura Samuels (*Library Assistant*)

Mathematics:
*Ms Kalpana Patel, MBA, BA Hons
Mr Daniel Littlestone, MSc (*Second in Department, Head of GCSE Further Mathematics, Assistant Director of Studies (Performance Data Management)*)
Mrs Orly Selouk, BEng Hons (*KS3 Mathematics Advisor*)
Mrs Sara Wolman, BSc Hons (*Virtual and E-Learning Coordinator*)
Mrs Ruth Davis, BA Hons (*KS5 Mathematics and Further Mathematics Coordinator*)
Mr Peter Fleeman, BSc Hons
Mrs Pinki Ojha, BEng, BEd
Dr Sapna Somani, MSc, BSc Hons
Miss Tanja ten Have, BSc

Media Studies:
*Mr Brandon Alford, BEd, BA Hons
Mrs Dawn Goulde, MBA, BA Hons

Modern Foreign Languages:
*Mrs Nicola Fahidi, BA Hons (**Spanish*)
Mr Paul Abrahams, BA Hons (*Director of Academic Operations*)
Ms Naomi Amdurer, BA Hons (*Head of Middle School/ Charity & Social Action*)
Ms Sarah Perlberg, BA Hons (**French, Assistant Head of Upper School*)
Mrs Vardit Sadeh–Ginzburg, MA, BA Hons (**Modern Hebrew*)
Ms Ariella Eshed, BEd, MA (*Modern Hebrew*)
Mrs Lili Schonberg, BA Hons, BSc Ed Hons (**Preparatory MFL*)
Mrs Deborah Clayden, BA Hons (*French, Spanish*)

Mrs Mónica Palenzuela, BA Hons, MA (*Spanish*)

Mrs Na'ama Fialkov, Montessori Certified (*Ivrit*)

Miss Dalia Freedman, BA Hons (*Spanish, French*)

Performing Arts:

*Mrs Nicola Stimler, BA (*Director of Drama*)

*Mr Stephen Levey, LLB Hons (*Music*)

Mrs Joanna Fleet, BA Hons (*Assistant Head (Director of Studies)*)

Mr Adam Gooch, BSc Hons (*Assistant Head (Middle School)*)

Mrs Carole van der Watt, BA Hons (*Head of Behaviour for Learning, Drama*)

Miss Amreen Rajulawalla, BA Hons (*Learning Support Assistant (Music)*)

Physical Education:

*Mr Philip Monaghan, BA Hons

Mrs Lorraine Conetta, BEd Hons (*Head of Girls' PE, Head of Preparatory School PE*)

Mr Robert Hammond, BSc Hons (*Assistant Head of Sixth Form*)

Miss Lauren Burns, BA Hons

Mr Nick Freeman, BA Hons

Mr Adam Gooch, BSc Hons (*Assistant Head (Middle School)*)

Ms Helen Lord, BSc Hons

Miss Emily Balsam (*Sports Assistant*)

Psychology:

*Mrs Helen Stephenson-Yankuba, BSc Hons

Mrs Melisa Resnick, MPhil

Science:

*Mrs Vanessa McClafferty, BA Hons

Mr Felix Posner, BSc Hons (*Biology*, *Director of Management Information Systems*)

Dr Ben Tabraham, MSci, PhD, BSc Hons (*Chemistry*)

Ms Kirsti Cullen, BSc Hons (*Electronics*)

Mrs Moniza Abbas, BSc Hons

Ms Yewande Ajayi, BSc Hons, MSc

Mrs Shahed Alsharifi, BEd Hons

Mrs Julyanne Burgess, BSc Hons

Ms Bharatiben Desai, BSc Hons (*Biology*)

Mr Chris Wright BSc Hons (*Physics*)

Mrs Michelle Sacker, BSc Hons

Mr Robert Tunwell, BSc Hons (*KS3 Science Coordinator*)

Mr Jonathan Fitzsimmons (*Senior Exam Invigilator/ Assistant Science & Engineering Technician*)

Miss Sheena Murphy, BA Hons (*Senior Science Technician*)

Mr Muhummad Rahman, MSC, BSc Hons (*Science Technician*)

Sociology:

*Mrs Melisa Resnick, MPhil

Mrs Helen Stephenson–Yankuba, BSc Hons

Miss Julia Bromage, BA Hons

Immanuel College Preparatory School

Head of Immanuel College Preparatory School: Mrs Alexis Gaffin, BEd Hons Cantab (*Designated Safeguarding Leader – Safeguarding and Child Protection for Preparatory School including EYFS*)

Deputy Heads:

Rabbi Moshe Braham, BSc Hons (*Director of Jewish Life and Learning*)

Ms Jacyn Fudge, BSc Hons (*Head of EYFS, Deputy Designated Safeguarding Leader – Safeguarding and Child Protection for Preparatory School*)

Mrs Shelley Peysner, LLB Hons (*Preparatory School Administrator*)

Class Teachers:

Mrs Jill Ducasse, BEd Hons

Mrs Katie Fisher, BSc Hons

Mrs Lara Goldstein, BA Hons

Mrs Lucy Handelsman, BA Hons

Mrs Danielle Kingsley, BEd Hons

Mr Jonathan Sumroy, BA Hons (*Deputy Designated Safeguarding Leader – Safeguarding and Child Protection*)

Mrs Suzy Kennedy, BA Hons

Mrs Shoshanna Berkley, BSc Hons

Mrs Carli Pruchnie BSc Hons

Jewish Studies:

Mrs Tova Bamberg, BSc

Mrs Rochel Levine

Miss Leah Katanka

Modern Foreign Languages:

Mrs Lili Schonberg, BA Hons, BSc Ed Hons

Music:

Mr Lewis Fisher, BA Hons, ATCL (*Pianoforte*)

Physical Education:

Mrs Lorraine Conetta, BEd Hons (*Head of Girls' PE, Head of Preparatory School PE*)

SENCO:

Mrs Vicky Arnold, BA Hons

Teaching Assistants:

Mrs Gemma Buckland, BSc Hons

Mrs Niki Cotsen

Miss Claire Franks, BSc Hons

Mrs Naomi Goldberg, BA Hons

Mrs Nicole Greenwold, BA Hons

Miss Vanessa Lawee, BA Hons

Mrs Jane Marks

Miss Hannah Rosenberg, BSc Hons

Miss Lauren Sherman

Breakfast Club Assistants:

Mrs Pam Young (*First Aid Officer*)

Mrs Annette Wright

Lunch Time/After School Assistants:

Mrs Hayley Goldman

Mrs Leila Peterman

Support Staff (for Senior and Prep School)

Administration:

Mrs Shelley Peysner, LLB Hons (*Preparatory School Administrator*)

Mrs Ann Stern (*Sixth Form Administrator*)

Administrative Assistants: Mrs Louise Cohen; Mrs Lisa Fisher; Mrs Lesley Gold; Mrs Hayley Goldman; Mrs Debbie Myers

Admissions:

*Mrs Sarah Greenfield, BA Hons (*Head of Admissions and Marketing*)

Mrs Celia Rabstein (*Deputy Head of Admissions*)

Bursary:
Mr Antony Berkin, BA Hons, FCA (*Bursar*)
Mr Navnit Popat (*Finance Officer*)
Mrs Helen Rowbottom (*Sales Ledger Controller*)

Business Development:
Mrs Lynda Dullop, BA Hons (*Director of Business Development*)

Counsellor: Mrs Zoe Ingram, BSc Hons

Examinations:
Mrs Debbie Fitzsimmons (*External Examinations Administrator*)
Mr Jonathan Fitzsimmons (*Senior Exam Invigilator/ Assistant Science & Engineering Technician*)

First Aid:
Mrs Alison Buike (*School Nurse*)
Mrs Pam Young (*First Aid Officer (Prep School)*)

Head Master's Office:
Mrs Simone Garfield (*PA to the Head Master and Deputy Heads, Safeguarding Administrator*)
Mrs Elaine Essex (*Senior School Secretary*)

Human Resources:
Ms Rachelle Hackenbroch, BA Hons (*Director of HR*)
Miss Maureen O'Shea (*HR Administrator & Administrator i/c Appointments*)
Miss Faye Westbrook, BA Hons (*HR & Compliance Officer*)

IT:
Mr Pardeep Karwal (*IT Support Administrator*)
Mr Radostin Yordanov (*IT Technician*)

Marketing:
Mrs Sarah Greenfield, BA Hons (*Head of Admissions and Marketing*)
Mr Tom Warner (*Marketing Assistant*)

Pastoral Office:
Mrs Rochelle Freedman (*Pupil Wellbeing Coordinator & Advisor*)
Mrs Simone Garfield (*PA to the Head Master and Deputy Heads, Safeguarding Administrator*)

Behaviour Support:
Mrs Carole van der Watt, BA Hons (*Head of Behaviour for Learning*)
Mrs Romi Baron, BA Hons (*Behaviour and Pastoral Administrator*)

Site Team:
Mr Gary Hanscomb (*Director of Estates*)
Caretakers: Mr Luis Fidalgo; Mr Keiron Richens; Mr Jayson Pillay
Mr Jonathan Kramer (*Assistant Caretaker*)

Ipswich School

Henley Road, Ipswich, Suffolk IP1 3SG

Tel: 01473 408300
email: enquiries@ipswich.school
website: www.ipswich.school
Twitter: @ipswichschool
Facebook: @ipswichschool
Instagram: @ipswich_school
LinkedIn: /school/ipswich-school

Motto: *Semper Eadem*

The School was founded in the fourteenth century by the Ipswich Merchant Guild of Corpus Christi. Its first Charter was granted by Henry VIII and this was confirmed by Queen Elizabeth I.

At Ipswich School we pride ourselves on a passion for learning, and the care and attention we give to our pupils. Through these we help our pupils to unlock their potential and develop their talents. We are consistently ranked in the top 150 schools nationwide and are considered as the top Independent School in our area.

Ipswich School occupies an attractive site adjacent to Christchurch Park. The cricket field lies within the perimeter of the school buildings and a further two sports sites, Notcutts playing fields and Ipswich School Sports Centre (Rushmere) – with its three astroturf hockey pitches and six netball courts – are owned by the School locally. In total, students benefit from 60 acres of pitches and fields.

The Boarding House stands in its own grounds a short distance from the school. There is a choice of full, weekly and occasional boarding for pupils in the Senior School. There is a new Sixth Form boarding house, fully ensuite, also minutes from the main School.

All academic subjects have been housed in new or refurbished rooms in the last few years and visitors comment on the quality of the buildings, which are grouped around one of the School's playing fields.

The Preparatory School is housed in purpose-built accommodation on an adjacent campus; it benefits from all the amenities of the Senior School including the Sports Hall, Swimming Pool, Performing Arts Centre and Playing Fields. (*For further details, see entry in IAPS section.*)

Admission. Entry to the Preparatory School after Nursery is by means of age and stage-appropriate assessments consisting of English, Mathematics, Non-Verbal Reasoning and appropriate behaviour. At age 11, admission is by means of the Entrance Examination which is held at the end of January or early February. This consists of a Reasoning Test and papers in Mathematics and English. Practice papers are available and the examination is set to assess potential. At age 13, admission is by means of either the Common Entrance Examination in June or our own Entrance and Scholarship Examination in March. Admission to the Sixth Form for girls and boys from other schools is by attainment of the required grades at GCSE, a report from the previous Head and an interview in November. Application forms may be obtained from the Admissions Manager. A registration fee of £50 is payable (£25 for brothers or sisters).

Religious Education. There is religious education throughout the age range and weekly chapel services for different sections of the school; there are also occasional Chapel Services on Sundays and after School at which pupils and their parents are most welcome.

Careers. Computer analyses of interests and aptitudes complement carefully planned advice about GCSE, A Level choices, higher education and professional training. There is also a wide variety of talks, seminars and work experience options throughout the year.

Curriculum. In the Preparatory School, pupils study English, Mathematics, Languages, Computing, History, Geography, Religion, Science, Music, PE, Games, Art and Design Technology, PSHE and Outdoor Education.

Senior School pupils follow a common curriculum in the first two years with a choice between French and Spanish, plus Classical Civilisation in Year 7 and Latin in Year 8. German or Russian are introduced in Year 9. Mathematics is taken at IGCSE, one or more Modern Foreign Languages and at least two sciences through to GCSE level. Apart from these compulsory subjects, pupils are examined in four other subjects chosen from French, Latin, History, Geography, German, Russian, Spanish, Drama, Design and Technology, Classical Civilisation, Art and Design, Computer Science, Philosophy, Religion and Ethics, and Music.

In the Sixth Form, A Level subjects are chosen from the following:

Mathematics, Further Mathematics, Physics, Chemistry, Biology, Computer Science, Latin, Economics, Business, Art, Fine Art, Art Textiles, Design Technology, Music, History, Geography, English Literature, French, German, Russian, Politics, Psychology, PE, Philosophy, Religion and Ethics, and Theatre Studies. The School also runs Level 3 BTEC in Sports and Exercise.

In addition to their A Level studies, Sixth Formers participate in a Life Skills Programme called The Edge, designed to complement and broaden the conventional curriculum in areas such as Cooking, The Law, Digital Lifestyle, Travel and Health and Fitness for Life. Students are also able to gain an ILM qualification as well as the Extended Project Qualification (EPQ).

Clubs, Trips and Activities. All are encouraged to participate in a variety of co-curricular activities which take place in lunchtimes, after school, at weekends and during the holidays. One afternoon a week is devoted to a host of community service activities, such as music and drama in the community, volunteering at local Primary schools and Special schools, journalism for internal publications, CCF (Army and RAF contingents) and a variety of sports and other pursuits. Sixth Formers may participate in the School's Leadership Programme at this time.

Drama in the school is particularly strong; continuous activity in this sphere maintains a succession of productions throughout the year, in all age groups. Productions have included: *Little Shop of Horrors, Amphibious Spangulatoas* and *Dark Tales* and in early 2020 our Sixth Form production was the play *Road*.

Ipswich School's Britten Faculty of Music has an impressive reputation as a place where musicians thrive, finding unstinting support from expert staff. Opportunities abound for enjoyable music-making, including Symphony, Intermediate and Chamber Orchestras; Chapel Choir; Wolsey Consort; Show Choir; Choral Society; Intermediate String Ensemble and various Chamber Music Groups; Big Band, Stage Band and Sax Ensemble. We have an annual concert at the world renowned Snape Maltings concert halls,

featuring ensembles from the Senior School and Prep School; our concerts have included Elgar's 'Pomp and Circumstance March, No. 4' and Elgar's 'Serenade for Strings'. We have a popular annual music competition which culminates in a 'Young Musician of the Year' final, and the Preparatory School runs its own Summer Strings course. Our annual Festival of Music brings world-renowned musicians into the school environment. Highlights of the Festival have included jazz musician Courtney Pike, The Swingles and Sara Dowling and the Chris Ingham Trio. Our state-of-the-art Music School was officially opened in March 2016 by Julian Lloyd Webber.

Duke of Edinburgh's Award. The School runs a successful Duke of Edinburgh Award scheme. In 2020, 75 of our Year 10 pupils entered the Bronze Award and participated in an expedition that saw them exploring the Suffolk countryside to the North and East of Ipswich. In 2020, we also saw pupils enrol on to the Silver and Gold Awards. Two of our overseas students continued their Gold Skill activities, via the internet, whilst residing in Hong Kong during the lockdown period. This year saw two of our Year 12 pupils become Regional Duke of Edinburgh Award Ambassadors, one of the tasks they have taken on is helping the Bronze participants complete their award.

Games. Our key aim is to support the development of individuals at every level, whatever their sport of choice. In line with the school's core values, our sports ethos centres around passion, potential and performance. We aim to develop an environment where athletes set realistic but challenging goals, are encouraged to be curious, creative and take risks, and are given opportunities to express themselves without fear of failure. Success is judged and celebrated not just on the outcome, but on the process and the spirit of sport. It is our goal that every pupil who participates in sport at School feels important, supported and has a sense of belonging to not just their team, but Ipswich Sport as a whole. The termly sports for boys are rugby, hockey and cricket and for girls, hockey, netball and cricket in the summer. These take place on our excellent Notcutts playing fields and our Sports Centre at Rushmere, which boasts 3 hybrid hockey pitches and 6 netball/tennis courts. In addition to termly sports, pupils have the opportunity to be involved in a range of other sports including indoor hockey, athletics, golf, tennis, Eton fives, football, squash, sailing, badminton and swimming. Ipswich School has links with a number of external clubs and academies and we are proud of our range of sports touring opportunities on offer to our pupils.

Fees per term (2021–2022). Day: Senior School £5,641; Lower School £5,167; Preparatory School: £4,470 (Years 4–6), £4,712 (Year 3 inc lunch); Pre-Preparatory School (Years 1 & 2) £4,288 (inc lunch); Reception £3,638 (inc lunch).

Boarding (inclusive of tuition fees): Full Boarding: £11,419 (Years 9–13); Weekly Boarding: £10,365 (Years 9–13). Please note that we only accept full boarders in Year 7 and 8 under exceptional circumstances.

Scholarships. These are available for external candidates at Years 7, 9 and 12 entry.

Academic scholarships of up to half fees are awarded at Years 7 and 9 entry on the basis of examinations and an assessment visit. Our very top Academic Scholars are known as Queen's Scholars, commemorating the Royal Charter granted to the School by Queen Elizabeth I in 1566. Art, Music and Sport scholarships are awarded at Year 7 entry. All-Rounder, Art, Sport and Music scholarships are awarded at Year 9 entry. Music and Art scholarships are awarded on the basis of excellence in these areas as demonstrated by audition or portfolio. Music auditions for promising instrumentalists entering Years 7 and 9 are held in January. Sport scholarships are awarded to pupils who will make a significant contribution to the quality of sport at the School.

Sixth Form Scholarships are awarded for academic excellence, for exceptional musical talent and for an all-rounder who will do well academically and contribute outstandingly in other areas of school life such as sport, art or drama. Academic Scholarships are awarded on the basis of school reports, predicted GCSE grades, interview, group activity and scholarship essay. Sixth Form Music scholarship auditions are held in November. A Sports scholarship is also available at 16. We also support Arkwright Scholarships, which focus on Design Technology.

Awards may be supplemented by bursaries in cases of proven need.

Bursaries. These are available on a means-tested basis, up to full fee remission, for entry at 11, 13 and 16 years.

The Old Ipswichian Club. The alumni association for former pupils of Ipswich School. Annual dinners are held in London and Ipswich, and many less formal socials are held in a variety of venues each year. Sports gatherings are held for cricket, fives, golf, rugby and cross-country.

Charitable status. Ipswich School is a Registered Charity, number 310493. It exists for the purpose of educating children.

Visitor: Her Majesty The Queen

Governing Body:
H E Staunton, BA, FCA (*Chairman*)
N C Farthing, LLB (*Vice Chairman*)
Dr E Alimeta, MB, BS, MJePer, MRCGP, DFSRH
Prof M Bailey, BA, PhD
W D Coe, BSc
The Revd Dr G M W Cook, MSc, PhD, FIBiol, FRSC
R Cooper, BSc, MS
Mrs J Crame, BSc, ACA, PGCE
J S Davey, BA, MBA
Dr R E Gravell, PhD, BMEdSci, BSc, MRCSLT, MUKCP
E B Hyams, BScEng, ACGI, CDIPAF, MIET
C Oxborough, BSc, FCA
A C Seagers, BA
Rt Revd M A Seeley, MA, STM, Bishop of St
　Edmundsbury & Ipswich (*ex officio*)
M Taylor, BA, ACA
Dr R A Watts, MA, DM, FRCP
Dr T A H Wilkinson, MA, PhD
R P E Wilson, MA, ARCM

Headmaster: **N J Weaver**, BA, MA

Senior Deputy Head (*Pastoral*): Mrs A Cura, BSc
Deputy Head (*Academic*): T Allen, BSc
Head of Sixth Form: B Cliff, MA
Head of Middle School: A R Bradshaw, BA
Head of Lower School: Ms A Caston, BSc
Chaplain: The Revd Holly Crompton-Battersby, BA, BTh

Heads of Houses:
J W Orbell, BSc
S J Blunden, BA
D J Beasant, BA

J Steward, BSc
Mrs H L Steele, BSc
L Morgan, BSc

Heads of Department:
Art and Design: R J Parkin, BA
Biology: Mrs H Blee, BSc
Sixth Form Careers: A M Calver, BSc
Computer Science: S J Dove
Chemistry & Science: D J P Halford-Thompson, BSc
Classical Civilisation: Miss K Hutton, BA, MEd
Design Technology: M A J Molenaar, BEng
Drama: Mrs S Pitt, BA
Economics & Business Studies: E R Wilson, BEd
English: Ms N S Carter, BA
Geography: R G Welbourne, BA, FRGS
History: Mrs O E Tollemache, BA
Learning Support & EAL: K F Allen
Life Skills: S J Duncombe, BA
Mathematics: M J Core, BSc
Modern Languages: J A Thompson, MA
Music: Mrs B Steensma, BEd (*Director of Music*)

Physical Education:
Mr B H Edmondson (*Director of Sport*)
Mrs S M Carvell, BA (*Curriculum PE*)
Mrs C J Ward, BSc (*A Level PE*)

Physics: S A Arthur, MSc, BEng
Psychology: Mrs N Smith, BSc
Philosophy, Religion & Ethics: Ms T Walker, MSci Ed

Head of Preparatory School: Mrs A H Childs, BA QTS,
　PGC PSE, DipEd, MA

Bursar: P Wranek, BSc, ACA
Admissions Manager: Mrs L J Trainer
Headmaster's PA: Mrs Y R Gills

James Allen's Girls' School (JAGS)

144 East Dulwich Grove, London SE22 8TE

Tel:　　　　020 8693 1181
email:　　　enquiries@jags.org.uk
website:　　www.jags.org.uk
Twitter:　　@JAGSschool
Facebook:　@JAGSschool
Instagram:　@JAGSschool

JAGS is set in 22 acres of grounds in North Dulwich, with extensive playing fields and long-established Botany gardens. The school buildings include a community music centre with purpose-built practice rooms, well-equipped modern library, 13 science laboratories, a purpose-built suite of language laboratories, 6 art rooms, 4 computer rooms, design technology workshops, swimming pool, floodlit artificial turf pitch, dance studio, sports hall with squash court, fitness studios and a climbing wall and a professionally-managed theatre. The Sixth Form Centre has its own tutorial rooms, common rooms and lecture theatre.

JAGS Senior School has approximately 800 pupils with 200 in the Sixth Form. About a third of girls come up from our Junior School, James Allen's Junior School, with about two-thirds entering from other preparatory and state primary schools.

Girls follow a broad curriculum with a wide choice of GCSE/IGCSE and A level options.

The co-curricular programme is a key part of a JAGS education. The excellent Prissian Theatre enables first-class, full-scale drama productions, while the active music department plays a central role, offering some 30 ensembles including 6 choirs, 4 orchestras, brass ensembles, wind ensembles plus jazz and big bands. A great variety of other interests is encouraged, from The Duke of Edinburgh's Award, debating, photography, and the Literary Society, to Politics and Amnesty International. Study visits to Russia, France, Italy, Spain and the USA are regularly organised. The choirs, orchestras and sports teams also visit overseas. Community Action plays an important part in school life, and there are extensive partnership activities with other local schools and community groups.

There are a multitude of sports taught including hockey, netball, football, cricket, basketball, gymnastics, dance, tennis, rounders, swimming and athletics. There are also opportunities to do yoga, badminton, rowing, sailing, golf and BMX biking.

Fees per term (2021–2022): £6,615

Admission. Girls are mainly admitted at 11+ and also into the Sixth Form. Casual vacancies at other ages.

Entrance Examination: For details and method of admission, please visit www.jags.org.uk.

Scholarships and Bursaries. JAGS strives to attract intellectually curious girls, regardless of their economic background, and so they have their own means-tested bursary scheme for all year groups from 11+ entry upwards. They also offer scholarships to pupils who show exceptional potential academically and in Art, Music and Sport at 11+, deferred 13+ and 16+ entry. Sports scholarships are also offered at 11+ and deferred 13+ entry.

Their **bursaries** are crucial in making them accessible to everyone, not just to those whose families can afford the fees. They provide financial assistance for up to 100% of fees as well as the costs of uniform, travel, trips and lunches. Bursaries cover well over 80% of all fees for the 130 pupils whose families currently receive them. Bursaries may be awarded on entry across all year groups and may also help current pupils continue their education at JAGS should their families' financial circumstances change.

Charitable status. James Allen's Girls' School is a Registered Charity, number 1124853 and exists for the purpose of educating girls.

Governors:
Mr David Miller, MA, FCSI (*Chair*)
Mr Alan Bird, BA Cantab, MSC
Richard Collins, MA Oxon, FCA, CF
Sarah Drennan-Jones
Milind Dhuru, FCA, MBA
Adrian Floyd, BSc Hons, PGCE
Victoria Hyndman, MBA
Alexandra Loydon
Ms Gerri McAndrew, OBE, Hon MLitt, BA Hons
Dr Jane Marshall, FRCPsych
Dame Erica Pienaar DBE, BA Hons, MBA, FRSA
The Hon Dr Rema Kaur Wasan, MA Cantab, MBBS Lon, MRCP, FRCR UK
Ms Sonia Watson OBE, MBA, Hon FRIBA
Mr Nick Wood, MA, MEng

Head: **Mrs Alex Hutchinson**, MA Oxon, PGCE

Head of Junior School: Miss Finola Stack, BA Hons, MA Ed, PGCE, Mont Dip

Director of Finance & Clerk to the Governors: Mr Jason Peck, Chartered Accountant, Member of the ICAEW, BSc Hons

Deputy Head, *Academic*: Laurence Wesson, BSc Hons

Deputy Head, *Pastoral*: Samantha Payne, BA Hons

Deputy Head, *Community & Co-Curricular*: Rhona Muir, MA Oxon, MSc

Director of Operations: Justine Addison, MA

The John Lyon School

Harrow-on-the-Hill, Middle Road, London HA2 0HN

Tel: 020 8515 9400
email: admissions@johnlyon.org
website: www.johnlyon.org
Twitter: @JohnLyonHarrow
Facebook: @johnlyonharrow
Instagram: @johnlyonharrow
LinkedIn: /school/johnlyonharrow

Motto: Stet Fortuna Domus

John Lyon is an academically selective, coeducational independent day school in Harrow-on-the-Hill in North West London.

2021–2022 marks the beginning of coeducation at John Lyon, with girls joining the School in Year 7 for the first time in our 145-year history. We also now offer an all-through education from Nursery, aged 2½, to A Level, aged 18, thanks to our coming together with Quainton Hall School in central Harrow, which now becomes John Lyon's Prep School.

Academic excellence is at the very heart of what pupils who study here seek to achieve. With the opportunity to explore a broad curriculum and gain a solid grounding in all the major academic subjects, pupils work alongside dedicated teachers to develop learning skills, creativity and the ability to fully apply themselves in all areas of life.

Building on this platform, pupils perform well from the point they join the School – whether at age 11, 13 or 16 – and achieve excellent results in public examinations at GCSE and A Level. Most students are rewarded for their hard work by gaining places at leading UK universities, before moving on into the workplace in a huge and varied range of valued professions.

John Lyon pupils also gain from their time outside the classroom. The School has a strong reputation for opportunities and success in Music, Art, Drama and Sport. Add to this an exciting Co-Curricular Programme focusing on each pupil's sense of community, achievement and wellbeing, a range of more than 100 extra-curricular activities, and pastoral care that is second to none, a John Lyon education is designed to nurture high-achieving and happy children.

Admission. John Lyon offers a broad education to pupils who aspire to achieve excellence in all they do. As such, the admissions procedure is designed both to reveal applicants' ability as well as to judge their potential. The School offers places to able young pupils who have a great attitude to learning combined with a desire to be the best that they can be.

Pupils typically join John Lyon in Years 7, 9 and the Lower Sixth, largely from a North West London catchment area, including the Boroughs of Harrow, Hillingdon, Ealing, Brent, Barnet, Camden, Westminster, Kensington & Chelsea and Hammersmith & Fulham, as well parts of Middlesex, Berkshire, Buckinghamshire and Hertfordshire.

The School prides itself in its welcoming and helpful approach to admissions, for children at 11+, 13+ and at 16+ into the Sixth Form.

11+ selection is based on English and Mathematics examinations, participation in a group activity and an interview. 13+ selection includes examinations in English, Mathematics, French and Science, as well as an interview with the Head. 16+ entry is by interview and results at GCSE.

Curriculum. The academic curriculum is at the heart of every working day at John Lyon – it forms the core of all the School seeks to achieve as a leading place of learning. English, Mathematics, the sciences, humanities, creative arts, languages and digital learning form a curriculum designed to educate and inspire, giving knowledge and a desire to want to know more.

The School places a large emphasis on Learning Skills, which apply to all areas of a pupil's experience and success at John Lyon, both inside and outside the classroom. With a focus on reading, the chance to work on extra projects and through the wide range of activities on offer, Learning Skills enhance each pupil's communication, self-reflection and evaluation, logical and critical thinking, independent learning, academic writing and transferable skills.

John Lyon is also a proudly digital school, recognised as one of the leading 50 digital innovation schools in the UK and praised for its use of technology in the classroom to enhance learning outcomes. A School Managed Device policy means all students have a laptop or tablet with them during the School day, allowing them to access content and complete assessed work online while taking more ownership and responsibility for their learning. Pupils in Years 7, 8 and 9 follow a Digital Learning curriculum beginning with essential skills such as online safety training to understand how to use the internet and digital technology responsibly.

Scholarships. All pupils who take the 11+ or 13+ entrance examination will be considered for an Academic Scholarship. Their performance in the examination, their school reference and their interview will all be taken into consideration. Sixth Form Scholarships are awarded dependent on GCSE results. The School also awards a small number of Scholarships to candidates of outstanding ability and potential in Drama, Music, Sport, Art and STEAM.

Bursaries. In line with the purpose of the School at its founding almost 150 years ago, John Lyon remains committed to widening access for local families. Each year, the School makes available a number of means-tested bursaries to pupils who demonstrate exceptional talent and potential.

School Buildings. The main School buildings house the Science and STEAM laboratories, Drama studios, Art studios, gallery and the Boyd Campbell Hall. The Music School has a 120-seat recital hall, a recording studio and eight individual practice studios. The sports complex comprises a 25-metre indoor swimming pool, fitness studio and sports hall.

Games. A floodlit multi-use games area allows for all-weather Hockey and Tennis at the 25-acre Sudbury Playing Fields, a short distance from the main School site. There are four main Cricket squares, seven Football pitches, a challenge course, pavilion and Archery range. Pupils also use sporting facilities at Harrow School including Cricket nets, Athletics track, nine-hole Golf course, Tennis, Squash and Badminton courts.

The main Sports are Association Football and Hockey in the Autumn and Spring Terms, and Cricket, Athletics, Tennis and Swimming in the Summer Term, supported by Badminton, Basketball, Archery, Water Polo, Golf and other games.

Co-Curricular Programme. On Friday afternoons at John Lyon all pupils put their Academic timetables to one side and participate in the School's broad, engaging and fascinating Co-Curricular Programme.

The Co-Curricular Programme offers something different to pupils beyond the classroom and is aimed at developing a sense of achievement, wellbeing and enjoyment, while gaining practical skills and engaging with the eight School Values. The John Lyon Co-Curricular Programme is an important and integral part of the School timetable and wider School life, designed to add to pupil learning and introduce pupils to exciting new ideas and opportunities, which will help them in School, outside School and beyond into higher education and the workplace.

Extra-Curricular. John Lyon's extra-curricular sports practices, clubs and activities are a much-loved element of School life, aimed at encouraging curiosity, furthering knowledge and nurturing passions outside the timetable. The School's extra-curricular activities are second to none and allow every pupil to flourish as an individual. John Lyon believes that options beyond the classroom are essential to balance the learning in class. They help pupils build resilience, teamwork and leadership, and are seen by many as a distinguishing feature on a university application form and then on a CV. But above all, a well-rounded pupil is a happy pupil. John Lyon typically offers more than 100 clubs and societies every week that provide a wealth of experiences and opportunities to every pupil.

Charity and Community. The charitable ethos that has run through John Lyon since its founding in 1876 shows no sign of slowing, and this generation of pupils, like their predecessors, engage in numerous charitable and community projects, giving time and raising money for projects in Harrow and beyond.

John Lyon's public benefit objectives are to support the wider community through the sharing of expertise and facilities in Sport, the arts and academia. The School has strong links with schools in the maintained sector, who regularly join events; facilities are used by local schools and community groups; pupils raise significant sums for local, national and international charities; access to a John Lyon education is widened through scholarship and bursary awards; and pupils are seen out in the community all year round, giving their time to local initiatives.

The School is part of John Lyon's Foundation, an educational foundation also consisting Harrow School and John Lyon's Charity. The Foundation aims to maximise the opportunities for children and young people by enabling them to realise their potential, broaden their horizons and ultimately enable them to experience and enjoy a better quality of life.

Careers. Specialist advice concerning entrance to Higher Education is given and there is a team of specialists in the Sixth Form Centre to offer guidance and support with UCAS, university choices, Oxbridge preparation and careers.

Entry to University. 2021 university destinations included a broad range of Russell Group universities such as Oxford, Durham, Warwick and Imperial, and especially institutions within the University of London, notably UCL and KCL.

The Lyonian Association. All pupils leaving the School become life members of the Association. The Association has shared use of the School's sports ground, and its own pavilion at Sudbury Fields.

Fees per term (2021–2022). Years 7 to Lower Sixth: £6,637 (including lunch); Upper Sixth: £6,393 (lunch optional).

Charitable status. The Keepers and Governors of the Free Grammar School of John Lyon is a Registered Charity, number 310033.

Governors:
Mr G Goodfellow, QC, MA, LLM (*Chairman*)
Mr N Enright, MA Oxon, MBA, NPQH, FRSA [OL]
  (*Deputy Chairman*)
Mr R Fox, LLB Hons [OL]
Mr G Stavrinidis, BSc Eng, MBA, DipM [OL]
Dr S Jollyman, MB ChB, MRCGP
Mr I Kendrick, BEd Hons, MA
Mr D Tidmarsh, BSc Hons, PGCE
Mr J Graham, BSc Hons, MRICS [OL]
Mr L Halligan, MPhil Econ, BSc Hons [OL]
Mr R Winter, CBE, FCA
Mrs C Southgate, B Bus Acc, FCA
Mr A Smith, BA, DipRAM, ARAM
Professor J Greenwood, PhD, FRCPath
Mr Anup Vyas, LLB Hons [OL]
Mr Gary Grant, BA Hons [OL]
Mrs Kay Burnaby

Clerk to the Board of Governors: The Hon Andrew Millett, MA [OL]

[OL] *Old Lyonian*

Head: **Miss K Haynes**, BA Warwick, MEd Birmingham, NPQH

Deputy Heads:
Mr J Pepperman, MA Cantab
Mr A Sims, MA, MEng Cantab

Assistant Heads:
Mr T Lewis, MA, MEng Cantab (*Academic*)
Mr J Rowe, MA UEA (*Pastoral*)

Senior Teachers:
Mr R Lokier, BA Cantab (*Director of Studies*)
Dr F Weinberg, BSc, MSc, PhD Imperial (*Director of Admissions*)

Chief Operating Officer: Mr G Mawdsley, MA Cantab

Kelvinside Academy

33 Kirklee Road, Glasgow G12 0SW

Tel: 0141 357 3376
email: rector@kelvinside.org
website: www.kelvinside.org
Twitter: @kelvinside1878
Facebook: /KelvinsideAcademy

Motto: ΑΙΕΝ ΑΡΙΣΤΕΥΕΙΝ

Kelvinside Academy was founded in 1878. Since May 1921, it has been run by the Kelvinside Academy War Memorial Trust, which was formed in memory of the Academicals who gave their lives in the War of 1914–18. The affairs of the Trust are managed by a Board of Governors.

Kelvinside Academy is a co-educational day school for some 650 pupils, aged 3 to 18.

The main building is in neo-classical style and Grade A listed but has been extensively modernised within. Further buildings and extensions provide excellent facilities for all subjects and interests, and are symptomatic of the school's progressive approach. Recent additions include Scotland's Innovation School, state-of-the-art IT and multimedia suites, custom-built nursery, library upgrade and sports pavilion.

Curriculum. Junior School pupils (from J1) benefit from specialist input in Nuvu Innovation, Art, Music, PE and Modern Languages. The Senior Prep (P7) year is a transitional year with a core curriculum taught by the class teacher but science, languages, art, music and PE are delivered by secondary specialists. Computing is a core compulsory subject up to S4.

Senior 3 and 4 pupils follow eight National 4 or 5 courses, followed by Higher and Advanced Higher courses in Senior 5 and 6.

Combined Cadet Force. The hugely popular CCF is compulsory for one year in Senior 3. Pupils also embark upon The Duke of Edinburgh's Award scheme at this stage.

Games. Rugby and hockey are the principal team games in the winter terms with athletics, tennis and cricket in the summer. A range of additional sports and games, from handball and football to basketball and dance, is offered.

Activities. A rich programme of extracurricular and House activities contributes significantly to the broad educational experience enjoyed by all pupils.

The Expressive Arts. Music, drama, dance and the visual arts have a central role in both the curriculum and the co-curriculum.

Fees per term (2021–2022). Nursery £820–£3,060, Junior School £3,000–£4,100, Senior School £4,390–£4,630.

Admission. For Nursery and P1, children undergo an informal assessment. For P2 to Senior 3, children sit an entrance test and informal interview. For Senior 4 to Senior 6, entry is by interview, school report and exam results.

Bursaries. Financial support with fees (ranging from 10%–100%) is available to P7 and Senior School pupils.

Charitable status. The Kelvinside Academy War Memorial Trust is a Registered Charity, number SC003962. The purpose of the Trust is to run a combined primary and secondary day school in memory of those former pupils of the school who gave their lives in the war of 1914–18.

Board of Governors:
Mr D Wilson, BAcc, CA (*Chairman*)
Mr A Tear (*ex officio*)
Professor W Cushley, BSc, PhD, FSB
Mr C J Mackenzie, LLB, Dip LP, NP
Mr A Palmer, BAcc, CA
Mrs S Taylor
Mr A McKendrick
Mr D Morwood
Mrs J MacGeachy
Mrs N Hinde
Mr Mel Scott
Ms L Baxendale
Ms M Carey

Rector: **Mr D J Wyatt**

Chief Operating Officer: Mr D Pocock
Deputy Rector: Ms D Gallacher
Academic Deputy: Mr C Derrick
Assistant Deputy: Mr J I Cuthbertson
Head of Junior School: Mrs C Sweeney
Director of Admissions & Communications: Mrs K Bottomley

Kent College

Canterbury, Kent CT2 9DT

Tel: 01227 813906
email: admissions@kentcollege.co.uk
website: kentcollege.com
Twitter: @kentcollegehm
Facebook: @kentcollege
LinkedIn: /Kent-College-Canterbury

Motto: *Lux tua via mea*

This outstanding boarding and day school is situated on the rural edge of the beautiful City of Canterbury. Students come to the school from the age of three through to eighteen. The majority of students live within an hour of the school. However, the school also has a strong and fully integrated boarding community of children from the age of seven; these children come from all over the world and add an exciting international aspect to the school. Academic, sporting and musical achievements are nationally acclaimed. Parents choose the school for its warm, friendly and welcoming nature where their children are encouraged to achieve all that they can, in a happy and supportive environment.

Facilities. The Junior and Senior schools occupy two independent sites. All of the six boarding houses are situated on site. Both of the schools are surrounded by extensive playing fields which are used throughout the school day. Modern classrooms and provision of laptops to senior school students, distinguishes Kent College as a market leader in education. Excellent sport, music and drama facilities are augmented by the highest level of teaching and coaching.

The Great Hall is an impressive 600-seat auditorium that provides cutting-edge facilities for worship, concerts and the performing arts. The Great Hall is an important step for Kent College in building a world-class campus, and it is used as a versatile and practical space for the school's highly regarded Drama and Music departments, as well as for the wider local community. The school also runs its own farm and equine unit.

Curriculum. The curriculum is aligned to the National Curriculum but a greater range of subjects is provided. It is not the aim to specialise in any one group of subjects but to provide a balanced curriculum which will give full opportunity for students to get a good grounding of general knowledge and later to develop particular talents to a high standard. We pride ourselves on being able to provide a personalised learning experience, where we can organise the curriculum to suit the child.

The International Baccalaureate is offered alongside A Levels in the Sixth Form with outstanding results in both.

Learning Support Centre. The Learning Support Centre is a haven of help for those amongst the school intake that need extra support. Students are taught all the mechanisms that they need to access the whole curriculum. Support remains a constant throughout the child's time here.

International Study Centre. Small group lessons and specific language assistance provide a useful platform for those students who arrive without an adequate level of English. These students are then integrated into the mainstream classes at a pace that suits them.

Pastoral Care. The school operates closely with each student and the student's parents to ensure that there is an open line of communication. Each student is individually supported by a strong team: house parents; heads of house and lower school heads of house; tutors; teachers and peer mentors all of whom take a significant interest in looking after the needs of each individual.

Religion. As a Methodist school a strong Christian ethos purveys all that the school does. Students of all faiths and no faith are welcomed in the school.

Games and Activities. The school possesses 28 acres of playing fields and a floodlit all-weather hockey pitch. The major games for boys are Rugby, Hockey, Tennis, Cricket and Athletics and for girls Netball, Hockey, Tennis, Cricket, and Athletics. Hockey is a particular strength with teams regularly attaining National championship status. Representative honours are common occurrence in all sports. The boarding community enjoys full use of the facilities in the evening with regular activities in Basketball, Football and Fitness Training. Senior pupils take part in various forms of community service in the City and the school also has its own Duke of Edinburgh's Award group. There is a full range of optional school activities, including Art, Debating, Chess, Conservation, CDT and Photography. The School has its own farm and developing equine unit which provides countless opportunities for outdoor adventure and agricultural experiences.

Music and Drama. Music and drama play an important part in the life of the school.

There are four choirs, two orchestras, a jazz band, rock groups and a variety of other specialist ensembles and singing groups. Many concerts are given each year, including the annual Carol Service in Canterbury Cathedral. The last whole-school production was *My Fair Lady*, which was a great success!

Admission. The usual ages of admission to the Senior School are 11, 13 and 16. Entrance Examinations usually take place in the Spring Term for admission the following September.

Fees per term (2021–2022). Day Pupils: £5,797–£6,665; Boarders: £8,967–£12,339 (full). International Study Centre: £1,350 extra.

Entrance Scholarships. The school awards academic, music, sport, drama and art scholarships to pupils for entry into Years 7, 9 and 12. Scholarships normally carry a value equivalent to a percentage remission of the tuition fees which would not exceed a maximum of 50% and would be at the discretion of the Head Master. Full particulars may be obtained from the Registrar.

Academic scholarships for Years 7 and 9 are awarded as a result of performance in our Entrance Test, usually held in the Spring Term, for entry the following September. Sixth Form academic scholarships are awarded on the basis of existing performance, a detailed report from the Head of Year or current school, and confirmation of high levels of performance in the final GCSEs. The school also offers specific scholarships for the International Baccalaureate.

Music/Drama GTX scholarships of up to half the tuition fee are offered in conjunction with the Entrance Test to candidates for entry into Years 7, 9 and 12. Free tuition on two instruments is offered to Music Scholars.

Sports GTX scholarships of up to half the tuition fee are awarded to pupils for entry into Years 7, 9 and 12. For Years 7 and 9 these will be awarded in the Spring Term in conjunction with the Entrance Test and on the basis of assessment at Kent College. For Year 12, Sports scholarships will be based on current performance and other assessment methods during the year. Scholars receive 1:1 coaching, physiotherapy support and enjoy a programme of nationally recognised motivational speakers.

Bursaries will be awarded in accordance with, and after consideration of, the financial circumstances of parents. Parents will be invited to complete a financial assessment form and the scale of bursary awarded will be based on the information provided and the financial criteria which the school applies to all bursary awards. All bursaries are reviewed annually.

In addition, the school operates an awards system for the children of HM Forces, NATO and War Graves Commission personnel, whereby the parents pay a set figure, normally 10% of the inclusive fee, plus the amount of Boarding School Allowance which they receive. The balance is treated as a Bursary Award.

Honours. Most school leavers go on to Russell Group and other top universities both in the UK and abroad. Each year a number of pupils secure offers of places at Oxford and Cambridge.

Charitable status. Kent College, Canterbury is part of the Methodist Independent Schools Trust, which is a Registered Charity, number 1142794. The School was founded to provide education within a supportive Christian environment.

Governors:
Chair: Mrs L Cocking, BA
Secretary to the Governors and Bursar: Mrs K Simpson

Executive Head: **Mr M Turnbull**, BA Liverpool, MA London

Deputy Head: Mr G Letley, BA Kent

Chaplain: Revd Dr P Glass, BA Leeds, MA Cantab, PhD Leeds

Director of Marketing and Admissions: Mrs Andrea Warden
Executive Head's PAs: hm@kentcollege.co.uk

Head of Junior School: Mr S James
Head of Junior School's PA: Miss H Bayly
(See entry in IAPS section)

Kimbolton School

Kimbolton, Huntingdon, Cambs PE28 0EA

Tel: 01480 860505
email: headmaster@kimbolton.cambs.sch.uk
website: www.kimbolton.cambs.sch.uk
Twitter: @KimboltonSchool
Facebook: @KimboltonSchool
Instagram: @Kimbolton_School

Motto: *Spes Durat Avorum*

The School was founded in 1600 and was awarded Direct Grant status as a boys' day and boarding school in 1945. Girls were first admitted in 1976. The Preparatory School (ages 4–11) and the Senior School are fully co-educational with day boys and girls (4–18) and boarding boys and girls (11–18). As a result of the withdrawal of the Direct Grant the School assumed fully independent status in 1978. There are around 300 pupils in the Prep School and 760 pupils in the Senior School. There is almost a 1:1 ratio of girls to boys.

Mission Statement. Kimbolton School creates a caring, challenging environment in which all pupils are encouraged to fulfil their potential and are given opportunities to flourish in a wide variety of curricular and extra-curricular interests.

It provides a close family environment where young people are educated to be tolerant, socially responsible and independent of mind, equipping them for our changing world. It is a community that challenges pupils to discover their talents, develop socially and excel.

Facilities. The Senior School facilities are situated in and around the main school building, Kimbolton Castle, once the home of Queen Katharine of Aragon and for three centuries the home of the Dukes of Manchester. Now, with its Vanbrugh front and Pellegrini murals, it is a building of considerable beauty and architectural importance. The former State Rooms are study areas for senior pupils and the Castle Chapel is used each day for prayers.

The Queen Katharine Building is a state-of-the-art teaching and learning centre, complete with a 120-seat multimedia lecture theatre. Its two-storey Science and Maths wing provides outstanding facilities including 12 laboratories and a digital learning suite. The Lewis Hall caters for the performing arts and daily assemblies and provides modern theatre and concert facilities. The Design Technology Engineering Centre is up-to-date and well-equipped, as is the Music School.

A large sports complex, incorporating squash courts, gymnasium, sports hall, multi-gym and changing rooms stands in the Castle's parkland. Closer to the Castle itself, lie a modern Art Centre, Library and a 25m indoor swimming pool. The School has two fine all-weather hockey pitches, one of which is floodlit.

Our separate girls' and boys' boarding houses stand adjacent to the grounds in the picturesque Kimbolton High Street. The boarding community is an important part of the School.

The Prep School is located to the west of Kimbolton village, at the opposite end of our 120 acres of parkland and playing fields. It has, on site, a dining hall, library, digital suite, assembly hall, music teaching and practice rooms, science laboratory, art and design technology room, and sports hall, as well as large, light and airy classrooms.

We are very much one school: the curricula of the Prep and Senior Schools are aligned, our warm caring ethos starts at Reception Year and continues through to the Upper Sixth; and some of our staff teach at both the Prep and Senior Schools.

Admission and Organisation. The Prep School admits children at 4+, 7+ and 9+ (as day pupils) with the expectation that they will complete their education in the Senior School. Entry at other ages is sometimes possible. Tests for entry at the Prep School are held in February. Entry into the Senior School at the age of 11 is open to boarders and day pupils; the Senior School Entrance examinations are also held in February. There are also entries at 13+, usually by the Common Entrance Examination in June. Those not preparing for Common Entrance may sit the School's own 13+ examination in February. Entry into the Sixth Form is based on interview and GCSE/IGCSE results.

Arrangements can be made for overseas candidates to take the entrance examination at their own schools.

Pupils are accepted in September at the start of the academic year, but a few places may be available for entry in other terms.

The relationship between the Prep and Senior Schools is a close one and contributes to the strong 'family' atmosphere of the whole School. In the Senior School, there are four senior houses and one junior house. It is an important element of our pastoral care that boarding pupils and day pupils are together – there are no day houses. Housemasters/Housemistresses, assisted by Tutors, look after the general well-being and progress of their charges.

Work and Curriculum. For the first two years in the Senior School there are four or five parallel forms; in each of the third, fourth and fifth years there are five or six smaller forms with sets for some subjects. Boys and girls entering at 13 join one of the Third Forms. An option scheme is introduced in the Fourth Form. In the Sixth Form specialisation occurs, and pupils will usually study three subjects from the following list: English Language; English Literature; History; Geography; French; Spanish; Maths; Further Maths; Physics; Chemistry; Biology; Music; Art (Fine Art); Art (Photography); Art (Critical and Contextual); Design Technology and Engineering; Drama and Theatre; Physical Education; Economics; Business; Politics; and Philosophy, Religion and Ethics.

Each A Level has a 7th period of subject enrichment, allowing students to explore topics beyond the curriculum. To widen their interests and experience, all students also choose to take an Extension Course in subjects including Astronomy, Classics, Robotics, Cooking For Life, Creative Writing, Debating, Digital Media, Ethical Philosophy, Music Technology, Political Ideas, Psychology and World of

Wine. All Sixth Formers follow a 'Preparing for Citizenship' series of lectures, seminars and debates. Almost all leavers gain places at the universities of their choice, with many heading to Oxbridge colleges and Russell Group universities

Religious Teaching. Our school is non-denominational with a Christian ethos and attracts children of all religions and none. Pupils attend Chapel once a week and have RS lessons each week in the First to Third Form. Other services are held in the School Chapel during each term for pupils and parents to attend. Sunday Services are held in the Chapel and occasionally the School worships in the Parish Church.

Sport and Activities. The School owns over 120 acres of land, more than 20 of which are laid out as playing fields. The major sports for boys are association football, hockey and cricket. For girls the main sports are hockey, netball and tennis. Other sports include girls' cricket, girls' football, athletics, gymnastics, dance, climbing, archery, swimming, golf, fitness training, rifle shooting, clay pigeon shooting, squash, badminton, basketball and rounders. Swimming is popular with before and after school sessions and numerous galas. Extensive use is also made by the sailing club of nearby Grafham Water, both for recreational sailing and inter-school matches. Canoeing is popular and each year a team competes in the highly demanding 125-mile Devizes–Westminster challenge. The equestrian club competes in around twenty fixtures during the course of the year. The aim is to find a sport that each pupil loves and will continue to enjoy long after leaving Kimbolton.

Music and drama play an important part in the life of the School and almost half of the pupils take lessons in a great variety of instruments. There is a Choral Society, two orchestras, several bands and many ensemble groups. The School stages plays, musicals or concerts each term.

The School contingent of the CCF is a voluntary, keen and efficient body, divided into Navy, Army and RAF Sections with a national reputation for excellence; Community Service is an alternative. There is a successful Duke of Edinburgh's Award scheme with a large number of participants.

There are many other activities and societies that meet on a regular basis, such as debating, public speaking, forensic science, photography, chess, robotics, motor vehicle engineering, bookworms, dance, beekeeping, gardening, medical society, modelling, pottery and philosophy.

All pupils are able to participate in the large number of trips in the UK and abroad.

Careers. Advice can be sought at any time by pupils or their parents from the Careers staff and we have excellent resources in the Careers Room. All pupils undertake an online profiling test at the end of the Fourth Form, which results in a personal careers guidance report. This is the basis for an individual, half-hour interview with a visiting Careers Guidance Institute-qualified interviewer early in the Fifth Form. Morrisby membership gives our pupils access to a lifelong range of resources and guidance. An annual HE, Gap and Careers Fair is held for Fourth to Sixth Formers.

Dress. The School colours are purple, black and white. Boys wear blazers and grey flannels (shorts until the final year in the Prep School). The girls' uniform includes a standard skirt, blouse and blazer. Sixth Formers wear a black suit.

Scholarships and Bursaries. A number of scholarships are awarded at 11+ and 13+ to candidates who perform with distinction in the Entrance Examination or in Common Entrance.

In addition, William Ingram Scholarships are awarded for 13+ entrants who excel at Music, Art or Games and Leadership.

Sixth Form Scholarships and Exhibitions are awarded to those who achieve outstanding results in GCSE.

There is a bursary scheme for deserving candidates aged 11 or over; bursaries may be awarded on their own or in addition to scholarships.

Fees per term (2021–2022). £3,433 (Lower Prep), £4,675 (Upper Prep), £5,725 (Senior Day), £9,520 (Senior Full Boarding), £8,950 (Senior Weekly Boarding). These figures include a 2% discount which is applied if fees are paid by termly direct debit.

The fees are inclusive of lunches and there is no charge for laundry, books and stationery.

There is a reduction of 2½% in tuition fees when siblings attend at the same time.

Music tuition Fee: £255–£300 per term for individual lessons. (Half a term's notice must be given in writing before a pupil discontinues music lessons.)

Old Kimboltonians Association. All correspondence to: Ms V Wakefield, Alumni Officer, OKA, Kimbolton School, Kimbolton, Huntingdon, Cambridgeshire PE28 0EA; email: alumni@kimbolton.cambs.sch.uk.

Charitable status. Kimbolton School Foundation is a Registered Charity, number 1098586.

Governing Body:
Cllr J A Gray (*Chairman*)
Mr J W Bridge, OBE, DL (*Vice Chairman*)
Mr P F R D Aylott, MA, MNI
Mrs S M Brereton
Mrs J L Doyle
Mr P J Farrar
Cllr I D Gardener
Cllr Mrs D Hellett
Mrs K E S Lancaster, MC Cantab, LPC/CPE
Dr P Loughna
Ms B E Madson
Mr S J F Page, BA Hons, Cert Ed
Mr G K Peace
Mrs T Reid
Mrs J L Rice
Mr D J Suckling
Mr G R Yeandle

Headmaster: **Mr J Belbin**, BA, FRSA

PA to the Headmaster: Mrs J Nelson-Lucas

Senior School:

Senior Deputy Headmaster: Mr M J Eddon, BSc
Deputy Head (Academic): R H Taylor, MA
Assistant Head (Extension & Enrichment): Mr J C Newsam, MA, MEd
Assistant Head (DSL): Mrs C A Stokes, BEd
Assistant Head (Staff): Mrs L A Hadden, BA
Director of Activities: Mr R E Knell, BA
Head of Sixth Form: Mr M S Gilbert, BEd

School Chaplain: Mr P J Crawford
Head of Careers: Mrs A J Bates, BA

Heads of Departments:
Art: Mrs L D Bamford, BA, MA
Biology: Mr P M Gillam, MA
Chemistry: Mr E C Drysdale, BSc
Design, Technology & Engineering: Mr K Spencer, BEd, MSc, MInstMI
Digital Learning: Mr M Reed, MEng
Drama: Mrs J C Webber, BA
Economics & Business Studies: Mr J R Saunders, BA
English: Mrs A E O'Donnell, MA
Food & Nutrition and Textiles: Mrs L King, BSc
Geography: Mr S Wilson, BA
History: Mr O J Chipperton, MA
Maths: Mr A S Jessup, BSc, MA
Modern Foreign Languages: Mrs M Viruete Navarro, MA
French: Mr R E Knell, BA
Spanish: Mrs M Viruete Navarro, MA
Music: Mr D Gibbs, MA, FRCO
Philosophy, Religion and Ethics: Mrs C E Thomas, MA
Physical Education: Miss T M Lloyd, BSc
Physics: Mr C M Holmes, BSc, BA
Politics: Mr F W B Leadbetter, MA, BD, AKC, FRSA, FRHistS
Academic Support: Ms R Stewart, BEd
Director of Sport: Mr C K Lawrence, BSc
Boys' Games: Mr A S Lawless
Girls' Games: Mrs E L R Lawless
Outdoor Pursuits: Mr J Sweet, BA

Preparatory School:

Headmaster of Preparatory School: Mr J P Foley, BA
Senior Deputy Head (DSL): Mr O C Stokes, BEd, MEd
Deputy Head (Academic): Mrs R L Lambert, BEd
Head of Lower Prep: Mrs L K Collins, BA

Bursar & Clerk to the Governors: Mrs J F Agnew, LLB Hons, LLM
Registrar: Mrs R White

King Edward VI School
Southampton

Wilton Road, Southampton, Hampshire SO15 5UQ

Tel: 023 8070 4561
email: registrar@kes.hants.sch.uk
website: www.kes.hants.sch.uk
Twitter: @KESSouthampton
Facebook: @KESSouthampton
Instagram: @kessouthampton

"After seven years of being a KES student, I can say for certain that I made the right choice of school. I was never the most academically able or sporty student but the culture here is one of developing existing skills, encouraging new talent and never leaving any individual to settle for anything less than that of which they are capable." – *Upper Sixth Student*

King Edward VI School was founded in 1553, making it the oldest in Southampton, with a long and distinguished history stretching back over 460 years. We are extremely proud of these traditional roots, but we are prouder yet to be recognised as a vibrant, modern institution, dedicated to equipping our pupils with the skills to thrive in the 21st century.

Admission. An entrance examination is held in January for boys and girls seeking to enter the First Year at age 11 or the Third Year at age 13 that September. Applications from able under-age candidates will also be considered. Smaller numbers of entrants are accepted into the other school years if there is space, provided the applicants are of suitable academic ability. Students may also apply to join the Sixth Form. In order to qualify for entrance to the Sixth Form a student will normally be required to have grade B (or a 6) or above in six subjects at GCSE, including English Language and Mathematics, and A grades in the subjects to be studied at A Level.

Registration for entry may be made at any time on a form obtainable via the school website or from the Registrar, who can supply current information about fees, bursaries and scholarships.

Class sizes average 22; the average size of Sixth Form sets is 8.

Curriculum. All pupils follow a common course in the first two years: this includes French or German or Spanish with Latin or Classical Civilisation, Mathematics, Science and an Extended Studies programme. In years 3, 4 and 5 all pupils study eight 'core' subjects to IGCSE: Biology, Chemistry, English Language, English Literature, a Modern Foreign Language, Mathematics, Religious Studies and Physics. In addition there is a range of 'option' subjects: Art, Computer Science, Design and Technology, Economics, Dance, French, Geography, German, History, Italian, Music, PE, Philosophy, Spanish, Sports Science and Theatre Studies. The syllabus leading to the IGCSE Examinations, in which most pupils take eleven subjects, is designed to avoid any premature specialisation. In the Sixth Form, students study four A Level subjects in the Lower Sixth and then at the end of this year choose to continue with all four or just to continue with three of the subjects. In addition, all have an afternoon of Games in both years and follow a Foundations Studies programme in both the Lower and Upper Sixth Year.

On entering the First Year, pupils join a form of about 22, with a Form Tutor responsible for their general welfare and progress. The other years are organised on a system of pastoral groups of about 16. Each group has its own Year Head. In addition there is a Head of Lower School who has general responsibility for the first three years; a Head of Upper School and a Director of the Sixth Form have similar responsibilities in their respective areas.

Our aim is to provide a congenial atmosphere and a disciplined environment in which able pupils can develop as individuals.

Academic. As a leading co-educational independent day school, King Edward's undoubtedly has high academic standards and expectations. Under the guidance of expert teaching staff, our pupils consistently excel in public examinations, and both GCSE and A Level results are exceptional. As a result, Sixth Form students regularly gain admittance to leading universities in this country and abroad; this year 87% of our students secured places at the UK's top 25 universities (including Russell Group and medical schools).

School Activities. 10% of a student's timetable is devoted to physical education as sport and games are regarded as forming an integral part of life at King Edward's. The major sports played in the three terms are rugby, hockey, cricket and tennis for boys; and netball, hockey, tennis and rounders for girls; other sporting activities include athletics, basketball, badminton, fencing, squash, swimming and a number of other games. The School has a large sports hall, a dance studio, and a fully equipped fitness studio and an all-weather pitch for hockey and similar games which provides twelve tennis courts in summer. There are a further 33 acres of off-site sports fields which include a second astro pitch and floodlit netball and tennis courts.

A considerable range of clubs and societies meets during lunchtime, after school, at weekends and in school holidays, catering for pupils of all ages and many differing tastes. All are encouraged to join some of these societies, in order to gain the greatest advantage from their time at the School.

In addition to a large number of sporting teams representing the School, there are such activities as charitable and community work, dance, drama, debating, chess, Duke of Edinburgh's Award scheme, international expeditions, sailing and numerous superb musical opportunities. The School has flourishing choirs, as well as orchestras and a large number of smaller instrumental groups. We have a brand new bright and large Art department and vibrant and well-equipped Design and Technology premises. The studios and workshops are usually open during lunchtimes and after school. Over the past 6 years the whole school has been expanded and refurbished with modern classrooms and specialist rooms. The Dobson Theatre was remodelled and refurbished in 2017, the dining room extended in 2018, and our central library was remodelled and extended in September 2019.

Fees per term (2021–2022). £5,877. Fees can be reduced in appropriate cases by the award of Bursaries and Scholarships. Scholarships are available on entry at age 11, 13, and 16. Further Scholarships may be awarded during a pupil's career in the School. Some Scholarships are awarded for proficiency in the Creative Arts. Foundation Bursaries are available at age 11, 13 and into the Sixth Form.

Charitable status. King Edward VI School Southampton is a Registered Charity, number 1088030. The object of the Charity is to advance education and training in or near Southampton or elsewhere, including the carrying on of school or schools or other educational establishments and ancillary or incidental educational or other associated activities for the benefit of the community.

Patron: The Lord Lieutenant for the County of Hampshire, Mr Nigel Atkinson

Governors:
Chair: A J Morgan, MA Oxon, FCA, ATII
Vice-Chair: I H Rudland
Mr N Challis, CEng, BEng, MIStructE
Cllr M Chaloner, MA Cantab, Barrister-at-Law
Mrs M L Chant
Mr A Connell, BSc
Reverend J M Finch
Mr B E Gay, BA
Mr J J Gray, BSc, FCA
Ms A Holden
Mr A Jones
Miss P S Kirk, BEd, CertEd
Mr A Knibb, BA Hons, B Arch, ARB, RIBA
Mrs S J Mancey
Cllr K Mans, FRAes, BA
Dr J E Mitchell, MA Cantab, MBBS, DRCOG, DCH

Mrs C G Musker, Chartered MCIPD
Mrs H V Nicholson, MA Oxon, MSc
Mr W A Oscoft, BSc
Mrs W P Swinn, BDS, LDS, RCS
Dr A L Thomas, MA PhD Cantab, CBiol, MRSB
Mrs J L Wadsworth

Bursar and Clerk to the Governors: Mr Ray Maher, BA
Econ, ACA

Head: Mr Neal Parker, MA Ed, MBA

Senior Deputy Head: Mr Adrian Dellar, BSc (*Chemistry*)
Deputy Head (*Academic*): Dr Bruce Waymark, BA, MA
Ed, PhD (*Geography*)

Assistant Head (*Pastoral*): Mr William Collinson, BA
(*English*)
Assistant Head (*Registrar*): Mrs Emma Sheppard, BSc
(*Chemistry*)
Assistant Head (*Teacher Development and Pedagogy*): Mrs
Paula Burrows, BSc (*Physics*)
Assistant Head (*Co-Curriculum*): Miss Hilary Smith, BSc
(*Biology*)
Assistant Head (*Digital Strategy and ICT*): Mr Oliver
Rokison, MEng (*Engineering*)

Director of Sixth Form: Mr Nick Culver, MA (*Economics*)
Head of Upper School: Dr Emma Thomas, BSc, PhD
(*Chemistry*)
Head of Lower School: Mrs Lisa Henderson, BEd (*PE*)
Director of Student Guidance: Mrs Lem Millar, BSc
(*Biology*)

Teaching Staff:
* *Head of Department*

Art:
*Mr Graham Piggott, BA
Miss Alex McGinn, BA
Mrs Nicola Moxon, BA
Mr Ed Lewis, BA

Biology:
*Mr Simon Aellen, BSc
Mrs Josephine Barnes-Wardlaw, BSc
Mrs Laura Burnett, BSc
Miss Lucinda Downing, BSc (*Junior Science Coordinator*)
Mr Stephen Hall, BSc
Mr James Hyder, BSc
Miss Gemma McGregor, BSc
Mrs Lem Millar, BSc
Mr Mark Miller, MA, DPhil
Miss Hilary Smith, BSc
Miss Katrina Yerbury, BSc

Chemistry:
*Mrs L Millington, BSc
Mrs Jan Collinson, MChem
Mrs Claire Costello-Kelly, BSc
Mr Adrian Dellar, BSc
Mrs Georgie Dellar
Dr Stuart Gamblin, BSc, PhD
Dr Viv Green, MSc, PhD
Mr Chris Jackson, BSc
Mrs Emma Sheppard, BSc
Dr E Thomas, BSc, PhD

Classics:
*Mrs Jacqui Meredith, BA
Mr Stuart Ayers, BA
Mr Chris Giles, BA

Mr Julian Halls, BA
Miss Alice Rieuf, MA

Computer Science:
*Mr D Cutler, MPhys
Mrs Kayla Chen, BA
Mr Oliver Rokison, MEng
Mr Mark Willis, BSc

Design & Technology:
*Mr Simon Barker, MA
Mrs Amelia Blow, BSc
Mr David Blow, BSc
Mrs Sarah Peterson, BSc
Mrs Helen Sheridan, BA

Economics/Business Studies:
*Mr Paul Sheppard, BSc
Mr Nick Culver, MA
Mr Matthew Laverty, BA
Mrs Sue Quinn, BA

English:
*Dr Alistair Schofield, MA
Mrs Hannah Arnold, BA
Mr Alan Chandrachud, MA
Mr William Collinson, BA
Miss Emer Cullen, BA
Mrs Sam Evans, BA
Miss Hannah Goodsell, MA
Mrs Joanna Gunton, BA
Mrs Julia Hardwick, BA
Mrs Catherine Lane, BA
Mrs Ellen Rawson, MA
Mr Benedict Reekes, MA

Geography:
*Miss Laura-Jane Grant, BA
Mr Andy Gilbert, BA
Mr Geoff Havers, BSc
Ms Teresa King, BA
Mrs Alice Penfold, BA
Mrs Emily Walls, BA
Dr Bruce Waymark, BA, MA Ed, PhD

History:
*Mr Nick Diver, MA (*Head of Humanities*)
Miss Jacky Barron, BA
Mrs Shona Burt, BA
Mr Kevin Coundley, MA
Dr David Filtness, MA
Mrs Rosemary Potter, BA

Mathematics:
*Mr Gerard Eyssens, BEd
Mrs Catherine Asiki, BA
Mr Simon Barley, MSc
Mrs Laura Matthews, BSc
Mr Richard Nichols, BSc
Miss Emma Ridley, BSc
Mr Paul Robinson, BEng
Mr Ian Rosenburg, BEd
Mr John Singleton, BSc
Mrs Jennifer Thimbleby, BSc
Mr Mark Willis, BSc

Modern Languages:
*Mr Alastair Sinclaire, MA
Mrs Karen Clement, BA (*French*)
Mrs Elisa Ladislao, BA (*Spanish*)
Mr Stuart Ayers, BA

Mrs Rebecca Hall, BA (*German Coordinator*)
Mrs Hong Deng, MA
Mr Gavin Lawson, MA
Miss Victoria Pastor, MA
Miss Alice Rieuf, MA
Mrs Sophie Rugge-Price, MA

Music:
*Miss Charlotte Forsey, BMus, PG Dip (*Director of Music*)
Miss Stacey Barnett, BA
Mr James Belassie, MA
Mrs Tara Hayden, MA

PE:
*Mr Daniel Kent, BA (*Director of Sport*)
Mr Lloyd Powell, BSc (*Sport Science*)
Mrs Jessica Ferrand, BA (*Deputy Director of Sport*)
Mr Matt Mixer, BSocSc (*PE & Games*)
Mr Calum Crichton, BA
Mrs Lisa Henderson, BEd
Mr Josh Richardson
Miss Lucy Lister, BSc
Mrs Clare Kelly, BA
Mrs Janis Kent, BA
Mr Alex Penn, BA
Mrs Hannah Penn, BA (*Performance & Fitness Coordinator*)

Psychology:
*Mrs E Brindley-Ewan, BA
Mr Mark Miller, MA, MPhil
Miss Hilary Smith, BSc

Physics:
*Mr Rob Simm, BSc
Mrs Paula Burrows, MSc
Dr Helen Dean, BSc, PhD
Mr Lawrence Herklots, BSc (*Head of Science*)
Mrs Maryam Mahdavi, BSc
Dr Magdalena Mayor, MSc, PhD

RE:
*Mrs Catherine Lane, BA
Mr David Field, MA
Mrs Helen Searles, MA
Mr Tim Tofts, MA, Dip Phil

Theatre Studies:
*Mrs Lisa Gilmour, BA (*Director of Drama*)
Mrs Hayleigh Hawker, BA

Curriculum Support:
*Mrs Z Ramshaw, BA
Ms Catherine Boyle, BEd
Mrs Georgina Dellar, BA
Mrs R Whitfield, BA

King Edward's School
Bath

North Road, Bath BA2 6HU

Tel:	Senior School: 01225 464313
	Junior School: 01225 463218
	Pre-Prep School: 01225 421681
email:	reception@kesbath.com
website:	www.kesbath.com
Twitter:	@KESBath
Facebook:	@kesbath
Instagram:	@kesbath

As the city's former grammar school, founded in 1552, KES has a very healthy tradition of nurturing academic excellence and ambition, reflected these days in the School's outstanding results which consistently place us in the top five independent schools in the South West. The ethos of the School is one that encourages all pupils to play as hard as they work and to make the most of all the wonderful opportunities here, both in and out of the classroom, that enable them to grow and thrive within a supportive and caring framework. We set the bar high, but we also give our pupils all the tools that they need to reach those ambitious standards. We aim to foster talent in all its forms and to open doors to enquiry and discovery. Independent-mindedness and creative spirit are strong suits, but so too is the sense of community that seeks to respect and value all its members.

As a family of three schools, the Pre-Prep, Junior and Senior sections of King Edward's offer an inspiring and supportive environment for children age 3 to 18. Some join us just for the Sixth Form, many stay for their entire school career. All pupils are encouraged to be the best they can be and all are nurtured along the pathway to leading happy, fulfilled and successful lives at school and beyond.

ISI Inspection report. In 2015 the School was inspected by the ISI and was judged as 'excellent' across all eight aspects of school life under review including pastoral care and co-curricular provision. The report noted that "The success of the school lies in the strength of the ethos which permeates it from the EYFS to the sixth form. All three sections of the school encourage the pupils to strive for excellence and to achieve to the best of their ability in a stimulating environment so that they acquire a love of learning which goes beyond the formal curriculum."

Organisation. King Edward's is a co-educational day school. The School consists of a Senior School of 843 pupils, a Junior School of 187 pupils and Pre-Prep & Nursery of 87 pupils.

Facilities. The Senior School is situated on a 19-acre campus with stunning views across Bath. A further 17-acre site at nearby Bathampton is home to the School's playing fields and sports pavilion. Senior School buildings include the Wroughton Theatre, extensive laboratories for Biology, Chemistry, Physics and ICT with a new Modern Foreign Languages building which opened in the Autumn Term 2019. The newly refurbished Holbeche Centre includes an extensive Sixth Form Centre with adjoining café, an extended Careers and Higher Education Centre, a refurbished Design Suite and Design Technology studios. There is also a modern Sports Hall, together with an all-weather sports pitch. One of the most iconic buildings on the site is the stunning Wessex Building: a three-storey, glass-fronted structure with a dining room and servery on the first floor, a multi-purpose second floor for assemblies, presentations, concerts and social gatherings, and a state-of-the-art Library on the ground floor. The Senior School also recently opened a purpose-built Drama Centre.

Admission. King Edward's Pre-Prep and Nursery is non-selective upon joining. Thereafter, children progress to Reception and then on to Years 1 and 2. Space allowing, children are also welcomed throughout the academic year.

Junior School: Children joining from our own Pre-Prep do so via internal assessment. They do not sit an entrance examination. Pupils from other primary schools and preparatory schools are offered places based on assessment and interview. The main entry is in Year 3 but other vacancies may occur.

Senior School: All potential Year 7 pupils are interviewed and assessed via an entrance examination testing Verbal Reasoning, Mathematics and English. Older pupils may enter the Senior School, if and where places are available, by sitting an entrance examination appropriate to their age.

Pupils may also seek direct entry into the Sixth Form. Such pupils are expected to acquire a sound set of GCSE passes before transfer for advanced study. Applicants are interviewed and a reference is sought from their present schools.

Application forms and further information concerning entry are obtainable from the Registrar or available online. Open Days are held in the Autumn and Spring terms.

Fees per term (2021–2022). Pre-Prep starts from £2,990, Junior School £4,015, Senior School £5,075–£5,165.

Scholarships. Scholarships are awarded in Year 7, either for academic excellence or for an outstanding special talent in art, drama, music and sport.

Bursaries. Income-related entrance Bursaries may be awarded to children entering Years 7 and 12, whose parents are unable to pay the full fee. A general Bursary fund is also available to assist parents during times of unforeseen family circumstances, when they may find themselves unable to fund full school fees. Further details are obtainable from the Bursar's office.

Senior School Curriculum. We start in Years 7 and 8 with a broad range of subjects, to which we add choice and greater range in Year 9. By the time pupils are choosing their GCSE options, they will have a clearer idea of their strengths and enthusiasms and be able to select the best range of subjects to go alongside the core subjects of English, Maths, all three sciences and a modern foreign language.

For A Level, further specialisation and greater focus on personal interest and academic strengths come into play as pupils look to their education and potential careers after life in the Sixth Form. We offer careers guidance and testing to support these fundamental choices and then UCAS and Higher Education guidance as they look to make the move to their chosen degree subject from the A Levels they will complete in Year 13.

No two pupils are the same and so we work to provide as much choice and flexibility as we can in our options schemes for Years 9, 10 and 12. All combinations are possible in principle and a broad mix of subjects is as supported as more traditional routes of sciences, languages or humanities.

Throughout, there is an underlying appreciation that pupils succeed best when taught interesting and engaging lessons by enthusiastic, specialist staff. We want our pupils to leave here with valuable study skills, having found their intellectual and academic passion and having fulfilled their potential in that area.

Music and Drama. There is a healthy musical tradition in the School, with over 20 instrumental and choral groups affording opportunities to explore differing musical styles. Partnerships with Bath Abbey and Bath Philharmonia Orchestra help to further extend the experience of our musicians and choirs.

King Edward's is known for producing exceptional theatrical work and is regarded as a centre of excellence for its creative and challenging performance work, the professional standards of its productions, and its consistently outstanding academic results. In addition to two big productions each year, the Senior School also offers inter-form competitions, Duologue performances, drama clubs, drama tech club and an end-of-year 'Spectacular'. The School has also introduced LAMDA exams and taken several shows to the Edinburgh Fringe.

Sport. Sport plays a significant role in the life of King Edward's School. The School enjoys a strong sporting tradition, where all pupils are encouraged to take an active role in the curricular and co-curricular opportunities available to them. Each pupil is encouraged to develop their potential, creating the opportunity to allow later involvement at recreational level or within a competitive environment. We aim to nurture teamwork, leadership, commitment and a passion for sport through the opportunities available to all pupils at KES. The major games are rugby, hockey, cricket and netball. Minor sports include athletics, cross-country, tennis, soccer, badminton, golf, dance, gymnastics, table tennis and trampolining.

School Societies and Activities. The School aims to challenge and stimulate all pupils by offering a wide range of activities and experiences beyond the classroom. The 2015 ISI Report found our extra-curricular provision to be "outstanding", and we truly believe that there is something for everyone from among the 100 clubs and societies running each year.

Outward bound opportunities include joining the School's CCF, founded in 1896, or taking part in the Duke of Edinburgh's Award scheme. The School also enters the Ten Tors Competition each year. Lunchtime clubs include Lego Robotics, KES Amnesty Club, the Socrates Debating Club and IFS Student Investor Club.

Pastoral Care The Deputy Head (Pastoral) coordinates the pastoral team. Every child has a Form Teacher who is at their foremost contact during daily life at school. Tutors work in teams managed by Heads of Year or Senior Tutors who are in turn assisted by Heads of Sector (Lower, Middle School and Sixth Form). The pastoral staff are ably supported by a School Nurse and Counsellor. The School prides itself on its family atmosphere and the excellent relationships between pupils of all ages and staff.

Honours. In 2020 pupils performed exceptionally in their A Levels: Over 90% A*–B grades. At GCSE: 81% of grades awarded 9–7.

King Edward's Junior School and Pre-Prep and Nursery. For further details please see separate entries for the Junior School and Pre-Prep and Nursery under IAPS.

The Association of Old Edwardians of Bath. c/o The Development Office.

Charitable status. King Edward's School Bath is a Registered Charity, number 1115875. It is a charitable trust for the purpose of educating children.

Chair of Governors: Mrs W Thomson, MEd, BEd Hons, LLCM TD

Headmaster: Mr M J Boden, MA (*German & French*)[2]

Second Master: Mr M J Horrocks-Taylor, BSc, MEd (*Geography*)[2]

Acting Bursar: Mr T Davies, BA, FCA

Deputy Heads:
Academic: Mr T Burroughs, BA (*History & Politics*)[2]
Pastoral: Ms C Losse, MA (*German & French*)[2]
Curriculum & Digital Strategy: Mr D Middlebrough BA (*Mathematics*)[2]

Assistant Heads:
Communications, Events & External Relations: Mr D Chapman, BA (*Mathematics*)[2]
Head of Sixth Form: Mr P Simonds, BSc (*Geography*)[2]
Co-curricular: Mr J Tidball, BSc (*Geography*)[2]

Teaching Staff:
* *Head of Department*
[1] *Head of Year/Sixth Form Senior Tutor*
[2] *Professional Review and Development Manager*
[…] *Staff on leave*

Mrs A Baker, MA, BSc (*Chemistry*)
Mr M Barber, BA (*Economics & Business Studies*)[1]
Mrs H Bateman, BA (*Learning Support*)
Mrs R Bird, MA (*Psychology*)
Mrs S Bird, BA (*Drama/Theatre Studies*)*
Mr D Blake (*Economics & Business Studies*)
Mr M Boden, MMus (*Music*)
Mr G Brown (*Physical Education & Games*)
Mrs C Bruton, BA (*English*)
Mr M Bull, MA (*Classics*)*
Mrs J Burchell, MA (*Classics*)
Mr M Buswell, ME (*Religious Studies & Philosophy*)*[1]
Mr G Butterworth, BA (*Economics & Business Studies*)*
Mrs B Charlton (*Spanish*)*
Mrs S Chubb, BA (*English*)
Mrs C Corrie, BSc (*Chemistry*)
Mrs S Cox, BSc (*Learning Support*)
Mr P Davies, BSc (*Mathematics*)
Miss H Dawes, BA (*Religious Studies & Philosophy*)
Mrs T Dawson, BSc (*Mathematics*)
Mrs L Dias, BSc (*Economics & Business Studies*)
Mr T Dore, BSc (*Biology*)
Mr R Drury, BA, LRAM (*Music*)*
Dr C Enos, BSc, PhD (*Chemistry*)
Mr M Evans, MMath (*Electronics*)
Mr P Feeney, MA (*Classics*)
Mr C Ferguson, BA (*German*)*
Dr A Fewell, BSc, PhD (*Biology*)
Mr T Fisher, MA (*English*)
Mrs R Flay (*Art & Photography, Design & Technology*)
Mr J Garner-Richardson, BSc (*Chemistry & Biology*)
Mrs E Gil (*Spanish*)
Mrs H Graham, MA (*History & Politics, Head of Upper School*)
Mrs E Grainger, BA (*French & Spanish*)
Dr C Gruzelier, MA, PhD (*Classics*)

Mrs L Gwilliam, BSc (*Physical Education* & Games*)
Mr D Hacker (*Physical Education & Games*)*
Mr T Hager, BA (*English*) [Acting]*
Mr M Harrison, BSc, MSc, CPhys, MInstP (*Physics*)
[Miss C Hartley, BA (*English*)]
Mr R Haynes, MA (*Electronics*)*
Mrs F Hughes, MA (*Art & Photography*)
Mr E Hume-Smith, BA (*Art & Photography*)*
Mr A Hutchings, BEd (*Design & Technology*)
Mrs S Hutchings, BEd (*Mathematics*)
Mrs L James, BSc (*Computing & ICT*)*
Mrs C Jones, BA (*German & French*)
[Miss Z Kayacan, BA (*English*)*]
Mrs A Kean, BSc (*Biology*)
Mr J Kean, MA (*English*)
Mr L King, BA, MSc (*Physical Education & Games*)
Miss P Kirby, BSc (*Biology*)*
Dr J Knight, BSc, PhD (*Geography*)*
Mr B Lang, BSc (*Physics*)
Mrs R Lang, BSc (*Mathematics*)
Mr D Lehmann, BSc (*Mathematics*)
Mr S Lilley, BSc (*Physical Education & Games*)
Mrs C Livesey, BEd (*Physical Education & Geography*)[1]
Mr P Livesey, BEd (*Physical Education & Games*)
Mr S Lomon, BA (*History & Politics*)*
Mrs P Mason, BSc (*Biology & Chemistry*)
Mr J Mawer, BSc (*Geography*)
Miss S McCrorie, MA (*Mathematics*)
Miss L Miners, MSc (*Chemistry*)
Miss S Moon, BA (*History*)
Mrs A Munn, BA (*Learning Support*)* Head of Lower School
Mr M Oehler, BSc (*Chemistry* & Science**)
Miss N Organ (*Spanish*)
Mr R Pagnamenta, MEng (*Mathematics*)*
Miss L Perris, BMus (*Music*)I
Mr P Perry, BA (*English*)[1]
Mrs J Rees-Roberts, MSt (*Religious Studies*)
Mr E Rice, MA (*English*)
Mrs S Richardson, MSc, MA (*Physics*)*
Mrs M Roy (*Design & Technology*)*
[Mrs A Salako, BA (*Economics & Business Studies*)]
Mrs K Simonds, BSc (*Learning Support & Geography*)
Mr T Sneddon, BSc (*Mathematics*)
Ms S Stanford-Tuck, BScEd (*Biology*)
Mrs C Stevens, BSc (*Physics*)
Mrs V Stevens-Craig, BA (*Drama/Theatre Studies*)
Mrs D Tamblyn, BEd (*Drama/Theatre Studies*)
Mr R Thomas, MA (*History & Politics, HE/UCAS**)
Miss K Trump, BA (*Physical Education & Games*)I
Mrs A Tse, BSc (*Biology, Head of Middle School*)
Mrs S Utton, BSc (*Psychology*)*
Mr A Vass, MA (*French*)*
Ms S Vernon, BA (*English*)[1]
Dr L Wainer, MSc, PhD (*Mathematics*)
Mr T West, BA (*Computing & ICT*)
Mrs S Williams, BSc (*Physics*)
Mr D Willison, BA (*Art*)
Miss E Young, BEd (*Physical Education & Games*)

Examinations Officer: Mrs C Cameron-Davies
School Chaplain: Revd Caroline O'Neill
School Librarian: Miss L Bowman, BA, MLS
SSI KES CCF: 2Lt P H Jones

Finance Manager & School Accountant: Mrs N Rowlands, AAT

Headmaster's PA: Ms L Wolfe, BA
Bursar/Second Master's PA: Miss H Barnes, BSc
School Secretary (Academic): Mrs K Tedstone
School Secretary (Pastoral): Mrs B Lascelles, BSc
School Receptionist: Mrs A Budgett
Registrar: Miss A Rashid
Admissions Administrators: Miss H Lane; Mrs L Thomas
Development Officer: Mrs C Davies, BA
Communications Officer: Mrs K Gentle, MA
Marketing Communications Officer: Mr G Goold, BA
Music Administrator: Mrs S Walker
PE Administrator: Mrs R Worsdall, BA
School Nurses:
Mrs C Turner, RGN, BSc
Mrs S Nicholson, RGN, BSc
Mrs V Rutherford, RGN

Junior School Staff:
Head of Junior School: Mr G Taylor, BA Ed, NPQH
Deputy Head (Pastoral): Mrs R Hardware, BEd
Deputy Head (Academic): Mr M Innes, BA, PGCE
Lower School Co-ordinator: Mrs F Dore, BSc, PGCE
Director of Activities: Mrs E Pike, BA, PGCE

Miss L Atkinson, BSc, MEd, PGCE
Mrs R Barrett, MA Oxon, PGCE
Mr C Carter, BEd
Miss L Chapman, MA, PGCE
Mrs S Cook, BA, GTP
Mr J Corp, BSc, PGCE
Mrs E Heaney, BEd
Mrs C Hutchings, BMus, PGCE
Mrs A Jabarin, BA, PGCE
Mr J Roberts-Wray, BA, PGCE
Mrs C Webb, BA, PGCE
Miss A Young, BSc, PGCE

PA to the Head/Junior School Administrator: Mrs C
  Garner-Richardson

Pre-Prep School Staff:
Head of Pre-Prep & Nursery: Ms J Gilbert, BEd Hons,
  NPQH

Mrs J Carter, BA Hons
Miss S Cullen, PGCE, EYTS
Mrs H Blakey, BSc, PGCE (*Head of Early Years*)
Mr S Boydell, BA Hons, PGCE, MEd, MRHistS, CTHist
Mrs S Knight, MA, PGCE
Ms E Rocksborough-Smith, BA, PGCE
Miss L-M Williams, BSc, PGCE (*Head of KS1*)

Pre-Prep Administrators: Mrs A Foxall; Mrs H Leek

King Edward's School
Birmingham

Edgbaston Park Road, Birmingham B15 2UA

Tel:	0121 472 1672
email:	admissions@kes.org.uk
website:	www.kes.org.uk
Twitter:	@KESBham
Facebook:	@KESBham
LinkedIn:	/company/king-edwards-school-birmingham

Motto: *Domine, Salvum fac Regem*

King Edward's School, Birmingham, was founded in 1552 and occupied a position in the centre of the city until 1936 when it moved to its present 50-acre site in Edgbaston, surrounded by a golf course, lake and nature reserve and adjacent to the University. It is an independent day school with 878 boys aged 11 to 18. Approximately 35 in each year receive financial assistance with fees, from scholarships and the Assisted Places Scheme. The School belongs to the Foundation of the Schools of King Edward VI in Birmingham (two independent, six grammar schools and four academies), and its sister-school, King Edward VI High School for Girls, is on the same campus. Academically one of the leading schools in the country, King Edward's is also renowned for the scale of its provision and its excellence in sport, music, drama, outdoor pursuits and trips and expeditions.

Admission. Most boys enter the school at 11+, although a small number join at 13+. In addition, applications at 16+ to enter the Sixth Form are encouraged. At both 11+ and 13+ candidates take papers in Mathematics, English and Verbal Reasoning at a level appropriate to the National Curriculum. A large number of pupils are also interviewed as part of the admissions process. At 16+ entry is decided by interview, report from current Headteacher and predicted GCSE grades.

The names of candidates must be registered at the School before the closing date as stated on the School's website. A recent photograph must be produced when the name of a candidate is registered for the examination.

Term of Entry: Autumn term only.

Scholarships and Assisted Places. Approximately 25 academic scholarships varying in value from 5% to 50% of the fees are awarded each year. Most of these scholarships are awarded at 11+, but awards are also made to outstanding candidates at 16+ and, very occasionally, at 13+. Music scholarships are also available.

The Assisted Places Scheme offers means-tested support to up to 20 boys a year. The scheme targets primarily 11+ entrants but 16+ entrants are also eligible to apply.

Fees per term (2021–2022). £4,885.

Academic Success. The School's 2021 International Baccalaureate Diploma results were excellent, with an average point score of 40.3. 62% of the boys gained 40 points or above, and 91% of Higher Level subjects were graded 7 or 6 (the equivalent of A*/A at A Level). Almost all leavers go on to university, some after a gap year.

At GCSE, 74% of results were graded 9/8 grades and 89% were 9–7. Furthermore, 45 boys achieved 10 or 11 9/8s and a further 21 achieved nine 9/8s.

Curriculum. *Lower School*: The following subjects are studied by all boys to the end of the third year: English, Mathematics, French, Geography, History, Physics, Chemistry, Biology, (General Science in first year), Latin, Art, Design, Drama, Music, PE and Religious Studies. All boys study one of German, Spanish or Classical Greek in the third year and may take their choice to GCSE or IGCSE and beyond. In addition, boys are required to undertake familiarisation courses in Information Technology. In the Fourth and Fifth year, boys take 10 subjects. All boys must study Mathematics, English Language, English Literature, a Modern Foreign Language and at least two sciences, plus three or four other optional subjects at GCSE or IGCSE.

Sixth Form: Since September 2010, A Levels have been replaced entirely with the International Baccalaureate Diploma. The School believes that this diploma provides a more challenging and broad Sixth Form education with greater opportunity for independent learning and is a better preparation for university study and life thereafter.

The School's curriculum goes beyond preparation for examinations. For example, PE and games are compulsory for all and Friday afternoon is set aside for the entire school to pursue non-academic activities: Combined Cadet Force, Leadership, service in the community, outdoor pursuits, Art, Information Technology etc.

Music and Drama. The School has a very rich musical and dramatic life. Many of the musical groups and theatrical productions take place jointly with King Edward VI High School for Girls. There are over ten different musical groups and choirs. The School's Performing Arts Centre has main hall seating for up to 500 and excellent facilities for music and drama.

Games. Rugby, cricket, hockey, and water polo are the major team games in the School. However, many other games prosper including archery, athletics, badminton, basketball, chess, cross-country, cycling, fencing, fives, golf, kayaking, squash, swimming, table tennis and tennis. The School has extensive playing fields for all these activities plus its own swimming pool, international-standard athletics track, sports hall, gymnasia and squash courts. In 2015 the School opened a new hockey pavilion and astro pitch, and in 2019 it opened a new sports centre, which includes a sports hall, cardiovascular fitness room, multipurpose space, classroom and changing rooms.

Societies and Clubs. The School has a very wide range of clubs and societies including Christian Union, Islamic Society, Literary Society, History Society, Bookworms, Economics and Business Society, Senior and Junior Dramatic Societies, Art Society, Geographical Society, Debating Society, Mentoring Society, Mathematical Society, Modern Languages Society, Sustainability Society, Writers' Society, Lifeguarding, Chess Club, Model United Nations, Spectrum, School Chronicle and Hillwalking.

CCF, Outdoor Pursuits and Expeditions. The Royal Naval, RAF and Army Sections of the Combined Cadet Force are very popular amongst pupils. In addition, the KES Award and the Duke of Edinburgh's Award scheme have grown substantially in recent years, so that the majority of pupils in the third year gain the KES Award and over 40 each year undertake the Gold Duke of Edinburgh's Award. All of this forms part of a strong tradition of trips and expeditions, ranging from cycling and caving and walking and skiing trips, to language trips to Europe, to major expeditions to Ecuador and the Galapagos Islands, Guyana and Madagascar. There have also been very successful rugby tours to Australia, India, Canada, South Africa and China.

Forms and Houses. In the first five years, each form has an average of 25 pupils. In the Sixth Form, forms are on average 12 in number, and often comprise pupils together from the Lower and Upper Sixth. There is also a house system, comprising eight houses, which continues to provide an important element of pastoral support and competition in sport, music, drama, debating and general knowledge.

Charitable status. The Schools of King Edward VI in Birmingham is a Registered Charity, number 529051. The purpose of the Foundation is to educate children and young persons living in or around the City of Birmingham.

Governing Body:
Chairman: Mr Tim Clarke
Vice Chair: Mrs G Ball, OBE

Prof G Brodie	Mr I Metcalfe
Mr P Burns	Ms G Sehdev
Mr O Choudhry	Mrs A Smith
Mrs C Hosty	Prof H Thomas
Mr B Lenon	Prof S West
Mr G Marsh	

Bailiff: Mrs Sharon Roberts

Chief Master: Dr Katy L Ricks, MA, DPhil

Deputy Chief Master: Mr K D Phillips, BA
Deputy Head (Director of Post-16 Education): Mr H M Coverdale, BSc Econ
Deputy Head Academic: Dr R J Evans, BSc, PhD
Deputy Head (Pastoral): Ms D E McMillan, BSc

Assistant Heads:
Mr M J Bartlett, BA
Mr G J Watson, MA

Assistant Teachers:

Mr L M Roll, BA	Mr T J Wareing, BA
Mr E J Milton, BA	Mrs G J Babb, BA, MA
Mrs G A Ostrowicz, BA	Dr C S Arico, MSc, PhD
Mrs C M L Duncombe, BA	Dr M Romon-Alonso, MSc,
Mr C D Boardman, BSc	PhD
Mr S J Tinley, BSc	Miss F C Lee, BA
Mr J Porter, BSc	Mr J J W Fair, BSc
Mr M J Monks, GRSM,	Dr T S Miles, MSc, PhD
Dip RCM	Mr J M Pavey, BSc
Mr R W James, BA	Ms D K Poole, BA
Mr S L Stacey, MA	Dr J Fennell, BSc, PhD
Mr D J Ash, MA	Mrs C L Gillow, BA
Mr J P Smith, BSc	Mr E J Aston, BSc
Ms R Leaver, MEng	Mr T Burdett, BSc
Mr D M Witcombe, MSc	Mr N A Shepherd, BSc
Mr P A Balkham, BA	Mr A M Dutch, BMus
Mr I J Connor, BSc	Dr M D Leigh, MA, PhD
Ms S-L Jones, BSc	Dr S P Kulkarni, BSc,
Mr R D Davies, BSc	MPhil, PhD
Ms E K Sigston, BA	Mr J M Butler, BA
Dr J L Amann, BA, PhD	Ms P K Higgins, BA
Mrs P J R Esnault, MA	Dr A D Webb, MChem
Mr C A P Johnson, BA	Mr C R Turford, BA, MA
Dr M R Follows, BSc, PhD	Mr A W J Petrie, BA
Dr D C Wong, BEng, PhD	Mr A D Langlands, BSc
Mrs K S Charlesworth-	Mr B A Coates, BSc
Jones, BA	Mr J M Benge-Abbott, BSc
Ms H A Ferguson, BSc,	Mr J W Brogden, BA
MSc	Ms H E Falkner, BA, MA

Mr A J Pearson, BA
Mr G Adams, BSc
Mr R D Orchard, BSc
Mr G Macdonald, BSc
Mr T G A Wyndham, BSc, MSc
Mrs K C Linehan, BA, MA
Miss C V Bayley, BA, MEd
Mrs O Zamaniego, BA
Mrs R J Froggatt, BSc
Mr P D J Moore-Bridger, BA
Mr M S Narwal, BSc
Dr S Carta, BA, PhD
Dr P Mason, MSc, PhD
Mr T M J Woolley, BA
Ms R J Miszkurka, BSc, MEd
Dr A C Brown, BA, MA, DPhil

Mr D A Jones, MA
Mr J Lloyd, BSc
Ms J V Orchard, BA
Dr M E Otero Knott, MA, MLitt, MPhil, PhD
Ms R A Sykes, BA, MSt
Mrs J L Putt, BA
Miss K J Bancroft, BA, MA
Dr J S Bendall, MChem, PhD
Mr D J Leigh, BA, MA
Miss G McKinley, BA
Mr J Ramsay, BA, MA
Dr N Strabic, PhD
Dr M G Yeo, MA, PhD, MEd
Miss R V Morris
Mr N W Round

Part-time Teachers:

The Revd D H Raynor, MA, MLitt
Mr R J Deeley, MA
Mrs C R Bubb, BA
Mrs H J Cochrane, BA
Mr P W L Golightly, BA
Ms L C Seamark, BA

Mrs E J Wareing, BA
Mrs C Smith, BA, MA
Mrs S L Behan, BSc
Ms B Dehame-Hare, MA
Ms A Havel, BA
Ms C R Shuker, BSc

Librarian: Ms K A Fletcher-Burns, BA, MSc Econ; Mrs L Beckett [maternity cover]
School Medical Officer: Dr M Forrest, MBChB, DRCOG, MRCGP

King Edward's Witley

Petworth Road, Godalming, Surrey GU8 5SG

Tel: 01428 686700
email: admissions@kesw.org
website: www.kesw.org
Twitter: @KESWitley
Facebook: @KESWitley
LinkedIn: /king-edward's-school-witley

King Edward's Witley, a Bridewell School, was founded in 1553 by King Edward VI as Bridewell Royal Hospital. Originally housed at the Bridewell Palace, which was given under Royal Charter to the City of London, the School moved to Witley in 1867, simultaneously changing its name; it became co-educational again in 1952. The School is an independent boarding and day school for girls and boys aged 11–18. The School has 423 pupils; approximately 65% are day pupils. There are a substantial number of bursaries, currently around 50, available to help girls and boys whose home circumstances make a boarding style of education a particular need.

The School is situated in a 100-acre campus in an Area of Outstanding Natural Beauty in the Surrey countryside, approximately ten miles south of Guildford, with Heathrow and Gatwick international airports both within a 45-minute drive.

King Edward's Witley is steeped in history, but combines its traditional strengths with a modern outlook. The School prides itself on its ability to provide a school community that reflects the real world admitting pupils from a broad range of academic, social, economic and cultural backgrounds – 70% are English native speakers and 40 countries are represented. All children are nurtured to encourage independent thinking and a spirit of respect and understanding for others, resulting in a mature and well-rounded outlook on life and a commitment to upholding the strongest moral values.

King Edward's takes pride in its academic, socio-economic and cultural diversity. The School ensures that all pupils are congratulated for their effort and dedication to achieving personal success. King Edward's Sixth Form offer the International Baccalaureate Diploma Programme (IB) and A-levels. In 2021, IB pupils achieved an average score 35.9 out of a possible 45; the world average is 33.02. We had a very small cohort of two pupils this year so we are not reporting overall percentages.

In 2021, at GCSE, 96.7% of pupils achieved 5 or more grades at 9–4 (A*–C) including English Language and Mathematics. 64.5% of grades were 9–7 (A*–A), 81% of grades were 9–6 (A*–B).

The School also runs a one-year Pre Sixth Form course for overseas pupils, representing an opportunity to improve English language skills and trial both IB and A Level subjects on offer, allowing for more Sixth Form choices.

Renowned for its ability to nurture pupils so they excel in their academic studies, King Edward's Witley also provides a highly motivating and inspiring environment for children to equally thrive in other sporting / creative activities. The School has an excellent reputation for its welcoming community and the provision of high-quality pastoral care.

Year 7 and Year 8 constitute the Lower School and are accommodated in Queen Mary House with shared communal facilities for boys and girls. From Year 9 upwards boys and girls live in six modern, purpose-built paired houses where the accommodation and study areas are completely separate but everyone can come together in the shared communal facilities on the ground floor.

Facilities at the School are second to none and include a state-of-the-art Business and Finance Centre, indoor swimming pool, gym, all-weather hockey and tennis playing fields and a central dining hall, which delivers an outstanding standard of catering. The School pioneered paired boarding houses with communal areas, where everyone can come together in their spare time to enjoy games, TV, music and conversation in the common rooms, kitchen, music and television rooms. For the Sixth Form, a lively common room, Sixth Form prefects room, study area and careers library provide an environment for independent learning and recreation.

Admission. Children are normally admitted at 11+, 13+ and 16+ but if there is room they may be admitted at other times, and occasionally a child who should clearly be working alongside older children is admitted at 10+. Admission is by pre-testing or by the School's own entrance examination and interview taken normally in the January prior to entry.

Fees per term (2021–2022). Boarders: Lower School £11,225, Year 9–11 £11,225, (Pre) Sixth Form £11,665, including all boarding and tuition fees, books and games equipment, and the provision of school uniform and games clothing.

Day Pupils: Lower School £5,595, Year 9–11 £6,840, (Pre) Sixth Form £7,195, including meals and uniform. Individual music tuition in piano, organ, singing and all orchestral instruments is available.

Bursaries. Bursaries are available for both boarding and day pupils. The School has an endowment providing support for children whose circumstances make boarding a particular need. Awards are reviewed annually with regard to parental circumstances and to school fees. They may be given in conjunction with Local Education Authority grants or help from a charitable trust. The School has a dedicated Bursaries Officer who works with applicants to source the financial support needed to enable worthy candidates to join the School.

Scholarships. Academic, Art, Drama, DT, Music and Sports Scholarships are offered at 11+, 13+ or 16+ for entry to the Sixth Form. These awards will be up to a maximum of 30% of full fees but may be augmented in case of financial need. Children of serving members of the armed forces will be considered for a discount.

Charitable status. King Edward's Witley is a Registered Charity, number 311997. The Foundation exists to provide boarding education for families whose circumstances make boarding a particular need, though the excellent facilities and the high standards of academic achievement and pastoral care make it attractive also to any family looking for a modern and distinctive education.

Treasurer and Chairman of Governors: Mrs J Voisin, BA

Head: Mrs Joanna Wright, BA, PGCE

Deputy Head: D Corran
Deputy Head Co-Curriculum: M Harrison
Assistant Deputy Head (Academic): R Davies

Academic Staff:
* *Head of Department*
† *Housemaster/mistress*

J AJ Allen, BA (*English*)
Mrs S Antill, NatDip (*ICT*)
R Arch, MA, MSc (*Economics & Business Studies*)
Ms R Archer (*Design & Technology, Food & Textiles*)
B Arthey, BA (*Guitar*)
Dr P Attwell, BSc, PhD (*Science*)
A Bardell (*Technician – Art & Photography*)
A Baynes, MA (*Modern Languages*)
Ms H Browning (*Learning Support & EAL*)
Mrs A Butler (*School Office Administrator*)
Dr C Brockhaus, MA, PhD (*Language Assistant*)
T Campbell, BA (*Geography*)
E Cathro (*Chemistry*)
Miss E Cattle, MA (*Classics*)
Dr P Cave, LRAM, GRSM, ARAM, PhD (*Piano*)
Mrs L Cleaves, BA, MA (*Drama*)
Miss S Condy, BTh, MA (†*Elizabeth, Religious Studies & Philosophy*)
Miss T Cowell, BMus, MMus (*Brass*)
J G Culbert, BSc, Dip Comp Sc (*Science, *Physics*)
R Davies, BSc, MLitt, MA (*Mathematics*)
Mrs M Davies (*Careers and Higher Education*)
Miss F de Bray (*Music*)
Miss J Dibb-Fuller, BSc (*Learning Support and EAL*)
Mrs S Ellison, BA, LRAM (*Bassoon*)
N Emsley, BSc, Dip Com (†*Grafton, Mathematics, Science, Theory of Knowledge and Critical Thinking*)
Mrs F Fitch, BA (*Head of Hockey*)

M Fox, BSC (*Science*)
Mrs E Francis, BA (*History*)
T Frazer, BA (*Assistant Director of Music*)
Mr A Guthrie (*Science Technician*)
Ms C Harding, BA, ACRM (*Double Bass*)
Mrs E Harman, BSc (†*Ridley, Economics & Business Studies*)
Mrs J Harris, BA (*Library & Resources, Extended Essay Coordinator*)
Mrs L Harris-Jones, BA, MA, MBA, (*Religious Studies & Philosophy, *Theory of Knowledge & Critical Thinking*)
Ms R Harris, PGDip, BMus (*Voice*)
M Harrison, BA (*Director of Co-Curriculum and Leadership, Modern Languages*)
G Haylock, BA (*Head of Football*)
P W Head, BEng, MPhil (*Mathematics*)
J Hennessey-Brown, ARCM, BMus (*Cello*)
Mrs A Hill, BSc (*Science Technician*)
Mrs R Hillage, PGCE, BA (*Learning Support and EAL*)
Mrs S J Hinde-Brown, BA (*Modern Languages*)
Mrs J A Hinton, BSc (*Modern Languages*)
Mrs A Hobbs (*Sports Coach*)
Miss R Hodges, MA (*Science*)
Mrs G Holtham, BA (*Modern Languages*)
Mrs J Hooker (*Design & Technology Food and Textiles*)
Miss S Hughes, MChem (*Science*)
Ms U John, GMD, RNCM (*Violin and Viola*)
A N K Johnson, BSc, MSc (*Design & Technology Resistant Materials*)
Mr S Laurent (*Teacher of Sports, Cricket specialism*)
D Laurence, BA (*Economics & Business Studies*)
Dr A Lennard, PhD, BSc (*ICT*)
Mrs J M Lyttle, BA (†*Tudor, English & Drama*)
A Macmillan, BA (†*Wakefield, Design & Technology Resistant Materials*)
Mrs Z Marsden, BA (*Learning Support and EAL*)
Ms R McNaught, BA, MA, Dip RAM
Mrs A Meyer, BSc, BEd (*Mathematics, Assistant Head of Sixth Form, Pre Sixth Coordinator*)
P Miller, MSc, BSc, (*Director of Sport*)
Dr H Mir, PhD (*Mathematics*)
Mrs L Moore, BA (*Art & Photography*)
Miss N Nishizono-Miller (*Organist in Residence*)
Ms A Ochoa-Fagan, BA (*Language Assistant*)
Mrs M Pevreall, BSc, MSc (*Biology*)
Mrs M Phillips, BA (*History*)
Mrs D Pickering, MA (*Teacher of French and Subject Co-ordinator*)
Mrs M A Plana Duran, BA (*Language Assistant*)
Ms O Pocock, MA (*Classics*)
Reverend J Radcliffe, MA (*Religious Studies & Philosophy*)
C Robinson (*Technician, Design & Technology Resistant Materials*)
Mr A Ryman (*Teacher of Sports*)
Mrs C Shouksmith, BA (*Art & Photography*)
A Sibacher, BSc (*Mathematics*)
B Simmonds, BMus, Dip ABRSM, LLB, MPerf (*Piano*)
D Slater, BA (*English*)
S Sliwka, BMus, FRCO, LRSM (*Director of Music*)
D Standing, MA RAM (*Voice*)
Mrs S Styles, BEng (*Science*)
Mrs H Thorpe, BA (*Geography*)
D Tobias, BA (†*Edward, English, Theory of Knowledge and Critical Thinking*)
Mrs J Todd (*Examinations Officer*)

Mr F Tontoh (*Percussion and Drums*)

Ms E Trussler (*Artist in Residence*)

Mrs E Turnbull, BSc (*Mathematics*)

Mrs A Valentino, BA, MEd (*English*)

Mrs C van der Vijer, BA (*Language Assistant*)

Mrs A Webster, BA (*Learning Support and EAL*)

Ms J Webster, BMus (*Flute*)

H Wiggin, BMus, Grad Dip, MPerf (*Clarinet, Flute & Saxophone*)

Mrs C Wickramasinghe De Silva, BA QTS (*Learning Support and EAL*)

Mrs S Witherby, BA, MSc (*Learning Support and EAL*)

Mrs J Worrall (*Science Technician*)

King William's College

Castletown, Isle of Man IM9 1TP

Tel: 01624 820400

email: admissions@kwc.im

website: www.kwc.im

Twitter: @kwciom

Facebook: @kwciom/

Instagram: @kwcandthebuchanschool

LinkedIn: /school/king-william's-college

Motto: *Assiduitate, non desidia*

King William's College owes its foundation to Dr Isaac Barrow, Bishop of Sodor and Man from 1663 to 1671, who established an Educational Trust in 1668. The funds of the Trust were augmented by public subscription and the College was opened in 1833 and named after King William IV, 'The Sailor King'.

In 1991, the College merged with the Isle of Man's other independent school, The Buchan School, Castletown, which had been founded by Lady Laura Buchan in 1875 to provide education for young ladies. The Buchan School has been reformed as the junior section of the College for boys and girls up to age 11. (*For further details of The Buchan School, see entry in IAPS section*).

The Isle of Man, being internally self-governing, has a very favourable tax structure and the independence of College would not be affected by changes in UK legislation.

The College is set in superb countryside on the edge of Castletown Bay and adjacent to Ronaldsway Airport. The Isle of Man is approximately 33 miles long and 13 miles wide and is an area of diverse and beautiful scenery. The Isle of Man is an unusually safe environment with a very low crime rate.

There are approximately 380 pupils at College and a further 160 pupils at the Preparatory School. There is also a Nursery School for 2 to 4 year olds on the Buchan site. Both King William's College and The Buchan School are fully co-educational.

Entry. New pupils are accepted at any time, but most begin at the start of the September Term. Boys and girls are admitted to the Preparatory School up to the age of 11 at which point transfer to King William's College is automatic. Entry to College, including Sixth Form level, is by Head's report and interview.

Further details and a prospectus may be obtained from the Admissions Office to which applications for entry should be made.

Organisation. The school is divided into three sections: Fourth Form (Years 7 & 8), Fifth Form (Years 9, 10 & 11) and Sixth Form (Years 12 & 13). Each section is led by a Head of Year, assisted by a team of tutors who monitor the academic progress and deal with all day-to-day matters relating to the pupils in their charge. In addition, all pupils are placed in one of three co-educational Houses for internal competitive purposes, which provides an important element of continuity throughout a pupil's career at the School.

Boarders. There are two houses: one for boys and the other for girls. The living and sleeping accommodation is arranged principally in study-bedrooms for senior pupils with junior pupils sharing with one other student. Each House has its own Houseparent who is responsible for the pastoral welfare of the pupils. He or she is assisted by two or three tutors, of whom at least two are resident.

Chapel. The College is a Church of England foundation but pupils of all denominations attend Chapel; the spirit of the services is distinctly ecumenical.

Curriculum. Pupils at both Schools follow the National Curriculum in its essentials.

The curriculum is designed to provide a broad, balanced and challenging form of study for all pupils. At 11–13 pupils take English, Mathematics, French and Spanish or Latin, Science, History, Geography, Design Technology, ICT, Art, Music, Drama, Religious Studies, Physical Education, PSHE. Pupils then go on to study typically 9 or 10 subjects at (I)GCSE level from a wide number of options.

In the Sixth Form King William's College offers the **International Baccalaureate**. Students choose 6 subjects, normally 3 at higher level and 3 at standard level, which must include their first language, a second language, a science, a social science and Mathematics. In addition, students write an extended essay (a research piece of 4,000 words), follow a course in the Theory of Knowledge (practical philosophy) and spend the equivalent of one half day a week on some form of creative aesthetic activity or active community service (e.g. Duke of Edinburgh's Award fulfils this requirement).

Music and Drama. There are excellent facilities for Drama with House plays and at least one major school production each year, together with regular coaching in Speech and Drama. There are Junior and Senior Bands and Choirs, and a very flourishing Chapel Choir. The House Music competition is one of the many focal points of House activity.

Games. The College has a strong tradition and a fine reputation in the major games of rugby, hockey, netball and cricket. There are regular fixtures with Isle of Man schools and schools in other parts of the British Isles. Athletics, football, cross-country and swimming all flourish and there are both House and College competitions. Senior pupils may opt to play golf on the magnificent adjoining Castletown Golf Links or to sail as their major summer sport. There are approximately thirty acres of first class playing fields, an indoor heated swimming pool which is in use throughout the year, a miniature rifle range, a gymnasium for basketball and badminton, hard tennis courts, two squash courts and an all-weather pitch and outdoor cricket nets.

Other Activities. There is a wide range of societies and activities to complement academic life. The Duke of

Edinburgh's Award Scheme flourishes and expeditions are undertaken regularly both on the Island and further afield. There is a thriving Combined Cadet Force and Social Services group. There are strong links with the Armed Services who help regularly with Cadet training. There are regular skiing trips, choir tours and educational trips to the UK and abroad.

Travel. King William's College is easily accessible from the UK and abroad. Some boarders come by sea from Heysham or Liverpool using the regular service to Douglas but the majority of boarding pupils and parents come by air from the British Isles and much further afield. There are direct flights to London, Belfast, Birmingham, Dublin, Liverpool, Manchester, Bristol and other UK cities. Boarding House staff are fully experienced in arranging international flights and younger pupils are met at the airport.

Health. The health of all pupils is in the care of the School Doctor. There is a sanatorium supervised by a qualified nursing staff and high standards of medical care are available at Noble's Hospital in Douglas.

Fees per term (2021–2022). Day: £7,500 (Years 7 & 8), £8,300 (Years 9–11), £9,600 (Years 12 & 13). Boarding Fee: £4,620 in addition to Day Fee.

A reduction of one-third of the fee for boarders and one half of the fee for day pupils is allowed for children of clergy holding a benefice or Bishop's licence and residing in the Isle of Man. There is a similar arrangement for children of Methodist Ministers.

A reduction of 15% is allowed for serving members of the Armed Forces of the Crown. Once a pupil is accepted, the reduction continues even though the parent may leave the Services.

A reduction is allowed for the second, third and fourth child.

Scholarships and Bursaries. Year 7 Academic Scholarships are offered up to the value of 10% of the current tuition fee and examinations take place in January. There are papers in English and Mathematics and an interview.

Drama, Music and Sports Awards to the value of 10% of the tuition fee are also available to candidates entering Lower Fourth who demonstrate exceptional talent or potential.

There is also a Bursary fund to support students if the financial circumstances of parents make this necessary.

Further details of all scholarships may be obtained from the Principal's Office and on the website.

Charitable status. King William's College is a Manx Registered Charity, number 615 and is operated as a Company limited by guarantee.

Visitor:
The Most Reverend and Right Hon Dr J Sentamu, Lord Archbishop of York

Council Members of Bishop Barrow's Foundation:
His Excellency Sir John Lorimer, Lieutenant Governor of the Isle of Man (*Chairman of Council Members*)
Mr S Billinghurst, BA Hons, ACA
Mr A C Collister
Mrs A Craine
Mr T W B Cullen, MBE, MA
The Lord Bishop, Rt Revd P Eagles
Mrs E J Higgins, BSc, ACA

Dr M J Hoy, MBE, MA, PhD
Mr G Kinrade, Chief Executive Officer, Department of Education and Children
Mr N H Wood, ACA, TEP

Governors:
Mr P B Clucas, BA, BSc Hons (*Chairman*)
Mr S Billinghurst, BA Hons, ACA
MR Y C D Chan, BA Hons, MEd, ACA, DChA
Mr A C Collister
MRS S M Dean, BA Hons, FCCA
MRS C Edmundson, BMus, MBA, PGCE, LRAM, ARCM
Mr R W Flower, BSc Hons, MEd
Mr M Grace, BSc Hons, MRICS
Mr P L Harwood, BSc Hons, FIA
Mrs E J Higgins, BSc, ACA
Dr L V Hulme, LRCP, MRCS
Miss S J Leahy, LLB, Dip LP
Mr R Raatgever, BCom, BAcc Hons, CA SA, ACA

Bursar and Clerk to the Governors: Mr J V Oatts, BA, MSc, Dip Surv

***Principal: J H Buchanan**, BA Hons*

Deputy Head Academic: Miss C L Broadbent, MA
Deputy Head Pastoral: Mr S L Corrie, BMus Hons

* Head of Department
† Housemaster/mistress

Full Time:
Helen Allan, BSc Hons
John M Allegro, BA*
Lee Batchford, BSc Hons*
Amy L G Beesley, BA Hons, PGDip
Amy Benziane, BA Hons
Catrin Beswick, MSci
Karen E Brew, MSc
Katharine M Brown, MPhys*
Madeleine J Burger, BEd
Amy-Jayne Clark, BA Hons, MA
Stephen N Cope, BA Hons*
Matthew Crabtree, BSc
Emma Craine, BA
Denise Currie, BA*
Colin Davidson, MA Hons
Steven Daykin, BMus, PgDip, MISM*
Esther Drane, BA Hons
Bernadette Dunn, BEd Hons
Sonja M Ellson, MA*
Carolina Ganzo-Perez, MA
France Heckel, MA
Lauren Hewes, BA
Vikki Hope, BSc Hons
Niall A Howell-Evans, BA
Edmund J Jeffers, BA†
Sara A Jeffers, BA Hons
Stephen B Jelly, BA Hons*
Stephen P Kelly, BA*
Amanda Kerr, BA, MA*
Bethan Kirkham, BA
Bethan Kneen, BSc
Duncan M C Matthews, BSc Hons*
Anya L Morgans, BA Ed, BSc*
Paul H Morgans, CChem, CSci, PhD, MRSC
Jacqueline Munro, BA Hons, CPT3A, DipEd SEN, RQTU
Susie Parry, BA Hons
Riaan Riekert, BComm

Alison M Schreiber, BA, MA
Kirry K Shimmin, BSc
Zoe E Shimmin, BSc, MSc
Clare V Singleton, BA*
Alasdair D Ulyett, BSc
Philip Verschueren, MSc
Zoe E A Watterson
Madeleine P Westall, BSc

Part-Time
Amanda Barber, PhD
Joanne A Busuttil, BA
Helen Field, BA Hons
Heather Savage, BA
Erica J Scott, BA Hons (*Chaplain*)
Elena Sinclair, BA
Elaine Smith, BSc

Principal's PA: Mrs Jo Bateson
Admissions Registrar: Mrs Marion Taggart
School Medical Officer: Dr Marijtje Drijfhout, MRCGP, DRCOG, DFFP, DPalMed, DOcMed

King's College School

Wimbledon Common, London SW19 4TT

Tel: 020 8255 5300 (Senior School)
        020 8255 5335 (Junior School)
email: admissions@kcs.org.uk (Senior)
        jsadmissions@kcs.org.uk (Junior)
website: www.kcs.org.uk
Twitter: @KCSWimbledon
Facebook: @kingscollegeschool

Motto: *Sancte et Sapienter*

King's College School was founded as the junior department of King's College in 1829. According to the resolutions adopted at the preliminary meeting of founders in 1828, 'the system is to comprise religious and moral instruction, classical learning, history, modern languages, mathematics, natural philosophy, etc., and to be so conducted as to provide in the most effectual manner for the two great objects of education – the communication of general knowledge, and specific preparation for particular professions'. In 1897 it was removed from the Strand to its present spacious site on Wimbledon Common.

Organisation. King's College School is a day school. Boys only are admitted below the sixth form whilst the sixth form is co-educational. The school consists of a senior school of 1,192 pupils aged 11 to 18 and a junior school of 202 pupils aged 7 to 11 who are prepared for entry to the senior school.

Pastoral care is delivered in forms until year 8. From year 9 (fourth form), pupils are allocated a tutor in a house who is responsible for their progress and welfare throughout the rest of their school career.

Admission. Entrance at 11+ into year 7 is via an entrance exam which boys sit in year 6.

Entrance at 13+ into year 9 is via a pre-test which boys sit in year 6 followed by the CE or scholarship in year 8. Should a boy's prep school no longer be preparing pupils for

CE, the conditional year 9 place is subject to satisfactory reports from his prep school head.

Places for girls and boys are available each year for entry to the sixth form via 16+ entrance tests. Preliminary enquiries about entry should be made to the admissions registrar.

Please note that in the context of Covid-19, we have made some changes to our admissions procedures for 2020/21: more information is available on our website.

Junior School. Entrance examinations, graded according to the ages of the pupils, are held in the January of the year of entry. Enquiries should be made to the junior school secretary. (*For further details of the junior school refer to entry in IAPS section.*)

Scholarships. A number of academic, music, sport, drama and art scholarships are available at 11+, 13+ and 16+ entry points. For further details, visit the school website or contact the admissions registrar.

Bursaries. Means-tested bursaries of up to 100% fee remission are available at 11+, 13+ and 16+ entry points. A bursary award may in addition include provision for extras such as school trips and uniform. For further information, please visit the school website.

Fees per term (2021–2022). The senior school (year 9 onwards) £7,665; the lower school (years 7–8) £6,930; the junior school (years 5–6) £6,930; the junior School (years 3–4) £6,435.

The Curriculum – Junior School. The curriculum of the junior school is designed to lead naturally into that of the senior school in content and style. All boys within a year group follow the same timetable.

Transition and first form (years 3 and 4):

English; Mathematics; Science; History; Geography; Religious Studies; Music; Drama; Art; Technology (year 3 only); ICT; Personal, Social, Health and Economic Education (PSHEE); Think Tank (in years 3 and 4); three double sessions of Physical Education and Games.

Second and third forms (years 5 and 6):

English; Mathematics; Science; French; Latin; History; HOTEL (History of the English Language); Geography; Religious Studies; Music; Drama; Art; Design and Engineering; ICT; Personal, Social, Health and Economic Education (PSHEE); Physical Education and two afternoons of Games. Boys are set French and Mathematics from year 6.

The Curriculum – Senior School. The lower and middle school curriculums offer a wide range of options which enable the maximum choice of subjects in the sixth form. A very wide range of subjects is available at GCSE and IGCSE (International GCSE). In the sixth form, pupils choose to study either A Levels or the International Baccalaureate Diploma Programme (IBDP).

Religious Education. King's is an Anglican foundation but welcomes pupils from all churches and faiths, and the practice of other faiths is encouraged. The school has a Chaplaincy through which pupils are prepared for confirmation and there is a Chapel for voluntary worship and communion

Music. A new state-of-the-art music school, with a 200-seat concert hall, was opened in September 2018 by HRH The Duchess of Gloucester. Four orchestras, six choirs, big band, chamber ensemble, as well as various smaller groups and jazz groups, perform a number of major choral and orchestral works each year. There are regular performances at major London venues including Westminster Abbey, Cadogan Hall, St Paul's Cathedral and St John's Smith Square. The choir and orchestra also undertake international tours. Approximately 30% of the pupils have individual music lessons at the school.

Games. A new multi-function sports and swimming complex was opened in September 2019. It provides a six-court sports hall, a 25m swimming pool, aerobic areas, a strength and conditioning room and a large studio amongst other facilities. There are two all-weather surfaces for hockey and tennis at the Kingsway ground. The school's boathouse is on the Tideway at Putney Bridge. After an introduction to a range of games in the fourth form, pupils have a free choice of termly sports. The major sports are rugby, hockey, netball, football, tennis and cricket and the games programme also includes athletics, badminton, basketball, cross-country running, fencing, golf, rowing, squash, swimming, table tennis and water polo.

School Societies and Activities. Every pupil is encouraged to take part in extracurricular activities. Societies meet in the two extended lunch breaks and after school. Friday school finishes early to allow pupils to participate in a range of activities such as the CCF and community service. The school runs an impressive outreach programme supporting a number of neighbouring state schools. There are active drama and debating societies, together with a wide range of other clubs.

Honours. Places offered at Oxford and Cambridge for 2016: 57, 2017: 51, 2018: 44, 2019: 46; 2020: 39, 2021: 25

Charitable status. King's College School is a Registered Charity, number 310024. It exists to provide education for children.

Governing Body:
The Archbishop of Canterbury (*Visitor*)
The Rt Revd Christopher Chessun, Bishop of Southwark
  (*Ex Officio*)
Lord Deighton, KBE (*Chairman*)
G C Slimmon, MA, MBA (*Vice Chairman*)
S A Bennett, BA
O L Carlstrand, BSc, CEng, MICE
C G Hale, MA, LLM
S A B Hobbs, BA, PGCE
D G Ingram, MA
Sir Robert Jay, QC
Professor D A Lievesley, CStat, AcSS, CBE
I A Macmillan, BSc, ACA, MBA
A Ng, BSc, FCA
Dt C Okelo, BSc, MD
R J Parker, MA
J L Robinson, BA, PGCE, MEd
J G Sarpong, BSc, MBA
M D J Sharp, BA
P J L Strafford, BA, MBA

Bursar & Secretary to the Governing Body: Mrs A M
  Clarke, MA

Senior School Staff

Acting Head: **Ms J F Lowson**, MA

Deputy Heads:
Mr R H Amlot, MA
Miss M J Clarke, MA
Mr K Gross, BEd
Mr J A Short Ring, FCCT, BA

Assistant Heads:
Mr B M Baulf, MA (*Head of Teaching and Learning*)
Mr W C Forse, MA (*Head of Admissions and Marketing*)
Mr J S Gibson, BA (*Head of Lower School*)
Mrs J M Lawton-Cook, BSc (*Head of Sixth Form*)
Mr D Miller, BSc (*Head of KCS Online*)
Mr J H Renwick, MA (*Head of Middle School*)
Mr C P Sandels, MSc (*Acting Head of Sixth Form*)
Mr M Stables, MA (*Director of Studies*)

Directors:
Mr T J Davies, BA (*Digital Learning and Innovation*)
Miss R M Davis, BA (*Staff Welfare*)
Miss O R Harman, BA (*Equality, Diversity and Inclusion*)
Mr P A Hatch, MusB (*Partnerships and Outreach*)
Mr L B D Kane, BSc (*Co-Curricular Education*)
Miss C A Ramgoolam, MA (*Public Occasions*)
Mr J M Stanley, BSc (*Mental Health and Wellbeing*)
Mrs S Willis (*Safeguarding*)

Teaching Staff:

* *Head of Department*

Art:
*Miss G A Joyce, BA
Mr N Pollen, MA
Miss E J Schofield, BA
Miss C van Oosterom, BA

Biology:
*Mr A P Hedges, BSc (*Acting Head of Biology*)
Miss E M Arnold, BSc
Dr J E Blythe
Miss J Brown, MA
Mr J E Grabowski, BSc (*Head of Layton*)
Miss A M Lethbridge, BSc
Mrs R G O'Brien, MA
Mr J F Painter, MA
Miss E J C Witney-Smith, BSc

Chemistry:
*Dr A M Hayes
Dr I I F Boogaerts (*Deputy Head of IB*)
Ms C M Burke, MSc
Miss A M Dawe, BSc
Dr P M Lloyd (*Deputy Head of IB*)
Mr J W McGarey, MA (*Acting Deputy Head of Sixth Form*)
Mr R J Mitchell, MA
Ms M E Sanford, BSc
Dr R A L Winchester
Miss R Y Yang, BSc

Classics:
*Mr S L C Young, BA
Miss F T I Barwick Ward, BA
Mr B M Baulf, BA (*Assistant Head, Head of Teaching and
  Learning*)
Mr G E Bennett, BA (*Deputy Head of IB*)
Miss V R Casemore, MA
Miss E A Garnett, MA
Mr A L V Karski, BA
Mr J A Pinder, BA

Computer Science:
*Mr D Haxton, BSc
Miss C A Ramgoolam, MA (*Director of Public Occasions*)

Design & Engineering:
*Miss L E L Spicer, MSc
Mr J D Broderick, MA

Mr R W Entwisle, MEng
Mr D Hopwood, BSc
Mr M Jones, BSc

Drama:
*Ms D J Barron, MA (*Director of Drama*)
Miss H Feeny, MA
Mr J L B Trapmore, MA (*Head of Curricular Drama*)

Economics & Social Sciences:
*Mrs S M Danaher, BA (*Head of Economics*)
Mr F R C Jones, BA
Mrs H E Marion, MA
Mr H S J Poole, BA
Mr G J A Simpson, BSc
Ms A M Troy, BA (*Deputy Head of Economics*)
Mrs S Williams, BCom

English:
*Dr J P D Cannon
Mr R H Amlot, MA (*Deputy Head*)
Miss S L Bailey, BA
Mrs K L Bird, MA
Ms J A L Blunden, MA [maternity leave]
Mr B L Bransfield, MA
Mr D I Cass, BA (*Deputy Head of English, Deputy Head of Staff Development*)
Miss C F Crothers, BA
Miss A V Eilert, MA (*Deputy Head of IB*)
Miss O R Harman, BA (*Director of Equality, Diversity and Inclusion, Deputy Head of Sixth Form*)
Mr H R Trimble, BA
Mr R C Yule, BA

Geography:
*Mr M V Christou, MA
Mrs M J Clarke, MA (*Deputy Head, Academic*)
Mr J A Galloway, BA (*Senior Teacher*)
Mrs J M Lawton-Cook, BSc (*Assistant Head, Head of Sixth Form*)
Miss L M Nahorniak, BA (*Acting Deputy Head of Sixth Form*)
Mr J F Odling, BSc
Mrs K E Potts, MA
Miss F L M Smart, BA
Mr J M Stanley, BSc (*Director of Mental Health and Wellbeing*)
Mr K H Tipping, BA

History:
*Mrs F A Ring, MA
Miss R M Davis, BA (*Director of Staff Development*)
Mr J G Lawrence, MA, MLitt
Ms J F Lowson, MA (*Acting Head*)
Mr B E F Reekes, BA
Mr T D Rendell, BA
Mr J A Short Ring, FCCT, BA (*Deputy Head*)
Mr M A Stephenson, MA
Mr O H Wheatley, BA (*Deputy Head of History*)
Mrs S E Wiseman, MA (*Head of PSHE*)

Learning Enrichment:
*Miss E Sadler
Mrs A L J Sandwell, BA
Mrs K M Winter, MA

Mathematics:
*Mr S J Nye, BSc
Dr C G Bell
Miss R Bhattacharya, BA

Mr H Bond, BSc
Mr S J Bradley, BEng
Dr A Charfi
Miss L K Cooke, BSc
Dr S Coury
Mr W G Forse, MA (*Assistant Head, Admissions and Marketing*)
Mrs S Y Han, BSc
Mr A Haria, MA (*Deputy Head of Higher Education and Careers*)
Miss J E James, BSc
Mrs E C Nicholl, BSc [sabbatical]
Mr M J Poole, BSc
Dr T R Squires, BA (*Head of Alverstone*)
Mr M Stables, MA (*Assistant Head, Director of Studies*)
Mr M J Stenning, BSc (*Deputy Director of Studies*)
Mr A M R Trosser, MSci & ARCS
Mr O Vella, MSc
Mr S A Williams, BSc (*Deputy Head of Mathematics*)

Modern Languages:
*Mrs H M Mulcahy, BA
Mrs A J Ansbro, MA
Miss B P Cerda Drago, BA (*Deputy Head of Modern Languages, Head of Spanish*) [maternity leave]
Mr H Chapman, MA
Mr S A Etienne, MA (*Deputy Head of Education, Overseas Schools*)
Mr K Gross, BEd (*Deputy Head, Director of Overseas Schools*)
Mr S C Kent, MA (*Head of Higher Education and Careers, Head of Chinese*)
Miss M M E Kidwell, MA (*Acting Head of Spanish*)
Miss J A Maxwell, BA
Mrs P Liberti
Mrs H M Lindsey-Noble, BA (*Acting Deputy Head of Modern Languages, Head of German*)
Miss R C Peel, BA (*Head of Major*)
Ms C O H Robinson, BA
Mr J M A Ross, BA (*Acting Head of French, Italian Coordinator*)
Mr J R C Saxton, BA
Ms R Serrano Ramirez, BA
Mr D Starrett, BA
Mrs L Tremayne, BA

Music:
*Mr D G Phillips, MA (*Director of Music*)
Mr N E Bricht (*Head of Wind & Brass*)
Mr W S Ford, BA
Mr P A Hatch, MusB (*Director of Partnerships & Outreach, Assistant Director of Music*)
Mr M L Nixon, BMus (*Head of Keyboard*)
Mr T J Smedley, BMus (*Head of Strings*)

Physical Education:
Mr R P McCluskey, BA (*Director of Sport*)
Mr J S Gibson, BA (*Assistant Head (Head of Lower School)*)
Mr T Gwynne, BSc (*Head of Year 8 (Lower School), Head of Cricket*)
Mr L B D Kane, BSc (*Director of Co-Curricular Education, President of Common Room*)
Miss K McGinley, BA (*Head of Girls' Games*)
Mr G McGowan, BA (*Head of Football*)
Mr T P Rogers, BSc (*Head of Middle School, Head of Rugby*)
Mr B D Tibble, BSc (*Head of Hockey*)

Physics:
*Miss J L Dunscombe, MPhys (*Acting Head of Physics*)
Mr G Cawley, BSc
Mr M J Cole, MEd (*Head of Kingsley*)
Mr T H Davies, MA
Mr A J Foster, MA
Miss E L Geraghty, MA (*Head of Education – Overseas Schools*)
Mr D Miller, BSc (*Assistant Head, Head of KCS Online*)
Dr K A Ralley
Mrs R F A Rose, BSc (*Head of Year 7 (Lower School)*)
Mr C P Sandels, MSc (*Acting Head of Sixth Form*)
Ms M A G Spottiswoode, BSc

Psychology:
*Mrs E S Britton, MSc
Miss J Li, MSc
Miss A McGarvey, BSc (*Deputy Head of Middle School, Deputy Director of Professional Learning*)

Theology & Philosophy:
*Mr A J Wood, MA
Mr F J Barber BA
Dr H M Cocksworth, MA (*Deputy Director of Partnerships*)
Rev Dr J W Crossley (*Chaplain*)
Mr T J Davies, BA (*Director of Digital Learning and Innovation; Head of Glenesk*)
Mr J H Renwick, MA (*Assistant Head (Head of Middle School)*)
Miss E R Tozzi, BA (*Deputy Head of Sixth Form (Head of New Pupils)*)

Junior School Staff

Headmaster: Mr E H Lougher, BA, MSc

Deputy Heads:
Mrs H J Morren, MA (*Pastoral*)
Mr D Jones, BA (*Academic*)

Assistant Heads:
Mr E J M Borton, BA (*Academic and Public Occasions, Head of Geography*)
Mr J E A Hipkiss, BSc (*Communications, Head of Science*)

Head of Rushmere: Mrs C Madge, BEd

Teaching Staff:
Mr R D Anderson, BCom (*Head of Mathematics*)
Miss V J Attié, BA (*Head of Tudor House, Modern Languages*)
Mr G S W Baird, MA (*Head of History and Religious Studies*)
Mr A Baker, BEd (*Rushmere Teacher*)
Mr J J Barrington, BSc (*Head of Football and Cricket*)
Miss C M Bitaud, BA (*Head of EAL*)
Mr A J Blackburn, BA (*Mathematics*)
Mrs J C Blight, BEd (*Rushmere Teacher*)
Mrs C Bourne, BEd (*Head of Second and Third Forms, Mathematics*) [maternity leave]
Mr P K Brady, BA (*Acting Head of Second and Third Forms, Head of Stuart House, Geography*)
Mr D Cheers, BEd (*Head of Rugby*)
Mrs S J de Montfort, BTheol (*Professional Tutor (Induction)*)
Ms M M Downes, BA (*Learning Enrichment Coordinator*)
Miss L S Gillard, MA, ATC (*Head of Art & Design*)
Mrs E E Gordon, MA (*English and Drama*) [maternity leave]
Mr R O Graham, BA (*Mathematics*)

Mrs O M Hamilton, MA (*Head of Religious Studies, Classics*)
Mr M J Hortin, MA (*Head of Classics*)
Miss S R Hunter, BSc (*Head of Lower School Maclear, Science*)
Mr B D James, BSc (*Head of Rushmere Games*)
Mr N A Jay, BA (*Professional Tutor (Qualifications)*)
Mrs J C Lewis, BA (*Rushmere Teacher*)
Mr H A C Manger, BSc (*Head of Windsor, Rushmere Teacher*)
Mrs S J Martineau Walker, BA (*Art*)
Ms C McGregor, BA (*Head of Drama*)
Ms H F Montgomery-Massingberd, BA (*Head of Modern Foreign Languages*)
Mrs J Morley, MEd (*Learning Enrichment, Junior SEND Coordinator*) [maternity leave]
Mr M L Nixon, BMus (*Head of Keyboard*)
Mr C Norman, MA (*Head of Norman, History*)
Mr L O'Sullivan (*Head of Lower School Glenesk, Head of Swimming and Water Polo*)
Mr I R Parker, MA (*Music*)
Mrs L J Pearson, BA (*Learning Enrichment Coordinator*)
Mrs S K Phillips, BEd (*Rushmere Teacher*)
Ms R L Prescott, BA (*English with Drama*)
Mrs R F A Rose, BSc (*Head of Year 7 (Lower School), PSHEE, Science*)
Mr P P Thomas, MA (*Head of ICT*)
Mrs S J Walker, BA (*Rushmere Teacher*)
Miss R Walshe, BSc (*Rushmere Teacher*)
Mr R Weber MMus (*Head of Music*)
Mrs S Zeqiri, BA (*English with Drama*)

Support Staff:
PA to the Head Master: Mrs S Carrett
Admissions Registrar: Ms S J W Dowling, BA
PA to Junior School Headmaster: Mrs S Richards

King's College, Taunton
A Woodard School

South Road, Taunton, Somerset TA1 3LA

Tel:	Headmaster: 01823 328210
	Reception: 01823 328200
email:	admissions@kings-taunton.co.uk
website:	www.kings-taunton.co.uk
Twitter:	@KingsTaunton
Facebook:	@kingscollegetaunton
LinkedIn:	/company/kingsschoolstaunton

Motto: *Fortis et Fidelis*

King's College, Taunton is an independent co-educational boarding and day school for boys and girls aged 13 to 18 years.

Situated on the outskirts of Taunton, the county town of Somerset, on a splendid 100-acre site, King's College offers high academic standards, a friendly and caring day and boarding community, and has an enviable reputation for music, drama and sport. Kindness, consideration for others, honesty and self-discipline are the values which King's hold dear, providing its pupils with the inner resources not just for school, but for life.

A Woodard school, Canon Nathaniel Woodard renamed the school King's College in memory of King Alfred, when he bought it in 1879, but its historical links go back to the medieval grammar school which was founded by Bishop Fox of Winchester in 1522.

King's College, Taunton, delivers success at all ages whilst offering a friendly, happy and safe living and working environment. The school provides an extraordinary breadth of opportunities to pupils and has very high academic standards. As well as the school's academic success, pupils also enjoy the highest levels of achievement in sports, art, drama and music. The school is a regular on the national circuit for rugby, hockey, cricket and football, and in the past has won such things as the BBC Songs of Praise Senior School Choir of the Year title. The co-curricular offering includes an off-site equestrian centre, leading CCF department, as well as a thriving performing arts scene and academic enrichment societies, all of which are just a taste of the breadth of opportunity available to pupils.

King's College has produced a large number of Oxbridge entrants over the years and is well regarded by the top universities in the UK. Pupils can join the Third Form (Year 9) at 13, going on to take GCSE exams, or in the Sixth Form (Year 12) at 16 or 17 to study for A Levels. The school is blessed with highly-qualified and committed members of staff who see their role as ensuring the happiness and successful development of each individual member of the school community. The word community is very prominent at King's: boarders and day pupils benefit from a strong Christian ethos in an environment where self-respect and kindness to others are highly-regarded qualities.

Admission. All entries are made through the Director of Admissions. Pupils normally enter at 13 years in the Michaelmas Term and are admitted via Common Entrance or the Scholarship Examination.

The registration fee is £100.

Fees per term (2021–2022). Boarders £11,790, Day Pupils £7,960. The fees are inclusive of all extra charges of general application.

Scholarships. Scholarships are available to boys and girls going into the Third Form (13+) and Sixth Form. Major Academic scholarships are awarded, as well as scholarships for music, drama and performing arts, art, DT and sport.

Auditions for music and drama scholarships and awards are held in February (13+), and in November for Sixth Form.

Applicants for art and DT scholarships are invited to visit the school during the Lent Term with a portfolio of work.

13+ sports scholarships are available for competition each February and Sixth Form sports scholarships are available in November.

Charitable status. Woodard Schools Taunton Ltd is a Registered Charity, number 1103346. King's College exists to provide high quality education for boys and girls aged 13–18.

Headmaster: **R R Biggs**, MA Rhodes Scholar Pembroke College Oxford, BSc Cape Town

Deputy Head (*Pastoral*): Mrs K L McSwiggan, BA Reading

Deputy Head (*Academic*): Mr J J B Lawford, MEd Open, BA Birmingham

Head of Sixth Form: Mr O R Ridley, BA York

Head of Boarding: Mr J H Griffiths, BTech Brunel

Director Finance & Operations: Mr S C Worthy, BA, MBA

Director of Admissions & Marketing: Mrs K J Rippin

Director of Development: Mr J J Mack

PA to the Headmaster: Mrs F Byrne

King's Ely

The Old Palace, Palace Green, Ely, Cambridgeshire CB7 4EW

Tel: 01353 660701 (Principal's PA)
           01353 660707 (Admissions)
email: admissions@kingsely.org
website: www.kingsely.org
Twitter: @Kings_Ely
Facebook: @KingsElyOfficial
Instagram: @kingselyofficial
LinkedIn: /kingselyofficial

Energy, Courage, Integrity

King's Ely is a leading independent, co-educational day and boarding school in Cambridgeshire which serves the academic and pastoral needs of children aged 2 to 18, with boarders from 8 years old.

Nestled in the beautiful and tranquil cathedral city of Ely, King's Ely is a vibrant, nurturing, inclusive and forward-looking community which has prepared children's futures for a millennium, making it one of the oldest schools in the world.

Ely is just 15 minutes from Cambridge and 1 hour from London, with direct rail links to both. The school is a 5 minute walk from Ely train station and King's Ely's privately-run school buses stop at key locations around Cambridgeshire, Suffolk and Norfolk.

King's Ely is delighted to be a finalist in the recent Independent Schools of the Year Awards, and its latest Independent Schools Inspectorate (ISI) inspection (November 2021) resulted in the school achieving the highest grading possible in every single category.

Inspectors said that "pupils throughout King's Ely make excellent progress across all areas of learning and at all ages and ability ranges", and that "pupils show a keen appreciation, respect and support for the diverse nature of their community".

King's Ely is a school where learning really is an adventure. Students are encouraged to take risks in their learning, pushing themselves beyond the boundaries of their expectations, discovering more about the world around them, and, in doing so, more about themselves. What makes King's Ely special is its determination to instil in the young people in its care a real enthusiasm for learning and a belief that all students can achieve if the teaching is approached in a way that suits the learning style of each pupil. This is not easy necessarily; it is challenging, often uncomfortable, but King's Ely students know that they are well supported, that their teachers believe in them, and so they are willing to step out of their 'comfort zone' and take the very risks that will bring about high-level learning.

Whether a student shines in a classroom, in a laboratory, on a stage, on a pitch or on a mountainside, King's Ely promises an abundance of opportunity for personal development, both academically and socially.

Organisation. King's Ely is fully co-educational from the ages of 2 to 18. The total roll is 1,050 and around a quarter of pupils over the age of 8 are boarders.

The school is divided into four parts: King's Ely Acremont, the Nursery and Pre-Prep for children aged 2 to 7, which stands in its own grounds at Acremont House; King's Ely Junior for children aged 7–13 (Years 3–8); King's Ely Senior for students aged 13–16 (Years 9–11) and King's Ely Sixth Form for students aged 16–18 (Years 12–13).

Buildings. The Old Palace on Palace Green, home for centuries to the Bishops of Ely, serves as the entrance to the school, housing the Sixth Form Centre, the Head's Offices and Admissions, as well as the Development Office. The school still uses many of Ely's medieval monastic buildings – as boarding houses, as classrooms and as the dining hall. The 14th century Porta, the great gateway to the monastery, has been converted into a magnificent Senior School Library. Other recent buildings show the continuing and substantial investment in modern facilities: the renovated Georgian villa that now houses the Nursery and Pre-Prep section of King's Acremont; a new Art School and Performance Studies block, housing the new Dance Studio and 'Black Box' Drama Studio; a Technology Centre; a Senior Music School and Recital Hall and a self-contained, two-storey accommodation including seven classrooms and a science laboratory for Years 7 and 8.

King's Ely Acremont. At King's Ely Acremont, children thrive in a happy, safe environment where they feel secure and valued and quickly develop a sense of belonging. Children from the ages of 2 to 7 are encouraged to question, explore and have the confidence and security to take risks in their learning. A rich, creative curriculum sets the children on the road to becoming lifelong thinkers and learners. Courage and courtesy are valued, encouraged and celebrated publicly.

Children may start in King's Ely Nursery in the term in which they turn 2. The Nursery is sessional and it is recommended children attend three sessions a week from the outset. However, flexibility to suit the needs of each individual child is important. As children progress through the Nursery, the number of sessions should increase to a minimum of five sessions per week. The children are very well prepared for a smooth transition into Reception through regular visits ensuring that they are very familiar with both staff and setting in the next stage of their journey through King's Ely. Please contact Admissions to discuss suitable sessions for your child.

Children start Reception in the September following their 4th birthday. Reception, Year 1 and Year 2 are all taught in Acremont House. Small class sizes, with a Teacher and Teaching Assistant in each, allow children to flourish, preparing them well for the transition to King's Ely Junior.

King's Ely Acremont offers working parents the option of an 8am Breakfast Club, After School Care until 6pm and Holiday Club. Forest School, Science Club and Musical Sparklers are just some of the clubs on offer.

King's Ely Junior. King's Ely Junior celebrates the many ways that students learn and is keen to embrace different learning styles. Students are encouraged to develop their autonomy as they mature and there is an expectation of an ever-increasing use of information literacy, technology and study skills during the students' time at King's Ely Junior. Individual responses, such as films being made for homework, or a computer generated response to a task are equally as welcome as a formal written piece of work. Students can be characterised by their flexibility of approach and it is seen as an important life skill for the next generation.

Ensuring that every student is challenged to fulfil their potential and encouraged along the way, requires that the progress of each student is measured and supported well at all times. Form Tutors shoulder this role on a day to day basis. However, each student has a Head of Year who monitors their work and considers how well they are progressing against the school's predictions. Weekly meetings ensure that speedy intervention is offered to support or extend students appropriately.

From Year 5 onwards, students are set for Maths and English. At this point the students are split between four sets of about 14. These groups are reviewed frequently by the subject teachers and the Head of Year and any adjustments to the sets are made by the Director of Studies, following discussion with parents. As students progress through the school more subjects are set, such as Languages and Science. In Years 7 and 8, subjects are linked according to the English, Maths and Science or Language sets. Students are taught in four or five groups, depending on subject.

Every term is punctuated by a host of academic challenges that serve to inspire the pupils and encourage them to push the parameters of their learning. Examination results are high and the school prides itself on being at the forefront of developments in the educational world.

During the school day all children are divided among four co-educational Houses for pastoral and competitive purposes; each of these Houses is staffed by male and female members of the teaching staff. King's Ely Junior has one co-educational boarding house and one for the boy choristers of Ely Cathedral who are all pupils of King's Ely Junior. There is a wide range of extra-curricular opportunities both at lunch times and after school – Archery, Pottery, Golf, Engineering Club – the choices are endless!

King's Ely Senior. The amount of academic choice that pupils can exercise grows as they move through the Senior School. Options in the Sixth Form are very flexible and the sets are often small. Up to GCSE (Year 11) there is a compulsory core of English, Mathematics, Religious Studies and Sciences. In addition, every pupil chooses up to four option subjects from: Art, Business Studies, Classical Civilisation, Design and Technology, Food and Nutrition, Drama, English as a Foreign Language, French, Geography, German, History, Latin, Music, Physical Education, Spanish. Inter-House competitions in disciplines such as singing, Ely Scheme and debating are keenly participated in.

King's Ely International. At King's Ely International, students are welcomed from all over the world to engage with the unique community that is King's Ely. The aim is to ensure a smooth and successful transition into the vibrant environment of a UK boarding school, steeped in history but offering an innovative educational experience.

Although fully integrated with the main school, King's Ely International offers effective support academically for international students between the ages of 14 and 16 who may be studying for the first time in the UK. The one-year intensive GCSE course suits students who wish to complete their GCSEs in a year. The Pre-GCSE programme is for students between the ages of 14 and 15 who need support in their English. It is also a "stand-alone" course and may be seen as a sabbatical year, especially for European students who wish to return to their home countries after a year abroad improving their English.

Extra-Curricular Activities. King's Ely has a holistic approach to education and this is reflected in the school's thriving co-curricular scene, for which it is renowned. Music, Art, Drama, Ely Scheme (outdoor education), Sports, practical hobbies and interests – all are catered for in a large range of lunchtime and after-hours activities.

Ely Scheme. All pupils in Year 9 are introduced to the school's distinctive outdoor pursuits programme, Ely Scheme, which provides a training in practical and personal skills and in teamwork, initiative and leadership. For some pupils it leads on to the Duke of Edinburgh's Award Scheme or to specialised activities such as climbing, kayaking or pioneering.

Art, Drama and Music. Music is strong, as one would expect in a school that is so closely linked to the cathedral. There is a full programme of performances for school and public audiences, and regular tours overseas. Nearly half of all pupils have personal tuition in a musical instrument; many learn two or even three. An outstanding Art School, opened in March 2010, inspires Fine Art, Sculpture, Photography and Textiles. All parts of the school present plays every year in addition to productions by year or ad hoc groups.

Games. The school's main sports are Rowing, Rugby, Football, Netball, Hockey and Cricket. Athletics, Badminton, Basketball, Tennis, Sailing, Squash, Swimming, Golf, Clay Pigeon Shooting and Horse Riding are also available. All pupils are encouraged to take part in team games, and there is a full programme of fixtures against other schools.

Religious Worship. The Junior and Senior Schools worship regularly in Ely Cathedral. Other services weekly are also in accordance with the principles of the Church of England. The Bishop conducts a confirmation service for pupils in the Lent Term. However, all denominations (or none) are warmly welcome.

Exeats. Boarders are granted weekend exeats on the written request of a parent or guardian. Weekly and flexi boarding are increasingly popular.

Admission. Registration forms can be obtained from the Admissions Department and a £100 (£150 for non-EU) fee is payable at first registration.

Admission to King's Ely Acremont is by interview.

Admission to King's Ely Junior is by interview and INCAs in English and Maths. There is also Lucid screening for dyslexia. King's Ely Junior entrance assessments are held in January prior to the following Michaelmas Term. Small groups of children are invited to attend assessments throughout January. Offers are made for the beginning of February.

Admission to King's Ely Senior at 13+ entrance is by the school's entrance examination consisting of English, Maths, Science and Lucid in late January.

Admission to Year 12 at 16+ is by interview with the Principal and predicted GCSE grades. The entry qualification for the Sixth Form is not less than six C grades with B grades in subjects selected for A Level. Twenty-seven AS/A2 Level subjects are offered in Years 12 and 13. Taster Days are held throughout November and December.

Pupils may enter the school at any time, depending on availability of space and assessment.

Scholarships and Exhibitions. Entrance Scholarships and Exhibitions up to a cumulative total of 10% of tuition fees are awarded for achievement and potential in academic work, music and sport, and 5% in art, design technology, drama.

A competitive examination is held in January each year and successful candidates enter Year 9 the following Michaelmas Term. These Scholarships will be continued until the end of Year 11, subject to satisfactory progress, after which an application for a Sixth Form Scholarship may be made.

King's Ely Senior:

Academic Scholarships are for the three years from Year 9 leading to the GCSE examinations and are made on the basis of a competitive examination set by the school in January. Successful candidates are also interviewed.

Music Scholarships are available for choral and/or instrumental excellence, including organ-playing, and may include free weekly tuition on two musical instruments. Candidates for entry into Year 9 are invited to the school for auditions in January.

All boy Choristers of Ely Cathedral are full boarders of King's Ely Junior and receive a choristership worth 50% of fees while they remain in the choir and a bursary worth 33% of fees on transfer to King's Ely Senior. Members of the Cathedral Girls' Choir are all boarders in King's Ely Senior and receive a bursary worth 33% of boarding fees. Additional means-tested funding may be available. Chorister auditions are held in February for boys who will be aged 8 and for girls who will be 13 by the following September.

Sports Awards, for entry into Year 9, are open to boys and girls with potential for major county, regional or national representation or with all-round sporting excellence. Reports will be sought from the candidates' coach(es) and practical tests, if required, will be held at the school in January.

Art, Drama and Design Technology Exhibitions are available for entry into Year 9 and assessments are held in January.

Sixth Form:

Academic Scholarships are for the two years of the A Level course and are made following an examination in November and an interview with the Vice Principal (Academic) and Head of Sixth Form (Academic). Candidates should be on course for at least six A* or A passes at GCSE.

Music Scholarships are available for choral and/or instrumental excellence, including organ-playing, and may include free weekly tuition on two musical instruments. Candidates for entry into Year 12 are invited to the school for auditions in November.

Sports Awards, for entry into Year 12, are open to boys and girls with potential for major county, regional or national representation or with all-round sporting excellence. Reports will be sought from the candidates' coach(es) and practical tests, if required, will be held at the school in November.

Art, Drama and Design Technology Exhibitions are available for entry into Year 12 and assessments are held in November.

Full particulars of all awards are available on the King's Ely website.

Bursaries. Awards may be supplemented by a means-tested Bursary if there is genuine financial need. Bursary support may be available to new pupils over the age of 7 whose parents are unable to pay the full tuition fee.

Fees per term (January–July 2022). King's Ely Acremont Nursery and Pre-Prep: Nursery places are booked by the session; Daily rates range from £29 (mornings)–£68 (extended day). The fee for Pre-Prep Reception to Year 2 is £3,703 per term (no boarding). Pre- and after-school care and holiday club are available at extra charge.

King's Ely Junior per term: Years 3 and 4: £5,320 (day); £8,339 (boarding); Years 5 to 8: £5,707 (day); £8,805 (boarding).

King's Ely Senior per term: Years 9 to 13: £7,888 (day); £11,415 (boarding).

Flexi boarding: It may be possible to offer overnight accommodation for day pupils on an occasional basis at a cost of £50–£60 per night. The cost of extended flexi boarding will be quoted in advance upon application to Admissions.

Concessions: A generous discount in fees is available from age 4 for children of clergy serving the Christian faith and boarders who are children of Services personnel in receipt of CEA and also for children of FCO employees. Sibling discount on the third child is available. Bursaries are available to those entering Year 7 or beyond.

Old Eleans. Former pupils receive news of the school and of their contemporaries and are invited annually to events.

Charitable status. The King's School, Ely is a Registered Charity, number 802427. Its aims and objectives are to offer excellence in education to day and boarding pupils.

Chairman of Governors: Mr David Day

Principal of King's Ely: Mr John Attwater

Head of King's Ely Acremont Pre-Prep and Nursery: Mrs Faye Fenton-Stone
Head of King's Ely Junior: Mr Richard Whymark
Head of King's Ely Senior: Mr Jonathan Shaw

Vice Principal Academic (Whole School): Mrs Jane Thomas
Director of Boarding: Mr Andy Thomas
Director for International Students: Mr Matthew Norbury
Director of Admissions and Marketing: Mr Nick Tappin

The King's School

Canterbury

25 The Precincts, Canterbury, Kent CT1 2ES

Tel: Reception: 01227 595501
              Bursar: 01227 595544
              Admissions: 01227 595579
email: info@kings-school.co.uk
website: www.kings-school.co.uk
Twitter: @KingsCanterbury
Facebook: @KingsCanterbury
LinkedIn: /the-king's-school-canterbury

St Augustine's foundation of a monastic school in Canterbury in 597 AD marks the origin of The King's School: hence, its claim to be the oldest school in the country. It was re-founded by King Henry VIII in 1541. More recently, a Junior School has been established on the former estate of Lord Milner outside the city. The close relationship with the Cathedral Foundation has been there throughout.

King's Scholars. Many schools cherish the notion that they are the oldest school in the country, but there is little doubt that there has been a school on the present World Heritage site of King's School, Canterbury since the Augustinian mission to England in 597 AD. The name of the school and its intimate relationship with the Cathedral community of the mother church of the Anglican Communion date from the Henrician settlement, as do the King's Scholars who, along with the Headmaster and the Senior Deputy Head, form part of the original Foundation of Christchurch, Canterbury. So much for the history, the King's Scholars continue to occupy buildings and be taught in classrooms that predate the Reformation. Besides their function in the Cathedral, the King's Scholars are at the heart of the vibrant and open-ended academic life of the school. Each year, some of the King's Scholars are on full means-tested bursaries, keeping alive the original vision of the school. The modern King's Scholar discovers a school which is fully co-educational, diverse in its catchment and intentions, as well as in tune with the wider life of the city of Canterbury and national/international context beyond its immediate compass.

Scholarships and Bursaries. Up to twenty King's Scholars and Exhibitioners are elected each year following competitive examinations and interviews in February. A further group of King's Scholars are added at the Sixth Form entrance stage (competitive examination and interviews in the November preceding entry). These academic awards have a meritocratic value of 10% of the fees, but the crucial thing is that they can be augmented by means-tested bursaries up to 100%. The extremely strong tradition of music at King's, both instrumental and choral, means that Music Scholarships (about 20 are awarded annually) are generously provided for. The school is particularly welcoming for those who have come on to King's from the choir schools of Cathedrals and Colleges. There are further Music Scholarships made for Sixth Form entry.

There are further Scholarships and Exhibitions at 13+ for exceptional ability in Art and Sport – the Gower Sports Scholarships named after the former England cricket captain

– and the school also grants awards for DT, Drama and Dance.

Academic Life. The King's curriculum is distinct for its combination of striving for the very highest standards in the most appropriate Public Examinations (IGCSEs at the end of Year 10 for a few subjects, but mainly at the end of Year 11; A Levels and Pre-U courses in the Sixth Form) on the one hand, and the pursuit of learning and the development of the intellect for its own sake (self-standing courses, tutorials and lectures in the evenings and extended project qualifications, as well as independent research). The school puts particular emphasis on studying Mandarin, German and Russian, as well as 'new' subjects like Photography and Computer Science. A wide degree of choice of subject in the Sixth Form (Earth & Planetary Sciences and Philosophy, for example) is often an engine for academic success.

Some 20–25 offers of admission to Oxford and Cambridge are received each year.

All-round Vision. Christopher Marlowe, William Harvey and Thomas Linacre number amongst King's pupils and the pursuit of the Renaissance ideal still resonates in the contemporary school. The strongest encouragement is given to Music, Drama, Sport, CCF and the Visual Arts. This stems from belief in the value of these activities in themselves, but also since recreation and success in these fields leads to growth in self-confidence and better academic performance. Alongside these activities are opportunities to get involved in Partnership projects and pursue the Duke of Edinburgh's Award.

Numbers and Organisation. There are currently 903 pupils on the school roll, 444 boys and 459 girls, of whom 80% are boarders. There are 6 boys' boarding houses, 7 girls' boarding houses and 3 (mixed) day houses. To the east of the main school buildings in the Cathedral Precincts is St Augustine's, home to 5 boarding houses, the original Medieval Hall and magnificent school library. There are 2 major sites for sport, Birley's and Blore's, each with extensive sports facilities. Junior King's School, the prep school of King's, occupies a site on the River Stour, in Sturry, three miles from Canterbury. There are currently 367 pupils at Junior King's, 193 boys and 174 girls of whom 81 are boarders.

Admission. Application should be made to the Assistant Registrar. It is advisable to register pupils at an early age. Admission is normally through the Common Entrance Examination, the King's School entrance examination (for non-CE candidates) or, if academically appropriate, through the King's Scholarship Examination. The age of entry is about 13.

Fees per term (2021–2022). Senior School: £13,285 for boarders and £8,375–£9,300 for day pupils. Junior School: ££9,090 for boarders and £5,500–£6,525 for day pupils.

OKS (Old King's Scholars). *Coordinator*: Molly Burgess, OKS Association Office, Tel: 01227 595669; email: oks@kings-school.co.uk.

The King's Society exists for all parents, past and present. A termly programme of social and cultural events is open to all members and is published on the school website.

Charitable status. The King's School of the Cathedral Church of Canterbury is a Registered Charity, number 307942. It exists to provide education for boys and girls.

Visitor: The Lord Archbishop of Canterbury

Governors:
Chairman: The Very Revd Dr R A Willis, DL, DCL, DD, Dean of Canterbury Cathedral
Revd Canon Dr E Pennington
Revd Canon Dr T Naish, MA, PhD
Revd Canon A Dodd
R C A Bagley, LLB
Count Benoit De Vitry D'Avaucourt
M L Sutherland, BSc, MSc, PhD, Fellow of Corpus Christi College, Cambridge
Mrs E McKendrick, BA
Sir Roger De Haan
J D Tennant, MRICS (*Vice-Chairman*)
Dame F J Judd [OKS], QC
M W S Bax [OKS], FRICS
Dr H Hughes, OBE, FRCGP
W Kolade

Clerk to the Governors: M R Taylor, FRSA

Governors Emeriti:
The Very Revd J A Simpson, OBE, MA, DD
The Lady Kingsdown, OBE, DCL

[OKS] *Old King's Scholars*

Headmaster: P J M Roberts, MA

Headmaster's PA: Mrs L Hutchinson
PA to Senior Deputy Head & Lattergate Office Administrator: Mrs A Goodier
Lattergate Receptionist: Miss A Comber

Senior Deputy Head: Mrs E A Worthington, MA

Deputy Head Academic: L G Bartlett, BA, MRSC
Deputy Head Pastoral: Miss T Lee, BA
Deputy Head Co-Curricular: G Hunter, BEng, Grad Dip Ed

PA to Deputy Head Pastoral/Deputy Head Co-Curricular: Mrs F Bird
Academic Assistant: Mrs G V Hone, BSc Econ
Examinations Officer: Mrs S Reid

Head of Sixth Form: A J Holland, BSc
Heads of Middle School: D Galmes Gazapo BA; J M Maréchal BA, MSc
Head of Lower School: R T M Harrison
Head of Oxbridge: H L Warwicker MA
Head of Extended Projects: Miss A K Fraser, MA, MPhil

Bursar: M R Taylor, FRSA
Capital Projects Director: G Merryweather
Deputy Bursar: J Hadlow, BA, Associate CIPD

Directors of Development: Mr J Underhill; Mrs S Tingle

Head of Marketing: K L Orwin, BA

Registrar: J W Outram, BA
Assistant Registrar: Mrs B Skilton

Senior Chaplain: The Revd L R F Collins, BD, AKC, MTh
Graduate Assistant Chaplain: S Thorne

Librarian: Miss P K Rose, FDA, MA, PGCHE, ACLIP

Medical Officer:
Dr T Crook, MB BS, MRCGP, DRCOG

* *Head of Department*
† *Housemaster/mistress*

Art:
Mrs G C Burrows, BA
*Mrs I A Dutton, BA
M McArdle, BA
Mrs G Farrell, BA
D K Willis, BA
Mr J Dutton

Classics:
*M W Browning, BA
W Corbyn, BA
Miss H L Warwicker, BA

Design & Technology:
*M J Rolison, BEd
V Caspary, MFA

Drama:
*Mrs R J Beattie, BA, FRSA
Ms R Frances, BA

Economics:
*J Pope
Mrs L A Horn, BSc
J Hounsell, BA
A Rodriguez, MSc
M D Bell, BCOM, CIMA

English:
Dr H Barton, MA, PhD
Mrs L Carlyle, BA, DPhil
†Mrs J M Cook, BA
*Dr L Grindlay, MA, PhD
A J W Lyons, BA, MA, FRSA
Dr J P Wilper, BA, MLitt, PhD
†Mrs A L Young, MA
L J Benson, BA, MA

Geography:
A J Holland, BSc
†M E Lister, BSc, MSc
J A Lloyd, BSc
†R P Sanderson, BA
Mrs S J Sensecall, BSc
*Ms Freyja Dolan, BA

History:
*Miss C E Anderson, BA, MA
†G W H Harrison, MA
Dr D J C Perkins, BA, MA, Dip Law, PhD
Mrs E A Worthington, MA
I Bannerman, BA

History of Art:
*Dr H Barton, MA, PhD

ICT and Computing:
†Mrs L M Cousins, BA
A J Holland, BSc
B D M Katz, BA, MSc
*C P Wooldridge, BSc

Mathematics:
†Mrs E R Bell, MSci

M O Cox, MA, MEng, Dip ITEC
Dr R A B Johnson, MSc, PhD
Mrs J Gorman, BSc
B D M Katz, BA, MSc
A McFall, BSc
*S P Ocock, BA
Dr K J Palmer, BSc, PhD
M Henderson, BA
Ms E Berry, BA
Ms F Walton, BA
E Triffault, BA

Learning Support:
Mrs D J Ardley, BA
Mrs S Burke, MA
Ms G R Moorcroft, BEd, MA
Mrs M L Orders, BA
*Mrs C R Titterton, BA
Mrs B Raffety, BA
Mrs K Rothwell, BA

Modern Languages:
Mrs Z T Allen, MA
Miss L N Bernardo Otamendi, Lda, MPhil, MA
*Miss H C Davies, MA
Mrs M B Garcés-Ramón, Lda
Mrs N Geoffroy, L-ès-ScEd
R T M Harrison, BA
†Mrs R E Heskins, BA
Dr J R Karolyi, BA, PhD
*Mrs L Liu, BA, MPhil
Miss J M Maréchal, BA, MSc
Miss F Zanardi, MA
D Galmes-Gazapo
S A Bird, MA
E McCaffery, BA
A A T Blum
N Madeley
J Bao, BA, MA

Music:
K Abbott, Dip RCM
*W Bersey, BMus
Mrs A Caldon, BA, PDM
G R Swinford, BA
N G Todd, MA

Politics:
Mrs D J Ardley, BA
E N Nilsson, BA, MA

Physical Education:
*Miss K V Batty, BSc
†M E Lister, BSc, MSc
†R A L Singfield, BEd (*Sport)

Religious Studies and Philosophy:
*Dr D Cardinal, MA, PhD

The Revd L R F Collins, BD, AKC, MTh
Mrs C A Cox, BA, MPhil
Miss A K Fraser, MA, MPhil
Mrs C A Hayes, BA
*Miss T Lee, BA
J W Outram, BA

Science:

Biology:
Ms K Budden, BSc
J M Hutchings, BA
*Mrs E H Lockwood, MA, BSc
Dr M A McVeigh, MSc, PhD
†M J W Smiley, MA
M J Thornby, BSc
B A Landymore
E Rooms, BA

Chemistry:
L G Bartlett, BA, MRSC
R P Cook, BSc

*Dr S T Hayes, MSci, PhD, MRSC
Dr L W Hynes, BSc, PhD
Dr L E J Jones, MChem, PhD
D A Scott, BSc, MSc, MA Ed, MRSC (*Science)
†A S D Stennett, BSc
Mrs H Hunter

Physics:
*Miss L M Comber BSc (*Science)
F Elias, Ldo, PhD
Miss L M Kendrick, BSc
†Mrs E S Ladd, BEng
†M C Orders, BSc

Earth & Planetary Sciences:
*M R Mawby, BSc

Psychology
*J M Hutchings, BA
I Williamson, BSc, MA, MSc

Houses and Housemasters/mistresses:

School House: A Vintner
The Grange: C Orders
Walpole: Mrs A L Young
Meister Omers: R A L Singfield
Marlowe (*day*): G W H Harrison
Luxmoore: Ms L Cousins
Galpin's: R P Sanderson
Linacre: M Lister
Tradescant: A S D Stennett
Broughton: Dr D McVeigh
Mitchinson's (*day*): Mrs E S Ladd
Jervis: Mrs R E Heskins
Harvey: Mrs J M Cook
Bailey (*Sixth Form*): Mrs E Bell
Carlyon (*day*): M J W Smiley
Kingsdown: Mrs C A Hayes

The Junior King's School
Milner Court, Sturry, Nr Canterbury, CT2 0AY
Tel 01227 714000

Headmistress: Mrs E J Károlyi, MA

(For further details see Junior King's School entry in IAPS section.)

The King's School
Chester

Wrexham Road, Chester CH4 7QL

Tel: 01244 689500
email: info@kingschester.co.uk
website: www.kingschester.co.uk

Motto: *Rex Dedit, Benedicat Deus*

The School was founded AD 1541 by King Henry VIII, in conjunction with the Cathedral Church of Chester. It was reorganised under the Endowed Schools Act in 1873, and by subsequent schemes of the Ministry of Education. The School is now Independent. The aim of the School is to prepare pupils for admission to Universities and the professions, and at the same time provide a liberal education.

Organisation. The School, which at present numbers 1100, consists of (i) an Infant School for pupils aged 4 to 7 years, (ii) a Junior School for pupils aged 7 to 11 years, and (iii) the Senior School. The Infant and Junior Schools are housed in separate buildings, but are run in collaboration with the Senior School. On entry to Shells (2nd year of the Senior School) pupils are placed in one of eight houses; every student has a tutor who oversees their progress and welfare throughout their school career.

Admission. Please refer to our admissions policy which outlines the criteria and selection process for entry: www.kingschester.co.uk/policies. Selection is by academic merit alone.

Academic. Departments are grouped into four Faculties whose Heads report to the Academic Deputy Head. The subjects offered for study in the Sixth Form are – on the Arts side: Art, Business, Classical Studies, Drama, Economics, English, English Language, French, Geography, German, History, Latin, Music, Philosophy, Politics, Religious Studies, Spanish; and on the Science side: Biology, Chemistry, Computing, Further Mathematics, Mathematics, Physics, Sports Science and Design Technology. It is possible to take most combinations of subjects in the Sixth Form.

Spiritual life. The School is part of the Cathedral Foundation and regularly holds its own services in the Cathedral. Spiritual assemblies are held regularly in school.

Music. Music is part of the general curriculum for all pupils up to the age of 14. After this music may be taken at GCSE and A Level. Private tuition in orchestral instruments, piano and organ is available. There are many musical ensembles and choral groups including the Schola Cantorum which leads the worship in Cathedral services.

Cadet Corps. There is a CCF contingent which gives pupils opportunities to develop leadership skills and to undertake adventurous training.

Outdoor Education. Opportunities are provided both within and outside the curriculum for outdoor education, and all pupils in each of the first three years of the senior school spend some days away at centres specialising in outdoor activities. In addition many pupils participate in the Duke of Edinburgh's Award Scheme at all levels.

Games. Football, Hockey, Netball, Rugby, Cricket, Rowing, Swimming, Badminton, Basketball, Athletics, Netball, Tennis, Squash, Golf, Rounders.

Buildings. Formerly situated adjacent to the Cathedral, the school moved into new buildings in 1960 situated in rural surroundings nearly 2 miles from the centre of Chester. Since then there has been an impressive programme of additional building development. These include the Wickson Library, a new Music School, the Vanbrugh Theatre and extensions to the Sixth Form Centre. In September 2014 the Junior School was extended to provide a new Junior School Library and Learning Centre, and in September 2015 a purpose-built Infant School was opened by the Duke of Westminster. A state-of-the-art Sports Centre opened in April 2019.

Alumni associations. Please see the website (www.kingschester.co.uk/alumni) for details of OAKS (the Organisation for the Alumni of the King's School) and CAOKS (Chester Association of Old King's Scholars).

Fees per term (2021–2022). Tuition: Senior School £4,673; Junior School £3,583; Infants £3,161.

The School offers a small number of bursaries annually.

Scholarships. Academic scholarships of up to £500 are awarded to pupils during their early years in the Senior School. Scholars carry the title 'King's Scholar' throughout their time at the school.

Tenable in the Sixth Form: A number of scholarships are awarded to students on entry to the Sixth Form and during their Sixth form years. These include: (1) Keith Oates Scholarship: £1,000; (2) Investec Scholarship: £1,000; (3) King's School Parents' Association Scholarship: £500.

Tenable at Universities: (1) Old King's Scholars Exhibition: £750; (2) Robert Platt Exhibition: £500; (3) John Churton Exhibition: £500; (4) Haswell Exhibition: £500; (5) Finchett Maddock Exhibition: £500.

Charitable status. The King's School, Chester is a Registered Charity, number 525934. The aim of the charity is to provide a sound education to all boys and girls who can benefit from it regardless of their economic and social background.

Governors:
D K Rowlands (*Chairman*)
R N Arnold, BSc, ACA
Mrs J M Carr, BA, FCA
S E Docking, BA
Mrs C A Edwards, MA
The Venerable T R Stratford, BSc, PhD, Dean of Chester
Mrs S J Verity, BSc
J Walsh
J B Ebo
A J Bartley
Professor F S Fahmy
Miss C Gillies
Mrs D Leonard

Clerk to the Governors: Mrs H A Jordan, FInstML, MCGI

Headmaster: G J Hartley, MA Cantab, MSc

Deputy Head (*Operations*) T M Gill, MA
Deputy Head (Academic): J E Millard, BA
Deputy Head (Pastoral): M J Harle, BSc
Head of Sixth Form: J P Carter, MA
Director of Studies: A J Dewbery, MA
Senior Tutor: R G Wheeler, BA
Director of Learning Support: Mrs S Glass, BA

Assistant staff:
* *Head of Department*

Art and Design:
*S Downey, BA (*Head of Faculty – Creative Arts & PE*)
Ms L Black, BA
Mrs A L Hollingworth, BA (*Assistant Head of Sixth Form*)

Biology:
*R H Jones, BSc, PhD
J A Dunn, MSc

Dr H C Faulkner, BSc, DPhil (*Head of Faculty – Science*)
L A Parkes, BSc, MSc (*Head of Dutton House*)

Chemistry:
*A Cook, BSc, PhD
Dr C A Gleave, BSc, PhD
Dr J R Macnab, BSc, PhD
Mrs K L Russon, BSc
Dr S Wharton

Classics:
*P R Wilcock MA
Mrs S H Gareh, BA, MA
M J P Punnett, MA

Design Technology:
*R J Curtis, BSc
Ms L Black, BA
Miss S J Champion, BA
Mrs A Crump, BSc

Drama:
*Mrs C L Howdon, BA
Mrs J Williams, BA, MA

Economics & Business:
*S D Walton, BA, MSc
Miss R Hillier, BA, MSc
Mrs C A Rule, BA

English:
*R J Aldridge, BA, MBA
M A Boyd, BA
Dr K F Mair, MA (*Head of Lester Smith House*)
R G Wheeler, BA

Geography:
*M J Prestshaw, BSc MEd, MRes
Mrs R H Aldridge, BA (*Head of Walsh House*)
J A D Blackham, BA (*Head of Grosvenor House*)
Mrs A M McNabb, BA (*Head of Bradbury House*)

History & Politics:
*P G Neal, BA
J P Carter, MA (*Head of Sixth Form*)
Mrs G K Chadwick, BA
R J M Hensman, BA, MA, PhD
S Neal, BA (*Head of Faculty – Languages & Humanities*)

Information Technology:
*O Hall, BA
A J Dewbery, MA
Mrs E E Simpson, BA, MBA
D Hughes, BSc

Mathematics:
*Mrs C E Lanceley, BSc
S D Bibby, BSc
C J Canty, BSc
Mrs S Cooper, BSc

Head of Junior School & Infant School: Mrs M A Ainsworth, LLB, MEd

Deputy Head (Junior School): A Griffiths, BA

Director of Studies (Junior School): T W Griffin, BA

A J Dewbery, MA
Mrs A Ignata, BSc
Mrs C Plass, BSc
Mrs C N Ranson, BSc
Miss D Roberts, BSc
Mrs H E Sugarman, MMath

Modern Languages:
*Miss L E McCutcheon
M D Bircham, BA
Mrs K Bowden, BA [Maternity Leave]
Mrs M Rowley Williams, BA, MEd
Mrs R E Webb, BA (*Head of Gladstone House*)
R West, MA
Mrs C Irvine, BA

Music:
*Ms D L Neal, BMus, MA (*Director of Music*)
Mrs K Bannerjee, BMus
Mrs V L S Latifa, BMus
J E Millard, BA

Personal & Social Education:
*M S Lee, MA

Philosophy & Theology:
*J R Rees, BA
M S Lee, MA
Ms J E Rutberg, MA (*Head of Faculty – Social Sciences & Maths*)
D Taylor, BA

Physical Education:
*R Lunn, BEd (*Director of Sport*)
*Mrs C Sumner, BA (*Assistant Headteacher, Pastoral*)
Mrs K Jones, BA (*Assistant Director of Sport; Head of Fox House*)
B Horne, BSc (*Director of Football*)
Miss E L Halstead, BA
S Egerton, BA
R I Hornby, BA

Physics:
*S Bosworth, MA, DPhil, FRAS
Ms H M Davies, BSc, MSc
N Heritage, MSc, PhD, MInstP, CPhys
B Horne, BSc
Mrs K Scutter, BSc

Deputy Head (Infant School): Mrs J C Callaghan, BEd

Assistant Staff (Junior School & Infant School):
Miss J M Anderson, BA, CertEd
Mrs J Benson, BA
T Blakemore, BA Ed
H J Duncalf, BEd
Mrs D Grove, BA
Miss J M L Hartley, BA
K A Hollingworth, BEd
Miss S Ley, BA
J B Melville, BEd
Mrs N C M Moffatt, BA
Mrs L Morrice Evans, BA
Mrs M D O'Leary, BA
D M O'Neil, BSc
Mrs S Parker, BEd
Miss K A Savage, BA
J N Spellman, BEd
Mrs N J Stevens, BMus
Mrs A Stevenson, BEd
Mrs N M Tomlinson, BA
Mrs S Tomlinson, BEd
Mrs K Williams, BEd

Visiting Music Teachers:
W Armstrong, BA, PGRNCM (*Oboe*)
Ms S Boryslawska, BA
S J Hall, BSc (*Bass Guitar*)
G Macey, ATCL (*Woodwind*)
Ms S Marrs, FTCL (*Voice*)
N Middleton, BA (*Drums*)
Mrs R Mulholland, ARCM, LRAM (*Cello*)
D Ortiz, BMus (*Head of Brass*)
A Parker, MA (*Saxophone*)
M Reynolds BA (*Piano*)
Mrs J Richardson, CT ABRSM, ATCL (*Flute*)

Extra-Curricular Staff:
Director of Rowing: J A D Blackham, BA
Contingent Commander, CCF: Maj M S Lee, MA
Duke of Edinburgh's Award Coordinator: D A Brown
Educational Visits Coordinator: R I D Hornby, BA

Director of Finance & Operations: Mrs H Jordan
Directors of Human Resources: Mrs E R Davidson, BA, CIPD & Mrs A H Millard, BSc, MCIPD
Director of Marketing, Communications & Partnerships: Mrs S O'Donnell
Director of Development: Mrs E E Gwyther, BA
Director of ICT: J K Warne, BSc, MCSA
Admissions Manager: Mrs E R Sears, BA
Head Librarian & Archivist: Mrs R Harding, MA
Examinations Officer: Miss J Davies, BSc
School Nurse: Mrs L Jones, RN
Care Scheme Manager: Miss K McKean

Headmaster's PA: Mrs K E Paul, BSc

The King's School
Macclesfield

Alderley Road, Prestbury, Macclesfield, Cheshire SK10 4SP

Tel: 01625 260000
email: mail@kingsmac.co.uk
website: www.kingsmac.co.uk
Twitter: @kingsmac
Facebook: @kingsinmacc

The King's School is the top performing independent school in Cheshire East for both GCSE and A Level results and has appeared in *The Telegraph* Top 200 Independent Schools for exam results in 2014–2020.

Founded in 1502, King's has recently re-located to the country's newest school campus. The purpose-built school sits on a stunning 80-acre rural campus just outside Macclesfield.

King's offers an exciting co-educational learning environment for boys and girls aged 3–18. It strives for excellence across all areas of teaching and learning, as well as in sporting, musical and creative endeavours. Exceptional pastoral care is a defining feature of the school. The last ISI Inspection awarded King's the highest grading of 'excellent' in all aspects.

Number in School. Infants age 3–7: 140 boys and girls. Juniors age 7–11: 240 boys and girls. Senior pupils age 11–16: 700 boys and girls. Sixth Form: 220 boys and girls. Total: 1,300.

Organisation and Curriculum. The King's School is a co-educational day school and is organised into three Divisions: the Infant & Junior Division; the Senior Division; and the Sixth Form. Each Division is run by a Principal, who is responsible for day-to-day organisation and welfare of pupils. Girls and boys from 3–18 enjoy a broad curriculum and the same extensive range of opportunities.

The King's School has one Board of Governors and one Head of Foundation, plus a Senior Management Team, who manage the school.

King's aims include 'to challenge our pupils to aspire, work hard and achieve' and 'to develop lively and enquiring minds'. The curriculum is broad and rich throughout all year groups offering pupils of all ages choice and a range of experiences.

The School's most recent ISI Inspection Report (2015) graded King's as 'excellent' – the highest ranking – in all eight aspects. As well as teaching and pupils' achievements being excellent, so too is Pastoral care, which is a high priority within the school. The divisional structure is key to enabling each unit to be small and operate as a community. Coupled with the aim of 'fostering a friendly, polite and caring community', King's is definitely a happy place to be a pupil.

Infant & Junior pupils enjoy the highly engaging 'Learning Challenge Curriculum', which is an enquiry-based approach to learning and delivers cross-curricular learning in humanities, languages, science and creative subjects.

Senior pupils enjoy a broad and balanced curriculum, which covers English, Maths, three humanities, four languages, four creative subjects, Computer Science, Critical Thinking, PHSE, PE, Games and three Sciences. Senior pupils are able to study 10 or 11 GCSEs.

Sixth Form students are assigned to a personal tutor responsible for a group of 10–15 pupils throughout their Sixth Form course. Any justifiable combination of available A Level subjects may be pursued, complemented by an IGCSE Global Perspectives (in Year 12), and a wide range of options from the Extended Studies Programme in Year 13, including the EPQ, Japanese, the Arts Award, Sports Leadership and others. Students choose from these options, which are designed to extend their breadth of cultural interest and intellectual inquiry, whilst Recreational Activities are designed to encourage the positive use of leisure time and offer initial experience in sports and activities new to the individual. Pupils are supported by an excellent Careers service and are well prepared for University Entrance Examinations, competitive entry to university and higher-level apprenticeships.

New campus. The King's school moved to its new £60m campus in the summer of 2020. All pupils are taught co-educationally at the new campus, which offers state-of-the-art facilities to enhance the educational experience of all pupils, from 3–18 years old. The new campus contains a dedicated Sports Centre, with a 25m swimming pool, indoor cricket facilities, large indoor hall with six-courts, a martial arts studio, gym and cafe.

Arts and Craft. Well-equipped, spacious Art rooms and Design & Technology (DT) workshops include an Innovation Suite and are used for teaching and are also available for use by the members of the Art Club, STEM Club, Textile Club and Craft societies outside the timetable.

Music. Over 400 pupils receive tuition in the full range of orchestral instruments, the Piano, Organ, Classical Guitar and Singing. An introductory tuition scheme enables all new entrants to assess their talent. There are three orchestras, a Concert-band, two Jazz bands, three Choirs and many ensembles, all of which provide regular performing experience. The Foundation Choir was the first BBC Songs of Praise Choir of the Year in 2003. Choir tours to Europe take place alternate years. Pupils regularly enter the music profession in addition to those pursuing academic training. Music Scholarships are available.

Drama. Theatre Studies is an important creative option at GCSE and covers all aspects of the theatre. Great importance is attached to the regular production of school plays and musicals, which involve large numbers of pupils and enjoy a distinguished reputation. Facilities include a large Performance Hall, as well as a drama studio and main hall (950 seats). Pupils regularly take examinations and study for LAMDA qualifications in performance and public speaking.

Sport. The school has extensive sporting facilities and a large Games Department with around 20 staff. The school offers Sports Scholarships and has an Elite Athlete Programme (KEAP). All pupils take part in Games and PE activities appropriate to the season. Junior School sports include Football, Cricket, Netball, Hockey, Tennis, Rounders, Rugby, Swimming, Athletics and a wide range of individual games. In the Senior School, boys' sports include Rugby, Hockey, Cross-Country, Squash, Badminton, Cricket, Tennis, Athletics and Basketball; the girls' sports include Hockey, Netball, Tennis, Football, Cross-Country, Volleyball, Cricket, Rounders, Gym and Athletics. In addition there is a varied programme of sports in the Sixth Form, including activities such as Caving, Fell Running, Sailing and Rock Climbing which are actively pursued by boys and girls.

Outdoor Pursuits. This is a thriving part of the school. There is a regular programme of activity weekends including canoeing, gorge scrambling, surfing, coasteering, etc. In addition, numerous expeditions are arranged in the many favourable areas near the school and also abroad. Sailing and Orienteering are popular and The Duke of Edinburgh's Award scheme attracts around 300 pupils each year. King's is one of the largest DofE authorising centres in the north of England.

Clubs and Societies. There is a wide range of clubs catering for most interests and hobbies, ranging from Astronomy, Debating, Dance, Chess and Squash to Sailing, STEM Club, Equestrian Society, Electronics Club, Coding Club and Taekwondo.

Fees per term (2021–2022). Senior School and Sixth Form £4,530, Infants & Junior School £3,670. Sibling discount scheme available.

Scholarships and Bursaries. Bursaries are available for entry at 11 and 16 years of age. In addition a number of Academic Scholarships are awarded based on performance in the Entrance Examination. Senior School Music Scholarships are available for pupils joining Year 7 (in instrument or singing). Music and Organ scholarships are also available in the Sixth Form. Senior Sports Scholarships are available to pupils joining Year 7.

Admissions. King's is a selective school. Admission to the Infant & Junior Division, as well as the Senior Division, is normally for September each year through competitive examination of age-appropriate entrance assessments. Girls and boys are admitted to the Sixth Form subject to academic attainment at GCSE, interview and course requirement: a minimum of two grades 7 or above (A*/A) and four grades 6 or above (B) is standard. Further details of Admission arrangements are available on the website and upon request. Immediate admission, e.g. for new arrivals in the area, is possible if places are available.

Former Pupils' Association. Chairman: David Barratt; email: formerpupils@kingsmac.co.uk. An annual magazine and termly newsletter are provided to former pupils alongside a full programme of events.

Visit the Website. The award-winning website is found at www.kingsmac.co.uk.

Charitable status. The King's School, Macclesfield is a Registered Charity, number 1137204. It exists for the education of boys and girls between the ages of 3 and 18.

Chairman of the Governors: Mr A Higginson, BSc Hons, FCMA

Vice-Chair of Governors: Dr J Kennerley, BPharm, MRPharmS, PhD

Senior Management Team:

Headmaster: Mr Jason Slack, BSc Hons, MA Ed

Deputy Headmaster (*Academic*): R Griffiths, MA Cantab
Deputy Head (*Operations*): Mr P J Cooper, BSc
Director of External Relations: Mrs C Johnson, BSc, DipM
Director of Finance: Mr J M Spencer Pickup, BSc Hons), ACA
Senior Teacher: Mrs R Roberts, BA, PGCE
Principal of Seniors: Mrs H L Broadley
Principal of Infants & Juniors: Mrs R Cookson, BA
Principal of Sixth Form: Mr R Davies, MA

Vice-Principal of Seniors (*Lower School*): Mrs E Smith
Vice-Principal of Seniors (*Middle School*): Mr S Mattingly
Vice-Principal of Infants & Juniors: Mrs E L Warburton, BEd

Heads of Departments:
Art & Design: Mrs D Inman, BA

Classics: Mr A Mallin, BA
Computing: Mr P Mackenzie, BSc
Design & Technology: J Nichols, BEd
Drama: Mr D A Forbes, BA
Economics & Business Studies: Mr J S MacGregor, MA
English: Mr R Kellett, BA, PGCE
Geography: Mr A S Puddephatt, BA
Geology: Dr J A Fitzgerald, BSc, MSc, PhD
History: Miss L Hughes, BA

Learning Support: Mrs C Edge

Modern Languages: Mr I E Dalgleish, BA
German: Mrs Slack
French: Mdm Schue
Spanish: Ms S Bailey

Director of Music: Mr I Crawford, BMus
Physical Education (*Director of Sport*): Mr C S Thompson, BA, PGCE
Physics: Dr S J Hartnett, BSc, DPhil, PGCE
Politics: Miss Hughes
Psychology: Mrs C Bell, BSc, PGCE, MA Ed
Religion & Philosophy: Mr R N Jackson, BA

Science: Mr J Street, BSc, PGCE
Biology: Dr Patrick
Chemistry: Miss L C Watkins, BSc

King's Rochester

Satis House, Boley Hill, Rochester, Kent ME1 1TE

Tel: 01634 888555
email: admissions@kings-rochester.co.uk
website: www.kings-rochester.co.uk
Twitter: @Kings_Rochester
Facebook: @KingsRochester
LinkedIn: /king-s-school-rochester

The School traces its history to 604 AD, when St Justus, the first Bishop of Rochester, formed a school in connection with his Cathedral; it was reconstituted and endowed by Henry VIII as the King's School in 1541. The School has been fully co-educational since 1993.

The School is situated in the Cathedral Precinct of Rochester and sits in the shadow of the Castle on the bank of the River Medway; it enjoys the open spaces of the Esplanade, Vines and the Paddock, which is one of the School's playing fields. The Alps, a multi-sport playing field, is just 5 minutes from the School. Further up the road is the King's Rochester Sports Centre, which is home to 9 external tennis/netball courts, a large gymnasium, a fitness gym, physio suite and changing rooms, in addition to the indoor swimming pool and playing fields already on the 1,400-year-old school's town-centre site.

The Main School dates from the mid-nineteenth century, but the School also has a number of fine listed buildings from the eighteenth century and considerable extensions of more recent date, including a Conference Centre and dining facility, a girls' boarding house, and a Pre-Prep building with Sports Hall and a modern, self-contained Nursery.

The School numbers about 650 pupils, including a small but significant community of 60 boarders from the local area, London and overseas. The School is fully co-educational and divided into a Pre-Preparatory School of approximately 140 pupils (4–8 years), plus 33 in the Nursery, a Preparatory School of approximately 200 pupils (8–13 years) and a Senior School of approximately 300 pupils (13–18 years); this provides 3 units of an intimate size, which are regarded as a single community working closely together. While catering for the whole of a pupil's career from 3 to 18, there is a large entry of pupils at 11, 13 and 16 who bring experience from other backgrounds and enjoy the advantages of coming into a stable community with a strong family atmosphere.

The boarders, some of whom are weekly, play an important part in the life of the School. Although a small community, they are a large enough part of the School to make a very significant contribution of their own and enjoy a more intimate atmosphere than is possible in a larger boarding environment.

King's is the world's oldest Cathedral Choir School. The Dean and Chapter are ex officio Governors, the Principal and King's Scholars are members of the Cathedral Foundation, and the Cathedral Choristers are members of the Preparatory School. The School uses the Cathedral for worship.

Work. In the Pre-Preparatory School, the pupils follow a four-year curriculum of Maths, Science, English, Religious Studies, Geography, History, Computing, Art and Craft, Design & Technology, Music, Physical Education and PSHEE. Daily spoken German lessons taught by native German teachers form part of the curriculum from the age of 4.

In the Preparatory School, the curriculum covers Art, Religious Studies, English, General Science, History, Geography, Mathematics, Computing, Latin, French, German, Spanish, Music, Drama, Physical Education, Design & Technology and PSHEE.

In the Senior School, the curriculum is as broad as possible to enable a wide choice of option subjects for the Fifth Form, including: Art, Classical Civilisation, Computer Science, Design and Technology, Drama, French, Geography, German, History, Latin, Music, Physical Education, Russian and Spanish. Games, CCF or TechSoc, and PSHEE are also on the curriculum.

In the Sixth Form, a wide range of A Level subjects are available and most pupils study three. Some pupils also take the Extended Project Qualification as additional study alongside their A Levels and sometimes a fourth A Level such as Further Mathematics.

All Sixth Formers who wish to, go on to university or other further education, and are encouraged to think carefully about their ultimate careers. Careers talks are given by outside speakers during the GCSE year, and the advice of specialist careers advisers and the careers teachers is available at all stages.

Activities. The School aims to develop pupils through a wide range of activities, both within the School programme and outside it.

There is a large CCF contingent, with Army, Navy and Air Force sections. Strong Service connections locally give a particularly wide scope for CCF activities.

Pupils also undertake a variety of activities in Voluntary Service, Charity Fundraising, Enrichment Programmes and The Theatre Production Society. Pupils also participate in the Duke of Edinburgh's Award scheme.

Out of School there is a range of over 25 school societies in all three parts of the School, and in the holidays there is a strong tradition of annual cultural and outdoor expeditions in this country and abroad for Preparatory and Senior School pupils.

Art, Drama and Music. The School sets great store by the Arts, and uses the comparative proximity to London to take pupils to art exhibitions, concerts and the theatre. The School stages major drama productions each year, the 2019 production of *Titanic The Musical* was the largest production ever produced with a cast and crew of 160 pupils. There is a strong musical tradition enhanced by visiting music staff, and pupils are encouraged to learn instruments. In addition to concerts in the School and the Cathedral, the Orchestra gives a number of outside performances each year, some by invitation. The choral tradition is strengthened by the presence of the Cathedral choristers in the School who regularly undertake overseas tours. Many pupils are in the national theatre and orchestra groups, the BBC Young Chorister of the Year 2016 was from King's Rochester.

Games. The boys' games are Rugby, Hockey, Football (Preparatory School), Cricket and Tennis and for girls' Hockey, Netball, Cricket and Tennis. Other team sport options are Rowing (from our River Medway boathouse), Athletics, Cross Country, Fencing and Swimming, and there are opportunities in addition for Squash, Badminton and Sailing. Physical Education is a regular part of the School curriculum and all pupils are required to take part in games. 80% represent the School competitively.

Religious Education and Worship. Although there is no denominational requirement for entry to the School, religious instruction is in accordance with the principles of the Church of England. All three parts of the School begin the day with an assembly or chapel service, some of which are held in the Cathedral.

Admission. Pupils can enter the School at any age from 3 to 18, although the main entry points are: 4+, 7/8+, 11+, 13+ and 16+. Entrance to the Senior School is either by Common Entrance at 13 or by the School's own examination for pupils who have not been prepared for Common Entrance.

Sixth Form entry is on the basis of interview and School report, together with satisfactory GCSE results (Pupils should attain a minimum of a grade 6 in the subjects they wish to study at A level).

Choristers. Choristerships are awarded to boys and girls aged 8 following voice trials and satisfactory performance in the Preparatory School Entrance Examination. Under normal circumstances, the choristership will continue until a boy transfers to the Senior School or until a boy or girl leaves the choir.

Scholarships and Bursaries. Scholarships are offered in the Senior School and Preparatory School in recognition of talent and commitment in the following categories:

• Academic 11+, 13+ and 16+ entry
• Music 11+, 13+ and 16+ entry
• Sport 11+, 13+ and 16+ entry
• Drama 13+ and 16+ entry
• Art 13+ and 16+ entry

The following Scholarships are also available offering varying generous fee remission:

• Cathedral Choristerships
• Dame Susan Morden Choral Scholarship for boys aged 8
• Chesterfield Organ Scholarships 13+ and 16+ entry only
• The Peter Rogers' Music Scholarship for Senior School pupils

External candidates should liaise with the Registrar for details of entry assessment and process. Internal candidates should always discuss applications with the Head of the Preparatory or Senior School as relevant, prior to application. All Scholarships are reviewed annually and their continuation is subject to satisfactory progress being maintained.

Bursaries offer means-tested financial support to able pupils who would otherwise be unable to attend King's.

- They are only available to assist those in financial need
- They are available to current pupils whose financial circumstances have significantly changed
- They are generally only offered to external pupils in addition to a Scholarship Award and also on the assessment of the mutual benefit to the child and the School

Fee Remissions. Children of Church of England ministers are given an annually means-tested reduction in tuition fees.

Children of Service Personnel are given a 20% reduction in tuition fees.

Where parents have three or more children at the school a reduction after the second child is given, amounting to 10% of the third child's tuition fees, 20% for the fourth child and 40% for the fifth and subsequent children.

Fees per term (2021–2022). Senior School: Boarders £11,280, Day Pupils £6,900. Preparatory School: Boarders £7,840, Day Pupils £4,705–£5,340 (inc lunch). Pre-Preparatory School (Day only): £3,625–£3,930 (inc lunch).

Charitable status. King's School, Rochester is a Registered Charity, number 1084266; it is a charitable trust for the purpose of educating children.

Patron: The Lord Bishop of Rochester, The Right Reverend James Langstaff

The Governing Body:
Acting Chair of Governors: The Very Reverend Dr P Hesketh, PhD, BD, AKC

Governors:
Mr B Bell, BSc Hons, CIMDIP, FCIM
The Revd Canon S Brewer
Mr M J Chesterfield
Mr P Coen, MBA, FCCA, FPFS
The Reverend Canon C Dench
The Reverend Canon Dr G Giles, PhD Middx, MLitt Cantab, BA Hons Lancaster, CTM, ARSM
Mr D R Graves, BA Hons, FCA
Mrs R A Olley, CEd
The Reverend Canon M Rushton, MA Oxon, MA
Mrs J E Shilling, BA Hons
Mr M G Snoswell
Mrs E Whitlam, MSc

The Executive Board:

Principal of King's Rochester and Headmaster of the Senior School: Mr B P H Charles, BA Hons, PGCE, Exeter & Durham

Headmaster of the Preparatory School: Mr T H Morgan, BMus Hons RCM
Headmistress of the Pre-Preparatory School: Mrs K Crozer, BEd Hons Greenwich
Bursar and Clerk to the Governors: Ms D J Godwin, BA Hons, CIMA University of Central England
Deputy Head (Pastoral) and Designated Safeguarding Lead: Mr C H Page, BA, PGCE Royal Holloway, London
Director of Operations: Miss K J Petts, Level 7 Advanced Professional Certificate in School Financial and Operational Leadership, The Chartered Institute of Public Finance and Accountancy

Director of External Relations: Mr K France, BA Hons Edge Hill

Senior School Academic Staff:
Principal of King's Rochester and Headmaster of the Senior School: Mr B P H Charles, BA Hons, PGCE, Exeter & Durham
Deputy Head (Academic): Miss N J Steel, BSc, PGCE Sheffield
Deputy Head (Pastoral): Mr C H Page, BA, PGCE Royal Holloway, London
Deputy Head (Co-Curriculum): Miss H L Catlett, BA Hons Canterbury & Chichester
Assistant Head (Head of Sixth Form): Mrs S L Miles, MA, BA Hons, PGCE Kent
Chaplain: The Revd S J Padfield, MA Hons Bristol
PA to the Principal and Office Manager: Mrs V Howard

Academic Staff:
Mr O Bailey, BA Hons, PGCE Angela Ruskin
Miss N Bent, MA College Falmouth
Miss V Burgess, MSc, BSc Hons, Edinburgh & Greenwich
Mr C J E Carroll, MA, PGCE, Swansea & Cambridge
Mr C Coetzee, BA South Africa
Miss C Coop, BSc, PGCE Wales
Miss L E Costelloe, BA Royal Holloway, London
Mr M E Drury, BSc, MA, UCL, Greenwich
Mr S Fish, BA Hons, Westminster, London
Mr A Glashan, BSc, PGCE, Loughborough & Buckingham
Mrs N Gould, MSc, BSc East Anglia
Mrs E A Hanson, BSc St Andrews
Mrs Y Z Harkin, MA, BA Hons, PGCE, SpLD, York, South Wales & Cambridge
Mr G T Haslett, BSc Kent at Canterbury
Mr M J Hebden, BA Hons Lancaster
Mrs Y Jackson, BEng Hons Heriot Watt
Mr S J Johnson, BEd Hons Nottingham Trent
Miss F Lowe, BA Hons Exeter
Mrs C McCabe, Cert TESOL, HLTA, New South Wales & Northampton
Mrs E M McCarthy, BA Hons, PGCE Reading
Ms M McIntyre, BA, MPhil Robert Gordon, Aberdeen
Miss A Morrice, BA, MPhil, PGCE Cambridge
Mr J Mountford, BA Hons Bristol
Miss C O Kelly, Licence Langues Université Aix-Marseille 1
Mrs R J Oliver, BA Hons, PGCE, Kent (KIAD), West Surrey College of Art and Design & Greenwich
Mr S Owen, BEd Wales Caerleon
Mrs E L Parren, BSc Hons Birmingham
Miss S Pembroke, BSc Hons, HND, Nottingham Trent & Wales
Mrs A J Richter, BSc Loughborough
Mr B W Richter, BA Newcastle
Mr B C Rivers, BA Hons Brunel
Mr A J Robson, BA Central St Martin's College, Liverpool
Mrs L A Rogers, BA Hons Brighton
Miss G Snook, BSc Loughborough
Mr P G Stevens, BSc Hons Southampton
Mr D G Taylor, BA Hons Chichester
Dr K Thomson, PhD, MA Hons, St Andrews & Edinburgh
Mrs A J Warne, MA Hons St Andrews
Mr C J White MSc, BSc, PGCE York
Mr C White, BSc, PGCE East Anglia
Miss L J Williams, BA Hons Open University
Mrs N Wiltshire, BA Hons, PGCE, Pau and The Adour Region & Lancaster

Miss K Zielinska, MA, BA Hons, PGCE, Oxford, Canterbury Christ Church & Exeter

Librarian: Mrs X Guo, MA Northwest Normal, China

Combined Cadet Force Contingent Commander: Major S Short, RE

Director of Sport (Senior School): Mr M J Hebden, BA Hons, PGCE, Lancaster & Buckingham

The King's School Worcester Foundation

Senior School
5 College Green, Worcester WR1 2LL

Tel: 01905 721700
email: info@ksw.org.uk
website: www.ksw.org.uk
Twitter: @KingsWorcester
Facebook: @KingsWorcester

King's St Alban's Prep
Mill Street, Worcester WR1 2NJ

Tel: 01905 354906
email: ksa@ksw.org.uk

King's Hawford Prep
Hawford Lock Lane, Claines, Worcester WR3 7SD

Tel: 01905 451292
email: hawford@ksw.org.uk

A Cathedral School appears to have existed at Worcester virtually continuously since the 7th century. In its present form, however, The King's School dates from its re-foundation by King Henry VIII in 1541.

This Foundation of Schools has a history dating back to the 7th Century and close links to the Cathedral. The King's School has a strong sense of tradition combined with a modern and successful approach to learning, inspiring pupils to aim higher, shaping the character to go further, and instilling the values to lead lives of purpose. The King's School is well known locally for its friendly atmosphere and excellent relationships between staff and pupils.

Today, The King's School, Worcester is a Foundation comprising two preparatory schools and a senior school – all three are co-educational day schools.

The Senior School, for pupils from 11–18, still occupies its original site adjacent to Worcester Cathedral and sits on the banks of the River Severn. The buildings are grouped around College Green and the School Gardens. They range in date from the 14th century College Hall and Edgar Tower through the 17th and 18th century buildings surrounding College Green, to a range of modern, purpose-built buildings including an award-winning boat house, a modern ECO Sports Hall and Performing Arts Centre, an enviable well-resourced School Library and a recently refurbished Modern Languages Department.

King's St Alban's stands in its own grounds adjacent to the main school site, offering education from age 2–11, with a purpose-built pre-prep department for girls and boys aged 4–7 and a teacher-led nursery for children from 2 years. The

school has a large hall, a dedicated Science Laboratory, an IT suite, an Art and Technology Room, Libraries, Music Rooms, Sports Hall and 25 metre Swimming Pool. In the grounds stand the Chapel, the main buildings of the Prep School with the Nursery and Pre-Preparatory Department on an adjacent, self-contained site. Frequent use is made of the Senior School facilities, such as the 300-seat Theatre and Dance and Drama Studios.

King's Hawford is set in a spacious rural setting just to the north of the city and offers education from age 2–11. The school has a strong focus on outdoor learning and holds the LoTC (Learning Outside the Classroom) Award, for its outstanding outdoor learning provision. The school is accommodated within an elegant and recently refurbished Georgian house surrounded by playing fields, a heated enclosed swimming pool, a multi-purpose sports hall and performance space and secure play area for younger children. The school has a double-decker bus that has been converted into an amazing library. The children's weekly radio show is posted on the website.

The nurseries at the Prep Schools are well regarded and rated highly amongst parents. In 2021 they received the UK Top 20 Group Award.

Numbers and Admission. The King's School is fully co-educational. King's St Alban's has 182 pupils. King's Hawford has 283 pupils. The Senior School has 881 pupils, including 269 in the Sixth Form.

Entrance to the King's School is by the Prep Entrance Test at 7, 8 or 9, or by the School's Examination at 11, 12 and 13. Boys and girls also join the School at Sixth Form level; this entry is by test, interview and GCSE results.

Religion. The King's School has an historic connection with Worcester Cathedral. Religious education, given in accordance with the Christian faith, is non-denominational. Pupils of all denominations and faiths are welcomed.

Curriculum The Senior School offers GCSE and A Level examinations in preparation for Higher Education. The curriculum is designed to give all pupils a general education and to postpone specialisation for as long as possible. Further details will be found in the Prospectus and on the School's website.

Games. The major sports are Rugby, Netball, Hockey, Football, Rowing and Cricket. Other sports include Tennis, Athletics, Cross Country, Badminton, Rounders, Fencing, Golf, Swimming, Sailing and Canoeing. PE and games are compulsory for all: a wide choice is offered to Sixth Formers.

Other Activities. The Senior School organises a contingent of the Combined Cadet Force (CCF) and provides an outstanding programme to enable pupils to engage in the Duke of Edinburgh's Award scheme.

Pupils undertake Community Service within and beyond Worcester and our Charity Committee organises a series of events across the year to fundraise and raise awareness of wide-ranging issues.

Regular drama performances are of an exceptional standard and our accommodation for them is superb with a fully equipped theatre seating 320, a black box studio which seats 80, and also a dance studio complete with mirrors and a sprung floor. Music is similarly impressive with a broad range of ensembles, choirs, orchestras, bands, quartets and groups.

Sport is very strong among both boys and girls and benefits from some outstanding facilities, including a swimming pool, three-storey climbing wall and an industry-standard Boathouse.

As well as a thriving Lego Robotics Club, School Radio and participation in the Engineering Education Scheme and Young Enterprise, pupils are offered the chance to undertake Model Union Nations (MUN) and debating.

Scholarships and Bursaries. Both Music and Academic Scholarships are available at 11+, 13+ and 16+ in the Senior School, value up to one third of tuition fees. Academic scholarships at 11+ and 13+ are awarded on the basis of the Entrance Test and an interview: at 16+ on the basis of an aptitude test and interview.

Fees per term (2021–2022). Senior School £5,068, Prep Schools £2,538–£4,789

Charitable status. The King's School Worcester Foundation is a Registered Charity, number 1098236. It exists to provide high-quality education for boys and girls.

Chair of Governors: Mrs P Preston, MA Oxon, DipM

Chief Executive and Headmaster of The King's School Worcester Foundation: **Mr G E Doodes**, MA, FRSA

Senior Deputy Head and Deputy Head Pastoral: Mr J Ricketts, BSc
Deputy Head Academic: Mrs K Beever, MA, CEng
Deputy Head (Staff and Co-curricular): Miss A Oliver, MSc

The King's Prep Schools:

King's St Alban's:
Head: Mr R A Chapman, BSc
Assistant Head Pastoral: Mrs L Kilbey, MA, LRSM
Director of Studies: Mr D Braithwaite, BEd
Assistant Head, Pre-Prep: Miss B Cartwright, BEd

King's Hawford:
Head: Mrs J Phillips, BA, BEd
Deputy Head: Mrs C Knight, BEd
Assistant Head: Mrs A Marshall-Walker, BA
Head of Lower School: Mr O Roberts, BEd
Head of Early Years: Miss A L Kingston, BA

Kingston Grammar School

London Road, Kingston-upon-Thames, Surrey KT2 6PY

Tel: 020 8546 5875
email: enquiries@kgs.org.uk
website: www.kgs.org.uk

Motto: *Bene agere ac laetari*

A school is believed to have existed in the Lovekyn Chantry Chapel since the fourteenth century. However, in 1561, Queen Elizabeth I, in response to a humble petition from the Burghers of Kingston, signed Letters Patent establishing the 'Free Grammar School of Queen Elizabeth to endure for ever'. In 1944 the School accepted Direct Grant Status and became fully independent in 1976. Two years later it became co-educational, initially with girls in the Sixth Form, but in the following year joining in the First Year, to progress through the School. There are still close links with the Royal Borough of Kingston upon Thames, but no residential qualification for entry to the School. There are

around 850 pupils and the proportion of boys to girls is approximately 52%–48%.

Buildings. Starting with the medieval Lovekyn Chapel, the site of Kingston Grammar School has been developed over 450 years. The refurbishment of the Fairfield Building has provided modern, energy-efficient classrooms and science laboratories. The Queen Elizabeth II building, opened by Her Majesty in 2005, has a Performing Arts Centre, a Music Technology Suite, Sixth Form Centre and classrooms. Pupils have access to an extensive networked computer system which they can access from home. The school is easily accessible by road and rail links to Kingston. The 22-acre sports ground includes an indoor sports pavilion, 4 cricket squares, 6 netball courts, 8 tennis courts, 6 cricket nets, 2 hockey pitches plus practice area, 4 football pitches, an Olympic gym and the KGS boat house.

Entry to the School. Admission to the School at 11+ and 13+ is by examination and interview and at 16+ by assessment, interview and GCSE results. Candidates sit the School's own examination papers; for 13+ in November prior to year of entry and for 11+ in January of the year of entry. We also hold a 10+ deferred entry exam for candidates in Year 5 at primary school to join the School in Year 7.

Term of Entry. Pupils enter in September. Occasional vacancies are considered.

Fees per term (2021–2022). £7,045; this covers all charges excluding public examination fees, trips and lunch.

Scholarships and Bursaries. The Governors award scholarships (on merit) and means-tested fee assistance to pupils entering the School at 11+, 13+ and 16+.

At age 11 the School offers Academic Scholarships that are awarded based on the results of a scholarship examination and interviews, which are by invitation only following the the entrance examination.

Academic Scholarships are also awarded to entrants into Third Year, at the discretion of the Head Master following entrance examinations and interviews and, to the Sixth Form, following entrance examinations, interviews and successful GCSE results.

Art Scholarships may be awarded at 11+, 13+ and 16+ following practical test, an interview and submission of a folder of work.

Design & Technology Scholarships may be awarded at 16+ following an interview and submission of a folder of work.

Drama Scholarships are also available at 16+, based on auditions and an interview.

Music Scholarships, plus free tuition on one instrument, are available. Auditions are in January for candidates who are applying for entry at 11+, and November for candidates who are applying for entry at 13+ or 16+.

Sport Scholarships for candidates demonstrating outstanding sporting potential are available at 11+, 13+ and 16+, based on practical assessment.

Curriculum. The academic curriculum through to GCSE emphasises a proper balance between varied disciplines and a range of intellectual experience, with all taking Maths, English, the three sciences and at least one modern foreign language as part of 10 IGCSE/GCSE subjects. Maths IGCSE may be taken early by the most able candidates. There is a Learning Support Department and mentoring for pupils with specific needs. A full Careers Programme is offered with support for university entry as well. Pupils are encouraged to view academic pursuit as a desirable end in itself, using a profiling process to develop their commitment to study. In the Sixth Form, students choose 4 A Level subjects in the Lower Sixth and normally continue with 3 into the Upper Sixth. In addition, students in the Lower Sixth undertake an academic enrichment programme, designed to develop the skills necessary to learn independently and to broaden their horizons. They are able to choose from courses such as the Extended Project Qualification (EPQ), MOOCS, OU courses or Critical Thinking. They also engage in community service. All Sixth Form students attend fortnightly lectures on wider social issues and international themes. Almost 100% of the Sixth Form elect to proceed to higher education, including Oxford and Cambridge, with a high proportion gaining entry to Russell Group institutions.

Care. A pupil's Form Tutor is responsible for welfare and progress. Experienced Heads of Year, supported by Assistants, coordinate the work of Form Tutors. There is a full-time qualified nurse plus a healthcare assistant working in a dedicated medical area and a school counsellor visits two days a week to support any pupils who have concerns in and out of school. Parents' meetings are held regularly and pupils receive a number of written reports per year, in addition to twice-termly grade cards. Pastoral evenings are also held covering a wide range of outside topics using a variety of external and internal speakers. Sessions are also held where parents can discuss with each other and staff the difficulties and anxieties faced by young adults. Pastoral education takes place in all year groups through a dedicated bi-weekly lesson, supplemented by high-quality outside speakers on a wide range of subjects.

Games. The School's sports grounds are beautifully situated at Thames Ditton, next to the River Thames, opposite Hampton Court Palace. Kingston Grammar School not only prides itself on the high percentage of pupils engaged in competitive sport, but the large number who go on to obtain county, regional and international honours. Cricket (summer term), hockey (winter/spring terms) and rowing (all terms) are the focus sports with teams/crews competing at all levels in friendly fixtures as well as county, regional and national championships. The School also has representative sides in athletics, cross country running, golf, netball and tennis, with an emphasis on creating sporting opportunities for all as well as focussed training and support for its performance athletes.

Societies. The School is proud of its extensive co-curricular provision and its programme of House-based activities. A large number of School societies provides for the interests of pupils of all ages. They range from Chess and Debating to STEAM and Young Enterprise. The Duke of Edinburgh's Award scheme is popular and overseas travel is a regular feature of many activities. The Music Department has a vigorous programme of concerts and tours, and a flourishing Drama Department provides a wealth of opportunity for pupils in all aspects of dramatic production.

Community Service. A large number of pupils volunteer at a dozen local organisations through the Community Service Programme at KGS, including Richmond MENCAP, the Joel Community Project, three local primary schools, Kingston Museum, St Stephen's homeless drop-in, Elmbridge Community Link and Wingham Court Care Home. While older pupils are directly involved in the projects, younger pupils also support groups through activities which take place within school. Volunteering is challenging and rewarding, and helps to foster compassion, empathy and a sense of social justice, while enabling students to develop skills such as teamwork, responsibility and resilience. Although KGS already offers a wide range of activities to choose from, staff are also willing to help pupils find other projects. In addition, the School has a partnership with a school in Ghana; gap year pupils undertake periods of work experience, whilst younger pupils are involved in fundraising activities and co-curricular links.

Careers. The Careers Staff assist students with their options at all levels, are available at parents' evenings and give advice on possible future careers. They are in close contact with employers in professions, commerce and industry through a strong alumni department. All pupils undertake the Morrisby Profile at the end of Fourth Year to assist with career and study choices whilst in Fifth Year pupils spend a week or more involved in work experience after their GCSE examinations. An annual Careers Fair and other specialist careers seminars are offered during the academic year. Particular attention is given to the advice on entry to universities to which the majority of Sixth Formers go and students are encouraged to explore apprenticeship routes as well.

Parents' and Staff Association. The Association exists to further the interests of the School in the broadest possible way and does much to strengthen the links between staff, parents and students. The Sherriff Club (rowing), The Hockey Society, Music Society, and Drama Society also support school activities.

KGS Friends (our alumni society) does much to foster a spirit of unity and cooperation. All pupils and their parents automatically join the Friends on leaving the School.

Honours. Around 10% of the cohort achieve places at Oxford and Cambridge

Charitable Status. Kingston Grammar School is a Registered Charity, number 1078461, and a Company Limited by Guarantee, registered in England, number 3883748. It exists to enable children to adapt their talents to meet the needs of an ever-changing world, whilst holding fast to the principles of self-reliance, a sense of responsibility and a determination to seize opportunity.

Governing Body:
Mr R O'Dowd, BSc, RSA (*Chair*)
Mrs L Adam, BSc (*Vice Chair*)
Dr N Ahmed, BSc
Mrs C Chevallier, MA, CIPD
Mr N Cole, MA, MPhil, DPhil Oxon
Mrs L Dux, LLB
Mr A D Evans, BSc, ACA
Mr J Harchowal, MRPharmS, MSc, BPharm Hons
Mr N Khandan-Nia, BSc
Ms F C Le Grys, MA
Mrs J Mikardo, BA, CQSW, Member of ACP
Mrs D Rose, MA Cantab

Clerk to the Governors: Ms D Coomes

Head Master: S R Lehec, BA

Deputy Head Pastoral: Mrs V S Humphrey (*Geography*)
Deputy Head Academic: Mr W Cooper, MPhil (*Religion & Philosophy*)
Assistant Head: Mrs D M Sherwood, BSc (*Geography*)
Assistant Head: Mr A J Beard, MA (*History*)
Assistant Head: Mrs A Lett, BSc (*Chemistry*)
Assistant Head: Ms A Williams, BSc (*Biology*)

Assistant Head: Mr N Hudson, BA (*English*)

Staff:
* *Head of Department*

Miss L S Andrews, BSc (*Mathematics*)
Mrs A Angell, BA (*History*) [maternity leave]
Miss A Arcos Villanueva, BA (*Spanish*)
Mrs J Barkey, BA (*Art*)
Mr D Bartram, BSc (*PE*)
Mr T Beaumont, BSc (* *Boys' Hockey*)
Miss C Beckford, BA (*Design Technology*)
Mr A Beggs (*Contingent Commander CCF*)
Mr M Behnoudnia, BSc (*Second in Physics, Assistant Head of Academic Scholars*)
Mr T G Benson, MSci (*Physics, Head of STEAM*)
Mr C Bequignon, MA (*French & German*)
Mr A Brown, BSc (*Economics*)
Mrs J Butcher, BA (*History & Politics, Assistant Head of Year*)
Miss S J Butler, BA (*PE, Head of First Year*)
Mr B Campbell, BA (*English*)
Mr N Casasanto, BA (*Chemistry*)
Mr I Chiew, MSc (*Mathematics*)
Miss S E Christie, BA (*Art*)
Miss M Christmas, MA (*Drama*)
Miss A Clarkson, BA (*Chemistry*)
Ms S Clifford, BSc (*Mathematics*)
Miss D Collins, BA (*English*)
Mrs M Collins, MA (*History*)
Mr K Connor, MEng (*Second in Mathematics*)
Mr M Cooney, BA (* *Classics, Hockey*)
Miss M Cope, BA (*History*)
Mrs S J Corcoran, BEd (* *Learning Support*)
Dr A Crampin, BSc, PhD (*Physics, Head of Lower Sixth*)
Mr S R Crohill, BA (*Drama*)
Miss E Cuthbertson, BSc (*Biology*)
Mr M Daly, BSc (*Hockey, PE*)
Mr B Day (*Boatman*)
Mr I Deepchand, BSc (* *Physics, Assistant Head of Year*)
Mr J A Dyson, BA (* *Art*)
Mrs A L Edwards, MA (* *Psychology*)
Miss L Emm, BA (*Design Technology*)
Mr M B Emmerton, MEng (*Mathematics*)
Mrs A Evans, MA (*German*)
Mr D Farr, BA (* *Design Technology*)
Mr A R Fitzgerald, MA (*Director of Careers & Universities*)
Mr N S Forsyth, BSc (*Biology, Head of Wellbeing*)
Mr O P Garner, BA (*French & Italian, Head of Fifth Year*)
Mrs P S Garside, BA, MA (* *English*)
Mr A Gautam, MA (*Computer Science*)
Mr R M Gee, BA (* *Drama*)
Mr M S Grant, BA, MA (*History, Head of Third Year*)
Mr E Green (*Director of Rowing*)
Mr M Hall, MSc (*Head of Football*)
Mr J Halls, BA (*Design Technology*)
Mr S Hardy (*PE*)
Mrs S Hassan, MSc (*Mathematics*)
Miss A Henderson, BA (*History*)
Mrs R L Hetherington, BA (*Design Technology, Head of Third Year*)
Miss A L Hicks, BSc (*Biology, Head of Fourth Year*)
Miss L Hobbs, MA (*English*)
Mr A S House, MSc (* *Geography*)
Mrs L Hruska, BSc (*Geography*)
Mrs H Hunt, BA (*Religion & Philosophy*) [maternity leave]

Miss O Jackson, MA (*English*)
Ms M Jimenez, BA (*Spanish*)
Mrs C A Jones, BSc (*Mathematics*) [maternity leave]
Miss J Kaur, BSc (*Geography*)
Dr K Kennedy, DPhil (* *History, Young Enterprise*)
Mr M Laflin, BA (* *Director of Music*)
Mr S Lavery, MSc (*Assistant Director of Sport*)
Mr H R Lawrence, BSc (*Religion & Philosophy*)
Mrs L M Macfarlane, MSc (*Geography, Head of Second Year*)
Mrs P Mayor, BSc (*Physics*)
Ms F McBride (*Librarian*)
Mr S R Morris, BSc (*Mathematics, Deputy Director of Careers & Universities*)
Miss H M Naismith, MSc (* *Girls' Hockey, PE*)
Mr C O'Collins, BSc (*Chemistry*)
Miss L Parkes, BSc (*PE*)
Miss V Paterson, MA (*Classics*)
Miss M Parry, BSc (*Mathematics*)
Mrs K D Pinnock, BA (*French & Italian, Head of Community Service*)
Mrs E Pytel, BA (*Classics, Head of Academic Scholars*)
Mrs N A Reilly, MSci (*Mathematics*)
Mrs L Rhys, BSc (*Mathematics*)
Mr P J Ricketts, MA (*Economics*)
Mrs M Robinson, BSc (* *PSHE*)
Mr M J C Rodgers, BSc, MSc (* *Biology, Golf Programme*)
Mrs T M Russell, Mag Phil (* *Modern Foreign Languages*)
Miss R J Sharp, BA (*French & Spanish, Second in Modern Foreign Languages*)
Dr P Sheehy, MA, PhD (*Religion & Philosophy*) [maternity cover]
Mr P J Simmons, BSc (*PE, Assistant Head of Year*)
Mr J W Skeates, MA (* *Mathematics*)
Mr D A R Sorley, BA (* *Politics, History, Professional Tutor*)
Mrs J Stapleton (* *Netball*)
Mrs P W E Stones, MA (*Second in English*)
Mr S Symington, MSc (* *Economics*)
Miss K Tamblyn, BA (*English*)
Mr J J Tierney, BMus (*Music*)
Mrs R Wakely, BA (*Art*)
Mr A Watts, BA (*Director of Sport*)
Mr C G Wenham, BSc (*Second in Chemistry, Head of Upper Sixth, Head of CU*)
Miss O Wilkinson, BA (*Spanish*)
Mrs C Williams, BA (* *Religion & Philosophy*)
Dr L H Winning, MChem, DPhil (* *Chemistry*)

Director of Finance & Operations: Mr D Leen
Director of Human Resources: Mrs N Sloan
Facilities Manager: Mr J Farmer
Head Master's PA: Mrs C Pink
Head of Marketing: Mrs N Man
Senior Registrar: Mrs J Shalgosky

Kingswood School

Lansdown, Bath BA1 5RG

Tel:	01225 734200
email:	admissions@kingswood.bath.sch.uk
website:	www.kingswood.bath.sch.uk
Twitter:	@KingswoodSchool
Facebook:	@KingswoodSchool
Instagram:	@kingswoodschool
LinkedIn:	/kingswoodschool

Motto: *In via Recta Celeriter*

Kingswood Senior School is a thriving independent co-educational day and boarding school like no other, welcoming children from 11–18 years old. As a busy boarding and day school, we offer a staggering range of co-curricular opportunities, celebrating both cultural and sporting achievement.

Whilst some pupils continue their journey from Kingswood Prep School, we welcome many new students at our various entry points and they settle into life at Kingswood seamlessly which is testament to the strength of our inclusive community.

Pastoral Care. Pastoral care is central to everything we do at Kingswood and we all want our pupils to feel good about themselves, recognise their strengths, constantly develop any areas that they find challenging and have a positive impact on the community and world around them.

Site and facilities. With an abundance of space on our 200-acre site in Lansdown, Bath, we are within easy reach of the M4 and M5 motorways, as well as having great transport links to Bristol and London. The School sits alongside original Victorian buildings and a host of modern developments, including boarding houses, a theatre, a sports hall, a sixth form centre and dining area. In addition to the sports hall, sporting facilities include a swimming pool, two floodlit AstroTurfs, extensive playing fields and a modern pavilion. The seven boarding and day houses are located within the school campus.

Curriculum. Our curriculum is engaging and interactive, enabling us to build on our pupils' past educational experiences and allows them to achieve a deeper understanding of, and greater competence in, each aspect of the curriculum as they move through the School. At Sixth Form level students take either three or four subjects from over twenty options, as well as participating in a programme of General Studies, and many pursue an Extended Project Qualification.

Co-Curricular. Pupils benefit from a vibrant and extensive co-curricular programme which enhances their learning experience at Kingswood. Whether it is participating in Hockey with the Deputy Head at 7am or Cooking at 8pm, pupils develop passions that last well beyond their time at Kingswood.

Sports and Games. Kingswood is widely recognised as one of the top schools for sport in the South-West, with students competing at both national and international levels. We are fortunate to have strong links with various professional clubs such as Bath Rugby; we work with Team Bath at Bath University so that we can support gifted and talented sportsmen and women in fulfilling their athletic potential. However, our games philosophy at Kingswood is very much "sport for all", and we believe in encouraging all students, whether they be on the A, B, C or D teams, to be the best they can.

Sustainability. At Kingswood, we are passionate about the future and contributing to a fair and sustainable future for all. We recognise that we have a unique opportunity to educate and empower our pupils and wider community to share this vision and deliver this future. To this effect, the School offers a wide variety of activities, projects and programmes that engage with the many facets of sustainability.

Leavers. The vast majority of Kingswood sixth formers go on to university, either immediately after school or after a gap year. Much support is given to all Upper Sixth students, including guidance on writing personal statements and interview practice. As a result of this support, the overwhelming majority of Kingswood students achieve a place at their first-choice university.

Fees per term (2021–2022). £5,471 (day), £9,845–£11,792 (full boarding), £8,600–£10,654 (weekly boarding).

EAL teaching is provided for students who do not speak English as their first language – this is invoiced separately as required. HM Forces families receive a reduction in boarding fees of up to 20% for each child.

Entry Requirements. Entry at 11+ and 13+ is based on Kingswood's own entrance examination, a report from the candidate's current school and, where possible, a personal or group interview. Sixth Form entry is dependent on performance at interview, current school report and GCSE achievement.

Scholarships and Bursaries. Academic and Special Talent scholarships (up to a maximum of 25% of the basic fees) are available annually to day and boarding pupils entering Years 7, 9 and Lower Sixth. Special Talent scholarships are awarded for excellence in a particular field: Art, Drama, Music, Sport, Design Technology. John Wesley All-Rounder Awards are also available for boarders only. Means-tested bursaries, worth up to 100% of fees, are available in Years 7, 9 and 12.

Charitable status. Kingswood School is a Registered Charity, number 309148.

Chairman of the Governing Body: Mr S Holliday

Clerk to the Governors & Bursar: Mr S Vickery

Headmaster and Principal of the Kingswood Foundation:
Mr A Gordon-Brown

Deputy Head (Pastoral): Mr G D Opie
Deputy Head (Academic): Mr J M Davies
Director of Co-Curricular: Mr J W Davies
Assistant Head (Academic): Mr P MacDonald
Assistant Head (Pastoral): Mr J Matthews
Head of Lower School: Mr S Pentreath
Assistant Head (Pastoral): Mrs C Sergeant
Head of Sixth Form: Mr C Woodgate
Head of Boarding: Mr D Harding

Head of Marketing & Communications: Mrs S Patten
Head of Admissions: Mrs D W Patterson

Kirkham Grammar School

Ribby Road, Kirkham, Preston, Lancashire PR4 2BH

Tel: 01772 684264
email: info@kirkhamgrammar.co.uk
website: www.kirkhamgrammar.co.uk
Twitter: @KirkhamGrammar
Facebook: @kirkhamgrammarschool
Instagram: @kirkhamgrammar
LinkedIn: /school/kirkham-grammar-school

Kirkham Grammar School, founded in 1549, is a co-educational independent School of 850 pupils aged between 3 and 18. The Senior School of 654 pupils, 80 of whom are boarders, incorporates a Sixth Form of 182, and the Junior School, for day pupils, has 230 on roll.

Kirkham Grammar School prides itself on developing well-balanced and confident young people, the vast majority of whom go on to University. As well as excellent academic results and a good Oxbridge entry record, the School introduces pupils to as wide a range as possible of cultural, sporting and creative activities and encourages them to participate in those which appeal to them. Great emphasis is placed on preparing pupils for life beyond university.

The School has a strong Christian ethos, with an emphasis on care for the individual, traditional family values, inspirational teaching and each child fulfilling their potential.

It is a friendly close-knit community where staff and pupils work closely together, fostering leadership and self-discipline, and encouraging cheerful, friendly and supportive relationships within the framework of 'one family'.

Facilities. Occupying 30 acres of its own grounds, Kirkham Grammar School boasts some excellent facilities, which include a large multi-purpose hall, a superb floodlit all-weather pitch, Lawrence House Pavilion, a Sixth Form Centre, an outstanding Technology Centre and Languages Centre, and a magnificent Dining Complex. The Senior School has undergone a transformation over the last decade and boasts a host of magnificent new facilities. In addition, we have completed phase one of a planned development programme. This included the refurbishment of the Summerlee Hall, a multi-purpose space available for use by the whole foundation; a new psychology classroom; a new conference room and an upgrade to the rugby pitches and sports facilities. The teaching provision includes twelve interactive classrooms and a science block designed to meet the needs of the large number of pupils who pursue studies in this area. Significant developments have also been made to both Music and Sport facilities.

Boarding. The School is a member of the Boarding Schools' Association. The refurbished Boarding House is pleasant and comfortable and is run by a House Parent (Academic), whose residence is attached to the boarding wing of the School. The House also has a team of full-time support staff and tutors.

Academic Programme. The courses lead to GCSE, A Level and BTEC. In the first three years, the basic subjects studied are English, French, Mathematics, German, Spanish, Geography, History, Physics, Chemistry, Biology, Music, Art & Design, Drama, Computing, Design and Technology, Religion, Philosophy & Ethics and an enrichment programme including Philosophy. The first stage of specialisation takes place on entering the Fourth Year where the core subjects of English, Mathematics, Physics, Chemistry and Biology are taught in sets, and there is a further choice of subjects from four option blocks, which include: Art & Design, Computer Science, Design and Technology, Drama, Business Studies, French, Geography, German, History, Latin, Music, Physical Education, Religious Studies and Spanish.

In the Sixth Form, A Level subjects are chosen from the following: Art & Design (Fine Art and Photography), Biology, Business Studies, Chemistry, Computer Science, Design & Technology, Drama & Theatre Studies, Economics, English Language, English Literature, French, German, Geography, Government & Politics, History, Latin, Mathematics, Music, Physical Education, Physics, Psychology, Religious Studies and Spanish. BTEC programmes are also available in Applied Science, Business and Sport.

In addition many Sixth Form students voluntarily continue in the CCF and the Duke of Edinburgh's Award, Young Enterprise or Community Service. Extra tuition is provided for Oxbridge candidates. Students are also offered the opportunity to undertake an Extended Project Qualification (EPQ) alongside their A Levels. A comprehensive careers service is available.

Sport. There is a strong sporting tradition at Kirkham Grammar School and it ranks among the very best schools in the country for rugby and girls hockey. The other main sports played are cricket, athletics, tennis, netball, cross-country, badminton, squash, swimming, rounders, volleyball and basketball.

Music. There is a very active musical life at the School, with regular Concerts both at lunchtime and in the evening, providing a platform for the Orchestra, Choir, various ensembles and Soloists.

Co-Curricular Activities. An impressive range of co-curricular activities is offered by a School renowned for its sporting prowess, but with strength across the board in music, art and drama. There is a strong and popular Combined Cadet Force contingent, with Army and RAF sections, and a flourishing House System. A large number of societies cater for a wide range of interests including astronomy, drama, the very popular Duke of Edinburgh's Award scheme, chess, badminton, climbing, science, young engineers, Sixth Form discussion group, music and many others.

Admission to Senior School. Four Year entry. Pupils are usually admitted at 11 years old after passing the entrance examination held in February each year. Admissions to the School in other year groups, especially the Sixth Form, are possible. Day and Boarding applications should be made to the Registrar who will be glad to provide further details.

Fees per term (2021–2022). Day (excluding lunches): Senior School £4,190; Junior School £3,130; Pre-School: £248.40 (full week), £55.20 (full day).

These fees cover tuition, use of class, text and library books, school stationery, scientific equipment, games apparatus.

Senior School Boarding: £3,890 in addition to the Day fee. The boarding fee is discounted by 5% for children resident Monday to Friday (weekly boarders) and for children whose parents are current members of HM Forces.

Scholarships and Bursaries. The School offers an impressive number of Scholarships and Bursaries at 11+ and 16+. Further details are available from the Registrar.

Junior School (3–11 years). An integral part of the School, under the same Board of Governors, this section of Kirkham Grammar School comprises of a Junior, Infant and Pre-School department housed in excellent, purpose-built accommodation. The curriculum is organised to ensure that the education is continuous from the age of 3 to 18.

The curriculum in the Infant and Junior department promotes the development of pupils morally, culturally, mentally and physically, ensuring that they are prepared for Senior School, and also amply prepared for the responsibilities of later life. An emphasis on the importance of physical engagement, creativity and opportunity pervade the day-to-day experience at Kirkham Grammar School.

The teaching in Pre-School and Reception is equally as ambitious and stimulating, provided in a caring and supportive environment. There is a strong emphasis on preparing pupils for the rigour of education in future years to ensure that they fulfil their potential. As a result, the curriculum is designed first and foremost to focus on the strong development of every pupil's social and emotional needs. The daily educational diet constitutes a planned curriculum with an emphasis on language, mathematics and design and technology. In addition, as in the Junior and Infant department, importance is placed upon physical exercise, modern foreign languages and music lessons, all delivered by specialists.

The School guarantees that a Kirkham Grammar Junior, Infant and Pre-School pupil will thrive and succeed through opportunity, inspirational teaching and their renowned family ethos.

Application should be made direct to the Headmistress's PA from whom a separate prospectus may be obtained.

Old Kirkhamians Association. For further details contact the Secretary via the School.

Charitable status. Kirkham Grammar School is a Registered Charity, number 1123869. The object of the Charity shall be the provision in or near Kirkham of a day and boarding school for boys and girls.

Chairman of Governors: Mrs L Wareing

Headmaster: **Mr D H Berry**, BA, MA, NPQH (*History*)

Senior Deputy Head: Mrs D C Parkinson, BSc, NPQH (*Physics*)
Deputy Head: Mr M J Hancock, BEd, MA, MBA (*Design Technology, Economics*)
Deputy Head: Mr M P Melling, BA, MA Ed (*Government & Politics*)
Deputy Head: Mrs H Shuttleworth, GMus, RNCM, PGCE (*Philosophical Enquiry, PSHE*)
Deputy Head: Mrs N Walter, BA (*PSHE*)
Deputy Head: Mr S R Taylor, BSc, MRes (*Biology, Chemistry*)

Heads of Year:
Sixth Form: Mr S R Taylor, BSc, MRes
Assistant Head of Sixth Form: Mrs J Stanbury, BA
Assistant Head of Sixth Form: Mr S R Whittle, MA Cantab
Fifth Year: Mr S Duncan, BA
Fourth Year: Mrs T Marsh, BEng
Third Year: Mr G S Partington, BA
Second Year: Mr D Gardner, BEng
First Year: Mrs G R Latham, BA

Heads of Departments:
Art: Mr S P Gardiner, BA
Boys' Sport: Mr J P Roddam, BA
Business Studies & Economics: Mr M J Percy, Ba
Biology: Ms P E Halloran, BSc
Chemistry: Dr A B Rollins, BSc, PhD
Design & Technology: Mr D Gardner, BEng
Drama: Mrs G R Latham, BA
English: Mrs E L Hiller, BA, PGCE, MEd
Geography: Mr S R Whittle, MA Cantab
Girls' Sport: Mrs L D Osborne, BA
History: Mrs H L Atkinson, BA
Latin: Mrs S P Long, BA
Learning Support: Mrs B P Batty, BSc
Mathematics: Mr J Procter, BA
Modern Foreign Languages: Ms A C Johnson, BA
Director of Music: Miss J Z Crook, BMus
Physics: Mrs C A Smith, BSc
Politics: Mr M P Melling, BA, MA Ed
Psychology: Mrs J Stanbury, BA
Religion, Philosophy & Ethics: Mrs L Bowles, BA

Houses & House Parents:
House Parent (Academic): Mr A E Trenhaile, BA, MEd
House Parents (Pastoral): Mrs J Dinsley, Miss B Rawcliffe
Kirkham House: Mr M Percy, BA
Fylde House: Mr S R Whittle, MA Cantab
School House: Mr J R Lyon, HND
Preston House: Mrs J M Glover, BEd

School Business Manager: Mr M H Thomson
Finance Controller: Mr D I McNeillie
Headmaster's PA: Mrs J Hunt
Registrar: Miss S J Potts
Head of Communications and Publicity: Mrs M C Tickle
Examinations Officer: Mrs S Morton

Junior, Infant and Pre School:

Headmistress: Mrs K L O'Donoghue, BA

Deputy Head (Academic): Mrs K Aldeen, BA Hons, QTS, MA, NPQSL
Deputy Head (Pastoral): Mr S Lewis, BA

Pre-School Manager: Mrs S Anyon, BTEC
Junior School Headmistress's PA: Miss J Stewart
School Secretary: Miss B Sharman

Lancing College
A Woodard School

Lancing, West Sussex BN15 0RW

Tel: 01273 452213
email: admissions@lancing.org.uk
website: www.lancingcollege.co.uk
Twitter: @lancingcollege
Facebook: @lancingcollege
Instagram: @lancing_college
LinkedIn: /company/lancing-college

Motto: Beati mundo corde

Founded in 1848 by the Revd Nathaniel Woodard, Lancing College is one of the first schools of the Woodard Foundation.

There are 600 pupils in the school, accommodated in ten houses.

Location. The school stands on a spur of the Downs, overlooking the sea to the south and the Weald to the north, in grounds of 550 acres, which include the College Farm.

By train, Lancing is 10 minutes from Brighton, 30 minutes from Gatwick Airport and 75 minutes from central London.

Buildings and Facilities. The main school buildings, faced with Sussex flint, are grouped around two quadrangles on the lines of an Oxford or Cambridge College.

The Chapel, open to visitors every day, has the largest rose window built since the Middle Ages.

The College has extensive laboratories, a purpose-built Music School, a Theatre with a full-time technical manager and a modern Design and Technology Centre with computerised design and engineering facilities. Alongside this, a strikingly modern Art School provides vast studio space and a photography suite. A café is located in the centre of the school for use by pupils and staff. There are over 350 private studies for boys and girls, many of which are study-bedrooms. There is a sports hall, indoor swimming pool and a miniature shooting range. Sporting facilities also include Squash, Tennis and Fives courts and an all-weather surface and full-sized AstroTurf hockey pitch. The Equestrian Centre, opened in 2017, provides livery as well as additional centre horses for co-curricular activities.

Admission. Boys and girls are normally admitted at the beginning of the Autumn Term in their fourteenth year. The Advance (Pre-Test) Programme provides an early entry route for pupils, who can apply in the Advent Term of Year 6 and Year 7.

A registration fee of £200 is paid when a child's name is entered in the admission register. Entries should be made via the Director of Admissions, who will assign a House, following as far as possible the wishes of the parents. After a pupil has joined the school, parents usually correspond with the Housemaster or Housemistress directly.

Sixth Form Entry. Applications for entry should be made to the Director of Admissions one year prior to the year of entry. Testing takes place in November or by private arrangement.

Curriculum. Designed as far as possible to suit every pupil's potential with a wide range of subjects on offer including over 20 at A Level. Pupils work closely with academic staff and personal tutors to help them consider future options, entry to universities and to a wide range of professions. The College prides itself on the individual support available for pupils.

In a pupil's first three years, the curriculum provides a broad, balanced education without premature specialisation. The total of subjects taken at GCSE is limited to about nine or ten, the object being to promote excellence in whatever is studied and to lay firm foundations for the Sixth Form years.

The following subjects are studied in the Senior School: English Language and Literature, Religious Studies, Mathematics, Physics, Chemistry, Biology, French, Spanish or German, Geography, History, Physical Education, Music, Art, Design and Technology, Photography, Latin, Greek or Classical Civilisation, and Drama.

In the Sixth Form there is a choice of over 20 subjects which can be studied to A Level. A BTEC qualification is also available in Business and Sport. Pupils are also encouraged to carry out an EPQ (Extended Project Qualification) to enhance their studies.

A close connection has been established with schools in Germany and Spain, with which individual and group exchanges are arranged.

Tutorial System. In addition to the Housemaster or Housemistress, there are pastoral Tutors attached to each House who act as Academic Tutors to individual pupils. The Tutors' main functions are to supervise academic progress and to encourage general reading and worthwhile spare time activities. A pupil usually keeps the same Tutor until he or she moves into the Sixth Form, where this function is taken over by an Academic Tutor chosen from one of the specialist teachers.

Music and Art form an important part of the education of all pupils. There are orchestras, bands, ensembles and choirs. Organ and Choral awards to Oxford and Cambridge and Colleges of Music are frequently won. There is a full programme of extra-curricular **Drama**. The **Art School** and **Design & Technology Centre** provide for a wide range of technical and creative work.

Other Activities. Boys and girls in their first year are given the opportunity to sample the many activities on offer at the College. A well-organised co-curricular programme is followed by pupils of all age groups and participation is strongly encouraged under the supervision of the Assistant Head, Co-curricular.

Several plays are produced each year and pupils are able to write and perform their own plays and to learn stagecraft.

In the Advent Term the main sports are Association Football for boys and Hockey for girls; in the Lent Term Hockey for boys and Netball for girls. Squash, Fives, Badminton, Basketball, Volleyball, Cross Country and Shooting (the College has an indoor range) take place during both terms for boys and girls. Rugby Sevens is played in the Lent Term. Cricket, Tennis, Sailing, Athletics and Rounders take place in the Summer Term. There is Swimming all year round in the College's indoor heated pool; Lancing College Swimming Club, affiliated with Swim England, supports the development of county, regional and national swimmers.

The College has a CCF contingent (with Army and RAF sections) and takes part in the Duke of Edinburgh's Award scheme. The option to join Explorer Scouts has been recently set up to focus on life skills, leadership, teamwork and volunteering. There is also a flourishing Outreach group, which works in the local community. Pupils help to run a small farm (including sheep, goats, pigs, alpacas and chickens) and participate in conservation projects under the supervision of the Farm Manager. Links have been established with local industries and pupils are involved in business experience through the Young Enterprise scheme.

Careers and Higher Education. A number of the teaching staff share responsibility for careers advice and there is a well-equipped careers section in the Gwynne Library. Popular universities include Imperial College, Manchester, Bristol, Durham, UCL, LSE and Sheffield; three to Oxbridge in 2021; several to other international universities. All members of the Fifth Form attend the annual Careers Fair and enrol in the 'Morrisby' online profiling programme. Pupils in the Sixth Form take part in the 'Leaving Lancing' programme with activities to help pupils develop practical, team working and leadership skills.

Scholarships and Exhibitions. Candidates for the following awards must be under 14 years of age on 1st

September in the year of the examination. The age of the candidate is taken into account in making awards. A candidate may enter for more than one type of award, and account may be taken of musical or artistic proficiency in a candidate for a non-musical award; but no one may hold more than one type of award, except in an honorary capacity.

A number of scholarships in Academic subjects, Art, Drama and Sport are offered every year, ranging in value up to a maximum 10 per cent of the annual school fee. In very exceptional cases, awards of up to 25 per cent are made.

A number of Music and Choral Scholarships ranging in value up to a maximum 10 per cent of the annual school fee (25 per cent in very exceptional cases). Scholarships may be offered to pupils from schools where the time for Music is less than in some others, and where a candidate may have less musical experience but greater potential.

One Professor W K Stanton Music Scholarship for a Chorister from Salisbury Cathedral School, or failing that any Cathedral School. A Stanton Exhibition may also be awarded. There is one Peter Lewis Scholarship for a promising horn player.

The Peter Robinson Cricket Scholarship is awarded to an outstanding young cricketer at 13+ and 16+ entry.

A number of Ken Shearwood Awards, ranging in value up to a maximum 10 per cent of the annual school fee (25 per cent in very exceptional cases), are made to pupils of all-round ability and potential who have made outstanding contributions to their present schools.

Entry Forms for Academic, Art, Music, Drama, Sport and All-Rounder (Ken Shearwood) awards are obtainable from the Admissions Office.

Sixth Form Awards: Scholarships are available for new entrants to the Sixth Form with special proficiency in Academic subjects, Art, Music, Drama and Sport. There is also one Organ Scholarship. The candidate's general ability to contribute to the life of a boarding school community will also be taken into account. A small number of Scholarships is also available internally on the strength of GCSE results.

The value of all Entrance Scholarships may be augmented by bursaries, according to parental circumstances.

Fees per term (2021–2022). Boarding £12,850; Flexi-Boarding £10,800 (for incoming Years 9 &10); Day £8,780.

Further details about fees, including the scheme for payment in advance of a single composition fee to cover a pupil's education during his/her time in the school, are available from the Bursar.

Charitable status. Lancing College is a Registered Charity, number 1076483. It exists to provide education for boys and girls.

Governing Body:
The Provost and the Directors of Lancing College Ltd

Visitor: The Archbishop of Canterbury

Governors:
Mr Martin Slumbers, BSc, ACA [OL] (*Chairman*)
Mrs Anne-Marie Edgell, LLB (*Deputy Chairman*)
Mr David Austin, BSc
Mr Robert Crawford Clarke, BSc Agric, MRICS
Baroness Cumberlege, CBE, DL
Mr Freddie Dennis, BA, MA
Mr Andrew-Dane Fairclough, BA

Professor Michael Farthing, MD, DScMed, FRCP, FMedSci
Dr Sally Godward, MRCGP
Mr Tim Hancock, MA [OL]
Mr Justin Higgo, MA Oxon, Dip. Law [OL]
Mrs Charlotte Houston, BSc, ACMA, CGMA [OL]
Ms Helen Hunter, MA Oxon [OL]
Mr Henry Lawson, MA Cantab, MBA Harvard [OL]
The Rt Revd Jonathan Meyrick MA Oxon, OL (*Provost*)
Dr John Scott, BA Oxon, PhD, MBA [OL]

Clerk to the Governing Body: Mrs Hannah Betts, BSc

[OL] *Former Pupil*

Head Master: **Mr D T Oliver**, BA, MPhil

Bursar: Mr M B Milling, CA
Senior Deputy Head: Mrs H R Dugdale, MA
Deputy Head: Mr J R J Herbert, BA, PhD
Executive Director of External Relations and Communications: Mrs Diana Cree, BA, MBA, MRS, CIM
Assistant Head (Academic): Mrs P S Faulkner, BSc
Director of Admissions: Ms Maggie Roberts, BA, MEd
Director of IT: Mr A C Brown, MBCS
Chaplain: The Revd R K Harrison, BA, MA
Foundation Director: Ms Catherine Reeve, BA [OL]

Common Room:
Miss S Airey, BSc Loughborough (*PE*)
Ms D Alacorn, BA Universidad Valle del Bravo, Mexico (*Spanish*)
Mrs K Andrew, BA De Montfort (*Director of Sport*, *Head of Academic PE*)
Mr T P Atkinson, BA Lancaster (*History*)
Mr T S Auty, BA Norwich School of Art (*Head of Photography*; *Art*)
Dr C N M Baldock, BA Cantab, PhD Yale (*History*)
Mr N D D Beeby, BA London, LGSMD (*Director of Drama and Dance*)
Mr L Benson, BA Winchester (*Head of Football*)
Mr G D Bird, BSc, MSc Wellington (*Psychology*)
Ms D Blease, BSc, BA, MA Oxon (*Joint Coordinator of Science, Head of Chemistry*)
Mrs K J Blundell, BA Photography Westminster, BA Textiles Chelsea College of Art and Design (*Head of Art*)
Mrs F Britnell, BSc, PGCE Keele (*Chemistry*)
Mrs M Brookes, Referendarstudium 2, Münster (*German*)
Mr N A Brookes, BSc Manchester, MSc Newcastle (*Mathematics*)
Mr J J Bullen, BSc Bristol (*Head of Mathematics*)
Dr R Bustin, BSc Exeter, PhD UCL (*Head of Geography*)
Mrs E Campbell, MA Oxford, BTh South Africa (*Mathematics*)
Mr A Carter, BSc Coventry (*Head of Hockey*)
Mr A M Chappell, BSc Durham (*Assistant Head, Pastoral*; *Biology, Chemistry*)
Mr D J Collins, BSc Exeter (*Physics*)
Mr G Costarella, BA L'Aquila (*Spanish, French*)
Dr A Currie, BSc Royal Holloway, PhD (*Learning Support*)
Mr R P Dolan, Assistant Head, Safeguarding (*Economics*)
Mr S A Drozdov, BEd Russia (*Head of Languages, German*)
Mr G A Drummond, BSc Bath (*PSHE Co-ordinator, Economics, Politics*)

Mrs H R Dugdale, MA Cantab (*Senior Deputy Head, English*)

Mr A M Durkan, MPhys Southampton (*Physics, Psychology*)

Ms C Dutton (*Classics*)

Mr J R J East, BSc Manchester (*Mathematics*)

Ms C L Edwall, BS Greenville College USA, BA Oxon, MPhil Cantab (*English*)

Ms K V Edwards, BA de Montfort (*Assistant Director of Sport*)

Ms M Espiga-Gomez, BA Malaga (*Head of Spanish*)

Mr C J Eustace, MA Cantab (*Assistant Head, Co-Curricular*; *Classics*)

Mrs P S Faulkner, BSc Edinburgh (*Assistant Head, Academic*; *Biology*)

Mrs L Fryer, BA Newcastle (*Assistant Head of Languages, French*)

Miss L J Gaukroger, BA, MPhil Kent (*Classics*)

Mr T A Grant, MA St Andrews (*English*)

Mr J A Grime, BSc Liverpool (*Geography*)

Miss E Harlow, BA Durham (*Music*)

Mr D J Harman, BA Exeter, MA Sussex (*Head of English and EAL*)

The Revd R K Harrison, MA Oxford, BA Leeds (*Chaplain*)

Mr D J Harvey, BSc Reading (*Biology*)

Mrs H L Harvey, BA Gloucestershire (*Mathematics*)

Dr J R J Herbert, BA, PhD Birmingham (*Deputy Head, English*)

Miss R A Hopkinson, BSc Birmingham (*Joint Coordinator of Science, Head of Biology*)

Dr E P Keane, BA College of the Holy Cross, PhD Cambridge, MA New York (*Head of Politics, History, Joint Head of Junior Scholars*)

Dr D A Kerney, MA Cantab, PhD Sheffield, FRSA (*Head of History, Head of Sixth Form Enrichment*)

Ms L Langford, BA Cantab (*Library Supervisor*)

Mr C Langworthy, MusB LRSM (*Head of Academic Music, Assistant Director of Music, Joint Head of Junior Scholars*)

Mrs Q Liang, MA Sussex (*Head of Chinese*)

Mrs K Lindfield, HND Northbrook College of Art and Design (*Art*)

Mr D Loe, BSc Sussex (*Mathematics*)

Mrs S E Marchant, BA Brighton, MCLIP (*Librarian*)

Mr R J Maru, NCA Advanced Coach & ECB Level III (*Director of Cricket*)

Mr A E Mason, BA, MA Oxon, MMus The Royal College of Music (*Director of Music*)

Miss E McElnea, BSc Surrey (*Mathematics*)

Ms A McKane, BA, MA, Dip.Ed Monash (*English*)

Ms A M McKeown, BA King's College, London (*Head of EAL, English*)

Mrs R J McNamara, BA Brunel, MA UCL (*Head of Learning Support*)

Mr T J Meierdirk, BFA Illinois (*Head of Design and Technology*)

Mr R P Mew, MA, BA LitHum Oxford (*Head of Classics*)

Mr T A Miller, BSc Manchester (*Mathematics*)

Mr C M Mole, BSc Manchester (*PE*)

Mrs C R Mole, BA UCL (*Head of Economics and Business Studies*)

Ms J Nixon, BA Oxford Brookes (*Assistant Librarian*)

Dr S R Norris, BSc, PhD Southampton (*Chemistry*)

Dr M S W Palmer, BA Sussex, PhD Edinburgh, MIL (*German, Italian*)

Mr N L Payne, BA London (*English, University Applications Co-ordinator*)

Mr K Perrault, Masters Nanterre Paris-Ouest la Défense (*French*)

Mrs M S Porter, MSc Southampton (*Physics*)

Mr E Prager, MA Cantab (*Mathematics*)

Dr G A Preston, BSc Portsmouth, PhD Southampton (*Head of Science, Physics*)

Dr A J H Reesink, MSc Utrecht, PhD Binghamton, New York (*Geography*)

Mr P C Richardson, MA Cantab, MA London (*Head of RS, History*)

Mrs H M Robinson, BSc Newcastle (*Chemistry, Head of Overseas Universities Applications*)

Miss D Sellers, BA, PGCE Nottingham (*History, RS*)

Mr M J H Smith, BA Durham (*RS, English*)

Miss E Staddon, BSc Middlesex (*Psychology*)

Mr P W Tarbet, BSc Durham (*Mathematics, Computing*)

Ms D Taylor, BTec Chichester (*Art*)

Mr G C Thomas, BEng Bristol, MInstP (*Head of Computing, Physics*)

Mr A W Tobias, BA York, MA Exeter (*Economics*)

Mr E D Watson, BSc Hull (*Economics, Business Studies*)

Mrs R M Wren, MBA Lancaster, BSc York (*Biology*)

Mr A P Williamson, MA Oxford (*Chemistry*)

Houses & Housemasters/mistresses:

Boys:
Head's: Mr G D Bird
Second's: Mr D J Harvey
School: Mr C M Mole
Gibbs': Mr M J H Smith
Teme: Mr T P Atkinson

Girls:
Field's: Mrs E Campbell
Handford: Ms A McKane
Manor: Ms K V Edwards
Sankey's: Mrs F Britnell

Co-ed:
Saints': Mrs M S Porter

Head Master's PA: Miss A Bargione, BA
Admissions Manager: Mrs S L Linfield
Deputy Admissions Manager: Miss B Williams

School Medical Officers
Dr V Figuera, DM, MRCGP
Dr C Huckstep, MB BS, DRCOG, DCH
School Dental Officer: Mrs J M Edwards, BDS, DOrth, MOrth [Orthodontics only]
Counsellor: Ms J Painter, BA Sussex, Dip Psychodynamic Counselling
Counsellor: Ms C Morris, BA Beds, MA Essex, PG Dip Brighton
Health Centre Manager: Mrs A Brennan, BA, RGN
Nursing Sisters: Mrs A Hill, RGN, BSc; Mrs C Johnson, RGN; Mrs G Johnston, RGN, BSc; Mrs J Line, RGN

Langley School

Langley Park, Loddon, Norwich, Norfolk NR14 6BJ

Tel: 01508 520210
email: admissions@langleyschool.co.uk
website: www.langleyschool.co.uk
Twitter: @Langley_School
Facebook: @LangleySchool
Instagram: @langleyschooluk
LinkedIn: /langley-school-1960-limited

Langley School is blessed with a 110-acre site, in the market town of Loddon, 10 miles south of Norwich, Norfolk. Originally based in Norwich itself – founded in 1911 – the school moved to its current site after the Second World War. The first girls arrived at Langley School in 1978, with three girls joining the Sixth Form. Langley School and Taverham Hall merged in 2017, creating a new site for the Prep School, which now provides a through-school education from ages 2 to 18.

Our educational environment is inclusive, supportive and allows every individual to flourish and succeed. We provide a first class, aspirational education rooted in intellectual development, nurture, challenge and empowerment through creativity, activity and service to others.

The character of the individual is also central to the Langley education – we want our young people to embrace important values such as kindness, confidence (with humility), curiosity and integrity.

Age Range. 10–18

Number of Pupils. 430

Academic Development. The Langley intake is inclusive and allows the young person to develop at their own speed. The classroom curriculum has excellent support and allows everyone to be stretched and challenged. We have a wide range of subjects that cater for a variety of interests: Mandarin, Psychology, Photography, BTEC sport. In 2021, 95% of Langley pupils achieved 9–4 grades at GCSE, and 94% achieved A*–C at A Level.

Whether Oxbridge or a local apprenticeship is the goal, the Langley education allows students to get there; we celebrate the success of each individual, whatever that is. Our students receive guidance at every step of their journey from the Sixth Form Team and the Head of Careers. Students are also encouraged to participate in academic challenges; Oxbridge support, public speaking, UCAS days, University visits and courses for part-time jobs to acquire transferable skills and experience.

Pastoral Care & Boarding. The boarding facilities, which have separate houses for boys and girls, include matrons and qualified nurses who provide 24-hour care, plus on-site resident teachers.

The accommodation offers excellent facilities, including newly refurbished common rooms, kitchens, laundry and study areas.

During weekends, resident staff offer a programme of activities, including visits, events and outings to encourage students to make effective use of leisure time.

Langley School is committed to prioritising wellbeing through excellent pastoral care, a proactive approach towards promoting resilience, openly communicating about wellbeing issues and providing support where needed. The school was recently awarded a National Wellbeing award.

The community of boarding pupils at Langley plays a vital role in the life of the school. It offers the perfect environment to live and learn together, giving pupils the chance to make lifelong friendships. Although it's never easy to leave the comfort of family and friends, every effort is made to ensure that Langley feels like a home away from home for pupils. The utmost is done to cater for the needs of the boarding community, including providing them with a safe, friendly and supportive environment.

Co-curricular & Personal Development. Life at Langley focuses on a holistic education. Academic lessons are at the core, but every pupil will be involved in Co-curricular activities at the end of every day. This programme adds diversity and enrichment to a pupil's daily routine, allowing them to participate in activities that are important to them.

Boys and girls from all Senior School year groups are assigned a house on arrival and stay there throughout their time at school. Each house has its own culture, and support will be given by Head of House and house staff when students need it. The school offers an unprecedented amount of enrichment activities for students and all students are encouraged to take a full and active part in the sports offered through the curriculum.

The Model United Nations group and Debating Society are at the centre of Langley enrichment. We enter national conferences and our pupils are always dynamic, consultative and direct when needed. Confidence gained through all the activities at school allows the Langley leaver to be ready for the world.

The creative arts are a real focus at the school with facilities and opportunities in Music, Drama and Art. We have been awarded a Gold Artsmark award that recognises this excellence. With outstanding indoor and outdoor sporting facilities, including a fully equipped gym, the School is a sporting one. Langley is particularly good at Football, and runs a Football Academy headed up by former professional football player Grant Holt. Students have the opportunity to continue with their academic studies while achieving a BTEC in Sports Performance and Excellence, alongside weekly football coaching and training. Rugby is the main winter sport for boys at Langley School and the Leicester Tiger Academy coaches visit Langley students regularly as part of the Good2Great partnership, so students can enjoy high quality rugby coaching. A new Netball Academy at Langley has just launched for, not only our own girls, but those from other schools as well, to offer enrichment in sport.

Inspection Reports and Awards can be viewed via the school's website: www.langleyschool.co.uk. Langley School Open Mornings take place in March, May, September.

Fees per term (2021–2022). Full Boarding: UK Residents £11,250, International Student (including Tier 4 Visa management charge) £11,250. Weekly Boarding (4 or 5 nights per week, Sunday to Friday) £9,600. Flexi Boarding: 2 nights per week (Sunday to Friday) £7,250, 3 nights per week (Sunday to Friday) £8,050. Day Pupils £5,700.

Charitable status. Langley School is a Registered Charity, number 311270.

Chair of Governors: Lt Col Mark Nicholas, MBE

Headmaster: **J E Perriss**, BA Hons, MEd, PGCE

Deputy Heads:
Deputy Head, Pastoral: Mr Paul Clark
Deputy Head, Academic: Mrs Rachel Ayres
Deputy Head, Co-curricular: Mr Andrew Walker

Latymer Upper School & Latymer Prep School

Upper School
King Street, Hammersmith, London W6 9LR

Tel: 020 8629 2024
email: head@latymer-upper.org
website: www.latymer-upper.org
Twitter: @LatymerUpper
Facebook: @latymerupper
LinkedIn: /latymer-upper-school

Prep School
36 Upper Mall, Hammersmith, London W6 9TA

Tel: 020 7993 0061
email: principal@latymerprep.org
website: www.latymerprep.org
Twitter: @latymerprep

The Latymer Foundation governs two schools – Latymer Upper School and Latymer Prep School. The Schools' ethos of social inclusivity is as strong today as it was 400 years ago when our founder, Edward Latymer bequeathed his legacy to ensure an education for disadvantaged children, which remains firmly at the heart of the School.

Situated on the banks of the River Thames in West London, it is one of the country's leading co-educational, independent day schools. Visitors frequently refer to the 'palpable buzz' and energy they experience when they come on site and this vitality is one of the many characteristics of Latymer that makes studying and working here so stimulating. Latymer values and respects diversity; it is modern and forward-thinking; it promotes a global outlook; and has a dynamic community of talented people who combine the highest academic achievement with excellence in the arts and sport.

In 2018, Latymer Upper School won three TES Independent School Awards, including Independent School of the Year and became the first school ever to be nominated for a Social Mobility Award. Our long-running bursary scheme ensures a first class education to academically able students from all walks of life. Currently over 240 pupils (1 in 5) are in receipt of a bursary, which are funded wholly through donations by members of the Latymer community. The Inspiring Minds campaign aims to raise enough funds to be able to offer one in four of our pupils a means-tested bursary by 2024, making Latymer one of the most inclusive independent schools in the country.

The vibrant student body consists of more than 1,400 girls and boys from all walks of life, of which 392 students are in the Sixth Form and 174 are in the Prep. The two schools share the same grounds and excellent sports, music and theatre facilities.

Admission is by competitive examination and interview.

Candidates for the Prep School are required to sit a 7+ entrance exam and, once in the Prep School, are not required to sit the 11+ entrance exam, being automatically accepted to the Upper School.

For candidates hoping to join the Upper School, the 11+ examination is usually taken in the January of Year 6. Successful candidates are then invited for interview, which takes place in late January/early February.

Entry to the Sixth Form is based on an exam, followed by an interview in November of the year before entry, and conditional offers at GCSE.

Details of Open Days and Entry are on the School's website.

Fees per term (2021–2022). Upper School: £7,153; Prep School: £6,515.

Bursaries. A number of means-tested bursaries are awarded every year assessed on academic merit and family circumstances. These range from 25% to 100% of fees and are available at 7+, 11+ and 16+.

Scholarships. *11+ Entry:* Music Scholarships of varying amounts are offered, together with music awards of free tuition on two instruments. Scholarships will only be offered to candidates who are successful in the school's competitive entrance examination.

16+ Entry: Scholarships for Music, Drama, Art and Sport. Candidates who have satisfied the academic requirements will be invited to an interview and assessment in December of the year preceding entry.

Further details are available from the Director of Admissions and Bursaries (020 8148 4519; admissions@latymer-upper.org).

Curriculum. A full range of academic subjects is offered at GCSE and A Level. Languages include Spanish, Mandarin, Latin, French, German and Greek (European Work Experience and exchanges are run every year). Science is taught as separate subjects by specialists from Year 7. Form sizes in the Prep and Lower School of around 22 and smaller teaching group sizes ensure the personal attention of staff. Our own World Perspectives Course, now UCAS accredited, comprising elements of Geography, History, RS, Politics, Philosophy, and Economics is enjoyed by Years 10 and 11. Year 9 students take our 'Global Goals' sustainable development course.

Pastoral Care. The School takes pastoral care very seriously. Each pupil has a tutor, and tutor groups are small, meaning that each pupil can receive individual care and attention. Tutors see their pupils very frequently, monitor their academic progress and help them with day-to-day issues. Form Tutors deliver a coherent PSHCE programme which promotes involvement in the community, charity work, and the personal, social and academic development of the Form. Tutors are supported by experienced Heads and Assistant Heads of Year, who have significant pastoral expertise and, along with tutors, are the first port of call for parents' and pupils' concerns. Three Heads of Division (Lower School, Middle School and Sixth Form), a Pupil Welfare Officer and the Deputy Head (Pastoral) complete the pastoral team. Additionally, many specialists also support the teaching staff in caring for our pupils including a team of three counsellors, two registered nurses in our Medical Centre, our Chaplain and the Head of Wellbeing and PSHCE.

Much of this is echoed in the Prep, which also has access to the on-site counsellors and nurses. The Prep provides a caring, happy and safe environment, promoting high quality personal development alongside independent learning. While Form tutors have primary pastoral responsibility – in terms of pupils' academic and social life at the school – wellbeing is a whole school responsibility. As we are a small school, the staff all know the children and their families well and there is a continuous sharing of information among staff.

The Academic Mentoring Department (AMD) is integral to the academic and pastoral structures at both Latymer Prep and Upper School. With a deep understanding of current thinking on neurodiversity and growth mindset, the AMD team embraces a creative approach to teaching and learning. Using assistive technology – iPads, laptops and a range of software – AMD support enhances the academic work of pupils across the age ranges, providing an education that will enable all our pupils to achieve the highest academic standards, while simultaneously maintaining excellent mental health. There is also a highly effective Prefect and peer mentor system where the more senior students provide advice and a listening ear for our younger pupils, as well as demonstrating leadership across the school community.

Music and Drama. The Performing Arts play a large part in the life of the School. The Latymer Arts Centre houses music practice rooms and a 300-seat theatre in addition to increased facilities for Art. The Latymer Performing Arts Centre houses a 100-seat recital hall, music classrooms, and more practice rooms and a dance/drama studio. The installation of a 5-metre-wide drop screen, laser projector and surround-sound system in the Recital Hall means that at the 'click of a button' the Recital Hall transforms into a Cinema. This supports the School's new courses and competitions in film-making and history of film.

Across Prep and Upper schools there are several orchestras and bands and a number of major concerts each term, both in-school and in Central London venues. There are a number of major drama productions each year, and opportunities for all pupils to perform in events. The School also has its own recording studios and record label.

Science and Library. A state-of-the-art building, housing three floors of science laboratories. The spacious library on the ground floor is popular with all year groups and is overseen by a dynamic and multi-award-winning Librarian.

Sport. Moving towards a substantially co-ed programme in the Upper and Prep Schools, the emphasis is on engagement, inclusion, participation, and opportunity at every level.

Upper School teams enjoy great success in the major sports of rugby, football, hockey, netball, rowing, fencing, cricket and tennis; with other sports such as athletics, basketball, badminton, dance, climbing, swimming and water polo, volleyball, triathlon, pilates and yoga providing for individual interests. The School maintains an excellent fixture card for all major sports.

The major sports played at the Prep School are football, rugby, cricket, athletics, hockey and netball, in addition to various PE activities such as basketball, badminton and gymnastics. Each year the whole school participates in the 'Bandstand Cup' cross country race. There is also a thriving swimming club.

The Sports Centre – opened by Sir Steve Redgrave in 2017 – features outstanding facilities including a 6-lane, 25m pool with an adjustable floor, a large sports hall, fitness suite, climbing wall and three studios all providing a full programme of indoor sporting activities and fitness training throughout the year for pupils in both schools.

In addition, the School has netball courts and an on-site Boat House with direct river access and a large pontoon installed in 2021. The Wood Lane complex (a short coach drive away) features all-weather, floodlit playing surfaces, including 4 rugby/football pitches, 3 cricket squares, a floodlit AstroTurf for hockey, netball, football and tennis and a modern pavilion with changing rooms. Out of school hours the facilities are used for training by the England Rugby Team and visiting international teams.

Sixth Form. The large co-educational Sixth Form offers around 35 A Level choices; students opt to take three or four subjects at A Level in addition to the very popular Extended Project. Students have the opportunity to undertake work experience in Paris or Berlin and receive extensive Careers and Higher Education guidance. All students expect to go on to university or art college. In 2021 86% of students got a place at their first choice university; 20 students took up places at Oxbridge and 30 went to universities overseas – MIT, Princeton, UPenn, Bocconi and Trinity College, Dublin – and 15 students went on to study medicine and veterinary science. The newly refurbished Sixth Form Centre opened in September 2021; the new Centre includes quiet study spaces, a café and an attractive area for socialising and relaxing. Students also have access to expert advice in the University and Careers Centre.

Extra-Curricular Activities. There is a fantastic choice of around 150 clubs and societies for pupils to enjoy at lunchtime and after school. From chess to dance, aerospace to Japanese puzzles, life-drawing to water polo, each student is encouraged to try new activities, be it for one term or longer – with some going on to become lifelong passions. All pupils are encouraged to join at least two different clubs and societies.

In addition, every pupil in Upper School has the opportunity to have residential experiences and to take part in outdoor pursuits as part of the annual Activities Week. The Prep runs residential courses and an annual overseas trip.

The Duke of Edinburgh's Award scheme flourishes with a number of students achieving the Gold Award each year.

Fundraising by a very active Parents' Gild ensures that nobody is excluded from an activity for financial reasons. The Parents' Gild is an integral part of the school community, organising a variety of fundraising and social events ensuring opportunities occur frequently to meet with staff socially.

Community Partnerships. Latymerians are 'academic, rounded and grounded' and they care about each other as well as those who may need help in the local and global community. Community service is an important part of a Latymer education and for many years the School has been working in partnership with 200 local schools, charities and community organisations to deliver a wide variety of projects both in the UK and abroad. The partnerships with local schools benefit more than 600 children each year and holiday camps now run every holiday as part of the school's mission to tackle holiday hunger in the local area.

Alumni. Upon graduation, Latymerians join a successful global network of nearly 6,000 alumni. This lifelong relationship with the School provides career opportunities, mentoring, an exclusive alumni networking platform, regular news updates and a popular programme of events.

The Alumni team is part of the Foundation Office based within the School.

Charitable status. The Latymer Foundation is a Registered Charity, number 312714. It exists to provide an opportunity for able pupils from all walks of life to develop their talents to the full.

Chairman of Governors: Ros Sweeting, LLB

Co-opted Governors:
Tracey Scoffield, BA
Alex Plavsic, MA Oxon, FCA
Gubby Ayida, MA, FRCOG, DM
Charles Wijeratna, BA
Annamarie Phelps, MA, CBE
Mark Brewer, BA
Chantal Free, MBA Imperial
Robert Lewis, BA Oxon
G David Price, PhD, FGS
Bobby Uberoi, BSc Econ, ACA
Kieran Murphy
Pauline Campbell
Lucinda Evans
Jamie Grant

Ex officio Governor: The Revd Simon Downham, LLB, DipMin, MA

Clerk to the Governors: Lucinda Evans

Head: **Mr David Goodhew**, MA Corpus Christi College Oxford, FRSA

Deputy Heads:
Matthew Chataway, BA, MA King's College London (*Pastoral*)
Ian Emerson, MA, BSSc Newcastle (*Academic*)

Assistant Heads:
Charles Ben-Nathan, BA Exeter, MBA Middlesex (*Director of Studies*)
Lucy Cole, BSc, MA Durham (*Co-curriculum*)
Rachel Marley, BSc Birmingham (*Middle School*)
Yuvraj Nirwal, BSc LSE, MA UCL Institute of Education (*Director of Teaching and Learning*)
Dr John Roberts, BA, MA Newcastle, PhD Warwick (*Sixth Form*)
Amy Sellars, BSc Cardiff (*Lower School*)

Prep School Principal: **Andrea Rutterford**, BEd Hons, Dip SpLD

Prep School Deputy Principal: Victoria Penney, BEd
Director of Studies: Charlotte Hurst, BA, MA

Heads of Year:
Sam Adams, BA Birmingham, MA Surrey (*Upper Sixth*)
Sarah Fordyce, BSc Bath (*Lower Sixth*)
Debbie Kendall, BA Leeds (*Year 11*)
Lucy Snooks, BA Loughborough (*Year 10*)
Kat Burns, BA Manchester (*Year 9*)
Gareth Cooper, BSc Port Elizabeth (*Year 8*)
Katie Temple, BA Durham (*Year 7*)

Heads of Departments:
Academic Mentoring: Ceri Ellis, BA Sussex, Dip SpLD Hornsby
Art: David Mumby, BA Wolverhampton, PGCE Goldsmiths
Biology: Elizabeth Hansford, BSc Durham, MSc London School of Hygiene & Tropical Medicine
Chemistry: Ed Forbes, MChem Edinburgh

Classics: Marcel Lewis, BA Durham
Computing: Jackie Price, BA Huddersfield
Design: Elizabeth Green, BA Loughborough
Drama: Justin Joseph, BA London (*Director of Drama*)
Economics & Politics: Paul Goldsmith, BA Leeds, MBA Cass Business School, FRSA
English: Jon Mitropoulos-Monk, BA Lady Margaret Hall Oxford
Extended Project: Helen Doyme, MSci UCL
Geography: Mike Ashby, BA Middlesex, MSc King's College London, FRGS, CGeog
History: Jonathan White, MA Selwyn College Cambridge
History of Art: Ruth Taylor-Bell, BA Bristol, PGDip Manchester
Mathematics: Patrick MacMahon, MA Emmanuel College Cambridge, MSc OU
Modern Languages: Cameron Palmer, BA, MA UCL Institute of Education
Music: Tony Henwood, MA Exeter College Oxford, ARCO, FRSA (*Director of Music*)
Physical Education & Games: Natalie Maclean, BSc Bath (*Director of Sport*)
Physics: Alex Birchmore, MSci Nottingham
Religion & Philosophy: Elizabeth Fletcher, BA Durham
World Perspectives: Laura Leicester, BA Nottingham

The Grammar School at Leeds

Alwoodley Gates, Harrogate Road, Leeds LS17 8GS

Tel:　　　　0113 229 1552
email:　　　enquiries@gsal.org.uk
website:　　www.gsal.org.uk
Twitter:　　@TheGSAL
Facebook:　@TheGSAL
LinkedIn:　/the-grammar-school-at-leeds

The Grammar School at Leeds is one of the UK's leading independent, co-educational schools. It enjoys the heritage of both Leeds Grammar School and Leeds Girls' High School with a lineage traceable back to 1552 with a long history of academic excellence. It benefits from a magnificent site on the outskirts of the north of Leeds.

We are committed to caring for our pupils as well as educating them. Our aim is to help them develop their individual abilities and talents within an ethic of teamwork, friendship and mutual respect.

We teach with pleasure and our pupils learn with enjoyment. That essentially sums up our mission. How well we accomplish it depends on much more than just excellent exam results. Our satisfaction lies in guiding children and young adults to become, quite simply, the best of their generation.

Structure. Pupils are taught using the structure that has come to be known as the 'diamond model'. Classes are fully co-educational from age three to eleven and again in the Sixth Form. Between the ages of eleven and sixteen, boys and girls are taught separately, but enjoy mixed extracurricular and pastoral activities. Pupils therefore have both the social benefits of co-education and the academic benefits of single-sex teaching in the adolescent years.

Junior School pupils progress to Senior School, in most cases automatically. Primary School begins with Nursery, Senior School Year 7 and Sixth Form Year 11.

Religion. The School has a Chaplain and its own Chaplaincy centre which serves as a focus for worship and pastoral care. Although an Anglican foundation, the School welcomes boys and girls of all faiths and separate meetings are held for Jewish, Muslim, Hindu and Sikh pupils.

Facilities. The Grammar School at Leeds occupies a modern, purpose-built site whose facilities are unrivalled anywhere in the country. They include:

- Specialist suites of teaching rooms for all subjects with the necessary support systems for each faculty.
- Centres for each section of the School, with generous common rooms, locker and cloakroom areas.
- A large assembly hall.
- A newly extended Junior School, having its own identity, specialist resources and operating an independent timetable.
- A library incorporating multimedia facilities.
- IT centre with three interlocking suites.
- A dedicated art, design and technology unit with computer aided design suite.
- Seventeen specialist science laboratories.
- A fully resourced music school.
- Theatre with fully-equipped lighting gantry.
- A new Food Technology Suite.
- Extensive playing fields with changing facilities and hospitality areas.
- A large indoor sports complex with 2 sports halls, climbing wall, squash courts, conditioning room, a 25m swimming pool of competition standard.
- Extensive grounds with pitches, tennis courts, athletics track.
- Large play and recreation areas for each section of the School.
- Refectory for breakfast, lunch and snacks.
- Provision for a wide variety of indoor and outdoor extracurricular pursuits.
- Conservation areas.
- A versatile Chaplaincy Centre.
- A new Sixth Form Centre with its own cafeteria, study area and IT and leisure facilities.

Curriculum. Nursery and Pre-Prep establishes the foundation for a long and rewarding education – pursuing a broad and balanced curriculum, which builds upon the natural aptitudes, learning skills and interests of each child, whilst enabling each to develop at his/her own pace. We use our own schemes of work, broadly based upon the early years of the National Curriculum, but refined by our own expertise and experience.

In the Primary School pupils concentrate upon the core subjects of English, Mathematics and Science. History, Geography, French/German, Religious Studies, Music, Art and Technology are also taught.

Pupils follow a broad curriculum, including two foreign languages in Years 7–9.

At the end of Year 11 pupils are presented for the GCSE examination.

In the Sixth Form students choose to study up to 4 A2 Level subjects and are encouraged to choose a broad range of subjects.

Games. Rugby, Football, Cricket, Athletics, Swimming, Tennis, Basketball, Badminton, Cross-Country, Volleyball, Hockey, Netball, Rounders, Squash, and Golf. There is a running track, swimming pool and a sports centre, including squash courts.

Other Activities. The School's many clubs and societies offer pupils the opportunity to participate in a wide range of out-of-school activities from Mountaineering and Skiing to Choral Singing, Dancing and Drama. There are regular tours and visits abroad and there are long-established exchanges with French and German schools.

The School has an extensive Arts Programme which covers music, film, drama, debating and creative art and includes visiting groups with national reputation as well as the students' own contributions.

The School provides a contingent of the CCF (Army & RAF sections), and has a Scout Troop, with Cub Pack and Venture Scout Unit. The School participates in the Duke of Edinburgh's Award scheme and Community Service is compulsory in the Sixth Form.

Admission. The entrance procedure takes place in the Spring term for entry the following September and is based upon an examination, an interview and school report. Very young boys and girls are assessed through a series of observed activities. The usual points of entry are 3+ for Nursery, 4+ for Reception, 7+ for Junior School and 11+ for Senior School, although applications can be made at any time for any age. Entry to the Sixth Form is based upon interview and report and the attainment of good GCSE grades.

Details of the entrance procedure together with copies of sample papers are available from the Headmaster's secretary.

Fees per term (2021–2022). Senior School £4,917; Primary School Y3–Y6 £3,672; Reception–Y2 £3,366; Nursery FT £3,000, 4 days £2,400, 3 days £1,800

Bursaries. A number of means-tested bursaries (some full fee) are currently awarded each year to pupils entering the school at 11+ and 16+ (Sixth Form).

GSAL Alumni. This includes the Old Leodiensian Association – Leeds Grammar School and the Old Girls Club – Leeds Girls' High School. See Alumni section of school website, email: alumni@gsal.org.uk.

Charitable status. The Grammar School at Leeds is a Registered Charity, number 1048304. It exists for the advancement of education and training for boys and girls.

Governors:
Mr A M Martin, MA, FCA (*Chairman*)
Mrs C Lyons, BA Hons (*Vice Chair*)
Mr J Woodward, MA (*Vice Chair*)
Mrs E E Bailey, BChD, LDS, RCS, DOrthRCS
Sir Stephen Brown, KCVO
Mr J Cross, BA Oxon, ACA
Mr M Curle, LLB, Chartered MCSI
Ms J A Harper, MBE, MA, Hon Fellow
Professor A Harrison Moore, MA Hons, AGMS Dip, PhD
Mr I Jones, MA, ACA, MBA
Mrs D Kenny, BEd
Mrs J Semple, BSc, MSc
Mrs C Vilarrubi, BSc Hons, MSc, MBA, CPsychol

Mr M A Waldron, MA Cantab
Mr A J Walsh, ACIB

Teaching Staff:

***Principal & Chief Executive*: Sue Woodroofe**

Head of Junior School: Gabrielle Solti
Vice Principal & Head of Senior School: Graham Purves
Senior Deputy Head (Pastoral Care): Helen Stansfield
Deputy Head (Academic): Debbie Danks
Director of External Relations: Helen Clapham
Director of Finance: Steve Kingston

Director of Sixth Form: Ben Harding
Head of Student Development: Christine Jagger
Head of Upper Sixth: Jane Pratt
Head of Lower Sixth: Milly Stead
Head of Year 11: Maria Collins
Head of Year 10: James Veitch
Head of Year 9: Rachel Purell
Head of Year 8: Paul Rushworth
Head of Year 7: Stephen Gibbin

Heads of Department:

Art: Stewart Kelly
Design & Technology: John Bagshaw
Biology: Lynne Gilbert
Chemistry:Geoffrey Huband
Classics: Martin Gibson
Drama: Roz Bendelow
Economics/Business Studies: Rob Stephenson
English: Laurel Rees
Food Technology: Yvonne Wilson
French: Nick Hele
Geography: Simon Knowles
German: Emma Whittaker
History: Keith Milne
ICT: Tim Street
Mathematics: Orla Weaver
Music: Philippa Sidwell
Physics: David Dee
Politics: Andrew Stodolny
Psychology: Alison Wilson
Religious Studies: Fiona Fishburn
Spanish: Rowan Reed-Purvis
Sport: Loran O'Brien

Admissions: Alice Gibbons
Principal's Secretary: Elaine Green

Leicester Grammar School

London Road, Great Glen, Leicester LE8 9FL

Tel: 0116 259 1900
email: admissions@leicestergrammar.org.uk
website: www.lgs-senior.org.uk
Twitter: @LGS_Senior
Facebook: @Leicester-Grammar-School
LinkedIn: /leicester-grammar-school

Leicester Grammar School was founded in 1981 as an independent, selective, co-educational day school to offer able children in the city and county a first-class academic education. Its founders sought to create a school which would maintain the standards and traditions of the city's former grammar schools lost through reorganisation and develop them to meet the demands of a rapidly changing environment. The School moved to a new state-of-the-art building on the south-east side of Leicester in September 2008.

There are 860 day pupils in the Senior School, of whom 230 are in the Sixth Form. A further 400 pupils, aged 3–11, attend the Junior School.

Admission. An entrance examination is held in the Lent Term for boys and girls seeking to enter the Preparatory (10+) and Year 7 (11+) forms in the following September. Papers are taken in Non-verbal Reasoning, English and Mathematics. In addition, admission into Years 9 and 10 takes place at ages 13 and 14 and there is provision for direct entry into the Sixth Form, offers of a place being conditional upon the GCSE grades gained. The normal entry requirement to the Sixth Form is a minimum of three GCSEs at Grade 7 or better accompanied by a minimum of three further GCSEs at Grade 6 or better. Visitors are always welcome to make an appointment to see the school and meet the Headmaster. All applications are handled by the Head of Marketing & Admissions, from whom all Registration forms are obtainable. Candidates at all levels may be called for an interview.

Scholarships and Bursaries. The School offers a range of scholarships for pupils of outstanding academic, musical, sporting or artistic talent. These are awarded on the basis of examination and assessment. Awards cover entry at all ages from Year 7 including sixth form entrants.

The fee remission associated with scholarships is not means dependent and is usually worth no more than 5–10% of the termly fee.

Bursary support is available either for new applicants to the School or for existing pupils whose circumstances have changed. Bursaries are available only to pupils in Year 7 and above at Leicester Grammar School. Bursaries of up to 95% of the termly fee are available, subject to rigorous testing of financial need and limited by the overall bursaries budget.

Curriculum. Class sizes are about 20 to 24 in the first three years; the average size of a GCSE group is 19, of a Sixth Form group 12.

All pupils in the first three years (and those entering the preparatory form) follow a balanced curriculum covering the National Curriculum core and foundation subjects, Religious Studies and Latin (Classical Studies in the preparatory form). Classes are split into smaller groups for the creative and technological subjects, so that all pupils can gain practical experience, whether in the School's ICT suite or on its extensive range of musical instruments. From Year 8 the three science subjects, Biology, Chemistry and Physics, are taught separately. There is no streaming and setting occurs only for Mathematics and French from Year 8. In Year 9 an element of choice is introduced and pupils must opt from a choice of third languages and from a list of five creative subjects.

In Years 10 and 11 pupils prepare for GCSE or GCSE equivalent examinations in ten subjects, as well as doing PE/Games. All study a 'core' of three subjects: Mathematics and English Language and Literature. The range of 'options' includes Art, Biology, Chemistry, Classical Civilisation, Computing, Design and Technology, Drama, French, Geography, German, Greek, Religious Studies, History, Latin, Music, Physics, Spanish and PE. Students will normally follow at least two Science subjects and at least one Modern Foreign Language.

Students in the Sixth Form normally study 3 A Levels from a choice of 21 subjects, including Further Mathematics, Economics, Physical Education, Politics, Computing and Theatre Studies. There is no rigid division between arts and science sides. To ensure that breadth of education does not suffer, a proportion of the Sixth Form complete an Extended Project. The school has an excellent record of success at public examinations and university admissions, including Oxbridge. The Careers Department is very active in giving help and advice to students.

School activities. A broad range and variety of activities complements the academic curriculum. Participation rates are high.

Music, drama and sport form an integral part of life at LGS. Every pupil in the First Year learns a musical instrument and a high proportion continue afterwards with private weekly lessons. The School Orchestra gives two major concerts a year, whilst a training orchestra, a jazz band, a dance band, recorder groups and various chamber ensembles explore other avenues. The School Choir is the resident choir for the Crown Court Services and tours regularly. Links are strong with the Leicestershire School of Music orchestras and several pupils play in national orchestras. Senior and junior drama clubs function throughout the year, a major play or musical and a junior play are staged regularly and house drama extends the opportunity to act to most pupils.

Games are seen as an important means not only of promoting health and fitness but also of inspiring self-confidence. Major winter games are hockey, netball and rugby and in summer athletics, cricket and tennis. Opportunities occur for individuals to follow their interest in badminton, basketball, squash, golf, table tennis, gymnastics, dance, sailing and cross-country running whilst swimming is an integral part of the PE programme. The school's own facilities are extensive and meet all modern standards for sport. Teams represent the School in the main games at all age groups and several students achieve recognition at county or even national level. The school is proud of the fact that it is one of only eight other schools to have been awarded the Sportsmark Gold with Distinction, for the quality of the delivery of sport within the school.

Societies and clubs complement these activities, ranging from chess to The Duke of Edinburgh's Award scheme, history and Lit Soc to model aeroplanes, debating to art, design and technology, for which the workshop and art rooms are usually open during lunchtimes and after school.

Religion. The school espouses the principles of the Church of England, teaching the Christian faith, its values and standards of personal conduct, but also prides itself on welcoming children of all faiths, who play a full part in the life of the community. Very strong links exist with Leicester Cathedral and there is a flourishing Guild of Servers and University of Leicester clergy participate in school life and prepare confirmation candidates.

Pastoral Care. Responsibility for a wide-ranging system of pastoral care and for the creation of the caring, friendly and disciplined environment, resides in eight Heads of Year, assisted by form teachers, personal tutors and a very active house system.

Junior School. Entry to the Junior School is by interview and, where appropriate, assessment at 3+, 4+, 7+ and into other school years, when places are available. Pupils are prepared for entry to the Senior School. A balanced curriculum is followed covering National Curriculum Key Stages 1 and 2 and beyond; French (from 5 years), classical studies and ICT are also taught. A wide range of activities complements the academic curriculum, with a strong stress on music and a rapidly growing games programme. The School is a Christian foundation and lays great emphasis upon the pastoral care of young children. (*See also Junior School entry in IAPS section.*)

Fees per term (2021–2022). Senior School £4,710; Junior School (Years 3–6) £4,071; Kinders to Year 2 £3,831.

Old Leicestrians Association. All correspondence to the OL Secretary, c/o the School.

Charitable status. Leicester Grammar School Trust is a Registered Charity, number 510809. Its aims and objectives are to promote and provide for the advancement of education and in connection therewith to conduct, carry on, acquire and develop in the United Kingdom or elsewhere a School or Schools to be run according to the principles of the Church of England for the education of students and children of either sex or both sexes.

Senior Leadership:

Headmaster of Leicester Grammar School and Principal of the Leicester Grammar School Trust: Mr John Watson, MA Hertford Oxon

Director of Finance and Operations: Mr Stephen Jeffries, LLB Leeds (*Law*) FCA
Senior Deputy Head: Mr Magnus Anderson, MA Pembroke Cantab (*Physics*)
Deputy Head Curriculum: Mr Carl James, MA Girton Cantab (*Mathematics*)
Deputy Head Pastoral: Miss Jennifer Young, MA Exeter (*History*)
Director of Wellbeing and Co-curriculum: Mrs Angela Ewington, MA Nottingham (*Biology*)
Head of Sixth Form: Mr James Hunt, BA Reading (*English*)

Academic Staff:

Art and Design:
Miss Katie-May Driver, BA University of the Arts (*Head of Art and Design*)
Mrs Amanda Davies, MA De Montfort
Ms Sally Haywood, BEd Worcester College, BA OU (*History of Art*)
Miss Jennie Knight, BA De Montfort

Biology:
Dr Kathryn Fulton, BSc Dunelm, PhD Nottingham (*Head of Biology*)

Mrs Philippa Clare, B Sc, ARCS Imperial College, MSc Leicester

Mr Peter Cox, *BSc Wales*: University of Wales, Bangor (*Duke of Edinburgh Award, Learning Technologies Co-ordinator*)

Mrs Angela Ewington, MA Nottingham (*Director of Well-being and Co-curriculum*)

Mr Paul Lawrence, BSc Leicester

Business & Economics:
Mr Peer Moore-Friis, BA De Montfort PGDIP Oxford, CIM DIP (*Head of Business & Economics, Young Enterprise Co-ordinator*)

Mr Khuzema Esmail, BA Portsmouth (*Head of PSD Careers*)

Mrs Clare Scott, BA Hons, Careers Leader

Chemistry:
Dr Simon Ainge, BSc, PhD Newcastle, CChem, FRSC, ARSM Organ (*Head of Chemistry, School Organist*)

Dr Adrianne Kendall, MA, DPhil Wadham and Linacre Oxon

Mr Andrew King, MChem Loughborough (*Assistant Timetabler*)

Miss Angela Patterson, BSc Sunderland Polytechnic (*Head of House – Duke's, Community Service Co-ordinator*)

Classics:
Mr Philip Pratt, MA Harvard (*Head of Classics*)
Mr Peter Donnelly, MA Durham
Mr Christopher Gilham, BA London
Dr Anastasia Vassilliou-Abson, BA Athens, MPhil, PhD Birmingham

Computing:
Mrs Maskean Sian, BA Middlesex (*Head of Computing*)
Mr Lee Kelham, BEng Cranfield

Design, Engineering and Technology:
Miss Katie Campbell, BA Nottingham Trent (*Head of Design, Engineering & Technology*)
Mr Will Burns, BSc Edinburgh Napier
Mr Nathan Grimadell, BSc Derby (*Head of Year 8*)

Drama:
Ms Annette Hulme, BA Essex, MA Loughborough (*Head of Academic Drama*)
Miss Rachel Adams, BA Italia Conti Academy (*Head of Performance Drama*)
Dr Julian Griffin, *M A Cantab*: Fitzwilliam, PhD OU (*Head of English, Theatre Studies*)

English:
Dr Julian Griffin, MA Fitzwilliam Cantab, PhD OU (*Head of English, Theatre Studies*)
Mrs Rachael Kendall, BA Dunelm, MA Goldsmiths (*Deputy Head of English*)
Mrs Catherine Barnes, BA De Montfort, MA Birmingham
Miss Rebecca Hadfield, BA Exeter (*Charity Co-ordinator*)
Mrs Marlene Higginson, BEd, MA Toronto (*Editor of Leicestrian*)
Miss Nicola Hughes, BA London (*Head of Initial Teacher Training*)
Mr James Hunt, BA Reading (*Head of Sixth Form*)

Food and Nutrition:
Mrs Elaine Nisbet, BEd Trent Polytechnic
Mrs Rebecca Pole, BSc Sheffield Hallam

Geography:
Mr Richard Campbell, MA Edgehill (*Head of Geography*)

Mr Craig Cumming, MSc Edinburgh
Mrs Heather Feasey, BA Cape Town
Miss Emma Hill, BSc Reading
Mrs Marie McNally, BA Westminster (*Head of Year 9*)

History:
Mr Andrew Picknell, MA University of London (*Head of History*)
Mr Trevor Allen, BA Kent
Mrs Vicky Hird, BA Leicester
Mrs Amanda McHugh, MA Anglia Ruskin
Miss Jennifer Young, MA Exeter (*Deputy Head Pastoral*)

Learning Development:
Miss Joy Clapham, BA Hons, MBA Ed, PGC SpLD Leicester, PGC SENCO Northampton, SpLD and TPC Patoss (*Director of Learning Development*)
Mrs Clare Charles, BTh Selwyn Cantab, SpLD ATS BDA (*Life Education*)
Mr Khuzema Esmail, BA Portsmouth (*Head of Life Education*)

Mathematics:
Dr David Crawford, MA, DPhil Jesus Oxon, MEd Bristol, MA Ed, MSc OU (*Head of Mathematics*)
Mr Graham Inchley, BSc Hull, MSc Bristol (*Deputy Head of Mathematics*)
Miss Lorraine Howd, BSc East Anglia
Mrs Kate Hyde, BSc Leicester
Mr Carl James, MA Girton Cantab (*Deputy Head Curriculum*)
Mrs Roxanne King, BSc Birmingham
Miss Hannah McCleery, BSc Loughborough
Mr Neil Murray, BSc Imperial, MA London, MSc Sheffield Hallam
Mrs Kerry Pollard, BSc Loughborough
Mr Joey Radford, BSc Sheffield (*Head of House – Judges*)
Mrs Zoe Village, BSc Leicester (*Assistant Head of Sixth Form*)

Modern Foreign Languages:
Mrs Sylvie Lopez-Correia, MA Université de Picardie Jules Verne (*Head of Modern Languages*)
Mrs Emma Nelson, BA Northumbria (*Deputy Head of Modern Foreign Languages*)
Miss Alex Chell, MPhil Trinity Dublin (*French, German*)
Mrs Amy Dewe, BA Warwick (*French, Charities Co-ordinator*)
Mrs Katharine Douglas, BA Liverpool (*French, Italian, EAL*)
Miss Charlotte Julian, BA Birmingham (*French, Spanish*)
Sra Irma Manktelow, BSc Instituto Politécnico Nacional, Mexico (*Spanish*)
Mrs Francoise Paton, DEUG and Licence Bordeaux (*French*)
Mrs M Siegfried-Brookes, MSc Zurich (*German Assistant*)
Miss Hatice Torun, BA Manchester (*French, German*)

Music:
Mr John Barker, BMus, MMus RCM, PGCE, MTeach UCL IOE (*Director of Music*)
Mrs Amy McPherson, BA St Anne's Oxon (*Deputy Director of Music, Able, Gifted and Talented Co-ordinator*)
Miss Eleanor Graff-Baker, MA Queen's Oxon

Physical Education:
Mr James McCann, MA Bath (*Director of Sport*)

Mr Geraint Davies, MEd, BSc De Montfort (*Head of PE and Games*)

Mrs Aneska Button, BA Loughborough

Mrs Charlotte Calland, BA De Montfort

Mr Harry Ellis, BSc Loughborough (*Charity Co-ordinator*)

Miss Christina Feeney, BA Dunelm (*Head of House – Vice Chancellors*)

Miss Caitlin Jeffries, BSc West of England

Mrs Nikki Laybourne, BSc Hons, MSc Loughborough

Mr Laurie Potter (*Head of Year 7*)

Miss Amy Rothwell, MSc Loughborough

Miss Milly Scotchbrook, BSc Nottingham (*Sports Graduate*)

Mr Matt Stubbs, BEd Sheffield Hallam (*Head of Academic PE*)

Mr Troy Thacker, BEd Crewe & Alsagar CNAA (*Head of Year 10*)Physics

Mr Philip Reeves, BSc Manchester (*Head of Physics, Director of Rugby*)

Miss Ellen Allcoat, BSc Bristol (*Senior House Co-ordinator*)

Mr Magnus Anderson, MA Pembroke Cantab (*Senior Deputy Head*)

Mrs Fiona Johnston, BSc Thames Polytechnic

Miss Kate MacLeod, BSc University London (*EPQ Co-ordinator, Assistant Head of Sixth Form*)

Politics:

Dr Sarah Yeomans, MA, PhD Loughborough (*Head of Politics*)

Psychology:

Ms Kat Lovelock, BA Warwick (*Head of Psychology*)

Mrs Emma Mason, BSc Warwick

Religious Studies:

Ms Jane Ford, BA Newcastle (*Head of Religious Studies*)

Mrs Eva Brookes, BA Sheffield, MA London

Mrs Jane Tompkins, BA Leicester, MA Heythrop: London (*Head of Year 11*)

Mr Duncan Whitton, BA Leicester Polytechnic

Science:

Mrs Emma Mason, BSc Warwick

Textiles:

Mrs Amanda Davies, MA De Montfort

Miss Jennie Knight, BA De Montfort

Leighton Park School

Shinfield Road, Reading, Berkshire RG2 7ED

Tel: 0118 987 9600

email: admissions@leightonpark.com

website: www.leightonpark.com

Twitter: @LPSchool

Facebook: @leightonparkschool

Instagram: @leightonparkschool

LinkedIn: /leighton-park-school

Leighton Park is a leading co-educational day and boarding school for students aged 11–18 based in Reading, Berkshire.

Leighton Park exists to form young people of real character and confidence, with a determined desire to change the world, reflecting the school's Quaker values and forward-looking approach. We are a school that inspires Achievement with Values, Character and Community and academic excellence is the consequence of our approach.

Our vibrant learning community empowers each student to achieve excellent outcomes, through supporting their choices, nurturing individuality and encouraging talent in whatever direction it may lie. Ours is an education for succeeding in life, as well as in academic assessments. Set in 65 acres of beautiful parkland, our students have an enriching environment in which to learn, reflect and grow.

With Quaker values held strongly at the centre of all that we do, our emphasis is on our students loving their learning, encouraging them to try a huge range of new experiences and developing their greatest talents. You will be struck on visiting us by the warmth of relationships that characterise the school, the wealth of opportunities for development of body and mind, and the sense of calm and space in which that development takes place.

Academic. The success of our approach is demonstrated by UK Government 16–18 league tables, which place the school in the top 100 in England, or top 1%, for the academic progress made by our students. Despite being among the top performing schools in the country we are no results factory. We believe a school must be judged by the full range and depth of achievements of its students, and at Leighton Park we develop young people who understand, cherish, and make a difference to the world which they inherit. Leighton Park is particularly known for STEAM (Science, Technology, Engineering, Arts and Maths), with a particular emphasis on creative problem solving and interdisciplinary approaches.

Sixth Form. In Sixth Form, students can choose between the International Baccalaureate Diploma Programme (IB) and A Levels with or without an Extended Project Qualification (EPQ) which carries UCAS points worth half an A Level.

Hobbies and Other Activities. Our wraparound provision, which welcomes day students from 7.20am to 9.00pm, offers all our pupils the time to discover and develop their greatest talents. The school's curriculum, which includes a compulsory iGCSE in Global Perspectives, positions students for success in a fast-changing world, where many of today's jobs will not exist in 30 years' time. Students have the time and space to understand and enjoy their learning and extend their passions through our 90 different co-curricular hobbies. Central to the school's approach, we teach leadership, creative thinking and risk-taking, empowering students to be a force for good in the world and reflecting the school's Quaker ethos. The range of choice and the school's focus on the individual create a fun, supportive and nurturing experience.

Sports. Sport plays an important role in life at Leighton Park with many individual performers and teams reaching county and regional level in sports. The school's Advanced Performer Programme supports elite athletes. While the School does very well in traditional sports such as rugby, netball, cricket and hockey it also offers alternatives such as yoga, basketball and parkour. The School is very supportive of individual talents and interests from equestrian sports to gymnastics. First-rate coaching and superb facilities ensure that talented and enthusiastic students can develop their sporting abilities to the full.

Music. Music is another particular strength of the School with a stunning Music and Media Centre providing students with exceptional facilities, including a Yamaha Live Lounge recording studio and a media production suite. Our Music department is accredited as a Flagship Music Education Partner, the only school in Europe to hold this status, with 50% of students studying an instrument and 27 music teachers on staff.

Location and School Life. The school is set in 65 acres of beautiful parkland in Reading, 25 minutes from London and 30 minutes from London Heathrow Airport. A significant proportion of the Park is dedicated to sport and outdoor learning opportunities, but it also provides that all-important space in which your child can take some time for peaceful reflection.

Facilities. Leighton Park has the facilities you would expect of a leading independent school, including an impressive library, swimming pool and historic buildings. Our new Music and Media Centre provides fabulous music and creative media facilities for students, including a Live Lounge, music practice rooms and performance spaces. In recent times, investments have been made to support the school's Science, Technology, Engineering, Arts and Maths focus, placing the creative arts at the heart of the traditional STEM approach. This includes modern science labs, a wonderful Design Technology centre and impressive mathematics facility. The school's innovative use of the latest teaching and learning technologies is supported by continuous investment in technology, including Google Classroom, Clever Touch screens in classrooms and personal Chromebooks.

Boarding. Our Weekly or Full Boarding students enjoy the very best of Leighton Park, benefiting from a wonderful sense of calm, balanced with an incredible amount of activity and dynamism. There is a co-educational Lower School Boarding House for Years 7 and 8, Fryer House, with two Senior Houses for boarders in Year 9 and above; School House for boys and Reckitt House for girls. Students come from 39 different countries, with strong UK representation.

Housemasters and Housemistresses create homely environments supported by tutors and matrons, ensuring each student feels relaxed and comfortable. With a dedicated staff and plenty of opportunity to socialise with other students, each house is very much its own community.

Entry. Entry to the school includes consideration of school reports, tests in English, Maths, essay writing and an interview, with an additional English test where appropriate. Pupils are normally admitted at one of three points: Year 7 (age 11); Year 9 (age 13), and the Sixth Form. Entry to the Sixth Form requires 5 GCSE passes or equivalent at Level 6 / Grade B or above, with a Level 7 required in certain subjects. We also offer a Pre-Sixth course of 5 GCSEs in one year.

Fees per term (2021–2022). Full Boarding £10,565–£13,110; Weekly Boarding £9,175–£11,070; Day £6,745–£8,220

Scholarships and Bursaries. We award academic, art and design, dance, drama, music and sport scholarships to students entering Years 7, 9 and Sixth Form based on a competitive exam. These typically represent 10% of a day student's fees. We also offer Majors Scholarships, representing up to 25% discount on fees in STEAM, Ethical Enterprise and Music. Just as important as the financial incentive is the support they receive to develop their talents and excel in their field. Candidates may apply for any combination of scholarships, but can only receive the financial benefits of one. Bursaries may be available, in cases of financial hardship, to existing and prospective pupils. Bursaries are always means-tested and subject to annual review. Additional awards may be made by the David Lean Foundation.

Old Leightonians. Website: www.leightonpark.com/old-leightonians.

Charitable status. The Leighton Park Trust is a Registered Charity, number 309144. It exists to provide education for young people.

Governors:
Jan Digby (*Chair*)

Eme Dean-Lewis	
Azka Desousa	Bruce Johnson
Lottie Dodwell	Marion Mitchell
James Gazet	Andrew Nind
Philip Griffin	Liza Phipps
David Hickok	Matt Winkless
Chris Houston	Nick Wood

Head: **Matthew Judd**, BA, PGCE, QTS

Deputy Head: Edward Falshaw, BA, MA, PGCE, QTS
Deputy Head (*Pastoral*): Nicky Hardy, BA MA, QTS
Deputy Head (*Academic*): Alex Wallace, BSc, PGCE, QTS

Bursar: Keith Eldridge, BA, FCA

Teaching Staff:
* *Head of Department*
§ *Part-time*
† *Housemaster / Housemistress*

Sam Bates, BSc, PGCE, QTS (*Biology, Resident Tutor*)
Jeremy Belas, BSc, QTS (§**Director of Sport*)
Monica Bolsover, BSc, NQ (*Mathematics*)
Simon Booth, MEng, PGCE, QTLS (*Physics)
Mary Boyd, BSc, MA, PGCE, QTS (*Assistant Head (Director of Studies), *Mathematics*)
Mark Budge, MEng, QTS (*STEAM Coordinator, Mathematics*)
Beth Butler, BA, PGCE, QTS (§*Dance*)
Tom Cartmill, BSc (§*English as a Second Language*)
Bridget Clarke, BSc, QTS (§*Mathematics*)
Jon Clarke, BSc, PGCE, QTS (*Physics*)
Natasha Coccia, BA, PGCE, QTS (*Assistant Head (Director of Co-curricular and Outreach)*)
Imogen Cook, BA, PGCE (*History, Philosophy and Religious Beliefs & Values*)
Harriet Custance, BA, MA, PGCE (**English as a Second Language*)
Didier Descamps, BA, MA, QTS (**Modern Foreign Languages*)
Richard Duckett, BA, PhD, PGCE (**Politics and Global Perspectives*)
Rebecca Edwards, BA, QTS (*PE and Games, †Reckitt House*)
Beverley Eldridge, BA, MBA, QTS (*Head of Year 10 & Year 11, Economics*)
Daniel Fisher-Wienesen, BMus, MMus, QTS (*Music*)
Anne Fitzsimons, PGCE (§*Mathematics*)
Carol Gainlall, BSc, Cert Ed (§*Mathematics*)
Andrew Gallacher, BA, PGCE, QTS (*PE and Games, Resident Tutor*)
Pablo Gorostidi Perez, MBA, QTS (*CAS Coordinator, Modern Foreign Languages*)
Claire Gulliver, BSc, PGCE, QTLS (§*Psychology)
David Hammond, BSc, MSc, QTS (§*Science)
Jennifer Hatton, BA, PGCE, QTS (§*Food Technology*)

Emilia Hicks, BSc, QTS (§*Chemistry)
Nicholas Hill, BSc, PGDipEd, QTS (Chemistry, Resident Tutor)
Deborah Ince, BA, PGCE, QTS (Art and Textiles)
Nicola Jenkins, BSc, PhD, PGCE, QTS (Physics)
Duncan Laurie-Pile, BSc, PGCE, QTS (Second i/c Mathematics)
Isabelle Lauzeral-Bataille, BA, MA, NQ (§Modern Foreign Languages)
Alexander Leighton, MA, PGCE (English, †School House)
Michael Liggins, BA, PGCE (*Business and Economics)
Zoe Macpherson, BA, PGCE, QTS (PE and Games, *Netball)
Jakki Marr, Bed, QTS (*Girls PE and Games, †Field House)
Leana Mikula, BEd, QTS (English, Additional Tutor)
Rachel Milhofer, BSc, PGCE (§Science/Chemistry)
Jane Morris, BEd, QTS (§Learning Support)
Anna Murgett, Spanish Degree, Spanish PGCE, QTS (Senior School Enrichment Coordinator, Second i/c Modern Foreign Languages)
John Murray, BA, QTS (§Latin)
Myles Nash, BA, QTS (†Director of Boarding)
Sarah Owen, BSc, MA (§Business)
Jonathan Porter-Hughes, BA, PGCE, QTS (English, †School House)
Jenny Powlesland, BA, NPQSL, PGCE, QTS (Assistant Head (Teaching and Learning))
Christopher Price, BSc, QTS (*Computing and ICT)
Lara Rawlings, BA (Assistant Director of Music)
Lisa Reskalla, BA, QTS (Learning Support)
Matt Richards, BSc, QTS (Chemistry, *Hockey)
Leni Samuel, BSc, QTS (Assistant Head of Year 10 and Year 11, Mathematics)
Sally Saunders, BA, QTS (§*Careers & PSHE, Head of Year 9)
Rosemary Scales, BA, MEd, NQ (*Director of Music)
Peter Scoggins, BA, PGCE, QTS (*Drama and Theatre Studies)
Caroline Semeyn, BA, PGCE, QTS (Modern Foreign Languages, Senior Resident Tutor)
Saima Shabir, BSc, DPhil, PGCE, QTS (Chemistry)
Mark Simmons, Bed, QTS (§Assistant Head (Senior Master))
Gemma Sims, BSc, MSc, PGCE, QTS (*Biology)
Ellie Smales, BSc, QTS (Geography)
Graham Smith, BA, NQ (*Tennis, Geography)
Mark Smith, BEng, BSc, QTS (*Design and Technology, Senior Resident Tutor)
Oliver Staines, BA, QTS (*Geography, Additional Tutor)
Adrian Stewart, BPrimEd, NQ (Georgraphy, †Fryer)
Alasdair Stuart, BSc, PGCE, QTS (Computer Science)
Helen Tatlock, BA, PGCE, QTS (*History, Resident Tutor)
Helen Taylor, BSc, PGCE, QTS (*Sixth Form, IB Coordinator)
Matthew Taylor, BA, PGCE (*English)
Merion Taynton, BA, Australian Teaching Qualification (Assistant Head of Fryer, English)
Stephen Taynton, BA, Australian Teaching Qualification (*Philosophy and Religious Beliefs & Values)
Chloe Tibbatts, BA, PGCE (Art)
Keeley Toms, BA, PGCE, PGCE SENDCo, QTS (*Learning Support – SENDCo)
Jo Toovey, BSc, MA, MSc, PhD, PGCE, QTS (Psychology)

Jacqueline Tree, BA, PGCE, QTS (English, Resident Tutor)
Roy Vigus, BA, GTP, QTS (Learning Support)
Mark Wood, BA, PGCE, QTS (*Art)
Lan Worrall, BA, MA, QTS (Chinese)
Damon Young, BA, MA, QTS (Deputy Housemaster, Drama)

Registrar: Claire Elmer
Head's PA: Virginia Cashin
Librarian: Grace Ritchie

The Leys

Trumpington Road, Cambridge CB2 7AD

Tel: 01223 508904
email: admissions@theleys.net
website: www.theleys.net
Twitter: @LeysCambridge
Facebook: @TheLeysSchoolCambridge

Motto: *In Fide Fiducia*

The Leys is situated half a mile from the centre of the university city of Cambridge, close to the River Cam and Grantchester Meadows. The School was founded in 1875 on the initiative of a group of leading Methodists to provide a liberal Christian education, establishing a tradition which has continued unbroken to this day. The School was incorporated as a Charitable Trust in 1878. All the buildings are grouped around the Main Field and lie within the estate originally acquired for the purpose; there is a second extensive playing field nearby.

The Leys is a friendly, caring and happy community, large enough to offer many opportunities, but not so large as to lose sight of the individual. The School is fully co-educational; of a total of over 560 pupils, 200 are in the Sixth Form. Girls and boys are accommodated in separate houses. 70% of the pupils are accommodated in the boarding houses, but all, including the 160 day pupils, are able to enjoy all the opportunities offered by boarding school life.

Buildings and Facilities. There is a continuing development programme involving all areas of the School. A state-of-the-art Music School was opened in 2005. There is an excellent Humanities Building with first-class facilities for Geography, History, Classics and Divinity together with a Museum and Archives Centre, and an award-winning Design Centre, which contains workshops (metal, plastic and wood), a 3D printing and laser cutting area, Art School, Ceramics Studio, Computer Centre, together with facilities for Design, Photography, Cookery and an Exhibition Centre. A Sports Hall and all-weather pitch were built in 1995. In 2008 the Sports Hall was extended to include a superb fitness suite and cricket pavilion, and a second Astroturf pitch was added. A new climbing wall was constructed in summer 2007. A major capital development has been added, which provides a new theatre, Assembly Hall, Drama and Dance Studios, Drama Department, School Café and three new Science Laboratories. This project, known as Great Hall, was completed in summer 2013. There are 40 acres of playing fields, an indoor heated swimming pool open all the year, a recently refurbished boat house on the Cam shared with King's, Selwyn and Churchill Colleges, and synthetic as well as grass tennis courts. A radical redesigning and refurbishment of all boarding houses began in summer 2006, with the aim of providing the most comfortable and homely of boarding facilities. To date six of the seven Senior Boarding Houses have been refurbished. The School Library underwent a major refurbishment in 2008.

Admission. Admission for girls and boys is mainly at 11+, 13+ and 16+. Entrance tests for 11+ and 13+ entry are held in the January prior to entry. Places in the Sixth Form are available for both girls and boys who have successfully completed their GCSE or equivalent courses elsewhere. Application for admission should be made to the Admissions Office in the first instance.

Scholarships. Scholarships are available for entry at 11+, 13+ and to the Sixth Form, valued at a maximum of 5% fee remission, which can be supplemented by means-tested bursaries up to a total concession of 100%.

Academic Scholarships are available for entry at 11+, 13+ and for entry to the Sixth Form at 16+. Scholarships are also available for entry at 13+ in Music, Art, STEM, Sport, Drama and all-rounders, and for entry to the Sixth Form at 16+ in Music, Art, Sport and Drama.

The School also participates in the Arkwright Scholarship Scheme, which is an external examination offering Scholarships for those wishing to take Design and Technology in the Sixth Form and who are aiming to read Engineering, Technology or other Design-related subjects in Higher Education.

The Scholarship Examinations at 11+ and 13+ take place in the Spring Term and the Sixth Form Scholarship Examination takes place in the November of the year prior to entry.

Bursary awards are made on a means-tested basis, and applications for bursaries must be made before entrance tests are taken.

Special awards for children of Methodist Ministers and members of HM Forces are available. Special consideration is given to the sons and daughters of Old Leysians.

Further particulars may be obtained from the Registrar.

Curriculum. The academic curriculum broadly conforms to the National Curriculum but is not restricted by it. Each pupil has an Academic tutor who, in conjunction with the Director of Studies and the Housemaster or Housemistress, works to tailor the pupil's programme to suit the needs of the individual wherever possible. Pupils follow a broad programme in the first three years (Years 7, 8 and 9). At the end of Year 9 they choose three from a wide range of options to add to the basic core of IGCSE English Language and Literature, separate Sciences and a Modern Foreign Language, and GCSE Mathematics and Religious Studies. The GCSE examinations are normally taken at the end of Year 11, but Religious Studies is taken by all pupils in Year 10.

In the Sixth Form, a similar option scheme operates with pupils choosing from a total of 25 subjects to take normally 3 A Levels in the Sixth Form. Double Maths (Maths and Further Maths) is regarded as one subject leading to two A Levels.

There is considerable flexibility of combinations possible at both levels, and choices are made after consultation between parents, tutors, careers staff and subject teachers. The most able pupils are given an enrichment programme under the guidance of the Director of Academic Development, including extension projects, visits to Gifted and Talented seminars, and seminars with Cambridge undergraduate or postgraduate students. In addition, departments organise extension groups and societies and the school has a thriving Debating Society and a Model United Nations group. The school runs its own Independent Research Project to help senior pupils develop independent study skills.

About 95% of the A Level candidates proceed to degree courses. A Reading Party for potential Oxford and Cambridge candidates is held during the Summer Term.

Personal and Social Education forms an integral part of the curriculum at all levels. In the Sixth Form this is supplemented by a year-long programme that draws on the cultural resources of Cambridge University and the city as a whole.

The Chapel. The School Chapel is at the heart of the community in every sense. From the time of its Methodist foundation The Leys has been firmly based on non-sectarian Christian principles. It welcomes boys and girls of all denominations and religions, encouraging them to see the relevance of a personal faith of their own. Religious Education forms part of the curriculum. Preparation is also given for Church membership, and a combined confirmation service is held.

Physical Education. The physical education/games programme aims at introducing a wide variety of physical activities. Sports available are Rugby, Hockey, Cricket, Tennis, Athletics, Netball, Badminton, Basketball, Gymnastics, Golf, Rowing, Sailing, Dance, Shooting, Climbing, Squash, Swimming, Volleyball, Water Polo. Outdoor activities such as Camping, Orienteering, Canoeing, and Climbing are also encouraged through CCF and The Duke of Edinburgh's Award. PE is offered at GCSE and A Level. The School has close links with many Cambridge University Sports Clubs, with the Sixth Form competing in University Leagues.

Careers. In the Lower School, careers guidance forms part of the PSHE programme and is carried out by tutors and members of the Careers Department. Year 9 are supported in their option choices by tutors and Careers staff and are introduced to the Careers Library. Year 11 take the Preview Careers Selection Programme. It matches pupils' interests and abilities to appropriate career fields and is followed up by two individual interviews with career specialists. Year 11 pupils are also encouraged to participate in the Work Experience scheme. Support continues into the Sixth Form with all Lower Sixth being interviewed by Careers staff. An annual Careers Forum is organised in the Lent term, enabling pupils to investigate various career paths before embarking on their UCAS applications. Work experience is organised throughout the Sixth Form.

Societies. All are encouraged to participate in out-of-school activities of their choice. These range from Literary, Philosophical, Scientific, Mathematical, Languages, Debating, Music and Drama societies to any of the activities available in the Design Centre, which are available after School and at weekends. The life of the School is enriched by its proximity to Cambridge; distinguished visiting speakers are available, and pupils are encouraged to go to plays, concerts and lectures in the town. The programme of visiting speakers is largely run by the pupils themselves, overseen by a member of staff. A programme entitled the Cambridge Experience ensures that all Sixth Form pupils avail themselves of the cultural opportunities afforded by the school's location.

Combined Cadet Force. Except in special circumstances, pupils in Year 10 join the CCF (Army or Navy section) and also follow The Duke of Edinburgh's Award scheme. CCF camps take place annually. There is a miniature range, and a Rifle Club exists for small-bore shooting. The School is an authorised centre for the organisation of activities within The Duke of Edinburgh's Award scheme and pupils work towards the Bronze, Silver or Gold awards in the four sections: community service, expeditions, physical recreation and skills or hobbies.

Fees per term (2021–2022). Years 7 and 8: £8,655 (Boarders), £5,735 (Day); Years 9–13: £11,870 (Boarders), £8,930 (Home Boarders), £7,945 (Day)

St Faith's Preparatory School is part of the same Foundation. It was founded in 1884 and acquired by the Governors of The Leys in 1938. There are 570 boys and girls, aged 4–13 years. The buildings, which include the Keynes Building opened in 2006 and a new Sports Hall opened in May 2011, stand in 10 acres of grounds. *For further details, see entry in IAPS section.*

The Old Leysian Society. *Secretary*: Andrew Erby The Leys School, Cambridge CB2 7AD.

Charitable status. The Leys and St Faith's Schools Foundation is a Registered Charity, number 1144035. It aims to enable boys and girls to develop fully their individual potential within a School community firmly based on Christian principles.

Governors:
Chairman: Sir Tony Brenton, KCMG
Mrs H Arthur, Cert Ed
M D Beazor, BA, FRSAHH
HH Judge Revd M A Bishop, MA [OL]
Mrs A M Brunner, BA
Miss J H E Burton, BA
M A Elliott, BSc [OL]
Mrs P M Graves, MA, Dip S W
B Haryott, BSc, FREng, CEng, FICE, FIStructE, FRSA, CRBCCC [OL]
R B Hewitson, LLB
Mrs E Hooley
C M Kidman, ACIOB [OL]
P R Lacey, MA, PGCE, FRSA
A S MacGregor BSc CertEd
Mrs M E Mackay, RGN
T C Moore [OL]
R Norfolk
Mrs J Plows, BA
Revd J M Pursehouse
R C Sadler, FRICS
A V Silverton, BSc, FCSI [OL]
D Unwin, MA, ACA [OL]
Dr R D H Walker, MA
R B Webster, FCA
R J Willmott, MCIOB

[OL] *Old Leysian*

Headmaster: M J Priestley, MA Oxon

Deputy Head: Mrs C E Mayo, MA Cantab

R Adamson, BSc, PhD	D R Bell, MA
B A Barton, BA	A Bennett-Jones, BSc
A R C Batterham, BA	Ms E Bonnaud, BA, MA
Miss C E Battison, BA	N R Born, MA

M A Brown, BSc
Miss S J Byrne, MA, PGCE
D Cassidy, BPhEd
Ms H S Clark BA
Ms L J Clark, BA
Miss L Corble, BA
Mrs K J Cox, BSc
P J Crosfield, BA
Mrs E R Culshaw, MA
T Dann, BSc
P M Davies, BSc
G J Deudney, BSc, BEd
D A Divito, BSc, MSc, PGCE
N J Dix-Pincott, BA, MA
R J Driscoll, BA, BEd
T P Dunn, BA, MSc, MEd Cantab, CPsychol, FRSA
Mrs C M Earl, BSc
W J Earl, BSc
Miss K E Eaves, MA
Miss H Edmondson, BA
M A Egan, BSc
A S Erby, BSc
J W Fawcett, BA, MA
D K Fernandes, BSc
R Fielden, MA, DPhil, PGCE
R Francis, MA, MEd
Revd C I A Fraser, BA, MA Ed, MCMI, PG Dip, FRSA
M C Gale, BEd
Miss G H Jefferies, BA
S G Hancock, BA, MA
A P Harmsworth, MA, FRAS
Ms J L Hebden, BA, MA

R A D Hill, BA
Mrs A Hodges, BSc, RSA Cert SpLD
Ms C C Howe, BA
Mrs C L Howe, BSc, PhD
G K Howe, BSc, MSc, MA, MEd
R I Kaufman, BA
M J Kenworthy, BMus
Miss C A Knights, BA
Mrs A Lainchbury, BA, MCLIP
S N Leader, BA
Mrs C E Leigh, BA, MEd
Mrs G L Lester, MA, BA, Dip SpLD
M P J Lindsay, MSc
A C R Long, BA
Mrs C E Mayo, MA Cantab
R S McAlinden, BA
Ms S J McEwan, BA
S A Newlove, BSc, PhD
Ms E F Prosser, BSc
T L Reed, MA, MSc
Mrs L A Reyes, MA
N P Robinson, BSc, MBA, CEng
R T Roe MA PGCE
Mrs J A Samuel, BSc
Mrs J Schofield, BSc
Mrs J Stobbart, BA
B R Stuttard, BA
W P Unsworth, BSc, PhD
P R Wallace, BSc, MPhil, DPhil
A J Welby, BA
P White, BEd
Mrs H Williams, BA

[OL] *Old Leysian*

Housemasters and Housemistresses:
Barker House: Mr N Robinson
Barrett House: Mr M C Gale
Bisseker House: Miss E F Prosser
Dale House: Mrs C Earl
East House: Mr. N. Dix-Pincott
Fen House: Mrs C Emery
Granta House: Mrs H Williams
Moulton House: Miss A Macpherson
North A House: Mr B A Barton
School House: Mr J Fawcett
West House: Mr A C R Long

Director of Studies: O E Peck
Director of Pastoral Care: Mrs Helen Hynde
Senior Tutor: W R Davidson
Director of Wider Curriculum: W J Earl
Chaplain: Revd S Coleman
Director of Sport: J G Clarke
Examinations Officer: Miss Anna Hunt
Head of Careers: N P Robinson
Head of Outdoor Education: R S McAlinden
Bursar: P D McKeown, BA
Finance Bursar: Mrs M Cooksey, FCCA
Bursar's PA: Ms Kerry Bishop
Headmaster's PA: Ms Helen Hammond
Registrar: Ms Nathalie Edge-Partington

Deputy Registrar: E A Munro
Head of Marketing: Mrs A M Cox, CIM
Medical Officers:
Dr A J Stewart, MA, MB BCh, DRCOG, DCH, MRCGP, AFOM
Dr C Lea-Cox, BSc, MB BS, MRCGP, DCH, DFFP
Nursing Staff:
Sister M A Williams, SRN, SCM
Sister L Gate, RGN
Sister J Rhodes, RGN

Lincoln Minster School
Part of United Learning

The Prior Building, Upper Lindum Street, Lincoln, Lincolnshire LN2 5RW

Tel: 01522 551300
email: admissions@lincolnminsterschool.co.uk
website: www.lincolnminsterschool.co.uk
Twitter: @MinsterSchool
Facebook: @LincolnMinsterSchool
LinkedIn: /Lincoln-Minster-School

Lincoln Minster School is an independent co-educational HMC day and boarding school for pupils aged 4–18 years. We aim to provide an inspirational all-round education that combines academic achievement with a wealth of co-curricular opportunities.

We offer an all-through education, where the nurturing, stimulation and development of our pupils in all areas of school life, overseen by inspiring and caring staff, is at the heart of what we do.

Our 'I AM ME' principle refers to how we celebrate our pupils as individuals and what they bring to Lincoln Minster School in their own special way. From Prep through to Senior, the levels of participation of our pupils across many areas of school life is a real joy to see. We strongly believe that a very important part of our mission is to inspire pupils to develop interests beyond the classroom and also develop a sense of balance in their lives.

Our intention is to provide an inspiring 'Education for Life', from Reception all the way through to our A Level pupils. Individual needs are catered for across all age groups where boys and girls, of differing abilities and interests, excel in our vibrant community and where pupils have the opportunity to develop their leadership, mentoring and communication skills.

Structure and Organisation. Set in Lincoln's Historic Quarter our Preparatory and Senior School sites are fully equipped to prepare our pupils for the careers of tomorrow, providing pupils with an inspiring environment in which to fulfil their potential.

The Preparatory School is a short walk from Lincoln's Bailgate, has been extensively redeveloped and was opened in September 2014.

Our Senior School site is made up of a number of buildings, both new and old. The main Prior Building was purpose built and opened in 2002 by the former Archbishop of Canterbury, Lord Carey. The sweeping, curved building overlooks the city and boasts fully equipped science labs, art studios, IT suites and our dedicated Sixth Form Centre. Our latest addition, the Harper Building, is dedicated to music and performance and includes an impressive Recital Hall, music practice rooms and a fully-equipped Drama Studio, as well as a Sports Hall.

The sight of our pupils in their distinctive blazers and staff in their academic gowns processing to the Galilee Porch at Lincoln Cathedral for our End of Term Services and Prize Giving Ceremonies is a special one; a reminder of how important a sense of tradition is in a modern world and a modern school.

Lincoln Minster School is a member of United Learning, which owns and manages independent schools and academies across England. There is no doubt that membership of a group of this size gives Lincoln Minster School strength and breadth of contact.

Curriculum. A full range of subjects is offered and the school is proud of its excellent track record of examination success.

We specialise in finding the best in every pupil and place equal value on cultural, technological, scientific, linguistic and creative subjects.

The curriculum is supported by a wealth of trips, visits and activities. We offer over 150 different clubs and activities to pupils including a comprehensive sports programme to cater for all tastes.

We are proud to offer a number of exciting specialist programmes in Golf, Tennis and Squash. In partnership with industry specialists, our exclusive Sport Performance Programmes offer young potentially elite players the opportunity to train on world-class facilities.

Pupils on these tailored programmes benefit from high-quality coaching and opportunities to compete alongside their studies.

We encourage all of our pupils to stretch and challenge themselves, to test new skills outside their comfort zone, and not to worry when they make a mistake, but to learn from it. This way, our boys and girls develop a resilience, grow in self-esteem and become more equipped to face the challenges that lie ahead.

Music. Music is a key component of the school's curriculum throughout all year groups. Whether it is the Year 5/6 orchestra, strings ensemble, jazz band or Pre-Prep choir, our pupils are encouraged to involve themselves fully.

Our Harper Building benefits from individual practice rooms, classrooms and a purpose-built Recital Hall – the ideal venue for concerts, performance rehearsals and workshops.

We also hold memorable concerts throughout the year in the nave of Lincoln Cathedral.

Boarding. We have three spectacular boarding houses in the heart of Lincoln's Cathedral Quarter.

All of our boarding houses are just a short walk to school sites and are overseen by highly experienced and approachable boarding staff. We pride ourselves on making every pupil's boarding experience a happy and productive one and have a range of boarding options to suit every family.

We have an inclusive boarding culture where each boarder, whether termly, weekly or flexi, are all treated as equal members of our boarding family.

We have a blend of day pupils and boarders, both from overseas and from the UK. This broad social and cultural mix ensures the school has a truly national and global outlook.

Admissions. Once you have decided to join the Lincoln Minster family, our staff will support you throughout the entire application process.

We are a proudly non-selective school with no entrance exams. We welcome pupils who will support the aims, ethos and expectations to which we aspire. We are confident that we can fully provide any child with a true education for life in line with their potential.

Scholarships. Each year, we are proud to award Scholarships to pupils who are capable of extremely high levels of achievement and who we believe will make a significant contribution to the life of the school.

Scholarships are offered at entry into Years 7 through to 12 and existing pupils can also apply in Year 9. Awards vary and are dependent on a variety of factors, including references and assessment performance. Once awarded, they will be reviewed on a termly basis. If the criteria are met at every review, scholarships will continue for the duration of another term during the pupil's time at Lincoln Minster School.

Fees per term (2021–2022). Day (including lunch): Pre-Prep £3,378, Prep £4,345, Seniors £4,965. Termly Boarding: £8,381 (Up to Y6), £9,730 (Y7–13), £11,310 (Overseas Boarders); Weekly/Flexi Boarding: £7,613 (Up to Y6), £8,809 (Y7–13).

Charitable status. Lincoln Minster School is part of United Learning which comprises: UCST (a Company Limited by Guarantee, Registered in England, number 2780748, and a Registered Charity, number 1016538) and ULT (a Company Limited by Guarantee, Registered in England, number 4439859, and an Exempt Charity).

Chair of Local Governing Body: Neil Davidson

Members:
Mrs Alison Baptie
Dr Barry Devonald
Mr Steve Gelder
Mr Chris Jackson
Mr Jim Kirkby
Mr Phill King
Mr John Latham
Mrs Sharon Stone
Mr John Weitzel
Mr Robin Wright (*Vice Chair*)

Senior Leadership Team:

Headmistress: **Mrs Maria Young**, MA, PGCE

Deputy Head (Academic): Mr R Eastham, MEd, BSc Hons, PGCE
Deputy Head (Director of Studies): Mr S Grocott, BSc Hons, PGCE
Assistant Head (Pastoral): Mrs J Muir, BA Hons, PGCE
Head of Preparatory School: Mr M Burton, BEd Hons, NPQH
Bursar: Ms Jane Stone

Heads of Department:
Mrs K Cook-James, BEd (*Learning Support*)
Mr M Barrett (*IT*)
Mr N Boot, BA Hons, DipLaw, QTS (*History*)
Mr J Cochrane, BSc, PGCE (*Mathematics*)
Mr T Eves, BSc Hons, PGCE (*Acting Head, PE & Games*)
Mr C Freckelton, BSc Hons, GTP (*Food Science*)

Mrs R Hewitt, MEd, BA Hons, PGCE (*English*)
Mrs J Fellows, BA Hons (*Modern Foreign Languages*)
Mrs R Gladwin, BA Hons, PGCE (*Social Sciences*)
Mrs J Glenn-Batchelor, BA Hons, GTP (*Geography*)
Mrs H Mason, BSc Hons, PGCE (*Science*)
Mr D Osborne, BSc, QTS (*Acting Head, Geography*)
Mrs N Hutchinson, MEd, BMus Hons, PGCE (*Music*)
Mrs C Servonat-Blanc, BA Hons, PGCE (*Art, Graphics & Photography*)
Miss A Tweedale, BA Hons, PGCE (*Business Studies*)
Mrs J Wafer, BA Hons, PGCE (*Drama*)

Executive Assistant to the Headmaster: Miss L Shammon
Examinations Officer: Mr J Hart, MSc, BSc Hons, PGCE

Lingfield College

St Piers Lane, Lingfield, Surrey RH7 6PH

Tel:	01342 832407
email:	office@lingfieldcollege.co.uk
website:	www.lingfieldcollege.co.uk
Twitter:	@LingfieldColl
Facebook:	@LingfieldCollege
Instagram:	@lingfieldcollege
LinkedIn:	/company/lingfield-college

Age Range. 2–18.

Number in School. 893

Fees per term (2021–2022). £3,825–£5,940. Nursery according to sessions attended.

Situation. The School is located just outside the village of Lingfield on the Surrey, Sussex, Kent border. Lingfield station has a line to London Victoria via Hurst Green, Oxted and Woldingham and is 5 minutes' drive or ten minutes' walk. The School also operates an extensive bus service.

Entry. Senior School: at 11+ and 13+ by Entrance Examination and report from previous school. At 16+ by 6+ GCSEs results and school report.

Scholarships. Prep School: available from Year 4. Senior School: at 11+, 13+ and 16+ (Academic, Art, Drama, Music and Sport). Means-tested Bursaries may also be available to Scholars.

Academic. In Years 7–9, the pupils study the core subjects and a range of other options within the Lower School Curriculum. Pupils typically take 10 GCSEs which consist of English Language and Literature, Triple Science (although some may take Dual Science), at least one Language and 3 other subjects of their choice which include Computing, Media and Economics. IGCSEs are taken in the majority of subjects. The top Maths set takes Additional Maths as well as IGCSE Mathematics. 23 subjects are offered at A Level and many students also sit the Extended Project Qualification.

The School offers an extensive Scholars' Programme for its Academic Scholars and Award Holders. Seminars are held and special excursions planned as part of the Scholars' enrichment programme. Headmaster's Lectures are held every term. The School is dedicated to a progressive and innovative approach to learning and has invested heavily in digital learning (including refurbished Media Suites and iPads plus an interactive lecture theatre), whilst valuing traditional methodology.

Pastoral. Pastorally, the School was considered 'outstanding' in its last inspection. Since then, improvements such as smaller tutor groups, more parent focus groups, regular school council and House meetings have further enhanced the feel of a forward-thinking, family-focused school. Communications between the Lingfield village community, staff, students and parents are both open and honest. The School has a 'Whole School' approach to support wellbeing and mental health, working in a proactive and preventative way to support every student to stay emotionally healthy, as well as supporting specific needs. The School employs a comprehensive team of welfare support including a School councillor.

Sport. The School has a sporting ethos of 'Opportunity, Participation and Excellence' and students have access to a wide range of sporting activities which take place at lunchtime and after school. Students represent the School across a full range of sports at all levels and age groups, as well as participating in regional and national competitions. Hockey, netball and football form the core of major team sport representation in the autumn and spring terms whilst cricket, athletics, tennis and rounders provide the main options for the summer term.

The Rugby Club runs for both the autumn and spring terms and provides an option for those who want to play rugby to represent the School. Golf, equestrian, swimming, cross country, badminton, basketball and table tennis are some of the other competitive team sports available.

Pupils who hold Sport Scholarships benefit from the Elite Sports Mentoring Programme which helps aspiring young athletes fulfil their potential.

Co-curricular. The School has an extensive co-curricular programme with over 140 clubs on offer, taking place both at lunchtime and after school. The clubs vary from arts and crafts to sporting and practical activities and have been designed to assist pupils develop their hobbies, strengths and skills. Recent additions to the program include Fencing and Bouldering clubs. There are also numerous trips for the students to go on; these include departmental trips, language exchanges and sports tours.

The Duke of Edinburgh's Award programme is particularly popular. More than 90% of pupils take the Bronze Award in Year 9 & 10 and about 40% of them proceed to the Silver and Gold Awards.

In the Sixth Form a wide programme of activities is arranged such as Zumba, Ballroom Dancing, Self Defence, Car Maintenance, Orienteering, Cooking, Youth Parliament, Debating, Public Speaking, Critical Thinking and Safe Driving Talks. In addition to this, an extensive range of outside speakers visit the School to hold seminars and lectures, offering pupils the chance to broaden their horizons.

Music. A substantial number of students subscribe to instrumental lessons and participate in the numerous ensembles available to them. The School maintains two orchestras, three choirs, a jazz band, ukulele group and various chamber ensembles, including String, Flute, Percussion, Woodwind and Brass Ensembles, which are run by a team of specialist instrumental tutors. As well as the main school concerts and productions, regular informal recitals are given.

Drama. The Drama Department offers a full range of theatrical experience to its actors and audiences alike. The Department explores challenging texts from the classics and from modern writers which push both the academic and performance boundaries of the students. All pupils are taught Drama in the Lower School and it is a popular and successful option at both GCSE and A Level. They are all accommodated in the School's newly extended and refurbished teaching suite which includes two fully equipped studio spaces, technical, costume and make-up workrooms as well as a specialist Speech and Drama room.

Religion. Lingfield transferred to a lay management in 1987. It maintains its Christian ethos and welcomes students and staff of all faiths, and of none. Its philosophy is based on a strong belief in the development of the whole person. The School has a tradition of providing a caring, friendly and disciplined environment.

Buildings. The School has experienced substantial redevelopment in the last 15 years. Recent improvements include a new Sports Hall, Drama Centre, Science Rooms and Art and Photography facilities. A state-of-the-art Sixth Form Centre was opened in September 2014, offering a university-style lecture theatre, modern, interactive classrooms, atrium coffee shop and student-designed common room. A new Performing Arts Centre opened in September 2017. There are 40 acres of grounds which include 4 football pitches, a floodlit astro and cricket nets.

Charitable status. Lingfield Notre Dame is a Registered Charity, number 295598. It exists to provide education.

Chair of Governors: Mrs F Halpin

Headmaster: **Mr R W Bool**, BA Hons, MBA
Headmaster's PA and Clerk to Governors: Mrs T Unwin

Deputy Heads:
Mr C Fast, BEd, BSc
Mrs A Folkard, BSc
Mrs A Brown, BSc

Assistant Heads:
Mr S Hofmann, BSc
Mr S Casey, BA Hons

Prep School:
Head of Prep School: Mrs J Shackel, BA Hons (*SENDCO*)
Prep School Head's PA: Mrs S Wood
Director of Studies, Prep School: Mrs C Hubbard, BA Hons

Head of Finance: Mrs A Brassett
Head of Organisational Development: Mrs C Wren, Chartered MCIPD
Registrar: Mrs J Armstrong
HR Manager: Mrs C Marsden, HND, MCIPD
Marketing Manager: Miss C Whitlock, BA Hons, CIM cert

A full list of teaching staff is available on the website.

Lomond School

10 Stafford Street, Helensburgh, Argyll and Bute G84 9JX

Tel: 01436 672476
email: admin@lomondschool.com
website: www.lomondschool.com
Twitter: @LomondSchool
Facebook: @LomondSchool
Instagram: @lomond.school
LinkedIn: /school/lomond-school

A superb quality of life. Lomond School is a co-educational independent school, for children aged 3 to 18, positioned in the elegant suburbs of Helensburgh, a coastal town located only 10 minutes from Loch Lomond and the Trossachs National Park. We make the most of our unique location by providing and encouraging participation in a wide range of opportunities for outdoor learning, sports and activities. Our young people enjoy a superb quality of life in a beautiful and safe environment.

Personalised Education. At Lomond School we believe passionately that education should be about supporting our young people to develop and grow, both academically and personally, as rounded individuals with strong values who are ultimately prepared to embark confidently and successfully on their life beyond Lomond School.

We uphold this commitment with six **Guiding Principles** which are delivered throughout our curriculum and co-curriculum. These include: Internationalism; Environmentalism; Adventure; Leadership; Lifelong Learning and Service. To find out more visit our website at www.lomondschool.com.

As an International Baccalaureate World School we are proud to offer our sixth form pupils the choice of studying the IB Diploma Programme, IB Career-related Programme or SQA Highers and Advanced Highers, ensuring a pathway for all.

Inclusive Ethos. Our focus is on preparing our students for their future by ensuring that they learn the skills necessary to be successful in the 21st century whilst developing the traditional values and qualities that they require to be responsible and active global citizens.

We provide small class sizes, an extensive programme of extra-curricular activities, attention to the individual and a strong record of academic achievement which opens the door to allow new experiences, skills and talents to be explored. All aspects of development are accorded importance, be they academic, musical, dramatic, sporting or in wider outdoor activities.

The Lomond Family. Our experienced pastoral care team ensures the welfare and onward progression of all of our students. Our young people are well known by staff and teachers and we see ourselves as a large family where any issues or problems are identified and dealt with promptly and effectively.

Extra-curricular and Outdoor Learning. Our location means that there is a particular emphasis on outdoor pursuits. The Duke of Edinburgh's Award is, without doubt, a significant feature and we have enjoyed great success carrying out expeditions both locally and abroad. Many of our trips and excursions revolve around our passion for the outdoors and have included trekking in Morocco, canoeing in Norway, skiing in Austria and travelling to Africa to help a number of educational charities there.

We also build many cultural and educational trips into the school year with visits to Paris, Berlin, Brussels and Iceland, as well as Hockey and Rugby tours to South Africa or more locally. We support and encourage our young people to make the most of the opportunities available, recognising both the immediate and long-term benefit of the personal development these experiences and activities can offer.

Living at Lomond. Our boarding facility adds a distinctive dimension to the school; the mix of cultures and backgrounds enriches our curriculum and co-curriculum, supporting all of our pupils to develop their global awareness and understanding.

Our infrastructure boasts a mix of modern, purpose-built structure and characterful listed buildings, which make for an inspirational setting for our young people. We continually invest in our facilities and take a cutting-edge approach to every new project we initiate.

Entry and Scholarships. Means-tested bursaries are available for entry between T2 and S6 with fee assistance ranging from 10% to 100% depending on circumstances. In addition, we offer discounts for the Armed Forces and are a CEA approved school. Scholarships are also available in the fields of academic excellence, creative arts, music and sport.

Lomond is a non-selective school. Part of our admission process, however, is an assessment in Mathematics and English for 11 to 18 year-olds. For younger pupils, placement in classes is the main requirement, whilst for senior pupils reports and examination results are given due weighting.

Fees per annum (2021–2022) – monthly amount by direct debit over 10 months. Tuition: Nursery – Local Authority Funded with priority given to those entering our Junior School. £941 (Junior 1–2), £1,117.50 (Junior 3–5), £1,215 (Transitus 1), £1,291 (Transitus 2), £1,327.50 (Senior School).

Boarding (inc Tuition Fees): £3,046

All fees are inclusive of the annual Capital Levy (£210).

Charitable status. Lomond School Ltd is a Registered Charity, number SC007957. It exists to provide education for boys and girls.

Board of Governors:
Chair: Mr A Hart

Staff:

***Principal*: Mrs J Urquhart**

Academic Depute: Mrs C Chisholm
Pastoral Depute: Mr A B H Minnis
Head of Junior School: Mrs A Lawn

Director of Finance: Mr J Guy
Marketing: Mrs J Scullion and Mrs L Mathis
Admissions: Mr J Hewat

* Head of Department

Subject Teachers – Secondary:

Art & Design:
*Mrs D Aitken
Mrs L Jack

Business Studies & Economics:
*Mrs K Ferguson
Mr E Hall

Drama:
Mrs M McCann

EFL:
Dr M Cotter-MacDonald

English:
*Mrs E Kydd-Corr
Dr M Cotter-MacDonald
Mrs C Bremner
Mrs C Chisholm

Geography:
*Mrs N McKenzie
Mrs C Hoole

Graphic Communication:
Mr J Stewart

Health & Food Technology:
Mrs N Harwood

History and Modern Studies:
*Mrs S Guy
Mr J Forrest
Mr A B H Minnis

Learning Support:
*Mr S McKenzie
Mrs S Bell

Mathematics:
*Mr G Macleod
Mrs E Cameron
Mrs L McGarry

Modern Languages:
*Mr N Mackay
Miss C Cuthbert
Mr D Vescio

Music:
*Mr D Fleming
Miss M-C Brown

Physical Education:
*Mr C Dunlop
Mr S Louden
Miss L Hems

RME:
Mr D Vescio

Science:

Biology:
*Mr T Chambers
Miss M Devillers
Chemistry:
Miss M Ward
Miss M Devillers
Physics:
*Dr A MacBeath
Mr A Meikle

Careers Advisor:
Mrs N McKenzie

School Nurse:
Mrs I Krsmanovic

Head of Junior School:
Mrs A Lawn

Class Teachers – Junior School and Transitus:

Class Teachers – Transitus:
Mrs R Ballance
Mr K Muggoch

Class Teachers – Clarendon
Mrs J Fullarton
Mr J Grafton
Mrs J Macleod
Mrs S Melvin
Mrs L LeGood

Nursery/Pre-School Group:
Head of Nursery: Mrs L Canero
Mrs G Thomas
Miss J Wardle
Mrs E Nelson

Lord Wandsworth College

Long Sutton, Hook, Hampshire RG29 1TB

Tel: 01256 862201 (Main Office)
            01256 860385 (Admissions)
email: info@lordwandsworth.org
website: www.lordwandsworth.org
Twitter: @LordWandsworth
Facebook: @LordWandsworth
Instagram: @lordwandsworth

Motto: *Vincit Perseverantia*

Lord Wandsworth College is a co-educational secondary school for 660 pupils between the ages of 11 and 18. Approximately 60% of the pupils are boarders, either full, weekly or flexi.

LWC is thriving under the leadership of Adam Williams who became Headmaster in 2015. Its increasing popularity has been reflected in rising pupil numbers, and a transformational vision for education has led to major investment in the campus and facilities. The latest, and most significant, of these capital projects is an £8 million state-of-the-art Science Centre, due to open early in 2022. This is a dynamic and highly successful school on a clear upward trajectory.

Location and accessibility. Situated in a magnificent 1,200 acre campus of rolling countryside, woodland and a working arable farm, Lord Wandsworth College provides and inspiring education to 660 boarding and day pupils, aged 11–18. LWC is just five miles from Junction 5 of the M3 and only one hour from London by road or rail.

History. Lord Wandsworth College is named after Baron Sydney Stern, a Liberal MP and the son of a City banker. Granted a peerage after winning the seat of Stowmarket in 1891, Stern took the title of Lord Wandsworth in reflection of his many links with the area. When Lord Wandsworth died in 1912, he left a generous bequest to educate the children of agricultural workers – children who had lost one or both parents and needed the support of a boarding environment. Lord Wandsworth's Trustees purchased the site on which the College now stands and the first

Foundationers arrived in 1922, followed by fee-paying pupils in 1945.

Committed to upholding the wishes of Lord Wandsworth, every year the Lord Wandsworth Foundation offers approximately 50 assisted Foundation places. 2,500 Foundationers have passed through the College since its inception. The Foundation exists to help children who have lost the support of one or both parents through death, divorce or separation and require a caring and supportive boarding environment in which to thrive.

Mission statement. LWC is a socially inclusive non-denominational boarding and day school for boys and girls. We focus on the needs of each individual, while developing in each child a concern for others and a love for and loyalty towards the school community. We ensure that each pupil shapes their values and aspirations within a stimulating and supportive environment, and strive constantly to improve the quality of teaching and learning. We aim to equip pupils with character attributes, passion, resourcefulness, independence, skills, knowledge and qualifications so they can become the best possible version of themselves and make a great contribution to a changing world.

The outstanding features of the school are

- that almost all academic staff live on campus allowing them to provide a high level of pastoral care;
- that Character Education is imbedded into the curriculum and co-curriculum. By promoting Character Education, we believe we will give all pupils the best chance of realising their full potentials.
- that all pupils, whether full, weekly, flexi boarding or day, belong to one of the eight houses and are fully integrated into the social life of the school;
- that the school is purpose-built with an outstanding range of facilities for both academic and extracurricular activities;
- that the school is an unusually unpretentious, happy and caring community.

Curriculum. The aim of the curriculum is to provide a full and flexible range of subjects to fit the needs of each individual. The school's policy is to follow closely the National Curriculum.

Subjects taught to GCSE are: English (Language and Literature), French, Geography, Mathematics, History, Latin, Classical Civilisation, Drama, Physics, Chemistry, Biology, Spanish, German, Art, Music, Design & Technology, Computer Science and Religious Studies.

Most pupils continue into the Sixth Form where the subjects taught at A Level are: English, History, Geography, Economics, Business Studies, Classical Civilisation, Music, French, Spanish, Politics, Physics, Chemistry, Biology, Mathematics, Further Mathematics, Art, Design, Theatre Studies, PE, Psychology and Photography. We also offer the EPQ and BTECs in Sport, Enterprise and Entrepreneurship and Creative Digital Media.

Games. The school provides incredible sports facilities and has a local and national reputation for many of its pursuits. The main boys' games are rugby, hockey and cricket and for girls hockey, cricket and netball with many pupils reaching County and National level. In addition swimming, athletics, tennis, football, golf, cross-country running, horse riding and canoeing are all on offer.

Drama. Drama has a high profile and several shows are staged each year. There is a musical production every other year as well as showcases, reviews and workshops. Pupils are encouraged to participate in all fields of drama either acting, writing, set design, tech support, lighting, stage management, prop-making or sound.

Music. There is a large variety of instrumental ensembles, including a swing band, concert band and rock groups. Pupils have the opportunity to sing in various choirs. Tuition is available in singing, all orchestral instruments, piano, percussion and guitar. Musicians regularly perform formally and informally both within school and at local venues.

Other activities. There is an extensive extracurricular programme. Some of the activities on offer are: Mandarin, Cookery, Chess, Community Service, Pottery, Drama clubs, Mountain Biking, Dance, Photography, Art Clubs, Riding, Life-saving, Debating and Climbing.

The Duke of Edinburgh's Award scheme is thriving and the College has its own licence to run the scheme. There is an active CCF programme for Year 10 pupils and above which has an Army and Air Force Section.

Organisation. There are three main entry points to the College: 11+, 13+ and 16+. Students are accepted at other entry points provided there is a vacancy. The completion of a Registration Form is the first step for all years. A £225 non-refundable registration fee is charged to cover the cost of administration and entrance testing.

Scholarships and Awards on offer are:

First Form (Year 7): Academic, Performing Arts (Music, Drama and Dance) and Sport.

Third Form (Year 9): Academic, Performing Arts (Music, Drama and Dance), Art, Sport and All-Rounder

Sixth Form (Year 12): Academic, Performing Arts (Music, Drama and Dance), Art, Sport and All-Rounder

Foundation Awards are available for children who have lost the support of one or both parents through death, divorce or separation.

Further details for all scholarships and awards may be obtained from the Admissions Office.

Fees per term (2021–2022). Senior Full Boarding £12,280, Senior Weekly Boarding £11,690, Senior Flexi Boarding £10,470 Senior Day £8,630, Junior Full Boarding £10,970, Junior Weekly Boarding £10,420, Junior Flexi Boarding £9,400, Junior Day £7,340.

Charitable status. Lord Wandsworth College is a Registered Charity, number 1143359. It exists to provide education for boys and girls.

Chairman of Governors: R J Hannington

The Governing Body consists of 12 governors.

***Headmaster*: Adam Williams**, MA

Senior Deputy Head: Alex Battison, MA
Deputy Head, Teaching and Learning: Stephen Badger, MA Cantab
Deputy Head, ISI Compliance, Inspection & Academic Systems: Jackie Davies, MA
Chief Operating Officer: Baz Bennett

Teaching Staff and Assistants:
† *Houseparent*

Marie-France Allen (*French Assistant*)
Chris Andrews, BA (*Computing, Head of Digital Strategy*)
Sarah Badger, MA (*Head of French and MFL*)
Pippa Battison, BA (*History*)
†David Beven (*Assistant Director of Sport*)

Kazuko Copeman, (*Business Studies*)
Diane Crichton, BSc (*Chemistry & Head of 4th Form*)
†Kate Cuff, BA (*Drama*)
Rachel De La Cruz, MA (*Head of Spanish*)
Alice Greer, MA (*English*)
Lauren Griffin, BMus, MA (*Director of Music*)
Sally Dawson-Couper, MA (*Head of Mathematics, Assistant Deputy Head, Academic Systems*)
Natalie Eley, BSc (*Chemistry*)
Alison Fisher, BA (*EAL*)
†Russell Fisher, BA (*Design and Technology*)
†Max Gaulton, BEcon (*Mathematics*)
Alex Hamilton, MA (*Head of Latin and Classics*)
Esther Haydock, BSc (*Physics*)
Ben Hazell (*Sports Assistant*)
James Hine, BA (*History*)
Nicole Jinadasa, BSc (*Chemistry*)
Richard Kimber, BEng (*Mathematics*)
Beverley Lane, BSc (*Mathematics*)
Claire Liggins, BA (*Head of Design & Technology, Assistant Deputy Head, Pastoral*)
Jonathan Lilley, BA (*Head of History*)
Rebecca Lodge, BA (*Design and Technology*)
Jeni Loud, BSc (*Physics & Chemistry, Assistant Deputy Head, Teaching & Learning*)
Audley Lumsden, BSc (*Physics*)
Pete Maidment, BA (*Chaplain*)
Chris Millington, BA (*ICT & Computer Science*)
Jane Mitchell, BA (*Head of PSHEE, Director of Wellbeing*)
Graham Mobbs, BA (*Head of Art*)
Veronique Morris-Aloni, MA (*Curriculum Support*)
Vincent Murtagh, BSc, PhD (*Head of Chemistry*)
Jan Norgaard, BSc (*Head of Geography*)
Aaron Parker, (*Assistant Head of Music*)
Harriet Paskell, BSc (*Geography*)
Robin Pyper, BSc (*Deputy Head Pastoral, Designated Safeguarding Lead*)
Chris Radmann, BA (*Head of English, Head of 6th Form*)
†Lesley Radmann, BA (*English*)
James Rayner, BA (*Sports Assistant, Head of Rugby*)
Gemma Reeks, BA (*Head of Performing Arts*)
Tim Richardson, BA (*Head of PE & Co-Curriculum*)
Helen Shedden, BA (*English & EPQ*)
†Tom Shedden, BA (*History*)
Soma Singh, BA (*Head of Sport*)
Richard Thorne, BA, MSc (*Head of Science*)
Jonathan Turney, MA (*Head of Biology*)
Ian Watson, MEng (*Head of 3rd Form, Mathematics*)
Christian White, MA (*Head of Philosophy & Ethics*)
David Widdowson, BSc (*Mathematics*)
Louis Yates, BSc (*Head of Psychology*)

Director of Admissions & Marketing: Pete German

Loretto School

Linkfield Road, Musselburgh, East Lothian EH21 7RE

Tel: School: 0131 653 4444
             Headmaster: 0131 653 4441
             Admissions: 0131 653 4455
email: admissions@loretto.com
website: www.loretto.com
Twitter: @LorettoHead
Facebook: @LorettoSchool
Instagram: @LorettoSchool
LinkedIn: /company/loretto-school

A small School, big on heart, big on ambition.

- One of Scotland's leading schools.
- Scotland's oldest boarding school, founded in 1827.
- An independent, private boarding and day school for girls and boys, from 3 to 18 years.
- Set in a safe, leafy, spacious, 85-acre campus in Musselburgh; the school enjoys all the advantages of its rural setting.
- Globally connected, with the convenience and opportunities of being just 9 kilometres/ 6 miles from Edinburgh, its international airport, rail and road networks.
- Offering the traditional British/ English curriculum of GCSEs and A Levels, one of the leading independent schools in the UK.
- More than 9 out of 10 pupils enter the University of their choice, such as Oxford, Cambridge, St Andrews, and Durham.
- Welcoming about 525 pupils: 375 in the Senior School, 150 in the Junior School and Pre-School.
- An excellent staff to pupil ratio (1:7).
- Every pupil is known personally, and can grow and develop wherever their interests lie.
- A distinctive emphasis on the full development of the individual in mind, body and spirit.
- Exceptional facilities, bespoke to learning and teaching, sport, drama, dance, art and music.
- Extensive Sports programme with specialised coaches in major sports including Cricket, Hockey, Lacrosse, Rugby and more.
- An industry-leading Golf Academy with indoor and outdoor centres, providing every pupil with an unmatched opportunity to develop their talent.

Find out more through a virtual tour of Loretto – Follow pupils on a guided tour of the School and listen to what they say about life at Loretto. Find out more from the School's Headmaster and teaching staff about their ambition for young people.

Start your tour now at www.youtube.com/playlist?list=PLoszjy4tbL3soo2FA1nsG1vAHHsSrHFFL

Fees per term (2021–2022). Boarding: £7,750–£11,900; Flexi Boarding (3 nights p/w): £6,600–£9,875; Day (including meals): £5,900–£8,100.

Admission. Loretto School's Admissions procedure aims to ensure that girls and boys who join Loretto are able to be happy, successful and secure within its academic, cultural and pastoral environment, whether they are boarders or day pupils.

Applications are accepted for entry into most years in the School except Upper Sixth (Year 13).

The selection criteria include provision of satisfactory evidence, through the School's own age-appropriate assessment tests, of academic ability sufficient to access the School curriculum, and a satisfactory reference from the applicant's current school. Loretto is academically selective but also recognises the central value of co-curricular activities, and enthusiasm in these fields is expected and encouraged.

Scholarships and Bursaries. Academic, Art, Drama, Golf, Music, Piping and Sports Scholarships are available. Means-tested bursaries up to 105% are also available.

To find out more, please visit www.loretto.com or contact the Admissions Department, Tel: 0131 653 4455, email: admissions@loretto.com.

Loretto Junior School. Please see Loretto Junior School's entry in the IAPS section.

Chairman of Governors: Mr Peter McCutcheon

Headmaster: **Dr Graham R W Hawley**, BSc Hons, PGCE, PhD

Head of Junior School: Mr Andrew Dickenson

To view Loretto Senior School's Staff Directory, please visit www.loretto.com/senior-school-staff-directory

Loughborough Grammar School

Burton Walks, Loughborough, Leicestershire LE11 2DU

Tel:	01509 233233
email:	grammar.admissions@lsf.org
website:	www.lsf.org/grammar
Twitter:	@LboroGrammar
Facebook:	@LboroGrammar
Instagram:	@LboroGrammar
LinkedIn:	loughborough-schools-foundation

Motto: *Vires acquirit eundo*

Loughborough Grammar School was founded in 1495 by Thomas Burton, Merchant of the Staple of Calais. The School is part of the Loughborough Schools Foundation, a foundation of four schools comprising: Fairfield Prep School (boys and girls 3–11), Loughborough Grammar School (boys 10–18), Loughborough Amherst School (boys and girls 4–18) and Loughborough High School (girls 11–18). The schools operate under one governing body and are situated on two neighbouring campuses in the town. The Foundation also includes The Loughborough Nursery for children from 6 weeks to 4 years.

There are just under 1,000 boys in the School, including 60 boarders.

The School moved to its present site of some 27 acres in 1852 and is situated away from the centre of the town in attractive grounds containing the beautiful avenues of trees known as Burton Walks. At its centre is a handsome Victorian College quadrangle. There has been an impressive development programme in recent years – a new Music department was opened in September 2006; a new state-of-the-art Chemistry building in September 2009; a refurbished and extended Biology building in September 2011; a new Physics building in September 2012 and a new Mathematics building and boarding provision in 2013, completing the Science Park.

Admission. Entry to the School is by the school's own examination at all levels and also by Common Entrance at 13+. Sixth Form entry is dependent on GCSE results and interview with the Headmaster and other senior staff.

Boarding Arrangements. Boys are admitted to Denton House at the age of 10 or over; Sixth Form boys are in School House. Termly and Weekly boarding is available.

Fees per term (2021–2022). Day without EAL £4,640–£4,735, Weekly Boarding £9,915–£10,010, Full Boarding without EAL £11,400–£11,495, Full Boarding with EAL £11,725–£11,820. Music (individual instrumental lessons): £247.50 (for 10 lessons).

The School offers a 25% boarding fee remission to sons of HM Forces and sons of Clergy.

Scholarships and Bursaries. A number of Scholarships are offered, based on performance in the Entrance Examination. Sixth Form scholarships are based on GCSE results. Music Scholarships are also awarded at 11+, 13+ (Common Entrance), and 16+ (Sixth Form). There are also a number of bursaries, dependent on parental income.

Foundation Bursaries. School Assisted Places (up to 100% fee remission) are based on financial need and Entrance Examination performance. Such places are means-tested and an application for one requires the completion of a form declaring income and a home visit.

Religious Teaching. The School is non-denominational though there is a strong Christian tradition. The Chaplain teaches Religion and Philosophy but is available for boys at any convenient time. On Wednesdays, Boarders attend the School Chapel and, on request, are prepared for Confirmation by the Chaplain.

Curriculum. The aim of the School is to give a broad and balanced general education to GCSE with greater specialisation afterwards. In Year 6, boys follow a curriculum similar to that of their last year of junior school; subjects included are English, Mathematics, French, Art, Sciences, Drama, Design and Technology, Geography, IT, History, Music, PE, RE. In Year 7, all boys study English, Mathematics, Science, French, History, Geography, Latin, and Music. Additionally, all boys have lessons in RE, PE, PSHE and Games. In Year 8, Design and Technology is introduced and, in addition to French, boys choose a second language from either German or Spanish. In Year 9 pupils continue with both MFLs, and make some choices from their existing subjects as well as Ancient Greek and Drama.

In Years 10 and 11, for GCSE, boys study English Language and Literature, Mathematics, a modern Foreign Language, and at least two sciences. They also choose three subjects from an extensive options list. Some more able boys study a tenth subject.

The Sixth Form contains 300 boys. A wide range of A Level subjects and combinations is available, along with General Studies, EPQ, Games and other activities. There are some joint teaching lessons with the Girls' High School.

Learning support is available to pupils with diagnosed Special Educational Needs or Disabilities (SEND). We offer targeted support from our experienced and well qualified Learning Support teachers and assistants.

Games. The School has an excellent First XI field and a junior field of over 13 acres within its precinct and within two miles are well-equipped playing fields extending to nearly 70 acres.

The School runs teams in Rugby, Soccer, Hockey, Cricket, Athletics, Tennis, Cross Country, Swimming, Badminton, Fencing and Squash. In addition, there is a Sailing and Canoe Club. The School prides itself in an array of Mind Sports, with teams in Bridge, Chess, Go and Chinese Chess.

Combined Cadet Force. There is an efficient and keen CCF of about 250 boys from Year 10 onwards, run on an optional basis, with 17 Officers, an SSI and a RQMS. Boys have the choice of joining the RAF, Army or Royal Navy Sections. The CCF complex is purpose-built with excellent facilities and many varied and Adventurous Training courses are available to members.

Scouts. There is a flourishing Scout Troop of 35 boys and 1 Scouter.

The Duke of Edinburgh's Award. Over 250 boys are actively involved in the scheme and each year a large number earn Gold, Silver and Bronze awards.

Music (of which much is joint with the Girls' High School) takes place in our award-winning Music department, which has "All-Steinway School" status, and instrumental ensembles involve all the schools in the Foundation. For boys at LGS, there are 4 Choirs and 26 instrumental ensembles, including 3 Orchestras, 2 Wind Bands, 2 Jazz Bands and nearly twenty smaller instrumental ensembles, which each rehearse weekly. Our top ensembles perform on the national stage regularly, including in the MfY Schools' Prom at the Royal Albert Hall (2017), and there are annual music tours for instrumental and vocal groups alike: recent tours have taken in Barcelona (2014), Truro (2015), Prague (2016) and Belgium (2017). Our sacred choirs sing services regularly at cathedrals around the UK, having performed in Southwell Minster, as well as Coventry, Birmingham, Leicester, Gloucester and Worcester Cathedrals in the past couple of years. We put on a large-scale concert each spring at De Montfort Hall, involving all Year 7 pupils and other choirs performing a choral masterpiece (Carmina Burana, Mozart's Requiem, Verdi's Requiem) with our symphony orchestra.

Drama. The School has a fine Studio/Theatre and all boys in Years 6, 7 and 8 participate in a dramatic production. After that, there are productions for other age groups in conjunction with the Girls' High School each term.

Careers. Careers advisors are available to inform boys on options for their futures, with special regard to University or Professional careers. The School is a member of the Independent Schools Careers Organisation.

Academic Successes. An average of 10 boys per year gain admission to Oxford and Cambridge, and over 98% each year begin degree courses at Universities.

The Loughburians Alumni Association. All former pupils of the Loughborough Schools Foundation have automatic free membership to the alumni association. All enquiries to loughburians@lsf.org.

Charitable status. Loughborough Schools Foundation is a Registered Charity, number 1081765, and a Company Limited by Guarantee, registered in England, number 4038033. Registered Office: 3 Burton Walks, Loughborough, Leicestershire LE11 2DU.

Chairman: Admiral Sir Trevor Soar, KCB, OBE, DEng Hon, FCMI

Headmaster: **Dr Christopher Barnett**, MBE, MA Oxon, DPhil, Chevalier, Ordre des Palmes Académiques

Senior Leadership Team:
Senior Deputy Head DSL & Head of Boarding: Mrs HM Foster, BA Greenwich, MEd Buckingham
Deputy Head Academic: Mrs M C Herring, BSc St Andrews
Assistant Head Academic: Dr T G Willmott, BSc, PhD London, MBA Leicester
Assistant Head Wellbeing & Learning: Mr R B Parish, BSc, MSc Bristol
Assistant Head Pupil Experience: Dr A D Waters, BSc Cambridge, PhD Bristol

Magdalen College School
Oxford

Cowley Place, Oxford OX4 1DZ

Tel: 01865 242191
email: enquiries@mcsoxford.org
website: www.mcsoxford.org
Twitter: @MCSOxford
Facebook: @MCSOxfordUK
Instagram: @mcsoxford
LinkedIn: /school/magdalen-college-school-oxford-limited

Motto: *Sicut Lilium*

Magdalen College School consists of 637 boys aged 7–16 with a co-educational Sixth Form of 326. Academic standards are amongst the highest in the country and there is a strong emphasis on study beyond the syllabus, especially in the Waynflete Studies programme. This allows Sixth Formers to develop a personal project, which is finally supervised by university academics. Almost all pupils go on to higher education with about a third each year progressing to Oxford or Cambridge. The school seeks to develop the individuality and interests of each pupil. There is a strong emphasis on extracurricular activity, with particularly proud traditions in sport, music and drama.

History. Founded by William of Waynflete, Magdalen College School opened in 1480, and rapidly acquired an international reputation. Early Masters included Thomas Wolsey, early pupils Richard Hooker, John Foxe, Thomas More and William Tyndale. The school, which from an early stage provided choristers for the College choir, was accommodated entirely in College until the late 19th Century, when expanding numbers led to the acquisition and erection of buildings on the other side of the Cherwell, opposite the University Botanical Gardens and adjacent to St Hilda's College. Today's school still occupies this picturesque site.

Buildings. The school buildings include a Chapel which also serves as a theatre, a library, classrooms, science laboratories, Music School, Sports Complex, Design and Technology Rooms and an art department. In June 2001, a £2m sports complex was opened and in 2005, the school opened its new Sir Basil Blackwell Library. In Autumn 2008

The Michael Peagram Building was opened which houses a modern dining hall, the Art and Design department, Senior Common Room and reception area. In 2012, the Sports Hall was extended to incorporate a studio and additional classrooms, and a climbing wall was added. The state-of-the-art Richard Record Sixth Form Centre was completed in October 2017, including a cafeteria, study space and offices as well as the central social space.

Pastoral. From 7–11, boys are in form groups. Their Tutor is responsible for day-to-day care, pastoral welfare and academic progress. Boys from age 11 and Sixth Form girls are allocated to one of the six Houses. A Housemaster or Tutor in charge of each section is responsible for the pastoral and academic welfare of pupils in his or her Houseroom. The Heads of Departments, SENCO, Chaplain and Matron also play key roles in the pastoral organisation.

Organisation and Curriculum. All boys study a core of subjects to GCSE level, consisting of English, Maths, Science and at least one modern foreign language. In addition, there is a wide variety of options taken by pupils in their GCSE years including Latin and Greek, Geography, German, Spanish, History, Computing and Art. There is no streaming and very little setting.

Pupils study four subjects in the Lower Sixth and sit rigorous internal exams in the Trinity Term. Pupils have the opportunity to focus on three subjects in the Upper Sixth, but a significant proportion sit four or even five A Levels. MCS has a busy curriculum in the Sixth Form; as well as their A Levels, all pupils complete an independent research project (Waynflete Studies), have Games sessions and take part in our Community Service Programme. The provision is further enriched by a Thinking Skills programme and by regular seminars and lectures delivered by members of the MCS community and visiting speakers.

Careers. Careers Aptitude Tests are offered to all boys in the Upper Fourth Form, and there is a regular programme of careers workshops with support programmes for specific careers, e.g. Medicine. Most pupils undertake a work experience placement at the end of the Fifth Form; an extensive programme offering entrepreneurship opportunities from Year 9 upwards is in development.

Sports and Societies. In addition to Physical Education, which is taught in the curriculum, games play a major part in the School. Major sports are rugby in the Michaelmas Term, hockey and rowing in Hilary, and cricket, rowing and tennis in the Trinity Term. Other sports include basketball, netball, football, fencing, cross-country, sailing and athletics. There are Army and Air Force sections of the CCF and a Community Service Organisation. Many pupils participate in the Duke of Edinburgh's Award scheme.

The main playing field, surrounded by the River Cherwell, adjoins the grounds of School House and covers 11 acres. The school also enjoys the daily use of the adjacent Christ Church playing fields and regularly uses a number of other university sporting and cultural facilities. In addition, the school has use of the Magdalen College sports fields one mile from the School. Rowing takes place on the Cherwell from the school grounds.

Music is extremely important in the school and there is a large Choral Society, a Madrigal Group, Senior and Junior Orchestras, a Jazz Band and other ensembles. Many pupils are involved in drama and there are several productions in the year, including performances at theatres around Oxford. There are many other societies and clubs covering cultural and recreational activities. The main school concert is held annually in the Sheldonian Theatre. The school is the founder and main sponsor of the Oxford Festival of the Arts, an annual multi-disciplinary celebration, which features events, performances and community projects throughout the City.

Admissions. The main entry points are at 7, 11, 13 and 16. Around 25 boys are taken at 7, a further 15 or so at 8 and 9, and about 70 at the age of 11. Up to 25 boys are taken at 13. Around 60 boys and girls join the school directly into the Sixth Form.

Admission at ages 7, 8, 9 and 11 is by a School Entrance Examination held in January or February each year.

Admission at age 13 is by pre-test at 11 followed by the Common Entrance Examination for most candidates at preparatory schools and by a School Entrance Examination held in March each year for candidates at maintained schools.

Offers of Sixth Form places are made after interview, and are conditional on GCSE grades.

Candidates can be registered at any age. Full particulars can be obtained from the Registrar, email registrar @mcsoxford.org

Term of Entry. Pupils enter the school in September. Exceptionally, for example if parents move into the Oxford area, other arrangements can be made.

Fees per term (2021–2022). £6,358 (Year 3 to 4); £6,600 (Year 5 to Sixth Form). They are payable in advance and are inclusive of textbooks and stationery. The Registration Fee (non-returnable) is currently £100 or £200 for overseas candidates. For the latest fees look at www.mcsoxford.org/fees

Scholarships, Exhibitions and Bursaries. Scholarships, Exhibitions and Governors' Presentation Awards are awarded at all points of entry.

Bursaries are available subject to testing of parental means and many bursaries are supported through alumni gifts.

At age 13, up to 16 Scholarships of up to £300 are awarded each year based on the results of a two-day scholarship examination in February. Candidates should be under 14 on the subsequent 1 September. Closing date for entries: 11 January.

Music, Art, Drama and Sports Scholarships are awarded each year on the results of assessments held in January (Music), February (Art and Drama) and November (Sports). Music award holders also receive free tuition in one instrument.

Further information can be obtained from the Registrar.

Choristerships. There are 16 Choristerships. Entry is by Voice Trial and candidates should normally be between the ages of 7 and 9. For a Chorister two-thirds of the tuition fee is remitted. All enquiries about Choristerships should be addressed to the *Informator Choristarum*, *Magdalen College*, *Oxford OX1 4AU*. Choristers normally continue at the school after their voices have broken. In deserving cases, further financial help may be available.

Honours. Almost all pupils go on to higher education when they leave – to Oxford, Cambridge and other universities.

Old Waynfletes. The school has an active alumni network which supports social and professional activities and fundraising projects. Representative Old Waynfletes of the 20th century include Olympic athlete and soldier, Noel

Chavasse, VC and bar; bookseller Sir Basil Blackwell; Nobel Prize winner Sir Tim Hunt; composer Ivor Novello; educationalist Tom Wheare; theatre director John Caird, film and theatre director Sir Sam Mendes, visual artist Julian Opie and sports commentators Nigel Starmer Smith and Jim Rosenthal.

Contact: Waynflete Office, Magdalen College School, email: waynfleteoffice@mcsoxford.org.

Charitable status. Magdalen College School Oxford Limited is a Registered Charity, number 295785. Its aims and objectives are to promote and provide for the education of children.

Governors:
Dr P N Withers (*Chairman*)
Professor S R MacKenzie (*Vice Chairman*)
Mr A D James (*Vice Chairman*)
Professor M R Bridson
Professor C C Coussios
Mr J M Hawker [OW]
Mr S R Hope
Mrs A F La Trobe Weston
Ms J A Phillips
Dr R R Phillips
Mr R J Price
Dr R A Saldanha
Mr B A M Vessey

Master: **Miss Helen L Pike**, MA Oxon, MA Michigan, MA London (*History*)

Usher: Mr T G Beaumont, MA Catab (*History, Safeguarding Officer*)
Deputy Head (*Academic*): Mr B D White, BA Oxon (*Mathematics*)
Deputy Head (*Education Development*): Dr S R Crawford, BA Oxon, PhD (*Biology*)

Clerk to the Governors and Bursar: Mrs A H West, MA
PA to the Master: Mrs A Sweeney, BA
Registrar: Mrs A. Green, BA
Director of the Waynflete Office: Mrs S J Baker, MA

The Manchester Grammar School

Old Hall Lane, Manchester M13 0XT

Tel: 0161 224 7201
email: general@mgs.org
website: www.mgs.org
Twitter: @MGSMagic
Instagram: @manchestergrammarschool
LinkedIn: /the-manchester-grammar-school

Motto: *Sapere Aude ~ Dare to be Wise*

The Manchester Grammar School was founded in 1515 to promote 'godliness and good learning', and it has endeavoured throughout its history to remain true to these principles, while adapting to changing times. It is now an independent boys' day school with around 1,500 pupils. Almost all leavers go on to university, and there is a strong tradition of boys progressing to Oxford and Cambridge and other leading Russell Group universities. A number of pupils each year obtain offers from prestigious US

universities. Over 150 qualified teaching staff provide all pupils with a broad, traditional and flexible curriculum; for example, boys may study up to five languages at GCSE, from a choice of Latin, Greek, French, German, Italian, Mandarin, Russian and Spanish. Arabic and Czech are available as part of the options programme in the Sixth Form. The School offers a vast and diverse range of co-curricular opportunities.

The tradition of offering places to clever pupils regardless of their background is maintained by MGS bursaries. Approximately 220 pupils in the school receive means-tested bursaries. Our pupils come both from primary and preparatory schools and represent a wide variety of cultural, ethnic and religious backgrounds.

Registration and Entry. Entry to the Junior School is considered at age 7, 8, 9 and 10, subject to availability at any stage during the academic year. Junior School pupils progress automatically to the Senior School. Entry for most other boys joining the School is at age 11, although entry at other ages is considered, subject to availability and applicants for Sixth Form entry are particularly welcomed. At all levels the normal assessment for entry involves prospective pupils spending a day in School, being taught and assessed in small groups. Alongside these assessment days, there is an entrance exam for entry at age 11. Sixth Form entrants have to meet GCSE grade requirements. Further details are available from the Admissions Office.

Fees per term (2021–2022). £4,460 (£13,380 per year).

Bursaries. The School offers means-tested bursaries of up to 100%. There are currently approximately 220 boys in receipt of financial support from the School and the majority receive full-fee support (the average fee support is currently 91%). The School does not offer academic scholarships.

Junior School. The Junior School opened in September 2008 in award-winning accommodation. It admits boys from age 7 and currently has approximately 240 pupils. There is a strong focus in its curriculum on creativity, academic enrichment and skills-based learning. Specialist teachers from the Senior School contribute to the academic enrichment in Years 5 and 6.

Senior School Organisation and Curriculum. During the first two years, the boys will study English, Mathematics, a modern foreign language (French, German, Russian, Spanish and Mandarin Chinese are offered), Classics (including Latin) History, Geography, General Science, Religious Studies, PSHE, Computing, Music, Art & Design, Drama, PE, Swimming and Games. Greek, Italian and Electronics are introduced as options in Year 9; there is also the opportunity for pupils who have not already done so to take up languages offered in Year 7. In Year 10, pupils may opt to study for an AS Extended Project Qualification; Classical Civilisation is also offered. Pupils make GCSE choices towards the end of Year 9 and typically take ten subjects, including Mathematics, English, English Literature, a language and at least one science subject.

In the Sixth Form, A Level and Pre-U courses are offered, with each department selecting the course which offers the best preparation for university; in addition, all students participate in the School's own non-examined enrichment programme, which includes a philosophical and critical thinking course (Perspectives).

Pastoral Care. Each form in the school is looked after by a Tutor, who is responsible, with the appropriate senior members of staff, for the academic and general progress of each pupil. In the Senior School Tutors work with no more than 13 boys. Regular written reports are supplemented by Parents' Evenings. The School Medical Room is staffed by a part-time doctor and two full-time Nursing staff. The older pupils selected as prefects are encouraged to help younger pupils in running societies and other co-curricular activities.

Creative Arts. All pupils experience Music, Art & Design and Drama within the curriculum; in addition, each of these areas offers activities to large numbers of pupils during the lunch-hour and after school. There are choirs, orchestras and instrumental tuition; plays, drama workshops and musicals; clubs for art, pottery, and computer design. There are regular exhibitions and public performances both in school and in public venues. The School has a well-equipped theatre and drama studios, providing many opportunities for pupils both to perform and provide technical support for productions.

Sport. All boys take part in timetabled games and the school produces successful teams in most sports. A new sports hall opened in 2015 and a water-based hockey pitch was added in 2018; there are extensive playing fields, a gymnasium, indoor swimming pool, squash courts, tennis courts and fitness suite. The choice of sport increases with age, to include rowing, climbing and golf in addition to mainstream sports.

Outdoor Pursuits. The school has a long tradition of camping and trekking and there are numerous weekend and holiday excursions. The School is the largest centre for D of E in the North West. Mountain activity days are offered most weekends, free of charge. Four annual camps cater for the full age range and offer a wide choice of activities. In recent years expeditions have visited the Alps, the Pyrenees, Morocco and Scandinavia. The School has two centres in Cumbria and one in Derbyshire.

Foreign Visits. Many trips abroad are organised each year, providing enjoyable holidays of broad educational value. Destinations include France, Germany, Spain, Russia, Italy, Greece, Mexico, Argentina, Peru, Mexico, Egypt, Tunisia, South Africa, India and China.

Societies and Activities. There are over 200 clubs, societies and activities catering for a variety of interests, including Chess and Bridge Clubs, and a school newspaper produced by pupils. The School is active in charitable fundraising and has a very extensive community action programme, including projects in Manchester and Salford, as well as in Kenya.

Prizes and Scholarships. In addition to bursaries, funds are provided for grants to help deserving pupils with the expense of a range of co-curricular activities. Prizes are awarded in all subjects in the curriculum.

Old Mancunians' Association and MGS Parents' Society. The Old Boys' Association has a well developed network all over the world. There is an annual Old Boys' Dinner in Manchester with further events in the UK and overseas. The Development Office Administrator is Julie Wright, who can be reached at the School.

The MGS Parents' Society has a membership of parents and friends and exists to support school activities and promote a programme of social events.

Charitable status. The Manchester Grammar School is a Registered Charity which provides Public Benefit. The aim of the School is to prepare able boys from the Manchester area, regardless of their financial background, to proceed to university and make a positive contribution to society in their adult life.

Governors:
Dr David Barker
Mr Allan Beardsworth
Mrs Clare Bolton
  (*Treasurer*)
Professor David A
  Cardwell
Professor Tom A
  Hinchcliffe

Ms Joy Kingsley
Mr Brandon Leigh
Mrs Jane Luca
Dr Helen Moore
Dr Jonathan R W Prag
Mr Robert Race
Mr Michael Robinson
Mr John Young

Ex officio Governors:
The Dean of Manchester
The Lord Mayor of Manchester

Bursar and Clerk to the Governors: Mrs G M Batchelor, BSc

High Master: Dr M A Boulton, BEng, PhD

Deputy High Master: Mrs M A S Lowe, BA, MPhil, MEd

Academic Deputy Head: B Bowles, MEng, MMath
Academic Deputy Head Teaching and Learning: D O Lacey, BA, MEd
Pastoral Deputy Head: A N Smith, BA
Surmaster & Head of Co-Curriculum: J W Mangnall, MA
Head of Junior School: E R Losse, MA
Director of Development: S P Jones, BA, MBA
Head of Lower School: P W Freeman, BSc, MSc
Head of Middle School: S G Crawshaw, BSc, PhD
Head of Sixth Form: M D Corbett, BSc
Assistant Head: S Foster, BA, MA
Proctors: S E Jones, BA; D M Taylor, BA
Director of Admissions: D L Virr, BSc
Director of Studies: D Jeys, BSc, MA

Academic Staff:
* *Head of Department/Subject*
[1] *Language Assistant*
[2] *Teaching Assistant*

Art & Design:
R E Berry, BA
K Davidson, BA, MA
J Dobbs, BA, MA Ed
*L J Murphy, BA
S Taylor, BA

Biology:
*J Blair, BSc
S G Crawshaw, BSc, MA, PhD
P W Freeman, BSc
E Loh, BSc, MSc, PhD
N A Loughlin, BSc
C Morgan, BSc
M J Smedley, BSc, PhD
A Wicking, BA

Chemistry:
T Ahmed, BSc
I Airth, BSc
C Buckley, BSc
M Facchini, BSc, MSc
S Graham, MSci, PhD
H M Hughes, BSc
T C James, BSc
*F C Roberts, MChem
G M Tinker, MEng

Classics:
L D Hopkins, BA, MPhil, DPhil
F E Hunt, BA
*C A Owens, BA, MA
S R Sharma, BA MPhil
N G Williams, BA
R G Williams, BA, DPhil

Computing:
R Brown, BSc
B J Charlton, MSci
*D E Millington, BSc, MSc
D Soon, BSc, MBA, MBCS

Duke of Edinburgh:
*M D Rollinson, BSc, MEd

Drama:
S Abbs, BA, PGDipEd
S L Bell, BA
*M J Nichols, BA
J Sherratt, BA
K Tetley, BA

Economics:
G R McSherry, BSc
A E Rigler, BA
J A Shirlin, BA
*A C Thornton, BA, MPhil

Electronics:
*D P Smith, MEng, PhD

English:
R E Adams, MA, MA
E C Appleton, BA, MA
J L Geldard, BA, MA, MA
J Grant, BA, MEd
M M Howard, BA, MA
R Keep, MA Cantab, PGDipEd
A Lloyd-Hughes, BA
C E McCarthy, BA, MA
C A Ramtuhul, BA
H Sargeant, BA, MA
B Townsend, BA
S Van der Ouderaa, MA
J Welsh, BA, MA
*L F Williamson, BA

General Science:
L R Harris, BSc
*D W Inglis, BSc, PhD
D L Virr, BSc

Geography:
F C G Baker, BA
M D Corbett, BSc
A Curry, BSc
P J Higgins, BSc
J W Mangnall, MA
C G McKernan, BSc
M A Nowell, BSc
S P G Spratling, BA
*P J Wheeler, BSc
J O Wilkowski

History:
G R Barker, MA
N Carter, MA
S F Carter, BA, MA
*A R T Hern, BA, MPhil, MPhil
J Hopkins, BA, MA PhD
D O Lacey, BA, MEd
M A S Lowe, BA, MPhil, MEd
S Orth, BA, MA, PhD
C L Pearson, MA, MA
W B Pye, BA
A M Smith, MA
M G P Strother, MA, MPhil, MSt
D M Taylor, BA

Junior School:
C T Ashurst, BA, MEd
J M Aspinall, BA
K V Atty, BA
D R Barnett, BEd
J M Barnett, BA
A J Bentley, LLB
A G Bird, BSc
²L L Birch
C E Boddington, BSc
²C M Burke, BSc, MSc
²S Butt
S M Callaghan, BA
²J S Caverly

C Daly, BA
D D Freeborn, BA
T O Glennie, BA
N J Grundy, BA
F E Jones, BSc
²G Knight
*E R Losse, MA
²E Malik
²C Mercer
T C Neild, BA
²M Parker
²S Reed
²N Reynolds
²J Robinson, BA
E M Shercliff, BA
²V J Tierney
Z L Ward, LLB

Mathematics:
J K Allinson, BA, MA
J P Barker, BSc
B Bowles, MEng, MMath
J J Burke, BSc, PhD
A E Carolan, BSc
A R Davies, BSc, MSc
T J Dessain, MMath, PhD
L Devlin, MSci
*A C Hunter, BSc, MSc, PhD
D Jeys, BSc, MA
I Z Khan, BSc
S J Leigh, BEng
O W J Llewellyn-Smith, BSc
J L McMillan, BSc, MA
G J Morris, BSc
D V Naughton, MM, PhD
J Parkinson-Jones, MMath
T J Pattison, BSc, MIMA, CMath
R T Watt, BSc

Modern Foreign Languages:
P J Chadwick, BA, MA, DPhil
¹E Ciufini
A P Dobson, BA, MA
¹I Feindt
E A Garnett, BA, GDL, LPC
¹M A Harkati
L Hegarty, BA, BA
*A V Hemsworth, BA
*J A Houghton, BA
A Jacinto, BA
S E Jones, BA
¹I L Kilpatrick
*R Lan, BA, MA
S Lu, BA
D Minguito-Pantoja, BA
R J Neal, BA, MA, MEd
S J Paulson, BA
L M Rigby, BA
G Rrugeja
*N J Sharples, BA, MA
C J Shaw, BA

*L Speed, Mosc Dipl
K J Tinslay, BA
¹N Vazquez Miro
¹E Velardi
¹M Zhao

Music:
G Blackwell
F A Bradley, BMus
H Butchart, BA, LTCL, ARCM
*R M Carey, MA
E L Jackson, BMus

PSHE:
*C E McCarthy, BA, MA

Physical Education:
T A Grainger, BSc, MA
R F Jennings, BA
A Khares
J L Leggett, BA
D R Paddon
M J Roe, BSc
S Swindells, RFU II, RFU III
D J Taylor
W J Van Zyl, BSc
*M Watkinson, Levels 1–4 Coaching Cricket
G Wilson, Euro I
T C Young, BA

Physics:
M A Boulton, BEng, PhD
N W Davenport, BEng
*P Holt, BSc, DPhil

A J Marsden, MSc, PhD
S H McGarry, BEng, MSc
R W Morley, BSc, MA
S U Riley, BEng, PhD
M Saghir, BSc, MSc, PhD
Dr D P Smith, MEng, PhD
L Thewles, BSc

Politics:
S Foster, BA, MA, LLB
*R N Kelly, BA, MA, MPhil
E C Kilheeney, BA, MA, PhD
D O Lacey, BA, MEd

Religion & Philosophy:
M Bolton, MA
*A Brower Latz, BA, MD, PhD
M P A Coffey, MA, MA
D Farr, MA
A Greggs, BA
J Kenny, BA, MA
N D Raven, BD, MTh
A N Smith, BA

SEND:
A V Batchelor, BSc, MA
*H Butchart, BA, LTCL, ARCM
R Daws, BSc, MEd
L Merlo, BA, MA
H E Sargeant, BA, MA
R Q Shone

Medical Officer: Dr J L Burn, FRCP, FRCPCH
PA to the High Master: J Lloyd
Admissions Office Manager: K Heathcote

Marlborough College

Marlborough, Wiltshire SN8 1PA

Tel: Main Switchboard: 01672 892200
            The Master's Office: 01672 892400
            The Bursary: 01672 892390
            Admissions: 01672 892300
email: master@marlboroughcollege.org
            admissions@marlboroughcollege.org
website: www.marlboroughcollege.org
Twitter: @marlboroughcol

Founded 1843. Incorporated by Royal Charter.

The College is fully co-educational and full boarding. There are 1,011 boys and girls in the 16 Houses and the usual age of entry is either 13 or 16.

Registration. For entry to the College at 13+ registrations are accepted no earlier than four years before entry. The College assesses the majority of applicants in the January of Year 6 and offers are made for approximately 75% of places. There is a second entry point in the January of Year 7 when approximately 20% of places will be offered. The final 5% of places will be offered in Year 8. All applicants to the College must meet our entry criteria and take either the Academic Scholarship or the Common Entrance examination. Children whose schools do not prepare them for Common Entrance will have alternative arrangements and parents should contact the Admissions Department directly. Please see our website for details of this policy: www.marlboroughcollege.org. The 13+ Scholarship examinations take place in March prior to entry in September. Sixth Form entry and Scholarship examination is in the November before entry. Registrations for entry at 16+ must be made before the 1st of October in the year before entry.

Bursaries. Bursaries of up to 110% of the fees are available for candidates for both 13+ and 16+ entry and the College offers a limited number of bursaries for the children of Clergy. All bursaries, including those for Clergy places, are awarded on a means-tested basis and applications must be submitted by the September of the academic year in which the child takes their entry assessment. While the College is committed to expanding its bursary provision, unfortunately the number of applications often exceeds the funds available. Places for candidates requiring a bursary grant are awarded via our standard assessment procedures according to our Bursary Policy, which is available on the website.

Scholarships. There are up to 8 academic scholarships at 13+ and a further 22 Awards in Music, Art, Design Drama and Sport. William Morris All Rounder Awards may be awarded to candidates who just fail to gain an award in two or more of Academic, Sport, Art, Drama or Music Scholarships. Up to 20 awards are made at Sixth Form entry.

A Scholarship Prospectus and copies of past papers may be obtained from the Admissions Office. Applications and enquiries about entries and scholarships should be addressed to The Director of Admissions, tel: 01672 892300; email: admissions@marlboroughcollege.org.

Academic. The Collége's curriculum follows and extends the National Curriculum to allow for a proper combination of breadth and specialisation. It is designed to stimulate, challenge and support all pupils and to ensure that they maximise their potential. There is a clear focus placed upon success in public examinations, where standards are very high, but the College prioritises pupil success at university and in their subsequent careers.

Almost all pupils go on to study at university either in the United Kingdom (approximately 80% annually to Russell Group universities) or, increasingly, overseas with destinations ranging from Europe to North America and beyond.

In the Lower School a wide-ranging curriculum is followed. Central to this is "Form", an innovative and unique humanities course which embraces English, History and Religious Studies. It gives pupils a sense of the history and evolution of human culture, and our place within it. It aims to develop the skills and habits of mind that will lead to success at the College and beyond – wide reading, critical analysis, synthesis and evaluation of ideas, the confidence to have a go and voice their opinions. Choices are made at the end of the Shell (Year 9) leading to 10 or 11 GCSEs and IGCSEs. In the Sixth Form, pupils choose from over 30 A Levels, as well as having the option to take on an Extended Project (in which the College is a large and successful centre) and further language options, including Mandarin, Arabic and Hebrew. The College does not offer AS examinations in any subject.

The curriculum is supported by an enormous range of academic extension and enrichment activities through societies, lectures, theatre trips, museum and gallery visits, debates, poetry readings, conferences, concerts, creating a full co-curriculum which recognises that qualifications alone do not produce an educated person.

Careers. Nearly all pupils who come to Marlborough go on into the Sixth Form and virtually all proceed to degree courses. The well-resourced Guidance Department is located at the heart of the College and assists Housemasters and Housemistresses in advising boys and girls and their parents about Sixth Form subject selection, higher education options, gap year projects, work experience and careers. Each year, a good number of pupils take up Oxbridge and medical places, and around 10% move on to universities overseas. The College is an ACT testing centre (for those considering North American universities).

Co-Curricular. Sports facilities are outstanding. There are two first class floodlit AstroTurf pitches, acres of sports pitches, allowing for at least 20 simultaneous games in the field sports, a newly re-laid athletics track, a sports hall, an 8-lane 25m swimming pool with hydraulic floor, 24 tennis courts, six fives courts, four squash courts, two rackets courts and nine netball courts. The main sports for boys are rugby, hockey, cricket, athletics, tennis and football, and for girls, hockey, netball, tennis, lacrosse and athletics. Alternative sports include aerobics, badminton, basketball, beagling, clay pigeon shooting, fencing, fishing, fives, girls' cricket, golf, jiu jitsu, rackets, riding, rugby sevens, shooting, squash, swimming, water polo, watt biking, yoga and Zumba. There are regular fixtures in many of these sports and several run sports tours and pre-season trips. Pre-Covid tours included boys' and girls' cricket to South Africa, netball to Barbados, lacrosse to the USA, rugby to France and hockey to the Netherlands and Spain (both boys' and girls'). The shooting team enters both the Schools' Cup and the Imperial Cup at Bisley each year.

An Outdoor Activities Department offers the Gold and Silver Duke of Edinburgh's Award, canoeing, climbing, kayaking and mountain biking. The annual Devizes to Westminster kayak race has become a feature of the Lent Term for up to 10 Upper School crews. The school has its own indoor climbing wall and there is a weekly Climbing Club. There are numerous OA activities each Sunday in term-time in House groups and more adventurous trips further afield in the school holidays. Recent trips have been to the Brecon Beacons and Snowdonia, but pre-Covid destinations included Nepal, Peru and Iceland. The Gold Duke of Edinburgh's Award Training, Practice and Assessed Expeditions take place in school holidays and half-terms.

The College's Combined Cadet Force is thriving. It is compulsory for part of Year 10 and optional thereafter. It provides excellent leadership training and there is a strong record of College pupils winning Sixth Form Army Scholarships. All year groups take part in Field Days or CCF Camps both in the UK and abroad; the Upper School cadets have visited the US Navy Seals in California on four recent occasions.

The College also offers a comprehensive Outreach Programme in the local community. The mantra "with privilege comes responsibility" is the underlying philosophy. Many of the pupils are involved with local primary schools, a special school, Riding for the Disabled and local environmental projects, amongst others. The College has a partnership with Swindon Academy which involves College staff and pupils providing academic support. Swindon Academy pupils also attend some themed residential weekends at the College in normal times. The Swindon Academy Year 7 and Year 8 pupils visit the College weekly. A more recent partnership with Pewsey Vale School is growing. In the Summer Term the Lower Sixth pupils help to run a Primary Club for local 4–7 year olds.

Recently the College has started to provide maths mentoring to pupils in Slough and Swindon, using the Colet Mentoring platform. In addition, pupils use TWIN science kits (and during lockdowns, the associated app) to capture the interest of talented local primary school children in STEM subjects. EdClub, an online mentoring scheme with children in Kenya, was founded at the College and pupils in the Hundred and Lower Sixth are in contact with their mentees on a weekly basis.

The College has a large array of thriving academic and intellectual societies which complement and support the academic programme, attracting impressive speakers each term from across a broad section of disciplines. These continued via Zoom during lockdown.

There is a programme of Day Trips in term-time and, usually, Study Trips in the holidays, which support and enrich the academic curriculum. Whilst this has not been possible over the past academic year, recent examples include Geography to China, Iceland and Tenerife, History of Art to Italy, Politics to Bosnia, Classics to Greece, English to Ireland and Physics to CERN and Florida. The Modern Languages Department runs a series of exchanges and trips to language schools in the target country.

Drama. Drama at Marlborough is all about collaboration, creative debate, experimentation and excellence. With many productions every year, diversity of style is at the heart of what we offer; from contemporary productions of classical tragedy to musicals and farcical comedy. Independent productions give the opportunity for pupils to write, direct and produce, working alongside visiting practitioners and influenced by the wide range of touring productions that visit our three well-equipped theatres. Trips to the theatre are enjoyed frequently being within visiting distance of London, Bristol, Oxford and Stratford. Drama is offered as an option in the Shell (Year 9) and then is a popular choice at both GCSE and A Level.

Fine Art and Photography. Art at Marlborough has been respected nationally and internationally across the last half century for the delivery of visual excellence. Our success lies in the fact that Art staff believe in every pupil's individuality and potential to fully realise their artistic ambitions. Furthermore, Art is encouraged through an investigative outlook and fortified by the opportunity to explore contemporary and traditional making techniques, via the teaching expertise and resources within the Art School.

The cornerstones of our Art Department philosophy are to encourage pupils to strive for excellence and build long lasting skills for future development and achievement. Art Staff develop personal schemes of work to enrich curriculum-based projects and find much of the most exciting work that students create often emerges through teachers inspiring and communicating their own particular skills. Students are able to steer their creative journey through an exploration or 2 & 3D processes including sculpture, ceramics, textiles, drawing, printmaking, painting and film, along with digital and traditional darkroom photography.

Our aim is to foster the pursuit of artistic enjoyment and discovery; to observe carefully, describe precisely and keep an open mind to all possibilities, these are the skills of adventurers! In term time, the Art studios remain open well beyond the timetabled day and at weekends, enabling pupils to seek 1:1 support and further pursue their work and ideas outside of class time.

Co-curricular Art goes hand-in-hand with and enriches taught lessons. The Art School is a happening place with a plethora of Activities: Visiting Artists, Exhibitions and Trips. We have forged strong and lasting links with the British Museum, the Royal Society of Painter-Printmakers in London, Verso Art Charity, Preshute Primary School, Aberystwyth University St Barbe Museum and Art Gallery and Eames Fine Art.

Art Scholarships are awarded annually to individuals of exceptional ability and promise. Extra tuition on a weekly basis is given to Art Scholars. There are 34 Art Scholars across the five years presently.

Our Art department has an exceptional track record in preparing pupils for first choice destinations in higher education. Over the past two years we have placed 28 pupils on a range of leading foundation and degree courses all over the world.

Opened in 2005, our purpose-built Art School houses five open-plan studios for painting, drawing, relief and intaglio printmaking, screen printing, a photography darkroom and studio; lecture room and a computer suite and a well-resourced Art library. Two buildings adjacent to the Art School accommodate the ceramics and sculpture studios as well as a 'large scale drawing' studio. A particular bonus for our Upper Sixth Art pupils is that they are each given their own individual studio work-station. We also have a dedicated gallery and archive space in 'The Mount Gallery'. Pupils, teachers, parents and the wider community are able to regularly view a diverse programme of curated exhibitions within the Mount House Gallery and, at times, around College buildings and grounds.

We generate a dynamic and creative centre of learning for all pupils; from Shell to GCSE and A level, emphasising visual tradition and contemporary innovation, and encourage each individual to create quality visual and written work and in doing so, learn much about themselves.

Design and Technology. The design department recently located to the Beko Innovation Centre and consists of a large multi-disciplinary design studio with integrated digital design tools. The main studio offers a flexible space for large scale prototyping and focused design education, as well as a base for engineering, computer science, entrepreneurship and other disciplines to engage with the space. We also have a separate workshop area with our new CNC machine and an array of more manufacturing-focused equipment. The department has invested in 3D printing equipment which is used across all year groups and by wider members of the Marlborough community and this is housed in our Design Study; a space intended for sixth form to engage in independent design practice which also houses our design library. We also have outbuildings which accommodate our wood preparation equipment, spray booth, metalworking and heat treatment areas.

Fees per term (2021–2022). £13,310

The Marlburian Club. www.marlburianclub.org

Charitable Status. Marlborough College is a Registered Charity, number 309486 incorporated by Royal Charter to provide education.

Visitor: The Most Revd The Lord Archbishop of Canterbury

Council:
President: The Rt Revd The Lord Bishop of Salisbury
G I Henderson, CBE, BA, BCL,MA (*Chairman*)
Professor Sir J Bell, GBE, FRS, HonFREng, PMedSci
Mrs P Cameron Watt, MA Hons, PPE
J P W Coleman, LLB
Mrs A J Cooke, LLB
P Denton, MSc, ACA
E Elliott, MA
Mrs T Freeman, BA
The Revd S Gray, BA, MA, PGCE
T D Martin-Jenkins, MA, MBA
Professor S D Mordant, AO
R Perrins, BSc, FCA
The Revd Lindsay Yates, MA, MTh

International Council:
Y A M Tunku Ali Redhauddin ibni Tuanku Muhriz, BA, MC/MPA
J K Baker, BSc, FCA

***Master*: Mrs L J Moelwyn-Hughes**, MA, MEd

Second Master: W D L Nicholas, BEng, MSc
Deputy Head (Academic): D T Clark, MTheol
Deputy Head (Pastoral): E C Nightingale, MA
Deputy Head (Co-Curriculum): J R B Scragg, MA
Director of Admissions: Dr N G Hamilton
Director of Safeguarding: Mrs C Kane
Assistant Head (Teaching & Learning): Mrs B E A Nightingale, BA
Assistant Head (Inspection): T C M Lauze, BA, MBA
Head of Boarding: Mrs J A Hodgson, BA

Assistant Staff:
* *Head of Department*
† *Housemasters/Housemistresses*

Miss A L Adderley, BA (†*New Court*)
B R Allen, MA
M W Alleyne (*Cricket*)
N M Allott, BSc
D I Andrew, MA, MSci (*Economics & Business*)
A J Arkwright, BA (*Instrumental Studies*)
D R Armitage, MA (†*B House*)
C E Barclay, BSc, FRAS, FRSA (*Director of the Observatory, Director of EPQ*)
Miss S H Bingham, BA
J M Birchall, BSc
T A Birkill, BSc (*Biology*)
M B Blossom, MA
Ms V R Brown, MA
Mrs R L T Bruce, BA
A A Burke, MA
M P L Bush, BA
M Butterfield, MA (*Organist*)
J P Carroll, BEd (*Upper Sixth*)
D T Clark, MTh (*Religious Studies*)
S C Clayton, BA
M Conlen, BSc
Mrs H A M Cox, BSc (†*Elmhurst*)
J R Cox, BA
Ms M A D'Angelo, BA (*Spanish*)

Miss J Darby, BA, GMus
R G De Rosa, BSc (*Geography*)
A H de Trafford, MA (†*Turner House*)
Miss V G M Delalleau, BA
S J Dennis, MBE, MSc (*Remove*)
T J Dolan, MSc (*Computer Science*)
Dr G A Doyle, MSc, PhD, DIC, CChem, MRSC (*Science*)
P T Dukes, FGSM, ARAM (*Artistic Director*)
J J Duplock, MA
S Earwicker, MPhil
O P Elton, BA (*Mathematics*)
M A Eysele, BSc
Mrs A J Finn, MSc (†*Morris House*)
Dr S D Flatres, MSci, PhD
C A Fraser, MA
Mrs J L Fruci, BA
Miss O Gallagher, BSc
W H Gibbs, BSc
B W Giles, MA
T P Gilmour (*Rugby*)
A Gist, MA
N O P Gordon, MA (*English*)
M A Gow, BA (*Politics*)
Miss L S Gray, BSc
P E D Green, MA
Miss O F Grimley, BSc
C L Harrison, BSc (†*Summerfield*)
S R Hawthorn, BSc (†*Preshute*)
Mrs E R Hayes, MA (*French*)
J Hodgson, BSc (*Lower Sixth*)
Mrs R F Horton, MA (*Director of Sport*)
Miss K J Hvass, BA
Miss J C Isitt, BA
Miss R K James, BA
Mrs R L Jerstice, BA (*Psychology*)
Dr R J Justice, MA, DPhil
P N Keighley, BEng
Mrs A L Keighley, BA
D Kenworthy, BA, MFA (*Drama*)
Mrs K J Kiggell, MA (†*Dancy House*)
T A Kiggell, MA
G D M Lane, BSc (†*C3*)
Mrs J E Lane, BSc
J T W Lane, BA
Miss A C Langdale, MSc
Ms Q Li, MA (*Mandarin Chinese*)
Mrs D L Lilley, MA (†*Mill Mead*)
J F Lloyd, MPhil (*Classics*)
M C J Loxton, MA
Mrs J L Luker, BSc
J J Lyon Taylor, BSc (†*Littlefield*)
G I Macmillan, BA (†*Cotton House*)
D J Madden, BEng (*Design and Technology*)
Miss I C M Marks, MA (*Form*)
Mrs H J C Marvin, BSc (*Lacrosse*)
T G R Marvin, MA
Mrs J McClean, BA (*Learning Support & Study Skills*)
Dr F S McKeown, BA, PhD (*History of Art*)
M McNally, BSc
G J McSkimming, BSc (†*Barton Hill*)
A O J Meehan-Staines, BA (*Choirmaster*)
Mrs H L Meehan-Staines, BSc (*Hundred*)
B H Miller, BSc
S R Molyneux, MA
W J Molyneux, BA
Mrs Y Momota

J J L Moore, MA
N J L Moore, MA
P N Morley-Fletcher, MA (*Italian*)
C A F Moule, MA (*History, Academic Scholarship &
  Leadership Programme*)
Mrs E J P Moule, MA
J N Newman, BSc
P J Newman, BA
E G Nobes, MA (*Careers*)
P J O'Sullivan, BA
A G Oxburgh, BA (*Oxbridge*)
J H Parnham, MA
Mrs C N Pembroke, BA (†*Ivy House*)
Mrs E J Penrose, MA
G R Playfair, MA (†*C2*)
J M Quinn, BA
Miss T C Rainer, MA (*German*)
M S Ramage (*Hockey*)
Dr L J Richards, BSc, PhD
Dr D G Roberts, MSc, PhD
J L Roberts, BA, BEd
Dr E Ryder, BSc, PhD
Mrs M C Sandall, BA
R A Sandall, BCom, BA (*Shell*)
Mrs R Scott, MA
M J Sharrad, BSc (*PE*)
C S Smith, BEng, MSc
Mrs E C Smith, BA
K G A Smith, BA
Dr J P Swift, BSc, PhD (†*C1*)
Ms R C Thomas, BA
I R Thorp, MMath, PhD
H L R Tilney, BA
R Tong (*Outdoor Activities*)
Miss C Toomer, GGSM
E F J Twohig, MA, MFA (*Art*)
Mrs C A Walsh, BSc (*Chemistry*)
C J Wheatland, MPhys (*Physics*)
R D Willmett, BA (*Lower Sixth*)
Mrs A T Woodford, BA (*Modern Languages*, *Upper
  School French*)
Miss B L Woods, MSc
J Wright, BSc

Senior Chaplain: The Revd T W G Novis, BA, Mdiv
Medical Officer: Dr A Collings MB, BS, DCH
Librarian: J E Burton, BA
Master's Assistant: Mrs S Nicholas

Merchant Taylors' School

Sandy Lodge, Northwood, Middlesex HA6 2HT

Tel: Head Master's PA: 01923 821850
          Reception: 01923 820644
          Admissions Officer: 01923 845514
          Bursar: 01923 825669
email: info@mtsn.org.uk
website: www.mtsn.org.uk
Twitter: @MerchantTaylors
Facebook: @MerchantTaylors
Instagram: @merchanttaylorsschool
LinkedIn: /merchanttaylorsschoolnorthwood

Motto: *Concordia parvae res crescunt*

The school has enjoyed a distinguished history since its foundation by the Merchant Taylors' Company in 1561. It was one of the nine original "Clarendon" public schools and its pupils have achieved distinction throughout its history. The school enjoys close links with the Company, which, to this day, constitutes its Governing Body. In 1933 the school moved from central London to its present superb, rural setting of 280 acres at Sandy Lodge, Northwood. We are within easy reach of parents in Buckinghamshire, Hertfordshire, Middlesex and North-West London by car, train or school coach service, as well as a mere half hour by tube from Baker Street.

Four distinct boys' day schools share the campus. The nursery school, pre-prep and prep cater for 330 boys from 3 to 13 years of age (the prep school shares some of its facilities with the senior school, but is a separate school in its own right), while the senior school has approximately 890 pupils from 11–18, with over 300 in the sixth form.

All pupils have an individual tutor who looks after them during their school career in small House tutor groups. They are encouraged to cultivate interests at which they can excel, to have confidence in their abilities and to gain self-knowledge as well as knowledge. The academic achievements of the school are first-rate and are achieved in a humane, civilised and unpressured atmosphere. We place a great emphasis on encouraging boys to organise many activities themselves and to take responsibility for others.

Admission. Entry to the senior school at 11+ and 13+ is by the School's own Entrance Examinations, together with an interview; for entry to the Prep school, see Merchant Taylors' Prep entry in the IAPS section. 16+ applications are invited after the publication of GCSE results. Applicants should have at least seven top grades at GCSE.

Term of entry. September unless there are very special circumstances.

Scholarships and Bursaries. There are no separate Scholarship papers in the Entrance Examinations. We make awards to boys who perform exceptionally well in these examinations and at a separate interview; we take into account information received from the boy's current school.

11+ entry: At least 5 major Academic Scholarships are awarded, each up to a maximum value of 50% of the School fee. Up to 5 minor Academic Scholarships each to the value of £200 per annum. Up to 2 All-Rounder scholarships, each up to a maximum value of 50% of the School fee. Scholarships for Sport, Art, Design Technology & Drama (a maximum of 2 per subject) each to the value of a £200 department programme and associated materials.

13+ entry: At least 5 major Academic Scholarships are awarded, each up to a maximum value of 50% of the School fee. Up to 12 minor Academic Scholarships each with a minimum value of £200 per annum. Up to 2 All-Rounder scholarships each up to a maximum value of 50% of the School fee. Up to 8 scholarships for Sport, Art, Design Technology & Drama (a maximum of 2 per subject) each to the value of a £200 department programme and associated materials.

16+ entry: Entrance Scholarships are available across the disciplines of Engineering; Bio-Medicine; Finance and Economics; Languages; Humanities; Creative Arts and Technology. Each up to a maximum value of 50% of the School fee. One bursary up to the value of the full School fee is available.

Music Scholarships: Four Music Scholarships (one of up to 25% of the School fee; one of up to 15% and two of up to 10%) awarded across 11+, 13+ and 16+. A Scholarship includes free instrumental and/or singing tuition on two instruments (or instrument and voice). Additional awards of free tuition may be made if there are boys of sufficient merit.

All Scholarships can be supplemented by means-tested bursaries should there be a proven need.

Bursaries: The School welcomes applications from parents whose sons would benefit from attending Merchant Taylors' School, and who will contribute strongly to the life of the community, but who require financial assistance. Means-tested bursarial support is available up to the value of 100% of the School fee; further details can be obtained from the Admissions Office.

Scholarships at Oxford and Cambridge Universities. At the end of their first undergraduate year, Old Boys are eligible for election to a maximum of three Sir Thomas White Scholarships at St John's College Oxford, a Matthew Hale Scholarship at The Queen's College Oxford and a Parkin & Stuart Scholarship for Science or Mathematics at Pembroke College Cambridge.

Curriculum and Organisation. The curriculum in years 7, 8 and 9 (Thirds, Upper Thirds and Fourths) is a broad one: Art and Design, Biology, Chemistry, Computing, Design Technology, Drama, English, French, Geography, History, Latin, Mathematics, Music, Physical Education, Physics, PSHCE, and Religious Studies. Greek, German, or Spanish are started when 13+ boys enter the school. All boys take nine or ten GCSEs, chosen from the subjects above. Boys are entered for IGCSEs and GCSEs. A student entering the Lower Sixth embarks upon a two-year course in which all boys initially study four subjects to A Level, with most certifying three and some four. An extensive choice of super-curricular options is available, including the EPQ, Thinking and Study skills and Careers Preparation.

Music. All orchestral and band instruments, piano, organ, percussion and guitar are taught to boys throughout the school. Choirs, orchestras, bands and chamber groups give frequent concerts throughout the year.

Games and Physical Education. Magnificent playing fields include over 55 acres dedicated to rugby, cricket, soccer and hockey. There are fives, squash and tennis courts; an athletics track and two floodlit, all-weather pitches. The Sports Hall accommodates four badminton courts, a multi-gym, a climbing wall, a fencing salle and indoor cricket nets. The school's lakes provide a marvellous facility for our sailing club, canoeing and windsurfing. Physical Education is compulsory for all pupils, and all pupils learn to swim. There is an indoor swimming pool and water polo is offered. Coaching in fencing, basketball, judo and karate is excellent. MTS is one of only two schools in the country to host first-class cricket fixtures and is the home of Middlesex Youth Cricket.

Service Sections. The school has a Contingent of the Combined Cadet Force with RN, Army, and RAF Sections. The CCF includes girls from St Helen's School, Northwood. There is a rifle range for the use of the Contingent (and we send a team to Bisley every year). The Duke of Edinburgh's Award scheme allows boys to achieve Bronze, Silver and Gold Awards, and the Community Service programme provides an opportunity for a wide range of activities in the local area. All boys in Years 10 and 11 take part in the CCF, The Duke of Edinburgh's Award scheme or Community Service teams.

The school places great emphasis on charitable endeavour and the boys run a great many societies to support good causes. A special feature of the school's charity work is Phab, a week-long residential holiday for handicapped children held every Easter and organised by Sixth Form boys together with the girls of St Helen's School. The school also has a charitable partnership with two schools in India.

School Societies. A large number of societies cover a wide field of interests and activities.

Careers. There is an outstanding Careers Advisory Service, which organises annual Careers and Higher Education Conventions at the school and a range of work experience.

House and Tutorial Systems. The school is divided into eight Houses. Each House is under the care of a Head of House and a team of tutors, who are responsible for the pastoral care of boys in that House.

Fees per term (2021–2022). £8,912 (Autumn Term), £6,684 (both Spring Term & Summer Term); these cover not only tuition, games, and lunch but also a lifetime alumnus subscription (OMT). There is a non-refundable registration fee of £100; separate admission fee deposits are charged later.

Merchant Taylors' Prep, the Preparatory school to Merchant Taylors', adjoins the senior school.

(For further details see Merchant Taylors' Prep entry in IAPS section.)

Charitable status. Merchant Taylors' School Charitable Trust is a Registered Charity, number 1063740. It exists to provide a first-class all-round education for boys, irrespective of their background.

The Governors of the School:
Chairman: D G M Eggar

G B M H du Parc Braham	R Newall
R J Brooman	J Oram
Dr J M Cox	L E Orr
Commodore A Cree, CBE	V Paul
A Eastwood	Mrs J Redman
D Haria	Sir M Tomlinson, Kt, CBE
Mrs S Morgan	J Twining
A G Moss	

Clerk to the Governors: E Valletta

Head Master: S J Everson, MA

Bursar: I D Williams, MBA, CMgr, GCMI, MAPM, MCIL
Second Master: M C Husbands, MA
Deputy Head (Academic): R C Garvey, MA
Senior Master: C R Evans-Evans, BA, MEd, NPQH
Registrar: J G Taylor, MA
Deputy Head, Information Services: Dr A R H CLARKE, MA, DPhil
Development Director: N J Latham, LLB Law
Head Of Upper School: Dr C L Harrison, PhD
Head Of Middle School: Mrs L P Pruden-Lawson, MA
Head Of Lower School: T W Jenkin, MA
Head Of Pupil and Staff Well-Being: T C H Greenaway, BSc
School Chaplain: The Reverend J T Fields, MA, STM

Assistant Staff:

* *Head of Department*

Art & Design:
*Ms I Lumsden, BA
A C Cataldo
S N Leech, BA

Biology:
*Mrs S N Stuteley, BSc
Dr C L Harrison, PhD
Dr A Komissarova, MA, PhD
T C H Greenaway, BSc (*Assistant Head, Staff and Pupil Well-Being and SCR President*)
B C Oxenham, BSc
Mrs L P Pruden-Lawson, MA (*Head of Middle School*)
B J Simpson, BSc (*PSHCE)

Careers:
Ms S Grice, BSc (*Careers)
Mrs K Richards, Associate CFA (*UK Careers Co-ordinator*)
Mrs M Thobani (*Work Experience Co-Ordinator*)

Chemistry:
*M P Powell, MA
R I M Alexander, BSc (*Director of Hockey & Deputy Leader of Co-Curricular Activities*)
M S T Hughes, BSc
Dr M M Lohr, PhD (*Assistant Staff Tutor*)
Dr M Lomas, BSc, PhD (*Assistant to Head of Lower School*)
Mrs F A Rashid, BSc (*Science)
J R Talboys, BSc

Classics:
*P D Harrison, MA (*Deputy Director of Teaching & Learning*)
Miss M A Bergquist, BSc (*Joint Deputy Director of Communications*)
Ms C D Drew, BA (*Staff Tutor*)
E H Gazeley, BA
M C Husbands, MA (*Second Master*)

Computing:
G N Macleod, BA (*Head of Academic Computing*)
J E Firestone, MA (*Head of CCF and Outdoor Education*)
E E W Williams, MA

Design & Technology:
*A C Duffey, BA
N J Kyriacou, BEd
Miss H M Park, BSc
S J Reid, BSc
G A Wilson, BA

Drama and Theatre Studies:
Miss C L Clarke, BA (*Director of Drama*)

Economics & Politics:
Dr M I Beacham, BA, MSc, PhD (*Economics)
A R Fraser, MSc
R C Garvey, MA (*Deputy Head Academic, Religion and Philosophy*)
Mrs H C Hall, BA
C J Oey, MA
Mrs S F Pearson (*Subject Leader for Politics and Assistant Head of Upper School*)

English:
*M G Hilton-Dennis, BA
Miss M J Fitzpatrick, BA
Dr M I Hetherington, MA PhD
T W Jenkin, MA (*Head of Lower School*)
J D Manley, MA (*Head of Mulcaster House*)
I J Mitchell, BA, BSc (*Psychology)
A J Richardson, BA
D G Robinson, BA
Ms D M Scott, MA
Mrs K Shockley, BA,
Ms L V Smith, MA (*Director of Teaching & Learning, SCR Representative – Governing Body*)
Miss E K Trafford, MA (*Deputy Director of Co-Curriculum*)

Geography:
*A Murray, MA
Mrs E J Lemoine, BA (*Head of Raphael House, Joint Deputy Director of Communications*)
Miss H J Maxfield, BA (*Assistant Head of Middle School*)
Mrs S A Riddleston, BA (*Senior Teacher*)
R Simmonds, BSc (**PSHCE & Head of Andrewes House*)
Miss S R Watson, BA
D A Westcott, MSc

History:
*M W S Hale, MPhil
Mrs F E Blatchford Pace, BA
M Flower, BA (*Head of White House, Head of Phab*)
M T Herring, BA (*Assistant Head of Upper School*)
P A Hoyle, MSt
J G Taylor, MA (*Registrar*)

Information Services:
Dr A R H Clarke, MA, DPhil (*Deputy Head, Information Services*)
J P Beck (*IT Manager*)
P A J Gregory (*Senior Network Engineer*)
R Dixon (*Network Engineer*)
E J Roberts (*IT Technician*)
I Rudling (*Webmaster*)

Learning Support:
*Ms E J Sadler, BA, MEd Head of Learning Support
Mrs D N Desai, BSc (*Teaching Assistant*)
Mrs D D Kotecha, MSc (*Teaching Assistant*)
F Murphy-O'connor, BA (*Graduate Assistant*)
Miss I E Roberts, BA (*Specialist Teacher*)

Library:
Mrs A J South, BSc, Dip Lib (*Senior Librarian*)
Mrs P J Jones, BA, PG Dip (*Part-time Library Assistant*)
Mrs R J L Millard, BA, MA (*Assistant Librarian*)

Mathematics:
*A S Miller, BSc
A P Carroll, BA
N J Cleaver, MSci
S J Coles, BSc
J T Coren, MA
M A Fothergill, BSc (*Head of Manor House*)
Mrs H E Ezomo, BA
Mrs D C Gedalla, BA
Mrs S M Hale, BSc, MSc (*Assistant to Head of Upper School*)
S F Hardman, BSc (*Second in Mathematics*)
Mrs G M Hazan, BA

Mrs N Manek, BA (*Examinations Officer*)
Ms N C Monteiro, MSc
Mrs T A Omert, BEng (**Charities*)
S L Rowlands, BA

Modern Foreign Languages:
*R P Bailey, BA
Mrs M C R Castro, BA (*Spanish*)
Miss R G Haye, Licence LCE (*Joint Acting Head of French*)
Ms V M Kotsuba, BA, MA (*French*)
M W Pacey, BEd (*Subject Leader for German*)
Miss D E Rabbette, BA (*French*)
J M S Rippier, BA (*Director of Communications & French*)
Ms A Troletti, MA (*Joint Acting Head of French*)
Mrs C E Udell, MA (*German & French*)

Music:
S J Couldridge, Dip TCL (*Director of Music*)
Dr R L Couchman, BA, MPhil, PhD (*Head of Academic Music*)
Mrs J H Stubbs, MusB ARCO, ALCM (*Assistant Director of Music*)
D T Tonks, MSt
Miss S A Walsh, MA
J D Collins, BMus (*Graduate Assistant*)

Physical Education:
L D Foot, BSc (*Director of Sport*)
P J B Davies, MSc (**Sport Science*)
C R Evans-Evans, BA, MEd, NPQH (*Senior Master*)
I McGowan, BSc, MSc (*Director of Cricket*)
J O Middleton, BSc (*Director of Hockey*)
A J Mills, BSc (*Director of Rugby, Head of Walter House*)
M J Penny, BSc

Physics:
*Mrs A Mayadeen, MPhys
R Aniolkowski, BSc
Dr A R H Clarke, MA, DPhil, CPhys, MInstP (*Deputy Head, Information Services*)
C P Hull, BSc (*Assistant Head of Middle School*)
Miss K N Hustwitt, BSc
D J Spikings, BA, MEng (*Director of Studies*)
B Waterhouse, BSc

Psychology:
*I J Mitchell, BA, BSc

Religion & Philosophy:
*I L Regan-Smith, MA
L J Charman, MA (*Head of Hilles House*)
R C Garvey, MA (*Head of Upper School & Teacher of Economics*)
J King, MA

School Counsellor:
Ms P Llewellyn, BSc Hons, PG Dip (*Lead School Counsellor*)
A Mullen, BACP (*Accredited Counsellor/Psychotherapist*)

Visiting Teachers:
W Alexander, DipTCL (*Guitar*)
J Atkins, DipRAM (*Trumpet*)
Miss C Barry, BA (*Cello*)
S Byron, BMus Hons RCM (*Trombone*)
Miss S Clark, MA LRSM, ARCM, DipRCM, CTABRSM (*Piano*)
Mrs N S Coleman, CertEd (*Flute*)
Miss K Cormican, GTCL, PDOT (*Violin*)

Mrs R Couldridge, GTCL (*Violin, Viola and Piano*)
A Gathercole, GGSM (*Trumpet*)
M Gibbs, BMus
Ms N Hawkins (*Guitar*)
R Halford
D Hester, LTCL, DipTCL (*Bassoon, Music Technology*)
R N Hobson
J Lawrence, BA (*Percussion*)

Sports:
A Bruce (*Strength and Conditioning*)
N Buckman (*Tennis*)
J Burley (*Rugby – Performance Analyst*)
G Calway (*Cricket*)
A Chowdhury (*Tennis*)
E Conway (*Rugby*)
J Cumming (*Watersports*)
S Dokic (*Athletics*)
D Emms (*Tennis*)
L Fazekas (*Fencing*)
A French (*Watersports*)
S Galloway (*Cricket*)

Mrs N Manington, BMus, LGSM (*Piano and Jazz Piano*)
B Marshall, MMus
N Martin (*Percussion*)
D Robb (*Clarinet*)
D Saunderson, GGSM (*Singing*)
J Shiner, MA
Mrs M Stone, MMus (*Piano*)
Mrs N Tait, LRAM Hons (*Cello*)
R Wainwright (*Organ*)

J Jones (*Judo*)
R Kerr (*Hockey*)
M Khalifa (*Squash*)
R Lawrence (*Rugby*)
N Li (*Table Tennis*)
J Ling (*Hockey*)
P Loudon (*Hockey*)
D Manley (*Athletics*)
J Moore (*Cricket*)
R Patel (*Cricket*)
D Samuel (*Rugby*)
G Summerfield (*Cricket*)
L Wooldridge (*Cricket*)

Head Master's PA: Mrs J Jolliff
Admissions Officer: G McCann
Bursar's Secretary: Mrs A Johnson

Merchant Taylors' Prep:
Head of School: Dr Karen McNerney, BSc Hons, PGCE, MSc, EdD
Senior Deputy Head: Antony McConnell, MA Hons, PGCE, FHA
Deputy Head: Andrew Crook, BA Hons, PGCE

Merchiston Castle School

294 Colinton Rd
Colinton, Edinburgh EH13 0PU

Tel: 0131 312 2200
Headmaster: 0131 312 2203
Admissions: 0131 312 2201
email: headmaster@merchiston.co.uk
website: www.merchiston.co.uk
Twitter: @MerchiNews
Facebook: @MerchistonEdinburgh
Instagram: @merchinews
LinkedIn: /merchistoncastleschooledinburgh

Motto: *Ready Ay Ready*

The School was established in 1833 and moved in 1930 from the centre of the city out to its present spacious and attractive site, bordered by the Water of Leith and close to the Pentland Hills.

There are 400 boys in the School, of whom 260 are boarders.

Admission. The normal ages of entry are 7–14 and 16, though from time to time there may be vacancies at other ages. Entry at 7–12 is by entrance assessment, interview and current school report; entry at 13 by the Common Entrance or Merchiston entrance examinations and current school report. Entry at 14 is by Merchiston entrance examinations. Entry to the Sixth Form at 16 depends on a successful showing in GCSE or National 4 and National 5 examinations as well as on interview and a school report. There are approximately 140 pupils in the Sixth Form. Entry is possible in all three terms where vacancies permit.

A prospectus and further details may be obtained from the Admissions Office. Prospective parents are encouraged to visit the School. Information may be also found on our website (www.merchiston.co.uk) and via these links:

Admissions: www.merchiston.co.uk/admissions

Personalised Virtual Tour: www.merchiston.co.uk/admissions/open-events/personalised-virtual-tour

Order a Prospectus: www.merchiston.co.uk/admissions/order-a-prospectus

News Centre: www.merchiston.co.uk/about/news-centre

Courses of study. In the Juniors the curriculum comprises English, English Literature, Mathematics, Biology, Chemistry, Physics, History, French, Latin, German, Spanish, Mandarin, Geography, Religious Studies, Art and Design, Music, PE, Electronics, Design and Technology, and Information Technology.

In the Middle School a 2-year course leading to GCSEs is followed, consisting of a core curriculum: English, English Literature, Mathematics, a foreign language (French, Spanish, Mandarin), IGCSE Biology, Chemistry and Physics, and a wide range of optional subjects, including History, a second foreign language, Electronics, Information Technology, Geography, Latin, Religious Studies (Philosophy and Ethics), Art and Design, Design and Technology, and Music.

A Level options include English Literature, Mathematics, Further Mathematics, Biology, Chemistry, Physics, French, German, Spanish, History, Geography, Economics, Government and Politics, Classical Civilisation, Religious Studies, PE, Information Technology, Latin, Design and Technology, Electronics (AS only) and Art. Other languages at A Level (including Classical Greek, Italian and Russian) are available on request and at additional charge. In addition to his main subjects, each boy follows a General Studies course offering Moral and Social Studies and Careers Guidance. Classes are small throughout the School, and all subjects are set by ability. The School prepares boys for entry to Oxford and Cambridge.

The School makes provision for specialist ESOL teaching for International students, including an opportunity to study GCSE English in the Upper Sixth year.

In 2021, university destinations included Glasgow, Aberdeen, Durham, Exeter, Imperial College, Newcastle, Sheffield, University College London (UCL) and Warwick. In addition, seven went to universities overseas (six in the US) and two secured Oxbridge places.

Support for Learning Provision. Able boys with learning difficulties, including dyslexia, enjoy successful careers at Merchiston. Our aim is to enhance self-esteem through genuine praise. We encourage each pupil to find success in his area of strength, whether inside or outside the classroom. The objective is that all pupils have access to a wide and varied curriculum, and that, as a result, each

discovers his own personal strengths and talents, and enjoys the resulting success. All are expected to follow mainstream GCSE courses.

Houses. Each of the boarding houses caters for a particular age group and the atmosphere and activities are tailored accordingly. The modern purpose-built Sixth Form boarding house offers 126 en-suite bedrooms, with kitchens, a multi-gym and open plan social spaces with stunning views of Edinburgh. The Housemaster, Housemother and House Tutors pay special attention to the care of the individual and to the development of both his studies and interests.

Day boys. The life of day boys is fully integrated with that of the boarders.

Games. The principal games are rugby, played in the Autumn and Lent Terms, and in the Summer Term cricket and athletics. There is a large indoor heated swimming pool and a sports hall, and there are good facilities for other sports including hockey, tennis, football, squash, fives, shooting, sailing, skiing, basketball, golf and badminton. Merchiston prides itself on fostering the pursuit of excellence in a sport-for-all environment. The School is currently represented nationally and internationally in many sports, such as athletics, cricket, golf, rugby and target shooting.

Music. Music plays an important part in the life of the School. Tuition is available in all keyboard and orchestral instruments; currently about fifty per cent of the School learn a musical instrument, and two choirs flourish. There is also a School orchestra, a close harmony group, a jazz band and two pipe bands. The choir and instrumentalists frequently go on tour, e.g. to the USA, the Far East, and Europe.

Drama. There is at least one major drama production a year, jointly staged with our sister school, as well as frequent House plays or drama workshop productions in a well-equipped, purpose-built theatre.

Art, Craft, Design and Technology, and Ceramics. The Art and Design Centre offers scope both within the curriculum and in the pupils' free time for painting, pottery, metalwork, woodwork and design work. Courses in Computing and Electronics are also available both within the curriculum or in free time.

Societies. There is a wide variety of clubs, including chess, debating and electronics. Visits to theatres, concerts and exhibitions are a frequent part of a boy's life at Merchiston. The Enlightened Curriculum uses Edinburgh as a prime resource for cultural experiences for all age groups.

CCF participation is voluntary. CCF includes outward bound activities such as climbing, hillwalking, canoeing and camping. All senior boys at Merchiston also undertake a Bronze Duke of Edinburgh's Award expedition, with participation at Silver and Gold level on a purely voluntary basis.

The School is also very active in community service work.

Girls. The School does not accept girls but has a special relationship as brother/sister school with St George's School for Girls, Edinburgh and Kilgraston School in Perthshire. This includes joint expeditions, concerts, tours, seminars, debating, drama, social events and study courses. Merchiston operates a joint fee scheme with both schools.

Careers advice. An expert careers adviser supplements the advice of the Academic Leadership Team, Housemasters and Academic Tutors. In the LVI year, pupils attend timetabled lessons in Careers as part of the General Studies Programme of the Sixth Form, where they are also encouraged to take a Work Experience placement and to visit local universities in the month of June. When pupils start in the Shell, they undertake Cambridge Occupational Analysts (COA) Preview and Profile assessments. These assess each individual's interests and abilities in several key cognitive areas. In the Fifth Form each individual has a discussion with the Head of Careers, during which interests are explored and feedback from the COA assessments is given. The discussion is focused on career areas of interest – as identified by the individual and the COA feedback – and identifying areas to be investigated, as well as touching on potential A Level programmes. There is an annual HE & Careers Fair to which other local schools are invited.

Links with parents. There are regular parent/staff meetings and parents are fully briefed and consulted with regard to all academic and career decisions. There is also a parents' forum, which holds regular meetings.

Health. There is a medical centre in the charge of the School Nursing Sisters and the School Doctor visits regularly.

Fees per term (2021–2022). Junior School: Boarders £7,360, Day boys £5,110; Forms 2 and 3: Boarders £8,560, Day boys £5,770. Senior School (Forms 4 and above): Boarders £11,960, Day boys £8,680.

Sibling, Forces and Teaching Profession (means–tested) fee reductions are available.

Scholarships and Bursaries. Scholarships are offered for competition from 10+ up to 16, with an emphasis on 13+ entry from Prep Schools.

Junior (10+–12+): Academic, Music (including a Piping Exhibition), All-Rounder.

Senior & Sixth Form (13+, 14+, 16+): Academic, Music (including a Piping Exhibition), Sports, All-Rounder, Art & Design, Design & Technology.

Scholarships no longer carry an automatic fee concession.

For further information see: www.merchiston.co.uk/admissions/scholarships.

Means-tested financial assistance: where parental income is not sufficient to allow the pupil to attend Merchiston, parents may apply for means-tested financial assistance, which may be up to 100% of the day or boarding fees.

Forces: 10% fee remission is available to the sons of serving members of HM Forces.

Trust Applications: The School can apply to charities on behalf of prospective candidates who can demonstrate financial need.

Old boys. The Secretary of The Merchistonian Club, c/o the School. Former pupils include: The Rt Hon Lord John MacGregor, MP; Sir Peter Burt, former Chief Executive, Bank of Scotland; The Rt Hon Lord Kenneth Osborne PC, longest-serving judge of the current Scottish bench; Air Marshal Sir John Baird, Surgeon General of the British Armed Forces between 1997 and 2000; International Rugby Union players: N G R Mair, W S Glen, I H P Laughland, A C W Boyle, A H W Boyle, Q Dunlop, G R T Baird, J Jeffrey, P Walton, C Joiner, B R S Eriksson, D W Hodge, N J Mayer, I A Fullarton, P J Godman, F J M Brown, Sam Hidalgo-Clyne, Zach Mercer; Shane Corstorphine, former Senior Vice-President Skyscanner.

Charitable status. Merchiston Castle School is a Registered Charity, number SC016580. It aims to give each boy in his way the capacity and confidence to live in an uncertain world and to make that life as rich as possible; more specifically, to encourage him to work hard and to take pride in achievement, to think independently, to face up to challenges, to accept responsibility, to show concern for others and the environment, and to develop wider skills and interests.

Governors:
G T G Baird, HND, FRAgS (*Chairman*)
D C M Moore, BSc, MPhil, PhD
G R T Baird
S P Abram
R W Nutton, MBBS, MD, FRCS
R S Elliott
Mrs P Abrahams, OBE, MA
A Fraser, LLB, DIPLP, NP, WS
D E L Johnston, QC, MA, PhD, LLD, FRSE
Dr A Connan, MBBS, MRCGP, FSRH, MIPM
Ms G Hinton
N Mitchell
Mrs P Axon, BEng (*Clerk to the Governors*)

Staff:

School Leadership Team:

**Headmaster*: J Anderson*, BA Queen's Belfast

Deputy Head Teaching & Learning: Dr D D J Cartwright, BSc, PhD Edinburgh
Deputy Head Wellbeing: D Rowlands, MA Cambridge
Bursar: Mrs P Axon, BEng Reading
Director of Admissions: Mrs K Wilson

Pupil Support Leadership Team:
Senior Deputy Head: A W Johnston, MA Edinburgh
Assistant Head Pupil Support: W Ogilvie-Jones, BSc Brunel

Housemasters/mistresses:
Pringle: Mrs R MacLennan
Rogerson: B Aitchison
Evans: S Buchanan
Laidlaw: N Leibermann; M Raikes

Heads of Academic Departments:

Art & Design and Design & Technology: J M V Cordingley, MA London
Biology: Mrs H J Williams, MSc Glasgow
Chemistry: R R Greenwood, MSc London
Classics: M R Hillier, MA Cambridge
Computing: D H Thomson, MA Glasgow
Design & Technology: Mrs C L Nugent, BSc Northumbria, MEd PhD Edinburgh
Economics: W Donkin, BEd Cape Town
English: Mrs S J Binnie, MA Edinburgh
English as an Additional Language: Mrs S J Hardman, BA Sheffield
Entrepreneurship: F Newham, MA Oxford
Geography: Mrs T A S Bower, BA London, MSc Toronto, DPhil Oxford
History and Politics: S R Thompson, MA Edinburgh
Mathematics: Ms F Vian, PhD Parma
Modern Languages: Ms C Flanagan, MA Glasgow, PhD Cambridge

Music: S M Dennis, BMus Edinburgh
G Campbell, MA Aberdeen (*Master i/c Pipe Bands*)

Physical Education: C R Harrison, BSc Napier
R C Deans, BSc Abertay (*Director of Rugby*)
R D McCann, BSc Ulster (*Director of Sport*)

Physics: J Mayoh, MPhys St Andrews, PhD Cambridge
Religious Studies: Revd N G D Blair, MA Edinburgh
Support for Learning: Mrs I Stewart, BEd Glasgow

Administration:
Mrs J Thynne (*Executive Assistant*)
Mrs E Firoozi (*Academic Secretary*)
Ms J Cunningham (*Administrative Assistant*)

Admissions:
Mrs K Wilson (*Director*)

Marketing:
Mrs K J Nicholls, BA Warwick, MA Falmouth

Library:
Ms R E A Gibb, BSc OU (*Librarian*)

Medical Staff:
Mrs SA McLean, RSCN, RGN (*Director of Health Services*)
Mrs N Fallowfield, RGN (*School Nurse*)
Mrs J N Fisher, RGN (*School Nurse*)
Mrs B Officer, RGN (*School Nurse*)
Mrs D Marshall (*Health Assistant*)

Specialist Sports Coaches:
K Sanford (*Basketball*)
A Evans (*Cricket*)
S Gilmour, MSc Edinburgh (*Cricket*)
J Hay (*Squash*)
A Murdoch (*Golf Academy Director*)
S Pender (*Tennis Academy Director*)

Support Staff:
Mrs F Blair, BSc Edinburgh, BA Queen Margaret's (*School Counsellor*)
Mrs M Cordingley, BA Roehampton (*School Shop Manager*)
Mrs K Coyne, BA Glasgow (*Housemother*)
Major A D Ewing, BSc Napier (*CCF Instructor*)
Mrs C Haston (*Housemother*)
Mrs M Lucas, BA Edinburgh (*Masterchef*)
Mrs A McGregor, BA Edinburgh (*Housemother*)

Mill Hill School

The Ridgeway, Mill Hill Village, London NW7 1QS

Tel: 020 8959 1176
email: office@millhill.org.uk
           registrations@millhill.org.uk
website: millhill.org.uk
Twitter: @MillHillSenior
Facebook: @MillHillSenior

Overview. Mill Hill School is at the heart of a Foundation dating back to 1807, which also includes our Pre-Prep, Grimsdell; our Prep, Belmont, The Mount, Mill Hill International and our most recent addition, Cobham Hall School, Kent.

The Mill Hill School Foundation educates boys and girls aged 3–18 and offers day places, weekly and full boarding for pupils aged 13–18.

History. Mill Hill was founded by Samuel Favell (1760–1830) and Revd John Pye Smith (1774–1851) as a grammar school for the sons of Protestant dissenters and opened in 1807. The School became fully co-educational in September 1997.

Location. The School is situated in Mill Hill village, a conservation area on the borders of Hertfordshire and Middlesex, approximately 10 miles from the centre of London. Set in 120 acres of parkland originally formed by the famous botanist Peter Collinson, the grounds provide a spacious setting for the academic buildings and boarding and day houses, and offer extensive facilities for sports and activities.

Houses. There are 848 pupils in the school, of whom 110 are boarders. Weekly and full boarding is available for entry at Year 9, Year 10 and Sixth Form. There are five Boarding Houses and eight Day Houses, all of which have been recently refurbished. Day pupils take a full part in the activities of the school. Full boarders have a full range of activities and workshops on Saturday mornings. These sessions are optional to day and weekly boarding pupils. Housemasters/mistresses and House Parents, together with their teams of Tutors, aim to provide an environment that is both caring and supportive. The welfare of each pupil is supported throughout their school career by a Housemaster/mistress or House Parent and Tutor team who get to know them well and liaise closely with their families.

Each House provides a social space and pastoral focus for pupils. Pupils are looked after by a named Tutor attached to their House, who works closely with the Housemaster/mistress or House Parent to ensure that all pupils are well supported academically and pastorally. The Tutor is the first point of contact for routine, day-to-day matters. The Tutor works together with the Housemaster/mistress or House Parent to provide pastoral and academic support and development, including advice on GCSE or A Level option choices, UCAS applications and references, and ensuring that pupils balance and manage their activities and commitments.

Admission. The majority of boys and girls enter at the age of 13, and candidates are selected on the basis of interviews, examinations and a Head's reference.

Pre-testing is offered in Year 6 for unconditional places at Year 9 (13+) entry. For Year 6 Track candidates, the test is a computer-based assessment of aptitude in reading comprehension, verbal, non-verbal and numerical reasoning. Results are age-standardised, enabling us to accurately compare candidates born at different times of the year. Only chance vacancies apply to Year 8 Track prospective 13+ pupils, with candidates registering their interest in the Autumn Term and a waiting list being drawn up based on computer-based assessment.

Scholarship candidates are identified through entrance tests in English, Mathematics, Science, French and Latin. Candidates are called back for interviews on the basis of their scores. Single-subject awards may be made. Awards are also made for Art, Music, Drama, Sports and Design Technology.

There are two other methods of entry:

(a) A limited number of places may be available at 14+. Candidates are selected on the basis of interview, performance in the 14+ Entrance Examinations (English, Maths, Science and French) and a Head's reference.

(b) Sixth Form Entry: Admission to the Sixth Form is based on an entry requirement of five GCSE passes, at least two at Grade 7 plus three at Grade 6, together with at least Grade 6 in Mathematics and English, or equivalent qualifications or written examinations for overseas pupils, as appropriate. More detailed entry requirements for specific A Level courses are given in the school's Sixth Form Curriculum Guide. Candidates unable to offer the range or number of subjects required (e.g. some overseas candidates) will be considered on their individual academic merit.

Selection is made on the basis of an interview or an examination in each of the subjects the pupil wishes to take at A Level, a general interview with a senior member of the school, and a reference from the candidate's present school. Offers made are conditional on meeting the entry requirements detailed above. International candidates are interviewed either in person or online. All pupils with English as a second language will be asked to sit an EAL paper and a spoken English interview. Scholarships are awarded on the basis of examinations and interviews in January.

Pastoral Care. The Mill Hill School Foundation and its staff are committed to safeguarding the welfare and safety of children. This has long been recognised as a strength within its community, with pupils being supported throughout their school career in an environment that is caring, supportive and understanding of the challenges of adolescence.

In the school's most recent full ISI Inspection in 2020, the overall quality of pastoral care was rated as 'Excellent', and genuine pride is taken in maintaining and developing this aspect as a real strength of the school as a whole. The report also portrayed teachers and tutors as 'knowing their pupils very well' and described pupils' behaviour as 'showing a high degree of maturity'. The provision of boarding was also rated as 'Excellent', and the school received praise for providing a 'lively, supportive and caring environment that allows boarders to grow in confidence, independence and sensitivity to the needs of others, in line with its aims'. The diverse make-up of the school was also recognised as a strength, and the report noted that 'pupils of all nationalities work most effectively with one another' and that they 'respect and value the cultural diversity within their school.'

Mill Hill School believes that wellbeing can simply be defined as being well in body, mind and spirit, acknowledging that achieving such a state is difficult and maintaining it is even harder, especially when dealing with the day-to-day pressures and expectations from peers, family members, teachers, exams and social media. With this in mind, they have created numerous support avenues for their pupils to access to assist them in keeping themselves mentally and physically well. All pupils are educated on how best to look after both their physical and mental health throughout their time at the school, with a focus on wellbeing embedded into all that they do, from PSHE, the Tutor Programme, assemblies and Chapel to whole school initiatives such as 'Wellbeing Week.' Pupils also have access to the Wellbeing Wing; a quiet space to go during the day should they need a moment away from the hustle and bustle of a busy school day.

Another particularly notable element of Mill Hill's pastoral care is the wide range of dynamic Pupil Councils, who meet regularly to discuss areas such as anti-bullying, mentoring, boarding, charity, environmental issues, food,

Fourth Form (new Year 9 pupils), inter-faith and Sixth Form specific issues. In addition, there is a Full School Council, which offers pupils an opportunity for their voices to be heard on key whole-school issues.

There are three School Counsellors, all of whom are qualified Child and Adolescent Psychotherapists.

Curriculum. The School's academic curriculum is broad, flexible and forward-looking and is designed to encourage among pupils intellectual curiosity, sound learning and a spirit of enquiry in the pursuit of academic excellence. It seeks to enable pupils to acquire core knowledge and skills in English, Mathematics, Science and a Modern Language and, in addition, to develop their own particular academic interests. It also incorporates a full programme of Personal, Social and Health Education, appropriate guidance and information for pupils on subject choices, higher education and careers. Detailed information on the curriculum for each Key Stage is set out in a series of three curriculum guides, which are available on the School website and from the Admissions Office.

Provision for Pupils with Special Educational Needs and/or Disabilities (SEND) and Learning Difficulties and/or Disabilities (LDD). The school provides those pupils with SEND or LDD with support to meet their individual needs and to help ensure the pupils reach their potential. The Learning Support Department plays a key role in this work, seeking to identify, through screening and ongoing monitoring, the particular needs of individual pupils and putting in place strategies and, where necessary, additional support designed to help them fulfil their potential. Where a pupil has an Education Health Care Plan (EHCP), the requirements of the EHCP are closely followed in order to ensure the school provides an effective and accessible educational experience. The progress of all pupils on the school's Learning Support Register is regularly reviewed and support is amended as appropriate.

Academic and Careers Guidance. Through the tutor system, presentations and information evenings, pupils are helped to make the best possible choices of GCSE and Sixth Form courses and to make well-informed and appropriate higher education choices. In the Sixth Form the School arranges visits to universities, as well as presentations, workshops and information evenings. The School has a full-time Head of University and Post-School guidance and an active Careers Department which provides information and advice on possible future careers paths. Careers Education is included within the School's Personal, Social, Health and Religious Education programme, and careers interviews are arranged for pupils in the Fifth Form (Year 11) and in the Lower Sixth, and also on request for other pupils.

Pupils with English as an Additional Language. EAL pupils are prepared for IGCSE English as a Second Language in Remove and the Fifth Form (Years 10 and 11). IELTS is taken in the Lower Sixth. Individual EAL tuition, in addition to class lessons, can be arranged if required. Cross-curricular support is also offered if requested by a pupil or subject teacher. For pupils whose first language is not English, EAL support is provided as appropriate, to enable them to maximise their academic opportunities and to enjoy all of the social and cultural aspects of life at the School. Some EAL pupils follow a modified curriculum in order to accommodate their needs.

Academic Enrichment. The school prides itself on offering a diverse array of opportunities for pupils to pursue their curiosity and extend their knowledge and skills outside the formal curriculum. There is a wealth of subject societies operating in both the Lower School (Years 9–11) and in the Sixth Form. Academic departments enter pupils of all ages for external competitions, such as essay prizes in Humanities and Classics, Olympiads in Science subjects and national debating competitions for Modern Languages. A number of current and past pupils have held Arkwright Engineering Scholarships. Sixth Form pupils can opt for the Extended Project Qualification. The school uses its proximity to central London to take pupils to lectures, plays, concerts, exhibitions and special events. There is a wide variety of academic trips on offer, such as Modern Languages exchanges and study visits to many destinations in Europe, Art trips to New York and the Venice Biennale, Design Technology trips to the Centre for Alternative Technology in mid-Wales, Geography field trips to Iceland.

Art, Drama and Music. The Creative Arts have a long and successful tradition at Mill Hill and are a key part of the academic curriculum. In addition to achieving excellent results in public examinations, relevant academic departments have a high success rate in preparing students for further study in the Arts.

Alongside academic successes, there is a substantial and varied programme of co-curricular activities in these subjects. The Art Department offers facilities and expertise for pupils to develop their interest and skills in painting and drawing, alternative media, film, illustration, multimedia, photography (including digital photography), printmaking, sculpture, textiles, theatre design and video.

In addition to the extensive range and number of Drama performances relating to examination courses, there is a biennial Inter-House Drama Festival, which alternates with the biennial Inter-House Music Festival; both attract a high level of pupil participation. There is a regular programme of school plays, ranging from Shakespeare to musicals. The school's musical ensembles include an orchestra, wind band, string ensemble, two jazz bands, four choirs and numerous ad hoc pupil bands and chamber ensembles. Individual tuition in most instruments and in singing is available from high-quality specialist teachers. There is an extensive programme of concerts, competitions, and recitals throughout the year, some of which include recitals by professional performers.

Sport. Mill Hill School is renowned for its sporting excellence, aiming to equip Millhillians for a healthy life now and in the future. We achieve this through our dual stream approach; Fit for Performance and Fit for Life. Every pupil, regardless of physical ability or experience, is encouraged to participate in both competitive and non-competitive sport and activities. The core sports for boys are rugby, hockey, football and cricket, and for girls are hockey, netball, cricket, rounders and tennis. Elective sport opportunities include athletics, badminton, basketball, cross country, Eton Fives, golf, horse riding, soccer, swimming, table tennis, triathlon and volleyball. For our most able pupils, we run an innovative Sports Scholarship programme where pupils have access to our Performance Department, which includes a full-time Physiotherapist, Nutritionist, Mental Skills Coach and two Strength & Conditioning Coaches. Junior Sports Scholars work alongside the Performance Department during their time-tabled sessions in the week, whilst our Senior Sports Scholars have their own individual mentors who work with them on a one-to-one basis, designing individual programmes and workshops.

There is a range of awards and Bursaries (including full Bursaries) available for talented sporting pupils, designed to supplement our home-grown talent. Through our continued commitment to delivering an outstanding coaching provision, and our drive for pupil progression, we have developed a unique portfolio of partnerships with professional clubs and coaches across many of our sports. Our impressive list of full-time coaches includes an England & Mavericks netball player, Saracens Premiership rugby player, Middlesex County Cricket Coach, Tottenham Hotspur Premiership Academy Coaches, Great Britain Hockey Coach, Great Britain athlete, and PGA Advanced Golf Pro, alongside our club partnerships, which include Saracens Rugby, Middlesex Cricket, Hampstead & Westminster Hockey Club and Tottenham Hotspur FC. The links our pupils have with professional players and coaches ensures that they receive the highest level of support, driving innovation and collaboration.

The school's facilities are both extensive and impressive; they include: a modern sports complex incorporating a recently refurbished indoor sports hall; indoor cricket nets; a fully-equipped fitness suite and conditioning centre. There is also a newly laid floodlit AstroTurf; 25 metre swimming pool; three fives courts; six outdoor tennis courts; four netball courts; an indoor golf teaching suite incorporating a golf simulator and an outdoor golf centre; and numerous cricket, football and rugby pitches across the 120-acre site.

Co-curricular Activities. The Fourth Form (Year 9) pupils are introduced to the range of core and elective sports (as above), and take part in a six-week programme designed specifically for new pupils to fully integrate in the school and participate in aspects of adventure training. All pupils are also offered a range of over 200 other activities, include Debating, extensive Drama and Music opportunities, Computing and many more. In the Remove (Year 10) the focus is teamwork and leadership. Pupils choose from a number of options including the CCF (Army, Navy and RAF), Duke of Edinburgh Award, Sports Leaders programme, Charity, Sustainability and Business Enterprise. In addition, there are many societies to cater for a variety of out-of-school interests.

Fees per term (2021–2022). Day (including lunch) £7,610, Full Boarding £12,300, Weekly Boarding £10,380. Fees include additional charges for curriculum expenses and additional contributions towards basic sports trips and visits.

Scholarships and Bursaries. Scholarships, which attract a maximum of 10% fee remission in total, are available to pupils showing exceptional talent in a variety of areas, both in the classroom and on the sports field. Academic, Music, Drama, Art, Design Technology, and Sports Awards are available at 13+ and Academic Scholarships are available to candidates entering the Sixth Form. In addition to major awards, there are a number of minor awards or exhibitions on offer.

Bursaries are available for those entrants able to demonstrate a financial need. Parents will be asked to complete a detailed statement of their financial circumstances. Applicants for Bursaries will be selected through the normal admissions process. There is provision for the award of full-fee Bursaries for entrants at all levels. It is possible for Bursary funds to be used to top up Scholarship Awards. As with Scholarship queries, the Head, Deputy Head or the Assistant Head (External Relations) & Registrar are happy to offer advice.

There are also various special Scholarships and Bursaries available, further information of which may be found on the school's website: millhill.org.uk.

Charitable status. The Mill Hill School Foundation is a Registered Charity, number 1064758.

Court of Governors:

Chair of Governors: Mr E Lipton BSc Hons, MBA, FRSA, FRICS

Vice Chair of the Court of Governors: Mrs S J Miller, BA Hons

Governors:

Professor E W F W Alton, MA, MB, BS, MD, FRCP, FHEA, FERS, FMedSci

Mrs C Avery, MA Oxon

Mr Simon Bayliss, BSc Hons, PGCE, MSc

Mr K A Doble, BA, PDM, PGCE, FRSA

Mr P Dunleavy, BA Hons, CISSP-ISSAP, CISM, CDPO, MBCS

Mr R A Eliott Lockhart, MA, MPhil

Mr A Millet, BA, MBA, FCA

Mrs M Moore, MSc Dist, BA Hons, FCIPD

Mr N Nihat

Dr K O'Neill-Byrne, BA Hons, MB, BCh, BAO, Dip Clin Psych, FRCPsych

Mrs M Patel, MBA

Mr M Skelly, BEng Hons, PhD, RAEngVTF

Mrs S Stoneham, LLB Hons, LPC

Clerk to the Court of Governors: Mrs M Bassingthwaite, BA Hons

CEO of The Mill Hill School Foundation: Mr Antony Spencer, MA Oxon

Director of Operations: Mr Sean Ryan, MSc

Director of Finance and Resources: Mrs Nicky Marlow, BA, ACA

Head: Mrs Jane Sanchez, BSc

Deputy Head (Academic): Mrs Sam Bernstein, BSc

Deputy Head (Pastoral): Mr James Dickin, BEd, MPS

Assistant Head (Sixth Form): Mr John Barron, BSc, MA

Assistant Head (External Relations) & Registrar: Mr Anthony Binns, BA

Assistant Head (Pupil Development & Wellbeing): Miss Jade Boyle, BA

Assistant Head (Staff Development & Wellbeing): Dr Adam Morton, BSc, MEd, PhD

Assistant Head (Teaching and Learning): Mr Luke Stubbles, MSc

Assistant Head (Co-Curricular and Sports): Mr Tom Vercoe, BSc, MA

Foundation Head of Boarding: Mr John Taylor, MA, FRSA

Head, Mill Hill International: Ms Sarah Bellotti, BEd

Head, Belmont: Mr Leon Roberts, MA

Head, Grimsdell: Mrs Kate Simon, BA

Millfield

Street, Somerset BA16 0YD

Tel: 01458 442291
email: generaloffice@millfieldschool.com
website: millfieldschool.com
Twitter: @millfieldsenior
Facebook: @MillfieldSchool

The school was founded in 1935 by R J O Meyer with the philanthropic aim of using its resources to generate places for boys who were gifted but not wealthy. The school became co-educational in 1939. Millfield's vision is to be leading the global arena for the development of children, offering an environment where students are immersed in limitless academic, artistic and sporting opportunities and individually supported to discover their brilliance. Set in over 100 acres of grounds, the facilities are unmatched in the UK: an Olympic-sized swimming pool, an Indoor Equestrian Centre, stabling for 53 horses, a 500-seat Theatre, golf courses, an art gallery and a music school complex housing the 350-seat Johnson Concert Hall. State-of-the-art cricket and golf centres opened in Spring 2020.

The school is fully co-educational with approximately 1,300 students, 57% boys and 43% girls; 75% of whom are boarders.

Housing. There are 16 single-sex, Year 10 to Upper Sixth, boarding houses. Most Sixth Formers have their own rooms whilst younger students share either in pairs or fours. As part of the Nine at Millfield programme, Year 9 have dedicated boarding and day houses. All Year 9 houses lie in the heart of the campus and have a higher staff to student ratio to oversee every aspect of each student's well-being and academic progress. There are four day houses for Year 10 to Upper Sixth; they have their own base on site and may stay in the evenings to do supervised prep.

The Curriculum. We have a broad, unrivalled choice for GCSE, BTEC and A level options.

All students entering Year 9 (at age 13), regardless of ability, study English, Mathematics, three Sciences, at least one language, Art, Design and Technology, IT, Food and Nutrition, Geography, History, Religious Studies, Physical Education and Music. The student to teacher ratio is 6.5:1. Students have a structured co-curricular programme.

In Years 10 and 11, students follow courses leading to GCSEs in the core subjects of English, Mathematics, Science and a Modern Language. In addition, there is a wide choice of options: Art & Design, Business Studies, Chinese, Computer Science, BTEC Tech Award in Digital Information Technology, Drama, Economics, BTEC Tech Award in Enterprise, Food & Nutrition, French, Geography, German, History, BTEC in Digital Information Technology, Italian, Latin, Music, Physical Education, Product Design, Religious Studies and Spanish. The Learning Support Centre provides individual support for all students in need of this.

At Sixth Form level, a wide range of A Level subjects are on offer. These include Art, Biology, Business, Chemistry, Chinese Mandarin, Drama, Economics, English Literature, French, Further Mathematics, Hospitality and Catering, Geography, German, Politics, History, IT, Italian, Latin, Mathematics, Media Studies, Music, Philosophy, Physical

Education, Physics, Product Design, Psychology, Religious Studies and Spanish. Also on offer are the vocational courses of BTEC Business and BTEC Enterprise and Entrepreneurship (both equivalent to two A Levels), BTEC National Diploma in Art & Design (equivalent to three A Levels), BTEC Diploma in Sport (equivalent to two A Levels), Leiths Introductory Certificate and the British Horse Society Complete Horsemanship certificate. Most students will study three A Level courses (or the equivalent curriculum loading) in the Lower Sixth and continue with all of these courses into the Upper Sixth. Wider enrichment opportunities are available to all Sixth Formers. The curriculum offers breadth, depth and flexibility in course choice. Students are also prepared for STEP papers and Scholastic Aptitude tests for American Universities. English as an additional language (EAL) and Learning Support is available at all levels.

Sport and Activities. Millfield runs an unparalleled range of sports and activities to engage all students. Those in Years 9, 10 and 11 generally choose from one of the core games of the term, including athletics, basketball, cricket, dance, football, hockey, netball, riding, rugby and tennis depending on term and gender. In Sixth Form, the range extends to include all of the above plus badminton, canoeing, chess, clay shooting, climbing, karate, sailing, skiing, squash, trampolining, triathlon, and various fitness activities such as aerobics, pilates and yoga. Throughout the School, students may also specialise in one of our high-performing programmes including athletics, cricket, fencing, golf, modern pentathlon, squash, swimming and tennis.

Students in Years 9, 10 and Lower Sixth take part in the school's Activities Programme where they can further broaden their experiences through a choice of more than 100 activities, ranging from athletics and British Military Fitness to film clubs, dissection, lacrosse, beekeeping and falconry.

Fees per term (2021–2022). Boarding £13,785; Day £9,055.

Scholarships and Bursaries. Scholarships of up to 10% are awarded for exceptional talent in Academic, All-rounder, Art, Drama, Dance, Design & Innovation, Music and Sport. A limited number of Headmaster's Scholarships of up to 50% are also available. Where parental resources are limited, these may be augmented by means-tested bursaries of up to 100%.

Charitable status. Millfield is a Registered Charity, number 310283. Its aim is to provide independent boarding and day education for boys and girls, and to maintain an extensive system of bursary aid to gifted students or those in financial need.

Governors:

Chair of Governors: R Rudd

W Bushell	C Macdonald
R Clark	J Maudslay
Mrs N Della Valle	Mrs J Mitchell
Mrs F Dickens	D Pinto
S East	M Simon
R Exley	R Soluade
T Griffiths	R Tovey
Mrs K Griggs	O Welsby
C Harvey	P Warner
C Hirst	

Clerk to the Governors: Mrs R Summerhayes

Headmaster: **Gavin Horgan**, MA Oxon

Finance Director: Mrs M Johnson, BSc Hons, ACA
Deputy Head (*Academic*): Mrs A Haydon, BSc, MSc, PGCE
Deputy Head (*Pastoral*): Mrs K Weston, BSc Hons, MSc, PGCE
Assistant Head (*Academic*): Dr A Gutteridge, MPhil, PhD
Assistant Head (*Housing*): A Collins, BA, Dip, QTS
Assistant Head (*Sixth Form*): E James, BA Hons, MSc
Assistant Head (*Middle School*): R Furlong, BSc Hons, MEd, PGCE
Director of Sport: Dr S Drawer, MSc, PGCE, PhD
Registrar: J Postle, BA Hons, PGCE, FRSA
Head of Marketing: Mrs L Webb, BA Hons
Director of IT: G Henderson, BA Hons, MA

Heads of Department:
Art, Design & Technology: P Maxfield, BA Hons, PGCE
Biology: Mrs L McEwan, BSc
Chemistry: D Armour, BSc
Computing and ICT: M Shields, BSc Hons, PGCE
English as an Additional Language (*EAL*): H Winkley, MA
Economics: A Shaw, MA Oxon, PGCE
English, Drama and Media: J C Baddock, BA Hons
Equine Studies: D Anholt, BHSI HT
Geography: Miss A Starling, BA Hons, PGCE
History: A Arbuckle, MA Cantab, PGCE
Food and Nutrition: P Reeves, BA Hons, DTLLS, MA
Languages: M Nash, BA Hons, MA, ATCL, PGCE
Learning Support Centre: Ms J White, BSc Hons, MEd, QTS, PG Dip, MDG
Library: S Bull, BA, PGDE
Mathematics: Dr C Fiddes, BA Oxon, PhD
Music: M Cook, MA Music Cantab, PGCE Secondary Music
Physical Education: S Maddock, BA Hons, MEd
Physics: J Hudson, MA Hons Cantab, PGCE
Religious Studies: T Churchill, BA Hons, MA, PGCE
Sciences: Mrs R Landrigan, BA Hons, MA Oxon, PGCE

Houses and Housemasters/Housemistresses:

Boarding Houses:
Abbey: Mrs C Shelver
Acacia: Miss J Moore
Butleigh: Mrs E Watambwa
Etonhurst: Ms K Lloyd
Holmcroft: Mr R Owlett
Joan's Kitchen: Mr M Speyers
Keen's Elm: Mr and Mrs T Sawrey-Cookson
Kernick: Ms C Coutand-Moore
Kingweston: Mr D Askham
Martins: Ms C Garcia
Millfield: Miss E Tait
Orchards: Mr S Robertson
Portway: Mrs C Trainor
Shapwick: Mr T B Kingsford
St Anne's: Mr P Williams
Southfield: Ms T Allen
The Grange: Mr B Pender
Walton: Mr J Lewis
Warner: Mrs C Rose

Day Houses, Boys:
Great: Mr J Bishop
Mill: Mr G Catto

Day Houses, Girls:
Overleigh: Mrs A Brade
The Lakes: Mrs J Gray

Day House (*Year 9 Girls & Boys*):
Ivythorn: Mrs K Butt

Heads of Sport:
Director of Athletics: A Richardson, BA Hons, IAAF Level 5 Elite coach
Tutor i/c Badminton: K Lloyd, BSc
Head of Basketball: C Seeley
Director of Cricket: M Garaway, ECB Level 4 Coach
Master i/c Cross Country: J Allen
Director of Dance and Drama: R Fox
Director of Fencing: M Cleary
Head of Football: S Perkins
Director of Golf: K Nicholls, PGA/LET member
Director of Hockey: R Keates, HA Coach Level 2
Head of Karate: T Cheung, purple belt in Washinkai Karate and Kickboxing, blue belt in Shotokan karate
Director of Modern Pentathlon: T Parris, BAF Advanced Coach
Director of Netball: J Adamson
Director of Outdoor Adventure: N Mortley
Director of Equestrian Sport (*Riding & Polo*): D O Anholt, BHSI, HT
Director of Rugby: J A Mallett, RFU Level 4
Skiing: L Beaumont
Director of Squash: I Thomas, High Performance Coach
Director of Swimming: E Dale, BSc
Director of Tennis: L Beaumont
Head of Trampolining: J Boyd
Master i/c Triathlon: P Guthrie, BTF Level 3 Cert Coaching

Monkton Combe School

Monkton Combe, Bath BA2 7HG

Tel:	01225 721102
email:	admissions@monkton.org.uk
website:	www.monktoncombeschool.com
Twitter:	@MonktonBath
Facebook:	@MonktonCombeSchool

Monkton Combe School, just a mile from the World Heritage City of Bath, is an independent, co-educational boarding and day school for pupils aged 2–18. We pride ourselves on our lively Christian ethos, excellent exam results and our strong pastoral care. At Monkton, we set standards for life; giving young people the qualities of character they need to become trusted employees, inspiring leaders and valued friends.

Organisation. The Prep School has its own Head and the Principal has overall responsibility for both schools.

(*For further details see Monkton Prep entry in IAPS section.*)

Number of pupils. *Senior*: 372 (215 boys, 157 girls); 211 of these are boarders and 135 are sixth formers.

Admission for those from a Prep school is usually via abilities test data or test, plus an assessment day during Year 6. A reference is sought from their existing school.

Admission at age 14 is by an abilities test, a reference from the candidate's current school and an interview.

For Year 12 entry, candidates usually sit an abilities test and attend an interview. A school reference will be sought and any place then offered is subject to pupils obtaining an average score of at least 6 in all GCSE subjects taken. Progression to Year 13 depends upon a satisfactory performance throughout Year 12. For certain A Levels, a minimum grade at GCSE in that subject may be a prerequisite.

Chapel. There is a full-time resident Anglican Chaplain. A short service is held three times each week. There is a Confirmation Service annually.

Houses. The three boys' Houses and three girls' Houses are all under the care of Houseparents, who, together with the Tutors, are responsible for the pupils' general welfare. Day Pupils are fully integrated into boarding house life.

Tutor System. Each pupil has a Tutor who keeps in touch with parents and provides guidance and advice.

Curriculum. There is a broad-based curriculum in the years leading to GCSE.

In Year 9 all pupils study English, Mathematics and the Sciences with a foundation course normally comprising two Foreign Languages, Art, Design Technology, Drama, Geography, History, Information Technology, Music, PE and Religious Studies.

In Years 10 and 11 pupils study core subjects of English, Mathematics and usually two Sciences and can choose up to six additional optional subjects from a list of 18.

In the Sixth Form 28 subjects are offered. All pupils take the Extended Project Qualification. A notable feature of the Sixth Form programme is a wide variety of lectures and presentations delivered by visiting speakers.

University. Over 80% of leavers go to their first-choice university, including Oxford, Cambridge, UCL, Edinburgh, Durham, Exeter and Warwick.

Sport. The major sports are Rugby, Hockey, Netball, Cricket, Rowing and Tennis. Other sports include: Athletics, Badminton, Basketball, Cross-Country, Football, Golf, Swimming and Squash.

The School has extensive playing fields, an all-weather AstroTurf for Hockey and Tennis, Boathouses on the River Avon, 3 Netball Courts, 18 Tennis Courts, a covered Rifle Range, a Rowing Tank, 2 Squash Courts, a Sports Centre, 25m indoor pool and Fitness Centre.

CCF and Community Service. There are sections for all three Services, as well as Bronze and Gold Duke of Edinburgh's Award and an active Community Service group.

Leisure All School facilities are available to pupils during their free time. There is a Choir, Orchestra, Jazz band and other music groups and tuition is available in all orchestral instruments. There is a School drama production in the Michaelmas and Lent Terms and concert and theatre trips to nearby Bath and Bristol. The 30 clubs and societies include Outdoor Education, the Literary Society and a popular Christian Union, attended by 70–100 pupils weekly.

Scholarships are awarded on entry to the School for candidates at Year 9 and 12. The Principal reserves the right to award up to two Year 10 Scholarships. All awards are conditional on a continued contribution to the area of School life recognised in the award.

Bursaries are given to pupils who would otherwise not be able to come to the School. Special consideration is given to the children of clergy and missionaries.

Fees per term (2021–2022). Senior: £10,315–£11,670 (boarders); £6,960–£7,315 (day).

Old Monktonian Club. Details from the School Development Office.

Charitable status. Monkton Combe School is a Registered Charity, number 1057185. Its aims and objectives are to provide education for girls and boys combined with sound religious training on Protestant and Evangelical principles in accordance with the doctrines of The Church of England.

Governors:

Chair: Prof H Langton, RGN, RSCN, ACNT, RNT, BA Hons, MSc

Revd S Barnes, BA QTS Hons, MA, Cert BA

Mrs R Coates, BA Hons

C B Fillingham, MA

Mrs E S K Hubbard, BA Hons

A Lyttle

Mrs J J Perry, BPharm Hons, MRPharmS, Dip Clin Pharm

R J Pringle, BSc Hons

A Reid, MA, PGCE, NPQH

D Rosser, BSc Hons, MRICS

E J J Shaw, BA Hons

M Thomas, CMG

Mrs M White, MA, PGCE

S B M Young, BA, FCA, ACA

Senior Leadership:

Principal: **Mr C J Wheeler**, BA Dunelm, PGCE, FRSA

Head of Prep: Mrs C Winchcombe, BEd Hons, MA Ed

Vice Principal: Mr J Goodman, MA Oxon, PGCE

Bursar: Mr J Kempton

Monmouth School for Boys

Almshouse Street, Monmouth, Monmouthshire NP25 3XP

Tel: 01600 713143
email: boys.enquiries@habsmonmouth.org
website: www.habsmonmouth.org
Twitter: @Habsmonmouth
Facebook: @Habsmonmouth

Motto: *Serve and Obey*

Monmouth School for Boys guides day and boarding pupils aged 11–18 through this crucial stage of their educational and emotional development. We provide a positive, constructive and inspiring single-sex community from Years 7 to 11 within which boys thrive and flourish.

Monmouth Schools Sixth Form brings day and boarding boys and girls together at this final stage of their educational journey with us, recognising their greater maturity and focus.

The school was founded in 1614, by William Jones, a merchant of the City of London and a Liveryman of the Worshipful Company of Haberdashers, who was born near Monmouth and bequeathed a large sum of money to found a school and almshouses in the town.

The school has derived immense advantage from this unusual association with the City of London.

The school is controlled by a Board of Governors appointed variously by the Haberdashers' Company, the Universities of Oxford, Cambridge and Wales, and local representative bodies.

Mr James Murphy-O'Connor became the first overarching Principal of Haberdashers' Monmouth Schools in September 2019. Formerly Principal of Prior Park Schools in Bath, Mr Murphy-O'Connor's role has an emphasis on academic and co-curricular provision, marketing, fund-raising, outreach and community relations working with the three schools' heads to provide the best possible provision for pupils.

Through our unique Monmouth Model, our boys benefit from the invaluable interaction with Monmouth School for Girls, sharing many trips and expeditions, events and community projects.

Our boys' talents are nurtured and they make the most of the area's wonderful natural resources and the excellent facilities on offer for sports, culture and the arts.

There are approximately 500 boys in the senior school, of whom 140 are boarders. The fully co-educational Monmouth Prep School caters for 240 boys and girls aged 3 to 11, with boarding available at age 7. (*For further details see entry in IAPS section.*)

Facilities. Over the past decade, a new sports complex, a studio theatre, an all-weather pitch, a 500-seat theatre and a stunning sports pavilion have all been added to the suite of historic buildings.

A £2m upgrade of boarding at Monmouth saw a complete redevelopment of the largest house, Weirhead, while a new health and wellbeing centre was created in the summer of 2021.

The William Jones Building (opened to mark the 400th anniversary) provides excellent facilities in classrooms for maths, English and modern languages as well as a completely new reception and administration area. This move has allowed the school to release space to expand and further enhance the boarding accommodation.

Boarding. The boarding community forms the core of the school. Junior boarders (7–12 year olds) are accommodated in Chapel House for their first few years and benefit from the care of a dedicated house team who also provide an ambitious and popular programme of extra-curricular activities, tailored to the interests of the age group.

There are three middle-school boarding houses for boys between 13 and 17: New House (13–16 year olds); School House (14–17 year olds); and Weirhead (14–17 year olds). The school has a flexible boarding policy which provides a considerable degree of freedom for families to make boarding arrangements which fit in with their lives, but which encourages boys to take full advantage of the many sporting, cultural and extra-curricular activities for which the school is renowned.

September 2011 saw the opening of Buchanan House, a sixth form boarding house for boys aged 17–18, with single study-bedrooms and en-suite facilities

Admission. The main admission points are 7, 10, 11, 13 and 16, but other stages will be considered if places are available.

Due to current restrictions on social distancing, we are streamlining our whole entrance process, with the emphasis placed firmly on looking for potential not just test-performance.

Details of these new steps for academic assessments, scholarships and awards from: www.habsmonmouth.org/virtual-admissions/online-assessments

Candidates from overseas are welcome. Those whose first language is not English take a preliminary test of proficiency in English before proceeding to the appropriate entrance test.

The school accepts pupils with dyslexia or similar specific learning difficulties. They are taught in mainstream lessons and additional study support is available.

Curriculum. The curriculum is designed to provide both flexibility and breadth and to be in step with the National Curriculum without being constrained by it. Those in Years 7 and 8 study a wide range of subjects including Latin, French and combined science. In Year 9 the three sciences are taught separately and pupils have the option of starting Greek.

Pupils normally take 9 or 10 GCSE subjects, 4 of which are of their own choosing.

We offer a Foundation 1 Year GCSE course in up to 6 GCSEs including English, maths and the three sciences.

The school is enriched by close cooperation with Monmouth School for Girls in many areas of school life, especially at Sixth Form level. Co-educational teaching is offered from a range of 26 A Level subjects along with an enrichment programme.

A particular feature of the curriculum is the extensive range of Modern Languages. French is taught at all levels and Spanish and German are available from Form III.

The Chapel. The school is an Anglican foundation and the Chapel plays an important part in its life. All pupils attend Chapel at least once each week and there is a weekly service for boarders. A varied programme of preachers is organised, including clergy and lay people of many denominations. The Bishop of Monmouth officiates at the annual Confirmation Service.

Games. The main sports are rugby, rowing, cricket and soccer. Many other sports are also available at a highly competitive level including athletics, cross-country running, golf, softball, squash and swimming. Several members of staff have international sporting honours and pupils regularly gain places to represent Wales in a variety of sports.

Activities. There is an extensive programme of activities throughout the school. Pupils in Form IV and above may join the CCF (Army and RAF sections) which enjoy excellent links with locally based regular and territorial forces. Community Service is a popular option and many boys participate in the Duke of Edinburgh's Award scheme. There is a very strong musical tradition with many pupils taking part in choirs, orchestras and bands which achieve high levels of success in competitions, and play to appreciative audiences locally and on the regular overseas tours which take place. Drama is also strong and good opportunities are provided for participation at all levels. A wide range of school Clubs and Societies further enriches the life of the school.

Fees per term (2021–2022). Day £5,533, Boarding £10,489–£11,389; Monmouth Prep School: Day £2,648–£3,881, Boarding (Years 3–6) £6,999.

Scholarships and Bursaries. A number of Entrance Scholarships are normally awarded to day boys or boarders on the basis of performance in the Year 7 Entry Assessments (11+), on the Foundation Scholarship Examination (13+) held in the Lent Term, and the Sixth Form Scholarship Examination (16+) held in November. In cases of need, Scholarships may be augmented by a means-tested Bursary.

- *Music Scholarships and Exhibitions* may be awarded at 11, 13 and 16 and carrying free instrumental tuition. Sixth Form organ or instrumental scholarships are also available.

- *Sports Awards* are available to suitable candidates at 11, 13 and Sixth Form entry.

- *Headmaster's Awards* are available for candidates who show all-round ability and potential.

- *The E F Bulmer Award* is available to suitable Sixth Form candidates living in Herefordshire; awards range in value from 50% to 100% of the fees. A new Sixth Form Boarding Scholarship is available, which is means-tested and can cover up to 75% of the fees.

Family fee support, by way of a bursary, can provide up to 100% remission of fees, in certain circumstances.

Service Bursaries are available for the sons of serving members of HM Armed Forces, who are in receipt of the CEA and this guarantees that no more than the minimum 10% of fees is payable by parents.

To arrange an individual bespoke tour or for more details about the new steps for academic assessments, scholarships and bursaries, please contact the Admissions Registrar, Miss Ellie Townsend; Tel: 01600 710433, email: boys.admissions@habsmonmouth.org

Old Monmothians. Past members of the school are eligible to join the Old Monmothian Club which enjoys a close relationship with the school. The Membership Secretary is Roger Atkins, c/o Old Monmothians, Monmouth School for Boys, Almshouse Street, Monmouth NP25 3XP.

Charitable status. William Jones's Schools Foundation is a Registered Charity, number 525616. Its aims and objectives are to provide an all-round education for boys and girls at reasonable fees; also to carry out the Founder's intention that local boys qualifying for entry should not be prevented from attending the school by lack of funds.

Board of Governors:
Chairman of Governors: Mr A Twiston-Davies

Mr P Alderman	Mrs H Moriarty
Mrs E Ashford	Lord Moynihan
Mrs J Booth	Councillor R Roden
Professor R Carwardine	Mrs R Rose
Mrs S Clayton	Mrs L Russen
Mr T Haden-Scott	Mr N Waters
Dr S Honeywill	Dr R Weeks
Mr N Manns	Mr I de Weymarn
Mr R Miners	Mrs R Williams
Dr A Mohindru	

Clerk to the Governors: Mrs F Creasey, BCom, ACMA

Foundation Bursar: Mrs T Norgrove, MBA

Principal: Mr J Murphy-O'Connor, MA Oxon, PGCE

Headmaster: Mr S Dorman, MA Oxon, MPhil Belfast

Senior Deputy Head Pastoral: Mr D Edwards, BA Dunelm

Senior Deputy Head Academic: Professional Development:
  Mrs L Gregory, BA Reading
Senior Deputy Head Academic: Teaching & Learning: Mrs
  K Whiteman, MA Oxon
Director of Boarding (Assistant Head): Mr A Peace, BSc
  Wales
*Head of Academic Progress and Digital Learning
  (Assistant Head):* Mr D Evans, BA Coventry, MA Wales
Head of Wellbeing (Assistant Head): Miss S Fowler, BSc
  Swansea
Assistant Head Extra-Curricular Activities & Adventure:
  Mr G Stentiford, BSc, MSc Durham
Assistant Deputy Head (Academic): Dr E Evans BSc, PhD
  Cardiff

Chaplain: Revd C Swartz, BA Connecticut, MA Cantab

* *Head of Department*
† *Housemaster/Housemistress*

Assistant Staff:
Mrs E Aldridge, BSc
Mrs E Arrand, BA (**English*)
Miss E K Barson, BSc, MSc (**Biology*)
Mr J Bateman, LLB (†*Town House*)
Mr J Boiling, BA
Mr D Briggs, BSc
Mr C Bassett-Jones, BSc
Miss M Campos Moreno
Mrs J Cardenas, MSc, MA
Mr K Chaplin, BSc (†*Monmouth House*)
Mrs E Cole, BSc
Mrs A Copley, BEd, PGDipTOD
Mr P Daley, BA, MStud
Dr J Danks, BSc, DPhil (†*Dean House*)
Mrs G Davis, BA
Mr J Despontin, BSc, MSc
Dr E Evans, BSc, PhD
Dr H Evans, BSc, MSc, PhD (**Mathematics*)
Mr N Goodson, BSc
Miss L Goupil, BA, MA
Mr P Griffin, BA (**Drama*)
Mr J Griffiths, BSc
Miss J Griffiths, BSc
Mrs J Gunn, BA
Mrs D Harding, BSc
Dr J Harrison, BA, PhD (**History*)
Mr A Hawley, BA
Mrs S Holmes, BEd
Mr D Hope, BA (†*Weirhead House*)
Mrs L Hope (**ICT*)
Mrs I Evers-Jones, BA
Mrs J Johnston, MA
Mr A Jones, BA (**Director of Sport*)
Dr D Jones, MPhys, PhD (**Physics*)
Mr I Lawrence, BSc, MSc (†*Buchanan House*)
Mr D Lawson, BA, ARCO (**Director of Music and
  Organist*)
Mrs L Lewis, BA
Mr M Lewis, BA (†*School House*)
Mrs L Livingston, BA (†*Severn House*)
Mr K Madsen, BA (**Economics,* †*Glendower House*)
Mrs R Marsh, BSc
Mrs T Matthews, BA
Ms S Mone, BA (†*Chapel House*)
Mr P Morris, BEd (†*Wye House*)
Mr D Murray, MA
Dr D Ogborne, BSc, MSc, PhD

Ms K Owens, BA
Mrs L Parr, BEng, BSc
Mrs L Parsons, BA (**Modern Languages*)
Mrs G Peace, BA, MA (†*Tudor House*)
Mr M Peake, BA (**Art*)
Mr D Pearson, BSc
Mr R Picken, BA
Mr S Rentell, BA
Mr A Shakeshaft, BA
Mrs K Sixtus Staatsexamen
Mr G Stentiford, BSc, MSc (**Geography*)
Mr C Stonier, BSc
Mr M Tamplin, BSc (†*Hereford House*)
Mr P Vaughan-Smith, BA (†*New House*)
Miss L Watkins, BA
Mr A White, BA (**Design Technology*)
Mr R Whiteman, BA (**Classics*)
Mrs R Widdicks, BA (**Study Support*)
Mr O Williams, BSc, MA
Mr P Williams, BA
Dr A Winter, BSc, PhD (**Chemistry*)
Mrs R Wynne Lord, MA (**Religious Education*)

Mr O Morris, BA, PG Dip CG (**Head of Careers*)
Ms S Williams, BA (**Head of Libraries and Learning
  Resources*)
Mr N Davidson (**SSI CCF*)

Monmouth School for Girls

Hereford Road, Monmouth NP25 5XT

Tel: 01600 711100
email: girls.enquiries@habsmonmouth.org
website: www.habsmonmouth.org
Twitter: @Habsmonmouth
Facebook: @Habsmonmouth

  Motto: Serve and Obey

  Monmouth School for Girls is one of the schools of the
William Jones Foundation, arising from a bequest in 1614,
and administered by the Worshipful Company of
Haberdashers.

  Mr James Murphy-O'Connor became the first
overarching Principal of Haberdashers' Monmouth Schools
in September 2019. Formerly Principal of Prior Park
Schools in Bath, Mr Murphy-O'Connor's role has an
emphasis on academic and co-curricular provision,
marketing, fund-raising, outreach and community relations
working with the three schools' heads to provide the best
possible provision for pupils.

  Mrs Jessica Miles took over the headship at Monmouth
School for Girls in April 2019. She was formerly the Head
of Queen Margaret's School in York.

  The school guides day and boarding pupils aged 11–18
through this crucial stage of their educational and emotional
development.

  There are 465 girls in the senior school, including a Sixth
Form of 110. The fully co-educational Monmouth Prep
School caters for 240 boys and girls aged 3 to 11, with
boarding available at age 7. (*For further details see entry in
IAPS section.*)

A thriving boarding community with accommodation on the school site includes a junior house and modern senior house with study-bedrooms and Augusta House, the Sixth Form boarding facility, with 47 en-suite bedrooms.

Our girls thrive and flourish within a positive, constructive and inspiring single-sex community from Years 7 to 11, set in the outstanding natural beauty of the Wye Valley. Education is carefully planned to motivate girls; we deliver a broad choice of subjects, with teaching specifically tailored to their learning styles and subject choices free from any gender stereotyping.

Through our unique Monmouth Model, girls also benefit from the invaluable interaction with Monmouth School for Boys, sharing many trips and expeditions, events and community projects.

Understanding the pressures of adolescence, our focused approach prepares girls for Sixth Form, where they have the confidence to aim high in their specialist academic subjects and to fulfil their particular sporting, musical or artistic ambitions. Monmouth Schools Sixth Form brings day and boarding boys and girls together at this final stage of their educational journey with us, recognising their greater maturity and focus. We offer the benefits of pastoral care within a co-educational academic environment.

Monmouth girls develop a can-do attitude and make the most of the superb facilities on offer for sports, culture and the arts. Full use is made of the ample sports facilities: spacious playing fields, all-weather pitch, tennis courts, indoor swimming pool and sports hall. All are adjacent to the school.

Main sporting activities include, netball, softball, rowing, fencing, hockey, dance and equestrian. Many girls play at County, National and International level. A newly established tennis academy makes the most of the impressive site.

A purpose-built Performing Arts Centre, housed over three floors, opened in Autumn 2018. This state-of-the-art facility replaced the old gymnasium and is linked to the existing theatre at stage and hall level. A new home to the music department and with a dance and drama studio on the top floor, it features a recital hall with space for an audience of up to 150 people and includes a viewing gallery.

The school has a Chaplain and is a Christian foundation. Girls are encouraged to attend the places of worship of their own denomination.

We teach classics throughout the school. At examination level, we offer Latin at GCSE and A Level, and Classical Civilisation at A Level. Classical Greek is offered by request as an extra-curricular activity. The school excels in a variety of STEM programmes, gaining many accolades in 'The Big Bang' and ESSW competitions.

Almost all our pupils progress to Higher Education. With excellent careers advice, girls are aware of the scope of degree subjects. More than 60% of our girls gain places annually at Russell Group universities, including Oxford and Cambridge.

We encourage creative and practical work, especially music and drama. Girls frequently attend concerts, plays and exhibitions, and take an active interest in industry and management. Local businesses lend support to the school's Young Enterprise schemes.

Girls participate in the Duke of Edinburgh's Award scheme, Combined Cadet Force, overseas expeditions and community projects and many also belong to local voluntary organisations.

Fees per term (2021–2022). Senior School: Day £5,169–£5,533, Boarding £10,122–£11,389. Monmouth Prep School: Day £2,648–£3,881, Boarding (Years 3–6) £6,999.

Entry Entry is usually at 7, 11, 13 or post GCSE, although occasionally other vacancies occur. Informal assessments for entry at 7+ to Monmouth School Girls' Prep are normally held in the Lent term. Entry to the senior school is normally by examination, interview and report from the current school. The interviews and entrance examinations are normally held for 11+ in January, 13+ in February/March (or Common Entrance Examination in June), and for 16+ in November.

Due to current restrictions on social distancing, we are streamlining our whole entrance process, with the emphasis placed firmly on looking for potential not just test-performance.

Details of these new steps for academic assessments are available from: www.habsmonmouth.org/virtual-admissions/online-assessments

Scholarships and Bursaries. A number of academic scholarships are normally awarded at 11+, 13+ and 16+ to the best candidates on the basis of the school's entrance examination, interview and report from the current school. Music scholarships, also available at 11+, 13+ and 16+, are normally awarded on the basis of audition and interview held in the Lent term for 11+ and 13+ and the Michaelmas term for 16+.

Sport and Dance scholarships are available at 11+, 13+ and 16+ entry and are normally awarded on the basis of assessment and interview, held in the Lent term for 11+ and 13+, and Michaelmas term for 16+. Creative Arts (art and drama) scholarships are normally awarded following an assessment day held at the school in the Lent term for 13+ and the Michaelmas term for 16+.

Means-tested Bursaries and Assisted Places of up to 100% of fees are also available at all entry points.

To arrange an individual bespoke tour or for more details about the new steps for academic assessments, scholarships and bursaries, please contact the Admissions Registrar, Mrs Karen Stafford-Smith; Tel: 01600 711104, email: girls.admissions@habsmonmouth.org.

Charitable status. William Jones's Schools Foundation is a Registered Charity, number 525616. The object of the Foundation shall be the provision and conduct in or near Monmouth of a day and boarding school for boys and a day and boarding school for girls.

Board of Governors:
Chairman of Governors: Mr A W Twiston-Davies

Mr P Alderman	Mrs H Moriarty
Mrs E Ashford	Lord Moynihan
Mrs J Booth	Councillor R Roden
Professor R Carwardine	Mrs R Rose
Mrs S Clayton	Mrs L Russen
Mr T Haden-Scott	Mr N Waters
Dr S Honeywill	Dr R Weeks
Mr N Manns	Mr I de Weymarn
Mr R Miners	Mrs R Williams
Dr A Mohindru	

Clerk to the Governors: Mrs F Creasey, BCom, ACMA

Foundation Bursar: Mrs T Norgrove, MBA

Principal: Mr J Murphy-O'Connor, MA Oxon, PGCE

Head: Mrs J Miles, MA Oxon, PGCE

Senior Deputy Head Pastoral: Mrs R Rees, BA Hons Manchester, PGCE

Senior Deputy Head Academic: Mrs K Whiteman, MA Oxon, PGCE

Head of Academic Progress and Digital Learning (Assistant Head): Mr D R Evans, BA Hons Coventry, MA Wales, PGCE

Director of Sixth Form (Assistant Head): Mrs G Peace, BA Hons Belfast, MA

Director of Boarding (Assistant Head): Mr A Peace, BSc Hons Wales

Head of Wellbeing (Assistant Head): Mrs S Fowler, BSc Swansea

Chaplain: Reverend C Swartz, BA Hons Trinity College, Connecticut, Anglican Ministry Training Cambridge, MA Cambridge

Art:
*Mr C Beer, BA, PGCE
Miss C Rushe, BA, PGCE

Business Studies:
*Miss M C Attrill, BTEC Dip Business Studies, Cert Ed

Careers:
Mr O Morris, BA, PgDipCG, Head of Careers
Mrs D Gray, BSc, Careers

Classics/Latin:
*Mrs L J Beech, BA, PGCE
Dr C Geisz, BA ICES, MA, PhD

Computing:
*Mr J Childs, BEng, PGCE
Mrs L Partridge, BA

Economics:
*Miss M C Atrill, BTEC Dip Business Studies, Cert Ed
Mr D Evans, BA, PGCE

English and Drama:
*Mrs Z Harvey, BA, PGCE
Ms K Bourne, BA, PGCE
Mrs J Harper, BSc, PGCE
Ms J Knight, BA, MA, PGCE
Mr D Murray, MA, PGACA RWCMD
Mr S Riordan, Professional Acting FdA
Mr A Shakeshaft, BA
Dr R Thompson, BA, MA, PGCE, PhD
Ms S White, BA, PGCE

Ethics and Philosophy:
*Miss J Johnson, BSc, PGCE
Dr H Whately, PhD, PGCE, MA, MSc, BA
Reverend C Swartz, BA, MA
Mrs M Wilkes, BA, PGCE

Geography:
*Mr N Meek, BA, MA, PGCE, MEd
Mrs J Harper, BSc, PGCE
Mr S Rentell, BA, PGCE

History:
*Mr M Seaton, BA, PGCE
Mr P Grant, BA, PGCE
Mrs K Whiteman, MA, PGCE

Mathematics:
*Mr A Skailes, BSc, PGCE
Miss J Griffiths, BSc, PGCE
Dr S Lawlor, BSc, PhD, PGCE
Mrs J Morris, BSc, PGCE
Mrs V Price, BSc Ed
Mrs C Skailes, BEng, PGCE, PhD

Modern Languages:
*Mrs H Smail, MA, PGCE
*Mrs H English, BA, PGCE
Mr D Edwards, BA
Mrs A Hutchings, BA, PGCE (*French & German*)
Mrs R Jenkins, MA, PGCE (*Spanish*)
Mrs R Rees, BA, PGCE (*French & German*)
Mrs C Takeuchi, MA, PGCE (*French*)
Mrs K Wellings BA, PGCE
Miss S Williams, BA MA

Music:
*Mr D Harris, GRSM Hons, DipRCM Advanced/Teachers, PGCE
Mrs R Friend, LRAM, LRAM TD

Personal, Social and Health Education:
*Ms K Bourne, BA, PGCE

Psychology:
*Mrs K Smith, BSc, Dip Teaching
Miss J Johnson, BSc, PGCE

Science:
*Miss L Woodburn, BSc, PGCE (*Science & Biology*)
*Miss D Crichton, BSc, PGCE (*Chemistry*)
*Mr G Dunn, BSc, MSc, PGCE (*Physics*)
Mrs D Clarke, BSc, PGCE (*Chemistry*)
Mr M Coffey, BSc
Mr P Jefferies
Ms C Levick, BA, PGCE (*Biology*)
Mrs V Lyons, BSc, PGCE (*Biology*)
Mrs H Moreby, BSc, PGCE (*Physics*)
Mrs C Natt, BSc, PGCE, MA Ed (*Biology*)
Mr A Peace, BSC
Mrs C Skailes, BEng, PGCE, PhD
Dr D Watson, MChem, PhD (*Chemistry*)
Mr I Westlake, BSc, PGCE

Speech & Drama:
Mrs A Baker, B Phil Cert Ed
Mr D Murray, MA, PGACA RWCMD
Mr A Shakeshaft, BA

Sport, Physical Education & Dance:
*Mrs C Jones, BSc, MSc, GTP
*Ms R Parry, BA, PGCE (*Dance*)
*Mrs K A Callaghan, BA (*Rowing*)
Mr R Fletcher (*Rowing Coach & Boatman*)
Mrs R Harris, BSc, PGCE
Mrs S Morgan, BSc, PGCE
Ms Z Pritchard, Teaching Certificate Royal Academy of Dance, Teaching Associate Imperial Society of Teachers of Dance, Dip Dance Education
Mrs S Rossiter, BSc
Mr K Williams, BA, IPGCE (*Rowing Coach*)
Mrs S Wilson, BA, PGCE
Mr D Wood BA

Technology:
*Mr S McCluskey, BSc, PGCE
Mrs K Lewis, BEng, PGCE
Mrs R Nieuwoudt, BSc, PGCE

Mr P Williams, BSc, QTS

Learning Support:

Mrs J Jefferies, BEd, PGCE Specific Learning Difficulties
Gloucestershire

Mrs C Bown, Joint Hons English and French Literature,
PGCE

Miss T May, BA, PGCE, MA

Mrs M Dorman, BSc, PGCE, PG Dip

MG CCF Contingent Commander: Mr D Edwards, BA

Moreton Hall

Weston Rhyn, Oswestry, Shropshire SY11 3EW

Tel:	01691 773671
email:	admin@moretonhall.com
website:	www.moretonhall.org
Twitter:	@moretonhall
Facebook:	@moretonhall

One of the UK's highest achieving schools, Moreton Hall was founded in 1913 by Ellen Lloyd-Williams (Aunt Lil) in Oswestry and moved to its present location in 1920. In 1964, the school became an educational trust. Although the school is predominantly boarding, a number of day pupils are admitted each year.

Member of HMC, GSA, The Society of Heads, IAPS, and AGBIS.

Admission. Moreton Hall Prep is the preparatory school of Moreton Hall, sharing not only its extensive facilities but also a commitment to nurture and celebrate the talents of each child. Moreton Hall Prep takes girls and boys from Transition (age 3) to Year 6 and offers a unique start to their education, ensuring academic rigour goes hand in hand with encouragement to achieve success in all creative and sporting fields.

Girls and boys are admitted to Moreton Hall, normally in September at age 11 by the School's entrance examination which is held at the end of January each year. This examination requires no knowledge of foreign languages and is designed to test potential ability rather than factual recall. This examination can be taken by pupils at 10+, with supplementary papers at 12 and 13. Sixth Form entrance is by entrance examination, current school report and interview, and numbers are limited. All applications should be addressed to the Principal.

Though predominantly boarding, day pupils are welcomed. Boys may board from the age of 8–13.

Scholarships and Bursaries. A number of Academic scholarships worth up to 20% of fees will be awarded to pupils at ages 11+, 12+, 13+ and 16+. Scholarships for Music, Drama, Art and for outstanding sporting talent are also available. Pupils may apply for more than one scholarship. Means-tested bursaries may be awarded up to the value of 100% of fees.

Fees per term (2021–2022). Boarders: £8,190 (Moreton Hall Prep), £11,910 (Years 7 and 8), £12,590 (Years 9–13). Day pupils: £3,550–£5,045 (Moreton Hall Prep), £9,570 (Years 7 and 8), £10,360 (Years 9–13).

Curriculum. Going well beyond the National Curriculum, some 20 subjects are available at GCSE, varying from traditional academic subjects such as Latin and the Sciences, to practical subjects such as Drama, Dance and Physical Education. Modern Languages available include French, German, Spanish, Mandarin Chinese and Russian. A Levels in History of Art, Social Biology, Business Studies and Theatre Studies extend the range of the curriculum. Information Technology is a compulsory subject up to Sixth Form, optional thereafter.

Examinations offered. GCSE, A Level, ABRSM, ESB (English Speaking Board). Over 95% of Upper Sixth go on to University.

Religious activities. Non-denominational. Weekday service, longer service on Sunday, visiting preacher.

Academic, Sporting and Extra-Curricular facilities. Moreton Hall is engaged in an ambitious development programme and has facilities of the highest quality designed to provide the right environment for the education of pupils in the twenty-first century.

Younger pupils are housed in the Stables building under the supervision of resident houseparents and assistants. The building is designed to create a family atmosphere with dormitories split into smaller units, close to common rooms, washrooms and staff accommodation.

As pupils progress up the school, the dormitories are gradually replaced by double and finally single study-bedrooms. The Sixth Form Houses provide single and double en-suite facilities. Here, within the structure of a boarding school, senior girls are given the necessary freedom to prepare for the next stage in their careers.

The Centenary Science Centre is a unique Medical Science Faculty. The Science Centre, Information Technology rooms and Art and Design Centre are housed within a short distance of the central classroom, careers and library complexes.

All classrooms, libraries and boarding houses are networked and all Sixth Formers have internet access from their study-bedrooms.

An exceptionally well-equipped Sports Centre comprising a sports hall and floodlit tennis courts along with a heated indoor swimming pool, nine-hole golf course, an all-weather surface, and playing fields are set in one hundred acres of beautiful parkland at the foot of the Berwyn hills. The school offers a wide range of sporting options including Lacrosse, Netball, Hockey, Cricket, Tennis and Athletics. Sailing and Riding are also popular.

The Holroyd Community Theatre, Musgrave Theatre, Outdoor Theatre and Music School stimulate theatrical and musical activities ranging from house plays, lunchtime shows and jazz evenings through to ambitious school plays and orchestral concerts. Great emphasis is placed on girls taking part in as wide a range of extra-curricular interests as possible.

The nationally acclaimed Moreton Enterprises offers students real business experience. Supervised by professional advisers, but all run by the students themselves.

Old Moretonian Association. Lorna Campbell, c/o Moreton Hall.

Charitable status. Moreton Hall Educational Trust Limited is a Registered Charity, number 528409. It exists to provide a high quality education for girls and boys.

Governing Body:

Chair: Mr J Dixey, MD, FRCP

Deputy Chair: Mrs K Neilson

Chair of Finance Committee: Mr A Stockdale

Ms E J Flynn, MA Ed

Ms A Foulger

Mr M Heath

Ms S Hincks

Ms C Jones, BEd Hons, NPQH, Dip Mus, PGCertSpLD
    Dyslexia, AMBDA

Mrs S Tunstall

Mrs L Yule, BSc

Principal: **Mr George Budd**, BA Hons

Head of Senior School: Miss S Hughes, MTheol

Head of Moreton Hall Prep: Mr J Bond, BA Hons, MEd

International Director: Mrs V Eastman, MA

Director of Operations: Miss E Beer, BA Hons

Development Director: Mrs L Campbell, BA Hons

Financial Controller: Mr I Davies, BA Hons

Morrison's Academy

Ferntower Road, Crieff, Perthshire PH7 3AN

Tel: 01764 653885

email: enquiries@morrisonsacademy.org

website: www.morrisonsacademy.org

Twitter: @macmorrisons

Facebook: @morrisonsacademy

Instagram: @morrisonsacademy

Motto: *Ad summa tendendum ~ Striving for the highest*

Morrison's Academy Boys' School was opened in 1860 with a Girls' Department in 1861, an arrangement which continued until 1889 when a separate school for Girls was opened within the ten acres of the original site. In 1979 these two schools were brought together to become Morrison's Academy. The original foundation was possible through the generosity of Thomas Mo(r)rison, a native of Muthill who became a builder in Edinburgh and who in 1813 executed a Trust Deed directing that the fee of the reversion of his estate should be used to found and erect 'an institution calculated to promote the interests of mankind, having particular regard to the Education of Youth and the diffusion of useful knowledge …a new institution which may bear my name and preserve the remembrance of my good intentions for the welfare and happiness of my fellow men'.

The School. Morrison's Academy is a vibrant co-educational day school located in Crieff, Scotland. An integral part of the community in Crieff, the school comprises a 10-acre main campus supplemented by 45 acres of sports fields and main hall. Morrison's Academy provides a quality education for approximately 500 boys and girls from 2 to 18 years. Morrison's Academy delivers a contemporary Scottish curriculum. The school's strong academic foundations are supplemented by numerous skills based educational programmes including Forest School, our Outdoor Adventures and Activities programme, Morrison's Academy's unique Learning for Life programme and the Peter Jones Enterprise Academy, the first in Scotland. Each programme has been carefully developed to provide pupils with life skills: resilience, perseverance, problem solving and social skills – preparing Morrisonians for big futures.

Morrison's Academy's Nursery is housed in a purpose-built facility with an extensive garden on the main campus. The Nursery benefits from access to the school's extensive campus, facilities and specialist teaching staff. There is a well established transition programme for pupils leaving Nursery and entering into Primary school, preparing them for Primary One.

The Primary School, housed in a separate building on the main campus, educates pupils in small classes. Pupils also benefit from access to the wider school facilities and specialist subject teaching. Transfer between primary and secondary is helped by our Transitional Year (P7), which provides teaching in the primary school by a class teacher supplemented by lessons in the secondary school taught by subject specialists.

The Secondary School supports pupils to fulfil their academic potential, gain Scottish qualifications and entry to universities in both the UK and abroad. Academic expectations and achievements are high and small groups encourage individual learning and development. Over 97% of our S6 go on to university.

Staff and pupils mix easily and the scale of the school allows for every individual to be known and valued by all throughout their time at Morrison's Academy.

Virtual Learning Environment and Hybrid Learning. Pupils in our Primary and Secondary School utilise our well established Virtual Learning Environment. Morrison's Academy became a Google School in 2018/19 and this forms the backbone of our Virtual Learning Environment. Coursework is set up in the Virtual Learning Environment's online classrooms, where work is submitted, marked and commented on. Our early focus on digital citizenship helped our pupils to navigate remote learning during the COVID-19 lockdown and we were able to continue to deliver our classes successfully throughout our Primary and Secondary School. Weekly assemblies continued, classes were delivered via a mixture of virtual classrooms, face-to-face online meets and recorded lessons. We were able to continue to support every child with their coursework and their wellbeing. Hybrid learning is available to any pupil who is shielding loved ones or isolating at home. They can follow their timetable, participate in class discussions and submit work using our Virtual Learning Environment.

Situation. Morrison's Academy is situated in the beautiful market town of Crieff on the edge of the Scottish Highlands in Perthshire. Strathearn is a beautiful area of mountains, rivers, lochs and rich agricultural land. Pupils attend from the local area and travel from Perth, Pitlochry, Dunkeld, Aberfeldy, Auchterarder, Stirling, Dunblane and Falkirk, roughly two thirds of whom utilise the school's bus service.

Curriculum. Morrison's Academy follows a modern, Scottish curriculum; its dynamic and varied teaching methods support pupils to fulfil their academic potential and encourage every individual to strive for their highest. Pupils in Primary and lower Secondary follow the Scottish 5–14 programme of study, leading in upper Secondary to National 5 and then to Higher and Advanced Higher National Qualifications. Emphasis is placed upon academic achievement, but is coupled with numerous enriching educational skills-based programmes including Forest School, our Outdoor Adventures and Activities programme, Morrison's Academy's unique Learning for Life programme (which focuses on the 'non-academic' skills young people need to get on in the world) and, more recently, the Peter

Jones Enterprise Academy, the first in Scotland which develops entrepreneurial skills. Pupils are encouraged to develop broad skills and interests outside the classroom. Co-curricular activities (available to primary and secondary pupils) are extensive and Morrison's Academy makes good use of its glorious location.

Houses. All pupils are placed in one of the four houses named after local families: Campbells, Drummonds, Grahams and Murrays. There is healthy, competitive rivalry between the houses and senior pupils are encouraged to take charge of teams for sporting, music, debating and other events.

Games and Activities. Morrison's Academy encourages pupils to participate in a wide range of co-curricular opportunities, offering over 90 different sports, activities and clubs to its Primary and Secondary pupils. All pupils use the playing fields and facilities on the main campus or walk to the 45 acres of playing fields, including an artificial pitch and cricket wicket for all-weather playing, and pavilions at Dallerie. There is also a Strength and Conditioning Suite for pupils. Main sports are rugby, hockey, cricket, tennis and athletics. From upper primary fixtures against other schools take place, generally on Saturday mornings. Other sporting activities include football, basketball, netball, swimming, golf, weight training, sailing, short tennis, skiing, climbing, mountain biking, karate and more. To complement the sporting activities, pupils are active in The Duke of Edinburgh's Award Scheme, the Combined Cadet Force, drama, music – with a variety of choral, ensemble, band and orchestral opportunities available, debating, chess, Pipe and Drum Band, environment group, Enterprise club, charity fundraising, art, photography and more. Pupils are challenged to make the most of their time and all within the wonderful environment of Perthshire.

Fees per term (2021–2022). Day: Primary £3,307–£4,710, Secondary £4,983.

The fees include tuition, textbooks, stationery, external examination fees, sports and curriculum-related travel.

Where 3 or more children are enrolled coterminously, families will be awarded the following sibling discounts: 3rd child at school – 25% discount & 4th and subsequent children – 50% discount.

Admission Procedure. Admission to the school is by entrance test and school report and/or exam results and entrance interview. Entrance testing can take place throughout the year as required.

For a prospectus pack and any queries, please contact the Admissions Registrar on admissions@morrisonsacademy .org.

Scholarships and Financial Assistance. Morrison's Academy believes that every talented child should be able to receive a Morrison's Academy education and the opportunities that presents. Consequently, a number of Bursaries are means-tested and awarded each year. Bursaries are primarily available for pupils entering Primary Six and upwards although, depending on the number of applicants and exceptional circumstances, younger years of entry can be considered. Bursaries are awarded using a combination of academic merit (as tested in the Admission's Entrance Assessment) and financial need. Awards are in the form of a discount on tuition fees and will be subject to repeat testing of parental means every other year, with changes to financial circumstances required to be notified in between. In exceptional cases, full fee awards may be

available, but the majority of awards fall in the range of 20% to 60% of the tuition fee.

There are also a number of Sixth Form Scholarships which are awarded after examination and interview in May. The awards, which carry a nominal financial value, recognise both achievement and potential.

Charitable status. Morrison's Academy is a Registered Charity, number SC000458. The school is a recognised charity providing education.

Board of Governors:
Chairman: Mr D Glen

Mrs I Beveridge	Mr E McLellan
Ms S Brooks	Ms T Moran
Mrs L Butler	Mr J O'Neill
Mr D Cloy	Cllr C Reid
Mrs K Cook	Mr J Stewart
Mr C Dolby	Mr J Taylor
Mr G Martin	Mr R White

Clerk to Governors: Mr G Sutherland

Staff:

Rector: Mr A McGarva

Depute Rector: Mr D Johnston
Assistant Rector: Ms E McCormick
Assistant Rector: Mr C Nicoll
Head of Primary: Ms M Bulloch
Head of Nursery: Mrs N Connelly
Head of External Relations: Mrs M Gardi McGregor
Head of Finance: Mrs T Totten
Head of Operations: Mrs M Butler
Admissions Registrar: Mrs C Elliott

Teaching Staff:

Art & Design:	*Mathematics*:
Ms P O'Neill	Mr I Barnett
Ms G McLaren	Mr A Jack
Ms E Hamilton	Mrs J McConville
Business Studies:	*Modern Languages*:
Mrs A Dunphie	Mr A Fynn
Ms S Anderson	Mrs K Buick
	Mrs E Candlish
Computing & IT:	Ms M Nimmo
Mrs P Boal	
	Music:
Drama:	Mrs P Kennedy (*Director*
Ms L Kirk	*of Music*)
	Mrs P Benbow
English:	Mrs S Smart
Mrs L McNaughton	
Mrs G Marshall	*Physical Education*:
Mrs L Staines	Mr S G Weston (*Director*
Mrs R Veevers	*of Sport*)
	Mr A Dodge
Geography:	Mr L Howell
Mr A Wylie	Mrs J Lee
Mr R Anderson	Miss E McCormick
	Mrs D J McMillan
History/Modern Studies:	Mr C Nicoll
Mr M Clayton	Mr D Sanderson
Ms N Bales	Mr A Sutherland
Mr D Johnston	
Ms H Rowan	*Science*:
	Mr N Gwynne
Home Economics:	Ms C Piggot
Ms E Constable	Mr R Armstrong

Mr F Black
Mr M McKeever
Mrs S Steven

Primary:
Mrs L Anderson
Mrs C Armstrong
Mrs W Clark
Mrs M Douglas
Ms B Kemp
Mrs G Lauchlan
Mr B Leadbetter
Mrs C Robertson
Ms J Swarbrick

Nursery:
Ms N Christie
Mrs S Legger
Mrs G Mills
Ms A Senior
Mrs C Senior
Mrs M Thomson

Learning Support:
Mrs K Fetter
Mrs R Blake
Mrs J Corbett
Mrs G Wilkie

Mount Kelly

Parkwood Road, Tavistock, Devon PL19 0HZ

Tel: 01822 813193
email: admissions@mountkelly.com
website: www.mountkelly.com
Twitter: @Mount_Kelly
Facebook: @MountKellyFoundation
Instagram: @mount.kelly
LinkedIn: /mount-kelly

If you like the outdoors, have a sense of adventure and are keen to take advantage of every opportunity that comes your way then Mount Kelly is the school for you. Read below to also find out more about our performance swimming programme, girls' football academy and our award winning chamber choir.

Our spectacular location means that we are well known for our strong commitment to co-curricular activities and we encourage all pupils to take part whether it be camping out on the moor, paddling a canoe, riding the waves on a surf board or enjoying an overnight sail in our 50 foot pilot cutter 'Olga'. We call it the 'Mount Kelly Spirit' an attitude to life that develops here, one that allows pupils to really experience the life-defining educational experience that we promise.

With a high standard of academic schooling and a proven track record in public examination results, over 85% of our pupils gain places at their top choices of universities.

The School has an internationally recognised coaching facility for swimming with a 4 lane 25m pool and an 8 lane 50m pool and has had alumni at the last five Olympic and Paralympic games. In 2020 Mount Kelly won the prestigious Arena League confirming our place as the top school for swimming in the UK.

In association with Chelsea FC Foundation, the School runs a girls' football programme for 16–18 year olds. Two fully FA licensed coaches offer at least 16 hours coaching a week and the squad is the current ISFA Sevens U18s champions.

Our swimmers and footballers board and are taught alongside their contemporaries.

The College Chamber Choir is the flagship ensemble of the School. The group perform a wide range of challenging music from all periods and in a huge variety of styles, but mostly a cappella. They won the Barnardo's School Choir of the Year Competition in London in 2020, and compete internationally every year.

The success of our swimmers and singers create a culture in which the level of commitment and dedication required to excel are not considered out of the ordinary but are qualities to which everyone can aspire.

The School was selected as a finalist for the *Independent School Parent* magazine's Independent School of the Year Award in 2019 and was a finalist in the Performing Arts category in 2020.

Site and Buildings. Mount Kelly is set in over 100 acres of green fields and woodland on the edge of Dartmoor National Park and on the outskirts of the historic town of Tavistock, Devon. The buildings comprise the School Chapel, Assembly Hall, Performing Arts Centre, Dining Halls, Libraries and ICT Centre, Art Studios, Technology workshops, Science Laboratories, Swimming Pools (50m, 25m indoor and 25m outdoor), Sports Hall, Gym, Climbing Wall, Fives and Squash Courts, floodlit All-Weather Pitches.

Term of Entry. Pupils may be accepted at any stage in the school year from the nursery though to the Lower Sixth Form.

Scholarships. Each year, Mount Kelly makes available a number of scholarships and awards to pupils hoping to join us in Year 9 or the Sixth Form. Scholarships and awards are competitive on entry, and provide exceptional opportunities for able pupils. Awards may be given in the following disciplines: Academic, Art, DT, Music, (inc Choral) Sport, Football and Swimming.

Curriculum. The GCSE curriculum is flexible and aims to stretch each pupil appropriately. The core subjects are Mathematics, English (Language and Literature), Science and a Modern Foreign Language. The range of option subjects include Art & Design, Business Studies, Computer Science, Drama, DT, EAL, Geography, History, Music, Physical Education and Philosophy, Religion and Ethics (PRE).

Pupils entering the Sixth Form need to possess 6 GCSE passes. Mount Kelly pupils study for 3 A Levels. A Level option subjects include Mathematics, Further Mathematics, English Literature, Biology, Physics, Chemistry, Fine Art, Photography, Business Studies, Economics, Geography, History, Computer Science, Music, Physical Education, Product Design, Psychology, Religious Studies, Modern Foreign Languages and EPQ. All pupils in the Lower Sixth year receive tuition in Public Speaking.

Co-Curricular Activities. Mount Kelly has a strong commitment to co-curricular activities and the majority of College pupils are involved with the Combined Cadet Force, Duke of Edinburgh's Awards, the Devizes to Westminster International Canoe Race, the Ten Tors Challenge or sailing the school's pilot cutter.

Academic staff run the innovative Learning Outside the Classroom Programme from Year 3 to Year 10. Children in the Pre-Prep attend forest school on a daily basis as weather permits.

All pupils are encouraged to explore new interests and to make the most of their spare time. Societies and Activities include LAMDA, Debating, Current Affairs, Drama, Choir, Orchestra, Ensembles, Chess, Computer Programming, Photography, Chess, Fine Arts, Surfing and Textiles.

Sport. Mount Kelly has a strong sporting tradition. Sports undertaken are Rugby, Hockey, Cricket, Football,

Tennis, Athletics, Swimming, Netball, Cross Country, Squash, Basketball, Sailing, Surfing and Yoga.

Fees per term (2021–2022). Day Pupils £2,540 to £6,180 and Full boarding: £6,820 to £10,990.

Charitable status. The Mount Kelly Foundation is a Registered Charity, number 306716.

Chairman of the Governors: Dr Kevin Wilson

Head Master and Principal of the Foundation: Mr Guy Ayling, MA

Principal Deputy Head: Mr Adam Reid, MSc, PGCE

Deputy Head (*Academic*): Mr James Dixon, MA, PGCE

Deputy Head (*Pastoral*): Mr Drew Bott, BA, PGCE

Head of Prep: Mr Dominic Floyd, BA, PGCE, QTS

Mount St Mary's College

College Road, Spinkhill, Nr Sheffield, Derbyshire S21 3YL

Tel: 01246 433388
email: head@msmcollege.com
website: www.msmcollege.com
Twitter: @MountSpinkhill
Facebook: @MSMBHS
Instagram: @mountstmarys_barlboroughhall
LinkedIn: /mount-st-mary-s-college-barlborough-hall-school

Motto: *Sine Macula*

Mount St Mary's College, a co-educational boarding and day school, and its preparatory school and nursery, Barlborough Hall, educate children from age 3 to 18 in the Jesuit tradition.

Mount St Mary's College was founded in 1842 by the Society of Jesus. The manor of Spinkhill in North East Derbyshire was the first home of the College, forming the nucleus of the present school. The Elizabethan manor of Barlborough Hall, 1¼ miles away, is the home of the Preparatory School to the College (*see also Barlborough Hall entry in IAPS section*).

Educating children since 1842, we have over a century of teaching and pastoral expertise as well as long-standing traditions that embed charm and character in school life. Boys and girls excel during their time with us, growing in knowledge, confidence, humility and aspiration.

We follow a traditionally robust GCSE and A Level curriculum and the quality and quantity of our music and sporting departments is immense. In addition, we offer a varied range of popular co-curricular opportunities; Combined Cadet Force, fencing and Latin, to name but a few. Our teaching nursery ensures children are school-ready when they join Reception.

Numbers. College 347 (11–18); Preparatory School (3–11 years) 202. Boarders, Weekly Boarders and Day Pupils (girls and boys) are accepted at the College.

Aims. Mount St Mary's College is a Jesuit Catholic school and seeks to develop the whole person and encourages an appreciation of the needs of others, both in the College community and the world at large. The College seeks to produce young men and women for others. Pupils of other and no religious denominations are most welcome.

Special Features. Mount St Mary's College is well known for its family atmosphere. Pupils benefit from the close interest and encouragement which they receive throughout their time at the College and parental involvement is particularly encouraged. The strong emphasis on extra-curricular activities illustrates the Jesuit commitment to developing each pupil's individual talents in all areas – academic, spiritual, cultural and physical.

Location. Situated in beautiful private grounds in villages in north east Derbyshire, between Chesterfield, Worksop and Sheffield, the schools are easily accessible from Junction 30 of the M1. A fleet of school minibuses operates throughout the region.

Boarding. Full and flexi boarding options are available for pupils in Year 7 upwards. Boarders live in the boys' or girls' houses, under the care of a Resident Boarding Pastoral Leader and Senior Boarding Tutor, assisted by resident House Tutors. The majority of rooms are en-suite, with either 2–3 sharing or in single rooms. Boarders, both domestic and international, enjoy a full evening and weekend programme incorporating studies, the arts, sport and social time.

Curriculum. Pupils at Mount St Mary's are prepared for GCSEs, AS and A Levels, and University entrance. The curriculum for the first three years (ages 11–13) broadly follows National Curriculum at KS3 with opportunity to pursue a second foreign language and a range of creative arts subjects. The standard GCSE package is nine GCSEs, although more or less is negotiable according to ability; this includes a core of English, Mathematics, a foreign language and between one and three separate Sciences. Several subjects follow the IGCSE curriculum. Other subjects are chosen from a range of options. In the Sixth Form pupils choose from a variety of A level subjects and vocational qualifications.

In addition to an extensive academic programme, all pupils engage in a full programme of Games and Physical Education at every level. Specialist tuition is available in a variety of musical instruments and in speech and drama training. Assessment and monitoring of work is built into the tutorial system and there is a regular timetable of reports, pupil progress interviews and communication with parents. Academic excellence and breadth of knowledge are characteristics of Jesuit education and the curriculum is constantly reviewed to ensure that the widest opportunities are available to each pupil.

Religion. Mount St Mary's College is a distinctively Jesuit school, that welcomes children of all denominations to share its ethos. Ignatian principles inform the College's work in fostering a realistic knowledge, love and acceptance of self and of the world in which we live and this underpins our main objective: the formation of young men and women for others. The College maintains a strong link with Jesuit missions in different parts of the world, finding ways to further the work of the Society in this area. Pupils have the opportunity to be involved in gap year projects supported by the Jesuits.

Sports. The College has extensive playing fields for rugby, hockey, cricket and football. It also has a Grade A accredited athletics track. Rugby, for which the College has a strong regional and national reputation, is the major boys' sport. Cricket facilities are excellent with all-weather practice wickets and indoor practice nets. The main girls' sport in the winter term is hockey, for which there is a floodlit all-weather hockey pitch. There is a full-time Level 4 Athletics Coach. Other sports include swimming, tennis, shooting, netball and fencing.

Art, Drama and Music. There are many opportunities to be involved in the Arts within the school, both within the curriculum and as part of the extra-curricular activities. Within the Art and Design department pupils can study fine art, textiles, resistant materials within the workshop, and photography. On Saturday mornings activities are run involving sculpture, textiles, art and photography.

Music is particularly strong, and popular at all levels. Pupils are encouraged to take up a musical instrument, and can participate in a wide number of musical activities. Drama is also strong in the College, and several Senior and Junior productions are put on every year. The music and drama departments collaborate to produce a whole-school musical.

Combined Cadet Force and other Extra-Curricular Activities. All pupils in Year 10 participate in the Combined Cadet Force, in the Army or RAF section. They can continue to be a member, if they choose, in Year 11 and the Sixth Form. The CCF gives opportunities for external leadership courses and adventure training and fulfilling Duke of Edinburgh's Award options. There are extensive opportunities for extra-curricular activities at lunchtime, after school and on Saturday mornings. Pupils can pursue interests in drama, music, sports, the Duke of Edinburgh's Award and many other clubs and societies.

Facilities. Facilities include a Sixth Form Centre, a Drama Studio, ICT suite of three fully-equipped rooms, Music School with practice rooms, Recital Hall and Music Studio, College Theatre, Library with ICT facilities, various pupil common rooms, Fitness Centre, heated indoor swimming pool, Sports Hall, Rifle Range, Outdoor Pursuits Centre, all-weather tennis courts and 30 acres of games fields. The athletics track was opened in 2007.

Admissions. Entry to the College at age 11, 12 and 13, is via the College's entrance assessment, taken early in the Spring term at the College. At other ages, pupils are accepted on the basis of school reports, with College entry tests as appropriate and in the Sixth Form, pupils are accepted on the basis of GCSE results, or their equivalent.

The Headmaster, Daniel Wright, extends a warm welcome to families to get in touch with Mount St Mary's College or its Preparatory School. Call the Admissions team on 01246 433388 or email: admissions@msmcollege.com.

Fees per term (2021–2022). Full Boarders: £10,815 (Years 9–13), £8,260 (Years 7 and 8). Weekly Boarders: £8,660 (Years 9–13), £6,740 (Years 7 and 8). Day Pupils: £4,930 (Years 9–13), £4,290 (Years 7 and 8). Barlborough Hall: £3,780 (Years 5 and 6), £3,700 (Years 3 and 4), £2,780 (Reception–Year 2).

Scholarships. Academic scholarships are awarded at 11+, 13+ and Sixth Form on the basis of the College's Scholarship Assessment papers. GCSE results also form an aspect of Scholarship awards at Sixth Form. Music and sports scholarships are also available and the College will be happy to provide further information on these. In keeping with the College's ethos, bursaries are awarded in cases of demonstrable need. The Old Mountaineers offer postgraduate scholarships to former pupils of the College and applications are considered annually for these. All scholarships take place early in the Spring Term at the College.

Charitable status. Mount St Mary's is a Registered Charity, number 1117998. The College was founded in 1842 to provide an education for children.

Leadership Team:

Chief Executive: Gareth Chapman

***Headmaster*: Dan Wright**

Headteacher, Barlborough Hall School: Karen Keeton

Deputy Head (Pastoral)/Head of Boarding: Jack Murphy

Head of Admissions: Caroline Routledge

Resident Jesuit Priest: Fr Michael Beattie, SJ

New Hall School

The Avenue, Boreham, Chelmsford, Essex CM3 3HS

Tel: 01245 467588
email: admissions@newhallschool.co.uk
website: www.newhallschool.co.uk
Twitter: @NewHallSchool
Facebook: @newhallschool
Instagram: @newhallschool_1642
LinkedIn: /school/new-hall-school

Pupil numbers. Senior Divisions (11–16): 637. Sixth Form (16–18): 240. Preparatory Divisions (4–11): 377. Nursery (1–4): 98

Day 1,025, Boarding 327.

Location. New Hall School benefits from a magnificent campus and stunning heritage setting, with a grade I listed main building part of a former Tudor palace occupied by King Henry VIII.

We aim to educate the whole person: academically, creatively and socially, in a community which also nurtures the spiritual dimensions of human life. All benefit from the outstanding facilities on offer within our stunning 70-acre campus.

New Hall is set in an idyllic and convenient location, just 25 minutes by train from London Stratford and within easy reach of all major airports. We offer a distinctive education of real quality that is designed to give students the best start in life.

Diamond Model. At New Hall, students are educated in co-educational classes up to age 11 and again at Sixth Form, however, from 11 to 16 they are taught in single-sex lessons.

The main benefits of the 'diamond model' and five years of single-sex teaching derive from the ability to tailor pastoral and academic provision more sensitively and expertly to the needs of young people going through the physical, emotional and social upheaval of adolescence. Young teenagers are liberated from the negative peer pressure of having to perform in mixed classes.

Gender stereotyping of subjects is also removed. Girls and boys follow an identical curriculum and do not learn to perceive subjects as being more suited to either girls or boys.

Curriculum. New Hall Preparatory Divisions curriculum is enriched by specialist subject teachers for French, Computer Science, Latin, Drama, Music, Physical Education, Art and Dance. Their expert knowledge and passion for their subjects greatly enhance the children's learning experience.

The extensive co-curricular activities on offer set New Hall Preparatory Divisions apart; from Philosophy and Latin, to Mandarin and Poetry, there is always something to do.

Creative subjects including Music, Drama, Dance, Art and Design Technology all form part of the mainstream academic curriculum, and also feature in activities offered outside normal lessons. We have three choirs, infant, junior and chamber, as well as a Preparatory Orchestra. Our pupils regularly perform at prestigious venues, which include the O2 Arena and the Royal Albert Hall.

The Senior Divisions curriculum is distinctive in its breadth and academic rigour. An imaginatively taught and well-balanced curriculum is appropriately tailored to the needs of the individual. The experienced and dedicated staff endeavour to bring out the best in everyone.

New Hall has its own Most Able and Talented programme, which is proven to add exceptional value at GCSE and A Level. We believe that giftedness can be created and that students' academic skills can be developed at ever higher levels if they are given intellectual challenges.

New Hall encourages able students to apply for Oxford or Cambridge universities. The school has a good track record of students winning Oxbridge places in a wide range of subjects, including sciences, arts, humanities and languages.

We are proud that our examination results are consistently among the best of any independent school in the area.

Co-Curriculum. Our co-curricular programme is designed to add breadth to the New Hall education, which enables us to develop the well-rounded young men and women of whom we can be proud.

Our educational philosophy is reflected in the extensive array of challenging co-curricular activities. Educational visits in the Senior Divisions to countries such as India and China, alongside our societies and clubs, create a stimulating environment for your son or daughter to develop his or her passions, learning and talents.

Through activities such as debating, Model United Nations and political philosophy, students can become independent thinkers with a broad and rich experience of social and academic life.

Our Ethos. Our Catholic foundation and ethos is central to all that we do, supported by the work of our lively Chaplaincy Team. At New Hall, a special value is placed on love and forgiveness, which encourage relationships based on trust, kindness, self-respect and care for those in need.

All students participate in our award-winning New Hall Voluntary Service (NHVS), where they gain confidence, leadership and team-working skills and a desire to serve others. They will develop a sense of charity and community that will remain with them beyond their years at New Hall.

Boarding. We have a thriving full boarding community and options for full or flexible boarding. The four boarding houses offer their members a strong sense of identity and opportunities to forge new friendships. There are dedicated boarding provisions for students aged 7–16 and for Sixth Form students.

Although each of our boarding houses has its own individuality, a common theme throughout is the exceptional pastoral care and dedication of the residential team. This is a significant strength of our school.

Music and Performing Arts. Our dedicated Performing Arts Centre and theatres allow students opportunities for group or individual performances, which develop talent and encourage confidence.

Music has a long and fine tradition at New Hall. There is a host of performing groups, including choir, chapel choir, senior orchestra, strings academy and jazz band. Students can participate in the Trinity Drama programme, which develops presentation and public speaking skills. Drama performances range from Shakespeare to modern plays and musicals. Dance is a particular strength, with the annual dance show attracting a cast of more than 200 girls and boys.

Students take part in regional and national festivals and competitions and groups regularly perform in major venues across Europe.

Sport. New Hall students are able to develop their team spirit and physical development through our rich programme of sporting opportunities.

Under the guidance of expert coaches, including former international sportsmen and women, New Hall balances first-class training for those with particular sporting talents, with an inclusive 'sport for all' approach.

Our elite sportsmen and women compete at county, regional and national levels, at which they have enjoyed individual team success.

Our facilities set us apart and the rich variety of sports on offer include rugby, hockey, netball, cricket, swimming, athletics, golf, skiing and tennis.

Fees per term (2021–2022). Senior Divisions: Day £6,312–£6,765; Full Boarding £8,946–£10,824.

Preparatory Divisions: Day: £3,207–£4,425; Full Boarding (from age 7): £7,059.

Nursery Division: £1,602–£3,645.

Sixth Form: Day £6,834; Full Boarding £10,824.

Entry requirements. ISEB Common Pre-Test assessment, school report, supplementary piece of creative writing, and interview.

Scholarships and Bursaries. Scholarship candidates follow the normal entrance procedure and, dependent on the type of scholarship, a further assessment. All candidates for Year 7 entry are entered for the Academic Scholarship, which is awarded to the highest achieving student from the ISEB Common Pre-Test results. Other scholarships at Year 7 entry 2022 are available in Music, Modern Languages, All-Rounder and Sport. There are also scholarships available for Catholic students. Similar scholarships are available for Year 9 entry. For Sixth Form entry, there are scholarship awards available based on GCSE examination results as well as an All-Rounder scholarship, Modern Languages, Classical Languages, Music, Sport and STEM.

Further information on Admissions, Scholarships and Bursaries is available from the Admissions Team and on the school website.

Charitable status. New Hall School Trust is a Registered Charity, number 1110286. Its aim is the education of children within a Christian environment.

Chair of Governors: Dr Miriam Edelsten

Senior Leadership & Management Team:

Principal: Mrs K Jeffrey, MA Oxon, PGCE Surrey, BA Div PUM, MA Ed Mgt OU, NPQH

Deputy Principal: Mr A Fardell, BA Kent, LRAM
Vice Principal, Boarding: Mr J Sidwell, BSc Loughborough, PGCE London
Vice Principal: Dr P Tiffen, BSc Warwick, PhD Cambridge, PGCE ARU
School Chaplain: Fr M Hardy BA Ulster, STB, STL
Head of Sixth Form: Mr J Alderson, BA Manchester, PGCE Cantab
Head of Girls' and Boys' Divisions: Mrs S Minnis, BA Chelsea
Head of Preparatory Division: Mrs S Twomey, BA, PGCE Wales
Head of Pre-Prep Division: Mrs R Tagoe, BSc Soton, MA Netherlands, PGCE CCCU
Director of Studies: Mr P Bray, BA MA Dunelm, GTP
Director of Learning & Teaching: Mrs A Hilder, BA Southampton, PGCE Bath
Head of Theology: Miss M Webb, BA Soton, PGCE St Mary's
Executive Assistant, Clerk to Governors & Company Secretary: Mrs E Murphy
Estate Manager: Mr S Hall, BSc Essex, Dip RSA, Grad IOSH

Newcastle-under-Lyme School

Mount Pleasant, Newcastle-under-Lyme, Staffordshire ST5 1DB

Tel:	01782 631197
email:	info@nuls.org.uk
website:	www.nuls.org.uk
Twitter:	@NuLSchoolUK
Facebook:	@NewcastleunderLymeSchool
Instagram:	@nulschooluk

Newcastle-under-Lyme School, which attracts pupils from a large area of Staffordshire, Cheshire and Shropshire, is a co-educational day school for 800 pupils aged 3–18. The present School was formed in 1981 through the amalgamation of Newcastle High School and the Orme Girls' School, two schools which were endowed under an educational charity scheme for children in Newcastle-under-Lyme which has its roots in the 1600s. The two schools enjoyed a reputation for scholarship and for service to the community throughout North Staffordshire, a reputation which has continued with the formation of Newcastle-under-Lyme School. The School is also well known for its high standards in sport, music and drama, which play a major part in the co-curricular life of the School. The Prep School is adjacent to the Senior School and has some 300 pupils aged 3–11. The School is rated as Excellent by ISI in both inspection categories.

Buildings and Grounds. Set in 30 acres, the School is pleasantly situated in a quiet conservation area close to the centre of Newcastle-under-Lyme. The original buildings still form part of the School and extensions have been added from time to time. A fine dining hall was opened in one of the wings of the original building, part of the continuing programme of development and refurbishment which was begun when the School reverted to full independence in 1981. The Millennium Sixth Form Centre opened in 2000 affording spacious new accommodation for senior students. The new Stinton building was opened in September 2014. The excellent sports facilities, including pool and Astroturf will be further enhanced in 2022 with a new £3.5 million sports centre. The School has a Language laboratory, workshops, a Music School, an Art and Design Centre and a gymnasium. There are also tennis and netball courts and extensive playing fields adjacent to the School.

Organisation. The School is organised in two sections: the Preparatory School – Nursery (2004), Pre-Prep (2004) and Prep (1982) – which has up to 300 pupils in the age range 3 to 11, and the Senior School of some 500 pupils, including the Sixth Form numbering more than 150 students.

Form Tutors and Heads of Year have particular responsibility for pastoral welfare.

Curriculum. A broad curriculum in the first five years has English (Language and Literature), Mathematics, Biology, Chemistry, and Physics as core subjects. All pupils also take a Modern Foreign Language, Latin, Greek, History, Geography, Religious Education, Music, Art, Food and Nutrition, Design and Technology, Computer Science, PE, Swimming and Games. Pupils have the option of taking Biology, Chemistry and Physics as a dual-award GCSE or as three separate GCSEs in Year 10 and Year 11.

Pupils take nine GCSEs and the great majority will proceed to take three A Level subjects in the Lower Sixth Form. There is the possibility of taking the Extended Project Qualification.

Choices in the Sixth Form include A Level Business Studies, Psychology, Philosophy, Economics, British Government and Politics and Physical Education in addition to the subjects available at GCSE. Pupils access our Aspire programme for Oxford and Cambridge Entrance and a specialist programme for Medicine, Dentistry, Veterinary Science applications.

Co-Curricular Activities. The main school games are Rugby, Cricket, Hockey, Athletics, Tennis and Cross-Country for the boys and Hockey, Athletics, Netball, Tennis and Rounders for the girls. Swimming and Life Saving also feature strongly and there are opportunities for Aerobics, Basketball, Badminton, Golf and other physical activities in the Sixth Form.

There are also strong traditions in both Music and Drama and standards are very high. More than 200 pupils receive instrumental tuition and there are a number of concerts in each year with major performances being given locally. There are three major drama productions each year including one each at Upper School and Lower School levels plus a whole-School production.

The flourishing Combined Cadet Force has naval, army and air-force sections and there is also a Scout troop. Pupils also participate in the Duke of Edinburgh's Award scheme with great success.

Clubs and Societies meet during the lunch hour and after school.

Careers. The School places much emphasis on the importance of careers guidance, both in the GCSE years and in the preparation for higher education.

Admissions. Entry to the Nursery is on a first-come first-served basis. Entry to the Prep School and Years 7, 8, 9 and 10 of the Senior School is by examination/assessment only. Pupils moving into the area may be considered for entry at any time.

Entry at Sixth Form level is by interview and GCSE qualifications.

Registration forms are available on request.

Scholarships and Bursaries. The offer of a number of prestigious Scholarships has recently been enhanced with a range available at Year 7 and Sixth Form entry. They include academic, sports, music, art and drama Scholarships and Exhibitions.

Bursaries: A number of Bursaries are available for pupils applying for entry to the Senior School and Sixth Form. Bursaries offer assistance with School Fees, depending upon parental income.

Further details may be obtained from the Registrar.

Fees per term (2021–2022). Senior School £4,482; Prep School: Prep £3,664, Pre-Prep £3,263, Nursery £44.50 per day.

Charitable status. Newcastle-under-Lyme School is a Registered Charity, number 1124463. The object of the Charity shall be the provision and conduct in or near Newcastle-under-Lyme of a day or a day and boarding school or schools for boys and girls.

Chair of Governors: Mr D P Wallbank, BA

Headmaster: **Mr M Getty**, BA Hons, NPQH

Deputy Heads:
Mrs J A Simms, BA, MSc (*Pastoral*)
Mr I S Dicksee, BA, MA (*Academic*)

Head of Sixth Form: Mr A Poole, BSc, MA

Finance Bursar: Mr A Cryer

Newcastle-under-Lyme Preparatory School:

Acting Head: Mrs K Thomson, BA, MEd
Deputy Head: Mr M J Erian, BA, MA

Nursery Manager: Mrs A Smith, NNEB, NEBS

Norwich School

70 The Close, Norwich, Norfolk NR1 4DD

Tel: 01603 728430
email: admissions@norwich-school.org.uk
website: www.norwich-school.org.uk
Twitter: @NorwichSchool
Facebook: @NorwichSchool
Instagram: @norwich_school

Norwich School is a co-educational, independent day school for pupils aged four to eighteen. Currently there are 1,152 pupils attending the school. Set in the Cathedral Close, Norwich School is a traditional, yet lively place where boys and girls enjoy a rounded and stimulating education. The school is characterised by strong, warm relationships and a profound appreciation of scholarship.

The school achieves exceptional results but we believe that an education for life is about more than statistics. Here

we enjoy local character, beautiful surroundings and a remarkable history. Staff and pupils together create a supportive atmosphere and boys and girls benefit from specialised facilities and a broad curriculum.

Ethos. Learning is at the heart of the broad education we offer at Norwich School. This invaluable asset is underpinned by strong Christian values, especially those of love, care and compassion; which we emphasise in all activities and relationships within our community.

Aims. Norwich School is committed to: Nurturing and developing knowledgeable, reflective young people who are capable of understanding difficult concepts and expressing complex and profound ideas; Providing a rich, broad and varied education that develops the diverse talents of all; Equipping our young people for a lifetime of leadership and service.

Pastoral. The Senior School is organised by Houses. Pupils are allocated to a House upon joining the school, and stay with that House as they move up through the year groups. Many of a pupil's first and firmest friendships will be forged within the House.

Each of the eight Houses is managed by a housemaster – a senior member of staff who comes to know the pupils and their parents very well during their years of association with the House, and who brings compassion and continuity to a pupil's life. If a problem arises, the tutor will involve the housemaster in its resolution; they are familiar figures in the school who offer a blend of experience and encouragement.

Sixth Form. Life in the Sixth Form is a busy and rewarding experience, combining rigorous academic scholarship and commitment to a range of extra-curricular activities, as well as leadership and service roles. Our aim is to ensure that all pupils reach their potential and are able to apply for the university courses and career paths of their choice.

Extra-curricular activity. There are many areas of life beyond the classroom that serve to fulfil the aim of a broad and varied education. Encompassed within the programme are challenges, opportunities for service, group cooperation, team participation and leadership. All are seen as central to the educational experience of each school member.

It is hoped that every pupil will find something from the programme which will influence and stay with them far beyond their school days.

Bursaries. Norwich School sets aside generous funds to enable pupils to attend the school who would otherwise not be able to do so without financial help. Bursaries are available in the Senior School only.

All bursaries are means-tested and can result in a reduction in fees of up to 100%; there is a sliding scale based on family income and finances and resources of the school.

Scholarships. The school offers a range of awards for excellence in five areas: academic excellence (11+, 13+ & 16+), music (11+, 13+ & 16+), sport (11+, 13+ & 16+), drama (16+ only) and art & design (16+ only). A place on one of our scholarship programmes is made available to Senior School pupils with outstanding ability, potential and flair, which the school assesses by examination, interview, portfolio and audition, as appropriate.

Means tested financial support is also available to candidates applying for these awards.

Admission. The main points of entry are at ages 4, 7, 11, 13 and 16. Applications to other year groups are also considered.

Fees per term (2021–2022). Senior School £5,990; Lower School (Years 3–6) £5,460; Lower School (Reception–Year 2) £4,063.

Old Norvicensians. All enquiries should be made to Mrs R Lightfoot, Norwich School, 71a The Close, Norwich NR1 4DD.

Charitable status. Norwich School is a Registered Charity, number 311280. It exists solely to provide education.

Mr P J E Smith (*Chair of Governors*)

Head: **Mr Steffan D A Griffiths**, MA Oxon

Nottingham High School

Waverley Mount, Nottingham NG7 4ED

Tel:	0115 978 6056
email:	info@nottinghamhigh.co.uk
	enquiries@nottinghamhigh.co.uk
website:	www.nottinghamhigh.co.uk
Twitter:	@NottsHigh
Facebook:	@nottshigh
Instagram:	@nottshigh
LinkedIn:	/nottshigh

Motto: *Lauda Finem*

This School was founded in 1513 by Dame Agnes Mellers, widow of Richard Mellers, sometime Mayor of Nottingham. The first Charter was given by Henry VIII, and supplementary Charters were given by Philip and Mary, and by Queen Elizabeth. The School, which remains independent, is now administered under the terms of a scheme issued by the Charity Commissioners.

Organisation. There are 1,157 day pupils, of whom 332 are in the Infant and Junior School and 240 in the Sixth Form. Nearly all Junior School pupils go on to complete their education in the Senior School. (*For further details about the Infant and Junior School, see entry in IAPS section.*) From 2015 the school became co-educational in the Sixth Form and Infant school, followed by the other year groups from 2016.

Curriculum. The Senior School curriculum leads to examinations at GCSE in the normal range of subjects. The Sixth Form are prepared for AS and A Levels. The range of subjects is wide: Latin, Classical Civilisation, Drama, Modern Languages, English, History, Economics, Politics, Design Technology, Geography, Mathematics, Physics, Chemistry, Biology, Music, Art, Philosophy, Psychology, RS, Classics, Music Technology and Computer Science.

Admission. Entrance Examinations and assessments are held in January each year. Applicants for the Infant School should be between the ages of 4 and 7 years, for the Junior School between the ages of 7 and 11 years, and for the Senior School/Sixth Form between 11 and 16 years on 1 September of the year of entry subject to places being available and a successful interview (entry to Sixth Form is also dependent upon a minimum of 5 7s at GCSE).

Fees per term (2021–2022). Tuition: Senior School £5,349; Junior School £4,261; Lovell House Infant School £3,662.

Entrance Scholarships and Bursaries. The Entrance Examination for the Senior School is held in January each year for the award of Entrance Scholarships. Part-Scholarships of a fixed sum may be awarded based on exam performance. They are not linked to parental finances and will normally continue throughout a pupil's school career. Application does not have to be made for part-scholarships as these are awarded at the discretion of the Headmaster, subject to entrance examination performance and interview.

Nottingham High School also has its own means-tested Bursaries to be awarded to pupils entering the Senior School at age eleven. All Bursaries will be awarded at the Headmaster's discretion and will normally continue until a pupil leaves the School.

Games. The Playing Fields, covering 20 acres, are situated about a mile and a half from the School with excellent pavilion facilities. There are also indoor cricket nets at the school. The School games, in which all pupils are expected to take part unless medically exempted, are Rugby, Hockey, (together with Association Football in the Junior School) in the winter, and Cricket or Tennis and Athletics in the summer for boys. Girls play Hockey (The School has 2 brand new purpose built Hockey pitches), Netball and Rounders in the winter and summer terms respectively. Other alternatives provided for seniors include Cross Country, Squash, Association Football (Sixth Form), Badminton, Golf, Shooting, and Basketball. Swimming (the School has its own 25m pool) forms part of the Physical Education programme.

Combined Cadet Force. The School maintains a contingent of the CCF based on voluntary recruitment and consisting of Navy, Army and Air Force sections. There is a small bore range, and the School enters teams for various national competitions.

Societies. Individual interests and hobbies are catered for by a wide range of Societies which meet in the lunch break or at the end of afternoon school. These include and are not limited to Drama, Modern Languages, Mathematics, Chemistry, Biology, English, Politics, Arts, Music and Debating Societies, the Chess Club, the Bridge Club, Christian Union, and the Scout Troop. Over 160 pupils a year participate in the Duke of Edinburgh's Award scheme. The Community Action Group and the Explorer Scouts are alternatives to this.

Music. Apart from elementary instruction in Music in the lower forms, and more advanced studies for GCSE and A Level, tuition is offered by 3 full-time and 18 part-time teachers in the full range of orchestral instruments. There are 2 School orchestras of 50 and 30 players, 2 Choirs, a concert band (wind) of 50, a Training Band and Big Band and choral and orchestral concerts are given each year. There are a number of instrumental bursaries, covering fee tuition on one instrument, available to pupils entering Year 7.

Honours. 10 Places at Oxford and Cambridge in 2019.

Charitable status. Nottingham High School is a Registered Charity, number 1104251. It exists to provide education for pupils between the ages of 4 and 18 years.

Governing Body:
The Lord Lieutenant of Nottinghamshire
The Lord Mayor of Nottingham

Two Representatives of the City Council
One Representative of the Nottinghamshire County Council
Four Representatives of the Universities
Eleven Co-optative Members

Chairman of the Governors: Mr Steven Banks

Headmaster: Mr Kevin Fear

Deputy Head (Academic): Mr Paul Spedding
Deputy Head (Individuals): Miss Lisa Gritti
Assistant Head (Co-Curricular): Mr Richard Alexander
Assistant Head (Director of Studies): Dr Katharine Linton
Assistant Head (Teaching and Learning): Mrs Angharad
  Simpson
Assistant Head (Individuals): Ms Michaela Smith
Head of Sixth Form: Mr David Gillett
Head of Infant & Junior School: Mrs Clare Bruce
Director of Finance and Estates: Mr Stuart Ramsey

Learning Support Coordinator: Mr Mark Glarvey

Headmaster's EA: Miss Rebecca Winch
Director of Finance & Estates: Mr Stuart Ramsey
Head of Marketing: Mrs Claire Sneddon
Head of Admissions and Partnership: Miss Rebecca Russ

Head, Infant and Junior School: Mrs Clare Bruce
Deputy Head (Academic): Miss Lucy Thorpe
Deputy Head (Pastoral): Mr Christian Cordy

Oakham School

Chapel Close, Oakham, Rutland LE15 6DT

Tel: 01572 758500
         Admissions: 01572 758758
email: admissions@oakham.rutland.sch.uk
website: www.oakham.rutland.sch.uk
Twitter: @OakhamSch
Instagram: @oakhamschool
LinkedIn: /oakhamschool

Motto: *Quasi Cursores Vitai Lampada Tradunt*

The possibilities for learning really are limitless at Oakham. As a large co-educational boarding and day school with over 1,000 pupils (540 boys, 484 girls) aged 10–18 and a 50:50 split of boarders and day pupils, we are proud to be able to offer a truly staggering range of experiences, activities and opportunities.

Whilst academic excellence lies at the heart of everything we do, our focus goes far beyond helping our students to achieve outstanding examination results. The Arts flourish and we have an enviable reputation for excellent coaching in a variety of sports. Activities are also an integral part of life beyond the classroom.

Oakham is an exceptionally caring community. Our unique House structure ensures we nurture all aspects of our pupils' well-being throughout their Oakham journey; students are surrounded by staff who are expertly trained to both support their needs and to challenge them to become independent, thoughtful, and responsible young adults.

Oakham is well known and loved for being a friendly and unpretentious school. Whilst we are proud of our 400-year heritage, our priority is always to be at the forefront of educational developments. We were one of the first

independent schools to move to co-education in 1971 and we were also one of the first schools to introduce the IB Diploma, alongside A Levels. We continue to look to the future and our focus now, in today's digital world, is on effectively teaching students Information Literacy.

Facilities. Oakham's facilities include one of the best school libraries in the country, state-of-the-art Science and Design Technology facilities, an art gallery, a new Faculty of Social Sciences, a theatre, and a music school. The sports facilities are extensive with 40 acres of superbly maintained fields, all-weather pitches for hockey and tennis, a sports complex with an indoor swimming pool, squash courts, fives courts and fitness centre, and access to nearby Rutland Water for sailing and Luffenham Heath for golf. The sports hall has recently undergone an extensive programme of refurbishment, which includes a viewing gallery for parents to enjoy the sport in action on our world-renowned pitches. A new Medical and Pastoral Centre opened in 2017.

Organisation and Curriculum. Oakham has 16 houses: four in the Lower School (ages 10–13), 10 in the Middle/Upper School (ages 13–17), and two houses for final year girls and boys, where they can concentrate more closely on their studies and enjoy increased freedom in preparation for university. The Housemaster or Housemistress is responsible for pastoral support. Each pupil has a tutor, who is responsible for pupils' personal and academic development, and for keeping a balance between academic, creative and social activities.

The curriculum is tailored so that an education at Oakham develops the potential of all our pupils, opening up academic and commercial opportunities around the world. The Lower School offers a unique and exciting programme combining the full range of traditional subjects with the development of essential learning habits. In the Middle School, pupils can choose their GCSEs and IGCSEs from a comprehensive range of subjects. In the Upper School Oakham is unusual in offering a choice between A Levels or the highly-regarded IB Diploma Programme.

GCSE/IGCSE: All pupils take English Language, English Literature, Dual-Award Science (which comprises Biology, Chemistry and Physics), with the possibility of studying separate Sciences, and Mathematics. They also choose from History, Geography, Religion and Philosophy, French, Spanish, German, Drama or Music and a variety of Creative Arts subjects (Fine Art – Painting and Mixed Media, Textile Design or Sculpture, Design Technology or Electronics). Other options include: Citizenship Studies, Classical Civilisation, Computer Science, Creative iMedia, Greek, Latin and Physical Education. We expose pupils to a rich cultural environment, providing an exciting programme of projects and visits to enhance learning beyond the classroom and the exam syllabus.

16+: Upper School pupils may opt either for A Levels and equivalent stand-alone qualifications or the International Baccalaureate Diploma. A Level subjects on offer include: Art: Critical and Contextual Studies, Art and Design, Biology, Business (A Level and BTEC), Chemistry, Classical Civilisation, Computer Science, Design Technology, Drama and Theatre Studies, Economics, English Literature, French, Geography, German, Classical Greek, History, Latin, Mathematics, Further Mathematics, Music (Cambridge Pre-U), Philosophy, Physics, Politics, Psychology, Spanish, Sport Science (A Level and BTEC). The International Baccalaureate Diploma Programme offers a similar range, but students study six subjects: three subjects are studied at Higher Level and three at Standard Level. Additionally, all students take the three Core Elements of the Diploma: Theory of Knowledge, the Extended Essay and a programme of Creativity, Activity and Service.

Music. Around half of all pupils play in musical ensembles, choirs, bands, orchestras, and musical theatre productions. Over 80 concerts each year present a wide variety of performing opportunities both in and out of School, as well as international tours. Pupils are regularly selected for national youth ensembles and the School Chamber Choir have a national reputation for excellence.

Drama plays an important part in the life of the School with five major productions each year. A majority of pupils at all levels takes part in at least one dramatic production a year.

Art, Design and Technology. The Richard Bull Centre and the state-of-the-art Jerwood School of Design together offer an extensive array of creative and Design Technology opportunities, including painting, pottery, sculpture, textiles, print-making, photography, computer-aided design and electronics, working in wood, metal and plastics. Pupils regularly compete for and win nationally recognised awards and scholarships, such as the Arkwright Scholarship.

Sport and Activities. Our major sports are rugby, hockey, cricket, athletics, netball and tennis. Some 30 other sports options are also offered. A typical year will see over 100 pupils progress to the national finals in 10 different sports. Oakham is proud to be a well-recognised training ground for national squads.

We offer a comprehensive activities programme (over 125 on offer) and each week pupils follow an activity (or hobby) and, from the Middle School upwards, a Service Option. They can try something new or pursue an existing passion. Our Service Options develop skills and values for life. Pupils choose from an extensive volunteering programme, the Combined Cadet Force or the Duke of Edinburgh's Award.

Entry. Normal entry points are 10+, 11+, 13+ and 16+. Pupils are accepted mainly in September at the start of the academic year. Full admissions information is available from the Director of Admissions.

Scholarships and Bursaries. The following scholarships are available: Academic and Music (11+, 13+ and 16+), All-rounder (13+), Art, Design and Technology, Drama and Sport (13+ and 16+). The basic value of a scholarship is up to 10% and top-up means-tested support may be available. For further information, including bursaries, please request an information booklet from the Director of Admissions, Tel: 01572 758758.

Fees per term (2021–2022). Lower School (age 10–13): £9,400–£10,270 (full boarding), £7,395–£9,760 (transitional boarding: 2 to 5 nights), £6,150–£6,745 (day).

Middle and Upper Schools (age 13+): £12,600 (full boarding), £11,950 (flexi boarding: up to 5 nights), £7,610 (day).

Honours 2021. Overall 65% of all exams taken at A Level, Pre-U, BTEC or in the IB Diploma were awarded A* or A or equivalent. At A Level 59% of pupils gained A*/A grades and 85% gained A*–B grades or equivalent. In the IB Diploma our average point score was 35, compared with the worldwide average of 30. More than a third of pupils (37.5%) achieved 40 or more points (equivalent to 4 A*s at A Level) and two pupils achieved a near perfect score of 44

points. At GCSE, 66% of pupils gained A*/A/9–7 grades. 93% of leavers went to a university of their choice, with the remaining 7% choosing other options. These included: studying at international universities, following specialist Art, Drama, and Music courses, or taking a Gap Year. Four students gained places at Oxbridge; seven students left to study Medicine and Medical courses.

Charitable status. Oakham School is a Registered Charity, number 1131425, and a Company Limited by Guarantee, registered in England and Wales, number 06924216. Registered Office: Chapel Close, Market Place, Oakham, Rutland LE15 6DT. It exists for the purpose of education.

History: J N J Roberts, MA
Languages: E J Milner, MA
Learning Support: Dr E Stanley Isaac
Mathematics: Mrs W Singhal, BSc
Music: P Davis, MA, ARCO
Religion and Philosophy: Mrs K Brett, BA
Social Sciences: P Nutter, BA
Science: Dr J A Chilton
Sport: I Simpson, BSc

Chaplain: The Revd T F Tregunno, MTh

Housemasters/Housemistresses:

Lower School:
Ancaster: Mrs A Petit, LLB
Lincoln: Mrs M P Northcott, BA
Peterborough: M M Fairweather, MA
Sargants: D Williams, BA

Middle School:
Barrow: A S Denman, BA
Buchanans: Mrs C L Latham, BEd
Chapmans: O Hughes, BA, MA
Clipsham: S Dachtler, BA
Gunthorpe: Mrs Lydia Dunbavand, BSc
Hambleton: Miss S Angove, MA
Haywoods: G Gelderbloom, HDE Dip RSA
Rushebrookes: Mrs K M Robinson, MA
Stevens: Mrs E Roe, BEng
Wharflands: T Dixon-Dale, BA

Upper School:
Round House: Mrs E L Durston, BSc
School House: D M Taylor, BA

Oldham Hulme Grammar School

Chamber Road, Oldham, Lancs OL8 4BX

Tel: 0161 624 4497
email: admin@ohgs.co.uk
website: www.ohgs.co.uk
Twitter: @OhgsPrincipal
Facebook: @OldhamHulmeGrammarSchool

Motto: *Fide sed cui Vide*

The school, founded in 1611, was reconstituted in the 19th century under the Endowed Schools Act. The main buildings of Oldham Hulme Grammar School were opened in 1895 on a commanding south-west facing site overlooking the city of Manchester.

The Oldham Hulme family of schools is renowned for delivering outstanding levels of education at each stage of a child's development. With unbeatable standards and outstanding achievements, the schools cater for boys and girls aged 2 to 18 and offer a caring, orderly and academically stimulating environment.

At the age of 2 school life begins in the Nursery which has recently moved into new modern premises. Confidence is then built throughout the infant, junior and secondary years and great care is taken in the sixth form to create extremely capable, well-balanced young adults.

The schools' primary aim is to provide a caring, friendly and lively school environment that fosters a desire to learn

and at all times, pupils are encouraged to think and work independently. With a reputation for academic excellence and outstanding extra-curricular activities, pupils benefit from the right environment which enables them to achieve their full potential in life so that they go on to become successful, happy and confident young men and women.

Oldham Hulme Grammar School values academic achievement and standards are high. Consequently there is an excellent record of examination success at GCSE and A Level. Pupils are taught within small classes by a team of dedicated, well-qualified staff.

The schools also offer an excellent pastoral care system which guides and supports pupils, promoting their personal development within the wider school community.

The comprehensive careers education programme on offer widens each pupil's understanding of the opportunities available in the changing world of work, while equipping them with the skills to manage their future career.

A stimulating range of extracurricular activities provides opportunities for fun, challenge, initiative, leadership and service, while activities within the wider community encourage active involvement and promote a genuine concern for the needs for others.

Fees per term (2021–2022). Nursery (see website), Infants and Juniors £2,924; Senior School and Sixth Form £3,995; International Students £16,500 per annum payable in advance.

A number of bursaries are awarded annually to pupils entering at the ages of 11 and 16. These awards are based on parental income and academic ability and will remain in place for the time in school subject to satisfactory progress by the pupil.

Charitable status. The Oldham Hulme Grammar School is a Registered Charity, number 526636. It exists to provide a balanced academic education for pupils aged 3 to 18.

Governors:
Chair: Mr V A K Srivastava, LLB Hons (*Chair of the Finance and General Purposes Committee*)
Contactable via the School's Clerk to the Governors.

Vice Chair: Mrs A Richards, BSc Hons (*Child Protection Governor*)
Hon. Treasurer: Mr D M Meredith, ACIB

Elected Governors:
Mrs R Freeman, ATT
Mr J Greenwood, BA Hons, MRICS, MCIOB
Mr R S Illingworth, BSc Hons
Mr W Ley, ICAA, BCOM
Mr R Lobley, MRICS (*Chair of the Health & Safety Committee*)
Mr K Sanders, DipM
Mrs V Stocker, LLB
Mr J Williams, BSC Hons (*Chair of the Education Committee*)

Representative Governors Metropolitan Borough of Oldham:
Dr Z Chauhan, MD, MRCGP
Mr J Sutcliffe, BA Hons, MEd

Academic Staff 2021–2022:

Principal: C J D Mairs, MA Edinburgh

Deputy Principal (DSL): J C Budding, BEd Sheffield Hallam

Assistant Principal (Academic): M C Jones, MPhys Manchester

Assistant Principal (Pastoral, DDSL): A H Marshall, BSc Hull

Head of 6th Form (DDSL, Head of Lees House): Mrs A Longley, MA Manchester

Director of Studies: Miss R L Turner, BSc Loughborough

Director of External Relations: Mrs C Brownlie, MA Sheffield

* *Head of Department*

S P Adamson, MA Manchester (*English, Duke of Edinburgh's Award Scheme, Careers, Head of Booth/ Platt House*)

Dr A Altimeemy, PhD Manchester (**Physics*)

W L M Atkins, BSc Keele (**Biology, CCF*)

Mrs C Bailey, MSc Leicester (*EAL Coordinator*)

Mrs A Begum, BSc Salford (*Computer Science*)

Mrs A Berry, BSc Nottingham (*Psychology*)

D Berry, BSc Huddersfield (**Psychology*)

Mrs N Bibi, BSc Manchester (*Mathematics*)

Miss J C Brown, BA Liverpool (*Physical Education*)

N P Buckley, BA Sheffield (*Business Studies and Economics, Head of Year 11*)

N J Chesterton, BA Leeds (*Physical Education and Games, Head of Assheton House*)

Ms L J Cowan, MA Dundee (*History, Duke of Edinburgh's Award Scheme, Head of Year 9*)

Mrs N L Cross, BSc Manchester (*Mathematics, Duke of Edinburgh's Award Scheme*)

M N Dowthwaite, BA Manchester (**History and Politics, School Functions Officer*)

Miss C W Duffy, BA, MPhil Aberystwyth (*History*)

Mrs S Eckhardt, BA Salford (**Drama*)

Mrs A E Eden, BA Manchester (*i/c Politics*)

Mrs C A Eliot, BA Heriot Watt (**Textiles, PSHE Coordinator*)

Mrs R Ford, BA Leeds (*Physical Education*)

O M Gandolfi, BSc Bangor (*Biology, Duke of Edinburgh's Award Scheme, Head of Year 10*)

Mrs H Garside, BA North Wales (*Modern Languages*)

M J A Grant, MA Newcastle (*Modern Languages, Head of Hulme House*)

Miss J V Graystock, BA Liverpool (**Art*)

J J W Gumpert, MA Cambridge (**Religious Studies*)

D J Hadfield, MSc Cranfield (*Maths, Physics*)

A P Henson, BSc Loughborough (*PE*)

J R Hesten, BA Manchester (*i/c Physics*)

Miss R L Hampson, BA Manchester Metropolitan (*Drama*)

Mrs D Howarth, BSc Manchester Metropolitan (**Home Economics, Charities Coordinator*)

A H B Hurst, BA Manchester Metropolitan (*Director of Sport*)

Mrs C J Jones, BA Manchester (*English*)

Mrs T A Kershaw, BA Salford (**Modern Languages*)

Miss R Khanom, BSc Aston (*Mathematics*)

Mrs J A Lamb, BSc Liverpool (**Mathematics*)

Miss L Lavin, BSc Manchester Metropolitan (*Biology, Head of Year 7*)

Mrs J Leach, BA Hull (*English*)

Mrs D Maders, BSc Leeds, MRSC (**Chemistry*)

Mrs L Manton-Howard, BSc Leeds (*second i/c Mathematics*)

Miss G McCarrick, BSc, Manchester Metropolitan (*Geography, Head of Year 8*)

Mrs J McCarthy, MA, PG Dip Liverpool (*Art, Design Technology*)

Dr C R Millington, BSc Durham, DPhil Oxford, MEd Cambridge (*Chemistry*)

Ms E Mills, BA Manchester (**English*)

S J Murray, BMus Manchester, RNCM (*Music*)

S Norbury, BSc Liverpool John Moores (**Computer Science*)

Mrs H M North, BSc Liverpool (*Chemistry*)

A Peacocke, BA Glamorgan, (**Geography*)

Miss H R Plews, BA Liverpool, M Phil Cambridge (*Classics, Academic Tutor 6th Form, CCF, G&T Coordinator*)

J M Procter, PhD UMIST (*Chemistry, Physics, ECT/ITT Coordinator*)

S G Rawlings, BEng Aston (*Deputy Head of 6th Form, Mathematics, Physics*)

D R A Rees, BSc Bradford (**Business Studies and Economics*)

M Richmond, BSc Leeds (*Mathematics, Master i/c Football*)

Mrs K Roach, MA Sheffield (*English, Peer Mentor Coordinator, i/c Newsletter*)

D G Robertson, BMus Aberdeen, ALCM (*Director of Music*)

Miss S E Shepherd, BA London (*i/c French*)

C R Sykes, MA Manchester (*Geography, Psychology, Cover Supervisor*)

Mrs L Tanner, BA Leeds (*Physical Education*)

Mrs J Travis, DipM (**Careers, Food Technology*)

M Turner, BEd Leicester (*Mathematics*)

Mrs A Vose, BA Liverpool Hope (*Religious Studies*)

R B Williams, BSc Leeds (**Learning Support*)

Hulme Nursery, Infants & Juniors:

Head of Nursery and Infants (DDSL): Miss C Barnett, BA Edge Hill

Deputy Head of Nursery & Infants (DDSL): Mrs H Whitwam, BA Bradford College (*PSHE Coordinator*)

Nursery Manager: Ms D Smith, HLTA

Head of Juniors (DDSL): Mrs R Knott, BA Surrey

Deputy Head of Juniors: A Booth, BA Central England

Mrs R L Christodoulides, BEd Birmingham (*Literacy Coordinator*)

P S Coulson, BSc Edge Hill College (*ICT Coordinator*)

S Davies, BA Edge Hill University (*PSHE Coordinator*)

Mrs S Dockerty, BA Huddersfield (*DDSL*)

Miss K V Evans, BA Sheffield Hallam (*PSHE Coordinator*)

Mrs K Faulkner, BA Manchester Metropolitan (*Art*)

Miss C Goodwin, BA Manchester Metropolitan

S J Murray, BMus Manchester RNCM (*Music Coordinator*)

Miss A Rees, BA Edge Hill

Mrs H Russell, BA York, CSLPS OU, HLTA, QTS

Miss M Wall, BA Manchester/Lancaster (*SEND*)

Mrs E White, BA Durham (*SEND*)

Visiting Music Teachers:

Miss C Babington, BMus, PG DIp, MMus RNCM, MusM VU Manchester (*Cello*)

Mrs V Eastham, MA, FTCL, LRSM (*Piano*)

Mrs L Edge, PG Dip Perf, RNCM, BMus (*Flute*)

K Heggie, GRNCM (*Guitar*)

Mrs M Hulme, BSc, LTCL (*Violin*)

Mrs J Kent, CT, ABRSM (*Brass*)

B McNamee, BA Hons, PGCE, PGDIP, MMus, BMus
(*Voice*)
Miss E Owen, BMus Hons, Dip ABRSM (*Piano*)
Miss J Puckey, BMus (*Clarinet & Saxophone*)
M Walton, MMus Wales, BMus Hons RCM (*Violin*)
A Wares (*Drums & Percussion*)

Business and Operations Department:
Mrs N Duncalf, AAC, ACCA (*Head of Finance & Support*)

The Oratory School

Woodcote, Reading, South Oxfordshire RG8 0PJ

Tel: 01491 683500
email: enquiries@oratory.co.uk
website: www.oratory.co.uk
Twitter: @oratoryschool
Facebook: @TheOratorySchool
Instagram: @theoratoryschool
LinkedIn: /company/the-oratory-school

Motto: *Cor ad cor loquitur*

The Oratory School was founded in 1859, by Saint John Henry Newman. It is an HMC Co-educational Catholic boarding and day school for pupils aged 11–18.

Location. The School is situated in an 'Area of Outstanding Natural Beauty' (AONB) in grounds of approximately 100 acres, in South Oxfordshire, yet is within easy travelling distance of London, major motorways and airports.

Ethos. The Oratory has high academic standards, but an Oratory education is about developing young people in a much deeper sense than exam results alone can demonstrate. An Oratory education gives our young people every opportunity to draw out and find their individual innate talents and qualities, and instils in them a sense of joy and a genuine love of learning. At The Oratory everyone will find their place to shine, encouraged through our vast array of co-curricular activities. The Oratory is not a large school and this enables each and every pupil to be known, valued and stretched as an individual within our nurturing community. Strong pastoral care is at the heart of what we do. As a Catholic school that welcomes pupils of all faiths or none, visitors often comment on the inclusive family atmosphere of our school; it is this supportive environment that nurtures the confidence, self-expression, and resilience that are vital for success and happiness in the world of today.

Organisation. Four Senior Houses and one Junior House, St Philip House, both day and boarding. There are currently 357 pupils: 92 boarding, 38 weekly boarding, 14 flexi boarding and 213 day pupils.

Health. The school's Medical Centre is permanently staffed during term time by a team of Registered Nurses and a duty nurse is present night and day.

Admission. Pupils enter at 13+ through the Scholarship or Common Entrance Examinations, or at 11+ or 16+ by entrance exam. Pupils also enter in the 6th Form and in other year groups subject to availability. All pupils are expected to take an assessment prior to entry.

Academic. All pupils follow the internationally recognised and intellectually rigorous GCSE (or IGCSE in a

number of subjects) and A Level curricula, with the Extended Project Qualification (EPQ) also offered at 6th Form. We have a rich and varied curriculum that is enhanced by master-classes, workshops, lectures and field trips to inspire and enthuse our pupils.

All academic subjects are taught in small classes by specialist teachers who have a real drive to instil a genuine love of learning in all our pupils. As The Oratory is a smaller school, the pupils have the benefit of developing excellent relationships with their teachers and tutors, who know their strengths and their weaknesses, and who can support them throughout their entire school journey, ensuring that all our pupils are set challenging targets.

We are a selective school. Academic endeavour is very much encouraged; we want our pupils to work hard, take responsibility for their own learning, and strive to achieve everything of which they are capable. Having reached their academic potential, the majority of our pupils gain entry to their first choice of university, including many Russell Group universities. They then go on to pursue a wide range of exciting careers.

Religious Education. The school is an HMC Catholic school which welcomes pupils of all faiths or none. There is a resident Chaplain who looks after the spiritual needs of both pupils and staff.

Art, Drama and Music. *The Good Schools Guide* describes our Art Department as a 'creative oasis – the words "art department" simply don't do justice', and The Oratory has won top accolades both for A Level and GCSE Art and Design, confirming our place nationally as one of the top schools for Art in the country. In 2021, A Level exam results were 100% A*–A in both Art and Photography A Levels. The department believes that anyone can be an artist, and here film-making, textiles, coding and animation are all possible alongside traditional Art media. In an age where creative thinking is becoming increasingly important in the workplace, The Oratory Art Department is well placed to equip our pupils for the future.

The Drama Department is an active, flourishing department at The Oratory and Drama provision is outstanding, helping pupils to develop their imagination and self-expression, confidence and public speaking skills. All pupils have the opportunity to perform in our state of the art Theatre and Performing Arts Centre. If they are not involved in LAMDA, GCSE, or A Level Drama performances, pupils can still participate in the main school production or in our popular inter-house Drama Competition. There is also a Drama club that focuses on improvisation techniques, and we run regular theatre trips.

Music touches the lives of everyone at The Oratory and is an integral part of life at the school. Our aim is to build a musical journey for every pupil in the school, whatever their level of musical ability or particular musical interest. There are rehearsals for ensembles every day of the week, and individual lessons on instruments ranging from the piano to the bagpipes. We have a strong tradition in both choral and jazz music; however, the repertoire encountered by our pupils encompasses everything from plainsong to punk. There is a strong emphasis on performance and providing abundant opportunities to shine at all levels of ability. The choir has toured New York and Hong Kong in recent years. There are frequent concerts in London and prestigious venues such as St George's Chapel, Windsor Castle. The Jazz Band have had the opportunity to play alongside members of Ronnie Scott's Jazz Orchestra, and there are frequent enrichment visits to venues such as the Wigmore Hall and English National Opera

Sports. The Oratory has a 9 hole golf course and a Sports Centre that includes a 25m swimming pool, indoor sports hall, gym, ergo room, indoor cycling studio, 2 squash courts, 6 lawn tennis courts and we are one of only five schools in the country to have a Real Tennis court. We also have a boathouse on the River Thames for our rowers.

In addition to the main games of Rugby, Football, Cricket, Hockey, Netball and Rowing, pupils take part in Athletics, Cross-Country Running, Swimming, Tennis, Badminton, Basketball, Squash, Golf and Real Tennis. There is a coeducational cricket programme, swimming and rowing sessions and horse riding available.

Co-curricular. Enrichment activities take place three or four times every week, with a vast array of activities to choose from, encouraging our pupils to try new things.

Leadership skills are encouraged by our flourishing contingent of Oratory CCF, which includes Army, RN, RAF and Adventure Training. The Duke of Edinburgh's Award scheme is popular with the Gold expedition going to various locations in the UK and overseas.

Careers Guidance. Almost all students at The Oratory go on to higher education. Advice and guidance is readily available for our students, who are helped through the process by their tutor, as well as the rest of the 6th Form team. We provide guidance to achieve smooth and successful applications to the institutions and courses to which our students aspire: Careers advice; UCAS preparation and advice; Specialised Oxbridge preparation; Medic preparation.

There is also guidance on careers (including visiting guest speakers and a Careers Fair), apprenticeships and more vocational courses.

Fees per term (2021–2022). Boarders: £12,612 (Junior House £8,630); Day Pupils: £8,918 (Junior House £6,250).

The fees include board, tuition, consolidated extras and games. Means-tested bursaries are offered on a discretionary basis.

Scholarships. A number of Academic Scholarships and Awards in Art, Music, Drama, DT and Sport are offered. Awards are of varying values. All-rounder Awards are made on the recommendation and reports from a pupil's current Headteacher. 6th Form Scholarships are also available.

Alumni. Oratory School alumni are called Old Oratorians. There is a Development Office that keeps in touch with the 5,500 alumni through a programme of events and communications.

Charitable status. The Oratory Schools Association is a Registered Charity, number 309112. It is a charitable trust dedicated to continuing the aims of its Founder, Saint John Henry Newman.

Governing Body:

President: The Rt Hon Lord Judge, MA Cantab, PC

Vice-Presidents:

Rt Revd R J Byrne, BD, AKC, Cong Orat

His Eminence Cardinal Vincent Nichols, PhL, MA, Med STL

Chairman: P Lo, BA, PGCE
Vice-Chairman: M E Edwards

Clerk to the Governors & Bursar: F Yates, MA Oxon, ACA

Head Master: **J J Smith**, BA, MEd, PGCE

Deputy Head Academic: M Syddall, MA Oxon, MSt
Deputy Head Pastoral: M B Fogg, BA

Bursar: F Yates, MA Oxon, ACA
Chaplain: Fr D Rocks, OP

Oundle School

Oundle, Peterborough, Northamptonshire PE8 4GH

Tel: 01832 277125 (Admissions Office)
email: admissions@oundleschool.org.uk
website: www.oundleschool.org.uk

Motto: God Grant Grace

Oundle School is one of Britain's leading co-educational boarding and day schools, situated in the charming market town of Oundle, Northamptonshire. Travel from London is less than an hour by train yet the School enjoys a beautiful setting in the heart of the UK countryside. The School's buildings, dating from the 17th to the 21st centuries, are dispersed throughout the town, giving the school a unique and distinctive character. Oundelians take their place within the community of Oundle town, not isolated from it.

Oundle has long been associated with the very best of modern independent education. The School welcomes 20% of its pupils from countries across the world as well as pupils from all corners of the UK, resulting in a rich and diverse community with an international outlook. Its full boarding ethos is one of its greatest strengths. For boarders, this offers a wealth of opportunity across a seven-day week, with a full and varied weekend programme throughout term time. For day pupils, this breadth of opportunity both within and beyond the School day greatly enriches their experience and gives them access to a boarding-style education.

Laxton Junior School, a co-ed day School in Oundle for pupils aged 4–11, also comes under the Corporation of Oundle School.

Number of Pupils (2021–2022). 840 boarders and 270 day pupils.

Admissions. Main entry is at 11+, 13+ and 16+ with a small number of places available at other stages, including boarding places at 12+.

11+ Entry (Boarding and Day)

Each year, over fifty pupils join Oundle at 11+. Boarders enter The Berrystead, the junior boarding House and day pupils enter Scott House, adjacent to The Berrystead. After two years, pupils who wish to board transfer to a senior boarding House and day pupils transfer to Laxton.

Entry is by written examination in the January before entry in September. Applicants take entrance papers in Mathematics, English, Science and a Cognitive Ability Test alongside an interview. Boarding and Day places are awarded on the basis of performance in the exams and interview. Academic and Music Scholarships are available at this level of entry.

12+ Entry (Boarders only)

Places permitting, we offer a small number of boarding places at 12+ into The Berrystead. Entrance examinations, similar to those for 11+, are taken in January of the year of entry.

13+ Entry (Boarding and Day)

Most of Oundle's boarders join in the Third Form from a wide range of Prep Schools, either through Common Entrance examinations sat in June each year or the Academic Scholarship examination sat in January. Candidates who are not at a Prep School sit Oundle's own entrance tests in the January before entry in September. The examination consists of papers in Mathematics, English, Science and normally a Modern Foreign Language (French/Spanish/German).

There are five girls' boarding Houses and eight boys' boarding Houses, each admitting approximately twelve pupils a year. The Registrar can provide help with choosing an appropriate House but it should be noted that houses fill up at least three years ahead of entry. A number of day places are available each year. Candidates sit Common Entrance, the Academic Scholarship examinations or Oundle's own tests depending on which type of school they are moving on from.

Facilities. Oundle has sixteen houses: eight boys' boarding houses, five girls' boarding houses, a junior boarding house, junior day house and senior day house. A continuous cycle of renovation and refurbishment is in operation. Each house has its own distinct community, with in-house dining a hallmark of the School's character.

Academic departments are situated in the Cloisters, the Needham building, the Adamson Centre, the Gascoigne building, Old Dryden and SciTec.

The Adamson Centre for Modern Languages is equipped with two state-of-the-art language laboratories, six language assistant pods, fourteen teaching rooms and an International Suite. SciTec Oundle's impressive home of science opened, with enhanced Design, Technology and Engineering facilities and a new purpose-built Mathematics department, bringing together the STEM subjects and embracing developments in new fields such as nanotechnology and mechatronics.

Art, Music, Drama and Design, Engineering and Technology are all very strong and well provided for. The Art Studios are large, airy and well equipped and the department includes the Yarrow Gallery. Facilities in Music include the Frobenius Organ and an electronic Music Studio. The Drama Department is centred on the Rudolph Stahl Theatre, a cleverly converted chapel in the middle of the town, where numerous productions of both the School and visiting companies take place.

The teaching areas are very well equipped; the Information Technology Centre includes two fully-equipped computer rooms and there are 'cluster networks' around the School. Thin Client terminals are located for each boarder in the Houses. Electronic whiteboards and computer-driven projectors feature in most teaching rooms.

The most recent development focus has been on resourcing a modern, thoughtful vision of sport. A new Sports Centre housing a 50m pool, an 8-court sports hall, a fitness suite and multiple studios opened last year alongside the existing Sports Centre. The new facilities, which include an athletics track, tennis courts, AstroTurfs, cricket nets and netball courts, support sport at a top competitive level whilst catering for a multitude of sports and leisure activities at all levels.

The Chapel was built as a memorial shortly after the Great War and its East windows, designed by John Piper, were installed in 1956. Thirty-two stained glass windows by Mark Angus, added in 2005, compliment Piper's original vision. Religious instruction accords with the Church of England, but other faiths are welcomed.

Academic Curriculum. Third Formers (Year 9) take a general course consisting of English, Mathematics, French, Latin, Physics, Chemistry, Biology, History, Geography, Theology, Philosophy and Religion (TPR), Art, Design and Technology, PE, Music, Drama, Computing, and German or Spanish or Chinese or Greek. Our Third Form curriculum is complemented by our unique Trivium course that is studied by all pupils with the intention of placing learning for its own sake at the heart of an Oundle education. The First and Second Form curriculum is similar. The traditional importance of Science and Technology is still maintained, with all pupils being taught the three Sciences to IGCSE level (both Triple Award and Dual Award on offer) and all Third Formers spending time in both the Art and the Design and Technology Departments. Computing and Microelectronics are available at all levels.

The two-year GCSE/IGCSE courses begin formally at the start of the Fourth Form. The core curriculum comprises English Language and Literature, Mathematics and the three Sciences. In addition, each pupil selects five subjects from Art, Chinese, Computing, Design Engineering Technology, Drama, French, Geography, German, Greek (Classical), History, Italian, Latin, Music, Physical Education, Theology Philosophy and Religion, Russian and Spanish. All pupils must choose at least one modern foreign language (eight are timetabled), many study two or more.

In the Sixth Form, pupils choose four subjects from Art, Biology, Chemistry, Chinese, Classical Civilisation, Classical Greek, Computing, Design, Engineering and Technology, Economics, Electronics, Literature in English, French, Geography, German, Government and Politics, History, History of Art, Italian, Latin, Mathematics, Further Mathematics, Music, Philosophy and Theology, Physical Education, Physics, Psychology, Spanish and Theatre Studies. Of these, Chemistry, Chinese, Literature in English, German, History, History of Art, Italian, Physics and Spanish are assessed by the linear Cambridge Pre-U qualification; other subjects are assessed as A Levels.

Studies in the Sixth Form are enhanced by an extension block, in which is available the School's bespoke *Quadrivium* course – which is a selection of different courses divided into four topics looking at a central theme, and other options, such as one-year *ab initio* courses in Italian and Russian, Music Technology, preparation for Music Diplomas, and Projects. The last of these leads to AQA Extended Project Qualification.

Honours. Almost all Oundelians proceed to university; in 2021 fourteen pupils secured places at Oxford and Cambridge.

Sport. Pupils participate in a minimum of three sports afternoons per week, and can train up to five times per week with their team on top of individual training programmes. We provide competitive and recreational opportunities for our pupils and support those who show great potential through our 13+ and 16+ Scholarships.

The main School sports are Rugby, Hockey, Cricket, Rowing, Netball and Tennis, but others available include

Aerobics, Athletics, Badminton, Clay Shooting, Cross Country, Cycling, Fencing, Fives, Golf, Horse Riding, Sailing, Shooting, Soccer, Squash, Swimming and Volleyball.

Activities. A full range of activities take place which are an integral part of the wider school curriculum. Events in Drama and Music feature prominently in the School calendar, and Art Exhibitions are held regularly in the Yarrow Gallery. A large number of Societies meet on a regular basis. Links have been established with schools in France, Germany, Spain, Hungary, the Czech Republic, Russia, China, America and Australia, with annual Exchanges taking place. Pupils are able to participate in the very large number of expeditions and trips in the UK and abroad. There is a flourishing CCF comprising Army, Navy, RAF, Fire and Adventure Training sections and a thriving Duke of Edinburgh's Award scheme is in operation. Community Action plays an important part in school life and contributes significantly to the wider community. Much time and energy are devoted to fundraising activities in support of national charities, international aid programmes and holidays run at Oundle for MENCAP and inner-city children.

Scholarships. An extensive series of entrance scholarships is offered each year.

Scholarships at 11+:

- Junior Academic scholarships for entry to The Berrystead or Laxton. Examination in January.
- Junior Music scholarships. Audition and interview in January.

Scholarships at 13+:

- Academic scholarships. Assessment in May.
- Oundle scholarships. Assessment in March.
- Music scholarships. Assessment in January.
- Drama scholarship. Assessment in March.
- Art scholarships. Assessment in March.
- Design, Engineering and Technology scholarships. Assessment in March.
- Sports scholarships. Assessment in November.

Scholarships at 16+:

- Academic scholarships. Assessment in November.
- Music scholarship. Assessment in November.
- Art scholarship. Assessment in November.
- Design, Engineering and Technology scholarship. Assessment in November.
- Sport scholarships. Assessment in November.

Full details about these and all other awards are available from the Registrar on 01832 277125 or the Assistant to the Deputy Head, Admissions on 01832 277116, email: admissions@oundleschool.org.uk.

Bursaries. Bursaries vary in size according to circumstance; it may be that a ten percent remission makes all the difference to a family, whilst others may require 100 percent or more to ensure a pupil does not miss out on the broad range of co-curricular opportunities Oundle offers. Whilst a pupil must comfortably satisfy the academic entry requirements, bursaries are not solely dependent on scholastic merit. Priority is given to those who are likely to gain most from an Oundle education and who will contribute fully to the life of the School.

Parents who feel that they may need the support of a bursary are encouraged to discuss the matter with the School, through the Admissions Office in the first instance, well in advance of the due date of entry. Decisions regarding bursary assistance are made approximately two years ahead of entry and confidentiality is assured every step of the way. Judgements are dependent on a supporting reference from a previous school, an informal interview and on analysis of a family's financial circumstances.

Fees per term (2021–2022). Boarders: First Form (Year 7) £9,960, Second Form (Year 8) £11,560 and Third Form to Sixth Form £13,105.

Day Pupils: First Form (Year 7) £6,385, Second Form (Year 8) £7,405, Third Form to Sixth Form £8,395

Details of extras are given in the School prospectus.

The registration fee is £250.

Laxton Junior School caters for 4 to 11-year-old boys and girls and has 250 pupils on roll. *(For further details, see entry in IAPS section.)*

Charitable status. Oundle School is a Registered Charity, number 309921.

The Governing Body:
Mr R H Ringrose (*Chairman*)
Mr D A Hutchinson (*Vice Chairman*)
Mr N Chippington
Mr H Clayden
Mrs J C Kibbey
Mr M C B Spens
Mrs R Lawes
Mr T W Stubbs
Mrs Suzanna D'Oyly
Mr C G McAndrew
Mrs D McGregor
Mr I Hodgson
Mr C McAndrew
Mr C Tyler
Mr J Whitmore

Ex-Officio:
Mr Tim Coleridge (*Master*)
Mr James Thomson (*Second Warden*)
Alderman Charles Bowman (*Third Warden*)

Mr D J Toriati, OBE (*Secretary and Bursar*)

Leadership:

Head: Mrs S Kerr-Dineen, MA Cambridge

Deputy Head: Mrs D L Watt, MA Oxford
Deputy Head Academic: Mr I C Smith, MA, MSci Cambridge
Deputy Head Pastoral: Mrs A E Meisner, BA Nottingham
Deputy Head Co-Curricular: Mr A J Sherwin, MA Edinburgh
Deputy Head Admissions: Mr A B Burrows, MAEd Open, BSc York
Deputy Head Partnerships and Outreach: Mr G Montgomery, MSci Queen's, MA Bath
Senior Chaplain: Revd B J Cunningham, MA Oxford

Bursary:
Bursar: Mr D J Toriati, MA King's College
Director Finance: Mr P Lamb, ACMA

Admissions:
Registrar: Mr J Hammond Chambers, MA Nottingham
Assistant Registrar: Miss S Johnson, BA Durham

Pangbourne College

Pangbourne, Reading, Berkshire RG8 8LA

Tel: 0118 984 2101
email: admissions@pangbourne.com
website: www.pangbourne.com
Twitter: @PangbourneColl
Facebook: @pangbournecollege
Instagram: @pangbourne_college
LinkedIn: /pangbourne-college

Motto: *Fortiter ac Fideliter*

About Us. Pangbourne College is a small, independent boarding and day school with a unique history and a bright future. It's a community where you can flourish; our small size allows us to get to know each student individually, ensuring that they are nurtured as they grow academically and socially.

Our Flag Values of kindness, selflessness, moral courage, initiative, industry, resilience, and integrity underpin all we do as a College. They are rooted in our Christian ethos and go a long way to prepare our pupils for life's challenges and the responsibilities of adulthood. Our aim is to equip Pangbournians with the strongest possible foundations for their future.

Providing a challenging academic curriculum, we also offer plenty of co-curricular opportunities for sport, music, art, drama and adventurous training, so that each individual fulfils their potential and develops confidence, values and skills to make a positive difference to the world.

Ideally Located. The campus is set in 203-acres of beautiful West Berkshire countryside, in an Area of Outstanding Natural Beauty, and yet we are just 10 minutes from Junction 12 of the M4 motorway. We are also on the mainline rail network between Oxford (30 minutes) and London Paddington (45 minutes). Daily school transport services are available from Ascot, Basingstoke, Henley/Wargrave, Maidenhead, Newbury and Wantage.

Highly Rated. In November 2019, the Independent Schools Inspectorate (ISI) rated the college as 'Excellent' for both the academic and personal development of its pupils. It said: 'Pupils demonstrate exemplary attitudes to learning: they respond to academic challenge with energy and purpose.'

In June 2021, we were shortlisted for the 'Co-educational Independent School of the Year' category in the *Independent Schools of the Year 2021 Awards.*

The Good Schools Guide describes us as: 'A small, distinctive, grounded and family-oriented school that puts huge emphasis on self-discipline, teamwork and leadership. Caring and supportive, Pangbourne buzzes with activity and encourages every pupil to have a go.'

Admissions. We welcome applications from children from a variety of backgrounds and educational experience, who demonstrate the potential to make the very best of the opportunities that Pangbourne offers. We want our community to be inclusive and reflect the world outside of school.

We are not an academically selective school, but we are discerning in our selection process. Therefore, our assessment process is designed to identify your child's core strengths and skills, both inside and outside of the classroom.

Scholarships & Exhibitions. Pangbourne College offers a limited number of scholarships and exhibitions to pupils who demonstrate exceptional academic ability or excellence in a major co-curricular domain. Registered pupils who have completed their admissions process are welcome to apply for a scholarship in the academic year before they enrol into the College. Scholarships given to Year 7 pupils are known as exhibitions. We offer awards in a range of areas, all of which should be applied for on the appropriate form and sent to the Head of Admissions:

- Academic
- Music
- Sport
- Design Technology
- Art
- Drama

For more information, please contact the Head of Admissions, email: admissions@pangbourne.com or visit www.pangbourne.com/admissions/scholarships-exhibitions.

Visit Us. The only way to experience the authentic Pangbourne is to visit us and enjoy a tour of the College and speak to pupils and staff here. They will give you real insight into what Pangbourne is today. We would encourage you to join us on one of our Open Mornings, held in Autumn and Spring, or one of our popular Head's Breakfasts.

Parents say… 'As we looked at other schools it became really clear to us that Pangbourne educates and nurtures your child as an individual, for who they are. Pangbourne really sees your child and understands and nurtures them, both academically and pastorally, in a way that works for them and for the wider family.' *Abi Williamson, A Parent*

Fees per term (2021–2022). At age 11 and 12: Boarders £9,050; Weekly Boarder £8,210; Part Boarders £7,910; Day Pupils £6,300. At 13 and above: Boarders £12,680; Weekly Boarder £11,510; Part Boarders £11,060; Day Pupils £8,540.

Charitable status. Pangbourne College Limited is a Registered Charity, number 309096. The objective is to provide an excellent all-round education for boys and girls between the ages of 11 and 18.

Governing Body:
Chairman: Mr P Roberts, MBE
Vice-Chairman: Revd A T Bond

Headmaster: Mr T J C Garnier

Deputy Head Academic: Mrs S Greenwood

Deputy Head Co-Curricular: Mr R Follett

Deputy Head Pastoral: Mr R Bancroft

Bursar: Mr N Walne

Assistant Head Boarding: Mr T Cheney

Assistant Head Pupil Mental Wellbeing: Mrs C Bond

The Perse Upper School

Hills Road, Cambridge CB2 8QF

Tel:	01223 403800
email:	office@perse.co.uk
website:	www.perse.co.uk
Twitter:	@ThePerseSchool
Facebook:	@theperseschool
Instagram:	@theperseschoolcambridge
LinkedIn:	school/the-perse-school-cambridge

The Perse School is Cambridge's oldest secondary school, founded in 1615 by Dr Stephen Perse, a Fellow of Gonville and Caius College. The School still maintains close links with both Gonville and Caius and with Cambridge University.

The Perse Upper School is a co-educational independent day school for pupils aged 11–18.

Ethos. The Perse is a very special school which is both traditional and innovative, academic and caring, understanding and structured, industrious and fun. While our excellent academic results are well-known, prospective pupils and their parents can be surprised to discover the exciting extra-curricular opportunities also on offer. Beyond the classroom there is a wealth of opportunity in music, drama, sport and outdoor pursuits, along with a vibrant programme of over 100 clubs and societies. The Perse is a supportive community characterised by mutual respect, encouragement and care. Our diverse pupil body sets us apart from the stereotypical image of independent schools. Students come from a wide range of backgrounds thanks to our significant bursary programme and a commitment to delivering an outstanding education whilst keeping a downward pressure on fee increases. The School's vision is: 'To love learning and strive for excellence'.

History. The School remains true to its historic roots, with close links to the University of Cambridge and a £1 million a year means-tested bursary programme that supports more than 90 pupils.

Admission. There are approximately 1,220 students in the Upper, including 360 in the Sixth Form. The main entry points are Year 7, Year 9 and the Lower Sixth. For Years 7 and 9 candidates are examined in maths, English and verbal reasoning, and undertake a short humanities video/questions exercise. Sixth Form applicants sit entrance tests and offers are conditional on I/GCSE results.

Facilities. The Perse has invested more than £40 million in new facilities over the last decade. In 2021 a new Sixth Form Centre opened, together with a refurbished lecture theatre and dining facilities. The Upper occupies an attractive 27-acre greenfield site with extensive on-site playing fields and recreational areas. In addition, the School has recently acquired and developed a 45-acre site at Abington, 6 miles from the School, for additional sports and outdoor pursuits activities. Pupils enjoy high specification science labs and classrooms; a purpose built sports centre, fitness suite and studio, extensive netball and tennis courts and 3 all-weather Astroturf surfaces; a recently extended music centre including a rehearsal hall; art studios and a gallery; a lecture theatre; and an outdoor pursuits centre, climbing wall and shooting range. In the heart of the School, the Rouse Library and the award winning Peter Hall Performing Arts Centre overlooks Ellison Court.

Academic Excellence. Perse pupils learn in a purposeful and supportive environment where they are taught to think independently and to make sense of a diverse and complex world. The School achieves some of the best A Level and Pre-U results of any co-educational school in the country, regularly appearing in the top 10 schools nationally. In 2020, 93% of A level entries were awarded an A* or A grade (or the Pre U equivalent). Pupils regularly excel in science and maths Olympiads, economics and business challenges, drama and poetry contests and essay and fiction writing competitions.

Rounded Education. There is a buzz about daily life at The Perse. There are more than 100 clubs and societies on offer. Nearly 450 pupils, several of whom are involved in national ensembles, take part in 70 school ensembles, with 60 concerts, masterclasses and competitions organised throughout the year, including recent high-profile performances at Saffron Hall, Ely Cathedral and Westminster Abbey. There are at least 10 drama productions each year led by a Theatre Practitioner in Residence and based in a state-of-the-art Performing Arts Centre. A wide range of other performance, literary and debating opportunities are also available. The main sports are cricket, hockey, netball, rugby and tennis. There is an extensive fixtures list; the School fields more than 160 teams in 30 different sports and regularly enjoys regional and national success. More than 600 pupils are involved in the Outdoor Pursuits programme, developing personal confidence, team working and leadership skills. There are a wide range of trips on offer from weekend outings in the UK's national parks to adventurous international expeditions. Popular groups include the Perse Exploration Society, Paddle-sport Club and Climbing Club.

Supportive Community. The Upper is a happy school where pupils feel safe, secure and supported. The School works hard to strike the right balance of work and play, comfort and challenge, instruction and discovery, rules and common sense, and guidance and independence. Each student has a pastoral tutor who monitors their progress and there are peer listeners, form prefects and a system of heads of year, heads of section, senior tutors and school counsellors. The Perse has a very active programme of charitable fundraising and outreach, and pupils have the chance to become involved in the wider community. Perse pupils work with children from over 20 local primary schools and support charitable fundraising projects such as Christel House and East Anglia's Children's Hospices.

Global Perspective. The Perse has strong international links including foreign language and cultural exchanges, a partnership with Christel House (a charity that educates some of the world's poorest children) and membership of the SAGE global alliance of leading schools. Pupils regularly travel overseas and increasingly collaborate remotely through the latest technology.

Fees per term (2021–2022). £6,175, excluding lunch. Lunch £289 per term.

Bursaries and scholarships. Means-tested bursaries are available, ranging from 5% to 100% of annual tuition fees. Scholarships are limited in financial value, worth £450 as a one-off payment. At Year 7 and Year 9 the School offers a small number of academic and music scholarships to pupils of exceptional merit. Sixth formers are able to apply for a maximum of two scholarships. All sixth form applicants who sit our entrance tests are automatically considered for an academic scholarship and general scholarship.

The Perse Prep is a co-educational preparatory school for pupils aged between 7 and 11. Tel: 01223 403920; email: prephm@perse.co.uk. (*See The Perse Prep School entry in IAPS section.*)

The Perse Pelican School is for children aged 3 to 7. Tel: 01223 403940; email: pelicanschoolsec@perse.co.uk. (*See The Perse Pelican School entry in IAPS section.*)

Alumni & Development. The Perse develops relationships with Old Perseans and Friends around the world. Tel: 01223 403808; email: perseado@perse.co.uk.

Charitable status. The Perse School is a charitable company limited by guarantee (company number 5977683, registered charity number 1120654) registered in England and Wales whose registered office is situated at The Perse School, Hills Road, Cambridge CB2 8QF.

Governing Body:

Nominated by Gonville & Caius College:
Prof A D Oliver, MA, MPhil, PhD, LittD

Nominated by Trinity College:
Dr L Merrett, MA, PhD

Co-opted:
A Y-C Au, MA, FCA
Dr H Bettinson, MA, PhD
S A Boyle, MA
K A Davies, MA, FCA
W M R Dawkins, BA
N Finlayson-Brown, BA
S Freestone, OBE, DL, MEd, GRSM, LRAM, ARCM
C P Hancock, QC, MA, LLM [OP]
S D Lebus, MA
Dr R Mason, BSc, MBBS, MRCP, MBA
G J Proudfoot, MA
S C Roberts, MA
J W Scott, MA (*Chair*)
M Singh, MBA, Master Mariner
S L Steele, CTA
C J Stenner, LLB (*Vice-Chair*)
D Williams, MB, BCh, FRCP, FRCPH

Clerk to the Governors: G A Ellison MA

Head: Ed Elliott

Bursar: Alison Shakespeare
Senior Deputy Head: Dan Cross
Deputy Head (*Pupil Development and Welfare*): Ed Wiseman
Deputy Head (*Operations and Outreach*): Gavin Richards
Deputy Head (*International and Educational Opportunities*): Simon Armitage
Deputy Head (*Teaching and Learning*): Tanya Khimyak
Director of Communications: Claire Ziwa
Deputy Bursar and Chief Financial Officer Ginni Carroll
Director of HR: Cheryl Few
Business Development Director: Kathy Sawtell
Director of ICT: Fraser Robertson

Plymouth College

Ford Park, Plymouth, Devon PL4 6RN

Tel: +44 (0)1752 505100
email: admissions@plymouthcollege.com
mail@plymouthcollege.com
website: www.plymouthcollege.com
Twitter: @PlymouthCollege
Facebook: @PlymouthCollege
Instagram: @plymcollege

Plymouth College, based in the maritime city of Plymouth with the moorland, countryside and coastal landscapes of Devon and Cornwall close to hand, has been at the forefront of education in South West England since its foundation in 1877. It amalgamated in 1896 with Mannamead School for boys in Plymouth, founded in 1854. The School became fully co-educational in 1995 and in 2004 merged with St Dunstan's Abbey for Girls.

Numbers. Currently there are 540 pupils in the school (310 boys and 230 girls) from ages 3 to 18.

Buildings. The Senior School stands on high ground in Plymouth. The buildings include Science Laboratories, Art and Craft rooms including extensive facilities for photography and print-making, the Dining Hall, an Assembly Hall in which concerts and plays are performed as well as a well-equipped Design and Technology Block. The grounds in Ford Park include a rifle range and an indoor, 25m heated swimming pool. Playing fields at Ford Park are supplemented by two other fields close by. There is an on-site astro surface and the school has use of a full-size AstroTurf pitch for hockey nearby. In 2004 a hospitality suite and Music School opened and in 2011 two new boarding houses were established. The Boarding Houses have undergone a two-year refurbishment programme since 2016. The Sixth Form has its own dedicated Centre with its own Bistro and 2016 saw the opening of the Michael Ball Drama Studio, opened by its namesake who is an old boy of the school. Another old boy, Tom Daley, opened the new Strength & Conditioning Gym in 2018. There is also an outdoor education centre located on Dartmoor.

The Preparatory School, for pupils aged 3–11, is on the same site as the Senior School and benefits from the extensive facilities.

Organisation. Below the Sixth Form, pupils are set in some areas so that pupils may proceed at a pace best suited to their abilities. Pupils are organised in 4 Houses and participation in house events is actively encouraged. Each pupil is under the supervision of a Tutor and Head of Year who report to the Assistant Head. In Years 7–10 Form Prefects are appointed. Every pupil is expected to play a full part in games and other school activities outside the classroom. Pupils in Years 10 and above also take part in our enrichment programme which includes The Duke of Edinburgh's Award, CCF (all 3 sections), Sports Leaders Award and a wide range of other activities. All pupils take part in a PSHEE programme, with careers advice starting in Year 7. English (Language and Literature), a Modern Language, Mathematics, Physics, Chemistry and Biology are taken by all to GCSE. Normally three more are chosen by the pupils

Sixth Form. The Sixth Form is based on tutor groups with approx. twelve pupils in each group. Pupils usually study three subjects at A Level, with four being studied in exceptional circumstances. In addition, our Sports Baccalaureate is an alternative to A Levels and includes a BTEC in Sport & Outdoor Education as well as qualifications in other sporting and outdoor activity areas. Tutors keep a pastoral and academic watch on the pupils' performance, feeding information to the Head and Assistant Heads of Sixth Form.

Sixth Formers are well prepared for universities and careers both in the UK and overseas, including scholarship advice for the US, with detailed university advice starting in Year 9.

Games. Rugby, Football, Cricket, Hockey, Netball and Swimming are the major sports. There is also Athletics, Badminton, Basketball, Cross-Country Running, Fencing, Sailing, Shooting and Tennis. Games are compulsory but more senior pupils have a wide range of options available to them.

School Activities. Pupils take part in a very good range of activities. There is a contingent of the CCF with Navy, Army and Air Force Sections. There is also The Duke of Edinburgh's Award scheme and adventure training as well as participation in Ten Tors each year. Pupils in Year 10 participate in a Sports Leaders scheme with local primary schools. A number of overseas expeditions are also organised each year. School Societies cover a range of activities from Mountain Biking to Young Enterprise. There is also a very good and active Outdoor Education department which offers pupils opportunities in such activities as Bushcraft, Caving and Kayaking.

Music & Performing Arts. There is an excellent school choir that sings at all major school events, concerts, and church services throughout the school year. The school orchestra, like the choir, provides music at school events and concerts. In addition to these groups the school has various small ensembles that are run by the visiting specialist instrumental teachers. The school has a thriving house drama and music competition that attracts whole school support. As well as the formal/organized music making there are innumerable student-led bands that help to ensure that the music department is a vibrant environment. Tuition is provided on all orchestral instruments, including percussion. Voice, piano, organ and all types of guitar lessons are also available. Speech and drama lessons (LAMDA) are offered to all students. The music and drama departments work together on large-scale productions. The drama department offers drama clubs to all year groups. Both departments work with a number of visiting performers/practitioners throughout the year; these are usually focused on specific year groups or examination groups. There are annual music and drama scholarships and instrumental exhibitions.

Boarders. With pupils from all over the world, the boarding houses are run by an enthusiastic, experienced and friendly team who are responsible for all aspects of boarders' welfare. There is also a good mix of activities at the weekends including ten-pin bowling, ice skating, beach visits, cinema trips, surfing, moorland walking and horse riding.

The Boarding Houses are situated on the senior school campus: one for boys, one for girls (approximately 40–50 in each) and two smaller houses for quarantine purposes during the pandemic.

Admission. Admission to the Senior School is normally based on the College Entrance Examination for boys and girls over 10½ and under 12 on 31 August of the year of entry, but it is also possible to enter at other points during the academic programmes. Admission to the Preparatory School is from the age of rising 3. For admission to the Senior and Prep School, please contact admissions@plymouthcollege.com.

Scholarships and Bursaries. There are a variety of Scholarships and Awards for Academia, Art, Music, Drama and Sports and High Performance Sports. These are typically awarded for Year 7, 9 and Sixth Form Entry. In addition to scholarships, means tested bursaries of up to half fees are available. Further information, email admissions@plymouthcollege.com.

Bursaries are means tested.

Fees per Term (2021–2022). Prep School from Reception £2,730 to years 5 & 6 £3,698. Senior School: Day: Years 7–8 £4,794, Years 9–11 £5,462, Sixth Form £5,676. Boarding: Years 7–8 £9,562, Years 9–11 £10,450, Sixth Form £10,960. Weekly Boarding: Years 7–8 £7,670, Years 9–11 £8,338, Sixth Form £8,553. Occasional boarding is available at £50 per night and for up to a maximum of 14 nights a term.

Fees include stationery and games. There are no supplementary lunch charges for full boarding pupils. Music lessons are extra.

Armed Forces and sibling discounts are available.

Charitable Status. Plymouth College is a Registered Charity, number 1105544. Its aim is to provide private education for boys and girls.

Head: **Mrs J Hayward, MA Downing College Cambridge**

Deputy Head (Pupil Welfare And Development): Mr C Irish, BSc Birmingham
Deputy Head (Teaching And Learning): Mr A Carr, MA St Andrews
Director of Studies: Mr P Grey, BSc Open, AMInstP
Bursar: Mr T Williams (*Prep and Senior School*)

Teaching Staff:

Mr E S Agobiani, LLB Leicester (*Head of Year 9*)
Miss P J Anderson, MA Emmanuel College Cambridge (*Head of Classics*)
Mr R Atkinson, BA Exeter
Mr M Bennett, BA Exeter (*Head of Music, Joint Head of English*)
Mrs A C Blunden-Currie, BA Exeter
Mr K C Boots, BA Wales, MEd Exeter, AMBDA
Mr B Bryan, BSc Northampton (*Head of Psychology*)
Mr M Byrne, BSc Loughborough (*Head of Boarding & Director of Cricket*)
Mr C Chilcott (*OED Tutor*)
Mrs A-L Chubb, BA Wolverhampton (*Head of History*)
Mrs R L Connor, BA Nottingham (*Head of EAL, Deputy Head of Sixth Form*)
Mr J Dickin, BA Warwick, PDGE (*Head of English*)
Mr R L Edwards, BA Wales (*Director of Rugby*)
Mrs J Eglinton, BMus Royal Northern College of Music, MMus (*Director of Music*)
Mr S Fenwick, BA Exeter (*Head of Hockey*)
Mrs B Field, BSc York (*Head of Chemistry, Head of Girls' Boarding*)
Mrs N E Glasgow, BA Aberystwyth

Mrs A E Green, BSc Nottingham

Dr A Hawker, BSc Plymouth, PhD

Miss N S L Husband, BA Queen Margaret

Mr D A Jones, BSc Birmingham (*Head of Mathematics*)

Dr S Jordan, PhD Dundee

Mrs N Lilley, BA Nottingham Trent (*Head of Business & Economics*)

Mrs N Lisney, BA Plymouth (*Head of Design Technology*)

Mr G J Llewellyn-Rees, BEng Brunel, MEng Heriot Watt, MBA Imperial College (*Head of Physics*)

Mr D J Martin, BA Warwick (*Head of Religious Studies*)

Dr A Miller, BSc, PhD Bristol, CChem, MRSC, CPhys, MinstP (*Head of Computer Science*)

Miss I Moore, BEd Plymouth Marjon

Mrs R Moore (*Head of Lower School and Joint Head of English*)

Mr P M Mutlow, BA Durham (*Director of Sport*)

Mr C G Nicol, Dip. Duncan of Jordanstone College of Art (*Head of Art*)

Dr A Norris, BSc Liverpool, PhD

Miss L M Odendaal, BA Stellenbosch

Mrs N Paice, BA College of St Mark & St John (*Head of Geography*)

Mr D P Prideaux, BSc Bristol (*Head of Biology*)

Mr P J Randall, BA Oxford Brookes (*Head of MFL*)

Mr O Rees (*OED Manager*)

Mrs C Riley-Harling, BSc St Mark & St John (*Head of Year 11*)

Miss L M Russo, MSci Imperial College

Miss C P Sherratt, BSc Plymouth

Mrs L E Smith, BSc Exeter

Mrs S Sullivan, BA Glasgow School of Art

Mr A G Summons, BSc, MSc Exeter (*Head of Sixth Form*)

Miss E D Tremaine, BEd De Montfort (*Head of PE*)

Miss F Venon, Licence D'Anglais Universitie de St Etienne, Maitrise (*Exams Officer*)

Mr M P Wesley, BSc Nottingham Trent (*Head of Year 10*)

Mrs V J Willden, BA Plymouth

Pocklington School

West Green, Pocklington, York, East Yorkshire YO42 2NJ

Tel: 01759 321200

email: admissions@pocklingtonschool.com

website: www.pocklingtonschool.com

Twitter: @PockSchool

Facebook: @PocklingtonSchool

LinkedIn: /pocklington-school

Pocklington is an inclusive, family focussed and academic school that offers incredible experiences inside and outside the classroom. We believe in encouraging pupils to seize opportunities from the broad range of activities we offer. Along with our approach to teaching and learning, these help to form the bedrock of our young Pocklingtonians' character and grow the qualities that support our values. Our sense of community, care for each other and pride in the school is tangible. This is no more evident than in our outstanding boarding provision. At the heart of this ethos lie our Values and Virtues. They drive all that we do at Pocklington and mean our pupils leave with a deep sense of social responsibility and the ability to shape their own future.

Pocklington School lies 12 miles east of York on the edge of a vibrant, friendly market town, on a 50-acre campus with good public transport links and its own bus service. The school, founded in 1514, blends strong traditions with innovation and flexibility, encouraging pupils to have the courage to take chances with their learning and achieve the best that they can.

Numerous co-curricular activities for day and boarding pupils take place every day until 5pm, and each pupil is encouraged to pursue their own interests to help develop the depth of character and self-awareness to tackle life's challenges on their own terms. Facilities include a 300-seat theatre, an indoor sports hall, strength and conditioning room and swimming pool, plus 21-acres of grass sports pitches and two full-sized synthetic pitches. Full, weekly and part-time boarding options are available, in outstanding boarding houses that create a home from home for all our boarders.

Right through from Prep School, with its emphasis on nurturing children's natural curiosity, imagination and enthusiasm for learning, to the Sixth Form where independent thought is prized, our pupils are encouraged to be resilient, resourceful learners. Our new 'working week' supports the school's strategic goal of further improving academic performance, increasing pupils' independence and meeting the needs of modern family life. Pupils engage in a 5-day academic week, Monday to Friday, with Saturdays reserved for sports fixtures and a new boarders' weekend programme.

We employ the best educational tools and new technology to ensure youngsters are enthused and inspired by the world of knowledge available to them. Our Art and Design Technology Centre has every facility to encourage the pursuit of traditional arts and crafts, as well as providing cutting-edge equipment for digital and computer design, and manufacturing technology. An individual approach, supported by flexible learning platforms, allows each pupil to progress at his or her pace, boosting their confidence and self-esteem so they often exceed their expectations.

Our Sixth Form has spacious communal areas, a study centre and a comprehensive library. Students are encouraged to work both collaboratively and independently as they begin to make the transition to university study and/or workplace success.

Recent former pupils who retain links with the school include Davis Cup winner Kyle Edmund, England rugby star Rob Webber and world-renowned concert pianist Alexandra Dariescu.

We aim to instil the Pocklington Values and Virtues into all our pupils, to engage with our families and support them in raising the Pocklingtonians of tomorrow and to be open to innovation, conscious of tradition and so secure our Foundation's future.

Fees per term (2021–2022). Day £2,992–£5,463, Boarding £8,110–£10,027, Weekly Boarding £7,529–£8,601). Other boarding options are available – see website for details.

Chair of Governors: Mr T A Stephenson, MA, FCA

***Headmaster*: Mr T Seth**, MA Cantab

Head of Pocklington Prep School: Ms S Ward, LLB PgDip

The Portsmouth Grammar School

High Street, Portsmouth, Hants PO1 2LN

Tel: 023 9236 0036
email: admissions@pgs.org.uk
website: www.pgs.org.uk
Twitter: @PGS1732
Facebook: @ThePortsmouthGrammarSchool
Instagram: @theportsmouthgrammarschool
LinkedIn: /school/pgs1732

Motto: *Praemia Virtutis Honores*

The Portsmouth Grammar School is a happy and vibrant independent school located in the historic heart of Portsmouth and only a few minutes' walk from the Solent.

The Portsmouth Grammar School was founded in 1732 by William Smith: Mayor of Portsmouth and Physician to its Garrison. Of humble origins, Smith flourished through spirit, vision, and learning. He was determined that, like him, the young people of Portsmouth should have access to a transformative education. And so, in his will, he asked his Oxford college, Christ Church, to establish a school in the town where he had prospered.

We remain true to William Smith's vision today. A forward-looking school located in the historic heart of Portsmouth, we encourage our pupils to envision their life at 25, and we prepare them to make a positive contribution in whatever pathway they choose. Portsmouth is, after all, a city concerned with destinations.

We do this by nurturing the individual potential of each of our pupils. Our success in public examinations and in securing places at first-choice universities is combined with attention to personal flourishing and to the joy of lifelong learning. In our caring, family community, pupils develop through academic challenge, an astonishing breadth of co-curricular activity, and opportunities both to lead and to serve. Our guiding commitment is to support every pupil to be happy and successful; in that order.

The Portsmouth Grammar School is a fully co-educational independent day school. There are 1,269 pupils in the School.

The Pre-School offers outstanding care for girls and boys from age 2½ to 4, supporting them to become confident and happy children who are active, independent learners.

The Junior School at The Portsmouth Grammar School is a happy and dynamic place for children aged 4–11 (Reception–Year 6) to learn. We like to think of it as a 'Eureka' school, where every day our children are challenged to 'find things out'. Children in the Junior School excel academically and grow into happy, confident, individuals. The main ages of entry are 4 and 7, however there are places available for intermediate entry.

Pupils in the Junior School no longer sit the 11+ entrance assessments for entry in to the Senior School. The Head of the Junior School will recommend entry to the Senior School following its programme of continuous assessment.

The Portsmouth Grammar Senior School offers girls and boys aged 11–16 outstanding academic, pastoral and co-curricular opportunities. Pupils flourish in a supportive and caring environment, achieving excellent results at GCSE. Pupils are enthusiastic and committed learners. They enjoy

supporting others in their learning, using information and communication technology to enhance their understanding. Admission is by the School's Entrance Assessment at 11+ and at 13+. Entrants at 13 are usually pre-tested at 11 to accommodate high demand for places. Pupils are admitted at other ages, should vacancies occur, subject to assessments and satisfactory reports from previous schools.

PGS offers a broad Sixth Form curriculum, which places a strong emphasis on academic challenge and enrichment. Admission to the Sixth Form is subject to satisfactory standard at GCSE and interview.

Curriculum. The Portsmouth Grammar School aims to create an environment in which pupils are keen to develop a range of analytical skills and creative talents. We encourage pupils to be enquiring and independent in their learning. We want our learners to evaluate their progress critically and learn to optimise their potential by setting themselves challenging goals and adopting effective study techniques. They should be willing to work collaboratively, with proper respect for each other's different talents and mindful at all times of academic honesty. The Sixth Form A Level curriculum offers all pupils the opportunity to undertake an Extended Project Qualification (EPQ), which may be essay-based, creative or practical. They will have access to a wide range of taught academic enrichment courses, to extend their learning beyond their core subjects, through our Ignite! programme. Students may choose from a broad range of community partnership projects and work experience, receiving skills coaching and opportunities for leadership development.

A Level subjects include: Art, Biology, Business Studies, Chemistry, Classical Civilisation, Design and Technology, Drama, Economics, Electronics, English Literature, French, Geography, German, Government and Politics, Greek, History, Latin, Mathematics, Further Mathematics, Music, Physical Education, Psychology, Religious Studies and Spanish. The Personal Enrichment Curriculum offers pupils the resources, opportunities and coaching to develop and build personal qualities, personal perspective and ideas, extended thinking, confidence, the ability to take control of life and an understanding of what they enjoy. It is focused on personal development through exciting, rewarding and hugely enjoyable opportunities, providing an inspiring platform for the future.

The Sixth Form prepares candidates for entry to Higher Education, and the Universities and Careers Department provides excellent support with UCAS applications and close relations with various forms of employment.

Religion. The Portsmouth Grammar School is non-denominational.

Pastoral Care. We firmly believe that a child's happiness is an essential foundation for their wellbeing and to their progress in learning. It is also vital to their preparation for a flourishing and fulfilled life beyond school, as individuals, as lifelong learners, as citizens and within the world of work. Individualised care is at the heart of PGS life; our staff are enormously dedicated and go above and beyond to support the pupils in their care.

Sport. Rugby football, netball and hockey are the main games in Winter and Spring; cricket (boys and girls), tennis and athletics in the Summer. Cross-country running, squash, judo, badminton, gymnastics, basketball, aerobics, swimming and sailing are also available. The School has enjoyed national success in recent years in sports such as football, hockey, netball, athletics, and cricket.

The Co-Curriculum. There are significant opportunities for co-curricular involvement at the school. Music, Sport, Drama, CCF and Outdoor Pursuits including Ten Tors and participation in the Duke of Edinburgh's Award scheme, play a huge role in the development of pupils and provide them with a diverse and popular range of activities. Service to the local community and charity work is also an important feature of the school's ethos. Many clubs and societies cater for a considerable range of co-curricular interests from the Model United Nations to Wildlife Club. Numerous expeditions, holiday activities and trips are actively encouraged and include many foreign tours for sports teams and music ensembles. The School has a flourishing exchange scheme with French, German and Spanish schools. Sports teams have recently gone on tour to Singapore, Malaysia and South Africa. Recent expeditions have seen pupils travel to Madagascar, Uganda, Cambodia, Argentina and Cuba.

Fees per term (2021–2022). Senior School £5,754; Junior School £3,692–£4,096. (Fees quoted include direct debit discount.)

Scholarships and Bursaries. An extensive programme of scholarships and means-tested bursaries is offered in the Senior School from 11–18 years and we are extremely grateful to all those whose generosity makes it possible for a growing number of pupils to join PGS each year, regardless of their financial situation.

Scholarships are non means-tested and awarded to recognise exceptional academic or co-curricular ability. Where appropriate, these awards may be augmented by a bursary.

Bursaries are entirely means-tested and reflect the outstanding academic potential of an individual pupil regardless of ability to afford the school's fees.

All candidates are automatically considered for academic scholarships at 11+, 13+ and 16+.

Additionally, scholarships can also be awarded for excellence in Art, Drama, Music and Sport at 11+, 13+ and 16+. Existing PGS pupils may also apply for consideration for these awards once they become eligible during their time at the school.

Full details of all scholarships and bursaries are available on the School's website.

Buildings. The School is located within the historic quarter of Portsmouth. The Grade II listed buildings of the Junior and Senior School sit comfortably next to modern developments, including a new Sixth Form Centre, a state-of-the-art Science Centre, a Music School, a modern dining and theatre complex and a fully refurbished library. The School sports facilities are located at the Hilsea Playing Fields and include an all-weather pitch and Sports Pavilion.

Honours. Just under 90% of pupils win a place at their first or insurance choice university and we have frequent success in helping our pupils secure offers for prestigious degree apprenticeship schemes with organisations such as Dyson, Rolls Royce and Unilever.

Sportsmen include England Cricket Captain Wally Hammond, Athletics International Roger Black, and Paralympian Ross Morrison. Military distinction in abundance, including 3 VCs (one the first VC submariner), several Admirals, Generals and Air Marshals. Medicine is also a continuing theme – from pioneer ophthalmologist James Ware to Viagra researcher Ian Osterloh. Arts are well and diversely represented: dramatist Simon Gray, poet Christopher Logue, novelist James Clavell, film director James Bobin, Sky News entertainment reporter Joe Michalczuk, cathedral organist Christopher Walsh, and pop singer Paul Jones. Civil Servants, Judges and barristers galore, plus entrepreneur industrialist Alan Bristow.

Charitable status. The Portsmouth Grammar School is a Registered Charity, number 1063732. It exists to provide education for boys and girls.

Governing Body:
Chairman: Mr W J B Cha, BA
Vice Chairman: Mrs M Scott, BSc
Mrs S Baker, MA
Mrs K Bishop, BA
Mr T W Burden, MA
Mr M R Coffin, BA Econ, FCA
Mrs V Durham, MA Oxon
Mrs S Gingell, MSc, DIPSW
Dr M Grossel, BSc, MA, PhD
Mr N D Latham, CBE, MSc, CEng, FIMarEST, FIMechE
His Honour Judge Lodder QC, LLB
Mr J Nicholls BA, ACA, FCT
Mr P G Parkinson, BA, Dip Arch
Mr J D Poulton, BA Cantab
Dr S Ross, MB ChB, MRCGP

Senior Team:

Head: Dr A K Cotton, BA, MSt, DPhil, MA Ed

Senior Deputy Head: Mr D M L Payne, MA
Deputy Head (Academic): Mrs S Haslam, BA Hons, MA, QTS
Deputy Head (Teaching and Educational Development): Mr H R Wiggins, MA
Deputy Head (Innovation): Mr L F Rees, BA
Assistant Head (Sixth Form): Mrs R Clay, BA
Assistant Head (Pastoral): Miss F E A Bush, BA
Assistant Head (Admissions and Partnerships): Mrs J Jackson, BSc
Assistant Head (Co-Curriculum): Mr C Ellis, BSc
Assistant Head (Pupil Progress): Mr Martin Hill, BA Hons, MEd

Bursar: Mr S R Merriam, BSc, CDir, FLoD

Examinations Office:
Assistant Head of Examinations: Mrs D Valentine, BA

Junior School and Nursery

Head of the Junior School: Mrs A Wilson-Smith, BA, PGCE
Deputy Head: Mr J Ashcroft, BSc, PGCE
Head of Early Years & Infants, Mrs J Millward, BEd

Assistant Heads:
Mr C Ellis, BA, QTS (*Co-curriculum*)
Mrs R Evans, BA, QTS (*Pastoral*)
Mrs G Radford, BA (*Academic*)

Pre-School Lead: Mrs C Eastburn, BA, PGCE

Princethorpe College

Princethorpe, Rugby, Warwickshire CV23 9PX

Tel: 01926 634200

email: post@princethorpe.co.uk

website: www.princethorpe.co.uk

Twitter: @PrincethorpeCol

Facebook: @princethorpecollege

Instagram: @ThePrincethorpeFoundation

Princethorpe College is a Catholic, co-educational, HMC independent day school and welcomes members of all faiths and backgrounds. The school was founded as a boys' school in 1957 in Leamington Spa by the congregation of the Missionaries of the Sacred Heart (MSC), moving to its present site, a former Benedictine monastery, in 1966. The College became co-educational in 1996, and in September 2001 formed a partnership with Crackley Hall School in Kenilworth in order to provide continuous education from 2 to 18 years. A further merger took place in September 2016 with the Crescent School, Rugby. All schools are members of an independent trust – The Princethorpe Foundation.

Number in School. The school has around 900 day pupils from 11 to 18 years with some 200 in the Sixth Form. An extensive network of private coaches transports pupils from a wide area.

Aims. The College provides a caring, Christian environment for children where their needs can be met and their talents, confidence and self-esteem developed. There is a healthy balance between freedom and structure and an emphasis on self-discipline through responsibility and trust, which develops confidence and independence.

The College draws on a rich tradition of Catholic teaching and the spirituality of the Missionaries of the Sacred Heart, whose ethos is central to its character. In welcoming families of a variety of faiths and none, the school community is a living example of ecumenism. The College motto, *Christus Regnet* – let Christ reign – is a reminder of Christ's love, service, forgiveness and generosity of spirit.

Academic. A broad-based, stimulating curriculum satisfies a wide range of ability and fosters a love of learning. A favourable pupil to teacher ratio, permitting personal attention, contributes to impressive value-added achievements. High fliers are stretched and provided with intellectually challenging assignments through our da Vinci Programme, ensuring that they achieve at the highest possible levels. The curriculum is well supported by a magnificent library and ICT. Qualified specialists give tuition to pupils with special educational needs.

Pupils in Years 7 to 9 have a broad-based curriculum which avoids early specialisation and usually go on to take nine or ten GCSEs.

Supervised homework and free extended day are offered until 6.00pm.

The Sixth Form. Students in the Sixth Form are prepared for A Level examinations after which the vast majority proceed to university. The Head of Sixth Form and the team of tutors monitor the academic progress of Sixth Formers through regular discussions with the students and their teachers. Visits to university Open Days, together with professional careers advice enables students to make the best choices about their next stage of education.

Our Sixth Form enrichment programme puts a strong emphasis on the acquisition of key skills and the education of the whole person. Sixth Formers are offered residential outward bound courses, training programmes and retreats which provide an opportunity for reflection and exploration, to develop a mature and balanced perspective. Guest lecturers, debates and trips all enhance Sixth Form life.

All Sixth Formers enjoy privileges and have the responsibilities of leadership and example; certain members are elected to perform prefectorial duties. Prefects attend a leadership course and learn valuable management skills. They organise activities for younger pupils and chair the School Council, which offers a forum for lively discussion and gives the students an influential voice in the running of the College. The House Captains have a pivotal role in the organisation of inter-house events.

Princethorpe Diploma. Open to all Sixth Form students the innovative Princethorpe Diploma brings together six components (work experience, community and ethos, service to others, extra-curricular, academic studies and attendance and punctuality) that we believe are critical in today's world, helping our students leave us as mature, confident, resilient, well-rounded young adults, with a strong set of moral values to guide them through adult life.

Careers. The Careers Advice Programme commences in Year 9 and regular tutorials are held concentrating on option subject choices and developing careers awareness. Interview technique is developed and students are assisted with work experience placements which are undertaken at the end of Year 10 and Lower Sixth. The College also holds a biennial Careers Fair for pupils in Year 10 to Sixth Form and their parents.

Art & Design. A feature which immediately strikes all visitors to the College is the outstanding display of canvases. Superb examination results and successes in national competitions are commonplace. The study of drawing, painting, graphics and ceramics are central and they are enhanced by using the work of great artists as stimulus material.

Technology includes Food, Graphics, Resistant Materials, Textiles and Electronics. Pupils can work with a variety of materials, realising their technical designs in the well-resourced workshops, which includes CAD/CAM facilities.

Music and Drama. Music is studied by all pupils in their first three years and as an option at GCSE and A Level. The College choir gives regular performances and tours. Many pupils learn instruments and are encouraged to join the orchestra. Peripatetic staff offer tuition in most instruments. There is a state-of-the-art studio with digital recording facilities for Music Technology and there is an acclaimed Binns organ in the magnificent Chapel built by Peter Paul Pugin.

The College has a theatre and regular productions are staged including musicals and revues. Productions involve a large number of pupils and staff and provide an excellent way for pupils of different years to get to know each other. There are thriving Dance and Drama Clubs. Theatre Studies is offered in the Sixth Form.

Physical Education. All pupils participate in games and Physical Education classes. Physical Education can also be studied as an examination subject at GCSE and A Level as can a BTEC in Physical Education. The major sports are rugby, netball, hockey, cricket, rounders, tennis and athletics; they are run in tandem with badminton, soccer, squash, basketball and trampolining.

The Sports Centre has a sports hall, fitness gym and a climbing wall. Extensive outdoor facilities include an internationally recognised cross-country course, floodlit all-weather pitch, tennis courts and over sixty acres of games pitches.

Sports Clubs include Rugby, Football, Hockey, Netball, Climbing Wall, Badminton, Archery, Golf, Fitness, Running, Trampolining, Cycling, Athletics, Rounders and Tennis.

Co-curricular Activities. There is always a wide range of clubs, societies and activities such as Airgineers, Art, Beekeeping, Book Club, Chess, Cookery, Craft, Creative Writing, Dance, Darts, Debating, Drama, Electric Car Club, Equestrian Club, Film Review, Green Team and Wildlife Club, History Club, ICT, Language Conversation – Spanish and French, MEDSOC, Mindfulness, Model UN, Photography, Poetry, Project Club, Psychology, Science, Technical Theatre, Textiles, Young Designers, Youth Chaplaincy and Youth St Vincent de Paul. The Duke of Edinburgh's Award, World Challenge, Camps International and Outward Bound courses are also offered. The Arts Society provides a cultural programme of lectures, poetry evenings, music recitals and play readings.

Admissions. Admission is by examination, in November, for entry the following September, generally at 11 and 13 and at other ages as space allows. Students from other schools join the Sixth Form after their GCSE courses.

Scholarships. There is a variety of Scholarships available for particularly able or talented candidates ranging from Academic, Art and Music to All-Rounder. Additionally, for the Sixth Form there are Academic, Art, Music, Organ and Sports Scholarships available. Scholarships to a maximum reduction of 50% of tuition fees are on offer.

Academic Scholarships: Candidates applying for entry in Years 7, 8, 9 and 10 will be considered automatically for an academic scholarship when taking the Entrance Examination.

All Rounder Scholarships: Sometimes there are students who are both academically able and gifted in a variety of areas and the most outstanding of these can be awarded an All Rounder Scholarship. Supportive evidence is required, such as references from team coaches or activity leaders.

Art Scholarships: Candidates must submit a portfolio and attend an Art Scholarship day. Further details and an Art Scholarship application form are available from the Registrar.

Music Scholarships – Instrumental and Choral: Candidates must attend an audition. Further details and a Music Scholarship application form are available from the Registrar.

Sixth Form Academic Scholarships: Sixth Form Academic Scholarships are open to all external candidates who are expected to achieve 9–7 grades at GCSE. Applicants will be invited to the Academic Scholarships Day where they will sit a Verbal Reasoning examination and have an interview with the Headmaster. More details are available from the Registrar.

Sixth Form Sport Scholarships: Senior Sport Scholarships may be awarded to internal or external candidates entering the Sixth Form. Full details are available from the Registrar.

Sixth Form Music – Instrumental, Choral and Organ Scholarships: Candidates must attend an audition. Full details are available from the Registrar. In the Sixth Form there is also an Organ Scholarship of up to 50% of tuition fees available to candidates who have a high level of ability and are committed and enthusiastic performers. Again details are available from the Registrar.

Sixth Form Drama Scholarships: Students will be required to attend an audition. Further details available from the Registrar.

Sixth Form Art Scholarships: Students will be required to attend an Art Scholarship Day. Further details available from the Registrar.

Fees per term (2021–2022). £4,617 excluding transport and meals. Instrumental tuition, external examinations and some targeted support for those with learning needs are charged as extras.

Charitable status. The Princethorpe Foundation is a Registered Charity, number 1087124. It exists solely for the education of children.

Governing Body:
Trustees:
Chair of Trustees Mrs Elizabeth Griffin, BSc, PGCE, CTC
Deputy Chair: Colin Russell, IEng, ACIBSE, MBA
Jatinder Birdi
Mrs Caroline Cook
Quintin Cornforth, BSc
John Fisher
Michael Fletcher, BSc
Mrs Barbara Forster, Cert Ed
Mr Richard Harcourt, MBA
David Jackson, MInst AM, HNC Business Studies
Charlie Jenkinson, BA, CIPS, MILT
Mrs Elizabeth Kenward, BA, PGCE, CTC
Mrs Marie Kerrigan Cert Ed
Mrs Caroline McGrory, MA Oxon, LPC
Ms Teresa McNamara, BPhil, Cert Ed
Kieron Shaw, MBE, MSc, FCIS
Commodore Bernard Warner

Staff:

Headmaster: Ed Hester, MA Oxon, PGCE (*Mathematics*)

Deputy Heads:
Pastoral: Mrs Beth Sharpe, BSc, PGCE, PGCert Ed (*Special Needs and Inclusion, Design and Technology, Designated Safeguarding Lead*)
Academic: Tom Marriott, MA Cantab (*History*)

Assistant Heads:
Co-curricular: Neil McCollin, BA, QTS
Director of Digital Strategy: Andy Compton, BA, PGCE, MA (*Modern Languages*)
Director of Studies: Michael Spencer, BSc, PGCE (*Physics*)
Teaching and Learning: Dr Liz Pyne, BA, MA, PGCE, PhD (*History*)
Marketing, Admissions and Communications and Old Princethorpians Secretary: Mrs Melanie Butler, BA

Head of Sixth Form: Ben Collie, BSc (*Biology*)

Foundation Assistant Head: Alex Darkes, BEd
Foundation Bursar, Company Secretary and Clerk to the Trustees: Eddie Tolcher, BA, ACIB, MCMI, TechIOSH

Foundation Development Director: Steve Kowal, BSc

Art:

Paul Hubball, BA, PGCE (*Head of Art; also Head of Photography*)

Mrs Rebecca Blunsom-Washbrook, BA, GTP (*also Photography*)

Mrs Jackie Clark, BA, MA, QTA

Mrs Susan Harris, BA, PGCE (*Head of Transition and Induction*)

Miss Helen Plenderleith, BA

Careers:

Mrs Jacqui Quinney, BA, PGCE (*Head of Careers*)

Mrs Kerry Low, BA, Dip CG (*Careers Adviser*)

Mike Taylor, BA, PGCE (*Head of Geography; Work Experience*)

Classics:

Mrs Rachel Taylor, BA, QTS (*Joint Head of Classics*)

Mrs Laura Rindler, MA Oxon, PGCE, MBA (*Joint Head of Classics*)

Computer Science:

Adam Depledge, BSc (*Head of Computer Science; also CoRE Programme*)

Ms Jenny Andrews, BEng, MSc. LLB, PGCE, QTS

CoRE Programme:

Mrs Anne Allen, BSc, PGCE (*Assistant Head of Sixth Form; also Geography*)

Adam Depledge, BSc (*Head of Computer Science*)

Mrs Louise Harrison, BSc, PGCE (*Head of Academic PE*)

Roderick Isaacs, MA Cantab, MA, CertEd (*Assistant Head of Sixth Form; also Religious Studies*)

Kieran McCullough, BA, PGCE (*House Activities Coordinator Fisher; also Religious Studies and Games*)

Mrs Helen Pascoe-Williams, BA, PGCE (*Leader of Learning, Innovation and Character Development; da Vinci Coordinator*)

Adam Rickart, BSc, PGCE (*Head of Austin House*)

Design and Technology:

Paul Scopes, BEd, AST (*Head of Design and Technology*)

William O'Hara, BSc, PGCE

Mrs Miranda Porter, BSc, PGCE (*also Games*)

Ms Jacqui Scott, BSc, PGCE (*also Games*)

Tom Walton, BSc, PGCE

Mrs Beth Sharpe, BEd, PGCE (*Deputy Head – Pastoral and Designated Safeguarding Lead*)

Drama and Theatre Studies:

Ms Aileen Cefaliello, BA, PGCE (*Joint Head of Drama and Theatre Studies; also English*)

Miss Vicky Roberts, BA, PGCE (*Joint Head of Drama and Theatre Studies*)

Mrs Celia Scott, BA, ALA Associate

Economics and Business:

Mrs Elizabeth Gane, BA, PGCE (*Head of Economics and Business*)

Mrs Helen Baker, BA, PGCE (*also Geography*)

Ms Helen Essery, LLB, PGCE (*also Head of Law*)

Mrs Louisa Fielding, BA, PGCE (*Senior Head of House; also Head of Fisher House*)

Daniel Lumb, BA

Mrs Laura Wilford, BSc, QTS

English:

Chris Kerrigan, BA, MA, PGCE (*Head of English*)

Miss Becky Forde, BA, MA, PGCE

Miss Rachael Mack, BA, QTS (*also Games*)

Mrs Fiona Moon, BA, PG Cert Dyslexia and Literacy (*Second in Department; also Special Educational Needs*)

Mrs Jessica Newborough, BA, PGCE (*House Activities Leader*)

Mrs Helen Pascoe-Williams, BA, PGCE (*Leader of Learning, Innovation and Character Development; also da Vinci Coordinator and Coordinator of Extended Project Qualification*)

Mrs Jessica Proudlock, BA, PGCE

Geography:

Mike Taylor, BA, PGCE (*Head of Geography; also Careers – Work Experience*)

Mrs Anne Allen, BSc, PGCE (*Assistant Head of Sixth Form; also CoRE Programme*)

Mrs Helen Baker, BA, PGCE (*also Economics and Business*)

Stewart Dear, BSc, QTS (*also Games*)

Mrs Sarah Evans, BSc, PGCE

History:

Peter Bucknall, BA, MA (*Head of History; also Head of Rugby*)

Mrs Katharine Darwood-Bredin, BSc, GTP (*Head of Politics; also History and Games*) [maternity leave]

Peter Harris, Trainee Teacher

Mrs Tracey Hester, BA Oxon, PGCE (*Oxbridge Coordinator*)

Miss Julia Lindsay, BA, MA, PGCE (*House Activities Coordinator for Fisher; also Politics and Games*)

Greg Lyttle, BA, MA, PGCE (*also Politics*)

Tom Marriot, MA Cantab (*Deputy Head – Academic*)

Dr Liz Pyne, BA, MA, PGCE, PhD (*Assistant Head – Teaching and Learning*)

Law:

Mrs Helen Essery, LLB, PGCE (*Head of Law; also Business*)

Mathematics:

Mrs Sharon McBride, BSc, PGCE, ALCM (*Head of Mathematics*)

Mrs Christina Baxter, BSc, QTS

Mrs Tanya Cowan, BSc, PGCE

Ed Hester, MA Oxon, PGCE (*Headmaster*)

Miss Sophie Jones, MEng, PGCE

Ms Helen Lewis, BA

Ms Davinya Munford, BSc, PGCE

Alex Phillips, BSc, PGCE (*also Games*)

Mrs Leanne Rickart, BEd (*Second in Department*) [maternity leave]

Alef Rosenbaum, MA Oxon, PGCE

Theodoros Scoutas, PGCE (*KS5 Mathematics Coordinator*)

Mrs Isobel Turner-Pryce, MA, PGCE

Modern Languages:

Mrs Stella Keenan, MA, PGCE (*Head of Modern Languages; Spanish Subject Leader and French*)

Andy Compton, BA, MA, PGCE (*Assistant Head – Director of Digital Strategy*)

Mrs Sarah Duran, Licence LLCE Anglais, PGCE (*Second in Department*)

Mrs Bérénice Galano, Licence LLCE Anglais (*House Leader – Austin; French and Spanish*)

Mrs Michele Gawthorpe, MA Oxon, QTS

Mrs Katherine Parsons, BA, MA, PGCE (*Spanish*)

Mrs Natalie Shedden, BA, PGCE

Music:
Gil Cowlishaw, BMus (*Director of Music*)
Mrs Alison Wakeley, BMus, MMus, PGCE (*also REAL Time Coordinator*)

Photography:
Paul Hubball, BA, PGCE (*Head of Photography; also Head of Art*)
Mrs Rebecca Blunsom-Washbrook, BA, GTP (*also Art*)

Physical Education and Games:
Lee Cassell, BA, PGCE (*Foundation Director of Sport*)
Miss Sinead Birks, MPhysEd (*Graduate Sports Coach and Teaching Assistant*)
Will Bower, BSc, PG Dip with QTS (*Head of Outdoor Education*)
Peter Bucknall, BA, MA (*Head of Rugby; also Head of History*)
Miss Ellie Callan, BSc, NQT (*House Leader – Fisher*)
Ms Hannah Carminati, BSc, QTS (*House Leader – Benet; also Primary School Sport Liaison*)
Lewis Clarke, BSc, PGCE
Ben Collie, BSc (*Biology; also Head of Sixth Form*)
Ms Suzanne Cox, MSc (*Trampoline Coach*)
Stewart Dear, BSc, QTS (*also Geography*)
Adam Depledge, BSC (*Head of Computer Science; also CoRE Programme*)
Mrs Sarah Evans, BSc, PGCE (*also Geography*)
Stuart Friswell (*Rugby Coach*)
Mrs Elizabeth Gane, BA, PGCE (*Head of Economics and Business*)
Mrs Louise Harrison, BSc, PGCE (*Head of Academic PE and CoRE Programme*)
Ross Holtom, BA (*i/c BTEC Sport*)
Rod Isaacs, MA Cantab, MA, Cert Ed (*Assistant Head of Sixth Form; also CoRE Programme and Religious Studies*)
Miss Jen Law, BSc, PGCE (*Head of Girls' Games*)
Neil McCollin, BA, QTS (*Assistant Head – Co-curricular*)
Miss Rachael Mack, BA, QTS (*Hockey Coach; also English*)
Dr Dominic Phelps, BA, MA (*also History*)
Alex Phillips, BSc, PGCE (*also Mathematics*)
Mrs Miranda Porter, BSc, PGCE (*also Design and Technology*)
Gavin Rooney (*Sports Coach*)
Ms Jacqui Scott, BSc, PGCE (*also Design and Technology*)
Cyprian Vella, BA, MA, PGCE (*Assistant Head of Sixth Form; Acting Head of Religious Studies*)
Tom Walton, BSc, PGCE (*also Design and Technology*)
Mrs Clare White , BSc, PGCE (*Science; also Psychology and Sociology*)
Paul Whitehead (*Hockey Coach*)

Politics
Mrs Katharine Darwood-Bredin, BSc, GTP (*Head of Politics; also History*)
Greg Lyttle, BA, MA, PGCE (*also History*)
Mrs Julia Lindsay, BA, MA, PGCE (*also History and Games*)

Psychology and Sociology:
Mrs Fionnuala Schofield, BSc (*Head of Psychology and Sociology*)
Miss Lizzie Caisey, BA, MA, PGCE
Ms Jo Powell, BA, PGCE
Adam Rickart, BSc, PGCE (*Head of Austin House; also CoRE Programme*)

Mrs Clare White, BSc, PGCE (*also Science and Games*)

Religious Studies:
Cyprian Vella, BA, MA, PGCE (*Head of Religious Studies; also Assistant Head of Sixth Form; Games*)
Rod Isaacs, MA Cantab, MA, CertEd (*Assistant Head of Sixth Form; also CoRE Programme*)
Kieran McCullough, BA, PGCE (*House activities Coordinator Fisher; also CoRE Programme*)
Miss Megan O'Gorman, BA, QTS
Dr Dominic Phelps BA, MA (*also Games*)

Special Educational Needs Department:
Ms Lorna Prestage, BSc, PGCE, PG Dip, ADG (*Special Educational Needs Coordinator*)
Mrs Kayley Arkesdon, MBA (*Learning Support Assistant*)
Ms Kat Brittain (*Learning Support Assistant*)
Mrs Clare Callaghan, BSc, PGCE (*SEN Mathematics Support; also Mathematics*)
Mrs Caroline Hardware (*Learning Support Assistant*)
Mrs Anna Jelec, MEd, PATOSS (*Learning Support Teacher and Specialist Assessor*)
Mrs Amanda Kelly (*Learning Support Assistant*)
Mrs Fiona Moon, BA, PG Cert SpLD (*also English*)
Mrs Lee O'Gorman (*Learning Support Assistant*)
Mrs Angela Ritson, BA, QTS (*Learning Support Teacher*)

The Sciences:
Miss Emma Cooper, BSc, PGCE (*Head of Science; Head of Chemistry*)
Ben Collie, BSc (*Biology; Head of Sixth Form; Games*)
Mrs Sam Curtis, BSc, PGCE (*Chemistry*)
Dan Lee, MEng, PGCE (*Second in Science; Head of Physics*)
Dr Emilie Onyekwe, BSc, QTS (*Chemistry*)
Miss Faye Roberts, BSc, MSc, PGCE (*Biology, also Head of Benet*)
Simon Robertson, BSc, PGCE (*Head of More House; Biology*)
Mrs Sophie Rose, BSc, PGCE (*Physics*)
Mrs Joanne Smith, MChem, PGCE (*Chemistry*)
Rob Southern, BSc, PGCE (*Physics*)
Michael Spencer, BSc, PGCE (*Physics; also Assistant Head – Director of Studies*)
Mrs Catherine Warne, BSc, PGCE (*Biology*)
Mrs Clare White, BSc, PGCE (*Science; also Psychology and Sociology*)
Dan White, BSc, PGCE (*Biology and Chemistry*)
Ms Francesca Wright, BSc, PGCE (*Chemistry and Biology*)

Prior Park College

Ralph Allen Drive, Bath BA2 5AH

Tel: 01225 835353
email: info@priorparkschools.com
website: www.priorparkcollege.com
Twitter: @priorpark
Facebook: @prior.park.37

Motto: *Deo Duce, Deo Luce*

Prior Park College is a fully co-educational Catholic Boarding and Day School. Founded in 1830 by Bishop Baines, it was under the control of the Bishops of Clifton until 1924, when it passed to the Congregation of Christian

Brothers. Since 1981, Prior Park has been under lay management and has more than doubled in size. Prior Park is a friendly, thriving community of around 600 pupils, with a strong boarding community, excellent academic standards and a strong devotion to educating the whole person.

The College is housed in magnificent Palladian architecture, built by John Wood for Ralph Allen, with glorious views of the World Heritage City of Bath. The 57-acre site combines an elegant setting for boarding and day education with access to Bath and its numerous cultural attractions. Proximity to the M4 and M5 motorways places the College within easy reach of London, the Midlands, the South-West and Wales. Good rail links and proximity to Bristol, Heathrow and Gatwick international airports allow easy transfer for our international students.

Structure of the School. Prior Park is a friendly, thriving community of approximately 600 pupils. The two boarding houses are home to approximately 140 full and weekly boarders. Flexi boarding is also available if space is available.

Objects of the College. The school's primary aim is to provide a genuine all-round education and whilst academic endeavour remains at the school's core, Prior Park encourages its students to embrace all the opportunities on offer. It is a school that cares. The school's renowned pastoral system provides space and support for each of its students and enables our leavers to be capable, confident and compassionate adults.

Buildings and Grounds. Ranked by the Oxford Royale Academy as the UK's most beautiful boarding school. The Houses, Administration and College Chapel are to be found in the fine 18th-century architecture grouped around Ralph Allen's celebrated Palladian Mansion. A major refurbishment programme of boys' and girls' boarding accommodation has provided comfortable study-bedrooms, quiet areas and recreational rooms. On-site facilities are excellent and include a state-of-the-art sports centre with fitness suite, indoor swimming pool, all weather pitches, 150-seat theatre, recording studio, Chapel and an industry standard A Level DT workshop.

Curriculum. The academic curriculum conforms to and goes beyond the requirements of the National Curriculum. The curriculum in Year 7–9 is broad. Great care is taken to ensure that careful guidance is given to pupils in Year 9 and Year 11 when GCSE and A Level choices are being made. The majority of pupils will study ten GCSE subjects. In Sixth Form students mostly take three A Level subjects plus another qualification, e.g. an Extended Project Qualification (EPQ).

Music. The College has a highly-deserved reputation for musical excellence. Two chapel choirs provide high quality music for the weekly sung Mass in the glorious surroundings of the Chapel of Our Lady of the Snows. The John Wood Chapel, within Prior Park Mansion, offers a further concert and rehearsal venue for the many musicians in the school.

The Music Department, also in the Mansion, houses a recording studio and teaching and practice rooms. Around half the pupils learn a musical instrument and there are several thriving orchestras, chamber groups and bands. Several Prior Park musicians have gone on to Oxbridge. Other graduates go to major conservatoires and play in NYO, NCO, etc.

Performing Arts. The students stage around fifteen drama productions a year. Recent performances include:

Hedda Gabler, *Hamlet*, *Daisy Pulls It Off* and *The Crucible*. The Julian Slade Theatre is a wonderful setting for this extensive and diverse performing arts programme. It has been extended to provide a Dance Studio and further teaching and technical-support areas.

Physical Education and Games. Physical Education is included in the curriculum. Games are an important part of school life. Main school games are Rugby, Hockey, Cricket, Netball and Tennis. Provision is made for Swimming, Badminton, Cross-Country, Football, Basketball, Table Tennis, Athletics.

Clubs and Societies. There are daily clubs ranging from African Drumming to Sci-Fi. Students are required to choose one activity per week and the choice can vary each term.

The voluntary Combined Cadet Force includes Navy and Army Sections. Adventure training takes place both in the UK and overseas. Cadets are encouraged to participate in the Service and Contingent Camps and Courses.

The Duke of Edinburgh's Award scheme operates at Bronze and Gold Award level. Participants work on the four sections: volunteering, skills, physical, and expeditions; plus a residential project section at Gold Award level.

Saturday Active is a programme of courses that take place every Saturday morning. There are over 20 courses to choose from, including Sailing, Golf, Street Dance, Archery and Robotics.

Boarders and day pupils alike participate in a wide range of activities after school. Public speaking and debating thrive. All younger full-time boarders take part in Saturday Active.

Careers. Our careers guidance programme combines the traditional strength of the House system with the benefits of a specialised central careers department. Every pupil receives individual guidance through the five years from Form 4 (Year 9) to Upper Sixth, with particular support at the three critical stages of choice for GCSE, A Level, and university entrance. At the same time, professional careers advice is available from an independent Careers Advisor, who provides objective information and guidance.

Admission. Main points of admission are at 11+, 13+ and 16+ but pupils may transfer into the College at 12 and 14 if places are available. Early registrations are encouraged. Prospective families are encouraged to visit the College on Open Days or by arranging an individual visit.

Entrance and scholarship examinations for 11+ and 13+ take place in December and January prior to entry in September. 16+ scholarship examinations and interviews take place in November. Please contact the Registrar, admissions@priorparkschools.com, for the relevant entrance/scholarship admission booklet.

Scholarships and Bursaries. Academic Scholarships are available at 11+, 13+ and 16+. Art, DT, Drama, Music and Sporting Excellence awards are available at 11+, 13+ and 16+. Awards can carry with them a fee remission.

Bursaries are available, including HM Forces Bursaries. The Bursar is pleased to discuss individual cases. Sibling discounts apply.

Fees per term (2021–2022). Full Boarding £8,663–£11,667; Weekly Boarding £7,686–£9,056; Day £5,314–£5,865

The Paragon School, Bath – Junior School of Prior Park College. The Paragon School is part of Prior Park Educational Trust. Housed in an impressive Georgian mansion, the co-educational school for 3–11 years is set in beautiful wooded grounds, only a few minutes drive from Prior Park College. A broad and balanced curriculum is delivered within a happy, caring environment.

Head: Mrs Rosie Allen

For further details, see entry in IAPS section.

Prior Park School, Gibraltar. Opened in September 2016, Prior Park School is the first Independent co-educational senior school in Gibraltar for children 12–18 years.

Headmaster: Mr Peter Watts

For further details please visit: www.priorparkschools.com

Charitable status. Prior Park Educational Trust is a Registered Charity, number 281242.

President:
Sister J Livesey, CJ, MA Cantab

Patrons:
Miss J Bisgood, CBE
Mr C J B Davy, CB
Mr D R Hayes
The Rt Revd D R Lang BA, Bishop of Clifton
Mr F J F Lyons, KSG
Sir Cameron Mackintosh
The Rt Hon the Lord Patten of Barnes, CH, PC
The Revd Monsignor Canon R J Twomey, VF
Commodore C B York, FCMI, Royal Navy

Trustees:
Mr J Shinkwin, MA Oxon, PGCE (*Chair of Trustees*)
Mr T Alves, BSc
Mrs S Hall, ACMA
Mr S Head, MA Cantab
Mr B Hutchison, BA Hons
Mr J Jarvis, LLB Hons, BVC Barrister-at-Law
Mr L McKell, MA Hons, MEd
Mrs M Moore, BA Hons
Revd Prebendary N Rawlinson, MA, MB, BChir, FRCS, FRCEM, Cert Pall Med Dip
Ms A Shepherd, MBE, BA Hons
Mrs J Singleton, BA Hons, Dip TEFL
Mr J Webster, BA, BArch, MCD, RIBA, MRTPI

***Headmaster*: Mr Ben Horan**, MA

Deputy Head Academic: Mr C Gamble, MSci Hons
Deputy Head Pastoral: Mr S Cane-Hardy, BA Hons, MEd
Assistant Head (Activities): Mr M Bond, BSc Hons, PGCE, RM
Assistant Head (Compliance): Miss E Wickham
Assistant Head (Director of Studies): Mr K Chard, BSc Hons, PGCE
Assistant Head (Pupil Intervention): Mrs I Burton
Assistant Head (Teaching and Learning): Miss N Cordon, MA Cantab, PGCE
Assistant Head (Tracking): Miss R Childs, MA Cantab
Assistant Head (Wellbeing): Mr D Sackett, BA Hons

Heads of Departments:
Art: Ms S Seville, BA Hons, BA Fine Art
Biology: Dr R Trott, BSc, PhD
Chemistry: Dr R Archer, PhD, MSci
Classics: Mrs S Hearn, BA Oxon
Design & Technology: Mr R Faulkner, BSc
Computer Science: Mr J Gibbons, BA, MA
Drama & Theatre Studies: Mr D Langley, BA
Economics and Business: Mr M Jones, BCom

English: Dr K McGowran, BA, MA, PhD
English as an Additional Language (EAL): Mr P Stroud, BA, MSc
Eurasian Studies: Ms B Main, BA Hons
Geography: Mr S Burt, BSc
History: Mr M Bishop, BA Hons
Learning Development Programme (LDP): Mrs L Knibb, BA Hons, PGCE
Mathematics: Mrs J Jones, BSc Belfast
Modern Languages: Mr T Barrat, PGCE
Music (Academic): Miss D Prosser, BMus Hons
Physical Education & Sports Science: Mr R Gwilliam, BA Hons
Physics: Miss R Childs, MA Cantab
Psychology: Mrs F Evans, BA Hons
Theology and Philosophy: Mr T Maxwell, BA

Visiting Music Staff for Acoustic/Electric Guitar, Bass Guitar, Bassoon, Cello, Clarinet, Drums, Flute, Oboe, Piano, Saxophone, Trumpet, Violin, Viola, Voice.

Executive PA to Headmaster and Director of Operations and Finance: Ms D Miller
Registrar: Mrs Vicki Quinn
Lay Chaplain: Miss Theresa Gibson
Director of Development: Mr Declan Rainey

Queen Anne's School

6 Henley Road, Caversham, Berkshire RG4 6DX

Tel:	0118 918 7300
email:	office@qas.org.uk
website:	www.qas.org.uk
Twitter:	@QASCaversham
Facebook:	@QASCaversham
Instagram:	@qas_caversham
LinkedIn:	/school/queen-anne's

An innovative education for an ever-changing world.

Set in 35 acres and just a short walk from the River Thames, Queen Anne's School, Caversham, is an independent boarding and day school for girls between the ages of 11–18. The school prepares over 450 students for an ever-changing world through an exciting and continually evolving education, steeped in excellence and innovation.

"There's something magical about the place, it's as much about life preparation as academics. With such an array of first class facilities, tip top pastoral care, plus a culture of female empowerment, we think it's definitely one for the list of any parent for whom happiness & roundedness are top priorities." – **Good Schools Guide**

In 2021 Queen Anne's School was awarded the prestigious Microsoft Showcase School Award for the third year running. This award acknowledges the extensive digital teaching and learning that has become integral to the school's approach. The leading girls' day and boarding school became one of just a small group of schools in the UK to be recognised by the international tech giants as leaders in digital learning.

With over 100 co-curricular activities available, the school offers a holistic approach to the girls' learning, both in and outside the classroom. From animation to swimming and The Duke of Edinburgh's Award to Debate Club, there is a wealth of opportunities for students to discover their passions and their strengths.

The outstanding facilities include the Scott Music Centre, boasting a state-of-the-art recording studio, a suite of 24 iMacs and an impressive recital hall. The award-winning Sixth Form Centre that could be mistaken for a Google office, with themed breakout spaces, tech-filled study pods and a café, provides Sixth Formers with a dedicated space to learn, revise and relax.

The 2021 GCSE results saw 59% of students achieve 9/8 (A**/A*) and 100% achieve 9–4 (A**–C) across 25 subjects. An impressive 16 students achieved a full set of 9/8 (A**–A*) grades with five of these girls receiving straight 9s. At A Level, 72% of all grades awarded were A*/A and 99% received A*–C. The 2021 cohort went on to attend top universities, including Oxford, Warwick, Manchester, Durham, Exeter and Bath, studying a range of subjects including Medicine, Law, Animation & Games, Psychology, English, Fine Art and Architecture.

Queen Anne's School strives to support busy families and offers and an extensive transport network with buses covering areas in Berkshire, Oxfordshire, Buckinghamshire and London. The flexibility of day, flexi and full boarding options allow families to choose the right balance for their needs.

Visit www.qas.org.uk or contact the admissions team on 0118 918 7333.

Student Wellbeing. Queen Anne's has an excellent reputation for pastoral care. The staff believe that students perform best when they are happy and secure, and Queen Anne's has effective pastoral systems in place to ensure this. The support network includes House Parents and the House Pastoral Team, Academic Staff and Tutors as well as Heads of Year.

Curriculum. All girls follow a broad and varied curriculum up to GCSE. Separate subject sciences are taught, along with English Literature, English Language and Mathematics; French, Spanish, German or Mandarin may be taken from Year 7. Music and Technology, Art and Drama form part of the girls' timetable until the end of Year 9. Computer Science is taught throughout the school. A programme of personal, social and health education is followed by all girls. A wide range of A Level subjects is offered, with Music Technology, Film Studies, Media Studies, Criminology, Sociology and Environmental Science being introduced in September 2022.

Careers. Girls go on to Higher Education courses at many top universities in the UK and overseas and also take up places on Degree Apprenticeship schemes, for example at Dyson and Coca-Cola.

Co-curricular activities. Queen Anne's is reputed for many of its achievements. It offers a full extra-curricular programme and excellent opportunities for sport, including tennis, lacrosse, swimming and netball. Students interested in music, drama and art can pursue their passions with a number of clubs available to join and performance opportunities each term. The Duke of Edinburgh's Award, Young Enterprise, public speaking and debating, Model United Nations events, dance, riding, socials and many more activities are available.

Admission. Girls are admitted at 11+, 13+ and at Sixth Form by Queen Anne's Entrance Examination or by Common Entrance. Sixth Form places are offered on the basis of GCSE predictions and results. For further information please contact the Head of Admissions.

Scholarships are offered for entry at 11+, 13+ and 16+ and are awarded for excellence in one or more fields of school life. Awards may be made for Academic Excellence, Sport, Art, Drama, Music or All-Round Contribution

Fees per term (2021–2022). Full Boarding £13,590; Flexi Boarding £12,250–£12,920; Day pupils £8,370.

Charitable status. Queen Anne's School is part of The United Westminster and Grey Coat Foundation, which is a Registered Charity, number 1181012.

Board of Governors:
Chairman: Miss M Corbally, FCCA, CTA

Board members:
Mr C Booth, BA, FRSA, FCIPR
Mr D Charles, BSc, ACA
Mr M De Mello, BSc
Mrs C Gray, BA
Mrs I Millard, BA, PGDip, PGCE
Mr R F Penfold, MBE
Ms P Vanninen, MA Cantab, ACA
Mrs C Pampe, MBA, BA Hons

Senior Staff:

Leadership Team:

Head: Ms Elaine Purves, BA Hull, PGCE Durham

Senior Deputy Head (Academic): Mr Mark Richards, BMus Wales, MMus King's London, Research Fellowship Cardiff, FRSA, MCCT
Deputy Head (Pastoral): Mrs Lindsey Bryant, BSc, Nottingham, PGCE Hertfordshire, MEd Cambridge
Director of Finance and Strategy: Mr Edward Hellings, BA, ACA
Human Resources Manager: Mrs Judith Tremayne, Dip Performance Management, Dip Advanced Performance Management, Dip Change Management

Senior Managers:
Assistant Head (E-Learning): Mr Thomas Lange, Dipl-Ing FH, BEng Germany
Director of Lower School: Mrs Rebecca Croll, BSc Southampton, PGCE IOE, UCL, Msc Oxford
Director of Middle School: Mrs Linda McGrenary, BEd Strathclyde
Director of Sixth Form: Mr Ben Stephenson, BSc Warwick, MSc Loughborough, GTP
Head of Teaching and Learning: Mrs Anna Spellman, BA, PGCE Reading
Head of Monitoring and Tracking: Mr Derek Bottomley, BSc Leeds, PGCE Oxford

Queen Elizabeth Grammar School
Wakefield

Senior Section (Boys 11–18)
154 Northgate, WF1 3QX

Tel: 01924 373943
email: qsoffice@wgsf.net

Junior Section (Boys 7–11)
158 Northgate, WF1 3QY

Tel: 01924 373821
email: qjoffice@wgsf.net

website: www.wgsf.org.uk
Twitter: @QEGSYorkshire
Facebook: @QEGSYorkshire
Instagram: @QEGSYorksire
LinkedIn: /school/queen-elizabeth-grammar-school-
           wakefield

Motto: '*Turpe nescire*'

Steeped in over 430 years of history, yet recognised as a school at the forefront of educational thinking, QEGS is continually refreshing and growing its facilities and resources, to enable students to excel in every area of academic and sporting achievement.

Facilities. The Junior Section is housed in its own building and enjoys specialist facilities, including a purpose-built STEM block, a recently renovated swimming pool and the school's very own Forest School.

Across the drive in its inspiring Senior Section building, boys enjoy access to specialist areas for 25 academic departments. Students also have access to an indoor gym, fitness suite, sports pavilion and sports fields.

Curriculum. At QEGS boys follow a wide-ranging curriculum, tailor-made to each student's specific needs.

In the Junior Section boys enjoy active, well-paced practical learning with frequent brain breaks and opportunities for movement. Every lesson in and out of the classroom is buzzing with curiosity and enthusiasm.

In the Senior Section, there's a palpable sense of discovery and exploration as boys from 11–18 enjoy a broad range of unique learning experiences. The school's unique enrichment and development programme provides no fewer than 96 enrichment activities, enabling boys to customise a corner of their timetable and add that vital edge to an already high-octane academic diet.

Pastoral Care/Wellbeing. QEGS creates a secure environment where students gain a true sense of their own worth and feel a real sense of belonging, fostered through small personal tutorials, affiliation to a house, twice-weekly assemblies and dependable peer and staff support.

In addition to its in-school counsellor and matron, boys enjoy a number of wellbeing initiatives, including a weekly enrichment afternoon as well as a dedicated wellbeing day complete with lessons, online resources and mindfulness practices.

Physical Education and Games. Countless opportunities exist at every level of sport at QEGS. All boys can get involved either individually or as part of a team in Athletics, Badminton, Basketball, Climbing, Cricket, Cross-Country, Fencing, Fitness Training, Football, Gymnastics, Hockey, Judo, Mountain Biking, Rugby, Swimming, Table Tennis, Tennis and Volleyball.

The school's excellent sports facilities include a sports hall with fitness suite, games fields, swimming pool, athletics track, sports pavilion and all-weather Astroturf, providing the perfect environment for sporting achievement.

Athletics, Cricket, Hockey and Rugby teams regularly reach regional finals and latter stages of national competitions, as well as competing at international level.

Music and Drama. The school has a full programme of musical and dramatic activities. Throughout the year, all age groups in the Junior Section take part in a stage production, and the Senior Section stages major productions jointly with Wakefield Girls'.

Students can also access individual instrument or singing lessons, with a team of over 30 visiting instrumental musicians working with the school's music department.

There are three choirs in the Junior Section and a highly talented barbershop group in the Senior Section. The school's ensembles take part in local festivals and the latter in National Competitions.

The school's orchestras and swing band involve boys from Year 3 upwards and give performances of the highest standard at musical events throughout the year within school and in the local community.

Clubs and Societies. Over 50 clubs and societies are held during the school week, encouraging involvement, firing passions and igniting new interests. The various music groups include brass, woodwind, string ensembles and choirs. The school also participates in the Duke of Edinburgh's Award Scheme and is now officially recognised as an official DofE Centre. There is also a significant programme of charity collections and related activities.

Admissions. Entry into the Junior Section is usually at 7, although places are retained for entry at 8, 9 and 10 years.

Entry into the Senior Section is normally:

- at 11 based on each boy's performance in his entrance exam and how he presents himself in his personal interview. Or as a result of good academic performance in the Junior Section

- at 16 after a satisfactory performance in the GCSE examinations and personal interview.

Enquiries about entrance to the school should be made to the Admissions Manager (astuart-brown@wgsf.net).

Fees per annum (2021–2022). Junior Section: Years 3 & 4 £10,202, Years 5 & 6 £10,770. Senior Section (Years 7+): £13,623

Scholarships and Bursaries. The school is committed to helping students from all backgrounds to explore their full capabilities and enjoy the best educational start in life. Each year, the Governors award a limited number of academic scholarships to boys entering the Senior Section at 11.

Means tested awards are also available to students joining at Year 3, Year 7 or Year 12, covering up to 75% of their school fees under the Wakefield Grammar School Foundation Awards Scheme. Enquiries about awards should be made to the Admissions Manager (astuart-brown@wgsf.net).

The Old Savilians' Club. President: Mr R Ackroyd

Charitable status. Wakefield Grammar School Foundation is a Registered Charity, number 1088415.

Chair of Governors: Mr S Chamberlain, MSc, BA Hons, ACIArb

Bursar and Clerk to the Governors: Mr L Perry

Head: **Dr R Brookes**, MChem

Deputy Head (*Pastoral*): Mr J Palin, BEng

Assistant Head (*Co-curricular*): Mrs C Palin, BA

Director of Studies (*Operations*): Mr M Fitzsimons, MA
Director of Studies (*Staff*): Mrs A Eggleston, BA, MEd

Queen Elizabeth's Hospital (QEH)

Berkeley Place, Clifton, Bristol BS8 1JX

Tel: 0117 930 3040
email: headofqeh@qehbristol.co.uk
           office@qehbristol.co.uk
website: www.qehbristol.co.uk

Motto: Dum tempus habemus operemur bonum

Patron: Her Majesty The Queen

By his Will dated 10 April 1586, John Carr, a Bristol merchant, founded Queen Elizabeth's Hospital, a bluecoat school in Bristol on the lines of Christ's Hospital which was already flourishing in London. The Charter was granted to the School by Queen Elizabeth I in 1590. Originally composed entirely of boarders, the School continued so until 1920 when foundation day boys were admitted. Direct Grant status was accorded in 1945. The School is now independent and day only and, as of September 2017, has a co-educational Sixth Form.

Admission. There are 672 pupils in the Senior School, ranging in age from 11 to 18. Entrance examinations for both Year 7 and Year 9 applicants are held in January each year; Sixth Form and other Years by arrangement. Girls are able to join the co-ed QEH Sixth Form.

Term of Entry. Usually September.

Entrance Scholarships. A significant number of scholarships are offered at Year 7, Year 9 and Sixth Form. These are awarded purely on academic merit for outstanding achievement in the entrance procedures and may also carry with them generous assistance for applicants whose parents' means are limited. Sixth Form Scholarships are available for Maths, Science (including Computer Science), Languages (Ancient and Modern), Literature, Art and Social Sciences, Sport, Art, Drama and Music.

Academic, Music and Sports scholarships are available at Year 7 and Year 9.

Assisted Places. There are many School assisted places available. The School has a substantial foundation income and is able to give generous support to parents whose means are limited.

Buildings. The School was originally close by the City Centre but moved to new premises on Brandon Hill in 1847. A major building and improvement programme has included the building of the QEH Theatre (1990), refurbishment of the Art School (2000), new Mathematics rooms and heavy investment in ICT (2004). An 80-strong Junior School opened in 2007 (increasing to over 100 in 2012) along with a new Sixth Form Centre. In 2008 a multimillion pound development programme, in conjunction with Bristol City Football Club, saw new football pitches on 23 acres at the Sports Ground at Failand. A further £2.7 million has been invested at the Failand for a 3G artificial surface for rugby and football, sand-dressed artificial surfaces for hockey and tennis as well as tarmac surfaces for netball and tennis. A new £3 million Science and Art Building was opened in October 2016 and future development plans include improvements to Music and Art facilities and other areas of the school. An expanded Sixth Form Centre opened in September 2017.

Curriculum. Students are prepared for the GCSE (IGCSE in Mathematics and English) and GCE A Level, and for university entrance. The usual school subjects are offered at GCSE level, and the A Level subjects are: English Literature, English Language, Drama, Economics, Classics, Classical Civilisation, History, Geography, French, German, Spanish, Art, Photography, Film Studies, Music, Mathematics, Further Mathematics, Music Technology, Physics, Chemistry, Biology, PE and Sport, Business Studies, Computer Science, Ethics and Philosophy, Government & Politics and Psychology.

Music & Drama. There is a School Orchestra, Choir, Jazz Band, Brass Group, and Wind Band among the twenty or so ensembles. Music is included in the timetable for all the junior forms. GCSE and A Level music are part of the School curriculum, and tuition is arranged for a wide range of instruments. The Choir and Instrumentalists perform regularly and also undertake joint ventures with other schools in Bristol. Drama flourishes and the school has its own high-tech purpose-built theatre which seats 220.

Art. The Department is well equipped and offers ceramics, screen printing, photography and computer imaging.

Religious Studies. The School is a Christian one which welcomes students of all faiths, or none. Religious Studies is part of the curriculum and students attend two services a year in Bristol Cathedral.

Games. Rugby, Football, Athletics, Cricket, Swimming, Tennis, Hockey, Netball, Badminton, Sailing, Squash, Fencing, Judo, Climbing and Mountain Biking. A large number of students also participate in The Duke of Edinburgh's Award and Ten Tors.

Dress. Boys wear either grey trousers and a blazer or a plain dark suit. Sixth Form student wear smart business dress. Traditional bluecoat uniform is worn by some for special occasions.

General. All parents are encouraged to join the Friends of Queen Elizabeth's Hospital, a society whose aim is to promote a close relationship between parents and staff and to further the welfare of the School. There is a flourishing Elizabethan Society for alumni, which holds regular meetings and circulates a newsletter. A panel of former pupils, formed from all professions, and working with the Head of Futures, is available to give advice on careers to students.

The School has long been known in Bristol as 'The City School' and its links with the Lord Mayor and Corporation are strong. Students read the lessons and sing in the Lord Mayor's Chapel, and groups are in attendance for such occasions as Mayor-making and Council Prayers.

The central position of the School, close to the University, the Art Gallery and Museum, the Central Library, the Bristol Old Vic and the Bristol Beacon, affords ready access to a wide range of cultural facilities which students are encouraged to use.

Junior School. 110 Boys aged 7–11. (*For further details see QEH Junior School entry in IAPS section.*)

Fees per term (2021–2022). Senior School £5,100, Junior School £3,420. Fees include text and exercise books, and essential educational trips but do not include public examination fees or lunches (which are £236 per term).

Charitable status. Queen Elizabeth's Hospital is a Registered Charity, number 1104871, and a Company Limited by Guarantee, number 5164477. Queen Elizabeth's Hospital has existed since 1590 to provide a first class education.

Governing Body:
Mr P A Keen, FCIB (*Chairman*)

Mrs C Bateson, MA, BA Hons	Mr T Davis, BSc, MRICS
Ms S Blanks, MSc	Mr J Hirst
Mr J Buchanan, LLB Hons, CTA	Mr J Hollingdale, MA Oxon, FCA, MCIArb
Mr A Cherry	Mr M Jones, BSc
Mr E Corrigan, BA, FCS, MAE	Mr J Milne, MA, MBA
Mrs S Cosgrove, BSc	Mr K Riley, BA Hons, MA
	Mr C Woodford, FRICS, BSc Hons

Bursar: Mr M K Suddaby, MA, ACA

Head: Mr R D Heathcote, BSc

Deputy Head (*Academic*): Mr J Martin, MA
Deputy Head (*Pastoral*): Mr N Pursall, BA
Assistant Head (*Staff Development*): Mr C Brotherton, MA
Assistant Head (*Sixth Form*): Mr R Porter, MA
Assistant Head (*Logistics and Co-curricular*): Mr T J Dunn, BSc
Head of Marketing and Communications: Ms E A Down, BSSoc, LLB

Mr S Albon, BSc	Mr S Hofkes, BMus, PG Dip
Mr P M Amor, BA	
Mr T Appleby, BA	Mrs N Holcombe, BA
Mrs A L Baker, BA	Mr K M Holmes, BA
Ms C R Bernstein, MA	Mrs K Izzard-Clark, BSc
Ms H Bosson, BSc	Mr A Jarvis, BA
Miss J Bowkett, BSc	Dr J Jönsson, MSc, PhD
Mr R D Carr, BA	Mr P E Joslin, BEd
Mr D J Chalmers, BSc	Mr J Kelly, BSc
Mr A C Clements, BSc	Dr H L Kyle, BSc, PhD
Ms C Coleman, BA	Ms S K Liddle, BSc
Mrs E Conquest, BA	Mrs H Mann, MA
Mr C B Conquest, BEd	Miss L Mantle, BA, MA
Mr J Cox, BSc	Mr R Martineau, MEng
Ms O Darkes-Sutcliffe, BA	Mrs A Masom, BA
Mrs M M Dimes, BSc	Mrs M McGowan, BA
Mr A Donald, BA	Ms H McKellar, MA
Dr M Dutton, BEd, MA, EdD	Mr S Mitchell, BSc
Miss L Fenner, BA	Mr P C Moore, BEd
Mrs C Gardner, BA	Mrs S Moritz, BSc
Mr E M Gent, BA	Mr S J Munnion, BA
Mrs D Guthrie, BSc	Dr V Neild, BA
Mr R J Harris, BA	Mrs A Pegg, BA
Mr S A Harris, BSc	Mr W G Plowden, BA
Mr T Harrison, BA	Mrs I Porter, BA
Mr D T Hawkes, BSc	Ms C A Rostron, MA
Mrs P Hockenhull, BA	Mr C Ryan, BSc
	Ms K E Ryan, BA

Mrs L Shaw, BA	Ms E Taylor, BSc, MSc
Mrs H Shields, BA	Mrs N Taylor, BA
Mr M Sloan, BSc	Mr Z Verry, BA
Mrs R Steven, BA	Mrs F Waite-Taylor, BA
Mr A W H Swithinbank, BA	Mr R J Waldron, BA
	Mr G S Westwater, BSc

Junior School:
Headteacher: Mr D M Kendall, BA

Visiting Teachers:
Mr J Bacon, MMus
Mr P Barrett, BA, PG Dip
Mr R Grist, BA Hons, BMus Hons
Miss C Lindley, BA
Mr N Malcolm
Mr B Mullan, BMus
Mr A Purnell, BMus Hons RWCMD
Mr N Shipman, BMus, LGSMD
Mr A Stewart, BMus
Miss L Tanner, BMus, MMus, PG Dip
Mr J Whitfield, BMus

Chaplain: The Revd C M Pilgrim
Headmaster's Secretary: Mrs E Davies
Admissions Registrar: Mrs C Matthews
Librarian: Mr L Matiscsak

Queenswood School

Shepherd's Way, Brookmans Park, Hatfield, Hertfordshire AL9 6NS

Tel:	01707 602500
email:	admissions@queenswood.org
website:	www.queenswood.org
Twitter:	@QueenswoodSch
Facebook:	@QueenswoodSch

Motto: 'In Hortis Reginæ' – 'In the Queen's Gardens'

Queenswood is a progressive boarding and day school for around 450 girls, aged between 11 and 18, where boarders make up half of the School. The School was founded in 1894 in Clapham Park and moved to its current site in Hertfordshire in 1925. An all-round education focuses on equipping the girls with all the life skills required of women in the 21st century. Within a caring and supportive framework, the girls enjoy a dynamic academic curriculum, supported by a diverse and exciting co-curricular programme.

Queenswood has exceptional value-added results, with our pupils always performing beyond their predicted grades, particularly at GCSE. This is due to Queenswood's bespoke approach to education, developing a personalised learning plan for each pupil, so that her learning is tailored to her individual needs. The Personalised Learning Team works with our teaching staff to integrate the personalised plans into lessons, whilst simultaneously providing 1:1 support for girls with a high standard of academic achievement and for those who need a little more assistance in certain subjects.

It is a warm and friendly community where everybody knows each other. Girls thrive within a nurturing House structure tailored to meet their needs as they progress from the Lower School, through the Middle School, and on into the Sixth Form. Day girls are fully integrated within the Houses, are able to enjoy all the facilities and opportunities available to the boarders, but choose to go home at night after a packed school day. There is a flexible approach to boarding to meet the varying needs of individual families; girls may choose to flexi board for 1, 2 or 3 nights, weekly board or be full boarders. They can also flexi board for ad hoc nights.

Here at Queenswood, we know that happy girls are successful girls and so we place paramount importance on pastoral care. The Good Schools Guide states that, according to parents, our pastoral care is 'phenomenal'. The Guide also states that Queenswood parents rave about the 'proactive approach to mental health', highlighting our mentoring programme. On entrance to the school, Year 7 girls are mentored by a fellow pupil in Year 8 and Year 13, with these girls going above and beyond to help one another. This peer-support complements our fantastic pastoral staff, such as our boarding assistants and resident full-time counsellor, who ensure that someone is always looking out for your daughter.

Queenswood is proud to be an international community with an outward-looking approach; overseas girls make up around 20% of the pupils. We welcome girls of all faiths and none, recognise and support an individual's adherence to her own faith, but expect all girls to embrace the School's broad spiritual ethos.

The girls are ambitious high achievers, winning places at the top universities both at home and abroad prior to embarking upon a range of exciting careers. Individual talent also flourishes in sport and the creative and performing arts. The extensive co-curricular programme helps develop the girls' soft skills in a wide variety of ways and significantly contributes to their excellent academic results. As important as individual achievement is the development of a sense of responsibility for each other and the world in which they live. Queenswood girls are thoughtful young people with a secure set of values and self-confidence.

The beautiful Queenswood estate provides the perfect educational environment. Being just 20 minutes from central London, it also has the advantage of easy access to the cultural richness of the capital. At the same time, its proximity to major international airports provides ease of travel for both our overseas girls and for those participating in the School's foreign exchange and visit programmes.

Curriculum. With over twenty-five subjects in the curriculum and more than seventy co-curricular activities available, girls have every opportunity to discover their strengths and to become exceptional learners and leaders. We offer a holistic educational experience which supports and encourages intellectual, physical, moral and spiritual development.

Life. Queenswood encourages intellectual curiosity, of which the spiritual dimension is an important part. Girls are therefore welcome to discuss their thoughts, feelings and faith in an open and supportive context. Since true education is holistic it includes spiritual and moral development. All pupils of the School, whatever their religion, are encouraged to explore and develop their own faith in an atmosphere of tolerance. We accept girls of all faiths and none.

Boarding. We strongly believe that fun and friendship should be the foundation of our boarding community. So, we invite you to enter a world where your daughter will be able to embrace diversity, firmly establish her independence while still fostering a sense of care and concern for the community, sample more to achieve more and certainly make friends for life.

Lower School. Our ultimate aim in the Lower School is to help girls to become independent students with enthusiasm for learning and the ambition to develop their skills and qualities to their fullest extent. Beyond the classroom, there is a wealth of opportunities for younger girls to enrich their education. These include a wide range of over seventy co-curricular clubs and activities and a diverse programme of House outings and excursions.

Entry. Entrance to Queenswood is by examination (Common Entrance Exam or Queenswood's papers), interview and a report from the pupil's current Headteacher. For 11+ entrance, candidates will also take part in a team activity.

Scholarships. Queenswood Scholarships are awarded in recognition of outstanding achievement or promise in a particular sphere. The majority of our Scholarships are honorary and do not attract financial support; however, a small number of awards with fee remissions may be available for candidates applying for a music Scholarship who demonstrate exceptional potential.

Fees per term (2021–2022). Day: Years 7–8 £7,330; Years 9–11 £8,540; Sixth Form £8,540. Boarders: Years 7–8 Flexi boarding (1–3 nights) £7,550–£7,915, Weekly boarding £8,220, Full boarding £8,815; Years 9–11 Flexi boarding (1–3 nights) £9,150–£10,150, Weekly boarding £10,825, Full boarding £12,020; Sixth Form Flexi boarding (1–3 nights) £9,150–£10,150; Weekly boarding £10,825, Full boarding £12,020.

Old Queenswoodians' Association. The OQA has 4,000+ members and an active young membership that supports current Queenswoodians after their time at School has come to an end.

Charitable status. Queenswood School Limited is a Registered Charity, number 311060, which exists to provide high-quality education for girls.

Governors:
Mr H J de Sausmarez, BA, FCIS (*Chair*)
Mr T C Garnham, BSc (*Vice Chair*)
Mr R Baines, BSc, CIMA, CEng, MICE
The Reverend Dr D M Chapman, BSc, MA, MPhil, PhD
Mrs K Belshaw, LLB Hons, PGLDip, LLM, AKC
Dr O McGuinness, BSc, MB BS, FRCP, DCH, DRCOG
Mr S Morris, MA, PGCE, NPQH
Mrs C Norman, BSc, CIMA
Mrs N Penny
Mr J Phelan, MA Ed, BA Hons, PGCE
Mr A D Poppleton, BEng, CEng, AKC, FIET, FBSC
The Honourable N Stamp
The Reverend T Swindell, FCA
Mrs P M Wrinch

Principal: **Mrs J Cameron**, BSc Hons Surrey, PGCE

Bursar and Clerk to the Governors: Mr I Williams, BEng Hons RMCS Shrivenham, CEng
Director of External Relations: Mrs D Cresswell, BA Hons York, DipM
Deputy Head Academic: Mr I Sheldon, MChem Oxon, PGCE, MRSC
Deputy Head Pupils: Mrs H Mackay, BA Yale, MA London, BTh Liverpool, PGCE, MEd UCL

Assistant Head, Pupil Data, Teaching and Learning: Mr S Daughton, BA Hons, PGCE, MRHS, MA London

Assistant Head, Boarding: Mrs V Ludwick, BA Hons, PGCE

Head of Sixth Form: Mr C Fox, BA Hons Sheffield, MA Warwick, MSc Oxon

Chaplain: Rev V Maraj-Ogden, BSC Hons UWI, DipTh Middlesex, MA Theology London

Head of PR, Digital and Print: Mr N Kelley, BA Hons Oxon

Admissions Team:

Head of Pupil Recruitment: Mrs S Harris

Senior Admissions Assistant: Miss C Noone

Admissions and Marketing Assistant: Mrs V Leigh

Student Visa Co-ordinator: Miss H Langdon

Further details can be found at:
www.queenswood.org/explore/staff-and-governors

Radley College

Abingdon, Oxfordshire OX14 2HR

Tel: 01235 543127 (Warden)
       01235 543122 (Bursar)
       01235 543174 (Admissions)
       01235 543000 (General Enquiries)
email: warden@radley.org.uk
website: www.radley.org.uk
Twitter: @RadleyCollege
Facebook: @RadleyCollege
Instagram: @radleycollegeoxon

Motto: *Sicut Serpentes, sicut Columbae*

St Peter's College, Radley, was founded by the Reverend William Sewell, Fellow of Exeter College, Oxford, to provide an independent school education on the principles of the Church of England. It was opened on 9 June 1847 and incorporated by Royal Charter in 1890. It stands in a park of some 700 acres.

General Arrangements. There are 760 boys in the school, all of whom board. On admission, boys enter one of the 11 houses known as Socials. All are close together within the grounds. All meals are served in Hall on a cafeteria system. There is a daily Chapel Service for all boys.

Admission. The 13+ admissions process is held when boys are in Year 6. Boys are assessed using the ISEB Common Pre-Test, a current school report and an interview with the Warden or Senior Master at Radley. Those who have registered early on the Radley List (generally before a boy is 3 years old) will go through this process in the Michaelmas Term of Year 6 with offers being made in March of Year 6. Those who have not registered, or who are on the waiting list, go through the same assessments from November to March in Year 6, with offers being made by March of Year 6. This process is called Open Entry. Offers will be unconditional, but boys are required to sit 13+ Common Entrance (or Maths and English exams for those abroad) and Radley reserves the right to refuse entry in exceptional circumstances.

Places are also available for Sixth Form entry and, occasionally, in Year 10 (Removes): details are available on our website.

Scholarships and Bursaries. Academic, Music, Sport, Drama and Art Awards (Scholarships and Exhibitions) are all available every year. All awards may be supplemented by a means-tested bursary. Details are available on our website or from the Registrar, admissions@radley.org.uk. Further means-tested bursaries (11+ Funded Places) of up to 100% of the fees are available for boys who would otherwise be unable to afford to come to Radley and are assessed in Year 6.

Academic: Around 10 Academic Awards are offered annually.

Music: On average five Instrumental Scholarships and several Exhibitions are offered annually with free tuition.

Sport: At least five sport awards are offered annually.

Drama: Around two awards will be offered annually.

Art: Around two awards will be offered annually

Work. In the Shells, Removes and Fifth Form a broad curriculum is followed. There is some choice at GCSE with boys generally taking nine or ten subjects.

In the Sixth Form a boy can specialise in a combination of Classics, French, Spanish, German, Theatre Studies, English, History, Religious Studies, Geography, Geology, Biology, Chemistry, Physics, Mathematics, Economics, Politics, Economics and Business, Music, Art or Design, leading to A level qualifications. An AS in Art is also available, being part of a Sixth Form Curriculum Extension Programme, which also includes the Extended Project Qualification (EPQ), a mini-MBA and an International Relations Course.

Futures. Radley Futures is our comprehensive careers programme which runs through all years and is designed to prepare students for higher education and work. This includes writing CVs, psychometric testing and profiling, UCAS and international university application support and interview practice. All students can access professional advice and gain exposure to a wide variety of careers through talks, visits and work experience. In the 6th Form, boys are given the opportunity to join our business networking platforms where they can interact with Old Radleians and Radley parents, developing their early networking skills and starting to build their lifelong network before they leave.

Games. In the Michaelmas Term rugby football is the major school game. In the other two terms the 'wet-bobs' row; the 'dry-bobs' play hockey (the major game) and soccer in the Lent Term, cricket (the major game), athletics and tennis in the Summer. There are also numerous minor sports which involve boys in competition with other schools. The playing fields are close to the main buildings.

The College has its own boathouse, and the use of a stretch of the River Thames between Sandford and Abingdon. The VIIIs compete in regattas and Head of the River races.

There are three all-weather hockey pitches, an athletics track, five squash courts, a Real Tennis court, a rackets court, two covered Fives courts, 20 hard tennis courts and a 9-hole golf course. There is a large, well-equipped gymnasium and an indoor, heated swimming pool attached to a multi-purpose sports hall and a state-of-the-art rowing tank.

CCF and Duke of Edinburgh's Award. All boys, in their fourth term, join the Radley College Contingent, Combined Cadet Force (Army, Navy and Air sections). They work for the Proficiency examination, which takes three terms. When they have passed Proficiency and done a week's Corps Camp in the holidays they either stay on in a special section for further training or join one of the many Community Action Projects on offer. There is a thriving Duke of Edinburgh's Award scheme.

Fees per term (2021–2022). £13,900 (inclusive of medical attendance). There is available a system of insurance against loss of fees caused by illness, accident, or infection. Particulars can be obtained from the Bursar.

Charitable status. St Peter's College, Radley is a Registered Charity, number 309243. It exists for the purpose of the education of youth in general knowledge and literature and particularly and especially in the doctrines and principles of the Church of England.

Visitor: The Rt Revd The Lord Bishop of Oxford

Council:
Chairman: D C S Smellie, MA
Vice-Chairman: G A Kaye, BSc

N J Henderson, MA, FRCS	H J R Willis, MA
M J W Rushton, MA	S J B Shaw
D J Pluck, FCA	Revd Dr S Hampton
T M Durie, BA, ACA, FSI	H J R Morris
J C Bridcut, MA	W J L Maydon
R H Warner, MA, ACA	M Breen
Sir J Holmes	C M A Sweetnam
R N L Huntingford	C H Palmer
E J Martineau, FRGS	

Warden: J S Moule, MA

Sub Warden: B J Holden, MA, BTech
Academic Director: S R Rathbone, MA, MA

Senior Masters:
R D Shaw, MA
N Murphy MA
S Langdale
E Anderson

Under Master:
R M C Greed, BSc
T R G Ryder, BA, MFA

Teaching Staff:

G Wiseman, BA	†G R King, BA (*G Social*)
S Barlass, BA	D J Pullen, BSc
C M Bedford, BA, PhD	R K McMahon, MA, MPhil, DPhil
I S Yorston, MA	
J M Sparks, BSc	J E Gearing, BA
M R Jewell, BA	G C Dalrymple, MA, MSc
R Johnson, BSc	†S R Giddens, BSc, MSc, PhD (*C Social*)
I K Campbell, BA	
M C Hart, BA	†T C Lawson, BA (*E Social*)
B R Knox, BEd	
P M Fernandez, MA	†C E Scott-Malden, BA, MA (*B Social*)
D W S Roques, MA	
K A Mosedale, MA, MSc	A D Cunningham, MA, PhD
K J Knox, BA	
†H Crump, LLB, BA (*D Social*)	P J Miron, BSc, DPhil
	M P Hills, MMath
S H Dalrymple, BA	E O Holt, BA
†G H S May, MA (*H Social*)	†C A San Jose, BA (*F Social*)

J W Schofield, BA, MSc	J A D Wilson, MChem
K C Ison, BA	O W Choroba, MPhil, PhD
M G Noone, MA	†A M H Hakimi, BSc, MPhil (*L Social*)
R D Woodling, MChem	
S J Perkins, BSc	E Gearing, BA
M E Walker, BA, MA, PhD	A Davies, BA Hons
M M Carter	C R Mason, MMath Hons
M C F Brown, BA	A P Pancrazi, Lycee
†R E P Hughes, BSc (*A Social*)	M I Rumbold, BA
	O Astley, BA Hons
T C H Norton, MA	J de Ritter, BA
M G D Glendon-Doyle, BA (*K Social*)	Dr M Lebedeva, MSc
	Dr C Ploix, DPhil
†K W S Willis-Stovold, BSc (*J Social*)	C Robinson, BA
	A Wiles, BA
M Hurley, BA	Dr D Zimmer, MChem
P Asbury, BA	R J Grice, BA
A F C Nash, BA	A A Vaan, BSc
A C N Norman, MSc	T J Deasy, BA, MA
L P Robinson, BA	W A Jolly, BSci
D Scott, BA	Dr P J Langman, BSc
R Tufnell, BA	S R Ramsden, BA
C P McKegney	F E Taylor, BA
L J Clogher	B L Wilson, BA Hons
J A Gaunt	Dr D I Robinson, MEng
E Ellis	A C Bibby, BA
J A S Sheldrake	J Lemke-Jeremy
S W Townsend	C D Lloyd, BSc
R Beattie, BA	W Swain, BA
V K Buse, BA	O J Purslow
A J Hibbs, MPhys	R Catmull
B T Knowles, BA	T Horacek
L Ryan, BSc	S Matthews
O D Wills, MEng	E Simpkins

Chaplain: The Revd D Wilson, BSc, BA, MLitt, PhD
Assistant Chaplain: The Revd P J Taylor, MA, BTh
Librarian: Ms A K Muhlberg

Music:
Precentor: S J Gladstone, MA
A J A Williams, MMus, Dip RAM, GRSM, LRAM
Miss S-L Naylor, MA
T M Morris, MA, DPhil, FRCO

There are 36 peripatetic music staff.

Bursar and Secretary: A Ashton, MA, ACIB
Medical Officer: Dr J N B Moore, BSc, MB BS, DRCOG, MRCGP
Development Director: E Anderson
Registrar: S Langdale

Ratcliffe College

Fosse Way, Ratcliffe on the Wreake, Leicester, Leicestershire LE7 4SG

Tel: 01509 817000 School Office
01509 817072/817031 Registrar
email: enquiries@ratcliffecollege.com
website: www.ratcliffecollege.com
Twitter: @RatcliffeColl
@RatcliffePrep
@RatcliffeSport
Facebook: @RatcliffeCollege
Instagram: @RatcliffeCollege
LinkedIn: /school/ratcliffe-college

Motto: '*Legis Plenitudo Charitas*'

Ratcliffe College is a Catholic independent school for boys and girls, based in Leicestershire that welcomes all from the ages 3–18, with boarding from age 11. Here at Ratcliffe, Encouraging Big Ideas is at the heart of everything we do!

Age Range. 3–18.

Number of Pupils. 862: 424 girls, 438 boys. Sixth Form 148; Boarders 60.

Aims. The vision of the College is to educate young people in the spirit of the Gospel, seeking to nurture the God-given talents and potential of each individual, so that each one may become a confident and responsible member of society who is seeking to give back to the community. Whilst Ratcliffe is a Catholic school, it welcomes children of all denominations and faiths or none, whose parents feel they can share in and benefit from the School's ideals and environment.

Location. Ratcliffe College is set in over 200 acres of rolling parkland on the A46, seven miles north of Leicester. It is easily accessible by road and benefits from being free of congestion at peak times. The M1/M6 motorways, main line railway stations and airports of Birmingham and East Midlands are all within easy travelling distance. For day pupils, school buses operate daily from Leicester, Loughborough and Nottingham.

Site and Buildings. The main Senior School buildings surround a beautiful Pugin-designed quadrangle and contain the Administration offices, Chapel, Refectory, Library, Medical Centre, Media Rooms and pastoral areas, together with a number of subject departmental areas. In addition, there is a Music Department with Concert Hall; a fully-appointed Theatre; and a Science Centre with additional classrooms for Food Science. Sporting facilities include extensive playing fields, synthetic athletics track and two floodlit all-weather hockey pitches; the state-of-the-art Sports Centre comprises a swimming pool and sports hall with a modern fitness suite and squash courts. A complex of recently refurbished buildings nearby provides departmental bases for Geography, Modern Languages and Mathematics. Modernised Boys' and Girls' boarding accommodation is situated on the upper floor of the main building, in separate wings, with individual study bedrooms for older students.

The Rosmini Sixth Form Centre, named after our founder Blessed Antonio Rosmini, has an upper floor wholly dedicated to academic study with full IT accessibility. The ground floor hosts a canteen for meals, as well as a brand new Sixth Form Lounge for social gatherings and events. The Centre provides a flagship modern setting for Sixth Form study.

In 2014, the College invested £4.5 million opening a purpose-built Preparatory School building on the school site, which includes a dedicated technology and languages centre, art, science and food science laboratory, library, central assembly hall and music room for the young pupils. Next to our Preparatory School is an additional £2.3 million sports hall.

The Nursery is adjacent to the Prep School in purpose-built accommodation.

Organisation. The College is divided into 2 sections: Senior School (11–18 year olds) and Preparatory School (3–11 year olds, including the Nursery for 3–5 year olds). The sections are closely integrated, allowing continuity of education from 3 to 18. Boarding girls and boys are accommodated in separate wings within the main Senior School building, under the supervision of the resident Senior Housemistress and Housemaster, together with their Assistants. There is a strong emphasis on pastoral care for all pupils. The teacher to pupil ratio in the Senior School is 1:18 (the ratio in the Sixth Form is much lower).

Curriculum. In the Nursery, the emphasis is on early Literacy, Numeracy and the development of personal and social skills, all of which contribute to a child's knowledge, understanding and skills in other areas of learning. Programmes of study are based on the Early Years Foundation Stage Curriculum, but extend well beyond these guidelines to develop a child's interests, talents, outlook and general knowledge and understanding of the world.

The Prep School offers small class sizes, well-resourced classrooms, a clear focus on the National Curriculum, an extended school day and a varied co-curricular activities programme. The curriculum is broad and balanced including extensive provision for Drama, Music, Modern Foreign Languages, Physical Education and Latin, taught by specialist teachers. Each classroom has the most up-to-date teaching and learning resources, with specialist classrooms for Art, Music, Science, Food Technology, ICT and Performing Arts. As the children move into Year 6, approximately half their timetable is taught by Senior School specialists. This enables the highest academic standards at the end of Key Stage 2, which means that all pupils move very happily into Year 7 and the Senior School building.

In the Senior School a broad and balanced curriculum is followed, which aims to identify and provide for individual needs. Most students take at least nine GCSEs. Core subjects consist of English Language, Mathematics, Religious Studies, a Modern Foreign Language and Science (Core and Additional or Triple Award). This is augmented by up to three further option subjects.

In the Sixth Form, students study 3 A Levels; some are studying 4. During the autumn term of Year 12, the large majority of students will then decide which three of these subjects they wish to continue to A Level, perhaps with an Extended Project Qualification (EPQ) to be completed in Year 12. In addition, students may opt to study the EPQ and the European Computer Driving Licence (ECDL) Level 3 along with two A Level subjects. To ensure a balanced programme, Games lessons and the Enrichment Programme are also part of the curriculum.

Games. The playing fields, which surround the College buildings, cover 200 acres. All pupils participate in Games, including Cricket, Hockey, Rugby, Tennis and Athletics for boys, and Hockey, Netball, Tennis and Athletics for girls.

Co-Curricular Activities. Pupils' talents and interests are developed through an extensive programme of activities on weekdays and at weekends. As well as many sporting opportunities, 25% of pupils learn a musical instrument; there are many musical groups, including brass ensemble, orchestra and choirs; all Year 4 pupils have free year-round orchestral instrumental tuition. Many pupils are involved in school productions and film-making, and other media activities are popular. The Combined Cadet Force and The Duke of Edinburgh's Award both flourish with numerous workshops and field trips. Students are encouraged to be caring and to have consideration for others through Chaplaincy groups and Voluntary Service activities.

Admissions.

Prep School (Nursery 3–5 year olds): Children spend the morning in the Nursery and are informally assessed during this time.

Prep School (Years 1–6, 5–11 year olds): Children spend a half day in School and, during this time, take assessments in English and Mathematics. Entry is normally at Year 3 and Year 5 (when additional classes of 18 pupils are admitted), but a small number of places may be available for entry to other year groups if there are vacancies.

Senior School (11–16 year olds): Entry is normally at age 11+ and 13+ (when an additional form of entry is admitted), but a small number of places may be available for entry to other years if there are vacancies.

11+, 12+, 13+ and 14+ Entrance Examinations are held on a Saturday morning in the first half of the spring term, prior to entry in September. Papers are set in English and Mathematics, and Science, for some year groups. Students also have an informal meeting with a member of the Leadership Team.

Sixth Form (16–18 year olds): All applicants are interviewed and entry is also based on successful performance in GCSE (or equivalent) examinations. Applicants should obtain at least 6 good passes at GCSE, including Mathematics and English. For any subject to be studied in the Sixth Form, applicants should have at least GCSE grade 6 in that subject or a related subject. GCSE grade 7 or higher is normally required to study the following subjects in the Sixth Form: Mathematics, Sciences, Languages and English Literature. Specimen English and Mathematics papers for entry into Years 7–10 are available on request from the Registrar.

Students with a Specific Learning Difficulty, who have evidence within a professional assessor report, are allowed extra time. Acceptable evidence will be in the form of an Educational Psychologist or Specialist Assessor report which clearly indicates speed scores for reading, writing or cognitive processing falling below SS85. Medical reports will also be considered. Such reports will need to be current, i.e. they will have been completed within two years of the Entrance Examinations.

Non-Native Speakers of English from Overseas: It is strongly recommended that overseas applicants should provide an IELTS or Cambridge Assessment English examination certificate to confirm their ability in English language. However, applicants for entry to Years 9 and 10 do have the option of sitting our own English examinations, but will have to provide an IELTS or Cambridge Assessment English examination at the end of their first academic year in order to progress through the School.

Students may also be tested in subjects such as Mathematics and Science.

Overseas applicants are also interviewed via Skype, if a personal visit to the School cannot be arranged.

Scholarships and Bursaries. Ratcliffe College offers a wide range of scholarships to recognise academic, sporting, musical, dramatic and artistic talent amongst applicants for the Senior School.

Each scholarship is worth up to 50% of the fees and are offered in Years 7 and 12.

Bursaries are available on entry to Years 7 and 12, for up to 80% of a student's School Fee and in exceptional circumstances up to 100%. All awards are subject to parental means-testing. Sixth Form Talent Bursaries are also available in Sport, Music, Drama, Art and Design. For further details, please contact the Registrar.

Fees per term (2021–2022). UK Students: Full Boarding (Years 6–13) £9,304; Weekly Boarding (Years 9–13) £8,294; Weekly Boarding (Years 6–8) £7,411. Boarding fees include the full cost of the programme of boarding weekend trips throughout the year.

Overseas Students: Full Boarding £11,137. Boarding fees include the full cost of the programme of boarding weekend trips throughout the year and the cost of additional teaching of English as a Foreign Language where necessary.

Day: £3,333–£3,760 (Nursery aged 3–5); £3,760–£4,245 (Years 1–5); £4,903–£5,782 (Years 6–13).

Fees are subject to such termly increase as may prove necessary. Additional charges are made for: private Music lessons at £245 per term for 10 half-hour sessions (for individual tuition for each instrument); Where additional teaching of Learning Skills is required and agreed with parents, this will be charged at £46 per lesson. There is a non-refundable registration fee of £99 (£125 overseas) On acceptance of an offer, a deposit of £1,000 (£500 refunded during the second term) for students entering Ratcliffe College from the UK and of £5,000 (£3,000 refunded during the second term) for students from overseas, is payable on entry to the Preparatory School and Senior School. A deposit is not payable on entry to the Nursery, but will be required when the child moves to the Preparatory School. The deposit is not refundable if the student subsequently fails to take up the place. As fees are payable termly in advance, the deposit will be held until the student leaves and may be used to offset charges incurred during the final term. Any balance remaining will be refunded at that time.

Charitable status. Ratcliffe College is a Registered Charity, number 1115975, for the education of children.

Governing Body:
Consists of two members of the Board of Directors of the Company Limited by Guarantee which owns the College (Ratcliffe College Ltd), together with up to 10 additional governors, appointed by the Directors, who hold office for a period.

Chair of Governors: Mrs L Marsden
Vice-Chair of Governors: Mrs T Gamble
Dr Mary Riley
Mrs Sam Spillane
Mrs Karen Colville
Mrs Joanne Linnett
Fr Philip Sainter

Mr Graham Sharpe
Mr Simon Burns
Mr Mike Cummins
Mr Paul Rudd

Headmaster: **Mr J Reddin**, BSc, MSc

Deputy Head Academic: Mr K Ryce, BA, MSc
Deputy Head Pastoral: Mr C Donegan, BSc, MA
Assistant Head, Head of Sixth Form: Mr B Harrison, MPhil, MA
Assistant Head Academic: Ms J Davis, BA
Head of Preparatory School: Fr C Cann, MA, MA Oxon, Cert Theol
Deputy Head of Preparatory School: Mrs J Cartwright, BA
Assistant Head, Head of Boarding: Miss A Da Costa, BA
Father President: Fr P Sainter, IC, BSc, BPhil, MA, STL
Bursar: Mr C Bellamy, HND
Development Director: Mr A Yell, BSc

Teaching Staff:
* Head of Department

Mrs L Arnold, BSc, MPhil (*Information & Communication Technology*)
Miss E Bakewell, BA (*Physical Education*)
Mr W Ballard, BSc, MA (*Chemistry**)
Ms E Battrum (*Geography*)
Mr M Bobath, BA (*Latin**)
Mr J Box, BA, MA, CELTA (*EAL*)
Mrs K Burton, BA (*Food Technology**)
Mr J Cantrill, BA (*History**)
Miss M Casas-Ojeda, BA, MA (*Spanish*)
Miss P Charvong (*EAL*)
Mr A Chorley, MSc (*Science*, Physics*)
Mrs S Clarke, BA (*Mathematics*)
Mrs C Cole, MA (*Mathematics, DofE*)
Mrs L Cook, MA (*English*)
Miss A Corbinzolu, BA (*Head of Year 9, Religious Studies*)
Mrs A Crebbin, Licence (*French, Spanish*)
Mrs S Cushing, BA (*Languages**)
Mrs D Darlington, BSc (*Science*)
Mr M Darlington, BSc (*Physics*, Curriculum Director*)
Mrs L Davids, BSc (*Learning Support*)
Mr C Doherty, BEng (*Mathematics*)
Mrs K Donegan, BA (*Director of Music**)
Mrs A Dungey, BSc (*Science, Food Technology*)
Mr P Enoux, BA (*Key Stage 2*)
Mr W Faulconbridge, BSc (*Preparatory School Sport**)
Mr A Ferrari, BSc (*Key Stage 1/2*)
Mr J Finn, BA (*Key Stage 1/2*)
Miss D Gatt, BSc (*Biology*)
Miss L Gentle, BSc (*Physical Education*)
Mrs N Gilchrist, BEd (*Preparatory School*)
Mr P Gilchrist, BSc (*Boys Senior Housemaster, Extra-Curricular Coordinator*)
Mrs K Grace, BA (*Careers**)
Mrs D Grant, BEd (*Key Stage 1*)
Miss R Green, BSc (*Head of Nursery*)
Miss E Hall (*Lay Chaplain*)
Mr G Higham, BSc (*Mathematics**)
Miss V Hobbs, BA (*English*)
Miss C Jeyes, NNEB (*Nursery School*)
Ms E Johanson, BA (*Learning Support**)
Mr C Jones, BA, MA (*Economics and Business*)
Mr M Jones, BSc (*Head of Year 9, Information Communication Technology**)
Dr S Jones PhD (*Mathematics*)

Mr M Kaye, BA (*Physical Education, History, Boarding Assistant*)
Mr D Kent, BA (*Key Stage 2*)
Dr S Kyle-Ferguson, PhD (*Biology*)
Mr M Lambert, BSc (*Geography**)
Dr C Latham, BSc, MSc, PhD (*Preparatory School Learning Support*)
Miss C Llewelyn, BA (*Key Stage 2*)
Mr M Lucas, BSc (*Academic Physical Education**)
Mr P McCrindell, BA (*Head of Year 11, German*)
Mrs M Markham, BA (*Preparatory School Music*)
Mrs C Milligan, BCom, CELTA (*EAL*)
Mrs A Mullan, BA (*French*)
Mrs J Munton, BA (*Drama**)
Mr M Newman, BA (*Head of Year 13, History*)
Mrs Y O'Connor, BA, Med (*Religious Studies*)
Mrs S Owen, BA (*Early Years Practitioner*)
Miss L Phillipps, BA, MA (*Religious Studies*)
Mr B Plummer, BSc (*Key Stage 1/2*)
Mrs J Reddin, BA (*French*)
Mrs M Reeves, BA, MSc (*EAL**)
Dr A Robinson, BSc, PhD (*Science*)
Mr P Rogers, BA (*Head of Year 8, Design and Technology*)
Miss C Sapiano, BA (*Drama*)
Mr A Seth, BSc (*Design and Technology**)
Miss C Simms, BA (*Media Studies**)
Mr M Sleath, BSc (*Head of Year 13, Mathematics*)
Mrs E Smith, BSc (*Physics*)
Mrs P Smith, BA (*Religious Studies*)
Mr P Spencer, ACIB (*Head of Year 12, Business/Economics**)
Miss T Spencer, BA (*Business/Economics*)
Dr S Standen, BSc, PhD (*Head of Year 8, Science*)
Dr L Stannard, BA, MA, PhD (*English**)
Ms G Taylor, BSc (*Key Stage 1/2*)
Mr S Thorpe, BSc (*Head of Year 11, Science, Assistant Housemaster*)
Miss S Tidy, BA (*English*)
Mr P Trotter, CChem, MRSc (*Science*)
Mr D Turner, BEd (*Preparatory School, Assistant Boys' Housemaster*)
Mrs A Turns, BSc (*Director of Sport**)
Miss K Vickers, BMus (*Music*)
Ms W Walker (*Librarian*)
Mr N Walsh LLB (*Religious Studies**)
Mrs E Waters BEd (*Learning Support*)
Mrs L Wetton, BA (*Key Stage 2*)
Mrs L Whieldon, BA (*English*)
Mr E Woodcock, BA, MSc (*Head of Year 7, Physical Education, Boarding Assistant*)
Mr W Wong, BSc (*Mathematics*)
Miss A Wright, BA (*Art and Design*)

Sports Coaches:
Mr K Hill, Miss S Griffin, Miss J Thomas, Mr J Chapel, Mr M Birr, Mrs S Maclaine-Freeman, Mr N Taylor, Mr J Nightingale, Mr P Sign

Peripatetic Music Staff:
Mr P Bennett, Mrs C Bhabra, Dr M Bonshor, Mr J Boyd, Mrs S Cheeseman, Mr C Earp, Mr R Finn, Mrs S Forrester, Miss S Hall, Mr G Henderson, Mrs C Lee, Mr B Matthews, Mrs R Reedman, Mrs K Thompson

Teaching Assistants:
Mrs A Batten, BSc
Mrs S Pascoe, BSc

Mrs W Zaragoza de Vale
Mr T Mears, BA

Graduate Assistants:
Mr D Deery
Mr H Stamper
Miss A Ridley
Miss C Waldiin
Miss S Croizer (*Languages*)
Mr M Glaser (*Languages*)

Teaching Assistants (*Preparatory School and Nursery*):
Mrs S Allen
Miss E Angus, NVQ III
Miss C Croxall
Mrs R Deacon
Mrs L Finn, NVQ III
Mrs M Karanja
Miss E Lacey, NVQ III
Mrs A Leake
Mrs R Muse, NVQ III
Mrs Nilanthi Senavirathna-Yapa
Mrs E Sleath
Mrs K Smith
Mrs S Wereszczyinski

Administrative & Support Staff:
Mr J Teviotdale (*Finance Manager*)
Mrs C Govan (*Headmaster's Assistant*)
Mrs J Orton, CIPD (*Human Resources Manager*)
Miss K Smith, BSc (*Registrar*)
Mr I Blackmore-Allen, BA, MA (*Marketing & Communications Manager*)
Mrs S Patel (*School Secretary*)
Mr D Charlish (*Examination and Data Manager*)
Mrs L Liston (*Development Manager*)

School Nurses:
Mrs H Bogwandas, RGN
Mrs C Lang, RGN
Mrs D Warburton, RGN (*Senior Nurse*)

Science Technicians:
Mrs P Standen, Mrs S Widger, Mr M O'Hara

Technicians:
Mrs T Bradshaw (*Art & Design*)
Mr J Hoult (*Media Studies*)
Mrs K Toon (*Food Technology*)
Ms F Viccars (*Drama*)

Reading Blue Coat School

Holme Park, Sonning, Berkshire RG4 6SU

Tel: 0118 944 1005
email: reception@rbcs.org.uk
website: www.rbcs.org.uk
Twitter: @ReadingBlues
Facebook: @ReadingBlueCoatl
Instagram: @readingbluecoatschool

The School was founded in 1646 by Richard Aldworth, a merchant of London and Reading, and a Governor of Christ's Hospital. There are 820 pupils (aged 11–18) including a co-educational Sixth Form. From September 2023, the School will be extending its co-educational provision to welcome girls into Year 7. By 2027, it is hoped that there will be an even number of boys and girls in each year group.

Aims. The School aims to provide a stimulating and friendly atmosphere in which each pupil can realise his or her full intellectual, physical and creative potential. Pupils are encouraged to be self-reliant and adaptable and we hope that they will learn the basis of good citizenship founded on honesty, fairness and understanding of the needs of others.

The School is a Church of England Foundation, and emphasis is placed on Christian values and standards.

Buildings. The School is set in an attractive 46-acre site by the banks of the Thames in the village of Sonning. School House, originally built in the eighteenth century and extensively remodelled in the Victorian era, stands at the heart of the School. The School's facilities have undergone a continuous programme of improvement over the last decade, including a new IT Centre, a new Design Technology Centre, improvements to the School's entrance and dropoff/pickup area, a new Geology and Psychology block, a 23-classroom teaching facility, a cricket pavilion, improvements to the swimming pool and a boathouse on the banks of the Thames. More recently, Blue Coat has opened its dedicated Grounds, Maintenance and Activities Centre, which provides a shooting range and CCF and Adventure Education facilities. The three-classroom Coach House was also opened in 2021, and provides space for pupils to work collaboratively. The School has recently expanded its facilities for the Sixth Form and has plans for the further development of a Performing Arts Centre.

Curriculum. In Years 7 to 9, pupils study a broad range of subjects, including Classics, modern foreign languages and Religious Studies. In Years 10 and 11, pupils follow courses in Mathematics and Science and also opt to complete four further courses in a wide range of additional subjects, such as History, Geography, Geology and Physical Education. A wide range of subjects is offered at A Level, including Psychology, Economics, Business, Politics and Drama, with nearly every pupil going on to university, including Oxford and Cambridge. Adventure Education has also been introduced as a compulsory part of the curriculum, and is providing pupils with opportunities to flourish away from the classroom.

Sixth Form. The co-educational Sixth Form Centre accommodates more than 250 students. Girls are fully integrated into all activities. In addition to A Level courses, all Sixth Formers follow compulsory careers and enrichment programmes.

Games and Activities. A wide range of sports and activities is offered within the curriculum and regular school fixtures for all year groups are arranged. Full advantage is taken of the River Thames and Rowing is a popular sport for both boys and girls. The main boys' games are Rugby in the Autumn Term, Football in the Spring Term, and Cricket and Athletics in the Summer Term. Girls play Netball, Rounders and Hockey. Other sporting activities include Basketball, Tennis, Golf, Table Tennis, Climbing, Swimming, Archery, Cross Country, Badminton, Mountain Biking, Yoga and Sailing.

The Cadet Force includes Army, Royal Air Force and Royal Navy Sections. Camping and adventure training activities take place during holidays and at weekends. There is a wide range in the Activities Programme, as well as The Duke of Edinburgh's Award, overseas expeditions, community service and sports leadership.

Music and Drama enjoy a high profile in the life of the School. Well over a third of the pupils receive individual instrumental lessons and pupils are encouraged to join in activities such as the Choir, Chamber Choir, Piano Trio, String Ensemble, Concert Band, Saxophone Group, Brass Group, Swing Band, Wind Band, Junior Strings, Treble Choir, Rock Bands, Senior Brass Group and Blue Coat Big Band. Concerts, plays and musicals are presented regularly.

Admissions. The three main points of entry in September are at 11+, 13+ and 16+. 11+ entry is by assessments taken in the previous Autumn term, and 13+ assessments take place during the Autumn term of Year 7. Entry at other levels is by assessment and interview and is subject to vacancies. Entry to the Sixth Form for girls and boys is by assessment, interview and conditional on GCSE results. From September 2023, the School will be extending its co-educational provision to welcome girls into Year 7.

Scholarships and Bursaries. The Foundation makes provision for awards of scholarships and bursaries, including academic, music and art awards, based on merit and need. Foundation Scholarships up to 100% of fees are available according to financial need.

Fees per term (2021–2022). £6,013.

Charitable status. Reading Blue Coat School is a Registered Charity, number 1087839. Its aim is the provision of secondary education for pupils aged 11 to 18.

Chairman of Governors: P Bertram

Headmaster: **P J Thomas**, BSc Hons, GTP

Second Master: E Trelinski, BA, MA (*Politics*)
Deputy Head, Academic: R Tidbury, MSc Hons, PGCE (*Mathematics*)
Deputy Head, Staff: Dr K J Magill, MPhil, BA, PGCE, PhD, FCCT (*Religious Studies*)
Deputy Head, Pastoral: Dr G J Williams, BA, MPhil, DPhil, PGCE
Bursar: Mr T Tabrah, BA, ACA
Director of Marketing and Admissions: Mrs J Jarrett
Director of Development: Mrs S Bunnell-Pyper, BA Hons

* *Head of Department*

Mrs E J Archbold, BA, PGCE (*Biology*)
Mrs E J Ashley, QTS, BSc (*Geography*)
Miss E H Atherton, MChem, PGCE (*Chemistry*)
Mr M J Baker, BA Hons, PGCE (**Geography*)
Mrs C E Bamforth, MA, PGCE (*Biology*)
Mr S D Bateman, BA (*Business, Economics*)
Mrs K E Bayliss, BA (**Business, *Economics*)
Miss S Beaveridge, BA, QTS (*English*)
Mr T Bellinger, BSc, ECB (*Head of Cricket*)
Mrs L J Bennett, BEd Hons (*Religious Studies*)
Mrs S E Berry, BA, PGCE, Dip SpLD, AMBDA (**Learning Support, French*)
Mr O Blandford, BSc, IPGCE (*Graduate Sport and Physical Education Assistant*)
Mr C Bond (*Drama*)
Mr J Bowler, BA Hons, PGCE, LTCL, ARCM (**Director of Music, Performance Studies/Drama and Theatre*)
Mr K Buckland, BSc, MSc, PGCE, UEFA A (*Head of Football*)
Mr E J Clark, BA Hons, QTS (*Mathematics**)
Mrs M A Clews, BA, PGCE, PG Cert (**Psychology, Classics*)
Mr A W Colville, BSc Hons, BSc (**Biology*)
Mrs R L Crossland, MESci, PGCE (*Geology*)

Mrs C Dance, BA Ed Hons (*Mathematics, *Girls' Games*)
Mr J C Dance, BA Hons (*Sport and Physical Education*)
Mrs A M Dewar, BA Hons, PGCE (*French, German, Spanish*)
Mr R N Ennis, BA, PGCE (*Art*)
Mrs G R Finucane, BSc, MSc (**Geology, Geography*)
Mrs J L Forward, BSc (*Mathematics, Physics*)
Mr A J French, BA Hons, PG Dip (*Head of Rowing*)
Mr J Fuller, BEng, PGCE (*DT**)
Mr M Halicioglu, BSc, MSc, PGDE (*Physics*)
Miss D Harris, BA, PGCE (*English*)
Mrs E Harvey, BA Hons, PGCE (*Art**)
Mrs S A Head, MA (**Modern Foreign Languages, German, French*)
Mrs R Heffernan, BSc (*Economics and Business*)
Miss C A Holliday, BA, PGCE (*German, French*)
Mr P A Hoy, BSc, MSc (*Strength and Conditioning Coach*)
Mr T Jacobs, BA, PGCE (*Classics*)
Mr M J Jerstice, MSc, MA, PGCE (**Integrated Science, *Chemistry*)
Mr L B Johnson, BA Hons, PG Law Diploma (**Government and Politics*)
Mrs G M Kelly, BA Hons, PGCE (*Religious Studies, French*)
Mrs R Kennedy-George, MA, MPhil, PGCE (*English*)
Mrs A Lambourne Moss, BSc, PGCE (*Mathematics*)
Dr S R Langdon, MChem, PGCE, PhD (*Chemistry*)
Mr J Leigh, BA Hons, MA (*History*)
Miss C Loveday, MusB (*Technical Theatre Apprentice*)
Mr A J Maddocks, BA Hons (**French, German*)
Miss J Malpas, BSc, PGCE (*Psychology*)
Dr S A Manning, BSc, MA, PhD (*Biology*)
Mrs T A McConalogue, BEd (*Mathematics*)
Mrs I A McGough, BA, PGCE (*Design Technology*)
Mr R Meehan, BA Hons, BA Hons, PGCE (**Music*)
Mrs G Mitchell, BA Hons, PGCE (*Information Technology, Religious Studies*)
Mr W E Mitchell, BA Hons, PGCE (*Geography*)
Mr D Möller, BA Hons, PGCE (**Drama*)
Mr M Montague (*DT Technician*)
Mr W Nash-Wortham, BA Hons, PGCE (*Business, Economics, *Careers*)
Miss S Nicholl, BSc, PGCE (*DT*)
Mrs H J Oliver, BA Hons, PGCE (*French*)
Miss A Pegler, BA, MA, PGDipEd (*English*)
Mr M J Pink, BA Hons, MSc (*Psychology, Sport and Physical Education*)
Miss G Plowman, BA Hons (*History*)
Mr S L Pritchard, BSc, PGCE (*Mathematics*)
Mrs H E Rancombe, BSc Hons, PGCE (*Psychology, Biology*)
Mr D L Salmon, MA, Computing Dip, PGCE (*Physics, Electronics*)
Dr F B Santos, BSc, MSc, PhD (*Chemistry*)
Mr T E Seward, MSc (*Sport and Physical Education*)
Mr B J Shuler, BEng, MEd (**Physics*)
Mr J R Slack, BSc Hons, PGCE (*Mathematics*)
Mr R P Starr, BA Hons, PGCE (*Spanish, French*)
Mr M J Stewart, BA Hons, MA, PGCE (**English*)
Mr H A Stone, BA, MA, PGCE (**Religious Studies*)
Mr J Stone, BA Hons, PGCE (*English, Drama*)
Mr S Sydenham, ITT, MA, MSc (*Physics*)
Mrs A D Tapley, BSc Hons (*Biology*)
Mr I Teague, BSc (*Geography*)
Miss A R Thomas, BSc, PGCE (*Mathematics*)

Ms C R Thomas, MA, PGCE (*History*, *Government and Politics*)

Miss J L Thompson, BA, PGCE (*Geography*)

Miss B A Truman, BA Hons, MA, PGCE (*English*, *French*, *Film Studies*)

Miss T van der Werff, MA, PGCE (**History*)

Mr W Voice, BA Hons, PGCE (*Information Technology*)

Revd K L Wakeman-Toogood, BSc Hons, PGCE, BA Hons (*Mathematics*, *Chaplain*)

Mr T C Walford, BSc, PGCE (*Information Technology*)

Mrs N Watmough-Starkie, BMus Hons, PGCE (*Music*)

Mr C Wicks, BA, PGCE (*History*)

Mrs J M Wilkins, BSc, PGCE (*Mathematics*)

Mr G A Wilson, BSc (**Sport and Physical Education*)

Mr S Yates, BSc Hons, PGCE (**Information Technology*)

Mrs J F Zambon, BA Hons, PGCE (**Spanish*)

Mr P Zambon (*Information Technology*)

Headmaster's Secretary: Mrs K Abbott

Admissions: Mrs A Fernandes, BA Hons; Mrs M Bell, BSc; Mrs R Hardman, BSc

Marketing Officer: Mr T Strudwick, BA Hons

Librarian: Miss C Knight, BA Hons, MA, PG LIS

School Nurse: Mrs G F Montgomery, RGN

Sports Centre Manager: Mr R D Cook

Archivist: Mr P J van Went, MA, CertEd

Reigate Grammar School

Reigate Road, Reigate, Surrey RH2 0QS

Tel: 01737 222231
email: info@reigategrammar.org
          admissions@reigategrammar.org
website: www.reigategrammar.org
Twitter: @ReigateGrammar
Facebook: @ReigateGrammarSchool

Reigate Grammar School is a co-educational day school for pupils aged 11 to 18.

It is a multi-award winning school being named School of the Year for 2020–2021 in the Tatler School Awards and the winning school/college of the year in the UK Social Mobility Awards 2021. This follows awards as School of the Year for Pastoral Care, Community Engagement and for our ongoing contribution to social mobility – awards coming from the TES and ISSP. It is regularly listed in the Times league tables as amongst the highest attaining schools in the country. In 2021, 97% of students received university offers from Oxford, Cambridge, Russell Group or medical schools.

The school is situated in the historic market town of Reigate, just outside the M25, yet with easy transport links into London, Surrey and Sussex.

Reigate Grammar School has a strong tradition of excellence in a wide variety of extracurricular activities, including an enviable reputation in sport, music and drama; large numbers of pupils participate in the Combined Cadet Force and in The Duke of Edinburgh's Award. The school raises a significant amount of money each year for local and national charities and students give thousands of hours to volunteering locally.

Admissions. Pupils are normally admitted to the School at 11+, 13+ or 16+, although vacancies occasionally occur at other ages.

Fees per term (2021–2022). Years 7–8 £6,775; Years 9–13 £6,875. Sibling discounts are available.

Scholarships and Bursaries. The school offers a wide range of scholarships and bursaries.

Junior School. Reigate St Mary's Preparatory and Choir School and Chinthurst School, Tadworth (*see entries in IAPS section*) are the junior schools of Reigate Grammar School.

Charitable status. Reigate Grammar School is a Registered Charity, number 1081898. Its aim is to provide high quality education for boys and girls.

Governing Body:
Chair: Mr J Dean
Deputy Chair & Chair Elect: Mr E Elsey

Dr S Banerjee	Mrs M Edmunds
Mr M Benton	Mr L Herbert
Mr C Cobain	Mrs M Hulme
Mr D Cole	Miss L Page
Mr B Day	Mr N Weber
Mr C Dixon	Mr E Wheeler

Headmaster: **Mr S A Fenton**, MA Oxford, MEd Oxford

Deputy Head: Mrs M A Collins, BEng Bristol
Deputy Head: Miss S J Arthur, BA Durham
Deputy Head: Dr B P Stones, BSc PhD Edinburgh

Assistant Head: Mr R J Bristow, BA Oxford
Assistant Head: Mrs A L Crook, BSc Edinburgh, MSc Bristol
Assistant Head: Mrs C M Hosegood, BSc Durham
Assistant Head: Mrs C H Lawson, BA Liverpool
Assistant Head: Miss L J Robertson, BA East Anglia, MA Lancaster

Head of Upper Sixth Form: Mr R T James, BSc Bristol
Head of Lower Sixth Form: Miss C Green, BA East Anglia
Deputy Head of Sixth Form: Mrs L C N Budden, MA Edinburgh, MA Queen Mary

Head of Upper School: Mr M H Hetherington, BA Nottingham
Head of Fifth Form: Mrs A M Hetherington, BA Birmingham
Head of Fourth Form: Mrs E J Mitchell, BEd Exeter
Head of Third Form: Mr N R Newman, BA Newcastle

Head of Lower School: Mrs S L Leck, MA Cambridge
Head of Second Form: Mrs C L Cline, BSc St Mary's
Head of First Form: Ms C D Case, BA Canterbury

Chaplain: Rev P M Jackson, BA Cheltenham, BA Bristol
Bursar & Clerk to the Governors: Mr S P Douty, FCMA
Head of Foundation and Business Development: Mr S P Davey, MA

Heads of House:
Bird: Mrs A Fullalove, BA South Carolina, MA Queen's Belfast
Cranston: Mr J M C Leck, BA East Anglia
Hodgson: Miss S Shah, MPharm King's College London
Williamson: Mr M O'Donnell, BSc Kent

Teaching Staff:
A list of teaching staff is available on the website.

PA to the Headmaster: Mrs B G Eustace

Rendcomb College

Rendcomb, Cirencester, Gloucestershire GL7 7HA

Tel:	01285 831213
email:	admissions@rendcombcollege.org.uk
website:	www.rendcombcollege.org.uk
Twitter:	@RendcombCollege
Facebook:	@Rendcombcollege
Instagram:	@rendcombcollege
LinkedIn:	/rendcomb-college

Rendcomb College is a co-educational, independent day and boarding school for children aged 3 to 18 in the heart of the Cotswolds, UK. The College was founded in 1920 by Noel Wills and is set within a stunning 230-acre parkland estate which is equidistant from Cheltenham and Cirencester.

Our Mission. Our mission is to develop thoughtful, adventurous and academically ambitious young people who are lifelong learners. We aim to prepare them with the character and skills to succeed in the ever-changing world after school. Our pupils have the freedom to experience, explore and enquire about the world around them. We aim to encourage independence and tolerance in a safe, caring community and magnificent natural environment.

To achieve this we will:

- Promote a growth mindset, where abilities can be developed through dedication and hard work;
- Provide a co-curriculum that will challenge and support character development, leadership and teamwork;
- Encourage individualism, creativity and contribution to a nurturing and collaborative community;
- Engender physical, spiritual and mental wellbeing through a strong pastoral system;
- Prepare pupils for a life beyond school;
- Develop an appreciation for and responsible attitude towards their environment and surroundings.

Admission. Pupils join the Junior School from Nursery or Reception or join the Senior School at age 11, 13 or 16. The entrance examination at 11 is taken at Rendcomb and comprises three papers: English, Mathematics and Verbal Reasoning. At 13, pupils are admitted by Common Entrance or Rendcomb Examination and at 16 by interview, school reports and GCSE results.

Curriculum. Rendcomb College's curriculum extends well beyond the confines of the classroom and the core teaching day. Our small size in both the Junior and Senior schools enables all students to participate in a number of sports, in addition to a wide range of activities which begin after the end of formal lessons each day. Our philosophy is to consider these to be co-curricular, aimed at combining with the academic elements to genuinely develop the whole person and ensure that we provide a fully-rounded education.

University Entrance. In the last three years, leavers have gone on to a number of prestigious universities including Oxford, Bath, Exeter, Nottingham, Birmingham, Imperial College, London, Royal Holloway, Durham and Swansea. One student has gone on to study Veterinary Medicine and Science at Surrey while another secured a place at Coventry to join their BEng Motorsport Engineering course.

Houses. Both Day pupils and Boarders share the same Houses, enabling strong friendships and comradery to flourish among all pupils throughout the College.

Pupils can board when they join the Senior School in Year 7 through to Sixth Form. From Year 10 upwards, all Boarders have their own study bedrooms which can be personalised, whilst the younger pupils share dormitories with two or three other students.

Our boarding is very flexible, especially at weekends; from Saturday teatime onwards, Boarders choose to stay at school to work, relax or join in family life at home. There are beds for Day pupils too if they wish to try boarding, or if they need to stay over.

In September 2019, the Year 7–9 house, Godman, opened following an extension and refurbishment. In Years 10 and 11, pupils are split by gender until they reach Sixth Form when they join the co-educational Park House.

Boarders' weekends are full, busy and purposeful through the provision of an extensive programme of activities run by our Boarding Activities Coordinator.

The four Houses at Rendcomb College are located on the school's campus and within easy reach of classrooms and sports facilities. The Houses offer an ideal setting for all pupils to thrive and develop under the guidance of the Houseparents and their pastoral and domestic teams.

Bursaries. A number of bursaries are awarded in keeping with the original charitable aims of the College's Founder. The amount of the bursary award is not influenced by the level of the child's academic ability but by the extent of need and each case is assessed on its own merits with awards being made accordingly.

Scholarships. A number of Scholarships (Academic, Art, Music, Drama and Sport) are awarded each year at Year 7, 9 and 12 with additional Scholarships awarded in Year 3. Scholarships are based on the assessment of a pupil's potential and the value that we believe they will add to the life of our school. We also award the Noel Wills Scholarship and the Rendcomb Scholarship at Year 7.

Rendcomb celebrated its 100th birthday in 2020 and the Governors secured the launch of a number of 100% fully-funded scholarships for entry into Year 4 and Year 12.

Fees per term (2021–2022). Senior School: Boarding £8,700–£12,650, Day £5,800–£8,150. Junior School: Day £2,250–£4,315. We accept the Government's 30 hours scheme in Nursery and Reception for qualifying families.

Charitable status. Rendcomb College is a Registered Charity, number 1115884.

Chairman of Governors: Mr Nicholas Ford

Head of College: **Mr Rob Jones**, BA, MEd

Head of Juniors: Mr Gavin Roberts, BA, PGCE

Bursar: Mrs E Sharman, BSc

Repton School

Repton, Derbyshire DE65 6FH

Tel: 01283 559222 (Admissions)
          01283 559200 (Reception)
email: admissions@repton.org.uk
website: www.repton.org.uk
Twitter: @ReptonSchool
Facebook: @ReptonSchool

Founded in 1557, Repton School was established on the site of a 12th century Augustinian Priory in the Derbyshire village of the same name. Today Repton is a modern community with a clear sense of purpose and momentum. As a pre-eminent co-educational boarding and day school in the heart of England, Repton provides a balanced, broad-based education, blending heritage with the pursuit of excellence in a 21st century context, offering world-class facilities alongside high quality teaching and pastoral care.

Repton is home to around 620 pupils, making it large enough to achieve excellence in and out of the classroom, yet small enough for individuals to grow and flourish. Each pupil, whether day or boarding, is a member of a House, of which there are 10 (six for boys and four for girls). Repton Prep is situated two miles from the Senior campus and is home to enviable, age-appropriate facilities set in the beautiful 55-acre grounds of a Palladian manor house.

Academic standards are high and because most of the teachers, tutors and coaches live in the village, Reptonians never have to prioritise academic achievement over their love of the theatre or rank their aptitude for sport above their passion for music. Repton's considerable strengths were recognised in the 2020 ISI Inspection which found the School to be 'Excellent' in each of the areas examined.

Both campuses are situated in picturesque locations whilst offering extensive travel links. Repton and Repton Prep can be easily reached by road from the M1, M6 and M5 via the A50, by rail from East Midlands Parkway and Lichfield, or from nearby Birmingham and East Midlands airports.

Admissions. Pupils from a wide range of prep schools are admitted to Repton at 13+ (Year 9), 14+ (Year 10) and 16+ (Year 12). Repton invites prospective pupils to take part in GL Assessment's CAT4 Tests that focus on a pupil's potential, skills and abilities. Along with completion of these assessments, Repton will also request school reports and a reference from your child's current school.

Fees per term (2021–2022). Boarders £12,721; Day pupils £9,437. Some additional expenses (for trips, sports kit, pocket money etc) will be incurred.

Houses and Pastoral Care. There are ten Houses – six for boys and four for girls, each home to approximately 60 pupils. Day pupils are fully integrated with the boarders, who make up around 70% of the Repton community.

In-House dining is one of the most highly treasured aspects of Repton life and day and boarding pupils dine with teachers and staff in their own House three times each day. Each of the Houses has its own in-House catering team, including a Head Chef, providing delicious home-cooked food sourced from local producers.

The House is in a true sense every Reptonian's home in the School – the place where pupils eat, sleep, work and live. The Housemaster or Housemistress has overall responsibility for an individual pupil's work and development, lives in the House with their own family and is supported by a resident Matron, resident Tutor and team of Duty Tutors. The size of the House is carefully calibrated to allow for individualised care. Repton's pastoral care combines the best of traditional care with a systematically proactive approach aiming to pre-empt problems and support each pupil. By interweaving scientific and data driven measures the Pastoral team has developed highly tuned pastoral care provision; an inspection in 2020 called it 'leading edge'.

Curriculum. The Curriculum at Repton includes both the Academic Curriculum and Co-Curriculum. It gives pupils experience in linguistic, mathematical, scientific, technological, human and social, physical and creative education. It also provides for the spiritual, social and cultural development of pupils.

The Co-Curriculum provides a rich programme of activities appropriate to pupils' educational needs in relation to personal, social, emotional and physical development. It is Repton's aim to run a varied programme of sport and other extracurricular activities and all pupils are expected to participate.

Pupils joining Repton in B Block (Year 9) study Biology, Chemistry, Digital Literacy, English, Geography, History, Mathematics, Physical Education, Physics, PSHE and Religious Studies. They also opt to study a combination of modern foreign languages and classical subjects. The Creative Studies programme provides lessons in Art, Design Technology, Drama, Music, and Digital Literacy.

In A and O Block (Years 10 and 11) the core subjects taken by all pupils are Mathematics, English Language, English Literature and the Sciences. Most pupils also take a core Modern Foreign Language and all pupils in A Block study PSHE. There is an option system which enables a pupil to take three additional GCSEs. This includes Art, Business, Classical Civilisation, Design Technology, Drama, French (for those who wish to take this subject in addition to either German or Spanish as a core Modern Foreign Language), Geography, History, Latin, Music, Physical Education and Religious Studies. Art, Textiles, Photography and Music can also be studied "off timetable".

Most Sixth Formers study three subjects at the start of Lower Sixth, though some take four. Pupils can opt from the following subjects: Art, Biology, Business, Chemistry, Classical Civilisation, Design Technology, Drama, Economics, English Literature, French, Geography, German, History, Latin, Mathematics and Further Mathematics, Music, Physical Education, Photography; Physics, Politics, Psychology, Religious Studies, Spanish, Sport (BTEC), and Textiles.

Pupils have the opportunity to take the Extended Project Qualification and in the Lower Sixth pupils follow a programme devised by the School, "Future Learning, Future Skills" which covers public speaking, personal finances, geopolitics and prepares Sixth Formers for life beyond Repton.

Across all year groups specialist learning support lessons are also offered, including English as an additional language (EAL).

Beyond Repton. In 2021, 29% of pupils achieved an A* and 63.7% of pupils achieved A*/A with three pupils securing Oxbridge places. Reptonians go on to study at a wide range of universities with US universities proving increasingly popular. Six pupils in 2021 secured offers to study in the US including a prestigious music scholarship to Berklee College of Music and a field hockey scholarship to the Ivy League Yale university. They form a growing cohort of Old Reptonians in the US at prestigious universities including Harvard and Stanford.

Facilities at Repton are of a world-class standard and significant investments in recent years give pupils, partner schools and the wider community access to state-of-the-art facilities. This includes the newly refurbished Sports Centre and the Science Priory which offers pupils access to an observatory, outdoor classrooms and a university-style lecture theatre.

Repton is fortunate to possess outstanding all-weather water-based hockey pitches, indoor hockey, an indoor swimming pool, strength and conditioning suites, and a cricket ground that is the envy of many schools and clubs; a Music School with a plethora of practice rooms, concert hall, performance areas and recording studio; the 400 Hall Theatre with a versatile, purpose-built Studio space; and a stunning Art School with two art galleries, dedicated workshops for 3D work, ceramics, and photography.

Creative Arts. Music is at the heart of Repton and all pupils are encouraged to participate in a wide variety of classroom and extra-curricular music activities. The Music Department is housed in an impressive building which features a purpose-built concert hall, a fully equipped recording studio, a computer suite specifically for composition and a variety of academic and instrumental teaching spaces. The department's six full-time members of staff are joined by Heads of Strings, Wind & Brass and Singing and there are 30 specialist Visiting Music Teachers. In 2021 Repton appointed Mr Richard Yarr, FRSA as their first Music Fellow to provide pupils with career advice and contribute to masterclasses and workshops.

The Drama department offers many opportunities for all pupils to perform and work backstage in the vast array of productions that take place during the School year. It is housed in the award-winning 400 Hall Theatre with an auditorium, studio theatre, and a number of dressing room spaces. The theatre facilities were designed specifically as learning spaces for independent practice, thus allowing pupils to be heavily involved in production as well as in performance. Extra-curricular activities include all aspects of theatre production including acting, assistant directing, stage management, sound, lighting design and operation, hair and make-up and costume design.

The LAMDA qualification is offered to pupils to improve their confidence and self-efficacy and lessons are available flexibly to fit around pupils' individual programmes.

In addition to its timetabled curriculum, the philosophy of the Art School encourages 'Art for all' outside formal lessons. The department organises a bi-annual Fashion Show of collections made by the pupils, in addition to numerous exhibitions including works from both national and local art companies. The Artists-in-Residence scheme enables pupils, both on and off the academic timetable, to benefit from the expertise and inspiration of recent graduates and practising artists.

The Design and Technology Centre is home to two workshops, a CNC and 3D printing area, alongside a lecture room and classroom teaching spaces. The department encourages O Block (Year 11) pupils to apply for the Arkwright Scholarship every year; a prestigious national scheme which rewards excellence in design and engineering

disciplines and leads to exciting opportunities with local and national industry leaders.

Sport. At Repton, you will find a balanced approach to sporting success. Achieving in sport at the highest levels of performance and participation for all are in no way mutually exclusive. Over 80% of Reptonians represent the School in at least one sport and every Reptonian participates in sport at least three times per week. The School's illustrious sporting heritage is matched by the achievements of their pupils today. It is Repton's aim to discover and develop the sporting and athletic potential within every pupil, as part of a balanced and challenging curriculum encouraging a lifelong love of sport and the benefits it brings.

Repton has amassed an enviable collection of silverware across their focus sports (cricket, football, hockey, netball, swimming and tennis), but above all it is about what sport brings out in pupils: teamwork, dedication, resilience, leadership and a sense of achievement – both collectively and individually.

The redeveloped Sports Centre includes two floodlit water-based Astroturf hockey pitches, a state-of-the-art, full size indoor hockey facility, a 25m indoor swimming pool with spectator area, two indoor and 12 outdoor tennis courts, netball and squash courts as well as a specialist strength and conditioning suite.

Combined Cadet Force. All pupils join the CCF in A Block, joining either the Army, Navy or RAF section for a year's basic training. The Navy section makes good use of the local reservoirs for sailing. Repton also has excellent in-house facilities for the CCF including an indoor 0.22 rifle range, a climbing wall and the Old Trent for rafting. After A Block, continued membership of the CCF is voluntary, either as part of The Duke of Edinburgh's Award or as Community Service.

Scholarships. A range of scholarships and exhibitions are offered annually at 13+ and 16+, these include:

The Repton Scholarship is an academic award available to pupils in Year 8 prior to entry to Repton in Year 9. It rewards academic excellence and a commitment to academic progress, enrichment and a lifelong process of learning.

C B Fry All-Rounder Award is an award worth up to 20% of the Repton boarding fee offered at 13+ to candidates exhibiting outstanding all-round leadership potential. Assessments take place in March when candidates are in Year 7.

16+ Scholarships: The examination for both academic and non-academic awards takes place in November for entry the following September. A number of awards are available for pupils joining Repton from both the maintained and independent sectors.

Music Scholarships and Exhibitions are awarded at 13+ and 16+, with examinations taking place in November.

Drama Scholarships and Exhibitions are also offered at 13+ and 16+ with auditions and interviews taking place in November.

Art Scholarships and Exhibitions are offered at 13+ and 16+. Examinations take place in November (16+) and January (13+). Candidates will be assessed by examination, interview and an assessment of their portfolio.

Design and Technology (DT) Scholarships and Exhibitions are offered at 13+ and 16+. Examinations take place in November (16+) and January (13+). Candidates will be asked to complete a practical session, interview and to provide a folder of work for assessment.

Sports Scholarships and Exhibitions are offered at 13+ and 16+, to pupils of exceptional talent. Assessments are held in October (13+) and November (16+).

For further information email: admissions@ repton.org.uk

Bursaries may be available to those who would not otherwise be able to attend an independent school. These may, in appropriate circumstances, be used to supplement Academic or non-academic awards. Means-tested bursaries are also available to Forces families.

Charitable status. Repton (1093166) is a Registered Charity. The School exists to provide high quality education for boys and girls.

Headmaster: **Mr M Semmence**, BA Durham, MA, MBA Warwick

Principal Deputy Head: J G Golding, BA King's College London
Deputy Head (Academic): A Currie, MPhys, MEd, DipLCM, Durham
Deputy Head (Pastoral): T H Naylor, BSc Reading
Deputy Head (Outreach): Mrs S A B Tennant, MA Late Scholar of Somerville College Oxford
Deputy Head (Admissions and Marketing) & Director of Digital Development: J D Wilton, MA Lady Margaret Hall Oxford.
Assistant Deputy Head (Pastoral): Mrs A F Parish, BA Durham
Assistant Head (Sport): M M Carrington, BSc Loughborough
Director of Operations: A J Smith, BSc Loughborough
Chief Operating Officer: Mrs E Bateman, MPhil Birmingham
Chief Commercial and Development Officer: A J Cook, BA, MBA Gloucester

Heads of Department:
Business: Mrs M K Court, BA Durham
Chemistry: R G Dexter, BSc Royal Holloway
Classics: Mrs S A B Tennant, MA Late Scholar Somerville College Oxford
Design and Technology: Miss G L Hill, BA Nottingham Trent
Director of Art: I J Whitfield, MA Royal College of Art
Director of Music: O M Walker, BA Late Scholar of Keble College Oxford
Director of Science & Biology: Dr S M Ingleston-Orme, BSc, PhD Nottingham
Drama: J P Cooper-Richards, BA Wales
Economics: D A Exley, BSc York
English: B Miller, BA St Anne's College Oxford
Ethical & Religious Studies: Ms B Eades, BA Kent
Geography: Mrs L E Wilbraham, BA Queen Mary College London
History: Dr N F Pitts, BA, PhD Leeds
Mathematics: Dr M L Lawley, PhD Birmingham
Modern Languages: B Page, BA Warwick
Physical Education: C Lawrence, MA, MSc Loughborough
Physics: T M Lewis, MEng Cardiff
Politics: Dr M Lakin, DPhil, Oriel College Oxford
Psychology: Mrs G K Ritchie, BSc Loughborough

Boys' Boarding Houses:
The Cross: M R Wilson

Latham House: M W T Hunt
New House: R G Embery
The Orchard: I M Pollock
The Priory: N F Pitts
School House: W G Odell

Girls' Boarding Houses:
The Abbey: Mrs L E C Bispham
The Garden: Mrs K J Walker
Field House: Mrs C R Watson
The Mitre: Mrs C J Jenkinson

Admissions Manager: Mrs J Bird
Executive Assistant to the Headmaster: Mrs D Cameron

RGS Worcester

Upper Tything, Worcester WR1 1HP

Tel:	01905 613391
email:	office@rgsw.org.uk
website:	www.rgsw.org.uk
Twitter:	@RGSWorcester
Facebook:	@rgsw.org.uk
Instagram:	@rgs_worcester

School Aims. RGS Worcester Family of Schools provides an excellent all-round education for children aged 2–18 years, developing character, intellect, physical and emotional well-being and cultural understanding within a supportive community.

The Schools aim to cultivate an ethos in which each pupil is cared for individually, valued equally and achieves their potential by:

• Encouraging the growth of intellectual curiosity, creativity and a positive attitude to learning, through a broad, coherent and balanced curriculum, the use of digital technology to enhance teaching and learning, and educational and enrichment opportunities

• Developing in every child quiet self-confidence, aspiration, responsibility, resilience, spiritual values and a personal moral code, consideration for others, tolerance and understanding of other cultures

• Offering a wide range of co-curricular activities which children can develop their social, sporting and cultural interests, explore and enhance their leadership skills and learn the importance of working together

• Promoting opportunities for higher education and career options, and creating an awareness of the world beyond the School and a sense of service to the local and wider community

History. The Royal Grammar School Worcester was founded ante 1291, received its Elizabethan Charter in 1561 and was granted its 'Royal' title by Queen Victoria in 1869. The Alice Ottley School was founded in 1883 as Worcester High School for Girls. The two schools merged to form RGS Worcester & The Alice Ottley School in September 2007 and was renamed RGS Worcester in September 2009.

Location and Buildings. The Senior School is situated a few minutes' walk from the centre of the City and is convenient for rail and bus stations.

Educational facilities are outstanding: Sports Halls, specialist Art, IT, Technology and Textiles rooms, a Theatre,

Library, Science Block, Music Technology room, and a Lecture Theatre, as well as several assembly halls. The playing fields and boathouse are close by.

There are three co-educational Preparatory Schools: RGS The Grange, set in 50 acres of grounds to the north of the city; RGS Springfield, housed in a beautiful Georgian building in the centre of the nearby Britannia Square, secluded and secure, it benefits from its close proximity to the Senior School; and RGS Dodderhill in Droitwich Spa, Worcestershire. All three have a co-ed nursery from the age of 2.

Curriculum. Pupils follow a common curriculum for the first three years in the Senior School which includes the usual academic subjects, plus IT, Design Technology, Music, Drama and PE. The GCSE option arrangements (Years 10 and 11) allow a wide choice, giving a balanced curriculum which does not prejudice subsequent career decisions. Most members of the Sixth Form study four subjects to AS Level and at least three to A2 Level. In addition to those subjects studied at GCSE Level, PE, Classical Civilisation, Business Studies, Economics and Politics may be taken up. The Digital Learning Programme is an integral part of the teaching and learning experience.

Careers. A member of Inspiring Futures, the award-winning careers service is readily available and the Head of Careers is responsible for ensuring that all pupils receive basic careers education, and subsequently, access to all the necessary information and experience on which a sound decision may be made regarding future career and Further or Higher Education.

Physical Activities. A wide range of sporting interests and abilities is catered for. Sports include: Rugby Football, Association Football, Cricket, Athletics, Netball, Hockey, Cross-Country Running and Rowing.

Outdoor Pursuits. Combined Cadet Force comprises Royal Navy, Army and Air Force sections. Good opportunities exist for attachments to regular units in the UK and abroad for flying, leadership and adventure training. Those who choose The Duke of Edinburgh's Award scheme may work for their Bronze, Silver and Gold Awards, and undertake adventure training and community service.

Other Activities. There is a wide range of clubs and societies, with school productions taking place each term. School music is also strong: there is a Big Band, several brass ensembles, choirs and smaller vocal ensembles, and a very popular Jazz Band. The School fosters a range of international links including regular exchanges with schools in France, Germany, Spain, China and the USA.

September Admission. This is by examination held in January/February, mainly at 11+ but also at 12+ and 13+. Admission into the Sixth Form is on the basis of a test, interview and GCSE results. Exceptionally, pupils may also be examined and admitted at other points in the year. Admission to the Preparatory Schools is by an assessment from age 6+ and by classroom visit before this age.

Scholarships and Bursaries. Scholarships are offered for academic achievement as well as for music, art, design, textiles, drama and sport of up to 50% remission of fees. Bursaries of up to 100% are also available according to parental means and academic potential.

Charitable status. RGS Worcester is a Registered Charity, number 1120644. The aim of the charity is the education of boys and girls.

Chair of Governors: Mr Quentin Poole

Director of Finance & Operations and Clerk to the Governors: Mrs Joanna Monro

Headmaster: **Mr John Pitt**

Deputy Heads:
Senior: Mr Lloyd Beecham
Academic: Ms Rebecca Roberts Gawen

Preparatory Schools:
RGS The Grange:
Headmaster: Mr Gareth Hughes

RGS Springfield:
Headmistress: Mrs Laura Brown

RGS Dodderhill:
Headmistress: Mrs Sarah Atkinson

Robert Gordon's College

Schoolhill, Aberdeen AB10 1FE

Tel: 01224 646346
email: enquiries@rgc.aberdeen.sch.uk
website: www.rgc.aberdeen.sch.uk
Twitter: @robertgordons
Facebook: @robertgordonscollege
Instagram: @robertgordonscollege
LinkedIn: /robertgordonscollege

Motto: 'Omni nunc arte magistra' Be all you can be

Robert Gordon's College offers children from age three the very best start in their educational journey. The core values of Community, Leadership, Curiosity, Innovation and Resilience underpin the learning experience at Robert Gordon's College and are built into the DNA of a Gordon's pupil. From the beginning of their journey of discovery, pupils are encouraged to find out what they are good at and supported to do it to the best of their ability, providing pupils with the skills and tools they need to navigate an increasingly complex world.

At Robert Gordon's College, the community is passionate about imparting knowledge, sparking curiosity and inspiring appetites for growth through positive learning environments where pupils can explore and be all they can be.

Emphasis on learning through quality play experiences is key in the Nursery where the youngest learners in the College foster curiosity. These experiences are further enriched by specialist subjects including Art, French, Mandarin, Music and Physical Education which continue as they transition through the Junior School curriculum and co-curricular programme.

Mrs Sarah Webb, Head of Nursery and Junior School shares: "We encourage all children to be active in their learning whether in the classroom or outdoors at Countesswells. The exciting opportunities available to our pupils are extensive, enabling all our children to be eager and inquisitive. They are confident learners who are able to express themselves in a wide range of different situations preparing them for the next step in their educational journey."

When pupils enter Senior School they are encouraged to expand their horizons, and discover new subjects as they explore new languages, technology and their creative side.

Mrs Clare Smith, Head of Senior School highlights: "Our pupils build their knowledge and confidence as they begin to discover more about themselves as learners, exploring options for new pathways for the future."

"Leadership is a key element of these final years at school, where pupils are supported by the wider Gordon's community of alumni and partners across the world. We believe that exposing pupils to others who have experienced life beyond school, perhaps moving to a new city or region of the world, experiencing new industries and perhaps even connecting with alumni for work experience, is a critical part of preparing them for the future."

Stretching far beyond the end of their time at school, the values of a Gordon's education are intrinsic with pupils, who take them far into their futures, which is evident in the global Gordonian community.

Representing Great Britain in the Olympics and Scotland in the Commonwealth Games, Swimmer David Carry, has made great strides since leaving the College in 1999. Now CEO of Track Record Coaching, which enhances global business leadership teams, David reflects on how the ethos of the College helped shape his future: "The environment the school created encouraged me to believe in myself, dare to dream and explore beyond my limits. This has laid the groundwork for both my sporting and professional careers."

Register for the next virtual open event or contact the Admissions team to learn more about what a Robert Gordon's education can offer your child via admissions@rgc.aberdeen.sch.uk or visit www.rgc.aberdeen.sch.uk.

Number of Pupils. Nursery (age 3–5): 52 children; Junior School (Primary Classes 1–7): 419 pupils; Senior School (Secondary Forms 1–6): 1,071 pupils.

Admission. The main entry points are Primary 1, Primary 6 and Secondary 1. Entry to Primary 1 (age 4½–5½ years) is by interview held in January/February, and to Primary 6 (age 9½–10½ years) by Entrance Test held in January. Entry to Secondary 1 is by an Entrance Examination held in January. Entry at other stages depends upon vacancies arising, and the offer of a place is subject to satisfactory performance in an Entrance Test and interview.

Nursery Fees per annum (2021–2022).

Year round (48 weeks) All day £14,280

Year round (48 weeks) Half day (session 1 or session 2) £7,140

Term-time (37 weeks) All day £11,390

Term-time (37 weeks) Half day (session 1 or session 2) £5,695

Nursery fees are inclusive of lunches and snacks.

School Fees per annum (2021–2022).

Primary 1: £8.995 (excl lunch), £9,490 (incl lunch

Primary 2: £8,995 (excl lunch), £9,510 (incl lunch)

Primary 3: £12,215 (excl lunch), £12,730 (incl lunch)

Primary 4–7: £12,215 (excl lunch), £12,855 (incl lunch)

Senior: £13,995 (excl lunch)

Bursaries. Robert Gordon's College offers free places and reduced fee places to pupils every year for entry into Secondary 1. These Bursaries are awarded after jointly assessing financial need and academic merit. Burnett Scholarships offer up to half-fee discounts to pupils of outstanding talent in academic subjects, in music, or in sport and are available to pupils currently in Fourth or Fifth Year at other schools.

Charitable status. Robert Gordon's College is a Registered Charity, number SC000123. It exists to provide education for boys and girls.

Chairman of Governors: Professor James Hutchison

Head of College: **Robin Macpherson**, BA, MSc, FRSA

Head of Junior School: Sarah Webb, BEd
Deputy Head of Junior School: Sally-Ann Johnson, BEd, MEd
Deputy Head of Junior School: Varie MacLeod, BEd
Head of Senior School: Clare Smith, MA
Deputy Head (S1–S2): Anne Watson, BA
Deputy Head (S3–S4): Neil Buchanan, BSc
Deputy Head (S5 and Curriculum): Claire Cowie, MA, MLitt
Deputy Head (S6 and Pastoral): Robin Fish, MA
Director of Finance: Andrew W Lowden, MA, CA
Director of Development, Marketing and Admissions: Laura Presslie, BA
Director of ICT: David Stone, BSc, MSc

Roedean School

Roedean Way, Brighton, East Sussex BN2 5RQ

Tel: 01273 667500; Admissions: 01273 667626
email: info@roedean.co.uk
website: www.roedean.co.uk
Twitter: @RoedeanSchool
Facebook: @RoedeanSchool

Introduction. Roedean is an all-girls day, flexi-, weekly and full boarding school for 675 students aged 11–18, situated between the English Channel and a national park, on a cliff overlooking Brighton Marina.

The three Lawrence sisters founded Roedean in Brighton in 1885 and the School was Incorporated by Royal Charter in 1938. Their original aims were to give due emphasis to physical and outdoor education, to encourage independence and self-reliance, 'to give as much liberty as can be granted with safety' and to supply a sound intellectual training.

The school has grown from 360 girls in the last ten years, and, due to increased demand from UK parents, it now has a four-form entry into Year 7. Today the school community is made up of 30 different nationalities and remains committed to the founders' emphasis on independent learning and the development of self-confidence in readiness for professional life. The school buildings are set on a spacious, yet safe, 45-acre site surrounded by a further 70 acres of farmland. The campus looks out over the English Channel; with its stunning position by the sea in Brighton, Roedean is one of the UK's leading girls' schools.

Philosophy. As an academic school, we seek to inspire curiosity and a love of learning in all our girls. The strength of teaching at Roedean is that discussion and debate sit at the heart of learning. Lessons are thought-provoking and meaningful; the Sciences are as popular as the Humanities, and in all lessons girls thrive through collaboration, cooperation, challenge, and discussion with each other. Our girls are keen to think, to learn, to explore, and to develop intellectually, socially, and emotionally. The success of this approach is borne out by the fact that the girls achieve very highly, and go on to pursue their education at top institutions in the UK and beyond.

Our holistic vision of education also places a very high value on all the experiences that take place beyond the classroom, in Sport, Art, Drama, Music, and Dance, all of which make up an essential part of life at Roedean. The opportunity for girls to be able to excel in a number of different fields is one of the great gifts of Roedean, since it provides them with the space and time to devote to their passions, and all in one place. On-site facilities include the Chapel, cloisters, a flood-lit all-weather pitch, indoor swimming pool, professional theatre, cafés, dance studios, libraries, tennis and netball courts, cricket and football pitches, the Farm with sheep and goats, and acres of grounds and fields.

Roedean offers the kind of teaching, learning, and all-round experiences that enable every single girl to find her passion and voice, meaning every one leaves Roedean feeling that anything is possible. It is precisely this rounded education which produces independent and creative young women who will make their mark in the world. A Roedean education is a unique and wonderful experience.

Curriculum. Girls are given a structured grounding in basic skills and offered a very broad programme of knowledge and experience. Subject specialists work together in a coordinated approach to achieve maximum reinforcement and continuity across 30 subjects. The benefits of traditional subjects, including Latin, are balanced by Psychology, Russian, and Philosophy. Girls in KS3 take part in an academic enrichment programme called HHH (Heads, Hands, and Hearts), which includes self-defence, cookery, and Sign Language, among others. Class sizes are consistently small, ranging between 14 and 21 girls in the Senior School, with smaller groups in the Sixth Form.

Each girl's GCSE programme is individually tailored to provide a broad, balanced education and to ensure that requirements for higher education are met. The girls are strongly encouraged to undertake an independent academic project, with the support of specialist, in order to allow them to pursue their passions.

The strong Sixth Form offers an extensive range and combination of A Levels, covering over 24 subjects. Over time, the school has developed a strong link with the University of Sussex, enabling the most able Sixth Form mathematicians to study undergraduate geometry alongside their A Level courses.

Roedean girls consistently achieve outstanding A Level results, and this year was no different. Despite 2021 being another difficult year for our Year 13 cohort, after finding out that public examinations were, again, cancelled, the girls showed great determination to continue perform to the best of their abilities throughout the year. We are incredibly proud of our Leavers who, therefore, achieved very impressive and well-deserved A Level results, which were awarded based on a combination of academic merit, a broad range of work completed throughout their two years in the Sixth Form, and the professional judgment of their teachers about what they would have achieved if the examinations had gone ahead. Twenty girls achieved 4 or more A* grades and forty-nine achieved straight A*–A grades, meaning that 85% of students in the year group will be taking up places at their first choice UK universities and 67% of our students

are going on to top Russell Group Universities. The range of subjects they have chosen highlights the sheer breadth of academic interests within our student body and it is wonderful that all five students holding offers from Oxford and Cambridge have met the requirements and will be taking up their places. Furthermore, at a time when society's reliance on our medical services has been so high, we are incredibly proud that 5 of our students are going on to study Medicine.

In a climate when young women pursuing STEM subjects is very low nationally, Roedean is extremely proud that 40% of this year's leavers are going on to study STEM courses at university.

In the context of increasing rigour and challenge at GCSE level, Roedean is immensely proud of the GCSE cohort this year – the girls achieved excellent results under, once again, very difficult circumstances, particularly given that they were expecting to sit their examinations as normal until early January, when they were cancelled, and the precise nature of how they were going to be assessed was not entirely clear until March. The opportunity for continual and modular assessment allowed the girls to prepare thoroughly and demonstrate what they had learnt – while it is true that these results are different to those from examination years before the pandemic, they certainly are an accurate reflection of the girls' efforts, achievements, and hard work; their success reflects their consistently positive and diligent attitude over the two years of their GCSE courses. Very many students have exceeded expectations, and their positive approach has meant that they have been able to push grades over boundaries to achieve higher grades and realise their potential. Particular congratulations go to fifteen students who have achieved unbroken strings of Grade 9s, of whom ten were awarded a remarkable clutch of eleven or more Grade 9s. Furthermore, 21 students were awarded ten or more Grade 9s, and 40% of the group achieved Grade 9 or 8 in every one of their subjects, and this includes one who took 13 GCSEs in total. These achievements are simply outstanding, and a testament to the girls' exceptional work-ethic and focus.

Co-curricular Activities and Physical Education. The range of music, art and design, speech, debating, drama and dance opportunities within the curriculum are further supported by optional private tuition and club activities. The school is particularly strong in the performing arts: music (choirs and orchestras), drama, and dance.

Roedean is particularly excited about the refurbishment of its Theatre which has always been at the heart of Performing Arts at Roedean. This year, the Theatre been has returned it to its former glory, while adding more capacity, greater accessibility and improving sound quality and energy efficiency. Our Theatre is a top-class, professional facility, with 355 seats, which is supported by a Theatre Manager and a full-time technician, meaning girls can not only gain experience performing on stage, but they can also be trained in the operation and use of equipment; all performances are stage-managed by students.

The school has an excellent record in The Duke of Edinburgh's Award and Young Enterprise Business Scheme which offer girls opportunities to develop a spirit of discovery and independence and encourage links with the wider community.

In 2018, the School also opened a floodlit all-weather pitch on site, along with new netball and tennis courts, and this facility has already transformed sporting opportunities at Roedean. Netball, hockey, swimming, cricket, athletics and tennis are the principal sports, with lacrosse, football, badminton, basketball, volleyball, trampoline, gymnastics, fencing, golf and karate also available. Inter-school fixtures are part of all the major sport programmes and girls are encouraged to enter local, county and national tournaments.

Boarding. Your family might live ten time zones away, or perhaps in London or the local area – whichever is the case for you, you will be fully integrated into a House at Roedean, and it will be your home away from home. To make sure that you will be happy and relaxed here, we have invested over £11 million on all the Houses in recent years, and the results are truly spectacular.

There are four Houses in the main school, and two Houses for girls in the Sixth Form, where the girls have more independence, so that they can develop some of the skills they will need after they leave School.

Boarding comes in different shapes and sizes at Roedean. Many girls are full boarders – there are over 250 girls on site at the weekends, and there are lots of activities which take place on Friday evenings, Saturdays, and Sundays.

In addition to your bedroom, there are a variety of spaces where you can work or relax, play games or practise the piano. In each house, there is an ODR (the Old Dining Room), perhaps the symbolic heart of each house, where you can catch up with your friends at the end of the day. There is also the GDR (the so-called Girls' Dining Room, although it is now a common room), where there is a television and DVD player, and the Hobbies' Room which has a selection of games and puzzles for you to enjoy in the evening.

You will be fed very well in the Main Dining Room for all meals, but you also have the option of making toast or preparing pasta in the evening, and this can be done in the pantry kitchen which is next to the ODR, where there are cookers, hobs, and fridges, or in the 'snug areas' on the lower and middle corridors.

The Weekend Programme is full and varied, and it caters to the interests of the girls – there are trips up to museums and galleries in London, sporting activities such as horse-riding and windsurfing, and pottery painting, ice-skating, and the Christmas market local to Brighton, to name just a few.

Health. The School Health Centre is run by a Registered General Nurse who is assisted by a team of similarly qualified nurses. A doctor visits the School and holds clinics regularly each week. She is "on call" in case of an emergency. There is also a Counsellor who runs sessions in school each week.

Religion. The School welcomes students of all faiths, or none. Arrangements can be made for Anglicans to be prepared for Confirmation, for Roman Catholics to attend Sunday Mass locally, and for Jewish girls to receive instruction.

Facilities. Set in 118 acres of grounds, Roedean is very excited about its inspirational flood-lit all-weather pitch, 5-a-side football pitch and the resurfacing and floodlighting of existing courts which took place in 2018. This transformational investment has already improved the standard of sport at Roedean through greater training and playing time and the girls' confidence in matches is growing. Roedean also sports a heated 25m indoor Swimming Pool, Sports Hall and Gym.

At Roedean, we are lucky enough to have a top-class facility in the Roedean Theatre. The completion of two brand new dance studios last summer, on top of another two dance studios and a performing arts studio, allows us to offer pupils a chance to develop dance skills for enjoyment or for a career in dance or the Performing Arts.

All subjects are taught in specialist rooms, and students have Wi-Fi access throughout the school to support their studies. There is a Main Library and Resources' Centre to support individual study. There are two Art Studios adjacent to a Design & Technology Centre, a multimedia Language Centre, and a Science wing with nine laboratories for Biology, Chemistry and Physics.

The Roedean Sixth Form is truly a college within a school. After a £1.5 million refurbishment, the Sixth Form Centre at Keswick offers a more independent and focused space, with study areas to suit different learning styles, spaces for relaxing and catching up with friends, as well as for enjoying social events, and dedicated Sixth Form staff.

Roedean also plays host to music practice rooms, a chapel, an on-site café, a pitch and putt and also our own secret tunnel to the sea.

School Year and Leave Out. There are three terms, beginning in September, January and April. The summer holidays last eight weeks and Christmas/Easter up to four weeks each. Girls go home for half term and there are two weekend exeats each term. All boarders are free to go home at weekends and weekly boarders are escorted back to London on the train. The school provides a full boarding programme, but there is considerable flexibility to accommodate the individual needs of families.

Admission. Entry at 11+, 12+, 13+ and 16+ is through Roedean Entrance Examination papers in English, Mathematics, and Non-Verbal Reasoning, which can be taken at any time up to two terms before entry. A good number of suitably qualified girls are admitted each year to the Sixth Form.

Scholarships and Bursaries. Academic, Art, Dance, Drama, Music, Performing Arts and Sport scholarships (worth up to 10%–20% of fees) and exhibitions (worth up to 5% of fees) are available for girls entering Year 7, Year 9, and the Sixth Form.

Sixth Form Scholarship examinations are held in November; Junior Scholarship examinations are held in January.

Means-tested Bursaries are available. Details of scholarships and bursaries may be obtained from the Director of Admissions.

Fees per term (2021–2022). Full Boarders £11,660–£14,045; Weekly Boarders (5 days) £10,590–£11,810; Flexi-Boarders (3 days) £8,610–£10,410; Day Girls £5,990–£7,830. For girls entering the Sixth Form from other schools, there is an additional supplement of £1,510 per term (boarding). Parents who wish to pay a single composition fee should apply to the Director, Finance and Administration.

Extra fees are charged for individual tuition in musical instruments, speech training, ballet and some athletic activities.

For further details, please contact the Director of Admissions.

Charitable status. Roedean School is a Registered Charity, number 307063. It exists to provide quality education for girls.

President:
vacant

Vice-Presidents:
vacant

Chair of Council (*interim*):
Mrs V Smiley, BA, MA, DipIPR [OR]

Vice-Chair of Council (*interim*):
Ms D Patman, FRICS, ACIArb

Council:
Miss S de la Mare, FRSA [OR]
Mrs S Ellis, BA Hons, PGCE [OR]
Dr H Fajemirokun, BA Hons Oxon, PhD
Miss F Graham, BSc, PGCE, MCIPD [OR]
Mr S Hepher, BEd Hons
Miss C Jenkins, MTheol [OR]
Miss V Jenkins, MA, PGCE, MEd [OR]
Ms S J Louis, SA [OR]
Miss P McGivern [OR]
Ms K Molberg, BA Hons [OR]
Mrs T Outhwaite, BA, PGDip [OR]

[OR] *Old Roedeanian*

Clerk: Mr Richard Poffley, BA FCCA
ORA President: Ms M Henderson [OR]

Staff:

Headmaster: Mr O Blond, BA Essex

Head of School: Miss T Keller, BSc Manchester, PGCE, NPQH
Senior Deputy Head, Pastoral: Mr R Chamberlain, BA Newcastle, PGCE
Deputy Head, Academic: Dr J Hobbs, BA Leeds, PhD King's, PGCE
Deputy Head, Co-Curriculum and Outreach: Dr R Barrand, BA Durham, PhD Leeds, PGCE
Director of Finance and Administration: Mr R Poffley, BA Sussex, FCCA
Associate Deputy Head, Senior School: Mrs D Robins, BA Brighton, QTS Brighton
Associate Deputy Head Director of Sixth Form: Dr G Hannan, PhD London, MA, PGCE with QTS Durham
Assistant Head, Co-Curricular and Scholarships: Ms H Boobis, MA Cantab, BA Cantab, MEd Open, PGCE
Associate Assistant Head: Educational Guidance: Mrs J Sharp, BSc Manchester, MSc London, PGCE
Head of Sixth Form: Miss C Carragher, BSc Southampton, PGCE
Head of Middle School & Transition: Miss R Allen BA Manchester, MA Manchester
Director of Boarding: Miss C Le Bihan, BA Provence, PGCE

Heads of Department:
Art: Ms S Strachan, BA Kingston, PGCE Cambridge
Business: Mr S Low, BA Brighton
Classics: Miss C Hindle, MA St Andrews, MEd Cambridge, PGCE
Dance: Miss S Abaza, BA Chichester
Design Technology: Mrs Helen Quirk, BA Surrey Institute of Art & Design, PGCE
Drama: Mrs S Woodbridge, BA Bristol, PGCE
Economics: Mr P Clingan, BA Nottingham, PGCE
English: Mr D Woodhouse, BA Anglia, MA Sussex, PGCE Brighton

Geography: Mr G Carter
History: Mrs S Black, MA Edinburgh, MEd Cantab, PGCE
Learning Support: Mrs L Brunjes, BA Loughborough, PGCE
Mathematics: Mr D Orys, BSc London, PGCE Sussex
Modern Languages: Mr J Sampieri, MA France, PGCE Kingston
Music: Mr B Rous, BMus Royal College of Music, MMus King's College London, QTS
Philosophy & Religious Studies: Ms E Earl, BA Oxford, QTS
Physical Education: Miss K Wakeling, BSc Southampton, MA Bedfordshire, PGCE
Psychology: Mr P Harrison, BA Middlesex, PGCE
Science: Mr M Staniford,
Biology: Mrs P Borsberry, BSc Durham, MSc London, PGCE
Chemistry: Ms F Walker, BSc London, PGCE
Physics: Miss L Bryne (*interim*)

Director of Admissions: Mrs A Wienekus

Rossall School

Broadway, Fleetwood, Lancashire FY7 8JW

Tel:	01253 774201
email:	admissions@rossall.org.uk
website:	www.rossall.org.uk
Twitter:	@RossallSchool
Facebook:	@RossallSchoolUK
Instagram:	@RossallSchool
LinkedIn:	/RossallSchool

Motto: '*Mens agitat molem*'

Rossall has been described by the Good Schools Guide as 'a warm, inclusive and remarkably happy place to be'.

Set on an historic 160-acre campus on the picturesque Lancashire coastline, Rossall is one of the country's leading independent co-educational boarding and day schools, where boys and girls aged 0–18 are nurtured in a safe, secure and supportive environment.

With a history dating back to 1844, Rossall combines a traditional British education with a modern approach which focuses on developing the whole child.

With nearly forty different nationalities living and learning together, Rossall is a truly global village. The combination of UK day students and students from right across the world creates an exciting international dimension and an appreciation of diverse cultures, religions and politics.

Academic Curriculum. Rossall delivers a broad, balanced curriculum and outstanding results. At Nursery level, Rossall follows the Early Years Foundation Stage (EYFS) learning goals. From the age of 3 to 11, Rossall offers a bespoke and challenging curriculum.

Students from 11–16 follow the National Curriculum for England, culminating in GCSE and IGCSE examinations at the end of Year 11 (age 16). Students then have the option to choose either the IB or A Level route in the Sixth Form.

For 2021 Rossall students achieved 98% A*–C (9–4) at GCSE with 55% achieving A*–A (9–7). At A Level students achieved 93% A*–C with 61% of results in the A*–A range. IB students had a 100% pass rate and an average score of 35.

All subjects are equally valued at Rossall, giving students the freedom to experience a broad and balanced portfolio of learning up to the age of 16 so they can make informed choices about their Sixth Form studies.

Facilities. Rossall's generous facilities support the aims for teaching and learning excellence. From the dedicated Science building and state-of-the-art Design Technology workshops to the bright, spacious art studios complete with a computer-rich Graphics suite, Rossall provides every student with space and resources to pursue their academic studies and outside interests.

For those with musical ambitions Rossall is an All-Steinway School; the Beecham Music School, with its own practice organ, orchestra rehearsal room and Sibelius suite, offers students the opportunity to develop their skills, whilst our theatres, performance and exhibition spaces provide budding singers, actors and artists with the chance to explore their talents.

With the recent renovation of the Sixth Form study room (based on designs created by the students themselves) and the enhanced kitchen classroom to support the development of Food Studies skills, Rossall is a school which is constantly evolving to meet the needs of its students as well as the curriculum.

Beyond the classroom, the spacious 160-acre campus has extensive sports and recreation facilities, including a purpose built £4 million sports hall, a top-ranked golf academy – complete with GC2 simulator and putting green, a 25-metre indoor heated swimming pool, squash courts, tennis courts, fives courts, a modern all-weather sports pitch, a multi-use games area, 45 acres of sports pitches and a fitness room. Rossall offers an Elite Football Programme for girls and boys, working in partnership with Fleetwood Town, to develop the student by challenging the athlete.

Rossall also has its own beach, which is put to good use for our own exclusive sport of Ross Hockey, and is proud to be one of the few schools in the country with an on-site Astronomy Centre.

The House System. For younger pupils (aged 7–13), Anchor House, our dedicated Junior Boarding House, has a home-from-home family atmosphere.

Anchor House is full of fun and laughter; from baking in the kitchen to celebrating a birthday or taking part in one of our many house trips, there's always something to do and someone to do it with. As well as a varied activities programme, all of the house staff are committed to developing and supporting all students with their academic needs, ensuring that all of our children succeed and reach their maximum potential.

There are eight Houses for Senior boarders: three for girls (Rose, Wren and Dolphin) and five for boys (Dragon, Maltese Cross, Mitre Fleur de Lys, Spread Eagle and Pelican).

All Houses have triple, double and single bedrooms, a common room, a large games room, a kitchen for snacks and weekend baking and a library with computer workstations and internet access.

While each House has its own unique history and personality, all foster an environment in which boarders are encouraged to achieve their true potential and develop valuable skills and qualities such as communication, teamwork, leadership, empathy and cultural understanding.

Religious Instruction. Rossall was founded as 'the Northern Church of England School' and Chapel remains central to the well-being of the community. Pupils of all faiths are encouraged to share in this community, and the School has its own Chaplaincy with resident Chaplain.

Games. 45 acres of playing field and a brand new sports centre, a golf academy, floodlit Astroturf, multi-use games area, an indoor 25-metre swimming pool, along with squash, tennis, and fives courts allow all pupils to pursue a sporting interest.

The boys play hockey, cricket, football, basketball and rugby, with the girls playing football, hockey, netball, rounders, and tennis. All pupils are taught to play the unique game of RossHockey on the sandy beach owned by the School. The new Golf Academy boasts state-of-the-art technology, and with close links to major golf clubs, including Royal Birkdale and Royal Lytham and St Annes, students have the opportunity to play at some of the most prestigious golf clubs in the world.

The school also has an Elite Football Programme in association with League One football team, Fleetwood Town Football Club. There are full programmes of competitive fixtures against other schools and clubs. House matches occur in all major games, including football, and cross country in the Lent Term. Archery, athletics, shooting, horse riding and many other activities are also offered.

The CCF. Rossall's CCF contingent is the oldest in the country. All Year 8 students are either in the Army, Navy or Air Force sections. The school has a shooting range, keeps boats on the Wyre and there is the opportunity to fly at RAF Woodvale.

Activities and Clubs. Rossall is pleased to offer its biggest selection of extra-curricular activities to date.

Through our Activities Programme, Rossall students have the opportunity to learn new skills, socialise with other students and, most importantly, have fun.

The School encourages its students to try new activities, to help them broaden their horizons so that they can meet the challenges of the wider world.

The extensive range of clubs we offer at Rossall include: Debating Club, Scuba Diving, The Duke of Edinburgh's Award, Robotics and Electronics, Creative Writing, Volleyball, Choir, International Cookery, Hockey, Photoshop and Creative Graphics, Knitting, Rugby, Ceramics, Basketball, Orchestra, and Climbing.

Admission. Any term in the year for boys and girls aged 0–16, September preferably at 16+ or 17+. All applications for entrance should be made to the Admissions Team. On registration, a fee of £75 will be charged to UK applicants and £195 to international students.

Fees per term (2021–2022). Day £2,955–£4,810; Full Boarding £7,575–£12,280; Weekly Boarding £5,095–£8,280.

The school operates on a three-term year.

Scholarships and Bursaries. Scholarships are offered for academic, music, art, drama, sport and all-round achievement. Scholarships are awarded solely on merit and range in value. In exceptional circumstances, the School may award up to 100% fee remission.

A number of clerical bursaries are awarded on a means test to sons of Clergy who can sustain a proportion of the

Fees themselves but who need extra help. Bursaries are also available to families from the British Armed Forces.

All enquiries about Scholarships and Bursaries and other awards should be addressed to the Admissions Team.

Rossall Junior School. Rossall has its own Junior School for children aged 4–11 situated within the same grounds. There is also a Nursery School for day boys and girls aged 0–14.

Access. Motorway: 15 minutes from M55 (spur off M6). Railway: Blackpool North (6 miles). Air: Manchester International Airport (55 miles by road).

Alumni. Rossall has an active network of Old Rossallians who support the school, more can be found online at: www.rossall.org.uk/alumni/rossall-foundation

The Rossallian Club. This club for former pupils keeps a record of more than 5,000 members and coordinates the activities of eight Branches. A Newsletter is published twice each year.

Charitable status. The Corporation of Rossall School is a Registered Charity, number 526685.

Life Governors:
The Earl of Derby, DL
Mrs H N Trapnell (*Finance and General Purposes Committee, Trustee Trapnell Scholarship Fund*)
Mr A N Stephenson, MA (*Trustee Trapnell Scholarship and other trust funds*)

Governors:
Chairman: Mr Chris Holt, BSc, MBA, ACMA
Vice Chair: Mr S J Fisher, MA
Secretary of the Corporation and Clerk to the Council: Mr B E Clark, MBE
Mr M J Reece, MA
Mrs C M Preston, BSc, ARICS
Mr M Craven
Dr H O Fajemirokun
Dr D M Elliott, BSc MBChB
Mrs L Croston, BSc, PGCE, ALCM
Mrs K Thomas, MIFST, BSc, RSci
Mr D H Ewart, BA, PGCE, MA, DMS
Mr R A Wilson, MA
The Revd G Ashton, BA
The Revd Canon J M Hall, MA
Mr D K Gill, FCA
Mrs G Austin-King, BA, FCA, MBA, LLB, MCISI, MCIBS
Mr A C Potts, BSc, PGCE, C.Biol

Headmaster: **Mr Jeremy Quartermain**, BA, MA, MPhil

Deputy Head: Ms Dina Porovic, MSci
Bursar: Mrs Emma Sanderson, PGCE, MA Hons, MBA
Head of Boarding and Designated Safeguarding Lead: Mrs Emma Williams, BSc, PGCE
Head of Nursery and Juniors, and Designated Safeguarding Lead (Juniors including EYFS): Mr Matthew Turner, BSc, PGCE
Director of Logistics and Operations: Mrs Katie Lee, MA, CPP, CertEd
Head of Lower School (Year 7, 8 & 9): Mrs Catherine Stacker, BSc Hons, PGCE
Director of Studies: Mr Christopher Payne, MEd, PGCE, MA
Director of Public Benefit: Mr Mark Bradley, BSc Hons, PGCE

Head of Learning Development: Mrs Fiona Quartermain, BA, MA, PGCE
Head of Nursery: Mrs Nikola Stott, BA, MA, PGCE
Staff Mentor: Mr Ky Hutchinson, BSc, PGCE
Head of HR/Compliance: Mrs Stephanie Capstick
Head of Health and Wellbeing: Mrs Rachel Magowan
Head of International Courses (and EAL): Mrs Cheryl Wolstencroft, MEd TESOL, BA Hons
Chair of Common Room: Mr Anthony Fairhurst

Heads of Departments:

Art: Miss Laura Heap BA Hons, PGCE
Business Studies: Mrs Sharon Wright, LLB Business Law, PGCE
Classics: Mr Benjamin Clark, BA, PGCE
Drama: Mr David Newell, BA
Design & Technology: Mr Lee Hodgetts, BA Hons
EAL: Mrs Cheryl Wolstencroft, MEd TESOL, BA Hons
English: Mr Hugh Fitzherbert Brockholes, BA Hons, PGCE
Geography: Mr Matthew Hall, BSc, PGCE
History: Mr David Clarke, BAHons, MA, M.Phil, PGCE
Mathematics: Mr Alex Shaw, MPhys, MA, PGCE
MFL (Spanish, French and Mandarin): Dr Louisa Adcock, BA, MA, PhD
MFL (German): Dr Doris Dohmen, I.Staats-examen, DrPhil, PGCE
Music: Mr Adam Dobson, PGCE, BMus
Physical Education Academic: Mr Jack Cropper, MA, BA
Psychology: Ms Charlotte Lane, BSc
Religion, Philosophy and Ethics: Dr Philip Mallaband, PGCE, PhD, MA, BA
Science (Biology): Dr Jill Bradburn, BSc, PhD, PGCE
Science (Chemistry): Mrs Lauren Laid, MSc, PGCE
Science (Physics): Mr Andrew Millington, BSc, PGCE
Learning Support: Mrs Fiona Quartermain BA, MA, PGCE

Houses/Houseparents:
Anchor House: Mr Lee & Mrs Helen Gair
Dolphin House: Mrs Sharon Wright
Maltese Cross House: Mr Richard Symons & Mrs Isabelle Freeman
Mitre Fleur de Lys House: Mr Samuel Roberts
Pelican House: Mr Christopher & Mrs Rebecca Payne
Rose House: Dr Jill Bradburn and Mr Peter Bradburn
Spread Eagle House: Miss Nicola Pentelow & Mr David Newell
Wren House: Mrs Emma Williams

Instrumental Music Teachers for:
Brass, Flute, Guitar, Composition, Piano, Organ, Clarinet, Saxophone, Violin, Voice, Percussion

Admissions: Ms Gillian Leggett
Data Manager & Examinations Officer: Miss Kirstie Allen
Head of Marketing and Communications: Mrs Amy Pendlebury

Rougemont School

Llantarnam Hall, Malpas Road, Newport, South Wales NP20 6QB

Tel: 01633 820800
email: registrar@rsch.co.uk
website: www.rougemontschool.co.uk
Twitter: @rougemontschool
Facebook: @RougemontSchool

Rougemont was founded in a house of that name immediately after the First World War as a co-educational day school taking children through to grammar school entrance at 11. It moved to Nant Coch House just after the Second World War and grew to about 200 pupils.

In 1974 the school was re-founded as a Charitable Trust. Since then it has bought extensive new buildings and has approximately 570 pupils on roll in the Preparatory School (Infant Department – Nursery to Year 2 and Junior Department – Years 3–6) and Senior School (Years 7–13).

The Preparatory Junior Department and Senior School moved to a new site at Llantarnam Hall, a large Victorian mansion set in 50 acres of grounds, between 1992 and 1995, with the Infant Department joining them in April 2004. The grounds have been landscaped to provide playing fields and an extensive building programme has taken place on the site. During 1998 a Liberal Arts area including Sports Hall, Music suite and Drama Studio was completed. In 1999 a new classroom block and library was completed and in 2000 additional classrooms together with Art studio were built. New Science and Technology buildings were completed in 2009. In January 2019 a new Auditorium, Refectory and Sixth Form Centre were added.

Admission to the Preparatory and Senior Schools is by interview and assessments. Entry to the Sixth Form is dependent on GCSE results.

The following paragraphs refer to the Senior School although peripatetic specialists work in both and there is some interchange of teachers.

Curriculum. Pupils follow a wide syllabus to age 14. For the two years to GCSE pupils normally study ten subjects of which English Language and Literature, Mathematics and Numeracy, a language, science and a humanities subject are normally compulsory. 18 subjects are available.

Sixth Form. 19 AS/A2 Levels are available. Sixth Form pupils have their own common room and study area. Sixth Form pupils can also take part in a range of extracurricular activities and games.

Religion. Rougemont School has no direct affiliation to a Christian Church or denomination. However, the religious instruction, corporate worship and moral value system of the School is based on that of the broad tradition of the mainstream Christian Churches.

Careers. The School belongs to the Independent Schools Careers Organisation. The Senior teachers advise on all aspects of further education and careers.

Music. In addition to specialist teachers of music, a large number of peripatetic teachers cover the range of orchestral instruments. There are choirs and instrumental ensembles for all ages.

Drama. In addition to the Infant Department's Spring Festival and the Senior School Eisteddfod, two major plays and two musical events take place each year.

Elocution and Dance. Visiting staff hold weekly classes for LADA courses, ballet and modern dance.

Sport. The School has developed a high standard of performance in most major sports. There is a wide fixtures programme for both boys and girls, as well as the opportunity to participate in numerous coaching courses.

Clubs. A wide variety of extracurricular activities and clubs are available at lunch time and after school, as is supervised prep.

The Duke of Edinburgh's Award. This is a very successful activity within the school and over 60 pupils have gained the Gold Award in the last twenty years.

Fees per term (2021–2022). Preparatory School: Infant Department £3,376, Junior Department £3,849; Senior School: £4,453 – £4,818.

Scholarships. Academic Scholarships are available for entry into Year 7, up to the value of 25%. A limited number of means-tested bursaries are offered from Year 7 upwards. The School offers Academic, Sporting and Creative Arts Scholarships to the value of 10–20% for Sixth Form entry.

Further information. A prospectus and other details are available from the Registrar (Tel: 01633 820800, email: registrar@rsch.co.uk).

Charitable status. Rougemont School is a Registered Charity, number 532341. It exists to provide education for boys and girls.

Governors:
Chair: Mr P Harris
Vice-Chair: Mr M Cordner
Mrs A C Thomas
Mrs J Clark
Mr I Hoppe
Mr H Clark
Mr R Green
Mrs C McNamara
Mr D McClelland
Mrs M Tribbick
Mr D Lunt
Dr A Kotecha
Mrs W Williams
Mrs F Bennett

Headmaster: Mr R Carnevale, MA Ed, BSc, PGCE

* *Head of Department*
§ *Part-time*

Head of Preparatory School: Mrs L Pritchard, BA, PGCE
Deputy Head of Senior School: Mrs S Archer, BSc, PGCE (*Biology*)
Director of Staffing: Mrs S Roberts, BSc, PGCE (*Mathematics*)
Deputy Head (Academic): Mrs P Rogers, MA Ed, BSc, PGCE (*Director of Studies*, *Geography*, *ICT Coordinator*)
Academic Registrar: Mr M James, MA Ed, BEd, BA, BSc, CBiol, MIBiol, Cert Maths Open (*Biology*)
Business Manager: Mr A Knight, ACA
Facilities Manager: Mr A Watts

Senior School:
Mrs L Bateman, BA, PGCE (*Art)
Mr K Bell, BA, PGCE (**Boys PE and Games*)

Mrs S Boon, BA, PGCE (*Art, DT*)

Mr M Bowman, BSc, PGCE (*Mathematics*)

Mrs K Bridges, BSc, PGCE (*Science, Maths, IT*)

Ms C Bromley, BSc, PGCE (*Mathematics*)

Dr S Brown, BA, BSc, PhD, PGCE (*Senior Laboratory Technician*)

Mrs J Caddick, BA, PGCE (*English, UCAS & HE Coordinator*)

Ms A Clason-Thomas, BA, MA, PGCE (*Assistant Head of KS3, Pupil Coordinator KS3, French, English*)

Mrs L DeCruz, BA, PGCE (**Religious Studies, Curriculum Coordinator*)

Miss C Dugdale, BA, PGCE (§*PE, Religious Studies*)

Mrs K Elms, BA, PGCE (*English, Film Studies, House Tutor Coordinator*)

Mrs S Elson, LLB (§*Latin*)

Mrs R Garrod, BA, PGCE (§*History, KS3 History Coordinator*)

Mr A Griffiths, BEng, PGCE (*ALNco*)

Mr M Grimes, MSc, BSc, PGCE (*Head of Physics*)

Mr J Hardwick, BSc, PGCE (*Biology, Science, Careers*)

Mr J Hawkins, BSc (*Physical Education*)

Miss R Hayes, BA, PGCE (*Head of Design & Technology, DofE*)

Mrs E Hughes, BA, PGCE (*English*)

Mrs K Hughes, BSc, PGCE (**Geography, Clubs Coordinator*)

Ms J Jones, BA, PGCE (**English*)

Ms L Jones, BA, PGCE, (*Physical Education*)

Mrs A Jenkins, BSc (*Assistant Head of KS5, Chemistry, Physics*)

Mr M Jenkins, MA Cantab, PGCE (**History, Geography, House Tutor*)

Ms E Keddie, BSc, PGCE (*Mathematics, ICT, Pupil Support Coordinator Years 8 and 9*)

Mrs C Langford, BSc, PGCE (*Head of Chemistry, Curriculum Administrator*)

Mr S Mansfield, BSc, PGCE, (*Head of Biology*)

Ms K Marshall, BSc, PGCE, (*Director of Sport*)

Mr P McMahon, MSc, BSc, QTS (**Computing and IT, Google Administrator, ECDL Coordinator*)

Miss A Mintowt-Czyz, BA, PGCE (*English, KS3 English Coordinator*)

Mrs D Morgan, BA, PGCE (*French*)

Mrs S Munro, DEUG, Licence, PGCE (**French, Year 7 Pupil Progress Coordinator*)

Mrs L Nepean, BA, PGCE (*Head of Drama, House Tutor, Performance Coordinator*)

Miss C Owen, BA, PGCE (*Assistant Head of KS4, *Business Studies*)

Mr W Price, BA, PGCE (*Head of KS4, Head of Spanish*)

Mr A Richards, BSc, PGCE (**Mathematics*)

Mr M Savery, BA, PGCE (**Economics, Spanish, EPQ Coordinator*)

Mr J Steadman, BSc, PGCE (*Physical Education*)

Mr H Singer, MA Ed, BA, PGCE (*Assistant Head (Pastoral), Head of KS3, Design & Technology*)

Mrs T van der Linde, MA Ed, BSc, PGCE (**Head of Sixth Form, Chemistry*)

Preparatory School, Junior Department:

Miss L Hallas, BA, PGCE (*Deputy Head of Prep School, English, History*)

Mr A Bevan, BA, PGCE (*Director of Studies in the Prep School, Junior Department Class Teacher*)

Ms C Burdett, BA, PGCE (*Junior Department Class Teacher, Leader of Digital Learning*)

Mrs A Burridge, BSc, PGCE (*Junior Department Class Teacher, DofE*)

Mrs R Carroll, BA, PGCE (*Director of Creative Curriculum in Prep School, Junior Department Class Teacher, Able and Talented Coordinator*)

Mr C Dobbins, BMus, DipMus, LRSM, PGCE (*Director of Music, Games*)

Mrs A Exley, NNEB (*Teaching and Learning Assistant*)

Mrs K Galloway, KS2 (*Teaching and Learning Assistant*)

Ms R King, BA, QTS, (*Junior Department Class Teacher, Mat Cover*)

Mrs R Morgan, BA, PGCE (*Learning Development Centre*)

Mrs R Payne, NNEB (*Teaching and Learning Assistant*)

Mr A Pritchard, BSc, PGCE (*Mathematics, PE*)

Mr S Rowlands, BA, QTS (*Junior Department Class Teacher, House Tutor*)

Mrs L Singer, MA Ed, BSc, PGCE (*Junior Department Class Teacher, PE, Girls Games Coordinator for the Prep School*)

Mrs K Williams, BEd (*Junior Department Class Teacher*)

Preparatory School, Infant Department:

Mrs H Ashill, NNEB (*Teaching and Learning Assistant*)

Mrs Z Bennett, NNEB (*Teaching and Learning Assistant*)

Ms C Burdett BA, PGCE, QTS (*Infant Department Class Teacher, Leader of Digital Learning and Innovation*)

Mr C Dobbins, BMus, DipMus, LRSM, PGCE (*Director of Music*)

Mrs C Devine, BA, QTS (*Infant Department Class Teacher*)

Mrs L Kelley, BA, QTS (*Infant Department Class Teacher, Coordinator of Science*)

Mrs T Mountford, BEd (*Infant Department Class Teacher*)

Mrs N Noor, BA, PGCE (*Infant School Class Teacher*)

Mrs J Vineall (*Teaching and Learning Assistant*)

Preparatory School, Rougemont Nursery:

Mrs J Forouzan, NNEB (*Nursery Teacher*)

Mrs A Exley (*Teaching and Learning Assistant*)

Mrs E Mian, NNEB (*Teaching and Learning Assistant*)

Registrar: Mrs N Bates

Royal Grammar School
Guildford

High Street, Guildford, Surrey GU1 3BB

Tel:	Headmaster: 01483 880608
	School Office: 01483 880600
email:	office@rgsg.co.uk
website:	www.rgsg.co.uk
Twitter:	@RGSGuildford
Facebook:	@RGSGuildford
Instagram:	@rgs_guildford

Located in the centre of the historic town of Guildford, the RGS is an independent day school for around 970 boys aged 11 to 18, some 280 of whom are in the Sixth Form. As a flagship for boys' education, the School has a national reputation for academic excellence but also prides itself on its traditional values of decency and respect, supported by outstanding pastoral care. RGS boys have the opportunity to experience the widest range of enriching activities providing them with a broad and balanced education. Academic excellence is at the very heart of the School's philosophy. The RGS aims to encourage the growth of intellectual curiosity and creativity and to inculcate a life-long love of learning in the boys. The RGS is consistently one of the top five boys' schools in the country at both A Level and GCSE and is extremely proud of its Oxbridge record; in the last decade 301 places have been secured.

Buildings and Facilities. The Tudor buildings in Guildford's High Street have been at the very heart of the RGS for over five centuries. The School was founded by Robert Beckingham in 1509 and established by King Edward VI's Charter of 1552, which decreed that there should be "…one Grammar School in Guildford …for the Education, Institution and Instruction of Boys and Youths in Grammar at all future times for ever to endure". Among the first in the country to be purpose-built, the original buildings contain a remarkable Chained Library, which is now the Headmaster's Study. The School enjoys facilities appropriate to education in the 21st century, including a state-of-the-art Music School, Art School, purpose-built Sixth Form Centre, Sports Hall and the John Brown Building which houses the innovative Design and Technology centre. The Sports Ground at Bradstone Brook provides twenty acres of pitches, tennis courts and a pavilion overlooking the pitches. The School also benefits from the use of nationally renowned sports facilities in the immediate proximity, including Surrey Sports Park.

Curriculum. The school day is from 8.45am to 4.00pm; there are no lessons on Saturdays. Many co-curricular activities and clubs take place after school, however. In the first two years (Years 7 and 8 nationally), all boys follow a common curriculum embodying the programmes of study for Key Stage 3 of the National Curriculum. The subjects studied are English, French or Spanish, Geography, History, Latin, Maths, Information Technology, RE, PE, Art, Music, Drama, Design and Technology, and Science. In the Second Form, the boys study the separate sciences.

In the Third Form (Year 9) the boys continue to follow a core curriculum of study for Key Stage 3, but also begin to specialise by choosing to study from a pool of options, providing the opportunity to explore subjects in more depth. These optional subjects include additional languages – German and Ancient Greek. In addition, all pupils study Computational Thinking.

GCSEs and IGCSEs are offered with boys taking ten subjects out of the 23 available. At GCSE additional subjects include PE and Computer Science, as well as a range of ancient and modern languages. The opportunity exists to study Arabic, Mandarin, Japanese and Russian off timetable.

All Sixth Form boys take four subjects in the Lower Sixth Form and then three or four at A Level. A broad range of subjects are offered, all of which are well-regarded by the leading universities. The Sixth Form curriculum also includes a rigorous, in-house research project and a General Studies programme organised in conjunction with Guildford High School.

Religion. The ethos of the RGS is firmly based on traditional Christian principles and the School has strong links with Holy Trinity Church in the centre of the town and Guildford Cathedral; however, as a non-denominational school, boys from all faiths are welcomed. A diverse, stimulating assembly programme provides the opportunity for collective worship and broadens the boys' horizons while establishing a tolerant set of values. Religious Education lessons, which are an integral part of the School's curriculum, further contribute to developing each individual's moral compass.

Pastoral Care. Respect, tolerance and understanding of others characterise daily life at the RGS and the very strong rapport between boys and teachers makes for a vibrant environment. The boys establish lasting relationships within the year group; in addition, the house system, mentoring, and role of all senior boys as prefects ensure friendships are forged throughout the School. The outstanding pastoral care on offer from dedicated form tutors, heads of year and personal tutors, all overseen by the Deputy Head (Pupils), enables the boys to thrive in a mutually supportive environment where every boy can flourish as an individual.

Co-curricular Activities. The exceptional range of co-curricular activities offered is one of the greatest strengths of the School; there are currently over seventy societies at the RGS. These range from air rifle, chess, Christian Union, drama, Model United Nations, music, philosophy, squash to Young Enterprise. Boys have the opportunity to take Bronze, Silver and Gold Duke of Edinburgh's Award through the Combined Cadet Force or Outdoor Pursuits. Over 30% of students learn a musical instrument and they can join a variety of instrumental groups including Big Band, School Orchestra, Choir and a strong Choral Society. There are many opportunities for boys throughout the School to get involved in drama productions, both for the School and their house.

Games. The School's principal games are rugby, hockey and cricket, although as boys move up the School their sporting options widen considerably. Sports available include athletics, badminton, basketball, cross-country running, fencing, football, golf, sailing, shooting, swimming and tennis. Professional coaching and outstanding facilities develop the skill levels of boys of all abilities; the School takes pride in providing competitive sport and opportunities for all while also nurturing the very best of sporting talent. The School currently has a significant number of boys who are competing for county, national and international honours.

Admission. Boys may be considered for entry to the RGS at any age between 11 and 18. The usual ages of entry, however, are at 11+, 13+ and 16 into the Sixth Form. All applicants wanting a place at 11+ or 13+ take the entrance examinations in the November of Year 6; those for holding a deferred place for 13+ entry will also take the Common Entrance examination or Scholarship papers in Year 8. New boys are admitted in September of each year. The Headmaster is pleased to meet parents in small groups, arrange for them to see the School, and discuss the possibility of their son's entry to the School. Small group appointments are made through the Head of Admissions (Registrar and Marketing), who can supply a hard copy of the School's prospectus; it is also available on the RGS website.

Fees per term (2021–2022). £6,520 (plus £296 for lunches, which are compulsory for First and Second Forms), inclusive of all tuition, stationery and loan of necessary books.

Scholarships. Scholarships of up to 10% fee remission are awarded in recognition of outstanding academic merit. For boys entering the First Form at 11 there is a competitive examination in English and Mathematics, held in January. For boys entering the Third Form at 13, the Common

Academic Scholarship Examinations (CASE) are taken in May. The top scholar of a year group is designated the King's Scholar.

Music scholarships of up to 10% fee remission are available at 11 and 13. It is hoped that a King's Scholarship can be awarded each year to a boy of outstanding musical potential.

One Art Scholarship and one Sports Scholarship of 5% fee remission at 13+ is available annually.

Full details of Scholarships and Fee Assistance (Bursaries) are available from the Head of Admissions (Registrar and Marketing).

Charitable status. Royal Grammar School Guildford is a Company Limited by Guarantee. Registered in England, Company Number: 10874615. Registered Office: High Street, Guildford, Surrey, GU1 3BB. Registered Charity Number 1177353

Governing Body:
Chairman: Mrs S K Creedy, MA
Vice-Chairman: Mr C D Barnett, MA
Vice-Chairman: Mr P G Peel, FCA
Mrs K T Atkinson, BDS
The Revd Canon RL Cotton, MA, DipTh
Mr D J Counsell, FCA [OG]
The Earl of Onslow, High Steward of Guildford
Mr J D Fairley, BA
Mr P Fell, BA, FCA
Mr S G S Gimson, MSc
Professor M Humphreys, MBE, PhD, LLB, PFHEA
Dr L S K Linton, MA, MB ChB, MRCP
Mr T E Lingard, BSci, MInstP [OG]
Mrs M-L Logue, MA
Mrs N Nelson-Smith, BA
Professor S Price, MSc, PhD, FBTS, ERT, FHEA
Mr C T Shorter, CEng, MIStructE, FConsE, FFB
Mrs H Styche-Patel, BSc, MBA
Professor H E Treharne, BSc, MSc, PhD, SFHEA, FBCS
Mr N E J Vineall, QC, MA Cantab and Pittsburgh [OG]
Mr M J Windsor, BA, MA

[OG] *Old Guildfordian*

Chief Operating Officer: Mr R A Ukiah, MA
Bursar and Clerk to the Governors: Mrs C M Perceval, BA

Headmaster: Dr J M Cox, BSc, PhD (*Biology*)

Deputy Head (*School Development*): Mr G T Williams, MA (*History*)
Deputy Head (*Pupils*): Mr A U Woodman, BSc, MA (*Biology*)
Senior Master: Mr J W Pressley, MA (*Classics*)

Assistant Head (*Teaching and Learning*): Miss N S Goul-Wheeker, MA (*Classics*)
Assistant Head (*Partnerships*): Mr T W Shimell, MChem (*Chemistry*)
Assistant Head (*Operations*) : Mr N E Wild, BA (*Religion and Philosophy*)
Assistant Head (*Curriculum*): Mr D S J Wright, BA (*Economics*)
Assistant Head (*Co-curricular*): Mr S J H Yetman, BSc

* *Head of Department*

Art:
*Mr A N Rozier, BA
Mrs R F Shepherd, BA
Mr K A Trim, BA
Mrs A A Wood, BSc, MPhil

Biology:
*Mr S Burns, MBiochem
Mr A H Dubois, BSc
Dr E J Hudson, MA, MSc, PhD
Mr J J Richards, BSc [OG]
Mrs J S Thorpe, BSc

Chemistry:
*Mr W-S Lau, MChem, MRSC
Miss K P C Anderson, BSc, MSc
Dr J S Braithwaite, BSc, PhD
Mr E D Eburne, MSci [OG]
Mr H J Gray, MChem [OG]
Dr L A Whall, BA, PhD

Classics:
*Mr E K D Bush, MA
Mrs S E Besly-Quick, BA
Dr G Fanti, MA, MA, PhD
Mr P G Nathan, BA, LIB
Mr P I Palmer, BA
Mr D J Woolcott, BA

Design & Technology:
*Mr J B Kelly, BA, MA, MA RCA
Mr M Bailey, BSc [OG]
Mr A J Colebrook, BSc
Mr K A Trim, BA

Drama:
*Ms N C McClean, BA, MA
Miss S J Cox, BA

Economics:
*Mr J D Stratford, BSc
Mr D T Chapman, BSc
Mr N W Gough, BSc, MSc
Mr R E Presley, MA
Mr H H H Xuan, BA [OG]

English:
*Ms T T Wijesinghe
Mr D Amis, BA
Mrs H M Curtis, BA
Dr E A McEwan, BA, MA, PhD
Mr J G Muchmore, BA
Ms M A O'Gorman, BA
Mr N M Patel, BA, MSt

Geography:
*Mrs R G Waters, MA
Mr W D Cowx, BSc, MSc
Mr T E Fishpool, BA
Mr G S Oliver, BSc, MSc
Mrs G M Richards, BA
Mr J C Witts, BSc

History:
*Mr J M Davies, MA
Mr A C Dodd, BA, MA [OG]
Mr F C B Evans, BA
Miss C E Hayes, BA
Mr D N Holliday, BA

Mr T J J Owens, BA (**Politics*)
Mr W H N Spouge, BA, MA

Mathematics:
*Mr S G Black, MMath
Mrs I E Busby, BA
Mr J A Casale, BSc, MBA
Mr R D Crew, BTech
Mr S L Dennett, BSc
Mr P J Dunscombe, BSc
Mr C George, BSc
Mr A R Gyford, MSc
Mr M Hanak-Hammerl, MSc
Dr D J Jackson, MSc, PhD
Mr M R Jenkins, BSc
Mr A W J Jessett, MMath
Mr A B Kirkland, BSc
Mr N C Pinhey, BSc
Mr C Wakeling, BSc
Mrs D B Webster, BA
Mrs C A Wellard, BSc
Mrs F M Wimblett, BSc

Modern Languages:
*Ms A V E Tournier, Lic
Mr S J Baker, BA
Dr M M Creagh, BA, MSc, PhD
Mr R J A Lemaire, BA
Mr A R Lowe, BA
Mr J Marchiafava, Lic
Miss M-L McCarter, Lic, MA
Mrs R J Rathmell, BA
Mrs C E Smith, BA
Miss G E Spencer, BA
Mrs N Wilson, BA
Mr R G Yardley, MA, MEd

Music:
*Mr S J Orchard, BMus, MMus (*Director of Music*)
Miss L A Eaton, BMus, MMus
Mr D H Chambers, BMus, PCASS
Ms I Garvie, BMus, MMus, PGDip
Miss J Newman, AGSM, CRD
Miss L J A Wild, Lic, MMus
Mr P H White, MA

Physical Education:
* Mr G D G Cover, BSc (*Director of Sport*)
Mr R C Black, BSc (*Cricket*)
Mr B Dudley, BSc (*Rugby*)
Mr J D N Lythgoe, BSc
Mr C R Mullon, BSc (*Hockey*)
Mr T Remke, BCom

Mr T M Vickers, BA
Mr I Wilkes, BEd

Physics:
*Mr J P Hood, MA, MSci
Mr M A Burbidge, BSc, BA
Dr A P Calverley, MSci, PhD, FRAS
Mr L M Holland, BSc
Mrs N L Odhams, MA, MEng
Dr D Patel, BSc, PhD
Mr M R F Royds, BSc

Mr M D Unsworth, MEng
Mrs D Whitehead, BTech, RSci

Religion and Philosophy:
*Mr R B Meadowcroft, BA, MA
Mr T F Foster, BA [OG]
Mr S T Herman-Wilson, BA
Mr K Tayar, BA [OG]
Mr J C Winterburn, MA

Head of Admissions (*Registrar and Marketing*): Mrs K L Sweet, BA, MCIPD

Royal Grammar School

Newcastle upon Tyne

Eskdale Terrace, Newcastle-upon-Tyne NE2 4DX

Tel: 0191 281 5711
email: communications@rgs.newcastle.sch.uk
website: www.rgs.newcastle.sch.uk
Twitter: @RGSNewcastle
Facebook: @newcastleroyalgrammarschool
Instagram: @rgs_newcastle
LinkedIn: /school/royal-grammar-school-newcastle

Thomas Horsley, the original settlor of the Royal Grammar School Newcastle (RGS) pledged his legacy to the School in 1525. Almost 500 years later, RGS continues to flourish as the premier independent school in the North East of England and as one of the country's leading schools. The Sunday Times' *North East Independent School of the Decade*, we regularly lead all northern schools in national league tables and pride ourselves on academic excellence, a high level of pastoral support, involvement in a wide range of sports and other co-curricular activities, and our commitment to bursaries and partnerships.

The RGS has grown substantially in recent years. There are now some 1,340 students, over 270 of whom are in the Junior School. The Sixth Form of 355 students is one of the largest in the independent sector. We became co-educational 20 years ago and girls now comprise 46% of the school.

The school is based in the heart of the City, immediately opposite Jesmond Metro station. The school occupies over 30 acres of land and has state-of-the-art facilities, including five brand new art studios, a new library, a new Sixth Form Centre, a 25m swimming pool, two Sports Halls, a Performing Arts Centre, outdoor football/rugby pitches at Mooracres, an artificial turf pitch for hockey and the former County Cricket Ground.

Curriculum. The aim of the curriculum up to Year 11 is to offer a general education, culminating in GCSE in a wide range of subjects. All students study English (Language and Literature), a Modern Language (French, German or Spanish), Mathematics, Biology, Physics and Chemistry to this level and three further examination subjects are taken at GCSE level from Ancient History, Art, Computing, Economics, Geography, German, Greek, History, Latin,

Music, Spanish, Engineering Design & Technology and Drama. Additionally there is a programme of Art, Drama, Music and Technology for all in Years 7 to 9.

Sixth Formers will normally choose three A Level subjects. In addition, students will be required to select either a fourth A Level or a combination of two complementary courses from EPQ or non-examined subject. The range of A Level subjects currently: Ancient History, Art, Biology, Chemistry, Computing, Engineering Design Technology, Economics, English, Film Studies, French, Geography, German, Greek, History, Latin, Mathematics, Further Mathematics, Music, Philosophy, Physics, Physical Education, Politics, Psychology, Spanish and Theatre Studies. There is also a compulsory series of lectures and talks/workshops designed to provide cultural and personal broadening and development.

Almost all Sixth Formers go on to University, and success in gaining entry at Oxford and Cambridge, and medical schools, has been an outstanding feature of the school's record.

Physical Education. All students are required to take part in a Physical Education programme which, up to Year 10, includes Rugby, Football, Cross Country, Cricket, Athletics, Gymnastics, Hockey, Netball, Tennis, Rounders, Swimming. At the upper end of the School a wider range of activities is offered: in addition to the above students may opt for Badminton, Basketball, Climbing, Fencing, Fitness training, Karate, Orienteering, Squash, Tennis, Table Tennis, Volleyball and Dance. A wide range of activities is available to all through voluntary membership of various Sports Clubs.

Activities. Art, Drama and Music are strong features in the life of the School, all of them overflowing from scheduled lessons into spare-time activity. There is a large number of wide-ranging music groups and ensembles from choirs and orchestras to bands, jazz ensembles and rock groups. There are several productions in the theatre each term. Numerous societies meet in the lunch-break, before or after school, some linked with school work but many developing from private enthusiasms. There is a thriving Duke of Edinburgh's Award scheme. There is an entirely voluntary Combined Cadet Force Contingent. Annual overseas visits include ski-parties, sporting tours, Classics trips, visits to art galleries and to the battlefields of World War I.

Supervision and Pastoral Care. Each student is within the care of (a) Form Supervisor and (b) Tutor. The latter will normally be associated with the student throughout their school career, and the aim is to forge a personal link with students and their families.

The Careers programme begins in Year 9; in Year 11 and the Sixth Form every possible care is taken to advise each student individually about Careers and Higher Education.

The School's Medical Officers are available regularly for consultation; there are also male and female School Counsellors.

Buildings. Some of the School's buildings date from 1907 and are described by Pevsner as "friendly neo-Early-Georgian". Recent years have seen many developments and improvements, including the opening in February 1996 of a new Sports Centre, a new Science and Technology Centre which opened in 1997, and new Maths and ICT departments in 1998. A new Junior School extension opened in 2005 and a Performing Arts Centre opened in 2006. A new 6-lane, 25m swimming pool was completed in August 2015 as part of an additional sports complex which includes a second sports hall, a dance and fitness suite and new indoor and outdoor changing facilities.

A new building on the main site was completed in September 2019, and houses a new library, a suite of rooms for Art, Maths, Science, Engineering Design Technology, and a home for the new Digital Technology and Computing Department. Similarly, a new Pastoral Centre will link this new building with the rest of the School.

In January 2020, we opened our new Sixth Form Centre, which saw the combination of the old Sixth Form Common Room and old Library into a much larger, and modern area. The open-plan style centre comprises individual study pods, a Sixth Form only bank of computers, a space for collaborative working, printing facilities and a new coffee bar.

Junior School. Years 3 and 4 of the Junior School are separately housed in Lambton Road opposite the Senior School playing fields. Years 5 and 6 are housed in a purpose built extension on the main school site. Junior School students use the Sports Centre, Swimming Pool, games fields and dining hall. English and Mathematics are taught by Form Teachers, while History, Geography, French, Science, Religious Education, Music, Art and Physical Activities are taken by specialists.

Entrance. Entry is by examination. Application is via an online form: www.rgs.newcastle.sch.uk/prospective-families/admissions/how-to-apply.

Junior School at 7+ and 9+. Prospective students attend Assessment Days held in November (9+) and January (7+) when they take part in a number of activities and sit a number of short tests. A reference is sought from previous/current school.

Senior School at 11+. The Senior School examination is held each January for prospective students who will be 11 on 1 September of the year in which entry is desired. Applications by Friday 11th December 2022 (later application at School's discretion). A reference is sought from previous/current school.

Sixth Form at 16+. Applicants are considered for direct entry to the Sixth Form if their GCSE results are likely to form an adequate basis. A reference is sought from the previous/current school, prior to interview.

Each year a small number of places may be available at entry points other than the main ones listed. Please contact the Head of Admissions for details.

Term of Entry. Autumn, although a small number of places may become available throughout the year.

Fees per term (2021–2022). Senior School £4,833, Junior School £4,071.

Bursaries. Some bursaries, awarded on the basis of parental income, are offered. Details are available from the Head of Admissions

Charitable status. The Newcastle upon Tyne Royal Grammar School is a Registered Charity, number 1114424.

Governing Body:
Mrs J Berry
Mrs J Drummond, BA, MA
Mr R H Fell
Mr A Fletcher, LLB (*Chair*)
Mrs A Gupta
Mrs S Green
Professor M Haniffa, BSc, MBBCh, MRCP, PhD

Mrs T Hartley, MRICS, BSc Hons, MSc, MBA (*Vice Chair*)
Mr A Lamb, BA, CA
Mr N McMinn
Ms S Milligan, LLB
Mr T Murphy
Mr M Robinson
Councillor T Thorne, BA
Mrs C Stonehouse
Mrs S Woodroofe

Headmaster: **Mr G Stanford**, MA, MBA, FRGS

Deputy Head: Mr T E Keenan, BSc, MSc, PGCE
Deputy Head (*Academic*): Mr R C M Loxley, BSc, MEd, PGCE
Deputy Head (*Pastoral*): Miss S J Longville, BA, PGCE
Head of Sixth Form: Mrs N McGough, MSc, PGCE, MRes
Director of Partnerships: Mr J A Smith, BSc, MEd, PGCE
Director of Finance & Operations: Mrs R Amey, MEng, ACMA
Ms S Beck, MSc, InstFCert

Assistant Staff:
* *Head of Department*
§ *Part-time*

Art:
*Mr G P Mason, BA
Miss H C Bray, BA, MA
Mrs C Egan-Fowler, BEd
Ms R Harvey, MFA, BA
Mrs K Nowicki, BA (*Head of Upper Sixth*)
Miss K Riley, BA, PGCE

Biology:
*Mr P J Heath, BSc
Mrs L Astley, BSC
Dr M H Bell, BSc, PhD
Mr S Hall, BSc
Mrs S F Hutchinson, BSc
Dr C J Murgatroyd, BSc, DPhil (*Head of Year 7*)
Mr L Shepherd, BA

Careers and Higher Education:
*MR M G Downie, BA,
Mrs R J L Laws, MA (*Assistant Head*)
Mr S M F A Belfield, BA, MA (*Oxbridge Coordinator*)
Miss B Milburn, BSc (*Careers Coordinator, medical*)
Dr M B A Read, BA, MA, PhD (*North American Universities Coordinator*)
Mrs C Towns, Staatsexamen, GTP (*Careers Coordinator, non-medical*)

Chemistry:
Dr A J Pulham, BA, DPhil (*Science)
*Dr E A Smith, BSc, PhD

§Dr R Campbell, BSc, PhD
§Mrs S L Coates, MSc
Dr J L Greenhalgh, BSc, PhD
Mrs C J Hutton-Stott, BSc
Mr T Kelso, BSc (*Head of Year 10*)
§Mrs M C Slack, BSc
§Mrs M Wiggins, BSc
§Mr R W Wiggins, BSc
Mrs N Wright, BSc (*Head of EPQ*)

Classics:
*Mrs V C Mee, BA, MA
Mr S M F A Belfield, MA
Mrs P R Coningham, BA, MA
Dr L E Hope, PhD, MA, BA
Dr D A MacLennan, BA, MA
Miss P L Whitworth, BA

Digital Technology and Computer Science:
*Mr C J Wilde, BA
Miss J K Lynn, BSc
Mr M Moore, ME

Drama:
*Ms S G Davison, BA
§Miss J Blacklock, BA
§Mrs R A Shaw-Kew, BA

Economics/Politics:
*Mr J D Neil, MPhil
Mrs L E Davison, MA, BA
Mr R C M Loxley, BSc, MEd
§Mr S O'Dwyer, BA
Mr P Shelley, BA, MSc
Mr M J Smalley, BA

Engineering, Design & Technology:
Mr P M Warne, MEng
Mr M Lowe, BA
Mrs C A Pipes, BA, PGCE
Miss O Kenny, BA, MA

English:
*Dr S J Barker, BA, PhD
Miss H Chandy, MA
Dr C Goulding, BA, MLitt, PhD
Mrs K J Keown, BA
Mr A R D King, BA, MA
Dr S C Masters, BA, MA, PhD (*Film Studies*)
§Mrs L A Stadward, BA, MA

Food and Nutrition:
Mrs M Aitchison, BSc

Geography:
*Mr D A Wilson, BSc
Ms S Buist (*Head of Digital Strategy*)
Mr M G Downie, BA (*Careers & HE*)
Mrs K E Hammill, BA (*PSHE*)
Mrs R J L Laws, MA (*Asst Head of Careers*)
Mrs R A Leigh, MA
Miss Z C Morrow, BSc, MA

History:
*Mr D Tyreman, MA
Mr O L Edwards, BA (*Oxbridge Coordinator*)
Mr D C Greenhalgh, BA, MA (*Head of Year 8*)
Dr E S Matthews, MA, PhD
§Mrs L Crowley, MA, MLitt
§Mrs A J Palmer, MA

Mathematics:
*Mr N Hamilton, ME
Dr J Argyle, BSc, MSc, PhD
Mr H M W Bingham, BA
Mr A Delvin, BSc, MSc
Dr P M Heptinstall, BSc, PhD
Mr D A Jardine, BSc
Mr T Keenan, BSc, MSc (*Deputy Head*)
Mr A Pearson, BSc, MEd
Mr H Rashid, BSc, MSc
Mrs S Sharp, BA, MA
Mr A Snedden, BSc
Miss R M Watterson, BSc
Miss Z Winn, MMath
§Mr G D Dunn, BSc
§Mrs J Gwillim, BSc

Modern Languages:
*Miss K E Sykes, BA
Mr M S Bailie, BA, MA (*Head of Year 11*)
Miss S Demoulin, DEUG
Senora B Membrado-Dolz (*Spanish*)
Mrs D Williams, BA (*German*)
Miss J Budd, BA (*Head of Lower Sixth*)
Mrs C L Diaz-Crossley, BA
Mr T Harman, BA (*French*)
Miss E L Hayes, BA
Mr M Metcalf, BA, MPhil (*Head of Year 9*)
Mrs C Towns, Staatsexamen
Mrs D Williams, BA (*German*)
§Mrs Xing Wang (*Mandarin*)

Music:
*Mr N Smith, BM, MM (*Director of Music*)
Miss S L Bolt, BA
Mrs K Clappison, MA (*Head of Junior School Music*)

Personalised Learning:
Ms A E Lee, MSc, BA (*Director of Student Progress*)
Mrs H J Hardy, BA, MA (*Learning Support Assistant*)
Mrs N Kyle, BA, MSc (*Learning Support Assistant*)
Mrs S Huck, BA (*Learning Support Assistant*)

Philosophy and Religion:
Dr M B A Read, MA, MPhil, PhD (*North American Universities Coordinator*)

Physical Education:
*Mrs A J Ponton, BSc
Mr W Angus, BA
Mr A G Brown, BSc
Mr J Ingle, BSc (*Assistant Director of Sport*)
Miss N Harkness, BSc
Miss H Larsen, BSc
Miss A Lill, BSc
Mr A E Watt, BA
Mr J A Wood, BA
§Miss J Harrison, BSc
§Mr R V MacKay, BSc

Physics:
*Dr R M Houchin, MSci, PhD

Mr E T Rispin, BSc (*Head of Exams*)
Mr J L Camm, BSc
Mrs N C McGough, MSc, MRes (*Head of Sixth Form*)
Mr S McMenzie, BSc

Junior School

Headmaster: Mr J N Miller, BA

Deputy Head: Dr A J Spencer, BSc, PhD
Assistant Head Academic: Mrs K Clappison, MA
Assistant Head Pastoral: Mrs K Wall, BA

Mrs C Baker, BA
Miss H Close, BSc
Mr A Cragg, BA
Mrs C M Cree, BSc
Mrs H Dean, BEd
Mr T G Lloyd, BA
Miss S J McCulloch, BA
Miss M A Noble, BA
Miss R S Scott, BA

Mrs L M Stairmand, BA
Mrs R S Towers, MEd
Ms A J Whitney, BA
Mr B Woolerton, BSc
Miss L R B Wood, BA, MA
§Mrs C A M O'Hanlon, BA

Teaching Assistants:
Mrs A Gilmore, CACHE Level 3
Mrs L M Johnston, STA,
Mrs H Sisterson, BA, CACHE Level 3

Personal Care Assistant: Miss K Hobson, BA

School Medical Officer: Dr R Pedlow
Head of Admissions: Mrs A Perry

Miss B Milburn, BSc (*Careers Coordinator*)
Mr T Williams, BSc

PSHE:
Mrs K E J Hammill, BA

Psychology:
*Dr C M Bone, PhD, BSc
Miss K A Jacques, BSc

Royal Hospital School

Holbrook, Ipswich, Suffolk IP9 2RX

Tel: 01473 326200
email: admissions@royalhospitalschool.org
              reception@royalhospitalschool.org
website: www.royalhospitalschool.org
Twitter: @RHSSuffolk
Facebook: @RoyalHospitalSchool
Instagram: @royalhospitalschool
LinkedIn: /Royal-Hospital-School

The Royal Hospital School was founded in 1712 in Greenwich, London, to 'improve navigation' through education and, as it prepared boys for a life at sea, many went on to become explorers and pioneers of their time. The school is immensely proud of these historic links and discovery, exploration and challenge continue to shape its ethos. The traditional values of loyalty, commitment, courage, respect, service and integrity have underpinned the school's core aims and philosophy from the very beginning. Three hundred years later, they are still as relevant to the education it provides as they were then. Today the school is set in 200 acres of Suffolk countryside overlooking the Stour Estuary and it is a co-educational HMC boarding and day school for 730 pupils providing a full and broad education, fit for the modern world. It aims to inspire its pupils to have the courage and commitment to be ambitious for their futures, whichever path they choose, challenging pupils of all academic abilities, steering them to look beyond the moment, and beyond the confines of the classroom, and to approach life with an open and receptive mind.

House System. 57% of pupils board and there is a strong diamond-shaped House System. An ongoing programme of refurbishment and development provides superb facilities and accommodation for both boarders and day pupils.

Pupils joining the school at 11+ are accommodated in the Junior House purpose-built with 4/6-bedded rooms and facilities, routines and pastoral care that assist the transition between junior and senior school. Weekly boarding and the opportunity to stay overnight on an ad hoc basis are available.

At Year 8 (13+) pupils join one of nine Senior Houses. Two are co-educational day houses and one is a boys' day house with flexi boarding facilities enabling the boys to board up to 3 nights per week. There are also 3 boys' and 3 girls' Senior Boarding Houses which are each home to approximately 60 full and weekly boarders. Boarders in Years 8 and 9 share rooms with up to four other pupils and older pupils have double or single studies with en-suite facilities.

In the Upper Sixth both boarding and day boys and girls join Nelson House, where they learn to live more independently in preparation for university.

Curriculum and Academic Development. The school's curriculum shadows the National Curriculum Key Stages 3 and 4. On joining the school, pupils are placed in forms based on assessed ability from entrance testing or at 13+ the results of Common Entrance examinations. The school subscribes to the Durham University Value Added Measuring Scheme at all levels, allowing tutors to map pupil progress. In core subjects setting takes place from the outset and at GCSE level setting occurs in all core curriculum subjects. There are 66 x 55 min periods over a two weekly timetable.

Lower School (Years 7–8): The subjects studied are English, mathematics, science (biology, physics and chemistry), modern foreign languages (French and Spanish), Latin, geography, history, design technology, art, drama, music, religious studies, RHS Compass (digital literacy, Personal, Social and Health Education, Computing and study skills) and PE. There are four forms in Years 7 and 8 and the average class size is 18 pupils. Homework is set daily and completed within supervised sessions during the working day by both boarders and day pupils. All junior pupils must take part in at least three co-curricular activities after lessons.

Middle School (Years 9–11): The subjects studied in Year 9 are the same as in the Lower School and a further intake of pupils from prep schools means that there is an additional class. GCSE courses start in Year 10 and most pupils will study 9 subjects including English language and literature, mathematics, physics, chemistry, biology (either as three separate sciences or as the dual award) as the core subjects and four options from science (if taking separate sciences), history, geography, PE (Physical Education and Sports Science), French, Spanish, media studies, religious studies, art, music, theatre studies, design technology and business studies.

Sixth Form (Years 12 and 13): Pupils choose three from approximately 27 A Level and BTEC subjects. Subject choice depends upon average point scores at GCSE and

grades gained in specific subjects. As well as three A Level or BTEC subjects, pupils must choose one from a range of academic Elective subjects which can range from an Extended Project Qualification to a BTEC Level 2 First Award in Information and Creative Technology. RHS+ provides sessions on careers, managing finances, cooking on a budget, digital effectiveness and safety and coping with stress and mindfulness. RHSXtra runs a series of talks and seminars on topics aimed at broadening horizons and inspiring curiosity. Around 90% of pupils go to the University or Higher Education institution of their choice and approximately 50% to Russell Group and other top-class universities. An increasing number of pupils are gaining places on Higher Degree Apprenticeship schemes with leading corporations.

Pupil progress is formally monitored by means of at least two assessments or reports per term which grade the academic performance of the pupil against their target or challenge grades, as well as looking at their attitude to learning. Every pupil has a personal tutor and daily tutorial meetings are an opportunity to deal with any problems and check on progress.

All pupils have access to an electronic device, a suite of mobile learning apps and Wi-Fi throughout the site. Additional networked computers are available in Boarding or Day Houses as well as in computer suites around the school. Mobile learning is embraced by the teaching staff with the aim of enhancing teaching and learning. Recent remote and hybrid learning allowed a full, unadapted timetable of lessons to be delivered during the pandemic via MS Teams and OneNote.

Through high quality, enthusiastic teaching, excellent resources and dedicated tutorial support, every pupil is encouraged to aim high and achieve his or her personal best. The most able pupils' potential is realised through the mentoring of scholars, the Riddle and Studd Societies for gifted and talented pupils and Oxbridge preparation for those pupils requiring it, led by a dedicated Head of Academic Challenge.

Sport and Leisure. Facilities include ninety-six acres of playing fields, a golf course, shooting range, sports hall, fitness suite, gym, climbing wall, large heated indoor swimming pool, squash courts, tennis and netball courts and an all-weather sports surface.

The school has a strong sailing tradition and all pupils joining in Year 7 receive sailing instruction to RYA Level 2. Through the school's RYA-accredited Sailing Academy, pupils have access to a fleet of 40 racing dinghies on adjacent Alton Water reservoir, as well as traditional Cornish Shrimpers on the River Stour and Orwell. The school is widely known as one of the top in the country for both fleet and team sailing and offers an elite training programme for those wishing to follow Olympic pathway.

The Graham Napier Cricket Academy aims to provide a centre of cricketing excellence developing aspiring young cricketers to reach their full potential and promoting participation by girls and boys at all levels and ages.

The other main sports are rugby, hockey and netball where the school has an excellent group of coaching staff as well as strong links to academy and high performance centres in the region. Kayaking, athletics, cross country, climbing, basketball, football, tennis, riding and swimming are also sports on offer and are popular with a number of pupils at the school. The swimming pool also offers opportunities for kayak-polo, life-saving training and sub-aqua.

Music and Drama. The school has a particularly strong musical tradition and the state-of-the-art Music School provides a recital hall, specialist rooms, recording studio and technical suite. Almost half the pupils in the school are involved in music on a regular basis. The Chapel is of cathedral proportions and has one of the finest organs in Europe, much used by pupils as well as professional performers. Peripatetic teachers offer tuition in a wide range of instruments and the choir and chamber choir perform both nationally and internationally. As well as drama in the curriculum and LAMDA classes, productions are often combined with the music department for whole-school performances and there is a full programme of plays, competitions and festivals each year.

CCF and Community Service. All pupils participate in the Combined Cadet Force in Years 9 and 10 and are able to choose between Army, Navy, RAF and Royal Marine sections. The emphasis is on adventure training and personal development. More than 300 pupils take part in The Duke of Edinburgh's Award scheme and 100 of these to Gold Award. The Community Action Team promotes the school's social responsibility and is actively involved in a wide range of charitable activities in the local community.

Religion. The core values of the school are based on the Christian faith but pupils from a variety of religions and cultural backgrounds attend the school and all beliefs are respected. The magnificent Chapel, that holds over 1,000 people, is the spiritual hub of school life and the whole community gathers twice weekly for morning worship.

Admission. Entry to the school is normally at 11, 13 and 16 years. Pupils are asked to sit an entrance examination, comprising papers in English, mathematics and verbal reasoning, in the January prior to the September of the year of entry unless following Common Entrance for entry in Year 9. Entry into the Sixth Form is subject to a minimum average GCSE point score and specific grades in chosen A Level subjects. Entry is also subject to an interview and satisfactory reference from the pupil's current school.

Fees per term (2021–2022). Full Boarding: £9,143 (Years 7 and 8), £11,773 (Years 9–13). Weekly Boarding: £8,709 (Years 7 and 8), £10,811 (Years 9–13). Day: £5,699 (Years 7 and 8), £6,339 (Years 9–13). 3-Night Boarding: £7,664 (Years 7 and 8), £9,098 (Years 9–13).

A Boarding Bundle is available to parents of day pupils or 3-Night Boarders who want to take advantage of the flexibility of buying units of 15 nights purchased in advance. A maximum of three 15-night Boarding Bundles can be purchased per pupil in each academic year.

Discounts are available for services families eligible for the MOD Continuity of Education Allowance (CEA) and siblings where two or more children are in the School at any time.

Scholarships, Exhibitions and Awards are awarded annually for academic excellence, musical talent, drama, art, sport and sailing. All scholarship candidates are required to sit the school entrance examination (unless taking Common Entrance or GCSE examinations), have an interview and undergo an assessment in their relevant field. Full details from the Admissions Office, Tel: 01473 326136 or email: admissions@royalhospitalschool.org.

Bursaries. Pupils in receipt of a scholarship or award are eligible to apply for additional assistance by way of a means-tested bursary, should the financial circumstances of the family necessitate it. The school's parent charity, Greenwich Hospital, can award generous means-tested bursaries to the children of seafarers, particularly serving or retired Naval or Royal Marines personnel.

Charitable status. The Royal Hospital School is owned by Greenwich Hospital which is a Crown Charity.

Director, Greenwich Hospital: Mr A Turner

Governors:
Chair of Governors: Mr M Pendlington

Mr J Agar	Mr A Kerr
Mr T Arulampalam	Mr J Lynas
Ms J Dow	Mrs N Probert
Mr N Gallop	Mr P Smith
Mr J Gamp	Mr T Stenning
Prof R Harvey	Mr P Torrington

Leadership Team:
Headmaster: Mr Simon Lockyer, BSc, MEd
Second Master: Mr S J Dixon, MA
Director of Finance and Strategic Development (*Bursar*): Mrs J P Bromley, ACMA
Deputy Head (*Academic*): Mrs C A Stevens, BSc
Deputy Head (*Pastoral*): Mrs Z S King, BSc
Director of Learning: Mr M R Routledge, BA
Assistant Head (*Pastoral*): Mr L M Corbould, BSc
Assistant Head (*Co-curricular*): Mr B Martineau, BA Hons, PGCE, MBA

Chaplain: Revd J W P McConnell, BEd, MA, BD, DASE

Directors and Programme Heads:
Head of Middle School: Mr A Wynn, BSc
Head of Sixth Form & Careers: Mr C Graham, BSc
Head of Digital Learning: Mr M Vickers, MA
Examinations Officer: Mr A J Loveland, ACGI, MA
Academic Challenge Co-ordinator: Mr G N G Johnson, BA
Director of Music: Mr E C Allen, BA
Director of Sport: Mr N L Cooper, BA
Director of Sailing and Water Sports: Mr E M G Sibson, MSc
Head of Graham Napier Cricket Academy: Mr G R Napier
Head of Ceremonial: Lt Cdr (Retd) N M Griffiths, QGM
CCF Contingent Commander: Maj J F Pooley
Assistant Head of Sixth Form: Mrs M Price

Heads of Department:
Art: Mrs H L Barber, BA
Biology: Mr BA Raybould, BSc
Business and Economics: Mrs A S Williamson BSc
Chemistry: Mr M Coventry, BSc
Classics: Dr P Taraskin
Climbing: SSgt P Ryan
Head of Cricket: Mr P M Cohen, BA
Design Technology: Mr O Millington, BA
Drama: Mr D Kerr, BA
Duke of Edinburgh's Award & CCF: Sgt P Ryan
English: Ms J L Stone, BA
English as an Additional Language: Mr D P Coleman, BA
French: Mrs A Barth, BA
Geography: Mrs H Izod-Miller, BSc
History and Politics: Mr O Roe, BA
Learning Support: Mrs E Burge, MA
Librarian: Miss R Gitsham, BA
Mathematics: Ms S C Botley, BSc
Media Studies: Mr K Gurur
Netball: Miss L J Adams, BSc

Science: Dr A L Clayton, BSc, PhD
PE (Academic): Mrs S J Williams, MA, BEd
Physics: Dr M R Gibbs, BSc
PSHE: Ms M R Hemmens, MA
Psychology and Sociology: Mrs M R Price, BA
Religious Studies: Mrs K O'Callaghan, MA
Science: DR A L Clayton BSc PhD
Spanish: Mr A E Gutierrez-Aldana, BA

CCF School Staff Instructor: WO1 (RSM) K Weaver

Support Staff:
Deputy Bursar (Finance): Mr P Philips
Deputy Bursar (Operations): Mr J Reid, OBE, MA
Headmasters PA: Mrs F Stratford
Head of Administration and Compliance: Ms T Fairbairn
Commercial Manager: Mrs C Fitzpatrick
HR Manager: Mrs J Roberts
IS Manager: Mr A Davison
Transport Manager: Ms D Hodgson
Senior Registrar: Mrs S Walker
International Registrar: Mrs E Allinson
Community and Alumni Relations Manager: Mrs L
   Pembroke
Health Centre: Sister D Sweeney, RGN

The Royal Masonic School for Girls

Rickmansworth Park, Rickmansworth, Herts WD3 4HF

Tel: 01923 773168
email: enquiries@rmsforgirls.com
website: www.rmsforgirls.com
Twitter: @RMSforGirls
Facebook: @RMSforGirls
Instagram: @RMSforGirls
LinkedIn: /school/rmsforgirls

There are 970 pupils in school between the ages of 2 and 18. Around 100 of the current school population are boarders; day girls and boarders are fully integrated through the Houses.

Premises and Facilities. Founded in 1788, the School came to Rickmansworth in 1934. Purpose-built, the school stands in over 300 acres of parkland on an elevated site overlooking the valley of the River Chess. The buildings are spacious and well-appointed. They include excellent ICT facilities, a well-equipped Science building, a Planetarium, an Observatory, Chapel and Resource Centre.

The Sports Hall is equipped to the highest international standards and includes a gym and fitness suite. There is a heated indoor swimming pool, 12 tennis courts, four squash courts, superb playing fields and an All-Weather pitch, funded by the Campaign for Excellence. The School has been awarded Sportsmark status. The state-of-the-art Performing Arts Centre includes a recording studio and green room facilitating learning about production, as well as performance.

Location. Central London is 15 miles to the south and Amersham is just north of the town. The M25 is one mile from the school and links it to London (Heathrow) – 30 minutes, London (Gatwick) – 50 minutes, and Luton Airport – 30 minutes. London Underground services (Metropolitan Line) and British Rail from Marylebone enable Central London to be reached by train in 30 minutes.

General Curriculum and Aims. The first three years of Senior School provide a broad general education that fulfils the requirements of the National Curriculum and reaches far beyond it. Students cover a wide range of subjects including English, Mathematics, Science, History, Geography, Philosophy, Ethics and Religion, Design Technology, Computer Science, Food and Nutrition, Art, Textiles, Performing Arts, Physical Education and Life Skills. Language Studies begins with French, Spanish, German, and Mandarin, Latin is also offered. The academic curriculum is supported by a vast range of co-curricular opportunities and Sixth Form Studies are enhanced with the RMS Edge programme designed to provide a bespoke timetable for each student.

GCSE options are chosen from among all the subjects taught in Years 7 to 9 and new possibilities, such as Child Development, Performing Arts, Drama and Business are introduced at this stage. We also offer additional GCSE subjects such as iMedia and Astronomy. Most pupils take nine or ten GCSE subjects and girls are guided in their choices by subject teachers, in full consultation with parents. Triple Science is available.

The Sixth Form. The School offers 29 subjects in flexible combinations. Politics, Economics, Classical Civilisation, Photography, Sociology and Psychology are all new additions to the curriculum at this stage. There are also practical and vocational courses leading to qualifications in Performing or Production Arts, Business and Health and Social Care. Virtually all Sixth Formers go on to higher education.

Religion. Girls of all faiths and none are welcome. School assemblies are traditional and inclusive in nature and Chapel Services for boarders are held according to the rites of the Church of England.

Health. The School Doctor attends the Health Centre regularly. There are three nurses on duty every day.

Admission. Please contact the Admissions Department admissions@rmsforgirls.com or visit the school website for further information. The main entry points are 3+, 4+, 11+, 13+ and 16+, although students may join in other year groups subject to assessment and space being available. Families can book private tours at any time.

Scholarships and Bursaries. Scholarships are offered by the School to encourage and reward excellence. Scholarships are awarded in recognition of outstanding achievement, or promise in a particular area. Scholarship awards do not exceed 25% of the annual fee.

A number of scholarships are available at 11+, 13+ and 16+, and may be supported with means-tested bursaries.

At 11+: Awards are given in recognition of excellence with regard to academic achievement in the entrance examination, Sport, All-Rounder potential, Art, Drama and Music.

At 16+: Awards are given for academic excellence, Music, Art, Sport and Performing Arts.

Additional Scholarship Support may be available for those girls who are successful in the scholarship assessments, but whose parents could not otherwise afford the fees, to benefit from an education at RMS for Girls. These awards are subject to means-testing. The number of awards made in any one year will vary according to the quality and circumstances of candidates and the availability of funds.

Fees per term (2021–2022). Senior School: Full Boarders £11,060; Weekly Boarders £10,203; Day Pupils £6,365; Sixth Form £6,426.

Cadogan House Prep School: Full Boarders: £7,658 (Years 5–6); Weekly Boarders: £7,262 (Years 5–6); Day Pupils: £3,940 (Reception), £4,141 (Years 1 and 2), £4,909 (Years 3–6). Ruspini House Nursery School (boys and girls aged 2–4): please visit our website for range of fees.

Charitable status. The Royal Masonic School Limited is a Registered Charity, number 276784. Its aims are the advancement of education.

Board of Governors:
Professor John Brewer (*Chair*)
Mr K S Carmichael, CBE (*Honorary Life President*)

Mr S Brew	Mr S Staite
Mrs S Brophy	Mr A Wauchope
Mrs P Dyke	Mr I Williams
Mr J Knopp	Mrs H Wilson
Mrs T Lemon	Ms J Pardon
Ms S Shackell	Mr B Saini

Clerk to the Governors: Mrs D Robinson BSc Bristol, ACA

Head Teacher: Mr K Carson, BA Liverpool, MPhil Cantab, PGCE

Head of Senior School: Ms R Bailey, BSc York, PGCE
Head of Sixth Form: Mrs C Freeman BSc Durham, PGCE
Head of Cadogan House: Mrs M Horn, BA
Head of Ruspini House: Mrs V Greig, BA

Director of Finance and Operations: Mrs E Gosht
Director of Marketing and Admissions: Mrs A Nicoll

Deputy Head, Academic: Mrs Sophia Hardy, BA
Deputy Head, Pastoral: Mrs A Davies, BA

Assistant Head, Academic: Mrs H Roberts, BA Durham, PGCE
Assistant Head, Co-Curricular: Mr D Cox, BEng Brunel, MEd Cantab, PGCE

Head of Admissions: Mr M Carter

Head's PA: Mrs S Clifford

Royal Russell School

Coombe Lane, Croydon, Surrey CR9 5BX

Tel: 020 8657 4433
email: headmaster@royalrussell.co.uk
website: www.royalrussell.co.uk
Twitter: @Royal_Russell
Facebook: @RoyalRussellSchool
LinkedIn: /royal-russell-school

Motto: *Non Sibi Sed Omnibus*

Royal Russell is different by design. We are a co-educational family school, for children aged 3 to 18 years with boarding and day facilities, set in 110 acres of beautiful woodland, enjoying excellent access to London and Gatwick and Heathrow airports. We are proud to have enjoyed Royal Patronage from our foundation in 1853 and Her Majesty, Queen Elizabeth II is our current Patron.

Royal Russell's motto is '*non sibi sed omnibus*' which translates as 'not for oneself, but for all' and our commitment to each other is to help our happy and vibrant community to strive for their vision of success. Our extensive campus facilities and state of the art technology blend effortlessly to inspire learning and personal growth. We encourage pupils to extend their learning beyond the curriculum through enrichment activities and cultural experiences learning together in an open community that reflects the real world and celebrates both individual and collective achievements. As a school with a truly international outlook, we are proud of our links with campuses in China and South Korea.

Number in School. There are 1,126 pupils in the school: 830 pupils in the Senior School; 651 day pupils and 179 boarders. There are 258 in the Sixth Form, and 296 in the Junior School.

Admission. Pupils enter in the Autumn term at the age of 3+, 11, 13 or 16. Space permitting, pupils may be considered and admitted at other ages, and there is a direct entry into the Sixth Form for eligible pupils.

Curriculum. Our broad and stimulating curriculum combines to spark imaginations, inspire creative thinking and broaden horizons. We know that at Royal Russell, the best progress takes place with girls and boys learning together, problem solving and benefiting from different interpretations, perspectives and approaches.

Facilities. Our campus provides excellent academic and sporting facilities which include a well-resourced School Library, a new Science block, a Performing Arts Centre, spacious areas for Art, Design Technology, Food Science and Photography, a Media Studies Suite, a multi-million pound sports complex including a full-size floodlit Astroturf pitch, three all-weather training pitches and a swimming pool. Sixth Form pupils enjoy use of a Sixth Form Study Centre and Drapers' Cafe.

Organisation. Pupils perform best when they feel secure, accepted and supported. Our pastoral approach is highly valued by our pupils and their parents and is strengthened by our House System. The houses are at the centre of school life, with each pupil allocated to one of nine houses, led by a dedicated team including a personal tutor who gets to know each child well and understand their interests, aspirations and concerns.

Games. We offer an extensive range of sports for quality participation, fitness and fun including football, hockey, cricket, netball, tennis, swimming and athletics. Badminton, basketball, table tennis, trampolining and volleyball are also played.

Music, Drama and Art. Music and Drama play a prominent role at Royal Russell. Activity centres on our Performing Arts Centre at the heart of our campus. Our Drama department is lively and dynamic, offering all pupils the opportunity to take part, both within the curriculum and as a co-curricular activity and our thriving Music department has a reputation for excellence with many pupils achieving significant musical success. Pupils have opportunities to perform in many concerts, with Jazz, Swing and Samba Bands, Orchestra and the Chamber Choir and Barbershop. Our Art, Photography, Media, Food and Design Technology departments nurture the creative streak in every pupil.

Careers. The Head of Careers coordinates careers advice, giving individual counselling and helping with university applications and the School is a member of the Career Development Institute whose services are available to all pupils.

Clubs and Activities. With a programme of over 100 clubs and activities, all pupils are encouraged to participate. The school's involvement in the Model United Nations programme is renowned, with our annual International MUN conference, attracting over 500 student delegates from all over the world. There is a flourishing voluntary Combined Cadet Force and Duke of Edinburgh's Award scheme; the Theatre Society takes advantage of the school's proximity to London's theatres, and the annual ski trip is always over-subscribed.

Junior School. The aim in the Junior School is to instil a lifelong love of learning with a strong academic focus and extensive range of clubs and activities. Breakfast Club and after-school care is available. The Junior and Early Years Section provides a happy, secure and purposeful environment and the majority of children transfer to the Senior School after Year 6. (*For full details please see our entry in the IAPS section.*)

Scholarships. A number of scholarships are available each year to pupils aged 11+ to 13+, in music, drama, art or sport. Sixth Form scholarships are also awarded annually.

Fees per term (2021–2022). Senior School: Boarders £13,168 (Years 7–13); Day £6,662 (Years 7–13 inclusive of lunch). Junior School: Years 5–6 £5,126 and Years 3–4 £4,926 (inclusive of lunch, after-school clubs and supper), Reception to Year 2 £4,023 (inclusive of lunch), Nursery £2,415–£4,023.

Religion. The school's religious affiliation is to the Church of England but pupils of all faiths and none are welcome. Our approach to daily life is founded on Christian principles and we maintain an atmosphere of mutual respect and understanding.

Charitable status. Russell School Trust is a Registered Charity, number 271907. It exists solely for the education of boys and girls.

Patron: Her Majesty The Queen

Board of Governors and Trustees:
Chair: Mr A Merriman

Mrs V Agyei-Boateng	Mr J D Lacey
Prof A Ansari	Mr A Lorie
Mr N Cobill	Mrs A Martin
Mr P Dawson	Mr A Roach-Bowler
Dr A Fernandes	Sir Philip Moor
Mrs L Jessup	Mrs M Norris
Ms J Smith	Mr J Penny

Senior School:

Headmaster: Mr Christopher Hutchinson, BMet, FRSA

Deputy Head People: Mrs Nathalie Hart, Licence D'Histoire, PDC
Deputy Head Learning: Mrs Nikki Snelgrove, MSc, MA

Director of International Relations: Mr Graham Moseley, BEd Hons, MA
Director of International Relations: Mr David Selby, BA Hons

Director of Operations & Clerk to the Governors: Mr Neil Cufley
Admissions Registrar: Mrs Katie James

The Royal School Dungannon

2 Ranfurly Road, Dungannon BT71 6EG, Northern Ireland

Tel: 028 8772 2710
email: info@rsd.dungannon.ni.sch.uk
website: www.royaldungannon.com
Twitter: @RoyalDungannon

Motto: *Perseverando* (*Excellence through Perseverance*)

In 1608 James I made an order in Privy Council establishing six Royal Schools in Ulster of which Dungannon became, in 1614, the first to admit pupils. In 1983 plans were first drawn up to incorporate the neighbouring girls' grammar school and to use both campuses' excellent facilities for co-educational purposes. This development came to fruition in 1986. A £9 million building and refurbishment programme began in 2000 and was completed in 2003, providing very high-tech specialist accommodation in science, technology and IT. In 2007 an international standard Astroturf hockey pitch was completed with flood lighting and four new all-weather tennis courts were opened. Annual investment by Governors in the school's infrastructure has continued allowing RSD staff and pupils to enjoy excellent facilities.

For nearly four centuries the Royal School has aimed at providing an education which enables its pupils to achieve the highest possible standards of academic excellence and at developing each pupil into a mature, well-balanced and responsible adult, well-equipped for the demands of a highly complex and technological world.

There are four Houses which foster the competitive instincts and idiosyncrasies of young people. Pastorally, each year is supervised by a Head of Year who guides his/her pupils throughout the child's career in a caring school environment.

The Boarding Department provides accommodation for 54 Boarders with the Girls and Boys housed in separate wings of the modernised Old School building dating from 1789. The recently refurbished facilities include a new kitchen/dining area, recreation area with flat screen TV and games console, new furniture in all dormitories and fully regulated wireless internet throughout. There are a number of staff who assist in the Boarding Department, including a Head of Boarding, a team of seven resident teaching staff, a team of 5 day and evening matrons, and a large number of support staff. These staff all work together to ensure that high standards of care and support are maintained. The School is also serviced by a team of local doctors and dentists who support the Boarders. A major hospital is less than 30 minutes from the campus.

The extensive buildings are a mixture of ancient and modern, with recently opened technology and science accommodation. Eight well-equipped Science Laboratories, Audio/Visual Room, two Libraries, Sixth Form Centre and Study Rooms, Technology, two Music and Art Studios and two Information Technology Suites are supplemented by a

Boarding Department housed in well-appointed accommodation which has been completely renovated in the recent times. Boarders are able to make use of a wide range of facilities such as Sports Hall, Computer Laboratory, Multi-gym, Badminton Courts, Television Lounges, satellite TV, high-speed broadband (including Skype) and nearby facilities such as the local swimming pool and extensive parkland walks. Situated in its own spacious grounds in a quiet residential area of this rural town, the School is linked directly by motorway to Belfast (40 minutes), two airports, cross-Channel ferries and railway stations.

The establishment of good study skills and practices is considered to be of crucial importance. The size of the School ensures that no child is overlooked in any way.

At A Level new subjects are offered such as Economics and, in collaboration with partner schools, Media Studies, Politics, Psychology and Business Studies.

Pupils are prepared for GCSE and A Levels under all the major UK Examination Boards and there is a tradition of Oxbridge successes as well as a high rate of entry to the University of Ulster, Queen's University Belfast and other leading British Universities. In most years around 95% of the Upper Sixth Form proceed to Higher Education. The School's overseas students typically choose to enrol both at UK universities and universities in their home country.

Many co-curricular pursuits are encouraged during lunchtime or after school, such as Choir, Orchestra, Duke of Edinburgh's Award scheme, Chess, Charities, Debating, Public Speaking and many more.

Alongside the School's academic achievements in both Arts and Sciences may be placed its record in the sporting world: in Rugby, Hockey, Cricket, Badminton, Shooting, Table Tennis and Tennis.

Fees per annum (2021–2022). Day: £150. 7-Day Boarding: £11,700, £21,000 (non-UK/non-EU citizens). 5-Day Boarding: £8,400.

Charitable status. The Royal School Dungannon is a Registered Charity, number XN46588 A. It was established by Royal Charter in 1608 for the purpose of education.

Board of Governors:
Chairman: Dr G Walsh, BEd, PhD, ALCH, FHEA
Vice Chairman: R Patton, BA

Members:
Mrs J Anderson, BA Hons, MCIPD
K Black, BEd
Mrs T Boyd
D N Browne, MIB, MIMgt
Mrs W Chambers, BSc, MEd, PGCE, DipIT
R J Clingan, BSc, MEd, PGCE, PQH NI
Dr B A Curran, BA, MA, PhD, PGCE
J C M Eddie
R Eitel
Mrs R Emerson, BSc, CSP
G Ferry, BSc
Mrs Y Halliday, BEd Hons
Mrs E Harkness, BL
Mrs G Leonard
Lord Maginnis of Drumglass, PC
Dr D Maguire, BDS
Mrs L McDonald
K McGuinness, BSc, PGCE
N H McLean, LLB, MBA
Dr H G McNeill, BA, MB, FFARCSW

Dr P G Steen, PhD, BSc, CPhys, MInstP
Revd A S Thompson, MA, BD
Mrs J Williamson, BA, MSc, PGCE, CPsychol AEP, HPCP
J G Willis LLB
I A Wilson, BSc, PGCE

Secretary to the Governors: The Headmaster

Headmaster: Dr D A Burnett, BA, PhD, NPQH

Teaching Staff:
* *Head of Department*
[1] *Head of Year*
[2] *Head of House*

Deputy Head: R J Clingan, BSc, MEd, PGCE, PQH NI

Senior Teacher: *G R Black, BSc, PGCE
Senior Teacher: *Miss A E Chestnutt, BSc, MEd, PGCE
Senior Teacher: Mrs C L Kerr, BA, MEd, PGCE

Head of Boarding: Miss S Winslow

Mrs A Best, BA, PGCE
*N J Canning, BEng, PGCE
*R E Chambers, BSc, PGCE
*Mrs W Y Chambers, BSc, MEd, PGCE, Dip IT
Miss K L Clarke, BMus, PGCE
Miss S A Colgan, BSc, PGCE
*S J Cuddy, BMus, PGCE
[1]Mrs A Gilkinson, MSc, PGCE
Mrs G S Glenn, BSc, PGCE
J R Graham, BA, MSc, PGCE
*Mrs R L Hampton, BSc, PGCE
*[1]J W Hunniford, BA, MA, PGCE
*Mrs S J Jackson, BA, MEd, PGCE
*P S Kerr, BA, MSc, PGCE
[1]G S R Lucas, BSc, PGCE
[2]Mrs P L Matthews, BEd, PGCE
*[2]G W McClintock, BSc, PGCE
Miss D McCombe, BSc, PGCE
Mrs C E McMcCormick, BA, PGCE
[1]Mrs S J McCullough, BA, PGCE
M McDowell, BA, MA, PGCE
*K McGuinness, BSc, PGCE
Mrs L McGurk, BSc, PGCE
*Miss H Montgomery, BSc, PGCE
*P G Moore, MA, PGCE, GC, TEFL
Mrs N G Peden, BEd
*Ms A M Prescott, BEd, MEd
[2]A S Ritchie, BSc, PGCE
*[2]Mrs D Robb, BSc, PGCE
Mrs L Shaw, BA Hons, PGCE
Mrs A V Simpson, BSc, PGCE
*Mrs J Stewart, BSc Hons, PGCE, DIS
[1]Mrs E V Stitt, BA, PGCE
*Mrs A R Straghan, BSc Econ, PGCE
Mrs V I Troughton, BA, PGCE
A T Turner, BSc, PGCE
[1]G T Watterson, MSc, PGCE
[1]J W Willis, BEd Hons
I A Wilson, BSc, PGCE

Chaplain: Vacant

Administrative Staff:
Bursar: Mr D Wheeler, BSc Econ, FCA
Headmaster's Secretary: Mrs A Cullen

Matrons:
Mrs M Willis, SRN (*Day*)
Mrs C Saygi (*Evening*)
Mrs J Caddoo (*Evening*)
Ms M Campbell (*Evening*)

Rugby School

Rugby, Warwickshire CV22 5EH

Tel: 01788 556201 (Executive Head)
          01788 556216 (Head)
          01788 556260 (COO)
          01788 556274 (Admissions Registrar)
email: head@rugbyschool.net (Head)
          executivehead@rugbyschool.net (Executive
          Head Master)
          coo@rugbyschool.net (COO)
          admissions@rugbyschool.net (Admissions
          Registrar)
website: www.rugbyschool.co.uk
Twitter: @RugbySchool1567
Facebook: @RugbySchool1567
Instagram: @rugbyschool1567
LinkedIn: /school/rugby-school

'*Results of the staff and pupils innovative thinking and hard work are seen through sky rocketing results in academia, sport and the arts*' *(Tatler Schools Guide 2021).*

Ethos. Rugby, probably more than any other school in the land, focusses on helping our students become 'whole' people – people who are multi-faceted in their interests, talents and ambitions. Here, we do not just say 'the whole person is the whole point', we live it, every hour of every day.

Here, students flourish in a supportive and spiritually aware community which challenges learners, develops resilience and encourages intellectual risk-taking. We foster academic excellence and nurture individual talents enabling our students to develop a lifelong love of learning, while achieving outstanding results.

Executive Head Master, Peter Green, believes responsiveness, intellectual agility, flexibility and rigour will be the potent weapons for our students as they enter their post-school world.

"As a full boarding school, with an impressive staff: pupil ratio, we aim for the outstanding, in breadth and in depth. For example, our students continue with their sport, music, drama throughout their exams because they love doing these things and it gives both balance and perspective," he said.

Head, Gareth Parker-Jones, said he believes Rugby to have succeeded when a spark is created in the mind of the student, be it in the classroom, on the sports field, in the music rooms, on stage, in the art studios, or around any sort of activity.

"What I see here, time and time again, is that once a student becomes good at one thing and enjoys doing it, they soon become good at something else. And then something else again. In this way Rugby helps our students form the habit of doing things well – of being good at life," he added.

This, of course, owes a huge amount to Rugby being a true seven-day-a-week boarding school, along with two day

houses open from 7.00am to 10.00pm, there is the space and time to accommodate hundreds of activities – some academic, many not. Rugbeians are very busy, and that teaches vital life skills of prioritisation and organisation.

Academically, the last six years of exam grades have been Rugby's best yet, but while excellence is celebrated nobody is ever on bench. If 32 netball teams are needed to ensure every student gets to play a fixture, that is what happens.

And this is why we are the leading co-educational boarding school in the country.

Number of students. 868 (45% girls, 55% boys).

Location. Enjoying a central location just 48 minutes by train from London and close to the M6, M1 and Birmingham Airport, Rugby School offers the best of all worlds – a leafy green 150-acre campus of the edge of the countryside but still part of the town.

Facilities. A rich, cultural heritage runs through the core of the School with many buildings of architectural distinction from the impressive Chapel to the splendid Temple Speech Room. Step away from the town and enter another world of ancient cloisters and elegant quads punctuated by swathes of green.

The facilities are, however, state-of-the-art including a purpose-built Modern Languages building, an impressive Science Centre, a Design Centre featuring The Lewis Gallery with its dedicated art and exhibition space and a huge new sixth form centre for A Level subjects and the IB Diploma Programme, new from 2021.

The Music Schools have also been extended and refurbished to include 40 teaching/practice rooms, technology classrooms, recording studio and a small concert hall. Students regularly get to perform with the School's professional orchestra.

Sports facilities are equally impressive including a modern Sports Centre, with its 25m pool, fitness suite and courts, three new AstroTurf hockey pitches, soccer and rugby fields and hard courts for tennis and netball. Our polo fields mark the boundary of this wide-reaching campus. Sport at Rugby includes athletics, badminton, basketball, cricket, cross-country, fencing, fives, football, golf, gymnastics, hockey, netball, polo, rackets, rugby, sailing, squash, swimming and tennis. Every student has access to professional sports coaching and conditioning and there is a dedicated athletes programme.

Boarding Houses. The House structure at Rugby is central to our strong sense of community. Ideas flourish best where they were originated and it was our pioneering Head Master, Dr Thomas Arnold, who initiated the boarding house system to ensure exceptional pastoral care and provide the ideal social environment in which young people could thrive.

Much copied but never bettered, more than 200 years of 'House' experience has resulted in a genuine and uncompromised care plan which supports every single student.

The 15 Houses at Rugby, each with their own unique character, in different locations and of varying sizes, but all offering a true home away from home, a real family to which every pupil belongs and is rightly proud of. An ambitious programme of improvements is currently under way.

The ethos at Rugby that the whole person is the whole point is undeniably apparent within this perfected and seamless House structure. The role of Housemaster or mistress as head of the 'family' is to create and maintain a happy and balanced home with the able support of their deputy and the Matron, who importantly are all resident. Totally committed to the well-being of their young people, this nucleus of staff provides 24-hour care that is second to none.

Day Houses. Rugby's two Day Houses, one for girls and one for boys, were expanded in 2019 to provide even better facilities and space to meet increased demand for places. They now accommodate 200 day students who all benefit from the depth and breadth of a boarding experience.

Academic. *GCSE*: All the usual subjects are offered as well as Computing, German, Spanish, Latin, Greek, Design, Art, Music, PE, Theatre Studies and Religious Studies.

IB and A Level: Rugby now offers the IB Diploma. Alongside the core, CAS, Theory of Knowledge, Extended Essay and the traditional subjects, the list extends to far more including Theatre, Literature and Performance, Mandarin and Italian *Ab initio*, Psychology, Global Politics and Environmental Systems and Societies. A Level is offered in all the GCSE subjects as well as in Business Studies, Economics, Graphics, Textiles and Politics and students have the opportunity to pursue an Extended Project. All go on to Higher Education with an impressive number of students achieving Oxbridge places during the past three years.

A diverse programme of academic enrichment is an integral part of a Rugby education with all students attending at least three clubs and societies each week. Academic societies, many of which are student-driven, invite a wide range of eminent figures to the School – speakers have included Rowan Williams, Ambassador Frank Wisner, Anthony Horowitz, Poet Laureate Carol Ann Duffy and Dame Tanni Grey-Thompson.

Spiritual Life. A well-balanced individual needs a sense of spiritual awareness along with academic achievement and physical ability. The experience of holiness, an understanding of right and wrong, and respect for the worth of each human being; these things are the invisible glue holding our community together. These values are learned in every part of our lives, but the School Chapel and the activities connected with it are a particular focus for our spiritual development.

The Chaplains get to know the boys and girls by sharing meals, visiting the Houses and involving themselves with all the School's activities. They also share the teaching of the younger students, giving them regular contact with the entire Lower School.

Co-curricular. The co-curricular programme plays a huge part in the meaning of 'Whole' in our Whole Person Whole Point ethos. Our community is thriving, exciting, inclusive and full of opportunities for students to find inspiration, fun, challenge, curiosity, confidence and fulfilment. We believe growing as a person, developing into the type of adult students want to be, involves making choices, especially in how you spend your time. We offer as many opportunities as possible, not only on the academic route through school, but in our wide range of other activities. Every year the list gets longer as students make their own suggestions for new enterprises.

There are some incredible trips organised annually such as hockey, netball and rugby tours to Australia; World Challenge programmes have included Madagascar and Bolivia, cricket tours to India and Dubai, debating in Croatia, a Spanish trip to Costa Rica and Philosophy expeditions to Northern India.

Admission. At 11+ local boys and girls may be assessed for entry into Year 9 as day students. At 13+ offers of boarding places are made on the basis of previous school's report and interviews during Year 7, subject to CE at average 55% at least, or the School's own Maths and English tests, or scholarship entry.

At 16+: offers of places for boarders and day students on the basis of previous school's report, interview and written entrance tests during Year 11, subject to at least three A (or 7) grades and three B (or 6) grades or above (including English and Mathematics) and in the subjects chosen for A Level (and IB from 2021).

Scholarships. Our scholarship provision is designed to attract boys and girls of outstanding talent and skill in a variety of fields. We value scholarship of all sorts. Through the excellence of our academic provision and of our facilities we aim to foster high achievement at all levels and to challenge expectations. The interplay of teaching and learning, and the experiences to be gained from being part of a rich and diverse community, encourage all students to develop their talents and to emerge as confident, well-rounded individuals.

13+ (Year 9) Academic Scholarships: Examinations are held in February of Year 8.

16+ (Year 12) Academic Scholarships: Scholarship interviews are held in mid-November of Year 11. Candidates must first take the Sixth Form Entrance Examination and those showing scholarship potential will be called for Scholarship interviews.

Music Scholarships: Awarded each year at 13+ and 16+. At 13+ with assessment auditions held at Rugby School in late January of the year of entry. At 16+ the audition is held in November as part of the 16+ entrance procedure.

Art Scholarships: Awarded each year at 13+ and at 16+. At 13+ the assessment takes place in March of Year 8. At 16+, it is in November as part of the 16+ entrance procedure.

Design and Technology Scholarships: Awarded each year at 13+ and at 16+. At 13+ the assessment takes place in March of Year 8. At 16+ it is in November as part of the 16+ entrance procedure.

Sports Scholarships: At 13+ and 16+ for candidates with outstanding ability or potential in the major team games for boys (rugby, hockey, cricket and tennis) or girls (hockey, netball and tennis). At 13+ the assessment takes place in November of Year 8. At 16+ it is in October of Year 11.

Performing Arts Scholarships: A number of Performing Arts Scholarships are awarded each year at 13+ and 16+ to candidates with outstanding acting ability or potential. At 16+ there are also scholarships for technical ability in performing arts. At 13+ the assessment takes place in October of Year 8. At 16+ it is in October of Year 11.

Computing Scholarships: Awarded each year at 13+ and 16+. At 13+ the assessment takes place in May of Year 8. At 16+ it is in November as part of the 16+ entrance procedure.

Foundation Awards: Several Foundation Awards are made annually to day boy and day girl candidates at 13+ and 16+. These candidates must live within a radius of 20 miles from the Rugby Clock Tower – excluding the city of Coventry.

Awards and Augmentation: The value of a Scholarship Award or a Foundation Award (including more than one award) is a maximum fee concession of 5%. Support can be augmented up to 100% of the day fees subject to means assessment.

The Arnold Foundation aims to raise funds through charitable donations to support the education of talented boys and girls whose families would not be able to fund boarding school fees. Funds are available for several awards for entry to the sixth form and at 13+. Students offered a place through this scheme may be awarded up to 100% of the full boarding fee plus extras. The final selection is through interviews. Candidates are expected to pass the school's normal entrance requirements. Initial enquiries should be made via the Admissions Office

For further information and details of all Scholarships, Foundation Awards and The Arnold Foundation please contact the Admissions Registrar, Tel: 01788 556274, email: admissions@rugbyschool.net.

Fees per term (2021–2022) The consolidated termly fee for boys and girls: £12,818 (boarding), £8,042 (day).

Further Information. Visit: www.rugbyschool.co.uk. Enquiries and applications should be made in the first instance to the Registrar.

Charitable status. The Governing Body of Rugby School is a Registered Charity, number 528752. It exists to provide education for young people.

Governing Body:

B J O'Brien (*Chairman*)
R J A Elmhirst, LLB (*Deputy Chairman, Finance & Audit*)
P Smulders, BA, MBA
Ms C J Marten, MA
Ms G Woodward, BA
Mrs J Eastwood, BA
Mrs H Jackson, BSc
J R Moreland, MA, PGCE, NPQH
General Sir Tim Radford, KCB, DSO, OBE
R C Fletcher, FRSA, MBA, MPhil
J C F Barwell, BA, FCSI, OBE
D Skailes, BSc, FCA
Mrs C Wills
N Bacon, FCA, CTA
Mrs A Pantelis, BA, NPQH
The Reverend Canon Dr R M Pryce
S R T Penniston (*Associate Governor for RS Thailand*)
T B Cox (*Honorary Governor*)

Chief Operating Officer and Clerk to the Governing Body:
P A Nicholls, MA, FCA

Medical Officer: Dr H Collier, MB, ChB, DRCOG, MRCGP

Rugby School Group

Executive Head Master: P R A Green, MA, PGCE

Deputy Executive Head Master: Dr N G Hampton, MA, PhD, PGCE

Rugby School

Head: G Parker-Jones, MA, PGCE

Deputy Heads:
Mrs S A Rosser, BEd (*Pastoral*)
E S Davies, BA, MSc, PGCE (*Academic*)
Mrs L M Hampton, BEd, MSc (*Co-Curricular*)

Assistant Heads:
Dr G C E Joyce, BSc, PhD, PGCE (*Upper School*)
Miss R J Force, BSc (*Middle School*)

Dr J D Muston, MA, MPhil, DPhil (*Formation*)
P K Bell, MA, MSc, PGCE (*Houses*)

Admissions Registrar: H G Steele-Bodger, MA, PGCE

Teaching Staff:
* *Head of Department*

Chaplaincy:
The Revd R M Horner, BSc (*Chaplain*)
Miss L Greatwood, BSc, DipMin, PGCE
D R Shaw, MA, PGCE

Classics:
W D Nicholl, BA, MA*
Dr F B Chesterton, BA, MA, PhD, PGCE
T J Day, BA, PGCE
Ms S R Harris, BA, MSt, PGCE
X J Pollock, BA, MA, MPhil

Computer Science:
I Kurgansky, MSc, PGCE*
T E Rennoldson, BSc, PGCE
Mrs L A Bell, BEng

Design:
B J Welch, BEng, PGCE (*D&T*)*
J Ryan, BA, BTech, PGCE, MFA (*Art*)*
M Cuff, BA, PGCE (*Art*)
J Brown, BA, MA, PGCE
Miss E. Hampson, BA
Miss A K Janulewicz, BA, PGCE (*D&T*)
Mrs S E Phillips, BA, QTS (*Art, Ceramics*)
O Selfridge, BA, MA
D H Wright, BA, MA, PGCE

Economics and Business:
Mrs H L McPherson, BSc, MSc, PGCE*
A M Burge, BSc, PGCE
Miss H Burrows, BA, PGCE
Miss A Dudhia, BSc, MSc
J Oberst, BA, MBA

English:
T Eyre-Maunsell, MA, MA, PGCE*
Mrs M Baker, BA, PGCE
H Dhesi, MA, BA, PGCE
Mrs N B Lockhart-Mann, BA, HDipEd, MSc
Mrs E M Moyle, BA, MA
Dr J H Moyle, BA, MA, PhD
Ms A Scott-Martin, MA, MA, PGCE
Dr A T Shaw, BA, MA, PhD, PGCE
A N Smith, MA, MTeach, PGCE
Dr J A Sutcliffe, PhD

Geography:
R Ghosh, BSc, PGCE*
Miss A Abrahams, BA, PGCE
Miss P Battison, BSc, PGCE
J C Evans, BA, PGCE
Dr L E Milner, MA, MSc, PhD
Mrs S A Rosser, BEd
L D Shepherd, BSc, PGCE
D W Wood, BA, PGCE

History:
Dr T D Guard, MA, MSt, DPhil, PGCE*
Miss C V Barnett, BA, PGCE, NPQH
E S Davies, BA, MSc, PGCE
Dr M E Fowle, BA, MA, PhD, PGCE
Miss K Hollings, BA
Mrs M H Mahalski, MA, GDL, LPC, PGCE

Dr J D Muston, MA, MPhil, DPhil
G Parker-Jones, MA, PGCE
Dr T W Smith, BA, MA, PhD, PGCE, FRHistS, FRAS
J M Stedman, BA

IB Co-ordinator:
Mrs N B Lockhart-Mann, BA, HDipEd, MSc

Learning Development:
Mrs L J E Stevenson, LLB, Dip SpLD, Adv Dip, CPT3A*
Miss A G Bedson, BA, MA, PGCE
Mrs A L Cunningham-Batt, MA, OCR Cert SpLD, CPT3A
Mrs B Green, MA, MEd, Level 7 Diploma SpLD, PGCE

Mathematics:
N Jones, MA, MEng, PGCE*
W Uglow, BSc, PGCE (*Second i/c*)
M R Baker, BA, PGCE
P K Bell, MA, MSc, PGCE
Ms H C S Casson, BA, MA, FIA, FRSS, PGCE
Miss R J Force, BSc
Mrs N Good, MA, MMath, PGCE
I Kurgansky, MSc, PGCE
B L Lane, MA, MSc, PGCE
A Langstone, MA, BSc, PGCE
Mrs S C McGuirk, BEng, PGCE, NPQML
B J Rigg, MA, ACA
D R Shaw, MA, PGCE
Mrs L J Sheehan, MA, BA, PGCE
A J Siggers, BSc, PGCE

Modern Languages:
C M Brown, BA, PGCE*
Dr A C Leamon, BA, MA, PhD (*French*)*
Mrs C A O'Mahoney, BA, PGCE (*Spanish*)*
Dr B Parolin, BA, MA, PhD, PGCE (*Italian*)*
G Arnoux, MA
J Cerezuela Ortega, BA, MA
S Foulds, BA, PGCE
Ms C Piquard, MA
Ms B S Sanchez Alonso, BA, BA, PGCE
R Sanchez Saura, BA, MA, PGCE
Dr J C Smith, MA, DPhil, PGCE

Music:
R J Tanner, MA, FRCO, ARAM, Hon FGCM (*Director of Music*)
Miss V Brandwood, BMus, PGCE (*Academic Music Teacher*)
A R Davey, LTCL (*Contemporary Music*)
I Foster, BMus, PGDip (*GSMD*), QTS (*Music Partnerships*)
Miss R Taylor, MA, MA, Dip ABRSM, LRAM, ATCL
M Sandy, MMus, MA (*Cantab*) DipABRSM (*Vocal Studies*)
I Wicks, BSc, PGCE (*Keyboard*)
J A Williams, MA, BA, Dip ABRSM, PGCE (*Academic Music*)

Philosophy and Theology:
Mrs P Hollebon, BA, PGCE*
Revd R M Horner, BSc
Miss L J Greatwood, BSc, Dip Min, PGCE
Miss R James BA, PGCE

Sports Science:
Miss E M Watton, BA, PGCE (*PE*)*
Mrs D L Skene, BSc, PGCE (*Director of Sport*)
H Burke, BSc
H C Chamberlain, BSc, PGDip, PGCE

Mrs L M Hampton, MSc, BEd

Politics and International Relations:
P Teeton, BA, MA*
Miss A F Griffiths, BA, MSc

Psychology:
Mrs B Green, MA, MEd, Level 7 Diploma SpLD, PGCE

Science:
S P Robinson, BSc, PGCE, MRes*
Dr D Tchakhotine, BSc, PhD, PGCE (*Biology*)*
Dr S R Belding, MChem, DPhil (*Chemistry*)*
R Parker, BSc, PGCE (*Physics*)*
Dr M A Thompson, BSc, PhD, PGCE (*Science Enrichment & Outreach*)
Dr S A Crabb, BSc, PhD
Dr A G Davies, BSc, PhD, PGCE
R Dhanda, BSc, QTS
N A Fisher, BSc, MSc, MA, FInstP, PGCE
M Forth, MA, MChem, PGCE
Miss L J Greatwood, BSc, Dip Min, PGCE
Dr L M Hampton, BEd, MSc
Dr N G Hampton, MA, PhD, PGCE
Dr G C E Joyce, BSc, PhD, PGCE
Mrs R Lam, BSc PGCE
R B McGuirk, BSc, MSc, PGCE
M A Monteith, BSc, PGCE
Dr N J Morse, BSc, PhD, CChem, FRSC
Mrs E A Robinson, BSc, PGCE, MEd
Mrs E L Sale, BSc, PGCE
Dr P Thill, MEng, PhD, PGCE
Dr A A Wheatley, MA, MSci, PhD, PGCE
T M White, BSc, PGCE

Theatre Studies & Performing Arts:
Dr T D Coker, BA, MMus, MPhil, PhD (*Artistic Director*)
Dr S L Hancox, BA, MA, PhD (*Drama*)*
C J Browning
A K Chessell, BA, MSc, PGCE
Miss K C Thompson, BA (*LAMDA*)*

Careers and Higher Education:
Mrs D J Horner, BA*
Ms L Waweru, BPhilEd, PQCG
Mrs C Wheeler, BSc, PG Dip, QCG

Keeper of Scholars (and Oxbridge):
Dr A G Davies, BSc, PHd, PGCE (*Science & Mathematics*)
Dr T W Smith, BA, MA, PhD, PGCE, FRHistS, FRAS (*Arts & Humanities*)

PSHE Education:
Miss L J Greatwood, BSc, Dip Min, PGCE*

Sport:
Mrs D L Skene, BSc, PGCE (*Director of Sport*)
M Bayley, BSc (*Director of Rugby*)
M J Powell (*Director of Cricket*)
J M Stedman, BA (*Director of Hockey*)
C Folker, BCom (*Acc*) (*Director of Rackets Sports*)
N T Atley, MSc (*Strength & Conditioning Coach*)
Mrs A Canning (*Netball Development Officer*)
N Tester (*Head of Co-curricular Recruitment*)

Houses and Housemasters/mistresses:

Boarding Houses (boys):
Cotton: Mr Michael Powell
Kilbracken: Mr Saul Foulds
Michell: Mr Tim Day
School Field: Mr Mindy Dhanda

School House: Mr Andrew Smith
Sheriff: Mr Maurice Monteith
Whitelaw: Mr Chris Evans

Day Boy House:
Town: Mr Andrew Chessell

Boarding Houses (girls):
Bradley: Mrs Liz Sale
Dean: Dr Leanne Milner
Griffin: Mrs Liz Robinson
Rupert Brooke: Miss Katie Hollings
Stanley (Sixth Form only): Ms A Scott-Martin
Tudor: Mrs Debbie Horner

Day Girl House:
Southfield: Mrs Michelle Baker

Director of Development: Mrs K Wilson, BA

Ryde School with Upper Chine

Queen's Road, Ryde, Isle of Wight PO33 3BE

Tel: 01983 562229
email: school.office@rydeschool.net
website: www.rydeschool.org.uk
Twitter: @RydeSchool
Facebook: @RydeSchool
Instagram: @rydeschoolwithupperchine

Motto: '*Ut Prosim*'

Ryde School with Upper Chine is a day and boarding school providing education for boys and girls aged 2 ½ to 18. It is situated on the South Coast of England, a ten minute boat ride from Portsmouth on the Isle of Wight. Ryde School was founded in 1921 to provide a Christian education for boys. Upper Chine was founded as a Girls' School in Shanklin on the Isle of Wight in 1914. The two schools merged in 1994 to form Ryde School with Upper Chine and in 1996 the School acquired the buildings of Bembridge School. As a result of these acquisitions and mergers the School is now fully co-educational. Boarding provision is on the main school site in Ryde in two new boarding houses; a beautifully renovated Victorian villa for pupils to age 15 and a new purpose-built and award-winning building for Years 11 to Upper Sixth.

Situation and Buildings. The School stands in its own grounds of 17 acres in Ryde with stunning views over the Solent and is easily accessible from all parts of the Island and the near mainland. It is within walking distance of the terminals which link Ryde to Portsmouth by hovercraft (10 minutes) or catamaran (25 minutes) and a number of pupils travel daily from the mainland. In recent years there have been many additions to the School buildings with modern Art and CDT departments, eight science labs which have all been recently fully refurbished, a new Health and Wellbeing Centre, new tennis and netball courts, a new coffee shop for parents, staff and pupils, a new gym and a dedicated Sixth Form centre.

One boarding house has been stylishly refurbished to preserve the Victorian identity of the building whilst the second is a completely contemporary build overlooking the sea.

Organisation and Curriculum. As an IB World and Round Square School, the School aims to provide a world class education on the Isle of Wight enabling boarders and day pupils to flourish in mind, body and soul, nurturing the character, skills and values to help them make a positive difference and embrace the opportunities of the wider world.

In the Junior School, strong emphasis is placed on core skills, proficiency in reading, writing and number work and strong focus on STEM, sports and outdoor learning. All pupils in the Junior School get the opportunity to sail. Pupils are prepared for entry into the Senior School, and, following a recommendation from the Junior School, they are offered places in the Senior School at the age of 11. We also prepare pupils to move to specialist mainland schools and pupils have recently won scholarships to Winchester and Millfield.

In Years 7 and 8 we run a two-year diploma programme authorised by the PSB (Pre Senior Baccalaureate), "Ryde Global". The programme of work in the Senior School is designed to provide a broad but challenging education up to the end of Year 11 with all pupils working towards the Ryde EBacc. The subjects taught to IGCSE/GCSE level are English Language and Literature, Mathematics, Physics, Chemistry, Biology, French, German, Latin, Mandarin, Spanish, ESL, Geography, History, Business Studies, Art, Music, Academic PE, Drama, Computer Science and Design Technology. All pupils select an Elective subject from: Global Perspectives, Arts Award, Science CREST Award, Informatics or additional English and Maths to add breadth. All pupils also follow a programme of Personal Development (PD) and Games.

In the Sixth Form, pupils choose from three routes: the IB Diploma, 'A Level Plus' (3 A Levels plus various enrichment and extension options) and the IBCP (An IB certificate that combines academic courses alongside vocational qualifications in one of Business, Art or Sport). In addition, pupils are encouraged to take the Extended Project Qualification, designed to add breadth to their academic studies. Courses lead to entrance to universities, the Services, industry and the professions. The careers team provides advice and guidance to all pupils who go on to a variety of universities and careers, including Oxbridge, medical schools, arts colleges and other Russell Group Universities.

Tutorial System. Each pupil has a tutor who is responsible for his or her academic and personal progress and general pastoral welfare. The tutorial system encourages close contact with parents, which is further reinforced by parents' meetings which are held at regular intervals and a parent portal. The School aims to maintain sound discipline and good manners within a traditionally friendly atmosphere and encourages pupils to live up to the School motto "Ut Prosim".

Games. The main games in the Senior School are hockey, rugby and cricket for the boys, and hockey, netball and cricket for the girls with sailing and athletics also a big focus. Girls' football and rugby are also offered. In the Junior School, football is also played. Other games include basketball, rounders, croquet, squash, golf, swimming, rowing and tennis. Regular matches are arranged at all levels against teams both on the Island and the mainland. There are many opportunities for sailing, both keel boat and in the School's own fleet of dinghies. Many pupils compete for the School and for local clubs and nationally.

Music and Drama. The Music Department incorporates practice and teaching facilities and a well-equipped recording studio. The School has a flourishing choral tradition, with opportunities for participation in a variety of choirs and instrumental groups. Concerts and musical plays are performed in both Senior and Junior Schools, and concert tours abroad have taken place in recent years. Full-length plays are produced each year by both Senior and Junior Schools, and special attention is given in the English lessons of the younger forms to speaking, lecturing and acting. Musical Theatre is a particular strength. The School has its own theatre and studio theatre and a School Poet. Last year a music scholar won the Keyboard section of the BBC Young Musician 2020 and May 2022 will see the opening of a new Performing Arts Centre within the school grounds.

Activities. Pupils are expected to take part in extracurricular activities and there is a wide range to choose from, including the Combined Cadet Force, Duke of Edinburgh's Award scheme, a flourishing debating and public speaking programme, riding, art & design clubs, sports clubs, numerous trips and the opportunity for exchange visits. The school is particularly proud of the number of pupils undertaking Gold DofE.

Boarding. Boarding for both boys and girls is available from Year 6. Full, weekly and flexi boarding options are available in two boarding houses in the school grounds.

Fees per term (from January 2022). Tuition: Foundation Stage – please see School website; Pre-Prep £2,645–£3,765; Junior School £4,575; Senior School £4,730.

Boarding (inc. tuition): Junior / Senior School: £10,265–£10,420 (full), £9,140–£9,295 (weekly).

Rates are for payment by Direct Debit.

Scholarships and Bursaries. Scholarships may be awarded on merit to external or internal candidates for entry at 9+, 11+, 13+ and 16+. All scholarships may be supplemented by bursaries, which are means-tested.

Charitable status. Ryde School is a Registered Charity, number 307409. The aims and objectives of the Charity are the education of boys and girls.

Governors:
Chairman: Mr C Lees
Vice-Chairman: Dr M Legg
Hereditary Governor: Mr A McIsaac
Chair of Finance & General Purposes: Mrs D Haig-Thomas
Chair of Education Committee: Mrs J Bland (*also Inspection*)
Mr A Crawford
Ms C Doerries, QC
Mrs M Esfandiary
Mr P Hamilton
Mrs Caroline Jacobs (*Safeguarding*)
Mr A Ramsay
Mrs J Wallace-Dutton
Mr P Weeks (*Health and Safety Committee*)

Clerk to the Governors: Mr J Marren

Head Master: Mr M A Waldron, MA Cantab, MEd

Head of the Senior School: Mr P R Moore, MA
Deputy Head: Mr B Sandford-Smith, BSc, MEd
Head of Prep: Mr E Marsden, BEd
Head of Pre-Prep: Mrs E Willetts, BA
Bursar: Mr J A F Marren, BSc, ACA
Director of Learning: Mr D Shapland, MEd

Head of Sixth Form: Mr M J Windsor, BSc
Head of Pastoral Care: Miss C B Vince, BA
Assistant Head (Academic) : Miss G S Stenning, BA
Assistant Head (Curriculum): Dr G Speller, PhD Cantab
Head of Years 7 & 8: Mr M Whillier, BSc
Head of Year 9: Mrs P Ball, BA
Head of Years 10 & 11: Miss J Dyer, BA

Senior Teachers:
Mrs E Burgess, BSc (*Geography*)
Mr A Graham, BA, HNTD (*Mathematics*)
Mr A Jackson, BA (*Head of Modern Languages*)
Mr P Pavlou, BA (*Head of Group 5/Mathematics*)

§ *Part-time*

Senior School:
Mr M Alderton, MPhys (*Physics*)
Mr F Bagnall, BSc (*Director of Sport & Fitness, PE, Head of Rugby*)
Mr H Bagnall, BSc (*Millfield Housemaster, Head of Round Square, Science & Mathematics*)
Mrs J Bagnall, BA (*Round Square Conference Coordinator, Gold Duke of Edinburgh's Award, Geography*)
Mrs P Ball, BA (*Head of Year 9, Silver Duke of Edinburgh's Award, English*)
§Ms Annika Belgrano (*English as a Second Language, Languages*)
Ms K E Bishop, BSc, BA (*Head of Psychology, Science*)
Mrs N Broughton (*Design Technology*)
§Miss S Broyé, BA, MA (*Languages*)
Mr T Bull, BA (*Head of Academic Drama, i/c Global Rock*)
Mrs M E Burgess, BSc (*Senior Teacher (Prizes), Head of Geography*)
Mr D Buyanov-Taylor, BSc (*Mathematics*)
§Mrs L Chalmers, BA (*Religious Studies*)
Mr M G Chalmers, BSc (*Head of Chemistry, Rowing*)
Mr J C Comben, BA (*Head of History, Bronze Duke of Edinburgh's Award*)
Ms V Coughlin, BA, PG Cert Special Needs (*Head of Learning Support, History*)
Mr T Dumbach, AB Harvard, MSt Oxon (*i/c Latin, US University Entrance/Scholarship*)
Miss G Dye, BTEC, PE (*Sports Coach*)
Miss J A Dyer, BA (*Head of Years 10 & 11, Languages, i/c Spanish*)
Mr H Edwards, BSc (*Assistant to Head of Years 10 & 11, Head of Hockey, Head of Academic PE*)
Dr Flaherty (*i/c Politics*)
Dr B Foreman (*Head of Science*)
Mr A M Graham, BA, HNTD (*Mathematics, Senior Teacher*)
§Mrs N Green-Appleton, BSc MSc (*Science*)
§Mrs K Hayter, BA (*History, Politics*)
§Mr J Henson, BSc DipHE (*Music*)
Mr M Hooper, BA, MA (*Head of Economics & Business Studies, BTEC Programme Leader*)
Mr L Ilott, BEd (*Centenary Housemaster, PE*)
Mrs N Ilott, BA (*English*)
Mr A Jackson, BA, PGCE, NPQH (*Head of Modern Languages, Senior Teacher – NQTs & PGCE*)
Mr A Johnston, BA (*Head of ICT*)
Ms E C Jones, BA (*English*)
Ms J Jones, BSc, MA (*EE Coordinator, Geography, English, Learning Support*)

Mr N Jones, BSc, MSc (*EPQ Coordinator, KS3 Science Coordinator, Physics*)
§Ms L Kirkby, OND (*Art*)
§Miss A Lengersdorf, BA (*Languages, i/c German*)
Miss M Lopez-Vilar (*Languages*)
Mrs C Manser, BSc, PTLLS (*Director of Sailing, Economics & Business Studies*)
Miss S Masterson, BSc (*Head of Girls Games, Head of Seaford, PE*)
Mr P R Moore, MA (*Head of Senior School, Mathematics*)
Ms A J Newman, BA (*i/c Mandarin*)
Mrs L E O'Sullivan, BSc Ed (*Head of Trinity, Mathematics*)
Mr J Parry (*Graduate Teacher, Music & Sport*)
Mr P Pavlou, BA (*Senior Teacher – Timetable, Mathematics*)
§Miss J Rann, BA (*Art*)
Mrs J Ratcliff, BA (*Art*)
Miss A Richardson (*Graduate Art & DT Teacher*)
Ms C Rose, BA (*Head of Design Technology*)
Mr B Sandford-Smith, BSc, MEd (*Deputy Head, Psychology, Ryde Global*)
Mr D Shapland, MEd (*Director of Learning, IB Coordinator, RE, Politics*)
Dr G R Speller, BSc, MPhil, PhD Cantab (*Assistant Head – Curriculum, Head of Section 7–9 – PSB*)
Miss G S Stenning, BA (*Assistant Head – Academic, Head of English Faculty*)
Mr P G Swann, BSc (*Head of Physics*)
Mr C Thornton, (*Graduate Teacher, History & Sport*)
Mr C G S Trevallion, BSc (*Head of Biology, Duke of Edinburgh's Award Coordinator*)
Mrs R F Tweddle, GTCL, LTCL (*Head of Music, Choral Director*)
Miss C Verleure, BA (*Head of Chine, Languages*)
Miss C Vince, BA (*DSL, Head of Pastoral Care, English*)
Mrs L L Waldron, BA, MEd (*2nd in Dept, Mathematics, Internal Exams*)
Mr M A Waldron, MA Cantab, MEd (*Head Master, Politics*)
Mr G Watson, BA (*History*)
Mrs J J Whillier, BSc (*Mathematics*)
Mr M Whillier, BSc (*Head of Years 7 & 8, Chemistry*)
Mr G Whitehead (*Head of Art*)
§Mr J Willetts, BSc (*Head of Religious Studies, Economics, Careers & HE Advisor*)
Mr M J Windsor, BSc (*Head of Sixth Form, Geography*)
Mr A Woodward (*Cricket Professional*)
Mr C Youlten, BA (*Head of Arts Faculty, Performance, Drama*)
Mrs W Youlten, BA (*2nd in Dept, English*)
Ms H Young, BSc (*Assistant Head of Pastoral Care – SS, Head of Hanover, Chemistry*)

Junior School:

Head of Prep: Mr E Marsden, BSc
Head of Fiveways (*Nursery and Pre-Prep*): Mrs E Willets, BA

Mrs M Bradfield, NVQ	Ms L Mattey, BSc
§Mrs S Burgess, BA	§Miss O Newnham, BEd
Mr A Gallerwood, BA	Mrs G Owen, BA
Mrs G Gallerwood, BA	Mrs E Shaw, BA
Mrs D Grubb, BA	Miss R Shaw, BEd
Mrs J Jeffery	§Mrs T Simons, BEd
Mr J Mathrick, BSc	Mrs H Vann, BA
Mr J McGouran, BA	Mrs M Walker

Fiveways (*Nursery and Pre-Prep*):
Head: Mrs E Willetts, BA (*DSL*)

Miss K Clarke, NNEB	Mrs G Marsden, BA
Mrs F Curtis, MA, EYPS	Mrs P Ong, DPP
Ms P Evans, BEd	Miss A Townson, NVQ3
Mrs S Lea, NTD	§Miss E Wheeler, BSc
Miss V Lovell, BEd	

St Albans High School for Girls

Townsend Avenue, St Albans, Hertfordshire AL1 3SJ

Tel: 01727 853 800
email: admissions@stahs.org.uk
website: www.stahs.org.uk
Twitter: @STAHS
Facebook: @stalbanshighschoolforgirls
Instagram: @stahsgirls

St Albans High School for Girls is a selective, independent day school for girls aged 4–18 years. It is uniquely placed in being able to offer all the advantages of a continuous education in two very different settings; the Prep School is based in the picturesque village of Wheathampstead whilst the Senior School enjoys a more urban setting in the heart of the historic City of St Albans.

Mission. Fostering scholarship and integrity, the High School provides inspirational and adventurous opportunities and strong support to develop a lifelong love of learning and respect for others.

Values.

STAHS is ambitious:

We pursue bold ideas in an environment where creativity, innovation and success is encouraged and celebrated. We nurture and value relationships and partnerships that foster a global outlook. We inspire and support students and staff to achieve their potential and meet the challenges of society. We challenge ourselves and each other to strive for excellence in all we do.

STAHS is open:

We work in consultation and collaboration to benefit from new perspectives. We share ideas and maintain transparency. We are trustworthy and do what we say we will do. We listen and respond to the needs of our students and staff. We value open communication with parents.

STAHS is responsible:

We act with integrity for the greater good. We insist on upholding the highest academic and professional standards, and take personal accountability for our individual and collective performance against those standards. We respect and celebrate diversity and equal opportunity through fostering inclusivity. We aim for all our activities to be sustainable and ethically sound.

Academically curious, girls here have high expectations of themselves; results are exceptional and learning fun, with the majority of girls going on to their first-choice university.

Excellent facilities for all subjects include: the Jubilee Centre – a Performing Arts Centre and Art & Technology block; a Music school, a recently-refurbished and expanded Science block, and a new state-of-the-art Sixth Form Centre.

Girls are encouraged to embrace broad horizons through participation in an extensive programme of co-curricular activities and a wealth of wide educational opportunities. Sport and music feature strongly, as do an impressive selection of clubs and societies.

Outstanding pastoral care, based on a thriving house system, ensures that girls flourish with firm support around them. They are encouraged to feel valued for their contributions to the life of our outward-looking community. Inter-house sporting, drama and public speaking competitions are held throughout the year.

We are experts in girls' education and believe that they learn best in an all-girls environment. Our aim is that they leave the school as strong, resourceful young women, equipped with the skills of independent learning and enriched by the friendships they have made here.

Fees per term (2021–2022). Reception (age 4) £5,185 (inc Lunch); Years 1 and 2 (age 5–6) £5,475 (inc Lunch); Years 3–6 (age 7–11) £5,530 (exc Lunch); Senior School £6,565 (exc Lunch).

Private music lessons, special tennis coaching, school lunch (from Year 3) and daily school coaches are all optional extras.

Scholarships. Academic, Choral, Drama, Music and Sport Scholarships are awarded annually at entry to Year 7 and Sixth Form. In addition to these, scholarships are also available for both internal and external candidates on entry to Sixth Form in Art/DT. Fees Assistance up to 100% may be awarded in cases of hardship.

Admission. Pupils are normally admitted in September at 4+, 6+ and 7+ to the Prep School and at 11+ and 16+ to the Senior School. However, applications for places occasionally available in other year groups are welcome. Girls are required to have a minimum of grade 7 or above in subjects to be studied at A Level in most subjects. We would normally expect candidates to have at least 5 grade 7s, but this is not essential as a willingness to contribute to the life of the school is also important.

Charitable status. St Albans High School for Girls is a Registered Charity, number 311065. It exists to provide an education for girls "in accordance with the principles of the Church of England".

Visitor: The Right Reverend The Lord Bishop of St Albans

Council:
Ms Alison Arnold
Mr Paul Brewster
Ms Maria Carradice
Mr David Cotter
Ms Ellie De Galleani
Mr Neil Enright
Mr Tim Gardam
Ms Nishma Gosrami
Mrs Heather Greatrex (*Chair*)
Mrs Carol Jewell
Mr Matthew Keen
Mr Simon Martin
Mr Chris Murray
Mr Daniel Roe
Mr Robert Ward

Executive Team:

Head: Mrs Amber Waite

Deputy Head Pastoral: Mrs Rachel Parker

Deputy Head Academic: Mr Drew Thomson
Bursar: Mr Paul Daly
Head of Prep School: Mrs Judy Rowe
Director of Marketing, Admissions and Development: Mrs Claire Schofield

Senior School Leadership Team:
Director of Studies: Mr Henry Cullen
Assistant Head, Co-curricular: Miss Laura Hicks
Assistant Head, Head of Sixth Form: Mrs Helen Monighan
Assistant Head, Academic Development: Mr Jonathan Marshall
Assistant Head, Operations: Miss Kirsty Eddison

Senior Management Team:
Senior Teacher, Mathematics: Mrs Rosemarie Frost
Senior Housemistress, English: Mrs Jennie Douglas
Director of HR: Mrs Gillian Lusby
Director of Professional Development: Mr Stephen Ramsbottom
Secondment to SMT: Mrs Anju Jallport

Prep School Leadership Team:
Head of Prep School: Mrs Judy Rowe
Head of Pre Prep, Form Teacher: Mrs Elizabeth Courtney Magee
Senior Deputy Head Academic & Development: Mr Martyn Vandewalle
Deputy Head Pastoral & Co-curricular: Mrs Lucy Still
Assistant Head Curriculum: Miss Hillary Ennett

St Albans School

Abbey Gateway, St Albans, Herts AL3 4HB

Tel:　　　01727 855521
email:　　hm@st-albans.herts.sch.uk
website:　www.st-albans.herts.sch.uk
Twitter:　@SASHerts
Facebook: @stalbansschoolherts
Instagram: @sasherts
LinkedIn: /school/st-albans-school

The origins of the School date back to the monastic foundation of 948, and today, St Albans School is a day school of 860 pupils. Girls have been admitted into the Sixth Form since 1991. Whilst maintaining a high standard of academic achievement, the School aims to foster the development of talent and responsibility, along with the fulfilment of individual potential.

Buildings. For more than three centuries, the School was located in the Lady Chapel of the Abbey. It moved in 1871 into the Monastery Gatehouse, a building of considerable historic and architectural interest, where teaching still continues. There were extensive additions made to the campus during the twentieth century, which in recent years has been extended significantly by the purchase of a very large building on an adjacent site and its conversion to a superb Art school, Sixth Form Centre and a suite of classrooms and the building of a Sports Centre.

The School's new Mathematics and CCF building, the Corfield Building, opened in January 2020, which, as well as significantly improving the home of the School's ever-popular CCF unit, provides the Maths Department with a new building worthy of its outstanding results. The Corfield building houses a brand new CCF shooting range and office space on the lower ground floor, and a bespoke two-storey Maths Faculty on the upper ground and first floors.

Additionally, the School's new Computer laboratories opened in September 2020 and new, open plan Science laboratories opened in September 2021.

The School has close historical and musical ties with the Cathedral and Abbey Church of St Alban. By permission of the Dean, morning prayers take place twice weekly in the nave, where the School Choir sings regularly and an annual oratorio is performed in collaboration with St Albans High School for Girls.

Admission. The majority of boys enter at the age of 11 or 13, as well as into the Sixth Form at 16, when girls are also admitted; candidates are accepted occasionally at other ages. For the main entry at 11, an examination in basic subjects is held at the School each year in January, and parents of interested candidates can find all information on the School's website, along with online registration. Most candidates at 13 enter through the Common Entrance examination, and conditional offers of places are normally made about one year before entry, following a preliminary assessment. Ideally, parents should apply to the School at least 2 years in advance for entry at 13.

Pupils are admitted only at the start of the Autumn Term unless there are exceptional circumstances.

Fees per term (2021–2022). £6,630.

Bursaries and Scholarships. Assistance with tuition fees may be available in cases of proven need from the School's own endowments. Such Bursaries are conditional upon an annual means test and will be awarded according to a balance of merit and need.

Numerous scholarships are awarded on academic merit at each age of entry. Scholarships in Art, Music and Sport are offered to existing pupils or new entrants at 13+ who show exceptional talent. Choral Scholarships are offered only at 11+.

Curriculum. The curriculum for the first three years is largely a common one and covers a wide range. All boys study three sciences and French and Latin, with taster courses in German, Mandarin Chinese and Spanish as part of a carousel of languages, and devote some part of their timetable to Art, Drama, Music, ICT and CDT. Mathematics IGCSE is taken in the January of the Fifth Form (Y11), and in the Fourth and Fifth Forms a system of compulsory subjects and options leads in most cases to the taking of at least a further nine GCSEs or IGCSEs. In the Sixth Form, pupils study four subjects taken from the start of the Lower Sixth. In the great majority of cases, students will choose three subjects to study in the Upper Sixth to A Level, along with an Extended Project. Virtually all Sixth Form leavers go on to universities or other forms of higher education, with the vast majority going to Russell Group universities, as well as Oxford or Cambridge.

Co-curricular activities cover a wide range and there are clubs and societies to cater for most interests. Musical activities are many and varied and include regular concerts and recitals by the School Choir, Choral Society and ensembles and by professional artists. Plays are produced three or four times a year, and there is ample opportunity for creative work in the Art school and the Design Technology Centre. There is a strong contingent of the CCF with sections representing the Army and RAF. Many pupils join the Duke of Edinburgh's Award scheme and do various forms of social service and conservation work in and around St Albans. The School owns a Field Centre in the Brecon Beacons in Wales, which is used for research and recreation in holidays, as part of the Lower School curriculum and as a base for field studies and reading parties.

Games. The School competes at a high level in Rugby Football, Hockey, Cross-country, Cricket, Tennis, Athletics, Netball and Lacrosse, in addition to a range of other sports including Association Football, Squash, Shooting, Sailing, Swimming, Orienteering, Basketball, Golf and Table Tennis. The School's Sports Centre offers a swimming pool, sports hall, fitness centre, dance studio and climbing wall. The School also owns the Woollam Playing Fields, comprising an Astroturf all-weather pitch and a superb state-of-the-art pavilion. A video of Woollams' facilities can be viewed on the School's website. There are good links with Saracens RUFC, whose training is based at the Woollam Grounds.

The playing fields are within easy reach of the School, and the spacious and pleasant lawns on the School site, stretching down to the River Ver, give access to the open-air theatre, tennis courts and shooting range.

Charitable status. St Albans School is Registered Charity, number 1092932, and a Company Limited by Guarantee, number 4400125.

Board of Governors:
Chairman: Mr Neil Osborn, MA Oxon
Vice Chairs:
Ms L M Ainsworth, MA Oxon
Mr C McIntyre BA

Lt Col M W S Cawthorne, RM (*retd.*)
Mrs F Lightowler
Prof J P Luzio, MA, PhD, FMedSci
Mr S Majumdar, BA
Mr N C Moore, LLB, MA, CNAA
Mr C Oglethorpe, BCom
Miss A Philpott
Mrs C Pomfret, MA Oxon, ACA
Mr M E Punt, MA Oxon, MSc, PGCE
Mr A Woodgate, BA, MRICS

Advisory Council:
The Mayor of St Albans
The Dean of St Albans
The President of the Old Albanian Association
Mr P G Brown
Mr O King, MRICS
Mr P M Rattle, BA
Mr L Sinclair, BSc, MRICS
Mr B C Walker, BA, PGCE, CELTA
His Honour Keith Wilding [retd. Circuit Judge]

Bursar and Clerk to the Governors: Mr R J Hepper, MA Cantab, FCA

Staff:

***Headmaster*: Mr J W J Gillespie**, MA Cantab, FRSA

Second Master: Ms M Jones, BSc

Deputy Head – Teaching and Learning: Mrs V J Saunders BA, MEd Cantab

Deputy Head – Staff: Mr G D Nichols BA, MEd

Head of Sixth Form: Mr G J Walker, MA, FRSA

Head of Middle School: Mr C C Johnston MA, FRGS

Assistant Head – Co-Curricular and Head of Third Form:
Mr G S Burger, HDip Ed SA, MEd

Head of Lower School: Mrs R C Harris, MA Oxon

Assistant Head – Higher Educations and Careers: Dr R G
Hacksley, BA, FRSA

Assistant Head – Safeguarding and Wellbeing: Mrs H J
Robertson, BEng

Director of Marketing, Admissions and Communications:
Ms A J Crombie, BA

A full staff list is available on our website:
www.st-albans.herts.sch.uk/about-us

St Aloysius' College

45 Hill Street, Glasgow G3 6RJ

Tel: 0141 332 3190
email: mail@staloysius.org
website: www.staloysius.org
Twitter: @StAlsGlasgow
Facebook: @StAlsGlasgow
LinkedIn: /st-aloysius'-college

Motto: *ad majora natus sum* (I was born for greater
things).

Founded in 1859, St Aloysius' College is a Catholic
school for boys and girls aged 3 to 18. The school is fully
co-educational at all stages (Kindergarten to S6) with a roll
drawn from a wide catchment area in and around Glasgow.

As Scotland's only Jesuit school, St Aloysius' College
shares in a tradition of educational excellence which is
almost 500 years old. It is part of a worldwide network of
schools and universities whose mission is the "*Improvement
in living and learning for the greater glory of God and the
common good*" (*St Ignatius Loyola*).

The College creates an environment that is underpinned
by mutual respect, friendship and care for others. It prides
itself on upholding a clear set of religious, moral and
spiritual values.

Five Jesuit values underpin life at the College: Delight in
Learning, Personal Excellence, Make a Difference, Care and
Respect, and Faith and Values.

Great importance is placed upon educating the whole
person, with pupils encouraged to develop confidence,
leadership and teamwork through sport, outdoor activity,
music, drama, and many other activities.

Buildings. St Aloysius' College is located in the historic
Garnethill area of central Glasgow with additional facilities
in Millerston. The College's main Garnethill campus is
made up of a number of school buildings and is well served
by public transport.

The College campus is varied, providing examples of
both award-winning modern architecture and construction,
as well as historic listed buildings. The original Jesuit
residence, now part of the school, is a listed building, as is
The Mount where Art and Music are taught, and the
magnificent St Aloysius' Church which the College uses
regularly.

Two further additions to the St Aloysius' College
campus, The Junior School and The Clavius Building used
for Maths, Science and Computing, have attracted
widespread critical acclaim. Not only have the buildings
been the subject of great praise, but they have won many
architectural awards, including the Best New Building in
Scotland 2004.

The Kindergarten building is located beside the Junior
School and is the ideal place for younger pupils to learn and
play.

Completed in 2017, the state-of-the-art sports complex is
situated adjacent to the original College building. It
comprises a large games hall, dance studio, cardio and
weights room, viewing gallery and a café.

Curriculum. The Junior School and lower years of the
Senior School follow internally devised courses that are
suitable for academically able children. All Junior School
pupils study specialist subjects such as science, art, music,
IT and languages from Kindergarten and P1. National 5 is
taken at the end of S4 and pupils take five Highers in S5. A
wide range of Advanced Highers and other courses are
available in S6.

Music and the Arts. At St Aloysius' College, pupils are
taught the art of self-expression through the development of
the imaginative, the affective and the creative. These three
elements of Jesuit education are essential to the formation of
the whole person. Art is taught from Junior School by
specialist teachers and there is an established music
department with instrumental lessons from P3, orchestras,
and the unique Schola Choral Programme.

Sport and Outdoor Education. St Aloysius' College
offers an outstanding programme of sport and physical
education. Rugby and Hockey remain the College's
principal sports from P6 to U18 level. Cross-country and
athletics are also offered at all levels, whilst Senior School
pupils have the opportunity to represent the college in
basketball, football and swimming.

The College also offers opportunities to learn wider
Outdoor Education and pupils have enjoyed great success in
the Duke of Edinburgh's Award programme.

Co-Curricular. As well as Music and the Arts and Sport,
St Aloysius' College has an extensive co-curricular
programme designed to encourage personal excellence and
a delight in learning. This begins at Junior School, where
children can participate in the likes of STEM club, and
continues in Senior School where pupils are involved in
Public Speaking and Justice and Peace to name but a few.

Admission. Entrance assessments are held in January
and informal meetings with parents form part of the
application process at all stages. Pupils from Primary 4
upwards will also be asked to send in a 'Your Green Blazer
Story' as part of their application.

Fees per annum (2021–2022). £7,938–£14,130.

Bursaries are available on consideration of parents'
income.

Charitable status. St Aloysius' College is a Registered
Charity, number SC042545.

Board of Governors:
Fr Damian Howard SJ (*College President*)
Dr Isabelle Cullen (*Chair of Governors*)
Fr Simon Bishop SJ
Mrs Angela Doris
Mrs Natalie Finnegan

Ms Nicola Gallen
Mr Greg Hannah
Mr Nigel Kelly
Mr Ben McLeish
Mr Martin Morris
Mr Matthew Reilly
Mr Mike Smith
Prof Jane Stuart-Smith
Mrs Angela Vickers

Bursar and Clerk to the Board: Mrs Kathleen Sweeney, FCCA

Head Master: **Mr Matthew Bartlett**, MA, PGCE, NPQH

PA to the Head Master: Mrs Monica Harper

St Bede's College

Alexandra Park, Manchester M16 8HX

Tel: 0161 226 3323 (Senior School)
            0161 226 7156 (Preparatory School)
email: headteacher@sbcm.co.uk
            enquiries@sbcm.co.uk
            prepschool@sbcm.co.uk
            admissions@sbcm.co.uk
website: www.sbcm.co.uk
Twitter: @StBedesCollege
Facebook: @St-Bedes-College-Manchester
LinkedIn: /Bedian-Alumni

Motto: '*Nunquam otio torpebat*'

St Bede's is a Catholic HMC Independent Co-educational Grammar School welcoming Catholic and non-Catholic children from Nursery to Sixth Form. We are celebrating over 140 years of history set in a magnificent Grade II listed building in the heart of Manchester.

The College is widely recognised for the calibre of its students who leave as well-rounded, polite and articulate young adults who are academically successful and ready to meet the demands of life at university and beyond. Each year there are one hundred coveted places available ensuring each student is guaranteed individual attention and personalised support.

We believe passionately in the importance of traditional family values and in encouraging every pupil to develop genuine friendships. Each child in the College is known and valued in a community where there are no barriers to learning. Whilst academic success is a high priority, focus on developing lifelong learning is of greater significance. Ultimately we want to develop young men and women who are constructive and compassionate members of our society.

Admission. Children may join the College at different stages in their academic journey, where children can enjoy an all-through education, joining our co-educational Nursery for 3 year olds before moving up to our co-educational Prep School. and then on to the main College. It is assumed that all Prep pupils will transfer automatically into the Senior part of the College.

The College Entrance Examination for external candidates wishing to join the College at 11+ takes place in January each year. Details of the examination may be obtained from our Admissions team, email: admissions @sbcm.co.uk There is also direct entry to the Sixth Form. Interviews are held from the beginning of the Easter Term.

Curriculum. Curriculum provision is constantly monitored to ensure the best possible educational provision for all students.

The Lower School curriculum offers the core subjects of English, Mathematics, Sciences and RE together with Latin, Computer Science, Technology, History, Geography and PE/Games and tutor time. In the Middle School four subjects are chosen from French, German, Spanish, Latin, Classical Civilisation, Economics, Business, Computer Science, Design & Technology, Art and Music for a one-year course to further enhance GCSE options.

At GCSE/IGCSE, ten subjects are taken in varied combinations supported by a programme of academic enrichment.

Students must achieve 7 GCSE passes (grades 9–4) to be admitted to the Sixth Form. At A Level approximately 23 different subjects are currently on offer. Many students also opt to study the increasingly popular Extended Project Qualification. Flexibility ensures that any desired combination of subjects can be offered.

A strong learning support department ensures that all pupils fulfil their educational potential.

Co-Curriculum. There is an extensive weekly programme of extra-curricular provision that complements learning from outside the classroom and all pupils are encouraged to try new activities or extend their leadership by organising new ones for their peers.

Our goal is to develop wider skills for lifelong learning as well as helping to prepare students for the major ideas, innovations and challenges that they face in a rapidly-changing society. Bedians are confident in their ability to make a difference once they have left the College fully prepared for top universities and the world of work.

Fees per term (2021–2022). Senior School £4,024, Prep School £2,880.

Charitable status. St Bede's College Limited is a Registered Charity, number 700808. Its aims and objectives are the advancement and provision of education on behalf of St Bede's College.

Governance: The School is governed by a board of trustees. The Chairman of the Board is Mr Xavier Bosch

Headteacher: **Mrs S Pike**, BSc Hons, DipEd, MEd

Academic Deputy Head: Mrs T Davie, BSc Hons, MSc
Deputy Head: Mrs M Kemp, BA Hons, UNED
Assistant Head – CFA: Mr C Woan, BA Hons, MA
Assistant Head – Safeguarding: Mr T Sanders BA Hons
Head of Sixth Form: Mr D Rose, MA PGCE Cantab
Strategy and Innovation Director: Mr F Calmaestra, BA Hons, MA, MBA, MSc

Preparatory School:
Head of Prep: Mrs C Hunt, BEd Hons

St Benedict's School

54 Eaton Rise, Ealing, London W5 2ES

Tel: 020 8862 2000 (School Office)
          020 8862 2010 (Headmaster's Office)
          020 8862 2254 (Admissions)
          020 8862 2183 (Finance Director)
email: seniorschool@stbenedicts.org.uk
          admissions@stbenedicts.org.uk
website: www.stbenedicts.org.uk
Twitter: @stbenedicts
Facebook: @StBenedictsSchool
Instagram: @StBenedictsSchool
LinkedIn: /st-benedicts-school

Motto: *a minimis incipe*

St Benedict's is London's leading independent Catholic co-educational school, situated in leafy Ealing. The School is a successful blend of the traditional and the progressive; proud of its heritage but also forward thinking and innovative. A seamless education which can begin at the age of 3 and continue through to the Sixth Form, in a caring, happy community, enables our pupils to thrive.

Academic standards are high: inspirational teaching, tutorial guidance and exceptional pastoral care are at the heart of the education we offer, allowing children to develop their full potential.

The Junior School and Nursery provide a supportive and vibrant environment in which to learn. Sharing excellent facilities with the Senior School and a programme of cross-curricular activities help ease the transition at 11+ to the Senior School, which is on the same site.

At St Benedict's, there is a vital focus on personal development, and our outstanding co-curricular programme helps pupils to thrive by enabling them to find and develop their unique gifts and talents. St Benedict's has a distinguished sporting tradition, and Music and Drama are both excellent, with a strong choral tradition and termly drama productions.

We encourage principled leadership, resilience and character in our pupils, and promote the Christian values of integrity, fairness and generosity to others. This is a hallmark of the School and there could be no better way of equipping young people for the future.

Recent developments include a new Nursery and Pre-Prep Department, providing our youngest pupils with a first-rate learning environment. This is in addition to a new Sixth Form Centre and Art Department.

St Benedict's School is unique. Come and visit, and see what we have to offer.

Fees per term (2021–2022). Senior School £6,110, Junior School £5,185, Pre-Prep £4,665, Nursery £3,375–£5,075.

Charitable status. St Benedict's School Ealing is a Registered Charity, number 1148512, and a Charitable Company Limited by Guarantee, registration number 8093330.

Governing Body: The Governing Board of St Benedict's School

Headmaster: Mr Andrew Johnson

Deputy Heads:
Mr L Ramsden
Ms F Allen

Finance Director: Mrs C Bedwin

Headmaster's PA: Mrs R Wynne

Registrar: Mrs L Pepper

St Columba's College

King Harry Lane, St Albans, Hertfordshire AL3 4AW

Tel: 01727 855185
email: admissions@stcolumbascollege.org
website: www.stcolumbascollege.org
Twitter: @StColumbasHerts
Facebook: @StColumbasCollege
Instagram: @stcolumbascollege
LinkedIn: /school/stcolumbascollege

Motto: '*Cor ad Cor Loquitur*'

St Columba's College was founded in 1939, and has been a school in the tradition of the Brothers of the Sacred Heart (United States) since 1955. It is a Catholic, selective school, with over half of its pupils coming from all faiths and none. In September 2021, the school welcomed girls into the Lower Prep (Reception, Year 1 and Year 2) and the Lower Sixth Form. From September 2022, girls will be welcomed into Year 3, Year 4 and Year 7, followed by a phased transition to co-education for ages 4 to 18. The predominantly lay staff works together with pupils and parents to provide a Christian education based on traditional values, balancing a friendly community with sound discipline and academic rigour.

St Columba's College stands in its own grounds overlooking the picturesque St Albans Abbey. In 2013, a major building development at the heart of the College was completed and in recent years extensive improvements have been made to Science, English, Music, Drama, Sixth Form and Preparatory facilities.

Entry. St Columba's College admits pupils from 4–18, and there are currently 800 students in the Prep and Senior School. The main entry for the Senior School is at 11+, by entrance test and interview, with a smaller group being offered deferred entry at 13+.

Scholarships. Academic and music scholarships are awarded at 11+, 13+ and for the Sixth Form, as well as means-tested Bursaries. Sports Scholarships are offered in the Sixth Form.

The Curriculum. This is kept as broad as possible up to GCSE, pupils usually taking 9 to 11 subjects from the traditional range of Arts and Science options. There are 22 A Level subjects, and the Sixth Form is complemented by an enrichment course which prepares students for extra qualifications including the Extended Project and Personal Finance. Almost all of the Sixth Form students go on to universities, including Oxbridge.

Careers. A full-time Head of Careers and Higher Education works from a fully-equipped Careers Centre to ensure that all students receive high-quality guidance in order to make informed decisions about subject choices and university courses with subsequent career options in mind.

Pastoral Care. St Columba's is a Catholic foundation welcoming students from all faiths and none. The spiritual and moral well-being of our pupils is a matter of primary importance for all of our staff, the majority being tutors. The six Housemasters and their teams are supported by a Ministry Team. Relations between the College and parents are open – a strength of the College – and they are in regular contact with each other in monitoring the progress of the students. The College seeks to nurture the academic and personal talents of each individual.

Sport. All students participate, and the College has a strong sporting reputation. A rich variety of sports is available at all levels, including Rugby, Basketball, Football, Tennis, Cricket, Athletics, Swimming, Cross Country and Golf. Facilities include a large gymnasium and sports field on site. The Sports Department makes extensive use of soccer and rugby pitches, an athletics track, swimming pool and a golf course which are all immediately adjacent to the College site.

Extended and Extra-Curricular Activities. The College offers a wide variety of activities both at lunch-time and after school. These include clubs such as; rugby, football, basketball, cricket and athletics, drama, art, chess, computing, Young Enterprise, CCF, Duke of Edinburgh's Award and many others, as well as a variety of academic and social clubs. There is a number of music ensembles, including a choir, barbershop group, orchestra, flute quartet, jazz band and bell choir.

Preparatory School. The Preparatory School is on the same site as the Senior School and shares many of its facilities. The College has a strong family atmosphere, providing a secure and purposeful environment in which expectations are high. It admits students by assessment into the Lower Prep and Upper Prep. In their final year, most Preparatory School pupils are offered unconditional places at St Columba's College Senior School, following recommendations by Prep School staff.

(*See also St Columba's College Preparatory School entry in IAPS section.*)

Fees per term (2021–2022). Senior School £5,703, Prep 4–6 £4,925, Prep 3 £4,466 Reception–Prep 2 £3,808

Charitable status. St Columba's College is a Registered Charity, number 1088480. It exists to provide a well-rounded Catholic education for pupils from 4–18 years of age.

Governors:
Chairman: Mr K McGovern, BSc, MRICS

Bursar and Clerk to the Governors: Mr K Evans, CMgr, FCMI

Headmaster: **Mr David Buxton**, BA, MTh, MA

Deputy Head: Mrs K Marson, MA
Academic Deputy Head: Mr I Devereux, BEd
Head of Sixth Form: Mr D Waters, BA
Assistant Head: Mrs L Cronin, MA Cantab
Assistant Head: Mr J Tatham, BA
Head of Preparatory School: Mr R McCann, BA
Deputy Head of Prep: Mr K Boland, BA
Prep Assistant Pastoral Deputy: Miss K Leahy, BA
Prep Assistant Academic Deputy: Miss C Maton, BA

Administration:
Admissions Registrar: Mrs R Wilson

Headmaster's PA: Mrs R Coakley
Head of Prep's PA: Mrs E McConachie

St Columba's School

Duchal Road, Kilmacolm, Inverclyde PA13 4AU

Tel: 01505 872238
email: admissions@st-columbas.org
website: www.st-columbas.org
Twitter: @StColSchool
Facebook: @stcolumbasschool
Instagram: @stcolumbasschool
LinkedIn: /st-columba-s-school-kilmacolm

Motto: *Orare Laborare Literisque Studere*

Founded in 1897, St Columba's School is a non-denominational day school for boys and girls aged 3–18 years and is renowned for its first-class education and academic excellence. Situated at the heart of Kilmacolm, yet within easy reach of the city of Glasgow and the surrounding areas, it is a forward-looking, vibrant and dynamic school.

The first thing you notice at St Columba's is the warm welcome and the strong sense of community. This is in part the result of its size where teachers know each pupil by name. Indeed, considerable effort is made to create an environment which allows the School to identify and nurture the unique talents and skills of each pupil, and encourage each one of them to realise their full potential, grow and flourish.

St Columba's success is evident not only in its excellent academic results, regularly placing St Columba's as one of the highest-achieving schools nationally, but in the impressive young people you will meet in a classroom, at an international debate, or on a rugby field: they are polite, articulate and quietly self-assured. The School combines the pursuit of academic excellence with a range of opportunity and challenge to develop self-confident and independent young people who have a strong sense of community and who will become responsible and reflective future leaders. High-quality teaching, a strong sense of belonging and the space for pupils to grow and achieve their full potential is what St Columba's offers. The School is the first school in Scotland to be awarded the Queen's Award for Voluntary Service.

St Columba's offers wraparound care from 7.30am to 6.00pm, financial assistance and a dedicated coach service.

Facilities. Our school campus sits within the heart of the village of Kilmacolm and easy travelling distance of Glasgow. Junior School is nestled in a woodland setting filled with light and colour and caters for our children in Early Years to Junior 6. Senior School is located a third of a mile from Junior School and caters for pupils in Transitus (J7) to Senior SVI.

Over the last 5 years we have invested £7 million to provide the Senior School Girdwood Building that houses Transitus, English, Languages, the Pastoral Care Suite, a Library and 13 classrooms; revamped our 6 science laboratories; and landscaped our Junior School grounds. Our most recent investment is our modern Wellbeing Centre. This new resource at the heart of the school reflects the values of St Columba's where we recognise that, for children to flourish and for staff to support them, health and wellbeing is paramount.

Sports facilities include: gym area for gymnastics and dance, large purpose-built sports hall including fitness suite, all-weather floodlit hockey/tennis ground, access to three rugby pitches and a large playing field used for athletics and cross-country running.

Curriculum. St Columba's School follows the Scottish Curriculum at all stages. Junior School pupils are taught French, music, drama and PE by specialist staff. Transitus (P7) is a transitional year with core curriculum taught by the class teacher and science, languages, art, music and PE delivered by specialist secondary teachers. Pupils in Senior IV are presented for National 5 examinations followed by Higher Grade and Advanced Higher Grade examinations in Senior V and Senior VI.

Games. Rugby, hockey, tennis, athletics, badminton, gymnastics, swimming, volleyball, basketball, soccer, dance (girls), orienteering. Optional: netball, squash, cricket, golf, skiing/snowboarding, curling, street dance, weight-training.

Extra-Curricular. Throughout the whole school there are approximately 60 clubs and societies. They range from athletics and orchestra, gardening and science, STEM and enterprise, debating and history film, through to coding and philosophy covering most letters of the alphabet. There is truly something for every child. Individual tuition in a wide range of instruments is available. Public performances and school shows are arranged on a regular basis.

We offer a range of nationally recognised, progressive outdoor education awards which allow pupils to develop resilience and the ability to problem solve; and learn to work as part of a team in some of Scotland's most beautiful locations – Duke of Edinburgh's Award, National Navigation Award Scheme, British Canoeing and the John Muir Award. We are proud to be sector leaders running one of the most successful DofE Award programmes in Scotland, with 76% of our Gold participants going on to achieve their award. Mini Duke and Junior Duke Awards are also offered to children in Junior 2–6.

There is a very strong tradition of fundraising for charity and community service within the School.

St Columba's has strong links with schools in France and Canada.

Organisation. The school is organised into four Houses for both pastoral and competitive purposes. Each house has a Head of House as well as pupil Captain and Vice-Captain. Career guidance is supported by Inspiring Futures.

Admission. Entry to St Columba's is by a combination of entry test, interview and, where applicable, a report from the applicant's previous school. Open events are held in November and entrance tests are held in January. The main entry points are Early Years, Junior 1 and Transitus, however, pupils are taken in at other stages as places become available.

Fees per annum (2021–2022). Early Years 1,140 hours of free EYC in partnership with Inverclyde Council, J1 & J2 £9,625, J3 £10,545, J4 £11,205, J5 & J6 £11,780, Transitus–Senior VI £13,206.

A number of bursary places, ranging from 10–100% of fees are available.

Charitable status. St Columba's School is a Registered Charity, number SC012598. It exists to provide education for pupils.

Chairman of the Board of Governors: Mr D Girdwood, DL, BSc, MEd, SQH

Rector: **Mrs V Reilly**, MA Edinburgh

Head of Junior School: Mrs A Duncan, MA St Andrews, Dip EdMan, SQH

Depute Rector: Mr M J McLaughlin, MA Greenwich, BA Thames

Depute Rector: Ms A Berry, BA MRes Kent, MEd Buckingham

Depute Rector: Ms J Fulton, MA Stirling, MA Durham

Head of Finance and Operations: Mrs U Telfer
Admissions Registrar: Mrs M McWhirter
Rector's PA: Mrs A Maxwell

St Dunstan's College

Stanstead Road, London SE6 4TY

Tel: 020 8516 7200
email: collegeoffice@stdunstans.org.uk
            admissions@stdunstans.org.uk
website: www.stdunstans.org.uk
Twitter: @StDunstansColl
Facebook: @StDunstansColl

Motto: '*Albam Exorna*'

The College was founded in the 15th Century in the Parish of St Dunstan-in-the-East, part of the Tower Ward of the City of London. In 1888 the school was re-founded in Catford, South East London. It became co-educational in 1994.

Buildings. The College is located on a 15-acre site three minutes' walk from Catford and Catford Bridge railway stations. Facilities include an imposing Great Hall, a well-equipped Learning Resource Centre, Performing Arts Centre, three state-of-the-art ICT suites and a brand new Junior School, STEM block and Sixth Form Centre which opened in 2021. There is also a Wellness Centre for physical and mental first aid, counselling, chaplaincy and peer mentoring. To complement extensive playing fields on site, St Dunstan's has a sports hall, fully-equipped fitness rooms, floodlit netball/tennis courts, rugby fives courts and an indoor swimming pool, along with a 20-acre sports facility on nearby Canadian Avenue called the Jubilee Ground. This site provides playing fields, multi-use games areas, a gym, dance studio and function rooms, further enhancing the sporting and other facilities available to its pupils and the wider community.

Organisation and Curriculum. The College educates boys and girls from the ages of 3 to 18. The Junior School comprises a nursery class for 20 children (3+), a Pre-Prep Department for 120 children aged 4–7 and a Prep Department of 160 children aged 7–11.

In the Junior School great emphasis is placed on letting children learn in a friendly, caring and stimulating environment. Pupils study a broad curriculum and participate in a wide variety of extra-curricular activities. The Head of the Junior School is a member of IAPS (*see entry in IAPS section*).

The Senior School, with a total of 702 pupils, comprises Key Stage 3 (Years 7–9), Key Stage 4 (Years 10 and 11) and Key Stage 5 (Years 12 and 13). A considerable choice of subjects is on offer – Art & Design, Biology, Business Studies, Chemistry, Classical Civilisation, Computing Science, Design & Technology, Economics, English, Drama, Geography, History, Latin, Mathematics, Modern Foreign Languages, Music, Philosophy, Religion and Ethics, Physics, Psychology, Sport and Exercise Science along with Personal, Social, Health and Emotional Education (PSHEE).

The College is a vibrant, academic community with a friendly atmosphere. It values cultural diversity and has a reputation for high academic standards and excellent pastoral care. This continues into the Sixth Form where students are supported to achieve outstanding academic results (84% A*–B in 2018), whilst developing each individual's distinctive talents and skills. This philosophy has been the basis for the College's flagship St Dunstan's Diploma programme – a flexible, innovative and exciting programme designed to inspire, challenge and assist all Sixth Formers achieve their unique ambitions and potential.

Pupils have the opportunity to join a very wide range of co-curricular activities through its Forder Programme. This allows all pupils to immerse themselves in creative, active and service activities along with opportunities to develop leadership skills and a greater understanding of the wider world for the older year groups.

Combined Cadet Force. The CCF is extremely popular and comprises the Royal Navy Section, the Army Section and the Corps of Drums. Typically, cadets join the CCF in Year 9 and by Year 11 become responsible for training younger cadets. The activities undertaken are designed to develop qualities of leadership, resourcefulness, self-reliance, responsibility, confidence and a sense of community service.

Community Service. The College has a strong tradition of Service and involvement with the local community. Pupils from Year 9 upwards form a Community Service group that provides various types of help and support to the local community.

Drama. There are opportunities for pupils to be involved in drama productions to suit all ages and abilities. These range from small scale informal performance to larger whole College musicals. Pupils can study towards and be entered for LAMDA examinations. The College hosts an annual week-long Arts Festival in the summer.

Duke of Edinburgh's Award scheme. The College has very strong numbers of pupils involved at all Award levels.

Music. Pupils from all parts of the school participate in a variety of choirs, orchestras and instrumental ensembles. There is an annual Choral & Orchestral Concert for the whole College at St Pancras Church.

Sport. The chief sports are cricket, hockey, netball, rounders, rugby, soccer and swimming. Pupils also have opportunities to take part in cross-country running, fives, tennis, basketball, badminton, sailing, golf, fitness training and yoga.

Entrance. The main entrance points are at the age of 3, 4, 7, 11, 13 or 16. Admission to the College is competitive in all years with the exception of the Nursery, and depends on academic ability and the demonstration of potential. At 11+ an Entrance Examination is held annually in January.

Entrance Scholarships. Scholarships are offered for academic merit and also for excellence in Music, Sport, Art & Design and Drama. Means-tested bursaries are available.

Fees per annum (2021–2022). Nursery £12,501; Reception & Years 1–3: £14,319; Years 4–5 £16,374; Year 6: £18,039; Senior School £19,068.

The Dunstonian Association. The DA has 4,000 members. All pupils subscribe to the DA while at school and automatically become life members when they leave.

The Friends of St Dunstan's. This parent–school association works to support the educational, social and extra-curricular activities of the school for the benefit of all pupils. All parents are automatically members of the Friends of St Dunstan's.

Charitable status. St Dunstan's Educational Foundation is a Registered Charity, number 312747.

Governors:
Chairman: Mr P Durgan, BA, FCA
Deputy Chairman: Mr I Davenport, Esq
Ms V Alexander, MSc, BACP, FHEA
Dr Y Burne, JP, OBE
Dr A Cairns, PhD
Ms J Clements, BA Hons, LLB, OBE
Revd K Hedderly
Ms L Kiernan, MA, DipEd
Mr N Lyons, MA
Mr K L Marshall, RD, FICS, ACII
Mr D Probert, BA Hons, MBA
Miss D Robertshaw, BSc Hons, RGN, RSCN Dip
Mr J Ronan
Mr S Rahman, BA, LLB, LLM
Mr N Sheera, MA, MBA

Clerk to the Governors and Bursar: Mrs C Wilkins

Senior School Academic Staff:

***Headmaster*: Mr Nicholas Hewlett**, BSc

Deputy Head (Academic): Mr J R H Holmes, BA
Deputy Head (Pastoral): Mrs J McLellan, BA; Mrs G Davies, BSc [maternity cover]

Assistant Heads:
Head of Lower School: Mrs G Davies, BSc
Head of Middle School: Mr P O'Dwyer, MA
Head of Sixth Form: Mr A Brewer, BA
Co-curricular and Staff Development: Mr D Gower, BSc
Director of Studies: Mrs E Latham, BSc

* *Head of Department*

*Mrs J Anderson, BSc	Mr L Corbin O'Grady
Mr J Apweiler, BSc	Mr A Currie, BSc
Miss S Arajian, BSc	*Miss L Clewley, BSc
Mr R Austin, BSc	*Mrs N Crivellari, BA
Mrs H S Baptiste, BSc	Mrs G L Davies, BSc
Mr J Bell, BA	Mr R W Davies, BA
Miss E Bocarro, BSc	Mr P Dawson, BA
Mr M Bradley, BA	Mr W Diamond, BA
Mr A Brewer, BA	Mr J P H Elmes, MA
Mr H Burke, BA	Miss G Entwisle, BMus
*Mrs P Butler, BA	Miss A Esposito, BA
*Ms R E Butryn, MA	*Mr B Ford, BSc
Dr J Bunzl, PhD	Mr J Galbraith
Miss Z Chen	Mr G Gibb, BSc
*Miss L Clewley, BSc	Mr D Gower, BSc
Miss A Collard, BA	Mr R Gregg

Mr R Grocock, BA
Miss L Haddington, BSc
Mr G Hart, BSc
Mrs L Hartwell, BSc
Ms D Hernandez-Alarcon, BA
Mr J Holmes, BA
Mr S Hoffman, BSc
*Mr T Hofmeyr, MA
Miss H Hughes, BA
*Miss A Jordon, BSc
Miss A Karmock-Golds, BA
Miss L Kilbey, BA
Mr I Kimuli, BSc
Mrs E Latham, BSc
*Mr J Lavery, BA
Miss M Lopez, BA
Mr J Loveridge, BA
Miss F Margaroli
*Mr M McClune, BSc
Miss R McKay-Pryce
Mrs J McLellan, BA
*Mr R McStravick, BSc
Ms K Melhorn, BA

Miss T Miah, BA
Miss R Money, BMus
Ms M Moore, MSc
Mr P O'Dwyer, MA
*Mr D Oldfield, BA
*Miss E Partridge, BSc
Ms V Permanand, SENDCo
Dr R Qadiri, PhD
*Mr J Randall
Ms S Reece, BA
*Miss J Restivo, BA
Ms N Rich, BA
Mr T Scambler, BA
* Mr G Stewart, BA
Mr T Swan, BSc
*Mr M Thain, BA
Mr G Trainor, BA
Miss W Tseng, BA
Mr A Walls, BA
Miss D M Warren, BEng
*Miss R Watkins, BSc
Mr D J Webb, BA
Ms C Winder, BSc
Miss G Wright, BA

PA to the Headmaster: Mrs V Hearn
Director of Marketing, Admissions and Development: Mrs I Blake-James
Head of Admissions: Miss A Kothari
Head of Marketing: Mr J L Squibb
College Chaplain: Revd C Boswell
Junior School Secretary/Registrar: Miss D Jackson

St Edmund's College

Old Hall Green, Ware, Hertfordshire SG11 1DS

Tel: 01920 824247
email: admissions@stedmundscollege.org
website: www.stedmundscollege.org
Twitter: @StEdmundsWare
Facebook: @stedmundscollege.org
Instagram: @stedmundscollegeandprep

Motto: '*Avita Pro Fide*'

St Edmund's College, England's oldest Catholic school, is a leading Independent day and boarding, co-educational Catholic School for boys and girls aged 3–18. From the Nursery to the Sixth Form St Edmund's College offers an education that challenges and stimulates, developing the whole person in the intellectual, physical, emotional and spiritual areas of life; the richness of our extracurricular provision and our high academic standards are testament to the College's success and popularity.

Located on a beautiful site in rural East Hertfordshire, only 40 minutes to London by train, St Edmund's has outstanding transport links to the surrounding area and makes full use of the excellent facilities on its 450-acre site including floodlit astroturf pitches and indoor swimming pool.

Scholarships are available at 7+, 11+ and 16+ and we welcome applications for entry to all years if places are available. St Edmund's welcomes students from all faiths who support our ethos.

Admission. Students are mainly admitted at the ages of 11, 13 and 16, although entry is always considered at other ages if there are spaces available.

Scholarships. The College offers the following scholarships:

St Edmund's College 11+ Scholarships:

Douay Academic Scholarships are decided by the mark in the 11+ Entrance Exam, the school report, the confidential school report and the interview with the Headmaster.

Old Hall Academic Scholarships are restricted to Catholic students who are in a Catholic school (and have been for the last two years). As above, this award is decided by the mark in the 11+ entrance exam, the school report, the confidential school report and the interview with the Headmaster or Registrar.

All Rounder Scholarships are decided by interview, school report, confidential report and mark in the Entrance Exam. For this award, the child will be competent academically and also be able to make a substantial contribution to other areas of life at St Edmund's. This will be as agreed with the Headmaster but contributions might be to one or more aspects, such as drama, music, technology, the Catholic life of the College, specialised sports or outdoor pursuits.

Art Scholarships are decided by examination of a portfolio and a test. Scholars are required to make a significant contribution to the artistic life of the College.

Music Scholarships are decided by audition and include the provision of free tuition in two instruments. Scholars will normally be required to play two instruments with at least one to a high standard (voice can be counted as one instrument).

Music Exhibitions may also be awarded which give free tuition in either one or two instruments. Those in receipt of Music Scholarships and Exhibitions are required to make a significant and sustained contribution to the musical life of the College.

Sport Scholarships are decided by open competition and references from sports clubs or teachers where the child is already involved in sport at a very high level, for example, County level. Scholars will be expected to play a full and sustained role in the sporting life of the College.

The closing date for Year 7 scholarship applications is in November for entry the following September.

Sixth Form Scholarships:

At 16+, the Cardinal Allen Academic Scholarships are decided by open competition using the results of specially set scholarship examinations, interview and previous school reports. Candidates for these scholarships would be expected to achieve all A/A* grades in their GCSEs. Music, Sport and Art scholarships may also be offered through competitive test.

The closing date for Year 12 scholarship applications is in early November for entry the following September.

Bursaries. We also offer a limited number of means-tested Bursaries at 11+, of up to 100% of fees. The closing date is in November.

Further details are available from the Admissions Office on 01920 824247.

Fees per term (2021–2022). College: Day Pupils: £5,870–£6,330; Weekly Boarders: £8,340–£9,534; Full Boarders: £9,767–£11,202.

There are reductions for siblings and for sons and daughters of serving members of the Armed Forces.

Curriculum. All pupils follow the National Curriculum. At the end of Year 11, pupils take GCSE examinations in all courses that they have followed, usually more than is required by the National Curriculum.

In Rhetoric (Sixth Form), students study A Levels and the majority leave St Edmund's to progress to Russell Group universities including some to Oxford and Cambridge.

Religious Instruction. St Edmund's is a College for all those who appreciate the values of a Catholic Education. All students receive instruction in Christian doctrine and practice from lay teachers. Importance is attached to the liturgical life of the College and the practical expression of faith. All faiths and denominations are welcomed.

Sport. Great importance is attached to sport and physical education throughout the College. All pupils are required to participate in a variety of sports. The major sports for boys are rugby, football, cricket and athletics, while for girls they are hockey, netball, rounders and athletics. The other sports available are cross-country, tennis, swimming, basketball and badminton. A floodlit astroturf pitch, large sports hall, indoor swimming pool, tennis courts and Cardiovascular Fitness Suite, together with 450 acres of grounds, provide excellent facilities.

Extracurricular Activities. At St Edmund's we believe our responsibility reaches far beyond the academic success of our students. We have a commitment to the whole person, which is reflected in the broad range of activities on offer to everyone and we wish to encourage the notion that success can be achieved in many ways, not just in the classroom.

Each day between 3.30pm and 4.30pm, time is set aside for students to pursue an interest or activity. Wednesday afternoons are also dedicated to our activities programme.

The CCF (RAF and Army sections), Community Service and The Duke of Edinburgh's Award play a prominent part in developing a self-reliant and confident individual.

Careers. There is a Head of Careers and Careers Library. Careers advice is available to pupils from the age of 13. There are regular careers lectures and visits to industry and Universities.

Prep School. St Edmund's also includes a Prep situated on the same estate. It consists of a Nursery, Infants and Junior School for pupils from age 3 to 11, which feeds into the Senior School at 11. The pupils are able to make use of many of the amenities of the Senior School such as the Refectory, Chapel, Swimming Pool and Sports Hall. There is no boarding at the Prep School.

(*For further details, see entry in IAPS section.*)

Charitable status. St Edmund's College is a Registered Charity, number 311073. It aims to provide a Catholic Education for students of all faiths between the ages of 3 and 18.

President & Patron: His Eminence Cardinal Vincent Nichols, Archbishop of Westminster

Governors:
Mr Paul Raynes, MA Cantab (*Chair*)
Mrs Jane Ranzetta (*Deputy Chair and Chair of Academic Sub-Committee*)

Mr John Bryant (*Chair of Prep School Sub-Committee*)
Mr Stephen Grounds, BSc, DPhil
Fr Alban McCoy, OFM Conv, BA, MLitt
Ms Nichola Walsh, BA Hons, MA

Clerk to the Governors: Mrs K Pugsley

Senior Leadership Team:

***Headmaster/DSM Child Protection*: Mr M Mostyn**, BA Hons Exeter, MA Ed

Headmaster of Prep School: Mr S Cartwright, BSc Surrey
Bursar: Mr B Tomlinson, BA Hons London ACMA
Senior Deputy Head: Mrs K, MacDonald, BA Hons, PGCE, PQH NI Queen's Belfast
Deputy Head Pastoral: Mr P Curran, BSc Hons Reading, PGCE Swansea
Deputy Head St Edmund's Prep/DSL Child Protection: Dr F J F McLauchlan, MA, PhD Cantab (*Director of Music and Performing Arts*)
Assistant Head Academic Timetable, Curriculum & Data: Mrs R A K West, BEd Hons Exeter
Assistant Head Academic Teaching and Learning: Mrs C Noble, BA Hons Exeter, PGCE Canterbury
Assistant Head Community Life/Deputy DSL Child Protection: Mrs L Dunhill, BSc Hons, PGCE Nottingham [Maternity Leave]
Assistant Head Pastoral/DSL Child Protection: Mr G West, BSc East Anglia
Assistant Head of St Edmund's Prep: Mr G Duddy, BEd Wales (*Year 5, RE, Activities*)
Senior Teacher in Charge of Religious Life/Charities Co-ordinator: Mrs P Peirce, BD, AKC London

Admissions and Marketing Director: Mrs M Burke
Head of Boarding: Mr A Smerdon, BSc Hons St, Mary's, Twickenham, PGCE South Bank
Human Resources Directors:
Mrs H Duffy, LLB Hull, PGDL
Mrs L Nice, BA Hons Herts [Maternity Leave]
Priest in Residence: Revd Father P H Lyness, MA Rhodes
Technical Projects Director: Mr S Winfield

Heads of Department:
Art, Design and Technology: Miss A M Healy, BA Luton
Business Studies and Economics: Mr W Fulford-Brown, BA Hons Leeds Beckett, PGCE Nottingham
Drama: Mrs N Schiff, MA Herts, BA Plymouth, PGCE Reading
English: Mr D Fenrych-Fahy, MEd Cantab, MA London, BSc Hons Reading, PGCE Reading
Geography: Mrs E Barnard, BA Hons Manchester, PGCE London
History and Politics: Mrs C Barkham, MA Glasgow, PGCE Glasgow
Information Technology and Computing: Mr K R Fry, BSc Brunel, MSc Herts, PGCE Exeter (*Director of E-Learning*)
International Department: Miss Z Hibbert, BA Hons Portsmouth, PGCE Cantab, Delta M1 & M2 Seville Cert, TESOL UCL
Languages: Ms L Hill, BA Sussex, PGCE Reading
Mathematics: Mrs H Fraser, BSc, PGCE East Anglia
Media Studies: Mr L Woodward, BA Hons Bournemouth (*Housemaster of Douglass House, Edmundian Editor*)
Music: Mr J Woodhall, MEd St Mary's Twickenham, PGCE Roehampton, MM Surrey (*Director of Music*)

Physical Education: Mr P Kelly, BPhEd Hons Otago, MSc South Wales (*Director of Sport*)

Psychology: Mr N Eliasson, MA Birmingham, PGCE Canterbury, BSc Hertfordshire (*Intervention and Achievement Co-ordinator*)

Religious Studies: Miss A Moloney, BA Hons Surrey, PGCE Roehampton

Science: Miss M Towns, BSc UWE Bristol, PGCE London

Cardinal Hume Centre, Learning Support: Mrs N Wells, BSc Hons Hertfordshire, PGCE Greenwich

Careers: Mr B Snell, MA Lancaster, BA Hons Hull, PGCE Chichester

A full staff list is available at: www.stedmundscollege.org/information/staff-and-vacancies/who-we-are/staffing.

St Edmund's School Canterbury

St Thomas Hill, Canterbury, Kent CT2 8HU

Tel: 01227 475601 (Admissions)
  01227 475600 (General Enquiries)
email: admissions@stedmunds.org.uk
website: www.stedmunds.org.uk
Twitter: @StEdsCanterbury
Facebook: @StEdsCanterbury
Instagram: @stedscanterbury

Motto: '*Fungar Vice Cotis*'

St Edmund's is an independent, co-educational day and boarding school for pupils aged between 2 and 18 years, comprising the Pre-Prep, Junior and Senior Schools. Its aim is to provide varied opportunities for academic, sporting, artistic, musical and dramatic achievement. The school has excellent teaching facilities and numerous options for extracurricular activities.

First established in 1749 as the Clergy Orphan School in Yorkshire, the School later moved to London and settled in its present location in 1855. The School's commitment to its origins endures, as does its Christian ethos. However, the School welcomes pupils from all backgrounds and places a particularly strong emphasis on pastoral care.

St Edmund's is situated on a beautiful site at the top of St Thomas Hill, adjacent to the University of Kent and overlooking the historic city of Canterbury. It is within easy reach of the towns of East Kent, and is just over an hour from London. The proximity to London's airports, the Channel ports and Eurostar stations at Ashford and Ebbsfleet gives international pupils convenient access to the School.

St Edmund's is a distinctive and historic boarding and day co-educational school where a family atmosphere is fostered, individuals are valued, the spiritual element is explored, and pupils enjoy a rich academic and cultural experience. We are committed to producing happy and successful pupils who can access a high quality education, while enjoying a wealth of stimulating and exciting extracurricular activity. Set within a beautiful and extensive green field site affording spectacular views of the city and Cathedral of Canterbury, St Edmund's not only enjoys a stunning location, but also offers a happy, vibrant and creative environment within a supportive community.

The school offers a nurturing, yet challenging, environment where an emphasis is placed upon academic rigour and co-curricular involvement. Its co-curricular provision is broad, but also encourages excellence in each individual area. Its tradition of housing and educating the Choristers of Canterbury Cathedral brings much to the richness and diversity of our community.

Academic standards are set high. Its dedicated and talented teaching and support staff work alongside pupils to encourage them to develop into caring, resourceful and confident young men and women who are well equipped to tackle the demands of the modern world.

Organisation. The Nursery, Pre-Prep, Junior and Senior Schools are on the same site and are closely integrated, using the same Chapel, music and art facilities, theatre, dining hall, science laboratories, sports facilities, and so on. However, for practical day-to-day purposes the Junior School is led by the Head of the Junior School and the Nursery and Pre-Prep under the Head of Pre-Prep. St Edmund's derives much of its strength and its capacity to work efficiently and economically from its close-knit structure.

The Senior School is divided into four Houses: Baker, Wagner, Warneford and Watson, the respective Housemasters each being assisted by a team of Deputies and Tutors.

The Chapel. All pupils attend at least two of the morning services a week. Confirmation is conducted annually by the Archbishop of Canterbury (as Patron of the School) or by the Bishop of Dover acting on his behalf; the candidates are prepared by the School Chaplain. The School Carol Service is held in Canterbury Cathedral, by kind permission of the Dean and Chapter.

Buildings and Facilities. Over the past twenty years there have been extensive additions to and modernisation of the school's buildings and facilities: a new Junior School building; a purpose-built music school; a new Sixth Form Centre; the main hall with tiered auditorium and exhibition area; the sports hall; the technology department; additional classrooms and major extensions to science, art, IT and the Pre-Prep School; as well as the conversion of all Senior School boarding accommodation to study-bedrooms and refurbishment of Junior boarding premises. Recent additions include: phase one of the Academic Hub with 8 classrooms; new recreational facilities for Senior School boarders; a refurbished theatre and library; an AstroTurf pitch; a new medical centre; upgrading of classrooms, boarding and House facilities.

Academic Organisation. At St Edmund's, the academic expectations are high. The breadth and balance of the academic programme exceeds the requirements of the National Curriculum and pupils begin to be grouped by ability while they are in Junior School. This approach encourages children to apply their talents and aptitudes with diligence and perseverance. Comprehensive reports are sent regularly throughout the school year. A system of interim reports, as well as regular parents' meetings, ensures close communication with parents.

Nursery and Pre-Prep Schools: The Nursery and Pre-Prep Schools have their own classroom buildings and playground, creating a warm, secure and friendly learning environment in which pupils can develop to the full. The happy and purposeful atmosphere helps pupils develop their confidence.

The School has a wide range of excellent activities and teaches a broad-based curriculum that emphasises academic development as well as art, music, drama, outdoor education and sport. The teachers have many years' experience of working with Early Years' children and the small classes allow staff to focus on the needs of every pupil.

Junior School: The aim of the Junior School is to produce independent learners who are confident and motivated. In Forms 3 to 5, the National Curriculum is broadly followed and, while placing particular emphasis on English, Maths and Science, there is also focus on subjects such as Art, Drama, French, Geography, History, Information Technology, Latin and Music. Subject specialists teach Forms 6 to 8, helping to prepare pupils for Senior School. Music (from Form 3), Drama, Technology and Art (from Form 6) and Science (from Form 7) is taught in specialist facilities.

The House system gives older pupils the opportunity to experience the skills of organisation, cooperation and leadership, by helping and encouraging younger members of their Houses and assisting with the organisation of House teams and events. Taking on more responsibility and developing greater initiative is valuable in smoothing their passage to Senior School.

Choristers: The choristers of Canterbury Cathedral are all members of the Junior School. They board in the Choir House (in the Cathedral Precincts) in the care of Houseparents appointed by the school. All their choral training is undertaken in the Cathedral by the Master of Choristers and Cathedral Organist; the remainder of their education takes place at St Edmund's.

Senior School: In the first year of the Senior School (Year 9) pupils follow a core curriculum in English, Mathematics, French, Physics, Chemistry, Biology, History, Geography, Art, Music, Information Technology, Religious Education, PSHEE, Physical Education, and Technology. Drama, Spanish and Latin are options.

GCSE core subjects are: English, English Literature, Mathematics and the three (separate) Sciences. Options include French, German, Latin, Spanish, History, Geography, Art (Ceramics), Art, Food Technology, Product Design, Computer Science, Music, Drama, Dance, Physical Education and Religious Studies.

The following subjects are offered for A Level examinations: Art, Biology, Business Studies, Ceramics, Chemistry, Classical Civilisation, Design and Technology, Economics, English Literature, Film Studies, French, Geography, German, Government and Politics, History, Mathematics and Further Mathematics, Music, Music Technology, Photography, Physics, Psychology and Theatre Studies. In addition to their A Level choices, Lower Sixth pupils have the option to undertake an EPQ (Extended Project Qualification) and the Leiths Academy Diploma.

Careers and Higher Education. The School is affiliated to the Independent Schools Careers Organisation and the Careers Research and Advisory Centre. Pupils have the opportunity to undergo careers aptitude testing in the GCSE year, and all pupils are assisted in finding a placement for a week or more of work experience in the GCSE year. The careers and higher education staff give all possible help in the finding of suitable careers and in selecting appropriate universities and colleges of further education. Most A Level candidates go on to degree courses after leaving school; others join Art or Music conservatoires, or Drama schools.

Music. Music is woven into the fabric of school life at St Edmund's, reinforced by the presence of the Canterbury Cathedral Choristers. In the purpose-built Music School, specialist teachers give lessons to pupils from Pre-Prep through to the Sixth Form. Pupils of all ages participate in numerous musical ensembles which cater for a range of vocal and instrumental abilities. As a result, there is an exceptional practical examination record, with more than 80% of entrants achieving Distinction or Merit. Over twenty-five concerts and performances take place each year, from small lunchtime recitals in the Recital Hall to large gala concerts in Canterbury Cathedral. The school acts as a focus for musical excellence for children throughout East Kent and enjoys a creative partnership with the Tippett Quartet.

Performing Arts. Dramatic performance is included in the curriculum from the earliest years. Every term, the Pre-Prep School holds thematic drama workshops. Pupils in Junior and Senior Schools participate in school plays and other performances with vitality and enthusiasm, as an outlet for expressing their talents in acting, dancing, singing, music, choreography and technical production. The consistently outstanding GCSE and A Level results are testament to the emphasis placed on drama within the curriculum and school life in general.

Art. The emphasis St Edmund's places on creative subjects means that art is embedded in the curriculum across the three Schools. Pupils studying Art and Design enjoy excellent facilities and teaching. Drawing, painting, print-making, photography (traditional and digital), sculpture and ceramics are offered to pupils in the Junior and Senior Schools.

Sport. Association football, hockey, cricket, athletics, tennis, squash and (for girls) netball and rounders are the principal sports but there are opportunities for many other forms of exercise, including cross-country running, indoor rowing, golf, badminton, basketball, volleyball, swimming and gym-based fitness training. There is an AstroTurf pitch and large playing fields that adjoin the school buildings. There is an open-air heated swimming pool. The sports hall is well-equipped. There are eight tennis courts (both hard and grass), a compact golf course and a rifle range.

Activities. For those in the first four years of Senior School one afternoon a week is given over specifically to a broad range of activities. A number involve helping the local community, while other pupils learn new skills, e.g. archaeology, broadcasting, Eco-Schools, Japanese language and culture, kite making, literary and debating societies, photography, Rotary Interact and yoga.

In the second year all Senior School pupils join the Combined Cadet Force, a highly successful unit commanded by a member of the teaching staff and administered by an ex-soldier. There is an annual camp in the summer and an adventurous training camp at Easter, attendance at which is voluntary. Cadets may remain in the CCF for the duration of their school career if they wish, and are encouraged to do so if contemplating a career in the armed forces.

Pupils may also participate in The Duke of Edinburgh's Award scheme and the British Association of Young Scientists. There are regular field trips, choir and music tours, sports tours and many other one-off trips.

In Junior School, too, there is a diverse range of extracurricular activities, many of which draw on the school's excellent facilities for sport, music and drama.

There is a Year 8 outdoor activities week in Spain, an annual sports tour and skiing trip.

Health. The School Medical Centre is staffed by state registered nurses and provides medical care at all times. The health of the pupils is supervised by a senior local general practitioner under the NHS. A counselling service is available.

St Edmund's Festival of the Arts. Established in 2017, the Festival was planned and delivered with a clear and single aim: to celebrate the fantastic talents of young people by bringing to Canterbury an event as new and fresh as it was creative and innovative with a line-up of world-class artists. To date guest artists have included Freddy Kempf, Tasmin Little, Jess Gillam and Curtis Stigers and it has become a fixture in the Canterbury arts calendar.

Admission. *Pre-Prep School:* Entry at any age from 3–7. Once registered, children are invited to visit the School for informal assessment.

Junior School: Entry at any age from 7–12. Candidates will sit entrance tests and all prospective pupils will be interviewed or attend an assessment day.

Choristers: St Edmund's is the school of the Canterbury Cathedral choristers. For details of the voice trials please contact the Junior School Secretary.

Senior School: Entry at 13 from preparatory schools is through the Common Entrance Examination. Candidates from other schools will be tested appropriately or sit the School's own entrance tests. There is also a large entry of pupils into the Sixth Form, usually on the basis of interview and GCSE grade estimates from their present school.

Fees per term (2021–2022). Senior School: Boarders £12,846; Weekly Boarders £11,974; Day pupils £7,400. Junior School: Boarders £9,782, Weekly Boarders £8,915, Choristers £8,606, Day pupils £5,639–£5,459. Pre-Prep: £3,395–£3,925. Nursery £27.88 per day in receipt of Free Early Education. Extras have been kept to the minimum.

Entrance Scholarships. Competitive scholarships of up to 25% of tuition fees are offered in academic achievement, music, drama and sport at 11+, 13+ and 16+. In addition, art scholarships and choral exhibitions are available at 13+ and 16+. At the discretion of the Head an All-Rounder scholarship may be made to a candidate whose combination of talents merits an award. Such a candidate will have sat the academic scholarship paper and been assessed for a scholarship in at least one other discipline.

Bursaries and Fee Concessions. Originally founded to provide a free education for the fatherless sons of the clergy of the Church of England and the Church of Wales, St Edmund's now accepts applications from boys and girls for Foundationer status. Bursaries to provide a temporary (no more than 12 months) cushion are granted on a means-tested basis to existing pupils. Fee concessions, also means-tested, can be provided to the children of the clergy, members of the armed forces and to the third and subsequent children of the same family in the school at the same time.

Charitable status. The school is owned by St Edmund's School Canterbury, which is a charitable company limited by guarantee, registered in England and Wales, and a Registered Charity, number 1056382. It exists to educate the children in its care.

Patron: The Lord Archbishop of Canterbury

Governors:
Chairman: Air Marshal C M Nickols, CB, CBE, MA, FRAeS
Deputy Chair: Dr L Naylor
Dr M Carnegie, MB BS
Mr R Dodgson
Dr P Eichorn, MD
Mr C Harbridge, FRICS
Mrs N Leatherbarrow, BSc, MBA
The Revd Canon Dr T J N Naish, BA, MA, PhD
Mr Q L Roper, BA Hons, MA, NPQH
Mr S M Sutton, BA, FCA
Councillor P A Todd

Head: **Mr E G O'Connor**, MA Cantab, MPhil Oxon, MEd Cantab

Head of The Junior School: Mr Andrew De Silva, BAQTS, NPQH

Head of The Pre-Prep School: Mrs J E P Exley, BEd Hons CCCU

Chaplain: The Revd Joy Atkins

Bursar: Mr N C Scott-Kilvert, FCCA

Deputy Head: Mrs C J Shearer, BA Bangor, PCGE Leeds

Assistant Head Co-Curricular: Mr L A Millard, BSc Loughborough, PGCE

Please refer to the school website for the full staff list.

St Edward's, Oxford

Woodstock Road, Oxford OX2 7NN

Tel:	Warden: 01865 319323
	Bursar: 01865 319321
	Registrar: 01865 319200
email:	registrar@stedwardsoxford.org
website:	www.stedwardsoxford.org
Twitter:	@TeddiesOxford
Facebook:	@TeddiesOxford
Instagram:	@stedwardsoxford

Motto: '*Pietas Parentum*'

St Edward's was founded in 1863 by the Revd Thomas Chamberlain to educate the sons of middle class clergy in the Anglican tradition. The somewhat cramped original premises in the centre of Oxford soon proved inadequate for the growing School, so the decision was taken in 1873 to move to what were then the farmlands of Summertown. Today, the School sits on a vast 100-acre estate, complete with the Christie Academic Centre, the impressive Olivier Hall, the innovative North Wall Arts Centre, the high-specification Ogston Music School, a fully-equipped sports centre, a riverside boat house, pitches, courts, elegant Quad, golf course and canalside towpath. It is unusual to find such extensive grounds in a city boarding school; St Edward's is less than a mile from the university city of Oxford and only a 2-minute walk from the busy urban village of Summertown. The School has around 775 pupils, 83% of whom board, and 40% of whom are girls. Pupils live in one of 13 houses (five for girls, five for boys and three co-ed houses), and enjoy outstanding academic and co-curricular opportunities.

Ethos. We seek to educate pupils at St Edward's in a liberal and open community, in which scholarship is promoted, in which there is excellence in every area of school life, and in which there is a culture of service within and outside the School. We celebrate scholarship not only for the acquisition of knowledge through study but also for the development of a life-long interest in the life of the mind. We seek excellence for pupils in learning and in teaching, in pastoral care, in co-curricular opportunity, in diversity, in sustainability and in all school facilities. We believe that real public benefit comes not only from the sharing of resources and from working in partnership with others outside the School, but also – and more importantly – from the commitment to serving others which pupils will develop during their time at Teddies. We also believe in allowing pupils to be themselves and to chart their own course through the many opportunities available to them at Teddies, as the School is also affectionately known, so developing the confidence and the independence to thrive at university and in their professional and personal lives. At the same time, we ensure that pupils take full advantage of the facilities and opportunities available to them at the School, because we know that academic success and personal fulfilment follow from breadth of interest and engagement.

Pastoral Care. The comprehensive pastoral care system at St Edward's has long been regarded as one of the School's great strengths – a point highlighted by successive ISI reports. The system is underpinned by a highly-effective network of relationships offering distinct but interwoven levels of care. Each pupil sits at the centre of his or her network, surrounded by a range of people who can offer guidance and support. The Housemaster or Housemistress is a vital member of that architecture for pastoral care, and in this role they are supported by an Assistant HM and a Matron. Also key are Tutors who monitor the academic and pastoral life of six to 10 pupils, meeting with them regularly to offer advice and guidance across the full range of a pupil's experience of living and learning at Teddies. Within the school community, Sixth Formers are trained to offer a peer listening service and a great many other leadership and support roles; the two Heads of School meet regularly with senior staff to discuss all aspects of school life. School Nurses, the Health Centre, the Chaplaincy Team and School Counsellors are also part of the comprehensive pastoral care network.

Academic Work. Academically, it would be hard to overstate the importance to St Edward's of being in Oxford, within easy reach of the stimulating academic life of the university. Academic endeavour lies at the heart of the School; pupils are expected to work consistently hard, to take responsibility for their own learning and to engage actively in the many opportunities open to them for broadening their intellectual horizons. The school offers GCSE/IGCSE, A Level with the Extended Project and the IB Diploma. The GCSE programme is enhanced by St Edward's own Pathways and Perspectives courses – designed to stretch and inspire – two of which are taken alongside eight or nine GCSEs. The Sixth Form community is split 50/50 between A Levels and the IB. The Learning Support Department ensures the provision of support for pupils with special educational needs and disabilities, both through direct support of pupils and their parents and through the teaching staff.

In 2021, nearly two thirds of the Sixth Form grades were A*–A or Levels 7–6 (A Level or the IB Diploma), and just under 30% were at the highest grade (A* or 7). Just under 90% of all Sixth Form grades were A*–B or Levels 7–5, as they were when pupils last took examination papers in 2019. Some 60% of GCSE grades were Levels 9–7. Most Sixth Form leavers take up places at Russell Group or equally prestigious universities, including Oxford and Cambridge and, increasingly, pupils look to study overseas. In recent years, pupils have gone on to study at US and Canadian universities, including Harvard, Brown, Columbia, Dartmouth and UCAL Berkeley. Pupils have also been successful in their applications to universities in Hong Kong and Japan, and to universities in a number of European cities including Dublin, Amsterdam, Leiden and Madrid. Their success comes partly from the specialist support which we provide for them in their applications to universities outside the UK.

To extend academic opportunities for all pupils, outstanding university-level facilities have just opened at the heart of the School in the Quad. The Christie Centre features The Oxley Library, The Roe Reading Room, flexible new classrooms and a social learning space. Alongside the academic facilities is the stunning new Olivier Hall which hosts countless concerts, performances and gatherings for our growing community.

Higher Education and Careers. The Careers Education Department is firmly rooted in the real world of work. Our Head of Careers, a former Head Hunter with first-hand knowledge of a wide range of industries, runs a structured programme. Every Fifth Former benefits from a termly, compulsory careers session to help them identify and secure the most relevant work experience placements. Informal careers receptions are organised each year covering everything from financial services, law, engineering and fashion to marketing services, manufacturing and design.

Higher Education advice is highly personalised and quite exceptional. The Shell Curriculum and our Pathways and Perspectives courses are designed to feed directly into pupils' career planning by teaching explicitly the skills required for today's workplace: research, self-regulation, innovative thinking, presentation, collaboration and teamwork. Pupils are given every assistance in choosing the right course of further study and in preparing a strong application, including visits by representatives of UK and US universities, mock interviews and personal statement workshops. Tailored advice is given to Oxbridge and Ivy League candidates and to those aiming for highly-competitive courses, such as Medicine or Veterinary Science.

Music, Drama and the Arts. The cutting-edge programming of the award-winning North Wall Arts Centre enriches the cultural life of both the School and the wider community, placing St Edward's at the forefront of developments in arts education. As a result, the arts are highly valued and enormously successful at St Edward's. The Drama Department is flourishing: main school productions, including musicals, are complemented by devised pieces, House plays, Shell plays and a Speech and Drama programme. The Art Department is strong and vibrant, benefiting from recently enhanced facilities and a stream of visiting exhibitions to The North Wall. The Dance programme is extensive, with over 100 classes every week for more than 150 pupils – covering styles from ballet to hip hop – generating a range of material for regular dance shows. The Music Department, housed in the elegant Ogston Music School, delivers about 500 lessons every week, taught by a team of 40 visiting specialists. The main school groups include the Orchestra, Chamber Orchestra, Chapel Choir, Chamber Choir, St Edward's Singers (a choir for the School and the local community), Concert Band, Big Band, Jazz Band and various Chamber Music groups. There are around 60 concerts a year, in School and further afield, with occasional foreign tours.

Sport, Games and Activities. A wide variety of sports, games and activities is on offer. We compete at the highest level in several sports and can boast of county and national representatives. We encourage all our pupils to participate and to enjoy playing at all levels. We have fielded as many as 27 teams on one day – over 400 children representing the school. These sports, games and activities include rugby, football, hockey, cricket, rowing, athletics, netball, squash, tennis, swimming, cross-country running, sailing, golf, football, canoeing, ceramics, theatre crew, filmmaking, debating, investment, textiles, cycle maintenance, volunteering, charitable challenges, community service – and much more. We operate a Combined Cadet Force with Navy, Army and RAF sections, and offer The Duke of Edinburgh's Award.

Admission to the School. Formal registration, for which a fee is charged, takes place online via the school website. All applicants applying for 13+, Year 9, are asked to sit the ISEB Common Pre-Tests, ideally in the autumn of Year 6. Applications from all schools are encouraged, and separate routes are available for pupils registering later in the process, coming through the state system and from overseas. Place offers are conditional on a satisfactory school report, performance at interview and in the Common Entrance Examinations, Pre-Senior Baccalaureate (PSB) or our own 13+ entrance examinations. The Lower Sixth 16+ assessment interviews and scholarships take place in November prior to entry; place offers in the Sixth Form are subject to good performance at GCSE (at least six grades 9–6, and at least grade 7 in the subjects chosen for A Level or in the IB at Higher Level) and a satisfactory report from the previous school.

Scholarships. Academic and Music Scholarships, and Art and Sports Awards are available at both 13+ and 16+ entry. At 13+ entry, Arts Awards cover Art, Dance, Drama and Design Technology; and at 16+, Arts Awards cover Art, Dance and Drama.

Academic Scholarships: 16+ academic scholarships take place in the November prior to entry in the September, 13+ academic scholarships take place in the March prior to entry.

Music Scholarships: Most candidates perform on two instruments, and many offer singing as one of these options. Composition can also be considered. We look for potential rather than attainment to date, although the minimum standard required is about grade 5 for 13+ and grade 8 for 16+.

Dance and Drama Awards: Candidates for both these awards will be expected to demonstrate considerable natural ability and should be able to confirm that they have begun to reach high standards on the stage.

Music Scholarships, and Dance and Drama Awards for 13+ entry take place in the January/February prior to entry, 16+ in the November prior to entry.

Art Awards: Candidates must submit a digital portfolio of work prior to the assessment. On the day of the award they will be asked to complete an observational drawing task.

13+ scholarships take place in the January/February prior to entry, 16+ in the November prior to entry.

Sport Awards for both 13+ and 16+ entry take place in the November prior to entry. At 13+ candidates will show considerable natural ability and will have achieved county level for one of our major sports. At 16+, successful candidates will be competing regularly for their county or at national level. They may specialise in one or more of our major sports but will be expected to make a year-round contribution to the competitive games programme at St Edward's.

Bursaries. Any pupil applying to St Edward's in Years 9 or 12 may apply for means-tested fee assistance up to 100% of fees through our Bursary programme. Applications should be made by 1st September in the year of assessment for entry to the School. Bursaries are unrelated to scholarships and other awards.

Fees per term (2021–2022). Boarding £13,489; Day £10,794.

Charitable status. St Edward's, Oxford, is a Registered Charity, number 309681. The aim of the School is, for the benefit of the public, to promote and provide for the advancement of education of children and young people in a liberal and open environment which values creativity and innovation. The School aims to develop pupils equipped to face the opportunities and uncertainties of life with intelligence and curiosity, creativity and innovation, integrity and honesty, resilience and enthusiastic participation, moral courage and responsibility for their actions, a sense of compassion and service, and an understanding of and respect for other people.

Visitor:
The Right Revd The Lord Bishop of Oxford

Governing Body:
Chris Jones, MA. FRSA [OSE] (*Chairman*)
Wilf Stephenson, MA (*Vice Chair*)
John Adedoyin MA, MBA
Sarah Ainsworth, MA, MSc, CQSW (*Churchill Fellow*)
Caroline Baggs, BSc
Joe Burrows, MA
Georgina Dennis, MA [OSE]
Professor Louise Fawcett-Posada, MA, DPhil
David Jackson, LLB
Kenneth MacRitchie, MA, BD, LLB
Clare Robertson, MBChB, MRCP Paeds, FRCPCH
Michael Roulston, MBE, BPhil, MEd
Mike Stanfield [OSE]
Philip Winston, MA, PhD

[OSE] *Former Pupil*

Warden: A J Chirnside, MA Oxford

Sub-Warden: A J Darby, BA Durham

Deputy Head Academic: D J Flower, BA, MA Oxford
Deputy Head Pastoral: R Bellamy, BA Loughborough, MA Open

Chaplain: Revd E A Lennon, MA National Ireland, MA Oxford

Assistant Head Academic: L L H Tao, BA Durham
Assistant Head Pastoral: J E B Cope, BA Oxford, MA Open

Assistant Heads Extra Curricular:
N H C Coram-Wright, MA St Andrews
J Young, BSc Warwick

Director of Sport: E Singfield

Director of Music and the Arts: A C W Tester, MA late Organ Scholar of Fitzwillam College, Cambridge

Teaching Staff:

J Adlam, PhD Hamburg
D A Aldred, BA Exeter
S K Arbuthnot, BA Queen's Belfast
A Badri, BA Cambridge
S C S Barns, BSc Durham
L Barr, BA London
O J Barstow, MEng Nottingham Trent
O S Bartholomew, MA Oxford
N J Bond, BSc Cardiff Metropolitan
L Bowen, BSc, PhD Dundee
J Bowen, BA Camberwell School of Art
L Bray, MA York
M E Bunch, BA, MA Durham
J J Burbidge, MA, PhD Ohio
S Cabello Malfetano, BA Malaga
D Caro Solano, BA Western Australia
J A Cazabon, MSc Wales, Aberystwyth
H Chistenga, BSc Instituto Superior Pedagogico EJ Varona, Cuba
J E Clampham, MAM Edinburgh, MSc Kingston
L E Compton, BSc Warwick
R F Cottrell, BA Southampton
R F Craze, BSC Exeter
N C Creed, MA Late Choral Exhibitioner of Trinity College, Cambridge
G Damiani, BMus Guildhall School of Music & Drama, ARCO
A-L Davies, MA Pua
C A Davies, BA York, MA Open
J C Davies, BA Durham
J M Davies, MA, BA Swansea
A J Davis, BSc, PhD Leeds, FLS, FRGS
D Del Strother, MSc Durham
M-L Delvallée, Licence d'Anglais, MA Université du Littoral, MA Canterbury
P Diaz Rogado, MA Salamance
R E Drury, BSc Leeds
L C Duffy, BA Hull
I Dunn, PhD Liverpool
K J Eden, BA Winchester, MA City, London
L Elkins, Italia Conti Academy
A N Elliott, BA Oxford
J Fairbrother, BSc Surrey
J F E Ferguson, BA Newcastle
A Fielding, BA York, MSc Oxford
D Finamore, BSc Bath
M D Fletcher, MA Cambridge, PhD Bath, CSciTeach, CSci, CChem, MRSC
L K French, BSc Bangor
M Gillingwater, MSc, BSc Edinburgh, MEd Cambridge
A M Goldsmith, BA Newcastle
M J Golesworthy, MChem Oxford, FRSM, FTCL
P C Gowen, BSc Leeds
A R Griffiths, BSc Loughborough
A J Grounds, BA Brunel, MSc Oxford
A R Hahn, BA Glasgow School of Art
A J T Halliwell, BA Loughborough

L Hamblin-Rooke, BSc St Mary's Twickenham
C Hamilton, MSc Southampton
M J Hanslip, BEd Greenwich
P Herring, BA Hons Cambridge
C Holder, BA Brighton, MFA Slade School of Fine Art
T E Holdsworth, BEng Cranfield
S C Holland, BSc Nottingham Trent
C M Holliday, BA Bournemouth
M Hubert, BA Waterloo, Canada
N F Hunter, BA Courtauld Institute, London
H E Hyams, BSc West of England
J E Ingram, MMath Warwick, MEd University College London
M Islam, BSc Imperial College
M P Jackson, BA Manchester
R K James, BSc Liverpool
C M James, BSc Kent
F Q Livingstone, MA Cambridge
L M Mackrell, BA Royal Holloway
A E Moffatt, BA Oxford Brooks
H S Murphy, BSc Nottingham
G E Nagle, MA, DPhil Oxford
F C H Nelson, BA, MSt Oxford
K L Newson, BA Sheffield
S J T Palferman, BA Leeds, MPhil Oxford
R Perry, BA Oxford
M J Phillips, BA St Martins
J R Powell, GRSM, LRAM Royal Academy of Music, ARCM
H V Pumfrey, BA Durham, MA Birbeck
Y S Ramadharsingh, BSc University of the West Indies
K J Reid, MSc St Andrews
C V Riddle, BA Exeter
S J Roche, BA, MEd Leeds
L M B Rudolf, BMus London
A R Rush, MSc Loughborough
E P Scates, BA Bournemouth, MA Canterbury Christ Church
C S Schofield, MA Cambridge
J Sephton, BA Oxford
J E Sinclair, BA Oxford
N M Simborowski-Gill, MA Oxford
R M Simmonds, BA Exeter
J R McK Simpson, BEng Bristol
R H Stephens, BSc Southampton, MA Durham
R M Storey, BSc Edinburgh
G M Strachan, BA Durham
P O B Swainson, BA Exeter
A K S Talbot, BA Royal Holloway, PGCE Oxford
F S C Tao, MSc London School of Economics
M J Taylor, MA Durham, ALCM
H D Thomas, LLB Birmingham, MEd Cambridge
J W Thompson, BA Durham, MMus, Organ Scholar of Corpus Christi College, Cambridge, PGCE, FRSA
J E Thomson, BA Durham
P Torri, MA Milan, PhD Leuven
W H Truter, BSc Stellenbosch
L R Turley, BA, PGDip Glasgow School of Art, PGDip Oxford Brookes
C M Tyer, BA Royal Holloway
C Valente, MA Caen, France
P R Waghorn, BSc Bradford, MSc Open
C A Wallendahl, MA Oxford
A P Waring, BSc Birmingham
B R Watts, BSc Bristol, PhD Oxford
S J Wheeler, BSc Leeds, PhD Sheffield

F L Wickens, MA Oxford
A J Wiggins, MA Oxford
T Wyatt, BA Oxford

Post-graduate Teachers:
O Allison-Dogar, BA London
L Ayers, BSc Loughborough
M Blackham, BSc Solent
L A L Paul, BA Manchester
F Ronan, BSc Oxford Brooks
A A Sargent, BA Oxford
P Simmonds, BA Bristol
A Winter, BSc Exeter

Bursar: E G B Hayter, BSc
Registrar: N Jones, BEd
Examinations Officer: K Craven, BA
Assistant Examination Officer: V Abigail
Head of Careers Education: J Vaughan-Fowler, FRSA
Finance Bursar: D Thomas, MA, MSc, MBA, BA, FCA
Head of HR: O Pounderge, MSc, MBA, MCIPD, CMgr, FCM
Estates Bursar: R A Hayes
CCF, Contingent Commander: Sqn Ldr N H Coram-Wright, RAFAC, MA
CCF, School Staff Instructor: Captain O Perera

Medical Officers:
L Bennett, BA, MBBS, MRCGP, DFSRH
M Cheetham, BA, MB, MS (*2001*) UK
D Tiffitt, NBBS, DRCOG, MRCGP, MSc

Librarian: S A Eldred, BA, MSc

St George's College, Weybridge

Weybridge Road, Weybridge, Surrey KT15 2QS

Tel: 01932 839300
email: contact@stgeorgesweybridge.com
website: www.stgeorgesweybridge.com
Twitter: @sgweybridge
Facebook: @stgeorgescollegeuk
Instagram: @stgeorgesweybridge
LinkedIn: /company/st-george-s-weybridge

Motto: *Amore et Labore*

Founded by the Josephite Community in 1869 in Croydon, the College moved in 1884 to its present attractive grounds of 100 acres on Woburn Hill, Weybridge. Within its particular family orientated ethos, the College seeks to encourage a wide, balanced Christian education in the Catholic tradition, encouraging excellence and achievement across a broad spectrum of academic, sporting and extra-curricular activities. Almost all pupils move on to higher education, the vast majority gaining places at Russell Group universities, including Oxford and Cambridge.

The College is co-educational throughout, and there are approximately 1,000 students.

Admissions. Entry is mainly at age 11 (First Year), with smaller cohorts at 13 (Third Year) and 16 (Sixth Form). Students are accepted in September each year after successfully completing entrance examinations and interviews the previous winter. Entry is occasionally possible during an academic year.

Full details on the admissions process can be found on our website or by contacting our Admissions team.

Entrance Scholarships. Academic Scholarships are awarded at 11, 13 and for the Sixth Form. Additionally, at age 11, Music, Art and Sports Scholarships are offered, and at 13 and 16 Music, Drama, Sport and Art Scholarships are offered.

Details of the number of scholarships at each year group, process for application and guidance on expected standards are to be found on our website under the Admissions section. A certain number of scholarships are allocated to our Junior School candidates each year.

Bursaries. St George's offers financial assistance of up to 100% relief on fees via its means-tested Bursary Scheme. The scheme allows families who would not normally be able to consider the independent sector to seek a St George's education for their academically able child. Places are awarded from the age of seven at the Junior School and 11 at the College. At 11, we are able to confirm the award of a bursary prior to a child sitting the entrance examinations. As with all applications, children will need to reach the academic entry standards required at both schools to be offered a place.

Short term financial assistance. The College provides short-term financial assistance for existing families who find themselves in difficult financial circumstances. Further information is available from the Bursar.

Facilities. Our world-class Activity Centre was built to mark our 150th anniversary, opening in 2019 and offering an exceptional array of facilities for dynamic use. This ambitious building was designed to provide several flexible and varied environments to cater for many different types of activity, now and in the future. Spaces include a glassfloor in the main hall for multi-sport use, dance studio, climbing wall, mental performance studio, and a gym; all helping to inspire our students to excel throughout their school life and beyond. Our modern Sixth Form building provides group and silent study rooms, social space, five History and five Geography classrooms, staff offices and meeting areas. Refurbishment over the past three years has provided modern facilities for Science, Music, Languages, English, Mathematics, Theatre and Technology. There is an extensive Arts Centre, and an impressive Library. The College has 19 tennis courts, including three international standard grass courts, clay courts and an impressive four-court Indoor Tennis Centre. In addition, there are floodlit netball courts, an all-weather athletics track and two astroturf hockey pitches. The College Boat Club is situated nearby on the Thames, and is currently the subject of extensive redevelopment plans to replace the current building with a new facility by September 2022.

The Curriculum. This is kept as broad as possible up to GCSE, with a balance between Arts and Science subjects. Students usually take a maximum of 10 GCSEs, while A Level candidates may choose from over 20 subjects. The vast majority of our Sixth Form students go on to Russell Group universities, including Oxford and Cambridge.

Careers. Guidance is given throughout a student's career at St George's, but particularly while students are making GCSE, A Level and university choices. The Careers Coordinator has a contemporary, well stocked Careers Room and makes effective use of testing, portfolios, work experience, trial interviews, Challenge of Industry days and computer software to support students.

Art. The Art Department attracts large numbers of students at GCSE and A Level who achieve consistently high results in their examinations. A large proportion of A Level candidates successfully apply to Art Colleges, often each receiving several offers in this highly competitive field.

Music. Music plays a vital part in school life. There is a wide range of music-making encompassing early music, madrigal groups, jazz, rock, African Drumming as well as more traditional ensembles, orchestras and wind bands. The choir and orchestra give regular performances (including radio broadcasts), and usually tour Europe annually. Tuition is available on all orchestral instruments from a team of 36 visiting specialists who teach over 400 students each week. Students play in youth orchestras and have gained scholarships to the major conservatoires.

Responsibility and Service. While some of our work in this area was impacted by the pandemic, much has continued.

Many students engage in care for elderly people at home or in care homes, as well as those with disabilities. When able to, groups of Sixth Form students accompany people with disabilities to Lourdes in the Easter and Summer terms. Students find these activities a rewarding exercise in Christian service. More recently, Sixth Form students have supported refugee children with online weekly tutoring to support their transition to British schools. The Prefect system and the mentor system offer positions of responsibility to the oldest students. The Duke of Edinburgh's Award scheme is encouraged and there is a flourishing College Council.

Pastoral Care. The spiritual, moral and academic wellbeing of the students is the concern of every member of staff at the College. Nearly all staff act as Group Tutors with particular responsibility for the daily care of their students and for forging links with parents. Each Year Group is led by a Head of Year, and the Chaplain has a general pastoral role. All groups have a day of retreat away each year. The College also has six Houses to which the students are affiliated and all students have one period per week as part of their PSE programme.

Extracurricular Activities. A very wide range of clubs and societies take place both at lunchtime and after school. In addition to music and sport, a broad range of interests is catered for. Some examples include the Science, Cookery, Young Enterprise, Philosophy and Model Clubs.

Sport. All students participate in the wide variety of sports offered at St George's: rugby, hockey, netball, cricket, tennis, rowing, and rounders, plus a wide range of other activities such as golf, athletics, badminton, basketball and cross country. Each student has the opportunity to develop their own talents in small coaching groups. The College has its own Activity Centre, Boat House on the Thames, 19 tennis courts (including four indoor), two floodlit artificial pitches with viewing stand, floodlit netball courts, six artificial cricket nets, one main pavilion and two smaller cricket pavilions, and eight rugby pitches. The College has access to the Junior School heated outdoor swimming pool. Attendance at national hockey finals is an annual event and the College hosts a very popular Under 18 Hockey Sixes every year. International honours have recently been gained in hockey, cricket, rowing and tennis.

Junior School. St George's Junior School is located nearby in Thames Street, Weybridge, and is co-educational for children aged 3 to 11.

(*For further details*, *please see Junior School entry in IAPS section.*)

Fees per term (2021–2022). First Year to Upper Sixth: £7,250. Lunches (compulsory for First and Second Years) £360.

Charitable status. St George's College Weybridge is a Registered Charity, number 1017853, and a Company Limited by Guarantee. The aims and objectives of the Charity are the Christian education of young people.

Governing Body:
Chair: Mr D Nowlan
Mrs S Allom
Mr D Bicarregui
Mrs T Bowden
Mrs C Burnham
Dr L Gordon
Mr J Hood
Mr T Kirkham
Mr N Lemmon
Prof A Muggeridge
Mrs S Munk
Mr C Prescott
Mrs M Satchel
Mrs C Shevlin
Clerk to the Governors and Bursar: Mr G Cole

Headmistress: **Mrs R F Owens**, MA Oxon, PGCE, NPQH

Deputy Head, Academic: Ms F M May, MA, BA, PGCE
Deputy Head, Pastoral: Miss S L Hall, BSc, PGCE
Deputy Head, Staff: Mr C Kendall-Daw, MA, BA Hons, BPhil, STB, QTS, FCCT, FRSA

Assistant Head, College Entry: Mr L Chu, BA, PGCE
Assistant Head, Pastoral: Mrs T A Hall, BSc, MSc, PGCE
Assistant Head, Academic: Mr J E Davies, BA, PGCE
Assistant Head, Sixth Form: Mr J D Carr, BA Hons, PGCE
Assistant Head, Curriculum: Mr R H Cheney, BSc, QTS

College Chaplain: Fr Martin Ashcroft, CJ, MA, MA, STB, BPhil, BA CertEd
Assistant Chaplains: Mrs J Mall; Mr K Mendes

Heads of Department:
Academic Support: Ms T E Medhurst, BA Hons, PGCE, Dip Dyslexia
Art: Mr T A McIlwaine, BA Hons, PGCE
Biology: Mr M T Stather, BSc Hons, PGCE
Business & Economics: Mr D P Danaher, MTL, BA, PGCE
Chemistry: Ms S E Goodfellow, MA Oxon, BA Hons, PGCE
Computing: Miss D A Stansfield, BSc Hons, PGCE
Design & Technology: Mr D M Hoyle, BA Hons, PGCE
Director of Drama: Mr M A Schofield, MA
English: Mr N Waight, BA Hons, PGCE
Food & Nutrition: Mrs J B Weaver, BA Hons, PGCE
Geography: Mr G D Boyes, BSc, QTS
History: Mr M J Barham, BA Hons, PGCE
Languages: Mr T Deive, BA, PGCE (*i/c Spanish*)
Latin: Mrs S Carpenter, BA Hons, PGCE
Mathematics: Miss S H Arif, MEd, BSc Hons, PGCE
Director of Music: Miss K B Wardil, BA Hons, PGCE
Physics: Mr B J Peake, BSc, PGCE
Politics: Mr P Gillingham, BA Hons, PGCE,
Psychology: Mr W B Harrison, BA Hons, PGCE
Religious Studies: Mr S W McAndrew, BA Hons, PGCE, QTS
Director of Sport: Mr A Cornick, BA Hons, PGCE

St Helen and St Katharine

Faringdon Road, Abingdon, Oxon OX14 1BE

Tel: +44 (0) 1235 520173
email: admissions@shsk.org.uk
website: www.shsk.org.uk
Twitter: @SHSKSchool
Facebook: @StHelenStKatharine
LinkedIn: /school/st-helen-and-st-katharine

Founded in 1903, St Helen and St Katharine is an independent day school for girls aged 9–18 in Abingdon, just south of Oxford. Our 700+ students study in a campus-style environment with both beautiful Edwardian and modern buildings, set in 22 acres of grounds. The School aims to offer students the best possible experience at each stage of their educational journey, from Junior Department through to Sixth Form.

St Helen's is a school for bright girls with enquiring minds, a place where success is celebrated but not revered. Eager to learn and motivated to do their best, our students take advantage of the many opportunities on offer. We encourage them to challenge themselves and take risks academically and beyond. Our aim is to ensure that every student achieves success as she defines it, so that she can believe in herself, her talents and abilities, and feel prepared and equipped for life beyond school.

Academic. Our outstanding academic record makes us one of the leading girls' schools in the country. The curriculum offers a broad range of subjects as well an extensive range of opportunities for academic enrichment beyond lessons, such as attending lectures and conferences outside school, visiting specialist speakers, discussion dinners and Oxbridge preparation.

Our vision for St Helen's Sixth Form is to create an environment for our students that will spark their intellectual spirit and imagination. We offer students the chance to create a programme of four individual elements of study where they choose three to four A Levels out of 20+ subjects, offered as the core of their academic work, some taught jointly with Abingdon School. They can then add a St Katharine's study option – for example an EPQ, Ethics for Scientists or Mandarin – to complement or contrast their A Level subjects.

IGCSE and A Level results are consistently outstanding. In 2021, 95.8% of A Level grades were A*–B, and 79.7% were A*–A. 94.9% of IGCSE grades were 9–7, while 81.0% were 9–8.

Pastoral. Recognising the enormous change that our students undergo as they pass through school, our form tutors and support tutors are at the heart of a strong and accessible pastoral network. Every member of staff plays a role, including the Director of Students, Heads of Section, counsellors, the Chaplain and Health Centre staff, so that students have the support they need to talk through the trickier things. We allow students the space to explore their individuality in an environment that is big enough to celebrate a wide range of personalities and interests, whilst small enough to know, to care and to spot when someone is having a good, or a bad, day.

Beyond: extracurricular activities, trips and visits. Our broad and varied Beyond programme of extracurricular activities and clubs play a central role within school life. Students are offered opportunities to explore and extend their interests as we actively encourage them to give new things a go. We host sports clubs for elite competition as well as for leisure, 300+ music lessons per week and at least six drama productions every year. There are clubs and societies from cricket and photography to philosophy and Minecraft, as well as activities such as DofE and the Tycoon Enterprise competition.

Overseas expeditions, whether playing lacrosse in the USA, going on a language exchange across Europe or doing community work in Eswatini, provide experiences of a lifetime and play their part in developing self-reliance.

Facilities. Over the last decade an extensive building programme has been undertaken with many new additions to the school, including our Sport Centre, Performing Arts Centre, state-of-the-art Library, Science Centre, featuring 12 new laboratories, and a 3D Design Centre Towards the end of 2022, the School will have a brand new Sixth Form Centre, providing students with the space and opportunity to grow their academic and extracurricular interests in readiness for their future. The space echoes and anticipates the very best higher education institutions, smoothing the transition from school to university.

Admissions. Students are admitted to the Junior Department at either Year 5 or Year 6 and to the senior school at Year 7, Year 9 or Lower Sixth. It may be possible to admit students into other years should a place be available.

Scholarships. We believe that one of our most important roles as a school is encouraging our students to do their best, rewarding their achievements and celebrating their individual talents, both academically and beyond the classroom. Our scholarship programme seeks to recognise excellence and potential across academic ability, music, art, drama and sport. Our scholarship programme is not subject to means testing and varies in duration and value.

Bursaries. Opening access for families who would not otherwise be able to afford school fees has always been central to our ethos. If a student has the ability, imagination and drive to grasp the opportunities on offer at St Helen's we would like to give her that chance. We offer means-tested bursaries from 20–100% of fees from Year 7, as well as transformational bursaries at A Level.

Fees per term (2021–2022). £5,995

Charitable status. The School of St Helen and St Katharine Trust is a registered charity, number 286892.

Governors:
Chair of Governors: Mr Kevan Leggett

Mrs Pauline Cakebread	Mr Dave Lea
Dr Manjari Chandran-Ramesh	Mrs Joanne Loveridge
	Mrs Jenny Mitchell
Ms Sharon Cooper	Ms Jacqualyn Pain
Mr Giles Crowe	Mr Graham Steinsberg
Ms Olivia Rathbone	

Clerk to the Governors: Mrs Liz Tyler

Headmistress: Mrs Rebecca Dougall, MA London, BA Bristol

Deputy Head: Mr John Hunt, MA St Andrews
Director of Finance and Operations: Mrs Nicola McAvoy, BSc London

Assistant Head, Director of Students: Mrs Elizabeth Bedford, MA Oxford Brookes, BA Durham

Assistant Head, Director of Academic Development and Partnerships: Dr Abbie Pringle, DPhil, MSc Oxon, BSc Oxford Brookes

Director of Communications and Marketing: Ms Lea Askgaard, MA Southern Denmark

Director of Studies: Mr Clive Morris, MA Oxon

Head of Sixth Form: Mrs Heather Darcy, MA Warwick, BSc London

Head of Middle School: Mrs Helen Nash, BA Southampton

Head of Lower School: Mrs Kay Taylor, BA Wales

Joint Heads of Junior Department: Mrs Nina Bass, BSc Nottingham; Mrs Rachel Green, MA Oxon

St Lawrence College

Ramsgate, Kent CT11 7AE

Tel:	01843 572900 (Head of College)
	01843 572912 (Junior School)
	01843 808080 (Bursar and General Office)
	01843 572931 (Admissions)
email:	hm@slcuk.com
	jsoffice@slcuk.com (Junior School)
	bursar@slcuk.com (Bursar and General Office)
	admissions@slcuk.com (Head of Admissions)
website:	www.slcuk.com
Twitter:	@slcMain
Facebook:	@slcukofficial

Co-educational, Day: age 3–18 years, Boarding: age 7–18 years.

Number of Pupils.

Senior School 438: 244 boys (98 boarders, 146 day), 194 girls (72 boarders, 122 day).

Junior School 145: 7 boarders, 138 day pupils (of whom 19 attend the Nursery)

Educating children from the age of 3 to 18 years, this safe and caring school is set in over 45 acres of spacious, stunning grounds which house beautiful old architecture combined with new modern builds and facilities. Founded in 1879, it is home to just over 575 day and boarding pupils from local, UK and international families and welcomes boarders from 7 years of age.

High Performance Learning is embedded in our supportive, caring environment, which is founded on traditional Christian values. We have small class sizes where each child is an individual, nurtured to succeed in all aspects of life, ranging from progress in their studies to empathy, resilience and leadership.

Academic. St Lawrence has a long record of providing an excellent academic education within a supportive community, but is also modern in its outlook and very well suited to preparing pupils for a rapidly changing world. Class sizes are small and pastoral support is strong. Academic standards are high and impressive results are achieved across all years in the school. An extensive choice of GCSEs and A Levels are offered, with an excellent success rate of pupils going on to their first-choice university, including Oxbridge.

In the Junior School pupils are given the opportunity to explore new experiences such as Forest School, Thinking and Learning Skills and STEAM enrichment subjects. Pupils are expected to become independent learners and participate in STRETCH homework projects; we do not have Gifted and Talented for the few but rather we have STRETCH for all.

Boarding. Boarding pupils enjoy a 'home from home' experience, both in terms of comfort and atmosphere. In recent years, a massive programme of investment has created some truly remarkable facilities for boarders. All senior boarders are housed in single or double rooms with en-suite facilities and younger boarders are placed in rooms of between two and five pupils with modern streamlined en-suite bathrooms and Junior boarders (from age 7–11) enjoy living in Kirby House, a modern, purpose-built development which offers en-suite accommodation of exceptional quality.

Facilities & Extracurricular. Continued investment saw a new Science, Art and Design Centre opened in May 2018. Sporting facilities are exceptional and expert coaching is provided at all levels in a variety of disciplines including hockey, rugby, netball and cricket. There is an Olympic-standard waterbased hockey pitch and the Sports Centre houses a fitness suite, squash courts, climbing wall, dance studio and a large sports hall for badminton, basketball, etc. Music and drama flourish, enhanced by a 500-seat Theatre. Alongside the traditional chapel and library sits the school's modern coffee shop and boarders are able to use all of the facilities in the evenings and at weekends. All pupils benefit from an extensive activities programme which includes the CCF (Combined Cadet Force) and the Duke of Edinburgh's Award scheme, as well as chess, climbing, archery, golf, fencing, horse riding, table tennis, musical theatre, and many more activities.

Membership of the wider College community gives Junior School pupils the best of both worlds, and they are able to share many of the Senior School's excellent specialist facilities, including the Sports Centre and Theatre. The wide range of sports on offer includes rugby, hockey, cricket, netball, football, athletics, cross-country and swimming. There are plenty of fixtures against other schools, but, most importantly, children learn the value of fitness, cooperative teamwork and good sportsmanship. There is a proud musical tradition, and plenty of scope for drama and the creative arts, including LAMDA lessons. Some extra-curricular activities take place at the end of the school day, but most are concentrated into the popular, informal varied Saturday morning programme.

Location. The school is set in a safe, self-contained campus situated within easy walking distance of the historic seaside town of Ramsgate, home to the stunning Royal Harbour – currently the only Royal Harbour in England. It has excellent transport links to the continent, being near both Dover and the Channel Tunnel. London is only 75 minutes away by high-speed rail link to St Pancras International. Both Gatwick and Heathrow are under 2 hours away.

Exam Results. Outstanding results are achieved by the most academic students who progress to top universities. In 2019/20 the school entered the High Performance Learning (HPL) Fellowship of World Class Schools, confirming that our approach enables students to develop the cognitive skills, values, attitudes and attributes needed for high academic performance and lifetime success.

2021 GCSE results: 9–4 grades in Maths and English: 99%; 9–6 grades (all subjects): 79%.

2021 A Level results: A*–B grades: 75%; A*/A grades: 55%.

Admissions.

Junior School

An initial parental tour with the Head or Admissions Officer will be followed by a Pupil Taster Day, which allows the prospective pupil to be assessed in numeracy and literacy as well as getting to know the school from the inside.

Subject to a satisfactory meeting and supporting documentation, the Head of the Junior School may offer a place.

All parents will be asked to complete and return a Registration Form and a £100 Registration Fee (non-refundable).

Upon receipt of the Registration Form, the Terms and Conditions of the School will be sent with an Acceptance Form. The Acceptance Form must be completed and returned together with a deposit. This will secure a place at the School.

The deposit will be held for the duration of the child's time here and will be returned when all outstanding accounts have been settled in full. It does not form part of the payment for school fees or boarding fees that are charged termly in advance.

Senior School

At 11+ admissions are based on an Interview with the Head of College. A copy of a recent school report will also be required. Testing will be carried out where appropriate.

At 13+ the offer of a place will be dependent on the Common Entrance Examination, internal assessments and/ or a recent school report.

At 16+ the offer of a place will be dependent on a minimum of 5 GCSE passes.

EU and Overseas Students will be admitted on the basis of current performance, references and a short language test (as interviews are not always possible). Our special EFL centre will assess and integrate overseas pupils into the curriculum by offering a range of English teaching options, including an intensive English course.

Fees per term (2021–2022).

Senior School: Boarders £10,295–£12,485, Day £5,355–£5,675.

Junior School: Boarders £9,440, Day £2,665–£4,170

Fees are due and payable before the commencement of the relevant school term. St Lawrence College offers generous sibling allowances.

Individual Private Tuition: £60 per hour. Individual Instrumental Music: £41 per hour.

Bursaries. Parents in HM Forces pay the MOD CEA (Continuity of Education Allowance) plus 10% of our main boarding and tuition fees. Bursaries are awarded annually to pupils in need of financial assistance and who are likely to make a positive contribution to the life of the school. Bursaries may be awarded to new or existing pupils of the College and pupils who have been awarded a scholarship that requires supplementing. Parents may apply to the Governors' Bursary Committee for assistance and will be required to complete a confidential grant application form. Bursaries are means tested.

Scholarships. Scholarships can be offered in Years 7–11 for outstanding academic ability, art, drama, music or sports disciplines, worth up to 25% off fees. Sixth Form scholarships are also available.

Charitable status. The Corporation of St Lawrence College is a Registered Charity, number 307921. It exists to provide education for children.

The Council:

President: C Laing

Vice-Presidents:
Sir Martin Laing, CBE, MA, FRICS
The Baroness Cox, BSc, MSc, FRCN
G H Mungeam, MA, DPhil
B J W Isaac [OL]
M Iliff, MSc
D W Taylor, MA Oxon, PGCE, FRSA
J B Guyatt, MA
J Challender, BEd, MA

Chairman: M J Bolton, MBE, BA
Vice Chairman: G E Page

Members:
A G Burgess, TCNFF, ACP
J H Tapp, BSc
N G Marchant [OL]
T L Townsend, LLB [OL]
J Laslett, BA Hons, FCMA [OL]
Rev S Rae, PG Dip, BA Hons
G Carter, FRICS, FCABE
M Millin, LLB Hons, LLM
Dr J W D Neden, MA, MSc, MB, BS, FRCGP, DCH, DRCOG
S Pullen, BA Hons, PGCE, NPQH

[OL] *Old Lawrentian*

Clerk to the Governors and Bursar: J A Connelly, MA, MBA, BEng, CEng, MIET

Head of College: **Barney Durrant**, MA

Deputy Head (*Academic*): B Pennells, BA Hons Leeds
Deputy Head (*Pastoral*): T Moulton, BA
Chaplain: Revd J P Goodwin-Hudson (*Religious Studies*)
Assistant Head, 6th Form: E Matthews, BA West of England (*Drama*)
Director of Marketing, Admissions and Development: E Taker, BSc Hons
Development Director: Dr A Medhurst, BA Hons, MPhil, PhD Cantab

Junior School
Head: Mrs E Rowe, BA Hons, PGCE

St Leonards School

St Andrews, Fife KY16 9QJ

Tel: 01334 472126
email: contact@stleonards-fife.org
website: www.stleonards-fife.org
Twitter: @StLeonards_Head
Facebook: @stleonardsschool
Instagram: @stleonardsschool
LinkedIn: /school/st-leonards-school

Motto: *Ad Vitam*

Situated in the heart of St Andrews, St Leonards offers an outstanding co-educational boarding and day education for pupils aged five to 18, combining high academic achievement and opportunity with an inspirational atmosphere.

There are approximately 575 pupils in the School, of 35 different nationalities, with an equal number of boys and girls and around 140 boarders.

St Leonards was named Scotland's *Independent School of the Year 2019* by the Sunday Times Schools Guide.

Ethos. Founded in 1877, St Leonards aims to prepare young people for the challenges of life ahead, in line with the School's motto 'Ad Vitam', and to provide them with the skills to step into the world with confidence and integrity. We offer a broad, rigorous education and exceptional opportunities, while instilling confidence, responsibility and independence.

Location and Campus. St Leonards combines a beautiful, historic campus with the cultural and academic buzz that comes from being in the heart of the seaside university town of St Andrews.

The School is situated in a secure campus within the medieval walls of the former St Andrews Priory. The site has served as a place of learning since the 16th century and contains several buildings of historical significance, including our library, a building once used by Mary Queen of Scots as lodgings.

Students at St Leonards have sandy beaches, historic landmarks and world-famous golf courses on their doorstep, as well as the friendly town of St Andrews itself, in which our pupils are made to feel very much part of the community.

St Andrews is less than an hour from Edinburgh and just 20 minutes from Dundee (a one-hour flight from London).

Curriculum. St Leonards was the first school in Scotland to be accredited as an all-through International Baccalaureate School, delivering the inspiring Primary Years Programme, Middle Years Programme and IB Diploma and Career-related Programme in the Sixth Form.

In Years 7–11, pupils follow the MYP, followed by IGCSEs – typically around ten. A one-year Pre-IB course is also offered (equivalent to Year 11).

Years 1–6 follow the PYP, with all our IB Programmes ensuring a seamless learner journey, from Year 1 up to Year 13.

University Connection. The School has close links with the University of St Andrews, which was named top UK university by The Times Good University Guide for 2022. Each year, St Leonards appoints an Associate Researcher, a postgraduate student who provides a link for the pupils to the research community at the University. St Leonards students also have access to the University Library and Sports Centre and attend a range of lectures.

Sport, Drama, Art and Music. Students regularly enjoy success on the playing field in sports including rugby, lacrosse, hockey, tennis and football. They are encouraged to make the most of living just a few hundred yards from the most famous golf links in the world. The School runs a leading five-tier Golf Programme, delivered in partnership with St Andrews Links Golf Academy, and catering to all levels, from the complete beginner to the scratch golfer.

Pupils have the opportunity to learn a wide variety of musical instruments, leading to ABRSM recognition, while Drama students can take part in a number of professional-standard productions, staged both in School and at the neighbouring Byre Theatre. Art students show off their inspiring work every year in an exhibition that is open to the public, as well as gaining national recognition in photography awards.

Co-Curricular. There is an extensive range of over 50 different activities, including the Duke of Edinburgh's Award, sailing, skiing and debating. Trips abroad are organised throughout the school year, with recent destinations including Venice and Verona, Salamanca, skiing in the French Alps and a German exchange in Dresden. Community awareness is important at St Leonards, with recent projects ranging from sewing scrubs for frontline workers during the Covid-19 pandemic, to cooking and distributing fresh meals to families in need. This year's school charity is the RNLI.

Boarding. St Leonards excels in its boarding provision. Thanks to an ambitious £5m refurbishment programme, students live in modern, stylish comfort in a country house setting. According to a recent Care Commission inspection report, St Leonards offers its boarding pupils, 'an outstanding, Scottish, boarding experience', with the quality of care and support and the quality of the environment rated as 'excellent'. Full, flexi and weekly boarding is available from the age of 10.

Fees per term (2021–2022). Years 1–3: £3,280, Years 4–6: £4,066 (day) or £8,114 (boarding), Years 7–9: £5,000 (day) or £9,863 (boarding), Years 10–13: £5,313 (day) or £12,640 (boarding). Weekly and flexi boarding fees are also available.

Admission. Applications can be considered for any year group, at any time during the school year. Financial assistance may be given, based on need. Full details are available from the Registrar.

Charitable status. St Leonards School is a Registered Charity, number SC010904.

Members of Council:
Chair: Col Martin Passmore, MA, GCGI, FRSA
Mr Philip Petersen, BSc, MBA
Ms Charlie Wilson, BSc, FCCA
Mrs Carole Arnot
Ms Christine Bowie, MSc, PQD, MDACP Accred
Mr Danny Campbell
Mrs Victoria Collison-Owen, MA
Mr Ken Dalton, BSc Hons, CEng
Mr Paul Dollman, BSc Hons, CA
Mr Neil Donaldson, MSc
Mrs Laura Jacks, JD

Mr Alistair J Lang, BLE Hons, LLB, Dip LP
Mrs Heidi Purvis, BA, PGCE
Mr Andrew Peddie
Mrs Fenella Taylor, BA Hons

Academic Staff:

Head: **Simon Brian**, MA Hons Edinburgh

Senior Deputy Head (Teaching and Learning): Dawn
  Pemberton-Hislop, BA Hons Sheffield, MBA Keele
Deputy Head (Wellbeing): Andrew Durward, BEd Hons
  Edinburgh
Deputy Head (Boarding): Gerry Young, BSc Strathclyde
Head of Sixth Form: Aileen Rees, MA Hons Cambridge
Head of Years 10 & 11: David Blair, BSc Hons Stirling
Head of Years 8 & 9: Fiona McGregor, BSc Hons St
  Andrews
Head of Years 4–6 & Head of Outdoor Learning: Duncan
  Barrable, BCOM South Africa, GDTO Queensland
Head of Years 1–3: Claire Boissiere, MA Hons Dundee
Diploma & Career-related Programmes Coordinator: Ben
  Seymour, BSc Hons UEA Norwich
GCSE Coordinator: Michael Dick, BSc Hons St Andrews
Middle Years Programme Coordinator: Kathryn
  McGregor, BA Hons Southampton
Primary Years Programme Coordinator: Catherine
  Brannen, MEd Aberdeen, MA Madrid

Art & Design:
Donna Rae, MA Glasgow, BFA Chicago
Margaret Behrens, BA Hons, Dip PG Edinburgh
Camilla Fyfe, BA Hons Oxford
Winsome Hardie, BA Hons DJCA Dundee
Linda Jackson, BA Hons DJCA Dundee
William Clark, MA Winchester, BA Hons Dundee

Classics:
Andrew Lang, MA Hons St Andrews
Rebecca Masson, MA Hons, MLitt St Andrews

Computer Science:
Gus Ferguson, MBChB Cape Town, MSc Heriot Watt

Economics:
Pablo Funcasta, BA Cambridge, MSc LSE
Paula Prudencio-Aponte, BSc Bolivia, PG Dip St Andrews,
  MSc Manchester

EAL and English B:
Dawn Cremonese, MA Hons St Andrews, MA TESOL
  Leicester
Nicola Greener, BA Hons Newcastle

English:
Alfonso Iannone, MA Hons, PG Dip Edinburgh
Nafeesa Abdul-Karim, MA St Andrews, MPhil Cambridge
Katharine Gilbertson, MA Hons St Andrews
Denise Johnston, BA Hons Cardiff
Vanessa Samuel, BA Hons Cambridge
Andrew Proudfoot, BA Hons Liverpool

Geography:
Amy Henderson, MA Hons Dundee
Jill White, BSc Hons Aberdeen
Victoria Sherwood, BEd Hons Manchester Metropolitan

History:
Damian Kell, BA Hons, MA Hons Oxford
Susannah Adrain, MA Hons Dundee
David McLeish, MA History Dundee

Lorna Greenwood, MA Hons Edinburgh, Cert Ed Studies
  London
Jennifer Murray-Turner, BEd British Columbia, BA Hons
  Toronto

Learning Support:
Gillian Greenwood, MA Hons Cambridge
Aisling Bonner, BA Dublin City
James Turner, BEd Toronto, BSc Hons Nottingham Trent,
  MSc Brunel
Ann Stephens, BEd Dundee

Library:
Angela Tawse, MA, PG Dip St Andrews, MA UCL,
  MCLIP

Mathematics:
Russell Hall, BSc Hons St Andrews
Jonathan Edwards, BEd Hons Wales
Hilary Ballantine, BSc Hons Edinburgh
Michael Dick, BSc Hons St Andrews
Stuart Reilly, BSc Hons, BA Hons OU
Kristina Struck, State Exam MA Berlin

Modern Languages:
Nora Gannon, MA Aix-Marseilles
Mary Bradley, BA Hons Durham
Rie Adya BA MA Rissho, MPhil PhD Delhi
Susana Aranzana-Gonzalez, BA, MA, CAP Valladolid
Anne Bavaj, First State Examination MA Bonn, Second
  State Examination Aachen
Anna Beck, BA Columbia, MBA Cornell
Marion Dalvai, MA Trento, MPhil Dublin, PhD Dublin
Andrea Morris, MA Hons Glasgow
Marije Sneddon, BEd Ede
Louise Lacaille, MA Hons St Andrews, MSt Oxford
Elena de Celis Lucas, BA Hons A Coruna
Eulalia Grifell, MA Hons Heriot-Watt
Rebecca Masson, MA Hons, MLitt St Andrews
Max Sutherland, BSc OU, MA Hons St Andrews
Haiyan Wang, BA MA Sichuan, Chengdu, MSc Dundee

Music:
Fiona Love, BMus Hons Glasgow
Kate Chisholm, GRNCM, PG Dip RSAMD
Douglas Clark, Dip Mus Ed RSAMD
Martin Dibbs, MA, MLitt, PhD St Andrews, DMS ARMC
Darryl Dick, BMus Hons Birmingham
Winston Emmerson, BSc Hons Rhodes, MSc, PhD UPE
Stuart Foggo
James Lind, BMus Hons, MMus RCS
Ruairidh Geddes, Dip ABRSM
Kenneth Letham, BMus Hons, PG Dip RCS
Kirstie Logan, BSc Hons OU, Graduate RNCM
Jessica Long, MA Hons St Andrews, Dip ABRSM, PG Dip
  RCS
Dorothy McCabe, GRSM, ARCM, ATCL, Cert Ed London
Mairi McCabe, BMus Hons Napier, ATCL, Dip ABRSM
Melanie O'Brien, Dip TCL TCM London, ALCM, LLCM
  Napier
Megan Read, MA Glasgow, PG Dip Mus RSAMD
Suzannah Rice, BA Hons Southampton
Lynne Ruark, DRSAM, LRAM, Glasgow, CertEd
  Edinburgh
Toni Russell, BA Hons Applied Music Strathclyde
Paul Shiells, BEd Hons Aberdeen
Sally Shiells, BEd Hons, MMus Aberdeen
Dorine Sorber, MA RC Brussels
Anthony White

Physical Education:
Mark Baxter, BEd Hons Edinburgh
David Blair, BSc Hons Stirling
Fintan Bonner, BA Ireland
Louise Carroll, BEd Hons Edinburgh
Rosie Dawson, BA Hons Bangor
Neil Hislop, BEd Hons Jordanhill
Duncan McIntyre, BSc Robert Gordon, PGDE Edinburgh
Callum Parsons, BSc Abertay, HNC Fife College, UKCC
   Level 2 Coaching (*Scottish Rugby*)
Andrew Turnbull, BSc Napier

Psychology:
Rachael Cave, BSc Aberdeen

Science:
Sophie Sprot, BSc Hons Plymouth, MSRC
Patrick Smith, BSc Glasgow
Rachel Deegan, BA Oxford
Emma Coyle, BSc Hons Edinburgh
Mary Kennovin, BSc Hons Portsmouth Polytechnic, PhD
   St Andrews
Charlotte Kirby, BSc Hons St Andrews
Fiona McGregor, BSc Hons St Andrews
Robert MacGregor, BSc Hons Edinburgh
Rebecca Patterson, BSc QMUC
Aileen Rees, MA Hons Cambridge
Sara Tedesco, MSc Taranton, PhD Cork
Mark Arnold, HNC Dundee
Alison Hill, MSc Glasgow, BSc Hons Aberdeen PhD
   Belfast
Lyall Smith

Theatre:
Nichola McQuade-Powell, BEd Hons London
Christian Olliver, BA London RCSSD, BA Hons
   Birmingham Trent, MA London City
Laura Stewart, MA Hons Kent
Eva Walker, BA Hons West of Scotland

St Leonards Years 1–6

Nicola Arkwright, BEd Hons Coventry
Marina Barclay, PDA (*Classroom Assistant*)
Ailsa Beebee, BEd Dundee
Dianne Cormack, BSc Hons St Andrews
Anna Fisher, MA Hons Dundee
Teresa Fynn, MA Hons Edinburgh
Annabel Lindsay, BA Hons Oxford Brookes
Georgina Majcher, BSc Hons Northumbria
Caz McIntee, MFA New York, BA Hons DJCAD
Louise McQuade, BEd Hons Glasgow
Adele Neave, BSc Hons Glasgow School of Art
Billie Paterson Herd, NC Childcare & Education
Caroline Souter
Laura Stewart, MA Hons Kent

Chief Operating Officer: Andrew Maitland
Head of External Relations: Sarah Proudfoot, MA Hons
   Edinburgh

St Mary's School Ascot

St Mary's Road, Ascot, Berks SL5 9JF

Tel:	01344 296600 (Main Switchboard)
	01344 296614 (Admissions)
email:	admissions@st-marys-ascot.co.uk
website:	www.st-marys-ascot.co.uk

St Mary's School Ascot is a Roman Catholic boarding school founded by the Religious of the Institute of the Blessed Virgin Mary. St Mary's today is a self-governing, self-financing school.

Founded in 1885, the school is set in 55 acres within easy reach of London and Heathrow and close to the M4, M3 and M25 motorways.

Numbers on Roll. Boarders 365, Day pupils 23.

Age Range. 11–18.

Method of Entry. 11+ and 13+ School's own examination and interview. There is a small entry at Sixth Form.

Scholarships and Bursaries. At 11+ and 13+, there are three Academic Scholarships available worth up to 5% of the fees.

At 16+, there is one Academic Scholarship available worth up to 5% of the fees and the Sixth Form Science Scholarship worth up to 5% of the fees.

One Music Scholarship, worth 5% of the fees and free of charge musical instrument or vocal tuition for up to three 30-minute lessons per week, is awarded annually to a pupil entering the School at 11+ or 13+. Candidates must have qualified to at least Grade V on the first study instrument at the time of application.

One Art Scholarship worth up to 5% of the fees is awarded annually to a pupil entering the School at 11+, 13+ or 16+.

One All-Rounder Scholarship is is awarded annually to a pupil entering the School at 11+ and another at 13+.

One Sports Scholarship worth up to 5% of the fees is awarded annually to a pupil entering the School at 13+.

Means-tested bursaries are available.

Fees per term (2021–2022). Boarders £14,260, Day pupils £10,155.

Curriculum. All pupils follow a broad curriculum to GCSE including Religious Education, English, History, Geography, Maths, Biology, Physics, Chemistry, French, German, Italian, Spanish, Latin, Music, Drama, Art and Design, Computer Science and Physical Education. Tuition is also available in Piano, most String and Wind Instruments, Ballet, Tap Dancing, Speech and Drama, Ceramics and Craft activities, Tennis, Photography.

All pupils are prepared for GCSE at 16+ and typically take 10 subjects.

Sixth Form pupils have a choice of 25 A Level subjects and normally study 4 subjects. Interview, CV and course choice preparation is offered to all Upper Sixth pupils, including Oxbridge candidates. They are encouraged to undertake some of the many extra activities on offer and develop skills outside their A Level curriculum. Sixth Form pupils also have their own tutor who liaises closely with the Careers Specialist. Careers advice forms an integral part of the curriculum. This is supported by work experience, work shadowing placements and talks from external speakers, including Ascot Alumnae. The majority of sixth form pupils go on to university, and preparation is offered to Oxbridge candidates.

The School is a member of Inspiring Futures, which provides careers information, advice and guidance.

Religious Education is an integral part of the curriculum and the chapel holds a central position in the life of the school.

Sport. A varied programme is offered depending on age group. It includes Netball, Hockey, Gym, Swimming, Rounders, Tennis, Squash, Badminton and Athletics.

Purpose-built sports complex with sports hall, dance studio, squash courts and fitness suite. A floodlit 400m athletics track and hockey pitch provides a year-round, all-weather sports facility.

Drama. Performing Arts Centre which includes a flexible auditorium with lighting catwalks and control room with teaching facilities, fully-equipped drama studio and make-up and dressing rooms.

Art, Drama, Music, Science, Modern Languages and English. Specialist buildings are provided for all of these subjects and all pupils are encouraged to develop their musical, artistic, scientific and linguistic skills.

Libraries. The senior and junior libraries form the academic heart of the school. The senior library was built to meet the specific needs of Year 11 and Sixth Form girls and includes seminar rooms, which are used for teaching and careers advice.

Other Activities. Senior pupils are encouraged to participate in Community Service Projects, and those interested may enter The Duke of Edinburgh's Award scheme. There is a wide range of club activities for all ages, and, as a termly boarding school, generous provision is made for evening and weekend activities.

Charitable status. St Mary's School Ascot is a Registered Charity, number 290286. Its aim is to provide an excellent education in a Christian atmosphere.

Board of Governors:
Chairman: The Hon Mr M Hunt
Mrs A Ayton
Mr C Beirne
Miss A Clementi
Mr M Hattrell
Mr E Horswell
Ms A Lee
Mr P McKenna
Ms S Meadway
Mr G Moore
The Revd Dr D Power
Sr M Robinson
Ms C Vaughan
Ms L Wilson

Council:
Chairman: The Lord Hemphill
Mr M Armour
Mr N Davidson
Mr P Davis
Baroness S Hogg
The Hon Mrs O Polizzi

Senior Management Team:

Headmistress: **Mrs D Staunton**, BA York, MA York, PGCE

Senior Deputy Headmistress: Mrs C Ellott, BA Oxon, MA London, PGCE
Pastoral Deputy Headmistress: Mrs J Devine, BMus Leeds, MMus RNCM, PGCE
Academic Deputy Head: Mrs B Breedon, BEd Queen's Belfast, MSc Ulster
Bursar: Mr G Brand, BA Leeds
Director of Sixth Form: Dr D Coughlan, BA Cantab, MSt Oxon, PhD Cantab
Director of External Communications: Mr C Ellott, LLB UCL, BA OU, PGCE
Director of Co-Curricular: Mr A Smith, BA Warwick, MA Royal Holloway, PGCE

Catering Manager: Mrs J Carrington
Estate Manager: Mr T Clark
Finance Manager: Mr I McShea
Registrar: Mrs S Young

A full staff list can be found on our website: www.st-marys-ascot.co.uk/staff-list

St Mary's Calne

Curzon Street, Calne, Wiltshire SN11 0DF

Tel: 01249 857200
email: admissions@stmaryscalne.org
website: www.stmaryscalne.org
Twitter: @StMarysCalne
LinkedIn: /st-mary's-calne

St Mary's Calne (founded in 1873) is an independent boarding and day school for girls aged 11–18, a happy, purposeful and flourishing community of around 360 pupils with an 80% to 20% boarding-to-day ratio. St Mary's welcomes cultural diversity and around 15% of the students come from overseas.

The school is located in the market town of Calne amidst the Wiltshire Downs, an area of stunning natural beauty and historical significance. The school is within easy reach of the university towns of Bath, Bristol and Oxford and just over an hour by train from London. This ideal location means that the girls benefit from a huge range of co-curricular opportunities.

Focus on the individual. Small by design, St Mary's provides exceptional all-round education in a warm, nurturing environment. It is the individualised approach to every aspect of school life that makes St Mary's Calne special. The pastoral care is outstanding. Every girl has a Tutor to support her through aspects of school life, from organisational skills and subject choices through to university application.

Academic Excellence. St Mary's Calne has a well-deserved reputation for academic excellence and is committed to providing an education that will challenge and inspire its pupils. In the *Sunday Times Parent Power Schools' Guide 2020*, St Mary's was ranked 1st independent school in Wiltshire and 2nd in the South West. St Mary's is also the first independent school in the UK to be awarded the Platinum Science Mark Award.

In 2021, the girls went on to study at a range of leading universities including Oxford, Cambridge, Durham, Edinburgh, Exeter, King's College London (KCL), London School of Economics (LSE), University College London (UCL) and also prestigious universities in the USA. They will be reading a broad range of subjects including Archaeology, Art, Classics, Economics & Management, Engineering, English, French, Medicine, Music, Musical Theatre & Cabaret Performance, Philosophy & Theology and Veterinary Science.

Co-Curricular Opportunities. Opportunities in sport, music, art and drama abound and the facilities are superb, including a £2.55 million sports complex and full-size astro, a purpose-built theatre, a Sixth Form Centre and a state-of-the-art new library, overlooking the orchard.

80% of girls play musical instruments and take part in a wide variety of ensembles. The girls perform at many events, both in the local community and further afield.

Drama productions in the purpose-built theatre are of the highest standard and have transferred to the London stage. The Drama Department has a unique relationship with RADA, offering a course in advanced communication skills and girls also perform annually at the Edinburgh Fringe. In Art, in addition to holding a triennial exhibition in London, the girls have received numerous awards, including having artwork selected for the Young Artists' Summer Show at the Royal Academy of Arts.

The girls excel at sport, and the school is represented at county level in several major sports, nationally in athletics and lacrosse and internationally in horse riding, with all girls taking advantage of the superb sports facilities.

The girls also enjoy many other sports, including tennis (the St Mary's Calne Tennis Academy was a National Finalist for 'School of the Year' 2021 at the LTA Tennis Awards), hockey, horse riding, fencing and ski racing.

Outreach. The girls are very active in the local community and have helped in local hospitals and schools, performed concerts for the elderly in residential care homes and read to younger children in the community library. In addition, the girls help to raise awareness of, and funds for, local charities, such as Doorway, a charity which helps the homeless in North Wiltshire.

Fees per term (2021–2022). Boarding £13,760, Day £10,265.

Scholarships and Bursaries. Scholarships and Exhibitions are available to new entrants at 11+, 13+ and at Sixth Form. Any girl who is awarded a Scholarship or an Exhibition may apply for a means-tested Bursary.

We also offer Foundation Scholarships at entry to the school at 11+ and Sixth Form for girls applying from the State sector.

Please contact Admissions for further details and key dates regarding our Scholarships and Bursaries on: admissions@stmaryscalne.org

Charitable status. St Mary's School (Calne) is a Registered Charity, number 309482 and exists for the education of children.

Chair of Governors: Mr S Adde

Headmistress: **Dr Felicia Kirk**, BA Maryland, MA & PhD Brown

Senior Deputy Head: Mrs D Harrison, MA Cantab, PGCE Bristol, CPP Roehampton

Deputy Head Academic: Mr M Smyth, BSc Newcastle, PGCE Cantab, MSc Oxon

Deputy Head Pastoral: Mrs S Toland, MA Cantab, PGCE Brunel, CPP Roehampton

Director of Development, Marketing & Admissions: Mrs C Depla, MA St Andrews

School Chaplain: Revd J Beach, BSc Essex, BA Bristol, MTh Cardiff

Bursar: Mr D Boswell, BEd Cantab, FILM

St. Mary's College

Everest Road, Crosby, Merseyside L23 5TW

Tel: 0151 924 3926
email: office@stmarys.lpool.sch.uk
website: www.stmarys.ac
Twitter: @stmarys_college
Facebook: @stmaryscollegecrosby
Instagram: @stmaryscollegecrosby

Motto: '*Fidem Vita Fateri*'

St. Mary's College is an Independent Catholic School for boys and girls of all faiths aged 0–18, rated 'Excellent' in all areas by the Independent Schools Inspectorate (ISI). We are a thriving community which places a high value on outstanding academic achievement and all-round personal development. Our school is built on strong values which emphasise the importance of caring for others and striving for excellence in all we do. Boys and girls can start at our Bright Sparks & Early Years department (0–4 years) soon after birth and progress to our Preparatory School (4–11 years) before moving on to the College (11–18 years), where typically they achieve up to 100% pass rates at both GCSE and A Level. Our rich programme of extracurricular activities equips our pupils with the skills and values which will guide and support them throughout their lives. Scholarships and bursaries are available.

Numbers. There are 460 pupils in the Senior School; 157 pupils in the Preparatory School and 194 children in the Early Years department. There are no boarders.

Preparatory School. St. Mary's Prep offers an outstanding and inspiring primary education to 4–11 year olds. We provide individual attention, challenge and support which enables each child to achieve their own personal excellence, whatever that might be.

The academic thrust of the school is central with a strong focus on the key enabling skills of reading, writing and mathematics. Our curriculum is designed to give our pupils the best opportunity to succeed academically and develop a lifelong love of learning. Pupils are given a solid foundation in literacy and numeracy whilst developing skills in Science, History, Geography, Art, Design and ICT. These skills are developed through 'themes' chosen to capture the pupils' imagination and offer them the opportunity to explore different ways of learning. Specialist tuition in French, Spanish, Music, PE and Games is also an integral part of our curriculum.

We also provide an extensive programme of extra-curricular activities, and pupils are encouraged to take advantage of these opportunities to develop their confidence and extend their experience.

The Head of the Preparatory School, Mr Jonathan Webster, will be pleased to meet you and show you round.

Senior School. At St. Mary's College, pupils benefit from small class sizes and excellent facilities, including specialist IT, design and technology and learning resource centres, a well-equipped sports centre and our specialist music school.

We pride ourselves on our inspirational approach to education, and the focus for our highly qualified and experienced teaching staff is a combination of academic excellence with modern and imaginative teaching methods. We teach pupils how to think, not what to think. A rigorous yet broad and balanced curriculum is provided across the range of the humanities and sciences. During their first three years our pupils study 14 distinct subjects including separate sciences, Classics, Latin and two foreign languages. In their fourth year – after thorough consultation with pupils and parents – they begin two-year GCSE courses in a minimum of ten subjects, which must include English, English Literature, Mathematics, Religious Studies, and Science (either 3 or 2 GCSEs). A foreign language is strongly recommended to be one of the choices.

As well as academic excellence, we place a lot of emphasis on the cultural life of our pupils, with every child entering the college being given the opportunity to play a musical instrument. Drama and dance are also important features of life at St. Mary's, and our pupils are not afraid to tackle the classics, from Ajax and Electra to Grease and Oliver!

Specialist coaching is provided in numerous sports, including Rugby, Cricket, Football, Hockey, Netball, Swimming, Athletics and Cross-Country, and we have excellent facilities at our 20-acre playing fields, sports centre and brand new state-of-the-art gym.

A wide range of other student interests are catered for by a large number of clubs and societies meeting at lunchtimes or after school. Our Combined Cadet Force (Army and Royal Air Force) offers opportunities including adventure training and air experience flying, while there is also strong participation in the Duke of Edinburgh's Award Scheme.

Another important objective of the college is to broaden the horizons of our pupils and we do this via regular foreign trips, language exchanges and sport and music tours which have, in recent years, ventured as far afield as the United States and Australia.

St. Mary's is easily accessible to pupils throughout Merseyside and West Lancashire thanks to our extensive transport network of school coaches.

The Principal, Mr Michael Kennedy, will be pleased to welcome you to St. Mary's College for an informal meeting and a tour of the school.

Fees per term (2021–2022). Senior School £3,928; Preparatory School £2,665.

Scholarships & Awards. We offer a number of Academic Scholarships, which can be worth up to half fees and will be tenable throughout a pupil's career in the senior school (including Sixth Form), provided the pupil's efforts and behaviour remain consistent with the standard expected of scholars. The awards are based on academic merit alone and will be irrespective of income. There is no need to make a separate application: offers will automatically be made to parents whose children come top of the field in the entrance examination. Our Edmund Rice Scholarships (Assisted Places) are won by academic ability but also take a family's earnings into consideration.

We also award scholarships for those gifted in art, music and sport although the financial value of these Excellence Awards, as they are collectively known, is more modest; our Art, Music and Sport Scholarships are typically worth a £1,000 discount off annual fees.

Sixth Form Scholarships. Edmund Rice Scholarships (worth approximately 10% of fees) are available on merit, and are awarded on the basis of a Scholarship Examination.

Charitable status. St Mary's College Crosby Trust Limited is a Registered Charity, number 1110311. The aims and objectives of the Charity are to advance religious and other charitable works.

Governors:
Mrs S Ward, FCMA, BSc (*Chair of Governors*)
Mr M McKenna, LLB Hons (*Deputy Chair*)
Mr A Duncan, BA Hons, MBA
Mrs L Martindale, MA, BEd Hons
Mr D McCaughrean, MSc
Mrs P Old, LLB
Mr C Platt, FIIRSM, CMIOSH
Mr A Symons, BSc Hons
Mrs H Thompson, ACA, BSc
Mr C Wright, BSc Hons, MRSC, MIoD
Mr J Wright, BA, MA Oxon, MBA

Principal: **Mr M Kennedy**, BSc, MA, NPQH, CChem, MRSC

Vice Principal: Mrs J Thomas, BSc

Senior Leadership Team:
Mrs S Bartolo, BEd (*Head of Lower School*)
Mr A Byers, BA (*Head of Middle School, Head of Music*)
Mr P Duffy, MPhil (*Head of Sixth Form*)
Miss A Fletcher (*Business Director*)
Mr J Quint, BA, PGCert (*Director of Marketing, Admissions & Development*)
Mr N Rothnie, MA (*Extended Learning Coordinator, Head of History*)

Preparatory School Headmaster: Mr J Webster, BA

Head of Early Years: Mrs A Haigh, BEd

St Paul's School

Lonsdale Road, Barnes, London SW13 9JT

Tel:	020 8748 9162
email:	reception@stpaulsschool.org.uk
website:	www.stpaulsschool.org.uk
Twitter:	@StPaulsSchool
Facebook:	@StPaulsSchool1509
Instagram:	@stpaulsschoollondon
LinkedIn:	/St-Paul's-School

Motto: '*Fide et literis*'

St Paul's School is one of the UK's leading independent schools, offering an outstanding all-round education for some of the brightest boys in the country.

Founded by John Colet, Dean of St Paul's Cathedral, in 1509 to educate boys "from all nations and countries indifferently," regardless of race, creed or social background, St Paul's School remains committed to his vision today.

Erasmus, the greatest scholar of the northern Renaissance, advised Colet in the original planning of St Paul's School and wrote textbooks for the School's use. Today, a sense of scholarship, a commitment to all-round excellence and a culture of venturing beyond the syllabus continues to pervade life at St Paul's, which is known for its inspirational and responsive teaching, and outstanding academic results.

University Destinations. The most recent year for which the school has a full list of the destinations of St Paul's leavers is 2020.

Of those that choose to study in the UK, the largest proportion go to Oxford or Cambridge, an average of 31.5% over the last five years. In 2020, 126 pupils gained places at other Russell Group universities including UCL and Imperial College which are within the top 10 in the 2020 QS World University Rankings. 23 pupils are heading to top North American universities including MIT, Stanford and the University of Chicago, which are also within the top 10 in the 2020 QS World University rankings, and three to other international institutions.

A small number of pupils choose to take GAP years, paid employment, apprenticeships or internships.

Admission. Application for Admission to St Paul's is made via online application form on the school's website. 13+ candidates can register when they are in Year 5. In the autumn term of Year 6, three years before entry, they must take the ISEB Common Online Pre-Test. The results of this, together with a detailed report from their current school, will be used to select candidates for interview. Following the interview, boys may be offered a Main List place which is conditional upon continued good conduct and academic progress at their existing school, including an unreserved reference of support from their Head Teacher in Year 8.

There is a registration fee of £175.

For 16+ applications should be made one year in advance. Further details can be found on the School's website. No registration fee is required at the time of applying. Successful applications will pay the fee when accepting their place.

A deposit of £3,000 is required when a parent accepts the offer of a place for his son after interview. The Deposit will be returnable only if the boy fails to reach the necessary standard prior to entry or when the final account has been cleared after the boy leaves St Paul's.

Fees per term (2021–2022). The Basic Fee for St Paul's is £8,852 and £7,076 for St Paul's Juniors. This covers tuition, games, loan books, stationery, libraries, medical inspection, a careers aptitude test in the GCSE year, certain school publications and lunch, which all boys are required to attend. Charges are made for the purchase of some books (which become the personal property of boys) and public examination fees.

There are facilities for up to 35 boarders (ages 13 to 18) and boarding is flexible allowing boys to go home at weekends as they wish. The Boarding Fee is £13,322 per term. Boys joining at age 13 can only be weekly boarders and must return to a family member or approved guardian at weekends. Boys joining at age 16 can be full boarders. Boarding is not available for pupils for Year 9. From October 2021, there is a second boarding house for 11 pupils to allow flex-boarding.

Assistance with Fees – Bursaries. St Paul's takes pride in giving the best possible education to talented boys, irrespective of their family's financial circumstances. Each year there are funds available for free and subsidised places for those with a household income below £120,000. Bursaries are means-tested each year and may change as a family's financial situation improves or deteriorates. More information can be obtained from the school's website.

Scholarships. St Paul's School offers a number of honorary Academic Scholarships annually at 13+ and 17+. These are worth £60 per year. For external candidates entering at 13+, the scholarship examination is held annually in May. There are also a number of music scholarships awarded annually at 11+ and 13+. Each Scholarship is worth £60 per annum, plus free tuition on two instruments. Exhibitions consist of free tuition on one instrument only.

Curriculum. All boys follow a broadly based course up to IGCSE/GCSE. Thereafter in Year 12 & Year 13, A Level subjects are so arranged that boys can combine a wide range of Arts and Science subjects if they so wish. In Year 12, nearly all boys take four subjects and may also undertake an Extended Project, followed by three or four subjects in Year 13. Subjects are all taken in a linear way and there are no public exams in Year 12.

Games. Physical Activities offered include: Aikido, Athletics, Badminton, Basketball, Cricket, Cross-Country, Fencing, Fives, Futsal, Golf, Judo, Rackets, Rowing, Rugby, Rugby Sevens, Sculling, Soccer, Squash, Swimming, Tennis, Table Tennis, Ultimate Frisby and Water Polo. In addition, Climbing, Cycling and Sailing take place off site. The school has its own Swimming Pool, Fencing Salle, Tennis, Squash, Fives and Rackets Courts, Dojo, Fitness Centre and its own Boat House. The Sports Centre also comprises a Main Hall and Gymnasium. The Sports Hall is equipped for Tennis, Badminton, Basketball and has five indoor Cricket nets.

Music. All boys are taught music in the classroom in the first year. In subsequent years, GCSE is taught as a two-year course, and A Level taught in the final two years. Additional tuition is available in piano, organ, all the standard orchestral instruments, jazz, music theory and aural. There are a wide range of ensemble activities – chamber music, jazz and big band, two full orchestras, two training orchestras and several choral/vocal groups. The music school contains a professional standard concert venue, the Wathen Hall, several rehearsal rooms, two large teaching rooms and a music technology suite. There are regular concerts and recitals, as well as music competitions, musicals and external engagements, workshops and festivals.

School Societies. There is a wide choice of more than 30 Societies, including Musical, Artistic and Dramatic activities, Debating, Historical and Scientific Societies, Politics and Economics, Bridge, Chess, Natural History, Photography, European Society, a Christian Union and Social Service.

St Paul's Juniors adjoins the school. (*For details see entry in IAPS section.*)

Charitable status. St Paul's School is a Registered Charity, number 1119619. The object of the charity is to promote the education of boys in Greater London.

Governors:

Chairman: Richard Cassell, BA, LLB
Deputy Chairman: Tim Haynes, BA

Sarah Barker, LLB
Nicola Doyle, BEd
Veryan Exelby, MA
Adam Fenwick, MA
Lord Grabiner, QC
Harry Hampson, MA, MEng
Sam Newhouse, MA
Alison Palmer, BSc
Sarah Thomas, MA
Chris Vermont, MA

Clerk to the Governors: Elizabeth Wilkinson

St Paul's Teaching Staff:

High Master: Sally-Anne Huang, MA Oxon, MSc Leicester, MA Roehampton

Surmaster – Head of Senior School: Fran Clough, BSc Dunelm, PhD Cantab
Deputy Head – Academic: James Gazet, MA Cantab
Deputy Head – Co-Curricular: Thomas Killick, MA, PhD Cantab
Deputy Head – Pastoral and Boarding: Nick Watkins, MA Oxon, PGCE IoE
Deputy Head – Mental Health, Wellbeing & Life Skills: Samuel Madden, BA Exeter, MA LSE
Director of Admissions: Andy Mayfield, BSc Manchester, MSc, DPhil Oxon
Director of Teaching and Learning: Tahmer Mahmoud, BA Oxon, PGCE Leeds, MA London
Director of Assessment And Data: Simon Holmes, MPhys, DPhil Oxon
Director of Careers & Universities: Neville Sanderson, BA, MA London
Director of Partnerships and Public Service: Stuart Block, MA Cantab

Undermasters:
Caroline Gill, MA Cantab, PGCE Chelteham (*Fourth Form*)
Glenn Harrison, BSc Brunel, PGCE Cantab (*Fifth Form*)
James Gilks, MSc, PhD Nottingham, PGCE KCL (*Sixth Form*)
Naomi McLauglin, BA Cardiff, PGCE Goldsmiths (*Lower Eighth Form*)
Hannah Warner, MA Cantab, MA Dunelm (*Upper Eighth Form*)

Head of Faculty – Creative and Performing Arts: Daniel Pirrie, MA Edinburgh
Head of Faculty – English: Matthew Gardner, MA Oxon, MA Manchester, MA London
Head of Faculty – Humanities: Alexander Isaac BSc, MSc Bristol, MA London, PGCE London, FRGS
Head of Faculty – Languages: Douglas Perrin, MA, PGCE Cantab
Head of Faculty – Mathematics: Andrew Ashworth-Jones, BSc North London, PGCE Exeter

Head of Faculty – Science, Technology, Engineering, ICT & Computing: Camille Shammas, BSc Sheffield, PhD Bristol
Chaplain: The Revd Matthew Knox, BSc Manchester, BA MA Dunelm, PGCE Newcastle

St Peter's School, York

Clifton, York YO30 6AB

Tel: 01904 527300
email: enquiries@stpetersyork.org.uk
website: www.stpetersyork.org.uk
Twitter: @stpetersyork
Facebook: @stpetersschoolyork
Instagram: @stpeters.york

Motto: Super antiquas vias

Founded in 627AD, St Peter's is one of the world's oldest schools. It provides outstanding boarding and day education for boys and girls from 13 to 18. Pupils at St Peter's School achieve some of the best grades in the North of England at GCSE and A Level. It has a co-educational prep school, St Peter's 8–13, which admits boarding and day pupils and a day pre-prep and nursery, St Peter's 2–8. (*see separate entries in IAPS section*).

St Peter's is a co-educational boarding and day school with 582 boys and girls aged 13–18. There are 118 boarders housed in four boarding houses, and all day pupils are assigned to a day house, all of which are on the campus. St Peter's offers full boarding and part-time boarding options.

Buildings & Facilities. The School occupies an impressive 47-acre site just a few minutes' walk from the historic centre of York. Playing fields stretch down to the River Ouse and the School boat house, and the sports facilities are further supplemented by three sports halls, a fitness suite, an astro pitch and a 25m 6-lane swimming pool.

There are three performance spaces of varying capacities, a music school, an outstanding art school with its own exhibition gallery and an extensive library. The school's sports pitches have been recognised for their excellence by the Institute of Groundsmanship, and a Maths and Modern Foreign Languages block opened in September 2018.

Entrance. Pupils are admitted through the School's entrance examinations held at the end of January for 13+ and in mid-November for 16+. The School is oversubscribed and application before the entrance exam is strongly recommended.

Scholarships and Bursaries. Honorary scholarships are awarded to those performing extremely well in the entrance examination.

Various music awards covering a proportion of the fees and free tuition on up to three musical instruments are available for entrants at 13+ or Sixth Form. Interviews and auditions for these awards are held in January or February.

Help with Fees is available at 13+ and 16+. Full particulars on Help with Fees and scholarships are available from the Admissions Officer, Mrs Gillian Bland, Tel: 01904 527305 or email: g.bland@stpetersyork.org.uk.

Curriculum. St Peter's offers a very broad middle school curriculum including Music, PE, Art, Design & Technology, Community Action and courses in personal and social education, among many others.

Nearly all pupils proceed into the Sixth Form, and A Level courses are available in all subjects studied for IGCSE/GCSE, and in Economics, Politics, Business Studies, Further Mathematics and PE.

Academic and pastoral care. A comprehensive house and tutorial system with interim assessments and reports during the term ensure the close scrutiny by all the teaching staff of pupils' academic and general development.

Religious education and worship. Religious Studies are part of the curriculum, and Chapel is seen as an opportunity for pupils to be made aware of the School's Christian heritage.

Careers and university entrance. The School is an 'all-in' member of the Independent Schools Careers Organisation. Careers staff are available for consultation, maintaining an extensive library relating to careers and higher education and organising a full programme of events for the Sixth Form. In 2015 the School's Careers Department was accredited by Career Mark, 'The mark of Quality for Careers Education and Guidance'. Approximately 90% of Sixth Form pupils go straight on to further or higher education study, with over two thirds of pupils progressing to elite and Russell Group universities in the UK (including Oxford and Cambridge).

Games and Physical Education. Physical education is a significant part of the curriculum. There is an extensive games programme, 250 sports teams and excellent sports facilities. Rugby, netball, hockey, cricket and rowing are major sports, and many other options including swimming, athletics, cross country, basketball, squash, yoga, badminton, tennis, fencing, golf, mountain biking, trampoline, fitness and weight training are available.

Combined Cadet Force. A flourishing and voluntary CCF contingent, with army and air sections, allows the pursuit of many activities including a full programme of camps, expeditions and courses.

The Duke of Edinburgh's Award is also on offer with expedition training for all levels as part of the activities programme and 150 pupils are currently participating.

Music. Musical ability is encouraged throughout the School. There is an orchestra, bands, choirs, choral society, Barbershop and Barbieshop groups and numerous smaller activities. Concerts and tours abroad are a regular feature of the school year. Tuition in all instruments is provided, and music is offered at GCSE and A Level.

Art. Drawing, painting, print-making, ceramics and sculpture may all be taken up both in and out of school hours in an outstanding department.

Drama. The School has three performance spaces: the Memorial Hall, the Shepherd Hall and the smaller, more flexible Drama Centre. There are various productions through the year giving opportunities for acting and backstage skills.

Clubs and societies. Over 80 flourishing clubs and societies are available, including chess, debating and Radio 627. The Community Action programme has over 100 regular participants.

Travel and expeditions. Opportunities for trips and tours have included skiing trips, Classics trips to Greece, trekking in Morocco, a Rugby tour to Canada and the USA, among many others.

The Friends of St Peter's. Parents are encouraged to join the Friends, a society whose aim is to promote a close relationship between parents and staff.

Fees per term (2021–2022). Full Boarding £10,670, Non-EU Full Boarding £11,500, Day £6,460. Tuition fees include the costs of stationery and textbooks. There are no compulsory extras except for examination fees. Lunches are included in day fees.

Further information. Prospectuses are available on request: tel: 01904 527305, email: enquiries@ stpetersyork.org.uk, or via the website: www.stpetersyork .org.uk.

Charitable status. St Peter's School, York, is a Registered Charity, number 1141329.

Visitor: The Rt Honourable the Lord Archbishop of York

Board of Governors:
Chairman: Mr W Woolley
Vice Chair: Mr P B Hilling

Members of the Board:

Mrs C Bailey	Rt Revd Dr J Frost
Mr M Calvert	Dr S Hinchliffe
Mrs J Copley-Farnell	Professor T McLeish
Dr N Durham	Mr A Taylor
Mrs T Flannery	Mr P Widdicombe

Clerk to the Board: Ms K Hodges

Head Master: **Mr J M P Walker**, MA Oxford, MA London

Chief Operating Officer: Mr M Carr, BSc, MBA, LLB
Senior Deputy Head: Mr M Walters, MA Oxon
Director of Admissions, Marketing and Communications: Ms S T Opie, BSc
Pastoral Deputy: Miss T M Mounter, BA
Academic Deputy: Mr D H Gillies, BA, MSc Oxon
Director of Finance: Mrs R Johnson, BA, FCA
Head Master's PA: Miss C E Frank
Admissions Officer: Mrs G Bland

The Prep School – St Peter's 8–13
Head: Mr A I Falconer, BA, MBA
Head's Secretary: Miss S Bath

Deputy Head: Mr M C Ferguson, HDE
Director of Teaching & Learning: Mrs C Lees, BEd Cantab

The Pre-Prep and Nursery – St Peter's 2–8
Head: Mr P C Hardy, BA, PGCE
Head's Secretary: Mrs C Fattorini

Deputy Head: Mrs A M Clarke, BA

A full staff list is available on the school website.

Seaford College

Lavington Park, Petworth, West Sussex GU28 0NB

Tel: 01798 867392
email: info@seaford.org
website: www.seaford.org
Twitter: @seafordcollege
Facebook: @seafordcollege
Instagram: @seafordcollege
LinkedIn: /company/seaford-college

Motto: Love to Learn

The College was founded in 1884 at Seaford in East Sussex and moved to Lavington Park at the foot of the South Downs in 1946 in West Sussex. The picturesque grounds cover some 400 acres and include extensive sports facilities. The campus includes a Prep School for pupils aged 6–13 (*see IAPS entry*), outstanding Performing Arts Centre and Sports Hall, a superb Art and Design department, a modern Sixth Form Centre, purpose-built boarding houses, a state-of-the-art Mathematics, Science and Music School.

Seaford is controlled by an independent non-profit making Charitable Trust approved by the Department for Education and the Charity Commissioners, and is administered by the College Board of Governors.

Pupils. Seaford College offers day and boarding facilities, with options of full, weekly and flexi boarding. There are over 900 pupils at the College with 210 plus in the Sixth form. There are two boys houses, a girls house, a junior house and two Sixth Form boarding houses.

Aims. Seaford College's aim is to bring out the best of each individual, by helping every pupil to reach their full potential and to achieve personal bests both inside and outside the classroom. The aim is to enable pupils to leave the College feeling confident in their own abilities and able to contribute in the external world.

Academic. The Prep School (incorporating Years 1–8) offers a wide-ranging curriculum, which includes the core subjects of English, Mathematics, Science, Spanish, French and Information Technology, as well as Geography, History, Art, Music, DT, Sport, Forest School and PSHCE.

Years 10 and 11 lead up to the GCSE examinations. Students study the core subjects of English Literature, English Language, Mathematics and Science and then choose four other syllabuses to follow from a comprehensive list of subjects, which include: Art, Business Studies, Computing, Drama, Design and Technology, Geography, History, Music, Physical Education, Religious Studies and Spanish.

The A Level subject list is comprehensive. In the Lower Sixth, pupils choose three subjects to study. Over and above this in their first year students may undertake The Duke of Edinburgh's Silver/Gold Award or start an EPQ (Extended Project Qualification). In the Upper Sixth students concentrate on their three A Level subjects or BTEC courses in Business, Sport, Countryside Management or Hospitality.

Music. is an important part of life at Seaford and the Music School offers the latest in recording and performing facilities. The College boasts an internationally-renowned College Chapel Choir, who have sung on tour with Gary Barlow and have performed many concerts for charity. The College also has an orchestra and offers lessons for all instruments. Music can be studied at GCSE and A Level.

Sports. With superb facilities available in the grounds and staff that have coached and played at international level, the College has a reputation for sporting excellence. Facilities include: eight rugby pitches, eight tennis courts, three cricket pitches, a water-based all-weather hockey pitch, enclosed swimming pool, a large indoor sports hall that allows tennis and hockey to be played all year round, and a 9-hole golf course and driving range.

Art. The College has an excellent Art department, which allows students to exercise their talents to the fullest extent in every aspect of art and design, whether it is ceramics, textiles, fine art, animation, or any other medium they wish to use. Many pupils from Seaford go on to study at design school and work for design and fashion houses or advertising companies. Students display their work throughout the year in the department's large gallery.

Combined Cadet Force. The College has strong ties with the Military and has a very well supported Combined Cadet Force (CCF) with each wing of the armed forces well represented. Weekend exercises and training are a regular feature in the College calendar and include adventure training, canoeing, climbing, sailing and camping.

Admission. Entry at age 7 consists of a visit to the school, reports and references from current school. Entry at age 10 and 11 is determined by reports, references, and cognitive ability testing. 13+ pupils will sit the ISEB pre-test in Year 6, there is a visit to the school, reports and references. Offers are made in the January of Year 6 and are unconditional and deferred until Year 9. Sixth Form entry is dependent upon GCSE results, Academic transfer meeting, reports and references and a conditional offer is made in the year of entry based on 40 points at GCSEs and these should include English and Mathematics. Overseas students are required to take a written examination to determine the level of comprehension in English.

Scholarships and Bursaries. Academic, Music, Drama, Dance, Art, Design Technology and Sports scholarships may be awarded to boys and girls entering the prep and senior school at 11+, 13+ and 16+, with the exception of DT which is only available at 13+ and 16+. These scholarships offer up to 10% discount on fees per annum; this is at the discretion of the Scholarship committee. Scholarship trials, auditions and examinations take place in January, February, March and May of the year of entry.

Bursaries are available on a means-tested basis. A potential scholarship recipient in need of further financial assistance may apply for a means-tested bursary.

Sibling and Forces discounts are also available. Please contact the Admissions Secretary for more details.

Fees per term (2021–2022). Years 9–13: £11,750 (Full Boarding), £10,290 (Weekly Boarding), £7,595 (Day). Years 7 & 8: £8,085 (4-Day Monday–Thursday Boarding), £6,080 (Day). Year 6: £7,635 (4-Day Monday–Thursday Boarding). Years 3–6: £3,665–£5,595 (Day).

Extras. Drama, Clay Pigeon Shooting, Fencing, Duke of Edinburgh's Award, Golf, Sailing, Kayaking, Museum & Theatre trips, Creative Writing, Drone Club, Debating Club, Rock Climbing, Martial Arts, etc.

Charitable status. Seaford College is a Registered Charity, number 277439. It exists to provide education for children.

Governing Body:
R Venables Kyrke (*Chairman*)
Mrs S Sayer, CBE (*Vice Chair*)

R Norton	A Hayes
J Cooper	J Scrase
Mrs E Lawrence	Mrs S Kowszun
N Karonias	Mrs V Padgham
J R Hall	Dr J Slater
H A Phillips	

Headmaster: J P Green, BA Hons, PGCE

Deputy Head: W Yates, BSc Ed
Assistant Head: A Arya, BEng Hons
Assistant Head: S D'Agar, BSc Hons
Head of Academic Access and Achievement: Mrs S Butler, BA, MA
Prep School Head: A Brown, BEd
Deputy Head Prep School: J Harte, BSc

Teaching Staff:
* *Head of Department*

Art & Design:
*A G Grantham-Smith, BA, PG Dip ArtEd
Miss L Arnold, BA
Mrs K Grantham-Smith, BA (*Photography*)
A Kirkton, BA Hons
Mrs J Weld, BA

Business:
M Pitteway, BComm Hons
Mrs M Mackenzie-Foster, BA Hons, MBA

Computing:
D Crook, BA
J Bradbury, BA

Design Technology:
*D Shaw, BEd
Miss A Prince-Iles, BA Hons, PGCE
P Harker, MDes Hons
Ms S Byrne, BA

Drama:
*J Johnson, BA Hons, MA
D Gray, BA

Dance:
A Bennett, BA Hons

Economics:
*E Reynolds, BA
K Naylor, BA

English:
*K Finniear, BA Hons
Mrs K Tomlinson, BA
Mrs S Hollis, BA
Mrs R Rivers, BA Hons
Miss E Silvester BA
Miss T Spicer, BA Hons
G Vernon, BA, MA
Mrs K Woolgar, BA Hons

Food Technology:
Mrs A Wilkins Shaw, BSc Hons, PGCE

Geography:
*J Kimber, BSc
F Desforges-Medhurst, BA
J Follows, BA Hons, PGCE

J Hart, BA, PGCE
Miss E LeBarth, BSc Hons

History:
*J Gisby, BA Hons, PGCE
S Hirst, BA
J Wilson, BA
Miss A Thomas, BA

Learning Support:
*Mrs S Butler, BA, MA
Mrs P A Angier, BA, Dip CG, Dip SpLD
Mrs M Gilbert, BA Hons, PGCE, OCR SpLD
Ms A Jensen, Dip SpLD
Mrs L Ferris, OCR SpLD
Mrs H Russell, BA, OCR Cert SpLD
Mrs E Jones, CE
Mrs B Vernon

Mathematics:
Dr F Adeniran, BA
A Arya, BA
Dr N Pothecary, PhD, BA
Mrs J Percival, BSc
Mrs E Bloem, BA
Mrs F Lovell

Modern Languages:
*Ms A Loten, BA Hons, PGCE
Ms H Martin, PGCE (*French*)
Mrs J Linford, BA Hons, PGCE
Miss M Molinero Quiralte
J Jones, BA
Miss C Apps, BA

Music:
Miss M Molas-Moss
Mrs J Hawkins, PGCE, BMus
Mrs S Reynolds, BA Hons (*Choirmaster*)

Physical Education:
*L Doubler, BA
T Cobb, BA
J Thompson, BA Hons
Miss E Teague, BA Hons QTS
J Halsey (*Golf Professional*)
D Barnes, BA, PGCE
Mrs G Hegarty, BA Ed, PGCE
D Joseph, PE
Miss J Horn, BA Hons
J Phimister, BA
C Adams (*Head of Cricket*)
J Bird (*Head of Tennis*)
B Barnes (*Hockey*)

Psychology:
Mrs A Yates, BS, PGCE

Religious Studies:
Mrs L Stitt, BA Hons

Science:
*C Hawley
Dr N Street, PhD, MBA, PGCE
A Plewes, BSc Hons, PGCE
P Whelpton, BA

KS2 Teachers:
A Cooper, BA
Mrs J Lyne, BA
Mrs S Lewis, BEd Hons
Mrs H Stevens, BA Hons

Mrs F Jones, CertEd
Mrs M Mitchinson, BA, PGCE

Exams:
Mrs L Goddard

CCF:
A Plewes, BSc Hons, PGCE
K Lomas

Chaplain: Fr Colin Datchler
Director of Finance: A Golding
Director of Estates and Operations: G Burt
IT Systems Manager: A Bond
Marketing Manager: S Twigger
Headmaster's Secretary: Mrs A Thornley
Admissions Secretary: Mrs J Mackay-Smith

Sevenoaks School

High Street, Sevenoaks, Kent TN13 1HU

Tel: 01732 455133
email: regist@sevenoaksschool.org
            admin@sevenoaksschool.org
website: www.sevenoaksschool.org
Twitter: @SevenoaksSchool
Facebook: @SevenoaksSchoolUK
Instagram: @sevenoaksschooluk
LinkedIn: /sevenoaks-school

Motto: *Servire Deo Regnari Est*

Sevenoaks (founded in 1432) is a co-educational day and boarding school for students aged 11 to 18. Just half an hour from Central London and Gatwick International Airport, its superb 100-acre campus is set in the Kent countryside.

Sevenoaks is one of the world's leading IB schools, having taught the International Baccalaureate for over 40 years.

Sevenoaks is among the top schools in the UK. It has twice received the distinction of being named *The Sunday Times Independent Secondary School of the Year,* and the UK Independent Schools Inspectorate (ISI) awarded Sevenoaks the rare accolade of 'Exceptional' for its pupils' achievement.

In 2021, its average IB Diploma score was 41.3 points, about eight points above the world average, and consistent with previous years. The Higher Education department supported successful applications by 224 students to universities in the UK, USA, Canada, Europe and Hong Kong. An outstanding 92 per cent progressed to their first choice university.

Sevenoaks proudly publishes the university destinations of leavers every year. Given its global perspective, it supports about 20% of students to universities in another country, with increasing numbers going to North America, specifically Ivy league and top universities in the United States.

The majority go to Oxbridge, London universities or other top universities in the UK, such as Bristol or Durham.

Sevenoaks students have access to world-class facilities for co-curricular pursuits, including sport, music, drama and art, at least 70 clubs and societies, a wide range of study trips and exchanges, and a well-established community service programme.

There is a strong emphasis on the co-curriculum, from sport to music, drama and art. Pupils are regularly selected for regional and national orchestras and choirs, the NYT, and compete at county, national and international level in a number of sports.

Sevenoaks was one of the first UK schools to incorporate voluntary service as a compulsory element of the co-curriculum, pioneering a local Voluntary Service Unit in the 1960s and continuing with a strong service programme today. There is also a CCF, an emerging programme of social impact entrepreneurship and strong involvement in The Duke of Edinburgh's Award scheme; with Gold expeditions abroad as well as in the UK.

In 2017 the school launched its Middle School Diploma for Year 9, which records pupils' academic and co-curricular achievements in creativity, action and service as well as in the enriching Sevenoaks core courses, Ten Ideas That Changed the World and Critical Perspectives.

There are lessons and sport for all pupils on Saturdays and a full programme of activities for boarders on Sundays.

The facilities are first-class. In 2018, a state-of-the-art science and technology centre opened, uniting the four core fields of science, with an innovative new Sixth Form Global Study Centre alongside, providing the school's first dedicated space for the IB and higher education. Other recent developments include a sports centre providing outstanding facilities and an award-winning, world-class performing arts centre.

With seven distinctive and comfortable boarding houses, and a new girls' boarding house planned for 2023, its boarding community is fun, friendly and busy.

The school's international outlook promotes the principles of tolerance and open-mindedness. Ambitious but principled, confident and compassionate, Sevenoaks pupils are prepared for leadership in an ever more complex world.

Admission. The main points of entry to the school are at 11, 13 and 16 years. A small number are admitted at other levels. At 11+, pupils are admitted on the basis of a competitive examination held in January, an interview and school report. At 13+, candidates take part in an assessment process in May of their Year 7. A reference from their current school is also required. Academic and Co-Curricular scholarship examinations are held in the May of Year 8. At 16+ students are admitted into the Sixth Form based on their performance in interview and academic entrance tests, and on the strength of their current school reports. All applications for entry should be addressed to the Director of Admissions (regist@sevenoaksschool.org).

Fees per term (2021–2022). Boarders £13,320; Day Pupils £8,340 (including lunch). Fees for pupils entering directly into the Sixth Form are £14,451 (boarding) and £9,471 (day).

Scholarships and Bursaries. Approximately 55 awards are available at 11+, 13+ and 16+ for outstanding academic ability or promise, as well as outstanding ability in music, sport, art and drama.

Scholarships are awarded to the value of £1,000 or 10% of the day fee.

Applicants are invited to apply for 11+ scholarships on the basis of performance in entrance tests and interviews, and for music scholarships when confirming their application. For 13+ awards, candidates may be invited to take part in the Academic Scholarship exams, or those who attend a UK prep school may be put forward by their school. Internal candidates may apply for co-curricular scholarships.

Sixth Form academic scholarships are offered on the basis of performance in entrance tests and interviews. Applications for Sixth Form Art, Music, Drama and Sport scholarships should be made by expressing an interest during the application procedure.

Means-tested bursaries are available for pupils who could not otherwise afford the fees. Priority is given to local candidates. Scholarships may be augmented by bursaries in cases of financial need.

Charitable status. Sevenoaks School is a Registered Charity, number 1101358. Its aims and objectives are the education of school children.

Governing Body:
Chair: Ms Alison Beckett, MA, MBS
Vice-Chair: Mr C Gill, MPhil, BSc

Governors:
Mrs K Allen, BSc, ACA
Mr R Best, LLB
Mr A Boulton, MA
Mr J Davies, LLB
Mrs E Ecclestone, LLB, Dip LP
Mr G Innes, BSc, ACA
Cllr J London, LLM
Mr P Luxmore, BA
Mrs M McInerney, BSc, ACMA
Mr M Merson, MA, ACA
Mr D Phillips, BA, ACA
Dr A Timms
Prof I Wilson, MA, MEng, PhD, ScD, FIChemE, CEng, CSci
Mrs A Yuravlivker, BSc, ACA

Bursar and Clerk to the Governors: Dr Brigid McClure, MA, MPhil, PhD, FHEA

Academic Staff:

Senior Leadership Team:

Headmaster: Mr J R Elzinga, AB, MSt, FCCT

Senior Deputy Head: Dr Clare Ives, MA, PhD
Deputy Head (Pastoral): Mr Jonathan Lidiard, MA
Deputy Head (Academic): Mr Chris Taylor, MA, PGCE
Deputy Head (Co-curriculum): Mrs Sally Walmsley, MA
Deputy Head (Staff): Miss Helen Tebay, MA
Deputy Head (Boarding): Mrs Nichola Haworth, MA

Director of Admissions: Mrs A M Stuart, BSc, MEd
Executive Director of Advancement: Mr M D Joyce, BA
Director of Institute for Teaching & Learning: Mr M P Beverley, BA, MA
Director of Institute for Higher Education and Professional Insight: Mrs W J Heydorn, MA
Director of Service and Social Impact: Miss C Davison, BA, MA
Director of International Baccalaureate: Mr N T Haworth, BA
Head of Sixth Form Admissions: Ms L A Dolan, BA
Head of Sixth Form: Mr M T Edwards, BA, MPhil, PhD
Head of Middle School: Miss R L McQuillin, MA
Head of Lower School: Mr P G de May, BA

Sherborne Girls

Bradford Road, Sherborne, Dorset DT9 3QN

Tel: Admissions: 01935 818224
School: 01935 812245
Bursar: 01935 818206
email: admissions@sherborne.com
website: www.sherborne.com
Twitter: @sherbornegirls
Facebook: @sherbornegirls
Instagram: @sherbornegirls
LinkedIn: /Sherborne-Girls

Sherborne Girls, founded in 1899, provides an outstanding education for 11 to 18 year olds in the beautiful county of Dorset and is proud of its co-curricular programme and exceptional pastoral care. Girls are welcomed at 11+, 12+, 13+ and into the Sixth Form. There are 474 girls: 451 boarders, 23 day girls. A close relationship with Sherborne School allows co-ed opportunities including music, drama, activities, clubs and societies and social occasions. The schools have the same term dates.

Terms. Three terms of approximately 12 weeks each. Christmas holidays 3 weeks; Easter holidays 3 weeks; Summer holidays 9 weeks. Term dates are in common with those of Sherborne School.

Admission. Common Entrance Examination to Independent Schools. Scholarship Examinations and interviews. The School's own entrance examinations where Common Entrance is not possible. Girls should be registered in advance and reports will be requested from their current school. Assessment for 13+ entry takes place in January. For entry into the Sixth Form, girls are required to gain six good passes (grade six or above) in relevant subjects. See the "entry at 16+" page on the website for more details regarding the GCSE points.

Registration fee £200. A deposit of £2,000 is required before entry (a term's fees for overseas pupils) and credited to the last term's bill.

Scholarships and Bursaries. Academic Scholarships are offered at 11+, 13+ and 16+ annually as a result of examination and interview. There are also scholarships offered for outstanding promise in Music, Art, Drama and Sport. All examinations are held in January and February apart from Sixth Form in November. Scholarship awards are made on merit with a maximum merit award of £3,000. Scholarships may be combined with means-tested bursaries which can raise considerably the effective amount of an award. Bursarial support (up to 100%) may be available in cases of demonstrable need.

Music Awards (Junior and 16+): Scholarships of up to £3,000 with free music tuition for up to three lessons per week. Music Exhibitions offer free music tuition for up to three lessons per week.

Art Scholarships (13+ and 16+): Awards of up to £3,000. Candidates will be required to bring a portfolio with them and would be asked to do some work in the Art Department whilst they are here.

Sport Scholarships (Junior and 16+): Awards of up to £3,000. Candidates will offer one or more sports, preferably reaching county standard or higher.

Drama Awards (13+): Scholarships of up to £3,000 with free drama tuition for one lesson per week. Drama Exhibitions offer free drama tuition for one lesson per week.

All-Rounder Award (Junior): Awards of up to £3,000 available. All-Rounder Awards take into account ability in two areas of activity outside the classroom (art, drama, music and sport) as well as academic potential.

Fees per term (2021–2022). 13+: boarders £13,170, day boarders* £10,290, day girls £7,920. 11+: boarders £10,550, day girls £7,920.

*Day boarders are girls who wish to stay overnight on the odd occasion and for whom a bed space will be made available on request.

Houses. There are five houses for 13–17 year olds and one Upper Sixth house. Girls who are 11 and 12 years old spend their first two years together in Aldhelmsted West house.

Religion. The School has a Church of England foundation, but it values the presence and contribution of members of all the Christian traditions and of other faiths. Regular services are held in the Abbey, some jointly with Sherborne School.

Examinations. Girls are prepared for I/GCSE and A Levels. There is a wide choice of subjects to be studied.

Games. Hockey and Lacrosse/Netball are played in the Michaelmas and Lent terms and Tennis, Rounders, Cricket and Athletics during the Trinity term. Oxley Sports Centre in partnership with Sherborne Girls contains a 25m pool and state-of-the-art fitness suite. There are Squash Courts, floodlit Astroturf, Sports Hall, Dance Studio and Climbing Wall. Riding, Badminton, Cross-Country Running, Golf, Aerobics, Judo, Sailing, Trampolining are some of the alternative games.

Sherborne Old Girls. All enquiries should be made to Mrs Fiona James at the School, Tel: 01935 818329.

Prospective parents and their daughters are invited to the School's Tour Mornings or private visits by appointment. Please visit the school's website or telephone Admissions on 01935 818224 for further details.

Charitable status. Sherborne School for Girls is a Registered Charity, number 307427. It exists to provide education for girls in a boarding environment.

Council:
Chairman: Mr R Strang
Vice Chairs: Lady Plaxy Arthur, Mrs L Hall
Members:
Ms J Blanch
Mrs I Burke
Dr S Connors
Mr W J A Gordon
The Rt Revd Karen Gorham
Mrs A Harris
Mr R A L Leach
Mrs J Massey
Mr P Pilkington
Mr M Taylor
Dr P Williams
Mr P Ward
Mrs M Wingfield Digby
Mr N Wordie
Life President: Mr S Wingfield Digby

Clerk to the Council: Mrs F Clapp

Senior Staff:

Head: **Dr Ruth Sullivan**, BSc, PGCE Edinburgh, MSc, PhD London School of Hygiene and Tropical Medicine

Bursar: Mrs Fiona Clapp, MBA, BSc Hons London, PGCE
Senior Deputy Head, Teaching and Learning: Mrs Louise Orton, BSc Swansea, PGCE
Deputy Head, Pastoral: Mrs Jessica Briggs, BA Hons Reading
Deputy Head, Planning & Co-curricular: Mr Ian McClary, MA St Andrews, PGCE Cambridge
Director of Sixth Form: Mrs Florence Corran, MPhil Oxford
Director of External Affairs: Mrs Katherine Massey, BA Hons Oxford Brookes
Director of Sport, Adventure & Leadership: Mrs Jayne Dart, BSc Hons Oxford Brookes

For full list of staff please go to the school's website www.sherborne.com

Sherborne School

Abbey Road, Sherborne, Dorset DT9 3AP

Tel:	01935 812249
	01935 810403 (Admissions)
email:	admissions@sherborne.org
website:	www.sherborne.org
Twitter:	@SherborneSchool
Facebook:	@SherborneBoysSchool
Instagram:	@sherborneschool

Royal Arms of Edward VI: Dieu et mon droit.

The origins of Sherborne School date back to the eighth century, when a tradition of education at Sherborne was begun by St Aldhelm. Edward VI refounded the School in 1550. The present School stands on land which once belonged to the Monastery. The Library, Chapel, and Headmaster's offices adjoin the Abbey Church, are modifications of the original buildings of the Abbey. Sherborne School merged with Sherborne Prep School in 2021.

Situation. The School lies in the attractive Abbey town of Sherborne with a direct train to London taking two hours.

Organisation. There are just over 600 boys at Sherborne with 90% of them being full boarders. Boys are accommodated in eight houses, all of which are within easy walking distance of the main school.

Admission. Entry is either at 13+ (Year 9) or 16+ (Sixth Form) with a small number of places available at 14+ (Year 10). Assessment days take place for 13+ entry when pupils are in year 7. Pupils may then sit scholarship examinations or Common Entrance in year 8. Late applicants may be assessed after this time subject to places being available.

Scholarships and Exhibitions. Sherborne offers a wide range of scholarships and exhibitions at 13+ entry: Academic, Music, Art, Design & Technology, Drama and Sport. Sixth Form Academic, Sports and Music awards are also offered annually.

Closed Awards: A Raban Exhibition of up to 10% of fees for the sons of serving or ex-services officers; a Nutting Exhibition of up to 10% of fees for sons of RN Officers.

Sixth Form Entry. Places are available for boys who wish to join the Sixth Form to study A Levels for two years. Scholarship and entrance examinations take place by arrangement with the Director of Admissions.

Curriculum. All pupils follow a broadly based curriculum for their first three years to GCSE. In the Sixth Form boys study at least three A Levels drawn from a wide choice of available courses. There is also a diverse and stretching enrichment programme as a part of the compulsory curriculum.

Careers and Universities. The Careers Department has an enviable reputation. Boys experience work shadowing programmes in the fifth and lower sixth forms – these are followed by careers conventions, university visits, parents' forums and lessons in interview techniques. Virtually all leavers go on to university.

Pastoral Care. The boys in each house are in the care of a Housemaster and their family, a resident tutor and a resident matron. In addition, a team of tutors assists the Housemaster in the running of the House and boys have many avenues of support and advice available to them. The School Chaplain also plays a major role and will talk with a boy whenever required. A School Counsellor is available, and boys may book appointments directly and confidentially.

Tutor. Each boy has a personal Tutor who monitors his academic progress and provides a useful contact point for parents.

Religion. The weekly pattern of Christian services in the school Chapel or Sherborne Abbey underpin the spiritual rhythm of the school. There is a wide variety of voluntary Christian groups and services including a Friday night candlelit Eucharist which is well attended. Boys can be prepared for Confirmation into the Church of England and the Roman Catholic Church.

Community Service. Boys take part in a busy programme aimed at encouraging a sense of responsibility towards the local community.

Art. The Art School is a dynamic and highly successful department achieving outstanding academic results at all levels. The core disciplines are based around the study of Fine Art, with an eclectic mix of approaches such as painting, photography, 3D, digital media, printing and performance.

Design and Technology. The subject is taught from year nine right through to A Level and pupils can go on to higher education courses in Product and Aeronautical Design, Architecture and Engineering. The department has developed links with local industries where pupils can see CAD/CAM production, commercial furniture design and precision casting in process.

Music. There is a strong music tradition in the School – over 400 music lessons take place every week. There are two full orchestras, various chamber music groups, many different types of jazz band, a brass group, a swing band, Chapel choir and a choral society, not to mention rock bands. Numerous concerts, recitals and musical productions are held throughout the year. Lunch time concerts take place every Friday.

Drama. Drama productions of all kinds are a major feature of school life, from large scale musicals to classical drama, substantial modern works and fringe performances, many staged with Sherborne Girls. The sophisticated technical resources of the Powell Theatre attract programmes from professional touring companies.

Information Technology. The school has a fast, wireless network that is available throughout the school, including in boarding houses. Safe filtering systems and time restrictions are in place to protect pupils and all pupils have their own devices.

Sports. There are over fifty acres of sports fields, where, at any one time, seventeen various games or matches can take place. Other facilities include two AstroTurf pitches, twenty tennis courts, Rugby fives courts and a shooting range. Within the School's sports centre there is a sports hall, a twenty-five metre swimming pool, a fitness suite and squash courts. A wide variety of sports and activities are offered including athletics, badminton, basketball, canoeing, cricket, cross-country, fencing, fives, golf, hockey, polo, riding, rugby, sailing, shooting, soccer, sub-aqua, swimming and tennis. A new state-of-the-art Sports Centre is being built, due for completion in 2022.

Societies and Activities. In addition to a full sporting, music and drama programme, numerous academic societies meet regularly throughout the term. Over 100 clubs are offered for boys including bridge, chess, computing, debating, photography, dining, life drawing, cooking for university, film making, community service, speech and drama and United Nations.

The school has a strong tradition of outdoor education and, in addition to The Duke of Edinburgh's Award scheme, there are walking, climbing, kayaking and sailing trips. These are local or further afield in Scotland, the Lake District, Wales, Exmoor, Dartmoor and occasionally abroad. Boys also take part in the annual Ten Tors Challenge.

Membership of the Combined Cadet Force is voluntary and the Army, Royal Navy and Royal Marine sections attract about 150 boys and girls from Sherborne Girls each year. A large number of trips and camps are arranged during the term time and the holidays.

Old Shirburnian Society. Mr John Harden, Secretary, tel: 01935 810557, email: OSS@sherborne.org.

Girls' School. Sherborne School's unique partnership with Sherborne Girls offers collaborative opportunities and social events for its pupils throughout the year.

Fees per term (2021–2022). Boarders: £13,375; Day Boys: £10,600.

Charitable status. Sherborne School is a Registered Charity, number 1081228, and a Company Limited by Guarantee, registered in England and Wales, number 4002575. Its aim and objectives are to supply a liberal education in accordance with the principles of the Church of England.

Governors of the School:

Chair: Lt Gen David Leakey, CMG, CVO, CBE
Vice-Chair: Guy Hudson

Isabel Burke	Dr Max Jonas
Aubrey Capel	Nigel Jones, BSc, RICS,
Vicki Cotter	ACIArb
Guy D J Hayward-Cole	Angela Lane
Michael French	Robin Leach
Tim Hague	George Marsh

John Pocock
Gilly Staley
Elaine Stallard
Robert-Jan Temmink, QC

Matthew Whittell (*Staff Nominated*)
Michael Wilson

Headmaster and CEO: **Dr Dominic Luckett**, BA, DPhil, FRSA, FHA, FCCT

Deputy Head (*Academic*): Dr Tim Filtness, BA, MA, PhD
Deputy Head (*Co-curricular*): Tim Bennett, BA Ed
Deputy Head (*Pastoral*): Allister Sheffield, BSc

Director of Operations: Matthew Jamieson, BA

Assistant Head (*Academic*): Lindsey Millar, BA
Assistant Head (*Sixth Form*): Robert Marston, BSc

Senior Housemaster: Ben Sunderland, BEng

Bursar: David Cole, BSc, MSc, PhD

Director of Admissions: Vanessa Hicks

For a full Staff List please visit:
www.sherborne.org/about-sherborne/staff

Shiplake College

Henley-on-Thames, Oxon RG9 4BW

Tel: 0118 940 2455
email: registrar@shiplake.org.uk
website: www.shiplake.org.uk
Twitter: @ShiplakeCollege
Facebook: @ShiplakeCollege
Instagram: @ShiplakeCollege
LinkedIn: /shiplakecollege

Motto: '*Exemplum docet*' (The example teaches)

Shiplake College is an independent boarding and day school for almost 500 pupils (boys aged 11–18 and girls aged 16–18), based in the Oxfordshire countryside on the banks of the River Thames. In 2023 it will welcome girls into Year 7 and transition to become fully co-educational.

Ethos. A Shiplake College education is transformational. The central pillars of Shiplake are its core values, the 3I's, 'Inclusive, individual, and inspirational'. We ensure that every pupil is challenged and supported according to their need and ability. We firmly believe that in addition to a solid academic grounding, sporting, social and cultural achievements are vital to a pupil's long-term development. Shiplake offers a wide range of challenging enrichment activities to ensure an all-round education.

Academic. We aim to admit a well-balanced intake of pupils with a variety of skills and talents. Pupils are selected on his or her potential to make the most of the opportunities that Shiplake can offer. We are proud of our superb value-added results.

Pastoral Care. Shiplake is renowned for delivering outstanding pastoral care – largely due to the belief in a holistic approach to education. Houses are a huge part of the Shiplake community. Each house is run by a Housemaster/mistress who is supported by a strong team of staff including the Matron, Tutors, Medical Staff and the Chaplain. The houses provide excellent support for the pupils in addition to ensuring a comfortable, homely environment for pupils to

study or relax. There is a strong house spirit in evidence with competitions organised for arts, games and academic progress.

Boys joining at 11+ enter the Lower School which houses Years 7 and 8. From Year 9 all pupils become a member of one five houses. Both day and boarding girls join a purpose-built girls' house, but are attached to one of the boys' houses for social purposes, duties and inter-house competitions.

As a Church of England school there is an extensive programme of worship, very often provided in the neighbouring Parish Church. The Chaplain, whose role is purely pastoral, is always available to any member of the College community. Shiplake also welcomes pupils of other faiths or no particular faith.

Boarding. Boarding is an integral part of life at Shiplake. Full, weekly, flexi boarding and overnight stays (all available from Year 7) allow pupils to fully benefit from all the academic and co-curricular opportunities offered. 130 weekly and full boarders enjoy a busy weekend and evening programme, which covers a mixture of cultural, social and sporting trips and activities. International pupils, including a balance of British and non-British students resident abroad, represent approximately 5% of the current school population.

Location. The College is situated in 45 acres of beautiful Oxfordshire countryside, two miles upstream of the famous Henley Royal Regatta town of Henley-on-Thames. Shiplake is conveniently placed for access to the M4 and M40 and the railway stations at Henley and Reading. This idyllic countryside location is just an hour from London and within easy reach of Heathrow and Gatwick airports.

Facilities. Shiplake House, built in 1889 as a family home, is at the heart of the school. The College uses the twelfth-century Parish Church for assemblies and worship. In addition to the main school buildings, Shiplake boasts a range of facilities including the innovative 'Thinking Space', Lecture Theatre, Recording Studio, Tithe Barn Theatre, Sports Hall, Fitness Suite and award-winning sports fields. A Sixth Form Centre and a multi-activity centre with boathouse, two-storey climbing wall and indoor archery and rifle range both opened in September 2020.

Academic Structure. Boys entering the College in Year 7 follow the specially designed curriculum for Years 7 and 8. Boys enjoy the broad and balanced Year 9 curriculum which provides a strong foundation for GCSE. Sixth Form pupils select three subjects from a choice of 28 and also complete a qualification such as an EPQ.

Learning Development. Shiplake has a dedicated Learning Development Department to provide tailored additional help for both those who are academically gifted and those who find certain subject areas difficult to access. About 12% of pupils receive additional support, to improve pupils' confidence and self-esteem and equip them with the necessary skills. All pupils are able to approach their subject teachers for additional support whenever necessary.

Sport. Sport is an integral part of life at Shiplake College. The College has an excellent sporting reputation and most pupils take part in a sporting activity every day. The College enjoys direct access to the river, hockey, cricket and rugby pitches, tennis courts and an outdoor swimming pool. The sports hall offers a variety of indoor sports, a weight-training gym and a fitness room.

Almost all boys play rugby in the autumn term. In the spring term boys play football or row, and in the summer term there is the choice of cricket, tennis or rowing. The girls enjoy hockey, netball, rounders, tennis and rowing. Basketball, badminton, judo, yoga, cross-country running and athletics provide additional activities to develop skills and fitness.

Music, Art and Drama. The College has a thriving mixture of Arts activities and performances and all pupils are encouraged to enjoy the Arts. The annual House Music Competition ensures that every pupil in the school is involved in preparing for a performance and every term there is at least one concert. The Drama Department provides a range of opportunities for the theatrically inclined, to explore and experiment with the subject beyond the constraints of the curriculum.

Activities. Two afternoons are dedicated to a Co-Curricular programme where pupils choose from a wide range of activities including art, cookery, debating and canoeing. The College has a thriving CCF with Air Force, Army and Navy sections. Pupils take part in community service activities and the school has links to a Kenyan School for which fundraising activities are regularly undertaken. The College also runs a Duke of Edinburgh's Award scheme with a number of pupils each year collecting Gold Awards.

Careers. There is an experienced Head of Careers and particular attention is paid to the choice of university and career from Year 11 onwards.

Admission. The Registrar is the first point of contact for all admissions enquiries. Boys are admitted at 11+ into Year 7 and at 13+ into Year 9. There is an intake into the Sixth Form for boys and girls. Places are offered following an assessment day. Please contact the Registrar for further details. Occasional places arise in other years.

Scholarships. Means-tested scholarships and bursaries are offered for academic excellence and to outstanding sportsmen, artists, actors or musicians at Year 7, Year 9 and in the Sixth Form.

Fees per term (2021–2022). Full Boarders £12,450; Weekly Boarders: Years 7–8 £9,350, Years 9–13 £11,690; Flexi (2 nights): Years 7–8 £7,875, Years 9–13 £9,575; Day: Years 7–8 £6,670, Years 9–13 £8,375.

Alumni. The Old Viking Society has a programme of sporting and social events and sends frequent e-newsletters.

Charitable status. Shiplake College is a Registered Charity, number 309651. It exists to provide education for children.

Chairman of Governors: Sir David Tanner, CBE

Headmaster: Tyrone Howe

Bursar and Clerk to the Governors: J Ralfs
Deputy Headmaster (*Academic*): P Jones
Deputy Headmaster (*Pastoral*): N Brown
Director of External Relations: Mrs K Green

Shrewsbury School

The Schools, Shrewsbury, Shropshire SY3 7BA

Tel:	01743 280500 (Switchboard)
	01743 280525 (Headmaster)
	01743 280820 (Bursar)
	01743 280552 (Director of Admissions)
email:	admissions@shrewsbury.org.uk
website:	www.shrewsbury.org.uk
Twitter:	@ShrewsburySch
Facebook:	@ShrewsburySchool
Instagram:	@ShrewsburySchool
LinkedIn:	/school/shrewsbury-school

Motto: '*Intus si recte, ne labora*'

Founded by Edward VI by Royal Charter in 1552, Shrewsbury School combines tradition with a vibrant, modern co-educational vision and a strong sense of community.

The School sits on a 110-acre campus perched above the banks of the River Severn, overlooking the historic market town of Shrewsbury, approximately 50 miles west of Birmingham. It is surrounded by glorious unspoilt countryside, close to the Shropshire Hills and the nearby Welsh Marches and just a short drive away from Snowdonia National Park. All offer countless opportunities for walking, rock-climbing, field trips and expeditions, whilst the School's grounds host pitches described as 'the most beautiful playing fields in the world' (Sir Neville Cardus).

Shrewsbury is fully co-educational, with a seven-day boarding heartbeat and an integral day community. There are 13 houses: nine boys' houses (of which two are for day pupils); and four girls' houses (boarding and day).

It is associated with Packwood Haugh, a co-educational prep school for pupils aged 3 to 13 (*see IAPS entry*).

Number in School. There are 820 pupils in the School (618 boarding and 202 day).

Admission. Most admissions are in September. Girls and boys are admitted at 13 or 14 or into the Sixth Form at 16. Registration forms and other information can be obtained from the Admissions Office. The registration fee, which is non-returnable, is £100.

Entry at 13: Pupils usually take the Common Entrance Examination or the Scholarship Examination in the term preceding that in which they wish to come. The School has its own entrance test for pupils who have not followed the Common Entrance syllabus.

Sixth Form Entry: Direct entry into the Sixth Form depends on examination at Shrewsbury, an interview, and a favourable report from the applicant's present school.

Scholarships. Shrewsbury School has had a tradition, since its founding Charter in 1552, of making generous scholarship awards. Scholarships fall into various categories – Academic, Music, Art, Drama, Design & Technology, Sport and All-Rounder. Awards are made either to pupils under the age of 14 joining the School in the Third Form, or to those entering the School at Sixth Form level.

Statement of Aims. Shrewsbury School has a strong vision, derived from its position as a major co-educational boarding school of international reputation. It aims to instil a rigorous approach to academic work, based on the encouragement of independent thinking and intellectual curiosity. The School believes that learning should be a habit that is inculcated for life, not only a means to short-term examination success.

Through its diverse opportunities, Shrewsbury School aims to encourage and enable pupils to become caring, thoughtful, confident members of society. Ambitious yet not arrogant, generous in spirit, interesting, interested and able to respect and communicate effectively with people of all backgrounds.

To this end, Shrewsbury will always strive to achieve the highest possible standards in the breadth and quality of its curriculum, the provision of its facilities and resources, and the achievements – whether academic, sporting, musical, theatrical or artistic – of its pupils and staff. Shrewsbury delights in the uniqueness of its education; a blend of values, traditions, inspiring people, a beautiful location, participation in the world beyond school, and a strong belief that life is what you make of it.

Academic Curriculum. Shrewsbury's academic provision endeavours to be exciting, challenging, responsive and versatile. We want pupils to be engaged in a learning process that combines inspirational experience with the sort of rigour and precision that will prepare them not only to produce excellent results in public examinations, but also to be empathetic, innovative and leading contributors to the world beyond the school gates.

We actively encourage cross-curricular thinking – synthesising ideas between Faculties and encouraging the transference of skills. Our classrooms are warm, welcoming environments in which pupils can expect to have their thoughts and opinions heard and in which they will certainly be pushed to meet and exceed their potential. Above all else, we aim to engender excitement and enjoyment and to cultivate a love of learning for its own sake both in the classroom and well beyond it.

An academic programme entitled 'Origin' has been introduced for pupils in their first year at Shrewsbury (Third Form). The key motivator for this is a desire to ignite a passion for learning that will transcend the mechanics of examinations and remain with the pupils long after they have left the school. Alongside the core disciplines from which pupils make their GCSE selections, there are also 'Reading the World' sessions during the year which offer them the opportunity to consider problem-solving, current affairs, social change and the world of economics. In order to promote independence in learning, pupils undertake a key project, the Third Form Portfolio, which requires them to make a presentation and produce a written report on two self-selected areas about which they feel passionate. Pupils also follow a fortnightly programme of Personal and Social Development which promotes self-esteem, respect and tolerance.

All pupils take English, Mathematics, French, Physics, Chemistry, and Biology to GCSE. They are required to take at least one Modern Foreign Language, chosen from French, German and Spanish. Study of a second (or third) modern language can be undertaken in the option blocks, where the other choices are Latin or Ancient History, Greek, German, Spanish, History, Geography, Art, Design, Philosophy & Theology (RS), Music, Computer Science, Astronomy and PE. All pupils also study a non-examined course in Personal and Social Development.

All pupils in the Lower Sixth embark on four qualifications leading to at least three A Level qualifications at the end of their two years in the Sixth Form. The fourth option choice may be an Extended Project Qualification, a further A Level course, or the Global Perspectives Qualification. Subjects offered at A Level are: Art, Biology, Business Studies, Chemistry, Classics (Latin, Greek, Classical Civilisation), Design and Technology, Drama, Economics, English, French, Geography, German, History, History of Art, Mathematics, Further Mathematics, Music, Philosophy and Theology, Physical Education, Physics and Spanish.

For those pupils who need it, there is a well-equipped team of Learning Support specialists who work with teachers and pupils. English Language support is available for those for whom English is an additional language.

The Moser Library was extensively refurbished in 2017. It houses the School Library, the Moser collection of watercolours and the Ancient Taylor Library, which contains a large and important collection of medieval manuscripts and early printed books.

Sport. With nine full-size grass pitches, two AstroTurf pitches, an indoor Cricket Centre, two boathouses with an indoor tank and ergos, 14 fives courts and an indoor 25-metre deck-level pool, the sports facilities at Shrewsbury are of an exceptional standard.

Shrewsbury has a reputation for sporting excellence and all pupils are encouraged to play and compete at a standard relative to their abilities. School and house teams at every level train and play on most afternoons. There is a wide range of sporting options, from 'participation' sports focused on maintaining a healthy lifestyle, to 'performance' and 'podium' sports focused on achieving regional or national success.

Salopians compete internationally, particularly in rowing and cricket, and we are one of the strongest football schools in the country. Shrewsbury is also one of the top schools in the country for boys' and girls' running and for Eton fives. Pupils also achieve great levels of success in hockey, netball, rugby lacrosse, racket sports, fencing, athletics, basketball and swimming.

Music. Inclusivity is central to the ethos of Shrewsbury School's Music Department. The Music Faculty aims to give as many pupils as possible the opportunity to take part in the rich musical life on offer, and music of all styles and genres is encouraged. Approximately 45% of pupils receive individual music lessons, often in more than one instrument. Teaching is available in any orchestral instrument, as well as in singing, percussion, piano (classical and jazz), organ, guitar, harp and music theory. There are a large number of instrumental and choral groups and pupils are given regular opportunities to perform in public, ranging from Friday lunchtime concerts, chamber music evenings and pupil-led open mic nights in the Music School's own 200-seat auditorium, through to full orchestral concerts in Birmingham Town Hall or Cadogan Hall in London

A purpose-built music school provides a small concert hall, 20 practice and teaching rooms, two classrooms, and an IT suite equipped with the latest hardware and software. Larger concerts are held in the School's main assembly hall, the Alington Hall, which seats 500.

Drama. Drama is an important part of school life, with four major school productions, dance showcases, student-directed work, new writing and a range of house plays every year. Alongside the many opportunities for pupils to perform on stage as actors or dancers, they can also learn the technical theatre skills of designing and operating lighting and sound, and supporting with costume, hair, make-up and stage-management. Additionally the School hosts at least one professional visiting company or artist in the theatre each year.

Shrewsbury has built up a strong reputation for producing original musicals, with lyrics and music written by members of staff. On alternate years since 1994, these have toured to the Edinburgh Fringe Festival, where they have attracted great critical acclaim. *The Great Gatsby* is currently in development.

All pupils in the Third Form experience a module of Drama as part of the English syllabus, and pupils may study Drama as an academic subject at GCSE and A Level.

Our brand new Barnes Theatre features a 250-seat auditorium with state of the art equipment, a dance studio, a new entrance foyer and further studio spaces for drama.

Other Co-Curricular Activities. Co-curricular activities are a fundamental part of life at Shrewsbury and an extensive range of possibilities are offered to pupils, with one afternoon each week and a full day each term dedicated to these. Many of the activities make use of the unspoilt countryside on the doorstep and the easy access to the Welsh hills: the Combined Cadet Force, leadership courses, the Duke of Edinburgh's Award scheme, mountain biking, gliding, scuba diving, the Rovers (adventure club), the Natural History Society.

Arts-based activities include dance, creative arts, creative writing, film and video, music technology, and there are also opportunities to learn skills such as lifeguarding, judo, cooking, horse riding. Many pupils volunteer in the local community and many devise projects of their own through the pupil-led Global Social Leaders programme.

Societies. There is a wide variety of thriving clubs and societies at Shrewsbury. These range from Literary, Historical, Political, Debating, Model United Nations, STEM, Drama and Language societies to those catering for practical skills, including Beekeeping and Technical Theatre. Most academic faculties run their own societies, and their meetings often welcome distinguished academics to give lectures at school. These are also open to members of the public.

Field Study Centre. Shrewsbury owns a farmhouse in Snowdonia, which is used at weekends throughout the year as a base for expeditions and house trips.

Careers. The Futures Department plays an important part in preparing pupils for the world beyond Shrewsbury School. Led by the Head of Futures and the Head of Higher Education, the Department works as part of the whole school team, supported by the Salopian Club, to provide advice to pupils on course choices, universities, work experience and co-curricular activities. Old Salopians also benefit from access to support from the Department.

Careers education at Shrewsbury is embedded within the Third Form through the Personal and Social Development (PSD) and Tutorial programmes. The focus at this stage is on self-discovery and exploration, and enabling pupils to link the key skills they are developing through school life to the world of work. In the Summer Term they undertake pupil-led social action projects which benefit the local community.

Careers education through the PSD and Tutorial programmes continues in the Fourth Form. Pupils are introduced to external speakers from several contrasting professional areas and take part in the National Enterprise Challenge as part of National Careers Week and. During the Easter holidays, they are expected to take part in work experience.

At the beginning of the Fifth Form, pupils take a careers profiling test. The detailed personalised reports provide the stimulus for one-to-one interviews with qualified advisers, and the Tutorial and PSD programmes enable further exploration and support.

The focus in the Sixth Form is on supporting pupils to research information on all the options open to them. The Higher Education Adviser and the Head of Futures, with support from external speakers, deliver a full range of advice through lectures, workshops and one-to-one guidance to enable pupils to identify their strengths, vocations and ambitions. These include presentations and workshops on UCAS, Degree Apprenticeships / School Leaver programmes, LNAT, UCAT, BMAT, studying abroad and gap years. Upper Sixth pupils are guided through the application processes for universities, including Oxbridge, and are given assistance to plan effective and fulfilling gap years if they choose that option.

Community Service. Through an extensive range of volunteering opportunities and projects, including the pupil-led Global Social Leaders initiative, pupils play an active part in the local community. These include volunteering at Shrewsbury Food Bank, in the local hospital, in primary schools, care homes, charity shops and at Shrewsbury Ark for the homeless.

Shrewsbury House. Founded in Everton, Liverpool as a Club for boys in 1903 by masters from Shrewsbury School, Shrewsbury House was rebuilt as a Youth and Community Centre in association with the Local Authority and the Diocese in 1974. It runs Junior and Senior Clubs for local young people throughout the week. Links between Shrewsbury School and Shrewsbury House are strong, and the Headmaster and three members of staff sit on its Committee. Fundraising takes place at the School throughout the year and there are regular exchange visits, including opportunities for Lower Sixth Formers to take part in residential Social Studies courses at Shrewsbury House.

Shrewsbury International Schools. The school has close links with Shrewsbury International Schools in Bangkok and Hong Kong. Shrewsbury International School Bangkok opened in 2003 and an additional primary school was opened in the city centre in Bangkok in September 2018. Shrewsbury International School Hong Kong opened its doors to primary school children in September 2018. Teaching and pupil exchanges take place between the schools, and Governors of Shrewsbury School serve on the boards of management of the International Schools.

Fees per term (2021–2022). Boarders: £12,835–£13,584 including tuition, board and ordinary School expenses. There are no other obligatory extras, apart from stationery. Day Pupils: £8,805–£9,280.

Application for reduced fees may be made to the Governors through the Headmaster.

Old Pupils' Society. Most pupils leaving the school join the Salopian Club, The Schools, Shrewsbury SY3 7BA; email: oldsalopian@shrewsbury.org.uk.

Charitable status. Shrewsbury School is a Registered Charity, number 528413. It exists to provide secondary education.

Governing Body:

Chairman: T H P Haynes, MA

S R Baker, BSc, FCA, CF
R Boys-Stones, BSc, FCA
D Chance, MBA
J R Clark, MA, PGCE
Sir P Davis
Diana Flint, DL (*Appointed by the Lord Lieutenant of Shropshire*)
Carla Howarth, LLB, MA
Dr S Jones-Perrott, MBBS, FRCP, BA Hons Oxon
Professor A J McCarthy, BSc, PhD
J M H Moir, BA, MBA
Councillor CM Motley, BA Hons (*Appointed by Shropshire Council*)
J Pitt, BSc Hons, MBA,
Mrs F Schofield, BA Hons, PGCE
D Stacey, DL
Mrs G Walters, BBLS
Mrs S Hankin, BA
Councillor D Morris, BA

Headmaster: **N L Winkley**, MA, MEd

Bursar and Clerk to the Governors: M J Ware, MA, ACA

Senior Deputy Head: K Brennan, MSc, PGCE [from August 2022]
Senior Master and Director of Admissions: M J Cropper, MA
Deputy Head (*Academic*): R A Kowenicki, MSci, PhD
Deputy Head (*Pastoral*): Ms A R Peak, BA
Acting Deputy Head (*Co-Curricular*): H R Brown, MA, PhD, FTCL
Head of Partnership and Community Engagement: S H Cowper, MA
Director of Shrewsbury School Foundation: O A Jackson-Hutt, MA, MSt
International Development Director: Dr M Tamilarasan, BEng, PhD, FRAeS
Director of Marketing and Communications: G Ferriday, BA, FCIM

Assistant Masters/Mistresses:
* *Head of Faculty*
† *Housemaster/Housemistress*

Mrs R Adams, BEc, BEd (*Business, Politics*)
Mrs G Ansell, MA, Cert ES TESOL (*Head of English as an Additional Language (EAL), Chinese*)
Miss M Fernandez Aragon, MA (*Hispanic Fellow*)
J C Armstrong, MA (*Maths*)
Ms R Arrol, BA (*English as an Additional Language (EAL)*)
G G Bandy, MA (*English*)
A S Barnard, BA (*Geography, †Port Hill*)
M W D B Barrett, BSc (*Economics, Business Studies, †Rigg's Hall*)
R Barrett, MSc, PhD (*Physics, Safeguarding Team*)
G J F Bell, BA (*Philosophy & Theology, Senior Admissions Tutor*)
H O M Bennett, MA (*Philosophy and Theology*)
M C Bird, BA (*MCB, Philosophy & Theology, †School House*)
A D Briggs, BSc, PhD, MRSC, ACIEA (**Science, *Chemistry*)
Ms H R Brown, MA, PhD, FTCL (*Acting Deputy Head (Co-Curricular), *Director of Drama*)

Mrs L A Caddel, BA (*Art)
R A J Case, BSc, PhD (*Biology, †Radbrook*)
M D H Clark, MA (*Classics, Sixth Form Admissions Tutor*)
Miss C L Cissone Hunter, BA, PgDip (*Drama*)
C E Cook, MA (*History*)
S K P Cooley, MEng (*Maths, Physics*)
Mrs L A E Corcoran, BA (**Politics, History*)
S H Cowper, MA (*Spanish, French, Head of Partnership & Community Engagement*)
M Cropper, MA (*Senior Master & Director of Admissions, Maths*)
A R Currie-Jordan, MSc, PhD (*Biology*)
N P David, BSc, MRICS (**Director of Activities*)
Miss G M Davies, BSc (*Head of Girls' Cricket*)
Mrs J Davies, BSc (*Maths*)
Miss E Davis, BA (**Physical Education, Safeguarding Team*)
A R Duncan, BA (*Economics, †Severn Hill*)
M S Elliot, MA, PhD, CPhys, MInstP (**Astronomy & EPQ, Physics*)
Mrs C English, BA (*CE, Learning Support*)
R F Evans, BSc (*Geography*)
H S M Exham, BSc (*Biology, Head of Digital Learning, †Oldham's Hall*)
Miss C D Fagan, BA, MA (*English*)
H P Farmer, BA (*Modern Languages, Head of Pupil Welfare (PSD), Safeguarding Team*)
R T Fitton, MEng (*Maths*)
P G Fitzgerald, MA (*Classics)
Mrs S Fletcher, BSc (*Biology*)
S A A Fox, BA (*Geography*)
J R Fraser-Andrews, MA, MMus (*English*)
J A Gabbitas, BA, MA (*Art*)
Mrs H L Gale, BSc (*Chemistry*)
S Grant, BSc, MSc (*Senior Rowing Coach*)
S C Griffiths, BA, MSc (*History, Politics, †Ingram's Hall*)
M H Hansen, BSc, BA (*Maths*)
A F Harden, MA, PhD (*Classics*)
M J Harding, BA, ACA (*Economics and Business Studies*)
S M Harrison, BA, MA (*History of Art*)
I P Haworth, MA (*History*)
E C Higgins, BA (*Modern Languages*)
W A Hughes, BA (*PE, †Ridgemount*)
A T Hundermark, BSc (*Geography*)
M D B Johnson, BA (*Maths, Head of Pupil Behaviour*)
M P Johnson, MA, MSc (*Maths)
D M Joyce, DipRCM, ARCM (*Music*)
P A Kaye, BEng (**ICT & Computing*)
C W Kealy, BComm (*Business)
Revd A Keulemans, BSc, BTh (*Chaplain, Philosophy & Theology*)
Mrs V L Kirk, BSc (*Chemistry*)
Mrs S G Latcham, BA (*Classics*)
D A Law, BA, MA, PhD (*English*)
Mrs K Leslie, BA (*English)
Mrs A H Livingstone, MA, RSA (*Deputy Head of Learning Support*)
K M Lloyd, BA, MA (**Design & Technology*)
J V Lucas, LLB, BSc (*Mathematics, Head of Third Form*)
H G Mackridge, MA (*History, Head of Academic Innovation*)
Mrs J A Matthews, BSc (*Biology*)
F Matthews-Bird, BSc, PhD (*Geography*)
Mrs K M Maw, BA (*Assistant Director of Sport*)
Mrs M L McKenzie, BMus, MMus, LTCL (*Assistant Director of Music*)

Ms H L McClelland, BA, MA (*German*)

P A Merricks-Murgatroyd, BA (**Economics*)

Miss E D Micklewright, BA, MA (*Biology*)

P J Middleton, BA (*Acting Senior Deputy Head, English*)

Mrs K V Mitchell, MA, Dip Ed, APC (**Learning Support*)

S Mitchell, MSc (*Lead Athletic Development Coach*)

A P Morris, BA (*Spanish*)

T S Morgan, BSc, PhD (**Biology*)

A X Murray, BSc (*Chemistry*)

Mrs G E Murray, BSc, PGCertSpLD, AMDBA, APC (*Learning Support*)

D A G Nicholas, BA, MA (*History, Classics, Prep School Liaison*)

Miss E Nieper, BSc (*Graduate Sports Coach*)

C W Oakley, MMath, DPhil (*Maths, Head of Academic Administration*)

Dr J L Pattenden, MA, DPhil (*Physics*)

P Pattenden, MA, DPhil, C Phys, MInstP (*Physics, Head of Elite University Application*)

I W Payne, BSc, MA (*Maths*)

H R W Peach, BA (**German*)

Ms A R Peak, BA (*Deputy Head (Pastoral), Geography, Designated Safeguarding Lead*)

Mrs S E Pearson, BA, MA (*English, Safeguarding Team*)

Ms A P Pedraza, MA (**Spanish*)

A S Pembleton, BSc (**Director of Sport*)

Ms A P Pergod, MA (*French Fellow*)

T P Percival, MA (*Classics, Head of Higher Education*)

Miss N J Perkins, BSc (*Design and Technology*)

Miss E A Pitchford, BA (*Art, Photography*)

Mrs H E Pook, BA, OCR Dip SpLD (*Learning Support*)

D Portier, MA, DEA (*French, Head of Sixth Form*)

Mrs N M Pritchard, BA, PGDip (*Business Studies, Admissions Tutor*)

W R Reynolds, BSc (*Design & Technology, †Emma Darwin*)

D M Roberts, BSc, MEd (*Mathematics & Computing*)

T F Rudkin, BSc (*Head of Girls' Rowing*)

P J B Rudge, BA, BA (**History*)

Mrs A Z Schmaller-Russell, BA, MSc, PGDip (*German*)

O J Russell, MA, MPhil, FRGS (**Geography*)

M Schofield, BSc (*Chemistry*)

A J Shantry, PGDip (*Cricket Professional*)

Mrs S L M Shantry, BSc (*Maths*)

C Shelley, BA, HNC, MinstAM Dip (*Music, Music Technology*)

W M Simper, BSc (*Biology*)

M S Skipper, BMus (**Music*)

A Smiter, MSci (*Physics*)

Mrs A E Smiter, MSci (**Physics*)

Miss R R Southcott, BA (*Art Fellow*)

Miss A M Stevens, BSc (*Graduate Sports Coach*)

Mrs L R Temple, BA (*English, †Moser's*)

F W Tickner, BA (*English*)

Mrs J H Till, BA, RSA/OCR DipSpLD (*Learning Support*)

M J Tonks, BA (*Philosophy & Theology, Head of Guardianship and International Family Liaison*)

T D J Warburg, MA (*Modern Languages*)

Miss R B Weatherstone, BA (**French*)

N J Welch, BSc (*Maths*)

Miss E J Wheeler, MA, MA (**Philosophy & Theology*)

T C Whitehead, BA (*French, *Modern Languages*)

S P Wilderspin, BEd (*Physical Education, Master i/c Football*)

J E O Williams, MSc (*Science Fellow*)

Ms S E Williams, MChem (*Chemistry, Head of Middle School*)

S J Williams, BA (**Director of Music*)

B J Wilson, BA, MMus (*Head of Choral Music*)

Mrs C H Wilson, BA (*CHLW, Philosophy & Theology, †The Grove*)

R M Wilson, MEng, MA (*Maths*)

Miss R Witcombe, BSc (*Design & Technology*)

Miss G Y Y Woo, MSc (*Chemistry*)

Mrs C I U Wordie, TEFL, ACES (*German Assistant*)

D M Wray, MA (*Chemistry, Head of Science Outreach*)

J J C Wright, BSc (*Geography; †Churchills*)

Mrs A J Wyatt, BA (*Art, †Mary Sidney*)

N N Zafar, BA, MA (*Economics, Politics*)

School Doctors:
The General Practitioner Team, Mytton Oak Surgery, Racecourse Lane, Shrewsbury

Dental Adviser: R J Gatenby, BDS, DGDP, RCS

Headmaster's Personal Assistant: Mrs F Nicholas

Solihull School

Warwick Road, Solihull, West Midlands B91 3DJ

Tel: 0121 705 0958
email: admin@solsch.org.uk
website: www.solsch.org.uk
Twitter: @solsch1560
Facebook: @SolihullSchool
Instagram: @solsch1560
LinkedIn: /SolihullSchool

Motto: '*Perseverantia*'

Solihull School was founded in 1560 with the income from the chantry chapels of the parish of Solihull. The school is particularly proud of the richness and diversity of the education that it provides. The school has always been closely involved with the community, making its sporting and theatrical facilities available for local schools. In September 2020, the school merged with Saint Martin's to create a leading independent coeducational 3–18 day school across two campuses. Solihull Senior School on the Warwick Road campus and Solihull Preparatory School on the Saint Martin's campus.

Organisation. Solihull provides education for over 1,500 children aged between 3 and 18. The Headmaster of Solihull School is Mr D E J J Lloyd. Mr M P Penney is Head of the Preparatory School, which occupies a 20-acre campus on Brueton Avenue and has more than 440 pupils aged from 3 to 11. Mr S A Morgan is Head of the Senior School attended by 1,100 pupils aged 11–18. In 1973 girls were accepted into the Sixth Form. In September 2005 the school became fully coeducational.

Site and Facilities. Solihull moved to its present site in 1882 and the original school building, School House, survives. The Senior School campus now comprises over 50 acres of buildings and playing fields. Over the last 20 years there has been a very substantial building programme. This originally involved the extension of the Science Department and Design and Technology Centre, the laying of an artificial turf pitch and three squash courts, and the redevelopment of School House. In 2002 a new theatre, the Bushell Hall, was built, which can accommodate an audience of 600 and an assembly for 1,000. At the same time, the old hall was transformed into a library and IT rooms. In 2003, the Alan Lee Pavilion, was completed. In September 2005 a new teaching area, the George Hill Building, was unveiled to provide 16 classrooms and an extensive social space. A music school was unveiled in September 2009, The David Turnbull Music School. In September 2015 a four-floor, state-of-the-art Sixth Form centre, The Cooper Building, opened. It was designed to transform the Sixth Form teaching and learning and to incorporate the latest multimedia technology. A second artificial turf pitch was completed in 2017. In November 2019 the school opened a refurbished refectory. In September 2020, Solihull merged with Saint Martin's school and opened Solihull Preparatory School on the Saint Martin's campus. During the summer of 2020, The Junior School building on the Warwick Road campus was repurposed for Senior School use and renamed The Mark Hopton Building. The Preparatory School on the Saint Martin's campus has been redeveloped as a 3–11 school with substantial building work and modifications such as bespoke specialist teaching rooms for Art, Design and Technology, ICT, Music and Science and Clevertouch boards. Prep School facilities include a full sized floodlit artificial pitch, a 25m swimming pool, a large recently built library of over 8,000 books and a SMArt Performing Arts Centre that incorporates an auditorium and a dance studio. In October 2021, development work commenced on a car park expansion and new playing fields. This latest construction project on the Saint Martin's campus is due to be completed by September 2022.

Curriculum. In the Prep School particular emphasis is placed on establishing high standards in core subjects and key skills that permeate the children's learning across the curriculum. The Prep School has specialist teaching rooms for Art, Design and Technology, ICT, Music and Science. EYFS and Infant pupils enjoy the 'Alice House Guide to Living Well' programme – covering Happy, Engaged and Meaningful Living – and Junior School pupils learn resilience skills as part of the Prep School's Wellbeing and Personal Development programme.

At the beginning of the Senior School, all pupils take at least one year of Latin and Spanish. In the second year French and German are optional subjects. English Language and Literature, Mathematics, a Modern Foreign Language, Physics, Chemistry and Biology remain compulsory subjects to GCSE. Three other subjects are chosen from a wide range of options.

The size of the Sixth Form enables the school to offer a very wide range of subjects and combinations. These subjects are Art, Biology, Business, Chemistry, Classics, Dance, Design and Technology, Economics, English Literature, French, Greek, Geography, German, History, Latin, Mathematics, Further Mathematics, Music, PE, Physics, Psychology, Religious Studies (Philosophy and Ethics), Spanish and Theatre Studies. There is also a substantial programme of Enrichment for all pupils in the Sixth Form, ranging from Mandarin Chinese to Cookery.

Academic Success. In 2021, Solihull recorded another set of outstanding A Level results with 100% pass rate; 94% A* to B grades and 71% of all grades falling into the A* or A category. 90% of students went to their chosen university. At GCSE, 77% of the 2021 grades were at 9–7.

Games. Games are an integral part of the school curriculum and all pupils in the school are involved. PE is compulsory until Year 11 and all pupils in the school have a games afternoon. The school has a very strong tradition in the major team games, but also offers a very wide range of other options. The principal team games are rugby, cricket, hockey and netball. The Prep School pupils play football in addition to these sports. The school also has teams in tennis, athletics, swimming, clay-pigeon shooting, cross-country, badminton, basketball and fencing to name but a few. In recent years the school has organised very extensive tours for pupils of differing ages: in 2018 our senior rugby teams toured Singapore and New Zealand, and our senior girls' netball and hockey teams visited Singapore and Malaysia. Individual and team national success is a regular feature of Solihull sporting life.

Music, Drama and Dance. The school has a very strong tradition in Music and Drama, which has been enhanced since the building of the Bushell Hall, The David Turnbull Music School on the Warwick Road campus and the SMArt performing arts centre on our Saint Martin's campus. Over a third of all pupils learn a musical instrument and there are over 25 different musical groups in the Senior School. This ranges from orchestras, bands and choirs to piano, string and wind ensembles. Several of these groups are very successful in competition at local festivals. There are many opportunities for pupils to perform at concerts, both formal and informal, throughout the year. A busy programme of masterclasses is given by visiting professional musicians. There is also an excellent Chapel Choir that performs during the school week and at the chapel services each Sunday. Each term the choir sings Evensong in a cathedral (including an annual visit to St Paul's in London) and performs on BBC Radio 4's Daily Service. In 2015 the school joined the Steinway Initiative, purchasing three new Steinway grand pianos.

The Drama and Music departments come together each year for the staging of an ambitious musical, which always involves a large number of pupils. There are two major dramatic performances each year: a school musical (*Tommy, Joseph and the Amazing Technicolor Dreamcoat, Made in Dagenham, Twelfth Night, Nell Gwynn* and *Little Shop of Horrors*) and a school play (*Fuente Ovejuna, The Royal Hunt of the Sun* and *Goodnight Mr Tom*). In addition, there are several smaller productions in the course of the year.

Solihull expanded its Performing Arts offering with the addition of Dance in 2020.

Outdoor Education. Outdoor Education plays a major part in the school's life. In the Third Form pupils take part in an outdoor activities programme called Terriers. In the Shell Form every pupil spends a week at the school's mountain cottage in Snowdonia. From the Shell Form pupils are able to participate in the CCF, which has an Army and an RAF section, and from the end of the Fourth Form, they can pursue the Duke of Edinburgh's Award scheme. There are approximately 80 pupils in the CCF and 160 are involved at different stages of the Duke of Edinburgh's Award scheme. The school has a popular Mountain Club and organises biennial major expeditions: Cambodia in 2013, Ladakh India in 2015 and Alaska in 2017.

Admissions. Pupils are accepted into Solihull School through assessments at 3+, 4+, 5+ and 6+ and examination at 7+ to 14+. A major point of entry to Senior School is at 11+ (Year 7). Places are awarded on the basis of written exams in English and Mathematics and, in some cases, an interview. Some pupils are also accepted to enter the school at 12+, 13+ and 14+. A substantial number of pupils enter the school at Sixth Form level. Offers for admission to the Sixth Form are made on the basis of an interview, predicted GCSE grades and a personal profile. Such offers are conditional on receiving a pupil's school report which should indicate high levels of effort and attainment, excellent conduct and a positive attitude to school life plus achieving a minimum of two grade 7s and four grade 5s at GCSE, normally including grade 5 in Mathematics and English. For further Mathematics, a grade 8 in GCSE Mathematics is required. For Biology, Chemistry, Mathematics, Physics or a Modern Foreign Language a grade 7 in the subject is required. For all other subjects a grade 6 in the appropriate facilitating subject for each subject is required; however, a grade 7 is recommended.

The dates for entrance examinations and the Sixth Form scholarship examinations are available on the school website.

Fees per term (2021–2022). Nursery fees are available on our website. Reception/ Infant 1/ Infant 2 £3,585; Junior School £4,095–£4,255; Senior School £4,890.

Scholarships and Bursaries. The number of awards and their value is at the discretion of the Headmaster. As well as Academic, there are Art, Music and Sport Scholarships which are awarded at 11+. At Sixth Form Solihull awards Academic, Sport, Music and Theatre Arts Scholarships.

In addition to scholarships, means-tested bursaries are available to offer opportunities to pupils with financial needs. Applicants for such assistance are considered at Senior School and Sixth Form entry.

The Development and Alumni Relations Office at Solihull School. Solihull School Community Network https://alumni.solsch.org.uk is a network bringing together alumni, parents past and present, former and current staff and friends of both Solihull and Saint Martin's schools. It is a place to share memories, forge careers and social connections and offer support to current students and recent leavers. Email moseleyl@solsch.org.uk or call 0121 703 2963.

Old Silhillians Association. The Old Silhillians Association support and maintain links with the school. They also have their own clubhouse and extensive sports facilities. Website: www.silhillians.net; email: osa@silhillians.net.

Charitable status. Solihull School is a Registered Charity, number 1120597. It exists to provide high-quality education for pupils between 3 and 18 years old.

Chairman of the Governors: Mr Damian Kelly, BA

Bursar and Clerk to the Governors: Mr Richard Bate, MA Cantab, ACMA

Headmaster: Mr David E J J Lloyd, BSc

Head of the Senior School: Mr Sean Morgan, BA
Head of the Preparatory School: Mr Mark Penney, BA
Senior School Deputy Head (Academic): Mr David Morgan, BA, MA
Senior School Deputy Head (Teaching & Learning Innovation): Ms Daniele Harford-Fox, BA
Senior School Deputy Head (Pastoral): Mrs Rachael Speirs, BA
Preparatory School Senior Deputy Head (Pastoral & Staff Welfare): Mr Michael Jones, BA, MA

Preparatory School Deputy Head (Academic): Mrs Janet Humphreys, BEd

Director of Development and Alumni Relations: Ms Lucy Lunt, BA, PGDip

Assistant Head (Data & Assessment): Mrs Laura Blackburn, BSc
Assistant Head (Pastoral) and DSL: Mr Thomas Emmet, BSc
Assistant Head (Co-Curricular): Mrs Hannah Fair, BA, MA
Assistant Head (Staff Welfare): Mrs Emma Jones, BA
Assistant Head (ICT Strategy): Mr Matthew van Alderwegen, BA, MA
Preparatory School Assistant Head: Mrs Emma Inglis, BEd
Head of EYFS: Mrs Julie Litwinko, BPhil
Head of Infants: Miss Hannah Hicks, BA, QTS

Head of Sixth Form: Mrs Katherine Robinson, BSc
Head of the Middle School: Miss Natasha Evans, BA, MA
Head of the Lower School: Mr Michael Gledhill, BA, LLB

Assistant Staff:
* Head of Department

Mr Gareth Affleck, BA (*History & Politics*)
Miss Rachel Airdrie, BA
Mr Oliver Anderton, BSc
Mrs Joanne Ashton, BA
Mrs Nicola Atkins, BEd
Mr Matthew Babb, BSc
Mrs Katie Baden, BSc
Mr Owen Bate, BSc
Mrs Rebecca Beavon, BA
Miss Claire Bednall, BSc, MSc
Mrs Jennifer Bernamont, BSc
Mr Mark Bishop, BSc, MSc (*Mathematics*)
Mrs Claire Black, BA
Mrs Laura Blackburn, BSc
Mr Mark Briggs, BSc
Mr Darryl Brotherhood, BSc
Mr David Brough, BSc
Mrs Julia Brown, BSc
Mrs Julie Brown, BA, MA
Mr James Brown, BA
Miss Tracy Bryan, BA
Mrs Alison Burt, BSc
Ms Libby Campbell, BA
Mr Edward Carne, BA
Mr Samuel Chillcott, MSci, MEng (*Physics*)
Mrs Jackie Clark, BA, MA
Mr Neal Corbett, BA (*Design Technology*)
Miss Alexia Coste, BA, MA
Mr Martin Covill, BSc
Miss Lydia Cross, BSc
Mr Geddes Cureton, BSc
Mrs Hannah Davidson, BSc
Mr Mark Davies, BEng
Mr Paul Delaney, BA (*French*)
Mrs Pelvinder Deu, BSc
Mrs Nicola Dickerson, BA
Ms Claire Dignon, BA, MA
Mr Chris Dossett, BSc, MSc (*Director of Sport, Health & Fitness*)
Dr Amy Eagleton, PhD
Mr Alex Eden, BSc
Mrs Janine Elkington, BSc
Mr Jake Everling, BA

Mrs Suzannah Farnan, BSc
Mrs Tracey Farnell, BSc (*Prep School Sport, Health & Fitness*)
Mr Francisco Fernandez-Valverde
Dr Sian Foster, MA, MPhil, DPhil, MBA
Mrs Joanne Francis, BA, MPhil
Mrs Tracy Gallagher, BEd
Mrs Corinne Goodman, BSc (*Chemistry*)
Mr Simon Grove, LLB
Mr Christopher Guy, BSc
Mrs Helen Hallworth, BSc
Mr James Hands, BA
Mrs Lucy Harper, BA
Ms Katherine Harris, BA, MA
Mrs Jennifer Hart, BA, QTLS
Mr Stuart Hart, BA, MPhil, PhD (*English*)
Mr Heath Harlow
Mrs Mieke Hartland, BA
Mrs Saranne Haley, BSc, MA
Mr Stephen Hifle, QTS
Mrs Kim Higginson, BA
Mrs Kate Hull, BSc
Revd Canon Andrew Hutchinson, BA, MEd
Mrs Iryna Igoe, BEd
Mrs Elzabe Jansen van Rensburg, BSc
Mr Gareth James, BA
Dr Amelia Jennings, BA, DPhil
Dr Richard Jennings, BSc, PhD
Mrs Joanna Johnson, BA, MPhil (*Classics*)
Mr Tim Kermode, MA (*Director of Music*)
Mrs Karine Lacote, CRPE
Ms Natalie Leeson, BSc
Mr Nick Leonard, BEd
Mr Nicholas Linehan, BA
Mrs Alexandra Longden, BA
Mrs Gabrielle Lowe, BSc, PGDip
Dr Michela Luiselli, BA, PhD
Miss Lydia Lynch, BSc
Mr Andrew MacArthur, MMath
Mr Andrew MacKenzie, BA
Mr Darren Maddy
Mrs Jane Mander, BA
Mrs Hanlie Martens, MMus
Mrs Julie Massarella, BEd (*Food & Nutrition*)
Mr Philip May, BSc
Mr Tim Mayled
Mr Christopher Mayer
Mrs Colette McArthur, BA
Dr Sufia McGuire, PhD, MSc
Mrs Wendy Meigh, BEd (*Economics & Business*)
Mrs Hayley Middleton, BEng, BCom
Mr Stephen Mitchell, BSc
Mr Junaid Mohammed, BA
Mrs Clare Mollison, BA
Mrs Gabriella Morby, BA
Mr Paul Morgan, BA (*Spanish*)
Mrs Rachel Morgan, BEd
Mrs Ulrike Mynette, MA
Miss Rebecca Noon, BA
Mrs Dawn Parker, BSc (*Biology*)
Dr Mary Partridge, DPhil, MA, BA
Mr Owen Parsons, MSci
Mrs Zoe Patching-Jones, BA
Mrs Vanessa Patel, BA (*Computer Science*)
Mrs Helen Peat, BMus (*Prep School Music*)
Mrs Donna Penney, BSc, NASENCo

Mr Simon Phillips, BA, MMus (*Academic Music*)
Mrs Emma Pimlott, BSc
Miss Jessica Platt, BA, MA
Mr Alex Poole, BSc
Mr Ali Raza
Mr David Rice, BA, MA
Mrs Carol Rich, BA, MSci
Mrs Catherine Ridout, BEng
Mrs Helen Roberts, BMus, MMus
Mrs Alex Roll, BA
Mrs Louise Rooney, Level 5 Dip Ed, MBACP (*Wellbeing & Personal Development, Anti-discrimination Lead*)
Mrs Abigail Rudge, BA (*Dance*)
Miss Laura Rutherford, MA Cantab, MEd (*Religious Studies*)
Dr Fran Ryland, BSc, MPhil, PhD (*Combined Science*)
Mrs Elizabeth Shearing, BA, SENCo, APC, AMBDA (*Learning Support*)
Mrs Jane Sixsmith, MA & Honorary Doctorate
Mr Keith Slade, BMus, RNCM
Mrs Helen Smith, NVQ, QCF L3
Miss Rebecca Smith, BSc
Mrs Julie Spraggett, BMus
Mrs Laura Spratley, BA
Mrs Kirsteen Stafford, BA, MA (*Drama*)
Mrs Shirley Stout, BSc (*German*)
Mr Dan Super, BA (*Academic PE*)
Mrs Lucy Super, BA
Mr Leo Tat, MSc
Miss Amy Thacker, BA, MA
Mrs Sharron Thomas, BSc, Adv Dip SpLD
Mr Steve Thompson, BSc (*Sport*)
Mrs Raminder Trainor, BSc
Mrs Donna Trim, BA (*Art & Photography*)
Dr Jeremy Troth, PhD
Mrs Danielle Wana, BA (*Health & Fitness*)
Miss Steph Waldron, BSc
Mr Joseph Walker, BA
Mrs Sarah Watton, BA
Mrs Laura Webb, BA
Mrs Ruth Whaley, MA
Mr David Whiting, BSc
Miss Anna Wilkie, BSc (*Psychology*)
Miss Rebecca Windmill, MSci, MA (*Geography*)
Mrs Helen Winn, LLB
Ms Sarah Vaughan, BA, MEd
Miss Zhe Zhou, BSc, MSc

Human Resources Manager: Mrs Hayley Miles, MCIPD MA, BA
Assistant Human Resources Manager: Mrs Joanna Barrett, CIPD

Admissions Registrar: Mrs Nicolette Mullan
Admissions Officer: Mrs Allison Morris
Admissions Administrator: Mrs Linda Bevan

Assistant Bursar (Operations & Staff): Ms Julie Henrick, ILM
Assistant Bursar (Facilities, Compliance & Transport): Miss Gemma Deery, BSc, IOSH
Headmaster's PA: Mrs Lisa McGann
PA to the Bursar: Ms Suzanne Baldwin
PA to the Head of the Senior School: Mrs Tracey Duggan
PA to Head of the Preparatory School: Mrs Jessica Harris

Director of Post-School Pathways and Academic Guidance: Mrs Rhian Chillcott, MA

Alumni Events & Communications Manager: Mrs Lynn Moseley

Head of Technical Support: Mr Martin Moseley

Head of Marketing: Mrs Lucie Ray-Barrett

SSI & DofE Manager: Mr Philip Dean, MBE

Medical Officer: Dr Sunil Kotecha, MBChB, FRCGP, MSc
School Nurse Team Leader: Mrs Helen King, RGN
School Nurse: Mrs Liz Munro, BSc, RGN, DN, QN
School Nurse: Mrs Claire Evans, RGN

Librarian: Mrs Alison Vaughan, BA

Stamford School

Southfields House, St Paul's Street, Stamford, Lincolnshire PE9 2BQ

Tel: 01780 750300
email: headss@ses.lincs.sch.uk
website: www.stamfordschools.org.uk
Twitter: @SpedeNews
Facebook: @stamfordendowedschools
Instagram: @StamfordSchools

Motto: *Christ me spede*

Founded by William Radcliffe, of Stamford, 1532.

Introduction. Stamford School is one of three schools within the overall Stamford Endowed Schools Educational Charity, along with Stamford High School (girls) and Stamford Junior School, the co-educational junior school.

Buildings and Grounds. Stamford School dates its foundation to 1532. The grounds include the site of the Hall occupied by secessionists from Brasenose Hall, Oxford, in the early 14th century. The oldest surviving building is the School Chapel, which was formerly part of St Paul's Church, but which from 1548 until restoration in 1929 was used as a schoolroom. Extensive additions to the School continued to be made throughout the nineteenth and twentieth centuries. In 1956 the Old Stamfordians gave the School a swimming pool as a war memorial. The science school was built in 1957 and extended in 1973 when a new dining hall and kitchens also came into use. These were subsequently completely redesigned and upgraded in 2003. A music school was built in 1977 and extended in 1984. A further extensive development programme was begun in 1980 and included the building of one new senior boarding house (Browne), opened in 1981, and extensive and comparable provision in the other (Byard). Development works in 2009 saw the creation of a new Research and Learning Centre in the School House building, providing a library, study space and additional IT facilities. The Sixth Form Common Room is now located in a newly-renovated section of Brazenose House, containing quiet study areas, recreation and IT facilities. A glass atrium linking School House and the Hall has been erected, providing a new focal point for the School in a unique architectural style. The Science rooms were also upgraded. A new Sports Centre, which includes a fitness suite, gymnasium and 25m swimming pool, has been completed and forms a central part of the curricular and extracurricular sports provision.

The old gymnasium was subsequently renovated to become a state-of-the-art Performing Arts Centre.

School Structure and Curriculum. The school consists of around 680 boys divided into Lower School (11–14), Middle School (14–16) and Sixth Form. The Heads of each section, with their assistants and Form Tutors monitor the academic progress of each boy and manage the pastoral arrangements.

The National Curriculum is broadly followed but much more is added to the curriculum to make it stimulating and rewarding. Information Technology, Art & Design and Design Technology form an integral part of the curriculum and from Year 8 boys may begin German, Spanish or Russian. All boys are prepared for a complete range of GCSE examinations; the great majority of them continue into the Sixth Form and then on to higher education.

In the co-educational Sixth Form, of approximately 380 students, the timetable is arranged so that a wide range of combinations of subjects is possible. In partnership with Stamford High School all Sixth Form students can choose from the full range of 27 subjects and two BTECs available across the two schools.

Activities. Art, Music, Drama, Games and Physical Education form part of the normal curriculum. There is a choral society, an orchestra, a band and a jazz band, and a chapel choir. The musical activities of the school are combined with those of the High School under the overall responsibility of the Director of Music for the Endowed Schools. The school maintains RN, Army and RAF sections of the CCF and there is a rifle club. A large number of boys are engaged at all levels of The Duke of Edinburgh's Award scheme.

The school plays rugby, football, hockey, cricket, tennis, golf. The athletics and swimming sports and matches are held in the summer term. In winter there is also badminton, cross-country running and basketball. There are squash courts and a full-sized, floodlit AstroTurf hockey pitch.

There are many school clubs and societies and a thriving weekend activity programme.

Close links are maintained with the local community. The school welcomes performances in the hall by the music societies of the town and uses the excellent local theatre in Stamford Arts Centre for some of its plays.

Careers. The school is a member of Inspiring Futures and has a team of careers staff. There is an extensive new careers library, computer room and interview rooms.

House Structure. Boarding: Byard House; St Paul's; Browne House.

Weekly and three-night boarding are available, as well as full boarding.

Competition in games, music and other activities are organised within a house system. Housemasters with their assistants monitor boys' commitments to the wider curriculum and act as counsellors when boys need to turn to someone outside the formal pastoral and disciplinary system.

Admission. The main point of entry is at age 11, but boys are considered at any age. A number join at age 13 or directly into the sixth form. Application forms for admission may be obtained from the school office. The school's entrance examinations take place in late January, but arrangements may be made to test applicants at other times. Entry into the sixth form is considered at any time. Boys who enter through the Stamford Junior School progress automatically on to Stamford School at age 11 without having to take further entrance tests.

Fees per annum (2021–2022). Day £17,460; Boarding: 7 Day £31,300, 5 Day £27,170, 3 Day £23,605.

These fees include all stationery, textbooks and games. School lunches for day boys are at additional charge.

Application Fee £100. Acceptance Fee £500; overseas students pay an additional deposit.

Scholarships and Bursaries. The Schools offer a range of scholarships for pupils entering into years 7, 9 and 12 (Sixth Form). Scholarships are less common for pupils entering into other years but may at times be available. There are scholarships for Academic, Music, Art, Sports and All-Rounder performance. Means-tested bursaries can be applied for by families of pupils who would otherwise not be able to benefit from a Stamford education. Please see our website for full details.

Charitable status. As part of the Stamford Endowed Schools, Stamford School is a Registered Charity, number 527618.

Chair of the Governing Body: Nicholas Rudd-Jones

Bursar and Clerk to the Governing Body: Dean White

Principal: **William Phelan**, MBA

Headmaster: **Nicholas Gallop**

Deputy Head: Nicholas Davies

The Stephen Perse Foundation

Union Road, Cambridge, Cambridgeshire CB2 1HF

Tel:	01223 454762
email:	admissions@stephenperse.com
website:	www.stephenperse.com
Twitter:	@SPFSchools
Facebook:	@stephenpersefoundation
Instagram:	@stephenpersefoundation
LinkedIn:	/stephen-perse-foundation

We are a family of schools in Cambridge, Madingley and Saffron Walden educating boys and girls aged 1 to 18.

By recognising our pupils as individuals – with unique hopes, talents and ambitions – we unlock their true potential.

We enjoy learning for its own sake. Our teachers ignite curiosity, encourage critical thinking and creativity. By learning to think for themselves our pupils go on to achieve exceptional results. But for us, education is not just about grades. It is about strength of character, a sense of social responsibility, learning to innovate, communicate and collaborate.

Education needs to prepare youngsters for life beyond tests, exams and certificates. Our pupils gain an exceptional skill set, one that prepares them for life in tomorrow's world. They leave us ready to make their mark and achieve their dreams.

Our history. Founded in 1881 as the Perse School for Girls, our history is part of Cambridge's rich academic past. Since evolving into the Stephen Perse Foundation in 2001, we have grown significantly, opening our doors to boys as well as girls and providing a complete educational pathway to inspire and guide young learners from the age of 1 to 18.

In 2008, we successfully set up a co-educational Sixth Form; in 2010 we acquired our Madingley site; in 2013 we merged with Dame Bradbury's School in Saffron Walden; and in 2014 we introduced the diamond model co-educational community into Rosedale House, followed by our Senior School in 2017.

Our outstanding leadership and strategic vision has been acknowledged through awards and accolades including, in 2014, being named both Independent School of the Year at the TES Independent School Awards and taking home an award for Outstanding Strategic Initiative.

Their future. Today's young learners will go on to shape tomorrow's world. We believe that is our responsibility as teachers and parents to equip them with the tools they need to make their mark, whatever future they choose.

Through our forward-thinking vision for education and our creative curriculum, we foster a global outlook, digital citizenship, individuality and independent thought – empowering our pupils to succeed in tomorrow's world and the workplace of the future.

As well as being committed to academic excellence, we understand the importance of an education which values the immeasurable as well as the measurable. Our distinctive Learning Wheel illustrates our forward-thinking approach to education, putting our learners at its core.

As you may expect, we offer great facilities and one-to-one attention from brilliant teachers. What makes us different is the way we encourage young people to think: independently, analytically, logically, creatively and imaginatively – in an unusually friendly, relaxed atmosphere.

As an Apple Distinguished School, we are now leading the digital learning revolution, with our pupils using iPads as virtual satchels and unlocking new ways to learn and collaborate.

Dynamic and inspiring learning spaces are an important piece of our toolkit. We make use of Cambridge as our campus and enjoy first class facilities within our schools. We have most recently completed a transformational building project on our Senior School site in the heart of Cambridge, enjoyed by students across all our schools: a five-storey building with a rooftop sports pitch (the first of its kind in Cambridge), a Sport England standard four-court sports hall, activity space with viewing area, ten classrooms and an additional learning hub.

Admissions. Our pupils and students are as mixed as any group of young people – but they all have bright, enquiring minds, whether they're artistic or academic, sporty or in need of educational support.

There are many entry points across our schools, ranging from 1 to 18. Please see our website for details, dates and FAQs. We hold our own entrance tests and interviews, held annually, usually in January for a September start. Entry is available outside of these testing dates if places allow; please contact the Admissions office if you would like more information.

Boarding is available for our Sixth Form students.

Scholarships, Exhibitions and Bursaries. Academic Scholarships and Music awards are available in the Senior School. Sixth Form Scholarships are awarded on academic merit based on written papers and interviews. Sixth Form Music and Art Scholarships are also offered. Bursaries are available for pupils throughout the Foundation. Information about these may be obtained from the Bursary.

Pastoral Care. We place a great emphasis on pastoral care and the well-being of all our students. Established pastoral structures support the students and foster personal development, responsibility and informed choices. Subject teachers and year staff care for the academic progress and individual welfare of each student.

All schools tell you they're wonderful but the only way to know if they're right for you is to see for yourself. At the Stephen Perse Foundation you'll find pupils and students who bubble with enthusiasm, teachers who love what they do and a place where young people blossom and have amazingly good fun. They'll be delighted to show you what being here is really like.

Results. Our students achieve top results and go on to study at world-leading universities. Just as importantly, they are encouraged to pursue their dreams and follow the path that's right for them. Last academic year's results were outstanding with 72% of GCSE entries graded at 8 to 9; 81% of all A Levels graded at A* or A and 89% of all IB grades awarded at level 6 or 7.

Our leaver destinations represent the best, most exciting opportunities the world has to offer. In 2021, this included Classics at Cambridge, Economics at the University of Warwick and Engineering at the University of Edinburgh.

Fees per term (2021–2022). Nurseries £67 per full day (Ages 1–2) and £65 per full day (Ages 2–3); Stephen Perse Junior School Rosedale House £4,240–£5,360; Stephen Perse Junior School Dame Bradbury's £4,240–£4,950; Stephen Perse Senior School £6,200 and Stephen Perse Sixth Form £5,950.

Please see our website for our Sixth Form boarding fees.

Charitable status. The Stephen Perse Foundation is a Registered Charity, number 1120608, and a Company Limited by Guarantee, number 6113565.

Governors:
Mr J Dix (*Chairman*)
Dr V Christou
Dr M Ellefson
Prof R Foale
Mr D Gill
Dr D Needham
Mrs K Ollerenshaw
Dr H Shercliff
Dr J Tasioulas
Mr S Töpel
Mrs S Oliver
Dr Vicky Mills
Mr Munish Datta
Prof. Jason Robinson
Dr Claus Bendtsen
Mr Ray Anderson

Principal: **Mr R Girvan**

Bursar: Ms H Richardson

Vice Principal: Mrs T Handford

Head of Early Years: Mrs S Holyoake

Head of Dame Bradbury's: Mrs L Graham

Head of Rosedale House: Mr D Hewlett

Head of Senior School: Mr R Girvan

Head of Sixth Form: Mrs J Paris

Stockport Grammar School

Buxton Road, Stockport, Cheshire SK2 7AF

Tel: 0161 456 9000 Senior School
          0161 419 2405 Junior School
email: sgs@stockportgrammar.co.uk
website: www.stockportgrammar.co.uk
Twitter: @stockportgs
Facebook: @stockportgrammar
LinkedIn: /Stockport-Grammar-School-Alumni

Motto: *Vincit qui patitur*

Founded in 1487, Stockport Grammar School is one of England's oldest schools. The founder, Sir Edmond Shaa, was a goldsmith, 200th Lord Mayor of London and Court Jeweller to three Kings of England. The School's rich history and traditions are celebrated in the annual Founder's Day Service in Stockport.

A co-educational day school, Stockport Grammar School is non-denominational and welcomes pupils from all faiths and cultures. Almost all leavers go on into Higher Education, including many to Oxbridge. Although academic performance is formidable, it is not the be-all and end-all of life at Stockport Grammar School.

Stockport Grammar School aims to provide the best all round education to enable pupils to fulfil their potential in a friendly and supportive atmosphere. The backbone of the school is academic excellence, with a clear framework of discipline within which every activity is pursued to the highest level. Entry is at 3, 4, 7, 11 and 16, but vacancies may occur at other stages. There are over 1,400 pupils aged 3–18 years, with 350+ in the Junior School and over 250 in the Sixth Form.

The Senior School. Admission at age 11 is by competitive entrance examination. This is held in January, for admission in the following September. There are several open events: see website for details. Occasional vacancies are considered on an individual basis and a few places are available in the Sixth Form each year. Visitors are always welcome to make an appointment to see the school.

Curriculum. The emphasis is on how to learn effectively and these philosophies are introduced in the first three years as part of a broad general education. The sciences are taught as separate subjects and all pupils study Latin, French and German. On entering the fourth year, at the age of 14, pupils retain a core of subjects but also make choices, so that individual aptitudes can be fully developed. GCSE examinations are taken in the fifth year. In 2021, 76% of entries were graded 7 or higher and 27% at grade 9. On entering the Sixth Form, pupils begin with four subjects. The pass rate at A Level was 100% in 2021, with 86% of all entries gaining A* to B and 59% of entries at A* or A.

Art. A high standard is set and achieved. There are facilities for all aspects of two-dimensional work and textiles, plus a fully equipped ceramics area and a sculpture court. There are regular exhibitions in School and pupils' work is displayed annually at The Lowry.

Music. The curriculum provides a well-structured musical education for all pupils for the first three years. GCSE and Advanced Level are offered for those who aspire to a musical career as well as for proficient amateurs. Three main areas of musical ensemble – choirs, orchestras and wind bands – are at the centre of activities with opportunities open from First Year to Sixth Form. Emphasis is on determination, commitment and a sense of team work. All ensembles are encouraged to reach the highest standards.

Drama. A particularly strong tradition has been fostered over many years and regular productions involve all year groups. There are drama clubs, trips to local theatre groups and workshops in school. Drama is a GCSE subject option.

Physical Education. The Physical Education curriculum is diverse, with activities including aerobics, ball skills, badminton, basketball, dance, gymnastics, health-related fitness, squash, swimming and volleyball. The main winter games for boys are rugby and football, and for the girls hockey and netball. In the summer, boys concentrate on cricket and athletics, whilst the girls focus their attention on tennis, athletics and rounders. Extracurricular clubs provide further sporting opportunities including archery, climbing and fencing. Up to 400 pupils represent the school at Saturday fixtures and the teams have an excellent reputation, gaining success in regional and national competitions. Almost fifty pupils have represented their country, region or county in the last year.

Houses. Every pupil is a member of one of the four Houses, each led by two Heads of House staff assisted by a team of senior pupils. The Houses organise and compete in a wide range of sporting and non-sporting activities.

Clubs and Societies. The School has many active clubs and societies covering a wide variety of extracurricular interests, for example, debating, where Fifth and Sixth Formers have the opportunity to participate in up to four Model United Nations Assemblies around the world each year.

Development. In the summer of 2020 the School completed a major redevelopment of the Sixth Form facilities as well as providing a new purpose-built nursery.

Visits. Well-established language exchange visits are made every year to France, Germany and Spain in addition to hillwalking, camping, mountaineering, skiing, sailing and cultural trips.

Assembly. Formal morning assemblies are held for all pupils; there are separate Jewish, Hindu and Muslim assemblies. House assemblies, which sometimes include Junior School pupils, are on Wednesdays; the Sixth Form have an additional weekly assembly.

Pastoral Care. Form Tutors get to know each pupil in the form individually, and are supported by Year Heads, by the Head of Lower School (years 1 to 3), the Head of Middle School (years 4 and 5), the Head of Sixth Form and the Deputy Head (Pastoral).

Discipline. This is positive and enabling. Much importance is attached to appearance and to uniform, which is worn throughout the school.

Fees per term (2021–2022). Senior School £4,041 plus lunch fee of £234 per term; Junior School £3,120 plus lunch fee of £201 per term.

Bursary Scheme. The School's own Bursary Scheme aims to provide financial assistance on a means-tested basis to families who have chosen a Stockport Grammar School education for their children. Details available from the Bursar.

Stockport Grammar Junior School. (*See also entry in IAPS section.*) With its own Headmaster and Staff it has separate buildings and a playing field on the same site. The Junior School has boys and girls between the ages of 3 and 11 years.

Boys and girls join the Nursery when they are three. In its own building and with a designated play area, the Nursery is very well resourced. The children are looked after by qualified and experienced staff.

Entrance is by observed play at the age of 4 years into two Reception forms, and by assessment in February for an additional form at the age of 7. All pupils are prepared for the Entrance Examination to the Senior School at the age of 11.

The Junior School buildings provide special facilities for Art, Technology, Music and Computing. The winter games are soccer, rugby, hockey and netball, with cricket and rounders in the summer. There are swimming lessons every week; other activities include the gym club, life saving, athletics and chess. There are clubs running each lunchtime and after school for both infants and juniors. Matches are played every Saturday against other schools in the major sports. Many pupils have instrumental music lessons and there is an orchestra, band, recorder group and a choir. The musical, held in May each year, is a very popular event in which all pupils participate. Visits are made annually to the Lake District in May. Short annual residential visits are introduced from age 7.

Charitable status. Stockport Grammar School is a Registered Charity, number 1120199. It exists to advance education by the provision and conduct, in or near Stockport, of a school for boys and girls.

Patron: The Prime Warden of the Worshipful Company of Goldsmiths

Governing Body:
Professor A J C Bloor, MA, MB, BChir, PhD, FRCP, FRCPath
N Booth, LLB
A P Carr, MA (*Vice Chairman*)
Miss S E Carroll, BA
C Dunn, MA (*Chairman*)
A Gardiner, BSc
Dr L Gholkar
Mrs S Lansbury, LLB
J M R Lee, BA, MBA, DipM, MSt
J Mason, LLB, PGDip
Mrs C S Muscutt, BA
J A Shackleton, MA
A C Simpson, BSc, ACA

Clerk to the Governors and Bursar: Ms J Clague, FCA, CTA

Headmaster: **P M Owen**, MA, PhD Cantab

Deputy Headmaster – Academic: Mr I W Kendrick, BA, MA
Deputy Headmistress – Pastoral: Mrs J White, BA
Deputy Headmaster – Staffing & Co-Curricular: Mrs J L Smith, BA
Head of Lower School: Mrs H R Lawson, MA
Head of Middle School: Mrs J Fitzgerald, BSc
Head of Sixth Form: D J Stone, BA, MEd

Assistant Masters and Mistresses:
* Head of Department

Art:
*R A Davies, BA, MA
Mrs T Kampelmann, MA, PhD
Miss R J Upton, BA

Biology:
P K Allen, BSc
Miss K L Chandler, BSc
*P J Grant, BSc
Mrs E V Niven, BSc
Mrs A R Reid, BSc
Mrs J White, BA
Mrs M Whitton, BSc
Mrs L J Withers, BA

Chemistry:
Miss J J Berry, BSc
Mrs K L Britton, BSc
P Clear, MChem, MSc
E Eeckelaers, BSc, MA
*Mrs A L Glarvey, MChem, PhD
Mrs R F Grey, MChem
R D Heyes, BSc
Mr I McGeough, BSc

Classics:
Miss L E McAllister, BA
Ms R L Jones, BA
*A C Thorley, BA
Mrs E Zanda, BA, PhD

Drama:
*M J King-Sayce, BA, MSc
Mrs A K Moffatt, BA

Business & Economics:
*Miss L Curl, BA, MA
A J Phillips, BA
Mrs A M C Thomson, BA
Mr T Quinn, BA

English:
Mrs R V Cross, BA
*Mrs G A Cope, BA
A J O Johnson, BA
Mrs H R Lawson, MA
Miss E MacDonald, BA, MA
Mrs S L Moore, BA
Mrs A Mullholland, BA
Miss S Nichols, BA
Ms H E Roberts, BA
Ms R Walsh, BA, ME

French:
Mrs S L Belshaw, BA
*Miss S M Gibson, BA, MA
D Lorentz, BA, MA, DEA
Miss C L Stevenson, BA
J D Wilson, BA

Geography:
*A Cooke, BSc
Mrs H J Crowley, BSc

Mrs J Fitzgerald, BSc
Mrs G N Miles, BA
Miss K E Owen, BSc, MA, PhD
Mrs J Pass, BSc
Mrs J L Smith, BA

German:
Mrs S A Boardman, BA
Mrs K Christmann, MA

History:
Mrs H R Ashton, BA
Mrs K J Chesterton, BA, MA
*T Leng, BA
S A Moore, BA
D J Stone, BA

Computer Science:
N S Clarke, BA
*M J Flaherty, BSc

Life Studies:
*A G Ehegartner, BA
Miss H M Morgan, BA

Mathematics:
*G D Frankland, BSc
M Hamilton, MSc, PhD
Miss M E Higgins, BSc
Mrs L Lammas, BA
Mrs A S Larkin, BSc
Mrs A L Marsden, BSc
Mrs C L Marshall, BSc, MSc
Miss C A Mills, BSc
S. Olsson, BSc, MSc
K F J Prudham, BSc
Mrs R Reevell, BSc, MA
Mrs R C Taylor, BSc

Music:
*M G Dow, MA, ALCM
S Newlove, BA, MMus
Mrs J Matthews, BA

Religion, Philosophy & Ethics:
Revd L E Leaver, MA, BTh
Mrs A C Neale, BA
*J Swann, BA, MA

Physics:
Mrs R H Beare, MSc
Miss A Curtis, MEng
Mrs Z Dawson, MSc
*Mrs H M Fenton, BSc
Mrs C M Hird, BSc
I H Killey, BSc, BEng
P M Owen, MA, PhD
C M Shaw, BSc

Physical Education:
R Bowden, BA
E H Corbett, BA
Mrs L E Goddard, BSc
A S Hanson, BEd
Mrs J Maskery, BEd

*D A Thomson, BA
Mrs K Wilkinson, BA
Miss S Withington, BEd
C J Wright, BA

Psychology:
Mrs H K Larkin, BSc
*T J Buxton-Cope, BSc
N Serifin, BSc

Spanish:
I W Kendrick, BA, MA
Miss K A M Psaila, BA
Mrs A V Cole, MA

Food & Nutrition:
Miss S Hodkinson, BSc
Mrs H Oddy, BA

Design & Technology:
Mrs K Gate, BA
Mrs H Tadman, BEng
G M Whitby, BSc
*N Young, BA, MA

Learning Support:
Mrs S Boardman, BA
Mrs D H Meers, BA, MEd, AMBDA

School Chaplain: Revd L E Leaver, MA, BTh
Director of Music: M G Dow, BA, MA
Director of External Relations: Mrs R M Horsford, BA
Headmaster's Secretary: Mrs J E Baker
Admissions Officer: Mrs M Connor
Librarian: Ms J Pazos Galindo, BA, MA
School Nurse: Mrs P Ward, RGN, DipHE

Junior School

Headmaster: Mr M J R Copping, BEd, NPQH, FRSA, NPQEL
Deputy Head: S Milnes, B
Assistant Head (Curriculum): Mrs C Nichols, BEd
Assistant Head (Infants): Mrs C Bailey, BA

Teaching Staff:
Miss H Baker, BEd
Mrs S Barrowman, BA, MSc
J Bowden, BA
M Burns, LLB
Mrs H Carroll, BEd
Mrs L Carr, BA
M Cooke, BA
Miss B Corr, BA
Mrs K Ehegartner, BSc
Mrs C Hampson, BA (*DSL*)
Mrs L Hudson, BA
Mrs N Hurst, BEd
Mrs V Hutchinson, BA, MA

D Jones, ASA
Miss S Knowles, BSc
Miss A Micklethwaite, MA
Mrs J Noble, BA
Miss J Pepper, BA, ASA
Mrs K Roberts, BEd, MA
Mrs C Smith, BA
Mrs A Sullivan, BEd
A Taylor, BSc
Mrs L Turner, BEd
Mr M Vernon, BA
Mrs K Wells, BA
Mrs C Woodrow, BA

Headmaster's Secretary: Mrs B Cheyne

Stowe School

Stowe, Buckingham, Bucks MK18 5EH

Tel: 01280 818000
email: enquiries@stowe.co.uk
website: www.stowe.co.uk
Facebook: @stoweschool
Instagram: @stoweschool

Motto: '*Persto et Praesto*'

Our purpose is to create a community of Change Makers ready to transform the world.

We are opportunity-led and believe that schools must equip pupils to thrive in a fast-moving, ever changing world. We prepare Change Makers for jobs that don't yet exist, using technology which hasn't yet been invented, to solve problems which we haven't yet thought about. We can't compete on labour costs or raw materials, but we can set the pace in intellectual capital, creativity and entrepreneurial flair. Yes, we teach pupils numeracy and literacy and how to excel in exams, but we also teach them how to collaborate, to solve problems, to think critically and to reflect. We equip them with the skills, resilience and ideas they need to adapt and flourish.

It is what pupils do with the knowledge they acquire which will turn them into Change Makers. Emotional intelligence, team work and thought-leadership enable pupils to take advantage of new technologies, limitless access to information and advances in engineering, robotics and artificial intelligence. With empathy, versatility, originality and creativity, Stowe's inclusive community is transforming how young people are prepared to enter the world beyond the school gates. We have created a fully integrated programme of interventions: putting Change Makers at the centre of everything we do and providing transformational opportunities in and outside the classroom.

We offer co-curricular breadth and depth with a sports programme which encourages full participation while developing the talents of our elite athletes (which include Olympic medallists such as James Rudkin for rowing and Marilyn Okoro for track and field). Music, art, drama and creative writing encourage Change Makers to express themselves in diverse ways, transcending political, social and cultural boundaries while bringing a greater understanding of human experience.

We catalyse change by providing generous Change 100 bursaries, inspirational teaching and coaching, infrastructural investment, treating our work force as valued colleagues and prioritising social and environmental impact. By promoting equality and inclusion we move forward to realise our dream, every pupil at Stowe should go into the world to make positive change, create new opportunities and build a better future for all.

Stowe is a boarding and day school with boys and girls from 13 to 18. The School roll is 888, comprising 654 boarders and 234 day pupils. Pupils are also accepted each year for 2-year A Level courses.

Houses. There are nine boys' and six girls' Houses.

The Curriculum. The academic experience at Stowe is designed to encourage intellectual curiosity, a thirst for knowledge and understanding and independence of thought and expression. Stoics are asked to be committed and enthusiastic learners, to embrace challenge and to see failure as a necessary step in achieving progress. They are urged to be ambitious, make the most of their academic opportunities and to continually strive to improve their skills.

Art, Design and Information Technology. All pupils are introduced to these subjects in their first year at Stowe. Art and Design are popular both for those pursuing hobbies and for those studying for formal examinations. Traditional skills are covered alongside more modern techniques such as computer-aided design and desktop publishing.

Music and Drama flourish as important and integral parts of the School's activities both within and outside the formal curriculum. There is plenty of scope to get involved in the School Orchestras, Jazz Band, Clarinet Quartet, Choirs, School plays, House plays and House entertainments. The timetable is sufficiently flexible to allow special arrangements to be made for outstanding musicians to study outside school. Drama Clubs and Theatre Studies groups have a fully-equipped theatre at their disposal. The refurbishment of the Theatre and classrooms, alongside a new Music School, allows these creative arts to flourish.

Careers Guidance. Careers education forms a continuous thread throughout a Stoic's time at Stowe. It aims to provide a framework within which each can develop the self-awareness and experience necessary to make balanced decisions at each stage during their time at the school and, hopefully, after they leave. Stowe's Careers Education & Guidance Programme begins when pupils join the Third Form at 13. It aims to provide increasing contact with the world outside, throughout a Stoic's time at school and to help reach those decisions which affect their future in as well-informed and balanced a way as possible. Every encouragement is given to discuss the various options with Houseparent, Tutor and Careers Staff.

Religion. The School's foundation is to provide education in accordance with the principles of the Church of England and this is reflected in its chapel services on Sundays. Pupils of other faiths and other Christian Churches are welcomed and, in some cases, separate arrangements are made for them on Sundays. Every pupil attends the chapel services on weekdays.

Games. The main sports for boys are rugby, hockey and cricket; for girls, hockey, netball, lacrosse and tennis. Stowe also offers an exceptionally wide range of other sports, giving everybody the opportunity to take part in an activity they enjoy.

Significant investment has been made in our sports facilities in recent years and Stowe has some wonderful facilities which include:

- 8 Rugby Pitches
- 7 Cricket Squares
- Double floodlit AstroTurf
- 4 Football Pitches
- Eight-lane Athletics Track with comprehensive field event facilities
- Four-court Badminton Sports Hall
- BHS highly commended Equestrian Centre, including a cross country course and a floodlit show jumping arena
- 3 Lacrosse Pitches
- 11 lanes of turf cricket nets & 10 lanes of AstroTurf nets
- 3 Squash Courts
- State-of-the-art Gym
- 3 Fives Courts
- 25m six-lane Competition Pool
- Clay Pigeon Shooting Range
- 4 Netball Courts
- 27 Tennis Courts
- 12 Spinning Bikes
- 9 Hole Golf course and Teaching Studio

Other Activities. Pupils complement their games programme with a broad variety of extra-curricular activities, including clubs and societies.

On Mondays a special activities programme is based on Service at Stowe and at the heart of this is the Combined Cadet Force with all three service arms, the Duke of Edinburgh's Award scheme, Community Service (in the neighbourhood) and Leadership skills.

The Award at Stowe is designed to encourage Stoics to see the benefits of engaging fully in all areas of school life and to ensure that Stoics finish their time at Stowe with valuable experience and qualifications which will help them stand out in a fast-changing world, whilst also offering the opportunity to learn through positive experience. Stoics engage with The Award at three different levels during their time at Stowe. At all levels they will be expected to engage in eight key areas of school life; Academic Achievement, Achieving, Beyond Term-Time and Citizenship, Sport and Physical Activity, The Arts, In the Community and Thinking Differently.

Fees per term (2021–2022). Boarders £12,951, Day in Boarding pupils £9,311, Day House pupils £7,301 payable before the commencement of the School term to which they relate. A deposit is payable when Parents accept the offer of a place. This deposit is repaid by means of a credit to the final payment of fees or other sums due to the school on leaving.

Scholarships and Bursaries. A range of Scholarships and Exhibitions, up to the value of 25% of the School fees, is awarded annually. Scholarships may be supplemented by means-tested bursaries, with a limited number of fully-funded places, where there is proven financial need.

Academic Scholarships up to the value of 25% of the School fees are available for pupils at age 13+ entering Stowe's Third Form, and are awarded to gifted children already following the ISEB Common Academic Scholarship syllabus at their Preparatory School.

Stephan Scholarships are awarded to academically bright pupils from independent or state schools which do not follow the ISEB Common Academic Scholarship syllabus.

Academic Scholarships are also available to pupils wishing to join the School in the Lower Sixth Form after GCSE at 16+. Competitive Entry Examinations are held in the November of the candidate's GCSE year consisting of a Verbal Reasoning paper, two subject papers related to their AS Level choices, and an interview. Successful Scholarship candidates would normally be expected to gain A* and A grades in all their subjects at GCSE.

Music Scholarships: Candidates at age 13 should be at least Grade Five standard on at least one instrument and preferably nearer Grade Six. An Exhibitioner may be around Grade Four standard. Candidates at age 16 should be the equivalent standard of Grade Six or above on one instrument and be of a good standard on a second instrument or voice. A candidate gaining a Minor Scholarship of up to 10% or an Exhibition may be around Grade Five standard.

Drama Scholarships: Drama Scholars play a vital role at Stowe, contributing positively to the community through the Arts. Drama Scholars are expected to take the subject at GCSE and at A Level and to audition for all co-curricular school productions including Congreve and Junior Congreve. Scholars can expect an excellent education within the field of Drama, which becomes more personalised as pupils move through the School.

Design Scholarships: Not only will our Design Scholars develop their appreciation of design, but they will also consolidate it with the beautiful environment Stowe provides. Our Scholars will develop an appreciation of various architectural styles, an understanding of the Golden Ratio and they will learn about the precision involved in world-class engineering. The School has strong links with industry and a partnership with Silverstone UTC, which means that our Design Scholars can gain real-life experience and will learn beyond the examined syllabus. Our Design Scholars showcase their work each year at a major

exhibition on Speech Day. The School will also help Scholars to enter external competitions and scholarship programmes (for example, The Arkwright Scholarship programme). Design Scholars are expected to study GCSE Design in the Lower School and then A Level Product Design in the Sixth Form.

The Sixth Form Berry Scholarship for Original Thinking reflects the importance of original and creative thinking, not just in itself but, crucially, to the future needs of business and wider society. Macro-level changes to the world's economic make-up, coupled with technological advancement, changing workforce demographics, global integration and increased competition have meant that approaches and attitudes towards work have transformed – indeed, the world of work is almost unrecognisable compared with that of just a few years ago. We want pupils to leave Stowe, not only with an ability to adapt and thrive in that volatile world, but with the confidence to make positive change. Their ability to use the skills of original thinking will be key to that – and so we seek candidates who will be 'constructive non-conformists' within our community, and set an example for others to follow.

Sports Scholarships and Exhibitions may be awarded to exceptional candidates at 13+ and 16+ showing outstanding potential in at least one of Stowe's key sports: boys: rugby, hockey and cricket; girls: hockey, netball, lacrosse and tennis.

Roxburgh (All-Rounder) Scholarships at 13+ and 16+ are intended to enable any boy or girl of outstanding all-round ability and leadership potential to benefit from Stowe's unrivalled environment to develop fully his or her talents. In addition to strong academic potential, which will be demonstrated in Stowe's Entry Examinations, candidates would be expected to demonstrate a high level of ability in at least one of the following: sport, music, art and drama.

Change 100 Our ambition and mission is to raise an endowment fund of £100 million over the next ten years. This will transform our long-term ability to provide the life-changing chance of a Stowe education to talented and deserving children from socially diverse and financially disadvantaged backgrounds. This endowment will provide 100 free places in the School at all times, and forever, enabling 20 children in each year group to attend the School on a fully-funded place. To ensure that Change 100 has an immediate impact, we have also pledged to spend the first £1 million raised each year on places the following September. We are delighted that in September 2021, the first ten children joined us on our Change 100 programme and look forward to growing that number significantly in the years to come.

Full details may be obtained from The Registrar.

Admissions. Boys and girls can be registered at any age. Full details can be obtained from the Admissions Department (admissions@stowe.co.uk), who will supply registration forms. The School is always prepared to consider applications from pupils to enter the School at 14 if places are available. The date of birth should be stated and it should be noted that boys and girls are normally admitted between their 13th and 14th birthdays.

The Old Stoic Society. Director: Anna Semler. Old Stoic Society Office: Tel 01280 818252, email oldstoic@stowe.co.uk.

Charitable status. Stowe School Limited is a Registered Charity, number 310639. The primary objects of the charity, as set out in its Memorandum and Articles of Association, are to acquire Stowe House, which was achieved in 1923, and to provide education in accordance with the principles of the Church of England.

Governing Body:
Mr Simon C Creedy Smith, BA, FCA (*Chairman*) [OS]
Mr Christopher J Tate, BA, MIMC (*Vice Chair*) [OS]
The Rev Canon Peter Ackroyd MA, MBA, PhD
Mr Jonathan M A Bewes, BA, FCA [OS]
Mr Patrick Bradshaw, BA
Ms Rebecca Brown, BA
Ms Julie C Brunskill, BSc, MRICS
Ms Elizabeth J de Burgh Sidley, BA, FRICS
Mr Rupert Fordham, BA Cantab
Mr John Frost, BSc, MRICS, MNAEA, MARLA [OS]
Professor Guy Goodwin, BA, DPhil, FMedSci, FRCPsych
Mr Richard Greaves, BA
Mrs Joanne Hastie-Smith
Mr Sunjeewa Jayawardena, BSc, MBA
Mrs Andrea Johnson, BSc, PGCE
Mrs Catriona Lloyd, MA Cantab
Mr Doug Muirhead
Mr Andrew E Reekes, MA, MRes
Mrs Vanessa Stanley, BEng, MEd, AdvCertEdMgmt, NPQH
Lady Stringer, BSc, MB, BS, LRCP, MRCS
Miss Hannah Durden, MA Cantab, MRICS (*Chair of Old Stoic Society*) [OS]
Mr Michael B M Porter, BA, MSc (*Secretary to the Governors*)

[OS] *Old Stoic*

School Administrator: Annabel Lovelock

Head: A K Wallersteiner, MA, PhD

Senior Deputy Head: M D G Wellington
Deputy Head (Academic): Dr J A Potter
Deputy Head (Pastoral): L Copley
Assistant Deputy Head (Pastoral) & Designated Safeguarding Lead: M P Rickner
Director of Sport: C Sutton
Co-curricular Coordinator: G D Jones

* *Head of Department*

Art:
*Scott, Daniel
Brown, Peter
Greenwood, Melanie
Grimble, Chris J
Syrett, Cheryl J
Trelawny-Vernon, Elizabeth

Biology:
*Carter, Louise
Allen, Alison
Black, Georgina
Blake, Natasha
Crawford, Sarah
Gausden, Harriet
Lyons, Dr Sinéad
Newlin, Elspeth
Reinhold, Jessica H
Righton, Michael A

Business Studies & Economics:
*West, Dr Gordon D J

Ashfield, Anthony
Austen, Mark E L
Bristow, Angela
Corthine, Richard B
Freeman, William
John, Panos

Chemistry:
*Waine, Dr Alexandra
Broomhall, Mark
Gracie, Judie
Johnson, Roland G
Purves, Sally
Radley, Luke A
Ramshaw, Gemma
Rawlins, Sheilagh
Tearle, James
Teasdale, Matthew
Wakeford, Dr Joanna L

Classics:
*Murnane, Jonathan M
Blenkinsop, James

Computing:
*Gupta, Aditya
Martin, Glen
Mellor, Nick
Ramnarain, Prakaash
Sivalingham, Paulraj

Design & Technology:
*Quinn, Martin K
Peratopoullos, Costas
Treen, Victoria
Webster, Thomas
Wellington, Mark
Whitby, Stephen J
Williams, Samuel E

Drama & Theatre Studies:
*Clark, Rebecca E
Ackroyd, Emma
Baker, Keith

Games:
Director of Sport: Craig Sutton
Deputy Director of Sport & Head of Cricket: James A Knott
*Austen, Mark (*Cross Country*)
Blackmore-Beales, Dominic (*Hockey*)
Coote, George D (*Athletic Development, Sports Performance Programme*)
Compton, Simeone (*Netball*)
Corthine, Fiona E G (*Polo*)
Cuddy, Giles T A (*Lacrosse*)
*Davis, Cheryl S (*Swimming & Water Polo*)
Dias, Victoria L (*Head of Netball*)
Duckett, Jayne M (*Lacrosse*)
Dunkley, Sarah (*Netball*)
Gaunt, Harry (*Strength & Conditioning/Gym*)
George, Ben G (*Rugby*)
*Grimble, Chris (*Cycling*)
*Hancox, Andrew J (*Golf*)
Ingham Clark, Robert M (*Lacrosse*)
Jackson, Ella C R (*Hockey*)
Lewis-Williams, Megan (*Hockey*)
*Michael, Isaac (*Badminton & Basketball*)
Pynegar, Andrew (*Lifeguard*)
*Righton, Michael A (*Rowing*)
Rudkin, Andrew C (*Rowing*)
*Scott, Ben M O (*Hockey*)
*Seely, Grant L (*Rugby*)
Shepherd, Peter P (*Lacrosse*)
*Skinner, John (*Tennis & Fives*)
*Smith, Fitz (*Clay-Pigeon Shooting*)
*Syme, Duncan J (*Sailing*)

Geography:
*Murnane, Sarah A
Burch, Matthew
Campbell, Lorraine C
Copley, Liam
Elwell, Thomas
Rowley, Shelley

History:
*Griffin, Paul J
Cuddy, Giles T A
Green, Dominic J M
McNeill, Owain
Potter, Julie
Shah, Francesca L

Kenny, Alice R
Miller, Lucy I
Parker, Rob

EAL:
Johnson, Julie Y

English:
*Borman, Nicola
Ackroyd, Emma J
Cook, Jonathan M
Eisenhut, Heather J
McNeill, Owain
Pearson, Georgina
Peppiatt, James W H
Pickering Polláková, Vlasta
Rickner, Sophie C
Smith, Dr Fitzpatrick
Webber, Dr Andrew C

Stafford-Smith, Rhea

History of Art:
Atkinson-Wood, Meredith

Library:
Mrs L Foden
Miss L Stockley

Mathematics:
*Møller, Mikkel B
Adkins, Charles
Arnold, Andrew
Brown, Rebecca
Burton, Michael H F
Chitre, Smit

Handley, Lucia R A
Heaven, Leonie
Lee-Stevens, Victoria
Matthews, Michelle
Nichols, Jessica R
Paxton, Richard J
Penrhyn-Lowe, Sophie L
Stanworth, Alec M

Modern Languages:
*Tearle, Alice R G
Bernal-Guerrero, Andrea
Bolton, Elena
Danis, Emilie E N
Dobson, Simon G
Ferrero, Dr M Isabel
Fuentes Olea, Luis
Herrbach, Mathilde
Hutchin, Brigitte
Jones, Tracy L
Lamrabat Benkacem-Ziani,
   Nou
Moffat, Gavin R
Morales-Shearer, Julio
Pena, Liliana
Podesta, Desirée
Savage, Andrea
Stringer, Rowena
Thevenet, Pauline
Wheeler, Sandra
Windett, Emma

Music:
*Greene, Craig M T
Andrew, Ben
Bryden, Emma
Kingston, Jonathan
Nottage, Miles R H
Potts, Katie
Weston, Ben J

Houses and Houseparents:
Boys' Houses:
Bruce: P Arnold
Temple: B J Hart
Grenville: S Dobson
Chandos: A Ashfield
Cobham: R Corthine
Chatham: L Copley
Grafton: G R Moffat
Walpole: G D Jones
Girls' Houses:
Nugent: Mrs T Jones & Z Jones
Lyttelton: Dr S Lyons, Ross Deyzel
Queen's: Mrs S Rickner & M P Rickner
Stanhope: Mrs L M Carter
Sixth Form House:
West: Mr R Johnson & Mrs J Johnson
Day Houses:
Cheshire: Mrs S Sutton
Winton: J Peppiatt

Medical Officer: Dr Victoria Morrell, MA DFSRH,
   MRCGP
Director of Development: C Dudgeon
Group Director of Marketing and Admissions: T Roddy
Group Director of Finance: M Greaves
Group Director of Operations: M Kerrigan

Philosophy and Religion:
*Bray, Colin S
Adkins, Dr Imogen H
Holloway, Francesca L
Rickner, Michael P

Physics:
*Thompson, Paul A
Davis, Jonathan B
Fathulla, Kamaran
Gardner, Dean
Hart, Brian J
Matthews, Steven
Ramsay, Alison
Rose, Simon W

PSHE:
E Huxley-Capurro

Politics:
*Cole, Simon R
Floyd, J Paul
Shah, Francesca L

Skills Development:
*Carter, Sharon
Guntner-Jones, Luciane
Ivory, Rhian
Tait, Deborah
Walsh, Amy
Xiong, Jing

Sports Science:
*Dias, Victoria L
Arnold, Philip R
Compton, Simeone
Dias, Patrick J
Shepherd, Peter
Sutton, Sarah E
Taylor, Ruth

Strathallan School

Forgandenny, Perth, Perthshire PH2 9EG

Tel:	01738 812546
email:	admissions@strathallan.co.uk
website:	www.strathallan.co.uk
Twitter:	@StrathallanSchl
Facebook:	@strathallanschool
LinkedIn:	/company/strathallanschool

Motto: Labor Omnia Vincit

Strathallan School is an independent boarding and day school whose mission to provide an outstanding education for all stands true to its original foundation over 100 years ago. Harry Riley founded Strathallan in 1913 with the ambition to create a school where there would be opportunities for every pupil to excel, and the vision is one held true today.

The School is fully co-educational and numbers 553 pupils, of whom 248 are day pupils and 305 are boarders.

Situation. Strathallan School is located 6 miles south of Perth in the village of Forgandenny. It occupies an idyllic rural location, situated in 150 acres of richly wooded estate on the northern slopes of the Ochils and overlooking the Earn valley. At the same time, Strathallan is within easy reach of the international airports – Edinburgh (35 minutes) and Glasgow (1 hour).

At the centre of the School is the main building which dates from the 18th century and was formerly a country house and home of the Ruthven family. The School continues to invest in outstanding facilities, which have seen a £23m investment since 2005. These include modern laboratories, a Theatre, Computer Centre, Library, Design Technology Centre, Sports Hall, Fitness and Weight Training Room, 2 Floodlit Synthetic Hockey Pitches, Indoor Multi-Sports Facility, Dance and Drama Studio, Medical Centre, Art School and newly refurbished Boarding Houses. All boarding houses have been built within the last thirty years with modern facilities and a single study-bedroom for every boarder in their last four years.

Aims. The school's mission is to provide an outstanding education that gives opportunities for all pupils to perform to the very best of their abilities. Each individual, no matter their passion or interest, is supported and inspired to shine during their time at school. Our aim is to send pupils out into the world with close friends and the ability to make new ones, and with the knowledge and skills to succeed at university and beyond.

Organisation. The School is primarily a boarding school yet also takes day pupils who are integrated into the boarding houses. There are four Senior boys' houses (Ruthven, Nicol, Freeland and Simpson). There are three girls' houses (Woodlands, Thornbank and Glenbrae). All boarding houses have their own resident Housemaster or Housemistress, assisted by House Tutors and a Matron. Boys have single study-bedrooms from the Fourth Form and girls have single study-bedrooms from the Third Form.

Strathallan Prep School, launched in September 2020, has its own Head Teacher and has Riley as its boarding house. It is designed to cater for boys and girls wishing to enter the School at age eight. Riley is run by a resident Housemaster, assisted by House Tutors and two Matrons.

After Riley, pupils move directly to one of the Senior houses. Strathallan Prep School is the perfect balance of small classes with big resources. Its pupils enjoy the expertise of dedicated primary school teachers and the specialist input of subject teachers from the senior school. Strathallan Prep School and Riley House are situated within their own area of the campus, yet also enjoy the facilities of the main School.

The whole School dines centrally and there is a wide choice of hot and cold meals as well as vegetarian and vegan options. All boarding houses have small kitchens for the preparation of light snacks.

Religion. Strathallan has a Chapel and a resident Chaplain who is responsible for religious studies throughout the School.

Curriculum. Two of the keys to academic success are an ethos of continuous improvement and support from high quality, passionate teachers, and we pride ourselves on providing just such a learning environment. In addition, all pupils receive support from a tutor linked to their house and there is a full-time Careers Advisor to help with opportunities available beyond school. In 2020, the School became the first in Scotland to offer a triple pathway, including A Levels, one- and two year Highers, and Advanced Highers, providing choice and flexibility in the face of a diverse range of tertiary education and employment options after school. In 2021, 84% of A Levels awarded were A*–B grade, 83% A to B Higher and 74% 6–9 GCSE.

Junior. Boys and girls entering Strathallan Prep School follow a course designed for the transition between their previous school and joining the senior part of Strathallan School at the age of 13. The following wide range of subjects is taught: Art, Computing, Design Technology, Drama, English, French, Geography, History, Latin, Maths, Music, PE, Personal and Social Development, Religious Education and Science. Courses are generally based on English Key Stages Two and Three.

The aim is to ensure pupils have an appropriate basis in the core subjects to move on to further study whilst also providing experience in specialist areas taught by subject experts. Teachers are careful to take account of ability and previous learning, guaranteeing each pupil works at an appropriate level for them and progresses at the right pace.

Third Form. Pupils in the Third Form participate in the following wide range of subjects: Art, Biology, Chemistry, Computing, Design & Technology, Drama, English, French, Geography, German and Spanish, History, Latin, Mathematics, PE, Physics and Religious Education. They are given a grounding in the skills necessary to pursue the subjects in the future should they wish, and an experience which is worthwhile in itself. All subjects are taught by specialists.

Fourth Form and the start of GCSE study. The two year GCSE course begins in the Fourth Form. All pupils study English, Mathematics, at least one Modern Language and two of the three Sciences. In addition, each pupil studies History or Geography (and can study both), plus two other subjects from an extensive choice. The aim is to ensure that pupils keep their options open, pursue a well-rounded curriculum, and establish a good basis for Sixth Form study.

Pupils are supported in their study not only by the individual teachers and the Heads of Department but also by a tutor who is linked to their house. A system of Merits and Distinctions rewards both individual pieces of outstanding work and continuous hard work and achievement. It is a central aim of the academic programme that pupils' efforts and achievements are recognised.

Sixth Form. Nearly all pupils stay on into the Sixth Form where the normal entry requirement is five passes at grade C or above at GCSE level. It is a special feature of Strathallan's Sixth Form that there is the flexibility to choose either A Levels or Scottish Highers. The choice is determined by the needs of the individual pupil. There is a wide range of subjects (currently the widest curriculum in Scotland), including: Art & Design, Biology/Human Biology, Business Management/Business Studies, Chemistry, Classical Civilisation/Classical Studies, Computing Science, Design & Technology/Design & Manufacture, Drama, Economics, English, French, Geography, German, Graphic Communications, History, Latin, Mathematics, Modern Studies, Music, Music Technology, Physical Education, Physics, Psychology, Religious Studies/RMPS, Spanish and Theatre Studies, with the option to include an EPQ.

The formal academic curriculum is supplemented by an extension programme of talks, visits and exchanges. We have well-established links with continental schools, and visits to theatres, galleries, courses and conferences in the UK and abroad often take place. Extracurricular activities and societies complement academic study and enhance pupils' interest in learning and discussion through activity beyond the classroom.

Each pupil is allocated a tutor who is a member of the academic staff and one of the duty staff of the boarding house. The tutor monitors pupils' academic and social progress and is responsible for discussing their regular reports with them.

Games. The main School games are rugby, cricket, hockey, netball, athletics and tennis, and standards are high. Other sports include skiing, squash, rounders, football, fencing, judo, badminton, table tennis, basketball, swimming, golf, horse riding and cross-country running in all of which national and regional success have been achieved in recent years.

Strathallan has two squash courts, 15 hard tennis courts, three netball courts, two floodlit synthetic pitches, a heated indoor swimming pool, two sports halls, gymnasium, a fitness and weight training room and a dance and drama studio. One sports hall comprises a basketball court, three badminton courts, a rock-climbing wall as well as facilities for six-a-side hockey and indoor cricket coaching, while the other has three full-size indoor tennis courts, with a multi-play surface, allowing a multitude of sports to be accommodated. Sailing, canoeing and skiing are recognised pastimes, and pupils participate in School ski days in the Spring term. Strathallan also has its own nine-hole golf course as well as Tennis and Shooting Academies.

Activities. All pupils are encouraged to take part in a range of activities for which time is set aside each day. There are over 50 weekly activities to choose from including dance, drama, pottery, chess, photography, first aid, lifeguarding, judo, horse riding, shooting (both clay pigeon and small bore) and fishing. There are also many societies and a programme of external speakers who visit the School. Pupils can also work towards awards under The Duke of Edinburgh's Award and John Muir Award schemes and are encouraged to take part in community service.

Music. The Music department has its own concert room, editing suite, keyboard room and classrooms, together with a number of individual practice rooms. Music may be taken at GCSE, Higher and AS/A2 Level. Over 40 different ensembles rehearse every week, including choirs, traditional music ensembles, jazz band, wind band, an orchestra, folk bands and rock bands. A house music competition takes place annually and there are regular concerts throughout the term. Individual tuition is available for virtually all instruments.

Piping. The Piping and Drumming Department have two full-time piping instructors and a full-time drumming instructor, as well as visiting staff. Individual lessons take place in our designated department and are available throughout the year. Pupils can work towards SQA qualifications in Piping and Pipe Band Drumming. We have three prize winning Pipe Bands which take part in events across the world including the Barbados Celtic Festival and the New York Tartan Day Parade as well as appearances at Hampden Park and Murrayfield Stadium.

Art. Art is recognised as an important part of the School's activities and there are opportunities to study the subject at GCSE and AS/A2 Level. Pupils benefit from regular art trips abroad and have the opportunity to exhibit their work both locally and further afield. A purpose-built Art School features facilities for ceramics, sculpture and print-making. National awards reflect pupils' achievements in this area.

Drama. Drama thrives throughout the School and the department makes full use of the Theatre as well as the purpose-built Dance and Drama Studio. There are junior and senior performances each year and pupils are encouraged to become involved in all aspects of production. The School also provides tuition in public and verse speaking and pupils regularly win trophies at the local festivals. There is also an annual Musical and pupils enter musical theatre exams.

Combined Cadet Force. There is a large voluntary contingent of the Combined Cadet Force with Navy, Army and Marines Sections.

Careers. Careers guidance begins in the Third Form. The Careers Adviser maintains close links with universities and colleges and regularly visits industrial firms. We have exchange programmes with schools in Australia, New Zealand and South Africa. There is a dedicated Careers Library, well-stocked with prospectuses, reference books and in-house magazines. Strathallan is a member of the Independent Schools Careers Organisation, a representative of which visits regularly and of the Scottish Council for Development and Industry.

All pupils have the opportunity to gain work experience in the Fifth Form, after their GCSEs. There is also a GAP year programme which provides placements for pupils to work overseas prior to going to university. Strathallan has particularly strong links with charities in Kenya.

Pastoral Care. At Strathallan, there is a strong emphasis on pastoral care. The School has drawn up its own welfare guidelines in consultation with parents, governors and Perth and Kinross Social Work Department, and was rated 'Excellent' by the Care Inspectorate in 2019.

Health Centre. Strathallan has its own purpose-built Health Centre with consulting and treatment rooms. There are nursing staff at the Centre and the School's Medical Officers visit four times a week. Physiotherapy, chiropody, and relaxation also take place in the Centre during term time.

Entrance. Strathallan Prep School Entrance – Boys and girls are admitted to Strathallan Prep School at either age 7, 8, 9, 10, 11 or 12. An Entrance Day is held in early Spring each year for those who are available. Entry is based on a satisfactory school report and assessments in Maths and English.

Entry to the Senior School – Candidates for entry into the Senior School at age 13 may enter via the Open Scholarship examination in February, Common Entrance or a satisfactory school report.

Sixth Form – Boys and girls may also enter at Sixth Form level, either via the Sixth Form scholarship examination in November or on the basis of a satisfactory school report and GCSE/Standard Grade results.

Scholarships. Awards are made on the basis of competitive examination/assessment. Bursary help is available to supplement awards for outstanding candidates on a financial need basis.

Awards are available in the following categories to candidates entering the school at three levels:

Junior School: Academic, Music and Sport. Candidates should be under 13 years old on 1 September in the year of entry. Scholarship Examination: January.

Third Form: Academic, Music/Piping, Art, Performing Arts, Drama, All Rounder and Sports. Candidates should be under 14 years old on 1 September in the year of entry. Scholarship Examination: February.

Sixth Form: Academic, Music/Piping, Art, Performing Arts, Drama and Sports. Candidates should be under 17 years old on 1 September in the year of entry. Scholarship Examination: November.

Further information is available on the School's website, www.strathallan.co.uk, or from The Admissions Office, Tel: 01738 815091, email: admissions@strathallan.co.uk.

Bursaries. Bursaries are awarded dependent on financial circumstances and are available to pupils who have qualified for entry through assessment, scholarship or school report or a combination. It is not necessary for successful candidates for bursaries to have achieved scholarship standard but it may be possible to add a bursary award to a scholarship to enable a pupil to come to Strathallan.

Fees per term (2021–2022) Strathallan Prep School (Riley House): £8,573 (boarding), £5,351 (day), P3 & P4: £8,380 (boarding), £5,158 (day). Senior School: £12,012 (boarding), £8,158 (day).

Prospectus. Up-to-date information is included in the prospectus which can be obtained by contacting the Admissions Office or via the School's website.

Charitable status. Strathallan School is a Registered Charity, number SC008903, dedicated to Education.

Board of Governors:

Chairman: Mr M Griffiths, LLB Hons, CA
Mr N M Campbell, CA
Ms Alison Clark, BA Hons, MSc.
Professor J Crang, BA, PGCE, PhD, FRHist, FRSA
Mr K C Dinsmore, BA, LLB, Dip LP
Mr S Fairbairn, MA, LLB, Dip LP NP
Mr D Gillanders
Mr S J Hay, BA, MBA, MSc
Mr P Johnston, ACCA
Mrs E Lister, BSc, DipEd
Mrs P A Milne, BA, MBA, FCIPD
Professor G Paton, BSc, PhD

Mr A Sinclair, BSc
Mrs G M Wilson, MA Fine Art, PGCE
Mr A Wood, MRAC, FRICS

Headmaster: **Mr M Lauder**, MA

Assistant Staff:
Mrs T Ailinger, Staatsexamen, Cert TESOL
Mrs C Angus, MA, PGCE Primary
Mrs F Barker, MA, BD, MTh
Mr D J Barnes, BSc, PGCE, PGCG, FRGS (*Deputy Head Pastoral*)
Mr I Barrett, BA Hons, PGCE
Mr G J Batterham, BSc, PGCE (*Simpson Housemaster*)
Mr P Beeson, BA Hons
Mrs K Bergin, BEd Hons
Mr M Bergin, BSc, PGCE (*Nicol Housemaster*)
Ms S Birrell, BA Hons
Dr K E M Blackie, PhD, PGDE, BSc
Miss E de Celis Lucas, BA, CAP
Dr B Cooper, BSc, PhD, PGCE
Mrs M-L Crane, BA, PGCE
Mr S Dick, BEd (*Riley Housemaster*)
Mr A L M Dunn, MA, PGCE
Mrs Z Ettle, LLM, PGCE, PGDip (*Woodlands Housemistress*)
Mr D Foster, BA Hons, PGDE
Mr J Fraser, BMus
Mr N P Gallier, MBE, MA, MSc, PGCE
Mr G N Gardiner, BSc, PGCE
Mr D R Giles, BA QTS, Cert PP
Mr F Glancy, BA Hons, PGDE
Ms K Haddick, MA Hons, PGDE
Mrs S E Halley, BSc, PGDE
Mr R Halkett, BA, TEFLc
Mr S Hamill, BA (*Deputy Head Academic*)
Mr N A Hamilton, BMus
Mr B A Heaney, BSc, Dip Ed (*Freeland Housemaster*)
Mr A D Henderson, UKCC
Mr D M Higginbottom, MA, PGCE
Mrs J Higginbottom, MA, PGCE
Mrs R Hodson, MA, PGCE, MSc
Mrs C G Howett, BA, Dip Ed
Mr E Kalman, BSc, MPhil
Mr P J S Keir, BEd, Cert SpLD
Ms J Keller-MacBain, BA
Mr L Kent, BSc, PGCE (*Thornbank Housemaster*)
Mrs C Laird-Portch, BA Hons, PGCE
Mrs E C Lalani, BEd, Dip Man (*Head of Strathallan Prep School*)
Mr E Lee, MA, PGCE
Miss R Leese, BSc Hons, PGCE
Ms J Ling, BTech Ed Hons
Mrs C Marjoribanks. BSc Hons, PGCE
Mrs F MacBain, MA (*Assistant Head, Sixth Form*)
Mr R Macleod, BSc Hons, PGDE
Mr J McAuley, BA Hons, PGCE
Mr I McGowan, BCom Dip Teaching (*Ruthven Housemaster*)
Mr S McGuigan, BA Hons, PGDE
Ms S Mackay, BA, MSc, PGCE
Mr K McKinney, BSc, BEd
Mr B Miles, BA Hons
Ms G Miles, MSc PGCE
Dr I Mitchell, BSc, PhD
Mr S Mitchell, BSc, PGCE
Mr C Muirhead, BA

Mr T Ogilvie, LTA CC
Ms A Pfupajena, BSc Hons, PGDE
Mrs T Rankin, BSc Hons
Mr D Richardon, BA
Mr G S R Robertson, BA, DMS
Dr J D Salisbury, MA, PhD, PGCE
Mrs L Salisbury, BA, Dip Ed, PGCE, ALCM
Mr G Samson, BSc Hons, PGCE
Dr F Sapsford, MA Hons, MPhil Cantab
Dr T Sharples, MChem Hons, DPhil, PGDE
Miss A Sime, BEd (*Assistant Head, Co-curricular*)
Mrs S Simon, BMus Hons, PGCE
Mr C Swaile, MA Hons, PGDE
Mr J Thompson, BSc
Mrs A J Tod, MA, PGCE
Mr M R A J B Tod, BSc, PGDip
Mrs K Troup, BS, MA, PgCert
Mr P M Vallot, BSc
Ms A Wardlaw, BSc
Mr A Watt, BComm, HDE (*Assistant Head Organisation, Director of Studies*)
Mrs L Waugh, BA, PGDE
Ms K Wilson, BSc, PGCE (*Glenbrae Housemistress*)
Dr I Woodman, MA, MLitt, PhD, PGCE
Revd J Wylie, BSc, BD, MTh
Dr T Zhou, MSc, PhD

Bursar and Clerk to the Governors: Mr A C Glasgow, MBE, BEng, MSc, CEng

Director of External Relations: Mrs C Bath, BA Hons
Admissions Manager: Mrs A Johnstone, BA Hons
Alumni & External Relations Manager: Mrs A Wilson , BA Hons, MBA
Digital Media Manager: Mr D Glasgow, MA Hons
Marketing Manager: Mrs H Lewis-McPhee, MA Hons, MLitt

Medical Officers:
Dr L D Burnett, MBChB, BSc, DRCOG, MRCGP
Dr A M Lewis, MBChB, MRCGP

Streatham & Clapham High School GDST

42 Abbotswood Road, London SW16 1AW

Tel: 020 8677 8400 (Senior School)
020 8674 6912 (Prep School & Nursery)
email: senior@schs.gdst.net
prep@schs.gdst.net
website: www.schs.gdst.net
Twitter: @SCHSgdst
Facebook: @SCHSgdst

Motto: *ad sapientiam sine metu*

Streatham & Clapham High School is a distinguished historical foundation. It was founded as Brixton High School in 1887 by the Girls' Public Day School Trust as one of its earliest member schools. In 1895, HRH Princess Louise, Duchess of Argyll, opened its buildings in Wavertree Road, London SW2, now the site of the Prep School. In 1994 the Senior School moved to Abbotswood

Road, London SW16, into the imposing buildings of the former Battersea Grammar School.

The School offers an inspiring, enlightened and intellectually challenging education for its pupils in a lively, vibrant and warmly supportive environment. The family ethos of Streatham & Clapham High School enables its masters and mistresses to know, value and nurture each pupil as an individual. The School celebrates diversity and draws strength from its rich social and cultural mix.

The School's core belief is that all members of its community should be inspired to outperform expectations on a daily basis. The pursuit of excellence is thus the School's defining feature. It nurtures pupils to attain success across the widest spectrum of activity, extending far beyond the conventional 'academic' horizon. In so doing, they learn the beauty of reason, the allure of the aesthetic, and the vitality of the physical. The School's pupils thus learn to navigate the landscape of the human spirit and achieve beyond the realms of expectation.

The School's vision: to be unrivalled in empowering its young women to discover, nurture and project their unique identities and character.

The School's purpose: to enable every girl to achieve beyond the bound of expectation on a daily basis, across the spectrum of endeavour.

The School's salient and distinctive features:

- It nurtures, not coerces, excellence
- It is a family, not a factory, school
- It celebrates difference through its buzzy, diverse community, drawing strength from all that is great about London
- It has an unstinting commitment to innovation; the School does not stand still but is a trailblazer
- It draws strength from being part of the GDST family of schools, being pioneers in, and the shapers of, girls' education.

General Information. Streatham & Clapham High School is an independent, academically selective school for girls aged 3–18, with just under 900 pupils on the roll. Girls aged 3–11 attend the Nursery and Prep School, located in spacious buildings with outstanding facilities on Wavertree Road in Streatham Hill. The Senior School inhabits a four-acre site focused on a symmetrical 1930s building designed by J E K Harrison, FRIBA, in a delightfully tranquil and leafy oasis of south London, next to Tooting Bec Common, where the soundscape is dominated by birdsong. Many girls live locally and an increasing number walk or cycle to School, encouraged by the School's commitment to sustainable travel. The Senior School is ten minutes' walk from Streatham Hill National Rail station and seventeen minutes from Balham National Rail and Underground. Other pupils come from further afield, including Battersea, Clapham, Wandsworth, Dulwich, Tooting and Brixton. The School is also within easy reach of the theatres, museums and galleries of central London.

Facilities. The School has first-class facilities for learning, providing an environment that enables girls to develop their interests and strengths both inside and outside the classroom. The School keeps up-to-date with new teaching methods and innovative techniques, such as interactive online learning, and uses them to engage and extend its pupils. Its facilities include two ICT suites, a music suite including a dedicated music technology suite, a Recital Hall, two design & technology workshops, a full-size indoor Sports Hall, Dance and Art studios, and sports pitches and tennis courts. In 2017, the school occupied a stunning state-of-the-art sixth form centre on a new floor of the main building (which constituted the first phase of the £13 million building project), and the final phase of the building work, an architecturally innovative and spacious new dining hall and a striking new reception at the front of the school, together with a fountain atrium, was completed in March 2018. The new facilities have won a number of architecture awards, including the Building Design Awards, a RIBA Award, and the Architects' Journal Retrofit Awards (School Project of the Year)

Academic Matters. The ability profile of the school is significantly above the national average, with a proportion of pupils being far above the national average. The school is in the top tier of independent schools in terms of its public examination results. Pupils do well: in 2019 at GCSE, over 23% of results were Grade 9 and 72% of Grades 9 to 7; and in 2020 at GCSE, over 28% of results were Grade 9 and 78% were Grade 9 to 7; in 2021, over 38% were Grade 8, and over 86% Grade 9 to 7. At A Level, the percentage of grades at A*–B over the past five years has averaged around 79% and was 83% in 2020, 95% in 2021. Over 95% of SCHS pupils secured a place at their first choice of university in 2021.

The 2019 ISI Educational Quality inspection awarded the school the highest grade in both categories inspected; 'Excellent' for the quality of pupils' academic and other achievements and for the quality of their personal development.

Curriculum. The School offers a wide range of subjects. Pupils in the Upper Third, Lower Fourth and Upper Fourth (Years 7 to 9) study the core disciplines of English, Mathematics, and Science. Other subjects offered include Art, Mandarin and Sinology, Computing, Design & Technology, Drama, French, Geography, History, Italian, Latin, Music, Philosophy, Religion and Ethics, Physical Education, and Spanish. All of these subjects, as well as Ancient Greek, are available at GCSE or IGCSE in the Fifth Form (Years 10 and 11). The School offers a range of subjects for study at A Level, including Art & Design, Biology, Chemistry, Classical Civilisation, Latin, Critical Thinking, Design & Technology, Drama & Theatre Studies, Economics, English Literature, Geography, Government & Politics, History, French, Italian, Spanish, Mathematics, Further Mathematics, Music, Physical Education, Physics, Psychology and Religious Studies. The majority of sixth-form students also pursue the Extended Project Qualification to extend their interests and knowledge. Virtually all sixth-form students proceed to the most competitive Russell Group universities (including Oxbridge).

Enrichment Programme ('Kinza'). Kinza, an Arabic term meaning 'hidden treasure', is the School's unique enrichment programme of which there are timetabled weekly sessions throughout the year. Every Kinza course is designed to encourage a love and respect for learning for its own sake, utilising the interests and expertise of staff. The activities cover an extremely broad range of activities. In recent years, these have included Anthropology, Art History, Engineering, Crime Fiction, Fashion, Film and Society, Islamic Art, Young Money and much more. Opportunities to deepen aspects of the broad knowledge acquired through Kinza are afforded through individual research and collaborative working processes. Each girl participates in several different activities during the course of the year. At the same time of the week, the sixth-form students engage in the School's community service programme, 'Lux'.

Activities. The School has a thriving co-curricular life, with over 100 societies and clubs, ranging from academic fields to more specialised activities such as CCF. There are a very large number of activities in the performing arts; pupils having the opportunity to perform in a number of dramatic productions during the school year or to belong to around 15 music ensembles, including choirs and orchestras, which annually lead the School's Carol Service at Southwark Cathedral. Pupils may belong to a legion of sporting clubs (including hockey, netball, gymnastics, rowing, cricket, football, badminton, athletics and many more), and have the opportunity to participate in a number of outdoor educational activities, such as the Duke of Edinburgh's Award. A busy programme of trips and expeditions is scheduled, for instance a cultural trip to China, a flagship sixth-form expedition to Cambodia, geography trips to Iceland, sports tours and language trips abroad. The School's proximity to central London makes possible many excursions to concerts, museums, art galleries and theatres.

Pastoral Care. The School does not view outstanding pastoral care as an 'add-on' to its academic programme. Neither does it believe that a 'hothouse' atmosphere is desirable or healthy. The School's core belief is that girls achieve best if they are happy and settled in their social relationships. Hence the 'family' ethos of the School, which holds that the way in which individuals are nurtured and valued is intrinsic to the pupils' progress and success. All pupils are under the care of one of five Heads of House, and all members of staff, up to the Head Master, are easily accessible to pupils. To ensure that the School's social and emotional care is comprehensive and alert, the School has a Deputy Head Mistress with oversight of pastoral matters. In conjunction with the work of the Heads of House and the sixth-form mentoring scheme, this enables the School to identify challenges or problems early and then work with pupils and where necessary their parents to overcome them. It also helps the School to encourage and celebrate real progress and achievement every day. The strong prefectorial system and school council under the leadership of the Head Girl ensure that the pupil voice has suitable influence in shaping the life and work of the School.

Admission. There are six principal admission stages: by assessment for the Nursery (3+ years), 4+ and 7+, and by competitive entrance examination at 11+ and 13+ and at Sixth Form level. Occasional places sometimes arise at any age; interested parents are advised to contact the Registrar. 11+ candidates will undertake an interview and creative writing session. Applicants for 13+ entry will have individual interviews after the 13+ entrance examination. Applicants for 11+ entry sit the ISEB Common Pre-Test, comprising English, Mathematics, verbal and non-verbal reasoning exercises. Applicants for 13+ entry sit papers in English, Mathematics and Science. The transfer of a pupil from the Prep to the Senior School is contingent on the School's assessment of the pupil's suitability for admission into the Upper Third Form (Year 7).

Fees per term (2021–2022). Senior School £6,260, Prep School £4,864, Nursery £3,831. The fees are inclusive of non-residential trips and extras, but exclude the cost of lunch.

Scholarships. A number of scholarships, worth up to a maximum of 25% of fees, are available for 11+ and 16+

entrance. They are not means-tested. Academic scholarships are awarded on the basis of individual candidates' performance in the entrance examination and interview. A number of sixth-form academic scholarships are also available, on the basis of a written assessment and interview. Specialist scholarships, in Art, Drama, Music and Sport, are also available for 11+ entrance.

Bursaries. A small number of means-tested bursaries are available at 11+ and at 16+ for students applying for the Sixth Form. All requests are considered in confidence and application forms are available from the Registrar.

The Board of Local Governors:
Mrs F Smith, BA Durham, PGCE (*Chair*)
Mrs R Bailey Packard, BA
Mr R Brent, BA
Miss S Campbell, BA, MA
Mrs R Chowdhury, BA, MSc, CMRS
Mrs K Eldred
Mrs E Gibson, BA, LLB

Head Master: **Dr Millan Sachania**, MA Cantab, MPhil, PhD, FRSA

Second Master: Mr R Hinton, BSc Durham, PGCE (*Mathematics*)

Deputy Head Mistress: Mrs G Cross, BA Birkbeck, MA, PGCE (*English*)

Assistant Head Master (Co-Curricular and Partnerships): Mr A Christie, MA Oxon, PGCE (*Classics*)

Assistant Head Mistress (Sixth Form): Ms S Potter, BA Durham, PGCE (*Classics*)

Academic Director: Mr M Weatherhead, BEng De Montfort, MA St Mary's, NPQH

Head of Prep School: Mr T Mylne, BA Brighton, PGCE

Director of Finance & Operations: Miss A Bullock

Director of Marketing & Communications: Ms M Beer, BA Columbia, USA

Assistant Masters and Mistresses (Senior School):
Ms Sharon Akintunde, BSc UCL, MSc, GTP (*Head of Chemistry*)
Mr Paul Baker, BA Colchester, PGCE (*English*)
Miss Rebecca Baker, BA Falmouth, PGCE (*Head of Art*)
Mrs Anusha Burton, BA Birmingham, PGCE (*Philosophy, Religion & Ethics*) [maternity leave]
Mme Catherine Casset, BA Paris, MA, PGCE (*French*)
Dr Sadaf Choudhry, MEng QMW, PhD, PGCE (*Chemistry, Physics*)
Mrs Laura Cooper, BA Nottingham, QTS (*Head of Careers*)
Mr Andrew Doddridge, BSc UCL, PGCE (*Head of Geography*)
Mrs Rachel Duke, BA King's College, London, PGCE (*Philosophy, Religion & Ethics*) [maternity leave]
Miss Mariarosa Durello, BA Padua, Italy, PGCE (*Italian*)
Ms Lauren Eells, BA Sussex, MA, PGCE (*Assistant Head of Sixth Form* [maternity cover]*, History*)
Mrs Drina Evans, BSc Edgehill, PGCE (*Computer Science*)
Mrs Mary Evans, BA Exeter, PGCE (*House Mistress, Drama*)
Mrs Ciara Eves, BA St Mary's London, QTS (*Director of Sport*)
Ms Danielle Feehan, BA Sussex, MA Birkbeck, PGCE (*Assistant Academic Director, Head of English*)

Mrs Katherine Ferguson-Burke, MA Glasgow, PGCE (*Head of Biology*)

Mrs Rachel Ferguson, BA Manchester, PGCE (*English*)

Miss Sarah Fitzgibbon, BSc Leeds, PGCE (*Head of Science/Head of Physics*)

Mrs Jane Flanagan, BA Nottingham, MSc, QTS (*House Mistress, Geography*) [maternity cover]

Mr Stephen Flanagan, BA Edinburgh, QTS (*Charities Co-ordinator, Music*)

Mr Paul Frost, BA Lancaster, ACMA, PGCE (*Head of Digital Learning and Computing*)

Miss Carmen Garcia-Gomez, BA Southampton, PGCE (*Spanish*)

Mrs Rachel Grant, BSc Loughborough, PGCE (*House Mistress, Head of Jīhuì, PE*)

Ms Rowena Gray, BA Manchester, PGCE (*Assistant Head of English*) [maternity cover]

Mrs Sarah Harmer, BA Cardiff, MA, PGCE, CCET (*House Mistress, Head of Learning Support*)

Mr Tom Heaton, BAEd London Goldsmith's, QTS (*Head of Design & Technology*)

Ms Fiona Helszajn, BA Edinburgh, PGCE (*Second in Modern Foreign Languages, Spanish*)

Dr Nazish Khan, BSc Manchester, MSc Coventry, PGCE (*Chemistry*)

Mrs Juliana Kirby, BA Leicester, PGCE (*Head of Mathematics*)

Miss Alice Kirrage, MA St Andrews, PGCE (*Assistant Head of Sixth Form, Head of Classics*) [maternity leave]

Miss Katie Latham, BA King's College, MA UCL (*Classics*) [maternity cover]

Mr David Lee, BA Manchester, PGCE (*Head of History and Politics*)

Mr Patrick Lynch, BA London Metropolitan, PGCE (*Design & Technology*)

Ms Polly May, BMus Edinburgh (*Director of Music*)

Ms Thu Ha Nguyen, BSc Queen Mary's, PGCE (*Mathematics, KS3 Mathematics Co-ordinator*)

Miss Oyinsola Oreyomi, MSc Edinburgh, PGCE (*Mathematics*)

Mrs Caroline Pearman-Gibbs, BA Oxford (*Head of Modern Foreign Languages*)

Mr Phillip Powell, MSc Bristol, PGCE (*Biology*)

Mr Thomas Punt, BA Lancaster, PGCE (*Head of Philosophy, Religion & Ethics*)

Mr Duncan Reader, BA Cantab, MA, MSc, PGCE (*Mathematics*)

Ms Rose Ren, BA Shanghai, PGCE (*Lead in Mandarin & Sinology*)

Ms Kate Renshaw, BSc Leeds, PGCE (*Head of Upper Third Transition, Head of House, Biology*) [maternity leave]

Mr Thaddeus Rivett, BSc Brunel, PGCE (*Assistant Director of Sport, Head of Hockey*)

Miss Laura Ruffman, BA Bath, PGCE (*Head of Upper Third Transition (maternity cover), Physical Education*)

Miss Kathryn Shaw, BA Leicester, MA, PGCE (*Assistant Head of English*) [maternity leave]

Mr Michael Spooner, BSc Bristol, MA, PGCE (*House Master, Physics*)

Miss Charis Stubbs, BA Leeds Beckett, MSc, PGCE (*Physical Education*)

Ms Violet Tabrizi, BA Vancouver, PGCE (*History*)

Mrs Carol Tempestilli-Sarti, BA Kingston, MA, PGCE (*Learning Support*)

Ms Penelope Thane-Woodhams, BA Loughborough, PGCE (*Director of Drama*)

Mrs Laura Tuggey, MA Edinburgh, QTS (*Geography and History*)

Mr Calum Unsworth, BA Birmingham (*Head of Economics*)

Dr Esther van Heerden, BA Stellenbosch, SA, BA, BEd, MSc, MSc, DPhil, PGCE (*Head of Psychology*)

Ms Lily Vigor, BA Central Saint Martins, PGCE (*Art*)

Miss Hayley Walker, BA King's College London, PGCE (*Head of Classics*) [maternity cover]

Mr Frederic Ward, BSc Leeds, PGCE (*Mathematics, Science*)

Miss Sophie Westerby-Jones, BA Exeter, PGCE (*KS4 Co-ordinator, Mathematics*)

Mrs Emma Wheeler, BSc Birmingham, PGCE (*Biology*)

Mr Jack Williams, MA Oxon, QTS (*English*)

Head Master's Executive Assistant: Ms Shirley Halm
Registrar: Mrs Janine Funsch, BA London South Bank

Sutton Valence School

Sutton Valence, Maidstone, Kent ME17 3HL

Tel: 01622 845200
email: enquiries@svs.org.uk
website: www.svs.org.uk
Facebook: @SuttonValenceSchoolNews

Motto: *Where each cares for all and individuality is cherished*

Founded in 1576 by William Lambe, Sutton Valence School has over 425 years of proud history. Today the School is co-educational and includes a preparatory school on a neighbouring site. Both schools are situated on the slopes of a high ridge with unequalled views over the Weald of Kent in the historic, beautiful and safe village of Sutton Valence.

Our greatest strength is our community. The relationships we enjoy between staff, pupils and parents allow us to craft an educational journey that is individually suited to every pupil. During a family's association with the School we hope they will feel involved, listened to and informed.

Through the high expectations and standards we set, all our young people are encouraged and helped to go further than they had thought possible in their academic, co-curricular, community and leadership journeys. We want them to become confident, civilised, tolerant and open-minded individuals who possess a love of learning and a strong sense of self-discipline along with a set of values reflecting our principles as a Christian Foundation.

Ethos. A community where each cares for all and individuality is cherished.

Results. Sutton Valence School has an inclusive intake, however, our academic strength lies in enabling our students to achieve beyond their benchmarked potential, whatever their ability. On average, our students will gain results at A Level that outperform their predicted grade on entry to the School by 0.5 of a grade per subject. As measured by Durham University's Centre for Evaluation and Monitoring, Sutton Valence School has an outstanding record for adding academic value.

Curriculum. The academic curriculum is innovative and aims to achieve a balance between the needs of the individual and demands of society, industry, universities and the professions. Classes are small and the graduate teaching staff to pupil ratio is 1:9.

Our First and Second Forms (Years 7 and 8) follow our innovative, challenging and stimulating Junior Curriculum, which has academic excellence at its heart and continues to promote our pupils' love of learning. We also ensure that the fundamental study skills required for success are mastered so that our pupils can move on fully prepared to excel at GCSE and beyond. These pupils also pursue our excellent Junior Leadership programme.

Many pupils join us in the Third Form from other schools. In this Form we concentrate on developing a high level of competence in the essential numeracy, literacy and ICT skills across all subjects, in targeted-ability groups, in preparation for GCSEs which are then studied in the Fourth and Fifth Forms.

In Fourth and Fifth Form (Years 10 and 11) pupils usually study nine or ten subjects at GCSE level. These are divided between the core subjects – English and English Literature, Mathematics, a Modern Language (French or Spanish), Science, Religious Studies, PSHE and ICT – along with option groups. Each group contains a number of subjects, offering a choice which allows every pupil to achieve a balanced education whilst, at the same time, providing the opportunity to concentrate on his or her strengths.

Sixth Form Pupils, either progressing from our Fifth Form or joining us from elsewhere, pursue an A Level course in three or four carefully-chosen subjects, along with an extended project qualification (EPQ). They receive individual support and expert, bespoke, advice on appropriate Higher Education applications, interview practice, CV writing and careers in general. Whilst the vast majority continue their academic journey at university level, employment-based training routes are becoming an increasingly popular option for some.

Potential Oxbridge candidates are identified in the Lower Sixth year and suitable tuition is arranged.

Setting, Promotion, Reporting. In First to Fifth Form Mathematics and French are setted. Academic progress is monitored by tutors and, at regular intervals throughout the term, every pupil is graded for achievement and effort in every subject for their classwork and effort in their prep.

Higher Education and Careers. Sutton Valence School has a modern and well-equipped Sixth Form Centre which incorporates a careers library and the latest technology to help in degree and career selection.

Music. Music plays a very important part in the life of the school, and we have a deservedly fine reputation for the quality and range of our music-making. Approximately 40% of the pupils learn a musical instrument or have singing lessons; there are four choirs, an orchestra, wind band, string group, jazz band, and a full programme of concerts. Music tours to Europe are arranged, and the Music Society organises a programme of distinguished visiting performers every year.

Drama. As with Music, Drama is central to the life of the School and the creative expression of our students. Every year there will be a number of productions, in addition to theatre workshops and reviews. Pupils may choose to receive one-to-one drama coaching lessons in preparation for LAMDA exams. The Baughan Theatre provides an adaptable venue, seating up to 250 for Drama, Music and lectures, along with rehearsal rooms, technical gantry and scene dock.

Sport and Physical Education. Sutton Valence School has a deserved reputation as a strong sporting School, competing in 17 sports. On average, 40 pupils will have representative honours at County, Regional and National levels in the main sports as well as in other disciplines. On a typical Saturday afternoon, half the school will be engaged in matches.

Our 100-acre site has one of the best Cricket squares in Kent, two floodlit Astroturf pitches for Hockey, a six-lane indoor swimming pool, Tennis, Netball and Squash courts, a sports hall encompassing a full-size indoor Hockey pitch, sprung-floor Cricket nets and fitness suite, six Golf practice holes and a floodlit all-weather running track. Additional sports, such as Football, Judo, Dance, Horse riding, Badminton, Basketball, Fives and Fencing are offered through our activities programme.

Pastoral System. The School is arranged vertically in houses, with the Juniors (Years 7 and 8) in a separate house. Each House has a Housemaster or Housemistress and is divided into Tutor Groups containing pupils from each year and from day and boarding.

The School is a Christian foundation, however, our values are very much based on openness, tolerance and inclusivity. As such, we welcome students from all faith backgrounds, as well as those families who have no faith commitment.

Community Service, CCF and Duke of Edinburgh's Award. The CCF provides an organisation within Sutton Valence School which enables boys and girls to develop self-discipline, responsibility, self-reliance, resourcefulness, endurance, perseverance, a sense of service to the community and leadership. It complements the academic and other co-curricular aims of the School in preparing our pupils for adult life. All three services are offered – Army, Navy and RAF. Pupils are encouraged to join the Duke of Edinburgh's Award scheme where there is the opportunity for planning and undertaking expeditions. On average, 15 Gold Awards are achieved each year.

Clubs and Activities. Time is specifically set aside each week for clubs and activities. Every pupil spends time pursuing his or her own special interests, and with up to 40 clubs or activities from which to choose, the range and scope is very wide. In addition, various school societies and some other activities take place out of school hours, for example, the Kingdon Society for Academic Scholars.

Scholarships and Bursaries. Academic, Art, Design Technology, Music, Sport and Drama Scholarships are awarded at 11+, 13+ and Sixth Form entry. Candidates may apply for a maximum of two non-academic scholarships.

The Westminster Scholarship supports well-motivated and able pupils who enter Sutton Valence School at Sixth Form level and who are expected to achieve at least six GCSE passes at Grade 8 or 9.

Bursaries are awarded according to financial need at the discretion of the Scholarship and Bursaries Committee, and are reviewed annually. Forces bursaries are available.

Further details may be obtained from the Admissions Officer.

Fees per term (2021–2022). Tuition £6,100 to £7,550. Senior Boarding (in addition to Tuition): £4,325 (Full),

£3,390 (five nights p/w), £2,680 (four nights p/w), £2,120 (three nights p/w).

Lunch for Day pupils and occasional boarders: £307.

Instrumental Music: £278 per term (ten lessons).

Charitable status. The United Westminster Grey Coat Foundation is a Registered Charity, number 1181012.

Governing Body:
Mrs G Swaine, BSc Hons, MEd (*Chair*)
J C Baxter
R W Blackwell, MA
Mrs J D Davies, BSc
Mrs A F Dawson
Dr M J Heber, MB, BS, FRCGP
A J Hutchinson, MA Cantab
S C James, BA
Ms J Palmer
P P Sherrington, LLB, LLM, FCI Arb
Mrs A J Storey-Mason, MA
The Reverend A S Zihni, MA

Headmaster: **J A Thomas**, MA Cantab, MA London, NPQH

Deputy Headmaster: J J Farrell, MA Cantab, MEd Buckingham (*History*)
Academic Deputy Head: Mrs R K Ball, BA Wales Lampeter (*English, Media Studies*)
Assistant Head: D R Sansom, BSc Wales Swansea (*Geography*)
Assistant Head: Mrs S Rose, BEd Bishop Otter College (*Designated Safeguarding Lead, English*)
Bursar: S R Fowle

Administrative and Teaching Support Staff:
Headmaster's PA: Mrs S Bishop
Director of Marketing: Miss P Goodridge
Director of External Relations: W Radford
Admissions Officer: Mrs K Webster
Admissions Assistant: Mrs D Child

Tonbridge School

Tonbridge, Kent TN9 1JP

Tel: 01732 365555
email: schooladmin@tonbridge-school.org
website: www.tonbridge-school.co.uk
Twitter: @TonbridgeUK
Facebook: @tonbridgeUK

Motto: '*Deus dat incrementum*'

Tonbridge has a distinctive mixture of boarders and day boys and enjoys superb indoor and outdoor facilities on a 150-acre site, which lies only 40 minutes by train from central London. It currently has just over 800 boys, who come from a variety of backgrounds.

The school is highly respected, both in the UK and internationally, for providing a world-class education. Boys are encouraged to be creative and intellectually curious; to approach new opportunities with confidence; and to learn to think for themselves and develop leadership skills, while being mindful of the needs and views of others. A Tonbridge education includes a vibrant programme of co-curricular breadth and depth.

The school is renowned for its high-quality, innovative teaching and learning, and for academic achievement. Exam results at GCSE and A Level are outstanding, and each year an impressive number of Upper Sixth leavers gain places at the UK's leading universities, including Oxford, Cambridge and Russell Group institutions, with the large majority securing their first-choice destination. Those opting to study abroad also attend prestigious institutions, which in recent times have included Cornell, Columbia, the University of Pennsylvania, New York University, the University of Toronto and the University of Hong Kong.

Pastoral care is based around an outstanding House system. Strong and positive relationships between boys, staff and parents are central to its success, and the school strives to ensure that each pupil, whether a boarder or a day boy, feels fully at home and well supported.

Tonbridge was named as Independent Boys' School of the Year (Independent Schools of the Year Awards, 2019) in recognition of its record of academic and pastoral excellence and for the keen sense of social responsibility displayed by boys. The School was shortlisted in the same awards in 2020 for the Community Outreach award.

The School has a strong commitment to widening access and is striving towards doubling the number of boys who receive means-tested fee assistance.

Location. Tonbridge School is just off the M25, on the edge of the Kent / Surrey / Sussex borders, and attracts families from all over southern England and beyond. It lies in 150 acres of land on the edge of the town of Tonbridge, providing a good balance between town and country living.

Admissions. www.tonbridge-school.co.uk/admissions

About 160 boys are admitted at the age of 13 (Year 9) each year. An additional 20 or so places are available for entry to the Sixth Form at the age of 16 (Year 12). We also have up to 6 places for boys aged 14 (Year 10).

Registration for a boy at 13+ entry should be made, preferably, not later than three years before the date of intended entry. Boys will then be asked to complete the ISEB pre-test and to visit Tonbridge for an assessment afternoon, usually during the Autumn Term of Year 6. The information collected from these assessments, in conjunction with the current school Head's report, will determine whether the offer of an unconditional or provisional place may be made. Those receiving an unconditional offer will be required to complete no further assessment (although Tonbridge is pleased to receive and mark Common Entrance papers from those who wish to take these). Those receiving a provisional offer will be invited to take a further assessment (in Maths and English) during the Summer Term of Year 7, after which a provisional offer may be converted to an unconditional offer.

Later registration for Year 9 entry is possible during Year 7, with such candidates following a modified entrance procedure. Details of this procedure can be found on our website or obtained from the Admissions Office: Tel: 01732 304297; E-mail: admissions@tonbridge-school.org

Applications for 14+ (Year 10) and Sixth Form (Year 12) entry are best made by 1 September a year before entry, but may be considered later. Admission at 14+ is gained via our own Maths and English exams. Boys sitting for entry at 16+ will take papers in the 4 subjects they wish to study in the Sixth Form.

Please see the school website to view an online copy of the prospectus. The Admissions pages of the site give full details of the registration procedure.

Scholarships and Bursaries. Some 45 scholarships overall are offered each year to boys in either Year 6 (the Junior Foundation Scholarship) or in Year 8.

Up to 6 Junior Foundation Scholarships are available to candidates in Year 6 who are attending a state primary school or to those attending a prep school, but who would require financial support in order to attend Tonbridge. Candidates should register by early October during Year 6 and will be invited to attend an assessment afternoon in November, with the stronger candidates returning to take tests in Maths and English in February. Such scholarships, which are confirmed in Year 6, may provide financial support of up to 100% to allow boys not currently in the independent sector, attendance at prep school for Years 7 and 8, as well as at Tonbridge from Year 9.

In Year 8, a further 21 Academic Scholarships are awarded (following examination in early May) as well as 10 or more Music Scholarships (for which auditions are held in early February), up to 10 Art, Drama or Technology Scholarships (assessed in early February) and up to 4 Cowdrey Scholarships, for sporting ability and sportsmanship (also assessed in early February). The award of any scholarship opens up eligibility for a means-tested bursary of between 10% and 100% of school fees, as agreed by the Bursar following a confidential review of financial circumstances.

Entry forms and full particulars of all Scholarships and Foundation Awards are available on the school website.

Fees per term (2021–2022). £14,945 for a boarding place and £11,212 for a day place.

Charitable status. Tonbridge School is a Registered Charity, number 1097977.

Governors:
R J Elliott (*Chairman*)

T M Attenborough	Dr V Rangarajan
Mrs S Bishop	G M Rochussen
D P Devitt	Dr M S Spurr, DPhil
M Dobbs	Mr J Thompson
Professor H Gaunt	Mr J Thorne
Mrs S Huang	Mrs K Wheadon
Mr J G Leahy	Mr G White
Mrs J Naismith	

Clerk to the Governors: Major General A Kennett, CBE

Headmaster: J E Priory, MA Oxon

Second Master: J R Bleakley, BA
Bursar: A C Moore, MA, MBA, INSEAD
Deputy Head Academic: M J Weatheritt, MA
Director of Admissions: R Burnett, MA
Deputy Head Co-Curricular: J A Fisher, BSc
Deputy Head Pastoral: C J C Swainson, MA
Director of Learning & Academic Enrichment: Mr J Blake, BA, MSc
Tonbridge Society Director: A R Whittall, MA

Assistant Staff:
* *Head of Department/Subject*

Art:
*F J Andrews, MA, BA
T W Duncan, BA
Mrs E R Glass, MA

Mrs B L Waugh, BFA
Art Librarian: Mrs M P Dennington

Art Technician: Mrs J M Brent

Classics:
*Dr J A Burbidge, BA, MSt, DPhil
Mrs C C Campbell, BA
J A Nicholls, MA
A P Schweitzer, MA
R J M Stephen, MA
L F Walsh, BMus

Computer Science:
*Dr J E Robertson, BSc, MSc, PhD

Design Technology and Engineering:
*R L Day, BSc
W D F Biddle, BSc
Dr A O Cooke, MEng, DPhil
J M Woodrow, BA
Technology Technicians: R Davies; O Longson
Teaching Assistant: C Martin

Digital Creativity:
*P J Huxley, BSc
Technology Tutors: D P Love MIET; C D Walker

Divinity:
*J C F Dobson, MA
B C S Barber, BA
R Burnett, MA
P J North, MA, BA
The Revd D A Peters, MA
R T Scarratt, BA
Dr H J M Swales, MA, MPhil

Drama:
*G D Bruce, MA
K I Ssebandeke, BA
L Thornbury, Dip Drama

English:
*Dr J G Reinhardt, BA, MSEd, MA, PhD
J R Bleakley, BA
J E Coltella, MA
R H Evans, MA
S A Farmer, MA
Mrs S Pinto del Rio, BA
Dr J D Shafer, PhD, MA, BSc
N J Waywell, BA

Extended Project Qualification:
Dr M R Ackroyd, BSc, PhD

Geography:
*C M Battarbee, BA
C M Henshall, BA
Mrs J H McNeil, BA
Mrs J M Watson-Reynolds, MA, BA

History:
*N Hillyard, BA, MSt
Dr J M T Dixon, BA, MPhil, PhD
Mrs F C Dix Perkin, MA
C W Eades, BA
R W G Oliver, MA
N R V Rendall, BA
Dr C D Thompson, BA, MPhil, PhD

Mathematics:
*J M Ashton, BSc
T G Fewster, BSc
R J Freeman, MA, BSc
K A Froggatt, MA
Miss J A D Gent, BA
Dr I R H Jackson, MA, PhD
Dr J D King, MA, PhD
M J Lawson, BA
N J Lord, MA
V Myslov, BA
Dr A A Reid, MChem, PhD, AFHEA
A P Schweitzer, MA
S J Seldon, MA, MEng
Dr Z Wang, MMath, PhD

Modern Languages:
*W H C Law, BA
W H C Law, BA (*French)
S Kerr, BA (*German)
Miss D M McDermot, MA, MA, BA (*Spanish)
X J Wu, MA (*Mandarin Chinese)
R Burnett, MA
Mrs C Clugston, MA (*EAL)
R D Hoare, MA
J A Nicholls, MA
Miss M del Mar Ponce Galan
J A Storey-Mason, BA
Mrs R Thomson, BA, Dip HE, TESOL
J-P Vieu, BA, MA
C E Wright, BA
Mrs X Yu, BA

Music:
*M A Forkgen, MA, ARCO (*Director of Music*)
J R P Thomas, MA, FRCO (*Head of Academic Music & Choirmaster*)
D L Williams, GRSM, ARCM, LRAM (*Piano*)
S J Hargreaves, MA, MEd
L F Walsh, BMus

Physical Education:
Director of Sport and Head of PE: C D Morgan, BSc

Assistant Director of Sport & Hockey Coach: Mrs L Maasdorp

Science:
*P G Deakin, MEng, BA
*C T E Powell, BSc, MA, MRes (*Physics*)
G M Barnes, BSc
Dr A O Cooke, MEng, DPhil
P G Deakin, MEng, BA
R L Fleming, MA, MInstP
R J Freeman, MA, BSc
A G McGilchrist, MEng
Dr D S Pinker, PhD, MSci
M J Weatheritt, BSc, MA
*I A Roslan, MChem (*Chemistry*)
A T J Byfield, MA, BTh, PGDip
G C Fisher, BSc, MA
J A Fisher, BSc
A D Hoyland, MChem
Dr C R Lawrence, MA, PhD
Dr S X Sneddon, PhD, BSc
*H M Grant, MA (*Biology*)
Dr M R Ackroyd, BSc, PhD
Dr W J Burnett, BSc, PhD
Ms A R Cooper, MBiochem

Houses & Housemasters:

Boarding:
School House: K M Seecharan
Judde House: A G McGilchrist
Park House: A T Sampson
Hill Side: P J North
Parkside: Dr C D Thompson
Ferox Hall: C W Eades
Manor House: S J Hargreaves

Day:
Welldon House: R H Evans
Smythe House: G C Fisher
Whitworth House: W D F Biddle
Cowdrey House: N R V Rendell
Oakeshott House: G M Barnes

Librarian: Mrs H Precious, BA, MSc, MCLIP

Admissions Secretaries:
Miss R G Hearnden (*Senior Admissions Officer*)
Mrs V C Larmour (*Admissions Officer Lower Sixth Entry*)
Mrs R Griffiths (*Admissions Officer Pre-testing*)

Examinations Officer: Miss B J Shepherd

Administration:
Headmaster's PA: Mrs J T Bishop
PA to the Second Master & School Administrator: Miss E J Day
PA to the Bursar: Mrs D J Shepherd
Music Dept Administrator: Mrs J Marsh

P M Ridd, MA
A T Sampson, BSc
C J C Swainson, MA

Social Science:
*S M Cleary, BSc (*Social Science & Economics*)
Miss K E Moxon, MA (*Politics*)
C M Ashurst, BA (*Business*)
J Blake, BA, MSc
L U Masters
P J North, MA, BA
Dr J D W Richards, MA, PhD
K M Seecharan, BSc
A J Sixsmith, BA

Director of ICT Services: A W Milgate

Head of Communications: Mr N J Ellwood, MA
Media Content Producer: Mrs E R Sim, BA, MPhil

University Entrance and Careers:
Mrs A Rogers, BA

Learning Strategies:
*Mrs H F McLintock, BA
Mrs N M Gerard, BA
Mrs E Kirk-Smith, MB, BS, BSc

Trinity School
Croydon

Shirley Park, Croydon CR9 7AT

Tel: 020 8656 9541
email: admissions@trinity.croydon.sch.uk
website: www.trinity-school.org
Twitter: @TrinityCroydon
Facebook: @Trinity-School
LinkedIn: /Trinity-School

Motto: '*Vincit qui Patitur*'

The School was founded by Archbishop John Whitgift in 1596. The full title of the school is Trinity School of John Whitgift.

One of the three governed by the Whitgift Foundation, the School is an Independent Day School for boys aged 10–18 with a co-educational Sixth Form. The School aims to give a wide education to students of academic promise, irrespective of their parents' income.

Buildings and Grounds. Trinity School has been in its present position since 1965, when it moved out from the middle of Croydon (its old site is now the Whitgift Centre) to a completely new complex of buildings and playing fields on the site of the Shirley Park Hotel. The grounds are some 27 acres in extent, and a feeling of openness is increased by the surrounding Shirley Park Golf Club and the extensive views to the south up to the Addington Hills. There are additional playing fields in Sandilands, ten minutes' walk from the School.

The resources of the Whitgift Foundation enable the School to provide outstanding facilities. All departments have excellent and fully equipped teaching areas.

Admission. The main ages of admission are at 10, 11 and 13. Entry is by competitive examination and interview. A reference from the feeder school will also be required. The School attracts applications from over 150 schools, with approximately 60% entering from state primaries. Entries of boys and girls into the Sixth Form are also welcomed.

Fees per term (2021–2022). £6,366 covering tuition, books, stationery and games.

Bursaries. Whitgift Foundation Bursaries (means-tested) are available providing exceptionally generous help with fees.

Scholarships. Academic, Art, Design Technology, Drama, Music and Sport Scholarships are available annually to boys applying for entry at 10+, 11+ or 13+. Boys must be the relevant age on 1 September of the year of entry. Awards are based on the results of the Entrance Examination, interview and current school reference. They are awarded without regard to parental income and are worth a percentage (maximum 50%) of the school fees throughout a pupil's career.

Academic, Art, Music and Sport Scholarships are also available for entry to the Sixth Form, based on GCSE results.

Scholarships may be supplemented up to the value of full fees if there is financial need.

Music Scholarships of up to 50% fee remission include free tuition in two instruments. Applicants are required to play two pieces on principal instrument and show academic potential in the Entrance Examination. Awards are available for all instruments and singing ability can be taken into consideration. Further details from the Director of Music.

Organisation and Counselling. The School is divided into the Lower School (National Curriculum Years 6–9) and the Upper School (Years 10–13). The Pastoral Leader in charge of each section works with the team of Form Tutors to encourage the academic and personal development of each boy. There is frequent formal and informal contact with parents.

A counselling service is provided to pupils as part of the pastoral provision and a fully qualified School Counsellor is on hand to help students with their individual needs. Pupils can refer themselves to the Counsellor or they may be referred by staff.

There is a structured and thorough Careers service, which advises boys at all levels of the School and arranges work experience and work shadowing.

While the academic curriculum is taught from Monday to Friday, there is a very active programme of sports fixtures and other activities at the weekend, and all boys are expected to put their commitment to the School before other activities.

Curriculum and Staffing. The School is generously staffed with well qualified specialists. The organisation of the teaching programme is traditionally departmental based. The syllabus is designed to reflect the general spirit of the National Curriculum while allowing a suitable degree of specialisation in the Upper School.

The normal pattern is for pupils to take 9 or 10 GCSE subjects, and to proceed to the Sixth Form to study an appropriate mixture of AS and A2 level subjects, complemented by a wide-ranging General Studies programme, before proceeding to university.

Games and Activities. The main school games are Rugby, Football, Hockey, Cricket and Athletics, with the addition of Netball for girls in the Sixth Form. Many other sports become options as a boy progresses up the School. Games are timetabled, each pupil having one games afternoon a week.

At the appropriate stage, most boys take part in one or more of the following activities: Community Service, CCF, Duke of Edinburgh's Award scheme, Outdoor Activities. There are many organised expeditions during the holidays.

Music. Music at Trinity has an international reputation, and every year Trinity Boys Choir is involved in a varied programme of demanding professional work. The Choir has performed at the BBC Proms for the past seven years and sings at the Royal Opera House, the English National Opera, Glyndebourne or Garsington 3–4 times each year. Recently the choristers have travelled to Vienna, Brussels, Venice, Dusseldorf and Wachock Abbey, Poland. They also appear regularly on radio and television. Trinity Choristers, who specialise in religious music, hold an annual residential Easter Course at a British cathedral. Choral Scholarships are awarded annually and enable boys to receive additional professional voice training without charge.

Many boys learn at least one musical instrument, and a large visiting music staff teach all orchestral instruments, piano, organ and classical guitar. There are numerous orchestras, bands and other instrumental groups for which boys are selected according to their ability. Musicians recently travelled to Canada and instrumentalists are regular finalists in the Pro Corda National Chamber Music competition.

Drama. There are two excellently equipped stages in the school and a lively and developing programme of formal and informal productions directed by pupils, staff and members of the Old Boys Theatre Company. Drama forms part of the formal curriculum in Years 6–9 and can be studied for GCSE and A Level.

Art and Design Technology. As well as the formal curriculum, which has led to 70% of the School taking a GCSE in art or design technology, pupils are encouraged to make use of the excellent facilities to develop their own interests.

Charitable status. The Whitgift Foundation is a Registered Charity, number 312612. The Foundation now comprises the Whitgift Almshouse Charity for the care of the elderly and the Education Charity which administers three schools.

Visitor: His Grace the Archbishop of Canterbury

Chairman of the Court of Governors: Mr C J Houlding
Court Governors:
The Bishop of Croydon, the Rt Revd Jonathan Clark
Revd Canon Dr Andrew Bishop
Mr Michelle Bereaux
Mr N Edwards, BA Dunelm, ACA
Mr C J Houlding
Mr I Harley, MA, FCA, FCIB
Mr D McNeil
Dr A Mehta, FRCP
Ms D Payne, MA
Mr D Sutton, MA MLitt
Mr D Seymour, CB

Chief Executive of the Whitgift Foundation: Mr M C Corney

School Committee:
Chairman of the Trinity School Committee: Mr D Seymour, CB
Chris Butler
Marcie Buxton
Mr J Crozier
Mr S Jetha
Mr W Jones
Dr B MacEvoy
Mr A Patel
Mr T Perrin
Revd Canon Dr Andrew Bishop

Headmaster: Mr A J S Kennedy, MA Cambridge (*Physics*)

Senior Deputy Head: Mr T T Rounds, BA Birmingham (*Philosophy/Theology*)
Deputy Head, Pastoral: Miss S Ward, BSc Birmingham (*Psychology, Designated Safeguarding Lead*)
Deputy Head, Academic: Mr A J Corstorphine, MA, MPhil Cambridge (*Classics*)
Head of Lower and Middle Schools: Mr S Powell, BSc Durham, MEd Cambridge (*Geography*)
Deputy Head, Head of Sixth Form, Admissions & Marketing: Ms A M Geldeard, BA, MA Cambridge (*English*)
Director of Teaching & Learning: Mrs A C Cooper, BA, MA Leeds (*Fine Art*)

Director of Co-Curricular Activities: Mr M D Richbell, BSc Liverpool (*Physical Education*)
Bursar: Mrs J Stanley, BA CCAT, ACA

* *Head of Department*

Miss C Atkinson, BA UCL (*French*)
Mr M I Aldridge, BEd London (*Design Technology, Sixth Form Student Support, Head of UCAS*)
Mr S R Allison, BA Durham (*Spanish**)
Dr M S Asquith, BA, MA, PhD London (*English*)
Mr H Baggs, MSc UCL (*Maths*)
Miss R C Bainbridge, MA Durham (*Maths*)
Ms D S Bala, BDS Chennai (*Biology*)
Mr R Barlow, BSc Bristol (*Mathematics*)
Ms N M Beaumont, MA, MSc Oxford (*Mathematics**)
Mr E Beesley (*Saturday School*)
Mr O J Benjamin, BA Durham (*German*, Spanish, Junior Languages Coordinator*)
Mrs I M Bennett, BEd Leeds Beckett (*Biology, Head of Netball*)
Ms H A Benzinski, BSc London (*Mathematics, DofE Coordinator*)
Mr G C Beresford-Miller, BA Rhodes (*Physical Education, Head of Fourth Year*)
Mrs K A Beresford-Miller, BA King's London (*Religious Studies**)
Mr R M Biggs, BSc Cardiff (*Design Technology*)
Mrs N Blamire-Marin, BA Granada (*Lectora, Spanish*)
Mr P J Blanchard, BSc Exeter, MBA Warwick (*Chemistry*)
Miss V J Boorman, BA King's London (*Classics, Head of Lower Sixth*)
Mr N D Borley, BSc Manchester (*Chemistry*)
Mrs N Boyce, BA Rhodes (*Religious Studies*)
Mr M M Bright, MSc Bristol (*Physics*)
Mrs M Bromberg, MSc Imperial (*Biology*)
Ms Q Cao (*Mandarin*)
Mrs H C Carey, BSc Durham (*Religious Studies, Deputy Head of Lower & Middle Schools*)
Ms E Carson (*Spanish*) [Maternity Cover]
Mr C S Chambers, BA Cambridge (*Drama Productions**)
Mr S W Christian, BA Liverpool (*French, Spanish*)
Mr W A Coma, BA Leeds (*Art*)
Ms A Costello, BA Roehampton (*Learning Support*)
Mr D W G Currigan, BA, Chelsea, MA Kingston (*Design Technology**)
Miss A E Davis, BA Manchester (*Maths*)
Mr T J Desbos, LCE Lille (*French, i/c DLL*)
Mr F K Doepel, BSc Lancaster (*Economics & Business**)
Mr A B Doyle, MA Glasgow, MA Open (*English**)
Mrs R Doyle, BEd Glasgow (*SEN*)
Mr M A Edwards, BSc Loughborough (*PE and Games**)
Mr El Moudden, BSc London (*Computer Science*)
Miss J S Eminsang, BA Manchester (*Mathematics, Head of Junior Maths*)
Miss T Escacena, BA Seville (*Spanish*)
Mr N S Evans, BA Nottingham (*History, Politics, Head of Upper Sixth*)
Mr R E Evans, Dip Perf Royal College of Music (*Piano**)
Mr L M Flanagan, BA Cambridge (*Physics**)
Mrs K Fuge, BSc City University (*Music, Singing**)
Mrs A A Fulker, BA Oxford Brookes (*Art, Personal Development**)
Mr F J Gabbitass, BA Bath (*Physical Education*)
Mr N A Giles, BA Liverpool John Moores (*Hockey**)
Mrs A E Gilmour, BSc Loughborough (*Physics, Head of Diploma*)

Miss R M Goddard, BSc Portsmouth (*Biology*)
Mr B Goode, BA London (*English*) [maternity cover]
Mr M Hammond, BSc Hons Sussex (*Maths*)
Mr R D G Haythorne, BA, MA Oxford (*Maths*)
Mr T Heath, BSc Sheffield, MSc Bristol (*Biology, Junior Science**)
Mr T Heaton, BA Essex (*Sociology*)
Mr S M Hodge, BA Exeter (*Religious Studies, Head of Third Year*)
Mr R M Holdsworth, BA, MA Oxford (*Music**)
Mr O J Hutchings, BA, MA York (*History, Politics, & i/c Politics, Head of EPQ & SFP*)
Miss S J Justin, BA Reading (*Economics & Business, Head of Junior Year*)
Mr I Kench, BSc Loughborough, MSc Oxford (*Physical Education, Director of Sport*)
Mr G Kimmins, Exeter (*Physical Education*)
Mr S D King, BA Manchester Metropolitan (*Physical Education, Performance Sport*, Aquatics**)
Mrs R E Lattery-Lee, BA SOAS, London (*History*)
Ms P-S Lin, BA Taiwan, MA UCL (*Chinese**)
Ms A Long (*Physical Education, Girls' Games**)
Mr D J P Lydon, BA, MA Dublin (*English*)
Mr A E Magee, MA St Andrews (*English*)
Dr J Manchester, PhD Birmingham (*Chemistry*)
Miss K J Manisier, MSc Imperial (*Physics, Action Research Lead, ITT Coordinator, STEM Engagement Coordinator*)
Dr M Mariani, BSc Kent, PhD UCL (*Physics*)
Mr P Mazur, BA Wales, MA London (*Drama, Contingent Commander CCF*)
Mrs S J McDonald, MA St Andrews (*Head of Learning Support*)
Mr S A McIntosh, MA Oxford (*German, Timetabler*)
Mrs K Molteni, BA Hull, MA UCL (*History*)
Mr R D Moralee, BSc Johannesburg (*Biology**)
Mr S Munday, BA West of England (*Geography, Head of Second Year*)
Mr J C Munnery, BSc Nottingham (*Geography, Head of Fifth Year*)
Mr P D Murphy, BA Cambridge (*History**)
Mr S Orungbamade, BEd Nigeria (*Economics and Business*)
Mr S D Page, BSc Sussex (*Computer Science*)
Miss C A Parkinson, BSc Sussex, MSc UCL (*Psychology*, Science*)
Mr B J Patel, MA Cambridge (*Mathematics, Physics*)
Mr B Patel, MSc UCL (*Mathematics*)
Mr J A Paterson, BA Cambridge (*Classics*)
Mr C P Persinaru, DipRAM, LRAM (*Music, Strings**)
Mr J Pettitt, BMus Trinity College of Music (*Music, Jazz, Rock and Pop**)
Mr H P Petty, BA Bristol (*English, Clubs & Activities Coordinator*)
Mrs R J Petty, MA Oxford (*English, Drama, Deputy Designated Safeguarding Lead*)
Mrs X L Phasey, MA Schiller International (*Chinese*)
Mr J E Pietersen, BA Cambridge (*History, Politics, Deputy Head of Sixth Form*)
Miss E Poole, BA Exeter (*History*)
Mrs A Prestney, BA Durham (*Geography*)
Mr D K Price, BA Wimbledon School of Art (*Design Technology, Director of Admissions*)
Mrs S J Rapoport, BEd Twickenham (*Academic Mentor*)
Mr S Reck (*Music, Guitar**)

Mrs L Regan, BMus, LRAM (*Music, Assistant Director of Music*)

Mr T M G Richmond, BSc Manchester (*Biology, Head of S&C*)

Ms C Riddle (*Art*)

Mrs M F Roberts, MSc London (*Computer Science*)

Mr P J Roberts, BSc Bath (*Physical Education, Economics & Business, Rugby**)

Mr J Robertson (*Director of Art*)

Dr D P Robinson, MA, DPhil Oxford (*Chemistry**)

Miss L P Robinson, BA Birmingham (*Drama**)

Dr K R Rogers, BSc Cardiff, PhD London (*Chemistry*)

Mr C P Ruck, BSc Southampton (*Geography**)

Mr M P Ryan, BA Oxford (*English*)

Mr R M Salmanpour, BSc London (*Chemistry*)

Mr J B Savile, BSc Durham (*Geography, Sailing**)

Mr S D Schofield, BSc Worcester (*Physical Education, Cricket*, Cricket Academy*)

Mr A E Smith, BA York, MA, MSc London (*Religious Studies*)

Mr M Stacpoole, BA Twickenham (*PE*)

Dr E W Steer, PhD, MA Oxford (*Chemistry*)

Mrs B J Steven, BA Cape Town (*English*)

Ms T Stevens-Lewis, BA, MA Goldsmiths (*Art, i/c Photography*)

Mr J E Stone, BA Cambridge (*Classics*)

Ms C Story (*English*)

Ms E M Suarez, BA Juan Carlos 1, Rey de Espana (*Spanish*)

Miss A Sukiennik, BA, MA Paris X (*French*)

Mr D J Swinson, MA Cambridge, FRCO, ARCM, LRAM (*Director of Music**)

Mr P G Tattersall, BMus Hons RNCM (*Music*)

Mrs S Z Taylor, BSc Exeter (*Mathematics, Professional Coordinating Mentor*)

Mr J G Timm, BA Cambridge (*History, Politics*)

Mr C H Todd (*Music, Brass**)

Mr W S Tucker, BSc Exeter (*Physics*)

Mrs T A Upton, BSc Warwick (*Mathematics*)

Miss S T Van Dal, BA Cambridge, MA UCL (*Classics**)

Mr R van Graan, BA Canterbury Christchurch (*Director of Digital Strategy**)

Miss R M Walker, BMus Birmingham Conservatoire (*Music, Lower School Music*, Head of First Year*)

Mr M D Waller, St Andrews (*Religious Studies*)

Mrs Q Wang, BA Henan Institute of Finance (*Chinese*)

Mrs C E Webb, BSc Bath (*Maths*)

Miss G E Webber, BA, MA Nottingham (*Economics & Business*)

Mrs C-J Wilkinson, BSc Glasgow (*Biology*)

Mr F R Wilson, BSc Southampton (*Chemistry*)

Miss J Wiskow, MA Wuppertal, Berlin (*German*)

Admissions Registrar: Ms M-A Costart
Sixth Form Admissions: Ms S Redican
Headmaster's PA: Mrs K Walsh

Truro School

Trennick Lane, Truro, Cornwall TR1 1TH

Tel:	01872 272763
email:	enquiries@truroschool.com
website:	www.truroschool.com

Motto: *Esse quam videri*

Truro School was founded in 1880 by Cornish Methodists. In 1904 it came under the control of the Methodist Independent Schools Trust (MIST) and is now administered by a Board of Governors appointed by the Methodist Conference. Although pupils come from all parts of the country and abroad, the roots of the school are firmly in Cornwall and it is the only HMC school in the county.

The religious instruction and worship are undenominational though the school is conscious of its Methodist origins.

There are 830 pupils (499 boys, 331 girls; 751 day, 79 boarders) in the Senior School (age 11+ and above). There are another 290 pupils in the Preparatory School, where boys and girls may start in the Nursery at the age of 3.

The school is fully co-educational throughout and there is a strong Sixth Form of some 180 pupils.

Boarding. At the Senior School girl boarders live in Malvern (Sixth Form and 5th Year) and Pentreve; boy boarders live in Trennick House. All are supervised by resident teaching staff and families. Pupils eat in the central dining room with a cafeteria system. There is a School Medical Centre on site.

Campus and Buildings. The *Prep School* campus is built around a country house acquired by the school in the 30s. It has an indoor heated swimming pool and extensive areas for science, modern languages, computing, art and crafts, as well as a modern sports hall. A new Dining Hall was opened in 2013 and a new Assembly Hall and classroom block in 2018. The Pre-Prep is housed in a purpose-built unit.

The *Senior School* occupies an outstanding site overlooking the Cathedral city and the Fal Estuary; it is only five minutes from the centre of the city but the playing fields reach into the open countryside. The school is excellently equipped. There is a first-class Library, extensive science laboratories, excellent Technology and Art facilities, a computer centre, music school, Sixth Form centre, a Sixth Form cafeteria and a range of classroom blocks. The time block containing the Burrell Theatre, six classrooms and a drama centre has been extended to provide a Modern Languages Centre in The Wilkes Building. An attractive and newly-refurbished chapel provides a focus for the life of the school. The Sir Ben Ainslie Sports Centre, completed for September 2013, provides an eight-court multi-use sports hall, two county standard glass-backed squash courts with viewing gallery, large fitness suite with a range of aerobic, strength and conditioning equipment, a multi-purpose dance and exercise studio with a sprung wooden floor, adding to the existing excellent facilities of 25m swimming pool, cricket nets, tennis courts, 40 acres of pitches and cricket pavilion. Following a link with Truro Fencing Club in September 2014 the school has its own designated Fencing Salle. In September 2018 the School opened its new Cookery School, in association with Leiths of London – a state-of-the-art 10-bay facility for co-curricular cookery and delivery of the Leiths Introductory Certificate to Food and Wine during the Sixth Form.

Organisation and Curriculum. Our academic programme up to GCSE provides a balance between the three Sciences, Humanities, Creative Arts and Modern Languages. In the 1st to 3rd Year, pupils study English, Mathematics, Biology, Chemistry and Physics, French and German, Geography, History, Religious Studies, Art, Design & Technology, Drama, ICT and Music. Spanish is optional from 3rd Year. All pupils have PE as well as Games each week. Every pupil in the 1st Year is taught touch typing, and ICT lessons culminate in a City & Guilds certified qualification by the end of the 3rd Year.

At GCSE the norm is to study ten subjects at full GCSE. Compulsory subjects are English Language, English Literature, Mathematics, Religious Studies, Double Award or Triple Award Science; the options include French, German, Spanish, Geography, History, Art and Design, Design and Technology, Music, Drama, Computer Science, PE and Geology.

A Levels include the same subjects as at GCSE, but with the introduction of Further Mathematics, Religious Studies (with Philosophy and Ethics), Economics, Business Studies, Psychology and the Extended Project Qualification. Our Extension Studies programme includes modules on Photography, Philosophy and Film Studies. As part of this we provide advice on careers and university applications, with a specialised programme for potential Medics, Dentists and Vets and Oxbridge. Three subjects will be most commonly continued into the Upper Sixth at A Level and the vast majority of Sixth Formers go on to further education when they leave. From September 2018 we offer the five-term Leiths Introductory Certificate which carries UCAS points.

Out-of-School Activities. Co-curricular life is rich and varied. There is a choir, school orchestra, a jazz group, a brass band and many other ensembles. Facilities such as the ceramics room, the art room and the technical block are available to pupils in their spare time. A huge variety of activities includes fencing, squash, sailing, golf, basketball, debating, surfing, and many others. Many boys and girls take part in the Ten Tors Expedition, an exceptional number are engaged in the Duke of Edinburgh's Award scheme, as well as local Community Service.

Games. All the major team games are played. Badminton, cross-country, hockey, netball, squash and tennis are available throughout most of the year. Rugby and Girls Hockey are played in the Winter Term and Soccer and Netball in the Spring Term. In the summer, cricket, athletics and tennis are the major sports. The covered pool is heated. The School also has its own Fencing Salle.

Admissions. Truro School was once a Direct Grant Grammar School and most pupils join at the age of 11. There are vacancies for entry at other ages, particularly at 13 and 16.

Scholarships and Bursaries. Scholarships are available and the School offers a small number of means-tested bursaries up to the value of full fees. Truro School has linked with Truro Cathedral to offer chorister scholarships for girls (ages 13–18) and boys (ages 7–13).

Fees per term (2021–2022). Senior School: International Boarders £10,825, Boarders £9,925; Weekly Boarders £8,525; Day Pupils (including lunch): £4,995. Prep (including lunch): £4,415 (Years 3–4), £4,585 (Years 5–6).

Pre-Prep (including lunch): £3,110 (Nursery and Reception), £3,265 (Years 1 and 2).

Academic results. A number of pupils proceed to Oxbridge every year, along with overseas universities. Around 95% of the Sixth Form proceed to degree courses. In 2021 89% of A Levels were at A* to B grades with 74% at A*/A. At GCSE in 2021, over 67% were at grades A*/A, 9–7 and 28% at grade 9.

Former Pupils' Association. There is a strong Former Pupils' Association and it has its own webalumnus. The "Friends of Truro School" involves parents, staff, old pupils and friends of the school in social events and fundraising.

Charitable status. Truro School is part of the Methodist Independent Schools Trust, which is a registered Charity, number 1142794.

Visitor: The President of the Methodist Conference

Administrative Governors:
Chairman: R Thomas, BSc, MRICS
N Ashcroft, MBE
M Aliffe BA Hons, BSC, FRICS
R Cartwright CTA
B Dolan, LLb Hons
Mrs E Garner, BA Hons, MEd
R Griffin, MA
A Luck
M MacDonald, BEng, FCA
A Murray, MA
Mrs B Scarsbrook, BA Hons, BCL, BPTC
P Stethridge, CEng, FICE, FIHT
Mrs H Sullivan, MA
Mrs C White, MSc, BA Hons, FCIPD, FLPI
Dr J Williams, BSc Hons, MBBS

Headmaster: A Johnson, BA

Deputy Heads:
Mrs E Ellison, BSc
Dr S K Pope, BSc, PhD

Chaplain: A de Gruchy, MTheol

Boarding House Staff:
Mrs S Mulready, BA (*Malvern*)
T Copeland, BA (*Trennick*)
Mrs V Fiol, BA (*Pentreve*)

Heads of Year:
R Williamson, MA (*Head of Sixth Form*)
G D Hooper, PGCE (*5th Year*)
R T Picton, MPhys (*4th Year*)
Miss J R Egar, BA (*3rd Year*)
Mrs F L Thurlow (*2nd Year*)
Mrs C McCabe, BSc (*1st Year*)

Heads of Department:
D Meads, BA (*Art*)
Miss S E Finnegan, BSc (*Biology*)
Dr A Brogden, MChem, PhD (*Chemistry*)
B Oldfield, BA (*Drama*)
C Baker, BSc (*Design and Technology*)
J Whatley, BSc (*Economics, Business Studies and Politics*)
Mrs A L Selvey BA, MA (*English*)
Mrs J Wormald, BSc (*Geography*)
Ms J Hope, BSc (*Geology*)
Dr M H Spring, MA, PhD (*History*)
S J McCabe, MA (*Mathematics*)
N PIlborough, BA (*Modern Languages*)
M D Palmer, BMus, FRCO, LRAM (*Music*)

D J Sanderson (*Director of Sport*)
A L Laity, BSc (*Physics*)
Mrs B L Richards, BA Hons, PGCE (*Religious Education*)

Truro School Preparatory School
(see entry in IAPS section)

Head: Ms S Patterson, BEd

Business Director: K Topping

University College School

Frognal, Hampstead, London NW3 6XH

Tel: 020 7435 2215
email: seniorschool@ucs.org.uk
website: www.ucs.org.uk
Twitter: @UCSHampstead

University College School is a leading London day school providing places for approximately 500 boys aged 11–16, with a co-educational Sixth Form of approximately 300 places. UCS admitted its first cohort of girls into the Sixth Form in September 2008 and around 50 girls will join UCS each year.

University College School was founded in Gower Street in 1830 as part of University College, London and moved to its current location in Hampstead in 1907. The UCS Foundation comprises three separate schools offering education to children at each stage of their development from the ages of 3–18, founded to promote the Benthamite principles of liberal scholarship and education. Intellectual curiosity, breadth of study and independence of mind combine to achieve academic excellence; they are not subordinate to it.

Selecting children with no regard to race or creed, UCS fosters in them a sense of community alongside a tolerance of and a respect for the individual. By offering the fullest range of opportunities for personal and for group endeavour, it teaches the value of commitment and the joy of achievement. It is a place of study, but also of self-discovery and self-expression; a school that places equal value on learning with others as on learning from others.

Admission. UCS Pre-Prep accepts boys at the age of 4 to join Reception. Boys join the Junior Branch at the age of 7 and the Senior School at the age of 11. We invite both boys and girls to apply at 16 for places in our Sixth Form. We always advise parents to check the admissions pages on the UCS website for the most up-to-date information. Please note that all applications, whether to the Pre-Prep, the Junior Branch or the Senior School, are now made online through the website.

Curriculum. The UCS curriculum is designed to match the educational needs of pupils at all stages of their development. At the Pre-Prep, the mix of formal and informal learning develops independent and enquiring thinkers. At the Junior Branch, whilst the emphasis is on breadth, boys are also prepared for Key Stage 2 Tests in English, Maths and Science.

The Lower School: In the first years at the Senior School boys aged 11–13 follow a broad, common curriculum founded on the best features of the National Curriculum but enriched to develop a love of learning and positive study skills. These traits enable our pupils to develop their own academic specialisms as they go up through the school, whilst also ensuring that they receive a rounded academic education.

Mathematics is taught in banded groups related to boys' ability and progress. There is otherwise no streaming and subjects are studied within form groups. Homework is set each day, and usually takes between 45 minutes and one hour.

The Middle School. The curriculum is deliberately broad, in order to provide a suitable basis for further study leading to GCSE and Sixth Form courses. Pupils are divided into sets in Mathematics according to ability. More time is devoted to Science and boys may take up a further Classical or Modern Language (Greek, German, Spanish or Mandarin). In addition boys choose one option from Music, Drama and Computing. PSHE continues in Year 9 in the classroom and in the following two years, through a programme of presentations, discussions and visits from outside speakers. Homework tasks include a wider range of topics and activities than before.

For the two years leading to GCSE, boys continue with English and Mathematics. They may then choose freely a further seven subjects with the only proviso that, to maintain a sufficient breadth to their studies, they must include at least one Modern Language from those they have previously studied and at least one science subject. Boys in the top two Mathematics sets also take the Additional Mathematics qualification alongside their GCSE.

The GCSE subjects offered are: Biology, Physics, Chemistry, French, German, Spanish, Italian, Mandarin, Latin, Greek, History, Geography, Art, Design and Technology, Drama, Dance, Music and Computer Science.

The Sixth Form. Pupils may study any combination of four subjects in the Transitus (Year 12) and may freely mix Arts and Science subjects if they wish. Careful guidance is provided to ensure that the course upon which they embark will provide an appropriate basis for an application to the Higher Education course and institution of the individual pupil's choice. After one year of study, pupils may continue with three or four subjects in the Sixth Form (Year 13). Sixth Form sets normally include 8–10 pupils who, in preparation for Higher Education, are encouraged to take greater personal responsibility for study.

The A Level/Pre-U subjects available are: English, Mathematics, Further Mathematics, Biology, Physics, Chemistry, French, German, Spanish, Mandarin, Latin, Greek, History, Geography, Economics, Politics, Philosophy, Psychology, Drama and Theatre Studies, Computer Science, Design and Technology, Art, Music and History of Art.

Pastoral Care. We regard the personal, emotional and moral development of our pupils as a major priority at every single stage of the education that we offer. The aim of our pastoral system is to encourage pupils to develop their own identities and to express them with a proper regard for the feelings and sensitivities of others. Pupils are encouraged from an early age to develop a sense of responsibility for their own behaviour. Much stress is laid upon tolerance of and respect for one another. Considerable effort is made to build a sense of community within the school. To this end, two days a week the school starts with a whole school, deme or year assembly of a non-denominational character. Pupils and their parents know the identity and the responsibilities of the members of staff concerned for their care. Parents are involved as fully as possible in pastoral matters and will always be informed and consulted.

Careers. Pupils are guided by means of interviews and tests towards careers appropriate to their gifts and personalities. Pupils are given opportunities to attend holiday courses directed towards specific careers. Also, visiting speakers are invited to the School and there are frequent Careers events. There is a full Careers Library and a comprehensive programme of Work Experience. The Parents' Guild and Old Gowers' Club (alumni organisation) also provide advice and support.

Physical Education and Games. The state-of-the-art Sir Roger Bannister sports complex opened in December 2006. The pupils have periods of Physical Education within their normal timetable in the sports complex. The School playing fields cover 27 acres and are situated a mile away in West Hampstead. In addition to grass surfaces, there is a large all-weather pitch and two pavilions. An impressive new double pavilion, known as The Kantor Centre, was opened in 2019 and the fields have recently undergone major levelling and drainage works. The major sports for Lower and Middle school boys are Rugby, Football, Hockey and Cricket with increased choices from Year 9. The School has its own Tennis and Fives courts at Frognal, together with an indoor heated Swimming Pool. Other sports include Athletics, Squash, Badminton, Basketball, Climbing, Fives and outdoor pursuits. For sixth form boys and girls there is a wide choice of indoor and outdoor sports.

Music and Drama. There is a strong musical tradition at UCS and many pupils play in the Orchestras, Wind Band and a great variety of groups and ensembles. Choral music is equally strong and Jazz is a particular feature. Instrumental tuition is given in the Music School, opened in 1995, and this and Ensemble Groups are arranged by the Director of Music. The School's Lund Theatre, opened in 1974, is the venue for a range of Drama from major productions to experimental plays, mime and revue. An open-air theatre was completed in 1994. A regular programme of evening events is arranged for the Autumn and Spring terms.

Other School Societies. These cover a wide range of academic interests and leisure pursuits, including the Duke of Edinburgh's Award scheme. There is a very active Community Action Programme, which works in the local community and there are regular fundraising initiatives for both local and national charities.

Philanthropy at UCS. Philanthropy has played a significant role in modernising the UCS estate and providing exceptional spaces for its pupils. Three major new facilities have opened in recent years which provide modern and up-to-date environments for pupils and staff alike. The Kantor Centre delivers sporting facilities fit for the capacity of the school, visitors and the local community it serves. The AKO Centre for Innovation in Learning and Teaching saw the entire refurbishment of the school library along with establishment of a research fellow into cutting edge teaching methods. Philanthropy has always played its part in the site of the Sixth Form Centre, and some 50 years after the original appeal was made to build this, the AKO Foundation provided a much needed full refurbishment. The generosity of donors, alongside revenues from our commercial activities, has enabled UCS to commit significant sums to funding bursaries, the majority of which provide wholly free places to talented young people. It continues to be the mission of UCS to substantially increase these sums year on year, working to widening access to a UCS education wherever possible.

Fees per term (2021–2022). Senior School: £7,297, Junior Branch: £6,745, Pre-Prep: £6,096

Scholarships and Bursaries. UCS is firmly committed to promoting and increasing access to our unique education through fee assistance. From its beginning in 1830 UCS has had at its core a commitment to access, with a pledge that religion should be no bar to entry. In the 21st century, we add a further commitment – that the education we provide will not be restricted solely to those who can afford it and each year we commit £1.2 million to bursary support. We offer bursaries of up to 100% and UCS consistently ranks at the top of independent schools in London for the number of 100% bursaries awarded each year. The School also offers music scholarships which award the holder a reduction in the annual school fees of between 10% and, in exceptional cases, 50%. The precise value will depend upon the standard of applicants and the competition in any one year. Music scholarships entitle the holder to free instrumental tuition at school on an instrument (including voice) of the candidate's choice, which will remain in place throughout a pupil's time at UCS.

Alumni Association, the Old Gowers' Club. There are almost 9,000 current Old Gowers living in countries all across the world. Many are actively involved in helping current pupils prepare for the future, including supporting networking, interview preparation, attending careers events, and volunteering as speakers from universities and wide ranging professions. Amongst the Old Gowers are Nobel Prize winners, Olympic medalists, leaders in the arts, science and law as well as entrepreneurs in a diverse range of areas, to name but a few.

Charitable status. University College School, Hampstead is a Registered Charity, number 312748. Its aims and objectives are the provision of the widest opportunities for learning and development of students without the imposition of tests and doctrinal conformity but within a balanced and coherent view of educational needs and obligations.

Governors:
Chairman: S B Warshaw, BA, PGCE
Vice Chair: R Bondy [OG]
S A Adams, RIBA, FRSA
L Bingham, OBE, MIPA, MABRP, DBA
R A S Datnow, BA, MA, Dip LP
S Grodzinski, QC [OG]
N R Gullifer, MA
Dr S Rana, BA, MSc, PhD
E Riche, BSc, MBA
C Rodrigues, CBE, MBA, MA DUniv h.c.
S L Soskin
Professor C Tyerman, MA, DPhil Oxford, FRHistS
Dr P Wood, BA, MA, PhD

[OG] *Old Gower*

Senior School:

Headmaster: M J Beard, MA, MEd

Vice Master & Academic Director: M T English, BA, MA

Deputy Head (Pastoral): A R Wilkes, BA

Assistant Heads:
R H Baxter, BA, MA
S E Bennett, BA

S A P FitzGerald, BA
J E L Lewis, BA
P S Miller, BSc
E D Roberts, MSci
T P Underwood, BA

Deme Wardens:
Baxters: S C Walton, MusB
Black Hawkins: A M Mee, MA
Evans: S D Maze, BA
Flooks: J P Cooke, BA
Olders: M Foster, BSc
Underwoods: A H Isaac, BA, MA

Sixth Form:
Head of Sixth Form: R H Baxter, BA, MA

Lower School Wardens:
Head of Lower School: E D Roberts, MSci
Entry: E A Barnish, BA, MA
Shell: E R Orlans, BA, MA

Senior School Heads of Departments/Subjects:

Art: Mr L A Farago, BA
Art History: Mr A M Mee, MA
Biology: Mrs K R Ward, BSc
Chemistry: Dr S K Hoyle, MSci, PhD
Classics: Mr A R McAra, MA
Computer Science: Mr C Spence-Hill, BSc, MA
Design & Technology: Mr B Vliegen, BA
Drama: Mr C J Bhantoa, BA (*Director of Drama*)
Economics: Mr P Fernando, BA
English: Mr H Hardingham, BA, MA
Geography: Mr M B Murphy, BA
History & Politics:
Mr A G Vaughan, BA (*Head of History & Politics*)
Mr L Smith, BA (*Coordinator of Politics*)
Learning Support: Mr P G P Milton, BSc, MSc
Mathematics: Mr D J Armitage, MEng
Modern Languages:
Dr H L Lauremson, BA, PhD (*Head of Modern Languages & Head of Spanish*)
Miss C Bandera, BA, MA (*Coordinator of Italian*)
Mrs S Hess, BA (*Head of German*)
Miss M R Maggioni, BA (*Head of Mandarin*)
Ms Sophie Tobert, BA (*Head of French*)
Music:
Mr C R Dawe, BA, MA, MMus (*Director of Music*)
Mr I C Gibson, MA (*Head of Academic Music*)
Philosophy: Dr K S Viswanathan, BSc, MA, PhD
Physical Education: Mr E P Sawtell, BA (*Director of Sport*)
Physics: Dr P D Edmunds, MSci, PhD
Psychology: Mrs C E Hawes, BSc, MSc

Junior Branch:
Headmaster: Mr L Hayward, MA
Deputy Head (*Academic*): Mr M Miles, MSc
Deputy Head (*Pastoral*): Mr D J Edwards, BA
Assistant Head (*Admin*): Ms P Gaglani, BSc

Pre-Prep:
Headmistress: Dr Z Dunn, BEd, PhD, NPQH
Deputy Head (*Head of EYFS*): Ms N Watt, BEd
Director of Learning Support and SENCO (*Pre-Prep and Junior Branch*): Ms S Ryan, MA

Uppingham School

Uppingham, Rutland LE15 9QE

Tel: 01572 822216
email: admissions@uppingham.co.uk
website: www.uppingham.co.uk
Twitter: @UppinghamSchool
Instagram: @uppinghamschool
LinkedIn: /school/uppingham-school

Uppingham School's foundation dates from 1584, the year in which Archdeacon Robert Johnson, a local puritan rector, obtained a grant by Letters Patent from Queen Elizabeth I to found a free grammar school for the male children of poor parents. The boys were to learn Hebrew, Latin and Greek. In 1853 this small local school was transformed into one of the foremost public schools of its time by the remarkable educational thinker and headmaster, Edward Thring. His pioneering pastoral ideas and belief in the values of an all-round education shaped the School then and continue to define it now. Small, family-like boarding houses that offer children individual privacy; an all-round education that caters for a broad range of pupils, and inspiring surroundings in which children are happy and learn better – all of these lie at the heart of Uppingham's identity.

Uppingham is a fully boarding school for boys and girls aged 13–18. There are around 800 pupils in the School, of which some 360 are in the Sixth Form.

Uppingham is a Christian Foundation, and the whole School meets in the Chapel five days a week. The quality and volume of the congregational singing is legendary. Some pupils are members of other faiths, and every consideration is given to their needs. Pupils are prepared for Confirmation every year.

Situation. Uppingham is a small market town set in the beautiful Rutland countryside. It is about 100 miles north of London, roughly equidistant from the M1 and A1/M11, and midway between Leicester and Peterborough on the A47. The A14 link road makes connections with the Midlands and East Anglia easier and faster. It is served by Kettering, Oakham, Corby, Peterborough and Leicester train stations, and by Stansted, Luton, Birmingham and East Midlands airports.

The Buildings. At the heart of the School are the impressive buildings of the main quadrangle: the Victorian School Room and Chapel designed by the architect of the Law Courts in the Strand, George Edmund Street, the Library housed in a beautiful building dating from 1592, the Memorial Hall and the fine classroom blocks where the Humanities are based. The three Music Schools on this campus reflect the vitality of a musical tradition dating back to 1855. Edward Thring appointed the first Director of Music in any English public school. Nearby are the central Buttery, the Language Centre and the Sixth Form Centre.

At the western end of the town lies the Western Quad, the School's inspiring architectural vision of a space that unites Arts, Sciences, Theatre and Sport. The Science Centre contains 17 laboratories (including an environmental studies lab, outdoor classroom and project room), a lecture theatre, library, offices and meeting rooms. The Leonardo Centre for Art, Design and Technology, and Textiles looks across an open space studded with contemporary sculpture, and to the east sits the 300-seat Theatre with adjoining Drama Studio, workshops and Theatre Studies classrooms. To the north, overlooking an expanse of playing fields, lies the Sports Centre with a contemporary design that complements the central quad.

Academic Matters. Whilst the School is noted for its strong commitment to all-round education, the depth of its pastoral care and wealth of facilities, academic study is the priority. Pupils move around the School campus during the working day, and the 55-minute lessons encourage detailed and developed learning. A staff to pupil ratio of almost 1:7 caters for a wide range and ensures all subjects enjoy small class sizes.

Until GCSE, specialisation is minimal and pupils are taught in sets for most subjects. Most take a minimum of nine GCSE/IGCSE subjects. Members of the Sixth Form study three subjects alongside a parallel curriculum enriched by lectures and a variety of extracurricular activities. Extended Project Qualifications (EPQ) are also offered.

In 2021, 85.1% of all A Levels were graded A*/A, and 85.8% of all GCSEs were graded 9–7. At both A Level and GCSE the A*–C pass rate was 100%.

Each pupil's progress is monitored by a Tutor and the Housemaster or Housemistress – there are regular reviews of academic progress, in addition to pastoral reports.

At all stages of a pupil's career the Housemaster/ Housemistress and Tutor is in regular contact with parents. Parent-teacher meetings take place annually for all year groups, and additional discussions are held regarding GCSE and A Level options and higher education.

Nearly all pupils go on to further education. Parents and pupils may call on the School's Higher Education and Careers Advisers alongside additional professional services. Visiting speakers from universities and careers are featured throughout the year, and the School offers advice on GAP year planning.

Pupils have access to a beautiful, well-stocked central Library, the Science Library and other specialist libraries for most subject departments. For those with learning difficulties the School has trained staff to help with special education needs.

Beyond the Curriculum. As part of the School's enrichment programme Uppinghamians get involved in an extensive range of additional pastimes and hobbies, the Combined Cadet Force (CCF) and the Duke of Edinburgh's Award. They also participate in charitable outreach initiatives (locally, nationally and globally). All of these programmes are managed by experts in their fields who ensure that pupils aspire to, and are able to reach, their highest potential. We provide a multitude of experiences to enrich pupils' lives and cultivate new talents, passions and interests.

Music. Uppingham has always had a very distinguished reputation for music, being the first school to include music on its curriculum for all pupils. More than 50% of pupils learn an instrument, and a busy programme of weekly public recitals, house and year group concerts, and performances in the UK and abroad offer pupils of all abilities regular chances to perform. 45 visiting staff and 9 full-time staff enable pupils to receive conservatoire-style tuition at the school.

The Paul David Music School is an inspirational centre for learning and rehearsal, with cutting-edge music technology suites. The School has an outstanding Chapel Choir, accomplished orchestras and national prize-winning chamber groups, a slick and polished Jazz Orchestra, and a thriving Alternative Music Society promoting rock concerts.

Sports and Games. Uppingham has a strong tradition of sporting excellence, and pupils have gained county and national honours in a variety of sports. Sports on offer include rugby, hockey, cricket, tennis and athletics plus squash, badminton, swimming, football, sailing, aerobics and dance.

There is a full programme of formal house matches across all sports, providing an opportunity for all pupils to contribute within a team environment. The able are stretched and the very able are offered a high level of coaching from experienced coaches/professionals in all major sports, often going on to represent club, academy, county, regional or national teams.

The Sports Centre includes a sports hall, six-lane 25m swimming pool, fitness studio, gym, squash courts and dance studios. There are more than 65 acres of playing fields, three Astroturf surfaces (one floodlit), tennis, netball and fives courts, a shooting range and climbing wall.

The Leonardo Centre. The striking design of the Art, Design and Technology Centre allows the broad range of creative activities taking place to interact and stimulate each other. The Centre houses a fine art and printing space (with 3D printing), studios for design (including CAD design), textiles, ceramics, sculpture, photography and workshops primarily for wood, metal and plastic, and teaching rooms. The Warwick Metcalfe Gallery displays the work of pupils, staff and visiting artists.

Drama. Uppingham Theatre is a flourishing professionally equipped 300-seat theatre, with a stylish adjoining Drama complex with an 80-seat 'black box' studio, workshops, classrooms and offices. Major school productions open to all pupils are staged annually, ranging from big musicals such as *Oliver!* and *Legally Blonde* to opera and plays such as Shakespeare's *The Tempest*. There are Junior Drama Society productions, joint boarding-house productions, and pupils are an integral part of the running of the theatre. Drama and Theatre is taught at GCSE and A Level.

Boarding and Pastoral. There are fifteen boarding houses dotted around the town and School estate: nine for boys, one for Sixth Form girls and five for 13–18 year old girls. Houses are small, most being home to around 50 children, 45 in the case of the Sixth Form girls' house. All pupils eat their meals in their own house dining room, and are joined at lunch by teaching and non-teaching staff.

Much of the non-teaching life of the School is organised around the houses and they inspire strong loyalties. In addition to excursions and social events, there is a long-standing tradition of inter-house competitions (House Challenge, singing, debating and sports), house concerts, and some ambitious drama productions.

Pupils are supported by a wide-ranging pastoral network. The Housemasters and Housemistresses are resident, and lead a team of at least five tutors, including a Deputy Housemaster/Housemistress. Assigned to particular pupils, tutors help to monitor academic progress and social development. Each house is supported by experienced matrons providing medical support and supporting the pastoral care of the pupils. Any pupil may use the services of a professional psychologist or the School's qualified counsellor. The School's Medical Centre is open 24 hours a day in term time, with qualified medical staff in attendance.

Technological Environment. Uppingham provides outstanding technology facilities for pupils in both academic and boarding areas. Resources include the online Encyclopedia Britannica and JSTOR, an online collection of over 1,000 academic journals and one of the most trusted sources of academic content.

In the classroom academic departments have the tools to ensure that IT complements teaching and learning.

Admission. Most pupils are admitted to Uppingham in the September following their thirteenth birthday. Prospective pupils and their parents usually visit the School at least three years prior to entry. If not already registered, prospective pupils should register then. Two years before entry all registered pupils are given pre-tests and interviews at Uppingham. All applications must be supported by a satisfactory reference from their current school. The Headmaster offers places to successful candidates after this process has concluded. Parents then complete and return an acceptance form together with an entrance deposit. Receipt of the entrance deposit guarantees a place in the School subject to the pupil qualifying for admission. In completing the acceptance form parents also confirm that Uppingham is their first choice of school.

The final offer of a place in the School is conditional upon the pupil qualifying academically, and on his or her record of conduct (full details are available on the School's website).

To continue into the Sixth Form the minimum grade requirement is three 7s and three 6s at GCSE. It is recommended that pupils have at least 7 at GCSE in the subject they wish to continue at A Level. In some subjects (Mathematics, the Sciences and MFL) an 8 or 9 grade is required (full details are available on the School's website).

There are a limited number of places available for entry into the Sixth Form. Pupils may register an interest in Sixth Form entry to Uppingham at any time and formal registration should be completed by the end of September, eleven months prior to entry. The test, interview and offer procedures take place in October and November ten months before entry. Admission at this level is dependent on tests and interviews at Uppingham, and then achieving at least three 7s and three 6s at GCSE (or equivalent), excluding short course GCSEs.

Details about admissions can be found on the school website or may be obtained from the Admissions Office.

Scholarships and Bursaries. At 13+, Academic, Art/ Design & Technology, Drama, Music, Sport and Thring (All-Rounder) Scholarships are available. Scholarship exams are held in the February/March preceding entry, the deadline for applications is typically the end of December.

At 16+, Academic, Science, Art/Design & Technology, Drama, Sport and Music Scholarships are awarded in the November preceding entry. The deadline for applications is typically the end of September.

At Uppingham a candidate may only hold one scholarship award at any one time so that they can specialise in their area of talent. Candidates are not permitted to sit scholarships in more than two disciplines.

Where a family's financial means leaves them unable to afford a place at Uppingham they may be eligible to receive support via a means-tested bursary. All candidates seeking a bursary should be registered with the School and need to fulfil the same entrance criteria as described above.

Details of all scholarships and bursaries may be found on the school website or obtained from the Admissions Office.

Fees per term (2021–2022). Boarding £13,164; Day £8,150. There is a scheme for paying fees in advance.

Former Pupils. The Uppingham Association was founded in 1911 to maintain the link between OUs and the School. All pupils may become life members when they leave and a database of their names, addresses, school and career details is maintained at the School by the OU Administrator. In addition to a range of OU events that are organised each year for members, a magazine is published annually, which contains news about OUs and activities at the School, and all members are encouraged to make full use of the OU Website.

Charitable status. Uppingham School is a charitable company limited by guarantee registered in England and Wales. Company Number 8013826. Registered Charity Number 1147280. Registered Office: High Street West, Uppingham, Rutland LE15 9QD.

The Governing Body:

Chairman: Ms B M Matthews, MBE, BSc, FRSA [OU]
Vice-Chairs: R J S Tice [OU], BSc; K J Budge, MA, PGCE Oxon

The Very Revd Christopher Dalliston, Dean of Peterborough
Dr S Furness, PhD, LL, Lord Lieutenant of Rutland
C E V Colacicchi, MA Oxon
C F Ewbank, MA Cantab, MBA
J D R Fothergill [OU], MA Oxon, MBA
K J Gaine, MA Oxon
S A Humphrey, LLB Hons
C P M King, MA
R N J S Price [OU]
Professor J Scott
A E Timpson CBE [OU], MP
A W Y To, BSc, MRICS, MHKIS
D L C Wallis [OU], BA Hons Oxon
L J Womack [OU], BA Hons

[OU] *Old Uppinghamian*

Bursar/Finance Director, Clerk to the Trustees: S C Taylor, MA, ACA

Headmaster: **Dr R J Maloney**, MTheol St Andrews, MA, PhD King's College London

Senior Deputy Head: K M Wilding, BA
Deputy Head Academic: B Cooper, MA
Registrar: C S Bostock, MA, MSc
Chaplain: The Revd Dr J B J Saunders, BA, PhD
Assistant Head: Co-Curricular: Miss S E Delaney, BA, BA
Assistant Head: Teacher Development: Mrs R R Attenborough, MA, MA Ed
Assistant Head: Pastoral Care: Mrs R H Kay, BA, MA
Assistant Head: Sixth Form: Mr R J O'Donoghue, MA
Assistant Head: Data/Academic Management: Mr P J Nicholls, BSc

Assistant Staff:
* *Head of Faculty/Department*
† *Housemaster/mistress*

Art, Design & Technology: *H J Harrison, BA (*DT*)
*C P Simmons, BSc   S N Jarvis, BA, MA

J Luckhurst
*M E John, BA, MA
  (*Textiles*)
*E J Stokes, BA (*Art*)
†K Wells

Biology:
*H E Waymark, BSc
†N K de Wet, BSc, CBiol,
  MIBiol
Y L Guy, BSc
K Muller
Dr C L Pemberton, BSc,
  PhD
A Rajput-Buckland, BSc

Chemistry:
*R A King, BSc (*Science**)
Dr A J Dawes, MChem,
  MA, PhD
Y L Guy, BSc
A Kowhan, BSc
Dr N L Singleton, BSc,
  PhD

Classics:
*D W J Addis
S W Clark, BA, MA
S G Dewhurst, BA
D Draper, MA
Dr D C Oliver, PhD, MSc
†G S Tetlow, MA

Computer Science:
*S E L Webster, BSc

Drama and Theatre:
*J Holroyd, BA
S E Delaney, BA, BA
C J Hayes, BA (*Artistic
  Director*)
T R Tolond

Economics & Business:
*G R Matthews, BSc
N J King, BA
T G MacCarthy, BA
T Oakley, BA
G L Watt, BSc

English:
*Dr J C Methven, MA,
  MPhil, DPhil
N G Fletcher, BA
C Greenlaw, BA
G L Hardy, BA
V Kinmond, BA, MA
Dr E E Reddy, BA, PhD
M B Sherwin
K L Tetlow, BA

Geography:
*T P Davies, BSc
R R Attenborough, MA,
  MA Ed
†C C Breakwell, BSc, MSc
†T Hollyer BA
†A N Huxter, BSc
S J Kowhan, BA
R J O'Donoghue, MA
K M Wilding, BA

History:
*M J Patterson, BA
†J S Birch, MA
R H Kay
B M Kirkby, MA
I C Neilson
J A Reddy, BA
R A Stevens

History of Art:
*D S R Kirk, BA
Dr E E Wilce, BA, MA,
  PhD

Learning Support & EAL:
*G R Bruce, BA, MEd
  (*Learning Support*)
*A Rawlins (*EAL*)
J A Wilding, BSc

Mathematics:
*M J Melville-Coman, BSc
†L J Allen, BSc, MBCS
P Gomm, BSc
†K F Hanrahan, BSc
A S M Moosajee, BSc
N C Newell, BSc
P J Nicholls, BSc
A D Parker, BSc
J W Partridge, MA
L Whiteside, BSc
J A Wilding. BSc

Modern Languages:
*A J Dowsett (*German**)
M A B Davies, BA
*A Gadd (*Spanish*)
A J Hamilton, MA
Z J R Hunter, BA
†H M Johnstone, BA
I Miller
A Peltier
*L N Soto-Leroux (*French*)
K M Turney
R M B Wilkinson, MA
*Z B Zeng, BA, MA
  (*Mandarin*)

Music:
*P M Clements, MA,
  FRCO (*Academic
  Music**)
M P Ćwiżewicz, MEng,
  ACGI, PGDip (*Violin*)
A A Ffrench, MA, AGSM,
  PGDip (*Piano*)
C A Griffiths, GMus
  (*Voice*)
A J Kennedy, MA, PGDip
  (*Director of Music,
  Voice*)
S A Smith, BA, PPRNCM
W F J Smith, BMus, PGCE
  (*Bass Guitar*)
J Stevens, GGSM, MA
A P Webster, GGSM,
  ARCM, PDOT
  (*Clarinet*)

*Philosophy and Religious
  Studies*:
*Dr H D P Burling, BA,
  MPhil
B Cooper, MA
†R C Hegarty, MA
Dr R J Maloney, MTheol,
  MA, PhD
The Revd Canon Dr J B J
  Saunders, BA, PhD
†P M Shacklady, BA

*Physical Education &
  Sport*:
*H N Costello
B T Attenborough
J M Baker, BSc
†D J Bartley
†C C Breakwell, BSc, MSc
J J Cooke
N De Luca, MBA
A J A Hall
H E V Joseph
R Lalor, BA, MSc
D F Morris
K R Peters

Visiting Music Staff:
S Andrews (*Drums*)
M Ashford, GRSM Hons, LRAM (*Guitar*)
S Baker, BMus, MMus (*Trombone*)
M Braithwaite, BA Hons, AGSM (*Singing*)
J T Byron, BA, MA, PhD (*Piano*)
L Clements, BA, PGCE (*Flute*)
P Clements, MA, FRCO (*Organ*)
J Eddie, AGSM (*Horn*)
J Emmanuel, DipGBSM, DipABSM, LRAM (*Singing*)
D P Ferris, BMus Hons (*Jazz Piano*)
L H Ffrench, GRSM, LRAM (*Piano and Music Theory*)
N M France, GMus (*Drums*)
T M Gunnell, BMus (*Percussion*)
I Hildreth (*Bagpipes*)
C Le Page (*Violin and Viola*)
K Learmouth, ALCM, FRSA (*Guitar*)
R R E Leyton-Smith, MA, AdvPGDip RCM (*Cello*)
C Li, BMus, LRAM (*Flute*)
G K Lumbers, BMus (*Saxophone*)
R Lund, BMus Hons, MMus (*Violin and Viola*)
J Miller, BMus, LGSM (*Oboe*)
J A Moffat, DipRCM Perf, DipRCM Teach (*Singing*)
V F Morris, AGSM, LRAM (*Clarinet and Saxophone*)
E Neuhauser, BMus, LGSM (*Tuba*)
L Nolan, BA, MSt Oxon, PGCE (*Harp*)
E Pick, BMus Hons, MMus, DMA (*Piano*)
A J Pike, BA (*Music Technology*)
A M Reynolds, MusB, GRNCM (*Piano*)
R Reynolds, BA Hons (*Electric Guitar and Creative Music
  Technology*)
Y S Sandison, PPRNCM (*Singing*)
N Scott-Burt, BA, MMus, PhD, LRAM, ARCO (*Piano and
  Composition*)
A E Smith, BA Hons, MSTAT (*Alexander Technique*)
S Smith, BA, PPRNCM (*Piano, Accompanist in Residence*)
C Tanner, BMus, LRAM (*Bassoon*)
S Walton, BMus Hons (*Trumpet*)
P N Warburton, GBSM, ABSM (*Violin*)
P Waterfield, MSTAT, ARCM (*Alexander Technique*)

A P Siddall
T R Ward
S L Warwick-Smith, BSc,
  MA
A C Welch, BEd
†J R Welch, BEd

Physics:
*E L Ellis, BA
W S Allen, BEd
Dr D D Boyce, PhD,
  CPhys, CSciTeach,
  MPhys
G S Wright, BSc

Politics:
*H J Barnes, MA
†T Makhzangi, BA
T P Prior, BA, MA

Wellbeing:
*M Burder, BSc
†T C Hollyer, BA
R H Kay
D F Morris
M J Tetley, BA

T J Williams, MA (*Singing*)
V D Williamson, GMus, RNCM, PPRNCM, LRAM
  (*Singing*)

Houses and Housemasters/mistresses:
Brooklands: Nick de Wet
Constables: Katherine Hanrahan
Fairfield: Jo Welch
Farleigh: James Birch
Fircroft: Tom Hollyer
Highfield: Richard Hegarty
Johnson's: Lesley Allen
The Lodge: Helen Johnstone
Lorne House: Andrew Huxter
Meadhurst: Patrick Shacklady
New House: Christina Breakwell
Samworths': Kitty Wells
School House: Simon Tetlow
West Bank: David Bartley
West Deyne: Toby Makhzangi

Victoria College

Jersey

Mont Millais, Jersey, Channel Islands JE1 4HT

Tel: 01534 638200
email: admin@vcj.sch.je
website: www.victoriacollege.je
Twitter: @VictoriaCollege
Facebook: @VictoriaCollegeJersey

Motto: *Amat Victoria Curam*

The College was founded in commemoration of a visit of Her Majesty Queen Victoria to the Island and opened in 1852. It bears the Arms of Jersey and the visitor is Her Majesty The Queen.

There are currently 680 boys in College and 275 in the Preparatory School.

The College is situated in extensive grounds above St Helier and commands spectacular views south and west over the Bay of St Aubin.

The fine building of 1852 with its Great Hall, de Quetteville Library and administrative areas, is set at the centre of new teaching accommodation including classrooms, a music centre, an extensive Science suite opened by Her Royal Highness The Princess Royal, a Sixth Form Centre, Art and Design Technology suite, computer suites and the Howard Davis Theatre, refurbished in 1996 and updated in 2019. A suite of 4 new English classrooms were finished in 2014 along with a new Sixth Form Centre. House rooms (now Year Group rooms) were added in 2015.

College Field is adjacent to the main buildings and includes an all-weather hockey pitch.

Located in the grounds is a 25-yard shooting range, squash courts and CCF Headquarters. A multimillion pound sports complex with swimming pool was opened in 2003

Education. There is a strong focus on adding value in all aspects of educational provision. The Combined Cadet Force, The Duke of Edinburgh's Award and a wide-ranging co-curricular programme helps provide opportunities for all students, catering to all interests and skill levels. Academic excellence, focusing on supporting students to achieve their personal academic bests, is a core goal. The curriculum conforms to the requirements of the Jersey Curriculum. From September 2022 at GCSE, students study English Language and Literature, Mathematics and at least two Science subjects from Biology, Chemistry and Physics. They also select from Spanish, French, History, Drama, Geography, an additional Science, Music, Art, Computer Science, DT, Food & Nutrition, Sports Science and Classical Civilisation. Boys select their optional subjects from those which best suit their aspirations, passions and abilities, the choice being guided by teaching staff in consultation with students and parents.

Boys study three A Level subjects (from a choice of 23) suited to their interests and future career options. Students from 3 other collaboration schools on Island share provision at Key Stage 5, to widen the choice of subjects available, and students visit other schools for those lessons. A wide ranging Sixth Form enrichment programme is offered, including lecture series and careers programme, Extended Project Qualification, and a significant number of options, many of which carry formal qualifications outside of the traditional academic sphere (e.g. sports coaching).

Prizes. Her Majesty The Queen gives three Gold Medals annually for Science, Modern Languages and Mathematics as well as two Prizes for English History. The States of Jersey offers a Gold Medal and a Silver Medal annually for French.

Physical Education and Games. Sport is enjoyed and promoted across all Key Stages at the College, and consistent success in both on and off Island competitions is the norm. Many students represent the Island in chosen sports.

Winter games include Association Football, Rugby, Hockey and Squash. Summer games include Cricket, Swimming, Shooting, Tennis and Athletics. Matches are played against Elizabeth College, Guernsey and numerous English Independent Senior Schools.

Combined Cadet Force. The College has an excellent CCF Contingent with an establishment of approximately 135 across three sections: Army, Navy and RAF. It is commanded by Sqn Ldr S Blackmore.

Admission. The age of admission is 11 years though boys are considered for entry at all ages. Entrants that do not come directly from the associated Victoria College Preparatory School must pass the College Entrance Examination.

Fees per term (2021–2022). £2,240. A grant is payable by the States of Jersey to supplement fees.

Preparatory School. The College has its own Preparatory School which stands in the College grounds. Boys progress to the College at the age of 11. (*For further details see entry in IAPS section*).

Leaving Scholarships. There are a number of Scholarships for further education (of varying amounts). The Queen's Exhibition is tenable for three years at certain Universities; the Wimble Scholarship, the Sayers Scholarships and the De Lancey and De La Hanty Scholarship, tenable at British Universities, and the Rayner Exhibitions are recent additions to the rich endowment of Scholarships enjoyed by the College for its students.

Visitor: Her Majesty The Queen

Governing Body:
Chair: B Watt
Vice Chair: R Stevens

N Cawley	T Smith
P Willing	H Job
S Marks	G Hughes
R Bidmead	P Crossley
T Caldeira	D Pateman
R Kirkby	G Lumley
C Smith	

Headteacher: Dr Gareth Hughes, PhD, MPhil Cantab, MSc, MA Oxon, PGCE, NPQH (*Geography*)

Deputy Headteacher: Patrick Crossley, MA Cantab, MEd, BTh, FRSA (*RE*)
Assistant Headteacher (*Academic*): Karen Palfreyman, MA, BA Hons Cantab (*Geography*)
Assistant Headteacher (*Pastoral*): Anthony Griffin, BA Hons, PGCE (*English*)
Bursar: Carolyn Ferguson, CAT, MIAB

Teaching Staff:
Marianne Adams, BA Hons (*Head of English*)
Kieran Akers, BA Hons (*Senior Teacher Co-Curricular, Design & Technology*)
Miranda Blackmore, BSc Hons, PGCE (*Geography*)
Gareth C Bloor, MA, BD Hons (*Head of RE*)
May Brennand, MMaths, PGCE (*Head of Mathematics*)
Jacqueline Bryan, BA Hons (*Student Wellbeing*,)(*English*)
Brendan Carolan, BA Hons (*Head of Social Sciences*)
Samuel Coe, BSc Hons (*Chemistry*)
Steven Cooke, PhD, BEng Hons (*Head of Physics*)
David Cox, BA, BEd Hons (*Biology*)
Joseph Crill, BSc Hons (*Head of Hockey, Sports*)
Iain Durkin (*Mathematics*)
Emma Davies, BA Hons, PGCE (*Music*)
Lisa de Gruchy, MA Ed, BSc Hons, DPS, Assoc CIPD (*Head of Business Studies, Trident Co-ordinator*)
Nicole Edgecombe, MA, BA Hons (*Modern Foreign Languages*)
Elise Falla, BA Hons, PGCE (*Co-ordinator of Student Development, English*)
Alan Falle, BA Hons, PGCE (*Head of Sixth Form*)
Jodi Fowler, BEd Hons (*Design & Technology*)
William Gorman, BA Hons (*English*)
Samuel Habin, BA Hons (*Sports*)
Cristina Herrera-Martin, BA Hons, BEd (*Modern Foreign Languages*)
Daniel Hodder, BSc, PGCE (*Head of Geography*)
Maria Innes BA PGCE (*Modern Foreign Languages*)
Rebecca Kane, BSc Hons (*Biology*)
Stephanie Kellett, BA Hons, PGCE (*RE*)
Rachel Kemp, MA, PGCE (*English*)
Angela Matthews, BSc Hons (*Mathematics*)
Michel Morel, BA Hons, PGCE, AKC (*Chemistry*)
Vanessa McGrath, BSc Hons (*Mathematics*)
Dawn Murphy, BA Hons, PGCE (*Head of Economics & Deputy Head of Sixth Form*)
Francis Murton, BMus, LRAM, LTCL, ARCO, ACIEA, PGCE (*Director of Music*)
Lucy Ogg, BA Hons, LTCC (*Theatre Studies*)
Ozzy Parkes, BA Hons, PGCE (*Head of Computer Science*)
Monica Perestrelo, BA Hons, PGCE (*Head of Modern Foreign Languages*)
Richard Picot, BSc (*Co-ordinator of Celebrations & Rewards, Sports*)

Parmjeet Plummer, BA Hons, PGCE (*Senior Teacher Teaching & Learning, History*)
Orla Priestley, MSc, BSc Hons (*SENCO, Mathematics*)
Majella Raindle, MSc, BSc Ed Hons (*Mathematics*)
Jefferson Randles, BA Hons (*Head of Art & Display*)
Jane Richardson, PhD, BSc Hons, PGCE (*Head of Biology*)
Anna Robinson, BA Hons (*English*)
Andrew Royle, BSc Hons (*Sports*)
Helen Ryan, BA Hons (*Head of Photography*)
Holly Shrimpton, BA Hons (*Humanities*)
Matthew Smith, BA Hons (*Director of Sport*)
Rachel Smith, BA Hons (*History*)
Thomas Smith, BEng Hons (*Physics*)
Jamie Thomas, BA Hons, PGCE (*Design Technology*)
Olivia Varney, BA Hons (*Deputy Head of Sixth Form, English*)
Valérie Videt, Licence-ès-Lettres (*Modern Foreign Languages*)
Bram Wanrooij, MA, MEd (*Head of History*)
Adam Warburton, BA Hons (*Head of Theatre Studies*)
Susan Watkins, BEd Hons (*Head of Inclusion*)
Matthew Widdop, MChem, MRSC (*Head of Chemistry*)
Carys Williams, BEng Hons, PGCE (*Mathematics*)

Preparatory School
Headteacher: Dan Pateman, BA Hons

Wellingborough School

London Road, Wellingborough, Northamptonshire NN8 2BX

Tel:	01933 222427
email:	admissions@wellingboroughschool.org
website:	www.wellingboroughschool.org
Twitter:	@wboroschool
Facebook:	@WboroSchool

Motto: SALUS IN ARDUIS

Founded in 1595, Wellingborough School prides itself on its rich history and enduring traditions which are visible today in its architecture, House system and, most importantly, values. The School's mindset, however, is thoroughly progressive and, as an organisation, is keen to embrace innovations which strengthen the ethos and integrity of the School. Families are reassured by the School's longevity and the body of knowledge it has developed over time about how best to educate boys and girls.

Wellingborough School is a co-educational school for boys and girls from the age of 3 to 18, and is divided into a Preparatory School (age 3–11: 230 pupils), and Senior School (age 11–18: 600 pupils, including 150 pupils in the Sixth Form).

Curriculum. The Prep School follows the International Primary Curriculum which gives a thorough grounding in the core subjects, while offering the pupils a broad spectrum of experience in Languages, Art and Design, Music, Drama and Sports as well as an international perspective on global issues.

The School's academic standards and expectations are high, based to a large extent on the National Curriculum. In the Senior School, quality learning and teaching enables pupils to take ownership of their future as they make decisions about their curriculum. Pupils in Years 7 and 8 have the opportunity to study a full range of subjects before spending more of their time on the subjects they enjoy in Year 9 (through our mini-options system) before choosing from over 20 GCSEs for Year 10.

Students in Sixth Form can choose from 25 A Level options including an Extended Project Qualification.

Sport. The playing fields, over 40 acres in extent, are used for the main boys' sports of rugby, football and cricket, and hockey and netball for girls; cross country, athletics, and tennis are also highly popular. The School site also boasts two AstroTurf pitches, five all-weather tennis courts, a shooting range and Sports Hall. The latter has four badminton courts, indoor cricket nets and facilities for fencing, table tennis, basketball and a dedicated fitness suite.

Co-Curricular Activities. The School's Co-Curricular programme blends inside the classroom with outside the classroom and is an extremely important part of the life and ethos of Wellingborough School. Pupils can choose from a wide variety of co-curricular activities, which aim to accommodate all abilities and most interests, at lunchtimes, after school and at weekends for all year groups.

During their time in the Prep School, the children can experience specialist dance lessons, individual music lessons, ensemble practices and frequent plays. Other activities include; Art, Chess, Lego, Gardening, Cookery, Choir, Jigsaw, Touch-typing, Mindfulness, Reading and many more.

Pupils in the Senior School participate in lunchtime enrichment activities such as forensic science, chess, dance, first aid and public speaking, community cohesion projects are also popular.

The School's Drama Department produces an annual production each year, recent performances have included *Les Misérables*, *Oliver* and *Sweeney Todd*. The Music Department benefits from a variety of visiting music teachers offering individual lessons and ensemble practices in 25 different instruments.

Pupils from Year 9 onwards join one of four CCF Sections: Royal Navy, Royal Marines, Army or Royal Air Force, with the aim of developing cadets' personal qualities and leadership skills. The School also offers pupils the opportunity to achieve the Duke of Edinburgh Award at Bronze, Silver or Gold levels.

Admission. All applications for entry should be made to Admissions.

Pastoral Care. In the Prep School pupils in Years 1–6 are assigned to one of six Clubs. The vertical structure of the Club system means that pupils of all ages integrate with one another and older pupils can share their experiences and help and support our younger pupils.

In the Senior School, all pupils are allocated a House on entry. The single-sex House system includes 4 boys' Houses and 3 girls' Houses. Each House has its own character, colour, charity and history and is led by a Housemaster or Housemistress. The School also has an award-winning Wellbeing Team offering guidance and support to pupils of all ages and their families.

Scholarships are offered to external candidates for entry at 11+ and 16+. These Scholarships are awarded in the following subjects; Academia, Music, Drama, Art & Photography and Sports. Applications are required by the beginning of January and assessments take place in the following weeks.

Bursaries. Wellingborough is a diverse and welcoming community, a School which believes that its fees should not present a barrier to children who are in a position to benefit from the opportunities that it offers. The School offers eligible parents or guardians financial assistance with tuition fees, usually aimed towards the Senior School. Bursaries are awarded as a discount of between 10% and 100% of tuition fees, depending upon the financial, compassionate or other pertinent circumstances of the applicants. The parents of over 60 Wellingborough School pupils, aged 11 to 18, are currently in receipt of a means-tested Bursary.

Fees per term (2021–2022). Preparatory School: £3,289 (Nursery & Reception), £3,436 (Years 1–2), £3,723 (Year 3) £4,661 (Year 4), £5,092 (Years 5–6); Senior School: £5,323 (Years 7–8), £5,586 (Years 9–13).

Term of Entry. New pupils are accepted throughout the year. The largest entry is in September at the beginning of each academic year.

Old Wellingburian Club. All former pupils who have spent at least one year in the School are eligible for membership. Correspondence should be addressed to the OW Club Secretary at the School.

Charitable status. Wellingborough School is a Registered Charity, number 1101485.

Governors:
Mr P Tyldesley, Esq, BA, MRICS (*Chairman*)
Mrs D Line, BA, CA, CA SA
Mrs C Bruce, MA
Mr I M Cantelo, BEng Hons, CEng, MIET
Dr C Duncan, MBBS, DRCOG, MRCGP
Mr N M Lashbrook, BA Hons
Mr S Marriott, Esq
Mr J Smith, BSc Hons, MRICS
Mr R Thakrar, Esq, BSc Hons, MBCS
Miss R Turner, BA Hons
Mr D Waller, Esq, MA Oxon, MA London

Staff:

Headmaster: **A N Holman**, MA Cantab, MEd

Bursar: N A Johnson, MA Cranfield
Head of the Prep School: K Owen, BSc Exeter
Deputy Head (Academic): C A Gamble, MA Cantab
Deputy Head (Operations): R Spiby, MA Cranfield
Deputy Head (Pastoral): Q Wiseman, BA Newcastle
Head of Lower Prep: R M Girling, BEd Cambridge
Deputy Head (Prep School): C Petrie, BSc Loughborough
Director of Learning & Teaching: S R Medd, BSc Durham

Wellington College

Duke's Ride, Crowthorne, Berkshire RG45 7PU

Tel:	The Master: 01344 444101
	Director of Admissions: 01344 444013
	Group Finance Director & Bursar: 01344 444020
	Reception: 01344 444000
email:	info@wellingtoncollege.org.uk
website:	www.wellingtoncollege.org.uk
Twitter:	@WellingtonUK
Facebook:	@WellingtonCollege

Set within 400 acres of stunning parkland in leafy Berkshire and less than an hour's drive from London and Heathrow, Wellington College is one of the UK's and the world's great co-educational boarding and day schools. It seeks to provide young people with the knowledge, skills, and character to serve and help shape a better world. Its innovative and interesting use of technology in the classroom, combined with its emphasis on pupil-centred learning, ensures that Wellington is at the forefront of educational advance.

A wonderful fusion of heritage and modernity characterises our educational philosophy. Our curriculum, facilities and teaching methods are constantly adapting to the challenges of preparing young people for the ever-changing world of the 21st century. Wellington College is a school which is dynamic in every sense of the word, and yet all that we do is rooted firmly in our five College values – kindness, respect, courage, integrity and responsibility – values which underpin every aspect of life at Wellington.

Organisation. There are approximately 1,090 pupils, with 610 boys and 480 girls, spread across all age groups. All pupils belong to one of seventeen houses, seven of which are located in the main College buildings and ten in the grounds. Fifteen of the houses accommodate the 80%+ who board at Wellington as well as a handful of day pupils. There are also two specific day houses, one each for girls and for boys. 13+ boarders share rooms in their first year, and may do so in a second or third year, but then move on to their own room. There is a central dining hall with modern kitchens and serveries. Meals are taken here on a cafeteria basis by most of the pupils although some houses outside the main buildings have their own dining facilities. The V&A café is also open during school hours for drinks and snacks. The school has its own medical officer and a 9-bed health centre constantly staffed by fully-qualified nurses.

Pastoral. Wellington prides itself on the outstanding levels of pastoral support we offer our pupils. Pupil and staff-led Mental Health initiatives, alongside our nationally recognised Wellbeing curriculum not only help our pupils successfully navigate their teenage years, but also prepare them for healthy, happy and successful lives after school. House life lies at the heart of each pupil's experience, and it comes as no surprise that every Wellingtonian is convinced that their house is the best. Housemasters and housemistresses, dedicated tutor teams, matrons and housekeepers all ensure that the House truly is a home away from home.

Academic. Wellingtonians study GCSEs, followed by the IB Diploma or A Levels and, whichever route they take, results are superb: in 2021, 96% of A Level grades were A*–B and the IB cohort achieved an incredible 41.2 average, with 13 students achieving the maximum 45 points. At GCSE, 78% of grades were 9/8, 94% 9–7 and 99% 9–6. 100 Wellingtonians have been offered Oxbridge places over the past four years, while on average 25–30 move on each year to American universities, including several to Ivy League universities.

Sport. The College has an outstanding reputation for girls' and boys' sport with nearly 30 different activities offered with emphasis equally placed on both performance and participation. Despite the inevitable difficulties caused by the pandemic, 2020/21 was a year which saw the College community come together with an imaginative mixture of online activities during lockdown periods, and a range of internal fixtures and competitions when physically back at school, including the launch of 'The Wellington Premier League', an inclusive multi-sport rugby, football and hockey league hotly contested by all age groups in the school. The year still saw many individuals gain national or international honours across 14 different sports, with several going on to take up professional contracts, scholarships at US universities and places on UK-based performance squads, particularly in target shooting, rugby and hockey.

Performing Arts. Performing Arts are equally strong. Music and drama are stunning, with nearly two-thirds of pupils taking lessons in musical instruments or LAMDA. During the recent pandemic, the Arts have been as active as ever releasing content on our YouTube channel and performing concerts and competitions to audiences via live stream. Prior to the pandemic our choir went on tour to Germany and other activities included the recording of carols by the Chapel Choir, an orchestral recording, the annual musical, contemporary Shakespeare productions and imaginative and inclusive junior plays. Dance enjoys a purpose-designed studio and two spectacular shows each year play to packed houses. Wellington's impressive 900-seat Performing Arts Centre opened in 2018. It is no surprise that Wellington has been awarded Artsmark Gold.

Co-curricular. Leadership, service to others and developing an international outlook are also central to the College's core values which is why co-curricular activities include CCF, Duke of Edinburgh's Award, and a pioneering Global Social Leaders scheme, in which pupils learn to create and run innovative social action projects, tackling local and global issues

Clubs and societies range from Amnesty International to the fully co-ed Field Gun team, from WTV (Wellington's own television company) and its pupil-run radio station, DukeBox to a full range of more traditional pastimes such as Photography, Creative Writing and Model United Nations.

Admission to the School. Most pupils enter the school in September (at the start of Year 9) when they are between 13 and 14 years of age. There are occasionally places available for pupils at 14+ (Year 10). Around 50 pupils also join the College for the Sixth Form (applications open at the end of Year 10). Registration (with £300 fee) is online. Those registered for 13+ entry (by the end of Year 5) sit the ISEB Common Pre-Test in the Michaelmas term of Year 6. Selection for a subsequent assessment day (usually in the Lent term of Year 6) is based in small part on the results of the Pre-Test and in much larger part on a school reference. Those who are successful are then offered a place conditional on a satisfactory reference from their current school at the end of Year 8. A waiting list also operates. Where appropriate, an overseas deposit is also payable.

Scholarships. Detailed information about the scholarships available on entry at age 13+ or 16+ can be found on our website. Scholarships at 13+ are only awarded in Academics and Music. The most prestigious, named Academic scholarships and scholarships in other disciplines (Art, Drama, Dance and Sport) are awarded at the end of Year 9 to reward not only ability but also scholarly attitude. Students are invited to participate in Inspire Days in their areas of particular interest during Year 8.

For entry at 16+, scholarships are awarded in all of the above areas as part of the full application process.

As well as it being a great honour and accolade, pupils awarded scholarships upon entry to the College, and those awarded at the end of Year 9, are expected to be leaders and role models within their field of interest. They will also take part in a programme of extension activities and opportunities appropriate to their particular area of talent. Music scholars, for example, attend regular masterclasses with visiting professionals and Academic award holders partake in an extension programme of study designed by our Director of Academic Extension.

Scholarships do not carry any financial benefit. The only exception to this is Music Scholarships which allow for free tuition in two instruments and free composition and Alexander Technique lessons.

Fee-assisted Places. Widening access to Wellington is at the heart of the Governors' and Master's vision for the future of the College. All financial aid in terms of fee reduction is therefore awarded via a means-testing procedure (details on our website and from the Bursar's Office). Our aim is to enable an increasing number of families, who otherwise would not be able to afford the fees at Wellington, to send their son or daughter to the College. Means-tested bursaries may be up to 100% of College fees, depending on individual family circumstances.

Foundation Places. Very generous remission, including free places based on means-testing, are available for the sons and daughters of deceased military servicemen and servicewomen and of others who have died in acts of selfless bravery, subject to entry requirement and according to the rules of the Foundation. Further details are available from the Bursar's Office.

Fees per term (2021–2022). Boarders £14,210, Day (in boarding House) £11,920, Day £10,380. Separate charges totalling £332.50 per instrument are made for musical tuition (10 lessons). The school runs an attractive fees in advance scheme for parents with capital sums available.

The Wellington Community. Our role is to build a supportive, global professional and social network of students, Old Wellingtonians, parents (current and past), grandparents, staff and partner schools. We deliver a diverse programme of engagement events and offer careers support, guidance and mentoring opportunities by drawing on our incredible resources within the Community; we truly champion the diverse skill sets our unique Community has to offer. We also run Wellington College's own networking website, Wellington Connect, where all members of our Wellington Community can share expertise, find (or offer) mentoring opportunities, and make connections with friends past and present. To find out more please email the Wellington Community office on community@wellingtoncollege.org.uk or go to the Wellington Community website www.wellycom.net or sign up to Wellington Connect at www.wellingtonconnect.co.uk

The Wellington Group. A significant feature of Wellington is its outward-looking, expansive approach to education. Wellington's family of schools includes its prep school Eagle House, five schools in China and one in Thailand. Wellington was the first HMC school to be accredited as a Teaching School and now partners a broad range of local state schools. All of this provides pupils and staff with meaningful opportunities for partnership and service within national and international communities.

Further information including details of Visitors Days can be found on the website, and the Admissions Office can be contacted on 01344 444013.

Charitable status. Wellington College is a Registered Charity, number 309093. It exists to provide education for boys and girls aged 13–18.

Visitor: Her Majesty The Queen

President: HRH The Duke of Kent, KG, GCMG, GCVO, ADC, DL

Vice-President & Chairman of Governors: Mr William Jackson, MA

Ex officio Governors:
The Archbishop of Canterbury, MA, BA, DipMin
Arthur Charles Valerian Wellesley, 9th Duke of Wellington, MA, Hon DLitt, OBE, DL

Governors:
Ron Dennis, CBE
Mrs Gabriela Galceran Ball
James Garvey, BA, BAI, MA
Mrs Felicity Kirk, LLB
Dr Christie Marr, BA Hons, MSc, DPhil, MBA
Mrs Jill May, BA
Mrs Emma McKendrick, BA, FRSA
Mark Milliken-Smith, QC
Ms Virginia Rhodes, BA Hons
Duncan Ritchie, FCA
Ms Helen Stevenson, MA
The Rt Hon The Lord Strathclyde, CH
Lt Gen Sir Christopher Tickell, KBE, MA

Master: **James Dahl**, MA

Second Master: Mrs Cressida Henderson, BA
Senior Master: Matt Oakman, BA
Director of Admissions: Ed Venables, BA
Deputy Head (Academic): Benjamin Evans, BSc
Deputy Head (Co-curricular): Iain Sutcliffe, MA, MBA
Deputy Head (Educational Developments & Partnerships): Iain Henderson, BA
Deputy Head (Pastoral & Wellbeing): David Walker, BSc Hons
Deputy Head (Safeguarding): Mrs Delyth Lynch, BSc
Deputy Head (Teaching Staff Performance & Development): Mrs Katy Granville-Chapman, BA, MSc

Assistant Staff:
* *Head of Department/Year*
† *Housemaster/mistress*

Art:
*Mrs Alice Carpenter, BA Hons
Miss Sally-Anne Burt, BA
Mrs Bethan Carr, BA
Ms Amy Flanagan, BA
Jonathan Nickisson-Richards, MFA, BA Hons
Ms Janette Pyke, BA

Archie Wardlaw, BA
Miss Sara Wallis, BA (*Art History*)

Biology:
*Mrs Astrid Edmunds, BSc
Freddie Edmunds, BSc
Edward Hulbert, BA
Sam Laing, MSc
†Miss Kate Larkin, BA
Svend Larsen, BSc, MEd
Mrs Abigail Patterson, MA
Mrs Miranda Patterson, BSc (*Director of Science,
    Technology & Engineering*)
Greg Pienaar, BSc
Mrs Emma Poynter, BSc
Dr Harry Wright, BSc, PhD

Business:
*Simon Roundell, MA
Antony Adams, BA

Chemistry:
*Dr Caroline Evans, MChem, PhD
Dr Christopher Davison, PhD
Richard Gregory, BSc Hons
Ms Katherine Holder, MChem
†Mrs Rachel Loaring, BSc
Dr Julian O'Loughlin, MSc, PhD (*Director of Digital
    Learning*)
Stephen Simkin, BSc
David Wilson, MA

Classics:
*Dr Matthew Johncock, MA, PhD
†Simon Allcock, MA
Patrick Caffrey, BA Hons
Dr Rob Cromarty, MA, PhD
Mrs Alexandra Howe, MA, MPhil
Dr Emma Ramsey, MA, PhD (*Careers*)
Miss Caitlin Spencer, MA

Computer Science:
Stephen Barraclough, BSc
Miss Chelsey Cole
Paul Jennings, BSc (*Teaching School*)

Dance:
*Mrs Caroline Kenworthy, BA
*Mrs Clare Cooke, BA
Mrs Tory East
Ms Hannah Horton

Design, Engineering & Technology:
*Robert Winter, BSc
John Carrington, BEng
Mark Ellwood, BEd
Sam Wilson, BSc

Drama:
*Nick Huntington, BA Hons
Ms Claire Anderson, BA
Mrs Katie Hamilton, BA (*LAMDA*)
Alexander Mancuso, BA
Ms Melissa Price, BA

Economics:
*Dushy Clarke, BA, MSc
Mrs Emmie Bidston, BA (*Director of Wellington
    Leadership & Coaching Institute*)
Mrs Amanda Campion, MA (*Director of Academic
    Extension*)

Chris Ewart, MA
Thomas Massey, BSc
Mrs Julia Sutcliffe, BA (*Middle School*)
John Whitworth, BA

English:
*Ms Estella Gutulan, BA
†George Bilclough, MA
Miss Jessica Brown, BA
Ms Nancy Cho, BA Hons, MA, PhD
John Craig, MA (*Third Form*)
Tim Head, BA
Dr Carl Hendrick, MA, PhD
Miss Rachael Kirby, BA
Dr Ruth Lexton, BA, MPhil, PhD (*Oxbridge*)
Miss Erynn Oliver, MA
Miss Alexandra Russell, AB, MPhil
Miss Flora Sagers, MA
Ms Natalie Smith, BA
Dr Gavin Sourgen, MLitt, DPhil
Miss Kirsty Tyrrell, BA
Mrs Jo Wayman, BA
†Tom Wayman, BA, MPhil

Geography:
*Timothy Rothwell, MA
Jim Dewes, MA
Christopher Foyle, BA
†Jack Murray, BA
Miss Alice Taylor, BA

History:
*Ben Lewsley, BA (*HE & International Universities*)
Dr Victoria Gardner, BA, MLitt, DPhil (*Upper School*)
†Sam Gutteridge, MA
Philip Joy, MA
Tristan Macleod, BA
Hugh Pickering-Carter, BA, MSc (*& Politics*)
Miss Lucy Robb, MA
Mrs Chloe Whitelaw, BA, MPhil

Mathematics:
*Paul Cootes, MA, MSc
Richard Atherton, BSc, MPhil (*IB*)
Dr Narinder Basra, BSc, PhD
Gareth Benjamin, MMath
Justin Biggs, BCom
†Mike Cawdron, BSc
†Alexis Christodoulou, MA
Mrs Sarah Dalton, BSc Hons
Miss Clare Edwards, BA
Miss Helen Gray, BSc
Mrs Debbie Hathaway, BSc
Bob Jones, BSc (*Expeditions & Adventure*)
Kyle McDonald, BSc
Nathan O'Neill, BA
James Parrott, BA Hons
John Rawlinson, BSc
Qasim Sayed, MPhys, MEd
George Wells, BA (*HPQ*, *EPQ*)
Jonathan White, BA

Modern Foreign Languages:
*Dr Rachelle Kirkham, MA, PhD (*Director of Teaching &
    Learning*)
Mrs Sandra Aktas, BA, BSc (*French*)
Miss Katharina Auer, MA
Mrs Tanya Bateson, MA Hons
Mike Denhart, BA Hons

Mrs Sandrine Duff, MA
Ms Aurora Gomez, BA
Miss Georgie Grubb, BA
†Mrs Polly Gutteridge, MA
Mrs Christelle Hutchinson, BA
Ms Yasmine Jaoui, MA Hons
†Mrs Sophie Jobson, Lic d'Anglais, Dip d'Étude IFI
Mrs Katie Johnston, BA, MMus
Simon Kirkham, BA Hons (*German*)
Mrs Ningning Ma, MA (*International & Overseas
    Students*)
†Mrs Sarah MacKenzie, BA Hons
Charles Oliphant-Callum, MA
†Sam Owen, BA
†Oliver Peat, BA
Mrs Yunyun Tang, MA
Ms Emily Thomas, BA Hons
Mrs Catherine Willis-Phillips, MA (*Spanish*)

Music:
*Simon Williamson, MA, FRCO (*Director of Music &
    Arts*)
Anthony Bailey, BMus Hons, MMus
Nick Burrage, BA Hons
George de Voil, MA, FRCO
Michael Doran, ARAM
Sean Farrell, BA
Mrs Libby Fisher, MA
Jonathan Heeley, BMus Hons, MMus
Mrs Susanne Henwood, GRSM Hons, LRAM, ALCM

plus 50 visiting instrumental teachers.

Philosophy & Religion:
*Tom Kirby, BA, MSt
Mrs Jessica Goves, BA
Fr Adrian Stark-Ordish, BA
Dr James Tapley, BSc, MA, PhD (*Theory of Knowledge*)
Goulwenn Vincendeau, Diplome de Licence
Mrs Eleanor Winders, BA Hons

Physical Education:
*Dan Pratt, MSc (*Director of Sport*)
†Ms Adele Brown, BEd
Ms Brooke Cantwell, BPhEd
Mrs Jane Grillo, BEd (*PE*)
†Phillip Mann, BSc
Will O'Brien, BA
Mrs Kate Pratt, BSc
†Charlie Sutton, BA Hons
Ryan Tulley, BA, BSc

Physics:
*Adam Hicks, MEng
Mrs Tamara Christodoulou, BA
Dr Will Heathcote, MPhys, DPhil (*Director of
    Organisation*)
Tim Holmes, MSci, MSc
Solomon Lawes, BSc
Ms Jessica Lawrence, BSc
Ms Agnes Martin, MPhys
Joshua Webber, BSc
Mike Yuan, MPhys

Politics:
*Paul Dunne, BA, MSc
Dr Anthony Coates, MA, PhD
Daniel Richards, BA Hons

Psychology:
*Miss Sophia Candappa, BSc
Mrs Josie Long, BSc
David Rea, BSc

Wellbeing:
*Ian Morris, BA
†Gareth Carr

Academic Support:
*Mrs Kam Opie, BSc, MSc, SpLD Diploma
Ms Melissa Knight, BA, MSc

Houses and Housemasters/mistresses:
Anglesey: Mrs Rachel Loaring
Apsley: Alexis Christodoulou
Benson: Simon Allcock
Beresford: George Bilclough
Blücher: Sam Owen
Combermere: Mrs Sarah MacKenzie
Hardinge: Mrs Sophie Jobson
Hill: Phillip Mann
Hopetoun: Mrs Polly Gutteridge and Sam Gutteridge
Lynedoch: Mike Cawdron
Murray: Oliver Peat
Orange: Tom Wayman
Picton: Jack Murray
Raglan: Gareth Carr
Stanley: Charlie Sutton
Talbot: Ms Adele Brown
Wellesley: Miss Kate Larkin

CC CCF: Sam Wilson, BSc
Chaplain: Fr Adrian Stark-Ordish, BA
Chief Operating Officer: Stephen Crouch, BA, ACA
Operations Bursar: Brian Cannon, MSyl, MCGI
Estates Bursar: Edwin Wai, BA Hons, MSc
Director of Finance: Paul Thompson, MA, ACMA
Head of the Wellington Community: Murray Lindo, BA,
    MA, MSc, CIPD
Head of Prince Albert Foundation: Ms Sarah Miller
Legal & Compliance Director: Mrs Katherine Baker, MA
International Director: Scott Bryan
Director of IT Services & Development: Tony Whelton
Medical Officer: Dr Helen Rutherford
Health Centre Sister: Mrs Tracey Coles
Head of Student Emotional Health & Wellbeing: Dr Jenny
    Griggs
Head of Marketing: Mrs Vicky Williams
Registrar: Mrs Louise Peate, BSc
EA to the Master: Mrs Angela Reed
Bursary Assistant: Mrs Lisa Thompson

Wellington School

South St, Wellington, Somerset TA21 8NT

Tel:	01823 668800
	01823 668803
email:	admissions@wellington-school.org.uk
website:	www.wellington-school.org.uk
Twitter:	@wellingtonsch1
Facebook:	@WellingtonSchool
Instagram:	@wellingtonschool1

Motto: *Nisi dominus frustra*

Founded in 1837, Wellington School is a co-educational, academically selective school providing a friendly, disciplined environment and a wide range of co-curricular opportunities.

Situation. Located on the southern edge of Wellington, at the foot of the Blackdown Hills, this fully co-educational School is equidistant from Tiverton Parkway and Taunton Railway Stations. The M5 approach road (Junction 26) is within a mile. Currently there are 600 pupils in the Lower and Upper Schools (11–18 years), of whom 20% board.

Buildings. The School has witnessed an extensive building programme over recent years with a state-of-the-art study centre in the Duke's Building, brand new floodlit all-weather hockey pitch, refurbished Sixth Form Centre and cafe.

The John Kendall-Carpenter Science Centre has state-of-the-art laboratories and lecture theatre, a multimillion pound sports complex, a purpose-built Prep School and a new classroom block and examination hall. Major improvements to Performing Arts facilities, including a new foyer and theatre space, were completed in 2010. In 2017 a new junior girls' boarding house with en-suite rooms was opened.

Grounds. There are 35 acres of playing fields as well as a new floodlit all-weather hockey pitch, squash courts, an indoor swimming pool and a climbing wall.

Houses. There are mixed Houses including Day and Boarding pupils, with many inter-house competitions. In addition, there are 5 boarding houses in total.

There is a central Dining Hall and all meals are served on a cafeteria basis. The School also has its own well equipped laundry.

There is a fully equipped Health Centre, with a trained staff under the direction of the School Medical Officer.

Academic Organisation. The School is divided into the Lower School (Year 7–9), Upper School (Year 9–Year 11) and the Sixth Form. The Prep School (Nursery–Year 6) is on a separate, adjoining campus.

Most pupils enter the Senior School at Year 7, 9 or 12. The curriculum in Years 7, 8 and 9 is designed to allow pupils to develop the skills needed to succeed at GCSE and features a good range of practical and more academic subjects including Latin. At GCSE all pupils study English, English Literature and Mathematics as well as a Modern Foreign Language and a further five or six subjects. Pupils have a free choice of studying three sciences separately or as Dual Award Science. The Mathematics and Science courses lead to IGCSE qualifications. The most able mathematicians take IGCSE at the end of Year 10 before taking Additional Mathematics in Year 11. Students have a free choice from a wide range of subjects in the Sixth Form as well as the Extended Project Qualification. A system of grades every term and tutor groups ensure that academic monitoring of pupils is supportive and effective.

Religious Education is part of the curriculum in the Lower School and is an option for study at GCSE and A Level. The School is Christian in tradition and there is a short Act of Worship in the School Chapel on each weekday with a longer Sunday service. The content and form of these services are based on contemporary Anglican procedures. Attendance is expected although sensitivity is shown towards pupils of other faiths for whom alternative provision can be made.

Music. Tuition is available on all orchestral instruments, as well as piano, organ, drum kit and percussion, classical and electric guitars and voice. The department consists of 2 full-time, 1 part-time and 25 specialist instrumental staff. The School is equipped with Bosendorfer and Yamaha pianos. There is a large Rodgers Digital Organ in the Chapel. Some 30 ensembles rehearse each week, giving plentiful opportunities to performers of all ages and all instruments. The department currently runs a wide range of choirs of various genres including the renowned Chapel Choir. Concerts of all kinds take place throughout each term and world class musicians to the School to give recitals and masterclasses. Pupils are entered for ABRSM, Trinity Guildhall and Rockschool exams each term.

Physical Education and Games. Pioneering Sport and Wellbeing Department with all pupils playing games regularly, unless exempt for medical reasons. Wellbeing, which is also part of the curriculum for Years 7 to 11, takes place in the Sports Complex and includes nutrition, psychology and mental health alongside activities such as judo and body-pump with the aim of embedding physical activity as part of a healthy lifestyle. All pupils learn to swim and are given the opportunity to take part in as many sports as possible. In the winter term, rugby and hockey are the main sports; in the spring term hockey, netball and cross-country running; in the summer term athletics, girls and boys cricket, tennis and swimming. Team practices take place throughout the week with matches on Saturday afternoons.

Out of School and CCF Activities. All pupils from Year 10 upwards either join the large CCF contingent, with army, naval and RAF sections, or are engaged in Citizens Wellington with volunteering activities on a weekly basis, ranging from community services and conservation, to music, art and creative activities such as producing school radio podcasts. Outdoor Education, both within the CCF and as part of the School's extensive programme to introduce all students from Year 7 upwards, includes camping trips, Duke of Edinburgh's Award and climbing and caving clubs are very popular, with many trips organised for all year groups. The CCF also has a highly respected Corps of Drums, which frequently features in local ceremonial events. Societies, in addition to the above, include art, chess and drama at various levels, STEM, computing and others.

Careers. A careers and higher education coordinator offers a guidance service including visits to and from employers and universities, a careers speed-dating event, careers talks, a careers networking dinner and careers fair with local schools.

Entry. Entrance exam for Year 7, 9 and Sixth Form. There is a registration fee of £100 for all pupils and a refundable deposit of £400.

Scholarships and Bursaries. A number of academic and sport, drama and art and design scholarships are offered each year for entry at 11+ and 13+. Music scholarships are awarded for entry at 11+, 13+ and above. Awards may be increased by an income-related bursary. A small number of awards are offered for the Sixth Form.

Fees per term (2021–2022). Boarders £10,120–£10,930, Weekly Boarders £8,425–£8,865, International Boarders £10,930–£11,785. Fees include tuition, board, laundry, medical attention and Health Centre and books. Day pupils £4,935–£5,595 (excluding lunch).

Extras. Apart from purely personal expenses, the termly extras are private music lessons from £31.00 per 40 minutes; EAL lessons at various rates depending on need.

Charitable status. Wellington School is a Registered Charity, number 1161447. It aims to provide a happy, caring co-educational day and boarding community, where pupils are provided with the opportunity of making best use of their academic experience and the School enrichment activities, in order to enhance their overall preparation for life after the age of eighteen.

Governing Body:

Chairman: Mrs A Govey, MSc
Joint Vice Chairmen: Mr J Hester, BEd Hons Cantab
Mr R Palfrey, MA, PGC
Mrs S Page, MA, PGCE
Rear Admiral R Harding, CBE, FRAeS
Mr L Howell, OBE, QFSM
Mr D James, MEng, CEng, MiMechE, MBA Ess
Mr P Tait, MA
Mrs S Vigus-Hollingsworth, FCA, FALA
Mr J Vick, MA, PGCE
Miss S Merry, BSc, RGN

Headmaster: **Mr Eugene du Toit**, MA, MBA

Academic Deputy Head: Dr H Barker, BA Hons, PhD
Deputy Head (Pastoral): Mr R MacNeary, BA Hons, MA
Head of Sixth Form: Mrs L MacAlister, BA Hons
Head of Lower School and Co-curricular: Mr N Renyard, MSc, PGCE QTS
Head of Upper School: Mrs S A Dean, BA, PGCE
Head of Boarding: Mrs L Tabb, BSc, PGCE

Academic Staff:
Ms A Akhtar, PGCE, MA, BA
Miss E Argiros, BA
Mr C A Askew, BA, PGCE
Miss E Barclay
Dr H Barker, BA Hons, PhD
Mrs K Bishop, BA Hons, MA, PGCE
Dr S Bremner, BA, MA, PhD
Mr P J Buckingham, MA, PGCE
Mr S Campbell, CELTA, MBA, BA, PGCE
Mr J Caulfield, BA, QTS
Mrs N Clewes, BEng Hons, PGCE
Mr D A Colclough, BSc, PGCE
Mr D Cole, BA
Mr M Cole, BEng Hons, PGCE
Miss M Collins, BA, MA, PGCE
Mr S Costello, BA Hons, PGCE
Mrs V Daley, BSc, PGCE
Mrs C Davies, BA, PGCE
Mrs S A Dean, BSc, PGCE
Mr M E Downes, BSc, PGCE
Mr B Elkins, BD Hons, PGCE
Mrs S D'Rozario BA, MA, PGCE
Mr G Durston, BSc Hons
Mr T Fasham, BSc, PGCE
Mrs C Foster, BA Hons
Dr P T Galley, BSc, DIC, PhD, PGCE
Mr W Garrett, BA, PGCE
Mr A Gerolemou, BA, MA
Mr L Greany, BSc Hons, PGCE
Miss E Greenway, BSc Hons, PGCE
Mr E Grey, BSc Hons, PGCE, Prof GCE
Mrs E Gumbrell, FdA, BA, PGCE
Mrs L Gurney, BSc
Mrs S Harrod-Booth, BEng, PGCE, MA
Mr C Hamilton, MChem, ACA, PGCE
Mrs I Hare, BA Hons, PGCE

Mrs L Hayward, BSc
Miss F E Hobday, MA
Dr K A Hodson, BA, MA
Mr G Horner, BA
Mr B House, BSc
Miss A Howell, BSc, PGCE
Mr J Ilett, BA, PGCE
Miss M Jago, BA
Mrs C James, BA Hons, PGCE
Mr T Johns, MBA, PGCE, BSc
Dr A R Jolliffe, BA, MA, DPhil
Mr S Jones, BSc, PGCE
Mrs T Kaya, BA, TESOL
Mr P Lawrence
Mr J-M Legg, BA, PGCE
Mrs L E Leonard, BA
Mrs L MacAlister, BA Hons
Mr R MacNeary, BA
Miss R L Marsden, BA, PGCE
Mr R Marsh, BA, PGCE
Mrs C Merrett, PGCE, BA
Miss S Middleton, BA, PGCE
Mr D Millington, BA, MSc, PGCE
Mr A Moy, BSc Hons, PGCE
Mr A Phillips, BSc, PGCE
Mr H Phillips, BEd
Ms G Redman, BA Hons
Mr N Renyard, MSc, BA, PGCE
Miss H Richards, BSc Hons, QTS
Mrs T Robertson, BA Hons, MPhil, PGCE
Mr C J Sampson, BMus
Mr T Sampson
Mrs A Sands, MA Hons, PGCE
Miss K Sass, BA Hons, PGCE
Miss E Scott, BSc, PGCE
Mr I Schmidt, BA, PGCE
Mr A C Shaw, BA, MSci, PGCE, LCGI
Mrs R Shaw, LTCL, GTCL
Mr R E Stevens, BSocSc, PGCE
Mrs R Stratton, BA
Mrs L Tabb, BSc, PGCE
Miss S F L Toase, BSc, MSB, CBiol, PGCE
Mr A J Trewhella, BA, ARCO
Miss R Watson, MSc Hons, PGCE
Mr S West, BA, BSc, PGCE, MSc
Miss G Withers, LAMBA, BA, PGCE
Mr A Wilson, BA
Mr T Waller, BMus Hons, MA

Head of Admissions: Mrs R Debenham, BA, FCIPD
Medical Officer: Dr R Yates

Wells Cathedral School

The Liberty, Wells, Somerset BA5 2ST

Tel: 01749 834200
email: admissions@wells.cathedral.school
website: https://wells.cathedral.school
Twitter: @wellscathschool
Facebook: @wellscathedralschool
Instagram: @wellscathedralschool

In 909AD Wells Cathedral School was formed to provide education for the choir boys at Wells Cathedral. Today, Wells Cathedral School is a family-orientated co-educational boarding and day school for 2–18 year olds which provides an all-round education alongside world-class Specialist Music and Chorister training. Their vision is to inspire every individual pupil to nurture their talents in a vibrant, creative, spiritual and stimulating environment to become a responsible global citizen. Their core values are Creativity, Aspiration, Responsibility and Endeavour (CARE).

There is a Senior and Junior School with over 700 boys and girls aged from 2 to 18. Boarders number around 260, whilst the remainder are day pupils; there is a 50:50 split of boarders to day pupils in the Senior School, and a Prep School aged boarding option for pupils from Years 4–8. Once accepted, a child normally remains in the School without further Entrance Examination until the age of 18+.

Fees per term (2021–2022). Sixth Form: Boarders £11,404, Day £6,814. Years 10–11: Boarders £11,151, Day £6,658. Years 7–9: Boarders £10,738, Day £6,436. Years 4–6: Boarders £8,502–£9,438; Day £4,638–£5,573; Reception–Year 3: £2,770–£4,171. Nursery: various sessions available.

Scholarships and Bursaries. Scholarships are awarded to recognise current talent and potential in the fields of Academics, Art, Drama, Mathematics, General Music (for those not looking to join our Specialist Music Scheme) and Sport, for pupils joining the School in Years 7, 9, 10 and Lower Sixth. In addition to a financial award of up to 50% for truly exceptional candidates (the majority of Scholars are awarded 10%), Scholars receive enhanced educational opportunities and privileges to help them develop their talents. In addition, means-tested bursaries may also be available. The deadline to apply is early January. Scholarship Days are held later in the month, and decisions are announced in February.

For pre-professional musicians wishing to join our Specialist Music Programme, we offer a number of music awards based upon the standard and quality of applicants (assessed at Music Auditions held three times throughout the year) and individual financial circumstances. We also offer places to 'general' musicians who might wish to take advantage of the wealth of musical opportunity here, but who might not wish to enrol on the Specialist pathway.

The School is one of only four in England designated by the Department for Education to provide specialist musical education. The DfE therefore provides generous assistance (up to 100% of fees) with tuition, boarding and music fees for up to 80 gifted musicians per year. These grants are means-tested according to parental income, and are provided by the DfE Music & Dance Scheme.

In addition, all choristers automatically benefit from a 25% discount on tuition fees and a 50% discount on boarding fees, and may also be considered for further bursaries and financial assistance (on average, Choristers receive around 50% off their School fees). Once they have left the Choir at the end of Year 9 (or sometimes earlier if voice changes necessitate) they receive a discount worth 5% of their School fees for each year they were in the Choir, worth up to 20%, for the rest of their time at the School. Formal choral trials and academic entrance tests take place in October, although we welcome enquiries and applications at any point. Special arrangements can be made for children from overseas.

For further details of awards, contact the Admissions team, Tel: 01749 834441, email: admissions@wells.cathedral.school.

Situations and Buildings. The medieval city of Wells, with its famous Cathedral and a population of only 10,500, is the smallest city in England. It is just over 20 miles from Bath and Bristol where there is a good rail service, and easily accessed from the M4 and M5 motorways. Bristol International Airport is a 40-minute drive away.

The School occupies all but one of the canonical houses in The Liberty, keeping its medieval and 18th-century atmosphere, whilst providing for the needs of modern boarding education. There are modern classrooms and science laboratories built amongst walled gardens. There is a 25-metre covered swimming pool, tennis and netball courts, brand new astroturf pitch, three sports fields and an all-weather hard play area. A sports hall provides indoor facilities for tennis, badminton, cricket, basketball, volleyball, hockey, five-a-side football, climbing and a multi-gym. There are theatrical and concert facilities, including an award-winning concert hall, a music technology centre, a computer studies centre, art, design and technology department, drama studio, dance studio, library and sixth form centre.

There are eight boarding houses; one for prep boarders, one for Upper Sixth boarders and a further six in the Senior School, three for boys and three for girls, the most senior pupils having study-bedrooms. The aim is to give security to the younger pupils and to develop a sense of responsibility in the older pupils.

Organisation and Curriculum. Despite its national and international reputation, the School has retained close links with the local community, and its fundamental aim is to provide all pupils with an education consistent with the broad principles of Christianity. More specifically, the School aims to be a well-regulated community in which pupils may learn to live in harmony and mutual respect with each other and with the adults who care for them. The curriculum has been designed to enable all children who gain entry to the School to develop fully all their abilities, and to take their place in due course in tertiary education and the adult community of work and leisure.

The emphasis is on setting by ability in particular subjects rather than streaming. There is every attempt to avoid early specialisation. There is a Sixth Form of some 200 taking A Level courses in all major academic subjects.

The majority of pupils take up places at Russell Group Universities, with between 5 and 10% of the Upper Sixth being offered places each year at Oxford and Cambridge. The majority of Music Specialists will be offered places at the leading conservatoires in the UK and globally, often with scholarship awards.

Societies. There is a wide range of indoor and outdoor activities in which pupils must participate, although the choice is theirs. Outdoor education is an important part of the curriculum. Besides a Combined Cadet Force with Army and Navy sections, and a Duke of Edinburgh's Award scheme, activities as diverse as photography, sailing and golf are also on offer. Ballet and riding lessons can also be arranged.

Music. The School is one of four in England designated and grant-aided by the Department for Education (DfE) to provide special education for gifted young musicians, who are eligible for substantial financial assistance. Wells is unique in that both specialist and non-specialist musicians are able to develop their aptitudes within a normal school environment. These talents are widely acknowledged by audiences at concerts given by pupils from Wells throughout the world.

There are over 130 talented pupils following specially devised timetables which combine advanced instrumental tuition and ensemble work with academic opportunity. More than half of the School learns at least one musical instrument. Children in Year 1 are given the opportunity to learn a string instrument, usually cello or violin, as part of their music curriculum, which they can choose to continue in Year 2 as a paid lesson should they wish. Pupils receive the highest quality teaching, often leading to music conservatoires and a career in music. Central to specialist music training are the opportunities to perform in public and there is a full concert diary. There are also regular concerts by the many ensembles in the School.

The Wellensian Association. Old Wellensians, Wells Cathedral School, Wells, Somerset BA5 2ST.

Charitable status. Wells Cathedral School Limited is a Registered Charity, number 310212. It is a charitable trust for the purpose of promoting the cause of education in accordance with the doctrine of the Church of England.

Patron: HRH The Prince of Wales

Governors:
Chairman: The Very Revd Dr John Davies
The Revd Canon Nicholas Jepson-Biddle
The Revd Canon Dr Robert James
Prebendary Barbara Bates
Prebendary Harry Musselwhite
Mr David Brown, OBE
Mr Andrew Campbell-Orde
Mr Martin Cooke
Mr Andrew Gummer
Mr Tim Lewis
Mr Robert Powell
Mr Kris Robbetts
Mrs Elizabeth Shelton

Head Master: Alastair Tighe

Deputy Head (Pastoral): Martin Ashton
Deputy Head (Academic): Natalie Perry
Director of Music: Mark Stringer

Senior School

Teaching Staff:
Claudia Alabiso (*Modern Foreign Languages*)
Alison Armstrong (*Deputy Director of Music*)
Martin Ashton (*English, Media Studies, Christian Union*)
Lucy Balderson (*Music, Head of Year 10/11, Retention Officer*)

Julia Bird (*Head of EAL, Head of Upper Sixth Form, including WISC, Houseparent Ritchie*)
Danielle Blunden (*Learning Support*)
Jeremy Boot (*Head of Humanities, Geography*)
Neil Bowen (*Head of English*)
Harvey Brink (*Head of Academic Music*)
Simon Broderick (*History with Politics*)
Kate Brown (*Modern Foreign Languages*)
Ross Brown (*Coordinator of Brass Studies*)
John Byrne (*Head of Keyboard*)
Louise Cannon (*Dance*)
Glenn Channing (*Head of Rugby*)
Nicola Connock (*Head of Mathematics*)
Jack Coward (*Music Technology*)
Sarah Cowell (*EAL*)
Lou Cox (*Speech & Drama*)
Giles Crist (*Mathematics*)
Andrew Davies (*Religion, Philosophy & Ethics, Cross country*)
Shelley Deans (*Drama, Dance*)
Jules Desmarchelier (*Director of Languages*)
Mark Dignum (*Head of Learning Support*)
Christopher Dine (*Physics*)
Luke Dosanjh (*EAL*)
Victoria Dury (*MFL*)
Christopher Eldridge (*Head of History*)
Stuart Elks (*Director of Outdoor Learning*)
Mandy Fielding (*Head of Food Technology*)
Christopher Finch (*Leader of Vocal Studies*)
Janice Gearon (*English, History of Art*)
Helen Gray (*Head of Chemistry*)
Mark Grinsell (*Chemistry*)
Penny Hall (*Religion, Philosophy & Ethics, Learning Support*)
Stephen Harvey (*Private Learning Coordinator*)
David Heath (*Head of Art*)
Gemma Heath (*Art*)
Gill Hoadley (*Mathematics*)
Daisy Hunt (*Learning Support*)
Lauren James (*Learning Support*)
Teresa Jarman (*Business Studies & Computing*)
Echo Kenny (*Cantonese*)
Marcus Laing (*Head of Economics & Business*)
Stuart Langhorn (*Head of RPE & Chaplain*)
Edward Leaker (*Head of Instrumental Coaching, Woodwind Coordinator*)
Simon Lloyd (*Academic Music*)
Catherine Lord (*Senior Violin*)
Wendy Mahon (*Business & Economics*)
James Mayes (*History, Classics, Latin and Head of Hockey*)
Kathryn Mitchell (*Science*)
Bryan Moore (*Head of Computing, Mathematics*)
James Moretti (*Mathematics*)
Rebecca Murdoch (*Religion, Philosophy & Ethics, Geography, CCF*)
Robin Murdoch (*Mathematics, Head of EPQ*)
Eliana Nelson (*Head of Photography*)
Isabel Nixon (*Head of PSHE*)
Jayne Obradovic (*Percussion Coordinator, Summer Schools*)
Andrew O'Sullivan (*English*)
Kenneth Padgett (*Head of Science, Head of Biology*)
Claire Pattemore (*Boarders Activities*)
Natalie Perry (*Science*)
Lawrence Plum (*Head of Classics, CCF*)

Gemma Pritchard (*Head of Academic PE*)
Kimberley Richards (*EAL*)
Fiona Robertson (*Chemistry*)
Jenna Rowland (*Head of Psychology*)
David Rowley (*Geography, Geology*)
Sally Rowley (*English, Head of Sixth Form*)
Colin Sandison-Smith (*MFL*)
Deborah Searle (*Mathematics*)
Dr Janette Shepherd (*Biology, Head of Boarding*)
Matthew Shouler (*Mathematics*)
Constantine Sillem (*MFL*)
Geoffrey Smith (*Professor in Residence*)
Simon Smith (*Coordinator of Strings Studies*)
Saffron Stockall (*Psychology*)
Charlotte Tibbs (*Sport*)
Damian Todres (*Head of Creative Arts, Director of Drama & Theatre Studies*)
Tom Webley (*Director of Sport*)
Georgina Wheeler (*Physics*)
Laurence Whitehead (*Academic Music*)
Charlotte Wilde (*Head of Physics, Head of Academic Enrichment*)
Lara Williams (*English*)
Tammie Williams (*Head of Netball*)
Veronica Zausmer (*MFL*)

Junior School

Head of Junior School: Jody Wells
Deputy Head: Karl Gibson

Rebecca Allen (*Head of Pre-Prep*)
Diana Armstrong (*Chorister Coordinator*)
Laura Bain (*Games and PE*)
Sarah Jane Beats (*Mathematics, Head of Computing, Safeguarding*)
Steve Bratt (*Head of Sport & PE*)
Rebecca Bridgford-Whittick (*Head of SEND*)
Rachel Coling (*Art*)
Rhys Davies (*KS2*)
Kelly Fairey (*Head of KS1*)
Karl Gibson (*Science Coordinator*)
Naomi Hammerton (*KS2*)
Kateley Kinnersley (*KS2*)
Carina Morgan (*Dance*)
Clare Rowntree (*Head of Music & Performance*)
Emily Scott (*KS1*)
Fiona Shaw (*KS1*)
Sarah Swarfield (*PE and Sport*)
Lesley Wanklyn (*KS2, Head of Geography*)
Jonathan Ward (*Mathematics Coordinator*)
Rosie Warner (*History Coordinator*)
Charlotte White (*Head of EYFS*)
Clair Willis (*Drama*)

Bursar and Clerk to the Governors: P Knell
Admissions Registrar: J Prestidge
Head's PA: Mrs C Edwards
Director of Admissions and Marketing: J Fosbrook
School Doctor: Dr J Machling

West Buckland School

Barnstaple, Devon EX32 0SX

Tel: 01598 760000
email: admissions@westbuckland.com
website: www.westbuckland.com
Twitter: @westbuckland
Facebook: @wbsdevon
LinkedIn: /westbuckland

Motto: '*Read and Reap*'

West Buckland School is an independent day and boarding school set in 90 acres of beautiful North Devon countryside in the South West of England. Founded in 1858, the school has always stressed the importance of all-round character development alongside good academic achievement. Our size allows pupils to receive plenty of individual care and attention to their needs and talents.

West Buckland Preparatory School educates children between the ages of three and eleven. There is strong cooperation and support between the schools which share the same grounds, so making the transition as easy as possible.

West Buckland is fully co-educational.

Situation. The school stands in 90 acres of beautiful North Devon countryside on the edge of Exmoor. Barnstaple is 10 miles away and the M5 motorway can be reached in 35 minutes. Boarders arriving by train at Exeter station are met by coaches.

Buildings and Grounds. The central range of buildings, dating from 1861, still form the focus of the school, and now includes an arts centre. Other developments include a Library and Study Centre, Sixth Form boarding house, learning support centre and student cafe. The campus offers outstanding sports facilities, including an indoor heated 25-metre swimming pool, squash courts, 19 tennis courts and an Astroturf hockey pitch. The Jonathan Edwards Sports Centre opened in 2008 and the award-winning 150 Building for Art, Design Technology and the 150 Theatre opened in 2010. A new study centre for all senior school pupils and a co-educational Sixth Form boarding house with single en-suite bedrooms opened in 2015.

Admission. Boys and girls are admitted as boarders from Year 7 or day pupils. The present number of pupils is: 147 boarding, 520 day.

Entrance to the Preparatory School is by interview and assessment of school reports. Entry to the Senior School is by assessment or to the Sixth Form upon interview, GCSE results and school report.

Fees per term (2021–2022). Senior: Full Boarding £10,440–£11,245, Flexi Boarding £1,195 (5 night stay), Day £5,485. Preparatory: Day £2,770–£4,340.

Scholarships and Bursaries. A number of scholarships are awarded for entry at 11+, 13+ or 16+ (value at the discretion of the Headmaster). Candidates must be under 12, 14 or 17 years of age on 1st September for entry the following year. Applications are welcomed throughout the year – see our website for details.

Art, Music, Drama and Sports scholarships are available for entry at 11+, 13+ and 16+. At 16+ there is also an Art scholarship. Details and deadlines are available on our website.

With the support of the West Buckland School Foundation, means-tested bursaries are available for boarders and day students at all ages.

Curriculum. In the Preparatory School the main emphasis is upon well-founded confidence in English and Mathematics, within a broad balance of subjects that adds modern languages to the national curriculum. Particular attention is given to the development of sporting, artistic and musical talents.

In the Senior School breadth is complemented by specialisation. All students study the three separate sciences from Year 7, while both French and Spanish are the principal languages offered from Year 7. Our flexible options arrangements at GCSE respond to students' individual strengths and preferences. A wide range of A Level subjects is offered to sixth formers whose results uphold the high academic standards of the school.

Careers. The Careers Staff advise all pupils upon the openings and requirements for different careers. They make full use of the facilities offered by Connexions.

Games, The Performing Arts and other activities. One of the most impressive features of life at West Buckland is the quality and range of extracurricular activities, with a high level of involvement from pupils and staff.

The school has a strong sporting tradition. Rugby, hockey, cricket, netball, tennis, athletics, swimming, cross-country, squash, golf, shooting, badminton, basketball and many other sports offer opportunities for inter-school and inter-house competition and for recreation.

About a third of all pupils receive instrumental and singing tuition from specialist teachers. The wide range of choirs and instrumental groups give concerts at least once a week throughout the year. Drama is a strength of the school with productions of many kinds throughout the year. The Performing Arts are complemented by the exceptional facilities provided by the school's award-winning 150 Building which houses an impressive studio theatre.

Music. Tuition is available on all instruments. Pupils are encouraged to perform in concerts, in choirs and instrumental groups. Music Technology is also a strong feature of the department's work.

Outdoor Education. Much use is made of the proximity to Exmoor and the coast for climbing, kayaking, mountain biking, surfing, coasteering, scuba diving and other adventurous activities. All pupils receive instruction in camp craft, first aid and map reading. The Combined Cadet Force has Army and Royal Air Force sections, and offers a range of challenging pursuits. Our students succeed at all levels in The Duke of Edinburgh's Award scheme each year, and there is a regular programme of expeditions in this country and overseas.

Religion. The tradition is Anglican but the school welcomes children from all denominations and faiths – or none. Services of worship are held on a regular basis at East Buckland Church.

Attitudes and values. The school sets out to be a friendly and purposeful community in which happiness and a sense of security are the foundation on which young lives are built. At all levels, members of the school are asked to lead a disciplined way of life, to show consideration for others, to be willing to be challenged and to recognise that the success of the individual and the success of the group are inextricably linked.

Charitable status. West Buckland School is a Registered Charity, number 1167545. Its purpose is the education of boys and girls from 3 to 18.

The Governing Body:

Patron: P D Orchard-Lisle, CBE, TD, DL LLD [hc], DSc [hc], MA, FRICS

President: The Countess of Arran, MBE, DL

Chair: A Boggis, MA, PGCE

Vice Chairmen:
K Underwood
Mr I Blewett

Governors:
Dr T Brummitt, MBCHB, BSc Hons, MRCGP
Georgie Cotton
Dr R J Fisher-Smith, BA, MA, PGCE, PhD
Mr J Hall
P Hevingham, LLB Hons, MRICS, FCIARB
Mr G C James
N Kingdon, BDS, MOrthRCS
J Palk
Mrs S C E Salvidant, BEd Hons
P Stucley, BA Hons
Mrs N J Wild, BA Hons, MRICS
Mr J Wilson, MA

Bursar and Clerk to the Governors: Col G R Pearce, MBE

Headmaster: Mr Phillip Stapleton, BSc, MA Durham, MBA, PGCE, MRSC

Deputy Head: Mr D M Hymer, BSc University College London

Deputy Head Academic: Mr R Paler, BA Hons Kent, MA SOAS London, PGCE Institute of Education London

Deputy Head Pastoral: Mrs C Pettingell, BSc, MA Ed Plymouth

Headmaster, Preparatory School: Mr N Robinson, MSc, PGCE, DMS Portsmouth

Deputy Head, Prep: Mrs S Phillips, BA Hons, PGCE Kent at Canterbury

Day Houses & Housemasters/mistresses:
Brereton House: Dr E N D Grew, PhD Exeter
Courtenay House: D Brown, BSc Hons Bournemouth
Fortescue House: Ms K Venner, BSc Hons Loughborough
Grenville House: C Main, BA Hons Herriot Watt

Head of Boarding: Mr M F Robinson

Admissions Manager: Mrs M Tennant

Westminster School

Little Dean's Yard, Westminster, London SW1P 3PF

Tel: +44 (0)20 7963 1000

email: registrar@westminster.org.uk

website: www.westminster.org.uk

Twitter: @wschool

Instagram: @westminstergram_

LinkedIn: /company/westminster-school-london

Motto: *Dat Deus Incrementum*

Westminster School is an independent day and boarding school for boys aged 13–18 and girls aged 16–18, with a long history, a distinctive ethos, and a unique sense of place in the very heart of London.

About the School. Westminster is one of the leading academic schools in the country. Pupils achieve exceptional examination results and entrance to some of the top universities in the world. It is a busy, passionate and purposeful place where independent and deep thinking is enjoyed, encouraged and respected by all, and where holistic excellence is nurtured and valued. At the heart of London, adjacent to Westminster Abbey and the Houses of Parliament, the School's origins can be traced to a charity school established by the Benedictine monks of the Abbey of St Peter. After the dissolution of the monasteries in 1540, King Henry VIII personally ensured the School's survival. His daughter, Queen Elizabeth I confirmed royal patronage in 1560 and is celebrated as the School's Foundress. For several hundred years the School continued to be joined with Westminster Abbey, forming one collegiate foundation, until the 1868 Public Schools Act established the School as an independent body.

Academic. Westminster is one of the foremost centres of academic excellence in the country. However, our commitment to the academic life does not manifest itself in an educative style that revolves around the passing of examinations. Our pupils' success in public examinations and in gaining entry to leading universities, is a result of their enjoyment of academic enquiry and debate, as well as their curiosity and passion for subjects well beyond the content of the published syllabuses. The aim of the School is to instil in our pupils a deep love of learning and respect for the tradition of scholarship, as well as an openness to fresh ideas and innovative ways of thinking. Pupils are taught to appreciate and learn from the knowledge of those who came before them, yet we also ensure that they have ample opportunity to engage with current political, cultural and academic developments.

When pupils first arrive at the school, aged 13, they follow a common yet comprehensive programme of study. This includes English, Mathematics, the Sciences, Geography, History, Religious Studies, French and Classics, as well as Art, Drama, Music and Electronics, Design and Computer Science. They also benefit from a broad wellbeing (PSHE) programme and two afternoons of sport each week. In the Sixth Form boys and girls normally take four A Level or Pre-U courses.

Admissions. The two main points of admission at Westminster School are 13+ for boys and 16+ for boys and girls.

120 boys join each year at 13+, both boarding and day pupils. About half come from Westminster Under School with others from a wide range of schools, mainly in London. Entry for 13+ begins with visiting the School for the first time in Year 5. In Year 6, boys take ISEB Common Pre-tests in Mathematics, English, verbal reasoning and non-verbal reasoning. Interviews follow, as well as further tests in Mathematics and English, and a report from the boy's current school. Unconditional offers are then made for entry into Year 9 aged 13. The system described above is for boys who can remain at their prep schools until they are 13. Boys who attend primary schools, finishing in Year 6, should be registered for 11+ entry to Westminster Under School. Candidates who are not offered an unconditional place may be placed on a waiting list and they may sometimes be invited to sit further tests at the end of Year 7.

Registration for 16+ entry opens in the summer a year before entry. Entry is by competitive examination and interview. Candidates choose four entry examination subjects, usually the four subjects they plan to take for A Level. We also ask candidates to write a personal statement paper on the day. The offer of a place is conditional on a candidate achieving a minimum of eight (I)GCSE passes at A/7 grade, of which at least four are at A*/8, preferably in the subjects to be studied at A Level.

Boarding. Boarding has been central to life at Westminster since the School was founded. Between a quarter and a third of pupils choose to board and many members of staff live within the precincts to enable a flourishing boarding life. This means that activities continue into the evening, with a full programme of society meetings, lectures, school plays and concerts, and cultural trips to London events. There are six residential boarding Houses, including one which is a girls-only house. The Westminster Sixth Form is unique in London as the only co-educational Sixth Form with day and boarding pupils.

Bursaries and Scholarships. Since its foundation, Westminster School has made it possible for academically-able and musically-gifted pupils to attend the School, who would not otherwise have been able to do so without financial support. Bursaries of up to 100% are available and are awarded to pupils according to individual need, at both 13+ and 16+.

Queen's Scholarships are the School's much-coveted academic scholarships. There are 48 Queen's Scholars, with 12 chosen every year: eight boys at 13 and four girls at 16. Queen's Scholars board at the School and all belong to College, one of the six boarding Houses. An examination entitled 'The Challenge' is held annually to determine which pupils are elected as Queen's Scholars for entry at 13+. The Challenge consists of papers in Mathematics, English, French, Science, Latin, History, Geography and an optional Greek paper. For Queen's Scholarships awarded to girls entering at 16+, selection is based on the overall performance in the Sixth Form Entrance Exam papers and interviews. The School also awards up to eight Music Awards annually for 13+ entry and up to four Music Scholarships for 16+ entry.

Co-Curricular and Sport. To balance the academic pursuits of our pupils, Westminster offers a wide variety of activities to complement our curriculum. These provide pupils with new and different opportunities to engage with less familiar concepts, with one another and with the world around them. Pupils joining in Year 9 benefit from over 30 different classes and workshops, run by a combination of teaching staff and outside specialists. Pupils may choose the same activities throughout the year, or switch to new ones each term. Included are academic, musical and sporting activities, alongside such diverse pursuits as bookbinding, carpentry, robotics, board games, mythology and the Duke of Edinburgh's Award.

At Sixth Form our Options programme enables boys and girls to study an additional language such as Sanskrit or Arabic, take a practical course in cookery or bookbinding, learn a new skill such as electronics or computer programming, or complement their studies in a particular area of interest such as an Introduction to Political Philosophy, studying British Sign Language or Teaching English as a Foreign Language. A more intensive Community Service option also exists, where pupils can not only volunteer their time to local projects but also take specific courses to equip them for their chosen community outreach.

Westminster's programme of sport, known within the School as 'Station', offers pupils a choice of more than 25 different sporting activities. We have the unusual feature that all pupils have a free choice as to which sports they participate in. We are extremely fortunate, in the centre of London, to have a great deal of outdoor space for Station: pupils have a shooting gallery and several Fives courts, in addition to our playing fields at Vincent Square. We also have a Sports Centre that offers over 6,000m² of indoor space, housing a multi-use movement studio, a rowing training suite, fencing pistes, indoor cricket nets, a fully-equipped gym, two climbing walls, a dojo and a table tennis area and courts for basketball, netball, five-a-side football, volleyball, hockey and badminton.

Pastoral care. We strive to protect and support our pupils, helping them to develop into healthy, fulfilled and resilient people and make sure they feel safe and enjoy their time at Westminster. Yet we also want to nurture their own pastoral skills, encouraging them to care for others and to act thoughtfully and compassionately. We ensure that pupils receive both support and guidance from a variety of sources, primarily members of staff but also trusted peers. As well as a dedicated Housemaster, each pupil has a personal Tutor who has been assigned specifically and who knows and supports the pupil throughout their time at Westminster. Additionally, pupils can always access the wider pastoral resources of the School, such as our Chaplain, the School Counsellor and a team of pupils who have been trained as Peer Supporters. We also aim to keep the channels of communication between pupils, teachers and parents as open and straightforward as possible.

Community, Partnerships and Charity. At Westminster we are fortunate to enjoy some of the highest quality teaching and facilities in the country, so we are committed to making sure that less well-equipped schools have the chance to access and benefit from our resources. There are a number of established schemes in place to help children outside Westminster School. Platform is an academic programme created and provided by Westminster School and Westminster Under School that inspires Year 5 and Year 10 pupils who show exceptional academic potential and energy for learning. Primary school headteachers nominate participants every year, and the pupils then participate in a free one-year programme of Saturday morning sessions and a two-day course, to fuel their ambition and to allow their academic potential to flourish.

Westminster pupils enjoy a wide variety of volunteering opportunities and there is an emphasis on pupil-led fundraising to help to ensure that contributing to society in holistic and generous ways forms a key part of our pupils' educational experience.

Additionally, Westminster School maintains a close relationship with nearby Harris Westminster Sixth Form (HWSF), which was created in partnership with not-for-profit organisation The Harris Federation in 2014 to offer an outstanding education to students from all backgrounds and neighbourhoods in London. HWSF combines the Federation's experience of establishing outstanding academies in and around London with Westminster School's ability to teach and develop exceptional pupils.

Fees per term (2021–2022). Boarding: £14,424 for all year groups; £11,541 (13+ Queen's Scholars who joined from Play Term 2021); £8,655 (13+ Queen's Scholars who joined from Play Term 2017, and 16+ Queen's Scholars). Day: £9,987 (Years 9 to 11); £10,917 (Years 12 and 13). All day fees are inclusive of lunch.

Preparatory Department. Westminster Under School is Westminster School's preparatory equivalent. The Under School admits day boys only and currently has 292 pupils in attendance. Entry to the Under School is at 7+, 8+ and 11+. For further information, please see Westminster Under School's entry.

Charitable status. St Peter's College (otherwise known as Westminster School) is a Registered Charity, number 312728.

Visitor:
Her Majesty The Queen

Governing Body:
Mr Mark Batten [OW] (*Chair*)
The Dean of Westminster, The Very Reverend Dr David Hoyle, MBE (*Ex Officio Member*)
Ms Emily Reid [OW] (*Nominated Common Room Governor*)
The Reverend Canon David Stanton (*Nominated Abbey Governor*)
Mr Michael Baughan [OW]
Dr Priscilla Chadwick, MA, FRSA
Mr Richard Neville-Rolfe, MA [OW]
Dame Judith Mayhew Jonas, DBE
Ms Joanna Reesby
Mr Edward Cartwright [OW]
Mrs Ina De [OW]
Professor Maggie Dallman OBE
Mrs Vicky Tuck
Dr Sarah Anderson
Mr John Colenutt
Mr Nabeel Bhanji [OW]
Ms Jessica Cecil
Dr Tristram Hunt

Clerk to the Governing Body: Mrs Dawn Turpin

[OW] Old Westminster

Senior Management Committee:

***Head Master*: Dr Gary Savage**, PhD

Under Master: Mr James Kazi, MA

Bursar: Mr Martin Walsh, BComm, FCA

Deputy Head (*Academic*): Ms Clare Leech, MA

Deputy Head (*Co-curricular, Events and Planning*): Mrs Vivienne Horsfield, BA, MEd

Deputy Head (*Boarding and Educational Partnerships*): Mr Jeremy Kemball, BSc

Director of Upper School: Dr Tasos Aidonis, PhD

Director of Teaching and Learning: Ms Abigail Farr, MA

Winchester College

College Street, Winchester, Hampshire SO23 9NA

Tel:	01962 621247 (Admissions)
	01962 621100 (Office)
email:	admissions@wincoll.ac.uk
website:	www.winchestercollege.org
Twitter:	@WinColl
Facebook:	@WinchesterCollegeOfficial
Instagram:	@WinchesterCollege

Motto: '*Manners Makyth Man*'

Winchester College is a leading independent senior school in Hampshire, UK, set in beautiful, historic surroundings, and renowned for academic excellence. With boys full boarding throughout the school, for the first time girls and boys will be welcomed as day pupils into the Sixth Form in September 2022, with girls' boarding from September 2024. This exciting new development is part of the school's Vision for the 21st Century, which embodies a significant programme of change, and also includes increased bursary provision, broadening of the curriculum, and further investment in technologies and the school's facilities.

At Winchester there is a thriving culture of curiosity and exploration. Pupils are hand-picked for their ability to think; dons are selected for their enthusiasm, dedication and expertise. Put simply, inspiring teachers inspire learning.

Outside study time, pupils have a huge choice of extra-curricular activities, clubs and societies within which to find like minds and fresh challenges. Whether broadening or intensifying their interests, Winchester pupils take part in a stimulating range of activities that enriches their studies and their school life, including politics, rock climbing, natural history, scuba diving, literature, CCF, charities and expeditions.

Div. Div is at the heart of the education we offer. It defines the liberal character of Winchester academic life. Pupils engage in discussion and debate, and embrace the idea of learning for its own sake, unrestrained by any examination syllabus.

Div is multi-disciplinary in scope. In Years 9 to 11, it provides pupils with an introduction to the broad sweep of History, from classical times to the Early Modern period. It also encompasses English literature and language, the History of Science and Art, Religious Studies and PSHEE.

In the Sixth Form, each Div don determines the programme. The material selected for inclusion is equally likely to be artistic, literary, philosophical, political, sociological, art-historical, ethical, religious or musical.

Through this combination of disciplines, the school helps develop discriminating learners. Div helps pupils to think critically, to question and assimilate complex ideas, and to articulate their thoughts with clarity and confidence, both on paper and orally in front of their peers.

Academic. At Winchester College, academic expectations are high, and success is achieved through a genuine curiosity and love for learning. A Winchester education therefore combines cultural studies in Div with a conventional curriculum of examined subjects. Examined courses are taught by highly qualified subject specialists.

In addition to Div, pupils begin at Winchester in Year 9 studying Mathematics, Biology, Chemistry, Physics, French or German, Geography and Latin. They also study one of the following: Ancient Greek, Spanish, Russian or Chinese, and choose two subjects from Art, Design and Music.

GCSEs: Towards the end of Year 9, pupils express their preferences for GCSE study. The majority of pupils complete a minimum of nine GCSEs and IGCSEs (all graded 9–1). The compulsory subjects (in addition to Div) are English, Mathematics, Latin, French or German, and two or three Sciences. Pupils also choose from among the following to bring the total to nine: History, Geography, Ancient Greek, Art, Design, Music, Spanish, Russian and Chinese.

A Levels: Pupils ordinarily study three A Level subjects and, to foster independence and responsibility, an Extended Project Qualification (EPQ), alongside Div. Linear A Levels are complemented by the flexibility of the EPQ where pupils are able more deeply to explore their cross-curricular research interests. The EPQ encourages pupils to develop first-class research skills, to synthesise information from a variety of differing sources, and to become accustomed to the demands of independent study.

Sixth Form. We believe that Sixth Form should be the most interesting, enriching and academically demanding years of school life. There is no better place to spend these years than within the motivated and supportive community of Winchester College.

Learning alongside like-minded individuals, Sixth Form pupils enjoy inspirational teaching in small classes with outstanding resources. Each year, pupils join us with the intellectual spark and curiosity to take advantage of everything Winchester has to offer, and leave with the drive and determination to give something back. Winchester provides an intellectually stimulating environment in which conversation and debate are encouraged, and individual scholarship is nurtured. Subject specialists stretch individuals well beyond A Level syllabuses, providing the perfect preparation for university.

Fees per term (2021–2022). £14,445.

For more information see www.winchestercollege.org/admissions/fees.

Boarding. Boarding at Winchester offers an unmatched experience of focused learning and friendship. Discussions in class can continue in the house, instilling a lifelong love of debate. In consultation with parents and pupils, the school accommodates boarders with care, getting to know them first through a personal admissions process. There are approximately 60 boarders in each house.

Admissions. We spend time getting to know each prospective family during the admissions process. It is a unique system, focused on potential, not merely prior attainment. It is based substantially on interview and ensures that by the time a pupil joins Winchester, they will often have had a number of years to get to know us.

13+ (boys only). When your son reaches Year 4, attend one of our two Open Days or a weekly Registrar's Tour. Registrar's Tours will start in the summer term of Year 4. In Year 5, select from one of our two Open Days or a weekly Registrar's Tour, then explore your choice of boarding house with a 'Housemaster at Home' visit, which introduces you to up to three Housemasters.

16+ (boarding boys only, day girls and boys). The dedicated Sixth Form Open Day is held in September each year. Examinations and interviews take place in November.

For more information see the Admissions page on our website www.winchestercollege.org/admissions.

Scholarships and Exhibitions are awarded to pupils who successfully pass the Winchester College 'Election' for entry at 13+, a unique selection process involving written examinations and interviews.

Headmaster's Nominations may be awarded to pupils not previously offered a conditional place or Scholarship, but whose exam results are deemed strong enough.

Scholarships, Exhibitions or Headmaster's Nominations do not carry a remission of school fees.

Music Scholarships and Exhibitions are available to any candidate who shows exceptional musical talent. Scholarships offer free tuition in two instruments (including singing) and Exhibitions offer free tuition in one instrument.

In addition, up to three Choral Scholarships and one Organ Scholarship are available for 16+ entrants. These carry free tuition in two instruments, one of which must be singing or the organ.

Sports Scholarships offer successful candidates at 13+ and 16+ specialist coaching sessions, regularly assessed strength and conditioning programmes, and a dedicated Sports Department tutor.

More information on Scholarships: www.winchester college.org/admissions.

Bursaries. Winchester College is committed to maintaining the founder's intention of offering an education to any pupil who would benefit from it, regardless of their financial circumstances. Awards range from 5–100% of the school fee and are means-tested.

More information on Bursaries: www.winchester college.org/admissions/bursaries.

Charitable status. Winchester College is a Registered Charity, number 1139000. The objects of the charity are the advancement of education and activities connected therewith.

Visitor: The Lord Bishop of Winchester
Warden: Sir Richard Stagg, KCMG
Sub-Warden: Mr Andrew Sykes, MA

Fellows:
The Hon Sir Stephen Cobb, Hon LLD
Ms Clarissa Farr, MA
Mr Nicholas Ferguson, CBE, FSA Scot, BSc, MBA
Mr William Holland, BA, FCA
Mr Andrew Joy, MA
Mr Brian Li Man-Bun, JP, MA Cantab, MBA, FCA
Mrs Alison Mayne, MA, PGCE
Dr William Poole, MA, DPhil, FSA
Dr Magnus Ryan, MA, PhD
Mrs Laura Sanderson, MA, MPhil
Mr Roland Turnill, MA
Mr Miles Young, MA Oxon

Bursar and Secretary: P D Thakrar

Headmaster: **T R Hands**, BA, AKC, DPhil, FKC

Alumni, Winchester College Society Director: A J C Normand, Donovan's, 73 Kingsgate Street, Winchester SO23 9PE

Wisbech Grammar School

Chapel Road, Wisbech, Cambridgeshire PE13 1RH

Tel: 01945 583631
              01945 586750 Admissions
email: office@wisbechgrammar.com
website: www.wisbechgrammar.com
Twitter: @wisbechgrammar
Facebook: @wisbechgrammar
Instagram: @wisbech_grammar

Founded in 1379, Wisbech Grammar School is a co-educational day and boarding school, it draws around 600 pupils aged 3 to 18.

The School is set in 34 acres of magnificent grounds in a conservation area. Open, friendly and welcoming, the School is small enough for staff to know all the pupils individually, but large enough to provide an impressive range of opportunities. All members of the Senior School and Preparatory School are encouraged to develop their confidence and unlock their true potential, both inside and outside the classroom, as well as engaging with the wider community.

"On visiting for the first time, our immediate impression was of a school where pupils showed a real sense of purpose and where they were clearly enjoying their lessons and activities." This comment, by parents looking for a school, is typical of the feedback we are delighted to receive.

In the last year the School has been through a number of transformation projects which include:

• An upgrade of the whole school IT infrastructure in summer 2021 to support a more technological approach to teaching and learning. All new 1st Form pupils receive iPads as part of the everyday school toolkit and AI has been introduced into online and classroom teaching via platforms such as Century.

• The redesign of school classrooms based around Harkness tables – a method of teaching and learning that involves 12–14 pupils seated around a large oval table which encourages pupils to discuss ideas, work collaboratively and shifts the focus away from the more traditional, teacher at the front of the class, approach.

• A new 6th Form Centre which allows pupils to have a dedicated space for specialist 6th Form subjects, collaborative and silent working spaces, a lecture facility, plus a café and common room space; all with the aim of supporting academic success at A Level.

• The transformation of the old 6th Form house into a new International Boarding House for overseas pupils.

• The establishment of Science, Maths and Humanities Creative Hubs, so pupils benefit from having focused academic environments that utilise the expertise of specialist teaching staff and resources.

Senior School admission. The main entry is at age 11 by a competitive entrance examination. The test, which consists of verbal and non-verbal reasoning, spatial, quantitative tests and English, is designed to discover potential. Pupils can also enter at 2nd, 3rd and 4th Form levels. Offers of 6th Form places are made on the basis of interview and a report from a pupil's current school and final GCSE results.

Fees per term (2021–2022). Senior School (including 6th Form) £4,709; Prep School £3,299–£3,399.

Bursaries and Scholarships. Wisbech Grammar School offers a bursary programme which provides financial assistance to pupils who would not otherwise be able to take up the offer of a place, allowing them to achieve their full potential. Bursaries are means tested and will require the parents to make a detailed statement of their income and assets. Awards range from 5% to 85%. In exceptional cases, an award of 100% may be granted.

The School also offers Scholarships for children entering Year 7, Year 9 and Year 12. Scholarships are awarded to children who excel in a number of areas (Academic, Music, Art, Drama and Sport); this includes financial support and may be awarded alongside a bursary.

Application forms for Bursary Assisted Places are available from the Admissions Team: admissions@wisbechgrammar.com.

Travel to School. The School's catchment area embraces King's Lynn, Hunstanton, Downham Market, March, Whittlesey, Peterborough and Spalding and Long Sutton. School buses run from a number of these places, visiting villages en-route. The School is also well served by local buses.

The 6th Form experience. The School has a first-class track record in enabling pupils to realise their university and career aspirations. Entrusted with a greater degree of independence, 6th Formers are encouraged to make their mark and develop leadership qualities, both within the house system and at a wider level. The 6th Form centre has been transformed into a modern contemporary space for pupils.

Sport. WGS offers an all-inclusive sports curriculum that gives every pupil the opportunity to engage in sports at all levels. The School offers team sports including Rugby, Hockey, Netball, Cricket, and Athletics, as well as a range of individual sport and fitness sessions.

With the Elite Sports Programme, pupils can pursue sports at a higher level with expert coaching and player pathways with Northampton Saints and Northamptonshire County Cricket Club.

Performing Arts is an extremely popular element of our extended curriculum and many of our pupils take advantage of the variety of school productions and stage performances; *Joseph and the Amazing Technicolor Dreamcoat* and *Shout*, were a huge success and played to a nightly full house at The Angles Theatre in Wisbech.

The Music Department also plays a prominent role, with orchestras, choirs, steel bands, bespoke instrument tuition and performances throughout the year, showcasing the multitude of musical talents within the School. Our Dance Studio offers pupils access to top level coaching from visiting dance companies.

Co-curricular. We offer many options for pupils to enjoy an extensive array of clubs as part of their timetabled curriculum within the school day – from Archaeology to Astronomy, Philosophy to Politics, Shakespeare to Steel Band and Young Enterprise to Young Engineers.

The Art and Design department is a highly visible presence in the School, mounting exhibitions on-site and at the Reed Barn at the neighbouring National Trust property, Peckover House. Our talented artists and designers regularly win places at the top art colleges.

Around 130 pupils participate in the Duke of Edinburgh's Award, with those at the highest level mounting expeditions to the Lake District, Snowdonia and Mont Blanc. The Senior School adventure begins with an outdoor activity weekend for the 1st Form.

The Prep School at Magdalene House caters for pupils from Kindergarten to Prep 6. As well as access to many of the Senior School facilities, they also have their own library, dedicated computer room and a light and spacious hall.

Wisbech Grammar School is a trading name of Wisbech Grammar School Limited. The Company is registered in England and Wales with company number 11454188

Registered Office: Chapel Road, Wisbech, Cambridgeshire PE13 1RH

Senior Team:

Headmaster: Mr C N Staley, BA, MBA

Bursar: Mrs N J Miller

Senior Deputy Head – Magdalene House: Mrs K Neaves, BEd
Senior Deputy Head: Mr P W Timmis, BSc
Deputy Head Academic: Mr B J Rimmer, BSc

Assistant Head Teaching, Learning & Innovation: Mr R D Killick, BSc
Assistant Head Academic Administration: Mrs V Garment, BA, MA, NPQSL
Assistant Head Sports & Partnerships: Mr P J Webb, BA
Assistant Head Academic Leadership: Dr S J Miller, BSc, PhD, DIC
Assistant Head Co-Curricular: Dr K J Mann, BA, PhD

Head of Marketing and Admissions: Mr P A Lewis, MCIM

Withington Girls' School

Wellington Road, Fallowfield, Manchester M14 6BL

Tel: 0161 224 1077
email: office@wgs.org
website: www.wgs.org
Twitter: @WGSManchester
Facebook: @withingtongirlsschool
Instagram: @withingtongirlsschool
LinkedIn: /withington-girls-school

Motto: *Ad Lucem ~ Towards the light*

Since its foundation in 1890, Withington has remained relatively small and now has around 720 pupils, with over 150 in the Junior Department and a Sixth Form of a similar number. This size allows a friendly, intimate environment together with a broad and balanced curriculum. Withington provides a wide range of opportunities for girls, helping them to achieve their potential, academically, socially and personally. Withington attracts pupils from a wide geographical area and from many different social and cultural backgrounds, producing a diversity in which the school rejoices.

The School's A Level and GCSE results have been consistently outstanding. Girls who gain a place as a result of the entrance examination normally take GCSE/IGCSE examinations in 9/10 subjects, followed by 3 or 4 A Levels. An exciting and varied Enrichment programme offers Sixth Formers core elements such as PSHCE, financial literacy and professional skills plus a range of choices from computer coding and languages, to mosaics, mindfulness and cooking and preparing healthy meals. In addition to the Enrichment Programme, which all Sixth Formers follow, many also complete an Extended Project Qualification (EPQ). Studies are directed towards encouraging a love of learning for its own sake, frequently going beyond the confines of the examined curriculum, as well as towards the ultimate goal of University entrance, including Oxford and Cambridge (15% of the cohort in 2021).

The School enjoys excellent facilities and has an ongoing programme of major developments. Recent projects have included a purpose-built Junior School building, a central, enclosed 'Hub' area at the heart of the school and an expanded and refurbished suite of university-standard Chemistry laboratories, all of which were completed in 2015. During 2018 a significant new sports facilities development was completed, reflecting the school's ongoing commitment to the promotion of physical activity for girls, one of the school's founding principles. In 2019 the outdoor netball courts and all-weather pitch were resurfaced to a high specification, bringing Withington's sports facilities to an excellent standard across all areas. Outdoor fitness equipment – also installed in 2019 – has provided an innovative facility that will benefit fitness, wellbeing and social interaction for senior pupils. A project to extend and refurbish the dining room commenced in 2021 with completion expected early in 2022.

Withington fosters all-round development and the girls' academic studies are complemented by an extensive range of over 100 extra-curricular activities. Music is strong and very popular; there is a comprehensive range of choirs and orchestras, involving all age groups. Drama also thrives with regular productions including original works. Girls play a variety of sports, including hockey, lacrosse, netball, rounders, tennis, athletics and football. Pupils are selected to represent county and national squads and there are regular sports tours within Europe and further afield such as the USA and South Africa. In addition to fixtures with other schools, pupils compete in a variety of sports within the School's House system. The four Houses, named after Withington's founders, also provide a focus for dramatic, musical and other activities.

The Duke of Edinburgh's Award and the Young Enterprise scheme, Model United Nations conferences, voluntary work in the local community, science, mathematics, linguistics Olympiads and a wide range of academic extension activities, residential activity weekends, foreign trips and local fieldwork all feature prominently in the School's provision. Numerous extra-curricular clubs and societies include: Eco Society, debating, zumba, yoga, robotics, film making, app development, drama tech club, dance and chess. Awareness of the wider world is encouraged and girls have a strong sense of social responsibility, participating in many fundraising activities

and maintaining special links with a hospital and two schools in Kenya. Sixth Formers use their holiday time to participate in community projects in Uganda and The Gambia; others participate in World Challenge or similar expeditions (to Malaysia and Borneo in 2016, Sri Lanka in 2017 and Kenya in 2019). Preparation for life after school starts early and involves a programme of careers advice, work experience and UCAS application guidance. Older girls work with younger girls in numerous ways, through the House system, extra-curricular activities, peer support and mentoring.

Visitors are warmly welcomed and Open Days are held in the Autumn term. A number of means-tested Bursaries are awarded annually together with awards from various external Trusts. Entrance at age 7–11 is by Entrance Assessment/Examination, held in January, together with interview (11+ entry only) and a reference from current school. Admission to the Sixth Form is by interview and is conditional upon GCSE results. For entry at other points, please don't hesitate to contact the Admissions Team for further information.

The School has a thriving alumnae network with regular events and many alumnae offering help and inspiration to current pupils. The School engages in a number of partnership projects with local State schools and has strong links with the local community. Withington was named as The Sunday Times Parent Power Northwest Independent School of the Decade in 2021, Northwest Independent School of the Year in 2020, Top Independent Secondary School of the Year nationally 2009/10 and the Financial Times Best Value Independent Day School in 2012. Consistently ranked as the top secondary school in the Northwest, The Tatler Schools Guide named Withington as a Runner-Up for Public School of the Year 2015.

Fees per annum (2021–2022). Senior School £13,326, Junior School £9,999. LAMDA, individual instrumental music lessons and Arts Award are charged separately. Before and after-school care are not charged.

Charitable status. Withington Girls' School is a Registered Charity, number 1158226. It aims to provide an exceptional quality of opportunity, to encourage independence of mind and high aspirations for girls from seven to eighteen.

¶ *Alumnae*

Board of Governors:
Chair: Mr M Pike, LLB
Mr C Poston BSc, FCA (*Hon Treasurer*)
Dr J Allred, MB ChB, MRCGP, DRCOG, DFFP
Mr A Chicken, BA, MEd, FRSA
Dr R Dev-Jairath MBChB, MRCGP, DCH, DRCOG, DPD, FHEA
¶Miss M El-Gonemy, BA, MA
Mr M Griffin
¶Mrs D Hawkins, DL, JP, LLB
Prof D Leigh, BSc PhD CChem FRS FRSE FRSC MAE
Miss M Michael, BA, NPQH, LLE
Mr A Pathak, BSc
Mr H Sinclair
¶Mrs S Stuffins, BA, MSc, MRICS

***Headmistress*: Mrs S J Haslam**, BA Lancaster (*English*)

Deputy Head: ¶Ms J M Baylis, MA Manchester (*English and Drama*)

Director of Studies: Mr I McKenna, BA Manchester
(*Religious Studies*)
Assistant Head: Dr S E Madden, PhD Newcastle (*Biology*)
Bursar: Mrs A Cohen, LLB Liverpool

Full-time Teaching Staff:
* *Head of Department/Subject*

Mrs C Air, BA Oxon (*History)
Mrs L Bradshaw, MA Cantab (*Science, *Physics)
Miss K L Browning, BA London (*Geography*)
¶Miss D Bruce, BA Birmingham (**Religious Studies*)
Miss S Choudhury, BA Manchester (*English*)
Mrs E Corrigan, MSc Durham (*Biology)
Mr A Cumberford, BA Oxon (*German)
Mr K Eckersall, BSc Leicester, MA Durham (*Chemistry*)
Mrs C E Edge, MA Leeds (*English, Partnerships
Coordinator*)
Mr C Forrest, MPhys Manchester (*Physics*)
Ms A Furlong, MA St Mary's (*English*)
Mrs S E Hamilton, MA Aberdeen (*Geography)
Mrs S Hetherington, BA Leeds Beckett (*Physical
Education*)
Mrs J C Howling, MA Cantab (*Classics)
Mrs J Johnston, BA MMU (*Art*, *PSHCE)
Mrs N Kimpton-Smith, BA Durham (*History, Religious
Studies, Politics*)
Ms A Kusznir, Dip Mech Moscow (*Mathematics*)
Mrs K Michael, MA Open University (*Physics*)
Miss K Mottershead, BA Brighton (*Physical Education*)
Mrs S I Mounteney, BSc London (*Mathematics)
Miss A Noya, BA Santiago de Compostela (*Spanish*)
Mrs E O'Neal, BEd Leeds Polytechnic (**Physical
Education*)
Mrs M Parker, BA Leeds (*History*)
Mr A Parry, BSc Manchester (*Mathematics, Assistant
Examinations Officer*)
Mrs S J Rigby, BA Nottingham (*Learning Support)
Ms E K Robinson, MA Cantab (*Classics, Head of Sixth
Form, Enrichment*)
Mrs G E Sargent, BMus London (*Music)
Dr J Smiles, PHD Manchester (*Chemistry*)
Mr A Snowden, BSc Warwick (*ICT)
Mrs E Suttle, MSc Manchester Metropolitan (*English)
Miss R Thorpe, BSc Manchester (*Biology*)
Mrs N Toubanks, BSc Manchester (*Economics)
Dr C P G Vilela, PhD Lisbon (*Chemistry)
Mrs J Wagstaffe, BA Nottingham (*MFL, *Spanish*)
Mrs J C Wallis, BA Leeds (**Politics, Deputy Head of Sixth
Form*)
Mrs N Watson, BA Leeds (**Food & Nutrition*)
Miss F Whiteley, BSc Lancaster (*Psychology)

Junior School:
Head of Junior School: Ms Bridget Howard, BEd Exeter
Ms J Arschavir, MA Liverpool (*Year 5*)
Mrs S Birch, BEd Edge Hill (*Year 3*)
Mrs L Cordrey, BA York (*Deputy Head of Juniors, Year 4*)
Mr M Dunn, BSc Sheffield (*Year 6, Junior School
Coordinator of Assessment and Pupil Tracking*)
Miss L Gorman, BA Edge Hill (*Year 4*)
Mrs A Harris, MSc MMU (*Year 4*)
Mr J Lazenby, BA Liverpool (*Year 6*)
Mrs B Lowe, BSc Northumbria (*Year 3*)
Mrs K McCulloch, MA Manchester (*Year 5*)
Part-time Teaching Staff:
Mrs L Berry, BA Manchester (*Drama)
Mrs J W Bowie, MA Dundee (*English*)

Mr M Boyle, BSc Wales (*Biology*)
Miss H Brown, MA MMU (*Art*)
Mrs A Collard, BSc Durham (*Mathematics, Assistant
Partnerships Coordinator*)
Mrs R Corner, MA Exeter (*Drama*)
Mrs N Cottam, BSc Durham (*Biology*, *Careers)
Mrs F Cotton, BA Heriot-Watt (**Design Technology*)
Mrs D Da Silva, BA Portsmouth (*Design Technology*)
Mr C Eccles, MSc Manchester (*ICT & Computer Science*)
Mrs R Fildes, MA MMU (*Art)
Mrs S E Fletcher, BEd Brighton (*Mathematics*)
Ms A Godwin, BA Oxon (*Learning Support*)
Miss A Holland, BMus Birmingham (*Music*)
Miss R Hylton-Smith, MA Goldsmiths (*Music*)
Mr M Houghton, BA Oxford (*Classics*)
Mrs A Humblet, BA University of Dijon (*Spanish*)
Dr Z Kenny, PhD Edinburgh (*Biology*)
Mrs V Kochhar, BSc Exeter (*Mathematics*)
Mrs K Levene, BA Liverpool John Moore's (*Design
Technology*)
¶Mrs Y T Menzies, MA Salford (*French, *German*)
Mrs N Morgan, BMus Lancaster (*Music*)
Mrs D Odeyinde, BSc Queen's Belfast (*Learning Support*)
Ms C Ositelu, DEA-ès-L Nantes (*French*)
Dr L Pitts, PhD Leicester (*Science*)
Mrs S Roberts, MA Manchester (*Physical Education*)
Ms A Siddons, BA Bath (*German*)
Mrs R Statter, BSc Warwick (*Mathematics*)
Mrs J Stockton, BA Leeds (*English*)
Mrs Z Taylor, BA MMU (*Art*)
Dr E L Terrill, DPhil Oxon (*Mathematics*)

PA to Headmistress: Mrs A L Adams, BA Sheffield Hallam
Librarian: Mr D Whelan, BA MMU
Archivist: Miss H Brown, MA MMU
School Health Lead: Sister J Lees, RGN
School Counsellor: Miss S Horsfall, BSc Newcastle, Dip
GPTI
Examinations Officer: Mrs S Breckell, BSc Dundee
Development Director: Mrs L Dowdall, BSc Leeds
Director of Admissions and Marketing: Mrs C Dow, BA
Johannesburg
Admissions Officer: Ms J Ellis, BA Bath
Director of Digital Services: Mr A Lockett, BSc Bradford
Head of HR: Mrs L Ledson, BA Open University
Office Manager: Mrs V Brickhill
Site Manager: Mr M Morris, NEBOSH

Woldingham School

Marden Park, Woldingham, Surrey CR3 7YA

Tel: 01883 654206
email: registrar@woldinghamschool.co.uk
website: www.woldinghamschool.co.uk
Twitter: @WoldinghamSch
Facebook: @woldinghamschool.co.uk
Instagram: @woldinghamsch
LinkedIn: /company/woldingham-school

Woldingham is one of the UK's leading boarding and day
schools for girls aged 11–18. Set within 700 acres of the
most beautiful Surrey countryside, Woldingham provides an
inspiring and safe place for students to become confident,

compassionate and courageous young women. It's a place where students are helped to "write your own story" through excellent teaching, boundless opportunities and first-rate pastoral care.

Not only is Woldingham's location inspiring, it's remarkably accessible. London is just 30 minutes away by train and Woldingham is only 30 minutes from Gatwick Airport and 45 minutes from Heathrow Airport.

Main House, the stunning 19th century mansion at the centre of the school, sits alongside purpose-built science labs, humanities and language hubs, studios for art, drama and music, and a professional standard 600-seat auditorium.

Students achieve outstanding GCSE and A Level results to secure places at leading universities opening doors to exciting careers. Students can choose from a wide range of academic enrichment opportunities, from societies for debating, law and philosophy through to extra qualifications in areas such as mathematics and sports leadership.

Sitting alongside this is an exceptional co-curricular programme of sport, clubs, performing arts and outreach into the local community, enabling students to develop a wonderful range of skills, expertise and interests.

Sport is very important at Woldingham, with excellent indoor and outdoor facilities. The hockey and netball teams compete locally and regionally with first-class training from specialist coaches. The tennis dome means tennis can be played year round, as well as on outside courts in the summer. There is an indoor swimming pool, squash courts, fitness suites, dance studio and sports hall.

The beauty and peace of Woldingham in the Surrey Hills makes it the perfect place to board. Boarders live with their own year group in comfortable and well-equipped boarding houses, and there is a great sense of community. The fantastic and experienced team of housemistresses really understand how to help new girls settle in quickly and make the most of school life.

As one of the UK's oldest girls' schools, Woldingham is proud to be a pioneer of women's education. Our single-sex environment is supportive and stimulating. It enables students to be themselves and to grow into independent women who will make a positive contribution to the world.

Woldingham is a Sacred Heart Catholic school. We warmly welcome students of all faiths and none.

Admissions. Main entry is via the Woldingham School Assessment in the autumn prior to entry for 11+, 13+ (standard and deferred entry) and 16+ candidates.

Scholarships. We offer the following academic and co-curricular scholarships, designed to recognise exceptional achievement, intellectual curiosity and persistence:

Academic, Art, Music, Drama and Sport Scholarships are offered at 11+, 13+ and 16+. In addition, a Local Girl Scholarship (means tested) is offered at 11+, Performing Arts Scholarships at 11+ and 13+ and Science Scholarships at 16+.

Bursaries. We are committed to providing bursaries, depending upon the financial and other pertinent circumstances of applicants. They are intended for girls who demonstrate strong academic potential and where the financial circumstances of the family will make attending Woldingham impossible.

Fees per term (2021–2022). Full boarding £12,465–£13,570; Weekly boarding £10,950–£11,950; Day (tuition) £7,570–£8,250; Flexi-boarding: £64 per night (max. 2 nights per week).

Charitable status. Woldingham School is a Registered Charity, number 1125376.

Chairman of Governors: Mr Robert Parkinson, MA Oxon

Headmaster: Dr James Whitehead, MA Oxon, MPhil, PhD, FRSA

Senior Deputy Head: Ms Kerri Fox, MA Cantab
Deputy Head Operations & Co-curricular: Mrs Suzy Woolaway, BSc Open
Deputy Head Academic: Ms N Weatherston, BSc Newcastle
Head of Sixth Form: Mr P Abbott, BSc Cardiff
Head of Marden: Miss C Owen, BA Royal Holloway London
Director of Finance & Operations: Mrs J Wood, BA Exeter
Director of Communication: Ms J Rawlinson, BA Hull, MA Florida
Foundation Director: Mrs C Mair, BA London

Registrar: Mrs L Underwood

Heads of Departments:
Art: Miss S Campbell, BA London Metropolitan
Biology: Mrs E Petty, BSc Birmingham
Chemistry: Mr P Currie, Graduate RSC Kingston
Classics & Latin: Dr J Dixon, PhD Manchester, BA, MA Liverpool
Computer Science: Mr T Rattle, BA Exeter, MA Brighton
Design & Technology: Mr D Wahab, BA Brighton
Drama: Miss S Williams, BA Middlesex
EAL: Mrs T Carrilero, BA Spain
Economics & Business: Mr W Bohanna, BA UEA
English: Ms B MacLean, BA, MA Canada
French: Mrs C Maillot, BA equiv. France
Geography: Mr D Lock, BA London
German: Mr V Ceska, BA Czech, MA France
Higher Education & Careers: Miss J Gallagher, BSc Bristol
History: Mrs A Housden, BA Kent
History of Art: Mr A Cullen, BA SOAS
Learning Enhancement: Ms R Moorvan, BA S. Africa, MEd OU
Mathematics: Mrs R McKenna, BSc Cardiff
Media Studies: Mr S Maunder, BA Sheffield
Music: Mr J Hargreaves, BA York, MMus, FRSA
Physical Education: Mrs C Treacy, BSc Gloucestershire
Physics: Mr N Hillier, MSc LSE, BA Oxon
Politics: Mrs K Payne, BA Durham
Psychology: Mrs R Deaney, BSc OU, BMus, PG Dip RCM
Science: Mr P Rickard, BSc Bristol, BSc Liverpool
Spanish: Mr A Lopez, BA Oviedo
Theology: Mr A Ross, BA Lancaster, AIDTA [B]

Wolverhampton Grammar School

Compton Road, Wolverhampton, West Midlands WV3 9RB

Tel: 01902 421326
email: info@wgs.org.uk
website: www.wgs.org.uk
Twitter: @WGS1512
Facebook: @WolverhamptonGrammarSchool
LinkedIn: /company/wolverhampton-grammar-school

Wolverhampton Grammar School was founded in 1512 by Sir Stephen Jenyns – a Wolverhampton man who achieved success as a wool merchant, became a member of The Merchant Taylors' Company then Lord Mayor of London. He decided to benefit his home town by founding a school "for the instruction of youth in good manners and learning". The school retains close links with the Company.

Wolverhampton Grammar School is an all-through independent, selective day school for boys and girls aged 4–18 from a wide catchment area throughout the West Midlands, Staffordshire and Shropshire.

In 2011, the school opened a junior school (Wolverhampton Grammar Junior School) for students aged 7–11. The Junior School has proved exceptionally popular with parents, with waiting lists in some years. Families are advised to apply early to avoid disappointment. In 2021, Wolverhampton Grammar School expanded its junior school provision to incorporate Reception, Year 1 and Year 2 for students aged 4–7.

The school's mission is to deliver education that transforms lives as well as minds. It does this by delivering an education as individual as every child, within an environment that's like no other. The school delivers a personalised curriculum to provide an education and learning experience that is unique. Students achieve excellent GCSE and A Level exam results alongside an experience that includes the largest range of co- and extra-curricular activities available in the area.

The school was inspected in February 2017 and was judged to be 'excellent' in all areas. The report can be read on the ISI website: www.isi.net.

Buildings. The stunning 25-acre site includes a purpose-built Sixth Form Centre and Learning Hub. The £3.8 million Arts & Drama Centre is home to the Viner Gallery and Hutton Theatre. A Sports Centre and floodlit all-weather AstroTurf pitches provide some of the best sporting facilities in the area, with a Sports Pavilion providing panoramic views of the sports fields. Chemistry, Physics and Biology laboratories have been refurbished to the highest modern standards. State-of-the-art ICT facilities provide Wi-Fi internet access to all parts of the school and all teachers use iPads and app technology to enhance the learning experience.

Admission. The School accepts applications to the Junior, Senior and Sixth Form (Reception to Year 13) throughout the year, although new students usually join the school in September. The school's own Year 7 entrance tests are held in the preceding January. For the Sixth Form: offers of places are made subject to GCSE results and interview.

Fees per term (2021–2022). Reception £2,500; Years 1 & 2 £2,995; Years 3 to 6 £3,633; Senior School and Sixth Form £4,785.

Entrance Scholarships. There are a number of options available which offer support with fees, including a range of Bursaries and Scholarships. The awards vary according to the level of family income and are reviewed annually so please contact Jane Morris, Admissions Registrar on 01902 421326 or email jam@wgs-sch.net for further details.

Assistance with Fees. The School offers a number of means-tested bursaries to children from less affluent families who can demonstrate that they will benefit from the opportunity of an education with Wolverhampton Grammar School. Bursaries are reviewed annually so please contact Jane Morris, Admissions Registrar on 01902 421326 or email jam@wgs-sch.net for further details.

Curriculum. The curriculum is delivered using a two-week timetable. Supported by over 100 termly extra and co-curricular activities, it covers a broad range of academic subjects that includes language choices and Computer Science. Sixth Formers have a large choice of A Level subjects and Cambridge Technical qualifications. Sixth Formers usually take 3 or 4 subjects and this can also be supported by an Extended Project Qualification (EPQ) as well as structured work experience and HE/UCAS advice and guidance. Students go on to excellent universities including Oxford, Cambridge and other Russell Group institutions.

Games and Outdoor Activities. Wolverhampton Grammar School offers the largest range of extra-curricular activities, clubs, societies, trips, international expeditions and sport tours of any independent school in the area. Sport has a long tradition at the school and students compete at city, regional and national level. The 25-acre site includes rugby, cricket, hockey and football pitches, netball courts, an all-weather Astroturf and athletics track as well as a fully equipped sports centre with dance studio, multi-gym and indoor courts for badminton, squash and nets. A 'sport for all' attitude exists in games and PE, where the staff endeavour to match the student to a sport or activity in which they can succeed. There is a commitment to the highest standards of skill and sportsmanship but the emphasis is also placed on enjoyment. The school participates in The Duke of Edinburgh's Award scheme and there are opportunities to undertake field trips and foreign exchanges. There is a rigorous outdoor education programme. The School also boasts Fives Courts as well as a purpose-built climbing wall and sports pavilion offering panoramic views of large outdoor sports fields.

Dyslexia. The School's OpAL (Opportunities through Assisted Learning) department is designed to allow bright children with Specific Learning Difficulties (Dyslexia) to enjoy the challenge of a first-rate academic education. OpAL students have consistently achieved exceptional GCSE and A Level grades – consistently above the national average. Students also have access to additional 121 and small-group teaching around core curriculum subjects.

Arts and Other Activities. Purpose-built facilities for art, music and drama provide the best venues possible for exhibitions and school productions. The school boasts a purpose-built art gallery known as the Viner Gallery, which is used by students and commercial artists alike. A large contemporary theatre known as the Hutton Theatre is home to exceptional performances by students from across the School. The location of the music department at the heart of the school ensures the sound of singing, ensemble and band music is always heard on campus. There is a wide variety of extra-curricular clubs and activities giving students the opportunity to discover and cultivate new interests, both inside and outside the classroom. A Community Service programme and an active student Charity Fundraising Committee ensure that all students are involved in working for the good of others.

Pastoral Care. The school's first priority is the happiness of its students. Overseen by an Assistant Head with responsibility for Pastoral Care, the school has a dedicated, expert pastoral team, a school counsellor and Sixth Form mentors. The school also tracks student happiness using the latest digital tools. An important forum is the Student Parliament which consists of elected representatives from all year groups who are encouraged to voice concerns and suggest improvements to the running and organisation of the school.

Charitable status. Wolverhampton Grammar School Limited is a Registered Charity, number 1125268.

Chairman: Mr J E Sage

Directors, Council and Trustees:
The Mayor of Wolverhampton (*ex-officio*)
Mr S Aldis
Mr N Berriman
Mr C Bill
Mrs E Bloch
Mrs A Brennan
Rev S Cawdell
Mr R Cooper, [OW] (*ex-officio USA*)
Ms E Forde MBE
Dr M Gowan-Gopal
Dr S J L Gower [OW] (*appointed by the University of Birmingham*)
Mr J Harper
Mr P A Hawthorne, CBE [OW]
Mr D Hughes
Mr M Hughes
Mrs K Lawrence
Mr P Magill (*appointed by the Merchant Taylors' Company*)
Mr Y Malik
Mr A Phillips [OW] (*appointed by the Old Wulfrunians Association*)
Mr J Patel
Mr S Ross
Mr C Tatton
Mrs C Wood

[OW] *Old Wulfrunian*

Head: Mr A Frazer, MA, Christ's College Cambridge University

Deputy Heads:
Mr N J C Anderson, BSc, Leeds
Mr T R Hughes, MA, MPhil, PGCE, Queens' College and Homerton College, Cambridge

Assistant Heads:
Teaching & Learning: Mr A P Yarnley, BSc Hull
Pastoral: Miss C Jones, BA Nottingham Trent, Dip RSA
Academic Administration: Mr J R Wood, BA Royal Holloway, London, MA Ed Bangor

Head of Junior School: Mr D Peters, BMus Birmingham

Assistant Heads of Junior School:
Mr T J Cothey, BSc Lancaster
Mr J Griffiths, BA Liverpool John Moore's
Mrs E Stanton, BSc Hons Birmingham

Teaching Staff:
Miss L Austin, BSC Psychology Oxford Brookes
Mr T Baker, BSc Edinburgh
Miss A Bassett, BA Hons Worcester
Mr J Birch, MSc Birmingham
Mr M Blything, BA Sheffield
Mr R Bostock, PhD Aston
Mr R Bourne, MBA Aston
Miss E A Bowater, BA Birmingham City
Dr N J Bradley, BSc, PhD, Nottingham
Mr N Brown, BSc Hons Exeter
Mrs K Brown, MA Cambridge
Miss R Challoner, BA Hons Birmingham City
Mrs R E Clancy, BA Birmingham
Mr S M Clancy, BSc Loughborough
Mrs V J Clarke, BA Cambridge
Mr N H Crust, BA College of North Wales, Bangor
Mrs M Cuthbert, BA UCE
Mrs L D'Arcy, BSc Wolverhampton
Mrs A L Dalton, BA Nottingham Trent
Mr J G David, BA Newcastle-upon-Tyne
Mrs L Dixon, BSc Cardiff
Mr C Doman, BSc Hons Newman College, Birmingham
Ms E Duncan, BEd Hons Warwick
Mrs K A Dyer, BSc Gloucestershire
Ms A Fellows, BEd Birmingham
Mrs K L Finn, BA Manchester
Mr A Fowler, MA Magdalen College, Oxford
Mrs D S Gibbs, BA Bristol
Mrs A Grant, BSc Open
Ms C Green, PhD Birmingham
Mrs P D Grigat-Bradley, Erstes und Zweites Staatsexamen Ruhr-Universität, Bochum
Mrs G Guest, BA Hons Central England, Birmingham
Ms N T Guidotti, BA Anglia Polytechnic
Mr E D Hamill, BSc Glasgow
Mrs E S N Harris, BA Southampton
Mrs A Hughes, BEd Cambridge
Mr H Humphreys, BMedSc Birmingham
Mr S M Jackson-Turnbull, BA, MA, Huddersfield
Miss N Jacobs, BA Birmingham
Mr R Jagger, BA Liverpool
Mr T Jeavons, BSc Birmingham
Mr P Johnstone, BA Hull
Mr A Jones, BSc Hons Birmingham
Mr T King, ICC (*Senior Coach*)
Mrs P Manzai, BA Turin
Mr R W Mason, BA Nottingham
Mr N P Munson, BSc Birmingham
Mrs R E Munson, BA Leeds
Mr S L J O'Malley, BA Wolverhampton
Mr S P Palmer (*Senior Coach*)
M R Payne, BA Warwick
Mr J Piggott, BA Wolverhampton
Dr R Pounder, MChem, PhD Warwick
Mrs H Povey, BA Hons Birmingham
Mrs R Powell, BSC Hons Cardiff Metropolitan
Ms J Preston, Licence First Class Degree Lille III, France
Mrs C L Ray, BA Luton
Miss M Rattoo, BSc Coventry
Mr A Reddish, BA Sunderland
Mr G L Smith, BEd Loughborough

Mr T D Smith, BA Strathclyde

Mr L Taylor, BA Reading, MA Birmingham

Mr I H M Tyler, BA Saskatchewan, MEd Birmingham, Dip DA RADA

Mr J P Villafrati, BSc Birmingham

Mrs F E Wainwright, BSc Hertfordshire, PGCE Wolverhampton

Mrs K Wainwright, MSc Birmingham

Mrs D M Ward, BA, MA Birmingham

Miss E L Watson, BSc Manchester

Miss E Yates, MA Leicester

Miss R Young, BSc Warwick

Mrs B Young, BA Reading

Finance Director: Mrs S Hemmings

Head's PA: Mrs Caroline Harris

Woodhouse Grove School

Apperley Lane, Apperley Bridge, Bradford, West Yorkshire BD10 0NR

Tel: 0113 250 2477

email: enquiries@woodhousegrove.co.uk

website: www.woodhousegrove.co.uk

Twitter: @woodhouse_grove

Facebook: @woodhousegroveschool

Motto: '*Bone et fidelis*'

Woodhouse Grove was founded in 1812 and is a co-educational day and boarding school for pupils aged from 2 to 18 years. Boarding pupils are taken from the age of 11 years.

Our hard work has been recognised by the latest Independent Schools Inspectorate inspection which rated Woodhouse Grove as Excellent. The inspectors came away with very clear evidence of the Grovian Values that we seek to promote. They recognised our outstanding academic and co-curricular programme and our aim to ensure that all our pupils reach their full potential.

At Woodhouse Grove, we appreciate that every child is a unique individual and this is at the heart of everything we do. We aim to motivate pupils academically and beyond the classroom and to provide an educational environment designed to allow students to fully participate in school life.

We offer a rich, challenging and dynamic curriculum and want our students to ask questions of the world around them with an open mind; to have the character to listen to others, but also to stand up for their beliefs. We encourage our pupils to 'give back' to their community and we believe that this well-rounded, diverse approach is the key to building academic and personal confidence. Ultimately, our objective is to provide our students with the drive and aspiration to become the very best version of themselves that they can be.

Set in idyllic grounds near Leeds, the school is opposite Apperley Bridge train station and within four miles of Leeds Bradford Airport. We have high standards and an all-encompassing approach to education and our outstanding facilities reflect this. A recording studio, 230-seater theatre, sports halls, swimming pool and climbing wall are all within our 70-acre campus.

Numbers. There are 762 pupils in the Senior School including 68 boarders and a Sixth Form of 198 students. Brontë House (age 2–11 years) has 285 pupils.

Buildings. Our facilities include a purpose-built sports centre with a multi-functional sports hall, a fully-refurbished fitness suite, a dance studio, a 25m competition swimming pool, squash courts, floodlit outdoor courts, floodlit all-weather pitch, performing arts centre and climbing wall. We have fully equipped science laboratories, a state-of-the-art DT and Art centre, a spacious music and drama block, language suite and fully-equipped IT rooms. We have a modern spacious Sixth Form centre and refurbished boarding houses to provide a separate sixth form annexe for boys.

Sport. We have approximately 40 acres of playing fields including grounds for Cricket, Rugby, Football and Athletics as well as indoor Squash, Basketball and Swimming facilities. There are several all-weather Tennis Courts, a floodlit outdoor court for Netball and Tennis and a floodlit all-weather pitch.

Music. A high percentage of pupils have instrumental or vocal tuition and pupils can perform in a wide variety of music, drama and dance groups. Accredited exams offered include ABRSM & Trinity Guildhall Speech and Drama. There are a number of high-profile annual performances taking advantage of the dedicated theatre and recording studio. Music tours take place every two years. Sixth form courses are available in Music and Music Technology.

Curriculum. Boys and girls can enter the Senior School at any age but mainly at the age of 11, 13 and 16 and the curriculum is arranged to provide a seamless transition through from Brontë House and upwards through the Sixth Form to University entrance. A wide range of GCSE (and IGCSE) courses are offered and currently we are offering 24 subjects at A Level plus additional BTEC options and the opportunity to gain work experience within local business partners as part of the sixth form experience. Specialist support is offered to meet EAL, dyslexia and other learning needs. All students get the chance to study French, Spanish and German. The campus is served by full-site Wi-Fi.

Sixth Form Entry. Places are available for students who want to come into the School at the Sixth Form stage subject to entry requirements.

Scholarships and Bursaries. Scholarships can be applied for directly from the headmaster for academic, all-rounder, art, sport and music. In addition, bursaries can be awarded following the offer of a place, in cases of financial need (plus allowances for children of ministers and of service personnel). Extras include excursions and extra tuition, such as music.

Admission. Places are offered subject to availability and based on our own entrance exam, in-school interview and previous school report. Pupils are usually accepted in September, although arrangements can be made for entry throughout the school year.

Brontë House is our Preparatory School and takes boys and girls from the age of two years old. Ashdown Lodge Nursery & Reception takes pupils, on a day or part-day basis, all year round.

Fees per term (2021–2022). Main School: £10,185–£10,240 (full boarders), £4,830–£4,898 (day). Brontë House: £3,570–£4,326 (day). Ashdown Lodge Nursery and Reception: £3,255 (full day). Fees include all meals, books, stationery, examination fees and careers tests.

Extra Subjects. There is a wide range of extra subjects available including individual music lessons, singing, speech and drama, extra sports coaching, debating, Duke of Edinburgh's Award, photography and fencing.

Old Grovians Association. email: oga@ woodhousegrove.co.uk.

Charitable status. Woodhouse Grove School is part of the Methodist Independent Schools Trust, which is a Registered Charity, number 1142794.

Governors:

Mr A Wintersgill, FCA (*Chairman*)
Mr C Allen, LLB
Mr M Best, ACA
Mr S Bickerton, BDS, MFGDP, RCS
Mr S Burnhill, BSc
Mrs A Cook, BA
Mr R S Drake, LLB Hons, ACIArb
Rt Revd C P Edmondson
Mrs P M Essler, BSc
Mr R C Hemsley, FCA, MA
Ms P Kaur, MSc
Mr F J McAleer, BA Arch, Dip Arch, RIBA
Prof M Manogue, BDS, MDSc, PhD
Mr S Morris, MA, PGCE, NPHQ
Mr M Pearman, MA
Revd K Tankard, BA, MA
Revd P Whittaker, BA
Mrs G Wilson, CertEd

Staff:

Headmaster: J A Lockwood, MA

Deputy Head: Mrs E Nulty, BA
Deputy Head (*Academic*): E J Wright, BSc
Deputy Head (*Pastoral*): A M Cadman, BSc

Assistant Head (*Curriculum*): Mrs C Nott, MA
Assistant Head (*Organisation*): K D Eaglestone, BSc
Assistant Head (*Pupil Welfare*): Mrs F L Hughes, BEd
Assistant Head (*Teaching and Learning*): Mrs D L
   Shoesmith-Evans, MA

Chaplain: Revd V Atkins, BA
Operations Director: Mrs V Bates, ACA
Director of Marketing and Commerce: Mrs S Cadman, BA

* *Head of Department*
† *Head of House*

Miss F Alimundo, BA (*Geography, Geology*)
Mr J Allison, BA (**Design Technology*, †*Vinter*)
Mr S Archdale (*Speech and Drama*)
Revd V Atkins (*School Chaplain, RS*)
Miss A Barron, BA (*German*)
Mr N Barr, BA (*PE and Games, Mathematics,*
   †*Stephenson*)
Mr E Bean, BSc (**Physics*)
Mr P Borrington, BSc (*PE and Games*)
Mr A Cadman, BSc (*PE*)
Mrs P N Charlton, MA (*Art & Design*)
Miss E Corson, BA (*Modern Foreign Languages*)
Mr A N Crawford, BA, ARCO (*Music, Mathematics,*
   †*Findlay*)
Miss C Couper, BA (**Drama and Theatre Studies*)
Mrs K Curtis, BSc (**Academic PE, Games*)
Miss B Dawson (*Learning Support*)
Mr T Davis, BA (**Chemistry*)
Mr M Dawson, BA (*History*)

Mrs S Dawson, BA (*Mathematics*)
Mr M Dobson, BSc (*PE and Games*)
Mr K Eaglestone, BSc (*Mathematics*)
Mrs J L Edger, BSc (*Physics*)
Miss E Emmott, BA (*Art*)
Miss K England, BSc (*Chemistry*)
Miss L Evers, MA (*English, Media*)
Mr T Exeter (*Science*)
Mrs H Fisher, BSc (**Psychology*)
Miss L Follos, BA (*Design Technology*)
Mr C Garbutt, BSc (*Biology, Chemistry*)
Mr M Gill, BSc (*Information and Technology*)
Mrs K L Goodwin-Bates, MA (*English*)
Miss S Harder, BSc (*Science*)
Miss L Holloway, BA (*History & RS*)
Mrs F L Hughes, BEd (*French*)
Miss L Hughes, BA (*English*)
Dr A Ingham, BSc (*Biology*)
Mrs H Innes, BA (*Business Studies, Economics*)
Mr A Jarvis, BA (*Modern Languages*)
Miss C D Jemmett, BA (*English*)
Mr A Jennings, BA (*Religious Studies*)
Mrs K Jennings, BEd (*Assistant Director Sport, PE*)
Mr R Jones, BA (*PE and Games*)
Mr M Keegan, BA (*English*)
Mrs A Kerr, BSc (**Mathematics, IT*)
Mr D King, MA (**Director of Sport*)
Mr P Lambert, BA (*Modern Foreign Languages*)
Miss E Landy, MA (*Chemistry, Biology*)
Mrs V Limbert, BA (*English*)
Mr P Madden, BA (**History*)
Mr O Mantle, BA (*IT, *Business Studies, Economics,*
   †*Atkinson*)
Mrs H Mitchell, BA (**Modern Foreign Languages*)
Mr P J Moffat, BA (*Geography*)
Miss B Monk, BA (**ESOL, *Learning Support*)
Mr M F Munday, BA (*Geography*)
Mrs C Nott, MA (**Mathematics*)
Mrs E Nulty, BA (*Business Studies, Economics*)
Miss L Oakley, BA (**English*)
Miss C Pearce, BA (*PE and Games, Geography*)
Mr A J Pickles, BA (**Art & Design*)
Mrs H Priestley, BA (*Drama and Dance*)
Mrs L Richardson, BSc (**Biology*)
Mr J B Robb, BA (**Religious Studies*)
Mrs R Sharpe, BA (*English*)
Mrs D L Shoesmith-Evans, MA (**History, Politics*)
Mrs D Smith, BA (*Design and Technology*)
Mrs E Smith, BSc (*Mathematics*)
Mrs L Smith, BA (*Modern Foreign Languages*)
Mr C Softley, BA (*Director of Sixth Form, PE*)
Mrs C Spencer, LLM (*Business Studies, Economics,*
   †*Towlson*)
Miss H Spiller, BA (*Art*)
Mr D Sugden, BSc (*Mathematics*)
Mr J P A Tedd, MA (**Performing Arts, Music*)
Miss G Thompson BA (*PE and Games*)
Mrs R Vernon, BSc (*PE*)
Mrs R Warner, BA (*Politics, History*)
Mrs P L Watson, MA (*Business Studies, IT*)
Mrs L Watmough BA (**Business Studies*, †*Southerns*)
Miss K Webb, BA (*PE and Games*)
Mrs R Wickens, BA (**Geography*)
Mr E Wright, BSc (*Mathematics*)

Headmaster's Secretary: Mrs R Dodds
Admissions Manager: Mrs J Amos

Brontë House
Head of School: Mrs S Chatterton, BEd
Assistant Head (*Ashdown*): Mrs A Hinchliffe, BA
Assistant Head (*Upper School*): Mrs F Pearson, BA
Assistant Head (*Lower School*): Mrs H J Simpson, BA

Worth School

**Paddockhurst Road, Turners Hill, West Sussex
RH10 4SD**

Tel: 01342 710200
email: admissions@worth.org.uk
website: www.worthschool.org.uk
Twitter: @worthschool
Facebook: @worthschool
Instagram: @worth.school
LinkedIn: /worth-school

Worth is a Catholic Benedictine boarding and day school for boys and girls aged 11–18 where those of any faith, or none, are welcome. It is a truly distinctive school, known for its strong community values, friendly atmosphere and the excellence of its all-round education. The school has been under the leadership of Mr Stuart McPherson (formerly at Eton College) since September 2015 and in the Head Master's words is: "a place where we seek to uncover and ignite children's passions and talents. The path a life takes often begins at school, and this is why we do not just provide education, we offer learning with heart and soul, and this gives Worth a difference of kind that sets us apart."

This magnificent school is in the heart of the Sussex countryside, about halfway between London and Brighton, and less than 15 minutes from Gatwick airport. We are ideally placed to allow students to sample some of the cultural highlights that Britain has to offer, while providing a beautiful environment in which to learn.

In an Independent Schools Inspectorate (ISI) Report in November 2017, Worth was judged to be excellent – the highest possible grade – for the quality of the pupils' academic and other achievements and personal development. In January 2011 we had a full Ofsted inspection on provision for Boarders at Worth. The school was found to be 'Outstanding' and no recommendations were made. A review by the *Good Schools Guide* in 2017 concluded that "This school has everything going for it..."

The school offers a broad curriculum, where students can opt for the International Baccalaureate Diploma or A Levels. The School has offered the IB since 2002 and a pre-IB course was introduced for non-UK students in Year 11 in 2015. Examination results are excellent and pupils enter the best universities in the UK and abroad, including Oxford, Cambridge, Russell Group universities and Ivy League institutions.

The wider curriculum is rich and varied with a huge range of activities, societies, lectures and trips from which to choose. There is also a lively sporting programme which has produced students of national and county standard, and the school's reputation for performing arts is outstanding.

History. Worth welcomed girls into Years 7 and 9 in September 2010. They joined other girls in an already thriving co-educational Sixth Form, and the school has been fully co-educational since 2012 with girls integrated into all aspects of school life.

Courses of study. At GCSE level, students usually take ten subjects. The compulsory core is: English, Mathematics, Sciences, French or Spanish or German (plus PE and SMSC).

There is a wide choice of subjects at A Level and there is also the opportunity to take the Extended Project Qualification (EPQ). A BTEC in Business is available subject to demand. Full details of subject choices can be found on the School website.

Alternatively, Sixth Form students may study the International Baccalaureate. This involves the study of six subjects, three at Higher Level and three at Standard Level. Details can be found in the Sixth Form Subject Options booklet on the Worth School website.

Thanks to the generosity of a former student, a multi-million pound new Sixth Form Centre opened in the Autumn Term of 2021. Sixth Form students may also choose to study for Oxbridge entrance and a number gain places at either Oxford or Cambridge.

Pastoral Care. Care of each student is of central importance throughout the school, as evidenced by our 'Outstanding' Ofsted grading for Boarder provision. Each pupil is a member of a House and has a personal tutor who monitors work progress and assists the Housemaster/Housemistress with overall care. The House support structure also includes a Chaplain and a matron, supported by an assistant matron in each of the Boarding Houses. There is a counsellor available to pupils.

Sport. Worth loves its sports. The main sports are: rugby, football, hockey, netball, cricket, tennis and athletics. Other sports played at competitive level include fencing, squash, golf, basketball, lacrosse and swimming, and sports are also available through school clubs and activities (see below). There is a floodlit Astropitch, a nine-hole golf course, squash courts, tennis courts, fencing salle, dance studio and fitness suite. The school also makes use of the excellent athletics facility and 50m swimming pool at a multi-sports centre nearby.

Performing Arts. Music is important at Worth. There is a flourishing choir, the *Schola Cantorum*, that is involved in tours and makes regular appearances in the Abbey Church. The school orchestra performs regularly, as does the Jazz Band. The annual House Music and Young Musician of the Year competitions provide all pupils with an opportunity to perform and encourage an interest in music.

Drama also flourishes with regular dramatic and musical productions at all levels and the standard of performance is exceptional. There are three major productions a year, taking place in the purpose-built Performing Arts Centre which comprises a 250-seater theatre, box office, drama office and workshop, dressing rooms, recording studio, a sound-proofed 'rock room', rehearsal rooms, a recital room and music classrooms.

Extracurricular activity. On Wednesday afternoons every pupil participates in one or more activities, ranging from Age Concern and photography to sailing, clay pigeon shooting and website design. There is a horse riding school for students nearby and there are stables on the campus. Worth is also a centre of excellence for The Duke of Edinburgh's Award scheme. There are lectures by external speakers and a wide array of trips, visits and exchanges both at home and abroad.

Weekends. From September 2022 Saturday morning academic lessons, currently compulsory for all pupils in the senior school, will instead move into the Monday to Friday timetable. This change presents a range of new opportunities for boarders and an exciting new structure for the weekend boarding experience at Worth with a dynamic programme of activities, Games, revision classes and more.

Admissions Policy.

Entry at 11+: Entrance tests in English, Maths and Non-Verbal Reasoning are held in January each year. Offers are based on test results, a report from the student's current school and an interview with the Head Master. Annual promotion is subject to the pupil having shown satisfactory academic performance as determined by the Head Master, and a good disciplinary record.

Entry at 13+ (Year 9) for 2022–2023: Admission at 13+, after visits and registrations, is via the ISEB Common Pre-Test, taken either at Worth or at Prep schools in the Autumn Term of Year 7, and Worth's additional assessment days. Admission for overseas candidates is via separate assessment tests and interviews held in their own countries.

Entry at 16+: Admissions is by means of reports and references from the candidate's current school, assessments and interviews held at Worth during the year prior to entry. Entry is competitive, and successful applicants will usually be predicted to gain top grades in most of their GCSEs or equivalent examinations, but we recognise the central value of Art, Drama, Music, Sport and other co-curricular activities, and enthusiasm in these fields is expected and encouraged.

For further information on Admissions please contact the Registrar on 01342 710231.

Scholarships. Scholarships at Worth are highly prestigious awards available to students demonstrating outstanding talent and ability in the spheres of Academic Study, Art, Drama, Music or Sport. Candidates must be registered with the school prior to entering the scholarship process and applications for bursaries should be made at the same time as applications for scholarships.

For all types of scholarships, awards can range in value and a candidate may also hold one or more awards, so that Academic, Art, Drama. Music or Sport awards may be held concurrently. Additionally, at the Head Master's discretion, exceptional awards with a fee concession may be made where, during the assessment process, we identify exceptional potential or need. Tenure of any award depends upon continued satisfactory progress. The school reserves the right to vary the number of awards according to the strength of applications. The level of fee concession provided can be augmented by bursary support which is subject to means assessment.

For further information on scholarships and bursaries, please see the school website.

Fees per term (2021–2022). Years 9–13: Boarding £12,160, Day £8,360; Years 7 & 8: Day £5,630.

Friends of Worth. The parents of children at Worth run their own programme of social events to which all parents are invited. Typical events are coffee mornings, drinks receptions and a bi-annual ball.

Worth Society. All Old Worthians are entitled to join the alumni society which organises events as well as assisting with individual work experience and ongoing careers guidance. Contact Mary Lou Burge at worthsociety@worth.org.uk.

Charitable status. Worth School is a Registered Charity, number 1093914. Its aims and objectives are to promote religion and education.

Rt Rev Abbot Mark Barrett OSB, MA Cantab, MA, PhD (*President*)
Mr Tim Pethybridge, MA (*Chair*)
Mrs Brenda Alleyne, LLB
Ms Mary Coller, BSc
Dr Bridget Dolan, QC
Mr Jeremy Fletcher, BA
Mr Peter Green, Cert RE, MA
Mr Gavin Hamilton-Deeley, FCA
Dom David Jarmy, Cert Theol, PGCE
Ms Alison Palmer, BSc
Mrs Helen Parry, BSc

***Head Master*: Mr Stuart McPherson**, MA

Second Master: Mr André Gushurst-Moore, MA
Deputy Head (*Academic*): Mrs Alice McNeill, MA
Deputy Head (*External*): Mr Gordon Pearce, MA
Deputy Head (*Pastoral*): Ms Louise Chamberlain, BSc
Deputy Head (*Co-Curricular and Partnerships*): Mr Julian Williams, BSc, MA, Dip TESL
Assistant Head (*Pupil Progress*): Mrs Sarah Flint, BA
Assistant Head (*Sixth Form*): Dr Bruna Gushurst-Moore, BA, MSt, PhD
Director of Mission: Mr Will Desmond, BA
Chief Operating Officer: Mr Paul Bilton, MA, FCA

Teaching Staff:
* *Head of Department/Subject*

Mr Paul Ambridge, BA (*Physics*)
Mrs Esme Mustian Atkinson (*Librarian*)
Mr Garry Backshell, BSc Hons, MSc (*Physics*)
Mrs Frances Baily, MSc (**Physics*)
Mr Timothy Baldwin, BA, BSc Hons (*Economics*)
Mrs Andrea Beadle, BA, MA (**German*)
Mrs Sophie Belloul, BA (**French*)
Mr Jonathan Bindloss, BA (**Christian Theology and Philosophy, Theory of Knowledge*)
Mr Stuart Blackhurst, HND (*Head of Digital Strategy*)
Mrs Myfanwy Bournon, BA (*English, Austin Housemistress*)
Mr Lewis Brito-Babapulle, MA (*Director of Music*)
Mr William Burch, BSc (*Maths*)
Mrs Alexandra Burnham (*St Mary's Middles Housemistress*)
Mrs Caroline Burton, MSc (*Biology*)
Mr David Burton, BEd (*Director of Sport*)
Mrs Lucinda Button, BA (*Art & Design*)
Mrs Katie Camp, BA (*Art*)
Mrs Olivia Carter, BSc (*Mathematics*)
Mr Geoffrey Chapman, BA (*Religious Studies*)
Mr Raj Chaudhuri, BCom, ECB Level 4 (*Master in charge of Cricket*)
Mr Paul Cheeseman, BA (*Design and Technology*)
Miss Sarah Clarke, BA (**History*)
Mrs Dawn Clubb, BA, MA (**English*)
Mr Daniel Collins, LLB (*Head of Football*)
Miss Isabelle Collis, BSc (*Sports Coach*)
Mr William Crénel, LLCE (*French, St Bede's Housemaster*)
Miss Maria Isabel Del Valle, BA Hons (*Spanish, French*)
Mrs Jayne Dempster, BSc (*Mathematics*)
Mr John Dent, MEng (*Mathematics*)
Mr Matthew Doggett, MA, MSci (**Mathematics, Science*)

Mr Charlie Douglas-Hughes (*Director of Lettings and Wider Curriculum*)

Mr Jeremy Dowling, BEd (*Mathematics*)

Mr John Everest, BA (*Photography*)

Mr Neil Everest, MA (*Christian Theology*)

Mr Simon Faulkner, BA (*Head of Hockey, Games & Physical Education, Economics*)

Mr Jonathan Fry, BA (*Economics, Farwell Housemaster*)

Dr Barbara Gehrhus, Diplomchemiker, PhD (*Chemistry*)

Mrs Sarah George, BEd (*Learning Support*)

Mr Jamie Gostlow, BA, History

Mrs Jo Harvey-Barnes (*Games & Physical Education, Biology, St Catherine's Housemistress*)

Miss Hannah Higgins, BSC Hons, MSc (*Physics*)

Miss Juley Hudson, BA, MA (**Art*)

Mr Joseph Huntley, BA (*Religious, PSHE Coordinator*)

Mrs Siobhan Isaacs, BA (*Games & Physical Education, Assistant Director of Sport, St Anne's Housemistress*)

Ms Melanie Kendry, MA (*English*)

Mrs Andrea Kirpalani, BSc (**Science, Chemistry*)

Miss Naomy Larkin, BA (*English*)

Mrs Catherine Latham, BSc, MSc (*Head of Learning Support and SENCO*)

Mr Andrew Lavis, BA (**Geography*)

Mr Alex Leadbeater, BA (*Assistant Director of Music*)

Mrs Rachel Le Mare, BA, MA (*Business Studies*)

Miss Lucy Lockwood, BA (*Music Technology*)

Mrs Natalie Lynch, BA (*Director of Drama*)

Mr Mark Macdonald, BSc (*Geography, Chapman Housemaster*)

Mr Alick Macleod, MSc (*Geography, Gervase Housemaster*)

Mrs Helen Macleod, BA (*History*)

Mr David Marks, MA, BA (**English as an Additional Language*)

Mrs Sigrid Moiseiwitsch (*German*)

Mrs Maria Molinero, BA (**Modern Foreign Languages, Spanish*)

Mr Bruce Morrison, BEd (*Games & Physical Education, Mathematics, Butler Housemaster*)

Mr Robin Moss, BSc (*Chemistry & Science*)

Ms Sheena Nasim, MA (*Economics & Business Studies*)

Mrs Fiona Norden, BA (*English*)

Miss Tola Olawuyi, BEng (*Mathematics*)

Mr Andrew Olle (*Games & Physical Education*)

Mrs Emily Pearcy (*Sports Coach*)

Ms Elizabeth Peters, BA (*History & Politics*)

Mr Richard Phillips, BSc (**Economics and Business Studies*)

Ms Alessandra Pittoni, Laurea in Lingue (*Italian*)

Miss Kate Reynolds, BSc (*Biology, Games & Physical Education*)

Ms Linda Rice, BA, MA (*Learning Support*)

Mr Thomas Richardson (*Head of Rugby*)

Mr Liam Richman, BSc (*Mathematics, Rutherford Housemaster*)

Mr Philip Robinson, MA (*Classics*)

Miss Eleanor Ross, BSc (*Chemistry, Extended Essay Coordinator*)

Miss Charlotte Rule, BSc (*Geography, St Mary's Sixth Form Housemistress*)

Ms Victoria Sadler, MA (*Geography*)

Dr Peter Scott, MA, PhD (**Biology*)

Mrs Geeyoung Steele, BA (*Religious Studies*)

Mr Hugo Sutton, BA (*History, IB Coordinator*)

Dr Bianca Thomas, BSc Hons, MSc, PhD (*Biology*)

Mr Philip Towler, MA (**Classics*)

Mr Ryan Vaughan (*Computer Science*)

Mr Dan Weaver, BA (**Design Technology, *ICT*)

Mr Peter Webb, BA (*Mission Project Manager, Religious Studies*)

Miss Imogen Whyte, BA (*English*)

Ms Naomi Williams, BSc (**Psychology*)

Mr Ben Young, BA (*Spanish*)

Miss Bei Yu (*Mandarin*)

Registrar: Mrs Lucy Garrard

Head Master's Secretary: Mrs Samantha Braund

Head of Pupil Healthcare: Miss Tania Murphy

Wrekin College

Wellington, Shropshire TF1 3BH

Tel: Main: 01952 265600
          Headmaster's Office: 01952 265602
          Admissions: 01952 265603

email: admissions@wrekincollege.com

website: www.wrekincollege.com

Twitter: @WrekinCol

Facebook: @WrekinCollege

Instagram: @wrekincollege

LinkedIn: /school/wrekincollege

Motto: '*Aut vincere aut mori*'

Wrekin College was founded in 1880 by Sir John Bayley and in 1923 became one of the Allied Schools, a group of independent schools.

Wrekin is a highly successful independent co-educational day and boarding school for children aged 11–18. Boasting an extensive campus in a beautiful part of Shropshire, Wrekin opened a new Dance Studio in September 2021, and its state-of-the-art Music School in January 2020. These additions come after the launch of Wrekin's enviable Business School, in January 2017, which has the future of Wrekin's pupils at its heart. The recent and future developments reflect the school's guiding principle to help every child achieve the most they are capable of, prepare them for the competitive world they will enter, and give them a lasting sense of the joy and value of learning that will enrich their future lives. Other facilities include a purpose-built Theatre, a double Sports Hall, Astroturf (a second all-weather playing surface opened in autumn 2021), 25m indoor swimming pool, together with all the expected classrooms, ICT facilities and a dedicated Sixth Form Centre. Co-educational since 1975, there are seven Houses, which cater for both day and boarding pupils, and these include dedicated junior Houses for the 11 to 13 intake. Everyone eats together in a central dining room and a Health and Wellbeing Centre is available to all pupils. The Chapel is central to the school both geographically and in the impact it makes on the ethos of the school.

Admission. Wrekin is non-selective; boarders and day pupils are admitted at 11+ and 13+ after sitting the Entry Examination or Common Entrance. There is also a Sixth Form entry based on GCSE achievement. Entry into other years is possible, dependent on places being available.

Term of Entry. The normal term of entry is the Autumn Term but pupils may be accepted at other times of the academic year.

Academic Matters. The core purpose of the school is teaching and learning to support each child in reaching his or her academic potential. Wrekin is proud of its academic record, based on stimulating intellectual curiosity, providing excellent and inspiring teaching, and making learning exciting.

Classes are small and teachers are experienced, expert and approachable, and give a great deal of time to pupils both inside and outside the classroom. Our tutoring system means each pupil has personalised academic support throughout the year. Our Support for Learning staff can help those with additional needs, and our enrichment programme stimulates and stretches our more able students.

Our curriculum is constantly reviewed in the light of changes in educational policy and philosophy, but we are committed to offering our pupils a solid and broad academic foundation. We offer a wide range of subjects for GCSE, A Level and BTEC exams, and guide pupils in choosing subjects that suit their interests, abilities and future plans. Our Head of Careers advises pupils throughout their time at school, and the Head of Sixth Form offers expert advice on life after Wrekin, including university applications.

Sport. For a 'small' school, our sporting prowess is remarkable. We aim for very high standards in our core sports and a very wide range of options. We believe in excellence but also in participation – sport for all, and for life.

Educating the Whole Person. The outdoors is one of Wrekin's most valuable classrooms. The skills learned and adventures experienced during pupils' participation in the Combined Cadet Force and the Duke of Edinburgh's Award scheme stay with them for life. Both are enthusiastically supported by highly dedicated staff, and the take up among our pupils is impressive. We are very proud that Wrekin's 'completion rate' at all levels of the scheme is substantially above the national average.

What happens on the sports pitch and in the music rooms, the theatre and the art studios is just as important a part of a Wrekin education. The range and quality of activities available to every pupil is outstanding, especially for a school of this size. Our pupils' development and achievements in these areas are supported by wonderful facilities and highly dedicated staff.

Scholarships and Bursaries.

Academic Scholarships are awarded at our normal entry points of 11, 13 and 16.

Music and Art/Design Scholarships: As for all other scholarships, Music and Art Awards will not exceed twenty five per cent of the fees. However, Music Scholarships carry with them a specified amount of free instrumental and/or vocal tuition. Candidates must also satisfy the school's normal academic entry requirements.

Sports Awards: Sports Scholarships may be awarded to candidates with outstanding ability in Sport. Applicants must attend a sports assessment day and satisfy the school's normal academic entry requirements. Candidates should be capable of a very significant contribution to the sporting success of Wrekin College. Typically candidates will have representative success at regional or National level.

Pendle Awards may be offered to all-rounders who have high academic standards and excellence in other areas such as sport, music or art. Those seeking a Pendle Award must sit the academic Scholarship Examination, either at 11+, 13+ or 16+ level and meet scholarship standard in at least one other area.

Bursaries may be awarded on entry and can be awarded in addition to a scholarship. All bursaries are means tested.

For further information please visit our website www.wrekincollege.com.

Fees per term (2021–2022). First and Second Forms: £5,230 (day); £7,380 (weekly boarding); £9,810 (full boarding). Third–Sixth Forms: £6,320 (day); £8,690 (weekly boarding); £11,480 (full boarding).

Music lessons £25.75 per 30-minute session; Extra Tuition £25.75 per 30-minute session.

Sibling discounts are available when three or more siblings are enrolled in the Trust; details on request.

Old Wrekinian Association. A flourishing Wrekinian Association of over 3,500 members exists to make possible continuous contact between the School and its old pupils, for the benefit of both and to support the ideals and aims of the school. It is expected that pupils will become members of the Old Wrekinian Association when they leave Wrekin.

Charitable status. Wrekin Old Hall Trust Limited is a Registered Charity, number 528417. It exists to provide independent boarding and day co-education in accordance with the Articles of Association of Wrekin College.

Visitor: The Rt Revd The Lord Bishop of Lichfield

Governors:
R J Pearson, BSc (*Chairman*)
Revd M Beer
E Crawford, MB, ChB, BSc, MRCP
A J Dixon, LLB
J A Grant, BSc [OW]
A J Herber-Davies
P A T Hunt
A B Huxley [OW]
R M L Jones, FCA, BA Hons
P Mack, BSc, ACA, CTA
R Mottram
M Samra, FRGGP
D Styles
T Shaw, BSc, MRICS [OW]

[OW] *Old Wrekinian*

Headmaster: T Firth, BA Hons

Senior Deputy Head: Mrs A Wright, BSc

Deputy Head (*Teaching and Learning*): B Smith, BA, MPhil

†*Assistant Head* (*Planning*): Dr G Roberts, BSc, PhD
Assistant Head (*Co-Curricular*): D Winterton, BA

Head of Sixth Form: T Southall, BSc

Bursar: D Brown, BA, ACMA, CGMA

Assistant Staff:
† *Housemaster/mistress*

T Asch, BA	†H S R Brown, BA
†H Bibby, BA	K Carter, BSc
†L Boffey, BSc	S Carter, BEng, MBA
J Boulter, BA	L Castree, BA
A J I Brennan, BA	S E Clarke, BA, FRGS
R Brock, BSc	T Corbett, BSc

M Crone, BA
K Davies, BSc
R Edge, BSc
R Evans, BA
J Harris, BSc
P Harris, BSc
A Jagger, BA
A Knight, BSc
M Koepke
†J D Kotas, BA
T Lintern, BSc
K B Livingstone, BA
J Longfellow, BA MEd
  (*Cantab*)
†J Mather, BSc
†H Milton, BA
F Milton, BA
R B Nayman, BA
R Norval, BSc
J G Phillips, BA

S Platford MBE, BA LTCL
  ABSM
Revd L Plummer BA, LTh
C A Ritchie-Morgan
R Salano Marin, BA
J Shaw, BA
J Shindler, BSc
P M Stanway, BSc
D Szwarc
H Tarver MEng
C Tonks, BA
C Thust, BSc
P Trahearn, BA
S Trask, BEng
A Walsh, BA
†M N J Warner, BSc
A E Wedge, BSc
A Williams, BSc
Dr A Woodshore-Gray,
  BA, MA, PhD

Deputy Bursars:
Facilities: B C Crone
Operations: H Hyde

Chaplain: Revd L Plummer, BA, LTh

Head of Marketing: C Hendy, BA
Head of Admissions: R Curel
Headmaster's Personal Assistant: K Daniels BSc

Support for Learning:
D Tunnah, BSC, QTS, NASENCO, CPT3A
M Beattie, BA, TEFL
J Firth, BA, PGDip
H Ingoldby, BA, TEFL
J Roberts, BA, BSc, TEFL
French Assistant: F Kennedy
German Assistant: K Nayman

Visiting Music Staff:
L le Boutiller (*Voice*)
J Burgess (*Flute*)
R Ellis (*Voice*)
C Hickman (*Brass*)
Dr M Hall (*Piano*)
O James (*Percussion*)
C J Jones (*Piano, Clarinet and Saxophone*)
L Jones (*Violin*)
Y Kagajo (*Piano*)
J Magee (*Cello*)
P Parker (*Guitar*)
A Pinel (*Organ*)
F Stubbs (*Bassoon*)
M Svensson (*Head of Strings*)
G Wilkes (*Brass*)

Games:
C A Ritchie-Morgan (*Head of Girls' Games*)
J Shaw (*Head of Boys' Games*)

Sports Coaches:
Mrs K Bennett (*Girls'
  Games*)
Mrs G Bush (*Athletics*)
D Clarke (*Swimming*)
B Crump (*Hockey*)
G Davies (*Cricket*)
Mrs P Dean (*Netball*)
J das Gupta (*Rugby*)
S Floyd (*Hockey*)
T Gough (*Hockey*)

V Harrhy (*Boys' Games*)
J Mostyn (*Senior Options*)
A C Sammons (*Rugby*)
M Strangwood (*Cross
  Country*)
J Wodja (*Cricket*)
I Williamson (*Cross
  Country*)
Miss V Woodman (*Netball*)

CCF:
SSI & Outward Bound Activities Instructor: RQMS, E J
  Fanneran, late RA
Secretary OWA: M de Weymarn
Archive OWA: M Joyner MSc

HMC International

ALPHABETICAL LIST OF SCHOOLS

HMC Schools in Europe

The British School of Brussels

Pater Dupierreuxlaan 1, 3080 Tervuren, Belgium

Tel: 00 32 2 766 04 30
email: admissions@britishschool.be
website: www.britishschool.be
Twitter: @BSB_Brussels
Facebook: @britishschoolbrussels
Instagram: @bsb_brussels
LinkedIn: /the-british-school-of-brussels

Creation. The British School of Brussels (BSB) was founded in 1969 as a non-profit making organisation in Belgium and was opened in 1970 by HRH The Duke of Edinburgh. It is run by a Board of Governors, comprising distinguished British and Belgian citizens from both the professional and business worlds, together with parent and staff representatives.

Site. The school occupies a beautiful site of ten hectares, surrounded by woodlands and lakes near the Royal Museum of Central Africa in Tervuren, which is 20–25 minutes by car from the centre of Brussels. The site belongs to the Donation Royale, the Foundation which manages the estates left to the Belgian people at the beginning of the 20th century by King Leopold II.

Facilities. The school has excellent modern specialist facilities, situated on a green and spacious campus. These facilities include dance and drama studios, a university standard music suite as well as eleven science laboratories, four art studios and seven technology workshops. The campus is also home to an Early Childhood Centre for children of 1–3 years. The sporting facilities of the school have been extensively developed to include world class amenities such as a multi-purpose sports hall, gymnasium, and fitness suite. In addition, the BSB is the only international school in Belgium to have its own competition standard swimming pool. The school's outdoor sports facilities were redesigned in 2019 and now include multiple sports pitches, tennis courts and the largest free-standing bouldering wall in any school in Europe. As well as the exterior sports grounds, students also enjoy outdoor learning in the campus grounds and the adjoining forest. To aid learning at most stages of their development, students in most year groups are issued with either their own iPad or laptop computer.

Organisation. The British School of Brussels is an independent, fee-paying, non-profit-making international school. The School is a co-educational, non-selective day school for students from 1 to 18 years of age, with a roll of approximately 1,350. Around 30% of the students are British and there are approximately 70 other nationalities represented. The curriculum, both in the Primary School and Secondary School, is a British-based curriculum up to age 16, adapted to suit the needs of our European context and international students. In the Secondary School, students sit GCSE/IGCSE examinations at the end of Year 11 (aged 16). Senior students then have the choice of three pre-university qualifications: The International Baccalaureate (IB) Diploma (with English/French or English/Dutch bilingual options), GCE A Levels or BTEC courses in business,

sports, applied science, and hospitality prior to moving on to Higher Education in the UK, USA, Belgium and beyond. Provision is also made for Oxbridge tuition and US university applications. Our examination results, year on year, are very impressive and place us in the top performing schools globally. In 2021 our students achieved 100% pass rates in all three systems: in A Levels, in IB Diploma and in BTEC. Our IB average was 40.0 points. Students successfully graduate to some of the top universities around the world.

BSB has an established French/English bilingual programme for children aged 4–14 years to complement its English-medium teaching. We introduce the teaching of Spanish, German or Dutch as optional additional languages in the Secondary School. We have developed programmes to help students with specific learning needs and to help students who join us with little or no English skills. The school also employs a counsellor.

Enrichment Activities. In addition to curricular activities, we run one of the largest extra-curricular programmes in Europe. Our dedicated teachers and coaches offer around 200 different clubs and activities, from tennis to tag rugby and choir to creative writing.

With a three-tier approach, covering all aspects of participation, we offer after-school recreational sports (dance, netball, hockey, water polo, synchronised swimming and many more), competitive sports (our ISST and SCIS seasonal formats – basketball, cross-country, golf, athletics, volleyball) and our tier 1 academy sports that run year-round (football, swimming, and gymnastics).

Elsewhere, among many other options, students can follow their artistic passions in our music, drama, art, and design clubs, and feed their curiosity through our extra-curricular science and technology programmes.

Music and Drama. The Music Department houses an extremely well-equipped music technology studio, a recording studio, and a rehearsal studio for the school's orchestras, concert bands and instrumental ensembles. Individual instrument lessons are available from visiting specialist teachers, and take place in the suite of music practice rooms. The school is the largest Associated Board centre in Europe. Each year up to fifteen drama productions – including student-directed performances – are presented across the full student age range. The 240-seat Brel Theatre has its own workshop and Green Room, as well as a more intimate studio space that seats 80.

Careers. The school has the highest expectations of its student population and advice on careers, as well as higher and further education opportunities, is of vital importance to the further development of the students. The school takes part in many careers conventions and has its own international higher education and careers team.

Fees per annum (2021–2022). From €29,100 (Reception) to €37,235 (Years 10–13).

Past Students' Association. The school has a growing association of Alumni and has its own official BSB Alumni Facebook page. Please visit the Alumni section of the school website (www.britishschool.be) to see how to subscribe to the alumni newsletter and follow the school on Twitter and LinkedIn.

Patron: Her Excellency the British Ambassador to the King of the Belgians

Chairman of the Board: Mr Ian Backhouse

Principal: **Ms Melanie Warnes**

Vice Principal and Head of Primary School: Mr Neil Ringrose

Vice Principal and Head of Secondary School: Mr John Knight

The British School of Paris

38 quai de l'Ecluse, 78290 Croissy sur Seine, France

Tel:	00 33 1 34 80 45 90
email:	info@britishschool.fr
website:	www.britishschool.fr
Twitter:	@BritishSchParis
Facebook:	@BritishSchParis

Age Range. 3–18.

Number of Pupils. 600 (Boys and Girls)

Fees per annum (2021–2022). Senior School €27,139–€29,635; Junior School €17,753–€24,616.

The BSP provides, in a caring environment, a high-quality British-style education for British and international students, to enable them to become caring citizens and to lead fulfilling lives.

Located just 15 kilometres from Paris, the School caters for English-speaking children of over 50 nationalities (about 30% are British) from ages 3–18. It is a not-for-profit association in France and is presided over by a governing body under the patronage of His Excellency the British Ambassador to France.

The **Junior School** provides education for primary aged children from 3–11 years. The purpose-built Junior School is located very close to the Senior School along the leafy banks of the river Seine. There are 35 classrooms accommodating up to 480 pupils, as well as 4 bespoke classrooms and 2 activity areas that are dedicated to our foundation stage/nursery section. Studies are based on the English National Curriculum with emphasis on English, Maths and Science, and of course, the French language. Being a holistic educator the BSP has a strong co-curricular base with a special focus on music and drama as well as a large variety of sports. (*For further information about the Junior School, see entry in IAPS section*).

The **Senior School**, which caters for pupils aged from 11–18 years, is situated beside a beautiful stretch of the Seine in Croissy sur Seine. The buildings, with the exception of two nineteenth century houses, have been built since 1990. The Science and Technology block provides excellent facilities for Science, Information Technology, Electronics and Design. There are six large, well equipped science laboratories. The other classroom blocks house Humanities, Art, Business Studies, Modern Languages, Music, English and Mathematics. Other facilities include a generously staffed and resourced student career guidance programme, a library, IT labs, a refectory, a large sports hall and fitness centre. Students enter at the age of 11 and for the first three years, a broad general education is maintained in line with the National Curriculum. Pupils are prepared for the GCSE and A Level examinations in a comprehensive range of subjects.

Music and drama are an integral part of school life; the music centre includes teaching and practice facilities as well as a well-equipped electronic studio. Specialist teachers visit the School to provide individual lessons in a wide range of instruments. Children take the Associated Board exams at regular intervals.

The School has had considerable sporting success over the years, winning the International Schools' Sports Tournament competition in girls' field hockey, and boys' rugby. Our international fixture lists provide an incentive to gain a place in school teams. As well as local matches our teams travel regularly to Belgium, Holland and the UK.

Small overall numbers, modest class sizes and a supportive pastoral system all help new pupils integrate quickly. Our examination results are outstanding. At A Level over 55% of all grades were A* and A and 99% of all grades at GCSE were between A* and C in 2021. These results compare very favourably with high-calibre schools in the UK. Most students continue their education at prestigious universities in the UK, USA, France and worldwide. BSP students have been successfully admitted to the Universities of Cambridge and Oxford, London School of Economics, University of Pennsylvania, Stanford University, McGill University, Universidad de Madrid, Seoul National University, L'Université de la Sorbonne, to mention but a few.

Chairman of Governors: Mr E Coutts

Headmaster: **Mr N Hammond**

Head of Senior School: Ms A Brooking

Head of the Junior School: Mr M Potter

Registrar: Mrs K Dufraisse

Other HMC International Schools

Africa

Kenya

Peponi School

PO Box 236, Ruiru 00232, Kenya

email: office@peponischool.org
website: www.peponischool.org

Headmaster: **Mark Durston**

South Africa

Michaelhouse

Balgowan 3275, Kwazulu-Natal, South Africa

email: angjon@michaelhouse.org
website: www.michaelhouse.org

Rector: **Antony Clark**

Zimbabwe

Peterhouse

Private Bag 3741, Marondera 00263, Zimbabwe

email: rector@peterhouse.co.zw
website: www.peterhouse.co.zw

Rector: **Jon Trafford**

Asia

Brunei Darussalam

Jerudong International School

Jalan Universiti, Kampong Tungku, Bandar Seri Begawan BE2119, Brunei Darussalam

email: enrol@jis.edu.bn
website: www.jerudonginternationalschool.com

Principal: **Nicholas E Sheehan**

Hong Kong

Harrow International School

38 Tsing Ying Road, Tuen Mun, New Territories, Hong Kong

email: info@harrowschool.hk
website: www.harrowschool.hk

Head: **Ms Ann Haydon**

Kellett School

7 Lam Hing Street, Kowloon Bay, Kowloon, Hong Kong

email: mss@kellettschool.com
website: www.kellettschool.com

Principal & CEO: **Mark S Steed [HMC]**

Head of Kowloon Bay Prep School: Samantha Steed [IAPS]

India

The British School, New Delhi

Dr Jose P Rizal Marg, Chanakyapuri, New Delhi 110021, India

email: thebritishschool@british-school.org
website: www.british-school.org

Director: **Vanita Uppal**, OBE

The Cathedral & John Connon School

6 Purshottamdas Thakurdas Marg, Fort, Mumbai 400 001, India

email: principal@cathedral-school.com
website: www.cathedral-school.com

Principal: **Mrs Meera Isaacs**

The Doon School

The Mall, Dehradun 248001, Uttaranchal, India

email: hmdosco@doonschool.com
website: www.doonschool.com

Headmaster: **Dr Jagpreet Singh**

The International School Bangalore

NAFL Valley, Whitefield-Sarajapur Road, Near Dommasandra Circle, Bangalore – 562 125, Karnataka State, India

email: school@tisb.ac.in
website: www.tisb.org

Principal: **Dr Caroline Pascoe**

Indonesia

The British School Jakarta

Bintaro Jaya Sector 9, Jl Raya Jombang - Ciledug, Pondok Aren, Tangerang 15227, Jakarta, Indonesia

email: principal@bsj.sch.id
website: www.bsj.sch.id

Principal: **Mr David N Butcher**

Malaysia

Kolej Tuanku Ja'afar

Mantin, Negeri Sembilan 71700, West Malaysia
email: principal@ktj.edu.my
website: www.ktj.edu.my

Principal: **Dr Glenn Moodie**

Marlborough College Malaysia

Jalan Marlborough, 79200 Isjander Puteri, Johor, Malaysia
email: marlborough@marlboroughcollege.my
website: www.marlboroughcollegemalaysia.org

Master: **Alan D Stevens**

Singapore

Tanglin Trust School

95 Portsdown Road, Singapore 139299
email: admissions@tts.edu.sg
website: www.tts.edu.sg

Chief Executive Officer: **Mr Craig Considine [HMC]**

Head of Infant School: Mrs Paula Craigie [IAPS]
Head of Junior School: Mrs Clair Harrington-Wilcox [IAPS]
Head of Senior School: Mr Allan Forbes

(*See entry in IAPSO section*)

Thailand

Harrow International School Bangkok

45 Soi Kosumruamchai, 14 Don Muang, Bangkok 10210, Thailand
email: enquiry@harrowschool.ac.th
website: www.harrowschool.ac.th

Head: **Jon Standen**

Shrewsbury International School

1922 Charoen Krung Road, Wat Prayakrai, Bang Kholame, Bangkok 10120, Thailand
email: enquiries@shrewsbury.ac.th
website: www.shrewsbury.ac.th

Principal: **Christopher Seal**

Australia and New Zealand

Australia

Anglican Church Grammar School

Oaklands Parade, East Brisbane, Queensland QLD 4169, Australia
email: reception@churchie.com.au
website: www.churchie.com.au

Headmaster: **Dr Alan Campbell**

Camberwell Grammar School

PO Box 151, Balwyn, VIC 3103, Australia
email: headmaster@cgs.vic.edu.au
website: www.cgs.vic.edu.au

Headmaster: **Dr Paul Hicks**

The King's School

87–129 Pennant Hills Road, North Parramatta, NSW 2151, Australia
email: headmaster@kings.edu.au
website: www.kings.edu.au

Headmaster: **Anthony L George**

Methodist Ladies' College

207 Barker Road, Kew 3101, Melbourne, Australia
email: college@mlc.vic.edu.au
website: www.mlc.vic.edu.au

Principal: **Miss Diana Vernon**, BA, PGCE, MACE, MACEL

St Leonard's College

163 South Road, Brighton East, Victoria 3187, Australia
email: stleonards@stleonards.vic.edu.au
website: www.stleonards.vic.edu.au

Principal: **Mr Stuart Davis**

Scotch College

1 Morrison Street, Hawthorn, VIC 3122, Australia
email: scotch@scotch.vic.edu.au
website: www.scotch.vic.edu.au

Principal: **I Tom Batty**

The Scots College

Victoria Road, Bellevue Hill, NSW 2023, Australia
email: reception@tsc.nsw.edu.au
website: www.tsc.nsw.edu.au

Principal: **Dr Ian P M Lambert**

Central, North and South America

Argentina

St George's College North

Mosconi y Don Bosco s/n, Los Polvorines, Buenos Aires B1613 FTR, Argentina
email: info.north@stgeorges.edu.ar
website: www.stgeorges.edu.ar/north

Headmaster: **Oliver Proctor**

St George's College Quilmes

Guido 800, Quilmes, CP: 1878, Buenos Aires, Argentina
email: infoquilmes@stgeorges.edu.ar
website: www.stgeorges.edu.ar

Headmaster: **James Diver**

Brazil

St Paul's School

Rua Juquiá 166, Jardim Paulistano, São Paulo SP 01440-903, Brazil

email: spshead@stpauls.br
website: www.stpauls.br

Head: Titus Edge

(*See entry in IAPSO section*)

Chile

The Grange School

Av Principe de Gales 6154, La Reina, Santiago, Chile

email: rectoria@grange.cl
website: www.grange.cl

Headmaster: Mr Nicholas Eatough

Europe

Cyprus

The English School

1 Presidential Palace Avenue, PO Box 23575, 1684 Nicosia, Cyprus

email: info@englishschool.ac.cy
website: www.englishschool.ac.cy

Headmaster: Mr David Lambon

Czech Republic

The English College in Prague

Sokolovska 320, 190-00 Praha 9, Czech Republic

email: office@englishcollege.cz
website: www.englishcollege.cz

Headmaster: Dr Nigel Brown

The Prague British International School

K Lesu 558/2, 142 00 Praha 4, Czech Republic

email: info@pbis.cz
website: www.pbis.cz

Principal: Niki Meehan

Greece

Campion School

PO Box 67484, Pallini, Athens 153 02, Greece

email: mhenderson@campion.edu.gr
website: www.campion.edu.gr

Headmaster: Mike Henderson

St Catherine's British School

Sofokil Venizelou 77, 141 23 Lykovrissi, Athens GR 145 10, Greece

email: headmaster@stcatherines.gr
website: www.stcatherines.gr

Headmaster: Mr Stuart Smith

Italy

The British School of Milan

Via Pisani Dossi 16, 20134 Milan, Italy

email: info@bsm.school
website: www.britishschoolmilan.com

Principal & CEO: Dr Chris Greenhalgh

St George's British International School

Via Cassia, La Storta, 00123 Rome, Italy

email: secretary@stgeorge.school.it
website: www.stgeorge.school.it

Principal & CEO: David Tongue

Netherlands

The British School in The Netherlands

Boerderj Rosenburgh, Rosenburgherlaan 2, Voorschoten 2252 BA, The Netherlands

email: admissions@britishschool.nl
website: www.britishschool.nl

CEO: Heath Monk

Headteachers:
Junior School Diamanthorst: Mr Chris Wathern
Junior School Leidschenveen: Mrs Karren van Zoest
Junior School Vlaskamp: Ms Sue Aspinall
Senior School Leidschenveen: Mr James Oxlade
Senior School Voorschoten: Mrs Vicki Hallatt (*interim*)

Portugal

St Julian's School

Quinta Nova, 2775-588 Carcavelos, Portugal

email: info@stjulians.com
website: www.stjulians.com

Interim Head: Paul Slocombe

Spain

The British School of Barcelona
Cognita Schools Group

Carrer de la Ginesta 26, 08860 Castelldefels, Barcelona, Spain

email: school@bsb.edu.es
website: www.britishschoolbarcelona.com

Principal: Mr Jonathan Locke

King's College
The British School of Madrid

Paseo de los Andes 35, Soto de Viñuelas, Madrid 28761, Spain

Headteacher: **Mr Matthew Taylor**, MA Oxon, MA London, PGCE, FRSA
Head of Primary Department: Paula Parkinson, BA Hons Newcastle, PGCE Manchester

Switzerland

Aiglon College

Avenue Centrale 61, Chesières 1885, Switzerland

email: info@aiglon.ch
website: www.aiglon.ch

Head Master: **Mr Richard McDonald**, MA Oxon, PGCE

Middle East

Bahrain

St Christopher's School

PO Box 32052, Isa Town, Kingdom of Bahrain

email: office.principal@st-chris.net
website: www.st-chris.net

Principal: **Dr Simon Watson [HMC]**

Head of Infant School: Ms Nat Dickinson
Head of Junior School: Mr Ian Fellows [IAPS]
Head of Senior School: Mr Nick Wilson

Oman

British School Muscat

PO Box 1907, Ruwi, Muscat PC112, Sultanate of Oman

email: principal@britishschoolmuscat.com
website: www.britishschoolmuscat.com

Principal: **Mr Kai Vacher**

Qatar

Doha College

PO Box 7506, Doha, State of Qatar

email: principal@dohacollege.com
website: www.dohacollege.com

Principal: **Dr Steffen Sommer**

Senior Vice Principal, Head of Secondary: Ruth Sanderson
Vice Principal, Head of Primary: Mrs Ruth Whymark

United Arab Emirates

Brighton College Abu Dhabi

PO Box 129444, Abu Dhabi, United Arab Emirates
email: headmaster@brightoncollege.ae
website: www.brightoncollege.ae

Head Mistress: **Mrs Helen Wilkinson [HMC]**

Head of Prep: Mr Daniel Cummings [IAPS]

The British School Al Khubairat

PO Box 4001, Abu Dhabi, United Arab Emirates
email: headmaster@britishschool.sch.ae
website: www.britishschool.sch.ae

Headmaster: **Mr Mark Leppard**, MBE

Dubai College

PO Box 837, Dubai, United Arab Emirates
email: dcadmin@dubaicollege.org
website: www.dubaicollege.org

Headmaster: **Mr Michael Lambert**

GEMS Wellington Academy – Silicon Oasis

Silicon Oasis, Dubai, United Arab Emirates
email: contactus_wso@gemsedu.com
website: www.gemswellingtonacademy-dso.com

CEO & Principal: **Kevin M Loft**

JESS, Dubai

PO Box 24942, Dubai, United Arab Emirates
email: jess@jess.sch.ae
website: www.jess.sch.ae

Director: **Shane O'Brien [HMC]**

Head Teacher, JESS Jumeirah Primary: Mr Asa Firth [IAPS]
Head Teacher, JESS Arabian Ranches Primary: Mr Jose Diez [IAPS]
Head Teacher, JESS Arabian Ranches Secondary: Mr Michael Waller

Headmasters' and Headmistresses' Conference

Associates

In addition to Full membership (open to Heads of independent schools in the UK and Ireland) and International membership (open to Heads of independent schools overseas), HMC also elects a small number of Associates each year.

HMC Associates are either heads of high-performing maintained sector schools proposed and supported by HMC divisions or influential individuals in the world of education, including university vice-chancellors and academics, who endorse and support the work of HMC.

The following is a list of current HMC Associates:

MARK HANLEY-BROWNE
Alpha Plus Group, London W1
website: www.alphaplusgroup.co.uk

ELIZABETH HUDDLESON
Bangor Grammar School, Bangor, Northern Ireland
website: www.bangorgrammarschool.org.uk

DR STUART D SMALLWOOD
Bishop Wordsworth's School, Salisbury, Wiltshire
website: www.bishopwordsworths.org.uk

ANDREW MOSS
Gordon's School, West End, Surrey
website: www.gordons.school

J SCOTT W NAISMITH
Methodist College, Belfast, Northern Ireland
website: www.methody.org

DAVID HUMPRHEYS
Methodist Independent Schools Trust, London NW1
website: www.methodistschools.org.uk

JANE SANCHEZ
Mill Hill Senior School, London NW7
website: www.millhill.org.uk

JESSICA MILES
Monmouth School for Girls, Monmouth, Wales
website: www.habsmonmouth.org/girls/

RUSSEL ELLICOTT
Pate's Grammar School, Cheltenham, Gloucestershire
website: www.pates.gloucs.sch.uk

JON WOODS
The Judd School, Tonbridge, Kent
website: www.judd.online

DAN BROWNING
Wymondham College, Wymondham, Norfolk
website: www.wymondhamcollege.org

JILL BERRY
Educational Consultant

DR BRENDA DESPONTIN
Former Head

PART II
Schools whose Heads are members of the Girls' Schools Association

ALPHABETICAL LIST OF SCHOOLS

The following schools, whose Heads are members of both GSA and HMC, can be found in the HMC section:

Benenden School
Berkhamsted Schools Group
Bromley High School
Bury Grammar Schools
Cheltenham Ladies' College
City of London School for Girls
Downe House
Francis Holland School, Regent's Park
Francis Holland School, Sloane Square
Godolphin and Latymer School
James Allen's Girls' School (JAGS)
Monmouth School for Girls
Moreton Hall

Queen Anne's School
Queenswood School
Roedean School
The Royal Masonic School for Girls
St Albans High School for Girls
St Helen & St Katharine
St Mary's School Ascot
St Mary's Calne
Sherborne Girls
Streatham & Clapham High School
Withington Girls' School
Woldingham School

GSA
GEOGRAPHICAL LIST OF SCHOOLS

448

Individual School Entries

Abbot's Hill School

Bunkers Lane, Hemel Hempstead, Herts HP3 8RP

Tel: 01442 240333
email: registrar@abbotshill.herts.sch.uk
website: www.abbotshill.herts.sch.uk
Twitter: @AbbotsHill
Facebook: @AbbotsHillSchool
LinkedIn: /abbot's-hill

Motto: *Vi et Virtute*

Founded 1912.

Abbot's Hill School is an Independent Day School for girls aged 4–16 years. Our Day Nursery and Pre-School caters for girls and boys from 6 months. The school is situated in 76 acres of parkland on the edge of Hemel Hempstead.

A great emphasis is placed on providing a complete and balanced education. We have a strong record of academic success. Throughout the school, pupils are taught in small classes in which excellent teaching and personalised support ensure that everyone is inspired to exceed their potential.

We pride ourselves on our pastoral care. The sense of being part of an extended family is frequently commented on by pupils, parents and staff alike. In such a nurturing environment, pupils grow naturally in confidence, are happy to embrace new challenges and eagerly take on increasing responsibilities. Pupils leave Abbot's Hill fully equipped to take on with passion the challenges and opportunities life has to offer.

With small classes and a high teacher to pupil ratio, the school aims to develop the academic and creative talents, social skills and confidence of each pupil. Every pupil benefits from being known personally by the Headmistress and teaching staff who seek to create a happy and caring environment.

Senior School. The Senior School is based in a spacious and comfortable 19th Century house, which, combined with purpose-built teaching blocks, Science, Sport, Performing Arts and ICT suites, provides our pupils with first-class facilities.

Curriculum. During the first three years, a broad programme based on the National Curriculum is followed, encompassing both academic and creative subjects. Each girl's potential and progress is carefully monitored by both teaching staff and a personal tutor. Subjects studied include English, Maths, Science, French, Spanish, Geography, History, Media Studies, Information and Communication Technology, Religious Studies, Music, Personal, Social, Health, Economic and Citizenship Education, Art and Design, Drama, Food Technology and Physical Education.

In Years 10 and 11, a core GCSE curriculum of up to 8 subjects is followed with girls choosing up to three further subjects.

Music and Performing Arts. The school has very strong Music and Performing Arts Departments with excellent facilities. The Performing Arts building includes studios for dance, drama and music as well as a theatre. The School Choirs and Orchestra perform regularly in concerts, recitals, plays, musicals and various functions throughout the year and there is a school production each year.

Sports. The school has a strong sporting tradition. There is a well-equipped Sports Hall, lacrosse pitches, grass and hard tennis courts, and a swimming pool. The main sports played are Lacrosse, Netball, Athletics, Tennis, Rounders and Swimming. All girls are encouraged to participate in the sporting opportunities at Abbot's Hill and currently there are a number of girls who have reached County and National standard in selected sports.

Extracurricular Activities. Many activities and clubs are held outside of school and these vary in range from Dance, Art, The Duke of Edinburgh's Award scheme, Music, Speech and Drama and all sports.

Admission. Admission to Abbot's Hill is by Entrance Examination, interview, and a report from the previous school.

Scholarships and Bursaries. Academic, Art, Drama, Music and Sport scholarships are available giving 5–10% reduction in fees. Means-tested Bursaries are also available.

Fees per term (2021–2022). Reception–Year 6: £3,863–£4,870; Year 7–11: up to £6,691.

Prep School. Abbot's Hill Prep is situated in the same grounds as the Senior School. The Prep School provides Pre-Preparatory and Preparatory education for girls aged 4 and above. Abbot's Hill Nursery and Pre-School welcome boys and girls from 6 months of age. The Prep mixes the formal setting of the classroom with the wealth of opportunity provided by our physical surroundings. Children are given the freedom in which to grow, learn and play. Classrooms and corridors are bright and well decorated with children's work reflecting the diversity of the curriculum.

The Prep School plays a very important role within our school community and is an integral part of the school as a whole. It is our aim at Abbot's Hill to nurture the whole child, thus enabling our pupils to develop their talents whether they be academic, artistic or sporting. Specialist teaching is introduced from a child's earliest days; French, Music and PE are introduced in the pre-school year. This is added to as a child progresses to include Drama, Games, ICT and Geography. By the time a girl reaches Year 5 she is being completely subject taught and is able to adapt to moving around whilst being supported by a class teacher.

The small class sizes at Abbot's Hill Prep enable individual needs to be recognised and met early with the minimum disruption. For those who need extra support this is offered within the classroom setting or one-to-one as appropriate. Gifts or talents for a particular area of learning can be extended and developed to their potential.

The wider curriculum plays a key role. Educational visits are an integral part of the teaching programme and children are regularly taken on visits to galleries and museums to enhance their learning experience. Outside visitors lead workshops at school for year groups or the whole school as appropriate. The extracurricular programme is wide ranging and ever changing. It currently includes such wide-ranging pursuits as languages, trampolining, gardening and board games as well as a wealth of musical and sports clubs.

Further information. Abbot's Hill welcomes visits from prospective parents and pupils. If you would like to visit the School, please contact the Registrar for an appointment on 01442 240333 or email registrar@abbotshill.herts.sch.uk.

Charitable status. Abbot's Hill Charitable Trust is a Registered Charity, number 311053, which exists to provide high quality education for children.

Chairman of the Governing Body: Mrs J Mark, BA Hons, QTS

Headmistress: **Mrs Kathryn Gorman**, BA Birmingham, MEd Cantab

Head of Prep School: Miss K Bluck [from Spring 2022]
Acting Head of Prep: Mrs Claire Worrell

Bursar: Mrs C Korniczky, BA Hons, ACA

Registrar: Miss A Cooper

Alderley Edge School for Girls

Wilmslow Road, Alderley Edge, Cheshire SK9 7QE

Tel: 01625 583028
email: schoolmail@aesg.co.uk
website: www.aesg.co.uk
Twitter: @schoolforgirls
Facebook: @aeschoolforgirls
Instagram: @aeschoolforgirls

Age Range. 2–18.
Number in School. 439

Fees per term (2021–2022). Nursery £3,280; Pre-School £3,280; Reception–Year 2 £3,180; Years 3–6 £3,750; Senior £4,680; Sixth Form £4,680.

Alderley Edge School for Girls provides girls with outstanding pastoral support, innovative teaching, a broad curriculum and a fantastic array of extra-curricular opportunities. Each girl is nurtured and supported in small classes and it is our priority that each girl reaches her individual potential and becomes the best she can be.

We value the successes and achievements of all our girls; both academically and in other contexts, from dance to drama, music to sport. Girls leave as confident, articulate and mature young women who can achieve in the world beyond our school gates.

Alderley Edge School for Girls is a community. All our girls, from those in Nursery at the age of two, through to Sixth Form at the age of 18, feel safe and secure and benefit from being in a school positioned in a vibrant village environment.

The School is a high-achieving, academic and dynamic school which fosters the well-being of each individual within an exciting, challenging and supportive environment. We recognise commitment, hard work and success, setting the girls the challenges they need to develop their talents to the full.

We are proud of our school and its Christian values, yet respect the beliefs of others in our community. We believe in social justice for all and feel a sense of responsibility for those less fortunate, for whom we provide support both locally and globally through our fundraising and community service.

The School has recently been awarded *Apple Distinguished Status* and is also a Regional Training Hub for Apple after a huge development in Technology Enhanced Learning. Girls bring their own iPads into school to enrich their learning experience. Each teacher is also given his/her own iPad to support their teaching. The School has also integrated Apple TVs into classrooms, corridors and the newly-built fitness suite.

In June 2021, the Independent Schools Inspectorate (ISI) undertook a Regulatory Compliance Inspection and Educational Quality inspection at Alderley Edge School for Girls. We are delighted to report that the School was found to be fully compliant with all ISI regulations with no recommendations. For EQ, we were awarded an 'Excellent' judgement for both pupils "Academic and other achievements" and "personal development." This is the highest grade.

We are a proud member of the Girls' Schools Association and we value the importance of an all-girls education and the benefits this provides for our students. There are numerous opportunities for girls to develop both team working and leadership skills and to help guide the school and their peers. In this way our students learn important life skills which prepare them for the world of work and they leave us as impressive young women who make a difference.

Admissions. The Early Years Department caters for girls from 2 years. Admission for girls to the Junior School is at 4/5 years old. Admission to the Senior School is at 11 years by Entrance Examination and interview.

The Arts.

Music. A very large percentage of pupils learn a musical instrument and examinations may be taken. The school runs 4 choirs, 2 orchestras, a jazz band and numerous smaller instrumental ensembles including string groups, a brass group and 5 different woodwind groups. Many cups have been won in local festivals and pupils perform in local youth orchestras.

Drama and Dance. Both are offered. The majority of pupils are involved in school productions and all pupils participate in House and other productions. There are four dance squads which rehearse weekly and holiday courses in Dance and Drama are also on offer.

Facilities. In creating a new school we achieved our objective to remain small enough to care for every child's needs and yet the school enjoys all the benefits and resources of a much larger school. A multi-million pound investment programme has provided a new Senior School and a completely refurbished Junior School. Facilities include a climbing wall, fitness suite, six superbly equipped science laboratories, brand new netball courts and pavilion, four ICT suites with online facilities throughout the school, language suite with language laboratory, Humanities block with Business Studies centre, competition-size sports hall, gymnasium, Performing Arts centre, chapel and a library with breathtaking views over the Cheshire Plain. In addition there is a modern and well-appointed Sixth Form centre – including a brand-new ICT suite and silent study zone and modern Sixth Form Coffee Bar – to accommodate the increasing number of girls in our Sixth Form.

Scholarships and Bursaries. We offer several Academic scholarships. Scholarships for Music are awarded at 11+, 13+ and 16+. Art, Performing Arts and Sport scholarships are available at 11+. Bursaries are also available (income linked).

Charitable Status. Alderley Edge School for Girls is a Registered Charity, number 1006726. It exists to provide education for children.

Chair of Governors: Mrs S Herring

Headmistress: Mrs Nicola Smillie

Deputy Headmistress: Mrs C Wood
Deputy Head, Academic: Mrs C Millar
Junior School Deputy Headmistress: Mrs Tracy Bains
Head of Year 7: Ms R Stokwisz
Head of Year 8: Mrs C Foster
Head of Year 9: Mrs S Waite
Head of Upper School: Mr D Wilson
Head of Sixth Form: Ms J Billington

Bursar: Mr S Malkin
Admissions Officer: Mrs A Dean

Heads of Department:

Art: Mrs M Billington
Business Studies: Mrs R Hilsley
Chemistry: Miss Annika Hall
Classics: Mr P Tandler
Design Technology: Mrs K Bryan
Drama: Mrs C Foster
English: Mrs C Polley
Food Technology: Mrs C Leigh
Geography: Ms N Johal
History: Mr D Wilson
ICT: Mrs L Gardiner
Mathematics: Mr S Cunliffe
Modern Foreign Languages: Mrs M Coltman
Music: Mrs A Pattrick
Physical Education: Miss L McConville
Physics: Mr Nigel Garfield
Psychology: Mrs Amanda Jackson
Religious Education: Miss R Stokwisz
Science: Mrs M Moss

Badminton School

Westbury-on-Trym, Bristol BS9 3BA

Tel: 0117 905 5200
email: admissions@badmintonschool.co.uk
website: www.badmintonschool.co.uk
Twitter: @BadmintonSchool
Facebook: @BadmintonSch
Instagram: @BadmintonSchool
LinkedIn: /school/badminton-school-limited

Motto: *Pro Omnibus Quisque Pro Deo Omnes*

Founded 1858. Non denominational.

Badminton is an independent girls' day, boarding and weekly boarding school situated in a 15-acre site in Westbury-on-Trym on the outskirts of the university city of Bristol.

Age Range of Pupils. 3 to 18.

Number of Pupils. 550.

Number of Staff. Full-time teaching 37, Part-time teaching 16. Teacher to Pupil ratio is currently 1:7.

Educational Philosophy. Whilst the school retains an outstanding academic record, its focus continues to be on nurturing the girls' natural curiosity and fuelling their passion for learning. The enduring excellence that Badminton girls achieve, stems from the positive atmosphere in the School and the holistic approach to education, as well as the exceptional relationships between staff and pupils, which are mature, friendly and based on principles of courtesy and mutual respect. Teachers are highly-qualified specialists in their field and encourage girls to develop academic confidence and to become independent learners by taking responsibility for their work and progress.

It is a characteristic of Badminton girls that they are thoughtful individuals, able to evaluate information and decide for themselves. This approach extends beyond their studies and into the day-to-day life of the School, where girls are given a wide range of opportunities to grow, develop and express themselves in an enormous range of activities. Staff also enjoy sharing their enthusiasm for their subject and often involve girls in projects and competitions in the local community and nationally.

The Badminton community gives girls a chance to develop an understanding of the viewpoints of others and to think about contributing to the world around them. Girls leave Badminton ready to face the changing and challenging wider world and, when they do, they take with them a strong network of lifelong friends developed through a wealth of shared experiences.

Boarding. The size of the campus and community at Badminton gives a homely and vibrant feel to the School. This, coupled with excellent pastoral care, leaves no scope for anonymity, but rather lends itself to strong mutually supportive relationships between girls as well as between girls and staff.

The boarding accommodation is split into three areas (junior, middle and Sixth Form) so girls get a good sense of progression and development as they move up through the school. Full-time, weekly or flexi boarding are offered and day girls are welcome to flexi board, allowing girls to easily combine their academic schedules with the many activities that are on offer after school and at weekends.

Bartlett House offers cosy bedrooms for boarders in Years 5–8 and easy access to gardens and play areas. Sanderson House, a modern boarding house opened in 2008, accommodates boarders in Years 9, 10 and 11. The Sixth Form Centre provides the Lower Sixth and Upper Sixth with a more independent environment in double or single study-bedrooms. In each House, boarders have the support of a resident Housemistress, Assistant Housemistresses and Resident Tutors and there is a broad range of clubs and activities on offer every day as well as a full weekend programme.

The School's enrichment programme is extremely important in the overall development of the pupils and girls participate in many activities and are encouraged to do so. The activities offered vary depending on the interests of the girls; some have an academic bias, others let the girls explore their creative interests. Girls are very much encouraged to enjoy and value their own and their peers' successes and triumphs in every area of life.

Curriculum. The School's broad curriculum provides a rich and varied experience for the girls. Through Art, Drama and Music programmes, each girl has many opportunities to express her individuality and develop her own unique identity. In an increasingly global society, the importance of languages has never been greater and girls have the opportunity to study Mandarin and Greek in addition to more traditional languages such as French and Latin.

Small classes ensure that all the girls receive individual help and attention from their teachers. Badminton girls are proactive and independent learners; they are not afraid to take intellectual risks and are always happy to ask questions. The emphasis at Badminton is on a holistic education, not narrowly academic, and both the curriculum and the timetable are constructed to create a balance between academic achievement, personal development, life skills and other enterprising activity.

Academic Record. Badminton has a fine academic record at GCSE and A Level. Sixth Form leavers go on to study at some of the top universities and Music Conservatories in the UK and overseas, including Oxford, Cambridge, the Royal Academy of Music and further afield.

Facilities. All facilities are situated on site and include: a new Sports Centre opened in 2018 complete with fencing piste, four court sports hall, climbing wall and fitness suite; a 25m indoor swimming pool; international-sized astro pitch; tennis and netball courts; as well as a fully-equipped Science Centre, Creative Arts Centre and self-contained Sixth Form Centre. There are extensive fiction, careers, music and art libraries as well as a Music School.

Music, Drama and Creative Arts. All girls are involved in the Arts, both within the curriculum and as extracurricular activities, and the School attaches great importance to the development of musical and artistic talent.

Music is extremely popular at Badminton with over 85% of all pupils studying at least one musical instrument. There is a wide range of choral and instrumental groups to join including Junior and Senior Choir, Schola (choral group), orchestra, swing band, string ensembles, woodwind ensembles and other mixed musical groups. With visiting peripatetic teachers, all of whom are professional musicians, the students can study any instrument of their choice. There are a wide variety of performance opportunities including informal concerts and concerts for the local community.

There are several drama productions every year including plays directed and produced by the girls. Many girls take optional Speech and Drama lessons and LAMDA examinations.

There is an excellent Creative Arts department, with a wide choice of subjects for the girls to pursue including Fine Art, Pottery and Sculpture, Textiles, Design, Jewellery-making and Photography.

Clubs and Societies. A wide range is offered including: Extended Project Qualification, The Duke of Edinburgh's Award, Italian GCSE, Sports Leaders Award, Leith's Cookery Course, Modern Languages, Debating, Drama, Musical Theatre, Mandarin, Young Enterprise, Art and Crafts, Science Outreach and The Prince's Trust.

Games and Activities. Specialist PE teachers and coaches offer timetabled and optional sport including Hockey, Tennis, Netball, Swimming, Athletics, Rounders, Gymnastics, Badminton, Basketball, Self-Defence and Judo.

Optional extras. All girls participate in activities which include the full choice of Games, Creative Arts and Clubs as above and boarders have the opportunity of additional activities at weekends.

Badminton is fortunate in being sited on the outskirts of the university city of Bristol; regular visits are arranged to concerts, lectures and theatres and there is considerable contact with Bristol University. Community and voluntary work is strongly encouraged, with girls assisting with Science Outreach and reading in local primary schools, volunteering in local hospitals and charity shops.

Admission. Girls sit the Senior School entrance assessments in the November or January prior to year of entry. Entrance assessments are taken in English, Mathematics as well as an online reasoning test. Girls are also interviewed by a senior member of staff and the girl's current school is asked to provide a reference.

Girls sit Sixth Form entrance papers in the November in the year prior to joining. They choose two academic subjects they are intending to study for A Level and also sit an online reasoning test. They too will be interviewed by a senior member of staff and the girl's current school is asked to provide a reference.

Prospective Junior School pupils are assessed by spending a day in the school during which they are observed and assessed informally by staff and the Junior School Headmistress. This also helps the girls to make initial relationships with their prospective peers and gives them a real taste for life at Badminton. From Years 3–6 the tests are more formal and written papers in English, Maths, Reading and a Reasoning test are completed during the assessment day. Entry for Little Acorns (our pre-reception class) is by appointment with the Junior School Headmistress, and girls will also have a short observation session in our Little Acorns class.

Prospective parents are encouraged to visit the school individually or attend one of our Open Mornings. To obtain a prospectus and arrange a visit, please contact the Admissions Department via email at admissions@badmintonschool.co.uk or call 0117 905 5271.

Scholarships. Academic, Music, Sport and All-Rounder scholarships are available for girls entering Badminton in Years 7, 9 and 12. A STEM Scholarship is also available in Years 7 and 9 and an Art Scholarship is available in Years 9 and Year 12. Scholarships for entry into the upper end of the Junior School are also available. Parents of girls who are awarded scholarships are also eligible to apply for a means-tested Bursary. Other Awards are also available.

Scholarship application forms and more information can be obtained by emailing our Admissions Department at admissions@badmintonschool.co.uk.

Bursaries. Bursaries are means-tested and awarded on the basis of parents' financial circumstances. Application forms may be obtained by emailing admissions@badmintonschool.co.uk.

Fees per term (2021–2022). Day: Juniors £3,465–£3,975, Seniors £5,810. Boarding: Juniors £7,900–£9,070, Seniors £11,565–£13,500

Forces families in receipt of CEA or an equivalent civilian allowance receive 20% remission of fees.

Charitable status. Badminton School Limited is a Registered Charity, number 311738. It exists for the purpose of educating children.

Chairman of Governors: Mr Justin Lewis MDA, BSc Hons

Director of Finance and Operations: Mr M Waymouth, MA

Headmistress: Mrs R Tear, BSc Hons Exeter, MA London, PGCE London

Head of Junior School: Ms H Welch, BSc Hons, MSc Loughborough, PGCE Warwick

Bedford Girls' School

Cardington Road, Bedford, Bedfordshire MK42 0BX

Tel: 01234 361918
email: admissions@bedfordgirlsschool.co.uk
website: www.bedfordgirlsschool.co.uk
Twitter: @BedfordGirlsSch
Facebook: @BedfordGirlsSch
LinkedIn: /bedford-girls'-school

Foundation – The Harpur Trust.

"Let me keep an open mind so I understand as much as I can in my lifetime and not reach the limits of my imagination."

Bedford Girls' School is a dynamic, forward-thinking selective independent day school for girls aged 7–18. We value creativity, technology and innovation highly, as we prepare our students to make a difference to the world around them. From Year 3 to Sixth Form, it is our belief that learning should be exciting and lifelong, so that students leave us fully equipped academically, personally, and emotionally with the desire to be the creative-thinkers, the change-makers and the problem-solvers of the future.

Part of the Harpur Trust, we offer both the International Baccalaureate and A Level to Sixth Formers. Whichever course of study our student elect to take post-16 our philosophy lies in equipping them with critical thinking skills and the attributes of the IB learner profile from the moment they join us, whether in the Junior or Senior Schools. As a result, we find that the natural curiosity of the girls is heightened and sharpened and they are extremely engaged with their own learning. Our girls excel academically; we are an outstanding sports school and have an excellent reputation for Music and the Creative Arts.

The atmosphere of our school is unique and exciting. Classrooms fizz with energy and enthusiasm and each day brings forth new discoveries and achievements. We would be delighted to welcome you to visit, either for one of our Open House events or a private tour, to experience at first hand a true flavour of life at Bedford Girls' School. Please visit www.bedfordgirlsschool.co.uk for further information or contact our Admissions Team: Tel: 01234 361918, email: admissions@bedfordgirlsschool.co.uk.

Admissions. Entry to the Junior School is based on online Cognitive Ability Assessments (CAT) and a creative writing task. Entry to the Senior School is based on interview and online Cognitive Ability Assessments (CAT). Sixth Form entry is based on interviews, CAT assessments and GCSE results. A reference from the Head of the student's current school is required for all candidates.

Fees per term (2021–2022). Junior School (7–11 years) £3,340; Senior School (11–16 years) £4,695; Sixth Form (16–18 years) £4,695.

Charitable status. Bedford Girls' School is part of the Harpur Trust which is a Registered Charity, number 1066861.

Chair of Governors: Ms T Beddoes

Head: Mrs Gemma Gibson

Senior Deputy Head: Mr J Gardner

Deputy Head – Pastoral: Ms E Teale
Assistant Head: Mrs J Axford
Assistant Head: Mrs P Hooley
Director of Sixth Form: Mrs H Woolley
Bursar: Mr J-M Hodgkin

Head of Bedford Girls' School Junior School: Mrs C Howe
Deputy Head: Mrs T Copp

Blackheath High School
GDST

Vanbrugh Park, London SE3 7AG

Tel: 020 8853 2929
email: info@bla.gdst.net

Junior Department:
Wemyss Road, London SE3 0TF

Tel: 020 8852 1537
email: info@bla.gdst.net

website: www.blackheathhighschool.gdst.net
Twitter: @BlackheathHigh
Facebook: @BlackheathHighSchool
LinkedIn: /Blackheath-High-School

Founded in 1880.

Blackheath High School is part of the Girls' Day School Trust (GDST), the UK's leading network of independent girls' schools. As a charity that owns and runs 23 schools and two academies, it reinvests all its income in its schools. For further information about the Trust, visit www.gdst.net.

Blackheath High School is a selective, independent day school for girls aged 3–18 situated in Blackheath, South East London. We enjoy an enviable 'village' like location, within the Royal Borough of Greenwich and have a long history of educating a rich social and cultural blend of students, that reflects the cosmopolitan character of London itself.

Rated 'excellent' in all areas in the latest ISI inspection, academic success is at the heart of what is offered at Blackheath High School. Fuelled by our aspirational culture, students make exceptional progress, with excellent public examination results and a range of ambitious and interesting university destinations. This is achieved through the provision of an innovative and interesting curriculum that challenges and inspires students, encourages critical thinking and nurtures a love of learning. Alongside our core curriculum there are unique opportunities such as Astronomy GCSE at the Royal Observatory in Greenwich Park next door to the school, and our bespoke academic enrichment programme – The Wollstonecraft Enrichment Programme. Optional courses are designed to engage and inspire, covering topics as diverse as: the culture and history of Tibet; an introduction to architecture and designing a radio programme for Radio 4 Woman's Hour.

Within the core curriculum, girls are able to choose two languages from Mandarin, German, French and Spanish and study these all through to Year 13 and great value is placed upon the girls broadening their horizons beyond the school with a range of exciting trips and work experience opportunities. A strong focus on science and technology subjects ensures that our students defy the national trends in terms of numbers of girls applying for science and technology subjects. Strong role models and a curriculum that is well supported by the latest technology, including iPads, digital radio stations and 3D printing, inspire ever-growing numbers of girls to pursue ambitions related to computing, science, and design. This is a school where girls are encouraged to discover their passions and teachers support and challenge girls in pursuing their aims.

Located between beautiful Royal Greenwich Park and stunning Blackheath, the school is located over three sites: separate Junior and Senior Schools and a dedicated sporting facility in Kidbrooke Grove that enables us to ring-fence curriculum time for the girls' sporting activity. With an £18m investment in our Senior School facilities completed, the opportunities available to the girls continue to grow. Adding to our recently refurbished dedicated Sixth Form Centre 'Westcombe House', the redevelopment includes a state-of-the-art library, creative arts centre, science labs and entrance building to enhance the opportunities already on offer through our theatre, dance and drama studios, language lab, science suite and teaching rooms.

Individuality is cherished and there is a culture of open-mindedness and harmony. Teachers pride themselves on their superb knowledge of the girls and the positive relationships that are fostered in the school. This is a community where older girls mix readily with younger and the atmosphere of open-mindedness and tolerance is genuine and tangible. These excellent relationships are founded upon the staff's willingness and desire to provide a superb and wide-ranging co-curricular programme. From overseas trips to exotic destinations like Peru and Beijing, to clubs designed to appeal to every girl, like 'crochet collective', 'Samba Band' or 'Iron Woman running club', the co-curricular programme builds vital life skills and cements positive and productive relationships. Our strong and empowering focus on 'girls first', as part of our founding mission, ensures this is a school where girls take pride in their talents and ability, ignore gender stereotypes, and are supported to achieve their dreams.

As described in the ISI report, the school provides an educational experience that is "stimulating and extraordinarily supportive, conducive to the highest standards of teaching and learning".

Admission to the school is by examination and interview; scholarships and bursaries are available. This year, the school has created a Virtual Open Day experience, available on our website. The Head likes to discuss each girl's particular needs individually with pupils and parents. Please telephone our Admissions Officer on 020 8557 3009 if you would like to arrange to speak to us, or for a prospectus.

Curriculum. We offer a broad choice of subjects at GCSE and an even wider choice at A Level. An education at

Blackheath High School inspires and equips girls to strive for personal excellence in all their endeavours: intellectual; physical; creative; cultural; social and moral. We prepare and empower girls for the future by providing an atmosphere in which academic curiosity is cultivated, confidence is built and a balanced, open-minded outlook is nurtured.

As an all-through 3–18 school, we have the luxury of being able to design a curriculum entirely tailored to these aims in every key stage.

Fees per term (2021–2022). Senior School £5,713, Junior Department £4,664, Nursery £3,630. The fees cover the regular curriculum, school books, stationery and other materials, choral music, and games, but not optional extra subjects, school visits or lunch.

Bursaries. The GDST makes available to the school a number of bursaries. The bursaries are means tested and are intended to ensure that the school remains accessible to bright girls who would profit from our education but who would be unable to enter the school without financial assistance.

Scholarships. A number of scholarships are available to particularly gifted girls for entry at 11+, 13+ or the Sixth Form. These are awarded on academic or sporting, musical and artistic merit as measured by the entrance examination and scholarship assessment days. Particulars of the examination are available from the Admissions Officer, email: admissions@bla.gdst.net.

Charitable status. Blackheath High School is part of The Girls' Day School Trust, which is a Registered Charity, number 306983..

Chair of Local Governors: Ms Elizabeth Little

Head: **Mrs C Chandler-Thompson**, BA Hons Exeter, PGCE

Deputy Head (*Staff and Students*): Mr C Alaru, BA, BEd Queensland University of Technology

Deputy Head (*Academic*): Mr S Henderson, BMus Hons London, PGCE

Deputy Head (*Learning, Enrichment & Student Progress*): Mrs N Argile, BSc Newcastle, MSc, PGCE

Director of Finance & Operations: Mr R Ryan, AAT, DSBM

Head of Junior School: Mrs S Skevington, LLB Hons Sheffield, PGCE EYP

Admissions Team: admissions@bla.gdst.net

Bolton School Girls' Division

Chorley New Road, Bolton, Lancs BL1 4PB

Tel:	01204 840201
email:	seniorgirls@boltonschool.org
website:	www.boltonschool.org/seniorgirls
Twitter:	@BoltonSchool
Facebook:	@boltonschool.org
Instagram:	@bolton_school_foundation
LinkedIn:	/bolton-school

Bolton School Girls' Division was founded in 1877 as the High School for Girls and quickly gained a reputation for excellence. In 1913 the first Viscount Leverhulme gave a generous endowment to the High School for Girls and the Bolton Grammar School for Boys on condition that the two schools should be equal partners known as Bolton School (Girls' and Boys' Divisions).

Bolton School – the TES' 2019 Independent School of the Year – is a family of schools, where children can enjoy an all-through education, joining our co-educational Nursery or Infant School before moving up to our single-sex Junior and Senior Schools with Sixth Forms. We are strong believers that girls and boys from 7+ perform best in a single-sex environment, but one where there are co-educational activities – the best of both worlds.

The School occupies a stunning 32-acre site and the Girls' Division Senior School contains over 770 day pupils. The co-educational infants' school, Beech House, offers an education for 225 pupils aged 4–7 and up to a further 200 girls are educated in the Junior Girls' School (age 7–11). In the Senior School, 200 girls typically attend the Sixth Form.

Bolton School Girls' Division seeks to realise the potential of each pupil. We provide challenge, encourage initiative, promote teamwork and develop leadership capabilities. It is our aim that students leave the School as self-confident young people equipped with the knowledge, skills and attributes that will allow them to lead happy and fulfilled lives and to make a difference for good in the wider community.

We do this through offering a rich and stimulating educational experience which encompasses academic, extra-curricular and social activities. We provide a supportive and industrious learning environment for pupils selected on academic potential, irrespective of means and background.

Facilities. Housed in an attractive Grade II listed building the school has an impressive Great Hall which seats 900 people, spacious corridors, a theatre, two Resistant Materials workshops, two Textile studios, two Food Technology rooms, four computer rooms, seven laboratories, three Art studios and two fine libraries staffed by two qualified librarians and their staff. In September 2013, the Sixth Form moved into the purpose-built £7m Riley Sixth Form Centre, where girls and boys share a Common Room, cafe and learning areas equipped with the very latest technology. The girls' dining room was completely redeveloped in the Summer of 2015.

Besides its own fully equipped gym, the Girls' Division shares the new £1m all-weather sports surface, an award-winning Careers Department, the Arts Complex and Sports Hall, a 25-metre swimming pool, extensive playing fields, the Leverhulme Sports Pavilion and an outdoor pursuits facility at Patterdale Hall in the Lake District. Pupils also have the option of spending a week undertaking sailing lessons on Tenacity of Bolton, a ketch built by pupils in the Boys' Division.

Beech House Infants' School. The curriculum, though based on the National Curriculum, extends far beyond it. Specialist teaching is provided for older pupils in Physical Education and Music and all children are taught French. The school has recently moved to purpose-built state-of-the-art premises and in addition to its own resources, Beech House benefits from the use of Senior School facilities such as the swimming pool, playing fields and Arts Centre.

The Girls' Junior School. There are 2 classes in each of Years 3–6. In September 2010, the junior girls moved into their new £5m school which has its own hall, laboratory, art

and design facility, IT suite and library, as well as large classrooms. Besides following the National Curriculum with Senior School specialists teaching PE, Music and French, pupils have additional opportunities. The many clubs and wide range of extra-curricular activities ensure a full and well-balanced programme.

The Senior School. The curriculum encompasses all the National Curriculum but also offers the study of up to three modern languages, the classics and a wide range of modules in Technology. At age 11 all girls follow a similar weekly timetable. The range of subjects offered cover: Art, English, French, Geography, History, Classical Studies, Mathematics, Music, PE, Religious Studies, Science and Technology. All pupils in Year 9 begin to study GCSE Biology, Chemistry and Physics. The above list does not fully show the great variety of opportunities available which also include: Athletics, Biology, Chemistry, Computer Graphics, Dance, Drama, Earth Science, Electronics, Food and Nutrition, Gymnastics, Information Technology, Lacrosse, Netball, Sailing, Climbing, Orienteering, PSHE, Resistant Materials Technology, Rounders, Swimming, Waterpolo, Tennis and Textiles Technology. This breadth is maintained to GCSE with a second language, German, Latin or Spanish, being offered in Year 8. In Years 10 and 11 we also offer Archery, Badminton, Basketball, Climbing, Fitness/Gym sessions, Football, Rounders, Unihoc and Volleyball.

GCSE. There is extensive choice at GCSE. All follow a common curriculum of English, English Literature, Mathematics, Biology, Chemistry and Physics (with an option to take Trilogy Award Science from Year 10) together with non-examined courses in Information Technology, PE, and Religion and Philosophy. Personal aptitude and inclination are fostered by allowing a maximum of 11 GCSEs: the core subjects plus options chosen from Art, Biology, Business and Communication Systems, Chemistry, Computing, Drama, Food and Nutrition, French, Geography, German, Greek, History, Information Technology, Latin, Music, Physics, Religious Studies, Resistant Materials Technology, Spanish and Textile Technology. Essential balance is maintained by encouraging all to include one Humanity and one Modern Language, but the choice is otherwise entirely free.

The Sixth Form. Flexibility is a key feature of the Sixth Form. Teaching in the Sixth Form is in smaller groups and single-sex teaching remains the norm, although in a very few subjects co-educational arrangements are in operation. Students choose from a list of approximately 30 AS courses. Breadth is promoted further by our complementary Curriculum Enrichment Programme. All students have the opportunity to follow a range of non-examined courses as well as Physical Education (sports include golf, football, life-saving, rugby, self-defence, tennis and yoga). Links beyond school include the Community Action Programme and Young Enterprise scheme, as well as opportunities with Business Awareness and Work Experience.

Students in the Sixth Form have greater freedom which includes wearing their own smart clothes, exeat periods and having their own Sixth Form Centre away from the Senior School. Joint social and extracurricular events are regularly organised with the Boys' Division. There are opportunities for students to assume a variety of responsibilities both within the school and in the wider community. Increasing personal freedom within a highly supportive environment helps students to make the transition to the independence of the adult world. Some students stretch themselves by taking the AQA Extended Project Qualification.

Almost all students (98%) go on to Higher Education or Degree Apprenticeships (5% typically to Oxford and Cambridge).

Music and Drama are popular and students achieve the highest standards in informal and public performances. The wide variety of concerts and productions may take place in the Arts Centre, the Great Hall or the fully-equipped Theatre, all of which make excellent venues for joint and Girls' Division performances. The School regularly performs at Manchester's Bridgewater Hall.

Personal, Social and Health Education, and Citizenship. PSHE, RSE and Citizenship are targeted in a variety of ways and coordinated centrally. Some issues may be covered within departmental schemes of work while others will be discussed in the informal atmosphere of form groups led by the form tutor. Those areas which require specialist input are fitted into longer sessions run by experts from outside school.

Careers. The Careers Department helps prepare students for adult life. It has a resource centre giving access to all the latest information. The extensive programme starts at age 11 and includes communication skills, work sampling, and support in making choices at all stages of schooling. In addition, girls prepare their CVs and applications to Higher Education with the individual help of a trained tutor.

Extra-curricular Activities. Patterdale Hall, our outdoor pursuits centre in the Lake District, offers many activities including abseiling, gorge walking, orienteering and sailing on Lake Ullswater. Awards are regularly made to enable individuals to undertake a variety of challenging activities both at home and abroad while every year, the whole of Year 9 as well as many older girls embark on The Duke of Edinburgh's Award scheme. In 2017 the School won the Queen's Award for Voluntary Service, the MBE for organisations. In addition to the annual exchanges for Modern Languages students, we also offer a wide range of educational and recreational trips both at home and abroad. All have the opportunity to follow a wide range of non-examined courses of their choice, including Physical Education.

Admission. Entrance to the school is by Headteacher's report, written examination and interview in the Spring term for girls aged 7 and 11. New girls are also welcomed into the Sixth Form. Applications to other year groups are welcomed and spaces may be available depending upon migration.

One in five Senior School pupils receives assistance with their fees through the School's own bursaries. Non-means-tested Scholarships are also awarded to those pupils who achieve highly in the Entrance Examination.

Fees per term (2021–2022). Senior School and Sixth Form £4,237; Infant and Junior Schools £3,389. Fees include lunches.

Charitable status. Bolton School is a Registered Charity, number 1110703.

Chairman of Governors: Mr I Riley, MEng, MBA

Head of Foundation: P J Britton, MBE, MEd

Head of Girls' Division: Mrs L D Kyle, BSc

Assistant Head: P Linfitt, BSc, MEng
Assistant Head: Ms H Bradford-Keegan, MA (*Curricular and Extracurricular Achievement*)

Assistant Head: Mrs C Winder, MA (*Head of Sixth Form*)
Assistant Head: Ms M Teichman (*Head of Upper School*)
Assistant Head: Mrs A Field, BA (*Head of Middle School*)

Senior School:

Heads of Departments:

Art, Design & Technology: Ms Peri Rogers, BA
Business Studies: Mrs S Foster, BA (*Acting Head*)
Careers and Higher Education: Miss L Jones, BA
Classics: Mrs J Hone, BA
Economics: Miss L Jones, BA
English: Mrs A Martin, MA
Food Technology: Mrs N James, BA
Geography: Ms S Noot, BA
History: C Owen, MA
ICT: Mrs S Brace, BSc
Learning Support Coordinator: Mrs A Elkin, BA
Mathematics: G Heppleston, BSc

Modern Foreign Languages:
D O'Neill, BA
Ms E Xerri, BA (*Second i/c*)
Ms R McQuillan, BA (*German*)

Music: Mr P Lovatt, MA
Physical Education: Mrs K A Heatherington, BA
Religion and Philosophy: Mrs K E Porter, BA
Resistant Materials: Miss R Langley
Science: Dr A Fielder, BA
Science Coordinator: Mrs K Power, BSc (*i/c Middle School & Trilogy Science*)
Biology: Mrs A D Furey, BSc
Chemistry: Mrs S Rich, BSc
Physics: Mr R Ball, BSc
Psychology: Mrs J Sanders, BSc

Instrumental Music Staff:
Brass, Cello, Clarinet, Flute, Guitar, Oboe, Organ, Percussion, Piano, Saxophone, Singing, Violin.

Lower Schools:

Head of Primary Division: Mrs S A Faulkner, BA, MA

Junior Department (Age 7–11):
Head: Mrs C Laverick, BSc
Deputy Head: Mrs H Holt, BEd

Beech House (Age 4–7):
Head (2021–2022): Mrs S A Faulkner, BA, MA
Deputy Head: Mrs J Mees, BSc

Bruton School for Girls

Sunny Hill, Bruton, Somerset BA10 0NT

Tel:	01749 814400
email:	admissions@brutonschool.co.uk
website:	www.brutonschool.co.uk
Twitter:	@BrutonSchool
Facebook:	@Bruton-School-for-Girls

Established in 1900 and set in beautiful Somerset countryside, overlooking Glastonbury Tor, Bruton School for Girls is a day school for girls and boys aged 2–7 and a day and boarding school for girls aged 7–18. Around 40% of the pupils board and full, weekly and flexi boarding options are available. The teaching week is Monday to Friday with no Saturday lessons, however there are sports and activities across the weekend for boarders and day pupils.

Sunny Hill Prep comprises the Nursery, Pre-Prep and Prep years. Boarding is available for girls from the age of 7 years old. The supportive environment enables creative and dedicated teachers to make the most of the inquisitive childhood years and ensures that every pupil receives individual attention. In a broad curriculum, they explore the exciting world of science, IT, humanities, French, music, DT and creative arts. Mathematics and English programmes build firm foundations for purposeful learning. The Early Years Foundation (Nursery to Reception) has an 'Outstanding' Ofsted rating. A weekly enrichment programme broadens the pupils experience and includes outdoor education and forest school, drama, cooking and problem solving.

The Senior School is a thriving community of girls age 11–16 years who are taught in separate year groups. Girls come from a wide variety of local, national and international schools, as well as from Sunny Hill Prep. Offering a broad and balanced curriculum, girls usually study 9–10 subjects at GCSE. We have an excellent academic reputation, which is especially notable as we are a non-academically-selective school. We consistently score highly on the 'added value' measure which shows that each girl significantly exceeds her expected grades. Additional learning support is available from specialist Skills Development teachers where appropriate.

The Sixth Form offers excellent preparation for university, with tutorial support and individual study programmes and a weekly lecture programme in the Autumn and Spring terms. An extensive range of A Levels is complemented by the Extended Project Qualification (EPQ), extension studies and extra-curricular activities which include public speaking and the Leiths Certificate in Food and Wine. Career and Higher Education advice feature prominently at this stage. Many girls entering the Sixth Form transfer from the Senior School and are joined by students from local and international schools.

Why choose BSG? We are passionate about, and experts in, girls' education. We believe in offering our girls an education that will equip them to grow intellectually, think independently and become confident and responsible young women. What really sets us apart is our focus on each girl as an individual. We are proud that our size means we get to know each and every girl personally. It is this academic and pastoral support that means we can help each girl to reach her full potential and become the most amazing person she can be. With over 50% of ALL girls achieving an A*/A, followed with 79% A*/A and 94% A*/B across all A Levels, we are extremely proud of our success.

Academic and Personal Expectations. Academically, the school has high expectations and most girls gain places at their first-choice universities, many of which are Russell Group and other prestigious establishments including Oxford and Cambridge. The girls are encouraged to have self-belief, to set challenging goals, display independence of thought and enjoy learning for its own sake.

There are many opportunities for leadership and the development of personal and social skills, particularly in the Sixth Form, where students may take up the role of prefect or hall captain.

Location. Set on a 45-acre campus in beautiful countryside, the school is close to the Somerset, Wiltshire and Dorset borders, and has easy access to the M3/A303 corridor between London and the South West. Bristol, Bath, Salisbury and the south coast are all within approximately one hour's travel. Castle Cary station, served by London Paddington–Exeter express trains, is 4 miles away. Transport can be arranged from London Heathrow, Bristol International and other airports. A network of daily buses serves the school from surrounding areas.

Boarding. Our boarding houses provide comfortable accommodation and facilities include common rooms, kitchens and dining areas. All the houses have Wi-Fi. Younger girls share a room with two/three other girls, while Senior girls either share a room of two or have their own study-bedroom. Sixth formers all have individual study-bedrooms and enjoy an increased degree of independence that aims to bridge school and university. The boarding houses are situated on the school campus and girls are cared for by experienced Housemistresses and house staff. A variety of weekend activities is offered and, as many of our boarders are full boarders, there is always lots going on at weekends.

Extracurricular Activities. Art, Drama, Music and Sport feature strongly. The outstanding success of the Art department is reflected in work displayed around the school. The Hobhouse Studio Theatre provides a professional-standard performance space for productions and 'speech and drama' presentations. There is a wide range of opportunities for both instrumental and choral performance, with choirs performing music across a range of styles and numerous instrumental groups, including a school orchestra and chamber groups. There is also the popular Duke of Edinburgh's Award programme. In the Prep, all pupils from Reception to Prep 6 participate in Forest School.

Entry. There is open entry into the Pre-Prep and Prep from which pupils normally progress seamlessly into the senior school. The senior school entry process includes the school's own diagnostic assessments or Common Entrance. Entry into the Sixth Form is by interview and GCSE or equivalent qualifications.

Fees per term (2021–2022). Prep: Day £2,835–£4,372, Full Boarding £8,022–£9,033; Senior: Day £6,232, Full Boarding £10,616–£11,508.

Scholarships and Bursaries. Bruton School for Girls has a range of scholarships which are offered on entry to the Senior School at 11+ upwards and Sixth Form including academic, all-round, music, art, sport and drama.

Means-tested financial assistance is available to support those pupils whose families would find difficulty in meeting the full fees.

Charitable status. Bruton School for Girls is a Registered Charity, number 1085577, and a Company Limited by Guarantee. It exists to provide education.

Chairman of Governors: Mr D H C Batten

***Headmistress*: Mrs Jane Evans**

Deputy Head: Mrs Rachel Robbins

Director of Learning & Teaching: Mrs Alice Taylor

Head of Prep: Mrs Helen Snow

Director of External Relations: Mrs Tessa Howard-Vyse

Burgess Hill Girls

Keymer Road, Burgess Hill, West Sussex RH15 0EG

Tel: 01444 241050
email: admissions@burgesshillgirls.com
website: www.burgesshillgirls.com
Twitter: @BHillGirls
Facebook: @BurgessHillGirls
LinkedIn: /burgess-hill-girls

An independent day and boarding school or girls age 2½ to 18 years, founded in 1906 by Miss Beatrice Goode. Our school has a Nursery (accepts boys), Prep School, Senior School and Sixth Form. To fully appreciate our school come for a visit and talk to the students, they will be delighted to show you around. (*See also Burgess Hill Girls Prep School entry in the IAPS section.*)

General. The ethos of the School is to provide a caring, challenging and supportive atmosphere which encourages young people to use their initiative, be inquisitive and creative and develop responsibility and independence. Boys are welcome in the nursery. Our school is a community in which girls flourish; from age 4 the focus is firmly on girls and the way they learn. They develop self-esteem and confidence and go on to make a positive contribution in their chosen professions. We have small classes with fully qualified, professional staff dedicated to catering for the needs of each individual child. The School has established a reputation for excellence in Music, Sport, Art, Textiles and Drama and achieves impressive academic results. We are consistently highly ranked nationally and regularly lead the field in Sussex. We believe that education for life involves much more than academic success alone. Girls can, and do, strive for excellence wherever their talents lie.

School Facilities. The Senior School offers specialist teaching rooms including: a state-of-the-art language suite equipped with computers and specialist software for personalised listening and speaking; a Music room equipped with the latest Apple Mac composition software; Music practice rooms; two Art studios with an exhibition area, Art library and a kiln area; a Drama studio; a fully-equipped Media suite; two modern Chemistry labs; a specialist Textiles room and Technology workshop; a Learning Resource Centre and enhanced outdoor PE facilities with tennis courts and an Astroturf training area. The Performing Arts facilities have been extended with a glazed, curved entrance foyer.

The Prep School's facilities include a Learning Hub which incorporates a library, large learning space and access to iPads and interactive electronic screen. The Prep School also offers fully-equipped subject-specific classrooms rooms for Music, ICT, Art, Science and Technology and access to all the sports facilities on the main school campus. The Pre-Prep are based in a building with bright, open classrooms and have their own hall and library. The Pre-Prep and Prep School have an exciting playground with a wooden adventure trail and outdoor classroom.

The Sixth Form centre includes a seminar room, contemporary classrooms, a study room with ICT facilities, a higher education library, a music practice room, two common rooms and a new student kitchen. All curriculum areas are well served with appropriate specialist accommodation, either in the Sixth Form Centre or in the Senior School complex for Art, Drama, Music, Media, PE, Science, Technology and Textiles. All classrooms are equipped with interactive whiteboards, and suites of laptop computers ensure that technology is available when and where needed.

The school has two Edwardian boarding houses with bedrooms and common rooms which are spacious, light and pleasantly furnished.

Curriculum. The curriculum is broad and challenging and relevant to the needs of young people. There is a wide choice of subjects both at GCSE and A Level with many extracurricular activities.

"The School is almost non-selective and yet achieves better results than many more competitive schools. The holistic approach to education, where equal value is placed on academic achievement and softer skills, produces extremely confident young women who grow up to believe they can be whatever they want to be." *Good Schools Guide 2019*

Entrance Procedures. Entrance to either the Prep or Senior School is by assessment and school reference. Senior girls are also interviewed by the Head. Scholarships are awarded each year for academic and/or musical excellence into Years 3–6 inclusive, 7, 9 and the Lower Sixth. Sport/Creative scholarships are available for students entering Year 7, 9 and the Lower Sixth. The Margaret Morris All-Rounder Scholarship is available to girls entering Year 9.

Fees per term (2021–2022). Senior School: £5,300–£6,950 (day girls); £10,600–£12,250 (boarding). Prep School: £2,270–£5,150 (day girls).

Bold Girls' Association. Now operates through the school. Please contact the school for further information.

Charitable status. Burgess Hill School for Girls is a Registered Charity, number 307001.

Chairman of Governors: Dr Alison Smith, MB ChB, MRCGP

Head: Mrs E Laybourn, BEd Hons

Bursar: Mr G Bond
Head of Pre-Prep and Prep School and Deputy Head of School: Mrs H Cavanagh, BA Hons QTS
Assistant Head, Academic (Teaching & Learning): Ms R Flint, MA Hons, PGCE
Assistant Head, Pastoral & Boarding: Miss N Donson, BMus Hons, PGCE

Assistant Head, Head of Sixth Form: Mr W O'Brien-Blake, BA Hons, MSc, QTS
Deputy Head of Prep School: Mrs S Collins, BA Hons, PGCE
Nursery Manager: Mrs S Roberts, BA Hons, PGCE

Heads of Departments:
Art & Design: Ms E Levett, BA Hons, PGCE
Biology: Mrs A Robinson, BSc Hons, PGCE
Chemistry: Mrs J Medcalf, BSc Hons, PGCE
Classics & Latin: Mr B Roberts, MA Hons, PGCE
Computer Science: Mr R Stanway, BSc Hons, PGCE
Drama & Speech and Drama: Mrs E Cassim, MA Hons, PGCE
Economics, Business and Politics: Ms D Flatman, MA Hons, PGCE
English: Mrs S Kruschandl, BA Hons, PGCE, MA Ed
French: Miss E Titley, BA Hons, PGCE
Geography: Mrs J Ponting, MA, BSc Hons, PGCE

German: Miss I Lester, MA, BA Hons, PGCE
History: Mrs T Jackson, BA Hons, MPhil, PGCE
Learning Resource Centre: Ms Y Akehurst, BA
Mathematics: Mr R Stanway, BSc Hons, PGCE
Music: Mr D Black, BEd, QTS, BMus, MMus,
Physical Education: Miss S Clapp, BA Hons QTS
Physics: Mr A Gillaspy, BSc Hons, PGCE
Psychology: Mrs J Scopes, BSc Hons, GTP
Religious Studies: Miss S Cull, BA Hons, PGCE
Spanish: Mr J Montesinos, BA Hons, PGCE

Head of Events: Mrs J Fleming
Registrar: Miss R McEvoy
Housemistress: Mrs S Beels (*Head of House*)
School Nurse: Mrs L Hall, RGN

Channing School

The Bank, Highgate, London N6 5HF

Tel:	020 8340 2328 (School Office)
	020 8340 2719 (Bursar)
email:	info@channing.co.uk
website:	www.channing.co.uk
Twitter:	@ChanningSchool
Facebook:	@ChanningSchool

At Channing everything is possible!

Channing School is unique in providing an education based on the principles of two Unitarian sisters who, more than 130 years ago, founded a school for girls in Highgate, North London.

In a changing world of uncertainty and pressure, girls find at Channing an oasis of calm purpose, where pupils are encouraged to think for themselves, and to keep an open mind. Our academic results are among the best in the country and our most recent Independent Schools Inspectorate (ISI) awarded Channing the highest possible ratings in all categories, concluding that 'The quality of pupils' achievements and learning is exceptional'.

Each girl is treated as an individual and valued for her achievements and efforts, whether they be sporting, musical, theatrical, intellectual, spiritual or academic …or none of the above. Sometimes the greatest lessons are learned from the kindness of others and we recognise and encourage this, too.

Every member of the school belongs to a warm, supportive community and this includes all our pupils, staff, parents, alumnae and many friends. Many visitors comment on the indefinable 'feel' of the school, its very special atmosphere and unique ethos.

Number of Pupils. 1,000, 133 in the Sixth Form.

The School is situated in Highgate Village, in attractive grounds, and offers a balanced education combining a traditional academic curriculum with modern educational developments. The complex of old and new buildings has been constantly adapted to provide up-to-date facilities, and there are strong links with the local community and local schools.

Girls usually take nine or ten subjects to GCSE and there is a wide range of A Level choices, including Physics, Further Maths, Politics and Theatre Studies. The Junior School has its own building – the elegant family home of Sir Sydney Waterlow, one-time Lord Mayor of London – set in spacious gardens, and is notable for its happy and secure atmosphere.

Most girls learn at least one musical instrument and there are frequent concerts and theatrical productions. The school is fortunate in its gardens, open space and its facilities. The school has invested £13m in new facilities including a Sixth Form Centre with bespoke study facilities, a state-of-the-art Sports Centre, a Music School and a magnificent Performing Arts Theatre.

Entry is by assessment at 4+, an examination/assessment and interview at 11+ and predicted GCSE results and interview at 16+. In addition, entry is subject to a satisfactory report from the applicant's current school. Entry assessments for occasional vacancies that arise for other years are age appropriate.

Further information can be obtained from the School prospectus and the Sixth Form prospectus available from the Registrar and the school website (www.channing.co.uk).

Scholarships and Bursaries. All candidates who sit the 11+ entrance examination are automatically considered for a Year 7 Academic Scholarship. They do not need to make a separate application. To be considered for a Sixth Form Academic Scholarship candidates (including current pupils) must sit the Sixth Form Academic Scholarship exam which takes place in November of every year.

Music Scholarships are offered at 11+ and 16+. These cover up to 50% of the tuition fees and lessons in school on one instrument for a year (renewable). Art Scholarships are offered to Sixth Form entrants based on submission of a portfolio of work. Bursaries are offered at 11+ and 16+. Please see the school website for further details.

Fees per term (2021–2022). Junior School £6,550; Senior School £7,240.

Charitable status. Channing House Incorporated is a Registered Charity, number 312766.

Governors:
Mrs C Leslie, LLB (*Chair*)
Mr J Alexander, FCA
Mr A Appleyard, BSc
Ms C Chandler-Thompson
Revd D Costley, BA
Mrs L Cristie, BA
Mr R Hirji
Ms C Hulme-McKibbin
Mr D Oliver
Mrs J Otterburn Hall
Mrs P Peck, BA Hons Cantab, MBA Oxon
Ms B Rentoul, MA
Mr W Spears, BA, MBA, FRGS
Dr A Sutton, MB, ChB, DRCOG, MRCGP, DFSRH
Mr K Van der Sande, MA Hons, DipArch RIBA, RIAS, FRSA

Bursar & Clerk to the Governors: Mr R Hill

Headmistress: Mrs L Hughes, BA Warwick

Acting Deputy Head: Mrs G Bhamra-Burgess, MSc SOAS
Deputy Head (*Academic*): Ms J Newman, MA UCL

* *Head of Department*
§ *Part-time*

Ms P Allkin (*Learning Support*)
Miss C Arnold, BSc Nottingham (*Biology*)
§Ms S Beenstock BA Leeds (*English*)

*Mrs G Bhamra-Burgess, MSc SOAS (*Economics*)
*§Mrs S Blake, BSc Bristol, MA London (*Geography*)
*Mr P Boxall, GRSM, ARCO Royal Academy of Music
(*Music*)
Mr A Boardman, BA Hons Durham (*Geography, Assistant
Head Teaching and Learning*)
§Ms J Bramhall, MA Oxon (*Geography*)
§Mr A Brand (*Mathematics*)
Ms A Cann, MPhil Bristol (*English, Oxbridge
Coordinator*)
*Ms T Cooper, MEng Imperial (*Second in Mathematics,
STEM Coordinator*)
Ms K Cronk, BA New York (*Learning Support Assistant*)
Mr P Daurat, MA Essex (*Mathematics*)
*Mrs W Devine, BA Reading (*Politics, MUN Coordinator*)
*Ms S Della-Porta, BEd Wollongong, Australia (*Physical
Education and Sport, Head of Year 10 and Sharpe
House*)
§Dr N Devlin, DPhil Oxon (*Classics, EPQ Coordinator*)
Miss S Donington, MA Leeds (*Second in English*)
*Mrs S Elliot, MA Cantab (*Classics*)
§Miss C Evans, BA Hons Southampton (*Physical
Education*)
*Miss P Evernden, MA Cantab (*English*)
*Mr S Frank, BSc Birmingham (*Biology*)
Miss S-L Fung, BSc Coventry (*Physics*)
Mrs C Garrill, BA Leicester (*French*, Politics*)
Mr P Gittins, BA Wolverhampton (*Art, PSHE*, Head of
Year 9 and Spears House*)
Ms H Gjertsen, BA Hons Birbeck (*Head of Sixth Form*)
Ms J Gomez (*Spanish, French*)
*Mr D Grossman, BSc Hons Manchester (*Assistant Head
Director of Digital Learning and Technology*)
*Mr A Haworth, MA RCA (*Art*)
*Mr G Headey, MA Kent (*Religious Education*)
§Mrs B Hernandez, BA Hons Alicante, Spain (*Spanish,
French*)
*Ms J Hill, BA Hons Royal Conservatoire of Scotland
(*Drama and Theatre*)
*Mr M Holmes, BSc Hons City (*Information and
Communication Technology*)
§Miss A Hosseini, BSc UCL (*Chemistry*)
Ms Y Hume, BFA Hons UNSW, Australia (*Art*)
§Ms K Hurst, MA East Anglia (*Drama and Theatre*)
*Mr R Jacobs, BA Oxon (*Physics*)
Mrs H Kanmwaa, BA Oxon (*English*)
§Mrs K Kavanagh, BA Sheffield (*English*)
§Mrs A Kennedy, MSc London (*Chemistry*)
Ms J Kung, BA USYD, Australia, DipEd MU, Australia
(*History, Director of Sixth Form*)
§Ms A Lam (*Art*)
§Mrs M Levontine (*Library Assistant*)
Miss R Lindsay, BA Arts, BA Ed, UNSW, Australia
(*Physical Education*)
Miss Z Lindsay, BA Leicester (*History*)
Miss R McNamara, MPhil Cambridge (*Classics*)
§Ms S Mackie, BA Oxon (*Art*)
§Mrs S Mahmood, BEd University of Alberta, Canada
(*Chemistry*)
Ms S Melvin, BA Oxon, MA MPhil Columbia (*Classics,
More Able Coordinator*)
*Mr P Martini-Phillips, BA Hons Leicester (*History,
Assistant Director of Sixth Form*)
Miss E Moor, BA Durham FRGS (*Geography*)
§Ms E Pavlopoulos, LLB Kings/Paris I, MA Ed Open
(*Careers, French, German*)

Ms N Quow (*Chemistry, Year 7&8 Science Coordinator*)
Miss I Ramsden, MA Oxon, MSc City London (*Senior
School Librarian*)
Mrs A Reece, BA Liverpool (*Physical Education*)
*Ms N Rehmat (*Psychology*)
§Mr D Riggs-Long, BSc Imperial (*Mathematics*)
*§Miss A Romero-Wiltshire, BA Nottingham (*French*)
§Ms A Rozieres, MA Grenoble, France (*French*)
§Mrs D Shoham, MSc LSHTM (*Biology*)
§Mr M Smith (*Economics*)
*Dr C Spinks, PhD Manchester (*Science and Chemistry*)
§Ms A Stöckmann, MA Westfaelische Wilhelms, Germany
(*German*)
Mrs S Walker, BA Durham (*Humanities*)
*Mr C Waring, BS Strathclyde (*MFL and Spanish*)
§Ms K Wilkinson, BA East Anglia (*English, Assistant
Head of PSHE*)
§Miss L Wilkinson, MA City (*Drama*)
Miss C Williams, BSc West of England (*Mathematics,
Psychology*)
Mrs R Williams, BSc Hons UCL (*Mathematics, Assistant
Director of Sixth Form*)
§Mr P Williamson, BEd Huddersfield (*Mathematics*)
*Mrs H Wootton, BSc Exeter (*Mathematics*)
Ms M Yun, BSc London (*Mathematics, Duke of Edinburgh
Manager*)
Miss L Zanardo, BA, BMus Ed, Grad Dip Australia
(*Assistant Director of Music, Head of Year 11 and
Waterlow House*)
Ms N Zekan, BEd RMIT Australia (*Physical Education,
Head of Year 8 and Goodwin House*)
§Mrs D Zuluaga De La Cruz, MA Valenciennes, France
(*French*)

Junior School Staff:

Head of Junior School: Miss D Hamalis, BEd Hons

Deputy Head: Mrs L Broughton-Williams, BSc Hons,
PGCE [maternity leave]
Director of Studies: Miss R McGinnety, BA Hons, PGCE
Head of Early Years and Key Stage 1: Mrs G Eliad, BA
Hons, PGCE
Acting Deputy Head and Head of Key Stage 2: Miss D
Wright, BA Hons, PGCE
Acting Assistant Head: Miss C Bolton, BA

Miss A Alfaro, MA, PGCE
Miss C Bolton, BA (*Physical Education*)
Miss C Clancy, BEd Hons, PGCE
§Miss A Conway, BA Hons, BSc, PGCE (*Drama
Coordinator*)
Mrs G Eliad, BA Hons, PGCE
Miss E Evans, LLB Hons, PGCE
Mr R Fellows, BA Hons, PGCE (*Art & DT Coordinator*)
Miss A Frost, BEd
Ms S Grimstead, BA Hons, PGCE
Mr C Headey (*Music*)
*Mrs J Jarman, BSc, GTP (*Physical Education*)
Ms A Jimenez, BA Hons, PGCE (*MFL Coordinator*)
Ms J Kilanko, MA Dip OCR SpLD (*Learning Support*)
Miss R McGinnety, BA Hons, PGCE
§Mrs C Marley, BMus Hons, PGDip (*Music*)
Miss K Marshall, MSc, PGCE
Mrs K Miller, BA Hons, PGCE
Miss R Newell, BA, PGCE, MEd
Miss D Parmar, BEd Hons
Miss A Phipps, BEd

Mr C Rich, MA, PGCE
Mrs C Siltoe, BA, PGCE
Miss S Snowdowne, BEd
Miss D Wright, BA Hons, PGCE

Plus 13 Teaching Assistants and 29 Visiting Music
Teachers.

Cobham Hall

Brewers Road, Cobham, Kent DA12 3BL

Tel: 01474 823371
email: enquiries@cobhamhall.com
website: www.cobhamhall.com
Twitter: @CobhamHall
Facebook: @CobhamHall

Dive into an education at Cobham Hall, where we aim for each student to discover there is more in them than they thought.

Cobham Hall is a Round Square Boarding and Day school for girls aged 11–18 situated near Rochester, Kent and on the doorstep of London. Offering a range of flexi-Boarding options as well as full boarding and day places, Cobham Hall provides flexibility for family life.

At the heart of Cobham Hall's educational experience are the core values of Trust, Respect, Honesty, Kindness and Tolerance. These values, along with our Round Square ideals, provide the structure for our Personal Discovery Framework – a journey of growth and development that each student will undertake at Cobham Hall.

There is More at Cobham Hall. Education should be about preparing students for life after school. Personal and academic success, health and wellbeing, and focus on community go hand-in-hand. It is our responsibility to provide each student with the knowledge, skills and opportunities to become the best version of themselves. A combination of high teaching standards, small class sizes and a wide range of co-curricular activities help to achieve good results and develop skills and interests for life. We encourage our students to challenge themselves – both their abilities and their perceptions – and believe that by taking part in everything Cobham Hall has to offer, students discover more about themselves. Our Key Skills lessons specifically focus on the develop of crucial life skills, especially those identified by the World Economic Forum as those required for life in the 21st Century, such as resilience, communication, determination and teamwork. We enable today's students to step into tomorrow's world ready to embrace and adapt to new challenges.

There's more to our Sixth Form. Complementing Cobham Hall's broad A Level subject options are courses that encourage all-round development. Sport, Tutorial and Global Critical Thinking provide balance, promote good physical and mental health, and encourage awareness and discussion of the world and their place in it. The Duke of Edinburgh's Award, service opportunities and the Ivy House Leadership Award allow students to step out of their comfort zone, try new things, and support their community. With the Extended Project Qualification, students can immerse themselves in a subject they are passionate about in a way that suits their abilities and develops research and analytical skills.

There's more opportunity to be an individual. Cobham Hall's small class sizes mean each student gets the support needed academically, and the care needed pastorally. Looking after students' emotional and physical wellbeing forms the essence of our pastoral care practices. Wellbeing is central to School life, with timetabled lessons and a dedicated Wellbeing Centre. As Sixth Form student Maisy explains, "Each Department is extremely supportive to all students, and I believe no student would go unseen if struggling, due to the small class sizes and passionate teachers."

There's more opportunity to explore. Students are encouraged to explore the world around them, either through activities such as Model United Nations, or on national and international trips. As a Round Square school, students can attend conferences both in the UK and globally. Closer to home, we are nestled in a 150-acre site: plenty of space to reflect amongst the bluebells and daffodils, to collect data for science lessons, to be inspired for Art lessons, to boost stamina and fitness in PE, or simply to run around and enjoy being a child.

Cobham Hall students become inquisitive, inspiring young people ready for life after school.

Fees per term (2021–2022). Day girls: £6,804–£8,246 Boarders: £10,279–£12,831.

Charitable status. Cobham Hall is a Registered Charity, number 1064758. It exists to provide high quality education for girls aged 11–18 years.

Governing Body:
Mr E Lipton (*Chairman*)
Court of Governors

Staff:
Headmistress: Mrs Wendy Barrett, BSc Hon London, PGCE

Bursar: Mr D Standen, BSc Bradford
Deputy Headmistress: Mrs S Carney, BEd Exeter
Director of Studies: Dr Patrick Drumm, BMus, MA, DPhil
Head of Boarding and Pastoral: Mrs Anna Lenton, FCCT, MBA, BA Hons
Head of Upper School: Mrs M Thompson, BSc London
Head of Lower School: Mrs E Wilkinson, BA London

* *Head of Faculty*

Arts Faculty (including Music and Physical Education):
*Mrs K Walsh, BA Kent Institute of Art & Design
Miss L Mayell BA PGCE Cardiff, MA Rochester
Mr L Green BMus, DipEd Sydney, PGDipRAM, ARAM Royal Academy of Music
Mrs C Moore, BA
Miss D Fautley, BSc Herefordshire

English and Languages Faculty (including Drama and Film Studies):
*Mrs V Kipling BSc Canterbury Christ Church and Mrs R Puri MBA Sheffield
Miss J West, BA Oxford, MA Oxford
Mrs K Bonner, BA, MA Canterbury Christ Church
Mrs F West-Lindsay, BA Reading
Mr J Malcomson
Mrs C Gorman, MA Exeter
Mr A Mangan, BA Winchester

Miss J Caro Quintana, Licenciada en Filologica Inglesa, Valencia, Spain, PGCE Exeter
Mrs E Wilkinson, BA London
Mrs M Gutierrez, Licenciada en Lenguas Extranjeras Columbia, GTP Christ Church
Mrs F Louvez
Dr P Marin, BA, MA USA, MPhil Oxon, PhD Dublin
Mr M Janowicz, BA, PGCE, PGDip Canterbury Christ Church

Humanities Faculty (including Geography, History, Economics, Psychology, Politics and Wellbeing):
*Miss A Williams, BA Oxon
Mrs S Carney, BEd Exeter
Miss V Kipling, BSc Canterbury Christ Church
Mrs R Keys, BA Hons Plymouth
Mrs K-A Hickmott, BSc Middlesex
Mrs R Puri MBA Sheffield
Mrs J Gavin
Ms C Russo Tomassi

Mathematics and Science:
*Miss S Ryder BSc, PGCE Canterbury Christ Church
Mrs W Barrett, BSc London
Mrs C Sheehan, BA Greenwich
Mrs N Youseman-Taylor
Mr P Hosford, BSc Thames Polytechnic (*Physics*)
Mrs M Thompson, BSc London (*Biology*)
Mr A Kirkaldy, BSc Wales, PGCE Southampton (*Chemistry*)
Mr R Kipling

Student Support Department:
*Ms J Harding, BA
Ms Kirsty Paterson, BA
Miss M Frost, BA Hons Canterbury Christ Church (*Teaching Assistant*)
Mrs J Balson, BTEC Level 3 (*Teaching Assistant*)
Mrs K Topps

Boarding Staff:
Mrs C Russo Tomassi
Miss A Ukachi-Lois, BSc Plymouth, MSc Loughborough (*Housemistress*)
Miss N Shipton, BA Chichester (*Senior Housemistress*)
Miss S Shipton

Croydon High School
GDST

Old Farleigh Road, Selsdon, South Croydon, Surrey CR2 8YB

Tel: 020 8260 7500
email: admissions@cry.gdst.net
website: www.croydonhigh.gdst.net
Twitter: @CroydonHigh
Facebook: @CroydonHighSchoolGDST
Instagram: @croydonhighschool

Founded in 1874, the school's original site was in Wellesley Road Croydon but is now situated in the leafy suburb of Selsdon.

Croydon High School is part of the GDST (Girls' Day School Trust). The GDST is the leading network of independent girls' schools in the UK. As a charity that owns and runs 23 schools and two academies, it reinvests all its income in its schools. For further information about the Trust, see p. xix or visit www.gdst.net.

For over 140 years, Croydon High School has provided a superb all-round education for girls around the Croydon area and further afield. The school combines tradition with a forward-looking, supportive and nurturing atmosphere where every girl is encouraged and supported to achieve her personal best. The school welcomes girls from a wide range of backgrounds; excellent pastoral care ensures that each girl is known as an individual.

Croydon High offers girls a wide range of co-curricular opportunities ensuring that each can find something she enjoys. The school regularly achieves local, regional and national success in Sport; its Arts are also outstanding, with a vibrant Music department offering opportunities to musicians at varying ability levels to develop their talents in all musical genres. Termly productions involve students across all year groups and young artists are motivated and inspired to develop their creative talents in different media.

The school aims to develop confident young women with wide-ranging interests and abilities who have also achieved excellent academic results. Emphasis is placed on ensuring that girls are happy and fulfilled in whatever career path they choose for the future.

Number of Pupils. Senior School (aged 11–18): 453 girls; Junior School (aged 3–11): 235 girls (excluding Nursery).

Facilities. The purpose-built school has outstanding facilities; including specialist music rooms with a high-spec Mac Suite and recording studio, drama studio, language laboratory, computer suites, 10 science laboratories, design technology room and a fully equipped sports block incorporating sports hall, gym, indoor swimming pool, fitness room and dance studio. The school is surrounded by spacious playing fields with netball/tennis courts, athletics track and an all-weather hockey pitch.

The Junior School, which has its own Nursery, is in an adjacent building on the same site, sharing many of the excellent facilities. Refurbishment, completed in December 2020, greatly enhances the Main Hall and provides additional space for the school's subject specialist teaching in Music, Drama, MFL and Computer Science, which is a specialty. It also boasts a state-of-the-art 4D immersive learning room, where girls can experience sound and sights that inspire them to produce highly imaginative written and verbal work.

The Sixth Form have their own suite of rooms, including a common room and quiet study area, adjacent to the school library and excellent Further Education, Mentoring and Careers resources are available on site. This is a real strength of the school.

Curriculum. Most girls take 9–10 GCSE subjects with the aim of providing a broad and balanced core curriculum which keeps career choices open. Over 23 subjects are offered at A Level including Government & Politics, Psychology, Economics, Latin and Business. Almost all girls proceed to University, and, each year, a number are offered places at Oxbridge or to read Medicine.

Admission. A whole school Open Day is held annually in October and a Sixth Form Open Evening also in October. An Open Event for both Junior and Senior Schools is held in May. Tours and private visits are welcome and can be arranged at any time through the Junior and Senior Admissions Registrars.

The school admits girls to the Junior School on the basis of either individual assessment (younger girls) or written tests (girls of 7+ and above). Selection procedures are held early in January for Juniors and assessments for Infants are held during the Autumn and Spring Terms for entry in the following September.

For entrance to the Senior School in Year 7, the school holds bespoke Entrance Tests in December for entry the following September. References are taken up for all successful applicants.

Entrance Tests are held in February for Year 9 entry in September.

For the Sixth Form, the school interviews applicants and requests reports from the present school. A Sixth Form Open Evening is held in October and Scholarship and Bursary applicants sit an examination in late November.

Further details on the admissions process are available on the website or via the Registrar, admissions@cry.gdst.net.

Fees per term (Spring and Summer Terms 2022). Senior School: Years 7–9 £5,721, Years 10–13 £5,934; Junior School: Nursery (full time) £3,448, Reception £4,118, Years 1–2 £4,229, Years 3–4 £4,618, Years 5–6 £4,695.

Scholarships and Bursaries. Following the ending of the Government Assisted Places Scheme, the GDST has made available to the school a number of scholarships and bursaries.

Academic scholarships are available for entry at 11+ or to the Sixth Form. Music, art & design, drama and sports scholarships are also available at 11+ and 16+.

For entrance at Year 9, the school offers two Academic Plus scholarships to applicants joining from other schools, who have chosen to be assessed academically and in one of the following subjects; art, music, drama or sport.

Bursaries are means tested and are intended to ensure that the school remains accessible to bright girls who could not otherwise benefit from the education we offer. These are available to Senior School girls only.

The school has a vibrant and active Old Girls Network – The Ivy Link – which supports the school in numerous ways, including offering careers and mentoring connections.

Charitable status. Croydon High School is part of The Girls' Day School Trust, which is a Registered Charity, number 306983.

Chairman of Local Governors: Ms L Lipczynski

***Headmistress*: Mrs E L Pattison**

Deputy Head, Pastoral: Mr D King

Deputy Head, Academic: Dr Philip Purvis

Deputy Head, Sixth Form and Operations: Mrs S Bradshaw

Assistant Head, Co-Curricular: Mrs E Webb

Head of Junior School: Mrs S Raja

Deputy Head of the Junior School: Miss L Threadgold

Director of External Relations: Mrs F Cook

Director of Finance: Mr J Nelson

Derby High School

Hillsway, Littleover, Derby DE23 3DT

Tel:	01332 514267
email:	headsecretary@derbyhigh.derby.sch.uk
website:	www.derbyhigh.derby.sch.uk
Twitter:	@DerbyHighSchool
Facebook:	@derbyhighUK
LinkedIn:	/derby-high-school

Derby High School is an independent day school conveniently situated in the Derby suburb of Littleover which educates boys and girls aged 3 to 18.

Academically, the school regularly achieves the best results in the county, however a Derby High education is about much more than academic results. Whether your child is musical, creative, analytical or sporty, at Derby High each student's individual strengths are identified to help them achieve their potential in a fun, friendly and supportive atmosphere.

There are 598 pupils in school of whom 306 are in the Senior School, and 214 are in the Infants and Juniors.

The Primary Department follows an enhanced national curriculum course. KS1 and KS2 take internal assessments. ASPECTS are used for pre-school and INCAS for Year 5. There is considerable enrichment in the curriculum with a wide variety of sports, music, drama and other activities available both within the curriculum and at club time.

The Senior School offers courses in Art and Design, Biology, Chemistry, Design Technology, Drama, Business, Economics, English Language and Literature, French, General Studies, Geography, German, History, Food & Nutrition, Mathematics, Further Maths, Music, Physical Education, Psychology, Physics, Religious Studies, Spanish and Theatre Studies. The curriculum is enhanced by activities such as the Engineering Education Scheme, Young Enterprise, The Duke of Edinburgh's Award and World Challenge. Sports, drama and music are also strengths, with pupils gaining recognition at county and national level.

The main points of entrance are at pre-school, Reception, Year 3, 11+ and 16+ where Scholarships and Assisted Places are available. Entrance is by examination and interview. Entrance at other ages is by assessment and takes place by arrangement.

The school has an active Christian ethos and broadly follows the teaching of the Church of England, but pupils of all faiths are welcomed and valued.

Examinations. Pupils are entered for ASPECTS, INCAS, GCSE and A Level examinations, some Sixth Form pupils take the EPQ. The school takes part in INCAS and MidYIS testing. Many pupils have individual music lessons and take music examinations through the Associated Board of the RCM. LAMDA is offered in the Junior School, leading to examinations. The Young Enterprise examination may be taken by Company members.

Games. Hockey, Netball, Rounders, Tennis, Swimming, Athletics, Short Tennis, Tag Rugby, Football and Trampolining are major sports.

Fees per term (2021–2022). £2,332–£4,630.

Charitable status. Derby High School Trust Limited is a Registered Charity, number 1007348. It exists to provide education for children.

Foundation Governors:
Chairman: Mr B Lad
Mr M Hall
Dr R Faleiro
Ms H Barton
Co-Opted Governors:
Ms R Chahal
Ms F Apthorpe
Mrs S Sandle
Miss S Hughes
Miss S Chittim
Mrs R Stajak

Head: **Mrs A Chapman**, MA Open University, BA Hons Nottingham, PGCE Warwick

Deputy Head: Miss A Jordan, BA Hons Wolverhampton, PGCE Keele (*History*)

Assistant Head, Co-Curricular: Mr A Lee, BA Hons Salford, PGCE Leicester (*French, German, EPQ, *Careers, Sociology*)
Assistant Head, Data & Curriculum: Mr A Maddox, MMath, PGCE, PGDES Oxford (*Mathematics*)
Assistant Head, Pastoral: Mrs C Bellman, BA Hons, MA, PGCE Oxford (*English, EPQ*)

Chaplain: Dr J Whitehead, MA Sheffield, BA Hons Nottingham

Bursar: Mrs M Mitchell, BA Hons, ACA, ICAEW

* *Head of Department*

Miss A Allum, BSc Hons, PGCE Brunel (*Physical Education*, **PSHE*)
Mrs K Aydi, BSc Aberdeen, PGCE Bath (**Science, *Biology*)
Dr G Bhattacharyya, BA Hons Cambridge, PhD Cambridge, PGCE Oxford (*Physics*)
Mr J Bournon, BA Hons Wimbledon School of Art, Teach Cert Central Institute London (*Art*)
Mrs J Bower-Gormley, BA Hons Hull, PGCE Warwick (*History*)
Mrs E Davies, BA Hons Nottingham Trent, PGCE Loughborough (*Food & Nutrition*)
Mr R Dodson, MEng Hons Bristol (**Mathematics*)
Mr J Gallagher, BA Hons Durham, PGCE Nottingham (**Geography*)
Mrs S Goodman, BSc Hons, PGCE Sheffield Hallam (*Physical Education, Deputy Head Sixth Form*)
Mrs J Hancock, BEd Hons Manchester Metropolitan (*Physical Education*)
Mrs K Hewitt, BSc Hons Birmingham, PGCE Leeds (*Biology, Food & Nutrition*)
Mrs S Hilton, BA Hons Brighton, PGCE Brighton (**Business, ICT, Young Enterprise*)
Mrs R Huskisson (*Information Resources Manager*)
Mr P Ince, BA Hons Staffordshire, PGCE Wolverhampton (*German, French*)
Mrs S Ince, BA Hons University of Central England (*Design Technology, Art & Design Graphics*)
Miss S Kelliher, BA Hons Dublin, PGCE Birmingham (**German, *French, *MFL*)
Mrs R Lesley, BM Hons Birmingham, PGCE University of Central England (**Music*)

Mrs N Ley, BSc Hons, PGCE Loughborough (*Mathematics*)
Mrs M Martinez Hernandez, BA Hons Salamanca, PGCE Madrid (**Spanish*)
Mrs S Martin-Smith, HND, BA Hons Swansea, PGCE Swansea (**Art, Textiles*)
Dr S Mathews, BA Hons Sheffield Hallam, MSc, PhD Manchester (**History*)
Mrs C McBeth, BA Hons Derby, MSc Loughborough (*SENCO*)
Mr R Moorhouse, BSc Hons, MSc, PGCE Loughborough (*Physical Education*)
Dr J Myers, BSc York, PGCE Leicester, PhD Heriot-Watt (**Chemistry*)
Dr S Ngwerume, MChem Leicester, PhD Nottingham, PGCE Leicester (*Chemistry*)
Mrs J Orr, BSc Hons Ulster, PGCE Nottingham Trent (**Physics*)
Mrs S Peake (*Examinations Officer, DofE*)
Mr C Quichaud, BA Hons Birkbeck London, PGCE King's College London (*French, Spanish*)
Miss M Render, BA Hons, PGCE Hull, Cert TESOL (*English*)
Miss C Riley, BSc Hons, PGCE Leeds (*Chemistry, Head of Key Stage 4*)
Mrs M Roe, BA Hons, PGCE Nottingham (*Geography*)
Mrs A Saunders, BA Hons Leeds, PGCE Canterbury (*Religious Studies*)
Mrs J Seddon, BA Hons Sheffield, PGCE Durham (**Psychology*)
Mrs L Seymour, BA Hons, PGCE Nottingham (*German, French*)
Mrs M Steer, BA Hons Wales, PGCE Leicester (*English*)
Miss B Stirland, BA Hons Cumbria (**Director of Sport*)
Mrs F Supran, BA Hons Manchester, PGCE Oxford, Cert TEFLA Oxford Brookes (**Drama, English*)
Mrs J Webster, MA Hons, PGCE Cambridge (**English*)
Mr S Williams, BSc Hons Birmingham, PGCE Nottingham (*Mathematics, *ICT*)
Miss L Wilson, BA Hons, PGCE Manchester (*Religious Studies, History*)
Mrs C Wood, BSc Hons Manchester, PGCE Nottingham (*Biology, Chemistry*)

Primary School:
Head of Primary: **Mr J Harper**, BA Hons with QTS, Nottingham Trent
Assistant Head, Primary: Mrs R Youngman, BEd Hons Derby, NPQML

Mrs S Cooke, BMus Hons RNCM (*Music*)
Mrs J Coward, BA Hons Strathclyde, PGCE Derby
Mrs G Cureton, BA Hons Derby, PGCE Birmingham City
Mrs A Dowell, BSc, QTS Birmingham
Mrs L Earp, BA Birmingham City
Mrs S Evans-Bolger, BA Hons QTS, MA Ed BG University College Lincoln
Mrs J Foster, BEd Hons Derby
Mr R Gould, BA Hons Wolverhampton
Mrs R Hamilton, BSc Hons Edinburgh, PGCE Strathclyde
Miss S Holmes, BA Hons QTS, Leeds Beckett
Mr C Horne, BEd Hons Derby, EdD Leicester
Miss D Hyland, BA Hons, PGCE Birmingham
Miss H Law, BA Hons, PGCE QTS Manchester
Mrs C Miller-Odell, BA Hons Newcastle, PGCE QTS Brighton

Miss K Shore, BEd Wolverhampton, PGCE Birmingham City (*EYFS Coordinator*)

Mrs J Swainston, BEd Hons Sheffield (*Primary Coordinator*)

Mrs A Trindell, BSc Hons QTS BG University College Lincoln

Edgbaston High School

Westbourne Road, Edgbaston, Birmingham, West Midlands B15 3TS

Tel: 0121 454 5831
email: admissions@edgbastonhigh.co.uk
website: www.edgbastonhigh.co.uk
Twitter: @Edgbaston_High
Facebook: @Edgbaston-High-School-Official-430788326941674
Instagram: @edgbastonhighschool

This independent day school, founded in 1876, attracts girls both from the immediate neighbourhood and all over the West Midlands. They come for the academic curriculum, the lively programme of sporting, creative and cultural activities, and for the individual attention and flexibility of approach.

Personal relationships at EHS are of paramount importance. Parents, both individually and through their association, give generously of their time to support our activities; while staff, through their hard work and good relationship with the girls, create an atmosphere at once orderly and friendly.

Organisation and Curriculum. There are three departments working together on one site which caters for over 850 day girls aged two and a half to eighteen. One of the features of EHS is the continuity of education it offers. However, girls can be admitted at most stages. Staff take special care to help girls settle quickly and easily. Pupils enjoy a broadly based programme which substantially fulfils the requirements of the National Curriculum and much more.

The **Pre-Preparatory Department, known as Westbourne,** offers facilities to girls aged two and a half to five in a spacious, purpose-built, detached house. The staff aim to create an environment in which they can promote every aspect of a girl's development. A brand new Nursery (part of the £4 million Octagon building) was opened in February 2005.

The **Preparatory School** accommodates over 350 girls from 5+ to 11 in up-to-date facilities, among them a new IT suite, Science Laboratory, Library and Design Technology Centre. A full curriculum, including English, Mathematics, Science and Technology, is taught throughout the department.

The **Senior School** caters for about 500 girls aged 11+ to 18. Girls follow a well-balanced curriculum which prepares them for a wide range of subjects at GCSE and A Level.

Examination results are very good with high grades distributed across both Arts and Science subjects. The vast majority of girls in the Sixth Form of over 100 proceed to Higher Education. Every year girls obtain places at Oxbridge and Russell Group Universities.

Co-Curricular Activities. Girls can take part in a broad range of activities including art, ceramics, Mandarin, drama, Duke of Edinburgh's Award, music, sport and Young Enterprise. There are clubs during the lunch hour and after school. Instrumental music lessons are available. There is a strong music tradition in the school. Girls go on visits, expeditions and work experience in this country and abroad. We encourage girls to think of the needs of others.

Accommodation. There is a regular programme of improvements to the buildings. An exciting new multi-purpose hall, The Octagon, was opened in February 2005. A floodlit all-weather surface was opened in Summer 2006. The school has its own indoor swimming pool, 12 tennis courts and 8 acres of playing fields. Work on extended Sixth Form accommodation, a new library and fitness suite, at a cost of £3.5m, was completed in January 2011. In August 2016 the school completed a building development designed to enhance the Preparatory School. At a cost of £1.6 million, the project has resulted in a newly extended library, Art room and large welcoming Reception space. A multi-purpose building, the Hexagon, was completed in early 2018. In September 2018, the Sports Pavilion underwent a refurbishment.

Location. The school is pleasantly situated next to the Botanical Gardens in a residential area, 1½ miles south-west of the city centre. It is easily accessible by public transport and also has its own privately run coaches.

Fees per term (2021–2022). Pre-Prep £3,012.75 (5 days); Prep £3,106–£4,695; Senior £4,621, Sixth Form £4,695.

Scholarships and Bursaries. Academic Scholarships are available at 11+, awarded on the basis of performance in the entrance examination. Sixth Form Subject Scholarships are awarded based on examination and interview.

Two Music Scholarships are also offered annually: one at 11+ and one at 16+. 11+ candidates must sit the main entrance examination in October and then have written, aural and practical tests. Candidates at 16+ attend an audition and interview in January.

At 16+ there are further subject scholarships awarded to girls of outstanding ability. Assessments take place in January.

A Bursary fund exists to help girls of good academic ability in financial need to enter at Reception, Year 3, 11+ and the Sixth Form and to assist those whose financial circumstances have changed since they entered the School. Bursaries may cover part or full fees. All scholarships can be combined with means-tested bursaries in cases of need.

Further information. Full details may be obtained from the school. Parents and girls are welcome to visit the school by appointment.

Charitable status. Edgbaston High School for Girls is a Registered Charity, number 504011. Founded in 1876, it exists to provide an education for girls.

President: Sir Dominic Cadbury, BA, MBA

Vice-Presidents:
Mr Duncan Cadbury, MSc
Mr I Marshall, BA
Her Honour Judge Sybil Thomas, LLB

Council:
Chairman: Mr J D Payne, BSc, MRICS
Deputy Chairman: Mrs C Fatah, RGN

Ms H J Arnold, BSc Hons
Mr M Chitty, MA
Mrs A E S Howarth, Cert Ed, Dip Ed
Mrs V J Nicholls, Chartered MCIPD
Mr G I Scott, MA Oxon
Mrs S Shirley-Priest, MA MRICS
Mrs P Tilt
Mrs J Tozer

Representing the Old Girls' Association:
Ms E Hartley and Mrs A Lacey

School Staff:

Headmistress: Mrs C Macro, MA Oxford

Deputy Head Academic: Mrs S-E Rees, MA Oxford, NPQH
Deputy Head Curriculum: Mrs J Crimp, BSc Manchester, MEd Birmingham
Deputy Head Pastoral: Mrs A Cirillo-Campbell, BA UCE Birmingham

School Management Team:
Mrs L Batchelor (*Director Co-Curricular*)
Dr A Rajp (*Director Teaching & Learning*)
Mr P Smith (*Director Academic Enrichment*)
Miss H Welsh (*Director Learning Support*)
Mrs G Parsons (*Head of Year 13*)

* *Head of Department/Subject Leader*

Ms G Ajmal, BA Wolverhampton (*English, Head of Year 9*)
Miss M Aznar-López, BA Birmingham (*Spanish, French, DofE Bronze Coordinator*)
Mr J Ball, BSc Birmingham (*Assistant Head of Department Mathematics*)
Miss M Barbet, Licence D'Anglais Université de Clermont-Ferrand, France (**French*)
Mrs L Batchelor, BSc Birmingham (*Director Co-Curricular*)
Mrs A Bennet, BA Keele (*French, German*)
Mr D Berman, MA Oxford (*Science; Octagon Technician*)
Mrs C Cardellino, BA Leicester (**MFL, *German*)
Mrs A Coley, BA Northampton (*Food & Nutrition and Textiles, Charity Co-ordinator*)
Dr E Cruice, BSc Sussex, PhD Birmingham (*Science*)
Mr A Deeley, BSc Royal Holloway and Bedford College London (*Science*)
Mrs C Doble, BA De Montfort, Leicester (*Art*)
Mr M Dukes, BA Wolverhampton (*Director of Visual Communications*)
Mrs K Egan, BA Liverpool (*Geography*)
Mrs Z Ehiogu, BA University of East London (*Head of Year 12, *Wellbeing, Mindfulness and Study Skills*)
Mrs S Flitter, MA Oxford (*Classics*)
Mr A Flox-Nieva, Licenciado En Filología Inglesa Universidad De Castilla, Spain (**Spanish*)
Miss J Fones, MA Birmingham, MSci Birmingham (*Chemistry*)
Mrs J Forrest, BSc Open University (*Biology*)
Miss S Glover, BA Nottingham (**History, Assistant Head of Year 9*)
Mrs E Goulbourne, BEd Wolverhampton (*Food & Nutrition and Textiles*)
Ms D Graham, BSocSc Birmingham, Grad Dip Psych Aston (**Psychology*)
Mr P Gray, MA Ohio, USA, BA Leeds (**English*)

Miss J Harrison, BA Southampton, MA Birmingham (**English, Extended Project Higher Education Advisor*)
Miss M Hayday, BA Hull (**Religious Studies, Head of Year 10*)
Mrs S Hewison, BA (*Ed*) Exeter (*Physical Education, Assistant Head of Year 7*)
Mr M James, BA Northumbria (*Art*)
Mrs Y Jin, BA Xi'an, China, MSc UCE Birmingham, MPhil Xi'an, China (*Mandarin*)
Miss N Jones-Owen, BA Manchester Metropolitan (*English, *Media Studies, Head of Year 7*)
Miss N Khodabukus, M Biochem Oxford (*Science, Chemistry*)
Mrs J Lambert, BSc Birmingham (**Mathematics*)
Mr S Lane, BA Plymouth (**Drama*)
Miss K Lawrence, BA Bath Spa (*Dance and PE*)
Mrs A Lee, BSc Birmingham (*Mathematics, Assistant Head of Year 11*)
Mrs L Lucas, BA Birmingham (*Academic Support*)
Mrs S Lynch, BSc Sheffield, MA Sheffield (*Chemistry*)
Mr P Malone, BA Sheffield (*ICT, Business Studies*)
Miss K Massey, BSc Reading (**Geography*)
Mrs R Matthews, BSc Aberystwyth (**Biology*)
Mrs K McAlister, MA Oxford (**Classics*)
Miss M-P Monet-Rossetti, BA Open University (*French, German*)
Mrs L Mooney, BA Wolverhampton (**D&T Textiles, Head of Year 8*)
Miss A Mortimer-Lane, BSc Loughborough (*PE*)
Miss S Mullett, BA Nottingham (**Art*)
Mrs K Newling, BSc Birmingham (*Mathematics*)
Mrs R Norman, BSc Liverpool (*Mathematics*)
Miss S O'Hare, MA St Andrews (*English, Head of Year 11*)
Mrs S Park, BA Cardiff, MPhil Cardiff (*English*)
Mrs G Parsons, BSc University of Wales Institute, Cardiff (**Physical Education, Head of Year 13*)
Mrs L Parsons BSc Coventry, MSc Coventry (**Psychology*)
Mr C Proctor, BA Swansea (*English*)
Dr A Rajp, BSc Birmingham, PhD Birmingham (*Biology, Director of Gifted & Talented*)
Mrs H Reene, BA Essex (*Sociology*)
Mr M Rees, BA Cambridge, MMath Cambridge (*Mathematics*)
Miss R Richardson, BA Reading (*History, Higher Education Advisor*)
Miss E Roberts, BA King's College London (*Classics, Music*)
Mr K Robson, BMus Conservatoire Birmingham, MA Huddersfield (**Music*)
Mrs S Rowntree, BA Salford (*Drama*)
Dr D Royal, BSc UCL, PhD UCL (*Physics*)
Miss C Roye, BSc Loughborough (*Assistant Head of Physical Education*)
Mr J Sabotig, BSc Birmingham (**Physics, Head of Houses*)
Mrs H Sahota, BSc Birmingham (*Mathematics*)
Mrs J Scriven, BA Newcastle Upon Tyne (*Religious Studies*)
Mrs J Shutt, BA Keele (**Business and Economics, Head of Careers*)
Mr R Shutt, BA Bournemouth (*Business, Economics and ICT, Head of KS3 Computer Science, Assistant Head of Year 10*)
Mr R Skilbeck, BA Leeds College of Music (*Music, Ensembles Coordinator*)

Mrs A Smith, BA Birmingham (*English, Assistant Head of Sixth Form*)

Mr P Smith, BA Staffordshire (*Director of Academic Enrichment*)

Mr N Southall, BSc BCU Birmingham, MA BCU Birmingham (*Music Deputy Director, Music Examinations Secretary*)

Mrs C Syer, BSc Oxford Polytechnic (**Food & Nutrition and D&T Textiles*)

Mr M Tomaszewicz, BSc Birmingham (*Science*)

Miss S Vann, BEd De Montfort, Bedford (*Physical Education*)

Miss H Welsh, BSc Portsmouth (*Director of Academic Support*)

Mr M Wiggins, BA Birmingham (**Religious Studies, *Sociology*)

Miss E Wood, MA Edinburgh (*Classics, Assistant Head of Year 9*)

Mrs H Zhang, Shandong Norman University Jinan, China (*Mandarin*)

Librarian: Miss S Lee, BA Aberystwyth

Examinations Officer/Library Assistant: Mrs J Hall, BSc Surrey

Head of ICT Systems, Development and Management: Mr A Matloob, BSc BCU Birmingham

Network Manager: Mr A Ijaz

ICT Technician: Mr A Atkins

School Systems Administrator: Mr J Coley, BSc Northampton

Language Assistants:

French: Ms M Romero

German: Mrs A Tack-Benton, MA Osnabrück, Germany

Spanish: Ms L Garcia Rodriquez, MA Cadiz, Spain

Technicians:

Art: Miss A Birch, BA Southampton

Food & Nutrition and Textiles: Mrs C Harris

Science:

Mrs A Duvnjak, BSc Coventry, MSc Birmingham

Miss V Gutzmore, HND, BSc Open University

Mr P Shillito, BSc Birmingham

D of E Silver and Gold Coordinator: Mrs S Griffiths

Extra Curriculum Service Providers:

Music:

Pianoforte/Oboe:

Ms E Cockbill, MA, LLCM, ALCM

Pianoforte:

Mrs H Howell, GBSM, ABSM

Miss M Morris MMus, LRSM

Mrs C Purkis GBSM, ABSM, LRAM

Flute/Recorders:

Miss H Jones, BA

Mrs S Wilson, BA

Clarinet/Theory:

Miss M Harper, GRNCM, ARMCM

Clarinet/Saxophone/Pianoforte:

Mr J Meadows, BA, ABSM

Bassoon:

Mr P Brookes, ABSM, GBSM Dip

Violin/Viola:

Miss A Chippendale, BMus

Mr M Owen, LRAM

Cello/Double Bass:

Miss J Carey GRSM, ARCM

Guitar:

Miss E Larner. BMus

Brass:

Mrs M Brookes, DRSAMD

Percussion:

Mr J Powell

Voice:

Ms E Cragg, BMus

Mr G Stuart, B Mus, ALCM

Fencing:

Professor P Northam, BAF

LAMDA Teachers:

Mrs T Bolt

Ms C Fidler, BA, LRAM, FETC, IPA

Mrs J Foley BA, PGDip, BSSD

Life Saving: Mrs R Link

Gym Club: Mrs S Hewison

Admin Staff:

Headmistress's PA: Ms G Franchi

Reception/Administration: Mrs Y Crawford; Ms J Flynn; Mrs D Hartley

Finance Director/Company Secretary: Mrs B Kail, CIMA

Finance Manager: Ms M Andrews, MAAT

Bursary: Mrs S Blankson; Mrs A Nicholson

Director of Admissions and Communications: Mrs A Rowlands, BSc Lancaster

Admissions & Communications Manager: Mrs A Jackson

Admissions & Communications Assistant: Mrs H Smith, BSc BCU

Holiday Provisions Manager: Miss A Sanzari

School Nurses: Mrs M Al-Ani; Mrs H Heyes; Mrs C Willson

Facilities Manager: Mr W Heyes, MHCIMA

Assistant Facilities Manager: Mr W Hayes

Catering Manager: Mr N Hall

Housekeeper: Miss A Toy

Caretaker: Mr V Johnson

Assistant Caretaker: Mr E Cronin

Groundsmen: Mr P Rees; Mr M Whitehouse

Preparatory School:

Head: Mrs S Hartley, BEd Bristol

Deputy Heads:

Mrs A Aston, BSc Birmingham

Miss C Robinson, BA Exeter

Mrs A M Collins, BEd Birmingham

Mrs S Crompton, BSc Leeds

Mrs A Dawes, BSc Cardiff

Miss S Dawes, BSc Leeds

Miss R Deacon, BSc Newman College

Mrs S Donelly

Mrs S Draper, BSc Swansea

Miss C Dugdale, BSc Leeds Metropolitan

Mrs C Eveleigh, BSc Bath

Mrs S Flitter, MA Oxford

Mrs J Goodyear, BA Ed Worcester College of Higher Education

Mrs C Hennous, BA

Mrs L Hobbs, BSc Birmingham

Miss S Howarth, BSc Worcester College of Higher Education

Mrs L Humble, BA Swansea

Mrs H Jones, BA Swansea

Mrs J Knott, BA Birmingham
Miss K McKee, BA Sussex
Miss V Nelsey, BA Hull
Miss F O'Connor, BEd Wolverhampton
Mrs M Poade, BA Reading
Mrs F Scott Dickins, BA London
Mrs G Villiers Cundy, BEd Bath
Mrs F Watson, BA Leeds
Mrs V Woodfield, BEd UCE Birmingham

Teaching Assistants:
Mrs D Audley
Mrs M Bracey
Mrs G Draysey
Mrs N Mohamed
Mrs J Russon

Preparatory School Nurse: Mrs H Heyes
Preparatory School Technician: Mr P Flynn

Before School Care Supervisor: Mrs C Harris
School Support and After School Care Supervisor: Mrs M
   Henry
School Support and After School Care Assistants:
Miss E Clinton
Mrs J Eyres
After School Care Assistants:
Miss L Osborne
Mrs M Rees

Administration Staff:
Preparatory School Secretaries: Miss S J Bent; Mrs K
   Williams

Pre-Preparatory Department:
Mrs L Bowler, BA Leicester
Miss V Brenner, BA St Martin's College, Lancaster
Mrs J Goodman, BA Birmingham
Mrs D A Kennedy, BEd West Midlands College of Higher
   Education
Mrs H Robinson, BEd University of Wales
Mrs H Skidmore, BA Trinity College, Carmarthen

Teaching Assistants:

Mrs R Aulak	Mrs F Green
Miss S Collins	Mrs C Holliday
Mrs J Corbett	Mrs A Knight
Mrs E Cornelius	Mrs J Redden
Mrs H Coulson	Miss A Sanzari
Mrs D Deakin	Mrs P Varma

Before School Care Supervisor: Mrs H Coulson
Before School Care Assistant: Mrs C Holliday

After School Care Supervisor: Mrs R Aulak
After School Care Assistants:
Miss E Clinton
Mrs M Hart
Mrs P Varma

Visiting Staff:
Ballet: Miss D Todd

Farnborough Hill

**Farnborough Road, Farnborough, Hampshire
GU14 8AT**

Tel: 01252 545197
email: admissions@farnborough-hill.org
website: farnborough-hill.org
Twitter: @FarnboroughHill
Facebook: @Farnborough-Hill
Instagram: @farnborough.hill

Motto: Wholeheartedly

Farnborough Hill, founded in 1889, is a leading Catholic independent day school for around 575 girls aged 11–18 years. The School welcomes girls of all faiths and none, who are happy to support the School's ethos. Located on the Hampshire/Surrey border, the School has excellent transport links, both by train and road, while enjoying a beautiful and inspiring setting in over 65 acres of parkland.

Farnborough Hill is a vibrant community. The vision for pupils is simple: to help them become the very best version of themselves. Teachers believe in the gifts and talents of each individual and value the uniqueness of each person. From this diversity and belief comes a unity of purpose: to develop young women, each strong, compassionate and courageous, each going into the world to play a positive role.

Farnborough Hill girls are engaged, committed and fun-loving. They are achievers but not paralysed by perfectionism. They are risk-takers and carers. These fabulous girls are buoyed up by all the adults at Farnborough Hill, each in their specific role, sharing responsibility for the development of character and nurturing the spirit of the girls in their care.

Superb resources and facilities combined with the energy and expertise of highly-motivated staff ensure that the girls have the opportunities and self-belief to succeed in a wide variety of fields. This is a place where pupils thrive, are nourished, and are allowed to develop their individual character before launching into the world as agents of change.

Admission. Entry is by examination taken in January for the following September.

Scholarships and Bursaries. The school offers academic, music, sports and art and design scholarships and also bursaries for parents who are in need of financial assistance. Academic scholarships are offered for entry at 11+. One of these is reserved for a Roman Catholic student. In addition music, sport and art and design scholarships are awarded at 11+. Sixth Form scholarships are awarded for academic achievement, excellence in the performing arts, the creative arts and sports. An additional scholarship is awarded by Farnborough Hill Old Girls' Association.

Fees per term (2021–2022). Tuition: £5,253.

Further information. The prospectus is available from the Director of Admissions. The Head is pleased to meet prospective parents by appointment.

Charitable status. The Farnborough Hill Trust is a Registered Charity, number 1039443.

Mrs Pippa Sutton, BA, PGCE Oxon (*Mathematics*)

Mrs Colleen Swire, BEd St Mary's Belfast (*Religious Education, Philosophy & Ethics*)

Mrs Ceri Symonds-Keates, BA Brighton, PGCE Chichester (*History, Politics*)

Dr Ian Taylor, BA, MSt, DPhil Oxon (*Music*)

Mr Scott Temple, MChem, PGCE Sussex (*Chemistry*)

Mrs Marimar Tyler, BA, PGCE OU (*French, Spanish*)

Dr Andrew Tytko, BSc, PhD Leeds, MA Dunelm, PGCE Kingston (*Business, Economics*)

Mrs Hannah Van Klaveren, BA Exeter, PGCE, MSc Oxon (*Geography*)

Miss Lucy Warwick, BMus DipABRSM Manchester, PGCE Sherborne (*Music*)

Miss Polly White, BA UCL, PGCE King's (*French, Spanish*)

Miss Naomi Wilcock, BA, PGCE Chichester (*Physical Education*)

Mrs Lucy Willis, BA Oxon, PGCE London, QTS (*English*)

Mrs Lori Winch-Johnson, BA Hertfordshire, MSc, PGCE Surrey, CCRS DipPerfCoach Newcastle (*English, Drama, Learning Support*)

Mrs Katherine Wood, BA Staffordshire, PGCE Canterbury Christ Church (*English*)

Mrs Taryn Zimmermann, BA Leeds, PGCE Manchester (*German, Spanish*)

Matrons: Mrs Lucinda Forster-Knight, RGN; Mrs Nicola Condren, RGN

Bursar: Cmdr Mike Robertson, BSc Hons, ACIPD

Director of Admissions: Mrs Lindsey Lovegrove, BA, MCIPR

Chaplain: Mrs Nelle Dalton, BA, MDiv

Haberdashers' Girls' School

Aldenham Road, Elstree, Herts WD6 3BT

Tel:	020 8266 2300
email:	office@habsgirls.org.uk
website:	www.habsgirls.org.uk
Twitter:	@habsgirlsschool
Facebook:	@habsgirlsSchool
Instagram:	@habsgirlsschool

Haberdashers' Girls' School is situated on a site of over 100 acres, shared with their neighbours Habs Boys, and has an excellent reputation for academic, sporting and musical achievements. Entry to the Junior School is at 4+ or at 7+; and to the Senior School, at 11+ and Sixth Form. The academic results are outstanding, a reflection of able pupils who enjoy learning and thrive on a full and challenging curriculum.

Facilities are first-class with a brand new STEM building and Drama studio and a very wide range of co-curricular activities. Sport, music, drama, art and debating thrive and there are many other opportunities for leadership within the school community, including the Duke of Edinburgh's Award and Arts Award schemes and a very active community service programme. Life at Habs is busy and challenging, embracing new technology alongside old traditions, which include the celebration of St Catherine's Day as patron of the Haberdashers' Company and an annual Carol Service held at St Martin-in-the-Fields in London.

Over 110 coach routes, shared with Habs Boys, bring pupils to school from a thirty-mile radius covering north London, Hertfordshire and Middlesex. The provision of a late coach service ensures that pupils can take part safely in the wide range of the many clubs and societies organised after school. The St Catherine Parents' Guild, the school's parents' association, provides enormous support to the school through fundraising and social events.

Junior School. There are approximately 315 day pupils in the Junior School, with two parallel classes from Reception to Year 6.

Pastoral Care: Class teachers and Learning Support assistants maintain close contact with pupils and their parents. It is very important that our pupils feel happy and comfortable. Every adult has a responsibility for the pupils' welfare and security and there are many layers of care in place. From the outset, through the behaviour code, pupils are encouraged to be friendly, polite and caring to everyone else in the community, whether adults or children, and there is strong peer support. There are two nurses, a counsellor and two individual needs specialists, all of whom are able to provide support and to ensure each pupil understands her unique importance in the school community. Where appropriate, older pupils have responsibility for younger ones and Senior School Sixth Formers regularly help Juniors in the classroom. A programme of PSHCE (personal, social, health and citizenship education) lessons covers important issues of self-development and allows pupils to reflect on their responsibilities to each other and the wider community. Many parents are involved in the classroom, clubs and outings.

Spiritual and Moral Education: Habs is a school with a Christian tradition which welcomes the rich diversity of faiths within the community. Assemblies are held for the whole school at least twice a week and on other days are separate for Key Stage One and Key Stage Two. Values, themes, stories and reflections are drawn from a range of sources including cultures, traditions and faiths. Once a year selected classes perform an assembly to which their parents are invited. Parents are also very welcome to attend assemblies on major occasions such as St Catherine's Day and are often invited to speak to the pupils in assemblies on an area of their expertise or experience relevant to the pupils. Pupils also take part in many charitable ventures throughout the year, raising money and enhancing their awareness of lives in the wider world.

Enrichment: There is a wide range of clubs covering our pupils' interests in sport, music, arts and crafts, languages, science, maths, creative writing, reading, games and puzzles, cookery and gardening. Visits linked to the curriculum are arranged for every class and there are regular visitors to school such as theatre companies, historical re-creations, authors, illustrators, musicians and scientists. Joint events with the Boys' School occur at intervals throughout the year for the different age groups.

Sport: We have first-class sports facilities, including a sports hall, gymnasia, netball and tennis courts, a swimming pool and ample playing fields. The curriculum provides a core of gymnastics, dance, swimming, netball, tennis, athletics and rounders. Teams in netball, cricket, football, gymnastics, rounders and pop lacrosse compete against other schools.

Performance Arts: Concerts and drama productions are a major part of school life, showcasing the wide range of creative talent amongst our pupils. Our Performance Space provides many opportunities to explore and extend their interests in the performance arts. There are two major drama productions annually: an Infant production for all those in Reception and Key Stage One, and a dramatic production for Year 6. The annual Spring Concert showcases all the musical groups and ensembles as well as a massed choir of all Key Stage Two pupils. The summer Chamber Concert features performances from many of our musical ensembles. Informal lunchtime concerts occur at least once a term for Year 4 to 6 soloists or duets. Our pupils' own art and design work is displayed around the school.

Curriculum: There is a broad and challenging curriculum with the provision of opportunities for outdoor, active and independent learning, with plenty of practical tasks and problem solving, to enable pupils to develop their bright young minds. Fun is a vital ingredient. There are curriculum evenings for parents to learn about the school's approach to particular subject areas and how they can best support their daughters at home and work in true partnership with the school.

The Early Learning Goals of the Foundation Stage are met through a balance of child-initiated opportunities and teacher-led activities. There is a daily range of stimulating, play-based activities which prompts pupils to ask questions, to discover, to wonder and to learn new skills. No homework is set in Reception or Year 1 so that pupils can enjoy the precious childhood pleasures of imaginative play and being read to by a parent when they get home. Music, French and daily PE lessons are taught by specialist teachers. Phonics teaching enables pupils to make rapid progress with reading and to gain an easy independence in their writing, while the foundations of mathematical thinking are laid through carefully selected practical tasks.

Extensive use is made of IT throughout the Junior School, with a dedicated IT Suite enabling an exciting Computing curriculum, including coding and robotics. In addition, all pupils have an iPad which they can use in class under the supervision of the teacher. The use of mobile technology is not meant to replace traditional learning but to supplement and enhance it and, in some cases, to open up whole new ways of learning for the pupils.

Creativity is fostered in music and dance, in art, design technology, literacy activities, drama and role play. The school grounds provide a rich environment for building knowledge about the world of nature as well as space to develop physical skills and pupils spend one afternoon a week in our on-site Forest School.

At Key Stage One, curriculum subjects are English, Mathematics, Science, History, Geography, Religious Studies, French, Spanish, ICT, Art, Design Technology, Music, PSHCE and Physical Education, including swimming. Fostering a love of reading is paramount.

As pupils progress through Key Stage Two they encounter more subject specialists. Science lessons, which are taught in the well-equipped laboratory, strongly feature practical and investigative work. The Art Room is a magnificent space for the creation of stunning works of art, while pupils can feel transported to another culture as soon as they step into the Languages Room and they are introduced to German for the first time.

Senior School. There are approximately 870 students aged 11–18 in the Senior School.

Pastoral Care: In such a big and busy school, care for each individual is deeply important so that all can flourish and fulfil themselves in every way. Looking after them is a pastoral team consisting of the Deputy Head (Pastoral), Assistant Head (Pastoral), Heads of Year, Form Tutors, a School Nurse, a Counsellor and an Individual Needs Specialist. The provision of pastoral care is designed to help students make decisions and to care about others within the framework of a very diverse community. There is an outstanding range of opportunities for their personal development and to help them consolidate a system of spiritual beliefs and a moral code. The welfare of students is of paramount importance and it is the responsibility of all members of staff, teaching and support staff, to safeguard and promote this. From the moment a student joins the school, emphasis is placed on the partnership with parents so that, hand-in-hand, school and parents can support each child, operating on a basis of trust and with people they know from the start.

Spiritual and Moral Education: Haberdashers' is a school with a Christian tradition which welcomes the rich diversity of faiths within the community. The day begins with the whole school assembly or House meeting to reinforce the school's values and its sense of community. These meetings are often led by the students themselves. Once a week there are separate faith assemblies: Christian, Hindu, Jain and Sikh, Humanist, Jewish or Muslim. Students can choose which one they attend. Holy Communion takes place at the Boys' School. Roman Catholic Mass is celebrated each half term, either in the Girls' or the Boys' School. Students may pray at lunchtime in a room set aside for them to do so. Students organise and run many charitable events within their Houses throughout the year. This enhances their awareness of the wider world as well as raising funds for charities small and large, at home and abroad.

Enrichment: There is a wide range of clubs on offer in the Senior School, including Art, creative writing, Dance, debating, Design Technology, Drama, football, Maths, Philosophy, Science, and synchronised swimming. Trips and visits include a Year 7 adventure holiday and various trips abroad, with language exchanges, work experience, and study visits. Subject specific trips in the UK and abroad include field trips, theatre visits, trips to sites of historical importance, museums and art galleries, music and sports tours.

Sport and Performance Arts: The core curriculum includes gymnastics, dance, swimming, lacrosse, netball, tennis, athletics and rounders. For older students, there are additional options in self-defence, badminton, football, trampolining, etc. There are clubs in a range of sports for recreational enjoyment as well as for the teams. There are major drama productions in all sections of the school and symphonic concerts showcasing a variety of ensembles, including three orchestras, wind and jazz bands, percussion groups, flute choirs, and rock bands, as well as recitals and chamber concerts. There are annual Drama and Music Festivals; occasionally, there are joint productions and orchestral concerts with the Boys' School. Students' painting, sculpture and design installations are displayed around the school.

Opportunities for leadership and challenge are valued and encouraged. Activities include: The Duke of Edinburgh's Award; Community Service; European Youth Parliament; Model United Nations; etc.

Curriculum: The school follows its own wide-ranging academic curriculum tailored to the needs of its very able pupils. It preserves the best of a traditional education whilst responding positively to curricular developments. Much emphasis is placed on developing the students' ability to think and learn independently, nurturing an intellectual resilience and self confidence which will prepare them for the world beyond school. In all subjects, the curriculum aims to be something that inspires the students and stimulates discussion and ideas. A high value is placed upon creativity, imagination and the opportunity to pursue topics beyond the confines of the exam specifications. The school is not required to follow the National Curriculum but draws upon the best practice of what is happening nationally and in other schools. In the first three years of the Senior School, students follow a set curriculum, studying French, Spanish and German on a carousel and then choosing two to continue with into Year 8. As they progress through the school they are given greater choice and the opportunity to personalise their curriculum to suit their needs and interests. Thus the GCSE curriculum has space for up to four optional subjects. In the Sixth Form the students have a free choice of subjects from the subjects on offer. At each level, the curriculum is designed to prepare them for the opportunities, responsibilities and experiences of the next stage of their education and their lives.

Fees per term (2021–2022). Senior £6,690; Junior £6,031 (R–Y2), £6,172 (Y3–Y6). A number of scholarships are awarded annually and means-tested financial assistance (up to full fees) is also available for students entering at 11+ or 16+.

Charitable status. The Haberdashers' Aske's Charity is a Registered Charity, number 313996. It exists to promote education.

Chair of the Board of Governors: Simon Cartmell, OBE

Headmistress: Mrs R Hardy, MA Oxon

Principal Deputy Head: Mrs S Wright, MEd Cantab

Deputy Head (Academic): Mr D Sabato, BA Nottingham
Deputy Head (Pastoral): Miss A Jones, MEd Cantab

Assistant Head (Academic): Mrs M Hall, BSc St Andrews
Assistant Head (Admissions, Marketing and Development): Mr T Scott, MA Cantab
Assistant Head (Pastoral): Mrs C Milsom, BA Brunel

Academic Head of Sixth Form: Mrs L Mee, BSc London

Director of Co-Curricular: Mr S Turner, BSc Brunel
Director of Partnerships: Mr J Plotkin, MA Oxon

Staff lists can be found online at www.habsgirls.org.uk/ about/staff-lists.

Harrogate Ladies' College

Clarence Drive, Harrogate, North Yorkshire HG1 2QG

Tel:　　　01423 537045
email:　　admissions@hlc.org.uk
website:　www.hlc.org.uk
Twitter:　@HLCNews
Facebook:　@HarrogateLadiesCollege
Instagram:　@harrogateladiescollege
LinkedIn:　/harrogate-ladies'-college

Harrogate Ladies' College is a Boarding and Day school for 300 girls aged 11–18. Situated within the College campus, Highfield Pre-School is a pre school for over 70 boys and girls between the ages of 2–4. Highfield Prep School, which opened in 1999, is a Day Prep school for over 230 boys and girls between the ages of 4–11.

Location. The College is situated in a quiet residential area on the Duchy Estate about 5 minutes' walk from the town centre and is easily accessible by road and rail networks. Leeds/Bradford airport is 20 minutes' drive away. Harrogate itself is surrounded by areas of natural interest and beauty.

Accommodation. Approximately 40% of the pupils are full boarders. Houses are arranged in mixed age groups from Year 7 to Year 12. Year 13 pupils enjoy a greater sense of independence in their own accommodation called Tower House. This contains a large, modern kitchen, comfortable lounges and relaxation areas and girls have individual study-bedrooms. Each house has a Housemistress and Assistant Housemistress who are responsible for the well-being of the girls. There is a well-equipped Health Centre with qualified nurses.

Curriculum and Examinations. The College aims to provide a broad-based curriculum for the first three years in line with National Curriculum requirements. This leads to a choice of over 28 subjects at GCSE, IGCSE and A Level. Each girl has a form tutor who continuously monitors and assesses her development.

Facilities. The central building contains the main classrooms, hall, library, and dining rooms, and a Sixth Form Centre with studies, seminar rooms, kitchens and leisure facilities. The College Chapel is nearby. An extension provides 8 laboratories for Physics, Chemistry, Biology and Computer Studies. Three dedicated computer suites, provision in the boarding houses and throughout the school, form an extensive computer network. Sixth Formers have network access using their own laptops from studies and bedrooms. Additional facilities for specialised teaching include Art, Textiles, Photography, Design and Technology, Drama and Home Economics/Food Technology.

Our award winning Business School is where girls are able to enjoy the academic study of Economics, Business Studies and Psychology in a state-of-the-art business-like environment which helps prepare young women of today for the global world of tomorrow.

Sport. The College has its own sports hall, a full size indoor swimming pool, gymnasium, fitness centre, playing field, netball courts, 9 tennis courts and 2 squash courts. Girls are taught a wide range of sports and may participate in sporting activities outside the school day. Lacrosse and netball are played in winter, and tennis, rounders, swimming and athletics are the main summer physical activities. Extra-curricular sports include badminton, basketball, fencing, golf, horse riding and gymnastics.

Wellbeing. Wellness is at the heart of our school community and our wellness initiative is designed to support pupils, staff and parents. Our Wellness Centre is the hub for a wide range of activities to support and encourage all-round physical, social and mental wellbeing, including Yoga and dance classes.

Sixth Form. The College has a thriving Sixth Form Community of 100 pupils. Girls have a choice of 26 courses at A level. There is a broad range of general cultural study. In preparation for adult life, Sixth Formers are expected to make a mature contribution to the running of the school and many hold formal positions of responsibility. Personal guidance is given to each girl with regard to her future plans and most pupils choose to continue their education at University.

Religious Affiliation. The College is Christian although pupils of other religious denominations are welcomed. We focus on inclusion, mutual respect and understanding of people of all faiths and of no faith.

Music. A special feature is the interest given to music and choral work both in concerts and in the College Chapel, and the girls attend frequent concerts and dramatic performances in Harrogate. There are Junior and Senior choirs, orchestra, string, wind and brass groups.

Scholarships. Academic, Art, Textiles, Music, Choral, Drama and Sport scholarships are available.

Fees per term (2021–2022). Boarding £11,000, Day £5,840. Fee remissions are available for girls with a sibling at Harrogate Ladies' College or at Highfield Prep School.

Entry. Entry is usually at age 11, 13 or at Sixth Form level. Entry is based on the College's own entrance examination and a school report. Sixth Form entry is conditional upon GCSE achievement and an interview with the Principal.

Charitable status. Harrogate Ladies' College Limited is a Registered Charity, number 529579. It exists to provide high-quality education for girls.

Chair of Governors: Dame Francine Holroyd

Principal: **Mrs Sylvia Brett**, MA London, BA Dunelm

Director of Finance: Miss Rebecca Henriksen, MA Edinburgh, ACA
Director of Admissions and Marketing: Mrs Sarah Bowman, MSc Stirling, BA UWE
Head of Highfield: Mr James Savile, BEd Southampton
Senior Deputy: Mrs Joanna Fox, BA OU
Senior Master: Mr Peter Massey, BA, MA Cambridge
Head of Boarding: Miss Laura Brookes, MA St Andrews
Assistant Head, Head of Lower School: Mrs Joanna Griffin, BA Bristol
Assistant Head, Head of Middle School: Mrs Fran Irvine, BEd Bedford
Assistant Head, Joint Head of Sixth Form (*Academic*): Mr Paul Dwyer, BSc Warwick
Assistant Head, Joint Head of Sixth Form (*Pastoral*): Miss Bonnie Horgan, MEd Leeds

Headington School

Oxford, Oxfordshire OX3 7TD

Tel: 01865 759100
         Admissions: 01865 759 861/113
email: admissions@headington.org
website: www.headington.org
Twitter: @HeadingtonSch
Facebook: @HeadingtonSch
Instagram: @headington_sch
LinkedIn: /school/Headington-School

Headington is a highly successful day and boarding school in Oxford for 815 girls aged 11–18 with a Preparatory School for 262 girls aged 3–11 occupying its own site just across the road. (*See Headington Preparatory School entry in IAPS section.*)

The School offers girls from Nursery to Sixth Form an unrivalled opportunity to pursue academic, sporting and artistic excellence in a caring and nurturing environment.

Founded in 1915 and set in 23 acres of playing fields and gardens, our superb facilities provide the perfect backdrop for teaching and learning that extends way beyond the classroom and curriculum. We encourage participation in all aspects of sport and culture, teamwork and leadership, challenging girls to discover and explore their own potential and achieve more than they thought possible.

Consistently in the premier league of academic schools in the UK, life at Headington is about much more than exam results. Through the sheer breadth of subjects and activities at Headington, we aim to educate the complete individual, giving girls the confidence and self-awareness to compete, contribute and succeed at school, university and in their adult lives.

Facilities. Headington offers a superb range of facilities to day girls and boarders to support and enhance their learning. Our Music School has fantastic acoustics, along with teaching rooms, a recording studio and electronics studio. The 240-seat Theatre, run by a professional team who provide expertise in set design, lighting and sound design, is home to the School's Drama Department. Our Dance and Fitness Centre benefits from a fully-equipped gym, training rooms and a large dance studio. Other sports facilities include a floodlit all-weather pitch, sports hall and 25m indoor swimming pool. In 2016, the School opened its award-winning Library, and an extended and refurbished Sixth Form Centre opened in early 2019. A new Creativity and Innovation Centre, the Hive opened in 2021 and features light and airy art studios, a lens suite, 3D workshop and 3D printers, photographic studio, lecture theatre and gallery space.

Curriculum. In Years 7 and 8 girls are taught in four classes of around 20 each, which increases to six slightly smaller classes in U4 after 13+ entry. They study Art, Biology, Chemistry, Computing, Dance, Drama, English, Fashion and Textile Design, Food and Nutrition, French, Spanish and German (there is an introduction to all three languages in Year 7 then girls choose two of these languages to continue in Year 8), Games, Geography, History, Latin, Mathematics, Music, Physical Education, Physics, Religious Studies. By Year 9 they choose two subjects from Art, Dance, Drama, Fashion & Textile Design and Music.

Most girls study nine or ten GCSE subjects, from a choice of 26 subjects and the HPQ, with girls being given freedom to choose their own programme of study. The majority of students move into the Sixth Form where they can choose from 29 A Level subjects along with the EPQ. Many new girls, both day and boarders, also join us at this stage.

Physical Education. From Olympic rowers to recreational dancers, Headington offers a genuinely inclusive approach to PE and extracurricular sport and encourages each girl to enjoy sport at the level that suits her. PE is taught throughout the school and many girls choose to study PE to GCSE. They can choose from more than 30 different sporting activities, from Dance and Fencing to Equestrian and Trampolining. Sports such as Hockey, Netball and Athletics are played competitively against other schools and girls have the chance to represent the School across a range of abilities. Around 70 girls currently compete at county level and beyond and the School enjoys national success in a wide range of sports. Headington rowers compete at the very highest level, with the School consistently triumphing at the National Schools' Regatta. More than 150 girls row and regularly go on to represent Great Britain at international competitions.

Music. At Headington every girl has the opportunity to enjoy music both within the curriculum and beyond. More than 350 individual music lessons take place each week and visiting teachers offer girls the opportunity to learn a wide range of instruments. The Senior School has numerous orchestras, choirs and ensembles, from junior orchestras to the exceptional Chamber Choir, which has made numerous recordings and toured overseas.

Drama. There is a busy programme of productions each year and girls of all ages become involved in all aspects of theatre, from writing and producing their own plays, to lighting, costume and make-up. Drama is an option at GCSE and A Level. Many girls also elect to take Trinity Speech and Drama exams in school.

Dance. At Headington, the state-of-the-art Dance facilities provide a multitude of opportunities for every girl. Dance is part of the curriculum in the Lower School and girls may select it at GCSE and A Level. Outside the classroom there is a huge range of dance options, from Ballet to Street Dance and Contemporary. As well as annual Dance Shows, the Headington Dance Company competes in local and national competitions.

Extracurricular Activities. More than 120 extracurricular activities take place every week during lunchtime, before and after school. A wide choice of subjects, sports, interests and hobbies ranges from The Duke of Edinburgh's Award and Drama to Astronomy and Young Enterprise. Headington has a very successful Combined Cadet Force, with around 60 cadets from L5 and above in our Army detachment.

Higher Education and Careers. Each year girls head off to leading universities in the UK and abroad or to competitive school leaver programmes. A significant number of girls choose Oxbridge each year; some head for medical or veterinary college and others take up Art Foundation courses. Girls graduate from a wide range of arts and science degrees in subjects as diverse as civil engineering, architecture, classics and natural sciences. Detailed assistance on choice of universities is given in the Sixth Form along with special programmes for Medicine, Veterinary Science, Oxbridge, Law and Architecture. A careers programme is in place throughout the School.

Boarding. Just over a quarter of the School – around 200 girls – are boarders. The boarding houses provide girls with a 'home from home' where, supported by a team of highly experienced staff, they learn to develop into mature and independent young people. Many boarders come from the UK and the School is also very proud of its international boarding community, made up of more than 30 nationalities from all over the world. There is a choice of flexible boarding options for girls aged eleven and upwards with full, weekly and half-weekly boarding all on offer.

Entrance. The main entry points to the Senior School are at 11+, 13+ or, for the Sixth Form, 16+. Girls are occasionally able to join at other ages if places become available. Girls enter the School at 11+ via Headington's own examination day and interview in December. Girls at UK prep schools sit the ISEB pre-tests in Year 6 or 7 for entrance at 13+. Other 13+ candidates sit the School's own examination papers in Year 8. Sixth Form entrance examinations and interviews are held in the November before the proposed year of entry and include a general entrance paper, a critical thinking skills assessment and an academic interview.

Registration fees are £125 (UK) and £250 (overseas based families). For information about admissions, please check the website, www.headington.org, or contact the School's friendly admissions team who will be happy to help.

Fees per term (2021–2022). Senior School: Full Boarders: £12,455–£13,655; Weekly Boarders: £10,680–£11,810; Half-Weekly Boarders: £8,445–£9,285; Day Girls: £6,210–£6,760.

Scholarships and Bursaries. Scholarships are awarded for academic achievement, art, dance, drama, music and sport. These awards recognise talent and achievement and most do not provide any fee reduction or financial reward, although there are a small number of special academic and music scholarships available to the highest achieving candidates at 11+, 13+ and 16+ entry. The Headington Access Programme (HAP) supports talented girls who would benefit from all that the School has to offer but who may not be able to access a Headington education without some form of financial assistance. Means-tested bursaries of up to 100 per cent of fees are available for local day girls who achieve high marks in our entrance examinations and are awarded at 11+ and 13+. Exceptional candidates at 16+ may be eligible for our Special Awards programme, worth 10 per cent of fees.

Charitable status. Headington School Oxford Limited is a Registered Charity, number 309678. It exists to provide quality education for girls.

Governing Council:
Chair of Governors: Mrs Sandra Phipkin ACA
Vice Chair of Governors: Mrs Carol Oster Warriner, MA Oxon

Dr Charlie Foster, OBE
Mrs Kiki Glen, MA Hons
Mrs Penelope Lenon, BA Hons
The Rev Darren McFarland, BA Hons, BTh
Miss Bryony Moore, MBA
Mr Richard Nicholson, MA Oxon, ARCO, PG Cert, QTS
Dr Kate Ringham, BA Hons, PhD
Mrs Sallie Salvidant, Cert Ed, BEd Hons
Mr Stephen Shipperley

Company Secretary: Mr Richard Couzens, MBE, MA Cranfield

Clerk to the Council: Miss Emma Saville

Headmistress: Mrs C Jordan, MA Oxon

Head of Prep: Mrs J Crouch, BA Keele, MA London, NPQH

First Deputy Head (Staff & Operations): Mr S Hawkes, BA Brunel

Deputy Head (Academic): Dr A-M Stanton-Ife, MA Cantab, MA UCL, PhD UC

Deputy Head (Pastoral): Miss A Proctor, BA Oxon, MSc Dunelm

Bursar: Mr R Couzens, MBE, MA Cranfield

Heathfield School
Ascot

London Road, Ascot, Berkshire SL5 8BQ

Tel: 01344 898343
email: admissions@heathfieldschool.net
website: www.heathfieldschool.net
Twitter: @HeathfieldAscot
Facebook: @HeathfieldSchool
Instagram: @heathfieldascot
LinkedIn: /heathfield-school

Introduction. Pioneering high standards in girls' education since 1899, this boarding (weekly and full) and day school provides an outstanding all-round education for girls in beautiful surroundings less than an hour from London in the heart of Berkshire near the world-famous Ascot Racecourse.

The school combines exemplary standards of pastoral care with a personalised academic curriculum which adds value to every girl's achievements to provide a truly holistic education for girls aged 11–18.

Not only is Heathfield firmly on the academic map but it also produces county and national sportswomen and talented artists, photographers, actors, musicians and dancers.

Heathfield is headed by Sarah Wilson, who has an MA in Educational Leadership and Management, as well as a first-class degree from Brunel University in Secondary Education with Geography and Physical Education. Ms Wilson was appointed Head in January 2021.

The school also boosted its growing reputation for the STEM (Science Technology Engineering and Maths) subjects with the completion of a state of the art STEM facility, officially opened by Lord Robert Winston.

Atmosphere and Ethos. The school's aim is to help every student excel, and to get the most out of life by providing the very best intellectual stimulation, physical challenges and pastoral care. The school is founded on Church of England principles but welcomes all faiths.

Pastoral Care. Heathfield's strength is in its size meaning each girl is supported throughout her school career and can never slip under the radar. Pupils are overseen by a dedicated team of academic staff, Heads of Year, Tutors, Housemistresses, Heads of House and prefects. They work together to provide the highest level of pastoral care. Teachers will meet with your daughter regularly to discuss her particular needs and to ensure she is achieving her maximum potential.

Curriculum. Heathfield offers variety in terms of the subjects on offer as well as fundamental excellence in all the traditional subjects. At A Level, girls can choose from twenty-four subjects plus EPQ (Extended Project Qualification). Extras such as the Leiths Basic Certificate in Food and Wine and the Duke of Edinburgh's Award are also offered. The school is famous for its excellence in the creative arts and enjoys a close relationship with the University of the Arts, London and a new creative partnership with Falmouth University. It has also won a record five Good Schools Guide awards for Art and Design Photography at A Level.

Activities. The St Mary's Theatre, Sports Hall, playing fields and swimming pool are always hives of activity and there are many other co-curricular activities including frequent museum, art gallery and theatre trips, field trips and overseas visits.

Sport. Heathfield's outstanding facilities include a large multi-purpose sports hall, a dance studio, five lacrosse pitches, six tennis/netball courts and a 25m indoor heated swimming pool. The school competes successfully at lacrosse, netball, swimming, rounders, athletics and various equestrian disciplines including polo. Girls have represented the school regionally, nationally and internationally in a variety of sports.

Boarding Accommodation. Boarding accommodation is first-class. From Form IV onwards, all girls have single rooms. For more freedom and independence, the Upper Sixth live in Wyatt House which contains two fully-equipped kitchens and areas in which to study and socialise.

Medical Welfare. Three nursing sisters and the school doctor are in charge of the girls' medical welfare, supported by Heads of House, Housemistresses and Tutors. The Heads of House or Housemistresses are available at all times for any parental concerns.

New Facilities. A state-of-the-art STEM (Science, Technology, Engineering and Maths) block opened in January 2016 and a digital recording studio opened in 2017. A new Sixth Form Centre is underway for 2022.

Admission. Admission points are 11+, 13+ and Sixth Form. Occasional places may be available in other year groups. Applicants are assessed using an online CEM test along with an interview with the Headmistress. Common Entrance examinations are also used as a guide, if they are taken. Entry into the Lower Sixth Form is via predicted GCSE grades and interview. Deferred entry is also available and international students wishing to apply are guided through the procedure step by step by our Admissions team. For further information see: www.heathfieldschool.net

Scholarships and Bursaries are awarded. Scholarships are worth £750 per annum. Bursaries are means-tested and are awarded at the Headmistress's discretion.

Fees per term (2021–2022). Senior (Forms III–UVI): Boarding £12,950, Day £8,000. Lower (Forms I–II): Boarding £12,650, Day £7,840.

Charitable status. Heathfield School is a Registered Charity, number 309086. It exists to provide a caring boarding education leading to higher education for girls aged between 11 and 18.

Chair of Governors: Mr Tom Cross Brown, MA Oxon, MBA Insead

Senior Leadership Team:

Headmistress: Sarah Wilson, BSc Hons Brunel, MA Open

Bursar: Mrs M Frier, BSc Hons Bristol, BFP, FCA

Director of Studies: Mr D Mitchell, MA Hull, MSc York, BA Hons Warwick, PGCE UWE

Director of Pastoral & Boarding: Mrs R Whitton, BSc Hons, PGCE Liverpool

Director Of Sixth Form: Mr J Hart, MA, BA Hons London

Director of Marketing & Admissions: Ms A Morgan, MCIM, MIDM

Director of Co-Curricular: Miss W Reynolds, BEd Hons Liverpool

Director of Development: Mrs E Boryer, BSc Hons Bristol

A current full staff list can be found on our website: www.heathfieldschool.net/about-us/staff.

Howell's School Llandaff
GDST

Cardiff Road, Llandaff, Cardiff CF5 2YD

Tel:	029 2056 2019
email:	admissions@how.gdst.net
website:	www.howells-cardiff.gdst.net
	www.howellscoedcollege.gdst.net
Twitter:	@HowellsSchool
Facebook:	@Officialhowells
Instagram:	@howellsschoolgdst

A magnificent Victorian gothic building right on the edge of the great, green expanse of Llandaff Fields, Howell's School Llandaff GDST has a tremendous sense of roominess for a city school, with a swimming pool, tennis courts, sports pavilion and all-weather sports pitch on the five-acre site.

Visionary Principal Sally Davis presides over excellent academic results, and in August 2021 results at Howell's were outstanding. At GCSE, 70% of all grades were at A* or level 9–8, and 86% were at A*–A or level 9–7. Truly exceptional results in exceptional times. In the Co-Ed College, over 30% of students achieved an impressive A* at A Level, with 78% of grades at A*–A. Students took up places at leading universities across the UK, including Oxford, Cambridge, Warwick, Durham, Edinburgh and Central Saint Martins.

Student numbers. 670: Nursery 13; Prep School 214; Senior School 287; Co-Educational Sixth Form College 156.

Founded in 1860 as a school for girls, the school was built by the Drapers' Company from the endowment left in 1537 by Thomas Howell, son of a Welshman, merchant of London, Bristol and Seville and a Draper.

Howell's School Llandaff is part of the Girls' Day School Trust GDST. The GDST is the leading network of independent girls' schools in the UK. As a charity that owns and runs 23 schools and two academies, it reinvests all its income in its schools. For further information about the Trust, visit www.gdst.net.

Howell's School puts great value on a rich and varied life outside of the classroom, with enrichment activities running from the Pride group to Poetry Club, Silent Discos to Synchronised Swimming. The extensive Enrichment Programmes, together with impressive Wellbeing and Laureate Programmes, make Howell's a special place to learn and develop in an exciting, creative and thriving environment. The school's strong Leadership Team, talented and dedicated teaching and support staff, wonderful young people and committed and interested parents are what make Howell's unique.

The Nursery at Howell's is situated in Roald Dahl's childhood home and takes inspiration from its famous former occupant. Girls who enter the nursery experience a safe, family atmosphere, making the transition from home to nursery a relaxed and happy one. The Prep School radiates an atmosphere in which every child is valued and nurtured. Great emphasis is placed on developing the self-identity, self-esteem and self-confidence of every girl.

When entering the Senior School, girls are encouraged to develop skills of self-analysis and reflection, and choose the learning methods that suit them best, whilst teachers challenge and motivate them towards an appetite for lifelong learning. Howell's aims to help students acquire skills essential to tackling a competitive and rapidly changing world. The established co-educational college has a proven track record for excellence in and out of the classroom, and offers students an exceptional learning experience with flexible teaching styles designed to manage the transition between school and university.

Curriculum. All National Curriculum subjects including Welsh are taught at Key Stages 1, 2 and 3. From Year 3, French, Spanish and Welsh are all taught. Latin is introduced in Year 8. First language Welsh is taught on demand. There is a broad range of subjects available in the College. Examinations in a number of AS subjects are taken at the end of Year 12. Active learning styles are an essential part of the classroom experience, and the curriculum is made more diverse by:

- Educational visits, locally and abroad
- Visiting authors, poets, musicians, artists and lecturers
- Special activity weeks focusing on particular areas of the curriculum

Extracurricular activities. The school's aim is to fulfil the potential of all the students in all areas, which it achieves through a rich extracurricular programme. Extracurricular opportunities include:

- Orchestras, choirs and jazz groups
- Reading and reviewing, eco, science, mathematics, history, geography, language and cultural clubs
- Concerts, plays and eisteddfodau
- Tennis, hockey, cricket, swimming, athletics, cross-country, netball, rugby and football teams
- The Duke of Edinburgh's Award, Rotary, public speaking and debating teams, Community service and fundraising for charities

The school seeks to support the widest range of students' needs through specialist dyslexia teaching and through an extensive and comprehensive careers programme.

Admission. A selection process operates for all points of entry. Contact Admissions for further details.

Fees per term (2021–2022). Co-Ed College: £4,843; Senior School: £4,798; Prep School: Years 3–6 £3,702, Reception–Year 2 £3,633, Nursery £2,875.

Fees quoted are inclusive of non-residential school trips and lunch.

Scholarships and Bursaries. Bursaries, which are means-tested, are available in the Senior School and in the Co-Ed College; these are intended to ensure that the school remains accessible to bright students who would benefit from a Howell's education, but who would be unable to enter the school without financial assistance.

Academic, Sports, Art and Design, Drama and Product Design Scholarships are available to students going into Year 7 and 12. Details of how to how apply for scholarships and bursaries are available, on request, from the school.

Charitable status. Howell's School Llandaff is part of The Girls' Day School Trust, which is a Registered Charity, number 306983.

Chairman of Governors: Mrs S Thomas

Principal: **Mrs S Davis**, BSc London

Deputy Principal: Mrs J Ashill, BEd Swansea

Deputy Principal: Mrs N Chyba, BA London

Assistant Principal: Mrs C Darnton, BEd Hons West Glamorgan, MSc Leicester

Director of Finance and Operations: Mr G Dyer, BA Brighton

Kilgraston School

Bridge of Earn, Perthshire PH2 9BQ

Tel: 01738 812257
email: admissions@kilgraston.com
website: www.kilgraston.com
Twitter: @kilgraston
Facebook: @kilgrastonschool

Kilgraston is an independent boarding and day school for children aged 5 to 18 years. It is an all-through school comprising Junior Years, Senior School and Sixth Form.

Kilgraston is set in a Georgian mansion house located in 54 acres of stunning parkland three miles from the centre of Perth with Edinburgh and Glasgow only an hour away. The school has fantastic facilities including a state-of-the-art science centre, a sixth form study centre, a 25m indoor swimming pool complex, and floodlit astroturf hockey pitch and tennis courts. Kilgraston is also the only school in Scotland with an on-site equestrian centre incorporating a 60m x 40m floodlit arena with show jumps.

Visitors to Kilgraston are struck by its warm and welcoming atmosphere, and the sense of community and friendship across the year groups. Staff know each pupil individually, and are proud of the well-rounded girls who thrive in a range of curricular and co-curricular activities. Kilgraston's Sacred Heart ethos is central to school life, providing a firm foundation for personal growth and individual contribution, whilst welcoming girls of all faiths and none.

The Curriculum. Kilgraston follows the Scottish educational system with all the girls studying a broad curriculum before selecting subjects to continue at National 5 (GCSE equivalent). Over 18 subjects are offered at Higher/Advanced Higher (A Level equivalent). Kilgraston has a record of high academic achievement and the girls gain entrance to top UK and international universities including Oxbridge. In 2021, 77% of pupils obtained a Grade A at Higher level with 87% achieving a Grade A at Advanced Higher level.

Music, Art and Drama play an important part of life at Kilgraston. The Music Department has 14 individual teaching rooms, a recording studio and two large music rooms designed to suit all needs. There are also many opportunities for pupils to perform throughout the year by participating in orchestra, string orchestra, fiddle, woodwind and brass groups or one of several choirs.

The Art Department is housed in the top of the mansion with superb views across the Ochil Hills and the school boasts an impressive number of past pupils who are practising artists.

Sports and recreation are catered for within a superb sports hall including a climbing wall and fitness gym. The extensive grounds incorporate the indoor 25m swimming pool, nine floodlit all-weather courts, playing fields and athletics track. Whilst the main sports are hockey, netball, tennis, rounders, swimming and athletics other sports include football, touch rugby, skiing, cricket, badminton, yoga, karate, fencing, aerobics, ballet, modern dance and highland dancing. Fixtures and competitions are also arranged against other schools throughout the year. Kilgraston also hosts the Scottish Schools' Equestrian Championships every Spring.

Kilgraston is divided into houses which compete against each other in games, music and debating. The girls can also take part in The Duke of Edinburgh's Award scheme and are encouraged to use all the facilities not only for curriculum lessons but also for leisure activities.

Kilgraston Junior Years, for pupils aged 5–12, is located in its own building within the same stunning parkland.

Girls are able to progress to Kilgraston Senior School, or prepare for scholarship exams for Kilgraston and Common Entrance exams for other schools. The academic standard is high with all pupils completing the Junior Years and achieving a place in their senior school of choice.

From age ten, the curriculum becomes more specialised with increasing input from specialised subject staff and use of facilities in the Senior School. Pastoral care is the responsibility of a tutor.

The Junior Years core academic curriculum is enhanced by a wide range of co-curricular subjects. Art, drama and music flourish and opportunities are provided throughout the year for pupils to perform and compete in local festivals and events. LAMDA, Associated Board and Trinity examinations are offered and there is an annual production.

Admission is normally interview and school report. Entry to the Junior Years is by interview and assessment.

Means-tested bursaries are available on application. Scholarship Examinations are held in early February. Scholarships are honorary with no remission of fees. Awards are also offered each year as a result of outstanding performance in the Academic Scholarship Examinations.

Scholarships are also offered in Art, Music, Drama and Sport.

"Happy, articulate and kind children and young people who are very proud of their school. They thrive in the stimulating environment for learning, and make the most of the extensive range of enriching activities and learning experiences offered to them." Her Majesty's Inspectorate Report, February 2019

Fees per term (2021–2022). Boarding: Senior School (Lower Fourth–Upper Sixth) £11,845, Junior School (Upper Second–Upper Third) £9,050. International: Senior School (Lower Fourth–Upper Sixth) £12,800; Junior School (Upper Second–Upper Third) £10,410. Day: Senior School (Lower Fourth–Upper Sixth) £6,935; Junior School: (Lower Third–Upper Third) £5,425, (Reception–Upper Second) £4,080.

Charitable status. Kilgraston School Trust is a Registered Charity, number SC029664.

Chair of Governors: Mr David Beal

Senior Leadership Team:

Headmistress: Mrs D MacGinty, BEd Hons, NPQH, DipMonEd

Deputy Head: Mrs C A Lund, BA Hons, MA, MA Ed Man, PGCE

Head of Finance: Mrs M Mackie, ACCA

Head of Boarding & Pastoral Care: Mrs S Muller, Bachelor of Social Work, PGCE

Head of Sixth Form: Mrs D McCormick, BSc Hons

King Edward VI High School for Girls

Birmingham

Edgbaston Park Road, Birmingham B15 2UB

Tel:	0121 472 1834
email:	enquiries@kehsmail.co.uk
website:	www.kehs.org.uk
Twitter:	@KEHSBham
Facebook:	@KEHSBham

Independent, formerly Direct Grant.

Founded in 1883, the School moved in 1940 to its present buildings and shares its 50-acre site with King Edward's School (a leading boys' independent school). There are 650 girls from 11 to 18 years of age, all day pupils, of whom 190 are in the Sixth Form.

Ranked first for academic results among independent schools in the West Midlands by The Sunday Times Schools Guide 2022, Parent Power.

Curriculum. KEHS is a school synonymous with intellectual ambition, offering an unrivalled education to the brightest girls in and around Birmingham. It provides outstanding teaching through a forward-looking and challenging curriculum and culture of scholarship, going beyond the confines of exam specifications and making connections across disciplines. It seeks to impart the joy of learning and enquiry together with intellectual courage, with the resilience and adaptability requisite for this. The

consistently outstanding results are a by-product of the all-round education on offer, with a highly-prized co-curricular programme at the heart of the school and bespoke courses that complement the traditional curriculum – including Leadership and PPE (Politics, Philosophy and Economics) – on offer.

In **Year One,** all girls take English, Mathematics, separate Sciences, Religious Studies, French, Latin, History, Geography, Music, Art and Design, Drama, Computing, Food Studies and Physical Education.

In **Years Two and Three,** all girls take English, Mathematics, separate Sciences, Religious Studies, Latin, History, Geography, Music, Art and Design, Drama and Physical Education, together with two languages from French, German, Mandarin and Spanish and an enrichment carousel including Food Studies, Computing, Design Technology and Leadership. In Year Three, girls choose two out of the creative subjects (Art, Design Technology, Drama and Music).

Core subjects in **Years Four and Five** are English Language, English Literature, Mathematics, at least two Sciences, but they can take three, and Physical Education. Girls then choose their other GCSE subjects from Art, Drama, Design Technology, French, Geography, German, Greek, History, Italian, Latin, Music, Physical Education, Religious Studies and Spanish. In Year 4, girls have a rotation of enrichment options including PPE, Food Studies, Computing and Wellbeing.

In the **Sixth Form,** girls choose four A Levels from a wide range of subjects – all Arts, all Sciences or a mixture of the two. Emphasis is placed on breadth at this level. The school also offers the Extended Project Qualification. All Sixth Form girls take a Friday afternoon enrichment option ranging from Life Saving to Art Appreciation and all take Physical Education. Girls in the Lower Sixth have additional enrichment sessions.

All girls follow a course in personal decision-making in which they explore and discuss a wide range of issues which call for personal choice and which helps develop life skills.

Religious and moral education are considered important. Academic study of them is designed to enable girls to be informed and questioning. There is no denominational teaching in the school in lessons or morning assembly. Girls of all faiths or of none are equally welcome.

In Sport, world-class coaching and outstanding facilities across multiple sports, both in lessons and as part of the co-curricular programme, enable girls to chase their own personal bests. All girls take part in PE, including in the Sixth Form. Sports on offer include gymnastics, hockey, netball, tennis, rounders, dance, fencing, badminton, cricket, squash, swimming, athletics, basketball, volleyball, self-defence, aerobics and health-related fitness. KEHS has its own indoor swimming pool, sports hall, well-equipped fitness suite with a strength and conditioning area, extensive pitches, including two astropitches, tennis courts and an international-standard athletics track.

In addition to the music in the curriculum, there are opportunities for girls to perform individually, in small groups or larger ensembles with co-curricular music being offered jointly with King Edward's School. There are around 40 concerts a year, with some in venues such as Birmingham Symphony Hall and the Barber Institute. Individual (or shared) instrumental lessons, at an extra fee, are arranged in school in a great variety of instruments.

Some instruments can be hired. Individual singing lessons can also be arranged.

Rich co-curricular opportunities enable girls to develop leadership and other practical skills as well as character and perspective. A large number of clubs (many joint with King Edward's School) are run by pupils themselves with help and encouragement from staff. Help is given with activities relating to The Duke of Edinburgh's Award scheme. Some activities take place in lunch hours, others after school and at weekends.

Proactive pastoral support promotes the development of balanced, self-reflective and assertive pupils with a strong moral compass. Pastoral care is focused on knowing girls as individuals, as well as being proactive about the issues they are likely to experience collectively.

The compassionate approach that characterises life at KEHS means that pupils and staff have myriad opportunities to help others, particularly through the thriving community service and outreach programmes. Each year, significant funds are raised for a variety of charities, and girls also offer practical support to local organisations such as care homes. The school's outreach programme sees free activities and use of facilities offered to local primary schools.

A spacious careers room is well stocked with up-to-date information. Individual advice and aptitude testing is given at stages where choices have to be made. The Careers Adviser has overall responsibility but many others are involved with various aspects. Girls are encouraged to attend conferences, gain work experience, make personal visits and enquiries. Old Edwardians and others deliver talks about their careers either in school or online. There is good liaison with universities and colleges of all kinds. Virtually all girls go on to higher education. A wide range of courses is being taken by Old Edwardians.

Admission of Pupils. Entry is normally for girls of 11 into the first year of the school in September. Applications must be made by September the year before they are due to start secondary school. The entrance examination is held in early October. Girls should have reached the age of 11 years by 31st August following the examination. Girls are examined at the school in English and Mathematics. The syllabus is such as would be normally covered by girls of good ability and no special preparation is advised.

Girls from 12 to 15 are normally considered only if they move from another part of the country, or in some special circumstances and only on the rare occasions when a space opens up in a year group. Applications should be made to the Director of Admissions.

There is an entry into the Sixth Form for girls wishing to study four main A Level subjects. Application should be made to the Director of Admissions by the end of January in the preceding academic year.

Fees per term (2021–2022). £4,759.

Scholarships and Bursaries. KEHS offers academic scholarships to the most able girls at 11+ and 16+ at the discretion of the Principal. Academic Scholarships are available each year and there is no separate scholarship examination. Music Scholarships are available to girls joining the school at 11+ and Music and Sports Scholarships are available to girls joining the Sixth Form.

Means-tested Assisted Places are available for girls entering the school at 11+ and Sixth Form.

Charitable status. The Schools of King Edward VI in Birmingham is a Registered Charity, number 529051. The purpose of the Foundation is to educate children and young persons living in or around the city of Birmingham mainly by provision of, or assistance to its schools.

Governing Body: The Independent Schools Governing Body

***Principal*: Mrs Kirsty von Malaisé**, MA Cantab, PGCE

Vice Principal (Academic): Mr Martin Lea, BSc Sheffield, PGCE
Vice Principal (Pastoral) DSL: Mrs Sarah Shore-Nye, BA Swansea, PGCE
Assistant Head (Community): Mr Andrew Duncombe, MA Cantab, PGCE
Assistant Head (Pastoral) Deputy DSL: Mrs Gemma Hargraves, BSc Cardiff, PGCE

Director of Enrichment: Mrs Kam Sangha, BA De Montfort, MBA UCE, PGCE
Director of Sixth Form: Mrs Joanna Whitehead, BSc Birmingham, PGCE
Director of Admissions: Mrs Catherine Oakes

The Kingsley School

Beauchamp Hall, Beauchamp Avenue, Royal Leamington Spa, Warwickshire CV32 5RD

Tel:	01926 425127
email:	schooloffice@kingsleyschool.co.uk
website:	www.thekingsleyschool.co.uk
Twitter:	@Kingsley_School
Facebook:	@thekingsleyschool
Instagram:	@thekingsleyschool
LinkedIn:	/company/thekingsleyschool

Independent Day School for Girls aged 3 to 18, and boys up to 11 years, founded in 1884.

For over 135 years The Kingsley School has had an excellent reputation for high academic standards and first class pastoral care. What sets The Kingsley School apart from other schools is its distinctive family ethos and friendly atmosphere. We are immensely proud of the fact that everyone who visits us remarks on the happy staff–student relationships and the sense of community it fosters. At Kingsley, pupils have a positive and purposeful approach to learning. The atmosphere is unique; enthusiastic and approachable teachers inspire pupils to learn; behaviour is excellent and pupils are challenged and supported according to individual need. Where practical, we aim to personalise the curriculum so that pupils can reach their potential whatever their gifts and talents.

The Kingsley **Preparatory School** is friendly and purposeful and offers a rich, vibrant and creative curriculum for girls and boys aged 3–11. Outstanding teaching encourages a love of learning by providing a balance between the sound foundations for academic progress with character-building creativity. Kingsley has a well-established core curriculum in which the focus is on excellence within English, mathematics and science, supported by bespoke teaching in music, drama, modern foreign languages and physical education. In support of the core curriculum we have developed an exciting Creative

Curriculum which sets our pupils a challenge; to explore and discover the real world. Most girls progress to The Kingsley Senior School, and boys move on to the next stage with self-assurance, some having been awarded scholarships for entry into local schools.

The **Senior School** provides continuity of academic and pastoral care. We offer a broad, balanced and stimulating academic experience. The curriculum at Kingsley is structured to maximise progress, building on girls' prior learning to encourage creativity, intellectual curiosity and independence. Our GCSE results are excellent, with high attainment year on year. At GCSE our curriculum provides opportunities for girls to study examinations in the core subjects of English, mathematics and the three separate sciences, as well as in the humanities subjects, the performing arts, physical education and modern foreign languages. The school delivers an academically rigorous timetable, yet has the flexibility and scope to offer additional subjects such as Latin and classical civilisation. Girls also experience a range of design subjects, for example food technology and textiles. Academic standards are high, as demonstrated by the 2021 GCSE results, with top marks awarded across the board in all subjects. Of all grades, 35% were awarded at level 9–8, 52% at level 9–7 and 99% at level 9–4.

The Kingsley School's **Sixth Form** provides a wide range of opportunities for all students. We offer a high-quality A Level curriculum and cater for a wide range of interests and post-16 aspirations. Students' academic achievements are outstanding and the diversity of their goals is embraced, with most progressing to their first-choice university, choosing to take apprenticeships within prestigious commercial organisations or studying further Higher Education courses. In the 2021 A Levels, 37% of all grades were awarded at A*, 68% at A*–A and 97% at A*–C, with a 100% pass rate. Destinations of recent leavers include Medicine at UEA, Law at Birmingham, Leeds and Liverpool, Medieval and Modern Languages at Cambridge, Neuroscience at Manchester, Dentistry at Bristol, English at Cardiff, Geography at Leeds, Maths at Swansea, Music at Edinburgh and Leeds, Marine Zoology at Newcastle, Zoology at Exeter, Business Management at Exeter, Veterinary Science at Liverpool, Pharmacology at Leeds, Agriculture with Animal Science at Harper Adams, Nursing at Leeds, Conservation and Forestry at Bangor, Fashion with Marketing at Southampton and a Pharmaceutical Apprenticeship at Boots PLC.

The school operates a tiered system of Learning Support where pupils benefit from a broad and balanced curriculum, with small classes and excellent relationships with teachers. Lessons provide opportunities for challenge and extension, as well as scaffolded learning, with teachers making dynamic assessments of need on an individual basis. In every area of school life, pupils are supported to be the very best version of themselves and fulfil every aspect of their potential.

Kingsley runs a formal Enrichment Programme which aims to extend and enhance the core curriculum. The inclusive programme takes place within the school day, enabling all pupils to enjoy new experiences and develop essential life skills. Many of the clubs and activities are tailored towards particular year groups or Key Stages and themed by skill base. Academic clubs are generally subject specific, while STEM clubs – aimed at developing enquiry skills – focus on exciting scientific and technological advances. Pupils also have access to a wide range of performing arts clubs – including choirs, instrumental groups and drama workshops – and wellbeing activities. Our affiliation with Round Square enables us to offer clubs with more of an international focus, giving pupils greater exposure to different cultures and languages and the opportunity to develop their communication skills, leadership abilities and more. Aligned to our formal Enrichment Programme are wider opportunities for character development such as the Duke of Edinburgh's Award and Young Enterprise and World Challenge schemes. There are also a variety of both local and international trips.

Sport and physical education are a vital part of life at Kingsley; each child is encouraged to achieve their personal best. We recognise that mental and physical fitness go hand in hand with developing wellbeing and academic potential. Sport helps to develop resilience, teamwork and leadership skills and lifelong health and fitness. Each week there is an inclusive programme of extracurricular sports offered, and we compete regularly against local and regional opposition, with thriving sports teams. Kingsley also runs its own competitive riding squad and an award-winning ski team.

We offer tuition in the performing arts leading to national music and drama qualifications. There are Kingsley choirs, musical ensembles and bands with regular opportunities to perform and showcase talent; both Prep and Senior School have annual musical theatre and drama productions.

Fees per term (2021–2022). Preparatory School: £3,749 (Reception to Year 2), £4,365 (Years 3–6). Senior School & Sixth Form: £4,688.

Scholarships and Bursaries. Academic, all-rounder, art, music, drama, sport and performing arts scholarships are available at 11+. Academic, all-rounder, drama, music, art, photography, textiles and PE scholarships are available in Sixth Form.

Bursaries are available.

Our fleet of school minibuses serves a wide area and before and after-school care is available.

Charitable status. The Kingsley School is part of the Warwick Independent Schools Foundation, a Registered Charity (number 1088057).

Warwick Independent Schools Foundation Governors:
Mrs Sally Austin (*Foundation Chair*)
Mr David Loudon (*Foundation Vice-Chair*)
Mrs Marie Ashe (*Chair, Finance & Regulatory Committee*)
Prof Simon Barnes
Ms Jo Broughton
Mr Chris Gibbons
Mrs Lynne Greaves
Prof Damian Griffin
Mrs Maureen Hicks
Mr Stephen Jobburn
Mr Adrian Keeling
Mr Tim Keyes (*Chair, Education Committee*)
Mrs Catherine Robbins
Mr Jonathan Wallis (*Chair, Resources & Estates Committee*)
Dr Ruth Weeks
Mrs Anne Wilson
Mr Tim Cox (*Ex-Officio as Lord Lieutenant of Warwickshire*)

Principal of Warwick Independent Schools Foundation: Mr R Nicholson, MA Oxon

Headteacher: **Mr J Mercer-Kelly**, MChem, PGCE, PGDES

Deputy Head (Pastoral): Mrs C McCullough, BA QTS SENCO

Assistant Headteacher (Academic): Mrs R Rogers, BSc, PGCE, MA

Head of Sixth Form: Mrs D Morgan, BA, PGCE

Interim Head of Preparatory School: Mrs M Gamble, BA, DipEd Secondary, ATQ Primary, NCSL Head

* *Head of Department*

Art:
*Mr E Lax, BA, PGCE

Classics:
*Ms I Peace, BA, PGCE

Design and Technology:
*Mrs C Dempsey, BEd
Mr E Agnew-Morley, BSc, PGCE

Economics and Business Studies:
*Mrs M Bennett, BEd, MA
Mrs K Ahmed, BA PGDipEd
Mrs R Rogers, BSc, PGCE, MA

English and Drama:
*Mrs A Alton, BA, PGCE
Mrs C Bowler, BA, PGCE
Mrs D Morgan, BA, PGCE
Mrs E Smith, BA, PGCE

Food and Nutrition:
Mrs K Hughes-O'Sullivan, BEd, MA

Geography:
*Mrs K Ahmed, BA, PGDipEd
Mrs C McCullough, BA QTS, SENCO
Mrs R Rogers, BSc, PGCE, MA

Health and Social Care:
Mrs S Mace, BA, PGCE

History:
*Mrs C Partridge, BScEcon, PGCE

ICT:
*Mrs M Bennett, BEd, MA
Dr A Smith, BA PhD PGDE
Mr M Thompson, MSc, PGCE

Mathematics:
*Mr T Spillane, BSc, PGCE
Mrs P Davies, BSc, PGCE
Mrs L Laubscher, HED SA, QTS
Dr A Smith, BA, PhD, PGDE

Modern Languages:
*Mr I Stickels, BA, PGCE
Mrs C Cocksworth, BA
Mrs T Connor, BA
Mrs H Foulerton, BA, PGCE
Miss M Mahé, Licence de Langues, Maîtrise de Littératures et Langues

Music and LAMDA:
*Mr J Smith, BMus, PGCE
Mrs B Morley, BA (*LAMDA*)
Mrs B O'Reilly, BMus, MMus, PGDip (*Prep Music*)
Mrs A Vallance, BA, QTS (*LAMDA*)

Personal and Social Education:
*Mrs K Hughes-O'Sullivan, BEd, MA

Mrs K Ahmed, BA PGDipEd
Mrs C Dempsey, BEd

Physical Education:
*Miss S Windsor, BEd
Mrs S Bates, BA CertEd
Miss C Mason, BSci, PGCE
Mrs C McCullough, BA QTS, SENCO
Mrs J Purdy, BA, PGCE

Psychology:
*Mrs S Mace, BA, PGCE
Mrs K MacLeod, BSc, CertTeach

Philosophy, Ethics and Religion (PER):
*Miss R Bubb, BA, PGCE
Mrs K Ahmed, BA, PGDipEd
Mrs K MacLeod, BSc, CertTeach

Science:
Dr C Robertson, BSc PhD, PGCE (*Biology*)
Mrs S Bains, MSc, PGCE (**Chemistry*)
Mrs A Hawthorn, BEng, MSc, PGCE (**Physics*)
Mrs S Bacon, BSc Hons, PGCE
Mrs S Baker, BSc, PGCE
Mr M Thompson, MSc, PGCE

Duke of Edinburgh, Manager: Mrs L Laubscher, HED SA, QTS

Head of Careers: Mrs S Bennett, BA

Academic and Learning Support:
*Mrs L Payne, BA, SEND PG
Mrs R Athwal, BSc, MEd, PGCE
Mrs C Cocksworth, BA
Mrs B Freeman, BA, QTS
Mrs Y Raja, Dip

Preparatory School:
Mrs G Adair BN, PGCE
Mrs R Bhangal, BA NCFE
Miss C Bray LLB LLM, PGCE
Miss H Fennell, BA Primary with QTS, PGSENCO
Mrs N Finnegan, BA, PGCE
Ms C Gardner, TA Qual
Mrs L Hartog, NPQICL, EYPS, BA
Ms C Hayward, NNEB
Mrs S Holmes, BA QTS
Miss M Knight-Adams, BSc, PGCE
Ms C Lopez, BA, MA
Mrs A Norris, BEd QTS
Mrs B O'Reilly, BMus, MMus PGDip Perf (*Music*)
Mrs S Whittle, BA, PGCE

Finance Office:
Senior Finance Assistant: Mr D Falp
Finance Assistants: Mrs M Adamo; Mrs S Punj

Administration:
Alumnae & Development Officer: Mrs S Bennett
PA to Headteacher: Mrs J Bostock
Admin & Receptionists: Miss L Biddlecombe; Mrs K Lewis (*Prep School*); Mrs S Lihou; Mrs K Parker (*Prep School*)
LRC Assistant: Ms P Tudway
Exam Officer/Cover Administrator: Mrs S Tsang

Marketing and Admissions:
Registrar: Mrs J Durham
PR & Marketing Manager: Mr J Farrington-Smith
Digital & Marketing Assistant: Mrs A Gardner
Admissions Assistant & Events Coordinator: Mrs C Hunt

School Nurse: Mrs T Ball SRN, BSc Hons

Wellbeing Counsellor: Mrs P Thomas, BSc Dip, Psch PGDip, Registered MBACP

Instrumental Staff:
Mr C Bowen, BA, PGCE (*Guitar*)
Mr N Jones (*Drums*)
Mr C Langdown, MMus RCM, GRSM DipRCM, ALCM (**Keyboard Studies*)
Mrs L Martin, BMus Hons, QTS (*Flute*)
Miss B Morley, BA (**Vocal Studies*)
Mrs E Murphy, BA, PGCE (*Piano, Recorder*)
Mrs B O'Reilly, BMus, MMus, PGDip (*Strings*)
Mr J Smith, BMus, PGCE (*Brass/Electric Guitar*)
Mrs C Wimpenny, GBSM, ABSM (*Cello/Double Bass*)

Lady Eleanor Holles

Hanworth Road, Hampton, Middlesex TW12 3HF

Tel: 020 8979 1601
email: office@lehs.org.uk
website: www.lehs.org.uk
Twitter: @LEHSchool

This Independent Girls' School is one of the oldest in the country, founded in 1710 in Cripplegate under the Will of the Lady Eleanor Holles. In 1937, the school moved to purpose-built premises in Hampton. Numerous additions to the building have enabled the school to increase to some 990 girls, aged from 7 to 18 years, who enjoy a wealth of specialist facilities and the use of 24 acres of playing fields and gardens. Nine science laboratories, Learning Resources Centre, Sixth Form Library, a Product Design suite, extensive computing and multimedia language facilities and a dedicated Careers area are complemented by grass and hard tennis courts, netball courts, 5 lacrosse pitches, track and field areas and a full-sized, indoor heated swimming pool refurbished in 2017. A Boat House, shared with Hampton School, was opened in October 2000 and a large Sports Hall, adjacent to the swimming pool, in September 2001.

September 2012 saw the opening of a new Arts Centre consisting of a 300-seat theatre, new Music and Art Departments, and Sixth Form Common Rooms, followed in September 2013 by a new dining room, a new suite of classrooms, two dedicated Drama Studios, and a Conference Room.

In 2018 the Gateway Building opened with a state-of-the-art Computing suite, and Product Design facilities. Both of these subjects are now offered at A Level.

Both the Junior and Senior Schools are equipped with a lift for the disabled.

The School's Statement of Purpose embodies the original aim, to encourage every student to develop their personality to the full so that they may become a person of integrity and a responsible member of society. It also emphasises the value of a broad, balanced education which gives due importance to sport, music and the creative arts in general, whilst providing the opportunities for students to achieve high academic standards within a framework of disciplined, independent study.

The Curriculum. In Years 7–9 girls take two modern foreign languages (with the option of Mandarin in Y9), Latin, separate sciences, dedicated computing lessons and a PSHE programme which continues throughout the school. Selection rather than specialisation for GCSE allows girls to respond to individual abilities and attributes, and every student continues to experience a broad education in which as few doors as possible are closed. A large sixth form of about 200 students means that a wide choice of Advanced Level subjects is offered. Most students study four or five subjects in L6, proceeding to A Level with three or four. They have the option of taking the Extended Project Qualification, and emphasis is placed on leadership roles and extra-curricular activities. All sixth form students move on to further training, the majority to universities, and there is a sizeable Oxbridge and North American contingent annually. The formal Careers programme, which begins in Year 9, continues throughout the school and uses external specialists, parents, past pupils, ECCTIS and other computer programmes, as well as the School's own, trained staff.

Extra-Curricular Activity. A key strength of the school is the range and diversity of its flourishing extra-curricular provision. Some 120 clubs run each week ranging from Music, Drama and Sports to Outward Bound, CCF and subject clubs, all aiming to stimulate further and inculcate a love of learning outside the classroom. Sixth Formers lead a number of groups which focus on various political, environmental and ethical issues, including 'Model United Nations', 'Amnesty' and Eco-Squad. Sixth Formers are encouraged to take the initiative and form their own clubs with a Medic Group, Law Society and Book Club formed in the recent past. The School is very much at the heart of the local community and has developed a wide range of activities to ensure that students are aware of their social responsibilities, including Service Volunteers which works with disadvantaged local school children and the elderly, and running numerous activities in local primary schools, including language and drama clubs. Pupils are strongly encouraged to participate in extra-curricular activities.

The Junior School (192 pupils aged 7–11) is accommodated in a separate building in the grounds. It is an integral part of the whole school community and uses many of the specialist facilities available for Seniors.

(*See entry in the IAPS section for more details.*)

Entrance. Pupils may enter the Junior School from the age of 7, and the Senior School at 11 years. LEH Junior School pupils are guaranteed places in the Senior School (other than in exceptional circumstances). Students with good academic ability may apply for direct entry to the Sixth Form. All external applicants must sit the School's competitive entrance examinations, which are held in November for Sixth Form entry and December (7+ and 11+) each year, for admission in the following September. There are no internal hurdles for entry to Sixth Form. Registration and Entrance Examination Fee is £125, or £200 for overseas applications.

Scholarships and Bursaries.

11+ Entry Academic Scholarships: On average ten awards are offered each year. These are expressed as percentages of the full fee and will thus keep pace with any fee increases. Awards are non-means-tested and usually 10%. The awards are based solely on performance in the school's own Entrance Examinations and subsequent interview.

Governors' Bursaries: Candidates who sit entrance papers at any stage from 11+ onwards may be considered for a bursary award. These are available for up to 100% of fees, plus extras, and are means tested and subject to annual review.

Sixth Form Academic Scholarships: Ten Scholarships worth 10% of fees over the two years of Sixth Form study are offered to internal and external candidates who sit the Sixth Form Entrance and Scholarship Examination in November before the year of proposed entry.

Music Scholarships: Both Major and Minor Awards for Music are available at 11+ and 16+. These are for 10% and 7.5% of fees respectively, plus free tuition on one instrument. Candidates must satisfy academic requirements in entrance papers before being invited to a music audition. Full details are available from the school.

At 16+ only, Scholarships are also available in Art, Sport, Drama and STEM (one in each).

Fees per term (2021–2022). £5,999 in the Junior School; £7,246 in the Senior School. Fees are inclusive of books and stationery and exclusive of Public Examination fees.

Former Pupils' Association. Holles Connect. Address for communications: Alumnae Administrator c/o Lady Eleanor Holles; email: alumnae@lehs.org.uk

The Cripplegate Schools Foundation

Chairman of the Foundation: Mr D H King, BSc, FCA

Vice-Chair: Sister P Thomas, BEd, MA

Governors:
Ms S Bhasin
Ms A Blair, LLB
Mr M George
Mr R J Milburn, MA, FCA
Ms C Millis, Chartered FCIPD
Mrs B Parson, CertEd, BEd Hons
Mr S Pitchford, LLB
Mr R Price, LLB
Mrs C Thomas, BA Hons
Miss C V Thomas, BSc, AA Dip, ARB, RIBA

Clerk to the Governors: Mrs S Whitehouse, BA

Head Mistress: Mrs Heather G Hanbury, MA Edinburgh, MSc Cantab

Deputy Head: Dr D James, PhD King's College London
Deputy Head Pastoral: Mrs A Poyner, BSc Exeter, MBA
Head of Junior School: Mrs P Mortimer, BEd Oxon
Director of Finance and Operations: Mr M Berkowitch, BSc, JD
Senior Assistant Head (Academic Systems): Mr M Williams, BA City of London Polytechnic
Director of Teaching & Innovation: Mr D Piper, BA King's College London
Head of Sixth Form: Mr M Tompsett, MA Cantab
Head of Upper School: Ms F Ellison, MA Cantab
Head of Middle School: Mrs K Sinnett, BA Cantab
Director of Development & Communications: Mrs J Blaiklock, MA Oxon

Senior School

Art and Design:
Mrs D Howorth, BA Hons Staffordshire (*Head of Art*)
Mr L Curtis, BA Slade School of Art, MA Royal College of Art
Miss E Hollaway. MA Wimbledon College of Arts

Ms A E Seaborn, BA Winchester School of Art
Miss S White, BA University of the Arts

Classics:
Miss K C Eltis, BA Oxon (*Head of Classics*)
Mrs R Brown, BA Durham (*Head of Year U5*)
Ms Flora Ellison, MA Cantab (*Head of Upper School*)
Miss E Lewis, BA. MA UCL
Mr D Piper, BA King's College London (*Director of Teaching & Innovation*)

Computing:
Miss S Bruin, PGCE Reading (*Head of Computing*)
Miss R Crisa, BSc Brunel, MSc St Mary's London
Mr S Hughes, PGCE Bristol
Mrs V Whiffin, MEng Southampton (*Manager of Digital Teaching & Learning*)

Drama and Theatre Studies:
Miss Victoria Bedford, MA Royal Holloway (*Director of Drama*)
Miss A Lindsell, BA University of London
Miss S Torrent, BA Greenwich
Mrs P Tate (*Music and Drama Administrator*)

Economics:
Miss A J Matthews, BA Leicester (*Head of Economics and Careers*)
Miss D A Self, BSc Brunel

English:
Mrs E Gwynne, MA Durham (*Head of English*)
Mrs K Mackichan, BA Leeds (*Deputy Head of English*)
Miss H Barnett, BA Durham (*Head of L6*)
Mrs V Davies, MSc Kingston
Dr D James, PhD King's College London (*Deputy Head*)
Mrs C Moon, BA, MA UCL
Mrs U Renton, MA Aberdeen
Mrs C Richardson, BA Reading
Miss A-M Wright, MA Aberdeen
Dr B Westwood, DPhil Wadham College Oxford

Food and Nutrition
Mrs H Boczkowski, BSc Bath Spa (*Head of Food and Nutrition*)
Ms M Swinbank, BA Hons Leeds Metropolitan

Geography:
Mr L M O'Rourke, BA Southampton (*Head of Geography*)
Mrs H Hanbury, MA Edinburgh, MSc Cantab (*Headmistress*)
Mrs K Hanna, PGCE London [Maternity cover]
Miss R Ling, BA Oxon [Maternity leave]
Mrs R Lockett, BA Southampton (*Head of Year L4*)
Miss A Perlowska-Goose, BSc Reading
Ms J Noble, BSc Middlesex [Temporary cover]

History of Art:
Miss A Lindsay, BA Manchester (*Head of History of Art*)

History and Politics:
Miss N Randall, MA York (*Head of History and Politics*)
Mr N Allen, BA Nottingham
Mrs A M Bradshaw, MA St Andrews
Mrs B Farthing, PGCE Goldsmiths College London
Ms J FitzGerald, BA Newcastle, MA Central School of Speech & Drama (*Initial Teacher Training Coordinator*)
Mrs L Harding-Anderson, BA Warwick

Mathematics:
Mrs J Manns, BSc Sheffield (*Head of Mathematics*)

Mr C Ralphs, BEng Birmingham (*Deputy Head of Mathematics*)
Mrs N Banerjee, BA Delhi
Mr M Deacon, BSc Exeter
Mrs H Doshi, BSc City London
Mrs M Najjar, BSc UCL
Miss R Nicholl, BSc King's College London (*Head of L5*)
Mr U Patel, BSc Hons Sussex, MA Ed Open University
Mrs A Poyner, BSc Exeter, MBA (*Deputy Head Pastoral*)
Mrs M Read, BSc Durham
Miss T Saunders, BSc University of Southampton
Mr C Sin, BSc MSc Cardiff
Mrs K Sinnett, BA Cantab (*Head of Middle School*)
Mr M Williams, BA City of London Polytechnic (*Senior Assistant Head (Academic Systems)*)

Modern Languages:
Mr M Russell, BA Oxon (*Head of MFL and German*)
Mrs U Arrieta, BA Deusto, Bilbao (*Head of Spanish*)
Mrs A Buck, Licenciada en Filología Anglogermanica Valencia, Spain (*German and Spanish*)
Miss M Castello (*Spanish Assistant*)
Miss E Devern (*French Assistant*)
Mrs R Hart, BA, MA Oxon (*Spanish*)
Mrs V Kean, BA Leeds (*Head of French*)
Ms M-C McGreevy, BA Leeds, MA Bath (*German and French*)
Ms N Murray, BA, MA Leeds (*French*)
Mr H Ng (*Mandarin*)
Mrs N Rees, MA Cantab (*Spanish*)
Miss D Robbins, MA St Andrews (*French*)
Mrs A Rowe, BA Nottingham (*French and German*)
Mr M Tompsett, MA Cantab (*German, Head of Sixth Form*)

Music:
Mrs M Ashe, MA Oxon (*Director of Music*)
Mr B G Ashe, BA York, LRAM (*Composer-in-Residence*)
Miss C Overbury, MA Oxon
Miss N Redman, BMus Manchester, MMus, GSMD (*Head of Thirds*)
Mrs P Tate (*Music and Drama Administrator*)
Mrs C Zuckert, BMus Birmingham, MMus

Natural Sciences:
Miss L Mercer, BSc Edinburgh (*Head of Science and Biology*)
Miss A Boland, BSc St Mary's London (*Head of Psychology*)
Mr A Hayter, BSc Durham (*Head of Chemistry*)
Mrs V Whiffin, MEng Southampton (*Head of Physics*)
Mrs F Rosier, BSc Bath, MRSB (*Biology*)
Mr A Brittain, BSc Canterbury Kent (*Physics*)
Mrs N C Camilleri, BSc Manchester (*Physics*)
Mrs J Crook, BSc Nottingham (*Chemistry*)
Mrs V Davies, MSc Kingston (*Psychology*)
Mrs P Earl, BSc Swansea (*Biology*)
Mrs T Hayter, BSc King's College London (*Chemistry*)
Mrs S Jansz, BSc Bangor (*Chemistry*)
Mr N Johnson, MSc Nottingham (*Physics*)
Mrs H Lenox-Smith, BSc UCL (*Biology*)
Miss G Liu, BA Newnham College Cantab
Mr R Mangion, BSc King's College London (*Chemistry*)
Miss K Millar, BEng Queen's Belfast (*Physics*)
Ms L Monteil, BSc Manchester (*Psychology*)
Mrs C R Nicholls, BSc Cardiff (*Biology, Head of Year L4*)
Ms C Packer, BSc UCL (*Chemistry, Head of U6*)
Miss V Ranjan, BSc Durham (*Biology*)

Mrs F Rosier, BSc Bath, MRSB (*Biology*)
Miss C Shum, BSc UCL (*Biology*)

Philosophy, Religion and Ethics:
Mrs L Garcia, MA UCL (*Head of Philosophy, Religion and Ethics*)
Mr I Jakeway, BA Oxon, MA Reading
Mr T Lightfoot, BA Reading, MPhil Regent's Park College

Physical Education:
Miss D Mugridge, BA Hons University College Chichester (*Director of Sport and Outward Bound Activities*)
Miss K Hoffman, BA Hons North Carolina, USA (*Assistant Director of Sport & Head of Lacrosse*)
Miss E Affleck, BA Chester (*PE Graduate Assistant*)
Mrs R Crane, BA St Mary's Twickenham (*Head of Gymnastics*) [Maternity leave]
Mrs N Crowther, PGDip Roehampton (*CCF School Staff Instructor*)
Miss E Curtis, BA Brighton
Miss E Harrison, BA Durham
Mr T Lewis, BA Brighton
Miss L Preece
Mrs E Searle, BEd Hons Exeter (*Head of Netball*)
Mrs T Sedgbeer (*Duke of Edinburgh Coordinator, CCF Contingent Commander*)
Mr C Summers, MSc Chester

Product Design:
Mr S G Bicknell, BSc Brunel, PGDip (*Head of Product Design*)
Mrs A-M Angliss, BEd Trinity College Dublin (*Teacher i/c Textiles*)
Mrs A Pollard, MSc Leeds (*Textiles*)
Mr D Smeaton, BEng Southbank Polytechnic
Ms M Swinbank, BA Hons Leeds Metropolitan (*Food and Nutrition, Textiles*)

PSHE:
Ms R Hart, BA Hons and MA Oxon (*Head of PSHE, Spanish*)
Mrs A Bradshaw, MA St Andrews
Barney Brew, Pets As Therapy Centre (*Pro Bonio*)

Rowing:
Mr A Smith (*Head of Rowing*)
Mr S Larner, BSc Imperial College London, MOst British School of Osteopathy, PGDip (*Assistant Head of Rowing*)
Mr T Gale
Mr A Johnston, BA Newcastle
Ms A Leake, BA Newcastle
Mr J Moon

Learning Support:
Miss M Christodoulou, BA Middlesex, MA Durham, PG Cert Dyslexia and Literacy (*Head of Learning Support*)
Mrs N Rees, MA Cantab
Mrs S Woodhouse, Diploma Kingston Polytechnic

Learning Resources Manager:
Miss G Pearce, BA Bath Spa (*Head of Library Services*)
Mrs C Didiot-Cook

Senior School Administrative Staff:
Head Mistress's Personal Assistant: Ms E Clinton, BA, PGCE
Registrar: Mrs A Siddiqui, BSc, MSc [Maternity leave]
Acting Registrar: Mrs M Bradley
Director of HR: Ms N Dimitrova, Assoc CIPD
School Office Manager: Mrs S Austyn

Estates Manager: Mr P Sisodiya
Finance Manager: Mrs M Seraphimova-Spasova, BSc Oxford Brookes, ACCA Member
Director of IT Services: Mr M Taylor, BSc London, PGCE, CITP

Junior School

Head of Junior School: Mrs P Mortimer, BEd Oxon
Deputy Head of Junior School: Mrs R Yates, BA Cantab, LLM

Teaching Staff:
Mrs J E Allden, BSc London Chelsea College, MSc Kingston (*Assistant Academic Coordinator & Head of Computing*)
Mrs M Bass, BEd Natal
Miss S Connor, BA Hons Kent at Canterbury
Mrs J Deverson, BEd Oxford Brookes
Miss J Dunckley, BA Brighton (*Head of Junior School PE*)
Mr J Estorninho, BEd Melbourne, Australia (*Head of Junior School Music*)
Mrs M Frampton, BEd Exeter
Mrs S Harding, BEd De Montfort
Mr A Hopkins, BSc Portsmouth
Mrs K Hurley, BA Middlesex
Mrs K Keightley, MA Edinburgh
Mrs L Kent-Skorsepova, MA Comenius, Bratislava
Mr J Miller, BSc Durham, MSc UCL
Mrs N Rees, MA Cantab
Mrs K Sehgal, BA St Mary's London
Mrs M Walker, BA Canterbury Christ Church (*Director of Studies Junior School*)
Mrs L Wright, BA Kingston
Mrs L Cowin (*Teaching Assistant*)
Ms P Evans (*Teaching Assistant*)

Junior School Administrative Staff:
Junior School Secretary & Personal Assistant to the Head of Junior School: Mrs A Rahman, BA Thames Valley
Junior School Office Administrator: Mrs R Thomas Jones, BA Wales

School Nurses:
Senior School: Sister S Brew, RGN
Junior School: Nurse L Parker, RCN

School Counsellors:
Senior School: Mrs G Young, BA, MBACP, Higher Diploma in Counselling
Senior School: Ms K Lacy MA East London, Diploma in Counselling
Junior School: Mrs R Ticciati, SRCN, SRN, MBACP

Leicester High School for Girls

454 London Road, Leicester LE2 2PP

Tel: 0116 270 5338
email: enquiries@leicesterhigh.co.uk
website: www.leicesterhigh.co.uk
Twitter: @LeicesterHigh
Facebook: @Leicester-High-School-For-Girls

The school is a Trust with a Board of Governors in membership of AGBIS and the Headmaster belongs to the GSA.

Leicester High School is a well-established day school for girls situated in lovely grounds on the south side of the city. Founded in 1906 as Portland House School, it now comprises a Junior Department of approximately 100 girls (3–9 years) and a Senior School of approximately 250 girls (aged 10–18) sited on the same campus.

The Headmaster is responsible for both the Junior Department and Senior School. The staff are well-qualified specialists and the school is renowned for both its academic excellence and extra-curricular programme. At present 18 subjects are offered at GCSE Level and 21 subjects at A Level.

Facilities. The premises are a combination of modern purpose-built units and the original Victorian house, skilfully adapted to its present purpose. The facilities of the School have been systemically improved and updated over recent years. The school has a Junior Department and a Senior School in separate buildings on one site. The Junior Department has its own hall, library, IT suite, garden, playground and outdoor learning area. The Senior School has a central gym, library, drama/dance studio, ICT suites, language computer suite, 6 science laboratories, art and design studio, separate sixth form area and food studies room set around an award-winning courtyard garden. The school benefited from a £3.7m extension in 2010. The 3-acre grounds of the school have tennis and netball courts within extensive gardens. Most recently a specialist music centre has been added.

Religion. The school has a Christian foundation but welcomes girls of other faiths or of none.

Admission. All candidates over the age of 7 are required to pass an entrance examination for admission into the Junior and Senior sections. Direct entry into the Sixth Form is dependent on GCSE results. Entrance into the Early Years Unit is by assessment. A registration fee of £85 is payable for all applicants.

The Headmaster is always pleased to meet parents of prospective pupils and to show them around the school. All communications should be addressed to the Admissions Officer from whom prospectuses, application forms and details of fees may be obtained.

Fees per term (2021–2022). £3,210–£4,340.

Extras. Individual Music lessons, Speech and Drama, Ballet and Taekwondo are offered.

Scholarships and Bursaries. The Headmaster's Scholarship is a five-year scholarship for entry into Year 7 for an academic girl. All those interested must sit the January Entrance Examination. Registering for the examination costs £85.

Scholarships are awarded to any student – either existing Year 6 or external candidates – on the basis of performance in the Year 7 examination papers in English and Mathematics sat on Entrance Examination day in January.

The Margaret Bowler Scholarship: A scholarship of 5–25% for Year 10 students.

The LHS Sixth Form Scholarship: A scholarship of up to 25% is available to one, exceptional girl joining the Sixth Form. A personal statement, grades and references will be requested and shortlisted girls will be invited to attend an initial interview with the Head of Sixth Form and the subject heads of her chosen A Levels. If successful at this initial interview, girls will be invited to attend a final interview with the Headmaster.

Girls entering the Sixth Form from a state school, and resident in Leicestershire or Rutland, have been invited to apply for a Sir Thomas White Scholarship, which is 100% fees-only funded for two years. The School has had seven Sir Thomas White Scholars in recent years.

A small number of Bursaries are available from Year 6 onwards up to the value of full fees.

Charitable Status. Leicester High School Charitable Trust Limited is a Registered Charity, number 503982. The Trust exists to promote and provide for the advancement of education based on Christian principles according to the doctrines of the Church of England.

Board of Governors:

Chair: Mr M Dunkley, LLB, TEP
Vice-Chair: Mr T Leah, BA, NPQH

Mrs J Carroll
Mrs M Neilson, BEd
Mrs S Webb, BA, PGCE, MBA, NPQH

Clerk to the Governors: Mrs E Mackay, AAT

Headmaster: Mr A R Whelpdale, BA, NPQH

Deputy Head: Mr J M Partridge, MA, BSc, NPQSL

Assistant Head: Mrs D Solly, MSc, BSc

Head of Years 6 and 7: Mrs K McCarthy, BSc
Head of Years 8 and 9 (*with overview of KS3*): Mrs D Morgan, BSc
Head of KS4: Mrs J Rose, BEd
Head of Sixth Form: Ms K Purewal, BSc

Teaching Staff:
* *Head of Department*

Careers:
*Miss E Tyler, BSc

Computing and Information Technology:
*Mrs K Madlani, BSc

English:
*Mrs K Penney, BA
Dr N Taylor, BA, MA, PhD

Expressive Arts:
Mrs E Bott, BA (*Art and Design*)
Miss E Ikin, BA (*Art and Design/Photography*)
Mrs P Parrans-Smith, BA (*Music*)
Mrs J Rose, BEd (*Drama, Head of KS4*)

Food Studies:
*Mrs J Whalley, BSc

Geography:
*Mrs K Haresign, BA
Miss S Leaning, BA, MSc, MA

History and Politics:
*Miss A Paul, MA
Mrs F Lodder, MA

Mathematics:
*Mr M Pinnick, BSc
Mrs K Keary, BSc
Mr A Stewart, BEng
Mrs D Solly, MSc

Modern Languages:
*Mrs M Watkiss, BA (*Spanish and French*)
Mrs R Congreve, LLB (*Spanish and French*)

Mrs G Wheeler, BA (*French*)

Personal, Social, Health and Citizenship Education:
*Mrs D Morgan, BSc (*Head of KS3 Years 8–9*)

Philosophy and Belief (*RS*):
*Mr D Ingram, BA, MA, DipMM

Physical Education:
*Mrs K McCarthy, BSc
Mrs J Prasad-Smith, BSc
Miss S Watson, BA
Mrs D Solly, MSc

Science:
*Mr A McMurray, BSc, MBA (*Physics*)
Mrs K Greenwood, BSc (*Chemistry*)
Mrs D Morgan, BSc (*Chemistry*)
Mrs H Rai, BSc, MSc (*Biology*)
Miss E Tyler, BSc (*Biology and Physics*)

Social Science:
Mrs K Haresign, BA (*Economics*)
Miss K Purewal, BSc (*Psychology* and *Sociology*)

Special Educational Needs and Disabilities Coordinator:
Mrs P Oaten, MA

Highly Able Coordinator:
Mrs K Penney, BA

Head of House:
Mrs E Bott, BA

Duke of Edinburgh's Award/Adventure Service Challenge/ Outdoor Education:
Miss S Watson, BA

School Bursar: Mrs E J Mackay, AAT
Accountant: Mrs K Allen, BA, FCA
Finance Officer: Mrs J Garner, AAT
Headmaster's PA and School Administrator: Mrs I Evans
Admissions Officer: Mrs L Jaiya, BEd
Admin Officer: Mrs K Kotadia
Examinations Officer: Mrs Y Chan
Head of Marketing and Admissions: Ms A Costello, BA, MSc, PG Dip CIM
Librarian: Mrs S Timms
ICT Network Manager: Mr A Collins
IT Technician: Mr R Rai
School Nurse: Mrs E Powdrill, BSc, Dip HE
Laboratory Technician: Miss C Baylis, MSc, BSc
Site Manager: Mr D Parmar
Caretakers: Mr G Neary, Mr M Panter
Groundsman: Mr P Dunn

Visiting Staff:
Mrs H Barwell (*Dance*)
Mrs W Boswell (*Piano*)
Mr N Bott, BA (*Drums, Electric Guitar*)
Ms J Bound (*Singing*)
Mrs J Bound, GBSM (*Piano*)
Mrs S Griffiths (*Oboe*)
Mrs K Loomes, FIDTA (*Ballet*)
Ms A Mee (*Violin*)
Mr J Pagett, BA (*Guitar*)
Mrs C Pitchford, LRAM (*Violin*)
Miss E Stanier, BA (*Speech & Drama*)
Miss C Sullivan, BA (*Speech & Drama*)
Mr M Wells (*Taekwondo*)

Junior Department:

Head of Department: Mrs S J Davies, BA Ed
Assistant Head: Mrs P Gascoigne, BA
Early Years Coordinator: Mrs N Weller, BSc, PGCE

Class Teachers:
Y5: Mrs C Dryland, BA
Y4: Mrs L Walton, BSc, PGCE
Y3: Mrs P Gascoigne, BA (*and Junior PE Coordinator*)
Y2: Mrs S Neuberg, BA
Y1: Miss E Stell, BA
YR: Mrs N Weller, BSc, PGCE
YF: Mrs J Jethwa, NVQ5

Part time:
Miss S Williams, BEd

EYFS:
Mrs L Boyer, NNEB
Mrs L Dunn

Learning Support Assistants:
Mrs R Dye
Mrs N Sturmey, NVQ5

Administrator: Mrs M Singh, NVQ

Loughborough High School

Burton Walks, Loughborough, Leicestershire LE11 2DU

Tel: 01509 212348
email: high.office@lsf.org
website: www.lsf.org/high
Twitter: @LboroHigh
Facebook: @LboroHigh
Instagram: @LboroHigh
LinkedIn: @loughborough-schools-foundation

Loughborough High School, one of the oldest girls' grammar schools in England, is part of the Loughborough Schools Foundation, a foundation of four schools comprising: Fairfield Prep School (boys and girls 3–11), Loughborough Grammar School (boys 10–18), Loughborough Amherst School (boys and girls 4–18) and Loughborough High School (girls 11–18). The schools operate under one governing body and are situated on two neighbouring campuses in the town. The Foundation also includes The Loughborough Nursery for children from 6 weeks to 4 years.

Loughborough High School is an 11 to 18 school of approximately 550 day girls with a large Sixth Form. Established in 1850, the School is located on a delightful 46-acre site close to the town centre with many first-rate facilities, which are being added to and improved continuously.

We have an excellent reputation for our academic, cultural and sporting achievements, and for the quality of our pastoral care. Pupils are encouraged to be kind, adaptable and resourceful individuals and are presented with opportunities that enable them to become the best version of themselves.

Since we are a comparatively small school, we are able to know our pupils as individuals and this leads to a strong community spirit. In providing a strong academic education

in a disciplined atmosphere we hope to enable each girl ultimately to enter the career of her choice. We believe that our academic curriculum and extra-curricular activities nurture our pupils and encourage them to become active citizens of a modern world.

Further details about the school can be obtained by contacting the school's Registrar.

School Curriculum. Applied Science, Art, Biology, Business, Chemistry, Classical Civilisation, Computer Studies, Drama, Economics, English, French, Games (hockey, netball, tennis, rounders and athletics), Geography, German, Greek, Gymnastics, History, History of Art, Latin, Mathematics, Modern Dance, Music, Physical Education, Physics, Politics, Religious Studies, Sociology, Spanish, Food, ICT, Psychology and Theatre Studies. Careful note is taken of the National Curriculum with additional subjects included within the curriculum to provide breadth and depth.

Fees per term (2021–2022). £4,640–£4,735. Music (individual instrumental lessons): £247.50 (for 10 lessons).

Scholarships and Bursaries.

Academic Awards: The Governors offer a number of awards at 11+ which are made on academic merit. All candidates are considered for these awards without the need for any further application.

Music Awards: Music Scholarships are available to musically promising and talented pupils who are successful in the Entrance Examinations. Auditions are held around the time of the Entrance Examinations.

Bursaries: Means-tested Foundation Bursaries of up to 100% remission of tuition fees are available. These awards are normally made only to those entering at 11+ and 16+.

Further details of all these awards are available from the School.

Charitable status. Loughborough Schools Foundation is a Registered Charity, number 1081765, and a Company Limited by Guarantee, registered in England, number 4038033. Registered Office: 3 Burton Walks, Loughborough, Leics LE11 2DU.

Chairman: Admiral Sir Trevor Soar, KCB, OBE, DEng Hon, FCMI

Head: **Dr F Miles**, BA Hons Cambridge, MBBS King's College London

Senior Leadership Team:
Senior Deputy Head: Mr S Thompson, GRSM Hons, LRAM, ARAM, MBA London
Deputy Head (Academic): Dr S Reid, BA Hons Durham, MA Bristol, PhD Huddersfield
Assistant Head (Staffing and Professional Development): Mrs L Simpkin, BA Hons Leicester
Assistant Head (Pastoral): Miss V Standring, BSc Hons, MSc Chester
Assistant Head (Co-curricular): Mr C Nicholls, BA, Hons Liverpool
Director of Sixth Form: Mr J Travis, BSc Hons Leeds

Manchester High School for Girls

Grangethorpe Road, Manchester M14 6HS

Tel:	0161 224 0447
email:	administration@mhsg.manchester.sch.uk
website:	www.manchesterhigh.co.uk
Twitter:	@ManHighGirls
Facebook:	@ManHighGirls
Instagram:	@manhighgirls
LinkedIn:	/school/manhighgirls

Established in 1874, Manchester High School for Girls (MHSG) has a long and proud history of educating women who have gone on to change the world.

Its alumnae include the famous suffragette sisters, Sylvia, Christabel and Adele Pankhurst, through to present-day business leaders such as Nicola Mendelsohn, Vice-President of Facebook EMEA, and Clara Freeman, the first female Executive Director of Marks and Spencer.

As a 'through' school, for girls aged 4–18, Manchester High enables pupils to enjoy a seamless and settled education from their infant years through to the early days of adulthood. Whatever stage of school life they are at, students find Manchester High a vibrant and stimulating environment, where their classmates, not just the teachers, support and encourage them.

The School is committed to developing fulfilled and balanced individuals through diverse extra-curricular activities, and exceptional Wellbeing and Futures programmes.

Girls benefit from a wide and varied learning experience that is full of opportunity, and they are challenged and supported to achieve their personal best. This is a testament to the school's public examination results which are, year on year, some of the best in the country.

At MHSG, artistic and sporting talents are nurtured and students enjoy a diverse range of extracurricular activities. These are complemented by superb modern facilities which include a state-of-the-art Sixth Form Centre with lecture theatre, common room and study area, a sports complex, a fitness suite, a dance studio, all-weather sports pitches, a multi-purpose auditorium, a drama studio and a purpose-built Music House. Instrumental and Speech & Drama lessons are optional extras.

Highly skilled and committed staff strive to ensure that every MHSG student leaves the School a well-educated young woman, with highly-developed interpersonal skills and a broad range of interests. The School encourages girls to respect themselves and others; developing responsible global citizens who have a positive impact on the world.

Students at Manchester High come from a wide range of backgrounds and this rich social and cultural mix gives the School a warm and friendly feel. The girls learn about the importance of social responsibility with charity, voluntary and community work strongly encouraged.

Entry to the Reception class is by assessment while an entrance examination is set for the Juniors and Year 7. From time to time vacancies in other year groups can become available, but the main entry levels are at ages 4, 11 and 16. Sixth Form assessment is by interview and GCSE qualifications.

MHSG is committed to providing education to academically gifted girls regardless of circumstance. In the Senior School financial assistance is offered through a limited number of part or full means-tested bursaries. One or more scholarships may be awarded for excellence in performance in the entrance tests taken at the age of 10 or 11 for admission to the Senior School in September. Such scholarships will be awarded on merit only, not on the basis of parental income, and will provide part remission of fees. Music, Sports and Dance scholarships are also available.

Further details and a prospectus are available from the Registrar.

The Reports of the ISI Inspections from 2016 and 2019 can be viewed on the School's website.

Fees per term (2021–2022). Seniors £4,200, Juniors £3,130, Infants £3,080

Charitable status. Manchester High School for Girls is a charitable company limited by guarantee, Registered Charity, number 1164323, Company number 9665070. The aim of the charity is the provision and conduct in Manchester of a day school for girls.

Chair of Governors: Lady R Cooper, OBE, PhD

Head Mistress: Mrs H F Jeys, BA, PGCE

Senior Leadership Team:
Mrs A P Goddard, BA, PGCE (*Deputy Head*, *Pastoral*)
Ms J L Hodson, MA, PGCE (*Deputy Head*, *Teaching and Learning*)
Mrs S Norton, BA, MA, PGCE (*Assistant Head*, *Director of Sixth Form Studies*)
Mrs S Gibbons, BA, PGCE, NPQH (*Head of Preparatory Department*)
Mr J P Moran, FCCA (*Bursar*)
Mrs L Barnwell (*Director of Development & Marketing*)

Manor House School, Bookham

Manor House Lane
Little Bookham, Leatherhead, Surrey KT23 4EN

Tel:	01372 457077
email:	admissions@manorhouseschool.org
	admin@manorhouseschool.org
website:	www.manorhouseschool.org
Twitter:	@ManorHseSchool
Facebook:	@manorhousesch
Instagram:	@manorhouseschool_bookham
LinkedIn:	/school/manor-house-school-bookham

Motto: "To Love is to Live."

Established in 1920, Manor House School, Bookham is an independent (private) school for girls aged 4–16 with a co-educational (boys and girls) nursery. A member of the GSA (Girls' Schools Association), Manor House School is a smaller, nurturing through-school delivering great academic results alongside a thriving extra/co-curricular programme. For more information on recent academic results, please visit www.manorhouseschool.org/academic-results

Seven school values form the foundations of school life: Academic Excellence, A Love of Learning, Happy and Healthy, Individual Challenge, Creative and Collaborative,

Unforgettable Experiences and Future Leaders. The school motto 'To Love is to Live' was chosen in 1921 by the Bishop of Plymouth, Dr Masterman, who was a close friend of one of the school's original founders.

Manor House pupils enjoy high levels of success across academic subjects as well as Sport (boasting some future world-class soccer players, cyclists, triathletes and tennis stars in its midst) and the creative and expressive arts, with additional music, singing and drama lessons a popular choice. An extensive co-curricular enrichment programme provides clubs and activities every term for every student to enjoy.

Facilities include an award-winning Nursery, Wellbeing Centre, Forest School, a large indoor hall which hosts sporting events and professional level theatre productions, an outdoor swimming pool, a Tennis Academy, netball courts and purpose-built science blocks.

Admission at Year 3 and Year 7 is by the School's own Entrance Examinations. Other main entry points are at Reception Class, although the school welcomes mid-year applications to other entry years, subject to the availability of places. Selection is determined by successful completion of an age-appropriate taster and assessment day. Offers are made following the outcome of this process at the discretion of the Headteacher.

Academic, Art, Drama, Music and Sport Scholarships are awarded at Year 7 and Academic Scholarships at Year 3.

All Scholarships are awarded based on performance in the Entrance Examinations (preceding September entry) and attendance or submissions at our Scholarship Day. For an application pack, please contact: admissions@ manorhouseschool.org.

Means-tested bursaries may also be applied for and further details are available from bursar@manorhouseschool.org

Fees per term (2021–2022). £3,249–£6,105.

Further details can be found at www.manorhouse school.org/admissions/fees

Charitable status. Manor House School is a Registered Charity, number 312063. It exists for the promotion of children's education according to their academic, social, sporting and musical abilities.

Open Mornings are typically in October, February and May subject to social distancing guidelines or visit our Virtual Open Day at www.manorhouseschool.org/virtual-open-day.

Email: admissions@manorhouseschool.org and visit www.manorhouseschool.org for details of local minibus services.

Senior Leadership Team:

Headteacher: **Ms T Fantham**, BA Hons, MA, NPQH

Deputy Head: Mr S Hillier, BSc Hons, PGCE, NPQH
Director of Admissions and Marketing: Mrs K McSweeney, BA Hons
Bursar: Mr A Ellison, MSP, PRINCE2, IOSH
Head of Key Stage 4: Mrs T Williams, BA Hons, PGCE
Head of Key Stage 3: Mrs R Waterhouse, BSc Hons, PGCE, MA Ed
Head of Key Stage 2: Mrs H Redward, BSc Hons, QTS
Head of Early Years and Key Stage 1: Mrs Y Ferrey, BA Hons, PGCE, EYPS, NNEB

For a full staff list please visit www.manorhouseschool.org/about-us

The Marist School – Senior Phase

Kings Road, Sunninghill, Ascot, Berkshire SL5 7PS

Tel: 01344 624291
email: admissions@themarist.com
website: www.themarist.com
Twitter: @TheMaristSchool
Facebook: @TheMaristSchool
Instagram: @themaristschool

Independent Day School for Girls aged 11–18 founded in 1870 by The Marist Sisters. The school has been at the current site since 1947 and is set in 55 acres of private woodland in the village of Sunninghill near Ascot.

Number of Pupils. 285 girls.

Mission Statement. The school mission statement "Living life in all its fullness", seeks to realise the unique potential of each student rooted in our core Marist values: Simplicity, Love of Work, Presence, Family Spirit and In Mary's Way.

Statement of Aims

• Create a distinctive and vibrant community that promotes academic excellence within an ethos of strong values.

• Create confident, happy young adults ready for success.

• Provide an environment where pupils develop the voice to challenge misconceptions and the confidence to shape the world in which they live.

• Provide a broad and balanced curriculum which develops a life-long love of learning and a commitment to aspirational goals.

This is in line with the overall ethos of The Marist order which has a worldwide presence, providing a truly international dimension to a girl's education.

Facilities. Indoor swimming pool, Multi-purpose Sports Hall, dedicated Sixth Form suite, comprehensive ICT suite, Music and Drama block, Music Recording Studio, Language Laboratory, Ceramics Studio & Darkroom, AstroTurf Multi-Sports Surface and Learning Resource Centre.

Academic Curriculum. Art, Biology, Business Studies, Classical Civilisation, Chemistry, Computing, Drama/Theatre Studies, Economics, English, Extended Project Qualification, Food & Nutrition, French, Geography, Government & Politics, History, Latin, Mathematics (also Pure & Mechanics, Pure, Statistics, Pure & Statistics), Music, Personal, Social & Health Education, PE, Photography, Philosophy & Ethics, Physics, Psychology, RE, Science, Spanish and Textiles.

Sixth Form. The school offers a total of 24 subjects at A Level. While the majority of students take 3 A Levels, it may be possible for some students to take 4 A Levels if appropriate.

Extracurricular Activities. All pupils are actively encouraged to take part in the huge wealth of activities on offer including sports, drama, computing, orchestra, choir, STEM, and a whole variety of subject-based clubs and activities. Please check the school website for up-to-date lists.

Results. 2021: 86% A*–A grades achieved; GCSE: 75% 9–7 grades achieved.

Admission. Entrance examination tests in (1) Mathematics (2) English Comprehension & Creative Writing Paper and (3) CEM Verbal and Non-Verbal Reasoning Paper, (4) Personal Portfolio, (5) Interview with the Principal and (6) Reference from Primary/Preparatory Headteacher.

Sixth Form Entry. All students will need to achieve a minimum of 8 GCSEs at grades 9–5 including English and Maths. For their chosen A Level subjects, students should achieve grades 9–6 in subjects chosen AND related subjects.

Fees per term (2021–2022). £5,465 (Years 7–9), £5,245 (Years 10–13). Extra benefits: Generous sibling discount scheme (4th and any subsequent children free), after school care provided.

Scholarships. Year 7 and Sixth Form Academic, Art, Drama, Music and Sport scholarships are available.

Preparatory School. The Preparatory Phase of The Marist School is on the same campus which is for girls aged 2–11 and boys aged 2–4. *(For further details, see The Marist School – Preparatory Phase entry in the IAPS section.)*

Affiliations. Girls' Schools Association (GSA), Catholic Independent Schools Conference (CISC), Silver Artsmark, Eco-Schools award and Healthy School.

Charitable status. The Marist School is a Registered Charity, number 225485. The principal aims and activities of The Marist School are religious and charitable and specifically to provide education by way of an independent day school for girls between the ages of 2 and 18 and boys aged 2–4.

Chair of Governors: Mrs Ann Nash

Principal: **Mrs Joanne Smith**, BA Hons Oxford Brookes, PGCE Brunel

Heads of Department:
Art: Mrs R Ellwood
Classics: Mr J Walker
Drama: Miss A Messina
Economics/Business Studies: Miss S Knight
English: Mrs L Lutton
Food Technology: Mrs M Holloway
Geography: Mr E de Grande
History: Mr A Baker
Information Technology: Miss C Broderick
Mathematics: Miss C Vardon
Modern Foreign Languages: Mrs R Beckh
Music: Mrs L Crozier
Psychology: Mrs J Cope
Physical Education: Mrs J Bishopp
Religious Education: Miss L Vaughan-Neil
Science: Mrs A Costello

Head of Sixth Form: Mrs H Major

Marymount London

George Road, Kingston-upon-Thames, Surrey KT2 7PE

Tel: 020 8949 0571
email: admissions@marymountlondon.com
website: www.marymountlondon.com
Facebook: @MMILondon

Marymount London is an independent, day and boarding school for girls which nurtures the limitless potential of curious, motivated students (ages 11 to 18) of diverse faiths and backgrounds. Founded in 1955 through the charism of the Religious of the Sacred Heart of Mary (RSHM), the School proudly stands as the first all-girls' school in the United Kingdom to adopt the International Baccalaureate curriculum (IB MYP and Diploma), where girls are inspired to learn in a creative, collaborative, interdisciplinary, and exploratory environment.

Students are empowered to build their confidence, leadership skills, and sense of self on a seven acre garden campus conveniently located just twelve miles from Central London. The campus offers outstanding facilities, including a STEAM Hub, sports hall, dance studio, modern dining hall, and tennis courts. The School's challenging academic program is based on the International Baccalaureate curricula:

- The Middle Years Programme (MYP), offered in Grades 6 to 10, encourages students to draw meaningful connections between eight broad and varied subject groups. With a central focus on the development of conceptual understanding and effective approaches to learning (ATL) skills, the MYP is a student-centred, inquiry-based programme rooted in interdisciplinary learning.

- The International Baccalaureate Diploma Programme (DP) for Grades 11 and 12 builds on the strong foundation of the MYP, leading to independent research opportunities as well as exceptional university placement within the UK and around the world.

- Marymount's 2021 results are exceptional: 100% pass rate and an average of 38.22 points; the School's bespoke, student-centred college counselling programme leads to successful placements in top universities in the UK and around the world.

Marymount's holistic approach to learning delivers a well-rounded education that encourages critical thinking, intercultural understanding, and participation in a wide array of interesting extracurricular offerings. Robust transport service from London/surrounding areas and boarding options (full, weekly, and flexi) are available.

Marymount offers year-round rolling admission as space allows. The admissions section of the website, featuring an online application portal, provides all of the information necessary to get started. Applicant families are encouraged to learn more about the School's strong tradition of excellence by exploring the website and making contact with the Admissions team by phone/email.

Headmistress: **Mrs Margaret Giblin**, BA St Patrick's Pontifical University, Ireland, Higher Diploma in Teaching National University of Ireland, MA St Mary's Twickenham

Mr Alan Fernandes, MBA Oxford Brookes, BSc St Mary's Twickenham

Mr Nicholas Marcou, BA Hons York, PGCE Roehampton, MA St Mary's Twickenham

Ms Annah Langan, MA Hons Glasgow, MA St Mary's Twickenham, PGCE Roehampton

Miss Adriana Williams, MSc Warwick

Ms Victoria Mast, BA Hons Durham, PGCE Buckingham

Admissions and Communications Team:

Ms Hannah Connell, BA Nottingham, MA University of the Arts London

Mrs Joy Duval-Koenig, BA American University of Paris, MSc Boston

Miss Juliette Bloom, MA Edinburgh, MSc Bath

Heads of Departments:

Ms Momoko Aoe, MA Master of Education, Curriculum & Teaching, Boston, BA Health & Exercise Science/ Teaching, New Jersey

Mr João Barroca, BSc Hons Portugal, MBA Spain

Mr Jonathan Bridger, BA Hons Sussex, PGCE with QTS

Mrs Emma Burke, BA Hons, PGCE St Mary's Twickenham

Mr Stephen Clarke, MA Hons, PGCE Glasgow, TESOL

Dr Sandra Forrest, BA Denison, US, MA NYU, PGCPSE Open

Ms Dolores García-Suárez, BA Spain, MA King's, London

Ms Lauren Gregory, BA Mississippi, USA, MEd North Texas, USA

Mr George Marshall, MA Cantab, MSc Kings College, QTS, PGDip

Mr Jim Robertson, BA Hons Kingston, QTS

Ms Helen Szymczak, BA Dramatic Art Hons AFDA South Africa, ATCL, MA London

Residential Houseparents:

Mrs Paula Horton (*Head of Boarding*)

Mrs Annabel Plumridge, PGCE Secondary Science, BSc Biochemistry Southampton

Mayfield School

The Old Palace, Mayfield, East Sussex TN20 6PH

Tel: 01435 874623 (Headmistress and Secretary)
            01435 874600 (School)
            01435 874642 (Admissions)
email: enquiry@mayfieldgirls.org
website: www.mayfieldgirls.org
Twitter: @mayfieldgirls
Facebook: @mayfieldgirls
Instagram: @mayfieldschool

Mayfield is a leading independent boarding and day school for girls aged 11 to 18 set in the beautiful, and easily accessible, Sussex countryside less than an hour from central London. Awarded the top grade of "excellent" by the Independent Schools Inspectorate and described by Country Life as "one of the finest schools in the land", a Mayfield education combines academic rigour, breadth of opportunity and a strong sense of community. The School has an excellent academic record, exceptional pastoral care and an extensive co-curricular programme. Individuality, independence of thought and intellectual curiosity are nurtured and the School encourages equally the intellectual, creative, physical, emotional and spiritual development of each pupil.

Mayfield is successful in unlocking and developing the unique potential and talent of each girl. Every pupil is accepted for who she is and is instilled with the confidence to find her strengths, wherever they may lie, and develop them in an inspiring and nurturing environment. Mayfield's ethos reflects its Catholic foundation and encourages integrity, initiative, respect and a commitment to be the best you can be within a vibrant and inclusive community, which welcomes all. Mayfield is a lively, happy and successful School and Mayfield girls develop a lifelong love of learning, a range of transferable skills that will prepare them for their future, and friendships that will last a lifetime.

Founded in 1872 by Cornelia Connelly and her Society of the Holy Child Jesus, the School continues to fulfil its Founder's vision to educate young women to respond to the needs of the age. This is achieved through an innovative and stimulating curriculum, an extensive range of co-curricular opportunities and a strong and supportive pastoral foundation.

Curriculum. Mayfield's curriculum, both within taught lessons and beyond them, is designed to create an environment in which questioning, reflection, risk-taking and the freedom to learn from mistakes are all encouraged. Inspirational teaching, from highly-qualified and dedicated staff, enables girls to flourish and excel, reflecting the equal value placed on every subject and the breadth of curriculum offered. In Years 7, 8 and 9 pupils enjoy a broad curriculum with core subjects – English, Maths, the sciences, Religious Studies, Geography, History, Physical Education and ICT – complemented with a variety of languages and lessons in Art, Music, Drama, Textiles (to Year 9), Ceramics and Food and Nutrition. In Lower School (Years 7 and 8) the curriculum is structured within a Lower School Diploma programme. This provides the opportunity for girls in Year 7 and 8 to develop soft skills, such as teamwork, problem solving and resilience, alongside their academic education. Time each week is also specifically dedicated to the spiritual and pastoral education of the girls in the form of assemblies, liturgies and Mayfield's innovative Life Skills Programme.

To ensure an excellent basis for further study and a wide variety of career options, all pupils in Years 10 and 11 follow a compulsory common core, comprising English Language and English Literature, Mathematics, at least one language, Religious Studies and Science (separate or trilogy). Most pupils study 10 subjects at GCSE, selecting from a wide range of optional subjects including Art & Design, Drama, Geography, History, Greek, Latin and Spanish. During Year 10, all pupils also study for an ICT qualification in effective IT user skills (BCS Level 2 Certificate).

Sport is also an integral part of the timetable. Options range from traditional sports including Hockey and Netball, Cricket and Tennis to other activities including Water Polo, Fitness Room, Circuit Training, Volleyball and Badminton. In addition, there are clubs in Hockey, Netball, Swimming, Dance, Tennis, Athletics and Football.

The guiding principles of Sixth Form study (Years 12 and 13) at Mayfield continue to be breadth and depth and it is not unusual for girls to combine Mathematics and Science subjects (consistently the most popular choices at A Level) with Ceramics, Art or a language. Pupils choose up to four A Levels from a wide selection of over 30 options. In addition, the Sixth Form benefits from the School's Enrichment Programme, enabling girls to develop valuable life and critical thinking skills from a wide variety of options, including Art, Music and Revolution; Photography and Photoshop; Farming and Land Management; Certificate in Culinary Skills and The Art of Effective Communication. Pupils also have the opportunity to complete an Extended Project Qualification (EPQ) on a topic of their choice, which is excellent preparation for higher education. The School's state-of-the-art Sixth Form Centre is an inspirational learning space, with an individual study area allocated to each pupil, dedicated group work spaces and excellent resources, providing a first-rate transition to university.

Mayfield has an excellent record of outstanding examination results and girls invariably perform well above expectation, however, the School's focus is not exclusively to this end and it encourages a balanced approach to academic studies and the development of the whole person.

Mayfield girls receive excellent careers advice and guidance throughout their school career as an integral part of the curriculum and this prepares them very well to make excellent, informed choices. Almost all pupils progress to higher education, the vast majority to Russell Group universities including Oxbridge and, increasingly, to overseas universities particularly in the USA and Europe. They study a wide variety of subjects, from Architecture to Zoology, with a regular stream of engineers, medics and vets, lawyers and economists. The School has a highly engaged alumnae community throughout the world, which is a valued support network for advice on further study and career options.

Co-curricular Activities. An extensive co-curricular provision at Mayfield accompanies learning in the classroom and girls are positively encouraged to try new activities, ranging from Riding (in the School's first class equestrian centre), Fencing and Kick Boxing to Textiles, Debating and Journalism, Cricket, Astronomy and Dance. The School's 'Actions Not Words' Programme, reflecting Mayfield's motto and incorporating the Duke of Edinburgh's Award scheme, provides opportunities to be involved in service in both the local community and overseas, ensuring that faith in action continues to be an important part of Mayfield life.

There are significant opportunities to become involved in the creative and performing arts. Mayfield has outstanding Arts, Ceramics and Textiles facilities and teaching and has produced award-winning artists. Pupils benefit from a variety of exhibitions and workshops throughout the year.

Mayfield has an impressive reputation for music and, with a significant number of girls learning a musical instrument, there are opportunities to perform in the School Orchestra and in the many ensembles. In addition, Mayfield's acclaimed school choir, Schola Cantorum, performs regularly in prestigious venues in the UK and internationally, including the Vatican, Westminster Cathedral, St Paul's Cathedral and Westminster Abbey.

Pupils also have the opportunity to develop their drama skills performing in the wide variety of drama productions throughout the year, together with Drama Club, LAMDA and theatre workshops.

Admissions. The main entry points are at 11+, 13+ and 16+, with applications considered for occasional places in other years. Entry at 11+ is based on the ISEB Common Pre-Test, and 13+ and 16+ entry is based on the School's own Entrance Assessments.

Registration fee: £150

Fees per term (2021–2022). Full Boarders £12,250, Day girls £7,750.

Scholarships and Bursaries. Academic Scholarships and Creative Arts, Drama, Dance, Music, Sport and Riding Scholarships are available for entry at 11+, 13+ and 16+. Scholars are identified through a programme of examination and assessment and are expected to show a high degree of aptitude in their chosen discipline. Scholarships are offered on merit.

Means-tested bursaries up to 100% of the cost of a day or boarding place are available.

Charitable status. Mayfield School is a Registered Charity, number 1047503. It exists to provide education for girls in keeping with its Catholic foundation.

Governors:
Chairman: Lady Davies of Stamford, MA Oxon, MBA
Deputy Chairman and Chairman of Governance Committee: Dr Christopher Storr, KSG, MA, PhD
Deputy Chairman and Chairman of Finance and General Purposes Committee: Mr Chris Buxton, BA, ACA
Chairman of Education Committee: Mrs Marion McGovern, BA, Cert Ed
Chairman of Ethos Committee: Dr Rhona Lewis, MA, PhD
Miss Julia Bowden, BA, MBA, MA Oxon, PGCE
Mrs Angela Drew, BA, PGCE, MBA
Mr Andrew Larsson, MA Cantab, MEng, MCISI
Mrs Maureen Martin, BA, PGCE
Mrs Marlane Mellor, BSc, ACMA
Mr Tim Reid, LLB
Mrs Karen Sorab, OBE
Mrs Caroline Wood, BSc
Fr Dominic

***Headmistress*: Miss A M Beary**, MA, MPhil Cantab, PGCE

Deputy Head (*Pastoral & Boarding*): Mrs N C Green, BA, MA, PGCE, MBA

Senior Managers:
Director of Studies: Mrs A R Bunce, BSc, PGCE
Bursar: Mr R Gordon, MA, MBA
Head of Sixth Form: Mr J Doy, BA, PGCE
Head of Middle School: Mrs J M Stone, BSc, MSc, GTTP
Head of Lower School: Mrs C Baker, BSc, PGCE
Director of Development: Mrs C A Saint, BA Dublin, PG Dip

Teaching staff:
* Head of Department

Art:
*Miss J Thackray, BA, PGCE
Miss J Alcaraz, BA Textile Design, CELTA, QTS
Miss H Oliver, BA
Mrs A Sivyour, BA, PGCE
Mrs J Day, BA, PGCE

Ceramics:
*Mr T Rees-Moorlah, BA, PGCE, QTS
Mrs Y McFadyean, BA
Mr D Stafford, BA 3D Design Ceramics, MA Ceramics

Classics:
*Mrs D Downing, BA, MA
Mrs E Aherne, MA, BA Oxon

Mrs G Fytili, BA, MA
Mr S Oliver, BA, MLitt, PGCE

Digital Literacy & Technology:
*Mrs L Bartlett, BA Hons, QTS, Dip RSA (*Years 7–10*)
Mrs J Jones, BA, QTS

Drama & Theatre Studies:
*Mrs S Gerstmeyer, BA, GTP, QTS
Mr D Smith, BA, PGCE
Miss S Watikss, BA, CertEd, MA

Economics & Business Studies:
*Mrs A Cox, BSc, PGCE

English:
*Miss J Staunton, BA, MPhil, PGCE
Mr J Doy, BA, PGCE
Mrs J Leslie, BA, PGCE
Mrs L Parrett, BA, PGCE, MSc
Mrs L Misiewicz, MA Oxon, MA
Ms E Bell, BA, PGCE

Food & Nutrition:
*Mrs S Smeaton, BSc Hons, PGCE, DipSEN
Mrs C Davies, BEd, AFH Cert, Cert Boarding Education

Geography:
*Mr S Gough, BSc, PGCE
Mrs V Williams, BA, MA, MSc, PGCE, QTS
Mrs F Morris, BEd

History:
*Mr D Warren, BA, PGCE
Mr J Davis, BA, MA, MSc, ARHistS, PGCE, Dip
   Counselling, MBACP
Mrs L Lawson, BA, PGCE
Miss I Ewing, BA, PGCE

History of Art:
*Dr J Weddell, BA Arch Hons, MA, PhD
Mr J Davis, BA, MA, MSc, ARHistS, PGCE, Dip
   Counselling, MBACP

International English:
*Mrs K Kilvington, BA, MA Oxon, MSc, DipTEFLA
Mrs C Gibson, BA, CELTA
Mrs A Maimi, BA, CELTA, QTS
Miss M Whittle, BA, MA PGCE, DELTA

Learning Support:
*Mrs E Martin, BA, PGCert, PAPAA, MA
Ms M Curran, BEd, PGDip Dyslexia, PGDip Special
   Needs, PGAdv Cert Language Impairment
Dr M-S Reijers, PhD, MSc
Miss M Whittle, BA, MA, PGCE, DELTA
Mrs N Lancaster, BSc, PGCert Direct Learning

Librarians:
Mrs J Gabriel, BA, MA
Miss P Kotesovska, BSc, CELTA

Mathematics:
*Ms A Demetriou, BSc, PGCE
Mr W Clarke, BSc, PGCE
Mrs S Howie, BSc, PGCE (*Deputy Head of Department*)
Mrs L Motoc, BSc, PGCE
Mrs J Stone, BSc, MSc, PGCE
Mr H M Whittle, BSc
Mr J Marshall, MPhys
Mrs J Carpinato, BEng

Modern Languages:
Mrs R Testa, BA, PGCE (*Head of French*)
Mrs M Criado, BA, PGCE (*Head of Spanish*)
Mrs A Boyle, BA
Mrs E Edwards, BA, PGCE
Mrs A Fernandez, BA, CAP
Mrs A, Maimi, BA, CELTA, QTS
Mrs N, Maslova PGCE
Mlle C Richard, BA, MA, MA, PGCE
Miss J Ruival

Music:
*Dr M J C Ward, MA Cantab, MPhil, PhD (*Director of
   Music*)
Mrs L Le Riche, ATCL, BMus, MMus, PGCE
Mr M Dowgan, BMus, DipArts, PGCE
plus c.20 visiting music teachers

Physical Education:
*Mrs G Fletcher, BA, MA, PGCE (*Director of Sport*)
Miss S Auer, BA, PGCE
Mrs C Baker, BSc, PGCE
Miss I Jones, BSc
Mrs J Jones, BA, QTS
Mrs F Morris, BEd
Miss E Nixon, BA, PGCE
Miss E Starr, BSc
Mrs P Whitby, BA, QTS

Politics:
*Mr P Ferguson, BA, PGCE

Psychology:
*Miss C Holmes, BA, PGCE, MSc

Religious Studies:
*Mrs G McGovern, BA, MA, PGCE
Mrs C Kimber, BA, PGCE, QTS
Mr S Oliver, BA, MLitt, PGCE
Mr C Pierce, BA, PGCE
Mrs K Sunderland, BRelSc, Cert Ed, QTS

Riding:
Miss J Barker, BEd, BHSII J, CertEd (*Director of Riding*)

Sciences:
Mr M Rich, MA, PGCE (*Head of Biology*)
Mrs C Baker, BSc, PGCE
Mr R Cowan, MA Oxon, PGCE, PGCES (*Head of
   Chemistry*)
Mrs A Bunce, BSc, PGCE
Dr D Corvan, BSc, PGCE, MSc, PhD (*Head of Physics*)
Mrs R Davies, BSc, PGCE
Miss S Gilpin MSCi
Miss R Jackson, BSc Dunelm, PGCE
Mr S Senior, BSc, PGCE
Ms E Garcia Claramonte, BSc, PGCE
Mr D Turner, MChem, PhD, PGCE

Textiles:
*Mrs T Budden, Dip Fashion Design & Construction
Miss J Alcaraz, BA Textile Design, CELTA, QTS

Technicians:
Mrs S Chapman (*Food & Nutrition*)
Miss H Oliver, BA (*Art*)
Mr A Smith (*Physics*)
Mrs H Robertson (*Textiles*)
Mr D Stafford (*Ceramics*)
Mrs E Furlong (*Chemistry*)
Miss M Wolmarans (*Biology*)

Careers Coordinator: Mrs A C Glubb, BA, CIM DipM,
PGCE, OCN Level 3 Dyslexia, QCF Level 4 Diploma
Career Info & Advice, Level 6 Cert Career Leadership
Examinations Officer: Mr A Welford
Gifted & Talented Coordinator: Mrs K Kilvington, BA,
MA Oxon, MSc, DipTEFLA
STEM Coordinator: Mrs R Davies, BSc, PGCE

Housemistresses and Pastoral Staff:

Leeds House (*Years 7 and 8*):
Miss P Kotesovska, BSc, CELTA (*Housemistress*)
Miss J Alcaraz, BA, CELTA, QTS (*Assistant
Housemistress*)

St Gabriel's House (*Years 9 and 10*):
Mrs P Whitby, BA QTS (*Housemistress*)
Mrs H Robertson (*Assistant Housemistress*)
Mrs C Jones (*Day Matron*)

St Michael's House (*Year 11*):
Mrs J Ruival (*Housemistress*)
Miss S Gilpin, MSCi (*Assistant Housemistress*)
Mrs C Jones (*Day Matron*)

St Dunstan's House (*Years 12 and 13*):
Mrs K Sunderland, BRelSc, CertEd, QTS (*Housemistress*)
Miss K McCulloch (*Assistant Housemistress*)
Mrs C Jones (*Day Matron*)

Graduate Assistants:
Miss S Qureshi
Mr J Walser
Miss M El Adel

Sixth Form:
Head: Mr J Doy BA, PGCE
Deputy Head: Mrs R Davies BSc, PGCE

Middle School:
Head: Mrs J Stone, BSc, MSc, PGCE
Year 9 Senior Tutor: Miss S Auer, BA, PGCE
Year 10 Senior Tutor: Mrs C Gibson, BA, CELTA
Year 11 Senior Tutor: Mrs A Maimi, BA, CELTA, QTS

Lower School:
Head: Mrs C Baker, BSc, PGCE
Deputy Head: Mr D Smith, BA, PGCE

Chaplaincy:
Lay Chaplain: Mr R Lavery

The Maynard School

Denmark Road, Exeter, Devon EX1 1SJ

Tel:	01392 355998
email:	admissions@maynard.co.uk
website:	www.maynard.co.uk
Twitter:	@MaynardSchool
Facebook:	@MaynardSchoolExeter
Instagram:	@maynardschoolexeter
LinkedIn:	/company/the-maynard-school

The Maynard School in Exeter is the South-West's
leading independent school for girls aged 4–18 years
(Reception–Year 13). As one of the oldest girls' schools in
the country, we pride ourselves on being experts in
educating girls. Statistically it is a proven fact that girls in

single-sex schools outperform their peers and The
Maynard's long history is testament to this success. League
tables consistently place us as one of the highest performing
schools in the South-West and our latest ISI Inspection
deemed us as 'excellent' in all five main categories.

However, a Maynard education isn't just about academic
achievement. It is about so much more; we boast numerous
individual and team champions in the sporting arena with
access to some of the best facilities available; we are proud
to offer Food & Nutrition and Textiles & Fashion classes as
a life-skill; we are one of the highest achieving schools for
music and drama in the county; we relish our timetable
packed with trips and workshops to be enjoyed by the whole
school.

We are the first and only school in Devon to be awarded
the Wellbeing in Schools Award in recognition of the sheer
breadth of provision and robustness of support that we offer
to all of our students and staff. The Maynard is a warm place
where everyone is nurtured individually and encouraged to
carve for themselves successful futures whilst creating
everlasting friendships and enduring childhood memories!

Ethos. Our vision is to be a leading school in the UK,
committed to educational excellence in a caring and happy
environment that fosters a lifelong love of learning. Our
mission is that our team of inspiring teachers will instil in
each individual the confidence to excel academically,
socially and morally. Through an educational experience
designed specifically for girls, we are able to give them the
skills and the courage to go out into the world and make a
real difference.

Numbers. There are approximately 450 day girls in the
School, of whom 100 are in the Pre-Prep and Junior School
and 100 in the Sixth Form.

School Buildings. The School is set in a leafy area of
central Exeter in Devon, five minutes from the centre of the
city. The extensive buildings include a separate Sixth Form
Centre; a purpose-built block for Science, Mathematics, and
Computing; well-equipped Food & Nutrition and Textiles
Rooms; Music and Art Rooms and a Performing Arts
Theatre which also serves as a gym, and an impressive
Sports Hall which provides full-scale indoor facilities. The
Junior School and Pre-Prep are situated within the grounds
and are fully equipped for the education of girls aged 4–11
years.

Curriculum. The curriculum is academically rigorous
and maintains a good balance between Arts and Science
subjects. English, Mathematics, the Sciences and Sport are
particular strengths; full scope is given to creative and
practical activities, as well as ICT skills. The School
prepares all girls for University, including Oxford and
Cambridge. A carefully developed programme of careers
advice, begun at 11+ and continuing through to the Sixth
Form, ensures that all pupils are individually guided in
subject options with their long-term career interests at heart.
The Maynard Aspire programme is an enrichment initiative
for high achieving students in Upper 5 (Year 11) and the
Sixth Form who are ready to develop their skills in a wider
context as they make decisions about their future career
paths.

Examinations. Candidates normally take 9 subjects at
GCSE and 3 at A Level. Students are fully prepared for
Oxford and Cambridge University Entrance.

Physical Education. Hockey (outdoor and indoor),
Netball, Badminton, Basketball, Volleyball, Fencing, Dance
and Gymnastics are offered in the winter terms; Tennis and

Rounders are played in the Summer Term. Training is given in Athletics and Swimming is part of the normal timetable for all girls during the Summer Term. Besides its excellent indoor facilities and the three hard courts in its own grounds, the School has access to a playing field a short walk away and is close to three swimming pools and an Astroturf playing area. The school has an extensive fixture programme in Netball, Hockey, Indoor Hockey, Badminton, Basketball, Tennis, Swimming, Athletics and Rounders. Teams have regularly reached national standard. In addition, The Maynard has a strong extra-curricular programme of outdoor pursuits including the Ten Tors, the Duke of Edinburgh's Award and Exmoor Challenge.

Admission. All admissions, except Pre-Prep, are subject to an Entrance Assessment graduated according to age and held in January each year for entry in the following September. Pre-Prep admissions attend a Taster Day where they are informally assessed. Entry into the Sixth Form is by interview.

Fees per term (2021–2022). Pre-Prep: Reception £2,352, Years 1–2 £2,710; Junior School: Years 3–5 £4,108; Senior School: Years 6–13 £4,910. Fees include wraparound care from 8.00am to 5.30pm. Reception fees include lunch.

There is a generous Sibling Discount Scheme.

Scholarships and the Maynard Award Programme. A range of Academic, Sport, Music and Creative Arts Scholarships are available for senior school entry at 11+, 13+ and Sixth Form. In addition, the Maynard Award Programme is a new initiative which offers opportunities to girls from all sectors of the community. Two 100% Scholarships are available for entry into our Lower 6th as part of the Programme.

Further Information. The Prospectus and Scholarship and Maynard Awards information are available from the Admissions Office. Visitors are very welcome by appointment, and tours and taster days can be arranged for girls considering the school. Email: admissions@maynard.co.uk; Tel: 01392 355998.

Old Maynardians. Email: LucyMcNally@maynard.co.uk

Charitable status. The Maynard School is a Registered Charity, number 1099027. It exists to provide quality education for girls.

Governors:
Lady Jan Stanhope (*Chair*)
Lady Emma Birkin
Mr Nick Bruce-Jones
Mrs Jane Chanot
Mr James Dart
Mr Christopher Gatherer
Mr Henry Luce
Miss Wendy Manfield
Mrs Sara Randall-Johnson
Ms Lynn Turner
Ms Sarah Witheridge
Ms Christina Walton
Ms Adele Westcott

Senior Leadership Team:

Headmistress: Miss S Dunn, BSc Hons NPQH Exeter

Head of Junior School: Mr S Smerdon, BEd Exeter
Director of Sixth Form: Mr T Hibberd, MA Cambridge
Director of Studies: Dr P Rudling, MA Cambridge, MSc, PhD Exeter

Assistant Head: Mrs C Leigh, BSc Hons Birmingham, MEd Exeter
Assistant Head: Mr M Loosemore, BA Hons Southampton (**English*)
Marketing & Communications Manager: Mrs R Board, BA Hons Warwick

Teaching Staff:

* *Head of Department*

Mrs S Bean, BA Hons Oxford (*English*)
Ms J Bellamy, BA Hons Manchester (**Drama*)
Miss A Blackwell, BA Hons, MA, LTCL Durham (*Director of Music & Performing Arts*)
Miss T Boillet (*EAL*)
Mr T Bowler, BSc Hons Exeter (*Mathematics*)
Miss A Cunningham-Johns, BA Hons Bristol, MA Cardiff, PGCS Bristol (*English*)
Miss P Daniel, BSc Hons Mathematics Lancaster, PGCE Exeter (*Mathematics Teacher*)
Mrs E Darcy (*PE*)
Mrs K Dell, BA Hons Oxford, PGCE London (*MFL*)
Mrs W Dersley, BSc Hons Open (*Mathematics*)
Mrs L Douglas, BA Rhodes, South Africa (*Geography*)
Mrs R Fabian, BSc Hons Exeter (*Physical Education*)
Mrs S Fanous, BEd Keele (**Food & Nutrition, Textiles*)
Mrs C Finnegan, BA Hons Central Saint Martins (*Food & Nutrition, Textiles*)
Mr J Friendship, BSc Hons Bristol, MBA Exeter (*ICT teacher*)
Mrs K Fry, BEd Exeter (*Junior School*)
Mrs C M Gabbitass, BSc Hons Loughborough (*Director of Sport*)
Mr A Ganley, BA Hons Nottingham (*Drama*)
Mrs C Gorrod, BA Hons Surrey (*Junior School*)
Mrs K Greenwood, BSc, PGCE Surrey (*Year 2 Teacher*)
Miss K Gwynne, MTheol St Andrews, ThM Princeton (*Religious Studies*)
Mrs M Harland, BA Hons Nottingham, PGCE Exeter (*History*)
Miss E Hartopp, BA Hons York (*English*)
Dr R Henderson, Math Hons Durham, PhD East Anglia (*Mathematics*)
Mr T Hibberd (*SLT, Director of 6th Form, Religious Studies*)
Mr M Hoile, BA Hons Winchester (*Primary Education*)
Ms A M Hurley, MA London (**Art*)
Dr L Keen, MA, PhD Exeter, MA St Andrews (**Classics*)
Mrs R Khreisheh, BA Hons Oxford (*Junior School*)
Mrs J Kingdon, BA Hons, PGCE Durham (*Year 3 Teacher*)
Mrs K Mears, BSc Hons, MA Birmingham (*Physical Education, i/c of House System*)
Mrs C Leigh, BA Hons Birmingham, PGCE, MEd Exeter (*SLT, Assistant Headteacher, Physical Education*)
Mrs D Lewis, BA Hons Cheltenham (*Careers, Exams Officer*)
Mr J Lodge, Bsc Hons Sussex (*Physics*)
Mr M Loosemore, BA Hons Southampton (**English*)
Mr I Macdonald, BSc Hons Sussex (*Chemistry, Physics*)
Mrs A Meaton, BA Ed Southampton (**Pre-Prep*)
Dr P Merisi, MPhil, PhD Exeter (**Mathematics*)
Mrs R Merritt-Biggs (*Geography*)
Mrs K Rymer BSc Hons Nottingham (*Geography*)
Mrs E Pinkerton-Smith (*Year 6 Teacher*)
Miss N Pursglove (*Biology*)
Mr P Richards LLB Southampton (*Lead Teacher Economics*)

Mr C Ridler, MA Hons Warwick (*Science)

Mrs K Riley, BEd Hons Plymouth (Reception Teacher)

Mrs A Rowley, BA Hons Liverpool (English, Head of Upper 3)

Dr P Rudling (SLT, Director of Studies, *Psychology)

Mrs L Smart, BA Hons Exeter, PGCE Oxford (French and German)

Mrs C Smith, MA Tours (*Modern Foreign Languages)

Mrs R Smith, BA Hons, PGCE (Junior Music)

Mrs K Spelman, BA Hons Oxford, MA London (Classics, History)

Miss K Stylianidou, BA Hons Greece, MA Exeter (Year 1 & 5 Teacher)

Mrs L Stanton, BA Hons Sheffield, PGCE Exeter (Spanish and French)

Mr J Tabb, BA Hons London (*Humanities)

Mrs Z Vingoe, BA Hons Manchester Metropolitan (Art)

Miss K Williamson, BSc Hons Bristol, MEd Exeter (*Geography, Deputy Head of Sixth Form)

Mr A Wood, BA Hons Exeter (Physics)

Mrs S Wood, BA Ed Exeter (Physical Education)

Mrs T Wood, BA Hons, MSci Cambridge (Natural Sciences)

Mrs V Woulfe, BSc Hons Keele (Mathematics)

Ms J York, BSc Hons Bath (Biology)

Key Support Staff:

Mrs E Bremner (Marketing Assistant)

Mrs Z Cunningham (Human Resources Advisor & PA to Headmistress)

Mrs M Davey, DipHE Exeter, BSc Hons Plymouth, BA Hons Kent (School Nurse)

Miss M Ellis (Archivist)

Mrs J Hourihan, BSc Birmingham, 2 x BA Hons Open, PgDip Information and Library Studies Robert Gordon (Librarian)

Mrs K Munro (School Registrar)

Peripatetic Staff:

Mrs F Austen (Harp)

Mrs S Barlow (Dance)

Mrs D Broomfield (Singing, Piano)

Mrs E Bucci (Netball Coach)

Mr M Cann (Piano)

Dr H Catterick (Kick-Boxing, Martial Arts Instructor)

Mr D Cottam (Guitar)

Mrs C Cox (Netball Coach)

Mrs H Edwards (Netball Coach)

Mrs N Fitzgerald (Badminton Coach)

Ms J Gall (Clarinet Teacher)

Mrs A Higgins (Piano, Bassoon, Concert Orchestra)

Miss M Hiley (Percussion)

Ms K Howard (Creation Station – after school club)

Miss A Kettlewell (Singing)

Mrs P Leonard (Speech & Drama)

Mr J Martin (Outdoor Education)

Miss M North (Piano)

Mr A Nuthall (Brass, Saxophone)

Mr T Ross (Flute)

Mr J Rycroft (Lead Tennis Coach)

Mr W Scudder (PT Instructor)

Mr T Stinton (Martial Arts)

Mrs C Thomas (Oboe)

Mrs A Tillson-Hawke (Violin, Viola)

Ms I Woollcott (Double Bass)

Mr C Worcester (Basketball Coach)

More House School

22–24 Pont Street, London SW1X 0AA

Tel: 020 7235 2855
email: registrar@morehousemail.org.uk
website: www.morehouse.org.uk
Twitter: @morehouseschool
Facebook: @morehouseschool
Instagram: @22morehouse

More House is an independent Catholic day school of 200 girls, aged 11–18. The school was founded in 1953 by the Canonesses of St Augustine; since 1969 it has been under lay management as a charitable trust.

Located in the heart of Knightsbridge in central London, the school provides an advantageous proximity to some of the city's best museums and galleries.

Aims of the School.

- To establish an environment where pupils flourish in a caring environment that recognises and cherishes each one as an individual.

- To foster an ethos of spiritual growth, not only for those within the Roman Catholic Church, but also for those who adhere to other faiths or no faith.

- To develop the spiritual, academic, and cultural potential of each pupil to the full at every stage of their school career in such a way that this development will continue throughout their life.

- To encourage intellectual curiosity and pride in achievement.

- The school expects all its members to act with integrity, to display a concern for justice, and to be sensitive to the needs of other people.

Ethos. More House is a small and happy community, in which a generous pupil to teacher ratio ensures each student is fully supported, nurturing their talents and abilities so that they may reach their full academic and personal potential.

Pupils leave More House armed not only with the qualifications they need to pursue the courses and careers of their choice, but with a confidence, composure, and grace that will stay with them and carry them through the rest of their lives.

Religious Affiliation. Although the school has a Catholic foundation, pupils of all faiths or no faith are welcome. More House provides a safe and inclusive environment that fosters mutual respect and understanding of all faiths or the absence of one.

Curriculum. The maximum class size at More House is normally sixteen. Class sizes decrease further up the school, numbering between one to ten students in A Level classes. This ensures the needs of each individual student are catered for. The school curriculum is academically rigorous and broad. In the first two years, all pupils study English, Maths, Sciences, History, Geography, Religious Studies, Art, ICT, Music, Drama, Physical Education and Enrichment. Students will study French in Year 7 and add either Spanish or German as a second language in Year 8.

The A Level courses offered at More House are varied and diverse and include Art & Design, Business & Economics, Drama & Theatre Studies, Psychology and History of Art in addition to more traditional subjects.

Further breadth of study is achieved through an enrichment programme, which includes study for the EPQ (Extended Project Qualification), Leadership & Team Building, Core Religious Studies and Core Physical Education.

Most girls leaving the sixth form proceed to higher education and have left to go on to universities that include Durham, Imperial College London, King's College London, Nottingham, St Andrews and Exeter.

Extracurricular. More House offers an impressive number of extracurricular clubs that take place before, during, and after school, including dance, debating, circuit training, science, foreign film, drama, band, percussion, retro games, dream catcher crafting, multi-skills, ukulele, eco, guitar, art, Horrible Histories, prayer, chess, book, scrabble, Italian, and Mandarin, to name a few.

The PE department's extracurricular activities include climbing, swimming, rowing, netball, rounders, hockey, football, and cricket.

The music department runs several talented choirs and chamber choirs, who perform in concerts regularly throughout the year. Furthermore, the combined choirs go on a yearly tour in the Autumn term – recent destinations have included Tuscany, Madrid, Paris, Malta, New York, Vienna, and Budapest.

The drama department stages several productions throughout the school year and a school musical every two years at an external venue. Recent productions have included *A Little Princess: The Musical, Macbeth, A Midsummer Night's Dream,* and *Little Women.*

Facilities. The school occupies two adjoining, nineteenth-century, Queen Anne style houses. The buildings retain many of their original architectural features and charm, but have been modernised to include purpose-built facilities. These include four science laboratories, two computer rooms, a chapel, a library and a drama and dance studio. The recently renovated sixth-form centre features a bright and spacious common room, communal kitchen, and two study rooms.

Physical education and extracurricular sport take place in Battersea Park, Hyde Park, Imperial College London, Fulham Reach Boat House, and Latchmere Leisure Centre – all a short walk or short coach ride away.

Admission. Admission is primarily for entry in Year 7, with occasional places available across other years. More House is part of the London 11+ Consortium – details can be found on the school website. Entry at 11+ is by examination, coupled with an interview with one of the Co-Heads. £125 registration fee.

Fees per term (2021–2022) £7,250 including school meals.

Scholarships and Bursaries. Academic, Music, Drama, Art & Design, and Sports scholarships are awarded at 11+ and sixth form, based on merit. Bursaries are also available, based on means-testing for girls joining in Year 7 and occasionally in other year groups.

Charitable Status. More House Trust is a Registered Charity, number 312737. It exists to provide an academic education for girls aged 11 to 18 within the framework of a Catholic Day School.

Governing Body:
Chairman: Mr J J Fyfe, BSc Birmingham
Vice-Chairman: Mrs M S Shale, BA Birmingham, FCA
Mrs S J Sturrock, BMus London, ARCM

Mr L Mayol-Navarrete, LLB Granada, PhD Cardiz
Mr K Lake, BA London
Mr I Bogle, BA RCH Glasgow, RIBA, ARIAS, CKA, SKA, FRSA

Clerk to the Governors: Mrs C Ralston Boyle, BA Exeter

Head: Ms F Hagerty, BA Bristol, PGDip LAMDA

Associate Head: Mr M Keeley, BMus London

Deputy Head, Academic: Mrs J Brett, BA Hons Witwatersrand
Director of Pastoral Care: Miss D Reid, BA Belfast

Senior Teachers:
Mr T Robertson, BSc Leeds
Miss O Henvey, BEd Belfast

Registrar: Ms J Day
Marketing Officer: Miss S Xiberras
School Secretary and PA to Head: Mrs K Macmillan
School Counsellor: Mrs J Gaylor, BSc, MA

Teaching Staff:
* *Head of Department*

Ms E Aldous, MA Austria, MBA Leicester
*Mr W Benskin, BA Sussex, PGCE Brighton
*Miss E Calderwood, BMus London
Mrs S Fischer, BA Birmingham
Ms J Frith, BA Exeter, MPhil Cambridge
*Mrs L Garwood, BA Durham
Ms C Godfrey, BA East Anglia
Mr P Hegarty, BA, PGDip, ED Open University
*Ms B Hunt, MBA Scotland
Ms A Inchenko, MSci Bristol, MSc Imperial
Mr S James, BSc Durham Cantab
Ms F Khizar, BSc London
Miss E Lorch, BSc Plymouth, MSc London
*Mrs J Majewski, BSc, MSc Massey
Mr J Millard, BA York, PGCE UCL
Ms S Naidu, BSc, MSc London
*Miss S O'Callaghan, BA, BEd Australia, RCSSD London
Miss M Ormesher, BA Newcastle
*Ms C Phelps, BSc East Anglia
*Mrs P Revell, BA Wellington
Mr J Rodriquez, BMus London
Mrs O Soltani, BSc Ternopil
Miss A Stanbury, BSc Loughborough
Miss N Stojanovic, MA Paris
Ms R Sym, Cantab
Mrs R Tunnicliffe, MA London
Ms K Wallace, BA Leeds
*Mrs K Wilson, BA, PGCE Edinburgh
Ms H Yate, BA, MA London

Support for Learning:
*Mr J Roberts, SENCO
Mrs J Courtney, DIPCOT Brunel, MRCOT HCPC (*Occupational Therapist*)
Ms V George
Ms E Gillies (*Educational Psychiatrist*)
Miss S Gunner, BA Roehampton
Mrs C Ward (*Speech & Language Therapist*)

North London Collegiate School

Canons, Canons Drive, Edgware, Middlesex HA8 7RJ

Tel: Senior School: 020 8952 0912
          Junior School: 020 8952 1276
email: office@nlcs.org.uk
website: www.nlcs.org.uk
Twitter: @NLCS1850
Facebook: @nlcs1850
Instagram: @nlcs1850

North London Collegiate School is a top independent day school for girls aged 4–18. Since its founding in 1850, generations of girls have received an ambitious academic education and formed a bond with NLCS, which lasts forever. We provide a carefully judged blend of support and challenge, a friendly and warm atmosphere, glorious facilities and extensive extra-curricular activities.

We are proud of our tradition of producing independent-minded young women with the drive and confidence to make the most of opportunities and make a difference in the world. That was the vision of the school's founder and it remains true of the school today.

We have a strong track record of enabling students to gain entry to their first choice of university, but examination success is only part of the picture and passionate teachers inspire pupils with a love of their subject which goes beyond the examination syllabus.

NLCS celebrates the individual and creative spirit of the pupils. We provide the springboard for our students to find their place in a world which will require not only technical skills, but also creative and communication skills to thrive. This is why we continue to invest in and enhance our music and arts provision and offer a wealth of sporting opportunities. Over 50 clubs and societies create a vibrant atmosphere that enables students to develop a relaxed self-confidence and enjoy their time at school.

NLCS has a global perspective that is unique amongst London day schools. In the Sixth Form, students can study the International Baccalaureate Diploma – a highly regarded qualification that is particularly prized by Ivy League, Russell Group and European universities. In addition to this, the opening of our sister schools in Jeju, Dubai and Singapore benefits our students through exchange and collaboration opportunities.

We believe that happy students are successful students. Our pastoral care is focused on individual support for every student, developing resilience and a sense of perspective, so that girls are able to tackle challenges head-on, learn from set-backs, and have the confidence to try again if things don't work out initially. We aim to provide an environment which promotes self-confidence, a feeling of self-worth and the knowledge that pupil's concerns will be listened to and acted upon.

There are approximately 1,080 girls at North London Collegiate School: 120 in the First School aged from 4 to 7, 190 Juniors aged 7–11 and 770 in the Senior School aged 11–18, of whom 235 are in the Sixth Form.

The school's academic record is outstanding. It has twice been named as *The Sunday Times* "Independent School of the Year" and *The Daily Telegraph* has described it as the most consistently successful academic girls' school in the country. Results in 2021 were again consistent with the school's academic profile. 100% of A Level entries were awarded A*–A grades, with 91% of students gaining straight A* grades.

Another superb set of IB results in July 2021 with an average point score of 43, and four students gaining the maximum score of 45 points, something usually only achieved by around 150 students out of 160,000 candidates across the globe. In 2021 the School was ranked No. 1 in the UK for the International Baccalaureate (IB) by *The Sunday Times*. NLCS has offered the IB programme as an alternative to A Levels since 2004, and since then, has had a consistent record of success, ranking NLCS as one of the highest-achieving IB schools not only in the UK but in the world.

In 2021, 20 girls secured offered places at either Oxford or Cambridge, with 100% of students who applied receiving offers from Russell Group institutions. Students also secured offered places to study at Ivy League or equivalent institutions in the US.

The GCSE 2021 results were the school's best ever, with 95% of all entries awarded grade 9.

The facilities at the school are first class, designed to offer the girls every opportunity to develop themselves both academically and socially. These facilities include lacrosse pitches, all-weather tennis courts and a Sports Centre with an indoor swimming pool, climbing wall and fitness centre.

The Performing Arts Centre, with a 350-seat auditorium, orchestra pit, galleries and rehearsal rooms, hosts over 35 productions a year. There are many Music and Drama opportunities including productions, choirs and orchestras. On the campus are a Music School, Drawing School and an Engineering & Technology Block, all situated around the lake, where waterlilies in the summer make it the ideal place to relax during the long lunch interval. Alternatively, girls may visit the beautifully light and spacious four-floor library.

There is an extensive school coach scheme.

Full details of Open Days and Taster Afternoons are on the school's website.

Bursaries. Enabling bright girls from all backgrounds is central to the ethos of the school. Many bursaries are offered to girls who do well in the 11+ test and those entering the Sixth Form, whose parents can demonstrate financial need.

Scholarships. Music Scholarships are awarded at 11+ and 16+

Fees per term (2021–2022). Senior School: £7,049; Junior School: £5,956.

Charitable status. The North London Collegiate School is a Registered Charity, number 1115843. It exists to provide an academic education for girls.

The Governing Body:
Mr R Hingley (*Chair*)
Mrs S Carter, BSc Hons, Associate CFA (*Vice Chair*)
Mr P Needleman, MA, FIA (*Vice Chair*)
Mrs S Dar, BSc, MA
Mrs E Davis, BA, Dip
Ms V Godfrey, MA Oxon, MBA, FRGS
Ms R Herdman-Smith, BA
Ms C Marten, BA, MA, PGCE
Dr T Maruthappu, MA, MBBS MRCP PHD
Miss V Savage, BMUS, PGDIP, PGCE
Dr D Toh, PhD, CPA, PGHE

Mrs L Tyler, MA, NPQH
Mrs E Watford, MCHEM, MBA
Dr A Weller, MA, PhD
Professor B Young, BA, MA, DPhil
Mr D Baille, BSC, MSC, FRICS (*Associate Governor*)

Chief Operating Officer: Mr I Callender, BA Oxon

Headmistress: Mrs E S Clark, MA Cambridge, PGCE

Deputy Head – Academic: Mrs C Hitchen, MA
    Nottingham, MEng Newcastle

Deputy Head – Pastoral: Dr H Bagworth-Mann, BA
    Brunel, PhD Brunel

Director of Studies and Administration: Mr M Burke, BA
    Newcastle, MA Durham

Head of Junior School: Mrs J M Newman, BEd Cantab

Assistant Heads:
Teaching and Learning: Mrs J Bedi, MA Cantab
Enrichment: Mr J Majithia, BA Oxon
Senior Tutor: Dr C Jackson, PhD Glasgow
Professional Development: Mr H Waddington, MA Cantab,
    MPhil Cantab, FRGS
Head of Sixth Form: Miss D Gibbs, BA Surrey
Head of Upper School: Mrs E Wells, BSc York, MPhil
    Cantab
Head of Middle School: Mr B Tosh, BA Greenwich

Director of University Admissions: Mr D James-Williams,
    BA London, MA Open

SEN Advisor: Mrs K Cowan, BA Sussex, PGCE, OCR
    APC SpLD CELTA

Director of IB Diploma: Mr H Linscott, BA London, MA
    London

Head of Careers: Dr R Silverman, BSc, MSc Nottingham,
    PhD Bristol

Head of Examinations: Mrs A Evans-Evans, BSc
    Manchester

Heads of Academic Departments:
Art and Design: Mr N Price, BA Coventry, MA Wales
Classics: Dr G. McCormick, DPhil Oxon
Computing: Mr Z Qureshi, BSc Hertfordshire
Drama: Miss H May, BA Princeton
Economics: Mrs S Dean, BSc London, MSc London
Engineering, Design & Technology: Mr H Hutchings, BA
    Lancaster
English: Ms M Henson, BA, MA Cork
Geography: Miss J Payne, BA Manchester
History and Government & Politics: Dr W Van Reyk, BA,
    MSt, DPhil Oxon
Mathematics: Mr W Galton, BSc Cambs
Modern Languages & Spanish: Ms D Mardell, MA Cantab,
    MEd Cantab
French: Miss K Bonnal, Maîtrise Avignon
Italian: Dr N Ibba, MA Bologna, PhD London
Russian: Miss E Makower, BA Oxon
German: Ms A Venter, MA Paris
Mandarin: Ms A Hickman, BA Durham
Music: Mr C Ham, BA Cantab, MMus Royal Northern
    College of Music
Physical Education: Miss G Aldcroft, BA Liverpool
Religious Studies & Philosophy: Mr J Holt, BA Durham,
    MA Open
Biology: Mr M Reeve, BSc Newcastle

Chemistry: Miss M Siddiqui, BSc London
Physics: Mrs N Timoshina, MSc Moscow

PA to the Headmistress: Mrs D Daum

Notre Dame School

Burwood House, Cobham, Surrey KT11 1HA

Tel: 01932 869990
email: office@notredame.co.uk
website: www.notredame.co.uk
Twitter: @NotreDameCobham
Facebook: @NotreDameSchoolCobham
LinkedIn: /notredamecobham

Notre Dame School is an independent Catholic day school for girls aged 2–18 and boys aged 2–4 and welcomes families of all faiths and none.

Notre Dame School is unashamedly holistic and students are at the centre of everything we do. Their physical and mental wellbeing is every bit as important as their wonderful academic, sporting and creative achievements. The focus at Notre Dame is on happiness and success – in that order. We are profoundly committed to this educational philosophy and through it we fulfil our aim of providing an exemplary all-round education. The academic, creative, physical, moral and intellectual challenges expected in all good schools complete with state-of-the-art facilities, are balanced with fun and laughter in a trusting and compassionate atmosphere, which enables everyone within our community to become the best versions of themselves.

Our staff are encouraged and supported in continually striving to enrich the educational experience for our students. We have a range of dynamic strategies which together assure the delivery of an exemplary all-round education, as recognised across the board in our 'Excellent' ISI Inspection Report in 2017. A detailed teaching and learning quality assurance programme is in place, which focuses on five categories; teaching, learning, differentiation, behaviour and assessment. Year-on-year tracking shows impressive rises in all five areas. 'Learning walks' and marking reviews allow middle and senior managers to monitor standards and share good practice. The focus on assessment and collaborative marking has included pupils in the process and given them greater ownership over their own academic progress.

Wellbeing at Notre Dame is not an 'add-on' but is about an attitude that has been embedded in our school for the last 400 years. Across our entire school community we have formalised and wide-reaching strategies in place to promote wellbeing and resilience and ultimately happiness, self-confidence and a wider spiritual awareness – our Lestonnac Approach.

Creativity is embedded in the teaching of all subjects at Notre Dame and art, music, drama and sport offer particular scope for personal expression, exploration, inspiration and growth. All students are encouraged to cultivate a passion for at least one of these areas. At Notre Dame our students are hugely supportive of each other and are always excited to celebrate each other's success.

It is the integration of all these strands – academic challenge, quality of teaching and learning, student and teacher collaboration, wellbeing and resilience and excellence in Sport and the Arts, which allows us to fulfil our aim of providing an exemplary holistic education. Our academic value added (in top 8% nationally) and examination results (70% A*/A grades at A Level) speak for themselves and are particularly impressive given our broad intake.

Notre Dame is built on 400 years of educational experience: The Company of Mary Our Lady was founded in Bordeaux in 1607 to educate girls, and Notre Dame is one of some 300 educational foundations around the world that now come under this umbrella. To ready our pupils for the wider world, to live life to the full, we believe that our shared mission and purpose help our children to aspire to be the best they can be in in all their endeavours, during their school years and beyond.

ISI Inspection 2017. The full report can be viewed on the school website: ISI-Inspection-Report.

Transport. Notre Dame is excellently located – two minutes from the A3/M25 junction, 10 minutes from Walton, Weybridge, Cobham or Esher, and 20 minutes from Guildford, Wimbledon and Putney. Private school coaches for girls from Year 3 upwards – flexible single/return journeys – from Clapham, Putney and Fulham to Esher, Woking and Weybridge and many stops in between.

Admission. Usual entry points: Year 7 (age 11), Year 9 (age 13) and Year 12 (Sixth Form). Occasional places are sometimes available in other year groups.

Registration: Registration Form and payment of £125 registration fee.

Assessment: The 11+ entrance examination held in November – Maths, English and Non-Verbal Reasoning. Closing date for entries late October. Approximately two-thirds of intake at 11+ comes from Notre Dame Prep.

11+/13+/Sixth Form scholarships awarded in Art, Music, Drama and Sport. Academic scholarships also awarded based on performance in entrance examination.

For occasional places: candidates invited to attend Taster Day, to include assessments and time with prospective classmates. Assessments can be arrange overseas as necessary.

As a rough guide, intake sits in the top third of the ability range.

Prep School. For further information about Notre Dame Prep School, please see entry in IAPS section.

Fees per term (2021–2022). Senior School £6,050; Prep School £3,868–£4,909.

Charitable status. Notre Dame School Cobham is a Registered Charity, number 1081875.

Chair of Governors: Mrs Wanda Nash

Executive Team:

Headmistress (*Senior School***): Mrs Anna King**, MEd, MA Cantab, PGCE, FRGS

Headmistress (Prep School): Mrs Amélie Morgan MA, BA Hons, PGCE

Bursar: Ms Louise Ayling, BSc Hons, MA Oxon, PGCE, FCA

Senior Leadership Team:

Assistant Head (Curriculum): Ms Sarah Badger, BSc Hons, PGCE

Assistant Head (Teaching and Learning): Mr Michael Coackley, BA Hons, PGCE

Head of Sixth Form: Ms Sian Lewis, BSc Hons, PGCE

Assistant Head (Pastoral): Mrs Amanda Windibank, BA Hons, PGCE

Assistant Head of Prep: Mrs Clare Barber, BSc Hons, PGCE

Pastoral Director (Prep): Miss Rebecca Golding, BA Hons, PGCE

Head of EYFS & Assistant Head: Miss Melanie Lehmann, BA Hons, EYPS

Head of Infants: Miss Geraldine Deen, BA Hons, QTS

Director of Admissions and Marketing: Mrs Beccy Johnson, MA Oxon, Dip Stat

Alumnae Manager: Mrs Ros Roberts, NUJ, BACB, IoD

Notting Hill and Ealing High School

GDST

2 Cleveland Road, Ealing, London W13 8AX

Tel:	020 8799 8400
email:	enquiries@nhehs.gdst.net
website:	www.nhehs.gdst.net
Twitter:	@nhehs
Facebook:	@nhehsGDST
Instagram:	@nhehsgdst

Founded 1873.

Notting Hill and Ealing High School is an academically selective, independent day school for girls aged 4 to 18. It is part of the GDST (Girls' Day School Trust) which is the leading network of independent girls' schools in the UK. For further information about the Trust, see p. xix or visit www.gdst.net.

Pupils and Location. Approximately 900 pupils. 590 in the Senior School (153 in the Sixth Form) and 310 in the Junior Department. Transport links are excellent (Ealing Broadway station is nearby and several buses stop outside the school) and the School runs its own Bus Service. Students come from Ealing and all over west London.

Ethos. This is a school with a long tradition of academic excellence and creativity within an exceptionally warm and supportive environment. Notting Hill & Ealing girls are well grounded, confident and independent. They are proud of their school and value kindness and laughter, fun and friendship. This is a place where tolerance and mutual respect are nurtured; where you can be yourself. With a wide variety of activities and opportunities, and a strong emphasis on charitable giving, everyone can enjoy being part of a vibrant community and express their passion for learning, and for life.

Pastoral Care. The system of pastoral care is overseen by the Deputy Head – Pastoral working through the Heads of Year and Form Tutors. A well-structured system that is sufficiently flexible, supports every girl and ensures she is treated as a whole person with individual strengths and needs. In the Sixth Form the tutor team is led by the Head of Sixth Form.

Curriculum. Throughout the Junior and Senior Schools our curriculum is broad and balanced and encourages independence of learning and thought. In Years 7–9 everyone follows courses in English, History, Geography, Mathematics, Physics, Chemistry, Biology, Design Technology, Computer Science, Religious Studies, Art, Music, and Drama. In Year 7 all girls study Mandarin plus a second modern language (French, German or Spanish). In Year 8 Latin also becomes available. Girls usually take ten subjects at GCSE, including a compulsory core of English Language and Literature, Mathematics, 3 Sciences and a Modern Language. 26 subjects are offered at A Level. Most girls take 3 or 4 subjects. Those who wish may also take the Extended Project Qualification which is highly regarded by university admissions tutors. Each department runs a special programme to support UCAS applications and there is additional support for those applying to Oxbridge or particularly competitive universities. There are also lessons in personal health, ethical and social issues, appropriate to each age and stage. Physical Education is taught throughout the school.

The Sixth Form. Our sixth formers play an important role in the school. They enjoy the independence of their own new Sixth Form Centre with common rooms, outdoor space for relaxing, café and fitness centre. They take responsibility for many extra-curricular activities such as organising clubs and act as mentors for girls in the lower years. Additional leadership opportunities are offered by the House system, and voluntary and charity work. All go on to Higher Education and, with excellent results (typically 94% achieving grades A*, A or B, with 65% of grades being A*/A and 26% of grades being A*), successfully secure places at their choice of university (including Oxford and Cambridge).

Extra-Curricular Activities. Students can choose from over 100 clubs and activities, covering an extensive range of sport, drama and music – as well as over 50 special interest clubs.

We take full advantage of everything London offers, with visits to theatres, museums, galleries, performances, and conferences incorporated into the curriculum. Trips abroad are arranged and there is an annual ski trip.

Careers Advice. All girls are enrolled in our careers programme which entitles all students to help and advice until the age of 23. Sixth formers receive extensive support with university applications, including mock interviews. The GDST Alumnae Network, the unique resource from the GDST, offers each student access to a database of former GDST students, who will give advice and support on careers (including helping with work experience) and universities. An annual Careers Evening typically featuring senior representatives from almost 70 different professions and occupations is organised by the Parents' Guild.

Creative Arts. There are three orchestras, three choirs, and many chamber and ensemble groups as well as two rock bands and a jazz band. School productions offer opportunities either to perform or to work with production, lighting, sound, costume and staging. Art thrives within the curriculum and through various art clubs. It also contributes to work in design technology and various aspects of ICT, such as web design and animation projects.

Sport. Sport is taken seriously with success in local fixtures and championships, and we encourage participation and enjoyment at all standards. On-site facilities include all-weather pitch, four-court sports hall, dance studio and indoor swimming pool. Lifeguard training is available for sixth formers. Aerobics, self-defence, kick boxing and football are among the extra-curricular sports clubs currently available.

Fees per term (2021–2022). Junior School £5,084, Senior School £6,593.

Scholarships and Bursaries. Academic, music and sports scholarships are available at 11+. At 16+ there are academic awards as well as awards for Physical Education, Drama, Art, and an All-Rounder scholarship.

Bursaries are available at 11+ and 16+ and we actively encourage applications.

Admission. Usually at 4+, 7+, 11+ and 16+, by appropriate test and/or interview.

Occasionally, vacancies may become available in other year groups.

Charitable status. Notting Hill & Ealing High School is part of The Girls' Day School Trust, which is a Registered Charity, number 306983.

Chair of Local Governing Board: Mrs Charlie Parkin Altman

Head: **Mr Matthew Shoults**, MA, PGCE

Senior Deputy Head – Pastoral: Mrs Rebecca Irwin, BA, PGCE

Deputy Head – Academic: Ms M Copin, MA, MMath, BA

Head of Junior School: Ms Kate Bevan, BA, PGCE, MA

Nottingham Girls' High School GDST

9 Arboretum Street, Nottingham NG1 4JB

Tel:	0115 941 7663
email:	enquiries@not.gdst.net
	admissions@not.gdst.net
website:	www.nottinghamgirlshigh.gdst.net
Twitter:	@NottmGirlsHigh
Facebook:	@FriendsofNGHS
LinkedIn:	/Friends of Nottingham Girls High School

Founded 1875.

Nottingham Girls' High School is part of the GDST (Girls' Day School Trust). The GDST is the leading network of independent girls' schools in the UK. As a charity that owns and runs 23 schools and two academies, it reinvests all its income in its schools. For further information about the Trust, see p. xix or visit www.gdst.net.

Additional information about the school may be found on the school's website and a detailed information pack may be obtained from Central Admissions at the school.

Number of Pupils. Senior School 521 (including 151 in the Sixth Form); Junior School 204.

A selective day school for girls aged three to 18, NGHS is on a single site adjacent to a park in the middle of Nottingham. The original Victorian houses have been modernised and there have been extensive additions to create a well-resourced school. The Junior School, including a Nursery for three to four year olds, is housed in separate buildings on the same campus as the Senior School, and has been extended to include a library and ICT learning resources centre as well four additional classrooms. A major programme of refurbishment in the Senior School has included refitting the science laboratories, food technology and design technology. A state-of-the-art performing arts centre was opened in December 2016.

There is a self-contained Sixth Form Centre providing a large coffee shop-style common room and recreational area. The tutorial rooms are light and airy, and fully equipped with the latest technology.

The school grounds include an all-weather sports pitch, climbing wall, woodland area for outdoor learning activities including a fire pit, pizza oven and low ropes course, gymnasium, sports hall and fitness suite. The modern dining hall has excellent facilities for providing a wide choice of snacks and home cooked meals throughout the day including vegetarian, Halal and non-Halal options.

Examination results are among the best in the country, featuring in the top 100 schools for A Level results for all schools and the top 50 for GCSEs for girls schools. NGHS educates girls by empowering them with the skills they need for life in addition to excellent results. Leadership, confidence, passion and resilience are among the qualities increasingly demanded in today's ever-changing society. Everyone is encouraged to embrace adventure, seize opportunities to participate fully in a wide range of enrichment activities to develop skills and qualities that will lead to a happy, successful and fulfilling life with no sense of gender stereotypes or limits to what they can achieve.

Curriculum. The curriculum is designed to give a broad academic education and due regard is paid to the National Curriculum. In the Junior School, as well as following a pattern of work designed to help develop a confident grasp of core skills, the girls benefit from a stimulating and challenging integrated creative curriculum with enrichment experiences firmly embedded into teaching and learning. Girls are tested regularly and there are assessments for all girls wishing to join the school. There is liaison with the Senior School staff, helping to ensure continuity for pupils at 11+. In the Senior School girls are prepared for GCSE, A Levels, EPQs as well as Advanced Mathematics and a Performing Arts Technical Award. Almost all girls proceeding to university and individuals are encouraged to play to their strengths and do what is right for them. The personalised curriculum available for Senior School girls enables this.

Girls at all ages follow a comprehensive programme of personal and social development including aspects of careers, citizenship, health and sex education, current affairs and environmental issues.

Throughout the school girls are encouraged to develop their physical skills and the school has an excellent sports record; teams regularly win trophies at City and County level with many being selected to compete at regional or national level.

Music and Drama is also an important part of the school, with many choirs, bands, orchestras and performing arts groups taking place across all year groups.

Admissions. For Nursery, girls are visited at home to assess their readiness for the NGHS environment. At 4+ entry, small groups of girls are invited to come into school and take part in a number of activities together to see if they are ready for school. Entry at 11+ is by interview and written tests which includes English, mathematics and verbal reasoning and is designed to determine potential and understanding. Most of the existing students stay on at 16+ if they meet the entrance criteria and a number of students are admitted into the Sixth Form from other schools. The entry requirement is 8 GCSE subjects at an average of grade B, with grades A or B in any subject to be studied in the Sixth Form as specified by the department. This is supported by individual interviews and a report from the current school. The school will consider applications for admission into most year groups if there are available places and girls pass the entrance assessments.

Fees per term (2021–2022). Nursery: £33.75 per morning session and £54.00 per all day session (including lunch). Juniors: Rec (including lunch) £3,550; Years 1–2 (including lunch) £3,584; Years 3–6 (including lunch) £3,650; Seniors (excluding lunch): Years 7–13 £4,766. The fees cover non-residential curriculum trips, school books, stationery and other materials, games and swimming, but not optional extra subjects.

Scholarships and Bursaries. The GDST makes available a substantial number of bursaries. These are means tested and intended to ensure that the school remains accessible to bright girls who would profit from our education but who would be unable to enter the school without financial assistance. Up to 100% of the tuition fee may be awarded. Bursary application forms are available from the Admissions team at the school.

A limited number of scholarships are available for Year 7 and Sixth Form based on academic merit. Performing Arts, Sports and Music scholarships are also available. The value of a scholarship is up to a maximum of 10% of the current tuition fee.

Charitable status. Nottingham Girls' High School is part of The Girls' Day School Trust, which is a Registered Charity, number 306983.

Chairman of Local Governors: Mrs Jean Pardoe, OBE, DL

Head: **Mrs J Keller**, BA

Deputy Head: Ms K Handford-Smith, MEd

Assistant Heads:
Mrs R A Halse, BSc
Mrs L M Wharton-Howett, BA

Head of Junior School: Mrs L Fowler, BA Ed

Director of Finance and Operations: Mr J C Dunn, ACA

Director of Marketing: Mrs C Bale, MA

Admissions: Mrs C L Haddow

Oxford High School GDST

Belbroughton Road, Oxford, Oxfordshire OX2 6XA

Tel:	01865 559888
email:	oxfordhigh@oxf.gdst.net
website:	www.oxfordhigh.gdst.net
Twitter:	@OxfordHighSch
Facebook:	@OxfordHighGDST
Instagram:	@oxfordhighschoolgdst
LinkedIn:	/school/oxford-high-school

Motto: *Ad Lucem*

Oxford High School is an independent day school for girls aged 4 to 18 years. Founded in 1875, it is Oxford's oldest girls' school. The school is located across three sites in Summertown in north Oxford, all within walking distance of each other. It is part of the Girls' Day School Trust (GDST) which is at the forefront of educational innovation, teaching over 20,000 girls across the UK in 25 schools as the country's leading network of independent girls' schools.

At Oxford High School, we empower each and every student to be whoever they want to be. Those who find their way here are curious, outward-looking, and sparky; they delight in learning and questioning, they care about the world in which we live in and are fearless in the pursuit of their passions. Whether a Sixth Former organising a virtual conference and extending the invitation to other schools throughout the UK, or a Year 7 stepping up to their very first leadership role, our students embrace challenge and take every opportunity to realise their goals and aspirations, whatever they might be. With the unwavering support of their teachers and peers, OHS students forge their own paths in the world and continually push themselves to go beyond.

The school achieved 'Exceptional' in its 2016 ISI inspection, with an 'Excellent' rating on all areas of the inspection.

Pupil numbers. 832: Prep School 230, Senior School & Sixth Form 602.

The Senior School is extremely well-resourced with a sports hall, indoor swimming pool, The Mary Warnock School of Music, separate purpose-built centres for all other subjects, and well-equipped ICT areas. Our new Sixth Form, Arts, and Well-being Centre – the Ada Benson Building – has state-of-the-art teaching and learning spaces, dedicated campus-style areas for Sixth Formers, an auditorium for talks, lectures, NT-Live events, and new teaching and gallery spaces for the Art Department. Students from the Prep sites have regular access to facilities in the Senior School.

Curriculum and Co-Curriculum. The OHS Curriculum is one that inspires as well as challenges, and girls are well-prepared for their GCSEs and A Levels. With 24 subjects to choose from, there is always something to suit a student's interests and their timetable is individually tailored around their choice of subjects. The school offers eight languages including Latin and Ancient Greek. About 90% of our Year 13s secure places at top Russell Group universities, with 10% of the year group going on to study Medicine and 1 in 4 girls regularly proceed to Oxbridge, as well as leading institutions for art, music, and the performing arts.

Many girls take examinations in Music and Speech & Drama, and multiple productions are staged each year alongside concerts at venues including the Sheldonian Theatre and Oxford Town Hall. Girls also participate in a wealth of co-curricular activities, including the Duke of Edinburgh's Award, Young Enterprise and the school's own sporting partnership, Girls on the Ball. Clubs are offered in robotics, poetry, astronomy, genome analysis and bee-keeping, to name a few. In the Sixth Form, the 360 Programme offers an innovative and academically challenging programme to prepare girls for life at university and beyond, supported by the GDST's extensive alumnae network.

Girls at the Prep and Pre-Prep also enjoy a highly varied and engaging curriculum, such as the Singapore Mathematics programme and their weekly Global Studies lessons. The PE curriculum introduces girls to a multitude of sports such as gymnastics, athletics, hockey, and cricket, to name a few. Drama and Music are a key part of life at OHS Prep School. Every girl is encouraged to participate in one of the many ensembles and to perform in the school plays. The girls develop great confidence and they thoroughly enjoy it.

In Autumn 2021 the Prep School launched its Future Ready Programme, which aims to build well-rounded young people with many different passions, who have a broad knowledge base, strong work ethic, self-belief and confidence. Pupils work through progressive levels and complete a series of age-appropriate tasks, working towards the achievement of badges. The tasks are varied and wide-ranging, spanning academia, sustainability, life skills and personal development.

Admissions. The main points of entry are at Reception, Year 3, Year 7, Year 9 and Year 12. Applicants are also able to join the school at other entry points if there are places available Please contact our Admissions team for details (admissions@oxf.gdst.net or 01865 318500).

Fees per term (from January 2022). Reception: £3,089 (plus lunch £247); Years 1 & 2: £3,629 (plus lunch £247); Years 3 & 4: £4,144 (plus lunch £296); Years 5 & 6: £4,184 (plus lunch £296). Senior School (Years 7–13): £5,521 (plus lunch £296 for Years 7–11). Lunch is compulsory for girls from Reception to Year 11 and optional for Sixth Form girls only, who have the freedom to go to Summertown in Oxford or eat in school.

The fees cover the regular curriculum textbooks, stationery and other materials, compulsory educational visits, choral music, games and swimming, but not optional extra subjects.

Bursaries. The school offers means-tested bursaries and ensures that it remains accessible to bright girls who would profit from the education provided, but who would be unable to enter the school without financial assistance. Bursaries are available at Year 7, Year 9 and Year 12 entry to the Senior School and a confidential application can be made to the GDST. If your family's assessable income and resources are below £87,500 a year, you may be eligible for some support.

Scholarships. Scholarships are available for Year 7, Year 9, and Year 12 entry in Art, Drama, Sport, Music, Academic and the Head's Scholarship. These scholarships are held for the duration of a girl's time at Oxford High, subject to satisfactory progress and behaviour.

Charitable status. Oxford High School is part of The Girls' Day School Trust, which is a Registered Charity, number 306983.

Chairman of the School Governing Board: Miss Katherine Haynes

Head: Mrs Marina Gardiner Legge

Deputy Heads:
Dr Ed Batchelar (*Academic*)
Miss Laura Knowles (*Pastoral*)

Head of Prep School: Mrs Jessica Williams

Deputy Head of Prep School: Mr Nick Dawson

Registrars:
Gemma Tuckey (*Senior School*)
Maria Blick (*Prep School*)

Palmers Green High School

104 Hoppers Road, London N21 3LJ

Tel: 020 8886 1135
email: office@pghs.co.uk
website: www.pghs.co.uk
Twitter: @PGHSGirls
Facebook: @palmersgreenhighschool
Instagram: @palmersgreenhighschool
LinkedIn: @palmers-green-high-school

Motto: *By Love Serve One Another*

Palmers Green High School, founded in 1905 by Miss Alice Hum, has provided an exceptional education for over 100 years. At PGHS we specialise in educating girls, challenging them to achieve their full potential within our warm and friendly school environment.

The school motto, "By Love Serve One Another" was carefully chosen and it still epitomises our special ethos where individuals are nurtured, successes are celebrated and their contribution to the community is greatly valued.

We provide an inspiring, challenging and supportive environment through which all pupils are given opportunities to be inquisitive, independent and develop a lifelong love of learning.

PGHS is a very special 'through-school' where pupils progress in a familiar setting and benefit from seamless transitions across the key stages in the Lower and Senior Schools. There is an authentic feeling of being one family where strong friendships are formed and extend beyond year groups.

All sections of the school, from the Nursery through to the Seniors, enjoy being part of our 'one school' community. Preps use the same facilities as the GCSE pupils in some subjects e.g. Art, Music, PE and D&T, and Years 5 & 6 enjoy Science in the laboratories. Throughout, small class sizes and excellent teaching enable rapid progress, whilst exciting extra-curricular activities encourage pupils to develop into well-rounded individuals.

Our purpose-built Nursery is designed for 3–4 year old girls, most of whom transfer to Reception at PGHS. Lower School classes from Reception through to Year 6 benefit hugely from the encouragement and expertise of their class teachers and teaching assistants. Favourable teaching group sizes, light and airy classrooms and access to Senior School facilities all lead to an inspirational learning environment. This is enriched by specialist teaching in Art, Design & Technology, Drama, French, Spanish, Music and PE – frequently in half-class groups.

In the Senior School, small class sizes (an average of only 10 at GCSE) and a broad range of extra-curricular activities enriches the pupils' experience. In 2021, 72% of GCSE/IGCSE grades were A*/9/8 and 93% were A*/9–A/7. The School is currently, and is frequently, ranked number one in *The Sunday Times* national league table for small independent schools.

Former pupils enjoy coming back to share their news with current pupils. Recent leavers have followed Sixth Form courses at Henrietta Barnett, St Michael's, Latymer, Dame Alice Owen's, Woodhouse College, Haberdashers, North London Collegiate, Aldenham, Channing, Haileybury and Roedean. Popular university destinations include Birmingham, Bristol, Cambridge, Durham, Exeter, Glasgow, King's College London, Liverpool, London School of Economics, Manchester, Nottingham, Oxford, University College London, University of East Anglia and Warwick.

Palmers Green High School is recognised for its all-round excellence in a small and nurturing environment and parents can be reassured that PGHS pupils not only attain excellent results in relation to their abilities and aptitudes, but also grow in confidence and poise as members of this very special school community.

Fees per term (2021–2022). Nursery £3,430 (Full time) Nursery £2,100 (Part time); Reception–Year 2 £3,980; Years 3–6 £4,260; Years 7–11 £5,700.

Scholarships. Academic, Sport, Art and Drama Scholarships; Music Awards and Bursaries, are available to candidates aged 11+ for entry in September.

Entrance. Admission to all year groups is by assessment and interview, the main intakes being at 3+, 4+, 7+ and 11+.

Charitable status. Palmers Green High School Limited is a Registered Charity, number 312629. It exists for the education of girls.

School Governors:
Chair: Mrs Melanie Curtis
Vice Chair: Mr Anthony Frankal
Governors:

Mr John Atkinson	Mr Jason McKinlay
Miss Anna Averkiou	Mr Jeremy Piggott
Miss Alexia Eliades	Mrs Karen Tidmarsh
Mrs Bronwen Goulding	Miss Devkee Trivedi
Mr Dermot Lewis	

Headmistress: Mrs Wendy Kempster, BSc Reading, PGCE

Bursar: Mrs Angela Monty, MAAT
Deputy Head, Designated Safeguarding Leader: Miss Hannah Lucas, MSc KCL, BSc Sussex, PGCE, NPQSL
Teaching Staff:
* *Head of Department*

*Mrs L Aghassi, CertEd Middlesex (*Computing*)
*Miss A Akkari, ATCL, BA Hons, MA Bristol, PGCE (*Music*)
*Mrs L Ayling, BA Hons, QTS Middlesex (*Careers and PSHEE*)
Miss M Ayling (*Learning Support Assistant*)
*Miss R Begum, MA Cantab, PGCE (*English*)
Mrs H Bhundia, Dip Playgroup Practice (*First Aid Coordinator, Teaching Assistant*)
Mrs E Christodoulou, BA Middlesex PGCE (*Lower School Class Teacher*)
Mrs K Conlon, MSc London, BSc London (*Librarian*)
Mrs A Davey, BA Leeds, PGCE (*English*)
Mr A Desai, BEng, BEd India, OTTP, PGCE (*Mathematics*)
Mrs H Dodi, NCFE CACHE Level 3 (*Teaching Assistant*)
Mrs A Fowler, BA Brighton, QTS (*Physical Education*)
Miss L Gelsthorpe, BA Manchester, MSc Salford, PGCE (*Lower School Class Teacher*)
Mrs K Gil, CACHE Level 3 (*Nursery Assistant*)
*Miss S Govani, BA London School of Economics, PGCE (*History*)
Mrs S Hagi-Savva, NVQ3 (*Assistant School Secretary, Teaching Assistant*)

Mrs S Harney, BEd Cantab (*Head of Nursery and Early Years Coordinator*)

Mrs E Hassan, NVQ3 (*Reception Teaching Assistant*)

*Miss J Henry, MA, BA Newcastle, PGCE (*Art*)

*Ms E Hopley, BA MPhil Oxon, PGCE (*Geography*)

*Mrs B Kennedy, BSc Loughborough, PGCE (*Physical Education*)

Senora M Larotonda, MA London, BEd Buenos Aires, PGCE (*Spanish*)

Mrs E Logan, BA Middlesex, PGCE (*Art*)

Mrs M Louca, BSc Brunel, PGCE Middlesex (*Lower School Class Teacher*)

Mrs L Matthew, BA Royal Scottish Academy of Music, PG Dip [Maternity Cover]

Ms F Medlicott, MA Guildhall School of Music and Drama, BA Bristol, PGCE (*Music*)

Mrs M Mehran, BSc North London (*Science Technician*)

Mrs A Michael, NNEB (*Nursery Assistant*)

Miss R Mohabeer, BSc King's College London (*Science*)

*Mrs A Morison, BA Hons Manchester, PGCE (*Drama*)

Mr S Morris, MA Cantab, PGCE, PGCert SEND (*Individual Needs Coordinator*)

Miss J Newman, BA London, PGCE (*French, History*)

Mrs M Nicolaou, NVQ3 (*Teaching Assistant*)

Mr R Odell, BSc Keele, PGCE Keele (*Science*)

*Mme K Parry-Garnaud, Licence Anglais Tours, France, BA Sunderland (*Modern Foreign Languages*)

Mrs J Pauk, BA Aberystwyth, PGCE (*Lower School Class Teacher*)

*Mr A Pepper, BSc Loughborough, CertEd (*Design and Technology*)

Miss V Rich, BSc Bedfordshire, PGCE Institute of Education (*Lower School Class Teacher*)

Miss L Selley, BA Brighton, QTS (*Physical Education*)

Mrs S Sharma, MA UCL, PGCE (*Lower School Class Teacher*)

Mrs M Sinfield, CACHE Level 3 (*Lower School Teaching Assistant*)

Ms A Singh, BA London (*Examinations Officer & Individual Needs Teaching Assistant*)

Mrs R Stern, BEd, University of KwaZulu-Natal

Ms O Tennant, BA Manchester, GTP Middlesex (*Lower School Class Teacher, French*)

*Mrs S Turanli, BSc London, PGCE (*Physical Education*)

*Mrs M Wing, BSc Transylvania, PGCE Middlesex (*Mathematics*)

Mrs S Wood, BSc London, PGCE (*Science*)

Mrs K Woods-Shelley, BA Middlesex, PGCE, LLAM (*Drama*)

Visiting Staff – Instrumental Tuition:

Miss A Akkari, ATCL, BA Hons, PGCE, MA (*Singing/ Piano*)

Miss G Austin, LRAM, Dip RAM (*Violin/Viola*)

Miss L Bell, BA, MMus (*Piano*)

Mrs B Cimen, BA Hons, LGSM (*Piano*)

Miss V David, AGSM (*Violin/Viola*)

Mr M Hurley, BMus (*Guitar*)

Miss E Jeffery, BA, PGCE, (*Voice*)

Mr J Matthews, BMus, LTCL (*Saxophone*)

Ms M Tyler Brown, Prof Cert Hons, RAM, LRAM, PG Dip RNCM, MA City, PGCHE, QTLS (*Cello*)

Administrative Staff:

PA to the Headmistress/Admissions Secretary: Mrs L Mount

Office Manager and Admissions Secretary: Ms V Bennett-Gayle

School Secretary: Mrs A Dudley

Assistant School Secretary: Mrs S Hagi-Savva

Assistant to the Bursary Department: Ms M Soudah

Data Manager: Mrs K Thompson, BA Denver, Colorado, GTP Hertfordshire

Marketing Officer: Mrs L Clarke, BCOM Hons Birmingham, DipM MCIM

Site Manager: Mr D Skornag

Lunchtime and Outdoor Supervisor: Mr F McLoughlin

Pipers Corner School
High Wycombe

Great Kingshill, High Wycombe, Bucks HP15 6LP

Tel:	01494 718255
email:	theschool@piperscorner.co.uk
website:	www.piperscorner.co.uk
Twitter:	@PipersCornerSch
Facebook:	@PipersCornerSchool
Instagram:	@PipersCornerSch

At Pipers Corner all girls, from Pre-Prep through to Sixth Form, are supported and challenged to achieve their full potential. In our nurturing and encouraging environment personal development is as important as academic success and every girl is stretched as much outside as inside the classroom. We aim to know each girl as an individual and identify, develop and support her talents and strengths.

Academically successful, our students progress to further study at some of the country's top higher education institutions. In 2021, 61% of all A Level results were at grades A*/A, and 89% at grades A*–B. At GCSE there was a 99% pass rate, with 73% at grades 9–7 (A*/A).

Fees per term (2021–2022). £3,125–£6,580.

Facilities. The School is set within 96 acres of picturesque Chiltern countryside, 4 miles north of High Wycombe and 2 miles from Great Missenden. The Arts Centre is the home of our 280-seat theatre, with state-of-the-art sound and lighting facilities, and a café serving nutritional and delicious food at break and lunch. Sixth Form students benefit from the modern Sixth Form Centre, with a separate quiet study room. Pipers Radio is our bespoke station, broadcasting live shows every day. Sporting facilities include the sports hall, swimming pool and triple-court astro pitch. Wraparound care is available from 0730–1800 hours.

Pastoral Care. Student welfare is at the forefront of our school, we offer exceptional pastoral care with an extensive network of support. Pastoral care is enriched by a Christian ethos, encouraging the exploration of personal values and beliefs whilst retaining fundamental respect for the views of others. The School is made up of four Houses, consisting of students from all year groups, allowing students to integrate and make connections beyond their immediate peer group.

Enrichment. Learning is enhanced with a range of visits and excursions, both nationally and abroad, for Pre-Prep through to Sixth Form. We have a wide variety of extra-curricular activities, encompassing physical, intellectual and creative pursuits. Our students are encouraged to seize every opportunity afforded to them, to take on leadership and organisational responsibilities and to be open to trying new activities.

Admissions. Girls can join Pipers at the beginning of most year groups, from Reception through to Sixth Form. The Admissions Team are the first point of contact for enquiries regarding spaces. For most year groups, an interview and day visit or assessment day will form the basis of an offer, subject to the receipt of a satisfactory reference from a current school.

Scholarships and Bursaries. We are keen to encourage girls with talent and potential, and to widen access to allow as many girls as possible to take advantage of the excellent education we provide. Means tested bursaries are available up to a maximum of 100% of fees (including any Scholarship award).

There are Academic, Art, Drama, Music and PE scholarships available for Year 7 applicants, in addition to the Jessie Cross Award which is a mean-tested scholarship for students currently educated in a state primary school. Students joining Reception can apply for the Jessie Cross Foundation Award, which is means-tested and awarded for the duration of Pre-Prep education (Reception – Year 2). For Sixth Form entry, there are subject specific scholarships in addition to the broader Academic Scholarship. Students already at Pipers and those from other secondary schools can apply.

Charitable status. Pipers Corner School is a Registered Charity, Number 310635. It exists to provide high-quality education for girls.

Visitor: The Rt Revd The Lord Bishop of Buckingham

Chair of Governors: Ms H F Morton, MA, MSc, CEng
Mr A Cannon, BA Hons
Ms E J Carrighan, MA, MBA
Mr M F T Harborne, CBII
Mrs J B Ingram, BA, JD
Mr F W Johnston, BA, FCA (*Vice Chair*)
Reverend H E Peters, BSc, FdA
Lady Redgrave, BSc, MBBS, MSc SEM
Mr H B P Roberts, BSc Eng, FCA
Miss H J R Semple, MA
Mr M Stepney, MA
Mr P B Wayne, MusB, NPQH

Headmistress: **Mrs H J Ness-Gifford**, BA Hons, PGCE

Deputy Head Academic: Mrs T Smith, BA Hons, MA, PGCE

Deputy Head Pastoral: Ms R Tandon, BA Hons, MSc, PGCE, PGDip

Assistant Head Operations: Mrs E Cresswell, BA Hons, PGCE

Assistant Head Academic: Mrs C Derbyshire, BSc Hons, PGCE

Head of Prep: Mr R Urquhart, BSc Hons

Bursar and Clerk to the Governors: Mr J D Clarke, BA Hons

Director of Admissions & Marketing: Mr G Ranford, BA Hons

Director of Digital Strategy: Mr A Rees, BSc Hons, PG Dip, MSc

Portsmouth High School
GDST

25 Kent Road, Southsea, Hampshire PO5 3EQ

Tel: 023 9282 6714
email: admissions@por.gdst.net
website: www.portsmouthhigh.co.uk
Twitter: @portsmouthhigh
Facebook: @PortsmouthHigh
Instagram: @portsmouthhighuk

Portsmouth High School, founded in 1882, is part of the Girls' Day School Trust (GDST), the leading family of independent girls' schools in the UK. As a charity that owns and runs 23 schools and two academies, the GDST reinvests all its income in its schools. For further information about the Trust, see p. xix or visit www.gdst.net.

Additional information about the school may be found on the school's website and a digital prospectus can be downloaded via the 'Request a Prospectus' button.

Number of Pupils. 360 are in the senior school (11–18), 160 in the prep school (rising 3–11).

Portsmouth High School is committed to the wellbeing of each individual pupil and enabling each girl to become the best version of herself. Each girl is encouraged to develop her own voice and her own views and to understand and build on her strengths. There is an atmosphere of achievement across the curriculum and examination results are consistently excellent.

Just a 5 minute walk from the sea, the school attracts pupils from an extensive area of Hampshire, West Sussex and the Isle of Wight. All major transport providers serve the area and the school also runs its own extensive minibus service throughout the local catchment area.

The senior school provides a broad and balanced education that prepares girls to specialise at A Level and the sixth form provides the perfect bridge to higher study. The senior school is accommodated in the original building; a capital investment programme has seen the development of a sport, design technology and geography building on the senior school site plus a state-of-the-art food technology centre. The separate science department has undergone refurbishment and has 7 well-equipped teaching laboratories.

A partnership with the University of Portsmouth gives the school joint use of the University's Langstone sports ground facilities, including a floodlit synthetic turf pitch and a multi-use games area; the site is just 2 miles from the school. In addition, facilities on-site include a Sport England standard sports hall with climbing wall, 3 tennis and 3 netball courts.

Sixth form students do not wear uniform, but have a smart 'Dress for Work' code. Sixth Form House has a large common room, kitchen and separate rooms for private study.

The Prep School. This is a school where intellectual curiosity is developed and girls enjoy learning through a range of opportunities both inside and outside the classroom with a unique explorer approach. The prep school is located 2 minutes' walk away in a wonderful Thomas Ellis Owen period house with extensive gardens including 2 netball courts, an all-weather sports pitch, an outdoor classroom and a range of other indoor and outdoor facilities.

The Curriculum. The aim at Portsmouth High School is to foster in each girl the confidence to take risks and tackle new challenges, within an atmosphere of ambition and enterprise, through providing appropriate teaching, advice and support. The focus on girls' learning is reflected in the design of learning spaces; the use of digital technology; a challenging and rewarding curriculum and a focus on pupils taking responsibility for their learning and having the confidence to take intellectual risks.

Co-Curricular Activities. There is an extensive programme of co-curricular activities in both the prep and senior schools. The lunchtime and after-school clubs range from climbing to public speaking and the programme is responsive to the interests of the pupils themselves.

There is an enthusiastic involvement in music, art, sport and drama with many performances and fixtures throughout the school calendar for prep and senior girls. Senior girls have the opportunity to become involved in The Duke of Edinburgh's Award scheme as well as a sixth form enrichment programme. There are regular overseas trips, sports and music tours.

Admission Procedures/Entrance Examinations. At 11+ and 13+ entry the examinations in mathematics and English are designed to test potential rather than knowledge. Prior to the 11+ examinations all girls take part in a series of team activities in school. At 13+ girls take part in a taster day and are interviewed by the Headmistress.

Sixth form entry is based on having at least English, mathematics and science GCSE and applicants are invited for interview. Entry into the prep school is based on taster days, observations and reports from current schools.

Fees per term (2021–2022). Senior School £4,800; Prep School: Years 3–6 £3,394, Pre-School to Year 2 £2,574. Please note these fees are subject to review for the spring term 2022.

The fees in the prep school include wraparound care from 7.30am to 6.00pm daily. The fees also cover the regular curriculum, school books, non-residential curriculum trips, stationery and other materials, public examinations, choral music, games and swimming. The fees for extra subjects, including individual lessons in instrumental music and speech training, are shown in the Admissions Handbook which can be downloaded from the school website.

Scholarships and Bursaries. Bursaries are means tested and are intended to ensure that the school remains accessible to bright girls who would be unable to enter the school without financial assistance.

Academic, sport, music, art and drama scholarships are available for 11+ and 13+. At sixth form (16+) art, drama and sport scholarships are available. Please see the scholarships and bursaries page on the school website for further details.

Charitable status. Portsmouth High School is part of The Girls' Day School Trust, Registered Charity number 306983.

Chair of the School Governing Board: Mrs K Butwilowska, JP, BA, MEd

Headmistress: Mrs J Prescott, BSc Cardiff, PGCE, NPQH

Deputy Head (Pastoral): Mrs H Trim, MSc Leicester, BSc Southampton

Deputy Head (Academic): Mrs Sarah Parker, MA Hons, PGCE

Headmaster, Prep School: Mr P Marshallsay, BA Ed

Admissions Registrar: Mrs C Thompson, BSc Hons

Queen Mary's School
A Woodard School

Baldersby Park, Topcliffe, Thirsk, North Yorkshire YO7 3BZ

Tel:	01845 575040
email:	admissions@queenmarys.org
website:	www.queenmarys.org
Twitter:	@QueenMarysSch
Facebook:	@Queen-Marys-School

Queen Mary's is an outstanding day and boarding school for girls aged 4 to 16 and boys aged 4 to 7. Academic excellence and exceptional extra-curricular opportunities are on offer within in a nurturing environment, where education is truly tailored to the individual. The school has a unique family atmosphere with friendliness and concern for others being an important part of the school's ethos. The country setting provides a safe haven for pupils to thrive and develop self-confidence.

Location. Queen Mary's is situated at Baldersby Park in a beautiful Grade 1 Palladian mansion, with 40 acres of grounds, including formal gardens, playing fields, sports facilities and Queen Mary's Equestrian Centre. Despite its idyllic surroundings, it is only 2 miles from Junction 49 of the A1 and within ten minutes of Thirsk station. York and Harrogate are within easy reach and so are Leeds/Bradford and Teesside airports. Minibuses transport pupils to and from home on a daily basis with 32 drop-off points.

The Curriculum. Pupils at Queen Mary's are offered a great deal in terms of breadth and depth of learning. Generous time is given to core subjects, English, Mathematics, Science and Modern Languages, but strong emphasis is also placed on the supporting subjects – Geography, History, Religious Studies, Latin, Classics, Design Technology, Music, Art and a varied programme of Physical Education. Classes are kept deliberately small, which means that every girl can receive plenty of support from her teachers. The school has an excellent scholarship programme and a learning support department for those pupils who have specific learning difficulties. The two years leading up to GCSE are full and focused, with most girls taking ten subjects at GCSE. The public examination results are excellent, with 40% of entries being awarded Grades 8–9 in 2021.

Pastoral care. All girls in school have personal tutors who oversee the academic, social and emotional development of each of their tutees. Building self-confidence and developing the individual talents of each pupil is seen as a vital aspect of the education offered. Each girl is encouraged to be self-reliant from an early age and pupils are taught a real concern for the needs of others. Girls in their final year at Queen Mary's undertake a number of important responsibilities to help the school community function smoothly.

Boarding. Queen Mary's offers a number of boarding options to suit the needs of parents and their daughters. Those who choose to board may be flexi, weekly or full boarders. The boarding community is thriving. The full boarders, who stay at weekends, enjoy a broad range of activities and trips.

Extracurricular Activities. An impressive range of extracurricular activities is available to all members of the school community. Choral and orchestral music are both huge strengths of the school, as is sport, with Hockey, Lacrosse, Swimming, Netball, Gymnastics, Football, Dance, Tennis, Rounders and Athletics all on offer. Facilities include an indoor swimming pool and full sized AstroTurf pitch and sports pavilion. Performing Arts, Drama, Debating and The Duke of Edinburgh's Award are highly popular choices and the all-weather outdoor Riding facilities allow more than 90 girls to ride each week. Children enjoy the opportunity to tackle the climbing wall, canoe on the adjacent River Swale or participate in other Outdoor Adventure activities.

Religious Affiliation. The school is part of the Woodard Corporation, an Anglican foundation which promotes Christian education and high academic and pastoral standards within all its schools. The school has its own Chapel. The school Chaplain prepares girls for confirmation. Girls of other denominations are welcome.

What happens after GCSE? Specialist careers advice is offered throughout the senior school and well-informed staff support the girls as they seek to make applications and progress on to some of the most prestigious sixth forms in the country. Every senior girl was awarded a place at her first choice of sixth form destination in 2021 and a healthy proportion of the girls each year join their new schools as scholars.

Scholarships. Scholarships are offered in the Senior School to those candidates who show particular academic flair or have special talent in Art, Music, Riding or Sport. Assessments are held during the Spring Term.

Entrance. By interview with the Head. Entry can be at most stages, subject to availability. An up-to-date prospectus can be sent upon request. Visit www.queenmarys.org for more information.

Fees per term (2021–2022). Reception £3,010 (day); Pre-Prep: Years 1–2 £3,295 (day); Year 3–6 £5,450 (day), £7,455 (weekly boarding), £7,790 (boarding); Senior: Years 7–8 £5,910 (day), £7,950 (weekly boarding), £8,295 (boarding); Years 9–11 £6,705 (day), £8,800 (weekly boarding), £9,155 (full boarding).

Charitable status. Queen Mary's School (Baldersby) Ltd is a Registered Charity, number 1098410. It exists to educate children in a Christian environment.

Chair of Governors: Mr T E Fielden, BA Hons, FCA

Head: Mrs Carole Cameron, MA, PGCE, NPQH, FRGS

Deputy Head: Mrs Deborah Hannam Walpole, BEd Hons

Queen's College, London

43–49 Harley Street, London W1G 8BT

Tel: 020 7291 7000
email: queens@qcl.org.uk
website: www.qcl.org.uk
Twitter: @queenscollegew1
Facebook: @QueensCollegeW1
Instagram: @queenscollegew_1
LinkedIn: /school/queens-college-w1

Queen's College was the first institution to provide an academic education and qualifications for young women. It was founded in 1848 by F D Maurice, Professor of Modern History at King's College, and was housed originally at 45 Harley Street.

Today it is a thriving girls' school of 385 pupils aged from 11–18, of whom around 90 are in the Sixth Form. Queen's College Preparatory School (020 7291 0660), which opened in 2002 at 61 Portland Place, takes girls from age 4–11.

Queen's College is situated in Harley Street, combining the beauty of four eighteenth century houses with modern facilities for science, languages, art, drama, music and computer science, as a well as a Hall and gymnasium. Three libraries, in the care of a graduate librarian, offer the students some 10,000 books, and there is also a unique archive recording the history of the College.

Curriculum. Class sizes rarely exceed twenty and the normal size of a year group is 60–65, divided into three forms. The year group is streamed for Mathematics and French during the first year and at a later stage for English, Latin and science.

Pupils usually take nine or ten subjects at GCSE, and the three sciences are taught separately. At A Level it is possible to study History of Art, Economics, or Government and Politics as well as the subjects already taken at GCSE.

There is a comprehensive programme of sport offered for all year groups. There is a gym on site and outdoor games take place at Paddington Recreation Ground. Younger pupils play netball, football, rounders, hockey and tennis, while seniors can choose from a wide range of activities including Taekwondo; there are thriving clubs before and after school for swimming, running and other leisure pursuits. Dance is offered to GCSE. Regular sports fixtures are arranged against local schools. The Duke of Edinburgh's Award is organised at bronze and silver levels. Individual music lessons are offered in all instruments including voice, and the musical or dramatic productions and jazz concert are highlights of each year.

The location of the College means that theatre and other educational visits in London are an integral part of the curriculum, complemented by opportunities to travel abroad or to other parts of the country. In recent years groups of girls have visited France, Greece, Germany, Italy, South Africa, the USA and Japan. There are regular ski trips, usually run jointly with Queen's College Preparatory School.

Almost all pupils leaving Queen's proceed to university, including Oxford or Cambridge, and several students each year choose to take an Art Foundation course at one of the London colleges. Former students are prominent in medicine, education, writing and the media; they retain contact with each other and the college through the Old Queens' Society, which also gives bursaries to families in financial need.

Pastoral Care. Queen's prides itself on its friendly and informal atmosphere, highly valued by pupils, parents and staff. Pastoral care is strong and we have a full-time nurse to support the work of form tutors and pastoral staff. A specialist in various special educational needs works individually with pupils once the need has been identified. We send reports to parents every half-term and hold regular Parents' Evenings. Parents also support the College through membership of the Parents' Association, giving practical and some financial assistance to College functions.

Admission. The College is a member of the London 11+ Consortium. Candidates for Year 7 entry sit the London 11+ Consortium entrance examination and are invited to attend an interview. As well as high academic standards we value enthusiasm and creativity, and academic, music and art awards are available to 11+ entrants.

If vacancies arise we also welcome applicants at other ages, particularly after GCSE, where there is a long-standing tradition of accepting students to undertake their A Level education at Queen's. Some scholarships are available on entry at this stage. Means-tested bursaries are available at all points of entry.

Fees per term (2021–2022). £6,895.

Charitable status. Queen's College, London is a Registered Charity, number 312726. It exists to provide education for girls. It is an Anglican foundation, open to those of all faiths or none who are prepared to subscribe to its ethos.

Patron: Her Majesty The Queen

Visitor: The Rt Revd and Rt Hon the Lord Bishop of London

Council:
Chairman: Professor Alison While, BSc MSc PhD London, RGN, RHV
Vice Chairman: Mr Matthew Hanslip Ward, MA Cantab
Mrs Jenny Blaiklock, MA Oxon
Mrs Catherine Brahams-Melinek, BA UCL, MA Durham
Mr Richard Ford, BSc LSE
Mrs Alexandra Gregory, BA Exeter, ACA
Mr David Imrie, MA Durham
Mrs Dina Mallett, BA Reading
Mrs Rae Perry, BA Trinity Washington, MBA New York, MSc Liverpool
Ms Holly Porter, MA Cantab, MA RCA, RIBA, FRSA
Mr Paul Reeve
Mr Joe Silvester, BA Bristol, MA London
Mrs Sarah-Jane Watson, LLB Durham
Mrs Linda Wei, BA Harvard, MBA INSEAD
Mrs Patricia Wilks, BA Oxon

Bursar and Clerk to the Council: C P Morton, BA Durham, MBA Cranfield

Principal: R W Tillett, MA Cantab

Headmistress of Queen's College Preparatory School: Mrs L Hall, BA Hons Bristol, MA Herts

Senior Deputy Head – Pastoral: Dr S J Abbott, BA, MA, PhD Reading

Deputy Head – Academic: K B Shapiro, BA Manchester, MA College of Europe

Deputy Head – Operations & Co-curricular: E A Wilkins, MA Oxon, MA Cardiff

Registrar: Ms Barbara Porter, LLB Open

Queen's Gate School

131–133 Queen's Gate, London SW7 5LE

Tel:	020 7589 3587
email:	info@queensgate.org.uk
website:	www.queensgate.org.uk
Twitter:	@QueensGateSch
Facebook:	@QueensGateSch
Instagram:	@QueensGateSchool
LinkedIn:	/queen-s-gate-school

Queen's Gate School is an independent day school for girls between the ages of 4–18 years. Established in 1891, the School benefits from an abundance of history on its doorstep. The V&A, Natural History Museum and Science Museum are all a short walk from the School, allowing for weekly visits for younger pupils and access to the private gardens at Stanhope and Kensington Gardens for outdoor activities. We aim to create a secure and happy environment for girls to realise their academic potential and explore their interests and talents. In addition, an exceptional art, music and drama department allows us to present plays at RADA and Carol concerts at Holy Trinity.

Academic work at Queen's Gate is essential at all stages, but our idea of education extends far beyond the classroom. We encourage all girls to pursue their interests through the various clubs organised at lunchtime or before and after School. As well as music and sport, we offer clubs for gardening, debating, drama, The Duke of Edinburgh, songwriting, bridge, stem club, creative writing, drone engineering and many more.

Emphasis is on courtesy and concern for others. Girls are encouraged to participate in charitable work in their local community and further afield, enabling them to become responsible citizens in a small school and a larger world.

Academic work at all stages at Queen's Gate is essential, it is at the heart of our School, but our idea of education goes far beyond the classroom. We want to provide an education that is much more than just academic success. We aim to produce confident, self-disciplined and motivated young women.

Junior School. We are a small, friendly school, but we enjoy all of the benefits of a broad community. Both the Junior and Senior Schools take advantage of shared resources, and many lessons, such as Science, STEAM and our six languages, are taught by specialist teachers.

Academic standards are high, and a love of learning is evident throughout the School. The Junior School Curriculum at Queen's Gate School includes a well-balanced range of diverse and exciting subjects taught by specialist teachers, with excellent enrichment opportunities.

Specialist teachers teach the sciences in our well-equipped laboratories, and we also have specialists in all six languages, art, music, design technology and PE.

Teaching groups are small, and learning is 'hands-on' investigative and collaborative; teaching methods are vibrant, dynamic and challenging. Maths challenges, entrepreneurial projects, English Speaking Board Examinations, art exhibitions and creative writing competitions run throughout the School and add extra excitement to our busy curriculum.

Junior School Pastoral Care. At Queen's Gate Junior School, we are renowned for our exceptional pastoral care. However, we understand that the wellbeing of our girls is just as important as their outstanding academic education.

Queen's Gate is a small school, with just one class for each year, enabling us to give our pupils a great deal of individual attention. Our family ethos ensures that each child is valued and nurtured; support and extension derive naturally from the built close relationships.

Senior School. Girls enter the Senior School at the age of 11–18, from both our Junior School and independent and maintained feeder schools from across the capital. We aim to create a secure, happy, and stimulating environment where each girl will enjoy her time and flourish academically and personally. Teaching methods combine modern technology with traditional rigour at all stages.

Senior School Pastoral Care. Each pupil has a Form member and meets with her Form Tutor or deputy each morning, afternoon and end of the day.

Our Heads of Years also oversee progress and the girls' general wellbeing in their care.

Our Learning Support Department plays an integral part in the wellbeing of our girls and liaises closely with our subject and pastoral staff to ensure that any difficulties are recognised and supported in the best way possible. We also have EAL support. In addition, our School Counsellors visit the School each week to support girls, staff and parents.

Sixth Form. The Sixth Form is a time for pupils to build on their experiences, to think and plan for life after School. In addition to the academic subjects offered in Sixth Form, we also offer a wide range of other opportunities. These include our:

Wider World Programme – a rolling, two-year enrichment programme of weekly lectures during the Autumn and Spring Terms, designed to widen knowledge of important issues and debates. In addition, we also offer help with topics that girls may be required to discuss at their university interviews, and we also introduce them to university-style lectures.

Past speakers have included:

- Dr Helen Pankhurst, women's rights activist and author of *Deeds Not Words*
- Dame Helena Morrissey DBE, a British financier and campaigner
- Prof. Lyndon Da Cruz of Moorfields Eye Hospital
- Penny Marshall from ITN News

Duke of Edinburgh – The Gold Award is a fantastic opportunity to participate in physical activity, volunteer, and learn and improve skills.

The Gold programme involves:

- Volunteering for 12 months
- Doing physical activity and skill; one for 12 months, one for six months
- A residential section (four nights away from home)
- A practice expedition

- The qualifying expedition

Inspiring Women Series – was developed to provide an opportunity for staff, students, members of the local community and other interested parties to hear from women who have been successful within their field.

The diverse range of high-profile speakers has encouraged engagement and discussion, and the series is now a regular and essential feature in the Queen's Gate events calendar.

Speakers have included: Sally Gunnell OBE; TV presenter and vlogger, Venetia Falconer; Adventurer, Pip Stewart; and Film producer, Kate Pakenham.

Enrichment – All girls in Lower Sixth will attend a weekly enrichment tutorial chosen from various options available.

Available Enrichment includes:

- Model United Nations (MUN)
- Extended Project Qualification (EPQ)
- Oxbridge essays and competitions
- The ARTiculation Prize
- Logical Reasoning
- SAT Preparation
- Becoming a Mental Health Ambassador
- A history of Europe through European cinema
- Current Affairs

Curriculum. Girls follow as broad a curriculum as possible and generally take GCSE in ten subjects, including English, Mathematics, Science, and a modern language.

We offer an extensive range of AS/A Level subjects; four AS Levels in the first year and three taken at A2 Level.

Games. Netball, Hockey, Tennis, Swimming, Rowing, Athletics, Basketball, Horse Riding, Cross-Country, Biathlon and Dance.

Admission. By test and interview in the Junior School; by London 11+ Consortium entrance examination; by the School's entrance examinations for entry to other years in the Senior School.

Applicants for the Sixth Form require a minimum of six GCSEs at A Grade with A grades required in those subjects they wish to pursue to A Level.

Registration fee: £125.

Fees per term (2021–2022). £6,690–£7,410.

Board of Governors:
Mr Michael Cumming (*Chair*)
Mrs Laura Marani (*Deputy Chair*)
Dr Alexandra Cran-McGreehin
Mr Jonathan Dobson
Mr William Gillen
Mrs Reica Gray
Dr Jill Harling
Mr Gary Li
Mr Peter Trueman
Mrs Manina Weldon

Principal: Mrs R M Kamaryc, BA Hons, MSc, PGCE

Senior School:

Director of Pastoral Care: Ms C De La Pena
Director of Teaching, Learning & Assessment: Mr M Crundwell, BSc Hons, MPhil Lon, MEd Dist, QTS
Director of Operations & Academic Development: Mrs Z Camenzuli, BA, MA Oxon, PGCE

Director of Curriculum: Mr P Williams, MA
Director of Sixth Form & Outreach: Dr M Lee, BSc, PhD Lon

Head of LVI: Miss C E Adler, BSc Hons, QTS
Head of UV: Mrs S Sexon, BA, MA, QTS
Head of V: Mr A Cohen, MA, PGCE
Head of IV: Mr R Moss, BA Hons, PGCE
Head of LIV: Mrss M Miah, BSc Hons, PGCE
Head of Remove: Miss C Spencer, BSc Hons, PGCE

Junior School:
Director of the Junior School: Mr J Denchfield, BA Hons PGCE
Preliminary & EYFS Coordinator: Miss E Allan, BA, BEd, PGCE
Transition: Mrs Y Dhaliwal, BA, BEd, MEd [Maternity Cover]
Mrs G McCarter, BA [Maternity Leave]
IB & Acting KS1 Coordinator: Mrs M MacDonnell, BA, PGCE
Mrs E Russell, BA, MA, PGCE [Maternity Leave]
IA: Mr P Dawson BA Hons, PGCE
IIB & Senior Tutor: Mrs C Makhlouf, BEd Hons
IIA: Mr M Molero Segura BA
III Form & Director of Studies: Miss L Coles, BA, PGCE

Redmaids' High School

Westbury Road, Westbury-on-Trym, Bristol BS9 3AW

Tel: 0117 962 2641
email: admissions@redmaidshigh.co.uk
website: www.redmaidshigh.co.uk
Twitter: @RedmaidsHigh
Facebook: @redmaidshighschool
Instagram: @redmaidshigh
LinkedIn: /redmaids'-high-school

With a history dating back to 1634, we understand how valuable single-sex education can be in giving girls a great start in life. Supportive, inspirational staff, a progressive mind-set, excellent pastoral care and wide ranging opportunities, mean we develop inspirational young women, who are fully equipped for whatever path they choose in life.

Our academic record is excellent and our students excel in a diverse range of subjects. But we are so much more than the sum of our exam results. By prioritising development of the whole girl, giving breadth and depth of knowledge and experience, as well as an international mindedness, we aim to equip girls to become the leaders of tomorrow.

Redmaids' High became the first International Baccalaureate (IB) World School in Bristol, winning accreditation in 2008. More than twelve years on, we have guided our Sixth Formers to world-beating IB Diploma results, alongside our established and successful A Level programme. Both courses are highly valued by universities and employers and generate rich and diverse learning throughout the school.

Opportunities here extend far beyond the classroom. Girls are given the chance to become exceptional public speakers who excel in local and national competitions; future game-changing scientists, engineers and mathematicians; adventurers, who spend time caving, kayaking and competing in local and national sporting fixtures. We support and encourage them to be whoever they want to be.

We have the experience and expertise that enable our girls to shine whilst helping them understand the importance of curiosity, collaboration and possibility.

Our first-class facilities provide the very best learning environments, allowing girls to excel not only academically but also in sport, drama, art and music. Technology makes a central contribution to the way students work and learn – we use iPad technology in the classroom to create dynamic and independent learning environments. In addition, the international links developed over recent years and the thriving alumnae network are an integral part of the school and a hugely valuable asset for the students.

All this adds up to Redmaids' High School being one of the finest girls' schools in the UK for girls aged 7 to 18. The opportunities and facilities – combined with excellent teaching – equip young women with the skills and confidence to truly make their mark in today's world.

Character. The school provides a positive and purposeful learning environment where everything is focused on the girls; where there is no dilution of attention to their needs as young women; and where they are offered all the opportunities and hold all the responsibilities.

Facilities. The 12-acre site at Westbury-on-Trym, Bristol, just beyond the Clifton Downs, provides an inspirational backdrop for learning, with space for girls to relax and enjoy. The campus has a spacious, rural feel, despite being just a few miles from the city centre.

At the centre of the Senior School is Burfield House, built in the 19th century as a private family home. Today it houses classrooms, offices, the Pearson Library, Dining Hall and main school reception.

Redland Hall, opened in September 2017, provides a modern performance space and auditorium, complete with flexible seating, first-class lighting and acoustically engineered sound systems. It also houses new classrooms, additional music practice rooms and an area for serving refreshments at key school events.

The contemporary, self-contained Sixth Form Centre, opened in 2011, provides a university-style, independent learning space for Years 12 and 13.

Exceptional sports facilities are a hallmark of the school. There is an ethos of 'sport-for-all' balanced with elite competition. The recently redeveloped off-site sports ground, The Lawns at Cribbs Causeway, offers an International Hockey Federation certified pitch, a new multi-purpose area used for both netball and tennis and an extensive athletics, cricket and rounders space. On site at Westbury-on-Trym on our hockey pitches, netball courts and in our sports hall, girls take part in netball, basketball, fencing, judo, dance and gymnastics.

A detached former stable block is home to the music department, and includes teaching and rehearsal space. Students can also access specialist recording equipment and individual workstations with keyboards and Apple computers.

Six fully-equipped, modern laboratories provide everything the Science Department needs, while the Art Department has room to be creative with two large studio spaces, a computer suite and a library.

Extended Day. Senior girls can arrive from 7.45am and stay until 6.00pm, at no extra charge. Breakfast can be bought on an ad-hoc basis and supervised homework and extra-curricular activities take place until 5.30pm. Clubs and societies include: current affairs, choirs, orchestras, Harry Potter club, the Duke of Edinburgh's Award scheme, film production, drama and many sports clubs.

School Life. The School Council and Sixth Form leadership positions encourage students to take responsibility for others. Peer support systems, clubs run by older students and staff, and charitable fundraising demonstrate the pupils' involvement in their community. Assemblies celebrate pupils' all-round achievements, examine topical issues and offer opportunities for thought, reflection and spiritual exploration.

Curriculum. For the first three years, all Redmaids' High students follow a broad and balanced curriculum. Setting takes place in Mathematics from Year 7 and separate Sciences from Year 9. In Year 7, all girls study two modern languages chosen from French, German, Russian and Spanish. In Years 10 and 11, we select the best mix of qualifications from GCSE and IGCSE to prepare the girls for the next steps in their education.

Sixth Form. Redmaids' High offers Sixth Formers the choice of A Levels or the International Baccalaureate (IB) Diploma. Students take three or four linear A Levels, with exams at the end of Year 13. Most girls enrich their A Level experience by taking an additional qualification such as an EPQ, Creative Writing course, Astronomy GCSE, or a Level 3 Food Science or Sports Leaders award. IB Diploma students select six subjects, three each at Higher and Standard level, which they take together with compulsory core topics of Theory of Knowledge, Creativity Activity Service, and the Extended Essay. Final IB Diploma exams also take place at the end of the two-year course.

Redmaids' High Sixth Formers enjoy the independence of a modern, purpose-built centre with dedicated teaching, seminar and common rooms, café, quiet study area, ICT facilities and careers library. Students achieve their full academic potential through high-quality teaching and developing habits of independent study and academic rigour. Almost all students go on to study at university, including Oxbridge. Sixth Formers take on many leadership roles within school and develop a broader understanding of the wider world through a varied community service programme. They also follow a Futures Programme to prepare them for life beyond school and receive individual careers advice.

Fees per term (2021–2022). Years 7 to 13: £5,150. Curricular school trips are included in this fee. Lunch is compulsory for Years 7 to 11 and is invoiced termly. Other extras are individual music lessons, speech and drama lessons, optional non-academic trips, and any one-to-one tuition for those with individual needs.

Admission to Senior School. All students are admitted on the basis of an entrance examination, interview and headteacher's report. Key points of entry are at Year 7, 9 and 12. The entrance exam for Years 7 and 9 is held in January for admission the following September. Entry can take place into other years, subject to availability.

Scholarships. Scholarships are available to girls who show true potential, a dedication to learning and a lot of ambition in any subject. They are available for entry into Years 7, 9, 10 and 12 for both internal and external

candidates. They may also be awarded to exceptional students entering at other stages.

Bursaries. The unique founding origins of Redmaids' High mean the school can offer a number of fully and partially-funded places.

Junior School. *See Junior School entry in IAPS section.*

Charitable status. Redmaids' High School is a Registered Charity, number 1105017. It has existed since 1634 to provide an education for girls.

Governing Body:
Chairman: Mr Andrew Hillman
Vice-Chairman: Mrs Elizabeth Clarson and Mrs Rosemary Heald

Mrs Katie Atkins	Mrs Elizabeth Fry
Mr Richard Bacon	Mr Mike Henry
Ms Sally Dore	Mr Richard Page
Dr Bisola Ezobi	Mrs Gillian Rowcliffe
Dr Abdul Farooq	Mrs Anne Taylor
Mr James Fox	Mrs Juliet White

Senior School:

Head: **Mr Paul Dwyer**, BA Hons Oxon, FCCT

Deputy Head: Mrs Laura Beynon, MA Durham
Deputy Head: Mrs Kate Doarks, BSc Hons Bristol

Assistant Head Sixth Form and International: Mr Jon Cooper, MA Hons St Andrews
Assistant Head Co-curricular: Dr Alice England, PhD Sheffield
Assistant Head Staff: Mr Tom Johnston, BA Hons Bath College of Higher Education
Assistant Head Pastoral: Mrs Jacklyn Turner, BSc Hons Aston

Director of Finance and Operations: Mr M Marshall, FCMA

Junior School:

Headteacher: Mrs Lisa Brown, BSc Hons Leicester

PA to Headmistress: Mrs Jenny Bell
PA to Director of Finance and Operations: Mrs Susannah Wooldridge

Admissions Registrars:
Mrs Lynn McCabe (*Juniors*)
Mrs Sarah Baker-Patch & Mrs Antonia Firebrace (*Seniors and Sixth Form*)

Rye St Antony

Pullen's Lane, Oxford OX3 0BY

Tel:	01865 762802
email:	enquiries@ryestantony.co.uk
website:	www.ryestantony.co.uk
Twitter:	@RyeStAntony
Facebook:	@RyeStAntony

Motto: Be Ambitious, Be Curious, Be Yourself.

For over 90 years, Rye St Antony has offered first-class teaching, excellent facilities and a wide programme of enrichment opportunities to support Rye St Antony pupils in discovering who they are and who they have it in them to become – to be their own unique individual.

Recent inspections have given the school top rankings: 'Outstanding' by Ofsted and 'Excellent' in all areas inspected by the Independent Schools Inspectorate (ISI Inspection Feb 2017). Set in a beautiful twelve-acre site only one mile from the centre of Oxford, Rye helps pupils seek excellence in the recognition that every pupil is an individual with their own unique talents, skills and interests to be developed. Academic standards are high, and we never forget that wider life skills are also important to prepare our pupils for a happy, fulfilling and successful life.

Rye St Antony is a school of 300 pupils that provides a safe and stimulating environment in which every individual is considered a valued member of the community. Each young person is encouraged to be ambitious in their aspirations and goals, curious in their learning and themselves in every walk of life. We respect others and pupils are challenged to consider their opinions; no one is overlooked. Pupils have access to the best and most varied opportunities for enrichment which challenges them, develops their character and helps them to be independent, determined and resilient. Each year almost every member of Sixth Form achieves her preferred university place, and destinations range from Veterinary Science at Bristol, Radiography at University of West England, and Paramedic Science at Coventry to English Literature at Cardiff, Occupational Therapy at the University of East Anglia and History at York. The school really does bring out the best in each pupil, helping all girls to discover the subjects they are passionate about and enabling them to take their first steps towards a rewarding future.

We have day places for girls aged 3–18 years and boys aged 3–11 years. Rye St Antony offers full, weekly and flexible boarding options for girls in year 5 and above, including occasional boarding to help each pupil to fully participate in all that the school has to offer.

The school is highly regarded for its happy and purposeful atmosphere and its strong sense of community and has been successfully educating the individual for over 90 years. The school's aim is to help each pupil develop the intellectual curiosity and skills, the emotional understanding and resources, the ability to work independently and with others, and the personal, social and spiritual values that will lead to personal fulfilment and the ability to contribute something of value to the world. Our pupils leave us as confident young people sure of their ability, and well equipped and excited for the future that lies ahead.

Religious Life. Founded with a Catholic Ethos, the Christian values of respect, dignity and tolerance continue to underpin school life today. Rye pupils have faith in each other and faith in themselves and their abilities. They are fully involved in all aspects of the school community, leading societies, activities and school council to name a few. The nurturing and inspiring environment that is Rye means that everyone is welcome, and everyone is successful.

Senior School Curriculum. Our girls are encouraged to challenge themselves, push boundaries and achieve their maximum potential. The small class sizes means that lessons are tailored to each girl's unique learning style and each individual has the freedom to express themselves. Whether independently or as members of a team, our pupils are curious, questioning and confident in their ability to analyse, investigate and evaluate ideas. Above all, we develop a thirst for learning which stays with our pupils for life.

Girls have access to a broad and balanced common course for the first three years comprising English, Mathematics, Physics, Chemistry, Biology, Religious Education, French, History, Geography, Technology, Information and Communications Technology, Art, Graphic Communication, Music, Drama and Physical Education. There is a full PSHE programme.

Seventeen subjects are offered as GCSE subjects. For the two-year GCSE course pupils usually study 10 subjects, a mixture of options and core subjects.

In Sixth Form three or four A Level subjects are chosen from over twenty options. We also offer Leiths Extended Certificate in Professional Cookery and BTEC Business.

Careers Guidance. The school's careers advisory service provides help and guidance for all pupils, and there is a formal programme of careers advice throughout Years 9, 10 and 11 and Sixth Form. Almost all pupils go on to university and are helped to investigate thoroughly the Higher Education and careers options open to them, careful guidance being given concerning their applications and interviews. The support of the Head and other senior staff is available at all stages. Work experience placements are supported, and pupils are encouraged to make particular use of this option at the end of their GCSE courses. Visiting speakers give lectures on various higher education and careers topics and visits to appropriate conferences and exhibitions are arranged regularly.

Prep School Curriculum. The Prep School and Senior School are closely linked, and Prep School pupils are steadily introduced to the specialist teaching and facilities of the Senior School.

In Early Years, the teaching of most subjects is undertaken by the class teachers. Additionally, children enjoy specialist weekly teaching in Music, French, PE, Cookery and Drama. Children also take part in weekly Forest School sessions.

In Years 5 and 6 pupils are taught by subject teachers, some of whom also teach in the Senior School. This arrangement gives them the benefit of specialist teaching and encourages them to develop a feeling of confidence and continuity when the time comes for them to move into the Senior School. It also allows those girls to build positive classroom relationships before moving into the Senior School. The use of the Senior School facilities by Prep School pupils is particularly valuable in Science, Art, Music, Physical Education and Drama. There is a Prep School Library in Langley Lodge, and older Prep School pupils may also use the King Library in the Senior School.

Performing Arts. The school has a strong tradition of debating and public speaking, and pupils have many successes to their credit in city, county and regional competitions. A major drama production each year, and various smaller presentations give pupils the opportunity to develop their skills in performing, directing, lighting, sound, stage design, costume design and make-up. There are frequent visits to Stratford, London and regional theatres, including the Oxford Playhouse.

The majority of pupils learn one musical instrument and some learn two or more; there are two choirs, one orchestra and several smaller ensembles, and some pupils are often members of local ensembles outside School. Instruments studied include piano, violin, viola, cello, flute, oboe, clarinet, trumpet, bassoon, saxophone, french horn, guitar and percussion. Through musical productions, concerts, and the liturgy there are many opportunities for pupils to contribute to the musical life of the school.

In Drama pupils prepare for the examinations of the London Academy of Music and Dramatic Art (LAMDA), and in Music, they prepare for the examinations of the Associated Board of the Royal Schools of Music (ABRSM).

Sport. The school has an indoor sports centre and well maintained playing fields, Astro courts that can be played on throughout the year, and there is an outdoor heated swimming pool. The principal winter sports are netball and hockey; the principal summer sports are tennis, swimming, athletics and rounders. Girls compete regularly in local, county and regional tournaments.

Duke of Edinburgh's Award. The school has an outstanding record in The Duke of Edinburgh's Award, each year about 20 girls achieving the Bronze Award, 10 girls achieving the Silver Award and several more girls achieving the Gold Award. The purpose of the Award is to give challenge, responsibility and adventure to young people, thus encouraging them to develop initiative and team skills.

Visits. Fieldwork, conferences, lectures, art exhibitions, plays and concerts give girls an interesting programme of visits within the UK. Visits abroad include study courses, exchanges, sports tours and skiing holidays, and the school regularly hosts visiting groups from schools overseas.

Health. The School Nurse works closely with the School Medical Adviser who sees girls at the nearby Health Centre. Dental and orthodontic treatment can be arranged locally, and the John Radcliffe Hospital is five minutes away.

Admissions. Applicants to the Prep School are invited for a taster day and during the day will sit a Mathematics and English assessment in the classroom setting. 11+ and 13+ applicants will be invited for an entrance day during which they will take assessments in English and Mathematics. All other applicants to the Senior School will sit assessments relative to their year.

Admission to the Sixth Form is by interview, school report and GCSE results. International applicants will be assessed by interview, level of English and assessments relative to their year.

Scholarships. Scholarships are available at 11+, 13+ and 16+ in 5 subjects. We recognise that individuals may have a particular set of skills or a talent that may fall outside of these categories, and to these pupils we can award an all-round scholarship or exhibition.

Fees per term (2021–2022). Senior School: Full Boarders £9,805; Weekly Boarders £9,325; Day Pupils £5,685. Prep School: Full Boarders £8,400; Weekly Boarders £7,940; Day Pupils £3,425–£4,525.

Charitable status. Rye St Antony School Limited is a Registered Charity, number 309685, to provide for the education and welfare of pupils, in accordance with the school's aims.

St Augustine's Priory School

Hillcrest Road, Ealing, London W5 2JL

Tel: 020 8997 2022
email: admissions@sapriory.com
website: www.sapriory.com
Twitter: @staugustinesp
Facebook: @StAugustine's_Priory
Instagram: @st.augustines.priory
LinkedIn: /st-augustine-s-priory

Motto: *Veritas*

St Augustine's Priory is a Catholic, independent day school for girls aged 3–18 and also welcomes boys in the nursery. The school was founded in France in 1634 by Lady Mary Tredway to provide a haven where young English women could be provided with an independent education. Moving to Ealing in 1914–15, to its current location, the School follows the philosophy expounded by its Patron, St Augustine of Hippo: children (and for that matter adults) achieve their best when they are happy.

Our vision is for girls to leave St Augustine's equipped with an outstanding academic education and also with the full range of skills required to lead an effective and fulfilling life as women. As part of their journey, in a girls' school environment, they will acquire the skills of self-knowledge, of reflection, of intellectual risk-taking, of persuasiveness and team-building and of emotional strength as well as a cultural fabric for their enriched enjoyment of life. Our team of dedicated and enthusiastic teachers, teaching assistants and support staff care for the girls and encourage them in all aspects of their education and development.

Number of Pupils. There are approximately 480 girls aged from 3–18 across the school.

Location. The School is well served by public transport, with Central and Piccadilly line connections within a ten-minute stroll, Ealing Broadway Underground and main line station approximately 20 minutes' walk away and buses stopping nearby. The School sits in an idyllic setting of thirteen acres, with views across to the South Downs.

Admission. St Augustine's Priory is a unique and vibrant community; the best way to understand it is to come and look around the school and meet the pupils, Headteacher and staff. During the application process we invite Parents to visit us on Open Morning during the Michaelmas and Lent Terms and you are also warmly invited to visit the school for a private appointment at other times.

St Augustine's Priory operates a selective entry procedure. Selection is based upon academic merit and potential, which is assessed through an entry examination, an interview at the school and references from the candidate's previous school. Our selection process is designed to identify pupils who are able to benefit from our balanced and well-rounded education and to make a positive contribution towards the life of the school. Admission to the Prep is via interview and assessment in the Michaelmas Term. Girls in the Junior School move up seamlessly into the Senior School. External candidates for 9+, 11+, and 16+ sit entrance examinations on our various Selection Days in the Lent Term.

Those wishing to join the Sixth Form are invited to visit the school and meet with the Director of Sixth Form. Interviews are then conducted by the appropriate Heads of Department along with the Headteacher and offers are sent out with conditional GCSE pass requirements.

Faith. St Augustine's Priory is a Catholic Independent Day School for Girls. The Chapel is at the heart of school life and is used for assemblies, weekly Masses and as a place for moments of quiet reflection and prayer. We also welcome girls from other religions and faiths and learn from them.

Pastoral Care. Children from all backgrounds and all races, with a wide range of gifts, make up the community which is St Augustine's Priory. From their first day, girls become part of a community which respects the beliefs and customs of its members and learns to work together. When problems arise and questions need to be asked, we encourage a very personal approach.

Curriculum. We offer an extensive and balanced curriculum including PSHEE, and offer 20 subjects at GCSE and IGCSE and 24 subjects at AS and A2 Level. Girls will usually take ten or more subjects at GCSE.

Priory 6 (Sixth Form) and Careers. Priory 6 facilities include a common room, ICT suite, kitchen and balcony overlooking the South Downs. The Head Girl and Deputy Head girls have their own office.

We expect girls to think about their next steps and to make informed decisions at every stage of their development. Priory 6 students are supported by the Careers Coordinator and Head of UCAS who provide advice and guidance. We work with the students to consider their many future options, assisting with university and course selection, preparation for Oxbridge and other university applications and subsequent interviews. This process is supplemented by a fortnightly programme of guest speakers and a biennial Careers Evening.

Working with Form Tutors and the Director of Priory 6, every girl is expected to examine her own strengths and to explore possibilities suitable for her interests and personal abilities. Talks, conferences, seminars, courses and University Open Days allow all our students to keep abreast of opportunities on offer.

All of this support builds on the guidance received throughout the school. When our girls leave here for university, they take with them not only impressive qualifications but also kindness, an understanding of, and the ability to adapt to, the world in which they live, the confidence to succeed in whatever they choose to do and above all, friendships which will last them through life.

Co-curricular Activities. A wide variety of co-curricular activities aim to ensure spiritual, moral, social and cultural development of all pupils, and to enable students to develop their talents to the full by searching for excellence. Girls will develop and practise new skills, integrate with children across year groups and be challenged and encouraged to take risks. Clubs on offer include fencing, yoga, life drawing, cake decorating, photography, Cipher & ink illustration and Poetry. The school excels in its extremely popular sports activities fielding winning teams in hockey, netball, swimming and cross country.

Whilst Drama forms part of the curriculum we also stage a biennial major production in the Spring at Questors Theatre, which allows involvement by the whole Senior School. We offer LAMDA, qualifications in Acting, Speaking Verse and Prose and Speaking in Public. A Musical Theatre club is run for Preps and a Drama club for Juniors.

Music flourishes throughout the school with girls taking part in school orchestras, ensembles, choirs and concerts. A wide range of private musical instrument lessons are also on offer.

Art is outstanding and the girls' work is displayed throughout the school. An annual Art Exhibition is held each summer and is open to the public, and the department makes use of visits to the many theatres, museums and galleries in London.

A majority of girls complete The Duke of Edinburgh's Bronze, Silver and Gold Awards. Visits to Iceland, New York and Salamanca enrich Modern Foreign Languages and Geography learning, as well as History visits to Berlin, sports tours to Paris and Holland and ski trips to Italy and Canada.

Facilities. St Augustine's Priory offers superb amenities including a full-size floodlit all-weather astroturf pitch, floodlit competition-sized netball court and indoor sports hall set in stunning 13-acre grounds. In 2017 the school enhanced, expanded and modernised its School Hall complete with acoustics and sound-proofing.

In addition to sporting facilities, our 13 acres include a dedicated Prep meadow, orchards, Sixth Form Rose Garden, outdoor stage and Priory Farm which homes chickens, micro-pigs and sheep. The state-of-the-art Science Wing opened in 2007 with four laboratories and dedicated Senior and Junior music and drama rooms. A new Nursery block was completed in 2011. To complement this there are two IT suites, music practice rooms, Senior and Junior Art rooms, a Sixth Form Art studio and separate photography studio, Modern Languages Academy, dedicated Sixth Form areas, private studies and seminar rooms, and Scriptorium. Kitchens are on site and the Chef and catering staff serve fresh cooked lunches daily.

Fees per term (2021–2022). Nursery: £1,797 (5 mornings/afternoons), £3,978 (full time), Preparatory Department £4,224, Junior Department £4,725, Senior Department £5,658.

Additional information may be found on the school's website and a more detailed prospectus may be obtained from the School.

Charitable status. St Augustine's Priory School Limited is a Registered Charity, number 1097781.

Board of Governors:
Mr P D'Arcy (*Chair*)
Mrs C Phillips (*Vice Chair and Chair of Health & Safety Committee*)
Mr R Beeston
Miss M Bowler
Mr B Cassidy (*Chair of Academic Committee*)
Mrs C Copeland
Mr J Davies (*Chair of Safeguarding Committee*)
Dr B Marino
Mr H Parmar (*Chair of Finance & Capital Projects Committee*)
Mrs A Sparks
Dom M Stapleford
Mr F Steadman
Mr J Philpott (*Clerk to the Governors*)

Senior Leadership Team:

Headteacher: Mrs S Raffray, MA, NPQH, Chair of The Society of Heads

Deputy Head (*Pastoral*) *Seniors*: Mrs M George, MA, PGCE (*Designated Safeguarding Lead*)
Deputy Head (*Academic*) *Seniors*: Ms C MacAllister, ALCM, BA, ACA, PGCE
Deputy Head (*Pastoral*) *Juniors*: Mrs K Mackay, BA, PGCE (*Deputy Designated Safeguarding Lead – Juniors & Co-curricular Coordinator, Juniors & Seniors*)
Deputy Head (*Academic*) *Juniors*: Miss E Keane, BA, NPQH (*Deputy Designated Safeguarding Lead*)

Director of Priory 6 & UCAS: Mrs H Maclennan, MA Cantab, MEd

Bursar: Mr J Philpott, BA, MA
Registrar and Head of Communications: Mrs G Savic, BA
Director of Operations & Marketing: Miss L Masih, BSc, CSBM

Welfare Staff:
School Nurse: Mrs R Finnegan, RGN
Counsellor and Play Therapist Consultant: Mrs R Good, BSc, PGCE, Dip Therapeutic Counselling

Key Administration Staff:
Mrs K Bhatti, MSc Econ, ACLIP, DipLis (*Librarian*)
Ms N Chandler (*PA to the Bursar & HR Officer*)
Miss S Masih, BA (*Admissions & Communications Assistant*)
Miss L Naylor, MAAT (*School Office Manager, Finance and Examinations Assistant*)
Mrs T Sumpter, RGN, AMSPAR (*PA to the Headteacher*)
Mrs G Vymeris MA (*Assistant Bursar*)

Please see our website for a full Staff List.

St Catherine's School
Bramley

Station Road, Bramley, Guildford, Surrey GU5 0DF

Tel: 01483 893363
email: schooloffice@stcatherines.info
           admissions@stcatherines.info
website: www.stcatherines.info
Twitter: @stcatsbramley

Founded as a Church of England School for Girls in 1885, welcoming both day girls and boarders, St Catherine's is one of the UK's premier girls' schools. The location, just three miles south of Guildford and surrounded by miles of countryside offers space and green vistas and yet, is within one hour of central London and Heathrow Airport.

In The ISI Report, October 2016, We were pleased to receive '*Excellent*' in all three focus areas. Wherever the Inspectors visited from PP1 to the U6, and from Day to Boarding, they encountered girls and staff who were proud to represent St Catherine's. A recurring theme of the Report was the close teamwork between the girls and their teachers. '*Pupils attitude to learning are exemplary. Teachers create an ambience of encouragement in which learning thrives*'.

Superb examination results are testament to the quality of teaching and learning, where students are not afraid to show enthusiasm and ambition. Lessons are taught in well-appointed classrooms by subject specialists. In 2021, 94% of girls achieved A*–B at A Level and 91% achieved Grades 9–7 at GCSE.

With extensive playing fields, superb sports facilities and an auditorium which boasts better acoustics than many London venues, it is no surprise that St Catherine's is always buzzing with life after the teaching day is over.

A well-established House system underpins the whole School, allowing new girls to feel at home very quickly, encouraging an ethos of care and concern for others as well as a friendly competitive spirit.

The outstanding results gained by our students in public examinations secure them places at the top universities, in competitive disciplines like medicine and veterinary science, law and languages. This success comes not only as a result of the fine quality of the teaching, but is also due to the individual attention received by every girl. St Catherine's places great emphasis on creating a happy environment where every girl is encouraged to work hard to maximise her talents. The atmosphere is friendly and one in which children can develop and grow in a very stimulating environment.

Pivotal to the life of St Catherine's are the six school Houses. The girls' loyalty and affection for their Houses is impressive with memories of inter-house plays, competitions and matches enduring long after School days have ended.

A broad and varied curriculum allows all pupils to participate in many challenging and rewarding extracurricular activities. As a Church of England School girls are encouraged to think of others and impressive sums of money are raised for charity each year. The School has its own beautiful chapel which is used by the girls on a daily basis.

The School's flexible approach to boarding makes it increasingly attractive to busy, professional families; the ISI team picked out boarding as one of the outstanding features of St Catherine's. The School welcomes both weekly and full boarders who enjoy a busy and exciting programme. The Four cornerstones of boarding at St Catherine's: Expert care from experienced and highly trained boarding staff; a huge raft of on-site activities with superb facilities; a friendly and welcoming community; and, last but not least, boarding at St Catherine's represents excellent value for money.

Facilities include 3 lacrosse pitches, a multi-purpose sports hall, fitness suite and indoor pool. The auditorium provides superb acoustics for our musical and theatrical productions, better than many London venues. The Sixth Form girls have their own Library which provides a perfect study environment right at the heart of the School. The Anniversary Halls and the Speech Hall Library were officially opened by the School's patron, HRH The Duchess of Cornwall; the first Baron Ashcombe, the Duchess's Great-Great Grandfather was one of the original founders and benefactors of St Catherine's.

Activities Week is held each year in the Summer Term when every girl in the School participates in a variety of programmes organised to both support the curriculum and offer challenges not normally met in the classroom. Pupils participate in outward bound ventures, an industrial heritage tour to the north and midlands, modern language courses in France, Germany and Spain, whilst Sixth Formers focus on university choices. Activities Week costs are included in the fees.

International links are also very important. St Catherine's has an exchange programme with St Catherine's Melbourne, Australia and there are also links with schools in Kenya and South Africa.

St Catherine's has an unrivalled reputation in art, music, sport and drama; photography and textiles are popular options amongst the Sixth Form, and younger girls are encouraged by an enthusiastic Art and Design department to take advantage of the superb facilities, and join many after-school clubs.

Music is an important feature of school life, with numerous choirs, orchestras and concert bands rehearsing each week and performing regularly. There are in excess of 600 individual music lessons taking place each week where over half the girls learn to play a musical instrument. There are flute choirs, string quartets, recorder groups and ensembles to cater for all levels of ability. Concerts and recitals are held regularly. The Jennifer Bate Organ Academy and the Jennifer Bate Organ Scholarship in conjunction with Guildford Cathedral. The School boasts two organs, one in the School Chapel and a second in the Preparatory School.

Many girls go on to represent their county in netball, lacrosse, swimming, squash and athletics. Every girl is encouraged to take part in sport at school, whatever her level of expertise. The PE Department regularly fields four or five teams for lacrosse and netball, allowing every girl who wishes to play competitively the opportunity to do so.

Drama and Theatre Studies are extremely popular options; girls are encouraged to audition for the annual middle and senior school plays. As well as acting opportunities, pupils are also offered the opportunity to help backstage and front of house and learn many valuable skills as a result. LAMDA classes are offered to all year groups.

With the opening of the impressive new performance halls including state-of-the-art lighting and acoustics, facilities for Theatre are second to none. St Catherine's also has its own very popular School of Dance.

The Preparatory School: most girls join at 4 with a limited number of places available in other years. It aims to support families in helping younger pupils develop a strong sense of values, high standards of behaviour and consideration to others, as well as achieving excellent academic success. The girls benefit from specialist teaching, combining the best of traditional methods with modern technology to prepare them for the Entrance Examinations to all Senior Schools at 11+, including St Catherine's.

St Catherine's is situated in the heart of the attractive Surrey village of Bramley, three miles south of Guildford which has a main line station (Waterloo 35 minutes). The school operates a return bus service to Guildford Station Monday to Friday and there is a Friday evening bus service to London for weekly boarders. There is easy access to Heathrow and Gatwick and travel arrangements are made for overseas boarders. Close proximity to London allows frequent visits to theatres and galleries and the miles of countryside on our doorstep is an asset to the many girls who take part in The Duke of Edinburgh's Award scheme.

The successful completion of The 6, a Sixth Form centre, now offers modern boarding accommodation and a contemporary Common Room for day girls and boarders alike. Also planned are an extension to the creative arts facilities and a new science and digital learning space.

Fees per term (2021–2022) Day Girls: £3,255 (Pre-Prep 1), £3,900 (Pre-Prep 2), £4,610 (Pre-Prep 3), £5,440 (Prep School), £6,585 (Senior School).

Boarders: Middle and Senior Boarding and Tuition £10,955.

Fees include the Activities Week programme for Senior School girls and lunches for all pupils aged 4–18.

Entry. This is by Entrance Examination held in January. The Preparatory School also holds its entrance assessments in January.

Scholarships and Bursaries.

11+ (Year 7): There are four Academic Entrance Scholarships available for pupils at age 11. These are awarded on the results of the Entrance Examination. Two scholarships are for 20% of the fees payable and the other two are for 10% of the fees. These are for the first five years of Senior School and are extended through the Sixth Form at the discretion of the Headmistress and in consultation with the teaching staff.

Upper 5 and Sixth Form (Year 11): The following scholarships are awarded during the Summer Term to pupils already in the School in the L5 (Year 10) and in the Autumn Term U5 (Year 11). Selection for the awards is based on the results of the June examinations at the end of the L5, performance throughout the L5 year and a rigorous panel interview.

The available Sixth Form Scholarships are:

- *Margaret Kaye Scholarships*: These are scholarships of 20% of the fees payable to run for three years, through U5 (Year 11) and the Sixth Form.
- *Sixth Form Scholarships*: These are scholarships of 10% or 20% of fees. The number can be extended depending on the performance of the candidates and the recommendations of the awarding panel.

- *The Sixth Form Music Scholarship*: There are two Music Scholarships. One, to the value of 20% of the School fees is awarded during the Autumn Term of U5 to a girl who intends to study Music A Level alongside her practical music-making. The second is to the value of 10% of the School Fees and is awarded to a girl who makes a significant contribution to School music-making but will not take Music A Level.

- *The Sixth Form Art and Textiles Scholarship*: There is an Art and Textiles Scholarship to the value of 20% of the School Fees, awarded during the Autumn Term of U5 (Year 11).

- *The Sixth Form Drama Scholarship*: There is a Drama Scholarship to the value of 20% of the School Fees, awarded during the Autumn Term of U5.

- *The Clare Gregory Memorial Sports Scholarship*: This is awarded for sporting prowess and is for 20% of the day fees in the Sixth Form and is awarded internally at the end of the Spring Term in U5.

- *Scholarships for New Entrants to the Sixth Form*: There are up to three external academic, Art/Textiles and Music scholarships of up to 20% of fees and these are awarded at the discretion of the Headmistress, to new pupils joining the School in the Sixth Form. The Art/Textiles and Music scholarships are conditional upon the applicant studying Art/Textiles or Music A Level.

Music Scholarships and Awards:

An 11+ Music Scholarship of 20% of the fees and tuition on one instrument, with music and exam entry fees paid, may be awarded annually upon entry to an 11+ candidate judged by the Director of Music and an adjudication panel to have strong musical talent. A second Music Scholarship of 10% of fees and tuition on one instrument can be awarded in years where the field of applicants is particularly strong. Applications should be made by November and auditions are in January. There is an expectation that the successful candidates will take Music GCSE and A Level.

Jennifer Bate Memorial Organ Scholarship is offered in conjunction with Guildford Cathedral to a girl who is already a good organist or shows potential. This award is typically for 20% of fees payable and includes tuition on the organ and one other instrument, with music and exam entry fees. It may also involve a Bursary/Help with Fees if appropriate. Ideally, Jennifer Bate Memorial Organ Scholars are boarders who can take a full part in the Boarders' Evening Chapel Service each week.

Further Music Awards which cover music tuition, exam fees and sheet music on a range of musical instruments including chapel organ and voice are available to pupils in the Senior School. Some are specifically for those wanting to take up instruments which tend not to be the popular choice of most students, but which contribute greatly to the impact and success of the School's musical ensembles. e.g. euphonium, double bass, viola, bassoon, French horn, tuba. Auditions for Awards take place at the same time as Music Scholarship auditions.

Bursaries/Help with Fees: The School offers a number of means-tested places to girls at age 7 (Year 3), age 11 (Year 7) and at Sixth Form entry. Help can be provided for up to 100% of the fees.

For further information about any of the above Scholarships/Awards/Bursaries, please contact the Senior School Registrar or see www.stcatherines.info/admissions/bursaries-and-scholarships

Charitable status. St Catherine's School Bramley is a Registered Charity, number 1070858. It exists to provide education for girls in accordance with the principles of the Church of England.

Governing Body:
Chairman: Brigadier M P Lowe, MBE, MA, RCDS
A Alonzo Esq, BSc, PhD
J Blauth Esq, BA, FRSA, MCMI, MRAeS
Prof F Cotter, MBBS, FRCP[UK], FRCPath, FRCP[I], PhD
Mrs P Crouch, LLB
Mrs K Farrell
Mrs S Fitzsimons MA
Mrs C Good
Mrs H Hounsell
Mrs C S Johnstone, MRCS, LRCP, MBBS, MD, FRCP
Dr J McGowan, MBBS, FRCA
A Pianca Esq, FCA
Mrs S E Shipway
J C M Tippett Esq, BSc, FCA, TEP
D Ulyet Esq, BSc

Headmistress: Mrs Alice Phillips, MA Cantab

Head of Boarding (Acting): Mrs Helen Harkness
Director of Studies: Mrs Jacki Deakin, BSc UCL, PGCE
Senior Housemistress: Mrs Kirsty Meredith, BA Hons London, AKC, PGCE
Director of Staff: Mrs Claire Wyllie, MA Dunelm, PGCE
Head of Sixth Form: Mrs Kate Hawtin
School Administrator: Mrs Sheila Kelsall, MA Open, BSc Hons Open, PGCE
Head of Prep School: Miss Naomi Bartholomew, MA London, BEd Cantab, QTS, MA London
Deputy Heads – Curriculum: Mrs Julie Micklethwaite, BEd Hons Roehampton; Mr Matthew Parry, BSc, MSc Wales, PGCE
Deputy Head – Pre-Prep: Miss Emily Jefford
Deputy Head – Staff: Mrs Wendy Gibbs, BEd Hons Winchester

Administration:
Senior School Registrar: Mrs Clare Woodgates
Prep School Registrar: Mrs Sally Manhire
Marketing Director: Ms Pippa Carte, BD, MA
PA to the Headmistress: Miss Toppy Wharton

St Catherine's School
Twickenham

Cross Deep, Twickenham, Middlesex TW1 4QJ

Tel:	020 8891 2898
email:	admissions@stcatherineschool.co.uk
website:	www.stcatherineschool.co.uk

Motto: Not Words But Deeds

Age Range. Girls 4–18 years.

Number in School. 420 Day Girls.

Founded in 1914 by the Sisters of Mercy, independent since 1991. St Catherine's is a Catholic School which warmly welcomes girls of all faiths.

Aims. We are proud of our Catholic ethos, which informs our commitment to a values-based education that builds character and confidence. Our broad and exciting curricular and co-curricular programmes operate within a friendly and supportive environment which encourages and challenges girls to strive to be the best they can be. Emphasis is placed on care and respect for others, self-discipline, and the nurturing of both leadership skills and the compassion to serve. Staff know the pupils as individuals and there is a strong sense of community which promotes academic success and creates a happy, purposeful school.

Situation. The school enjoys an enviable position, located next to the River Thames. It is a short distance from the centre of Twickenham and a short walk from Strawberry Hill and Twickenham Stations. Both have regular services to London (Waterloo), Surrey, Berkshire and Middlesex. There are also a number of local bus routes.

Entrance. The main point of entry is at age 11 and 16 but girls, especially those seeking a Prep place, are accepted at any stage, subject to availability. Places at the school are usually awarded on the basis of an interview, a report and reference from the candidate's previous school and an assessment or examination, depending on the pupil's age.

Scholarships and Bursaries. Academic Scholarships are awarded annually for Year 7 and for Sixth form. Art, Drama, Music and Sport scholarships are also awarded annually following an audition/assessment and are conditional on the applicant achieving the school's academic requirement for entry. The Siena scholarship is an all-rounder scholarship awarded for Years 10–13.

A limited number of means-tested Bursaries are offered depending on need and funds available.

Curriculum. In the Senior School pupils follow courses in English, Mathematics, Biology, Chemistry, Physics, Religious Education, French, German, Spanish, History, Geography, Drama, Music, Art, Food and Nutrition, Computing and Physical Education. All of these subjects are offered at GCSE, when most pupils study ten subjects. All of the above subjects are available at A Level, with the addition of Politics, Graphics, Further Mathematics, Economics, Psychology, Photography, Sociology and Textiles.

There is a strong commitment to Sport, Music, Drama and extracurricular activities. The school has its own hockey pitch and indoor swimming pool as well as tennis and netball courts. Sports include swimming, netball, athletics, hockey, tennis, gymnastics, trampolining and rounders and our pupils achieve considerable success at county, regional and national level.

Music plays an important part in the life of the school; all pupils are encouraged to participate in choirs, orchestras and ensembles, and there is a varied programme of concerts and informal performances each term.

Drama is popular and, as well as opportunities to perform in school productions, regular theatre visits take place during the year.

Buildings. The Preparatory and Senior departments are on one site. The buildings include a large multi-purpose hall as well as a smaller assembly hall, attractive Prep and Senior Libraries, ICT Suites, a spacious Art and Photography Suite and a Food and Nutrition Room. The Music Centre includes classrooms and individual practice rooms. There are fully-equipped laboratories for Physics, Chemistry and Biology. A large programme of new building has recently added extra teaching blocks, a Sixth Form Centre, Drama Studio, Fitness

Suite and a Chaplaincy Room, and further development is planned.

Co-curricular Activities. These play a significant role in the life of the school. Activities include the Duke of Edinburgh's Award scheme, Badminton, Science Club, Football, Rugby, Rowing, Cross-Country Running, Zumba, Chess and Photography. Trips, both locally and abroad, add to the extensive range of activities on offer. Pupils also take part in community service and fundraising activities.

Fees per term (2021–2022). Inclusive of lunch: Reception £4,160, Years 1 and 2 £4,270, Years 3 to 6 £4,490, Years 7 to 13 £5,375 (excluding examination fees).

Charitable status. St Catherine's School, Twickenham is a Registered Charity, number 1014651. It aims to provide for children seeking education in a Christian environment.

Chair of Governors: Ms Sylvia Hamilton

***Headmistress*: Mrs Johneen McPherson**

Senior Deputy Head: Miss Amy Wallace

Bursar & Clerk to the Governors: Mr Andrew Ferguson

Admissions Manager: Mrs Julie Harris

St Gabriel's

Sandleford Priory, Newbury, Berkshire RG20 9BD

Tel:	01635 555680
email:	info@stgabriels.co.uk
website:	www.stgabriels.co.uk
Twitter:	@StGabrielsNews
Facebook:	@stgabrielsnewbury
Instagram:	@stgabrielsnews
LinkedIn:	/company/st-gabriel's-newbury

Independent Day School for Girls, in membership of GSA and IAPS.

Number of Pupils. 450.

St Gabriel's offers an innovative, inspiring and balanced education, in an established, vibrant and cohesive day school community. Pupils and staff are full of enthusiasm and purpose, such dedication enables pupils to develop effectively, enabling them to move on to the next stage of their education with a lifelong intellectual curiosity, the ability to question and challenge and a confidence and belief in their ability.

Curriculum. The curriculum is broad and well-balanced, providing an education that is both traditional and forward-thinking. Small class sizes, an outstanding system of pastoral care and dynamic teaching assist pupils to form strong relationships ensuring they achieve their full potential both academically and holistically.

A choice of 26 subjects is offered at GCSE of which English, English Literature, Mathematics, all three Sciences, and a Modern Foreign Language (MFL) are compulsory.

At Sixth Form, students choose three subjects to study to A Level from the 26 offered. All students also study for the Extended Project Qualification.

Results. Securing the best possible examination results is the key focus at St Gabriel's. Examination results at both A Level and GCSE are consistently excellent. In 2021, 80% of

GCSE results were grade 9–7 and 62% of A Level grades were A*–A. St Gabriel's are justly proud of their students' achievements and it is not surprising that they go on to study a wide and diverse range of courses at their chosen universities.

Inspection. The latest Independent Schools inspection took place in November 2019. St Gabriel's was rated Excellent & Outstanding, they reported: "At all stages in the school, pupils make excellent progress in terms of their attainment".

Extra-Curricular Activities. The school provides a wide range of opportunities outside of the classroom. Numerous activities and visits extend and enrich pupils' learning experience throughout the school. The performing and creative arts, sport and a wide range of clubs and societies ensure that girls progress to the next stage of their education with confidence. Whether it is through The Duke of Edinburgh's Award or World Challenge, the girls constantly rise to meet new challenges.

Music. A variety of choirs, orchestras and instrumental groups ensure able musicians have the opportunity to perform at the highest levels. Most orchestral instruments may be learned with bespoke guidance, and tuition is given to pupils who show a considerable aptitude for composition.

Sport. Netball, Hockey, Swimming, Rounders, Athletics, Cricket, Cross-Country, Dance, Equestrian, Gymnastics, Rugby and Tennis.

Facilities. Specialist IT suites, state-of-the-art science laboratories and MFL rooms, multi-disciplinary sports hall, theatre and dance studio.

Christian Community & Ethos. The school welcomes children of all faiths and combines traditional Christian values with strong pastoral care to provide a progressive, 'real world' safe, happy and supportive environment. A strong moral code ensures pupils leave the school as well-balanced, unpretentious individuals with the confidence to be assertive and decisive with warmth and without arrogance.

Supervised Prep. This is provided on a daily basis between 4.00pm and 6.30pm.

Scholarships & Bursaries. Academic, Sport, Art, Dance, Drama and Music scholarships are awarded at 11+ and 13+. Sixth Form scholarships are also awarded at 16+. Bursaries covering up to 100% of fees are available through the Montagu Award scheme, which aims to ensure that St Gabriel's is accessible to girls who would otherwise not be able to enjoy the unique education the school offers.

Admission. Entry to the Junior School for children aged 6–10 years is by assessment. An entrance examination is held in November for entry at 11+ and 13+ and girls are accepted in to the Sixth Form on the basis of their GCSE results and an interview. From September 2022, the school will accept boys into Year 7 and by 2026 the school will be co-educational throughout.

Fees per term (2021–2022). £6,040–£6,260.

Junior School. (*See entry in IAPS section*).

Charitable status. The St Gabriel Schools Foundation is a Registered Charity, number 1062748. It exists to provide education for girls.

Governing Body:
Chairman: Mr N Garland, BSc Hons

Mr S Barrett	Mrs J Heywood
Mrs S Bowen	Mrs S Hutton
Mr D Peaple	Mr M Scholl
Mr N Rankin	Mrs J Whitehead
Mr S Ryan	

Principal: **Mr R Smith**, MA Hons, MEd, PGCE

Vice-Principal: Mrs A Chapman, BA Hons, PGCE, QTS (*Spanish*)
Bursar & Clerk to Governors: Mrs Penny Setter, BA Hons
Head of Sixth Form: Mrs H Trevis, BSocSc Hons, PGCE (**Psychology, Religion, Philosophy & Ethics*)
Head of Junior School: Mr P Dove, BA Hons, PGCE (**Thinking Skills*)
Head of Upper School (*Years 9, 10 & 11*): Mrs E Hammons, LLB, PGCE (*History, Politics*)
Head of Lower School (*Years 7 & 8*): Mrs R Wright, BSc Hons, PGCE (*Physical Education*)
Deputy Head of Junior School: Miss A Smith, BEd Hons, QTS (*Form Tutor Year 2, *Mathematics*)
Director of Studies: Mrs A Chicken, BA Hons, PGCE (*Mathematics*), Mrs Jennifer Wellard-Hughes, BA Hons, PGCE, QTS (**English*)
Sandleford Nursery Curriculum Manager: Mrs C Lawrence, BA Ed, QTS (*Form Tutor Year 2*)
Sandleford Nursery Manager: Mrs K Noonan, BA Hons, EYTS
Sandleford Deputy Manager: Mrs M Bullock, NVQ Level 3
Compliance Coordinator: Mrs V Vaughan, BSc Hons, QTS (*Mathematics*)
Challenge & Extension (*Senior School*): Mrs A Chicken, BA Hons, PGCE (*Mathematics*)
Challenge & Extension (*Junior School*): Miss A Smith, BEd Hons, QTS (*Form Tutor Year 2, *Mathematics*)

Senior School Teaching Staff:
* Head of Department

Mrs K Ali, BSc Hons, PGDip, PGCE (*Chemistry*)
Mrs N Archer, BA Hons, PGCE (*English*)
Mrs N Bailey, BA Hons, QTS (*Mathematics*)
Mrs L Bainbrigge, BA Hons, PGCE (*Art*)
Mrs V Brazendale, BA Hons, QTS (**Physical Education*)
Mrs A Beake (*Science Technician*)
Mr A Beverly, MA, PGCE (**Religion, Philosophy & Ethics*)
Mrs C Causer, MA, BA Hons, QTS (*Classics*)
Mrs R Chaplin, BA Hons, QTS (**Drama*)
Mrs G Clarkson, MA, PGCE (*Mandarin Chinese*)
Mrs K Cook (*Art Technician*)
Mrs Rosamund Cox, MA, BA Joint Hons, PGCE (*Spanish, French*)
Dr R Dennis, PhD, BSc Hons, PGCE (*Biology*)
Ms S Ferretti, Laurea in Lingue, PGCE (**Modern Foreign Languages, Italian, French*)
Mrs C Gwilliam (*Science Technician*)
Mrs R Golding, BA Hons, PGCE (*English*)
Miss E Halstead, BA Hons, QTS (*Classics*)
Ms J Hammett, MSc, BSc Hons, PGCE (**Science*)
Mrs R Harvey, BSc Hons, PGCE (**Geography*)
Mrs K Hastings, BA Hons, PGCE (**Dance*)
Mrs S Haywood Smith, BSc Hons, JEB (*Computer Science*)
Ms M Hunter, MA RCA, BA Hons (*Art, Textiles, Photography*)
Mr M Ives, MA, BA Hons, PGCE (**Classics, Latin, Greek*)
Mr R James, PGCE (*Physical Education*)
Mrs T Johnson, MEng, QTS (*Mathematics*)

Mrs P Joseph, MEd, BA Hons, PGCE (*Physical Education*)
Dr R Kitto, MA, QTS (*Business Studies*)
Mrs J Knott, BSc Hons, PGCE (**Design Technology*)
Mrs F Lavasani, MSc, BA Hons, PGCE, QTS (**Business Studies*)
Mrs J Lee-Delisle, BA Hons (*Drama*)
Mr B Lewis, MA Cantab, PGCE (*History, Politics*)
Mr J Lloyd, BSc Hons, PGCE (*Mathematics*)
Mr J Mannion, BA Hons, PGCE (**Computer Science, History*)
Mrs D McLaughlin, BSc Hons, PGCE (*Physics*)
Mr E Verdejo Moreno (*Language Assistant*)
Ms H Rayner, BA Hons, PGCE (*Physics*)
Mrs C Reseigh, BA Hons, PGCE (*French*)
Miss A Roe, MA, BA Hons, PGCE (*Geography*)
Mr R Shah, BSc Hons, PGCE (*Chemistry*)
Mrs J Shillaw, BA Hons, PGCE (**History, *Politics*)
Mr A Sousa (*Language Assistant*)
Mr P Spurrett, BA Hons, PGCE (**Art*)
Dr P Tebbs, DPhil Oxon (*Music*)
Mrs H Trevis, BSocSc Hons, PGCE (**Psychology, Religion, Philosophy & Ethics*)
Mrs L Tyler, BA Hons, PGCE (*Spanish*)
Mrs J Wellard-Hughes, BA Hons, PGCE QTS (**English*)
Miss C Woodhouse, BMus Hons, PGCE (**Music*)
Mrs S Yeoman (*Technology Technician*)
Mrs T Zogaj, MA, RCA, BA Hons, PGCE, QTS (*Food & Nutrition*)

Junior School Teaching Staff:
* *Subject Leader*

Miss E Bloomfield, BA Hons, PGCE (*Form Tutor Year 2, *English*)
Mrs S Bloxsom, BA Hons, QTS (*Form Tutor Reception, *Music*)
Mrs R Chaplin, BA Hons, QTS (**Drama*)
Mrs G Clarkson, MA, PGCE (*Mandarin Chinese*)
Mrs M Davidson, BEd Hons (*Form Tutor Year 5, *English*)
Mr P Dove, BA Hons, PGCE (**Thinking Skills*)
Mrs R Dye, MA, PGCE, QTS (*Form Tutor Year 4, *Mathematics*)
Mrs K Hastings, BA Hons, PGCE (**Dance*)
Miss N Hart, BA Hons, QTS (*Form Tutor Year 5,*Outdoor Education, *Physical Education*)
Mrs L Hayes, BA Hons, PGCE (*Form Tutor Year 4, * French*)
Mrs J Knott, BSc Hons, PGCE (**Design Technology*)
Mrs C Lawrence, BA Ed Hons, QTS (*Form Tutor Year 2*)
Mrs R Lonsdale, BSc Hons, PGCE (*Form Tutor Year 3,*Science*)
Mr J Mannion, BA Hons, PGCE (**Computing*)
Miss H Moth, BA Hons, QTS (*Form Tutor Year 3, *Science*)
Mrs A Pasternakiewicz, BEd Hons (*Physical Education*)
Miss J Pearmine, BA Hons, PGCE (*Form Tutor Year 6*)
Miss A Smith, BEd Hons, QTS (*Form Tutor Year 2, *Mathematics*)
Mrs T Thrower, NVQ Level 8, QTS (**Art*)
Mrs S Webb, BSc Hons, PGCE (*Form Tutor Year 1, *PSHE*)
Mrs D Wilkinson, BA Hons, PGCE (*Form Tutor Year 6, *Humanities, *Religion, Philosophy & Ethics*)
Mrs T Zogaj, MA, BA Hons, PGCE (**Food & Nutrition*)

Teaching Assistants:
Mrs C Adams, NVQ Level 3, MFA University of Texas
Mrs Y Brown, CACHE Level 3 (*Reception*)
Mrs T Chen, MSc, PGCE, QTS
Mrs S Ducker, NVQ Level 3
Mrs S Hamilton-Stubber
Mrs G Livingstone, BA Hons, NCFE Level 3
Mrs Z McAlister, NVQ Level 3
Mrs S Morris, BSc Hons, HLTA
Mrs Z Stafford, QTS

Sandleford Nursery Staff:
Miss L Barrett, NVQ Level 3
Miss A Brewer
Mrs S Bradbury, QTS
Miss K Grineau, CACHE Level 3
Miss M Hamm, NVQ Level 3
Miss F Hughes, CACHE Level 2
Mrs N Kelly, NVQ Level 3
Miss K Lee, NVQ Level 3
Miss J Magpusao, NVQ Level 3
Mrs L Mannings, FdA
Miss T Marsh, Apprentice
Miss S Milligan, CYPW Level 3
Miss E Philpott, NVQ Level 3
Miss K Pontin, CACHE Level 2
Miss C Taylor
Mr D Taylor, NNEB
Miss M Townsend, NVQ Level 3

Visiting Music Staff:
Mr D Birnie, BMus Hons (*Guitar*)
Mr T Bott, BMus Hons, PG Dip (*Violin*)
Miss L Chinn, BMus Hons (*Brass*)
Mr B Copeman, BA Hons (*Flute, Recorder*)
Mr S Daruvala, BMus Hons (*Drum Kit, Percussion*)
Ms L Hayles, BA Hons, PG Dip (*Singing*)
Mr M Lijinsky, CT ABRSM (*Piano*)
Mrs H Page, BMus Hons, PGCE (*Piano*)
Mr S Parker, ALCM, LLCM, CT ABRSM (*Clarinet, Saxophone*)
Mr N Reeves, MMus, BMus Hons (*Piano*)
Mrs S Riddex, BA Hons, PGCE, LTCHM, LESMD (*Cello*)

Individual Needs:
Mrs C Cockar, QTS (1:1 LSA)
Mrs T Chen, MSc, PGCE, QTS (1:1 LSA)
Miss L Durling, PGCE (1:1 LSA)
Miss D Humphries, BSc Hons, PGCE, Dip SpLD
Mrs C Oxley, BSc Ed Hons, Dip SpLD (**Individual Needs*)

Administrative, Support & Facilities Staff:

Bursar's Office:
Mrs A Austin (*Payroll & Accounts Administrator*)
Mr T Britten (*Site Manager*)
Mrs K Frampton (*Accounts Assistant*)
Mrs J Goodman-Mills, OCR Level 3 (*Transport Coordinator*)
Mrs A Morris, BA Hons (*HR & Operations Advisor*)
Mrs A Williams, AAT Technician NVQ Level 4 (*Accountant*)

School Office:
Mrs J Benney, BSc Hons (*Director of Marketing & Admissions*)
Mrs H Corkhill, BEd Hons (*Examinations Officer*)
Mrs T Harpwood (*School Secretary*)
Mrs C Herbert (*School Secretary*)

Miss C Jackson (*Executive Secretary*)
Miss E Jennings, BA Hons (*Marketing Assistant*)
Mrs A Kail (*Data Manager*)

Support:
Ms C Adams, NVQ Level 3, MFA University of Texas
    (*After School Club*)
Mrs A Borzoni, BA Hons, PG Dip (*Librarian*)
Mr L Hammond (*After School Club*)
Miss A Joseph (*After School Club*)
Miss L Keen, BA Hons, NMCR (*School Nurse*)
Mrs Z McAllister, CACHE Level 3 (*After School Club*)
Mrs Z Stafford, QTS (*Breakfast Club & After School Club*)

St George's, Ascot

St George's School, Wells Lane, Ascot, Berks SL5 7DZ

Tel: 01344 629900
email: office@stgeorges-ascot.org.uk
website: www.stgeorges-ascot.org.uk
Twitter: @stgeorgesascot
Facebook: @stgeorgesschoolascot
Instagram: @stgeorgesascot
LinkedIn: /school/stgeorges-ascot

Member of GSA, AGBIS, BSA.

St George's Ascot, is a vibrant Boarding and Day school for girls aged 11–18 providing an excellent academic education in a supportive and caring environment.

The school is set in 30 acres of stunning grounds, only 30 minutes from central London and located just off the High Street in Ascot.

St George's is not a narrowly academic school – reaching each of our pupil's academic potential is our priority but this alone is not what makes a great education. St George's prides itself on offering a much more in-depth approach to learning; preparing our pupils beyond school by developing good communication skills, a love of learning and a willingness to get involved. According to Government School performance tables, the value St George's adds to girls' grades every year at A level places the school in the top 5% of all Sixth Form schools and colleges in England.

A markedly friendly atmosphere, small class sizes, strong pastoral care and a wide range of opportunities for individual development make St George's stand out from the crowd.

Curriculum. Small class sizes ensure that every girl is given the right balance of academic challenge and support by inspirational teaching staff, who deliver a wide-ranging and varied curriculum. Girls are given opportunities to excel, not only in traditional subjects but also in Art, Drama, Music and Sport. Team sports are offered in Lacrosse, Netball, Swimming, Tennis, Rounders, Athletics, Squash and Polo.

Academic results at St George's are strong, with the majority of the girls going on to Russell Group universities. All Sixth Form girls take the Extended Project Qualifications in addition to A Levels, and typically one third of the candidates achieve three or more A grades.

Entrance. Entry at 11+ is by our own assessment. A reference from the current school, combined English and Mathematics examination and an online CEM (Centre for Evaluation and Monitoring) test, together with a short presentation to a senior member of staff take place in the November of Year 6. For entry at 12+/13+, testing takes place in the January preceding entry and applicants will sit papers in English, Mathematics, Science and an online CEM test. Girls will also make a short presentation to a senior member of staff.

Girls considering an application to the Sixth Form will be invited for an interview with the Head of Sixth Form or another senior member of staff. Any offer of a place made will be contingent on meeting our minimum admissions criteria of achieving at least six, 9 to 4 grades at GCSE, with at least a 6 in any subject to be taken at A Level. A wide range of scholarships are available at 11+, 13+ and 16+.

Fees per term (2021–2022). £12,660 Boarding, £8,065 Day.

Scholarships. Scholarships are available at 11+, 13+ and 16+ for outstanding potential, as evidenced by examination results. Academic, Art, Performing Arts, Sport, Swimming, Music and All Round scholarships and instrumental awards are available at 11+, and Academic Art, Music, Drama, Performing Arts, Swimming, All Round and Sport scholarships at 13+ and 16+.

Extra Subjects. Other languages (including Mandarin), Music (most instruments), Speech and Drama, Ballet, Modern Stage and Tap Dancing, Individual Tennis, Polo, Riding, Zumba, Pilates, and Acro.

Charitable status. St George's School Ascot Trust Limited is a Registered Charity, number 309088. It exists to provide independent secondary girls' education.

Governors:
Mr A Mackintosh, BSc Aberdeen, MBA City (*Chairman*)
[1]Mrs D R Brown, MBE [OG]
[1]Dr J M Gibbons, BA, MPhil, DPhil
[2]Mr P James
[2]Mr E Luker, FRICS
[1]Mr A Miles, BSc Durham, PGCE
[2]Mrs R E S Niven Hirst, BArch Newcastle, RIBA [OG]
[2]Mr P Sedgwick, MCSI
[1]Ms A Triccas, MA, BA London
[2]Mrs K Trueman Alexander, BA Exeter, MLitt Christie's
    [OG]

[1] *Member of Education sub-committee*
[2] *Member of Finance and Marketing sub-committee*

Headmistress: Mrs E M Hewer, MA Cantab, PGCE

Bursar and Clerk to the Governors: Mr J F Anderson

Deputy Head Academic: Mr J V Hoar, BA Hull, PGCE
Deputy Head Pastoral / Designated Safeguarding Lead:
    Mrs H L Simpson, BA Ed Exeter
Deputy Head Co-Curricular and Connections / Deputy Designated Safeguarding Lead: Mr A J Wright, MA Oxon, MA London, PGCE

Teaching Staff:

* *Head of Department*

Art, Textiles, Photography and Cookery:
*Miss O Antolik, BA Kingston, PGCE
Ms K Gilbert, BA Chichester, PGCE
Mrs H Jones
Mrs A Morgan, BA Dundee, PGCE
Ms E Townsend, BA East Anglia, PGCE

Business and Economics:
*Mr D Wilkins, BSc London, PGCE

Classics:
*Miss L Fontes, BA Leeds, PGCE
Miss M Kalsi, BA, MA Sussex, PGCE

Drama:
*Mr A Carroll, BA St Mary's, PGCE
Mrs E Gregan, BA Liverpool, PGCE

English:
*Mrs S Rutherford-Gibb, BA Liverpool, PGCE
Ms L Baker, BA Sheffield, PGCE
Mrs E Gregan, BA Liverpool, PGCE
Ms M Johnston, BA East Anglia, MA London, PGCE

EAL:
*Mrs N Anderson, MA East Anglia, PGCE
Mrs S Davies, CTESOL

EPQ:
*Ms A Kennedy, BA, MSc Strathclyde

Geography:
*Mrs S Johnson, BSc Exeter, PGCE
Miss N Stepp, BSc St Mary's, PGCE
Mr J Schofield, BA Hons Exeter, PGCE

History and Politics:
*Mrs D Kratt, BA Reading, PGCE
Mr J Hoar, BA Hull, PGCE
Mr A Wright, MA Oxford, MA London, PGCE
Mr J Schofield, BA Hons Exeter, PGCE

History of Art:
*Dr A Haughton, BA Open University, PhD Warwick

ICT and Computing:
*Mr J Kundi, BSc Brunel, PGCE

Learning Support:
*Ms M Johnston, BA East Anglia, MA London, PGCE

Modern Languages:
*Miss E Pierre, Licence de Langue Rennes, France, PGCE
   King's College, London
Miss L Fontes, BA Leeds, PGCE
Mrs R Martinez, BA Portsmouth, PGCE
Mrs C Tea, BA Birmingham, PGCE

Mathematics:
*Mr P Wilson, BEng Nottingham, PGCE
Mr Naeem Mohammad, BSc, MA Punjab, HDipEd Dublin
Mrs S Scholefield, BSc Birmingham, PGCE
Mr B Tang, MA Harvard, PGCE

Music:
*Mr I G Hillier, GLCM, FLCM, FCSM, FGMS, PGCE
Miss K Tomsett, BA Music Industrial Leeds
Mrs C Thomson, LLB Bristol, PGCE

Physical Education:
*Miss K Wooldridge, BSc Loughborough, GTP with
   PGCE
Mrs L French, BA Oxford Brookes
Mrs K Hammond, BEd Chichester
Miss C Gillatt, BA Chichester, PGCE
Miss L Myers, BA Leeds Met, QTS (*& Designated
   Safeguarding Lead*)
Miss N Stepp, BSc St Mary's, PGCE (*Swimming*)
Mrs R Tune, BSc Loughborough, PGCE

Psychology:
*Mrs E Shingles, BSc Brunel, GTP

Philosophy, Ethics and Religion:
*Mrs M Magill, BA Bristol, MA London, PGCE
Miss M Kalsi, BA, MA Sussex, PGCE
Revd S Watts, BA, BDiv

Science:
*Mrs V Allan, BSc Bristol, PGCE
Dr C Alsop, BSc, PhD Durham, PGCE (*acting i/c
   Chemistry*)
Mr Naeem Mohammad, BSc, MA Punjab, HDipEd Dublin
Mrs E Shingles, BSc Brunel, GTP
Mrs A Sutton-Jennings, BSc Sheffield, MSc Birmingham,
   QTS
Mrs D Ferrer, BA Lincoln, PGCE (*i/c Physics*)

SGA Stretch Co-ordinator:
Dr C Alsop, BSc, PhD Durham, PGCE

SMSC:
*Mrs H Simpson, BAEd, Exeter
Mrs N Anderson, MA East Anglia, PGCE
Miss K Wooldridge, BSc Loughborough, GTP with PGCE
Ms E Townsend, BA East Anglia, PGCE
Miss L Myers, BA Leeds Met, QTS
Ms A Morgan, BA Dundee, PGCE
Ms M Johnston, BA East Anglia, MA London, PGCE

Heads of Year:
First Year: Ms E Townsend
Second Year: Miss L Fontes
Third Year: Mrs M Magill
Fourth Year: Mrs D Kratt
Fifth Year: Miss L Myers
Sixth Form: Mr A Carroll

Boarding and Pastoral Staff:
Deputy Head Pastoral: Mrs H Simpson, BAEd
School Chaplain & Charities Coordinator: Revd S Watts,
   BA, BDiv
School Nurse: Miss N Kvik, BSc

Housemistresses:
Markham: Mrs S Harmon, BA, MA, PGCE
Knatchbull & Deputy Designated Safeguarding Lead: Miss
   L Myers, BA, QTS
Loveday: Miss N Stepp, BSc, PGCE

Assistant Housemistresses:
Knatchbull: Miss T Alford, BSc Oxford Brookes
Markham: Miss N Conde, BA, MSc

Director in Residence: Miss S Ash, MA Surrey, QTS
Tutor in Residence: Miss K Tomsett, BA Music Industrial,
   Leeds
Artist in Residence: Miss Y Amer, BA UAL
Head Librarian in Residence: Ms A Kennedy, BA MSc
Teacher of PE in Residence: Miss C Gillat, BA Chichester,
   PGCE
Counsellor: Mrs T Curtis
Listener: Ms E Manners

Co-Curricular Staff:

Heads of Houses:
Alexander: Miss N Stepp, BSc, PGCE
Becket: Mrs K Hammond, BEd
Churchill: Mr Naeem Mohammad, BSc, MA, HDipEd
Darwin: Ms A Kennedy, BA, MSc

Duke of Edinburgh's Award: Mr D Moran, BA, PGD

Partnerships and Outreach Co-ordinators:
Miss N Conde, BA, MSc
Mrs L French, BA

Visiting Staff:
Arabic: Mrs M Elssadi, BA Damascus
Chinese: Miss T Y Joyce, MA Hong Kong, PGCE
French: Ms M Boussaid, BTS
German: Mrs S More, DLL Goethe Institut, PGCE, QTS
Italian: Mr R Somma, BA Italy, PGCE
Japanese: Mrs K Forrester, BA
Russian: Mrs M Strain, MA
Spanish: Mrs I Fanning, BA, MA
Learning Support: Mrs R Baxter, BA; Mrs J Hooper, BComm
Percussion: Mr R Smith
Guitar: Mr P Williams, BA
Violin: Mr S Perkins, BMus
Double Bass: Mr Charlton, BA
Singing: Mr A Thompson, BA; Miss N Parker, BA
Piano: Miss E Krivenko, MMus; Mrs K Stanley, BMus
Harp: Mrs E Elliott, BA RSAMD
Flute: Mrs S Dunsdon
Trumpet: Mr G De Rezende Dias, BA, MA
LAMDA:
Ms R Moir, BA, PGCE
Ms N Hammond-Betts, MA [maternity leave]
Mrs S Thomas-Lane, BA
Tennis: Mr N Ingham
Modern and Zumba: Ms A Lewis
Pilates: Ms K Keeling
Squash: Mrs N Leader, BSc
Dance: Miss R Findlay; Miss H Fowler; Miss R Herszenhorn; Miss Z Pembroke

Support Staff:
Bursar: Mr J Anderson
Operations Manager: Ms J Quinn
Finance Manager: Mrs L Foster
Estates Compliance & Enterprise Manager: Mr P Lewis
Accounts Assistant: Mrs L Young
Resources Officer: Mrs T Barber
Personal Assistant to Head: Mrs J Witt
Secretary to the Senior Leadership Team: Mrs C Reader
Administrative Assistant: Miss H Austin
Director of Admissions and Marketing: Mrs K Bertram
Marketing, Design and Communications Co-ordinator: Mrs E Little
Marketing Assistant Digital: Mrs E Davies
Admissions Assistant: Mrs S Holloway
Admissions Co-ordinator: Mrs S O'Brien

Receptionists:
Mrs S Davies (*Mon–Wed*)
Ms L Glimmerveen (*Thur–Fri*)

Data Manager: Mrs R Smith
Examinations Officer: Mrs C Barlow
Alumnae Co-ordinator: Ms L Glimmerveen
Domestic Bursar: Mrs A Craciun
Deputy Domestic Bursar: Mrs J Burns
Head Chef: Mr C Leisten
Network Manager: Mr A Attan
IT Technician: Mr M Merry
Art Technician: Mrs A Older
Theatre Technician: Mr R Pearn

Science Technicians:
Mrs J Bhandal

Mr P Goldsbrough
Mrs K Hicks

Head Librarian: Ms A Kennedy
Deputy Librarian: Mr D Moran

Clerk of Works: Mr R Cotterell
Groundsman: Mr P Thompson
Electrician: Mr C Smith
Maintenance: Mr R MacRobbie
Gardener: Mrs P Shepherd

Minibus Drivers: Mr K Baldwin; Mr C Stephens; Mr B Fejza; Mr C Kerton; Mr A Sidhu; Mr G Buckner

St James Senior Girls' School

Earsby Street, London W14 8SH

Tel: 020 7348 1777
         Admissions: 020 7348 1748
email: admissions@sjsg.org.uk
website: www.stjamesgirls.co.uk

Motto: *Speak the truth. Live generously. Aim for the best.*

Founded in 1975, St James Senior Girls' School is a day school with 259 pupils aged from 11–18. We are situated on a spacious site in Olympia, West Kensington, shared with St James Preparatory School.

We offer an education which nurtures and enriches the physical, intellectual, emotional and spiritual development of our pupils. Our happy, united atmosphere provides the ideal environment for every girl to discover her own unique combination of strengths and talents and to 'be the best she can'.

St James girls are industrious, open-hearted and courageous; they work together, enjoying others' successes as well as their own. They achieve the highest academic standards and are also encouraged to develop strength through self-discipline and an ability to live according to an intelligent understanding of what is wise and true. Regular opportunities for stillness and quiet enable pupils to learn to be at ease with themselves, to appreciate the value of being fully present and to develop their ability to concentrate.

Our teachers have excellent subject knowledge and give their time generously to support the well-being and development of their pupils. Relationships throughout the school are extremely positive and are characterised by a spirit of love, trust and mutual respect.

Whilst admission to the school is through a selective procedure, the school seeks to admit those candidates who are able and willing to make good use of the education offered. We aim to foster creativity and intellectual curiosity, challenging our pupils to achieve excellence. Standards in public examinations are high: nearly all leavers proceed to Higher Education degree courses either at university, a specialist music college or to pursue an art foundation course.

The Curriculum offers a wide-ranging education including PSHEE, citizenship, philosophy and religious studies as well as leadership training, public speaking and debating. Community Service runs throughout the school. Careers Guidance is offered to all pupils from Years 7–13.

Subjects available to GCSE/IGCSE: art, biology, chemistry, Classical Greek, computer science/applied IT, drama, English language, English literature, French, geography, history, Latin, mathematics, music, physical education, physics, religious studies, Sanskrit and Spanish. Year 7 are taught General Science prior to commencing the three separate sciences in Year 8. Year 7 receive lessons in textiles and, as well as Year 8, receive cookery lessons in the newly refurbished on-site teaching kitchen.

Subjects offered at A Level: art, biology, chemistry, Classical Greek, drama and theatre, Economics, English literature, French, geography, Hinduism, history, History of Art, Information Technology BTEC Level 3 NEC (equivalent to one A level), Latin, mathematics, further mathematics, music, physics, psychology, religious studies and Spanish. Students also take the Extended Project Qualification, a project which develops research and independent learning skills.

The Sixth Form. Most pupils stay on to complete their education in the Sixth Form. This is treated as a very distinct stage and pupils' growth in initiative and responsibility is supported and encouraged. The PSHEE and SMSC programme is continued in order to provide support for personal development through a series of talks, debates and workshops. Emphasis is placed on academic excellence and the cultivation of social awareness and, in particular, leadership skills which are developed through assuming responsibility for younger pupils in the school. Students are offered a community service project abroad to South Africa to trek in the wilderness and do volunteer work in a Zulu village.

Creative Arts. The performing arts are strong features of the school. There is a tradition of choral and solo singing, as well as instrumental music making. Most of our productions take place in our assembly hall, fully equipped with lighting and sound. There are several choirs, orchestras and instrumental ensembles and girls are strongly encouraged to take up individual instruction with one of our visiting instrumental and/or vocal teachers. There are performance opportunities for all pupils every year: the Lower School (Years 7–9) perform a play one year, a musical the following year and vice versa for the Upper School (Years 10–13). Recent Lower School productions include: *Mary Poppins* (2019), *The Lion King* (2017) and *Arabian Nights* (2016). Recent Upper School productions include: *Dido and Aeneas* (2018), *Les Misérables* (2017) and *The Wizard of Oz* (2015). Pupils also have the opportunity to perform in the school's Youth Dance Company and music, speech, debating, choreography and other artistic competitions. There is also an annual Arts Week during which pupils have the opportunity to take part in various workshops.

Physical Education. PE is an important part of school life. Athletics, cricket, cross country, football, health related fitness, handball, lacrosse, netball, rounders, and team-building are all offered. We have a playground and gymnasium on site and use the facilities at nearby Hammersmith Fitness and Squash Centre, Linford Christie Stadium, Will to Win in Chiswick House Grounds and King's House Sports Ground in Chiswick. There is also an annual Sports Week during which pupils take part in various trips and hear presentations from high profile sportswomen.

Extra-Curricular Activities. Pupils are offered a wide range of clubs including art, classics, cookery, creative writing, dance, drama, Female Lead, football, karate, lacrosse, netball, LAMDA, STEM, zoology, The Duke of Edinburgh's Award, ICT, choirs and orchestras. Years 7–12 attend an annual Activity Week with their own class at a variety of locations within and outside the UK. There are also optional trips to Berlin and Iceland as well as skiing or sporting excursions.

Admission. For entry at 11+ girls sit the London 11+ Consortium Entrance examination; at Sixth Form candidates are required to sit an entrance exam and to attain the necessary GCSE grades for A Level study. For occasional vacancies in Years 8, 9 and 10 candidates will need to take an entrance examination.

Fees per term (2021–2022). £7,160

Bursaries. There are limited funds available for Bursary assistance. Awards are discretionary and based on a full financial enquiry into parents' means by the Bursary Fund Committee. The funds are primarily to assist children already attending St James, but some help may be available to new parents in specific circumstances.

Charitable status. The Independent Educational Association Limited is a Registered Charity, number 270156. It exists to provide education for children.

Board of Governors, Olympia:
The St James Senior Girls' and Prep Schools share a single governing body which meets as the Board of Governors, Olympia. The Board's role is to ensure that the schools provide its pupils with the very best education and opportunities, oversee developments at the school and generally support the Heads and the school. The Board of Governors sets the school's plans and policies.

Chair of Governors, Olympia: Mr Hugh Venables, BSc, MBA

Governors:
Mrs Annabel Lubikowski, BA Hons, MPhil, PGCE (*Vice Chair*)
Mrs Angela Bowman, BA Hons, MPhil, PGCE
Mr Stephen Lehec, BA Hons Soton, PGCE Oxon
Mr Raghu Nandakumara, MA Cantab, MSc

Director of Education: Mrs Laura Hyde, Cert Ed, MEd

Headmistress: Mrs Sarah Labram, BA

Deputy Heads:
Pastoral: Mrs Michelle Holder, BA, MSc, PGCE, Dip Couns
Academic: Mr Alastair Horsford, BA, QTS

Assistant Head, Staff Development: Miss Anna Holliss, BA, QTS, MEd, CMgr, FCM
Head of Sixth Form: Mrs Yolanda Saunders, BA, PGCE
Assistant Head of Sixth Form: Mr Stephen Allen, MA Cantab, MSci, PGCE
Head of Lower School (Year 7): Mrs Jane Mason, MA Oxon, PGCE
Head of Middle School (Years 8 & 9): Mrs Brooke Kenwright, BEd, MEd
Head of Upper School (Years 10 & 11): Miss Niamh Somers, BA, PGCE

Teaching Staff:
* Head of Department

Mr Stephen Allen, MA Cantab, MSci, PGCE (*Chemistry*)
Miss Ana Amador, BSc Hons (*Science*) [maternity leave]
Ms Sarah Ashbolt, BA, MA, PGCE (*Psychology*)
Mr Paul Bahia, BSc, QTS, PGCE (*Economics*)

Ms Lara Basma, BSc, MSc, PCGE (*Second i/c Mathematics*)

Mr Robert Bateman, Dip Hons, BA, MA (**Drama*)

Mrs Pauline Bath, BA, PGCE (*History*)

Miss Lauren Berridge, BA, PGDE (*Physical Education, i/c lacrosse*)

Miss Joti Birdi, BA, MA, PGCE (*English*) [maternity cover]

Mrs Suzie Brown (*St James Teaching Kitchen*)

Ms Theresa Brown, BSc, PGCE (*Science*) [maternity cover]

Ms Myra Brunton, MA Oxon, ARCM, PGCE (*Director of Music*)

Mrs Rebecca Candy, MA Cantab, PGCE (**Careers, *Religious Studies*)

Miss Janine Cetin, BTh/BA (**English*)

Mr Leo Chan, MA, PGCE, QTS (*Mathematics*)

Mlle Mylène Chaudagne, Licence, MA, PGCE (**Modern Foreign Languages, Senior Teacher Pastoral*)

Ms Julia Childs, Dip, BA, MA (*English and Learning Development*)

Dr Josef Craven, BA, MPhil, PhD (**History and *Citizenship*)

Mr Fraser Dawson, BSc, PGCE (*Chemistry*)

Mr Nicholas de Mattos, BA, PGCE (*Classics*)

Ms Emily Ford, BA (*Art*)

Ms Ioanna Georgiou, MSc, MPhil, QTS, FIMA, CMathTeach (**Mathematics, Senior Teacher, *Academic Enrichment and EPQ Coordinator*)

Miss Lisa Hayat, MA, PGCE (**History of Art*)

Miss Anna Holliss, BA, QTS, Med, CMgr, FCM (*Director of Physical Education*)

Mrs Elena Jessup, BSc, MA (*Sanskrit*)

Mr Warwick Jessup, BA Oxon, MA, MPhil (**Sanskrit*)

Mrs Brooke Kenwright, BEd, MEd (**PSHEE and Physical Education*)

Ms Rebecca Landon, BA, PGCert NASENCO, PGCert Psychometric Testing, Assessment & Access Arrangements CPT3A (*SENDCO*)

Mr Kenneth MacLean, BSc, MSc, PGCE (**Science and Biology*)

Mrs Jane Mason, MA Oxon, PGCE (**Classics*)

Miss Eileen McDonagh, BA, PGCE (*Geography*)

Miss Julie Menon, Licence Maîtrise, PGCE (*French*)

Miss Thu Nguyen, BA (**ICT & Computer Science*)

Mrs Imogen Riley, BA Oxon, PGCE (**Geography and *Outdoor Pursuits*)

Mrs Yolanda Saunders, BA, PGCE (*Classics*)

Miss Niamh Somers, BA, PGCE (*Biology*)

Miss Priya Soni, BA, MA Oxon, PGCE (*English*) [maternity leave]

Mrs Gordana Tarundzioska, BEd, BSc (*Mathematics*)

Mr David Treloar, BA, PGDip (**Art*)

Ms Jennifer Watts, BD, PGCE (*Religious Studies*)

Mrs Montserrat Wight-Rahona, BA, QTS (**Spanish*)

Mr Stuart Young, BSc, QTS (**Physics and *ICT Strategy*)

Support Staff:
Librarian: Mrs Katharine Boddy, BA, PGCE
Assistant Librarian: Ms Nuría Sole-Bonet
Examinations Officer: Mrs Alison Buchanan

Technicians/Assistants:
Mrs Vinita Thatte, RSci Tech (*Senior Laboratory Technician*)

Miss Viktoria Boyko, BA (*Art*) [maternity cover]

Mrs Carla Escoto Montero, Lic Psic (*Science, Art*) [maternity leave]

School Nurses:
Mrs Amanda Fryer, RN, RSCN
Ms Bernadette O'Gorman, RN

Meditation Programme Coordinator and Wellbeing Coach:
Mrs Emily Johnston, AMI Mont Dip, ITEC Dip

Administrative Staff:
Registrar: Mrs Patricia Snowdon, BPhil
Marketing Manager: Mrs Olivia Blake, BA, MA
Events Manager: Mrs Leah Murray
School Secretary: Miss Abigail Davies, BA
PA to Headmistress / Director of Education:
Mrs Isabella Olley, BA [maternity leave]
Miss Caleigh Pearson [maternity cover]
PA to Deputy Heads: Miss Kelly Farrell
Receptionist: Ms Alejandra Diaz Garcia
Sixth Form Receptionists: Ms Sinit Goitom; Ms Marva Lewis

Bursary:
Chief Operating Officer: Mr William Wyatt
Bursar: Mrs Eve McCann
Interim Finance Manager: Mr Donald Hamilton, BSc
Credit Controller & School Fees Administrator: Mrs Alla Edwards
Accounts: Ms Milena Herrera Barios
PA to the Chief Operating Officer: Miss Sinead Costello

HR Manager: Mrs Nadia Bonomo, Assoc CIPD, BA

Property Management:
Estates Manager: Ms Antonietta Cappasso, IWFM
Caretakers: Mr Karl Graham; Mr Dusan Jokic; Mr Mio Lazic; Mr Franco Pegoraro

Development Office:
Development Manager: Miss Ellie Mello, BA, MA

St Mary's School
Colchester

91 Lexden Road, Colchester, Essex CO3 3RB

Tel: 01206 594180
email: registrar@stmaryscolchester.org.uk
website: www.stmaryscolchester.org.uk
Twitter: @stmaryscolch
Facebook: @stmarysseniorschoolcolchester

Motto: *Scientia et Veritas*

St Mary's – a happy, high achieving school

St Mary's is an independent school in Colchester, Essex for girls age 3–16 and boys age 3–4. The school is proud to have charitable status, meaning all fees are reinvested into the school. Being truly independent, with no owners or shareholders, and overseen by a committed governing body who help ensure a high-quality education and happy learning environment is provided.

Beautiful settings

The Lower School and Senior School are both situated in impressive historic buildings, set within beautiful grounds.

Academically outstanding

St Mary's is an academic school and students' exam results are impressive, despite the fact the school is not academically selective.

The Lower School is ranked in the top 25 highest performing Preparatory Schools in England by the *Sunday Times*. Many girls achieve scholarships to senior school, and there is an impressive 11+ pass rate for those who choose to sit the exam.

At the Senior School GCSE results are also regularly amongst the best in the country. In 2021, overall, 99% of GCSEs at St Mary's were graded at four, or above. Such success is achieved by tailoring the education to suit the needs of each individual in small classes and by giving the girls the encouragement and support they need to aim high.

A wealth of opportunities

St Mary's strongly believe that success in life comes from more than just impressive exam results. A brilliantly balanced education is offered in order to develop exceptionally well-rounded individuals.

With a huge variety of clubs, enrichment activities, music and drama productions, visits and international travel experiences on offer, there's ample opportunity to learn new skills and develop talents.

There are numerous positions of responsibility available to the girls, which help develop their leadership skills, and foster team spirit through initiatives such as the School Council and School Houses.

Positive environment

For young people to thrive they must feel confident, relaxed and secure. Every child is known and understood at St Mary's and the girls feel comfortable challenging themselves and asking questions.

Before children even start at St Mary's time is taken to get to know them and their families, and there are initiatives in place from induction programmes to buddy systems to help students settle in. There's a very positive culture at St Mary's and visitors often comment on how staff and students are always smiling.

The school believes in instilling the values of respect and courtesy, and through its charity and outreach work, the students develop a strong sense of community. St Mary's is a leading Eco School and the students get a strong sense of caring for the environment as a result. As a global member of the Round Square Organisation, those who attend St Mary's benefit from international links, which helps to broaden their horizons.

In this positive environment, young people develop the strength of character and the self-belief they need to make the very most of the life that lies ahead.

Fees per term (2021–2022). Kindergarten: from £55.55 per day; Lower School: £3,490–£4,340; Senior School: £5,085–£5,295. Fees are inclusive of lunches, drinks (including milk at the Lower School), accident insurance and certain books.

Charitable status. St Mary's School (Colchester) Limited is a Registered Charity, number 309266.

Chair of Governors: Mr Adam Hildred

Principal: Mrs N Griffiths, MA, PGCE, NPQSL

Head of Lower School: Mrs E Stanhope, GMus, NPQH

Head of Senior School: Miss A Jones, BEd, NPQH

Head of Finance and Operations: Mrs E Bevan

Registrar: Mrs J Tierney

St Mary's School
Gerrards Cross

Packhorse Road, Gerrards Cross, Buckinghamshire SL9 8JQ

Tel:	01753 883370
email:	registrar@st-marys.bucks.sch.uk
website:	www.stmarysschool.co.uk
Twitter:	@StMarysSchoolGX
Facebook:	@St-Marys-School-Gerrards-Cross
Instagram:	@stmarysgx
LinkedIn:	/company/st-mary-s-school-gerrards-cross

Badge: *Ecce Ancilla Domini*

Founded by Dean Butler in 1872. Formerly at Lancaster Gate. Established in Gerrards Cross in 1937 as an Independent Day School catering for 400 day girls.

The School is situated in the attractive residential area of Gerrards Cross which is surrounded by beautiful countryside, 20 miles from London, close to the M25 and A40/M40, on the main bus routes and 10 minutes from the Railway Station.

The aim of the School is to provide an excellent academic and rounded education leading on to University for day girls between the ages of 3 and 18 and to enable each of them to develop their own talents and personalities in a happy, caring and purposeful environment, and to become successful, fulfilled adults.

Curriculum. Subjects offered include English Language and Literature, History, Geography, RE, Drama, French, German, Spanish, Business Studies, Economics, Information Technology, Computer Science, Mathematics, Psychology, Sociology, Politics, Textiles, Dance, Chemistry, Biology, Physics, Music, Art & Design, History of Art, Media Studies, Food & Nutrition, Extended Project Qualification, Equestrian Team, Gymnastics, Hockey, Netball, Tennis, Rounders, Football, Badminton, Swimming, Personal, Social, Cultural and Health Education, and other sporting activities.

Regular trips are made to places of educational interest, field courses are undertaken, foreign visits including a ski trip to Canada are arranged, and there is highly successful participation in The Duke of Edinburgh's Award scheme and Young Enterprise. There is an excellent staff to pupil ratio.

Examinations. Girls are prepared for Entrance to the Universities and Colleges in all subjects; for the General Certificate of Education at A Level and GCSE/IGCSE Level; Associated Board Examinations in Music and examinations in Speech and Drama (LAMDA). The School is an 11+ centre.

The Buildings are a highly attractive mixture of old and new and include two Libraries, Dining Hall, a Science Block with Laboratories, a large open-plan Art Studio, a Home Economics Room, Textiles Room, two Computer Suites, a modern Sixth Form Centre, Cedar House which opened in 2016, two Music Rooms, Drama Studio, Chapel and two

Assembly Halls/Gymnasiums equipped to the highest standards. Cherry Tree House, a new classroom block with state-of-the-art technology, opened in 2018.

The Prep Department, in the grounds of the Senior School, comprises Little St Mary's, a new build opened in 2020 for Nursery and Reception girls, Paddington House, and two modern purpose-built blocks, with a Science Laboratory, Hall, Gymnasium, Textiles/Art room and ICT suite.

The lovely grounds include tennis and netball courts, a hockey pitch and an athletics field. There is a Sport England full-size Sports Hall and a Multi-use Games Area is to be completed in October 2021.

School Hours. The hours are 8.30am–3.45pm. The School year is divided into 3 terms. Wraparound care is provided from 7.45am and after school until 6.00pm.

Reports are sent to Parents at half terms and at the end of each term and there are regular Parent/Staff meetings. The School also communicates with Parents via SchoolPost on Firefly.

Fees per term (2021–2022). £2,220–£6,290.

Scholarships and Bursaries. Academic scholarships are available at 7+, 11+ and at 16+ in the Sixth Form. There are also Art, Drama, Music and Sports scholarships at 11+ and Sports and Expressive Arts at 16+. A means-tested Bursary scheme is in operation.

Charitable status. St Mary's School (Gerrards Cross) Limited is a Registered Charity, number 310634. It provides education for girls from Early Years to A Level in a well-structured, academic and caring environment.

Governors:
Chairman: Mr D R Wilson, BA, FCA
Mrs C Bayliss, CertEd
Mrs D Campkin, ACA, BSc Hons
Mrs S Clifford, BSc
Mrs M Hall, MA Cantab, CPA, EPA
Mr N Hallchurch, LLB Hons
Mrs R Martin, Med, NPQH, FRSA
Mr N Moss, MNAEA
Mrs H Phillips, BA Hons

Senior Leadership Team:

***Headmistress*: Mrs Patricia Adams**, MA Oxon (*French, Spanish*)

Senior Deputy Head: Mrs Jo Kingston, BSc Hons Cardiff, MPhil Bath (*Chemistry*)

Deputy Head (Acting): Mrs Jacqui Deadman, BEd Hons Exeter, PSHCE

Head of Preparatory Department: Mrs Mairead Carney, BA Hons Galway (*Year 6 Class teacher*)

Bursar, Mrs Lisa Andrews, BA Hons Hertfordshire

Assistant Head Marketing and Communications: Mr James Dodd, BSc Hons Lancaster, MTL Birmingham City (*Business, Economics*)
Assistant Head Teaching & Learning: Mr Andy Gibb, BA Hons Queen's (*English*)

Head of Sixth Form: Mrs Katie Cork, BA Hons Durham (*Psychology*)

Heads of Department:
Mrs J Barber, MA Ed Oxford Brookes (*Business & Economics*)

Ms R Brereton, MA Auckland (*History (acting)*)
Mrs K Cork, BA Hons Durham (*Psychology*)
Mr S Cox, BA Hons East Anglia (*Politics*)
Mrs J Deadman, BEd Hons Exeter (*PSHCE*)
Mr T Evans, BA Hons Brunel (*Media Studies*)
Mr C Haydn-Slater, BA Hons Manchester (*Religious Studies*)
Mr J Heath, BSc Hons Loughborough (*Geography/ Humanities*)
Mr J Hopkins, BSc Hons Durham (*Science*)
Mrs L Jenkinson, MA St Mary's Twickenham (*Food & Nutrition*)
Mrs K Kalinowski, BA Royal Central School of Speech & Drama (*Drama*)
Mr A Keenan, BA Hons Queen's Belfast (*Modern Foreign Languages*)
Miss K Lasocki, BA Hons Leeds (*Dance*)
Mr P Martin, MA Cambridge (*ICT*)
Mrs E McNally, MA OU (*English*)
Miss J Newton, BA Hons The London Institute (*Art & Design*)
Mrs J Phillips, MA Beds (*Director of Expressive Arts*)
Mrs F Qureshi, BSc Hons Royal Holloway & Bedford New College, London (*Maths*)
Mrs K Stansfield, MA York (*History*) [Maternity Leave]
Mrs B Taylor, PGD Leeds, BA Hons de Montfort, OCR L7 SpLD (*LEAPS*)
Mrs R Webster, BA Leeds (*Physical Education*)

St Nicholas' School

Redfields House, Redfields Lane, Church Crookham, Fleet, Hampshire GU52 0RF

Tel: 01252 850121
email: headspa@st-nicholas.hants.sch.uk
website: www.st-nicholas.hants.sch.uk

Motto: *Confirma Domine Serviendo*

St Nicholas' School is a small independent day school for girls aged 3–16 and boys aged 3–7. Founded in 1935 in Branksomewood Road, Fleet, the school moved to Redfields House, Redfields Lane, Church Crookham in 1996. Redfields House, a Victorian Mansion, is set in 30 acres of glorious parkland and playing fields.

Branksomewood, the Nursery and Infant department, retains the original name of the road where the school was founded. Being built of natural wood with a wonderful airy atmosphere this building gives light and space to our younger children, creating a calming environment in which they thrive. With an adventure playground set in the woods, a large hall fitted with PE equipment overlooking the grounds, and our experienced teaching staff, it is no wonder the children are so happy.

St Nicholas' Junior department is based in Redfields House itself which keeps the charm of the old family house with its oak panelling and the senior department is located in the newer part of the school behind. All three departments have benefited from several building projects. Both Infant and Junior pupils have Forest School sessions throughout the year that take advantage of the beautiful outdoor learning space.

Facilities include an Olympic-size sports hall with courts, showers, changing rooms and a viewing gallery. This has enhanced the sports lessons and enabled even more sports competitions as well as extra-curricular activities. Badminton, tennis, netball, volleyball and basketball may be played throughout the year.

Our Art, Design Technology and Textiles Centre, offers three spacious rooms with large work benches, and a kiln for pottery. By having this wonderful building it has opened an opportunity for the school to adapt the old art centre into several music practice rooms. Tuition is offered in the violin, piano, guitar, harp, drums, singing, woodwind and brass.

The Pritchard Hall, named after the school's founder, was unveiled in 2009. The performing arts centre has raked seating for over 330, in the semi round and contains with an orchestra pit where concerts and plays are staged regularly. In addition, the drama department has two studios.

September 2013 welcomed the opening of state-of-the-art laboratories for juniors and seniors. The classrooms include teaching areas as well as practical learning spaces in a bright and welcoming environment.

In 2016 the addition of an all-weather pitch and two new tennis courts complemented the sports facilities. The new sand-based AstroTurf is floodlit and provides pupils with a multi-use sports facility including hockey, tennis and netball. The tennis courts are also floodlit. Hockey, athletics, football and rounders take place on the games field and the floodlit courts are used all year round. In 2018, the Junior Department benefited from a new play area. An outdoor classroom in the woodland provides Forest School lessons for all Infant and Junior pupils.

Pupils come to St Nicholas' from Hampshire, Surrey and Berkshire. School buses operate from Farnham, Odiham, Fleet, Basingstoke, Camberley, Yateley, Aldershot and Farnborough. Situated just off the A287, the Hook to Farnham road, junction 5 of the M3 is approximately 4 miles short away.

Religion. The school is a Christian foundation but children of other faiths are welcomed. Assemblies or hymn practices are held each morning. Children are encouraged to show tolerance, compassion and care for others.

Curriculum. St Nicholas' offers an extended day, from 7.30am to 6.00pm. Academic standards are high and a balanced curriculum is offered. Small classes place greater emphasis on the individual and pupils are encouraged to achieve their full potential in every area of school life. The curriculum is kept as broad as possible until the age of fourteen when choices are made for GCSE. The option choices vary by year depending upon the girls' abilities and talents. On average each girl sits ten subjects at GCSE. More than twenty subjects are offered at this level. A carefully structured personal development course incorporates a careers programme. Our girls move confidently on to enter sixth form colleges or scholarships to senior independent schools. Choir, drama and music thrive within the school and there are frequent performances which enable the girls to develop self-confidence.

Co-Curricular Programme. Our Co-Curricular programme refers to the academic, personal, spiritual, creative and physical development of every pupil, alongside a sound understanding of community. As a through school we have the unique opportunity to monitor and support the progress of every pupil according to their strengths and abilities at each key stage. Our focus is to offer experiences that are meaningful and child-centred; whether that be mindfulness walks, relaxation classes or exploring Forest School, participating in our Duke Of Edinburgh scheme or the girls running their own lunch time club and working alongside teaching specialists during Activity Weeks.

Physical Education. Pupils take part in inter-school and local district sports matches across a large number of sports including netball, hockey, basketball, football, tennis, swimming, volleyball, badminton, tag rugby, cross-country, athletics, ultimate frisbee and Taekwondo.

Entry. Children may enter at any stage subject to interview, school report and waiting list. Scholarships and Bursaries are available. For 11+ candidates there is an entrance examination.

Fees per term (2021–2022). Infants: £3,685 (Reception), £3,865 (Year 1), £3,884 (Year 2); Junior School: £4,341 (Year 3), £4,362 (Year 4), £4,425 (Year 5), £4,425 (Year 6); Senior School: £5,201 (Years 7–11). Nursery: £10.00 per hour.

Further Information. The prospectus is available upon request from the Registrar. The Headmistress is pleased to meet parents by appointment.

Charitable status. St Nicholas' School is a Registered Charity, number 307341. It exists to provide high quality education for children.

Chair of Governors: Stephen Mellor

Headmistress: **Dr Olwen Wright**, PhD Winchester, MA, BA Hons, PGCE

Deputy Head – Academic: Caroline Egginton, BEd Hons London

Deputy Head – Pastoral: Claire Huyton, BSc Hons Liverpool, PGCE, QTS

Head of Infants and Juniors – Lee Render, BA Hons, QTS Surrey

Bursar: D T Canning, FCCA

Teaching Staff:
Josephine Allen, BA Hons QTS West of England (*Key Stage 2*)
Florence Ayache, BA Hons Glamorgan, QTS (*Spanish & French*)
Helen Barnes, BA Ed Hons Exeter (*Deputy Head of Juniors*)
Jenny Brackstone, BA Hons Nottingham, PGCE (*Key Stages 3 & 4*)
Sarah Carter, BEd Hons Southampton (*Key Stage 2*)
Emma Chambers, BSc Hons Southampton, QTS, PGCE (*Director of Sport*)
Gemma Cross, BSc University of Wales, PGCE, OTS (*Science*)
Rebecca Cunliffe, BA Hons Kingston, BTEC, QTS (*Head of Art*)
Josie Downer, BA Hons Leeds, MA King's (*Head of Drama and ELSA*)
Joanne Edwards, BA Hons Brunel, PGCE (*Head of History*)
Rachel Firth, BA Hons Bath (*Textiles*)
Katie Francis, MA Kingston, BA Hons Nottingham, PGCE, QTS (*Stage 2*)
Amy Franke, BMus Hons, MMus Surrey (*Music*)
Dianna Gair, BEd Hons Wales, QTS (*Stage 2*)
Katherine Head, PhD, BSc Hons Bristol, PGCE, QTS (*Head Of Biology*)

Rebecca Hoddinott, BA Hons South Bank (*Food Prep and Nutrition*)

Laura Homer, BA Hons Wales, PGCE (*Key Stage 2*)

Hannah Hopkins, City & Guilds, Level 3 (*LSA and ELSA*)

Pilar Kimber, MA Reading (*Latin & Classical Civilisation*)

Alexandra Lawrence, MA Oxon, PGCE (*Head of Modern Languages*)

Stella Lawson, BA Nottingham Trent, QTS (*Teacher of English/Phase Leader*)

Val MacFarlane Travers, BEng Hons Liverpool, PGCE (*IT*)

Deborah Martin, BA Hons Surrey (*Mathematics and ELSA*)

Lyndon Martin, BSc Surrey, QTS (*Mathematics*)

Julie Merker, BA OU, CertEd (*PE*)

Wendy Moller, BEd University South Africa (*Foundation Stage Teacher*)

Helen Molloy, BA Hons Sheffield, PGCE, QTS (*Head of Curriculum Support and Exams Officer*)

Sarah Moore, BA Hons, University of the West Of England Bristol, PGCE, QTS

Paul Nicholls, BA Hons London (*Director of Co-Curricular Activities*)

Sarah Park, BA Hons Keele, QTS (*Activities, Head of English*)

Virginia Pearson, Perf Cert RAM, LTCL, ARCM (*Music*)

Jo-Lesley Paxford (*LSA*)

Mary Porter, MA UCL, BSC Hons Southampton, QTS (*Geography*)

Benjamin Pont, BMus Hons (*Director of Music*)

Joanna Pont, BMus Hons (*String Tutor*)

Lisa Ruffell, BA Hons, QTS Surrey (*Key Stage 2*)

Lucy Sartori, Bsc Hons Royal Holloway and Bedford New College, QTS

Julia Tiley, MA, BA Hons, QTS Kingston (*Deputy Head of Infants*)

Jane Tomlinson, BA Hons London, PGCE (*Modern Languages*)

Louise Wallace, BA York, PGCE, QTS (*Curriculum Support*)

Steve Warriner, BA Hons Trent Polytechnic (*Forest School and D of E*)

Dan Wileman, PE Assistant

Xinsheng Zhang, MEd Johannesburg SA (*Chinese Mandarin*)

Peripatetic Music:

Eleanor Bowyer, PGCE Middlesex (*LAMDA, Speech and Drama*)

Wendy Busby, BMus Hons (*Voice*)

Sylvia Ellison, BA Hons, PG Dip RCM (*Oboe*)

Vanessa Gynn, BA Hons, PG Dip RCM

Claire Hickling, BMus Hons (*Piano, Flute*)

Claire Hasted, BMus Hons (*Violin*)

Oksana Maxwell, LTCL (*Piano*)

Valerie Mitchell, LRAM (*Piano, Cello*)

Austin Pepper, ALCM (*Brass*)

Rachel Riordan, Adv Teaching RSM (*Saxophone, Clarinet*)

Rebecca Whittock, BA Hons University of London (*Violin*)

Administration:

Catering: David Clayton, Chartwells, Compass Group PLC

Headmistress's PA: Dawn Brown, FInstAM, FGPA

IT Network Manager: Darren Arnold

Head of Admissions & Marketing: Paula Stelfox, AMCIS in Admissions Management

Assistant Registrar: Frances van Heerden, BSc Natal UED

Infrastructure Technician Apprentice: Rio Elms BTEC, Level 2 IT

Laboratory Technician: Michele Axton, BA OU

Teaching Assistant: Tania Negus, Level 3 Diploma EYFS

Lunchtime Supervisor: Marcia Barrington, NVQ in Childcare

Librarian: Sarah Stokes

Payroll and Pensions Administrator: Debbie Smitherman, Dip in Pensions & Payroll Management

School Assistant: Amanda Bullock

School Secretary and Medical Officer: Sarah Watkins, RGN, NNEB

Maintenance:

Head of Maintenance: Paul Rippingale, Midas Trained

Assistant Maintenance Officer: Bruce Sharp, City & Guilds Levels 2 & 3

Groundsman: Maurrice Readman, Nebosh Certificate, Health & Safety, Midas Trained

Bus Drivers: Trevor Mills; Glenn Shearer, Midas Trained

Afternoon Caretaker: Peter Attwood

Morning Caretaker and Bus Driver: Timothy Hunt, Midas Trained

St Paul's Girls' School

Brook Green, Hammersmith, London W6 7BS

Tel:	School Office: 020 7603 2288
	Admissions: 020 7605 4882
	Business Directorate: 020 7605 4881
email:	admissions@spgs.org
	communications@spgs.org
	frontoffice@spgs.org
website:	www.spgs.org
Twitter:	@SPGSMain
Facebook:	@StPaulsGirlsSchool
Instagram:	@stpaulsgirlsschool
LinkedIn:	/stpaulsgirlsschool

Founded in 1904 as one of the first purpose-built schools for girls, St Paul's embraces both tradition and innovation. The emphasis on liberal learning established by the first High Mistress, Frances Gray, and Director of Music, Gustav Holst, finds expression today in an academically adventurous curriculum, which encourages intellectual freedom, discovery and the joy of scholarship. This is matched by supportive and individual pastoral care, vibrant co-curricular life and a busy programme of partnership and service activities.

Results and Destinations. St Paul's is committed to providing an outstanding academic education within a highly encouraging environment. Students regularly achieve exceptional results (87.5% A* at A Level or the Pre-U equivalent, and 97.1% at GCSE in 2021), but the school aims to teach far beyond the prescribed curriculum, endowing students with a lifelong love of learning and the necessary tools of scholarship and enterprise. Our teaching places emphasis on creativity, innovation and entrepreneurship, while our broad and progressive curriculum is rich in opportunities to learn about new technologies, preparing students to navigate an increasingly interconnected world with ease. Students take GCSE and IGCSE examinations in Year 11; alternative school directed courses in art, drama and music are also offered for this age group. Senior students are offered 23 subjects at A Level or

Pre-U, and are prepared for university entrance by our specialist higher education and careers advisory team. Students go on to study at major universities in the UK and the USA, with over 30% going to Oxford or Cambridge annually.

Co-curriculum. It is also the opportunities outside the classroom which make a St Paul's education distinctive. Many of the 100+ clubs and societies on offer are run by students for other students, and new ones are created every year to reflect passion and demand. Students are given leadership opportunities and an environment in which to experiment, innovate and push boundaries. The creative and performing arts flourish at St Paul's. Since its foundation, music has always been a particularly strong feature, with well over half the student body taking instrumental lessons; there are also multiple orchestras, choirs and ensembles on offer. Art and design benefit from studio and workshop facilities and there are several major exhibitions of students' work every year. Drama enjoys a purpose-built theatre and drama studio and any student can direct her own production. Volunteering is also an important feature of wider school life, with students spending time at homeless shelters, food rescue and redistribution centres, local primary schools and residential care homes.

Pastoral Care. A focus on wellbeing is also central to our ethos. Our top priority is enabling our students to learn and thrive in a happy and supportive environment. All students from Year 7 are placed in small tutor groups of between 13 and 15 students to ensure the highest standards of pastoral care. Strong systems of support mean students always have somewhere to turn when they need a listening ear, from peer supporters to in-house school counsellors. Our pastoral curriculum aims to introduce students to a diverse range of perspectives and demonstrate the importance of collaboration, diversity and inclusion, empowering them to make a difference in the world beyond school.

Sport. There are extensive sporting facilities on site and sport is played with verve and distinction. Indeed, facilities are some of the best offered by a central London school. These include a 50m swimming pool, four outdoor netball courts, two lacrosse pitches, an athletics track including field events, and five tennis courts. At our Sports Hall and newly built Pavilion, we also house three dance and fitness studios and a multi-gym. The physical education department prides itself on delivering a broad, balanced and exciting curriculum, offering a wide range of both traditional and varied sporting opportunities. We aim for every student to strive to discover a sport that they love and in which they can achieve. The three main sports at SPGS are lacrosse, netball and rowing, but students are also able to take part in extra-curricular sporting clubs to broaden their participation in sport. Fixtures are played throughout the year, ensuring every student who wants the opportunity is able. In the Autumn and Spring terms alone, there are over 500 fixtures played.

Sixth Form. The Senior School (Sixth Form) is housed in our wonderful Garden Building opened in 2018. Students have a large and comfy common room, kitchen, group working space and quiet study room at their disposal. Tutor groups are small, enabling first class pastoral support. Students are further supported by the Senior School team and they are guided through the university application process by a personal higher education co-ordinator and an academic advisor. One of the highlights of the Senior School

is the weekly lecture by invited speakers. Sitting alongside the Friday lecture is the St Paul's Programme which offers a range of non-examined courses including *Flexible Thinking* and *Decision Making*.

Alumnae. St Paul's Girls' School is proud to have a supportive global network of over 7,000 alumnae which are supported by a dedicated team in the school's Development Office. They remain connected to each other and the school in a myriad of ways including through an exclusive alumnae networking platform, monthly bulletins, publications and frequent in-person and online events. As a vital part of the community, alumnae assist in supporting students with mentoring, careers and university guidance.

Partnerships. Partnerships play a key role in school life at SPGS. Each year we share our Higher Education and Careers programmes with over 150 students from numerous schools. Students at local schools join group sessions and receive tailored advice, interview practice and personal statement guidance. This summer, year 10 and 12 students from Hammersmith Academy, West London Free School and Cardinal Vaughan Memorial School attended a week-long aspirational STEM Summer School. Music Junction, Book Clubs in School and working with the West London Zone are some of the ways that we support local primary schools. We formed a network of independent and maintained schools through the West London Partnership, as part of which we share ideas, online sessions and make connections across London.

Admissions. The main ages of admission are 11 and 16. There are currently 788 girls on the roll. The school is committed to making a St Paul's education available to the brightest students whatever their means and has an active development campaign dedicated to raising funds for the bursary programme.

Scholarships

Junior Music Scholarships (11+), to the value of lessons in two instruments/voice, currently worth £1,680 per annum, tenable for five years when scholars will be able to apply for a 16+ scholarship in Year 11 for their final two years at St Paul's. Music exhibitions may also be awarded following auditions at the discretion of the Director of Music. They are based on the value of lessons in one instrument/voice, currently worth £840 per annum and tenable for five years.

Senior Music Scholarships (16+), to the value of lessons in two instruments/voice, currently worth £1,680 per annum, tenable for two years *(choral awards up to the value of one lesson in voice may be available)*. External candidates must be successful in the Senior School entrance examination.

Senior Art Scholarships (16+), of the value of £250 per annum are offered to up to two internal and two external candidates who are currently in their final GCSE year and who, if applying from another school, have previously been successful in the Senior School entrance examination. Candidates take part in a workshop and are also required to submit a portfolio.

Senior Drama Scholarships (16+), of the value of £250 per annum are awarded on the basis of an audition, workshop and interview with our Director of Drama and other drama staff to candidates who show outstanding potential as an actor or director. Please note that scholarship candidates will often study drama at A Level; however, those able to demonstrate a significant commitment to co-curricular drama will also be considered.

Bursaries

Junior Bursaries (11+) to a value of up to full fee remission, based on proven financial need and subject to annual review, are available. Candidates must be successful in the 11+ entrance examination. The number of junior bursaries available each year will vary.

Senior Bursaries (16+) to a value of up to full fee remission, based on proven financial need and subject to annual review, are available for candidates who have been successful in the Senior School entrance examination and who are currently in their final GCSE year at another school.

Fees per term (2021–2022). £8,802, including lunches and personal accident insurance, and excluding textbooks. The fees per term for new entrants entering at 16+ are £9,463.

Registration & Examination Fee £125.

Charitable status. St Paul's Girls' School is a Registered Charity, number 1119613, and a Company Limited by Guarantee, registered in England, number 6142007 and is governed by its Memorandum and Articles of Association. It exists to promote the education of girls in Greater London. The sole member of the charitable company is the Mercers' Company.

Governors:

Chairman: Mr Simon Wathen
Deputy Chairman: Mrs Zeina Bain

Ms Justine Archer	Mrs Clare Hebbes
Ms Lisa Barclay	Mrs Geeta Khehar
Mr Nicholas Buxton	Mrs Gillian Low
Mr Nicolas Chisholm, MBE	Professor Jane Ridley
Mr Tim Haywood	Dr Julia Riley

High Mistress: **Mrs Sarah Fletcher**, MA Oxford

Senior Deputy Head, Director of Studies:
Mr Andrew Ellams, MA Oxford

Deputy Head, Director of Pastoral Care:
Mrs Lizzie Beesley, MA Oxford

Deputy Head, Director of Co-Curriculum:
Mr Fred Hitchcock, BA Bristol

Deputy Head, Director of Senior School:
Ms Josephine Lane, BA Leeds

Deputy Head, Director of Partnerships:
Mr Leigh O'Hara, BA York, MMus London

Deputy Head, Director of Strategic Development:
Mr Ellis Whitcomb, BSc Birmingham, PGCert Cambridge

Bursar:
Mr Gerard Hickie, BEng UCC, MBA INSEAD

Director of Operations:
Mrs Barbara Sussex, MPhil Birmingham

Assistant Head, Teaching and Learning:
Mr Giles Bennett, BA Middlesex, BSc Open, MSc Oxford, MIMA

Assistant Head, Teaching and Learning:
Miss Mary Wenham, BA Oxford, MA London

Director of Admissions:
Ms Melinda Armitage, BBus Victoria

Heads of Department:

Art: Mr Matthew Bunning, BA Cambridge
Biology: Miss Rosalind Orchard, BSc Cambridge
Chemistry: Ms Marianna Doria, MChem Oxford, MSc London
Classics: Dr Matthew McCullagh, BA, MPhil, PhD Cambridge
Computer Science and Creative Technologies: Ms Melissa Bustamante-Jenke, BSc, PGCE London
Drama: Miss Isabel Foley, BA, MA London
Economics: Mr Nicholas Hazell, BA Leeds, PGCE Brighton
English: Dr Joanna Bratten, BA Steubenville, OH, MLitt, PhD St Andrews
Geography: Miss Rhiannon Cogbill, BA, MPhil Cambridge
History: Mr Rupert Try, MA, MSt Oxford
Mathematics: Dr Damon Vosper-Singleton, MMath Oxford, PhD London
Modern Languages: Ms Marjorie Delage, BA Limoges
Music: Mr Leigh O'Hara, BA York, MMus London
Physical Education: Miss Jessica Basch, BA, MA St Davids, PA
Physics: Ms Agniete Geras, BA Oxford
Politics: Mr Thomas Peck, BA Manchester
Religion and Philosophy: Miss Cat Graham, BA Oxford

St Swithun's School

Alresford Road, Winchester, Hampshire SO21 1HA

Tel:	01962 835700
email:	office@stswithuns.com
website:	www.stswithuns.com
Twitter:	@StSwithunsGirls
Facebook:	@StSwithunsGirls
Instagram:	@StSwithunsGirls
LinkedIn:	/company/StSwithunsGirls

St Swithun's is a modern and flourishing educational organisation. The school is set on an impressive and attractive campus of 45 acres in the South Downs National Park on the outskirts of Winchester. It offers girls excellent teaching, sporting and recreational facilities. St Swithun's is a World Class High Performance Learning (HPL) School

The school offers weekly boarding, full boarding and day options for girls aged 11–18. At present the senior school (girls aged 11–18) has 300 day girls and 216 boarders. There is an adjoining Prep School for girls aged 4–11 with a co-ed pre-school (*see Prep School entry in IAPS section*).

Ethos. St Swithun's is an 'appropriately academic' school which means that we celebrate intellectual curiosity and the life of the mind, but not to the exclusion of all else. We expect our pupils to develop individual passions and through them to acquire a range of skills and characteristics. These characteristics will include a willingness to take risks, to question and to debate, and to persevere in the face of difficulty. In the words of Samuel Beckett: "Ever tried. Ever failed. No matter. Try again. Fail again. Fail better." If a girl can immediately excel at everything we ask of her, we as educators must set the bar higher.

We want all girls to learn about life beyond the school gates, to appreciate the rich variety of our world, to develop an understanding of compassion and to value justice. We encourage all pupils to become involved in fundraising and community work. They should appreciate how their decisions and their actions can affect those around them.

St Swithun's was founded by Anna Bramston, daughter of the Dean of Winchester, and Christian values underpin our approach to education. We provide a civilised and caring environment in which all girls and staff are valued for their individual gifts and encouraged to develop a sense of spirituality and of kindness. We believe that kindness and tolerance are at the heart of any fully functioning community.

Location. The school is on a rural site in Winchester's 'green belt' but only a short distance from the city centre. It is easily accessible from Heathrow and Gatwick airports and is one hour from London by car (via the M3 motorway). There is a frequent train service to London Waterloo (one hour). We also offer a popular London taxi service from St Swithun's School to London on a Friday evening and a return journey on Sunday.

Curriculum. Girls at St Swithun's benefit from a broad and balanced curriculum that promotes individual choice and achievement. The timetable is designed to enable each pupil to fulfil her intellectual, physical and creative potential through a dynamic range of purposeful lessons and activities.

From their first years here girls are taught to examine social, cultural and moral issues so that they can make informed decisions about their own way of living as well as respecting the values of each individual. The PSHEE & citizenship programme is tailored for each year group and is delivered through a range of school activities and specialist speakers.

All girls follow an enrichment programme known as Stretch. This consists of taught short courses and lectures from visiting speakers. Courses are wide-ranging and topics such as magic and mathematics, biblical Hebrew, cryptic crosswords and French cinema. M5 girls will use Stretch to undertake community service.

Games and PE are taught throughout the school so that girls can participate in a wide range of team and individual sports. Both in lessons and as recreational activities, the emphasis is on personal enjoyment and the development of a healthy, active life, but all pupils receive expert coaching and the most talented individuals and teams are entered into county, regional and national competitions.

Learning support provides bespoke support for individual girls who may be experiencing difficulties in aspects of their academic studies.

Girls take 9 or 10 GCSE exams to allow time for other interests and activities. Everyone takes English language, English literature, mathematics, at least two sciences and one modern foreign language. The girls then choose a further three or four subjects from a choice of 13. Girls are encouraged to take at least one humanity or social science to ensure a breadth of knowledge and skills.

In the sixth form girls are offered 22 subjects from which they choose four at A Level (five if maths and further maths are chosen). Advice is given about the implications for their choice of university, degree course and career to ensure sensible combinations. Some girls choose to follow courses in subjects which are not offered at GCSE. Over half the sixth form study at least one science subject at A Level.

Girls normally continue with three of their lower sixth subjects to complete three full A Levels.

In addition, all sixth-formers may choose to do the Extended Project Qualification (EPQ). This is worth half an A Level and is graded from A*–E. The qualification gives girls the opportunity to research an area of personal interest. Universities recognise the value of the skills required for the qualification and it attracts UCAS tariff points. Italian GCSE is also available in the sixth form.

In 2020 St Swithun's became accredited as a High Performance Learning (HPL) World Class School. The philosophy and principles of HPL, that everyone can perform highly, are embedded across the curriculum and all areas of school life for all students in the school. Our unique academic enrichment programme, delivered in lunchtime and break sessions, is also open to the whole school.

Religion. The school is a Church of England foundation. There are close ties with Winchester Cathedral, where termly services and the annual confirmation and carol services are held. A full-time chaplain prepares girls for confirmation. There is a newly converted chapel at the heart of the school.

Music. From the first hymn in the morning to the final applause on concert nights every day is enriched by music and the school enjoys a fine reputation for the excellence and variety that girls achieve. Through lessons, practice, rehearsals, exams, competitions, performances and cathedral services, the girls are drawn together to make the most of a busy and ambitious musical life: 75% have instrumental lessons and there is a choice of twenty-two instruments to study. Twenty flourishing school ensembles create a wealth of music and everyone is welcome to join in. Our most accomplished musicians are also cathedral choristers or play in county and national groups. There are endless possibilities at St Swithun's whether it is Renaissance church music, African drumming or 21st century pop music that girls wish to study, listen to, compose or perform. They are taught to appreciate many different styles of music from all over the world and from different historical eras. Learning to compose enables some to express themselves through music and we encourage performing as an integral part of what we offer. Learning a musical instrument and sharing this with an audience requires a high standard of creativity, commitment, technique and courage.

Sports. All girls are encouraged to be involved in sport throughout their time at the school. Sport at St Swithun's has so much to offer, emphasising cooperation, leadership, teamwork, competition and respect. Our girls learn how to deal with success and failure, how to be self-disciplined and how to communicate with each other. We expect every girl to try her best in every area of school life and sport is no exception. Many girls represent their county, region or even country in sports as diverse as lacrosse, fencing, diving, athletics and tennis and we are naturally very proud of these individuals. However, whilst we celebrate success and our teams aspire to excellence, we value effort and sportsmanship as much as winning and we are proud to run first, second and sometimes third teams for all age groups.

Of supreme importance to us is identifying at least one sport to suit each girl so that she will acquire a lifelong enjoyment of exercise. Our Team Orange sports performance programme provides an individually tailored pathway for each student to achieve her full potential at whatever level that might be: from being motivated to live a healthy and active life to achieving elite athletic performance and everything in between.

Facilities. The original school building contains the main teaching rooms and libraries and has been extended and developed to provide specialist areas for languages, information technology, food and textiles and careers. The science wing contains eight fully equipped modern laboratories and project rooms. In addition, there is an art, design and technology centre and a performing arts building was opened in 2003. This has a 600-seat main auditorium and two smaller performance spaces. A new library, careers and ICT facility was opened in 2007. A new further education study centre for sixth form students opened in late 2021.

School Houses. There are 6 boarding houses and 4 day girl houses, each staffed by a housemistress or housemaster and assistant who take pride in the high level of pastoral care offered to each girl. The junior house is for day girls and boarders aged 11 who are then transferred to one of the senior houses after a year. They remain in the senior house until they have completed one year in the sixth form. The upper sixth house is for boarders and day girls together, with study-bedrooms for boarders, study facilities for day girls and common rooms and kitchen for all.

Careers. Most girls continue to university, including Oxford and Cambridge, and all continue to some form of higher education and training. Each girl is counselled by one of the team of careers staff in a well-resourced department. Lectures and video presentations are organised frequently and a careers fair held annually. St Swithun's is the Oxbridge hub in Winchester.

Leisure Activities. There is an extensive range of co-curricular activities and an organised programme of visits and activities at the weekend. Girls participate in the Duke of Edinburgh's Award scheme, Young Enterprise and local community service work. The sixth form are able to assist with Stretch activities and this can count towards their UCAS tariff. Each year there are drama productions as well as regular drama activities. There are many overseas study and activity trips which include volunteer work, language trips, ski trips and watersports holidays.

Health. The school health centre forms part of the main buildings. It is staffed by qualified RGNs and visited by the school doctor twice a week.

Entrance. Entry is by means of a pre-test and the Common Entrance examination for Independent Schools. The majority of girls enter the senior school at the age of 11 or 13 years, but girls are accepted at other ages, including the sixth form, subject to satisfactory tests.

Scholarships and Bursaries. Academic scholarships, carrying a fee subsidy of up to 20%, are available for day girls and boarders entering the school at 11+, at 13+ and to the sixth form.

Music scholarships carry a subsidy of up to 20% and provide free tuition on two instruments; exhibitions provide free tuition on one instrument. Music scholars can apply for a means-tested award of up to 100% of school fees.

Sports scholarships are awarded at the end of year 9 when all girls, whether they joined the school at year 7 or year 9, will have had the opportunity to develop skills in all of the sports which the school offers. Sports scholarships are also available for internal and external candidates at 16+. These scholarships have a maximum value of 20% fee remission.

Bursaries of up to 100% of school fees are available for girls who meet the school's entrance criteria. All bursaries are subject to means-testing. In addition, the school offers a number of 20% boarding bursaries to new HM Forces families joining the school.

Fees per term (2021–2022). Senior School: Boarders £12,113; Day Girls £7,306. Prep School: £3,890–£5,060.

Charitable status. St Swithun's School Winchester is a Registered Charity, number 307335.

Chairman of School Council: Mrs Alison McClure

Headmistress: Ms Jane Gandee, MA Cantab

Deputy Head Pastoral: Mr Graham Yates, MA Brunel
Deputy Head Academic: Mr Charlie Hammel, AB Princeton, MLitt St Andrews

Admissions Registrar: Mrs Kate Cairns
Deputy Registrar: Mrs Mhairi Bennett
Assistant Registrar: Mrs Liz Turner

Sheffield High School for Girls
GDST

10 Rutland Park, Sheffield, South Yorkshire S10 2PE

Tel:	0114 266 0324
email:	enquiries@she.gdst.net
website:	www.sheffieldhighschool.org.uk
Twitter:	@SheffieldHigh
Facebook:	@sheffieldhighschool
LinkedIn:	/Sheffield-High-School

Sheffield High School for Girls is the leading South Yorkshire private school, offering an engaging and enriched education for girls from age 4 right through to 18. At Sheffield Girls' we aim to bring out the best in all our pupils and encourage them within a happy, structured and nurturing environment. Our ethos is one of mutual respect and care: every girl is valued for her own talents and interests and encouraged as an individual so that she can thrive.

Sheffield High School for Girls is part of the Girls' Day School Trust (GDST). The GDST is the leading network of independent girls' schools in the UK. As a charity that owns and runs 23 schools and two academies, it reinvests all its income in its schools. For further information about the Trust, see p. xix or visit www.gdst.net.

Number of Pupils. 770 (145 in sixth form).

The school was opened in 1878 and has occupied its beautiful leafy site in the suburb of Broomhill since 1887. It draws its pupils from all parts of the Sheffield City region. Transport to and from school is available from a wide area.

The Infant School, which relocated back to No. 4 Melbourne Avenue in summer 2021, is home to Reception, Year 1 and Year 2 girls. They benefit from specialist teachers and teaching facilities, enabling them to develop an early love of music, languages, sport and drama. The facilities include the Infant School Library, music rooms, a science room and an art room where we deliver our unique fusion curriculum. Our outdoor play area was fully refurbished in 2021.

The Junior School, based at No. 5 Melbourne Avenue, is surrounded by outdoor learning spaces as well as easy access to the wider facilities in the Senior School, including indoor and outdoor sports facilities. Learning is enhanced by enrichment beyond the curriculum, which includes speakers and visitors into school, and trips to theatres and museums. In 2020 we were named as the first World Educational Robotics (WER) UK robotics HUB for Primary School children and we offer our robotics curriculum from Year 5 onwards.

In the Senior School a £3.5 million development programme over the past three years has seen the development of a new cookery room, a new drama studio and a complete refurbishment of the gym, which now incorporates a state-of-the-art fitness suite and accommodation for trampolining, gymnastics and dance. We installed brand new Biology labs in summer 2021.

A separate Sixth Form building, close to the Senior School buildings, offers well-furnished and comfortable common rooms for Years 12 and 13, a Learning Resource Centre with laptops, printers and high-speed Wi-Fi, and a fully equipped kitchen. We are very proud of our national reputation for achieving excellent results academically, but also for our outstanding success in sport, music, art and drama and for our work within the local community.

Beyond the School Day. Food and refreshments are available in the dining hall from 7.30am every morning. In the Infant and Junior School, after-school care is available daily from 3.15pm until 6.15pm in Tea Time Club.

Between 3.30pm and 5.30pm every Monday to Friday during term time, Senior pupils can stay in school to devote time to homework tasks or revision. We offer over 100 co-curricular clubs and programmes and many pupils stay in school after 3.30 pm to take part in a wide range of activities led by staff and senior students.

Curriculum. School life at Sheffield Girls' centres on an exciting and challenging curriculum. As well as the core subjects of English, Mathematics and Science, the broader Infant and Junior School curriculum includes History, Geography, Drama, Religious Studies and PSHE with specialist teaching in Music, Modern Foreign Languages (French, Spanish or German), Art and Design Technology and Physical Education.

In the Senior School, a challenging and up-to-date curriculum combines the best of traditional, modern, scientific, creative and practical subjects to provide a broad, balanced and inspiring Secondary School education. From Year 7, girls study three separate sciences, two modern foreign languages and Latin (from Year 8) in addition to the standard national curriculum. There is a full range of options in languages, humanities and technical and aesthetic subjects. Most girls study nine GCSE subjects. We are one of the only providers of the Pre-Senior Baccalaureate in the region, offered to girls in Year 7 and Year 8 in preparation for their continued studies in the upper school.

In the Sixth Form, the school offers a bespoke curriculum tailored to the needs of each individual, with a personalised timetable for each girl. The majority of Year 12 students study 3 or 4 A Levels. Students can also opt to do the Extended Project Qualification (EPQ). Our Forging Futures programme provides timetabled courses and stand-alone events for Year 12 and 13 pupils throughout the year, focussing on skills for life and skills for success.

The school has received a string of prestigious national awards for the exceptional quality of its extra-curricular provision, such as PE Quality Mark with Distinction, Artsmark (Gold), GO4it, ICT Quality Mark, Eco-Schools Award and Career Mark, making it the only school in South Yorkshire to be so accredited for the quality of its careers provision.

The school's sporting teams often compete in national finals and teams regularly reach national competition finals in STEM subjects and debating. The School's many lunchtime and after school clubs encourage excellence in sport, music, drama and art, and we offer the full Duke of Edinburgh's Award scheme. A varied programme of residential trips and expeditions at home and abroad is available, including Sport, Music, Foreign Language and Art tours. The School has strong community links and has recently received four Independent School Awards as well as being shortlisted in two further years. Awards have been for: Best Independent-Maintained School Collaboration, Outstanding Community Initiative and Best Leadership Team.

Fees per term (2021–2022). Senior School and Sixth Form £4,542, Junior £3,349 Reception and Infants £3,227

The fees cover the regular curriculum, school books, stationery and other materials, most extra-curricular activities, but not school lunches. Girls are required to stay for school lunches up to Year 7 and these are charged separately per term.

Scholarships and Bursaries. The GDST makes available to the School a substantial number of scholarships and bursaries. In particular, it aims as far possible to focus its support on girls for whom the chance of a GDST education would be a transformative, life-changing prospect.

Bursaries are awarded to pupils in the top 30% of performance in the entrance examinations. All bursaries are means-tested.

Scholarships are awarded on merit, irrespective of financial means. Offers are made based upon performance in the entrance examinations or audition for Year 7, or in the case of Sixth Form scholarships for outstanding ability demonstrated in individual subjects and disciplines. A Scholarship can be combined with a bursary where there is financial need.

Charitable status. Sheffield High School is part of The Girls' Day School Trust, which is a Registered Charity, number 306983.

Chair of Local Governors: Mr Jon Dunn

Headmistress: Mrs N Gunson, BSc MSc Huddersfield

Deputy Head: Mrs S White, BA Sheffield

Senior Teacher, Assistant Head (Academic): Mr Carl Adams, MChem Sheffield

Assistant Head (Pastoral): Mrs A Reed, BA Sheffield Hallam

Assistant Head (Co-Curricular): Mrs E Rodgers, BEd Liverpool John Moores

Head of Junior School: Mr C Hald, MA York

Director of Finance and Operations: Mr I Kane, BSc Open University

Director of Marketing and Communications: Mrs Rebecca Mills, BA Hull

South Hampstead High School
GDST

3 Maresfield Gardens, London NW3 5SS

Tel: 020 7435 2899
email: senioradmissions@shhs.gdst.net
website: www.shhs.gdst.net
Twitter: @SHHSforgirls

Founded in 1876, South Hampstead High School is a selective, independent day school for girls aged 4 to 18 in North West London – a buzzing academic powerhouse with kindness and curiosity at its core. Although excellent results and university destinations place it among the country's top schools, South Hampstead is known for its forward-looking ethos and an approach that aims to ignite a genuine joy in learning – this is a school that opens doors, hearts and minds.

The school is well-connected to most London postcodes, close to Finchley Road and Hampstead underground stations (Jubilee, Metropolitan and Northern lines), several overground stations and numerous bus routes. It has approximately 930 pupils, including around 130 in the Sixth Form and 265 in the Junior School. Entry is competitive: at 4+ and 7+ to the Junior School, and 11+ and 16+ to the Senior School. Occasionally vacancies arise at other ages. Full details of the admissions procedures are available at www.shhs.gdst.net.

The Junior School occupies two large houses a few minutes' walk from the main Senior School site. The Senior School is housed in a bright, modern building, designed by Hopkins Architects. Sixth Form students have their own home in Oakwood – complete with its own common room and cafe – in a beautiful, Victorian house, connected to the Senior School. A four-acre sports ground with excellent facilities is a short walk away.

At South Hampstead, the curriculum is designed to provide a secure and imaginative basis for academic progress at each key stage of a pupil's development. The intention is that all girls develop their own enthusiasms and initiative within a broad educational framework and a balanced range of academic, cultural and aesthetic subjects. In the Junior School there is a clear focus on developing literacy and numeracy skills and an integrated approach to the curriculum whereby the focus is on learning across several subjects around a theme. In this way girls develop real depth of knowledge, as well as confidence in key skills such as research, analysing results and interpreting and presenting information. In the Senior School the curriculum has a strong academic spine. The Head teaches Philosophy to all Year 7 pupils, while other subjects on offer include Critical Thinking, Design & Technology, Drama and a choice of French, German, Mandarin and Spanish.

The Sixth Form offers a range of 24 subjects at A Level and students have a strong track record in the Extended Project Qualification (EPQ). A rich and varied programme of speakers, leadership opportunities, international trips and co-curricular activities ensure that every student has the chance to grow, to give back and to shine. The school's Futures Programme provides a comprehensive framework for supporting pupils with higher education and career choices, while a dynamic Free Thinking Fridays programme encourages independent thought and debate. The vast majority are offered their first choice university – primarily to Russell Group universities, including Oxbridge, but with good numbers to medical school, prestigious art colleges and Ivy League destinations.

Pupils throughout the school participate enthusiastically in an enormous number of co-curricular clubs, societies and activities. Creativity in art, writing, music and drama is strongly encouraged at all stages. There are many orchestras, ensembles and choirs. Tuition in almost any instrument and singing can be arranged and girls are prepared for the examinations of the Associated Board of the Royal School of Music. Large numbers of pupils participate in the Duke of Edinburgh's Award and Young Enterprise business scheme.

Fees per term (Spring/Summer 2022). Senior School £6,690, Junior School £5,466.

The fees do not include school meals or instrumental/singing lessons.

Scholarships and Bursaries. A number of scholarships and bursaries are available to internal or external candidates for entry at 11+ and to the Sixth Form. The bursaries are means-tested to ensure that the school remains accessible to bright girls who would benefit from a South Hampstead education but require financial assistance. Scholarships are currently awarded for academic, musical and sporting excellence (11+) and academic, art, drama and music in the Sixth Form.

Charitable status. South Hampstead High School is part of the Girls' Day School Trust, a leading network of independent girls' schools, Registered Charity, number 306983. As a charity that owns and runs 23 schools and two academies, it reinvests all its income into its schools. For more information, please visit www.gdst.net.

Board of Governors:
Chairman: Ms A Dewinter, BA, MSc, GDL
Mr N Chandra, MA
Mrs K Fear
Mrs V Fox, BSc
Mrs L Frank, BA
Mr R Freeman, BA, MBA
Ms A Gooch, OBE
Miss D Navanayagam, BA
Mrs J Solomon, MA
Mrs J Todd, BA
Mrs M Trehearne, MA, BEd
Dr V Wass, OBE, BSc

Headmistress: Mrs Victoria Bingham, BA Oxon

Senior Leadership Team:
Senior Deputy Head Pastoral: Ms Z Brass, BA Queen's University Canada
Director of Finance and Operations: Mr R Jones, MA Oxon
Director for Employability & Partnerships: Dr R Osborne, MEng Oxon, PhD Imperial
Head of Junior School: Ms C Spencer, MSc Sheffield, BSc Leeds
Deputy Head of Junior School: Miss L Szemerenyi, BSc Sussex
Deputy Head Academic: Mr A Westwood, BSc Nottingham
Director of Sixth Form: Mr R White, BA Leeds
Director of Philanthropy & Alumnae: Mrs S Whitworth, MA Edinburgh

Stamford High School

St Martin's, Stamford, Lincolnshire PE9 2LL

Tel: 01780 484200

email: headshs@ses.lincs.sch.uk

website: www.stamfordschools.org.uk

Twitter: @SpedeNews

Facebook: @stamfordendowedschools

Instagram: @StamfordSchools

Motto: *Christ me spede*

Founded by Browne's Hospital Foundation, of Stamford, 1876.

Introduction. Stamford High School is one of three schools within the overall Stamford Endowed Schools Educational Charity, along with Stamford School (boys) and Stamford Junior School, the co-educational junior school.

Numbers and Boarding Houses. There are 618 girls aged 11–18 years including boarders. The main point of entry is at age 11 though applications are welcomed at any stage up to the Sixth Form. Girls who enter through the Junior School progress automatically on to the High School without further competitive entrance testing. Boarders are received from the age of 8 (in the Junior School). There are two Boarding Houses for girls including a Sixth Form Boarding House where the girls have single or shared study bedrooms. The School accepts full, weekly and three-night boarders.

Fees per annum (2021–2022). Day £17,460; Boarding: 7 Day £31,300, 5 Day £27,170, 3 day £23,605.

These fees include all stationery, textbooks and games. School lunches for day girls are at additional charge.

Application Fee £100. Acceptance Fee £500; overseas students pay an additional deposit.

Extras. Individual music lessons, Speech and Drama, Dancing, (Riding for boarders only).

Curriculum. All pupils follow the National Curriculum with the addition of modern foreign language teaching, excellent sports and music provision. There is a broad GCSE curriculum choice, with the majority of girls entered for at least 9 GCSE examinations and students are encouraged to maintain a breadth to their experience. They then continue on to A Level examinations leading to university entry. In partnership with Stamford School, all Sixth Form girls have access to the full range of A Level subjects offered across the two schools providing an exceptionally wide choice of 27 A Level subjects, plus 2 BTECs.

Throughout their time in the school, many girls are prepared for the examinations of the Associated Board of the Royal Schools of Music in music and The London Academy of Music and Dramatic Art for speech and drama. There is much scope for creative activities in Music, Art and Drama and state-of-the-art facilities for Information & Communication Technology. The Director of Music for the Stamford Endowed Schools ensures that the Music Department works very closely with Stamford School providing access to a wide range of activities for orchestras, bands, Chapel Choir and choirs. There are joint drama productions and a Performing Arts Studio.

Sport and Physical Education include Hockey, Netball, Tennis, Swimming, Golf, Judo, Athletics, Volleyball, Basketball, Badminton, Trampoline, Gymnastics and Squash. There is a very full programme of co-curricular activities including Olympic Gymnastics, Athletics and Taekwondo. There is a heated, indoor swimming pool, a Sports Hall and a floodlit artificial hockey pitch. The Duke of Edinburgh's Award Scheme operates at Bronze, Silver and Gold levels with a considerable number of girls taking part each year. There is a thriving, mixed CCF offering RN, Army and RAF sections. There are many school clubs and societies and a thriving weekend activity programme.

Entrance Examinations are held in January.

Scholarships and Bursaries. The Schools offer a range of scholarships for pupils entering into years 7, 9 and 12 (Sixth Form). Scholarships are less common for pupils entering into other years but may at times be available. There are scholarships for Academic, Music, Art, Sports and All-Rounder performance. Means-tested bursaries can be applied for by families of pupils who would otherwise not be able to benefit from a Stamford education. Please see our website for full details.

Charitable status. As part of the Stamford Endowed Schools, Stamford High School is a Registered Charity, number 527618.

Principal: **William Phelan**, MBA

Head: **Victoria Buckman**

Deputy Head: Andrew Murphy

Chairman of Governors: Nicholas Rudd-Jones

Bursar and Clerk to the Governing Body: Dean White

Sydenham High School
GDST

19 Westwood Hill, London SE26 6BL

Tel: 020 8557 7000

email: senior@syd.gdst.net

website: www.sydenhamhighschool.gdst.net

Twitter: @SydenhamHigh

Facebook: @sydenham.high.gdst

LinkedIn: /sydenham-high-school-gdst

Founded in 1887 by four pioneering women, Sydenham High School is an independent day school for girls aged 4–18 and is part of the GDST (Girls' Day School Trust). The GDST is the leading network of independent girls' schools in the UK. As a charity that owns and runs 23 schools and two academies, it reinvests all its income in its schools. For further information about the Trust, see p. xix or visit www.gdst.net.

Pupil numbers. Senior School 477, Prep School 241.

Sydenham High is a school bursting with warmth, creativity, talent and, above all, excellence in all that we do. We pride ourselves on enriching young minds in a way that will endure a lifetime. Providing a first-class education for girls was the aim of our founders and it remains our aim today. The outlook and opportunities for girls may have changed, but our educational goals have not. Our school motto, 'Nyle ye Drede' (Fear Nothing), lies at the heart of all we do. A Sydenham High education is centred on the girl, and academic and pastoral excellence go hand in hand. We want our pupils to have a 'can do' approach and inner strength, empowered to use their voice, so that they are enabled to thrive, succeed and be happy.

Our pupils have independence of mind, the courage to take risks, a strong moral compass as well as a social conscience, and are accepting and respectful of themselves and others. They have been described as having 'self-confidence without arrogance' which is a perfect description of a Sydenham High pupil.

We are a school which is small enough to ensure that every pupil is visible, but large enough to have lots going on, and the education on offer here is both aspirational and personalised. We want to empower our girls to face potential challenges with confidence and be resilient in all that they do, so that in an ever-changing world they are able to respond positively to the ever-increasing demands placed on them, both at school and in their future lives.

Curriculum. The school offers a broad curriculum, ensuring all our pupils are stimulated and excited by learning. English and Maths provide solid foundations while languages offered include French, German, Spanish, Italian and Latin. Pupils study Biology, Chemistry and Physics as separate sciences. Creative and practical subjects include Design Technology, Art, PE, Music and Drama, as well as Computer Science. Humanities include History, Geography, Religious Studies and Classical Civilisation.

In the Sixth Form, there are 26 subjects to choose from: Art, Biology, Chemistry, Computer Science, Design Technology, Drama & Theatre Studies, Economics, English Literature, French, Geography, German, Government & Politics, History, History of Art, Italian, Latin, Mathematics and Further Mathematics, Music, Philosophy, Physics, PE, Psychology, Religious Studies, Sociology and Spanish. Our 'Next Steps' programme ensures that sixth formers own their future and are equipped with the knowledge and skills to thrive in higher education and beyond. Following what is right for each individual is key. There is no one mould for our pupils. Our Oxbridge and Competitive Courses preparation provide targeted and focused guidance to support in making applications to Oxford or Cambridge, alongside applications for medicine, veterinary, dentistry and law. Degree apprenticeships and Art Foundation courses are increasingly popular. Another key feature is our Active Citizen Programme, incorporating a Professional Skills programme which ensures that students are well versed in the soft skills required for the workplace, Volunteering to reflect pupils' strong social conscience and Enrichment to develop skills beyond the curriculum. Alongside this, we offer a huge range of additional opportunities including the chance to take part in the Young Enterprise programme and leadership responsibilities within the school.

Personalised subject guidance at both GCSE and A Level ensures that our pupils are fully informed when choosing their options. Bespoke timetabling means we are able to offer pupils the widest range of subject combinations to suit their interests. Regular careers events and opportunities broaden pupils' knowledge of career options and sixth form students go on to read a range of subjects at competitive universities. The breadth of co-curricular opportunities ensures there is something for everyone, encouraging pupils to get involved and develop key skills. Performing Arts are an integral part of school life, whilst we offer over 20 sports,

including rowing. Involvement in the wider community is encouraged through our successful involvement in The Duke of Edinburgh's Award scheme and charitable activities.

Fees per term (2022–2023). Senior School £5,946, Prep School £4,675.

School fees include examination fees, textbooks, stationery and other materials, choral music, PE and swimming, Careers counselling. They do not include instrumental music, speech and drama, and externally-run after-school clubs.

Scholarships and Bursaries. A number of scholarships are available each year for entry to the Senior School at 11+ and the Sixth Form at 16+. Scholarships are awarded on merit for Academic, Art, Drama, Music and Sport (plus Rowing at 16+) and no financial means test is involved.

The GDST provides means-tested bursaries which are intended to ensure that the school remains accessible to bright girls who would benefit from our education, but who would be unable to enter the school without financial assistance. Bursaries are awarded on the basis of financial need and academic merit. Details can be obtained from our Registrar. It is recognised that occasions will arise when some form of short-term assistance is required – a small fund exists to help pupils in such cases.

Charitable status. Sydenham High School is part of The Girls' Day School Trust, which is a Registered Charity, number 306983.

Chair of Local Governors: Miss B Holbrooke, MSc Oxford, MSc Oxford Brookes

Headmistress: Mrs K C Woodcock, BA Bristol, PGCE

Deputy Head (Academic): Mr C Batty, BSc Bangor, Wales, PGCE

Deputy Head (Pastoral): Dr E Waites, PhD Birmingham, Maitrise Poitiers, BSc Liverpool, PGCE

Deputy Head (Operational): Ms S Munday, MA London, BA Bristol, PGCE

Head of Prep School: Ms V Goodson, MA Durham, BA Durham

Deputy Head of Prep School: Mrs G Panton, MA St Andrews, PGCE

Head of Sixth Form: Ms R Parrish, BA Southampton, PGCE

Director of Finance & Operations: Mr J Nelson, BA Napier

Director of Marketing & Communications: Miss L Hooper, BAEcon Manchester, PGDip

Talbot Heath

Rothesay Road, Bournemouth, Dorset BH4 9NJ

Tel:	01202 761881 Senior School Admissions
	01202 763360 Junior School Admissions
	01202 755410 Finance
email:	office@talbotheath.org
website:	www.talbotheath.org
Twitter:	@TalbotHeathSch
Facebook:	@TalbotHeathSch
LinkedIn:	/Talbot-Heath-School

Motto: *Honour before Honours*

Talbot Heath is an Independent School for Girls, founded in 1886, and is among the longest-established schools in the Bournemouth area, with over a century of success. It is a Church of England Foundation and pupils of all denominations are welcome. This School is committed to safeguarding and promoting the welfare of children and young people and is also committed to a policy of equal opportunity.

There are some 347 girls in the Main School, of whom 80 are in the Sixth Forms and 40 are Boarders. There is a Junior Department for about 147 girls between the ages of 7 and 11. The Pre-Preparatory department caters for 120 girls aged 3+ to 7.

The school enjoys an attractive wooded site and outstanding facilities for Art, Drama, Music and STEAM subjects, they are an Apple Distinguished School and Apple Regional Training Centre, with outstanding ICT provision, 1-to-1 iPad provision from Y1 and extensive modern accommodation for a wide range of sports activities. Talbot Heath have high performing Tennis and Swimming Academies.

Many believe that the future will be powered by STEAM (Science, Technology, Engineering, the Arts and Maths). The STEAM Hub, which opened in September 2019, is the heart of our vision for the future and provides an extensive flexible learning centre, dedicated to interdisciplinary learning with a creative focus. The centre includes a large auditorium, gallery space, graphic design, robotics, technology, textiles, art, drama and food studios, as well as flexible learning spaces for the use of pupils of all ages. In addition the school has a covered pool and sports facility as part of this inspirational new complex.

The school follows the best practice of the National Curriculum but does not undertake Key Stage testing at levels 1, 2 and 3.

Examinations. 21 subjects are offered to GCSE (including Core Subjects) and A Level, and girls gain places at a variety of universities, including Oxford and Cambridge, or go on to other forms of higher education or professional training.

Admission. Girls are admitted into the Junior School by examination at 7 and above and into the Main School by examination at 11+, 12+ and 13+. The Entrance Examination is held annually in January and girls must be capable of working with those of their own age. Entry to the Pre-preparatory Department requires no examination.

Boarding House. St Mary's Boarding House is located in the School grounds.

Fees per term (2021–2022). Tuition: Senior School: £5,138; Junior School: £2,355–£4,193; Kindergarten according to sessions. Boarding (in addition to Tuition Fees): £3,964 (full); £3,537 (weekly); flexi: £50 per night; 3 nights £120.

Scholarships and bursaries are available and there is also a discount for daughters of Service families and the clergy.

Charitable status. Talbot Heath is a Registered Charity, number 283708. It exists to provide high quality education for children.

Governing Body:
Chair: Mrs C Sutcliffe
Vice Chair: Dr R Day

Mrs C Edwards	Mrs S Richards
Mrs A Ewins	Dr D Sadd
Revd R Higgins	Mrs C Saunders
Mr A Main	Mrs K Thompson
Mrs R Newton	Mr D Townend
Mrs C Norman	

Head: Mrs A Holloway, MA Oxon, PGCE

Deputy Head, Pastoral: Mrs C Stone
Head of Junior School: Mrs E Pugh

Assistant Heads:
Teaching and Learning: Mrs H Chapleo
Academic Management: Mr I Cradick
Curriculum and Progress: Mr M Gibson

Assistant Heads, Junior School:
Academic: Mrs S Breeze
Pastoral: Mrs L Marks

Director of Support Services: Mr A Poole
Director of Finance: Mr G Ives
Head of Senior School Admissions: Mrs K Wills
Head's PA/Office Manager: Miss D Marshall
HR Manager: Mrs D Flynn
Marketing Manager: Mrs H O'Shea

Tormead School

Cranley Road, Guildford, Surrey GU1 2JD

Tel:	01483 575101
email:	admissions@tormeadschool.org.uk
website:	www.tormeadschool.org.uk
Twitter:	@tormeadschool
Facebook:	@TormeadSchool
Instagram:	@tormeadschool

Established in 1905, Tormead is one of the leading independent day schools for girls aged 4–18 and a member of the GSA (Girls' Schools Association). Located close to the town-centre of Guildford, Surrey, Tormead benefits from pleasant grounds combined with the practicalities and local resources of a busy and thriving town nearby.

As an academically selective school, we achieve excellent results; 89% of students achieved grades 9–7/ A*–A at GCSE and 91% of students achieved A*/A at A Level in 2021, but most importantly, we celebrate achievement of all kinds at Tormead – hence our belief that 'all results matter'. Almost all Tormead students progress to higher education, reading for degrees at some of the best universities across the country. On average, 10% of students gain an Oxbridge place. Whilst standards and expectations are high, the teaching and learning environment at Tormead is one of fun and enthusiasm; students leave the school as confident, articulate and self-reliant young women, ready to meet the challenges of life beyond secondary school.

Our curricular enrichment programme is extensive and boasts over 108 clubs and co-curricular opportunities for girls to take part in and discover. Activities such as the Duke of Edinburgh Award, Lamda, 3D Printing Club, Rowing, Forensics Society, Rugby and Technical Theatre Club give each girl the opportunity to experience new activities and find their niche. Tormead has a lively and active musical life, with orchestras, various chamber groups, ensembles and choirs on offer, as well as our highly popular Jazz Band that has undertaken tours to various European countries and the introduction of Glee Club in the past year.

Tormead excels at Sport, with a busy programme of fixtures in Hockey, Netball, Rounders, Athletics and Swimming taking place throughout the school year for every age group in the secondary school. Gymnastics has been a particular strength at Tormead for many years, with our teams competing successfully at national level and bringing home national championships.

We are also one of the select few schools to hold Apple Distinguished School Status meaning girls benefit from the use of iPads and Apple technology to enrich their learning and extra-curricular activities. By exposing students to a vast array of apps, we feel we foster the importance of creativity within our curriculum.

Fees per term (2021–2022). Reception £2,935, Years 1 & 2 £3,240, Years 3 & 4 £4,800, Years 5 & 6 £4,865, Years 7–13 £5,570.

Scholarships. Prep – Academic scholarships are available at 7+.

11+ – Academic, Art, Drama, Music and Sports scholarships are available.

16+ – Academic, Art, Drama and Music scholarships are available.

Bursaries. Available at 11+ and 16+ and based on the level of parental income.

Alumnae. Email alumnae@tormeadschool.org.uk or visit www.alumnae.tormeadschool.org.uk.

Charitable status. Tormead Limited is a registered charity (312057). It exists to advance education for girls aged 4–18.

Board of Governors:
Mrs Rosie Harris, BA, ACA (*Chair*)
Mrs Anne Cullum, BA, PGCE, NPQH
Mrs Anne Geary
Mr Matthew Howse, LLB
Mr Robert Jewkes, BEng, FIE Aust
Dr Caroline Kissin, MB ChB, MRCP, FRCR
Professor Graham Miller, BSc Hons, MSc, PGCE, PhD
Mrs Suzanne Newnes-Smith
Mr Peter O'Keefe, RIBA, MCIOB, MIMgt
Miss Anna Spender, BSc, FIA
Mr John Watkins, FCA

Head: **Mr David Boyd**, MA Oxon, MA UCL, PGCE Cantab

Executive Group:
Mrs Karen Dabill, BSc Bangor, PGCE Surrey (*Deputy Head Academic*)
Mrs Nicola Fry, BA Ed Exeter (*Head of Prep School*)
Mrs Stella Lawton, CSBM NCTL (*Bursar and Clerk to the Governors*)

Senior Management Team:
Mrs Mary Fowell, HNDip Marketing, CiAM/DiSM AMCIS, CDMP DMI (*Head of Marketing and Admissions*)
Mr Christopher Ives, BA Warwick, PGCE Reading (*Assistant Head – Teaching, Learning and Mentoring*)
Mrs Samantha Jones, BSc Surrey, PGCE SWELTEC (*Assistant Head – Adventure and Service*)
Miss Marie Langlet, Licence d'Anglais, Maitrise d'Anglais Toulouse, PGCE Oxon (*Assistant Head – Wellbeing*)
Mrs Michelle O'Brien, BA Chichester (*Head of Development and Alumnae Relations*)
Miss Imogen Painter, BA Dunelm, PGCSE Nottingham Trent (*Assistant Head – Academic Performance*)
Mr Gary Press, BSc, CertEd Brunel (*Assistant Head – Data, Systems and Logistics*)
Mrs Catherine Williams, BA Cantab (*Assistant Head – Careers*)

Prep Senior Management Team:
Mrs Mary Price, BA York, MA IoE, PGCE Leicester (*Deputy Head*)
Miss Salaidh Insch, BEd Surrey (*Director of Studies*)
Mrs Elizabeth Alderman, BSc Leeds, PGCE Bristol (*Head of Pre-Prep*)

Tudor Hall

Wykham Park, Banbury, Oxfordshire OX16 9UR

Tel: 01295 263434
email: admissions@tudorhallschool.com
website: www.tudorhallschool.com
Twitter: @TudorHallSchool
Facebook: @TudorHallSchool
Instagram: @tudorhallschool
LinkedIn: /school/tudor-hall-school

Motto: *Habeo Ut Dem*

Tudor Hall is an Independent Boarding and Day School for Girls aged 11–18 years. The school was originally founded in 1850 and moved to Wykham Park in 1946. It is situated in spacious grounds 1½ miles from Banbury Station and is within easy access of London, Oxford, Bicester and Stratford-upon-Avon – M40, Junction 11. This enables the girls to enjoy a wide range of cultural and educational activities.

The school accommodates approximately 250 boarders and 75 day girls. Its buildings comprise a 17th century and an 18th century manor with a modern purpose-built house for Sixth Formers and extensive new facilities which include 5 science laboratories; designated modern languages department with a language laboratory; purpose-built drama studio, music school and sports complex; art studio and design technology workshop. The latest addition is a Teaching Centre, opened in 2019, which provides designated English and Mathematics Departments, ceramics and textiles studios and a professional kitchen. Sports facilities include floodlit tennis, netball courts, gym and AstroTurf hockey pitch, a swimming pool, grass athletics track and pitches for lacrosse, rounders and cricket.

The curriculum and co-curriculum at Tudor Hall are extensive, providing students with intellectual challenge and the opportunity to expand their horizons. Lessons are delivered in a manner which encourages confidence, gives satisfaction and enjoyment, and allows all students to learn, make progress and be successful. They develop a love of lifelong learning and acquire the necessary skills needed for university and adult life. A comprehensive careers programme ensures that students leave armed with pertinent and relevant information and experience to continue to be successful in life beyond school.

Admission is by internal examinations at 11+ and internal examinations and Common Entrance at 13+. Entry may also be made to the Sixth Form where all girls pursue courses leading to higher education or vocational training. Entry is by assessment, interview and predicted grades at GCSE. Boarders joining at 11 live in a separate and smaller house within a family environment to help them become accustomed to being away from home. Girls are divided into four competitive Houses, but residence is with their own age group.

Tudor Hall places great importance on having a friendly atmosphere, a lively and united spirit and high standards. Girls are expected to take an interest in a wide range of activities as well as following a broad educational programme. Involvement in the local community through the Duke of Edinburgh's Award and social service, and participation in events with other schools are encouraged. Debating and public speaking are strong and there is keen involvement in the Young Enterprise Scheme, Model United Nations and European Youth Parliament. Tudor Hall is an Anglican school but members of all religious groups are welcomed. There is a small chapel.

Scholarships and Bursaries. Every pupil is encouraged to aim high in all areas of Tudor life, in order to fulfil their potential. The school's Aim Higher Programme offers all pupils the opportunity to broaden their horizons and excel in areas of particular interest to them. Scholarships are one element of this programme, and any pupil may apply at the appropriate entry point. Scholarships are offered in recognition of an individual's current performance and potential in a particular discipline. The value of all awards is up to £1,000 per annum, with the exception of the 13+ All-Rounder award which carries a value of up to £2,000 per annum. Academic scholarships are awarded for the duration of the pupil's time at Tudor Hall. Other scholarships awarded at 11+ and 13+ are subject to review at 16+.

The following scholarships are available:
- 11+: Academic, Drama, Music, Visual Arts
- 13+: Academic, All-Rounder, Drama, Music, Sport, Visual Arts (Art, Design Technology or Textiles)
- 16+: Academic, Dance, Drama, Music, Sport, Visual Arts (Art, Design Technology, Photography or Textiles)

Bursaries are separate to scholarships and are awarded to support new and current students who are in financial need.

Fees per term (2021–2022). £13,150 for boarders; £7,900 for day pupils.

Board of Governors:
Chairman: Mrs Debbie Chism

Chairman of Finance & General Purposes Committee: Mr John Elliot
Chairman of Education & Welfare Committee: Mrs Alison Darling
Chairman of Audit Committee: Mrs Kathy Fidgeon
Chairman of Carrdus School Committee: Mr Duncan Bailey
Mr Simon Beale
Mrs Sally Bowie
Miss Alice Carson
Mr Simon Davis
Mr Jonny Hammond-Chambers
Miss Mary Kinnear
Mr Bob Lari
Mr Charlie Newsome
Mrs Jennifer Scarfe
Mr Mark Sewell
Miss Elizabeth Style
Mrs Nicky Wilson

Senior Management Team:

Headmistress: Julie Lodrick

Bursar & Clerk to the Governors: Neil Urquhart
Deputy Head: Emma Bell
Deputy Head (Pastoral): Kate Simlett
Head of Sixth Form: Justine Stephens
Director of Staff: James Wakeley
Director of Studies: Lucy Keyte
Director of Co-Curriculum: Sadie Lapper

Boarding Staff:
Boarding Coordinator: Jackie Webb
Ashtons Housemistress: Sarah Neale
Ashtons Deputy Houseparent: Lindsey Pickering
Ashtons Deputy Houseparent: Ryan Pickering
Inglis Housemistress: Sarah Belcher
Inglis Deputy Housemistress: Hazel Rhodes
Vs Housemistress: Pippa Duncan-Jones
Vs Deputy Housemistress: Anya Diaz-Cebreiro
IVs Housemistress: Ceri Angell
IVs Deputy Housemistress: Scarlett Embury
IIIs Housemistress: Liz Saunders
IIIs Deputy Housemistress: Caroline Rimmer
Todd/IIs Housemistress: Elizabeth Buckner-Rowley
Todd Deputy Housemistress: Lauren Nightingale
IIs Deputy Housemistress: Claudette Povey
Boarding support: Rebecca Coles; Penny Davies; Carol Edginton; Rachael Knapman

Pastoral:
School Chaplain: Alison Richardson
School Counsellors: Mahwish Qamar; Sarah Whitehouse

Administrative and Support Staff:
PA to the Headmistress: Jennifer Lewis
PA to the Deputy Heads: Amelia Chubb
Data Manager: Brian Wray
Examinations Officer: Katie Donald
Senior Administrative Secretary: Helen Mascall
Administrative Secretaries:
Katie Donald
Joanne Twelvetrees (*Music*)
Rachael Knapman (*PE*)
School Reception: Annabelle Coombs; Kate Greaves; Philippa Drinkwater
Educational Visits Coordinator: Alex Simlett
Travel Administrator: Marilyn Harris

Admissions, Marketing and Communications:
Registrar: Daniel Roberts
Assistant Registrar: Fiona Gaskin
Director of Marketing and Communications: Daryn Castle
Community & Events Officer: Rebecca Butler
Graphic Designer: Nicola Mawle

Bursary:
Financial Controller: Kenneth Iredale
HR & Compliance Manager: Nicole Hamilton
Finance Assistants: Diane Cook; Louise Sollis; Carol
   Edginton

Development and Alumnae Relations:
Head of Development & Alumnae Relations: Rachel Graves
Development & Alumnae Relations Office Administrator:
   Bethan Leyshon-Smith
Alumnae Communications Manager: Lindsay Silver

Grounds, Maintenance and Domestic Services:
Property Services Manager: Ben Stowe
Head of Gardens and Grounds: vacant
Facilities Administrator: Caroline Thomas
Domestic Services Manager: Linda Tubb

ICT Systems and Network:
ICT Systems & Network Manager: Paul Smith
ICT Senior Network Engineer: Luke Harris
ICT Technician: Melanie Bolton

Technicians:
CDT: Steven Price
Science: Sarah Carolan; Julie Brown
Textiles: Amy Harris
Textiles & Art: Hope Talbot

Librarian: Lara Price

Medical:
School Doctor: Dr Nicola Elliott
Nurse-in-Charge: Janet Bonham, RGN
Nurses:
Lindsey Pickering, RGN
Milena Krupinska, RGN

Teaching Staff:
Lucy Andrews, BA UAL, MA BCU, PGCE Exeter
   (*Photography*)
Emma Bell, MA Oxon, PGCE London (*History*)
Jo Benlalam, BMus, AKC, PGCE London (*Head of
   Careers, Head of Academic Music*)
Elizabeth Buckner-Rowley, BA Portsmouth, PGCE Leeds
   (*Spanish*)
Lucinda Burton-Sims, BA Leeds, PGDipEd Birmingham,
   PSHEE [Maternity Leave]
Alan Christopher, MA Essex, BTEC Kingshurst, HND
   Coventry (*Drama*)
Jason Conduct, BSc UCL, PGCE Sussex (*Head of Science
   and Physics*)
Iona Corbett, MA Dundee, PGCE MMU (*Business Studies*)
Sheila Craske, BA Oxon, PGCE MMU (*Head of Art*)
Lindsey Cullen, MA Oxon (*Head of Classics*)
Bernard D'Souza, BA Nottingham Trent, PGCE Warwick
   (*Mathematics*)
Jane Drake, CertEd Bedford (*Head of Food and Nutrition*)
Gerard Duncan, PGDSST, BPE University of Otago, New
   Zealand (*Physical Education*)
Pippa Duncan-Jones, BSc Loughborough, PGCE Leeds
   (*Physical Education*)
Ian Edwards, BSc Newcastle, PGCE UEA (*Mathematics,
   Academic Administrator*)

Scarlett Embury, BSc Newcastle, PGCE Chester
   (*Mathematics*)
Sara Fordy, BA Winchester, PGCE Oxon (*Head of
   Textiles*)
Jonathan Galloway, BA Middx, PGCE London (*Head of
   Philosophy, Theology and Ethics*)
Alison Gamble, MA London, CPE Law (*Head of Senior
   History & Politics*)
Marie Genot, MA Provence, France, PGCE UWE (*French/
   Spanish*)
Shazia Gleadall, BA Birmingham, PGCE Chester (*Head of
   KS3 Religious Studies*) [Maternity Leave]
Victoria Gross, BA Brunel, PGCE Middlesex (*Head of
   Design and Technology*)
Elizabeth Gulliver, BA Oxon (*Head of Psychology*)
Kerri Hadfield, BA Leeds, PGCE Canterbury (*Head of
   Geography*)
Louise Harper, BA Dunelm, PGCE Oxon (*Head of KS3
   Geography*)
Matthew Harper, BA Oxon, PGCE Warwick (*French/
   Spanish*)
Marilyn Harris, BA London, PGCE Bulmershe (*French*)
Kate Hart, BA MMU, PGCE Birmingham (*Head of
   PSHEE*)
Charlotte Harwell, BA, MA Lancaster, PGCE Oxon
   (*Religious Studies*) [Maternity Cover]
Susie Jeffreys, BSc Plymouth, PGCE Exeter (*Geography*)
Monica Jimenez, BA La Rioja, Spain, PGCE Canterbury
   (*Head of Spanish*)
Kathryn Joel, BA Warwick, DELTA, TESOL (*EAL
   Coordinator*)
Matthew Kent, BA Keele, MA, PGDip Ed Birmingham
   (*2nd i/c English*)
Kate Kettlewell, BVSc Bristol, PGCE Oxon (*Biology*)
Lucy Keyte, BA Nottingham, PGCE Warwick (*French*)
Rachael Knapman, Netball Level 1 Coach UKCC (*Netball*)
Sadie Lapper, BSc Worcester, PGCert Gloucester, MSc
   Oxford Brookes (*Physical Education, Head of Lower
   School*)
Lindsey Lea-James, BMus, LTCL, ALCM, PGCE
   Huddersfield (*Director of Music*)
Mark Lee, BMus Royal Birmingham Conservatoire (*Music,
   Learning Support*)
James Long, BA, PGCE Liverpool (*Head of Hockey*)
Victoria Marsh, BSc Keele, PGCE Exeter (*Head of
   Mathematics*)
Harry Mitchell, BSc Bristol, PGCE Loughborough
   (*Mathematics*) [Maternity Cover]
Bev Murphy, BA Wales, MA, PhD, PGCE UEA (*History,
   Deputy Head of Learning Support*)
Sarah Neale, BA Worcester (*Dance*)
Lauren Nightingale, BA Brighton (*Physical Education,
   Dance*)
Pervin Özkan, Licence Tours, France, PGCE Exeter (*Head
   of French*)
Charlotte Pemble, BSc, PGCE Worcester (*2nd i/c Physical
   Education*)
Jonitha Peterpillai, BSc, Warwick, MSc, PGCE Oxon (*2nd
   i/c Mathematics*) [Maternity Leave]
Ryan Pickering, NPLQ, NUCO (*Sporting Facilities &
   Physical Education*)
Claudette Povey, BA Brighton (*Physical Education*)
Jack Prentice, BSc Central Lancashire, PGCE Warwick
   (*Head of Chemistry*)
Bob Roberts, BA, MA Warwick, PGCE Lancaster (*Head of
   English*)

Ian Robinson, BEng, PGCE Lancaster (*Physics*)

Jez Ross, BA Cantab, MA Warwick, PGCE Leicester (*History/RS*)

Kate Simlett, MSc Loughborough (*Physical Education*)

Amelia Simonow, BA Nottingham, MA Courtauld, PGCE Cape Town (*Head of History of Art*)

Catherine Simpson, BA, GDL, MPhil Cantab, PGCE Belfast (*English*)

Rachel Smith, BA Wales, PGCE Leicester (*Psychology*)

James Stead, BA Cumbria, PGCE Wales (*Art*)

Justine Stephens, BA London, PGCE Middx (*Head of Drama, Head of Year V*)

Holly Thomas, BA Bath, PGCE Coventry (*Head of Modern Languages*)

Richard Thompson, MA Oxon, PGCE London (*Head of Economics, Head of Business Studies*)

Julia Thorn, BA Reading, MSt Oxon (*Classics*)

Emma Thornton, BSc De Montfort, PGCE Liverpool (*Director of Sport*)

Sarah Upton, MSc Birmingham, PGCE Cambridge Partnership, (*Chemistry*)

Katie Viggers, BSc Loughborough (*Physical Education*)

Henry Vigne, BA London, MA Kent, PGCE Buckingham (*Head of Junior History*)

James Wakeley, BSc OU, PGCE Bath (*Head of Computing & IT*)

Rebecca Warrington, BA MMU, MA, PGCE Middx (*Textiles*)

Georgina Way, BA Ed Exeter, PGCE Glos, AMBDA (*Head of Learning Support*)

John Whitty, BA Durham, MSt, DPhil Oxon (*Religious Studies*)

Layla Williams, BA London, PGCE De Montfort (*Head of Dance*)

James Woodward, BSc Wales, PGCE Exeter (*Biology, Head of Year IV*)

Additional Subject and Coaching Staff:

Helen Fryer (*Lacrosse*)
Ginny Steven (*Ballet*)

Tennis:
Godwin Abah
Annabelle Bailey
Mark Boden
Pamela Eagles
Lee Morton

Learning Support:
Daniel Carrington (*Mathematics & Science*)
Teaching Assistants: Stephanie Herbert; Isabel Rimmer; Sarah Skevington
Elizabeth Smith (*Learning Mentor*)

Modern Foreign Languages:
Camille Morand (*French Assistant*)
Kubra Özkan (*French Assistant*)
Belen Sainz-Pardo (*Spanish*)
Nadine von Paledzki (*German Assistant*)

Music:
Arthur Bocaneanu (*Graduate Assistant*)
Bob Evans (*Brass*)
James Foley (*Guitar*)
Sarah Haigh (*Singing*)
Kim Keeble (*Oboe*)
Becki Luff (*Harp*)
Veronique Matarasso (*Violin and Viola*)

Cliff Pick (*Percussion*)
Kate Pickin (*Piano*)
Miranda Ricardo (*Cello and Piano*)
Beverley Savidge (*Singing*)
Elisabeth Sharam (*Flute*)
Deborah Siepmann (*Piano*)
Kayleigh Skinner (*Singing*)
Lucy Tugwell (*Clarinet and Saxophone*)
Chris Windass (*Violin*)

Speech and Drama:
Pippa Phillips
Layla Williams

Walthamstow Hall

Senior School:
Holly Bush Lane, Sevenoaks, Kent TN13 3UL

Tel: 01732 451334

Junior School:
Bradbourne Park Road, Sevenoaks, Kent TN13 3LD

email: registrar@whall.school
website: www.walthamstow-hall.co.uk
Facebook: @walthamstowhall
Instagram: @walthamstowhall
LinkedIn: /school/walthamstow-hall

Walthamstow Hall is an Independent girls' day school founded in 1838, based on two separate sites in Sevenoaks. The Junior School in Bradbourne Park Road takes pupils from age 3–11 years and the Senior School in Holly Bush Lane takes pupils from 11–18 years.

The School has a long established history of preparing academically-able individuals for stimulating, purposeful and happy lives within and beyond school. The belief that every pupil given the right opportunities, encouragement and inspiring teaching can develop an incredible range of skills and talents, is central to the everyday life of the School.

The Headmistress is a member of the GSA (Girls' Schools Association).

The School was judged to be 'Excellent' in all categories by the ISI in 2019, excellent being the highest category awarded.

Facilities. Walthamstow Hall is set in its own grounds within the town of Sevenoaks. Pupils are taught in light and airy classrooms in buildings specifically designed for learning. The original 1882 Arts and Crafts building still lies at the heart of the Senior School. During the past 13 years, campus developments have included the building of the Swimming Pool complex, Music, Drama and Design Technology rooms, and a new additional Entrance Hub and Art Gallery. The Ship Theatre provides an exciting performance arena, and more recent additions have included the new Sports Centre opened in 2015, the expansion of provision of Art studios, and a new Sixth Form Centre with additional Science facilities opened in 2018. The Junior School offers wraparound care, and benefits from specialist facilities including an ICT Suite, Science Laboratory, Design and Technology, Art and Cookery Rooms and a dedicated Music Centre.

Curriculum. Walthamstow Hall delivers an enriched curriculum which is innovative and flexible, facilitating breadth and individual choice, without sacrificing depth of study. This is brought to life with inspirational teaching.

All pupils in their first three Senior School years (7, 8 and 9) follow a core curriculum of broad and balanced subjects, with a second language being added in Year 8. They also receive lessons in 'Q', which is a mixture of practical skills, critical thinking and personal qualities which aims to encourage creative and critical thinking.

Subjects taught from age 11 up to 18 include: Art, Biology, Business, Chemistry, Classical Civilisation, Computing, Computer Science, Creative Textiles, Drama, Economics, English, English Literature, Extended Project Qualification (EPQ), Fine Art, Food Preparation & Nutrition, French, History, Geography, German, Politics, Latin, Mathematics, Additional Mathematics, Further Mathematics, Music, Philosophy & Theology, Physical Education, Physics, Religious Studies, Sociology, Spanish, Art Textile Design, Theatre Studies and Three Dimensional Design.

Pupils are prepared for I/GCSE and A Levels, with the choice of A Level or Cambridge Pre-U for Music. The record of success in public examinations is excellent. In 2021 95% of A Level examinations were passed at grades A*–B, and 96% of GCSEs were passed at grades 9–6.

The breadth and flexibility of the curriculum, combined with expert teaching and encouragement to be ambitious, enables students to be highly successful in their post-Sixth Form choices. The vast majority secure their first-choice places at Universities, Drama and Art Colleges, and on Higher Level Apprenticeships.

Religious Teaching is interdenominational.

Co-curricular Activities. The high profile of Drama, Music, Sports, trips, careers and study skills and personal development, together with an excellent pastoral system, provides further opportunity and support for every pupil.

An active policy of 'sport for all' enables both team players and individuals to find the sporting activities that suit them best. Lacrosse, netball, swimming, athletics, cross country, badminton, hockey, cricket and tennis are all on offer, with many teams and individuals achieving highly at local, county and national levels.

A high proportion of pupils participate in the Duke of Edinburgh's Award scheme at Bronze, Silver and Gold level, the Enterprise Club, the School choirs and orchestra, ABRSM and Trinity Drama.

Pupils undertake voluntary service within the local community and abroad.

Admission. Admission to the Senior School for Year 7, as well as for those at prep schools who wish to defer entry to Year 9, is through the Independent Schools Examinations Board (ISEB) Common Pre-Test in the Autumn Term prior to entry. Admission for Year 9 (unless deferred at Year 7) and Sixth Form is through the School's own entrance examinations. At each level of entry candidates are also required to attend an interview and provide a Head's Report from their previous school. Parents are warmly invited to visit the School at Open Mornings in September and March, or on a personal visit.

Fees per term (2021–2022). Senior School and Sixth Form £7,070.

Scholarships. Academic scholarships are awarded to the candidates who show the greatest academic potential in the School's own Year 7, 9 and Sixth Form scholarship examinations.

Music and Sport scholarships are also available for Year 7 and Year 9 entry. Drama and Art are added to the choice of Awards that can be applied for at Year 9 and Sixth Form entry.

All awards are available to both internal and external candidates.

In addition, a means-tested bursary scheme in the Senior School provides financial help with school fees based on a family's financial circumstances. The scheme includes our Founders' Bursary, which pays nearly 100% of a pupil's school fees throughout their time at the school.

Charitable status. Walthamstow Hall is a Registered Charity, number 1058439. It exists to provide education for girls.

Headmistress: **Miss S Ferro**, MA Oxon, MA Lond, PGCE Surrey (*Designated Safeguarding Lead*)

Deputy Head: C Hughes Esq, BSc Hons, Cert Ed Loughborough, NPQH (*Deputy Designated Safeguarding Lead*)

Director of Studies: S Ledsham Esq, MA Oxon, PGCE Sussex

Head of Sixth Form: Mrs B Brown, BA Hons, PGCE Loughborough

Head of Key Stage 4: Mrs K O'Donnell, BA Hons Sheffield, PGCE Canterbury

Head of Key Stage 3: Mrs K Hofmann, MA St Andrews, QTS

Senior School Heads of Department/Teachers In Charge of Subject:

Biology: Miss T Cheney, BSc Hons Durham, MSc LSHTM, QTS

Careers: Mrs L Hayes, MA Canterbury, BCom Hons Cape Town, QCG, RCDP

Classics: N Buckingham Esq, BA Hons, MA Reading, PGCE London

Co-Curriculum: Mrs L von Kaufmann, MA, BA Hons Oxon, PGCE Bristol

Computer Science: Mrs L Rowell, BA Hons Surrey, PGCE King's College

Drama: Mrs V Bower-Morris, BA Hons Surrey, PGCE Goldsmiths

Duke of Edinburgh Award: Mrs K Fassnidge, BA Hons Cardiff, TEFL, QTS

Economics & Business: R Dewey Esq, BA Hons Heriot-Watt, PGCE Kent & Medway

English: Miss S Mehaffey, MA, PGCE Edinburgh

EPQ Coordinator: Mrs L Thomas, MA Open, BA Hons Wales, PGCE Bristol

Geography: C Sullivan Esq, HNC, BA Hons Sussex, NPQL

History & Politics: Ms O Windle, MA, BA Hons Edgewood College, USA

Learning Support: Mrs S Dalton, BSc Hons Keele, PGCE Canterbury, Dip SpLD Dyslexia

Mathematics: T Dakin Esq, BSc Hons Bristol, PGCE Sussex

MFL: Mrs R Hunt, BA Hons Exeter, PGCE King's College

Music: N Castell Esq, BMus Hons, PGCE Manchester (*Director of Music*)

Physics: R Hill Esq, BSc Hons Warwick, PGCE Sussex

Science & Chemistry: Dr E Doyle, BA Hons Cambridge, MSc Cambridge, MA Cambridge, PhD Cambridge, QTS

Sociology: S Wilson Esq, BA Hons Sunderland, PGCE London

Sport: Miss R Leggett, BA Hons with QTS Brighton (*Director of Sport*)

Theology & Philosophy: D Pollen Esq, BA Hons Bristol, MA UWE

Three Dimensional Design & Food Preparation & Nutrition: Mrs C Evans, BA Hons Greenwich, QTS

There are 40+ Specialist Visiting Staff (Music, Sport, Drama & Learning Support), as well as 20 Technical and Administrative Support Staff.

Bursar and Clerk to the Governors: P A Horner Esq, MBA, CMgr, FCMI

Admissions Registrar: Mrs A Knight

PA to the Headmistress: Ms K Lippiatt

Network & Data Manager: P Cole, Esq.

Head of Marketing: Ms S Pelling, BA Hons Keele

Lead Librarian and Archivist: Mrs L White, MA Brighton MCLIP

Medical Centre:

Mrs E Leisinger, Diploma in Nursing Brighton

Mrs L J Mottram, Undergraduate Diploma in Nursing Studies The City University

Mrs C Baker, MBACP Accred (*Senior School Counsellor*)

Wimbledon High School

GDST

Mansel Road, London SW19 4AB

Tel:	020 8971 0900 (Senior School)
	020 8971 0902 (Junior School)
email:	info@wim.gdst.net
website:	www.wimbledonhigh.gdst.net
Twitter:	@WimbledonHigh
Facebook:	@WimbledonHigh
Instagram:	@wimbledonhighschoolgdst
LinkedIn:	/school/wimbledon-high

Founded 1880.

Wimbledon High School is part of the GDST (Girls' Day School Trust). The GDST is the leading network of independent girls' schools in the UK. As a charity that owns and runs 23 schools and two academies, it reinvests all its income in its schools. For further information about the Trust, see p. xix or visit www.gdst.net.

Pupil numbers. Junior School: 340 aged 4–11; Senior School: 690, including 195 in the Sixth Form.

Wimbledon High School combines academic strength with a firm belief that learning should be fun. Fionnuala Kennedy became Head in September 2020, having been Deputy for 5 years prior. "This is a school with a strong sense of community – academically very successful, yet where laughter abounds. Our students live life to the full, taking themselves seriously while holding themselves lightly." Results at A Level and GCSE are consistently extremely high, music and drama are a vibrant part of school life and a Director of Sport and Head of Rowing have led the girls to national success in sport. Activities include World Challenge, Model United Nations and The Duke of Edinburgh's Award, alongside many smaller clubs and societies, from Coding social robots to Gardening. The older girls often run these themselves.

A holistic and innovative programme of pastoral care, GROW, underpins school life, with the aim for each girl to be known, supported and able to shine. The student leadership team includes an equality, diversity and inclusion rep – further broadening diversity is a key focus for the school. Partnership activities have expanded in recent years, with older students helping with Literacy, Maths, Latin and mentoring younger peers. The school runs SHINE, the outreach Serious Fun on Saturdays programme, as well as Teach Together and volunteering opportunities with local charities.

Junior and Senior Schools share one central Wimbledon site, with a swimming pool and sports hall, Performing Arts Centre and a new dining hall and STEAM tower (Science, Technology, Engineering, Arts and Maths). The school's Ex Humilibus building project is due for completion in September 2022, which will see a new Sixth Form Centre, auditorium and Junior playground in the sky. The playing fields are ten minutes' walk away at Nursery Road (the site of the original All England Club) providing a full-size, all-weather hockey pitch and five netball/tennis courts. Cricket and football are growing sports and a number of students represent their sport on a national stage, latterly: athletics, tennis, karate, gymnastics and hockey.

The **Junior School** provides a creative and academic education in a happy and stimulating environment, with specialist teachers for PE, languages, music and science. A new curriculum, Adventum, and an enhanced co-curricular offer, Arcadia, has brought a fresh focus to learning and a growing emphasis on outdoor education. An after-school club offers flexibility to working parents. Sports teams do well, as do the school's chess players and musicians.

The **Senior School** curriculum runs over a two week timetable. In Key Stage 3, girls study English, Mathematics and Sciences; they learn two of French, German and Spanish, as well as Latin, Geography, History, Religious Studies, PE, Music, Drama, Art, Design & Technology (graphics, textiles and product design on rotation), Computer Science, study skills and PSHE (Personal, Social and Health Education). Mandarin starts as an optional club in Year 9.

At Key Stage 4, girls choose 9 GCSE subjects, of which one must be a Modern Foreign Language (Mandarin is an option), with the possibility of adding Classical Greek as a 10th GCSE. PE and PHSE continue. A bespoke Politics, Philosophy & Economics (PPE) course in Year 10 brings breadth beyond the curriculum and new this year is the school's Civil Discourse programme. The school holds regular lectures for older girls, parents and staff.

In the **Sixth Form**, students may choose from the same subjects on offer at GCSE (except PE – compulsory in Year 12 but non-examined), plus Further Mathematics, Economics, Politics and Classical Civilisation. There is a high uptake of Maths and science subjects and in recent years the Extended Project Qualification has been popular. A comprehensive programme of careers and university entrance advice is offered, including specialist support for applications to overseas universities, medical and veterinary courses and Oxbridge.

Admissions. 4+ girls are assessed in groups in a nursery-style environment; indication of a girl's potential is the key at this stage, rather than evidence of what has already been learnt.

For 11+ entry, candidates sit papers in Verbal and Non-Verbal Reasoning (round 1). A creative assessment day makes up round 2, with group activities across a whole morning.

The occasional entry examination for other years tests Maths and English.

16+ assessment comprises entrance exam and interviews. Offers of places are conditional upon GCSE grade 8 or above (A* or A) in candidates' chosen A Level subjects, and a minimum of eight GCSEs (grades 6–9) overall.

Fees per term (2021–2022). Senior School £6,772; Junior School £5,264.

The fees cover the regular curriculum, school books, choral music, games and swimming, but not optional extra subjects.

Scholarships and Bursaries. Academic scholarships are awarded to girls who do exceptionally well in the 11+ exam, typically worth 5% of the fees. There are also music and sport scholarships at 11+. At 16+ there are scholarships in Art, Drama, Music and Sport, worth up to 10%, as well as Academic scholarships. Details and application forms are available online.

Bursaries take account of academic merit, but all are means-tested. The maximum value is the full fee, and bursaries cover other costs, such as uniform, too.

Charitable status. Wimbledon High School is part of The Girls' Day School Trust, which is a Registered Charity, number 306983.

Chair of the Local Governors: Mrs R McKinlay, BA Hull

Head: **Ms F Kennedy**, MA Oxon

Head of Junior School: Ms C Boyd, BA Royal Holloway

Director of Finance & Operations: Mrs K Jones, BA Exeter, ACMA

Deputy Head Academic: Mrs C Duncan, BSc Hons Sheffield

Deputy Head Pastoral: Mr B Turner, BA Hons, MA London

Director of Sixth Form: Dr J Parsons, BMus, MA, PhD Cardiff

Director of Digital Learning & Innovation: Mrs R Evans, BA York, MA UCL

Director of Co-curricular & Partnerships: Miss J Cox, MSc, BSc Brunel

Director of Marketing & Communications: Mrs R Brewster, BA Oxon, MA Leeds

Director of Studies: Mrs S Pett, MA Cantab

Wychwood School (Oxford) Ltd.

74 Banbury Road, Oxford, Oxfordshire OX2 6JR

Tel:	01865 557976
email:	admissions@wychwoodschool.org
website:	www.wychwoodschool.org
Twitter:	@wychwoodschool
Facebook:	@wychwoodschool
Instagram:	@wychwoodschool
LinkedIn:	/company/wychwood-school

Wychwood School (Oxford) Ltd. is a unique and friendly day and boarding school for girls aged 11–18, with excellent academic grades and outstanding pastoral care. Situated in the heart of Oxford, the school offers an exceptional education for pupils of all abilities through its small class sizes which allow for extensive individual attention without intense pressure. Established in 1897, individuality has always been more important than conformity at Wychwood and the girls have opportunities for success in many directions.

Curriculum. All girls are expected to take up to 10 subjects at GCSE; most go on to work for A Level and BTEC and University entrance. The lower school curriculum includes: English, Mathematics, Religious Studies, History, Geography, Biology, Physics, Chemistry, Psychology, French, Spanish, Computer Science, Textiles, Art, Drama, Photography, Music, PHSEE, PE and Drama. In addition, girls can also choose to study Business Studies, Economics, Film Studies, Politics, Sociology and History of Art for A Level. Visiting staff teach other optional foreign languages and musical instruments; there is a school choir, chamber groups and various ensembles.

School Council. Day-to-day life is largely controlled by the School Council which meets weekly and consists of staff, senior pupils (elected by the school) and form representatives. This is a type of cooperative government, the mature result of a long series of experiments, which trains the girls to deal with the problems of community life and gives everyone, in greater or lesser degree according to her age and status, an understanding of, and a voice in, the rules necessary for a sensibly disciplined life.

Sixth Form. Members of Wychwood Sixth have considerable freedom yet play an active part in the life of the school. The choice of subjects at A Level and BTEC is wide. Classes are small and stimulating. Individual help with university applications and careers is a key feature of Wychwood Sixth. Girls are allowed to be out of school during study periods and on a Friday, students do not start lessons until 9.30am. There are regular outside speakers and girls attend a variety of lectures, conferences, exhibitions and meetings. Their participation in school plays and concerts as well as School Council is greatly valued. Sixth Form girls may spend approximately two hours per week on community service. Sixth Form boarders have individual study-bedrooms.

Entrance. A personal interview between the Headmistress and the pupil is a key part of the selection process. There are entrance tests in English and Maths (for years 7–10) and in chosen A level subjects (for entry into Wychwood Sixth) to satisfy the staff that the girl will benefit from an education of this kind; the opinion of the girl's former school is also taken into account, particularly in relation to non-academic qualities.

Scholarships and Bursaries. Scholarships are awarded as academic, creative arts, drama, music sports and all-rounder.

Academic scholarships are awarded on the basis of results in the entrance examination papers at 11+ and 13+ and on the basis of the results of scholarship papers at 16+. Girls take three scholarship papers in subjects of their choice at 16+ as well as a general paper. We award major scholarships of £1,000 p.a. and minor scholarships of £500 p.a.

Dates for scholarship auditions for non academic subjects will be advised to applicants at each entry point. Creative Arts Scholarships are offered at 11+, 13+ and 16+ to candidates with outstanding ability in either Art or Creative Writing (11+ and 13+) or both. We award major scholarships of £1,000 p.a. and minor scholarships of £500 p.a.

Art: Candidates are asked to bring 6 artistic compositions or craft items which will be discussed with the Head of Art. A short unprepared task will also be undertaken.

Creative Writing: Candidates are asked to bring 6 different pieces of writing, including poetry, a story and a description. These will be discussed with the Head of English. A piece of creative writing will also be set.

Drama scholarships are offered at 11+, 13+ or 16+ to candidates with outstanding ability and potential in drama. We award major scholarships of £1,000 p.a. and minor scholarships of £500 p.a. Drama scholars are expected to be LAMDA or equivalent grade 3 or 4 level at 11+, grade 5 or 6 level at 13+ and grade 6 or 7 level at 16+. Candidates are asked to perform a prepared piece and discuss their love of drama with the Head of Drama at audition.

Music Scholarships are offered at 11+, 13+ and 16+ to cover instrumental tuition of up to two instruments including voice. Music scholars are expected to be ABRSM or equivalent grade 3 or 4 level at 11+, grade 5 or 6 level at 13+ and grade 6 or 7 level at 16+. Candidates are expected to play two prepared pieces on their instrument(s) and to do aural tests and sight reading as well as have an interview with the Director of Music. There is also a single organ scholarship available to cover organ tuition which is awarded to a high-level pianist.

Sports scholarships are offered at 11+, 13+ and 16+ to candidates with outstanding ability and potential in sports. We award major scholarships of £1,000 p.a. and minor scholarships of £500 p.a. Candidates will take part in a practical session. They will also have an individual interview with the Director of Sport when they will have the opportunity to discuss their achievements and their favourite sports. Candidates are also requested to provide a reference from the Head of PE at their current school or from their coach at the highest level in whichever sport they participate.

All scholarship awards are intended for the support of the pupils' interests. All scholarship award holders are expected to be fully involved in the area of school life in which they have their award.

Bursaries. There are means-tested bursary funds available for a limited number of pupils in particular financial need.

Fees per term (from January 2022). Full Boarders UK £10,700, Full Boarders (Overseas) £11,700, Weekly Boarders £9,440, Day Girls £5,950.

Directors:
Board of Directors of Wychwood School Oxford Ltd.
Mrs D Pluck, BA, FCA [Old Girl] (*Chairman*)
Ms A Stewart, MA, ACA
Mr Simon Tyrrell, BSc Hons, MRICS
Mrs Abigail Tyrrell, BA Hons, PGCE
Mr James Weedon, BSC, MRICS

Staff:

Head: **Mrs A Johnson**, BSc Dunelm, PGCE

Deputy Head Academic: Mrs A Stacey, BA Hons, PGCE
Deputy Head Pastoral: Ms B Sherlock, BA, PGCE, MEd (*English*)
Head of Wychwood Sixth: Mr M Pennington, BA Hons, MA

Miss J Bettridge, TESOL Cert (*EAL*)
Mlle M Boubkari, BA, PGCE (*French*)
Mrs K Britton, BSc Hons, MBA QTS (*Biology*)
Miss F Centamore, BSc, PGCE (*Director of Sport*)
Mrs M Constance, BEd Hons, MA (*Drama*)
Mrs C Crossley, BA Hons, PGCE (*RS*)
Dr M Donald, BA Hons, PhD (*Psychology/EPQ*)
Miss O Goodrich, BA Hons, MA, PGCE (*EAL*)
Mr P Humphreys, BSc, PGCE, MEd, BSA Cert (*Geography*)
Mr P Ilott, BEng (*Physics*)
Mrs T Jarrett, BA Hons, PGCE (*Careers, EAL*)
Mr L Jimenez, LLB, MA (*Spanish*)
Mrs H Kirby, BA Hons, PGCE (*English*)
Mrs S McCullagh, HND, OND (*Textiles*)
Mr M Pennington, BA Hons, MA (*Photography*)
Mr R Pleming, MA (*English*)
Miss Y Roberts, BA Hons, PGCE (*TA*)
Mrs J Sherbrooke, BSc Hons, MSc, PGCE (*History*)
Mrs M Stephenson, BSc Hons, PGCE (*Computing, SENDCo*)
Miss V Stone, BSc, PGCE (*Mathematics*)
Mrs Rebecca Cooper, BSc, PGCE (*Mathematics*)
Mrs G Troth, BSc Hons (*Business, Economics, PSHE*)
Mrs B Walster, BMus Hons, PGCE (*Music*)
Miss A Wardell, BA Hons, MA (*Art*)
Dr J Williams, BA Hons, PGCE, SRN, RSCN (*History of Art*)
Mrs C Au Yeung (*Marketing and Admissions Assistant*)
Mrs J Bridge (*Office Manager*)
Mr R Constance (*Technician*)
Mrs L Escott (*Junior Housemistress*)
Mr P Granville (*Finance and Support Staff Manager*)
Mrs L Henk (*Senior Housemistress*)
Mrs I Howes (*Office and Finance Assistant*)
Mrs J Hunt, BA Hons (*Head of Marketing and Admissions*)
Mrs C Legg, BA, MSc (*Librarian*)
Mr J Mott (*Network Manager*)
Mr Phil Partington (*Catering Manager*)
Miss S Phipps (*School Counsellor*)
Miss E Varley (*Assistant Housemistress*)
Miss T Werger (*Assistant Junior Housemistress*)

PART III
Schools whose Heads are members of
The Society of Heads

ALPHABETICAL LIST OF SCHOOLS

The following schools, whose Heads are members of both The Society of Heads and HMC, can be found in the HMC section:

Bedales School
Birkdale School
Bristol Grammar School
The Cathedral School Llandaff
City of London Freemen's School
Cokethorpe School
Gordonstoun
Halliford School
Kirkham Grammar School
Langley School

Lincoln Minster School
Moreton Hall
Mount Kelly
Reading Blue Coat School
Rendcomb College
St Columba's College
Seaford College
Shiplake College
Wisbech Grammar School

The following schools, whose Heads are members of both The Society of Heads and GSA, can be found in the GSA section:

More House School
St Augustine's Priory School

THE SOCIETY OF HEADS
GEOGRAPHICAL LIST OF SCHOOLS

Individual School Entries

Abbey Gate College

Saighton Grange, Saighton, Chester, Cheshire CH3 6EN

Tel: 01244 332077
email: admin@abbeygatecollege.co.uk
website: www.abbeygatecollege.co.uk
Twitter: @AbbeyGateColl
Facebook: @AbbeyGateCollege
Instagram: @abbeygatecollege
LinkedIn: /company/abbey-gate-college

Motto: *Audentior Ito*

Founded in 1977, Abbey Gate College is a co-educational day school for pupils from 4–18 years of age.

Location and Facilities. The senior school is set in 20 acres of beautiful grounds at Saighton Grange some three miles south of the City of Chester. The history of Saighton Grange goes back long before the Norman Conquest, although most of the present building is Victorian. From 1853 the Grange was a residence of the Grosvenor family. Additional facilities include a large Sports Hall, playing fields and an Arts and Media Centre opened in March 2004 by HRH the Duchess of Gloucester. A purpose-built Art and Design & Technology Centre and new science laboratory were completed in Spring 2008 and opened by His Grace the Duke of Westminster. In 2013 developments included a new multi-purpose classroom and drama studio. In 2016 a Sports & Teaching Pavilion was opened, followed two years later by the opening of an all-weather pitch. Future developments include two fully-equipped and cutting-edge laboratories and a new Sixth Form Centre with personal study zones and a range of seminar classrooms.

The Infant and Junior School is situated in Aldford, a picturesque village only two miles from Saighton. Facilities here include a new Foundation and Infant School building opened in 2018, with three spacious classrooms with covered outdoor areas, a library area, and a space for Learning Enrichment, along with excellent playing fields, an ecology and wildlife area plus a number of other outdoor learning spaces. The Infants and Juniors benefit from shared use of the senior site facilities and specialist staff that teach throughout the age range.

Aims and Mission. "We are committed, within our safe and caring community, that each one of our pupils will become the best that they can be and have the self-belief to go forward into this changeable world with courage and with compassion."

We pursue our whole College mission, guided by three defining and aspirational aims:

- Self: each pupil is mentally and physically well, learns and achieves to their individual potential, and is comfortable and confident to be who they are in our diverse and inclusive College.
- Service: each pupil makes a positive difference to the lives of others in our College, as well as in our local and in wider, global communities.
- Sustainability: each pupil contributes towards preserving and protecting the planet we all inherit and share, and has the opportunity to be creative and innovative; to help further humanity's progress in the future.

In achieving these aims, the College builds the self-confidence of pupils and prepares them for the opportunities, responsibilities and experiences in the next chapters of their lives.

Academic Programme. The curriculum is balanced, broad, and challenging to help pupils maximise their potential, empowering them with intelligence, resilience, and the attitude to succeed. Exam results are strong across the board, with significantly positive value-added at each key stage. Pupils are constantly stretched and challenged. Small class sizes, the attention they deserve, and the school's friendly, caring approach ensure they discover and develop their personal talents.

The College is well equipped with the latest technology: interactive touch screens in every classroom, access to a range of iPads, tablets, laptops and PCs, blended learning with Bring Your Own Device in the Senior School, 3D printers, computer-aided design (CAD) equipment, Wi-Fi, and a Virtual Learning Environment (VLE), all help to develop the skills that pupils will need to succeed in the jobs of tomorrow.

The stunning woodland, gardens, and natural, green spaces on both sites contribute to pupils' curricular learning and engagement with sustainability, as well as supporting the context of wellbeing, calm, and respect.

Creativity is well-nurtured by the College's specialist Art and Design Departments, in addition to the Music Department, which enjoys an excellent reputation in the region for the quality of its choir in particular, who delight audiences in the Chester area and beyond on a regular basis.

Many pupils of all ages take music lessons and with visiting staff are prepared for the Associated Board Examinations.

Sport. All pupils participate in physical education and games. Boys play rugby, soccer, cricket and tennis; girls play hockey, netball, tennis and rounders. Athletics is popular for both boys and girls and all sports provide full fixture lists for the various College teams. The local swimming pool is reserved each week for sessions with a fully-qualified instructor for the younger pupils.

Other activities. Pupils visit all corners of the world, including History Department trips to the First World War battlefields, the USA and Poland, Geography Department trips to Iceland, Switzerland and Costa Rica and cultural trips to France. There is a well-established service project with a school in Eswatini and award-winning Young Enterprise teams. The College also have large numbers of pupils completing the Duke of Edinburgh's award at bronze, silver, and gold level.

Admission.

Senior School: Most pupils enter the College at age 11 following an Entrance Examination held in the Spring Term, although where occasional places occur in other year groups, assessments can be made mid-year. Each pupil is allocated to one of the Senior School Houses; the house system encourages competition, community and positive attitudes through the allocation of home points.

Junior School: Pupils are admitted to the Junior School by means of short assessment and interview at ages 7, 8, 9 and 10, dependent on spaces being available. It is expected that children already in this part of the school will move directly into the College at age 11.

Infant School: Entry at ages 4, 5 and 6 is also available. Reception places are limited and assessments run on separate occasions throughout the year.

Sixth Form: Priority is given to existing pupils but places are offered to others and are conditional on good results at GCSE.

Scholarships. Academic scholarships are available following the results of the Entrance Examination. A comprehensive Bursary Scheme also operates at 11+ and Sixth Form entry offering places to pupils with proven ability or talents who would normally not be able to afford the school fees.

For musical talent awards are offered, including the Daphne Herbert Choral Scholarship and the Music Exhibition Scholarship at Year 7.

Fees per term (2021–2022). Tuition: Infant and Junior School £3,174; Senior School £4,551.

Abbey Gate College Alumni. All pupils are encouraged to join the Alumni Association. Further details of the Association can be obtained from the Registrar at the College.

Charitable status. Deeside House Educational Trust is a Registered Charity. number 273586. It exists to provide co-education for children in the Cheshire, Wirral and North Wales areas.

Visitor: His Grace The Duke of Westminster

Chair of Governors: Mr A Grime

Head: Mr C Jenkinson, MA Oxon, PGCE, MInstLM

Deputy Head: Mr G Allmand

Academic Staff:

Mr J Andrews	Mrs L Hornby
Mr A Austen	Mrs C Houghton
Mr T Baglole	Mrs G Hudson
Mr K Bailey	Miss G Johnson
Dr S Ball	Miss E Jones
Mrs K Baty	Mr D Kebell
Mrs C Bennett	Mrs H Kitchin
Mr M Booth	Ms F Lawrence
Miss K Burdon	Dr E Leatherbarrow
Mr K Burdon	Mrs Z Leonard
Mrs A Byers	Mr D Luckwell
Mr P Carter	Dr J Lloyd-Johnson
Mr M Cavallini	Mrs P McClean
Mr C Cutler	Miss H Milloy
Mr G Darbey	Mrs N Moses
Mr M Dickins	Mrs A Neal
Mrs S Dolan	Mrs L Poyser
Ms S Donarski	Mrs A Prestwich
Mrs S Dorricott	Mr M Richardson
Ms Z Dunn	Mr D Rowett
Mrs C Faithfull	Mr S Rowson
Mrs V Grey	Mrs E Sanders
Mr A P Green	Mrs N Stammers
Mrs S Hall	Mr D I Stockley

Mrs S Storrar	Miss H Wood
Mrs G Thomas	Mrs E Worth
Miss S Toosey	

Infant & Junior School:

Head of Infant & Junior School: Mrs A M Hickey

Mr P Butcher
Mrs J Dukes
Miss L Green
Mrs E Newman
Mrs S Parry
Mrs W Richards
Mrs S Tomlins
Mrs C Travis
Mrs A Williams

Teaching Assistants:
Mrs G Foulkes
Mrs W Jones
Mrs A Higgins
Mrs A Kinsey

Director of Finance and Operations: Mrs R Kennedy
Registrar: Mrs S Boyd
HR & Compliance Manager: Miss C Duffy
Finance Manager: Mrs P Rees, FCCA
Finance Assistant: Mrs J McBride
Marketing and Promotions Manager: Mrs F Hodgkinson

Librarian: Mrs J Littler

School Nurse: Miss P Sheckley

Technicians:
Mrs R Freeman (*Art*)
Mr S Horsefield (*DT*)
Mr S Huxley
Mrs H Rawson

PA to Head of Infant and Junior School and Receptionist/ Administrator: Mrs A Ivory
PA to Leadership Team & Alumni Officer: Mrs S Knowles
School Secretary: Mrs D Roxborough
Examination Officer: Mrs A Owen
Attendance Officer: Mrs A McCleary
Network System Admin Manager: Mr P Rowlands
ICT Technician: Mr M Millar

Estates Manager: Ms D Coakley
Gardener: Mr T Frodsham
Caretakers: Mr M Healy; Mr R Tyrrell; Mr P Hamilton; Mr P Walker
Cleaners: Mrs S Jennerway; Mrs S Okoth
Mini Bus Driver: Mr D Owen

Abbotsholme School

Rocester, Uttoxeter, Staffordshire ST14 5BS

Tel: 01889 594265 (admissions)
         01889 590217 (main number)
email: enquiries@abbotsholme.co.uk
website: www.abbotsholme.co.uk
Twitter: @AbbotsholmeSch
Facebook: @abbotsholmeschool
Instagram: @abbotsholmeschool

Abbotsholme School is an independent day and boarding school for boys and girls aged 2 to 18, situated in wonderful rolling hills and meadows on the border of Staffordshire and Derbyshire, close to the magnificent Peak District, in the UK. Our 140-acre campus offers the perfect environment to learn, achieve and enjoy a special education that focuses on academic success and character development. With superb facilities, all of our pupils from Nursery through to Sixth Form, have the opportunity to participate and excel in an extensive programme of sports, outdoor education, agriculture and equine activities as well as the creative arts, music and drama. Abbotsholme aims to prepare each pupil for the whole of life through a balanced, flexible and challenging curriculum fostering a sense of self-worth, enthusiasm for learning and ambition for the future.

ISI Inspection. Following the recent inspections by the Independent Schools Inspectorate, it was reported that at Abbotsholme the *'quality of the pupils personal development is excellent'*, *'pupils have positive attitudes towards learning'* and *'academic and other achievements are good'*.

Special Characteristics. Membership of the *Round Square* organisation (www.roundsquare.org) provides a strong international perspective. A worldwide and unique association of schools committed to personal growth and responsibility through service, challenge, adventure and international understanding, members share one aim – the full and individual development of every pupil into a whole person. Abbotsholme offers an IDEALS programme where pupils understand and learn more in-depth about these values.

Our *outdoor education* programme is both well known and well regarded. Its pioneering principles inspired such organisations as The Duke of Edinburgh's Award scheme. With adventures both close to home and internationally, it presents pupils with personal challenges, both physical and mental, and teaches them the importance of taking responsibility for themselves and others. Many pupils are involved in The Duke of Edinburgh's Award scheme and all participate in summer camps and autumn hikes each year.

Abbotsholme is one of the very few schools in England to have a working *farm* upon which pupils are able to learn about animal husbandry and crop management and gain a healthy respect for the environment. In addition to the 70-acre farm, our British Horse Society approved *Equestrian Centre* is a popular place to be for our horse enthusiasts, who happily involve themselves in the upkeep of the stables and yard and can study for BHS exams.

We believe that the physical and mental disciplines of working together in a team are very important. *Sport* teaches the art of winning and losing with equally good grace, self-reliance and leadership, and the opportunities to compete are grasped by many of our pupils. The main sports at Abbotsholme include: hockey and cricket, with additional sports being football, netball, rugby, tennis, swimming, athletics, cross-country, badminton and basketball.

All pupils are encouraged to appreciate *Music* in some way, either by learning to play an instrument, entering the Musician of the Year competition or joining in with the inter house school singing competition.

Performing Arts flourishes, in and out of the classroom, with performances in the 120-seat theatre always oversubscribed. All pupils who are keen to be involved, whether on stage or behind the scenes, find regular opportunities to experience the fun and self-discipline characteristic of performance and improvised theatre.

The influence of the *Art* department is evident throughout school, where pupils' painting, drawing, pottery and ceramics are permanently on display. In addition many pupils enjoy the facilities of the *Design and Technology* department, which provides excellent opportunities for developing creative design into quality manufacture and 3D creations. There is an opportunity to help build electric cars in the *Automotive Engineering Club* and race them at places like Silverstone and Rockingham. Photography is a real strength of the Art department and pupils have access to a traditional darkroom as well as cutting-edge editing equipment.

Curriculum. Abbotsholme caters for a broad ability range. Academic standards are high with the majority of sixth formers going on to their first-choice university. Breadth and balance shape the curriculum, which aims to develop critical and creative thinking and self-discipline across a wide range of subjects at GCSE and A Level.

Activities. Abbotsholme firmly believes that a school should have a greater purpose beyond preparing students for College or University. As a result we seek not only to help all pupils realise their individual academic potential but also to develop in everyone a sense of responsibility for themselves and others through active participation within the community as well as a sense of adventure through challenges in and beyond the classroom. A comprehensive range of compulsory activities is integral to the curriculum as part of our carousel programme. Each half-term's activities alternately include Outdoor Education, Farm/Equestrian work, Performing Arts and the recent introduction of Mandarin. Wednesday afternoons are home to sports fixtures and an array of other activities, such as fencing, equestrian, walks, rock climbing, mountain biking and dance etc.

Home from Home. The boarding experience at Abbotsholme is a happy one, where staff and pupils know each other well and where every individual shares equal responsibility for the community's well being and progress. Small, friendly homes are run by resident houseparents as family units. Younger boarders share bright and comfortable dormitories in threes and fours whilst older pupils have single or shared study-bedrooms. A log cabin village has been added for sixth formers giving them opportunities to experience a greater degree of independence and privacy. Weekly boarding has become a popular option for families with busy lives and for our full boarders, a full programme of weekend activities provides plenty of choice and lots of fun, balancing academic work with social time. Our modern approach to boarding means that sleepover and flexi boarding are also options.

Facilities. These include: dedicated classroom areas for each subject, including specialist science laboratories, art, music, design and IT centres (two suites), a purpose-built studio theatre for performing arts, sixth form centre, log cabin complex, indoor climbing wall, 70-acre working farm, equestrian centre and manège, a modern, multi-purpose sports hall, synthetic pitch, extensive playing fields and outdoor swimming pool, traditional dining hall and a chapel, which combines as the venue for morning assembly as well as concerts.

Fees per term (2021–2022). Day £3,085–£7,720; Weekly Boarding £6,360–£9,425; Full Boarding £8,440–£11,585; Occasional Boarding: £52 per night.

The Abbotsholmians' Club. The Club currently has some 2,000 members and is run by a Committee of Old Abbotsholmians, elected yearly. Members receive regular mail-outs, which give contact addresses and details of the adventures of OAs, young and old. There are also regular invitations to events, to help them keep in touch with each other and with current developments at the school. An enormous amount of networking takes place between OAs, often facilitated by the Club, ensuring that friendships are sustained and memories are relived. Website: www.abbotsholmians.co.uk.

The Club operates a small Bursary fund specifically aimed at helping to educate sons and daughters of OAs at Abbotsholme.

Abbotsholme Arts Society. The School is host to one of the most respected concert presenters in the country. Although embracing jazz, poetry and drama performances, its core programme of chamber music has brought a Who's Who of big-name musicians to the school over the years – Ashkenazy, Brendel, Galway, Hough, the Amadeus Quartet to name just a few. Pupils are able to attend any of the Arts Society concerts free of charge. Website: www.abbotsholmeartssociety.co.uk.

Abbotsholme Parents' Association. Run by parents, for the benefit of parents, children and school, the Parents' Association (APA) aims to help new families settle in and become quickly familiar with Abbotsholme and all that it has to offer. Keen to promote active parental involvement in the school, members regularly organise social activities and fundraising events.

Headteacher: **Mr Simon Ruscoe-Price**

Deputy Headteacher: Mrs Amy Thornton

Head of Prep School: Mrs Kristy Hankin

Director of Curriculum: Mr Gareth Pardoe

Headteacher's PA: Mrs Julie Noon

Registrar: Mrs Juliette Sheldon

Austin Friars

Etterby Scaur, Carlisle, Cumbria CA3 9PB

Tel: 01228 528042
email: office@austinfriars.co.uk
            admissions@austinfriars.co.uk
website: www.austinfriars.co.uk
Twitter: @AustinFriarsSch
Facebook: @austinfriarsschool

Motto: *"In Omnibus Caritas"*

Austin Friars is a co-educational day school, founded by members of the Order of St Augustine in 1951. It is the UK's only Augustinian school and pupils of all denominations are welcome into the School which provides education for boys and girls aged 3–18.

The 3–18 profile of the School allows pupils more time to respond to the core Augustinian values of Unity, Truth and Love which are enshrined in the way the School goes about its business on a daily basis. The 3–18 model also facilitates a seamless transition from Pre-School to VI Form and presents younger pupils with access to facilities usually the preserve of secondary pupils, such as science laboratories, music suites, specialist sports facilities and design technology workshops.

The quality of pastoral care is one of the School's greatest strengths. Both the Junior and Senior Schools are divided into three Houses with the House being central to the strong sense of a community in which older and younger pupils mix freely.

Studies. The curriculum at all levels is broad and balanced which encourages academic achievement alongside sporting, musical, cultural and creative development, thus allowing each child's talents and potential to be fully pursued. Pupils are encouraged to become increasingly independent learners as they progress through the School with excellent support mechanisms available, on an individual or small group basis, for those pupils with specific learning difficulties who require specialised provision. From age 3 in the Pre-School, pupils benefit from specialist teaching. In the Senior School, class sizes are small and high standards are expected and achieved through careful monitoring of progress and a commitment by all to outstanding teaching and learning.

Activities. The School is an excellent centre for developing new and existing interests and talents. Some 50+ extra-curricular activities are available to pupils both during the School day, and in after school clubs. Music, Speech and Drama have a high profile across all phases of the School. There are regular concerts, musical performances, plays and musicals.

Sport. The school has a full-sized AstroTurf which is utilised throughout the year and various sports pitches. The range of sporting options available is vast. Gymnastics and fitness are all offered within the activities programme. The pupils regularly achieve county status in their various sports. Qualified and enthusiastic staff provide coaching in team sports from the Junior School upwards, and the School's record in inter-school competition is acknowledged far beyond Cumbria. Annual skiing trips take place.

Admissions. Children are admitted into the Pre-School in the three to four age range following a successful taster session. Entry into the Junior School at all levels, except Kindergarten, is by assessment during taster days. Entry into Kindergarten is by interview and a taster session.

The Senior School adopts a three-form entry policy. The majority of places are offered at 11+ where pupils sit the Senior School's entrance assessments; entry to the VI Form is on the basis of performance at GCSE. Admissions at other ages are considered, subject to availability of places and completion of the entrance assessment. All prospective pupils spend a taster day(s) with their prospective year group.

Fees per term (2021–2022). Pre-School: £6.65 per hour, plus £2.15 for lunch (the EYFS offers government funded hours). Junior School: £2,835 (R–Year 2), £3,100 (Years 3–4), £3,895 (Years 5–6). Senior School: £5,225 (Years 7–8), £5,250 (Years 9–11), £5,330 (Years 12–13).

Charitable status. Austin Friars is a Registered Charity, number 516289. It exists for the purpose of educating boys and girls.

Chairman of Trustees: Mr John Little

Headmaster: Mr M F Harris, BSc, PGCE

Deputy Head: Mrs J Thornborrow, BSc, PGCE
Deputy Head (*Academic*): Mr D Harte, BSc, PGCE
Head of VI Form: Mr S Parry, MEd, BSc, PGCE, Dip RSA
Head of Junior School: Mr Chris March, BSc

Bursar: Mr D Strawbridge, MSc
Admissions and Marketing Manager: Miss A Burns, BA

Bedstone College

Bucknell, Shropshire SY7 0BG

Tel: 01547 530303
email: admissions@bedstone.org
            reception@bedstone.org
website: www.bedstone.org
Twitter: @BedstoneCollege
Facebook: @BedstoneCollege
Instagram: @BedstoneCollege

Motto: *Caritas*

Bedstone College, founded in 1948, is a fully co-educational, independent, boarding and day school catering for children between the ages of 4 and 18 years. The school enjoys a beautiful 40-acre campus within an idyllic setting amongst the south Shropshire hills, close to the ancient and beautiful market town of Ludlow, and within a 30 minute drive of both Shrewsbury and Hereford.

The school comprises the Junior School (for children aged 4 to 11 years), Senior School (for ages 11 to 16 years) and Sixth Form (for ages 16 to 18 years), all integrated within one campus. Students from the age of 9 are welcome to board at Bedstone.

Bedstone offers a broad and balanced curriculum with a wide range of subjects available at GCSE, BTEC, AS and A Levels, as well as being a candidate school for the International Baccalaureate for introduction in September 2022. Bedstone is proudly non-selective and offers the opportunity for students of all ability levels to achieve

beyond their expectations, including securing places at the University of their choice.

The College aims to fulfil the potential of every child wherever that potential may lie and, with an average teacher to pupil ratio of 1:8, the smaller class sizes allow individual needs to be catered for. The well-qualified and highly-motivated staff believe that each child has a unique talent which it is their job to find and to nurture.

Bedstone is very aware of the problems that learning difficulties, such as dyslexia, can cause and the nationally recognised Learning Support Department, led by its full-time director with the aid of fully-qualified staff, is central to the help provided. Bedstone is one of a small number of schools in the UK to be accredited by CReSTeD as a Specialist Dyslexia Unit.

Character of the College. Many children who join Bedstone have done so because their parents feel that the individual strengths of their child will thrive best at Bedstone, that the challenges and opportunities for fulfilling their child's unique talents do not exist at their current school, or that they wish for greater pastoral support and guidance for their child. Every parent knows that what they want is the education of the whole child – mind, body and spirit – and Bedstone provides that with its academic and extracurricular programme coupled with its outstanding pastoral care and boarding ethos. Bedstone prides itself on its supportive environment that students are proud to be a part of, including the free provision of a Health and Wellbeing App for every student.

Accommodation. The main house, Bedstone Court, is a listed building of fine architectural merit and accommodates the Junior and Senior boys' houses. In addition, it houses the administration offices, library, dining hall and sixth form area. The two girls' boarding houses are on the opposite side of the campus with the senior girls accommodated within a purpose-built boarding house and the junior girls within the homely surroundings of a 19th century manor house. All boarding houses have been completely refurbished. All boarding houses have resident staff and their families as houseparents. There is seating for 300 people in the Rees Hall Theatre with full AV facilities. There is a modern well-equipped Sports Hall, Design Technology and Art Centre, Music School, a Medical Centre staffed by RGNs, Fitness Suite, Performing Arts Studio, Learning Support and Counselling facility, and a wide range of additional facilities. The College has a campus-wide wireless LAN.

Religious Education. The formal classroom teaching of Religious Studies follows the National Curriculum which covers all the major world religions. More broadly, the college follows the teachings of the Church of England though other denominations, and children without any religious affiliation, are most warmly welcomed. Children, whose parents wish it, are also prepared for Confirmation by the Chaplain. The College enjoys a strong choral tradition and the Choir enjoys an excellent reputation.

Senior College Curriculum. From the First Form (Y7) to the Third Form (Y9) (when a number join from other Preparatory and Primary Schools) the subjects taught are: Religious Education, English Language and Literature, History, Geography, French, Spanish, Mathematics, Biology, Physics, Chemistry, Design Technology, Art, Music, Physical Education and ICT.

In the Fourth and Fifth Forms, in addition to the Core Curriculum of English, English Literature, Mathematics, one modern foreign language (French or Spanish), the three

Sciences, Religious Studies, (and non-examination Physical Education), options are: History, Geography, Art, Business Studies, Music, French, Spanish, Design Technology and Sports Studies.

Throughout the College, in all classes, we help students achieve the very best that they are capable of and surpass their own expectations. With the aid of close tutorial support, industry mentor scheme, career pathways, a well-qualified staff, an excellent staff/pupil ratio, plus, of course, determined effort on the part of the students, good progress and examination success are assured. A Level courses are offered in English, History, Geography, French, Spanish, Business Studies, Art, Design Technology, Mathematics, Further Mathematics, Music, Physics, Chemistry, Biology, Psychology and Sports Studies. BTECs in Agriculture and Physical Education are also available as options.

The College has its own Learning Support Department. Excellent EAL provision is available for those who require it in addition to pre-sessional intensive English courses, a three-year A Level programme, IELTS, IGCSE and subject-specific language support.

Careers. There are specific careers staff and a well-resourced Careers Room. Bedstone makes full use of Inspiring Futures' careers services and all members of the Fifth Form take the Inspiring Futures Psychometric tests and have the opportunity to undertake work experience. Our individual guidance means that, typically, 90% or more of Sixth Former leavers gain entrance to their university of first choice.

Games and Physical Education. There are 15 acres of playing fields, with an excellent Sports Hall, fitness suite, performing arts studio and netball & tennis courts plus an astroturf. The success of the boys and girls in physical activity at school, county and district level has been nothing short of remarkable. The school holds several ISA National Championships in various disciplines including Rugby 7s, Cross Country, Tennis and Hockey.

Rugby, Football, Athletics, Cross-Country and Cricket are the main sports for the boys and Hockey, Cricket, Netball, Rounders, Cross-Country and Athletics for the girls but they can join in many more. A rotation system ensures that all students, to a greater or lesser degree, have their share of such activities as Basketball, Swimming, Badminton and Tennis. Nor are the individualists forgotten. Horse riding is popular, and there are facilities for Table Tennis and Mountain Biking, whilst the South Shropshire and Powys hills provide excellent opportunities for Duke of Edinburgh's Award activities.

Clubs and Activities. The Duke of Edinburgh's Award scheme flourishes and there is a wide range of out-of-class activity, including splendid dramatic and musical productions, debating, individual music tuition. There are twice weekly 'activities' sessions which offer some 40–50 different clubs over the course of any one year. Pupils are expected to know and observe all College rules and parents to cooperate in seeing that this is done. Prefects play an important part in the pastoral system of the College. There are also a number of trips and visits that take place throughout the year, including visits to some of the most beautiful cities in Europe. Every two years there are major international sports tours for both the boys and the girls.

Bedstone Junior School is for boys and girls aged 4 to 11 years. The school is housed in its own separate accommodation and yet shares all the facilities of the senior school. Science, Modern Foreign Languages, Sport, Art and Music are all taught by senior school subject specialists within specialist areas. There is a specialist gifted and talented mathematics programme for the most able junior school students and talented sports players are developed through specialist coaching from the teachers in the senior college and entry into regional and national competitions.

The Junior School is an integral part of the College and children find the transition to the Senior College seamless. Any child accepted within the Junior School is automatically accepted into the Senior College.

Scholarships. For the academically talented, there is an opportunity to attend a Scholarship Assessment with awards available to successful students for entry into the School.

Fees per term (2021–2022). Junior School: Day: Reception to Year 2 (age 4–7) £1,725, Years 3–6 (age 7–11) £3,640; Boarding (Years 5–6, age 9–11) £6,115. Senior School: Day: Year 7 £4,320; Years 8–13 £5,030; Boarding £10,000; International Boarding (age 9–18) £12,500.

Head: **Mr T Mullins**, BA, MBA

Deputy Headteacher: Mr C Braden, BEd, PG Dip

Houseparents:

Boys Boarding:
Pearson House: Mr and Mrs A Whittall
Rutter House: Mr and Mrs O Downing

Girls Boarding:
Bedstone House: Mr and Mrs P Singh
Wilson House: Mr and Mrs M Rozée

Members of Common Room:
Ms C Beddow, BSc PGCE (*Sport/PE, Science*)
Mrs S Crabtree, BA, QTS (*English, Junior School teacher*)
Mrs J Crouch, BA, PGCE (*DT, Maths, i/c Art*)
Mr O Downing, BA, PGCE (*Head of 6th Form, Head of English, Exams Officer*)
Ms C Evans, BMus, PGCE (*Head of Music*)
Dr D Foreman, PhD, PGCE (*Head of Biology/Psychology*)
Miss C Higgins, BA, PGCE (*Junior School Teacher*)
Mrs C Hunter, CDMVA La Sorbonne (*Head of MFL*)
Mr L Kouniakis, BA, TESOL, QTS (*Head of EAL*)
Mrs A Lawrence, MA, PGCE (*Junior School teacher*)
Mr J Lowe MA, DipRSA Dyslexia, PGD SEN + Inclusion, PGCE, CPT3A, SpLD APC Patoss (*Head of Learning Support*)
Mr D P Marsh, BSc, PGCE (*Head of Geography*)
Mr R Martin, BSc, PGCE (*Head of Mathematics*)
Mrs C Newnham, BSc, PGCE (*Biology*)
Mr E Olive, BSc, PGCE (*Head of Physics*)
Mr J Percival, MA, PGCE (*Head of History*)
Mrs J Richards, MA Ed, PGCE (*Junior School teacher*)
Miss S Ross, BA, QTS (*i/c PE & Games*)
Mr D M Rozée, BSc, PGCE, MRSC (*Head of Science/Chemistry*)
Ms C Simmons, MA Oxon, PGCE (*Mathematics*)
Mrs C Spencer, MA, PGCE (*Head of RE*)
Mr A Whittall, BA, PGCE (*Head of Boarding, Mathematics*)
Mrs J Williams, BEd (*Junior School teacher*)
Mrs N Williams, BSc Econ, PGCE (*Head of Business Studies*)

Teaching Assistants:
Mrs L Meredith, NNEB
Mrs K Singh, BA

Learning Support:
Mr J Lowe, PGD Inclusion & SEN, PGCE

EAL:
Mr L Kouniakis

School Medical Team:
Mrs N Stead, RGN; Mrs J Jackson, RGN

Visiting Music Staff:
Ms J Hudson (*Drums*)
Mr D Luke (*Guitar*)
Mrs J Whittle (*Musical Theatre*)
Mr J Hymas (*Violin*)
Mr J Nicholls (*Piano*)
Mr C Lacey (*Woodwind*)

Competitive Houses:
Hopton: Mr R Martin
Stokesay: Miss S Ross
Wigmore: Mr J Lowe

Headmaster's PA: Mrs C Preston
Accounts Administrator: Mr P Downes
Admissions & Marketing Officer: Mrs Julia Mukho
Marketing & Communications Officer: Mr Tim Cozze-Young
Registrar, Librarian, EVC: Mrs A Whittall
Receptionists: Mrs W McKee-Wills; Miss J Goode-Naprous
Catering/Head Chef: Mrs M Hart
Domestic Supervisor: Mrs D Gough
Transport Manager: Mr P Singh

Beechwood School

12 Pembury Road, Tunbridge Wells, Kent TN2 3QD

Tel: +44 (0)1892 532747
email: info@beechwood.org.uk
website: www.beechwood.org.uk

Beechwood is an independent co-educational day and boarding school for pupils aged 3–18. Founded in 1915, there has been a school here for well over 100 years.

The Nursery School (age 3–5), Preparatory School (age 5–11) and Senior School (age 11–18) are located in 23 acres of landscaped grounds overlooking open countryside, close to the centre of the historic town of Royal Tunbridge Wells. The Main School is based in a Victorian villa with all facilities located on a single campus. There are 325 pupils on roll.

Boarding is offered for seventy boys and girls in modern and comfortable accommodation on the school campus. After a big refurbishment programme in 2021 our junior boarders often share in two or three bedded rooms whilst older students are allocated single study-bedrooms. We receive a large number of applications for boarding places each year, so an early application is advised. The School does not operate 'Exeat' weekends.

Beechwood is noted for its genuine family atmosphere. Consideration for others underpins the code of behaviour for all pupils, making Beechwood a happy school with high academic standards being achieved through expectation and challenge, rather than prescription. We are an ambitious, caring school and that sense of confidence and generosity of spirit permeates throughout the school. At Beechwood we prepare our pupils for the future but encourage them to enjoy the present.

Curriculum. In our small classes, teachers stimulate pupils to excel in what they are good at and build confidence in areas they find difficult, from the youngest child in the Nursery through to our oldest Senior School pupils. Our Learning Development department supports the individual needs of those pupils who require extra support.

Beechwood provides a broad education. At Key Stage 3 all pupils study a range of subjects. Most subjects are taught in mixed-ability classes of boys and girls. Mathematics is setted from Year 7. French is studied in Year 7 along with either Spanish or German. Academic standards are important and we challenge our pupils to achieve their best. We also encourage our pupils to participate in a wide range of extracurricular activities, trips, and visits.

At GCSE pupils can study from a wide range of subjects. Biology, Chemistry and Physics ('triple Science') are offered as single subjects and we offer French, German, and Spanish as Modern Foreign Language options. Mathematics, English Language, RS and English Literature are compulsory at GCSE as well as at least one science subject. This enables pupils to select from a wider range of options when they construct their GCSE portfolio. Additional English language lessons are provided for international pupils. Pupils participate in a diverse PE curriculum and study PHSCE as part of their personal development.

At A Level, more than twenty subjects are offered including three Sciences, Theatre Studies, Further Mathematics, Business Studies, Photography, Product Design, Psychology, Film Studies, History, Criminology and Textiles. The Sixth Form curriculum is enhanced by an enrichment course that includes Life Skills and comprehensive Careers and University application advice. We also offer the EPQ (extended project qualification) and the Arts Award.

Sixth Formers are encouraged to show initiative and take responsibility. They have opportunities for leadership as prefects and in organising activities for younger pupils. All leavers successfully gain places at university on a wide range of courses.

Examination Results. Beechwood's record in public examinations is particularly impressive for a wide ability school, with a pass rate (9–5) of around 90% at GCSE and 100% at A Level, and is in the top 25% of schools for value-added performance at A Level.

Sports. Pupils are encouraged to experience a wide variety of sports, the emphasis being on fun and participation. Sports facilities include a MUGA (multi use games area) hockey and football pitches, netball, basketball and tennis courts, cricket nets, sports hall, badminton and volleyball courts.

Preparatory School and Nursery. Our Preparatory School and Nursery provide an excellent beginning for every child in a supportive, family atmosphere. The curriculum stimulates enquiry, academic standards being maintained through regular monitoring and assessment. French is studied from Year 1 and all pupils also enjoy cookery lessons. In addition, by sharing the facilities of the Senior School, pupils participate in a wide variety of sports and can represent the school in matches. Extra-curricular activities include chess, crafts, gardening and drama. Many pupils have instrumental music lessons.

Entry Requirements. The school is non-selective academically, selection being based on interview with the Headmaster, previous school report, performance in entrance assessments and confidential reference. All enquiries and applications should be addressed to the Registrar.

Fees per term (2021–2022). Full boarders £10,200; Weekly boarders £9,175; Day pupils £2,895–£5,940.

Scholarships. Academic, Sports, Performing Arts and Creative Arts scholarships are available on entry to Year 7, 9 and 12. Entrance Days take place in November for entry to Year 7 and 9, prior to entry the following September. Year 12 are taken prior to GCSE results.

Beechwood School is part of the Alpha schools group.

Head: **Mr Justin Foster-Gandey**, BSc Hons, PGCE

Deputy Head: Mr Paul Kershaw, BSc Hons, PGCE, MA

Academic Deputy: Mr Jon Millward, BSc Hons, PGCE

Staff:

Heads of Division:
Mrs Rebecca Smith, BA Hons, PGCE (*Junior Division*)
Mr Joshua Rowe, BSc, PGCE (*Middle Division*)
Mr Michael Awdry, BA Hons, PGCE (*Sixth Form*)

Heads of Department:
Mrs Deborah Buckner, BA, MA (*Psychology*)
Mrs Michelle Burton, BA, PGCE (*Drama*)
Mrs Patricia Carey, BA Hons, PGCE (*Computer Science*)
Mrs Olga Clarke, PGCE, Maîtrise MA, Licence/Deug BA (*Modern Languages*)
Mrs Kim Cook, BEd Hons, Dip Ed, AMBDA (*Learning Development*)
Mrs Maria Heslop, MBA, BA Hons, Cert Ed (*History*)
Mr Gary Hatter, MEd, PGCE (*Art*)
Ms Karen Johnson, BA Hons, PGCE (*Media and Film Studies*)
Mrs Sarah Kershaw, BA Hons, PGCE (*Music*)
Mr Jonathan Millward, BSc Hons, PGCE (*Science & Maths*)
Mrs Louise Neill, BSc Hons, PGCE (*Geography*)
Ms Nicola Phipps, BA Hons, PGCE (*English*)
Mrs Candy Prodrick, BD, PGCE (*Religious Studies*, *PSHE*)
Mr Joshua Rowe, BSc, PGCE (*Physical Education*)
Mrs Helen Startup, BSc Hons, PGCE (*Design Technology*)

Preparatory School:
Head: Ms Dani Saffer, BEcon, BPsych, MEd
Head of Pre-Prep: Mrs Melanie Ireland

Registrar: Mrs Tiffany Hyatt
School Secretaries: Ms Sarah Goulden; Miss Grace Pugsley

Bethany School

Curtisden Green, Goudhurst, Cranbrook, Kent TN17 1LB

Tel: 01580 211273
email: registrar@bethanyschool.org.uk
website: www.bethanyschool.org.uk
Twitter: @bethanyschkent
Facebook: @bethanyschkent
LinkedIn: /Bethany-School-Kent

The School was founded in 1866 by the Revd J J Kendon. It is a Charitable Trust administered by a Board of Governors, a member of the Association of Governing Bodies of Independent Schools.

Bethany has 335 pupils, aged 11 to 18. Approximately 30% board on either a weekly or termly basis, with a varied weekend programme of activities available for termly boarders. A generous staff to pupil ratio of 1:8 ensures small classes and high quality pastoral care. Individuals are encouraged to develop their potential to the full in academic and all other respects. Most teaching takes place in modern classroom blocks, the result of an ongoing building development programme. Development in ICT has been a priority at Bethany: a wireless network enables pupils from Year 7 upwards to use laptops across the curriculum.

The Orchard, our dedicated Sixth Form Boarding House, offers single study-bedrooms with en-suite facilities, study rooms for day pupils and communal facilities. Recent additions to the School include a brand new six-lane, 25m indoor swimming pool, a state-of-the-art fitness suite and a new Sixth Form centre as an extension of The Orchard and an extension to the outdoor events facility. Our next major project will be the Performing Arts Centre.

Situation. The School occupies a scenic, 60-acre, rural campus in the heart of the Kent countryside, easily accessible from most parts of South East England: an hour from Charing Cross (Marden Station) and easy access to Gatwick and Heathrow Airports, the Channel ports and Ashford and Ebbsfleet International railway stations.

Admission. The normal age of entry is at 11 or 13 by the School's Entrance Assessment and at Sixth Form level based on predicted GCSE grades, but the School welcomes pupils to the Bethany community at other stages if places are available.

Fees per term (2021–2022). Year 7: £5,970 (day), £9,270 (weekly boarding), £9,995 (full boarding); Year 8: £6,175 (day), £9,485 (weekly boarding). £10,215 (full boarding); Years 9–13: £6,595 (day), £10,235 (weekly boarding), £11,250 (full boarding). Dyslexia and Learning Support £695 (full time), £350 (part time); English as an Additional Language Support £695 (Years 7–11), £350 (Years 12–13).

Scholarships and Bursaries. Academic Scholarships are awarded based on performance in the Entrance Examination. Scholarships are also available in Performing Arts, Creative Arts and Sport at the main points of entry, which are Years 7 and 9 and into the Sixth Form. The Christopher Jackson Scholarship is available for pupils who attend state primary schools local to Bethany, are particularly able and have a capacity for academic excellence. Means-tested bursaries are also available.

Children of members of HM Forces and the Clergy receive a 10% fee discount.

Curriculum. The broad curriculum is based on the National Curriculum. The full range of subjects is taught including Information Technology from 11+ and Spanish from 13+. We have also introduced Mandarin at Year 7 and GCSE Dance. There are 26 GCE A Level subjects, including Economics, Business Studies, Spanish, Government and Politics, Music, Photography, Politics, Textiles, Theatre Studies and Media Studies. We also offer BTECS and Applied A Levels in Business Studies, Finance, PE and Music. Almost all Sixth Form leavers proceed to degree courses at University.

Dyslexia. The Dyslexia and Learning Support department, which enjoys an international reputation, has been supporting pupils at Bethany for over 30 years.

Games and Activities. The School offers a wide range of sporting opportunities and enjoys an extensive fixture list, having established a long tradition of inter-school Sport. Facilities include a Sports Centre, climbing wall, fitness room, three squash courts, tennis courts, an indoor swimming pool and a floodlit AstroTurf. There is also a wide range of clubs and activities. The Duke of Edinburgh's Award scheme is well established at Gold, Silver and Bronze levels.

Music. There are wide-ranging opportunities for instrumental tuition. There are sectional instrumental groups including: a Symphony Orchestra, Rock School, Jazz Band, Concert Band, Brass Consort and a Choir, all making use of the fine Music School with its recording studio and music technology area.

Careers. The School is a member of Inspiring Futures and careers education is an important part of the Curriculum. Sixth Form pupils take part in the Coursefinder Analysis Scheme and receive detailed advice regarding Higher Education and Gap Year opportunities.

Chapel. The Chapel, built in 1878, is the focal point of School life. Bethany welcomes children of all faiths or none, and together they attend Chapel twice weekly.

Charitable status. Bethany School Limited is a Registered Charity, number 307937.

Governors:
Mr Jonathan Fenn, LLB (*Chair*)
Mrs Wendy Kent (*Vice Chair*)
Mr Peter Askew
Mrs Susan Bonell, OBE, BA, FCIS
Mr Keith Buckland
Mr Roger Clark
Mrs Elizabeth Connell, BA, LLB
Mr Andrew Cunningham
Dr Robert Hangartner, BSc, MB BS, MBA, FRCPath
Mr Matthew Harman, BSc Hons, MCIOB
Mr Nigel Kimber, BSc, FCA
Mrs Philippa Mackinnon
Mrs Gabby Power
Mrs Lindsay Roberts, BEd Hons
Mr Dan Shaw, BA, LLB

(To contact any member of the Governing Body please use the following address: c/o Bethany School, Curtisden Green, Goudhurst, Kent TN17 1LB Tel: 01580 211273)

Senior Staff:

Headmaster: Mr Francie Healy, BSc, HDipEd, NPQ

HR Manager: Miss Toni Carter, Chartered MCIPD
Bursar: Mrs Victoria Epps-Wood
Deputy Head Academic: Mrs Emily Hill BA Hons, PGCE (*English*)
Deputy Head Pastoral: Mr Alan Sturrock, BEd Hons (*DSL, Games, Geography*)

Teaching and House Staff:
Mr Ritchie Beckham, BA Hons (*English and Media*)
Mr Dariius Bell, BA Hons, MRes, PGCE (*English and Media, History*)
Mr Alex Bolton, BA Hons, NPQSL (*Director of Performing Arts, Head of Key Stage 4*)
Mr Jonny Brinson, BMus, PGCE (*Head of Music*)
Miss Leah Bullock, BA Hons (*Performing Arts Assistant*)
Mrs Nicola Clough, BDes, PGDE (*Art and Textiles, Assistant Head of Key Stage 4, Head of Kiplings*)
Mr Richard Clough, BA Hons, PGCE (*History, Assistant Head of Year 7 & 8*)
Mr Cliff Cooper, MSc (*Director of Outdoor Learning, Maths, Second Assistant Housemaster Kendon*)
Mr Simon Cuthbert (*Head of Religious Studies, Lay Chaplain*)
Mr Simon Davies, BA Hons (*Head of History & Politics, Housemaster The Orchard*)
Mr Simon Duff, BEd, TEFL, NPQML (*Head of Business Economics, Second Assistant Housemaster The Orchard, Head of 6th Form*)
Miss Mathilda Fuller (*Mathematics*)
Mrs Sarah Fuller, BSc Hons (*Speech Pathology and Therapy, Learning Support Assistant, Exam Access Arrangements*)
Mr Alejandro Garcia (*Spanish*)
Mr Sherrick Hamilton, BA Hons (*Head of Computing and IT Services*)
Mr Steve Hampton (*Food and Nutrition, Second Assistant Housemaster The Orchard*)
Mrs Kate Harper, BSc Hons QTS, PGCert SpLD (*School SENCo, Head of Dyslexia and Learning Success, Learning Support, Specialist Teacher*)
Miss Katie Hayward (*Art and Photography Technician, Trainee Teacher*)
Mrs Frances Healy, BA SpLD (*English*)
Mr Tom Henson, BA Hons (*Assistant Housemaster Kendon, Trainee Teacher*)
Mr Anthony Khan, BA Hons, PGCE (*Business Studies, Housemaster The Mount, Head of Student Enterprise*)
Miss Sam King, BA (*Head of Girls' Sport*)
Mr Adam Manktelow, BSc Hons, PGCE (*Joint Head of Maths*)
Miss Claire Mills, BEd Hons PGCert SpLD (*Learning Support Specialist Teacher, Head of Year 7 & 8*)
Mr Marcus Norman, BEd Hons (*Head of Design & Technology*)
Mr Matt Payne, BSc Hons, PGCE (*Director of Sport*)
Mrs Rachael Payne, BA Hons, PGCE (*Dance Lead*)
Mr Rob Philbin, BSc Hons, PGCE (*Biology Lead*)
Mr Devin Reilly, BSc Hons (*Science, Competitive House Coordinator*)
Ms Nicola Rendall-Jones, BA Hons, DTEFLA, PGCE (*Head of EAL*)
Mr Ceri Roberts (*Geography*)
Mrs Caroline Rowell (*Teaching Assistant Apprentice*)
Mrs Carly Shapland, BA Hons (*Head of English and Media*)
Miss Fleur-Estelle Shaw, MA PGCE (*Head of Geography, UCAS Coordinator*)

Mrs Sarah Smart, BA Hons, PGCE, NPQML (*Head of Art, Assistant Housemistress The Orchard*)

Mrs Anne-Marie Sturrock, BEd Hons (*DLS, EAL, PSHCE Coordinator*)

Mr Mike Thomas, MSc, PhD (*Head of Science, Physics Lead, Second Assistant Housemaster Mount*)

Mr James Vickerman, BSc Hons, PGCE (*Science, Housemaster Kendon*)

Mrs Jules Wareham, BEd Hons (*Maths, Games, Head of Year 9, Prep School Liaison, Second Assistant Housemistress The Orchard*)

Mr Michael Willis (*Head of Modern Foreign Languages*)

Ms Jada Woolf, BSc Hons, MEd (*Joint Head of Maths*)

Ms Leaf Ye Zhao (*Mandarin, Second Assistant Housemistress The Orchard*)

Key Support Staff:
Registrar: Mrs Sally Martorell, BA Hons
PA to Headmaster: Mrs Andrea Discombe
Finance Manager: Mrs Monica Beadsworth
Marketing Manager: Miss Caroline Webb, BA Hons, PGCE
Marketing Assistant: Mrs Sara Cooper
School Receptionists: Mrs Amy Mewse School; Mrs Ceri Mooney
Exams and Data Manager: Ms Katja Thornton
Librarian and Archivist: Mrs Claire Rendell
Senior Sister, Wellness Centre: Ms Rhiannon Eyre, RN, BSc Hons

Bournemouth Collegiate School

Senior School:
College Road, Southbourne, Bournemouth, Dorset BH5 2DY

Tel: 01202 436550
email: registrar@bcschool.co.uk
Twitter: @BCS_Senior
Facebook: @Bournemouthcollegiateschool
Instagram: @bcs_school

Prep School:
40 St Osmund's Road, Poole, Dorset BH14 9JY

Tel: 01202 714110
email: prep-admin@bcschool.co.uk
Twitter: @BCSPrep

website: www.bournemouthcollegiateschool.co.uk

Together we #achievetheextraordinary

Bournemouth Collegiate School offers the very best in independent co-education for ages 2–18 with boarding from age 11. Our Senior School is situated in a beautiful coastal location just a few minutes from Bournemouth beach and our Preparatory School is located in a spacious woodland setting in Lower Parkstone, Poole.

BCS provide a holistic teaching experience to all students, understanding that academic success is not the only principal factor in a child's education. Our mission is to equip our students with the tools and experiences for a successful and enriching future; helping them to realise their full potential for personal and academic excellence. We're proud to say the school saw record-breaking results at both GCSE and A Level for the academic year 2020–2021.

BCS provides a nurturing environment where the happiness of our pupils comes first. Our 'added value' extends to our variety of co-curricular opportunities and sporting and music programmes, that allow our pupils to cultivate new skills and develop into well-balanced, confident and versatile young people. BCS runs a successful Sports Academy for talented athletes that utilises our outstanding facilities across both sites, including indoor swimming pools at both schools, this was recognised at the Independent School's Association Awards 2021, when BCS were announced as winners of the award for Outstanding Sport (Large School).

We encourage independent learning and intellectual curiosity by providing pupils with a wide range of experiences including trips, seminars, talks by guest speakers and the opportunity for fun, expression and friendship in the many school events on offer. Our aim is to inspire each pupil to make the most of their talents. This way the pupils at BCS, of any age, grow in self-esteem, develop resilience, have a sense of adventure and are equipped to flourish as young adults.

Fees (2021–2022)

Prep School (termly): £1,810–£4,025.

Senior School (annual): Day Pupil £15,240, Weekly Boarder £28,740, EU/Full time Boarder £32,090, International Boarder £37,850.

For more information regarding fees please visit bournemouthcollegiateschool.co.uk.

Scholarships and Bursaries. Each year, we are proud to award a limited number of scholarships to pupils who are capable of extremely high levels of achievement and who we believe will make a significant contribution to the life of the school.

Bursary support is also available through a means-tested application process. For more information please visit our website or contact us at registrar@bcschool.co.uk

Headmaster: **Mr Russell Slatford**, BSc, MA Cantab

Senior Deputy Head: Mrs Maria Coulter, BSc Hons, PGCE, NPQH, Dip Ed

Head of Prep School: Miss Kay Smith, BEd, NPQH

Box Hill School

Mickleham, Dorking, Surrey RH5 6EA

Tel: 01372 373382
           01372 385002 (Registrar for Overseas Admissions)
           01372 384240 (Registrar for UK Admissions)
email: registrar@boxhillschool.com
website: www.boxhillschool.com

Affiliations: The Society of Heads, Round Square, BSA, AGBIS, ISBA, BAISC, IBO, DofE, NAGC.

Box Hill School is a co-educational school set in forty acres of grounds in the heart of the Surrey countryside, offering day, weekly and full boarding places for 11–18 year olds. We have a strong educational, artistic and sporting tradition; however, what makes us stand out is that we discover and nurture the talents and abilities of every individual student, so that they can unlock their potential and in doing so, develop confidence and resilience. Box Hill School is proud of its academic attainment and broad curriculum. Academic standards are high given the non-selective approach to education and students achieve above national averages in public exams.

In the Sixth Form, students can choose to study either the IB Diploma Programme or A Levels. Subject combinations are flexible within the constraints of our options timetable system, and we aim to cater for as wide a range of choices as possible.

Box Hill School is a proud founder member of Round Square, an international network of over 200 schools worldwide united by a set of 'IDEALS': Internationalism, Democracy, Environmental concern, Adventure, Leadership and Service which are at the core of the school's ethos.

All the Houses at Box Hill School are small and friendly, and the students often mention they enjoy the 'home away from home' environment. The Boarding Houses each board around 20–35 pupils with the majority of boarders' rooms being doubles and triples, particularly at Key Stage 4 and above. First-time Boarders are reassured by the family structure of our Houses and find them easy to settle into. To strengthen the bond between students even further, a central school dining room is provided and students are allocated to competitive group teams for school-wide competitions. Full-time Boarders also enjoy a variety of outings at the weekend. An on-site medical centre is provided, staffed by qualified nurses with two non-resident school doctors on call. Boarders may stay in school during term time, except at half terms. There are no 'exeat' weekends.

We provide strong pastoral support for each student, each one being assigned to a House, complete with common room and kitchen. The Houses are run by teaching House staff and each student is assigned to a personal tutor within their house – a member of teaching staff who supports their academic and pastoral development.

We believe that activities outside the classroom form an important part of education, and all students take part in the extensive timetabled activities programme. As well as this regular programme, younger students take part in expeditions around the UK twice a year. The Duke of Edinburgh's Award is particularly strong in the school. Students have the opportunity to participate in Round Square expeditions, carrying out community based projects in locations including Peru and South Africa. They also have the opportunity to go on an exchange to another Round Square school overseas.

The school has an active Parents Association, comprised of supportive parents and friends of the school who maintain links with the local community as well as running social functions and fundraising events. Parents are strongly encouraged to join.

Special features of the School:

- International opportunities through Round Square membership
- IB World School
- Small classes and a high level of academic support
- Outstanding pastoral care
- Weekly and termly co-curricular activities for all students from an exciting and wide range of options from Chamber Orchestra to High Ropes.

- International Study Centre

Courses offered. GCSE: Mathematics, English Language, English Literature, Biology, Chemistry, Physics, Geography, History, Business Studies, Computer Science, French, Spanish, Music, Art, Textiles Design and Fashion, Drama, Physical Education, Design Technology.

IB: Biology, Environmental Systems, Business and Management, Mathematics – Analysis & Approaches, Mathematics – Applications & Interpretation, Chemistry, Psychology, Economics, English Language and Literature, Visual Arts, Geography, History, Russian, Italian, French, Spanish, German, Physics. We aim to offer all other IB approved languages in any year, subject to demand.

A Level: Art, Biology, Business Studies, Chemistry, Economics, English, Further Mathematics, Geography, History, Mathematics, Physics, Psychology.

Sports. Athletics, basketball, cricket, football, hockey, netball, rounders, rugby and tennis as competitive sports but many others as part of the activities programme such as dance, kickboxing, pilates, golf, swimming, volleyball, mountain biking and multi-gym.

Drama, Music and Art. Art students gain excellent examination grades each year, with many going on to be accepted at major art schools. Our purpose-built Music School enables a wide range of musical opportunities within school, including a choir, Year 7 choir, rock band and performance opportunities for individual vocalists and instrumentalists. The school stages senior and junior productions each year and has performed *The Great Gatsby, Blood Brothers, Wendy & Peter Pan* and an innovative and original festival, *A Festival of Music and Mayhem,* to name a few. LAMDA coaching is available and the school has an excellent record in these examinations.

Fees per annum (2021–2022). Day from £18,525; Weekly Boarding from £23,985; Full Boarding from £30,750.

Scholarships. A variety of awards are offered for entry to Box Hill School; the latest information can be found on the school's website. Scholarships are available for those entering Years 7, 9 and the Sixth Form, under the following categories: Academic, Art, Drama, Music and Sport.

Bursaries are available on application following registration and are subject to means-testing and are offered on the basis of a formula laid out in the school's Scholarships and Bursaries Policy which is available on request from the school. All bursaries are reviewed annually.

Method of Entry. Entry is based on an interview, the two most recent reports from the pupil's present school, and written tests in Maths and English. Sixth Form entry is based on report, interview and GCSE predictions. For overseas pupils a personal interview on site is desirable but we are happy to conduct a virtual interview if necessary. Main school entrance ages are 11, 13 and 16 years. Under normal circumstances, we like to meet prospective pupils and their parents or guardians – this also gives you an opportunity to have a look around our campus facilities and meet key staff and students.

Charitable status. Box Hill School Trust Limited is a Registered Charity, number 312082. It exists to promote the advancement of education.

Chairman of Governors: Mr Trevor Johnson

***Headmaster*: Mr Cory Lowde**

Chief Operating Officer: Mr Stuart Ansell

Registrar for Overseas Students: Mrs Kirstie Hammond

Registrar for UK Students: Mrs Claire Jordan

Headmaster's PA: Mrs Kate Kench

Bredon School

Pull Court, Bushley, Tewkesbury, Gloucestershire GL20 6AH

Tel: 01684 293156
email: admissions@bredonschool.co.uk
website: www.bredonschool.org
Twitter: @BredonSchool
Facebook: @Bredon-School
LinkedIn: /bredon-school-2002-limited

Age Range. 7–18.

Number of Pupils. 240: Boarders 89, Day 151.

Bredon School is a co-educational independent boarding and day school located in the beautiful Gloucestershire countryside. The School supports children with dyslexia to achieve their potential in a caring, nurturing environment. The inspiring location, wide-ranging curriculum and vast outdoor environment enables all pupils to find an area in which to shine; whether that is on the school farm, within the forest school, out on the sports fields, taking part in outdoor education and adventure activities, or joining our thriving Combined Cadet Force. The opportunities are endless.

Ethos. Bredon educates the whole child through sound, realistic academic provision, sympathetic pastoral care delivered through a House system, regular leadership challenges and a varied sports programme. The small and friendly environment allows children of all ages to thrive and achieve academic success.

Learning Support. The school is internationally-renowned for its expertise in supporting children with dyslexia and is CReSTeD-accredited, holding Dyslexia Specialist Provision (DSP) status. Within its dedicated Learning Support Centre, an extensive range of specialist software and specialist tuition allows pupils to organise their thoughts, practice their skills and use voice-activation to enhance their individual progress.

Curriculum. Bredon provides a broad academic curriculum at all Key Stages through to GCSE and A Level. In addition Bredon offers extensive vocational programmes at Foundation, Intermediate and Advanced levels. The School Farm offers a vocational route for those interested in pursuing a career in agriculture or land-based studies. Class sizes across the school average 8–12 and the teacher to pupil ratio is 1:5.

Physical & Outdoor Education. In addition to the many sporting opportunities on offer; including frequent competitive fixtures with local schools, there is a fully-equipped gymnasium, a 30-metre sports hall, a climbing wall and bouldering course, a clay shooting ground, plus numerous outdoor sports pitches and cross country running trails. Bredon also has a swimming pool, a canoe launch onto the River Severn, a forest school and thriving School Farm with rare breed pigs, cattle, sheep, Shetland ponies and

fowl, which add to the amount of time children spend learning outdoors and engaged in practical activity. The school also organises an extensive range of trips and expeditions through the Duke of Edinburgh's Award scheme and dedicated overnight outdoor education activities.

Clubs and Activities. There are many thriving lunchtime clubs including model making and music activities. In addition, once a week, the afternoon lessons are given over to activities and the children can choose from activities as varied as sailing, cycling, dancing, music, art, cookery, magic club, fencing, engineering, farming and clay pigeon/air rifle shooting.

Boarders. There is provision for boarders from age 9 and they are cared for by house parents, creating a real home from home environment. Accommodation is in dormitory-style rooms until Year 11 when boys move into individual study-bedrooms. All girls have individual rooms. Boarders have an extensive range of after school activities to participate in and there is a lively schedule of weekend events too.

Pupils join us from the local area, the UK and the wider world, and come together to form a vibrant community of learners who are socially and morally responsible and who support one another on their journey towards becoming happy, healthy, confident and capable young people.

Admissions. Admission is by potential not just attainment, and all lessons are taught with dyslexia-friendly teaching in mind. There is no entrance examination, instead school reports and any specialist reports will be requested and assessed, followed by a 3 or 5-day 'taster' visit to the school to assess suitability. A place is usually offered upon completion of a satisfactory taster stay.

Fees per term (2021–2022). Day £4,000–£7,950; Boarding £8,785–£12,735.

Chairman of Governors: Mr Aatif Hassan

Headteacher: Mr Nick Oldham, BA Hons, QTS dip NLP

Bursar: Mr S Giles, BSc, FCCA

Senior Deputy Head: Mrs G Hamilton, PGCE
Deputy Head (Pastoral and Boarding): Mr T Butt, BSc Hons, PGCE, QTS
Deputy Head (Academic): Mr N Monk, BA Hons, PGCE, QTS, Level 7 Coaching and Mentoring

Director of Learning and Development: Mrs Kelly Weston, BSc Hons, PGCE, QTS, CPT3A, MEd SEND

Clifton High School

College Road, Clifton, Bristol BS8 3JD

Tel: 0117 973 0201 (School Office)
            0117 933 9087 (Admissions)
            0117 933 9083 (Finance)
email: admissions@cliftonhigh.co.uk
website: www.cliftonhigh.co.uk
Facebook: @CliftonHighSchoolBristol

Clifton High School is set in the beautiful surroundings of Clifton, situated in the heart of the village. Our central position in a city that is renowned for its culture and vibrant nature has helped to make Clifton High an exciting and dynamic School that embraces tradition but is unafraid of change.

Clifton High School was founded over 140 years ago as a girls' school, and today is a thriving co-educational 3–18 school of around 600 pupils. We pride ourselves on our family ethos, valuing the emotional and personal development of each child as much as the academic; fostering excellent relationships between staff, pupils and parents and enabling each pupil to reach their full potential.

Our small class sizes allow for a strong rapport between teachers and pupils, providing encouragement and support to every single child, pupil and student, creating an atmosphere where everyone can develop happily and progress successfully.

"Realising Individual Brilliance" is more than just a catchline for our School. Focusing on the individual child is embedded in everything we aim to do at Clifton High School. Whether it is developing a pupil's passion, catering for individual learning needs, stretching and challenging academic ability, exploring and enjoying sports and outdoor activities or embracing environmental issues, we are proud that the experience a Clifton High education provides is a bespoke offering, with no two pupils taking the same path through school.

Our Diamond Edge Model and focus on academic rigour, combined with outstanding pastoral care, means that the individual is at the centre of our work.

Aims, Ethos and Values.

Our overarching school aim is simple: *To realise individual brilliance.*

Our small class sizes and focused tutoring allows us to know our pupils in ways not always possible in larger schools. Our school ethos helps to create a community to support this:

At Clifton High School, we want to ensure that all pupils enjoy learning, see the worth in a holistic education and to try their very best. We want pupils to learn how to deal with success and defeat, and over time to discover their individual brilliance so that they can become passionate in their interests and, consequently, have fulfilling careers, providing the potential to live full and satisfying lives. Our School Ethos will celebrate the individual, in all the ways that we are different and ultimately all the ways each of us is unique. We should be proud of who each of us is; our sex, gender, gender reassignment, age, race, colour, nationality, ethnic or national origin, disability, sexual orientation, religion, faith or other beliefs. Clifton High School's ethos will look to create a safe culture in which our school aim, to realise individual brilliance, can be achieved.

Our aim and ethos are further supported by four key values which are embedded in our school community: Curiosity, Empathy, Love, and Direction.

- *Curiosity:* From curiosity comes learning, the bedrock of any school. We aim to promote a sense of curiosity in all our young people, to instil a love of learning in all areas of school life, promoting informed questioning and debate alongside self-motivation and the passion to explore new ideas independently.
- *Empathy:* You never really understand a person until you consider things from their point of view. We aspire to foster empathy in all our young people which will allow them to operate in a world which is dependent on human interaction and will give them the necessary skills and desire to change the world in positive ways. Empathy is

the foundation of kindness and kindness the route to a fulfilling life.
- *Love:* Love is the value that makes our relationships better, whether those relationships are with others or with oneself. Love for others means wanting what is good for them and can be achieved more effectively when one has love for oneself, providing self-confidence and resilience to face the challenges in the world. We also celebrate a love for the natural world, encouraging a passion for being outdoors and, consequently, nurturing a desire to preserve our planet for the generations to come.
- *Direction:* We value aspiration and achievement in all things, both within and beyond the curriculum. We encourage the highest ambition and personal commitment and aim to support individuals to achieve the goals they set themselves. Having direction gives purpose and drives motivation.

Facilities. The School is located on the edge of Clifton Village, which provides a wealth of resources for the children and young people – from local businesses and artists to outdoor spaces. The excellent facilities and accommodation include a brand new Sixth Form Centre, Science department with seven laboratories, a STEM room, well stocked libraries and over 250 networked workstations, a multimedia language laboratory and a performing arts theatre and cinema and Nursery Pre-School provision: The Hive. Sports facilities include a heated 25m indoor swimming pool with spectator's gallery, a gymnasium featuring a climbing wall and floodlit multi-games courts on site. Professional grade off-site sports facilities, in partnership with the University of Bristol, include an indoor tennis centre (with four courts), ten outdoor courts, newly refurbished 3G pitches and grass pitches for football, rugby and cricket.

Outdoor learning includes an environmental pond, eco garden and vegetable beds. The School is proud to hold the green flag Eco Schools Award. This encourages the children to make the most of the outdoor teaching space nurturing each child, not only to appreciate the environment, but also to provide the opportunity for imagination, social interactions and to learn about responsibility.

Curriculum. Class sizes average 16 in the Infants and Junior School and 18 in the Senior School.

The Hive Nursery Pre-School and Reception classes follow the Foundation Stage curriculum, focusing upon: personal, social and emotional development; communication; language and literacy; problem solving, reasoning and numeracy; knowledge and understanding of the world; physical development and creative development. The children enjoy a myriad of experiences in a safe and stimulating environment with highly experienced teaching staff, who place a strong emphasis on exploration, investigation, discovery and problem solving through teaching and free-play activities. The large and light classrooms within handsome Victorian buildings are a hive of activity; 'Busy Bees' will make use of the department's own wildlife pond, mud kitchen, fire pit and outdoor classroom as part of our onsite Forest School provision and a STEAM room.

Years 1 and 2, children are taught in large, bright, airy rooms which ensure plenty of space for creative, practical, lively activities. Boys and girls are taught by highly experienced and well-qualified teachers and teaching assistants who are always prepared to go that extra mile to increase the experiences and opportunities for the children.

The curriculum also includes English, Mathematics, French, IT, Science, History, Geography, Art, Music, Swimming and Games. Children in Years 1 and 2 enjoy regular visits to a nearby Forest School throughout the year. Happy, excited, secure learners leave Year 2 ready to embrace the challenges and opportunities that Junior School will bring.

The *Junior School* gives children a strong grounding in English, Mathematics, Science, ICT, History, Geography, Modern Languages, Music, Art, Drama, Religious Studies, PE, Swimming and Games (Netball, Hockey, Rugby, Football, Tennis, Rounders and Cricket). As children progress through the Junior School, a greater number of subjects are taught by specialist teachers, for example Modern Languages, Art, Mathematics, Science, Music, Swimming and PE. Learning in the Junior School is engaging, exciting, challenging and fun and children are encouraged to be curious, creative and confident. Boys and girls are taught the skills they need to become self-motivated, inquisitive, enthusiastic learners who embrace the opportunities life has to offer. Clifton High enjoys an enviable reputation for the breadth of extra-curricular activities that are available and their *Enrichment Programme* allows the children to experience a diverse range of activities outside the normal curriculum. including Choirs, Orchestra, Speech and Drama, Dance and Art and Craft, together with a wide range of sports clubs. Visiting speakers and regular trips to the local area and further afield enhance the curriculum in all departments. Children in the Junior Department also have the opportunity to enjoy a residential trip each year.

The *Senior School* is fully co-educational throughout. Boys and girls are taught separately for English, Mathematics, Physics, Chemistry and Biology in Years 7–9 and together in all other subjects before moving back into fully mixed classes for their chosen examination subjects when they reach Year 10. This is the pioneering Diamond Edge Model of education and Clifton High School is the only school in the Bristol area to adopt this approach. Year 7–9 pupils study a broad and balanced curriculum including English, Mathematics, Physics, Chemistry, Biology, Computing, History, Geography, modern languages (French, German, Spanish), Latin, Drama, Music, Art & Design, Food & Nutrition, Product Design, Textiles, PE and Personal, Social, and Health Education (PSHE). For study at GCSE there is a common and balanced core of English, Mathematics, separate sciences, humanities and a modern foreign language, in addition to which pupils may select subjects based on their interests and career plans. There is also a newly introduced programme of Life Skills and Competencies which runs alongside the GCSE courses and provides further opportunities for pupils to develop and identify extra skills, qualifications and interests. The school has an excellent academic record at GCSE and A Level. Throughout the Senior School and Sixth Form pupils have a personal tutor who monitors their academic and social welfare.

The co-educational *Sixth Form* is a thriving centre of excellence within the School. The students play an important part in the whole school community, developing their leadership skills through a peer support scheme with younger pupils, the House system, the Pupil Council, the Head's Team, the Eco Club Committee and many other opportunities. Students have a wide choice of A Level subjects. The most able are encouraged to submit Oxbridge and Russell Group University applications, and the vast majority of those who apply gain the offer of a place. All Sixth Form students take part in Futures and Skills which is an enrichment programme designed to offer a range of experiences and also have individual careers guidance sessions. All students have regular one-to-one tutorials. Sixth Form students holding scholarships are encouraged to manage the Scholars' Forum by producing an annual programme of debates and current affairs discussions with other pupils in the Senior School and for inviting speakers in to the school to talk on specific topics of interest.

International. Clifton High School has a successful track record in educating international students and is a sponsor for UK Visas and Immigration. Despite not being an international school, Clifton High embraces the cultural and social diversity that international students bring. For those parents looking for a first-class English education which offers a true integration into British culture and education then Clifton High School is the school for you. For international students whose parents will remain overseas, the School offers a unique home boarding service where students live with a local family. This is only available to students aged 16 or over.

Physical Education is a key part of the curriculum, not only for competitive sport, but for promoting a healthy lifestyle through the enjoyment of sport and exercise. The School has unique partnerships with sporting associations such as Bristol Rugby, the Lawn Tennis Association, the University of Bristol and Bristol Henleaze Swimming Club. The programmes that they run within the school provide pupils with elite coaching and player pathways up to international standard, forging links with the School's growing Talented in Sport programme. In addition to the School's traditional sports of hockey, netball, football, rugby, swimming, athletics, rounders, cricket, tennis and gymnastics, specialist staff also teach a wide variety of other activities including Olympic level synchronised swimming, squash, badminton, basketball, climbing, water polo and trampolining. Boys and girls regularly gain county and national honours and both boys and girls sports teams perform strongly in their relevant leagues and tournaments.

Music and Drama. Virtually any instrument, including voice, may be studied, with around 153 instrumental lessons taking place in school each week. Associated Board examinations are taken. There are opportunities to belong to orchestras, wind bands, drama groups and choirs who perform in a variety of concerts and productions throughout the year including some of the highest profile events in the school calendar. In Speech and Drama, a large number of pupils enter LAMDA examinations and consistently achieve outstanding results. Many Clifton High School pupils have gone on to study at top drama schools and are now working within the industry.

Charitable and Extra-curricular Activities. Pupils have a strong sense of social responsibility and are actively involved in various local and national charity fundraising events throughout their time at Clifton High School. Annual collections amount to several thousand pounds. The School also shares its expertise in a range of subjects with schools and groups across Bristol through its 'Masterclasses on the Move' initiative; a diverse programme that offers complimentary educational workshops to schools, nurseries, pre-schools and playgroups in Bristol and the surrounding area. There is an extensive extra-curricular activities programme throughout the school, responding to pupils' interests. Clubs are split into three categories: Skills Development, Academic Progress and Individual Brilliance.

There are over 100 clubs running in the three categories throughout the year, including Fencing, Dance, Water Polo, Tumble Club, Judo Club, Art Club, Orchestra, Climbing Club, Eco Club, App Building and 3D Printing Club. Clifton High School is particularly successful in running the Duke of Edinburgh's Award and World Challenge expeditions every year. There is a rich programme of trips both home and overseas.

Admission and Scholarships. Entry to The Hive Nursery Pre-School, Infants and Junior School is through in-class assessment by the class teacher and taster session with the relevant class. Entry to the Senior School is dependent on the results of an entrance examination, interview with the Head of School and school report. Pupils in Clifton High School Year 6 also sit the entrance examination to the Senior School. A good number of scholarships are awarded for Year 7 and Sixth Form entry, with flexibility for awards at entry to other year groups. Means-tested school-assisted places are available at all Senior School levels. Music and Sports awards are also available on entry to the Senior School, with sports, performing arts and creative arts awards available in the Sixth Form. Further details may be obtained from the School Registrar and Admissions Manager.

Fees per term (2021–2022). Tuition: The Hive Nursery Pre-School £61.50 per day; Infants: Reception £2,990 per term, Years 1–2 £3,620; Junior School (Years 3–6) £3,680; Senior School (Years 7–11) £5,285; Sixth Form (Year 12) £5,285 (fixed for the duration of the two years); Sixth Form (Year 13) £5,180 (fixed fees for the second year)

The Hive Nursery and Reception now accept 15 free hours per week for children under 5 years old.

Lunch: Years 1–6 £255, Years 7–13 £272.

Termly fees across the school are inclusive of all compulsory educational visits.

Reductions for siblings concurrently in the school (except where fees are paid by an authority or bursary): 2nd–7%; 3rd–15%; 4th–25%.

Charitable status. Clifton High School is a Registered Charity, number 311736. It exists to provide first-class education for pupils aged 3 to 18 years.

Patron: Dr Richard Gliddon Phd, BSc, FI Biol

Chair: Mr J Caddy BSc

Head of School: **Mr Matthew Bennett**, BSc, Ed Educ Hons Exeter, MSc Oxford

Director of Operations: Mrs Louise Brennan

Senior Master: Mr Manolis Psarros, BA Hons UCW Lampeter, MA, MEd Bristol
Deputy Head/Second Master: Dr Mark Caddy, BSc Hons, PhD Warwick
Deputy Head Academic: Mr Christopher Collins, MA Oxford, PGCE
Deputy Head Pastoral: Mr Luke Goodman, BA Hons Birmingham, PGCE
Assistant Head – Pupil Voice and Staff Development: Mrs Louise Brackenbury, BSc Hons UWIC, PGCE
Head of Sixth Form: Miss Katherine Rich, BA, Birmingham, PGCE

Child Protection and Safeguarding:
Mr Luke Goodman, BA Hons Birmingham, PGCE (*Designated Safeguarding Lead*)
Ms Alison Taylor, BSc Hons Reading, MEd Bristol, PGCE (*Deputy Designated Safeguarding Lead*)

Miss Claudia Mulholland, BSc Hons Swindon, PGCE (*Designated Safeguarding Lead Support – The Hive and Infants*)
Mrs Helen Tabb, BA Hons Surrey, QTS (*Designated Safeguarding Lead Support – Juniors*)
Miss Natasha Widdison, BA Joint Hons Nottingham (*Designated Safeguarding Lead Support – Years 7–11*)

Senior School Teachers:
* *Head of Department*

Art and Design:
*Mr Paul Ayers, BA Hons Cornwall, MA Falmouth, PGCE
Miss Lisa Davies, BA Hons Leeds
Ms Claire Jaques, BA Hons Plymouth, PGCE

Business Studies:
*Mr Peter Jackson, BA Hons Westminster, PGCE

Classics:
*Mrs Elizabeth Marriott, BA Oxford, MA London, PGCE
Mr Manolis Psarros, BA Hons UCW Lampeter, MA, MEd Bristol

Design and Technology:
*Mr Simon Francis BA Hons Bristol Polytechnic, PGCE (*School Curriculum Lead, Product Design*)
*Ms Angela Holland, BEd Hons, MSc Bristol (*Food and Nutrition*)
*Mr Bryan Murphy, MA Cambridge, PGCE (*Design and Innovation*)
*Mrs Emma Studd, BA Hons, MA UWE, PGCE (*Art and Textiles*)

Drama:
*Mr Craig Pullen, BA Hons Manchester Metropolitan, MA Leeds Metropolitan, PGCE
Mrs Susan Johnson-Martin, BA Hons Royal Holloway College London, PGCE

English:
*Mrs Philippa Lyons-White, BA Hons Bristol, PGCE
Miss Israel Gayton, BA Hons Exeter, PGCE
Mr Christopher Hope, BA Hons Hull, MA Birmingham, PGCE [Paternity Leave]
Mrs Siobhan Hosty, MA Kingston
Mr Manolis Psarros, BA Hons UCW Lampeter, MA, MEd Bristol
Mrs Catherine Quirk-Marku, BA Hons Lancaster, MEd Bristol, PGCE

Geography:
*Mrs Laura Giles, BSc Hons Loughborough, PGCE
Mr Luke Goodman, BA Hons Birmingham, PGCE
Mrs Amy Schmid, BA Hons Birmingham, PGCE

History:
*Mr Oliver Mullins, BA Hons Birmingham, PGCE
Miss Rachel Coleman, MA St Andrews, PGCE

Digital Learning:
*Mr James Webber, BA Hons Sheffield, PGCE
Mr Samuel Mazzarella, MMus Cambridge, PGCE
Mr Richard Shelswell, MEng Hons Bath, PGCE

Mathematics:
*Mr Andrew Hillman, BSc Hons Nottingham, PGCE
Dr Mark Caddy, BSc Hons, PhD Warwick
Mr Christopher Collins, MA Oxford, PGCE
Mr Andrew Harkin, MSc Dublin Institute of Technology, PGCE
Mr Matthew Izzard-Clark, MEng Hons Bristol, PGCE

Mr Richard Shelswell, MEng Hons Bath, PGCE
Ms Alison Taylor, BSc Hons Reading, MEd Bristol, PGCE

Modern Languages:
*Miss Natasha Widdison, BA Joint Hons Nottingham, PGCE
*Ms Rebecca Bartlett, BA Hons Exeter, PGCE (*Spanish*)
*Mrs Tara Harris, BA Hons Newcastle upon Tyne, PGCE (*German*)
*Mrs Eulalia Ribot-Bruno, BA Hons Université de Provence, PGCE (*French*)

Music:
*Mr Andrew Cleaver, BA Hons Lincoln and Hull, QTS
*Mrs Donia Pieters, BA Hons Brunel, MMus Goldsmiths, QTS (*Senior School Music – Academic*)
Mr Samuel Mazzarella, MMus Cambridge, PGCE

Physical Education:
*Mr James Taylor, BSc Hons Sheffield Hallam (*School Sport and Extra-Curricular*)
*Miss Rebecca McInnes, BSc Hons UWIC, PGCE (*Acting Head of Girls' Games*) [Maternity Leave]
*Mr Thomas Morison, BEd Hons St Mark and St John, QTS
*Mrs Lynne Reid, BSc Hons Cardiff, PGCE (*Head of School Girls' Games*) [Maternity Leave]
Mr Mike Wallington, BSc Hons Glamorgan, PGCE (*Games*)

Science:
*Miss Jennifer England, BSc Hons Exeter, PGCE (*Biology*)
Miss Rebecca Cole, BSc Hons Bath, PGCE (*Biology*) [Maternity Leave]
Mr Joseph Cozens, BSc Hons, Swansea (*Biology*)
Mr Henry Gauntlett, BSc Hons Cardiff (*Biology*)
Ms Louise Brackenbury, BSc Hons UWIC, PGCE (*Chemistry*)
*Mr Harry de Cothi, MChem Hons UCW, Cardiff, PGCE (*Chemistry*)
*Mr Paul Griffin, BSc Hons Birmingham, PGCE (*Physics*)
Mr Bryan Murphy, MA Cambridge, PGCE (*Physics*)

Enhanced Learning:
*Mrs Gabrielle Pilgrim BA Hons Reading, PGCE, BDA ATS, SpLD APC Patoss
Ms Vivienne Agoston, BSc UEA, PGCE
Mrs Lucie Bailey, BA Hons Lincoln, RSA CELTA TEFL
Ms Heidi Couper, BA Hons Bristol, PGCE
Mrs Faith Jameson BA Hons Warwick, PMP MA in SpLD/ Dyslexia
Mrs Sue Jones, BA Hons Bristol, PGCE
Mrs Amanda Swannell, BA Hons Hull, MA UWE, PGCE, PG Dip Dyslexia

The Hive and Infant School:
*Mrs Sarah Barker, BEd Hons UWE
Mrs Donna Andrews, BSc Hons Bath, QTS, EYPS
Miss Angharad Daker, BA Hons UWIC, EYTS
Mrs Sarah Manning, BEd Hons Kingston
Miss Claudia Mulholland, BSc Hons Swindon, PGCE
Mrs Caroline Pope, BA Hons London, PGCE
Mrs Olivia Price, BA Hons Kingston
Miss Kerry Quick BEd, Saint Mark and Saint John, Plymouth, QTS
Mr Samuel Rimmer, BSc Hons Leeds, MSc Brock Ontario, PGCE
Mrs Claire Shaw, BA Hons King Alfred's College, QTS

Junior School:
*Ms Alice Bagnall, BSc Hons UCW, Cardiff, PGCE (*Years 3–6*) [Maternity Leave]
Miss Lucy Buff, BA Hons University of Liverpool, PGCE
Mrs Hannah Crofts, BEd Hons Winchester
Miss Jesse Dyer, BA Hons Exeter, MSc Bristol
Mrs Pamela Eyles, BSc Hons Bristol, PGCE
Mrs Polly Gibbons, MA Hons St Andrews, PGCE
Ms Claire Jaques, BA Hons Plymouth, PGCE
Mr Charles Lowe, BA/Ed Joint Hons Goldsmiths
Mrs Bridget McDonnell, BA Hons Bristol Polytechnic, PGCE
Mr David Pye, BA Hons West London Inst of HE, PGCE
Mrs Helen Tabb, BA Hons Surrey, QTS

Teaching Assistants:
Mrs Lindsey Burch, NNEB, NVQ Level 3
Ms Alba Cirilo Cuadrado, Early Years Practitioner
Miss Debbie Clements, NNEB
Ms Karen Collins, Level 3 Supporting Teaching and Learning
Mr Alexander Minter-Swanell, BSc Warwick
Miss Hannah Pegler, BSc Hons Hartpury, Early Years Practitioner

Pupil Welfare Counsellor: Mrs Jackie Brangwyn, BEd Hons Sussex, MSc Bristol, Diploma

Business Support Staff:

Admissions, Development, Communications and Marketing:
*Miss Rebecca Brown (*Admissions, Development, Communications and Marketing Manager*)
Miss Bethany Curry (*Communications and Marketing Executive*)
Ms Carine Kenyon (*Development and Communications Officer*)
Mrs Sarah Maidment (*Admissions International Officer*)
Miss Rebekah Malvern (*Registrar and School Admissions Officer*)

Finance:
*Mr Michael Stewart (*Assistant Director of Finance and Operations*)
Mr Michael Richards (*Accounts Assistant*)

School Office:
*Miss Alice Bushell (*Events Manager*)
*Mrs Lucy Mansford (*Office Manager*)
Mrs Frances Avent (*Administrator Assistant, Quality Assurance, Facilities and Operations*)
Mrs Punam Kaur (*Administrator*)

Concord College

Acton Burnell Hall, Shrewsbury, Shropshire SY5 7PF

Tel:	01694 731631
email:	enquiries@concordcollege.org.uk
website:	www.concordcollegeuk.com
Twitter:	@ConcordCollege
Facebook:	@ConcordCollegeUK
Instagram:	@concordcollege
LinkedIn:	/concord-college-uk

Concord College is a highly successful, academic, co-educational international school for day and boarding students aged 13–18, providing GCSE/IGCSE and A Level courses. Set in 80 acres of Shropshire parkland, the College combines outstanding facilities with first-rate academic performance. The College is regularly rated in the top 10 schools in the UK. Students are cared for by a dedicated staff in a safe and beautiful environment. Concord is an international community dedicated to rigour, kindness and creativity and provides a vibrant and friendly environment in which students can flourish and fulfil their potential. Students are expected to display mutual respect and to promote harmony, decency and trust. The result is a happy and kind community in which students are polite, articulate and conscientious without ever losing their sense of fun.

Number of students. 600 (approximately equal numbers of boys and girls) of whom over 480 are boarders.

Facilities. The campus is centred around an historic hall which, with other college buildings, is set in beautifully maintained grounds. There has been considerable investment over the past 15 years with the addition of many modern facilities. Lessons are taught in well-equipped classrooms with excellent IT provision. The new state-of-the-art Science block comprises 22 laboratories including a special projects lab. The academic departments are well supported by a modern library complex in the Jubilee Building which students can access for their studies and reading for pleasure. There is a well-resourced theatre and music school, an excellent sports centre and indoor swimming pool as well as extensive grounds including sports pitches, tennis courts and a high ropes course. Most students have individual study-bedrooms, many with en-suite bathrooms. Meals are eaten in the College Dining Room where students can select from a variety of international cuisine. The wide range of facilities also includes common rooms and a student kitchen.

Wellbeing. All students have Tutors who have oversight of their pastoral wellbeing (as well as monitoring their academic progress). Boarding students also have boarding parents who focus on providing boarders with the emotional and practical support they need when they are away from home. Concord also offers support to students via Heads of Year in the Lower School and via our House system in the Upper School. Medical provision is available 24 hours-a-day, there is a modern and well-equipped medical centre and a dedicated nursing team. Mental health is taken very seriously, and support and counselling are available. The campus is secure and security staff are on duty at all times.

Education. Teaching groups average 16 students at GCSE and 14 students at A Level. Teachers are experts in their subjects. At GCSE, English, Mathematics and Sciences are compulsory. Optional subjects include Art, Astronomy, Computer Science, Economics, French, German, Geography, History, Music, Statistics, Religious Studies and Spanish. For GCSE sciences, Biology, Chemistry and Physics are taught as separate subjects and emphasis is placed upon laboratory experience.

Sixth Form students normally study at least three A Levels. There is also an opportunity to study for a further AS level or an EPQ which is an independent research project. Subjects include Art, Biology, Chemistry, Economics, English Language and Literature, French, Geography, History, Mathematics, Further Mathematics, Music, Physics and Spanish. All students who do not have a GCSE in English are expected to study English. There is a comprehensive careers programme to support all students with their university applications in the UK or overseas.

Reports to parents are sent at half term in the first term and subsequently at the end of each term. Parents also receive the results of weekly Saturday Tests.

Examination Results and University Entry. The College's students achieve excellent examination results; 2021 results were a new record for Concord College, 94% of grades at A level were A*/A (98% A*/B grade). The college has a particularly strong record of placing students into STEM courses at top universities, as well as into UK medical schools. 83% of 2021 leavers attained places at Top 10 universities (according to *The Times* World Rankings) or at medical school. In 2021, 11 students won places at Oxford or Cambridge, 19 at Imperial College London, 40 at University College London, 8 at the London School of Economics and Political Science and 15 at Kings College London. GCSE and IGCSE results are also impressive; in 2021 66% of GCSE grades were the highest possible grade, 9 or equivalent, and 94% were at grade 7 or more (A*/A).

Clubs, Sports and Extracurricular Activities. Students at Concord can choose from a multitude of activities. Many clubs and societies have an academic focus and are part of Concord's well-developed super-curriculum, for example the Medics Society, the Philosophy Club and numerous academic discussion groups.

Sports, music, dance and drama are also all available in our own facilities. There is a sports hall, squash courts and gymnasium as well as outdoor facilities including for football, athletics and tennis. A wealth of sporting activities are on offer ranging from archery to fencing and badminton to volleyball. There is a purpose-built dance studio and a range of gym equipment available for students to use after lessons and in the evenings.

Musicians can have individual instrumental tuition and join one of the chamber groups. Choir and singing lessons can develop all levels of vocal talent. Many other activities are also offered ranging from public speaking and chess to horse riding and charity fundraising. Students take part in Concord's outdoor education programme and the Duke of Edinburgh's Award scheme is also available. Whatever their talents, students are able develop them at Concord.

The School Week. Lessons run from 9.00am to 4.00pm Monday to Friday with Wednesday afternoon allocated to sport and an optional trip to Shrewsbury for senior students. There is compulsory supervised study (prep) each evening Monday to Friday.

Saturday mornings are used for subject testing. Subjects are tested in rotation allowing teachers and students alike to monitor academic progress. These tests are taken under examination conditions to help students to prepare for their GCSEs and AS and A Levels.

Selection for Entry. Applicants are selected on the basis of school reports, academic achievement, entry tests and interviews. Overseas applicants are required to sit Concord's entry tests to assess their potential for future study. Entry normally takes place into Year 9 (Form 3), Year 10 (Form 4) or Year 12 (Sixth Form).

Fees per annum (2021–2022). Full boarding fees are £47,500 per annum. Boarding fees are due for payment on a half yearly basis and invoices are issued accordingly. Day student fees are £15,600 per annum.

Scholarships and Bursaries. A fee reduction of between 5% and 10% of full fees may be available to Sixth Form students who have a particularly strong academic background. For entrants to GCSE classes, scholarship entry tests are administered. A number of means-tested bursaries are also available.

Charitable status. Concord College is a Registered Charity, number 326279. It exists to provide high quality education for secondary age students.

Chair of the Governors: Dr Iain M Bride

Clerk to the Governors and Bursar: Mrs Barbara Belfield-Dean

Principal: **Michael R Truss**, PhD, MPhys Oxon

Vice-Principal (Academic): Tom Lawrence, BA, PGCE
Vice-Principal (Pastoral): Jeremy Kerslake, MA
Head of Lower School: Mrs Rachel Coward, MEd, BEd
Assistant Principal: Phil Outram, PhD, BSc
Assistant Principal: Daniel Wilson, MA
Assistant Principal: Rob Pugh, PhD, BA

Principal's Personal Assistant & Admissions Registrar: Mrs Wendy Hartshorne

Dover College

Effingham Crescent, Dover, Kent CT17 9RH

Tel: 01304 205969
email: admissions@dovercollege.org.uk
website: www.dovercollege.org.uk
Twitter: @DoverCollege
Facebook: @DoverCollege
LinkedIn: /Dover-College

Dover College was founded in 1871 in the historic grounds of the old St Martin's Priory.

We are the closest school to continental Europe, one hour to Central London by train and within easy reach of London's airports.

We are a small, family-style school with a vibrant mix of local and international pupils. We expect academic excellence from our pupils, but also encourage them to find their talents in other areas such as art, drama, music and sport.

Co-education. Dover College (age 3–18) has been fully co-educational since 1975 and the 300+ boys and girls are integrated at all levels. There are 100 boarders.

Organisation. Our Muddy Knees Nursery & Prep School are located in their own comfortable building on the main College campus and accept day pupils aged 3–11. Our Senior School is for pupils aged 11–18 and we can accept day, weekly boarding and full boarding pupils. We have two boarding houses for girls and two for boys. Pupils in Shell and Remove have their own dedicated house, Priory, to help them with the transition from Prep to Senior School.

Catering. The catering team provides delicious, healthy, well-balanced homemade food and meals are taken in our historic Refectory.

Curriculum. We are academically ambitious. We take the time to really get to know each child so that the right balance of challenge and support is in place based on their needs. We recognise that success is as unique as the individual and we celebrate achievement where it represents the personal best for each child.

Our distinctive curriculum, connecting Early Years right through to Sixth Form, focuses on not only achieving results but also developing inquisitive and creative minds ready for the challenges ahead. We are a member of the Round Square organisation, a group of 150 worldwide schools, and share their commitment to an all-round education. We prize their values of Internationalism, Democracy, Environmentalism, Adventure, Leadership and Service.

Sixth Form. The Sixth Form is overseen by a Head of Sixth Form and pupils are able to choose A Levels and BTECs. Traditional academic subjects are provided, as are the practical subjects of art, design and technology, textiles, photography, drama and music.

Sixth Formers wear business attire and are given more choice and freedom than younger pupils, being expected to respond positively to their treatment as young adults. A well-equipped Sixth Form Centre is used as a meeting place and social club.

The School's Careers Adviser works in liaison with external agencies to plan, deliver and evaluate an integrated careers education and guidance programme. This enables pupils to gain the necessary knowledge, skills and understanding in order to make informed career plans before attending the universities of their choice.

International Study Centre (ISC). The International Department was started in 1957 and backed at the time by members of NATO, although international boarding has a far longer history than this starting point. The International Study Centre provides intensive English courses for pupils whose first language is not English. These courses vary in length and the aim is to enable all pupils to integrate fully into the life of Dover College as soon as possible after their arrival.

Individual Support. There is an Individual Needs Department in which pupils with learning difficulties (e.g. Dyslexia) receive 1:1 tuition. Each pupil has a member of staff as a personal tutor. The tutor supervises his/her pupils' general academic progress.

Learning Resources Centre. It provides cutting-edge facilities and resources to all pupils, including Careers information.

Sport. The School's main playing fields are a short distance away; on site are tennis courts, an astroturf, basketball court and an excellent Sports Hall with a fitness suite. Sports include Athletics, Badminton, Basketball, Cricket, Cross Country, Running, Football, Hockey, Netball, Rugby, Sailing, Tennis, Volleyball and various PE activities.

Swimming takes place at the indoor swimming pool in the local leisure centre. Golf may be played on local courses and horse riding is also offered locally through the School.

Extracurricular Activities. In addition to sport, pupils have the opportunity of taking part in a wide range of over 50 activities including Adventure Training, Art, Car Mechanic, Chess, Computing, Debating, Duke of Edinburgh's Award, Dancing, Fencing, First Aid, Horse Riding, Language Clubs, Music, Photography, Wine Tasting, Stage Management and Technology. The London West End theatres are within easy reach and regular trips to a variety of productions are made.

Pastoral Care. All pupils benefit from a carefully designed system of outstanding pastoral care. Every Dover College student belongs to a House and Boarders are provided with comfortable accommodation in one of four boarding houses. All Sixth Formers have single study-bedrooms. A Housemaster or Housemistress, supported by a team of tutors, runs each House; it is their role to give pastoral support as well as supervising the pupils' academic progress.

Pupils have access to a fully equipped and professionally staffed Medical Centre, which can accommodate pupils overnight.

Religious Life. College has its own Chapel and is a Church of England school. All pupils are encouraged to respect each other's beliefs and faiths from a position of tolerance and understanding.

Entry. Pupils are typically admitted into the Senior School at 11, 13 or 16 years old, but may come at any age. Most pupils join the College in September, but entry in January and April is possible.

Entry into Muddy Knees Nursery and Prep is by interview and an informal assessment carried out during a 'Taster Day' at the school. Entrance into the Senior School at 11+ and 13+ is dependent on previous school reports as well as an interview with the Headmaster. Provision is made for direct entry into the Sixth Form for boys and girls. This is normally conditional upon GCSE results. Further information can be obtained from Admissions.

Fees per term (2021–2022). Muddy Knees & Prep Day £3,075–£4,100; Senior Day £4,875–£5,950; Senior Weekly Boarding (up to 6 nights per week) £8,500–£10,050; Full Boarding £10,945–£12,250.

Scholarships. Academic Scholarships are awarded by competitive examinations.

Scholarships for Music, Drama, Art, Design Technology, Sport and All-Rounder are available by competitive interview.

Scholarships are available to pupils at 11+, 13+ and 16+ entry. Scholarships are not awarded to pupils in the Prep School.

Sibling Bursaries (5%) and Service Bursaries are automatically awarded. Members of HM Armed Forces and the Diplomatic Service who are eligible for the boarding allowance only pay a parental contribution of 10% of the full boarding fee.

Further details may be obtained on application to Admissions.

Old Dovorian Club. President: Mr Robert McAlpin, c/o Dover College.

Charitable status. Dover College is a Registered Charity, number 307856. The School exists to develop confidence and individual talents.

Chairman of Governors: Mr Michael Goodridge, MBE [Old Dovorian]

Headmaster: **Mr Simon Fisher**

Bursar & Clerk to the Governors: Mr Andrew Hodkinson, MBE

Deputy Head: Mme Therese Taylor

Deputy Head of Prep School: Mrs Tracey Mills

Head of International Study Centre: Mrs Clara Hebblethwaite

Director of Admissions & Marketing: Ms Alison Wilson

PA to the Headmaster: Mrs Jo Proctor

d'Overbroeck's

333 Banbury Road, Oxford OX2 7PL

Tel: 01865 688600
email: mail@doverbroecks.com
website: www.doverbroecks.com
Twitter: @doverbroecks
Facebook: @doverbroecksoxford
Instagram: @doverbroecks_oxford

Age Range. 11–18 (11–16: day only; 16–18: day and boarding).

Number in School. 702.

Fees per term (2021–2022). Tuition: £6,325 (Years 7–11); £8,300 (Years 12–13); £9,330–£10,150 (International School). Boarding: £4,150–£6,800.

d'Overbroeck's is a co-educational school in Oxford for students aged 11–18. We have day students only at the Years 7–11 site; a mixture of boarding and day students in the Sixth Form, and mainly boarding at our International School.

Our academic approach is characterised by small classes (maximum of 10 students per class in the Sixth Form and 15 up to GCSE) and a highly supportive and encouraging approach that builds on each student's strengths and enables outstanding academic achievements.

Teaching is highly interactive and seeks to generate enthusiasm for the subject, sound academic skills and effective working habits – while at the same time providing a thorough preparation for public examinations and ensuring that the learning experience is motivating and fun. The environment is friendly, stimulating and engaging with staff and students working together to achieve the best possible results.

A wide range of sporting and other extra-curricular activities is available to complement the learning in the classroom. Students can take part in numerous school events and performances as well as benefit from the wide range of educational, cultural and social activities which Oxford has to offer. We believe that happiness and success go hand in hand – and throughout the school we do our utmost to ensure that every student is given new opportunities to develop and is encouraged and rewarded – whether in the classroom, on stage or on the sports field.

Years 7–11, the Sixth Form and the International School are based on different sites, which allows each site to develop an individual sense of identity, as well as providing a clear sense of progression when students start their A Level studies and begin to make the transition towards university. Many students from other schools also join us for direct entry into our Sixth Form.

We expect high standards of commitment and effort from our students and have a track record of strong GCSE and A Level results, both in absolute terms and on a value-added basis. Students benefit from excellent teaching and a positive approach which enables them to maximise their potential. In 2021, for example, our students achieved 68% grade 9–7 (equivalent to A*–A) at GCSE and 67% grade A*–A at A Level. The overwhelming majority of students go on to university and we have an excellent record of success with entry to Oxford and Cambridge, as well as medical, law, veterinary and art schools.

Main Entry Points: at 11+, 13+ and directly into the Sixth Form, post GCSE.

Scholarships: Academic, Art, Music, Drama, Sport, Journalism.

***Principal*: Jonathan Cuff**, BA, MSc

Senior Vice Principal: Alastair Barnett, BA, PGCE (*History*)

Vice Principal (*Head of Years 7–11*): Jane Cockerill, BA, MEd, PGCE

Vice Principal (*Head of The International School*): Ted McGrath

Vice Principal (*Head of Sixth Form*): Alasdair MacPherson, MA (*English*)

Academic Director: Andrew Gillespie, MA

Pastoral Director: Sarah Squire, DPhil

Bursar: Georgina Paton
Assistant Bursar: Tammy Heavens

Chair of Governing Body: George Ghantous

Teaching Staff:
* *Head of Department or Departmental Coordinator*

Chris Almond, MChem, DPhil, PGCE (*Chemistry*)
Katie Amiri, BA, DELTA (*EAL*)
Nick Andrews, MSc, DPhil (*Maths*)
Louise Arnould, BA, PGCE (*Art*, *Textiles*)
Daniel Austin, BA DELTA (*EAL*)
Michelle Barratt, BSc, MA, DELTA (*EAL*)
Rebecca Bates, BSc, PGCE (*Biology*)
Rachel Bayley, BA, PGCE (*Music*)
Chrissie Beller, BTec, PGCE (*Photography**)
Shanti Bharatan, MSc, PhD (*Biology*)
Joe Bibby, BSc, PGCE (*Physics*)
Charlotte Bloomfield, BSc (*Physics*)
John Blythe, PTLLS (*Photography*)
Dave Borthwick, MChem, PhD (*Chemistry**)
Christophe Brinster, M-ès-L (*French**, *Film Studies**)
Kelly Bristow, MSc, PGCE, CPsychol (*Psychology**)
Hesper Bunch, MA, PGCE (*Art*)
James Burroughs, MChem, PGCE (*Chemistry*)
John Butler, BA, PGCE (*Sociology**)
Evelyn Campbell, BA, PGCE (*Mathematics*)

Michelle Cartey, MSc, PGCE (*Chemistry*)
Jennifer Clark, BSc, PGCE (*Chemistry*, *Science*)
Meghan Clarke, BA, MSc (*Computer Science*)
Alex Coburn, MA, PhD, PGCE (*History*)
Andrew Colclough, BA, MA (*Politics**)
Claire Coltellini, MA, PGCE (*French*)
Margaret Craig, BA, MA, FAETC (*History of Art*)
Stephen Creamer, MEng, PGCE (*Chemistry*, *Physics*)
Charles Currie, MPhys, PGCE (*Physics**)
Fraser Daly, BA, PGCE (*Economics*, *Business*)
Jon-Paul Davies, BSc, MA, PGCE (*Geography**)
Fleur Delany, MA, PGCE (*Geography*)
Kainan Dong (*Mandarin*)
Lynn Doughton, BSc, MA (*Biology*)
Kamar Finn, BScEd, BArch, NPQAL (*Art**)
Alison Fogg, BA, MA, MSt (*English*, *Drama*)
Kendell Fowler, BSc, PGCE (*Business*)
David Freer, BSc, PGCE (*Computer Science*)
Claire Gallagher (*EAL*)
Lucy Gallagher, MA, PhD, PGCE (*English**)
Nita Goriely, MS, PhD (*Mathematics*)
Agnieszka Gurbin, BA, MA, PhD, ESOL (*EAL**)
Nick Haines, MMathPhil (*Mathematics**)
Joanne Hall, BA, PGCE, TEFL (*Mathematics*)
David Hardwick, BSc (*Physics*)
Marianne Harlock, BA, PGCE (*Psychology*)
Simon Harrison, BA, MA (*Economics**)
Holly Hiscox, BA, MA, PGCE (*History*)
Christopher Holland, BA, MPhil (*English**)
Graham Hope, MA, DPhil (*Mathematics*)
Clare Horne, BSc, PhD, PG Dip (*Mathematics*)
Dominic Hunter, BSc, PGCE (*Computer Science**)
Fizza Hussain, BA, PGCE (*Drama*)
Arthur John, MA, PGCE (*German*)
Adam Johnstone, MA, MSt (*EPQ**, *Biology*)
Jo Kalies, BA (*Physical Education*)
Elena Kolpakova, MSc, PhD (*Russian*)
Christopher Lacy, BA, TEFL (*EAL*)
Andrew Latcham, BA, DPhil (*History*, *Politics*)
Jessica Leach, BA, PGCE (*Sociology*, *Media*)
Chloe Lewis, BA, PGCE (*Classics*, *Classical Civilisation*)
Mark Longbottom, MSc (*History**)
Kate MacDonald, BA, DSpLD (*Learning Support*)
David Mackie, BA, MA, DPhil, CPE, PGDL (*Classical Civilisation*, *Latin*, *Philosophy**)
Becky Mann, BA, PGCE (*Politics*, *History**)
Christine Martelloni, MSc (*French*)
Sandra Monger, BA, DELTA (*EAL*)
Rachel Moon, BSc (*Computer Science*)
Charlotte Moore, BSc, PGCE (*Chemistry*, *Physics*)
Llywelyn Morris, BA, PGCE (*Economics*)
Pamela Mossman, BA, MEd (*Business**)
Alex Newton, BA, MA, PGCE (*Art**)
Emily Nicholls, BA, PGCE (*English*, *Drama*)
Rachel Nicholson, MA, PGCE (*Italian*)
Jane Nimmo-Smith, BA (*Classics**, *Ancient History**)
Dearbhla Nutley, BA, PGCE (*Spanish*, *French*)
James O'Connor, BTEC HND (*Music Technology**)
Stephen O'Keeffe, MA (*Mathematics*)
Leon O'Rourke, BSc, PGCE (*Mathematics*)
Barbara Olla, BA, MA, PhD (*Italian*)
Catherine Orme, BA, PGCE (*Biology*)
Mikaela Parker, BSc, PGCE (*Chemistry*, *Biology*)
Lisa Pearson, BSc, MSc, PGCE (*Economics*, *Business*)
Mark Piesing, BA, PGCE (*Media**)
Robert Pollard, BA, TESOL, PGCE (*History*, *Politics*)

Richard Poyser, BA, PGCE (*Music**)
Martin Procter, BA, PGCE (*Physical Education**)
Nick Reeves, MA, PGCE (*Art**, *History of Art**)
Jonathan Richards, BSc, PGCE (*Physical Education**)
Naomi Richards, BA, PGCE (*History*)
Rowena Ritchie, BEd, MSc (*Biology*, *Science*)
Angus Roberts, BA, MA, MSc, PGCE, CEng
   (*Mathematics*, *Physics*)
Sara Roberts, BA, MA (*English*)
Ana Rodriguez Nodal, BA (*Spanish*)
Amy Rossiter, BA, PGCE (*Physical Education*)
Emily Rugg, BA, PGCE (*Mathematics*)
Becky Saxby, BSc, PGDE (*PE*)
Joan Shaw, MSc, PGCE (*Physics*, *Science*)
Sarah Shekleton, BA, MA, PGCE (*Mathematics**)
Lianne Skriniar, Dip TCL (*Music*)
Jennifer Skym, BA, PGCE (*Geography*)
Bethany Slater, BA, PGCE (*Mathematics*)
Aoife Squires, BSc, MSc (*Science*, *Chemistry*)
Janey Su (*Mandarin*)
Joe Swarbrick, BA, PGCE (*Drama**)
Jaimie Tarrell, BEd (*Biology**)
Sarah Terry, BA, PGCE (*English*)
Rachel Thanassoulis, MA, PGCE (*English*)
Emma Tinker, BA, MA, PhD (*Film Studies*)
Michael Vanden Boom, MSc, PhD (*Mathematics*)
Katie Vingoe, BA, PGCE (*Learning Development**)
Rie Wakayama, BA (*Japanese*)
Eleanor Walker, BSc, PGCE (*Psychology*, *EPQ*, *Science*)
Dominic Ward (*Geography*)
David Wareham, BA, MA, DELTA (*EAL*)
Ian Watkins, BA (*Mathematics*)
Rebecca Watkins, BA, MA, PGCE (*English*, *Drama*)
Jackie Watson (*Economics*, *Law*)
Victoria Wells, BA, MSc, PGCE (*REP*, *Geography*,
   Learning Support)
Natasha Wertheim, BA, PGCE (*Religion*, *Ethics and
   Philosophy**)
Paul Wheeler, BSc, PGCE (*Geography*)
Stephen Wheeler, BA, Dip TESOL (*EAL*)
Tricia Whitby, BA (*Geography*)
Henry Winney, MA, PGCE (*Chemistry**, *Biology**)
Phil Wintle, BA, MA, PGCE (*Media*)
Sharon Wyper, BA, PGATC, MA (*Art*)
Jonathan Young, BA, BSc (*Business**)
Elena Zambrano (*Spanish*)

Sport & Extra-Curricular Activities:
Years 7–11: Jo Kalies
Sixth Form: Jonathan Richards
International School: Becky Saxby

Registry:
Head of Admissions: Antony Bounds
Years 7–11: Rob Barker
Sixth Form: Rebecca Wood
International School: Nari Park

Boarding Office:
Head of Boarding: Felisa Deas
Head of Host Family Boarding: Emma Brett

School Counsellors: Charlie Morse-Brown, Kiki Glen

Higher Education & Careers Coordinator: Alex Coburn

Principal's PA: Sarah Hitchcox

Dunottar School
United Learning

High Trees Road, Reigate, Surrey RH2 7EL

Tel: 01737 761945
email: info@dunottarschool.com
website: www.dunottarschool.com
Twitter: @dunottarschool
Facebook: @Dunottar

The aim of Dunottar is to offer an outstanding education to boys and girls and, through excellent teaching and high levels of individual support, to enable our pupils to achieve added value comparable with what is achieved in the top schools in the UK. Dunottar is a vibrant, co-educational secondary school which, as part of United Learning's family of schools, shares the group's core values of ambition, confidence, determination, creativity, respect and enthusiasm along with the objective of bringing out the "Best in Everyone". Dunottar celebrates achievement in its broadest sense resulting in a community of happy, confident pupils who achieve their first choice ambition for their future education and employment.

The School was founded in 1926 and joined United Learning in 2014. It is situated in 15 acres of beautiful grounds on the outskirts of Reigate, convenient to mainline stations and bus routes. The main building is a handsome Palladian mansion and purpose-built wings include additional classrooms, art and design suites, the recently opened £4.5m Performing Arts Centre, the main hall, state-of-the-art Sixth Form Centre, a 25-metre heated indoor swimming pool and large sports hall with 4 lane cricket net system. Outdoor space includes a sports field, several netball courts, an outdoor classroom/theatre and arrangements with Old Reigatian RFC and Salfords CC extend the off-site sporting facilities.

Religion. The School holds the Christian ethos paramount and welcomes children from any denomination or none.

Curriculum. The School offers a broad education and preserves a balance between arts and science subjects. Early specialisation is avoided, though some subject options become necessary from the beginning of the GCSE year. Subjects include English Language and Literature, Mathematics, French, Spanish, History, Geography, Religious Studies, Biology, Physics and Chemistry, Business and Economics, Design and Technology, Computer Science, Physical Education, Drama, Food and Nutrition, Music and Art and Design. Dunottar has strong sporting and music traditions. Teaching is given in a wide range of musical instruments and pupils are encouraged to join the orchestras, music groups and choirs. A busy fixtures list offers many opportunities for competitive sport and 'sport for all' is encouraged within school and through the co-curricular programme. Rugby, football, athletics, netball, lacrosse, swimming and cricket are amongst the sports on offer. Co-curricular clubs are designed to broaden horizons and encourage new skills, hobbies and interests and range from current affairs debating to science-based groups such as 'dissection club' and sports including badminton and swimming. Students also participate in The Duke of

Edinburgh's Award scheme at Bronze, Silver and Gold levels.

Careers. Dunottar offers an interesting and varied careers programme for pupils, from online careers research tools through to careers networking lunches and suppers. The school welcomes a range of speakers from a diverse range of fields to offer our pupils an insight into application processes, daily life of employees and the skills employers are looking for.

Examinations taken. GCSE and A Levels, Associated Board of the Royal School of Music, London Academy of Music and Dramatic Art, Imperial School of Dancing, Royal Society of Arts.

Admissions. The admissions process at Dunottar is designed to identify those pupils who will thrive at the school. The admissions process is as friendly and relaxed as possible. The main intake is in Year 7 and Year 12. We are happy to consider pupils joining into other year groups where spaces are available. Prospective pupils can be registered at any time prior to the registration deadline. For Year 7 entry pupils should be registered before 30th September of the year prior to entry and assessments take place in the Autumn term. Applications for entry to Year 12 are usually required by 31st December in the year of entry. The Admissions Department are happy to answer any questions about the admissions process.

Fees per term (2021–2022). £6,207 (Years 7–13).

For Year 7 entrants, there is no application process for an Academic Scholarship. These are awarded to those pupils who reach the highest standard in the entrance assessments and show the greatest potential for growth.

Year 12 Academic Scholarship candidates will need to write one essay (chosen from a selection of titles provided by the school) and then discuss their essay with the Headmaster. Candidates will also sit a test paper in a subject selected by the candidate (November of Year 11). Some scholarships are also available in Year 7 and Year 12 for those who show exceptional promise and talent in Music, Art, Performing Arts and Sport. Further particulars may be obtained from the Admissions Department.

Charitable status. Dunottar School is part of United Learning which comprises: UCST (a Company Limited by Guarantee, Registered in England, number 2780748, and a Registered Charity, number 1016538) and ULT (a Company Limited by Guarantee, Registered in England, number 4439859, and an Exempt Charity).

Senior Leadership Team:

Headmaster: Mr M Tottman, MA Oxon, MBA, QTS

Deputy Head Pastoral: Mr M Broughton, BA Hons Worcester, MEd (*Designated Safeguarding Lead*)
Deputy Head Academic: Mrs J Hislop, BA Hons Southampton, PGCE
Deputy Head Operations: Mrs R Stringer, BA Hons Warwick, PGCE

Teaching Staff:
* *Head of Department*

Art & Design:
Ms B Horn, BA Hons WSCAD, PGCE*
Mr M Huxley, BSc Hons Westminster, PGDip PGCE
Mr J Kopiel, BA Hons UEL, MA RCA, PGCE

Careers:
Mrs K Hanlon, BSocSci Hons Keele*

Computing:
Mrs S Berry, BSc Hons Exeter, PGCE*
Mr K New, BSc Hons Manchester Metropolitan, PGCE

Design & Technology:
Mrs F Exley, BSc Hons Brighton, PGCE*

English:
Ms K Lewis, MBA De Montfort, BEd Hons*
Mrs R Ballantyne, BA Hons Keele, MA, PGCE
Mr M Broughton, BA Hons Worcester, MEd
Dr I McClure, BA Hons Oxon, MA, PhD, PGCE
Mrs S van Duijvenvoorde, BA Hons Central Lancashire, PGCE

Economics & Business and Government & Politics:
Mrs N Wintle, MA Oxon PGCE*
Mr S Whiteley, BSc Hons Manchester, MA, QTS

Food & Nutrition:
Ms A French, BEd HomeEc*
Mrs S Giblin (*Food & Nutrition Assistant*)
Ms R Macintyre, BA Hons UEL, PGCE

Foreign Languages:
Miss M O'Keefe, BA Hons Liverpool, PGCE*
Mrs A Coleman, BA Hons Bradford, PGCE
Mrs B Leonard, BA Hons Bristol, PGCE
Ms L Tanner, BA Hons Durham, PGCE

Geography:
Mrs S Thorne, BA Hons Leicester, PGCE*
Mrs T Bates, BA Hons Newcastle, PGCE
Mrs N Jackson, BSc Hons Sheffield, PGCE (*Director of Sixth Form*)

History:
Mrs J Boden, MA St Andrews, PGCE* (*Deputy Head of Sixth Form*)
Miss A Nawaz, BA Brunel, PGCE
Mrs R Stringer, BA Hons Warwick, PGCE (*Deputy Head Operations*)

Learning Support:
Mrs H Rutt, BA Hons Manchester Metropolitan, PGCE, NASENCO*
Mrs K Hanlon, BSocSci Hons Keele

Mathematics:
Mrs J Gentle, BSc Hons Loughborough, PGCE*
Mrs N Budgen, BComm Durban, SA, PGCE (*Head of Year 9*)
Mrs L Chessell, BSc Hons Durham, PGCE (*Head of Year 8*)
Mrs R MacTavish, BSc Hons York, ACMA, CSBM, PGCE
Mrs S Ryde, BSc Bristol, PGCE

Music:
Miss E Pettet, BMus Hons Surrey, PG Cert Guildhall School of Music & Drama, PGCE, DipABRSM (*Director of Music and Head of Co-Curricular*)*

Performing Arts:
Mrs S van Duijvenvoorde, BA Hons Central Lancashire, PGCE*
Mrs T Jago, BA Hons Hull, PGCE (*Assistant Head Staff Development, Acting Head of Drama*)

Physical Education:
Mr S Manning, BA Hons Exeter PGCE (*Director of Sport*)*
Mrs E Bambridge, BA Leeds, Sports Coach Dip, Level 3 CBT Dip, Level 3 Child Psych Dip, Mental Health First Aid Cert (*Sports Coach and Head of Wellbeing*)
Mr M Everett, BSc Hons Brighton, PGCE (*Director of Football, Head of Year 7*)
Mr T Lowe, BMus Hons Guildhall School of Music & Drama, MA, DipRam, PGCE
Mr D McColl, BSc Bristol, PGCE (*Head of Lacrosse*)
Mr J Myers, BSc Hons Chichester, PGCE (*Director of Cricket*)
Mrs E Pieters, BA Hons Brighton, QTS (*Head of Girls' Sport*)
Miss L Purvis, BA Hons Chichester, PGCE

Psychology:
Mr D Kokott, BA Stellenbosch, PGCE, CertCoun* (*Head of Year 11*)

Religious Studies & Philosophy:
Mr P Cooper, BA Nottingham, PGCE* (*Head of Year 10*)
Mrs H Bilham, BA Hons Liverpool, PGCE
Miss A Nawaz, BA Hons Brunel, PGCE

Science:
Mr M Carter, BA UBC, BEd, MSc, GradCert (*Physics*)*
Mrs R Bird, BSc Hons University College London, PGCE
Mrs R Pope, BSc Hons Nottingham PGCE (*Chemistry*)*
Mrs S Sagar, MSc Coventry, BSc Hons, PGCE (*Acting Head of Biology*)*
Mrs H Davison, BSc Hons Southampton, PGCE
Mr J Holland, BEng Hons Cardiff, QTS
Mr S Kaye, BSc Hons Imperial College, MSc, PhD, PGCE
Miss R Luke, BSc Hons Royal Holloway, London, QTS
Mrs J O'Dwyer, BSc Hons Durham, PGCE
Mr G Taylor, MA Ed Chichester, BA, QTS (*Assistant Head Learning & Innovation*)

Sociology:
Mrs J Boden, MA St Andrews, PGCE*
Mrs J Hislop, BA Hons Southampton, PGCE (*Deputy Head Academic*)

Support Staff:

Admissions & Marketing:
Mrs R Tottman, MA Hons Oxon, PGCert SpLD (*Head of Admissions*)
Mrs G Wiles, BSc Hons Aston (*Marketing Manager*)
Mrs S Edwards (*Admissions Manager*)
Mrs L Taylor (*Outreach Manager*)
Mrs K Tomlinson, BA Hons Queen Mary, London (*Social Media Officer*)

Administration Team:
Mrs C Kendrick, BA Kingston (*Executive Assistant to Headmaster*)
Mrs J Cullender (*Accounts Assistant/Reception*)
Mrs J Jones (*School Secretary*)
Mrs E Mason (*Personal Assistant to SLT*)
Mrs L Moon (*Accounts Assistant/Reception*)
Mrs K Ridgers, BA Hons Leeds (*Academic Projects Coordinator*)

Catering:
Mrs M Dennehy (*Catering Manager*)

Drama:
Mrs C Clark, Mountview Theatre School Diploma (*Drama Practitioner*)

Estates Team:
Mr J Aliperti (*Premises Apprentice*)
Mr T Crocker (*Premises Officer*)
Mr C Cure (*Premises Apprentice*)
Mr L Doe (*Weekend Premises Officer*)
Mr J Woods (*Premises Supervisor*)

Examinations:
Mrs L Longstaff (*Examinations Officer*)

Finance:
Mrs S Fribbance (*Finance and Admin Manager*)
Mr G Davies, BA Hons Queen Mary, London (*Finance Officer*)
Mrs P Vadher (*Finance & Marketing Assistant*)

Health & Welfare:
Mrs C Allison, School Nurse, RGN
Mrs J Gumm, BA Hons, PG Dip Couns, MA CBT, Adv Cert Sup, PG Dip Sup, MBACP Reg Accred, School Counsellor

HR:
Mrs L Wootton, BA Hons Essex MA, CIPD (*HR Manager*)
Mrs A Tarrant, BA Hons Reading, PGCE, QTLS (*HR Coordinator*)

IT, AV & DATA:
Mr T Stevens, BSc Hons Staffordshire (*Network Manager*)
Mr A Fernandez (*IT/AV Technician*)
Mr A Kerr (*Data Manager*)

Technicians:
Dr R Ashworth, BSc Hons Brighton, PhD (*Senior Science Technician*)
Miss N Osei, BSc Hons Nottingham (*Science*)
Mr M Exley (*D&T*)
Mrs S Machacek (*Art*)

Peripatetic Staff:

Drama and Performing Arts:
Mr C Watts (*Drama*)
Miss C Walford, AISTD Dip (*Dance*)

Music:
Mrs S Dembinska, BA Christchurch, Performance Diploma Trinity (*Piano*)
Mrs Z Eborn, BA MUS GRNCM (*Violin*)
Mr B Fisher, BA Hons Southampton (*Brass*)
Ms K Howells, BMusHons, DipABRSM (*Clarinet, Saxophone, Flute*)
Mr F Malafronte, BMus, Mmus, Art Dip RCM (*Guitar*)
Mr D McGibbon (*Voice*)
Miss L Nagioff, Dip NCOS (*Violoncello*)
Mr J Park (*Drums*)
Miss E Reynolds, BA Oxon (*Music Theory, Violin*)
Ms L Sánchez de Haro, BMus, MPerf GSMD (*Piano*)
Mrs C Stapel, BA Amsterdam Conservatorium (*Violin*)
Mr C Thompson, BA Hons East Anglia, MTC (*Voice*)

Sport:
Mr D McColl (*Lacrosse*)
Mrs E Bambridge (*Lacrosse, Netball*)
Mr B Small (*Rugby, Rugby Sevens*)
Mr S Ogilvie (*Football, Cricket*)
Mr K Childs (*Swimming*)
Ms P McCarthy (*Netball*)

Embley
United Learning

Embley Park, Romsey, Hampshire SO51 6ZE

Tel: 01794 512206 (Senior School)
            01794 515737 (Prep School)
email: info@embley.org.uk
website: www.embley.org.uk
Twitter: @EmbleySenior
Facebook: @EmbleyHampshire
LinkedIn: school/embleyhampshire

Embley is an independent day and boarding school for girls and boys aged 2–18. The school is nestled in 130 acres of private parkland, which includes woodlands, playing fields, tennis courts, AstroTurf pitches, a swimming pool and a golf course. It also runs a comprehensive sailing programme with its own boats moored at Lymington.

The school is academically ambitious for its children and motivates them to achieve their personal best. It encourages an appropriate belief in oneself while being mindful that the world does not end at the tip of one's nose and that happiness in life is through success in enriching the lives of others.

Constitution. Over 555 pupils, with 400 in the Senior School and Sixth Form and 155 in the Prep School.

Boarding. Flexi and full time boarding are available from 11+. The Heads of Boarding reside in the Boarding House. The house family includes dedicated nurses and matrons who specialise in the welfare and medical needs of all boarders.

Curriculum.

Prep School: A broad curriculum is offered, including French, Music, Computer Science, Design Technology and Physical Education taught by specialists. Throughout the school (when appropriate) children take part in lessons delivered outside the classroom.

Senior School: The GCSE curriculum offers a choice of many subjects (including separate subject sciences).

Sixth Form: More than 20 A Level subjects are available and a Pre-A Level for international students whose first language is not English. All students are expected to take an Extended Project Qualification (EPQ).

Further details can be found at www.embley.org.uk

Co-curricular and enrichment. The school has an extensive co-curricular programme which includes sailing, skiing, horse riding, golf, rugby, football, cricket, hockey, netball, cross country, basketball, swimming, tennis, athletics and golf. The school has a thriving drama, art and musical life. All Senior School pupils are encouraged to undertake The Duke of Edinburgh's Award scheme.

Higher Education & Careers. The school runs a regular series of industry career evenings, its own Higher Education Conference and International University Conference. Year 12 students benefit from an MBA Experience in partnership with Winchester University and all Sixth Form students attend termly Nightingale Lectures (black-tie events with eminent guest speakers).

Admission procedures.

Nursery: No formal assessment

Prep School: Entry at any age from 4 to 11. Informal assessment Reception and Year 1. Assessment Year 2 to Year 6.

Senior School: Entrance assessments, interview and a suitable reference from the head teacher of the pupil's current school.

Sixth Form: Offers made usually on the following conditions: A minimum of 5 GCSE grades 9 to 5 and at least grade 7 or 8 in the A Level subjects to be studied or equivalent. A suitable reference from the head teacher of the pupil's current school.

Scholarships. Scholarships are available at 11+, 13+ and 16+ and are awarded for: Academic, Art & Design, Music, Drama and Sport.

Fees per term (2021–2022). Nursery: £3,055 (full time). Prep School £3,632–£5,579; Senior School: £5,668 (day), £9,770 (UK boarding), £9,866 (EU Boarding), £11,006 (International Boarding), £11,212 (Pre-A Level). Please refer to www.embley.org.uk/admissions/fees for further information.

Local Governing Body:
Professor R Thomas (*Chairman*)
Mr C M Canning (*Headmaster*)
Mrs K Smith
Dr L Black
Mrs R Brooks
Mr R Butler
Mr R Page
Ms A Johnston

Headmaster: **Mr Cliff Canning**, BA Hons, BD Hons, HDipEd, NUI

Deputy Head: Mr Jose Picardo, MA, PGCE
Bursar: Mrs Claire Brighton, MBA
Head of Prep School: Ms Sheina Wright, BA, QTS
Assistant Head (Pastoral): Mrs Rebecca Clayton, BSc, PGCE
Assistant Head (Co-Curriculum): Mrs Elaine Morgan, BA, PGCE
Director of Marketing, Admissions & Communications: Mrs Charlotte Welland, BA

Ewell Castle School

Church Street, Ewell, Surrey KT17 2AW

Tel: 020 8394 3576 (Admissions)
            020 8393 1413 (Main Office)
email: admissions@ewellcastle.co.uk
website: www.ewellcastle.co.uk
Twitter: @EwellCastleUK
Facebook: @EwellCastleSchool
Instagram: @ewellcastleschool
LinkedIn: /school/ewell-castle-school

Ewell Castle is an independent, co-educational day school in North Surrey, twenty minutes from London. It was built as a castellated mansion in 1814. It offers a Nursery, Pre-Preparatory School, Preparatory School, Senior School and a Sixth Form.

The gardens and playing fields of the Senior School cover some fifteen acres and were once part of Nonsuch Park. The Senior School is accommodated at The Castle. The Preparatory School occupies two other premises in Ewell village: the Nursery and Pre-Preparatory School, a Georgian house minutes from the Senior School; and the Preparatory School, the former Rectory to the parish church, opposite the Senior School. The School, which was founded in 1926, is registered as an educational charity and is administered by a Board of Governors, which is in membership of AGBIS (Association of Governing Bodies of Independent Schools). The Principal is a member of The Society of Heads and the Head of the Preparatory School is a member of IAPS (Independent Association of Prep Schools).

The School comprises approximately 660 pupils in total with 480 pupils in the Senior School and 180 pupils in the Preparatory School.

Buildings. The School is located on three sites within the village of Ewell, Chessington Lodge accommodating The Nursery, and Pre-Prep: co-educational 3–7 years; Glyn House: co-educational 7–11 years) and the Senior School (The Castle: co-educational 11–16 years and the Sixth Form co-educational 16–18 years). Academic departments are well resourced and accommodated. Recent developments on the Senior School site include the Budgell Building, the Music Pavilion and the refurbishments of the PE/Games changing rooms.

School Mission. We will inspire our children and young people to thrive, engaging them to excel in a creative and academic environment. We will instill a growth mindset to develop: confidence, contentment and emotional intelligence.

Aims and Ethos. We are a vibrant learning community, inspiring every child to thrive: discovering strengths, deepening intellectual curiosity and cultivating wellbeing.

Values. Personal integrity, mutual respect, social responsibility and lifelong resilience.

Organisation. The Preparatory School is co-educational and accepts pupils from three years. Most pupils transfer to the Senior School, whilst others go to a range of Independent and selective/non-selective schools at 11+. The Sixth Form has been co-educational since September 2013 and the Senior School became fully co-educational in September 2015.

Curriculum. National Curriculum requirements are incorporated into Senior and Preparatory School schemes, although the broad and flexible curriculum extends beyond such criteria. Breadth at KS3 (11–13 years) is replaced at KS4 (14–16 years) by a core of Mathematics, English, Science and Religious Studies, supplemented by a wide ranging option scheme covering the languages, arts, humanities and technologies. There is an increased range of subjects available at A Level and BTEC in the Sixth Form

Work experience is undertaken by pupils in Year 11. Specialist HE/Careers guidance is available from Year 9 within the Senior School.

After the Sixth Form the majority of pupils proceed to universities and colleges, with most pupils achieving their first choice of institution.

Extracurricular Activities. The principal sports are rugby, football, hockey, netball and cricket. In addition there are numerous pursuits which include: athletics, badminton, basketball, table tennis, skiing, and tennis. There is an extensive music and drama programme and other activities such as The Duke of Edinburgh's Award scheme. Regular language, sports and field trips embarked for America, Austria, Belgium, France, Germany, Iceland, Ireland, Italy and Spain in recent years.

The school benefits from an active PTA.

Admissions. Girls and boys are admitted to the Preparatory School at the age of three. There are no entry requirements at this stage. Older children are invited to attend the school for a day's assessment in November for entry into the Senior School and Sixth Form.

At the Senior School the standard points of entry are at 11+, 13+ and 16+. Subject to availability, there may be places at other levels. Entry requirements include interview, report from previous school and written assessments.

Visitors are welcome to the school on scheduled Open Days or by appointment.

Scholarships. Scholarships are available for pupils entering the school at 11+, 13+ and 16+. At 11+ awards are made on the basis of competitive examination/assessment in the designated category. Awards are made for Academic excellence and also in the categories of Art, Design and Technology, Drama, Music, Performing Arts and Photography (both Sixth Form only) and Sport.

Fees per term (2021–2022). Senior School £6,047, Preparatory School £4,145, Pre-Preparatory School £3,668, Nursery & Reception £3,135.

Preparatory School. *For further information, see Ewell Castle Preparatory School entry in IAPS section.*

Charitable status. Ewell Castle School is a Registered Charity, number 312079. The aim of the charity is to achieve potential and excellence over a broad field: in academic, in sport, in the arts, and in numerous other extracurricular activities and aspects of school life.

Chairman of the Governing Body: Mr C Griffith

Principal: Mr Silas Edmonds, MA, NPQH

Head of Preparatory School & Vice Principal: Mrs L Macallister BA, PGCE, NPQSL
Senior School Deputy Head (Academic) & Vice Principal: Mrs H Blake, MA, NPQH
Senior School Deputy Head (Pupil Wellbeing) & Vice Principal: Mr S Leigh, BA, PGCE
Deputy Head of Preparatory School & Assistant Principal: Mrs S Fowler, BSc, PGCE
Deputy Head of Preparatory School & Assistant Principal: Mrs G Bean, MA, PGCE
Bursar: Ms J Abraham, BSc, FCCA
Marketing, Development & Alumni Manager: Ms C Hernandez, BA, CIM Grad Dip

Heads of Department:
Art & Design & Photography: Ms D Carrick, BA, QTS
Business: Mrs R Rudd, BA,QTS
Computing and Information Technology: Mr R Brooks, LLB, PGCE
Design Technology: Mrs D Sarmiento, MA, BA, GTP
Drama: Mr L Bader-Clynes, BA, RADA Dip
Economics: Mrs R Rudd, BA, QTS
English: Ms K Wallace, BA, PGCE
Geography: Miss S Earthrowl, BSc, PGCE
History & Classics: Mr J C W Blencowe, BA, PGCE
Learning Support: Mrs S Bailey, BEd, CELTA, Dip SpLD
Mathematics: Mr J Baldwin, BSc, QTS

Modern Foreign Languages: Miss P Hernandez, Licence LLC, PGCE (*Deputy DSL*)
Music: Mrs L Oldfield, BA, MA, PGCE
Performing Arts: Mr B Essenhigh, BA, QTS
Philosophy and Religious Studies: Mr T Stone, BA, MA, QTS
Physical Education: Mr N Turk, BSc, GTP
Politics: Mrs E Harrison, BA, PGCE
Psychology: Mr J D'Souza, BSc, PGCE
Science: Mr B Visser BSc, PGCE

Executive Assistant to the Principal : Mrs K El-Dahshan, BA Cantab

Farringtons School

Perry Street, Chislehurst, Kent BR7 6LR

Tel: 020 8467 0256
email: fvail@farringtons.kent.sch.uk
website: www.farringtons.org.uk
Twitter: @OneFarringtons
Facebook: @OneFarringtons

Farringtons School is situated in 25 acres of green belt land in Chislehurst, which provide attractive surroundings while still being within easy reach of London (25 minutes to Charing Cross), the South Coast and Gatwick airport (45 minutes) and Heathrow airport via the M25 (1½ hours).

The School is committed to providing a first-class education for pupils of all ages in a caring community which supports all its members and helps each pupil to achieve his or her full potential both academically and personally. After-school care is available until 6.30pm.

The curriculum offered is that of the National Curriculum, with a wide range of GCSE and A Level subjects available. Nearly 100% of Sixth Form leavers customarily go on to degree courses at Universities or Higher Education Colleges. Academic standards are high from a comprehensive intake of pupils and in 2021 a 99% pass rate was achieved at A Level.

The excellent facilities include a Technology building, a large Sports Hall with Dance Studio and Fitness Suite, splendidly-equipped Science and Modern Language departments, a well-stocked library, Careers Room, indoor heated swimming pool and extensive playing fields, as well as a School Chapel, where the School regularly comes together.

The main sports are netball, tennis, football, rugby, swimming and athletics, but badminton, volleyball and table tennis are also undertaken and other extracurricular activities available include The Duke of Edinburgh's Award scheme, various choirs and instrumental ensembles, gymnastics, dance, ballet, drama club, fencing, etc.

To obtain a prospectus and further information or to arrange a visit, contact the Registrar: admissions@farringtons.kent.sch.uk.

Fees per term (2021–2022). Day: £3,490 (Pre-Reception, full time), £4,310 (Junior), £5,420 (Senior); Weekly Boarding £9,040, Full Boarding £11,350.

Charitable status. Farringtons School is part of the Methodist Independent Schools Trust, a Registered Charity, number 1142794. It exists solely to provide a high-quality, caring education.

Governing Body:
Chairman: Mr A Harris
Vice-Chairman: Mr Ric Hinton

Members:

Mr D Baillie	Mrs J King
Revd N Cowgill	Mr A Raby
Mrs S Donaldson	Dr A Squires
Mr P Johnstone	Mr M Vinales

Bursar and Clerk to the Governors: Mrs Sally-Anne Eldridge

Headmaster: Mr David Jackson, BA, MEd

Deputy Head: Mr N Young
Assistant Head (*Curriculum*): Mr L Garwood
Assistant Head (*Pastoral & DSL*): Mr S Smith
Head of Sixth Form: Ms V Jackson
Head of Junior School: Mr R Boyjoonauth
Deputy Head of Junior School: Mrs J Cryan

Director of Marketing & Admission: Mrs F Vail
Registrar: Mrs B Thompson

* *Head of Department*

English:
*Miss S Bliss
Mr B Coulthard
Mrs V Denman
Mrs S DiStefano
Mrs S Freeston
*Mrs K O'Neil
Mr P Scowen
Ms Mingyue Yang
Mr K Jones
Mrs R Saunders
Miss A Sawyer
Mr S Smith

Mathematics:
*Mr F Gray
Mrs I Haider
*Mrs Z Hanson
Ms M Jeffrey
Mr T Kyle
Mrs M Mahil
Mr A Miah
Mr N Varley

Science:
Mrs J Daws
Miss F Evans
Miss M Finlay
Miss A Lester
Mrs V Owen
Mrs L Sriram
Mr L Templeman
*Mr D Worden

Modern Languages:
Mr J Hernando
Ms V Jackson
Mrs F Jackson
*Mlle I Mosqueron
Mr P Scowen

Humanities:
Mr D Barrett
Mr C Catling
*Mr G Curran
Mr A Essex

Business, Finance & Technology:
Mrs R Ashworth
Mr J Gardner
Mrs R Miah
*Miss K Ootim
Mr S Owen
Mrs L Williamson

Performing & Creative Arts:
Mrs G Allen
Miss R Azulay
Mrs S Freeston
Mrs D Humphrey
Miss N Lubrani
Mr R Matthews
Mr S Message
Mr N Raynor
Miss I Smith
Mrs S Watson
Mrs P White
*Mrs J Warburton

Learning Development:
Ms K Miles
*Mrs D Rabot
Mrs J Pyle

Sport:
Mrs E Broughan
Mr A Doherty
*Mr C Doyle
Miss B Farrant

Mrs J Sherwood
Mr B Suverkrop

Junior School:

Ms F Alexander	Ms H Kearns
Miss S Austin	Mrs L Long
Mrs G Bastos	Miss N Mensah
Mrs P Brookman	Mrs N Pasquie-Taylor
Mrs S Carter	Miss K Randall
Miss S Cox	Mrs H Reynolds
Mrs C Crouser	Mrs H Roberts
Mrs J Cryan	Mr T Ruffle
Mrs T Devaux	Miss S Seager
Mrs C Fitzpatrick	Mr J Shimmin
Mrs V Fox	Ms K Streeter
Mrs C Frisby	Mr B Suverkrop
Mrs H Hill	Mrs A Vinales
Mrs J Hurst	Mrs S Walker
Ms S Johnson	Ms S Watts

Fulneck School

Pudsey, Leeds, West Yorkshire LS28 8DS

Tel:	0113 257 0235
email:	enquiries@fulneckschool.co.uk
website:	www.fulneckschool.co.uk
Twitter:	@FulneckSchool
Facebook:	@FulneckSchool
LinkedIn:	/fulneck-independent-school

Fulneck School was established in 1753 by the Moravian Church, a very early Protestant Church which has two schools in England and many more abroad. It is situated within the historic Fulneck Settlement, located on the peaceful slopes of the beautiful Tong valley just outside Leeds. With short, ideal and reliable links to Leeds and Manchester airports and access to a wealth of culture and experience, Fulneck School is a traditional, rural school with a forward-thinking attitude.

The School is a registered charity and the Provincial Board of the Moravian Church is the Trustee of the School. The Governing Body provides a range of professional expertise and is in membership of AGBIS (Association of Governing Bodies of Independent Schools). The Principal is a member of The Society of Heads.

The School is co-educational and provides a modern, academic curriculum based on Christian principles. Fulneck Sixth Form offers 20 A Level and BTEC subjects and the school has an outstanding record of success in public examinations. Class sizes rarely exceed 20 and most teaching groups are smaller; in the Sixth Form groups seldom exceed 10.

Buildings. The main buildings of the School are part of the original settlement, yet other buildings on the campus have been added over the years – most recently a new self-contained Sixth Form Centre and Fitness Centre. Extensive playing fields and tennis courts are located on the site, which adjoins Fulneck Golf Club, and looks over to the Domesday village of Tong.

Pastoral Care. The staff work closely and effectively together, sharing in the duties and recreational needs of the School. The School Nurse, who is medically qualified, and other house staff take care of the boarders in conjunction with the resident teaching staff and the Principal, who also lives on the campus. Weekly and flexi boarding are offered in addition to full boarding.

Sport. Netball, Football, Cricket, Athletics and Tennis are the main games of the School, but Basketball, Badminton, Cross-Country Running, Golf, Rounders, Table Tennis and Martial Arts are all available to the pupils as part of a rapidly expanding programme of outdoor pursuits. Teams of various ages, in most sports, have full fixture lists with neighbouring schools. Dance classes are also run.

Activities. Music education is strong with choirs and orchestral groups in the junior and senior school. The Choirs perform often to the public.

There are a number of clubs and societies such as Art, Computer Coding, Languages, Golf, Netball, Table Tennis, Forensic Club, Science, Eco, Strength & Conditioning, Dance and Martial Arts.

The Duke of Edinburgh's Award scheme is available to pupils over the age of 14, together with a wide range of trips and residential visits, walking and skiing. The school has regularly participated in World Challenge expeditions.

Pre-School and Early Years. The Pre-School setting has recently benefited from full refurbishment and admits children in the term of their 3rd Birthday. Children from Pre-School transition directly into Reception Class which is housed in the main Junior School Building next door.

Junior School (Key Stage 2). The Junior School is self-contained and caters for pupils from the ages of 4–11. Once a pupil is admitted he or she will usually progress into the Senior School, after assessment at age 11. The Junior School has access to many of its own specialist facilities, including teaching staff for Science, Art, Technology, Music, IT and Library, as well as to the Senior School sports facilities.

Senior School and Sixth Form. In the Senior School students study GCSEs, A Levels and BTECs. The school also offers one-year pre-sessional courses prior to GCSE and A Level for students for whom English is not their first language. The school is able to offer short stay options for international students looking to experience the UK education system, these can range from visits of just a few weeks, to a full year of study.

Learning Support Unit. Specialist staff provide help on an individual or small group basis to children with dyslexia or other learning differences. The Unit is CReSTeD approved and has repeatedly confirmed its 'DU' status, the highest grade awarded to mainstream schools.

Parents and Friends Association. There is a flourishing organisation which acts as a fundraising body, and also supports the School in a variety of other ways. This is a living example of the belief that education is a partnership between home and school.

Admission. Admission to the school is welcomed at any age depending on the availability of places, although the main intake is at the ages of 3, 7 and 11. Direct entry to the Sixth Form is also possible. Means-tested academic bursaries and other scholarships are available.

Fees per term (2021–2022). Junior School Day: Nursery (mornings only) £1,600; Foundation Stage (full day) £2,591; Years 1 & 2 £2,810; Years 3–6 £3,518. Senior School: Day £4,686; Weekly Boarding £8,542; Full Boarding £9,545; Flexi Boarding £55 per night.

Fulneck Former Pupils' Association. Mr R Tordoff, Fulneck School, Pudsey, West Yorkshire LS28 8DS.

Charitable status. Fulneck School is a Registered Charity, number 251211. It exists to provide a traditional, Christian education for boys and girls between the ages of 3 and 18.

The Governing Body:
Mrs L Jordan (*Chair*)
Mr C J Stern (*Vice Chair*)

Mr C Smith	Mrs E Dawson
Miss C Pearson	Mr P Acton
Revd R Hopcroft	Mrs H Kernohan

Principal: **Miss F Smith**, BSc Hons Brunel, PGCE

Vice Principal, Senior School: Mrs Gemma Carver, BSc Hons

Vice Principal, Acting Head of Junior School: Ms K Marlowe, BA Ed Hons UWE

Bursar: Mrs K Thompson

Highclare School

10 Sutton Road, Erdington, Birmingham B23 6QL

Tel:	0121 373 7400
email:	enquiries@highclareschool.co.uk
website:	www.highclareschool.co.uk
Twitter:	@HighclareSchool
Facebook:	@highclareschool
Instagram:	@highclareschool
LinkedIn:	/company/highclare-school

Founded 1932.

Age Range. 2+ to 18 years. Co-educational.

Number of Pupils. 521

Fees per term (2021–2022). £3,065–£4,630.

Location. The School is situated on three sites on the main road (A5127) between Four Oaks, Sutton Coldfield and Birmingham. The Senior Department and Sixth Form are on direct train and bus routes from Birmingham city centre, Tamworth, Lichfield and Walsall as well as being serviced by our own buses. There are two preparatory schools, known as Highclare Preparatory School: Woodfield and Highclare Preparatory School: St Paul's. Wraparound care operates from 7.30am until 6.00pm for the parents who require it. Holiday cover is available for Pre-School only. The ethos of the school lies in the fulfilment of potential for each pupil, outstanding pastoral care and a belief in the education of the 'whole person'.

Organisation. Four departments:

Pre-Preparatory Department (age 2+ to 4 years, co-educational). An educational setting, with qualified teachers, integrated into the School, it has the support of facilities and resources of the Preparatory School. MFL, dance and music are taught from Pre-Prep 2.

Preparatory Departments (age 4+ to 11 years, two co-educational departments). The Preparatory School, with classes of up to a maximum of 22 pupils, follows National Curriculum guidelines. Pupils also have the benefit of specialist tuition in MFL, PE/games, music and science. Other foundation subjects are taught by subject and by class teachers. Entry by School's own assessment procedure.

Senior Department (age 11 to 16, co-educational). The full curriculum is covered at KS3. At GCSE all students study English Language and English Literature, Mathematics, Combined Science or separate sciences, and most study a modern foreign language, (French, German or Spanish) with a wide choice of options. In addition PSHCE, Physical Education, Music and Performing Arts form an important part of the curriculum. Through a wide programme of enrichment activities every child has the opportunity to enjoy activities beyond the academic. Entry by School's own assessment procedure.

Sixth Form (age 16+). The Sixth Form is co-educational and accepts external candidates as well as pupils transferring from Highclare Senior School. A wide range of A Level subjects is available for study alongside the extended project qualification. Excellent pastoral, higher education and careers guidance is also offered and timetables are structured to meet the individual requirements of each student.

All parts of the School participate in extensive lunchtime and after-school activities.

The School is multi-denominational. Further information may be obtained from the School or the website and prospective parents are always welcome to visit. Open mornings are held throughout the year including school-in-action days on all three sites.

Charitable status. Highclare School is a Registered Charity, number 528940.

Chair of Governors: Mrs L Flowith

School Leadership Team:

Headmaster: **Dr R Luker**, BA Hons, MA, PGCE Madeley, PhD Sheffield Hallam

Head of Preparatory School: Mrs P Bennett, BA Hons, PGCE Liverpool

Business Manager: Mrs M P A McGoldrick, BA Hons, MSc Manchester, MAAT, AInstAM Dip

Deputy Head of Senior School: Academic: Mrs S Cassell, BA Hons Oxford, PGCE Keele

Deputy Head of Senior School: Academic: Mr Matthew Coles, BSc Hons Warwick, PGCE Bristol

Deputy Head of Preparatory School: Mrs J Griffiths, BA Hons, QTS York, MA Wolverhampton

Designated Safeguarding Lead: Mrs H Good, BEd Hons Worcester

Senior School Staff:

Headmaster: Dr R Luker, BA Hons, MA, PGCE Madeley, PhD Sheffield Hallam

Deputy Head of Senior School: Pastoral: Mrs S Cassell, BA Hons Oxford, PGCE Keele

Deputy Head of Senior School: Academic: Mr Matthew Coles, BSc Hons Warwick, PGCE Bristol

Assistant Head of Senior School: Mrs H Bate, BSc Hons Bimingham

KS5 Coordinator: Mrs M Sharman-Everton, BA Hons Birmingham QTS

KS4 Coordinator: Mrs A de Sousa Bartlett, BEd Hons St Mary's College

KS3 Coordinator: Mr R Linfield, BA Hons, PGCE Birmingham

Heads of Departments:
Art: Mrs K Stott, BA Hons, PGCE Birmingham, QTS

Business Studies: Mrs A Green, BSc Econ Aberystwyth, PGCE Warwick

Design & Technology: Mrs H Good, BEd Hons Worcester

Drama: Mrs M Sharman-Everton, BA Hons Birmingham QTS

English: Mrs K J Dawson, BA Hons Exeter, PGCE Oxford

Geography & Religious Studies: Mrs J Palmer, BSc Hons Open, PGCE Birmingham

History: Miss M Watson, BA Hons Durham, MA Warwick, PGCE Glos

Food & Nutrition: Mrs A Smith, BEd Bath

Information Technology/Computing: Mr L Sneary, BSc Hons Brunel, PGCE Brunel

Law: Mrs N Stead, LLB Cardiff

Mathematics: Mr S Parkinson, BSc Hons Southampton, PGCE Birmingham

Modern Languages: Mrs J Lightfoot, BA Hons Newcastle, PGCE Warwick

Music: Miss A Cassells, BMus Hons Cardiff, PGCE Birmingham

Psychology: Mrs L Bradbury-Grubb, BSc Hons De Montfort, QTS

Physical Education: Mr R Linfield, BA Hons Birmingham, PGCE Birmingham

Science: Mr W Murray-Smith, BSc, MA Warwick, QTS Nottingham Trent

Sociology: Dr D Edwards, BA Hons Liverpool, PGCE Leics, MA, PhD Manchester

Posts of Additional Responsibility (*Senior*):

Learning Support Coordinator: Mrs C Roberts, BA Hons, PGCE Hull

Preparatory School Staff:

Head of Preparatory School: Mrs P Bennett, BA Hons, PGCE Liverpool

Deputy Head of Preparatory School: Mrs J Griffiths, BA Hons, QTS York, MA Wolverhampton

Highclare Preparatory School: *St Paul's*:

Assistant Head and KS2 Coordinator: Mrs J O Quigley, BA Hons Birmingham, PGCE UCB

KS1 Coordinator (Acting): Mr J Goddard, BA Hons History Nottingham Trent, PGCE Newman College

EYFS Coordinators:

Mrs J Harris, BA Hons, MA, PSC, ECS Birmingham, EYPS

Mrs P Mitchell, BEd Hons Wolverhampton

Highclare Preparatory School: *Woodfield*:

Assistant Head and KS2 Coordinator: Mr P Greenfield, BSc Hons Manchester, PGCE Cumbria

KS1 Coordinator: Mrs K S Tidman, BA Hons UCE, PGCE

EYFS Coordinators:

Mrs J Harris, BA Hons, MA, PSC, ECS Birmingham, EYPS

Mrs P Mitchell, BEd Hons Wolverhampton

Hill House School

Sixth Avenue, Auckley, Doncaster, South Yorkshire DN9 3GG

Tel:	01302 776300
email:	info@hillhouse.doncaster.sch.uk
website:	www.hillhouse.doncaster.sch.uk
Twitter:	@HillHouseSchool

Hill House was founded in 1912 and now occupies the site of the former RAF Officers' Quarters of RAF Finningley. The school provides a seamless, fully co-educational day education from age 3 to 18, and aims to provide a top-class holistic education where extra-curricular success and personal development stand alongside academic excellence. Hill House was named Independent School of the Year 2012–2013.

Number of Students. There are 700 pupils, with an equal number of boys and girls.

Education. Children enter the School at 3 years of age via Nursery where structured play and learning are the order of the day. As children progress through the School there is a gradual change to subject based teaching in specialist rooms, in preparation for GCSEs at 16 and A Levels at 18. Upon leaving the Junior School children enter a full house system for pastoral care. All main school subjects are offered, including individual Sciences, French, Spanish and Latin.

Facilities. The whole school is based in a historic building with new, purposely renovated classrooms. The site includes a large hall, dining room and theatre. In 2011 Hill House Sixth Form was launched, housed in its own new Sixth Form Centre, including classrooms, coffee shop and large common room. A new Music School contains practice rooms, a recording studio and a performing studio. 2013 saw the opening of the school's new sports grounds at Blaxton. In 2015, the blue AstroTurf Paver Hockey Pitch was opened, and in 2017 a new Dining Hall was created.

Extra-Curricular Activities. Music, Drama, Art and Sport play an important part in the life of the School. Throughout the year over 100 academic, recreational, musical and sporting activities per week are also offered in extra-curricular time. The major sports undertaken include rugby, netball, hockey, cricket, and tennis. There is a competitive fixture list including a number of overseas tours. There are two orchestras and five choirs within the school, who enjoy the newly-built Music School. Drama productions and concerts are undertaken on a regular basis. Residential trips and sports tours are undertaken at most age levels.

The School Day. School opens at 8.00am, with lessons from 8.40am to 4.00pm. Activities run from 4.00pm, and a before and after school club operates from 7.30am and until 6.00pm. The school operates a five-day week, with a full games afternoon for all ages above 7. There are some activities and fixtures at weekends. Sixth Formers also have an Internship Afternoon, where they spend time at local businesses, hospitals etc.

Fees per term (2021–2022). £3,040–£4,620 according to age. Fees include lunch and most extras.

Scholarships. Scholarships are available at 11+ for Academic, Sport, Art, Music and Performing Arts, and at 16+ for Academic and Leadership.

Charitable status. Hill House School Limited is a Registered Charity, number 529420.

Governors:
Mrs J Fearns (*Chair*)
Dr A Cooper

N Ebdon	A Ogley
A Joshi	J Pickering
Dr R Kersh	J Sprenger
R Leggott	M Wilson-MacCormack

Headmaster: **David Holland**, MA Cantab

Head of Senior School: Mrs Caroline Rogerson, BSc Hons
Head of Junior School: Mr Jonathan Hall, BEd Hons
Deputy Head: Mrs Belinda McCrea, MA Cantab
Second Master: Mr Simon Hopkinson, BA Hons
Deputy Head of Junior School: Mrs Charlotte Leach, BA Ed Hons

Bursar and Clerk to the Governors: Mrs Karen Kidney, ACMA Hons

Heads of Departments:
Miss K Barnes, BA Hons (*Sport*)
Mr Mark Brannan, BSc Hons (*Science*)
Mr Victoria Bodman, BA Hons (*Practical Music*)
Miss Jo Chappell, BA Hons (*Religious Studies*)
Mr Richard Dorman, BA Hons (*History*)
Mr Graham Green, MA (*Geography*)
Dr Kurt Johnson, PhD (*English*)
Ms Heather Lindsay, BA Hons (*Classics*)
Mrs Wendy Parkhurst, BA, MA (*Art*)
Mr Christopher Rose, BSc Hons (*Director of Rugby*)
Mr James Ross, BSc Hons (*Director of Hockey*)
Mrs Mahjabeen Thomas, BSc Hons (*Mathematics*)

Housemistress (*Field House*): Mrs Mahjabeen Thomas, BSc
Housemaster (*Master House*): Mr Peter Shipston, BA, MA
Housemaster (*New House*): Mr Christopher Barnett, BEng Hons
Housemaster (*School House*): Mrs Christine Havard, BA Hons

Kingsley School

Northdown Road, Bideford, Devon EX39 3LY

Tel:	01237 426200
email:	admissions@kingsleyschoolbideford.co.uk
website:	www.kingsleyschoolbideford.co.uk
Twitter:	@KSBideford
Facebook:	@KingsleySchoolBideford
Instagram:	@kingsleyschool
LinkedIn:	/company/kingsley-school-bideford

Kingsley School Bideford, a single campus Co-educational Boarding and Day school for pupils aged 0 to 18, is committed to discovering, nurturing and celebrating the talents and achievements of each and every one of its pupils. This commitment makes it the ideal school for families from the UK and overseas, who believe that every child is an individual, worthy of individual attention and encouragement.

As a relatively small school of around 420 boys and girls from Nursery to Sixth Form, Kingsley's atmosphere is like a large family where everybody knows each other well. The school's philosophy encourages personal qualities such as courage, generosity, honesty, imagination, tolerance and kindness. In addition, we develop the students' broader interests and skills in sport, music, art, and drama. Overall, a Kingsley education develops each student's individual character and talents both inside and outside the classroom.

Location. Kingsley School is situated in the beautiful North Devon market town of Bideford, a historic port beside the estuary of the River Torridge. The spectacular scenery of the North Devon coast and beautiful beaches are on our doorstep, and there is easy access to the National Parks of Exmoor and Dartmoor. The North Devon link road, which passes close to Bideford, provides a direct route to the M5 motorway.

Earth Centre. Our current project is the development of the Earth Centre offering; based in the heart of Devon's UNESCO biosphere we are aiming to become the destination for excellence in educating and developing our students to be future leaders and experts in environmental protection and sustainability. Environmental sustainability is of significant importance and is seen as an integral part of the curriculum and the way Kingsley School is run and operated. In particular, climate action, biodiversity restoration and nutrition from healthy food are at the forefront of the schools' policy on environmental sustainability. Through its investment in the Earth Centre concept, Kingsley is driving its school operations towards carbon neutrality; investing in ecology zones to restore and enhance biodiversity on its school sites; and developing commercial-scale market gardens to provide nutrient-dense healthy food for its pupils and the wider community. These activities are also aimed at cultivating a range of academic and vocational skills relevant to the environmental challenges we face and the new career opportunities becoming available.

Organisation. Kingsley School is entirely co-educational and comprises a Senior School with approximately 200 pupils, aged 11 to 18 years and a Prep School with approximately 130 pupils aged 2½ to 11 years, as well as 50 in our Pre-Prep, which offers wraparound care for children from 8 weeks to 3 years old. In addition, the Learning Development Centre, with a nationwide reputation for outstanding dyslexia provision, serves around 25% of the school's pupils.

Site and Buildings. Situated on a beautiful 25-acre site, the school has two Boarding Houses for boys and one for girls, all of which have immediate access to extensive playing fields, an all-weather hockey pitch, netball and tennis courts.

In recent years, an ambitious building programme has led to the provision of first-class facilities for sport, ICT, drama, gymnastics, art and science. The Library provides an excellent environment for study, research and career guidance.

Curriculum. Senior School, for GCSE study, the core of subjects include English, Mathematics, Biology, Chemistry, Physics, Modern Languages and Religious Studies. In addition, subjects such as Art and Design, ASDAN, Computer Science, Drama, Engineering, Geography, History, Hospitality, Music and Sports Science and PSE complete the programme of study. In the Sixth Form, there is a wide choice of A Level and vocational subjects including Applied Science, Art, ASDAN, Biology, Business Studies, Chemistry, Drama, Economics, EAL, English Literature, EOQ, Geography, History, Horticulture, Hospitality, Maths, Further Maths, Modern Foreign Languages, Music, Photography, Physics, Psychology and Sport. Tuition in English for speakers of other languages is also available.

Sport and Physical Education. All pupils, girls and boys, are encouraged to participate in various sports, including rugby, hockey, netball, cross-country, handball, cricket, gymnastics, badminton, basketball, football, rounders, tennis, judo, swimming and health-related fitness. The Judo Academy has a unique link with the elite Team Bath. The school's gymnasts compete at a local, regional and national level. Our cross country athletes compete at regional and national ISA levels. Kingsley School is also home to the Devon Handball Squad. Recently, the girls' handball team came second in the Handball Nationals. A number of our students achieve England and GB squad pathway for handball.

Clubs and Activities. There is an extensive range of extra-curricular activities organised and supervised by staff. The Duke of Edinburgh's Award scheme, Ten Tors, Eco club, gardening, filming, choir, orchestra, judo, computing, art, music, climbing, and surfing are among the most popular clubs available for our pupils to enjoy. Numerous expeditions and field trips are organised each year, both in the UK and abroad. Musicals, plays and concerts are regularly presented in the school's purpose-designed theatre.

Careers. From Year 9 onwards, pupils are offered a planned programme of careers education and guidance as part of the tutorial programme. This is complemented by presentations from visiting professionals, visits to careers events and close contact with Careers Advisers from Connexions Cornwall and Devon. All pupils have access to the latest careers information in the School Library.

Pastoral Care. In addition to their Year Heads, all pupils have a Personal Tutor responsible for monitoring their academic progress and personal wellbeing. For Boarders, care is also the responsibility of the Housemaster or Housemistress.

Admission. Boys and girls join the Nursery from 3 months. Entry to the Prep and Senior Schools is by interview and taster day. For pupils with recognised learning difficulties, entry is by interview and an up-to-date educational psychologist's report. 13+ admission is through our own Entrance Examination or Scholarship Examination. An interview and a report from their present school are required for older pupils.

Scholarships. Entrance Scholarships are offered annually for pupils joining Year 7, Year 9 and Year 12 based on the results of entrance tests held in the preceding January. Candidates may be considered for an academic scholarship along with individual scholarships in Music, Performing Arts, Sport, Art and the Kingsley Top Universities Programme. Scholarships will be awarded on the basis of an interview, audition or assessment at the School, together with a supporting portfolio of achievement in the relevant subject. Candidates who figure very highly in all three areas but do not gain an individual award may be considered for an All-Round Scholarship at the Headteacher's discretion. If an All Round Scholarship is offered it will be based on academic performance and performance in two other

scholarship areas. Assessment for Year 7, 9, 12 academic scholarships is made through written tests in Mathematics, English and Science, and a verbal reasoning test.

Fees per term (2021–2022). Prep School: Day £2,055 (Reception), £2,160 (Years 1 and 2), £2,685 (Years 3 and 4), £3,470 (Years 5 and 6); Boarding (from Year 4): £5,785 (weekly), £8,275 (full). Senior School: Day £4,360–£4,620 Boarding: £9,995 (full), £7,245 (weekly).

Prospectus. The Kingsley School prospectus is available from the Admissions team, email: admissions@kingsleyschoolbideford.co.uk, tel: 01237 426200 or online via the school's website: www.kingsleyschoolbideford.co.uk. Visitors are most welcome to tour the school by appointment.

Headteacher: Mr Robert Pavis, MA Ed

Assistant Headteacher (Pastoral): Mrs Sarah Gosai
Assistant Headteacher (Academic): Mrs Christine Hamilton

Head of Prep/Pre School/Nursery: Mr Andrew Trythall, BA

Head of Marketing: Mrs Lucy Goaman BA, MA, MCIM
Director of Admissions: Mrs Lou Wivell, BA
Head of Boarding: Mrs Laura Holt
Business Manager: Mr Stephen O'Brien

Leweston School

Sherborne, Dorset DT9 6EN

Tel: 01963 210691
email: admin@leweston.dorset.sch.uk
website: www.leweston.co.uk
Twitter: @LewestonSchool
Facebook: @Leweston
Instagram: @leweston1891

Leweston School is a co-educational boarding (full, weekly and flexi) and day school. The school has adopted the 'diamond model' with teaching in Science, Maths and some sport taking place in single-sex classes. With this model the school provides the opportunity to combine the academic benefits of single-sex education with the all-round advantages of co-education.

Situated in 46 acres of beautiful Dorset parkland, 3 miles south of Sherborne, the school offers all the advantages of both the traditional and modern in education with excellent facilities, particularly in the Sciences, Design & Technology and Sport. The school is also a Pentathlon GB Modern Pentathlon Training Academy, and one of only 9 in the country, thanks to its impressive record in the field of multisport disciplines. The school runs dedicated training programmes for these disciplines and hosts a number of popular training camps and competitions throughout the year. There is also a popular and successful Equestrian team who are NSEA Regional Points League winners for the third year running. Leweston pupils achieve outstanding results in many sports as representatives of the school, the county and Team GB.

Founded by the Religious of Christian Instruction in 1891, the school is a Catholic foundation but has a large percentage of pupils from other denominations. There are approximately 550 pupils in the whole school of whom around 80 are boarders. The ethos of the school is based on a wide social mix with a spread of talents, firm but friendly discipline and a keen sense of Christian and moral values. The Head is forward looking with a strong sense of leadership and vision. The school has a Lay Chaplain and pupils are expected to attend Chapel once a week. Preparation for confirmation is available for both Catholic and Anglican pupils.

The academic standard of the school is high. At both GCSE and A Level pass rates are consistently over 95% and the school's reputation for excellence in Music and Drama runs parallel with academic achievement in Sciences and the Arts. Each year pupils gain places at leading universities and go on to read a wide range of degrees. The real success of the school, however, is achieved by realising the full potential of each individual pupil; much emphasis is placed upon the rich extracurricular offering, which helps to discover and nurture a wide range of talents.

Teachers are dedicated and imaginative, including specialist teachers for Dyslexia and EAL. The school's special quality is its ability to encourage in each pupil a sense of their own worth and ability. Pupils are outgoing and well-mannered. While Leweston has a high proportion of day pupils, the school is fully committed to boarding, offering a wide programme of activities in the evenings and at the weekends.

Sherborne is an attractive historic abbey town with few of the distractions of a large city but at the same time, it is served by regular Network Express trains to and from London and good road links to Salisbury, Exeter and Bath.

Leweston Prep (IAPS) for girls and boys aged 3 months to 11 years, with boarding provision from age 8, is situated on the same campus, thus offering continuity of education to age 18. The early years provision includes French, Spanish and weekly swimming lessons from Nursery and was recently award outstanding in all areas by Ofsted. The school hosts a weekly Forest School Playgroup and Toddler Swimming Group. (*For further details, see entry in IAPS section.*)

Scholarships are awarded at 11+, 13+ and Sixth Form entry. Academic scholarships are available as well as Music, Art/Design, Drama, Sport, Equestrian and Pentathlon. Dates of examinations: Late November for Sixth Form scholarships, late January for others. Further details and entry forms can be obtained from the Registrar or found on the school website.

Fees per term (2021–2022). Senior School: Full Boarding £8,857–£9,823; Weekly Boarding (4 nights) £7,707–£8,534; Day £5,452. Flexi Boarding (including supper): £50 per night.

Charitable status. Leweston School Trust is a Registered Charity, number 295175. It is a charitable foundation set up for educational purposes.

Governing Body:
Mr I Lucas
Mr S Griffith
Mrs S Gordon Wild
Deacon Mark Brown
Mrs V de Fontanals Simmonds
Mrs D Martin
Mr D McKechnie
Mrs R Peacock
Mrs S Crowther

Mrs A Hughes
Prof T Meehan
Mr S Greenwood

Head: **Mr John Paget-Tomlinson**, BA Reading, MA King's College London

Deputy Head (*Teaching and Learning*): Mr S Whittle, BSc Hons Birmingham

Assistant Head Pastoral (*Wellbeing*): Miss J Atyeo, BA Hons Leeds, MA London, PGCE Oxon

Bursar: Lt Col Gus Scott-Masson

A full teaching staff list can be found on the School website.

Lichfield Cathedral School

The Palace, The Close, Lichfield, Staffordshire WS13 7LH

Tel: 01543 306170
email: admissions@lichfieldcathedralschool.com
website: www.lichfieldcathedralschool.com

Age Range. 2½–18.

Number of Pupils. 520 including 34 Cathedral choristers.

Fees per term (2021–2022). Tuition: £3,120–£4,890.

Lichfield Cathedral School is an outstanding co-educational day school for children aged 2½ to 18. Our mission is to be an internationally recognised school that serves its local area by creating an inclusive school community devoted to Christian ideals of learning, raising the aspirations of each of its members and fulfilling their potential in body, mind and spirit.

The ethos of the school is that of a community where Christian values are upheld and, whilst most pupils are members of the Church of England, children of other denominations and religions are welcomed.

The school occupies two main sites: the Junior Years are located 3½ miles north of Lichfield city centre in six acres of countryside at Longdon Green, while the Middle and Senior Years occupy several buildings in the Cathedral Close, one being the magnificent 17th century Palace, the home of the Bishops of Lichfield until 1952.

The link with the Cathedral remains strong with a twice-weekly school service, as well as concerts and services throughout the year. The 18 boy choristers (aged 7–13) and 19 girl choristers (aged 10–15) are supported by scholarships provided by the Cathedral Chapter and the School. Former choristers continue their choral training in Cantorum, the scholarship-based chamber choir and Sixth Form Choral Scholars rejoin the Cathedral Choir to sing with the Lay Vicars Choral. Academic, art, drama and music scholarships are available to internal and external students entering Year 7 and Sixth Form.

Learning in the Early Years Foundation Stage is planned around half-termly topics and the children take part in a range of activities which are balanced between adult-led and child-initiated opportunities. Activities are carefully structured to challenge children, encouraging them to develop confidence and the skills needed to solve problems. The outdoor facilities offer children an exciting environment in which to explore and investigate, and we ensure children have the time for free play.

Forest School is a popular element of the curriculum up to Year 9 that provides a holistic, individualised approach to outdoor learning, with a strong focus on developing self-esteem, confidence, resilience, communication skills and social and emotional awareness.

The spirit of intellectual enquiry is at the heart of teaching and learning at the school. Academic results are strong, particularly at GCSE and A Level. Throughout Key Stages 1 to 3, pupils follow a broad and balanced curriculum of English, Mathematics, Science, Computing, French, Spanish, German, Latin, History, Geography, Religious Studies, Art, Design, Music, Drama, Physical Education and Games and Personal, Social and Health Education. ICT skills are developed across every subject.

We offer a wide range of GCSE subjects, including Art and Design, Biology, Business Studies, Chemistry, Computing, Design Technology, Drama Studies, English Literature, English Language, French, Geography, German, History, Mathematics, Music, Physical Education, Physics, Product Design, Religious Studies and Spanish. The same subjects are offered at A Level, with the addition of Computer Science, Economics, Further Mathematics, Government & Politics, Law, Music Technology, Philosophy and Ethics, Psychology and Drama & Theatre. BTEC qualifications are available in Applied Law, Criminology and Business.

A co-curriculum of activities ensures students are well-rounded and gain valuable skills for higher education, employment and life outside school. Extra-curricular activities every day after school cover a wide range of subjects from chess to cooking and from Taekwondo to tennis. Several orchestras and ensembles are extremely active, as are the five main school choirs.

The unique, whole school Ethical Leadership Programme helps pupils and students to develop both the life skills and the strength of character to make a positive contribution to the world and do what is right, because they know it to be so.

All pupils have access to a rich variety of both residential and day trips as well as pupil exchanges, overseas expeditions and cultural immersion opportunities. Many are directly linked to the curriculum, but the benefits to pupils go far beyond the purely educational. The Duke of Edinburgh's Award scheme is thriving. Sixth Form students take part in overseas volunteer work through World Challenge.

Parents are welcome to contact the school for a tour and a meeting with the Head or to attend the any of the school Open Events held throughout the year.

Charitable status. Lichfield Cathedral School is a Registered Charity, number 1137481.

Governors:
Chair: Mrs N Dawes, OBE
Mrs C Shaw
The Very Revd A Dorber
Mrs R Hadley-Leonard
Mr E Lunt
Mrs J Mason
Mr R Oakley
Revd Canon Dr G Platten

Mr C Rickart
Mrs N Roy
Revd Canon A Stead

Bursar and Clerk to the Governors: Mrs P Sharratt

Head Teacher: Mrs Susan Hannam, BA Hons, MA, PGCE

Deputy Head: Mr A Harrison, BEd Hons
Head of Junior Years: Mrs J Churton, BSc Hons, PGCE

Assistant Head (Pastoral): Mrs J Owens, BA Hons, PGCE
Assistant Head & Head of DT: Mr R Hoddle, BA Hons, PGCE
Assistant Head & Head of Science: Mrs M Gardner, BSc Hons, PGCE

Associate Assistant Head & Head of Geography: Mr M Amison, BSc Hons, PGCE, MSc, FRGS
Associate Assistant Head & Head of Sport: Mr M Turner, BSc, MEd, PGCE

Heads of Year:
EYFS: Mrs W Williamson, MBA, PGCE
Years 5 & 6: Mr S Coleman, BA Hons, PGCE
Year 7 and Chaplaincy Lead: Mr D Lane, BEd Hons
Years 8 & 9: Mr M Mayne, BSc Hons, QTS
Years 10–11: Mrs M Goodwin, BA Hons, PGCE
Head of Sixth Form: Mr A Sherrington, LLB, PGCE

Heads of Department:
Mrs B Dunne, BA, PGCE (*Drama*)
Mr J Gardiner, BA Hons, PGCE (*Computing*)
Mr L Guffick, BSc Hons, MSc, MA, PGCE, GTP (*Mathematics*)
Mrs I Johnson, BA Hons, PGCE (*Religious Studies*)
Dr P Jones, BA, MRes, PGCE, PGCES, PhD (*History*)
Mrs C Lamb, MA, ARCO (*Performance Music & Director of Music Outreach*)
Mrs D Rice, BA Hons, ALCM, PGCE (*Music*)
Mrs N Smith, BA Hons, PGCE (*Languages*)
Mrs S Whatley, BA Hons, PGCE (*Art*)

Longridge Towers School

Longridge, Berwick-upon-Tweed, Northumberland TD15 2XQ

Tel: 01289 307584
email: enquiries@lts.org.uk
website: www.lts.org.uk
Twitter: @LongridgeTowers
Facebook: @LongridgeTowersSchool
Instagram: @LongridgeTowers

Motto: *Carpe Diem*

The school occupies a Victorian Mansion set in 80 acres of woodland in the beautiful Tweed Valley and enjoys excellent road and rail links with England and Scotland. Daily school bus services operate within a radius of 35 miles from the school.

Longridge Towers, refounded in 1983 under its founder and President, the late Lord Home of the Hirsel, has grown from 113 pupils to 313 pupils. It is probably unique in offering the close personal relationships between pupils, staff and parents which creates a genuine 'family atmosphere'. The school has a reputation for turning out well-rounded and confident young people, the vast majority of whom continue their education at university.

Alongside the excellent academic results, the school offers many opportunities through its sporting and extra-curricular enrichment activities. All of these combine to give all pupils the chance to participate and acquire a variety of skills.

Sport figures strongly in the life of the pupils and many gain representative honours at county and national level in a variety of sports, such as rugby, hockey, cross-country running, athletics, tennis and cricket. Art, Music and Drama are also very popular and successful activities.

Entry. The school caters for a wide spectrum of abilities among its pupils who are taught in small classes. Special provision is made for the needs of pupils with mild dyslexia and for the small proportion of pupils for whom English is their second language.

Assessments upon entry to the Senior School in Mathematics and English are diagnostic and have no fixed pass mark.

The school is divided into 2 departments, Junior and Senior, and caters for pupils throughout their school career, from three to eighteen years. Pupils may enter at any age provided that a vacancy exists. Classes are small with less than 20 pupils per teaching set, reducing to about half this in the Sixth Form.

Activities. Longridge Towers is a school where the development of the pupils outside the academic sphere is considered to be vital. Every afternoon there is an extensive Enrichment programme offering a wide range of activities including: archery, rocket making, lacrosse, football, computer construction, dance, karate, judo, drama, kick boxing, creative writing, wildlife and gardening, young engineers, science club, debating, along with many others. The major team games are rugby, hockey, tennis, cross-country running, athletics and cricket. Many senior pupils participate in the Duke of Edinburgh's Award scheme. The musical activities within the school are varied and numerous. There are five Choirs, two Orchestras and various instrumental groups. Almost a third of the pupils take private instrumental lessons and the taking of grade examinations is encouraged. Over half of the pupils also take LAMDA examinations. No visitor to the school could fail to be aware of the variety and excellence of the artwork on display which includes clay modelling and photography.

Public Examinations. Sixteen subjects are offered at GCSE level, including Physics, Chemistry and Biology and 19, including Economics, Psychology, Sports Studies and Drama, are offered in the Sixth Form at A Level.

Boarding. The Boarding House and pastoral care are in the hands of resident non-teaching house parents. There is medical and dental care. Pupils have access to telephones and email and may send or receive fax messages using the facilities in the school office. Boarders may attend on a weekly or termly basis from age 8 years onwards. At weekends the boarders participate in a wide range of activities.

Scholarships and Bursaries. Academic awards at various levels are available annually to pupils aged 9–14 and 16 (into Sixth Form). Music, Sports, Art and All-Rounder Scholarships are also available to pupils aged 11–14 and 16.

Bursaries are available to children of serving members of the Armed Forces.

Bursaries are also available to pupils; the value of these is determined after consideration of a statement of parental income.

Fees per term (2021–2022). Full Boarders: £9,150 (Junior), £9,650 (Senior). Weekly Boarders: £7,000 (Junior), £7,500 (Senior). Day pupils: Government funded Nursery with charges for extra hours, £3,390 (Junior age 5–7), £4,290 (Junior age 7–11), £4,850 (Senior age 11–18).

Charitable status. Longridge Towers School is a Registered Charity, number 513534. It exists to provide an academic education for boys and girls.

Board of Governors:
Chairman: Mr A E R Bell

Mr A Birkett	Dr E C Miller
Mr T Bramald	Mrs P Derries
Mrs D Dakers	Mrs S Dalrymple
Mrs A Marshall	Mr M Mole

Headmaster: **Mr J C E Lee**, MA Hons, ACA, PGCE

Deputy Head: Mr P Whitcombe, BSc, PGCE

Head of Junior Department: Mrs S Maddock, BEd

Deputy Head of Junior Department: Mrs S Bullen, BA, QTS, NASENCo

Senior Teachers:
Mrs I Cheer, BA, BSc, Cert HSC, Dip HSW (*Music, Pastoral, SENCO*)
Dr N Dalrymple, PhD, MLitt, BA, PGCE (*Director of Learning*)
Mr A Skeen, BA, QTS (*Pastoral, Economics, Games*)

Teaching Staff:
Ms D Bryden, BEd (*Junior Department*)
Mr M Caddick, BA, PGCE (*German*)
Mrs C Cairns, BA Hons (*Junior Department*)
Miss A Coulson, PGCE (*Junior Department*)
Mr D Crowe, BA, PGCE (*History*)
Mr R Davie, BSc, PGCE (*Mathematics, Computing, Head of Sixth Form*)
Mr P Dodd, BEng, DIS, PGCE (*Head of Maths*)
Mrs S Douglas, BA (*Junior Department*)
Mrs A Gettins, BA (*Librarian, English*)
Mrs N Green, BA, PGCE (*EFL*)
Mrs L Johnson, BA, MA, PGCE (*English*)
Mr R Johnson, BA, MA, PGCE (*English*)
Mr C Johnston, BA (*Geography*)
Mr B Jones, BA, BEd (*Art*)
Mr D Kendall, BEd (*Physics*)
Dr D Hardy, MA, PhD, LRSM, QTS (*Music*)
Mrs J Masey, BSc, PGCE (*Science*)
Mr D Massie, BEd (*Head of Sport*)
Mrs B Mayhew, BA, PGCE (*French/Spanish*)
Miss J McCalvey, BSc, PGCE (*Science*)
Mrs R Mole, BSc, PGCE (*Junior Department*)
Mr R Moscrop, BA, QTS (*Junior Department*)
Mrs S Murray, BA, PGCE (*Junior Department*)
Ms H Norbury, BA, PGCE (*Junior Department*)
Mrs L Peters, BEd (*Girls Games, Sports Studies*)
Miss K Phillips, BA (*Drama/Speech & Drama*)
Mrs E Shaw, BA, PGCE (*Girls Games, Sports Studies*)
Mrs G Skeen, BSc, QTS (*Junior Department*)
Mrs M Smith, BSc, PGCE (*PE, CDT*)
Mr A Westthorp, BEng, PGCE (*CDT, Computing*)

Mrs K Westthorp, MA, PGCE (*French*)
Mrs D Whitcombe, MA, PGCE (*English*)
Mr R Woodrow, MEng, PGCE

Teaching Assistants:
Mrs A Young, FDTA
Miss K Redpath, HLTA
Mrs C Handley, BA, HLTA
Miss C Alexander, FD Level 3
Miss D Bowers, BA
Mrs D Johnston, FD Level 5

Boarding Staff:
Mr G Hattle, Cert. of Prof. Practice (*Senior House Parent*)
Mrs L Patterson (*House Parent*)
Mrs A Ireland, BA, PGCE, Cert. of Prof Practice
  (*Residential Senior House Parent*)
Mr M Short, Cert. of Prof. Practice (*House Parent*)

Matron: Mrs M Hattle, RGN

Administration:
Bursar: Mrs V Bryson, BA, Chartered Accountant
Bursar's PA: Mrs E Crossan
Finance Manager/Assistant Bursar: Mrs J Aitchison, BSc
Head's PA: Mrs C Craze, BSc
PA to Head of Junior Dept: Mrs A Allis, BA
H&S Co-ordinator: Mrs S Fleming
IT Manager: Mr D Mulholland
IT Assistant: Mr M McCarter
Registrar/Marketing Manager: Mrs M Burns
Reception: Mrs R Faltman
Site Manager: Mr C Smith

LVS Ascot

London Road, Ascot, Berkshire SL5 8DR

Tel: 01344 882770
email: registrar@lvs.ascot.sch.uk
website: www.lvs.ascot.sch.uk
Twitter: @lvsascot
Facebook: @LVSAscot

LVS Ascot is a non-selective, co-educational day and boarding school of over 800 pupils aged 4–18. It is an all-through school so pupils can begin their school career at LVS Ascot at age 4 and remain there until they complete Sixth Form.

Exam results in 2021 saw 94.7% of GCSE students achieving A*–C (grades 9–4); 97.2% in 2020. A Level results saw an increase in A*–C grades at 81.5%, compared with 75.3% in 2020.

Numbers. Infant & Junior School 210, Senior School 607 (including 161 in Sixth Form), boarding approximately 223.

Organisation. Pupils aged 4 to 11 (Years R to 6) are taught in the Infant & Junior School, in separate classes each with a class teacher. Houses are used for sports and other competitions. Junior School pupils may board from Year 3 (age 7) and join a mixed House (Kew House), which is an integral part of the Junior School buildings.

Senior School pupils, aged 11 to 18 (Years 7 to 13), are placed in tutor groups and a school House, with a tutor who monitors their pastoral care and oversees their academic performance. Students are taught in ability groups with a maximum class size of 20. Boarders are accommodated in four separate boarding Houses, each supervised by Housemasters/mistresses: Kew (junior house) is mixed for pupils from Year 3 to Year 7; Osborne (girls' house) for pupils from Year 8 to Year 11; Hampton (boys' house) for pupils from Year 8 to Year 11; Blenheim (mixed sixth form house) for pupils in Years 12 and 13.

Location. LVS Ascot is north of the A329, close to Ascot Racecourse and Royal Windsor. The school is easily accessible from the M3, M4 and M25 motorways as well as Heathrow and Gatwick airports. The school bus service connects with trains at Ascot Station, as well many surrounding towns within a 20 miles radius including locations in West London.

Facilities. LVS Ascot is a modern day and boarding school in the UK. The purpose-built facilities, set in 25 acres of landscaped grounds, include: boarding accommodation and classroom blocks, a sports centre, all-weather pitch, indoor swimming pool, fully-equipped 250-seat theatre and a music technology suite. LVS Ascot hosts over five-hundred networked computer workstations, with every classroom equipped with ICT resources for digital and interactive learning. Wireless networking provides additional facilities for centrally-managed student laptops, eBooks and other devices in a secure environment. There is a dedicated Sixth Form Centre, and a Learning Resource Centre, that has an extensive range of books and journals.

Curriculum. The curriculum is broad and based on the national curriculum 'plus'. Pupils follow a common core curriculum of English, Mathematics, Science, one/two foreign languages, plus PE and PSHE. Science is taught as separate subjects. At GCSE, students select their choices from: Business Studies, Technology, Art & Design, Geography, History, Food Technology, Music, Drama, Media Studies, Economics, Physical Education, Computer Science, Spanish, German or French.

A wide range of A Level and vocational options are provided, including Mathematics, Physics, Chemistry, Biology, Music, Geography, History, Economics, Business Studies, English, Art & Design, Theatre Studies, Design & Technology, Media Studies, Photography, Psychology, French, Spanish, German, ICT, Computer Studies, Engineering and Physical Education.

Sport. The school has superb indoor and outdoor facilities with a large sports hall, dance studio with ballet bars, a 25-metre swimming pool and a well-equipped gym as well as rugby, football and hockey pitches, tennis courts and an all-weather pitch. The school has achieved considerable success in providing County, Regional and National standard players in a wide range of sports. Whilst all pupils play team games such as Rugby, Football, Cricket, Hockey, Tennis, Netball, Basketball or Athletics in their early years, the range of options widens as pupils become older to encourage fitness for life, with opportunities such as skiing, skating, polo, fencing and playing squash.

Clubs and Activities. LVS Ascot is an accredited Duke of Edinburgh's Award training centre and runs a vibrant and popular award scheme. Alongside this there is a range of co-curricular activities such as music ensembles, newspaper club, riding, canoeing, rowing, climbing, cookery, animation and film club. In September 2015 LVS Ascot Junior School introduced a range of 25 co-curricular after-school clubs.

Admissions. There is no entrance examination; reports are requested from a student's current school. All students are interviewed prior to acceptance. Prospective students and their families are welcome to visit the school. Personal tours can also be arranged by appointment.

Fees per term (2021–2022). Infants £3,720; Junior: £4,455 (day), £9,515 (boarding); Senior: £6,330 (day), £11,275 (full/weekly boarding); Sixth Form: £6,670 (day), £11,720 (full/weekly boarding).

Scholarships and Bursaries. Academic, Music, Art, Drama, Sport Scholarships are available at Year 7 entry and various Scholarships are available for entry to the Sixth Form (Year 12).

Fee discounts and Bursaries are available to assist parents working in the Licensed Drinks Trade, MoD and British Diplomats. Third child discount is also available.

Charitable status. The Society of Licensed Victuallers is a Registered Charity, number 230011. It exists to provide education for boys and girls.

Patron: Her Majesty The Queen

Executive Director of Education & Operations: Mr I Mullins, BEd Hons, MSc, MBIM

Principal: **Mrs C Cunniffe**, BA Hons, MMus, MBA

Head of Infant & Junior School: Mrs R Cox, BA Hons, NPQSL, FCCT

Assistant Heads/Heads of Faculty:
Academic/Languages & Linguistics: Mrs S Petrault, BA Hons, CELTA
Academic/Science & Technology: Mrs S Catlin, BSc Hons, MA
Boarding: Mr B Hunt, BSc Hons, BSA Certified MCCT
Compliance & Co-curricular/Sports Science & Outdoor Education: Mrs L Collins, BA Hons
Sixth Form/Arts & Visual Studies: Mr S Moore (*acting*)
Wellbeing/Neuro-Diversity & Wellbeing: Mr J Curtis-Nye, BSc Hons, MA, AHEA

Housemasters/mistresses:

Boarding Houses:
Blenheim: Mr B Cutler-Ames, BA Hons, PGCE
Hampton: Mr J Wilder, FASC, BMus Hons, PGCE, BSA Certified
Kew: Mr B Hunt, BSc Hons, BSA Certified MCCT
Osborne: Miss P Swiech, BA Hons

Day Houses:
Brake: Mr D Ryan, BA Hons (*acting*)
Buchanan: Mrs C Robinson, MA
Coburg: Mr S McDonnell-Roberts, BSc (*acting*)
Hart: Mrs R Sandford, BA Hons
Kennington: Miss L Betteridge, BSc
Melbourne: Miss J Clark, BA Hons

Designated Safeguarding Leads:
Mrs L Collins, BA Hons (*Senior School*)
Mrs R Cox, BA Hons, PGCE, NPQSL, FCCT (*Junior School*)

Child Protection Officers:
Ms R Wilde, BSc Hons (*Senior*)
Mrs F Izod, BA Hons (*Junior*)

Heads of Departments:
Art and Design: Mrs R Sandford, BA Hons
Biology: Mrs L Chappell, BSc Hons

Business Studies/Economics: Mr R Furse, BA Hons
Chemistry: Mrs S Sales Mint, BSc, MPhil
Computing: Ms G Els, BA
Design & Technology: Mr M Smith, BEng
Drama/Performing Arts: Miss J Clark, BA Hons
EAL: Miss S Petrault, BA Hons, CELTA
English: Ms N Rowley, MEd, BA, HDE
French: Mr D Key, BA
Geography: Mrs M McAuley, BA, H Dip Educ, FDE
History: Mrs T Bason, BA Hons
Law, Government & Politics: Mr K Towl, LLB
Mathematics: Ms G Els, BA
Media Studies: Mrs J Westwood, BA Hons
Music: Mr J Wilder, FASC, BMus Hons, BSA Certified
Philosophy: Mr S Martin, BA Hons
Physical Education: Mrs E Pearce, BA Hons
Physics: Mr W Gilbertson, MA, MEng
PSHE: Mr B Hunt, BSc Hons, BSA Certified MCCT
Psychology: Mr F Green-Nickel, 1&2 Staatsexamen Lehramt
SEN: Mrs S Reade, BSc Hons, OCR Dip
Science: Mrs C Robinson, MA (*acting*)
Spanish: Miss R Heath, BA Hons

Head of Learning Resources: Mrs E Keeler, MA Hons, PG Cert, MCLIP
Education Technology Specialist: Mr S Panayi, BSc Hons

Infant & Junior School:
Head of Infant & Junior School: Mrs Rachael Cox, BA Hons, NPQSL, FCCT
Deputy Head: Mrs K Mackrell, BA Hons, NPQSL

Administrative Staff:
Head of Admissions: Mrs S Ingram
Executive PA: Mrs C Clark, BA Hons
Examinations Officer: Mrs R Jacobs
Principal's PA: Mrs C Gedge
Senior School Administrator: Mrs N Smith
Senior School Receptionist: Mrs S Dillon
Junior School Secretary: Mrs D Pearce
Junior School Receptionists: Mrs V De Barros; Mrs R Johal

Milton Abbey School

Milton Abbas, Blandford Forum, Dorset DT11 0BZ

Tel:	01258 880484
email:	admissions@miltonabbey.co.uk
website:	www.miltonabbey.co.uk
Twitter:	@MiltonAbbey
Facebook:	@MiltonAbbeySchool
Instagram:	@MiltonAbbey

Founded in 1954, Milton Abbey comprised around 210 pupils at the start of the 2021–2022 academic year. In the 2019 Pearson BTEC Awards it was named 'School of the Year' for the breadth and quality of its vocational courses.

Milton Abbey offers an outstanding range of qualifications, chosen to inspire students and prepare them for adult life. The focus is not only on what a student needs to learn, but on developing attitudes and habits for lifelong success. The School has a track record of enabling young people to gain the self-belief and confidence necessary to achieve.

With a deliberately small size, strong pastoral care, and great partnerships with parents, the School quickly gains exceptional knowledge of its pupils, setting ambitious targets for all. Lasting and fulfilling friendships are forged between pupils.

The School recognises that all children 'learn differently'. Students benefit from the support, inspiration, challenge and encouragement of an extraordinary team of teaching and boarding staff, enabling each pupil to achieve 'personal bests' in and beyond the classroom.

Situation. Stunning surroundings offer space, yet safety and security, providing an inspirational setting for learning. The Dorset towns of Blandford and Dorchester are nearby, along with beautiful rural and coastal areas.

Buildings. The Abbey is the School Chapel, and the dining room, the Abbot's Hall, dates back to the medieval era. Alongside a mansion house, modern facilities include contemporary boarding houses, a music school, art studio, fashion studio and creative media suite, a 370-seat theatre, plus a farm and stables. Sporting facilities include all-weather pitches, an indoor pool, cricket nets and golf course.

Organisation. Milton Abbey is proud of its full-boarding status and the comprehensive co-curricular and recreational programmes this allows.

On joining the School, every pupil is assigned to a House. Each House is a close-knit community with a team of resident staff and matrons. Milton Abbey has five boarding Houses: Athelstan, Hambro and Tregonwell for boys, and Damer and Hodgkinson for girls. Day and boarding pupils integrate in the same houses.

Curriculum. An innovative 'rotation curriculum' allows joining Third Form pupils to study core subjects throughout the year, while sampling a huge range of courses usually only available as GCSEs or BTECs. This helps them make informed decisions about their GCSE and BTEC choices for the Fourth and Fifth Forms, which they study alongside a balanced curriculum of core subjects. The Sixth Form provides a wide range of academic, technical and vocational courses including traditional A Levels, BTECs and top-up GCSEs.

Music. A wide variety of individual tuition is available for singers or musicians. Singing is a popular part of school life.

Sport. Sport plays a vital role in the development of pupils. With excellent coaching for team and individual sports, Milton Abbey provides one of the country's broadest sporting offers. The School's small size means each pupil has the time and support to enjoy sports, whether they're aiming to excel in a sport they already love or gaining confidence to find a sporting talent they didn't even know they had!

Activities. The School runs a comprehensive programme of engaging and rewarding co-curricular activities. From cookery courses to Duke of Edinburgh's Awards, and fashion design to Farm Club, there is something for all to enjoy. The School's thriving Combined Cadet Force holds camps and expeditions. Weekends offer pupils a choice of adventurous, cultural and social activities. As a member of the Round Square network, pupils undertake additional activities every Wednesday afternoon, designed to broaden their interests.

Admission. Most pupils join the School at age 13 in the Third Form (Year 9). The School gives quick and unconditional offers to prospective pupils, after they undertake an individual Admissions Visit. This provides clarity and certainty for families. Students seeking to join the Sixth Form are judged on individual merit and suitability for their chosen courses.

Offers are dependent on a satisfactory current school reference, including CAT4 or equivalent cognitive test scores, and an interview with the Head or Deputy Head. Offers are not dependent on Common Entrance results, however all applicants receiving an offer must maintain high levels of effort and application at their current school.

Prospective pupils with Special Educational Needs will be assessed by the Head of Learning Development, to make sure that the School can offer them the correct level of support.

Fees per term (2021–2022). Lower School: Boarding £14,275, Day £7,500.

Supplement for Sixth Form entrants: £500 per term.

Charitable status. The Council of Milton Abbey School Limited is a Registered Charity, number 306318.

Governors:
Ian G Bromilow, MSc, PhD (*Chair*)
Neil S Boulton
Colonel Oliver J H Chamberlain
Matthew Noyce
Patrick W McGrath
Colonel Neil K H Tomlin OBE
Michael C R Lefort

Visitor: Revd Canon C W Mitchell-Innes, MA

Head: **Judith Fremont-Barnes**, MA, MEd

Senior Deputy Head: James Watson, MA Hons, FCA, PGCE

Deputy Head (Academic): Claudia Hindle, MA, PGCE, MEd
Deputy Head (Co-Curricular): Chris Barnes, BA Hons
Deputy Head (Pastoral): Ruth Butler, BA Hons

Director of Finance: Stephen Lane, BSc, ACA

SENDCo & Lead Practitioner: Laura Kleiser
Head of Operations: Tracey Edwards
Head of Marketing & Events: Nick Cloke
ICT Manager: Brendan Picknell
Milton Abbey Association (Alumni) Manager: Hugo Mieville, BA, MA, PG Dip

Mount House School

Camlet Way, Hadley Wood, Barnet, Hertfordshire EN4 0NJ

Tel: 020 8449 6889
email: reception@mounthouse.org.uk
website: www.mounthouse.org.uk
Twitter: @MountHouseSch
Facebook: @MountHouseSchoolBarnet
LinkedIn: /school/mount-house-school

Age Range. 11–18 co-educational.

Number in School. 212 Day Girls & Boys.

Fees per term (2021–2022). £5,825.

Our mission at Mount House School is to inspire lifelong learning within a nurturing, culturally creative and intellectually dynamic community.

At Mount House, every individual is valued and each child's unique talents will be identified and nurtured. Students leave as able, articulate, balanced, caring, and well-rounded individuals with a genuine love of learning, ready to take on life's challenges and opportunities, aware of the needs of others and confident in their ability to make a difference.

Mount House expects students to be the very best they can be and inspires them to make their best even better. Our overarching aim is that Mount House is a happy and successful School, with an excellent record of GCSE and A level results and an outstanding record of students achieving places at top universities. The School is equally concerned to foster the wide range of skills that help young students grow into capable adults with a sense of self-worth. Mount House supports students as they strive for academic excellence within a clear framework of personalised pastoral care and wellbeing that brings success without stress.

Board of Directors:
Dr Colin Diggory (*Chairman*)
Mr Emil Gigov, FCA
Mr Ian Davis, MA, PGCE

School Staff:

Head: Mrs Sarah Richardson, BA, PGCE

Senior Leadership Team:

Deputy Head Pastoral: Mr M Kerr, BSc, MSc
Assistant Head, Head of Lower School, Director of Sport & Co-Curricular Activities: Mrs N Hillcoat-Hyde, BA, MA, PGCE
Assistant Head, Head of Upper School: Ms P Smyth
Assistant Head, Head of History: Mr T Phillips, BA Hons, PGCE
Assistant Head, Academic: Mr C McCormick, BA Hons, MA, PGCE
Bursar and Clerk to the Board of Directors: Mrs N Nathwani

Mr Phillip Allman, BA Hons, PGCE (*Sociology & Politics*)
Mrs Satbir Allman, MA, PGCE (*Sociology*)
Ms Amy Baird, BA Hons (*Art*)
Ms Carole Berry (*French*)
Mr Jerome Boonzaier, BCom, HDE Post Grad (*Business*)
Mr Peter Brozny, BSc (*Science*)
Mrs Maria Christou (*Careers*)
Ms Sofia Clarkson, MA, BA, PGCE (*Classics*)
Mrs Sue Colebrook (*Learning Support*)
Mr Paul Conyers, MA (*Maths, Science*)
Mrs Abisoye Da Rocha, BA Hons, PGCE (*French and Spanish*)
Ms Fiona Dawson, PGCE (*Drama*)
Mrs Kathryn Fallon, BA Hons, MLDP, PGCE (*Classics*)
Mr Patrick Gallagher, BSc Hons, MSc (*Mathematics*)
Ms Nicky Graves, BA Hons, PGCE (*Textiles*)
Mrs Nikki Gur, BSc, PGCE (*Mathematics*)
Miss Samira Hassan, BA (*Humanities*)
Mrs Hillcoat-Hyde, BA, MA, PGCE (*PE*)
Mr Ali Hosseinian, BEng Hons, PGCE (*Mathematics*)

Ms Semra Kazim, PGCE, MSc (*Science*)
Ms Clare Kelly (*Drama*)
Mrs Melani Lazouras, BA Hons, PGCE (*MFL*)
Mrs Rebecca MacDonald, MA Hons, PGCE (*English*)
Ms Eleonora Mariottini, Class 3 University, Italy QTS (*Spanish*)
Mr Dan Mather, BA (*PE*)
Mr Craig McCormick, BA Hons, MA, PGCE (*History*)
Mr Aidan Mullins, EdSC (*PE*)
Mr Paul Nancarrow, PG Cert TEAL, PG Dip, MA (*English*)
Ms Anastasia Nicola (*English*)
Ms Elizabeth Overman (*Learning Support*)
Mr Peter Pandelis, BSc Hons, PGCE (*Computing*)
Ms Oriana Patel, PGCE, BSc (*Geography*)
Mr Siraj Peara, BSc (*Science*)
Ms Melissa Petinou (*Learning Support*)
Mr Tony Phillips, BA Hons, PGCE (*History*)
Mrs Solene Roy, BSc, PGCE (*Psychology, Science*)
Ms Meliz Shukru (*Learning Support*)
Ms Elizabeth Somerville, BA Hons, PGCE (*Art & Design*)
Ms Claire Valdonio (*Learning Support*)
Mr Ronald Van Leeven (*Science*)
Mr Sam Whitehouse, BA Hons, PGCE (*Music*)
Ms Melanie Wiltshire (*Learning Support*)
Mr Jordan Wooldridge (*Learning Support*)
Ms Gabrielle Wong (*Business, Economics, Maths*)

Newcastle School for Boys

Senior School:
34 The Grove, Gosforth, Newcastle upon Tyne NE3 1NH

Tel: 0191 255 9300

Junior School:
30 West Avenue, Gosforth, Newcastle upon Tyne NE3 4ES

Tel: 0191 255 9300

email: enquiries@newcastleschool.co.uk
website: newcastleschool.co.uk
Twitter: @NSB_Boys @nsb_sport
Facebook: @NewcastleSchoolforBoys

Age Range. 3–18.

Number of Boys. 380.

Fees per term (2021–2022). £3,453 (Reception), £4,028 (Years 1–2), £4,155 (Years 3–6), £5,088 (Year 7 and above).

Newcastle School for Boys is the only independent school in the north east providing continuous education for boys from ages 3 to 18. Situated in Gosforth, Newcastle upon Tyne, the Senior School site on The Grove covers 5 acres of playing fields and buildings that currently house Years 7 to 11. Opposite the Senior School Years 12 and 13 are now housed in their own dedicated Sixth Form Centre, opened in September 2017. Our Junior School is housed on nearby sites on West Avenue and North Avenue. The School currently has 375 pupils on role from Nursery to Year 13.

The academic curriculum starts in the Infants and provides boys with opportunities for stretch and challenge from the outset. This leads through the Juniors to GCSE and

A Level qualifications in a wide range of disciplines at the Senior School and Sixth Form.

Pastoral care is outstanding throughout the school and boys receive plenty of individual attention so that they grow in confidence and independence.

Newcastle School for Boys believes strongly in enhancing learning beyond the classroom and runs an extensive trips and visits programme with great emphasis being placed on this in the junior and infant departments. Residential and day visits are offered to all pupils from age 5 onwards and culminate in major overseas trips and Duke of Edinburgh's Gold Award expeditions in the Sixth Form.

Senior School. The Senior School starts at Year 7 (11+) and runs through to Year 13 (18+).

We offer an enhanced curriculum leading up to GCSE, where most boys sit 10 subjects. The Senior School provides an extensive co-curricular programme of music, drama and a wide range of sports, including a number of major overseas trips. The School enhances its sporting provision through the use of a number of excellent local facilities including at South Northumberland Cricket Club and Northern Rugby Club.

Sixth Form. The School has established a successful and growing Sixth Form offering students a wide choice from a traditional AS and A Level structure. The Sixth Form provides the learning and support the boys need to achieve their best possible academic and personal outcomes.

Entrance and Scholarship Examinations are offered in January for boys entering Year 7 (11+), Year 9 (13+) and Year 12 (16+). Entry at other points is possible following a full academic assessment and interview.

Junior School. The learning environment across our Junior School is tailored to the needs of the younger boys, taking into account their energy and enthusiasm for challenge and discovery. The curriculum offered is a blend of the traditional and the innovative, and is designed to balance the need for adventure and fun, while maintaining progress in numeracy and literacy. The boys are provided with opportunities to develop their individual academic talents and to pursue their creative goals. Excellence is also pursued in the sporting arena where boys have opportunities including soccer, rugby, cricket, golf and fencing.

Regular drama performances and musical productions encourage teamwork and build confidence from an early age.

Breakfast club and after-school clubs and activities provide full wraparound care.

Charitable status. Newcastle School for Boys is a Registered Charity, number 503975.

Chairman of Governors: T J Care

Headmaster: **D J Tickner**, BA, MEd

Deputy Heads:
G Hallam, BSc
A Newman, BA

Head of Junior School: T White

Bursar: C Dobson, FCCA

Director of Marketing and Admissions: A Kingsland, BA, MSc

Our Lady's Abingdon

Radley Road, Abingdon-on-Thames, Oxfordshire OX14 3PS

Tel: 01235 524658
email: office@ola.org.uk
website: www.ola.org.uk
Twitter: @OLAabingdon
Facebook: @OLAabingdon
Instagram: @OLAabingdon
LinkedIn: /our-ladys-abingdon

Motto: *Age Quod Agis – Whatever you do, do it well*

Founded in 1860 by Mother Clare Moore of the Sisters of Mercy, Our Lady's Abingdon (OLA) is an independent, Catholic day school, for boys and girls aged 7–18. The school welcomes pupils of all faiths and none who wish to benefit from its nurturing and outward-looking ethos. OLA offers outstanding pastoral care and a wide range of academic and co-curricular activities, ensuring that pupils are confident and engaged and leave school excited about their next steps in life.

Small class sizes allow staff to get to know every single pupil, giving them the support and encouragement they need to fulfil their academic and personal potential.

Numbers. There are 330 pupils aged 11–18 in the Senior school and 40 pupils aged 7–11 in the Lower section.

Facilities and Buildings. Bright, spacious classrooms and an excellent library provide a pleasant ambience conducive to study and learning. Extensive grounds surround the buildings, providing an attractive setting in which pupils can play and relax during breaks. Sports facilities include football and rugby pitches, a multi-use games area, tennis courts, a sports hall, hockey and athletics provision and a 25-metre indoor swimming pool. The school has benefited from new dining rooms and a 70-seat cafe, with other recent building projects including a Design & Technology centre, an auditorium and library, the latest in ICT equipment and additional Science laboratories. The Music department benefits from new facilities to aid composition and support the wide variety of instruments taught in the school.

Curriculum. The school teaches a balanced range of subjects both academic and practical during the first three years. Latin is a core subject in Y7 and 8. Pupils usually take 10 or 11 subjects at GCSE, including English Language and English Literature, Mathematics, Science (Combined Science or Biology, Chemistry and Physics), Religious Studies and French or Spanish. Options are chosen from the Humanities to Classics and Physical Education. Three subjects are studied in the Sixth Form (OLA 6th), with many students taking the opportunity to take the EPQ (Extended Project Qualification) in the Lower Sixth. Some take Further Mathematics as a fourth A Level. The great majority of OLA 6th students go on to Higher Education, but some have also succeeded in gaining places on highly competitive professional placement programmes. There is also support throughout the school for pupils with special educational needs and for pupils for whom English is not their first language.

Co-curricular activities. The school provides an extensive programme of co-curricular activities including drama, music, art, public speaking and many forms of sport. Sailing is particularly popular. Buses run later on three evenings a week to accommodate these activities and to allow for supervised homework. There is also a strong commitment to local community schemes and an impressive record in the Duke of Edinburgh's Award scheme. OLA has regularly been accredited with the British Council's International School Award for the links it has fostered with schools in Uganda.

Fees per term (2021–2022). Senior School: £5,715; Lower School: £3,835–£4,605.

Admission. Through the school's own Entrance Examination at 11 and 13; pupils require at least 5 GCSEs at Grade 5 for entry to OLA 6th, with at least Grade 6 in the subjects they wish to study at A Level. Pupils interested in entering OLA 6th for whom English is a second language, must in addition have achieved a minimum level of 6.5 in IELTS for each category. Pupils may join in any year if a place is available with the exception of Years 11 and Upper Sixth.

Pupils may apply for Scholarships for entry to Year 7, Year 9 and OLA 6th. Candidates may also apply for bursaries, which are awarded at the discretion of the Governors.

Charitable status. Our Lady's Abingdon Trustees Limited is a Registered Charity, number 1120372, and a Company Limited by Guarantee, registered in England and Wales, number 6269288.

Board of Governors:
Chairman: Mr F Elturk, BSc
Mr G Ayling, MA
Dr L Bergmeier, PhD, CBiol, MRSB, FHEA
Mrs A Freeman, BEd
Revd J McGrath, STB, MA
Ms L Mills, BA, BSc
Mr F Peck
Sr P Roke, MA Cantab
Mrs H Ronaldson
Mr P Williams, MA Oxon
Dr Jacqueline Woodman, MB ChB, MRCOG, MA, MEd Ed, DPhil

Leadership Team:

Head of OLA: Mr D Gibbons, HA Hons Leeds, PGCE, MMU

Chief Operating Officer & Executive Leader: Mr P Karian, CIPD
Deputy Head: Dr B Reynaert, BSc, PGCE, PhD
Assistant Head (DSL): Mrs C Sharkey, BA, PGCE
Assistant Head (Pastoral): Mr L Allen, BSc, PGCE

Heads of Sections:
OLA 6: Dr E Lawson, BA, MA, PhD
Upper School: Mr A Jackson, BA, MSc, PGCE
Middle School: Mr J Cooper, BA, PGCE
Head of Transition: Miss S Page, BSc, PGCE
Lower School Coordinator: Mrs L Ainsworth, BA Hons

Heads of Departments:
Art: Mrs H Holden, BA, BA, PGCE, MSt
Careers: Mr C Sissons, BEd
Classics: Miss P Smith, BA
Design & Technology: Mr N Humphreys, BEd
Drama: Dr E Lawson, MA, PhD

Economics & Business Studies: Mrs L Webster, BA, Grad Dip, MEd
English: Mrs R San José, BA Hons Leeds
Geography: Mr A Jackson, BA, MSc, PGCE
History: Mr A Weekes, BA, PGCE
Learning Support: Ms S Martin-Morrissey, BA, PGCE, NASENCO
Mathematics: Mrs A Knight, BSc, PGCE
Modern Languages: Mme H Pang, MA
Music: Mr N Farrow, MA Oxon
Physical Education (Girls): Mrs M Barnett, BA
Physical Education (Boys): Mr L Allen, BSc, PGCE
PSHE: Ms S Martin-Morrissey, BA, PGCE, NASENCO
Psychology: Mrs J James, BSc, PGCE, GTP
Religious Studies: Miss S Campbell, BEd
Science: Mr A Easton, BSc, PGCE
Textiles: Mrs C Sharkey, BA, PGCE

Head of Admissions: Mrs R Knowles, BA, MBA
Head of Marketing: Ms K Sutton, CIM Dip
Head's PA: Mrs J Braley, BSc, Assoc CIPD
School Business Manager: Ms T Wheatley, AAT
School Development Manager: Mrs Z Doy, FIOS

The Peterborough School
A Woodard School

Thorpe Road, Peterborough PE3 6AP

Tel:	01733 343357
email:	office@tpsch.co.uk
website:	www.thepeterboroughschool.co.uk
Twitter:	@PeterboroughSch
Facebook:	@ThePeterboroughSchool
LinkedIn:	/company/thepeterboroughschool

The Peterborough School is the City's only independent day school for boys and girls from Nursery to Sixth Form. Situated in beautiful surroundings in the heart of Peterborough, the School enjoys excellent road and rail links. The School is a member of the Woodard Corporation, the largest group of Church of England Schools in England and Wales.

Situation and Buildings. The School is located in beautiful secluded grounds, near the centre of Peterborough, 50 minutes by fast train from King's Cross and easily accessible by road from the A1, A14 and A47. The elegant Victorian house is the centre of a modern, purpose-built complex of classrooms, laboratories, Music School, Art Block, Sixth Form Centre, Library and a modern Computing Suite. The Sports Facility was completed in September 2012.

The Preparatory School. Boys and girls are admitted into the Reception Class from the age of 4+. The whole range of Key Stage subjects is covered in addition to a variety of other subjects and activities, e.g. Reasoning, French and other languages. Some subjects are taught by specialist staff from the Senior School. There is emphasis on academic standards, good manners, Physical Education, Music and Drama.

The Senior School. The curriculum of the Senior School is characterised by small classes and an emphasis on individual guidance and target-setting. A balanced programme leads to high achievement at GCSE. English, Mathematics, Sciences, Religious Education, Games and PE remain compulsory throughout; Languages, Computer Science, Food Tech, History and Geography, Art, Art Textiles and Design Technology, Music, Drama and Physical Education form the matrix of options. Spanish has recently been added to the curriculum.

External candidates are selected from the entrance examinations and opportunities for Scholarships exist at Year 7 and Sixth Form entry.

The School has a modern Computing Suite with state-of-the-art equipment, including iPads and laptops. All classrooms are networked.

There are specialist laboratories for all sciences and a new Sixth Form science lab.

In the Sixth Form students usually take three A Level subjects but may in some circumstances undertake four. These are linear qualifications, with examination at the end of the two-year course of study: there are no AS examinations available at the end of the Lower Sixth. In addition to their academic studies, Sixth Formers undertake a significant enrichment programme that includes volunteering, the Extended Project Qualification (EPQ) and an electives programme.

As a School with pupils from Reception and children in the Nursery from 6 weeks and above, older pupils have many opportunities to develop a sense of involvement and responsibility, and carry out valuable service in the wider School community. Business sense is developed through the Young Enterprise scheme, in which the School is very successful. The Duke of Edinburgh's Award Scheme is also prioritised.

The Nursery. The Peterborough School Nursery offers daycare for babies to preschoolers. Optional lessons include French, Ballet and Key Sports.

Religion. Weekly Chapel Services are held and attendance is compulsory, although participation is optional.

Music and Drama. The music of the School, in particular its choral tradition, is renowned and the School competes in festivals as well as singing at events across the city. Tuition in singing, piano and all orchestral instruments is available. Major theatrical and musical productions take place several times a year, and the School presents an Art & Design Exhibition each summer. Speech & Drama is a popular extra curricular activity, with many students gaining LAMDA or New Era qualifications.

Games and Physical Education. The pupils achieve outstanding success in team and individual sports and athletics. Many pupils have represented the county, the region, and Team GB. The School estate is spacious with several pitches and all-weather courts. The many and varied sporting facilities of the city are within easy reach for swimming, rowing and athletics. The School is benefiting from the major development of its Sports Facility, including a Fitness Suite and Climbing Wall.

Extra-curricular Activities. Many clubs and societies operate in extra-curricular time, and field visits and excursions illuminate classroom work. Many pupils undertake the Duke of Edinburgh's Award Scheme at both Bronze and Gold levels, with outstanding success and the School has its own St John Ambulance division. Cubs, Scouts and Beavers are also run from the School.

Fees per term (2021–2022). Reception £3,676; Years 1–2: £3,852 Years 3–6 £4,670; Years 7–13 £5,687.

Tuition fees include a mid-morning snack and lunch.

Scholarships. Academic, Art, Music and Sport are the main scholarships available to those entering Year 7. Woodard All-rounder Scholarships are also available for Senior students at the Headmaster's discretion. Sixth Form Academic Scholarships are also available. Please apply to the Admissions Team for more information.

The Peterborough School Alumni (Westwoodians' Association). Secretary: Miss Alice Brazier who is based at the School.

Charitable status. The Peterborough School Limited is a Registered Charity, number 269667. It is an independent school which exists to promote the education of children.

School Council:
Chairman: Mr K Craig, BA Hons, FCCA, CTA
Mrs P Dalgliesh
Ms L Ayres, LLB
Mr C Spinley
Mrs K Hart, BA Hons
Mr P Hayes
Prof C J Howe, MA, DPhil, FLS
The Rt Revd R Ladds, SSC, Provost of Woodard Schools
Mrs H Milligan-Smith, LLB Hons
Mrs E Payne
Mr P Simmons
Mr P Southern, FRICS
Dr J S Thompson, LMSSA, MBBS, DRCOG

***Head*: Mr A Meadows,** BSc Hons Manchester, NPQH

Bursar: Mr S Dharamraj, MBA, MA, BSc Hons, FCMI
Deputy Headmaster: Mr R Cameron, BA Hons Southampton
Head of the Preparatory School: Mrs A-M Elding, MA OU, BEd Hons Derby
Head of Pastoral Care: Mr M Pryor
Director of Sixth Form: Mr A Stroud, BA Hons Oxon
Chaplain: Revd T Sherring, MTh Oxon, BA Exeter

Staff:
Miss H Adams, BSc Hons (*Mathematics*)
Mrs L Andrew, BEd Hons (*Preparatory*)
Mr P Baldwin, BA Hons (*Preparatory*)
Mr K Bingham, BA Hons (*Preparatory*)
Mr D Bocking (*Maths*)
Mr C Brocklesby, BA Hons (*Geography*)
Mrs H Brookes, BA Hons (*English*)
Mrs Burgess (*Speech and Drama*)
Miss A Buxcey, BA Hons (*Religious Education*)
Miss Z Chappell, BA Hons Cantab (*Preparatory*)
Miss S M Clarkson, BA Hons Cantab (*History*)
Miss H Clisset, BA Hons (*Dance*)
Mr G Cloke, BSc Hons (*Preparatory*)
Miss S Cummings, BA Hons (*Chemistry, Head of Key Stage 4*)
Mrs K Davis, BSc Hons (*Chemistry, Head of Key Stage 3*)
Mrs R Ditcher, BSc Hons (*Preparatory*)
Mr S Dyer, BA Hons (*Economics, Business Studies*)
Dr L Fox-Clipsham, PhD, BSc (*Science*)
Mrs L Grinyer, BA Hons (*English*)
Ms A Garala, BSc Hons (*Preparatory*)
Mrs R Hampson, BA Hons (*Art, Textiles*)
Mr A Harwin, BA Hons (*Art*)
Miss M Johal (*Sociology/Psychology*)
Miss C Johnson, BSc Hons (*Biology*)
Mrs E Kay, BSc Hons (*Physical Education*)

Ms A Kupara, BA (*Computing & Digital Strategy*)
Mrs L Lane (*PE*)
Mr S Law, BSc Hons (*Physics*)
Miss L McChlery, BEd (*Preparatory*)
Mrs L McClarnon, BEd Hons (*Preparatory*)
Mr J Marsden, BSc Hons (*Physical Education*)
Mrs G Mason, OND Hotel & Catering (*Food Technology & Preparatory Teaching Assistant*)
Mrs S Noone, BEd (*Preparatory*)
Mrs E Porsz, BA Hons (*Physical Education*)
Ms E Potbury, BA Hons (*French*)
Mrs C Raitt (*PE*)
Mrs J Roberts, BA Hons (*English*)
Mr P Schavier, Masters Degree (*German*)
Mrs R Shang, BA Hons (*Drama, PSHE*)
Mrs M Silvester, BSc Hons (*Mathematics*)
Mrs A Skelton, BA Hons (*Preparatory*)
Miss C Steward, BA Hons (*Preparatory*)
Mr M Twigg, BA Hons (*Product Design*)
Mrs C Wagner-Lees, BA Hons (*German*)
Mrs S Ward, BSc Hons, PGCE (*Head of Individual Learning*)
Mrs L Wisdom, BSc (*Geography*)
Mrs J Young, BSc Hons (*Physical Education*)

Instrumental Music/Speech & Drama:
Miss K Birtles, BMus Hons (*Flute & Oboe*)
Mr R Brain, BA Hons, MA (*Director of Choral Music*)
Mr J Cranfield, BA Hons (*Guitar*)
Mr R Haylett, BA Hons Cantab (*Singing*)
Mr M Jewkes (*Jazz Piano & Saxophone*)
Mrs M McAuliffe, Dip ABRSM (*Violin*)
Mr J Nessfield, BA Hons (*Brass*)
Mrs P Samuels, LGSM Cert Acting GSMD (*Speech & Drama*)
Miss E Smith, BMus Hons (*School Accompanist*)

Administrative Officers:
Head's PA: Mrs L Hale
Head of Marketing & External Communications: Miss A Brazier
Development/Admissions Manager: Mrs I Zizza
Admissions Officer: Mrs N Abbott
Administrative Assistant: Miss D Abbott
Accounts: Mrs J House, BA Hons; Mrs R Forman
Domestic Bursar: Mrs Z Clark
Estate Manager: Mr C Lang
Laboratory Technician: Mrs A Albon, BSc
Art and Food Tech Technician: Miss A Prebble
Network Manager: Mr A Nicholls
IT Technician: Mr K Rossall
LRC Manager: Mrs C Thomson
Receptionist: Mrs R Adcock

Teaching Assistants & Supervisors:
Mrs A Brennan
Miss C Callow
Mrs W Cohen
Miss F Cupoli
Ms E Drew, BA Hons
Mrs Z Green
Mrs E Penniston, BA Hons
Miss D Pepper
Mrs J Reade
Mr C Howitt
Mr R Westbrook

Medical Staff:
Mrs F Aylmore, BSc Hons (*Senior Nurse*)
Mrs M Lay, BSc Hons (*School Counsellor*)

Pitsford School

Pitsford Hall, Pitsford, Northamptonshire NN6 9AX

Tel: 01604 880306
email: office@pitsfordschool.com
website: www.pitsfordschool.com
Twitter: @Pitsford_School
Facebook: @PitsfordSchool
Instagram: @pitsfordschool

Age Range. 3–18 Co-educational.
Number of Pupils. 290 boys and girls.
Fees per term (2021–2022). Junior School £2,917–£4,731; Senior School £5,061. Lunches £304.

The School was founded in 1989 to offer a traditional Grammar School standard education to boys in Northamptonshire. Today, the School still offers the same high standards of education but to boys and girls from 3–18 years of age.

Pastoral Care. The School's academic success is complemented by effective pastoral support. By keeping class sizes small, a friendly, family atmosphere is evident, allowing pupils to grow and develop in confidence as they progress through the School.

Admissions. Reception, Year 7 and Sixth Form are the most common years of entry to the School, although pupils may be admitted in other years when required, if space is available.

Entry to Key Stage 1: pupils are invited to spend a day with their current year group to ensure they are happy in their future surroundings.

Entry to Key Stage 2: pupils are invited in for an Assessment.

Entry to the Senior School: Prospective pupils are invited to sit the School's entrance assessment.

Learning support programmes are available where a need is identified and likewise stronger pupils can be challenged where needed. Pupils generally take 9 or 10 GCSEs before transferring to the Sixth Form at the end of Year 11.

The Sixth Form is structured to provide a stepping stone from the discipline of Senior School to the demands of Higher Education. Sixth Formers take a full part in the life of the School and have many positions of responsibility including mentoring younger years and leading House and Sporting events.

Sport and Extracurricular Activities. Rugby, netball, cricket, rounders and tennis are just some of the sports played throughout the School. In addition, the School's Cross Country Team enjoys ongoing success when competing against other Schools. The Pitsford Run is a well known local event.

Junior School activities range from the School Council, Eco Club, Choir, cooking, Rugby, Netball, Arts and Craft plus many others.

Senior School pupils have over 60 activities to choose from. Most Activities take place on site, such as Yoga, Tai

Chi, Marvel Club, Duke of Edinburgh, Film Club, Musical Theatre Club and many more. However, the School's excellent location means that a number of activities such as sailing, kayaking and fishing are also available just a short distance from the School. All are extremely popular.

Music. Music is an integral element of school life at Pitsford School.

Musical Recitals are held in Pitsford Hall every Wednesday lunchtime and in addition, the School holds Four Evening Concerts per year. Individual music lessons are available in a wide range of instruments and group participation and performance opportunities include; woodwind, guitar, percussion, strings, sax and flute ensembles and two choirs.

A number of Junior and Senior plays take place throughout the year, ranging from Shakespeare to Musicals.

Charitable status. Northamptonshire Independent Grammar School Charity Trust Limited is a Registered Charity, number 298910.

Governing Body:
Chairman: Mr A Tait

Mr M Adams	Reverend S Trott
Mr J Brown	Mrs S Burditt
Mr S Coleman	Mr M Gaskell
Mrs J Harrop	Mr J Weitzel
Mr A Moodie	Miss L Mohess

Headmaster: Dr Craig Walker

Deputy Head: Mrs F M Kirk, BA, MEd

* *Head of Department*

Mrs A Arroyo (*Modern Languages*)
Mr O Auckland, BA Hons (*Junior School*)
Mrs C Ball (*Junior School*)
Ms A Bridges (*EYFS Specialist*)
Mrs C Cabrera-Alvarez (*Modern Languages*)
Mrs F L Care, MA (*Mathematics*)
Mrs L A Chacksfield, BEd (*PE and Games**)
Mme M H Conroy, BA (*Junior School*)
Mrs A Cowling, BSc Hons (*Biology and Chemistry*)
Miss L Crews (*Head of English*)
Mrs R Davies (*History and Religious Studies*)
Mrs J M Drakeford, BSc (*Chemistry and Biology**)
Dr J Ewington, BSc Hons, MSc, PhD (*Physics**)
Mrs S E Goode, BSc Econ (*Junior School*)
Mr Harrison, MA, PGCE (*History**)
Mrs R Heard, BA, NPQH (*Head of Junior School*)
Mrs R Humphrey BMus Hons (*Director of Music**)
Miss S M Jackson, BSc (*Head of Sixth Form, Chemistry*)
Mr M Kefford, BA (*PE and Games*)
Mrs C King, BA (*EFL*)
Mrs F M Kirk, BA, MEd (*English, General Studies*)
Mr M J Lewis, BSc, FRGS, FRMetS, CGeog (*Geography**, *Careers & Higher Education*)
Mrs L M Lyon, BEd (*Modern Languages*)
Mrs G Montford (*EYFS*)
Mr P Pitt (*Economics**)
Mrs H Pitts (*Junior*)
Mrs P Smith BA (*Art**)
Mrs E Streatfield (*Junior*)
Mr C L Stoner, BSc, MSc, Dip CEG (*Mathematics**)
Dr A Templeton, BSc, MSc, PhD (*Physics*)
Mrs H Thorne, BA, PGCE, CTABRSM (*Junior School Music*)
Mr F B Vié, Licence d'histoire, PGCE (*Modern Languages**)
Mrs C Whiting, MA (*ICT**)
Miss L Woodford (*English*)

Bursar: Mrs S Sherlock
Admissions: Mrs O Smallwood
Marketing: Mrs K Pacheco

Portland Place School
Alpha Plus Group

56–58 Portland Place, London W1B 1NJ

Tel:	020 7307 8700
email:	admin@portland-place.co.uk
website:	www.portland-place.co.uk
Twitter:	@PortlandPlaceHd
Facebook:	@PortlandPlaceSchool
Instagram:	@PortlandPlaceSchool

Age Range. 10–16 year olds. Co-educational.

Number of Pupils. 200 (60% boys and 40% girls).

Fees per term (2021–2022).

Day School: £7,470

Portland Place Online (Hybrid or Full Online): £2,985

Aims and Philosophy. Portland Place School is a leading independent co-educational day school for children aged 10–16, located in the heart of central London. It was founded 25 years ago with a particular purpose in mind: to be an alternative to the intense, large, examination-focused independent day schools in London.

The ethos is to be small, nurturing and inspirational – enabling students to achieve their very best, with space to develop and express their creativity.

Portland Place School encourages aspiration, resilience and a love of learning within a supportive and inclusive environment. Aiming to ensure each pupil achieves their best personally, socially and academically.

Happiness Gets Results. Portland Place School believe the importance of happiness in education should never be underestimated. It is only when children feel comfortable that they are truly in the right frame of mind to welcome new ideas and actively engage in their learning. Portland Place School adds significant value with usually 1 or 2 grades added to those predicted by externally administered baseline testing.

Curriculum. Portland Place School believe that exceptional teaching, combined with a modern curriculum inside and outside the classroom, provides the best stimulus for children to become inquisitive, open-minded and creative learners and achieve beyond exams.

The school's creative approach to academic study helps the child find their own path to learning. The curriculum at Portland Place is developed from the English National Curriculum and taught in small classes of up to 16 students. Full advantage is taken of its central London location with its excellent local facilities. The school caters for a range of abilities and learning styles, achieving strong results at GCSE.

Class music is a compulsory part of the curriculum in Years 6–9 and free individual tuition is offered to all Year 7 students.

Sport. Portland Place School offers a wide range of sport including athletics, basketball, cricket, cross country, dance, fencing, football, hockey, netball, rounders, swimming, tennis and rugby. Outdoor sports take place in Regent's Park a short walk from the school. Indoor activities include basketball, swimming and fencing. Specialist facilities are used where required. The school offers after-school sports activities and clubs and participates in inter school competitions across London and the UK.

Extracurricular Activities & Enrichment. There is a wide and ever evolving range of extracurricular activities that are offered during lunchtimes and after school. These range from yoga, Arabic, Shakespeare and table tennis. Whole school productions, concerts, choirs and performances take place throughout the year. The Duke of Edinburgh award is facilitated and encouraged for the older years. The students enjoy regular outdoor activities, day trips, charity projects and overseas trips including Berlin, Paris, Iceland, Barbados, Washington, New York and even Tanzania.

The weekly Enrichment Programme allows the students to participate in activities not tied to examinations and explore and develop new interests. Activities range from horse riding to carpentry; boxing to forest school; LEGO design to musical theatre.

Pastoral. Portland Place has an emphasis on supporting students' mental health and improving their personal resilience. There are school counsellors, plus a coaching programme that is integrated into the curriculum.

Location and Buildings. Portland Place is ideally located in the centre of London, less than five minutes' walk from Regent's Park (where much of the outdoor sporting activities take place) and ten minutes' walk from Oxford Circus. The school is housed in two magnificent Grade II* listed James Adam houses in Portland Place with a separate Art, Drama and Science building in Great Portland Street. The buildings are refurbished to an exceptionally high standard with specialist faculty facilities.

Portland Place Online School. In 2020 Portland Place extended their ethos into a new, innovative hybrid learning offering that runs in parallel to the main school: Portland Place Online. A cost-effective blended learning approach, combining live online teaching with an optional one day a week on site to access facilities for practical subjects such as science and sport; creating a unique educational offering for ages 10–16.

Admission. Entry to the school, usually at 10+, 11+, and 13+, is by baseline assessment in English and Mathematics (along with Science for Year 8 onwards) and an interview. Interviews for September entry are held in the autumn term prior to entry and the school's assessments are held in January.

Governance. Portland Place School is part of the Alpha Plus Group of schools.

Senior Leadership Team:

Headmaster: Mr David Bradbury, MSc Keele, MA Open, MInstP, CPhys, FRSA

Deputy Head: Mr Jamie Whiteside, BSc, PGCE, Edinburgh
Assistant Head (Welfare): Mr Tom Maslona

Assistant Head (Co-Curriculum) and Director of Music: Mr Steve Hill, MA Ed, BMus Hons, PGCE, Cert GSMD (P), ALCM
Assistant Head (Student Support): Ms Patricia Pieri, BSc London, MA
Finance & Operations Manager: Ms Vicki Bromley

The Purcell School

Aldenham Road, Bushey, Hertfordshire WD23 2TS

Tel: 01923 331100
email: info@purcell-school.org
website: www.purcell-school.org
Twitter: @PurcellSchool
Facebook: @PurcellSchool
Instagram: @the_purcell_school

The Purcell School is Britain's oldest school for young musicians. Situated on the outskirts of London in Bushey, Hertfordshire, the co-educational boarding and day school is home to around 190 musically talented young people aged 10–18.

The School aims to provide young musicians, of remarkable ability and promise from all backgrounds, with the best possible teaching and environment in which to fulfil their potential. We deliver the very highest world-class musical instruction and hold the UNESCO Mozart Gold Medal in recognition of the School's unique contribution to music, education and international culture.

The school affords ideal opportunities for practising, performing and developing musicianship, while also providing a balanced academic education which helps to prepare our students for life-long careers as musicians. The high quality of teaching and outstanding pastoral support is further complemented by a nurturing environment in which students can form stimulating and mutually supportive friendships with similarly gifted children.

Music Department. The Music Department at The Purcell School aims to provide a stimulating and challenging musical environment, at the heart of which is an individually tailored programme for every student. A flexible timetable, designed to enable students to practise, sustains this. Students in Years 7 to 8 are able to practise up to 3 hours each day, with those in Years 9 and 10 between 3–4 hours, and Sixth Formers in the region of 4–5 hours, depending on academic commitments. Practice supervisors are provided, themselves graduate musicians, and work with students up to Year 11 to ensure practice time is used effectively. The School's expert instrumental teachers also set practice goals and teach practice strategies.

Students have twice-weekly contact with their first study instrumental teacher for up to 2 hours' tuition. All of Purcell's instrumental teachers have considerable experience of working with motivated young musicians and have proven ability in enabling their students to succeed. They are all active performers and practitioners, and many teach at the London conservatoires as well as those further afield. As such, they are distinguished industry professionals, who understand exactly what is necessary to succeed in the music business today.

In addition, the Music Department offers an enriched musical programme that includes chamber music, orchestras, piano classes, choirs and aural and theory training. Frequent performing opportunities range from daily lunchtime concerts at School and in the surrounding area to formal recitals around the UK and in the capital's leading venues. The School's proximity to London provides regular performance opportunities at some of the world's finest venues, an experience unmatched by any other musical school. Students, for example, can audition for the chance to play concertos with the School's orchestras, to give solo and chamber music recitals at Cadogan Hall, Wigmore Hall, Purcell Room, Milton Court Concert Hall, Kings Place and other prestigious venues.

The School also facilitates frequent visits from the world's leading musicians for masterclasses, recitals, courses and collaborative projects to enhance the work of our regular teachers.

The importance of providing an outstanding all-round educational experience is paramount at The Purcell School, so that students can leave with the skills they need to meet the challenges of an ever-changing and complex world. Purcell therefore endeavours to deliver an integrated curriculum in which music, academic, pastoral and social provision are treated equally. The School recognises that intellectual curiosity and social empathy are vital components of being a great musician, and that it is imperative to develop the whole person for a student to be truly happy and healthy.

Academic Studies. The School's curriculum allows students to fulfil their musical potential without limiting their choices. A range of subjects are offered including Mathematics, English, Sciences, Modern Languages and Humanities, which provide an essential complement to performing skills.

The size of the School ensures that classes are generally small, which allows for a great deal of individual attention from experienced and dedicated teachers.

All students are set homework each day and time is allocated in the boarding houses each evening for this to be completed. Students' academic progress is closely monitored and parents receive frequent progress reports.

Boarding. With approximately 79% of students boarding, the School feels like a home from home and boarders lead very full lives. As travel time is reduced there is more time to practise, to ensure academic work is completed to a high standard, to be involved in a breadth of musical and co-curricular activities, and to build life-long friendships. Boarding also prepares students for the independence they will have in further education.

The Purcell School has three boarding houses – Avison, New Boarding House and Sunley – which are run by a dedicated team of warm and caring boarding and pastoral staff, who are responsible for each student's welfare and wellbeing. Great care is taken to ensure a student's stay is safe, productive and most of all as enjoyable as possible.

All boarders eat together in the main dining hall, however there are also common rooms and small kitchens in each corridor of the boarding houses. Weekend activities, evening events and social gatherings are regularly organised, and students are able to travel into London to attend the junior departments of the capital's music colleges and conservatoires or enjoy concerts and events.

Boarders have access to school facilities, such as practice rooms and computers, at evenings and weekends.

In each half of the term there is normally an exeat weekend when all students go home or to their guardian or to friends. There is also a half-term period in each of the three terms.

Admission. Entrance is by musical audition and interview – please see the School website for further details. The Registrar, Ms Karen Eldridge, can answer queries.

Fees per term (2021–2022). Day £8,925; Boarding £11,396.

Bursary funding is available, for those students who meet the eligibility criteria, under the Department for Education Music and Dance Scheme, and there is the possibility of means-tested financial support from the School for those who do not. Parents are welcome to consult the Bursar for guidance.

Charitable status. The Purcell School is a Registered Charity, number 312855. It aims to offer specialist musical training, combined with an excellent general academic education, to children of exceptional musical ability.

Royal Patron: HRH The Prince of Wales

Patrons:
Sir Simon Rattle, CBE, OM (*President*)
Vladimir Ashkenazy, CBE
Sir Andrew Davis, CBE
Donatella Flick
Dame Kiri Te Kanawa, DBE
Evgeny Kissin

Governing Body:
Dr Bernard Trafford, MA Oxon, MEd, PhD Birmingham (*Chairman*)
William McDonnell, BA Oxon (*Chairman of Finance and General Purposes Committee*)
Kirsty Von Malaisé, MA Cantab (*Chair of Music of Education Committee*)
Joanna Van Heyningen, OBE, MA Oxon, MA Cantab, Dip Arch RIBA (*Chair of Building and Development Committee*)
Michele Burton, MA Cantab
Jeffrey Hewitt, MA Oxon, MBA Stanford
Sir Roger Jackling, KCB, BCE
Timothy Jones, MA, DPHIL, Hon RAM
Professor Colin Lawson, CBE, MA Oxon, PhD, DMus, FRCM, FRNCM, FLCM, Hon RAM
Dr Rebecca Mooney, DPhil Oxon, MSt Oxon, MA Cantab
Ian Odgers, MA Cantab

Senior Leadership Team:

Principal: Paul Bambrough

Vice-Principal: Thomas Burns
Director of Music: Paul Hoskins
Bursar: Adam Wroblewski
Director of Boarding: Kate Caley
Head of Sixth Form & DSL: Ziggy Szafranski

Music Department:

Strings:
Charles Sewart (*Head of Strings*, *Violin/Viola*)
Richard Jenkinson (*Assistant Head of Strings*)
Pál Banda (*Cello*)
Aiste Dvarionaite Berzanskiene (*Violin*)
Anna-Liisa Bezrodny (*Violin*)

Sascha Boyarsky (*Cello*)
Sarah-Jane Bradley (*Viola*)
Tony Cucchiara (*Violin*)
Ben J Davies (*Cello*)
Alda Dizdari (*Violin*)
Cathy Elliott (*Double Bass*)
Tanja Goldberg (*Violin*)
Sadagat Mamedova-Rashidova (*Violin*)
Francesco Mariani (*Guitar*)
Julian-David Metzger (*Cello*)
Joo Yeon Sir (*Violin*)
Nathaniel Vallois (*Violin*)
Bozidor Vukotic (*Cello*)
Jacky Woods (*Viola*)

Keyboard:
William Fong (*Head of Keyboard, Piano*)
Lidia Amorelli (*Piano*)
Gabriele Baldocci (*Piano*)
Stephen Coombs (*Piano*)
Ben de Souza (*Accordion*)
David Gordon (*Harpsichord & Improvisation*)
Caterina Grewe (*Piano*)
Morte Grigaliunaite Freitas (*Piano*)
Gareth Hunt (*Piano*)
Jianing Kong (*Piano*)
Alla Kravchenko (*Piano*)
Ching-Ching Lim (*Piano*)
Florian Mitrea (*Piano*)
Tessa Nicholson (*Piano*)
Vitaly Pisarenko (*Piano*)
Danielle Salamon (*Piano*)
Tatiana Sarkissova (*Piano*)
Deborah Shah (*Piano/Accompanist*)
Daniel Swain (*Accompanist*)
Patsy Toh (*Piano*)
Nafis Umerkulova (*Piano*)

Brass, Percussion, Harp & Voice:
Daphne Boden (*Harp*)
Tony Cross (*Trumpet*)
Timothy Ellis (*French Horn*)
Daniella Ganeva (*Percussion*)
Tom Marandola (*Voice*)
Ruth Molins (*Trombone*)
Charlotte Seale (*Harp*)
Jill Washington (*Voice*)
Stephen Wick (*Tuba*)

Woodwind:
Joy Farrall (*Head of Woodwind, Clarinet*)
Abigail Burrows (*Flute*)
Izzie Couch (*Clarinet*)
Amy Green (*Saxophone*)
Graham Hobbs (*Bassoon*)
Barbara Law (*Recorder*)
James Turnbull (*Oboe*)
Stephen Williams (*Clarinet*)

Jazz:
Simon Allen (*Head of Jazz, Jazz Saxophone*)
Sebastiaan de Krom (*Jazz Drums*)
Sam Dunn (*Jazz Guitar*)
David Gordon (*Jazz Piano*)
Olli Hayhurst (*Jazz Bass*)
Jacqueline Hicks (*Jazz Voice*)
George Hogg (*Jazz Trumpet*)
John Turvills (*Jazz Piano*)
Steve Waterman (*Jazz Trumpet*)

Composition:
Alison Cox (*Head of Composition*)
Philip Dutton (*Compositions Department Assistant*)
Jacques Cohen (*Composition*)
Daniel Fardon (*Composition*)
Silvia Lim (*Composition*)
Gareth Moorcraft (*Composition*)
Simon Speare (*Composition*)

Audio Production Department:
Aidan Goetzee (*Head of Audio Production*)
Matthew Calvert

Academic Music Staff:
Mary-Kate Gill (*Head of Department*)
Alison Cox (*Composition*)
Daniel Fardon
Ryan Hepburn
Edward Longstaff [Sabbatical]
Andrew Williams
Irina Walters

Academic Staff:
Adriana Blond (*English*)
John Brookes (*Head of PE*)
Margaret Brookes (*Chemistry, Head of Science*)
Svetlana Emelianova (*Science*)
Panos Fellas (*Science, Physics*)
Aidan Goetzee (*Head of Music Technology*)
Deborah Harris (*Juniors*)
Elizabeth Hannam (*English*)
Kinga Kozak (*EAL*)
Heloise Lille (*French*)
Seana McEvoy (*Artist in Residence*)
Robert Matthews (*Head of EAL, German*)
Stevie Mitchell (*KS4 Academic Co-ordinator, Mathematics*)
Nicky Morris (*Counsellor, Arts Therapist*)
Craig Nunes (*Drama, English*)
Ashvin Patel (*Science, Chemistry*)
Darrell Pigott (*Head of History*)
Nadine Sender (*Head of Art*)
Jyoti Shah (*Mathematics*)
Adam Simmonds (*English*)
Theresa Strydom (*Philosophy*)
Alexandra Stone (*Head of Mathematics*)
Martina Swift (*EAL*)
Ziggi Szafranski (*Drama*)
Sally-Ann Whitty (*Head of Learning Support*)

Boarding Houses:
Sophie Baxter (*Sunley Practice Supervisor*)
Adriana Blond (*Assistant Houseparent, NBH*)
John Brookes (*Avison Assistant Houseparent*)
Margaret Brookes (*Avison Houseparent*)
Kate Caley (*Director of Boarding*)
Annette Cook (*Avison Assistant Houseparent*)
Samuel Cubarsi-Fernandez (*Assistant Houseparent, NBH*)
Sam Every (*Sunley/NBH Practice Supervisor*)
Lorna Griggs (*NBH Houseparent*)
Susie Hunter (*Sunley House Day Matron*)
Charlotte Lee (*NBH Practice Supervisor*)
Katharine Mendes da Costa (*NBH Day Matron*)
Richard Montgomery (*Practice Supervisor*)
Albert Owen (*NBH Practice Supervisor*)
Rachel Price (*Sunley Houseparent*)
Lucia Svecova (*Sunley Practice Supervisor*)

Admin & Non-Teaching Staff:
Linda Abrraham (*HR and Compliance Manager*)

Hilary Austin (*School Nurse*)
Thomas Bell (*Technology Technician*)
Charlotte Buck (*School Office*)
Lisa Canosa (*Exams Officer*)
Shirley Clark (*PA to the Principal*)
Susannah Curran (*PR & Communications Manager*)
Fiona Duce (*Music Timetabler*)
Karen Eldridge (*Registrar*)
Celia Findell (*Fundraising Manager*)
Caroline Fletcher (*School Office/Overseas Coordinator*)
Linda Griffiths (*School Office*)
Toni Holmes (*School Data Manager/Payroll Administrator*)
Impact Food Group Ltd. (*Caterers*)
Simon Kingsbury (*IT Network Manager*)
Marie Lynch (*School Office*)
Emma McGrath (*Development Assistant*)
Hawreen Osman (*Science Technician*)
Susan Pickard (*Finance Manager*)
Ryan Bunce (*Librarian*)
Sarah Upjohn (*Physiotherapist*)
Jo Wallis (*Deputy Bursar, Operations Manager*)
Bethany Wright (*Concerts Coordinator*)
Nicole Holmes (*Senior Housekeeper*)
Neal Webber (*Estates Supervisor*)

The Read School
Drax

Drax, Selby, North Yorkshire YO8 8NL

Tel:	01757 618248
email:	enquiries@readschool.co.uk
website:	www.readschool.co.uk
Twitter:	@Read_School
Facebook:	@readschool
Instagram:	@read_school1667

Age Range. Co-educational 4–18, Boarding 8–18.

Number in School. Total 224: Day 210, Boarding 14; Boys 128, Girls 96.

The school is pleasantly situated in the rural village of Drax and is very convenient for main rail (Doncaster, York, Leeds) and road access (M62, M18, A1). Manchester is the nearest international airport (1½ hours distant). It is a relatively small school where children are well known to each other and to the staff.

The school has been a focal point for education in the Selby-Goole area since the 17th century and celebrated its 350th anniversary throughout 2017. There has been a school on the same site since 1667 and it is proud to be one of the oldest educational establishments in the UK. The school has been co-educational since 1992 and offers a wide range of academic studies at GCSE and A Level. Within school, our small class sizes, inspirational teaching and wide array of extra-curricular activities, including an excellent sports programme, Combined Cadet Force, Duke of Edinburgh programme and Leith's Food Academy sections, provide an outstanding education. There is one class in each Junior School year from Reception to Year 5; Year 6 has two classes. There are two classes in each of the Senior years (7–11); 3 classes in Year 8. There is a small Sixth Form (26 pupils) following AS and A Level courses. High standards are expected in all aspects of endeavour, and in behaviour and manners.

Facilities. While the school has a long history, there has been considerable development in recent years. We have undertaken a stunning major upgrade of the Sports Hall, with a new floor and improved heating and lighting; made major improvements to the boarding provision on the school site; refurbished the all-weather games area and opened a new music facility.

Fees per term (2021–2022). Boarders: £7,368–£10,255; Day: £2,889–£5,234.

Admission. An offer of a place in the school is made after interview (and verbal reasoning and mathematics tests for admission to the Senior School) and satisfactory report from the pupil's current school.

Charitable status. The Read School is a Registered Charity, number 529675. It exists to provide a proper education for boys and girls aged 4–18.

Chairman of Governors: Brian Watt

Head: **Mrs R A Ainley**, MA Oxon (*Modern Languages*)

Bursar: vacant

Deputy Head: M A Voisey, BA (*English*)

Teaching Staff:
Mrs P Anderson, BEd (*English*)
Mrs S Ashworth-Lilley, BSc (*Psychology*)
Miss J Bullock, BSc, MSc (*Head of Science, English Additional Language*)
Miss H Butterill, BA (*Lower Junior School*)
Mr J Calderwood, BSc, (*Mathematics*)
Ms S L Campbell, BSc (*Junior School*)
Mrs S Chambonnet, BA (*French*)
Mrs H Crompton, BMus (*Head of Music*)
Dr P Duggan, BSc, PhD (*Biology, Chemistry*)
Mrs L Fairhurst, BA (*EYFS Teacher*)
Mrs J Fildes, BA (*Mathematics*)
Miss L Fletcher BSc (*Mathematics*)
Ms H Hewson, BA (*English*)
Miss J Hutchinson, PGE (*History*)
Mr G Hill, BA (*Head of Junior School*)
Mrs K Ives, BA (*Spanish*)
Mrs E Jackson, BSc (*Mathematics, Science*)
Mr L Johnson, BSc (*PE & Games*)
Mrs P Kavanagh, BA (*Business Studies*)
Miss M Keenoy, BA (*Head of Inclusive Learning*)
Mrs L Li, MEd (*Mandarin*)
Mr J Matthews, BSc (*Head of PE*)
Mrs B J Maunsell, BA (*Drama*)
Mrs S Morrell, BEd (*History, Religious Studies, PSHE Coordinator*)
Miss F M Newman, BA (*Junior School, KS3 Art, Dance*)
Mrs S Prosser, BA (*PE and Games*)
Miss S Rothwell, BEd (*Head of Creative Arts, Design Technology, Food*)
Mrs S Scholefield, BSc (*Head of Humanities*)
Mr C Sharples, BSc (*ICT, Computer Science*)
Mrs E Stark, BSc (*Chemistry*)
Mr R Stark, BSc (*Physics*)
Mrs N Suttill, BA (*Art*)
Mrs R M Wake, BA (*Junior School*)
Mrs C M Wynne, BEd (*Deputy Head Junior School*)
Mrs X Zambrano BA (*Spanish*)

Rishworth School

Oldham Road, Rishworth, Sowerby Bridge, Halifax, West Yorkshire HX6 4QA

Tel: 01422 822217 (Main School)
email: admissions@rishworth-school.co.uk
website: www.rishworth-school.co.uk
Twitter: @Rishworth1724
Facebook: @RishworthSchool
Instagram: @rishworthschool
LinkedIn: /rishworth-school-trading-limited

Rishworth is an exceptionally friendly, caring community, in which pupils are as strongly encouraged to rejoice in each other's achievements as to take pride in their own. The School succeeds in combining a disciplined environment with a relaxed and welcoming atmosphere.

While pupils are at Rishworth, we try to ensure that, in addition to the knowledge and skills acquired through academic study, they develop:

- A love of learning and the will to succeed.
- A sense of responsibility, self-discipline, purpose and fulfilment.
- A capacity for both self-reliance and cooperation.
- An appreciation of certain personal virtues and spiritual values, such as honesty, dependability, perseverance, commitment, humility and respect for others.

General organisation. Founded in 1724, Rishworth is a co-educational day and boarding school comprising a nursery for children from age 3, a Junior School, Heathfield, which has its own separate site where children are taught up to the age of 11, and the Senior School up to age 18. Rishworth is a Church of England foundation, but welcomes children of all faiths, or of none. Numbers stand at about 480 pupils, of whom over 50 are boarders.

Facilities and Location. Superbly located in 130 acres of a beautiful Pennine valley, the School has a mix of elegant older buildings and excellent modern facilities including a capacious sports hall with fitness suite, a separate, newly-redeveloped Sports Club with 25-metre indoor swimming pool and squash courts, a large expanse of games pitches, a music block, 3 modern ICT suites, wireless (and cabled) Internet and Intranet connection across the whole site, a Performing Arts Theatre, a centre dedicated to sixth-form study, freshly-refurbished boarding houses and newly-installed, state-of-the-art science laboratories.

Access to the School by road is easy, with the M62 within five minutes' drive. School buses run to the Halifax, Todmorden, Rochdale, Oldham and Huddersfield areas.

Welfare and Pastoral. The unusually high degree of attention afforded to pupils by small teaching groups, the careful monitoring of progress, coordinated pastoral support and a close working partnership with parents enables pupils to build on their strengths and allows specific needs to be addressed. Each boarding pupil is under the direct care of a Housemaster or Housemistress, who is ably supported by assistant staff in each boarding house.

Teaching. Taught by a dedicated staff of qualified specialists, the curriculum, both academic and non-academic, is broad and stimulating, and offers every pupil the chance to be challenged and to excel. A general curriculum, broadly in line with the National Curriculum, is followed until Year 9, after which pupils select GCSE options in consultation with their parents, tutors and subject teachers. A Level, Diploma and BTEC options are also selected via consultation.

Support is given by qualified specialists for certain special needs including dyslexia and English where this is not the pupil's first language.

Academic. In 2021, at GCSE we achieved a 100% pass rate and 93% of our students attained grades 4–9.

At A Level we also achieved a 100% pass rate, with nearly half graded A*, more than two-thirds graded A*–A, and nearly 80% A*–B.

Enrichment and Extension. In order to help our pupils to become the confident, balanced and considerate young men and women we wish them to be, we encourage participation in a wide range of activities because at Rishworth we understand that learning doesn't just take place in the classroom.

Sports are well appointed and well taught, and each term boys and girls enjoy excellent results. The School also has a justly high reputation in music and drama.

Additionally we have nearly 90 enrichment and extension activities! From Duke of Edinburgh through to our Medical Society, from skiing through to podcasting. There really is something for everyone.

Boarding. We have no dormitories. Boarders (from age 10 or 11, and sometimes age 9) are accommodated in individual study-bedrooms, almost all single occupancy which allow pupils their personal space. These are located in spacious houses, overseen by house staff. The boarding houses are cosy and family-centric, the secure havens needed by young people away from home. The character of the historic buildings has been retained, alongside the provision of top-rate modern amenities. A full programme of activities is arranged for the evenings and weekends, and there are good recreational facilities reserved for the boarders, including dedicated social areas.

Admission. Places in the Junior School, Heathfield, are given, subject to availability, on individual assessments appropriate to each applicant's age and previous education. Entrants for Rishworth at Year 7 are asked to sit the School's own entrance assessment, which also forms the basis for the award of scholarships.

Those who wish to join the School at other stages are assessed individually.

Fees per term (2021–2022). Reception to Year 2 £2,266; Years 3 to 6 £3,316; Years 7 & 8: £4,066 day, £9,700 full boarding, £8,800 weekly boarding; Years 9 to 13: £4,433 day, £10,500 full boarding, £9,600 weekly boarding. The School operates a number of schemes, including monthly payments, to ease the financial burden on parents.

Scholarships and Bursaries. Scholarships & Bursaries are available, the former on merit, the latter for demonstrable financial need. The extent to which these awards can be offered will also be determined by other factors, such as the School's own circumstances and the nature of a given cohort of applicants.

Scholarships may be awarded, up to a value of 30% of Tuition fees, for excellence in academic work, sport, music or drama.

For Year 7 entry scholarships, applicants are formally assessed. For Year 12 entry, awards are made on the basis of an individual's past record (including examination results).

Most awards are made to applicants at these entry levels. However, suitable candidates at any stage will be considered.

Substantial discounts are available for siblings of pupils in the School, for children of serving members of the Armed Forces and of ordained members of the Church of England. Bursaries may also be available in cases of financial need.

The Old Rishworthian Club maintains a fund for the grant of scholarships to children of ORs.

For more information contact the Bursar.

Charitable status. Rishworth School is a Registered Charity, number 1115562. It exists to provide education for boys and girls.

The Governing Body:
Revd Canon H Barber (*Chairman*)
T M Wheelwright, Esq
Mrs D M Whitaker, JP
Mrs F Ellam (*Vice Chair*)
Mrs M Garbett (*Vice Chair*)
Dr R Viney
Mr C Bell
Dr A Gupta
Mr P Hudson
Mr B Moore, Esq

Senior Leadership Team:

Head: **Mr A M Wilkins**, BA, MA Lit, MA Hist

Deputy Head: Ms J Sheldrick, BSc (*DSL*)

Bursar and Clerk to the Board of Governors: Mrs C Walsh

Director of External Relations: Mrs L Horbury, BSc, QTS

Head of Heathfield Prep: Mr D Baker, BEd

Key Business Support Staff:
Head of Admissions: Mrs R Miller, BA, MA
Head's PA: Miss Hannah Lloyd
Matron: Mrs D K Robinson
Librarian: Mrs B Day

Ruthin School

Mold Road, Ruthin, Denbighshire LL15 1EE

Tel: 01824 702543
email: registrar@ruthinschool.co.uk
website: www.ruthinschool.co.uk
Twitter: @ruthinschool
Facebook: @RuthinSchool

Motto: *Dei gratia sum quod sum*

Ruthin School was originally founded in 1284. Refounded in 1574 by Gabriel Goodman, Dean of Westminster, and granted a Royal Charter, the School is a centre of academic excellence in North Wales.

The School is co-educational with around 300 Students, comprising approximately half boarders and half day students. Ruthin School is an international community committed to high academic standards, dedication and mutual respect. Safeguarding and wellbeing are at the core of the School's ethos and informs all decision making. The School is run on the principle of collegiality and provides a safe, modern and friendly environment in which students can fulfil their potential. Students are expected to behave in a way that promotes decency, harmony and trust. They should strive to achieve their best at all times. staff will support them in this goal.

Organisation. Places (both day and full boarding) are offered to boys and girls from the age of 11.

The four boarding houses – Goodman, Trevor, Wynne and Gladstone – have their own House system under the guidance of resident Houseparent, Boarding Assistant, Housekeeper and Graduate Assistant.

Admission. The normal method of entry to the School is by interview, examination and reports.

Activities. A wide range of non-curricular activities is provided and has included fitness training, basketball, swimming, yoga, drama, rock climbing, sailing and canoeing, mountain biking, table tennis, badminton, conservation, gardening and tennis. Boys and girls are encouraged to participate in the Duke of Edinburgh's Award scheme at the age of 14 until they have completed the Bronze Award; several go on to complete the Silver and a few aspire to the Gold Award. Many students receive individual instrumental tuition from the professional music staff. A programme of excursions is organised for boarders in the evenings and at weekends and these are open to all pupils.

Bursaries and Awards. In addition to academic awards, remissions are available for siblings, children of members of the armed forces, and of Old Ruthinians. All awards are means tested and reviewed annually.

Curriculum. A wide curriculum is offered and includes English, Mathematics, History, Geography, Latin, separate Biology, Physics and Chemistry, Art, Music, Computer Science, French, and Spanish. Astronomy and Economics are added at GCSE level. Further Mathematics and Politics are taught in the Sixth Form.

An option scheme operates for Form 4, but English, Mathematics, Physics, Chemistry, Biology are compulsory.

Pastoral. All Students have a pastoral tutor and in the Upper Sixth an academic mentor to support university applications. Careers guidance is also offered to all Sixth Form Students.

Games. Basketball, football, cross-country, netball, tennis, badminton and athletics all feature in the coaching programme.

Fees per annum (2021–2022). Day £12,400–£15,000; Boarding £38,700. Fees are payable twice-yearly, at beginning of August and February. British parents have the option to pay monthly by Direct Debit.

Transport. The School provides daily transport to and from the North Wales coast, the Chester area and the Wrexham area. Transport is provided for boarders from Manchester airport to the School, at the beginning and end of each term.

The Old Ruthinian Association fosters close links between past and present students of the School.

Charitable status. Ruthin School is a Registered Charity, number 525754. It exists to provide education for boys and girls.

Visitor: Her Majesty The Queen

Council of Management:
Chair: D A Booker

C W Conway
P Coups
Mrs T A Hewett
R March
J E Sharples
A Yeung

Head: **Miss S Frencham**, BSc, PGCE

Bursar: N Grenfell-Marten, FCMI

Deputy Head Pastoral: Miss K Tipton BSc PGCE NPQSL

*Assistant Deputy Head – Assessment, Inspection,
Procedures*: Dr A W Hughes, BEng, PhD, PGCE
Assistant Deputy Head – Universities, Careers, Alumni:
Mrs J I Morton, MA Hons, PGCE

Teaching Staff:
J S Bartlett, BSc, PGCE
Mrs S M Bellis-Whitworth, BA, MA, PGCE
N J R Blandford, BA, MA, PGCE
Mrs E T Brodzinska, LLB, MA, DELTA
Mrs E M Brown, BA, MA Ed, PGCE, TEFL, AMBDA
B Cribb, BA, PGCE, MEd
Mrs R Crowther, BA, PGCE
Dr D G Edwards, BA Hons, DPhil
I G Evans, BA, PGCE
Mrs S J Eve, BSc, PGCE
Dr N Fairbank, BSc, MA, PhD
Miss P Foster, BA, PGCE, DELTA
Dr G H Green, BSc, MA, PhD
J P Hamer, BA, PGCE
Dr M D Hannant, PhD, PGCE
Mrs I Haywood, BSc, MBA, PGCE
J R Henry, BA, PGCE
M H L Hewer, MA Oxon, DipEd
Miss R Howlett, BSc, PGCE
Mrs K Hughes, BA, PGCE
G N Johnson, BSc, MSc, PGCE
Dr K M Johnson, BSc, PhD
Mrs M Kenworthy, BSc, PGCE
Mrs S Morley, BEd, CELTA
M A Orchard, BSc, PGCE
D A Owen Booth, MGCI, BEd, DipHE
C Perry, BSc, PGCE
Mrs C Peters, BSc, PGCE
Dr J Roberts, BSc, MSc, PhD
M S Robinson, BA, MA Oxon, PGCE
S D Stark, BSc, MEng, PGCE
R A Wadon, BSc, PGCE
Miss H Webb, BSc, PGCE
Miss D A Williams, BSc, PGCE
Dr M Wilton, BSc, PhD, PGCE

Registrar and PA to the Head and Bursar: Mrs S E
Williams
Deputy Bursar: Mrs J Rainford
School Medical Officer: Dr T Kneale
School Nurse: Mrs T Beaver, RGN, RSCN
School Nurse: Mrs S Fitzsimmons, BSc, RSCN
School Nurse: Mrs J Wordsworth, RGN

St Christopher School

**Barrington Road, Letchworth Garden City,
Hertfordshire SG6 3JZ**

Tel:	+ 44 1462 650947
email:	admissions@stchris.co.uk
	hello@stchris.co.uk
website:	www.stchris.co.uk
Twitter:	@StChris_School
Facebook:	@StChrisLetchworth
Instagram:	@stchris_school
LinkedIn:	/company/st-christopher-school-letchworth

St Chris is a progressive co-educational school in Letchworth Garden City (Hertfordshire) that educates children from ages 3 to 18. Founded in 1915, each child is encouraged to meet their personal and academic potential in a relaxed but purposeful atmosphere.

There are over 520 students from the Nursery to Sixth Form. The majority of students are day pupils but there is a family focussed full and weekly boarding community for pupils from Year 7 to Sixth Form (ages 11 to 18).

St Chris is a champion for progressive education and is known for its forward-thinking, creative and kind environment. Pupils are supported to reach their potential academically, socially and in the activities that they pursue.

Facilities. St Chris is set on a large, leafy 25-acre campus. The main buildings date from the early 1900s with substantial new additions since that time, all based on a shared campus for children from Nursery to Sixth Form.

The Nursery and Junior School are located in bright and airy buildings, refurbished in 2019, with all classrooms having easy access to outdoor learning spaces. An on-site Forest School and plenty of outdoor play areas, including an orchard with climbing trees, gives children plenty of space to explore.

The Senior School and Sixth Form comprise of a mixture of historic and more modern buildings including a Theatre and drama studio, a purpose built Cookery centre, a dedicated music centre, extensive facilities for science and information technology and an excellent art and design department including multiple workshop and studio spaces, fitted with top of the range components.

There are large playing fields and astro pitches, an indoor swimming pool and gym, sports hall, climbing wall and half-pipe for skateboarding!

Location. The School is located on the edge of Letchworth Garden City (Hertfordshire), in walking distance of the town centre and railway station, with excellent transport links to London and Cambridge. The A1(M) is a mile away and there are direct train lines to London (King's Cross, 35 minutes) and Cambridge (25 minutes). Luton Airport is 25 minutes and Heathrow 60 minutes by car. The School runs bus services to surrounding areas including North London and Cambridge.

Fees per term (2021–2022). Day Pupils (Nursery to Sixth Form): £1,680–£6,648; Weekly Boarding (Senior School) £9,015; Full Boarding (Senior School) £11,515

Admissions Procedure: St Chris has a selection procedure that is designed to identify pupils who are able to benefit from its balanced and well-rounded education, and to make a positive contribution towards the life of the School.

Pupils are admitted between the ages of 3 and 16. The are different assessment steps for each area of the School – see website for details: www.stchris.co.uk/admissions/how-to-apply

There is a Registration Fee of £100.

Scholarships and Fee Assistance:

Art and Academic Scholarships are available for entry into Years 7, 9 and 12. Fee assistance is available to encourage applications from families who may otherwise not be able to afford the full fees at St Chris. More information here: www.stchris.co.uk/admissions/scholarships-bursaries

Chair of Governors: Peter McMeekin, MSc, PhD

Leadership Team:

Head: Emma-Kate Henry, BA Hons, PGCE

Bursar, Company Secretary & Clerk to the Governors:
   Martin Scoble, BEng Hons
Head of Sixth Form, DSL: Nat Baker, BA Hons, PGCE
Head of Senior School: Rich Jones, BA Hons
Head of Junior School: Katie Wright, BA Hons

Director of Activities: Byron Lewis, BSc Hons
Director of Marketing & Admissions: Rhiannon Butlin, BA
   Hons, MSc

St Edward's Senior & Sixth Form

**Cirencester Road, Charlton Kings, Cheltenham,
Gloucestershire GL53 8EY**

Tel: 01242 388555
email: reception@stedwards.co.uk
website: www.stedwards.co.uk
Twitter: @StEdwardsChelt
Facebook: @StEdwardsSchoolCheltenham
Instagram: @stedwardscheltenham

   Motto: *Quantum Potes Aude*

A wealth of opportunity exists for students at St Edward's Senior & Sixth Form. We teach that there is no ceiling to potential, focussing on the individual needs of each and every pupil, and valuing their unique gifts and talents.

Located in the heart of Cheltenham, with a range of creative and sporting facilities to enrich our academic provision, the School offers a strong and vibrant school community, based on Christian values, in which all children can thrive.

We have high expectations of all members of our school community. Excellent teaching and pastoral care in our nurturing and encouraging environment allows our pupils to flourish. Our small class sizes mean that our teachers really know pupils as individuals and can provide tailored support to maximise achievement. A broad range of subjects is offered at GCSE, together with 24 subjects at A Level. Our School motto means to strive for the best and that is exactly what we want for all our students.

We encourage our pupils to become fully involved in all aspects of school life, offering an extensive range of extra-curricular clubs, sporting and cultural activities. It is important to us that our pupils are challenged to step outside of their 'comfort zone' and realise that they can achieve beyond their perceived potential.

Most importantly, our aim is to provide an education that will last a lifetime and enable our pupils to develop into happy, confident, resilient, compassionate and aspirational individuals who are ready to become positive and life-long contributors to society.

Admission. The main entry to the Senior School is at Year 7 and at Sixth Form. However, pupils are welcome to join at any point, providing there are spaces in the year group. Entry into all year groups is subject to successful completion of an Entrance Examination.

Fees per term (2021–2022): £5,325–£6,305.

Scholarships are available for entry to Year 7 and Sixth Form in the following areas: academic, art, music, drama and sport.

Further information is available on the School's website, www.stedwards.co.uk. To request a prospectus or arrange an appointment to visit the School, please contact our Admissions Manager at senioradmissions@stedwards.co.uk or on 01242 388555.

Charitable status. St Edward's is a Registered Charity, number 293360.

Chair of Trustees: Dr Susan Honeywill

Principal: **Mr M Burke**, BA Hons, PGCE, Ad Dip Ed, NPQH

St James Senior Boys' School

Church Road, Ashford, Surrey TW15 3DZ

Tel: 01784 266 930
             01784 266 933 (Admissions)
email: admissions@stjamesboys.co.uk
website: www.stjamesboys.co.uk

St James Senior Boys' School, founded in 1975, is registered as an educational charity and is administered by a Board of Governors. The Headmaster is a member of The Society of Heads and the Independent Schools Association. The school is a member of the International Boys' Schools Coalition (IBSC). These Associations require that excellence is assured by regular inspections by the Independent Schools Inspectorate which is itself monitored by Ofsted.

The school has 389 students – all boys, aged between 11 and 18.

The school relocated from its site in Twickenham in 2010 and now resides in the magnificent Victorian/Gothic building which once housed St David's School in Ashford, Surrey, set in 32 acres of grounds. This move has provided the physical space necessary for every boy to develop his sporting, artistic and dramatic talents in addition to working in high-quality classrooms and state-of-the-art laboratories.

Aims and Values. St James Senior Boys' School offers a distinctive education that unites a unique philosophical ethos with academic excellence and outstanding skills for life.

At St James we believe that every child is a pure and perfect being; it is our job as educators to help the pupils in our care to discover and express their individual talents and reveal their brilliance. With this room to grow and blossom each boy develops in body, mind and spirit.

Although academic potential is important to us, pupils at St James are not selected solely on their examination performance; we are also interested in strength of character, future potential and emotional intelligence. We are looking for a boy with a spark, who gives freely of themselves whether in the classroom, on the stage or the sports field.

We are known internationally for our championing of Meditation and Mindfulness, something we have been successfully practising for 40 years. Each boy has the opportunity to connect with their inner being in periods of Quiet Time each day. This makes an enormous difference to pupil development and academic achievement.

We also like to offer the pupils in our care the opportunity to push themselves beyond any self-imposed limits, and our beautiful 32-acre site certainly enables a wealth of sports, drama, music and other extracurricular activities to flourish. Activities offered include: Cadets, The Duke of Edinburgh's Award, Sailing Club, Mountain Biking and Kayaking on our lake!

At St James we wish to produce young men who can question with sharp minds, who can contemplate in quietude, who can find their way ahead with wisdom and moral discrimination and who can meet others with open-hearted compassion.

St James is ideally located with easy access from Central London and the South West London Suburbs through to the Thames Valley.

Academic Standards and Successes. Academic standards are high, but we also measure success to the extent that boys surpass their own expectations. 2021 results were: GCSE: 100% pass rate, 9–7 59%, 9–4 98%; A Level: 100% pass rate, A*–C 96%.

Extracurricular Activities. Boys are offered an adventure pursuits programme designed to challenge the young men in terms of fitness, endurance, courage, leadership skills, service, self-esteem and confidence. Cadets (239 Para detachment), The Duke of Edinburgh's Award, Skiing, Sailing Club, Climbing Club, Community Service and Task force are among the activities offered.

Educational Trips. These are fairly regular and frequent for the Lower School, but there is an Activities Week in March when Year 7 enjoy an adventure break in the UK; Year 8 go to Greece to further their studies of Classical Civilisation; Year 9 travel the pilgrims way to Santiago de Compostela, and Year 10 spend some time in Lucca in Italy for leadership training and aspects of teamworking, then move on to Florence to study Renaissance art and architecture.

Philosophy. Each class throughout the school has one period of Philosophy per week. The boys are opened up to the great ideas relating to human values and relationships. Broadly, the themes prepare boys through different stages of development – Years 7 to 8: the correct use of mind, the power of attention; Years 9 to 11: aspiring to a great vision of Man and exploring human relationships and personal mastery; Years 12 to 13: living the philosophical life, making it practical, the importance of service.

Meditation and Quiet Time. The importance of inner stillness is recognised in the school, with two 5 minute periods of Quiet Time every day. During this time, boys can meditate, pray, read something of value or just be still. Every lesson begins and ends in a quiet moment of stillness and rest.

Admissions. The standard entry is at 11+, 13+ and 16+. Boys applying for entry to Year 7 take an Entrance Exam in January and also are all interviewed by a member of the Senior Management Team shortly afterwards. Boys are not judged solely on their exam results for the Headmaster favours selection by character and their ability to express themselves. At 13+, students are required to pre-test at either 11+ or 12+ level (in Y6 or Y7). We welcome applications to our Sixth Form at 16+. Very good GCSE performance and satisfactory interviews will be the basis of selection.

Fees per term (2021–2022). £6,780.

Open Days and Visits. Every year we hold Open Days in October. We also encourage parents to come and see the school in action at one of the school's tours. Please book by online at www.stjamesboys.co.uk.

Charitable status. The Independent Educational Association Limited is a Registered Charity, number 270156.

Chair of Governors: John Story, FRICS

Headmaster: **David Brazier**, BA Hons, PGCE, MSc (*English*)

Deputy Headmaster: David Beezadhur, BA Hons, MA, GTTP (*Ancient History*)

Deputy Head Academic: Dr Steven Roberts, BA, PGCE, MA, PhD (*English*)

Assistant Headmaster: David Hipshon, BA Hons, MPhil Cantab, PhD, PGCE (*History*)

Assistant Headmaster Pastoral: James Johnson, BSc Hons, PGCE (*Science*)

Data & Assessment Manager: Lorraine Soares, MSc Hons, PGCE (**Science Chemistry*)

Senior Teacher: Virginie Quartier, BA, GLSE Belgium (**Languages*)

* *Head of Department*

Heads of Year:

Sixth Form: Nic Lempriere, MA, PGCE (*English*)
Year 7: Arjun Deb, BSc (*Mathematics*)
Year 8: Terrance Radloff, BA Hons (*Geography & *Psychology*)
Year 9: Richard Fraser, BA Hons (*Mathematics*)
Year 10: William Jeffreys, BA (*Physical Education*)
Year 11: Christopher Hitchcock, BA Hons, PGCE (*Physical Education*)

Academic Staff:

Adam Atkinson-Young, BA Hons, CertEd, MA (**Design Technology*)
Gillian Bloor, MA, PGCE (*English*)
Frank Byrne, BEng Hons, PGCE (**Physics, DofE Coordinator*)
Anne-Helene Choimet, BA France, PGCE MFL (*French*)
Katie Cole (*Photography*)
Wesley Davies BEd S Africa (*Physical Education*)
Dana Dragomir, BMed, BSc, PGCE (*Chemistry*)
Rakhi Gajree, BSc, PGCE, QTS (*Mathematics*)
Conor Gallagher, BSc Hons, QTS (*Biology*)
Charles Gould, BSc Hons, MSc QTS (**English*)

Dr Rishi Handa, BSc Hons, PGCE, MA, PhD (*Sanskrit, Religious Studies*)

Vishal Handa, BSc Hons, MPhil Cantab, PGCE, MCCT (**Economics, Mathematics, EPQ Coordinator*)

Alexander Harrison, BSc, PGCE (*Science & Physics*)

Victoria Howard-Andrews, BSc (**PSHE*)

Lee Howson, BSc Hons, MA, PGCE (*Religious Studies*)

Justin Le Frenais, BSc Hons, PGCE (**Geography*)

Oliver Lomberg, BA Hons (**Classics, Latin and Greek*)

Pardeep Marway, BSc Hons, PGCE (**Biology*)

Jonathan Mawer, BA Hons, PGCE (*History*)

Andrew Michalski, BSc, PGCE (**Computing*)

Paolo Militello, MA (*Spanish*)

Frances Montgomerie, MA Cantab, MA Hons (*Geography*)

Mark Saunders, BA, HND Art & Design (**Art*)

Oliver Saunders, BA Hons, GTTP (**History*)

Hanan Sheegow, BA Hons, PGCE, QTS (*English*)

Louise Spriggs, BA Hons, PGCE (*Classics*)

Tammy Taylor, BA (*Librarian*)

David Terry, MA Oxon, ARCO, ARCM, FRSA (*Director of Music*)

Ben Wassell, BSc Hons, GTTP (*Director of Sport and Physical Education*)

Michaela Weiserova, MSc (**Mathematics, *IT*)

Sandra Williams, BEd (**Business Studies, Careers Coordinator*)

Carlene Williams-Harvey, BSc (*Mathematics*)

Jessica Yadav, BA Hons, QTS (**Drama, English*)

Learning Support:

Alice Wood, BA Hons, PGCE, NASENCO (*SENDCo*)

Cora Wren, CertEd, BA Hons, OCR Level 5, DipSpLD (*SENDCo*)

Christine Davies

Angela Dempster

Angela Hall

Sarah-Jane Hipshon, BA Hons

Lesley Munro

Carola Robinson-Tait (*Learning Support Specialist Teacher*)

Support Staff:

Headmaster's PA: Nina Patel

Assistant to the Deputy Head: Lisa Canderton

School Nurse: Susan Harman, BSc, RN

School Counsellor: Annette Door, BA Hons, MSc, UKCP, MBACP, MUPCA

Registrar & Marketing Manager: Sarah Harris, BA Hons

Bursar: Christopher King

St John's College

Grove Road South, Southsea, Hampshire PO5 3QW

Tel:	023 9281 5118
email:	info@stjohnscollege.co.uk
website:	www.stjohnscollege.co.uk
Twitter:	@sjcsouthse
Facebook:	@SJCSouthsea
Instagram:	@sjc_southsea

Founded in 1908 by the De La Salle Brothers, St John's College seeks to provide an excellent all-round day and boarding education to boys and girls of all abilities. Children of all Christian denominations, those of other faiths and those with no formal religious affiliation but who are in sympathy with the values of the school are welcome. The College became fully independent and decoupled from the De la Salle Trust in September 2015, but continues to provide an academic education based on the spiritual and moral ethos of the Founder John Baptist De La Salle.

St John's is a thriving co-educational day and boarding school for pupils aged 4 to 18 (boarding from Year 7). Number of Pupils: 400 including 60 Boarders.

Situation. St John's College campus is located in the heart of Southsea, an attractive and thriving seaside suburb of Portsmouth. The College's extensive sports fields are located on the outskirts of the city, with transport provided to and from that site.

Approach and Ethos. Academically, St John's College is a non-selective school, its aim being excellence for every pupil according to their personal potential. All children who are able and willing to benefit from the curriculum provided are welcome to join the school community. The school's academic record – by all measures – is outstanding.

The pastoral care offered to boarders and day pupils is of very high quality. The commitment of the staff to the welfare and progress of each pupil is second to none. In return, honest effort and application is expected from the children – in order to meet the challenging standards set in academic work, sporting endeavour, behaviour and self-discipline.

Lower School. The Lower School is located within the main College campus. This enables younger children to enjoy a safe and secure environment with easy access to the wider College facilities, including the sports hall, astro, theatre, Chapel and music rooms. The Lower School offers a challenging academic curriculum and a wide range of extra-curricular and enrichment activities. It crucially provides a child-centred education, where every child is truly valued.

Middle School. The Middle School is based in spacious and airy classrooms on the ground floor of the refurbished De la Salle block, with easy access to the Library and Learning Support. This new learning initiative is designed to bring out the very best in the young people of the Middle School. The children are able to foster and build their love of learning and enthusiasm for their studies, while developing independence at their own pace. An innovative curriculum lets students build their soft skills, preparing them for the academic rigours of the Senior School, whilst letting them be children in a supportive and engaging environment.

Senior School. The Senior School curriculum encourages students to start making subject choices for their GCSE exams, whilst keeping one eye open for their choices in the Sixth Form. The diverse co-curricular programme provides opportunities for each and every student to engage, develop and flourish. A plethora of enrichment opportunities are available, aimed at providing students with as much knowledge, fun and experience as possible. A wide range of GCSE subjects is offered alongside IGCSE Maths, English and Science. Instrumental tuition is encouraged and the Senior School Choir and Orchestra are open to all pupils. Sport – principally rugby, football, cricket, hockey and netball – is strong at all levels. Pupils' progress in all areas is assessed formally each half-term, with formal examinations being held twice yearly.

Sixth Form. As they progress into the Sixth Form, older students are enabled and encouraged to become independent and self-motivated learners – in preparation for Higher Education. The teaching and pastoral staff continue to work closely with parents, who are kept fully informed of progress and achievement. A wide range of A Level subjects is offered. The College ensures a good student to teacher ratio, allowing for close and constant monitoring of the performance and effort of each student. Preparation for Oxbridge entry is available, and students are also offered practice interviews for university and job applications and a full careers service.

Beyond the formal curriculum, a wide range of sporting, academic, dramatic, cultural and social activities is available. The Politics Society, administered predominantly by Sixth Form students, enjoys a national reputation, alongside the new Medical Society and Engineering Pathway.

Admission. Pupils are accepted and placed on the basis of a formal assessment and previous reports.

Fees per term (2021–2022). Reception, Years 1 & 2: Day £2,750; Years 3 & 4: Day £3,400; Years 5 & 6 Day £3,550; Years 7 & 8 Day £4,535; Years 9 to 13 Day £4,600; UK Boarding (including tuition fees) £9,975; Overseas Boarding (including tuition fees) £11,275;

Music fees are extra.

Scholarships and Bursaries. Academic and other scholarships and bursary awards are available.

Charitable status. St John's College, Southsea is a Registered Charity, number 1162915.

Chairman of Governors: Ms Zenna Hopson

Head of College: **Mrs M Maguire**, BSc Hons, PGCE

Deputy Head Teaching & Learning: Mr A Martin, Meng, ACGI, Fri, PGCE
Deputy Head Pastoral & DSL: Mr M Round, BSc Hons, MSc, PGCE, FCCT, FRSA
Head of Lower School: Mrs M Jeffrey, BA Hons
Head of Middle School: Mrs S Fairey, BA Hons, PGCE
Head of Sixth Form: Mr N Krys, BSc Hons, PGCE

Bursar: Mrs J Doyle
Head of Marketing & Admissions: Mrs J Hunt

Heads of Faculty:
Creative Arts: Mr B Horrod, BSc Hons, PGCE
Humanities: Mr McBeath, BSc
Mathematical Sciences: Mr N Cater, BSc Hons, PGCE
Sciences: Mr N Krys, BSc Hons, PGCE
Communication: Mrs M Elder

Head's PA: Mrs C Withers

St Joseph's College

Belstead Road, Ipswich, Suffolk IP2 9DR

Tel: 01473 690281
email: admissions@stjos.co.uk
website: www.stjos.co.uk
Twitter: @MyStJos
Facebook: @StJosephsCollegeIpswich
LinkedIn: /St-Joseph's-College-Ipswich

St Joseph's College is a lively and purposeful day and boarding school offering girls and boys aged 2 to 18 space to thrive. Its Nursery, Prep, Senior and Sixth Form provision offers a broad, well-rounded and all-through education.

Located on a 60-acre parkland site near to the centre of Ipswich, the College is situated just ten minutes' walk from Ipswich train station and a five-minute drive from the A12/A14 interchange.

Traditional values are at the heart of the school community which, at the same time, is forward-thinking as it meets the challenges of an ever-changing world. Pupils are provided with every opportunity to develop their talents to the full, growing up in a happy and fulfilling environment guided by Christian values, where all are valued and encouraged.

Ethos. St Joseph's feels different and that's the way we like it. Our uniqueness is shaped by our ethos, which combines Christian values with a distinctive approach to supporting and nurturing children individually within a friendly, family environment. Along with the pursuit of excellence, this approach is reflected in all aspects of life at the College: academic, sporting and cultural.

Developments. December 2019 saw the reopening of the College Chapel following a £750K refurbishment. Known as the 'heart of St Joseph's', the striking Modernist chapel, with its iconic verdigris roof, hosts assemblies, concerts, lectures and dramatic productions as well as services.

Whilst the refurbishment was underway, a new meeting space was created – The ARC. Named for the school's three core values (Aspiration, Respect and Confidence), The ARC provides a formal assembly area which can also be used for concerts, art exhibitions and social gatherings.

In summer 2019 The Pavilion opened, a multi-use space with dual-aspect views over sports fields. The Pavilion crowns a move to concentrating on four performance sports: rugby, cricket, football and netball. New cricket nets were also installed and an indoor cricket training facility updated.

The second phase of the College's ambitious Building for the Future plans came to fruition in September 2016 with the opening of a state-of-the-art Sixth Form Centre, combining 21st-century technology with light, space, serenity and colour.

Eight years earlier, the innovative Prep School building was formally opened. This fascinating curved building with its maltings-style wind-catcher towers provides a highly stimulating environment for pupils aged 2 to 11 and is equipped with the latest technological and physical resources.

In September 2015 a new Technology Centre opened. The College offers Engineering from Prep School to Sixth Form, including both academic and practical pathways. In

March 2014 a floodlit AstroTurf pitch and new changing room complex were added to the school's facilities.

ISI Inspection. St Joseph's College achieved the top rating possible from the Independent Schools Inspectorate for its EYFS, Prep School, Senior School, Sixth Form and Boarding. ISI rated the school 'Excellent' across both mandatory inspection judgement areas: the quality of pupils' achievement and the quality of pupils' personal development.

Following the three-day focused compliance and education quality inspection in March 2019, the report commended academic achievement, teachers' subject knowledge, student study skills, and pupils' self-discipline and social awareness.

Boarding. We offer flexible, weekly and full boarding in two family-run, spacious and warm boarding houses. Accommodation includes both single and shared rooms, with kitchens, studies and recreational facilities.

Curriculum. The curriculum is designed to provide a broad and balanced education for all pupils from 2 to 18. Strong foundations in the core skills of reading, writing and numeracy are laid down in the Infant Department through innovative programmes, such as Read Write Inc and Singapore Mathematics. The Junior section continues the process of preparing the children for their secondary education by concentrating further on the core skills. In addition to these subjects, Science, Spanish, Music and PE are taught and the children are introduced to a wider curriculum, including Engineering, Art, History, Geography, RE, IT and Games. There is an emphasis on STEM subjects.

The Senior School prepares pupils for entrance to universities, other forms of higher education and the professions. Pupils are set according to ability in certain subjects. In Years 7 to 9, the emphasis continues to be placed on the core subjects whilst developing knowledge, skills and experiences necessary for the GCSE courses.

GCSE studies maintain a broad and balanced curriculum, but with the introduction of a degree of specialisation. Mathematics, English Language & Literature and Double Science Award are compulsory, with PE and Faith, Life & Wellbeing also studied by all. Once again core subjects continue to be set by ability. To cater for developing interests and abilities, there is a wide range of further choices.

The majority of our pupils continue into the Sixth Form to complete their A Level or vocational courses before going on to university or into apprenticeships or the workplace. Subjects available in the Sixth Form include: Art (Fine Art), Biology, Business (A Level), Business Studies (BTEC), Chemistry, Digital Media (CTEC), Drama and Theatre Studies, Economics, Engineering (BTEC), English, French, Geography, History, Law, Mathematics, Further Mathematics, Mathematical Studies, Music, Photography, Physics, Psychology, Sociology, Spanish, Sport Coaching and Development (BTEC) and Textiles. St Joseph's also offers the Extended Project Qualification, IELTS and EAL. with diverse sporting and other leisure and cultural opportunities. We are a national test centre for SAT admissions tests.

A Learning Support department operates throughout the College to provide support individually or in small groups for students of all abilities with specific learning needs and differences.

There is comprehensive careers guidance from Year 9 and extensive help with university admissions in the Sixth Form from the College's highly experienced Futures Advisor.

Extra-Curricular Activities. Sport, Art, Music and Drama are strongly encouraged, as is participation in the Duke of Edinburgh's Award. The College stages a musical production annually, together with plays and concerts. A large number of extra-curricular clubs meets weekly. Regular ski trips, activity holidays and language exchanges are organised throughout the College, including a Year 9 exchange with two leading schools in Sydney, Australia, plus exchanges to Argentina and China.

Admission. Entry to the College is normally at 2+, 7+, 11+, 13+ and the Sixth Form, with applications for vacancies at other ages, subject to spaces being available. The entry process includes an interview, a Taster Day (where Covid-19 regulations allow), a formal assessment and a report from the applicant's previous school. For the Sixth Form, the academic assessment is replaced by GCSE results.

Fees per term (2021–2022). Nursery: £61–£63 (per full session); Infants (Reception to Year 2) £3,415; Juniors (Years 3–6) £4,430 (day); Senior School: Years 7–8: £5,240 (day), £9,195 (weekly boarder), £9,620 (full boarder/EEA), £9,620 (overseas boarder); Year 9–11: £5,575 (day), £10,045 (weekly boarder), £12,430 (full boarder/EEA), £12,790 (overseas boarder); Sixth Form: £5,575 (day), £10,045 (weekly boarder), £12,430 (full boarder/EEA), £12,790 (overseas boarder).

Scholarships and Bursaries. The College offers a number of scholarships each year at select points of entry into Prep, Senior and Sixth Form, including academic, all-round and subject specific, including Sport. Means-tested bursaries may also be available in cases of need. Please contact the Admissions team for further information.

Charitable status. St Joseph's College is a Registered Charity, number 1051688. It exists to provide high-quality education for children.

Governing Body:
Chair: Mr Perry Glading
Vice Chair: Mr Richard Stace, LLB

Mr John Button	Mrs Vicky Fox
Mrs Ann Maria Cawthorn	Mr Anthony Newman
Mrs Renata Chester	Mr Matthew Potter
Mr Kevyn Connelly	Mr Christian Ross
Mr Phil Dennis	

Senior Leadership Team:

Principal: Mrs Danielle Clarke, BA Hons, NPQH

Deputy Principal: Mr Sacha Cinnamond, BA Hons, MA
Vice Principal, Head of Prep School: Mrs Vanessa Wood, BA Hons, PGCE
Vice Principal, Pastoral: Mrs Gina Rowlands, BA Hons, PGCE
Vice Principal, Co-curricular: Mrs Vicki Harvey, BA, PGCE, Dip Ed MCCT
Director of Business Development and Sport: Mr Anthony O'Riordan, NPQSL
Director of Finance: Mr Benjamin Palmer, FCCA
Director of Admissions, Marketing and Communications: Mrs Sarah Edwards, BA Hons
Director of Academic and International Projects: Dr Jen Stimson, BA Hons, MSc, PhD, PGCE

Head of Sixth Form: Mrs Katherine Simpson-Jacobs, BA Hons

Senior School Heads of Faculty and Pastoral Leads:

Mrs M Frost (*Head of Technology*)
Miss L Cunningham (*Head of Learning Support*)
Ms S Hare-Price (*Assistant Director of Sport and ECA*)
Mr M Grigg (*Head of Boys' Sport, Head of Rugby*)
Mrs H Green (*Head of English*)
Mr C Fletcher (*Senior Pastoral Manager*)
Mr D Briffa (*Head of Science*)
Mr C McNicholas (*Head of Humanities*)
Ms M Strong (*Head of MFL & EAL*)
Mr M Greenaway (*Head of Mathematics*)
Mrs V Harvey (*Head of Creative and Performing Arts*)

Prep School:

Mrs L Dhanak (*Head of EYFS & Infant*)
Mrs D Searle (*Deputy Head*)

Scarborough College

Filey Road, Scarborough, North Yorkshire YO11 3BA

Tel: 01723 360620
email: admin@scarboroughcollege.co.uk
website: www.scarboroughcollege.co.uk
Twitter: @ScarboroughColl
Facebook: @ScarboroughCollege
Instagram: @scarboroughcollege

Motto: *Pensez Fort*

Scarborough College, founded in 1896, is a thriving co-educational day and boarding school for children aged 3–18 with an exceptional academic pedigree and an unrivalled reputation for making the most of every child's potential. The College, its Prep School and Pre-School all share the same site. Our beautiful campus overlooks the spectacular North Yorkshire coast and is ten minutes' walk from the centre of the stunning seaside town of Scarborough. The boarding houses are merely a 15-minute walk from the beach. The College has fine views overlooking the South Bay of the town and Scarborough Castle.

Although the ethos of the College is firmly based upon wholesome traditional principles, we have a progressive approach to education, which has led to us offering the International Baccalaureate in our Sixth Form since 2007, a qualification that is highly prized throughout the world. Our average staff to student ratio of 1:8 ensures we develop the full potential of every child.

Superb facilities including 20 acres of sports pitches, a fully floodlit AstroTurf, a performing arts centre with 400-seater theatre, sports hall and neighbouring 18-hole golf course all ensure a truly first-class education can be delivered to nurture the talents of all.

Scholarships for academic performance, sport, music and as an 'all-rounder' are awarded at all entry points. Means-tested bursaries are also available.

Admission. *Prep School:* Admission is by visit to the school and an interview with the Head of Prep School. Taster days can be arranged.

Senior School: Admission at age 11 is following an Entrance Assessment and interview. Admission at all other ages is subject to recommendation from the previous school, an interview and satisfactory performance in a general assessment.

Sixth Form: Admissions are subject to the achievement of a minimum of five GCSEs at Grades 9 to 6 and an interview with the headmaster. *Overseas Students* are required to submit: school reports for the previous two years; academic certificates, if appropriate (GCSE or equivalent and any other exams taken); written reference from the Head of current/previous school. They are also required to sit our English and maths assessments and undergo an interview either during a visit to the school or via Skype. Scholarships and bursaries are available.

Senior School. Students join us in all year groups with especially high numbers of new arrivals in Years 7, 9 and 10 for GCSE, Year 11 for our bespoke Pre-IB course and the Lower Sixth for the IB Diploma.

Students in Years 7, 8 and 9 study three modern languages and three sciences, providing them with a firm foundation for further study. Along with English and maths, they also study traditional subjects including history, geography, music, art, religious education, classics, ICT, drama, and design and technology. Further options appear as GCSE subject choices in Year 10.

A dedicated Learning Support and English as an Additional Language team of staff ensures all individual needs are fully met.

Sport, music, and drama are very important parts of the daily College life with over 50 clubs and societies on offer every year. Horse riding is particularly popular and the College has both a Cricket Academy and Golf Academy.

Prep School. Our educational vision is simple: the pursuit of excellence in every aspect of school life in an environment which will develop active, questioning, confident, thinking children.

At the core of our school is a traditional academic approach and a challenging curriculum. We provide the best pastoral care and support for every child. We also pride ourselves on the breadth of our education inside and outside the classroom. Dedicated subject specialists deliver a stimulating programme including art, drama, design technology, French and music, as well as daily games and outdoor pursuits. The enrichment programme is rich and varied and includes our own Forest and Beach school too.

In addition we offer free wraparound care before and after school for our busy working parents.

Sixth Form and the IB Diploma. The International Baccalaureate Diploma programme provides our Sixth Form students with a stimulating and challenging post-16 curriculum. Our experience has shown that the IB encourages the development of inquisitive, critical and reflective thinkers who engage fully in the learning process to acquire knowledge. 29 separate subject course options are available.

In our Sixth Form, students develop a new relationship with their teachers within a university-style tuition setting. They have many opportunities to show and develop their leadership skills and become very involved in the School Council, hosting and organising school, house and social events as well as prefect duties and helping younger students in roles such as mentors and sports coaches. There is a rich programme of visiting speakers and exchange visits, and they have their own dedicated Study Centre, Café and Common Room. This is a caring, friendly and warm environment which is a great place to develop and grow into inquisitive and confident young adults.

Boarding. There are three traditional and charming boarding houses at Scarborough College, offering boarding accommodation for pupils aged 11–18 years from all around the world. These really do provide a warm family environment with a home-from-home feeling for all our students, both British and foreign.

A busy programme of weekend entertainment is planned each term to keep the students active. More spontaneous events also include house barbecues, impromptu sports, trips to the beach, go karting, mountain biking, surfing and cinema trips, just to name a few.

Our boarding staff are all experienced members of staff with families of their own, so know how challenging and demanding teenagers can be from time to time, but also are very caring, understanding and sympathetic to the needs of each and every individual child.

Day Pupils benefit from all of the extras that being part of a boarding school brings, including the opportunity for occasional boarding. The school bus service operates daily to Bridlington, Whitby, Driffield, Malton and Pickering.

For further up-to-date information on the school, please visit the College's website.

Fees per term (2021–2022). Senior School Day: £4,707–£5,247; Weekly boarding: £6,387–£7,211; Full UK boarding: £8,176–£9,200; Overseas boarding: £9,719–£10,759.

Charitable status. Scarborough College is a Registered Charity, number 529686.

Governors:
Dr J Renshaw (*Chairman*)
Mr A S Green (*Deputy Chairman*)

Mrs R Clements	Mr R Guthrie
Mr J Cliffe	Mr R Marshall
Mr S Fairbank	Mr J Rowlands
Mrs V Gillingham	Mr J Swiers
Mr J M Green	Mr G Young

Senior Management Team:

Headmaster: Mr Guy Emmett

Head of Prep School: Mr Chris Barker

Deputy Head: Mr Timothy Cashell

Assistant Head (*Academic*): Ms Sarah Grice

Assistant Head (*IB*): Ms Katherine Cook

Assistant Head (*Boarding*): Mr Simon Harvey

Assistant Head (*Teaching & Learning*): Mr James Fraser

Business Manager & Clerk to the Governors: Miss Alison Higgins

Director of Marketing and Admissions: Mr Remco Weeda

Shebbear College

Shebbear, Beaworthy, Devon EX21 5HJ

Tel:	01409 282000
email:	admissions@shebbearcollege.co.uk
website:	www.shebbearcollege.co.uk
Twitter:	@ShebbearCollege
Facebook:	@ShebbearCollege
Instagram:	@ShebbearCollege
LinkedIn:	/company/shebbearcollege

Founded in 1841 and steeped in history, Shebbear College is a thriving day and boarding school for girls and boys aged 4 to 18. Our 85-acre campus is situated in the beautiful Devon countryside, close to Exmoor and Dartmoor National Parks and the fantastic surfing beaches of the North Cornwall coast. Life at Shebbear is busy, filled with academic purpose, co-curricular activity, creative discovery and outdoor adventure. We are a community where everyone is known and cherished and life-long friends are made within our supportive and caring environment.

Pupil Numbers. In the Senior School there are around 200 pupils, of whom around 50 are boarders, and around 70 pupils in our Prep School.

Situation and Location. Shebbear College borders on Dartmoor National Park and stands in 85 acres of unspoilt countryside. It can be easily reached by main road and rail links; only 40 miles west of Exeter and 40 miles north of Plymouth. Both cities have their own regional and international airport.

Buildings. Shebbear College boasts impressive facilities in all areas of the curriculum. The extensive buildings include a separate Sixth Form Centre; a purpose-built block for Science; a modern Computing suite; a superbly equipped modern Music Centre; Art Rooms and two Performing Arts halls. Our Sports Hall, gym and dance studio provide full-scale indoor facilities. The Pre-Prep and Prep School are situated within the grounds and are fully equipped for children aged 4–11 years. There are two boarding houses, Ruddle girls and Pollard boys.

Admission. Admissions into all year groups are accepted all year round, with an Entrance Day for those looking to join Year 7 and Year 9 taking place each January. We are a non-selective school and this day is simply designed to help us establish the academic ability and level of each child. Entry into the Sixth Form is by interview.

Houses. Every pupil belongs to a House – Pollard, Ruddle, Thorne or Way. These Houses organise activities and games competitions throughout the year. The House Tutors watch each child's progress academically as well as their general development.

Curriculum. All pupils at Shebbear College follow the National Curriculum until the age of 14. A wide choice of subjects is available in the following two years, leading to GCSE, but everyone is obliged to take English, Mathematics, Science and, usually, a foreign language. In the Sixth Form there is not only a wide choice of A Levels, but there is particularly flexible timetabling which enables students to mix Arts and Science subjects. We also offer a variety of BTEC courses which pupils can study alongside A Levels and/or the Extended Project Qualification (EPQ).

Sport. With more than 25 acres of playing fields, modern sports hall with multi-gym, dance studio, cricket nets, all-weather pitch, tennis and netball courts, pupils have the security to exercise within the school grounds confidently. The main games covered for the boys are rugby and football, and for girls, netball and hockey. We also offer mixed cricket, athletics and tennis. A variety of other sports are also on offer including rounders, volleyball, badminton, basketball, gymnastics and dance.

Outdoor Education. Shebbear College is well known for its strong Outdoor Education programme, and its vision is to become the best school for Outdoor Education in the South West. Pupils take part in weekly lessons which include Forest School, learning bushcraft skills, building, trekking and tree planting. Pupils take part in the Ten Tors Challenge and Duke of Edinburgh Award each year.

Music and Drama. Music and drama play a central role in life at Shebbear. Our choir has over 40 members and our orchestra, also with over 40 members, represents most instruments. Players perform regularly in concerts and instrumental ensembles. Every year, a theatrical or musical production is performed to a very high standard. Following successful completion of A Levels, we regularly have pupils going on to the Cardiff University School of Music and other prestigious Conservatoires.

Societies and Activities. All pupils participate in at least 4 afternoons a week of extra-curricular activities. This widens their interests and develops their self-confidence. The list of activities is endless and includes the usual and unusual. Many pupils enjoy getting involved in Ten Tors training, hillwalking, camping, sailing, canoeing, and surfing. Many pupils are involved in the Duke of Edinburgh's Award scheme.

Careers. Our innovative careers department, Horizons, prepares all of our pupils for their lives beyond school. In the Sixth Form, pupils have access to our excellent programme dedicated to university applications, apprenticeships and gap years.

Scholarships and Bursaries. We offer Scholarships at 11+, 13+ and 16+ for talented pupils in the areas of academia, sport, music, drama and art. Bursaries are available to all pupils but are based on parental income.

Fees per term (2021–2022). Prep 1 and 2 £1,985. Prep 3 and 4 £3,090. Prep 5 and 6 £3,415. Senior School: Day £4,475. Weekly Boarding £5,295–£5,570. Full Boarding £9,785–£10,250.

Charitable status. Shebbear College is a Registered Charity, number 1142794.

Chairman of the Governors: Mr M J Saltmarsh

Head: Mrs Caroline Kirby

Senior Deputy Head: Mr C Jenkins
Deputy Head Pastoral: Mrs F Lovett
Deputy Head Academic: Mr N Newitt
Head of Prep School: Mr M Foale
Bursar: Mr M Shaw
Head of Marketing & Admissions: Mrs J Conway
Clerk to the Governors: Mrs A Stairs

Heads of Departments/Senior Staff:
Academic Support: Miss L Body, BA Hons, PGCE, NASENCo Award
Art: Miss H Kaur, BA Hons, PGCE
Biology/Chemistry: Mr G Drake, BSc Hons
Digital Learning: Mr C Banyard, BSc Hons, MBCS

English: Mrs F Shamsolahi, BA Hons
History: Dr E Fox, PhD, MA & Mr L Wilson
Media: Mrs F Lovett, BA Hons
Drama: Mr J Pomroy, BA Hons, PGCE, MEd
Geography: Mr C Jenkins, BSc Hons, PGCE
Sport & Outdoor Education: Mr R Giles, MEng, MSc, QTS
Science (Physics): Mr S Clewley, BSc Hons, PGCE
Mathematics: Mrs C Cardoo, BSc Hons, PGCE
Modern Languages / UCAS / Careers: Mrs J Aliberti, BA Hons, PGCE
Creative, Digital and Performing Arts: Mrs R Sadler-Smith, BMus Hons, PGCE

Head's PA: Mrs A Stairs

Sibford School

Sibford Ferris, Banbury, Oxon OX15 5QL

Tel: 01295 781200
email: admissions@sibfordschool.co.uk
website: www.sibfordschool.co.uk
Twitter: @SibfordOxon
Facebook: @SibfordOxon
LinkedIn: /sibfordoxon

Founded 1842. A Co-educational Independent Boarding (full, weekly, and flexi) and Day School. Membership of The Society of Heads, BSA, AGBIS.

There are 398 pupils in the school aged between 3 and 18: 345 pupils in the Senior School and 96 pupils in the Junior School. There are 85 teachers plus visiting staff.

Curriculum. Sibford School offers an extensive, innovative and diverse education where pupils are encouraged to 'live adventurously'. Broad and balanced curriculum which reflects our view that while some may have talent for maths or history others may be gifted in the arts or horticulture. Renowned dyslexia tuition and support for a small number of pupils with other learning difficulties.

Junior School (age 3–11): wide-ranging curriculum with an emphasis on outdoor education. Literacy, numeracy, science and technology skills are emphasised alongside art, music, drama and PE. Enriched Curriculum in Year 6 with Senior School Staff. Specialist teachers help individual children with specific learning difficulties. No SATS.

Senior School (age 11–16): all pupils follow courses leading to GCSE, in a curriculum expanding on the National Curriculum. Information Technology is introduced at an early age and the use of laptop computers is widespread.

Dyslexic pupils have special tuition in small groups on a daily basis. Highly regarded Support for Learning Department provides specialised support within the timetable. Personal and Social Development runs through the school.

Sixth Form (age 16–18) students take A Levels and/or BTEC Diplomas. The Sixth Form curriculum leads to higher education and offers a particularly wide range of opportunities for further study.

Overseas pupils are welcomed into the school community. The school has a specialist ESOL department and English as an additional language is taught by ESOL qualified teachers.

Entry requirements. Admission is by interview and internal tests. Where applicable a report from the candidate's current school is required. No religious requirements.

Examinations offered. A Level, GCSE, BTEC Diploma, Associated Board Music Examinations, LAMDA, Oxford and Cambridge IELTS Examinations.

Academic and leisure facilities. Exceptional Performing & Creative Arts in purpose-built facilities. Multi-purpose Sports Centre, including a state-of-the-art Climbing Wall. 25m indoor swimming pool. Well-equipped Library and Information Technology Centres. Design Technology Centre. Separate Sixth Form Centre. Wide range of indoor and outdoor activities. 50 plus-acre campus set in beautiful North Oxfordshire countryside. Three boarding houses (for girls, boys and sixth form). Easy access to Stratford, Oxford, Cheltenham, Birmingham, London.

Religion. Established as a Quaker school, Sibford welcomes pupils of all faiths, backgrounds and nationalities, encouraging in each of them genuine self-esteem in a purposeful, caring and challenging environment.

Fees per term (2021–2022). Full Boarders £10,281– £10,489, Weekly Boarders £8,894–£8,995. Occasional Boarding £69 per night, Day Pupils £5,293– £5,397. Junior School: Day Pupils £3,362–£4,068. The fee for a full term of learning support is £1,750.

Scholarships and Bursaries. The School offers general Academic scholarships and specific scholarships in Art, Music and Sport. A limited number of bursaries is offered to both Quaker and non Quaker children.

Charitable status. Sibford School is a Registered Charity, number 1068256. It is a company limited by guarantee under number 3487651. It aims to give all pupils a vehicle to educational and personal success.

Head: **Toby Spence**, BA, MEd

Assistant Head (Pastoral) and Designated Safeguarding Lead: Tracy Knowles, BA Ed
Director of Studies: Anna Jo Mathers, BA
Co-Heads of Sixth Form: Helen Gormley and Darren De Bruyn
Head of Junior School: Edward Rossiter, BSc, PG Dip Social Sciences, MEd

Business Manager: Ally Lynch, Health and Safety, Estate & Business Management
Admissions: Elspeth Dyer
Marketing Manager: Harriet Canavan

Stonar

Cottles Park, Atworth, Wiltshire SN12 8NT

Tel:	01225 701740
email:	office@stonarschool.com
website:	www.stonarschool.com
Twitter:	@StonarSchool
Facebook:	@StonarSchool
Instagram:	@StonarSchool

Co-educational Day and Boarding School from Nursery to Sixth Form.

Ethos. Established in 1895, Stonar is a leading day and boarding school in a charming countryside setting, and home to the UK's finest riding academy. Our progressive curriculum transcends the purely academic, creating an enriching environment in which pupils discover and develop their individual talents and gain a deeper experience of the world.

Curriculum. A talented and committed staff offers pupils a broad and flexible curriculum. Prep Children follow the IPC. In Years 10 and 11, pupils study GCSEs, with an individual choice from wide-ranging options in addition to the core of Science, Maths and English. Over twenty subjects are offered in the Sixth Form, in both A Levels and Diplomas. Throughout the School our small class sizes ensure pupils are supported to achieve their very best.

Considering our broad academic intake, Stonar's results are outstanding and pupils go on to university courses ranging from Medicine, Law and Accountancy to Geology, Veterinary Science and Music. Talented artists proceed to a variety of Art Foundation Courses. Young riders take up careers in eventing or go for the Equine Studies option.

Stonar is in the top 2% of Schools within the UK for value-added in 2021.

Co-curricular Activities. The school's internationally renowned onsite Equestrian Centre provides tuition for all ages and abilities. Facilities include indoor and outdoor arenas, cross country training fields and a hacking track. The Equestrian Centre has the top level of BHS accreditation and is also a Pony Club centre.

The Sports Hall, indoor Swimming Pool, AstroTurf, Theatre and Music & Arts Centres offer first-class opportunities for sport, music and drama. An extensive programme of Stonar Clubs includes academic, sporting and life skills options which challenge and extend pupils' development, in addition to Adventure Training through Explorer Scouts, Duke of Edinburgh's Award and Ten Tors.

Boarding. Three boarding houses are set within the grounds offering a homely environment for boarders from 10 years old.

Admission. Individual Taster Days for Prep applications, with entrance assessment days for entry into Years 7 and 9 in January for the year prior to entry. Sixth Form places are offered based on projected grades and individual interview.

Fees per term (2021–2022). Prep Day £3,071–£4,147; Senior Day £5,530–£5,965; Prep Boarding £9,169; Senior Boarding £10,210–£12,444.

Scholarships and Bursaries. Year 7, Year 9 & Sixth Form Entry: Academic, Art, Drama, Sport, Music and Riding Scholarships are offered.

A limited number of means-tested Bursaries are available. A Forces discount is available to all pupils whose parents are current serving members of HM Forces.

Governance. Stonar is a part of the Globeducate School's Group, trading as NACE Educational Services Limited, Company Registration No. 8441252, Registered Address: 17 Hanover Square, London, United Kingdom W1S 1HU.

Chairman of Board of Directors:
Mr Daniel Jones (*Globeducate UK Ltd*)

Head: **Mr Matthew Way**, BSc Hons, MEd

Senior Deputy Head: Mrs Nicola Hawkins, MSc, BSc Hons, PGCE

Head of Prep: Mr Rob Cunningham, MSc, BSc Hons, PGCE

Deputy Head Academic: Mr Mark Ebden, MSci, PGCE

Deputy Head Pastoral: Mrs Tina Tilley, BSc Hons, PGCE

Head of Sixth Form: Mrs Charlotte Bennett, BA Hons, PGCE

Senior Staff:

Mrs S Abi Saad, BSc Hons QTS (*Maths*)

Mrs S Aikman, BA Hons, PGCE (*Head of Modern Foreign Languages*)

Dr R Beeching (*Subject Lead Biology*)

Mrs J Birkett-Wendes, BA Hons QTS, PG Dip (*Head of Learning Support*)

Mrs Z Bolton, BA Hons, QTS, MA (*English*)

Mrs K Bouchard, BSc Hons, PGCE (*Science*)

Mr S Boxall, MA, PGCE (*Subject Leader of History*)

Mr J Carlyle, MSc, BA Hons, PGCE (*Head of Humanities*)

Mrs J Carter, BA (*Drama*)

Miss A Catt, BA Hons (*EAL*)

Miss S Cholmondeley, MEng Hons, PGCE (*Head of Maths and Computer Science*)

Mrs S Cross, BA Hons, PGCE (*Art & Photography*)

Mr A Curtis, MSc, BSc Hons, PhD (*Head of Careers, Psychology*)

Mrs C Deans, MA, TEFL Dip (*Head of EAL*)

Mr J Dyde, BA Hons, PGCE (*Head of English*)

Mr J Eldred, BSc Hons, PGCE (*Maths*)

Mrs S Fisher, BA Hons, PGCE (*Assistant Director of Music, English*)

Mrs T Gates, BA Hons, PGCE, PG Dip (*Learning Support*)

Miss O Harris, BA Hons (*Art*)

Mr R Hobson, BSc Hons, PGCE (*PE & Games*)

Mrs S Holtom, HNC, HLTA (*Learning Support*)

Mrs K Leach, BSc Hons, PGCE (*Science*)

Mr D Messenger, BSc, PGCE (*Maths*)

Mr R Miller, BA Hons (*Director of Sport*)

Mr S Moore, BA Hons, PGCE (*Head of Rugby*)

Mrs L Noad, BA Hons (*PRE, Houseparent of York*)

Mr A O'Hanlon, BA Hons, PGCE, PG Dip (*Head of Creative & Performing Arts*)

Miss C O'Shea, BSc Hons, PGCE (*Maths*)

Dr A Passmore, BA Hons, MA, PhD, (*Music*)

Mrs K Rabbitt, BSc Hons, PGCE (*Equine Management & Riding Coach*)

Mrs A Rigby, MA, BA Hons, PGCE (*French and Spanish*)

Mrs B Russell, MLD, BA Hons, HLTA, ELSA (*Deputy Head Learning Support*)

Mrs J Slark, BSc Hons, PGCE (*Subject Leader of Business*)

Mrs E Small, BA Hons, PGCE (*EAL*)

Mrs C Toghill, BA Hons (*Subject Leader of Drama*)

Mrs F Villaba-Carrasco, MA, PGCE, PG Dip (*Spanish & French*)

Mrs R Wells, BSc Hons, PGCE (*Science/Chemistry*)

Mrs H White, BSc Hons, PGCE (*PE & Games*)

Mr D Wicks, MSc, BSc Hons, PGCE (*Head of Science, Physics*)

Ms J Wigley, BA Hons QTLS (*Subject Leader of Food and Nutrition*)

Mrs J Wilkinson, BA, PGCE (*English*)

Mrs R Windridge, MA Ed, PGCE (*Learning Support*)

Prep School Staff:

Mrs J Skinner, BA Hons, PGCE (*Year 6 Tutor & Lead Teacher Curriculum*)

Mr R Onyett, BA Hons, PGCE (*Year 6 Tutor*)

Mr D Gower, BSc Hons, PGCE (*Year 5 Tutor & Lead Teacher Co-curricular*)

Mrs K Osborne, BA Ed Hons (*Year 4 Tutor*)

Mrs H Saunders, BSc Hons, PGCE (*Year 2 & 3 Tutor & Lead Teacher English*)

Mrs H Pemberton, BMus, PGCE (*Year 1 Tutor*)

Mrs J Willis, BA Hons, PGCE (*Reception Tutor*)

Mrs V Clarkson, BTEC (*Learning Support*)

Mrs S Crouch, NNEB, EYFS (*Reception Class Teaching Assistant*)

Mrs N Passmore, MA, BMus Hons (*Music*)

Nursery:

Nursery Manager: Miss J Tyler, BA Hons (*SENCO*)

Mrs S Snook, Level 6 Dip (*EYFS Nursery Deputy*)

Mrs J Redsull, NNEB (*Forest School Leader*)

Equestrian Centre:

Miss E Halsey, BHSII (*Director of Riding*)

Miss J Chilcott, BHSII (*Senior Coach*)

Mrs J Chinn, BHSII (*Riding Coach*)

Mr N Hubbard (*Senior Yard Manager*)

Mrs E Sowels (*Equestrian Centre Secretary*)

Stover School

Newton Abbot, South Devon TQ12 6QG

Tel:	01626 354505 (Main switchboard)
	01626 359911 (Registrar)
	01626 335240 (Finance Office)
email:	schooloffice@stover.co.uk
website:	www.stover.co.uk

Stover School is a leading independent, co-educational, non-selective, day and boarding school for pupils aged 3 to 18. It is set in 64 acres of beautiful and historical grounds in the heart of Devon's glorious countryside between the foothills of Dartmoor and the South West Coastline. In the last ISI Inspection the School was judged as fully compliant and in the previous quality inspection as excellent in teaching, pastoral care, welfare, health and safety, quality of leadership and management and governance.

Stover School delivers a cutting edge Research Based Learning Curriculum across the entire age range while retaining a healthy focus on traditional Christian morals, values and manners. Happy children are at the very centre of the school's ethos, reflecting the robust system of pastoral care. Children who feel safe, valued, respected and who trust those around them are free to focus on learning to their maximum potential.

Pupils are encouraged, motivated and supported in achieving their aspirations in all areas of the academic and broader curriculum. Successes are celebrated wherever they occur, be that be in Bushcraft, French, Hockey, Science, Fencing, Art or Computer Programming.

The extensive activities and enrichment programmes ensure that everyone can enjoy, develop and challenge themselves. In this relatively small school every pupil is well known. The strong House system provides a framework for pupils to develop a sense of collectiveness within the supportive environment. Pupils learn respect for themselves and others through the teaching of moral values and good standards of behaviour.

The aim is to ensure that every child enjoys their experience at Stover School, having achieved the best they are capable of in the broadest education sense and having equipped themselves with the qualifications and skills required for future success and fulfilment.

Recent developments include a refurbished Art Studio, Sixth Form Centre and boarding accommodation, a newly established tennis academy, the creation of a music ensemble practice suite and recording studio, the establishment of a clay shooting and rifle range and the arrival of the first vegetable beds, chickens and beehives, coupled with an outdoor classroom.

Examinations. Public examinations set by all examination boards include GCSE, BTEC and A Level. Music examinations are set by the Associated Board of the Royal Schools of Music. Speech and Drama examinations are set by LAMDA. Sixth Form pupils can also take CoPE and CSL/HSL qualifications, set by ASDAN and Sports Leaders UK respectively.

Physical Education. Hockey, rugby, netball, table tennis, football, rounders and cricket are the core team games. Individual sports include athletics, gymnastics, golf, tennis, badminton and cross country. Other sports throughout the year include adventure development, orienteering, shooting and skiing.

The school has extensive grass pitches, six tennis courts (3 floodlit and one cover all-weather), a 9-hole golf course, cross-country tracks, clay pigeon and rifle range and cricket nets. We run a full range of school sports activities, clubs and fixture lists for both Senior and Prep.

Optional subjects. In addition to a wide variety of activities organised by Stover's own staff there are specialist peripatetic staff for instrumental and voice tuition, speech and drama, riding, fencing, judo, golf, clay pigeon and rifle shooting and tennis coaching.

Fees per term (2021–2022). Preparatory School: Day: Reception £2,820, Years 1–3 £3,303, Years 4–6 £3,770. Weekly Boarding: Years 4–6 £6,580. Full Boarding: Years 4–6 £7,600, International £7,990 (inclusive). Senior School: Years 7–13: £4,630 (day), £7,970 (weekly boarding), £9,625 (full boarding), £9,995 (International, inclusive).

Entrance and Scholarships. Compatibility of new pupils is assessed through a Head's interview, school tours, a series of taster days and submission of previous school's full written report. Academic, Music, Sport and Arts Scholarships are available and can be sat at point of entry or on our Scholarship Assessment Day in January. In addition, means-tested bursaries are available. Stover School, in association with Plymouth University, also offers the Excellence in Mathematics Scholarships to International students. This attracts a 10% remission of fees at Plymouth University for the duration of the Undergraduate Degree course (3 years).

Health. Nursing care is provided by our on-site Matron who is a Registered General Nurse. All boarders are registered with the school's GP.

Old Stoverites. c/o Stover School.

Charitable status. Stover School Association is a Registered Charity, number 306712. Stover School is a charitable foundation for education.

Headmaster: **Mr R W D Notman**, BCom Birmingham

Deputy Head Teacher: Dr J Stone, BSc Wales, MEd Open, PhD S'ton, HDipEd Dublin

Head of Preparatory School: Mr B Noble, BSc Hertfordshire

Senior Leadership Team:

Mr R W D Notman, BCom Birmingham (*Headmaster*)

Mr B Noble, BSc Herfordshire (*Head of Preparatory School*)

Dr J Stone, BSc Wales, MEd Open, PhD S'ton, HDipEd Dublin (*Deputy Head Teacher*)

Mr P Jenkins (*Bursar*)

Mrs H Notman, BSc, UMIST, MSc Ed Res Manchester (*Senior Teacher – Safeguarding, Welfare & Boarding*)

Mr M Mooney, BEd Cheltenham & Glos (*Senior Teacher – Pastoral*)

Middle Leadership Team Senior School:

Mrs S-J Avery, BA Plymouth (*Head of KS4, English*)

Mr S Griffin, BEd Cheltenham & Farnborough (*Head of KS3, Geography*)

Mrs D Robinson, BA Twickenham (*Head of Sixth Form*)

Mrs A Stone, BA Angers, HDipEd Dublin, CELTA (*Deputy Head of Sixth Form, Head of EAL*)

Senior School Teaching Staff:

* *Head of Department*

*Dr D Allway, BSc, MSc, PhD Manchester (*Science*)

Mrs H Bailey, MSc Swansea (*Mathematics*)

*Mr J Balfour, MA Exeter (*Drama*)

*Mr P Barter, BA Exeter (*Humanities, Duke of Edinburgh Award Coordinator*)

Mr J Brown, MA (*Science*)

Mrs C Carroll, BSc Nottingham (*Science*)

*Mr S Cocker, BSc, QTS Marjon (*Mathematics*)

*Miss R Cocks, BSc Southampton (*Humanities*)

*Mrs N Coen, BSc Cardiff (*Food & Nutrition*)

Mrs A Coster, BA Exeter (*Sport*)

*Mrs T Craven, BA, QTS Brighton (*Sport*)

*Mrs R Fenton, BA Manchester (*English & Media*)

Mr G Forsyth, BA Sheffield, TEFL (*English*)

*Mr G Foxley, BA Plymouth (*MFL*)

Mrs R Galvin, BSc Brighton (*Mathematics*)

Mrs K Gardner, BA Nottingham (*History*)

*Mr M Halse, BA Plymouth (*Boys' PE*)

Mr J Hartley, BA Exeter (*Business*)

Miss J Henwood, BSc Bath (*Mathematics*)

*Mrs C Howard, BA Wales (*Art & Photography*)

Mr B Kerr, BSc Derby (*Computer Science*)

Mrs E McEwen, BA Oxford Brookes (*English*)

Mrs J Mooney, PGCE Exeter (*Science, Mathematics*)

Miss A Morgan, BSc Wales (*Biology*)

Mrs H Rice, BA Wales (*MFL*)

*Mrs A Richards, BSc Ed Exeter (*Physics*)

*Mrs B Seward, BA Middlesex (*Philosophy & Ethics*)

*Mrs C Sewell, BA, MA Edinburgh (*Psychology, German*)

*Mr J Tizzard, BMus, DipEd Cardiff (*Music*)

Mrs C Wightman, BA Wolverhampton (*Art*)

Revd F Wimsett, BA Wales, Certificate in Theology Exeter (*School Chaplain & Teacher of Religious Studies*)

Tettenhall College

Wood Road, Tettenhall, Wolverhampton, West Midlands WV6 8QX

Tel:	01902 751119
email:	head@tettcoll.co.uk
website:	www.tettenhallcollege.co.uk
Twitter:	@TettColl
Facebook:	@TettColl

Motto: '*Timor Domini Initium Sapientiae*'

With a history dating back to 1863, Tettenhall College has played a significant role in educating young people from across the region, and today provides a stimulating learning environment for boys and girls, boarders and day pupils, from the age of 2–18.

The emphasis at Tettenhall College is on a personalised education that develops the whole person, both in and beyond the classroom with exceptional extra-curricular opportunities that complement the rigorous academic environment. The School ensures that everyone will find their niche and grow in confidence.

Life skills and preparation for life beyond school are important elements of the educational offering here and this permeates from Nursery through to Sixth Form. In the Preparatory School, the unique enrichment programme aims to deepen and widen the experiences of pupils with subjects ranging from Latin, Mandarin, and Philosophy to Engineering. English, reading and mathematics remain at the heart of the curriculum and are taught daily. Science classes, taught in the modern laboratory, now include an engineering focus.

Academic success is a major focus across the whole School, with consistently high GCSE and A Level grades above national averages. In 2021, at A Level an impressive 57% of grades were awarded at A*/A, 85% achieving A*–B grades and 96% gaining A*–C grades.

However, for a non-selective school, an equally important measure of success is 'value-added', which compares pupils' predicted grades at entry to the School with actual grades achieved at 16. On this measure, Tettenhall College is also above many of the highly selective state and independent schools in the country. Our small class sizes ensure that the most able pupils receive the necessary stretch to flourish whilst those requiring support are given this – at no extra cost.

Situation and Buildings. Set in over 30 acres of beautiful woodland grounds, with outstanding sporting facilities, Tettenhall College is a blend of historic buildings and modern amenities where pupils thrive within a caring family atmosphere. Located in the picturesque village of Tettenhall, yet only 40 minutes from Birmingham International Airport, the School is one of the leading independent day and boarding schools in the region catering for girls and boys from 2 to 18 years.

Amenities include a brand new Sixth Form and Study Centre, an indoor heated Swimming Pool, Sports Hall, Squash Courts, Sports Pavilion and floodlit artificial courts for football, netball, tennis and hockey. There are two cricket squares and playing fields for rugby, football and athletics.

Religion. Services in the College Chapel are interdenominational.

Entry. For the Preparatory School suitability is assessed during a taster day/session during which a number of informal assessments are completed. Those wishing to join the Senior School at Years 7, 8 and 9 will be invited to attend the College Entrance Assessment in the January prior to entry the following September. Entry to Year 12 is determined by GCSE results (or equivalent), school reports, and a successful interview with the Headmaster.

Organisation. Senior School (Years 7 to 11 and the Sixth Form) and the Preparatory School (Reception to Year 6) are divided into four Houses which compete in activities, work and games. The Nursery comprises Day Nursery and Pre-School from the age of 2 to 4.

Senior School & Sixth Form Curriculum. Years 7 to 9 in Senior School are designed to give our pupils a sound basis for studies at GCSE and beyond.

As well as a strong emphasis on the core subjects of English, Mathematics and Science we consider languages to be important, and so offer French and Spanish. Creativity abounds in our Art, Music and Drama programmes, and History and Geography lessons teach pupils about our world, both past and present.

Computing offers exciting possibilities to understand and control new technologies. Physical Education and Games encourage health and fitness, as well as providing opportunities to acquire and develop skills and attitudes to individual endeavour and teamwork. Add to the mix the moral and ethical dimensions discussed in PSHE and Religious Education and you have an academic programme that is broad and balanced, enjoyable and intellectually demanding.

In Year 9, Business and Electronics are introduced to ensure that pupils experience all of our GCSE subjects before choosing which subjects they wish to study further. EAL is offered as a specialist subject throughout Senior School.

The A Level years are academically challenging and entry into the Sixth Form (Years 12–13) is dependent on appropriate success levels at GCSE: the minimum entry requirement is 5 GCSEs at grade 5 or above. Our A Level curriculum offers a wide range of subjects, with small class sizes ensuring the best possible results.

For further information on the curriculum subjects offered in the Senior School and Sixth Form, please visit our website.

Careers. Extensive advice is given by the Head of Careers and every Sixth Former is assigned a Personal Tutor to guide and support them over the two years. This is enhanced by many visits and seminars throughout the year from external organisations such as universities and local companies. In addition the School is supported by Old Tettenhallians who will come in to host career talks and seminars.

Societies and Activities. All pupils are encouraged to become fully involved in the life of the community and to play a part in the social and cultural organisations.

Pupils take part in The Duke of Edinburgh's Award scheme, working for Bronze, Silver and Gold Awards. In addition to the sporting opportunities, school plays and musicals are produced each year; there is a house festival of Performing Arts and the Music Department has a deservedly strong reputation for its quality of performance and opportunities. All pupils from Year 6 take part in the extended day programme where activities range from climbing and mountain biking to the Extended Project Qualification for our older pupils

Preparatory School. The Preparatory School is housed separately in a purpose-designed building opened in 2002. It shares a number of the facilities with Senior School and Senior School Staff help with games and specialist teaching.

The curriculum goes far beyond the confines of the national curriculum. Younger pupils are taught by a form teacher with an emphasis on the acquisition of key skills in Literacy and Numeracy. As children move through the years they are introduced to teaching from subject specialists.

Athletics, Cricket, Netball, Hockey, Rounders, Rugby, Football, Swimming and Tennis are the main sports and all pupils have PE and two afternoons of games each week. Extracurricular activities change regularly but include clubs in all the previously mentioned sports.

Fees per term (2021–2022). *Boarding:* Years 5–9 £7,998 (full), £6,319 (weekly); Years 10–13 £11,500 (full), £9,101 (weekly). *Day:* Nursery £2,858 (full-time), Reception £2,643, Year 1 £2,956, Year 2 £3,200, Years 3–6 £3,780, Years 7–13 £4,998.

Scholarships and Bursaries. Senior School Academic Scholarships may be offered to outstanding boys and girls. Scholarships are also awarded for Music, Art, Performing Arts and Sport.

Means-tested Bursaries are available. There is a reduction in fees for the children of the Clergy and members of HM Forces as well as children of former pupils.

The Old Tettenhallians' Club. Membership is automatic on reaching 18 years of age.

Charitable status. Tettenhall College Incorporated is a Registered Charity, number 528617. It exists to provide a quality education for boys and girls.

Chairman of Governors: Mr Jeremy F Woolridge, CBE, DL, BSc Hons

Senior Leadership Team:

Headmaster: Mr Christopher McAllister, NPQH, BA Hons

Bursar: Mr C Way, BSc Hons
Senior Deputy Head: Mrs R Samra-Bagry, BSc Hons, PGCE
Head of Preparatory School Division: Mr J Gomersall, BSc Hons, PGCE, MCCT
Director of Admissions & External Relations: Mrs V McAllister, MA

Assistant Heads:
Pastoral: Mrs J Hollinshead, BSc Hons, PGCE
Academic: Mr D Matthews, BScEcon, LLM, PGCE
Preparatory School: Ms M Lofting, BA Hons, MA, PGCE

Thetford Grammar School

Bridge Street, Thetford, Norfolk IP24 3AF

Tel:	01842 752840
email:	office@thetgram.norfolk.sch.uk
website:	www.thetfordgrammar.co.uk
Twitter:	@ThetGram
Facebook:	@thetfordgrammarschool

Thetford Grammar School is a co-educational independent boarding school that teaches pupils aged 3–19. We are one of the oldest schools in the country and have been educating young people since the 7th century. Our pupils benefit from an academically robust, yet rounded education that includes a range of extracurricular activities and a strong pastoral system. We understand that children learn best when they are relaxed and at ease and our school is very much focused on providing an environment that encourages this. Children flourish at Thetford Grammar School because they feel safe and supported.

Buildings and Situation. Situated close to the centre of Thetford, the school occupies a well-established site graced by several buildings of architectural interest and the ruins of a medieval priory. There are extensive playing fields with a refurbished pavilion within walking distance of the main buildings, as well as an award-winning Sixth Form Centre built around the original Cloisters.

Organisation. Prep Department pupils (age 3–11) are taught in their own premises with independent facilities. Older Prep pupils have contact with specialist teachers in several subject areas and benefit from similar integration into many other aspects of school life. Main School education from 11 follows a two-form entry pattern in core subjects to GCSE. Sixth Form students play a full part in the life of the school.

Curriculum. Prep Department teaching follows National Curriculum lines with strong emphasis on the English/Mathematics core with the other curriculum subjects taught as part of the Exploration Curriculum, a project based learning style of teaching. Music, Art and Modern Foreign Languages are taught by subject specialists, while a full programme of PE and Games allows for the development of team sports and individual fitness.

Main School education through to GCSE is based on a common core of English, English Literature, Mathematics, a Modern Language (French, Spanish or German) and the Sciences. Options allow students to develop skills and interests in History, Geography, RS, Business Studies, Languages, the Expressive Arts, Physical Education and Technology. IT is strongly represented across the curriculum. AS and A2 courses are offered in all these subjects. Mathematics and Science lead a strong pattern of results at this level and Sixth Form students proceed to university degree courses.

Sport and Extracurricular Activities. The life of the school extends widely from the classroom into sport, community service, dramatic and musical presentation.

Winter sports are Rugby, Football, Hockey, Netball and Cross-Country with Cricket, Tennis, Rounders and Athletics in the Summer. Popular indoor sports such as Basketball, Aerobics, Badminton, Volleyball and Gymnastics are also followed. Sixth Form students are able to enrol in the local gym which is situated opposite the school.

A majority of pupils take part in training for The Duke of Edinburgh's Award scheme. A lively concert programme supports individual instrumental tuition and choral rehearsal while opportunities for theatre are provided termly by House and School productions.

There is a varied programme of curricular and extracurricular clubs and trips including expeditions and foreign visits.

Admission. Admission into the Prep Department follows a day in school with the appropriate year group during which an assessment is made. Admission into Main School is by formal examination with interview and school report. Sixth Form entrance is on the basis of interview and school report, with subsequent performance at GCSE taken into consideration. The main Entrance Examination is held in January but supplementary testing continues throughout the year. Full details from the Admissions Officer, admissions @thetgram.norfolk.sch.uk.

Fees per term (2021–2022). Prep Department: Reception–Year 2 £2,818, Years 3–6 £4,005; Main School £4,668, including books and tuition but excluding uniform, lunches, transport, examination entry fees and some specialised teaching such as instrumental music lessons. Nursery funding of 15 hrs per week is available and there are fee awards for Service families across the school. Sibling discount is applicable when a family has 2 or more children in the school at any one time from Reception year upwards and where the family is not in receipt of a bursary or other remission assistance. Fees are subject to an annual fee increase.

Scholarships and Bursaries. Bursaries can be available from Year 3 upwards. Scholarships of an honorary nature may be awarded to the top performers in the entrance examinations. Music scholarships are available on entry in Year 3, Year 7, Year 9 and Sixth Form. Academic Scholarships are available in Year 3, Year 7, Year 9 and Sixth Form. Art, Drama and Sport are also available in Year 7, Year 9 and Sixth Form for both internal and external candidates. Pathways Scholarships are available on entry into Year 12. Details of all awards may be obtained from the Head.

Head: **Mr Michael Brewer**, BA, PGCE

Deputy Head: Mrs A Faye, BSc, PGCE

Head of Preparatory Department: Mrs A Faye, BSc, PGCE

Head of Sixth Form: Mr A Ward, BSc London, PGCE
Deputy Head of Sixth Form: Miss D Dunsmore, BSc Cambridge, PGCE

Academic Staff:
Mrs A Alecock, BA Manchester
Mrs L Arbuthnot, BA University of the Arts Norwich
Mrs T Beukes, BSc Stellenbosch SA
Mr G Bone-Knell, BSc UWE
Mrs H Butler-Hand, BA, MEd Cantab
Mrs K Clark, BSC Kent, PGCE
Mrs S Collins
Ms S Cornell, BA Hons UEA
Mrs R Dimminger, Dip Ed Bulawayo
Mrs E Eden, MEd Cambridge, PGCE
Ms K Ehinger, MA Sheffield
Mrs J Foreman, BA Warwick
Mr M Foreman, BEd Nottingham

Mrs A Glassbrook, BA Hons Sheffield
Mr M Glassbrook, BSc Northumbria, PGCE
Mrs T E Granger, BSc Wolverhampton, PGCE
Miss C Griffiths, BA LCC, PGCE
Mr M Hill, BA Bedfordshire
Mrs J Hibbitt, BSc Hons Liverpool, PGCE
Mr D Mitchell, BA Hons Liverpool
Ms S Northmore, BEd Huddersfield Polytechnic
Mrs H Pringle, BA Teesside Polytechnic
Mr E Rose, BSc Maths, PGCE University of East Anglia
Mrs C Salt, BEd Exeter
Mr E Sedgwick, BEd Hons Greenwich
Mrs D Skeels, BEd Nottingham Trent
Mr J Snipe, BSc Bristol, PGCE
Miss F Travers, BA Nottingham Trent
Mrs M Trotter
Mrs A Vinciguerra, MA UEA, PGCE
Mrs P Weyers, MMus Wales, PGCE
Mrs L Wingham, BA London, PGCE

LAMDA:
Mrs S Cornell, BA Hons UEA

Teaching Assistants:
Mr A Bell
Mr B Doyle
Miss E Dunsmore
Mrs K Hill
Miss Emily Bell
Ms M Kheder
Mrs L Steeds
Miss S Wookey

Learning Support:
Mrs K Jones, BSc QTS, Dip SpLD, AMBDA, SpLD APC Patoss

Visiting Music Staff:
Mrs S Brotherhood (*Woodwind*)
Mr J Cushion
Ms F Levy, LLCM TD, ALCM (*Violin*)
Mr J Rowland (*Drum Kit and Jazz Piano*)

Administrative Staff:
Mrs F Brewer (*International Admissions*)
Mrs L Collings (*Admissions and Marketing*)
Mrs H Stocks (*Receptionist*)
Mrs C Huggins (*Accounts Secretary*)
Mr A Koch (*Accounts Assistant*)
Mrs A Faye (*Examinations Officer*)
Mrs C Reynolds (*Senior School Secretary/HR Admin*)
Mrs J Settle (*Librarian*)

Technicians:
Ms S Parlane
Ms L Aylward
Mr A Gatward

Maintenance and Compliance:
Mr D Ford
Mr R Gray
Mr J Lacey
Mr M Mosby
Mr M Reynolds

School Nurse:
Mrs J Theobald

Tring Park School for the Performing Arts

Mansion Drive, Tring, Hertfordshire HP23 5LX

Tel: 01442 824 255
email: info@tringpark.com
website: www.tringpark.com
Twitter: @TringParkSchool
Facebook: @TringParkSchool
Instagram: @tringpark_school

Tring Park School for the Performing Arts is the UK's leading vocational and academic boarding and day school. We offer an exceptional opportunity to young people aged 8–19, enabling them to study a dual curriculum with specialist training in the performing arts alongside an exceptional academic education.

Number in School. Boarders: Boys 114, Girls 256. Day: 121.

Pupils are provided with the necessary training required to forge influential careers in the performing arts; with notable alumni including Daisy Ridley, Lily James, Drew McOnie, Ella Henderson and Joe Griffiths-Brown. Alternatively, if pupils wish to do so, they can secure places at top Russell Group universities, with many of our alumni becoming lawyers, doctors and scientists.

Entrance is via audition. Scholarships are available for the dance course via the Government's Music and Dance Scheme and Dance and Drama Awards (DaDAs) for Sixth Form. School scholarships and bursaries are available for the Acting, Musical Theatre and Commercial Music courses.

Performance Foundation – Lower and Middle School Course

In Lower School, the course aims to build confidence and performance skills whilst consolidating basic technique. Pupils on the Performance Foundation Course take part in core technique classes in classical ballet, modern and tap dance, solo and group singing classes and acting classes which cover script work, voice work and improvisation.

In Middle School, pupils have the opportunity to develop their skills and talents in technique classes and live performances, so that they can make the right choices about the future direction of their career and education. Pupils will continue to study core classes in ballet, modern and tap dance, solo and group singing and acting.

Dance – Lower, Middle and Sixth Form Course

At Sixth Form level, students study classical ballet, contemporary and jazz dance. The curriculum is enhanced by additional classes in pointe work, repertoire, virtuosity, pas de deux, body conditioning, weights classes, Pilates and commercial dance. Second year students continue to develop their skills and contemporary improvisation is introduced. During the third year of training, dancers join Encore Dance Company and have the opportunity to work with internationally known guest professional choreographers.

Commercial Music – Sixth Form Course

The two-year Commercial Music Course focuses on Pop, Rock and Jazz music. The creative aspects of the Commercial Music Course allow students to write original material, create their own arrangements and write for commissions.

Acting – Sixth Form Course

The two-year Acting Course includes classes covering: voice, classical and modern text, physical theatre, movement for actors, acting study, improvisation, dance and singing. All students on the Acting Course also benefit from screen acting lessons and workshops. A strong theatre company ethos is fostered as part of the Acting Course activities, and students participate in a variety of performances throughout the year.

Musical Theatre – Sixth Form Course

The two-year Musical Theatre Course provides students looking to forge a career in the performing arts with a strong understanding and knowledge of technique in the three essential specialist skills. Students study an intensive two-year course focussed on singing, dance and acting.

Fees per term (2021–2022).

Prep Department (Years 4–6): Boarders £8,730, Day £5,135.

Lower School (Years 7–9): Boarders £11,540, Day £7,385.

Middle School (Years 10 & 11): Boarders £11,715, Day £7,495.

Sixth Form: Boarders £12,535, Day £8,295.

Sibling discount available: 10% of termly fees. Forces discount available – please enquire.

Charitable status. The AES Tring Park School Trust is a Registered Charity, number 1040330. It exists to provide vocational and academic education.

Board of Governors:
Chair: Mrs Angela Odell
Deputy Chairman: Mr Mark Hewitt
Mrs Alice Cave
Mr Daniel Zammit
Mr Edward Williams
Mr Eric Pillinger
Ms Jan Kitteridge
Mr John Clark
Mr Mark Taylor
Mrs Mary Bonar
Mr Michael Harper
Ms Rachel Joseph
Mr Robert Breakwell

Senior Management Team:

Principal: **Stefan Anderson**, MA Cantab, ARCM, ARCT, ARCO

Deputy Principal: Anselm Barker, MSt Oxon, BA Harvard, ARCM
Director of Vocational Studies: Elizabeth Odell, BA, AVCM, AISTD, FDI, QTS
Business Director: Stephen Robinson, MBA, MA, DMS

Vocational Directors:
Director of the Dance Course, Head of Dance: Lorraine Jones, LISD (MTH, Tap), AISTD CB NT
Artistic Director of Encore and Graduate Programmes: Antony Dowson, ARAD, PDTC Dip
Head of Drama and Director of the Acting Course: Edward Applewhite, BA Hons, Dip Acting GSA, QTS

*Head of Music and Director of the Commercial Music
    Course*: Harmesh Gharu, MA, BMus Hons, PGCE
Director of Musical Theatre Course: Donna Hayward,
    FISTD
Director of Performance Foundation Course: Louisa Shaw

Academic Management Team:
Deputy Director of Studies (Academic): Dr Anu Mahesh,
    PhD, MSc Hons, PGCE
Head of the Preparatory Department: Amanda Deer, BEd
Head of Lower School: Sarah Bell, MA, BA Hons, PGCE
Head of Middle School, Head of Careers and UCAS:
    Imogen Myers, BA Hons, CAP, MA
Head of Sixth Form: Dr Sarah Coren, PhD, BSc Hons, QTS
Head of Humanities: Robert Brown, MA, BA, IPGCE
Head of Arts: Jo Myers, BA Hons, PGCE

Head of Learning Support: Suzanne Kennedy, BA Hons,
    PGCE, MA, NPQH, SpLD, SENCOs

Trinity School

Buckeridge Road, Teignmouth, Devon TQ14 8LY

Tel:	01626 774138
email:	admissions@trinityschool.co.uk
website:	www.trinityschool.co.uk

Foundation and Ethos. With a joint Anglican/Catholic
foundation, Trinity School's Christian ethos and family
atmosphere are complemented by a commitment to
excellence in both academic and personal development.
With recent inspections by both ISI and Ofsted rating the
School as 'Outstanding' in many areas, the School has
successfully demonstrated a determination to deliver the
best education possible for the pupils in its care.

Pupil Body. 250 pupils from age 3 to 19 years, with
around 50 boarders.

Location and Facilities. The School offers excellent
facilities in a very attractive environment with panoramic
views of Lyme Bay. Facilities include a purpose-built
Design Technology building, IT laboratories, a Music
Centre, a Science block, a Food Technology Centre, en-suite
boarding accommodation for Sixth Formers, indoor and
outdoor tennis facilities, a 25m heated swimming pool, and
an Art Centre. The School is very well connected by road
and rail, with the nearest railway station being under a mile
away and on the London main line.

Academic Record. At the upper end of our ability
profile, we have a proven track record of sending pupils to
Russell Group universities. We have gained 6 Good School
Guide Awards for performance in English, Business Studies
and Science. Prep pupils' performance considerably exceeds
expectations at KS1 and KS2. 95% of Sixth Form students
in recent years have progressed to university or
apprenticeships. A mix of BTEC and A Level subjects are
taught (inc all facilitating subjects) in the Sixth Form.

Pastoral Care and Welfare. The quality of the School's
pastoral care is an established and considerable strength as
proven by the recent inspections. Our Anglican/Catholic
ethos permeates all that we do. We believe that for care to be
effective, it is essential that school and family work closely
together – the relationship needs to be dynamic, honest and
built on mutual trust and understanding. This approach, and

the fact that Trinity provides education for girls and boys of
all ages, helps to generate the School's warm, 'family'
atmosphere.

Personal Development. Extensive sporting, cultural,
charitable and leadership opportunities are available at all
ages: rich musical life with yearly musical productions
involving Prep and Senior department pupils; choir; one of
the most active CCF sections in the country; Ten Tors and
DofE regulars; Lawn Tennis Association centre of
excellence with one national LTA champion and regular
Independent Schools Association (ISA) champions; in
swimming, athletics, cross country, tennis – Prep and Senior.

Admissions. Trinity is a non-selective school, so there
are no entrance examinations required for entry.
Assessments are carried out for new students in order to
gauge ability and tailor education. Scholarships are by open
competition at 11+, 13+ and 16+, for academic, creative
arts, sport and all-rounder Notre Dame Awards (selection in
January). Bursaries and HM Forces Bursaries.

Fees per term (2021–2022). Tuition (day pupils)
£2,735–£4,335; Boarding: £7,340–£9,020 (weekly),
£7,905–£9,785 (full), £8,055–£10,495 (international
students).

Charitable status. Trinity School is a Registered
Charity, number 276960.

Patrons:
Rt Revd Robert Atwell, Bishop of Exeter
Rt Revd Mark O'Toole, Bishop of Plymouth

Proprietor and Director: Mr Ali Khan

Senior Leadership Team:

Headmaster: **Mr Lawrence Coen**, BSc Hons, PGCE

Deputy Head: Mrs Julia Bryant

Head of Preparatory Department: Mr Mike Burdett

Assistant Heads:
Miss Kate Ashfield
Mrs Lucy Atkins
Mrs Anna Brown
Mrs Jade Connelly
Mr Robert Larkman
Mr Sean Lovett

Director of Learning: Miss Jennie Moss

Bursar: Mr Shaun Dyer

Westholme School

Meins Road, Blackburn, Lancashire BB2 6QU

Tel:	01254 506070
email:	secretary@westholmeschool.com
website:	www.westholmeschool.com
Twitter:	@westholmeschool
Facebook:	@WestholmeSchool
Instagram:	@westholme_school
LinkedIn:	/company/westholme-school

Westholme School comprises: Infant School (Boys and
Girls aged 3–7), Junior School (Boys and Girls aged 7–11),

Senior School (Boys and Girls aged 11–16) and Sixth Form (Boys and Girls aged 16–18).

There are currently 631 day pupils at Westholme: 506 in the Senior School and Sixth Form, 125 in the Infant and Junior Departments.

Westholme School is administered by a Board of Governors which includes three nominated Governors representing current parents. Although the school is non-denominational, its Christian foundation is regarded as important, the emphasis being placed on the moral aspect of Christian teaching.

Senior School and Sixth Form. The aim of the Senior School is to provide an atmosphere in which each pupil can develop his or her abilities to the full and can excel in some field of activity. There is constant effort to widen interests and to instil a strong sense of individual responsibility. Most students continue to the Sixth Form and then move on to Higher Education. Most pursue degree courses, a significant number at Oxford and Cambridge.

The Senior School offers an academic curriculum in English Language and Literature, Mathematics, Biology, Chemistry, Physics, Geography, History, French, German, Mandarin, Spanish, Design Technology, Food Preparation, ICT, Textiles, Art, Photography, DT, Physical Education, Business Studies, Classical Civilisation, Drama, Latin, Music, Music Technology, Ethics, Philosophy & Religion (EPR), Psychology, Sociology and Theatre Studies. Most of these subjects can be taken for the GCSE examination and at A Level.

Set in the countryside to the west of Blackburn, Westholme School offers excellent facilities. The premises have been regularly upgraded to give purpose-built accommodation for specialist subjects such as Art, Design and Information Technology and Music; seven modern laboratories support the three separate sciences. Sporting facilities include a sports hall, indoor swimming pool, all-weather pitch and tennis courts and a large playing field with running circuit. The full-sized professional theatre seats 500 and offers students outstanding production resources. The Learning Resource Centre has open-access multimedia giving students full research facilities. The Sixth Form wing offering excellent facilities complete with lecture theatre, common room, computer workstations, café and classrooms.

The Performing Arts are a special feature of the school. There are several school choirs and students have the opportunity to learn a string, brass or wind instrument and to play in the school orchestras or wind ensembles. Co-curricular Drama includes the full-scale spectacular musical, in the round productions, club and house competitions, while make-up and costume design are popular options at GCSE.

School societies and house teams meet on most days during midday break and students are encouraged to participate in a variety of activities and in their house competitions. These provide younger students with opportunities beyond the curriculum and older students with the chance to assume a leadership role.

Infant School and Junior School. There is close cooperation between these schools and with the Senior School. A family atmosphere allows children to learn in a supportive and happy environment. Firm academic foundations are laid with the emphasis upon the basic skills of literacy and numeracy. Excellent facilities afford ample teaching space and resource areas; the Junior School has

three halls, music rooms and specialist provision for Information Technology. Co-curricular activities include public speaking, orchestra, choir, sports, societies and school visits. Music and sport are taught by specialists and all Departments use the swimming pool, sports hall, athletics track and outdoor pitches at the Senior School.

Admission. Pupils usually enter the school in September. Entry to the Junior and Senior Schools is by examination, and to the Infant School by interview. The normal ages of entry are at 4, 7, 11 and 16.

In view of the demand for places, parents are advised to make an early application.

The Principal is happy for prospective parents to visit the school during normal working hours; appointments may be arranged through the Registrar, from whom application forms are available. Annual Open Days are held in October and other open days are held in the spring and summer terms.

Private coaches run from Accrington, Blackburn, Bolton, Burnley, Colne, Chorley, Clitheroe, Darwen, Leyland, Preston, Standish, Ribble Valley, South Ribble, the Rossendale Valley and Wigan.

Fees per term (2021–2022). Senior School £4,020; Junior School £3,120; Infant School: £2,895;

Scholarships are available for entry into Year 7 and Year 12 for students who show good academic ability and various Bursaries are available (means-tested).

Charitable status. Westholme School is a Registered Charity, number 526615. It exists for the education of children between the ages of 2 years and 18 years.

Governing Body:
Chairman: Mr B C Marsden, FCA
Vice Chairman: Mr P Forrest, MRICS, FCIOB
Mr D J Berry, BA, FCMA, MIBM
Dr S Bhattacharyya, MBBS, FRCS Eng, FRCEM
Dr R Dobrashian, MBChB, FRCR
Mrs J Meadows, BSc Hons, ACA
Mr O McCann, BA Hons
Mr G O'Neill, BA Hons
Mrs L Robinson, BA Hons, MA
Mrs V Robinson-Hoy, BA Hons
Miss P Williamson LLB Hons

Clerk to the Governors: Mr J Backhouse, LLB Hons

Principal: Dr Richard G Robson, BA Hons, PGCE, MA, EdD

Commercial Director: Mrs Vivienne Davenport, MA Oxon

Deputy Headteacher, Pastoral: Mrs Jude Gough, BA Hons Wolverhampton, PGCE, MISTC

Assistant Head, Pastoral: Mrs Carla Hornby, BSc Hons Staffordshire

Headteacher, Infant and Junior School: Mrs R E Barnett, BA Hons, MA, PGCE

Windermere School

Patterdale Road, Windermere, The Lake District, Cumbria LA23 1NW

Tel: +44 (0)15394 46164
email: admissions@windermereschool.co.uk
website: www.windermereschool.co.uk
Twitter: @windermeresc
Facebook: @Windermereschool
LinkedIn: /in/winderemere-school

A visit to Windermere School or a look at our website tells you this is a very special place indeed. Our stunning location has been the inspiration for world-famous artists, poets, and authors, a sanctuary and the antidote to congested city life, a fascination to scientists, a home for adventurers as well as part of the masterpiece of human creative genius that affords us UNESCO World Heritage status. It is a daily inspiration to every one of us fortunate enough to call it our school.

Schools are what we build together and the Windermere community is as special as the place itself. Every child is different, talented, and special and every child matters. Here their differences are respected, their talents developed and their individuality encouraged. Our staff are dedicated to bringing out the very best in everyone and our examination results, university destinations, and the confidence of our pupils bear testimony to this commitment.

The beauty of our location, expertise of our staff, and wealth of facilities are enhanced by our size. Windermere is a deliberately small school. Pupils are known and cherished for who they are, every family is a vital part of our community and the voices of everyone are heard. Our classes are small, our pupils are happy, our education is bespoke and the results are stunning.

It is a rare privilege to be part of a school with Windermere's history and potential and we would be delighted to welcome you and your family to our school.

Numbers. There are approximately 320 pupils in total. The Senior School has approximately 243 pupils, of whom around 40% are boarders. The size of the community has the advantage of providing a friendly atmosphere of understanding and fosters good staff-pupil relationships. Many members of the teaching staff hold additional qualifications in outdoor adventure.

Curriculum. The curriculum offered at Windermere School reflects the belief that students should be exposed to as many opportunities as possible and leave the school as well-rounded individuals. It is tailored to the needs of each child, with small class sizes. Each pupil is provided with a personal tutor that stays with them throughout their years at the school, to oversee work on a daily basis and act as an advocate. One-year and two-year GCSEs and IGCSEs are taken in Years 10 and 11. Sixth Form students undertake the internationally recognised International Baccalaureate Diploma or International Baccalaureate Careers Programme. Sixth Form students also have the opportunity to study BTEC Business.

There are qualified staff and programmes in place for Special Educational Needs, English as an Additional Language, and Gifted and Talented pupils.

Music, Art, and Drama play an important part in the life of the school. There are two choirs, and individual instruction leading to chamber groups and orchestra. Students are prepared for the written and practical music exams of the Associated Board of the Royal Schools of Music. The school participates in regional Music Festivals. The Central School of Speech and Drama and LAMDA's examinations are also taken in Speech and Drama. Art and Design Technology provide considerable scope and opportunity. The Art Studios contain facilities for History of Art and an Art History Library. Drama classes are included in the curriculum, and there are several productions staged each year.

Extra-Curricular Activities. Windermere School's watersports centre, Hodge Howe, with over 160 metres of lakefront on the shores of Windermere, hosts a wide range of activities during the school's timetabled curriculum, and as part of the extra-curricular activity programme. The centre has accreditation from the Adventure Activities Licensing Authority, as well as being a Royal Yachting Association Training Centre. In 2018, the School was announced as a British Youth Sailing Recognised Club by the Royal Yachting Association for its race training. Windermere was the first school in the UK to be awarded this status.

There are traditional competitive sports teams in hockey, netball, tennis, athletics and more. Many students play for regional and national teams, as well as for the school.

Religion. The school is Christian in outlook and welcomes other denominations.

Boarding. There is a strong boarding tradition at Windermere School that benefits the whole school community. Each Boarding House has live-in staff supervised by a House Mistress or House Master. Each evening, academic staff oversee prep and are available for extra tuition and advice. There are weekend activities, we offer on-site activities along with staff-led excursions throughout the Lake District and beyond. It is a safe and caring extended family environment where pupils can excel both academically and personally.

Round Square. The School is a member of the international Round Square group of schools. Exchanges and Overseas Service Projects are regularly arranged between the schools involved in Australia, Canada, Germany, India, Switzerland, South Africa and USA and Brunei.

Infant and Junior School. The nearby Infant and Junior School is in the care of a Head, and takes boarders from age 8, along with day children up to Year 6. The Infant and Junior School is fully integrated with the Senior School giving continuity of teaching programmes and use of joint facilities.

Fees per term (2021–2022).

Average Day Fees (including lunch): Reception £2,840, Years 1–2 £3,260, Years 3–6 £4,820, Years 7–8 £5,620, Years 9–11 £6,240, Years 12–13 £6,350.

Average Weekly Boarding Fees: Years 3–6 £7,400, Years 7–8 £9,370, Years 9–11 £10,570, Years 12–13 £10,690.

Average Full Boarding Fees: Years 3–6 £8,080, Years 7–8 £9,910, Years 9–11 £10,995, Years 12–13 £11,105.

Discounts are available for Forces families eligible for the MOD Continuity of Education Allowance (CEA).

Charitable status. Windermere Educational Trust Limited is a Registered Charity, number 526973, with a mission to provide education of the highest quality.

Chair of Governors: Mr A Chamberlain

Headmaster: Mr Tom Hill

Deputy Head Pastoral: Mrs L Moses

Deputy Head Academic: Mrs E Vermeulen

Head of Elleray Campus: Mrs J Davies

Administrative Staff:
School Business Manager: Mrs S Ross
Head's PA: Mrs P Thistlewood
School Secretary: Mrs S Dougherty
Admissions: Mrs A McClure

The Yehudi Menuhin School

Stoke d'Abernon, Cobham, Surrey KT11 3QQ

Tel:	01932 864739
email:	admin@menuhinschool.co.uk
website:	www.menuhinschool.co.uk
Twitter:	@menuhinschool
Facebook:	@yehudimenuhinschool

The Yehudi Menuhin School was founded in 1963 by Lord Menuhin and is situated in beautiful grounds in the Surrey countryside, close to London and within easy reach of both Gatwick and Heathrow.

The School provides specialist music tuition in stringed instruments, piano and classical guitar for approximately 85 musically-gifted boys and girls aged between 8 and 19 and aims to enable them to pursue their love of music, develop their musical potential and achieve standards of performance at the highest level. The School also provides a broad education within a relaxed open community in which each individual can fully develop intellectual, artistic and social skills. We are proud that our pupils develop into dedicated and excellent musicians who will use their music to inspire and enrich the lives of others and into friendly, thinking individuals well equipped to contribute fully to the international community.

Music. At least half of each day is devoted to musical studies. Pupils receive a minimum of two one-hour lessons each week on their first study instrument and at least half an hour on their second study instrument. Supervised practice is incorporated into the daily programme ensuring that successful habits of work are formed. All pupils receive guidance in composition and take part in regular composers' workshops and concerts. Aural training and general musicianship studies are included in the music curriculum. To awaken feeling for good posture, training in Alexander Technique is provided. GCSE and A Level Music are compulsory core subjects for all pupils.

Regular opportunity for solo performance is of central importance to the musical activity of the School, and pupils also perform chamber music and with the String Orchestra. Concerts are given several times each week within the School and at a wide variety of venues throughout the United Kingdom and overseas. The most distinguished musicians have taught at the school, including Boulanger,

Perlemuter, Rostropovich and Perlman. Lord Menuhin visited the school regularly. Selection of pupils is by stringent audition which seeks to assess musical ability and identify potential. Special arrangements are made for applicants from overseas, who account for around half of the School's pupils.

The School opened a state-of-the-art Concert Hall in 2006 seating 315 with outstanding acoustics. Concerts and outreach programmes are now presented in this new facility. New purpose-built Music Studios opened in September 2016.

Academic Studies and Sport. The curriculum is designed to be balanced and to do full justice to both the musical and the general education of each pupil. Academic studies including the understanding of art, literature and science are considered vital to the development of creative, intelligent and sensitive musicians. All classes are small with excellent opportunities for individual attention, and as a result GCSE and A Level examination grades are high. To broaden their artistic and creative talents, all pupils work in a wide variety of artistic media including painting, ceramics and textiles. Pupils from overseas with limited English receive an intensive course in the English Language from specialist teachers.

The extensive grounds allow plenty of scope for relaxation and sport, including tennis, dance, badminton, football, swimming and yoga. An indoor swimming pool was opened in 2010.

An International Family. The international reputation of the School brings pupils from all over the world who find a happy atmosphere in a large musical family. Pupils live in single or shared rooms and are cared for by the resident House Staff and Nurse. New en-suite single rooms for senior pupils were provided in the girls' house in September 2015; similar facilities in an extension for the boys' house opened in September 2016. Special attention is paid to diet with the emphasis on whole and fresh food.

Fees and Bursaries. All pupils fully resident in the UK are eligible for an Aided Place through the Music and Dance Scheme which is subsidised by the Department for Education (DfE). Parents pay a means-tested contribution to the school fees based on their gross income assessed on a scale issued by the DfE. After two calendar years pupils from overseas may be able to obtain support through the Music and Dance Scheme. Until that time they pay full fees, although the school has some bursary funds available to assist with fees for pupils until they become eligible for the Music and Dance Scheme.

Admission. Entry to the School is by rigorous music audition, and prospective pupils are auditioned at any time during the year. Candidates may audition at any age between 7 and 16.

Charitable status. The Yehudi Menuhin School is a Registered Charity, number 312010. It exists to provide musical and academic education for boys and girls.

President Emeritus: Daniel Barenboim, KBE
Co-President: Tasmin Little, OBE

Vice-Presidents:
Barbara R-D Fisher, OBE
The Hon Zamira Menuhin Benthall

Governors Emeritus:
Daniel Hodson
Anne Simor

Examinations Officer: Jeanne Rourke, BA Hons, PGCE
Partnership & Outreach Officer: Keelan Carew
Music Admin Assistant: Dave Greenwood
Music Administrator: Emily Howell [maternity cover]

Bursary:
Assistant Bursar (Finance): Philippa Stanfield, ACA, BSoc
   Sci Hons
Assistant Bursar (Estates/Compliance): Alison Packman
PA to the Bursar and Business Development Co-ordinator:
   Niamh Poole, BA Hons
Accounts Assistant: Angeline Gao
IT Support Assistant: Victor Araujo
HR Manager: Lucy Flower, BA Hons, CIPD

External Relations:
Head of Individual Giving: Marion Chow
Trusts and Foundations Manager: Jonathan Hodgson
Membership and Events Administrator: Michelle Feeley
Marketing Manager: Sarah McDonald, BA Hons

Estates:
Estates Manager: Brian Harris
Assistant Estates Manager: Steve Foden

Catering:
Catering Manager: Jean Labourg
Weekend Chef: Jo Busby
Junior Sous Chef: Samuel Bartlett
Kitchen Porter: Arulanantham Gnanasegaram
Lunchtime Assistant: Julie-Ann Sage

Menuhin Hall Manager: Tamas Reti, BMus Hons
Menuhin Hall Technical Manager: Brian Fifield

Part-Time Assistant Technical Managers:
Alex Baily
Al Forbes
Dominic Mackie

Commercial Lettings and Hall Operations Coordinator:
   Jon Griffin

Menuhin Hall Bar Staff:
Charly Brough
Anna Larson
Adrian Whyte

The Society of Heads

Alliance Members UK

Berkhamsted Boys School, Berkhamsted, Herts
email: enquiries@berkhamsted.com
website: www.berkhamsted.com/boys/

King's Ely, Cambs
email: reception@kingsely.org
website: www.kingsely.org

Kingswood House School, Epsom, Surrey
email: office@kingswoodhouse.org
website: www.kingswoodhouse.org

The Moat School, London SW6
email:office@moatschool.org.uk
website: www.moatschool.org.uk

The Royal School, Wolverhampton, West Midlands
email: info@theroyal.school
website: https://theroyalschool.co.uk

Thorpe House School, Gerrards Cross, Bucks
email: office@thorpehouse.co.uk
website: www.thorpehouse.co.uk

Alliance Members Overseas

Brummana High School, Brummana, Lebanon
email: info@bhs.edu.lb
website: www.bhs.edu.lb

Leerwijzer School, Oostduinkerke, Belgium
email: info@leerwijzer.be
website: www.leerwijzer.be

Peponi School, Ruiru, Kenya
email: office@peponischool.org
website: www.peponischool.org

St George's International School, Luxembourg
email: info@st-georges.lu
website: www.st-georges.lu

The English School of Kyrenia
email: info@englishschoolkyrenia.org
website: www.englishschoolkyrenia.com

The Junior and Senior School, Nicosia
website: www.tjss.ac.cy

The Roman Ridge School, Accra, Ghana
email: enquiries@theromanridgeschool.com
website: www.theromanridgeschool.com

PART IV
Schools whose Heads are members of the Independent Association of Prep Schools

ALPHABETICAL LIST OF SCHOOLS

The following schools, who also have IAPS Heads, can be found in the HMC section:

Bedales School
Bromley High School
Campbell College
The Cathedral School Llandaff
Dulwich College
Elizabeth College
Eltham College
Frensham Heights
Gordonstoun
Ibstock Place School
Immanuel College
King's Ely
The King's School
King's Rochester
The King's School Worcester Foundation
Latymer Upper School & Latymer Prep School
The Grammar School at Leeds
Lincoln Minster School
Magdalen College School

Moreton Hall
Mount Kelly
Nottingham High School
Pocklington School
The Portsmouth Grammar School
Queen Elizabeth Grammar School
Ratcliffe College
Rendcomb College
Repton School
Rossall School
Royal Grammar School
St Edmund's School Canterbury
Solihull School
The Stephen Perse Foundation
Strathallan School
Wellingborough School
West Buckland School
Wisbech Grammar School
Wolverhampton Grammar School

The following schools, who also have IAPS Heads, can be found in the GSA section:

Blackheath High School
Bruton School for Girls
Derby High School
Harrogate Ladies' College
The Kingsley School
Notting Hill and Ealing High School
Pipers Corner School

Queen's College, London
St Catherine's School
St Mary's School
Sheffield High School for Girls
Sydenham High School
Tormead School
Wimbledon High School

The following schools, who also have IAPS Heads, can be found in The Society of Heads section:

Bournemouth Collegiate School
Hill House School
Newcastle School for Boys

St John's College
St Joseph's College
Scarborough College

The following schools, who also have IAPS Heads, can be found in the ISA section:

Ballard School
Belmont School

Cranford House
Duke of Kent School

IAPS
GEOGRAPHICAL LIST OF SCHOOLS

IAPS Member Heads and Deputy Heads

Individual School Entries

Abercorn School

Lower School
28 Abercorn Place, London NW8 9XP

Tel: 020 7286 4785
email: lower@abercornschool.com

Middle School
248 Marylebone Road, London NW1 6JF

Tel: 020 7723 8700
email: middle@abercornschool.com

Upper School
38 Portland Place, London W1B 1LS

Tel: 020 7100 4335
email: upper@abercornschool.com

website: www.abercornschool.com
Twitter: @abercornschool
Facebook: @abercornschool
Instagram: @abercornschool

Founder & High Mistress: **Mrs Andrea Greystoke**, BA Hons

Headmaster: **Mr Christopher Hammond**

Age Range. 2 to 14+ Co-educational.
Number of Pupils. 300.
Fees per term (2021–2022). £3,260–£7,250. Fees include all extras, apart from lunch and school transport.

Since 1987, Abercorn School has proudly offered children from the age of 2 to 14 years the perfect balance of a rigorous academic curriculum, delivered in a warm and nurturing environment in central London.

The school has gained an enviable record of achievement for both boys and girls graduating at 11+ and 13+. We guide both pupils and parents through the education process to ensure our pupils attain the highest standard and meet their potential. From September 2022, Abercorn will be accepting Year 9 pupils, with the capacity to expand to Year 11 and beyond.

The children are continuously evaluated, supported and challenged in order to foster their individual talents and skills. We are firm believers in traditional values and standards, including excellent pastoral care. However, we are committed to embracing the best of what the 21st century offers, and preparing each child to face the challenges of the modern world with confidence and competence.

Happiness is an essential prerequisite to the acquisition of knowledge. At Abercorn learning is serious but fun!

'Pupils are extremely well prepared for the responsibilities, opportunities and experiences of the next chapter of their lives.' *Independent Schools Inspectorate 2018.*

Discover Abercorn, discover their future.

Aberdour School

Brighton Road, Burgh Heath, Tadworth, Surrey KT20 6AJ

Tel: 01737 354119
email: enquiries@aberdourschool.co.uk
website: www.aberdourschool.co.uk
Twitter: @aberdourschool
Instagram: @aberdour_preparatory_school

The School is an Educational Trust run by a Board of Governors. Welcoming girls and boys from age 2 to 11.

Chairman of the Governors: Mr D Davie, MSc Dist, MBCS

Headmaster: **Mr S D Collins**, CertEd

Deputy Head: Mrs E Hoskins, BSc Hons

Head of Middle School: Mrs S Couper, BA Hons, QTS

Head of Pre-Prep: Mrs A Terry, BA Hons

Age Range. 2–11.
Number of Pupils. 330 Day Boys and Girls.
Fees per term (2021–2022). £1,570–£5,425 inclusive.

Children can start from 2 years old in Nursery, which is part of the Pre-Prep Department and transfer to Middle School, which comprises Years 2 and 3 (ages 6 to 7). Senior School follows, which includes Years 4, 5 and 6 (ages 8 to 11). Children are prepared for all the major 11+ Senior Schools and many scholarships have been won. There are ample playing fields, climbing wall, two all-weather areas, a large sports hall and indoor heated swimming pool. There are two science laboratories, a design technology room and an Arts & Innovation Centre with a STEAM room, languages studio, classrooms, music rooms, VR and Creativity studio and dance studios. All the usual games are coached and the general character of the children is developed by many interests and activities. Aberdour offers a uniquely personalised education with its own distinct curriculum. Finding the Brilliance in Every Child.

Charitable status. Aberdour School Educational Trust Limited is a Registered Charity, number 312033. Its aim is to promote education.

Abingdon Preparatory School

Josca's House, Kingston Road, Frilford, Abingdon, Oxon OX13 5NX

Tel: 01865 391570
email: admissions.manager@abingdonprep.org.uk
website: www.abingdon.org.uk/prep
Twitter: @abingdonprep
Facebook: @abingdonprep
Instagram: @abingdon_prep

The School was founded in 1956. In 1998 it merged with Abingdon School to become part of one charitable foundation with a single Board of Governors.

Chairman of the Governors: Professor Michael Stevens

Headmaster: **Craig Williams**, MA Oxon, PGCE

Age Range. Boys 4–13.
Number of Pupils. 250 Day.
Fees per term (2021–2022). £4,275–£5,995.

Main entry points are at age four and seven, although entry into other years is sometimes available. The majority of boys move on to the senior school, Abingdon. Abingdon Prep School pupils, for whom Abingdon School is an appropriate next step, receive an offer of a place for Year 9 at Abingdon School at the end of Year 5 at Abingdon Prep. The offer is based on the continuous assessment of each Abingdon Prep pupil. There is no separate entrance examination. The offer is subject to a boy maintaining his profile of achievement in Years 6 to 8 at Abingdon Prep. Boys not moving on to Abingdon are prepared for other senior school entrance examinations.

Abingdon Prep is a thinking and learning school – as well as a teaching school. Pupils enjoy a happy and stimulating environment where they are encouraged to develop self-reliance and a sense of responsibility. Considerable emphasis is placed on helping pupils to develop good working patterns together with sound organisational and learning skills.

The School enjoys facilities including dedicated art, drama, ICT, music, CDT and science suites and a multi-purpose sports hall and swimming pool. The School benefits from extensive grounds with woodland, gardens, adventure play areas, an all-weather pitch and acres of sports fields. Autumn 2022 sees the opening of a new development to house a Music School, a second science lab, purpose-built spaces for CDT and four additional classrooms for Years 6 and 7.

The extra-curricular activities are a major strength of the school outside the classroom. The excellent amenities enable every child to participate in a wide range of sports and activities. There are regular fixtures against local schools in the main school sports of rugby, football, cricket, tennis and athletics. All pupils swim at least once a week. There is a range of over 100 after-school clubs, which includes amongst many others, orchestra, choir, art, science, karate, golf, fencing, gardening, chess and drama.

A regular number of academic, music, drama and all-rounder awards are gained every year to senior schools – the majority to the senior school, Abingdon.

A large number of trips are organised for all year groups during the year and the oldest boys go abroad for a week on completing their examinations.

Charitable status. Abingdon School is a Registered Charity, number 1071298. It exists to provide for the education of children aged 4–18.

Aldro

Lombard Street, Shackleford, Godalming, Surrey GU8 6AS

Tel: 01483 813530 (Headmaster)
01483 813535 (Admissions)
01483 810266 (School Office)
email: hmsec@aldro.org
website: www.aldro.org
Twitter: @AldroSchool
Facebook: @AldroSchool

Chairman of the Governors: Mr T R Johns, BA, PGCE

Headmaster: **Mr Chris Carlier**, MA Oxon, MEd, PGCE

Age Range. 7–13.
Number of Pupils. 205: 65 boarders, 140 day pupils.
Fees per term (2021–2022). Boarding: Form 3 £8,066, Form 4 £8,898, Forms 5–8 £9,074. Day: Form 3 £6,024, Form 4 £6,855, Forms 5–8 £6,991.

Aldro is a co-ed independent day and boarding prep school set in a beautiful rural location yet within a mile of the A3 and 45 minutes of central London, Gatwick and Heathrow airports.

Aldro aims to offer an exceptional all-round education in a happy, purposeful community. It has a Christian foundation and this underpins the values and ethos of the school. Each school day starts with a short service in the lovely Chapel, beautifully converted from an eighteenth century barn.

The school is fortunate in having a spacious site including a lake and about 20 acres of playing fields. We have our own rowing lake, the new sports centre, four all-weather tennis courts, brand new netball court, two shooting ranges, swimming pool and a croquet lawn. The Centenary Building opened in 2000 and houses most of the classrooms, the ICT centre, an outstanding library and, in the basement, changing rooms and a large common room. The Crispin Hill Centre incorporates a Music School and Theatre. Two science laboratories and the Art and Design & Technology Centre have been developed in eighteenth century buildings either side of the Chapel. The Argyle Building including a new dining hall and kitchen was opened in late 2003. The dormitories in the main building have recently been refurbished. The boarders enjoy high-quality pastoral care and a varied programme of activities in the evenings and at weekends.

In the classroom, there is a balance between the best traditional and modern approaches, whilst firm and friendly encouragement of each individual has led to an outstanding academic record of success at Common Entrance and Scholarship level. Many academic awards have been won in the last four years (2019 being a record breaking year) to leading schools such as Charterhouse, Eton, Sherborne, Winchester, Radley, Tonbridge and Wellington College.

Aldro is committed to giving pupils real breadth to their education and much emphasis is placed on extracurricular activities. There are many opportunities for the arts, with a good record of success in Art and Music scholarships – 20 awards have been won in the past four years. An astounding 85% of our children learn musical instruments and there are three choirs, brass group, and numerous more ensembles. Drama also features prominently with several productions each year.

The major sports are football, netball, rugby and hockey in the winter, with cricket, tennis and swimming in the summer. Athletics, cross-country running, polo, sailing and shooting are secondary sports and high standards are achieved. A huge range of activities are available including badminton, dodge ball, pioneers, bottle digging and pétanque. The school has an enviable record for Chess with 9 teams winning National championships in the past six years.

Pupils at Aldro are treated as individuals with talents to develop. They lead cheerful and purposeful lives, and are well-prepared for a wide range of leading senior schools.

There is a focus on excellence and achievement, whether that is in the classroom, music room or on the sports field. Aldro prepares children for the rest of their lives.

Charitable status. Aldro School Educational Trust Limited is a Registered Charity, number 312072. It exists to provide education for boys and girls.

Aldwickbury School

Wheathampstead Road, Harpenden, Herts AL5 1AD

Tel: 01582 713022
email: office@aldwickbury.org.uk
website: www.aldwickbury.org.uk
Twitter: @aldwickbury
Facebook: @aldwickburyschool
Instagram: @aldwickburyschool
LinkedIn: /company/aldwickbury-school

Chair of Governors: J Bromfield, MBE, BA, PGCE

Headmaster: **P Symes**, BSc Hons Brunel

Deputy Head: C Schanschieff, BSc Hons Exeter

Age Range. 4–13

Number of Boys. Prep School: 265 Pre-Prep: 100

Fees per term (2021–2022). Day Boys: Pre-Prep £4,505–£4,770, Years 3–8 £5,145–£5,795. Flexi-Boarding Fee: £34.00–£41.50 per night.

Aldwickbury is a day and flexi-boarding school for boys set in 20 acres on the outskirts of Harpenden in Hertfordshire.

At the heart of the Aldwickbury community lies our belief that pastoral care should form the bedrock for academic success. Every boy is nurtured and encouraged to try their best, embrace challenge and most importantly; be kind.

We allow them to flourish as individuals in an environment that challenges and stimulates them whatever their interests, passions or talents. Our teaching mixes traditional approaches together with modern ideas and methods. We aim to equip all the boys with the skills to be happy and confident, build relationships with their peers and staff and develop strategies for coping with the challenges life presents.

The breadth of opportunities on offer at Aldwickbury is something we are incredibly proud of. The boys are challenged and engaged academically but also benefit from a wide-ranging co-curricular programme making full use of our extensive grounds and facilities. The school offers boys of all abilities a myriad of exciting opportunities to develop their confidence and unearth their talents in the arts, STEM, on stage, in music and on the sports field.

The journey through the school prepares the boys to leave at 13 when we believe they are truly ready for senior school education. The boys move onto a wide range of senior schools, both day and boarding. The recent results at Common Entrance, entry tests and scholarships have been a reflection on the excellent teaching that the boys receive.

Maximum class size for Pre-Prep is 16 and 20 for Years 3–8. Wraparound care is available in the form of breakfast and after-school clubs and flexi-boarding is also available from Year 5 upwards.

The school has excellent facilities based around a large Victorian House. Purpose-built teaching blocks, including a modern self-contained Pre-Prep department, ensure that the education is of a high standard. Other facilities include an indoor swimming pool, tennis courts and playing fields.

Over the last ten years there has been extensive redevelopment of the school's facilities, including a new hall complex, a new music department, refurbishment of the science labs and a total renovation of the Coach House providing a new Art and DT department. A new £3.8M sports centre is currently being built and is due for completion in 2022.

Charitable status. Aldwickbury School Trust Ltd is a Registered Charity, number 311059. It exists to provide education for children.

All Hallows School

Cranmore Hall, East Cranmore, Somerset BA4 4SF

Tel: 01749 881600 (School Office)
           01749 881609 (Admissions)
email: info@allhallowsschool.co.uk
website: www.allhallowsschool.co.uk
Twitter: @AllHallowsSch
Facebook: @allhallowssch

Head: **Dr Trevor Richards**, CPsychol

Age Range. 3–13 Co-educational.

Number of Pupils. 256: 140 Boys, 116 Girls.

Fees per term (2021–2022). Boarding £8,420; Day: £2,860 (Rec–Year 2), £4,900 (Year 3), £5,150 (Year 4), £5,460 (Year 5 & 6), £5,560 (Years 7 & 8). A range of scholarships and bursaries are available.

The all-round personal development of children has long been at the heart of the vision and ethos at All Hallows. The school passionately promotes an individualised and holistic approach to learning that seeks to inspire each child to fulfil their potential, with happiness and well-being at the heart of everything the school does. The dedicated and experienced team at All Hallows works in partnership with parents to prepare children for the ever changing world they are growing up in and for the lives they will lead, nurturing and encouraging them to live responsibly and compassionately and to embrace with energy and enthusiasm the fantastic opportunities that lie ahead. This approach is proving outstandingly successful with superb pupil outcomes and the children known for being exceptionally well-prepared for their senior schools.

All Hallows pioneered boarding co-education for preparatory school age children and the school continues to be innovative with the recent appointment of dedicated boarding staff who are fresh and ready to welcome the children into the boarding house at the end of the day. Boarding was rated '*Excellent*' in all areas in the latest integrated inspection report in 2014, with ISI recognising the school in all areas as "*of exceptionally high quality*" noting that "*children are exceptionally well cared for*".

Christian principles are integrated into daily life so that all faiths are welcomed into the life of this Roman Catholic foundation. Energetic and family-orientated staff, many of whom reside in the school, provide for the academic and pastoral welfare of the children.

The school has a mix of boarders and day pupils with many day pupils flexi boarding on a regular basis. There is an extensive programme of activities and prep for all children each evening after school, with weekend and holiday highlights. An innovative Saturday enrichment programme for Years 6, 7 and 8 comprises an ever broader range of extracurricular activities including photography, young enterprise, bush craft and more.

The school enjoys regional and national sporting success both at a team level and on an individual basis. A comprehensive programme of competitive fixtures enables children of all abilities to play against local opposition in the traditional team sports. Excellence within a framework of sport for all is the school's aim. Tennis is popular and the school has strong links with the Tennis Performance Centre in Bath.

Exceptional facilities for creativity allow the children and staff to discover talent and develop potential. A state-of-the-art Creative Centre offers the children fantastic design facilities including 2D and 3D design packages, 3D printing, laser cutting, animation, digital photography and fantastic 'making' opportunities. Music and the Arts thrive, ranging from the grace of the Chapel Choir to the creativity and performance of dance and drama. All Hallows also enjoys Forest School status, this fresh learning approach brings immense benefits and the outdoor environs are an integral part of the curriculum at the school, helping to foster the skills and wider perspective that truly encourage innovation, risk-judging and positive risk-taking, self-belief, ambition and a genuine sense of optimism.

All Hallows support parents in selecting the most appropriate senior school to suit a particular child's needs and talents. In the last few years, pupils have gone to over forty different senior schools with around 65% of the leavers, on a year-on-year basis, gaining a scholarship or award to their senior school.

Charitable status. All Hallows is a Registered Charity, number 310281. The school is a Charitable Trust, the raison d'être of which is the integration of Christian principles with daily life.

Alleyn's Junior School

Townley Road, Dulwich, London SE22 8SU

Tel: 020 8557 1519
email: juniorregistration@alleyns.org.uk
website: www.alleyns.org.uk

Chair of Governors: Mr Iain Barbour

Head: **Mr Simon Severino**, MA Hons, PGCE

Registrar: Mrs Felicity Thomas

Age Range. 4–11.
Number of Pupils. 244 boys and girls.
Fees per term (2021–2022). Reception to Year 2 £6,275; Years 3–6 £6,535 including lunches, most clubs, out of school visits and one residential trip per year for Years 3–6.

Alleyn's is a selective, co-educational school and we attract families and children from diverse backgrounds with a range of personalities, talents and interests which need to be met. So, we aim to create an environment for each child to achieve their best academic progress by developing the children's sense of confidence. To this end we offer small class sizes in a well-structured school where teachers work towards creating a calm, purposeful but vibrant atmosphere, so that high levels of participation are possible for all children.

Diverse interests and talents need to be nurtured outside the classroom too. So, there is a wealth of co-curricular opportunities for pupils to develop their individual strengths and passions. With around seventy clubs each term to choose from, the children can explore new interests, learn new skills, mix with different children and develop new passions.

Bright children with bright futures need to have opportunities to develop a sense of team spirit and to take individual responsibility for themselves and for others. The school's pastoral care is supported by a strong House system that extends from Reception all the way through school to Year 6. Our children love their school very much and this is because the relationships they have with each other, as well as with their teachers, are mutually supportive.

Alleyn's has a wonderful history that we cherish along with a desire to remain at the forefront of education. We aim to prepare our children for the demands of an ever-changing society and world. The school's origins can be traced back to Edward Alleyn in 1619, who was arguably the most famous Shakespearean actor of the Elizabethan age. From its origins, Alleyn's has continued to create a school where children and teachers respect each other in a friendly, safe and happy environment. In doing this we lay the foundations for future personal and academic fulfilment.

Charitable status. Alleyn's School is a Registered Charity, number 1161864, and a Charitable Company Limited by Guarantee, registered in England and Wales, number 09401357. Registered office: Townley Road, London SE22 8SU.

Alpha Preparatory School

21 Hindes Road, Harrow, Middlesex HA1 1SH

Tel: 020 8427 1471
email: sec@alpha.harrow.sch.uk
website: www.alpha.harrow.sch.uk

Chair of the Board of Governors: Ms K Brookes

Headmaster: **Mr Pádraic Fahy**

Age Range. 3–11.

Number of Pupils. 162 boys and girls (day only).

Fees per term (2021–2022). Inclusive of lunch, with no compulsory extras: Nursery £1,622–£2,621; Pre-Preparatory £3,676; Main school £4,051.

The School, situated in a residential area of Harrow, was founded in 1895, and in 1950 was reorganised as a non-profit-making Educational Charity, with a Board of Governors elected by members of the Company; parents of pupils in the School are eligible for membership.

The children enter the Main School at the age of 4 by interview and assessment, but there may also be a few vacancies for older pupils; entry is by written tests and a day at the school, dependent upon age.

There is a full-time staff of 16 experienced and qualified teachers, supported by well-qualified and experienced Teaching Assistants. Alpha also has some part-time teachers in instrumental Music. The main games are football, cricket, netball and rounders with cross-country, athletics, tennis and basketball. Extracurricular activities include Piano and Violin and Guitar instruction as well as Art Club, Science Documentary Club, Lego Club and Chess. Alpha is soon to enhance its extra-curricular offerings to include yoga, judo and more.

Religious Education, which is considered important, is non-sectarian in nature, but follows upon the School's Christian foundation and tradition; children of all faiths are accepted.

Outside visits to theatres and museums form an integral part of the curriculum and during the Lent Term pupils in Year 6 visit the Isle of Wight.

Regular successes are obtained in Entrance and Scholarship examinations, with many Scholarships having been won in recent years.

The School has its own Nursery (Alphabets) for children aged 3 in the term of entry.

Further details can be obtained from the Administrative Staff at the school.

Charitable status. Alpha Preparatory School is a Registered Charity, number 312640. It exists to carry on the undertaking of a boys and/or girls preparatory school in Harrow in the County of Middlesex.

Altrincham Preparatory School

Marlborough Road, Bowdon, Altrincham, Cheshire WA14 2RR

Tel: 0161 928 3366
email: admin@altprep.co.uk
website: www.altprep.co.uk

Headmaster: **Mr N Vernon**

Age Range. 2+–11.

Number in School. 300 Day Boys.

Fees per term (2021–2022). £2,446–£3,193.

With an engaging curriculum designed to capture the imaginations of its boys and a reputation for outstanding academic, musical and sporting achievements, Altrincham Preparatory School is widely regarded as one of the very best schools for 2–11 year olds in the North-West.

Altrincham Preparatory School believes in delivering academic excellence and its boys go on to some of the best selective grammar schools in the region, including Altrincham Grammar School and The Manchester Grammar School. Yet while recent examination results are hugely impressive, Altrincham Preparatory School is also a music school, an arts and technology school and a sports school. The culture of participation means the boys want to be part of everything and two full-time specialist PE teachers have guided the boys to national finals in a range of sports.

Altrincham Preparatory School was successfully inspected for Compliance by the ISI in February 2019 and the ISI Report (February 2016) identified the school as "excellent" with the broad overall provision "enriching the pupils' educational and personal experience, enabling them to develop their talents happily and fruitfully". The ISI was also impressed by the boys' positive approach to their studies, while the "high-quality teaching" was reflected in "good and often rapid progress and significant academic achievement". Pastoral care is at the centre of everything the School does.

Altrincham Preparatory School is committed to providing such high-quality education in a happy, safe and state-of-the-art environment. The Early Years Foundation Stage Centre at Bank Place opened in 2015 with a beautiful 16-place Nursery for boys aged 2 and above feeding into the Pre-School. Boys there are able to access the adjacent Bell Field for outdoor exploration, while the use of Bowdon Cricket, Hockey and Squash club's facilities means games can take place on high-quality artificial and grass surfaces. With bright, well-equipped and attractive classrooms, Altrincham Preparatory School is welcoming, nurturing, and most important of all, happy.

Amesbury

Hazel Grove, Hindhead, Surrey GU26 6BL

Tel: 01428 604322

email: L.Turner@amesburyschool.co.uk

website: www.amesburyschool.co.uk

Twitter: @amesbury_school

Facebook: @Amesbury School

Chair of Governors: Tarquin Henderson

Head: Jonathan Whybrow, BEd

Age Range. 2–13.

Number of Pupils. 361.

Fees per term (2021–2022). Prep School: £5,250–£5,750; Pre-Prep & Reception: £3,750–£3,775; Early Years (Pre-Nursery & Nursery): from £33.40 per session.

Amesbury is a co-educational day school founded in 1870 and is the only co-educational Prep school in the Hindhead/Haslemere area. The main building is unique, as the only school to be designed by Sir Edwin Lutyens, and stands in its own 34-acre estate in the heart of the Surrey countryside.

We are a family school, keen for siblings to study together and to feel equally valued irrespective of their aptitudes and abilities. There is no competitive entry. Entry is based on registration plus a visit – not a formal assessment but the opportunity for child and school to get acquainted.

Classes are small guaranteeing individual attention. Study programmes currently lead to senior school entrance and scholarship examinations at 11+ and at 13+. We have a proud tradition of academic, sporting and artistic achievement. The school has excellent purpose-built facilities with an award winning Visual Arts Facility which opened in September 2015 and a Library which opened in 2019.

We pride ourselves on sending children to the best senior schools in the country at both 11+ and 13+. Amesbury's academic record is excellent with an average of 20% of pupils receiving senior school scholarships. "Many a school may claim to be 'academically rigorous'. Not all would also make such a virtue out of also being 'relaxed' …this one does." (Good Schools Guide).

In addition to a compelling academic record, Amesbury has a thriving Performing Arts Department: "Music embraces everything from formal chapel choir to semi-secret bands formed each year, strutting stuff at annual concert. There's plentiful dance and drama including ambitious takes on Shakespeare" (Good Schools Guide). As for sport, the site is 34 acres, with an all-weather astro, indoor sports hall and an all-school tennis programme. Our Extra Curricular programme runs a whole host of activities including Judo, Golf, Chess, Music Technology, Drama and many more.

Amesbury understands its role as part of your family life. We believe weekends should be your time; there is no Saturday school and prep can be done at school. We offer Breakfast Club and After School Care. Our Pre-Nursery and Nursery offer early drop-offs, late pick-ups and holiday care.

ISI Inspection.

The quality of the pupils' academic and other achievements is excellent.

- Pupils of all abilities make excellent progress during their time at school.
- Pupils are highly independent and confident communicators, who keenly articulate their views and opinions to enhance their learning.
- Pupils have extremely well-developed study skills and relish opportunities for analytical and hypothetical thinking in their learning.
- Pupils have outstanding attitudes to learning and enjoy the breadth of the curriculum.

The quality of the pupils' personal development is excellent:

- Pupils develop high levels of confidence and warmly embrace new challenge.
- Pupils speak passionately about all that the school provides and the strong support that staff provide.
- Pupils have excellent moral awareness and a mature understanding towards the importance of positive behaviour.
- Pupils' empathy towards the needs of their peers is exemplary.

Focused Compliance:

Eight standards are reviewed and the highest accolade one can hope for is that the school will be found to be compliant in all eight areas. Amesbury was found to be fully compliant.

Open Mornings take place in October, February and May.

Charitable status. Amesbury School is a Registered Charity, number 312058. It exists to provide education for boys and girls. It is administered by a Board of Governors.

Ardingly College Prep School
A Woodard School

Ardingly, Haywards Heath, West Sussex RH17 6SQ

Tel: 01444 893200

email: registration@ardingly.com

website: www.ardingly.com

Chairman of School Council: Mr Robert Haynes Brown, BSc, MSc Econ

Head: Mr H Hastings, BA Hons, MEd Oxon

Age Range. 2–11.

Number of Pupils. Prep 254.

Fees per term (2021–2022). Reception–Year 2 £3,240–£3,335, Years 3–4 £4,727–£4,911, Years 5–6 £5,439–£5,655.

Ardingly College Prep School is the Preparatory School for Ardingly College Senior School (*see entry in HMC section*).

Ardingly College Prep School is set within 250 acres of glorious Sussex countryside, which it shares with the Senior School. The School is co-educational and has over 270 pupils from Pre-Nursery to Year 6 (ages 2–11). The Prep

School benefits from the College's Chapel, Music School, Dining Hall, Gymnasium, Sports Hall, Indoor Swimming Pool, 2 Astro Pitches, Medical Centre and School Shop. Girls and boys are admitted into the Prep from the age of 2. There is an extensive after-school care provision which includes activities that run until 7.00pm for all pupils. The School offers care from 8.00am to 6.00pm for 50 weeks of the year through Ardingly Active camps.

The extracurricular activities include Drama Club, Fencing, Swimming Clubs, Orchestra, Jazz Club, Chess Club, Mandarin Club, Forest School, as well as numerous Sports Clubs. The School has also recently launched a new Dance School.

Girls play hockey, netball and football. Boys play football, hockey and cricket. In the summer both girls and boys excel at athletics. Cross country and swimming take place throughout the year, along with the use of the Reservoir with Sailing Club in the Trinity Term. The School has had much success on a national scale in swimming and athletics with national champions in all sports.

Religious Education is in accordance with the teaching of the Church of England.

Details of Scholarships are available on the website and Bursaries can be applied for following the award of a a scholarship.

A new character and skills initiative known as 'Shaping My World' was launched in 2019 based on children being Generous, Adventurous, Ingenious and Curious. The School prides itself on encouraging independence, wanting to help the children learn how to prepare themselves for anything.

The Early years in the Prep School provides children with the perfect introduction to their education. Safely yet idyllically situated within the College estate, our Early Years are housed within carefully restored Grade 2 listed Victorian farm buildings. The school grounds provide us with a wealth of resources for many different purposes including Forest School.

Highly qualified staff work across our Prep school and our Nursery.

Charitable status. Ardingly College Limited is a Registered Charity, number 1076456. It exists to provide high quality education for boys and girls aged 2–18.

Ardvreck School

Crieff, Perthshire PH7 4EX

Tel: 01764 653112
email: office@ardvreckschool.co.uk
            admissions@ardvreckschool.co.uk
website: www.ardvreckschool.co.uk
Twitter: @ArdvreckSchool
Facebook: @ArdvreckSchool
LinkedIn: /ardvreck-school

Headmistress: **Mrs Ali Kinge**, BA, PGCE, BCAv

Chairman of the Governors: Jeremy Garrett-Cox

Age Range. Co-educational 3–13.
Number of Pupils. 107. Main School: 29 Full Boarding, 10 Step-up Boarding, 61 day. Little Ardvreck 17.

Fees per term (2021–2022). Main School: £8,550 (boarders), £5,690 (day); Little Ardvreck £2,720.

Ardvreck, an extraordinary boarding and day preparatory school, located in the heart of rural Perthshire and within an hour's reach of Glasgow and Edinburgh, offers a unique, educational experience to boys and girls from the age of 3 to 13.

Now, any school can provide excellent academic rigour, a strong pastoral ethos and a broad co-curricular programme, all of which we do very well indeed. What sets our school apart is most definitely the people, the characters, the personalities who are somehow, at Ardvreck, a rather rare and dedicated breed!

Ardvreck has an unbelievable team of staff, they are the movers and shakers, optimists, can doers, smilers and who all care, beyond belief, about the education and wellbeing of every single child in our school.

Known for our sense of adventure and creativity, we are most definitely the school every grown-up wishes they had attended as a child. It's where kindness, courtesy and good manners are at the forefront of every human interaction. It's an environment where working hard and playing hard are of equal importance and where good humour and fun permeate every undertaking.

We burst with pride at each speech day when we celebrate the achievements of the children whose lives we have helped to shape. They are happy, well-rounded and fulfilled children who are full of hope and ambition for their futures. It will come as no surprise then, that Head Teachers from public schools all over the UK are very keen to enlist Ardvreck pupils. Since 2019, 82% of our pupils have been awarded scholarships to a total of 27 of senior schools across the UK, including to Eton and to St Mary's, Ascot. Our pupils have secured scholarships for Music, Sport, Academic, Drama and Art to name a few.

Our dedicated boarding house, Dalvreck, accommodates up to 70 boarders on any given night. Refurbished in 2020, Dalvreck House is filled with the latest technologies as well as many home comforts taking into account your children's suggestions and needs.

We see time as the most important currency for our boarders who are given the time to enjoy being children within our beautiful 40-acre estate and beyond into our extended "garden", the foothills of the highlands. The boarders at Dalvreck benefit from our sector-leading outdoor provision, together with the weekend and evening activities which brim with fun and inspiration.

Boarders who live overseas can be escorted to and from Scottish airports; all necessary documentation can be handled by the School if required.

You will soon realise that we firmly believe classrooms do not need walls. As well as outdoor lessons, the entire school regularly adventures into the exciting, natural playground on our doorstep to undertake Barvicks (expeditions) and a regular Ard Challenge.

A modern and well-equipped Music School provides the best possible opportunities for music-making. There is an orchestra and choir, both of which regularly participate in both school and local music events. Visiting music specialists teach the full range of instruments including the bagpipes. Music and drama play an important part in the life of the school and a major production is staged annually with several smaller productions and numerous concerts taking place throughout the year.

There is a heated, indoor swimming pool (all children are taught to swim), an Astroturf surface for hockey, tennis and netball, and a superb sports hall.

This is not just a school; this is Ardvreck School. Here the children are prepared to be resilient and well equipped, with a daring spirit to succeed and to overcome anything that is thrown at them on their life journeys; they are courageous pioneers.

Admission is by a meeting with the Headmistress and an overnight or day 'taster'. Financial assistance is available through means-tested bursaries.

Charitable status. Ardvreck School is a Registered Charity, number SC009886. Its aim is to provide education for boys and girls.

Arnold House School

1 Loudoun Road, St John's Wood, London NW8 0LH

Tel: 020 7266 4840
email: office@arnoldhouse.co.uk
website: www.arnoldhouse.co.uk

Chairman of the Board of Governors: Dr M Badenoch, BSc, MBBS, DCH, DRCOG, MRCGP

Headmaster: **G F Tollit**

Age Range. 3–13.
Number of Boys. 358 (Day Boys only).
Fees per term (2021–2022) Reception to Year 8 £7,328, Pre-Reception £6,595

Arnold House School was founded in 1905 in St John's Wood, London. It is an independent preparatory school for boys aged 3–13, and a member of IAPS. A thriving school, with 350 boys, Arnold House aims to provide an education of breadth and excellence and to serve the boys' best interests across the ability range. The School aims to do so in a supportive, purposeful and stimulating environment, to provide a foundation for the boys' development within a generous Christian ethos, to help them mature into well-rounded individuals by developing their enjoyment of music, the arts and sport, and to promote good citizenship through the virtues of courtesy and industry.

The school works across three sites including 7 acres of playing fields at Canons Park, which also houses a 150-seat auditorium. More recently, the School acquired 38 Marlborough Place (The Huxley Building) in St John's Wood allowing for the expansion of an Early Years offering. The main point of entry is in Pre-Reception (aged 3). Occasional places may become available further up the school and bursary places are offered from Year 5.

Boys transfer to their chosen independent senior schools and Arnold House has an enviable record of success in placing each boy in the school that is right for him. More than half of the boys move on to the most sought-after London day schools: City of London, St Paul's, Mill Hill, UCS and Westminster. Others transfer to renowned boarding schools: Eton, Harrow, Marlborough, Bradfield, Radley, Rugby, Tonbridge and Winchester have been popular destinations in recent years.

Charitable status. Arnold House School is a Registered Charity, number 312725. It exists to provide education for boys in preparation for transfer to senior independent schools.

Ashford Prep School
United Learning

Great Chart, Ashford, Kent TN23 3DJ

Tel: 01233 620493
email: ashfordprep@ashfordschool.co.uk
website: www.ashfordschool.co.uk
Twitter: @AshfordPrep
Facebook: @AshfordSchool
Instagram: @ashfordschool
LinkedIn: /school/ashford-school

Ashford Prep School (part of Ashford School) is home to over 350 children from 3 to 11 years of age. Based in the leafy village of Great Chart on a site of 44 acres, the School provides an inspiring environment that encourages both personal growth and a sense of community.

Head of Ashford Prep School: **Mr Nick Tiley-Nunn**

Deputy Head, Teaching and Learning: Mrs R Clifford, BSc

Deputy Head, Pastoral: Mr C Neesham, BA

Fees per term (2021–2022). Nursery: £783 (one full day per week), £3,605 (full-time). Reception, Years 1 & 2: £3,605, Years 3 to 6: £5,200.

The School believes in the importance of focusing on the development of the individual through a broad education in which every child can find success whilst developing confidence, motivation, self-esteem and emotional intelligence.

The School enjoys both classroom-based and excellent specialist teaching with well-designed facilities for science, art, music, PE, ICT and Design Technology. The School is fully networked and has exceptional provision for ICT with ACTIVboards in all classrooms, iPads for each pupil, a computer room capable of accommodating entire classes and broadband access to the Internet throughout. Other facilities include the sports pavilion, a floodlit all-weather astro and sports fields (three cricket squares and four rugby pitches).

Team sports include rugby, hockey, netball, football, rounders, athletics and cricket. Regular fixtures are held with local and regional schools. Children also participate in PE and swimming as part of their curricular programme. An extensive range of co-curricular activities is provided during lunchtime and after school. Individual music tuition with a wide range of instruments is available. Music, drama, dance and public speaking are all important opportunities; productions and presentations are performed by all age groups to a high standard and take place throughout the year. The choir and orchestra meet regularly.

A programme of educational trips and visits provides a stimulating and important addition to the all-round education and development of the 'whole' child and the costs of these are included in the fees.

An inspection by the Independent Schools Inspectorate in March 2014 declared the whole school 'outstanding' or 'excellent' in every category, and described the School as 'exceptionally creative in all areas'.

The Ashford Prep School Nursery (3 to 4 years) offers an exciting and vibrant environment for engaging children in a broad range of learning activities. All children have the best possible individual care and education, supported by exceptional and experienced staff. They are encouraged to explore, play and learn whilst developing independence and resilience, amongst other skills.

The Nursery follow the Early Years Foundation Stage Curriculum, which covers the areas of Personal, Emotional and Social Development, Communication and Language, Physical Development, Literacy, Mathematics, Understanding the World and Expressive Arts and Design.

The thriving Nursery operates on a flexible basis and the Prep School offers full, wraparound care from 7.30am to 6.30pm for all our children. The School operates Mondays to Fridays. Holiday Clubs operate during school breaks.

Children normally progress to Ashford Senior School (*see* HMC entry) without the need to take an entrance test, unless they wish to sit scholarship exams. The Prep School has had considerable success in preparing children for scholarships at leading independent schools as well as other entrance tests including the 11+.

Ashford Prep School recently became a member of the Pre-Senior Baccalaureate (PSB), a prestigious charity that represents several world-class, forward-thinking Schools. The School has a strong commitment to adventurous learning and as such, is in a good position to embrace the PSB framework. The ability to award the Pre-Senior Baccalaureate at the end of pupil's time at Ashford Prep School will help celebrate and recognise the pursuit of becoming a true all-rounder.

The Head of the Prep School, Mr Nick Tiley-Nunn, believes that learning should be the ultimate adventure. In order for a Prep School to truly prepare its pupils for their onward journey, they need to experience an education that is broad and allows them the space to explore what it is that they are passionate about. His team's aim is for every child to leave Ashford Prep as a vastly skilled all-rounder with a kind heart and positivity running through their veins, with their eyes open wide to the inspiration that surrounds them.

Charitable status. Ashford Prep School is part of United Learning which comprises: UCST (a Company Limited by Guarantee, Registered in England, number 2780748, and a Registered Charity, number 1016538) and ULT (a Company Limited by Guarantee, Registered in England, number 4439859, and an Exempt Charity).

Avenue Pre-Prep & Nursery School

2 Highgate Avenue, Highgate, London N6 5RX

Tel:	020 8348 6815
email:	office@avenuepreprep.co.uk
website:	www.avenuepreprep.co.uk

Principal: **Mrs Mary Fysh**

Head: **Mrs Sarah Tapp**

Age Range: 3–7 Co-educational

Number of Pupils: 90

Fees per term (2021–2022): £2,800–£5,350

The ethos of the School is the happiness and success of every child through a secure, friendly and exciting environment. The provision of a wide and varied programme of activities, all of which are timetabled and included in the fee, contributes considerably towards achieving this aim. The high staff/child ratios enable children to learn and achieve in small groups thus progressing successfully throughout the curriculum. External assessments are introduced in the Nursery and continued through Reception, Year 1 and 2. The results are collated and provide a useful means of tracking the progress of each child: it also aids the planning and learning needs of different children. The School is non-denominational and children of all denominations or none are welcome. Children are made aware of major religious festivals including Christmas.

Pre-Nursery children enter the School when rising 3. The staff ratio is 1:7 and the children enjoy participating in many different activities designed to promote speech and language skills, hand/eye coordination and the development of social skills. The large garden provides many opportunities for physical activities, role play and social interaction.

The Nursery takes children from the age of 3+ for four and a half days a week and the staff ratio remains at 1:7. A new purpose-built nursery wing has recently been completed in the grounds which will enable nursery children to enjoy full days at school until 3 pm. The Nursery children build on the skills they have learned in Pre-Nursery and are also introduced to letters and numbers. Singing, using the Kodaly teaching approach, is introduced in the Pre-Nursery and continues throughout all the classes as does Drama. Visits to places of interest off-site are also introduced in the Nursery year.

The Reception Class is divided into two groups for Literacy and Numeracy, which are taught each morning. French and swimming are added to the curriculum along with Dance, Woodwork and Swimming. Children remain at school until 3 pm and either bring a packed lunch or sign up for a school lunch.

The Year 1 and 2 children's respective class teacher remains with them throughout Key Stage 1 to ensure a seamless transition from Year 1 to 2, greatly benefiting the children's preparations for their future 7+ assessments. The classes follow a curriculum based on the National Curriculum but designed to enable each child to progress towards a successful outcome at 7+. Learning the violin or cello is introduced and mandatory for all Year 1 children.

This is continued through Year 2. After School Clubs are available free of charge for all Year 1 and 2 children. These clubs are held on four afternoons a week and finish at 4 pm.

Children are prepared for the 7+ entry to their next school and advice and support is provided for parents throughout their child's time at The Avenue.

We have built up good relationships with other schools in the area and as members of the IAPS (since November 2009) enjoy meeting and visiting member schools.

Aysgarth School

Bedale, North Yorkshire DL8 1TF

Tel: 01677 450240
email: admissions@aysgarthschool.co.uk
website: www.aysgarthschool.com
Twitter: @AysgarthSchool
Facebook: @aysgarthschool
Instagram: @aysgarthschool

Chairman of Governors: P J S Thompson, Esq

Headmaster: Mr Rob Morse, BEd Hons De Montfort

Senior Deputy Headmaster and Deputy Head Pastoral: Mr Paul Barlow, BEd Hons De Montfort

Deputy Head Academic: Dr Ed Canning, BSc Leeds, PGCE Canterbury, PhD

Deputy Head Operations: Mr Guy Askew, BA Hons Leicester, PGCE Hull

Age Range. 3–13.

Number of Pupils. 203. Pre-Prep Department: 66 boys and girls aged 3–8. Prep School: 137 boys aged 8–13.

Fees per term (2021–2022). Boarders (full and weekly) £9,290, Day £7,140, Pre-Prep £2,820–£3,860.

The Prep School is a day and boarding school for boys set in 50 acres of grounds in North Yorkshire about 6 miles from the A1. It attracts boys from all over the UK, and boys go on to the country's leading independent senior schools, many of them in southern England. Some boys start as day boys or weekly boarders to enable them to adjust to boarding gently, some boys will remain as day boys throughout their time at the School. For exeats, boys can be escorted on trains from Darlington to the north and south and there are coaches to and from Cumbria and Lancashire.

Boys of all abilities are welcomed and academic standards are high. All boys are prepared for Common Entrance and several gain scholarships. Before entry, each boy is assessed to ensure that any special needs are identified early and given fully integrated specialist help where necessary. Class sizes are typically around 12. Recent developments include newly refurbished science labs and rifle ranges, and all pupils have access to Chromebooks, particularly at the top end.

The activities in which boys can participate are enormously varied. The facilities include a new heated indoor swimming pool, a state-of-the-art sports hall, a climbing wall, 17 acres of excellent playing fields and a floodlit all-weather pitch. Cricket, Football and Rugby are the main school sports, however there are opportunities to participate in a wide range of other sports including Tennis and Water polo. Music is one of the strengths of the school with more than 75% of boys playing a musical instrument and boys are regularly awarded music scholarships at their senior schools. There are three choirs and the school musicians have regular opportunities to perform both in the school and locally. Each term different year groups produce a play or musical. Art & Craft and Design & Technology are taught by specialist teachers.

The school has a fine Victorian chapel, and boys are encouraged to develop Christian faith and values in a positive, caring environment. Pastoral care is the first priority for all staff. The headmaster and his wife, a housemaster and his wife and three matrons, are all resident in the main building. A wide range of exciting activities in the evenings and at weekends ensure that boys are keen to board, and they are encouraged to do so particularly in their last two years as preparation for their next schools.

The school aims to encourage boys to be well mannered and courteous with a cheerful enthusiasm for learning and for life and a determination to make the most of their abilities.

There is also a flourishing Pre-Prep Department including a Nursery for day boys and girls aged 3 to 8.

Charitable status. Aysgarth School Trust Limited is a Registered Charity, number 529538. Its purpose is to provide a high standard of boarding and day education.

Bablake and King Henry VIII Prep and Pre Prep
Part of the Coventry School Foundation

BKHS Bablake Preparatory
Coundon Road, Coventry, West Midlands CV1 4AU

Tel: 024 7627 1260
email: info.bps@bkhs.org.uk
Twitter: @BKHSBablakePrep
Facebook: @BKHSBablakePrep

BKHS King Henry VIII Preparatory
Warwick Road, Coventry CV3 6AQ

Tel: 024 7627 1169
email: info.khps@bkhs.org.uk
Twitter: @BKHSKHVIIIPrep

BKHS Pre Prep
The Grange, Brownshill Green Road, Coventry, West Midlands CV6 2EG

Tel: 024 7627 1285
email: info.thegrange@bkhs.org.uk
Twitter: @BKHSBablakePrep
Facebook: @BKHSBablakePrep

website: www.bkhs.org.uk

Chair of Governors: Mr I Dunn

BKHS Head of Pre Prep: Mrs T Horton

BKHS Bablake Prep Headmaster: Mr L Holder

BKHS King Henry VIII Prep Headteacher: Miss C Soan

BKHS Admission. Enquiries about admissions should be addressed to the Admissions Office: admissions@bkhs.org.uk.

Scholarships are awarded to existing pupils based on formal and informal assessments at the end of Year 3 in the form of discounted fees.

Children may join BKHS Pre Prep in the September after they turn three. The Pre Prep offers a happy, homely and stimulating environment where thorough and considered preparation takes place for the education that lies ahead.

Later admission to the Pre Prep and Prep School is available at any time should space exist. An assessment of a pupil's potential takes place before entry.

BKHS Fees per term (2021–2022). Prep School £3,265; Pre Prep £2,810.

BKHS brings together the rich heritages of Bablake and King Henry VIII schools. The School continues the tradition of an exceptional education within the city, built upon outstanding opportunities, superb teaching and learning, and strong pastoral care.

The School is represented on the Headmasters' Conference and on the Association of Governing Bodies of Independent Schools. The governing body is the Coventry School Foundation, on which are represented Sir Thomas White's Charity, the Coventry Church Charities, Coventry General Charities and Birmingham, Coventry, Oxford and Warwick Universities. There are also several co-opted Governors.

Pupils enjoy coming to school and are given broad opportunities to develop and learn. They acquire skills and interests that will equip them for their future learning and for life.

We are a school where children are nurtured as individuals. This helps them to achieve all that they are capable of academically, creatively and on the games field. A strong tradition of pastoral care exists at the School. Fundamentally, the School seeks to be a happy place where individuals can grow and express themselves. We recognise that each child is unique and will have their own developmental path: we are committed to helping pupils to develop at the appropriate times, in the direction of their talents and interests, and to ensure that all children feel safe and secure.

Most of our pupils continue their education at either BKHS Bablake Senior or BKHS King Henry VIII Senior until they complete their A levels (*see Bablake and King Henry VIII School entry in HMC section*).

Throughout the school, we help our pupils make the most of their abilities and the outstanding opportunities that exist.

We follow a broad and balanced curriculum – lessons are interesting and our academic results are excellent. Our teachers' commitment to helping everyone achieve their potential is reflected in the support of our parents and the hard work our pupils put into their studies. All achievement – academic, creative or sporting – is recognised and celebrated. The support and respect of the community helps all children achieve their best.

Pupils receive expert coaching in a wide variety of sports and have the opportunity to take part in many activities. We believe in participation and the pursuit of excellence and all children have the opportunity to represent the school in fixtures. We share the swimming pools, fields, sports hall and astroturf with our Senior School and make use of the BKHS specialist facilities. Taking part in a wide variety of

activities builds confidence and reinforces positive child development.

There is a very strong music tradition at BKHS Preparatory and we offer many opportunities for children to develop their musical talents. Lessons are taught by a music specialist from Nursery upwards. Children in Years 3 and 4 participate in our choirs and optional choirs are run in Years 2, 5 and 6. In addition to classroom music and singing, children can learn solo instruments in school. We have a number of talented peripatetic music teachers who deliver high-quality tuition during the school day. Children learning solo instruments (in or out of school) have the opportunity to join one of the many co-curricular music clubs and groups which take place before, during and after school. There are also solo performance opportunities in concerts throughout the year.

The School has a vibrant co-curricular activity programme which may be accessed by pupils from Reception onwards, this includes both lunchtime and after-school clubs. Our broad and balanced sports curriculum, alongside a strong co-curricular programme of activities, provides opportunities for all children to succeed.

Charitable status. Coventry School Foundation is a Registered Charity, number 528961. It exists to provide education for boys and girls.

Badminton Junior School

Westbury-on-Trym, Bristol BS9 3BA

Tel:	0117 905 5271
email:	admissions@badmintonschool.co.uk
website:	www.badmintonschool.co.uk
Twitter:	@BadmintonSchool
Facebook:	@BadmintonSch
Instagram:	@BadmintonSchool
LinkedIn:	/school/badminton-school-limited

Chairman of Governors: Mr Justin Lewis MDA, BSc Hons

Head of Junior School: **Ms Heidi Welch**, BSc Hons, MSc, PGCE

Age Range. 3–11.

Number of Girls. 130.

Fees per term (2021–2022). Day: £3,465–£3,975 inclusive of lunch and extended day. Boarding (from Year 5): £7,900–£9,070.

Educational Philosophy. Children learn best when they are interested, happy and supported in their work. Our girls thrive in a stimulating environment where high standards of work and behaviour are expected. All subjects in the Junior School are taught by enthusiastic subject specialists in classes of no more than 16 girls. We provide a welcoming and friendly atmosphere so that all of our girls feel secure whilst we encourage them to develop their own particular talents and interests. Our philosophy is centred on the development of self-confidence, a healthy respect for one another and the nurturing of curious, critical minds.

We believe children enjoy being kept busy and acquiring new skills, so we try to create a balance between academic work in the classroom, plenty of physical exercise, a range of extra-curricular activities and opportunities for recreational and creative play. The girls are given the opportunity to explore and develop their language skills and study French, Latin, German and Spanish whilst additional languages, such as Mandarin and Italian, are offered in after-school clubs.

Facilities. The Junior School is well appointed with light airy classrooms, dedicated rooms for Art and Music, a Science laboratory, and an ICT suite. We have a well-stocked library and a Hall in which various activities including ballet, drama and musical concerts take place. There is a wonderful, secure adventure playground that the girls make the most of during break and lunch times.

Being on the same campus as the Senior School, the girls make use of all the facilities on site which include the 25m indoor swimming pool, the new Sports Centre complete with climbing wall, fencing piste, fitness centre and four-court sports hall, and the all-purpose sports pitch. There are excellent facilities for music, which plays an important part both inside and outside the curriculum.

With our extended day facilities we aim to provide a warm and caring environment to suit the needs of all our pupils and their parents. Every day clubs such as gardening, chess, drama, art or playground games take place after school and girls are welcome to stay on for prep or late stay until 5.45pm, at no additional cost

For further information on Badminton School, see entry in GSA section. A prospectus is available on request from our Admissions Department (admissions@badmintonschool.co.uk).

Charitable status. Badminton School Limited is a Registered Charity, number 311738. It exists to provide education for children.

Bancroft's Preparatory School

High Road, Woodford Green, Essex IG8 0RF

Tel:	020 8506 6751
	020 8506 6774 (Admissions)
email:	prepoffice@bancrofts.org
website:	www.bancrofts.org
Twitter:	@BancroftsSchool
Facebook:	@bancroftsschool
Instagram:	@bancrofts_social_media

Acting Chairman of the Governors: Mr E Sautter, MA

Head: J P Layburn, MA

Deputy Head, Pastoral: Mrs L Life, BA

Director of Studies: Mr T Paramour, BA

Assistant Head, Lower Phase: Mrs L Dalton, BA

Assistant Head Upper Phase: Miss A Adams, BA

Age Range. 7–11.
Number of Pupils. 128 girls, 138 boys.
Fees per term (2021–2022). £5,413

Bancroft's Preparatory School was established in September 1990 in the attractive grounds of Bancroft's School in Woodford Green (*see entry in HMC section*) and

in 2000 the Head at that time became a member of IAPS. Academic results are excellent and places are much sought after – the school is heavily oversubscribed with numbers of registrations rising year by year.

The Prep School has its own distinct character within the Bancroft's community and has the advantage of being able to use the excellent Senior School facilities. The Prep School is housed in an attractive modern building with its own performing arts studio for drama, music and dance, a science lab and a children's adventure play area. There are three classes of 22 (maximum) children in each of its four year groups.

The Prep School is a truly academic school but its vision of education is about much more than academic results. It's about character development, about the life of the school outside the classroom as well as in it. The Prep School believes the bright children it recruits can 'have it all': outstanding academic qualifications which will enable them to pursue their enthusiasms; rich and formative experiences from a wide ranging co-curricular programme which will help to develop them as people; and an active, reflective approach to learning which will set them up for life.

Children are assessed for entry at the age of six/seven, visiting the school in small groups and tested by the Head and the Deputy Head, Pastoral. The experience is friendly and low-key. Once accepted, pupils have guaranteed transfer to Bancroft's Senior School (on the same site) at the age of eleven. Bancroft's Prep School offers up to two assisted places for pupils entering the School at the age of 7 each year. These awards are based on family finances and performance in the entrance tests. The administration of the Prep School and Senior School are closely linked and the Head is a member of the Senior Leadership Team of Bancroft's School.

Charitable status. Bancroft's School is a Registered Charity, number 1068532. It exists to provide a rounded academic education for able children.

Barfield Prep School

Guildford Road, Farnham, Surrey GU10 1PB

Tel:	01252 782271
email:	admin@barfieldpst.org
website:	www.barfieldpst.org

Barfield School is part of the Prep Schools Trust.

Chairman of the Board of Trustees: Dr Ralph Townsend

Headmaster: **Mr Andy Boyle**

Age Range. 2–11 Co-educational.
Number of Children. 236
Fees per term (2021–2022). Reception–Year 1 £3,540; Year 2 £3,740; Years 3–4 £5,050; Years 5–6 £5,215; Nursery £1,200–£4,300.

Barfield Prep School, set in 12 acres of beautiful grounds, was awarded "Excellent" in all eight areas of inspection by the ISI in 2016. The school is co-educational and takes children between the ages of 2 and 11 years.

In 2021 we underwent a complete brand identity change. Headteacher Andy Boyle has now been at the school for two years and it seemed like the right time, alongside the school transitioning from a 13+ school to an 11+ school, to consolidate his vision for the school and to fully engage the staff, parents and pupils in the process.

Our brand defines our culture, so it's essential that it represents who we are, what we believe, and what we value. We have kept our owl that has been the school's emblem since it was founded in 1933, but modernised it and tried to capture the school's key values of Integrity, Compassion, Resilience, Tolerance and Enthusiasm in its creation.

The brand relaunch coincided with the official opening of a £1million+ investment building project which has provided the school with fantastic new classrooms, a science lab and food tech room.

Barfield School is a family-orientated school with an excellent reputation for high academic standards and caring staff. Facilities include an Outdoor Treehouse Classroom, Auditorium, ICT Suite, Library, Music and Music practice rooms, Cookhouse, Art and DT rooms. The school has a flourishing PE and Outdoor Pursuits Department, with a full-size climbing wall, high ropes course and zip line. There is a magnificent indoor heated swimming pool and children are encouraged to participate in a wide range of extracurricular activities. Activity courses are run throughout the school holidays and are enjoyed by children from Reception to Year 6.

Children are taught in small classes and are prepared for Common Entrance and Scholarship examinations, as well as Grammar School entry.

The Nursery is an integral part of the school and is bright and airy, with plenty of green free-flow space. Open 50 weeks of the year from 8.00am to 6.15pm, experienced and qualified staff nurture, encourage and support all the children, ensuring they feel both happy and secure. The children have use of all the school facilities and access to specialist teachers for swimming and music.

Visitors are always welcome. Please contact the school.

Charitable status. Barfield School is part of the Prep Schools Trust, which is a Registered Charity, number 309639.

Barlborough Hall School

Preparatory School to Mount St Mary's College

Park Street, Barlborough, Chesterfield, Derbyshire S43 4ES

Tel:　　01246 810511
email:　　headteacher@barlboroughhallschool.com
website:　www.barlboroughhallschool.com
Twitter:　@BarlboroughHall
Facebook:　@MSMBHS
LinkedIn:　/company/mount-st-mary's-college

Head Teacher: **Mrs Karen Keeton**

Deputy Headteacher: Mrs Cath Chadbourne

Key Stage 2 Coordinator: Mrs Fran Wilson

Key Stage 1 Coordinator: Mrs Cath Chadbourne

Early Years Coordinator: Mrs Andrea Booth

Admissions Officer: Alyson Temporal

Age Range. 3–11 Co-educational.

Number of Pupils. 210.

Fees per term (2021–2022). £2,780–£3,780.

Barlborough Hall School is a co-educational preparatory school in the Jesuit Catholic tradition, welcoming pupils aged 3–11 of all denominations. The preparatory school to nearby Mount St Mary's College (11–18), Barlborough is set in over 300 acres of parkland.

Barlborough started as a school in 1939 and is built around an Elizabethan manor house which now houses many of the teaching rooms. The school encourages children to develop their talents in many different areas: academic, social, spiritual and physical with a strong focus on the individual. Academically, pupils achieve success through small classes, low pupil to teacher ratios and setting from Year 3 onwards. Teaching facilities ensure that children receive a traditional preparatory school education and include a science laboratory, technology lab and ICT suite. Pupils learn French from Nursery and most pupils learn Latin in Years 5 and 6, taking this into Year 7 when they go up to the Mount.

All pupils receive pastoral care and academic tutoring from their Form Teachers, under the leadership of the Key Stage Coordinators. There is a clear sense of progression from Pre-Prep, situated in its own distinct area with its own playground, to the Upper School, which allows pupils to develop greater independence but still within a nurturing environment. There is a Jesuit chaplain who works closely with the teachers on the Chaplaincy team.

Emphasis is placed on developing the whole person, and the school enjoys an impressive reputation for its sport and music. There is an indoor heated swimming pool, dance studio and extensive games fields, and pupils enjoy a wide range of sports.

Barlborough Hall is well-established on the rugby, football, hockey and netball circuit and plays regular fixtures against other schools. Many pupils learn instruments from skilled peripatetic teachers and the School's Music Teacher leads prize-winning choirs and an orchestra. Drama also flourishes, with a major production every year in our theatre.

There are many extracurricular activities, allowing pupils to develop their interests in a wide range of fields. Pupils are encouraged to take part in at least two activities a week and have the option to attend Saturday school, where they are able to enjoy hobbies in a more relaxed environment or practise for team sports. The wide range of activities available includes Chess, Ballroom Dancing, Art, Drama and Touch Typing. Pupils can also stay after school every evening to do homework under teacher supervision.

For further details of the admissions process and a prospectus, please contact the Admissions Team at admissions@barlboroughhallschool.com.

Barlborough Hall pupils can automatically transfer at age 11 to Mount St Mary's College (*see entry in HMC section*).

Charitable status. Mount St Mary's is a Registered Charity, number 1117998.

Barnard Castle Preparatory School

Westwick Road, Barnard Castle, County Durham DL12 8UW

Tel: 01833 696032
email: prep@barneyschool.org.uk
website: www.barnardcastleschool.org.uk
Twitter: @barney_school
Facebook: @BarnardCastleSchool
Instagram: @barnardcastleschool
LinkedIn: /company/barnard-castle-school

Chairman of Governors: Mrs C J Sunley

Headmistress: **Mrs Laura Turner**, MA

Age Range. 4–11 years.
Number of Pupils. 187 girls and boys, including 9 boarders.
Fees per term (2021–2022). Prep: £7,036 (Boarders), £3,633 (Day). Pre-Prep: £2,399.

Barnard Castle Preparatory School is the junior school of Barnard Castle School and offers an all-round, high-quality education for boys and girls aged between 4 and 11 years. The School offers both day and boarding places and is situated in a beautiful setting on the edge of a traditional English market town.

The campuses of the two schools are adjoining, allowing shared use of many excellent facilities. At the same time the Preparatory School is able to provide a separate, stimulating environment, with small classes, a wide range of co-curricular activities and an exciting school excursion programme.

The School is well served by a bus network system, a breakfast club and after-school supervision is readily available. The boarders reside in a fully-functional boarding house, Old Courts, which creates a warm and friendly environment supported by a full range of facilities including the School's medical centre. Flexi boarding (minimum of 4 nights) is also available.

Sport, Drama and Music occupy important places in the life of the School. All children have numerous opportunities to participate in each of these, as well as an extensive co-curricular programme. The School also offers a qualified learning support service to those children who require further assistance.

Charitable status. Barnard Castle School is a Registered Charity, number 1125375. Its aim is the education of boys and girls.

Barnardiston Hall Preparatory School

Barnardiston, Nr Haverhill, Suffolk CB9 7TG

Tel: 01440 786316
email: registrar@barnardiston-hall.co.uk
website: www.barnardiston-hall.co.uk

Headmaster: **Mr K A Boulter**, MA Cantab, PGCE

Registrar: Mrs L P Gundersen

Bursar: Mrs A Gregory

Age Range. Co-educational 6 months–13 years.
Number of Pupils. Day 180, Boarding (full and weekly) 27.
Fees per term (2021–2022). Day Pupils £2,960–£4,920; Weekly Boarders £6,810; Full Boarders £7,385.

Barnardiston Hall, set in 36 acres of grounds on the borders of Suffolk, Essex and Cambridge, offers an individual all-round education for boys and girls, both day and boarding. High standards are achieved by small classes taught by graduate and teacher-trained staff, a caring approach and close liaison with parents.

The School has good facilities, including a Nursery, Pre-Preparatory Block and Art Room / CDT complex, a very modern and well-equipped computer room, assembly hall, Music Block, science laboratory, library, tennis/netball courts, AstroTurf and extensive sports fields. For the boarders, the dormitories are bright, uncluttered and home-like.

The curriculum is designed to allow pupils to reach Common Entrance standards in the appropriate subjects. The best of traditional methods are mixed with modern ideas to provide an enjoyable and productive learning environment. Spanish is taught from the age of 3; French from age 7. The School is CReSTeD registered. Pupils go on to a wide range of secondary schools, both in the local area and further afield.

Sports in the Michaelmas and Lent Terms are hockey, swimming (Pre-Prep only) and cross-country/orienteering for all pupils, rugby for the boys and netball for the girls. During the Summer, all do athletics, cricket and tennis/short tennis. The School has won the National Orienteering Championships many times over the past few years including 2021.

There is a wide range of clubs and societies including 3 choirs, an orchestra, recorders, chess, painting, drama, carpentry, cookery and pottery. Ballet, speech and drama, piano, guitar, woodwind, violin, brass, string and singing lessons are also offered.

Throughout the term, there are weekend activities for boarders (optional for day pupils) which include mountain walking. Derbyshire Dales at 6, Ben Nevis at 8, camping, visits to museums/historic buildings and other places of interest and theatre trips.

Barrow Hills School

Roke Lane, Witley, Godalming, Surrey GU8 5NY

Tel: 01428 683639
email: info@barrowhills.org
website: www.barrowhills.org
Twitter: @BarrowHills
Facebook: @Barrow-Hills-School

Chairman of the Governors: Mrs Justine Voisin

Headmaster: **Mr Philip Oldroyd**, BA, PGCE

Age Range. 2–13.

Number of Pupils. 200.

Fees per term (2021–2022). Tuition: £3,600–£5,595 (including meals). Nursery and Kindergarten according to sessions.

Barrow Hills School is an independent, co-educational day school and nursery.

We strongly believe that a happy child is a successful one. Children are challenged within a positive, diverse community of learners and are stretched at a time appropriate to them, helping them to aspire to achieve their individual best. Balanced with an ethos of strong pastoral care, children become well-rounded high achievers.

Teaching is based on the understanding that children vary in academic ability, learn and mature at different rates and discover areas of the curriculum which they enjoy and excel at. The family feel of the School is evident and the children clearly benefit from being members of a small community. Class sizes allow for more individual attention from staff, who value and understand every child and spend quality time with them to enhance their learning and confidence. The intimate atmosphere is a particular strength of the School and enables us to build warm relationships with our families.

Education at Barrow Hills is for life, not just the classroom and we are committed to being leaders in Prep School education; promoting mutual respect, curiosity of mind and independence of spirit; prepared for greater things. Our extensive grounds provide excellent facilities that encourage play and exploration. Children experience a wide variety of activities in order to develop their abilities without fear of failure.

We provide devices for every child in the Prep department. Access is also provided for younger children along with Wi-Fi, large screen digital displays and air printers across the school.

Music and theatre is in our DNA and our children are part of a culture that sees everyone, every year, be part of a production. Sport matters; by Year 3 all children have five hours of sport a week, including competitive matches against rival schools. Major team sports are: hockey, netball, rounders, tennis, cricket, swimming and some lacrosse for girls; football, rugby, hockey, swimming and cricket for boys. We have strong links with excellent senior schools, in particular with King Edward's Witley, our partner school. We are proud of our 100% success at Common Entrance with all children gaining entry to their chosen senior school at 13+. Many of our children are awarded scholarships. We offer a broad range of extracurricular activities and a comprehensive programme of educational and residential visits.

Our main building is an attractive Arts and Crafts house, with 33 acres of beautiful gardens, playing fields and woods. We are close to Guildford, Godalming and Haslemere.

Key entry points: Nursery, Kindy, Reception, Year 3, Year 7.

Charitable status. Barrow Hills School Witley is a Registered Charity, number 311997.

Bassett House School

60 Bassett Road, London W10 6JP

Tel: 020 8969 0313
email: info@bassetths.org.uk
website: www.bassetths.org.uk
Twitter: @bassetths
Facebook: @Bassett-House-School
Instagram: @bassetths
LinkedIn: /showcase/bassett-house-school

Motto: *Quisque pro sua parte ~*
From each to the best of his or her ability

Chairman of Governors: Libby Nicholas

Headmistress: **Kelly Gray**

Age Range. 3–11 Co-educational.

Number of Pupils. 120.

Fees per term (2021–2022). Nursery (5 mornings) £3,160, Pre-Prep £6,320, Prep £6,585.

Bassett House School was founded in 1947 and takes both boys and girls from the age of 3 or 4 until age 11. Entry is, in the younger years, non-selective and the school has some 120 pupils in 10 classes.

Kelly Gray, the headmistress, believes Bassett House is a warm, traditional school with an innovative soul, where children flourish in all areas of the curriculum. "One of the many elements that make Bassett so special is that we are small enough to ensure our educational approach and pastoral support are bespoke to the needs of our pupils, whilst being big enough to enable our pupils to spread their wings and thrive."

Bassett House School also teaches the value of endeavour and of staying power, of developing social skills and forming respectful relationships. It has an extensive programme of extra-curricular activities and clubs, day outings and residential trips, as well as a lively schedule of music, drama and sports.

Bassett House provides a thorough and broad educational grounding following the national curriculum and embracing different teaching techniques (including Montessori). The school has invested heavily in the latest classroom technology to give teachers additional tools to make learning lively, fun and effective. It has specialist teachers in maths, English, science, computing, French, music, physical education, art/design technology, eurhythmics, Latin and dance.

The school was built towards the end of the 19th century and what was originally designed as a large family house now provides modern spacious and airy classrooms. The school premises include use of a separate annex comprising an assembly hall with a stage and gymnasium, three classrooms, a kitchen and a garden. There is also a brand new building, with three Early Years classrooms, an interactive learning zone for child-initiated learning and a performing arts studio for music, dance and drama. The main school building has a playground and the school also uses excellent local play and sports facilities. Included in the school's facilities is an edible garden and new playground.

Beachborough

Westbury, Nr Brackley, Northants NN13 5LB

Tel:	01280 700071
email:	admissions@beachborough.com
website:	www.beachborough.com

Chair of Governors: Mrs S Barrett

Headmaster: **Mr Christian Pritchard**, MA, BA Hons QTS

Age Range. 2½–13.

Number of Children. Main School 225 (40% flexi boarding), Pre-Prep 150.

Fees per term (2021–2022). Prep School: Years 5–8 £5,970, Years 3–4 £5,476, Reception, Years 1 & 2 £3,802. Nursery from £319 for one session per week. Flexi boarding from £38 per night.

Beachborough is a friendly and energetic Independent Prep School ideally situated on the borders of Buckinghamshire, Oxfordshire and Northamptonshire. We provide an outstanding all-round education for around 300 boys and girls, a quarter of whom take advantage of our flexible boarding provision. We are large enough to have a diverse and lively community, yet small enough for each individual to be known and nurtured.

We believe that a good prep school education will give children opportunities that will equip them intellectually, physically, culturally and emotionally for the challenges of the twenty-first century. At whatever stage your child joins us, be it Early Years (pupils aged 2½ to 5), Pre-Prep (pupils aged 6 to 7) or Prep School (pupils aged 8 to 13) they will be warmly welcomed into the school. We are not obsessed with reflecting on past glories or the latest headline-grabbing news, but have an active desire to find each child's individual talent and help them surpass their personal best. Our parents use words such as inclusive, nurturing and rounded to define our school, so if you share in our belief that happy children thrive, please come and visit.

Charitable status. Beachborough is a Registered Charity, number 309910.

The Beacon

Chesham Bois, Amersham, Bucks HP6 5PF

Tel:	01494 433654
email:	office@beaconschool.co.uk
website:	www.beaconschool.co.uk
Twitter:	@Beacon_School
Facebook:	@beaconschoolamersham
Instagram:	@beaconschooluk
LinkedIn:	/the-beacon-school

Chairman of the Governors: Charles Miller

Headmaster: **William T Phelps**, MA New York, BA AKC King's College London

Age Range. 3–13.

Number of Boys. 521.

Fees per term (2021–2022). Upper School (Years 7 & 8) £6,175, Middle School (Years 5 & 6) £5,976–£6,175, Lower School (Years 3 & 4) £5,700, Pre-Prep (Years 1 & 2) £4,600, Reception £4,100, Nursery (Little Beacons) 1,700 (5 mornings); £2,300 (5 mornings & 2 afternoons); £3,200 (5 mornings & 5 afternoons)

The Beacon is an independent day school for boys aged 3 to 13 years. The Beacon prepares boys for secondary education through a curriculum that offers both richness and diversity of opportunity. From the earliest steps in initial learning, to independent success in competitive examinations, the priority is to ensure sound academic development, within a happy and stimulating environment. The Beacon is proud to prepare its boys for entry to over 26 senior independent day and boarding schools, with a variety of academic, music, drama, art, design and technology and sport scholarships being awarded each year. The school also enjoys impressive success at 11+ for entry into Buckinghamshire Grammar Schools.

The ethos of The Beacon is encapsulated in the words: Traditional Values, Contemporary Education, World-Class Experience. Over 500 boys are educated in extremely well-resourced buildings; a blend of old: 17th-century farmstead and barns; and new: including a 220-seat Theatre, a Design and Technology Suite, Cooking and Nutrition Room, Science Laboratories, newly-covered 25m Swimming Pool, Drama Studio, Music Technology Suite, two Libraries, a large Sports Hall and two AstroTurfs, set in attractive surroundings, with 16 acres of playing fields.

Each class in Pre-Prep (Nursery to Year 2) has a class teacher and an assistant, with a maximum of 18–20 boys.

There is a second entry point when the boys join the Prep School in Year 3 at age 7, and a fourth class is added. Class sizes are a maximum of 20. Boys study a broad range of subjects, including Modern Foreign Languages from Year 4, Self and Society and Science.

The third entry point is in Year 7 at age 11, where boys are prepared for The Pre-Senior Baccalaureate, Common Entrance and scholarship examinations to many leading independent senior schools. In Year 8, boys take on leadership roles and demonstrate greater responsibility and independence.

Wrap-around care is available for all boys from 07:30 (Breakfast Club) until 18:00 (Prep and After-School Care and Clubs).

Sport at The Beacon is all-inclusive and exemplifies teamwork, emphasising the school ethos that everybody matters. Boys regularly compete at County level in cricket, hockey, tennis, athletics, cross country, swimming and rugby. The Beacon has an excellent record of success in many national and regional competitions.

The Performing Arts Department has numerous instrumental ensembles and choirs, and a range of weekly music and drama clubs for all ages.

There are 24 visiting music and drama specialists with over 400 weekly lessons taking place. Every boy at The Beacon is given a chance to perform throughout the year in a range of musical productions, playlets, showcases and concerts, with international choir tours and performances at the Edinburgh Festival particular department highlights.

Charitable status. The Beacon Educational Trust Limited is a Registered Charity, number 309911. It exists to provide education for boys.

Beaudesert Park School

Minchinhampton, Stroud, Gloucestershire GL6 9AF

Tel:　　　01453 832072
email:　　office@bps.school
website:　www.beaudesert.gloucs.sch.uk
Twitter:　@beaudesertpark
　　　　　@beaudesertsport
Facebook:　@Beaudesert-Park-School
Instagram:　@beaudesertparksch
LinkedIn:　/company/beaudesert-park-school

Chairman of Governors: M C S-R Pyper, OBE, BA

Headmaster: **C Searson**, BA

Age Range. 3–13, boys and girls.

Number of Pupils. 400 (218 boys and 182 girls). 98 children in Pre-prep, and 302 in Prep. 160 children (from Year 4 upwards) board, the vast majority of whom flexi-board for between 1 and 3 nights per week. Most families live within 20 miles of the school.

Fees per term (2021–2022). From £2,050 per term in Nursery. All fees include lunch. Boarding and flexi-boarding fees also include breakfast and supper.

Thriving country prep. A thriving prep school with a family feel, Beaudesert sits in glorious grounds on the edge of 500 acres of National Trust common land, surrounded by Cotswolds countryside.

Parents speak of a happy, confidence-building school with excellent teachers and knockout facilities – a place where children are able to enjoy the important business of childhood for as long as possible. The School proudly adheres to a strongly all-round education ethos, with children encouraged to thoroughly enjoy all aspects of school life and take advantage of heaps of opportunities to experiment and excel in the arts, sport and beyond. There are thriving music, drama, art and sport departments.

Balanced, child-centred approach. The School is non-selective but there is a strong academic tradition, and all pupils are encouraged to work to the best of their ability. There is great emphasis on effort and all children are praised for their individual performance whilst being kept safe from too much pressure. When they leave aged 13, they move on to over 20 different senior schools, usually with an array of scholarships and awards under their belts. In 2021 over a third of Beaudesert's leavers moved on to leading UK senior schools with a scholarship or award.

Founded on a 'sport for all' premise, the School offers a huge range of sporting activities including cricket, football, rugby, hockey, netball, rounders, tennis, swimming, athletics, golf, badminton, fencing, dance, judo, riding, yoga and sailing. A wide number of societies and clubs meet each week, with a choice of 30+ extra-curricular activities on offer each term.

Knockout facilities. The School is very well equipped and includes a high-spec, multi-functional Performing Arts Centre (shortlisted for a RIBA award when launched), as well as three science labs, indoor and outdoor swimming pools, sports hall, Art Studio and Design Technology department – not to mention two wonderful Forest Schools in the forest areas. The Nursery and Reception class areas were refurbished in 2019 to include free flow inside-outside spaces to embed the child-led learning ethos. Our Nursery also features a creative studio for messy play and Beaudesert 'roleplay cottage'. There are also AstroTurf tennis courts and hard courts within the 30-acre site, as well as 15 acres of sports fields. The School stands high up in the Cotswolds adjoining 500 acres of common land and golf course. Despite its rural location, the School is within half an hour of the M4 and M5 motorways and within easy reach of the surrounding towns of Gloucester, Cheltenham, Cirencester, Swindon, Bath and Bristol.

Rich heritage brought bang up to date. Founded in 1908 in Warwickshire, the School moved lock, stock and barrel to its hill-top spot in Gloucestershire in 1918. In 2018, Beaudesert celebrated 100 years of being in glorious Gloucestershire. 2021 sees the launch of the School's new House System. Rooted in Beaudesert Park's environmental ethos, the new system aims to foster healthy competition, leadership and community across year groups.

Charitable status. Beaudesert Park is a Registered Charity, number 311711. It exists to provide education for boys and girls in a caring atmosphere.

Bede's Preparatory School

Duke's Drive, Eastbourne, East Sussex BN20 7XL

Tel:　　　01323 734222
email:　　prep.school@bedes.org
website:　www.bedes.org
Twitter:　@bedesprep
Facebook:　@bedesprepschool

Co-educational day and boarding school with Nursery and Pre-Prep departments.

Chair of Governors: Mrs Geraldine Watkins, JP

Headmaster: Mr Mark Hammond, MA, BA Hons, PGCE

Deputy Head: Mr David Newberry, BSc Hons, GTP

Age Range. 3 months–13 years Co-educational.

Number of Pupils: 336: Prep 219, Pre-Prep 30, Nursery 87; Boarders: 24.

Fees per term (2021–2022). Boarding £2,980 (in addition to Tuition); Tuition: Prep £4,880–£5,990, Pre-Prep £3,480 (Reception, Years 1 & 2). Nursery prices per session.

Bede's Prep School, founded in 1895, is situated in Eastbourne, on the South Coast with spectacular views of the sea. It takes a couple of minutes to reach the beach from the school and the principal playing fields are in a wide natural hollow nestling in the South Downs.

Boarders sleep in cosy bedrooms in a house that has a real family feel and are looked after by dedicated and caring staff. Both winter and summer weekends are filled with an exciting variety of activities and special celebrations take place on the children's birthdays.

Pupils are prepared for Common Entrance and the more able are tutored to sit scholarships to independent senior schools. Last year 95% of pupils chose to continue their education at Bede's Senior School (*see HMC section entry*).

Bede's offers academic, sport, music, dance, art and drama scholarships and bursaries for children from the ages of 7 to 12 years.

Pupils from the age of 4 are given Information Technology lessons at least once a week in a Computer Centre which is constantly updated to keep at the forefront of educational technology. French and Music, Short Tennis and other Sports are also introduced to children in this age group.

In January 2016, a newly expanded nursery facility opened with a state-of-the-art unit for babies from 3 months upwards and expanded provision for toddlers. This was followed by the launch of the school's Pre School Scheme with two classrooms, a messy activity area and free flow access to a new outside play area and Forest School.

The Art Department is very strong, opening for after-school activities to encourage young talent. Music also plays an important role at Bede's. There is a thriving orchestra and the majority of pupils learn one or more instruments, with children as young as six playing in recorder groups. Informal concerts take place during the school year and there are also several choirs.

Drama forms an integral part of the school. The Pre-Prep produces a Christmas play and there are frequent productions throughout the year for older children to take part in.

Sport at Bede's is taken seriously. Boys play soccer, rugby, hockey, cricket, tennis and athletics and the major sports for girls are netball, hockey, rounders, athletics, cricket and tennis. All the pupils use the indoor 20-metre swimming pool. The fixture list is very comprehensive and, whilst the top teams enjoy a high standard of coaching and performance, special emphasis is placed on ensuring that the other teams also have the opportunity to play matches against other schools. The Sports Hall covers two indoor tennis courts and is used to house a huge variety of sports. Wet weather activities include badminton, basketball, climbing and table tennis. Children also regularly use facilities at the Senior School nearby. Cricket and team sports are also played at the 'Hollow' playing fields next to the school at the foot of the South Downs National Park and with stunning views of the coastline and Eastbourne beyond. The Prep School also has a new astro court for hockey, cricket and other sports.

There is a Learning Enhancement department staffed by qualified learning support staff which can cater for pupils who require additional or particular support. The school also has an EAL centre which is run by highly trained and experienced staff. Gifted children are placed on a Curriculum Enhancement Programme to maximise their potential.

The School operates a comprehensive programme of activities after lessons which children are encouraged to participate in ranging from fencing to cookery and basketball to art masterclasses.

The school runs a comprehensive coach and minibus service locally and transport to and from Gatwick and Heathrow airports is arranged by the transport department.

Entry to Bede's Prep School is by interview.

Charitable status. St Bede's School Trust Sussex is a Registered Charity, number 278950. It exists to provide education for boys and girls.

Bedford Girls' School Junior School

Cardington Road, Bedford, Bedfordshire MK42 0BX

Tel: 01234 361918
email: admissions@bedfordgirlsschool.co.uk
website: www.bedfordgirlsschool.co.uk
Twitter: @BedfordGirlsSch
Facebook: @BedfordGirlsSch

Foundation – The Harpur Trust.

"Let me keep an open mind so I understand as much as I can in my lifetime and not reach the limits of my imagination."

Chair of Governors: Ms T Beddoes

Head of Bedford Girls' School: Mrs Gemma Gibson

Head of Bedford Girls' School Junior School: Mrs C Howe

Deputy Head: Mrs T Copp

Age Range. 7–11.

Number of Pupils. 215 in the Junior School (950 across the whole school)

Fees per term (2021–2022). £3,340

Bedford Girls' School is a dynamic, forward-thinking selective independent day school for girls aged 7–18. We value creativity, technology and innovation highly; we are preparing our students to make a difference to the world around them. From Years 3 to Sixth Form, it is our belief that learning should be exciting and lifelong, so that students leave us fully equipped academically, personally and emotionally, with a desire to be the creative thinkers, the change-makers and the problem-solvers of the future. We embrace the International Baccalaureate philosophy of education and are an accredited IB World School offering the IB Primary Years Programme in the Junior School and a choice of IB Diploma Programme or A Levels in the Sixth Form.

This journey begins in the Junior School where our expert teachers recognise and ignite the curiosity of every individual, harnessing her natural curiosity and fuelling her confidence to develop her own thoughts, opinions and talents. Students not only excel intellectually, but also as well-rounded, insightful, caring girls with a joy and passion for life and learning.

The atmosphere of our school is unique and exciting. Classrooms fizz with energy and enthusiasm and each day brings forth new discoveries and achievements. We would be delighted to welcome you to visit, either for one of our Open House events or a private tour, to experience at first hand a true flavour of life at Bedford Girls' School. Please visit www.bedfordgirlsschool.co.uk for further information or contact our Admissions Team: Tel: 01234 361918, email: admissions@bedfordgirlsschool.co.uk.

Admissions. Entry to the Junior School is based upon Cognitive Ability Testing (CAT) and a creative writing task. Entry to the Senior School is based on an interview with the Headmistress and Cognitive Ability Testing (CAT). Sixth Form entry is based on interviews, Cognitive Ability Testing, and GCSE results. A reference from the Head of the student's current school is required for all candidates.

Charitable status. Bedford Girls' School is part of the Harpur Trust which is a Registered Charity, number 1066861.

Bedford Modern Junior School

Manton Lane, Bedford, Bedfordshire MK41 7NT

Tel: 01234 332513
email: info@bedmod.co.uk
website: www.bedmod.co.uk
Twitter: @BedfordModern
Facebook: @BedfordModernSchool

Chair of Governors: Shirley Jackson

Head of Junior School: **Mrs J C Rex**, BA Hons, PGCE

Deputy Head of Junior School: Mrs P S Pacyna, BA Hons, QTS

Director of Studies: Mrs K Harpin, BA Hons

Junior School Head's Assistant: Mrs J Smith

Head of Junior School Sports Development; Mr T W Bucktin, BSc, PGCE

Age Range. 7–11 Co-educational.
Number of Pupils. 249 (M: 47%; F: 53%).
Fees per annum (2021–2022). £10,528.

The Junior School is housed in its own separate building adjacent to the Senior School. Facilities include specialist rooms for Art and Science, ICT, Design Technology and a newly refurbished Library, with designated Year 3 classrooms and play area and a superb state-of-the-art School Hall.

The whole site overlooks the School playing fields and the Junior School has extensive views over the Ouse Valley. Many of the Senior School facilities are available to the Junior School, including full use of the playing fields, Sports Hall, Gymnasium, covered and heated Swimming Pool and all-weather pitches. The Howard Hall provides facilities for full-scale drama productions and use is made of the Music School.

There is a strong musical, dramatic and sporting tradition.

Students are admitted to the Junior School at ages 7, 8, 9 and 10, after taking tests, some of them on computer, in January each year in English, Maths and non-verbal reasoning. Students proceed to the Senior School at 11, unless special circumstances prevent this.

(*See Bedford Modern School entry in HMC section.*)

Charitable status. Bedford Modern School is part of the Harpur Trust which is a Registered Charity, number 1066861. It includes in its aims the provision of high quality education for boys and girls.

Bedford Prep School

De Parys Avenue, Bedford MK40 2TU

Tel: 01234 362216
email: admissions@bedfordschool.org.uk
website: www.bedfordschool.org.uk
Twitter: @bedfordschool
Facebook: @Bedford-School
Instagram: @bedfordschool_uk
LinkedIn: /school/bedfordschool

Chairman of Governors: Sir Clive Loader, KCB, OBE, ADC, FRAeS

Headmaster: **Mr Ian Silk**

Age Range. 7–13.
Number of Boys. Day Boys 383, Boarders 11, Weekly Boarders 4, Flexi Boarders 3.
Fees per term (2021–2022). Day £4,525–£5,930, Full Boarding £8,056–£9,564, Weekly Boarding £7,676–£9,187.

Bedford Prep School is a thriving and vibrant independent day and boarding school for boys aged 7–13.

We believe that boys learn best when they're happy, confident, and their curiosity is stimulated, so we feel it's paramount that learning is fun, creative, inspirational and active. We also recognise boys learn differently from girls and this informs our teaching.

Whether it's music and the arts, science and technology, language and literature, or sports and games, boys are encouraged to learn new skills and embrace new experiences.

Visit our classes and you'll find boys thoroughly engaged in their learning, inspired by challenge, competition, high expectations and risk within a safe environment. Our expectations are high but achievable, and our curriculum encompasses and transcends the National Curriculum. Our bespoke Future Skills Curriculum teaches content and subject-specific skills for each subject whilst also explicitly developing **skills, attributes and characteristics** to ensure that every boy continually practises these skills and competencies, and reflects on our school values. We believe that this enables boys to achieve success not only in the Prep School, but also as they move up to the Upper School, as well as throughout life in general.

Our extensive campus offers boys outstanding academic, sporting, music, drama and art facilities. We share the swimming pool, recreation centre, playing fields, Astro and tennis courts with the Upper School and make use of the school's fantastic theatre and other specialist facilities.

Working with each and every boy, we help them to develop their sporting talents. We provide expert coaching in a wide variety of sports, including rugby, hockey, cricket, golf, skiing, horse riding, cross country, swimming, badminton and rowing.

Creative arts are a big part of school life, with boys taking part in concerts, exhibitions and performances throughout the year. In our dedicated music building, with a state-of-the-art music technology suite and well-equipped practice rooms, many of our boys learn to play one or more instruments.

Boys can also get involved in a broad range of extracurricular activities: from cookery to steel band, chess to climbing – there is something for every boy.

A full range of wraparound care options is available to working parents. Boys can stay at school, free of charge, until 5.45pm in our Late Room or join one of our before and after school 'Day Plus' sessions.

Eagle House, our purpose-built junior boarding house, is a real home from home for our boarders, who flourish in its warm, family atmosphere. Full, weekly, flexi and occasional boarding is available, enabling boys and their parents to find an option that is just right.

Admissions. Entrance assessments for the Prep School are held during the spring term and all boys are assessed in English, maths and underlying ability. We will also request a report from your son's current school.

We recommend that families come and visit us to see the school in action and meet the boys and staff. Please call admissions on 01234 362216 or email: admissions@ bedfordschool.org.uk to arrange a visit or request a prospectus.

Charitable status. Bedford Preparatory School is part of the Harpur Trust, which is a Registered Charity, number 1066861.

Number of Pupils. 531: 53 boarders (aged 9–13), 278 day boys and 189 day girls (aged 3–13), including pre-school children at the Woodlands Nursery which is housed in new purpose-built premises on the main school site.

Fees per term (2021–2022). Day pupils: Years 5–8 £6,055, Years 3 and 4 £4,890, Years 1 and 2 £4,785, Reception £4,095. Boarders (up to 4 nights per week in addition to day fees) £1,440. No compulsory extras. Fees are inclusive of lunches, most trips and visits.

Beechwood Park occupies a large mansion, with a fine Regency Library and Great Hall, in 37 acres of surrounding grounds, which provide ample space for the Forest School (complete with outdoor classroom). Modernisation has added Science laboratories, computer suites, Design Technology workshop, gymnasium and sports facilities, including a large sports hall and two squash courts, two netball courts, an all-weather pitch and an indoor swimming pool complex. Boarding House with modern facilities and spacious common rooms. Two purpose-built classroom blocks house the Middle and Junior Departments. The Music Department has a song room, 14 practice rooms and a newly-opened Music Technology Suite and Recording Studio. A large Performance Hall provides space for assemblies and the many music and drama productions.

Many day pupils use private buses serving Harpenden, St Albans and the surrounding villages. Many subsequently convert to boarding under the care of the Houseparents, Mr and Mrs R Humphreys.

Class size is around 20 (15 in Reception); Maths is streamed from Year 3 onwards, English from Year 5 and other major subjects from Year 6. There is a resident Chaplain. The Director of Music has a staff of visiting instrumentalists in a flourishing Music Department.

The number of scholarships gained each year and Common Entrance results affirm a high standard of work, against a background of wide ranging extracurricular activities.

Football, Rugby, Cricket (boys and girls) Netball, Hockey, Swimming, Athletics and a Sport for All programme, which includes an unusually wide range of minor sports, are all coached by well-qualified PE Staff.

Charitable status. Beechwood Park School is a Registered Charity, number 311068. It exists to provide education for boys and girls from 3–13.

Beechwood Park

Markyate, St Albans, Hertfordshire AL3 8AW

Tel: 01582 840333
email: admissions@beechwoodpark.com
website: www.beechwoodpark.com
Twitter: @BWPSchool
Facebook: @BWPSchool
Instagram: @bwpschool
LinkedIn: /company/beechwood-park-school

Chairman of Governors: Mr M Hammond

Headmaster: **Mr Edward Balfour**, BA Hons, PGCE

Age Range. 3–13.

Beeston Hall School

West Runton, Cromer, Norfolk NR27 9NQ

Tel: 01263 837324
email: office@beestonhall.co.uk
website: www.beestonhall.co.uk

Chairman of Governors: The Earl of Leicester

Headmaster: **W F de Falbe**, BA Hons, PGCE

Bursar: Mrs S Lubbock

Age Range. Co-educational 4–13 years.

Number of Pupils. 152: 36 Boarding, 116 Day Pupils; 72 Boys, 80 Girls.

Fees per term (2021–2022). Boarding: £6,930 (Year 3), £8,990 (Years 4–8); Day Pupils: £3,340 (Pre-Prep), £4,590 (Year 3), £6,690 (Years 4–8).

Beeston Hall was established in 1948 in a Regency house set in 30 acres in North Norfolk, close to the sea and surrounded by 700 acres of National Trust land. Beeston has a reputation for being a cheerful, family school, with a focus on achievement arising out of happiness and confidence. Kindness and courtesy, alongside hard work and awareness of others, underpin all aspects of life at Beeston, where children are encouraged to proceed with the three core values of purpose, resilience and empathy at the centre of everything they do – the Beeston Brief.

The scale, and strength, of the pastoral care system ensures that every child is closely watched over and cared for. Beeston has a boarding ethos, the majority full, with weekly or flexi for younger ones, or those progressing towards boarding; most children experience boarding before they leave. Relatively non-selective, Beeston is very proud of the value-added in children's development. Recent destinations have been: Ampleforth, Eton, Downe House, Framlingham, Gresham's, Harrow, The Leys Cambridge, Oakham, Oundle, Queen Margaret's York, Norwich School, Radley, Repton, Rugby, Stephen Perse, Shrewsbury, Stowe, Tudor Hall and Uppingham and Wycombe Abbey. The school enjoys great success at scholarship level, with an average of over 60% of leavers winning awards in the last 6 years.

In addition to the usual examinable subjects, art, music, DT, computing, PHSEE, reasoning and theatre studies are all timetabled, providing children with a wealth of opportunities to find activities in which they can excel. Qualified EAL staff support overseas pupils and the Learning Support is headed by an experienced educational psychologist, so learning needs are swiftly identified and acted upon.

Every child takes part in at least one production each year, with an emphasis on developing confidence through participation and presentation. Three choirs and ten music groups meet each week and over 80% of the school learn a musical instrument. The school is equally proud of its record on the sports field where all children are coached, regardless of ability, by a dedicated team of staff, and are given the opportunity to represent the school. In 2016 cricket was introduced for girls, now with several county players. The under 11 boys were national finalists in ESCA prep competition last year. Hockey is strong with both boys' and girls' teams regularly reaching IAPS national hockey finals. In addition to the usual major sports, children compete in cross country, athletics, swimming, tennis, fencing and sailing (IAPS champions in 2019), whilst a comprehensive activities programme provides opportunities to suit all tastes: shooting, martial arts, circus skills, archery, roller-skating, surfing, skiing, chess, Scottish reels, yoga, cooking or scouts, to name a few. Forest School is a timetabled part of the week for Year 5 and below.

The 2017 ISI Inspection Report comments thus: 'Pupils' attitudes to work are outstanding, nurtured by the high expectations of staff …many awards also reflect pupils' exceptional achievements in areas such as sport, music, art, drama …Pupils can apply their outstanding numeracy skills effectively across a range of subjects …Pupils show outstanding social skills and are highly respectful of people …'.

Religious denomination. Mainly Church of England; 15% Roman Catholic.

Charitable status. Beeston Hall School Trust Limited is a Registered Charity, number 311274. It exists to provide preparatory education for boarding and day boys and girls.

Belhaven Hill School

Belhaven Road, Dunbar, East Lothian EH42 1NN

Tel: 01368 862785
email: secretary@belhavenhill.com
website: www.belhavenhill.com
Twitter: @Belhaven_Hill
Facebook: @BelhavenHill
Instagram: @bebelhaven

Chair of Governors: Camilla Gray Muir

Headmaster: Olly Langton, MA Hons History Edinburgh

Deputy Head Academic: John Marriott, BA Hons, MA, PGCE, MBA

Deputy Head Pastoral: Katie Gale, BSc Hons, PGCE, CCRS

Age Range. 5–13 Co-educational.
Number of Pupils. 62 boys, 48 girls. Boarders 66, Day 44.
Fees per term (2021–2022). Boarding £8,975. Day: £6,870 (Form 1–3), £6,360 (Form 4), £5,480 (Form 5), £3,750 (Form 6–8).
Religion. Non-denominational.

Overlooking the sea in an idyllic East Lothian location, Belhaven Hill School is an independent boarding and day school for boys and girls from 5 to 13 years. Since its establishment in 1923, the school has focused on developing well-rounded, happy, confident children through a strong academic curriculum, lots of sport and a broad extracurricular programme. Ideally placed just off the A1, it is close to both a mainline London–Edinburgh railway station, is only 30 miles from central Edinburgh and less than an hour to Edinburgh airport.

A full boarding and day school, Belhaven Hill has a long tradition of providing a first class all-round education before sending its pupils far and wide to all the leading public schools in both England and Scotland. These include Ampleforth, Eton, Downe House, Fettes, Glenalmond, Gordonstoun, Harrow, Loretto, Marlborough, Merchiston, Oundle, Radley, Rugby, Sherborne, Stowe, Strathallan, Tudor Hall, Uppingham and Winchester. Committed and enthusiastic members of staff work with small classes of between 10–16 pupils. There is ample opportunity for scholarship and extended work, resulting in an impressive number of awards being gained every year. A strong learning support department with four dedicated, trained staff provides one-to-one and small group tuition.

Belhaven Hill pupils are renowned for being happy children and this is in no small part due to the outstanding pastoral care provided for day pupils and boarders alike. The majority of staff live on site and the policy of the governors has been to keep the school comparatively small in order to retain a family atmosphere. The boarding boys are housed in the original main building and the boarding girls in a separate, purpose-built house and are looked after by Houseparents. The pastoral system revolves around the four 'Patrols', with each day and boarding pupil being looked after by their form teacher in the junior years and a personal tutor higher up the school. A full-time School Nurse and a team of matrons (day and night) take care of the children around the clock. A newly-appointed Deputy Head Pastoral is in overall charge of pastoral care.

The school has an excellent reputation for sport with rugby, netball, hockey, cricket, rounders, tennis and athletics, making up the main part of the sporting programme. Swimming takes place from April to October in the school's heated outdoor pool. In addition, many opportunities abound for a wide variety of other recreational activities: skiing, surfing, horse riding, golf on the adjacent links course and gardening for those who want to grow their own produce in the school's walled garden. An extensive Activity Programme offers something for everyone to discover and enjoy such as charity work, debating, 'mastermind', knitting, model-making, computer programming and coding, cookery, crafts, chess, Taekwondo, fencing, Girls' rugby and cricket, mixed football, water polo, Highland dancing and reeling to name but a few.

Music and Drama flourish at Belhaven and every child has ample opportunity to perform in regular concerts and productions throughout the year. LAMDA tuition is available and Academic Music and Drama lessons are now included in the timetable. A stand-alone music building houses a vibrant department which caters for a wide range of instrumental ensembles including its own Pipe Band and three choirs. Over 90% of the children play one or more instruments, with specialist tuition provided by a team of peripatetic music staff. Outdoor Education has always been on the agenda at Belhaven, but is now taking on a more prominent profile, with a lesson a week for each class, regular 'Cook-outs' and 'Camp-outs', challenging Bushcraft courses and membership of the National Navigation scheme (NNAS).

The school is well resourced with purpose-built facilities, including an outdoor heated swimming pool, floodlit all-weather pitch, playing fields, sports hall, specialist music and art schools, a well-stocked library, attractive teaching rooms with large format display screens in each classroom to connect to the staff and children's individual iPads. Belhaven is now preparing for its next major phase of development which will form the focus of its forthcoming Centenary Campaign. Together with ambitious plans for bursaries, the developments include a new facility to further strengthen digital education and to build on the provision for swimming, indoor sport, drama and musical performance.

Belhaven begins with the belief that every child is an individual and the school's mission is to foster both their individuality and abilities. To achieve these aims, it places the child at the core of everything it does. By providing an environment that promotes enjoyment, exploration and nurtures curiosity, through its core values of Courtesy, Courage and Creativity, each child grows to understand that they are responsible for their learning and the world around them. As a result, they grow to value and respect others, delighting in the achievements of others as well as their own. Qualities such as tolerance, honesty and perseverance are all encouraged and celebrated via traditional and modern means, with the children understanding that it is better to

have had a go at reeling or coding and found them difficult, than never to have tried either at all. Whether they are day pupils or boarders, all children benefit from a boarding school ethos of community, fun and friendship. Ultimately, Belhaven aims to provide the children with the practical skills and the mindset to be able to shape the world around them.

Means-tested bursary support is available. Fee concessions are available for children of members of the armed forces. For a prospectus and more information please see our website www.belhavenhill.com or contact Olivia Reynolds our Admissions and Development Officer at admissions@belhavenhill.com.

Charitable status. Belhaven Hill School Trust Ltd is a Registered Charity, number SC007118. Its aim is to educate children in the fullest sense of the word.

Belmont
Mill Hill Preparatory School

The Ridgeway, Mill Hill Village, London NW7 4ED

Tel: 020 8906 7270
email: office@belmontschool.com
website: www.millhill.org.uk/belmont
Twitter: @MillHillBelmont
Facebook: @MillHillBelmont

Co-educational Preparatory Day School for 7 to 13 year olds. Awarded 'Excellent' in quality of education in academic achievement and personal development – ISI Inspection January 2020.

Chair of the Court of Governors: Mr Elliot Lipton, BSc Hons, MBA, FRSA, FRICS

Head: **Mr Leon Roberts**, MA, PGCE

Senior Deputy Head (*Pastoral*): Ms K Scanlan

Deputy Head (*Operations*): Mr J Fleet, BSc Hons, PGCE

Deputy Head (*Academic*): Mrs J Lumsden, BSc Hons, PGCE

Age Range. 7–13 Co-educational.

Number of Pupils. 286 Boys, 264 Girls. Total 550

Fees per term (2021–2022). £6,274 (£18,822 per annum).

Overview. Belmont Mill Hill Preparatory School is situated in the Green Belt on the borders of Hertfordshire and Middlesex, just ten miles from Central London. We are a part of a Foundation, dating back to 1807, which also includes our Pre-Prep, Grimsdell; our Senior, Mill Hill School, Mill Hill International, and our most recent addition, Cobham Hall, Kent. Belmont stands in about 35 acres of beautiful green space, with sports pitches, a nature reserve, woods to explore, and our own cross-country course; all of us feel better for such freedom to breathe. We take advantage of the truly rural environment by extending our learning through Forest Schools and our Eco Garden. We provide a happy, secure and rich learning environment for boys and girls aged 7 to 13, the majority of whom move on at the end of Year 8 to our senior, Mill Hill School, which educates boys and girls from age 13 to 18 and offers full and weekly boarding places from aged 13+.

Academic. We are proud to offer a curriculum that is both academically rigorous and engaging and goes far beyond the national curriculum, in order to instil a love of learning in our pupils. Our curriculum runs seamlessly through every school in the Foundation, and is designed to prepare your child for life in the 21st century. It teaches children to think creatively and critically, and builds flexible skills for a fast-changing world of new technologies. Our teachers are highly skilled, motivated and love their work. We use both traditional teaching and learning methods, and innovative approaches using IT, inquiry based projects and peer-to-peer learning.

Pastoral Care. We believe that a child who is happy and safe in their environment will flourish. Our excellent pastoral care underpins all aspects of school life. We actively deliver our school values of 'Be Kind, Try Your Best and Embrace Challenge' in every subject, activity, sporting or musical performance the children take part in. The backbone of our pastoral system is based on a team of outstanding tutors, who get to know every child and support them on each step of their journey through the school. Our pastoral care is individually tailored through our mentoring programme and additional support for pupils and families is available, if necessary, through our team of School Counsellors.

Activities and Sports. We run over 100 clubs each term, and always make sure we offer a breadth and variety of activities in each year group that guarantee that every child can find their niche. Our pupils perform with skill, energy and commitment. The school has its own sports hall with a climbing wall and cricket nets, secure play areas and an adventure playground. The sports grounds are second to none, and they are set in a stunning landscape. With 35 acres to ourselves, we have maintained rugby and football pitches, AstroTurf for hockey, netball courts and cricket squares (including artificial surfaces), cricket nets, tennis courts, a woodland cross-country course. In addition, the school makes use of further facilities on offer at Mill Hill School, including sports fields, Fives Courts, swimming pool and theatre.

Entry Points. The usual and main point of entry is at 11+ but 7+, 8+, 9+ and 10+ entry is considered as vacancies occur.

Charitable status. The Mill Hill School Foundation is a Registered Charity, number 1064758. It exists to provide education for boys and girls.

Belmont Grosvenor School

Swarcliffe Hall, Birstwith, Harrogate, North Yorkshire HG3 2JG

Tel:	01423 771029
email:	admin@belmontgrosvenor.co.uk
website:	www.belmontgrosvenor.co.uk
Twitter:	@BelmontGrosveno
Facebook:	@BelmontGrosvenor

Chair of Governors: Mr Gordon Milne

***Acting Headteacher*: Mrs Emma Shea**

Age Range. 3 months–11 years Co-educational.

Number of Pupils. 143.

Fees per term (2021–2022). Prep £4,021, Pre-Prep £3,395, Pre-Reception £1,560–£3,395. Nursery: Under 2s £35.00–£69.00 per session; Over 2s £32.50–£61.00 per session.

Belmont Grosvenor School is a magical place – a warm and friendly family school where every child is nurtured and made to feel special.

Along with its Magic Tree Nursery, Belmont Grosvenor welcomes boys and girls from three months to 11 years and is set in 20 acres of beautiful countryside just three miles from the centre of Harrogate, North Yorkshire.

One of our greatest strengths is the continuity of education we offer. We provide a rich, diverse, happy, and supportive learning environment, fostering each child's intellectual, creative, sporting, and personal development.

We encourage our children to enjoy and respect learning, to develop as effective communicators and as independent, critical thinkers and decision-makers, accept challenges, and appreciate and respect differences.

Each child at Belmont Grosvenor is valued both as an individual and as a member of the school community, and we offer them a range of educational opportunities to fulfil their ambitions and potential.

It is our goal that Belmont Grosvenor School children learn to live as informed, concerned and responsible members of society.

Our 20 acres of grounds ensure our children learn both inside and outside the classroom – our Forest Schools area is well used with weekly lessons on the timetable for Nursery youngsters to Year 2. We have the prestigious Silver Learning Outside the Classroom Mark which recognises how BGS uses its grounds, buildings and environment, and enhances the outdoor learning with clubs, trips and visits.

Learning outside the classroom is embedded in the school's curriculum and all children, from the youngest in Magic Tree Nursery to Year 6, make full use of its fields, woodland and outdoor facilities, which include an outdoor classroom and a logged Forest School area complete with parachute roof and campfire.

Berkhamsted Pre-Prep

Chesham Road, Berkhamsted, Hertfordshire HP4 2SZ

Tel:	01442 358188 (Pre-Prep)
	01442 358276 (Berkhamsted Day Nursery)
email:	preprep@berkhamsted.com
website:	www.berkhamsted.com/pre-prep
	www.berkhamsted.com/day-nursery
Twitter:	@BerkoPrePrep
Facebook:	@berkhamstedschool
LinkedIn:	/berkhamsted-school

Chairman of Governors: Mr G C Laws

Principal: Mr Richard Backhouse, MA Cantab

***Headteacher, Pre-Prep*: Ms Karen O'Connor**, BA, PGCE, NPQH

Age Range. Pre-Prep: 3–7 years. Day Nursery: 5 months–3 years. Co-educational.

Number in School. 102 Boys, 103 Girls.

Fees per term (2021–2022). £3,610–£3,790 (including lunch).

Berkhamsted Pre-Prep is a co-educational independent day school for ages 3–7. Berkhamsted Pre-Prep offers a balanced approach to learning where children are equally nurtured and challenged to extend themselves. Taking risks and being adventurous in all aspects of school life underpin an ambition to aim high with integrity, for every individual child. The extensive grounds and innovative approach to learning which develop not only knowledge but also the skills of being a learner, ensure that the children bound into school excited and hungry to learn more. The family atmosphere, where experienced staff place pastoral care and wellbeing at the heart of school life, provides children with a safe and secure environment to grow emotionally and socially. In addition, children have opportunities to learn French, music, drama, dance, sport and art, all taught by specialist teachers, as well as an outdoor education that takes full advantage of our exceptional grounds.

Knowing that future success is dependent on the firm foundations of academic and personal growth, the excellent educational start at Pre-Prep enable children to progress through the family of schools at Berkhamsted and beyond, with key skills of leadership, independence and high levels of communication. Pupil voice and placing the child at the centre is seen in all aspects of school life with the evidence being considerate, empathetic and confident children who embrace every day with curiosity and a smile.

After-school clubs, outings and trips further enhance an exciting curriculum and extend children's experiences. Wraparound care, from 07.30 to 18.00, supports parents and provides a healthy breakfast and home-from-home experience after a long day. Camp Beaumont, our holiday activities camp at the school designed for 3–11 year olds, is usually available every holiday from 08.00 to 18.00.

Berkhamsted Day Nursery (0–3+ years) is open 50 weeks per year from 07.30 to 18.00, and is situated on the school site. Children can join Berkhamsted Day Nursery from 5 months of age and can move on to Berkhamsted Pre-Prep, which is just next door. Berkhamsted Day Nursery caters for children up to the September that they begin in the Nursery class at Berkhamsted Pre-Prep (when they can use the school's out-of-hours clubs).

In June 2016, the Independent Schools Inspectorate found the quality and standards of the early years provision at Berkhamsted Day Nursery and Berkhamsted Pre-Prep to be '*outstanding*' across all five key areas. The ISI also concluded that 'All children make excellent, continuous progress in relation to their individual starting points and capabilities due to the nurturing and supportive environment that recognises each child as an individual'.

Berkhamsted Prep

Doctors Commons Road, Berkhamsted, Hertfordshire HP4 3DW

Tel: 01442 358201/2
email: prep@berkhamsted.com
website: www.berkhamsted.com/prep
Twitter: @berkhamstedprep
Facebook: @berkhamstedschool
LinkedIn: /berkhamstedschool

Chairman of Governors: Mr G C Laws

Principal: Mr R P Backhouse, MA Cantab

Head: **Mr J Hornshaw**, BEd Hons, MEd, NPQH, FInstLM

Deputy Head: Mr P D Whitby, BA, MA

Age Range. 7–11.

Number of Pupils. 167 boys, 163 girls.

Fees per term (2021–2022). £4,895–£5,285.

Berkhamsted Prep School is part of Berkhamsted School, a school with a 'Diamond' structure that combines single-sex and co-educational teaching. Boys and girls are taught together at the Pre-Prep (Haresfoot site) from age 3 to 7, and at the Prep (Doctors Commons Road site) from age 7 to 11. They are then taught separately from age 11 to 16 (Berkhamsted Boys and Berkhamsted Girls), enabling them to flourish academically, with numerous co-educational activities, trips and events, before coming back together again in a joint Sixth Form.

Berkhamsted Prep School offers first-class facilities for the 7 to 11 age group, in conjunction with the highest standards of teaching and educational development. All classes offer a happy, caring environment where children are encouraged to investigate and explore the world around them. Classes at all levels have access to computers. Key features include a multi-purpose hall, modern dining facilities and a full range of specialist classrooms (e.g. Science laboratory, a DT and an ICT suite with mobile device accessibility for all year groups, Drama Studio, new Food Technology and Art classrooms). The school has also added a netball court, Eton Fives courts and an outdoor learning area. The Prep School also has use of Senior School facilities including extensive playing fields, tennis and netball courts, a Sports Centre, a swimming pool and a 500-seat theatre.

All children are encouraged to develop to their full potential and grow in confidence and independence. The School's general approach is progressive, while retaining traditional values and standards; courtesy and politeness towards others are expected at all times. Academic achievement is of great importance, but the emphasis on other activities such as sports and music ensures that pupils receive a well-rounded education.

The most recent ISI Inspection Report (September 2017) found that the school was excellent in all areas, in particular in terms of the quality of pupils' academic and other achievements and also their personal development.

A wide range of voluntary extracurricular activities is offered at lunch-time and the end of the school day, including art, drama, music and sport. Choirs and orchestras perform in concerts and services throughout the year and school teams compete successfully in a variety of sports.

In addition, the school operates a holiday care facility with Camp Beaumont, with activity programmes available for 3–11 year olds, tailored by age group. There is something for everyone: craft a new creation in clay, take part in sports and games, relax and unwind with mindfulness and yoga, or have lots of fun with water-based games including aqua Olympics and Wet, Wild and Wacky. There is also extended care from 08.00 to 18.00 each day.

Charitable status. Berkhamsted Schools Group is a Registered Charity, number 310630.

Bickley Park School

24 Page Heath Lane, Bickley, Bromley, Kent BR1 2DS

Tel: 020 8467 2195
email: info@bickleyparkschool.co.uk
website: www.bickleyparkschool.co.uk
Twitter: @bickleyparksch
Facebook: @bickleyparksch

Chairman of Governors: Mr M Hansra

Head: **Ms Tammy Howard**, MA, BSc Hons, PGCE

Age Range. Boys 2½–13, Sibling Girls 2½–4.

Number of Pupils. 402 Boys, 5 Girls.

Fees per term (2021–2022). From £2,490 (Nursery) to £5,305 (Boys in Years 4–8). There are no compulsory extras.

Bickley Park School, founded in 1918, is a boys-only day school which occupies two spacious and attractive sites in Bickley: the Prep Department at 24 Page Heath Lane and the Pre-Prep Department at 14 Page Heath Lane. The school has excellent facilities to complement the original Victorian buildings, including a five-acre sports field, state-of-the-art new science labs, a large sports hall, swimming pool, Design Technology and Art Studios.

The EYFS Department (rated as outstanding in the school's last inspection) provides a first-class foundation before the children progress into Pre-Prep.

In the Prep Department, the children are introduced to more specialist teaching and setting for Mathematics, English, Science, Spanish and French. The curriculum is built around Four Quadrants of Learning that espouse academic rigour alongside exceptional opportunities in the wider curriculum.

The majority of children leave at 13+ to attend some of the UK's leading independent schools, whilst a small number leave at 11, usually to join local Grammar Schools.

The school is very outward-looking and enjoys a vibrant community feel.

Charitable status. Bickley Park School Limited is a Registered Charity, number 307915. It exists to provide a broad curriculum for boys aged 2½–13 and girls aged 2½–4.

Bilton Grange

Dunchurch, Rugby, Warwickshire CV22 6QU

Tel: 01788 810217
email: admissions@biltongrange.co.uk
website: www.biltongrange.co.uk
Twitter: @biltongrange
Facebook: @biltongrangeschool

Headmaster: **Gareth Jones**, BA Hons, PGCE, MEd

Deputy Headmaster: Paul Nicholson, BA Hons, PGCE

Assistant Head – Pastoral: Mireille Everton, BA Hons

Assistant Head – Academic: Greg Das Gupta, BSc, BCom, PGCE

Assistant Head – Boarding: Mark Tovey, BEd Hons

Assistant Head – Pre Prep: Katie Gedye, BA, QTS

UK Registrar: Liz Graham, BSc Hons

International Admissions Registrar: Caroline Morgan, MA Oxon

Age Range. 3–13.

Number of Pupils. 351 boys and girls of whom 45 are full, weekly, or flexi-boarders. Preparatory (8–13 year olds): 196 pupils; Pre-Preparatory and Early Years (3–8 year olds): 101 pupils.

Nestled in 90-acres of parkland and woods, Bilton Grange is a safe and wonderful place where a child's imagination can run free. Whenever and wherever a child's mind is thrilled, they will learn, and here, in this environment, each child can grow up better because they can stay younger longer. They can be the hero of his or her story because Bilton Grange makes learning the adventure it should be.

Pupils here benefit from a huge range of opportunities designed to support individual interests. Children share common values of respect, awareness of others and courtesy. They are usually 'all-rounders', willing to take advantage of all that is on offer – be it on the sports field, in the classroom or on an adventure weekend. The school demonstrates all the advantages of a traditional prep school curriculum with the benefits of an innovative approach to teaching and learning. Expect small class sizes, a broad range of subjects and specialist teaching staff, plus the '90-acre classroom' to enhance the learning landscape even further.

Bilton Grange is non-selective and yet maintains the highest standards across the board, delivered in a relaxed setting suited to the young learner. Children are entered for the Common Entrance Examination and take their next step to some of the top senior schools across the UK including Rugby, Oundle, Eton, Repton, Oakham, Bloxham and Uppingham. Every year many of our children achieve awards and scholarships to senior schools and, in recent years, all Year 8 leavers have moved up to the senior school of their choice.

Full, weekly and flexible boarding is offered with more than 50 boys and girls boarding on a full and weekly basis. A close knit team of house parents and matrons create a nurturing environment where children feel comfortable, safe and secure, whether they are staying for an occasional night a week or boarding full time.

Impressive facilities feature a purpose-built theatre and separate Music School, an atmospheric panelled library, chapel, sports hall, 25m indoor swimming pool, nine-hole golf course, shooting range and a floodlit artificial grass hockey pitch located within Pugin's walled garden. Sporting success is achieved at regional and national level, while creative arts are a big part of school life with scholarship successes and achievements across Music, Art, Drama and Design Technology.

Fees per term (2021–2022) Preparatory: Full Boarding £9,413, Weekly Boarding £8,730, Day £6,096–£6,909, Pre-Preparatory: £3,581–£4,295. (Fee discounts for Services' children.)

Bursaries and academic scholarships are awarded annually and open to both internal and external candidates in Year 6, to start in Year 7. Bursaries are awarded on a financial need basis – please see the school website for more information.

We encourage all prospective parents and children to visit and see why Bilton Grange is the first step in the adventure of life.

Charitable status. Bilton Grange is part of the Rugby School Group. Charity number 528752.

Birchfield School

Harriot's Hayes Lane
Albrighton, Wolverhampton WV7 3AF

Tel: 01902 372534
email: office@birchfieldschool.co.uk
website: www.birchfieldschool.co.uk
Twitter: @BirchfieldSch
Facebook: @Birchfield-School

Chair of Governance Advisory Committee: Sir Michael Griffiths

Headmistress: Mrs Sarah Morris, BA Hons, PGCE

Age Range. 4–16
Number of Pupils. 138
Fees per term (2021–2022). From £2,500 to £3,334.

Birchfield School is a preparatory and senior day school for boys and girls aged 4 to 16. It is in the process of extending its senior school provision to provide a GCSE programme of study for students aged 13–16. The latest Independent Schools Inspectorate Report in November 2021 highlighted the first-class all-round education delivered by the school and awarded Birchfield 'Excellent' in both 'The Quality of the Pupils' Academic and Other Achievements' and 'Personal Development', as well as full compliance.

Having joined the St Philip's Education Group in November 2021, Birchfield has seen a major investment in facilities with enhancements across all areas, especially in Science and Sport and the addition of an outdoor classroom for the youngest Reception pupils. A further Woodland Dell prioritises a focus upon learning in the natural world. Birchfield's subject specialist staff operate from well-equipped classrooms with modern facilities such as a Music Suite, Science laboratory, Design and Technology workshop, Art studio, 6,000 title Library and Food Technology room. There are two ICT suites with networked PCs and iPads which are used throughout the school.

Sport is a fundamental and much-valued part of school life at Birchfield and with extensive playing fields, a traditional cricket pavilion and floodlit astro-turf pitches, pupils are well placed to continue Birchfield's enviable sporting tradition and achievements.

Birchfield encourages self-expression through Music, Drama, Art and Design Technology. The Art department has a reputation for success in both regional and national art competitions. The Music department holds regular concerts and all pupils are encouraged to take up an instrument on joining the school. Birchfield also enjoys a vibrant community of singers who perform successfully in their ABRSM grade exams. In Drama, pupils are encouraged to join LAMDA through which they enjoy an enviable and consistently high rate of Distinction grades in their exams.

The school has a well-resourced Learning Enhancement department which provides excellent support for pupils with a range of special educational needs. For those demonstrating strong academic ability, gifted sessions and advanced groups are offered to provide challenge in core areas. A rich and challenging leadership programme for senior pupils facilitates teamwork and charity work.

The first Year 9 cohort will launch in 2023 and undertake a broad and balanced three-year GCSE programme within Beamish House, an impressive dedicated building offering modern state-of-the-art facilities, study centres, changing rooms and outdoor space for senior pupils.

Birchfield has a longstanding and fine reputation for its all-round holistic education and occupies a beautiful rural location within easy reach of Wolverhampton, Telford, Shrewsbury and Newport with excellent transport links. A separately owned nursery also operates on the Birchfield School site and welcomes children from 6 weeks to 4 years old.

Birkdale Prep School

Clarke House, Clarke Drive, Sheffield S10 2NS

Tel: 0114 267 0407
email: prepschool@birkdaleschool.org.uk
website: www.birkdaleschool.org.uk
Twitter: @BirkdalePrep
Facebook: @BirkdaleSchool

Chairman of Governors: P Houghton, FCA

Head of Prep School: C J Burch, BA, PGCE

Age Range. 4–11.
Number of Pupils. 250 day.
Fees per term (2021–2022). Pre-Prep Department £3,140; Prep Department £3,850. Lunch included.

Birkdale Prep School is a school specialising in quality education and care for children 4–11. Birkdale admit girls from Reception to Prep 2 (Y4) and this will progress year by year until the school is fully co-educational. Continuous education is offered from 11–18 at Birkdale Senior School (Co-educational Sixth Form).

Birkdale Prep School is based at Clarke House, situated in a pleasant area near the University, close to the Senior School. The school has a firm Christian tradition and this, coupled with the size of the school, ensures that pupils develop their own abilities, whether academic or otherwise, to the full.

The Pre-Prep Department is based in a new building, Belmayne House. The facilities are outstanding and designed specifically to meet the needs of 4–7 year olds. Specialist subject teaching across the curriculum starts at age 7 and setting in core subjects in the final two years enhances, still further, the pupil to teacher ratio.

The school has its own Matron and pastoral care is given high priority. Pupils are encouraged to join a wide variety of clubs and societies. Music plays a significant part in school life, both in and out of the timetable. There is a large choir, brass band and orchestra.

Cricket, Rugby and Football are played on the School's own substantial playing fields, which are within easy reach of the school. A broad range of activities is available as part of the extensive extracurricular programme.

The majority of pupils pass into the Senior School.

Charitable status. Birkdale School is a Registered Charity, number 1018973, and a Company Limited by Guarantee, registered in England, number 2792166.

Bishop's Stortford College Prep School

Maze Green Road, Bishop's Stortford, Hertfordshire CM23 2PH

Tel: 01279 838607
email: psadmissions@bishopsstortfordcollege.org
website: www.bishopsstortfordcollege.org
Twitter: @BSCollege
Facebook: @bishopsstortfordcollege
Instagram: @thebishopsstortfordcollege

Chairman of Governors: Mr G E Baker, BSc, MRICS

Head: **Mr W J Toleman**, BA

Age Range. 4–13.

Typical Number of Pupils. 50 boarders and 505 day pupils.

Fees per term (2021–2022). Full Boarders £8,566; Overseas Boarders £8,746; Weekly Boarders £8,314; Day £5,126–£5,576; Pre-Prep £3,320–£3,385. There are no compulsory extras.

Bishop's Stortford College is a friendly, co-educational, day and boarding community providing high academic standards, good discipline and an excellent all-round education.

There are 40 full-time members of staff, and a number of Senior School staff also teach in the Prep School. As the Prep and Senior Schools share the same campus, many College facilities (music school, sports hall, swimming pool, all-weather pitches, dining hall, medical centre) are shared.

The Prep School also has its own buildings containing a multi-purpose Hall, laboratories, IT centre, library, art room and classrooms. In 2013 the Dawson Building was opened, enhancing and extending the Prep School facilities.

The Prep School routine and curriculum are appropriate to the 7–13 age range, with pupils being prepared for Common Entrance and Senior School Scholarships, although most children proceed to the College Senior School. There are 23 forms streamed by general ability and setted for Maths. High standards of work and behaviour are expected and the full development, within a happy and friendly atmosphere, of each child's abilities in sport and the arts is actively encouraged. A strong swimming tradition exists and many of the staff are expert coaches of the major games (rugby, hockey, cricket, netball, tennis and swimming). The choirs and orchestra flourish throughout the year, and two afternoons of activities provide opportunities for pupils to participate in many minor sports, outdoor pursuits, crafts, computing and chess. Six major dramatic productions occur every year.

A Pre-Prep for 4–6 year olds was opened in 1995 and new purpose-built accommodation was opened in September 2005.

The Prep School is run on boarding lines with a six-day week and a 5.00pm finish on three days with Wednesdays and Fridays ending between 4.00pm and 4.30pm, and Saturdays between 2.30pm and 3.00pm. The 7 and 8 year olds have a slightly shorter day and their own dedicated building.

Entry tests for 7, 8, 9, 10, 11 year olds are held each January. Scholarships are available at 10+ (Academic and Music) and 11+ (Academic, Music, Art and Sport), as is Financial Assistance.

Charitable status. The Incorporated Bishop's Stortford College Association is a Registered Charity, number 311057. Its aims and objectives are to provide high quality Independent Day and Boarding education for boys and girls from age 4 to 18.

Bishopsgate School

Bishopsgate Road, Englefield Green, Surrey TW20 0YJ

Tel: 01784 480222 (Admissions)
             01784 432109 (School Office)
email: headmaster@bishopsgatesch.uk
             office@bishopsgatesch.uk
             admissions@bishopsgatesch.uk
website: www.bishopsgate-school.co.uk
Twitter: @BishopsgateSch

Chairman of Governors: Mr Tim Eddis, BA

Headmaster: **Mr Rob Williams**, BA Hons, MA, PGCE

Age Range. 3–13.
Number of Pupils. 375.
Fees per term (2021–2022). £5,601 (Years 5–8), £4,883 (Years 3–4), £4,088 (Years 1–2), £3,603 (Reception), Nursery: £3,535 (5 days), £1,975 (5 mornings).

Set in 20 acres of beautiful woodland, close to Windsor Great Park, Bishopsgate is blessed with a glorious learning environment. The heart of the school remains as a large,

Victorian house, but many additional modern buildings have been added offering parents outstanding on site facilities for their children.

The most recent, exciting projects that have just been completed are the new Science lab, the new Food Tech room, the sound clouds in the Dining Room and the new astro turf pitch that is situated next to the fabulous brand new state-of-the-art Sports Hall which opened in September 2020. These developments and other future projects are part of the Governors long term plan to ensure Bishopsgate continues to offer excellence in teaching along with progressive facilities.

The School also has a four-lane 25-metre swimming pool and swimming is included in the curriculum from Nursery. In addition, the school has a well equipped Design & Technology Suite and an upgraded IT Suite which includes touch-screen computers and the procurement of laptops and Chromebook for the pupils. The completion of a major upgrade of the School All Weather Facility, the Performing Arts Studio, the building of a new cricket square, and the redevelopment of the current all-weather surface has vastly enhanced the facilities.

Children may enter Bishopsgate from the age of 3 into our Nursery. Our trained staff and well-equipped Nursery ensure that each child is given the best possible start to life. There is a warm family atmosphere as we recognise how important it is for children to feel happy and secure. We place great emphasis on building a solid foundation of social skills and a love of learning, which will enable each child to settle confidently into school life. A wide variety of activities is on offer with plenty of opportunities for healthy outdoor learning for all year groups.

Beyond Nursery, a class teacher remains at the core of each child's learning. Emphasis is placed on establishing a firm foundation in literacy and numeracy, but the curriculum is broad with a range of educational visits planned to enrich and extend the children's learning. The teaching of French, Music, PE, Singing and Dance is provided by specialist teachers. Good use is made of our glorious grounds as an Outdoor Learning resource.

Form-based teaching continues in Years 3 and 4, but by Year 5 all teaching is by subject specialists. Programmes of study in Upper School are full and varied, covering the traditional academic subjects as well as Art, Design, Music, Computer Studies, PSHE and PE. The children are prepared carefully for entrance to a range of senior schools and we are proud of our record of success. We prepare children for 11+ entry to senior schools, but we also encourage our children to remain with us to age 13.

In Upper School, opportunities to represent the school in sports teams, plays, choirs and instrumental groups are all part of the 'Bishopsgate Experience'. In addition, a busy programme of extracurricular activities ensures that all children have the opportunity to shine at something.

Music plays an essential part in the life of the school with many of our pupils enjoying individual music lessons. There are choirs and ensembles. Participation by children of all abilities, with ample opportunities to perform, is our aim. Drama productions, dance and public speaking events all provide additional occasions when the children can develop their presentation skills.

Our vibrant Art and Design Department occupies a spacious studio equipped with a kiln for ceramics and a printing press for design projects. There is an annual ArtsFest for the whole School and the children's work is displayed proudly around the school and in our annual School magazine.

Team Games, Rowing, Athletics, Dance, Tennis, Gymnastics, Swimming and much more are all included in a varied and exciting sporting programme within the school day. An extensive programme of inter-school fixtures is arranged each term and we like to see as many parents in support as possible! We like to win, but our priorities are participation, enjoyment and teamwork.

A prospectus and further details can be obtained from the Admissions Office.

Charitable status. Bishopsgate School is a Registered Charity, number 1060511. It aims to provide a broad and sound education for its pupils with thorough and personal pastoral care.

Blackheath Prep

4 St Germans Place, Blackheath, London SE3 0NJ

Tel:	020 8858 0692
email:	info@blackheathprep.co.uk
website:	www.blackheathprep.co.uk
Twitter:	@BlackheathPrep
Facebook:	@blackheathprep
Instagram:	@blackheathprep

An outstanding co-educational day school in South East London

Chairman of Governors: Mr Hugh Stallard

Head: **Mr Alex Matthews**, MA, PGCE, MA Ed

Age Range. 3–11.

Number of Pupils. 163 Boys, 191 Girls.

Fees per term (2021–2022). Nursery: £2,890–£4,910; Reception–Year 2 £4,740; Years 3–6 £5,130.

The school is located close to Blackheath village, overlooking the heath itself and borders of Greenwich Park. The five-acre site includes attractive playing fields, cricket nets, tennis courts and two playgrounds, providing enviable sporting opportunities and room for children to play.

A well-equipped learning environment includes specialist rooms for Science, ICT, Art, DT, Maths and Music. A spacious multi-purpose hall and music suite enhance the opportunities for Music, Drama, Sport and extracurricular activities. Over 70 activities are offered in a wide-ranging extracurricular programme.

Most children join the school in the nursery at the age of three and progress through the Pre-Prep (4–7) and Prep (7–11) before leaving to transfer to selective senior schools. Academic standards are high and pupils are well prepared for selection at 11 and achieve consistent success in obtaining places at their first choice of grammar or independent senior school. On average over the last five years more than 50% of Year 6 pupils have been awarded academic scholarships each year and scholarships in Art, Music, Drama and Sport.

The form teacher of every class is responsible for the pastoral welfare of each child, supported by a robust pastoral framework across the school. In the Nursery and the

Pre-Prep the key worker and the form teacher are primarily responsible for teaching the children. However, there is a strong emphasis on specialist teaching from the very beginning. Music, French, PE, Drama and Dance are introduced in the Nursery. As the children progress through the school, specialist teachers are responsible for Art, ICT, Design Technology, Maths, English and Science. The quality of teaching is recognised as one of the many strengths of the school and pupils are encouraged to develop a sense of curiosity about the world around them and nurture a lifelong love of learning.

The school positively encourages parental involvement in the daily life of the school. The strong ethos and vision of the school of kindness, curiosity, ambition and courage is underpinned by the vibrant enthusiasm of all involved and by a strong sense of community.

The Blue Coat School

Somerset Road, Edgbaston, Birmingham B17 0HR

Tel: 0121 410 6800
email: admissions@thebluecoatschool.com
website: www.thebluecoatschool.com
Twitter: @bcsbirmingham
Facebook: @bluecoatbirmingham
Instagram: @bcsbirmingham
LinkedIn: /Blue-Coat-School-Birmingham

Founded 1722. Co-educational Day Preparatory School.

Chairman of Governors: Mr B H Singleton

Headmaster: **Mr N G Neeson**, BEd Hons, NPQH

Age Range. 3–11.

Number of Pupils. The total enrolment is 627 children. Nursery and Pre-Prep have 261 girls and boys from 3–7 years, while Prep has 366 from 7–11 years.

There is a graduate and qualified full-time teaching staff of 50, and 7 part-time teachers.

Fees per term (2021–2022). Pre-Prep: £3,053–£3,828; Prep: £4,457–£4,616. The fees quoted include lunches and morning and afternoon breaks. Over 80 co-curricular activities take place each week, some of which are charged as extras.

Assisted Places are available to children with a demonstrable need, entering Years 3 and 4.

7+ Scholarships are offered for academic and musical excellence (entry to Year 3).

The School is set in 15 acres of grounds and playing fields just 2 miles from the centre of Birmingham. Its well-designed buildings and facilities include a newly refurbished Dining Hall, AstroTurf pitch and cricket nets, Chapel, Year 6 Hub, spacious auditorium and a superb multi-purpose Sports Centre with a 25m indoor swimming pool and two air-conditioned studios. A Breakfast Club is offered to Years 2 to 6 from 7.30am. After care is available until 5.45pm for all year groups.

Additional features include a Forest School, Media Suite with green screen wall, library, specialist facilities for Science, Art, Design and Technology and Music. All the classrooms have an IWB, and the school is very well equipped with Apple and Windows computers including desktops, laptops and tablets.

Children are prepared for scholarships and examinations to prestigious local schools. The school enjoys particular success in the 11+ examinations to Birmingham's grammar schools and the schools of the King Edward VI Foundation. The Statutory Framework for the Early Years Foundation Stage is followed for children aged 3 to 5, and the National Curriculum is incorporated at Key Stages 1 and 2 as part of a wider academic structure.

The school is well known for its Music. The robed Chapel Choir is affiliated to the RSCM, and there are five further choirs and a significant number of instrumental groups and ensembles. Musicals, concerts and recitals feature in abundance, involving the great majority of the children. Over 300 instrumental lessons are given weekly.

The main sports are Hockey, Netball, Rounders, Rugby, Football, Cricket, Athletics and Swimming. The teams enjoy considerable success in inter-school competitions and all children have the opportunity to develop their skills.

An extensive Co-Curricular programme includes Gymnastics, Judo, Creative Arts, LAMDA, Fencing and Chess. Lessons in the classroom are complemented by outings including field courses and residential trips.

The Blue Coat School was shortlisted for *The Times* Prep School of the Year 2020 and 2021.

Charitable status. The Blue Coat School Birmingham Limited is a Registered Charity, number 1152244, and a Company Limited by Guarantee, registered in England, number 8502615.

Blundell's Preparatory School

Milestones House, Blundell's Road, Tiverton, Devon EX16 4NA

Tel: 01884 252393
email: prep@blundells.org
website: www.blundells.org

Chairman of Governors: Mr N P Hall, MA, FCA

Head Master: **Mr Andy Southgate**

Age Range. 3–11 years.

Numbers of Pupils. 246 (143 boys, 103 girls)

Fees per term (2021–2022). Nursery £828.25–£3,043.05, Prep £2,465–£4,355

Blundell's Preparatory School is a family school and all the staff adopt a personal interest in every child and work in partnership with the parents. The school places great emphasis on children being happy, secure and confident, thus offering individuals every opportunity to achieve their full potential within a caring family atmosphere. The rural setting is within easy reach of the market town of Tiverton and is conveniently placed less than ten minutes from the M5 motorway and Tiverton Parkway Station.

The School has an excellent reputation for providing sound academic standards which are based on providing the core subjects of Maths, English and Science taught to an extremely high standard. Added to this is the bonus of a wide range of supplementary subjects, well taught by specialist teachers in specialist teaching areas, including a fully-equipped Art & Design Centre and a Food Technology Suite.

Drama, music and art flourish at Blundell's Preparatory School with all the children participating fully both in lessons and as part of co-curricular activities. Specialist music teachers offer an extensive variety of different instruments. The drama and music departments have their own dedicated facility.

The sports department has an enviable reputation of producing good all-round sporting pupils, as well as nurturing and extending those with talent. Amongst the sports offered are rugby, football, netball, hockey and cross-country in the winter and cricket, tennis, athletics and swimming in the summer. The Preparatory School has access to the extensive sporting facilities within Blundell's senior campus.

There is a comprehensive choice of co-curricular activities offered to the pupils which includes ballet, chess, fencing, golf, art, judo, Bushcraft Club, Wild Wonders and woodwork.

(*See also Blundell's School entry in HMC section.*)

Charitable status. Blundell's School is a Registered Charity, number 1081249. It exists to provide education for children.

Bootham Junior School

Rawcliffe Lane, York YO30 6NP

Tel: 01904 655021
email: junior@boothamschool.com
website: www.boothamschool.com
Twitter: @BoothamSchool
Facebook: @BoothamSchool
LinkedIn: /bootham-school

Clerk to the School Committee: Cathy Woodbine

Head: **Helen Todd**, BA Hons, MA Ed, QTS

Age Range. 3–11 Co-educational.

Number of Pupils. 124.

Fees per term (2021–2022). £2,430–£3,630 inc. lunch for full-time pupils.

Bootham Junior School stands apart by treating each member of its community, in a practical application of Quaker principles, as equally important. We welcome all faiths or none, encouraging our children to develop their own convictions while learning to respect those of others. The Independent Schools Inspectorate reports '*A sense of calm and a quiet pace to the working of the school that enables individuals to flourish*'. Although our children are as boisterous as any others, and, indeed, enjoy a tolerance to behave as children, quietness is important. The values of cooperation, community, and quietness grow from the Quaker tradition, but they resonate with the modern world of work, where teams find solutions individuals can't, where knowledge is seen as interrelated and not separate, and where values-driven responses earn our respect.

At Bootham Junior School, we aim to encourage a lifelong love of learning and inspirational teaching is a good place to start. Equally important is the mutual high regard and understanding that children and teachers enjoy. This relationship provides the very best environment for learning to take place. High standards are achieved because children feel happy, confident, motivated and respected. Education is more than examination preparation; it is about unlocking potential skills and aptitudes. We want our children to find their particular strengths: through sport, through music, through the Arts, through outdoor education, through social debate and action.

Bootham Junior School has a beautiful sports field, a swimming pool at the senior school dating from 1912 and hard courts for tennis and netball. The range of sports taught include: gymnastics, dance, athletics, netball, tennis, swimming, football, basketball, cricket and rounders. Our Director of Music has a range of musical groups including: two choirs, orchestra, flute group, string group, clarinet group and recorder group. Individual music lessons are also available in all instruments should parents wish it. Engagement with the community is in line with a Quaker sense of responsibility and extends to children's activities too. Drama flourishes both within and beyond the formal curriculum. Regular productions of plays and musicals cater for different age groups and allow talents to be explored, nurtured and showcased. Children also take part in LAMDA schemes for recital and public speaking. Our Outdoor Classroom is an extremely well-used resource and all children have the opportunity to take part in residential experiences, from nursery age onwards. We believe in building adaptable, resilient young people who can respond to the world around them. Whatever their interests, this is the place where all our children can find inspiration and where they will be inspired. The small size of our school means that everyone has the chance to try something new. The result is a sense of personal achievement both in and outside the classroom.

Charitable status. Bootham School is a Registered Charity, number 513645.

Boundary Oak School

Roche Court, Wickham Road, Fareham, Hampshire PO17 5BL

Tel: 01329 280955
email: admissions@boundaryoak.co.uk
            office@boundaryoak.co.uk
website: www.boundaryoakschool.co.uk
Twitter: @boundaryoak
Facebook: @boundaryoak

Executive Head: **Mr James Polansky**, MA Cantab, PGCE

Headmistress: **Mrs Sophie Savage**, BA Hons, PGCE

Age Range. 2–16.

Number of Pupils. 51 Boarders, 238 Day Pupils.

Fees per term (2021–2022). Boarding Supplement (Years 3–11): £2,121 (Weekly boarding 5 nights); £2,802 (Full boarding 7 nights). Day Pupils: £3,149–£5,098 (Reception–Year 11), Pre-School: £60 for all-day session.

The school was founded in 1918 and moved to Roche Court in 1960. A new 99 year lease was secured in 1994. The school is set in 22 acres of pleasant, self-contained grounds between Fareham and Wickham in Hampshire and enjoys extensive views of the countryside around.

The Pre-School takes children from the age of 2 to rising 5 and this group is housed in a purpose-built centre offering the most up-to-date facilities. This department is structured to the needs of this age group and the day can extend from 7.40 am to 6.15 pm.

The Pre-Prep Department has its own purpose-built buildings and other facilities within the school, and caters for children from rising 5 to 8 years of age (Reception to Year 3).

At 8 years the children move to the Preparatory Department where they remain until they are 11 (Year 6). From here they move to Seniors in Year 7 and choose their GCSE options in Year 9 from a large array of subjects. Full and weekly boarding are offered to all from the age of 7 years and the school has a policy of admitting boarders in a flexible system that is of great benefit to all. Pupils are prepared for a wide number of independent schools throughout the United Kingdom in a friendly and caring environment.

Apart from the historic main house of Roche Court where the boarders live, there is the Jubilee Block of classrooms, three laboratories, the Widley Block, Library and the Music Centre. The School has an ICT Suite and a purpose-built Art and Design Technology Centre that incorporates work areas for Cooking, Photography, Pottery and Carpentry. The school has a fine Assembly Hall that is also used for Drama and Physical Education.

As well as extensive playing fields with woods beyond for cross country and an all-weather AstroTurf pitch which incorporates football, hockey, netball and tennis courts, there is a large sports hall, an outdoor swimming pool and the indoor Fareham Pool is within very easy reach.

Most sports are taught and there is a wide selection of clubs and activities run in the school for both day and boarding pupils including judo, horse riding, art, camp craft, chess, and many more.

For a copy of the prospectus and details of scholarships and bursaries, please apply to the Registrar, email: admissions@boundaryoak.co.uk or look at our website www.boundaryoakschool.co.uk.

Bradford Grammar Junior School

Keighley Road, Bradford, West Yorkshire BD9 4JP

Tel: 01274 553742
email: chsec@bradfordgrammar.com
website: www.bradfordgrammar.com
Twitter: @RRibeiro_BGS
            @bradfordgrammar
Facebook: @bradfordgrammarschool
LinkedIn: /bradfordgrammar

Chairman of the Board of Governors: Lady L Morrison, LLB

Headmaster: Mr R Ribeiro

Age Range. 6 to 11.

Number of Pupils. 82 boys, 65 girls.

Fees per term (2021–2022). £3,530

Bradford Grammar Junior School is a selective school for boys and girls aged 6 to 11, holding no catchment boundaries and a strong reputation for specialist teaching.

The school seeks to inspire happy, respectful and grounded children, who are ready for the transition to Senior School. The school's aim is to provide exceptional care in a nurturing atmosphere so that each child can thrive.

Location. Bradford Grammar Junior School is located at the same site as the Senior School at Keighley Road, Bradford. It is housed in an original seventeenth century manor house called Clock House.

Specialist facilities. The school offers pupils a wide range of specialist facilities, including a swimming pool, theatre, an outdoor classroom, instrumental music tuition and dedicated Computer Science and Design Technology rooms. Full use is made of the Senior School facilities including Science laboratories, Sports facilities and Art rooms.

Specialist teaching. In Years 2, 3 and 4 (age 6 to 9) pupils are taught the majority of subjects by form teachers and are based in their classrooms, with specialist teaching for Art, Modern Foreign Languages, Music, Computing, and Games. In Years 5 and 6 pupils have increasing input from specialist teachers utilising the extensive facilities throughout the whole school.

Co-curricular Activities. The Junior School offers a wide and varied range of co-curricular activities which mainly take place during the lunch break. All pupils are encouraged to participate in at least two different activities each week. These may include: netball, hockey, rugby, swimming, cross country, cricket, football, rounders, athletics, table tennis, dance, design technology, computing, Lego, craft, art, board games, gardening, choir, orchestra, wind band, string group, guitar group and samba band.

Pastoral Care. Form Teachers are closely involved with the wellbeing of the children in their form and all of our teachers have a good knowledge of, and relationship with, the pupils. We encourage open communication between school and home and hope parents will keep in close contact with us. A child's progress and happiness are our priorities. We promote good manners and respect for others throughout the School and believe that this is an important aspect of all pupils' education.

After Care. Bradford Grammar Junior School provides before and after school care from 7.45 am to 6.00 pm.

Transport Links. The school organises private coach transport for pupils travelling to and from Huddersfield, Halifax, Bramhope, Horsforth, Rawdon, Wharfedale and Oxenhope. It is situated a short walk from Frizinghall Railway Station, which is on the Airedale and Wharfedale lines. There are half-hourly rail services, taking approximately 30 minutes, to Leeds, Skipton, Ilkley and Apperley Bridge.

Entry. The school is selective and takes a number of pupils each year for entry from Year 2 (age 6 to 7) through to Year 6 (age 10 to 11). Entry to Years 2, 3 and 4 (age 6, 7 and 8) is by assessment. Entry to Years 5 and 6 (age 9 and 10) is by entrance examination and involves tests in Maths and English.

Pupils who progress from Bradford Grammar School Junior School to the Senior School are not required to sit the 11+ entrance exam. The close relationship between the two schools enables a smooth transition from Junior to Senior School.

Charitable status. Bradford Grammar School (The Free Grammar School of King Charles II at Bradford) is a Registered Charity, number 529113. It exists to provide education for children.

Brambletye

Lewes Road, East Grinstead, West Sussex RH19 3PD

Tel: 01342 321004
email: schooloffice@brambletye.com
website: www.brambletye.co.uk
Twitter: @brambletweet
Facebook: @brambletyeschool

Chairman of Governors: Mr P J Lough, MA, PGCE

Headmaster: **Mr Will Brooks**, BA, PGCE, MBA Ed

Age Range. 2–13 Co-educational.

Number of Pupils. 301 day/boarding pupils.

Fees per term (2021–2022). Boarders £8,860–£9,065; Day Pupils £6,675–£7,435; Pre-Prep: £3,585 (Years 1 & 2), £3,450 (Reception), Nursery £3,325 (5 full days) varied pricing if doing fewer sessions.

Brambletye is an independent day and boarding Preparatory School for boys and girls aged 7–13 years, situated in beautiful grounds in rural Sussex. There is a Pre-Prep/Nursery department which takes boys and girls from the age of 2 years to the age of 7 years.

Brambletye is a large country house in its own wooded estate of 140 acres, overlooking Ashdown Forest and Weir Wood Reservoir. The school stands one mile south of East Grinstead. Gatwick Airport is only 20 minutes by car and Heathrow is an hour away. London is 30 miles by road and 50 minutes by rail. There is escorted travel to and from London at the beginning and end of all exeat weekends and half-term holidays.

The school has outstanding academic, sporting, music, drama and arts facilities. These include a new modern classroom block, 2 redeveloped science laboratories, an up-to-date Arts Room and Design Technology workshop, a brand new Library, an ICT room, a large theatre and music rooms. There is also a Sports Hall, large astro pitch, tennis and netball courts, two squash courts, a swimming pool, a golf course and several playing fields. We aim to produce happy, confident, well-rounded children who work hard, enjoy drama, games and music, play a part in some of the numerous societies and hobbies, and take a full share in the daily life of the school. These facilities in conjunction with high quality teaching staff, generate regular awards for the children from the schools that inherit them.

Brambletye has always been run along family lines, with a distinctive warm and friendly atmosphere. Traditional values such as high standards of manners and good behaviour provide a platform for academic and personal development. As a co-educational day and boarding school, pupils enjoy and benefit from living and working in a community. At weekends, there is a full programme of activities for the boarders and children are encouraged to make constructive use of their spare time. The environment is inspirational and pupils develop a love of learning which creates a positive interaction with the staff and a curiosity about the world around us.

The Nursery and Pre-Prep Department is situated in a self-contained purpose-built state-of-the-art building. The main aim of the Department is to provide a secure, friendly and structured environment in which all children are encouraged to achieve their full potential and to develop at their own rate.

Children may join the Nursery class at the age of two before progressing to Reception at four. Boys and girls transfer to the Prep School at the age of seven. All children acquire the basic skills, while following the breadth of the National Curriculum. Religious Studies, Physical Education, Art, Music, Science and Technology are all integrated into the weekly timetable. Children have swimming lessons throughout the year in the indoor pool, and teachers from the Prep School visit regularly to teach Music and to coach games. The Pre-Prep has an exciting School in the Woods project.

Enquiries about admissions and our scholarships and bursary programme are welcomed throughout the year. Brambletye offers generous discounts for Armed Forces and Foreign Office Families.

Charitable status. Brambletye School Trust Limited is a Registered Charity, number 307003. It aims to provide an all-round education for the children in its care.

Brentwood Preparatory School

Shenfield Road, Brentwood, Essex CM15 8BD

Tel: 01277 243300
email: prep@brentwood.essex.sch.uk
website: www.brentwoodschool.co.uk

Chairman of Governors: Sir Michael Snyder, DSc, FCA, FRSA [OB]

Headmaster: **Mr K J Whiskerd**, BA, PGCE

Head of Early Years and Key Stage 1: Mrs V Audas, BEd

Age Range. 3–11.

Number of Children. Prep 589.

Fees per term (2021–2022). £5,245.

Brentwood Preparatory School has its own buildings and grounds and whilst quite distinct from Brentwood School, shares the use of its chapel, indoor swimming pool, Sports Centre and world-class athletics track.

It is a very exciting time for the co-educational Preparatory School, which opened in 1892, as the doors have opened on a major programme of improvement works which sees the School at the forefront of cutting-edge educational facilities. The multi-million pound investment includes new buildings, refurbishment and upgrading of existing buildings and improvements to external areas and landscaping.

Children, aged 3 to 7, are primarily taught in the spacious Higgs Building and South Prep with very well-equipped classrooms. Entrance is by an informal assessment at age 3.

Older children, aged 7 to 11, are mainly based in Middleton Hall, an elegant building which has its own extensive grounds, sports pitches and all-weather Astroturf. Entrance is at age 7 by an academically-selective test and candidates come from a wide range of schools. Small class sizes and a team of well-qualified, and often specialist teachers provide a caring and challenging environment. Designated rooms for art, design technology, drama, MFL (French, German, Mandarin), ICT, music and science provide outstanding facilities and a stimulating environment in which children can thrive.

There is an extensive programme of house and inter-school sports matches. Choirs, orchestras and a variety of ensembles perform regularly both in and out of school. Every child has the opportunity to take part in a major drama production. There is a wide range of co-curricular lunchtime and after-school clubs that are offered through our ACES programme. Older Prep pupils participate annually in Enrichment Week and weekly in our Activities Programme to complement school-based work. They also enjoy annual residential trips.

The Preparatory School has a strong academic tradition and a reputation for providing an excellent all-round education. The vast majority of pupils transfer to the Senior School (founded in 1557) at age 11.

The 2020 development has resulted in an increase in the Preparatory School roll; expanded and re-organised Early Years facilities; new Assembly and Dining amenities; and a suite of state-of-the-art specialist teaching areas. The Preparatory School offers various Foundation options and all Prep pupils, from 3 years of age, can extend their school day from 7.30am–6.00pm by using our Wraparound.

The 2019 ISI Report stated: 'Children entering the Early Years Foundation Stage (EYFS) make rapid progress from their starting points, with many achieving at levels beyond age-related expectations at the end of Reception. As they engage in well-planned and challenging activities, they develop high level skills and apply their knowledge to solve problems... Preparatory School pupils continue to develop excellent skills, knowledge and understanding, supported by exciting topics and high expectations. The evidence available from standardised assessments, lesson observations, interviews and work scrutiny shows that many pupils exceed age related expectations, and some achieve exceptional performance levels.'

Charitable status. Brentwood School (part of Sir Antony Browne's School Trust, Brentwood) is a Registered Charity, number 1153605. It exists for the purpose of educating children.

Brighton College Nursery, Pre-Prep & Prep School

Years 4 to 8:
Walpole Lodge, Walpole Road, Brighton, East Sussex BN2 0EU

Tel: 01273 704210
email: prepoffice@brightoncollege.net

Nursery to Year 3:
Eastern Road, Brighton, East Sussex BN2 5JJ

Tel: 01273 704259
email: prepprepoffice@brightoncollege.net

website: www.brightoncollege.net
Twitter: @BCNPPS
Facebook: @BCNPPS
Instagram: @BCNPPS

Chairman of Governors: The Lord Mogg, KCMG

Headmaster: **John Weeks**, BA Hons, PGCE

Senior Deputy Head: Joanne Wergan, BA Hons, PGCE

Deputy Heads:

Kathryn White, BA Hons, PGCE

Phil Smith, BA Hons, PGCE

Liz Kelly, MEd, PGCE, NPQSL [maternity leave]

Ant Falkus, BSc Hons [maternity cover]

Jonno Melia, BSc Hons, PGCE

Registrar: Alison Westbrook, BA Hons, PGCE

Age Range. 3–13.
Number of Pupils. 524
Fees per term (2021–2022). From £3,660 (Reception) to £7,020 (Year 8).

Brighton College Nursery, Pre-Prep & Prep School is a co-educational school, which offers a broad curriculum taught to high standards by dedicated and energetic staff. The Nursery & Pre-Prep cares for children from Nursery to Year 3 in a purpose-built building with playing fields, overlooking the sea. Years 4 to 8 are housed at on their own site situated adjacent to the College. Both sites are urban, but enjoy close proximity to the sea, the South Downs and the vibrant sports and culture of Brighton, where an annual arts festival is held in May. Some of the excellent facilities provided by Brighton College are shared, including the College Chapel, the School of Science and Sport, playing fields, a purpose-built Recital Hall and the Great Hall.

From Reception, our children benefit from specialist lessons in art, music, French, Mandarin, library, PE, games and swimming on its own well-equipped site. From Year 4 upwards, specialist teaching is broadened to include design technology, LAMDA, our innovative HEALTH curriculum, Spanish and German.

Pastoral care is strong and a culture of kindness is commonplace and reinforced in assemblies, within the curriculum and during form time. The motto from Nursery to Year 8 is 'Be Good. Be Kind. Be Honest. Be the Best You'.

Academic standards are high and are one of the foundations upon which school life is built, along with the broad range of subjects taught. A variety of teaching methods is used – the key principle being that children enjoy their lessons and thus develop a love for learning.

Learning Support teachers can provide specialist teaching on a 1:1 basis or in small groups for pupils with an identified need.

Sport is a very important part of the life at the school. Girls and boys games teaching begins in Year 1 and includes netball, hockey, football, rugby, cricket, athletics and swimming.

The school is well known for its strength across the performing arts. Thirty-five visiting music teachers provide tuition for a large number of pupils who learn a wide variety of instruments. There are two orchestras, a concert band and three choirs organised by the music department.

Drama clubs and lessons are available from Year 3 and there are opportunities for children to perform during the academic year through assemblies, recitals, Chapel services and annual drama productions and musicals. The Brighton College School of Dance is thriving and many pupils attend classes after school during the week and on Saturdays.

The school runs a large number of clubs and activities after school and at lunchtimes for pupils from Reception and there is a range of school bus routes for pupils from Year 4. Children attending Nursery can stay for optional, themed afternoons which include yoga, French and art.

The Admissions team hold regular events for prospective pupils and their families or can arrange individual visits. Open Mornings, taster days and themed mornings take place throughout the year, alongside taster and assessment days for pupils wishing to join the school. For more information contact prepadmissions@brightoncollege.net or 01273 704343.

Charitable status. Brighton College is a Registered Charity, number 307061. It exists to provide high quality education for boys and girls aged 3–18.

BGS Infants and Juniors

Elton Road, Bristol BS8 1SR

Tel:	0117 973 6109
email:	admissions@bgs.bristol.sch.uk
website:	www.bristolgrammarschool.co.uk
Twitter:	@bgsbristol
Facebook:	@bgsbristol

Chairman of Governors: Romesh Vaitlingam, BA Hons Oxon, MBE

Head: **Miss Heidi Hughes**, BA Hons, MEd, PGCE

Deputy Head: Mrs Veryan Rookes, BSc Hons, PGCE

Deputy Head: Mrs Vicky Drew, BA Hons, QTS

Assistant Head: Mrs Lucy Bendall, BA Hons, PGCE

Assistant Head: Mrs Kate Conway, BA Hons, PGCE

Age Range. 4–11.
Number of Pupils. 336. Infants 108; Juniors 228

Fees per term (2021–2022). Juniors: Years 3–6 £3,517. Infants: Years 1 & 2 £3,268, Reception £2,992. Fees include lunch.

BGS Infants and Juniors is an independent co-educational day school. It was founded in 1900 and since 2010 has offered Infant as well as Junior provision. The School occupies self-contained buildings on the same site as the Senior School, Bristol Grammar School (*see entry in HMC section*). The School's facilities include a Hall, Library, Music, Art, Science and Technology rooms. Some facilities are shared with the Senior School, particularly the Sports Hall, Performing Arts Centre and Dining Hall. The School now thrives on the happy and purposeful demands of approximately 340 girls and boys aged 4–11 years.

Entry into BGS Infants is by an informal assessment session. Entry for the Junior School is by test and is normally at seven or nine years old (entry to other age groups is subject to the availability of places). Peloquin bursaries are awarded annually and are means-tested. Children who have been members of the School since the start of Year 5 or earlier are offered places in the Senior School following continuous assessment of their progress; other children take the normal Senior School entrance test.

BGS Infants and Juniors aims to provide a rich, broad and balanced curriculum while also maintaining a nurturing environment for children to flourish. The School encourages all pupils to develop their own ideas, giving support so they gain skills and confidence and offering challenges to stretch their thinking. Many subjects are taught by subject specialists, including specialists from the Senior School. Music, art, dance and drama are particularly encouraged with the annual MADD Evening being a particular highlight. There are many clubs and activities including Lego, Gardening, Mindful Colouring, Russian, Board Games, Ukulele, and Coding, as well as extra sports and musical opportunities. One afternoon per week is dedicated to the Activity programme, where children can choose a new challenge or a favourite hobby. In addition, all children in the Infant School, and many Juniors, take part in Forest School and swimming lessons. The children have many opportunities to develop leadership and responsibility; the Infant and Junior School Councils meet regularly with the Head and there is a Charity Committee as well as an Eco-Committee.

A wide range of sports is offered to the pupils at the School's superb playing fields at Failand with its state-of-the-art pavilion. The impressive purpose-built Sports Hall on the main campus provides facilities for indoor PE and has a climbing wall. Pastoral care is provided by the Form Tutors and the Assistant Heads, supported by all teaching staff and the Head. Form Tutors take a lead in ensuring that children are learning and progressing well. A prosperous House system produces many friendships between age-groups, with mentors and buddies showing new pupils the ropes, making sure that things are running smoothly for them. This leads to a strong sense of family and community within the School owing much to the warm and trusting relationships between children, with each other and with their teachers.

Charitable status. Bristol Grammar School is a Registered Charity, number 1104425. The object of the Charity is the provision and conduct in or near the City of Bristol of a day school for boys and girls.

Brockhurst School

Hermitage, Newbury, Berkshire RG18 9UL

Tel: 01635 200293
email: registrar@brockmarl.org
website: www.brockmarl.org.uk

Headmaster: **D J W Fleming**, MA Oxon, MSc

Age Range. 3 to 13.

Number of Boys. 131 Boys (including 13 Boarders).

Fees per term (2021–2022). Full Boarding £9,000, Day £3,900–£6,500. International Boarders £9,250.

Established in 1884, Brockhurst is situated in 500 acres of its own grounds in countryside of outstanding beauty, but is only four miles from access to the M4. The school is located on the same site as Marlston House Girls' Preparatory School which occupies separate, listed buildings. Boys and Girls are educated separately, but the two schools join forces for drama, music and many hobbies. In this way, Brockhurst and Marlston House aim to combine the best features of the single-sex and co-educational systems: academic excellence and social mixing. The schools have built up a fine reputation for high standards of pastoral care given to each pupil within a caring, family establishment. (*See also entry for Marlston House School.*)

The Pre-Prep School, Ridge House, is a co-educational department for children aged 3 to 6½.

Boys are prepared for entry to all Independent Senior Schools and there is an excellent scholarship record.

All boys play Soccer, Rugby, Hockey and Cricket and take part in Athletics, Cross Country and Swimming (25m indoor heated pool). Additional activities include Riding (own ponies), Fencing, Judo, Shooting (indoor rifle range) and Tennis (indoor court and three hard courts). Facilities for gymnastics and other sporting activities are provided in a purpose-built Sports Hall. Year 7 pupils make a week-long visit to a Château in France as part of their French language studies.

Music and art are important features of the curriculum and a good number of pupils have won scholarships to senior schools in recent years. The school has a dedicated Music School and professionally designed Theatre.

Where appropriate, pupils can be transported by members of staff to and from airports if parents are serving in the armed forces or otherwise working overseas.

Bromsgrove Preparatory & Pre-Preparatory School

Old Station Road, Bromsgrove, Worcs B60 2BU

Tel: 01527 579679

Pre-Preparatory:
Avoncroft House, Hanbury Road, Bromsgrove, Worcs B60 4JS

Tel: 01527 579679

email: admissions@bromsgrove-school.co.uk
website: www.bromsgrove-school.co.uk
Twitter: @BromsSchool
Facebook: @BromsgroveSchool
Instagram: @bromsgroveschool

Chairman of Governors: Mr Paul West, QPM

Headmaster: **Mr M Marie**, BSc, PGCE

Age Range. 2–13.

Number of Pupils. Prep School (7–13): 208 day boys, 212 day girls, 61 boy boarders, 36 girl boarders. Pre-Preparatory & Nursery (3–7): 120 boys, 121 girls.

Fees per term (2021–2022). Nursery: £3,045 (full-time); Pre-Prep: £2,865–£3,155; Prep: £4,175–£5,415 (day), £8,700–£10,730 (full boarding), £6,345–£7,680 (weekly boarding).

Forces Bursaries and, from 11+, scholarships (academic, art and music) are available.

Bromsgrove Preparatory School feeds the adjacent 990-strong Senior School. (*See Bromsgrove School entry in HMC section.*) The sites covering 100 acres offer exclusive and shared facilities, with a combined Prep and Senior Performing Arts Complex opened in November 2017, which gives outstanding performance and rehearsal facilities to the School. Boarding at prep is thriving with a dedicated boarding house (Page House) for 85 boys and girls, this has recently been extended by the addition of Senior Page for pupils in Year 8. This allows the School's youngest boarders to live together in modern and comfortable surroundings. Other recent improvements include a new suite of classrooms, an upgrading of the dining hall, a new science laboratory, refurbishment of the library, main hall and sports hall. Pupils have access to a flourishing Forest School. Teachers working in both Senior and Preparatory Schools ensure continuity of ethos and expectation.

Academic, sporting and cultural facilities are extensive and outstanding.

Pupils are admitted at the age of 7+ with another substantial intake at 11+ but pupils, including boarders, are admitted throughout the age range up to 13. Admission to the School is by Entrance Test supported by a report from the current school. Year 5 and 6 pupils are assessed during the course of the year; the outcome of these assessments allow them to be guaranteed a place in Bromsgrove Senior School two years later. Pupils admitted at age 11 are also guaranteed entry to the Senior School.

Prep School boarding is flourishing and the junior boarding houses are lively, homely environments where pupils are cared for by resident houseparents and a team of tutors. The School aims to make a boarder's first experience of life away from home enjoyable and absorbing.

All academic lessons are timetabled from Monday to Friday, with Saturdays offering an optional and flexible programme of activities and sports fixtures, the majority of pupils attend for activities on a Saturday. The School has a national reputation in a number of sports.

The aim of the School is to provide a first-class education, which identifies and develops the potential of individual pupils, academically, culturally and socially. It prepares them to enter the Senior School with confidence. In the Preparatory School, there is a purposeful and lively atmosphere. Mutual trust, respect and friendship exist between staff and pupils. The high quality and dedication of the teaching staff, favourable teacher to pupil ratio and regular monitoring of performance ensure that the natural spontaneity and inquisitiveness of this age group are directed purposefully. The latest ISI Inspection (2016) found the School to be excellent in every category.

The pastoral care system is rooted in the School's Christian heritage and firmly founded on the form tutor. It is designed to ensure that every pupil is recognised as an important individual and that their development is nurtured.

The School has its own feeder Pre-Preparatory School which takes children from the age of 2. The clear majority of children transfer to the Prep School at the end of Year 2. Situated just a mile away in the spacious tree-lined grounds of an old manor house, the Pre-Preparatory School has spacious and light classrooms and delightful outdoor areas for the popular Forest School. The Headmaster is Head of both the Preparatory and Pre-Preparatory sections, giving good continuity and communication between the School. High teacher to pupil ratios and small class sizes ensure each pupil's individual needs are met.

Charitable status. Bromsgrove School is a Registered Charity, number 1098740. It exists to provide education for boys and girls.

Brontë House
The Junior School of Woodhouse Grove

Apperley Lane, Apperley Bridge, Bradford, West Yorkshire BD10 0PQ

Tel: 0113 250 2811
email: enquiries@brontehouse.co.uk
website: www.woodhousegrove.co.uk
Twitter: @BronteHouse_
Facebook: @brontehouseschool

Chairman of Governors: A Wintersgill, FCA

Head: **Mrs Sarah Chatterton**

Assistant Head (*Ashdown*): Mrs A Hinchliffe

Assistant Head (*Upper School*): Mrs F Pearson

Assistant Head (*Lower School*): Mrs H J Simpson

Office Manager: Mrs K Bedford

Admissions: Mrs J Amos

Age Range. 2–11 Co-educational.

Number of Pupils. 285 Boys and Girls.

Fees per term (2021–2022). £3,570–£4,326 (day). Ashdown Lodge Nursery and Reception: £3,255 (full day). Fees are graduated according to age. The day fee covers an extended day from 7.30 am to 6.00 pm; there are no extra charges for breakfast, tea or the majority of supervised activities after lessons. Options of term time only, term time plus 8 weeks and 51 week contracts are available for Nursery care.

At Brontë House we welcome children to Ashdown Lodge, our Early Years setting, from the age of two years old. In Pre-Nursery and Nursery, there are three types of child care options to meet the different requirements of our families: term time only, term time plus 8 weeks holiday care and 51 week contracts.

The School is situated in its own grounds, a short distance from the Senior School, close to both Leeds and Bradford and with easy access to Leeds/Bradford Airport and the Yorkshire Dales National Park.

Our hard work has been recognised by the latest Independent Schools Inspectorate inspection which rated both Brontë House and Woodhouse Grove as Excellent. The inspectors came away with very clear evidence of the Values that we seek to promote. They recognised our outstanding academic and co-curricular programme and our aim to ensure that all our pupils reach their full potential.

During their time in Foundation Stage, we aim to develop a child's ability and self-confidence, encouraging good behaviour and consideration for others. Children are provided with a stimulating programme of learning and play within a calm and relaxed atmosphere, providing a framework for every individual to fulfil their potential ready for the next stage of their education.

The EYFS curriculum is followed, beginning in Nursery and lasting for two years. Language and literacy, mathematics, knowledge and understanding of the world, physical and creative development are promoted in preparation for the transfer to Key Stage One.

By encouraging a child's intellectual, creative, sporting and personal development, we aim to get the best from our children in the classroom, on the games field, in music, drama and all other activities. We also offer bushcraft lessons to all pupils, appropriate to their age, where they learn about the outdoors, nature and survival skills. The broad academic curriculum covers a wide range of subjects, including foreign languages, but with particular emphasis on ensuring a strong foundation in reading, writing, mathematics and science.

As children progress through the school they are encouraged to take increasing responsibility and to show consideration for others. Friendship, trust and courtesy are promoted so our children have a sound foundation as they move up to Woodhouse Grove at the end of Year Six.

We aim to encourage every pupil to develop his or her potential by participating in a variety of activities both as part of the curriculum and extracurricular. As they progress through the school, sport plays an increasingly significant role in the life of the children and there are plenty of opportunities for pupils to be involved in team games and individual sports, which encourage not only physical achievement but also a healthy outlook for enjoying school life to the full.

As with sports, music and drama also play an important part of life at Brontë House. All children are encouraged to learn an instrument. The music curriculum is a mixture of traditional and modern with opportunities for composing and performing. There are many choirs and ensembles and the children are regularly offered the chance to take part in concerts and festivals. Housed in spacious rooms on the top floor of Brontë House, our children are given excellent opportunities to develop musically and creatively.

Charitable status. Woodhouse Grove School is part of the Methodist Independent Schools Trust, which is a Registered Charity, number 1142794.

Brooke Priory School

Station Approach, Oakham, Rutland LE15 6QW

Tel: 01572 724778
email: communications@brooke.rutland.sch.uk
website: www.brooke.rutland.sch.uk
Twitter: @Brooke_Priory
Facebook: @brookepriory

Headmaster: **Mr Duncan Flint**, BSc Hons, PGCE

Age Range. 2 to 11 years (co-educational).

Number of Pupils. 135: 119 (age 4+ to 11); 16 (Nursery, age 2 to 4).

Fees per term (2021–2022). £2,150–£3,650.

Staff. There are 17 qualified members of the teaching staff.

Brooke Priory is a day Preparatory School for boys and girls. The school was founded in 1989 and moved into its own purpose-built building in February 1995. Since then it has doubled its classroom provision, established a Nursery, fully-networked Computer Suite, state-of-the-art Resources Centre, Theatre, Art & DT Studios, individual Music Practice Rooms, Sports Hall and use of Oakham School's sports pitches, astroturf and swimming pool.

Brooke Priory provides a stimulating, caring environment in which children are encouraged to attain their highest potential. Class sizes average 16, in parallel forms, and children are grouped according to ability in Mathematics and English (reading and spelling).

The school delivers a broad and varied curriculum, where every child will participate in Art, Drama, French and Music. Over 60% of children in the Prep Department enjoy individual music lessons and are encouraged to join one of the Choirs and Ensembles.

The curriculum is enriched with a variety of trips, visits (and residential trips for Forms III–VI) which support learning in the classroom.

In recent years, the school has enjoyed 100% pass rate at 11+ to independent schools and local select entry grammar schools. Some children are offered scholarships to independent schools each year including academic, music and sport. In 2020, a record number of scholarships were awarded to children progressing to a variety of senior independent schools. Children progress to senior schools as confident and independent learners.

Sport is an important part of the curriculum. Children swim weekly throughout the year and are coached in a wide variety of games by specialist staff. The main sports are Soccer, Rugby, Hockey, Netball, Cricket, Rounders, Tennis and Athletics.

The original Brooke Priory, which is situated just 1 mile outside Oakham, is set in 30 undulating acres and everyone, from the Nursery to Year VI, visits regularly for Welly Days.

The school offers a wide choice of extracurricular activities.

Before and after school care is available and holiday clubs are enjoyed by many children. Many holiday courses specialise in sport, dance/drama and music.

Broughton Manor Preparatory School

Newport Road, Broughton, Milton Keynes, Buckinghamshire MK10 9AA

Tel: 01908 665234
email: info@bmprep.co.uk
website: www.bmprep.co.uk

Chairman of the Governors: Mr David Pye, BA Hons, Cert Ed, MA Ed Dist, HETC, SEDA III, FRSA, FFSC, FGMS

Headmaster: **Mr Jeremy Smith**, BA, QTS

Headmistress: **Mrs Rachel Smith**, BA, PGCE

Age Range. Nursery 2 months–2½ years. Pre-Prep 2½–7 years. Preparatory Department 7+–11 years.

Number of Pupils. 350 Day Pupils.

Fees per term (2021–2022). Nursery (per week): £305 (2 months–2 years). Pre-Preparatory: £4,240 (2–5 years), £4,412 (6–7 years). Preparatory £4,820 (8–11 years).

Broughton Manor Preparatory School is a well-established, family-owned school, with two sister Pre-Preparatory and Preparatory schools based across Milton Keynes.

Opening hours are 7.30am to 6.30pm for a 35-week academic year and a total of 46 weeks per year, enabling children of working parents to join play schemes in school holidays and to be cared for outside normal daily school hours.

Staff are highly qualified and committed to delivering the very best teaching and levels of care. Academic standards are "excellent", as rated in the most recent ISI Inspection, with pupils being prepared for entry to senior independent schools locally and nationally and to grammar schools. Teaching is structured to take into account the requirements of the National Curriculum, with constant evaluation and assessment for each pupil. Scholarships are offered for those with all-round academic and sporting abilities from the ages of 7+.

The Nursery can be found in the old Manor House, surrounded by spacious grounds.

The Pre-Preparatory and Preparatory Departments are housed in a modern purpose-built building. All departments have access to their own outside Spinney, soft play and extensive playground areas; there is a multi-purpose sports hall, a separate assembly hall and Astroturf court.

State-of-the-art facilities include an Art Studio, high-tech CTS Suite and Science laboratory.

Music and Sport play an important part in the life of the school. Concerts are held, and a wide variety of sport is played, with teams competing regularly against other schools, and additional clubs are held for those wanting to learn specialist activities such as karate, yoga, tennis and ballet.

The school aims to incorporate the best of modern teaching methods and traditional values in a friendly, caring and busy environment, where good work habits and a concern for the needs of others are paramount.

Bruern Abbey School

Chesterton House, Chesterton, Oxfordshire OX26 1UY

Tel: 01869 242448
email: secretary@bruernabbey.org
website: www.bruernabbey.org

Headmaster: **Mr J Floyd**, MA, PGCE

Age Range. Boys 8–16.
Number of Pupils. 154.
Fees per term (2021–2022). Day £8,990, Boarding £10,820, Flexi Boarding £63 per night.

Bruern Abbey School is unique in the marketplace because it is the only school in the country that caters exclusively for children diagnosed with learning difficulties and prepares them for Common Entrance to mainstream public schools; learning difficulties should not preclude academic success. ISI has stated that 'pupils are successfully educated in a secure and nurturing environment where they are given every possible help and encouragement to overcome the challenges presented by their specific learning difficulties'. Bruern provides a tailored education in beautiful surroundings and maintains high expectations for the academic future. We aim to enhance boys' self-esteem, in the firm belief that confidence is the key to academic success. A recent Crested report stated that 'Bruern Abbey is a unique school with its own special way of delivering an all-round education for its pupils. It successfully prepares boys for the Common Entrance Examination whilst at the same time developing each boy into a happy and confident individual'.

Bruern Senior School will open in September 2022, extending provision to provide boys with invaluable support throughout their GCSEs and beyond.

In most other respects, Bruern models itself on traditional preparatory schools, with breadth to the curriculum, including French to Common Entrance, full and varied sports, activities and cultural programmes, and the adherence to good manners, self-discipline and common courtesy. We encourage boys to share their aspirations and their anxieties. Ofsted has stated that 'the school has an incredibly warm and compassionate approach to all the boys' and also that 'pastoral care is exceptional – very understanding and caring staff'.

At Bruern we place great emphasis on experiencing all that prep school life has to offer; specialist teaching should not mean missing out on all the fun. We also make every effort, despite our somewhat diminutive size, to give the boys an action-packed time – be it musical, theatrical, cultural or sporting.

Bruern differs from traditional preparatory schools in many ways which allow our boys to succeed at Common Entrance and be ready for life beyond. These are regarded as the 'pillars' upon which the School's ethos and reputation, founded by the Principal in 1989, still stand, not to be compromised under any circumstances, and ingrained within the mission statement. They are not necessarily in any order of priority, but are:

- a clear focus on literacy and numeracy, with nine periods each of English and Mathematics a week. We have approximately twice as many English and Maths lessons as standard prep schools for all our Junior School boys, and there are two teachers in each class for these key subjects;
- small classes (eleven pupils or fewer) which allows boys more individual attention in class;
- limited withdrawal for remedial support, as boys needs are met in class;
- the extensive use of IT as a tool with which to deliver the curriculum;
- the use of laptops in lessons. For those who have difficulty in expressing themselves as swiftly or as coherently on paper as they do in speech, this is an absolute godsend;
- the teaching of reading as a distinct curriculum subject;
- the importance attached to good food and to finding the time for children within their busy schedule to eat, talk, play and relax together without the distraction of television or electronic games.

Bryanston Knighton House

Durweston, Blandford Forum, Dorset DT11 0PY

Tel: 01258 452065
email: admissions-bkh@bryanstonkh.co.uk
website: www.bryanston.co.uk/bryanstonkh
Twitter: @knighton_house
Facebook: @knighton.house.school
Instagram: @knighton.house.school
LinkedIn: /company/knighton-house-school

Chair of Governors: Mr Julian Greenhill

Head: **Mr Will Lockett**, BA, PGCE

Age Range. 3–13.
Number of Pupils. Prep School: 70; The Orchard, Pre-Prep and Nursery: 35.
Fees per term (2021–2022). Boarders £5,975–£7,828; Day: Prep £3,862.50–£5,098.50 Pre-Prep £2,781, Nursery: £2,395 (full time but excluding Early Years funding). There are no compulsory extras.

Established in 1950, Bryanston Knighton House is an exceptional friendly co-ed day and boarding school for pupils aged 7–13, with an 'outstanding' pre-prep for children aged 3–7.

In 2020, Bryanston Knighton House made the decision to move progressively towards co-education. Consequently, for the first time, the School is now accepting boys up to and including Year Six as boarding pupils and Year Seven and Eight as day pupils. Work is now proceeding on a planned refurbishment of the School's boarding accommodation in preparation for the move to a full co-education environment in September 2022.

Bryanston Knighton House keeps pace with the expectations of the 21st Century, while nurturing its unique traditional values. We pride ourselves on our pastoral care and the opportunities we offer children through a crucial developmental stage of their life. We encourage independent thinking and learning, and outdoor play is a key part of the school day. In a delightful country setting, the School provides a safe but challenging environment in which children can discover their strengths, take risks and make friends. Boarding is entirely flexible and ponies and pets are all welcome.

The small class sizes and high staff-to-pupil ratio ensures individual attention. The scholarships and awards won from Bryanston Knighton House reflect academic, musical, artistic and all-rounder prowess; there is a strong artistic and musical tradition. Team sports and swimming have an all-year-round place in the timetable. There are many extracurricular activities including riding, triathlon, tetrathlon, dance, drama and outdoor environmental pursuits.

This careful balance of academic subjects and extracurricular activities encourages all aspects of personal growth. The size of Bryanston Knighton House ensures that each pupil is known by everyone; each child has an identity and is respected for their individuality.

Bryanston Knighton House feeds a wide range of senior schools, both co-ed and single-sex.

Charitable status. Bryanston Knighton House School Limited is a Registered Charity, number 306316.

The Buchan School

Westhill, Castletown, Isle of Man IM9 1RD

Tel: 01624 820481
email: admissions@kwc.im
website: www.kwc.im
Twitter: @kwciom
Facebook: @kwciom
Instagram: @kwcandthebuchanschool
LinkedIn: /school/king-william's-college

Chairman of the Governors: Mr P B Clucas, BA, BSc Hons

Headteacher: **Mrs Janet Billingsley-Evans**, BSc

Age Range. 4–11.
Number of Pupils. 166 (87 boys, 79 girls).
Fees per term (2021–2022). Day only: £3,994 (P1–P3), £5,200 (Forms 1–4).

After more than a century of independence, mainly as a Girls' School, The Buchan School amalgamated, in 1991, with King William's College to form a single continuous provision of Independent Education on the Isle of Man.

As the Preparatory School to King William's College (*see entry in HMC section*), The Buchan School provides an education of all-round quality for boys and girls until the age of 11 when most pupils proceed naturally to the Senior School although the curriculum meets the needs of Common Entrance, Scholarship and Entrance Examinations to other Independent Senior Schools.

The school buildings are clustered round Westhill House, the centre of the original estate, in fourteen acres of partly wooded grounds. The whole environment, close to the attractive harbour of Castletown, is ideally suited to the needs of younger children. They are able to work and play safely and develop their potential in every direction.

Classes are small throughout, providing considerable individual attention. A well-equipped Nursery provides Pre-School education for up to 65 children. At the age of 4, boys and girls are accepted into the Pre-Preparatory Department. They work largely in their own building in bright, modern classrooms and also make use of the specialist Preparatory School facilities where they proceed three years later.

The School is particularly well-equipped with ICT facilities extending down to the Pre-Prep Department. There is a Pavilion with fields marked out for a variety of team games and a multi-purpose area which is used for Rugby, Football, Hockey and Netball.

There is emphasis on traditional standards in and out of the classroom, with an enterprising range of activities outside normal lessons. Music is strong – both choral and instrumental – and there is energetic involvement in Art, Drama and Sport.

The school strives for high academic standards, aiming to ensure that all pupils enjoy the benefits of a rounded education, giving children every opportunity to develop their individual talents from an early age.

Entry is usually by interview and school report (if applicable) and the children may join The Buchan School at any time, providing there is space. The School is a happy, friendly community where new pupils integrate quickly socially and academically.

Charitable status. King William's College is a Registered Charity, number 615. It exists for the provision of high quality education for boys and girls.

Buckingham Preparatory School

458 Rayners Lane, Pinner, Middlesex HA5 5DT

Tel: 020 8866 2737
email: office@buckprep.org
website: www.buckprep.org
Twitter: @BuckinghamPrep
Facebook: @buckinghamprep

Chairman of Governors: Mrs Lynn Grimes

Head Teacher: **Mrs Sarah Hollis**

Age Range. Boys 3–11.
Number of Pupils. 114.
Fees per term (2021–2022). £3,315–£4,250 (includes lunches).

Buckingham Preparatory School (BPS) is a small school which offers its pupils an extremely high level of academic education and pastoral care. An ISI inspection in May 2017 rated BPS as "Excellent" and "Outstanding" in each and every aspect of our offering in every part of the school.

Our teaching staff have been universally praised for their "constantly warm and encouraging guidance" and pupil progress is put down to our teachers' "highly effective use of clear explanations" and "because all teachers focus strongly on improving individual pupils' learning and achievement".

With a maximum class size of 18 throughout the school, individual attention is guaranteed.

BPS pupils consistently achieve excellent academic results due to the inspirational teaching, commitment and professionalism of its highly qualified teaching staff. Each year, Year 6 pupils gain offers to the major Independent and Grammar schools in the area and beyond. In the majority of cases, this is to the boys' first-choice schools, often with scholarships.

BPS also prides itself in its results in other areas of the curriculum; areas which are vital in building confidence and self-esteem. Achievement in sport, music and drama is excellent. The pupils regularly take part in local fixtures, often winning inter-school tournaments in cricket, unihoc, football, rugby swimming and cross-country, and other sports. A thriving choir and school plays allow the pupils plentiful opportunities for performance. Speech & Drama classes (LAMDA) and individual instrumental tuition are also on offer.

The Expressive Arts Week, when pupils have the opportunity of participating in approximately 14 categories of events, is also a focal point of the academic year allowing all boys from the very youngest to demonstrate their individual talents.

The School also believes in forging a strong Parent/Teacher partnership so that parents feel they have a vital role to play in the education of their child. A thriving Parent/Teacher Association also organises as many as three major fundraising events during the academic year which are always well supported and are highlights of the year.

At BPS we do not select pupils based simply on their current academic abilities, but on their desire to learn and achieve. We believe in potential. We believe that if your child wants to succeed, then we will enable him to do so.

Charitable status. The E Ivor Hughes Educational Foundation is a Registered Charity, number 293623.

Burgess Hill Girls – Prep School

Keymer Road, Burgess Hill, West Sussex RH15 0EG

Tel:	01444 241050
email:	admissions@burgesshillgirls.com
website:	www.burgesshillgirls.com
Twitter:	@BHillGirls
Facebook:	@BurgessHillGirls
LinkedIn:	/burgess-hill-girls

Chairman of Governors: Dr Alison Smith MB, ChB, MRCGP

Head: Mrs E Laybourn, BEd Hons

Deputy Head of School and Head of Pre-Prep and Prep School: **Mrs H Cavanagh**, BA Hons, QTS

Deputy Head of Prep School: Mrs S Collins, BA Hons, PGCE

Age Range. Girls 2½–11.

Number of Pupils. 125.

Fees per term (2021–2022). £2,270–£5,150.

Burgess Hill Girls is a day and boarding school for girls between 2½ and 18 years. We welcome boys into our Nursery (2½ to 4 years).

The school stands in 14 acres of beautiful grounds close to the centre of Burgess Hill town. It is a five minute walk from Burgess Hill railway station and transport is provided to collect girls from outlying areas of East and West Sussex.

It is small enough that pupils are known as individuals yet large enough to offer breadth, choice and opportunity. Girls are able to strive for excellence wherever their talents lie and the mix of ages, working together on the same site, gives the school a special character. The aim of the school is to provide each girl with the opportunity to realise her potential and the focus is firmly on girls and the way they learn.

The Prep School provides a broad, varied and stimulating curriculum within a warm and caring environment. Every girl is helped to reach her full potential socially, physically, emotionally and intellectually. Whilst academic achievement is important, the school aims to educate young people for life, providing education in the broadest sense.

The Prep School offers small classes and subject teachers for music, sport and languages. It has an excellent reputation for Music and the Prep School Choir have sung at St Paul's and Chichester Cathedrals.

All Prep School pupils take part in sports, with daily PE lessons. There are many opportunities to play against other schools in a range of sports and many pupils achieve sporting success at local, county and national level.

The Prep School offers fully-equipped subject-specific classrooms for Music, ICT, Art, Science and Technology and access to all the sports facilities on the school campus plus a Learning Hub incorporating a library – a large learning space with access to iPads and an interactive electronic screen.

The Pre-Prep and Nursery are based in the Little Oaks building with bright, open classrooms and its own hall and library. The Pre-Prep and Prep School have a playground with a wooden adventure trail and outdoor classroom. The Nursery has an equally exciting specific outdoor play area.

Entrance to the Prep School is by assessment and school reference. Scholarships are awarded each year for academic and/or musical excellence into Years 5–6 inclusive.

"The School is almost non-selective and yet achieves better results than many more competitive schools. The holistic approach to education, where equal value is placed on academic achievement and softer skills, produces extremely confident young women who grow up to believe they can be whatever they want to be." *Good Schools Guide 2019*

Charitable status. Burgess Hill Girls is a Registered Charity, number 307001 (formerly known as Burgess Hill School for Girls).

Bute House Preparatory School for Girls

Bute House, Luxemburg Gardens, Hammersmith, London W6 7EA

Tel: 020 7603 7381
email: mail@butehouse.co.uk
website: www.butehouse.co.uk

Chair of Governors: Mr Jonathan Beckitt

Head: **Ms Sian Bradshaw**, BEd Hons

Age Range. 4–11.
Number of Pupils. 309 Day Girls.
Fees per term (2021–2022). £6,380 inclusive of lunches.

Bute House overlooks extensive playing fields and is housed in a large, bright, modern building. Facilities include a science laboratory, an art room, a food technology room, a music studio, a drama studio, a multi-purpose hall and a spacious, well-stocked library which extends to separate reading pods. A well-qualified, enthusiastic and experienced staff teach a broad curriculum, which emphasises both the academic and the pastoral side of school life. Information Technology is an integral part of the curriculum and the Computing classrooms are all equipped with multimedia machines. Laptops, iPads and Chromebooks are also widely used for individual or class work. French and Spanish are taught from Year 1.

Sports include swimming, gymnastics, dance, tennis, football, netball, kwik cricket and athletics which are taught on our excellent on-site facilities. Full use is made of our local area and all that London has to offer. Residential trips further afield are also offered to the girls from Years 3–6.

Girls are encouraged to take an active part in school life from the start. There is a democratically elected School Council and regular school meetings, run by the girls, when all pupils are able to put their views forward, as well as to volunteer for key roles around the school. A wide variety of extracurricular activities are also available, such as cookery, Claymation, curve stitching, drama, knitting, Karate, musical theatre and unihoc, to name but a few.

The school aims to provide academic excellence in a non-competitive, happy environment where girls are encouraged to be confident, articulate and independent and where courtesy and consideration are expected. All girls are encouraged to 'run their own best race' and thrive in a nurturing and happy environment.

There is a flourishing Parents Association who are closely involved with events throughout the school year, as well as a very active Governing body who participate in the running of the school.

Entry is by ballot at age 4 and by assessment at age 7.

Caldicott

Crown Lane, Farnham Royal, Buckinghamshire SL2 3SL

Tel: 01753 649300
email: admissions@caldicott.com
website: www.caldicott.com
Twitter: @CaldicottSchool
Facebook: @Caldicott.School
Instagram: @caldicottschool
LinkedIn: /company/caldicott-school

Chairman of the Board of Governors: M S Swift

Headmaster: **Jeremy Banks**, BA Hons, MEd

Age Range. 7–13.
Number of Boys. 105 Boarders and 138 Day Boys.
Fees per term (2021–2022). Year 7 and 8 Boarding: £10,271; Year 5 and 6 Boarding: £9,244; Year 5 and 6 Day: £6,967; Year 3 and 4 Day: £6,246.

Caldicott is a thriving day and boarding prep school for boys aged 7–13 in South Buckinghamshire. Situated in 40 acres of magnificent grounds, we are located just 15 miles from Heathrow Airport and 30 minutes from West London where we operate a daily return bus service from Chiswick, Brook Green, Notting Hill and the local area.

Our founder, Mr J Heald Jenkins, believed decency, tolerance and humanity would enable each boy to 'shine their light on the world'. Today, his vision remains relevant and a source of inspiration.

At Caldicott we place each individual boy at the centre of our day and boarding experience and believe happiness is key to fulfilling potential. Offering flexi and occasional boarding to Years 3–6 allows our busy parents some manoeuvrability in their schedules, it also eases the boys' transition into weekly boarding in Years 7 and 8. We strive to keep Caldicott at the forefront of best practice and we work hard to be regarded as a leading light in education.

We have the reputation as one of the best prep schools in the UK with an excellent record in preparing boys for scholarships and Common Entrance to top UK public schools including Eton, Harrow, Radley and Wellington. We have a strong and dynamic staffroom of dedicated and inspirational teachers and professionals. As a result, we have high academic standards and expectations, an outstanding record in art, sport, music and drama scholarships, excellent pastoral provision and a wide range of extra-curricular activities in which all boys can take part.

We are committed to an education that has the wellbeing of each boy at its heart; to develop individuals who thrive and flourish in the fullest sense. We aim to equip our children to be happy and confident, form lasting relationships with others and develop strategies for coping with the challenges life throws at them – essential skills for succeeding in today's complex, fast-moving world. Our community is not only warm and welcoming from the staff and pupil body, but also our parents form the Friends of Caldicott who add another layer of friendship and happiness.

Most of all, we believe in excellence in education, treasuring tradition and cherishing childhood. We are a school where boys fulfil their academic potential and are guided to become all-rounders, with the character and grit to succeed.

Charitable status. Caldicott is a Registered Charity, number 310631. Its purpose is to provide education for the young.

Cargilfield School

45 Gamekeeper's Road, Edinburgh EH4 6HU

Tel: 0131 336 2207
email: admin@cargilfield.com
website: www.cargilfield.com
Twitter: @cargilfield

Chairman of the Board of Governors: Mr David Nisbet, BA Hons

Headmaster: **Mr Rob Taylor**, BA, PGCE

Assistant Headmaster: Mr David Walker, BA Hons

Deputy Heads:

Mrs Emma Buchanan, MEd, BEd

Ms Anjali Dholakia, MA Hons, LLB, Dip LP, PGDE

Mr Ross Murdoch, BEd Hons

Age Range. 3–13.

Number of Children. 290

Fees per term (2021–2022). Boarding: £7,050 (weekly). Day Pupils: £5,750, Pre-Prep £3,630, Nursery £2,107–£3,527.

Cargilfield is the oldest independent boarding and day prep school in Scotland, for more than 300 boys and girls, aged 3–13 years. Each child has an extensive range of opportunities to learn, explore and discover before they leave Cargilfield to join leading senior schools across Edinburgh, Scotland and the whole of the UK with no particular tie to any school. Children leave with confident, lively minds, secure values and a sense of identity and community spirit that serves them well for their future lives. We achieve this by delivering a broad and challenging education in a supportive and caring family-led environment. As a prep school, Cargilfield offers your child a chance to reap the benefits and flourish as one of the oldest pupils in the school with positions of responsibility and significance. Without the influence of much older pupils, we can limit the influences that force children to grow up faster than we want and develop instead, qualities of courtesy, self-reliance and assurance.

A small prep school means we get to know our pupils well so that we can guide them towards a senior school that will best suit their needs and reflect your priorities for their education. Small classes, good teaching and high expectations mean that we can achieve high standards for a range of abilities. In addition, a broad curriculum, both inside and outside the classroom, will develop your child's all-round abilities. We play sport every day from age 8 onwards and offer regular opportunities for music, art, design and drama. This is supported by over 40 different clubs, looking to inspire new talents and a wide range of

interests. Try fly-tying or snowboarding, highland dance or computer coding.

As your child grows through the school, there are opportunities to challenge and stretch them further with opportunities to join evening activities, to board on a weekly or flexible basis or to join us on weekend camps or school-based activity weekends.

Charitable status. Cargilfield School is a Registered Charity, number SC005757.

Carrdus School

Overthorpe Hall, Nr Banbury, Oxfordshire OX17 2BS

Tel: 01295 263733
email: office@carrdusschool.com
website: www.carrdusschool.co.uk
Twitter: @carrdusschool
Facebook: @carrdusschool
Instagram: @carrdusschool

Chair of Governors: Mrs D Chism

Headmaster: **Mr Edward Way**, BSc Hons

Deputy Head: Mr Mark Tetley, BA Hons

Age Range. Boys & Girls 3–11 (Nursery Class for children 3–4½)

Number of Day Pupils. 120

Fees per term (2021–2022). From £3,825–£4,335 (Sibling discounts available).

Carrdus School is a co-educational day prep school for girls and boys aged 3–11 years, nestled within 11 acres of beautiful grounds, located on the outskirts of Banbury, Oxfordshire and bordering nearby Northamptonshire, Buckinghamshire and Warwickshire. The Carrdus Pathway is a holistic approach to learning, forming strong relationships, instilling confidence and nurturing each child as they make their way through the school; ensuring they achieve their full potential and setting the foundations for academic success.

The teaching staff consists of highly qualified individuals, including the advantage of a plethora of specialist subject teachers from parent school, Tudor Hall. The school has an excellent record of success in examinations, regularly sending pupils to well-known independent senior schools, with many achieving Academic Scholarships.

The on-site facilities are vast for this modest school and include a heated outdoor swimming pool which the children use on a weekly basis, two full sized tennis courts, a purpose built Art Studio, Science Lab, a multi-use Sports Hall and new Sports pitches. Music, Sport, Drama and Art are highly valued in the curriculum. There are regular sessions of Outdoor Learning and STEM where children can get really hands-on and are encouraged to learn through doing. The girls and boys at Carrdus also have the advantage of daily use of Tudor Hall's extensive Sports, Arts and Science facilities.

The aim of the school is to produce confident, independent and resilient children, who are happy and engaged in all that they do, and who have the satisfaction of reaching their own highest academic and personal standards.

Charitable status. Carrdus School is part of Tudor Hall School, which is a Registered Charity, number 1042783.

Casterton, Sedbergh Preparatory School

Kirkby Lonsdale, Cumbria LA6 2SG

Tel: 015242 79200
email: prepoffice@sedberghprep.org
website: www.sedberghprep.org
Twitter: @Sedbergh_Prep
Facebook: @SedberghPrep
LinkedIn: /casterton-sedbergh-preparatory-school

Chairman of Governors: Mr Richard Gledhill

Headmaster: **Mr Will Newman**, MA

Age Range. 6 months–13 years Co-educational.

Number of Pupils. 213.

Fees per term (2021–2022). Day £2,953–£5,779, Full Boarding £7,178–£8,564, Weekly Boarding £6,701–£8,087.

Casterton, Sedbergh Preparatory School is situated in the spectacular rural location of the Lune Valley between the Lake District and Yorkshire Dales. The School offers space to grow and learn and lays the foundations for nurturing the resilience our children will need as young adults and the tenacity essential for achieving high standards. This is evident in the unrivalled activities' programme and around the clock pastoral care, available to all our pupils. Breadth of opportunity and depth of involvement is what sets us apart. Maths competitions, explosions and dissections in Science lessons, pony care at our stables and collecting eggs from the School chickens – all these create outstanding memories for the children at Sedbergh Prep.

Facilities at the School are first class and include a high-spec Design, Technology and Engineering Department, seven Science laboratories, floodlit astro and tennis courts, a theatre, heated pool, equestrian centre and several computer suites. We are excited by the curiosity and thirst for learning that each child, regardless of their academic ability, naturally displays. We work hard to allow each child the time to question and develop their thoughts independently, leading to fresh discoveries in an innovative learning environment. Our curriculum is ambitious; we believe this is the best way to prepare our pupils, not only for the remainder of their educational journey, but for the workplace and life itself. Our academic programme facilitates opportunities for the children to discover, apply and communicate what they have learned and we strive to make our pupils independent learners, well-prepared for the next stage in their development.

One of our strengths is a focus on the individual. We are not a School of rote and regurgitation. Rather, we understand that a child's future success is dependent upon their ability to use what they know in a variety of creative ways. Every area of School life, therefore, provides fantastic opportunities for creativity of all kinds. Day in, day out, we encourage pupils to live our ethos of 'give it a go and try

your best', supporting them to face and overcome challenges in all areas of their schooling and beyond.

Our three boarding houses – Beale, Thornfield and Cressbrook – are very much 'home from home' environments and our House Parents support and nurture our boarders, who provide the School with a unique family atmosphere. The Prep School's holistic approach to pastoral care aims to bring out the best in every child. We look to develop young people who are kind, responsible, creative, ambitious, collaborative and courageous – the values that make up our 'Ways of the Wolf' and guide the ethos of the entire Prep School.

The Cavendish School

31 Inverness Street, London NW1 7HB

Tel: 020 7485 1958
email: admissions@cavendish-school.co.uk
website: www.cavendishschool.co.uk
Twitter: @CavendishSchool
Facebook: @The-Cavendish-School
Instagram: @thecavendishschoolcamden

Chair of Governors: Mrs Alice Gotto and Ms Nicola Rushton, Co-Chairs

Headteacher: **Mrs Taryn Lombard**

Age Range. Girls 3–11.

Number of Children. 210 Day Pupils.

Fees per term (2021–2022). Nursery: from £3,050 (mornings only) to £5,250 (full time), flexible according to the number of afternoon sessions. Reception–Year 6: £5,350. Fees include lunch and day trips.

The Cavendish School is a friendly, happy IAPS school for girls aged three to eleven. The school is situated near Regent's Park in the heart of Camden Town with its excellent public transport links. The Cavendish welcomes pupils of all faiths and none.

The school is non-selective at entry and achieves remarkable results. We provide manageable class sizes and high teacher-pupil ratios so that the foundations of a good education and effective study habits are laid from the beginning.

Through a broad and balanced curriculum we provide personalised learning and much specialised teaching, including languages, music, sport and science, which allows our pupils to flourish. Many gain entry and scholarships to top senior schools at 11+. We pride ourselves on ensuring each pupil goes to the senior school where she will thrive and have an excellent record of girls going to their first choice school. (See our website for leavers' destinations.)

There is an extensive programme of extracurricular activities, an extended day including breakfast club and after-school care services and flexible arrangements for nursery-age pupils.

We are very strong in sports, music, drama and art. Class music is taught by specialists; instruction is available in a wide variety of instruments and we have a thriving orchestra and choirs.

The school is housed in well-maintained Victorian buildings and a modern wing with purpose-built ICT facilities. It has recently expanded into an additional new building containing five extra classrooms and a 230-seater multi-use auditorium. It has plenty of outdoor space for sport and recreation, and makes good use of the many resources on our doorstep including Regents Park and all that central London has to offer.

The school maintains close links with the local community in a variety of ways both charitable and educational.

Our most recent inspection report by the Independent Schools Inspectorate awarded us 'excellent' in all areas and is available to read via our website.

Charitable status. The Cavendish School is a Registered Charity, number 312727.

Charlotte House Preparatory School
Nursery, Pre-Prep & Preparatory School for Girls

88 The Drive, Rickmansworth, Herts WD3 4DU

Tel: 01923 772101
email: office@chpschool.co.uk
website: www.charlottehouseprepschool.co.uk
Facebook: @CharlotteHousePrepSchool

Chairman of Governors: Ms Catriona Smith

Headmistress: **Miss P Woodcock**, BA Hons QTS

Age Range. 3–11.
Number of Pupils. 120 Girls.
Fees per term (2021–2022). £1,675–£4,560

Charlotte House is a forward-thinking dynamic school built on traditional values. This winning combination means we instil in our girls all the social and academic tools they need to become independent, successful, confident and caring women.

Our pupils aspire to be the best. We help them discover their talents and encourage them to persevere when they meet challenges. To aid this we teach them a varied curriculum and they are fortunate to have specialist teachers right the way through the school commencing in Nursery.

We are passionate about the learning that goes on outside the classroom walls, whether it is their manners as they move around the school, discovering mini beasts in our beautiful garden or meeting up with their French pen pals in France; we provide the girls with a wealth of experiences to learn more about themselves and the world around them.

Charlotte House encourages the girls to be confident so that they meet challenges head on. We enter many academic and sporting inter-school competitions. We encourage the girls to be confident on stage with termly class assemblies and each girl is involved in an annual play.

At Charlotte House, we recognise the importance of strong links between home and school and provide many opportunities for parents to visit us and find out more about their daughter's progress.

Charlotte House has an excellent record at Secondary Transfer and we have a thorough programme in place to ensure both the girls and their parents feel supported and ready for the challenges secondary transfer poses. Our girls go on to a wide range of schools including state and private schools and the secondary schools often comment on how pleased they are to welcome our girls as they know they will be of a high calibre.

We are a dynamic school whose girls achieve great things!

Charitable status. Charlotte House School Limited is a Registered Charity, number 311075.

Cheam School

Headley, Newbury, Berkshire RG19 8LD

Tel: 01635 268242
Registrar: 01635 267822
email: registrar@cheamschool.co.uk
website: www.cheamschool.com
Twitter: @CheamSchool
Facebook: @CheamSchool
Instagram: @cheamschool
LinkedIn: /company/cheam-school-educational-trust

Cheam is a leading independent, day and boarding prep school, nestled in 100 acres of Berkshire countryside, for pupils aged 3 to 13 years.

Chairman of Governors: R Marsh

Interim Headmaster: **T C Haigh**, BA Birmingham, PGCE

Age Range. 3–13.
Number of Pupils. 90 boarders, 380 day children.
Fees per term (2021–2022). £9,445–£9,775 Boarders (5 nights per week); £3,975–£7,530 Day children.

The School became co-educational in September 1997. A merger with Inhurst House School, formerly situated at Baughurst, and which relocated to the Headley site in 1999, offers parents the opportunity for education from 3–13+ for their sons and daughters.

Bursaries are offered annually for 8 year olds.

Classes are small (maximum 18) and pupils are prepared for the major senior independent schools with Marlborough, Bradfield, St Edward's Oxford, Radley, Eton, Wellington, Sherborne Girls', Pangbourne, St Mary's Calne, Harrow, St Mary's Ascot and Downe House featuring frequently. Recent improvements include excellent facilities for Design Technology and Information Technology, a dedicated Science Building, a refurbished Chapel and Teaching Block, a Music School, a Sports Hall, AstroTurf pitches and much-improved boarding facilities. Dormitories are comfortable, carpeted and curtained.

Rugby, Soccer and Cricket are the major team games for boys; Netball, Rounders, Cricket, Tennis and Hockey for girls. A heated outdoor swimming pool, 6 all-weather tennis courts and a 9-hole golf course in the extensive 80-acre grounds allow a wide range of other sports and pastimes to be enjoyed.

The School is situated half way between Newbury and Basingstoke on the A339 and is within easy reach of the M3 and M4 motorways and the A34 trunk route from Portsmouth, Southampton and Winchester to Oxford and the Midlands. London Heathrow Airport is within an hour's drive.

Charitable status. Cheam School Educational Trust is a Registered Charity, number 290143. It provides high-class education for boarding and day pupils; traditional values; modern thinking; education for the 21st century.

Cheltenham College Prep School

Thirlestaine Road, Cheltenham, Gloucestershire GL53 7AB

Tel: 01242 522697
email: prepadmissions@cheltenhamcollege.org
website: www.cheltenhamcollege.org
Twitter: @cheltprep
Facebook: @cheltprep
Instagram: @cheltprep

President of Council: Mr Bill Straker Nesbit

Head: **Mr Tom O'Sullivan**, LLB Hons Durham, PGCE Cambridge

Age Range. 3–13.

Number of Pupils. 410 (41 boarders, 369 day boys and girls).

Fees per term (2021–2022). Boarders £6,540–£8,520; Day Boys and Girls £2,925–£6,555.

Cheltenham College Prep School is a co-educational preparatory school from 3 to 13. The Pre-Prep Department is located in a separate purpose-built wing. From September 2022, the school will have a brand new, purpose-built nursery school onsite, providing the perfect start to school life for its youngest pupils.

The school stands in a beautiful 15-acre site near the centre of Regency Cheltenham; the town itself being well served by both motorway and rail networks. Pupils enjoy a brand new, dedicated Science and Technology Centre with university grade Science labs and state-of-the-art technology equipment including a laser cutter and 3D printer. Around the school, other excellent facilities include: an art studio, extensive ICT suites, music school, large multi-purpose Assembly Hall, and woodland Forest School. It also benefits from the College's amenities including the stunning College Chapel, spacious sports complex with a 25m indoor swimming pool, floodlit astroturf all-weather pitches, athletics track, squash courts, tennis courts, and fully-equipped science laboratories.

The curriculum is wide and stimulating with all pupils being prepared for 13+ Common Entrance and Scholarship examinations. In addition to the normal academic subjects, all pupils study Art, Music, PE, Information Technology, and Design & Technology, all led by a team of professional and dedicated teachers.

A wide range of sports are available including: rugby, cricket, hockey, cross country, netball, badminton, athletics, golf, gymnastics, squash, ballet, sailing, skiing, horse riding, fencing, archery, swimming, tennis and orienteering. Sporting skills are taught from an early age by a large number of full-time sports professionals and include swimming for the whole school.

The Boarding House aims to provide a 'home from home', with excellent pastoral care and a wide range of extracurricular activities under the supervision of the House Parents. The boarding facilities themselves are large and airy, with plenty of pictures, toys and colourful duvets making the place warm and homely. Regular contact with parents is encouraged with frequent exeat weekends, with flexi-boarding being a popular option for children from Year 3 up. Progress reports are issued three times a term and either formal parent/teacher meetings are held or full reports issued at the end of each term.

Visitors are warmly welcomed and further information is available from the Prep Admissions team, who arranges school tours, Taster Days, entry assessments and meetings with the Head.

Charitable status. Cheltenham College is a Registered Charity, number 311720. It exists to provide education for boys and girls.

Chesham Preparatory School

Two Dells Lane, Chesham, Bucks HP5 3QF

Tel: 01494 782619
email: office@cheshamprep.co.uk
             registrar@cheshamprep.co.uk
website: www.cheshamprep.co.uk
Twitter: @cheshamprep
Facebook: @CheshamPrep

Chairman of Governors: Mr A Kinnier QC, MA Cantab

Headmaster: **Mr Jonathan Beale**, BEd Hons, PGCE

Age Range. 3–13.

Numbers of Pupils. 391 boys and girls.

Fees per term (2021–2022). £3,180–£5,140 (inc lunch).

Chesham Preparatory School has a well justified reputation for being an incredibly friendly school where boys and girls work hard, behave well and achieve wonderful things. The most recent ISI report (2016) is glowing in its praise for a school in which, "The quality of the pupils' achievements and learning is excellent. The pupils' attitude to their work and learning is exemplary."

Founded in 1938, Chesham Prep has developed into a flourishing co-educational school. As a partially selective school which educates pupils from 3 to 13 years of age, it champions the strong belief that boys and girls of Prep school age should be educated together. They thrive in the holistic, caring environment and there is a real emphasis on ensuring that every child fulfils his or her potential whatever his or her varied strengths.

In September 2011 the school was delighted to announce the opening of its nursery – extending the provision offered to children rising 3 years old. From that early age, the children are well prepared for a smooth transition into their Reception class and, very importantly, they feel part of the Chesham Prep family.

The school boasts excellent success rates at 11+ Grammar school entry, as well as 13+ Common Entrance to senior independent schools. All pupils benefit enormously from the wonderful years of personal development at Chesham Prep.

Sports teams are highly skilled and competitive, while there is a fabulous choir and orchestra, as well as a wide range of opportunities for involvement in the creative arts. Children are encouraged to express themselves with joy and passion!

Above all, it is the aim of Chesham Preparatory School to inspire children with a love of learning and a confidence to make the most of their abilities.

'*I knew as soon as I looked at it – it's just got a vibe about it and is the best decision I've ever made', said a parent, as did many others besides. More grounded, less pressured and softer around the edges than some of the other local offerings, this is a real community school that lives up to its promise of making learning fun, and the results speak for themselves.* The Good Schools Guide 2021/2

To find out more or to arrange to visit the school, please visit our website: www.cheshamprep.co.uk.

Charitable status. Chesham Preparatory School is a Registered Charity, number 310642. It exists to provide education for boys and girls.

Chinthurst School

52 Tadworth St, Tadworth, Surrey KT20 5QZ

Tel: 01737 812011
email: office@chinthurstschool.co.uk
website: www.chinthurstschool.co.uk
Twitter: @ChintSchool
Facebook: @ChinthurstSchool

Chair of Governors: Mr James Dean

Headteacher: Miss Cathy Trundle, BA Hons QTS

Age Range. 2–11.
Number of Pupils. 220.
Fees per term (2021–2022). Little Chicks: £1,155 (min 3 mornings). Kindergarten: £1,925 (min 5 mornings). Lower School £3,975; Upper School £5,420

Founded in 1908, Chinthurst is a coeducational day school and nursery for children aged 2½ to 11 and a junior school of the multi award-winning senior school, Reigate Grammar. Central to the school's ethos is a bespoke and comprehensive wellbeing programme called Wellbeing at Heart, which has been designed to help children understand how their bodies and minds work and give them the skills to navigate life's inevitable challenges.

Building strong relationships is a key part of this approach and ensures children know they are truly valued as individuals. This gives them the confidence to try new things and the resilience to learn from their mistakes. More importantly, the children are happy and visitors often comment on the buzz of energy, warmth of atmosphere and

sense of fun around the school buildings and grounds. Chinthurst was a 2020 Independent school of the Year Finalist in recognition of this.

Sport is an important part of life at Chinthurst and school teams are extremely successful in both local and county competitions in a variety of sports. Both girls and boys play cricket and there is an onsite cricket academy run by a top Surrey County Cricket coach. A strong extracurricular programme provides additional sporting opportunities, as well as a broad range of other popular clubs including dance, drama, martial arts and craft.

An emphasis on outdoor learning means the children spend as much of the timetable as possible learning outside in the grounds and younger children enjoy regular Forest School sessions in addition to this. Every child is a member of one of three well established Houses and this gives them a sense of belonging and peer support as well as providing plenty of opportunities for friendly inter-house competitions.

The school is renowned for their music, drama and art provision. The children gain outstanding marks in LAMDA drama exams and there is a strong peripatetic music programme. There are many opportunities to perform throughout the year at assemblies, musical showcases and drama productions as well as in choirs and ensembles. Standards are always extremely high and the children also enjoy performing in the community and at local festivals. A well-equipped art studio allows the children to explore their creative potential.

Academic outcomes are excellent and children leave as well rounded individuals with an enthusiasm for life which is very much a reflection of the Chinthurst spirit.

Charitable status. Chinthurst School is a Registered Charity, number 1081898.

Christ Church Cathedral School

3 Brewer Street, Oxford OX1 1QW

Tel: 01865 242561
email: schooloffice@cccs.org.uk
website: www.cccs.org.uk
Instagram: @cccsoxford

Chairman of Governors: The Very Reverend Professor Martyn Percy, Dean of Christ Church

Headmaster: Mr Richard Murray, BA, MA

Age Range. 3–13 (co-ed Nursery).
Number of Boys. 20 boarders, all are Cathedral Choristers and required to board, and 150 day pupils.
Fees per term (2021–2022). Day boys (including lunch) from £6,025; Pre-Prep from £4,040 (including lunch); Cathedral Choristers £3,800; Probationer Choristers: £4,205 (Chorister fees are subsidised by the Cathedral); Nursery £1,535 and Reception £3,330 (inc. EY Funding).

Christ Church Cathedral School is a day Preparatory and Pre-Preparatory School for Boys with a co-ed Nursery.

The School provides Choristers for the choirs of Christ Church Cathedral, Pembroke College and Worcester College, and is governed by the Dean and Canons of Christ

Church, with the assistance of lay members drawn from the city's professional community, some of whom are past or current parents.

It was founded in 1546 when provision was made for the education of eight Choristers in King Henry VIII's foundation of Christ Church on the site of Cardinal Wolsey's earlier foundation of Cardinal College. In the latter half of the nineteenth century, at the initiative of Dean Liddell, father of Alice Liddell, the inspiration for 'Alice in Wonderland', the boarding house was established at No 1 Brewer Street, and in 1892, during the Headship of the Reverend Henry Sayers, father of Dorothy L Sayers, the Italian Mediaeval scholar and creator of Lord Peter Wimsey, the present building was erected.

The School is centrally situated off St Aldates, two hundred yards from Christ Church. It therefore enjoys the unique cultural background provided by Oxford itself as well as beautiful playing fields on Christ Church Meadow. Buildings include a former residence of Cardinal Wolsey and the Sir William Walton Centre, which contains a recital hall and spacious classrooms.

Charitable status. Christ Church Cathedral School Education Trust is a Registered Charity, number 1114828.

Churcher's College Junior School and Nursery

Midhurst Road, Liphook, Hampshire GU30 7HT

Tel: 01730 236870
email: ccjsoffice@churcherscollege.com
website: www.churcherscollege.com
Twitter: @ChurchersJunior
Facebook: @ChurchersJunior
Instagram: @ChurchersJunior

Chairman of Governors: M J Gallagher, Dip Arch Hons, RIBA, MIoD, FIMgt

Head: Mrs F Robinson, BA, MA

Deputy Head: Mrs P Yugin-Power, BSc, MA Ed

Head of the Infant Department: Miss K M Humphreys, BEd

Senior Teacher – Middle School: Mrs S J Moore, ARCM, GRSM

Senior Teacher – Upper School: N Rushin, BSc, MSc

Director of Studies: Mrs R Drummond, BSocSc

Head of Nursery: Mrs A Knowles, BSc

Age Range. 2¾–11 Co-educational.
Number of Pupils. 250 (excluding Nursery)
Fees per term (2021–2022). £3,610–£3,855 excluding lunch.

Churcher's College Junior School and Nursery is the perfect place to start your child's learning journey.

We are a haven for learning and adventure with a 'have a go' philosophy and an overarching aim for each child to reach their personal best inside and outside the classroom. With a broad and rich curriculum, the children enjoy a range of subjects and fully seize the array of opportunities on offer. From the academic to the activities that feed the soul, the children love it here.

Set just off the South Downs in Liphook, Hampshire, your child can experience a real countryside childhood and then make a very smooth transition at eleven years old as she/he moves to the Senior School in Petersfield. We fully support each child at every step of the entrance process. Every child's happiness is paramount to their achievement and we pride ourselves on our high-quality pastoral care, excellent teaching and learning, all within a warm, family atmosphere.

The Nursery. Nestled in the grounds of our Junior School, Churcher's College Nursery is a warm and creative environment where children are encouraged to explore, question and discover. Every child is unique and we want to give each boy and girl every opportunity to grow and flourish in a safe and nurturing environment so that they become happy, self-confident and thoughtful children who respect each other and the wonderful natural space they are sharing.

Pastoral. Happy children make happy learners. We strive to create a secure and friendly place of learning in which our children feel valued and where they can grow personally, socially, spiritually and intellectually. Class teachers take responsibility for day-to-day pastoral care. Heads of School support pupils, parents and staff. Our close-knit community enables us to talk freely with parents and vice versa. We work hard to make sure pupils thrive here. The House system fosters great community spirit, allowing friendships to form between year groups.

Academic. Academic rigour is at the heart of our teaching.

Junior Curriculum: A broad and balanced curriculum, combining academic, creative and cultural elements, gives children a varied day and also develops a lifelong love of learning in preparation for Senior School and beyond.

Nursery and Reception: Pupils in the Nursery and Reception Class follow the Early Years Foundation Stage curriculum.

Sport. We offer a broad range of sports to help develop fitness and skills, teamwork and a healthy attitude towards competition through PE and Games. There are many opportunities to represent the school in a variety of matches from Year 2 onwards. The pupils learn a great deal from these: etiquette, collaboration, organisation, sportsmanship. They enjoy the experiences immensely.

Music and Drama. The Arts play a significant role throughout school life at the Junior School.

Music is integral throughout school life and is a dynamic and engaging department at the Junior School. Music is made accessible to all pupils, whatever their abilities, whether being inspired for the first time or developing existing skills. With plenty of performance opportunities, the pupils' confidence is positively built. From the harp to trombone, individual music lessons are available at extra cost.

Drama plays a key part in helping our pupils to gain confidence and to develop their imagination and communication skills. There are a number of dramatic performances throughout the year. The Infants are all involved in a wonderful Nativity performance and a summer production. At key points during their Junior years, year groups work together to perform a production. Assemblies and workshops also provide more opportunities for pupils to unleash their dramatic flair and build every child's confidence.

Adventure. Building confidence and self-esteem is important for all of our children. We do this by providing challenging and adventurous activities that include the opportunity to take risk in a controlled environment. This is achieved through our Outdoor Adventurous Activities Programme and embedding Learning Outside the Classroom throughout the curriculum. From onsite campfire events to residential trips off site, the children relish the opportunity to learn outside their comfort zone. Children remember these adventures and experiences fondly.

Clubs and After-school Activities. Pupils at Churcher's are encouraged to be involved in a wide range of activities, to broaden their interests and try new things. There is a great deal of choice, with activities ranging from sports and drama to music and dance. We love giving our children every opportunity to discover something a bit different or try out a new activity, and we find they thoroughly enjoy doing so.

Charitable status. Churcher's College is Registered Charity, number 1173833, and a Charitable Company Limited by Guarantee, registered in England and Wales, company number 10813349.

City of London Freemen's Junior School

Ashtead Park, Ashtead, Surrey KT21 1ET

Tel:	01372 822400 (School Reception)
	01372 822423 (Admissions)
email:	admissions@freemens.org
website:	www.freemens.org

A co-educational day and boarding school, located on a magnificent 57-acre site in Ashtead Park, Surrey.

Chairman of Governors: Mr Philip Woodhouse

Head: **Mr Matt Robinson**, BA Hons, MA, MEd

Age Range. 7–12.

Number of Pupils. 392

Fees per term (2021–2022). Tuition £5,067–£5,629.

The City of London Freemen's Junior School was established formally in 1988 as an integral part of Freemen's and it prepares girls and boys for entry to the Senior School. The School is located on a magnificent 57-acre site in Ashtead Park, Surrey, where the many outstanding facilities are available to all pupils (*see separate entry in HMC section*).

With its broad based curriculum and modern purpose-built facilities, the Junior School offers a challenging and unique atmosphere for all. There is a Junior School Head with specialist teaching staff and a clearly defined academic and pastoral structure to ensure that all pupils know what is expected of them. The Junior School encourages young pupils to develop their strengths and discover new skills and passions in an environment of kindness, honesty and fun. There are usually 20 pupils in each of the three parallel classes in each year group. In Year 7, the number of year

groups rises to four classes. Junior pupils benefit greatly from seeing their Form Prefects, who are Sixth Formers from the Senior School, on a daily basis.

For the first four years, in Key Stage 2, Heads of Year work in liaison with the subject coordinators and the Heads of Senior School Departments to ensure that the programmes of work are compatible and progressive. The aim is to establish a secure foundation in traditional core subjects within a curriculum which will broaden experience and excite the imagination of each child. In Years 7 and 8 the teaching programme is managed by the Heads of the Senior School Departments using specialist teachers for all of the subjects. Whilst academic excellence throughout the Junior School is still a major aim, there is also an enrichment programme and a very full programme of extracurricular activities including drama, music and sports.

Fully integrated into whole school routines, the Junior School takes full advantage of Ashtead Park's facilities. Extensive playing fields, the floodlit all-weather pitch, award-winning swimming pool and a large indoor sports hall, ensure that the sports facilities available are second to none.

There are three Houses in the School providing pastoral care and supervision whilst also promoting healthy competition in many activities. In both the Senior and the Junior School outstanding work and good progress, inside and outside the classroom, are recognised by the award of appropriate merits and distinctions.

Admission to the Junior School is through entrance examination, interview and feeder school report. Progression to the Senior School is based on continuous assessment with no separate qualifying entrance test and as such is almost always automatic for Junior School pupils. Pupils are constantly reviewed and can be assured that they will move through to the Senior School with many familiar faces around them.

Clifton College Pre-Preparatory School

Guthrie Road, Clifton, Bristol BS8 3EZ

Tel:	0117 315 7160
email:	prepadmissions@cliftoncollege.com
website:	www.cliftoncollege.com
Twitter:	@Clifton_College
Facebook:	@CliftonCollegeUK
LinkedIn:	/clifton-college

Chairman of College Council: Mr Nick Tolchard

Headmaster: **Mr Jim Walton**, BA

Age Range. 4–8

Number of Pupils. 136

Fees per term (2021–2022). Reception (full time) £3,560; Year 1 £3,780; Years 2–3 £4,160.

Clifton College Pre-Preparatory School is a vibrant co-educational school for children aged 4–8, children aged 3 months and older can register for the College's Butcombe Nursery, just next door. The College prides itself on creating an environment where children are fully engaged, and who are creatively immersed in their learning, making firm friendships along the way. The highest possible standard of education is provided for all, and places strong emphasis on building the core skills of literacy and numeracy, the essential foundations for future learning.

Life at the Pre-Preparatory is busy and exciting. Year 2 and 3 pupils may take part in a range of co-curricular activities at lunchtimes or after school, with around 16 clubs and societies taking place. These change termly and include a variety of sports, sewing club, craft club, science club, ukulele club, book club and Lego club. Services and concerts are held every term in the Chapel, and an annual musical is performed at the wonderful Redgrave Theatre. There is a full programme of educational visits and outings for all ages, including a youth hostelling trip for Year 3.

Each class benefits from a dedicated class teacher, along with support from a teaching assistant. Qualified specialist class teachers deliver a topic-based curriculum, with specialist teachers for Music, Dance, Sport, French and Mandarin.

Piano and instrumental lessons are available from Year 2, and all children in Years 2 and 3 learn the recorder, strings and sing in the choir.

The Pre-Preparatory benefits from aspects of the Preparatory school, it is governed by the same Council and enjoys the considerable advantages of sharing many of Clifton College's impressive facilities. These include the swimming pool, sports hall, library, multi-activity hall, Chapel and Theatre. The Pre-Preparatory school is situated in two buildings either side of a superb playground, with a variety of exciting play equipment available.

Recent investment has seen the creation of an outdoor area leading from the reception classrooms. This is designed to give reception classes easy access to an outdoor space which they can use to extend and enhance their learning.

Another exciting provision is the Forest School at our Beggar's Bush Sports Ground. All year groups, from Reception to Year 3, visit the Forest School, it provides a range of stimulating outdoor experiences for the children, enabling them to learn, achieve and develop confidence through curriculum-linked activities and free exploration of the natural woodland.

Charitable status. Clifton College is a Registered Charity, number 311735. It provides boarding and day education for boys and girls aged 0–18.

Clifton College Preparatory School

The Avenue, Clifton, Bristol BS8 3HE

Tel: 0117 315 7160

email: prepadmissions@cliftoncollege.com

website: www.cliftoncollege.com

Twitter: @Clifton_College

Facebook: @CliftonCollegeUK

Instagram: @CliftonCollegeUK

LinkedIn: /clifton-college

Chairman of College Council: Mr Nick Tolchard

Headmaster: **Mr Jim Walton**, BA

Age Range. 8–13

Number of Pupils. 262

Fees per term (2021–2022). Boarders (from Year 4) £8,635–£10,230; Flexi Boarders (3 nights from Year 4) £5,820–£7,345; Day Pupils £4,725–£6,200

There is no 'one size fits all' approach at Clifton College Preparatory School, a friendly and inspiring co-educational boarding and day school for boys and girls aged 8–13. Each child is considered and treated as an individual with a unique profile of skills, passions, talents and undiscovered potential. Clifton College offers a stimulating and challenging curriculum, which combines traditional methods with programmes of study relevant to the needs of the next century.

Clifton College Preparatory School aims to provide the highest possible standard of education, and to help pupils develop the key skills of literacy and numeracy, as well as observation, information-seeking, posing questions and problem-solving. In addition, we aim to develop their ability to co-operate and work productively with others, as well as to work and learn independently.

A wide range of subjects are studied, and pupils are supported and encouraged to become high achievers across the varied curriculum. Small class sizes, first-class facilities and teaching excellence enables pupils to aim high, reaching their academic potential, and beyond.

The vast majority of pupils move through to the Upper School, but those who choose to move elsewhere are prepared for, and often win, scholarships to other schools.

As part of Clifton College, the Preparatory School benefits from being governed by the same Council and enjoys the considerable advantages of sharing many of Clifton College's impressive facilities. These include the Redgrave Theatre, Sports Complex, Indoor Swimming Pool, Gymnasium, Squash and Rackets Courts, and over 90 acres of playing fields off-site at Beggar's Bush. This includes an Olympic-standard water-based Hockey pitch, a 3G pitch, an indoor Tennis and Netball Centre and Activity Centre. The School has its own impressive Science laboratories, Arts Centre, ICT suites, Music facilities and Chapel.

There are six Houses in the Prep School, three day Houses for Years 4–6, two day Houses for Years 7–8, and a boarding House for Year 4 upwards. Pupils benefit from a supervised environment where they can meet, work or relax, and provides a true home away from home. Each House is led by a Housemaster/Housemistress and their spouse, along with Tutors, Matrons and the occasional House dog. All Houses are beautifully renovated, and In 2012 two new Houses were opened, containing a large dance studio with light rigging, and a sprung floor for performances.

The excellent and well-rounded co-curricular programme encourages children to try something new, find new interests, and to engage with the world around them – boosting their confidence and self-esteem.

The youngest boys and girls (aged 2–8) learn next door at the Pre-Preparatory School, under the care of their own teachers. (See separate IAPS entry for Clifton College Pre-Preparatory School.)

Charitable status. Clifton College is a Registered Charity, number 311735. It provides boarding and day education for boys and girls aged 0–18 years.

Colfe's Junior School

Horn Park Lane, London SE12 8AW

Tel: 020 8463 8240 Junior Head
          020 8463 8266 Junior Office
email: junioroffice@colfes.com
website: www.colfes.com
Twitter: @ColfesSchool
Facebook: @ColfesSchool

Chairman of the Governors: Mr Matthew Pellereau, BSc, FRICS

Head of the Junior School: **Miss C Macleod**, MSc

Deputy Head and Head of EYFS: Mrs S Gurr, BEd Hons

Director of Studies: Miss L Kirkland, BA Hons, PGCE

Head of KS2: Mrs V Welch, BA, Cert Ed

Head of KS1: Mr M Heil, BEd

Head of Learning Support: Mrs G Fisher HND, OCR Level 7 Cert SpLD

Age Range. 3–11.
Number of Pupils. 460 boys and girls.
Fees per term (2021–2022). Junior School, KS2 £5,045 (excluding lunch); KS1 £4,770 (including lunch); EYFS £4,570 (including lunch).

Colfe's Junior School is an independent day school for boys and girls 3–11. Entrance is academically selective. The Junior School offers a broad curriculum and aims to provide an excellent all-round education. Small class sizes and a team of well-qualified teachers provide a caring and vibrant environment. Children normally enter at the ages of 3 or 4, although the occasional vacancy arises at other times.

For the children starting school it is the beginning of an exciting and inspiring journey; this begins in our Nursery and Reception classes which together form the Early Years Foundation Stage (EYFS). Children gain confidence and thrive in a warm, friendly and nurturing atmosphere where they feel secure and valued. Through a specialised play-based curriculum teachers plan for a rich learning environment which provides opportunities for the children to flourish in all aspects of their development. In Years 1 and 2 children begin to study all National Curriculum subjects, building on the skills, knowledge, understanding and experience gained during their time in Nursery and Reception. Moving into KS2 the focus shifts to three aspects of every child – talent, potential and character. Strong curriculum and expert teaching is underpinned by a rich programme of music, art, sport, drama, outdoor pursuits. Each pupil belongs to a House and they compete to earn the most points, helping them to develop a real sense of community.

The majority of Junior School pupils transfer to the Senior School at the end of Year 6, providing they achieve the qualifying standard.

The Junior School is housed in modern purpose-built accommodation with spacious and well-equipped classrooms. Excellent library facilities and specialist accommodation for art and design, ICT and science provide pupils with a stimulating environment in which to learn. Full use is made of the school's swimming pool, sports centre, visual and performing arts centre and extensive on-site playing fields.

PE specialists teach a wide range of sports and there is an extensive programme of House and inter-school sports matches. A school choir, orchestra, strings group and numerous ensembles perform frequently both in and out of school. Drama productions normally take place each term. There is a wide range of after-school clubs on offer (over 50 each week for the 7–11 year olds) and a Breakfast Club from 7.30am and Late School scheme until 6.00pm each day.

Charitable status. Colfe's School is a Registered Charity, number 1109650. It exists to provide education for children.

Colston's Lower School

Park Road, Stapleton, Bristol BS16 1BA

Tel: 0117 965 5297
email: admissions@colstons.org
website: www.colstons.org
Twitter: @ColstonsLower
Facebook: @ColstonsSchool
Instagram: @colstonsschool

Chair of Governors: Mr N Baker

Head of Lower School: **Mr D A H Edwards**, BEd, MA

Deputy Head: Mr M Weavers, BEd Hons

Head of Juniors: Mr O Barwell, BA Hons

Head of Pre-Prep: Miss S Evans, BEd Hons

Age Range. 3–11.
Number of Pupils. 230 Day Pupils.
Fees per term (2021–2022). £2,885 (Reception, Years 1 & 2), £3,480 (Years 3 & 4), £3,740 (Years 5 & 6) plus catering charge of £220 (Reception to Year 2) or £245 (Years 3 to 6).

Colston's Lower School is located in Stapleton village, which is within the city of Bristol. It is less than one mile from Junction 2 of the M32 and therefore easily accessible from north Bristol and South Gloucestershire. In addition to its own specialist facilities for Science, ICT, Music, Design & Technology, Art and Games, the Lower School has full use of facilities at the neighbouring Upper School including 30 acres of playing fields, theatre, concert hall and sports centre.

At the end of Year 6, pupils move from the Lower to the Upper School (see entry in HMC section). They work in small classes on a broad and engaging curriculum that extends and enthuses a community of highly active learners. It incorporates the full range of academic subjects together with French, Design and Technology, ICT, Art, Music, Forest School and competitive sports. A wide range of co-curricular activities such as climbing, golf and ballet are also available. The School benefits from a highly efficient Learning Support Unit for those needing additional support and a Gifted and Talented program for those who show particular strengths.

The creative arts flourish in the Lower School, with a choir and orchestra, regular concerts, school plays and music competitions. A large number of children also play musical instruments, with specialist teachers providing weekly tuition.

In addition to PE lessons, there are two afternoons of junior games each week. The boys principally play rugby, hockey and cricket, and the girls play hockey, netball and rounders. Pupils also enjoy opportunities to take part in football, tennis, athletics and badminton. All juniors are encouraged to take part in competitive sports fixtures, and sports tours are also arranged.

The school also has its own excellent Forest School site which is used every week for outdoor learning.

Colston's Lower School offers a wide range of clubs and activities, and pupils are able to stay on at school under supervision for an extended day or start with Breakfast Club. There are numerous visits and trips including skiing, camps and adventure activities.

Charitable status. Colston's School is a Registered Charity, number 1079552. Its aims and objectives are the provision of education.

Copthorne School

Effingham Lane, Copthorne, West Sussex RH10 3HR

Tel: 01342 712311
email: office@copthorneprep.co.uk
website: www.copthorneprep.co.uk
Twitter: @copthorneprep
Facebook: @copthorneprep

Chairman of Governors: K Bell

Headmaster: **N Close**, BA Hons, PGCE

Deputy Head: S Janman

Age Range. 2–13.
Number of Boys and Girls. 300
Fees per term (2021–2022). Day: Reception £3,325, Year 1 £3,430, Year 2 £3,485, Year 3 £4,595, Year 4 £5,045, Years 5–8 £5,790. Weekly Boarding £7,055. Occasional Boarding £35 per night.

Copthorne is a flourishing IAPS Prep School with approximately 300 boys and girls aged from 2 to 13. The school has grown by over 75% within the last 5 years. Children are prepared for Independent School Scholarships or Common Entrance. In the last 5 years Copthorne children have been awarded 48 Scholarships or Awards to a variety of Senior Schools.

We believe that, in order to learn, children must be happy and feel secure in their environment. Copthorne Prep School is full of happy children and the environment is caring but still allows children the freedom to develop as individuals.

The school helps to develop each child's confidence, to raise self-esteem and to make children feel good about themselves. Nothing does this more than children enjoying success in all areas of school life. This is why Art, Music, ICT, DT, Drama and Sport are all just as important as the pursuit of academic excellence.

We provide opportunities for children to achieve success in all areas of the curriculum and we always celebrate their achievements.

We recognise that all children have talents, and every child is encouraged to realise their true potential, whatever that may be, in whatever area of school life.

We demand and set high standards, and our children respond by always giving of their best.

Put simply, our mission is to:

Develop **C**onfidence – Provide **O**pportunity – Realise **P**otential – in every single child.

The school is very proud of its history of over 100 years, and retains all the important traditions of the past whilst developing a very forward thinking approach. The children receive a child-centred education, where their individual needs come first, in an environment that is parent-friendly, with very high levels of communication and pastoral care.

Charitable status. Copthorne School Trust Limited is a Registered Charity, number 270757. It exists to provide education to boys and girls.

Cottesmore School

Buchan Hill, Pease Pottage, West Sussex RH11 9AU

Tel: 01293 520648
email: admissions@cottesmoreschool.com
website: www.cottesmoreschool.com
Twitter: @cottesmoreprep
Facebook: @cottesmoreprepschool

Tatler School Awards '**Prep School of The Year 2020**' and TES '**Boarding School of The Year 2019**'.

Headmaster: **T F Rogerson**, BA Hons, PGCE

Age Range. 4–13.
Number of Pupils. 200
Fees per term (2021–2022). Prep: £6,290 (Day), £9,550 (Boarding); Pre-Prep: £3,360–£4,480.

Cottesmore is an award-winning co-educational Preparatory school for girls and boys in West Sussex, less than an hour from London.

Curriculum. Boys and girls are taught together in classes averaging 12 in number. Children are fully prepared for Common Entrance and Scholarship examinations. Cottesmore achieves excellent academic results. The strength of Cottesmore's academic programme lies within its breadth. There are 21 different curriculum subjects taught. Through this rich variety of intellectual experience, each girl and boy finds her or his particular strength and this in turn lifts their all-round potential.

Music. The musical tradition is strong – more than 90% of children learn a variety of instruments; there are three Choirs, a School Orchestra and several musical ensembles.

Sport. The major games are Football, Rugby, Cricket, Hockey, Swimming, Tennis, Netball, Athletics and Rounders. Numerous other sports are taught and encouraged. These include Archery, Riding, Basketball, Shooting, Short Tennis, Canoeing, Snooker, Cross-Country Running, Squash, Table Tennis, Gymnastics, Trampoline, Golf, Chess and Judo. The School competes at a national level in several of these sports.

Recent Developments. Our Technology Centre houses a constantly developing Information Technology Suite, a Design Technology room for metal, woodwork, plastic and pneumatics, a Craft room, Kiln, two Science laboratories and Art Studio.

Hobbies and Activities. These include Pottery, Drone Club, Photography, Bridge, Model-Making, Model Railway, Tenpin Bowling, Gardening, Rollerblading, Ballet, Modern Dancing, Drama, Craft, Carpentry, Printing, Cooking and Debating.

The boys and girls lead a full and varied life and are all encouraged to take part in as wide a variety of activities as possible. Weekends are a vital part of the school life and are made busy and fun for all.

Headmaster's Philosophy: Everyone has a talent. Whatever creative or academic outlet makes a child tick, Cottesmore finds and nurtures it. Endeavour and fun are the most important elements of intellectual life at Cottesmore. Success follows this explosion of discovery and purposefulness.

Entry requirements. Entry is by Headmaster's interview and a child's last three terms' school reports, if necessary. For a prospectus or more information, please contact the Registrar, Lottie Rogerson, at admissions@ cottesmoreschool.com or telephone 01293 520648.

Coworth Flexlands School
United Learning

Valley End, Chobham, Surrey GU24 8TE

Tel: 01276 855707
email: secretary@coworthflexlands.co.uk
          registrar@coworthflexlands.co.uk
website: www.coworthflexlands.co.uk
Twitter: @CoworthFlexSch
Facebook: @CoworthFlexSch
Instagram: @coworthflexlands

Chairman of Governors: Mr Paul Clarke

Headmistress: **Miss Nicola Cowell**

Age Range. Girls 2½–11 years; Boys 2½–7.
Number of Pupils. 125.
Fees per term (2021–2022). £3,666–£4,944.

Coworth Flexlands Prep School and Nursery is an independent school for girls, with a co-ed Nursery and Pre-Prep. Nursery starts at the age of 2½ and is fully immersed in school life. Nestled in between the villages of Sunningdale, Windlesham and Chobham, you discover a happy, high achieving school where children are inspired and nurtured. This approach brings out the best in the children and the girls move on to top Senior Schools with many gaining scholarships. The boys head off to local Prep Schools, well prepared.

A Prep School that Inspires Minds and Nurtures Spirit. A school where happiness gets results.

The school offers the convenience of optional wraparound care and clubs for busy parents from 7.30am to 6.00pm and a wide range of on-site holiday activities.

Charitable status. Coworth Flexlands School School is part of United Learning which comprises: UCST (a Company Limited by Guarantee, Registered in England, number 2780748, and a Registered Charity, number 1016538) and ULT (a Company Limited by Guarantee, Registered in England, number 4439859, and an Exempt Charity).

Crackley Hall School

Kenilworth, Warwickshire CV8 2FT

Tel: 01926 514444
email: post@crackleyhall.co.uk
website: www.crackleyhall.co.uk
Twitter: @CrackleyHallSch
Facebook: @crackleyhallandlittlecrackersofficial

Co-educational Nursery and Junior School.

Leadership Team:

Headmaster: **Mr Robert Duigan**, BComEd, MEd

Deputy Head: Mr Duncan Cottrill, BSc, PGCE (PSHCE)

Assistant Head – Early Years Foundation Stage and KS1: Mrs Susan Glen-Roots, BEd (English and Drama)

Assistant Head – Key Stage 2 and Academic: Ms Sharon McAloon, BA, ATS

Age Range. 2–11 years.
Number of Pupils. 236
Fees per term (2021–2022). Junior School: £3,370–£3,751. Nursery: £275.50 per week (full time, term time only), £268 per week (full time, all year).

Crackley Hall is a co-educational independent Catholic day school which welcomes pupils of all denominations. The school is part of The Princethorpe Foundation comprising Little Crackers Nursery, Crackley Hall School, Crescent School and Princethorpe College.

Crackley Hall continues to go from strength to strength following the merger with Abbotsford School in September 2010. Under the leadership of Headmaster, Robert Duigan, pupil numbers have risen considerably and we are now well known for our high academic standards, sporting provision and excellence in the performing arts.

In 2017 the ISI Inspectors judged the school to be 'excellent' in every area.

In 2019, in its Canonical Inspection Report, the Archdiocese of Birmingham rated the 'Catholic Life' and 'Collective Worship' at Crackley Hall School as 'outstanding'.

Building work that provided more classrooms, specialist teaching rooms for Art and Music, greatly enhanced IT, Science and Technology suites, and improved sports changing rooms was completed in 2013, and the second phase of major development, a new multi-purpose hall with additional teaching space, was completed in Spring 2016.

Situated on the outskirts of Kenilworth, Crackley Hall occupies a pleasant and safe setting with playing fields a short distance across the road. An extended day facility is offered; pupils may be dropped off from 7.45am and can stay at school until 6.00pm. Nursery attendance times are flexible, with term-time and year-round (51 weeks) places available.

Crackley Hall bases its care for individuals on the sound Christian principles of love and forgiveness; children become strong in the understanding of themselves and others. There is a keen sense of community between pupils, staff and parents. We encourage fairness, freedom, friendship and fun.

Small class sizes promote individual attention. The curriculum is based on national guidelines, but pupils are encouraged to achieve well beyond these targets. During the early years, great emphasis is placed on developing key skills in reading, writing, speaking, listening, mathematics and science. The learning of tables and spellings is actively developed through simple homework tasks. Specialists teach Art, Design Technology, French, Music, Games, ICT and RE. Recent investment has resulted in specialist teaching rooms for Art and Music, greatly enhanced IT, Science and Technology suites and improved sports changing facilities.

Sports are very strong with football, rugby, cricket, hockey, netball, tennis, athletics, swimming, rounders, trampolining, gym and karate all available. There is a strong and thriving music department and all pupils together with members of the choir, choral group and orchestra participate in concerts and stage productions to enrich their learning and to build confidence and self-esteem. Pupils have the opportunity to study a wide range of individual instruments under the guidance of a team of peripatetic staff and specialist teachers offer classes in music, theatre, speech and drama and dance. Other activities are offered before and after school as well as during lunch breaks including art, chess, craft, ICT, Mandarin, cookery, rock school, Lego, Latin, brass, climbing, sewing and mindfulness.

Admission is through interview with the Head, assessments in English and Mathematics, and a taster day at the school. We also ask for a reference from the child's current school. The admission information is considered as a whole so that as accurate a picture as possible of the child can be obtained. The pastoral elements are as important to us as academic ability.

Parents are welcomed into school for Friday morning assembly when the children's good work is celebrated. An active Parent Teacher Association organises social and fundraising events. Pupils are encouraged to maintain their links with the school by joining the Past Pupils' Association.

Charitable status. The Princethorpe Foundation is a Registered Charity, number 1087124. It exists solely for the purpose of educating children.

Chairman of Governors: Bill Farrar

***Headmaster*: John Gilmour**

Bursar: Tom Kerrigan

Admissions & Marketing: Jennifer Trueland

Age Range. 3–13.

Number of Pupils. 204: 114 boys, 90 girls.

Fees per term (2021–2022). £4,950.

Craigclowan provides a warm and nurturing environment for boys and girls aged 3–13 to learn and grow. Set in stunning grounds with magnificent views over Perthshire, the school has a distinguished history, a reputation for the highest standards and expectations and a passion for childhood.

Craigclowan delivers a modern education within a framework of traditional values. With a dedicated, caring and supportive ethos, the staff are very close to the children, and the families, in their care and treat them as individuals in all they do. Every child is encouraged to achieve their all-round potential, in the classroom, on the sports fields, on the stage and in the music and art departments.

The school aims to make the most of the world outside the classroom through a wide range of outdoor activities that build confidence and resilience, encourage creativity and problem solving and ensure rosy cheeks and muddy boots. Wellie boots and waterproofs are a must! When it comes to moving on to senior school, pupils go on to attend a wide variety of top UK schools, both north and south of the border, many with scholarships under their belts. The values that are instilled in children during their journey through Craigclowan, are the qualities that allow them to thrive after they leave.

School is a hive of activity from 7.30am until 6.00pm, with a family-friendly wraparound care programme before and after lessons. The school minibus fleet collects children from across the region and Craigclowan's ever-popular holiday activity camps operate throughout the year. Grant funding is available for nursery pupils setting out on their Craigclowan adventure.

Why not come along and find out what a Craigclowan education has to offer to your family? You will be assured of a very warm welcome and will find a school in a stunning location with tremendous spirit.

Charitable status. Craigclowan School Limited is a Registered Charity, number SC010817. It exists to promote education generally and for that purpose to establish, carry on and maintain a school within Scotland.

Craigclowan Prep School

Edinburgh Road, Perth PH2 8PS

Tel:	01738 626310
email:	head@craigclowan-school.co.uk
website:	www.craigclowan-school.co.uk
Twitter:	@craigclowan
Facebook:	@craigclowan
Instagram:	@craigclowan

Cranleigh Preparatory School

Horseshoe Lane, Cranleigh, Surrey GU6 8QH

Tel:	01483 542058
email:	cjs@cranprep.org
website:	www.cranprep.org
Twitter:	@CranleighPrep
Facebook:	@CranPrep

Chairman of Governors: Mr Adrian Lajtha, MA, FCIB

Leadership Team:

Head: **Mr Neil R Brooks**, BA Hons QTS

Mrs H Pakenham-Walsh, BA Ed Hons

Mrs C A Beddison, BMus Hons, PGCE

Mrs E F Lewis, BA Hons

Mrs A J Jolly, BSc, PGCE

Age Range. 7–13.

Number of Pupils. 340 (50 Boarders, 290 Day).

Fees per term (2021–2022). Boarders £8,680; Day Pupils: £5,540 (Forms 1 & 2), £7,190 (Forms 3–6). These are genuinely inclusive and there are no hidden or compulsory extras.

The School stands in its own beautiful and spacious grounds, set in 40 acres of stunning Surrey countryside, just 50 minutes from London. Cranleigh Preparatory School is a co-educational boarding and day school. A teaching staff of 59 enables classes to be small. The Head and his wife live just at the bottom of the school drive. The boarding Houseparents and their families both live on the school site. They are fully involved with the health and happiness of the boys and girls, together with pastoral staff, including matrons. A great source of strength is the close partnership with Cranleigh School 'across the road', with both schools sharing an innovative 7–18 programme across sport, music and computing. The Preparatory School has use of Senior School sports facilities, including an indoor pool, artificial pitches, the stables and golf course.

The boys and girls are prepared for Common Entrance and scholarships. Pupils have achieved over 200 scholarships in the last five years to some of the country's leading schools, including Cranleigh School, Brighton College, Charterhouse, Eton, KCS Wimbledon, Marlborough, RGS Guildford, Tonbridge, Wellington and Winchester.

Boarding life is busy and fun, with a wide array of exciting activities on offer. There is the opportunity to board all week or flexi board for one or more nights during the week; all pupils return home every weekend and there is a weekly bus service to and from London.

The curriculum is broad, balanced and covers all and more than that laid down by the National Curriculum. The School teaches Computing, and technological problem solving is encouraged. Art, Food Technology, Design and Music are included in the curriculum at all levels. Individual instrumental lessons are available and peripatetic music staff teach at both schools. There are choirs, orchestras, bands and several ensembles. Boys and girls are given every incentive to develop spare time interests and a choice of activities is built into the timetable.

The School is fortunate to have excellent facilities including a full-sized artificial pitch, a large Sports and Drama Hall, a Dance Studio, a Music School and very light, airy classrooms. The School has recently opened a brand new teaching block, housing three new Science laboratories, two Art Studios and state-of-the-art Design and Food Technology areas. Boarding numbers are steadily increasing, and the boarding facilities are being updated again later this year.

Rugby, football, hockey, netball, cricket, athletics, tennis, swimming, squash, cross country, basketball, fencing, riding, golf, Eton Fives, archery and badminton, are among the sports.

Main entry age is at 7 or 8, with limited availability at 11. Places are sometimes available in the intervening year groups.

Charitable status. Cranleigh School is a Registered Charity, number 1070856, whose Preparatory School exists to provide education for boys and girls aged 7–13.

Cranmore

Epsom Road, West Horsley, Surrey KT24 6AT

Tel: 01483 280340
email: office@cranmore.org
website: www.cranmore.org

Joint Chair of Governors: Mr Michael Henderson & Mrs Annette Turner

Headmaster: **Mr B Everitt**, BSc, MEd, PGCE

Deputy Head (*Academic*): Mr J Pulford, BSc, PGCE

Assistant Head (*Pastoral*): Ms J Schembri, BA, PGCE

Head of Lower Prep School: Miss Sarah Gallop, BA, PGCE

Age Range. 2+ co-educational diamond model.

Number of Pupils. 420 Day Pupils.

Fees per term (2021–2022). Nursery (5 full days/week) £3,300; Reception £3,995; Years 1 & 2 £4,425; Year 3 £4,685, Years 4 to 6 £5,300, Years 7 upwards £5,995.

On 1 September 2019, the school formed a partnership with St Teresa's Effingham, The Effingham Schools Trust, offering education to girls and boys aged 2 to 18. Cranmore is equidistant between Leatherhead and Guildford and is easily accessible from Cobham, Esher, Weybridge, Dorking and Woking with school transport available. Normal entry points are Nursery, Reception, Year 3 (7+), Year 7 (11+) and Year 9 (13+). Entry is non-selective in the early years and assessments are held for other year groups. There is a Scholarship programme for 7+, 11+ and 13+ entry offering Academic, Sport, Music, Art and Drama Scholarships. The most recent Inspection awarded the school top grades in every category including 'Outstanding' for the Early Years (Nursery and Reception).

Cranmore Nursery (from age 2) has its own dedicated accommodation which includes several rooms and outdoor learning area. The Lower Prep School (Nursery to Year 3) offers all children access to tremendous resources including the sports hall, gymnasium, swimming pool, forest school and music facilities. Pupils are taught by specialist subject teachers from Year 4. Cranmore's academic standards are high and pupil development enables all pupils to fulfil their individual potential.

Pupils in Years 7 and 8 are given significant additional opportunities with a broad curriculum including Philosophy, Politics, Decision Maths, Reasoning, Latin, Debating and Current Affairs.

An ongoing programme of investment over several years has given the school many outstanding facilities based on the extensive 25-acre site. These include a £250,000 redevelopment of the Cranmore Nursery outdoor learning area, Multi-Activity Games Area including netball court, complete car park redevelopment, a forest school, refurbishment of 25m swimming pool, new hospitality suite, teaching block with 3 large well-equipped science labs, and 2 ICT suites. The sports facilities include: a MUGA (multi-use games area), a sports hall, gymnasium, 25m swimming pool, 4 AstroTurf tennis courts and hockey pitch, 5-a-side astro, 9-hole golf course, large playground with rubberised surface, 3 squash courts and fitness room plus extensive playing fields. Plans are underway for the development of a dedicated science and technology building to be completed in 2022–23.

Sports teams compete in galas, tournaments at local and national level; Inter-School and Inter-House competitions allow all pupils to take part. All children have the opportunity to represent the school at one of the main sports: rugby, football, cricket, netball and hockey. Our swimming squads compete successfully at national level. There is also a long tradition of other sports including golf, tennis and rowing – with boats housed at a local rowing club on the Thames. Skiing is supported by weekly training at Sandown with plans to install a ski simulator within school. There is a thriving extracurricular programme as well as trips to support curriculum learning and to develop team building and leadership skills.

The Drama, Speech and Music school offers every pupil the opportunity to learn an instrument, sing in one of our choirs and play in a wide variety of ensembles and orchestras.

Cranmore is a Catholic school, welcoming families from all religious backgrounds and none. Our Christian ethos is central to supporting every child's development underpinned by our core values: Community, Faith, Character, Compassion and Intellect.

Charitable status. Effingham Schools Trust is a Registered Charity, number 1095103. It exists to provide education for children.

Crescent School

Bawnmore Road, Bilton, Rugby, Warwickshire CV22 7QH

Tel: 01788 521595
email: admin@crescentschool.co.uk
website: www.crescentschool.co.uk
Twitter: @CrescentSchRug
Facebook: @cres.school

Leadership Team:

Headmaster: Joe Thackway, BA, PGCE

Deputy Head, Head of Curriculum & Assessment: Ms Bryony Forth, BSc, PGCE, NPQH (Year 5 Teacher – Mathematics, Geography)

Finance Manager and Registrar: Mrs Helen Morley

Head of Wellbeing, Deputy DSL: Mrs Sam Stapleton, BSc, QTS (Year 1 Teacher – RE and PSHE)

Assistant Head, Head of Pre-Prep, Designated Safeguarding Lead, Head of Pastoral Care: Alan Webb, BEd (Year 2 Teacher)

Assistant Head, Educational Visits Co-ordinator, Events Manager: Mrs Sarah Webb, BEd (Year 6 Teacher – English)

Age Range. 4–11.
Number of Pupils. 157 Day Boys and Girls (73 boys, 84 girls).
Fees per term (2021–2022). £3,262–£3,558.

The Crescent School is an independent co-educational preparatory school for day pupils aged 4–11 years. It merged with the Princethorpe Foundation in September 2016 joining the other schools in the Foundation – Little Crackers Nursery, Crackley Hall School and Princethorpe College.

The school was founded in 1948, originally to provide a place of education for the young children of the masters of Rugby School. Over the years the school has steadily expanded, admitting children from Rugby and the surrounding area. In 1988, having outgrown its original premises, the school moved into modern, purpose-built accommodation in Bilton, about a mile to the south of Rugby town centre. The buildings provide large and bright teaching areas, with a separate annexe housing the Nursery and Reception classes. There are specialist rooms for Science, Art, Design Technology, ICT and the Performing Arts. In addition, there is also a spacious Library and Resource Area. The multi-purpose hall provides a venue for daily assemblies, large-scale music-making, is fully equipped for physical education and has all the necessary equipment to turn it into a theatre for school productions. The school is surrounded by its own gardens, play areas and sports field.

The requirements of the National Curriculum are fully encompassed by the academic programme and particular emphasis is placed on English and mathematics in the early years. All pupils receive specialist tuition in Information and Communication Technology, Music and Physical Education. Specialist teaching in other subjects is introduced as children move upwards through the school. Spanish is introduced in Reception, followed by French in Year 3. The pupils are prepared for the local 11+ examination for entry to maintained secondary schools, including local grammar schools, and specific entrance examinations also at 11+ for independent senior schools.

The performing arts are a particular strength of the school and lessons are given in speech and drama, singing, percussion, musical theory and appreciation and recorder playing. Instrumental lessons (piano, brass, woodwind and strings) are offered as an optional extra. There is a school choir, orchestra, brass, string and wind ensembles and recorder groups.

Charitable status. The Princethorpe Foundation is a Registered Charity, number 1087124. It exists solely for the purpose of educating children.

The Croft Preparatory School

Loxley Road, Stratford-upon-Avon, Warwickshire CV37 7RL

Tel: 01789 293795
email: office@croftschool.co.uk
website: www.croftschool.co.uk

Chairman of The Board of Directors: Mrs L Thornton, Cert Ed Lond, FRSA

Chairman of the School's Governing Committee: Mrs V Aris, MBE, MSc

Headmaster: **Mr M Cook**, BSc Hons, PGCE

Deputy Headmaster: Mr E Bolderston, BSc Hons, PGCE

Age Range: 3–11
Number of Pupils: 403: 215 boys, 188 girls
Fees per term (2021–2022): £516–£4,448

The Croft Preparatory School is a co-educational day school, for children from 3 to 11 years of age, situated on the outskirts of Stratford upon Avon. Founded in 1933, the school occupies a large rural site with superb facilities and extensive playing fields, offering children some of the most exciting educational opportunities in the area. There is also a nature conservation area with a lake.

A family-based school, The Croft provides specialist teaching in small groups, where good discipline and a wider knowledge of the world around us, both spiritual and geographical, is encouraged. Music, Sport and Drama each play an important part in the curriculum. The resulting high educational standards provide the all-round excellence which is at the heart of the school.

The scope of the grounds and facilities enable a wide range of activities and opportunities – sporting, creative and recreational. From the Sports Hall, swimming pool and games pitches, to the Music practice rooms, Performance Space, small arenas in the playgrounds and the 600-seat Theatre; the Croft Cabin and conservation area, to the imitation Motte and Bailey castle, Geology Museum and Train Shed. The opportunities are endless at The Croft.

The children are prepared for 11+ entry to the local Grammar Schools or Senior Independent Schools.

Entrance requirements. Children can be accepted in Little Crofters from the age of 3 years. Prospective pupils registered for Years 1–6, where a place is available, are invited into School for a taster day. They will spend a day in the classroom with their age group and be assessed by the Class Teacher. Parents provide a copy of their child's latest school report and if deemed necessary, an assessment of literacy, numeracy, and sometimes other appropriate tests will be given by the SENDCo.

Crosfields School

Shinfield Road, Reading, Berks RG2 9BL

Tel: 0118 9871810
email: registrar@crosfields.com
website: www.crosfields.com
Twitter: @crosfieldsnews
Facebook: @CrosfieldsSchool
Instagram: @crosfieldsjuniorschool

Chairman of Governors: Mr C Bradfield

Headmaster: **Mr Craig Watson**, BEd, MA

Second Master: Mr Simon Dinsdale, MA Ed Open, BA Hons Chichester, FLCM, LTCL, LLCM, FISM, PGCE Open

Deputy Head Academic: Mr Richard Ebbage, BSc Roehampton, MSc Southampton, QTS, NPQSL UCL

Deputy Head Pastoral: Mr Adam Mallins, BSc Birmingham, PGCE Buckingham

Age Range. 3–16.
Number of Pupils. 625.
Fees per term (2021–2022). £3,802–£5,750 inclusive of food, educational day visits, curriculum residentials, text books and many co-curricular sessions. There is an additional charge for children in Nursery, Reception and Year 1 who remain in school after 4.15pm.

Crosfields is an independent, co-educational day school in Shinfield, Reading, pleasantly situated in over 40 hectares of wood and parkland. Offering education to Nursery children through to Senior School, Crosfields is a modern, well-resourced school boasting an outstanding reputation for academic excellence, and holds a strong track record in preparing pupils for the most academically demanding of schools.

A recent Independent Schools Inspection awarded Crosfields 'excellent', with inspectors commenting that, "Academic attainment is in advance of that expected at the relevant levels of age and stage of development." Pupils benefit from small class sizes where they receive individual attention from experienced and dedicated teaching staff, all housed in purpose-built, spacious classrooms. With contemporary science labs and well-stocked libraries, the school offers a broad curriculum that develops confident and independent learning, enhanced by exciting day and residential trips.

Facilities at Crosfields are considered unrivalled in the Reading area, where children enjoy an abundance of green space. Forest School outdoor learning sites, age-appropriate play equipment and sports areas are just some of the many jewels in the Crosfields crown. A floodlit artificial turf pitch provides four netball courts or hockey pitches, and is complemented by many natural turf sports pitches, cricket wickets, nets and pavilion. Pupils enjoy an on-site sports centre that houses a sports hall and dance studio, as well as a state-of-the-art swimming pool with moveable floor so that children of all ages can learn to swim confidently.

Furthermore, Crosfields has recently extended its age range to 16, and will have its first cohort of Year 11 pupils completing their GCSEs in 2023. What's more, the school has constructed a brand new, state-of-the-art two-storey Senior School building comprising bright classrooms, performance space, library and café. Children in the Senior School also benefit from a number of academic enrichment opportunities and challenges, such as the Duke of Edinburgh Award and Model United Nations.

In addition to its outstanding academic reputation and facilities, Crosfields offers working parents wrap-around care that includes an early morning breakfast club that opens at 7.30am, and after-school collection times up to 5.50pm. A comprehensive, co-curricular programme caters for all children and interests, and has over 90 activities ranging from cookery, golf, drama classes, judo, dance, fencing, choir singing and music, science and most recently, rowing, to name but a few!

The school is easily accessible from junction 11 of the M4 and the A33 Basingstoke Road. A number of transport routes for pupils travelling into the school are available for families who may require additional support with the school run. Routes run between neighbouring towns, including Basingstoke, Maidenhead, Henley and Wokingham, plus villages in between including Caversham, Mortimer, Burghfield, Hartley Wintney, Hook and Tadley.

Charitable status. Crosfields School Trust Limited is a Registered Charity, number 584278. The aim of the School is solely to provide education for children between the ages of 3 and 16.

Culford Preparatory School

Bury St Edmunds, Suffolk IP28 6TX

Tel: 01284 385308
email: admissions@culford.co.uk
website: www.culford.co.uk
Twitter: @CulfordSchool
Facebook: @OfficialCulfordSchool
Instagram: @culfordschool

Chairman of Governors: Air Vice Marshall S Abbott, CBE, MPhil, BA

Head: **C Bentley**, MEd

Age Range. Co-educational 7–13.

Number of Pupils. 230 (Day), 40 (Boarders).

Fees per term (2021–2022). Day £4,125–£5,405, Boarding £7,990–£8,585 (full), £6,980 (3-night), £6,470 (2-night).

Admission is by entrance examination at all ages, though the majority of pupils enter at age 7 or 11 and scholarships are available at 11+.

Culford Prep School has its own staff and Head, but remains closely linked to the Senior School. This allows the School to enjoy a significant degree of independence and the ability to focus on the particular needs of Prep School age children while benefiting from the outstanding facilities and community spirit of Culford.

Facilities. Culford Prep is situated in its own grounds, within Culford Park. The heart of the School is the impressive quadrangle at the centre of which lies the Jubilee Library. Other facilities include two science laboratories and two state-of-the-art ICT suites which, in common with the rest of the Prep School's classrooms, have networked interactive whiteboards.

Outside Prep have a mix of playing fields for all the major sports and the perennially-popular adventure playground.

Teaching & Learning. Prep School pupils are given a thorough grounding in the essential learning skills of mathematics and English and the enhanced curriculum broadens beyond the confines of the National Curriculum. Work in the classrooms is augmented by an extensive Activities Programme which offers pupils a wide range of opportunities and experiences, including trips out and visits from guest authors and experts in their field.

Music & Drama play a significant part in Culford Prep School life, and a variety of theatrical performances, choirs and ensembles are performed each year, either in Prep's own hall or in Culford's purpose-built Studio Theatre. Specialist speech and drama lessons are also offered.

Sports Facilities. Culford Prep School have access to the fantastic Sports and Tennis Centre, a state-of-the-art facility, which comprises a four-court, championship-standard Indoor Tennis Centre, a 25m indoor pool, gym, strength and conditioning suite, golf swing studio and a large sports hall with a climbing wall and indoor cricket nets. Outside there are further tennis courts, two of which are seasonally covered, two artificial turf pitches (one in partnership with Bury Hockey Club) and numerous rugby and hockey pitches. Pupils can also pursue athletics, horse riding, archery, CCF and the Duke of Edinburgh's Award. Culford launched a new Football Academy programme in 2018 to sit alongside its already well-established tennis, golf and swimming programmes.

Boarding. Prep School boarders live in Cadogan House, a mixed boarding house located next to the School overlooking the playing fields. Boarders are able to take advantage of a comprehensive programme of weekend activities and are looked after by a team of dedicated staff under the direction of the Housemaster. Recent trips have included visiting Harry Potter World, the Oasis Camel Park and the North Norfolk Coast.

Religious affiliation. Methodist: pupils from all faiths, and those of none, are welcome.

Charitable status. Culford School is part of the Methodist Independent Schools Trust, which is a Registered Charity, number 1142794.

Cumnor House School
Cognita Schools Group

Boys School:
168 Pampisford Road, South Croydon, Surrey CR2 6DA

Tel: 020 8660 3445

Girls School:
1 Woodcote Lane, Purley, Surrey CR8 3HB

Tel: 020 8668 0050

email: admissions@cumnorhouse.com
website: www.cumnorhouse.com
Twitter: @wearecumnor
Facebook: @WeAreCumnor
Instagram: @cumnorhouseschool
LinkedIn: /company/cumnorhouseschool

Head of School, Cumnor Boys': **Miss Emma Edwards**

Headmistress, Cumnor Girls': **Mrs Amanda McShane**

Age Range. Boys 4–13, Girls 4–11. Co-educational Nursery 2–4 years.

Number of Pupils. Prep & Pre-Prep: 360 Boys, 185 Girls. Nursery: 149.

Fees per term (2021–2022). £3,990–£4,970 (including lunch and school trips).

Cumnor House School for Boys – shortlisted for Sporting Achievement, Independent School of the Year 2021 – is one of Surrey's leading Preparatory Schools and prepares boys for scholarships and common entrance examinations to leading senior independent schools and local grammar schools.

Scholarships have been won recently to Charterhouse, Epsom, Dulwich, Harrow, Tonbridge, Westminster and the local senior independent schools, Caterham, Trinity and Whitgift.

Music, Sports, Art and Drama play a large part in the life of the School and all contribute to the busy, happy atmosphere.

Choir, sports tours and matches, ski trips, regular stage productions and a broad spectrum of clubs and options, give the boys the opportunity to pursue a wide range of interests.

This school is located in a residential area in South Croydon with access to good transport links.

Entry requirements: Taster Day with Assessment.

At **Cumnor House School for Girls – shortlisted for Small Independent School of the Year 2021–** our main aim is to give parents and their daughters as much choice as possible when selecting their senior schools in Year 6. This journey starts in the Early Years; by developing confidence and a positive attitude to learning, we lay vital foundations for the future.

Practical experiences complement the curriculum and encourage the love of learning needed to embrace the academic, cultural, sporting and musical opportunities that Cumnor House School for Girls provides. The girls are encouraged to develop all their interests and talents, both within the extensive curriculum and through involvement in a wide range of clubs and activities.

Scholarships have been won recently to Caterham, Croydon High, Ewell Castle, Old Palace, Reigate Grammar, Royal Russell, Streatham and Clapham High, Sutton High and Woldingham.

The school is located in a quiet, leafy, private road in Purley – a hidden gem of a school!

Entry requirements: Taster Day with Assessment.

Cumnor House Sussex

Danehill, Haywards Heath, West Sussex RH17 7HT

Tel: 01825 790347
email: registrar@cumnor.co.uk
website: www.cumnor.co.uk
Twitter: @cumnorhouse
Facebook: @cumnorhouse
Instagram: @cumnorhousesussex

Headmaster: **Fergus Llewellyn**

Deputy Head Pastoral: Michael Matthews

Deputy Head Academic: Bruno Shovelton

Head of Pre-Prep: Jacqui Freeman

Head of Finance: Matt Mockridge

Age Range. 2–13.
Number of Pupils. 365: 195 boys, 170 girls
Fees per term (2021–2022). Boarding: Full £8,035, Weekly £7,820; Day: Years 5–8 £6,875, Year 4 £6,075, Year 3 £5,280 Year 2 £4,175, Year 1 £3,695, Reception £3,165 (£2,400 above free entitlement).

Cumnor House Sussex is one of the country's leading independent day and flexible boarding schools for children from the ages of 2 to 13. Situated at the heart of the Ashdown Forest in Sussex, we provide an empowering education for active and ambitious boys and girls.

Cumnor is a School that lives by its motto of "Aim High, Be Kind and Dare to be Different". It places the child at the centre of all it does, looking each day to help them become the very best version of themselves, in whatever area that might be. It aims to strike the balance between the modern and the traditional. It looks to include every member of its community, from the Nursery child through to its parents. It wants its children to be happy and to thrive.

Set in 60 acres of beautiful Sussex countryside, our award-winning Cumnor Nursery is a truly wonderful, bespoke space for young children to explore, investigate, create and discover through play. The Nursery is a caring, friendly and nurturing environment where children are encouraged to make the most of the joys of living and learning. We are the only independent school in Sussex offering truly flexible childcare from 7am to 7pm, 50 weeks of the year, for children aged 2 to 4, and offering up to 30 hours EYEE.

Cumnor House Pre-Prep provides a happy, safe and nurturing environment in which children can begin to develop a life-long love of learning and interest in the world around them. Our self-contained Pre-Prep is the hub of Cumnor, with easy access to the Prep school's wider facilities including Woodpeckers, the theatre, swimming pool, home economics, music barn, sports pitches and 60 acres of Sussex countryside to explore. Our dedicated, passionate and devoted teachers support and encourage pupils to become well-rounded, inspired and confident individuals who are kind, tenacious and eager to do their best.

We are focused on individuals and every child is known to us. The happiness and well-being of each child is of paramount importance and in all decision making the impact on the child is considered first. We are ambitious for every child in our care and offer a fully rounded education within a community that nurtures childhood. We value kindness – to others and ourselves – above all else and believe this is central to enabling children to achieve their full potential while at school and to succeed in later life.

The breadth and depth of our curriculum is evident through our long standing track record of academic achievement, scholarship success and an unrivalled range of destination senior schools. Our children consistently achieve impressive academic results, moving on to over 20 different senior schools, with over 50% in any one year doing so with an Award or Scholarship.

Cumnor is a warm, friendly community with family at its heart. We offer preparation for boarding life at senior school with flexible boarding options for children in Year 7 and 8 in a home-from-home environment where they can develop personally, socially and creatively alongside their friends.

A pioneering wellbeing curriculum is at the core of Cumnor's ethos and why we led the way as the UK's first school to introduce 'iSpace Wellbeing'; an exciting, child-friendly approach to children's wellbeing education. iSpace is incorporated into the daily routine for all children from Nursery to Year 6, supported by a staff Wellbeing Team and Ambassador Awards for those children showing a keen interest in wellbeing lessons and putting their learning into practice. The success of iSpace, which is now being adopted in schools across Sussex, Surrey and London has swiftly been followed by #iWonder for Year 7 and 8 pupils, helping teens to understand their emotional, physical, social and mental health.

Charitable status. Cumnor House School Trust is a Registered Charity, number 801924. It exists for the advancement of education.

Dair House School

Bishop's Blake, Beaconsfield Road, Farnham Royal, Buckinghamshire SL2 3BY

Tel: 01753 643964
email: admissions@dairhouse.co.uk
website: www.dairhouse.co.uk
Twitter: @DairHouseSchool
Facebook: @dairhouse

Chairman of Governors: Mrs Jane Masih

Headmaster: **Mr Terence Wintle**, BEd Hons

Age Range. 3–11 Co-educational.
Number in School. 135 Day pupils.
Fees per term (2021–2022). £1,018–£4,500.

Located on the A355 in Farnham Royal, we are conveniently placed for Farnham Common, Farnham Royal, Gerrards Cross, Beaconsfield, Stoke Poges, Burnham and Slough.

Dair House School offers an exciting and personalised education to boys and girls from 3–11 years old.

We take pride in our warm, friendly, individual care, catering for each child's abilities. We provide our children with a firm sense of belonging and a sure foundation from the start in classes which are no larger than 19.

The school has excellent facilities with a new Learning Resource Centre which the children love to visit. Each class is fully resourced with smartboards and iPads. Our Nursery is very much part of the school with the children attending Thursday assemblies and enjoying a fantastic outdoor play environment.

Dair House School is situated in 4 acres of wonderful tree-lined grounds with a large sports field and an all-weather sports surface.

We offer a breakfast club from 7.30am and an after-school tea club until 6.00pm, as well as a plethora of lunchtime and after-school activities.

Charitable status. Dair House School Trust Limited is a Registered Charity, number 270719. Its aim is to provide 'a sure foundation from the start'.

Dame Bradbury's School
Stephen Perse Foundation

Ashdon Road, Saffron Walden, Essex CB10 2AL

Tel: 01223 454762
email: admissions@stephenperse.com
website: www.stephenperse.com
Twitter: @DameBradburys
Facebook: @stephenpersefoundation
Instagram: @stephenpersefoundation
LinkedIn: /company/stephen-perse-foundation

The Junior School at Dame Bradbury's is one of two Junior Schools in the Stephen Perse Foundation educating boys and girls following the same curriculum and vision for education designed to encourage independent, creative and reflective thinking. Dame Bradbury's is located in Saffron Walden; the sister Junior School at Rosedale House is located in the centre of Cambridge.

Chairman of Governors of the Stephen Perse Foundation: Mr J Dix

Principal of the Stephen Perse Foundation: Mr R Girvan

Head of Dame Bradbury's: **Mrs L Graham**

Age Range. 1–11.
Fees per term (2021–2022). Nursery: Age 1–2 £62 per day, Age 2–3 £60 per day, Age 3–4 £60 per day; Reception £3,990; Years 1–2: £4,240; Years 3–4: £4,740; Years 5–6: £4,950.

Every child that joins us takes an individual journey at Dame Bradbury's, through which they flourish and succeed.

Set in the beautiful town of Saffron Walden, we pride ourselves on getting to know every child and their family.

We are not afraid to do things differently. Our approach encourages young people to become independent thinkers – preparing them for life way beyond school.

Whilst our school has a history dating back to 1317, our facilities in the heart of Saffron Walden are definitely 21st century, from our beautiful sports grounds, modern sports hall and AstroTurf to our inspiring library, theatre and art studio.

Creativity and fun is everywhere – in our Forest School and inspiring art facilities, as well as in our clubs. From ballet to photography, rugby to rock band – there's something to capture the imagination of every child.

From 1 to 11, our pupils share a willingness to experiment, to question and to take on new challenges. They leave us full of enthusiasm, equipped with a love of learning and ready to take their next steps in life.

As part of the Stephen Perse Foundation, we offer a natural route into the Senior School in Cambridge and our children are already used to visiting for joint activities, trips and projects.

Danes Hill

Leatherhead Road, Oxshott, Surrey KT22 0JG

Tel: 01372 842509
email: registrar@daneshill.surrey.sch.uk
website: www.daneshillschool.co.uk

Chair of Governors: **Mr Hugh Monro**

Acting Head: **Mr Rob Andrews**, BSc

Age Range. 3–13 co-educational.
Number of Children. 772.
Fees per term (2021–2022). £2,327–£6,780.

As a co-educational school, Danes Hill prepares boys and girls for Scholarship and Common Entrance examinations to senior schools. A high academic success combines happily with a strong tradition of sporting prowess, to ensure that all children are exposed to a kaleidoscope of opportunity on a peaceful 55-acre site set well back from the main Esher-Leatherhead road. The Pre-Preparatory Department takes children from 3 to 6 years and is situated separately, but within easy walking distance of the Main School.

Extensive facilities include 2 state-of-the-art IT suites, a science block with 5 fully-equipped laboratories, a high-tech Art and DT centre, and new studio theatre. Both Pre-Prep and Main School sites have covered swimming pools.

The curriculum is broad and a wide range of extra-curricular activity is encouraged. Languages are a particular strength of the school. All children learn French and Spanish from age 3.

Pastoral care and pupil welfare are closely monitored. The school's Learning Support Centre provides a high level of support both for those with specific learning difficulties as well as running a programme for the exceptionally gifted and talented.

Residential and day trips are seen as an essential part of the school experience. The school operates language trips to centres in Spain and France. The annual Trips Week is a very special feature of the school calendar with over 500 children leaving the site to a range of residential destinations in the UK and abroad. There are also annual ski trips, as well as choir, rugby, netball and hockey tours.

Sport is a major strength and specialist games staff ensure that all the major sports are expertly coached. A floodlit astroturf pitch allows all-weather training and team spirit is valued alongside ability. There are extensive programmes of inter-school fixtures for all age groups. Every child is encouraged to participate. We also arrange annual games dinners for the senior teams and their parents to celebrate the end of each season. In-house Easter and Summer holiday activity courses are also very popular options with the pupils.

Charitable status. Danes Hill School (administered by The Vernon Educational Trust Ltd) is a Registered Charity, number 269433. It exists to provide high-quality education for boys and girls.

Daneshill School

Stratfield Turgis, Hook, Hampshire RG27 0AR

Tel: 01256 882707
email: office@daneshillprepschool.com
website: www.daneshillprepschool.com
Twitter: @DaneshillPrep
Facebook: @daneshill
Instagram: @daneshillprep

Headmaster: **Mr Jim Massey**, BSc Hons

Age Range. 3–13.
Number of Pupils. Day Boys 155, Day Girls 155.
Fees per term (2021–2022). Nursery on application; Reception £3,850 Year 1 £3,950, Year 2 £4,280, Year 3 £4,610, Years 4–8 £5,205. Lunch included. There are no compulsory extras.

Founded in 1950, Daneshill has always prided itself on the collective qualities of its teaching staff and their ability to interact with pupils and deliver a stimulating learning experience.

Set in over 100 acres of beautiful Hampshire countryside, the School provides the perfect environment and atmosphere for each pupil to grow and prosper as an individual with a strong set of core values.

After the sad death of Simon Spencer in 2016, the school was acquired by the Wellesley family and now forms part of the Wellington Estate. The Wellesley Family have a specific expertise and experience in education and are committed to Daneshill's long-term future as an independent prep school with a focus on the same core values that have established its reputation.

Academically the Daneshill curriculum has always maintained the expectations of the national curriculum while also offering so much more in respect of what we would regard as real education. Traditional values form the basis of a learning experience that engenders an enthusiasm for knowledge and encourages hard work as a means to academic success. This broadly-based curriculum also allows the development of high academic achievement to sit comfortably alongside our enthusiasm for pupils to become actively involved in all areas of the performing arts as well as the pursuit of sporting excellence.

Our aim has always been to develop enthusiastic learners who will make a strong contribution to their senior schools as good citizens and as pupils who are prepared to work hard in order to achieve success. This is certainly made easier by the children at Daneshill who possess a self-confidence and natural carefree joy which makes them a pleasure to teach. Each of them is a living testament to our belief that self-esteem is crucial to their development and success. We are also justifiably proud of the way our pupils exude courtesy, honesty, warmth and respect for others. They develop responsible attitudes to learning and life, and are a credit to themselves and their families.

Visitors to the School will be made very welcome and straight away they will experience the atmosphere that makes Daneshill unique.

Davenies School

Beaconsfield, Buckinghamshire HP9 1AA

Tel: 01494 685400
email: office@davenies.co.uk
website: www.davenies.co.uk
Twitter: @DaveniesSchool
Facebook: @DaveniesSchool
Instagram: @daveniesschool

Chairman: Mr N Edwards

Headmaster: **Mr Carl Rycroft**, BEd Hons

Age Range. 4–13.

Number of Boys. 339 (day boys only).

Fees per term (2021–2022). Pre-prep: £4,035 (Reception), £4,695 (Years 1 and 2); Junior School: £5,720 (Years 3 and 4), £5,780 (Middle School, Years 5 and 6); Senior School: £6,085 (Years 7 and 8).

Davenies is a thriving IAPS day school for boys aged 4–13. Our ethos and philosophy enable the boys to make the most of their preparatory years, supported by high-quality pastoral care, a broad and stimulating curriculum and numerous extra-curricular opportunities.

Davenies has its own distinct character and from their earliest years children are encouraged to relish the learning experience.

We are committed to an education both in and out of the classroom, thereby enabling the academic, artistic, musical, creative and physical potential of each child to flourish. The school environment is a warm, caring and happy one, where self-esteem is nurtured and grown; we believe that by fostering a wide range of interests and passions we provide the boys with every opportunity to develop in confidence. Our high-quality teachers have an excellent track record of preparing children for life at the country's leading senior schools and beyond.

Enterprises such as unique Davenies Award Scheme and the permeation of technology in our teaching and learning ensure we offer a truly independent educational experience.

At Davenies, our outstanding facilities support us in providing a positive learning experience with our own language of learning that nurtures each boy's understanding of how he learns. Davenies' boys are polite and friendly with their own individual characters, personalities, passions and interests.

Davenies offers a wide range of Scholarships to those boys who display an outstanding talent. Exhibitions are also available for individuals who show tremendous potential in their chosen area. Areas where awards are offered include Academic, Music, Sport, Art, Drama and Design and Technology. As well as the accolade of receiving a Scholarship there is a fee remission of 10% from the published school fees, and an Exhibition receives a remission of £300 per term. Successful candidates are automatically enrolled onto our Gifted and Talented programme, which aims to help boys flourish within their specific talent.

The Governors of Davenies are committed to broadening access to the School in Years 7 and 8 by offering to eligible parents/guardians means-tested financial support with the payment of school fees. Bursaries may be awarded in the form of a discount of up to 85% on tuition fees payable, depending on the financial, compassionate or other pertinent circumstances of applicants. The child's suitability for the school is the first consideration in granting support.

Charitable status. Beaconsfield Educational Trust Ltd is a Registered Charity, number 313120. It exists to provide high standards and the fulfilment of each child's potential.

Dean Close Pre-Preparatory School

Lansdown Road, Cheltenham, Gloucestershire GL51 6QS

Tel: 01242 258079
email: squirrels@deanclose.org.uk
website: www.deanclose.org.uk
Twitter: @DeanCloseSchool
Facebook: @DeanCloseSchool

Chairman of Governors: Mrs K Carden, MPhil, BA

Headmistress: **Dr C A Shelley**, BEd, PhD

Age Range. 2–7 Co-educational.

Number of Pupils. 142.

Fees per term (2021–2022). £2,800–£3,000.

Dean Close Pre-Preparatory School is a co-educational, Christian, family school which occupies the same campus as Dean Close Preparatory and Dean Close School and is, therefore, able to share their outstanding facilities including the swimming pool, sports hall, tennis courts, theatre and art block.

The Pre-Preparatory School is based in a purpose-built school building opened by Lord Robert Winston in June 2004. The School has a large hall surrounded by classrooms on two floors. There are two playgrounds – one for the Nursery and Kindergarten and one for Reception and Years 1 and 2.

The curriculum within the Pre-Preparatory School offers a wide range of learning opportunities aimed at stimulating and nurturing children's development and interests in an intellectual, physical, spiritual, social and emotional sense. Speech and Drama, Dance, Tennis, Music, Orchestra and Choir are some of the extracurricular activities available. All children participate in Forest School, which inspires creativity, thinking skills and cooperation, together with a love of the natural world.

Charitable status. Dean Close School is a Registered Charity, number 1086829.

Dean Close Preparatory School

Lansdown Road, Cheltenham, Gloucestershire GL51 6QS

Tel: 01242 258000
email: dcpsoffice@deanclose.org.uk
website: www.deanclose.org.uk
Twitter: @DeanCloseSchool
Facebook: @DeanCloseSchool
Instagram: @deanclose_prepschool

Chairman of Governors: Mrs K Carden, BA, MPhil

Headmaster: **Mr Paddy Moss**, BA

Age Range. 7–13.
Number of Pupils. 298: Boarding Boys 35, Boarding Girls 40, Day Boys 111, Day Girls 112.
Fees per term (2021–2022). Boarders £6,875–£9,175, Day Boarders £4,890–£7,600, International Boarders £7,700–£9,700; Day Pupils £4,080–£6,850.

Dean Close Preparatory School is a co-educational, Christian, family school which occupies the same campus as Dean Close School and is, therefore, able to share the outstanding facilities. These facilities include: 25m swimming pool, amphitheatre, shooting range, performance hall, 550-seat theatre and chapel. There are also extensive playing fields and sports facilities including hard tennis courts, floodlit astroturf hockey pitches and the new sports hall, which houses indoor tennis and cricket nets, as well as a large gymnasium and dance studio.

The Prep School also has its own teaching blocks and Music School, and a £4.5m building which opened in autumn 2013. This contains an additional 360-seat theatre and 8 teaching areas located over two floors, with a dedicated IT suite and drama rooms.

The new building also contains a music suite, which links to the existing Music School, and comprises 6 music practice rooms including a dedicated guitar room. The building has a formal reception area where parents and visitors are welcomed into the School.

There are two additional classroom blocks. One consists of 10 specialist teaching rooms including 2 laboratories and a computer centre. The other has 7 purpose-built classrooms, together with day house facilities, a staff Common Room, a new Library and an Art and Technology block. There is also a separate dining hall and kitchens.

Although the Preparatory School is administered by the same Board of Governors as the Pre-Prep and the Senior School, it has its own Headmaster and staff. There are 48 teaching staff who either hold degrees or diplomas in education. As well as a dedicated Director of Music, Director of Sport and Director of Drama. The music department is also supported by a team of excellent peripatetic music teachers specialising in a variety of instruments.

Pupils in Years 7 and 8 are taught in ability based form classes. All pupils follow an Independent Curriculum, aligned to the Common Entrance for: English, Mathematics, Biology, Chemistry, Physics, French, History, Geography, Religious Studies and Spanish. Pupils in the top two forms study Latin from Year 7.

The School has three boarding houses one for girls, one for boys and a mixed boarding house for the younger children. Each boarding house has a team of resident Houseparents, 2 House Tutors and a resident matron.

The day pupils are accommodated in three purpose-built houses. Each is run by a Housemaster/Housemistress, assisted by House Tutors.

The main games for boys are rugby, hockey and cricket, and for girls, hockey, netball, cricket and tennis. Swimming, athletics and cross-country running are also taught and use is made of the School's covered playing area. Golf and horse riding are available nearby.

A wide range of additional activities is also available: camping, canoeing, hillwalking, orienteering, judo, climbing, cooking, watercolour painting and all forms of dance, to name but a few.

With a Prep School population of 298, the sense of family-like community is developed in such a way that it is possible for every child to know each other and to be individually known, valued and cared about. The Prep School offers Foundation, Art, Drama, Music, Academic and Sports scholarships at 11+ and educates the Choristers who sing Evensong at Tewkesbury Abbey.

Charitable status. Dean Close School is a Registered Charity, number 1086829. It exists to provide education for children.

Devonshire House Preparatory School

2 Arkwright Road, Hampstead, London NW3 6AE

Tel: 020 7435 1916
email: enquiries@devonshirehouseprepschool.co.uk
website: www.devonshirehouseschool.co.uk
Twitter: @DHSPrep
Instagram: @DHSPrep

"Pupils leave the School as confident, resilient young people who have a strong self-esteem." **ISI Inspection Report**

Headmistress: **Mrs Stephanie Piper**, BA Hons

Age Range. Boys 2½–13, Girls 2½–11
Number in School. 650: 340 Boys, 310 Girls.
Fees per term (2021–2022). £3,290–£6,825.

The co-educational preparatory and pre-preparatory school in Hampstead, with its own nursery.

Devonshire House is a place where families come together for their children's most formative years. The School's commitment is to outstanding care and education, to help discover, inspire and develop pupils' talents and to support them throughout their years at the School and in their move to their next schools.

The results for senior school entry are exceptionally good, with some forty scholarships and exhibitions to senior schools in the last three years. However, the School is perhaps proudest that this is achieved in such a creative and happy school with its broad curriculum and with so many extra-curricular activities.

The School aims to create adaptable and creative minds, for a changing world.

The Head, Senior Leadership Team and Staff are committed to an open, trusting dialogue with parents about their children and to be available to advise and help throughout each child's school career.

Pupils learn how to work hard for their own achievements and to work with others with commitment, understanding and co-operation. They learn many things – traditional and innovative – and above all they learn how to grow their talents and how they may want to apply them in their lives.

Devonshire House has fine buildings, with substantial grounds and games areas, in the heart of Hampstead.

The School seeks to inspire not only a love of learning, but a love of thinking for oneself and the strength and resilience to do so, to make the most of life and to help others along this journey.

"A wonderful experience for my children. I am truly thankful for all the teachers and friends in DHS." **Junior School Parent**

Dolphin School

Waltham Road, Hurst, Berkshire RG10 0FR

Tel: 0118 934 1277
email: enquiries@dolphinschool.com
website: www.dolphinschool.com
Twitter: @DolphinSch
Facebook: @dolphinschoolhurst
Instagram: @dolphinschoolberkshire

Founded in 1970.

Head: **Adam Hurst**

Age Range. 3–13.

Number of Pupils. 211: 121 Day Boys, 90 Day Girls.

Fees per term (2021–2022). Nursery £3,630 (9.00am to 3.00pm, 5 days); Reception £3,795; Years 1–2 £4,180; Years 3–4 £4,985; Years 5–8 £5,075.

We believe that all children have their own interests, skills and talents, but all too often these remain hidden. Dolphin School offers an environment which encourages individuality to flourish. Children leave Dolphin with confidence in themselves, a strong sense of identity, intellectual curiosity, and the ability to adjust sensitively to different schools and social situations. Throughout life, in a rapidly changing world, our students will have the skills and the confidence to successfully pursue their goals and interests, in order to lead happy and fulfilled lives.

Dolphin children are allowed to develop as individuals and are encouraged to fulfil their potential, in small classes, under the careful guidance of specialist teachers. Abundant academic, artistic, social and sporting stimulation is provided through a varied, broad, well-rounded programme. We encourage lateral thinking and the ability to link concepts and ideas across subject and topic areas. Expectations for all children are high and academic rigour is a key component in all lessons.

Dolphin School provides the friendly, family atmosphere of a small school. All members of staff are actively engaged in the pastoral care of all of our children, and form teachers assume special responsibility for the daily wellbeing and overall progress of their small group of children. In addition, children in Years 5–8 have their mentor, as another layer of pastoral and academic support. The average class size is 15, although this can vary year-to-year. Children learn to take part in constructive and dynamic dialogue, to consider and empathise with the opinions of others, and to take pride in their own achievements, but also the accomplishments of their peers. They are encouraged to accept responsibility and to develop leadership skills.

Courses offered. At Dolphin, children are taught by subject specialists from Year 3 and in some cases from Nursery! In Early Years we provide a firm grounding in literacy and articulacy. French begins in Nursery, Latin in Year Six, and Spanish in Year Seven. Laboratory based Science is taught from Year 3. English, Mathematics, Geography, History, ICT, Global Citizenship, Classics, Art, Drama, Music and PE are taught throughout the upper school. Teachers seek ways and create opportunities to link their own subject to others, with a strong cross-curricular approach integral to learning at Dolphin.

Activities. A unique feature of a Dolphin School education is our extensive residential field trip programme in which all children participate from the age of seven. Annual field trips include visits to East Sussex, Dorset, Ironbridge, North Wales, Northumbria and Italy, while the French and Drama departments organise residential trips to Boulogne and Stratford respectively. We also offer an extensive mountain-walking programme, with staff and children participating in graded fell-walking. Locations include the Lake District, Brecon Beacons, Snowdonia and the Alps.

We believe in 'hands-on' learning, whether in or outside the classroom, and all Dolphin students also benefit from an extensive range of inspiring and stimulating day trips throughout the year.

Almost all costs associated with field, walking and day trips are included in the fees, as are lunchtime and after-school clubs which include: athletics, tennis, rounders, cricket, computer programming, swimming, football, netball, gymnastics, arts and crafts, hockey, chess, cross-country, rugby, art, music, orienteering, gardening, cookery, team building and drama.

We field teams from Year 2 in football, hockey, cricket, netball, swimming, cross-country and athletics. We are well represented at county level and a large number of our students play with distinction for local clubs.

Facilities. Our hall offers a splendid venue for school concerts and plays. We stage several major productions each year. Grounds include a swimming pool, two all-weather tennis courts, netball courts and large playing fields. We also have our very own 'copse', where our highly acclaimed forest school takes place. Cricket matches are hosted at Hurst Cricket Club, with hockey matches played on the excellent facilities at Sonning HC.

Entry. We welcome new students into any year group and children can join us at any point in the school year. Our staff and pupils are open and friendly, providing a warm welcome. Nursery at age 3+, Reception at age 4+, and at any time throughout Years 1–8.

Examination results. Our examination results are very strong and we frequently win scholarships (academic, drama and sport) to senior independent schools, including Abingdon, The Abbey, Queen Anne's and Leighton Park. We have a thriving Old Delphinian organisation. Most past pupils gain good degrees with a disproportionately high number going on to study at Oxbridge.

The Downs Malvern

Brockhill Road, Colwall, Malvern, Worcs WR13 6EY

Tel: 01684 544 108
email: registrar@thedownsmalvern.org.uk
website: www.thedownsmalvern.org.uk
Twitter: @DownsMalvern
Facebook: @TheDownsMalvern
Instagram: @thedownsmalvern

Chairman of Governors: Mr Carey Leonard

Headmaster: **Alastair S Cook**, BEd Hons, FRGS, IAPS

Age Range. 3–13 years Co-educational.

Number of Pupils. 196 children.

Fees per term (2021–2022). Full Boarding £5,197–£7,995; Weekly boarding £4,555–£7,035; Flexi boarding £43.00 per night; Day £4,290–£6,040; Pre-Preparatory £2,510–£3,400; Early Years: £25.69 per am/pm session, £51.38 per day (8.30am–3.30pm), £56.27 per day (8.30am–5.00pm).

The Downs Malvern, part of the growing Malvern College worldwide 'Family of Schools', is a busy, vibrant and successful co-educational preparatory school for boarding and day children aged between 3 and 13 years, offering an exciting education in a very happy environment.

Located 3 miles west of Malvern, 4 miles east of Ledbury, 15 miles from the M5 motorway, on the main line from Paddington and served by Malvern College transport, the Downs is situated on the Herefordshire side of the Malvern Hills on a beautiful rural 55-acre campus in Colwall.

The Downs Malvern strives to exceed the confines of the National Curriculum in academic, as well as cultural, sporting and social accomplishments. The school offers a broad curriculum challenging the academically gifted and supporting those with special needs. Following the School's most recent Independent Schools Inspectorate (ISI) inspection, The Downs Malvern was considered to be 'an excellent School'. The full inspection report is available on the School website.

The Early Years and Pre-Prep have now settled into their newly refurbished building. Six years after a seamless move from the Pre-Prep to the Prep Department at 7 years old, pupils will move on to a variety of independent senior schools on the basis of scholarship or Common Entrance examinations. Whilst there is the option to go on to a wide variety of independent schools, The Downs Malvern is the main feeder school for Malvern College. The emphasis in Years 7 and 8 is not only a preparation for scholarships and Common Entrance, but also to allow a smooth transition to the College academically and socially.

Sports, especially team games, are a significant part of the curriculum, as are Music and Art. 80% of the pupils learn to play a musical instrument. There is also a wide and expanding Hobbies programme that includes Railway Engineering as well as Speech and Drama, Dance, Design Technology and Art. The school has its own 9.5 inch gauge miniature steam railway, a unique feature.

Boarding. The refurbished Boarding House provides a home for up to 60 boarders. Boarding can be full, weekly, regular-flexi or a one-off experience with a published programme of exciting and creative evening and weekend activities. All boarders are looked after by a caring staff, dedicated to their welfare. A boarding inspection carried out by the ISI found the provision of boarding care at The Downs to be 'excellent'.

Facilities There is a wide range of facilities including: a 300-seat capacity Concert Hall; self-contained Music and Art buildings; new Science laboratories; a new Design and Technology suite, Pottery studio and wireless computer network with whiteboards. The large sports complex is supplemented by an AstroTurf Hockey pitch, 3 Netball/Tennis courts and 55 acres of grounds set aside for games pitches, Forest School lessons and relaxation.

11+ Scholarships and Exhibitions, as well as being awarded to pupils who show academic excellence, are also awarded to pupils who have a particular talent in Art, Music, Drama or Sport.

Bursaries are available offering assistance to parents subject to completion of a means test form. Discounts are available for Forces Families and the School has a strong relationship with Her Majesty's Armed Forces.

Charitable status. The Downs, Malvern College Prep School, trading as The Downs Malvern, is a Registered Charity, number 1120616. It exists to provide education for girls and boys from 3–13 years.

Downsend School
Cognita Schools Group

1 Leatherhead Road, Leatherhead, Surrey KT22 8TJ

Tel: General 01372 372197
            Admissions 01372 372311
email: admissions@downsend.co.uk
website: www.downsend.co.uk
Twitter: @DownsendSchool
Facebook: @DownsendSchool
LinkedIn: /company/downsend-school

Headmaster: **Ian Thorpe**, BA Ed Hons Exeter, MA Ed Open

Head – Little Downsend: Vanessa Conlan, BEd Hons Southampton

Head of Senior School: Karl Newland, BSc Surrey, MEd Buckingham, PGCE

Head of Junior School: Clare Kirkham, BA Hons London, PGCE

Age Range. 2–16 co-educational.

Fees per term (2021–2022). Little Downsend (Nursery, Reception, Year 1): £1,069–£4,240. Downsend School: Year 2 £4,685, Years 3–6 £5,685, Years 7–8 £5,790, Years 9–11 £6,410. Sibling discounts apply for more than one child in reception or above.

Downsend is a co-educational day school for children aged between 2 and 16 years.

Downsend (Junior & Senior) is located at the Leatherhead Road site and stands on a pleasant, open site just outside the town, surrounded by its own playing fields, tennis courts, Astro pitch, cricket nets and sports pavilion. The Sports Complex includes a large indoor swimming pool and sports hall. The comfortable and vibrant library, expanded networked ICT provision, bespoke facilities for Design Technology, Textiles and Food Technology, a Music Suite (complete with sound proof practice rooms) and Drama Room extend the curriculum to support pupil's learning and development.

Little Downsend (age 2 to 6). There are three co-educational pre-preparatory school sites in Ashtead, Epsom and Leatherhead. Pupils work in a welcoming and stimulating environment, in small classes, where a strong focus on education builds solid foundations in Numeracy and Literacy. Dance and Drama, French, Music and Swimming are all taught by specialists and enhance the curriculum across all year groups. An enhanced afternoon programme, further supported by a wide range of after school clubs including Spanish, is also on offer. An extended day facility is available. At the age of 6 the children move on to Downsend Junior where they are joined by children from other local independent and state schools.

Downsend Junior & Senior (age 6 to 16). Founded in 1891, Downsend was an established academic prep school which extended its provision to age 16 from September 2020. The school is a thriving community where children are encouraged to develop their talents both in and outside the classroom. A huge variety of extra-curricular opportunities are offered to allow children to try new activities during and after school.

The standard of work is high and there is a broad and engaging curriculum. Our approach to learning sees English, Science, Maths, Languages, Humanities, Art and Technology being lifted off the pages of textbooks and worksheets through creativity and enthusiasm. In addition to the usual subjects, children study Art, Drama, Food Technology, ICT, Music, Design Technology, Textiles and PSHE. There is a termly curriculum collapse day for STEAM projects. Parents are kept informed of their children's progress through regular parents' evenings and termly reports and are welcome at all times to communicate with teaching staff and the management team.

The school has a strong reputation for music, with regular and varied concerts throughout the year, as well as orchestras and choirs for the Junior and Senior School. A large number of children learn musical instruments and all pupils in Year 3 enjoy the instrumental scheme where they try different instruments before choosing which one to learn for the rest of the school year. Drama is equally important and there is a production at the end of each term. Pupils can take part in a full range of sports not only in school but also at local, regional and national level. Regular visits occur outside school and trips abroad are also offered.

The holiday club scheme, Downsend+, gives pupils access to exciting and absorbing workshops, courses, themed days and thrilling days out. Run by qualified Downsend staff, this provision is available to children from age 5 (Reception) from 8.00am to 5.30pm, including breakfast, lunch and tea as appropriate. Little Downsend+ is also available as a dedicated facility for our younger children aged 2–5 and is held at Little Downsend Leatherhead.

Dragon School

Bardwell Road, Oxford OX2 6SS

Tel: 01865 315 405
email: admissions@dragonschool.org
website: www.dragonschool.org
Twitter: @thedragonschool
Facebook: @DragonSchoolOxford
Instagram: @dragonschooloxford

Motto: *Arduus ad solem* – 'reach for the sun'

Chairman of Governors: Andrew Webb, MA, MBA

Head: **Emma Goldsmith**, BA

Age Range. 4–8 (Pre-Prep), 8–13 (Prep).
Number of Pupils. 798
Fees per term (2021–2022). Prep Day £7,473; Prep Boarding £10,931; Pre-Prep £4,239–£5,573.

Founded in 1877, the Dragon is a co-educational boarding and day school in Oxford which offers an outstanding educational experience for both boys and girls from 4 to 13 years. The school's distinctive approach encourages enquiry, confidence and enthusiasm in a quintessentially English school environment. Recognised as individuals, children are encouraged to try everything and express themselves. Highly-qualified staff foster a culture of learning how to learn which promotes academic, sporting and creative excellence. Pupils progress to many of the top schools in the country and an impressive number obtain scholarships each year.

Dragon School's beautiful Prep campus and dedicated Pre-Prep are located just north of central Oxford – the oldest University City in the world.

The Curriculum. Teaching is tailored to the needs of each pupil and their learning styles and motivations. Teachers aim to inspire, motivate and challenge to help children take ownership of their own learning.

DragonQUEST is a new enrichment curriculum replacing academic lessons on Saturday mornings. Children choose from over 20 activities ranging from paddle boarding and bike mechanics, to visiting a working farm and cultural walks around Oxford.

Games & the Arts. The Dragon offers over 20 sports to both boys and girls including hockey, rugby, sculling, fencing, football, golf, cricket, equestrianism and judo. The Dragon supports children's development, coordination, movement and performance through sport and exercise. Children observe, explore and learn through drawing, painting, printmaking, sculpture and ceramics in Art, and experiment with a range of materials and electronics in Design Technology. Music and Drama are a real strength with a dual emphasis on participation and excellence.

Pastoral Care. The Dragon strives to create a happy, secure and stimulating learning environment in which all members of the school community can grow and develop as individuals. The Dragon follows a nurturing programme which enhances self-awareness, personal empowerment, self-esteem and empathy for all pupils. This whole-school approach extends beyond the classroom to all staff, children and parents.

Boarding. A range of flexible boarding options are available and begin from age 8, in small, family-run boarding houses.

Future Schools. 51 Scholarships and Awards were achieved by 2021 leavers. Dragons go on to around 30 different schools: Eton, Harrow, Headington, Magdalen College School, Marlborough, Oxford High, Radley, Rugby, St Edward's, St Mary's and Winchester. Preparatory years at the Dragon lay the firm foundations of a successful education at senior schools in the UK and beyond.

Head's Philosophy. It is important to harness the vitality, imagination and natural curiosity of young people to develop the mindset of 'why not?'. If this culture of questioning is embedded at an early age it will encourage an enthusiasm to lead a lifetime of learning. *Arduus ad solem* 'reach for the sun' is the School's motto and is as relevant today as it was when the school was founded. We want all of our children to become resilient and ambitious, ready to take on the challenges of being a global citizen of the 21st Century. The Dragon has a well-earned reputation of providing a community which will nurture these characteristics with the values of kindness, courage and respect underpinning all that we do.

Outstanding Characteristics. The 2014 ISI inspection rated Dragon School as 'outstanding' and teaching and learning as 'exceptional'. The School ethos promotes a warmly enthusiastic, genuinely respectful and a naturally unpretentious approach to learning. It fosters an intellectual curiosity, a strong sense of community and a keen pursuit of excellence in all its forms.

For further information or to arrange a visit please contact Dr Kate Heath, Registrar, on 01865 315 405 or admissions@dragonschool.org. Please visit www.dragonschool.org for more information. Personal tours available by appointment.

Charitable status. The Dragon School Trust Ltd is a Registered Charity, number 309676. Aim: to provide education for boys and girls between the ages of 4 and 13.

Dulwich Prep Cranbrook

Coursehorn, Cranbrook, Kent TN17 3NP

Tel: 01580 712179
email: registrar@dulwichprepcranbrook.org
website: www.dulwichprepcranbrook.org
Twitter: @DPCranbrook
Facebook: @DPCranbrook
Instagram: @dulwichprepcranbrook
LinkedIn: /dulwichprepcranbrook

Chairman of Governors: Mr Peter Anderson

Headmaster: **Mr Paul David**, BEd Hons

Age Range. 3–13.
Number of Boys and Girls. Day and Boarding: 279 (Upper School), 191 (Little Stream), 64 (Pre-Prep).
Fees per term (2021–2022). Day: £6,655 (Years 7–8), £6,570 (Years 5–6), £5,585 (Years 2–4), £4,230 (Year 1), £4,080 (Reception), Nursery: £3,425 (full day), £2,155 (mornings). Boarders: from £40 per night.

The School, which is one mile from the country town of Cranbrook, has extensive grounds (50 acres) and offers a broad and varied education to boys and girls from 3 to 13+. To ensure that children receive the personal attention that is vital for this age range the School is divided up into three separate, self-contained, departments. These are Nash House (3–5 year olds), Little Stream (5–9 year olds) and Upper School (9–13 year olds). Each department has its own staff, teaching equipment, sports facilities, playgrounds, swimming pools, etc. Pupils are prepared for Common Entrance or Scholarship examinations to any school of their parents' choice, and there is a strong emphasis on up-to-date teaching methods. The wide scope for sporting activities – Football, Rugby, Cricket, Hockey, Netball, Rounders, Athletics, Cross Country, Swimming, Tennis – is balanced by the importance attached to Art, DT, Drama, ICT and Music. Over 200 pupils learn the full range of orchestral instruments. There are two Orchestras, Wind and Brass Bands, Jazz Band, and four Choirs. The boarders are housed in the Manor House, boys and girls each under the care of House staff. The happiness of the boarders is a particular concern and every effort is made to establish close and friendly contact between the School and the parents. There is a flourishing Parents Association, and the school prides itself on its open door policy and friendly atmosphere.

The School is a Charitable Trust, under the same Governing Body as Dulwich Prep London, although in other respects the two schools are quite separate. The link with Dulwich College is historical only.

Charitable status. Dulwich Prep Cranbrook is a Registered Charity, number 1174358. It exists for the provision of high quality education in a Christian environment.

Dulwich Prep London

42 Alleyn Park, Dulwich, London SE21 7AA

Tel: 020 8766 5500
email: admissions@dulwichpreplondon.org
website: www.dulwichpreplondon.org

The School was founded in 1885 and became a charitable trust in 1957 with a board of governors.

Chair of Governors: Mrs K Kelleher

Head: **Miss Louise Davidson**

Age Range. Boys 3–13, Girls 3–5.
Number of Children. 828 boys, 13 girls.
Fees per term (2021–2022). Tuition: Day boys £4,760–£6,965 inclusive of lunch (there are no compulsory extras).

Dulwich Prep London is an independent prep school with a national reputation for excellence.

While we are essentially a boys' school, with about 840 pupils aged between 3 and 13, we start with the Early Years Department which also caters for girls. There are four other sections to the school: the Pre-Prep (Years 1 & 2), the Lower School (Years 3 & 4), and the Middle & Upper Schools (Years 5 & 6 and 7 & 8).

At 13+ our boys go on to more than fifty excellent day and boarding schools throughout the country. Alleyn's, Harrow, Dulwich College, Eton College, Marlborough College, Tonbridge, St Paul's, Wellington College, Westminster, and Winchester College are just a selection of our leavers' destination schools. In the 2019–2020 academic year our leavers gained more than 70 academic, musical, artistic, and sporting scholarships and awards.

Situated in SE21, we have the very best educational facilities. These include very spacious classrooms, a science block containing 3 labs, a DT suite, a cookery suite, and an observatory, a dedicated music school, a large sports hall, a studio theatre, 3 ICT suites, a superb art studio, a six-lane 25m swimming pool and more than 25 acres of playing fields, quite unique given our privileged location.

Some of the opportunities available to our pupils are:

- We run more than 25 sports teams each term with the top teams regularly doing well in national competitions. Recent sports tours include cricket to South Africa, football to Italy, rugby to Ireland.
- More than 700 individual music lessons take place every week and boys have the opportunity to perform regularly in a range of groups and ensembles.
- Approaching 30 groups perform regularly in our own 300-seat concert hall. Many also appear on the programme for our gala concerts at prestigious venues such as St John's, Smith Square, and Southwark Cathedral.

- We provide more than 100 clubs and extra-curricular activities, stimulating boys' intellectual and sporting interests.
- We run residential trips for pupils in Years 4–8 within the curriculum that are built into the fee structure. 15 more trips, ranging from cultural visits to skiing, are offered during the holidays.
- Drama productions are staged by forms and year groups from Reception to Year 8.

Charitable status. Dulwich Prep London is a Registered Charity, number 1174356. It exists to provide education for boys.

Dumpton School

Deans Grove House, Deans Grove, Wimborne, Dorset BH21 7AF

Tel: 01202 883818
email: secretary@dumpton.com
website: www.dumpton.com
Twitter: @dumpton
Facebook: @dumpton
Instagram: @dumpton_school

Chairman of Governors: Mr H Cocke

Headmaster: **Mr Christian Saenger**, BA Hons, QTS

Age Range. 2–13.
Number of Pupils. Girls and Boys: 218 aged 7–13 and 92 aged 2–7.
Fees per term (2021–2022). Prep School (Years 3–8) £5,763; Pre-Prep (Reception, Years 1 & 2) £3,224; Nursery charged at £7.35 per hour. The school week is from Monday to Friday. All fees include meals and there are no compulsory extras.

Dumpton School is a co-educational day school for pupils aged 2 to 13 years. The school is set in a beautiful rural setting with 26 acres of grounds but is nevertheless only one mile from Wimborne and school buses run daily to and from the nearby towns of Blandford, Bournemouth, Dorchester, Ferndown, Poole, Ringwood, Verwood and Wareham.

Despite record numbers in the school, class sizes are small. Children enjoy excellent teaching as well as incomparable opportunities for Music, Art, Drama and Sport in which the school excels. Dumpton is renowned for its caring approach in which every child is encouraged to identify and develop his or her abilities and personal qualities as fully as possible. This safe and supportive environment sees the children thrive and reach their full potential. The framework of family and Christian values emphasises the importance of teamwork and mutual respect that pervades the school. It is a very happy and successful school and children regularly win scholarships to their Senior Schools or places at the local Grammar Schools. Over the past twelve years, Dumpton pupils have been awarded over 278 scholarships to schools such as Bryanston, Canford, Clayesmore, Millfield, Milton Abbey, Talbot Heath and Sherborne.

Recent developments have included a new multi-purpose Performing Arts venue complete with music recital room, a new outdoor adventure playground for the Prep School, a new Science and Maths Block, a full-size floodlit Astroturf, a covered swimming pool, a new Art, Design and Food Technology Centre, an outdoor classroom, climbing wall and environmental area, complete with ponds, pontoons, beehives and pupil allotments. In addition, the school has been awarded Green Flag status by Eco-Schools for 4 years running as well as the South West Environmental Award for 2018. The building of a new state-of-the-art sports hall was completed in the summer of 2019.

The school motto 'You can because you think you can', lies at the cornerstone of teaching at Dumpton and our aim is for pupils to leave us having reached their full potential, as confident communicators and appreciating good manners and tolerance.

For a copy of the prospectus, please apply to the Headmaster's Secretary.

Charitable status. Dumpton School is a Registered Charity, number 306222. It exists to provide education for boys and girls.

Dunhurst

Bedales Prep

Alton Road, Steep, Petersfield, Hampshire GU32 2DR

Tel: 01730 711544
email: admissions@bedales.org.uk
website: www.bedales.org.uk
Twitter: @DunhurstSchool
Facebook: @bedalesschool
Instagram: @BedalesPrepSchool
LinkedIn: /bedales-school

Chairman of Governors: Stephen Nokes

Head: **Colin Baty**, BA Ed

Deputy Head (*Pastoral*): Graeme Thompson

Deputy Head (*Academic*): Andy Wiggins, BA Kent, PGCE Portsmouth

Age Range. 8–13.
Number in school. 190 pupils: 94 boys; 96 girls; 34 boarders
Fees per term (2021–2022). Boarders £8,735; Half-boarding (3 nights) £7,780; Day: £5,930–£6,575. Flexi-boarding available (£48 per night).

John Badley founded Bedales School in 1893 to educate through head, heart and hand. When Dunhurst was added in 1902 as the prep school, Badley's philosophy on education continued. Dunhurst is a unique school: a warm inclusive atmosphere in which relationships are built on trust, tolerance, respect, support and care; a stimulating curriculum that has breadth and depth; a school where children experience the joy of discovery and learning and a wealth of opportunity.

The academic curriculum aims to offer challenge through innovative teaching that inspires the pupil and focuses on the individual. Confidence grows as the children grow, and with it their desire to question and discuss. The school's distinctive approach to learning helps children excel academically. Learning through doing lies at the heart of the educational ethos.

The creative and performing arts, sport, the outdoor work programme and the diverse wealth of activities on offer ensure that every pupil can develop new interests and skills important to them.

Relationships throughout the Dunhurst community are warm and informal but this goes hand in hand with a strong philosophy of respect and courtesy. A global understanding is nurtured in the pupils through a wide range of outreach projects and fundraising initiatives; Dunhurst pupils are encouraged to see themselves through the context of a wider world.

Dunhurst engenders inquisitiveness in pupils so they are prepared for the academic rigour of IGCSEs, Bedales Assessed Courses (BACs), A Levels and beyond. It isn't all about getting results; there is depth to pupils' learning because of Dunhurst's diverse curriculum. The creative and performing arts, sport, the outdoor work programme and the wealth of activities on offer ensure that every pupil can develop new interests and skills.

Matches against other schools take place regularly in athletics, cricket, football, hockey, netball, rounders, rugby, swimming and tennis. A wide range of other sports and outdoor activities is also offered, including judo and golf.

Dunhurst makes full use of the first-rate facilities at Bedales which include a theatre, sports hall, floodlit netball and tennis courts, an all-weather pitch and indoor swimming pool. This and the similarity of ethos, makes for an easy transition for pupils moving from Dunhurst to Bedales Senior at the age of 13.

There is a strong boarding community at Dunhurst, with a range of options to suit the varying needs of its families, including full, half and flexi-boarding

Applicants for both boarder and day places sit residential entrance tests. The main points of entry are at 8+ and 11+. Entry at other ages is dependent on the availability of places.

For information about Dunannie, the Pre-Prep (3–8 years), see the Bedales entry in HMC section.

Charitable status. Bedales School is a Registered Charity, number 307332. It exists to provide a sound education and training for children and young persons of both sexes.

Durlston Court

Becton Lane, Barton-on-Sea, New Milton, Hampshire BH25 7AQ

Tel: 01425 610010
email: registrar@durlstoncourt.co.uk
website: www.durlstoncourt.co.uk
Twitter: @durlstoncourt
Facebook: @DurlstonCourt
Instagram: @durlstoncourt

Chairman of Governors: Mr Chandra Ashfield

Headmaster: **Mr Richard May**, BA, PGCE

Age Range. 2–13 Co-educational.

Number of Pupils. 270 Day Pupils.

Fees per term (2021–2022). Kindergarten £8.80 per hour (i.e. £39.60 per morning session – 4.5 hours including lunch, or £59.40 per day – 6.75 hours including lunch), Reception £2,800 (Fees for an eligible Reception child receiving EYE would be £2,031 based on an eleven-week term), Years 1 & 2 £3,185, Year 3 £4,765, Years 4–8 £5,935. www.durlstoncourt.co.uk/admissions/fees

Durlston Court is a wonderful school in a wonderful environment, situated on the border of Hampshire and Dorset, at the edge of the New Forest and by the sea!

Our purpose is to provide a first-class Prep School education for every child. This starts in our wonderful Kindergarten (age two upwards), through our Pre-Prep Department (Reception to Year 2) and then on to the Middle School (Years 3 to 5) and Senior School (Years 5 to 8). Whenever your child joins the school you can be sure that we develop happy, confident and successful children who flourish in an inspiring and nurturing environment where learning opportunities are limitless. Excellence, integrity and challenge are fostered as core values of the Durlston Family. Our children are prepared to face challenges and to fully engage and thrive in the world of today and tomorrow.

A preparatory school prepares a child for the next stage in his or her educational journey, and beyond. We are proud that we do this so well. Durlston Court has a long standing reputation for all-round educational excellence, confirmed by the highest inspection rating possible. We focus on good manners and behaviour whilst promoting ever-evolving tailor-made challenges for each child within the Durlston Family – a cohesive and mutually supportive unit. We look forward to encouraging the mindset and skills that will enable all to flourish post-Durlston.

Our children will be ready for the future – any future. In the world of endless opportunities that awaits them, our learning without limits philosophy will ensure that our pupils will be open to all possibilities and equipped to deal with the challenges ahead.

Our website will provide an overview of Durlston Court but to get a true taste of life at Durlston, I invite you to meet pupils and staff, and to view our impressive and ever-increasing facilities and to hear about our extended day provision. You can be assured of a very warm welcome.

Parents are most welcome to visit the school by making an appointment. Parents can also watch a virtual tour at: www.durlstoncourt.co.uk/tour-from-your-home

Further details of the school are available by visiting the school's website or by contacting registrar@durlstoncourt.co.uk.

Charitable status. Durlston Court School is a Registered Charity, number 307325, which exists to provide quality education for children from 2–13 years.

Durston House

12 Castlebar Road, Ealing, London W5 2DR

Tel: 020 8991 6530
email: info@durstonhouse.org
website: www.durstonhouse.org
Twitter: @DurstonHouse
Facebook: @DurstonHouse
Instagram: @durston_house_school

Co-Chairmen of Governors: Mr K Mahoney, BSc, MRICS & Mr D G Henshall

Headmaster: Mr G Entwisle, BA Hons

Deputy Head: Mr W J Murphy, BA, DipTch

Bursar: Mrs J Twyford

Director of Studies: Mr D Stock, BSc Hons, PGCE

Head of Complementary Curriculum: Mrs C Green, MA, BA, QTS

Head of Junior School: Miss P Orr, BEd

Acting Head of Pre-Prep: Ms D Finlayson, BSc Hons Middx, PGCE

Head of Studies Administration: Miss J Chisholm, BEd Canada, QTS

Age Range. 4–13.

Number of Boys. 350 Day Boys.

Fees per term (2021–2022). £4,490–£5,420.

Durston House is a vibrant, stimulating, energetic and forward-looking school. We have a proud and long history with a fine record of achievement, whilst we look forward with confidence and energy.

A boy's education here is shaped by the development of his **character** by giving him the confidence and skills to excel, his **curiosity** to learn and discover more, and his expanding **capability** to succeed in all he takes on. These three concepts, **Character, Curiosity** and **Capability** are the cornerstones of his success at Durston House and his success in life.

At Durston we are proud of our diverse community, one which values people through mutual respect, compassion and warmth. At Durston we welcome pupils from all ethnic, cultural and religious backgrounds; this is a school where pupils are taught from their earliest experiences, that a generosity of spirit, mutual respect and fairness really matter.

Pupils are recognised and appreciated for who they are as individuals. There is a wholehearted commitment to a holistic education, in which each individual and their talents come first. Our pupils shape the community and are supported and nurtured by teachers who really care. The excellent pastoral care at Durston allows for the school to flourish as the happy and relaxed place that it is.

An education here is based upon academic rigor through excellent teaching, encouraging our pupils to explore, question, take risks, and develop their creativity, communication and teamwork – all central to successful life-long learning. Our boys demand to be stimulated and challenged by their teachers, and in turn the expectations of our boys to be the best version of themselves is equally important. All of this is achieved through a spirit of humility and quiet determination.

At Durston we are proud of the academic achievements of our boys along with all they contribute to the broader aspects of the curriculum – the visual and performing arts, music and sport are all fundamental to a Durston education.

Charitable status. Registered Charity, number 294670.

Eagle House

Crowthorne Road, Sandhurst, Berkshire GU47 8PH

Tel: 01344 772134
email: info@eaglehouseschool.com
website: www.eaglehouseschool.com
Twitter: @EagleHouseSch
Facebook: @EagleHouseSch
Instagram: @eaglehousesch

Chairman of Governors: M Rickards, Esq

Headmaster: A P N Barnard, BA Hons, PGCE

Age Range. 3–13.

Number of Children. 386: 60 Boarders, 326 Day Children.

Fees per term (2021–2022). Prep School: £8,635 (boarders), £6,205–£6,425 (day pupils). Pre-Prep: £4,110. Nursery: £2,250 (5 mornings including lunch).

Eagle House is a co-educational, boarding and day Prep, Pre-Prep and Nursery located in Berkshire. The school's superb grounds and excellent facilities are the background to an experience where success, confidence and happiness are paramount. The school is proud of its academic record, preparing children for a host of top independent schools and boasting a diverse and robust curriculum. A new Pre-Prep and Music School opened in 2021.

Younger pupils follow the International Primary Curriculum and our older children have embarked on a new Curriculum 200 that links subjects through topics and themes. Great teaching, new technology and a focus on the basics mean that children make good progress and love to be in the classroom. Independent learning is a focus for all children and our Extended Project programme helps drive inquisitive minds.

Eagle House offers a diverse and varied extra-curricular programme and we unashamedly offer lots as part of our Golden Eagle activities experience. Children benefit from a huge range of opportunities in sport, music, drama, art, outward bound and community programmes. Busy children are happy and fulfilled children and we like to think that all pupils are Learning for Life.

Learning for Life means that children benefit from the best all-round education. They can feel confident in the classroom, on the games field, on stage, in the concert hall and in the community. Everyone is given the chance to stretch themselves in every area. Challenge is an important part of growing up and at Eagle House we learn that success and failure are both positive experiences.

Bright learning environments, outdoor learning areas and wonderful sporting facilities are important, but it is the community that shapes a young person. Through the excellent pastoral care and tutor system, coupled with a buddy structure, ensuring children have an older pupil to support them, Eagle House seeks to develop wellbeing from the youngest to the oldest.

Recognising how to be a positive influence within a community is also part of the Eagle House journey. Through our wonderful Learning for Life programme that teaches children about themselves and the wider community, we aim to make all our pupils responsible and independent as well as able to show empathy and understanding towards others. Time for reflection in chapel and assemblies also improves the way we look at the world and mindfulness sessions help us all take stock.

Boarding is a popular option and allows children to experience a varied evening programme of activities as well as being part of a vibrant and caring community. Boarding encourages independence, but it is also great fun and whether full, weekly or flexi, boarders have the most wonderful time.

We often say that Eagle House children have the time of their lives and we firmly believe this. Learning for Life at Eagle House opens the doors to all sorts of opportunities and this results in children who are highly motivated and enthusiastic in all they do. Eagle House buzzes with achievement and laughter – not a bad way to grow up!

Charitable status. Wellington College is a Registered Charity, number 309093. Eagle House School is owned by Wellington College and is part of the same charity registration.

Eaton House Belgravia Pre-Prep, Prep and Nursery

3–5 Eaton Gate, Belgravia, London SW1W 9BA

Tel: 0203 917 5050
email: sfielding@eatonhouseschools.com
website: www.eatonhouseschools.com
Twitter: @eatonhousesch
Facebook: @eatonhouseschools

Head: **Mr Huw May**

Age Range. 4–11, Boys; 2–4 Co-educational Nursery.

Number of Pupils. 240.

Fees per term (2021–2022). £6,895–£7,640. Nursery prices according to sessions attended.

Eaton House Belgravia has been in existence since 1897, and is part of the very fabric of Chelsea and Belgravia. It is a place where bright minds can excel in an environment which offers so many opportunities, opens minds to fluid thinking and instils a lifelong love of learning. Boys leave to join some of the best Prep and Senior schools in the country.

Boys will experience a happy, confident and ambitious start to their education, in a traditional yet modern and welcoming academic environment. Despite being non-selective at Nursery and 4+, in 2021 some 31 per cent of 7+ and 8+ pupils received offers for Westminster and St Paul's, with others choosing a range of other top schools, or remaining until 11+. Our first batch of 11+ results were also successful with pupils heading off to some of the top schools in the country including Westminster Under.

The Good Schools Guide points out, 'This would be an impressive record for a selective school, let alone one with EHB's broad intake.' *The Good Schools Guide* also comments that Eaton House provides 'Excellent preparation for the top academic Prep schools that the boys are aiming for' with a fast pace and boy-friendly teaching from 'excellent, nurturing' staff who 'know their boys and care for them.'

The happiness and wellbeing of the boys, which is a contributing factor to these outstanding results, is paramount under an energetic team, led by experienced Headmaster Huw May. New boys are welcomed by 'buddies', supported by a welcoming House structure, and presented with a clear code of good conduct to live by. This means that all the new Kindergarten boys soon find their feet, supported by children in other years that look after them, as they become part of such an energetic, action-packed and exciting community.

Mr May encourages all boys to behave with kindness, manners and team spirit at all times, becoming part of a mindful, supportive learning community. *The Good Schools Guide* (2020) says he is 'Ambitious for his school, shows vision and is full of enthusiasm for developing each boy's all-round potential, emotionally as well as academically.'

Individual potential is developed through a personalised learning plan created for each boy which looks at his life at Eaton House Belgravia in the round – both academically and socially. Mr May is determined that no boy shall ever feel overlooked or unsupported at his time at Eaton House Belgravia.

Parents are always involved in all aspects of their son's education, with the option to talk to teachers at collection and drop-off, and there are two week assessment plans for each boy in the run-up to exams.

The teaching strategy is to inspire and encourage creative, analytical thinking and to unobtrusively support the boys individually with any challenges that they may face. This means that every boy feels confident as he continues on his academic journey.

Boys take exams at 7+ or 8+, or they move up to the Prep School to take their exams at 11+. Eaton House Belgravia takes the view that if a boy is ready at 7+, he will sit his exams at that age, in close consultation with the parents. Alternatively, he may choose to sit at 8+ or stay on in the Prep and take the 11+. Each of these options depends on the child, as our boys blossom academically at different rates.

Eaton House Belgravia's Prep School has an excellent teacher-to-pupil ratio, offering a tutor group teaching model and an exceptional degree of 1:1 support towards exam preparation. This means that each pupil will receive a first-class education and achieve the senior school of his choice. The School has extremely high aspirations for every boy, and the progress that they make in the Prep is remarkable.

The day starts and ends in a traditional way, normally, with a handshake with the Headmaster. Pre-Prep boys learn Composition, Comprehension, Grammar, Daily Reading, Spelling, Daily Phonics, French, ICT, Mathematics, Music, Verbal and Non-Verbal Reasoning, Science, PSHE, RS, History, Geography and Verbal Reasoning. In addition, the boys will have lessons in Drama, Games, Art & Design and enjoy a number of educational trips each year.

For Prep boys, the subjects covered are Art, Computing, Design Technology, Drama, English, French, Geography, History, Latin, Maths, Music, PSHEE, Science, Robotics, Theology, and Philosophy & Religion.

Beyond academics, sport and the performing arts are both central to school life. A combination of onsite PE lessons and offsite games and swimming sessions enable boys to develop key sports skills.

Most of the boys have individual music lessons and some play several instruments to a very high standard by the time they leave. There are regular Music Assemblies in school and termly Music Competitions in which boys can showcase their talents. Belgravia's big annual musical production is enjoyed by many students, and boys can win Colours in music, singing, drama, the arts and sports for outstanding service to the school.

All pupils will engage in sports such as football, cricket, rugby and athletics every day as the School strongly believes that it is essential for a healthy lifestyle. Boys have a chance to enter competitions and challenges throughout the year. In addition, they can take advantage of over 30 clubs, which vary according to age.

In March 2020, Eaton House Schools appointed a new Head of Wellbeing, Ms Paula Kearney, who is available to help support all the Eaton House Belgravia parents and children. She established a Wellbeing Hub and offers 30-minute consultation sessions, which can be arranged face-to-face or online, by families or pupils who want to talk about any issue connected with wellbeing, learning or family life.

Eaton House Belgravia produces 'energetic and interesting boys' (Good Schools Guide 2020). The school harnesses this energy, encouraging every generation of boys to be recognisable for the strength of its intelligence and moral integrity. When they leave EHB, they should want to make a difference in the world and to lead by example.

Above all, during their time at the school, Eaton House Belgravia boys should thrive on trying new things, get involved and have lots of fun!

Eaton House The Manor Girls' School

58 Clapham Common Northside, London SW4 9RU

Tel: 020 3917 5050
email: sfeilding@eatonhouseschools.com
website: www.eatonhouseschools.com
Twitter: @eatonhousesch
Facebook: @eatonhouseschools

Headmaster: Mr Oliver Snowball

Age Range. 4–11.
Number of Pupils. 260 Girls.
Fees per term (2021–2022). £6,010–£7,020.

Eaton House The Manor Girls' School offers a happy, confident and ambitious start to your daughter's education. The main entry point is at aged 4, on a non-selective, first-come, first-served basis. There are English and Maths assessments for girls who wish to join the school in other years. Parents wishing to enrol their children in the school are advised to register them in the year following birth.

Eaton House The Manor Girls' School is outstanding academically and warm and caring in tone. It has now celebrated over a decade of success, academically and in every way, seeing a 12% increase in size in recent times. This year's leavers won an impressive 17 scholarships, including academic scholarships to Wimbledon High School, Putney High School, JAGS and Woldingham. Girls have been offered an impressive total of 61 scholarships over the last four years, from 2017–2021, in Academics, Music, Drama, Art and Sport.

Girls typically leave for a range of top schools including St Paul's Girls' School, Godolphin & Latymer, Wycombe Abbey, St Mary's Calne, St Mary's Ascot, James Allen's Girls' School, Putney High School, and many more. Beyond academics, the girls are happy, calm, emotionally intelligent, balanced and kind.

The School is currently strengthening its academic provision even further by adopting a more analytical, cross-curricular approach to the girls' learning. A stimulating classroom environment promotes intellectual curiosity and the girls prize both academic exploration and risk-taking highly. As a result, according to *The Good Schools Guide* (2020), parents believe that the main emphasis of the school is on academics, with a 'supportive and nurturing tone' complemented by the fact that 'Teachers are very enthusiastic which rubs off.' It also comments that the ethos of the school is 'Traditional without being remotely stuffy' and that 'There is a lovely feeling of girl power about the place!'

The Headmaster, Mr Oliver Snowball, wants the girls to have an adventure at school and to be intellectually challenged to their maximum potential. Beyond that, he would like each girl to feel that they are known, nurtured, challenged, and to have a genuine love of learning and a deep-rooted respect for people and places by the time that they leave the school. *The Good Schools Guide* (2020) comments that the Head is 'clearly engaged with the contemporary educational debate' with 'time for the girls as individuals.'

Sport is very important in the life of the school. Being regularly active enhances the girls' physical and emotional health and they have access to excellent facilities, both indoors and outdoors. They field teams in a range of sports such as hockey, netball, cricket and cross country, and are competitively placed in many inter-school competitions. In addition, House matches provide a great deal of excitement and healthy competition for the girls, as there is strong House spirit throughout the school.

In the arts, the school teaches girls how to generate original and meaningful ideas for themselves and actively encourages them to produce fresh, imaginative responses. There are always plays for the girls to shine in every year and they are held in a full-sized on-site theatre, complete with professional lighting and elaborate costumes. Specialist teachers in Drama, Music and the Arts bring the girls up to an exceptionally high standard very quickly. In addition, the school also offers speech and drama lessons leading to outside examinations.

The Art department is a very exciting place and girls are encouraged to experiment with a wide range of media. In Music, instrumental activities include a Musical Ensemble Club and an Orchestra with a string section which is setting a very impressive standard. Individual instrument playing is

strong with a theory club for keen musicians. The Form 2 Junior Choir includes every girl in the year, while the Senior Choir, open to years 3–6, now has over 50 members. The auditioned choir, Bel Canto, drawn from Forms 5–6, regularly performs at concerts, services and competitions.

The school day is very busy and the girls can take advantage of a range of up to 30+ clubs before and after school. Some of these are held with the Pre-Prep boys, such as Choral Club. There is truly something for everybody when it comes to clubs!

Pastoral care is very strong at the school. Mr Snowball feels that the school's mission is about understanding and supporting each individual girl and being there for her in every way. The House system, excellent form teachers and visible Senior Management Team all combine to ensure that each girl feels known and supported throughout her learning journey at Eaton House The Manor Girls' School.

There really is a 'sky is the limit' approach to learning and all pupils are encouraged to use their intelligence in a dynamic way to demonstrate quick, reasoned and engaged responses to the world about them. *The Good Schools Guide* (2020) praises 'the excellent, nurturing staff' who ensure that every child is treated as an individual and their talents noticed and celebrated.

In March 2020, Eaton House Schools appointed a new Head of Wellbeing, Ms Paula Kearney, who is available to help support all the Girls' School parents and children. She swiftly set to work to create a Wellbeing Hub and offers 30-minute consultation sessions, which can be arranged face-to-face or online, by families or pupils who want to talk about any issue connected with wellbeing, learning or family life.

Eaton House The Manor Pre-Preparatory School

58 Clapham Common Northside, London SW4 9RU

Tel: 020 3917 5050
email: sfeilding@eatonhouseschools.com
website: www.eatonhouseschools.com
Twitter: @eatonhousesch
Facebook: @eatonhouseschools

Headmaster: **Mr David Wingfield**

Age Range. 4–8.

Number of Pupils. 205

Fees per term (2021–2022). £6,010

Eaton House The Manor Pre-Prep is for boys aged 4–8. The School provides a happy, confident and ambitious start to their education in a traditional yet modern, fun and inclusive academic environment. It is based in modern buildings in the 1.5 acre grounds of Eaton House The Manor, directly opposite Clapham Common, with the Prep School (for boys aged 8–13) occupying the Georgian Manor House that gives the school its name.

Eaton House The Manor Pre-Prep's Cambridge-educated Headmaster Mr David Wingfield joined the school in September 2020. A mathematics specialist, he has been hailed as one of 'the most motivated teachers' that the *Tatler*

Good Schools' Guide 2020 has ever met and who is passionate about Early Years Education and Maths Mastery, which is also known as the Singapore Method. He has embarked on exciting plans for the school in the years ahead, which will result in an even fuller and more action-packed curriculum and pupil-led learning. He is a strong believer in wellbeing as the foundation of academic achievement, and has set to work empowering the staff and pupils to develop their leadership skills at every level of school life.

The majority of Pre-Prep boys move seamlessly to Eaton House The Manor Prep School, based on the same site, under Headmistress Mrs Sarah Segrave, where they stay until they are 13. Eaton House The Manor Prep School is outstanding academically and has sent generations of pupils to Eton, Westminster, St Paul's, Winchester, Harrow and others. Boys win many scholarships, including, in 2020, scholarships to Dulwich College and Sherborne. And in 2021, we saw an increase of scholarships awarded to our boys, to schools such as: St Paul's Cathedral Choir School, Charterhouse, Dulwich College, Harrow, Radley, Tonbridge and Westminster. The foundations of this success are built at the Pre-Prep, where younger boys discover a love of learning that lasts.

At Eaton House The Manor Pre-Prep, children are made to feel confident, secure and happy in their learning and personal development. The School's aim is to give the boys a smooth and confident transition into the Prep school.

An 'open door' policy means that parents can feel fully involved, confident in the knowledge that boys are being treated as unique individuals. Boys are taught to be kind, considerate, thoughtful and courteous, as well as to strive always to do their best both academically and personally.

Eaton House The Manor Pre-Prep's approach, which teaches in a child-first, inclusive fashion, with targeted tasks to challenge every boy across the attainment spectrum, means that it succeeds in bringing out the very best in each individual, attaining the highest academic results possible. The School encourages both independent and cross-curricular learning in topic work and lessons that are fun, exciting and active – perfectly suited to young boys. The School's four-strong Learning Enrichment team is on hand to ensure that no boy is hindered from achieving his academic potential by an unmet educational need; every boy is given the tools he needs to soar.

EHTM is a confidently sporty school, with Clapham Common providing the perfect venue for team games such as rugby, football and cricket. Sport is a central part of school life and there are a variety of sports and sports clubs beyond the core curriculum. Sport helps the boys' physical and emotional health as well as teaching them to be part of a team representing their school and their House.

Every boy is part of a team and that is very important for building team spirit and sociability. In addition, drama, art, and music are greatly enjoyed by all our pupils. They are all seen as fundamental in developing communication skills and confidence. The School has a full-size theatre with a technical rig and the boys (and parents) enjoy the many wonderful productions that are put on, complete with elaborate theatrical costumes and effects.

Exceptional pastoral care ensures that the years spent at Eaton House The Manor Pre-Preparatory are happy and inspiring, enabling every boy to fulfil his potential. The warm and friendly teaching staff understand and support the boys so that they grow in self-belief. The buddy system helps to integrate the newest boys into the school from the very beginning and the House system provides another layer of support and guidance. *The Good Schools Guide 2020* praises 'the excellent, nurturing staff' who ensure that every child is treated as an individual and their talents noticed and celebrated.

In March 2020, Eaton House Schools appointed a new Head of Wellbeing, Ms Paula Kearney, who is available to help support all Pre-Prep School parents and children. She swiftly set to work to create a Wellbeing Hub and to offer 30-minute consultation sessions, which can be arranged face-to-face or online, by families or pupils who want to talk about any issue connected with wellbeing, learning or family life.

Admission to Eaton House The Manor Pre-Preparatory School is non-selective and on a first-come, first-served basis into the Reception (Kindergarten) Year. Parents wishing to enrol their children in the school are advised to register them at birth.

Eaton House The Manor Preparatory School

58 Clapham Common Northside, London SW4 9RU

Tel: 020 3917 5050
email: sfeilding@eatonhouseschools.com
website: www.eatonhouseschools.com
Twitter: @eatonhousesch
Facebook: @eatonhouseschools

Headmistress: **Mrs Sarah Segrave**

Age Range. 8–13.
Number of Pupils. 510 Boys in the Prep and Pre-Prep.
Fees per term (2021–2022). £7,215.

Eaton House The Manor Prep School provides a happy, confident and ambitious start to your child's education, nurturing boys from ages 8–13 (and 4–8 in the Pre-Prep under Headmaster Mr David Wingfield).

Eaton House, which is housed in a 1.5 acre Georgian manor house site opposite Clapham Common, has sent generations of boys to Eton, Westminster, St Paul's, Winchester, Harrow, Dulwich, King's College Wimbledon and others. Boys win scholarships each year, including, in 2021, an academic scholarship to Westminster School, art scholarships to Charterhouse and Dulwich Prep and a sports scholarship to Tonbridge.

The School has great aspirations for every child, and the progress they make in their five years at EHTM Prep School is remarkable. *The Good Schools Guide* (2020) comments that the Manor is a 'friendly and happy' school with pastoral care 'high on the Head's agenda.' It concludes that, as a result, 'This is a school with excellent academic outcomes, very good value added... and consequently a school of really high expectations.'

Most of the pupils transition directly from the Pre-Prep where registration is open from birth. A good proportion of boys, however, join from other schools at age 8, and it is always worth asking about occasional places further up the school, including 11+ entry.

If the boys do brim with academic and social confidence, it's in part due to the exceptional pastoral care provided by the school. The Headmistress, Mrs Sarah Segrave, is committed in her belief that, on her watch, every boy will be recognised as an individual and his potential maximised.

Boys are prepared in all the core subjects for the finest day and boarding schools in the UK. They take a whole range of classes including Art, Computing, Design Technology, Drama, English, French, Geography, History, Latin, Maths, Music, PSHE, Science, and Theology, Philosophy and Religion.

With 40 staff for 225 boys, all pupils get the specialist input that they need, whether they are aiming for scholarships, Common Entrance or entry to London day schools at thirteen.

Eaton House The Manor wants the boys to be inspired academically. This is why the School provides stimulating, challenging lessons supported by an excellent wellbeing programme. It encourages boys to think for themselves, to engage fully in class discussions and to take pride in their work.

EHTM Prep offers a diverse range of extracurricular activities that go far beyond the classroom. The boys can often be seen out and about, whether exploring London's world-class museums and galleries, taking advantage of the school's prime location, or playing out on Clapham Common. In non-COVID times, the School works to combine fun and learning activities by planning regular trips both at home and abroad. One very special event involved a number of the oldest pupils completing the Three Peaks Challenge, climbing Ben Nevis, Scafell Pike and Snowdon in 24 hours, raising £11,243 for the Great Ormond Street Hospital children's charity.

Every day after school, the boys have a huge range of clubs on offer. As an example, they might include: Junior Art; Junior DT; Junior Basketball Club; Football Club; Running Club; Newspaper Club; Music Tech Club; Spanish for Beginners; Spanish for Intermediates; Musical Theatre Club; Performing Arts Club; 100th Wandsworth Cubs; Brilliant Public Speaking & Interview Skills; French for Advanced Speakers; Wallace Chess Club; Politics and Current Affairs Club; Construction Club – Lego; Music Tech Club; Shakespeare Project; Big Questions Breakfast Club; Model United Nations; Senior DT Club; Senior Basketball Club; Senior Art Club and Senior Science Club. When it comes to clubs, we can truly say there is something for everybody!

At Eaton House The Manor Prep, pastoral care is of the highest importance. Mrs Segrave makes it her personal mission to ensure that both she and the staff know the boys, share their highs and lows and are there for them in every way. Every day starts with the Head engaging in a few words of conversation with each boy. At the end of the day she is also there, and that means she comes to know the boys very well by the end of their time at Eaton House The Manor.

However, the cultural importance of treating all pupils as individuals runs far deeper than this important ritual; it is a fundamental cornerstone of the school's philosophy and intrinsic in everything that it does. There is a code of good conduct which the boys naturally follow, which encourages them to be thoughtful, kind, honest and team-spirited. Perhaps this is why the pupils follow their teachers in being so kind and caring. A recent ISI Report commented, 'The pupils have an excellent moral understanding. They demonstrate an outstanding natural courtesy and consideration towards everyone.'

In March 2020, Eaton House Schools appointed a new Head of Wellbeing, Ms Paula Kearney, who is available to help support all Prep School parents and children. She immediately built a Wellbeing Hub and began offering 30-minute consultation sessions to families or pupils who want to talk about any issue connected with wellbeing, learning or family life. These sessions can be face-to-face or online.

Sport is an integral part of life at school, whether representing School or House, or simply learning to be part of a team. In winter, EHTM Prep normally fields as many as 20 teams a week, for both home and away matches in football and rugby, and in summer The Manor excels at cricket, athletics and other field sports. This sporting prowess is nurtured by specialist coaches with formidable professional CVs, which proves useful beyond Prep School when boys are trialling for their senior schools.

Boys at Eaton House The Manor are as musical and artistic as they are sporting! The musical life at the Manor is vibrant, with nearly three-quarters of the boys playing at least one instrument, sometimes several, to a high standard. Musical boys can join our Choir, Vocal Ensembles, Brass Group, Orchestra or Woodwind Group, as well as take part in House Music Competitions, which include singing. There are also special Music Assemblies attended by parents, where boys can showcase their often quite exceptional progress on individual instruments.

In addition, there are Year Group Recitals where each boy has the opportunity to play their instrument or to sing. There are no auditions and they are open to all abilities, giving all the boys a chance to make music together, even if music is not their primary focus.

Every boy within the school has weekly drama lessons, and many become involved in complex and sophisticated theatrical productions, such as recent productions of *The Wind in the Willows* and *Lord of the Flies*. There are first-class facilities available for the arts, including a state-of-the-art theatre with full technical rig and the school always invests in lavish costumes and wonderful stage effects so that the boys can have the full theatrical experience.

In the Prep School, the boys perform at a high level. The wide range of performance opportunities available enable boys to share their talents with the community, allowing them to showcase what they have learned in their drama lessons. There is a well-established and popular Drama Club and regular concerts, musical ensembles and art exhibitions that allow the boys to develop self-expression and gain in confidence.

Mrs Segrave argues that a school is not a building, a curriculum or a timetable. Rather, it is a place where children grow intellectually and emotionally, guided by teachers who are determined that children succeed and are happy. *The Good Schools Guide* (2020) praises 'the excellent, nurturing staff' who ensure that the mission statement is fulfilled, with every child treated as an individual and their talents noticed and celebrated. As one former pupil wrote, 'The thing that I will miss the most is the atmosphere, how everyone is so happy and so encouraging.'

Eaton Square School

55–57 Eccleston Square, Pimlico, London SW1V 1PH

Tel: 0207 225 3131
email: registrar@eatonsquareschool.com
website: www.eatonsquareschools.com
Twitter: @ESS_Prep
Facebook: @EatonSquareSchool

Headmistress: **Mrs Trish Watt**

Age Range. 2–11 Co-educational Nursery and Prep School.

Number of Pupils. 316.

Fees per term (2021–2022). Reception & Year 1 £7,230; Year 2 to Year 4 £7,710, Year 5 & Year 6 £7,780.

Ethos. The School maintains high standards and encourages in every child an enthusiasm for learning, good manners, self-discipline and, in all things, a determination to do their best and realise their potential. The 2016 ISI inspection report found the school to be Excellent in all categories and highlighted the pupils' personal development as "outstanding". The School offers a stretching, challenging approach to learning that emphasises achievement and builds confidence. We make the most of our local London museums, galleries, theatres and concert halls to enhance the learning experience. In addition, each Prep year group participates in at least one trip outside of London annually.

Academic Life. The Class Teachers teach general subjects to their classes up to the age of 10. Thereafter, specialist subject teachers continue the curriculum in preparation for the Common Entrance Examinations for senior Independent Schools. A wide range of subjects are encompassed in the curriculum. ICT is introduced from the age of 3 and it is an integral part of the syllabus. In addition, all Prep School classrooms are equipped with interactive whiteboards and data projectors.

Pupils are prepared for entry into both selective London Day schools and leading Boarding schools through London Day School examinations and Common Entrance examinations at 11+. *See below* for information about our Senior School and Sixth Form.

Sport & the Arts. Sport and Physical Education include Swimming, Fencing, Gymnastics, Football, Rugby, Cricket, Hockey, Sailing, Skiing and Tennis and the School has successful teams competing against other London and national schools. The School regularly wins National Awards for its swimming success. Music is a flourishing department within the School. Appreciation of music, singing, composition, music theory and recorder tuition are taught by specialists at all ages. There are active School Choirs, an orchestra and a variety of ensembles that rehearse throughout the week. Instruction in Music, Art and Design Technology is included for all children from Nursery School upwards, as part of the Curriculum. Drama is integrated within the curriculum and each child takes part in at least two public productions every year.

Senior School & Sixth Form. An independent, co-educational day school for pupils aged 11 to 18, located in a beautiful Grade I listed building on Piccadilly, Mayfair opposite Green Park in the heart of London.

Eaton Square School is part of the Dukes Education Group. Dukes Education is a family of schools and education organisations based in the UK. We bring together schools that are diverse in their offering, and yet united as outstanding examples of teaching and learning.

Edge Grove

Aldenham Village, Watford, Herts WD25 8NL

Tel: 01923 855724
email: office@edgegrove.com
website: www.edgegrove.com
Twitter: @EdgeGrove
Facebook: @Edge-Grove
Instagram: @edgegrove

Chair of Governors: Mr Ian Elliott

Head: **Miss Lisa McDonald**, LLB Hons, PGCE

Age Range. 3–13.

Number of Pupils. 529

Fees per term (2021–2022). Day: Nursery (5 mornings only; optional afternoons are available every day) £2,485; Pre Prep (Reception–Year 2) £4,535; Lower School (Years 3 & 4) £5,035; Upper School (Years 5–8) £6,065.

Edge Grove is a vibrant and successful independent school for boys and girls aged 3–13 years. It is set in 48 acres of parkland, only 15 miles from central London and conveniently located close to the M1 and M25 motorways. Our wonderful setting and facilities ensure our children are exposed to a wide range of experiences and develop confidence in a challenging, fun and inspirational environment. The school was inspected by the Independent Schools Inspectorate (ISI) in September 2015 who rated it 'excellent' in all areas. The ISI stated that at all stages of the school "the quality of pupils' academic and other achievements is excellent. Key factors supporting high achievement are the extensive and innovative curriculum, pupils' understanding attitudes towards their learning and excellent teaching." They observed that pupils are "articulate and highly effective listeners. They are diligent in their approach to lessons and their behaviour is exemplary."

The Pre Prep at Edge Grove caters for children between the ages of 3 and 7. The Edge Grove Pre-School is located in a purpose-built building close to the main school site and can accommodate up to 40 children aged 3–4 years. The Pre Prep (Reception to Year 2) is situated within the main school grounds, close to the main Preparatory school. Class sizes are no more than 20, supervised by a teacher and teaching assistant. A broad curriculum is offered with French, Music, Sport and Forest School taught by specialist teachers.

Pupils move on to a wide variety of senior independent schools across the country and the school has an excellent record of Scholarship and Common Entrance success. Music and Art are also particularly strong and Edge Grove is a leading player in the world of prep school sport. There is a great range of after-school activities on offer every day until 6.00pm.

Facilities include an outdoor learning hub with a gazebo and stage; two Forest School sites; an adventure playground; a language classroom with a dedicated 'virtual language lab'; Chromebooks throughout the school and 1:1 from Year 5; iMacs for music technology; a fully-equipped textiles room and two science laboratories; and purpose-built and state of the art facilities for Home Economics. Sports facilities include a 20-metre heated swimming pool; vast playing fields with ten junior football fields; a 3-court badminton Sports Hall; an AstroTurf hockey pitch; two tennis/netball courts and six outdoor/four indoor cricket nets.

Charitable status. Edge Grove School Trust Ltd is a Registered Charity, number 311054.

Edgeborough

84 Frensham Road, Frensham, Farnham, Surrey GU10 3AH

Tel: 01252 792495
email: office@edgeborough.co.uk
website: www.edgeborough.co.uk
Twitter: @edgeborough
Facebook: @edgeborough
Instagram: @edgeboroughschool

Chairman of Governors: Mr Jeremy McIlroy

Acting Head: **Mr Rob Smith**

Age Range. 2–13.
Number of Children. Total: 363 Flexi-boarders 80, Day 283, Pre-Prep 83, Nursery 34.
Fees per term (2021–2022). Years 5–8 £6,263, Years 3–4 £5,648, Pre-Prep Years R–2 £3,857. Weekly Boarding (4 nights): £35 per night.

Edgeborough is a co-educational Independent School for children aged 2–13, with day and flexi boarding. The school is situated within 50 acres of rolling countryside in Frensham, Surrey.

Edgeborough offers a carefully balanced, all-round education with a focus on outdoor learning, which aims to develop skills, interests and an aspiration within pupils to do anything and everything to the best of their ability. A strong and enthusiastic team of experienced specialist teachers enrich the curriculum, while small class sizes ensure that each child's progress is recognised and encouraged.

Boarding at Edgeborough enhances the overall experience of pupils in the school and is a vital factor in creating a vibrant family atmosphere. Boarding at Edgeborough offers a modern take, providing a safe, home-from-home environment. It is an exciting opportunity to stay overnight with friends, while the schedule is as flexible as possible to tailor the experience to each family's needs.

Excellent educational opportunities at Edgeborough enable pupils to regularly gain scholarships to prestigious senior schools. During the past academic year, Edgeborough Year 8 pupils were awarded 13 scholarships to the senior school of their choice for excelling in sports, art, drama, music and all-round skills.

A range of extra-curricular activities and clubs provide the opportunity for teachers to nurture and develop pupils' self-esteem. Our vast outdoor space is ripe for discovering

and is a constant source of enjoyment for pupils. The specialist facilities help make learning fun, enriching the academic, social and cultural aspects of school life. Facilities include state-of-the-art ICT and science labs, music suites, an art and pottery studio, a fully-equipped indoor theatre, dance and drama studios, a large sports hall, floodlit astro pitches and a heated swimming pool.

Charitable status. Edgeborough is part of the Charterhouse family of schools (Registered Charity: 312054)

Elm Green Preparatory School

Parsonage Lane, Little Baddow, Chelmsford, Essex CM3 4SU

Tel: 01245 225230
email: admin@elmgreen.essex.sch.uk
website: www.elmgreen.essex.sch.uk

Principal: **Mrs A E Milner**, BTech Hons, MSc, PGCE

Age Range. Co-educational 4–11 years.
Number of Day Pupils. 220.
Fees per term (2021–2022). £3,270
Religious affiliation. Non-denominational.

Elm Green was founded in 1944 and enjoys a lovely rural setting, surrounded by National Trust woodland.

Children enter in the September after their fourth birthday and in their final year are prepared for scholarships, entry to other independent schools and for entry to maintained schools. Many of the pupils take the Essex 11+ and the school has an excellent record of success in this examination.

The school maintains a high standard of academic education giving great emphasis to a secure foundation in the basic subjects whilst offering a wide curriculum with specialist teaching in many areas.

Information technology and design technology form an integral part of the curriculum and there are flourishing art, music and PE departments. The school competes successfully in a wide range of sports – football, rugby, netball, swimming, cricket, gymnastics, athletics, rounders and tennis.

There are many extra-curricular activities and all the children are encouraged to work and to play hard in order to fulfil their potential.

The school aims to foster intellectual curiosity and to encourage individual and corporate work. Kindness and thought for others are given a high priority.

The Elms

Colwall, Malvern, Worcestershire WR13 6EF

Tel: 01684 540344
email: office@elmsschool.co.uk
website: www.elmsschool.co.uk
Twitter: @theelmsschool
Facebook: @ElmsSchoolColwall

Founded 1614.

Chairman of the Governors: S Townsend

Headmaster: C Hattam, BA Hons

Age Range. 3–13.

Number of Pupils. 156. Boys 91, girls 65

Fees per term (2021–2022). Full boarding £8,710; Flexi-boarding £7,685, Day Plus £6,665; Day £4,995, Pre-Prep (ages 3–7) £2,655–£4,440. Fees are payable termly.

The Elms is run as a charitable, non-profit making company with a Board of Governors. Children are taken in the Main School from the age of rising 8 and there is a Montessori and Pre-Preparatory Department for 3–7 year olds.

The Elms is a leading, independent, co-educational preparatory school for children aged between 3 and 13. Welcoming day pupils, flexi-boarders and full-boarders, we provide a special place of children to enjoy their education whilst receiving exceptional pastoral care and every opportunity to flourish. The strong values and ethos are evident throughout all areas of school life. The Elms seeks to find each child's talents by giving all children the freedom, space and endless opportunities to discover and develop themselves while growing in confidence. We recognise that all children are unique and hugely special and we provide a safe and secure environment for all children to be stretched to their potential.

'I can honestly say that what you have done for my daughter has been outstanding. Absolutely outstanding. What has been returned to me at the end of the process is a daughter who is confident, articulate, sports mad, and has an appetite for learning and is above all happy with herself and others. I couldn't have made a better choice…' *A Testimonial from the Parent of a Year 8 Leaver*

The Elms is situated in stunning countryside, surrounded by the Malvern Hills. There is a quiet ambition that emanates throughout the school and we enjoy celebrating the success of our children while embracing positive failure in a secure and nurturing environment. The curriculum is rich and diverse and delivered by our outstanding and dedicated staff. The house system and extensive extra-curricular programme provides vast opportunities in all of areas of school life. All children have the opportunity to care for our animals on the farm and they also have the chance to take riding lessons.

We are very lucky to have such fantastic facilities in all forums. Our children enjoy intensive sport sessions every day from our highly qualified staff. The sessions take place on the floodlit astroturf, in our recently refurbished indoor swimming pool and on the professionally prepared cricket, rugby and football pitches.

Bursaries are available and we offer scholarships for entry into year 7. The assessments are in academic, art, drama, music, musical theatre, sport, equine and all-rounder. Our year 8 leavers go on to a variety of leading senior schools that we ensure are carefully chosen for their individual needs and many achieve scholarships in a wide variety of areas.

At The Elms we pride ourselves on the strong community and family feel of the school. The relationship between staff and children is truly distinctive and allows children to flourish and have belief in themselves. Whilst recognising the absolute importance of academic achievement, we educate and nurture the whole child to ensure they are fully ready for their next school and life beyond.

Charitable status. The Elms (Colwall) Limited is a Registered Charity, number 527252. It exists to provide education for boys and girls.

Embley Prep School
United Learning

Embley Park, Romsey, Hampshire SO51 6ZA

Tel: 01794 515737
email: prep@embley.org.uk
website: www.embley.org.uk
Twitter: @embleyprep
Facebook: @EmbleyHampshire
LinkedIn: /school/embleyhampshire

Chairman of the Local Governing Body: Professor Richard Thomas

Headmaster: Mr Cliff Canning, BA Hons, BD Hons, HDipEd, NUI

Head of Prep School: **Ms Sheina Wright**, BA, QTS

Age Range. 2–11 Co-educational.

Number of Pupils. 170 day pupils

Fees per term (2021–2022). Nursery: £3,055 (full-time excluding EYE funding). Prep School: £3,632 (Reception, Years 1 and 2); £4,169 (Year 3); £5,579 (Years 4–6). Please refer to www.embley.org.uk/admissions/fees for further details.

Embley's Prep School provides an education with character that uncovers and nurtures each child's niche and inspires ambition and academic achievement. Children are encouraged to be independent and push themselves to find out more, giving a real sense of purpose to their learning adventures.

Specialist subject staff work across every year group to give children the very best learning experiences. Academic opportunities are combined with a diverse co-curricular programme including performing arts, drama and music alongside sports such as sailing, skiing, golf and tennis. Many varied initiatives and activities, such as the Prep School Stock Market Investment Club and Natural Sciences, provide a variety of complex, multi-layered, problem-solving experiences and develop articulate, reasoned and informed children with analytical minds.

The school is nestled in 130 acres of private parkland, which includes woodlands, playing fields, tennis courts, AstroTurf pitches, a swimming pool and a golf course. It also runs a comprehensive sailing programme with its own boats moored at Lymington.

Embley's Nursery operates for 48 weeks of the year, offering an exciting introduction to learning to ensure that each child will love going to school. From the early years, children are encouraged to be resilient in their approach and take responsibility for their learning adventures. They leave the Nursery with a calm confidence and independence: the perfect learning foundation.

At the end of Year 6, children progress to Embley's Senior School which is within the same campus.

Eton End School

35 Eton Road, Datchet, Slough, Berkshire SL3 9AX

Tel: 01753 541075
email: admin@etonend.org
website: www.etonend.org
Twitter: @EtonEndSchool

Board of Governors:

Chairman: Mr J Clark,

Deputy Chairs: Mrs N Brewster and Mr A Boothroyd

Headmistress: **Mrs Sophie Banks**, BA QTS, MEd

Age Range. 3–11 Co-educational.

Number of Pupils. 251: 145 girls, 106 boys.

Fees per term (2021–2022). Nursery: £1,875–£3,425; Pre Prep £3,525–£3,789; Prep £4,177–£4,505. Fees exclude lunch.

Eton End is a co-educational day school and nursery for children aged three to 11 years, situated on the fringes of Datchet and Eton and positioned in six acres of semi-wooded land. Having been established in 1936 to educate the children of Eton Masters, it is a school which successfully merges tradition with a forward thinking approach to teaching and learning. The links with Eton College continue to this day, enabling our pupils to experience numerous opportunities which extend and enrich their learning.

The children at Eton End achieve excellent academic standards, developing a life-long love of learning, in small classes. The highly qualified specialist staff bring the broad curriculum alive with their enthusiasm and expertise and use of the outdoor space is maximised to enhance this.

The Independent Schools Inspectorate (ISI) inspection report (May 2019) found Eton End to be 'Excellent' in all areas and with teaching and learning at the heart of all we do, excellent academic results are achieved. ISI stated that Eton End develops children's 'skills, knowledge and understanding to a high level and teaches them how to apply these skills across the curriculum'.

Eton End children are confident and articulate with strong communication skills, displaying excellent attitudes to learning from an early age. Encouraging the children to be resilient and to persevere, showing self-awareness and an ability to reflect on their progress is key. The children at Eton End display a strong sense of self-confidence, resilience and commitment to improve their learning and performance in readiness for the next stage of their lives. Empathising with peers, encouraging others and, most importantly, learning to respect one another are essential skills for life which are developed and nurtured at Eton End.

The opportunities available to the pupils at Eton End enable every child to find their strengths, both inside and outside of the classroom. With the wonderful space available and our bespoke 'Outdoor Learning Centre', the opportunities for outdoor learning are endless. An Eton End Education is not only about teaching the children a body of knowledge but also about preparing them for life in the 21st Century. This year we have revamped the Dining Room and built a bespoke Food Technology area, which will enhance the children's life skills further.

A full after-school programme of clubs and activities is available for pupils to enjoy, enabling them to develop alternative skills in the comfort of the school environment. Happiness and wellbeing are pivotal to an Eton End education and we work hard to ensure that our happy children thrive.

Eton End offers pupils an excellent all-rounded education, whilst ensuring they experience a childhood they will cherish.

Please contact us to chat to our Registrar or make an appointment to meet the Headmistress and tour the school on 01753 54107

Charitable status. Eton End School Trust (Datchet) Limited is a Registered Charity, number 310644. The aim of the charity is to provide a well-balanced education for children whose parents wish them to attend Eton End School.

Eversfield Preparatory School

Warwick Road, Solihull, West Midlands B91 1AT

Tel: 0121 705 0354
email: enquiries@eversfield.co.uk
website: www.eversfield.co.uk

Chairman of Governors: Dr T Brain

Headmaster: **Mr R Yates**, MA, BA, PGCE, LPSH

Age Range. 2¾–11 years.

Number of Pupils. 336 boys and girls.

Fees per term (2021–2022). Nursery and Kindergarten £1,200–£3,500 according to age and sessions, Middle School and Upper School £3,600–£4,100 inclusive of lunch, books and swimming lessons.

Eversfield is a Nursery and Day Preparatory School on an attractive five-acre site in the centre of Solihull preparing boys and girls for entry to the leading independent and grammar senior schools in the Midlands. The school was founded in 1931 and its mission is to provide an outstanding, broad education within a safe, caring, happy, family atmosphere where the talents of every child are valued and nurtured.

The curriculum focuses on academic excellence while retaining the breadth which nurtures the creative, sporting, technical and social skills of each child. The wide range of scholarships regularly awarded demonstrates the breadth of high-quality teaching across the school and children benefit by being individually guided through the process of carefully selecting the senior school that is right for them. The children are extremely happy and leave as confident, enthusiastic and inquisitive learners.

There is a rich variety of lunchtime and after-school extracurricular clubs on offer which provide opportunities to develop intellectual, creative and physical skills both inside and outside the classroom. The choice is impressive and includes choirs, chess, speech and drama, creative arts, dance, musical ensembles, STEM clubs and multiple sports disciplines.

Achievement in sport is strong and teams perform to a high standard against local opposition. Talented sports players are encouraged to attend trials for county teams and individual pupils compete at a very high level.

Eversfield promotes high moral standards and responsible attitudes based upon clear and relevant Christian teaching. A strong sense of community exists where small classes, a well-ordered routine and good pastoral support helps pupils to feel secure and develop their self-confidence.

On-site facilities include specialist rooms for teaching art, design and technology, science, food technology, music and computing. Sporting facilities comprise a gymnasium, extensive playing fields and all-weather courts. The sports and performing arts centre is an impressive state-of-the-art building featuring an indoor heated swimming pool, three badminton courts, indoor cricket nets and is also marked for netball. The customised lighting and sound system, theatre curtains, modular staging and retractable seating for over 200 make it the perfect venue for performances. Children in Kindergarten and Nursery have access to all the facilities on the site and are cared for in a warm and welcoming dedicated purpose-built building with its own secure outdoor all-weather play area.

Means-tested Bursaries are available for entry into Form 3 and 7+ Scholarships are offered for academic excellence for entry into Form 3.

Charitable status. Eversfield Preparatory School Trust Limited is a Registered Charity, number 528966. It is under the direction of a Board of Governors and exists to carry out the work of an Independent Preparatory School.

Ewell Castle Preparatory School

Glyn House, Church Street, Ewell, Surrey KT17 2AP

Tel: 020 8394 3579
email: enquiries@ewellcastle.co.uk
website: www.ewellcastle.co.uk
Twitter: @ECSPrep
Facebook: @EwellCastleSchool
Instagram: @EwellCastleSchool
LinkedIn: /Ewell-Castle-School

Chairman of Governors: Mr C Griffith

Principal: Mr Silas Edmonds, MA, NPQH

Head of Preparatory School: **Mrs L Macallister BA,** PGCE, NPQSL

Deputy Head of Preparatory School & Assistant Principal:
  Mrs S Fowler, BSc, PGCE

Deputy Head of Preparatory School & Assistant Principal:
  Mrs G Bean, MA, BA, PGCE

Age Range. 3–11.

Number of Pupils. 180 Girls and Boys.

Fees per term (2021–2022). £3,135–£4,145

School Mission. We will inspire our children and young people to thrive, engaging them to excel in a creative and academic environment. We will instill a growth mindset to develop: confidence, contentment and emotional intelligence.

Aims and Ethos. We are a vibrant learning community, inspiring every child to thrive: discovering strengths, deepening intellectual curiosity and cultivating wellbeing.

Values. Personal integrity, mutual respect, social responsibility and lifelong resilience.

Ewell Castle Preparatory School is an independent co-educational day school, located on two sites in the heart of Ewell Village. Nursery to Year 2 pupils (3–7 years) are based at Chessington Lodge in Spring Street, while Years 3 to 6 (7–11 years) are based at Glyn House in Church Street, opposite the Senior School (co-educational 11–18 years), with which a close liaison is maintained.

There are no entry requirements for Nursery children, but older pupils attend the school for a day's assessment, which will include assessment through lesson observation. The majority of pupils at the Preparatory School proceed to the Senior School and a number of bursaries and scholarships are available at 11+, 13+ and 16+ entry. The National Curriculum is incorporated within a broad curriculum.

The creative arts play an important part in school life. Apart from the timetabled music lessons, there is the opportunity for pupils to learn a variety of instruments under professional teachers. Drama productions take place regularly. Pupils' art work can be seen on display in the local community and is always to be found decorating the school walls. All pupils join in various sporting activities as part of the weekly curriculum. In addition, a wide variety of activities are available after school and during the holidays.

All pupils use the five acres of attractive gardens and playing fields at Glyn House for outdoor play and games lessons. In addition, Preparatory School pupils benefit from full access to the excellent sporting facilities, including a sports hall and playing fields, on the 15-acre site at The Castle. The main games are football, netball, hockey, cricket and tennis. There are also athletics and cross country events, including a school sports day. All pupils receive swimming instruction.

Outside speakers include police liaison officers and actors and authors who conduct workshops with pupils. A number of visits occur to places of interest which are relevant to a particular area of study. There are regular school visits abroad.

The school also enjoys close links with St Mary's Church, where regular assemblies are held throughout the year.

The Preparatory School aims to provide a caring, responsive and stimulating environment in which pupils are able to fulfil their potential. Hard work and high standards together with courtesy and consideration to others are of prime importance.

Charitable status. Ewell Castle School is a Registered Charity, number 312079. It exists to provide education for boys and girls.

Exeter Cathedral School

The Chantry, Palace Gate, Exeter, Devon EX1 1HX

Tel: 01392 255 298
email: reception@exetercs.org
website: www.exetercathedralschool.co.uk
Twitter: @ECSPrepSchool
Facebook: @ExeterCathedralSchool
Instagram: @ecsprep

Chairman of Governors: Mr Derek Phillips

Headmaster: **James Featherstone**, BA Hons, PGCE

Age Range. 3–13.
Number of Pupils. 8 full/weekly boarders, 20 regular flexi boarders, 247 day pupils.
Fees per term (2021–2022). Tuition: £2,823 (Reception–Year 2), £4,232 (Years 3–4), £4,382 (Year 5), £4,623 (Years 6–8). Full Boarding (6/7 nights a week) £2,722. Flexi-boarding is also available.

ECS is Exeter's oldest school, and the only school in the city to offer boarding. The earliest written reference to the School is 1179 and the School continues to educate the 40 boy and girl choristers of Exeter Cathedral. Now a thriving Prep School of some 260 boys and girls, ECS offers a broad and balanced education which has its roots in Christian values.

We are large enough to have the vibrancy, energy and expertise to be able to deliver truly first-rate educational opportunities; yet small enough to know each and every one of our pupils as individuals to ensure they are nurtured, excited, appropriately-challenged, valued and happy.

Pastoral Care and Pupil Wellbeing are at the forefront of all that we do, and we believe very firmly that happy children are best-placed to be successful learners and engaged members of the community.

Curriculum. We offer a curriculum that focuses on developing the whole child, aiming to ensure that each pupil leaves ECS ready for the challenges ahead and understanding their responsibility to others.

Music Founded as a choir school in the 12th century, and as one of today's 42 Cathedral Schools in the UK, ECS has music and music-making at its heart. We are known for the breadth of musical opportunity that we provide, and for being a school which promotes 'music for all' whilst providing high-calibre training and opportunities for our most gifted elite musicians.

The Choristers of Exeter Cathedral receive a Scholarship to attend the School, awarded by the Dean and Chapter of the Cathedral. As well as being fully involved in the life of the School, our Choristers are trained to a professional standard to sing alongside the adult members of the choir, benefiting from world-class musical coaching and unparalleled opportunities.

Sport. ECS is a school which is serious about its sport. The Director of Sport is Mrs Emma Ross (a former Hockey International), and our sporting philosophy is 'sport for all': the focus is on participation, development and enjoyment whilst still catering for our elite athletes.

We are proud of our long-standing association with some of the region's top sporting clubs and venues. We train and play at the world-class Exeter University Sports Hub, including the astroturf pitches and the Indoor Sports Hall; Exeter Cricket Club and County Ground; Exeter Athletics Arena; and Victoria Park Tennis Club. All of these first-rate venues are a few moments away in one of our minibuses, allowing our pupils and staff to make the most of the best sporting facilities in the city.

Charitable status. Exeter Cathedral School is a Registered Charity, number 1151444.

Exeter Junior School

Victoria Park Road, Exeter, Devon EX2 4NS

Tel: 01392 307080 Headmistress
01392 307080 Director of Admissions & Marketing
email: admissions@exeterschool.org.uk
website: www.exeterschool.org.uk
Twitter: @ExeterSchoolUK
Facebook: @ExeterSchoolUK
Instagram: @exeterschooluk
LinkedIn: /school/exeter-school

Exeter School is a co-educational day school. Exeter Junior School is situated in the grounds of Exeter School and provides for girls and boys aged 7–11.

The New School joined the Exeter School family in March 2021 and is a co-educational pre-prep from nursery to Year 2.

Chairman of Board of Governors: Mr James Gaisford, BSc, ACA

Headmistress: **Mrs Saskia van Schalkwyk**, BA Hons, QTS

Age Range. 7–11.
Number of Pupils. 193: 122 Boys, 71 Girls.
Fees per term (2021–2022). Form One/Upper One (Years 3 and 4) £4,040, Lower Two/Upper Two (Years 5 and 6) £4,120.

Exeter Junior School is housed in a spacious, Victorian building in the grounds of Exeter School. The close proximity of the junior school to the senior school enables the pupils to take full advantage of the facilities on site, which include a chapel, music centre, science laboratories, sports hall with dance studio, fitness suite and squash courts, indoor swimming pool, playing fields, all-weather astroturf arena and tennis courts. The junior school was extended in 2017 to provide additional changing room facilities and a STEAM room for DT, science and cookery.

The junior school retains its own playground and green space, therefore giving the school a separate and clearly recognisable identity. The playground benefitted from a substantial refurbishment over the summer of 2021 including bespoke wooden playground equipment and an outdoor classroom.

Liaison between junior and senior staff is a positive feature of this thriving junior school.

The school aims to offer, in academic, cultural and sporting terms, the widest possible range of opportunities thus helping each pupil to identify the activities which will give the greatest scope for development and fulfilment in years to come. Music, drama, art, sport and expeditions all have an important part to play in the life of the school.

The majority of pupils enter the school at age 7 or 9, and entrance is by informal assessment in January. This includes a report from the child's previous school, classroom sessions in the company of other prospective pupils, literacy and numeracy tasks. Pupils may enter the school at other ages where space is available.

Pupils are offered an academic programme which incorporates the National Curriculum model with the addition of French which is introduced from Year 3.

Exeter Junior School is offering free lessons on string instruments to all pupils entering Year 3 as a pilot scheme in 2021–2022.

Specialist teaching is offered from the outset, with the additional support of senior school staff in science, French, German, Spanish, music, sport and Latin.

A wide variety of clubs are available during the week including art & craft, dance, modern languages, calligraphy, sewing, football, hockey, netball, rugby, coding, Minecraft, chess and drama. After-school care is available until 5.30pm.

(*For further information about the Senior School, see Exeter School entry in HMC section.*)

Charitable status. Exeter School is a Registered Charity, number 1093080. It exists to provide education for children.

Fairfield Prep School

Leicester Road, Loughborough, Leicestershire LE11 2AE

Tel:	01509 215172
email:	Fairfield.office@lsf.org
website:	www.lsf.org/fairfield
Twitter:	@LboroFairfield
Facebook:	@LboroFairfield
Instagram:	@LboroFairfield
LinkedIn:	/loughborough-schools-foundation

Chairman of the Governors: Admiral Sir Trevor Soar, KCB, OBE, DEng Hon, FCMI

Head: Mr A Earnshaw, BA Lancaster, NPQH

Age Range. 3–11.

Number of Pupils. 233 Boys, 227 Girls (Numbers exclude Kindergarten).

Fees per term (2021–2022). Kindergarten £3,800 (5 days), Pre Prep £3,910, Upper Prep £3,995. Lunches and individual music lessons extra.

Fairfield is the prep school for the Loughborough Schools Foundation, a foundation of four schools

comprising: Fairfield Prep School (boys and girls 3–11), Loughborough Grammar School (boys 10–18), Loughborough Amherst School (boys and girls 4–18) and Loughborough High School (girls 11–18). The schools operate under one governing body and are situated on two neighbouring campuses in the town. The Foundation also includes The Loughborough Nursery for children from 6 weeks to 4 years.

Recently the School embarked on an ambitious building project to provide pupils with additional space and improved accommodation, including new classrooms for pupils in Reception and Years 1–3, an extended gymnasium with spacious changing rooms for pupils and staff, a specialist arts and craft room and an additional performance hall. Accommodation also includes a purpose-built Kindergarten unit for children aged 3+ during term time, which can cater for up to 44 children.

Fairfield's partnership with pupils, parents and the wider community ensures every child is given the ability to reach their full potential through a combination of academic, cultural, sporting and artistic opportunities.

Learning is extended through a wide range of activities, utilising iPads and other technologies, along with specialist teaching in science, ICT, modern foreign languages, PE, and music. Music is a vital part of the school's culture and the facilities available to pupils are second to none. All Year 2 pupils follow a course in instrumental playing, and children in the Upper Prep have the opportunity to have individual instrumental lessons with one of the Foundation Music department's peripatetic staff. In September 2015, the Music department became the only All-Steinway School in the Midlands, demonstrating the Foundation's commitment to providing pupils with the very best instruments on which to learn, practise and perform.

Fairfield provides access to an extensive range of extracurricular activities. There are a greater number of sports, and more teams, clubs and opportunities for extracurricular music on offer than ever before. Practically every single member of staff at the school runs at least one extracurricular session, ensuring that our programme of activities meets the diverse and ever-changing interests of our pupils.

In a nurturing, happy atmosphere, children are guided along their educational journey through purposeful, academic work and are constantly encouraged to succeed. Staff help develop each child's confidence, courtesy and self-worth so they grow stronger, not only as individuals, but also as members of their local community. By taking individual differences into account, the successful Fairfield Prep School pupil of today acquires the skills and values which allow them to make a valuable contribution to the success of the senior schools, and through their lives, to the society of tomorrow.

The Headmaster is happy to show prospective parents around the school by appointment. Further information can be found on the school website at www.lsf.org/fairfield.

Charitable status. Loughborough Schools Foundation is a Registered Charity, number 1081765, and a Company Limited by Guarantee, registered in England, number 4038033. Registered Office: 3 Burton Walks, Loughborough, Leics LE11 2DU.

Fairstead House School & Nursery

Fordham Road, Newmarket, Suffolk CB8 7AA

Tel: 01638 662318
email: registrar@fairsteadhouse.co.uk
website: www.fairsteadhouse.co.uk

Chair of Governors: Mr Jonathan Edge

Acting Head: **Mr Michael Radford**, BEd Hons, MEd

Age Range. 3 months–11 years Co-educational.
Number of Children. 207.

Fees per term (2021–2022). Tuition (including lunches): Reception, Year 1 & 2 £3,481, Years 3–6 £3,881. Please visit our website for information on current Nursery fees.

Fairstead House is situated in the heart of Newmarket and offers a combination of an excellent academic education with an emphasis on creativity and imagination in a caring, happy community with a unique family ethos, closely linked to the local community.

From Nursery onwards, we offer a broad and stimulating curriculum which provides the children with a solid foundation for their onward journeys to senior schools in both Independent and State sectors. The curriculum is complemented by Art, DT, Music, Drama and Sports.

Pupils take part in a variety of sports such as rugby, football, cricket, hockey and netball. All children play rounders and take part in cross-country running and athletics.

Extracurricular Speech & Drama lessons are available, as is private tuition in a wide selection of musical instruments. All children take part in the many theatrical productions that are held at School.

A programme of development has ensured the provision of first-class facilities throughout the School including a state-of-the-art Music & Drama Centre with specialist facilities, an ICT suite, iPads, interactive whiteboards in every classroom and a dedicated Science & DT area.

As well as a breakfast club and after-school care club providing wrap-around care, there is a diverse range of after-school activity clubs available. A Holiday Club is also available for all children out of term time.

Throughout the year, pupils go on a variety of trips and excursions, both day and residential. The residential trips to Norfolk and Snowdonia for the older pupils are designed to encourage independence and cultivate a spirit of adventure as well as personal responsibility and development.

Charitable Status: Fairstead House School Trust Limited is a Registered Charity, number 276787. It exists to provide education for boys and girls.

The Falcons Schools

Alpha Plus Group

Boys Nursery and Pre-Prep:
2 Burnaby Gardens
Chiswick, London W4 3DT

Tel: 020 8747 8393
email: admin@falconsboys.co.uk
website: www.falconsboys.co.uk

Boys Prep:
41 Kew Foot Road, Richmond, Surrey TW9 2SS

Tel: 020 8948 9490
email: admin@falconsprep.co.uk
website: www.falconsprep.co.uk

Peregrines Nursery and Falcons Girls:
11 Woodborough Road, Putney, London SW15 6PY

Tel: 020 8992 5189
email: admissions@falconsgirls.co.uk
website: www.falconsgirls.co.uk

Head Teacher, Girls School: **Mrs Sara Williams-Ryan**, L-ès-Lettres Geneva, MA, PCGE

Head Teacher, Pre-Prep School: **Ms Liz McLaughlin**, BSc, MEd

Head Teacher, Prep Boys School: **Miss Olivia Buchanan**, BSc Hons, MEd, PGCE

Age Range. Boys 2–7 and Girls 2–4 (Pre-Prep); Boys 4–13 (Prep); Girls 2–11 and Boys 2–4 (Peregrines Nursery and Falcons Girls).
Number of Pupils. 286 Boys; 96 Girls.

Fees per term (2021–2022). Nursery & Pre-Prep: £2,200–£5,390, Prep: £5,500–£5,945. Nursery & Girls School: £2,675–£6,325.

The Falcons Schools enjoy a well-deserved reputation for excellence. Results to the leading London Day Schools are impressive, as too is the specialist teaching on offer throughout the schools. The schools provide a safe outdoor space for play and sport and a school hall for gym, assemblies and lunch. Nearby sports facilities are used to enhance an exciting sports programme. There are well-equipped libraries, music rooms, ICT suites, with much-admired art and science facilities. Our overriding emphasis is on achieving excellence in numeracy and literacy whilst offering a broad and creative curriculum. The Falcons schools offer uniquely caring and stimulating environments, where learning is seen as fun and the pursuit of excellence is embraced by all.

Farleigh School

Red Rice, Andover, Hampshire SP11 7PW

Tel: 01264 710766
email: office@farleighschool.com
website: www.farleighschool.com
Twitter: @FarleighSchool
Instagram: @farleighschool

Chair of Governors: Mr Keith Abel

Headmaster: Fr Simon Everson

Age Range. 3–13. Boarding from age 7.

Number of Pupils. 462 (120 full and weekly boarders; 342 day pupils; 98 in Kindergarten and Pre-Prep).

Fees per term (2021–2022). Boarders: £9,280 (Years 7 and 8), £8,370 (Years 4–6), £8.010 (Year 3); HM Forces boarders £7,895 (Years 3–8); Day pupils: £7,135 (Years 4–8), £6,740 (Year 3).

Farleigh is a contemporary, Catholic, co-educational boarding and day school, which welcomes children of all faiths, or none. Situated in a stunning Georgian country house standing in 70 acres of magnificent parkland and landscaped woodland in the Test Valley of Hampshire, near Andover, Farleigh is just over an hour from London and within easy reach of Southampton and London airports.

High standards are achieved both in and out of the classroom and excellent academic results are the norm, with leavers going on to a large number of leading senior schools and more than a third each year gaining awards/scholarships to their chosen destination.

Farleigh has outstanding facilities, which include an all-weather pitch, a purpose-built music school with 12 practice rooms, Recital Hall, rehearsal room, sound-proof 'rock' room and recording studio. The Junior and Senior Boarding Houses have also undergone significant refurbishment. There is a spacious and light Art and Design Technology building, computer rooms with state-of-the-art technology, Theatre with tiered seating, a drama studio, spacious recreation rooms, a fine Chapel, gymnasium, 22-metre heated indoor swimming pool, tennis courts and separate purpose-built Pre-Prep and Kindergarten with its own landscaped and secure playground. In addition the school has three science laboratories and a food technology room, as well as additional circulation space with a well-lit ball play area and a small amphitheatre to the rear of the existing Farleigh Theatre.

The teaching staff is complemented by a committed pastoral team including Year Heads, House Parents, a Senior Nurse and a further Boarding Nurse and Day Matron. Many staff are resident, giving the school a welcoming family atmosphere, often commented upon by visitors. The latest Ofsted inspection of the school's boarding provision was "Outstanding" in all six areas inspected, "with no recommendations". The inspectors added, "This is a very caring school that is child-centred and achieves high standards throughout."

The school provides a vibrant and active evening and weekend activity programme for boarders. Regular dinner nights, barbecue parties, annual X-Factor competition, theatre trips, quiz nights, and bowling are just some of the weekend events organised for pupils. Weekday activities include bushcraft, forest school, cooking, cycling, community service, debating, golf, archery, yoga, winter cricket nets, swimming, water polo, tennis and additional sport sessions.

Drama, music and art play an important part in school life with two-thirds of the school learning at least one musical instrument and a quarter of the school taking up LAMDA drama lessons. A programme of major musical productions and informal concerts take place throughout the year and the children's artwork is displayed around the school.

The major sports for boys are rugby, football, cricket, athletics and cross country; for girls they are netball, hockey, cricket, athletics and cross country. Swimming lessons and extra tennis coaching are offered throughout the year.

Charitable status. Farleigh School is a Registered Charity, number 1157842. It exists for the purpose of educating children.

Felsted Preparatory School

Braintree Road, Felsted, Essex CM6 3JL

Tel: 01371 822610
email: prepadmissions@felsted.org
website: www.felsted.org
Twitter: @felstedprep
Facebook: @felstedschool
LinkedIn: /Felsted School

Chairman of the Governors: Mr R Brown

Head: Mr S C James, BA Hons, PGCE

Age Range. 4–13 Co-educational.

Number of Pupils. 490 pupils (of which 7 are full-time boarders, 6 weekly and 88 flexi boarders).

Fees per term (2021–2022). Day: Prep £4,800–£6,455, Pre-Prep £3,150. Weekly Boarding £8,355, Full Boarding £8,875, Flexi Boarding (1–4 nights) £54–£127.50 per week.

The staff, excluding the Headmaster, consists of over 50 full-time qualified teachers and there are additional part-time teachers for instrumental music and games. There are six matrons and two sisters in charge of the Medical Centre.

The School was rated 'excellent' in every category by the Independent School Inspectorate at its latest inspection in 2019, in addition to a legacy rating of 'Outstanding' by Ofsted for EYFS and Boarding. Shortlisted by TES for Prep School of the Year 2019.

The Prep School, set in its own area on the main Felsted School campus, has all its own facilities, including a modern well-equipped library, an excellent theatre/assembly hall, music practice rooms, a multi-purpose sports hall, open-air heated swimming pool and floodlit, multi-purpose, hard play/games area. Use is made of Felsted School's extra amenities at regular times so that indoor swimming, two Astroturf hockey pitches, small-bore rifle shooting, squash & tennis courts, a state-of-the-art Music School and another indoor sports hall are also available to the pupils. Pupils in Years 7 and 8 also lunch at the senior school every day as part of a smooth transition process to senior school.

Rugby, netball, hockey, cricket, tennis are core sports, with squash, swimming, athletics, cross country and football also played. Music plays an important part in the School's life, with an excellent Chapel Choir. Regular instrumental, orchestral and rock concerts are given and those children showing particular talent can study at the Junior Guildhall on Saturdays, subject to passing their auditions. The School has a deserved reputation for its drama productions, while Art, Design and Technology, Spanish, PSHE, and Computing are part of the weekly timetable. Out-of-class activities include public speaking and debating opportunities, horse riding, chess, football, golf, karate, cookery and dance/ballet, among others.

Pupils joining at 11+ can be guaranteed assured transfer to Felsted School at 13, as can pupils of a similar age already at the Prep School, following successful completion of assessment tests. The majority of pupils proceed to Felsted School itself, some move on to other major independent senior schools. There is an excellent record of academic, art, music, sport, drama and Design & Technology scholarships. (*For further information about Felsted, see entry in HMC section.*)

Scholarships and Awards are open to pupils joining Felsted Prep School at ages of 11+ in the September of the year of entry. Top-up bursaries may also be available on a means-tested basis. One 100% bursary is available each year to a child who meets the right criteria and is given at the discretion of the Head.

Charitable status. Felsted School is a Registered Charity, number 310870. It exists to provide education for boys and girls.

Feltonfleet School

Byfleet Road, Cobham, Surrey KT11 1DR

Tel: 01932 862264
email: office@feltonfleet.co.uk
          admissions@feltonfleet.co.uk
website: www.feltonfleet.co.uk

Chair of Governors: Mr Giles Ashbee

Headmistress: **Mrs Shelley Lance**, BD, PGCE

Registrar: Mrs Jackie Williams, BA Hons

Age Range. 3–13.
Number of Pupils. 488; of whom 37 are Boarders.
Fees per term (2021–2022). Boarders £7,475, Day Pupils £4,185–£6,150; Nursery £2,245 (5 mornings).

Feltonfleet School was founded in 1903 and became an Educational Trust in 1967. The School is situated in 25 acres of scenic grounds within easy reach of London and the southern Home Counties. There are 56 full-time and 4 Gap Year members of the teaching staff. The School became fully co-educational in September 1994 and offers both weekly boarding (Monday to Thursday) and day education, as well as a flexible boarding option. There is a flourishing, purpose-built Pre-Preparatory Department with two form entry.

Academics. Academic results are high, with outstanding results in Common Entrance. The staff team are 100% committed to drawing out the best in each and every child and this is really shining through in Feltonfleet's results.

Ethos. Feltonfleet is a community where "individuals really matter" – a core belief which shapes all we say and do. The school ethos is based upon positive learning, living and leading, alongside core values of Honesty, Responsibility, Respect and Kindness. Feltonfleet knows that the most enjoyable personal growth comes from developing a child's natural talents and skills. In nurturing this potential within a sharing community, with a strong sense of family, children are able to discover their gifts and grow in self-confidence, independence and compassion.

Pastoral. Feltonfleet is a happy, safe and caring environment where a very high priority is given to pastoral care. So much so that there is a dedicated Deputy Head (Pastoral Care). The division into Pre-Prep, Lower, Middle and Upper Schools means that, at each stage of a child's learning journey, their needs are met so that they can continue to grow in self-confidence and independence. Class teachers and form tutors take a close interest in their pupils' pastoral welfare. They are supported in their roles by the Year Leaders who are responsible for the welfare of children in each year group, and by the Deputy Head (Pastoral). Feltonfleet is an environment conducive to mindfulness and positive mental health. "Time To Think" sessions are an explicit part of the curriculum and form tutor system throughout the school.

Entry. Children are admitted from the age of three into the two-form Nursery in the Pre-Prep Department. Places are allocated on a first come first served basis with priority given to siblings. Moving into the Main School at the age of seven, pupils are joined by more children to create three forms. For entry into the Main School pupils are required to sit an entrance assessment and informal interview. Academic, Art, Music, Drama, DT, All-Rounder and Sports Scholarships are offered at 11+.

Facilities. A brand new, state-of-the-art, 400-seat Performing Arts Centre opened in May 2015, where dramatic productions, dance shows and music are performed by all year groups. Well-equipped Science, Art, DT and Digital Learning Departments and Library. 'Calvi House', for Pre-Prep pupils Nursery to Year 1, has its own hall, gardens and outdoor classrooms. 'Year 2 House' provides a dedicated space giving increased access to the extensive facilities and further specialist teaching available on the main campus. There are landscaped play areas throughout the school and a stunning tree house, pond and wildlife area with bird hide.

Sport. The Feltonfleet Sport aim is to 'create better athletes… for life'. The Department prides itself on its ability to encompass both excellence and sport-for-all within a very busy prep school environment. All pupils receive high quality teaching and coaching in a variety of sports and activities in a positive and safe learning environment. Facilities include a magnificent sports hall, sports fields, a 15m indoor swimming pool, a shooting range for air and .22 rifles, a large floodlit Astro pitch and a climbing wall.

Games played are rugby, football, hockey, netball, athletics and cricket.

Extra-Curricular Activities. The School has an active policy of preparing children for the challenges of today's world and an exceptional activities programme is offered to all pupils both during and after the school day. Pupils in the prep school are offered the opportunity to attend residential activity courses as well as subject-related overseas trips. In the final two years pupils attend residential leadership courses. After Common Entrance examinations, Year 8 pupils take part in a varied programme of activities, lectures and trips in preparation for leaving Feltonfleet and moving on to their senior schools.

Charitable status. Feltonfleet School Trust Limited is a Registered Charity, number 312070.

Fettes College Preparatory School

East Fettes Avenue, Edinburgh EH4 1QZ

Tel:	+44 (0)131 332 2976
email:	prepschool@fettes.com
website:	www.fettes.com
Twitter:	@Fettes_College
Facebook:	@FettesCollegeFettesPrep

Chairman of Governors: Lady M Wise

Chairman of Preparatory School Committee: H Bruce-Watt

Headmaster: **A A Edwards**, BA Hons, PGCE

Age Range. 7–13.

Number of Pupils. 208: 48 boarders, 160 day pupils; 108 boys, 100 girls.

Fees per term (2021–2022). Boarders £8,625, Day Pupils £5,880, including all meals and textbooks.

Fettes Prep School lies within the Fettes College grounds, on 100 acres of parkland in the heart of Edinburgh. The Prep School has its own separate campus adjacent to Fettes College and takes full advantage of all the excellent facilities on the site.

Learning. The curriculum is structured to reflect the strengths of the Curriculum for Excellence, the National Curriculum of England and Wales and IAPS guidance. A strong emphasis is placed on a thorough grounding in the traditionally important subjects of Maths and English. Class sizes are no larger than 18 and pupils from the age of 7 are taught by specialist Science, Language, Art, Music and Drama teachers.

Life. The two Boarding Houses are Iona for the girls and Arran for the boys. The pastoral teams of each house provide around the clock care to create a fun, happy and secure home away from home. We make the most of our fabulous location with plenty of action and adventure trips at weekends when we can be found visiting attractions far and wide.

Sport. We aim to balance 'sport for all' with our ethos of sporting excellence and each Prep pupil, irrespective of their sporting talents, has access to our state-of-the-art, on-site facilities. In addition to expanding their skills, we want our pupils to enjoy the camaraderie of playing in a team and to inspire them to develop a lifelong love of sport and physical activity.

The Arts. We firmly believe that art, drama and music are vital to every child's development, which is why specialists teach all three subjects from age 7. Our tailored curriculum gives the children the chance to explore their creativity, gain the confidence to perform, learn new techniques and experience the thrills and spills of shared endeavour.

Co-curricular. There are annual trips abroad to bring learning to life and other tours are regularly organised.

Every child is involved in a vast array of trips, talks, social events and activities, utilizing the beautiful city of Edinburgh, the surrounding countryside and beyond. The top two year groups are involved in a programme designed at the school to increase and improve resourcefulness, initiative and provide personal challenge.

Entry. Entry at the age of seven, eight or nine is by assessment tests and at 10+, 11+ and 12+ by the Entrance Examinations, taken in late Jan/early Feb. All applicants can apply for a means-tested bursary which can cover up to 100% of the fees. There is a finite amount of funding available each year and therefore not all applicants will be successful. Bursaries are awarded independently of any Scholarship or Award.

All candidates who are applying for entry into the 1st Form at 11+ years of age, will automatically be considered for a Junior Scholarship. The results of the Entrance Examinations will determine who receives a Junior Scholarship.

These Scholarships are awarded for academic or all-round excellence. They can also attract reductions of up to 5% of the fees and these reductions are not related to parents' financial circumstances. A Music award can also be applied for at 11+ and 12+ entry.

Further information and a prospectus can be obtained from the Registrar (Tel: +44 (0)131 311 6744, email: admissions@fettes.com) who will be very happy to arrange a visit.

Charitable status. The Fettes Trust is a Registered Charity, number SC017489.

Finton House

171 Trinity Road, London SW17 7HL

Tel:	020 8682 0921
email:	admissions@fintonhouse.org.uk
website:	www.fintonhouse.org.uk
Twitter:	@FintonHouseSch
Facebook:	@Finton.House.School
Instagram:	@fintonhouseschool

Terry O'Neill and Finola Stack founded Finton House in 1987 as a charitable trust with two principles in mind: firstly, that children joining in Reception should not have to face the pressures of a competitive entry system, and secondly that of an inclusive education where every child is able to shine.

Chair of Governors: Ms Liz Buckley

Headmaster: **Mr Ben Freeman**

Age Range. 4–11.

Number of Pupils. 175 Girls, 163 Boys.

Fees per term (2021–2022). £5,534–£5,570.

Entrance. Non-selective – first come/first served.

Exit. Boys and Girls at 11 for London Day, Prep or Boarding.

Aims to provide a broad education, embracing technology and outdoor learning, encouraging children to live a healthy life in order to flourish in a rapidly changing world. Academic subjects, music, art, computing, design and technology, languages and sports are all taught to a very high standard. High success rate in entrance exams to good 11+ senior schools, mainly London Day plus some boarding schools, and a third of leavers winning scholarships and awards. Strong policy of inclusion with a percentage of children with special needs. Employs a Speech and Language Therapist, an Occupational Therapist and teaching assistants in most classrooms. A stimulating environment which encourages all children to learn and gain confidence in their own abilities. Non-denominational but instils values such as respect, kindness, morality and resilience.

Charitable status. Finton House is a Registered Charity, number 296588. It exists to provide a broad, inclusive education for children.

Forest Preparatory School

College Place, Snaresbrook, London E17 3PY

Tel: 020 8520 1744
email: prep@forest.org.uk
website: www.forest.org.uk
Twitter: @ForestSchoolE17
Facebook: @ForestSchoolE17

Co-educational Day School.

Chairman of Governors: David Wilson, LLB

Head: James Sanderson, FRSA, FCCT, BMusPerf Hons Elder Conservatorium, BMus Adelaide

Age Range. 4–11.
Number of Pupils. 336
Fees per term (2021–2022). £4,916–£5,629.

Forest Preparatory School is part of Forest School (HMC), with which it shares a 50-acre site at the foot of Epping Forest on the East London/Essex border. Its aims are to offer an education of high quality, and to encourage and develop each child academically, physically and creatively. In the Pre-Prep, pupils are taught in small co-educational classes. From the age of 7, pupils are taught in single-sex classes, and at age 11 they proceed to the Senior Section of Forest School (*see separate entry in HMC section*).

Entry to the school is by selection, at 4+ by means of an informal assessment.

The Pre-Prep is co-educational, with 3 forms of 16 pupils in each year group who are taught predominantly by form teachers and supported by qualified teaching assistants. From the age of 7, forms become single-sex with 24 pupils in two forms in each year group. Starting in Reception, specialist teaching staff provide lessons in computing, music, drama, swimming, Forest Schools and PE/Games with the addition of dance, art, engineering, science and Mandarin as pupils progress through the school.

Academic standards, sport and music are all strengths of the school in equal measure. The main sports played are football, cricket, netball and rounders, and teams compete locally and regionally. Athletics, swimming and cross-country are all coached to a high standard. The musical life of the school is enriched by its choirs, orchestra and several chamber groups, and all pupils in Years 3 and 4 are provided with 2 years' free tuition in a musical instrument. There are endless opportunities for pupils to perform in concerts or recitals throughout the year, and Chapel services, form assemblies and school competitions provide occasions for public speaking and performance. Clubs take place at lunchtime, before school and after school, with a wide variety of extra-curricular clubs on offer. Breakfast club commences at 7.30am and after-school care is available until 6.00pm each day. Forest School also has an extensive school bus service in operation.

Charitable status. Forest School, Essex is a Registered Charity, number 312677. The objective of the school is education.

Fosse Bank School

Mountains Country House, Noble Tree Road, Hildenborough, Kent TN11 8ND

Tel: 01732 834212
email: office@fossebankschool.co.uk
           headteacher@fossebankschool.co.uk
website: www.fossebankschool.co.uk
Twitter: @FosseBankSchool
Facebook: @FosseBankSchool

Chair of Governors: Mrs Jenna Crittenden

Headmistress: Miss Alison Cordingley, LTCL, PGCE, NPQH

School Secretary/Admissions: Mrs Catherine Martin

Age Range. 2–11 Co-educational.
Number of Pupils. 110.
Fees per term (2021–2022). Nursery £3,470 per term (£3,585 including wraparound care 7:30am to 6:00pm). From £3,732 for Reception up to £4,708 for Year 6. Fosse Bank accepts 15 hours Government funding (please see website for details).

Founded in 1892, Fosse Bank School including Little Fosse Nursery (available from the term in which the child turns 2 years old) offers an excellent academic education combined with a truly supportive, friendly and stimulating environment in which children learn and flourish.

Wrap-around care is offered for fifty weeks a year from 7.30am to 6.00pm. With ample off-road parking, parents take advantage of the ten-minute walk to Hildenborough railway station, leaving cars in the ample school carpark.

Parents and children appreciate the excellent pastoral care. We celebrate each success and encourage every child to be the best that they can be. Our children have a reputation for being confident, articulate and well mannered. The school is a strong family community located in a beautiful Grade II listed building with 28 acres of parkland and boasting a range of wonderful facilities including an indoor heated swimming pool, tennis courts, sports hall, Mongolian Yurt and well-resourced Early Years. With research clearly demonstrating the link between physical learning and academic success, weekly Forest School sessions offer a unique educational experience using the outdoor environment of our woodland as a classroom,

Academic Studies. Our children achieve excellent academic results accepting offers of places at selective state and independent schools every year. Our Kent 11+ results are excellent. In the Early Years we give the children a solid foundation based on the Early Years Foundations Stage. Further up the school we extend the National Curriculum, offering many enriching learning experiences. Music, PE, Forest School and French are taught by specialists so that high standards are achieved in all subject areas. With recorder, violin and ukulele lessons as part of the curriculum, children are given frequent opportunities to perform and share their musical talents.

Extra-Curricular. A wealth of activities are available after school for all children, such as orchestra, science club, cookery, cross-country running, ballet, football, choir, karate, Lego and construction and many others. We also have a dynamic after-school care facility which provides lively activities from 3.30 to 6.00pm.

Entry Procedure. Fosse Bank is not academically selective at entry, although the Headmistress reserves the right to make a decision as to whether the applicant's learning needs can be managed within the School's normal provision. All children are required to attend a Taster Day before an offer may be made.

Charitable status. Fosse Bank New School is a Registered Charity, number 1045435.

The Froebelian School

Clarence Road, Horsforth, Leeds LS18 4LB

Tel: 0113 258 3047
email: office@froebelian.co.uk
website: www.froebelian.com
Twitter: @FroebelianS
Facebook: @FroebelianSchool
Instagram: @FroebelianSchool
LinkedIn: /FroebelianSchool

"We knew from our first visit to the school that it was perfect. Every day our instincts are justified, as we watch our little girl blossom into a confident, delightful and happy little person." A Parent

Chair of Governors: Mrs Rosey James

Head: Mrs Catherine Dodds

Deputy Head: Mrs Sharon Stratford

Admissions: Mrs Hannah Borkala

For full staff details, visit www.froebelian.com/about-froebelian/our-teachers-staff

Age Range. 3+ to 11+ years (3–4 years half days, optional afternoons).

Number of Pupils. 172 (86 boys, 86 girls).

Fees per term (2021–2022). £1,845–£2,985. Compulsory extras for full-time pupils.

A limited number of bursary-assisted places are available for eligible families.

Religious Affiliation: Christian, non-denominational.

Entry Requirements: Interview and assessment; written tests for older children.

Entry is usually at 3+ and limited places are sometimes available throughout the school.

The Froebelian School, Horsforth is one of Leeds' leading independent preparatory schools for children aged 3–11 years.

Children are at the heart of everything we do and we are passionate that all children enjoy a positive experience at Froebelian, in a caring, structured and secure environment. The time spent at the beginning of their journey in our Lower Kindergarten (Nursery) and Kindergarten (Reception) classes is crucial.

Therefore, to ensure we are laying the solid foundations for a lifelong love of learning, to gain knowledge and skills, and develop personal attributes, relevant to their futures, we have made significant investment in our provision in early years this summer; creating bespoke-designed classrooms and continuous access to an exceptional outdoor space.

At Froebelian we are enormously proud of our strong and closely-knit family community, and we work together to foster a life-long thirst for learning. We firmly believe that happy children make effective learners, and our school resonates with life and energy. The children and staff here apply themselves with dedicated enthusiasm in creating a stimulating and dynamic learning environment.

The Froebelian School strives to be truly innovative whilst maintaining our reputation for high standards. Quality classroom teaching and committed pastoral care ensure that our teachers really know and understand our children as individuals. Benefitting from a highly favourable staff to pupil ratio, we are able to provide plenty of focused support for pupils.

We set high expectations for effort and behaviour and the children always rise to meet this challenge. As a result, our children regularly secure a place at their first choice senior school and we enjoy an excellent scholarship success rate.

By cultivating a positive ethos built on strong relationships, our children can develop their skills across a wide range of opportunities available to them. Performance and participation are gently encouraged from the very beginning, and all our children have regular opportunities to perform in the sporting, theatrical, musical and public speaking arenas.

We nurture each child in a community based on fairness, respect and kindness where adults and children can trust and are considerate of each other, and we encourage children to build life-long friendships and equip them for success in a rapidly changing world.

Situated to the north-west of Leeds, and close to Bradford, the school is well served by major transport links. 'Wrap-around' care is available from 7.30am to 6.00pm in the form of Breakfast Club, Little Acorns and Homework and Activities Club and there is a holiday club during the summer break.

Our children adore their school and are justly proud of all they do. They love learning and there is a true sense of fun. We would love you to experience the warmth and politeness of our children for yourselves – please do come and meet them!

Charitable status. The Froebelian School is a Registered Charity, number 529111. It exists to provide education of the highest quality at affordable fee levels.

Garden House School

Turk's Row, London SW3 4TW

Tel: 020 7730 1652 (Girls)
020 7730 6652 (Boys)
email: info@gardenhouseschool.co.uk
website: www.gardenhouseschool.co.uk

Joint Principals: Mr Christian Warland and Mrs Sophie Strafford

Head, Girls' School: **Mrs Emma Studd**

Head, Boys' School: **Mr Dan Jameson**

Head, Early Years: **Mrs Julia Adlard**

Age Range. 3–11 Girls, 3–11 Boys.

Number of Pupils. 263 girls, 202 boys, taught in single-sex classes.

Fees per term (2021–2022). Kindergarten (all day) £6,000; Reception–Year 6 £7,650–£7,950. There is a 5% reduction for siblings.

Buildings and facilities. The School is housed in a light, airy building in Chelsea. Original artwork hangs in every classroom and facilities include libraries for different age groups, a ballet/performance/drama hall and dedicated science and art rooms.

Sport is played in various locations close to the School. The school has its own garden within the grounds of the Royal Hospital where children enjoy science lessons and attend a Gardening Club.

School drama productions are staged at the Royal Court Theatre in Sloane Square.

Aims, ethos and values. Garden House provides a stimulating and supportive environment in which our children gain an enthusiasm for learning. Our children achieve strong academic results in a calm, constructive manner, being encouraged to have inquiring and independent minds. We teach our boys and girls separately, delivered in teaching styles relevant to the difference audiences. Emphasis is placed not only on academic, sporting and artistic excellence but on manners and consideration to others. Our Kindness Code is adhered to and constantly re-emphasised.

Curriculum. English, Mathematics, Science, History, Geography, Religious Education, French (from Kindergarten), Latin, Computing, Life & Culture, Current Affairs, Art, Drama, Singing and Music, Dancing, Fencing and Physical Education (netball, tennis, rounders, gymnastics, swimming, athletics, cricket, hockey, rugby and football). We have many sports squads, sports clubs and matches. The Learning Support Department helps both children with special needs and those who are gifted, catered for in small groups, taught by two full-time and visiting specialist teachers. 80% of children learn at least one musical instrument. The School runs four choirs and a chamber orchestra.

A diverse range of early morning and after-school clubs include Chess, Coding, Debating, Harry Potter, Lego, Maths Monsters, Music Technology, French, Spanish and German to name a few of the fifty on offer every week.

Benefiting from our central London location, visits to museums, galleries and churches form an essential part of the Curriculum, as do annual field study and outward bound trips. Girls and boys spend a week in France after CE and boys enjoy a camping expedition among others including Outpost trip, a geography and science trip and a Bushcraft trip. The choir sings around the country; this year at Stratford-upon-Avon in a combined music/drama trip.

School Successes. Girls are prepared for the Common Entrance, with the majority leaving for the premier girls' Schools, 75% to leading London senior Schools, 25% to major boarding schools. Some boys leave us at eight, having been well prepared for entrance to leading London Prep Schools and 10% to top boarding Preps. Other boys remain at Garden House, being educated to the age of 11. Our children achieve several scholarships each year.

Entrance. We encourage you to visit the School. Girls and boys join Garden House in September after they reach 3 or 4 years of age. A Registration Form can be obtained from the School website and once completed and returned with the relevant fee, your child's name is placed on the Main List. Entry interviews are held one year before entry. We look forward to welcoming you and your children to Garden House School.

Gatehouse School

Sewardstone Road, Victoria Park, London E2 9JG

Tel: 020 8980 2978
email: admin@gatehouseschool.co.uk
website: www.gatehouseschool.co.uk
Twitter: @GatehouseSch
Facebook: @GatehouseSch

Headteacher: **Mrs S Korbay**

Age Range. 3–11 Co-educational.

Number in School. 492 Day Pupils.

Fees per term (2021–2022). £4,130–£4,353

Gatehouse School is an Independent Co-educational School for girls and boys aged 3 to 11.

Founded by Phyllis Wallbank, in May 1948, in the gatehouse of St Bartholomew, the Great Priory Church near Smithfield, London, the School was a pioneer of much that is now generally accepted in education. Gatehouse is based on the Wallbank plan whose guiding principle is that children of any race, colour, creed, background and intellect shall be accepted as pupils and work side by side without streaming or any kind of segregation with the aim that each child shall get to know and love God, and develop their own uniqueness of personality, to enable them to appreciate the world and the world to appreciate them.

Gatehouse is now located in Sewardstone Road, close to Victoria Park, and continues to follow this philosophy.

The Nursery is accommodated in a self-contained building with an outdoor play area. Pupils follow a balanced curriculum of child-initiated and teacher-led activities.

Lower Juniors are taught most subjects by their own qualified teacher and assistant, but have French, PE and Music with a specialist teacher.

In Upper Juniors from the age of 7, teaching is by subject and is conducted by highly qualified specialist staff. This is a special feature of Gatehouse and gives children from an early age, contact with subject specialists, not available to many children until secondary school.

We send children to schools such as City of London Boys and Girls, Forest, Bancroft's and Highgate, often with scholarships.

Charitable status. Gatehouse Educational Trust Limited is a Registered Charity, number 282558.

Gayhurst School

Bull Lane, Gerrards Cross, Bucks SL9 8RJ

Tel: 01753 882690
email: enquiries@gayhurstschool.co.uk
website: www.gayhurstschool.co.uk
Twitter: @GayhurstSchool
Facebook: @gayhurstschool
Instagram: @gayhurstschool

Chair of Governors: Mr Richard Thompson

Headmaster: **Mr G R A Davies**, BA Hons, PGCE, MEd

Age Range. 3–11 Co-educational.

Number of Children. 314

Fees per term (2021–2022). £4,175–£5,560 (inclusive of lunch). Nursery: from £2,265 per term.

Gayhurst is a happy, thriving and vibrant independent preparatory school for girls and boys aged 3–11. For over 100 years the school has endeavoured to bring out the best in every child in its care by focusing on individual talents and supporting children to achieve their full potential. Since becoming co-educational in 2008, Gayhurst has built a reputation as a family school, providing first-class co-education in Gerrards Cross.

Life at Gayhurst is engaging and exciting with regular activities organised to enrich the education of its pupils. Children are encouraged to participate in sport, with a busy programme of fixtures against other schools. Creativity is evident throughout the school with opportunities to learn an instrument, become a member of one of the many musical ensembles or take part in the annual year group drama productions. There are also numerous visits to places of interest on both day and residential trips.

Gayhurst strives to ensure that pupils are given every opportunity to achieve the best start in life. The school's commitment to continual improvement and development means that the children benefit greatly from the facilities offered on the school's five acre site, including IT rooms, Science laboratories, woodland adventure playground and an all-weather AstroTurf.

Pupils consistently achieve strong academic results progressing to both local Grammar Schools and to Senior Schools, day and boarding, in the Independent sector.

Headmaster, Gareth Davies says, "Pupils' social and personal development is enhanced by the co-educational experience that they get at Gayhurst. In my experience, boys and girls enjoy learning and socialising together and at such a young age, the elimination of gender stereotypes and access to different perspectives and ideas proves only to be beneficial. The family ethos, excellent pastoral care, support

and guidance from our caring staff and parent partnership also reinforce the children's positive experiences at school".

For more information about the school, or to arrange a visit, please contact the Admissions Coordinator on 01753 882690 or email admissions@gayhurstschool.co.uk.

Charitable status. Gayhurst School Trust is a Registered Charity, number 298869.

Glebe House School

2 Cromer Road, Hunstanton, Norfolk PE36 6HW

Tel: 01485 532809
email: ghsoffice@glebehouseschool.co.uk
website: www.glebehouseschool.co.uk
Twitter: @GlebeHS
Facebook: @GlebeHouseSchoolandNursery

Chairman of the Governors: Mr Nicholas Crane

Headmaster: **Mr Louis Taylor**, BA, PGCE

Age Range. 6 months to 13 years.

Number of Children. 198: 98 Boys, 100 Girls.

Fees per term (2021–2022). Prep £4,520; Pre-Prep £2,830.

Glebe House School and Nursery was founded in 1874 as a preparatory school and is surrounded by 12 acres of playing fields with a stunning new Nursery building.

The Junior School children are accommodated in a purpose-built building. The Senior School has specialist areas for all academic subjects and music, sport and drama are a significant part of a child's life at Glebe House. Our 25-metre indoor heated swimming pool, astroturf pitch for hockey, tennis and netball, adventure playground, gym, music school and performance hall all help to ensure that the core academic subjects are supported by a balanced and stimulating curriculum. Lessons finish at 3.30pm (Pre-Prep), 4.10pm (Prep) but breakfast club, after-school activities, cooked tea and supervised prep provide day care from 7.30am to 6.30pm.

Aims and Values. At the heart of Glebe House is our emphasis on supporting and valuing the individual. We encourage the traditional values of courtesy, consideration for others, self discipline and a desire to contribute to society.

Academic Life. We are committed to high academic standards, harnessing the best of modern educational practice. Class sizes remain small and every child is encouraged to achieve their full potential. Close supervision, with one-to-one support where necessary, is maintained and progress is carefully monitored through regular standardised testing and classroom assessments. The broad curriculum both incorporates and exceed national requirements, including offering a second modern language in addition to French from year six. Glebe House enjoys a high success rate at Common Entrance and in Independent Scholarship Examinations and with this solid foundation our pupils move confidently on to a wide range of senior schools.

Sport and Activities. We offer a wide sporting programme aimed to encourage fitness and a healthy enjoyment of sport that will remain with the children for life. Rugby, hockey and cricket are the main sports for boys and hockey, netball and rounders for girls. We also encourage involvement in many activities including athletics, cross country, football, golf, swimming and tennis. The lunchtime and after-school activity programme is varied and includes sporting, dramatic, artistic and musical groups as well as others such as Mandarin Chinese. We offer a wide range of activities during the summer holidays, including ball sports, swimming, craft, music and drama workshops, tennis, and sailing.

Pastoral Care and Boarding. Relations between children and staff are respectful but relaxed and the children know they are free to talk to all staff, one of the great advantages of a school this size. All pupils belong to one of three houses and have a tutor who sees them each morning and is the first point of contact for parents. Good communication is crucial and we operate an open door policy to parents. The school offers 35 weekly boarding places and flexibility in choosing from one to four nights.

Travel. Our minibuses pick up in the morning and take home at 4.15pm and 6.00pm to King's Lynn and surrounding areas.

Further Information. Prospective parents and children are most welcome to contact the School Registrar, email: tjf@glebehouseschool.co.uk, to meet the Headmaster and tour the school.

Charitable status. Glebe House School Trust Limited is a Registered Charity, number 1018815.

The Gleddings Preparatory School

Birdcage Lane, Savile Park, Halifax, West Yorkshire HX3 0JB

Tel: 01422 354605
email: admin@thegleddings.co.uk
website: www.thegleddings.co.uk

Headmistress: **Mrs Jill Wilson**, CBE

Age Range. 3–11 Co-educational.

Number of Pupils. 200

Fees per term (2021–2022). £3,430 including meals.

"The Gleddings is very special. It is precious to several generations of families in the locality and beyond. We are now educating the children of our past pupils. We consider it a great privilege to do so.

The staff and I remember, all of the time, the trust that parents bestow in us. We promise our best efforts for every child.

Our academic results speak for themselves but The Gleddings is about much more. We develop self-discipline, self-respect and confidence within The Gleddings' unique "YOU CHOOSE" ethos. We encourage children to THINK! and to learn how to learn."

Jill Wilson, Headteacher.

Godolphin Prep

Laverstock Road, Salisbury, Wiltshire SP1 2RB

Tel: 01722 430652
email: admissions@godolphin.org
website: www.godolphin.org
Twitter: @godolphinprep
Facebook: @godolphinschool
LinkedIn: /company/godolphin-school

Headmistress: **Miss Julia Miller**

Head of Admissions: Mrs Corinna Florence

To view a full list of the staff, please visit the website: www.godolphin.org.

Age Range. 3–11.

Number of Pupils. 80.

Fees per term (2021–2022). International £9,590; Full boarding £8,915; 5-day Boarding £7,610, 3-day Boarding £6,615; Day: £4,910 (Years 4–6), £3,910 (Year 3), £2,530 (Years 1–2), £2,520 (Reception).

Godolphin is a very special school, which offers a broad education for girls from 3–18. Our whole school ethos is unique in Salisbury and it ensures the girls move from one stage of their education to the next.

Godolphin Prep provides a supportive and stimulating environment with a strong academic ethos. Godolphin girls are happy and confident. They flourish because of the excellent pastoral care and the close partnership between staff and parents.

The whole school approach is reinforced through strong links with the Senior School and the three competitive Houses that girls belong to from Pre-Prep to the Upper Sixth.

Flexi and Full Boarding is available. Prep boarders, from the age of seven, are an integral part of the whole school boarding community and are supported by specialist boarding staff in a bespoke boarding house. The Walters House staff help and support them with every aspect of school life from homework and uniform to laundry and music practice.

Sharing the site with the Senior School means we offer outstanding facilities such as our art and design department, the swimming pool, theatre, science and technology labs and sports pitches.

We also share staff expertise an this enables us to offer a wide variety of after school activities which include fun cookery, Lego robots, kick boxing, choir, science club, Zumba, yoga and orchestra.

To find out more about Godolphin Prep, visit us on one of our Open Days when you can experience a typical school morning. For dates and further information visit www.godolphin.org.

Godstowe Preparatory School

Shrubbery Road, High Wycombe, Bucks HP13 6PR

Tel: 01494 529273
            01494 429006 Registrar
email: schooloffice@godstowe.org
website: www.godstowe.org
Twitter: @GodstoweSchool
Facebook: @GodstoweSchool
LinkedIn: /godstowe-preparatory-school

Motto: *Finem Respice*

Chair of Governors: T Leaver

Headmistress: Ms S Green, BSc Econ, PGCE

Age Range. Girls 3–13, Boys 3–7.

Number of Pupils. Preparatory: 334 (boarding and day). Pre-Preparatory: 115.

Fees per term (2021–2022). Boarders £8,500, Day Children £3,725–£5,740. Nursery: £1,787–£3,575.

Since its foundation in 1900, Godstowe Preparatory School has been at the forefront of education. It has a distinguished tradition as the first British boarding preparatory school for girls, in a foundation that includes Wycombe Abbey, Benenden and St Leonards.

Today, Godstowe is a flourishing boarding and day school with around 450 pupils, enjoying an unparalleled academic reputation. It has a Pre-Prep department for boys and girls aged between three and seven, and a Preparatory School for girls from seven to thirteen years old. Class sizes are small allowing children to benefit from individual attention.

A new indoor swimming pool opened in May 2019. The school underwent an ISI inspection in June 2018 and was regarded as 'excellent' in every respect.

Academic Record. Godstowe enjoys an excellent and unparalleled academic reputation amongst British independent schools. Despite its non-selective entry policy, Godstowe consistently achieves unrivalled academic results. In 2019, 33 scholarships and distinctions were awarded. By the age of nine, pupils are taught by specialists in 16 subjects across the curriculum. Language teaching includes French, Spanish and Latin. Sport, ICT, Art and Music are all outstandingly taught within first-rate facilities.

Boarding. Girls' boarding life is focused within three houses in the grounds, one of which is a dedicated junior house. Each has three resident staff and a warm and supportive atmosphere. A combination of professional and caring staff and beautifully refurbished accommodation ensures a safe and relaxing environment. Each house has its own garden, reinforcing the feeling of 'going home' at the end of the school day. Weekends are packed full of activity and fun, with many weekly boarders often choosing to stay at School for the weekend.

The **Enrichment Curriculum** offers 50 after-school activities each week, most of which run after school between 4.30pm and 6.30pm. The 'E-Curriculum' gives children the chance to try many exciting and challenging new pursuits including poetry writing, judo, cooking, Chinese Mandarin, football and debating. In addition, supervised homework sessions are offered every evening. Day children may join the boarders for breakfast and supper. Other than those sessions supervised by outside instructors all activities are offered free of charge. An Enrichment programme is also in place for Pre-Prep children.

Charitable status. The Godstowe Preparatory School Company Limited is a Registered Charity, number 310637. It exists to provide education and training for young girls and boys.

Grange Park Preparatory School

13 The Chine, Grange Park, London N21 2EA

Tel: 020 8360 1469
email: office@gpps.org.uk
website: www.gpps.org.uk
Twitter: @gpprepschool
Facebook: @grangeparkprep
Instagram: @grangeparkprepschool

Day School for Boys and Girls from 3–11.

Chair of Governors: Mr Amit Metha

Head: Mrs Flavia Rizzo, BSc, PGCE, MA

Age Range. 3–11

Number of Children. 144.

Fees per term (2021–2022). £3,570–£3,599.

Grange Park Preparatory School is a long established, happy and successful school that provides a broad and stimulating education. It is situated in the pleasant residential area of Grange Park.

We remain committed to educating boys and girls in a small school with small class sizes, thus allowing every child to be known as an individual. The children enjoy a broad curriculum taught by experienced staff who encourage excellence in all areas of school life.

We also have a Nursery class for boys and girls aged 3 and 4. Nursery staff and children have access to the excellent resources available at GPPS, including outside space, the gym and a cooked lunch for those children staying the whole day. The children follow the Early Years Curriculum with additional specialist teaching in French, Dance, Drama and Music.

In KS1 the children are taught mostly by form teachers with specialist teaching being introduced gradually in KS2. From Reception specialist teachers teach PE and Games, French, Music, Dance and Drama. Individual music tuition is available from Year 1.

In Key Stage 2 preparation for 11+ state selective and independent secondary schools starts from as early as Year 3, where children undertake verbal and non-verbal reasoning as part of the curriculum. In addition, from the spring term in Year 4, children wishing to sit for selective schools attend extra prep classes, thus equipping them with the tools to achieve their maximum potential in terms of academic attainment. Every year we are proud to announce that our Year 6 children do extremely well in the secondary school entrance exams, with some being awarded scholarships.

Children enjoy a very busy school life and benefit from an excellent variety of extra-curricular activities, including LAMDA, Judo, horse riding, tennis, cookery and chess to name a few, further enriching their experience and creating lifetime memories.

The school has a healthy eating policy. Lunches are cooked in school using only fresh ingredients; no processed food is used. There is always a vegetarian option and salads and fresh fruit are available daily.

Places for Reception are offered after the Headteacher has met with parents and their child. Children taking up chance vacancies in other classes will be invited to spend a day in school to ensure they will fit into the class successfully.

Before leaving GPPS every child will have been given a responsible role at some level, instilling in them a sense of duty and ingrained confidence, preparing them for today's challenges.

Grange Park Preparatory School is a part of The Inspired Learning Group, company number 11458444,

The Granville School

2 Bradbourne Park Road, Sevenoaks, Kent TN13 3LJ

Tel: 01732 453039
email: secretary@granvilleschool.org
website: www.granvilleschool.org
Twitter: @granville_prep
Facebook: @TheGranvilleSchool

Chairman of Governors: Mrs N Coll

Headmistress: **Mrs Louise Lawrance**, BPrimEd Hons

Age Range. Girls 3–11, Boys 3–5.

Number of Pupils. 200.

Fees per term (2021–2022). Kindergarten £2,095 (mornings only) or £3,615 (all day), Reception, Years 1 & 2 £4,260, Years 3, 4, 5 & 6 £5,425. Lunch included.

Breakfast Club (7.30am until the start of school day) £7.50 per session, After School Care £8.50 per session until 5.00pm, £16.50 per session until 6.00pm.

Extras: Private Lessons: Singing, Pianoforte, Violin, Cello, Oboe, Clarinet, Flute, Recorder, Brass £235 per term. LAMDA Individual Lessons £175 per term; Shared Lessons £130/£95. Ballet £85 per term.

The Granville School was founded on VE Day, 8th May 1945, with the Dove of Peace and Churchill's victory sign chosen to form the school crest.

The Granville is an exceptional school which combines the very best of a Prep school tradition with a vibrant, forward-looking outlook where change is embraced and innovation celebrated. Girls aged three to eleven, and boys aged three to four, thrive on individual attention and achieve their best in a happy, secure and stimulating environment. Our highly-qualified, specialist teachers make learning enjoyable, develop inquiring minds and raise levels of expectation.

The school maintains Christian principles and traditional values within a broad and stimulating curriculum. The Granville has a strong record of academic achievement and children are prepared for 11+ entry into independent schools and state grammar schools. Granville pupils excel in music, art, drama and sport. There is a wide range of extra-curricular activities available for all age groups.

The school is set in five acres of garden and woodland close to Sevenoaks Station. The original house and new buildings enable pupils to enjoy a high-quality learning environment with light and airy classrooms. The Granville has its own indoor heated Swimming Pool, a Sports Hall, Science Lab, Studio for Music and Drama, French room, ICT Suite, individual teaching rooms and Junior and Senior Libraries. A new building, opened in January 2014, provides high-quality Early Years facilities together with a large Art and DT room. Outside facilities include three netball/tennis courts, sports/playing field, junior activity playgrounds and a woodland classroom. Plans are under way to further develop the Hall, Computing Suite and Performing Arts Studio.

Means-tested bursaries are available on request.

Charitable status. The Ena Makin Educational Trust Limited is a Registered Charity, number 307931. Its aim is to run any school as an educational charity for the promotion of education generally.

Great Walstead School

East Mascalls Lane, Lindfield, Haywards Heath, West Sussex RH16 2QL

Tel: 01444 483528
email: GWmail@greatwalstead.co.uk
website: www.greatwalstead.co.uk
Twitter: @greatwalstead
Facebook: @GreatWalstead

Chairman of the Board of Governors: P Thurston

Headmaster: **C B Calvey**, BEd Hons

Deputy Head: W Fuller, BSc Hons, PGCE

Director of Studies: E Scotland, BMus Hons, PGCE, NPQSL

Age Range. 2½–13.

Number of Pupils. 325: Main School 229; Pre-Prep 44; Pre-School & Reception (EYFS) 49.

Fees per term (2021–2022). Tuition: Pre-School £460 per day (inc EYFE), Reception £2,895; Pre-Prep £3,435–£3,980, Main School £5,075–£5,550.

Founded in 1925 by Mr R J Mowll in Enfield, the school moved to its present location in the heart of Sussex two years later. Staff and pupils came to a large country house set in over 260 acres of fields and woodland, where children could learn and play in unspoiled surroundings.

From these beginnings, Great Walstead has developed into a thriving co-educational prep school, catering for children from 2½ to 13 years of age. It is a school which values children as individuals and regards it as vital that each child develops his or her potential – academically, creatively, socially and spiritually. Above all, the school is built on the strong values of Christian Faith, Success, Communication, Environment and Dedication, creating an essential foundation for the whole of a pupil's education and life.

The Early Years Foundation Stage incorporates Pre-School and Reception classes, welcoming children from the age of 2½ until it is time to enter the Pre-Prep at 5. It provides a full, rich and varied Early Years education, laying firm foundations in basic skills and understanding for future learning. They share a dedicated outdoor learning and play space with a giant covered sandpit, mud kitchen and music area.

The Pre-Prep covers the ages from 5 to 7 within its own section of the school. It has its own library, ICT suite and play area. The aim here is to ensure that the foundation skills of reading, writing and maths are taught while, at the same time, teachers add a breadth of interest through specialist lead classes in French, computer skills, PE and Music.

Children enter the Junior School at 7. For the next two years they will have a class teacher who supervises them closely for a good proportion of the day, but have specialist teachers for French, Music, ICT, Art, Craft, Design & Technology, Sport and PE. They have games or outdoor activities each day and gradually learn to become more independent.

Children in the senior age group, from 9 to 13 years of age, are taught by graduate specialist teachers in preparation for the Common Entrance examination and senior school scholarships at 13. In the past ten years, Great Walstead pupils have won over 200 scholarships or awards to senior schools and in the last four years over 50% of pupils gained such success. Facilities in the Senior School include two computer rooms with 21 linked PCs, a well-equipped science laboratory, and a fine Library.

The 269 acres of farmland, playing fields, and woodland make many outdoor activities possible. The woods host learning activities in Eco-School and Forest School and fun exercises in camp-building, as well as teddy bear picnics for the younger children. In the summer, the older children camp out overnight. In addition, the purpose-built challenge course gives enormous pleasure all year round for all ages.

The Art, Craft and Design Technology department is housed in old farm buildings, which have been adapted to make workshops and studios; the lessons form an integral part of the curriculum for all children. New in 2021, the Great Walstead Secret Garden is a wonderful addition to the curriculum, providing a fantastic walled garden space for academic and creative exploration using all of the senses.

The school's extensive grounds allow a wide range of major sports. Swimming is possible all year round in our own heated pool. We have a superbly equipped sports hall and facilities including a wonderful new AstroTurf. Match Day on Wednesdays for Years 5–8 and Thursdays for Juniors are weekly events with emphasis on sportsmanship, healthy competition and sport for all. All children (Years 3–8) have the opportunity to be involved in competitive sport at least once per season. Those children not involved in match fixtures on a particular week are able to access a carousel of indoor and outdoor activities, including: pottery, archery, art, ICT, woods games, gardening and a variety of sports.

The school has a Learning Enhancement department where specialist staff are able to give the extra support required. The department helps children with all their learning needs whether helping with a specific difficulty or extending those children who are gifted and talented.

Music has long been a strength at Great Walstead, with a high proportion of the children learning instruments and playing in groups, bands and orchestras. Singing is encouraged from Pre-School upwards. Drama is also an important part of the Arts here. All children are given the opportunity to act, with both major productions and form performances.

Matron, the school nurse, tends to the health of the children in the whole school. The school, through the Keep and Wrap Around Care, provides flexible holiday, pre- and after-school care, as well as other holiday activities to meet the needs of today's parents.

Parents are always made most welcome at the school. There is a thriving parents' organisation called FOGWA (Friends of Great Walstead Association) which provides a number of successful social events and raises substantial sums for the benefit of the school.

Academic, Music and Sports Awards are offered at 9+, and Academic, All-Rounder, Art, Drama, Music, Performing Arts and Sport Scholarships at 11+.

Charitable status. Great Walstead School is a Registered Charity, number 307002. It exists to provide a good education on Christian foundations.

Greenfield School

Old Woking Road, Woking, Surrey GU22 8HY

Tel: 01483 772525
email: admissions@greenfield.surrey.sch.uk
website: www.greenfield.surrey.sch.uk
Twitter: @GFSWoking
Facebook: @GFSWoking
Instagram: @greenfieldschoolwoking
LinkedIn: @greenfieldschoolwoking

Chairman of Governors: Mrs Janet Day

Headteacher: Mrs Tania Botting, MEd

Age Range. 6 months to 11 years.

Number of Pupils. 143 day girls, 186 day boys.

Fees per term (2021–2022). £2,032–£4,787.

Greenfield School is an academically non-selective, co-educational school and nursery for children aged from 6 months to 11 years. We aim to offer every possible opportunity for children to reach their full potential and recognise that all children have talents and strengths in many different areas. We are proud of our academic and non-academic successes and have a strong track record of achieving scholarships to a wide range of senior schools for music, art, sport, drama and academic excellence.

At Greenfield School we believe that a happy child will learn. Therefore, we provide a secure and caring environment working closely with our parents, to enable the children to develop their confidence and self-esteem and prepare them for the next stage of their education and future.

We attach importance to traditional values, promoting courtesy, respect, tolerance, empathy, humility and consideration for others, whilst ensuring the curriculum we deliver is both modern and relevant.

Greenfield School has high standards but we also appreciate the need to strike a happy balance between work and play and the formal and informal. There is an excellent ratio of adults to children throughout the school enabling children to receive individual attention and children are often taught in small groups. Parents are welcome to visit the school at any time and appointments can be made by calling the school office. To request a copy of the prospectus, please visit the school website or call the school office.

Charitable status. Greenfield School is a Registered Charity, number 295145. It aims to offer an excellent all-round education to children of all abilities.

Grimsdell

Mill Hill Pre-Preparatory School

Winterstoke House, Wills Grove, Mill Hill, London NW7 1QR

Tel: 020 8959 6884
email: office@grimsdell.org.uk
website: www.millhill.org.uk/grimsdell
Twitter: @millhillpreprep
Facebook: @millhillpreprep
Instagram: @millhillpreprep

Co-educational Pre-Preparatory Day School for 3 to 7 year olds. Presently there is no full-day option for the nursery.

Awarded 'Excellent' in quality of education in academic achievement and personal development – ISI Inspection January 2020.

Chairman of Court of Governors: Mr Elliot Lipton, BSc Hons, MBA, FRSA, FRICS

Head: **Mrs Kate Simon**, BA Hons, PGCE

Senior Deputy Head: Mrs Jenny Ticehurst, BEd Hons

Assistant Head Teaching & Learning: Miss Yuka Matsushita, BA Hons, QTS

Assistant Head Early Years: Mrs Emily Jenner, BA Hons, PGCE

Assistant Head Pastoral/SENCO: Mrs K Vanstone, BEd, MEdPsyc, PG Cert SpLD, ATS SENCO

Age Range. 3–7 Co-educational.

Number of pupils. 97 Boys, 106 Girls

Fees per term (2021–2022). Pre-Prep: £5,365. Nursery: £2,900 (mornings only), £2,475 (afternoons only).

Grimsdell, Mill Hill Pre-Prep is situated in the Green Belt on the boarders of Hertfordshire and Middlesex and just ten miles from Central London. A part of The Mill Hill School Foundation which is set in 160 acres of beautiful grounds, we make extensive use of the outdoors in all subject areas and 'Forest School' has a firm place within our curriculum. We provide a happy, secure and rich learning environment for boys and girls aged 3 to 7. Belmont, Mill Hill Preparatory School, is less than a quarter of a mile away and educates pupils from age 7 to 13, the majority of whom

move on to the senior school, Mill Hill, which educates boys and girls from age 13 to 18.

We pride ourselves on the exciting and creative curriculum we offer. The children who come here are inspired to learn whilst being encouraged to explore and enjoy their childhood. The boys and girls at Grimsdell learn through hands-on experience. With the support and guidance of professional, caring staff and excellent resources and equipment, each child is encouraged to reach their full potential. Our approach combines traditional skills of reading, writing and mathematics with the breadth and balance offered by an enhanced Early Years Foundation Stage and KS1 Curriculum. Every pupil can enjoy many opportunities offered by learning through Science, Technology and Computing, Art, Drama, Music, PE and French lessons.

The school is housed in a large Victorian building with its own secure play areas and adventure playgrounds, taking advantage of further facilities on the Mill Hill site including a Forest School area, sports fields, swimming pool and theatre.

The usual age of entry is at 3 and 4 years old, but 5 and 6 year olds are considered as vacancies occur. It is expected that most children will pass to Belmont at the end of Year 2.

Charitable status. The Mill Hill School Foundation is a Registered Charity, number 1064758. It exists to provide education for boys and girls.

Guildford High School – Junior School

United Learning

London Road, Guildford, Surrey GU1 1SJ

Tel: 01483 561440
email: guildford-admissions@guildfordhigh.co.uk
website: www.guildfordhigh.co.uk
Twitter: @guildfordhigh
Facebook: @GuildfordHigh
Instagram: @GuildfordHigh

Chairman of Local Governing Body: Ms Kate Richards

Head of Junior School: **Mr Allistair Williamson**, BPhEd Auckland

Deputy Head of Junior School: Mrs Kathryn L Hughes, BSc Hons London

Age Range. Girls 4–11.

Number of Pupils. 300.

Fees per term (2021–2022). Reception–Year 1: £3,800. Year 2: £4,367. Years 3–6: £4,934.

Awarded 'Best School for Pastoral Care' in *The Week* magazine 2018 and a top ten school in *The Sunday Times 2020 Parent Power*, the Junior School at Guildford High School is situated on the same site as the Senior School. It is a modern, bright, self-contained school with the third floor especially dedicated to Art, Music, Science, IT and the Library.

The girls normally start in the Reception classes (4 years) or at Year 3 (7 years), however, they are welcome in any year group depending on spaces available, and work their way through the Junior School with natural progression on to the Senior School at Year 7 (11 years).

The breadth and depth of the curriculum encompasses 15 fast paced subjects, with an embedded thinking skills programme. Three modern foreign languages are included, with Spanish starting in Year 1 for five year olds. Music, Drama and Sport play an important part in the curricular and co-curricular programmes. Specialist teachers and resources are employed throughout the Junior School. Parents and teachers work closely together to ensure excellent differentiation and a nurturing environment with strong pastoral care.

Guildford High School Junior School girls are confident, happy and well-prepared for entry to the Senior School. (*See Guildford High School Senior School entry in HMC section.*)

Charitable status. Guildford High School Junior School is part of United Learning which comprises: UCST (a Company Limited by Guarantee, Registered in England, number 2780748, and a Registered Charity, number 1016538) and ULT (a Company Limited by Guarantee, Registered in England, number 4439859, and an Exempt Charity).

Haberdashers' Boys' Prep & Pre-Prep School

Butterfly Lane, Elstree, Hertfordshire WD6 3AF

Tel:　　　020 8266 1779
email:　　prepoffice@habsboys.org.uk
website:　www.habsboys.org.uk
Twitter:　@habsboys
Facebook: @habsboys

Chairman of The Aske Board: Mr S Cartmell, OBE

Headmaster: Mr A R Lock, MA

Head of Prep School: **Mr M E Rossetti**, MA

Deputy Head (*Pastoral*): Mr G Thomas, BA Hons

Deputy Head (*Academic*): Mr P Swindell, BA Hons

Head of Pre-Prep School: Ms V Huggett, BSc

Age Range. Prep 7–11; Pre-Prep 5–7.
Number of Boys. Prep 215, Pre-Prep 73.
Fees per term (2021–2022). Pre-Prep £5,397 (including lunch); Prep £7,053.

The Preparatory School at Habs has been the top-performing independent boys' school in the country. It is vibrant with the energy and curiosity of over 200 boys aged 7–11 from a wide range of local schools and communities. It is a very special place to work and play.

It is housed in a purpose-designed building, opened by HRH The Princess Margaret, Citizen and Haberdasher, in 1983, on the same campus as the Senior School. The bright, cheerful classrooms provide a welcoming and stimulating environment. The Prep enjoys a unique mix of family

atmosphere and close links with the Senior School. The boys are able to share the wonderful facilities and grounds of the Senior School, including the Sports Centre, the heated indoor Swimming Pool, the Music School and the Dining Room. The Pre-Prep School is located six miles north of the school at How Wood, near St Albans.

The Prep building has completed an extensive refurbishment. This includes a brand new library and state-of-the-art teaching facilities.

The relationship between the Preparatory staff and their forms is close and friendly, within a context of firm discipline. In this environment, brimming with opportunities, the school ensures an education of breadth and depth extending well beyond national guidelines.

Sport and games play a major role in the boys' week, offering fitness and fun to all. Indeed, the sporting ethos of team spirit and fair play underpins the whole structure of Prep School life.

The arts spring to life in a wealth of musical, dramatic and artistic activity, guided by specialists whose passion for their subject is matched by the enthusiasm of their pupils.

Every boy is a musician for at least one year when he studies an orchestral instrument of his choice, free of charge, through the Music Scheme; many of these fledgling musicians eventually make their way into the Senior School's First Orchestra.

There are many clubs and societies; however boys with some special interest often start their own, supported by staff, and eagerly attended by those of like mind. Some boys also stay on to enjoy extra play time with their friends or to do their homework and to have tea. The After School Care Facility is equipped with bean bags, games and sports equipment.

Boys are admitted each September after assessments to the Pre-Prep at the age of 5+ and to the Prep at 7+. Boys are expected to move into the Senior School at 11. Most boys will flourish in the Senior School as they have in the Prep, and the transition is made as natural as possible. A qualifying examination assures candidates that the Senior School is right for them and they are given help preparing for the different pace and rhythms they will find there. (*For further details, please see entry in HMC section.*)

Charitable status. The Haberdashers' Aske's Charity is a Registered Charity, number 313996. It exists to promote education.

Hall Grove

London Road, Bagshot, Surrey GU19 5HZ

Tel:　　　01276 473059
email:　　office@hallgrove.co.uk
website:　www.hallgrove.co.uk
Twitter:　@hallgroveschool
Facebook: @hallgroveschool
Instagram: @hallgroveschool

Principal: Alastair R Graham, BSc, PGCE

Headmaster: **Neil Tomlin**, OBE, BA, MA

Age Range. 3–13.

Number of Children. Pre-Preparatory (age 4–7) 110; Preparatory (age 7–13) 320.

Fees per term (2021–2022). Day fees: Pre-School (mornings) £2,000; Reception–Year 2 £3,850; Lower Juniors (Years 3 & 4) £4,600; Upper Juniors (Years 5 & 6) £5,000; Seniors (Years 7 & 8) £5,300. Weekly boarding: £1,350 supplement per term. Pre-paid flexi-boarding: £40 per night. Sibling discount.

Hall Grove is a happy, vibrant school of over 400 boys and girls aged 3–13 with a separate pre-school in its grounds for those aged 3 and 4. Weekly/Flexi boarding is offered for up to 12 pupils. The main entry ages are 3, 4, 7 and 11.

The school was founded in 1957 by the Graham Family, Alastair Graham is Principal of the school. At its centre is a most attractive Georgian house set in beautiful gardens and parkland. Recent additions have provided some modern rooms and specialist teaching areas, an impressive computer facility and new classroom blocks. Despite this building programme, the character and atmosphere of a family home has been retained.

The academic standards are high and there is a very strong emphasis on Sport and Music. A wide range of activities flourish; woodwork, ceramics, food technology, drama and a host of major and minor sports including soccer, rugby, hockey, netball, rounders, cricket, tennis, athletics, swimming, golf, judo, basketball, badminton and dance. Riding and stable management is an added attraction.

Optional 'Half Boarding' extends the school day to 8.00pm for Years 6, 7 and 8. Some may stay overnight on a regular basis. There is also provision for after-school care and a full programme of evening activities.

Hall Grove has its own residential field study centre situated on the South Devon coast called Battisborough House and there are many field trips and expeditions both in Devon and overseas. Battisborough is available for hire by other schools and can accommodate up to 60 in comfort.

Halstead Preparatory School for Girls

Woodham Rise, Woking, Surrey GU21 4EE

Tel:	01483 772682
email:	registrar@halstead-school.org.uk
website:	www.halstead-school.org.uk
Twitter:	@halsteadprepsch
Facebook:	@halsteadprepsch
Instagram:	@halsteadprepsch

Chairman of Governors: Mr S Brookhouse

Headmistress: **Mrs S Maher**, BSc Hons, GTP, MBA

Age Range. 2–11 years
Number of Pupils. 220 Girls.

Fees per term (2021–2022). Nursery (flexible) from £790; Reception £3,725; Years 1 and 2 £4,165; Years 3 and 4 £5,095; Years 5 and 6 £5,245.

Halstead, a dynamic and unique school for girls who love to learn.

Described as a hidden gem, tucked away in a leafy suburb in Woking sits Halstead Preparatory School for Girls. Girls arrive from the age of two into Nursery and as they progress through the school with just two classes per year, the teachers are able to get to know the girls extremely well and deliver a personalised learning plan based on each girls' individual needs.

Headmistress Sharon Maher arrived September 2020 from a highly successful girls' preparatory school in London and explains "I was immediately attracted to Halstead as soon as I walked through the door, the girls were so bubbly, confident, bright and happy and the energy, laughter and buzz in the classroom and throughout the school was contagious".

The school boasts plenty of space outside and in, with multiple sports courts and green space for netball, hockey, tennis, rounders and athletics, to a hall for indoor sports and regular school productions in music and drama. Further purpose-built suites enable Art, Design and Technology, Food Technology and Science to be taught and all classrooms not only have whiteboards but iPads are in regular use across the school to support the girls' learning.

As the girls reach Year 5 and start thinking about their senior school, Halstead work very closely, and in partnership with parents to ensure that each girl gains entry to the right senior school for them and its long history of excellent results and scholarships reflect just that. As Mrs Maher explains "whilst we are incredibly and justifiably proud of our academic success, our focus remains on providing a solid foundation where Halstead girls are treated as individuals and are happy, well-rounded, intellectually curious girls with a genuine passion to learn, I could not be more proud to lead such a wonderful girls' school".

To book a place on Halstead's open morning to learn more about the school and to hear more from Mrs Maher visit www.halstead-school.org.uk

Charitable status. Halstead (Educational Trust) Limited is a Registered Charity, number 270525. It exists to provide a high quality all-round education for girls aged 2+–11.

The Hampshire School, Chelsea

15 Manresa Road, London SW3 6NB

Tel:	020 7352 7077
email:	info@thehampshireschoolchelsea.co.uk
website:	thehampshireschoolchelsea.co.uk

Head: **Dr Pamela Edmonds**, EdD, MEd, BEd Hons

Age Range. 2–13.
Number in School. 82 Boys, 55 Girls.
Fees per term (2021–2022). £4,600–£6,670.

Founded in 1928 and located in the London Borough of Kensington and Chelsea, The Hampshire School Chelsea is an independent, non-denominational day school that caters for boys and girls between the ages of rising 2 and 13+. The school is located in a characteristic grade two listed building in the heart of Chelsea, London just off the King's Road.

The Hampshire School Chelsea boasts exceptional facilities, including a spacious outdoor play and learning area in the heart of London, first-class learning facilities, a fully equipped music room, art room and original historic Chelsea library where classes take place. It's rich history only adds to the school's charm.

Through a Growth Mindset approach to learning, the School's Core Values of Respect, Resilience, Responsibility, Community and Excellence, the Pupil Voice programme and development groups, students are able to thrive. The broad array of over 40 extra-curricular activities per week support the pupils' development while sustaining a strong commitment to the emotional wellbeing of every child.

The EYFS curriculum taught in the Pre-School, with the addition of specialist teaching in French, music, PE, art, ballet and drama, places an emphasis on high levels of engagement which encourages rapid individual progress. Exceptional teaching and learning in all year groups and a broad, rigorous and coherent curriculum ensures a successful transition to selective senior schools at 11+ and 13+. Further emphasis is placed on developing each child's individual talents and the School's motto of 'Alte Spectemus' provides the focus for outstanding achievement.

Hampton Pre-Prep & Prep School

Gloucester Road, Hampton, Middlesex TW12 2UQ

Tel: 020 8979 1844
email: admissions@hamptonprep.org.uk
website: hamptonprep.org.uk
Twitter: @Hampton_Prep

Chairman of Governors: A J Roberts, CBE, BA, FRSA, FColl

Headmaster: **Mr Tim Smith**, BA, NZ Dip Tchg, MBA

Age Range. Boys 3–11, Girls 3–7.
Number of Pupils. 228.
Fees per term (2021–2022). Kindergarten (3–4 years): £2,205 (mornings), £4,410 (all day). Pre-Prep (4–7 years): £4,660. Prep (7–11 years): £5,095. All fees include lunch for full day pupils.

The Prep School moved into its new state-of-the-art building in March 2016. The School is situated in a quiet, leafy part of Hampton and is easily accessible by road and rail. The School merged with Hampton School in September 1999. Both schools are served by the same Board of Governors and the Headmaster of Hampton Prep reports to the Headmaster of Hampton School. The amalgamation produces economies of scale from which Hampton Prep benefits. Boys transfer to senior schools at 11+.

Although there is no expectation for pupils to select Hampton as their first-choice secondary school, approximately 50% of our boys transfer there each year. Since September 2004 Hampton has been offering Assured Places for 11+ entry. These can be gained from Year 2 through to the end of Year 5 via an ongoing programme of assessment of the boys. In addition, those boys who perform very well in the 11+ Hampton entrance examinations, but who do not gain an award from Hampton, will be considered for the W D James Award made by Hampton Prep, which will be in the form of a reduction in the child's first term's fees at Hampton.

The Pre-Prep is housed on its own site in the homely atmosphere of two linked residential houses offering space and security. Rooms are well-appointed and there is one class per year group of 22 pupils. The Prep School is two-form entry with 18 pupils per class. The Preparatory School, which backs onto an attractive public park, has undergone significant redevelopment, the old buildings have been demolished and the remainder of the site re-landscaped. The new facilities have played a large part in the transformation of the School, its academic life included. Major school sports are Football, Rugby and Cricket. An extensive programme of co-curricular activities includes: art club, chess, drama, judo, yoga, computing, Warhammer/Lego and a variety of minor sports. There is a School choir, an orchestra, and a flourishing tradition of drama. Individual music tuition is also provided.

Parents share in the life of the School as fully as possible and there exists a very active Parents' Association.

Please contact the School Office for a prospectus.

Charitable status. Hampton Pre-Prep & Prep School is part of the Hampton School Trust, which is a Registered Charity, number 1120005. It exists to provide a school in Hampton.

Hanford School

Child Okeford, Blandford Forum, Dorset DT11 8HN

Tel: 01258 860219
email: office@hanfordschool.co.uk
website: www.hanfordschool.co.uk
Twitter: @HanfordDorset
Facebook: @HanfordSchool

Chairman of Governors: Mr A Hussey

Headmaster: **Mr R Johnston**, BA

Age Range. 7–13.
Number of Girls. 100.
Fees per term (2021–2022). Boarders £7,850, Day Girls £6,250.

Hanford School, located between Blandford and Shaftesbury in Dorset, was founded in 1947 by the Revd and Mrs C B Canning. It is housed in a beautiful 17th Century Jacobean manor house set in 45 acres of land in the Stour valley. The amenities include a Chapel, Laboratories, a Computer Room, a Music School, an Art School, a Gymnasium, a Swimming Pool, a Handwork Room, two Netball/Tennis Courts (hard) and an indoor covered Riding School.

Girls arrive from the age of seven onwards and leave at 13 after taking Common Entrance. Hanford is non-selective and prides itself on bringing out the best in each and every girl. Pupils are prepared for entry to Independent Senior Schools including: Marlborough, Bryanston, St Mary's Shaftesbury and Sherborne Girls.

Hanford believes children should be children for as long as possible, climbing trees, building dens, riding ponies and playing in the garden. Giving girls free time is something Hanford has always believed in as it encourages girls to become lost in their own imagination and develop creatively. Hanford took the decision to switch off all 'Smart devices', iPhones, tablets etc. during term time. Unplugging the girls from social media, games and communications was not done to protect them but to encourage them to make their own fun; they will have plenty of time to use social media but a relatively short time in which to be silly, fun-loving children. The girls use their free time to play games such as British Bulldog, riding the Hanford ponies, tending the chickens, gardening or climbing trees.

Hanford teaches girls to combine having fun with working hard. A strong and committed teaching staff seeks to bring out the best in each and every girl. This combination of fun and hard work pays dividends when it comes to Common Entrance and Scholarships. Evidenced in year on year Scholarships for the past 27 years: academic, art, drama, sport and all-round. Class sizes are small, normally 10–12, and there is learning support available if required. Alongside the core curriculum girls are taught handwork, where they make their own school uniform skirt, and Art Appreciation (Art Apre) where they can begin to understand and appreciate the cultural world around them. Music has always been central to life at Hanford with almost all girls learning at least one instrument or joining one of the choirs or folk group; music composition is also offered as an activity.

Sport is also strong at Hanford. The rounders, tennis and athletics teams have all been county champions. Hanford is perhaps most famous for its ponies and stables with most girls choosing to have riding lessons and some testing their equestrian skills at local and national events including tetrathlons.

Hawkesdown House School

27 Edge Street, Kensington, London W8 7PN

Tel: 020 7727 9090
email: admin@hawkesdown.co.uk
website: www.hawkesdown.co.uk
Facebook: @hawkesdownhouse
Instagram: @hawkesdown

Outstanding Prep and Pre-Prep Day School for Boys and Girls with its own nursery.

Headmistress: **Mrs J A K Mackay**, BEd

Registrar: Mrs S Zazzarino

Age Range. 2–11.
Number of Pupils. 75.
Fees per term (2021–2022). £4,830 (age 2), £5,975 (age 3), £6,620 (age 4), £7,040 (age 5–11).

A love of learning and a nurturing environment are at the heart of Hawkesdown House. The School achieves academic excellence and first-class entry results to pupils' next schools, with a broad and exciting curriculum and in days filled with variety, laughter and busy purpose.

Parents are fiercely loyal to this educational philosophy, the success of which is borne out in the excellent results and in the creative, thoughtful, happy pupils. Many of the pupils coming to the School live within walking distance and the School is an important part of the Kensington community.

"Hawkesdown nurtures its pupils, encourages fun but also achieves academic success." Good Schools Guide

Hawkesdown ensures the development of the creative and adaptable thinking that is so vital in a fast-changing world. This is combined with dedicated teaching of the still important traditional subjects and teaching and inspiration towards kindness, initiative, courtesy, cooperative working, and persistence.

The School excels in matching pupils happily and successfully to future schools and spends time with parents, ensuring that the transition is smooth and free from stress. In 2020, leavers went to St Paul's, Westminster Cathedral Choir School, King's College Junior, Westminster Under School, Sussex House, Caldicott, Summer Fields and St Philip's School.

"The School maintains very high academic standards and promotes a clear set of morals and values, such as kindness, courtesy, persistence and taking responsibility. The school Motto "Endeavour, Courage and Truth" reflects this. Individual attention, personalised feedback and pastoral care for each pupil is also of great importance." Simply Learning Tuition

Hazelwood School

Wolfs Hill, Limpsfield, Oxted, Surrey RH8 0QU

Tel: 01883 712194
email: schoolsec@hazelwoodschool.com
website: www.hazelwoodschool.co.uk

Chair of Governors: Mr Roger Heaton

Head: **Mrs Lindie Louw**

Age Range. 6 months–13 years Co-educational.
Number of Pupils. 583.
Fees per term (2021–2022). Day Pupils from £3,600 (Reception) to £5,740.

Founded in 1890, Hazelwood stands in superb grounds, commanding a magnificent view over the Kent and Sussex Weald.

Pupils enter at age 4 into the Pre-Prep or at 7+ to the Prep School, joining those pupils transferring from the Pre-Prep to the Prep School. Entry at other ages is possible if space permits. Hazelwood School's Nursery and Early Years, open all year round for children from 3 months to 4 years, opened in September 2009 on the Laverock site which offers unrivalled accommodation and facilities.

A gradual transition is made towards subject specialist tuition in the middle and upper forms. Pupils are prepared for the Common Entrance examinations at 11+ and 13+, and also for Scholarships to Senior Schools. Over 200 academic, all-rounder, sporting, music and art awards have been gained since 1995. The school has a balanced curriculum with Forest Schools and Philosophy for Children sitting alongside the more traditional subjects of Maths, English, Science and Modern Languages.

Extracurricular activity is an important part of every pupil's education. Excellent sports facilities, which include games fields, heated indoor swimming pool, gymnasium and many games pitches, tennis courts and other hard surfaces, allow preparation of school teams at various age and ability levels in a wide range of sports. A fully-equipped Sports Hall was completed in May 2004. Our aim is that every pupil has an opportunity to represent the School. In September 2016 the Baily Building was opened containing 14 classrooms, a Recital Room, a Food Tech Kitchen, a Lower School Art Room and a 450-seat auditorium, The Bawtree Hall. In 2016 the school was crowned IAPS National Champions at U11 Netball. The U9 Rugby team was unbeaten in their National Finals.

Art, Technology, Music and Drama are also strengths of the school. Our Centenary Theatre incorporates a 200-seat theatre, music school and Chapel. All our pupils are encouraged to play an instrument and join one of the music groups catering for all interests and abilities. Further extracurricular activities include tap, ballet and jazz dance, judo, art, gymnastics, scuba, debating, fantasy football, Forest Skills, computing, Lego modelling and chess. In the summer term of 2017 the school introduced Ultimate Frisbee and Quidditch into its after-school club repertoire.

Our pupils develop a curiosity about the world in which they live and a real passion for learning. Most importantly of all they become confident learners, mature and articulate individuals who love coming to school each day. The school's Community Fund was set up to benefit from pupil and parent fundraising. Each year, grants totalling £8,000 are awarded to community organisations with an educational bias.

Charitable status. Hazelwood School Limited is a Registered Charity, number 312081. It exists to provide excellent preparatory school education for girls and boys in Oxted, Surrey.

Hazlegrove Prep School

Sparkford, Yeovil, Somerset BA22 7JA

Tel: 01963 442606
email: admissions@hazlegrove.co.uk
website: www.hazlegrove.co.uk
Twitter: @HazlegrovePrep
Facebook: @HazlegrovePrep

Senior Warden: Stephen Edlmann, MA

Headmaster: **Mark White**, MA Hons, PGCE

Deputy Headmaster: Matthew Bartlett, BSc Hons, PGCE

Head of Pre-Preparatory Department: Hannah Strugnell, BSc Hons, PGCE

Age Range. 2–13.

Number of Pupils. 364 boys and girls of whom 89 are boarders. Preparatory (7–13 year olds) 290 pupils; Pre-Preparatory (2–7 year olds) 57 pupils.

Fees per term (2021–2022). Preparatory: Boarders £7,235–£9,232 (fees are inclusive, with few compulsory extras); Day pupils £4,890–£6,237. Pre-Preparatory: £3,076. Nursery: Morning session £31, Afternoon session £20.50, Lunch £9.

Scholarships and Bursaries. Armed Forces Bursaries are available to serving members.

Hazlegrove is located within a 200-acre park and is based around a country house built by Carew Hervey Mildmay in 1730. The entrance to the school is situated on the A303 roundabout at Sparkford. The Preparatory School has a strong boarding ethos. This is reflected in the full days, Saturday morning lessons from Year Four and the full range of activities for boarders, and those day pupils who wish to join in, during the evenings and at weekends. The school was judged "Excellent" in all nine areas of assessment in its last ISI Inspection.

Hazlegrove is a happy and purposeful school with a strong tutor system. The curriculum provides a varied and exciting experience for pupils as they progress through the school and includes Art, Food Technology, Design and Technology, Drama, Music and Outdoor Education. Latin and Mandarin are introduced in Year 5. The main sports are Rugby, Hockey, Cricket, Netball, Rounders, Tennis, Athletics and Swimming. Squash, Golf, Horse Riding and Judo are also available among other activities.

Streaming and setting is introduced as pupils progress through the school with a scholarship stream in the top two years. Pupils are entered for Common Entrance or Scholarship Examinations. About 30% go to the senior school, King's School Bruton. Others move on to major senior schools such as Bryanston, Eton, Sherborne, Sherborne Girls, Millfield, King's College Taunton, Marlborough and Winchester. Between 25 and 30 scholarships and awards are gained by pupils each year. Extra support is available to those pupils who have specific learning difficulties or who are gifted.

Pupils have achieved considerable success at regional and national level in recent years through sport, in team and individual performances, in drama and in music.

Hazlegrove has outstanding facilities. These include a state-of-the-art Teaching and Learning Centre and Science Laboratories, a Theatre, a Sports Hall, a 25m Indoor Heated Pool, two Squash Courts, the Design Centre, three award-winning Libraries and an excellent Music School. Outside, the extensive playing fields are complemented by two synthetic pitches, tennis courts, eight all-weather cricket nets and for golf, a 6-hole course, a putting green and driving nets. A tennis coach ensures best use of the hard tennis courts and the second synthetic playing surface – both with flood lighting. The adventure playground is equipped with a timing device so pupils can compete for the Tarzan award.

Pastoral care for Boarders is provided by three sets of House Parents, four Matrons and a Nurse. Other resident staff provide additional support. The school has considerable experience of meeting the needs of pupils whose parents are in the Services or who live in expat communities working overseas. Flexible boarding can also be arranged to meet individual needs.

The school shop, which is on site, provides most necessary clothing and games kit.

Pre-Preparatory Department. Located in a purpose-built facility within the grounds, the Pre-Prep provides a carefully structured curriculum which encourages the development of the early skills within a balanced programme of learning and play. The children enjoy Forest School and specialist teaching for French, drama, music, games and tennis. In addition to making full use of the Prep School facilities, the Pre-Prep enjoys its own Rainbow Room dedicated to Science, Art and Investigation, an adjacent gardening area and extensive climbing equipment in the playground. After school care is available.

Charitable status. King's School, Bruton is a Registered Charity, number 1071997. It exists to provide education for children.

Headington Prep School

26 London Road, Headington, Oxford, Oxfordshire OX3 7PB

Tel: 01865 759400
            Admissions 01865 759855
email: prepadmissions@headington.org
website: www.headington.org
Twitter: @HeadingtonPrep
Facebook: @HeadingtonSchool

Chairman of Board of Governors: Mrs Sandra Phipkin, ACA

Headmistress: **Mrs J Crouch**, BA Hons Keele, MA Hons London, NPQH

Age Range. Girls 3–11.

Number of Pupils. 262

Fees per term (2021–2022). Day: £1,380–£4,880.

Headington Prep School occupies its own three-acre site just two minutes' walk from Headington School and one mile from the centre of Oxford.

The Prep School's friendly, family atmosphere means girls develop as happy individuals with a sense of responsibility and self-awareness, enjoying a wealth of experiences inside and out of the classroom as part of an outstanding education.

In September 2016, an outdoor play area was created for the Early Years Foundation Stage department. It includes a mound with a tunnel, extended climbing equipment with climbing wall, cargo nets and bridges and new all-weather flooring. This Centenary Campaign project also included a revamp of the nursery classrooms with new flooring, new lighting, redecoration and a two-storey role play area. A new playground for the older girls was opened in September 2018. A rolling programme of modernisation has seen classrooms refurbished for Year 6 this year, with more year groups to follow, and new kitchen facilities for Food and Nutrition were installed in October 2021.

We have a wide range of extracurricular facilities including a gym and specialist art and design facilities, as well as a substantial performance space for music and drama, and a refurbished library. Our adventurous art and design curriculum allows girls to explore their imaginations through painting, drawing, clay-work and model-building and there are many exciting opportunities for girls in drama and music. We want all our girls to enjoy a variety of musical activities and we are quick to spot and nurture talent. From the age of seven, girls have the chance to learn at least one musical instrument and many of our girls play at a very high standard. All girls are taught to read music in both treble and bass clef through our keyboard scheme which is for Reception and Year 1. Theory clubs are offered to continue and support their learning.

In sport, specialist staff deliver a broad and balanced programme with a total of 12 different sports on offer. Girls are encouraged to try new activities and discover new talents to achieve their full potential, with many taking part in county level tournaments.

The school day runs from 8.30am to 3.20pm for EYFS and KS1 and 8.15am to 3.45pm at KS2, with an extended day from 7.45am to 6.00pm. There are a large number of after-school clubs and activities from Fencing to Coding and Trampolining and aftercare runs every day incorporating a range of activities, tea and prep.

For girls entering the Nursery and Reception (EYFS), entry is by informal assessment at a taster session. Girls are assessed in small groups, with experienced staff supporting them as they play. For Reception age girls, emergent literacy and numeracy tasks are included in their activities. For girls entering Year 1 and Year 2 (Key Stage 1), entry is by informal assessment within the class setting. Literacy, numeracy and problem solving tasks are included within their activities.

For girls entering into Years 3 to 6, entry is by assessment in Mathematics, English and Non-Verbal Reasoning (NVR). Girls will also have a short interview and then spend the afternoon with their peer group at the Prep School.

The majority of pupils continue to Headington School, with a number of girls awarded scholarships every year. (*See Headington School entry in GSA section.*)

Charitable status. Headington School Oxford Limited is a Registered Charity, number 309678. It exists to provide quality education for girls.

Heath Mount School

Woodhall Park, Watton-at-Stone, Hertford, Hertfordshire SG14 3NG

Tel: 01920 830230
email: registrar@heathmount.org
website: www.heathmount.org
Twitter: @heathmountsch

The school became a Trust in September 1970, with a Board of Governors.

Chairman of Governors: Mrs J Hodson

Headmaster: **Mr C Gillam**, BEd Hons

Senior Deputy Head: Mr M Dawes

Age Range. 3–13.

Number of Pupils. 270 Boys, 222 Girls. Flexi/Sleepover boarding offered.

Fees per term (2021–2022). Boarding (1–4 nights): £500–£1,705 (Lent/Summer). Tuition: Nursery £2,480–£4,145, Pre-Prep £4,785, Years 3–6 £6,190, Years 7–8 £6,395.

There is a reduction in fees for the second and subsequent children attending the School at the same time.

Heath Mount School is situated five miles from Hertford, Ware and Knebworth, at Woodhall Park – a beautiful Georgian mansion with 40 acres of grounds set in a large private park. A dedicated Nursery, Pre-Prep and Lower

School are situated a short walk from the main house. The fabulous facilities are inspiring – a Performing Arts Centre and excellent sports facilities which include a sports hall, covered swimming pool, an all-weather pitch for hockey and tennis, netball courts and cricket nets. The main house contains an imaginatively developed lower ground floor housing modern science laboratories and rooms for art, pottery, textiles, film making, food technology and design technology. There is a further information technology room and well-stocked research and fiction libraries. The boys board in a wing of the main house and the girls in a dedicated house in the adjoining park. Resident boarding house parents provide a welcoming environment for both the boys and girls.

The School has an excellent academic record, as well as outstanding art and sport and some of the finest school music in the country. Illustrating this, in 2020 an outstanding 63% of our Year 8 leavers achieved scholarships to their senior schools across a range of areas.

Charitable status. Heath Mount School is a Registered Charity, number 311069.

Heatherton

Copperkins Lane, Amersham, Buckinghamshire HP6 5QB

Tel: 01494 726433
email: enquiries@heatherton.com
website: www.heatherton.com
Twitter: @HeathertonSch
Facebook: @HeathertonSchool
LinkedIn: /berkhamsted-school

Chairman of the Governors: Mr G C Laws (Chairman of Berkhamsted Schools Group)

Principal: Mr R P Backhouse, MA Cantab

Head: Mrs N Nicoll, MEd, BSc

Age Range. Girls rising 3–11, Co-Ed Nursery rising 3–4
Number of Pupils. 133 Girls, 7 Boys.
Fees per term (2021–2022) £3,565–£4,700 for Reception to Year 6 inclusive of all but optional subjects.

Founded in 1912, Heatherton is set in an attractive green and leafy location on the outskirts of Amersham.

Heatherton provides an excellent all-round education. An experienced staff of specialist teachers encourage each child's individual academic and emotional development. High standards are achieved across a broad curriculum with small classes (max 20), a caring ethos and a close relationship with parents.

At 11 pupils progress to both local independent girls' senior schools and Buckinghamshire grammar schools. Excellent results are produced at all stages of school performance tests and the girls are tracked from an early age, both pastorally and academically.

Musical, artistic and sporting talents flourish at Heatherton. A thriving orchestra, individual instrument lessons and many drama, ballet and music productions are an important part of life in a school year. Art and design skills are celebrated in displays and exhibitions, both

internally and externally. Each pupil is offered a wide range of sporting activities – swimming, netball, gymnastics, dance, athletics, tennis, lacrosse and cross country.

An extensive range of educational visits and activities in the UK and Europe are organised each year. The school has recently introduced an additional Enrichment Curriculum to its pupils' timetables, offering the girls exciting opportunities to expand their knowledge, with topics as diverse as mindfulness, team-building and Tudor cooking.

Heatherton offers wrap-around care from 07.30 until 18.00 for all pupils from Nursery to Year 6.

In September 2015, the Heatherton Nursery became Co-Educational, providing for both boys and girls. Heatherton has been recognised for its 'outstanding quality of provision' in the Early Years Foundation Stage. Its 'calm, purposeful environment' and 'a host of stimulating learning opportunities', were just some of the features highlighted by the Independent Schools Inspectorate who are now citing Heatherton's EYFS as an example of very best practice. Heatherton remains a girls' school from Reception class to Year 6.

Following a merger with Berkhamsted School in 2011, Heatherton pupils are increasingly enjoying the benefits of initiatives such as joint curriculum days, music and drama workshops, sports coaching and residential trips in partnership with Berkhamsted Prep, as well as access to the significant resources and infrastructure of the Berkhamsted Schools Group.

Charitable status. Heatherton School is a member of the Berkhamsted Schools Group, which is a Registered Charity, number 310630.

Heathfield Prep
The Preparatory School to Rishworth School

Oldham Road, Rishworth, Halifax, West Yorkshire HX6 4QF

Tel: 01422 823564
email: admin@heathfieldjunior.co.uk
website: www.rishworth-school.co.uk
Twitter: @HeathfieldPrep
Facebook: @RishworthSchool
Instagram: @rishworthschool
LinkedIn: /rishworth-school-trading-limited

Motto: *Deeds Not Words*

Chairman of the Board of Governors: Canon Hilary Barber

Head of Rishworth: Mr A M Wilkins, BA, MA, MA

Head of Heathfield: Mr D Baker, BEd

Age Range. 3–11 co-educational.
Number of Pupils. 100 day boys/girls and 30-place Foundation Stage Unit. Boarding is available from Year 5: details on request.
Fees per term (2021–2022). Day: Reception–Year 2 £2,266; Years 3–6 £3,316.

Staffing. 9 full-time teaching and 6 part-time teaching and a number of teaching assistants. Specialist teachers deliver: music, art, PE, French, dance and drama, with additional peripatetic staff providing further individual tuition in Music and the Arts.

Location. Heathfield stands in its own substantial grounds and enjoys an outstanding rural position in a beautiful Pennine location with easy access via the motorways to Manchester and Leeds.

Facilities. Well-equipped classrooms; Foundation Stage Unit and purpose-built Infant classes; designated teaching rooms for Music, Science, Art and Design Technology; modern ICT Suite; Library; a multi-purpose Hall for assemblies and productions; heated indoor swimming pool; netball court and football/rugby pitch; Pre/After School Care and Holiday School available. The extensive grounds are used for a wide variety of academic and other purposes with a fully developed Forest School.

Aims. To provide a stimulating and challenging environment in which individual attainment is nurtured, recognised and celebrated.

To ensure each child receives their full entitlement to a broad, balanced curriculum which builds on a solid foundation in literacy and numeracy.

Curriculum. An extensive programme of study which incorporates the Foundation Stage, Key Stage 1 and Key Stage 2. An emphasis on developing an independence in learning and analytical thinking through Literacy, Numeracy, Science, French, History, Geography, Religious Studies, Design Technology, Information and Communications Technology, Music, Art and Physical Education.

Extra-Curricular Activities. Includes activities such as: Drama, Choir, Orchestra, Baking, Brass, Recorder and String Groups, Steel Pans, Art and Board Games. Sports include Swimming, Rounders, Netball, Football, Rugby, Cross-Country, Cricket, Athletics, Gymnastics, Hockey and Biathlon.

Each term there are plays and musical concerts incorporating most children in the School. Residentials include Outdoor Pursuits, Camping and Environmental Studies.

Charitable status. Rishworth School is a Registered Charity, number 1115562. It exists to provide education for boys and girls.

Hereward House School

14 Strathray Gardens, London NW3 4NY

Tel: 020 7794 4820
email: office@herewardhouse.co.uk
website: www.herewardhouse.co.uk

Headmaster: **Mr P J E Evans**, MA

Deputy Headmaster: Mr P Cheetham, BA, PGCE

Director of Studies: Mrs H Martin, MA, PGCE

Head of Middle School: Ms K Hampshire, BSc, PGCE

Head of Junior School: Mrs R Batchelor, BSc, PGCE

Head of EYFS: Mrs N Scaffidi, BEd

Bursar: Mr A Jenne, BA

Headmaster's PA/Admissions: Mr J Jones, MSc

Age Range. 4–13.
Number of Pupils. 163 Day Boys.
Fees per term (2021–2022). £6,200–£6,360.

Hereward House provides a warm and welcoming atmosphere in which every child feels valued, secure and thrives. The school works hard to create a stimulating, purposeful and happy community, within which boys are encouraged and assisted to develop academically, morally, emotionally, culturally and physically. The school's aim is for boys to enjoy their school days yet at the same time be well prepared for the demands of Common Entrance and Scholarship examinations.

The school's academic success is built upon excellent teaching and the highly individual educational teaching programmes created to meet individual boy's needs. Great care is taken to ensure that a boy gains a place at the school which is right for him.

Boys are prepared for the Common Entrance and Scholarship examinations to highly sought after independent schools, both day and boarding. Two-thirds of boys proceed to top London Day Schools, such as City of London, Highgate, St Paul's, UCS and Westminster, others to leading boarding schools such as Eton, Harrow and Winchester. Scholarships and Awards have been won by our boys to several of the above schools.

The school takes pride in the breadth of education it offers. Music plays a major role in the boys' education. Almost all boys learn at least one instrument, most of them two or even three. There is a full school orchestra which gives a performance each term. Weekly concerts are held throughout the year.

Team Games play an integral part in the sports syllabus. We regularly field teams against other schools and have an enviable record of success in cricket, football and cross-country running. Swimming, tennis, hockey and athletics are included in our sports programme.

Art has a valued place in the syllabus. Chess, judo, fencing, coding, yoga, ICT and music theory are among the clubs available to the boys.

High March School

23 Ledborough Lane, Beaconsfield, Bucks HP9 2PZ

Tel: 01494 675186
email: office@highmarch.co.uk
admissions@highmarch.co.uk
website: www.highmarch.co.uk
Twitter: @HighMarchSchool
Instagram: @highmarch1

Established 1926.

Chairman of the Governing Board: Mr C Hayfield, BSc, FCA

Headmistress: **Mrs Kate Gater**, MA, PGCE Warwick

Age Range. Girls 3–11, Boys 3–4.

Number of Pupils. 277 day pupils.

Fees per term (2021–2022). £1,950–£5,395 inclusive of books, stationery and lunches, but excluding optional subjects.

High March consists of 3 school houses set in pleasant grounds. Junior House comprises Nursery and Key Stage 1 classes, ages 3–7 years, whilst Upper School covers Key Stage 2, ages 7–11 years. Class sizes are limited. Facilities include a state-of-the-art 20-metre indoor heated swimming pool, a well-equipped Gymnasium, as well as Science, Music, Art, Poetry, Design Technology, Drama, Information Technology rooms and a Library. Recent refurbishments include large extensions to the Art Room and Science Laboratory and re-landscaping of all the Upper School's outside space to include a new Adventure Playground, new Netball courts and an outdoor learning classroom. The playground at Junior House has also been re-landscaped and now includes a Sensory Garden as well as new play equipment.

High March is within easy reach of London, High Wycombe, Windsor and within a few minutes' walk of Beaconsfield Station.

Under a large and highly-qualified staff and within a happy atmosphere, the girls are prepared for Common Entrance and Scholarships to Independent Senior Schools and for the 11+ County Selection process. All subjects including French, Spanish, Latin, Music, Art, Technology, Speech and Drama, Dancing, Gymnastics, Games and Swimming are in the hands of specialists. The academic record is high but each child is nevertheless encouraged to develop individual talents.

Highfield & Brookham Schools

Highfield Lane, Liphook, Hampshire GU30 7LQ

Tel:	01428 728000 (Highfield Prep)
	01428 722005 (Brookham Pre-Prep)
email:	headspa@highfieldschool.org.uk
	admissions@brookhamschool.co.uk
website:	www.highfieldandbrookham.co.uk
Twitter:	@HighfieldSch
Facebook:	@HighfieldBrookham
Instagram:	@highfieldandbrookham
LinkedIn:	/highfield-and-brookham-schools

Chairman of Directors: Mr W S Mills

Headteacher, Highfield (*Prep*): **Mr Phillip Evitt**

Headteacher, Brookham (*Pre-Prep*): **Mrs Sophie Baber**

Age Range. 2–13.

Number of Children. 450.

Fees per term (2021–2022). Day Pupils £3,925–£7,575; Boarders £8,600–£9,475. Discounts are available for siblings and Forces families.

As with individuals, all schools have unique DNA. The strands that make Highfield and Brookham truly special are:

their *academic ambition*, their *co-curricular breadth*, the quality of their *relationships*, their sense of *community* and their beautiful *environment*. The school community is *full of life* and throws their *heart and soul* into everything they do.

Highfield and Brookham's outstanding *academic ambition* provides a supportive and collaborative process to parents to help them identify the right educational path for their child. Highfield feeds the country's top senior schools, including Marlborough, Winchester, Radley, Sherborne School for Girls and Eton, and enjoys a flawless track record of securing every child a place at their first choice senior school. They also have an excellent scholarship success rate at 11+ and 13+ to schools such as Canford, Charterhouse, Cranleigh, Harrow and Wellington.

Highfield and Brookham look beyond the curriculum to skills that children can learn through sport, music, drama and art. They have over 50 activities and sports on offer throughout the year. This *co-curricular breadth* broadens children's horizons and fosters lifelong passions.

The schools place huge importance on building *relationships*, and emotional wellbeing and resilience are at the very core of the schools' pastoral care. They are proud to be pioneers in the field with all teachers trained in well-being and mental health.

Their *environment* is made up of 175 acres of fields, sports pitches and woodlands to explore. It is a place where children learn beyond the walls of the classroom and teachers and children alike put their *heart and soul* into everything they do. To complement the numerous natural playing fields, and provide all year-round play, the schools also benefit from a floodlit all-weather pitch.

Choosing Highfield and Brookham, whether day or boarding, is your opportunity to make a positive impact on your child's educational journey, ensuring they leave as happy and well-rounded individuals, *full of life*, ready to tackle the next stage of their learning journey.

Highgate Junior School

3 Bishopswood Road, London N6 4PL

Tel:	020 8340 9193
email:	admissions@highgateschool.org.uk
website:	www.highgateschool.org.uk
Twitter:	@highgate1565
Facebook:	@HighgateSchoolLondon
LinkedIn:	/school/highgate-school

Founded over 450 years ago, Highgate is one of the UK's leading co-educational independent schools.

Principal of Junior School: **Mark James**, BA, MA

Principal of Pre-Preparatory School: **Katie Giles**, BA, MA, PGCE

Age Range. 4–11 Co-educational.

Number of Pupils. Junior (age 7–11): 400; Pre-Prep (age 4–7): 140.

Fees per term (2021–2022). Junior School (Years 3–6): £6,600; Pre-Preparatory School: £6,235 (Reception–Year 2).

Highgate Pre-Preparatory School is situated in a light, airy and colourful building at 7 Bishopswood Road, overlooking the open spaces of our sports grounds, with its own playground, separate music room and learning support room.

Pupils benefit from small class sizes, with qualified early-years teachers and assistants and specialists to teach sports, exercise, music and drama. Our pupils are closely supervised at all times and a friendly, tolerant and mutually supportive atmosphere is promoted across our Pre-Prep.

Highgate Junior School is in a new building that opened in September 2016. Built to the highest specification, there are specialist facilities for computing, science, art, DTE, drama and music, plus a retractable-seat hall, outside play spaces and a small amphitheatre.

Our broad and creative curriculum is planned around specific learning objectives for each subject area, within each year group. We promote high levels of achievement and effort, however we push the boundaries beyond mere acquisition of knowledge; we want our pupils to develop the confidence to investigate and enquire, to solve problems, and to take responsibility for their learning. We aim to enrich the learning experience of our pupils, broadening their social horizons and cultural interests.

We are exceptionally fortunate when it comes to sport at Highgate with extensive facilities, including an indoor pool.

Time is set aside, each week, for every pupil to take part in at least one co-curricular venture. Our wide co-curricular offering continues to evolve and develop in response to the changing needs of our pupils and the world around us and aims to:

- Develop qualities of self-reliance, endurance and leadership;
- Serve the community; and
- Develop interests and enthusiasms.

Highgate's pro-active pastoral care underpins all of our activities: pupil wellbeing is at the heart of all our thinking and teaching. We retain very close links across the three Highgate Schools to provide a secure continuity of education for the majority of pupils that transfer at age 7 and 11.

Admission. Entry to the Pre-Preparatory School is by individual assessment at 4+ (www.highgateschool.org.uk/pre-prep/admissions-3–4). Entry to the Junior School is by test and interview at age 7 (www.highgateschool.org.uk/junior-school/admissions-7) and transfer to the Senior School is at 11+ (www.highgateschool.org.uk/senior-school/admissions-11)

Bursaries are available from age 7+ and 11+: www.highgateschool.org.uk/bursaries

Charitable status. Highgate School is a Registered Charity, number 312765.

Hilden Grange School
Alpha Plus Group Ltd

Dry Hill Park Road, Tonbridge, Kent TN10 3BX

Tel: 01732 351169 / 01732 352706
email: office@hildengrange.co.uk
website: www.hildengrange.co.uk
Twitter: @HildenGrange
Facebook: @HildenGrange
Instagram: @hildengrangeschool

Headmaster: **Mr Malcolm Gough**, BA, LLB Rhodes, LLM Cape Town, PGCE OU

Deputy Head: Mrs R Jubber, BSc, HDE

Age Range. 2½–13 Co-educational.

Number of Pupils. 270: 190 Boys and 80 Girls.

Fees per term (2021–2022). Prep School (Years 5–8) £5,325, Prep School (Years 3–4) £4,790, Pre-Prep (Years 1 and 2) £3,885, Reception £3,370, Nursery: £1,175 per term (minimum five sessions per week). Lunches are provided at £245–£288 per term.

At Hilden Grange we provide a stimulating, friendly and secure environment in which an individual child's potential is developed in the academic, creative, physical and spiritual areas. Through encouragement, outstanding teaching and a positive, inclusive atmosphere, we aim to help pupils strive for high standards, both inside and outside the classroom, take a pride in their endeavours and enjoy participating in the life of the school with all its wide ranging opportunities. The wellbeing of each child underpins their success and is of paramount importance to us. Courtesy, good manners and mutual respect are expected at all times within our community. We aim for each individual to feel valued and very much a part of our school family.

Though links are especially strong with Tonbridge and Sevenoaks, boys and girls are prepared for all Independent Senior Schools and Grammar Schools at 11+ and 13+. We have an unequalled record of success in this area. Examination results rank among the highest in Kent, and in the past ten years, all pupils gained entry to their chosen school at 13. Boys and girls who show special promise sit for scholarships to the school of their choice, and our track record in this area is excellent. 176 scholarships have been gained in the past ten years in areas as diverse as music, drama, technology and sport as well as traditional academic scholarships. Pupils benefit from specialist teaching in all subjects from Year 3, dedicated staff, and class sizes that average 16.

The School stands in about twenty acres of attractive grounds in the residential area of North Tonbridge. Boys and girls are accepted into the Nursery at 2½+ or at 4+ into the Pre-Preparatory Department within the school grounds, and at 7 into the main school. Tonbridge School Chorister awards may be gained; at present there are nine Choristers.

There is an outdoor heated swimming pool, a dedicated Sports Hall, all-weather tennis courts, Science Laboratories, Music Rooms, an Art and Design area, a Library, a Learning Support Area, a dining hall and two Information Technology Rooms, with networks of personal computers. An extensive building program was completed in September 2012 providing new education and communal facilities which are enjoyed by the whole school.

The Headmaster, staff and children welcome visitors and are pleased to show them around the School.

Hoe Bridge School

Hoe Place, Old Woking, Surrey GU22 8JE

Tel: 01483 760018
email: info@hoebridgeschool.co.uk
website: www.hoebridgeschool.co.uk
Twitter: @HoeBridgeSchool
Facebook: @hoebridgewoking
LinkedIn: /company/hoe-bridge-school

Independent prep school in Old Woking for boys and girls aged 2 to 13 years old.

Chairman of Governors: Ian Katté

Headmaster: Christopher Webster, MA, BSc Hons, PGCE

Deputy Headmaster: Adam Warner, BA Hons

Head of Pre-Prep: Amanda Willis, BA Hons, QTS

Age Range. 2–13 years.

Number of Children. Prep 265, Pre-Prep 200.

Fees per term (2021–2022). Day: Prep £4,860–£5,510 (including lunch); Pre-Prep £1,650–£3,890 (including lunch).

We are very fortunate to enjoy the historic and inspirational site which is home to Hoe Bridge School. The 22-acre estate is a hidden gem in the heart of Surrey and a stone's throw from Woking town centre.

The school has invested strategically to ensure the best facilities in the area, with a high standard of classrooms from Nursery through to Years 7 and 8 to provide the perfect learning environment. These are complemented by specialist suites for subjects such as Art, Design & Technology, ICT, Science, Music and indoor exercise. Staff and children alike are justifiably proud of the recently built 110-seat Performing Arts Centre.

Sport and exercise are all-important in the school week, and are amply catered for with two sports halls, three large playing fields, all-weather pitch, heated outdoor swimming pool, outdoor and indoor cricket nets, cross country course and grass and artificial cricket squares.

Beyond, the Hideout outdoor classroom, pond with its own pontoon, meadow and woods provide a natural wonderland for outdoor learning, inspiration and exploration for inquiring young minds.

Within our estate, Pre-Prep enjoys its own purpose-built building with assembly hall, fully equipped gym, well-stocked library, ICT suite, art and music rooms, as well as modern classrooms with indoor and outdoor learning areas. All classrooms have interactive whiteboards and we make extensive use of iPads.

Transition to the Prep Department is seamless and as children mature they become increasingly independent learners in preparation for the move to senior school. The results achieved by the children across the ability range are outstanding leading to success at some of the country's leading schools. The pupils are inspired by dedicated staff, lessons are rigorous and interactive and achievement is excellent. 2021 Common Entrance Exam Results were outstanding with 93% A* to B.

Alongside the academics sport, music, art and drama play a major part throughout the school and children excel in many areas: end-of-year productions; sporting excellence achieving national success in netball and hockey, county success in cricket and football; individual musical success in national youth orchestras and choirs and a spectacular annual art exhibition. Scholarships in all these areas are won every year to a variety of schools across the country. "The pupils' successes in academic work, sport and music, both individually and in groups, are due to their excellent attitudes to learning." Latest ISI Inspection Report.

Senior pupils in Years 7 and 8 take part in regular extracurricular activities such as Bush Craft weekends, French trips, cricket and netball tours and are challenged by preparing and presenting a gourmet meal to their parents. It is at this stage of their time at Hoe Bridge that they take on extra responsibility becoming prefects and role models to the younger children.

We are passionate in the belief that the role of educators is to provide a wide-ranging framework in which children can grow and develop creatively in a continually changing and often unpredictable world. We have an unwavering commitment to empowering those within our community: inspiring, challenging and motivating both children and adults in all that we do. We have an environment, from Nursery through to Year 8, which grows and adapts, allowing all children to learn and understand from their many different strengths. Empathy and caring for others are our principal values, which are intrinsic within our ideology and shown in the special qualities within our community. Each child is known and valued for who they are.

In providing a safe and secure environment where children can explore their potential, confidence and self-esteem we nurture each individual enabling them to achieve the highest of standards. Learning is best achieved in a collaborative community which inspires and encourages ambitious minds with high quality and dynamic teachers being the driving force behind such a setting. We prepare 'Thinking Children', able to perform exceptionally well through the rigours of 11+ assessments and flourishing in Common Entrance and Public School Scholarships. Our children secure places at leading local and national independent schools, going on to flourish at top universities, within their successful careers and in life.

Charitable status. Hoe Bridge School is a Registered Charity, number 295808. It exists to provide a rounded education for children aged 2 to 13.

Holme Grange School

Heathlands Road, Wokingham, Berkshire RG40 3AL

Tel: 0118 9781566
email: school@holmegrange.org
website: www.holmegrange.org
Twitter: @holmegrange
Facebook: @holmegrange
Instagram: @holmegrange
LinkedIn: /company/holme-grange-school

Chairman of Governors: Mrs Sue Northend, Director of
    HR for REAch2 Academy Trust

Head: **Mrs Claire Robinson**, BA, PGCE, NPQH

Deputy Head: Mr Matthew Jelley, BA Hons, PGCE, MEd

Age Range. 3–16 Co-educational.

Number of Pupils. 662: 357 boys, 305 girls.

Fees per term (2021–2022). Little Grange Nursery
£2,100–£3,555; Pre-Preparatory: £3,795 (Reception),
£3,860 (Years 1–2); Prep: £4,890 (Years 3–4), £5,005 (Years
5–6), £5,225 (Years 7–8), £5,380 (Years 9–11) with an
option to pay over 10 months. Reductions for second and
subsequent children.

Holme Grange is a co-educational day school for girls
and boys aged 3–16 years. The school provides pupils with a
toolkit to live their lives and when they eventually enter the
adult world, they will do so well prepared with a real-life
foundation for every challenge they will face. Set in 21 acres
of Wokingham countryside, Holme Grange offers a unique
educational journey in an idyllic setting, delivering a
creative experience, sporting prowess and academic
excellence.

The School occupies a large country mansion, to which
many additional facilities have been added over recent
years, including outdoor classrooms, three additional
science laboratories, food technology room, common room
and additional classrooms. 2016 saw the opening of a 300-
seat Performing Arts Theatre, Music School and Drama
Suite and a new block housing a dining room, kitchens and
eight additional classrooms. The Sports Hall was also
extended, offering a fitness gym and changing facilities.
Further expansion saw the opening of a new senior building
in 2019 and this year a fourth science laboratory was added
to the senior facilities. Pre-Prep and Prep also have a
dedicated Science Laboratory. Reception pupils moved into
new classroom facilities in September 2019, with direct
access to an adventure playground. A Recording Studio was
introduced for the start of the 2020–21 academic year.

The School is set in an idyllic environment of just over 20
acres of grounds comprising grass pitches, all-weather
surfaces, swimming pool, Cricket, Football, Hockey and
Rugby pitches, Netball and Tennis courts, 3 Forest schools
and woodland walks for the children to explore. Specialist
teaching and facilities for Music, Art and Technology,
Dance, Performing Arts, Science, ICT and Sport enhance
our fully comprehensive provision and support the
individual development of all our pupils. Holme Grange is
one of the first schools in the area to have gained Forest
School status and has a number of qualified Forest Leaders
on the Staff, thus allowing opportunities for children to

achieve and develop confidence and knowledge through
hands-on learning in a woodland environment. The erection
of a second Polytunnel, together with a market garden shop,
provides opportunities for pupils to learn about sustainable
education whilst the development and expansion of the
School farm with its goats, pigs, chickens and ducks enable
the pupils to learn about life cycles and animal husbandry in
a very hands-on manner.

Little Grange is an established Nursery for 3 and 4 year
olds equipped to the highest standard located in its own safe
and secure environment within the School grounds,
providing flexible education either part or full day including
lunch and tea. There is the facility for all children to stay to
5.50pm.

We welcome and cater for pupils with a wide range of
ability. Entry is based upon an assessment day where
baseline assessment tests are taken in verbal and non-verbal
reasoning. This entry process is designed to identify pupils
who are able to benefit from our balanced and well-rounded
education. We aim to foster confidence and a love of
learning across the age range. Pupils are accepted from the
start of the term in which they turn 3 providing outstanding
continuous education up to and including GCSE, and also
preparing students for the Common Entrance examinations.
We celebrated another fantastic set of GCSE results in 2021,
with 17% at grade 9, 60% of all grades being 9–7 (former
A*–A). The pass rate across the board was 99%.

The Headteacher is assisted by a highly qualified and
experienced teaching staff with classroom assistants in the
Pre-Prep and NNEB assistants in Little Grange. There is an
Accelerated Learning Centre giving help to those children
with special needs.

The School's policy is to set high standards, to establish
good all-round personalities and to give inspiration for each
pupil's life. Our aim is to create an environment where every
child can thrive. Our Mission is to inspire achievement
beyond the bounds of expectation within an environment
where every child can succeed. A bold statement but one
that we believe every child deserves. We appreciate
children's differences and respond to their individual needs.
In 2013 we were awarded the prestigious NACE Challenge
Award for More Able, Gifted and Talented Pupils in
recognition of the high quality work by the whole school in
challenging all pupils to achieve their best, gaining re-
accreditation in 2017. Only 36 other schools in the country
have achieved this elevated status. In 2020 we were awarded
a Gold SMSC National Quality Mark, in recognition of the
spiritual, moral, social and cultural development Holme
Grange provides, and also an Artsmark Gold Award from
Arts Council England.

At Holme Grange we offer excellence in personalised
learning – a rare school that caters equally well for pupils at
both ends of the academic continuum. We believe in our
pupils and instil a belief in themselves.

We develop intellectual character through our learning
habits and the ethos throughout the school is one of warmth
and friendliness – questioning; divergent thinking and the
freedom to learn from mistakes are all encouraged. Pupils
are inspired to take responsibility for their own learning,
develop good work habits and gain a sense that learning can
thrill and invigorate.

We deliver a rounded education by providing
opportunities in sport, the arts, languages, technology and a
wide range of activities, maximising opportunities for
success for all. We hope to inspire your child both in and

outside of the classroom. At Holme Grange School, we foster self-reliance, self-discipline and self-confidence in a caring community where children gain interests and characteristics that give them a head start for life.

We will not only unlock your child's potential but will also foster within them, a passion for learning. Our pupils are prepared to succeed in an ever changing, competitive world. We offer challenge, we strive to inspire, develop confidence, provide opportunity and realise potential in every child up to the age of 16.

We are committed to providing the very best education. Academic standards are excellent. Life in our school is a journey of exploration and discovery. We are a holistic school offering an all-round education, bursting with life and vitality.

The School is a Trust, administered by a board of Governors who have considerable experience in education and business.

Charitable status. Holme Grange Limited is a Registered Charity, number 309105. It exists to serve the local community in providing an all-round education for boys and girls.

Holy Cross Preparatory School

George Road, Kingston upon Thames, Surrey KT2 7NU

Tel:	020 8942 0729
email:	admissions@holycrossprep.com
website:	www.holycrossprepschool.co.uk
Facebook:	@holycrossprepschool
Instagram:	@holycrossprepschool

Headteacher: **Mrs Sarah Hair**

Age Range. 3–11.

Number of Girls. 290.

Fees per term (2021–2022). £4,834.

Location. Holy Cross Prep is located on the private Coombe estate on Kingston Hill, just a short drive from the centre of Kingston upon Thames. The schools new pre-school opened September 2021 admitting girls from 3 years old into a newly refurbished and extended building within the grounds.

Educational Philosophy. Holy Cross Prep provides a warm, nurturing and stimulating environment for girls aged 3–11, welcoming all faiths and cultures. We offer two-form entry, with small class sizes to provide our pupils with the skills and knowledge they need to thrive and succeed in today's modern world. We are a compassionate, vibrant community, working together to inspire a true love of learning in our pupils.

Curriculum. Our broad and dynamic curriculum is delivered by exceptional, dedicated teachers, ensuring that our high academic standards are upheld across every subject. Specialist subjects include sport, music, drama, computing, art and French. Our staff take great pleasure in nurturing and guiding the girls on their individual learning journeys, and are justifiably proud of the great success they have with senior school entrance exams. Our girls engage and participate fully in school life, regularly performing academically above the national average. Academic success

not only enables access to highly selective senior schools, it also offers opportunities for academic scholarships, as reflected in the large number awarded to Holy Cross girls each year. Pupils are awarded scholarships based on their academic achievement, as well as their talents in sport, music, drama and art. Our pupils are happy, curious individuals, encouraged to nurture their natural inquisitiveness and a healthy attitude towards learning.

Our dynamic curriculum is supported by a diverse extra-curricular programme, with a wealth of activity clubs running before, during and after school. To support working parents, our wraparound care provision is available from 7.30am until 6.00pm on each full school day.

Facilities. Our state-of-the-art facilities are set in eight acres of beautiful, historic grounds, with plenty of outdoor space for the girls to explore. From our much-loved woodland walk and adventure playground, to our floodlit sports pitch and pavilion, pupils are actively encouraged to spend time enjoying the outside world. Completed in 2019, our tailor-made, all-weather facilities are perfect for a wide variety of sports, including hockey and football. We also have dedicated specialist classrooms and a spectacular multi-purpose hall, which hosts countless activities and events, including PE lessons, assemblies and drama productions, as well as our daily lunch provision. Large-scale productions benefit from a curtain theatre and retractable tiered seating for approximately 300 guests, which transforms the space into an auditorium.

Charitable status. Holy Cross Preparatory School is a Registered Charity, number 238426. It is a Roman Catholic School providing excellence in Christian education to local children.

Homefield Preparatory School

Western Road, Sutton, Surrey SM1 2TE

Tel:	020 8642 0965
email:	administration@homefieldprep.school
website:	www.homefieldprep.school
Twitter:	@HomefieldSchool
Facebook:	@homefield.school
Instagram:	@homefield_preparatory_school
LinkedIn:	/company/homefield-preparatory-school-trust-limited

"I don't believe we could have found a better school in the country to bring out the best in both our sons."

Chairman of Governors: Dr Inderpreet Dhingra, BSc Hons, PhD, MBA, FSI

Head: **Mr John Towers**, BA Hons, MA, PGCE, NPQH, FRSA

Age Range: 4–13

Number of Boys: 320

Fees per term 2021–2022: Senior Department: £5,015, Lower School, Years 1 & 2: £4,290, Lower School, Reception: £3,475

Homefield Prep is an academically selective day school for boy aged 4–13. Founded in 1870, we are one of the oldest prep schools in England and have been renowned for our academic success and family atmosphere for over 150 years, A safe and happy environment, with a real depth of specialist teaching ensures the fulfilment of our boys' individual potential. We offer a truly cosmopolitan school, our rich diversity a real strength. A generous education is provided, aimed at knowledge and skill, but also at building good character.

At Homefield we produce well-rounded boys who go on to some of the very best senior schools in the country. These expectations are not around undue pressure to pass exams. We encourage an enlightened individual who "can do all things if he will". Creative, inquisitive and inventive.

"Pupils make a strong contribution to their learning through their highly motivated and enthusiastic attitudes. The quality of pupils' achievements and learning is excellent." (ISI Inspection, March 2013.)

We are investing £8 million to provide the highest quality facilities for our boys now and for future generations. The first and second phases are now complete. These have provided a purpose built block of 14 new classrooms, to a very high specification, overlooking our playing fields and a brand new Performance Hall, Dining Room and Kitchen. At the same time we have also created new music facilities, a STEAM/Computing suite and a Library Hub.

Work is currently underway on the third and final phase of the project to create a brand new reception area plus administration offices. Finally, we will build a brand new all-weather sports pitch and all of this will be completed by the Summer of 2022. We expect to gain around 10% more green space. Our eco–credentials now include solar power, low energy underfloor heating and a 'green roof'. Our boys will have space, comfort and access to an excellent learning and recreational environment.

Throughout the school's development it has been very careful to preserve the original family ethos and intimacy, together with its reputation for academic excellence, the breadth of extra-curricular sporting, musical and artistic provision and first-class pastoral care. We pride ourselves on achieving fulfilment of individual potential, the openness of communication and the provision of specialist teaching from the earliest appropriate opportunity (French, Music and Sport from the Foundation Stage).

Awareness of others is encouraged and the boys are involved in many fundraising charity events. A wide range of opportunities are available to extend gifted boys and learning support is available for children with special needs. Wellbeing Wednesdays and Mental Health and Emotional Wellbeing are embedded into our school curriculum.

We offer academic, sporting, art and music scholarships as well as occasional bursaries.

Daily minibuses run to and from the Wimbledon, Carshalton and Worcester Park area.

Breakfast and after school clubs are available.

Charitable status. As a charitable trust since the 1960s, a keen sense of civic and community responsibility is important at Homefield. We believe that positive values influence character and attitude. In the 21st century it's more important than ever for our boys to feel rooted within a strong moral community. Homefield Preparatory School Trust Limited is a Registered Charity, number 312753.

Hornsby House School

Hearnville Road, London SW12 8RS

Tel: 020 8673 7573
email: school@hornsbyhouse.org.uk
website: www.hornsbyhouse.org.uk
Twitter: @hornsbyhousesch
Facebook: @Elementary-School/Hornsby-House-School-395996463883129
Instagram: @hornsbyhousesch

Chair of Governors: Ms Corinne Aldridge

Headmaster: **Mr Edward Rees**, BA Ed Hons

Age Range. 4–11.

Number of Pupils. 209 Girls, 226 Boys.

Fees per term (2021–2022). £5,300 (Reception to Year 2), £5,690 (Years 3 to 6). Lunch: £310 per term.

Hornsby House is a thriving IAPS co-educational prep school in Wandsworth, southwest London. At their most recent inspection in October 2016, the Independent Schools Inspectorate judged Hornsby House pupils' overall achievement as "excellent" and found that "pupils achieve highly from the wide ranging curriculum that provides for all abilities". Pupils' personal development was described as "excellent" and stated that "pupils have high levels of self-esteem, positive relationships, healthy lifestyles and social awareness". Hornsby House provides a nurturing environment where attainment and happiness are key aims and the children achieve outstanding educational outcomes as a result. In 2016 our Year 6 children won 40 scholarships and awards between them. There are three classes in each year group, a generous staff to pupil ratio and around 430 pupils in the school. Entry into Reception classes is unassessed and is on a first-come, first-served basis with priority being given to siblings. Children wishing to enter the school in year groups above Reception are required to attend an assessment.

There is an extensive co-curricular programme with over 50 clubs, as well as before and after school care. Over half the children in the school play a musical instrument and a third sing in one of the three choirs. Sport is a central part of the curriculum, the staffing level is excellent and the benefits of teamwork are seen clearly in school life as a whole. The school has an outstanding IT infrastructure, with four classrooms set up as e-learning suites and 120 iPads used to support the children's learning. The majority of leavers go to one of seven London day schools: Dulwich College, JAGS, Alleyn's, Emanuel, King's College School Wimbledon, Streatham & Clapham High School and Whitgift. The remainder move on to other day or boarding schools.

To arrange a visit to see the children at work, please contact the Registrar.

Charitable status. Hornsby House Educational Trust is a Registered Charity, number 800284.

Horris Hill

Newtown, Newbury, Berkshire RG20 9DJ

Tel:	01635 40594
email:	registrar@horrishill.com
website:	www.horrishill.com
Twitter:	@HorrisHill
Facebook:	@HorrisHillprofile
Instagram:	@horrishillschool

Headmaster: **Dr S J Bailey**, BEd, PhD, FRSA

Deputy Headmaster: Mr S J Moss, MA Hons, MLitt, GTTP

Chairman of the School: Mr J Forsyth

Age Range. 4–13.
Number of Boys. Boarders 60, Day 55.
Fees per term (2021–2022). Full Boarders from £9,975; Transition Boarders (3/4 nights per week) from £7,250; Day Pupils from £3,950.

Horris Hill is one of the leading prep schools in the UK. The school's emphasis is on the development of the whole child, without compromising the 130 year record of academic excellence. Horris Hill School has a unique ethos which develops every child as an individual and provides a rigorous and extensive academic, sporting, musical and artistic foundation.

We deliver success by achieving places and awards at the very best senior schools and developing children with impeccable manners, good humour, kindness and self-confidence. Recent awards to senior schools have included academic scholarship to Harrow and Winchester, Music Exhibition to Eton and Harrow, and sport scholarships at Cheltenham, Radley and Sherborne.

We nurture and challenge every child to see school as an exciting adventure and lessons are carefully planned to excite and interest with stimulating activities to foster each child's development.

Life outside the classroom is just as important to us at Horris Hill, enhancing your child's experience and enjoyment of their school days. Almost all of the children in the upper school take individual music lessons in our purpose-built music school, and, in the new dedicated theatre, pupils take part in weekly drama lessons, LAMDA classes and workshops with local theatre companies. The theatre also hosts quizzes, talks, lectures and movie nights.

Playing sport is a very important part of school life and we aim to give every child the confidence to participate on the games field, to provide high quality coaching for every age group and to see pupils develop a number of sports which they enjoy playing. Horris Hill pupils are very competitive on the pitch, but also understand the vital importance of playing fairly and of being great hosts.

With 65 acres of parkland and over 40 sports, activities, clubs and hobbies on offer there is no chance of your child being bored.

A significant proportion of our pupils, and nearly all of those in the lower school, are day pupils. Our local families form a considerable and vital part of our close-knit school community. In the upper school, day pupils all eat supper and complete their prep at school, just like their boarding counterparts. Boarding is a wonderful opportunity for your child to grow as an independent individual. Our younger boarders sleep in the heart of the school, where they learn how to thrive in a 'home away from home', in a nurturing and supportive environment. Life in our two senior boarding houses on the estate encourages their residents to develop the independence and confidence to prepare them for life at senior school. A variety of flexible boarding options are available, including as few as 3 nights at school for the youngest boarders, to weekly or full boarding.

To see for yourself what a difference a Horris Hill education could make for your child, please come and visit us. Simply email registrar@horrishill.com to arrange an appointment. We look forward to welcoming you to Horris Hill.

The school is owned and governed by Forfar Education who help to maintain the family-centred ethos whilst generating a safe, well-rounded education for its pupils. The proprietor of Horris Hill Preparatory School is Forfar Hampshire Ltd.

Hunter Hall School

Frenchfield, Penrith, Cumbria CA11 8UA

Tel:	01768 891291
email:	office@hunterhall.cumbria.sch.uk
website:	www.hunterhall.co.uk
Twitter:	@hunterhall_sch
Facebook:	@hunterhallschool
Instagram:	@hunterhallschool

Chairman of Governors: Mrs Natalie Harling

Headmistress: **Mrs Donna Vinsome**, BEd Hons, MA

Deputy Head: Mrs Kirsten Fletcher, BA Hons, PGCE, QTS

Foundation Stage Manager and KS1 Coordinator: Mrs Georgina Griffiths, B.Ed Hons

Bursar: Mr David White, BA Hons, FCCA

Age Range. 3–11 co-educational.
Number of Pupils. 95.
Fees per term (2021–2022). £2,902 Lower School (Reception to Year 2), £3,363 Upper School (Year 3 to Year 6) including after-school activities. Pre-School paid per hour.

Hunter Hall School has grown rapidly from its inception in 1986 into a thriving and vibrant community, providing high-quality education for children aged 3 to 11. Its location is idyllic, in imaginatively converted farm buildings on the outskirts of Penrith and only 1 km from the M6, providing easy access to the attractions of the Lake District and the north of England.

It is providing a range of experiences that is important at Hunter Hall and staff recognise that effective learning can take place in a variety of situations. Within the classroom, creativity and independence is encouraged, and the objective is to provide the children with the knowledge, skills and confidence to prosper, not only whilst at Hunter Hall, but also in the schools that they will subsequently join. In the Foundation Stage, the activities that are undertaken are determined in conjunction with the children, originating from their own interests and needs and facilitated by the staff. The aim is to stimulate curiosity, interest and excitement in learning, and to encourage self-discipline and develop confidence. These qualities extend as the children move through the school, with the emphasis on providing them with a range of skills to help them to recognise that they have the ability (and courage) to think for themselves. In addition, perseverance and cooperation are especially valued, creating a warm, friendly and almost tangible sense of community within the school.

The curriculum is broad, and specialist subject teaching is provided throughout the school. Class sizes are small. Teaching facilities are excellent. Pupils are encouraged to take responsibility for their own progress and to set themselves challenging targets.

Children at Hunter Hall spend a great deal of time outdoors and, indeed, beyond the school boundaries. The environment in the local area lends itself admirably to geographical and historical investigation, as well as providing an unrivalled stage for exploration and adventure as part of our weekly outdoor education sessions. Participation in Art, Drama and Music is extremely active, with extensive representation at local festivals. The variety and quality of sport that is on offer is equally remarkable, and Hunter Hall children have received wide-ranging recognition at local and national level.

This is a happy school, in which a Christian ethos of tolerance and respect for each other is dominant. Children (their parents), staff and governors enjoy spending time here and contributing to the development of the community.

Charitable status. Hunter Hall School Ltd is a Registered Charity, number 1059098.

Hurlingham School

Main School:
122 Putney Bridge Road, Putney, London SW15 2NQ

Tel: 020 8103 1083
email: office@hurlinghamschool.co.uk
website: www.hurlinghamschool.co.uk

Nursery:
The Old Methodist Hall, Gwendolen Avenue, Putney, London SW15 6EH

Head: **Mr Simon Gould**, BA Hons, QTS

Age Range. 2–11 Co-educational.

Number of Pupils. 411.

Fees per term (2021–2022). Main School: £5,975–£6,185; Nursery from £2,575.

Location and Facilities. Hurlingham is a non-selective independent preparatory school in Putney. The modern and spacious buildings provide excellent facilities which include bright classrooms, a large gym and dance and drama studios, as well as a science laboratory, art studio and several music rooms. Recreational space includes two large playgrounds, an adventure playground and the adjacent Wandsworth Park. The Nursery School is located at our new refurbished site in Gwendolen Avenue and provides families with the option of nursery provision for children aged 2 to 4.

Ethos. The School's ethos is to provide a happy, secure atmosphere in which children flourish both academically and personally. Experienced and enthusiastic teachers provide opportunities for the children that strongly promote creativity and independence of thought, essential attributes for a child growing up in the 21st Century. Self-confidence, self-discipline, self-motivation, self-esteem and above all a thirst and enjoyment for learning are nurtured.

Academic. The curriculum is broad, with the aim of providing a balanced and rounded education in which every child is treated as an individual and is encouraged to make the most of their particular talents. The important skills of reading, writing and numeracy are given a high priority in everyday teaching; these are delivered through many exciting cross-curricular topics which bring the children's learning alive and allow them to make sense of the world around them. All children on the main site learn French and Spanish in Reception, then choose one for the remainder of their time in school. Latin is taught from Form IV. Pupils are developed, nurtured and challenged to become critical thinkers who are thirsty for knowledge and can apply the skills that they have learnt.

Sport. All Hurlingham children participate enthusiastically in games and PE. Seasonal team games skills are taught in football, rugby, hockey, netball, cricket, gym and athletics. Numerous matches are organised with other local schools throughout the sporting year. Every Summer Term the whole school joins in with traditional Sports Day activities.

Music. Hurlingham has an excellent music department. The youngest children are encouraged to sing, play simple instruments and enjoy performing. The after-school Arts programme is open to all children from January of the Reception year through to the end of Year 6, enabling additional activities in music, art, drama and dance to be undertaken. For older pupils there are many extra opportunities to learn individual instruments, play in ensembles and participate in music concerts. There are several very popular choirs and ensemble groups.

Pastoral Care. The focus is ensuring a culture that cultivates a psychologically safe space for all to flourish and cares deeply about emotional well-being. Children are encouraged to consider their place in the world and seek opportunities to have impact in their community and care for each other. All staff foster an intimate and welcoming environment centred on family values, with a clear focus on good manners, kindness and respect for one another. The House System, School Council and various pupil committees provide the children with wonderful opportunities to support each other and express their views about their school.

Clubs. Children are encouraged to participate in a wide range of clubs which include: art, ballet, chess, drama, karate, music, modern dance, table tennis and science. Older children are able to do their homework in school if parents wish and after-school care is available.

Starting Out. A newly-refurbished nursery close to the main site provides cutting-edge pre-school experiences, including a unique 1:4 forest school option. Children begin their life on the main campus in Reception which, although contained within the school building, is a separate area allowing children to feel part of the whole school but not overwhelmed by it. The three parallel classrooms all have direct access on to the playground, thus enabling the teaching of the curriculum to extend outside. There is also a cosy dedicated activity hall for Reception pupils which provides space for all three forms to join together for group activities, regular access to computers and a quiet place for reading.

Entry. For entry to Nursery and Reception there is no entrance test or interview. Places are offered in order of registration, although all pupils attending the Nursery are guaranteed the offer of a place at the prep-school. Siblings, and those living within 1.2 km of the school, are also given priority. Older children are invited to spend a day at Hurlingham and take part in lessons in order to assess their academic ability.

School Visits. Appointments should be arranged with the School offices at either the main school or Nursery.

Hurstpierpoint College Prep School

A Woodard School

Chalker's Lane, Hurstpierpoint, West Sussex BN6 9JS

Tel:	01273 834975 (Prep and Pre-Prep)
email:	prepadmissions@hppc.co.uk
website:	www.hppc.co.uk
Twitter:	@Hurst_Prep
Facebook:	@HurstCollege

Chairman of Governors: Mr A Jarvis, BEd, MA, FRSA

Head of Prep School: Mr Ian D Pattison, BSc Southampton

Deputy Head of Prep School: Mr Nick J Oakden, BA Wales, NPQH, MEd Buckingham, NPQH

Admissions Officer: Mrs Christina Treadaway

Age Range. 4–13 Co-educational.

Number of Pupils. Prep 309; Pre-Prep 54.

Fees per term (2021–2022). £3,220–£5,835. There are no compulsory extras.

The Prep and Pre-Prep Schools of Hurstpierpoint College (*see entry in HMC section*) share a beautiful 140-acre campus with the College. Although both Schools operate independently of the Senior School, having their own timetable, staff, buildings and Heads, the schools work closely together to offer a first-class programme of education for boys and girls from the age of 4 to 18.

Hurst's Pre-Prep School for children aged 4–7 opened in 2001. It occupies a self-contained unit with well-equipped classrooms and a new outdoor play area, built in 2016. There is one class for each year group.

The Prep School has joint use of many of the College's superb facilities, including a 25m heated indoor swimming pool, theatre, drama and dance studios, music school, large sports hall, tennis courts and three full-size AstroTurf hockey pitches.

The aim of the Prep and Pre-Prep is to provide an outstanding education in a secure and happy environment.

The academic programme is exciting and innovative, with independent learning and mobile technology at the heart of our teaching and learning. The children are provided with an excellent grounding in the more traditional subjects and, as they progress through the school, they are encouraged to take more responsibility for their learning in order to develop the qualities and skills required for academic success in the Senior School.

The Sports programme is extensive with Netball, Hockey, Rugby, Football, Cricket, Swimming, Tennis and Athletics on offer. In addition there is a wide-ranging activity programme which caters for the interests of all pupils.

The Music, Drama and Dance Departments are also very strong; about half the pupils learn musical instruments. The Preparatory School choir performs at the weekly Chapel service. There are at least three musicals or plays each year involving many children throughout the School.

The College has a dedicated Medical Centre with fully-qualified staff.

Each year a number of scholarship awards are available for entry into Year 7 (11+).

Charitable status. Hurstpierpoint College is a Registered Charity, number 1076498. The College provides a Christian education to boys and girls between the ages of four and eighteen.

Ipswich Preparatory School

3 Ivry Street, Ipswich, Suffolk IP1 3QW

Tel:	01473 282800
email:	prepadmissions@ipswich.school
website:	www.ipswich.school
Twitter:	@IpswichPrepHead
Instagram:	@ipswichprephead

Chairman of Governors: Mr H E Staunton, BA, FCA

Headteacher: Mrs A H Childs, BA QTS, PGC PSE, Dip Ed, MA

Age Range. 4–11.

Number of Pupils. 233.

Fees per term (2021–2022). Years 4–6 £4,470; Year 3 (inc. lunch) £4,712; Years 1 & 2 (inc. lunch) £4,288; Reception (inc. lunch) £3,638;

At Ipswich Preparatory School we provide children with a supportive environment that encourages girls and boys to love learning, grow in self-confidence and acquire a wide range of worthwhile interests. The Preparatory School has its own staff and Head teacher, and is located across the road from the Senior School (see Ipswich School).

The Prep School is in three sections: Early Years, Lower Prep and Upper Prep:

In Early Years and Lower Prep, the staff aim to give every child a first-class start to their education through the opportunity to learn in a happy, relaxed atmosphere which encourages the development of confidence in all aspects of school life. Specialist teaching begins in Music, PE, ICT and French.

In the Upper Prep specialist subject teaching develops and teaching rooms are introduced; Music is taught by specialist musicians, as is Science, Art and DT and the Languages teacher will begin to inspire children to adopt a love of languages such as German, Russian, Spanish and French. The children are introduced more to the idea of moving from room to room, for more subjects, thus preparing them for the pattern of study they will experience at the Senior School.

At Ipswich Prep School we place key importance on the pastoral care of our pupils; care is one of our four core values at the school. Our pastoral care system is encompassed in all that we do from the moment a child enters the school until after they leave, ensuring that there us a smooth transition onto the next part of their schooling, and beyond.

Ipswich Prep School Head teacher, Amanda Childs believes "pastoral care is so much more than a form teacher knowing their children, it is about the whole community knowing what the children need and how to get the most out of a child both academically, and emotionally. This can only be done through investing a great deal of time, way beyond the school day."

The School enjoys the advantage of sharing Senior School facilities such as the extensive sports facilities, swimming pool, theatre/concert hall and the Chapel. The Prep School has its own Art, Design Technology, ICT and Science facilities.

In 2018, The Lodge Day Nursery was opened; the Nursery provides high quality care and learning for children aged three months to four years. There are spacious rooms where children can play and develop, providing them with stimulating spaces to learn and grow in – with new classes added, due to popular demand. Most of the children who join the Reception Class at Ipswich Prep School move into it from The Lodge Day Nursery preschool class, but children are welcomed from elsewhere from the September following their fourth birthday.

Charitable status. Ipswich Preparatory School is part of Ipswich School, which is a Registered Charity, number 310493. It exists for the purpose of educating children.

James Allen's Junior School

144 East Dulwich Grove, London SE22 8TE

Tel:	020 8693 0374
email:	prep@jags.org.uk
website:	www.jags.org.uk
Twitter:	@JAGS_Prep
Facebook:	@JAGSschool

Chair of Governors: Mr David Miller, MA, FCSI

Headteacher: **Miss Finola Stack**, BA Hons, MA Ed Open, PGCE, Mont Dip

Age Range. Girls 4–11.
Number of Pupils. Day: 302 Girls.
Fees per term (2021–2022). £5,995.

James Allen's Junior School is an independent day school for girls aged between 4 and 11, offering a high quality of education provided by a team of skilled, motivated and dedicated teachers and support staff. The curriculum is broad and well-balanced and enriched by a varied and

stimulating programme of extra-curricular clubs and activities.

Warmth, happiness and vitality are at the heart of everything we do at the Junior School. Children are encouraged to work to the best of their abilities, but we also want them to have fun and be curious in their learning. We see the primary years as vital to the success of all children's education.

The Junior School has an excellent staff-to-pupil ratio and provides specialist teachers in Art, DT, ICT, Music, PE and Science from Year 3. In French the children are taught from 4 years of age using the immersion method. Prep School girls enjoy specialist teaching for most of their subjects whilst regularly being taught by their Form Teacher. Our specially designed Computing suite, along with the Science, Design Technology and Art rooms, enable girls to enjoy their learning in a practical as well as a theoretical way. Enriching our exciting and diverse curriculum is an extensive range of extra-curricular activities to develop and extend the girls' own interests, teamwork and leadership skills.

The Pre-Prep School (for pupils aged 4–7) is housed in a separate Edwardian building with a large outside green space, including a sensory garden and Forest Schools activities. The Prep School (for pupils aged 7–11) is a large, modern building on the same site as the Senior School sharing their theatre, swimming pool and games fields. The contemporary Vaughan Williams Auditorium offers an exceptional musical performance and event space for the school and local community.

Pupils normally enter the school in the year in which they are 4 or 7 at the beginning of the Autumn Term. Assessments take place the preceding December and January. At 11, girls normally progress to JAGS where Prep girls regularly win scholarships.

Charitable status. James Allen's Girls' School is a Registered Charity, number 1124853. The purpose of the charity is the conduct at Dulwich of a day school in which there shall be provided a practical, liberal and religious education for girls.

Keble Prep

Wades Hill, Winchmore Hill, London N21 1BG

Tel:	020 8360 3359
email:	office@kebleprep.co.uk
website:	kebleprep.co.uk

Chairman of Governors: Mrs Christine Edmundson

Head: **Mr P Gill**, BA Hons

Age Range. 4–13.
Number of Boys. 142 Day Boys.
Fees per term (2021–2022). £4,330–£5,520.

As confirmed by the ISI Inspectors in 2012, the warm and friendly atmosphere that exists at Keble ensures that the boys are well-motivated, keen to learn and able to mature at their own pace. Strong pastoral care is regarded as a key element in the boys' overall development and well-being, along with the encouragement of courteous and considerate behaviour.

The academic staff comprises 21 qualified graduate teachers, 9 classroom assistants and 2 Learning Support teachers. The buildings are well maintained and facilities are regularly updated. The school has an ambitious ICT development programme.

The average class size in the school is 15, although many classes are taught in half-groups and sets as the boys progress through the school. Boys follow the Foundation Stage in Reception. General subject teachers cover the academic curriculum in Years 1 to 4, with subject specialists following on from Year 5 onwards. The National Curriculum is used as a guide to curriculum development. Art, Music, PE, ICT, PSHE and Games are introduced at appropriate stages and are included within the timetable. Boys are encouraged to learn a musical instrument, sing in the choir, perform in plays and concerts, and play an active part in the wide range of sports on offer.

Football, rugby and cricket are the major team games. Further opportunities exist to participate in hockey, swimming, basketball, athletics, cross country and tennis. There is a wide range of lunchtime and after-school activities and clubs, including drama, gardening and chess. There are also numerous educational outings and four residential trips.

Boys are not required to pass an assessment to gain entry into the school at Reception. Boys wishing to join the school at a later stage in Year 1 or above are assessed in order to ensure that they will fit comfortably into their new surroundings.

Boys are prepared for entry to senior independent schools through Common Entrance and Scholarship examinations at 13+. The school has a strong record of success in placing boys in the senior school which is right for them. In recent years, these schools include Aldenham, City of London, Haberdashers' Aske's, Highgate, Haileybury, Mill Hill, St Albans, St Columba's, University College and Westminster.

Charitable status. Keble Preparatory School (1968) Limited is a Registered Charity, number 312979. It exists to provide education for boys.

Kensington Prep School

GDST

596 Fulham Road, London SW6 5PA

Tel: 020 7731 9300
email: enquiries@kenprep.gdst.net
website: www.kensingtonprep.gdst.net
Twitter: @KensingtonPrep

Founded in 1873.

Kensington Prep School is part of the GDST (Girls' Day School Trust). The GDST is the leading network of independent girls' schools in the UK. As a charity that owns and runs 23 schools and two academies, it reinvests all its income in its schools. For further information about the Trust, see p. xix or visit www.gdst.net.

Head: **Mrs Caroline Hulme-McKibbin**, BEd Hons Cantab

Age Range. 4–11 years.

Number of Girls. 295.

Fees per term (2021–2022). £6,131

Since 1997 the School has been based in Fulham. The school is set in an acre of grounds and has large bright classrooms with specialist rooms for ICT, Art, Drama, Music, and Science. The large playground provides fantastic play facilities, netball and tennis courts and great resources for outdoor learning.

We have recently completed an innovative £2.7m building project 'Creating Spaces for Growing Minds' transforming the school, providing ground-breaking facilities for independent exploration, self-directed learning and collaborative work. These include spacious classroom breakout areas with retractable doors, a high-tech 'Explore Floor', multimedia recording studio, and an Eco-Greenhouse. The specialist Drama, Art, Science and ICT suites have also been refurbished and the school is fully accessible throughout for pupils with two new lifts. The latest development is the transformation of the school library which puts reading at the heart of the school, with a new more child-friendly design and an extensive range of books both fact and fiction.

The school focuses on growing great minds that are curious and creative, healthy and happy with an excellent, broadly-based but strongly academic curriculum. Independence, individuality and questioning thinkers are encouraged. Girls enjoy challenging and interesting work in a stimulating and caring environment, whilst being prepared for entry to leading boarding and day schools at 11+.

Kensington Prep was named 'Independent Prep School of the Year' in 2018 by Independent School Parent Magazine in recognition of its innovative 'Creating Spaces for Growing Minds' building programme. The School achieved the highest possible grades across the board in the recent Inspection by the Independent Schools Inspectorate, and the quality of pupils' achievements and learning was rated 'exceptional'.

Entry to the School is selective and the main entry point is at 4+. Occasional places do occur throughout the School from time to time.

Charitable status. Kensington Prep School is part of The Girls' Day School Trust, which is a Registered Charity, number 306983.

Kent College Junior School

Harbledown, Canterbury, Kent CT2 9AQ

Tel: 01227 762436
email: prepenquiries@kentcollege.co.uk
website: www.kentcollege.com
Twitter: @kcsimonjames
Facebook: @kentcollege
LinkedIn: /kent-college-canterbury

Chair of Governors: Mrs L Cocking

Executive Head: M M Turnbull, BA, MA

Head of Junior School: **S James**, BA Hons, MBA

(The full staff list can be found on the Kent College website.)

Age Range. 0–11 Co-educational.

Number of Pupils. Juniors (Day and Boarding) 200.

Fees per term (2021–2022). Juniors: Boarders £8,967; Day Pupils (including lunch): Year 6 £5,553, Year 5 £5,491, Year 4 £5,240, Year 3 £4,816, Year 2 £3,843, Year 1 £3,820, Reception £3,529, Pre-Reception £3,703 (full days, full week), Nursery: (0–3 years) £51.50 a day.

Kent College is a very happy and successful school for boys and girls aged 0–18, which is situated in the south east of England on the outskirts of the beautiful and historic city of Canterbury. Canterbury is less than one hour from the centre of London by train and very close to all of the London airports.

The Garden Cottage Nursery (0–3 years) and Prep School (3–11 years) are based in an idyllic 14-acre site, just one mile from the centre of Canterbury. This day and boarding school offers a British education with an innovative approach to learning, full of opportunities for children to grow and develop their skills and talents.

The school has a thriving Music Department and our Choristers regularly perform at national level; most recently seen on our TV screens in the BBC's 2019 Songs of Praise 'Junior Choir of the Year'. There are a wide range of sports on offer from hockey to football and the school hosts regular athletic and cross country events, as well as taking students on sports tours during the year. Art and drama are also well catered for with the installation of a new Art department in the main school house (which was previously owned by Sidney Cooper, the Victorian landscape artist) and with the development of an outdoor theatre, The Dell, in the grounds. Children thrive in this progressive environment where the emphasis is finding the right pace of education for each individual child.

We believe in making the timetable appropriate for each individual child. All children in the junior school take part in our Gifted, Really Enthusiastic, Able and Talented Programme, which enables the children to increase their performance even further in their chosen area. These lessons are given curriculum time and are delivered by specialist teachers who develop individual programmes for each pupil based on their needs and interests.

The areas of choice are geared towards maximising each child's chances of winning a scholarship to senior school and gaining entry to the school of their choice.

Boarding. Kent College has a long history of welcoming boarding pupils from abroad, as well as from British families resident in the UK or working overseas. The Junior school Boarding House takes children from the age of 7 upwards and is a cosy family environment. Boarders can participate in evening and weekend activities as well as joining up to 30 Sunday excursions over the school year, from ice skating at the Natural History Museum in London, to going to the theatre or paintballing. We have a popular range of innovative one-term or one-year residential courses available to boarders to develop talent and excellence in English language, music or sport.

Beyond the Classroom Our full range of 50 after school clubs offer a variety of interesting, challenging and fun activities for the children to enjoy whilst expanding their skills and knowledge.

There are clubs each evening from 4.10pm–5.00pm and 5.10pm–6.00pm which enable the children to be purposefully occupied until their parents can collect them. Many children choose to stay until six every evening, such is the range and variety.

For busy parents early care is also available in the mornings before school starts.

School Farm and Horse Riding. We are lucky to have a working farm where students can join the Farm Club and learn to care for and show animals at the Kent Show. Horse Riding lessons are also available in the school's riding arena and our NESA team successfully competes in events all over the country.

Charitable status. Kent College, Canterbury is part of the Methodist Independent Schools Trust, which is a Registered Charity, number 1142794. The School was founded to provide education within a supportive Christian environment.

Kew College

24–26 Cumberland Road, Kew, Surrey TW9 3HQ

Tel:	020 8940 2039
email:	enquiries@kewcollege.com
website:	www.kewcollege.com
Twitter:	@KewCollege

Chairman of Governors: Mr David Imrie

Head: **Mrs Jane Bond**, BSc, MAEd, PGCE

Age Range. 3–11 Co-educational.

Number of Pupils. 296.

Fees per term (2021–2022). £2,525–£4,400

Kew College was established in 1927 and was made into a charitable trust in 1985 by its founder, Elizabeth Hamilton-Spry, to ensure the long-term continuity of the school. The school's ethos is to ensure all pupils have an excellent grounding in the basics, but with a strong emphasis on areas such as art, music, drama and sport to develop the whole child.

Kew College's style is described as traditional, yet imaginative and the atmosphere is happy and lively with a team of enthusiastic, caring and dedicated staff to help fulfil each child's potential. Pupils enjoy excellent facilities including specialist ICT and science labs. The ISI inspection in October 2010 concluded that '*Pupils achieve well across the curriculum and extra-curricular activities, and standards are exceptionally high in all aspects of English and Mathematics. The quality of their reading, writing and mathematical skills is in advance of their years.*'

In the ISI Regulatory Compliance Inspection of November 2016 the school was deemed to have met all of the ISI standards, with no action points.

The welfare and happiness of the children is of primary importance. This was highlighted in the ISI Inspection report of October 2019 which concluded that, '*the quality of the pupils' personal development is excellent*'.

Beyond the core curriculum pupils enjoy a wide range of weekly after-school clubs including chess, computer, debating, Building Imagination, STEMKids, M:Tech –

music technology, fencing, handball and jazz dance, with arts and crafts and little golfers for the younger pupils. There are also school choirs, a wind band and string orchestra. The school takes full advantage of its London location for educational visits. There are residential field trips in Years 3, 4, 5 and 6. In their final term, Year 6 pupils enjoy a week-long stay at a château in France improving their language skills, cultural knowledge and doing outward bound team activities.

At 11+ pupils not only achieve places through competitive entrance examinations to selective London day schools but also win a good number of awards. Year 6 pupils this year gained 37 scholarships.

Charitable status. Kew College is a Registered Charity, number 286059.

Kew Green Preparatory School

Layton House, Ferry Lane, Kew Green, Richmond, Surrey TW9 3AF

Tel: 020 8948 5999
email: secretary@kgps.co.uk
website: www.kgps.co.uk
Twitter: @KewGreenPrep
Facebook: @KewGreenPrep
Instagram: @kewgreenprep
LinkedIn: /company/kewgreenprep

Headmaster: **Mr Jem Peck**

Age Range. 4–11 Co-educational.
Number of Pupils. 280.
Fees per term (2021–2022). £6,304.

Kew Green Preparatory School is housed in an attractive building and grounds directly next door to the Royal Botanical Gardens. The front of the school overlooks Kew Green, which is used for games and the back of the school has a good-sized playground which looks onto the River Thames.

In a non-pressurised, caring environment, KGPS produces excellent academic results, sending its pupils to London's best independent senior schools.

The children are encouraged to use philosophy and ethical thinking throughout the curriculum, which includes English, maths, science, French, RE, music, design & technology, art, games/PE and computer studies. All Upper School children attend a summer term Residential Week where cross-curricular studies are applied in a non-urban environment.

There are many after-school clubs and sports activities including three choirs, an orchestra and rock band. Individual tuition is offered in piano, violin, brass, woodwind, cello, saxophone, guitar, drums and singing.

An 8.00am to 6.00pm All-Day Care service is offered to parents at an extra charge.

The school is noted for its warm, happy atmosphere where parents play a full part in enriching the curriculum and social life. Off-site visits and guest workshops presented by noted visitors are a regular feature of education at Kew Green.

The school is always heavily over-subscribed and registration is recommended from birth. A prospectus can be downloaded on the school website and the registration form is now online.

Kimbolton Preparatory School

Kimbolton, Huntingdon, Cambs PE28 0EA

Tel: 01480 860281
email: prep@kimbolton.cambs.sch.uk
website: www.kimbolton.cambs.sch.uk
Twitter: @KimboltonSchool
Facebook: @KimboltonSchool
Instagram: @kimbolton_school

Motto: *Spes Durat Avorum*

Chair of Governors: Cllr J A Gray

Headmaster: **J P Foley**, BA, NPQH

Age Range. 4–11 Co-educational.
Number of Children. Approximately 300.
Fees per term (2021–2022). £3,433–£4,675 (including lunch). These figures include a 2% discount which is applied if fees are paid by termly direct debit.

Mission Statement. Kimbolton School creates a caring, challenging environment in which pupils are encouraged to fulfil their potential and are given opportunities to flourish in a wide variety of curricular and extra-curricular interests.

We provide a close family environment where young people are educated to be tolerant, socially responsible and independent of mind, equipping them for our changing world. We are a community that challenges pupils to discover their talents, develop socially and excel.

Our Preparatory School is located at the western end of Kimbolton village in a mix of modern and Victorian buildings, while our Senior School is based at the opposite end of the village in Kimbolton Castle, among 120 acres of parkland and playing fields. We are very much one school: the curricula of the Prep and Senior Schools are aligned; our warm, caring ethos starts at the Reception Year and continues through to the Upper Sixth; and some of our staff teach at both the Prep and Senior Schools.

Our normal entry points for the Prep School are 4+, 7+ and 9+, but we accept pupils into other year groups and/or at times other than September when space permits, subject to passing an appropriate assessment.

Pupils join our Reception year and are then split into two classes in Year 1 and Year 2. Years 3–6 have three classes each. Each has its own class teacher and pupils throughout the Upper Prep also benefit from a good deal of specialist teaching. We have provision for academically gifted children and provide one-to-one and small group tuition as needed.

We offer an extensive range of trips, visits and competitions to complement the curriculum, as well as regularly welcoming visiting speakers. From Year 4 onwards, children have the option of participating in residential trips.

There is a vibrant musical scene throughout Kimbolton School. The majority of children in Years 3–6 take individual music lessons in addition to class music; those in Years 1 and 2 may opt for small group string sessions. Performance opportunities abound, with formal and informal concerts plus an annual orchestral afternoon.

Lower Prep is located in Aragon House, a purpose-built facility for 4–7 year olds, refurbished and extended in 2019, which provides a safe, welcoming and happy environment. Children in Lower Prep also use the facilities on offer throughout the Prep School. Children automatically progress to the Upper Prep, with the expectation that at age 11 pupils will continue to the Senior School. (*See entry in HMC section*).

The Prep School has, on its own site, a dining hall, library, digital suite, assembly hall, music teaching and practice rooms, science laboratory, art and design technology room and sports hall, as well as large, light and airy classrooms. There is a full-time nurse on site.

Our outdoor facilities include tennis and netball courts, 400m grass athletics track, rounders fields, floodlit all-weather pitches, plus football, hockey and cricket pitches. Pupils also enjoy regular access to the first-class facilities at the Senior School, including a 25-metre swimming pool. We have a full programme of sports fixtures and tournaments and have achieved notable successes across a range of sports.

Out of hours options provide high-quality support to working parents. Children may arrive for breakfast at 7.30am and our 'Kim Club' facility is available after school until 6.00pm. There is also an extensive range of extra-curricular activities, clubs, and supervised prep to extend the school day. Many of our children use our daily bus service to travel to and from school.

Kimbolton Preparatory School was inspected by ISI in 2017.

Charitable status. Kimbolton School Foundation is a Registered Charity, number 1098586.

King Edward's Junior School
Bath

North Road, Bath BA2 6JA

Tel:	01225 463218
email:	junior@kesbath.com
website:	www.kesbath.com
Twitter:	@KESBathJunior
Facebook:	@kesbath
Instagram:	@kesbath

Chair of Governors: Mrs W Thomson, MEd, BEd Hons, LLCM TD

Head Teacher: **Mr G Taylor**, BA Ed, NPQH

Age Range. 7–11 Co-educational.

Number of Pupils. 187.

Fees per term (2021–2022). £4,015.

Our award-winning, purpose-built Junior School on the same North Road site as the Senior School is extremely well equipped for learning, with dedicated specialist teaching rooms for Science, Art, Design Technology and Music and a state-of-the-art ICT Suite and Technology Centre, all housed around a lovely central library. The School also includes a large multi-purpose hall and dining room.

Externally, the Junior School has its own adventure playground, dipping ponds, wildflower garden, multi-sport play area, an astro, Activity Trail, as well as access to the Meadow, a delightful and spacious area with beautiful views over Bath.

The Junior School is an integral part of the King Edward's foundation and is governed by the same Board. It joins with the Senior School in major events, such as the Founder's Day Service in Bath Abbey, and shares various games facilities and specialist teaching staff.

All children learn the strings (violin, viola, cello and double bass) in Year 3, recorder in Year 4, whole class orchestra/band and Gamelan in Year 5 and Steel Pans in Year 6. Well over half of the children learn additional instruments under the tutelage of a strong peripatetic music team. A mixture of French, German and Spanish is taught throughout the School while purpose-built facilities in Art, Science, Technology and IT, coupled with specialist teaching, ensure high standards of achievement in those areas. The School is a very busy one renowned for its co-curricular programme. The wide variety of activities on offer include table tennis, gymnastics, fencing, judo, chess, dance, Eco Club and Crafty Club. This is not to mention the various musical and instrumental groups and the many opportunities to play rugby, football, hockey, netball, cricket, tennis, cross country and athletics. Frequent educational trips are arranged in and around the local area and during the summer Activities Week; residential trips for Years 3–6, include destinations such as France and Devon. Sporting tours also take place each year.

The House system plays a central role in the life of the School. All children belong to one of four Houses and take part in many events and competitions during the year.

Pre-Prep & Nursery and Senior School. For details of the Pre-Prep and Nursery please see separate IAPS entry and for Senior School details please see King Edward's School's entry under HMC.

Charitable status. King Edward's Junior School is part of King Edward's School Bath which is a Registered Charity, number 1115875.

King Edward's School Pre-Prep and Nursery
Bath

Weston Lane, Bath BA1 4AQ

Tel:	01225 421681
email:	pre-prep@kesbath.com
website:	www.kesbath.com
Twitter:	@KESBathPrePrep
Facebook:	@kesbath
Instagram:	@kesbath

Chair of Governors: Mrs W Thomson, MEd, BEd Hons, LLCM TD

Head Teacher: **Ms J Gilbert**, BEd Hons, NPQH

Age Range. 3–7.

Number of Pupils. 87.

Fees per term (2021–2022). £2,990–£3,625

King Edward's Pre-Prep and Nursery offers an exciting and stimulating world in which to start school life. A desire to make learning 'irresistible' in a nurturing environment is at the heart of everything we do. Personalised learning, combined with academic rigour, ensures that every child thrives and is provided with the extension and support that they need. New initiatives, fresh challenges, concerts, trips, visiting experts and inspiring projects all help to enrich our broad and creative curriculum.

Ethos. *Child focused* – First and foremost we want every child to feel safe, encouraged and happy in school. We place children at the centre of learning, creating a close match between your child and the curriculum. This helps to increase a child's eagerness to learn, builds self-esteem and encourages positive attitudes.

Family focused – Visitors to the Pre-Prep often remark on the wonderful 'family feel' that they sense in the school. We work very hard to be as family-focused as possible and are very fortunate to have such supportive parents; we are never short of volunteers for the many school trips that the children enjoy and for all the varied events that take place. It is lovely to see not only parents but grandparents taking an active role in the school.

Outdoor focused – At King Edward's the outdoor environment is a natural extension of the classroom and we are proud of our status as a Forest School. As well as allowing children to engage directly with the environment, outdoor learning also brings together many different elements of the curriculum and enriches school life.

Facilities. Our Pre-Prep and Nursery is situated in a beautiful Victorian house close to Royal Victoria Park, Bath. In addition to the light and airy classrooms, we have a well-equipped gymnasium and school hall with stage. There is also an ICT suite, Teddy's Lodge for pre and after school care, an art room and library. Children make full use of the spacious and safe grounds to the rear of the main house, with a dedicated outdoor cedar lodge classroom, storytelling corner, surfaced playground, wooden fort, wooded area and an amazing adventure climbing frame. Recently completed is an extensively landscaped gardening area with greenhouse, where the children cultivate their own vegetables, as well as a dipping pond for Science investigation. There is also a magical sensory garden and newly-opened all-weather Astro pitch for team games.

Junior School and Senior School. For details of the Junior School please see separate IAPS entry and for the Senior School please see King Edward's School's entry under HMC.

Charitable status. King Edward's Pre-Prep and Nursery is part of King Edward's School Bath which is a Registered Charity, number 1115875.

King's College School, Cambridge

West Road, Cambridge, Cambridgeshire CB3 9DN

Tel: 01223 365814
email: office@kcs.cambs.sch.uk
website: www.kcs.cambs.sch.uk

Chairman of Governors: The Revd Dr S Cherry

Head: **Mrs Y F S Day**, BMus Cape Town, MMus London, GDL College of Law

Deputy Heads:

Mr T Coe-Hales, BA Hons Cantab, MA Cantab, PGCE Cambridge

Mr J Rist, MA Cantab, PGCE University of East Anglia

Age Range. 4–13 Co-educational.

Number of Pupils. 391 day pupils, 35 boy boarders including 27 choristers.

Fees per term (2021–2022). Weekly Boarders £8,820; Choristers £2,910; Day Pupils £5,695; Pre-Prep £4,485.

King's College School is a leading independent prep school with 400 boys and girls aged 4–13. We are large enough to provide a full range of options and facilities, but small enough to give a 'family feel' where the teachers can get to know all the children.

The school enjoys an excellent academic reputation, with a pleasing number of leavers winning scholarships to senior schools in various disciplines.

Situated close to the centre of Cambridge, the School is ideally placed to combine the strengths of traditional academic and cultural excellence with modern and innovative educational ideas.

Admission. Prospective parents are invited to come to King's for an individual tour of the School with the Registrar. Entry to all year groups is by assessment and by taking into account current school reports (Years 1–8).

Curriculum. Our curriculum embraces the Common Entrance and Independent Schools Scholarship syllabuses, as well as meeting the requirements laid down in the National Curriculum. We also teach French from the age of 4, Latin from age 9, and Ancient Greek to older children. Standards of literacy and numeracy are high at King's. While external examination success is the final goal, children are encouraged to develop a sense of achievement, enjoyment and attainment of potential in all subjects. The School has a history of winning numerous academic, art, music, drama and sports awards annually.

Choristers. In 1441 Henry VI founded King's College and decreed that there should be 16 choristers to sing at services in his chapel. Now over 550 years later, our choristers are famed throughout the world and each year millions of listeners and viewers tune in on Christmas Eve to enjoy the 'Festival of Nine Lessons and Carols' from King's College Chapel. For more information about the choir and choristerships at King's please visit our website: www.kcs.cambs.sch.uk/kings-choristers.

Schola Cantorum. From September 2020 a new choral training programme for girls in Years 6 to 8 was launched.

Facilities. A newly built Sport and Culture Centre is situated at the heart of the school. The Wiles Centre for

Technology has first-class facilities for ICT and DT. The Performing Arts Centre includes 16 music rooms and a multi-purpose hall used for plays and concerts; it also doubles as a fully-equipped gym.

A modern classroom block contains 2 well-equipped science labs as well as classrooms for modern languages, English and maths; our purpose-built library houses over 15,000 books.

Music. King's has a strong tradition of musical excellence and encourages pupils to participate on all levels. We have many choral and instrumental groups including jazz groups, 2 orchestras of some 80 players each and about 40 chamber groups.

Sports. Our new sports and cultural centre is now complete and includes facilities for badminton, netball, basketball, cricket, dance, concerts, lectures and assemblies. We also have two large playing fields, tennis courts, a heated outdoor swimming pool, floodlit astroturf, and two recently-built squash courts. Games include Rugby, Football, Hockey, Cricket, Girls' Cricket, Netball, Rounders, Athletics, Tennis, Squash, and Swimming.

Activities. Drama, Art, Computing, Craft, Touch-typing, Spelling, Gardening, DT, Gymnastics, PE, Chess, Science, Wildlife Explorers, Library, Orienteering, Yoga, Ballet, Spanish, Electronics, Karate, Jazz Dance, Street Dance, Airfix, Ballet, Cookery, Cross Stitch, Spelling, Board Games, French Films, and Mandarin Chinese.

Staff. The Head is assisted by 51 full-time and 22 part-time teachers. There are 40 full or part-time music staff.

Bursaries. Means tested bursaries are available for Primary School children applying for places in Years 3.

Leaving King's. Pupils are prepared for local senior school entrance assessments as well as for Common Entrance and academic scholarship examinations. Most children are offered places at their first-choice senior school and many achieve scholarship awards. Some pupils also transfer to local state schools.

Charitable status. King's College School is an integral part of King's College, Cambridge, which is a Registered Charity, number 1139422. Its aim is to provide an excellent education for girls and boys of mixed ability aged 4 to 13.

King's College Junior School

Wimbledon Common, London SW19 4TT

Tel:	020 8255 5335
email:	jsadmissions@kcs.org.uk
	HMJSsec@kcs.org.uk
website:	www.kcs.org.uk
Twitter:	@KCJSWimbledon

Chairman of the Governing Body: Lord Deighton, KBE

Headmaster: **Mr E Lougher**, BA, MSc

Age Range. 7–11.

Number of Boys. 286 (day boys only).

Fees per term (2021–2022). £6,435 (Years 3–4), £6,930 (Years 5–6).

The Junior School was established in 1912 as an integral part of KCS, to prepare boys for the Senior School. It shares

with it a common site and many facilities, in particular the Music School, the Art and Design Engineering School, the Dining Hall, the Sports Halls, the swimming pool and extensive playing fields. For the rest, Junior School boys are housed in their own buildings. The Priory, rebuilt in 1980, contains twelve classrooms, including specialist rooms for languages, mathematics, history, geography, information technology and multimedia work. The youngest age groups have their own special accommodation in Rushmere, a spacious Georgian house whose grounds adjoin the Junior School. The School also has its own purpose-built library, science laboratories and well-equipped theatre and assembly hall.

The School is separately administered in matters relating to admission, curriculum, discipline and day-to-day activities. There are thirty-nine members of staff in addition to those teaching in specialist departments common to both Schools.

The work and overall programme are organised in close consultation with the Senior School to ensure that boys are educated in a structured and progressive way from 7 to 18, having the benefit of continuity, while enjoying the range and style of learning that are best suited to their age.

Boys come from both maintained and pre-preparatory schools and are admitted at the age of 7, 8 or 9. Entry is by interview, activity session and examination.

Charitable status. King's College School is a Registered Charity, number 310024. It exists to provide education for children.

King's Hall School
A Woodard School

Kingston Road, Taunton, Somerset TA2 8AA

Tel:	01823 285920
email:	schooloffice@kingshalltaunton.co.uk
	admissions@kingshalltaunton.co.uk
website:	www.kingshalltaunton.co.uk
Twitter:	@KingsHallSchool
Facebook:	@KingsHallSchoolTaunton
LinkedIn:	/company/kingsschoolstaunton

Headmaster: **Mr J T S Chippendale**, BSc Joint Hons

Director of Finance and Operations: Mr S C Worthy, BA, MBA

Deputy Head (Academic): Mrs J Brazier, BSc Hons

Deputy Head (Pastoral): Mr S Watson, BA, BSc

Head of Pre-Prep: Mrs C Luckhurst, BEd Hons

Head of Boarding: Mrs A Hardy, BSc Hons

Director of Admissions: Mrs K Rippin

Chaplain: The Revd M A Smith, BA, Dip Th

Age Range. 2–13 Co-educational

Number of Pupils. 160 boys, 148 girls; including 70 boarders

Fees per term (2021–2022). Pre-Prep £2,755–£2,860, Preparatory £3,450–£5,890, Boarding £6,590–£8,565, International £7,650–£9,630

King's Hall School is a leading Pre-Prep and Prep school with around 308 girls and boys. Set in a beautiful countryside location surrounded by farmland, the school is only a couple of minutes' drive from the centre of Taunton.

The school respects traditional values and boarding is a strong feature which contributes to the tangible family atmosphere that exists in the school. Children enjoy a challenging all-round education in a progressive and stimulating environment.

Sporting facilities and opportunities are extensive, as is the School's co-curricular offering: Forest School, riding lessons at the school's off-site equestrian centre, archery, ballet, fencing, cookery, multi-sports and outdoor adventure are but some of the activities available.

Across the school site, pupils benefit from traditional and modern facilities: a bright modern science facility, new cookery school, adventure playground, outdoor swimming pool, astros and extensive grass pitches, a huge indoor sports centre and gym equipment, as well as an arts centre that acts as the hub for music and performing arts events. The school's 2.5km 'King's Loop' is popular for cross-country running at lunch times.

King's Hall has a partner senior school, King's College, Taunton, and the two schools benefit from having their own independent sites, furnished with excellent age-appropriate facilities and attitudes to maximise the opportunities for the children in their care.

There is a close working relationship between King's Hall and King's College and the majority of pupils progress to King's College at age 13. Scholarships are available for pupils with exceptional ability. These are awarded at 11+ and continue at King's College, Taunton up to age 18.

King's House School

68 King's Road, Richmond, Surrey TW10 6ES

Tel:	020 8940 1878
email:	info@kingshouseschool.org
website:	www.kingshouseschool.org
Twitter:	@kingshousesch
Facebook:	@kingshousesch
Instagram:	@kingshousesch
LinkedIn:	/company/kings-house-school

King's House School is a non-selective independent day preparatory school for boys aged 3 to 13 and girls aged 3 to 4 years in Richmond.

Chair of Governors: Mrs Christine Laverty

Head: **Mr Mark Turner**, BA, PGCE, NPQH

Age Range. Boys 3–13 (Co-educational Nursery).

Number of Pupils. 450.

Fees per term (2021–2022). Nursery Department £1,860–£5,000; Junior Department £4,740–£5,560; Senior Department £6,190 (all fees inclusive of lunch excluding Nursery).

King's House School is a mixed-ability inclusive independent day preparatory school for boys aged 3 to 13 and girls aged 3 to 4 years in Richmond. Founded in 1946, we are a thriving prep school and specialists in educating boys.

King's House provides a happy, lively and relaxed environment for our pupils, where the boys – and girls in our wonderful nursery – thrive and flourish. We offer a broad and balanced education to all our pupils, enabling them to discover their unique talents and passions.

Academic learning underpins the pupils' education, with an emphasis on the core areas of the curriculum in the early years. This widens to an increasing range of subjects by the time they reach the Senior Department (Years 4 to 8). Pupils are cherished as individuals and provided with the skills and mental resilience to succeed in whatever path they choose in life. Boys move on to a wide range of day and boarding Senior Schools, including Hampton School, St Paul's School and Epsom College.

We believe that King's House is a community; we pride ourselves on strong pastoral care and an environment where the children feel happy. The positive relationships that we enjoy with our parents, the local community and Rwanda Action are all key to the boys' sense of responsibility. We aim to ensure that the school keeps pace with global developments so that pupils are ready to take their place in an ever-changing world. When pupils graduate they are not only armed with outstanding academic results, but also with a sense of self-awareness, respectfulness and independence. Academic success is a result of the happy atmosphere of King's House, which allows pupils to simply be themselves.

The School is based on three sites on Richmond Hill and also benefits from its own 35 acre Sports Ground in Chiswick. The three main School sites have spacious state-of-the-art facilities. The School also enjoys the advantages of having close access to London with all the educational opportunities that affords.

King's House is a mixed-ability inclusive school at our two main entry points, Nursery and Reception. We believe that boys benefit from staying in the prep environment until they are 13 years old before moving on. Their final two years here allow them to take on leadership roles within a small year group, giving them the space to develop academically and emotionally.

King's House is proud of its traditions and history. Its principles and standards are founded on Christian values although the school is not aligned to any particular religion, and welcomes pupils of all religions and backgrounds.

For more information visit the school's website or contact our Registrar, Sally Bass, on 020 8940 1878 or admissions@kingshouseschool.org.

Charitable status. Kings House School Trust (Richmond) Limited is a Registered Charity, number 312669. It exists for the education of children.

Junior King's School

Milner Court, Sturry, Canterbury, Kent CT2 0AY

Tel: 01227 714000
email: office@junior-kings.co.uk
website: www.junior-kings.co.uk
Twitter: @JuniorKingsSch

Chairman of Governors: The Very Revd Dr R A Willis, BA, Dip Th, FRSA, Dean of Canterbury Cathedral

Headmistress: **Mrs Emma Károlyi**

Age Range. 3–13.

Number of Pupils. 365 (78 Boarders; 210 Day Pupils, including 77 Pre-Prep).

Fees per term (2021–2022). Boarders £9,090; Day Pupils £5,500–£6,525; Pre-Prep £3,880 (including meals).

Junior King's was founded in 1879 as the preparatory school to The King's School Canterbury, which can trace its roots back to the sixth century when St Augustine established a monastery in Kent.

Set in eighty acres of attractive countryside, just two miles from Canterbury city centre, Junior King's pupils enjoy a calm, happy and purposeful atmosphere drawing upon a rich Christian heritage. Girls and boys from the ages of three to thirteen years achieve their potential, both inside and beyond the classroom, whatever their ability.

The school has an outstanding reputation for academic excellence and scholarship due to a varied and stimulating curriculum. This is supported by first class teaching and opportunities to enjoy a wide range of sports, music, drama and extra-curricular activities.

The school is in the grounds of Milner Court, a 16th century Manor House This historic building, along with a Kentish Oast House used by the Pre-Prep, a newly-refurbished Tithe Barn used for theatre and musical productions, and a flint stoned church for services and assemblies has been sensitively augmented over the years. Other impressive facilities include specialist art, science, ICT and design suites.

Spacious and comfortable boarding accommodation for around 80 boarders with social rooms, kitchens and games rooms are at the heart of the school in the main building.

The school has a fine reputation for music, both instrumental and choral, as well as for art, design and drama. The school year includes a programme of concerts, recitals and exhibitions involving children of all ages.

In 2013, Mr Hugh Robertson, MP and Minister of State for Sport, Olympic Legacy and Tourism opened a stunning new all-weather sports pitch and tennis courts. In 2016, a magnificent new music school was officially opened by Dr Harry Christophers, CBE, OKS.

A large and modern sports hall is used for PE lessons, basketball, volleyball, badminton, and netball, as well as indoor hockey, soccer and tennis. Rowing and sailing take place on nearby lakes. Pupils make use of the large indoor swimming pool at the senior school.

For boys, cricket, soccer hockey and rugby are the main team games, while girls play netball, hockey and rounders. Athletics, tennis and fencing are joint pursuits.

Children can join the Nursery from the age of three in our impressive purpose-built 'Little Barn'. In its delightful Kentish Oast House setting, the Pre-Prep has its own spacious hall, library and seven bright classrooms complete with the latest ICT facilities. Outside, pupils have their own extensive adventure playground as well as sharing the main school facilities such as the sports hall, tithe barn, sports fields and dining hall.

Junior King's pupils progress at 13+ to The King's School Canterbury and other leading public schools, with a sense of achievement, maturity and self-confidence. Academic standards are high and the record of success in Scholarships and Common Entrance is outstanding.

(*See entry for The King's School Canterbury in the HMC section.*)

Charitable status. The King's School of the Cathedral Church of Canterbury is a Registered Charity, number 307942. It exists to provide education for boys and girls.

King's Rochester Preparatory School

King Edward Road, Rochester, Kent ME1 1UB

Tel: 01634 888577
email: prep@kings-rochester.co.uk
website: www.kings-rochester.co.uk
Twitter: @Kings_Rochester
Facebook: @KingsRochester
LinkedIn: /king-s-school-rochester

Acting Chair of Governors: The Very Reverend Dr P Hesketh, PhD, BD, AKC

Principal of King's Rochester and Headmaster of the Senior School: Mr B P H Charles, BA Hons, PGCE, Exeter & Durham

Headmaster of the Preparatory School: **Mr T H Morgan**, BMus Hons Royal College of Music

Headmistress of the Pre-Preparatory School: Mrs K Crozer, BEd Hons Greenwich

Bursar and Clerk to the Governors: Ms D J Godwin, BA Hons, CIMA, University of Central England

Deputy Headmaster: Mr P N Medhurst, MA, BA, Warwick & Greenwich

Second Deputy: Mrs C Green, BA, PGCE Sheffield

Age Range. 8–13.

Number of Pupils. 240.

Fees per term (2021–2022). Boarders £7,840, Day Pupils £4,705–£5,340 (including lunches).

Admission between 8+ to 12+ is by interview and report from present school as well as Entrance Examinations in English, Mathematics and Verbal or Non-Verbal Reasoning. Many children also join at 11+ and sit either our November or March 11+ Assessment Tests in English, Mathematics and Non-Verbal Reasoning.

Scholarships are awarded in Year 7 for academic attainment, sport, and music. Cathedral Choristerships are also available to pupils who are aged 8 by the September they start in Year 4.

The Preparatory School is an integral part of King's Rochester, founded in 604 AD by Justus, a Benedictine monk, the first Bishop of Rochester. The Cathedral is at the heart of the School's life with a weekly School service and every day the Choristers maintain the tradition of choral singing at the world's oldest Choir School. When the School is not in the Cathedral a religious assembly is held at the Preparatory School.

The School is a member of the Choir Schools' Association and was found to be "excellent in all areas" in the 2020 Independent Schools Inspectorate (ISI) report.

Set in Rochester Town Centre, the Preparatory School building overlooks the beautiful Paddock, one of the School's large playing fields. The teaching block consists of 12 classrooms, 2 Science Laboratories, a Computer Suite, Language Laboratory and a Library with over 6,000 volumes. Other facilities such as the Design and Technology Centre, Art Centre, Music School, Indoor Swimming Pool and Sports Halls are shared with the Senior School which virtually all pupils join following the internal Entrance Examination. The King's Rochester Sports Centre, just 10 minutes away, provides pupils with nine external tennis/netball courts, a large gymnasium, a fitness gym, physio suite and changing rooms.

The Preparatory School has a small number of boarders who are housed either in School House for boys, or St Margaret's House for girls. Boarding, both full and weekly, is available for boys and girls from 11+.

The curriculum is broad and balanced. In Year 8 science is taught as three separate subjects, French, German and Spanish are the modern languages, and Latin is taught to the A stream from Year 7. A full programme of CPSHE is given to all pupils. Individual educational support tuition and EFL is available if required.

All pupils enjoy the benefit of two full afternoons a week of Games in addition to a PE lesson for most year groups. Major sports include Rugby, Hockey, Cricket, Netball, Athletics, Tennis and Swimming. There is a wide range of extra-curricular activities at the end of the school day.

Choral and instrumental music is strong throughout the School. Many of our pupils learn one or more musical instruments and strong results are achieved in Associated Board examinations. Each year the Drama Club presents a play or musical held over three nights. Recently productions have required casts in excess of fifty and have been wonderful opportunities for pupils to show their dramatic and musical skills. Amongst latest productions have been *Peter Pan, The Roman Invasion of Ramsbottom, Honk!, The Caucasian Chalk Circle, Olivia, Bendigo Boswell, Homer's Odyssey, Under Milk Wood, Bugsy Malone, In Holland stands a House* and *Little Shop of Horrors*.

Charitable status. King's School, Rochester is a Registered Charity, number 1084266. It is a Charitable Trust for the purpose of educating children.

Kingshott

Stevenage Road
St Ippolyts, Hitchin, Hertfordshire SG4 7JX

Tel:	01462 432009
email:	pa2head@kingshottschool.com
website:	www.kingshottschool.com
Twitter:	@Kingshottsch
Facebook:	@kingshottschool
Instagram:	@kingshottschool
LinkedIn:	/school/kingshott-school

Chairman of Governors: Mr James Bentall

Headmaster: **Mr David Weston**, BA Hons, QTS

Age Range. 3–13.

Number of Pupils. (All Day) Prep (7–13): 156 Boys, 107 Girls; Pre-Prep (4–7): 81 Boys, 66 Girls; Nursery (3–4): 7 Boys, 11 Girls.

Fees per term (2021–2022). (including Lunch) Nursery £2,185 (5 mornings), Pre-Prep £3,855, Prep £4,705.

Kingshott, founded in 1931, occupies a large Victorian building, with major recent classroom additions, in 23 acres of attractive grounds on the outskirts of Hitchin. Luton, Letchworth, Baldock, Stevenage, Welwyn and the A1(M) Motorway are all within a 10 mile radius. The school has continued to invest in new facilities including a stand-alone Nursery building, Pre-Prep, purpose-built Prep School buildings and most recently a fabulous sports hall and drama theatre.

Kingshott, a Charitable Educational Trust, with a Board of Governors, welcomes all denominations. Children are encouraged to work towards and realise their individual potential – academic, creative, sporting – and to this end there is a happy friendly atmosphere, with strong emphasis on manners and being part of the wider community.

Kingshott offers a wide range of academic subjects including French, DT, Drama and ample curriculum time for PE and Games. This is complemented by a full and varied after-school programme.

There is a strong and successful sporting tradition which includes Football, Rugby, Cricket, Hockey, Netball, Rounders, Tennis, Swimming, Cross Country and Athletics. The School has a brand new sports and drama hall, its own covered, heated swimming pool, astroturf pitches, hard play areas and extensive playing fields.

Many pupils stay for Prep each evening, and there is opportunity for involvement in a wide variety of After-School Hobby activities. The School also offers a Breakfast Club and After-School Care is also available until 6.00pm for all pupils.

Academic, Music, Art and Sports Scholarships to Senior Independent Schools are gained each year, and Common Entrance results are very sound, with virtually all children accepted by their first-choice schools.

Entry for Reception and beyond is by assessment, appropriate to age.

Registration for Nursery and Pre-Prep is advisable several years before required admission.

Charitable status. Kingshott School Trust Limited is a Registered Charity, number 280626. It exists to provide education for boys and girls.

Kingswood House School

56 West Hill, Epsom, Surrey KT19 8LG

Tel: 01372 723590
email: office@kingswoodhouse.org
website: www.kingswoodhouse.org
Twitter: @kingswoodhouse
Facebook: Kingswood House
Instagram: @Kingswood_house

The school is an educational trust, overseen by a board of governors.

Chairman of Governors: Richard J Evans, BEd Hons, MEd

Headmaster: **Duncan Murphy**, BA Hons, MEd, FRSA

Age Range. 4–16; co-educational.

Number of Pupils. 250 day pupils.

Fees per term (2021–2022). Reception–Year 2 £3,500; Years 3–4 £4,975; Years 5–6 £5,190; Years 7–8 £5,250; Years 9–11 £5,570. Free after-school care provided until 5.00pm.

At Kingswood House, we have long enjoyed an outstanding reputation as a leading school for boys but we are embracing the future and moved to co-education in September 2021. Our Senior division opened in September 2016, thereby extending our exceptional academic and pastoral provision through to GCSE. We offer a genuine all-round education, underpinned by exciting curricular and co-curricular opportunities, with a strong emphasis on character development and preparation for life beyond the school gate.

Kingswood House is situated in a leafy suburb of Epsom with excellent transport links. We are ambitious for our pupils and challenge each individual to achieve their potential in a conducive environment of small classes and high expectations.

Accredited as "excellent in all areas" in our last ISI inspection, Kingswood House is also endorsed by the Independent Association of Preparatory Schools (IAPS) and the Society of Heads (SoH).

We are proud to be finalists for an ISY award in 2021. Furthermore, we won the National 'Best School Trip' Award in 2019 for our bespoke "Making of Modern Britain" residential.

Our values promote tolerance, respect and friendship and we welcome families from all faiths, or none. We offer a well-rounded education and a purposeful, supportive ethos in which each child will grow in independence, resilience and self-esteem. All boys and girls are encouraged to participate in every aspect of school life and this provides a wonderful platform for them to take themselves out of their comfort zone within a supportive environment. A rich variety of opportunities, both inside and outside the classroom, engenders an avid natural curiosity and propagates a willingness to try new things.

With the advent of our flourishing Senior Years, parents are able to consider their options carefully, secure in the knowledge that Kingswood House offers an excellent pathway for the pupils through to GCSE. We are also developing KHS for the future and have recently built an impressive Lower Prep and Upper Prep Department. The new Peter Brooks Building, boasting customised teaching accommodation for our Senior Years, opened in September 2018, and recent enhancements include a new Design Technology suite, Drama studio and Music Recording booth as well as the acquisition of superb playing fields off-site.

You are warmly invited to explore the benefits of a KHS education online, or better still, in person.

Charitable status. Kingswood House School is a Registered Charity, number 312044. It exists to provide educational support in the form of bursaries for the parents of children in need.

Kingswood Preparatory School

College Road, Lansdown, Bath BA1 5SD

Tel: 01225 734460
email: kpsreception@kingswood.bath.sch.uk
website: www.kingswood.bath.sch.uk
Twitter: @KWS_Prep
Facebook: @KingswoodSchool
Instagram: @kingswoodschool
LinkedIn: /school/kingswoodschool

Chairman of Governors: Mr S Holliday

Headmaster: **Mr Mark Brearey**, BA Hons, PGCE

Deputy Head – Pastoral: Ms Helen Worrall

Deputy Head – Academic: Ms Katharine Wilkinson

Head of The Garden Nursery and Head of EYFS: Mrs A Ballanger

Head of Year 1 and 2: Miss Rebecca Howe

Senior Teacher, Head of Year 3 and 4, Head of Performing Arts: Mrs Marie McGlynn

Senior Teacher, Head of Innovation, Health and Safety: Mr David Murphy

Senior Teacher, Head of Year 5 and 6, Academic Number 2: Mrs Alexandra St Quintin

Age Range. 9–11

Fees per term (2021–2022). £3,603–£4,314 (day), £8,498–£8,898 (full boarding), £7,138 (weekly boarding).

Kingswood Prep School is like no other, with an abundance of outdoor learning space and boundless opportunities. Here, we celebrate individuality and uniqueness in an unrivalled woodland setting in one of the safest cities in England.

We are a co-educational boarding and day school welcoming children between the ages of nine months to 11 years (up to age 18 in the Senior School), located in Lansdown, Bath. Providing a happy, secure and family friendly environment, our children are encouraged to fulfil their academic, artistic, sporting and musical potential. Each one of our exceptional teachers helps each child to develop their personality and finding the essence of what it means to be themselves; all with the Kingswood spirit and ethos.

The Garden At Kingswood. Our purpose-build nursery, nestled into our stunning grounds, welcomes children from nine months old for 50 weeks of the year. Learning comes through play, experimentation, investigation and discussion; starting from the children's own experiences and interests.

All children make full use of the outdoor spaces, and the curriculum is enriched by specialist teaching of Swimming, Games, Languages, Outdoor Learning, Music and Art in our Preschool and Reception rooms.

Opportunities. We provide opportunities to challenge and excite every one of our children both in and out of the classroom, including Bath's first education-based STEAM and Innovation Centre. This equips our pupils with the practical skills needed in an ever-changing workplace. Pupils have opportunities to explore a range of creative and innovative processes from Robotics and Programming in the STEAM rooms, to ceramics and printing in the Art room.

Co-curricular Activities. At Kingswood Prep, we aim to provide the best all round experience for your children, both in and out of the classroom. We offer an extensive and varied activity programme with more than 80 co-curricular activities each week, giving children experiences that go well beyond a normal school day.

We believe that every child has strengths and many have hidden talents; our challenge is to unlock and then nurture them. The activity programme is a key vehicle in enabling this process, as well as in helping our children to become more confident and self-motivated.

Boarding at Kingswood Prep. The boarding community is based in Westwood House, a large, bright boarding house situated on the main school campus. The House is shared with boarders from Years 7 and 8, with separate dorms and common rooms for our Prep School boarders. Our youngest boarders are in Year 4 with our oldest boarders in Year 6.

The House parents, supported by Assistant House parents, are resident in Westwood and support children each week by walking them to and from school, overseeing homework and downtime in the evening. Each Prep School boarder is also buddied with a Year 8 boarder to help develop a wider range of friendships and provide extra support. Weekends are filled with House activities and a variety of trips to local areas of interest, such as visiting the City of Bath, wildlife parks, adventure playgrounds and even boat trips on the river.

Charitable status. Kingswood Preparatory School is a Registered Charity, number 309148.

Knightsbridge School

67 Pont Street, London SW1X 0BD

Tel: 020 7590 9000
email: registrar@knightsbridgeschool.com
website: www.knightsbridgeschool.com
Instagram: @knightsbridge_school
LinkedIn: /company/knightsbridge-school

Principal: **Mr Magoo Giles**

Head: **Ms Shona Colaço**

Age Range. 4–16.

Number in School. 420.

Fees per term (2021–2022). £6,932–£7,770.

Knightsbridge School is a preparatory school offering a broad, balanced and challenging curriculum to prepare both boys and girls for entry to senior day and boarding schools. In September 2021, Knightsbridge School extended provision to Year 10 and will grow organically up until GCSEs.

Pupils are encouraged to play hard, work hard in the Junior School and work hard, play hard in the Senior School, and make the most of every opportunity open to them to achieve their full potential. They are taught all National Curriculum subjects to a high standard, and modern languages from nursery age upwards.

The school fosters a strong sense of community, and provides a supportive and warm environment. Small classes, overseen by highly qualified, dynamic and enthusiastic staff, will ensure that boys and girls benefit not only academically but also personally. By developing their self-esteem and confidence they will grow into happy, independent all-rounders of healthy body and healthy mind.

Located in the heart of Central London, the school is housed in two magnificent mansions. The premises have undergone an extensive renovation and upgrade programme. Teaching facilities include well-equipped and modern classrooms, a new science laboratory, an information and communication technology suite, music rooms, and a performing arts studio and a new library, as well as a fully catered kitchen and dining area.

Sports facilities include a gymnasium on site and the diverse and challenging sports programme makes use of local venues such as Burton's Court, Battersea Park, St Luke's recreational grounds, the Queen Mother Sports Centre and Hyde Park.

Entry to Knightsbridge School is by informal interview of both parents and children at the appropriate level. Prospective boys and girls for Year 1 and above will be expected to spend a day of assessment at the school in their relevant year group, and a report from the Head of the applicant's current school will be required.

Lady Eleanor Holles Junior School

Burlington House, 177 Uxbridge Road, Hampton TW12 1BD

Tel: 020 8979 2173
           020 8979 1601 (Registrar & Senior School)
email: junior-office@lehs.org.uk
website: www.lehs.org.uk
Twitter: @LEHSchool
Facebook: @LEHSchoolOfficial
Instagram: @lehjuniors

Chairman of Governors: Mr D H King, BSc, FCA

Head Mistress: Mrs H G Hanbury, MA, MSc

Head of Junior School: **Mrs Paula Mortimer**, BEd

Age Range. 7–11.

Number of Pupils. 192 day girls.

Fees per term (2021–2022). £5,999

Lady Eleanor Holles Junior School is housed in its own separate building in one corner of the school's spacious twenty-four-acre grounds. Junior School pupils make full use of the school's extensive facilities, such as the newly renovated heated indoor 25m pool, Sports Hall and floodlit netball courts. (*See The Lady Eleanor Holles School's entry in the GSA section for more details.*) They also take advantage of a fleet of school coaches serving most of West London and Surrey.

The school is academically selective, with most girls joining in Year 3. Entrance exams in English and Maths are held the December before entry. The vast majority of Junior School pupils are given guaranteed places in the Senior School.

The school's teaching is firmly based on the National Curriculum and there are specialist teachers for Science, Art, French, IT, Music and PE from the beginning. The school is very well resourced and staff use a wide variety of teaching styles and activities to ensure pace, stimulation and progression.

There is a wide range of extracurricular activities so girls can develop their own interests and abilities, and all achievements and progress are valued and praised.

Extracurricular clubs include Drama, Chess, Gardening and various Art, Music and Sports activities.

Whilst LEH is a broadly Christian foundation, it welcomes girls of all faiths, and none. School Assemblies, some of which are performed by the girls for their parents, may feature Hindu, Islamic Sikh or Jewish festivals and stories, as well as Christian.

In 2003, Burlington House, the home of the Junior School, was the subject of a very extensive programme of extension and renovation, and now boasts superb facilities for a 21st-century education. Amongst the main improvements were four spacious new Practical Rooms for Art, DT and Science; two new Computer suites; a well-stocked and welcoming Library; and larger, brighter classrooms.

The staff work hard to establish and maintain a caring, supportive atmosphere in which girls feel confident to be themselves, to respect and care for everyone in the community, to be proud of their achievements and to persevere with things they find challenging. Pastoral care is a priority and we are proud of the happy, lively, hard-working pupils of the Junior School.

Charitable status. The Lady Eleanor Holles School is a Registered Charity, number 1130254.

Lambrook

Winkfield Row, Nr Ascot, Berkshire RG42 6LU

Tel:	01344 882717
email:	registrar@lambrookschool.co.uk
	info@lambrookschool.co.uk
website:	www.lambrookschool.co.uk
Twitter:	@lambrookschool
Facebook:	@lambrook

Chairman of Governors: Paddy Burrowes, LLB Hons

Headmaster: **Jonathan Perry**, BA Hons, PGCE Cantab

Deputy Head: Daniel Cox, BA, MSc

Age Range. 3–13.

Number of Children. 610.

Fees per term (2021–2022). Middle and Upper School (Years 5–8) £6,999, Lower School (Years 3–4) £6,448, Reception–Year 2 £4,389, Nursery: £2,195–£4,389. Weekly Boarding (Years 5–8) £1,481 (in addition to day fees).

Lambrook is a thriving independent preparatory day and boarding school (weekly and flexi boarding), home to 610 boys and girls aged between 3 and 13.

From our children's beginnings in our Nursery through their Pre-Prep and Prep education, we immerse them in a world of experiences forging the academic and life skills they will need to soar into their young adult lives. Our children excel at their Common Entrance examinations, with many securing prestigious scholarship awards, enabling them to progress to the leading independent senior schools in the country.

The Lambrook experience offers inspiration at every turn: inside the classroom, in our expansive 52-acre grounds and within the architecture of our historic school site, which blends the beauty of our 19th Century buildings with state-of-the-art specialist facilities. We are proud of our rich history of success and to have received an 'excellent' rating across the board from the Independent Schools Inspectorate.

Academic rigour is married with an enviable list of extracurricular activities to feed young curious minds. On any day, the School is awash with activity on the sporting, musical and theatrical fronts that seek to draw the best out of each and every one of our pupils. Whilst opportunities abound at Lambrook, we recognise the vital role we also play in raising happy children. They have one opportunity for the education that will form the basis of their lives, and at the same time, one childhood: our aim is to keep a happy balance between the two.

We are situated in the Berkshire countryside near Ascot and are easily accessible from central London, the M4, M3 and M40 motorways. We provide transport services across the local area and also to and from West London.

Charitable status. Lambrook School Trust Limited is a Registered Charity, number 309098. Its purpose is to provide an excellent education for boys and girls.

Lancing College Preparatory School at Hove

A Woodard School

The Droveway, Hove, East Sussex BN3 6LU

Tel:	01273 503452
email:	hove@lancing.org.uk
website:	www.lancingcollege.co.uk
Twitter:	@LancingPrepHove
Facebook:	@LancingPrepHove
Instagram:	@lancingprep.hove

Co-educational school for children aged 3–13 years.

Chairman of Governors: Mr M Slumbers, BSc, ACA

Head: **Mrs K Keep**, BEd Hons

Age Range. 3–13 Co-educational.
Number of Pupils. 288
Fees per term (2021–2022). £2,620–£5,705 (including lunch).

Lancing College Preparatory School at Hove is situated on a superb 7-acre campus in the heart of Hove.

We aim to inspire a desire for excellence, to develop independent, searching minds and to foster creativity. We encourage the children entrusted to us to explore and achieve their potential, academically and creatively. Academia is rightly important to us but of equal importance is our pupils' personal development.

Whilst proud of our traditions, we are also a forward-thinking school, looking to build upon our past successes to achieve even greater heights in the future. By the time our pupils leave, they will have acquired a confidence and a self-belief, together with a set of values that will remain with them throughout their lives.

Our pupils are taught by our fully-qualified staff of 27 in our wonderful facilities, inside and out. A new school hall and library space opened in 2017, followed in 2019 by the relocation of our improved Pre-School within the heart of the Pre-Prep and new Music School with practice rooms and classroom/performance space. We have a fully-equipped science laboratory and art, design and technology room. Outside, our leafy grounds include an adventure playground, school garden, science garden, forest school area, grass fields and an all-weather area for sport: cricket, football, hockey, netball, rounders, rugby and tennis. Our pupils also access the extensive cultural and sporting facilities at Lancing College, where Years 7 and 8 also take part in the language programme, learning Spanish, German or Latin. Scholarships with means-tested bursaries are available for entry into Year 7.

Charitable status. Lancing College is a Registered Charity, number 1076483. It exists to provide education for boys and girls.

Lancing College Preparatory School at Worthing
A Woodard School

Broadwater Road, Worthing, West Sussex BN14 8HU

Tel: 01903 201123
email: worthing@lancing.org.uk
website: www.lancingcollege.co.uk
Twitter: @LancingPrepWthg
Facebook: @lancingprepworthing
Instagram: @lancingprep.worthing

Co-educational day school for children aged 2–13 years.

Chairman of Governors: Mr M Slumbers, BSc, ACA

Head: **Mrs H Beeby**, BH, PGCE, MA

Age Range. 2–13 Co-educational.
Number of Pupils. 188
Fees per term (2021–2022). £3,065–£4,210 (5 days including lunch). Wraparound care for Pre-Prep children is available at an extra charge and is free of charge for Prep children.

Lancing Prep Worthing is based in a lovely Georgian manor house on a site of two acres, with space to run and play, in the Broadwater area of Worthing. It is located some six miles from Lancing College.

Our ethos is made up three elements: Love Learning, Be Kind and Go out in the World and Do Good.

We nurture in all our pupils a love of learning to enable them to maximise their academic potential. Our broad and balanced curriculum is enriched with high quality creative and physical activities to provide a vibrant learning environment. Drama and Music are thriving; every year our children gain many awards in public competitions and have an impressive track record in external examinations.

Our pastoral care is excellent and the twin themes of loving learning and kindness to one another run throughout our school community. In working and playing together, within the framework of a Christian community, our children develop a sense of service to each other, and the world beyond the school gates, which will characterise their future lives. We hope they will learn that they can effect positive change and make a difference in the world.

The pupils are taught in bright and airy classrooms by our staff of 20, plus classroom assistants and visiting music and drama teachers. The school campus has undergone significant improvements since joining the Lancing College family of schools in 2014, with a refurbished hall, where freshly-cooked lunches are served daily, a popular Food and Nutrition room, new library and a new drama studio in 2017. Outdoor space comprises hard courts and a large grass field for the coaching of our main sports: cricket, football, hockey, netball, rounders, athletics and tennis. Our children also benefit from sharing the extensive cultural and sporting facilities at Lancing College. Children in Years 7 & 8 take part in a language programme learning Spanish, German or Latin led by Lancing College. Scholarships with means-tested bursaries are available for entry into Year 7.

Charitable status. Lancing Prep at Worthing is a Registered Charity, number 1155150. It exists to provide education for boys and girls.

Langley Prep School

Taverham Park, Taverham, Norwich, Norfolk NR8 6HU

Tel: 01603 868206
email: prepadmissions@langleyschool.co.uk
website: www.langleyschool.co.uk
Twitter: @Langley_Prep
Facebook: @LangleyPrepTH
Instagram: @langleyschooluk
LinkedIn: /taverham-hall-preparatory-school

Motto: *Conanti Dabitur ~ through effort we succeed*

Chair of Governors: Lt Col Mark Nicholas, MBE

Headmaster: **J E Perriss**, BA Hons, MEd, PGCE

Head of Prep: **M A Crossley**, BEd Hons, NPQH, MHFA Instructor

Head of Pre-Prep: **A Skipper**, BA Hons, PGCE in Primary Education

Deputy Heads:

E Wood, BSc, PGCE

S Menegaz, Maîtrise in English Literature & Language, PGCE

Age Range. 2–13.

Number of Pupils. 344 (30 in Nursery, 97 in Pre-Prep, 217 in Prep School)

Fees per term (2021–2022). Nursery day fee from £55. Pre-Prep £2,500–£3,700. Prep £4,350–£5,175 (inc lunch).

Langley Prep School, originally founded in 1921, is a co-educational IAPS and ISA day school set in 100 acres of beautiful woodland conveniently situated near Norwich whilst offering school transport for those living further afield. Scholarships are available from age 7 (Year 3) in the areas of music, sport, academic and art and open mornings take place each term. Under the leadership of its experienced Head of Prep, the School has received six outstanding inspection reports. The Head is also a mental health first aid instructor, a District Representative for 63 independent schools and a regular inspector of schools.

The School is proud to be known as a warm, friendly, welcoming school, where academic excellence flourishes alongside creativity and fun. Its aim is to develop empowered learners, and pupils are actively encouraged to think, plan and make decisions for themselves as well as showing kindness and consideration to others. They are given every opportunity, time and space to grow into independent learners and well-rounded citizens. Pupils recognise the value of their responsibility in the learning process, and via the School Council they are able to play an active role in the school's community. Langley Prep School and Taverham Hall School merged in 2015 and the result is that the pupils now have the opportunity for a seamless transition from the Prep to Langley Senior School.

Pastoral care and personalised learning. The school is dedicated to providing outstanding pastoral care for its pupils. Teaching staff will help identify a pupil's learning style, set personalised targets and tailor teaching to the individual, ensuring pupils have every opportunity to achieve their personal best. As pupils approach Year 8 and scholarship examinations, there is a greater move towards independence. Pupils take increased responsibility for their learning and conduct, as well as obtaining leadership roles within the school, including Prefect status and mentoring Year 3 pupils when in Year 8. From Year 6, pupils embark on the school's bespoke Wensum Award where the acquisition of life skills is rewarded with bronze, silver and gold levels. This award links in with the school's Pre-Senior Baccalaureate, an academic framework for pupils in Years 7 and 8 which seeks to celebrate achievement in a range of subjects as well as the development of lifelong skills such as resilience, collaboration and creativity. Their final year culminates in an exciting leavers' programme with a clear focus on fun, adventure, community action, teamwork and leadership. High pupil achievements contribute to the school's excellent record for Year 8 pupils obtaining scholarships each year.

Pre-Prep for ages 2 to 7. Children in the Pre-Prep department are heard to read every day and those in the Nursery and Reception classes follow the school's own bespoke curriculum. This curriculum draws on the strengths of the nationally recognised Early Years curriculum whilst crucially offering children, who are ready, the opportunity to read and write at a younger age and to develop their mathematical skills beyond the current levels of expectation.

Awards and wellbeing. The School is an active member of the Pre-Senior Baccalaureate, a framework focussing on the development of 21st century core skills alongside a vibrant and rigorous curriculum, which has been adopted by 30 excellent and innovative Prep Schools nationwide. The school has a dedicated Mental Health First Aiders team, led by the Head of Prep, which demonstrates the importance it places on wellbeing. The school recently attained a nationally accredited Wellbeing Award. Its holistic approach to education is further enhanced through fully integrated Outdoor Learning Centre lessons exploring the 100 acres of beautiful wooded parkland.

Art and drama. Creative thinking and imagination are further developed through a performing arts programme which offers a wide range of opportunities within Music, Drama and Art and is taught to all pupils in the school. A purpose-built Music and Art block houses the latest interactive whiteboards as well as music recording and composing equipment.

Extended day. Choice and flexibility are central to what the school is able to provide for families. This includes length-of-day options, after-school clubs and lift sharing/ school transport provision. Sibling discounts and means-tested bursaries may be available for some families, whilst scholarship opportunities exist for those in the Prep School.

Inspection Reports and Awards can be viewed via the school's website: www.langleyschool.co.uk.

Langley Prep School's Open Mornings take place in September, March and May.

Charitable status. Langley Preparatory School at Taverham Hall is a Registered Charity, number 311270.

Laxton Junior School

East Road, Oundle, Peterborough PE8 4BX

Tel:	01832 277275
email:	info@laxtonjunior.org.uk
website:	www.laxtonjunior.org.uk
Twitter:	@laxtonjunior
Facebook:	@laxtonjunior

Governors: The Worshipful Company of Grocers

Chairman, Oundle Corporation of Schools: Mr Robert Ringrose

Chair, Laxton Junior School: Mrs Debbie McGregor

Senior Leadership Team

Head: **Mr Sam Robertson**, MA Cantab, PGCE

Deputy Head: Ms Stacey Crump, BSc Hons Herts, PGCE Herts

Assistant Head Academic: Mrs Sumitha Hill, BA Hons Liverpool, PGCE Glos, MEd Glos

Assistant Head Admissions: Mrs Rachel Waterhouse, BEd Hons Derby

Assistant Head Co-Curricular: Mrs Claire Henderson, BSc Hons Trent, PGCE Plymouth

Assistant Head Pastoral: Mrs Jackie Ormston, BA Hons, QTS Northampton, MA Warwick

Age Range. 4–11.

Number of Children. 260

Fees per term (2021–2022). £3,360–£4,880

Part of the Corporation of Oundle School, Laxton Junior School (LJS), is an independent day school with 260 children aged 4 to 11. The school prides itself in providing an education of the very highest standard, with an approach that puts pupils' learning, happiness and wellbeing at its heart. It is a school that values community, quality and its strong relationships and, with class sizes of no more than 20, each child receives a learning programme that is individually tailored to their needs and interests. Positive communication and collaboration between home and school create a purposeful culture of support and challenge that enables all children to succeed.

Children engage with fantastic lessons which inspire a love of learning that, in turn, builds the resilience and confidence necessary to approach every new experience with optimism. The curriculum includes Art & Design, Computer Skills, MFL, Music, PE, Performing Arts, as well as the major academic subjects and is complimented by a vast range of music lessons and sports clubs delivered by highly qualified specialists. A tailor-made outdoor learning curriculum encourages a love of the outdoors with children enjoying the school's extensive outdoor space, including the recently constructed Woodland Garden, and the specific learning experiences this offers.

Five core values sit at the heart of an LJS education: care, a love of learning, opportunity, community and quality. These values are evident across everything the school does, ensuring pupils are equipped with the skills to thrive in all aspects of their future lives. LJS is proud of the high academic standards its children achieve, the vast majority moving up to Oundle School at the end of Year Six, but prouder still of the intellectually curious, open-minded, kind-hearted and well-rounded young people they become.

Charitable status. Laxton Junior School, part of the Corporation of Oundle School, is a Registered Charity, number 309921. It exists to provide education for boys and girls.

Leehurst Swan School

19 Campbell Road, Salisbury SP1 3BQ

Tel:	01722 333094
email:	registrar@leehurstswan.org.uk
	reception@leehurstswan.org.uk
website:	www.leehurstswan.org.uk
Twitter:	@LeehurstSwanSch
Facebook:	@Official-Leehurst-Swan-School-525934624132963
Instagram:	@leehurstswanschool
LinkedIn:	/leehurst-swan

Chairman of Governors: Mrs Victoria Hance

Headmaster: **Mr Terence Ayres**, BA Hons, PGCE

Age Range. 4–16 Co-educational.

Number of Children. 200.

Fees per term (2021–2022). Senior School £5,170–£5,275; Prep School £2,500–£3,995.

Leehurst Swan is an independent day school, just a 10 minute walk from Salisbury city centre, which has been inspiring and educating pupils for over 100 years. We are the only independent day school in Salisbury offering education for girls and boys from Reception to GCSE. The benefits of an all-through education are widely recognised, eliminating the problems of transfer between the stages of education.

Our mission is to encourage every pupil to find their voice. Everything we do is carefully sculpted to create a community of learners with character, passion, resourcefulness, independence skills, knowledge and qualifications. So everyone can become the best possible version of themselves and make a great contribution to a challenging world.

We love that every child is different. It's our privilege to help each child to find their voice and shine.

Children surprise themselves when they try something new. Seeing a bashful child confidently take to the stage, or an academic child take joy in sport, is rewarding for us all.

We encourage each and every child to take on challenges, to try new things, to be different, and to take pride in themselves, to become comfortable with who they are.

In the Senior school we choose which curriculum to follow based on what will provide the best educational experience for our pupils. In some subjects we believe the quality of the GCSE contents suits our pupils best; in others we choose the IGCSE.

IGCSEs are recognised all over the world and one of their greatest strengths is the option for pupils to complete coursework. Coursework provides pupils with the opportunity to practise their skills in essay and report writing, analysis, data presentation and creativity. The IGCSE prepares pupils for their next stage in education: A Level and university courses both demand independent learning and coursework-style tasks.

We believe that an excellent education should be grounded in variety, choice and outstanding opportunities. A diverse range of curriculum options and pathways allows us to create an exceptional education, preparing our pupils to deal with the challenges they will face in life.

The size of our school means that all of our staff get to know each of our pupils. We all work together to share information and insight and as a result, we're able to provide levels of individual support and guidance to pupils and their families.

School is an emotional as well as an academic journey and we are with you every step of the way.

In our last inspection Leehurst Swan achieved the grade of 'Excellent' in every aspect of educational quality; the highest possible outcome from the Independent Schools Inspectorate (ISI).

The inspectors reported, "The quality of the pupils' personal development is excellent. Pupils of all ages are happy and confident individuals who feel supported by the school community."

Further comments included: "The quality of the pupils' academic and other achievements is excellent. Pupils of all ages make excellent progress."

In 2020 the Regulatory Compliance Inspection found that Leehurst Swan was compliant in all components of the Compliance Inspection and that GCSE performances (for years 2017–2019) were reported to be 'above the national average for maintained schools'. Inspectors stated that our 'teaching enables pupils to make good progress, encompasses effective behaviour management and is supported by suitable resources'.

Leehurst Swan welcomes visitors to the school to come and see them at work and play.

Charitable status. Leehurst Swan Limited is a Registered Charity, number 800158. It exists to provide education for children.

Leicester Grammar Junior School

London Road, Great Glen, Leicester, Leicestershire LE8 9FL

Tel: 0116 259 1950
email: friell@leicestergrammar.org.uk
website: www.lgs-junior.org.uk
Twitter: @LGS_Junior
Facebook: @LeicesterGrammarJuniorSchool
Instagram: @lgs_junior

Chair of Governors: Mr S Gasztowicz, QC

Headteacher: Mrs S Ashworth Jones, BEd

Deputy Head (*Academic*): Mr D Fulton, BEd

Deputy Head (*Pastoral*): Mrs R Strong, BSc

Age Range. 3–11 Co-educational.

Number of Pupils. 390

Fees per term (2021–2022). Years 3–6 £4,071; Kinders to Year 2 £3,831; Kinders Part-time £2,528.

Leicester Grammar Junior School was founded in 1992 when Leicester Grammar School Trust took over educational responsibility for Evington Hall, an independent school run by the Sisters of Charity of St Paul.

The school is a selective, co-educational day school with a Christian Foundation. It acts as the junior school to Leicester Grammar School and is the first stage in a continuous education from 3 years through to A Level. In September 2008 both the Junior and Senior schools relocated to a new purpose-built campus SW of the city of Leicester. Thus, the school now encompasses the full 3–18 age range on the one site.

The school provides a stimulating, disciplined, happy environment where each child is encouraged to aim for the highest standards in everything they do and take a full and active part in all aspects of school life. It operates as an extension of the family unit within which the staff act with firmness and fairness. Respect and consideration underpin school life. Pupils are encouraged to develop a caring and responsible attitude to others, leading to good manners and acceptable behaviour.

The children benefit from not only academic success and development but also from excellent musical, sporting and dramatic involvement within a broad and well balanced curriculum.

Music is a particular strength of the school and plays an important part in the life of every child. From the beginning as 3 year olds, children are taught by a music specialist. Pupils have the opportunity to learn a variety of instruments and there is a particularly strong Infant String Scheme; children as young as five or six years of age learn to play the violin or cello. The school orchestra and ensembles perform at festivals, concerts and assemblies. There are also many choral opportunities within the Junior and Infant choir which are often linked with Drama. A number of boys and girls are also members of the Leicester Cathedral choir and enjoy weekly training sessions with the Cathedral Master of Music.

In 2004 the school received the Sportsmark Gold Award in recognition of the quality of sport within the curriculum and extracurricular. The PE and Games provision aims to develop skills in team and individual games, gymnastics, dance, swimming and athletics. The main team games are rugby, football and cricket for the boys and netball, hockey and rounders for the girls. After-school clubs offer additional sporting opportunities such as tennis, badminton, table tennis and cross country.

Admissions. Pupils are admitted at all ages between 3+ and 10+ although the vast majority enter in the September following their third or fourth birthday (Kinders or Reception). Following a visit to the school an Application Form is offered. When the form is returned a date for assessment is set. Parents wishing their children to be admitted to the Infant Department at times other than in September are invited to bring their child to school to spend part of a day with the class he or she would join. Class teachers then carry out an assessment to determine whether or not the child will be able to integrate into the year group.

Charitable status. Leicester Grammar School Trust is a Registered Charity, number 510809.

Leweston Prep School

Sherborne, Dorset DT9 6EN

Tel:	01963 210790
email:	admissions@leweston.dorset.sch.uk
website:	www.leweston.co.uk
Twitter:	@LewestonSchool
Facebook:	@lewestonprep
Instagram:	@lewestonprep

Clerk to the Board of Governors: Lt Col G Scott-Masson, Manchester School of Business

Head of Leweston Prep: **Miss Alanda Phillips**, BA Hons Winchester, PGCE, MA Ed

Deputy Head of Leweston Prep: Mrs E Winter, BA Hons Warwick, PGCE Bath Spa

A full staff list can be found on the School website.

Age Range. 3 months–11 years Co-educational.

Number of Pupils. 128 Girls, 112 Boys.

Fees per term (2021–2022). Day: Reception–Year 1 £2,095, Years 2–3 £2,753, Years 4–5 £3,415, Year 6 £4,073. Boarding: £6,105 (weekly), £7,320 (full). Nursery (per day): £57.00–£59.00 (all day 08:00–18:00 including food); £32.50–£33.50 (1 x 5 hr session 08:00–13:00 or 13:00–18:00); Breakfast Club 07:30–08:00; £5.50.

Setting. Leweston Prep School is an independent Catholic school for boys and girls with boarding provision from Year 4 and above. The school is situated in forty-six acres of Dorset parkland three miles south of Sherborne and occupies an enviable setting in a skilfully converted former Coach House providing a unique range of bright spacious classrooms. The beautiful rural site is shared with Leweston School, offering continuity of education right through to A Level. The Prep enjoys the benefit of many excellent facilities including a modern, well-equipped Art and Design Centre, an all-weather sports pitch, a swimming pool, a large sports hall, tennis courts and extensive playing fields. A new Prep Hall opened in September 2019 to support the school's expansion. Prep pupils take advantage of the specialist teaching in Languages, Art, Maths, Home Economics, Music and Sport. The parkland setting offers many opportunities for study and recreation. An accredited Forest School opened in September 2017 and every year group has a Forest School session once a week.

Ethos. Traditional excellence in teaching is combined with modern facilities and resources in a stimulating, happy and purposeful environment. The school motto 'Gaudere et Bene Facere' (Rejoice and Do Well) exactly reflects the importance of high academic standards together with artistic, musical and sporting excellence achieved in an atmosphere of joy and vibrancy. Each child is encouraged to develop individual talents within the caring and supportive school community. A friendly family ethos, and traditional values of work and behaviour are appreciated by parents. Full and flexi boarding options provide flexibility for pupils to enjoy a wide variety of extracurricular activities, whilst no Saturday morning school allows for rest and relaxation. Wrap-around care is available from 8.00am to 6.00pm.

Curriculum. Programmes of study encompass the National Curriculum without being constrained by it. Basic subjects are taught to a high standard concentrating on literacy and numeracy acquisition in the early years before expanding into a broader curriculum in Years 3–6. Well-qualified class teachers and specialist subject teachers foster independent learning and encourage the development of problem solving and investigative skills in all areas of the curriculum. Academic standards are high and many pupils gain awards to senior school.

There is a strong tradition in the creative arts and sport. Music and Drama are taught within the curriculum. A high percentage of pupils learn to play musical instruments and take additional Drama. There is a school orchestra and choir and many opportunities throughout the year for performance and grade examinations in both Music and Drama. All pupils in Years 4–6 undertake English Speaking Board assessments. Individual and team sports are considered important as part of the healthy, active lifestyle and the school enjoys a particular reputation for hockey and cross-country. The school is one of only nine Pentathlon Academies in the UK and is regarded as a centre of excellence by Pentathlon GB. Art, Ceramics and Design Technology are taught by specialist teachers using the exceptional facilities in the Art and Design Centre.

Charitable status. Leweston School Trust is a Registered Charity, number 295175. It exists to provide for children a contemporary education in the Catholic tradition.

Littlegarth School

Horkesley Park, Nayland, Colchester, Essex CO6 4JR

Tel:	01206 262332
email:	office@littlegarth.org
website:	www.littlegarth.org
Twitter:	@LittlegarthPrep
Facebook:	@LittlegarthPrep
Instagram:	@littlegarthschool

Chairman of Governors: Dr J Henderson, MA Oxon, PhD

Head: **Ms Kathy R Uttley**, BA Hons, PGCE, MEd

Deputy Head Curriculum: Miss Helen Smith, BA Hons, QTS

Deputy Head Pastoral: Mr Keith Dawes, BA Hons, QTS

Age Range. 2½–11.

Number of Pupils. Day: approximately 174 Boys, 144 Girls.

Fees per term (2021–2022). £964–£4,181.

Littlegarth has grown steadily following the School's move to our current premises of Horkesley Park in 1994. The Grade II listed Georgian house is situated in delightful Stour Valley countryside, designated as an Area of Outstanding Natural Beauty. The 30 acres of School land boast a number of purpose-built teaching rooms, including a multi-purpose Sports Hall, Science Laboratory, and numerous classrooms. A brand new purpose-built facility opened in January 2018, which provides outstanding specialist teaching rooms for music, drama and art, a large library incorporating a computer room, a learning support room and six substantial new teaching rooms. In 2019, existing rooms were refurbished to create outstanding facilities for Food Technology and Engineering. These facilities provide the children with increased opportunities to develop a wide range of skills, supported by our exciting and broad curriculum.

Outdoors, we make good use of our sports field with up to eight pitches and four outdoor cricket nets. Our outdoor play area has climbing and activity structures and a vegetable garden with a recent extension to the green area enhancing the natural space around our covered outdoor reading areas. Our innovative adventure woodland provides an excellent environment for nature walks and Forest School activities, which run from Nursery through to Year 4. This area has been enriched by the planting of wildflower meadows and the erection of an outdoor stage which has hosted productions and concerts by the children.

Children from the age of 2½ are provided with excellent specialist teaching in Drama, French, Music and Sport. Small class sizes ensure that children receive a high level of individual attention and the Early Years Foundation Stage (EYFS) framework provides a springboard for individualised learning which continues throughout the school. Pre-Prep teachers provide a firm foundation in the core subjects, supported by caring teaching assistants and learning support staff. In Year 3, the number of lessons taught by subject specialist teachers increases and from Year 4 all timetabled lessons are taught by subject specialists.

Pastoral care is one of the key strengths of Littlegarth, as highlighted in our inspection report. Year 6 children are given considerable opportunities to take on responsibilities and further develop their self-confidence as Prefects, supporting children and staff in a variety of ways.

The School produces many plays each year and strong drama links with the local community are being forged. As well as supporting the school library, parents are also actively involved in helping on school trips, running a wardrobe department and there is a flourishing 'Friends of Littlegarth' parent body.

A wide variety of clubs and extra-curricular activities are available each day and the School also provides pre and after school care which includes the provision of a Breakfast Club each morning.

Charitable status. Littlegarth School Limited is a Registered Charity, number 325064. It exists to provide education for children.

Lochinver House School

Heath Road, Little Heath, Potters Bar, Herts EN6 1LW

Tel: 01707 653064
email: registrar@lochinverhouse.com
website: www.lochinverhouse.com
Twitter: @LHSPrep

Chairman of the Governors: William Moores

Headmaster: **Ben Walker**, BA Hons

Age Range. 4–13.
Number of Boys. 341 Day Boys.
Fees per term (2021–2022). £4,020–£5,280 with no compulsory extras.

The academic staff consists of 36 qualified and graduate teachers, Laboratory, ICT, DT technicians, Teaching Assistants, a Matron and a Child and Family Support Worker.

The school, founded in 1947, is situated in a pleasant residential area on the edge of green belt land in South Hertfordshire, and yet is conveniently placed for access to London. At the heart of the school is a late Victorian house. Facilities on our 8½ acre site are extensive and include a purpose-built Pre Prep Department, separate Sports Hall, Gymnasium & Theatre, Music Centre, two Science Laboratories and specialist IT, DT, and Art rooms. Lochinver is fully advanced with IT including an exciting project which provides iPads to older boys.

Boys are prepared for Common Entrance and Scholarship examinations to a wide range of top day and boarding Independent Schools.

The school has its own extensive playing fields on site, including an all-weather, Astro pitch. The major sports: Football, Rugby, Cricket, Athletics and Basketball are complemented by opportunities to take part in a very wide range of further sports and physical activity. All boys learn to swim whilst they are at the School. Residential trips take place both within the UK and overseas, such as a European Football and Classics trip and a Rugby Tour to South Africa. During their time at the school each boy will spend some time in France as this is an important and much valued part of the French Curriculum. There are opportunities for the boys to also study Spanish, Latin and Russian.

Music, Art, Drama, Design Technology and PE are part of the timetabled curriculum for all boys. The school encourages boys to learn at least one musical instrument and currently 75% of the children are doing so. There is a School Orchestra, Junior and Senior Choir, together with a variety of instrumental Groups. Parents appreciate our provision of extended care at both ends of the day.

The school is a non-profit making Educational Trust administered by a Board of Governors.

Charitable status. Lochinver House School is a Registered Charity, number 1091045. It aims to provide a quality education.

Lockers Park

Lockers Park Lane, Hemel Hempstead, Hertfordshire HP1 1TL

Tel: 01442 251712
email: secretary@lockerspark.co.uk
website: www.lockerspark.co.uk

Chair of Governors: C Lister, BSc Hons, MBA

Headmaster: **G Taylor**

Admissions: Ms S Nash

Age Range. 4–13. Prep and Pre-Prep for Boys.
Number of Pupils. 170, of whom 45 are boarders or flexi boarders.

Fees per term (2021–2022). Boarders £8,775, Day Boys £3,835–£6,085. Day fees include the flexible day, which runs from 7.30am to 6.00pm/6.40pm (Pre-Prep/Prep) with the option to have breakfast, stay for supper and participate in evening activities at no extra cost.

Further details are outlined in the prospectus, available on application.

Lockers Park is a day and boarding school nestled in 23 acres of Hertfordshire woodland on the outskirts of Hemel Hempstead, with Berkhamsted, Harpenden and St Albans close by. The school is located near to excellent road and rail links serving London and the Home Counties as well as being in close proximity to London airports including Heathrow and Luton.

What makes Lockers Park particularly special is that it is a purposefully small school, where family spirit and kindness thrive. What's more, being purposefully small allows the pupils to achieve excellent results and develop an enthusiasm for life, and Lockers Park boys move on to the country's leading senior schools, with many achieving scholarships and exhibitions. Whilst the school pursues a programme of academic excellence, the Arts, Music, Sport and Co-Curricular success are also celebrated.

Treating boys as individuals is a central tenet, aiming to build independence and resilience, helping children discover hidden talents and initiate lifelong passions. The school's kinaesthetic approach lets boys be boys, ensuring pupils are highly engaged to achieve the best academic results.

Small class sizes (an average of 14 with a pupil to staff ratio of 8:1) and a staff of experienced teachers expect and encourage the best from every pupil, providing all the support and encouragement that growing boys need. The school's recent ISI evaluation concluded that "Pupils aspire to high achievement as a result of a culture where success is respected and celebrated."

A rich palette of opportunities is accessible to all at Lockers Park. Whether it's Sport, Science & Technology, Music, Art, Drama, Beavers, Cubs and Scouts or Chess and Debating, there really is something for everyone. Pupils are encouraged to try new things, to take on personal challenges and learn from their experiences. The school believes that trying out something new can help pupils to apply themselves, as well as developing teamwork skills and an appreciation of working towards goals.

At Lockers Park there are day boys, weekly boarders, flexi-boarders and full boarders, as well as many families who make the most of the school's popular inclusive wraparound care programme. Everyone is part of the Lockers Park family.

The flexibility the school offers is indispensable for many parents; approximately half of pupils board and many day boys also stay for activities and prep in the late afternoons and evenings. Wraparound care for Prep School pupils runs from 7.30am–6.40pm, including a cooked breakfast and supper. This exclusive feature is included within the termly fees and can be accessed on an ad-hoc basis with no need to pre-book.

Ask any boarder and they will confirm boarding at Lockers Park is a hugely enjoyable experience. With cheerful, homely dormitories, a well-equipped Common Room and a dedicated boarding team on hand to provide care, comfort and support, every boarder enjoys a secure family structure. Boys who board at weekends have an enviable array of activities including visits to sporting events, museums and theatre trips. The school's wonderful grounds are also well-used, especially in the summer when popular pursuits involve swimming in the outdoor heated pool and playing mini golf.

Bursaries & Scholarships. Lockers Park is committed to offering financial help to deserving candidates, subject to financial resources. Scholarships are available, which may be increased with a means-tested bursary.

Charitable status. Lockers Park School Trust Ltd is a Registered Charity, number 311061. It aims to provide an all round, high quality education on a non-profit making basis.

Longacre School

Hullbrook Lane, Shamley Green, Guildford, Surrey GU5 0NQ

Tel: 01483 893225
email: office@longacreschool.co.uk
website: www.longacreschool.co.uk
Twitter: @longacreschool
Facebook: @longacreschool
Instagram: @longacreschool

Headmaster: **Mr Matthew Bryan**, MA PGCE Cambridge, MA MSc Oxford

Age Range. 2–11.
Number of Pupils. 263 boys and girls.
Fees per term (2021–2022). £3,785–£5,750.

Longacre School is a thriving, co-educational preparatory school for boys and girls aged 2 to 11 years. Set in a beautiful rural location on the outskirts of the picturesque village of Shamley Green, between Guildford and Cranleigh, the school offers a wonderful environment for young children.

The school buildings comprise the original large 1902 house plus modern, purpose-built classrooms standing in nine acres of grounds. Facilities include a new dining room, sports hall and Astroturf, sports fields, woodland and an adventure playground. Longacre has a proud history and the motto of the school's founder, Ursula Fairfax-Cholmeley, "A happy heart goes all the way" is still very much part of the school's ethos.

The cheerful and purposeful atmosphere at Longacre is apparent as soon as you enter the school. Here, children are valued as individuals and are encouraged to fulfil their potential in every facet of school life. Personal and social development is highly valued, enabling pupils to grow in confidence as they mature.

At Longacre, we believe that children learn more effectively when they are happy, and that excellent academic results can be achieved without subjecting pupils to hothouse pressure. The fact that our pupils gain a range of scholarships, and that they transfer successfully to their senior school of choice, is evidence that this approach works.

Academic progress is closely monitored and regularly tested. Small class sizes enable pupils to be taught at an individual level, with increasing subject specialist tuition as children progress through the school. Alongside the core curriculum, Longacre offers a wide range of activities, sporting opportunities, stimulating off-site visits and exciting workshops. There are after school clubs every day, ranging from cooking to judo, and regular masterclasses for able pupils.

Longacre is a community where parents are welcome. The school has a thriving and supportive PTA and parents are kept well informed about school events and their children's progress through a weekly newsletter, formal and informal meetings and written reports. The Head and staff work closely with parents to ensure that their children are happy, successful and fulfilled.

Loretto Junior School

North Esk Lodge, 1 North High Street, Musselburgh, East Lothian EH21 6JA

Tel:	0131 653 4570
email:	admissions@loretto.com
website:	www.loretto.com
Twitter:	@lorettohead
Facebook:	@lorettoschool
Instagram:	@lorettoschool
LinkedIn:	/company/loretto-school

Chairman of Governors: Mr Peter McCutcheon

Headmaster: Dr Graham R W Hawley, BSc Hons, PGCE, PhD

Head of Junior School: Mr Andrew Dickenson

To view Loretto Junior School's Staff Directory, please visit www.loretto.com/staff-directory.

Age Range. 3–12.

Number of Pupils. 164.

Fees per term (2021–2022). Day: £2,833–£5,525; Year 7 Full Boarding £7,750; Year 7 Flexi Boarding (3 nights per week) £6,600.

Loretto has a whole-School approach and 'The Nippers' enjoy the same safe, supporting and stimulating environment as Senior School pupils, with closer adult supervision. They also benefit from the exceptional shared facilities such as the playing fields, Theatre, Sports Hall, Music School and Chapel. Occasional and Flexi Boarding are possible for pupils aged 11 and over.

A small School, big on heart, big on ambition.

- One of Scotland's leading schools.
- Scotland's oldest boarding school, founded in 1827.
- An independent, private boarding and day school for girls and boys, from 3 to 18 years.
- Set in a safe, leafy, spacious, 85-acre campus in Musselburgh; the school enjoys all the advantages of its rural setting.
- Globally connected, with the convenience and opportunities of being just 9 kilometres/ 6 miles from Edinburgh, its international airport, rail and road networks.
- Offering the traditional British/ English curriculum of GCSEs and A Levels, one of the leading independent schools in the UK.

- More than 9 out of 10 pupils enter the University of their choice, such as Oxford, Cambridge, St Andrews, and Durham.
- Welcoming 600 pupils: 400 in the Senior School, 200 in the Junior School and Nursery.
- An excellent staff to pupil ratio (1:7).
- Every pupil is known personally, and can grow and develop wherever their interests lie.
- A distinctive emphasis on the full development of the individual in mind, body and spirit.
- Exceptional facilities, bespoke to learning and teaching, sport, drama, dance, art and music.
- Extensive Sports programme with specialised coaches in major sports including Cricket, Hockey, Lacrosse, Rugby and more
- An industry-leading Golf Academy with indoor and outdoor centres, providing every pupil with an unmatched opportunity to develop their talent.

Admission. Loretto School's Admissions procedure aims to ensure that girls and boys who join Loretto are able to be happy, successful and secure within its academic, cultural and pastoral environment, whether they are boarders or day pupils.

Pupils can enter 'The Nippers' from age 3 and are prepared for entrance and scholarship assessments, mostly to Loretto at 12+.

The selection criteria include provision of satisfactory evidence, through the School's own age-appropriate assessment tests, of academic ability sufficient to access the School curriculum, and a satisfactory reference from the applicant's current school. Loretto is academically selective but also recognises the central value of co-curricular activities, and enthusiasm in these fields is expected and encouraged.

Scholarships and Bursaries. A range of Bursaries are available for entry to the Nippers, usually at 10+ and 11+.

To find out more, please visit www.loretto.com or contact the Admissions Department, Tel: 0131 653 4455 or email: admissions@loretto.com.

Loretto Senior School. Please see Loretto School's entry in the HMC section.

Charitable status. Loretto School is a Registered Charity, number SC013978.

Loyola Preparatory School

103 Palmerston Road, Buckhurst Hill, Essex IG9 5NH

Tel:	020 8504 7372
email:	enquiries@loyola.essex.sch.uk
website:	www.loyola.essex.sch.uk

Chair of Governors: Mrs A M Fox

Headmistress: **Mrs Kirsty Anthony**, BA Hons, PGCE

Age Range. 3–11.

Number of Boys. 179.

Fees per term (2021–2022). £3,695 (inc lunch).

Loyola Preparatory School is a long established school educating boys for over a century, originally as part of St

Ignatius College. As a caring Catholic School it welcomes boys of all denominations offering a weekly mass to celebrate faith, ethos and values.

As a boys-only school, Loyola focuses its teaching techniques to harness the attention of boys by applying the extensive studies made into 'the ways boys learn best'. These practices encourage greater stimulation and enjoyment which is demonstrated by their overall behaviour and results.

Loyola has a high teacher to pupil ratio, facilitated by enthusiastic and committed teachers, supported by a generous quota of quality teaching assistants.

Loyola boys are encouraged to be kind and respect each other, with the older boys acting as role models for the younger boys. Year 6 boys are given Prefect responsibilities as well as the opportunity to be elected to the position of Head Boy and Deputy Head Boy. All boys regularly take part in community events including fundraising for national and local charities.

Loyola supports their boy's progression for the next step in their learning journey by preparing them for entrance and scholarship exams with English and Maths being taught in small ability sets from Year 3 upwards.

The curriculum covers all the normal primary subjects and includes Spanish, science and computer studies. There are schola, choir and orchestra opportunities available in school, with additional tuition for piano, strings, woodwind, brass and guitar.

Loyola is proud of its range of sporting activities for the boys, aided by a large all-weather pitch on site. Sporting activities include soccer, cricket, rugby, swimming, athletics and sailing (Year 6) of which many are available during the school day and others offered as an after-school club.

During their time at the school, Loyola boys experience a wide range of trips and activities including a 5-day residential trip (Year 6), a 3-day residential trip (Year 5), together with many day trips across the school years selected to stimulate and enrich their learning experience.

The school prospectus is available on the school website and prospective parents are welcome to telephone for an appointment to be given a personal tour of the school.

Charitable status. Loyola Preparatory School is a Registered Charity, number 1085079. The school is established in support of Roman Catholic principles of education.

Lucton Prep School

Lucton, Leominster, Herefordshire HR6 9PN

Tel: 01568 782000
email: admissions@luctonschool.org
website: www.luctonschool.org
Twitter: @LuctonSchool
Facebook: @Lucton-School
LinkedIn: /lucton-school

Headmaster: Mr J Tyler, BA Hons, PGCE

Head of Prep School: **Mr David Bicker-Caarten**, MBA

Age Range. 6 months–11 years

Number in School. 140

Fees per term (2021–2022). Day £2,450–£3,440, Weekly Boarding £7,800, Full Boarding £9,295

Lucton Prep School From their first days at Prep School, Lucton provides an inspiring, happy and nurturing learning environment in which children acquire the fundamental skills that they need to flourish. Central to their growth at this stage is cultivating a genuine curiosity and enthusiasm for learning. Small class sizes, combined with excellent teaching staff mean that we are able to rigorously challenge the most gifted, and provide the support for those who might need it.

The school day at Lucton is well balanced, allowing children to be involved in a wide variety of activities both in and out the classroom, with busy days full of sport, forest school, drama, music, history, ICT, languages and much more.

The Lucton Nursery accepts babies from the age of 6 months and with the extra early and late sessions, nursery children may be dropped off from 8.00am and collected as late as 6.00pm.

The vast majority of Lucton Prep School pupils continue through to the senior part of the school. (*See full details in Lucton School's entry in the ISA section.*)

School Facilities. The school is set in 55 acres of beautiful Herefordshire countryside. Facilities on site include:

- Science laboratories
- Libraries
- ICT rooms
- Design and Technology workshop
- Theatre
- Tennis courts
- Indoor heated swimming pool
- Indoor sports hall
- Games fields
- Equestrian centre

Boarding pupils are housed in modern buildings and the Prep School boarders are all in dormitories in their own junior house. They have the opportunity to move into their own rooms in the Senior School.

Admissions. Admission can take place at any time of the year by interview and assessment. Prospective pupils are always invited to spend a taster day in the school without obligation. Examinations for Year 7 academic scholarships are held in January each year.

Affiliations. The Head of Lucton Prep School, part of Lucton School, is a member of the The Independent Association of Prep Schools (IAPS); the Headmistress of Lucton School is a member of the Independent Schools Association (ISA); and Lucton School is in membership of the Boarding Schools' Association (BSA).

Charitable status. Lucton School is a Registered Charity, number 518076.

Ludgrove

Wokingham, Berks RG40 3AB

Tel:	0118 978 9881
email:	office@ludgroveschool.co.uk
	registrar@ludgroveschool.co.uk
website:	www.ludgrove.net
Twitter:	@_Ludgrove
Instagram:	@Ludgrove_School

Chairman of Governors: C Butterworth

Head: **S W T Barber**, BA Durham, PGCE

Registrar: Mrs Rebecca Philpott

Age Range. 8–13.
Number of Boys. 188 Boarders.
Fees per term (2021–2022). £9,775.

Ludgrove is a thriving bi-weekly boarding boys prep school situated in 130 acres of beautiful grounds in Berkshire. It is a magical place to spend five years of childhood, where outstanding pastoral care lies at the heart of everything.

The principal aims of the school are for boys to grow and develop in a happy caring environment, to explore and expand their potential and to learn to develop an awareness and concern for others around them. We aim to prepare our boys to meet the demanding challenges they will experience at the next stage of their education with confidence and good humour.

We are unashamedly ambitious for every boy and are proud of our strong academic record. In recent years we have sent over 70% of boys on to Eton, Harrow and Radley, in addition to other distinguished public schools. The boys have a wealth of opportunities: a stimulating curriculum, exceptional facilities and a vibrant extra-curricular programme with exposure to music, drama, sport and art.

Our extensive facilities include a stunning 350-seat theatre, a refurbished sports hall and well-stocked library. An exciting addition in the 2020 academic year was the opening of a £2.5million, state-of-the-art Exploration Centre providing one of the finest prep school scientific and creative learning environments in the country. In addition to the impressive 130 acres of grounds incorporating numerous games pitches, a 9-hole golf course, squash courts, fives courts, an astroturf, tennis courts, a 20m indoor pool and adventure playground.

Charitable status. Ludgrove School Trust Limited is a Registered Charity, number 309100.

Lyndhurst House Preparatory School

24 Lyndhurst Gardens, Hampstead, London NW3 5NW

Tel:	020 7435 4936
email:	office@lyndhursthouse.co.uk
website:	www.lyndhursthouse.co.uk
Twitter:	@LyndhurstHouse
Facebook:	@LyndhurstHousePrepSchool
Instagram:	@lyndhursthouseprepschool

"A wonderful, nurturing and supportive environment. My son goes in every morning with a smile on his face." Year One Parent

Headmaster: **Andrew Reid**, MA Oxon

Age Range: 4–13
Number of Day Boys: 133
Fees per term (2021–2022): £6,120–£6,930

Lyndhurst House has an outstanding history of achievement and exceptional pastoral care. The boys win places, by scholarship or at Common Entry, particularly to the major London independent day senior schools. The School takes boys from the ages of four to thirteen.

The School's approach helps boys build self-confidence, easy, happy friendships and the key skills to discover, innovate and achieve. The boys have self-respect, respect for others and a very strong sense of commitment.

Individual attention to support academic progress and personal development have always been at the forefront at Lyndhurst.

The School seeks to understand what matters most to each family and encourages parents to visit as early as possible to meet the Head. It is a privilege for any school to have the care and responsibility of a child's early education and at Lyndhurst House, this is supported by the close open relationship with parents.

"Pupils are extremely considerate, caring and respectful of each other and all members of their school community. This is strongly encouraged by positive relationships with staff, firmly underpinned by strong values." ISI Inspection Report

The dynamic between exceptional academic education and the nurture and wider development of personality are complementary, and Lyndhurst House has a long record of success delivering this combination.

The School promotes the core values of decency, tolerance, understanding and sympathy and provides a very wide range of opportunities, in which pupils find fulfilment, enjoyment and the chance to excel.

Lyndhurst is a warm, friendly place where boys discover and grow their talents and initiative.

The School develops adaptable and innovative skills, but also helps the boys to understand that some things remain as important as ever: kindness and understanding others' perspectives; being able to be independent, but being kind to oneself; hard work. These all matter as much as ever, as does learning to find ways to relax.

In the coming years, much in society and the workplace generally will change radically, and the education at Lyndhurst emphasises adaptability, independent thought and the building of the skills and character, to be resilient at all stages of life.

"His confidence has grown and he has formed lovely friendships with his peers. We think the staff at Lyndhurst do an amazing job." Year One Parent

Maidwell Hall

Maidwell, Northampton, Northamptonshire NN6 9JG

Tel: 01604 686234
email: thesecretary@maidwellhall.co.uk
website: www.maidwellhall.co.uk
Twitter: @MaidwellHall
Facebook: @Maidwell-Hall

Chairman of the Governors: C D J Holborow

Headmaster: R A Lankester, MA Cantab, PGCE

Age Range. 4–13.
Number of Pupils. 140: 66 Day, 74 Boarders (58 Flexi, 16 Full).
Fees per term (2021–2022). £3,655–£9,600 dependent on age and whether a child is boarding or day. Please see our website for further details.

Maidwell Hall is a co-educational boarding school with some day pupils. Occupying a substantial 17th Century hall the school is situated in beautiful countryside and is characterized by its rural location and by 44 acres of grounds. It is a Christian school and the teachings of Jesus Christ are central to the moral and spiritual education of the children. Every Sunday morning the school worships in the parish church on the edge of the school grounds. The school aims to encourage all the children to discover and develop all their talents through the academic curriculum, the games programme, Music, Art, Drama and an impressive range of hobbies and activities.

The school is organized as a 7 day-a-week boarding school with a comprehensive programme of club activities in the evenings supplemented by a choice of outings or school based free-time activities on Sundays. Day children are fully involved in all aspects of school life, including all the after school clubs, for which there is no extra charge. Children from Year 3 to Year 6 can board for two or three nights a week or weekly board. The children benefit greatly from the freedom and security of the school's spectacular grounds including its famous arboretum (wilderness) and its large lake for fishing and boating. Leave-outs occur every 2 or 3 weeks and run from Friday midday until Monday evening and each term contains a long half-term break. Pastoral care for the boarders is the direct responsibility of the Headmaster and his wife, the Housemaster and the team of Matrons and other residential staff. In addition each pupil has an individual tutor.

Pupils are prepared for Common Entrance to the major independent senior schools (typically Eton, Harrow, Oundle, Radley, Rugby, Shrewsbury, Stowe and Uppingham) and every year several sit scholarships. In addition to core subjects all pupils study Art, Design, ICT, Latin, Music and Religious Studies and there are also timetabled lessons in PE, Swimming, PSHE, and Drama. There is a specialist carpentry shop which operates as a club activity.

The school has a strong reputation for sport. The major games for the boys are rugby, football, hockey and cricket and there are also matches against other schools in athletics, cross-country running, golf, squash, swimming and tennis. The major games for gir62 are hockey, netball, tennis and rounders. Teams are entered for riding events and the Pytchley hunt meets at the school every year. There is a successful school shooting team. In the Summer and Autumn there is sailing once or twice a week. In addition to impressive games pitches, sporting facilities include a multi-purpose sports hall with climbing wall, a squash court, a 6-hole golf course, astroturf, hockey pitch, tennis courts and a heated indoor swimming pool. There is particular emphasis on outward bound activities and leadership. There is a strong musical tradition and most pupils play one or two musical instruments; there is a thriving church choir and strings, wind and guitar groups. There are regular concerts throughout the year and each year there is a major school play.

Charitable status. Maidwell Hall is a Registered Charity, number 309917. It exists for the purpose of educating children.

The Mall School

185 Hampton Road, Twickenham, Middlesex TW2 5NQ

Tel: 020 8977 2523
email: admissions@themallschool.org.uk
website: www.themallschool.org.uk

Chairman of Governors: R J H Walker, BSc

Headmaster: D Price, BSc, MA, PGCE

Deputy Head: J Fair, BA

Age Range. 4–11
Number of Boys. 220 day boys.
Fees per term (2021–2022). Reception–Year 2 £4,407, Years 3–8 £4,958.

Founded in 1872, for over 140 years we have been preparing boys for a range of the leading independent London day and boarding senior schools. In the summer of 2020 the school completed a period of transition, phasing out Years 7 and 8 and now all boys leave us at the end of Year 6 aged 11. In September 2022 the school will open a day nursery for boys and girls aged 6 months to 4 years old.

Our 2019 and 2021 11+ leavers were offered places at over twenty senior schools. Between them, they were offered 41 scholarships including academic awards to Hampton, King's College Wimbledon, Kingston Grammar, Radnor House and St George's Weybridge and non-academic awards including St Paul's Juniors (music), Hampton (sport, music and chess) and Reed's (sport). Increasing numbers of boys are gaining entry to selective state grammar schools including Tiffin and Wilson's.

Boys are welcomed into Reception at 4+ where entry is non-selective. Places are allocated on a first-come-first-served basis. Boys also join at 7+ and 8+ and other year groups (subject to availability) where entry follows a successful assessment. Boys are taught by a well-qualified staff consisting of 22 full-time and 4 part-time members, in an average class size of 18. We teach a broad curriculum, including Art, DT, Music, and Drama, in addition to sport and PE.

Cricket, rugby, football, swimming and athletics are the main sports played at the school. We have our own 20m indoor swimming pool and a state-of-the-art Sports Hall. All boys have weekly swimming and PE lessons at school with specialist staff. From Year 3, boys have two afternoons of games each week at Sunbury Cricket Club including competitive fixtures against local schools.

We encourage boys to participate in our lively music and drama departments. All junior boys join the choir, performing in local events and there are many performance opportunities in school. 12 different ensembles rehearse every week: the string orchestra, the wind band, the brass ensemble, the samba band, 3 choirs, 3 recorder groups, and 2 rock bands. 11 visiting music teachers also give weekly lessons in all orchestral instruments plus piano, guitar, singing and music theory.

To help working parents, we provide wraparound care from 7.30am to 6.00pm with an extensive range of after-school clubs, such as chess, judo, cookery, computing and music technology.

In addition to bright modern classrooms, facilities include science laboratories, music practice rooms, IT suite, library and a creative and performing arts centre which provides a 160-seat theatre and large-sized art and design technology studios. Morning and afternoon minibus services are in operation and boys are collected from and returned to various locations in the Teddington, Kingston, Richmond, Isleworth and Chiswick areas.

The Mall School prospectus is available via the website or the Headmaster's PA who manages admissions to the school.

Charitable status. The Mall School Trust is a Registered Charity, number 295003. It exists to promote and provide for the advancement of the education of children.

Maltman's Green School

Maltmans Lane, Gerrards Cross, Bucks SL9 8RR

Tel: 01753 883022
email: office@maltmansgreen.com
website: www.maltmansgreen.com
Twitter: @MaltmansGreen
Facebook: @MaltmansGreenSchool

Headmistress: **Mrs Jill Walker**, BSc Hons, PGCE, QTS, MA Ed

Age Range. 2–11.
Number of Girls. Approx. 320.
Fees per term (2021–2022). Nursery (5 mornings and 1 afternoon) £2,444 rising to £5,370 in Year 6.

Our Approach. At Maltman's Green we believe in the pursuit of excellence whilst maintaining a sense of enjoyment. Girls are inspired to do their best inside and outside of the classroom through an exceptional academic curriculum and extensive extra-curricular opportunities. We prepare girls for the modern world through a relevant, adaptable and innovative approach that is supported by a foundation of traditional values. Our girls are given every opportunity to succeed across multiple disciplines, fostering confidence and self-belief, and empowering them for whatever future awaits.

We believe that the emotional, social and physical wellbeing of our girls is paramount. By providing a personalised learning experience in an encouraging and nurturing environment, we ensure our girls feel happy, confident and valued – a perfect foundation from which children can flourish. This ethos has been recognised by the ISI who applauded our "outstanding" pastoral care.

Games and The Arts. Our sports provision is an outstanding feature of the School, with dedicated facilities and daily lessons. All girls enjoy friendly tournaments between houses and within year groups where those with the talent and inclination can progress to squad level to compete locally, regionally or nationally with exceptional results.

Music is a very important part of life at Maltman's Green. Specialist teaching, exceptional facilities and lots of choice give our girls plenty of opportunity to explore and showcase their musical talents. Many girls participate in our various choirs and we have a variety of different musical instrument lessons available as well as instrumental ensemble groups to join. Drama too has a big part to play in school life where regular performances and workshops give girls a strong sense of confidence and creative expression. Our dedicated performance space with high-quality staging, lighting, costumes and props give our shows a professional feel.

Achievements. Our girls are encouraged to be independent thinkers, to challenge themselves and to always try their best. Maltman's Green provides a firm foundation, preparing girls to face senior school and beyond with confidence, determination and a lifelong love of learning. This is reflected in our impressive 11+ results (84% qualification rate in 2021) and a record number of scholarships awarded to Independent Senior Schools. This, combined with our girls' impressive achievements across sport, music and drama affirm our position as one of the foremost prep schools in the country.

Outstanding Characteristics. 2018 marked our 100th Anniversary and, since the School was founded in 1918, we have seen numerous developments and upgrades to our facilities, including dedicated subject classrooms, a 6-lane, 25-metre indoor swimming pool, a Science Lab, STEAM lab, IT hub, Art hub, Music hub a multi-use gymnasium, a state-of-the-art theatre space and a dedicated 2–3yr olds day-care centre. We place great importance on outdoor learning and have an extensive Woodland School as well as a discovery garden and landscaped grounds that offer a secluded, peaceful and nurturing environment. This excellent suite of facilities is complemented by our highly committed, well-qualified and experienced body of staff who enable us to provide an outstanding and unique breadth of challenging opportunities for our girls.

Charitable status. Maltman's Green School Trust Limited is a Registered Charity, number 310633.

Manor Lodge School

Rectory Lane, Ridge Hill, Shenley, Hertfordshire WD7 9BG

Tel: 01707 642424
email: enquiries@manorlodgeschool.com
website: www.manorlodgeschool.com
Twitter: @manor_lodge
Facebook: @ManorLodgeSchool
Instagram: @manorlodgeschool

Chair of Governors: Mr D Arnold, MBE

Head: **Mrs Alyson Lobo**, BEd Hons

Age Range. 3–11.

Number of Pupils. Nursery (age 3) 18; Infants (age 4–7) 181; Juniors (age 7–11) 222.

Fees per term (2021–2022). Nursery £3,640; Infants £3,900; Juniors £4,310.

There are three forms of 18–20 children in Reception to Year 6 inclusive. We have specialist teachers for French, PE, IT, DTECN, Art, Drama, Science (Years 5 & 6), and Music, as well as numerous instrumental teachers for piano, brass, woodwind, percussion and strings. All staff are fully qualified.

The main school building consists of an 18th century manor house with classrooms, a new Modern Foreign Languages section as well as a stunning new building dedicated specifically to STEAM subjects. There is also a building housing further classrooms for Year 6 and a sports hall/theatre provides additional space for sports, music and the performing arts.

The cottage at the end of the drive, houses our Nursery. The children must be siblings of pupils in the main school and are eligible to attend from the term in which they turn three.

Our classrooms are bright and well-equipped and the standard of work displayed is very high. We aim to provide excellent teaching and learning opportunities within a caring environment in which high standards of behaviour and good manners are encouraged and expected. We thus ensure that all pupils achieve their full potential and are prepared for entry to senior schools, both independent and state.

Music plays an important part in the life of the school. There are several choirs, an orchestra, jazz band and various ensembles and almost half the children in school learn an instrument. Music is of course linked to our Drama activities. Reception to Year 5 children take part in at least two performances a year, and in Year 6 the children all take part in the much anticipated Year 6 production. Art is of a particularly high standard and the children use a variety of media, producing excellent original work. We strongly believe in children being allowed a childhood and with this in mind, have created an all-weather Outdoor Learning area and will endeavour to create an environment that makes it simple to integrate traditional learning with an outdoor space. Our aim is to create physical spaces where students are able to develop key concepts that help meet their wellbeing needs as well as promote our ethos of a classroom without walls, leading children to understand that learning can come from any environment. The twelve acres of grounds also include pitches, an all-weather court and play areas with climbing activity equipment and other outdoor toys. The children are offered a wide range of sporting activities including football, rugby, hockey, cricket, netball, rounders, swimming and athletics.

Our caterers provide a delicious selection of fresh, healthy lunches and cater for a number of dietary requirements.

Extra activities available at the school include chess, drama and ju-jitsu. There are numerous clubs run by the staff after school until 4.30pm, for example, cooking, football, rugby, cricket, netball, dance, athletics and choir.

Charitable status. Manor Lodge School is a Registered Charity, number 1048874. The school exists to provide an education which will maximise the potential of the girls and boys in our care.

The Manor Preparatory School

Faringdon Road, Abingdon, Oxon OX13 6LN

Tel: 01235 858458
email: admissions@manorprep.org
website: www.manorprep.org
Twitter: @ManorPrep
Facebook: @ManorPrepSchool

Chair of Board of Governors: Mr Shaun Forrestal

Headmaster: **Mr Alastair Thomas**, BA Hons, PGCE

Age Range. Girls and Boys 2–11.

Number of Pupils. 372 pupils: 259 girls and 113 boys

Fees per term (2021–2022). £4,690 (Reception)–£5,720 (Year 6)

'To challenge, cherish and inspire'

Recently receiving the highest grade of 'excellent' in all areas by the Independent Schools Inspectorate, The Manor Preparatory School, situated in Abingdon, Oxfordshire offers children an unrivalled start to their education.

Welcoming children aged 2–11, The Manor creates an atmosphere of happiness and warmth where every individual is actively encouraged to give their absolute best so they can reach their potential and beyond. Children are delightfully self-confident and there are many opportunities for them to shine during their time at the school.

The children's personal development is further strengthened by staff who act as outstanding role models. By offering small classes, children receive the care and attention they need to flourish. Parents constantly praise the dedicated teaching staff, noticed also in a visit from the Good Schools Guide – 'There are far more people at The Manor that go the extra mile for every child than in other schools' (read the whole review at www.manorprep.org).

The school has an excellent record in ensuring leavers move on to the next school that is perfectly suited to each individual. Scholarships, awards and exhibitions feature highly in all areas. Aside from a wealth of enviable achievements academically, on the sports field and in creative and performing arts, the outstanding pastoral care is renowned for preparing children for life and not just for secondary school.

Beyond a stimulating start to school life, The Manor recognises that many parents are juggling busy lives and so offers fully flexible wraparound care which parents are able to change on a daily basis. Making the school easily accessible, children in Reception and beyond can take advantage of the Minibuses that run daily and have a dedicated supervisor on board. The in-bus supervisors really get to know the children and ensure a smooth and stress-free start and end to the day.

The school is very proud of the exceptionally happy, creative and colourful journey offered to the children. Come and see for yourself and learn how each child is challenged, cherished and inspired. To arrange a tour, please email Mrs Nicole Burroughs at admissions@manorprep.org or call 01235 858462.

The Marist School – Preparatory Phase

Kings Road, Sunninghill, Ascot, Berkshire SL5 7PS

Tel: 01344 624291
email: marketing@themarist.com
website: www.themarist.com
Twitter: @TheMaristSchool
Facebook: @TheMaristSchool
Instagram: @themaristschool

Independent Day School for Girls aged 2–11 and Boys aged 2–4.

Chair of Governors: Mrs Ann Nash

Principal: Mrs Joanne Smith

Vice Principal Preparatory Phase: **Mrs Jane Gow**, BEd Hons Twickenham, MA Reading, CCRS, NPQH

Age Range. 2–11.
Number of Pupils. 164 pupils.
Fees per term (2021–2022). £3,520 (Nursery & Reception), £4,040 (Years 1–2), £4,515 (Years 3–6).

Mission Statement. The school mission statement "Living life in all its fullness", seeks to realise the unique potential of each student rooted in our core Marist values: Simplicity, Love of Work, Presence, Family Spirit and In Mary's Way.

Statement of Aims
- Create a distinctive and vibrant community that promotes academic excellence within an ethos of strong values.
- Create confident, happy young adults ready for success.
- Provide an environment where pupils develop the voice to challenge misconceptions and the confidence to shape the world in which they live.
- Provide a broad and balanced curriculum which develops a life-long love of learning and a commitment to aspirational goals.

This is in line with the overall ethos of The Marist order which has a worldwide presence, providing a truly international dimension to a child's education.

The Marist Preparatory Phase is a thriving community of pupils, parents and staff, working together to provide an environment where each child is encouraged to make their mark on the world.

Our school values, based on Catholic tradition and The Marist Way, permeate every aspect of school life leading to an education that puts children firmly at its centre and builds meaningful, respectful, and authentic relationships between everyone.

Our approach encourages each child to engage with the world using their curiosity and creativity, to express their views and feelings with confidence, and to develop a life-long love of learning.

The Marist School consists of four phases – Early Years, Preparatory, Senior and Sixth Form – which are all on the same campus. *For further details, please see The Marist School – Senior Phase entry in the GSA section.*

Charitable status. The Marist School is a Registered Charity, number 225485. The principal aims and activities of The Marist School are religious and charitable and specifically to provide education by way of an independent day school for girls between the ages of 2 and 18 and boys aged 2–4.

Marlston House School

Hermitage, Newbury, Berkshire RG18 9UL

Tel: 01635 200293
email: registrar@brockmarl.org
website: www.brockmarl.org.uk

Headmaster: **Mr D J W Fleming**, MA Oxon, MSc

Age Range. 3–13.
Number of Girls. 105 Girls (including 14 Boarders).
Fees per term (2021–2022). Full Boarding £9,000, Day £3,900–£6,500. International Boarders £9,250.

Established in 1995, Marlston House is situated in 500 acres of its own grounds in countryside of outstanding beauty, only four miles from access to the M4. The school is situated beside Brockhurst Boys' Preparatory school and occupies separate listed buildings. Boys and girls are taught separately, but the two schools join together for drama music and activities. In this way Brockhurst and Marlston House combine the best features of the single-sex and co-educational systems: academic excellence and social interaction. The schools are proud of the high standard of pastoral care established within a family atmosphere. (*See also entry for Brockhurst School.*)

The Pre-Prep School, Ridge House, is a co-educational department of Brockhurst and Marlston House Schools for children aged 3–6 years, and is situated on the same site in new self-contained, purpose-designed accommodation.

Girls are prepared for entry to a variety of leading Independent Senior Schools through the ISEB Common Entrance and Scholarship Papers at 11+ and 13+.

All girls play Netball (outdoor and indoor courts), Hockey, Rounders and Tennis (outdoor and indoor courts) and take part in Athletics, Cross Country and Swimming (25m indoor heated pool). Additional activities include riding (own equestrian centre), fencing, judo, shooting (indoor rifle range), dance and ballet. Facilities for gymnastics and other sporting activities are provided in a purpose-built Sports Hall. Year 7 pupils make a week-long visit to a Château in France as part of their French studies.

Music and Art are important features of the curriculum and a number of girls have won scholarships and awards to senior schools in these subjects recently. The school has a dedicated Music School and professionally designed Theatre.

Transport is provided by the school to and from airports and between Newbury and Paddington stations. Pupils are accompanied by school staff to their destinations.

Mayfield Preparatory School

Sutton Road, Walsall, West Midlands WS1 2PD

Tel: 01922 624107
email: info@mayfieldprep.co.uk
website: www.mayfieldprep.co.uk
Twitter: @mayfield_prep
Facebook: @mayfieldprepschool

Administered by the Governors of Queen Mary's Schools.

Chair of Governors: Mrs J Aubrook

Headmaster: **Mr Matthew Draper**, BA, PGCE

Age Range. 2–11 Co-educational.

Number of Pupils. Day: 101 Boys, 106 Girls.

Fees per term (2021–2022). Main School £3,100; Pre-Nursery £1,860.

A co-educational day school for children aged 2 to 11+, set in a listed building with beautiful surroundings and playing fields. A purpose-built Science/Art building opened in November 2000.

The self-contained Nursery Department accepts children at 2+.

A fully qualified Staff with full-time ancillary support throughout KS1 ensures that the individual child receives maximum attention.

The main aim at Mayfield is to encourage intellectual excellence. Children experience a thorough grounding in literacy and numeracy skills.

Through stimulating courses of correctly-paced work the school specialises in the preparation of the children for Grammar and Independent School entrance examinations at 11+.

Our children achieve excellent results, but it is always borne in mind that the individual child's needs are met by matching achievement to potential. All children are expected and encouraged to develop daily in confidence and security.

We believe in a balanced curriculum, and at Mayfield practical and non-academic activities additionally provide interest and varied experiences in Sports, Art, Music, ICT, DT, Dance, Drama and Public Speaking.

Good manners are expected at all times, as well as a happy and whole-hearted participation in the life and studies offered by the school.

Merchant Taylors' Prep

Moor Farm, Sandy Lodge Road, Rickmansworth, Herts WD3 1LW

Tel: 01923 825648
email: office@mtpn.org.uk
website: www.mtpn.org.uk
Twitter: @MTSPrep
Facebook: @MerchantTaylorsPrep

Chair of Governors: Mr D Eggar

Head: **Dr Karen McNerney**, BSc Hons, PGCE, MSc, EdD

Deputy Head: Mr Tony McConnell, MA Hons, PGCE, FHA

Deputy Head: Mr Andrew Crook, BA Hons, PGCE

Age Range. 3–13.

Number of Pupils. 368 Day Boys.

Fees per annum (2021–2022). £11,648 (Nursery), £16,330 (Reception, Years 1 and 2), £17,139 (Years 3–8).

The School is located amidst 14 acres on a former farm in an idyllic park and woodland setting. The Grade II listed buildings have been stylishly converted to provide a complete and unique range of classrooms and ancillary facilities. The medieval Manor of the More, once owned by King Henry VIII and used as a palace by Cardinal Wolsey, was originally located within the grounds and provides some interesting and historical associations.

The School is divided as follows: an off-site Nursery & Reception School for children aged 3+ and 4 + based at Merchant Taylors' School; then on the Merchant Taylors' Prep School site, there is the Pre-Prep (Year 1 to Year 2) and the Prep Department (Year 3 to Year 8).

Pupils are admitted to the school after an assessment by Heads of Section. The main entry is into Nursery at 3+ when boys are admitted in the September after their third birthday. We also have a small 4+ and 7+ entry. Pupils are expected to remain until the age of thirteen. Parents of pupils at the Prep School will be given an assurance at the end of Year 5 as to whether their son will be able to progress to Merchant Taylors' School at the end of Year 8. Continuity scholarships are awarded to some pupils in the Prep School in Year 6.

Work of a high standard is expected of everyone. The curriculum is interpreted as richly as possible and includes Technology, Music, Art, Drama, Physical Education and Games. We focus on a genuinely holistic education that emphasizes values and dispositions as much as academic skills. The School has a fully-qualified and experienced staff team that complements modern teaching facilities including The Sir Christopher Harding Building for Science and Technology with two state-of-the-art laboratories, a new Art Design Technology workshop that opened in 2018, an ICT suite and a Library. A 200-seat theatre with tiered seating and a separate music school provide a Centre for the Performing Arts. A Centenary Trail and outdoor classroom accommodate a range of outdoor learning activities. A bespoke nursery school was opened in the grounds of Merchant Taylors' School in April 2008 known as The Manor. Additional classrooms were added as part of our centenary celebrations in 2010. In 2014 a new dining hall, kitchen and common room were added. In September 2016, the Reception Year joined the Nursery in The Manor to create a specialist Early Years Foundation Stage.

Swift access to London by train from nearby Moor Park Station (Metropolitan line) allows easy access to places of historical and cultural interest as well as concerts and lectures.

The school was originally founded as Christian, but children of all faiths have always been welcomed.

There is an extensive programme of extra-curricular activities in which all pupils are encouraged to take part. A key feature of the School's ethos is a strong tradition of caring, both for those within our community and for the wider community through regular charitable activities.

Rugby Football, Hockey, Association Football and Cricket are the principal team games. Athletics, Golf, Swimming, Table Tennis and other sports are also coached. The School has the benefit of a fully-equipped Sports Hall with indoor cricket nets and a floodlit AstroTurf facility.

The School has a flourishing Parents' Association which arranges social and fundraising activities, and an association for former pupils, The Old Terryers.

Charitable status. Merchant Taylors' School is a Registered Charity, number 1063740.

Micklefield School

10 Somers Road, Reigate, Surrey RH2 9DU

Tel: 01737 224212
email: office@micklefieldschool.co.uk
website: www.micklefieldschool.co.uk
Facebook: @MicklefieldSchoolReigate

Chair of the Council: Mrs J M Hamilton, LLB Hons, LLM

Headmaster: **Mr Ryan Ardé**, BA, NPQH

Bursar: Mr T Khan

Age Range. Rising 3–11.
Number of Pupils. 216 (100 boys, 116 girls).
Fees per term (2021–2022). £1,380–£4,645

'*Micklefield recognised the individuality in my twins and helped them realise their potential socially and academically.*'

'*Micklefield has helped my boys build confidence and self-esteem in a friendly and secure environment.*'

'*My children have flourished at Micklefield.*'

These quotes from current and former parents sum up the very special education offered at Micklefield School. Established in Reigate in 1910, we offer small classes, taught by qualified staff and qualified subject specialists. We cater for boys and girls from the age of rising 3 up to the age of 11, preparing them for Common Entrance and other examinations. The children enjoy academic success and have an excellent record in examinations for entrance to senior schools including Scholarship Awards.

In addition to the normal academic subjects, the curriculum includes design technology, computing, dancing, drama, French, netball, hockey, tennis, athletics, swimming,

football, rugby and cricket. The school also has its own Sports Ground within 250 yards in St Albans Road.

The children take an active part in a variety of musical and theatrical activities and excel in sports. Dramatic productions and concerts provide opportunities for everyone to display their talents. We encourage participation in drama festivals, sports fixtures, the School's orchestra and choirs. Visits to concerts, theatres and museums are organised together with residential activity holidays for the older children. After-school care is available for children from Reception age.

Visit the website or telephone for a prospectus on 01737 224212. Mr Ardé, the Headmaster, is always pleased to show prospective parents around by appointment.

Charitable status. Micklefield School (Reigate) Limited is a Registered Charity, number 312069. It exists to provide a first-class education for its pupils.

Millfield Prep School

Edgarley Hall, Glastonbury, Somerset BA6 8LD

Tel: 01458 832446
email: office@millfieldprep.com
website: millfieldschool.com
Twitter: @millfieldprep
Facebook: @millfieldprep

Chair of Governors: Mr Roland Rudd

Head: **Mr Dan Thornburn**, BA Hons, FCMI, MEd

Tutor for Admissions: Mrs Fiona Gordon

Age Range. 2–13.
Number of Pupils. 462; 245 Boys and 217 Girls
Fees per term (2021–2022). Prep: Full and Weekly Boarding £10,085; Day £3,825–£6,615; Flexi Boarding £1,170 (2 nights); £1,750 (3 nights); £2,335 (4 nights). Occasional boarding: £63 per night. Pre-prep: Day £3,010.

The school is administered by the same Board of Governors and on the same principles of small-group teaching as Millfield (made possible by a staff to pupil ratio of approximately 1:8) which ensures breadth and flexibility of timetable. It has its own attractive grounds of 185 acres some four miles from the Senior School, and its extensive facilities include games fields, art, design and technology centre, drama hall, music school, science laboratories, sports hall, AstroTurf, gymnasium, golf course, tennis courts, squash courts, sport pavilion, equestrian centre, 25-metre indoor swimming pool, three IT laboratories and chapel. The pupils also have access to some of the specialist facilities at Millfield including a water-based astro, Olympic-sized swimming pool, tartan athletics track and indoor tennis centre.

Small class sizes allow the individual pupil to be taught at his or her most appropriate pace. The range of ability within the school is comprehensive and setting caters for both the academically gifted and those requiring additional learning support. The curriculum is broadly based and provides a balance between the usual academic subjects and the arts. Junior pupils study French and in Year 6 there is a choice of Spanish or French, plus a taster in Latin for more able pupils. In Years 7 and 8 there is a choice of French, Spanish and Latin. Children may choose either one or two foreign languages, dependent on ability. Pupils are also given a choice of extra-curricular languages which vary depending on demand. Science is taught throughout the school and as three separate subjects from the age of 10.

There is a full games programme organised by qualified teachers of physical education, with the help of other staff. The programme includes Athletics, Basketball, Climbing, Cross Country, Cricket, Fencing, Football, Golf, Hockey, Netball, Riding, Rugby, Sailing, Squash, Swimming, Tennis, Outdoor Pursuits and Multi-Sports to name but a few. Over 70 different clubs are available.

Within Music the offering includes multiple Choirs and Orchestras, Wind Band and an exciting and ever-expanding range of ensembles, ranging from rock bands and brass bands to percussion ensembles and a guitar group. Over 250 pupils learn at least one musical instrument. There are regular opportunities for performance and all pupils are coached in performance and presentation skills. Highlight events include themed large ensemble evenings such as the annual Rock and Pop Concert, Summer Concert, Saturday morning breakfast masterclasses with visiting international artists and the whole school House Singing competition.

Admission usually depends on interview, assessment and reports from the previous school. A number of Academic, Art, Music and Sports Scholarships are awarded each year for entry into Years 6, 7 and 8. Applications for scholarships from good all-rounders: boys and girls who have reached a good standard academically and show promise in specific areas such as Art, Music or Sport are also welcomed.

There are five boarding houses for pupils aged 7 years and above (three for boys and two for girls). Each house is under the care of resident house parents and assistant house parents. The Medical Centre is staffed by three qualified nurses, a physiotherapist, and the School Doctor attends daily.

Charitable status. Millfield is a Registered Charity, number 310283. The Millfield Schools provide a broad and balanced education to boys and girls from widely differing backgrounds, including a significant number with learning difficulties, and many for whom boarding is necessary.

Milton Keynes Preparatory School

Tattenhoe Lane, Milton Keynes, Buckinghamshire MK3 7EG

Tel: 01908 642111
email: info@mkps.co.uk
website: www.mkps.co.uk
Twitter: @prep_mk
Facebook: @mkprepschool

Chairman of the Governors: Mr David Pye, BA Hons, Cert Ed, MA Ed Dist, HETC, SEDA III, FRSA

Proprietor/Principal: Mrs Hilary Pauley, BEd

Headmaster: Mr Simon Driver, BA, PGCE, QTS

Deputy Head: Mrs Katherine Foulger, BA Hons, PGCE, QTS

Age Range. Nursery 2 months – 3 years. Pre-Prep Department 3–7 years. Preparatory Department 8–11 years.

Number of Pupils. 330 Day Pupils.

Fees (2021–2022). Nursery (per week) £107 (2 mornings)–£302 (5 days). Pre-Preparatory Department (per term): £1,460–£4,280 (2–5 years), £4,380 (6–7 years). Preparatory Department (per term): £4,928 current pupils (8–11 years), £5,300 new pupils (10–11 years).

Milton Keynes Preparatory School is a well-established school, with two other schools in the group, both in Milton Keynes: one is a Preparatory School for children of 2 months to 11 years and one is a Pre-Preparatory school for children of 2 months to 4+ years.

Opening hours are 7.30am to 6.30pm for a 35-week academic year and an extra 11 weeks in school holidays, enabling pupils to join play schemes and to be cared for outside normal core school hours.

Staff are highly qualified and committed to delivering the very best teaching and levels of care. Academic standards are "excellent", as identified in recent inspections, with pupils being prepared for entry to senior independent schools locally and nationally and to local grammar schools. Teaching is structured to take into account, and extend, the requirements of the National Curriculum, with constant evaluation and assessment for each pupil. Scholarships are offered from Year 3 for those with excellent academic and sporting abilities.

Housed in purpose-built accommodation, specialist facilities include a CTS suite, a Music Technology studio, Sports Hall and AstroTurf courts, Science Laboratory, Design and Technology workshop and a large Art studio.

The Nursery and Pre-Preparatory Department have extended artificial grass gardens to enable year-round outdoor learning and activities.

The Environmental Studies Centre provides a state-of-the-art outdoor learning resource room and extensive outside areas for gardening and wildlife. There is a large Music and Drama Studio and a Fitness Room.

Music and Sport play an important part in the life of the school. Concerts are held, and a wide variety of sport is played, with teams competing regularly against other schools. A broad range of extra-curricular activities is offered in the Preparatory and Pre-Preparatory Departments.

The school aims to incorporate the best of modern teaching methods and traditional values in a nurturing and busy environment, where good work habits and a concern for the needs of others are paramount.

Monkton Prep School

Combe Down, Bath BA2 7ET

Tel: 01225 831200
email: mpsadmissions@monkton.org.uk
website: www.monktoncombeschool.com
Twitter: @monkton
Facebook: @MonktonCombeSchool

Chair of Governors: Prof. H Langton, RGN, RSCN, RCNT, RNT, BA Hons, MSc

Principal: Mr C Wheeler, BA Dunelm, PGCE, FRSA

Head of Prep: **Mrs C Winchcombe**, BEd Hons, MA Ed

Age Range. 2–13.

Number of Pupils. Boarders 49, Day 220

Monkton Prep School, for children aged 2–13, is a small school with a big heart. It's built on strong relationships, a Christian foundation and a culture of care designed to give each child a sense of belonging and firm roots from which to build and grow.

We are a school that celebrates childhood, where children are nurtured and cared for. Our staff forge close relationships with each child, and each parent, gaining insight and understanding to provide outstanding learning and pastoral care.

The School has a strong musical tradition and flourishing Art and DT Departments. There are numerous choirs, an orchestra, a band and various other instrumental groups. Drama also plays an important part in school life.

Rugby, Hockey and Cricket are the major boys' games; Netball, Hockey and Rounders are the major girls' games. All pupils take part in Gymnastics, Swimming, Athletics and Cross-Country. Squash, Badminton, Dance and football are also available. There is a full programme of matches. All pupils take part in a variety of hobbies and activities sessions which include gardening, cross-country running, cookery, gymnastics and fun science to name but a few.

Boys and Girls are prepared for Scholarship exams to Independent Senior Schools. At least three-quarters of them proceed to Monkton Senior School and the rest to a wide range of other Independent Senior Schools.

Over the years Monkton has educated many children from families who are working overseas, especially HM Forces families. We make special arrangements for them and are well used to meeting their various needs.

Site and Facilities. The School has full flexi-boarding arrangements that cater for both boys and girls from the age of 7. It stands in its own grounds on a magnificent site with the city of Bath on one side and the Midford Valley on the other. The buildings include a modern classroom block, a theatre for drama and music with 12 music practice rooms, a sports hall, an indoor 25-metre pool, science laboratories and dance studio. The Coates Building incorporates an art studio, design technology workshop, a learning resource centre, seminar room and ICT suite. There are 20 acres of grounds, 3 all-weather netball courts, extensive playing fields as well as an all-weather hockey pitch.

Fees per term (2021–2022). Kindergarten–Year 2 £3,407–£3,504; Years 3–8 (Day): £4,115–£5,995; Years 3–8 (Boarding) £7,650–£8,640.

There are reductions in fees for the children of clergy and HM Forces.

Monmouth Prep School

The Grange, Hadnock Road, Monmouth NP25 3NG

Tel:	01600 732426
	01600 732382
email:	prep.enquiries@habsmonmouth.org
	prep.admissions@habsmonmouth.org
website:	www.habsmonmouth.org/prep
Twitter:	@Habsmonmouth
Facebook:	@Habsmonmouth
LinkedIn:	/haberdashers'-monmouth-schools

Foundation Bursar: Mrs T Norgrove, MBA

Principal: Mr J Murphy-O'Connor, MA Oxon, PGCE

Director of Boarding: Mr A Peace, BSc

Head: **Mr N Shaw**, MA

Deputy Heads:
Mrs K Kirman, BSc
Mr T Evans, BA, PGCE

Nursery to Year 2:
Mrs J Cameron
Mrs S Chowns, BA
Mrs K Davies, BA
Mrs A Lewis, BEd
Mrs S Reynolds, BEd
Mrs L Shepherd, BA
Mrs V Taylor, BA

Mrs L Partridge, BA
Miss N Price, BEd
Miss R Forester-Bennett, BA
Mrs H Rees BA, PGCE
Mrs S Ridyard, BEd, MA Ed
Mrs A Roskilly-Green, BA PGCE

Years 3–6:
Mrs S Beaumont, BA, PGCE
Mrs A Copley, BHEd
M K Fradd, BSc
Mrs A Griffiths, BA
M S Holmes, BEd
Mrs S George, BA, PGCE
Dr T Murcott, BSc, PhD
Mr D Murray, MA

Miss R Sanderson, PGCE
Mr K Shepherd, BA
Mr F Somerset-Norris, BA, PGCE, MSc
Mr C Stonier, BSc
Mrs A Taylor, LRSC, PGCE
Dr S Wall, BSc, PhD
Mr J Walton, BMus

Age Range. 3–11.

Number of Pupils. 240 (boys and girls).

Fees per term (2021–2022). Day £2,648–£3,881, Boarding (Years 3–6) £6,999.

Monmouth Prep School is fully co-educational and welcomes day and boarding pupils aged 3–11, where we focus on developing enthusiastic, inquisitive, resilient girls and boys with high aspirations.

A child's educational journey at Haberdashers' Monmouth Schools begins at Monmouth Prep School, where boys and girls thrive and flourish with inspired and engaging subject-specialist teaching delivered across two sites.

Based at Agincourt, a delightful old rectory set in picturesque grounds, children in Nursery to Year 2 enjoy the beautiful, open spaces for learning and enrichment activities.

The Grange is modern and home to pupils from Years 3 to 6 where enhanced outside areas combine to create a dynamic and engaging space for children aged 7 to 11.

Pupils at Monmouth Prep School make the most of the outstanding facilities for science, languages, music, culture, sports and dance on offer across our family of schools.

Girls and boys immerse themselves in a breadth and range of educational opportunities, trips and expeditions, social and co-curricular events and shared community projects.

Children are motivated to learn with a sense of fun, enjoyment and excitement, both in and out of the classroom.

Carefully planned and coordinated, the curriculum focuses on developing enthusiastic, inquisitive and resilient boys and girls and provide a strong bedrock for learning across the whole of our integrated prep school.

Boarding, from the age of 7, creates a real sense of community throughout the school, where children thrive in a safe and friendly environment.

We will provide additional support for pupils who need it, confident that your child will flourish to their full potential.

There is a sense that anything is possible for children at Monmouth Prep School, ensuring a confident step up to the senior school.

Aims. We aim to provide an excellent education as the foundation for future achievement and to develop personal qualities of confidence, independence and social conscience.

Location. Nursery to Year 2 are based at Agincourt, a delightful old rectory set in picturesque grounds with beautiful, open spaces for learning and enrichment activities. Years 3 to 6 are based at modern premises at The Grange, next to Monmouth Schools Sports Club with its own 25-metre swimming pool, indoor sports hall and an all-weather pitch, with enhanced outside areas.

Facilities. We have well-equipped classrooms, hall, library, art studio, science laboratory, computer suite, music room and music studios. We have kitchens and the grounds provide a safe, spacious area for recreation, games and outdoor projects. In addition, we share the facilities of Monmouth School for Boys and Monmouth School for Girls, including the School Chapel, large playing fields, sports complex, gymnasium, artificial pitches, sports pavilion, drama studio, Performing Arts Centre and our professional theatre, The Blake Theatre.

Curriculum. Our curriculum is broad and varied and takes account of, though is not constrained by, the National Curriculum. We teach English, mathematics, science, Latin, humanities, information and communication technology and computing, history, geography, religious education, art, design technology, music, physical education, games, drama, French and study skills.

Extra-curricular Activities. We have a full programme of activities that take place both in the lunch break and after school. This includes hockey, rugby, netball, gymnastics, football, cricket, tennis, swimming, golf, karate, cross-country running, string orchestra, wind band, choir, fencing, art, gardening, computing and chess.

Entry is usually at 7+ following assessment, though recruitment is currently across all year groups.

We award a number of scholarships each year to pupils moving on to our senior schools. Various scholarships are available for girls and boys joining in Year 7 (11+) and Year 9 (13+) and applications are open for all candidates, whether boarders or day pupils. Scholarship allocation is based on entrance results, an interview, an audition or trial, and a clear display of outstanding potential. (For further details,

see Monmouth School for Boys and Monmouth School for Girls entries).

Charitable status. William Jones's Schools Foundation is a Registered Charity, number 525616. Its aims and objectives are to provide an all-round education for girls and boys at reasonable fees.

Moor Park School

Richard's Castle, Ludlow, Shropshire SY8 4DZ

Tel: 01584 876061
email: registrar@moorpark.org.uk
website: www.moorpark.org.uk
Twitter: @moorparkludlow
Facebook: @MoorParkSchool

Chairman of Governors: Julian Rogers-Coltman

Headmaster: **Mr Charlie Minogue**

Deputy Head: M. J-M Collin

Age Range. 3 months to 13 years.

Number of Pupils. 215.

Fees per term (2021–2022). Boarding £7,700–£9,225, Day £2,225–£6,215.

Founded in 1964, Moor Park is an IAPS, Catholic, co-educational boarding and day school accepting children from 3 months to 13 years of age. A family atmosphere pervades, resulting in happy, rounded and grounded children.

Children often start at Moor Park in the Tick Tock Nursery (from 3 months), which provides a secure environment for our very youngest children. The Nursery is located at the heart of the school and has been rated 'Outstanding' in all areas (Ofsted 2019). The learning environment (inside and outside) is maximised to allow real potential for exploration and creativity. The children transfer to the Pre-Prep Kindergarten in the term that they turn 3, where they are carefully prepared to start more formal schooling by a team of well-qualified and caring staff.

All our children make full use of the 85 acres of stunning grounds, but Moor Park is not just about getting muddy and exploring. Our schemes of work and teaching methods from Nursery to Year 8 have been designed to deliberately encourage the thinking skills, as well as the knowledge, that young people will need in a fast-changing world. Creativity, curiosity, critical thought, confidence, independence, and resilience are all deliberately fostered, and the results are plain to see. In the last five years, 118 leavers have won a total of 98 scholarships to senior schools, and this from a non-selective intake. Being a truly independent school has helped our children gain entry to the full range of schools nationally, and these scholarships include academic and extra-curricular awards to some of the top senior schools in the country.

It is also worth saying that Moor Park is emphatically not simply an academic hothouse and is a school where children of all abilities thrive. All of this is underpinned by a carefully maintained culture of kindness which ensures that all children are valued for who they are. Passionate teachers and an average class size of around 14 also make a difference, with specialist staff offering extra-curricular activities throughout the school.

Not every child can be good at everything but every child can be good at something and finding that something for every child we take seriously. Moor Park's facilities and, more importantly, enthusiastic and dedicated staff ensure that the school is well placed to get the best out of every child.

We have recently been shortlisted in the 2021 Independent Schools of the Year Prep School category and feature in the Tatler and Talk Education's top schools. We were rated 'Excellent' in all areas in our last inspection (ISI 2019).

Charitable status. Moor Park School is a Registered Charity, number 511800, which exists to provide education for young people.

Moorfield School

Wharfedale Lodge, 11 Ben Rhydding Road, Ilkley, West Yorkshire LS29 8RL

Tel: 01943 607285
email: enquiries@moorfieldschool.co.uk
website: www.moorfieldschool.co.uk
Twitter: @MoorfieldIlkley
Facebook: @MoorfieldSchoolIlkley

Moorfield is an Education Charitable Trust and the Headmistress is a member of IAPS.

Chairman of Governors: Mr Martin Alton

Head: Mrs Tina Herbert

Bursar: Mr Ian Findlay

Admissions Secretary: Mrs Debbie Firth

Age Range. 2–11 Co-educational.
Number of Pupils 108 Girls and Boys.
Fees per term (2021–2022). Nursery £27.00 per session; Main School £3,465 including lunch.
Staff: 8 full-time, 18 part-time.
Religious affiliation: Interdenominational.

Excellence in Education inspiring Kindness, Confidence & Creativity

Moorfield School is situated in a beautiful setting on the edge of Ilkley Moor. It prides itself in providing inspirational teaching within a giving and caring school. Independence and individuality are encouraged and confidence nurtured. The whole child is important and we work together to grow hearts, minds and strength of character.

Our child-led approach to teaching and learning from ages 2 to 6 is unique and results show that children at the end of Reception (90%) are way above the national average (67%) across the curriculum.

Further up the school, high standards in English and Maths are the bedrock of academic success enabling all our pupils to get into their secondary school of choice. Outstanding teaching from a vibrant staff gives pupils confidence to succeed in all subjects. With specialist teaching in many subjects, pupils are given the opportunity to develop skills and interests in Computer Science, Drama, Music and Sport, Art, Cookery and Bushcraft.

Support for working parents is provided by offering wrap-around care in term time from 7.45am to 6.15pm and throughout school holidays from 8.00am to 4.00pm.

Pupils leave Moorfield with a secure foundation of learning, a strong work ethic and the confidence to be successful.

Moorfield is recommended by *The Good Schools Guide*.

Charitable status. Moorfield School Ltd is a Registered Charity, number 529112.

Moorlands School

Foxhill Drive, Weetwood Lane, Leeds LS16 5PF

Tel: 0113 278 5286
email: info@moorlands-school.co.uk
website: www.moorlands-school.co.uk
Twitter: @MoorlandsHead
Facebook: @MoorlandsLeeds

Headteacher: **Jacqueline Atkinson**, GMus Hons, PGCE, MEd

Age Range. 2–11 Co-educational.
Number of Pupils. 144 Day Boys and Girls.

Founded in 1898, Moorlands is the oldest prep school in Leeds and is dedicated to providing a first-class education for girls and boys aged 2 to 11 years in a warm, friendly environment.

The school is conveniently located off the Ring Road at Weetwood Lane, yet sat in beautiful grounds providing all the outdoor space required for children to play in a safe and secure environment. The school boasts fantastic wrap-around care facilities, excellent teaching standards, an on-site swimming pool and small class sizes.

Our membership of the Methodist Independent Schools' Trust enables us to deliver outstanding value for money. Unlike many other schools, our inclusive fees, for children in Reception (starting the term after they turn 5) to Year 6, includes:

- Supervised breakfast club from 7.30am, after-school care and a sandwich tea from 5pm–6pm.

- Educational day visits, which form part of the learning experience on the curriculum.

- The choice of around 20 'free to attend' clubs, which take place between 4pm and 5pm.

- Regular learning support sessions, for those pupils who would benefit from it.

- For KS1 and KS2, regular bushcraft sessions, held within our extensive grounds and taught by specialists.

- For Reception, Forest Schools lessons held within the EYFS woodland area of the school grounds.

- Weekly swimming lessons, held onsite in our indoor pool, with qualified instructors.

- Specialist teaching in Music, Drama, Modern Foreign Languages, Sport and Art.

The aim of the school is to develop the full potential of every child within a happy and caring environment fostered by small classes and the professional skills of a highly qualified staff. Strong links between the parents and the school are encouraged to facilitate the provision of an effective education.

Admission is by assessment and observation. Pupils are accepted at 2 years old for entry into the Nursery and are expected to progress through the school in preparation for entry to senior independent day and boarding schools. The school has a well-developed specialist facility to provide assistance to pupils with any learning issue such as dyslexia or to gifted children.

Blended with this traditional core of academic work is offered a comprehensive range of sporting activities, outdoor education and a wide range of musical and extra-curricular pursuits.

At Moorlands, we have a simple yet beautiful motto, 'Intrepide', or 'be brave'! In school, we talk about how being brave or intrepid takes many forms. Being brave isn't always a grand gesture; sometimes it simply means 'having a go', such as attempting that difficult question, offering an answer in class when you're not quite sure or trying something new. This culture of intrepidness allows children to try new things in a safe, nurturing and stimulating environment.

Religious affiliation: Methodist.

Fees per term (2021–2022). EY £3,210, Reception £3,350, Years 1–2 £3,390 (lunch £210), Years 3–4 £3,765, Years 5–6 £3,790 (lunch £230)

Charitable status. Moorlands School is a Registered Charity, number 529216. It exists to provide children with the finest education possible, using the best resources in an environment of care.

Moulsford Preparatory School

Moulsford-on-Thames, Wallingford, Oxfordshire OX10 9HR

Tel: 01491 651438
email: heads.pa@moulsford.com
website: www.moulsford.com
Twitter: @Moulsford
Facebook: @Moulsford
Instagram: @moulsford

The School is a Charitable Trust controlled by a Board of Governors.

Chairman of the Board of Governors: Mr E L A Boddington

Headmaster: **B Beardmore-Gray**, BA Hons, QTS

Age Range. 4–13.
Number of Boys. 41 Weekly/Flexi Boarders, 318 Day Boys.
Fees per term (2021–2022). Day Boys £4,200–£6,275, Weekly Boarders £7,850. These fees are all inclusive, but individual coaching in music, judo, golf and fencing is charged as an extra.

The School has its own river frontage on the Thames, spacious games fields and lawns and is situated between Wallingford and Reading.

Boys are prepared for the Common Entrance and Scholarship examinations to the top independent schools in the country. An experienced and well qualified staff ensures that a high standard is achieved academically, musically, artistically and on the games field.

The principal games are rugby football, soccer, tennis and cricket. Other sporting activities include athletics, swimming, sailing, judo, golf and gymnastics. The school is proud of its fine academic and sporting reputation which has been built up over many years.

Charitable status. Moulsford Preparatory School is a Registered Charity, number 309643.

Naima Jewish Prep School

21 Andover Place, London NW6 5ED

Tel: 020 7328 2802
email: secretary@naimajps.co.uk
website: www.naimajps.org.uk

Chair of Governors: Mr Julian Levy

Headmaster: **Mr J W Pratt**, GRSM Hons, CertEd

Age Range. 2–11 Co-educational.
Number of Pupils. 152 girls and boys.
Fees per term (2021–2022). £4,005–£4,720.

Naima JPS is centred on the belief that an excellent secular education and strong Jewish grounding are mutually attainable. As such, our twin goals merge as we aspire to prepare our children for a successful life in society imbued with Torah values. We aim to provide a secular education on a par with the top national private schools with a curriculum that extends beyond the minimum guidelines provided by the National Curriculum. As a private school, we provide both the environment and teaching resources to monitor each individual, and to help children of all abilities to reach their full potential.

Naima JPS challenges all children, together with their parents, no matter what their level of religious observance, to pursue ongoing spiritual growth as individuals. We encourage children on their journey to spiritual maturity in a harmonious and nurturing community environment of tolerance, respect and care for one another.

The school has a one-form entry. Given that class sizes seldom exceed 22 and the favourable ratio of teachers and assistants to children – as little as 1:5 depending on the age and need – programmes of learning have the flexibility for differentiation. The school has a high number of particularly able children with specific intellectual gifts.

During the crucial early years at school it is important that children define themselves by things they can do well. Self-esteem, that essential by-product of success, empowers strength and gifts. Once children understand how their minds work, as they learn in many different ways, they can feel comfortable about entering any environment and mastering it. Children who truly understand, value and like themselves are better equipped to flourish and embrace fresh challenges. Confidence through success contributes to strong identities that welcome new horizons. Resiliency, discovery, independence and spiritual maturity are nurtured at all levels. At Naima JPS education is not about coveting garlands for the few, but ensuring that all children reach their full potential.

Charitable status. Naima JPS is a Registered Charity, number 289066.

The New Beacon

Brittains Lane, Sevenoaks, Kent TN13 2PB

Tel: 01732 452131
email: admin@newbeacon.org.uk
website: www.newbeacon.org.uk

Chairman of the Governors: Mr James Thorne

Headmaster: **Michael Piercy**, BA Hons

Age Range. Rising 3–13.

Number of Boys. 325 Boys (Girls in nursery only). Predominantly Day Pupils, but flexi boarding is available from Monday to Thursday.

Fees per term (2021–2022). £3,995–£5,750. Fees include lunches.

Boys are prepared for both grammar and senior independent schools, and enjoy considerable success at 11+ and 13+, with many achieving scholarships (including music, sport, art, design technology and drama) to a wide range of first-class senior schools.

The School divides into Senior, Middle, Junior and Nursery sections in which boys are placed according to age and ability. Initiative is encouraged by organising the School into 4 houses or 'companies'. The well-equipped main School building is complemented by several modern, purpose-built facilities: separate Pre-Prep and Junior School buildings for nursery girls and boys from rising 3, and for boys aged 4–9; a Sports Hall with modern changing facilities; a multi-purpose, AstroTurf sports pitch; a Theatre; a heated indoor Swimming Pool; a centre for Art and Music; and modern facilities for Science and Technology. Football, Rugby Union and Cricket are the major games. During the summer months Tennis and Athletics are available. Swimming and Shooting are available all year round. A very extensive range of extra-curricular activities is offered (including many interesting and exciting trips) together with a programme of pre- and after-school care. Music, sport, art and drama at the School are highly regarded.

Charitable status. The New Beacon is a Registered Charity, number 307925. It exists to provide an all-round education for girls and boys rising 3 in nursery and for boys aged 4–13.

New College School

Savile Road, Oxford OX1 3UA

Tel: 01865 285560
email: office@newcollegeschool.org
website: www.newcollegeschool.org

Governors: The Warden & Fellows of New College Oxford

Headmaster: **Dr Matthew Jenkinson**, BA Dunelm, MEd Buckingham, MSt, DPhil Oxon, FRHistS

Age Range. 4–13 years.

Number of Boys. 152 Day Boys, including 20 Choristers.

Fees per term (2021–2022). Reception £3,700, Year 1 £4,400, Years 2–4 £5,400, Years 5–8 £5,900, Choristers £2,200.

New College School was founded in 1379 when William of Wykeham made provision for the education of 16 Choristers to sing daily services in New College Chapel. Situated in the heart of the city, a few minutes' walk from the College, the school is fortunate in having the use of New College playing fields for sport and New College Chapel for school services.

The staff consists of some 22 full-time teachers and a full complement of visiting music teachers. In their final year all boys complete the Pre-Senior Baccalaureate, while there is also a separate academic scholarship form and pupils are prepared for their destination schools' entrance exams when applicable. The school broadly follows the national curriculum subjects, but also teaches French, Latin, Design Technology and Greek.

Sports, played on New College Sports Ground, include soccer, hockey, cricket, rounders, athletics and rugby. Activities include archery, art, craft, pottery, design, chess, sport, computing, drama, and science clubs. There is a Choral Society for parents.

Music plays a major part in school life with orchestra, ensembles, concert and junior choirs and form concerts, in addition to individual tuition in a wide range of instruments. An optional Saturday morning music education programme is followed by boys from Year 5 upwards.

Boys are admitted by gentle assessment to the Pre-Prep Department at 4 years and to the Prep School at 7 years. Potential Choristers are tested between the ages of 6 and 7 at annual voice trials.

Newbridge Preparatory School

51 Newbridge Crescent
Tettenhall, Wolverhampton, West Midlands WV6 0LH

Tel: 01902 751088
email: office@newbridgeprepschool.org.uk
website: www.newbridgeprepschool.org.uk

Chairman of Board: Mrs H M Hughes

Headmistress: **Mrs S Fisher**, BEd Hons

Age Range. Girls 2–11. Boys 2–7.

Number of Pupils. 147

Fees per term (2021–2022). £2,020–£3,080 including dance, recorder, drama, gym, netball, singing for various year groups.

Newbridge Preparatory School, founded in 1937, occupies a super site on the outskirts of Wolverhampton, convenient for parents travelling from Telford, Bridgnorth, Shropshire, and Stafford.

The school is divided into Lower School (Pre-Nursery–Year 2) and Upper School (Years 3–6). Upper School is housed in the main building which is a substantial house set in huge, beautiful mature gardens. There are specialist facilities in Art and Design, ICT, Science, Music and PE. The school also has netball and tennis courts.

The staff to pupil ratio is high. Specialist teaching takes place in Key Stage Two in English, Mathematics, Music, Science, French, PE, Dance and Drama. In Key Stage One: Dance, PE, Music and French.

Lower School enjoys a separate Nursery and purpose built accommodation for Pre-Nursery to Year 2. There is a multi-use sports hall.

Children with Special Needs are well supported and nurtured with 1:1 support and a SENCo.

Upper School girls take drama and dance and enter examinations. They also enter the annual local festival for Music and Drama.

The school offers a Breakfast Club (7.30 to 8.00am), an Early Club (8.00 to 8.30am), an After-School Club (3.15 to 6.00pm) and a Holiday Club (8.00am to 5.30pm).

Standards are high in all areas of the curriculum. Senior School results are excellent. Places are gained at local selective Independent and Maintained Schools but also Boarding Schools. Sporting, Academic and Speech and Drama Scholarships are attained for entrance into Senior School. Girls leave Newbridge well equipped to face the challenges of a Senior School.

Educational visits and visitors take place each term for Year 1 to Year 6. Nursery children enjoy a Forest School experience. Residential visits occur in Years 3–6. The visits vary from outdoor activities and challenges and cultural visits to London.

Emphasis is placed on traditional values, personal development and responsibility. The curriculum is very broad, including many opportunities in Sport, Dance, Drama and Music.

Our school mission statement is: *Aiming High, Building Bridges and Preparing for Life.* Our motto is: *Dare to dream it, Work to achieve it.*

Children are taught to do their best in all areas, strive for a challenge and succeed at their own level.

Emphasis is placed on self-discipline, inclusion, equal opportunity and respect.

Charitable status. Newbridge Preparatory School is a Registered Charity, number 1019682. It exists to advance the education of children by conducting the school known as Newbridge Preparatory School.

Newcastle Preparatory School

6 Eslington Road, Jesmond, Newcastle-upon-Tyne, Tyne and Wear NE2 4RH

Tel: 0191 281 1769
email: enquiries@newcastleprep.co.uk
website: www.newcastleprep.co.uk

The School was founded in 1885 and is now a Charitable Trust with a Board of Governors.

Chair of Governors: Mrs Susan Blair

Head Teacher: Ms Fiona Coleman

Deputy Head Teacher: Miss Gemma Strong

Bursar: Mrs Susan Easton

Age Range. 3–11.

Number of Pupils. 268 Day Pupils (168 boys, 100 girls).

Fees per term (2021–2022). £4,088.

The School is situated in a residential part of Newcastle with easy access from all round the area.

Newcastle Preparatory School is a fully co-educational day school for children aged 3 to 11 years. It is a warm, caring environment in which all pupils are encouraged to reach their full potential.

Children may join 'First Steps' at NPS from the age of 3 years. 'First Steps' is an exciting and colourful nursery with excellent resources and well qualified staff who look after the needs of each individual.

At age 4, children make the easy step into School where they experience many 'steps to success'.

The curriculum offered throughout school is broad and balanced so that children enjoy learning in a variety of ways. French is taught from the age of 4 with music and PE being taught by specialist teachers. As children progress through School they become independent learners, following a varied timetable and class sizes are small to provide individual attention.

Music is an important part of life at NPS. There is a choir and an orchestra.

Sporting achievements too are very good. There is a purpose-built Sports Hall and a wide range of sport is offered with extracurricular activities including rugby, football, cricket, hockey, netball, athletics, tennis and swimming.

Also there are many clubs and activities to enrich the curriculum, e.g. Drama, Dance, Chess, Philosophy, Art, ICT, Design, Food Technology and there is an effective School Council as well as a Buddy System.

Outdoor learning is offered throughout the school. In 2017 a dedicated Forest School area was opened and pupils also run a a local allotment.

The variety of opportunities ensures that the children leave NPS well equipped for an easy transition to senior school. The academic results are very good and the children receive an all-round education, so that they are confident, eager learners.

Charitable status. Newcastle Preparatory School is a Registered Charity, number 528152. It exists to provide education for boys and girls.

Newland House School

Waldegrave Park, Twickenham TW1 4TQ

Tel: 020 8865 1234
email: admissions@newlandhouse.net
website: www.newlandhouse.net
Twitter: @newlandhouse
Facebook: @Newland-House-School-Twickenham

Founded in 1897, the school was privately owned until 1971 when the Newland House School Trust was formed. It is a charitable Educational Trust with a Board of Governors.

Chairman of Governors: Mr Andrew Gumpert

Head: **Mr Chris Skelton**

Age Range. 3–13.
Number of Pupils. 267 Boys, 181 Girls.
Fees per term (2021–2022). Nursery from £2,382, Pre-Prep £4,226, Prep £4,716. Lunch is included in the Fees.

Newland House School is a co-educational day preparatory school set in a residential area on the Twickenham–Teddington border. In September 2017 the school also opened a nursery school for children aged 3 to 4. The school is ideally situated for parents in the Richmond, Kingston and Hampton areas and is very close to the river Thames.

The school currently occupies approximately 5 acres with grounds that provide sports facilities, including an all-weather pitch. The school is also fortunate to have daily access to the nearby National Physical Laboratory Sports Ground.

The school is divided into Nursery, Pre-Prep, which provides for children in Reception (EYFS) to Year 2, and Prep for children in Years 3 to 8. A new Pre-Prep school building was opened in autumn 2016 immediately adjacent to the Prep School providing an innovative and unique learning environment for pupils using leading sustainable design and the latest technology. Following the move to the new premises, the additional space has enabled the school to offer a three-form intake, with an additional 20 places available in Reception from September 2016.

The school's main intakes are at the age of 3 (Nursery) and age 4 (Reception) which are non-selective. Places may also become available in other age groups throughout the school year.

The Prep School has well-appointed, airy classrooms with a traditional feel, a large gymnasium/assembly hall, dining room, separate senior and junior libraries and two well-equipped science laboratories. There is an Art and Design Technology block, as well as a purpose-built Music block. The school has a substantial computer network, including a state-of-the-art computer suite.

The staff currently consists of 34 full-time teachers, and 10 classroom assistants, mostly in the Pre-Prep School. Children are well prepared for the Common Entrance and Scholarship examinations to Independent Schools. During the ISI Inspection in 2013, the school was found to be 'excellent' in many areas. In particular, the opportunities which the school provides for academic achievement and learning, as well as pastoral care and pupils' personal development, were clearly recognised.

There is a strong music department staffed by over 20 visiting music staff who teach a variety of instruments. There are 5 choirs, several wind and brass ensembles, 2 orchestras and a jazz band who have the opportunity to perform at a variety of external venues.

The main sports are Rugby, Football, Cricket, Netball, Hockey and Rounders. All children from the age of 7 have the opportunity to swim throughout the year. The teams take part in a range of leagues and competitions and there is an annual sports tour.

The school is committed to providing a broad and balanced curriculum and an environment that fosters enquiring minds. A wide variety of extra-curricular activities is available including, fencing, golf, chess, and badminton. The school also provides wrap-around care from 7.30am each morning and until 6pm in the evening.

Charitable status. The Newland House School Trust Limited is a Registered Charity, number 312670. It exists to promote and provide for the advancement of education for children of either sex or both sexes.

Newton Prep

149 Battersea Park Road, London SW8 4BX

Tel: 020 7720 4091
email: admin@newtonprep.co.uk
website: www.newtonprepschool.co.uk
Twitter: @NewtonPrep
Facebook: @NewtonPrepSchool

Chairman of Council: Dr Farouk Walji

Head: **Mrs A E Fleming**, BA, MA

Age Range. 3–13.
Number of Pupils. 618: 50% Boys, 50% Girls.
Fees per term (2021–2022). £3,325–£7,045.
Average size of class: <20.
The current teacher to pupil ratio is 1:11.
Religious denomination: Non-denominational.

Newton Prep is a vibrant school which offers a challenging education for inquisitive children who are eager to engage fully with the world in which they are growing up. The school aims to:

- inspire children to be adventurous and committed in their learning;
- provide balance and breadth in all aspects of a child's education: intellectual, aesthetic, physical, moral and spiritual;
- encourage initiative, individuality, independence, creativity and enquiry;
- promote responsible behaviour and respect for others in a happy, safe and caring environment.

Entry requirements. Siblings are given priority when allocating nursery places; other nursery places are awarded by lottery, while ensuring an even balance of boys and girls; children joining Reception are assessed individually: a gentle process, with offers made during October half term in the year before entry. Older children come to an assessment morning in the Spring Term (on a case-by-case basis at other times) during which they will be assessed in reading, maths and some diagnostic, age-appropriate reasoning tests. Scholarships and means-tested top-up bursaries are available in and after Year 3.

Examinations offered. All entrance examinations to senior schools, Common Entrance and scholarships at 11, 12 and 13. Children leave to go to top London day schools, with a significant minority now going up the boarding route. We pride ourselves on the quality of guidance offered by our dedicated Senior School Transfer Deputy Head and, every 2 years, we organise a Senior Schools Fair attended by over 75 schools. Throughout each school year, Heads from top public schools come for our popular Newton Forum evenings, along with an array of top-flight speakers from other fields of life: politics, the film world – even the spiritual sphere, as when the Dalai Lama hosted a children's conference at the school.

"Bright children, exceptional opportunities."

First-time visitors to the school are invariably impressed by the scale and range of the secondary-school-level facilities and by the wide open outdoor spaces enjoyed by the children on a large site so close to the centre of London. As well as the three school gyms there are two huge outdoor spaces for PE/Games and free play: behind the school, an all-weather pitch and, in front, a large, tree-fringed playground for the littler children. The school also has a large garden with a wildlife area and an activity area with a pirate boat.

Newton Prep occupies an early 20th-century elementary school building, which has been extensively remodelled internally, and behind which stands large modern extensions containing classrooms, the dining hall and kitchen, two gymnasiums, a 300-seat auditorium and a state-of-the-art recital hall (along with a recording studio and a music technology suite). The top floor of the Edwardian building provides one large general-purpose space as well as two art studios. Below are two floors of classrooms, including three collegiate-style science labs, three ICT suites and a library that is the envy of the many visiting authors, who all say it is one of the most vibrant and popular reading spaces they have come across in a school.

Despite the excellence of their education, Newton Prep children are notable for their lack of arrogance and entitlement. The kindness and generosity shown by the pupils towards their peers is remarkable and the engagement between the older children and the little ones is heartwarming, especially when it comes to inter-house events, when children up and down the school are united by their love for their house!

Newton is not a blazers and boaters kind of school. As one current parent put it, *"Newton combines a quirky nature and knowledge of families with great space and facilities ...All the teachers understand my (very different) children, the management is open to fresh ideas and the school is large enough to accommodate variety."*

Norfolk House School

4 Norfolk Road, Edgbaston, Birmingham B15 3PS

Tel:	0121 454 7021
email:	info@norfolkhouseschool.co.uk
website:	www.norfolkhouseschool.co.uk

Headmistress: **Mrs Susannah Palmer**

Age Range. 3–11.

Number in School. 154.

Fees per term (2021–2022). £2,539–£3,672.

Norfolk House School is an Independent day school, with a Christian ethos, situated in the pleasant suburb of Edgbaston and is ideally located for pupils and parents all over Birmingham and the surrounding areas.

The school aims to provide individual attention to each pupil, thus enabling each child to fulfil his or her potential. Small class sizes and favourable pupil to teacher ratios culminate in the best possible academic results. Many pupils move on to the various King Edward Schools, or to other Grammar Schools or senior Independent Schools as the direct result of the high standards achieved at Norfolk House.

The syllabus is designed to give each child a general academic education over a wide range of subjects – in line with the National Curriculum; the requirements of the Eleven Plus and the various Entrance Examinations are also taken into consideration.

A wide range of extra curricular activities and enrichment sessions ensure all the children receive a rounded education. Children are encouraged to pursue their interests, whether sporting, musical or artistic, alongside the rigorous academic work they encounter. This year, we have extended the curriculum to include the teaching of Engineering in KS2.

In addition, Norfolk House School aims to instil in each child good manners, consideration and respect for others, and recognition of personal responsibility. Norfolk House is a small school with an emphasis on caring and traditional values, yet forward thinking in outlook. It is a happy school with high attainment, competitive fees and a family atmosphere.

Norland Place School

162–166 Holland Park Avenue, London W11 4UH

Tel:	020 7603 9103
email:	registrar@norlandplace.com
website:	www.norlandplace.com

Headmaster: **Mr P Mattar**

Age Range. Girls & Boys 4–11

Number of Children. 222

Fees per term (2021–2022). £5,637–£6,265.

A thriving Preparatory School founded in 1876 and still standing on the original site in Holland Park Avenue.

Children are well-prepared for competitive London day schools and top rate boarding schools. The curriculum is balanced with an emphasis on English, Mathematics and Science. Music, Art and Games are strong. The school contains a Library in addition to specialist Music, Science and Art Rooms.

Early registration is essential.

Northbourne Park

Betteshanger, Deal, Kent CT14 0NW

Tel: 01304 611215
email: office@northbournepark.com
website: www.northbournepark.com
Twitter: @northbournepark
Facebook: @Northbourne-Park-School

Chair of Governors: Stephanie Loomis

Headmaster: **Sebastian Rees**, BA Hons, PGCE, NPQH

Age Range. Nursery–13, Co-educational.

Number of Pupils. 197 boys and girls, including 49 boarders.

Northbourne Park is a co-educational day and boarding school set in 100 acres of beautiful park and woodland in rural Kent, close to Canterbury and within easy reach of central London, Eurostar and Gatwick Airport.

We provide children with a first-class education focusing on the individual needs of every child, inspiring them to succeed across a wide range of learning experiences. We offer each child the freedom and space, together with countless opportunities, to grow in confidence and succeed.

Academic. From the Nursery and Pre-Prep through to the Prep School all our pupils gain confidence in their learning, and through inspirational teaching from dedicated staff, the pupils adapt well to an engaging and stimulating curriculum with a real sense of achievement. Although non-selective, we consistently achieve 100% pass rate in examinations – entry to top Independent Senior and local Grammar schools, LAMDA and the Associated Board of the Royal Schools of Music. Many of our pupils gain scholarships to prestigious Senior Schools.

Northbourne Park's unique Language Programme helps every child develop foreign languages in an integrated learning environment. French is introduced at 3 years and we have a unique Bilingual programme for French pupils joining Years 7 and 8 who study the French academic curriculum. The result is a clear advantage when they move on to Senior Schools.

Sport. We are passionate about sport and through an excellent sports programme the pupils develop key skills and learn the importance of teamwork and leadership. There are many opportunities to try a variety of sports from the traditional to the more diverse such as archery and trampolining. The school has recently installed a new all-weather sports pitch with floodlighting.

Creative Arts. We nurture a love for all the Arts. Many pupils learn one or more instrument in our purpose-built Music suite. They have the opportunity to take part in the choir, band, orchestra, string and brass groups performing regularly within the school and the local area. Other opportunities include LAMDA lessons, regular drama productions and Public Speaking that ensure pupils are articulate and confident in their performances. Artistic talents are encouraged through a range of media including sculpture, costume design, film-making on iMacs and pottery.

Community. Pupils are provided with a first-rate level of pastoral care in safe and nurturing surroundings with a real family atmosphere. Our welcoming boarding community provides a home-from-home environment and a continuous boarding service at weekends throughout the term. Boarders enjoy regular excursions and activities, and the accompanied services to London and Paris provide opportunities for weekends at home.

Extracurricular. We provide the pupils with a fun and extensive programme of clubs that help develop their interests and skills in hobbies that can endure long into adult life. Love of the outdoors and respect for the environment begins in the Pre-Prep and develops through into the Prep School with fun physical adventures. Whether they are playing in the woods, camping out overnight or following our pioneering Outdoor Education Programme, children love Northbourne Park life.

Fees per term (2021–2022). Boarders: £7,278 (weekly), £8,427 (full); French Programme £8,838. Day Pupils: £3,035–£3,696 (Pre-Prep), £4,306–£5,782 (Years 3–8), Flexi 3-night package £6,908. Fees include customary extras and many extracurricular activities. We offer bursaries and a wide range of scholarships. Sibling, HM Forces and Clergy discounts are generous and popular.

Charitable status. Northbourne Park is a Registered Charity, number 280048.

Norwich School, The Lower School

30 Bishopgate, Norwich, Norfolk NR1 4AA

Tel: 01603 728485
email: admissions@norwich-school.org.uk
website: www.norwich-school.org.uk

Chairman of Governors: P J E Smith, MA, FIA

Head of the Lower School: **J K Ingham**, BA

Age Range. 4–11.

Number of Pupils. 245.

Fees per term (2021–2022). £4,063–£5,460

The Lower School is the Infant and Junior Day School for Norwich School (*see entry in HMC section*). It is delightfully located in the Cathedral Close, between the East End of the Cathedral and the River Wensum. The Cathedral Choristers are educated at Norwich School, which is a member of the Choir Schools' Association.

The Lower School provides depth and breadth of education through a challenging curriculum. It seeks to recognise, nurture and develop each pupil's potential within an environment which encourages all-round emotional, physical, social and spiritual growth and to foster positive relations between pupils, teachers and parents. The dedicated teaching staff is committed to providing a stimulating programme of active learning which has rigour and discipline but avoids unnecessary pressure.

With one form in Reception and Year 1, two forms in Year 2, Year 3 and 4 and three forms in Years 5 and 6, the Lower School is the ideal size for ensuring a lively environment within a warm family atmosphere. The main building has bright, spacious areas for activities and lessons. As well as the library, there are specialised facilities for science, art, technology and ICT. There is an excellent play area in addition to the adjacent, extensive playing fields. A new Infant department opened in September 2018, offering bespoke facilities for the EYFS and Key Stage 1 curriculum.

A wide range of extra-curricular activities and school trips is offered. Music is a strong feature of school life. Many pupils choose to learn a musical instrument and participate in the various instrumental music groups. Rugby, netball, hockey, cricket and tennis are taught and the games programme is designed to encourage pupils of all abilities to enjoy games and physical activity.

The School aims to attract pupils who will thrive in a challenging academic environment and is therefore selective. All pupils are assessed by age-appropriate means. The principal entry points are at 4+, 7+ and 9+ with a smaller number of places available in other year groups.

Application forms and further details can be found on the website: www.norwich-school.org.uk

The vast majority of pupils from the Lower School progress to the Senior School at age eleven, and the curriculum is designed to prepare the pupils effectively for the next stage of their Norwich School education.

Charitable status. Norwich School is a Registered Charity, number 311280.

Notre Dame Prep School

Burwood House, Cobham, Surrey KT11 1HA

Tel: 01932 869990
email: office@notredame.co.uk
website: www.notredame.co.uk
Twitter: @NotreDameCobham
Facebook: @NotreDameSchoolCobham
LinkedIn: /notredamecobham

Chair of Governors: Mrs Wanda Nash

Head of Prep: **Mrs Amélie Morgan**, MA, BA Hons, PGCE

Assistant Head: Mrs Clare Barber, BSc Hons, PGCE

Head of EYFS: Miss Melanie Lehmann, BA Hons, EYPS

Head of Infants: Miss Geraldine Deen, BA Hons QTS

Pastoral Director: Miss Rebecca Golding, BA Hons, PGCE

Age Range. Girls 2–11, Boys 2–4.

Number of Pupils. 200 Girls, 18 boys.

Fees per term (2021–2022). Nursery please enquire, Reception £3,868, Prep 1 & 2 £4,535, Prep 3–6 £4,909.

Bursaries. A limited number of assisted places and bursaries are offered subject to income and asset tests.

Notre Dame School is an independent Catholic day school for girls aged 2–18 and boys aged 2–4. We welcome families of all faiths and none.

The 2017 ISI Inspection judged Notre Dame Prep School to be 'Excellent' across the board.

At Notre Dame School we have created a curriculum that encompasses the academic, creative, physical, moral, and intellectual challenges expected of all good schools, but also the fun, laughter and community needed to enable happy children to learn, to develop confidence and to feel fulfilled. A caring and trusting family relationship completes the balance, so that children can thrive and flourish.

Our children participate in many sporting activities, making full use of our on-site all-weather hockey, netball, tennis and athletics facilities, indoor arena, swimming pool and extensive fields. We encourage them to sing and play instruments in concerts and events in our wonderfully acoustic chapel, perform in our fully equipped 370-seat professional theatre, and enjoy our 26 acres of beautiful, rural parkland.

Prep School pupils benefit from a vibrant, bespoke humanities curriculum to develop thinking skills, moral foundation and knowledge. Meticulously planned and delivered English programmes and a 'mastery' approach to Mathematics are yielding excellent outcomes for our pupils. Girls are taught by specialist teachers for a number of subjects, including Music, Science (Juniors), Art, Drama, Dance, Spanish and PE. We are fortunate to have dedicated teaching spaces for Dance, Music, Drama, ICT and Art, as well as a fully-equipped Science Laboratory. Our girls leave the Prep School excellently equipped to take on their next challenge and nearly all progress to our Senior School.

Our outstanding Nursery welcomes boys and girls from the age of two and follows the Early Years Foundation Stage Guidance. As well as their own classrooms, outdoor play areas and Forest School, children access all of the school's sporting facilities and theatre and enjoy specialist teaching for Music, Dance, Spanish and Swimming.

Notre Dame is built on 400 years of educational experience: The Company of Mary Our Lady was founded in Bordeaux in 1607 to educate girls, and Notre Dame is one of some 300 educational foundations around the world that now come under this umbrella. To ready our pupils for the wider world, to live life to the full, we believe that our shared mission and purpose help our children to aspire to be the best they can be in in all their endeavours, during their school years and beyond.

ISI Inspection 2017. The full report can be viewed on the school website: ISI-Inspection-Report.

Transport. Notre Dame is excellently located – two minutes from the A3/M25 junction, 10 minutes from Walton, Weybridge, Cobham or Esher, and rarely more than 20 minutes from Guildford, Wimbledon and Putney. Private school coaches for girls from Year 3 upwards – flexible single/return journeys – from Clapham, Putney and Fulham to Esher, Woking and Weybridge and many stops in between.

Admission. Usual entry points: Early Years (age 2), Reception (age 4) and Year 3 (age 7). Occasional places are sometimes available in other year groups.

Registration: Registration Form and payment of £75 registration fee.

Assessment: Children are invited to attend a Taster Day, to include observation/assessment and time to get to know prospective classmates. As a rough guide, intake sits in the top third of the ability range.

Senior School. For further information about Notre Dame Senior School, *please see entry in GSA section*.

Charitable status. Notre Dame School Cobham is a Registered Charity, number 1081875.

Notting Hill Preparatory School

95 Lancaster Road, London W11 1QQ

Tel:	020 7221 0727
email:	admin@nottinghillprep.com
	admissions@nottinghillprep.com
website:	www.nottinghillprep.com
Twitter:	@NottingHillPrep
Instagram:	@nottinghillprep

Co-Chairs of Governing Body:

Mr John Mackay

Mr John Morton Morris

Headmistress: **Mrs Sarah Knollys**, BA Exeter, PGCE

Age Range. 4–13 Co-educational.

Number of Pupils. 380.

Fees per term (2021–2022) £7,308.

NHP is a co-ed Prep School, founded in 2003, in the heart of Notting Hill, West London. It was created through the cooperation of parents and teachers and this partnership with parents is a cornerstone of the philosophy of the school. It operates on a split site, Reception to Year 2 being housed in a fine Victorian School House and Years 3–5 in a magnificent modern building providing, in addition, a school hall/dining room, music practice rooms, science lab and computing suite. Years 6–8 have moved to exciting new premises on Portobello Green which also offer a music centre, an art and DT studio, an additional dining facility and a science lab.

Our aim is to educate children in the truest sense of the word – to light a fire, not simply fill the bucket. Driven by our Thinking School approach (we have been a Thinking School since 2014 and achieved Advanced Thinking School accreditation in March 2021), and delivered by dynamic and inspiring teaching, we strive to develop a passion for learning that will carry our pupils through their school years and beyond.

We create an environment where children's views and ideas are respected and encouraged. We believe that the classroom should be a place where pupils feel safe to challenge and be challenged.

When children do not fear being wrong, they are ready to express their own views, test out new ideas and take risks. At NHP, we celebrate making mistakes, and learning from them, as the path to deeper learning. We nurture the hardy attitudes and habits that will serve our children now and in later life. We develop in our pupils the ability to problem solve and become independent learners. We focus on their ability to cooperate, to think and act collaboratively and to show consideration for the feelings and needs of others.

We are a preparatory school and believe in academic rigour, preparing our pupils comprehensively for entrance exams to all the major London day schools at 11+ or 13+, as well as boarding schools at 13.

Alongside academic achievement, we also believe in the innate joy of childhood and we encourage children to follow their passions inside and outside of the classroom.

Music and performance are particular features at the school, with creative staff producing original material for plays and concerts. There are four choirs, an orchestra, chamber groups and bands and over two-thirds of the pupils learn a musical instrument.

A wide and varied sports programme using local facilities as well as our own on site gym ensures that children develop and perfect skills in the major sports (football, netball, hockey, rugby, cricket, athletics and swimming). Opportunities for displaying these skills are provided by frequent fixtures arranged with local schools.

Regular school trips enhance all aspects of the curriculum. Full use is made of the many and varied opportunities London offers to extend children's knowledge of their environment, their culture and their history.

NHP is noted for its open, friendly and happy atmosphere and its strong sense of being part of a wider community. Courtesy, kindness and appreciation of a diversity of talents, abilities and needs are defining values of the school's ethos.

The school is heavily oversubscribed and places are offered following a ballot.

Nottingham High Infant and Junior School

Waverley Mount, Nottingham NG7 4ED

Tel:	0115 845 2214
email:	juniorinfo@nottinghamhigh.co.uk

Lovell House Infant School:
13 Waverley Street, Nottingham NG7 4DX

Tel:	0115 845 2222
email:	lovellinfo@nottinghamhigh.co.uk
website:	www.nottinghamhigh.co.uk
Twitter:	@NottsHighIJS
Facebook:	@NottsHigh
Instagram:	@nottshighijs
LinkedIn:	/school/nottshigh

Chairman of Governors: Mr Steven Banks

Head: **Mrs C Bruce**

Deputy Head (*Academic*): Miss L Thorpe

Deputy Head (*Pastoral*): Mr C Cordy

Age Range. 4–11 Co-educational.

Number of Pupils. 332 Day pupils.

Fees per term (2021–2022). Infant School £3,662; Junior School £4,261.

Nottingham High Infant and Junior School has been co-educational since September 2016, with girls across all year groups.

The **Junior School** is housed in purpose-built premises on the main school site, having its own Classrooms, ICT Suite, Library, Art Room, Science Laboratory, Dining Hall and more. In 2018 our impressive new Junior School redevelopment was completed, expanding the number of classrooms, introducing a brand new spacious and contemporary library, improving our outdoor play areas, and much more.

Entrance Assessments are held in January, based around the core subjects of Mathematics and English, including reading, along with some measures of general ability. The tests are all set at National Curriculum ability levels appropriate for each age group.

The Junior School has an experienced and well-qualified staff. The curriculum is designed for those who expect to complete their education at Nottingham High School. The subjects taught are Religious Education, English, Mathematics, History, Geography, Science, French and PSHE. Full provision is made for Music, Art, Design Technology, Information Communication Technology, Swimming, Physical Education and Games.

The Junior School has its own Orchestra and about 100 pupils receive instrumental tuition. All Year 3 pupils play an instrument of their choice. A Concert and School Plays are performed annually. A wide range of supervised activities and hobbies takes place during every lunch time.

School games are Association Football, Netball and Rugby with some Hockey and Cross Country in the winter, Cricket and Tennis in the summer.

Lovell House Infant School opened in September 2008 for children in Reception, Year 1 and Year 2. Lovell House is situated across the road from the main High School in its own secure and self-contained grounds. The school has been completely refurbished and upgraded recently to provide state-of-the-art classrooms and facilities, and extensive play areas, all in a friendly, home-from-home surrounding. In fact, the main school building is very much like a large house, making the transition between nursery and the early stages of a formal school education so much easier.

Classes are deliberately kept small (a maximum class size of 18), so that our teachers are able to devote time to the children as individuals. The majority of subjects are taught by class teachers, although specialist teachers are used for ICT, Swimming, Music, French and Spanish. All subjects are taught in an integrated curriculum to allow time for play and problem-solving activities to take place.

Beyond the classroom we offer an excellent range of extracurricular activities, giving real breadth to our curriculum. We make full use of some of the Nottingham High School facilities, such as the swimming pool, the extensive games fields and both the music and drama facilities. Thus whilst Lovell House is largely self-contained we are also able to use the High School's wider facilities to expand the horizons of the children in our care.

Entry to Lovell House is by assessment; the admissions process is designed to assess the numeracy and literacy skills of the children applying for a place in Years 1 and 2, and a range of activities are used to assess the potential for learning for those applying for a place in Reception. In addition, all children are invited to school for a final classroom-based assessment where they are observed completing practical activities.

As part of Nottingham High School, Lovell House not only benefits from the continuity of education and community from entry at age 4 right through to A Level at age 18, but also from the extensive recreational and cultural facilities provided by the High School.

Charitable status. Nottingham High School is a Registered Charity, number 1104251. It exists to provide education for boys and girls between the ages of 4 and 18 years.

Old Buckenham Hall School

Brettenham Park, Ipswich, Suffolk IP7 7PH

Tel:	01449 740252
email:	admissions@obh.co.uk
website:	www.obh.co.uk
Twitter:	@OBHSchool
Facebook:	@OBHSchool
LinkedIn:	Old Buckenham Hall School

Chair of Governors: A McGregor, MA Cantab

Headmaster: **D Griffiths**, BA Hons, MEd, PGCE

Age Range. 3–13 years

Number of Pupils. 242 (Boarders: 31 Girls, 50 Boys).

Fees per term (2021–2022). Full Boarding £7,951–£9,052, Day pupils £5,505–£6,947, Pre-Prep £3,425, Nursery £28 per session

Give your child a third of an acre…

Old Buckenham Hall is recognised as one the leading preparatory schools in the UK. We have tremendous academic results with entry to many of the top public schools in the country. Our pastoral provision is outstanding, our boarding houses are beautiful and our facilities incredible. What really makes us special, though, is the happiness of our children, who bound around our magical setting. With each child having a third of an acre to play in they can climb the trees, fly down the zip wire or feed the chickens and ducks. If preferred, they can take on the challenge of the rope swings, have a round of golf or explore the big woods.

The staff to pupil ratio is approximately 1:8, giving an average class size of 14. All members of staff, including part-time staff, contribute to a wide range of afternoon, evening and weekend extra-curricular activities – where every child has the opportunity to participate. Activities on offer include arts and crafts, tennis, dance, drama, golf, music, climbing, cookery, gymnastics, clay pigeon shooting, fly-fishing and horse riding.

Winter sports include hockey, netball, tag rugby and lacrosse for the girls, and hockey, football, lacrosse and rugby for the boys. In the Summer girls and boys play cricket and take part in athletics. The school offers excellent tennis facilities with pupils receiving specialist tennis coaching on six tennis courts and a purpose-built, state-of-the-art AstroTurf. The school also has a squash court and a 9-hole golf course.

The boarding model is flexible, offering children the opportunity to board anything from 1 night a week to full boarding on an eleven-day cycle. Children boarding at the weekend enjoy a varied programme of exciting activities such as campfires, the 'Great OBH Bake Off', 'Bush Tucker

Trials', a Masquerade Ball and trips out to the coast and other local attractions. The junior boarding house, Spero, gives the youngest boarders at OBH a warm, nurturing boarding environment, whilst being in the care of very experienced and caring staff.

Children develop a wide range of life skills through the outdoor education programme – the OBEs (Old Buckenham Explorers) for pupils in Years 3–8 and the MBEs (Mini Buckenham Explorers) for pupils in the Pre-Prep. The construction of two outdoor classrooms has proved to be very innovative and exciting – where children learn to camp, shelter, cook and learn vital survival skills in preparation for Bronze, Silver and Gold expeditions.

Old Buckenham Hall was founded in Lowestoft in 1862 and moved in 1937 to Old Buckenham in Norfolk. In 1956, the school moved to its present site in Brettenham Park, Suffolk, which is 4 miles from Lavenham, 11 miles from Bury St Edmunds, 18 miles from Ipswich, 23 miles from Colchester and an hour and a half by direct train from London. The school became an Educational Trust in 1967.

The school prospectus can be obtained on application to the Registrar, Becky Griffiths.

Charitable status. Old Buckenham Hall (Brettenham) Educational Trust Limited is a Registered Charity, number 310490. It exists to provide education for boarding and day pupils.

The Old Hall School

Stanley Road, Wellington, Shropshire TF1 3LB

Tel: 01952 223117
email: admissions@oldhall.co.uk
         enq@oldhall.co.uk
website: www.oldhall.co.uk
Twitter: @oldhallschool
Facebook: @The-Old-Hall-School
Instagram: @theoldhallschool
LinkedIn: /company/old-hall-school

Chairman of the Governors: Mr R J Pearson, BSc

Headmaster: **Mr Martin C Stott**, BEd Hons

Age Range. 4–11.
Number of Pupils. 222: 120 boys, 102 girls.
Fees per term (2021–2022). Lower School: £2,950 (Reception), £3,300 (Years 1–2); Upper School (Years 3–6): £4,640.

Founded in 1845, The Old Hall School is a co-educational day school (4–11 years), which is housed in spectacular premises, located alongside Wrekin College. The school offers first-class facilities; a double sports hall, 25-metre indoor swimming pool, an artificial playing surface and grass pitches offer an excellent sports and games environment, whilst specialist music and drama areas help to promote high standards in the performing arts. A suite of specialist learning support rooms reflects the School's commitment to the needs of the individual.

The broad curriculum is enriched by a dedicated team of professionals who encourage pupils to fulfil their potential in a happy and secure environment.

Through the academic curriculum and caring pastoral system, the school aims to lay solid foundations in the development of well-motivated, confident and happy individuals who are always willing to give of their best on the road to high achievement.

Charitable status. Wrekin Old Hall Trust Limited is a Registered Charity, number 528417.

The Old School Henstead

Toad Row, Henstead, Nr Beccles, Suffolk NR34 7LG

Tel: 01502 741150
email: office@theoldschoolhenstead.co.uk
website: www.theoldschoolhenstead.co.uk
Twitter: @OldSchoolHstead
Facebook: @theoldschoolhenstead

Headmaster: **Mr W J McKinney**, MA Hons, PG Dip, MA Ed

Age Range. 2½–11.
Number in School. 100 Day Boys and Girls.
Fees per term (2021–2022). £2,459–£3,534; Nursery fees from £23.30 for 3 hours to £49.00 per day; early years funding accepted for under fives.

'Our children are so happy at Henstead …''Exceptional teaching standards and a wealth of opportunities across the whole academic, arts and sports spectrum.' '…inspiring staff whose dedication is reflected in such highly-motivated and well-rounded children.' – These are typical comments from the school's parents.

The school is committed to realising the potential of all its pupils, creating a place of learning that inspires children to excel in and make their own special contribution to the global environment that awaits them. Henstead children know not just what to learn, but how to learn it; they are interested and interesting and they have the words to prove it.

Whilst focusing on the core subjects, the teaching at The Old School Henstead ensures that every pupil maximises his or her potential. The curriculum is designed to inspire and challenge all pupils, with teaching adapted to meet their varying needs. The school's aim is to teach children how to grow into positive, responsible people, who can work and cooperate with others, whilst developing knowledge and skills in order to achieve their true potential. Above all, the school believes in making learning fun, to engender a love of lifelong learning in every child that passes through the school. Small class sizes, excellent teaching and an insistence on traditional values of hard work and good manners help all pupils at The Old School Henstead to achieve high academic standards. The school caters for pupils of all abilities, offering specialist support where needed at both ends of the ability spectrum. In Early Years (Reception) and the Lower School (Years 1 and 2), the children are taught in their class base by their class teacher for the majority of subjects. In the Upper School, from Year 3 onwards, the majority of subjects are taught by subject teachers. Assessment for learning plays a vital role in ensuring that every pupil makes excellent progress. Pupils are encouraged to take responsibility for their own learning, to be involved as far as possible in reviewing the way they learn, and to reflect on how they learn – what helps them learn and what makes it difficult for them to learn. Children learn French from Nursery up and Latin in Year 6.

In the Early Years Foundation stage the school aims to give each child a happy, positive and fun start, so that he or she can establish solid foundations on which to expand and foster a deep love of learning. This is done through the seven areas of learning and supported by the school's outstanding outdoor learning environment.

After-school clubs take place every day. The activities on offer – sports, science, art, dance and music clubs – vary from term to term.

There is an active house system that encourages pupils to interact and collaborate with pupils outside their own year group. The School Council has two elected representatives from every year from Reception to Year 6.

Music-making is a very important part of life at The Old School Henstead. The school choirs rehearse every week and lead the singing in the daily assembly and at regular services at St Mary's Church. In addition to this, the school has, over the years, been very proud of the achievements of the choir at local, regional and national music festivals.

The school believes passionately in sport for all. All pupils are expected to take part in competitive sport, representing the school in a range of sports. Outdoor Education is an important part of the curriculum, for it is inclusive, builds confidence and encourages supervised, sensible risk-taking and learning opportunities that are as varied and challenging as those enjoyed indoors. The culmination of this is the residential visit programme enjoyed by pupils in the Upper School. In sport, teams and individuals compete against local schools and further afield in both regional and national competitions.

In keeping with The Old School Henstead's focus on building pupils' confidence, social skills and awareness of others, the LAMDA syllabus provides an approach which is both structured and adventurous. With drama games, improvisations, role play and practice of specific elements of Drama, the children are equipped to meet not only the challenges of regular performance and presentation within the broader curriculum of the school, but also in their ensuing educational experience. The Junior and Senior Summer Shows, the traditional climax to the year, are produced at an exceptional level of professionalism by talented and dedicated staff and include every child from Nursery to the top of the Senior School, at an appropriate level of performance. LAMDA tuition is also offered in the Upper School.

Religious affiliation. The school is underpinned by a Christian ethos, but accepts children of all faiths and none.

Charitable status. The Old School Henstead Educational Trust Limited is a Registered Charity, number 279265. It exists to provide education for boys and girls.

Old Vicarage School

48 Richmond Hill, Richmond, Surrey TW10 6QX

Tel: 020 8940 0922
email: office@oldvicarageschool.com
website: www.oldvicarageschool.com
Twitter: @ovsrichmond
Instagram: @ovsrichmond
LinkedIn: /old-vicarage-school

Chairman of Governors: Mr G Caplan

Headmistress: **Mrs G Linthwaite**, MA Oxon, PGCE

Age Range. 3–11.
Number of Pupils. 240 girls.
Fees per term (2021–2022). £5,200 Reception – Year 6, £4,300 5 full days at Little Vic.

The Old Vicarage school is a non-selective girls' prep school based in a beautiful Grade 2* listed "castle" on Richmond Hill. The School was established in 1881 and became a Charitable Educational Trust in 1973. Whilst retaining traditional values, there is a clear vision for the future and teaching and facilities combine the very best of the old and the new. Girls are admitted into Little Vic pre-school in September following their third birthday. Older girls may be admitted further up the school if a vacancy arises, following a day spent at the school to ensure it is a good fit for them. Girls are expected to remain until the age of 11, being prepared for Common Entrance Examinations at 11+ and for entry to the London Day Schools. A good range of academic, sporting, drama and arts scholarships to senior schools has been awarded to girls over the years.

Work of a traditionally high standard is expected of the girls and they are challenged and supported in classes of up to 15 girls, encouraging self esteem and enabling them to fulfil their potential. Girls in the Lower School are taught by a Form Teacher, with some specialist input. Girls in the Upper School are taught by subject specialists who impart a real enthusiasm and love for their subject areas. They will also have a form tutor to provide the pastoral support the school is known for. A system of older buddies, prefects and the Student Council ensures that all girls feel an integral part of the school from the beginning.

Music and drama are active throughout the school. Individual music tuition is provided in a wide range of instruments in purpose-built facilities and active choirs sing at numerous competitions and collaborations. All girls take part in at least one dramatic production a year, as well as in assemblies to which parents are invited.

The major sports are netball, hockey, cricket, athletics and swimming and the school has sports facilities near Ham House as well as our own gym and playground. Girls compete in fixtures against other schools from Year 3 and have had notable successes in recent years in borough-wide championships.

Extra-curricular activities cater to a range of interests and include art, photography, sports, computing, cooking, craft and drama clubs. All girls in the Upper School attend a residential trip to Sussex, Dorset, Oxfordshire or France and up to fifty join the biennial ski trip to Italy.

Charitable status. The Old Vicarage School is a Registered Charity, number 312671.

The Oratory Preparatory School

Goring Heath, Reading, South Oxfordshire RG8 7SF

Tel:	0118 9844511
email:	office@oratoryprep.co.uk
website:	www.oratoryprep.co.uk
Twitter:	@OPS_OratoryPrep
Facebook:	@oratoryprepschool

Headmaster: **Mr Rob Stewart**, BA, MA

Number of Pupils. 353 (195 boys, 158 girls), including 27 full, weekly or flexi boarders and 100 in the Junior Prep department.

Fees per term (2021–2022). Boarders: £7,490 (weekly), £8,690 (full); Day: £5,800–£5,850; Junior Prep: Reception–Year 2 £3,400; Year 3&4 £5,650; Kindergarten (per day/session) £32 (morning), £60 (short day), £65 (full day); Nursery (per day/session) £36 (morning), £68 (short day), £75 (full day).

We provide an enriched education to boys and girls aged 2–13. Set within 65 acres of Oxfordshire countryside with outstanding facilities, we nurture happy, balanced, confident and inquisitive children. Our commitment to the pastoral care, wellbeing and all-round development of each child, with an ethos of broad-minded and inclusive learning are at the core of our education. We strive to strike a balance between encouraging children to step out of their comfort zone, seek adventure and develop resilience while ensuring that they feel stretched, fulfilled, secure and supported in being the very best that they can be.

Academic challenges and pursuits combined with self-expression through sport, music, art and drama are central to the confidence and self-discovery of our children and equip them with essential skills for life beyond school. In all that we do and teach, our children grow and learn under our founder St John Henry Newman's, motto 'Cor Ad Cor Loquitur' [Heart speaks to Heart]; encouraging our children to model the key values of kindness, compassion, humility and forgiveness. Such values are at the heart of our education, shaping the moral awareness and convictions of our pupils.

Pupils become ambitious and independent learners, immersed in a skills-based, interconnected curriculum, meaningful and highly relevant to their everyday experiences and life beyond school. We enable our children to make connections across subjects and think more deeply about their significance, applying their learning across different contexts and developing core, transferable skills, such as critical thinking and strong reasoning skills, to judge the value of ideas and knowledge presented to them. This includes Forest School from the age of two, science experiments in our woodlands and art classes in our gardens.

The school boasts an Astroturf for an array of sporting fixtures. The 25-metre indoor swimming pool for Year 3 onwards is the venue for galas and a starting point for Mini-Triathlons. The smaller pool for children from Kindergarten upwards allows for weekly lessons.

The children have so many opportunities to discover themselves and their talents through our after school activities programmes. Our Saturday Enrichment programme is open to pupils in Year 5 upwards and is designed to further develop skills in leadership, collaboration and critical thinking. Modules range from entrepreneurship and presentation skills to mock trials, gymnastics and beekeeping.

The school's Boarding House has a mix of nationalities with pupils in Year 3 upwards from China, Spain, France and Nigeria.

The Oratory Prep School is part of Bellevue Education (www.blvue.com).

Orchard House School

16 Newton Grove, London W4 1LB

Tel:	020 8742 8544
email:	info@orchardhs.org.uk
website:	www.orchardhs.org.uk
Twitter:	@orchardhs

Chairman of Governors: Mr Aatif Hassan

Headmaster: **Mr Kit Thompson**

Age Range. Girls and Boys 3–11.
Number of Pupils. 264: 139 Girls, 125 Boys.
Fees per Term (2021–2022). Nursery (5 mornings) £3,160, Pre-Prep £6,320, Prep £6,585.

Orchard House School is part of Dukes Education. It provides an excellent all-round education for boys and girls from 3 to 11, preparing them for the competitive entry examinations for the London day and country boarding schools whilst maintaining a happy, purposeful atmosphere.

There is an emphasis on teaching traditional values tailored for children growing up in the 21st century. Uniform is worn and good manners are expected at all times. Children shake hands with the staff at the end of each day and are encouraged to take part, with the deputy head or headmistress, in describing the school to prospective parents and other visitors. Appetising lunches are provided and all food is cooked freshly on site each day.

The main premises were designed by the well-known architect Norman Shaw and built around 1880; the building is Grade 2 listed. The school enjoys a corner site in Bedford Park and the classrooms have good natural lighting as well as overlooking a large playground.

Children aged 3 or 4 are admitted on a first come, first served basis. Occasional places higher up are filled following assessment. Selected aspects of the Montessori philosophy are used to deliver the Early Years Foundation Stage curriculum; at KS1 and KS2 the curriculum is based on the National Curriculum and the demands of the future schools. Specialist teachers are employed for many subjects and support teachers provide one-on-one or small group tuition where necessary. Staff turnover is low.

Orchard House is proud of the excellent results the children achieve at their future schools which include many of the most academic schools in this country. The school is within easy reach of St Paul's schools, Latymer Upper,

Hampton School, Notting Hill & Ealing High School and Godolphin & Latymer and many pupils have taken up places at one of these schools.

The school boasts state-of-the-art ICT resources and attractive playgrounds/garden with all-weather surfaces. The children make good use of additional local facilities to enhance their sport and drama lessons.

Orchard House participates in the Nursery Education Grant. There are occasional means-tested scholarships available through the House Schools Trust for children entering Year 4. Contact: info@orchardhs.org.uk for further information.

Orchard School

Higham Road, Barton-le-Clay, Bedfordshire MK45 4RB

Tel: 01582 882054
email: admin@orchardschool.org.uk
website: www.orchardschool.org.uk

Chair of Friends: Mrs Anna Gingell

Headmistress: Mrs Anne Burton, MEd Cantab, Cert Ed, HV SRN

Head of School: Miss Louise Burton, BEd Hons Cantab, QTS

Co-educational Day School.

Age Range. 4–11 years; Nursery for children aged 0–4.

Number of Pupils. Preparatory School 65; Nursery 30.

Fees per term (2021–2022). Tuition (including lunch) £2,987.27. Breakfast Club £4.16 per day. After School Club (including tea) £8.69 per day.

Location. Orchard School is a Preparatory School for boys and girls, ideally situated on the outskirts of a large village in south Bedfordshire.

The School has been established for 20 years, and the Nursery for 30 years. Located in a beautiful setting and backed by the Barton Hills (thought to be The Delectable Mountains in Pilgrim's Progress) both School and Nursery are surrounded by rolling countryside that hosts an abundance of wildlife.

Ethos. The school's motto – "to be the best that you can be" is reflected in all areas of school life. Orchard's aim is to enable each child to value and strive for the highest levels of achievement, and to nurture a pride in success. Praise and encouragement are the primary motivational tools employed, tempered by the recognition that every child develops at their own pace. Skillful and careful observations are undertaken by the teaching team to help the children meet and surpass key learning targets. The school also encourages an 'esprit de corps' and a sense of true belonging. Emphasis is placed on the moral, social and personal development of all pupils in order to expand their confidence and self-esteem.

100% academic success. The school boasts an exemplary academic record with (for example) a 100% pass rate into the nearby Harpur Trust schools in Bedford.

The combination of a progressive, structured, yet genuinely friendly family atmosphere creates an ideal environment for the children to thrive both academically and in other activities that they pursue.

Activities. We encourage each child to experience as wide a range of activities as possible; for example, music lessons, choir, ballet, dance and philosophy.

A comprehensive sporting programme including swimming and rugby is also included within the well-rounded curriculum. Further opportunities include craftwork, running, lacrosse, badminton and recorder are offered via lunchtime and after-school clubs. There are several visits a term across all year groups to complement topic learning and to provide a real-life context to the subjects being studied. Years 3 and 4 also enjoy residential trips to specialist adventure-based facilities where activities such as abseiling, kayaking and raft building help increase fun, team spirit and pupil confidence.

Friends of Orchard. Orchard is proud of its strong and supportive parent base and there is a well-established 'Friends of Orchard School' group which organises social gatherings and fundraising events, further enhancing the friendly and family inclusive atmosphere at the school.

Bursaries. Bursaries are available for year 3 and above.

Summary. Our aim is to develop well-motivated and confident children who are considerate to others, well-mannered, who know the value of hard work.

We are happy to say that virtually all Orchard School pupils have been proven to excel at their subsequent schools and seats of learning.

Orley Farm School

South Hill Avenue, Harrow on the Hill, Middlesex HA1 3NU

Tel: 020 8869 7600
email: office@orleyfarm.harrow.sch.uk
website: www.orleyfarm.harrow.sch.uk

The school is a Charitable Trust administered by a Board of Governors.

Chairman of Governors: Mr C J Hayfield

Headmaster: Mr T Calvey, BA Ed Hons

Age Range. 4–13 Co-educational.

Number of Pupils. 505 Day pupils, including 188 in Pre-Prep (age 4 to 7).

Fees per term (2021–2022). Pre-Prep £5,007; Years 3–4 £5,325; Years 5–8 £5,777 (inclusive of lunch).

At Orley Farm School we are in the fortunate position of being a London day school blessed with boarding school acreage and facilities. Founded in 1850, the school has grown and developed to become one of the leading and largest co-educational prep schools in Greater London. Entry is by assessment at 4+ and when occasional places appear in the rest of the school. The academic journey of the children begins in Reception and ends when pupils transfer successfully to their senior schools – at the end of Year 6 for our girls and at the end of Year 8 for our boys attending more traditional senior schools. Pupils enter a range of very impressive senior schools, including Aldenham,

Haberdashers' Aske's Boys and Girls, Haileybury, Harrow, John Lyon, Merchant Taylors', Mill Hill, Northwood College, North London Collegiate, Royal Masonic, Rugby, St Helen's, St Paul's and Westminster, to name but a few. However, most impressively, Orley Farm has served over 61 senior schools over the past 7 years. We pride ourselves in finding the right future step for every child. Scholarships are regularly awarded to our senior pupils – 36 awards were offered in 2020–2021 including a Queen's Scholar for Westminster.

Success, happiness and future fulfilment start with a deep love of learning. So firmly do we believe in this philosophy, that we have invested £9 million in our facilities (a Music and Drama School, three state of the art Science Laboratories, a new Humanities department, a new Dining Hall and at the very heart, a cutting-edge Library).

'Breadth, Balance & Excellence …The Orley Farm Way!'

Alongside academic excellence, we pride ourselves on giving pupils experiences and opportunities that foster a lifetime and love of learning. All pupils are expected to contribute to the broader curriculum and a packed programme of Drama, Art and Music and Design & Technology. Over 200 individual music lessons take place each week and are supported by many musical groups and choirs. Productions, concerts and competitions offer all pupils the chance to showcase their talents and dedication in a variety of different settings.

Sport plays a very large part in our school life. We have over thirty six acres of land and full use is made of this in providing a venue for training and matches. Pupils will compete internally and externally in athletics, cricket, football, hockey, netball and rugby. In addition basketball, cross-country, fencing, fives, gymnastics and tennis also thrive through activities, clubs and matches. A Gym, Sports Hall and full-sized AstroTurf pitch enable our strong PE and Games Department to help our pupils develop their sporting talents.

This rich blend of curricular and co-curricular education is exemplified by our Expeditions Week. All pupils and staff from Year 4 and above travel to a variety of venues to spend a week extending their curriculum in a host of new challenges and adventures.

We are privileged to be working with young learners at a point where we can 'hardwire' key traits and values that we believe are essential to happiness and success in an ever-changing world. Our 10 Thinking Skills are the bedrock of 'The Orley Farm Way' and we have no doubt that we are giving voice to the *ambitious*, the *creative*, the *curious*, the *focused*, the *resilient* and the *risk-takers* as they'll possess *empathy*, *flexibility of mind*, *initiative* and *good judgement* in all that they do!

We pride ourselves on preparing our young learners for life and, therefore, we go well beyond assessment preparation and this is reflected in an Alumni who know the power and value of an outstanding start in life but more importantly, how to find fulfilment, purpose, joy and wonder in making a difference to others. We are blessed and privileged to work with pupils, colleagues and parents who know the power of these years and who recognise this wonderful African proverb:

'*It takes a village to bring up a child*'

The Orley Farm Family is a special place and we would encourage anyone and everyone who might be searching for something a little more than the superficial to come and visit but be warned, there's no room for passengers, we are all committed to doing something with this privileged start…!

Orley Farm School is located in North West London close to Harrow on the Hill and is only twenty minutes on the Metropolitan Line from Baker Street Station.

Entry to this exciting place of learning is by assessment. For further details contact the Registrar, Mrs Julie Jago, on 0208 869 7634.

Charitable status. Orley Farm School is a Registered Charity, number 312637.

Orwell Park

Nacton, Ipswich, Suffolk IP10 0ER

Tel: 01473 659225
email: headmaster@orwellpark.org
website: www.orwellpark.co.uk
Twitter: @OrwellParkSch
Facebook: @orwellpark

Chairman of Governors: James Davison, BA

Headmaster: **Adrian Brown**, MA Cantab

Age Range. 2½–13.

Number of Pupils. 250 pupils including 33 full, 22 weekly, and 60 flexi boarders.

Fees per term (2021–2022). Nursery: £59 per day/£30 per session. Pre-Prep: from £2,961 (Day).
Prep: Day from £5,992, Weekly Boarding from £8,024, Full Boarding from £9,194.

Pupils are prepared for all Independent Senior Schools (local day and national boarding) via the Scholarship or Common Entrance Examinations. The school has a thriving Pre-Prep School, which is housed in a new, state-of-the-art building containing a large hall, six classrooms and music and ICT rooms.

The timetable is especially designed to be very flexible, with setting in most subjects, a potential scholars' set in Year 7 and a scholarship set in Year 8. The curriculum, both in and out of the classroom, is unusually broad. Children are encouraged to enjoy their learning and good learning support is offered. Thinking Skills and other opportunities for academic enrichment are also offered, including a weekly evening lecture programme to challenge the older children. There is a host of extracurricular activities (just under 100) run by permanent or visiting staff.

About 90% of the school learn a musical instrument and the school has a number of orchestral and ensemble groups. Drama is strong – all children have opportunities to perform regularly in school productions, and LAMDA lessons are offered as an extracurricular activity. All children take part in annual Reading and Public Speaking Competitions.

The very large Georgian style building and 110 acres of grounds (sandy soil) on the banks of the River Orwell have the following special features: 21 recently refurbished themed dormitories, 22 bright classrooms with modern audio-visual equipment, beautiful Orangery used as an Assembly and Lecture Hall, 2 ICT suites, large Design Centre including metal, wood and plastic workshop plus electronics, mechanics, home economics, radio and model-making areas, Music Technology Room, Music Room and 40 Practice rooms, Music Recording Studio, 2 Laboratories plus associated areas, brand new Library, Art Room including large pottery area and kiln, Observatory with 10' Refractor Telescope, Photographic Room, 17 Games pitches and one Astroturf pitch, one Multi-Use Games Area, large Sports Hall with permanent stage, Climbing Wall, Games Room, large heated Swimming Pool, 3 Squash Courts, 5 Hard Tennis Courts, Nine-hole Golf Course (approximately 1,800 yards) and a purpose-built Assault Course.

Good sports coaching is given and fixtures are arranged in the following sports: Rugby, Hockey, Cricket, Netball, Rounders, Tennis, Athletics, Squash, Sailing, Swimming and Cross-Country Running. Emphasis is also placed on individual physical activities and we offer a wide range including Gymnastics, Fencing, Ballet, Canoeing, Sailing, Modern Dance, Karate, Riding and Clay Pigeon Shooting. The school owns its own canoes and dinghies.

The School aims to introduce the pupils to a broad and varied set of experiences and opportunities. It tries to see that every activity, whether academic, sporting, social or character building, is properly taught using the best possible facilities and that each is conducted in an atmosphere which is friendly but disciplined. Children are encouraged to feel comfortable taking risks and to be confident without being arrogant. Under the overarching value of integrity, the school's core values are: kindness, collaboration, courage, spirit and respect.

Charitable status. Orwell Park School is a Registered Charity, number 310481. It exists to provide education for boys and girls.

Packwood Haugh

Ruyton XI Towns, Shrewsbury, Shropshire SY4 1HX

Tel: 01939 260217
email: admissions@packwood-haugh.co.uk
website: www.packwood-haugh.co.uk
Twitter: @packwoodhaugh
Facebook: @packwoodhaugh

Chairman of Governors: Mr T H P Haynes

Headmaster: **Robert Fox**, BSc Hons, PGCE

Deputy Heads

Roy Chambers, BA, MEd

Sue Rigby, BA Hons, PGCE, Dip SpLD

Age Range. Co-educational 4–13.
Number of Children. 210. Boarding: 45 boys, 16 girls. Day: 69 boys, 46 girls. Pre-Prep 34.
Fees per term (2021–2022). Boarding: UK £8,265, International £9,323; Day £4,593–£6,466, Pre-Prep (Acorns) £3,106. No compulsory extras. Extras available on request.

Set in the heart of the Shropshire countryside, between Shrewsbury and Oswestry, Packwood Haugh is a co-educational day (4–13) and boarding (7–13) school which provides an excellent all-round education in a happy and caring environment. Children benefit from a wide range of academic, sporting, musical, artistic and cultural activities which encourage them to develop enquiring minds and an enthusiasm for learning. The school espouses an atmosphere of cooperation and understanding between pupils, staff and parents and encourages good manners and consideration towards others at all times.

Packwood has always striven for academic excellence; class sizes are small (average 13) and children are prepared for all the major independent schools across the country winning a number of academic, music, sports, art and all-rounder scholarships and awards each year. Packwood is part of the Shrewsbury School family of schools and at least a third of pupils head to Shrewsbury. The school has a thriving pre-prep department (Packwood Acorns), which takes children from Reception.

The school's facilities are superb; a state of the art sports hall allows for fencing, indoor tennis, badminton, indoor cricket nets, judo, gymnastics and five-a-side football. Incorporated in the building are fully equipped DT and Art departments and a linked computer suite. A 280-seat theatre is used for assemblies, concerts and drama productions throughout the year.

As well as the classrooms in the main school buildings and a purpose-built new block, there are three science laboratories, two libraries, a Year 8 study area and two further computer suites. Park House, which accommodates Packwood Acorns and girls' boarding, is a short distance from the main school building.

Packwood has a very strong sporting tradition. Set alongside 66 acres of grass playing fields, there is a newly resurfaced full-size, floodlit AstroTurf pitch, an additional hard court area, tennis courts, squash courts, an indoor, heated swimming pool and a golf course. In the winter terms the boys play rugby, football and hockey while the girls play netball, hockey and lacrosse. There is also cross country running on a course within the grounds. In the summer both boys and girls play cricket as well as tennis, athletics and swimming.

Additional facilities include Forest School, a shooting range, cooking room and an adventure playground. Children can take part in over 70 activities throughout the year, including horse riding, sailing and gardening to name but a few.

Charitable status. Packwood Haugh is a Registered Charity, number 528413. It exists to provide day and boarding education for boys and girls from the age of 4 to 13.

Papplewick

Windsor Road, Ascot, Berks SL5 7LH

Tel: 01344 621488
email: schoolsec@papplewick.org.uk
       registrar@papplewick.org.uk
website: www.papplewick.org.uk
Twitter: @PapplewickAscot

Chairman of Board of Governors: Brigadier (Retd) A R E Hutchinson, JP

Headmaster: **T W Bunbury**, BA University College Durham, PGCE

Age Range. 6–13.
Number of Boys. 212: 87 Boarders, 125 day boys.
Fees per term (2021–2022). Boarding Fees £10,720; (Tier 4 £11,980) Day Boys: £5,930 (Year 2), £7,765 (Years 3–4), £8,235 (Years 5–6).

Papplewick is a boys only, day, weekly and full boarding school with an exceptional Scholarship record to top Independent Schools. Day boys do prep at school and come into board from the Summer term of Year 6. Happiness comes first and kindness is a priority here. Three very popular daily transport services run to and from London, one from Chiswick, one from Brook Green and one from near the Millennium Gloucester Hotel. Also, a daily service runs to and from Maidenhead/South Bucks. Situated between the M3 and M4, the school boasts easy access to London airports. A new Year 8 stand-alone boarding house has now opened with two Year 5 classrooms underneath and staff accommodation.

Papplewick exists to provide a high-quality education where – for all our academic, cultural and sporting success – the happiness of the boys come first, and kindness is a top priority.

Papplewick was awarded Tatler's Prep School of the Year 2018–2019

Charitable status. The Papplewick Educational Trust is a Registered Charity, number 309087.

The Paragon
Junior School of Prior Park College

Lyncombe House, Lyncombe Vale, Bath BA2 4LT

Tel: 01225 310837
email: reception.paragon@priorparkschools.com
       srees-jones@priorparkschools.com
website: www.paragonschool.co.uk
Twitter: @ParagonBath
Facebook: @TheParagonJunior
Instagram: @paragonjunior

Chair of Trustees: Mr John Shinkwin

Head of School: **Mrs Rosie Allen**, BA Hons, PGCE

Registrar: Mrs Susie Rees-Jones

Age Range. 3–11 years.
Number of Pupils. 135 Boys, 120 Girls.

Fees per term (2021–2022). Juniors: Years 5–6 £3,909, Years 3–4 £3,814. Infants: Reception, 1 & 2 £3,428. Pre-School: Full-time £3,200, Part-time £640 (per day 9am–3pm), £470 (per morning 9am until 1pm). Fees include lunch. Sibling discounts available. Registration Fee (non-refundable) £100.

60+ experienced and qualified teachers.

The Paragon is an independent, co-educational day school based in a beautiful Georgian house situated a mile from the centre of Bath. The school is set in eight acres of beautiful grounds with woodland, conservation areas, lawns and streams. It's the perfect 'outdoor classroom' and we use it right across the curriculum. We also enjoy regular access to the superb sport, science, D & T and drama facilities at our Senior School, Prior Park College.

Several factors help create the 'distinctive Paragon atmosphere'. One is undoubtedly the homely feel that comes from being based in a beautiful, former family home. Then there's our Christian ethos and strong pastoral care, as well as our belief that school at this age is about being stimulated and inspired, about laughter and spontaneity – in short, about having fun. We may be a private school and we certainly expect high standards of behaviour but we're anything but stuffy and grey.

We offer a broad curriculum taught in small classes by teachers with real passion. Academic life at The Paragon cultivates a love of learning and encourages independent and creative thinking. Our results are impressive. Our children consistently achieve well above the national average and many Year 6 children win senior school scholarships. Our facilities include a library, large gymnasium/dining hall, Pre-School with secure indoor and outdoor play areas, art studio, modern languages and dedicated Music Lodge.

Sport is particularly strong at The Paragon. Our sports teams take part, with considerable success, in a wide range of tournaments and festivals. We also offer a vast range of sports clubs that all children can join regardless of ability. Prior Park College offers us an indoor swimming pool, AstroTurf and grass pitches, tennis courts, athletics track and sports centre.

The Paragon's extracurricular programme is extensive. Staff run more than 60 lunchtime and after-school clubs that range from pottery and chess to drama and cross-country running. The school also enjoys an enviable reputation for Music. All children receive weekly music lessons from a specialist teacher. In addition, visiting instrumental teachers offer tuition in a wide range of instruments. We offer an excellent choice of extracurricular music activities including the orchestra, two choirs, a wind band, brass group, flute choir, string ensemble, African drumming group and an ever-growing Samba band.

The Paragon is proud of its consistently impressive academic results but we strive for much more than success in exams. We believe in developing the whole person – physically, spiritually, and emotionally as well as intellectually. As W B Yeats said: 'Education is not filling a bucket but lighting a fire.'

Charitable status. Prior Park Educational Trust is a Registered Charity, number 281242.

Parkside School

The Manor, Stoke d'Abernon, Cobham, Surrey KT11 3PX

Tel: 01932 862749
email: office@parkside-school.co.uk
website: www.parkside-school.co.uk
Twitter: @parksideprep
Facebook: @parksideprep
Instagram: @parkside_prep

Chairman of Governors: Robin Southwell

Head: **Ms Nicole Janssen**, BA Hons, PGCE, NPQH

Bursar: Mr A Fernando, BA Hons, CA

Deputy Head: Mrs M McMurdo, BEd Hons

Deputy Head: Mr W Gudgeon, BA Hons, QTS MEd

Age Range. Boys 2–13 years old. Co-educational Nursery 2–4 years old.

Numbers. Total 260: Prep 162, Pre Prep 53, Nursery 45.

Fees per term (2021–2022). Prep Boys £5,814, Pre Prep £4,238, Nursery £880–£3,520.

Parkside School is a wonderful environment where children's curiosity is awakened. Their journey is one of discovery; where talents and passions are nurtured and developed, and pupils are encouraged to take responsibility for their learning. It is an independent boys' school with a co-educational nursery set in 45 acres of beautiful Surrey countryside with school bus routes including to and from South West London.

Parkside was founded in 1879 and became a Charitable Trust in 1960. The School moved from East Horsley to its present site, The Manor, in 1979, its centenary year. Since the move, a continual development programme has seen the development of a purpose-built, well-equipped Science block, an extension of the main building to provide more Pre Prep classrooms, a Performance Hall, a Music School and six practice rooms. A new Food Technology Room and Forest School were opened in 2019, and an additional science lab was added in 2021 along with the new Outdoor Learning Area.

There is also a 20m indoor swimming pool and Sports Hall complex with a stage for drama, and a £2 million classroom block was added to further enhance the facilities in the school. The Design Technology Department, Nursery and new STEM ICT suite are housed in a delightful Grade II-listed barn which has been skilfully refurbished to provide spacious, well-lit classrooms and workshops. The newly refurbished second Computer Room 'CHQ' opened this Autumn 2021 with the Art and Music facilities housed in dedicated buildings.

The school is large enough to be flexible and offer setting in major subjects, yet small enough for each pupil to be known and treated as an individual. On average there are between 8–15 pupils in a 'set'. All teaching staff are highly qualified and are passionate about boys' learning; specialist teaching begins in Year 1 in Sport, ICT, Music and Forest School and for all subjects from Year 3 to Year 8. The children in Parkside's Nursery also enjoy individual swimming lessons, French and Forest School alongside the Early Years Curriculum. Each boy is a member of a House and this helps to stimulate friendly competition for work points and many other inter-house contests.

At Parkside, pupils develop the courage to rise to each challenge, persevere when the going gets tough and face their fears with confidence. The positive message of 'make it happen' underpins the whole approach to the learning journey and is at the forefront of all the pupils' minds. They are supported to take risks and persist with any obstacles they may encounter on their journey. Areas of improvement, as well as strengths, are celebrated and used to develop skills in order to achieve goals. The belief is that taking risks ensures complete development, resulting in a sense of pride and determination coupled with an unrivalled work ethic; invaluable in gaining success for their future.

The National Curriculum is a framework used to prepare all boys for entry to Senior Independent Schools at Year 9 by Common Entrance along with Scholarship examinations. All boys pass to their first choice Senior Schools and results in these examinations are impressive. **Parkside School achieved a 100% CE pass rate in 2021, with 100% scholarships gained to Tonbridge, RGS, Charterhouse, Reed's and commendation to Harrow.** The curriculum is broad based, and boys are taught Art, Music, PE, Food Tech, Forest School and Technology in addition to the usual Common Entrance subjects. There is a School Choir, Chamber Choir, Big Band, a School Orchestra and several smaller musical groups. During the year, there are many opportunities for boys to perform in musical and dramatic productions.

A Parkside education is forward thinking and based on a creative curriculum; however, traditional values are woven through all learning in day-to-day life. Success is supported by an emphasis on manners and etiquette; thus, ensuring the boys leave Parkside as outstanding and well-rounded gentlemen.

The School has a very well-known sporting record and many tournaments in different sports and at different age groups have been won, with Parkside coming in the top 10 in the country at IAPS Finals. In addition, a number of boys have gone on to represent their County and Country in various sports. The main sports are football (taught by Chelsea FC professionals), rugby, hockey and cricket, but boys are also able to take part in swimming, athletics, water polo, tennis, cross-country running, basketball and judo, as well as yoga. An extensive After School Activity Programme (including supervised homework sessions) is available, with over 40 different activities on offer, from gardening to kayaking, touch typing and coding to mindfulness with the newly added shooting club and bike trail club. Many boys have also represented the school at a high level (County and England) in chess. The 45 acre beautiful estate and the River Mole, which runs through the grounds, are also used to contribute to the all-round education each pupil receives both in and out of the classroom.

All children from Nursery to Year 8 can be supervised from 7.30am–6.00pm daily. Breakfast Club runs from 7.30–8.15am in the Nursery and Main School where a choice of hot and continental breakfast is offered. After school care is available for Nursery children from 3.00–6.00pm, Pre Prep boys from 4.00–6.00pm and Prep boys from 5.00–6.00pm. A hot meal is served between 5.00 and 6.00pm and sandwiches between 4.00 and 5.00pm.

Snacks are provided in Nursery between 3.00 and 4.00pm. Boys staying from 5.00–6.00pm will have the opportunity to complete their prep. After school care may be booked in advance or on an ad hoc basis by 9.00am in the morning.

Parkside was selected as one of five finalists in the UK as Best Independent Boys' School 2020 (ISOTY) as well as being finalists in the 2021 awards. This has been largely accredited, not only to the values, aims and ethos mentioned, but also to its colossal efforts in providing a continued outstanding education during the Covid-19 crisis. From the moment the government locked down the UK to the present day, the 'show must go on' approach to the children's education as well as the safety and wellbeing of Parkside's community has come first.

Virtual and individual tours are available by appointment only. For further details, contact Parkside's Registrar, Mrs Lindre Scott via email: admissions@parkside-school.co.uk or call 01932 62749

Charitable status. Parkside School is a Registered Charity, number 312041

Pembridge Hall School
Alpha Plus Group

18 Pembridge Square, London W2 4EH

Tel: 020 7229 0121
email: contact@pembridgehall.co.uk
website: www.pembridgehall.co.uk

Headmaster: **Mr Henry Keighley-Elstub**, BA Hons, PGCE

Age Range. 4–11.
Number of Girls. 418.
Fees per term (2021–2022). £7,815.

Pembridge girls take advantage of a vast array of learning experiences, both inside and out of the classroom. Pembridge Hall offers a 'three-dimensional education', believing that it is only by creating an environment in which teaching is inspiring and imaginative that girls will thrive. Sport and the Arts feature strongly on the curriculum.

Teachers, girls and parents work in a close partnership, ensuring that each girl is happy and achieving her maximum potential in every area of school life. Girls transfer at the end of Year Six to some of the finest senior day and boarding schools in the country.

Pennthorpe

Church Street, Rudgwick, Nr Horsham, West Sussex RH12 3HJ

Tel: 01403 822391
email: enquiries@pennthorpe.com
website: www.pennthorpe.com
Twitter: @PennthorpeSch
Facebook: @PennthorpeSchool
Instagram: @PennthorpeSchool
LinkedIn: Pennthorpe

Headmistress: **Mrs Alexia Bolton**, MEd, MA, BA Hons, QTS, PCPSE

Deputy Head: Mrs Lydia Waller, MA, BA Hons, PGCO, MPQSL

Bursar and Clerk to the Governors: Mr Brian Dempster, Assoc. CIB

Assistant Head (*Academic*): Mr David Cotmore, BA Hons, QTS, NPQSL

Head of Pre-Prep: Mrs Kylie McGregor, BA Hons, QTS

Head of Admissions & Communications: Mrs Catherine Pinder, MSc, BSc Hons

Age Range: Co-educational 2–13.
Number of Pupils: 250 Day Pupils.
Fees per term (2021–2022): £750–£5,780.

Whether it's academic achievement, consideration and kindness towards others, or an energetic and positive attitude – excellence underpins all that we do at Pennthorpe, and all that we strive to be.

Pennthorpe is a place of discovery, where the happiness of children takes precedence and the focus on learning, and dedication to every child's confidence and success, is relentless.

At Pennthorpe, children are uniquely valued for who they are, and for their individual strengths and passions. Whether in maths or textiles, cello or rugby, all skills are celebrated – everybody is somebody at Pennthorpe.

Children are deeply involved in their learning, demonstrated by their enthusiasm, their desire to learn new things and take risks, and their willingness to be in the driving seat of their own destiny. Children take responsibility for who, and what, they are becoming, in addition to who they aspire to be. Hopes and dreams become a reality at Pennthorpe.

Our broad and skills based curriculum requires our children to be authentic, independent learners; to trust their instincts and to be bold.

We teach our children *how* to learn, and then give them the tools and inspiration to challenge themselves. We embrace our failings; enabling our children to experience and overcome disappointment and fear, as well as gain perspective. Our innovative curriculum enables our children to dabble in everything, whilst giving them time to become thinkers, time to reflect, time to work slowly as well as quickly. We work hard to develop young people who can confidently take their place in the world, and prepare them to set about making it a better place for others.

Our exceptional staff team is integral to Pennthorpe's happy environment. The knowledge, passion, care and diversity of our team, complemented by our bespoke Wellbeing Curriculum, with its innovative elements such as our termly Happiness Tracker, creates Pennthorpe's very exciting atmosphere. We are committed to helping our children be happy, healthy and flourish. This is the foundation upon which academic success is built.

Topping it all off with our 26 acre, tardis-like campus, which is crammed with first rate, extensive facilities, means Pennthorpe offers a desirable education few could contend! The Independent School Inspectorate (ISI) agree; Pennthorpe achieved 'Excellent' in all categories in its latest inspection in October 2018. The inspectorate's report states "Pupils' attitudes to learning are excellent. As a result, they persevere, are resilient, confident and active learners who involve themselves fully in all they do."

Charitable status: Pennthorpe School is a Registered Charity, number 307043. It exists to provide an excellent education for boys and girls and to benefit the community.

Perrott Hill

North Perrott, Crewkerne, Somerset TA18 7SL

Tel: 01460 72051
email: admissions@perrotthill.com
website: www.perrotthill.com
Twitter: @perrotthill
Facebook: @PerrottHillSchool
Instagram: @perrotthill
LinkedIn: /perrott-hill-prep-school

Chair of the Board of Directors: Timothy Fisher

Chair of the Board of Governors: Lord Bradbury

Headmaster: **Mr Alexander McCullough**, BA Hons Dunelm, PGCE, NPQH

Age Range. 3–13.
Number of Pupils. 85 boys and 74 girls, of whom 20 are full, weekly or flexi boarders.
Fees per term (2021–2022). Boarders: £7,095 (weekly), £8,405 (full), £8,820 (international); Day pupils £1,880–£5,820.

Perrott Hill is an award-winning day and boarding school set in 28 acres of beautiful grounds in the heart of the countryside, near Crewkerne on the Somerset/Dorset border. It is served by excellent road and rail networks, being around two and a half hours from London. The school was awarded the Supporting Junior Boarders award at the prestigious BSA Awards 2020 and was named as one of only seven finalists for Prep School of the Year at the Independent Schools of the Year Awards 2020. The school was named Pre-Prep of the Year at the Independent Schools of the Year Awards 2019.

Perrott Hill is a thriving country preparatory school where children settle quickly and learn in confidence. Class sizes are small, with pupils being streamed from Year 5 onwards, where class sizes allow. Staff are dedicated and highly qualified. Sports facilities include an all-weather pitch, purpose-built sports hall, games fields, outdoor swimming pool and a four hole pitch and putt course. There is a theatre, an eco-build music school, Tinker Lab and extensive Forest School.

The award-winning Nursery and Pre-Prep are housed within the converted stable courtyard next to the main school buildings, which gives the younger children their own safe, secure environment whilst allowing them to take advantage of the grounds and facilities of the Prep School. There is an emphasis on outdoor learning including weekly on-site Forest School sessions.

Music, drama and art are taught within the timetable alongside core curriculum subjects. The choir and orchestra perform at charity concerts, in competitions and school functions and the school's recent Virtual Carol Service was broadcast to care homes across the county. There are drama productions throughout the school year.

Teaching is class-based until Year 5 and subject-based in the upper school, where all lessons are taught by specialist teachers. French, Music, IT and PE, however, are taught by specialists throughout the school.

Each child, boarding or day, has his or her own pastoral and academic tutor, while the welfare of the boarders is supervised by Mrs Layfield and Mr Sheldon. They are ably assisted by a dedicated and enthusiastic boarding staff (many of which live on site).

Sport is played every day, and matches take place on Tuesdays and Wednesdays as well as on Saturdays for the senior part of the school. Emphasis is placed upon skills and team work and games played include rugby, football, hockey, netball, cricket, tennis, rounders, swimming and cross-country running. The school takes part in national events, such as the National Small Schools Rugby Sevens. Optional extras include fencing, pinhole photography, carpentry, archery, karate, horse riding, ballet, speech and drama, cookery, Spanish, golf and craft. The school was named as 'great for extra-curricular' in The Week's Independent Schools Guide 2019.

Perrott Hill combines extremely high standards of academic and pastoral care and provides a 'home from home' for its pupils. The school has an enviable scholarship record, with 93 scholarships across the past six years, including an art scholarship to Harrow and a rugby scholarship to Millfield. Leavers' destinations include Blundell's, Bryanston, Canford, Downside, Eton, Harrow, King's Bruton, King's College Taunton, Marlborough, Millfield, Milton Abbey, Queen's College Taunton, Sherborne, Sherborne Girls, Taunton School, Radley and Winchester. Academic, music, sport, art, drama and all-rounder Scholarships are offered annually in February to children in Year 4 (9+) and Year 6 (11+).

The combination of countryside, space, a family atmosphere and a forward-looking academic programme creates an ideal environment for children to thrive both academically and in their leisure pursuits. Parents are encouraged to attend one of the school's Open Mornings which take place termly (including Virtual Open Mornings), and individual tours are available throughout the year.

The Perse Pelican Nursery and Pre-Preparatory School

92 Glebe Road, Cambridge CB1 7TD

Tel: 01223 403940
email: pelican@perse.co.uk
website: www.perse.co.uk

Chairman of Governors: J W Scott, MA

Head: **Mrs Francesca Heftman**, BA

Age Range. 3–7.

Number of Pupils. 150.

Ethos. We aim to awaken a thirst for learning, helping children to develop an understanding and enjoyment of the world around them. The children are enthusiastic and inspired by the opportunities on offer and delight in meeting challenges and taking risks whilst benefiting from a safe and secure environment. They learn through a range of play-based activities as well as more formal methods of learning and have many opportunities to develop their independence.

Our aim is to ensure that the children in our care are sociable, rounded, confident and inquisitive. We are proud of our broad, challenging, enticing curriculum and the spirit with which our pupils approach their learning.

Admissions. The main entry point for the Pelican is Nursery, which is for children who are three years old by 1 September in the year of entry. There are also a few spaces available for new children in Reception.

History. The buildings of the Nursery and Pre-Prep began life in 1911 as a boarding house for the Upper School. The School has been sympathetically extended inside and out, so that it provides exceptional space and excellent facilities, yet still feels like a home from home.

School Life. Our pastoral care is second to none. Every single child in the School is known to all and is valued for their individual characteristics. All achievements are celebrated.

Classroom routines are quickly established from the start of a child's time at the Pelican, and from day one they feel they belong. Every class benefits from a full-time teaching assistant who works alongside the teacher.

Dance, Games, Languages and Music are all taught by specialist teachers. An inclusive choir is open to everyone in Years 1 and 2 and a range of music ensembles are formed each year appropriate to the needs of the children in those year groups at the time. Our musicians regularly perform in regional and national festivals.

The children relish challenge and aim high, knowing that there is always someone to support them. We work in partnership with parents to nurture children's interests and provide opportunities to develop their potential. Pupils begin to acquire essential skills through play, topic work and a wide range of experiences and activities.

A Rounded Education. Regular school trips bring learning to life and being close to the centre of Cambridge, the School is able to take advantage of trips to local museums and wildlife parks.

Out of School Care. Children may be dropped at school from 8.00am and may stay until 5.30pm each day. We run an extended range of after school clubs catering to all tastes, from ballet to science, chess to football, and drama to gymnastics. In addition, children may attend our own holiday club, known as Club Pelican, which runs for 7 weeks of the year: five weeks in the summer holidays and one week in each of the Christmas and Easter holidays.

Moving On. By the end of Year 2, children are ready to move onto the Prep with confidence and enthusiasm. Their move is gradual and carefully managed.

Fees per term (2021–2022). Full-time (Reception, Years 1 and 2) £4,826, Part-time Nursery (six sessions per week) £3,252. Additional Nursery sessions: £43.84 per session. Nursery children attend a minimum of six sessions per week (two of which must be afternoons) but may attend up to 10 sessions per week.

Charitable status. The Perse School is a charitable company limited by guarantee (company number 5977683, registered charity number 1120654) registered in England and Wales whose registered office is situated at The Perse School, Hills Road, Cambridge CB2 8QF.

The Perse Preparatory School

Trumpington Road, Cambridge CB2 8EX

Tel: 01223 403920
email: prep@perse.co.uk
website: www.perse.co.uk

Chairman of Governors: Mr Jonathan W Scott, MA

Head: **James Piper**, BA Hons, PGCE, MEd

Age Range. 7–11.

Number of Pupils. 283.

Ethos. At the Prep we are committed to helping your child develop as a confident, smiling, interesting and interested individual. Our School has a strong academic edge, attracting an outstanding group of specialist staff who encourage in the children academic curiosity and a love of learning. Prep children thrive on challenges outside the classroom with great emphasis placed on developing breadth and balance through first-rate sport, clubs, music, art, drama and outdoor pursuits. Excellent pastoral care is at the heart of our work and ensures that our children feel completely at ease and secure in their surroundings.

Admissions. The main entry point to the Prep is Year 3 (7+) with about 25 places available. Admissions to Years 4, 5 and 6 is dependent on availability of places with about 3 places available in each year. Entrance tests assess the applicant's abilities in English, Maths and reasoning, and a reference from the child's current school is also sought. Selection for all year groups takes place in mid-January of the year of intended entry.

Facilities. The Prep is set in spacious mature parkland on Trumpington Road. Traditional and modern buildings are successfully combined on site, from the Victorian Leighton House to the 'New School' classroom block, and the Science block which opened in 2017. The Prep has nine acres of playing fields on its doorstep, including a full-size AstroTurf.

Educational success. The Prep is an academically selective school with pupils of above average ability who relish challenge. Most pupils progress to the Upper School in Year 7. Pupils follow a broad curriculum which promotes intellectual curiosity and a love of learning, and we nurture creativity through a vibrant programme of drama, music and art.

The depth of academic ability throughout the School allows intellectual curiosity to flourish and pupils thrive on challenges both inside and outside the classroom. Enjoyment of learning, mutual respect and the celebration of achievement characterise life at the Prep and as a result children become independent, confident and responsible.

A supportive environment. Pastoral care is first class: Form Teachers, Heads of Year and the Assistant Head (Pastoral) all support pupils, who have access to a medical room, with a qualified nurse, and to our counselling service.

A rounded education. We make good use of technology, based on our philosophy that it should be effective, meaningful and engaging. Resources include a dedicated ICT suite, a music technology room and bookable laptops and iPads. All classrooms are equipped with SMART boards and PCs. Staff can access the school Wi-Fi (with age appropriate filtering) and we use Teams and SharePoint as our Virtual Learning Environments.

We encourage every pupil to make the most of our extra-curricular provision. There is a wide range of lunchtime and after school clubs – more than 70 currently. Music is strong with over 30 different ensembles (including numerous choirs and an orchestra comprising of a quarter of the School). Sport is a major part of a Prep education, and all children compete, whether in House Matches or against other schools. The games programme (football, rugby, cricket, netball, athletics, tennis and hockey) is designed to encourage all pupils to enjoy games and physical exercise. Music plays an important part in the curriculum and wider life of the School. The majority of pupils learn a musical instrument and there are choirs, orchestras and numerous instrumental groups, where there are many opportunities for the children to perform publicly.

Moving on. The School plans carefully for a smooth transition to the Upper School. Year 5 and 6 pupils spend days on the Upper site as part of their subject learning, helping to prepare them for the move up.

Fees per term (2021–2022). £5,602.

Charitable status. The Perse School is a charitable company limited by guarantee (company number 5977683, registered charity number 1120654) registered in England and Wales whose registered office is situated at The Perse School, Hills Road, Cambridge CB2 8QF.

The Pilgrims' School

The Close, Winchester, Hampshire SO23 9LT

Tel: 01962 854189
email: admissions@pilgrims-school.co.uk
           info@pilgrims-school.co.uk
website: www.thepilgrims-school.co.uk
Twitter: @PilgrimsSchool
Facebook: @PilgrimsSchool
Instagram: @thepilgrimswinchester
LinkedIn: /the-pilgrims-school

Chairman of Governors: Ian Power

Head: **Dr Sarah Essex**, BA Cantab, PhD

Age Range. Boys 4–13.

Number of Pupils. 244 Boys (87 boarders/weekly boarders, 128 day boys, 29 boys in Pre-Prep).

Fees per term (2021–2022). Boarders £8,688, Day boys £6,819–£6,620, Pre-Prep £3,914.

Preparing boys for a broad portfolio of independent schools, with a significant number moving to Winchester College each year. Cathedral Choristers and Winchester College Quiristers are educated at the school and receive scholarships and bursaries up to the value of the full boarding fee together with free tuition in one musical instrument. All boys whether musical or not receive excellent academic and musical tuition, and the sporting tradition is equally strong. The school is noted for its happy family atmosphere, with a major focus on each boy finding his passion and talents, whether they be academic, sporting or artistic. Boarding is a popular option, either full or weekly. All enquiries about the school or singing auditions should be addressed to the Registrar.

Charitable status. The Pilgrims' School is a Registered Charity, number 1091579.

Pinewood

Bourton, Shrivenham, Wiltshire SN6 8HZ

Tel: 01793 782205
email: office@pinewoodschool.co.uk
website: www.pinewoodschool.co.uk
Twitter: @pinewoodprepsch
Facebook: @Pinewoodprepschool
Instagram: @pinewoodprepschool

Headmaster: **Neal Bailey**

Deputy Head: Colin Acheson-Gray, BEd

Age Range. 3–13.

Number of Pupils. 400 Boys and Girls (52% of year 5, 6, 7 and 8 are weekly or regular boarders) of which Nursery and Pre-Prep: 103.

Fees per term (2021–2022). Day £3,410–£6,565 inclusive, with no compulsory extras. Weekly boarding supplement: £1,600.

Pinewood is set in 84 acres of rolling countryside. The School offers a quality, family-based environment where children are encouraged to think for themselves and a strong emphasis is placed on self-discipline, manners, trust and selflessness. Resources include a purpose-built Music School and Science Labs, a flourishing Pre-Prep and Nursery, Art and Design Workshops, Research and Reference Library, ICT Rooms, AstroTurf and a state-of-the-art Sports Hall. Fortnightly exeats. Regular or weekly boarding from Year 5 upwards.

Excellent academic results are achieved through a mixture of traditional and forward-thinking teaching within a happy, friendly and stimulating learning atmosphere. Outside trips are frequent and visiting speakers prominent. Great success in Music, Art and Drama.

Sport is keenly coached and matches are played at all levels on our picturesque playing fields, which incorporate a nine-hole golf course. There is a wide range of activities and clubs both for day children and, in the evening, for boarders.

Pinewood is a school where staff, parents and children work together to find and realise the potential in every child.

Exit Schools: Marlborough, Cheltenham College, Bradfield, Radley, St Edward's Oxford, Cheltenham Ladies, Sherborne, Sherborne Girls, Rendcomb, Wellington College, St Mary's Calne, Dean Close, Monkton Combe, Tudor Hall.

Charitable status. Pinewood is a Registered Charity, number 309642. It exists to provide high quality education for boys and girls.

Port Regis

Motcombe Park, Shaftesbury, Dorset SP7 9QA

Tel: 01747 857800
email: admissions@portregis.com
website: www.portregis.com
Twitter: @PortRegisSchool
Facebook: @PortRegis
Instagram: @portregisschool

Chairman of the Governors: Mr James Hussey

Headmaster: **Mr Titus Mills**, BA, PGCE

Age Range. 2–13.

Number of Pupils. 320

Fees per term (2021–2022). Boarders £9,760 (full); Day £5,795–£7,250. Pre-Prep £3,330.

Port Regis is a co-educational day and boarding school for children aged 2–13. Located in the beautiful Dorset countryside, the school provides the perfect environment in which boys and girls can flourish and enjoy school.

Message from the Headmaster: "It is a tremendous honour to be the new Head of this wonderful school. Port Regis is steeped in history, founded as it was in 1881, and yet it remains a community that is, at its core, forward thinking and determinedly innovative in its approach to educating and nurturing young children.
Few other prep schools can provide the breadth of experience on offer at Port Regis. It is internationally renowned for its exceptional staff team and academic credentials, as well as our first-class facilities set within 150 acres of stunning grounds in rural Dorset. These facilities (that eclipse many at senior schools) enable Port Regis to deliver an outstanding holistic education that seeks to inspire the head, the hand and the heart together.
However, I believe it is the engagement of the *heart*, in education, that is of the most crucial importance. I have come to understand that the best schools not only focus on the expansion of pupils' intellects, artistic creativity or physical health. The best schools seek to go deeper still. They aim to nurture and steer the character and moral values of its children. As a preparatory school, not only are we preparing girls and boys for life at a senior school, we're preparing them for the great adventure of life itself. So, it seems entirely fitting for Port Regis to have such a compelling school motto: '*We seek higher things.*' This seems to get to the heart of the matter. Our passion here is to help our pupils hone an array of qualities – compassion and conviction, teamwork and empathy, resilience and curiosity, good manners and friendship. These things underpin a Port Regis education. These things propel Port Regians far in life.
And an educational journey such as this should not only be purposeful and stretching, but also great fun! The best schools should be joyful schools. Joy and wonder are integral parts of childhood and, I believe, these happy hallmarks should be clearly visible, and audible, in every corridor, classroom and playground.
We would love you to come and visit Port Regis. It is a special place. You will find a community in a stunning location, with a distinctive ethos and a tremendous spirit!"
Titus

Port Regis is located in 150 acres of parkland in the stunning Dorset countryside and enjoys a beautiful campus with facilities that are second to none in the Prep school world. Extensive woodland with nature trails sits alongside lawns, several ponds and a lake, so that the children can enjoy the space and freedom of the grounds. There are also 35 acres of games pitches, a nine-hole (18 tees) golf course, hockey pitch, hard tennis and netball courts, a 25m indoor swimming pool, a rifle range and an indoor sports complex, which includes two sports halls. An equestrian centre is conveniently situated close to the School.

The school's enviable reputation attracts the best teaching staff from all over the country. We are extremely fortunate to have an immensely accomplished team of staff dedicated to achieving this and who provide the happy, family atmosphere in which a child can realise their full potential.

Port Regis is extremely proud of its 100% Common Entrance success record and the high number of scholarships and awards won to senior schools every year. Learning Support is available for children with mild-to-moderate specific learning difficulties.

Extensive opportunities are provided for Music (about three-quarters of the School learn an instrument), Drama (there are up to six productions a year) and Art (in a wide choice of media), with Woodwork, Electronics, Riding, .22 Rifle Shooting, Karate, Gymnastics and Canoeing included in a list of over 70 hobby options. Major team games are Rugby, Hockey, Soccer, Netball, Cricket and Rounders. Inter-school, county and national standard competitions are entered. Home and abroad trips take place.

The high standard of boarding provision is an impressively strong feature of the school, which explains why so many boys and girls choose to board (awarded 'Outstanding' by Ofsted following their recent boarding inspection). The school was inspected by the Independent Schools Inspectorate (ISI) in June 2014 and was rated 'Excellent' in every single judgement.

Open Mornings take place each term and include tours of the school with pupils. Personal visits are also available.

Academic, Music, Gymnastic, Sport and All-Rounder entrance scholarships may be awarded annually. The School also has a wealth of experience in dealing with HM Services Families and offers special awards to children of HM Services Families.

Charitable status. Port Regis School Limited is a Registered Charity, number 306218.

Pownall Hall

Carrwood Road, Wilmslow, Cheshire SK9 5DW

Tel:	01625 523141
email:	headmaster@pownallhallschool.co.uk
website:	www.pownallhallschool.co.uk
Twitter:	@PownallHallSchool
Facebook:	@Pownall-Hall-School
Instagram:	@pownallschool

Chair of Governors: Mrs Eileen MacAulay

Head: **Mr D Goulbourn**, BA Hons, PGCE Distinction

Age Range. 2–11 Co-educational.
Number of Boys and Girls. 250 (Day Children)
Fees per term (2021–2022). £3,250–£3,750.

Pownall Hall, a preparatory day school for children aged 2 to 11 and set in its own beautiful and extensive grounds, has been established for over 100 years. It is situated on the north-western side of Wilmslow, 12 miles from Manchester and within easy reach of motorway, rail and air travel.

The school has highly-trained teaching staff, who prepare children for the Entrance Examinations to the Independent Day schools and Grammar schools in the area. A thorough grounding is given in all academic subjects extending well beyond the confines of the National Curriculum. An excellent mixture of traditional and modern techniques is used through the implementation of cutting-edge technology in and around every classroom. In Key Stage 2 each major subject has specialist teaching staff and subject rooms including a fully-equipped Science Laboratory, Art Studio, D&T Studio, Maths, English, Information Technology, and MFL rooms and, in addition, a computer-aided Library. Spanish, French and German are taught from the age of two.

Pownall Hall School has two pre-school years with children entering the Nursery from the age of 2 and transferring to Kindergarten at the age of 3. From January 2022 there will also be a room for children from 6 months–2 years From Kindergarten the pupils then enter Reception and go through the school to Year 6, by which point the school will have guided parents as to where best for their child to continue their education at the age of 11.

At Pownall Hall there is an excellent staff to pupil ratio throughout the school, ensuring that pastoral care is of a very high level and also supporting the learning of children of all abilities, in conjunction with a specialist SEND provision. Children are taught in small class sizes, gaining from the individual attention they receive.

Great importance is attached to Sport, Music and Drama in order to develop the rounded education that allows all children to achieve, wherever their ability lies. The school has its own well-equipped theatre where all children perform on stage during the year. Music is offered as part of the curriculum and also additionally through a full range of peripatetic teaching staff, providing chances for the children to perform in and outside school. As well as subject specialist rooms with an outstanding range of specialist equipment, the implementation of mobile technology for both staff and children provides opportunity for outstanding teaching and learning across the school.

The facilities for sport are very impressive with the school having its own extensive grounds, alongside a fully-equipped Sports Hall, Astro Pitch and both outdoor and indoor facilities for Netball, Hockey, Football, Rugby, Tennis and so much more.

All children experience outdoor learning, with Forest School, Extra-Curricular clubs, day and residential trips arranged as well as utilising our on-site woods for free-flow teaching and learning at all ages. Children in Years 3 to 6 also experience outdoor pursuits at a range of well-equipped sites which enhance their learning experiences. There is an extensive provision of co-curricular clubs, complementing our out-of-hours Breakfast Club and After School Care. Holiday Club runs on site throughout the year.

The school received an outstanding Full Inspection Report in 2017 and an outstanding EYFS Inspection in 2014.

Charitable status. Pownall Hall School is a Registered Charity, number 525929. It exists to provide education for boys and girls, aged 2–11 yrs.

The Prebendal School

52–55 West Street, Chichester, West Sussex PO19 1RT

Tel:	01243 772220
email:	office@prebendalschool.org.uk
website:	www.prebendalschool.org.uk
Twitter:	@theprebendal
Facebook:	@ThePrebendalSchool
Instagram:	@the_prebendal_school
LinkedIn:	/company/the-prebendal-school

Proprietor: Mr Ali Khan

Head: **Mrs Louise Salmond Smith**, BA, MMus, MBA, MA, PGCE, FRSA

Deputy Head: Mr I Richardson, BMus, MMus, FTCL, ARCO

Bursar: Mr M Chapman, MA, MBA

Chaplain: Reverend Dr I Smale, BA, MA, PhD

Age Range. 3–13.
Number of Pupils. 120 pupils in total (including 20 boarders): 82 in the Prep School (Years 3–8) and 38 in the Pre-Prep (Nursery–Year 2).

Fees per term (2021–2022). Full Boarders £7,900. Day Pupils: Years 5–8 £5,500; Years 3–4 £5,100. Weekly Boarding: £1,630 in addition to Day Fee. Reception–Year 2: £2,950–£3,420. Nursery: £8.50 per hour. Compulsory extras: laundry and linen for Full Boarders.

The Prebendal is the oldest school in Sussex and has occupied its present building at the west end of the Cathedral (though with later additions) for hundreds of years. The Cathedral Choristers are among the pupils educated at the school and they receive Choral Scholarships in reduction of fees. A range of scholarships and means-tested bursaries are available. Music and Academic scholarships are open to pupils entering the prep school and there are Academic, Art, Music & Sport scholarships available for Year 7 entry. Sibling discount, former Prebendalian discount and Armed Forces discount are also available. Year 8 Leavers achieve an impressive range of scholarship awards to a range of prestigious senior schools every September. In 2020, 82% of Year 8 leavers achieved awards.

There are excellent playing fields in the heart of the city. The sports are football, hockey, netball, cricket, athletics, tennis, rugby and rounders. Younger children enjoy Beach School and the school unveiled a new outdoor classroom and amphitheatre in September 2018. A new Pavilion is being built in 2022. The Pre-Senior Baccalaureate (PSB) and Quadrivium, a programme of academic excellence for children in Years 6–8, were also introduced in 2018. Pupils in Years 6–8 use iPads as an additional tool to enrich their learning.

Approximately 95% of the children learn to play musical instruments and the school has a large range of ensembles and choirs along with Concert Band and 1st Orchestra. There are many optional extras and after-school clubs, such as Forest School and Sailing. Flexi boarding is a popular choice and there is a growing demand for the extended day programme, from Breakfast Club to supper, for busy families. Pelicans Nursery opened in September 2019, with 7am to 7pm provision for three and four year olds so they can be Reception-ready.

Former pupils, parents and staff are known as The Prebendal Associates and events are held regularly throughout each academic year. The School also has its own thriving Toddler Group on Wednesday mornings during term time. The Head of The Prebendal School, Mrs Louise Salmond Smith, took up the post in September 2017.

Charitable status. The Prebendal School is a Registered Charity, number 1157782. Registered Company No. 09038149.

Prestfelde

London Road, Shrewsbury, Shropshire SY2 6NZ

Tel: 01743 245400
email: office@prestfelde.co.uk
website: www.prestfelde.co.uk
Twitter: @prestfelde
Facebook: @prestfelde
LinkedIn: /Prestfelde

Shrewsbury's Co-educational Prep School for all aged 3–13.

Chairman of Governors: Mr Stuart Hay, MB ChB, FRCS, FRCS Orth

Head: **Mrs F Orchard**, GTCL Trinity College, PGCE Reading

Age Range. 3–13.
Number of Pupils. 350 (201 boys, 149 girls).
Fees per term (2021–2022). Flexi Boarding: £34 per night, Day: Year 8 £5,730, Years 6–7 £5,700, Year 5 £5,630, Year 4 £5,410, Year 3 £4,630, Year 2 £3,540, Year 1 £3,460, Reception £3,400, Nursery £1,820 (5 mornings).

Supported by the nurturing environment that Prestfelde provides, children and their parents benefit from first-class facilities and a highly progressive and inclusive education. We pride ourselves on providing the best school experience a child can have, one that enriches their happiness in school, enables them to pursue their individual interests and develop confidence to grow into the person they want to be. Our excellent teachers build trusting relationships and impart their knowledge through inspirational teaching and learning experiences. Guiding and transforming pupils through a broad range of experiential learning; children at Prestfelde gain the skills, qualities and knowledge to set them up to succeed.

The site extends over 30 acres and backs onto countryside with top-class playing fields which form an integral part of the excellent sporting facilities.

Academic highlights are underlined by the level of success and quality of scholarships gained by pupils in the final year group. In 2021, Year 8 pupils achieved consistently high pass rates at Common Entrance despite COVID limitations and were 100% successful in gaining places to their first-choice senior schools. Each year pupils gain scholarships to a number of aspirational independent schools, covering every section of the curriculum from art, design, technology and drama to music and sport. Equally pupils choosing to progress to maintained schools are very well prepared for the next stage of their education, having been encouraged to adopt a positive work ethic.

Whilst many pupils maintain high levels of competitive sport in their disciplines, we recognise the importance of children enjoying the challenges of team sport at school. Outstanding coaching and mentoring in football, netball, rugby, lacrosse and cricket have encouraged pupils to become outstanding team players. Additional hours of coaching in these and other sports, together with physical education lessons, swimming (on site) and outdoor fitness by specialist coaches, enhance the physical well-being of Prestfelde pupils, resulting in the enjoyment of competition in a variety of sporting environments.

The extra-curricular offering at Prestfelde is designed to build on children's experiences with the aim of improving outcomes in all areas of their learning. Purposefully building on pupils' interests, we aim to light that spark for learning and to develop talents. Activities range from bushcraft and outdoor gardening to construction and minecraft. Pupils enjoy the many and varied inter-house competitions and the friendly rivalry enhances the will and enjoyment of achievement.

Charitable status. Prestfelde School is a Registered Charity, number 1102931. It aims to provide education for boys and girls.

Prospect House School

75 Putney Hill, London SW15 3NT

Tel:	020 8780 0456
email:	info@prospecths.org.uk
website:	www.prospecths.org.uk
Twitter:	@prospecths
Facebook:	@Prospect-House-School-163116433760812
Instagram:	@prospect_house_school

Managing Governor: Mrs L Nicholas

Head: **Mr Michael Hodge**, BPrimEd Rhodes QTS

Age Range. 3–11 co-educational.

Number of Pupils. 320 day pupils.

Fees per term (2021–2022). Nursery (5 mornings) £3,160, Reception–Year 2 £6,320, Years 3–6 £6,585.

Prospect House School occupies two large buildings on Putney Hill situated just a short walk apart. Children aged 3 to 7 years occupy the Lower School building at 76 Putney Hill and children aged 7 to 11 years are based in the Upper School at 75 Putney Hill. They both have large grounds, including an all-weather sports pitch. There are multi-purpose halls where assemblies, music recitals, gymnastics and drama productions take place. There are dedicated rooms for music, ICT, with art and DT also having provision within the school.

Most children join the school at 3 or 4 years of age, although occasionally there are places for older children. Selection for entry at 3 is by date of registration, with preference being given to brothers and sisters of children already in the school. An equal balance of boys and girls is kept throughout the school. There is also a good balance of male and female staff.

Although the school does not have selective entry at age 3 or 4, the academic track record is very strong. The curriculum includes all National Curriculum subjects, with the addition of French from the age of three. There are numerous specialist teachers and children from Nursery are taught by specialists for Music, PE, French, ICT and Art. Children are prepared for a wide range of leading day and boarding schools for entry at 11 years of age, with a high number of children taking academic, music and sports scholarships. There is a wide and varied sports programme with many fixtures against other preparatory schools and children from Year 2 upwards attend training sessions at a nearby sports ground under the guidance of qualified teachers.

The school was awarded 'Best Primary School' in the UK in 2009–10 for the teaching and use of ICT.

Clubs after school cater for many interests and visiting teachers also provide a wide range of individual music lessons. Children are taken on educational visits to London and the surrounding area every term, with residential field study trips being undertaken from Year 3.

Quainton Hall School

Hindes Road, Harrow HA1 1RX

Tel:	020 8861 8861
email:	admin@quaintonhall.org.uk
website:	www.quaintonhall.org.uk
Twitter:	@QuaintonHall
Facebook:	@QuaintonHallSchool
Instagram:	@quaintonhallschool
LinkedIn:	@quaintonhall

Quainton Hall is a thriving IAPS coeducational Preparatory School, dedicated to the education of boys and girls between the ages of 2½ and 11.

Chairman of the Board of Governors (*a committee of the John Lyon Governing Body*): Mr N Enright, MA Oxon, MBA, NPQH, FRSA

Headmaster: **Mr Simon Ford**, BEd Hons

Age Range. Boys and Girls 2½–11

Number of Pupils. 235

Fees per term (2021–2022). Reception to Year 2: £4,108; Year 3 to Year 6: £4,568 (fees include lunch). Nursery: £63/day, £32/half day. Breakfast and late sessions available.

For more than 120 years Quainton Hall has served families in and around Harrow. The 2021–2022 School year is of particular importance to Quainton Hall as it becomes John Lyon's Prep School, having joined with the nearby John Lyon School.

The life and work of the school is planned to enable children to shine in those areas and activities that they are good at and to reach their full potential. All members of staff have this objective as their aim. We also encourage the notion that learning is fun and that the acquisition of knowledge brings its own rewards. All that we do is conducted in an atmosphere and ethos that is personal, caring and family-orientated. We promote good order and self-discipline, consideration and tolerance towards others as well as personal motivation and group endeavour.

Curriculum. Children enjoy a broad and inclusive education, firmly centred on the core values of respect, integrity, determination and humility. With an emphasis on achievement, we believe in setting high expectations, leading by example and creating a secure, positive and inspiring learning environment where our pupils can feel challenged and supported to aim high and develop their individual talents.

Our results are consistently impressive and many of our leavers gain scholarships to the senior schools of their choice. In a recent ISI School Inspection, we were rated the highest possible 'Excellent', for both our pupils' academic achievement and personal development.

Nursery. As soon as children walk through the doors of our Nursery they become part of the caring Quainton Hall family. Set within a large, recently-refurbished and well-equipped building, with lots of access to outside space, our Nursery children are given the space to be inquisitive about the world around them while being supported to discover a love of learning that will benefit them for the rest of their lives.

Pre-Prep. From Reception to Year 2 our emphasis is on making our pupils feel excited about their learning and showing children how they can develop to the best of their ability in a caring yet challenging environment. We focus on building firm foundations in Literacy and Mathematics whilst ensuring children learn through cross-curricular themes and topics. The small classes have one class teacher and one teaching assistant, which means that each individual child is able to receive all the attention and support needed.

Prep. From Year 3 to Year 6, pupils begin to attend lessons with subject specialists in English and Mathematics, as well as other subjects including Science, Computing, Art and French, together with a full Games programme, which includes some competition against other schools. Great care is taken by form teachers and subject staff to develop in each child a good sense of purpose and drive, supported by sound and effective organisational skills. Each child's effort and attainment is regularly assessed and homework becomes a feature of school life. Children are also expected to have a reading book with them at all times. By the age of 11, Quainton Hall children are ready to make the leap into secondary education with great confidence.

Admissions. Choosing the right nursery and first school for your child can be a daunting prospect, so we are here to guide parents every step of the way.

Children typically join Quainton Hall in either Nursery or Reception years and continue to the end of Year 6, aged 11. However, some children do join us at other stages and we are always pleased to welcome them. We are proud to serve the families of Harrow and surrounding areas. Our families typically come to us from a North West London catchment area including the Boroughs of Barnet, Brent, Ealing and Hillingdon, as well as parts of Middlesex, Berkshire, Buckinghamshire and Hertfordshire.

As John Lyon's Prep School, the most common senior school destination for Quainton Hall pupils is John Lyon School, with unconditional places offered to all pupils without the need to sit an entrance examination. Other school destinations include Merchant Taylor's, the two Haberdasher's schools, and City of London.

Pastoral care. Quainton Hall is very much a family school where children are always our highest priority and where teachers and other staff operate an open-door policy. Our pastoral care is of paramount importance to us and our approach is rooted in a strong sense of community based on the belief that happy children can achieve great things.

Facilities. Through an ongoing desire to improve and enhance our provision, we are proud to boast first rate facilities including a recently refurbished swimming pool and Art and Design Centre, an AstroTurf pitch, a new ICT suite and modern classrooms with interactive whiteboards. We also have extensive use of sporting facilities at John Lyon School.

Charitable status. The Keepers and Governors of the Free Grammar School of John Lyon is a Registered Charity, number 310033.

Queen Elizabeth's Hospital (QEH) – Junior School

9 Upper Berkeley Place, Clifton, Bristol BS8 1JS

Tel: 0117 930 3087
email: juniors@qehbristol.co.uk
website: www.qehbristol.co.uk

Chairman of Governors: Mr P M Keen, FCIB

Junior School Headteacher: **Mr D M Kendall**, BA

Age Range. Boys 7–11.
Number of Pupils. 110 day boys.
Fees per term (2021–2022). £3,420 Fees include pre- and after-school supervision until 5.00pm.

The QEH Junior School was opened in September 2007 and is located in gracious Georgian town houses in Upper Berkeley Place backing onto the Senior School, which means it can share its first-class facilities including science, drama, music and sport. The cultural facilities of the city, such as the city museum and art gallery, are also on its doorstep.

Pupils travel to the school from across the region and there is a hub for public transport on the nearby Clifton Triangle. The school also offers timed parking facilities for parents in the adjacent NCP West End multi-storey car park, to pick up and drop off pupils, at no extra cost.

As the only boys' junior school in the city, QEH Juniors is unique in Bristol. Being small, it focuses on the individual, fostering a love of learning whilst nurturing the interests and talents of each boy. In addition there is a wealth of extracurricular activities available.

The school is a happy place with strong pastoral care, academic excellence, and high standards where the educational experience is designed to be relevant and meaningful for every single child. Each boy leaves recognising himself as a lifelong learner.

Boys can enter in Year 3 or Year 5 though places occasionally become available in other Years. Boys are expected to move into the Main School at 11. (*See QEH entry in HMC section.*)

Charitable status. Queen Elizabeth's Hospital is a Registered Charity, number 1104871, and a Company Limited by Guarantee, number 5164477.

Radnor House Sevenoaks – Prep School

Combe Bank Drive, Sundridge, Kent TN14 6AE

Tel:	01959 564320
email:	enquiries@radnor-sevenoaks.org
website:	www.radnor-sevenoaks.org
Twitter:	@radnorsevenoaks
Facebook:	@radnorsevenoaks
Instagram:	@radnorsevenoaks

Chairman of Board of Directors: Mr Colin Diggory, BSc Hons, PGCE, MA, EdD, CMath, FIMA, FRSA

Head: Mr Fraser Halliwell, BSc Hons, PGCE, MEd, FRSA

Head of Prep School: **Dr Emma Margrett**, BA Hons, MA, EdD, CCRS, FCCT

Radnor House Sevenoaks Prep School is a flourishing independent school with entry from the term in which pupils are 2½ up to the age of 11. In September 2014 the school became co-educational and in 2016 the school name was changed from Combe Bank to Radnor House Sevenoaks.

Aims and Ethos. As the world becomes more complex, diverse and fast paced, the school's mission is to future-proof its pupils to give them the very best start in life. Academic qualifications are an important aspect of this but so too are interpersonal skills such as emotional intelligence and leadership. Underpinning their approach to education is a set of core values – excellence, respect, courage and perseverance – which form the bedrock of the school and provide a moral compass for children from school through to adulthood. Pupil happiness is their first priority as a happy child is one who will thrive, grasp opportunities to learn and develop and will become a confident and well-balanced young person. One key focus is to be a pioneer in preparing the children for the digital age by working with Microsoft as one of their flagship schools as they aim to build adults who can thrive in the world of tomorrow by using technology to propel their learning forward.

Location. Situated in a Palladian Mansion and set in superb grounds with 28 acres of parkland just outside Sevenoaks, the school has excellent facilities. The Nursery and Prep School are on the same site as the Senior School and Sixth Form and there are many positive links between them, so that all pupils have guaranteed access through the school until they leave at 18. The Prep School is housed in an original stable block and affords a unique environment in which the students feel secure and comfortable.

Curriculum. A modern and broad range of subjects is taught at all age levels. The school boasts a strong Art Department with an innovative graphic design suite, alongside a popular Music Department with regular exhibitions and musical performances in which wide participation is achieved. Radnor House Sevenoaks has a well-earned reputation for competitive success in a wide range of sports. Swimming in the 25-metre covered pool is a particularly popular activity throughout the whole school. Outdoor Adventurous Education has taken a firm place on the curriculum in the form of Forest School and Bush Craft.

Transport. Coach transport is organized for pupils from Year 4 onwards for five significant routes, to be paid for on a termly basis.

Fees per term (2021–2022). Preparatory School £3,990–£5,150 (Lunch £265); Nursery: for the minimum of 3 sessions per week £1,140; Transition: for the minimum of 5 sessions per week £1,900 with additional sessions charged at £380 for both Nursery and Transition.

Ravenscourt Park Preparatory School

16 Ravenscourt Avenue, London W6 0SL

Tel:	020 8846 9153
email:	office@rpps.co.uk
website:	www.rpps.co.uk
Twitter:	@RPPSLondon
Facebook:	@RPPSLondon
Instagram:	@rppslondon
LinkedIn:	/company/rppslondon

Chairman of Governors: Mr Jok Dunbar

Headmaster: **Mr Carl Howes**, MA, PGCE

Deputy Head: Ms Lucy Bennison, BA Hons, QTS

Deputy Head (*Teaching and Learning*): Mr Sam Challenor, MA History of Art, MA Leadership, PGCE, QTS [maternity cover]

The full staff list is available on the school website.

Age Range. 4–11 co-educational.

Number of Pupils. 417 boys and girls.

Fees per term (2021–2022). £6,304.

Ravenscourt Park Preparatory school provides education of the highest quality for boys and girls, preparing them for transfer to the best independent schools at 11 years of age. The Lower School caters for pupils aged 4–7 and the Upper School for 7–11 years. All pupils are housed in one of the three main buildings that make up the RPPS site. The Gardener Building is home to a theatre, a state-of-the-art science laboratory and an art studio. The secure site includes a large play area, a newly refurbished outdoor learning area for Early Years and the school makes use of the extensive facilities of Ravenscourt Park which it adjoins.

The curriculum includes French, humanities, music, art and craft, RE and PE for all pupils in addition to the usual core subjects. In the Upper School the majority of subjects are taught by specialists. All Upper School pupils attend a Residential Week where studies across the curriculum are applied to a non-urban environment.

There are many after-school clubs and sports activities, as well as three choirs and two orchestras. Individual tuition is offered in piano, harp, violin, brass, woodwind, cello, saxophone, clarinet, flute, percussion and singing. The drama productions and concerts are a highlight of each school year.

A wraparound care service, before and after school, is offered to parents at an extra charge.

The school is noted for its warm, happy atmosphere where parents play a full part in enriching the curriculum and social life. Off-site visits and guest workshops presented by noted visitors are a regular feature of education at RPPS.

The school is very popular in the local area and registration is strongly recommended on the child's first birthday. A prospectus and registration form may be obtained from the school secretary and online. Open Mornings take place each month (dates are available on the school website).

The school was inspected by ISI in March 2016 and received 'excellent' in all the categories. The full inspection report is available on the school website.

Redcliffe Gardens School

A member of the Godolphin and Latymer School Foundation

47 Redcliffe Gardens, London SW10 9JH

Tel: 020 7352 9247
email: registrar@redcliffeschool.com
website: www.redcliffegardens.com
Twitter: @RedcliffeSchool
Facebook: @redcliffeschool
Instagram: @redcliffeschool

Chair of the Board of Governors: Mrs Alison Paines

Head: Mr Benedict Dunhill, BA

Age Range. Boys and Girls, rising 3–11
Number of Pupils. 85 Day Pupils (30 boys, 55 girls)
Fees per term (2021–2022). £6,500. Nursery: £3,600 (morning class), £2,400 (afternoon class), £6,030 (full day).

Easily accessible from all parts of central and West London, Redcliffe Gardens School is a small, friendly school with highly motivated, confident and happy children. Emphasis is placed on a combination of hard work, good manners and plenty of fun within a framework of traditional values of perseverance, courage and resilience. The balanced curriculum includes Maths, English, History, Geography, Science, IT, Art, Religious Education, Current Affairs, Music, Physical Education and Drama. French and Spanish are taught throughout the school.

Individual attention encourages the pursuit of high academic standards and we are proud that our children gain places at their first choice of senior or prep school, including Colet Court, Sussex House, St Philip's, Downe House, Benenden, St Mary's Ascot, Queen's Gate, Godolphin & Latymer, City of London, JAGS and Francis Holland. Every class has at least two hours of specialist-taught Physical Education each week including tag rugby, netball, rounders, cricket, judo, athletics and swimming.

After-school activities include Cookery, Gymnastics, Ballet, Coding, STEM, Plogging and LAMDA. Music is a strength of the school with visiting instrumental staff and a high standard of performance. Parents are encouraged to be involved with the school through Open Assemblies, Parents' discussion groups and workshops, the Parents' Committee and regular meetings with the teachers.

The Redcliffe Robins is our nursery class for children rising 3 and has access to all of Redcliffe's resources and facilities to help prepare the children for entry to the main school. Each day has a balanced timetable of Phonics, Mathematical Skills, Art & Craft, Music, Drama and PE with ample opportunity for structured free play and the development of social skills.

Children are assessed at three years of age for entry to the main school at four. Entry for subsequent years is also by assessment. Tours of the school are held during term time on Mondays, Tuesdays and Wednesdays at 9.30am, 10.30am and 11.30am. Booking is essential via the website.

Since 1st September 2020, Redcliffe Gardens School has been a member of the Godolphin and Latymer School Foundation.

Charitable status. Godolphin and Latymer School Foundation is a Registered Charity, number 1073924. It exists to provide a high standard of education for children within a caring environment.

Reddiford School

38 Cecil Park, Pinner, Middlesex HA5 5HH

Tel: 020 8866 0660
email: office@reddiford.org.uk
website: www.reddiford.co.uk

Chairman of Governors: Mr G Jukes OBE

Head: Mrs J Batt, CertEd, NPQH

Age Range. 2 years 9 months to 11.
Number of Pupils. Prep: 83 Boys, 63 Girls; Pre-Prep: 42 Boys, 33 Girls; Early Years: 37 Boys, 18 Girls.
Fees per term (2021–2022): Early Years (before Reception Year) £3,575, Reception £3,875, Pre-Prep £3,890, Prep £3,990.

Reddiford School has been established in Cecil Park, Pinner since 1913. Whilst the school maintains its Church of England status, children from all faiths and cultures are welcomed. Throughout the school the ethos is on respect for one another. Reddiford prides itself on being a town school based in the heart of Pinner; a few minutes' walk from local transport facilities.

Reddiford possesses a fine academic record, preparing its pupils for entrance at 11+ into major independent schools, many at scholarship level, and local Grammar schools. There is a high teacher to pupil ratio ensuring small classes leading to a friendly caring environment where all children are valued.

The Early Years Department is situated in its own building and caters for children from 2 years nine months to rising 5 years. It offers a stimulating and attractive environment where children are encouraged to be independent and active learners. The Early Years Department follows the Early Years Foundation Stage Curriculum.

The Pre-Prep Department builds on the knowledge and skills acquired in the Early Years placing the emphasis on developing confidence and the ability to learn and work independently and with others. The Pre-Prep Department has its own computer suite and interactive whiteboards in classrooms. There is specialist teaching in French, Music and PE from reception upwards and all children are taught to swim.

In the Prep Department children are taught by specialist teachers in properly resourced subject rooms. There is a fully-equipped science laboratory, dedicated art and music rooms and an ICT suite. Pupils are prepared for entry to the many prestigious senior schools in the area, a process which involves consultation with parents from an early stage.

There is an extensive programme of extra-curricular activities throughout the school including: sports (football, cricket, netball, gymnastics), languages (French, Latin, Mandarin), art and science. We also offer before and after school care (7.55am–6.00pm).

Assessments for Reception upwards require the child to be in school for the day. They complete English and Mathematics assessments and their ability to cope with the educational and social demands for the year group are evaluated.

Charitable status. Reddiford School is a Registered Charity, number 312641. It exists to provide education for boys and girls.

Redmaids' High Junior School

Grange Court Road, Westbury-on-Trym, Bristol BS9 4DP

Tel: 0117 962 9451
email: junioradmissions@redmaidshigh.co.uk
website: www.redmaidshigh.co.uk
Twitter: @RedmaidsHigh
Facebook: @redmaidshighschool
Instagram: @rredmaidshigh

Chairman of Governors: Mr Andrew Hillman

Headteacher: Mrs Lisa Brown, BSc Hons Leicester, PGCE Oxford Brookes

Headteacher's PA/Admissions: Mrs Lynn McCabe

Age Range. 7–11.
Number of Girls. 120 Day Girls.
Fees per term (2021–2022). £3,505 plus lunch.

At Redmaids' High Junior School, girls receive an outstanding educational experience. Our mission is for your daughter to wake up every morning eager to be at school. Small class sizes and a family atmosphere make that a reality.

We set the bar high academically, stretching our pupils to ensure they become the best they can be. Each week, time is given to all subjects in our broad curriculum. Alongside the core areas, the foundation subjects and creative arts are just as valued. Sport is integral to our timetable, instilling positive attitudes towards physical activity, and bringing teamwork and specific skills leading to success in competitive fixtures.

Our single-sex setting means no dilution of attention to the needs of the girls as young women. They are offered all the opportunities, hold all the responsibilities, and enjoy everything in their path without any self-consciousness or stereotypical judgement.

Extra-curricular activities are an essential part of the Redmaids' High experience. Girls learn resilience and determination through trying new things. Whether it is playing chess, football or hockey, taking part in a concert or book group, joining art or fencing clubs, caving on the Mendips or sailing in Bristol docks, they enjoy busy, active and purposeful days.

We value diversity and embrace internationalism; we are forward thinking in our teaching, preparing our pupils for an ever-changing technological future filled with careers that have not even been dreamed of yet.

The House system enables girls to work and make friends with children in all year groups. There is a happy and relaxed atmosphere within the school, with easy access for parents to speak to teachers, a regular discussion group with the headteacher and many social events bringing families, staff and pupils together.

Assessment of pupil progress is built into every subject area. We moved away from SAT testing some years ago, preferring Durham University's INCAS test for monitoring performance and progression, and individual target setting.

Pastoral care is one of our major strengths. New pupils are supported by a buddy system and through school meetings and class activities, pupils learn about good citizenship, taking responsibility for themselves, for each other and for the care of their community and their environment.

Close links are fostered between the Junior and Senior schools. Pupils benefit from use of a science laboratory, extensive PE facilities including an all-weather pitch, shared dining facilities and award-winning catering. At age 11, transition occurs to the Senior School (conditions apply) having sat the entrance examination and competed for academic, sport and music scholarships alongside those joining from other schools. (*See Redmaids' High School entry in GSA section.*)

The School occupies a spacious site nestled in a quiet residential neighbourhood. We have a mix of well-maintained traditional and purpose-built buildings including a library, music room, art studio and lofty assembly hall, plus a large garden for outdoor play complete with sports and climbing equipment.

Admission: All girls are assessed prior to entry. Potential Year 3 pupils are assessed in pairs, with girls spending half the day in class and half working alongside the headteacher. Year 5 and 6 taster days are conducted in groups. Interested families are encouraged to visit the school individually or at one of our collective events.

Charitable status. Redmaids' High School is a Registered Charity, number 1105017.

Reigate St Mary's Preparatory and Choir School

Chart Lane, Reigate, Surrey RH2 7RN

Tel: 01737 244880
email: office@reigatestmarys.org
website: www.reigatestmarys.org
Twitter: @rsmprepschool
Facebook: @ReigateStMarys

Chairman of Governors: Mr James Dean

Headmaster: **Marcus Culverwell**, MA Ed

Age Range. 2–11.
Number of Pupils. 373 (201 boys 172 girls).
Fees per term (2021–2022). Green Shoots £1,200 (min 3 mornings), Kindergarten £2,000 (min 5 mornings), Lower School (Reception, Years 1 & 2) £4,325, Upper School (Years 3–6) £5,420.

Reigate St Mary's (RSM) is a co-educational day school for children aged 2 to 11 years old. It is a junior school of Reigate Grammar School (RGS), the top co-educational day school in Surrey and typically, 80 percent of pupils transfer to RGS each year. RSM believes that a good education should be a challenging, inspirational and exciting journey, preparing children for happy and fulfilled future lives. The aim is to produce confident, resilient and creative young people who will one day become leaders who care deeply about a sustainable and equitable future for everyone.

This is achieved by a relentless focus on wellbeing, and by prioritising the building of strong relationships with the children and their families over everything else. From their earliest days, right through to their transition to senior school, each child is supported according to their individual needs and strengths. By doing this, the children know they are truly valued at school and this gives them the confidence to take challenges, learn from mistakes and ultimately reach their full potential.

The children enjoy busy days filled with imaginative teaching and exciting adventures focusing on teamwork, creativity, digital learning, and communication. Lessons are taken outside whenever possible and with 15 wonderful acres of grounds, there is plenty of space to roll down hills, explore dens and enjoy the school's many nature areas and playgrounds.

The youngest children joining Early Years are in the safe hands of warm and caring teachers and teaching assistants. The team focus on making sure each child feels happy and secure as they know that ultimately, happy children learn. Days in Early Years are designed to harness natural curiosity and ensure the children become enthusiastic and happy learners, eager to come to school every day.

As they move up through the school, the children learn to be good citizens, with the confidence to make the right decisions and the skills to thrive in the workplace of tomorrow. The school is passionate about teaching the children to be independent and resilient thinkers, fully equipped to reach their individual potential, whatever form that takes. An Education for Social Responsibility (ESR) curriculum is central to this and helps children to think about the core values that will lead to worthwhile and content lives, within stable and caring communities while protecting the planet for the future.

There is significant and ongoing investment in technology throughout the school and IT is embedded in all teaching. Classrooms are exciting and inspiring places where children use technology to explore. There is an impressive IT Lab and Mac Suite and the school's Lego robotics team have been UK finalists in the worldwide Lego robotics competitions many times.

Academic outcomes are excellent and approximately 80 percent of children transfer to the senior school, Reigate Grammar, which was voted Tatler School of the Year 2020.

Repton Prep

Milton, Derbyshire DE65 6EJ

Tel: 01283 707100
email: admissions@repton.org.uk
website: www.reptonprep.org.uk
Twitter: @reptonprep
Facebook: @repton prep
Instagram: @ReptonPrep

Chairman of Governors: E M Shires, BA, FCA

Repton Prep Interim Headmaster: **Mr Mark Brotherton**, BEd Hons, NPQH, FCCT

Deputy Head (Upper Prep): Mrs S Krbacevic, BSc

Deputy Head (Lower Prep): Miss K Cavill, BA

Deputy Head Pastoral & Boarding: M Casey BA

Age Range. 3–13.
Number of Pupils. 420
Fees per term (2021–2022). Pre-Prep: £3,291–£3,838; Prep: Boarders £7,750–£9,161; Day £5,662–£7,075

Repton Prep is the 3–13 campus of Repton School, a co-educational, boarding and day school providing an exceptional education for children aged 3 to 18 years. With over 400 pupils, around 40 of which board, the school offers a caring and productive environment with enviable facilities paired with excellent pastoral care.

Repton Prep firmly believes that learning is a collaborative endeavour. There is a strong community of pupils, teachers and staff, and a united belief that the most valuable education is one that is broad, balanced and allows children to enjoy their childhood whilst benefitting from a range of opportunities both in and out of the classroom. With a rich heritage and as part of Repton School, they enjoy enviable facilities and a plethora of resources enabling a curriculum where academic excellence and an enriching co-curricular programme provides a rounded education.

Set in the grounds of a Palladian mansion, nestled in the glorious Derbyshire countryside with its own lake and woodland, what makes Repton Prep truly special is the team of dedicated teachers and staff; a highly experienced, gifted and committed community who strive for each child to develop a lifelong curiosity in the world. During their time at Repton Prep, children benefit from deep and nurturing relationships that motivate and inspire them to succeed.

Repton Prep is located two miles away from Repton School and the close relationship between the two schools ensures a fluid transition from Repton Prep to Repton, although pupils who opt for other senior schools are fully supported to achieve CE. Both campuses offer fantastic travel links and can be easily reached by road from the M1, M6 and M5 via the A50, by rail from East Midlands Parkway and Lichfield, or from nearby Birmingham and East Midlands airports.

Admission. Repton Prep welcomes applications for both boarding and day places throughout the academic year, starting at age 3 and up to age 13. Boarding is available from Year 3, and from that point of entry upwards all candidates – day and boarding – must meet certain criteria before joining. A positive report from the child's previous school must be received, after which an informal assessment of Mathematics and English will be undertaken within a taster day at the School. Candidates for Year 7 and 8 entry have a more involved examination process.

Curriculum. A varied curriculum of academic and non-academic subjects are offered to pupils. The Lower Prep syllabus provides pupils with the skills and experiences that will form the foundation for their future learning, including the benefits of lessons taught by specialist teachers from an early age.

The Upper Prep curriculum builds on prior experience so that pupils become more independent and active learners. Teaching groups are streamed by ability with setting in place for Mathematics, English and French. This is designed to maximise the efficiency of teaching programmes and ensures that the work presented to pupils is 'just right'.

In Year 8, pupils are prepared for entrance examinations or, if applicable, scholarship examinations. However, it is the aim of Repton to produce young pupil at 13 who are well prepared for the senior phase of their education as well as being well on the way to being a major contributor to society in their lives beyond school.

Outdoor learning. Repton Prep's setting plays no small part in the broader education of its pupils. Lessons often spill out into the woods, spinneys, formal ponds (all the pupils are expert pond dippers!) or around the lake as teachers take full advantage of the glorious Derbyshire countryside. During playtime at Repton Prep the youngest pupils have their own Teletubbies-style playground, with tunnels, surfboards, blackboards and play equipment to spark their imaginations. Older pupils build dens, climb trees and explore the natural surroundings with unbounded curiosity. Every experience at Repton Prep is seen as a learning opportunity.

Beyond Repton Prep. With Repton offering pupils an education from 3–18, 90% of leavers move on to Repton, with a number of pupils also receiving places at other highly acclaimed schools.

Facilities. Repton Prep is surrounded by 55 acres of woodland, playing fields and a lake. The School has a plethora of facilities including a striking purpose-built dining hall, three science laboratories, and a sophisticated computer technology suite. The Quad development houses a contemporary Music facility, language laboratory, an Art department complete with kiln, and a Greenpower garage for Repton Prep's award-winning electric cars. An extensive library is situated in the main Hall, and there is an indoor competition-sized swimming pool, a sports hall and floodlit Astroturf. Pupils are fortunate to also have access to the world-class facilities at Repton School and shared resources across campuses.

Creative Arts. From Nursery onwards all pupils are given the opportunity to participate in a wide variety of classroom and extra-curricular music activities. The Music Department's two full-time members of staff are supported by 20 specialist Visiting Music Teachers offering over 200 lessons a week, and they work closely with the Director of Music at Repton School to deliver outstanding opportunities to pupils, from masterclasses to one-to-one tutorials with visiting musicians. Pupils are encouraged to take part in the School's wide variety of ensembles and choirs and they have an enviable number of pupils who are part of regional and national orchestras and ensembles.

The Drama department affords many opportunities for all pupils to design, direct and perform in the many productions that take place during the school year. Extra-curricular activities include all aspects of theatre production including technical and backstage.

Pupils are able to improve their confidence and love of performing without fear through LAMDA examinations. The personalised programme is tailored to individual needs and abilities from Year 2 upwards. Lessons are available within and outside of school hours. Repton Prep has enjoyed considerable success, with high uptake and consistently outstanding LAMDA examination results.

The Design and Technology Centre is home to a fully equipped workshop which enables pupils to develop a greater understanding of the real-world applications of Design Technology. It is the home of Greenpower, where pupils design, build and eventually race their own electric car.

Sport. Repton Prep recognises the importance of young people being involved in sport, whatever their ability and whatever their eventual chosen discipline. Pupils are actively encouraged to participate at the best level they can, and the aim is to equip every pupil with confidence and enthusiasm to enjoy sport and an active lifestyle both in school and beyond.

Squads are fielded in the major sports of football, hockey and cricket for boys and girls, with second, third, fourth and even fifth teams formed. There is a wide range of different sporting opportunities ranging from tennis, athletics, golf and kayaking to fencing and orienteering. The School also has its own equestrian team.

Houses. Day pupils join a House and throughout the year they can earn points by participating in various competitions, for positive behaviour and special accomplishments. This not only fosters a sense of community but also forms an integral part of life at the School. Boarders are assigned a boarding House and are welcomed into a warm, caring and fun environment, where they are looked after by Houseparents and House assistants in a relaxed setting where the emphasis is on enjoying a happy childhood.

Scholarships. Academic, Music, Sport and Drama Scholarships are available for new pupils joining Repton Prep at Year 7.

Bursaries may be available to families looking to access an independent education for their child, subject to means testing. These may, in appropriate circumstances, be used to supplement Academic or non-academic awards. Additional bursaries for are also available for Forces families.

Charitable Status. Repton Prep (1093165) is a Registered Charity. Repton Prep exists to provide high quality education for boys and girls.

RGS Prep

Maori Road, Guildford, Surrey GU1 2EL

Tel:	01483 880650
email:	rgsp-office@rgsg.co.uk
website:	www.rgsg.co.uk
Twitter:	@RGSprep
Facebook:	@RGSprep

Chairman of Governors: Mrs S K Creedy, MA Cantab

Head: **Mr T Freeman-Day**, BA Hons

Age Range. 3–11.

Number of Boys. 350 day boys.

Fees per term (2021–2022). £3,720–£5,330.

RGS Prep is the Preparatory School of the Royal Grammar School and the choir school for Guildford Cathedral. Cathedral choristers qualify for choral scholarships.

The main entry points are Nursery, Reception and Year 3. Many of the pupils gain entry to the Royal Grammar School at age 11.

The School is divided into four Houses for House competitions. Pastoral care and supervision of academic progress are shared by the Head, Housemasters, Form and subject teachers. Extra-curricular activities include music, art, chess, drama, computer club, judo, fencing, tennis, basketball, science and general knowledge.

Music is a strong feature of the life of the school, which is a member of the Choir Schools Association. In addition to the Cathedral Choir, there are senior and junior choirs, an orchestra, wind and string groups. Private tuition by qualified peripatetic teachers is available in most instruments. There are music concerts and the school Carol Service at the Cathedral has achieved wide acclaim. Music scholarships to Independent senior schools are gained each year.

Art plays an important part in the curriculum also, with boys receiving tuition throughout the school.

The well-equipped performance space further enhances drama productions.

Games are association football, rugby, cricket, athletics, swimming, basketball, hockey and badminton. There is a school field, gym and astroturf. A brand new, purpose-built Sports Hall opened in September 2016, and a bespoke performance space for drama and music.

Regular school visits are undertaken to local places of interest. School parties also go abroad, e.g. for skiing, watersports, football and on cultural visits.

The Pre-Preparatory department (for boys aged 3–7 and including a Nursery unit) is housed in a separate building, but shares many of the facilities of the main Prep School.

There is an active and very supportive Parents' Association.

Charitable status. Royal Grammar School Guildford is Registered Charity, number 1177353, and a Company Limited by Guarantee, incorporated in England and Wales, Company number 10874615. Registered Office High Street, Guildford, Surrey, GU1 3BB.

RGS Springfield

Britannia Square, Worcester WR1 3DL

Tel:	01905 24999
email:	springfield@rgsw.org.uk
website:	www.rgsw.org.uk
Twitter:	@RGSSpringfield
Facebook:	@RGS-Springfield

Chairman of Governors: Mr Quentin Poole

Headmistress: **Mrs L Brown**, BA Hons, PGCE

Age Range. 2–11 Co-educational.

Number of Pupils. 145

Fees per term (2021–2022). £2,949–£4,532 including lunch and wraparound care.

Introduction from the Headmistress. 'I am delighted to have this opportunity to welcome you to RGS Springfield, with its wonderful family atmosphere and nurturing co-educational environment, which together creates a uniquely friendly school.

Our aim is to ensure that children develop their full potential academically, socially and emotionally in a safe, caring environment.

All our pupils benefit from individual care, small class sizes, professional and dedicated teaching; all of which help children become confident, secure and considerate of the needs of others.

The school has scored highly in recent inspections, rated as consistently outstanding by Ofsted and ECERS and excellent in all areas by ISI inspectors (March 2015 and is fully compliant March 2018). There are a wealth of academic and extra-curricular opportunities to provide children with an enriching and stimulating environment, preparing them for the challenges of the 21st century, underpinned by traditional family values. The new digital learning programme adds a new dimension to classroom learning.

The school has wonderful grounds, which allow pupils to play outside in all weathers, learn from the natural environment and take part in all the fun that Forest School offers; wellies are very much encouraged!

The school, tucked away within the beautiful Georgian Britannia Square in the heart of Worcester, will provide a safe and happy place for your child to grow and develop. This website conveys only some of the ethos and spirit of RGS Springfield. Please visit us and see for yourself the happy, smiling faces of children having fun and learning in a stimulating environment. We are very much a happy family.

I look forward to welcoming you in person to our school.'

Overview. RGS Springfield is the co-educational junior school for RGS Worcester (*see HMC entry*). The school educates children between the ages of 2 and 11 and is situated within a large, beautiful Georgian Town House and gardens in the centre of Worcester.

High academic standards are expected as the children are prepared to enter RGS Worcester at 11. There is a wide range of extra-curricular activities on offer and, while the school is noted for academic, creative and sporting excellence, it is of the greatest importance that the children are encouraged to be kind, considerate and well-mannered.

In 2009 an extensive refurbishment was undertaken to restore and develop the original historic site, Springfield, providing excellent modern facilities including art, design technology, science and ICT rooms alongside large, airy and warm well-equipped classrooms.

The school is set in three acres of maintained grounds and offers fantastic games facilities and outdoor space, including an extended Forest School, Walled Garden and Paddock Play Area.

Charitable status. The Royal Grammar School Worcester is a Registered Charity, number 1120644.

RGS The Grange

Grange Lane, Claines, Worcester WR3 7RR

Tel:	01905 451205
email:	grange@rgsw.org.uk
website:	www.rgsw.org.uk/the-grange
Twitter:	@rgsthegrange
Facebook:	@RGS-The-Grange

Chairman of Governors: Mr Quentin Poole

Headmaster: **G W Hughes**, BEd Hons

Age Range. 2–11 Co-educational.

Number of Pupils. 375.

Fees per term (2021–2022). £2,949–£4,532 including lunch and wraparound care from 7.45am–6.00pm.

Introduction from the Headmaster. "Welcome to a nurturing school with a big personality.

Giving a child the best possible foundations for a bright future is a true privilege. Our fantastic facilities give pupils tremendous scope for achieving the academic, sporting and creative excellence that we encourage. Just as important is the safe, secure and caring framework that we provide, giving children the support and self-belief they need to make their own individual strides forward.

I get huge satisfaction from seeing each one cross barriers and shine in a way that is uniquely theirs and with two children myself, I know the pride parents feel when they see their child thriving.

I look forward to helping your child thrive too."

Overview. RGS The Grange is one of two co-educational junior schools for RGS Worcester (*see HMC entry*). The school educates children between the ages of 2 and 11 and is situated in open countryside three miles north of Worcester in Claines.

High academic standards are expected as the children are prepared to enter RGS Worcester at 11. There is a wide range of extra-curricular activities on offer and, while the school is noted for academic, creative and sporting

excellence, it is of the greatest importance that the children are encouraged to be kind, considerate and well-mannered.

The school has scored highly in recent inspections, being acknowledged as 'outstanding' and 'excellent' in all areas by ISI inspectors. The Digital Learning Programme adds a new dimension to classroom learning across all four RGS schools and RGS The Grange is a leading school of excellence for digital innovation.

RGS The Grange provides excellent modern facilities including specialist art, design technology, science, food technology, French and Computing & IT rooms alongside large, airy, well-equipped classrooms.

The school is set in 50 acres of grounds and offers exceptional games facilities and outdoor space, including a full-sized floodlit Astroturf, cricket pavilion, Forest School, traverse wall and adventure play area.

Charitable status. The Royal Grammar School Worcester is a Registered Charity, number 1120644.

The Richard Pate School

Southern Road, Leckhampton, Cheltenham, Glos GL53 9RP

Tel:	01242 522086
email:	hm@richardpate.co.uk
website:	www.richardpate.co.uk
Facebook:	@RichardPateSchool
Instagram:	@richardpate_school

Chairman of Trustees: Mrs Jane Williams

Headmaster: **Mr R A MacDonald**, MEd, BA

Deputy Heads:

Mrs S Wade

Mr P Lowe

Age Range. 3–11 Co-educational.

Number of Pupils. 300 (approximately an equal number of boys and girls).

Fees per term (2021–2022). Nursery: £1,285 (5 mornings), £1,710 (any 3 full days), £2,279 (any 4 full days), £2,849 (5 full days). Preparatory: £2,893 (Reception), £3,074 (Year 1), £3,273 (Year 2). Junior: £3,538 (Year 3), £3,695 (Year 4), £3,929 (Year 5), £4,103 (Year 6).

Hot lunches are provided and included in the fees, except for 'mornings only' nursery.

The School, occupying an 11½ acre semi-rural site at the foot of the Cotswold escarpment, is part of the Pate's Grammar School Foundation which is a charity founded by Richard Pate, a Recorder of Gloucester, in 1574.

It is a non-denominational Christian school which in its present form began in 1946. The aim of the school is to provide a high academic standard and continuity of education up to the age of 11 years. The curriculum is broadly based with strong emphasis being attached to music, art, drama and sport, for these activities are seen as vital if a child's full potential is to be realised.

Facilities include a music centre with individual practice rooms; a fully equipped computer suite; an all-weather astroturf with floodlights and a woodland area with enclosed pond for environmental studies. There is also a specialist wing with science labs, language suite and art studio. After-school care is available through until 5.30 pm.

At present the School is divided into three sections: Nursery 3–4 years; Preparatory Department 4–7 and Junior 7–11. Entrance is dependent upon the availability of places but most pupils join the school at the commencement of the Nursery, Preparatory or Junior Departments.

No entry tests are taken by younger pupils but assessment tests are conducted for pupils who enter at Year 3. A small number of 7+ scholarships are awarded each year.

The teaching takes full account of national curriculum guidelines with children in the upper part of the school following the normal preparatory school curriculum leading to Common Entrance and Scholarship at 11+. Pupils leave at age 11 for local Grammar Schools and a variety of independent secondary schools, particularly those in Cheltenham.

The Headmaster is assisted by two deputies and 22 fully qualified teachers including specialists in Latin, French, Art/ Design, Science, Music and Learning Support. The School employs music and dance teachers, who prepare children for participation in various competitions, in particular the Cheltenham Festival.

Charitable status. The Pate's Grammar School Foundation is a Registered Charity, number 311707.

Richmond House School

170 Otley Road, Leeds, West Yorkshire LS16 5LG

Tel:	0113 2752670
email:	enquiries@rhschool.org
website:	www.rhschool.org
Twitter:	@RHSchoolLeeds
Facebook:	@RHSchoolLeeds
Instagram:	@RHSchoolLeeds
LinkedIn:	/richmond-house-school

Chair of the Board of Governors: Mrs G Galdins

Headteacher: **Mr Chris Bouckley**

Age Range. 3–11.

Number of Day Pupils. 209 boys and girls.

Fees per term (2021–2022). Nursery: £2,092 (half days only), £3,270 (full time, including lunch), Reception to Year 6 £3,270, Lunches £225.

Richmond House School is an independent co-educational preparatory school providing an excellent standard of education for children aged 3 to 11 years within a happy, stimulating, family environment.

At Richmond House School, a team of dedicated staff is committed to giving each child the opportunity to develop into confident, hard-working and successful individuals.

All pupils are given the chance to learn and achieve across a broad range of activities and subject areas and the talents of each child are nurtured. The breadth of activities offered aims to challenge pupils, build self-confidence and lead pupils to discover new interests and skills.

The School boasts outstanding 11+ exam success with pupils having their choice of senior school and a substantial number being awarded scholarships.

In addition to strong academic credentials, Richmond House School is committed to providing all pupils with the opportunity to excel in other areas. The School is situated in 10 acres of land, providing excellent sports facilities and offering pupils a wide range of sports to choose from. The School also provides specialist teaching in Music, Art, Design Technology, ICT, Languages, Outdoor Learning and Science.

Pastoral Care is an important aspect of school life at Richmond House School. Our Assistant Head is responsible for leading Pastoral Care and works closely with staff, pupils and parents to ensure the well-being and progress of all pupils.

Excellent Pre and After School Care and an easily accessible car park and drop-off zone are available for busy families.

Charitable status. Richmond House School is a Registered Charity, number 505630. It exists to provide high quality education for boys and girls aged 3–11 years.

Ripley Court School

Rose Lane, Ripley, Surrey GU23 6NE

Tel:	01483 225217
email:	headmistress@ripleycourt.co.uk
website:	www.ripleycourt.co.uk
Twitter:	@RipleyCourtPrep
Facebook:	@ripleycourtschool1
Instagram:	@ripleycourt
LinkedIn:	@ripleycourtschool

Chairman of Governors: S Poole

Headteacher: **Ms A Clarke**

Age Range. 3–11 Co-educational.

Number of Pupils. Day: 100: Upper Court (Y3–Y6) 90 Little Court (R–Y2); Nursery and Transition (age 3+) 18.

Fees per term (2021–2022). Years 5–6 £5,220; Years 3–4 £4,950; Years 1–2 £3,850; Reception £3,580; Nursery/ Transition £3,390 full-time (10 sessions) or £1,695 part-time (min 5 sessions).

The main intakes are Nursery, Reception and Year 3. Scholarships are available from Year 3. Children may enter at other times if there is space. They are prepared for 11+ pre-testing and Common Entrance and Scholarship Examinations for a wide range of independent senior schools. There is a very high academic standard, and many Scholarships are won for academic performance as well as for sport, music and art.

Ripley Court School is renowned for its outstanding pastoral care and providing a warm and nurturing environment; children are encouraged to be themselves and grow into individuals able to explore their potential. The broad and balanced curriculum with subject specialist teaching, weekly enrichment programme and a wealth of extra-curricular activities, inspires children to reach their full potential and creates opportunities for independent learning, creativity, critical thinking and problem-solving skills.

In addition to the academic subjects, PE, Music, Art and Food Technology are a part of every child's timetable. Forest School sessions are also taught on-site from Nursery to Year 6. There are opportunities for all in orchestral, choral and dramatic productions – the school prides itself on ensuring every child can participate in all areas, including in competitive sports fixtures. The varied and enhanced curriculum, underpinned by our values of perseverance, aspiration, curiosity and kindness, further equips each individual to reach their full potential.

Facilities include a library, science laboratories, a gymnasium, computer suite, art, music and food tech rooms. There are banks of iPads to support learning. There are 19 acres of playing fields, on which Football (Association and Rugby), Hockey, Netball, Cricket, Tennis (2 hard, 2 grass courts), Athletics and Rounders are played in season. Swimming and Life Saving are taught in a large, covered, heated swimming pool.

Little Court uses all the facilities and much teaching expertise. The nursery, delivers specialist tuition in French, music, swimming and dance.

School transport serves Woking, Pyrford and West Byfleet.

Charitable status. Ripley Court School is part of The London Orphan Asylum (Reed's School), a Registered Charity, number 312008.

Rokeby School

George Road, Kingston upon Thames, Surrey KT2 7PB

Tel:	020 8942 2247
email:	reception@rokeby.org.uk
website:	www.rokebyschool.co.uk
Twitter:	@RokebyPrep
Facebook:	@rokebyprepschool

Maxim: Smart, Skilful and Kind

Chair of the Governors: Mrs Deirdre Davidson

Headmaster: **Mr J R Peck**

Age Range. 4–13.
Number of Boys. 403.
Fees per term (2021–2022). £4,991–£6,215 (including lunch and morning snack, books, day trips and some residential trips, personal accident and dental insurance and all compulsory extras).

Rokeby has an outstanding record of success in Common Entrance and Scholarships to leading Independent Senior Schools. Boys are accepted at 4+ to the Pre-Prep and at 7+ to the Prep School.

In recent years a fabulous two-storey, energy-efficient new building was opened by HRH Princess Alexandra. It has six spacious classrooms, a multi-purpose Performing Arts Hall, as well as other lovely spaces built to house Reception, Year 1 and Year 2 boys. The spacious and exciting playground area is enjoyed by all year groups and includes an outside classroom, an adventure playground

with balance wall and an area for gardening club to grow seeds and encourage wildlife.

Science is taught in three well-equipped Laboratories. There is a large Computer Room and a spacious Art and Design Technology Centre. Football, Rugby, and Cricket are played while other sports include Swimming, Athletics, Hockey and Basketball. There are two large Halls and an Astroturf. A full activities programme is available for boys from Chess Club to Golf. The Music Department provides Orchestra, Ensembles and four Choirs and there are fourteen visiting peripatetic teachers, who work within a sound-proofed music block.

There are a number of educational school trips arranged as well as trips overseas, including France, Italy, Iceland and a number of overseas sports tours, including Sri Lanka, Canada and Holland. The school operates a bus service to the Wimbledon, Putney, Barnes and surrounding areas.

Charitable status. Rokeby Educational Trust Limited is a Registered Charity, number 312653. It exists to provide an excellent education for boys aged 4–13.

Rose Hill School

Coniston Avenue, Tunbridge Wells, Kent TN4 9SY

Tel:	01892 525591
email:	admissions@rosehillschool.co.uk
website:	www.rosehillschool.co.uk
Twitter:	@rosehillschool
Facebook:	@RoseHillSchool

Chairman of Governing Body: Mr Nevil Phillips

Head: **Ms E Neville**, BA Hons, MEd

Age Range. 3–13.
Number of Pupils. 250.
Fees per term (2021–2022). Kindergarten £2,345–£2,805, Reception–Year 2 £4,025, Year 3–Year 6 £5,410, Year 7–8 £2,665.

Rose Hill School is an inspiring place to learn: a warm, caring school with inspirational teachers, an enriching curriculum, first-class facilities and creative indoor and outdoor learning spaces.

A modern school rich with tradition, we offer a rare mix: academic excellence; sporting achievement; exceptional pastoral care; and the freedom to explore the creative arts. Set in 18 acres of grass and woodland, the school has countryside on its doorstep and yet the town centre is just five minutes away.

With 250 pupils, everyone knows each other well. All the faces in the corridor are familiar and every teacher knows every pupil. This friendly and supportive family atmosphere means that children feel happy and secure and provides them with the confidence to embrace new challenges and opportunities with gusto.

A wide spectrum of co-curricular activities, including music, art, sport, drama and design, makes it possible for every child to fulfil his or her potential, whilst the school supports and nurtures their emotional and academic growth – helping them develop the leadership skills that will play a vital part in their future lives.

Expectations are high and pupils are encouraged to make the most of every day. Together, pupils, teachers and staff apply themselves with enormous energy to create a truly stimulating environment for learning.

Charitable status. Rose Hill School is a Registered Charity, number 270158. It aims to provide a high-quality education to boys and girls aged 3–13.

Rosemead Preparatory School and Nursery

70 Thurlow Park Road, West Dulwich, London SE21 8HZ

Tel: 020 8670 5865
email: admissions@rosemeadprepschool.org.uk
website: www.rosemeadprepschool.org.uk
Twitter: @RosemeadPrep
Facebook: @rosemeadprep
LinkedIn: /rosemeadprep

Headmaster: **Mr Philip Soutar**, BA Ed Hons

Age Range. 2½–11.
Number of Pupils. Day: 152 Boys, 152 Girls.
Fees per term (2021–2022). £2,620–£4,920.

Our school aims are at the very core of everything we do. They are:

- To encourage confidence from a young age, preparing children for the next stages of their own brilliant futures
- To meet the intellectual, physical and emotional needs of each child and embrace excellence across the curriculum
- To create an inclusive, nurturing community that enables children to be creative, reflective and compassionate
- To inspire a thirst for learning, providing opportunities that extend far beyond our curriculum
- To work in close partnership with our parents and the wider community

Our motto, Inspiring Brilliant Futures, reflects our desire to develop a passion for learning that will enable children to aim high and achieve their goals. The school's success is evident in our pupils' enviable record of entry to leading senior schools locally in both the independent and maintained sectors.

Although we set the highest academic standards, we are committed to providing a well-rounded and inclusive education. With bursaries and Academic scholarships available from Year 3, we work hard to identify and nurture talents in, for example, sport, the arts or leadership and allow all children to thrive. Outstanding pastoral support and the school's unique status under the auspices of the Thurlow Educational Trust, of which every parent is a member, results in an exceptionally strong school community.

All religious denominations welcome.

Charitable status. Rosemead Preparatory School (The Thurlow Educational Trust) is a Registered Charity, number 1186165. It exists to provide a high standard of education in a happy, caring environment.

Rowan Preparatory School
United Learning

6 Fitzalan Road, Claygate, Esher, Surrey KT10 0LX

Tel: 01372 462627
email: school.office@rowanprepschool.co.uk
website: www.rowanprepschool.co.uk
Twitter: @Rowan_Prep
Facebook: @RowanPreparatorySchool
Instagram: @rowanpreparatoryschool
LinkedIn: /rowan-preparatory-school

With a solid foundation of family and community and a progressive curriculum, Rowan Preparatory School provides a nurturing and inspiring learning environment that encourages girls (aged 2–11) to have a strong sense of self, a life-long love of learning and confidence in themselves to reach for the stars.

We see the best in every girl, embracing their individuality and the unique contribution they each make to school life. All we ask is that they trust in us to take them on the exciting educational journey that our school has to offer. And that they are willing to listen, learn and embrace our school motto of 'I can, I can, I know I can'.

Chairman of the Local Governing Body: Mrs Jo Marr

Headmistress: **Mrs Susan Clarke**, BEd, NPQH

Age Range. 2–11 (Pre-Preparatory age 2–7, Preparatory age 7–11).
Number of Pupils. 330 Day Girls.
Fees per term (2021–2022). Preschool (based on number of sessions attended), Reception £4,055 Years 1 & 2 £4,652, Years 3 to 6 £5,382.

In 1936, Miss Katherine Millar was determined to breathe new life into the English educational system. She wished to create an environment which inspired a passion for learning. The doors of Rowan were opened wide to enable girls to develop a strong sense of self and establish lasting friendships. Three quarters of a century on, Katherine Millar's core values are firmly established in the school. Girls achieve personal excellence in a warm, family environment.

As our motto says '*Hic Feliciter Laboramus*'; here we work happily.

The school is located on two sites very close to each other in a leafy part of Claygate. Rowan Brae accommodates the Preschool and Pre-Prep and Rowan Hill, the Prep.

Upon entering the Brae you cannot fail to notice the warm, friendly and happy atmosphere. The stimulating learning environment, both indoors and outdoors, creates an inspiring and engaging place to learn. Outstanding lessons and excellent resources allow all pupils to thrive and reach their potential. Girls in Year 2 are fully prepared for the seamless transition and exciting challenges which lay ahead at the Hill.

Girls at the Hill develop a thirst for knowledge, an appreciation of all subject areas and a deeper understanding of how to analyse and apply information across different areas of learning and in everyday life. The varied creative and outdoor curriculum continues to stimulate and inspire in all subject areas of day-to-day learning. Dynamic and challenging lessons, adapted to suit the girls' needs ensure that they can truly achieve personal excellence. There is a superb ICT Suite, which was funded by the very supportive parents association, The Friends of Rowan, and well-equipped playgrounds and adventure walkways with a wooded area called The Spinney, which is held in great affection by the girls.

Girls are prepared for entry to a wide variety of senior independent day and boarding schools. There is an excellent record of 100% of girls moving on to a first-choice senior school with over 30 scholarships being offered this year for academic, music, sports or art.

Rowan offers a broad-based curriculum of work so that each pupil is able to develop her own talents and maximize her potential through an adventurous learning approach. The school welcomes visiting speakers and performers to enhance the curriculum. Day trips are also included in each term and the annual residential trips to Sayers Croft, The Isle of Wight, European ski resorts and France are both popular and highly educational in content. In addition, a wide variety of clubs are offered before and after school and at lunchtimes; they include drama, chess, art, science, foreign languages and a host of sports and musical activities. In addition, breakfast club and after-school prep clubs are available to support families.

Rowan has an outstanding Music Department, with all girls singing in a choir and playing the recorder. In addition, three-quarters of girls at the Hill play a further instrument. There are various ensembles, which the girls can also join in preparation for the orchestra. Girls at Rowan Brae are invited to play the violin or cello as part of the school's String Initiative during Year 1, a fantastic opportunity to learn about music and performance.

The school has excellent sporting opportunities and achievements. Girls have the chance to represent the school both locally and nationally for sports such as swimming, gymnastics, tennis and biathlon. Games are developed throughout the school with girls taking part in their first matches from Year 2.

Rowan is very proud of its art, providing stunning displays around both the Brae and the Hill expressing the girls' individuality and excellent capabilities.

With small classes on both sites and strong pastoral care it is Rowan's aim to provide the essential early grounding in a happy, stimulating and secure environment where every child's needs are catered for.

Prospective parents are encouraged to attend one of the Open Mornings held each term or to make an appointment to view the school during a normal working day. Admission in the Early Years is non-selective and early registration is advisable if a place in the Preschool is to be assured. Girls entering the school at 7+ will be invited to take part in a Discovery Day which takes place in November.

Assisted places are available and details may be obtained upon request from our Head of Admissions.

Charitable status. Rowan has a Local Governing Body that plays an active and supportive role in the school. Rowan is part of United Learning which is an educational trust controlled by a Board of Governors and chaired by Mr Richard Greenhalgh which comprises: UCST (a Company Limited by Guarantee, Registered in England, number 2780748, and a Registered Charity, number 1016538) and ULT (a Company Limited by Guarantee, Registered in England, number 4439859, and an Exempt Charity).

The Royal Masonic School for Girls
Nursery School and Prep School

Rickmansworth Park, Rickmansworth, Herts WD3 4HF

Tel: 01923 725337 (Cadogan House Prep School)
           01923 725316 (Ruspini House Nursery School)
email: admissions@rmsforgirls.com
website: www.rmsforgirls.com
Twitter: @RMSforGirls
Facebook: @RMSforGirls
Instagram: @RMSforGirls
LinkedIn: /school/rmsforgirls

Chairman of Governors: Professor J Brewer

Headteacher: Mr K Carson, BA, MPhil Cantab, PGCE

***Head of Cadogan House Prep School*: Mrs M Horn**, BA

***Head of Ruspini House Nursery School*: Mrs V Greig**, BA

Age Range. Nursery School, Ruspini House: 2–4 (boys at 2+, girls only from 3+) Prep School, Cadogan House: Girls 4–11.

Number of Pupils. Nursery 54, Cadogan House 214.

Fees per term (2021–2022). Cadogan House: Boarders (Years 5–6): £7,658 (Full), £7,262 (Weekly); Day Pupils: £3,940 (Reception), £4,141 (Years 1 and 2), £4,909 (Years 3–6). Ruspini House: please visit our website for range of fees.

Ruspini House is a small, friendly, caring community within the larger RMS family, guided by the same inclusive and nurturing ethos.

Housed in totally refurbished, modern and bespoke facilities and sharing our stunning grounds, Ruspini House welcomes boys and girls from 2 to 4 years. The youngest RMS pupils quickly settle into the stimulating, happy and supportive environment where all children are encouraged to reach their full potential through a healthy balance of learning and play.

We follow the principles of the Early Years Foundation Stage Curriculum and focus on each child's individual needs and talents. We encourage each child to develop at their own pace and they are well prepared for entry into Cadogan House.

Recognised by the ISI as outstanding (2014), Ruspini House lays firm foundations for a love of learning. Boys and girls develop independence, curiosity and enthusiasm, learn good manners, courtesy and consideration for others within a busy and supportive framework, where they are challenged and have fun at the same time.

Cadogan House is the stunning, spacious and refurbished home of the RMS Prep for girls aged 4 to 11 years. Recognised as excellent in all areas, Cadogan House is a warm and vibrant community alive with the buzz of happy, enthusiastic and motivated young learners, each of whom is valued as an individual.

The girls benefit from all of the facilities afforded by our magnificent site, including a designated Outdoor Learning Area. We have Forest School status, giving pupils experiences that complement traditional classroom learning while building self-esteem, confidence, and wellbeing.

The learning opportunities are exceptionally broad with outstanding teaching from both subject specialists and class teachers. Small class sizes ensure that teachers quickly get to know the girls and focus on nurturing their individual talents and strengths to enable them to become well-rounded independent young people. In Pre-Prep, Reception to Year 2, English and Maths are taught each day as individual subject areas, whilst Science and Humanities are covered through cross-curricular work. In Years 3 to 6, girls study English, Mathematics, Science, Art, DT, French, Geography, History, Computing, Music, PE, PSHCE and Religious Studies, with several subjects taught by subject specialists.

Extra-curricular activities abound and sport and Performing Arts have a high profile; girls receive five PE lessons per week, including Swimming, Gymnastics and Dance, and all girls receive music and singing lessons each week, with most playing at least one musical instrument.

Above all, Cadogan House pupils learn to exemplify the core RMS values of which there are six: Inclusivity, Kindness, Courage, Perseverance, Ambition, and Integrity. The Values are the focus points for assemblies and Form time; pupils who demonstrate putting them into action in their daily life are recognised and rewarded.

Year 6 pupils transfer seamlessly onto RMS Senior School, where they are guaranteed a place in Year 7.

Charitable status. The Royal Masonic School Limited is a Registered Charity, number 276784.

Royal Russell Junior School

Coombe Lane, Croydon, Surrey CR9 5BX

Tel: 020 8651 5884
email: juniorschool@royalrussell.co.uk
website: www.royalrussell.co.uk
Twitter: @Royal_Russell
         @RRS_Sport
Facebook: @RoyalRussellSchool
LinkedIn: /royal-russell-school

Patron: Her Majesty The Queen

Chairman of Governors: Mr A Merriman

Headmaster: Mr John Evans

Deputy Head (*Learning & Teaching*): Mrs Ruth Bannon

Deputy Head (*Pastoral*): Mrs Sarah Pain

Head of EYFS: Ms Tanya Mawanda [from January 2022]

Age Range. 3–11.
Number of Pupils. 176 Boys, 122 Girls.
Fees per term (2021–2022). Upper Juniors: £4,926 (Years 3–4), £5,126 (Years 5–6); Lower Juniors: £4,023 (Reception–Year 2), Nursery £2,415–£4,023.

The Junior School stands on a magnificent campus extending to over 110 acres, which it shares with Royal Russell Senior School (11–18 years). (*See Royal Russell School entry in HMC section.*)

The school is well served by road, tram and rail links and is one of the few co-educational schools in the South London area.

There is a fully-qualified teaching staff of 35. The school has a broad curriculum which seeks to blend the highest standards of academic work with a wide range of co-curricular activities.

There are opportunities for all pupils to participate in football, netball, hockey, swimming, trampolining, gymnastics, cross-country and cricket as team sports. There is an extensive fixture list of matches against other schools and Royal Russell regularly competes regionally and nationally, with significant success.

Artistic development extends to include full dramatic and musical productions, and many pupils learn musical instruments. All forms of art, design and technology are actively encouraged.

There are excellent teaching facilities with the latest interactive technology, which are complemented by Science Laboratories, Music and Art Rooms, Computer Suite, School Chapel and a Performing Arts Centre with a 200-seat Auditorium. For sport, the impressive facilities include a large Sports Hall, Gymnasium, floodlit all-weather pitch for hockey and tennis, multi-use games area, netball courts, 4 grass pitches for athletics, football and cricket and an indoor swimming pool. There is also a Forest School and adventure playground.

The majority of the pupils join the school at 3 years into the Nursery, and transfer to the Senior School at 11+. Candidates for entry to the Lower Juniors and Early Years are assessed informally, while all other entrants sit assessments in English, Mathematics and Cognitive Ability appropriate to their ages.

Prospective parents are very welcome to come and meet the Headmaster and to tour the school, by appointment.

Charitable status. Royal Russell School is a Registered Charity, number 271907. It exists solely to provide education to girls and boys.

Ruckleigh School

17 Lode Lane, Solihull, West Midlands B91 2AB

Tel: 0121 705 2773
email: admin@ruckleigh.co.uk
website: www.ruckleigh.co.uk

Headmaster: Mr Dominic Rhys Smith, MA Oxon

Age Range. 3–11.
Number in School. Day: 120 Boys, 120 Girls.
Fees per term (2021–2022). £1,170–£3,335

Ruckleigh is an independent day school offering education to boys and girls between the ages of 4 and 11 with a Nursery catering for children from the age of 3.

Although a high standard of work is expected this is related to the individual child, and the school is able to provide opportunities within a wide range of academic ability. Each child has every chance to develop his or her talents to the full, often resulting in achievements beyond initial expectations.

The comparatively small classes mean that every child is well known individually throughout the school creating a friendly environment.

Pupils are guided into habits of clear thinking, self-reliance and courtesy. Sound practical judgement, sensitivity towards the needs of others, and a willingness to "have a go" are the qualities that the school seeks to promote.

Rupert House School

90 Bell Street, Henley-on-Thames, Oxon RG9 2BN

Tel: 01491 574263
email: office@ruperthouse.oxon.sch.uk
website: www.ruperthouse.org
Twitter: @ruperthouse
Facebook: @RupertHouseSchool
Instagram: @rupert_house_school

Chair of Governors: Mr C Lowe

Head: Mr N Armitage, BA Hons University of East Anglia, PGCE Cambridge University

Age Range. Girls and Boys 3–11.

Number of Pupils. 190.

Fees per term (2021–2022). £3,590–£4,960.

Rupert House School is a leading independent pre-prep and prep school situated in the centre of Henley-on-Thames. Welcoming boys and girls from 3 to 11 years old, the school provides first-class education with a broad curriculum and a wide range of extra-curricular activities. Children benefit from small class sizes with a focus on the individual pathway, in a creative, nurturing environment.

The school has a reputation for traditional values, good manners and strong academic standards, with 100% of their Year 6 girls this year achieving a place at their first choice senior school. The strength and breadth of the curriculum is reflected in range of scholarships the girls attain, including Academic, Sport, Art, Music and Drama. This year the school's sixteen Year 6 pupils won a very impressive fourteen scholarships between them. Of course, the progress made by all children is equally valued, with children moving forward with appropriate support in small classes to fulfil their potential, whatever their starting point.

A town school set in beautiful gardens, with playing fields and a Forest School to its name, Rupert House prides itself on its stimulating and varied curriculum, which includes Outdoor Education and many residential trips. Drama at the school is ambitious, with impressive productions at the Kenton Theatre, and Music is a joy and a strength. The sporting timetable allows for a good number of games lessons and their fixture list throws down the gauntlet to local prep schools with increasing success. Swimming happens year-round and other sports include Football, Rugby, Netball, Gymnastics, Tennis, Cross-Country and Hockey, Athletics, Cricket and Rounders.

The school's new all-weather pitch represents a significant expansion of sporting provision for all existing and prospective pupils, providing a top quality surface that can be used for hockey, netball, football, tag rugby and mini-tennis.

The school has successfully introduced an assessment model that focuses on the development of the values, skills, attitudes and behaviours required for children to succeed and flourish in an ever-changing world. Children are encouraged, recognised and celebrated in their achievements and directly prepared for the next step of their educational journey.

Rupert House's two minibuses cover Henley and Marlow, complementing the school's wrap-around care for working parents. This includes Breakfast Club from 7.30–8.15am and Homework Club/After-Care from 3.45–5.15pm.

Bursaries are offered to children from Reception through to Year 6 and a range of scholarships is available for places in the Upper School (Year 3 and above).

Charitable status. Rupert House School is a Registered Charity, number 309648. It exists to provide quality education for boys and girls.

Russell House

Station Road, Otford, Sevenoaks, Kent TN14 5QU

Tel: 01959 522352
email: head@russellhouse.kent.sch.uk
website: www.russellhouseschool.co.uk
Twitter: @RussellHouseSch
Facebook: @RussellHouseSchool
Instagram: @russell_house_school

Head: **Mr Craig McCarthy**

Age Range. Co-educational 2–11.

Number of Pupils. Approx. 200.

Fees per term (2021–2022). Russell Robins (Under 3s) £830 (2 mornings), Nursery Department £2,200 (5 mornings), Transition £2,280 (5 mornings), Reception £3,930, Years 1–2 £4,350, Year 3 £4,560, Year 4 £4,850, Years 5–6 £5,000. Fees are inclusive of lunch.

Russell House is a family-friendly school for girls and boys aged from 2 to 11.

We have a reputation for achieving excellent academic results in a warm, caring and inclusive atmosphere where every child has access to a myriad of opportunities for extra-curricular activities.

Many of our pupils are successful in the 11+ examination, gaining entry to the local grammar schools, and many pass on to independent schools such as Sevenoaks, Caterham and King's Rochester. We have a consistently good record in gaining scholarships, both academic and music which goes hand in hand with an ethos which encourages individuality, self-expression, curiosity to learn and the ability to challenge accepted wisdom.

The school is careful to cultivate a calm, happy atmosphere and there is also a strong emphasis on building skills for the future and developing a sensitive awareness of the world beyond the school.

Ryde School with Upper Chine Junior School

Queen's Road, Ryde, Isle of Wight PO33 3BE

Tel: 01983 612901
email: junior.office@rydeschool.net
website: www.rydeschool.org.uk
Twitter: @RydeSchool
Facebook: @RydeSchool

Chairman of the Board of Governors: Christoph Lees, MB BS, BSc, MD

Head of Prep: Mr E Marsden, BSc

Head of Pre-Prep: Mrs E Willetts, BA

Age Range. 2½–11.

Fees per term (from January 2022). Tuition: Foundation Stage – please see School website; Pre-Prep £2,645–£3,765; Junior School £4,575. Boarding (excluding tuition): £5,690 (full), £4,565 (weekly). Rates for payment by Direct Debit. Lunch included.

Scholarships may be awarded on merit to external or internal candidates for entry at 9+. Scholarships open up bursaries which are means tested.

The Junior School (Fiveways Nursery & Pre-Prep, Prep) provides an ambitious, happy and supportive environment, one in which children thrive and develop a lifelong love of learning. They benefit from a varied and relevant programme of study, supplemented by enriching extracurricular activities, as we seek to prepare our pupils for an exciting future in an ever-changing world.

The Junior School caters for children aged 2½–11 years. Fiveways, in its own separate building, is home to the Nursery and Pre-Prep. Through creative and imaginative teaching in new purpose-built classrooms, a sound foundation of key skills is established. Pupils receive the support of a well-qualified and dedicated staff, enjoying a full range of specialist facilities including a continually upgraded IT facility, with Internet access across the school, the new HIVE creative centre, including the Lego studio, Science Laboratory, Music room and Theatre.

A broad, balanced and rich curriculum is followed. Pupils have the unique opportunity to study and develop a love of languages from an early age. As the original host school for the Isle of Wight Literary Festival Schools programme, our children benefit from the thrill of visiting authors, poets and script writers. Pupils are encouraged to develop their full range of talents. In Music they are able to compose and perform. Many pupils undertake individual instrumental lessons. There are choirs, music groups and an orchestra. As well as weekly classroom drama lessons, we enter children into LAMDA examinations and they take part in shows and festivals across the Island. Art and Design Technology are taught as discrete subjects and clubs, competitions and exhibitions also allow the children to develop their talents. Sports teams start at U8 level and we compete successfully against Island and mainland prep schools in netball, hockey, rugby, football, athletics (indoor and outdoor), cricket, rounders and cross country. Every child will be able to sail by the end of Year 6 and swimming and tennis also make up part of our extensive sports programme. Our new outdoor education programme and outdoor classroom provides an inspirational environment for the children to learn, grow and develop. There is a full and wide-ranging programme of clubs and activities (which changes each term) during lunchtime and after school, offering something for everyone.

Our Senior School is on the same campus, enabling us to benefit from the use of a Sports Hall and pitches. Careful liaison between the staff and induction days in the Summer Term effect a smooth transition for our pupils to the Senior School (*see entry in the HMC section for Ryde School with Upper Chine*).

The Junior School takes flexi, weekly and full boarders from Year 6. The boarding community is run with an emphasis on family values and boarders enjoy a large range of extra curricular activities. Junior pupils board in a newly renovated Victorian Villa called Millfield; opened in 2020 within the school grounds, pupils enjoy twin and triple rooms, most with en-suite facilities.

Charitable status. Ryde School with Upper Chine is a Registered Charity, number 307409. The aims and objectives of the Charity are the education of boys and girls.

Rydes Hill Preparatory School

Rydes Hill House, Aldershot Road, Guildford, Surrey GU2 8BP

Tel: 01483 563160
email: admissions@rydeshill.com
website: www.rydeshill.com
Twitter: @rydeshillprep
Facebook: @RydesHill

Chairman of the Governors: Mrs Katie Cardona

Headmistress: Mrs Sarah Norville

Age Range. Girls 3–11, Boys 3–7. Pre-school Nursery for children 3–4

Number of Day Pupils. 132.

Fees per term (2021–2022). £3,128 (Reception)–£4,750 (Year 6) including lunch

Nursery. Term-time and all-year-round places are offered with flexible hours from 7.30am to 6pm

Rydes Hill is a Catholic Prep School educating girls from 3 to 11 and boys from 3 to 7. As a non-selective, one-form entry school, they are blessed with small class sizes in bright airy rooms, set in beautiful grounds in the Guildford suburbs. Rydes Hill is open to families of all faiths and beliefs and they are immensely proud of the deep bonds that unite their close-knit community.

The parents at Rydes Hill often coin a phrase that the School is 'small but mighty' as their achievements reach far beyond their small stature. Indeed, it is their small size that enables the teachers to have a genuine understanding of what makes every child tick, which, in turn, informs the individualised learning paths. Far from expecting the children to march to the beat of the same drum, Rydes Hill empowers the children to embrace their unique passions and talents and stay true to themselves. This is reflected in the breadth of scholarships awarded, with the 2021 leavers receiving 13 scholarships from academic to drama, music, Art and sport.

Rydes Hill emboldens their children to find their voice and public speaking is gently encouraged at every opportunity. All 210 children who sat Speech and Drama exams during the course of the last three years were awarded a distinction. Witnessing shy or timid children transform into confident orators through their Rydes Hill journey is one of the School's greatest sources of pride.

The School's 'small but mighty' spirit is evident on the sporting field where Rydes Hill frequently out-competes prestigious independent schools triple or quadruple their size. In 2020, Rydes Hill reached the IAPS National Championships in both Netball and Swimming spurred on by the collective roar from their supporters!

The undoubted heartbeat and driving force of Rydes Hill is the Headmistress, Mrs Norville who can be summed up in the words of one of the parents:

"By far and away the real understated (but somewhat self-effacing) gem at Rydes Hill is Mrs Norville. She is wonderfully passionate about what she does, she seems to emanate contagious energy, she is kind, she has good humour, and she has a profoundly holistic approach to the development of every single child at Rydes Hill. The School, under the leadership of Mrs Norville, is nothing short of magnificent."

Rydes Hill were recently ranked 22nd in the Top Independent Preparatory Schools in the Sunday Times Parent Power 2021, placing the School amongst the academically elite. Whilst they wear this accolade as a badge of pride, they know the real secret to their success is far from being elite. Their doors are open to all, they celebrate difference and they have both feet firmly planted on the ground.

Charitable status. Rydes Hill Preparatory School and Nursery is a Registered Charity, number 299411. It exists to ensure excellence in all aspects of education.

St Albans High School Prep

Codicote Road, Wheathampstead, Hertfordshire AL4 8DJ

Tel:	01582 839270
email:	Prep@stahs.org.uk
website:	www.stahs.org.uk
Twitter:	@STAHSPrep
Facebook:	@StAlbansHighSchoolPrep
Instagram:	@stahsgirls

Chair of School Council: Mrs H Greatrex, BA, MSc Hons, ACA

Head of the Prep School: Mrs Judy Rowe, BEd

Age Range. Girls 4–11.
Number of Pupils. 340.
Fees per term (2021–2022). Reception £5,185 (inc Lunch), Years 1 and 2 £5,475 (inc Lunch); Years 3–6 £5,530 (exc Lunch).

The Prep School for St Albans High School for Girls is a very popular, academically selective school, with a welcoming family atmosphere, offering outstanding pastoral care. St Albans High School is uniquely placed in being able to offer all the advantages of a continuous education in two very different settings. From the ages of 4–11, the girls have the freedom to grow and develop in an attractive rural environment, before moving on to the more urban setting of the Senior School, close to the heart of the City of St Albans.

The Prep School is set in 18 acres of grounds within the village of Wheathampstead. It has large playing areas, a meadow and school woods, where girls engage in forest school activities.

The curriculum is broad, embracing the National Curriculum and beyond. A central focus is placed on thinking skills, creativity and independent learning. Excellent facilities include an ICT suite, Science lab and outdoor classroom. New technologies are used to support learning, with SMART boards, laptops, iPads and Kindles, in addition to the computers in the ICT suite. Pupils at the Prep School use the school swimming pool located at the Senior School.

It is a happy and exciting school with a wide variety of activity days and educational visits throughout the school year. There is an extensive range of clubs including Art, Speech and Drama, Dancing, Sports, Orienteering, Karate, Fencing, Chess and Coding. Music is a real strength of the school and there are many music groups, choirs and an orchestra. Enrichment groups extend and support learning and there are opportunities for highly talented pupils to join with Senior School girls for events.

The School provides a supportive, challenging and creative environment, where girls work hard, are very successful academically and enjoy learning.

Charitable status. St Albans High School for Girls is a Registered Charity, number 311065.

St Andrew's Prep

Meads, Eastbourne, East Sussex BN20 7RP

Tel:	01323 733203
email:	admissions@standrewsprep.co.uk
website:	www.standrewsprep.co.uk
Facebook:	@StAndrewsprepEB
Instagram:	@standrewsprep_eastbourne
LinkedIn:	/st-andrew-s-prep

Chairman of the Governing Body: Mr P A J Broadley

Head: Mr Tom Gregory

Age Range. 9 months–13 years.
Number of Pupils. 243 (Prep School), 115 (Pre-Prep and Nursery).
Fees per term (2021–2022). Full boarding £8,915; Weekly Boarding £7,845; Flexible boarding – supplements from £27 per night; Day children: £6,250 (Years 7–8), £6,200 (Years 5–6), £5,925 (Year 4), £5,375 (Year 3), Pre-Prep £3,565. Nursery sessions: We offer the EYEE grant and sessions start from £26 for 3 to 4 year olds claiming the EYEE grant. For 2 to 3 year olds, sessions start from £35. For babies aged 9 to 24 months, sessions start from £36. Sessions run from 8.00am to 1.00pm, 1.00pm to 6.00pm,

8.00am to 4.00pm and 8.00am to 6.00pm. Please contact the Registrar for more details.

St Andrew's is positioned within 12 acres of beautifully tended grounds at the foot of the South Downs and is just a five minute walk to the beach. The school, founded in 1877, has a highly qualified teaching staff and children are taught in classes with a maximum size of 20 and an average number of approximately 16. A number of children in the Prep department are boarders and the school operates a popular scheme of flexi boarding allowing day children to stay any number of nights during the week on a flexible basis.

The Head is supported by the Deputy Head and a strong management team. All children in the school have a Form Teacher or Form Tutor who is responsible for their pastoral welfare and academic progress. Each section of the school has its own Head (Nursery and Pre-Prep, Junior, Middle and Senior), who coordinates, together with the Deputy Head and Pastoral Heads, the overall pastoral and academic work of the staff.

In addition to the expanse of playing fields, St Andrew's benefits from its own indoor swimming pool, newly refurbished netball and tennis courts and a new state-of-the-art sports hall and dance studio which was opened by Baroness Tanni Grey-Thompson in September 2016 to provide excellent sporting provision for its pupils. During the summer 2018 the boarding house was also refurbished together with the Pavilion which now forms a superb space for hosting events and presentations as well as a Senior Common room for pupils in Years 7 and 8.

There are three computer/iPad suites equipped with up-to-date software and hardware including a wireless network connection. There is an interactive whiteboard in every classroom. The equipment in the Pre-Prep suite is designed specifically for children from 3 to 7 years of age.

Other facilities include a modern purpose-built music block, an extensively equipped research and resource centre, a chapel, a Forest School and a creative arts centre with an art studio and design and technology facilities. The school strongly encourages music and drama and more than three quarters of the children play instruments and participate in orchestras, bands and choirs.

As well as music, drama is a timetabled subject and plays take place every term.

From the age of nine, children are taught by subject specialists. French is taught from the age of 5 and Latin is introduced from the age of 9. Children are introduced to working on computers from the age of two. The breadth of the curriculum means that, while the requirements of the National Curriculum are fulfilled, the children are able to experience a variety of other stimulating activities.

Accelerated sets exist from Year 5 to provide more challenging opportunities for those who are academically gifted. Academic, art, drama, music, and sports awards have been achieved to many major senior schools and over the past five years almost 140 scholarships have been won by St Andrew's pupils. The charity running St Andrew's Prep amalgamated with Eastbourne College in 2010 and the two schools are part of the Eastbourne College Incorporated Charity. The school benefits from the use of College facilities including astroturf pitches, a contemporary performing arts centre and specialist staff. Approximately 65–70% of St Andrew's Prep leavers each year progress to Eastbourne College. However, it should be noted that although the schools are inter-dependent, they are also independent of each other and the Headmaster of St Andrew's advises on any number of other schools too, as appropriate to each individual.

There is a wide range of activities on offer. The Co-Curricular programme, which runs for children in Years 5 to 8, offers opportunities for all children to develop areas of interest and strength or to discover new ones. Each activity offered has its own educational objectives and challenges designed to improve children's skills and broaden their horizons. Optional Saturday morning activities for Years 4 to 8 pupils are also very popular. An extensive programme of after-school activities has always been a strong feature of St Andrew's. This starts at the Pre-Prep and runs through to Year 8.

The school's strong sporting reputation manifests itself in national honours regularly achieved in many different sports. Specialist coaches are employed to teach the skills required for all to enjoy participating in team games and opportunities are available to anyone wishing to represent the school.

Charitable status. Eastbourne College Incorporated is a Registered Charity, number 307071. The aim of the Charity is the promotion of Education.

St Andrew's School

Buckhold, Pangbourne, Reading, Berks RG8 8QA

Tel:	0118 974 4276
email:	marketing@standrewspangbourne.co.uk
website:	www.standrewspangbourne.co.uk
Twitter:	@StAndrewsSch
Facebook:	@StAndrewsSch
Instagram:	@standrewssch
LinkedIn:	/company/st-andrew's-prep-pangboune

The School is an Educational Trust controlled by a Board of Governors.

Chair of Governors: Mrs Felicity M Rutland

Headmaster: **Mr Ed Graham**, BA Hons, QTS

Age Range. 3–13. Weekly Boarding Years 3 – 8

Number of Pupils. 315

Fees per term (2021–2022). Flexi Boarders £35 per night, £130 per week, £1,250 per term, Day Pupils £3,890–£6,525. Nursery from £1,945 (5 mornings).

The School is fully co-educational and set in over 50 acres of private wooded estate and parkland.

The Curriculum includes all the traditional CE and Scholarship subjects and there is emphasis on Music, Speech and Drama and Modern Languages. Senior School preparation and Study Skills are an important part of the senior pupils' timetable and Information Technology is well resourced.

Academic and Sporting standards are high. A brand new Sports Centre with indoor swimming pool was opened in January 2018 alongside a full-size Astro pitch.

Charitable status. St Andrew's (Pangbourne) School Trust Limited is a Registered Charity, number 309090. It exists to provide education for boys and girls.

St. Andrew's School, Woking

Church Hill House, Wilson Way, Horsell, Woking, Surrey GU21 4QW

Tel: 01483 760943
email: hmsec@st-andrews.woking.sch.uk
          admin@st-andrews.woking.sch.uk
website: www.st-andrews.woking.sch.uk
Twitter: @StAndrewsWoking
Facebook: @standrewsschoolwoking

Chairman of Governors: Mr Max Taylor

Headmaster: **Mr Dominic Fitzgerald**, BEd Hons

Deputy Head: Mr Jonathan Spooner, MA Hons

Age Range. 3–13 co-educational.

Fees per term (2021–2022). Prep £4,810–£5,515. Pre-Prep £1,401–£4,060.

St. Andrew's School was founded in 1937 and is an established, respected and thriving co-educational Prep school, set in 11 acres of grounds within a quiet residential area approximately half a mile from Woking town centre. The School seeks to create a nurturing and happy environment of trust and support in which all pupils are encouraged and enabled to develop their skills, talents, interests and potential to the full – intellectually, physically and spiritually, regardless of social circumstances, age or religion.

Within St. Andrew's walls children feel secure and confident and are highly motivated to perform to the best of their ability in all aspects of school life. They are competitive without losing sight of their responsibility to share and they are justifiably proud of their school and their own personal achievements. In a world of changing values, self-confidence and a solid grounding are essential building blocks for life. St. Andrew's hopes to provide all their children with this basic foundation as they prepare for the bigger challenges that follow. Children are prepared for entrance and scholarship exams to a wide range of independent senior schools and there are specialist teaching facilities for all subjects including science, ICT, music, drama and art. The curriculum is broad and the school places great emphasis on music, sport and the arts.

St. Andrew's is very proud of its excellent on-site facilities including an all-weather sports surface, sports pitches, tennis courts, cricket nets and outdoor heated swimming pool. We are very fortunate to enjoy the benefits of carefully designed school grounds that incorporate facilities to meet the needs of the children's physical and social development. Main school games are football, hockey, cricket and netball. Other activities include cross-country running, swimming, tennis and athletics.

Children can be supervised at school from 8.00am and, through our extensive after-school activities programme for Year 3 and above, until 6.00pm most evenings during the week. There is also an after-school club from 4.15pm to 6.00pm (chargeable) for Pre-Prep, Year 3 and Year 4 children.

Children are assessed for entry into Year 2 and above. Contact the School for more information regarding scholarships and bursaries.

Charitable status. St. Andrew's (Woking) School Trust is a Registered Charity, number 297580, established to promote and provide for the advancement of education of children.

S. Anselm's

Stanedge Road, Bakewell, Derbyshire DE45 1DP

Tel: 01629 812734
email: admissions@anselms.co.uk
website: www.sanselms.co.uk
Twitter: @SAnselmsPrep
Facebook: @s.anselms

The School is an Educational Trust.

Chairman of Governors: Mr S R Bowker, CBE

Headteacher: **Mr F Thompson**, MA, MPhil, NPQH

Age Range. 3–13.

Numbers. 207 (106 boys, 101 girls)

Fees per term (2021–2022). Boarders: £9,000. Day: Prep £5,900–£7,145; Pre-Prep £3,780–£4,295.

Welcome to S. Anselm's School, the only independent co-educational prep school in Derbyshire. Situated in the heart of the glorious Peak District it offers outstanding academic, sporting and extra-curricular opportunities to all pupils. We actively welcome children of all abilities to the school and pride ourselves on cherishing each individual child and allowing their full potential to shine through.

S. Anselm's sits on the crest of a hill in the heart of the Peak National Park – a beacon of excellence in all it does. All parents seek an environment where their children can remain children for as long as possible. Here at S. Anselm's it is just so. Through everything we do this ethos remains steadfast. We are proud of our tradition and are not ashamed to say that the values we hold dear are the very reason this school is quite unique.

With an 18-acre campus in the Peak District the children are surrounded by beauty and opportunities to explore. We have 5 netball courts, an indoor swimming pool, a recently renovated sports hall, a theatre with a permanent stage, a dedicated music block, 3 fully equipped science laboratories, 2 art rooms, a new innovations centre and a newly developed library. The school is forward looking in its approach to IT having invested heavily in it over the last 2 years with iPads for learning, fully interactive whiteboards and Wi-Fi throughout the school.

The boarders enjoy a varied programme of activities including the debating club and fiercely fought tournaments of dodgeball. Those who learn music practise for 20 minutes every evening and cocoa and toast every night give a homely feel to bedtime.

Here our pupils are encouraged to be themselves; they are genuinely excited about learning and have a real thirst for knowledge. They thrive in the music and art rooms, and on the games field and stage. Pupils adore this school and are justly proud of all they do. They love learning and there is a true sense of fun.

Our small class sizes mean our staff can plan their teaching to ensure every pupil is treated as an individual.

Each child is cared for and nurtured in every way they need. Our teaching staff simply want the very best for all our pupils and will do all they can to help them achieve their own personal best.

At the very centre of our values is creativity – whether through the individual or the community. It is creativity in thought and every aspect of life that sets a S. Anselm's pupil apart from others. We encourage our children to be creative in their thinking and their play and strongly believe in the importance of nurturing an environment where they can fully and confidently explore their individuality. This is a kind, caring and tolerant school and we are quite sure this wonderful environment will make a lasting impression on all who visit.

Charitable status. S. Anselm's is a Registered Charity, number 527179. It exists to provide an excellent all-round education for boys and girls.

St Anthony's School for Boys

Alpha Plus Group

90 Fitzjohn's Avenue, Hampstead, London NW3 6NP

Tel: 020 7435 3597 (Junior House)
         020 7431 1066 (Admissions)
email: PAHead@stanthonysprep.co.uk
website: www.stanthonysprep.org.uk
Instagram: @stanthonysprep

Headmaster: **Richard Berlie**, MA Cantab

Age Range. 4–13.
Number of Boys. 310 Day Boys.
Fees per term (2021–2022). £6,750–£6,950 including lunches.

Founded in the 19th century and now set in the heart of Hampstead village, St Anthony's is an academic IAPS preparatory school for boys between the ages of 4 and 13. It is Roman Catholic, but welcomes boys of other faiths. The majority of boys transfer at 13, via scholarship or CE, to leading independent senior schools including Westminster, University College School, KCS Wimbledon, Habs, Merchant Taylors', St Paul's, Mill Hill, Highgate, Harrow, Eton, City of London, Ampleforth, Stonyhurst, Sevenoaks, Bedales, Tonbridge, Winchester, Charterhouse and Oundle, The American School, Aldenham, St. Albans, Forest, Rugby, Haileybury, Sherborne, JFS and QE Boys. A number of boys also transfer to leading state Catholic schools such as The Cardinal Vaughan and The London Oratory. It is one of the prestigious Alpha Plus Schools whose CEO is Mark Hanley-Browne, a distinguished former Headmaster. A sister school, St Anthony's School for Girls, opened in 2016 and works closely to provide an equivalent excellent education.

The school accommodation consists of two large Victorian houses in close proximity. Both have their own grounds and separate playgrounds. There are eight forms in the Junior House, where boys range in age from four to eight, and ten forms in the Senior House, where boys range in age from eight to thirteen. The Senior House has a specialist Design and Technology room, a Music room, a Dance & Drama studio, a computer suite, a Science laboratory and a swimming pool.

All boys receive Religious Education lessons twice a week. The course, which centres on Catholic beliefs and practices, but includes aspects of other faiths, is followed by all pupils. The school's spiritual dimension is regarded as highly important and it exists within a liberal and inclusive atmosphere. Most pupils attend mass about three times each term.

The school curriculum is stimulating and challenging: for example, it is possible for boys to study five foreign languages. All pupils study French and Mandarin from Year 1; Latin and Greek are available from Year 6. The arts have an important place in the school with a majority of boys learning to play a musical instrument and all boys involved in drama. Sport is a further strength of the school with some pupils achieving success on a national stage. The school has use of a superb local sports club, at Brondesbury, with extensive facilities. It has recently introduced Computer Programming and Robotics courses have been very successful and pupils can study Philosophy from Year 4 upwards.

St Anthony's still retains its famous commitment to fostering individuality with alumni such as David Suchet, Anthony Gormley and Bombay Bicycle Club underlining its notable commitment to the liberal arts. Recently, pupils have been awarded Music, Arts and Academic scholarships to Westminster, Eton, Harrow, Highgate, Brighton College, Winchester, St Paul's, Habs, UCS, Merchant Taylors', Stonyhurst, City of London Boys, Cardinal Vaughan, St Albans, Shrewsbury and Mill Hill. Recently boys have also achieved Sports awards at Harrow, City of London Boys, Aldenham and Mill Hill.

The school works hard to instil in its pupils a sense of social responsibility and charity fundraising is a key feature of school life. A former pupil was awarded the Gusi Peace Prize (Asian equivalent of the Nobel). Much work is also done with local charities.

St Aubyn's School

Bunces Lane, Woodford Green, Essex IG8 9DU

Tel: 020 8504 1577
email: school@staubyns.com
website: www.staubyns.com
Twitter: @st_aubyns
Facebook: @St-Aubyns-School

The School was founded in 1884 and is governed by a Charitable Trust.

Chairman of the Governors: Mr A Botha

Headmaster: **Mr Len Blom**, BEd Hons, BA, HDE Phys Ed, NPQH

Deputy Heads:

Mr Marcus Shute, BEd Hons

Miss Helen Singleton, BSc Hons

Age Range. 3–13.
Number of Children. 525 Day.

Fees per term (2021–2022). £3,535 (Nursery) to £4,470 (Seniors) fully inclusive.

St Aubyn's provides an all-round preparatory education for children aged 3–13. The School is non-selective at its main point of entry for children aged 3. There are entry assessment tests for older children, principally at ages 4+, 7+ and 11+.

Classes are small, taught by well-qualified, dedicated staff. Nursery and Reception children are also supported by teaching assistants. Qualified nurses deal with all medical issues and emergencies.

The School offers a wide-ranging curriculum within a traditional framework, encompassing all National Curriculum requirements. French is introduced from Nursery onwards and Latin from Year 6. French, Music and PE are specialist-taught from an early age. All subjects are specialist-taught from Year 6.

Children progress to a range of selective, independent and state schools at 11+ and 13+. Pupils gain a range of scholarships at both 11+ and 13+. Recent awards include several academic scholarships as well as awards in Sport, Technology, Music and Drama. In 2021 a total of 7 awards were gained by a total of 4 children.

The School is pleasantly situated on the borders of Epping Forest, yet is close both to the North Circular and the M11. There are three departments within the School: Pre Prep including EYFS (3+, 4+, 5+, 6+); Middle School (7+, 8+, 9+) and Seniors (10+, 11+ and 12+) and each has its own base and resources. Facilities are extensive with 8 acres of grounds, large Sports Centre, all-weather pitches, fully-equipped Performing Arts Centre and Music School, Science Laboratory, Art and Design and Technology Studio, Library, Dance and Drama Studio and two IT Suites. A computer network runs throughout the school. Games include football, cricket, hockey, rugby, tennis, netball, athletics and swimming, all coached to a high standard.

The Director of Music leads a thriving department, with a School orchestra and various instrumental groups and choirs. Children are regularly involved in performances both within and outside the School.

In January 2017 a world-class, purpose-built, state-of-the-art Nursery facility was created and the School expanded and upgraded its changing room facilities in the Sports Hall in 2018. Most recently, an extension to the Performing Arts Centre and refurbishment of the Senior facilities and Science Laboratory were completed.

St Aubyn's School is a registered charity. All income from fees is for the direct benefit of its pupils. There is a means-tested assisted places scheme at 7+.

Charitable status. St Aubyn's (Woodford Green) School Trust is a Registered Charity, number 270143. It exists to provide education for children.

St Benedict's Junior School

5 Montpelier Avenue, Ealing, London W5 2XP

Tel: 020 8862 2250
email: juniorschool@stbenedicts.org.uk
website: www.stbenedicts.org.uk
Twitter: @stbenedicts
Facebook: @StBenedictsSchool
Instagram: @stbenedictsschool
LinkedIn: /st-benedicts-school

Governing Body:

The Governing Board of St Benedict's School

Headmaster: **Mr R G Simmons**, BA Hons, PGCE

Deputy Head: Mrs T Scott, BEd

Age Range. 3–11 Co-educational.

Number of Pupils. 273.

Fees per term (2021–2022). Nursery: £3,375–£5,075; Pre-Prep: £4,665; Junior School: £5,185.

St Benedict's is London's leading independent Catholic co-educational school, located in leafy Ealing. Within a caring, happy community, St Benedict's has strong academic standards. The Junior School and Nursery offers a holistic education for children aged 3 to 11, which continues through the Senior School and Sixth Form. St Benedict's, which welcomes children of other Christian denominations and faiths, is committed to supporting all children to develop their full potential.

Inspirational teaching and exceptional pastoral care are at the heart of the education we offer.

The Junior School and Nursery provide a supportive, friendly and vibrant co-educational environment in which to learn. In the Nursery a carefully-planned and child-centred programme enables and extends learning and development. The Junior School provides a broad and balanced curriculum based on a rigorous academic core. Sharing excellent facilities with the Senior School, and participating in a programme of cross-curricular activities, helps ease the transition at 11+ to the Senior School, which is on the same site.

There are extensive opportunities in music, art, sport and drama. St Benedict's has a proud sporting tradition, which promotes the highest sporting aspirations while encouraging everyone to enjoy sport, fitness and teamwork. Music is excellent, with several choirs (including the renowned Ealing Abbey Choir) and many instrumental ensembles. A wide range of co-curricular activities is offered, and an after-school club is available at the Junior School.

There has been huge investment in building and facilities at St Benedict's. Having opened our Sixth Form Centre and Art Department in 2015, a new Nursery and Pre-Prep Department opened in September 2017, providing our youngest pupils with a first-rate learning environment.

St Benedict's School is unique. Come and visit and see what we have to offer. You can be sure of a warm Benedictine welcome.

Charitable status. St Benedict's School Ealing is a Registered Charity, number 1148512, and a Charitable

Company Limited by Guarantee, registration number 8093330.

St Bernard's Preparatory School

Hawtrey Close, Slough, Berkshire SL1 1TB

Tel: 01753 521821
email: info@stbernardsprep.org
website: www.stbernardsprep.org
Twitter: @stbernardsprep
Facebook: @stbernardspreparatory
Instagram: @stbernardsprep

Acting Headteacher: **Mrs A Verma**, LLB Hons, NPQH, GTP

Deputy Head: Mr N Cheesman

Assistant Head: Mrs A Underwood

Age Range. 2½–11 co-educational.
Number of Pupils. 227
Fees per term (2021–2022). £3,195–£3,810

St Bernard's Preparatory has a unique ethos. We are a Catholic school, teaching the Catholic faith and living out the Gospel values which are shared by all faiths and are the foundation of all our relationships and the daily life of our school. We welcome and embrace children of all faiths and we recognise and celebrate our similarities and differences, developing mutual respect, understanding and tolerance.

We recognise the value and uniqueness of each individual, both child and adult. We celebrate the talents and gifts of each child and enable them to develop to their full potential spiritually, morally, academically, socially and physically. Our children are happy, courteous, confident, articulate young citizens, committed to the ideal of service to others.

We work in partnership with parents, recognising that they are the first and best educators of their child. We consider ourselves to be very privileged that parents have entrusted us with the care and education of their child. We ensure that parents are kept fully informed of their child's progress.

We are committed to offering a broad, balanced, creative and challenging curriculum, enriched by experiences and opportunities which enhance and consolidate the learning process. Small class sizes enable our team of highly qualified, caring, committed and enthusiastic teachers to be responsive to the needs of the individual child ensuring continuity and progression for all our children. We have developed a wide and varied range of after-school activities which broaden the curriculum and enrich the children's lives. Children are encouraged to develop new skills.

We are proud of our reputation as a school with a strong ethos and nurturing pastoral care coupled with academic excellence reflected in consistently outstanding results in local and national tests.

Our school motto 'Dieu Mon Abri' meaning 'God is my Shelter', is an inspiring reminder of God's love for each one of us. The three swords represent 'Love, Work and Prayer' which underpin and permeate the life of our school.

St Cedd's School

178a New London Road, Chelmsford, Essex CM2 0AR

Tel: 01245 392810
email: info@stcedds.org.uk
website: www.stcedds.org.uk

Chair of Governors: Mrs F Marshall

Head: **Mr M Clarke**, BEd Hons Cantab

Age Range. 3–11 Co-educational.
Number of Pupils. 400.
Fees per term (2021–2022). £3,080–£3,940 including educational visits, curriculum-linked extra-curricular activities, 1–1 learning support, lunch and the majority of after-school clubs.

St Cedd's School, founded in 1931, is a leading co-educational day school and Pre-School for children aged 3 to 11. The grounds and facilities create a vibrant and purposeful learning environment where children are encouraged to become independent, confident and caring individuals. A St Cedd's School education focuses on high standards of literacy and numeracy within an expansive academic broad and balanced curriculum, supplemented by a superb programme of sport and an extraordinary creative output of music and the performing arts. PE, Music, Art and MFL are taught by specialist teachers from Pre-School; Swimming and Recorders are introduced in Year 2 and International Studies is studied in Years 5 and 6. Following the 11+ entry and Independent School Examinations, a baccalaureate-style curriculum in Year 6 leads to the HOLDFAST Award which celebrates the breadth of children's achievements and talents. Music is a particular strength of the school with outstanding individual instrumental examination results. St Cedd's School is a Choir Schools' Association School and a member of the Chelmsford Choral Foundation. This link to Chelmsford Cathedral provides opportunity for our choirs to perform at Choral Evensong.

The grounded confidence the pupils have as a result of excellent teaching and differentiated learning in a happy and supported environment, where children have fun and are encouraged to take risks, results in great personal achievements. Our children aspire to the highest levels of attainment and we can boast a successful track record of outstanding results at entry to Grammar Schools and scholarships to Independent Senior Schools.

Breakfast is available from 7.30am and there is an extensive array of after-school activities with wrap-around care in our TLC provision until 6.00pm.

Charitable status. St Cedd's School Educational Trust Limited is a Registered Charity, number 310865. It exists to provide education for girls and boys.

Saint Christina's RC Preparatory School

25 St Edmund's Terrace, London NW8 7PY

Tel: 020 7722 8784
email: headteacherspa@saintchristinas.org.uk
website: www.saintchristinas.org.uk

Headteacher: **Mr Alastair Gloag**, BA

Age Range. Girls and Boys 3–11.
Number of Pupils. 121 girls, 39 boys.
Fees per term (2021–2022). £5,100 (inclusive).

Saint Christina's was founded in 1949 by the Handmaids of the Sacred Heart of Jesus. At Saint Christina's, children experience the joy of learning and the wonder of God and His Creation. Our purpose at Saint Christina's is to create an environment where children enjoy learning and where each individual experiences respect and acceptance enabling them to become the balanced person they are called to be.

As a School we take pride in the excellent examination results which we achieve. We value most of all our strong sense of community. We seek to ensure that children feel appreciated for themselves as individuals as much as their achievements. We believe that confidence can only grow in an atmosphere of trust and safety.

Boys and Girls are prepared for Common Entrance Examination and entrance exams to day and boarding schools.

The School is purpose built in a pleasant location within a short walk of Primrose Hill and Regent's Park. Prospective parents are warmly invited to visit the School.

Charitable status. Saint Christina's is a Registered Charity, number 221319.

St Christopher's School
Hove

33 New Church Road, Hove, East Sussex BN3 4AD

Tel: 01273 735404
email: office@stchristophershove.org.uk
website: www.stchristophershove.org.uk
Twitter: @stchrishove

Chairman of Governors: Mr A Underwood

Head: **Ms E Lyle**, BSc, QTS

Age Range. 4–13 co-educational.
Number of Pupils. 291.
Fees per term (2021–2022). £3,018–£4,611.

Since its foundation in 1927, St Christopher's School has expanded to become a highly successful academic preparatory school, located in the middle of Brighton & Hove, England's youngest and most vibrant city.

St Christopher's School aims to provide a traditional academic education within a supportive family environment where individual talents are developed to produce confident, articulate and well-balanced children. Pupils regularly obtain top academic scholarships and awards for art, music, drama and sport. St Christopher's is a Brighton College school and many of its pupils go on to Brighton College.

Entry to the School is at 4+, however, places are occasionally available in other age groups. In the Pre-Prep, pupils are taught mainly by their form teachers. Particular emphasis is placed upon reading, writing and mathematics, but the curriculum is broad and a wide range of subjects is taught by specialist teachers, including French, Latin, Science, Music, Art, ICT, PE and Games.

Pupils move into the Middle School in Year 4, where the curriculum reflects the syllabuses of the Common Entrance and Brighton College Academic Scholarship Examinations. Formal homework is introduced at this stage. In the Upper School (Years 7 and 8), all subjects are taught by specialists, who make full use of the interactive ICT suite, music technology suite, science laboratory, art studio and library. A variety of educational day trips, an annual residential visit to France and sports trips ensure that children receive a broad and stimulating educational experience.

The boys achieve an enviable record of success in football, rugby and cricket and the girls match that success in hockey, netball and rounders. The musical life of St Christopher's is enriched by three choirs and the choice of a wide variety of instrumental and vocal tuition. All pupils are encouraged to perform on stage as part of a wide programme of drama and the development of confidence is a central aim of the school. A wide range of extra-curricular activities is on offer. After-school care is available until 5.30pm each evening.

The Head is always delighted to welcome prospective parents. Please contact the Registrar to arrange a visit.

Charitable status. St Christopher's School, Hove is a member of the Brighton College Family of Schools and is a Registered Charity, number 307061

St Columba's College Preparatory School

King Harry Lane, St Albans, Hertfordshire AL3 4AW

Tel: 01727 862616
email: prepadmin@stcolumbascollege.org
website: www.stcolumbascollege.org
Twitter: @StColumbasHerts
Facebook: @StColumbasCollege
Instagram: @stcolumbascollege
LinkedIn: /school/stcolumbascollege

Chair of Governors: Mr K McGovern, BSc, MRICS

Head of Preparatory School: **Mr R McCann**, BA

Deputy Head of Prep: Mr K Boland, BA

Prep Assistant Pastoral Deputy: Miss K Leahy, BA

Prep Assistant Academic Deputy: Miss C Maton, BA

The Prep School is an academically selective Catholic day school open to students of all faiths and none. The school strives to create a welcoming community in which each pupil is valued as an individual, and endeavours to promote positive relationships based on mutual respect and understanding. There is a rigorous academic curriculum with an extensive range of extra-curricular opportunities. A full curriculum and sports programme is offered at Key Stage 1 and 2. From September 2022, the school will be welcoming girls into Reception, Prep 1, Prep 2, Prep 3 and Prep 4, followed by a phased transition to co-education from ages 4 to 18.

Age Range. 4–11.

Number of Pupils. 200 Students.

Fees per term (2021–2022). Reception–Prep 2, £3,808; Prep 3, £4,466; Prep 4–6, £4,925. Fees include personal accident insurance. Additional charges are made for coaches and consumables.

Entry. Admission to the Lower Prep is by an informal assessment, where children spend an hour with our teaching staff. Admission to the Upper Prep is by age-appropriate Maths, English and Reasoning assessments, and a reference and the latest report will be sought from the child's school.

Examinations. Most pupils progress at 11+ to St Columba's College, on the same site. In their final year, most Preparatory School pupils are offered unconditional places at St Columba's College Senior School, following recommendations by Prep School staff.

Facilities. Academic facilities include: modern form rooms with specialist facilities for Science, IT, ADT, Music, PE, Games, RE and French, and a professionally staffed extensive library. Sports facilities include: Rugby/Football pitches, Cricket nets and square. A swimming pool and athletics track are adjacent to the site.

There are a number of scholarships available to Prep School pupils on entry to St Columba's College Senior School. These include academic and music scholarships. Candidates for the music scholarships should be established performers on one or more instruments, are likely to have reached Grade 4 or above (or the equivalent), and will have good musical skills.

(*See also St Columba's College entry in HMC section.*)

Charitable status. St Columba's College is a Registered Charity, number 1088480. It exists to provide a well-rounded Christian education for pupils from 4–18 years of age.

St Dunstan's College Junior School

Stanstead Road, London SE6 4TY

Tel: 020 8516 7225
email: jsoffice@stdunstans.org.uk
website: www.stdunstans.org.uk

Chairman of Governors: Mr Paul Durgan, BA, FCA

Head of Junior School: Miss Laura Whitwood

Age Range. Co-educational 3–11.

Number of Pupils. Pre-Preparatory (Age 3–7) 140, Preparatory (Age 7–11) 240.

Fees per term (2021–2022). Nursery £4,167, Pre-Preparatory £4,773, Preparatory £5,458–£6,013. Fees include lunch.

We see that our ambitious, co-educational Junior School is the perfect starting point for pupils to make their first marks on their St Dunstan's shield as they begin their College adventure, learning who they are and discovering a true love of lifelong learning from the very earliest stages. Our academic ambition is cultivated by a balance of rigour, challenge, immersive real-life learning experiences and independent exploration.

Our pupils thrive from our forward-thinking and innovative approach to education, where they are well-prepared for the unexpected of tomorrow's world and ready to embrace any challenges that may come their way in the future. Pupils from Nursery to Year 6 are able to make excellent progress and achieve their academic potential in every area of our curriculum, whilst also reaping the benefits of the broad co-curricular programme available to them. The St Dunstan's curriculum is engaging, broad, balanced and unashamedly aspirational for each and every pupil, regardless of their starting point. We see that it equips them with the necessary skills they will need to thrive as proactive citizens within a rapidly changing world.

There is no better time to join St Dunstan's College Junior School. True to our forward-thinking and ambitious approach to education, we were absolutely delighted to move into our new building development in April 2021. Our new Junior School includes state-of-the-art, bright, modern and stimulating working environments, as well as dedicated specialist spaces for art, ICT, music and performance, along with a new library and Woodland Classroom. In addition, whether your child is in Nursery or Year 6, they will have their own dedicated outdoor learning space on each floor. Redesigned Junior School playing fields and two multi-use Games Areas will also ensure pupils have unrestricted access to age-appropriate, exceptional sporting facilities. With the new Junior School building as the first phase of a five-phase project, your child will reap the benefits of our first-class facilities from their very first day in school, through to their final day of Sixth Form.

Our pupils see that through learning, they gain a better sense of who they are, what they can achieve, and what they will be able to accomplish in the future. Learning at St Dunstan's does not just take place within our state-of-the-art classrooms; learning opportunities are embraced and appreciated in any setting, whether it is through our co-curricular 'Forder' Programme (with over 80 activities taking place each week), performing a production in our Great Hall or on the professional stage, by facing a fear on a residential visit, or playing a match to understand the benefits of teamwork and sportsmanship. Our pupils relish the learning for their own personal development and fulfilment.

We take pride in our broad and balanced curriculum which is taught by our highly-skilled teachers and provides children with the skills, knowledge and understanding they need to develop into curious, creative and courageous individuals. No day is ever the same at St Dunstan's and it is through our rich, exciting and vast selection of activities that we can focus on a holistic approach to education, in order that our pupils can thrive as well-rounded individuals, who feel happy and safe in school. They enjoy forming positive and trusting relationships with both their Form Teacher and specialist teachers in art, design technology, drama, music, ICT, swimming, PE, Modern Foreign Languages (Spanish in Prep-Prep and Spanish and French in Prep) and Stuart lessons (PSHE). As such, our pupils make rapid progress in every subject, and it is through exposure to a number of subject areas and enrichment opportunities that our pupils thrive. Our offering enables pupils to discover what sparks their interest, relishing new skills, but within a supportive environment, created by strong teacher/pupil relationships.

Boys and Girls are admitted at all ages from 3+ to 10+ but principally at 3+ and 4+ (Nursery and Reception) and at 7+ (Year 3). We also welcome applications for occasional place entry within the other Junior School year groups.

Charitable status. St Dunstan's Educational Foundation is a Registered Charity, number 312747. It exists to provide education for boys and girls.

St Edmund's Prep School

Old Hall Green, Ware, Hertfordshire SG11 1DS

Tel: 01920 824239
email: prep@stedmundscollege.org
website: www.stedmundscollege.org
Twitter: @stedmundsware
Facebook: @stedmundscollegeandprep
Instagram: @stedmundscollegeandprep

Chairman of Governors: Mr Paul Raynes, MA Cantab

Head: **Mr S Cartwright**, BSc Hons Surrey

Deputy Head: Dr F J McLauchlan, MA, PhD Cantab

Assistant Head: Mr G Duddy, BEd Wales

Head of EYFS: Mrs V Penfold, BA London Metropolitan

Age Range. 3–11 Co-educational.

Number of Pupils. 195.

Fees per term (2021–2022). Day (inc. Lunch): £1,680–£4,918.

St Edmund's Prep, founded in 1874, is a co-educational, independent Catholic Nursery, Pre-Prep and Prep school, situated in beautiful surroundings of wood and parkland in Old Hall Green, easily accessible from the main thoroughfares of Hertfordshire. The school embraces family values to lay the foundation for a happy and successful life. Education is seen as a joint venture involving staff, parents and children.

When you arrive at the Prep you will experience a welcome from us all that invites you and your child to be part of a very special community.

Guided by the principles of our Catholic faith and acknowledging Christ as our leader and teacher, we strive for excellence and creativity in forward-thinking education. We commit ourselves to the preparation of our children by instilling in them a sense of responsibility and strive to ensure that they leave St Edmund's Prep with a solid foundation on which to build their future in the College and beyond.

Small class sizes allow focused attention to ensure that your child becomes a confident learner both inside and outside the classroom. Our facilities shared with the College and our committed teachers ensure our pupils have the experiences they need to develop fully in all aspects of their lives. With a heritage and ethos deeply rooted in the Catholic tradition, we welcome families from all faiths who will appreciate the all-round education that we offer.

The school has a broad, balanced curriculum and it seeks to cater for the individual child at the different stages of their development. The curriculum offered is intended to improve the learners' knowledge, introduce them to a wide range of educational experiences and develop skills needed to deal critically and creatively with the world.

For students who join in or before Year 4, there is the possibility to not sit the entrance examination for the College at 11+, thus offering straight-through entry.

The Prep is a proud holder of the Gold sports mark for Sport and the England Arts Council Silver award.

The Prep is committed to healthy living and we deliver this through daily home-cooked, well-balanced meals; fresh fruit is provided at break times and sport and activity for all is a priority.

Co-curricular is the norm in the Prep with a stimulating, fun range of activities run every day from chess club to junior cadets; from cookery in dedicated facilities to sport.

A breakfast and tea-time club is offered and a school bus service runs for children over 7 in Year 3.

We are fortunate to share facilities with St Edmund's College and as a result, the Prep children have an opportunity to use the floodlit AstroTurf, all year round use of the indoor swimming pool, a large gymnasium as well as acres of grounds which the children, with supervision, can explore.

We are committed to being leaders in education in these changing times. We invite you to join us as a member of St Edmund's Prep.

Charitable status. St Edmund's College is a Registered Charity, number 311073.

St Edmund's School

Portsmouth Road, Hindhead, Surrey GU26 6BH

Tel: 01428 609875
email: admissions@saintedmunds.co.uk
website: www.saintedmunds.co.uk
Twitter: @excellentsteds
Facebook: @sainteds

Chairman of Governors: Mrs J Alliss

Headmaster: **A J Walliker**, MA Cantab, MBA, PGCE

Age Range. 2–16 Co-educational.

Number of Pupils. Senior, Prep and Lower Prep: 499 day pupils.

Fees per term (2021–2022). Lower School £3,495–£5,025; Prep and Senior £6,225; Nursery from £855 (three afternoons) to £3,400 (full week) not including EYFS funded hours.

The fees are inclusive of all ordinary extras including supervised prep, orchestra/choirs, games, swimming, lectures, optional Saturday activities etc, as well as a free hour of after-school care activities for children in the Lower Prep.

Scholarships and means-tested bursaries are available.

We are a fully co-educational school from age 2 through to 16. Through a rich curriculum, small teaching groups and exemplary pastoral care, St Edmund's seeks to provide an excellent all round education by encouraging its pupils to achieve their very best in all that they do. "I like St Ed's, I can be myself." These words, spoken by one of our pupils, capture much of what we strive to do at St Edmund's: to instil in every child a sense of self-esteem and belonging by building on their own talents, opening their eyes to new ones and giving them focused and personal support whenever it is needed. Academically, it is an approach that continues to pay dividends, with our pupils going on to a wide range of senior schools at both 11+ and 13+ and 16+ including St Edmund's Senior.

Yet of equal importance are the discoveries, excitements and good old-fashioned fun that St Edmund's Lower Prep, Prep and Senior create inside our 40 beautiful acres with facilities including professional MTB trails, an immaculate 9-hole golf course, indoor swimming pool, cross-country running course, games fields, rifle range, a floodlit all-weather sports pitch and Dance and Drama Studio. A brand new multi-use sports hall opened in January 2021. The list of co-curricular activities is endless at St Ed's, from mountain biking to cookery, scuba-diving to den building and from street dance to giant chess, including our unique optional Saturday Activity programme that allows us greater depth in the number of activities on offer to our pupils.

St Edmund's Senior School offers a rare and unique educational experience for those who join us. In contrast to the many larger institutions available, our dedication to small teaching groups and our strong sense of community creates an environment where pupils' confidence can be invigorated. Through high-quality teaching and resources, our aim is to provide our pupils with an inspiring and notable experience that naturally encourages an appreciation for lifelong independent learning. Our broad curriculum across Forms 7 to 11 presents a firm foundation upon which to make future educational choices, and our distinctive tutorial system enables our pupils a platform to discuss progress and achievements as well as any pastoral issues that require guidance and consideration. In 2020, our GCSE results posted a 100% pass rate (grades 4–9), with 72% of passes at grades 7–9 (old A*/A).

During our latest Independent Schools Inspection in June 2021, the report noted, "The quality of St Edmund's pupils' achievements and learning is 'Excellent'. Pupils' have positive attitudes to learning and they are well motivated. They show exemplary behaviour and their care for each other is special".

Charitable status. St Edmund's School Trust Limited is a Registered Charity, number 278301. Its aim is the education of children.

St Faith's School

Trumpington Road, Cambridge, Cambridgeshire CB2 8AG

Tel:	01223 352073
email:	info@stfaiths.co.uk
website:	www.stfaiths.co.uk
Twitter:	@St_Faiths
Facebook:	@StFaithsSchool
LinkedIn:	/st-faith's-school-cambridge

Chair of Governors: Mrs A Brunner

Headmaster: **Dr C Hyde-Dunn**, MA, PGCE, MA Ed, NPQH, PhD

Deputy Head: Mr J P Davenport

Age Range. 4–13.

Number of Pupils. 570

Fees per term (2021–2022). £4,560 (Pre-Prep), £5,600 (Years 3 and 4) £5,745 (Years 5 to 8).

Named *Prep School of the Year* in 2019 by The Times Educational Supplement, St Faith's, founded in 1884, is a co-educational day school for children aged 4–13 set in 9 acres of grounds on the south side of Cambridge, approximately one mile from the city centre. Our pupils also have access to a further 20 acres of sports fields just 2 minutes' walk away.

At St Faith's each child is taught, developed and nurtured, to equip them well for life, whatever path they choose to take. Passionate teachers share their knowledge, explore new ideas, challenge the status quo and instil a lifelong passion for learning. Teaching styles are tailored to meet each individual child's needs. Lessons are accessible, engaging and challenging for all pupils. Top-down excellence in all lessons ensures we continually stretch our pupils to achieve more than they thought possible. Our academic curriculum is ground-breaking in its innovative content and has been commended by institutions including Cambridge University, and the Times Educational Supplement awarded us 'Strategic Education Initiative of the Year' (2018) for the introduction of Engineering to the curriculum.

Exemplary, innovative and forward-facing academic subjects are interspersed each day with sporting endeavours, musical experiences, artistic creations and dramatic performances. Assemblies, tutor time and plenty of playtime ensure children have a chance to express themselves away from the classroom. Owing to small class sizes, exceptional teachers and the above average ability of our children all subjects follow an accelerated curriculum and the vast majority of pupils work at a higher level commensurate with their age.

Our green and spacious site, located in the heart of Cambridge, together with extensive playing fields, provide some of the best facilities of any prep school. Every classroom is equipped with modern teaching technology. The shelves in our library brim with over 12,000 volumes with relevance to our youngest and most mature readers. Engineering suites provide access to tools and equipment beyond many inventors' wildest dreams. Fully-equipped science laboratories and computer suites are used by all year groups. Our new £2m STEM Hub includes state of the art science laboratories, flexible large indoor spaces for interdisciplinary projects, a rooftop greenhouse and a night sky viewing platform.

Our broad sporting education is not simply a focus for sporting glory and trophy collection, though we are currently National Champions in Hockey, Athletics, Gymnastics and Trampolining. We believe sport is a conduit for developing mental as well as physical fitness. The losing as well as winning of sporting fixtures builds mental resilience and is an emotive demonstration of getting out of life what you put in. Of course team work is omnipresent in many sporting events and as such our pupils learn to revel in team as well as individual accolades, better preparing them for their futures. Drama and the performing arts are tools not only for teaching children a lifelong love of the arts but for promoting self-belief and confidence.

St Faith's pupils stand out as confident, articulate, grounded and courteous, attributes which will stand them in good stead for their futures.

St Faith's is part of The Leys and St Faith's Foundation and although each year approximately half of the children move on to The Leys at the end of Year 8, others prepare for entry to a variety of schools, mainly independent; on average 30 scholarships are awarded each year.

Charitable status. The Leys and St Faith's Schools Foundation is a Registered Charity, number 1144035. The aim of the charity is the provision of first-class education.

St Francis School

Marlborough Road, Pewsey, Wiltshire SN9 5NT

Tel: 01672 563228
email: admissions@stfpewsey.co.uk
            schooloffice@stfpewsey.co.uk
website: www.st-francis.wilts.sch.uk
Twitter: @stfrancispewsey
Facebook: @StFrancisSchoolPewsey

Chair of Governors: P Humphries-Cuff

Headmaster: **Mr David Lee**, BA, MA. PGCSE, QTS

Age Range. 0–13.
Number of Boys and Girls. 208: 104 Boys, 104 Girls.
Fees per term (2021–2022). Reception–Year 8: £2,535–£4,950 including lunch. Nursery Fees available on application.

St Francis is a co-educational day school for children age 0 to 13. Established in 1941, the School is situated alongside the Kennet and Avon Canal in the beautiful Vale of Pewsey, five miles south of Marlborough. Pupils travel from a wide area of Wiltshire; daily minibus services operate from Marlborough and Devizes and surrounding villages. Wrap-around care is available for all pupils, from 7.45am until 6.00pm.

Providing every child with the opportunity to fulfil their full potential is a feature of the School, and staff are positive and encouraging in their teaching. If a child needs additional support with their learning this is provided by the highly regarded Learning Support Department. The modern

Burden Block and George Cannon centre provides a Design Technology room, Art room, Science Lab, Drama loft and specialist subject teaching rooms, as well as form rooms.

The curriculum is diverse, which enables the older pupils to have, for example, STEAM, Art, Drama and Music in their timetable, alongside their lessons of English, Maths and Science. French is also a key part of the curriculum and is taught from the age of three. Pupils can take individual music lessons with specialist peripatetic music teachers, who offer a wide range of instruments. Many pupils enter local music, public speaking and choral competitions.

The pupils are offered plenty of opportunity to develop and excel in their sport. All the major sports are taught both outdoors on the playing fields and also inside the Hemery Sports Hall which is also used for drama performances. Swimming lessons are held weekly for pupils in Reception – Year 2 and there is a Swimming Squad for Year 3 and above. Regular matches take place against other schools and a policy of 'sport for all' allows all pupils to be involved.

Little Saints Nursery caters for children from 0 to 4 years of age for 51 weeks a year (both term time and full-time contracts are available). Little Saints Nursery makes use of all the facilities including the school's gardens, playground and woods.

The beautiful 17-acre school grounds include a Forest School and a wooden adventure playground, the St Francis Fortress, which was built in 2019, providing an exciting area for pupils to let off steam after their lessons.

Results are excellent. The pupils are mainly entered for the local senior schools, St Mary's Calne, Godolphin, Dauntsey's, Marlborough College, Stonar and Warminster, but scholarships and common entrance are also taken for boarding schools further afield. Awards are regularly achieved to all of the aforementioned.

Please telephone 01672 563228 or email admissions@stfpewsey.co.uk if you would like more information or to arrange a tour of the school with the Headmaster. Virtual Tours of the school and nursery are available on our website. Open Mornings are usually held during the Autumn and Spring terms.

Charitable status. St Francis is a Registered Charity, number 298522. It exists solely to provide education for boys and girls.

St Gabriel's
Junior School

Sandleford Priory, Newbury, Berkshire RG20 9BD

Tel: 01635 555680
email: info@stgabriels.co.uk
website: www.stgabriels.co.uk
Twitter: @StGabrielsNews
Facebook: @stgabrielsnewbury
Instagram: @stgabrielsnews
LinkedIn: /company/st-gabriel's-newbury

Chairman of Governors: Mr N Garland, BSc Hons

Principal: Mr R Smith, MEd, MA, PGCE

Head of Junior School: **Mr P Dove**, BA Hons, PGCE

Age Range. 6 months to 11 years Co-educational.

Number of Pupils. 242.

Fees per term (2021–2022). £3,834–£5,152.

Sandleford Nursery lies at the heart of St Gabriel's and provides high-quality nursery care and Early Years education for children aged 6 months to 4 years. Sandleford Nursery offers flexible full or part-time care with an extended day provision across 50 weeks a year. At the age of four, the majority of Sandleford Nursery children move through into the Reception class of the Junior School.

The Junior School is situated adjacent to the Senior School in 54 acres of parkland on the southern outskirts of Newbury.

Subjects taught include English, Mathematics, Science, Art, Computing, Dance, Drama, Humanities (History, Geography), French, Music, Outdoor Education, PE, Religious Studies, Technology (Food Technology, Design Technology) and Thinking Skills and PSHE.

The excellent range of facilities includes a multi-discipline sports hall, theatre, dance studio, junior science laboratory, library, orienteering courses and woodland trails. There are 2 computing classrooms and newly-refurbished, state-of-the-art science laboratories.

Sport plays an important and integral role in the life of the school and there is a comprehensive fixtures list from Year 3 to Year 6. In 2018 St Gabriel's Junior School achieved the *School Games Gold Award* for their commitment to sport. The wide range of sports includes: Athletics, Basketball, Cricket, Cross-Country, Dance, Football, Gymnastics, Hockey, Netball, Rugby, Rounders and Tennis, which are included in the curriculum for all pupils. Swimming takes place during the Summer Term in the outdoor heated swimming pool.

Music holds an equally high profile. As well as curriculum Music lessons, there is a wide range of co-curricular music-making for all pupils with an interest in the subject. Many pupils learn instruments in school and they are given numerous opportunities to perform at concerts, ranging from informal lunchtime events to major end of term extravaganzas.

In addition, pupils are offered a wide range of co-curricular activities, including Art Club, Ballet, Chess Club, Choir, Climbing Club, Creative Writing Club, Drama, Football, Film Making Club, Gymnastics, Judo, Music Theory, Recorder, Science Club, Trampolining Club and Training Orchestra. Pupils in Years 3–6 are also elected onto a School Council.

Pupils in Year 3 and above are provided with a managed school iPad as a tool to support teaching and learning in school and at home.

In 2021, the Junior School was awarded the Gold level from The Woodland Trust *Green Tree School Award*, demonstrating a commitment to using and improving the school grounds to develop pupils' environmental awareness.

Prospective pupils entering Year 1 and 2 are assessed by the class teacher and subject staff; prospective pupils entering Year 3 to 6 are assessed by the Individual Needs Department. Pupils who apply for entry to Year 6 will also be assessed on their ability to pass the 11+ entrance examinations to the Senior School.

From September 2022, the Senior School will also accept boys into Year 7 and by 2026 the school will be co-educational throughout. *(For further information about the Senior School, see St Gabriel's entry in GSA section.)*

Charitable status. The St Gabriel Schools Foundation is a Registered Charity, number 1062748. It exists to provide education for children from age 6 months to 11 years.

St George's Junior School, Weybridge

Thames Street, Weybridge, Surrey KT13 8NL

Tel: 01932 839400
email: contact@stgeorgesweybridge.com
website: www.stgeorgesweybridge.com
Twitter: @sgweybridge
Facebook: @stgeorgescollegeuk

Chair of Board of Governors: Mr D Nowlan

Headmaster: **Mr A J W Hudson**, MA Cantab, PGCE, NPQH

Age Range. 3–11.

Number of Pupils. 588

Fees per term (2021–2022). Nursery £2,040 (mornings only), £3,340 (full days); Reception–Year 2 £3,850; Years 3–6 £5,285. Lunches (compulsory): £280.

St George's Junior School is a fully co-ed Roman Catholic Day School, with a Senior School on a separate site nearby. The Junior School was established in 1950 by a Religious Order of Priests and Brothers known as "The Josephites" as a development of the educational provision of St George's College which celebrated its 150th Anniversary in 2019.

In September 2000, the Junior School moved from its previous co-located site a mile down the road, to its present 50-acre site on the outskirts of Weybridge close to the River Thames. Huge development has taken place since then, most notably, a new Kitchen and Dining Room, and a state-of-the-art Lower Years building for children aged 3–7 – The Ark – which was opened and blessed by Cardinal Cormac Murphy-O'Connor in 2016, at the same time as a new Performing Arts Centre. Along with the recent development of a Forest School and the Eco Garden, as well as new playing fields for cricket, rugby and rounders, the Master Plan has given the Junior School first-rate facilities which provide the children with a wonderful start to their education. The School operates a very extensive bus service and an option for parents using cars to drop off their children at either the Junior School using the 'Kiss and Drop' system, or the College, using the minibus shuttle service.

The Junior School has a genuinely happy atmosphere in which every pupil is respected and treated as an individual. The Headmaster considers the staff, pupils and parents to be constituent parts of an extended family – 'The Georgian Family'. The School has always placed great emphasis on the importance of maintaining excellent channels of communication between members of staff, parents and pupils.

Pupils who are 'rising three' are admitted into the Nursery, after which children can be admitted to any year group, subject to available spaces. The size of classes ensures that the School is a learning community by creating the correct balance between pupil interaction and pupil-teacher contact. The pupils in the top two years of the School are taught by subject specialists. French is offered to all pupils from Year 1. In November 2019, the ISI Educational Quality Inspection found the School to be 'Excellent' in all areas, following on from the Diocesan Inspection Report in May 2018 which noted that 'the school's pastoral care is a particular strength' and the 'teachers manifest an enthusiasm for sharing their love and knowledge of subject, and communicate high expectations'.

All pupils are assessed on entry and when they leave at the end of Year 6, the vast majority transfer to St George's College. In 2021, 7 Academic, 5 Sports, 4 Music and 1 Art Scholarship along with 1 Art Exhibition were awarded. While the pursuit of academic excellence is highly valued, the Mission Statement of the School stresses the importance of pupils being the very best versions of themselves. The School requires its pupils to have high moral values especially those of its school motto: "Honesty and Compassion".

The Junior School has four Houses which compete against each other across a wide range of activities inside and outside the classroom including Music, Public Speaking and Sport.

Extracurricular and other enrichment activities are, likewise, considered to play an important role in the educational development of children. The extensive range of activities include dance (ballet, modern and tap), gymnastics, and clubs based on the academic subjects taught in the School. Mandarin is offered to Upper Years pupils if they so wish, and pupils are taken to places of educational interest regularly, including theatre, music and art trips, and there is an annual Book Week during which pupils meet and listen to visiting authors and storytellers. The School recently hosted its own Literature Festival, inviting over 500 children from local schools to attend.

Considerable emphasis is placed on the Creative and Performing Arts. The school stages six major Drama Productions a year. All children in Year 2 learn the ukulele and recorder as part of the Music Curriculum. There is an orchestra, choirs and various ensembles. Individual music lessons are very popular, with over 50% of the children in Years 3 to 6 learning at least one additional instrument. Since September 2016 an Instrumental Tuition Scheme has been implemented which subsidises free peripatetic lessons for all children in Years 3 or 4, in order to encourage them to take up strings, woodwind or brass instruments, which has been a great success. Concerts take place at least once a term, and music lessons are supported by the use of the latest computer-based technology. Pupils have achieved considerable success at Public Speaking Competitions and achieve a very high level of attainment in their external Spoken English, LAMDA and instrumental music exams.

Apart from its own on-site sports facilities, comprising an artificial sports pitch, netball and tennis courts, a sprung floor gymnasium and a swimming pool, the School has use of outstanding sports facilities at the College including its brand new Activity Centre, a four-court indoor tennis centre, and a tartan athletics track. The Junior School has a track record of great sporting success with Hockey & Rugby teams regularly reaching the final stages of IAPS National Finals and more recently excelling at Boys' and Girls'

Gymnastics. In the midst of this tangible success, the Junior School prides itself on ensuring that all pupils from Year 3 upwards have the opportunity to represent the school at least once each term in one of the mainstream sports, i.e. Rugby, Hockey and Cricket for boys and Netball, Hockey, Rounders & Cricket for girls.

School lunches, which are compulsory for children in Upper Nursery staying on for afternoon activities and for all from Reception Year onwards, are prepared on site and eaten in the dining room which can seat 320 people. Since November 2020, the School has engaged the services of an external provider – 'The Gap Club' – for pre- & after-school care for all children who so wish from 7.30am – 6.30pm. Children in Years 1 & 2 can sign up for 2 after school clubs per week until 4.30pm, while those in Years 3–6 can sign up for clubs which continue until 5.00pm each day.

For the last few years, the School has usually had more applications for places than it can accommodate in all year groups. When vacancies do occur, pupils are admitted as long as they meet the School's entry criteria and successfully complete an assessment day at the School, as well as receiving a satisfactory report from their current school where this is appropriate. Priority is afforded to siblings and children from Roman Catholic families.

Charitable status. St George's Weybridge is a registered Charity, number 1017853. The aims and objectives of the charity are the Christian education of young people.

St George's School Windsor Castle

Windsor, Berks SL4 1QF

Tel: 01753 865553
email: enqs@stgwindsor.org
website: www.stgwindsor.org

Patron: Her Majesty The Queen

Chair of the Governors: Mr Martin Stanford

Head: Mr William Goldsmith, BA Hons Durham, MSC Oxford, FRSA, FCCT

Deputy Head, Head of Prep School: Mr Kevin Wills, BSc Hons, PGCE

Deputy Head, Head of Pre-Prep: Mrs Emma Adriano, BA Hons, PGCE, PG Dip

Age Range. 3–13 Co-educational.

Number of Pupils. 333 (24 weekly boarders) with over 50% opting to flexi-board

Fees per term (2021–2022).

Michaelmas 2021: Weekly Boarders £7,463, Prep School £5,364–£6,011, Choristers (Boarding) £3,865, Pre-Prep £3,866–£5,364, Kindergarten £1,894–£3,621.

Lent and Trinity 2022: Weekly Boarders £7,724, Prep School £5,552–£6,221, Choristers (Boarding) £4,000, Pre-Prep £4,001–£5,552, Kindergarten £2,323–£3,748

St George's School was established as part of the foundation of the Order of the Garter in 1348 when provision was made for the education of the first choristers. In 1893 the School moved into the Georgian building of the former College of the Naval Knights of Windsor situated between the mound of the Castle and the Home Park. Expansion followed with the admission of supernumerary (non-chorister) pupils. Extensions were made to the buildings in 1988 and 1996, the latter of which allowed for the opening of a Pre-Preparatory Department and Nursery. In 1997 girls were admitted to the School for the first time, entering both the Pre-Prep and the main school, and five years later the school became fully co-educational. A new building accommodating Music rooms, Modern Languages and Year 4 and 5 classrooms, was opened in Spring 2006 by HRH Princess Alexandra. The school is a central part of the Foundation of the College of St George, within Windsor Castle. The current structure of the school is divided into the Pre-Prep (EYFS to Year 3) and the Prep School (Year 4 to Year 8)

St George's School has a long and proud tradition of academic and musical excellence alongside impressive art, drama and sport. Many pupils gain academic, all-rounder and music awards to some of the country's leading independent schools; in recent years these have included Eton, Radley College, King's Canterbury, Bryanston, Rugby, Hampton, Sir William Perkins's and Wellington. The curriculum is stimulating, broad and varied. In addition to the teaching of core subjects, French is introduced to Kindergarten children with the addition of Latin and Spanish in Year 6. Specialist teaching in PE and Music is provided from the Nursery upwards and in Art, DT and Drama from Year 3.

Facilities for games are excellent with pitches and playing fields on the Home Park Private, an indoor swimming pool, a recently resurfaced tennis and netball court and a gymnasium. Several areas of the school buildings have recently undergone refurbishment, including the creation of a Design Technology workshop and new Science laboratories opened by HRH The Earl of Wessex. In 2013, a new Food Technology teaching room was opened and in 2015 there was a significant updating of the ICT suite. Enhanced Music facilities now include an Apple networked Music teaching room and recording studio.

The School seeks to pursue the highest standards and aims to develop happy, self-confident children who are encouraged to achieve their potential whilst at St George's. There is a strong family ethos within the school community where each child's talents and skills are identified and nurtured. Pastoral care is excellent and each class teacher and form tutor knows the children in their care extremely well. There are frequent parents evenings for all pupils in the school, and parents are regularly invited to support their children in plays, concerts and sports fixtures and to attend school services in St George's Chapel, Windsor Castle. Indeed, the ISI Integrated Inspection report in February 2016 rated the school as being 'Excellent' and the school was found fully compliant by ISI in all areas in 2019.

An exciting and innovative strategic plan launched in 2019, focuses on transformational learning; emotional wellbeing; global opportunities and first class creative arts. The Pre-Senior Baccalaureate, an inspiring and hugely popular philosophy of learning is being embedded in Key Stage 3, with a full Mindfulness programme from Kindergarten to Year 8. In 2021, the school adopted the progressive, International Baccalaureate PYP curriculum.

Communications are excellent: two railway stations, the M25, M3, M4 and M40 are all close by and Heathrow is just fifteen minutes away.

Charitable status. St George's School, Windsor Castle is a Registered Charity, number 1100392. Its purpose is the education, either as boarding or day pupils, of children of pre-preparatory and preparatory school age and of the choristers who maintain the worship in the Queen's Free Chapel of Our Lady, St George and St Edward the Confessor in Windsor Castle.

St Helen's College

Parkway, Hillingdon, Middlesex UB10 9JX

Tel: 01895 234371
email: info@sthelenscollege.com
website: www.sthelenscollege.com

Principals:

Mr D A Crehan, ARCS, BA, BSc, MSc, CPhys, MEd

Mrs G R Crehan, BA, MA, PGCE

Head Teacher: **Mrs S Drummond**, BEd Hons, MLDP, FCCT

Age Range. 2–11 co-educational.
Number of Pupils. 380 Day Pupils.
Fees per term (2021–2022). £3,400–£4,200.

St Helen's College has been described by inspectors as a 'Haven of Harmony' and was deemed 'outstanding/ excellent' in all 12 areas in its most recent educational quality inspection. It is a happy, family-run school, based on three enduring values: Love, Harmony and Growth.

The aims of St Helen's College are to develop as fully as possible each child's academic potential, to provide a wide, balanced, stimulating and challenging curriculum, and to foster true values and good character based on moral and spiritual principles. The children enjoy a purposeful and happy 'family' atmosphere and are taught by committed, professional, specialist teachers.

Children are prepared for independent senior schools and local grammar schools, and records of success are very good indeed. In addition to the academic subjects, sport, music and drama play an important part in the lives of the children.

An extraordinarily wide range of extra-curricular activities is offered, and pupils enjoy outings, day and residential, to many places of interest. There is a breakfast club, after-school club and summer school, and a holiday club which runs throughout the year.

Individual tours for prospective parents are run during term time and on regular Open Mornings. Please telephone 01895 234371 or contact susmith@sthelenscollege.com to make an appointment.

St Hilary's Preparatory School & Nursery

Holloway Hill, Godalming, Surrey GU7 1RZ

Tel: 01483 416551
email: registrar@sthilarysschool.com
website: www.sthilarysschool.com
Twitter: @StHilarysSchool
Facebook: @St-Hilarys-School-Trust
Instagram: @sthilarysschool

Chair of Governors: Mr Richard Thompson, BSc Hons, MBA

Headmistress: **Mrs J Whittingham**, BEd Cert, Prof Prac SpLD

Age Range. Boys and Girls 2–11.

Number of Pupils. 203 Day Pupils.

Fees per term (2021–2022). Including lunch: Reception £3,748; Year 1 £4,028; Year 2 £4,726; Year 3 £4,964, Years 4 to 6 £5,514. Kindergarten £32.50 and Nursery £34.00 per am/pm session with lunch extra.

St Hilary's is an independent preparatory day school which provides a stimulating, safe environment in which boys and girls can develop, be happy and flourish.

Situated in the heart of Godalming, St Hilary's prides itself in providing an outstanding all-round education, equipping pupils not only with strong academic standards but also the essential qualities and skills required beyond their time at our school. Ultimately we strive to ensure that all our pupils develop a real thirst for learning.

The Independent Schools Inspectorate judged our main school to be 'Excellent' in all areas in December 2016 and our Early Years Foundation Stage achieved 'Outstanding' at its last inspection. St Hilary's was also judged as 'Independent Prep School of the Year 2020', by the *Independent School Parent* magazine.

Every child enjoys the benefits of well-qualified, enthusiastic staff and a broad curriculum combined with splendid facilities. Amenities include well-equipped classrooms, music wing, spacious hall for the performing arts, science room, library, modern ICT suite, design & technology, art studios, all-weather pitch, the Hiorns Centre for drama and ballet and a newly opened Lego Innovation Studio. Small class sizes allow children to achieve their best in a dynamic and vibrant environment.

Outside the classroom, pupils can enjoy the woodland through Forest School and play opportunities with the very popular Trim Trail and exciting adventure play area. Pupils share a love of growing things in our gardens and appreciate the safe, beautiful surroundings.

Physical Education features highly at St Hilary's. The department gives all pupils equality of opportunity to participate in a broad range of activities. All pupils experience a variety of competitive and challenging situations. Our House system encourages healthy competition with matches, a swimming gala and sports days.

Children are given the opportunity to participate in a wide, varied number of extra-curricular activities, such as, gardening, football skills, drama, LEGO, science, art, pottery, textiles, debating, First Aid, French, chess, gym, cross country, judo, cricket, dance, tap, choirs, woodwind, string ensemble, percussion, orchestra, recorder groups and violin.

Speech & Drama is a highly popular option for many with pupils preparing for LAMDA (London Academy of Music and Dramatic Art) examinations. The school takes advantage of its ideal location and access to London for visits to galleries, museums and theatres.

Parents are guided in next school options and have the opportunity to make informed choices at a time when a child's true academic potential can be accurately predicted and talents in other areas identified. We have an excellent reputation in securing first-choice schools for our pupils when they leave. Our leavers successfully move on to prestigious schools; every year many obtain academic, art, music, sport and drama scholarships.

Please do come and visit us; we will be delighted to welcome you and discuss your child's education. We hold a number of Open Days throughout the year when you can see the school in action; please visit our website for more details.

Charitable status. St Hilary's School Trust Limited is a Registered Charity, number 312056. It exists to provide education for children.

St Hilda's School

High Street, Bushey, Hertfordshire WD23 3DA

Tel: 020 8950 1751
email: secretary@sthildasbushey.co.uk
            registrar@sthildasbushey.co.uk
website: www.sthildasbushey.com
Twitter: @StHildasBushey
Facebook: @sthildasbushey
Instagram: @sthildasprep

Chairman of Governors: Mrs Sarah Altman

Headmistress: **Miss S J Styles**, BA, MA

Age Range. Girls 2–11, Boys 2–4.

Number of Pupils. 183 Day Girls. Co-ed Nursery.

Fees per term (2021–2022). Prep School: £4,234–£4,511. Nursery fees upon application according to sessions chosen.

St Hilda's is an Independent Day School for girls aged 4–11, with a full-time nursery for boys and girls aged 2–4. It was founded in 1918 and has occupied its present 5-acre site since 1928. The Victorian house at the centre of the school has been continually improved, adapted and extended to provide an excellent educational environment. This includes a nature garden area, tennis courts, an indoor heated swimming pool, a large all-purpose hall, science laboratory, technology laboratory and computer suite.

We teach a wide range of subjects to a high academic standard in a secure and happy environment in which every pupil can develop their academic and personal potential. We offer a broad and challenging curriculum in which art, drama and music play an important role. There is also a wide range of extra-curricular activities, including ballet, seasonal sports activities, ICT, languages and drama. Pre-school and after-school care is offered from 07.30 until 18.30 Monday to Friday during term time.

Charitable status. St Hilda's School is a Registered Charity, number 298140. It exists to provide education for girls.

St Hugh's

Carswell Manor
Carswell, Faringdon, Oxfordshire SN7 8PT

Tel: 01367 870700
email: office@st-hughs.co.uk
         registrar@st-hughs.co.uk
website: www.st-hughs.co.uk

Chairman of Governors: P G Daffern

Headmaster: **Mr James C Thompson**, BA QTS St Mary's Twickenham

Age Range. 3–13.
Number of Pupils. 355: 199 Boys (70 Boarders), 156 Girls (61 Boarders).
Fees per term (2021–2022). Upper School: Weekly Boarders £8,640, Day £7,225; Middle School: Weekly Boarders £8,060, Day £6,645; Pre-Prep £4,185–£4,570. (All fees inclusive, with very few compulsory extras).

The School's main building is a fine Jacobean house with extensive grounds. Boys and girls are prepared for Pre-Test, Common Entrance and Scholarship examinations to senior independent schools. The school is organised into four departments: Nursery (3–4), Pre-Prep (4–6), Middle School (7–8) and Upper School (9–13). Careful liaison ensures a strong thread of continuity throughout the school. The main entry points are at 3, 4, 7 and 9.

The School is not academically selective and both welcomes and accepts children from all backgrounds and a wide range of academic abilities. We aim to foster confidence and a love of learning across this range: an impressive pre-test, scholarship and CE record and the provision of integral specialist support both bear testimony to our inclusive approach. The arts and sport feature strongly and pupils are encouraged to develop their talents and interests as broadly as possible.

St Hugh's is described by the Good Schools Guide as a school which "personifies what is best in prep school education".

Charitable status. St Hugh's is a Registered Charity, number 309640. It exists to provide a centre of excellence for the education of children.

St Hugh's

Cromwell Avenue, Woodhall Spa LN10 6TQ

Tel: 01526 352169
email: office@st-hughs.lincs.sch.uk
website: www.st-hughs.lincs.sch.uk
Twitter: @sthughslincs
Facebook: @sthughslincs
Instagram: @sthughswoodhall

Chairman of Governors: R Bussell

Headmaster: **Mr Jeremy Wyld**, BA Hons, PGCE

Age Range. 2–13.
Number of Pupils. 172. 54 boys, 49 girls. Pre-Prep: 24 boys, 22 girls. Nursery: 23 children.
Fees per term (2021–2022). Boarding £6,695; Day £4,798–£5,330; Pre-Prep £3,170. The fees are fully inclusive.

St Hugh's School was founded by the Forbes family in 1925 and today is fully co-educational, offering both day and boarding places. The Headmaster is assisted by 21 qualified and experienced teachers and is a member of IAPS (The Independent Association of Prep Schools) as well as the Boarding Schools' Association.

Pupils are prepared for the Common Entrance and Scholarship examinations. The school's academic record is excellent, with regular awards being gained to major Independent Schools, as well as 11+ and 13+ places at Lincolnshire Grammar Schools. Children with special learning needs are treated sympathetically within the mainstream, with support from specialist staff. The aim of the school is to give every child a good all-round education and to discover and develop his or her own particular talents.

The major school games for boys are rugby, hockey and cricket, and for girls netball, hockey and rounders. Pupils can also enjoy cross-country, tennis, athletics and swimming. All children have PE each week with time set aside for instruction in gymnastics and swimming.

The school lays heavy emphasis on extra-curricular activities including music, art, drama, forest school and sport. There is also a strong and continuing Christian tradition at St Hugh's.

The school has excellent facilities including a modern sports hall, an assembly hall with stage and lighting, a heated indoor swimming pool, extensive playing fields including an all-weather pitch, a fine library, dedicated classrooms and Music, Design and ICT studios.

Weekly and flexi boarders are accommodated in a well-appointed House under the close supervision of a Houseparent and dormitories and common rooms are bright and cheerful. Contact with parents and guardians is well maintained. Minibus transport for day pupils is provided from Boston, Louth, Skegness, Lincoln, Market Rasen and Sleaford.

The Pre-Preparatory department caters for approximately 40 children aged from 4 to 7 and is located in its own building with separate play area and staff.

The Nursery for children aged between 2 and 4 is attached to the Pre-Prep and accommodates approximately 45 children.

Charitable status. St Hugh's School (Woodhall Spa) Limited is a Registered Charity, number 527611. It exists to provide a high standard of education and care to pupils from the age of 2 to 13.

St James Prep School

Earsby Street, Kensington, London W14 8SH

Tel:　　　020 7348 1794
email:　　admissions@stjamesprep.org.uk
website:　www.stjamesprep.org.uk

Founded in 1974.

Chair of Governors: Mr Hugh Venables, BSc, MBA

Headmaster: **Mr Kris Spencer**, BSc, MA, FRGS

Age Range. 2–11
Number of Pupils. 230
Fees per term (2021–2022). £6,140

Admissions. Children can join the new nursery (opened September 2019) the term they turn three. Nursery children and siblings have priority for Reception places. All children are invited to a taster morning and are assessed from Year 3 upwards in English and maths.

For further information contact the Registrar, Miss Vicky Mitchell, 0207 348 1793, email: admissions@stjames prep.org.uk.

Head, Kris Spencer, is enthusiastic about the fully coeducational structure of the School having taught at some of the best single sex and mixed schools in the country. Previously, Deputy Head (Academic) of Notting Hill Prep, he worked for many years as Assistant Head at Latymer Upper and enjoyed teaching and management roles at St Paul's Girls' School, Westminster School, Abingdon and St Edward's.

An oasis of calm in bustling Kensington, the School is resourced with enviable outside space (including a Forest school), a fully resourced teaching kitchen, Science labs and a new ICT Suite.

St James Prep prides itself on adding value both to the academic results and the character of its pupils. Lessons start and end with The Pause – a moment of stillness that supports focus and well-being. Love of learning is the preferred route to success, so that pupils get great results for the right reasons, and without the stress of a hothouse atmosphere. Pupils can progress on to Senior Girls' or Boys' Schools – entry is automatic; but the emphasis is on choice with a robust 11+ programme which has seen recent leavers move on to top-flight schools such as St Pauls Girls' and Latymer Upper.

Strong in sports with over 18 different sports taught, including swimming, handball, cross-country running and squash, alongside traditional team sports. Girls are taught football, rugby and cricket, as well as netball, and both boys and girls compete with great success regionally and nationally. There is specialist teaching in all of the Arts, with

a packed schedule of performances including a Shakespeare Festival, weekly music assemblies and termly concerts.

The outstanding Art and Design department and on-site kiln, enables the children to produce first-class work and experience a range of different mediums and techniques including mosaic, printmaking and sculpture.

St John's Beaumont Independent Preparatory Boys School

Priest Hill, Old Windsor, Berkshire SL4 2JN

Tel:　　　01784 494053
email:　　sjb.admissions@sjb.email
website:　www.SJBWindsor.uk
Twitter:　@SJBHeadmaster
　　　　　@SJBAway
　　　　　@SJBBoarding
　　　　　@SJBSports
Facebook:　@SJBWindsor

Chairman of Governors: T R Cook

Headmaster: **G E F Delaney**, BA Hons, PGCE

Age Range. 3–13.
Number of Boys. 270 (50 Full, Weekly, Tailored Boarders; 220 Day Boys).
Fees per term (2021–2022). Boarding £10,415; Weekly Boarding £8,820; Tailored Boarding £8,245–£8,585; Day Boys £4,620–£6,820 Pre-Preparatory (Nursery–Year 1) £3,540.

St John's Beaumont is a Roman Catholic Jesuit boarding and day preparatory school for boys aged 3 to 13. The aim is to encourage well-rounded young men who can develop the confidence and open-mindedness to make the most of every opportunity and challenge that life will offer to them. It is important to us that boys demonstrate the same commitment to challenge as they do to areas that naturally inspire and interest them. Our curriculum is broad and invites the boys to think about life from a wider perspective: one that piques their interest and challenges them to see relationships and circumstances from a more sensitive and intelligent perspective. Classes are small and boys can receive individual attention according to their needs and abilities. There is a great emphasis on the academic and pastoral development of the boys and as a result the curriculum and teaching approach is planned very much with boys in mind. All boys study a rich variety of subjects within the curriculum and this is further supported by an excellent extra-curricular program for boys of all ages, including; rowing, rock climbing, philosophy, chef academy, golf and scuba diving. Boys are prepared for entry to a wide range of day and boarding schools including some of the top independent schools in the country and have won many scholarships in recent years.

The first purpose-built prep school in England, this pretty Victorian building stands on 70 acres on the edge of Windsor Great Park. It has a state-of-the-art sports hall and impressive ICT facilities endorsed by Microsoft awarding the school Beacon status. There is a dedicated science and art block, music school, concert hall and 25-metre indoor swimming pool. Games are played every day and the school particularly excels at rugby, cricket, tennis and swimming. The school's pool is also used by other schools and the local community. Wireless technology is available in classrooms enabling access to individual tablets and there are interactive whiteboards in all classrooms.

What others say:

'Happily, we left St John's blown out of the water, having spent the day at one of the most contented and civilised boys' preps we have ever had the privilege of visiting...' *The Good Schools Guide*

'Visitors are bowled over by the type of boys it is producing: well-rounded, socially intelligent young men with a strong moral compass...' *Muddy Stilettos – Berkshire*

An illustrated prospectus is available from the Headmaster, who is always pleased to meet parents and to show them around the school. Please email sjb.admissions@sjb.email.

Charitable status. St John's is a Registered Charity, number 230165. It exists to provide education for boys.

St John's College School

73 Grange Road, Cambridge, Cambs CB3 9AB

Tel: 01223 353532 Reception
           01223 353652 Admissions Secretary
email: shoffice@sjcs.co.uk
           bhoffice@sjcs.co.uk
website: www.sjcs.co.uk

Chair of Governors: Lindsay Dodsworth

Headmaster: **Mr Neil R Chippington**, MA, MEd, FRCO

Age Range. 4–13.

Number of Children. 448 girls and boys (including 19 Chorister and 7 Non-Chorister boy and girl boarders).

Fees per term (2021–2022). Choristers £2,975; Day Boys and Girls (4–13) £4,535–£5,640 (according to age); Boarders £8,905. Bursaries available for Choristers.

Profile. St John's prides itself on the quality of the academic and pastoral care it provides for each child. Through relaxed and friendly relations with children in a well-structured environment rich with opportunity; through close monitoring of progress; through communication and cooperation with parents; through expert staffing and, above all, through a sense of community that cares for the strengths and weaknesses of each of its members, St John's has consistently achieved outstanding results exemplified by over 70 scholarships during the last three years. Whilst its Choristers maintain the tradition of choral services and tour the world, St John's status as an Expert Centre for ICT, and other innovations, ensure the school's commitment to the future. Mr Neil Chippington joined St John's as the Headmaster in September 2016, having been Head at St Paul's Cathedral School in London.

Entry. At 4–7 by parental interview; at 7–12 by parental interview, report from previous school and, as appropriate, assessment.

Curriculum. The curriculum surrounds the core of formal skills teaching with a breadth of enrichment and extension for each child's talents. In addition to the usual subjects including specialist taught DT, ICT, Art, Music, Dance and Drama, and PE for all pupils, the following are also available: French (from 4+), Latin (from 9+), Greek (optional from 11+), Spanish (11+). Pupils prepared for CE and Scholarship examinations. Philosophy and Study Skills are now regularly taught to pupils in certain year groups and all pupils are being introduced to Mindfulness.

Leavers. Virtually all go to senior independent day or boarding schools. The School works closely with parents to assist them in finding the best school for their child.

Consultation. Tutorial system (1 teacher to 10 pupils) with daily tutorial session timetabled. Half yearly academic assessments, end of year examinations, termly Parents' Evenings and weekly staff 'surgery' times.

Sports. Athletics, Badminton, Basketball, Cricket, Cross Country, Football, Golf, Gymnastics, Hockey, Netball, Rounders, Rowing, Rugby, Short Tennis, Squash, Swimming, Table Tennis, Tennis. All games are timetabled and therefore given significant status. All major sports strong.

Activities. Numerous clubs including Art, Chess, Dance, Drama, Pottery, Sketching, Design Technology, Craft, Information Technology, Maths games and puzzles, Magic, Touch-typing, Cycling Proficiency, General Knowledge, Debating, Poetry, Sewing and Wardrobe. College Choir of international status, Chamber Groups, Orchestras, School Chapel Choir, Junior Chamber Choir, Parents' Choir, Major theatrical productions, e.g. *Oliver!*, *Hamlet*, and theatrical opportunities for all children. A range of visits relating to curriculum plus French, Classics, skiing and outward bound trips.

Facilities. School on two sites with facilities used by all pupils.

Byron House (4–8). Outstanding facilities including Science, DT Centre, two large suites of networked PCs, newly-designed Library, Drama Studio, Gym, Hall, and specialist Music wing. The Byron House site has also been redeveloped and the children can now use the newly landscaped and planted 'Forest Garden'. The site has completely redesigned classrooms and a large learning space for child-initiated learning and digital learning. The rooms are fitted with bespoke, streamlined storage. Investigative and collaborative skills have been fostered by the use of the new 'working walls' and 'writeable tables'.

Senior House (9–13). The Senior House site has been completely redeveloped. In addition to existing facilities such as the Chapel, Theatre, Gymnasium Science Laboratory, Art Room, ICT Room, Swimming Pool and Music School, the site boasts 14 new classrooms, an outstanding Library, a new DT and Computer Control and Graphics facility, a second Science Laboratory, a new Drama Studio, new Music facilities, a Quiet Garden, a new Multi-Sports Court and changing block, extensive storage and excellent staff facilities.

Boarding. From age 8. Girl and boy boarders form an integral part of life at St John's and benefit from all the School's facilities whilst living in the homely, caring atmosphere of a Boarding House which was completed in Spring 2011. The Boarding House accommodates up to 40 boys and girls and facilities include recreation areas, a library, TV, table tennis and use of all Senior House facilities. Day boarding and 'Waiters' facilities allow the School to be flexible to the needs of parents and children alike.

Charitable status. St John's College School is part of St John's College Cambridge, which is a Registered Charity, number 1137428.

St John's School

Potter Street Hill, Northwood, Middlesex HA6 3QY

Tel:	020 8866 0067
email:	office@st-johns.org.uk
website:	www.st-johns.org.uk
Twitter:	@stjsnorthwood

Chairman of Governors: Mr R A Robb

Headmaster: Mr M S Robinson, BSc, PGCE Loughborough

Age Range. 3–13.

Number of Boys. 350 Day Boys (Prep 221; Pre-Prep and Nursery 129).

Fees per annum (2021–2022): Nursery £11,260; Pre-Preparatory £15,190; Preparatory £16,340.

Facing south, on a 35-acre site, we have outstanding views over London. Since the Merchant Taylors' Educational Trust took the School under its wing, impressive development has taken place. St John's now has two completely refurbished science laboratories, a state of the art Design & Technology Workshop including 3D printer, a set of sewing machines and sublimation printing equipment, an ICT Centre and a large Music Department. Outside the classroom, we have an all-weather multi-purpose sports pitch, four rugby pitches and an athletics track, which have been levelled and provided with excellent drainage and irrigation. We also have an expansive nature trail and woodland area which is used by the Pre-Prep for Forest School on a daily basis and by older boys for ecological and environmental study. These areas are in addition to our extensive playing fields and formal gardens.

Our Pre-Preparatory Department provides dedicated Nursery facilities, an Information Technology Suite and Library. There are six purpose-built Pre-Prep classrooms in a self-contained area of the School leading to a covered outdoor play area and wooden climbing frame.

Nearing completion is a brand new two-floor sports hall with changing area and a dedicated site for our wraparound care providers. We are also looking forward to the construction of a purpose-built tree house which will benefit all pupils at St John's.

Most of the boys enter the School at either the age of three into the Nursery or at four into the Pre-Prep; there is a separate entry into the Prep School at seven. St John's has an excellent record of success in scholarship and senior school entrance examinations. Boys are prepared for all independent schools, but our links with Merchant Taylors' School, Northwood, are particularly strong.

Although the School was originally a Church of England foundation, boys of all religions and denominations are welcome.

Charitable status. St John's School, part of the Merchant Taylors' Educational Trust, is a Registered Charity, number 1063738. It exists for the purpose of educating boys.

St Leonards Junior Years

St Andrews, Fife KY16 9QJ

Tel:	01334 460470
email:	contact@stleonards-fife.org
website:	www.stleonards-fife.org
Twitter:	@StLeonards_Head
Facebook:	@stleonardsschool
Instagram:	@stleonardsschool
LinkedIn:	/school/st-leonards-school

Chair of the St Leonards Council: Col Martin Passmore, MA, GCGI, FRSA

Head: Simon Brian, MA Hons Edinburgh

Age Range. 5–11.

Number of Pupils. 128 (60 girls, 68 boys).

Fees per term (2021–2022). Day: £3,280 (Years 1–3), £4,066 (Years 4–6). Boarding (Year 6 upwards): £8,114.

St Leonards School in St Andrews spans Years 1 through to 13, with Years 1–6 classed as the 'Junior Years'. The school is administered by the St Leonards Council and educates children between the ages of 5 and 11, from Year 1 to Year 6.

Pupils typically continue on to Year 7, the first year of our Senior section of the school, and beyond to Year 13. With specialist teachers and small class sizes in the Junior Years, children benefit from individual attention. In addition to a strong academic tradition, drama, music, art, ICT and PE are included in the timetable.

St Leonards was the first school in Scotland to have been accredited to teach the inspiring International Baccalaureate Primary Years Programme, which encourages boys and girls to develop a love of learning. Since its accreditation for the PYP, St Leonards has become one of just two IB continuum schools in the UK, offering the PYP, MYP, CP and DP.

Pupils enjoy a dynamic and refreshing approach to teaching and learning both in and outside the classroom. A variety of sports are available, with rugby, hockey, lacrosse, tennis and cricket as the main team activities. Tuition in golf, dance and swimming is also offered. The leading St Leonards Golf Programme includes a 'St Leonards Minis' tier for beginners to the sport, who are looking to learn the basics and develop their game using state-of-the-art golfing technology.

Outdoor learning is a core part of the ethos in the Junior Years, including camping, bush craft, bee-keeping and Beach School at the East Sands, which is just a four-minute walk from the campus.

Charitable status. St Leonards School is a Registered Charity, number SC010904. It exists to provide education to children between the ages of 5 and 18.

St Martin's School

40 Moor Park Road, Northwood, Middlesex HA6 2DJ

Tel: 01923 825740
email: office@stmartins.org.uk
website: www.stmartins.org.uk
Twitter: @stmartinsprep

Chairman of Governors: Andy Harris

Headmaster: Mr Simon Dunn, BEd Hons

Age Range. 3–13.
Number of Boys. 400 Day Boys.
Fees per term (2021–2022). Main School £5,350; Pre-Prep £4,970; Nursery £4,125. Bursaries are available, details on request.

St Martin's aims to provide boys aged 3–13 with the breadth of education and experience necessary for them to realise their full potential in a safe and friendly environment. An enthusiastic staff of 40 experienced and well-qualified teachers maintains high academic standards and provides broad sporting, musical and cultural opportunities. The atmosphere is friendly and lively with great emphasis on pastoral care.

The School, which is an Educational Trust, administered by a Board of Governors, prepares boys for entry to all the Independent Senior Schools. One hundred and two Scholarship awards have been won to senior schools during the last five years. The School, which is in a pleasant residential area, stands in 12 acres of grounds. Facilities include a Kindergarten and separate Pre-Preparatory building; two Science Laboratories; a Performing Arts Centre; a Sports Centre including an indoor swimming pool; a playground; two ICT suites; an Art Studio with facilities for Design Technology; 3 Tennis Courts.

Computing, Art, DT, and Music are included in the curriculum for all boys, and a large proportion of the boys in the School learn a musical instrument. There is a varied after-school activity programme for boys to pursue their interests.

There is a pre-school and after-school club from Kindergarten age upwards enabling parents to work a full day.

The School is divided into Patrols for competitions in work and games, and senior boys make a responsible contribution towards the running of the School. Boys are taught football, rugby, cross-country running, hockey, cricket, swimming, athletics and tennis. The school has a fine reputation in inter-school matches.

Charitable status. St Martin's (Northwood) Preparatory School Trust Limited is a Registered Charity, number 312648. It exists to provide education for boys.

St Mary's School, Hampstead

47 Fitzjohn's Avenue, Hampstead, London NW3 6PG

Tel: 020 7435 1868
email: office@stmh.co.uk
website: www.stmh.co.uk

Chairman of Governors: Mr Sean Murphy

Headmistress: Mrs Harriet Connor-Earl, BA

Deputy Head: Miss Philippa d'Aquino, BA

Age Range. Girls 2¾–11
Number in School. 300 pupils.
Fees per term (2021–2022). Nursery £3,020 (5 mornings a week), £48.00 each additional afternoon per week; Reception to Year 6 £5,580.

St Mary's School Hampstead provides an outstanding and inspirational Catholic education to girls from 3–11 years.

St Mary's School celebrates the uniqueness of every pupil and their achievements. The rigorous, challenging curriculum places a strong emphasis on high academic achievement within a culture of care and support.

The School aims to instil four key habits of learning in their pupils. The children are encouraged to be risk-takers, not only in their play, but also in their learning. They are also taught to be resilient and not to fall at the first hurdle. Staff ask the children to make mistakes as through the process of challenging themselves, they make more academic progress and in turn excel not only in the classroom, but in their own self-confidence. The girls at St Mary's School are respectful, not just of each other, but of themselves. Finally, pupils are encouraged to be reflective on their faith, their behaviour and their academic work.

The School has recently invested in an extensive refurbishment programme to deliver the most up-to-date and stimulating learning spaces. The Global Learning Centre is a cutting-edge space that includes an Engineering and Robotics Lab, Virtual Reality Launch Pad, Art and Design Studio as well as a Green Room.

Another key priority has been incorporating the latest technology to bring learning to life with iPads and Google Chromebooks accessible to every pupil. The spacious classrooms are now flooded with natural light and offer innovative flexible seating.

The focus on technology is equally balanced with an emphasis on creative and physical development. Music, drama, art and sports are an essential part of school life and involve everyone. As part of the modernisation programme, the unique and extensive outside space has been enhanced. New climbing equipment has been installed and the full-size netball court has been upgraded allowing football, cricket and tennis to be introduced.

Used together – the integrated technology, the flexible seating and the broad curriculum – the girls at St Mary's are flourishing. They are adopting habits of learning and being encouraged to make independent choices which they can take forward into their secondary education.

Leavers achieve impressive results, gaining offers and Academic Scholarships from the best schools in the country, including Channing School For Girls, City of London

School For Girls, Francis Holland School, Highgate School, North London Collegiate, South Hampstead High School, St Mary's Ascot and St Paul's Girls' School.

St Mary's Preparatory School
Melrose

Abbey Park, Melrose, Roxburghshire TD6 9LN

Tel: 01896 822517
email: office@stmarysmelrose.org.uk
website: www.stmarysmelrose.org.uk
Twitter: @SchoolMarys

Founded 1895.

Chairman of Governors: Mr G T G Baird

Headmaster: **William J Harvey**, BEd Hons

Age Range. 2–13 co-educational.

Number of Pupils. 160.

Fees per term (2021–2022). Day: Pre-Prep £4,773, Prep £5,723. Weekly Boarding: £6,523.

Curriculum. A healthy variety of subjects including traditional core studies reflecting both the Scottish and English Curriculums (English, Maths, Science, Computer Studies, French, Geography, History, Classics, Latin, Spanish, RE, Art, Music, Drama and PE). The School's intention is to provide a genuinely nourishing environment allowing for the development of the whole child.

Entry requirements. Application by letter or telephone, followed by a visit to the school, if possible, and a tour guided by senior pupils. All pupils can be offered an 'In-day' to help with placement.

Examinations offered. Common Entrance to Scholarship for independent senior schools in Scotland and England.

Academic, sports, games and leisure facilities. Classroom computers, Science Laboratory and a big open Art Room. Theatre-Arts and Assembly Hall for concerts and drama. Spacious games pitches supporting a strong tradition in rugby, cricket, hockey, netball and rounders. There is a cross-curricular Study Support Programme for talented and gifted children as well as for children with Specific Learning Difficulties.

Religious activities. Morning Assembly with hymn-singing and readings, stressing pupil participation and contribution through drama and music.

Charitable status. St Mary's School, Melrose is a Registered Charity, number SC009352. Its aim is to provide education for primary school children.

St Michael's Preparatory School

La Rue de la Houguette, Five Oaks, St Saviour, Jersey, Channel Islands JE2 7UG

Tel: +44(0)1534 856904
email: clt@stmichaels.je
            tar@stmichaels.je
website: www.stmichaels.je
Twitter: @stmichaelsprep
Facebook: @St-Michaels-Preparatory-School-Jersey
Instagram: @stmichaelsschooljersey
LinkedIn: /company/st-michael-s-school-jersey

Headmaster: **M B S Rees**, DipEd, MEd, MSc (Psych), Member of the Independent Association of Prep Schools (IAPS)

Deputy Head: V B A Holden, BSc Hons, PGCE, MEd, FRSB

Academic Assistant Head: G S Green, BEd Hons

Pastoral Assistant Head: Mrs N C Mackereth, BA Hons

Age Range. 3–14.

Number of Pupils. 173 Boys, 153 Girls.

Fees per term (2021–2022). Pre-Prep (Reception, Years 1 and 2) £3,725–£4,191; Juniors (Years 3 & 4) £5,180; Middle School (Years 5 & 6) £5,725; Senior School (Years 7, 8 & Shell) £5,855. Lunch £360.

Boys and girls are prepared for scholarship and entrance to all Independent Senior Schools. Hockey, rugby, football, gymnastics, netball, rounders, cricket, athletics and tennis are taught on spacious playing fields with pavilion and hard tennis courts, which adjoin the school. The school also has a purpose-built Sports Hall (4 badminton court size), indoor swimming pool and gymnasium/dance/drama studio. Regular tours are made to Guernsey and England for sporting fixtures.

The school has flourishing and well equipped computer, art and engineering departments, in addition to networked computers in every classroom. A wide variety of clubs and hobbies function within the school, including activities such as Martial Arts, coding, engineering, yoga, cross-country and many other outdoor activities. Our Shell Year (Y9) take part in the Duke of Edinburgh's (Bronze) Award and play an integral role in the School's Social Impact programme.

Music, drama and art (including pottery), are all encouraged and a wide range of musical instruments are taught. There are three school choirs, two orchestras and a number of ensemble groups. The choirs participate locally and nationally in events and competitions.

For Middle and Senior School pupils there is an annual Activities Week, which takes Years 6, 7 and 8 to different locations in France; Year 5 take part in island-based activities. Every other year a party of children from Years 3 to 8 ski in Europe.

Care, consideration and courtesy form the School's Ethos and are important aspects of behaviour that the school holds dear.

The academic and physical development, in addition to the spiritual, moral and cultural growth of the whole child, is the main aim of the school and every child is encouraged to do 'a little better' than anyone thought possible.

St Michael's Preparatory School

198 Hadleigh Road, Leigh-on-Sea, Essex SS9 2LP

Tel: 01702 478719
email: office@stmichaelsschool.com
website: www.stmichaelsschool.com
Twitter: @StMichaelsLeigh
Facebook: @stmichaelsschool.co.uk

Chair of Governors: Mr Mark Stennett

Head Master: **Mr James Mobbs**

Age Range. Co-educational 3–11 years.

Number of Pupils. 255 day pupils (125 boys, 130 girls).

Fees per term (2021–2022). £1,709–£4,148 (all inclusive fee structure)

St Michael's is a Church of England Preparatory (IAPS) School founded in 1922 to provide pupils with a well-rounded education based on Christian principles, with children welcomed from other Christian traditions and faiths. The school has its own Chapel.

The school is situated in a popular residential area in Leigh-on-Sea within easy reach of public transport. London is accessible by rail and Fenchurch Street Station is approximately 40 minutes away.

The curriculum offered is broad, balanced and tailored towards the children's needs and it aims to contribute to the intellectual, physical, creative, social and spiritual development of each child. All the children, from Nursery through to Form 6, receive specialist teaching in Music, French, Drama and PE with additional specialist teaching in the Prep department. Pupils are prepared for the end of Key Stage standardised attainment tests, 11+ entry to local grammar schools and Entrance or Scholarship examinations for independent schools. High academic standards are achieved throughout the school and the children thrive in a happy but disciplined environment.

St Michael's has a dedicated and well-qualified staff team. Class sizes are small to enable personal attention to be given. The school is well resourced with many specialist areas. Nearby playing fields are used for Games. There is a wide range of extra-curricular activities available, with Music and Drama as particular strengths.

Visits to the school are warmly welcomed.

June 2015 ISI Inspection Report: 'Excellent' across all areas of its provision, 'Outstanding' EYFS provision.

June 2018 ISI Compliance Inspection Report: The School is compliant across all areas of its provision.

Charitable status. St Michael's Preparatory School is a Registered Charity, number 280688. It exists to provide education.

St Michael's Prep School

Otford

Otford Court, Row Dow, Otford, Sevenoaks, Kent TN14 5RY

Tel: 01959 522137
email: office@stmichaels.kent.sch.uk
website: www.stmichaels.kent.sch.uk
Twitter: @StMichaels_Prep
Facebook: @StMichaelsPrepSchool
Instagram: @stmichaelsprep
LinkedIn: /st-michael's-prep-school

Chair of Governors: Mr Rashid Chinchanwala

Head: **Mr Nik Pears**, BEd Hons Cantab

Head of Pre-Prep: Mrs Z Leech, BA Hons, PGCE

Age Range. 2–13 Co-educational.

Number of Pupils. 460

Fees per term (2021–2022). £842–£5,120.

St Michael's Prep School is a non-selective, co-educational school promoting a rich, varied, broad and balanced education within a Christian context. We challenge and stimulate pupils to achieve their best and strive for excellence in all that they do; fostering in them a sense of wonder and joy in learning, so that they take real pride in their accomplishments. Children are helped to understand themselves as individuals, their feelings and emotions, how they can affect others and to show tolerance and respect for the diversity of the world in which we live, as well striving for individual academic excellence. St Michael's has a strong record of pupils gaining scholarships into Senior Schools.

Culturally, the school provides a wide sporting, musical, artistic and dramatic programme to which all pupils are equally entitled and in which all children are encouraged to participate.

We recognise that every child is an individual and aim to promote their happiness, self-confidence and well-being as members of a caring community. Children are given opportunities to make a difference to their school and to the wider world. The school motto: *Perseverance, Wisdom, Gratitude* encapsulates the cornerstone of this education.

St Michael's has been judged excellent in both pupils' academic and personal development and we feel this is a welcome endorsement of what we believe about our school. We attract and retain some of the most excellent teaching and support staff who in turn ensure excellent outcomes for all children.

Pre-Prep is housed in a beautiful purpose-built eco-friendly building and our recently renovated Stable Court: here children learn and play with great joy.

St Michael's is set in 90 acres of the beautiful, rolling North Downs close to Sevenoaks town and the fast train service to central London. Our school is enhanced by a strong Parents and Friends Association and International Parents' Club who welcome international families.

A message from Nik Pears our Head:

"I would be delighted to welcome you to St Michael's and give you the opportunity to meet some of the extraordinary children and staff who make our school such a special place to grow up. In the first instance, please do visit our website where you will be able to take a virtual tour of our grounds and facilities and gain an insight into life at St Michael's."

Charitable status. St Michael's is a Registered Charity, number 1076999. It exists to provide education for boys and girls.

St Neot's Preparatory School

St Neot's Road, Eversley, Hook, Hampshire RG27 0PN

Tel: Office: 0118 973 2118
            Admissions: 0118 973 9650
email: office@stneotsprep.co.uk
            admissions@stneotsprep.co.uk
website: www.stneotsprep.co.uk
Twitter: @stneotsprep
Facebook: @stneotsprep
Instagram: @stneotsprepschool

Chair of Governors: Mr David Hertzell

Head: **Mr Jonathan Slot**

Age Range. 2–13 years co-educational.

Number of Pupils. 219

Fees per term (2021–2022). Years 5–8 £5,736, Years 3–4 £5,351, Reception–Year 2 £4,010, Nursery £73 per day (core hours), £47 per morning session, Tiny Tuskers £75 per day (core hours), £42 per morning session, additional hours charged at £9.60 per hour.

St Neot's, founded in 1888, is a happy, vibrant community for boys and girls from 2 to 13 years. The school is situated on the border of Hampshire and Berkshire and is set in 70 acres of beautiful grounds and woodland.

The school's educational philosophy is to inspire children to develop a love of learning in a supportive and happy environment, where each individual is encouraged to achieve their full academic potential and beyond. Children are motivated to discover their full range of talents and to develop the passion to pursue them. They are given the opportunity to embrace challenge, think creatively, develop self-confidence and foster empathy towards others, preparing them both intellectually and emotionally for success in the 21st Century.

We aim to provide the highest standards in teaching and learning, within a well rounded educational experience and St Neot's has a very strong record of success in achieving Scholarships and Awards to numerous Senior Schools.

St Neot's is committed to providing a world of opportunity in every aspect of school life. Stimulating learning environments ensure that engaged pupils work towards the highest academic standards, whilst also enjoying a breadth of experience in sport, music, art, drama and dance.

Emphasis is placed on developing independence, self-confidence, curiosity and collaboration. Forest School and

Outdoor Education programmes encourage children of all ages to develop these attributes, which are so vital in the modern world. The St Neot's journey culminates in the Years 7 and 8 leadership programme, which draws together a mix of skills through the Pre Senior Schools Baccalaureate (PSB).

Sport is a strength of the school and our state-of-the-art sports complex, comprising sports hall, 25m indoor swimming pool, all-weather astro, cricket nets, hard tennis and netball courts, significantly supplement the extensive playing fields. There is also an on-site mountain bike track and a traversing wall. Judo, dance and tennis are taught by specialist coaches and there are many after-school clubs and activities covering a wide range of interests. Holiday Clubs run in all school breaks and offer a wealth of opportunities, both sporting and creative.

St Neot's holds a Gold Artsmark award, giving recognition to our achievements in art, music, drama and dance. A number of plays, concerts and recitals take place throughout the school year for all age groups, either in the school grounds or in the Performing Arts Centre.

Open Mornings take place termly and details of these can be found on the school website: www.stneotsprep.co.uk. We would also be delighted to arrange an individual tour and a meeting with the Head. Please contact Admissions on 0118 9739650; email: admissions@stneotsprep.co.uk.

Charitable status. St Neot's (Eversley) Limited is a Registered Charity, number 307324. The aim of the Charity is to try to provide the best all-round education possible to as many pupils as possible, with bursarial help according to need.

St Olave's Prep School

106–110 Southwood Road, New Eltham, London SE9 3QS

Tel: 020 8294 8930
email: office@stolaves.org.uk
website: www.stolaves.org.uk

Chair of Trustees: Peter Houillon

Headteacher: **Miss Claire Holloway**, BEd QTS

Age Range. 3–11.

Number of Pupils. 215 Day Boys and Girls.

Fees per term (2021–2022). Nursery £2,008–£3,996; Reception & Year 1 £4,188; Years 2–6 £4,496.

In a single sentence, the school aims to bring out the best in everyone. It seeks to achieve this aim by providing an all-round education for both boys and girls aged 3 to 11 in a warm and caring environment in which each child can thrive and be happy knowing that each is accepted for who they are.

A Christian ethos permeates the pastoral life of the school, where care for others through thoughtful and responsible behaviour is expected. Praise and encouragement are emphasised and relationships between staff and pupils are relaxed and friendly. A close partnership with parents is sought.

The children in the EYFS (Nursery and Reception) and Pre-Prep (Year 1 and Year 2) are taught in mixed-ability classes where each child's progress is carefully monitored by the Class Teacher. In the Upper School (Years 3–6) the children are set across the year group for Mathematics. Throughout the school individual differences are appropriately met, with the very able and those with mild learning difficulties receiving additional support where this is thought beneficial. The school is noted for the broad curriculum it offers and for its excellent achievements in Music and Drama. A range of sporting activities is taught as part of the curriculum and there is a wide range of after school clubs and activities. Music and PE are taught by specialist teachers from the age of three, French is introduced at four years old and Latin at ten years old. The classrooms are equipped with computers and there is a networked suite which supports all areas of the curriculum. A specialist ICT teacher teaches all year groups from Reception to Year 6. Digital panels and portable devices are used to enhance learning.

St Olave's feeds a wide range of secondary schools and parents are given help in choosing the school most appropriate to meet the needs of their child.

Charitable status. St Olave's School is a Registered Charity, number 312734. It exists to provide high quality education for boys and girls.

St Paul's Cathedral School

2 New Change, London EC4M 9AD

Tel: 020 7248 5156
email: office@spcs.london.sch.uk
website: www.spcslondon.com
Twitter: @StPaulsCathSch

Chairman of Governors: The Very Revd Dr David Ison, Dean of St Paul's Cathedral

Headmaster: **Simon Larter-Evans**, BA Hons, PGCE, FRSA

Bursar: Martin Kiddle

Registrar: Clare Morgan

Age Range. 4–13 Co-educational.

Number of Pupils. Boarding Choristers circa 30, Day Boys circa 110, Day Girls circa 100, Pre-Prep circa 60.

Fees per term (2021–2022). Choristers £3,059; Day pupils £5,058–£5,446.

St Paul's Cathedral School has existed since the 12th century, originally established to educate the now world-class choristers of St Paul's Cathedral. Since moving to its present site, set to the east end of the Cathedral, it is also a vibrant day school, educating the children of professionals living and working in the City and local boroughs.

It is a school in high demand, and is noted for its friendly atmosphere, sense of purpose, care and kindness. Our response to COVID was innovative, and adapted quickly to provide the highest possible quality of education, even remotely.

Providing boys and girls with the firm foundations for the future and preparing them for the next stage in their education in a safe and comfortable environment is central to our aims and principles. There is real breadth to the educational experience here. We are just completing a substantial development to the school buildings, soon to be the envy of city based schools, and our location means that we can make the most of what London has to offer: trips to museums and galleries and other places of interest are a regular occurrence, not to forget our privileged access to the Cathedral, our school chapel.

Ultimately, the most important thing we aspire to do as a school is instil a life long love of learning.

The boys and girls go on to a wide variety of senior schools at 11+ and 13+: co-educational; single sex; boarding and day. We have a good record of scholarships, particularly music scholarships, to many of the top schools in London and beyond.

We pride ourselves on the high calibre of pastoral care given to all our pupils and resident staff take on the particular role of looking after the choristers who board in a separate building on the school's site.

All pupils are encouraged to play a musical instrument (most pupils play two) and there are music and theory lessons with school orchestras and chamber groups.

A wide variety of games is offered including field sports at local playing fields. The children have their own playground and the use of the hall for indoor games and gymnastics.

Admissions procedure. Prospective pupils of 7+ years in September are given academic tests in verbal and non-verbal reasoning, in January of the year of entry.

Pre-Prep children (4+) are assessed in an informal play situation in the November prior to entry.

11+ entry is becoming popular, and scholarships at 11+ offering 10% fee remission are available to exceptional candidates in music, art, sport and academic ability. For more information see: www.spcs.london/admissions/scholarships

Occasional places sometimes come up.

For prospective choristers, voice trials and tests are held throughout the year for boys in years 3, 4 and occasionally 5.

The Headmaster is always happy to invite prospective parents to see the school.

St Paul's Juniors

Lonsdale Road, London SW13 9JT

Tel: 020 8748 3461
email: spjheadpa@stpaulsschool.org.uk
website: www.stpaulsschool.org.uk
Twitter: @StPaulsSchool
Instagram: @stpaulsschoollondon
LinkedIn: /school/st-paul's-school

Chairman of Governors: Richard Cassell, BA, LLB

Head: **Maxine Shaw**, BSc London, PGCE Hull, PG Dip Brunel, NPQH

Age Range. 7–13.

Number of Boys. 505.

Fees per term (2021–2022). £7,076.

St Paul's Juniors is the junior division for St Paul's School (*see entry in HMC section*) and attracts bright, enthusiastic boys who are inquisitive and eager to learn.

Working closely alongside St Paul's seniors to inform the curriculum, ensures continuity and a more holistic learning experience, with some teaching staff working across both schools. Pupils at St Paul's Juniors hold a place at St Paul's School and transfer automatically at the end of Year 8, subject to ongoing good work and conduct, rather than a formal examination. Our aim is to offer a broad education to every pupil, along with the opportunity to enjoy a wide range of activities. Music, Art, Drama and Sport are all strong, but additional activities range from history and debating to chess, coding and cookery.

Boys join the School at 7+ and 8+ and 11+. Fifty-four boys join Year 3 into three classes of 18 and a further 18 join them at 8+. Thirty-six boys join in Year 7 creating a total of six classes in Years 7 and 8. Entrance at all levels is by competitive examination and interview. Means-tested bursaries are available at all points of entry.

St Paul's School sits on the south bank of the Thames. The Juniors are in separate but adjacent modern buildings and share many amenities, including the dining hall, sports complex, design & technology workshops and playing fields. St Paul's Juniors has its own main teaching block, hall/theatre, library, two computer rooms, drama studio and music school. Three science laboratories and art & design rooms are situated in a separate building.

Charitable status. St Paul's School is a Registered Charity, number 1119619. The object of the charity is to promote the education of boys in Greater London.

St Peter's 2–8

The Pre-prep School of St Peter's School, York

Clifton, York YO30 6AB

Tel: 01904 527361
email: enquiries2–8@stpetersyork.org.uk
website: www.stpetersyork.org.uk
Twitter: @stpetersyork
Facebook: @stpetersschoolyork
Instagram: @stpeters.york

Chairman of the Governors: Mr W Woolley

Head: **Mr Philip Hardy**, BA Northumbria, PGCE

Deputy Head: Mrs Antonia Clarke, BA Nottingham

Age Range. 2–8 co-educational.

Number of Pupils. 141 boys, 117 girls.

Fees per term (2021–2022). Nursery (full-time) £2,840; Reception, Years 1 & 2: £3,090; Year 3: £3,350. Nursery Education Grant accepted for 3 and 4 year olds.

A sense of belonging, infinite opportunities and unlimited possibilities is what it feels like to be a child at St

Peter's 2–8. As part of the St Peter's School family, the school represents the start of an exciting and rewarding learning adventure. In April 2021, St Peter's 2–8 was declared *Pre-prep School of the Year* in the national Tes Independent School Awards for its 'outstanding innovative and broad curriculum, which encourages curiosity in an ever-changing world'.

Curriculum. A vibrant and dynamic thematic skills-based curriculum is covered, which offers variety, challenge and opportunities for everyone to discover what they love. Small classes, individual attention, Forest School and a huge range of after-school activities enable high standards to be achieved. French is offered to all children from Nursery upwards.

Music and Drama. All children throughout the school have ample opportunity to be creative and express themselves. Nursery children have a session of music and movement, and all other classes have weekly lessons with a dedicated music teacher. From Year 2, children have the opportunity to learn to play a variety of instruments in personal lessons. Each year there are opportunities for children to participate in performances to a wider audience. All classes have weekly drama lessons, and there is the opportunity for Y2 and Y3 to do speech and drama as an after school activity.

Sport and Co-Curricular Activities. Physical Education starts in the Nursery. As children grow older, games and swimming are added. The pupils have access to the impressive sports facilities and 47-acre green campus at St Peter's School. Co-curricular activities include: Art, Drama, Animation, Ballet, Karate, Explorers, Lego and The Green Team

Assessments. Throughout Nursery and Reception, children work towards achieving the Early Learning Goals, culminating in the completion of the Foundation Stage Profile. Work is assessed continuously and children's progress is discussed at staff meetings. Incas is used in Years 1 to 3 for assessment purposes which informs future planning. There is ongoing communication between parents and staff through a reports system, invitations to visit the school and parent evenings.

An ISI Inspection in April 2017 found St Peter's School 2–18 to be 'excellent' in all areas for the quality of its education – the highest grading that any school can achieve.

Charitable status. St Peter's School, York, is a Registered Charity, number 1141329. It exists to provide education for boys and girls.

St Peter's 8–13

The Prep School of St Peter's School, York

Queen Anne's Road, York YO30 7WA

Tel: 01904 527416
email: enquiries8–13@stpetersyork.org.uk
website: www.stpetersyork.org.uk
Twitter: @stpetersyork
Facebook: @stpetersschoolyork
Instagram: @stpeters.york

Chairman of the Governors: Mr W Woolley

Head: **Mr A I Falconer**, BA Hons Lancaster, MBA Leicester

Deputy Head: Mr M C Ferguson, HDE Cape Town

Head's Secretary: Miss S Bath

Age Range. 8–13 co-educational.

Number of Pupils. 200 Boys, 184 Girls.

Fees per term (2021–2022). Day: £4,460–£5,420; Boarding: £8,180–£9,085. Non-EU Boarder: £9,800.

Tuition fees include the costs of stationery and textbooks. There are no compulsory extras except for examination fees. Lunches are included in day fees.

St Peter's 8–13 (formerly St Olave's) was founded in 1876. With its own halls, music school, practical subjects workshops, sports hall and magnificently appointed specialist teaching rooms, St Peter's enjoys some of the best facilities for a prep school of its type and is proud to be the Choir School for York Minster.

The school puts praise, encouragement and pastoral care of the individual as its highest priority. There is a demanding wide curriculum from the earliest age with specialist subject areas – modern foreign languages, information technology, science and music, amongst others – being taught by specialist teachers from Year 4. Progress is monitored through a regular system of effort grades, and attainment is measured through internal and externally moderated tests.

Boarding, available for children in Year 7 and above, is a flourishing aspect of the school, with a co-educational House under the constant care of resident Houseparents and their own family. Weekly and flexi boarding are also available. There are also five Day Houses.

Music plays an important part in the life of the school with 22 music teachers, two orchestras, a wind band and 14 ensembles playing and practising weekly. Over 200 pupils learn individual instruments, and all are encouraged to join larger groups. York Minster's girl and boy choristers are educated at St Peter's 8–13.

Sport has an equally high profile where football, hockey, cricket, netball, rugby, tennis and swimming are major sports. Athletics, cross-country running, squash, badminton, basketball and volleyball are also available for all. The boys have won the National Schools' Seven-a-Side Rugby tournament four times in the last twelve years and won the National Cricket JET cup. The school has 23 tennis courts, a synthetic pitch and a 25m 6-lane swimming pool.

Drama has an increasing profile, and out-of-school activities flourish through clubs such as eco club, science society, chess, photography, art and trampoline.

The vast majority of boys and girls move on to St Peter's 13–18.

Entrance assessments are held in January/February each year, and assessments can also be arranged at other times. Entry is possible in most year groups, although the school is heavily oversubscribed at most stages. Means-tested fee assistance is available from age 11.

Charitable status. St Peter's School, York, is a Registered Charity, number 1141329. It exists to provide education for boys and girls.

St Piran's

Gringer Hill, Maidenhead, Berkshire SL6 7LZ

Tel:	01628 594300
email:	registrar@stpirans.co.uk
website:	www.stpirans.co.uk

Chairman of Governors: Mrs Kate Taylor

Headmaster: **Mr Sebastian Sales**

Age Range. 2–11 Co-educational.

Number of Pupils. 405 day pupils.

Fees per term (2021–2022). £4,181–£5,924. Nursery – 5 full days: £268.87 per week (funded).

St Piran's is a thriving co-educational IAPS day school set amid 10 delightful acres just to the north of Maidenhead town centre. Founded as a small school in Blackheath, London in 1805.

Class sizes are small with a maximum of 20 children. Boys and girls benefit from individual attention in all subjects. They are provided with a wide range of exciting opportunities both inside and outside the classroom. Numerous trips to castles and museums, theatres and shows, history re-enactments, geographical fieldwork and religious sites extend the children's understanding of the world around them. In addition to the academic subjects, pupils take part in a wide range of other activities each week.

Academically, the school offers a broad curriculum at all levels in the school. French starts with our youngest classes where confidence in the spoken language is encouraged. By Year 6 we are introducing Latin and Spanish. The children enjoy specialist teaching in art, games and PE, IT, swimming and music from an early age. We support children with their entrance exams at 11+ to Grammar Schools or other Senior independent schools. Our results over the years have been excellent, supporting our desire to encourage independent thinkers, confident individuals and strong leaders of the future.

The main sports that pupils take part in are rugby, football, netball, hockey, cricket (both girls and boys) and swimming. The school has its own indoor swimming pool and large sports hall. St Piran's also has a dance studio and pupils are encouraged to take an active part in the performing arts. We are blessed with wonderful facilities which serve to enhance the varied sports programmes that we offer the children at all levels.

The school has its own Leadership programme and regular visits off site are arranged for all the children, including residential trips.

Pupils may enter the school at any age, although the main intakes occur at Nursery and Reception. Scholarships and bursaries may be offered after assessment. Please contact the school and an appointment can be arranged to talk to the Headmaster about financial support.

The school is proud of its outstanding record of achievement and the fully rounded education that it provides within a friendly caring atmosphere. We are proud of our Christian tradition and family ethos which foster high expectations and successful, happy children.

Children and parents are warmly invited to visit St Piran's to see for themselves the excellent facilities that we offer and to meet some of the staff and pupils.

Charitable status. St Piran's School Limited is a Registered Charity, number 309094.

St Pius X Prep School

200 Garstang Road, Fulwood, Preston, Lancashire PR2 8RD

Tel: 01772 719937
email: enquiries@st-piusx.lancs.sch.uk
website: www.stpiusx.co.uk
Twitter: @HeadStPius
Facebook: @StPiusXCatholicPreparatorySchool
Instagram: @stpiusxprepschool

Chairman of Governors: Mr Mark Hurst

Headmaster: **Mr Patrick Gush**

Age Range. 2–11.

Number of Children. 150 Day Girls and Boys.

Fees per term (2021–2022). Main School: £2,625–£2,825, Nursery: £25 per session.

The School is a non-profit-making charitable trust administered by a Board of Governors, providing education from 2–11, set in six acres of its own grounds in a pleasant suburb of Preston.

The children are prepared for the entrance examinations to independent schools and Grammar Schools and it has an excellent record of scholarships to senior schools and SATS results at KS1 and KS2.

The school has a large Nursery division which covers the EYFS in open-plan Nursery rooms.

All preparatory curriculum subjects are covered as well as sign language, Health & Wellbeing, and STEM.

Sports taught are Association Football, Cricket, Tennis, Hockey, Netball, Rugby, Rounders, Athletics and Cross Country.

Creative and Performing Arts, including Music and Drama, thrive alongside Outdoor Education and Forest School. Ballet, piano, wind, bass-guitar, percussion, string and singing lessons are some of the optional extras offered.

Charitable status. St Pius X School is a Registered Charity, number 526609. Its purpose is to equip the children with an outstanding academic and social education in a Catholic Christian environment, which will enable them to achieve their full potential – the school welcomes pupils of all faiths.

St Swithun's Prep School

Alresford Road, Winchester, Hampshire SO21 1HA

Tel: 01962 835750
email: prepoffice@stswithuns.com
website: www.stswithuns.com
Twitter: @stswithunsprep
Facebook: @StSwithunsPrepSchool

Established 1884. Girls day preparatory school with a co-ed pre-school. Church of England.

School Council:

Chairman: Mrs Alison McClure

Headmaster: **Mr Jonathan Brough**, BEd Cambridge, MA Roehampton

Deputy Head: Mrs Katherine Grosscurth, BSc Hons Plymouth, PGCE Exeter

Age Range. Girls 4–11, with a co-ed pre-school.

Number of Pupils. 180 pupils. Average class size 18. Pupil to teacher ratio 12:1.

Fees per term (2021–2022). Pre-school: £3,890 (all day including lunch); Reception, Years 1 & 2 £3,890; Years 3–6 £5,060.

Profile. Welcome to St Swithun's Prep School, a school in which every child is known, cherished and at the same time encouraged to be fearless.

Our modern, purpose-built prep school provides a simply spectacular and inspiring teaching and learning environment. It is an environment in which pupils and staff have warm, respectful relationships. The building includes specialist teaching rooms, a science laboratory, an art studio, a media/computing room, a performing arts space and a gym. Prep school children also have access to the school's athletics track and indoor swimming facilities, including a teaching pool. Swimming is part of the curriculum for all students. There is also a Forest School on campus. The children enjoy going to school and the staff relish having the opportunity to share adventures, interests and laughter.

While united in their enthusiasm and energy, the children are all individuals and we encourage them to sample a wide range of experiences so that they each develop individual passions. We look always to celebrate characteristics such as the ability to bounce back from disappointment, to show compassion for others, to rise to challenges and to keep a sense of perspective. We want your children to go home every evening with slightly grubby knees and tales of what they have done at school that day.

Entry. At 3.

Curriculum. Usual subjects taught plus French, art, technology, drama, ICT, music and PE, with due regard for National Curriculum requirements.

Leavers. Girls go on to a range of senior independent schools, with the majority going to St Swithun's Senior School.

Consultation. Biannual reports, regular parents' evenings and PTA.

Sports. Gymnastics, netball, pop lacrosse, rounders, tag rugby, tennis, short tennis, swimming, football, and athletics.

Activities. These include tennis, art, drama, gymnastics, judo, science, cookery, swimming, football and dance.

Musical concerts and productions are regularly held. Three annual residential trips in Years 4–6, and regular visits from Nursery to Year 6 take place.

Special needs. Qualified Learning Support teacher.

Charitable status. St Swithun's School Winchester is a Registered Charity, number 307335.

Salisbury Cathedral School

1 The Close, Salisbury, Wilts SP1 2EQ

Tel: 01722 555300
email: admissions@salisburycathedralschool.com
website: www.salisburycathedralschool.com
Twitter: @salisburycathsc
Facebook: @Salisbury-Cathedral-School
Instagram: @salisburycathedralschool
LinkedIn: /company/salisbury-cathedral-school

Founded in 1091. Co-educational Day and Boarding Preparatory, Pre-Preparatory and Choir School.

Chairman of Governors: Mrs J Monro-Higgs

Head Master: **Clive Marriott**

Age Range. 3–13.

Number of Pupils. Day pupils: 180; Boarders: 40.

Fees per term (2021–2022). Pre-Prep: £3,075 (Reception, Years 1 & 2), £4,610 (Year 3). Preparatory School: £5,540 (day), £8,140 (boarding).

'Warm', 'caring', 'happy' – these are the three most popular words used by parents to describe Salisbury Cathedral School. Our unique setting, adjacent to one of England's finest cathedrals, helps to cultivate a strong spiritual awareness and Christian values underpin everything that we do.

Our wonderful 21st century school is based in the 800 year old Bishops Palace within Salisbury Cathedral's grounds.

We believe a child's self-esteem is vital to their success. At SCS, we foster an unpressured environment where pupils are encouraged and congratulated every step of the way, celebrating their achievements and promoting a strong sense of self-worth. Our focus on the individual child means that all staff play a role in discovering strengths and areas that need guidance and support.

This approach works. Our academic results are impressive and consistently out-perform competing schools but, more than this, the children who leave us are confident, self-assured, well-rounded and comfortable in their own skins.

Facilities include: over 20 acres of beautiful grounds, an all-weather sports pitch, swimming pool, outstanding music facilities, a variety of performance spaces, specialist science laboratory, art, design technology and computer suites and extensive playground facilities.

Talented sports staff coach all the major team sports and every child plays in regular fixtures.

There are many after-school clubs open to all children in the Preparatory School. (Quality wrap-around school care is available for children in the Pre-Prep). The boarding house staff operate an "open door" policy to parents, organise many outings and activities and have achieved an enviable reputation for running a truly happy and caring boarding house.

For more information and/or to arrange a visit to the school, please telephone Jojo Orange, Registrar on 01722 555300 or visit our website.

Charitable status. Salisbury Cathedral School is a Registered Charity, number 309485. It exists to provide high quality education for children.

Sandroyd School

Rushmore Park, Tollard Royal, Salisbury, Wiltshire SP5 5QD

Tel: 01725 530124
email: admissions@sandroyd.com
website: www.sandroyd.org
Twitter: @SandroydSchool
Facebook: @sandroydschool
Instagram: @sandroydschool
LinkedIn: /company/sandroyd-school

Chairman of Governors: R G L Thomas, MRICS, FAAV

Headmaster: **A B Speers**, BSc, MEd

Age Range. 2–13 co-educational.

Number of Pupils. 140 boarders, 40 day, plus 50 in Pre-Prep, The Walled Garden.

Fees per term (2021–2022). Boarding: £9,260 (Years 4–8), £7,330 (Year 3), Day: £7,650 (Years 4–6), £5,690 (Year 3). Pre-Prep: £3,190, Nursery: £25 (per morning), £36 (all day including lunch).

Sandroyd has been a leading boarding Prep school since 1888 and offers an exceptional education in both the Walled Garden Pre-Prep (for children aged 2–7), and in the Prep School (for children aged 7–13).

It is a wonderfully unique family school, set in an idyllic environment, that 'prepares' children in the very broadest sense – offering academic excellence, and so much more. Sandroyd nurtures a child's confidence and self-esteem whilst encouraging each individual pupil to fulfil all aspects of their potential: academic, artistic, cultural, sporting and social.

Sandroyd is unequivocally proud of being a small school and the benefits it offers to all of its pupils. The school's size creates a wonderfully unique family atmosphere, in both the classroom and the boarding house, allowing staff to properly focus on the individual needs of each child at every stage of their education. Indeed, teachers and pastoral staff meet every morning to discuss how to best support each pupil that day.

Sandroyd offers an academically rich and rigorous education that goes far beyond preparing pupils to just pass entrance exams to the country's leading senior schools.

Whilst one in four pupils left with a scholarship to their Senior School, the School is focused on inspiring interests and developing talents – both inside and beyond the classroom – from music, dance and drama to a variety of sports which pupils play every day. Pupils are also encouraged to develop the qualities and skills they will need for life beyond their school days through the newly launched 'Strive' programme. This is an integral part of every child's curriculum, consisting of over 50 different activities delivered by specialists, as part of daily 'Strive' sessions.

Sarum Hall School

15 Eton Avenue, London NW3 3EL

Tel:	020 7794 2261
email:	admissions@sarumhallschool.co.uk
website:	www.sarumhallschool.co.uk
Twitter:	@SarumHall
Instagram:	@sarumhallschool

The School, which has a Christian (Church of England) foundation, is an educational trust with a Board of Governors.

Chairman of Governors: Dr C Sayer

Headmistress: Miss Victoria Savage, BMus Hons Edinburgh, PG Dip Royal Academy of Music, PGCE Buckingham

Age Range. 3–11.
Number of Pupils. 185 Day Girls.
Fees per term (2021–2022). £5,155–£5,575.

Founded in 1929, the school has, since 1995, been housed in new purpose-built premises which provide excellent, spacious facilities, including a large playground, gym, dining room and specialist art, IT, music and science rooms, in addition to a French room, changing room, multi-purpose room and individual music teaching rooms. The school has a purpose built Food Studio to support Food Technology teaching, as well as cross-curricular links and the opportunity to foster relevant and practical skills across the wider curriculum.

Girls are prepared for senior London day schools and for 11+ Common Entrance. Girls entering at age 3 are not assessed, but those joining from Year 1 are tested in English and Maths. The school is ambitious for its girls and believes that in a caring, supportive and imaginative environment, every girl can achieve her full potential. The pupils are encouraged to develop a set of transferable life skills that they can apply to a variety of scenarios, and develop as individuals with a sense of purpose in the school community and beyond. The school has a well-established record of scholarship and examination success; destination schools include Channing, City of London School for Girls, Downe House, Francis Holland, Godolphin & Latymer, Highgate, Mill Hill Foundation, North London Collegiate, Queen's College, Queen's Gate, Queenswood, South Hampstead High School, St Helen's, St Marylebone School for Girls, St Paul's Girls and Wycombe Abbey.

A broad curriculum is followed and a major investment in IT ensures that each girl has access to the latest technology, which expands and enriches their educational provision. French is taught from Reception and Mandarin from Year 4, and a comprehensive games programme, which primarily takes place on site, ensures that girls have the opportunity to experience a variety of sports. We believe in offering a broad and balanced curriculum, therefore there is a strong emphasis on music, art, design and drama. Woodwind, violin, piano, cello and singing are offered. There are also two choirs, an orchestra and ensemble groups. Other extra-curricular activities include theory of music, fencing, junior and senior football, gardening, modern art, nature, netball, tennis, ICT, yoga, philosophy, photography, drama, craft, chess, cooking, classical civilisations, board games, dance and performance.

Charitable status. Sarum Hall School is a Registered Charity, number 312721. Its purpose is education.

Seaford College Prep School
Wilberforce House

Lavington Park, Petworth, West Sussex GU28 0NB

Tel:	01798 867893
email:	wilberforce@seaford.org
	hrichardson@seaford.org
website:	www.seaford.org
Twitter:	@seafordcollege
Facebook:	@seafordcollege
Instagram:	@seafordcollege
LinkedIn:	/company/seafordcollege

Chairman of Governors: R Venables Kyrke

Head of Prep School: **Mr Alastair Brown**, BEd

Age Range. 5–13 Co-educational.
Number of Pupils. 241.
Fees per term (2021–2022). Day £3,665–£5,595; Weekly boarding: £7,635 (Year 6), £8,085 (Years 7 and 8).

Seaford College Prep School (Wilberforce House) is an integral part of Seaford College, having the same board of governors, but with its own buildings, playground and corporate organisation. There is very close cooperation between the two schools and there are many shared facilities such as the games fields, a new Sports Centre, the Music School, Science Department, and Art and Design Department. Wilberforce House is named after Samuel Wilberforce, the son of the anti-slavery campaigner William Wilberforce. Samuel is buried in the grounds of the School's chapel. The School is set in a magnificent 400-acre site adjacent to the South Downs National Park.

The Prep School educates boys and girls from the age of 5 and the vast majority of children continue their education at Seaford College until 16 or 18. The main entry points for the Prep School are at 7+ and 11+ although children are welcome to join the school at any age.

The school aims to nurture a love of learning through a broadly based curriculum and classroom activities are often complemented by day and residential visits. In Years 1–5, the majority of lessons are taught by form teachers with subjects such as Music, French, PE/Games and Design and Technology taught by specialist staff. Year 6 are form based for English, Maths, History and Geography with all other subjects taught by subject specialists. From Year 7 all subjects are taught by specialist staff, many of whom also teach in the Senior School. All classrooms are equipped with interactive whiteboards while a Special Educational Needs Coordinator oversees the school's learning support provision which further enhances learning and achievement. The majority of children complete most of their homework in school and the school day finishes at 5.20pm.

Boarding provision, from Year 6 upwards, is an important aspect of life in the school with the aim being to be as flexible as possible in order to meet parents' and pupils' needs as well as providing a warm and caring home-from-home atmosphere.

Pupils are able to benefit from the impressive range of games facilities on site, including the new Sports Centre, an AstroTurf hockey pitch, indoor swimming pool and a 9-hole golf course, with practice greens and driving range as well as the services of a golf professional. Expert coaching is provided in the main sports of football, rugby, hockey, cricket, netball, rounders, tennis, athletics and swimming. The school also has excellent facilities for music, art and design and technology.

The standard of pastoral care is high and the school has its own Chaplain who takes a weekly assembly. The Prep School aims to treat each pupil as an individual and to establish the firm foundations necessary for success in the Senior School and beyond. (*See Seaford College entry in HMC section.*)

Charitable status. Seaford College is a Registered Charity, number 277439.

Sevenoaks Preparatory School

Godden Green, Sevenoaks, Kent TN15 0JU

Tel:	01732 762336
email:	admin@theprep.org.uk
website:	www.theprep.org.uk
Twitter:	@Sevenoaksprep
Facebook:	@sevenoaksprep
Instagram:	@sevenoaksprep

Chairman of Governors: Jan Berry

Headmaster: **Luke Harrison**, BA Hons, PGCE

Head of Pre-Prep: Helen Cook

Age Range. 2½ to 13.
Number of Children. 400 pupils.
Fees per annum (2021–2022). Reception £11,244, Years 1–2 £12,828, Years 3–8 £15,540. Nursery & Kindergarten: £385 per term for one session per week.

Founded in 1919, Sevenoaks Prep School stands on a spacious 25-acre site of playing fields and woodland bordering the 1,000-acre Knole Estate. We welcome girls and boys from 2½ to 13 years of age. Our small class sizes and family atmosphere enables us to build special relationships with the children and their parents.

The curriculum is tailored to the needs of the pupils and their future aspirations. Whilst due regard is paid to the National Curriculum, our children are taught to the highest standard achievable by the individual. To this end, our teachers enhance their Programmes of Study to ensure that every pupil is motivated, challenged and prepared for 11+ or 13+ entry tests to local grammar schools or via Common Entrance examinations and scholarships to independent schools. Our academic achievements are consistently high and our pupils compete successfully for academic, sport, music and other scholarships.

Throughout the school all classes regularly participate in a programme of visits, workshops and field trips to support their learning. Education at Sevenoaks Prep is for life not just the classroom – it is the balance of academic study and co-curricular activities that prepare the children for their future.

The school comprises the Pre-Prep (Nursery–Year 2), and the Prep School (Years 3–8).

Nursery and Kindergarten are staffed by teachers who are specially qualified in Early Years education, with a high teacher to pupil ratio. The education provided is specifically designed to match each child's needs, so that child-initiated play and teacher-directed activities are thoughtfully planned and carefully balanced.

Full-time education starts in the Reception class in Pre-Prep and from this point, through Years 1 and 2, class teachers and their assistants provide a rich and stimulating environment where curiosity and enthusiasm to learn are fostered.

On entering the Prep school in Year 3, class teaching is continued for core subjects (with specialist teaching for drama, languages, music, ICT, PE and games). By the age of ten, our pupils are taught by specialist teachers in all subjects whilst each class continues to have a form teacher who monitors their progress. Years 7 and 8 are the secondary school years and this is reflected in the teaching and levels of responsibility offered to the children. At Sevenoaks Prep they are at the top of the school and are provided with leadership opportunities and responsibilities. Heads of our destination schools say that children from Sevenoaks Prep enter Year 9 as rounded individuals, confident both academically and socially.

Facilities include a large multi-purpose sports hall, a state-of-the-art drama and music suite, 'Forest School' outdoor education area, and modern Pre-Prep classrooms and hall. A new Centenary Centre housing science, art, humanities, ICT and a library opened in 2020. The location provides a useful and natural extension to the teaching facilities and a vast playground, where children are trusted and encouraged to explore safely.

The school provides after-school care until 6.00pm each evening and the extra-curricular activities are extensive. The school is supported by an active Social Events Committee who regularly arrange social events for parents to meet each other and to raise money for the school.

Sherborne Preparatory School

Acreman Street, Sherborne, Dorset DT9 3NY

Tel: 01935 812097
email: admissions@sherborneprep.org
website: www.sherborneprep.org
Twitter: @Sherborneprep
Facebook: @sherborneprepschool
LinkedIn: /sherborne-preparatory-school

Chair of Governors: Lieutenant General David Leakey
    CMG, CVO, CBE

CEO Sherborne Group: Dr Dominic Luckett

Head: **Mrs Natalie Bone**, BA Hons, PGCE

Age Range. 3–13.

Number of Boys and Girls. 194

Fees per term (2021–2022). Boarders: £8,250–£8,600. Day: Nursery £3,020; Pre-Prep £3,020; Prep: £4,675 (Year 3), £5,710 (Years 4–8). Generous discounts available for Forces families and a range of scholarships available from Year 3 upwards (scholarship assessments are held at the beginning of the Spring term each year). Bursaries available on a means-tested basis.

Sherborne Prep School aims to foster independent learning through the teaching of a broader enquiry-based curriculum with an emphasis on study and thinking skills, designed to meet the individual learning styles of the pupils.

The school, part of the Sherborne School Group, is a co-educational day and boarding school for children aged 3–13 years. Founded in 1858, it is set in twelve acres of attractive grounds and gardens in the centre of Sherborne and is well served by road and rail links. On 1st April 2021 Sherborne Prep merged with Sherborne School and now sits with Sherborne School and Sherborne International under the same governance. It also enjoys a long and close association with its neighbour, Sherborne Girls.

The Prep School (Years 3–8) offers a broad education, leading to Common Entrance and Scholarship examinations in the penultimate and final year groups. Despite being non-selective ourselves, a large proportion of pupils gain scholarships or awards to leading independent schools, including Sherborne School, Sherborne Girls, Blundell's, Bryanston, Canford, Charterhouse, Cheltenham Ladies' College, Clayesmore, Downside, Eton, Godolphin, King's Bruton, King's College Taunton, King's School Canterbury, Leweston, Marlborough, Milton Abbey, Monkton Combe, Queen's College Taunton, Radley, Rugby, Taunton and Winchester.

We encourage every child to embrace all the wonderful opportunities on offer and to discover and develop his or her talents and interests to the full. Our children grow to question and reason, so that they are fully prepared to embrace opportunity and fulfil their potential as resilient and responsible members of the community. Outdoor learning is integral within the curriculum, offering a great opportunity for pupils to develop curiosity, confidence and independence as well as enriching their knowledge of the natural environment. Sherborne Prep offers a full Saturday morning programme of various sporting, artistic, musical and cultural activities, including introductory language classes and informative lectures. At the end of each school day, the pupils can choose to attend an imaginative after-school enrichment and academic support programme until 6.00pm.

The Pre-Prep Department is housed in a fully-equipped and purpose-built classroom building, with experienced and well-qualified staff, providing an excellent ratio of teachers to children. The children enjoy weekly swimming lessons and a varied programme of after-school activities.

The School's ISI report in December 2015 stated The Prep as being 'outstanding' in all areas and praised the School for its success in developing independent learning and positive attitudes to work and study in both boarding and day pupils.

Charitable status. Sherborne Preparatory School is a Registered Charity, number 1081228. It exists to provide an all-round education for children.

Sompting Abbotts

Church Lane, Sompting, West Sussex BN15 0AZ

Tel: 01903 235960
email: office@somptingabbotts.com
website: www.somptingabbotts.com
Facebook: @somptingabbotts

Principal: Mrs P M Sinclair

Headmaster: **S J Douch**, MA

Bursar: D A Sinclair

Age Range. 2–13 Co-educational.

Number of Pupils. 120.

Fees per term (2021–2022). Day £3,350–£4,300 (including lunches).

The only independent, family-run school in the area!

Set in a magnificent site on the edge of the South Downs, Sompting Abbotts overlooks the English Channel with views towards Beachy Head and the Isle of Wight. The imposing Victorian house has some 30 acres of sports fields, woodlands, gardens and activity areas.

The aim of the school is to provide a well-balanced education in a caring environment, recognising and developing the individual needs of each child, so that maximum potential academic achievement may be gained. Within the community of the school an emphasis is laid on the cultivation of courtesy, self-discipline and respect for one another in order to engender a happy atmosphere.

The school has a vibrant Pre-Preparatory Department, which includes lively Early Years classes. In the Preparatory Department, well-equipped Science Laboratory and Computer Room are enjoyed by all ages. The Art and Drama departments offer wide scope for creativity, and peripatetic teachers provide tuition for a range of musical instruments. Free wraparound care is provided from 8.00am to 6.00pm.

Book your child in for a Taster Day to see what life is like at our wonderful school!

Spratton Hall

Smith Street, Spratton, Northampton NN6 8HP

Tel: 01604 847292
email: office@sprattonhall.com
website: www.sprattonhall.com
Twitter: @SprattonHall
Facebook: @sprattonhallschool
Instagram: @sprattonhall
LinkedIn: /company/spratton-hall-school

Chairman: Mr James Coley

Head Master: Mr Simon Clarke, BA

Deputy Head Master: Mr Robert Dow, BA Hons, PGCE

Age Range. 4–13 Co-educational.

Number of Pupils. 350+.

Fees per term (2021–2022). Prep £4,925–£5,425, Pre-Prep £3,575. Fees include wraparound care, most extra-curricular activities, stationery, lunch and all academic books.

Spratton Hall embodies the values of a traditional prep school, as academic achievement is always encouraged and rewarded. However, our motto is that we are 'more than just a school' and as such, we help children develop their strengths wherever they lie, be they in Sport, Drama, Art, STEM, or Music.

Recently recognised by *The Week* as being a "great all-round school", we have 50 acres of first-rate facilities, including: a purpose-built theatre, art studios, science labs, an indoor sports dome, floodlit AstroTurf and multiple sports courts, tracks, pitches and nets. Combined with our 65 extra-curricular activities, we definitely have something to delight and inspire every child.

In our Pre-prep, determination and kindness are woven into all areas of the curriculum, and children receive daily individual support from highly-experienced Early Years teachers. To complement their classroom-based learning, they also enjoy regular PE, Dance, Music, Art, Drama and Forest School sessions.

In 2021 the Pre-Prep School was proud to be shortlisted for 'Pre-Prep School of the Year'; following on from the Prep School which was shortlisted for 'Prep School of the Year' in 2020. With a 100% pass rate at Common Entrance and multiple annual scholarships to top public schools, the rigorous academic curriculum is offset with fun inter-house competitions, school trips and our exceptional pastoral care.

Our dedicated Head of Pastoral Care oversees the wellbeing and welfare of all pupils, and a well-resourced learning support team are always on hand to help children overcome any academic obstacles they may meet. Meanwhile parents are supported with extended school days, free wraparound care, and local minibus routes.

To experience a typical school day, the School holds Open Mornings in April and October. Alternatively, personal, safe school tours with the Head Master can be booked at www.sprattonhall.com. When you visit the website, you can also order a prospectus, or take a 360° virtual tour of our facilities.

Charitable status. Spratton Hall is a Registered Charity, number 309925. It exists to provide education for boys and girls.

Spring Grove School

Harville Road, Wye, nr Ashford, Kent TN25 5EZ

Tel: 01233 812337
email: office@springgroveschool.co.uk
website: www.springgroveschool.co.uk
Twitter: @SG_School
Facebook: @Spring-Grove-School-Wye
Instagram: @springgroveschool

Chair of Governors: Mrs Dawne Sweetland

Head: Mrs Therésa Jaggard, BA Hons, Cert Ed, NPQH
tjaggard@springgroveschool.co.uk

Bursar: Mrs Sarah Peirce
bursar@springgroveschool.co.uk

Head of Marketing and Admissions: Mrs Nicky Lee-Browne
admissions@springgroveschool.co.uk

Age Range. 2–11 Co-educational.

Number of Pupils. 216

Fees per term (2021–2022). £2,170–£4,430.

Spring Grove is a co-educational Day Preparatory School for children aged 2 to 11, widely known for its family ethos and feel. It is located in a stunning rural location just outside the village of Wye, between Ashford and Canterbury. The school offers a first-class education, preparing children for both grammar and senior independent school entry.

The facilities include an award-winning Nursery, School Hall, Art Room, Science Room, Music Room, well-equipped Classrooms, and Multi-Use Games Area. The grounds contain the main school buildings and 14 acres of playing fields.

Spring Grove has a strong tradition of academic excellence, exceptionally lively music, drama and art departments, accredited Forest School, and children who are inspired with a sense of wonder about the world. Emphasis is placed on innovative and creative teaching in a caring yet well-structured atmosphere with close contact maintained between parents and teachers. Numerous scholarships to senior independent schools have been awarded in the past two years.

The curriculum includes Music, Drama, Art, Dance, Forest School, PE and extracurricular activities. Athletics, Cricket/Kwik Cricket, Cross-Country, Football, Hockey, Netball, Tennis and Rugby are the principal games.

Enquiries concerning places and admissions should be made to the Registrar (email: admissions@springgrove school.co.uk, tel: 01233 812337).

Charitable status. Spring Grove School 2003 is a Registered Charity, number 1099823.

Staines Preparatory School

3 Gresham Road, Staines-upon-Thames, Surrey TW18 2BT

Tel: 01784 450909
email: admissions@stainesprep.co.uk
website: www.stainesprep.co.uk
Twitter: @StainesPrep
Facebook: @StainesPrepSchool
Instagram: @stainesprep

Staines Preparatory School has been 'Educating today's children for the Challenges of Tomorrow' for over 85 years and is a happy and welcoming non-selective school that prides itself on creating a genuine family atmosphere alongside a first rate education.

Chairman of Governors: Mr M Hall

Headmistress: **Ms Samantha Sawyer**, BEd Hons, MEd, NPQH

School Business Manager: Mrs R McLennan, BA Hons, Assoc CIPD

Age Range. 3–11 Co-educational.

Number of Pupils. 305: 160 Boys, 145 Girls.

Fees per annum (2021–2022). £10,520–£12,660.

At Staines Prep, our ethos of 'Educating today's children for the Challenges of Tomorrow' is more than our excellent academics. We will be with you and your child every step of the way throughout their first stage of education.

Our Staines Prep Way values, Growth Mindset approach and wellbeing initiatives define a culture of community and respect and your child will learn the importance of commitment to successful learning, develop discipline, self-esteem and a sense of responsibility. We are proud of how successful our pupils subsequently are in senior school entrance and scholarship exams

We were delighted to be shortlisted for Pre-Prep School of the Year 2021 in the Independent School Awards having been shortlisted for Prep School in 2020. This followed our ISI inspection in December 2019 where we were found to be excellent in all areas.

We offer state-of-the-art teaching, sporting, music and performance facilities to all of our pupils with our Upper School pupils also benefitting from dedicated senior school standard Science lab and Art Design Technology suites. Our new Digital learning suite not only caters for a full class to access their own desktop, it includes a dedicated space with green screen technology and lighting effects for multimedia learning and a flexible and larger space to enable coding with robotics and roamers and group work with iPads and laptops.

Our environmental area, The Sanctuary, allows the children to bring science to life and learn to safely explore the great outdoors. We use Forest School principles to teach skills that can be used in the classroom and beyond, encouraging team work, responsibility and communication as well as building self-esteem and independence. The children are not limited in what they can do but instead are taught how to access and manage the risks in nature. Our new Outdoor Classroom provides additional space for pupils to learn.

We understand how hard our parents work and we aim to support them by providing wraparound care from 7.30am until 6.00pm. We are less than 5 minutes' walk from Staines railway station and operate a school minibus service from the surrounding areas, making pick-up and drop-off that little bit easier.

To come and experience the school first hand, you can arrange a private tour to fit in around your commitments or visit us at one of our popular Open Events which run throughout the year. Details of these can be found on our website www.stainesprep.co.uk.

Stamford Junior School

Kettering Rd, Stamford, Lincolnshire PE9 2LR

Tel: 01780 484400
email: headjs@ses.lincs.sch.uk
website: www.stamfordschools.org.uk
Twitter: @SJS_Head
Facebook: @stamfordendowedschools
Instagram: @StamfordSchools

Stamford Junior School, along with Stamford High School (girls) and Stamford School (boys), is one of three schools in the historic market town of Stamford comprising the Stamford Endowed Schools. The schools are under a single Governing Body and overall management and leadership of the Principal and allow continuity of education for boys and girls from 2 to 18, including boarding from age 8. Each school has its own Head and staff.

Principal: William Phelan, MBA

Headteacher: **Matthew O'Reilly**

Chairman of Governors: Nicholas Rudd-Jones

Bursar and Clerk to the Governing Body: Dean White

Age Range. 2–11.

Number of Children. 350.

Fees per annum (2021–2022). Day: Reception £10,900, Years 1–2 £11,570, Years 3–6 £13,870; Boarding: 7 Day £24,100, 5 Day £21,725, 3 day £19,070.

The Junior School educates boys and girls up to the age of 11 (including boarders from age 8), when boys move on to Stamford School and girls to Stamford High School. Admission from the Junior School to the two senior schools is based on progress and without further entrance testing.

The Junior School occupies its own spacious grounds, bordering the River Welland, overlooking the sports fields and open countryside, the boarding houses, the sports hall, floodlit artificial hockey pitch and the swimming pool on the same site. It is on the south-west outskirts of Stamford within easy reach of the A1.

Entry to the School is according to registration at 4+ and assessment.

The lively and broad curriculum offers an ILIC-based (Independent Learning and Intellectual Curiosity) foundation to all academic, creative, and sporting subjects.

Lessons are stimulating, energetic, and fully engaging so that the natural curiosity of our pupils can flourish. Extensive facilities, sporting opportunities, and the wide-ranging co-curricular programme promote the rounded development that we believe is essential for our children.

In addition to teaching staff, the Junior School has a number of specialist teachers in physical education, swimming, art, music, and speech and drama, with a number of visiting teachers offering a variety of sports, dance and modern foreign languages.

There is a purpose-built nursery in the grounds of the school – Stamford Nursery School – offering first-class care and early learning for children aged 2–4. Pupils then head to the adjacent Early Years Reception Classes.

Boarding. The co-educational Boarding House (St Michael's) is run in a homely, family style. Boys and girls are accepted as full or weekly boarders from the age of 8. Occasional or flexi-boarding is accommodated where possible and according to family need. A full programme of activities takes place at weekends so that boarders enjoy a rich and varied week.

Stockport Grammar Junior School

Buxton Road, Stockport, Cheshire SK2 7AF

Tel:	0161 419 2405
email:	sgjs@stockportgrammar.co.uk
website:	www.stockportgrammar.co.uk
Twitter:	@stockportgs
Facebook:	@stockportgrammar

Chairman of Governors: Mr Christopher Dunn, MA

Headmaster: **Mr Matthew Copping**, BEd, NPQH, FRSA, NPQEL

Age Range. 3–11.

Number of Pupils. 356: 178 boys, 178 girls.

Fees per term (2021–2022). £3,120, plus lunch. Nursery £2,952, plus lunch.

Entry is mainly at 3+ and 4+ following assessment, with occasional places available at other ages. Stockport Grammar Junior School is a happy school, where children are encouraged to develop their strengths. A broad curriculum is taught and academic standards are high. There are specialist facilities and teaching in Science, ICT, PE and Games, Swimming, Music, Art and Design Technology. A large number of pupils learn to play a musical instrument and tuition is available for many orchestral instruments. French and Spanish are taught throughout. All children have swimming lessons in the School's pool. Children can choose to join in the numerous lunchtime and after-school clubs and activities.

The Junior School and the Senior School share the same site. The vast majority of pupils move into the Senior School at 11, having passed the Entrance Examination. (*See also Stockport Grammar School entry in HMC section.*)

Hockey, netball, football, rounders, cricket and athletics are the main sports. Swimming, tennis, cross-country, rugby, archery, canoeing and fencing are also offered. There is a full range of sporting fixtures and regular music and drama

productions. All Junior pupils have the opportunity to participate in residential visits, which include outdoor pursuits.

Before- and after-school care is available and holiday play schemes are run during the school holidays. A Breakfast Club is available from 7.30am each day.

Facilities are excellent. In addition to specialist teaching rooms, which include a computer room and a science room, the Junior School has its own large all-weather surface along with a sports hall and extensive playing fields.

Charitable status. Stockport Grammar School is a Registered Charity, number 1120199. It exists to advance education by the provision and conduct, in or near Stockport, of a school for boys and girls.

Stormont

The Causeway, Potters Bar, Herts EN6 5HA

Tel:	01707 654037
email:	admin@stormontschool.org
website:	www.stormontschool.org
Twitter:	@StormontSchool
Facebook:	@StormontSchool
Instagram:	@stormontschool

The school is administered by a Board of Governors.

Chairman of Board of Governors: Mr Andrew Newland

Headteacher: **Miss Louise Martin**

Age Range. 4–11.

Number of Pupils. 170 Day Girls.

Fees per term (2021–2022). £4,225–£4,480 (including lunch). There are no compulsory extras.

The School was founded in 1944 and has occupied its attractive Victorian House since then. There is a spacious, bright, purpose-built Pre-Prep building where the classrooms flow from a central play and study area, which adjoins the purpose built outdoor play area for EYFS, Year 1 and 2. Prep girls move to the main house in Year 3 and move around each area on their timetable. The well equipped Art, Pottery, Design Technology, Science and French rooms are housed in The Courtyard and provide inspirational learning areas for all the girls. The Millennium Building houses our Drama and Music Classroom and separate studios on the ground floor and our ICT Suite on the first floor. Within this building music is taught on the curriculum and individual music lessons are taught in the designated music studios by our peripatetic music teachers. The Johnston Sports Hall, with its own changing rooms, provides a fabulous space for gymnastics and a wide variety of team sports including netball, which take place whatever the weather. The school has outdoor tennis courts that double up as netball courts, a two-acre playing field and use of a swimming pool at Queenswood School.

The large and spacious Pearson Hall enables us to have whole school assemblies, class assemblies for parents to watch, concerts and various whole school activities or larger events. The stage is one that can be adapted depending on the occasion and some after school clubs also take place here.

Our Library has been relocated to the Dyson Room, within its high-vaulted ceiling and decorative woodwork panelling. Spaces for study, discussion or reading a good book have been created and new furniture installed.

Our well-qualified, specialist teachers and experienced staff prepare the girls for entry to a wide range of both independent and maintained senior schools at the age of eleven, many of whom gain Scholarships at their chosen school.

Charitable status. Stormont School is a Registered Charity, number 311079. It exists to establish and carry on as a school where children receive a sound education.

Stover Preparatory School

Newton Abbot, Devon TQ12 6QG

Tel:	01626 354505
email:	schooloffice@stover.co.uk
website:	www.stover.co.uk
Twitter:	@StoverSchool
Facebook:	@StoverSchool
Instagram:	@StoverSchool

Chairman of Governors: Mr S Killick, ND, ARB

Head: Mr Ben Noble, BSc

Age Range. 3–11 Co-educational.

Number of Pupils. 142.

Fees per term (2021–2022). Preparatory School: Day: Reception £2,820, Years 1–3 £3,030, Years 4–6 £3,770. Weekly Boarding: Years 4–6 £6,580. Full Boarding: Years 4–6 £7,600.

Stover Preparatory School enjoys a beautiful rural setting on the edge of Dartmoor National Park, close to the South Devon coast. Set in 64 acres there is ample space for pupils of all ages to experience the great outdoors, be that through play, nature walks, sport, orienteering, bushcraft, learning in our outdoor classroom or researching the history of our fine old buildings. Stover Preparatory School shares its fine site with Stover Senior School, making transfer at aged 11 years a smooth process for our pupils.

We pride ourselves on our warm, welcoming atmosphere where each individual is nurtured and encouraged to reach their full potential. Visitors frequently comment on the positive, happy feeling they experience upon entering the school. Teachers are aware of pupils' individual needs and provide support in an approachable and friendly manner.

We offer a broad, balanced curriculum with high academic standards, complemented by a wide range of extra-curricular activities. Spanish begins in Reception and French is also introduced at Year 3. Languages, PE and music are taught by specialist teachers across the school. All other subjects are taught by the class teacher to enable cross-curricular links to thrive. Underpinning everything we do is our firm belief in Research Based Learning, where pupils develop their inquiry skills, taking ownership of their learning from a young age. Sport and the Performing Arts play a vital role in each child's development. We have a full fixture list for our U9 and U11 teams as well as involvement with the local Schools' Sports Partnership. Our regular school performances and concerts are a highlight of the calendar. More than 80% of our Prep School pupils choose to participate in the Prep School Choir. In addition, we offer a Pre-Prep Choir and a Chamber Choir for talented pupils in Years 5 and 6. Residential and day trips into our beautiful local environment further complement the curriculum.

Facilities include an extensive Outdoor Classroom, Sports Fields, Tennis Courts, Art room, Music room, Multi-Purpose Hall, Library and ICT suite.

Flexi, weekly and full boarding are available from the age of 8 years. Scholarships are offered at 11+. The majority of our pupils move on to Stover Senior School.

See also Stover School senior entry in The Society of Heads section.

Charitable status. Stover School Association is a Registered Charity, number 306712.

Streatham & Clapham Prep School GDST

Wavertree Road, London SW2 3SR

Tel:	020 8674 6912
email:	prep@schs.gdst.net
website:	www.schs.gdst.net
Twitter:	@SCPSgdst
	@SCHSgdst
Facebook:	@SCPSgdst

Motto: *ad sapientiam sine metu*

Chairman of Local Governors: Mrs F Smith, BA, PGCE

Head: T Mylne, BA, PGCE

Age Range. Girls 3–11.

Number of Pupils. 240.

Fees per term (2021–2022). Prep School £4,724, Nursery (after EYS grant contribution), Full-time from £2,103.

Streatham & Clapham Prep School is a division of Streatham & Clapham High School GDST (*see entry in the HMC section*), situated on its own extensive campus in Streatham Hill, within a mile of the Senior School. The School provides a specialist academic curriculum as part of a liberal and challenging educational experience for its girls within a caring culture of warm relationships and diversity, all the while nurturing their personal development and confidence. Its facilities include a full-size gymnasium, all-weather pitch, state-of-the-art outdoor learning and play areas and specialist drama, music, IT and art and design rooms. Admission to the school is by selective assessment, with informal assessment of pupils for Nursery, Reception, Year 1 and Year 2, and an entrance examination for Year 3 candidates. Places in other year groups are occasionally available.

The school's distinctive features.

1. Its suffragist heritage: as a school where Millicent Fawcett sent her daughter and as a member of the GDST family of schools, the school is a pioneer in, and the shaper of, girls' education;

2. Its curricular specialisation from an early age;

3. Its trailblazing and innovative approach, supercharging its girls with life skills enabling them to embrace and instigate change;

4. Its family, not factory, environment, supporting individual families' needs; and

5. Its buzzy, diverse community, celebrating difference and drawing strength from all that is great about London.

Curriculum. The school's broad and varied curriculum benefits from leading specialist teachers in all areas. Girls enjoy distinctive and invigorating learning through programmes such as Philosophy for Children, the Learning Tree Programme, PE, Music, Art, Drama, Computer Science, Design & Technology, Mandarin, French and Latin.

Personal & Pastoral Development. Great emphasis is placed on nurturing well-balanced and considerate individuals, who are ready for the challenges of adolescent and adult life. Strong pastoral and House systems reinforce this ethos, as do lessons in philosophy, myriad opportunities to build resilience, and overseas residential trips.

Co-curricular Programme & Family Support. The school offers an extensive co-curricular programme with over 30 free clubs as well as other after-school activities, societies and events. Wraparound childcare is offered from 7.30am to 5.55pm, five days a week, during term-time. The school is conveniently located near major transport links and also offers eight minibus routes serving most of south London.

Stroud School
King Edward VI Preparatory School

Highwood House, Highwood Lane, Romsey, Hampshire SO51 9ZH

Tel:	01794 513231
email:	registrar@stroud-kes.org.uk
website:	www.stroud-kes.org.uk
Twitter:	@Stroud_School
Facebook:	@stroudschool

Chair of Governors: Mrs C Musker

Headmistress: Mrs Rebecca Smith, MBA

Deputy Head (*Pastoral*): Mr Jonty Stewart

Deputy Head (*Academic*): Mrs Sarah Mason-Campbell

Age Range. 3–13.
Number of Pupils. 325: 175 Boys, 150 Girls.
Fees per term (2021–2022). Upper School £6,159, Middle School £5,654, Pre-Preparatory £3,838, full-time Nursery £3,868 (without EYE funding).

Stroud is a co-educational day school for children aged 3 to 13 years. Pupils are prepared for entrance to Senior Independent or Grammar Schools.

The School stands on the outskirts of Romsey in its own grounds of 22 acres, which include playing fields, a full-sized sports hall, a heated outdoor swimming pool, tennis courts, riding arena, a new wellbeing centre, lawns and gardens and a brand new, purpose-built, KS2 building ready for pupils in September 2020. The main team games for boys are cricket, hockey, rugby and football, and for girls hockey, cricket and netball. Both boys and girls play tennis.

Music and drama play an important part in the life of the School. A wide variety of instruments is taught and children are encouraged to join the school orchestra. Each year there is a musical production and the Christmas Carol Service is held at the Romsey Abbey.

The Stroud School Association, run by the parents, holds many social activities and helps to raise money for amenities, but its main function is to generate goodwill.

The Study Preparatory School

Wilberforce House, Camp Road, Wimbledon Common, London SW19 4UN

Tel:	020 8947 6969
email:	admissions@thestudyprep.co.uk
website:	www.thestudyprep.co.uk
Twitter:	@thestudyprep
Facebook:	@thestudyprep

Chairman of Governors: Mr John Tucker

Head: Miss Vicky Ellis, BSc Hons, QTS, MA

Admissions: Ms Katie Salt

Age Range. 4–11.
Number of Girls. 320 (approximately).
Fees per term (2021–2022) £5,024.

The Study Preparatory School provides a happy and stimulating learning environment for girls from 4 to 11 on two very attractive and well-equipped sites adjacent to Wimbledon Common.

The girls enjoy a rich diversity of experiences, both in and out of the classroom. The school is renowned for its creative ethos, and has had Artsmark Gold status by Arts Council England since 2009. Each girl is encouraged to do her best academically, and excellent teaching standards encourage academic rigour and challenge. Music and sport are exceptionally strong, while drama, public speaking and a varied clubs programme play an important part. Guest speakers, fundraising events, workshops and school trips all help the children to understand important issues beyond the school gates. Good manners and consideration for others are encouraged at all times. Girls leave at 11+, very well prepared for the next stage of their education, with a zest for learning and many happy memories. Girls receive offers from leading day and boarding senior schools, many with academic or performance scholarships, with a total of 55 scholarships and awards offered in 2021.

Entry is by ballot at reception and by assessment thereafter. The Study has an assisted places scheme for girls aged 7+. For details contact Joint Educational Trust (JET) on 020 3217 1100.

Charitable status. The Study (Wimbledon) Ltd is a Registered Charity, number 271012. It exists to provide education for girls from 4 to 11.

Summer Fields

Mayfield Road, Oxford OX2 7EN

Tel: 01865 459204
email: admissions@summerfields.com
website: www.summerfields.com
Twitter: @SFSOxford
Facebook: @Summer-Fields-Oxford
Instagram: @summerfieldsoxford
LinkedIn: /Summer-Fields-Oxford

Chairman of Governors: A E Reekes, MA, FRSA

Headmaster: **David Faber**, MA Oxon

Age Range. 4–13.

Number of Boys. Prep: 163 boarders, 90 day; Pre-Prep: 72.

Fees per term (2021–2022). Prep: £10,945 Boarding, £7,628 Day. Pre-Prep: £4,326 Reception, £4,866 Years 1 & 2, £5,624 Year 3.

Set in 72 acres of delightful grounds which lead down to the River Cherwell and yet only a few miles from the city centre, Summer Fields is often known as Oxford's *Secret Garden*.

The School has always had a strong academic reputation with Summerfieldians regularly securing scholarships, awards and exhibitions to top independent schools including Eton, Harrow, Radley and Winchester. Each year, boys pass Common Entrance to a wide variety of top public schools.

Huge emphasis is placed on providing the highest standards of pastoral care. Each boy has a personal tutor, who is responsible for his academic progress and social welfare and will be in regular contact with the boy's parents. The boarders live in Lodges within the school grounds and are looked after by an experienced and dedicated husband and wife team of Lodgeparents. An exciting programme of Lodge refurbishment is currently underway, providing exceptionally comfortable and homely boarding accommodation. Around two-thirds of the staff live on site, making a significant contribution to school life both in and out of the classroom.

The Choir regularly sing Evensong in Oxford Colleges and tour abroad. At least one Drama production takes place every term in the Macmillan Theatre. Every summer an Art Exhibition of boys' work is held at the school.

The facilities are outstanding, including the recently refurbished chapel and the new Mark Shvidler Library, a wonderful new addition to the school's infrastructure. Outside in the grounds, a beautiful new tree house has recently been completed to enhance the outdoor learning provision throughout the school, but especially in the Pre-Prep. The Salata Pavilion includes purpose-built changing rooms for the boys and a large multi-functional space on the first floor. Within the school there is also a fine theatre, Art, Design & Technology, Music and ICT Centres and a magnificent Sports Hall, with squash and Eton fives courts, a shooting gallery and swimming pool. The extensive outdoor facilities include an astroturf and tennis courts and all-weather cricket nets, a nine-hole golf course, outdoor pool, adventure playground, the Plantation where the boys

camp, together with an outside classroom. A huge range of sports, activities and hobbies is on offer to the boys.

Summer Fields' Pre-Prep, opened in September 2018, offers an exceptional early education to boys aged 4–7.

Academic (for entry into Year 6 or 7) and Sport (for entry into Year 7 or 8) Scholarships and Bursaries are available up to a value of 100%. For further information or to arrange a visit, please contact Mrs Christine Berry, Tel: 01865 459204 or email: admissions@summerfields.com.

Charitable status. Summer Fields is a Registered Charity, number 309683.

Sunninghill Prep School

South Court, South Walks Road, Dorchester, Dorset DT1 1EB

Tel: 01305 262306
email: registrar@sunninghill.dorset.sch.uk
website: www.sunninghillprep.co.uk
Facebook: @SunninghillPrepSchool
Instagram: @sunninghillprep

Chair of Governors: Miss Jean Walker

Acting Head: **Mrs Nancy Sewed**, BSc Hons, PGCE, Dip SpLD, MA Ed

Age Range. 2 years 9 months – 13 years.
Number of Pupils. 160 (approximately).
Fees per term (2021–2022). £3,150–£5,555.

Sunninghill is a co-educational day school of approximately 160 children with single-form entry throughout the school from Nursery to Form 8. Classes are deliberately small so we can focus on the academic and personal development of the individual. This helps us fulfil our mission which is to find the unique brilliance of every child.

Founded in 1939, Sunninghill Prep became a Charitable Trust in 1969. It moved to its present site in January 1997 and has its own swimming pool, all-weather sports pitch, superb teaching facilities and extensive grounds. The surrounding local area and Jurassic coast is our extended playground.

In Form 6 children sit the ISEB 11+ in Maths, English and Science. Our bespoke Creative Curriculum then begins which takes children above and beyond Common Entrance. This helps facilitate entry to local Independent Senior Schools.

Over the years the school has attained many academic successes, but the broad curriculum also includes drama, art, craft, music and physical education. Friday Enrichments allow greater cross-curricular links for years 1–8, enhancing their learning further.

Team and individual sports are played with PE and Games taking place at least three times a week from years 3–8. These include hockey, netball, cricket and rounders for the girls, and hockey, rugby, football and cricket for the boys. In the summer term both boys and girls participate in athletics, swimming and tennis.

Out-of-school activities include academic clubs preparing for scholarships, such as the core subjects, humanities and art, plus debating, chess, creative arts, ballet, dance, LAMDA and various music clubs including choir and string quartet. We offer multi sports across a wide age group. Residential expeditions are a feature of the curriculum from Form 3 upwards and we are a member of the National Sailing Academy, with our own race team.

Sunninghill Prep prides itself on its nurturing, family ethos. The school's flourishing Parents' Association ensures that parents and staff all know each other and work together for the good of the children and the school.

The prospectus is available on request or downloadable from our website.

Charitable status. Sunninghill Preparatory School is a Registered Charity, number 1024774. It exists to provide education for boys and girls.

Sussex House

68 Cadogan Square, London SW1X 0EA

Tel: 020 7584 1741
email: schoolsecretary@sussexhouseschool.co.uk
website: www.sussexhouseschool.co.uk

Chairman of the Governors: John Crewe, Esq

Headmaster: Nicholas Kaye, MA Magdalene College Cambridge, ACP, Hon FCOT, FRSA, FRGS

Deputy Headmasters:

Martin Back, BA, PGCE Sussex (Pastoral)

Tony Chan, BA, LLB, Sydney, GradDipEd Wesley Institute Sydney (Academic)

Age Range. 8–13.
Number of Boys. 184.
Fees per term (2021–2022). £7,715.

Founded in 1952, Sussex House is situated in the heart of Chelsea in a fine Norman Shaw house in Cadogan Square. Its Gymnasium and Music School are housed in a converted chapel in Cadogan Street. The school is an independent charitable trust. At Common Entrance and Scholarship level it has achieved a record of consistently strong results to academically demanding schools. The school enjoys its own entirely independent character and the style is traditional yet imaginative.

There is a full-time teaching staff of 22. Creative subjects are given strong emphasis and throughout the school boys take Music and Art. Team sports take place at a nearby site and the school's football teams have an impressive record. Cricket is the main summer sport and there are opportunities for a variety of other sports, including tennis, swimming, athletics and golf. Sussex House is a centre of excellence for fencing and its international records are well known.

Cultural and creative activities play a major role, including theatrical productions in a West End theatre, a major annual exhibition of creative work featuring large-scale architectural models and an annual competition of poetry written by boys. There is a strong bias towards music and an ambitious programme of choral and orchestral concerts. A large number of pupils play musical instruments and there is an impressive record of music awards to senior

schools. The school provides a range of sporting and cultural trips.

The school has a Church of England affiliation. There is a school chaplain and weekly services are held in St Simon Zelotes Church, Chelsea. Boys of all religions and denominations are welcomed.

Charitable status. Sussex House is a Registered Charity, number 1035806. It exists to provide education for boys.

Sutton Valence Preparatory School

Church Road, Chart Sutton, Maidstone, Kent ME17 3RF

Tel: 01622 842117
email: enquiries@svprep.svs.org.uk
website: www.svs.org.uk
Twitter: @SVPS_News
Facebook: @SuttonValencePrepSchoolNews

Chair of Governors: Mrs G Swaine, BSc Hons, MEd

Head: Miss C M Corkran, MEd, BEd Hons Cantab

Deputy Head: Mr J Watkins, BSc Hons, PGCE Primary

Academic Deputy Head: Miss R Harrison, BEd Hons

Age Range. 2–11.
Number of Pupils. 300.
Fees per term (2021–2022). £3,325–£4,875. Lunch £275.

The values of our School community and the happiness of our children are central to everything we do. These provide pupils with a strong feeling of structure and security which enables them to work effectively.

At whichever point children join us they embark on their own journeys, each one different and each one with differing emphasis on the four areas we hold dear: Academic, Enrichment, Community and Leadership and Service.

By the time they leave us at the age of 11, it is our responsibility to have equipped the children during their formative years with the essentials of character to thrive in an increasingly competitive world. To put firmly in place the qualities which will make them clear thinking, lateral thinking, robust, hardworking, determined and yet kindly citizens, who will go on to influence many people in the coming years.

We have high expectations of ourselves and of our children, both inside and out of the classroom, and we have a long history of successful preparation of children for the next stage of their education, be that for our Senior School, the Kent grammars, or other schools.

None of this should come at the expense of childhood and what the School does so successfully is find that balance between delivering in terms of education, and yet doing so kindly and with many broad, interesting and high-quality opportunities. The School is very proud of its articulate and confident pupils who move on well-equipped to work things out for themselves, so crucial in an increasingly challenging world.

To achieve this we have dedicated Art, Science and ICT facilities and a new Library. Classes are small throughout the school. The 40 teaching staff are all well qualified and there is an extensive peripatetic staff for music. Special needs are addressed by the SENCO and three part-time teachers. The Kindergarten to Year 2 classes all have qualified classroom assistants.

The School is situated in 18 acres of countryside overlooking the Weald and includes a hard and grass play areas, heated outdoor swimming pool, four hard tennis courts, a Sports Hall, a 13-acre games field, a full-size Astroturf and a newly established 'forest school' area, all of which support our co-curricular programme.

A solid foundation in the core subjects of English, Mathematics, Science and ICT is supplemented by Languages, Music, Drama, Art, Design Technology and Sport which are all taught by specialist teaching staff. The co-curricular programme is wide and varied providing many opportunities for children to perform in drama productions and in concerts, occasionally in conjunction with the senior school. Children are prepared for our senior school, Sutton Valence, the local Grammar schools and other independent schools with an 11+ entry.

Cricket, football, hockey, netball, rugby and rounders are the major sports, with athletics, swimming and cross-country also being available. The proximity of the senior school, Sutton Valence, allows the children to benefit from their staffing and facilities, including the use of the Sports Hall, athletics track and the indoor swimming pool. After-school activities include chess club, art, 5-a-side football, gymnastics, drama, craft, croquet, science club, ballet and judo.

The school is a Christian foundation. Assemblies, for celebration, and the use of the local church are an important facet of our lives, with the school's Chaplain visiting regularly. The school provides a fulfilling education for all its children, a thriving network for its parents and a happy workplace for all who dedicate their lives to it.

Charitable status. The United Westminster and Grey Coat Foundation is a Registered Charity, number 1181012. It exists to provide education for boys and girls and provides valuable resources and support.

Swanbourne House
Part of The Stowe Group

Swanbourne, Milton Keynes, Buckinghamshire MK17 0HZ

Tel: 01296 720264
email: office@swanbourne.org
website: www.swanbourne.org
Twitter: @swanbournehouse
Facebook: @SwanbourneHouse
LinkedIn: /school/swanbournehouse

The School is a Charitable Trust, administered by a Board of Governors.

Chairman of Governors: Mr C Creedy-Smith

Head: **Mrs J Thorpe**

Age Range. 4–13.

Number of Pupils. Prep: 250 (40 boarders, mix of full, weekly and flexi).

Fees per term (2021–2022). Boarding: Full £8,904; Weekly £8,310; Day: Year 5–8 £6,487; Year 4 £5,500; Year 3 £5,000; Foundation–Year 2 £3,604–£3,752.

Established in 1920 and set within 55 acres of stunning Buckinghamshire countryside, Swanbourne House School is a Preparatory School with a difference. In January 2021, the school formed The Stowe Group with Stowe, giving pupils access to a combined site of over 800 acres with unrivalled educational and co-curricular facilities.

We aim to be a dynamic, diverse and forward thinking school offering an exemplary service in teaching and learning. Our pupils grow to understand the discipline of study as we ignite the fire for a lifelong love of learning, personal development and reflection. We aspire to develop well-rounded pupils, who rise to mental and physical challenge with optimism, open and enquiring minds, confidence and empathy. We teach children how to think and communicate responsibly and effectively and we give them the freedom and opportunity required to develop their capacity for independent, principled thought. Creativity is strongly encouraged in all areas of school life, not just in the expressive arts but across academics, art, computing, debating, DT and engineering, music and sport.

Enrichment opportunities abound at Swanbourne House. Pupils are able to choose from a broad range of inspiring and engaging clubs and activities, ranging in everything from sailing to ancient Greek lessons, fencing to fashion design, rugby tots to equestrianism (there's plenty of time for tree climbing and den building too!)

As a result of the breadth and depth of experience and learning at Swanbourne House, the number of scholarships our Year 8 children secure each year in academics, art, drama, DT, music and sport is very impressive indeed. Our Pre-Senior Baccalaureate results are consistently strong with very nearly all pupils securing their first choice of senior school. We tend to send the majority of our children to Stowe, Eton, Harrow, Cheltenham Ladies' College, Radley, Bradfield, Wellington College, Oundle, Rugby, Oakham, Uppingham, Bloxham, Cheltenham College, Concord, Repton, St Edward's and a number of other leading public schools.

A number of Old Swanbournians have gone on to be School Captains, Prefects and Sports Captains at their senior schools. They are well-grounded, well-mannered, emotionally intelligent and go on to become highly attractive candidates for the top universities and for future employers.

Swanbourne House is a school that continues to work very hard to earn and deserve its success and enviable reputation. We are there every step of the way on your child's journey through Prep School and we do our best to ensure that each and every child strives to do their best with confidence and determination, in a happy, safe and supportive environment.

Charitable status. Swanbourne House School is a Registered Charity, number 310640.

Talbot Heath Junior School

Rothesay Road, Bournemouth BH4 9NJ

Tel: 01202 763360
email: jsoffice@talbotheath.org
website: www.talbotheath.org

Chair of Governors: Mrs Clodie Sutcliffe

Head Teacher: **Mrs Elizabeth Pugh**

Number of Pupils. 250.

Age Range. Girls 3–11.

Our Ethos. Talbot Heath is a flourishing, vibrant and dynamic school, with a focus not only on high academic standards but outstanding pastoral care. It is unique in the area catering for girls aged 3–18.

Our pupils are confident, caring and articulate and have a genuine love of learning that permeates our school. We all strive to make sure that each girl reaches her full potential and every individual really matters, and is truly valued. The School's motto, 'Honour Before Honours', underpins everything we do. We care for each other and support one another with integrity and compassion.

Being selective, we value our academic tradition and encourage our pupils to be self motivated, hard-working, diligent and resilient in a nurturing and supportive environment. We have strong links and encourage clear communication with all our parents, which fosters a supportive community.

Our results, right from the first steps in EYFS, are outstanding, but the school places value on so much more than just results. Emphasis is placed on becoming rounded individuals, experiencing the full breadth of an extensive curriculum and becoming the very best they can be.

Facilities. The Junior School, housed in its own buildings on our woodland campus, is split into two departments, Pre-Prep (age 3–7) and Junior (age 7–11). Apart from large, spacious classrooms, Juniors have their own hall, two dining rooms, computer suites, a library, a studio, a science room and large outdoor play facilities including woodland trails, playgrounds and an adventure playground.

In addition to this, pupils make use of all the Senior School facilities as they progress through the school. These include the state-of-the-art STEAM Hub with interactive floors and walls, plus studios for DT, Art, Graphics, Textiles and Drama. A dedicated Music School, the Sports Hall, indoor swimming pool, athletics track, all-weather pitches, courts, gymnasium and Science centres. The girls are taught by subject specialists for Music and PE from Reception onwards. Once the girls reach Year 4, they are taught by academic subject-specialists for the majority of their curriculum. Every girl has a school iPad and benefits from STEAM lessons in our new state-of-the-art interdisciplinary hub.

Fees per term (2021–2022). £2,355–£4,193

Charitable status. Talbot Heath School Trust Limited is a Registered Charity, number 283708.

Terrington Hall School

Terrington, North Yorkshire YO60 6PR

Tel: 01653 648227
email: office@terringtonhall.com
website: www.terringtonhall.com
Twitter: @TerringtonHall
Facebook: @TerringtonHall
Instagram: @terringtonhall.school
LinkedIn: /company/terrington-hall-school

Chair of Governors: Mrs Katharine Lamont

Headmaster: **Mr Simon Kibler**, BA Hons

Age Range. 3–13 years.

Number of Children. 180

Fees per term (2021–2022). Day: £3,010 (Nursery and Reception); £3,195 (Years 1 & 2); £4,840 (Years 3 & 4); £5,180 (Years 5–8), Flexible boarding is available at £25 per night.

Terrington Hall is a vibrant and purposeful co-educational day, weekly and flexi-boarding school situated in the Howardian Hills, an Area of Outstanding Natural Beauty 15 miles north of York.

We blend forward thinking learning with a traditional prep school ethos to develop kind, confident and well-mannered children who have the courage to take calculated risks without fear of failure and the resilience to pursue their talents and interests.

Every day is aimed at expanding our children's horizons through a journey of discovery which makes learning fun and lights a spark in their hearts and minds. The high level of individual care and attention extended to every child is supported by small class sizes, an excellent staff/pupil ratio, specialist teaching staff and strong emphasis on wellbeing. Our nurturing yet focused environment develops children who are critical thinkers, self-directed and willing to seize opportunities.

Terrington's broad curriculum and excellent facilities are supplemented by an exceptional range of co-curricular activities and events, as well as the TALL programme which helps children acquire a depth of skills and experience outside their academic work. Collaborative leadership skills are prized, along with a clear sense of service and empathy. We aim to develop children who have an awareness of their social and environmental responsibility to the world around them.

As truly independent and not tied to any other school, we place special emphasis on preparing pupils for entry into the senior school that best suits each child, whether locally or further afield. We are particularly proud of the scholarships won by our pupils for academia, art, sport and drama.

The school has a strong boarding community, with over 90% of Years 3–8 pupils opting to stay for weekly or flexi boarding during the school year to make the most of the exciting evening activity programme.

Our excellent sporting facilities include eight acres of playing fields, AstroTurf pitches, tennis courts, an indoor heated swimming pool and sports hall. All major sports are played and an extensive fixture list ensures that every child has ample opportunity to represent the school. Specialist peripatetic tuition is available in Tennis, Cricket and Swimming (either 1:1 or small group sessions) throughout the year. All children have the opportunity to join residential adventure trips in the UK and beyond.

Teaching facilities are modern and well-equipped and include both computer and science suites. Music, art and drama are an integral part of the curriculum. Tuition is available for most instruments, voice and drama, with children prepared for exams with The Associated Board and Trinity College, London. The Junior and Senior choirs perform within school and at local venues, and our orchestra, jazz band and rock band ensembles run during enrichment throughout the year. All children have the opportunity to perform in recitals held in our Music Centre, as well as our more large-scale end of term concerts.

The Headmaster, his wife and children live in the school grounds and parents are fully involved in the life of the school. There is a flourishing 'Friends of Terrington Hall' parents' social committee.

Bursaries are available on a means-tested basis. Discounts are available to siblings and Old Terringtonians.

Charitable Status. Terrington Hall is a registered charity, number 532362. It exists to provide a quality education for boys and girls.

Thorngrove School

The Mount, Pantings Lane, Highclere, Newbury, Hampshire RG20 9PS

Tel: 01635 253172
email: admin@thorngroveschool.co.uk
website: www.thorngroveschool.co.uk
Twitter: @thorngroveprep
Facebook: @ThorngrovePrep

Proprietors: Mr Nicholas and Mrs Connie Broughton

Headmaster: **Mr A King**, BA Hons QTS Leeds, PDES Leadership and Management

Senior Deputy Head and Pastoral: Mr N Graham, BA Hons Oxford Brookes, PGCE

Deputy Head Academic: Mrs L Hanham, BEd Plymouth

Deputy Head, Head of Lower School and EYFS: Mrs V McSorland, BA QTS Bath Spa

Age Range. 2½–13 Co-educational.
Number of Pupils. 216 Day Pupils.
Fees per term (2021–2022). Reception–Year 2 £4,910; Year 3 and 4 £5,780; Year 5–8 £6,450.

Thorngrove School was founded in 1988 and is an IAPS co-educational day preparatory school for children aged 2½ to 13 years. The purpose-built facilities are set in former farmland in the village of Highclere, 5 miles south of Newbury and 12 miles north of Andover. Children are prepared for Common Entrance at 13+, from where their paths lead to a wide range of senior day and boarding schools.

The school is set in 25 acres of beautiful, Hampshire countryside. The extensive games fields provide numerous rugby, football and hockey pitches. In addition to this, there is an astro, two new hard courts which are used for tennis and netball and an impressive 3-lane cricket facility (installed Summer 2018). A multi-purpose hall was opened by Robert Hardy in 2007. This provides a wonderful space for music concerts and drama productions as well as indoor PE and games. Either side of the hall are four classrooms and changing facilities. We have a large IT suite and many of the classrooms have interactive whiteboards. Every child from Year 3 up has their own Chromebook and the school uses Firefly for its VLE. There is a dedicated music room in the Senior Block with several practice rooms. The Science laboratory is fully equipped. The Art room is well resourced and has recently been refurbished. Our well-stocked library is located centrally in the main building and we have a full-time librarian. All classrooms are modern, light and airy and some have direct access to the outside. There is also a D&T centre which was created in the old nursery. In September 2020 the Nursery was expanded to provide two rooms, linked to the Reception class and creating an impressive EYFS setting.

Thorngrove offers a unique environment where children can grow and learn independently. We value our intimate and friendly community, and the benefits that it brings; we are proud of our small class sizes and the individual attention we are able to offer to each of our pupils.

The school has a relaxed yet purposeful atmosphere, where working relationships between staff and pupils flourish. We are forward thinking in our approach – ready to adapt to change and technological advancement, whilst at the same time remaining true to traditional values.

Pupils are assessed continuously, and parents are always welcome to discuss their children's progress with staff on a regular basis or at parents' meetings. Above all, our aim is that all our pupils should reach their potential in terms of confidence, creativity and achievement.

In the most recent ISI inspection (March 2020) the school was rated 'excellent' in all available categories.

Thorpe House School

Oval Way, Gerrards Cross, Bucks SL9 8QA

Tel: 01753 882474
email: office@thorpehouse.co.uk
website: www.thorpehouse.co.uk
Twitter: @thorpehousesch
Facebook: @thorpehousesch
Instagram: @thorpehousesch
LinkedIn: /in/thorpehousesch

Independent Boys' School of the Year 2021 Finalist

Chairman of the Governors: Mr Richard Tufft

Headmaster: **Mr Nicholas Pietrek**, BA

Age Range. Boys 4–16.
Numbers of Pupils. 299 Day Pupils.
Fees per term (2021–2022). Y9–Y11 £6,275, Y7–Y8 £6,150, Y6 £5,350, Y5 £5,250, Y4 £5,200, Y3 £4,950, Y1–Y2 £3,950, Reception £3,500.

Thorpe House is an Independent boys' school based in the beautiful town of Gerrards Cross in Buckinghamshire. We offer education for boys from Reception to Year 11.

At Thorpe House our aspirations push us to achieve higher: there is no such thing as failure, only a desire to learn and become the best version of ourselves.

As soon as our boys start in Reception, we look to prepare them for the world to which we believe we should all aspire, one in which there is an emphasis on encouragement and recognition of our diversity and where we want the boys to consider not what they can do for themselves but what they can do for others.

Through an enrichment programme that runs throughout our three-year GCSE course, we build on the confidence that has already been nurtured in the earlier years to develop skills and empathy that will make them the leaders that we want and need; to direct the course of our society in the future.

Charitable status. Thorpe House School Trust is a Registered Charity, number 292683. It exists to provide education to boys.

Independent Senior Schools. We have an enviable success rate in delivering entry into their first-choice senior schools, with many being awarded scholarships in Academia, Sport, Music, Drama and Design Technology.

Nursery. Tockington Manor Nursery is set in a refurbished converted barn within the school grounds. Each child is encouraged to learn through 'hands on' experience overseen by their dedicated Nursery Practitioner who is specially trained to nurture and extend the development of every child. Children benefit from the wider school facilities, tending to their own "cottage style" vegetable garden, discovering nature and forest skills on "welly walks" or enjoying weekly swimming lessons in the school's indoor heated pool.

The School website has further details or a copy of the School's prospectus is available on request by emailing the Registrar, email: registrar@tockingtonmanorschool.com. The Headmaster will be delighted to give a tour of the School to prospective parents upon request.

Charitable status. Tockington Manor School is a Registered Charity, number 311716.

Tockington Manor School and Nursery

Washingpool Hill Road, Tockington, Bristol BS32 4NY

Tel: 01454 613229
email: admin@tockingtonmanorschool.com
website: www.tockingtonmanorschool.com
Twitter: @TockingtonManor
Facebook: @tockingtonmanorschool
Instagram: @tockingtonmanorschool
LinkedIn: /tockington-manor-school-limited

Chairman of Governors: Mr A Ramsay

Headmaster: **Stephen Symonds**, BA Ed Hons

Age Range. Boys and Girls aged 2–13+.
Number of Pupils. 137 Upper School, 64 Lower School, 48 Nursery.
Fees per term (2021–2022). Upper School Day £4,623–£5,360 (including meals and wrap-around care); Lower School £3,440; Nursery £56.18 per day.

Tockington Manor School and Nursery is an independent co-educational Preparatory school set in 28 acres of lovely countryside in the picturesque village of Tockington, South Gloucestershire. Pupils are welcomed from age 2 to 13+.

Our small friendly classes and family approach to education provides bespoke learning for every child. We pride ourselves in delivering a varied timetable geared to the needs of each pupil but with emphasis on the core subjects of English, Mathematics and Science. We aim to provide an environment that is positive, supportive and disciplined within a warm, caring family atmosphere. Pupils are encouraged to be confident, considerate and accomplished free thinkers. All pupils take part in all aspects of school life, academic or otherwise, making the most of every moment.

The school works closely with parents to prepare every pupil for Common Entrance and Scholarships to appropriate

Tower House School

188 Sheen Lane, East Sheen, London SW14 8LF

Tel: 020 8876 3323
email: admissions@thsboys.org.uk
website: www.thsboys.org.uk

Acting Chair: Mr Charles Pike

Headmaster: **Mr G Evans**, BSc, MA, PGCE

Age Range. 4–13.
Number of Boys. 181.
Fees per term (2021–2022). Reception and Year 1 £4,651, Years 2 and 3 £5,131, Senior School £5,273 (including residential trips and all school lunches).

Originally founded in 1931, Tower House School is now a 21st century centre of excellence for boys from the ages 4–13.

Our boys want to be part of everything. Whether it be sports teams, musical ensembles or our famous drama productions; pupils are enthusiastic because they know they are valued and have an important contribution to make.

Learning takes place both inside and outside the classroom. Weekly Forest School and frequent educational trips help to keep the fun aspect of education firmly in focus.

We are proud of our academic record and boys are prepared for a wide range of senior schools across the country, carefully chosen to suit their academic and extra-curricular strengths.

Tower House pupils characteristically approach the next stage of their educational journey with confidence, humility and distinction.

A prospectus is available online or from the School Secretary.

Charitable status. Tower House School is a Registered Charity, number 1068844.

Town Close School

14 Ipswich Road, Norwich, Norfolk NR2 2LR

Tel:　　01603 620180
email:　　admissions@townclose.com
website:　　www.townclose.com
Twitter:　　@townclose; @towncloseehead
Facebook:　　@towncloseschool

Chairman of Governors: Sarah Anthony

Headmaster: **Christopher Wilson**, BA Cantab, PGCE

Age Range. 3–13 Co-educational.

Number of Pupils. Prep 271, Pre-Prep 171.

Fees per term (2021–2022). £3,081–£4,673 including lunch and all single-day educational excursions. No compulsory extras.

Town Close School was founded in 1932 and became a Charitable Trust in 1968. The School is fully co-educational and is situated on a beautiful wooded site near the centre of Norwich. This location provides pupils with space and freedom and contributes substantially to Town Close's reputation as an outstandingly happy school.

There is a team of talented teachers who aim to produce well-motivated, balanced, confident children, who are caring and sociable and who know the value of hard work. The children receive excellent teaching and are prepared for all major senior schools. In recent years, pupils have achieved highly in entrance and scholarship assessments to a range of the country's leading senior schools.

A modern teaching building stands at the heart of the School, containing a large, well-equipped library, an art room, an IT centre and 16 purpose-built classrooms. There are many other outstanding facilities including an indoor heated swimming pool, a high-specification sports hall, a performance hall and a full-size, floodlit Astroturf. Science and DT are taught in specialist buildings and the school places a high value on innovation, engineering and scientific discovery. The Pre-Prep occupies a magnificent converted house on the campus and also contains a multi-purpose hall, kitchens, and a new and purpose-built Nursery wing that opens onto fantastic outdoor facilities.

Nursery and Reception classes follow the Foundation Stage curriculum, an important element of which is outdoor learning. Children progress through a broad and varied programme of activities with a strong emphasis on the development of personal and social skills and on establishing positive attitudes to learning and to school life. Swimming, music and dance are taught by specialist teachers, while the rest of the curriculum is delivered by class teachers, ably supported by well-qualified teaching assistants.

Throughout the children's time at Town Close particular attention is paid to the teaching of good handwriting and spelling. Traditional core skills are valued very highly in addition to promoting children's use of digital technology. IT provision is extensive allowing children to become confident and proficient users. The Pre-Prep pupils use a range of children's software to develop key skills and Prep Department children build on this foundation using more sophisticated software, either in the computer room or on laptops and tablets. All sections of the School have filtered access to the internet across the network. The School Intranet contains interactive activities, images, lesson material and links to carefully selected websites. Interactive whiteboards are used throughout the School to support the curriculum.

Town Close has an excellent academic reputation and is also known for the quality of its sport, music, art, drama and its extensive co-curricular programme. Trips and expeditions form a valuable part of what is offered, and provide the balance essential for a full and rounded education. Activities take place during the lunch hour, after school, and occasionally at weekends. In terms of music, the School has a full orchestra, a variety of choirs and a wide range of ensembles. All children are encouraged to perform with regular high-quality concerts and plays.

Physical Education plays an important part in the development of each child, be they in the Nursery or in Year 8. Emphasis is placed on fostering healthy exercise, as well as encouraging a positive, competitive attitude, individual skills and teamwork. As well as providing all the usual opportunities for the major sports (rugby, netball, hockey, cricket and athletics), coaching is offered in many other sports.

A visit to www.townclose.com will provide a fuller picture of the School, including a sight of the most recent inspection report, in which Town Close was given the highest rating in every area.

Charitable status. Town Close Educational Trust Limited is a Registered Charity, number 311293. It exists to provide education for children.

Truro School Preparatory

Highertown, Truro, Cornwall TR1 3QN

Tel:　　01872 272616
email:　　prepenquiries@truroschool.com
　　　　prepadmissions@truroschool.com
website:　　www.truroschool.com/prep

Chairman of the Governors: Mr R Thomas

Head of Truro School: Mr A Johnson, MA

Head of Preparatory School: **Miss S L Patterson**, BEd Hons

Key Stage I Coordinator: Mr P Sharp, BEng Hons

EYFS Coordinator: Ms Kate Williams, BEd Hons

Age Range. 3–11.

Number of Pupils. 288: 183 Boys, 105 Girls.

Fees per term (2021–2022). Prep (including lunch): £4,415 (Years 3–4), £4,585 (Years 5–6). Pre-Prep (including lunch): £3,110 (Nursery and Reception). £3,265 (Years 1 and 2).

Optional extras: Individual music lessons, fencing, ballet, judo, photography, Bushcraft, badminton, LAMDA (Speech & Drama), Pre-Prep tennis.

Truro School Prep was opened as Treliske School in 1936 in the former residence and estate of Sir George Smith. The school lies in extensive and secluded grounds to the west of the cathedral city of Truro, three miles from Truro School. The grounds command fine views of the neighbouring countryside. The drive to the school off the main A390 is almost 800 metres and Truro Golf Course also surrounds the school, so producing a campus of beauty and seclusion.

The keynote of the school is a happy, caring atmosphere in which children learn the value of contributing positively to the school community through the firm and structured framework of academic study and extracurricular interests. The approach is based firmly in Christian beliefs and the school is proud of its Methodist foundation.

Building development has kept pace with modern expectations and Truro School Prep has its own large sports hall, an indoor heated swimming pool, a design and technology workshop with a computer room adjoined and purpose-built Pre-Prep.

The games programme is designed to encourage all children, from the keenest to the least athletic, to enjoy games and physical exercise. Our excellent facilities and the diverse skill of our staff enable us to offer a rich variety of sporting and recreational pursuits. There are over 70 clubs that run before school, during lunch break or after school from 4.00pm to 5.00pm.

There is a strong school tradition in music and drama and the arts. Children may choose to learn a musical instrument from the full orchestral range. Each year the November concert, with Truro School, allows the school to show the community the excellent talents, which flourish in both schools.

Close links are maintained with the Senior School and nearly all pupils progress through at age 11 on the Head's recommendation to Truro School which is the only Independent Headmasters' and Headmistresses' Conference School in Cornwall (*see entry in HMC section*).

The prospectus and further details can be obtained from the Head's PA, and the Head will be pleased to show prospective parents around the school.

Charitable status. Truro School is part of the Methodist Independent Schools Trust, which is a registered Charity, number 1142794.

Twickenham Preparatory School

Beveree, 43 High Street, Hampton, Middlesex TW12 2SA

Tel: 020 8979 6216
email: admissions@twickenhamprep.co.uk
website: www.twickenhamprep.co.uk
Twitter: @twickenhamprep
Facebook: @twickenhamprepschool
Instagram: @twickenham_prep

Chairman of Governors: Mr H Bates

Headmaster: **Mr O Barrett**, BA Hons, QTS

Age Range. 4–13.
Number of Pupils. Boys 166, Girls 116.
Fees per term (2021–2022). £3,830–£4,255. Lunch £222–£245.

Founded in 1969, Twickenham Prep is an independent, co-educational school situated in Hampton. We are a happy, vibrant, and thriving school where every child is valued as an individual and inspired to achieve their full potential, personally, socially and academically. The pupils benefit from small classes, first-class facilities, specialist subject teaching and excellent pastoral care.

Our pupils achieve great success, both academic and extracurricular, moving on to excellent independent secondary schools with regular academic, sporting, musical, art and all-rounder scholarships. We are committed to working in partnership with our parents so that our pupils leave TPS as well-rounded individuals. The girls sit entrance exams at 11+ and the boys Common Entrance at 13+

Our curriculum is based on the National Curriculum with specialist teaching of PE, Games, ICT, French, Music and Think Tank (formerly Mind Lab, an innovative thinking skills programme) from Reception ensuring a balanced educational experience. Art/Design and Technology is introduced in Year 3 and from Year 4 pupils have specialist teaching in all subjects, with Latin being introduced in Year 5. Class sizes are about 18, developing each pupil to their full academic potential and promoting high academic standards. The school is well equipped to cover the full range of subjects, with purpose-built Art/DT, Science and Music facilities and a modern sports hall used for PE and termly productions.

Strong emphasis is placed on participation by all in sporting, musical and extracurricular activities. The school plays a wide range of sports and has recently formed an affiliation with Kempton Cricket Club to provide 10 acres of dedicated sporting facilities for rugby, football, cricket and athletics. The girls also play netball, hockey and cricket, with athletics and swimming also part of the sporting curriculum. Music and drama play a large part in the school with full-scale productions and concerts annually involving all pupils. There is a school choir and individual instrumental lessons are taught by visiting specialists.

TPS is a leading Chess school and we are also the current National Mind Lab Champions; we have represented the UK for the last 7 years at the International Mind Lab Olympics.

There are also many extracurricular clubs during and after school to choose from, including coding, dance, chess, DT, fencing and many sports options and we also provide on-site wraparound care from 7.30am to 6.30pm.

Located in Hampton we offer morning minibus services to children living in Kew, Isleworth, Richmond, Twickenham, Teddington, St Margaret's, Hampton Wick, Sunbury and East Molesey.

TPS has seen the exciting realisation of a new building project last year, with the opening of the Hub@51, a brand-new state-of-the-art facility. The Hub@51 houses a purpose built Art Studio, with facilities for Design and Technology and Textiles, along with two bright and airy new classrooms for our Year 7 and Year 8 boys. The Hub@51 is a statement of our aims to provide outstanding modern provision for the children and features a Digital Media Suite, including broadcast cameras and an editing suite. Further plans include opportunities for children to record and broadcast podcasts and short films, whilst the longer-term aspiration is to launch our very own radio station.

Entry to the school is non-selective at Reception with limited places available in other year groups subject to an assessment.

Regular Open Days are held and personal tours are available – the pupils and Headmaster would be delighted to show you around. Please contact the school office.

Charitable Status. Twickenham Preparatory School is a Registered Charity, number 1067572. It exists to provide education for boys and girls.

Twyford School

Twyford, Winchester, Hampshire SO21 1NW

Tel: 01962 712269
email: twyford@twyfordschool.com
website: www.twyfordschool.com
Twitter: @TwyfordSchool
Instagram: @twyfordschool

Chairman of Governors: Mr Colin Howman

Headmaster: Mr Andrew Harvey

Age Range. 2–13.

Number of Children. 394. Main School: 304, of whom 12 are weekly boarders, 73 are flexi boarders; Pre-Prep: 126.

Fees per term (2021–2022). Weekly Boarding: £8,745. Day: Prep Years 4–8 £6,949, Year 3 £5,796; Pre-Prep £1,061–£3,901. Fees are inclusive of all outings/trips run during the term.

Twyford School is situated at the edge of the beautiful South Downs just two miles from the historic city of Winchester and the M3. Twyford is a family school that aims to offer an all-round top-rate education with a Christian ethos. Most pupils are day pupils, but from Year 4, many board one or two nights a week through the school's flexi boarding system. By the final year, many weekly board, which makes an excellent preparation for their move to senior school. The contrast between the modern facilities (classrooms, laboratories, music school, creative arts and ICT block, swimming pool and sports centre) and the Victorian chapel and hall creates a rich and stimulating environment.

The school regularly achieves scholarships – 82 awards (academic, art, design, sport and music) in the last 6 years – to major senior schools such as Winchester College, St Swithun's, Canford, Marlborough, Wycombe Abbey, Godolphin, Wellington College, Bradfield, Radley, Bryanston, Eton, Sherborne Boys and Sherborne Girls.

Charitable status. Twyford School is a Registered Charity, number 307425. It exists to provide education for children.

Unicorn School

238 Kew Road, Richmond, Surrey TW9 3JX

Tel: 020 8948 3926
email: registrar@unicornschool.org.uk
website: www.unicornschool.org.uk
Twitter: @unicornschool

Chairs of Governors: Mr Geoff Bayliss and Mr Mark Byatt

Headteacher: Mrs Polly Fraley

Age Range. 3–11.

Number of Children. 171 Day Pupils: 87 boys, 84 girls.

Fees per term (2021–2022). £2,600–£4,770.

Unicorn is a parent-founded IAPS co-ed primary school founded in 1970. Situated opposite Kew Gardens, the school occupies a large Victorian house and converted coach house with a spacious, superbly-equipped playground and garden.

The school has free and unrestricted access to Kew Gardens and the sports facilities at the nearby University of Westminster grounds are used for games and Pools on the Park for swimming.

Our aim is for Unicorn to be a successful, forward-thinking school that embraces children, staff and parents in an evolving, exciting, dynamic and nurturing community, enriched with creativity and supported by excellent leadership and management. Pupils are encouraged to become independent, responsible, self-aware and confident young people, who reap the benefits of a very broad curriculum to achieve considerable success.

There are 22 children per class, where a variety of teaching methods are used and the children are regularly assessed. Importance is placed upon the development of the individual and high academic standards are achieved. The main point of entry is to nursery at 3+. Children are prepared for entry at 11+ to the leading London day schools, as well as a variety of boarding schools.

There is a specialist IT room and networked computers in every classroom and a bank of iPads to use; a Science and Design Technology suite with interactive whiteboard technology in all classrooms; music rooms, library and a state-of-the-art fully-equipped Art room.

The curriculum includes Drama, French (from age 5), Art and Music – with individual music lessons offered in piano, violin, cello, drums, clarinet, saxophone, flute, guitar and trumpet, as well as singing. Recorder groups, choirs, an orchestra and a wind band also flourish.

In addition to the major games of football, hockey, netball, cricket, rounders and athletics, there are optional clubs for tennis, squash, golf, riding, sailing, musical theatre and karate. Other club activities include arts and crafts, cookery, pottery, chess, riding, sailing and fencing. There are regular visits to the theatre and museums as well as the galleries of Central London. All children, from the age of seven upwards, participate in residential field study trips to Surrey, Devon and Cumbria.

An elected School Council, with representatives from each age group, meets weekly with the Headmaster and a weekly newsletter for parents is also produced.

A happy, caring environment prevails and importance is placed on producing kind, responsible children who show awareness and consideration for the needs of others.

Charitable status. Unicorn School is a Registered Charity, number 312578. It exists to provide education for boys and girls.

University College School – Junior Branch

11 Holly Hill, Hampstead, London NW3 6QN

Tel: 020 7435 3068
email: juniorbranch@ucs.org.uk
website: www.ucs.org.uk

Chairman of Council of Governors: Mr Stephen Warshaw

Headmaster: **Mr L R J Hayward**, MA

Age Range. 7–11.
Number of Boys. 251
Fees per term (2021–2022). £6,745.

The School was founded in 1891 by the Governors of University College, London. The present building was opened in 1928, but retains details from the Georgian house first used. It stands near the highest point of Hampstead Heath and the hall and classrooms face south. Facilities include a Science Laboratory, Library, Drama Studio, Music and Computer Rooms, and a Centre for Art and Technology. Boys receive their Swimming and PE lessons in the pool and Sports Hall at the Senior School, 5 minutes' walk away. The Junior School has full use of the 27 acres of playing fields on games days.

Boys enter at 7+ each year and they are prepared for transfer to the Senior School at 11+. (*See entry in HMC section.*)

Charitable status. University College School, Hampstead is a Registered Charity, number 312748. The Junior Branch exists to provide education for boys aged 7+ to 11 years.

University College School Pre-Prep

36 College Crescent, Hampstead, London NW3 5LF

Tel: 020 7722 4433
email: pre-prep@ucs.org.uk
website: www.ucs.org.uk/UCS-Pre-Prep

Chairman of Council: Mr Stephen Warshaw, BA, PGCE

Headmistress: **Dr Z Dunn**, BEd, PhD, NPQH

Age Range. Boys 4–7.
Number of Pupils. 100 Boys.
Fees per term (2021–2022). £6,096.

At UCS Pre-Prep, we firmly believe that happiness and self-esteem are the keys to success in every pupil's learning journey. The well-qualified and highly-supportive staff accompany each child on a voyage of educational and social discovery during the first years of school life.

The Pre-Prep fully supports the aims and ethos of UCS: intellectual curiosity and independence of mind are developed, self-discovery and self-expression are fostered and a cooperative and collaborative approach to learning is of great importance.

For every child in our care, we provide a continuously positive and creative learning environment that allows the individual the opportunity to develop personal qualities and talents. Children enjoy specialist teaching in Music, art and Physical Education and the full primary curriculum in well resourced classrooms. The outdoor learning programme takes advantage of the school's allotment and extensive space at the fields. At the end of Year 2, most boys transfer to the junior branch of UCS.

Charitable status. UCS Pre-Prep Limited is a Registered Charity, number 1098657.

Upton House School

115 St Leonard's Road, Windsor, Berkshire SL4 3DF

Tel: 01753 862610
email: info@uptonhouse.org.uk
              registrar@uptonhouse.org.uk
website: www.uptonhouse.org.uk
Twitter: @UptonHouseSch
Facebook: @UptonHouseSchool

Chair of the Council: Mrs V Barker

Headmistress: **Mrs Rhian Thornton**, BA Hons, NPQL, LLE, PGCE

Deputy Head: Mrs Kate Newcombe, BEd Hons

Head of Pre-Prep: Mrs Emma Pritchard, BSc Hons, QTS, NVQ3

Head of Early Years/Transition: Mrs Susi Broad, BSc Hons, QTS, DipTH

Age Range. Girls and Boys 2–11 years.
Number of Pupils. 266 Day: 176 Girls, 90 Boys.
Fees per term (2021–2022). £3,230–£5,400 (inclusive). Bursaries available.

Our aim at Upton House is to foster a happy and stimulating environment in which each child can prosper academically, socially and emotionally. The school prepares all children for their continuing education and equips them with life skills for the future.

Upton House School was founded in 1936 by benefactors and has evolved over the years to provide a well-equipped modern environment where children thrive.

At Upton House we aim to provide the best possible education for each child. We give encouragement and stimulation to develop their academic abilities and we develop pupils individual strengths, whether it is from our broad curriculum or from our wide range of extracurricular activities. This combined with a loving nurturing environment, develops a set of pastoral values which makes Upton very special.

Our newly-opened arts block houses a music room, an art studio and media room. Our kitchen serves freshly prepared, nutritious meals on site. Facilities also include a fully-equipped IT suite, a drama/dance studio, gymnasium and Nursery music room.

Specialist subjects include PE, French and Mandarin from 3 years old. Educational robots, iPads, laptops, and interactive whiteboards are used across the school to enhance learning. Diverse sporting activities include rowing on the Thames, judo, fencing and ballet.

Boys and girls leaving gain places at a wide range of excellent prep and senior schools and regularly win scholarships.

Entry is non-selective and means-tested bursaries are available for those entering the school.

We provide care from 7.45am in our Early Birds breakfast club as well as an extended day until 6pm for children from age 3. A wide variety of clubs are offered in the extended day programme as well as teacher-supervised prep for older children.

We have an active PTA which organises many fundraising events through the year and helps to forge close links between the school and parents. Please visit our website for details of forthcoming Open mornings. Personal tours are also welcome.

Charitable status. Upton House School is a Registered Charity, number 309095. It exists to provide an excellent all-round educational foundation for boys and girls.

The Ursuline Preparatory School Ilford

2–4 Coventry Road, Ilford, Essex IG1 4QR

Tel: 020 8518 4050
email: urspsi@urspsi.org.uk
website: www.urspsi.org.uk
Twitter: @URSPSI
Facebook: @URSPSI

Chair of Governors: Mr Simon Bird

Head: **Mrs Victoria McNaughton**

Age Range. 3–11 Co-educational.
Number of Pupils. 100.
Fees per term (2021–2022). Nursery: £2,673 (full-time including lunch, pre- and after-school care, net of government funding), Reception–Year 6 £3,510 (including lunch, pre- and after-school care).

The Ursuline Preparatory School Ilford is a Roman Catholic day school in the trusteeship of the Ursuline Sisters. The Ursuline Sisters first came to England in 1862 settling at Forest Gate from where they established the school in Ilford in 1903 at 73 Cranbrook Road. The school has since flourished. Formerly part of The Ursuline Academy, The Ursuline Preparatory School Ilford is now a fully independent school in its own right, but continues to share close and valued links with the Academy.

As a Catholic school, we firmly believe that Religious Education is the foundation of the entire educational process. Prayers and liturgical celebrations are an important aspect of school life, unifying the hearts and minds of all associated with the school and ensuring we are all working to achieve the best possible education for the children in our care.

We provide a safe, secure and stimulating environment for our pupils to thrive. We recognise each child's unique value and are committed to encouraging self-esteem and developing each child's potential. We encourage the children to become independent learners by building on their curiosity and desire to learn and developing their skills, concepts and understanding.

While the school continues to set its own high standards, we complement these with the integration of the best of the National Curriculum. English and mathematics form the core subjects together with Religious Education, science, history, geography, ICT, PE, drama, design technology, art, music, MFL and stimulating project work. The Performing Arts have a high profile in school and the children are regularly given the opportunity to develop their talents. Well-stocked libraries, audio-visual aids and a specialist Information Communication Technology department are all available throughout the nursery and school.

We offer a wide range of extracurricular activities including ballet, speech and drama and Irish Dancing. Other clubs and sports clubs including football, cricket, basketball, netball, gymnastics and trampolining are held weekly. Individual instrumental tuition can be arranged for piano, violin, guitar and ukulele. There is also an award-winning school choir.

All teaching staff are fully qualified, experienced and dedicated to the ideals of the school. They work in close partnership with parents to ensure that each child's special individual needs are recognised. In addition, we have the help of experienced general assistants. Our pupil to teacher ratio is excellent and we are able to engage in small group teaching.

Pre- and after-school care is available. Holiday club is run by an outside company at an additional cost.

Charitable status. The Ursuline Preparatory School Ilford is a Registered Charity, number 245661.

Ursuline Preparatory School Wimbledon

18 The Downs, Wimbledon, London SW20 8HR

Tel: 020 8947 0859
email: headteachersoffice@ursulineprep.org
website: www.ursulineprep.org
Twitter: @ursulineprep
Facebook: @Ursulineprep

Chair of Governors: Ms Merinda D'Aprano

Head Teacher: **Mrs Caroline Molina**

Age Range. Girls 3–11, Boys 3–4.
Number of Pupils. 160+.
Fees per term (2021–2022). £3,995 full-time, £2,450 for part-time Nursery.

The Ursuline Preparatory school is a Roman Catholic school that welcomes children of all faiths and none. Non-selective by choice, the school offers a values-driven, academic education to girls from 3–11 years of age and to boys in the Nursery class.

Established in 1892 to promote the values of St Angela Merici, OSU, the Ursuline Preparatory School places equal value on the an education of heart, mind and soul in the certain knowledge that only through the equal development of all three can a child truly excel. The school's mission is to develop a community that lives each day working together (*Insieme*) and united in harmony, valuing the contributions of all and championing the virtues of love, compassion, kindness and generosity. The children are encouraged to be grateful for the gifts they have been given and to develop these gifts to the full, in generous service to others. The school seeks to pass on the living and faith-filled tradition of Jesus Christ by having unswerving faith in every single one of our pupils and by encouraging them, in turn, to have faith and hope in others. A keen focus is to educate and create future leaders in the spirit of Serviam (*I will serve*), keeping justice at the centre of their lives.

The core provision of this school is three-fold:

- A strong Ursuline ethos;
- An academic provision, whether in the classroom or online, that prepares children fully for secondary school;
- A strong partnership between pupils, parents and staff.

Our children enjoy a rich diversity of experiences, both inside and outside of the classroom. Our 11+ preparation curriculum, full sporting programme, and developed range of extra-curricular activities, provides an enriching and engaging provision. We are ready and able to replicate this provision by distance learning, ensuring our children are fully prepared for the next step in their educational journey no matter the circumstances, as well as enabling them to look forward to the future with confidence, keen to make a difference in the world.

The girls at the Ursuline Preparatory School follow an academic curriculum and are fully supported, securing places in their senior school of choice. As a result of the Ursuline ethos, and the academic preparation process put in place, the girls here can face the 11+ with confidence. Last year girls received offers from the following schools: Claremont Fan Court School, Danes Hill School, Emanuel School, Kingston Grammar, Lady Eleanor Holles, Marymount, Nonsuch, Notre Dame, Putney High, St John's Leatherhead, St Paul's Girls' School, Surbiton High, Sutton High, Tiffin Girls, Ursuline High School and Wimbledon High.

An Ursuline education seeks to help the young people here grow and flourish in an environment in which every child is loved and valued. On such sure foundations, we help them become the very best that they can be.

Charitable status. Ursuline Preparatory School, Wimbledon is a Registered Charity, number 1079754.

Victoria College Preparatory School

Pleasant Street, St Helier, Jersey, Channel Islands JE2 4RR

Tel:	01534 723468
email:	admin@vcp.sch.je
website:	www.vcp.sch.je
Twitter:	@JerseyVcp
Facebook:	@VCPJERSEY
Instagram:	@victoriacollegeprep
LinkedIn:	/company/vcpjersey

Chair of Governors: B Watt

Headteacher: Dan Pateman, BA Hons

Age Range. 7–11.
Number of Boys. 275 Day Boys.
Fees per term (2021–2022). £2,219 (inclusive).

Victoria College Preparatory School was founded in 1922 as an integral part of Victoria College and is now a separate School under its own Headteacher, who is responsible for such matters as staffing, curriculum and administration. The Preparatory School shares Governors with Victoria College whose members are drawn from the leaders of the Island of Jersey with a minority representation from the States of Jersey Education Committee. Members of staff are all experienced and well-qualified teachers, including specialists in Art, Dance, Music, PE, French and Science. Entry to the Prep School is at 7 and boys normally leave to enter Victoria College at the age of 11. The school games are cricket, football, athletics, swimming, hockey, cross-country and rugby. Sporting facilities are shared with Victoria College. Special features of the school are exceptionally high standards of sport, drama, music and French. Many visits, both sporting and educational, are arranged out of the Island.

A separate Pre-Preparatory School (5 to 7 years) is incorporated in a co-educational school situated at Jersey College Preparatory School and offers places for boys whose parents wish them to be educated at both Victoria College and the Preparatory School. Candidates for Pre-Prep entry should be registered at Jersey College Prep, St Helier, Jersey.

Vinehall School

Robertsbridge, East Sussex TN32 5JL

Tel:	01580 880413
email:	admissions@vinehallschool.com
website:	www.vinehallschool.com
Twitter:	@vinehallschool
Facebook:	@Vinehall-School

Chairman of Governors: Mr John Giles, MBBS, FRCP, FRCR

Headmaster: Mr Joff Powis, BSc, QTS, NPQH

Age Range. 2–13 co-educational.

Number of Children. 200.

Fees per term (2021–2022). Prep: Years 6–8: £6,430 (day), £8,375 (full boarding), £7,700 (weekly boarding); Years 3–5: £6,230 (day), £8,175 (full boarding), £7,525 (weekly boarding); Pre-Prep: Reception, Years 1 & 2 £3,450; Nursery (without Early Years funding): £40 per morning session, £25 per afternoon session, £62.50 per full day session; Nursery (with Early Years funding): £34.30 per full day session.

Founded in 1938, Vinehall School is set within 47 acres of countryside in an area of outstanding natural beauty on the East Sussex/Kent border. A flourishing Nursery and Pre-Prep for boys and girls aged 2 to 7 is situated in a modern, well-resourced and purpose-built building on the same site as the Prep School.

The School's first-class facilities include a magnificent Millennium Building, comprising classrooms, IT suite and library, a science block, music building, art, design and technology centre, a purpose-built theatre with seating for 250, a sports hall and adjoining indoor swimming pool, an AstroTurf pitch, an adventure playground and a nine-hole golf course.

The curriculum, which is based on the National Curriculum but which extends far beyond, prepares pupils for Common Entrance, local grammar school entrance and scholarship entrance to a variety of independent senior schools. In 2018 25 senior school scholarships were awarded to leaving children. Leavers go on to a wide range of the UK's most prestigious senior schools. In 2018 children went on to 26 different destination schools.

The innovative 'Learning Journey' curriculum (which begins in Year 3), stimulates enquiring young minds. The academic day finishes at 4.40pm, with a wide range of clubs and enrichment activities until 5.20pm when school buses depart. On Saturday mornings (apart from exeat weekends) there are optional Clubs and Enrichment activities for pupils in Years 3 to 8. A dedicated learning support team is available for those children who require additional support.

Games and the Arts are an integral part of the Vinehall timetable. Pupils participate in all major team sports and everyone has a chance to represent the School. Girls' sports include netball, hockey, rounders and tennis and for boys, football, rugby, hockey, cricket and tennis. Swimming, gymnastics and athletics are also important sports throughout the year. Creative Arts are also strong, with flourishing Art, Music and Drama departments, all of which exhibit/perform regularly both inside and outside School. Carpentry and wood-turning are also offered.

Boarding is at the very heart of the School and Vinehall has a well-established boarding community, the majority being from Sussex, Kent and London. Temporary, weekly and full boarding are all available and we also offer an accompanied train service to and from London for weekly boarders each Friday and Sunday evening. There are regular exeat weekends and a full and varied programme of weekend activities.

Charitable status. Vinehall School is a Registered Charity, number 307014. It exists to provide a secure, quality education, in particular for those in need of residential schooling.

Walhampton School

Lymington, Hampshire SO41 5ZG

Tel:	01590 613300
email:	registrar@walhampton.com
website:	www.walhampton.com
Twitter:	@Walhamptonprep
Facebook:	@walhamptonprep
Instagram:	@walhamptonprep

Chairman of Governors: Mr Iain Rawlinson

Head: **Mr Jonny Timms**, BA, MA

Age Range. 2–13.

Number of Pupils. 357 pupils: 22 boarders, 234 Prep School.

Fees per term (2021–2022). Day £5,025–£6,465; Full Boarding £2,620 (in addition to day fees); Pre-Preparatory £3,250. The only extras are: After-School Activities, Riding, Sailing, Individual Music, Learning Support tuition, Wraparound Care and Expeditions.

Set within one hundred acres of lawns, lakes and woodlands in the idyllic New Forest, Walhampton is an independent day, flexi and full-time boarding school for boys and girls aged 2–13.

With small class sizes and outstanding teaching, Walhampton pupils achieve consistently impressive academic results and around 35% attain scholarships to top senior schools. Pupils are prepared for 13+ Common Entrance and the school has achieved 100% pass rate over many years. Over the last five years, pupils from Walhampton have gone on to: Canford, Bryanston, King Edward VI Southampton, Embley, Clayesmore, Sherborne, Ballard, Bedales, Sherborne Girls, Godolphin, Monkton Combe, Kings Bruton, Radley, Winchester, Marlborough, Eton and Harrow.

A Walhampton education allows children to be children for longer whilst also preparing them for their life after Walhampton and in the world of tomorrow. Pupils are encouraged to find their voice and develop the strength of character to be involved in society from the earliest age. Digital learning features highly with STEAM competitions and LEGO League challenges. And, the school's location and facilities enables Walhampton to offer a broad and dynamic curriculum, which stretches beyond the classroom. Lessons are also taught in the permanent outdoor classroom, in Forest School, by the lakes and in the kitchen garden bringing subjects like Maths, English, History and Science to life while making sure sports, music and the arts flourish alongside academic disciplines.

Walhampton has one of the ultimate prep school settings and offers over 35 different enrichment activities during the timetabled "SPARK" classes (Society/Service, Play, Adventure, Radical, Kindle/Create) as well as after school activities. The SPARK curriculum covers a broad rage of activities including bee keeping, bushcraft, conservation, cooking, drama, local history, orchestra, philosophy for children, plogging, pottery and sign language; as well as golf, rhythmic gymnastics and tennis with external specialist coaches; watersports and fishing on the school's lakes; sailing in partnership with the Royal Lymington Yacht Club;

specialist Rugby and Netball Academies; and riding in the on-site equestrian centre.

The network of daily bus routes for local day pupils; wraparound care (breakfast and supper clubs); and popular flexi boarding are all designed to support families with busy lives. For those considering a Walhampton education but living further afield, the Walhampton Express brings this remarkable country school closer. The escorted train service stops at mainline stations from Brockenhurst to London Waterloo. Boarding staff collect children on Sunday evening and escort them on Friday after chapel. Full, weekly and flexi boarders enjoy the relaxed and homely atmosphere of Bradfield House, surrounded by stunning grounds with views over the Solent to the Isle of Wight.

Walthamstow Hall Junior School

Bradbourne Park Road, Sevenoaks, Kent TN13 3LD

Tel: 01732 453815
email: registrar@whall.school
website: www.walthamstow-hall.co.uk
Twitter: @WalthamstowHall
Facebook: @Walthamstow-Hall
Instagram: @walthamstowhall
LinkedIn: /company/walthamstow-hall

Chair of Governors: Mrs J Adams, BA Joint Hons

Headmistress of Walthamstow Hall School: **Miss S Ferro**, MA Oxon, MA London, PGCE Surrey

Assistant Head of the Junior School: Mrs C Conway, BA Hons, MA Witwatersrand South Africa, PGCE Canterbury Christ Church

Senior Teacher: Mrs P Potter, BEd Southampton, Dip MEd Roehampton Institute

Head of Pre-Prep Department: H Andrews Esq, BA Hons, AKC King's College London

Day School for Girls.

Age Range. 3–11.

Number of Girls. 148.

Fees per term (2021–2022). Nursery £325 per session (2–10 sessions per week); Reception–Year 2 £4,045, Years 3–6 £5,180.

Walthamstow Hall Junior School is a happy and vibrant school with a proud tradition of providing the highest quality education for girls aged 3–11 years.

From Reception upwards pupils benefit from being in small classes (up to 15 per class) with two parallel classes in most year groups. Optimum-sized classes throughout the Junior School guarantee individual attention, with obvious benefits including a seamless and highly effective preparation for Senior School entrance exams without last-minute cramming and changes to routine.

A well-planned programme of education brings out the potential of each child as she progresses through the Junior School. A broad curriculum is enriched with many co-curricular activities and clubs. Wrap-Around care provision is available from 7.15am until 6.00pm Monday–Friday.

Girls are well prepared for a range of senior schools and have won awards to prestigious independent schools, including Walthamstow Hall Senior School (*see entry in GSA section*). Entry to our Senior School is from 11+, 13+ and 16+ with Awards, Scholarships and Bursaries offered. Equally, our track record in the Kent 11+ test is excellent.

Walthamstow Hall was founded in 1838 and is one of the oldest girls' schools in the country. It has built a reputation for all-round excellence and achievements by girls are outstanding. Over recent years, many facilities have been enhanced or added, and our specialist facilities include our ICT Suite and Science Laboratory, Design and Technology, Art and Cookery Rooms, well-stocked computerised Library, Tennis and Netball Courts and dedicated Music Centre. Girls also have access to facilities at the nearby Senior School including the Ship Theatre, Swimming Pool, and Sports Centre opened in 2018. The school is situated in the centre of Sevenoaks within easy reach of road and rail networks.

Warwick Preparatory School

Banbury Road, Warwick CV34 6PL

Tel: 01926 491545
email: admissions@warwickprep.com
website: www.warwickprep.com
Twitter: @WarwickPrep
Facebook: @warwickprep
Instagram: @warwickprep

Chairman of the Governors: Mrs Sally Austin

Headmistress: **Mrs Hellen Dodsworth**

Age Range. Boys 3–7, Girls 3–11.

Number of Children. c. 509.

Fees per term (2021–2022). Nursery: £2,933 (full time, after Nursery Education Funding, lunch included). Lower School (4–6 years) £3,546; Middle School (7–9 years) £4,094. Upper School (9–11 years) £4,347. Lunch £215 (Mid-morning fruit.)

Instrumental music tuition optional extra.

Warwick Preparatory School is an Independent School, purpose built on a 4½ acre site on the outskirts of Warwick. It is part of the Warwick Independent Schools Foundation, which includes Warwick School and the King's High School for Girls.

The Prep School has an exceptionally large staff, with specialist tuition in Art, French, Science, Music, Drama, DT, Physical Education and Computing.

Boys and girls are admitted from the age of 3+, subject to the availability of places. At the age of 7, the majority of boys continue to Warwick School, whilst the girls normally remain with us until they are 11.

Entry to King's High School is based on girl's progress at Warwick Prep and their aptitude, and girls may be offered a guaranteed place. If there are any concerns, the Entrance Examination will be used to determine a place, as with candidates outside the Foundation.

Early registration is advised if a place in the Pre-Prep Department is to be ensured. Entry to the School at the age of 7 and later requires a satisfactory level of attainment in the basic skills and may be competitive.

Charitable status. Warwick Independent Schools Foundation is a Registered Charity, number 1088057.

Wellesley House

Ramsgate Road, Broadstairs, Kent CT10 2DG

Tel: 01843 862991
email: admissions@wellesleyhouse.net
website: www.wellesleyhouse.org
Twitter: @wellesleyschool
Facebook: @wellesleyhouseschool
Instagram: @wellesleyschool

Chairman of the Governors: Mr P J Woodhouse

Headmaster: Mr Gavin Franklin, BA

Head of Pre-Prep: Mrs Hannah Brown, BSc

Age Range. 2–13.
Number of Pupils. 65 Boys, 40 Girls.
Fees per term (2021–2022). Boarding £8,777; Day: Years 6–8 £6,639, Year 5 £4,750, Year 4 £4,250, Year 3 £3,750; Years 1–2 £3,250; Reception £2,975.
Location. The school was purpose-built in 1898 and sits in 20 acres of extensive grounds.

A high-speed rail link runs hourly from St Pancras which takes as little as 1 hour 15 minutes, trains also run to Broadstairs from Charing Cross and Victoria. It takes under two hours from London by road. At the beginning of each term, and at most exeats and half-terms, the school operates coach services between Broadstairs and London via the M2 services.

Facilities. The school has a science and technology building, which includes modern science laboratories, an ICT laboratory and a craft room. Other facilities include a library, an indoor heated swimming pool, a chapel, four hard tennis courts, two squash courts, a modelling room, art room, a music wing, a recording studio, a .22 shooting range, fitness trail, outdoor stage and separate recreation rooms, all of which are in the school grounds. There is a spacious sports hall. The main team games are cricket, rugby, football, hockey, netball and rounders. Tuition is also given in fencing, squash, shooting, golf, tennis, archery, judo, scuba and swimming. Ballet, tap, modern dancing and riding are also available.

Education. Boys and girls are prepared for all independent senior schools. Those who show sufficient promise are prepared for scholarships and the school has a fine record of success on this front with 60% of leavers gaining scholarships in recent years. The curriculum is designed to enable all children to reach the highest standard possible by sound teaching along carefully thought out lines to suit the needs of the individual. In September 2019 Wellesley extended the educational provision and opened a Pre-Prep and in 2020, opened a Nursery.

The Headmaster and his wife are assisted by 21 teaching staff.

Charitable status. Wellesley House and St Peter Court School Education Trust Ltd is a Registered Charity, number

307852. It exists solely to provide education to boys and girls.

Wellington Prep School

South Street, Wellington, Somerset TA21 8NT

Tel: 01823 668700
email: prep@wellington-school.org.uk
website: www.wellington-school.org.uk
Twitter: @wellingtonsch1
Facebook: @WellingtonSchool
Instagram: @wellingtonschool1

Chair of Governors: Mrs Anna Govey, MSc

Head: Mrs Victoria Richardson, BSc, PGCE

Head of Pre-Prep: Mrs Jan Wheller, BEd Hons, PGCE

Head of Year 3 & 4: Mrs Angel Needs, BEd Hons

Head of Year 5 & 6 : Mr Roger Hitchen, BEd Hons, PGCE

Age Range. 3–11 Co-educational.
Number of Pupils. 200.
Fees per term (2021–2022). Day: £2,310–£4,195

Wellington Prep School opened in September 1999 in purpose-built accommodation to provide one of the most stimulating educational environments for children anywhere in the country.

Wellington Prep School provides an education of unrivalled quality which both complements and enhances the national reputation of Wellington School and enables us to deliver educational excellence from nursery level through to university entrance. Our school is a place of endeavour, teamwork, integrity and laughter; a place where each child is nurtured.

We believe whole-heartedly in our three core principles and these influence all we do in the classroom and out.

• Love of Learning

• Outstanding Relationships

• The Pursuit of Excellence

We value education in its widest sense; making the most of today in order that we can make even more of tomorrow and the days, weeks, months and years that lie ahead. This is 'Learning for Life.' Our education is unbounded, as we encourage our children to be curious, to be creative and to be compassionate. At WPS Learning is not a spectator sport.

We believe that every child deserves to be inspired every day. The qualities our children will need in life are as important as their skills. This is why we have high expectations for each child, nurture and support each child and develop each child's leadership skills. We encourage our children to think independently and to 'have a go', secure in the knowledge that they can learn from mistakes.

While the headline ratio of one fully-qualified and experienced teacher for every ten children in the Prep School is striking, it is the quality of these relationships that really matters and this cannot be gauged by a simple statistic. The range of experiences our teaching team provide for our children is superb. Every person cares deeply about the children in their care and each child's happiness and fulfilment.

Our children benefit from sharing some facilities with our Senior School, giving them access to:

- Eighteen purpose-designed, modern classrooms;
- A large, attractive, central school hall, the hub of our school;
- The most modern and up-to-date education resources;
- Purpose-built ICT suite and library;
- Spacious grounds including a large playground with wooden amphitheatre;
- Our forest school in the Blackdown Hills;
- The Princess Royal Sports Complex;
- Numerous sports pitches, hard courts and the astro;
- Music and drama resources across the whole school 3–18;
- Dedicated performance space;
- An indoor swimming pool.

School is open from 8.00am and there is an extensive clubs programme followed by STAR club, which is available to all children from 5.00 to 6.00pm during term time. For children in Reception and older, holiday clubs operate at Christmas, Easter and for six weeks during the summer holidays to accommodate busy working families. Our Nursery setting has a holiday club that runs during some weeks of the Prep School holidays.

Our prospectus is available from the School Registrar and can be requested via our website.

Charitable status. Wellington School is a Registered Charity, number 1161447.

Wells Cathedral Junior School

Jocelyn House, 11 The Liberty, Wells, Somerset BA5 2ST

Tel: 01749 834400
email: juniorschool@wells.cathedral.school
website: https://wells.cathedral.school
Twitter: @wellscathschool
Facebook: @wellscathedralschool
Instagram: @little_wellies_wcs

Chairman of Governors: Very Revd Dr John Davies, MA, MPhil, PhD

Head Master: Alastair Tighe

Head of the Junior School: **Mr Jody Wells**

Registrar: Joanna Prestidge

Age Range. 2–11 years.

Number of Pupils. 137 plus 44 in the Nursery. Girl to boy ratio approximately 1:1.

Fees per term (2021–2022). Day: £2,770–£5,573. Boarding: £8,502–£9,438. Weekly Boarding: £7,366–£8,300.

The Junior School is made up of the Pre-Prep department (age 2–7) and the Junior School (age 7–11). Pupils accepted into the Junior School normally make a smooth transfer to the Senior School at 11 and academic, music and sports scholarships are awarded.

Academic Work. The School prepares children for the academic demands in the Senior School. Pupils complete internal standardised baseline tests throughout each academic year. The School is not restricted by the National Curriculum; the aim is to ensure high academic standards within a friendly, creative and stimulating environment.

Children are assessed regularly for both academic achievement and effort and feedback is given to both children and parents. There are several opportunities throughout the year for parents to meet with teachers to discuss their child's progress.

As well as driving high academic standards, there is an important focus on developing 'Learning Powers' such as resilience, curiosity and motivation.

Boarding. We offer boarding for pupils in Years 4 to 8 (aged 8–13) in the beautiful house and grounds of Claver Morris. It is a priority to create a warm, caring family environment for this age range. The children are very well looked after by a resident family – community living lies at the heart of their daily lives. They all eat breakfast and most evening meals together; the house is extremely spacious and includes excellent facilities, including separate rooms for games, music and relaxing. The house has a lovely family feel and yet is large enough for the children to form lots of strong friendships.

Creativity. We have close ties to Wells Cathedral and all their boy and girl choristers attend our School, which is set in beautiful grounds just to the north of the cathedral. A number of pupils are specialist musicians who enjoy the expert tuition of the music department, which is one of the four in the UK designated and grant-aided by the Government's Music and Dance Scheme. Scholarships are available.

Drama, music and dance are considered vital activities to bring out the best in children. In our state-of-the-art Cedars Hall, we offer a full programme of concerts during the year for all age groups as well as big productions and small year group dramas. The School has established drama exchange links with schools in other European countries.

A whole school arts week each summer allows all aspects of creativity to come to the forefront for every pupil. Themes have included the Caribbean, Somerset and China; pupils experience workshops in the areas of art, dance, drama and music. Regular exhibitions and performances are a feature of the School.

Sport. The School has many excellent facilities, such as the sports hall, dance studio, astroturf pitch and swimming pool. Pupils experience a wide range of activities on the games field. Sport is played to a high standard with rugby, cross country, netball, hockey, cricket, swimming, athletics and gymnastics being the main sports; basketball and badminton are also available. A full programme of inter-school matches and house matches is available for all pupils in Year 3 to 6. Many clubs and activities run at lunchtimes or after school.

West House School

24 St James Road, Edgbaston, Birmingham B15 2NX

Tel: 0121 440 4097
email: secretary@westhouseprep.com
website: www.westhouseprep.com
Twitter: @westhouseschool

Chair of Governors: J Gittins

Headmaster: A M J Lyttle, BA Hons, PGCE Birmingham, NPQH

Age Range. Boys: 4–11 years; Co-educational Nursery: 12 months to 4 years.

Number of Pupils. A maximum 230 boys aged 4–11 (Reception to Year 6) plus 100 boys and girls aged 12 months–4 years.

Fees per term (2021–2022). 4–11 year olds: £3,009–£4,083 according to age. The fees include lunches and breaktime drinks. Under 4: fees according to number of sessions attended per week. Fee list on application.

West House was founded in 1895 and since 1959 has been an Educational Trust controlled by a Board of Governors. The school has a strong academic reputation and pupils are regularly awarded scholarships to senior schools at 11+. The well-qualified and experienced staff provides a sound education for boys of all abilities. The National Curriculum has been adapted to suit the aptitudes and interests of pupils and to ensure that it provides an outstanding preparation for entry into selective senior schools. Pupils are taught in small classes which ensures that they receive much individual attention. Specialist help is available for children with Dyslexia or who require learning support. Music teachers visit the school to give individual music tuition.

The school occupies a leafy five-acre site a mile from Birmingham city centre. As well as the main teaching blocks there are two well-equipped science laboratories and a sports hall.

The Centenary Building, opened in 1998, accommodates the art and design technology department, ICT room and senior Library. Extensive playing fields, two all-weather tennis courts and all-weather cricket nets enable pupils to participate in many games and sports. Pupils also enjoy a wide range of hobby activities, and drama and music play important roles in school life.

The school is open during term time between 7.30am and 6.00pm. On-site Holiday Clubs are run by members of staff during the holidays.

Charitable status. West House School is a Registered Charity, number 528959. It exists to provide education for boys.

Westbourne House School

Coach Road, Shopwyke, Chichester, West Sussex PO20 2BH

Tel: 01243 782739
email: admissions@westbournehouse.org
website: www.westbournehouse.org
Twitter: @WestbourneHse
Facebook: @westbournehouseschool
LinkedIn: /school/westbourne-house-school

Chairman of the Governors: Chris Keville

Headmaster: Martin Barker

Head of Pre-Prep and Nursery: Caroline Oglethorpe

Age Range. 2½–13.

Number of Pupils. 350: Boarders 50; Prep Day 210; Pre-Prep 90.

Fees per term (2021–2022). Prep: Day Pupils (Years 3–8) £5,575–£6,525; Boarding (in addition to day fees): Full Boarding £2,900 (7 nights), Part-Time Boarding: £1,555 (5 nights per week), £780 (2 nights per week), £470 (1 night per week, Years 3–6 only). Pre-Prep (Pre-Nursery to Year 2): £1,360–£3,900.

All I am, everything I can be

At Westbourne House, we uncover the magic in each child and ensure they make the most of the world of experiences offered to them here. We develop lifelong learners, cultivating curiosity and rewarding initiative in a kind, caring and happy environment.

Exceptional results

Westbourne House pupils go on to some of the most prestigious schools in the country, including Benenden, Brighton College, Seaford, Lancing, Canford, Eton, Harrow, Marlborough, Wellington, Winchester and Wycombe Abbey. Our scholarship record is second to none, with 33 scholarships achieved by our Year 8 leavers in 2020 for outstanding performance in academics, sport, music, choral, dance, art and drama, as well as awards for all-round achievement.

'Pupils here stay kids for longer than those in more urban schools.' – Good Schools Guide

Westbourne House is located in 100 acres of parkland in a picturesque location between the sunny South Downs and the south coast, just outside the beautiful city of Chichester. 1½ hours south of London, Westbourne House attracts many families seeking to enjoy the coastal lifestyle. It is easily accessible by train from London and only 45 miles from Gatwick Airport.

We makes sure we give children time to get out in the fresh air and explore the grounds, returning to lessons with muddy knees and renewed spirit; it's key to life here because we know that children who spend time outside are happier, healthier and more creative.

'Teachers have detailed knowledge of the children, allowing carefully-focused support to be provided.' – ISI Report

Thanks to small class sizes, our pastoral approach and an exceptional SEN team, we keep a close eye on each child's progress to identify when a child is ready for a challenge and to ensure that extra support is given where needed.

'Exceptional creative talents are evident in many areas.' – ISI Report

We give children endless opportunities to find their strengths and shine. Designed to be holistic and stimulating, our curriculum is an unforgettable journey of discovery: science experiments, outdoor adventures, drama, debates, chess, cooking, ceramics, poetry, music, kayaking and a variety of team and individual sports.

Confident, pro-active, collaborative leaders

A recent Independent Schools Inspectorate Report found Westbourne House pupils to "have exemplary leadership skills", to "demonstrate exceptional confidence" and to "show initiative" and "work remarkably well on their own, collaboratively and with their teachers".

'Founded as a family school and the atmosphere remains.' – Good Schools Guide

There is a deeply-felt sense of community here. Boarders live in one of seven family-style boarding houses. They enjoy a range of activities, but their favourite time is when they get to take advantage of the grounds, playing games, hanging out and creating lifelong bonds with their friends.

Charitable status. Westbourne House is a Registered Charity, number 307034.

Westbourne School

60 Westbourne Road, Sheffield, South Yorkshire S10 2QT

Tel: 0114 266 0374
email: enquiries@westbourneschool.co.uk
website: www.westbourneschool.co.uk

Chairman of the Governors: Mr D Peters

Headmaster: **Mr John Hicks**, MEd Kingston, BEd Hons Exeter

Bursar: Mrs Vina Khan

Age Range. 3–16.
Number of Pupils. 370 day pupils, boys and girls.
Fees per term (2021–2022). £3,120–£4,450.

The co-educational School, founded in 1885, is an Educational Trust with a Board of Governors, some of whom are Parents. The number of entries is limited to maintain small class sizes – with an average class size of 14 throughout the school and a staff to pupil ratio of less than 1:10.

A new £3 million development is set to open in 2022 for the expanding Pre-School and Junior School including three new classrooms, a gymnasium and a state-of-the-art hall for music and drama. French, Music, Drama and Games are taught by specialists, some in subject specialist rooms. Specialist Science and Technology are introduced from Year 4 (8+), as well as specialist teaching in Computing, Art and Design. French, Science, Computers, Drama and Sports are introduced from the age of 4.

In the Junior School, Forest School, in the school's historic Dell, provides an innovative programme of curricular outdoor learning. There are also ICT, Drama, Art and Music Rooms, Fiction and Reference Libraries, and a Hall with a Stage.

The Senior School provides teaching to GCSE from Year 7 to 11, up to age 16. It has its own campus immediately adjacent to the Junior School. Years 7 and 8 have the benefit of their own designated building with access to all the facilities available in Senior School. The school has a 3-form entry in Year 7 with a scholarship class. External and internal scholarships are taken in January of Year 6. All Senior School children are placed in sets in Maths (from Year 5), Science and English.

The school focuses on individualised learning, where close support and monitoring enable teachers to bring out the best in every pupil according to their ability. There is a tailored programme of additional curricular and extra-curricular activities for More-Able Pupils (MAPS) and a Special Educational Needs (SEN) team. Great emphasis is laid on courtesy and the school's values of respect, resilience, excellence and inclusion

An enrichment programme open to all pupils enables a wide range of cultural activities. Art, Music and Drama are strongly encouraged throughout the school, with regular concerts, plays and art exhibitions. Tuition in several instruments is available. A new Drama Studio opened in June 2015 and new Chemistry and Biology laboratories in September 2017.

The main sports are Rugby, Football, Hockey, Cricket, Athletics, Netball, Rounders and Cross-Country Running with regular matches against other schools. There are also opportunities for Short Tennis, Swimming, Basketball, Volleyball, Fencing, Skiing, Badminton, Climbing, Golf and Scuba Diving. Numerous educational visits are on offer with annual trips abroad.

A supervised breakfast club runs from 7.30am to 8.15am. While the length of day depends on the age of the child, there are after-school facilities for all pupils until 5.15pm, with some going on until 5.45pm. There is no school on Saturdays.

Charitable status. Westbourne School is a Registered Charity, number 529381. It exists to provide education of the highest quality for boys and girls.

Westbrook Hay Prep School

London Road, Hemel Hempstead, Herts HP1 2RF

Tel: +44 (0)1442 256143/230099
email: admin@westbrookhay.co.uk
website: www.westbrookhay.co.uk
Twitter: @WestbrookHaySch
Facebook: @Westbrook-Hay-Prep-School
Instagram: @westbrook_hay
LinkedIn: /westbrook-hay-prep-school

Chairman of Governors: Andrew Newland

Headmaster: **Mark Brain**, BA Ed Hons

Registrar: Kate Woodmansee

Age Range. Boys 3–13, Girls 3–11.
Number of Pupils. Day: 220 Boys, 138 Girls.

Fees per term (2021–2022). £3,818–£5,495.

Westbrook Hay is an outstanding independent prep school educating boys and girls from rising 3–13 years. The school's beautiful location boasts 26 acres of parkland overlooking the Bourne valley in Hertfordshire, and is just off the A41, between Berkhamsted and Hemel Hempstead. This unique setting offers a secure environment, within which children explore and enjoy all that childhood has to offer.

We know that our childhood is a most precious time. Here, at Westbrook Hay, we want it to be the best time of your children's lives. We believe that it is one filled with happiness, rich and varied experiences, in an ambitious, yet nurturing environment. This is what we strive to provide at Westbrook Hay and what make our boys and girls the confident, well-mannered young people of whom we are so proud.

The recent Independent Schools Inspectorate (ISI) carried out a very successful inspection and regarded our school as 'Excellent' in all area of the inspection:

"Pupils make excellent progress during their time at the school, as seen in their high attainment in senior school examinations."

"Pupils have excellent relationships with peers and adults and exhibit a strong sense of community through the school's ethos of 'happiness, confidence, success'."

Classes are small and each individual is encouraged and helped to achieve their potential. Individuality, honesty, a sense of humour and self-reliance are attributes which are stimulated and valued in this most friendly school, which maintains a caring, family atmosphere.

The wonderful Pre-Prep, for children in Nursery to Year 2, benefits from a modern purpose-built facility, a woodland school and outdoor classroom. Children in Years 3 and 4 are class taught primarily by their form teacher, before a move to a subject-based curriculum in Year 5. The academic focus is based on preparation for the pupil's chosen Senior Schools entrance and Scholarship examinations predominantly at the end of Year 8.

The facilities of the school have benefited from significant improvements including a £2 million lower school building, an art studio with pottery kiln, a fully equipped Information Technology room and a £3 million Performing Arts Centre, with 300-seat theatre and full music practice and performance facilities. The state-of-the-art Outdoor Classroom for our youngest children and the modernisation of the classrooms for our senior pupils are amongst the most recent additions to the outstanding facilities. We have further enhanced our outdoor play areas for the older children with a generously sized adventure playground.

Extensive playing fields give ample room for rugby, football, cricket, golf, and athletics. All-weather netball courts and a heated swimming pool are complemented by a Sports Hall which provides for POP lacrosse, hockey, badminton, table tennis, cricket nets, five-a-side football, gymnastics and many other indoor sports.

An exciting range of after school activities is provided by our Westbrook+ programme including Taekwondo, skiing, fencing, ballet, drama, shooting, golf, choir, knitting and sewing and model making, to name just a few. We offer breakfast club from 7:30am, supper club until 6pm and a school bus service is also available to accommodate the needs of working parents.

Our Westbrook Adventure is a range of exciting residential trips for children encouraging independence, courage, resourcefulness and teamwork. The trips become progressively more adventurous as the children get older. In Year 3 our children experience a first night away from home by camping in our Teepee style bell tents in the grounds of the school. By the time the children are in Year 6 they enjoy a 5-night language immersion, history and cultural trip to Normandy and in Years 7 & 8 the children can participate in the trip to Iceland, a language exchange, a geography trip to Wales and a national sports tour.

Charitable status. Westbrook Hay School is a Registered Charity, number 292537. It exists to provide education for boys and girls.

Westminster Abbey Choir School

Dean's Yard, London SW1P 3NY

Tel: 020 7654 4918
email: headmaster@westminster-abbey.org
website: www.abbeychoirschool.org

Chairman of Governors: The Dean of Westminster

Headmaster: Mr Peter Roberts

Age Range. 8–13.

Number of Boys. Up to 35 all chorister boarders.

Fees per term (2021–2022). £3,090 inclusive of tuition on two instruments. Additional bursaries may be available in cases of real financial need.

Westminster Abbey Choir School is the only school in Britain exclusively devoted to the education of boy choristers. Boys have been singing services in the Abbey since at least 1384 and the 35 boys in the school maintain this tradition.

Westminster Abbey Choir School is a special place, offering boys from eight to thirteen a unique and exciting opportunity to be a central part of one of our great national institutions. Boys sing daily in the Abbey and also take part in many special services and celebrations both in the UK and abroad.

The small size of the school, the fact that all boys are boarders and the high proportion of staff who live on the premises, allow the School to have an extended family atmosphere.

A full academic curriculum is taught by specialist staff and boys are prepared for the Common Entrance and academic scholarship examinations; most boys win valuable scholarships to secondary independent schools when they leave at 13.

Music obviously plays a central part in the school. Every boy learns the piano and at least one orchestral instrument and there are 15 visiting music teachers. Concerts, both inside and outside school, are a regular feature of the year.

Besides music and academic lessons there is a thriving programme of other activities and there are many opportunities for boys to develop interests outside music.

Sports played include football, cricket, athletics, hockey, sailing, canoeing and tennis.

Entry is by voice trial and academic tests. Further details are available from Jennifer Benjamin (Headmaster's PA and Admissions Officer). The Headmaster is always pleased to hear from parents who feel that their son might have the potential to become a chorister.

Charitable status. Westminster Abbey is a Registered Charity, number X8259. It is a religious establishment incorporated by Royal Charter in 1560.

Westminster Cathedral Choir School

Ambrosden Avenue, London SW1P 1QH

Tel: 020 7798 9081
email: office@choirschool.com
website: www.choirschool.com
Twitter: @WCCSLondon
Facebook: @wccslondon

President: HE Cardinal Vincent Nichols, Archbishop of Westminster

Chair of Governors: David Heminway

Headmaster: **Neil McLaughlan**, BA Hons

Age Range. 4–13.
Number of Boys. 264 (20 Choristers, 244 Day Boys).
Fees per term (2021–2022). Chorister Boarders £3,564; Day Boys (Reception to Year 2) £5,979; Day Boys (Years 3 to 8) £7,204.

Founded in 1901, Westminster Cathedral Choir School is a day prep and pre-prep school and boarding choir school. Choristers must be Roman Catholic, but day boys of all denominations are welcome.

The school forms part of the precincts of Westminster Cathedral and enjoys such facilities as a large playground and a Grade 1 listed Library. The school has recently undergone a £1.3 million refurbishment, including a brand new playground and boarding facilities.

Choristers and day boys alike achieve a high level of music making. The Choristers sing the daily capitular liturgy in the Cathedral and are regularly involved in broadcasts, recordings and tours abroad. There is also a day boy choir, two orchestras and a substantial programme of chamber music. Boys can learn the piano and any orchestral instrument in school.

The major sports include football, rugby and cricket and the boys travel to Vincent Square, Battersea Park and the Queen Mother Sports Centre for games.

There is a wide range of extracurricular activities available including: chess, computing, debating, fencing, football, judo, drama and a Saturday rugby club.

The school is justly famed for its fantastic food!

Assessment for Choristers is by academic assessment and voice trial, generally in November and February. Day Boy assessments are held in November (pre-prep) and January (7+ and 8+).

Charitable status. Westminster Cathedral Choir School is a Registered Charity, number 1063761.

Westminster Under School

Adrian House, 27 Vincent Square, London SW1P 2NN

Tel: +44 (0)20 7821 5788
email: sarah.long@westminster.org.uk
website: www.westminster.org.uk
Twitter: @WestminsterUS
Facebook: @westminsterUS

Westminster Under School is a busy, passionate and purposeful preparatory day school for boys aged seven to 13, where pupils greatly enjoy the pursuit of learning, and are given the support and guidance they need to develop as intelligent, compassionate and inquisitive individuals.

Chairman of Governors: Mr Mark Batten

Master: **Mrs Kate Jefferson**, LLB, LLM, NPQH

Deputy Master: Michael Woodside, BSc

Age Range. 7–13.
Number of Boys. 292.
Fees per term (2021–2022). £7,107 (inclusive of lunches).

About the School. Established by Westminster School in 1943, Westminster Under School is closely linked to the 'Great School', sharing the same Governing Body and the same ethos of a liberal education. The Under School's buildings overlook the beautiful school playing fields in Vincent Square, just a few moments' walk from the Great School and its site on the doorstep of Westminster Abbey and the Houses of Parliament. The Under School's premises were extended in 2011 with a new dining hall and a specialist suite of Art rooms located in an adjacent site, George House. The current site was also extensively refurbished.

Academic. While results are consistently outstanding, the School's focus is not solely aimed at learning for exams; instead the School aims to encourage the sense of wonder and curiosity that children at this age possess and to develop independent thought. The teaching programme is loosely based on the National Curriculum, but with much more flexibility for exploration. In the early years, English, Mathematics, Science, History and Geography are all taught by the pupil's form teacher, allowing boys to get comfortable in one familiar classroom and making the discussion and dissection of cross-curricular topics and ideas considerably easier. Boys then receive specialist teaching outside of their form classrooms in Art, Drama, Music, French, ICT, Religious Studies and Sport. As boys progress more of their lessons are taught by specialists, such as Latin and Greek, although the same broad range of subjects are available.

Admissions. The main entry points for Westminster Under School are at 7+, 8+ and 11+. Each year approximately 44 new boys are admitted to the Under School at 7+ and 8+, with 30 joining at 11+. At all ages the School looks for potential, and for boys who have natural ability and will, therefore, thrive here. Our challenge is to find that potential, rather than simply select intensely-tutored boys, and whose natural ability will grow with the challenges a Westminster education provides. At 7+ and 8+ the entrance assessment includes papers in Mathematics,

English, verbal reasoning and non-verbal reasoning. Based on the results of these, there is then a classroom activity and interview session at which we find out more about each boy as an individual. Entry at 11+ begins with ISEB Common Pre-tests in Mathematics, English, verbal reasoning and non-verbal reasoning, before selected boys sit further papers in Mathematics and English. Interviews with each boy then follow. Entry into the Under School at age 11+ guarantees a place at the Great School at 13+.

Bursaries and Scholarships. The purpose of a bursary is to give financial support to a child who has the academic ability to benefit from a Westminster education but whose parents would not be able to afford the fees either wholly or in part without unacceptable hardship. Means-tested bursaries up to 100% are available at 11+, as are Music scholarships, and many boys apply at this entry point from London primary schools. Bursaries that are awarded at 11+ entry will continue, subject to satisfactory academic performance, until a boy leaves the Great School, should he opt to stay at Westminster.

Co-curricular and Sport. Just as much emphasis is put on the non-examinable subjects as on the core curriculum. Consequently, the musical and cultural tradition is equally strong, with a junior and senior choir, an orchestra, and string, brass and jazz groups. Art is housed in a wonderful facility for all kinds of creative activity. The Art Department also organises competitions in photography and model-making. There are other school competitions in areas such as public speaking, creative writing, chess and Scrabble. The level of dramatic productions has risen in recent years and there are plays for each year group at different times of the year. Games are played on the ten-acre field at Vincent Square, or nearby in the Sports Hall. Seasonal sports such as football, cricket, hockey and rugby are played, but there are also opportunities to participate in athletics, basketball, cross country, swimming, skiing, rowing and tennis. There is vast array of after-school clubs in such activities as fencing, judo, karate, climbing and table tennis.

Pastoral care. Naturally we want to protect and support our boys, helping them to develop into healthy, fulfilled and resilient young people and making sure they feel safe and enjoy their time at the Under School. We also encourage the boys to look out for others and to act thoughtfully and compassionately at all times. Central to this are the School's six Core Values that underpin all that we do. These Core Values will enable the boys, not only to thrive academically, but to flourish both now and in their future lives. The School fully believes that nurturing the values of Compassion, Integrity, Resourcefulness, Service, Diligence and Commitment will ensure that all of our boys leave as good young men. All pupils have a dedicated form teacher and a form support teacher. The School has a BACP-accredited Child and Adolescent Counsellor, and we make time each week for personal, spiritual and philosophical reflection.

Charitable status. St Peter's College (otherwise known as Westminster School) is a Registered Charity, number 312728.

Wetherby School
Alpha Plus Group

11 Pembridge Square, London W2 4ED

Tel:	020 7727 9581
email:	learn@wetherbyschool.co.uk
website:	www.wetherbyschool.co.uk

Headmaster: **Mr Mark Snell**, BA Hons, PGCE

Age Range. Boys 2½–8.
Number of Pupils. 360
Fees per term (2021–2022). £7,980

Wetherby School is situated at 11 Pembridge Square and 19 Pembridge Villas. The four Reception classes and Little Wetherby (a boys-only nursery opened in September 2014) are based at 19 Pembridge Villas. Each class occupies a whole floor level and there is a playground at the back for the boys to run around in. The rest of the school in based at 11 Pembridge Square.

Whilst proud of its academic attainments for London Day School entry at 7+ and 8+ and top Boarding Schools, the priority is in producing happy, respectful, thoughtful, sociable and motivated boys. The curriculum is well balanced, with excellent sport, music and art opportunities including specialist teaching rooms for art, ICT, library and music. There is also a wide range of extra-curricular activities available. Wetherby operates a non-selective admissions procedure; registration is at birth.

Willington Independent Preparatory School

Worcester Road, Wimbledon, London SW19 7QQ

Tel:	020 8944 7020
email:	admissions@willingtonschool.co.uk
website:	www.willingtonschool.co.uk
Twitter:	@WillingtonHead
Facebook:	@willingtonprep
Instagram:	@willingtonprep
LinkedIn:	/company/willingtonprep

Chair of Governors: Mrs Meredith Brickwood

Headmaster: **Mr Keith Brown**, MA, BSc Hons, PGCE

Age Range. 3–11.
Number of Pupils. 180
Fees per term (2021–2022). £4,820–£5,415 according to age.

Based in the heart of Wimbledon, Willington Prep offers an education for life for girls and boys aged 3 to 11. It is an exciting time to be at Willington as we move, after 135 years of being an all boys school, to become a fully co-educational school. Welcoming girls into this fantastic learning community makes Willington a truly family friendly school. Offering a high quality education to all, where pupils are self-confident and happy, we instil the values of kindness, humility, respect and honesty in all that we do. Our quietly confident Year 6 pupils go on to a vast range of destination schools, many with scholarships from academic through to music, art and sport. A broad curriculum and rich co-curricular programme is offered from Nursery onwards, led by passionate, supportive teachers, who hold true to the school's motto, *non scholae sed vitae discimus* – we do not learn for school, but for life.

Charitable status. Willington School Foundation Limited is a Registered Charity, number 312733. Its aim is to devote itself to the continuation and development of the School.

Wilmslow Preparatory School

Grove Avenue, Wilmslow, Cheshire SK9 5EG

Tel: 01625 524246
email: secretary@wilmslowprep.co.uk
website: www.wilmslowprep.co.uk
Twitter: @wilmslowprep
Facebook: @wilmslowprep

Co-ed Day School founded 1909.

Chairman of Board of Trustees: Mr N Rudgard, MA Oxon

Headteacher: **Mr B Lavagna-Slater**, HDipEd, BA Hons, NPQH

Bursar: Miss S J H Davies, BSc Hons, IPFA Hons

Secretary: Miss L Kendal, BA Hons, PGCE

Age Range. 3–11.
Number of Pupils. 120 day pupils.
Fees per term (2021–2022). £1,104–£4,165 (lunches extra).

The School is registered as an Educational Trust. It is purpose built and is situated in the centre of Wilmslow in its own spacious grounds. The facilities include an Assembly Hall, modern Sports Hall, a Science Room, refurbished dedicated Music Suite, Computer Room with networked PCs, a specialist Art Room with a kiln, two well-stocked libraries and a Classroom Block with its own outdoor area for 3–5 year olds. There is a Tennis/Netball Court, a Sports field with its own stand-alone Sports Hall, outdoor long jump pit and new all-weather pitch, and ample play areas including an outdoor woodland/forest classroom.

The School aims to provide extensive educational opportunities for all its pupils. Class sizes are intentionally small, enabling all staff to know pupils individually and to provide tailored, focussed teaching. It has a long-established excellent academic record and caters for a wide variety of entrance examinations to Independent Senior Day and Boarding Schools.

Wilmslow Preparatory School offers a variety of activities which include Music, Art and Drama. Principal sports include gymnastics, netball, football, cricket, hockey, tennis, athletics and swimming.

There are thirteen qualified and experienced teachers on the staff, as well as a highly knowledgeable and expert team of teaching support staff and management.

Charitable status. Wilmslow Preparatory School is a Registered Charity, number 525924. It exists to provide full-time education for pupils aged between 5 and 11, and part-time or full-time education to kindergarten children from the age of 3.

Wimbledon Common Preparatory School

113 Ridgway, Wimbledon, London SW19 4TA

Tel: 020 8946 1001
email: info@wcps.org.uk
website: www.wcps.org.uk
Twitter: @_wcps

Chairman of Governors: Lord Deighton, KBE

Head: **Mr Andrew Forbes**, BA

Age Range. Boys 4–7.
Number of Pupils. 168.

Wimbledon Common Preparatory School is a pre-prep school for boys situated in Wimbledon village, south-west London. It was founded in 1919 as a preparatory school for King's College School and other public schools, and moved to its present site in 1957. In 2006 it was bought by King's College School and is now part of their foundation and run by their board of governors.

The school's aims are to provide challenging and exciting teaching; to develop a love of learning; to encourage good study skills; to offer a variety of extracurricular activities; to create a culture which encourages self-confidence and values tolerance, generosity, respect for others and a strong sense of community; to help boys acquire the social skills which will enable them to make a positive contribution to society; to develop sound parent partnerships, and to provide opportunities for boys to reflect upon their relationships with one another, the wider world and their God.

The school educates boys aged from four to seven years, offering Early Years Foundation Stage (EYFS) provision in its Reception classes.

Fees per term (2021–2022). £4,985.

Charitable status. Wimbledon Common Prep School is owned by King's College School, which is a Registered Charity, number 310024.

Winchester House School

44 High Street, Brackley, Northamptonshire NN13 7AZ

Tel: 01280 702483
email: office@winchester-house.org
website: www.winchester-house.org
Twitter: @WHSprepschool
Facebook: @winchesterhouseschool

Chairman of Governors: Mr Simon C Creedy Smith, BA, FCA

Head: Antonia Lee

Age Range. 3–13.

Number of Children. 297: 174 Boys, 123 Girls.

Fees per term (2021–2022). Pre-Prep: £3,635. Upper School: Day £5,200–£6,410; Weekly Boarding (Years 3–8) £8,110 inclusive.

"The quality of pupils' achievements and learning is excellent." ISI Inspection Report

"Low intensity, high academic standards and maximum happiness" Tatler Schools Guide

"A uniquely warm, welcoming environment where my children have truly flourished." Parent

Winchester House School is a friendly and outstanding prep school for boys and girls aged 3–13 with day, occasional and weekly boarding available. Small class sizes and outstanding teachers ensure each child is nurtured and receives individual care so they can thrive and be their best self.

Aim. The aim of Winchester House School is to develop lifelong learners with a spirit of resourcefulness and self-reliance within a warm and purposeful community.

The School. Winchester House School sits in its own 18 acres of sports fields and gardens in the market town of Brackley, midway between Oxford and Northampton and on the borders of Buckinghamshire, Oxfordshire and Northamptonshire. The school operates three minibus services for day children in the local area and wraparound care from 7.45am to 6.30pm.

Learning. Winchester House has outstanding facilities and small classes. It is non-selective and is proud of developing confident, inquisitive children. The leavers, in recent years, gained scholarships in all the disciplines (academic, sport, drama, music, computing and DT) to top independent senior schools in the country including Radley, Oundle, Rugby, Stowe, Bloxham, Malvern College and Millfield.

There is also a strong Learning Development department. Inspiring masterclasses and workshops offer an opportunity for the children to master a craft or have the opportunity to work with experts in a particular field. For the Year 8s there is an academic focus and for Year 7s an introduction to new skills and experiences.

Opportunity. Winchester House has magnificent facilities that include a newly refurbished ICT suite and Art & Design Studios, three separate science labs and two performance spaces. Sports facilities include a full-size AstroTurf, numerous rugby, hockey and cricket pitches, tennis courts, a heated swimming pool, squash courts and a fully-fitted sports hall with indoor cricket nets. Winchester House School offers riding lessons in the after-school curriculum.

There is an extensive after-school activity programme including skiing, golf, dance and STEM Club and it offers a broad range of instrumental music teaching, music groups and three choirs. Major dramatic productions have included *A Winter's Tale*, performed outside in the Upper Quad. The annual candlelit carol service in Hyde Park is a favourite amongst parents and alumni.

Confidence. The school understands that building a child's self-esteem is key to happiness and their ability and desire to learn. Their unique Learn to Lead programme teaches leadership and team-building and includes annual expeditions for all children from Year 4 including wild camping in Dorset.

Pastoral. Winchester House has strong pastoral care including a 'Circle of Support', a dedicated Wellbeing Mentor and buddy benches in the playground.

Ambition. Winchester House encourages children to take pride in everything they do and live by the school motto: "To be their best self".

Community. There is a strong community at Winchester House. Children are encouraged to show respect and kindness and parents are a valued part of school life, involved in school events such as the Christmas Fair and Easter Egg Hunts.

Charitable status. Winchester House School Trust Limited is a Registered Charity, number 309912.

Windlesham House School

Washington, Pulborough, West Sussex RH20 4AY

Tel:	01903 874700
email:	whsadmissions@windlesham.com
website:	www.windlesham.com
Twitter:	@WindleshamTweet
Facebook:	@windlesham
Instagram:	@windleshamhouse

Chairman of Governors: Douglas Moody-Stuart

Head: Ben Evans, BA Hons, PGCE

Age Range. 4–13.

Number of Pupils. 120 full boarders, 150 day (60/40 boys and girls). Children can board from Year 3.

Fees per term (2021–2022): Day £3,185–£8,174; Boarding (full) £9,578–£9,860, International fees vary depending on visa requirements. Flexible and weekly boarding available from Year 3.

Windlesham nestles in 65 glorious acres of the South Downs countryside in West Sussex and gives every child the opportunity to reach their potential in whatever sphere of life that may be. Established in 1837 and celebrating its 180th anniversary in 2017, Windlesham was one of the first schools in the country to be established as a preparatory school and in 1967 became the first IAPS co-educational school. Windlesham is one of the few prep schools to have no uniform and our children are not confined to a playground; they make dens, climb trees and camp in the woods and are free to choose what they want to do in their break times.

Today we educate approximately 310 pupils with a broad range of ability. Windlesham traditionally receives outstanding ISI reports which underlines our position as one of the leading prep schools in the world today. We give every child the opportunity to reach his or her full potential in whatever sphere of learning that may be. Although academic excellence is key we also encourage success in sport, music, drama and the arts whilst nurturing a friendly, family-oriented atmosphere with wonderful pastoral care. In

March 2018 a state-of-the-art sports hall and swimming pool were opened which enhance their sporting prowess.

With us children have the time and space to be children, away from the pressures of competition and urban hothousing. Windlesham is set in exceptionally beautiful grounds with magnificent buildings and facilities where children are encouraged to try a host of sports and extra-curricular activities after the academic day and at weekends. The children learn about independence, interdependence and cooperation.

At the top end of the school our overriding aim is to ensure that each child achieves the highest grades they can in their Common Entrance or Scholarship exams to some of the best senior schools in the country, as well as ensuring they follow a balanced and enjoyable curriculum. This year saw a record number of scholarships to senior schools and best ever Common Entrance grades, with all candidates gaining places at their first choice of school.

When the time comes to leave Windlesham, children do so as confident, curious, clever and – above all – kind people who are ready to make a difference in their world. Senior schools often comment on how well prepared Windlesham children are for the next stage. Some even admit they've got a hard act to follow.

Charitable status. Windlesham House School is a Registered Charity, number 307046. It exists to provide education for girls and boys aged 4–13.

Winterfold House School
Part of the Bromsgrove School Family

Chaddesley Corbett, Worcestershire DY10 4PW

Tel: 01562 777234
email: info@winterfoldhouse.co.uk
website: www.winterfoldhouse.co.uk
Twitter: @winterfoldhs
Facebook: @Winterfoldhs

Chairman of Governors: Mr Paul West, QPM

Headmistress: **Mrs Denise Toms**, BA, QTS, NPQH

Age Range. 0–13 Co-educational.
Number of Pupils. 337 Day Boys and Girls.
Fees per term (2021–2022). Preparatory £3,930–£4,590; Pre-Prep £2,865–£3,155.

Set in over forty acres of grounds with views to the Malvern Hills, Winterfold offers excellent facilities which meet the needs of a broad and balanced curriculum. The School is just half an hour from the centre of Birmingham, 10 miles away from Worcester, and a mere 10 minutes from the M5 and M42.

Winterfold is a non-selective school and there are no formal entry requirements or tests. It is a Roman Catholic co-educational day preparatory school but children of all faiths are warmly welcomed and made to feel valued members of the community. The nursery offers day care for babies and toddlers.

The School has an excellent academic record at all levels, including National Curriculum Key Stage Tests. There is a highly regarded Learning Support Unit which provides one-

to-one help for children with specific learning difficulties such as dyslexia. The majority of pupils continue to Bromsgrove School.

Winterfold places a great emphasis upon educating the whole child and aims to produce well rounded and confident boys and girls with high moral standards and good manners. In order to develop self-belief, every child is encouraged to achieve success in some area and thus the school fields a number of teams and not just in the main sports of rugby, soccer, cricket, netball, hockey and rounders; but also in sports such as golf, tennis, swimming, athletics, basketball and fencing. There are also a large number of clubs and societies and regular visits to theatres, concerts and other places of educational interest, providing fullness and breadth to the educational experience.

In recent years, there has been considerable investment into the School which has seen the development of a new classroom block with eight new classrooms, state-of-the-art Science labs and Art and CDT rooms. The School also boasts a splendid sports hall, new AstroTurf, hockey pitches and tennis courts, ICT suite, chapel and a library. Adventure playgrounds cater for the demands of the full age range of pupils. Music and Drama are real strengths of the School and a new Performing Arts Centre is at the heart of Music in the School.

Charitable status. Winterfold House School is part of the Bromsgrove School family which is a Registered Charity, number 1098740. It exists solely to provide education for boys and girls.

Witham Hall

Witham-on-the-Hill, Bourne, Lincolnshire PE10 0JJ

Tel: 01778 590222
email: office@withamhall.com
website: www.withamhall.com
Twitter: @withamprep
Facebook: @withamhallschool
Instagram: @withamhallschool
LinkedIn: /company/witham-hall-school-trust

Witham Hall is a happy and thriving boarding and day school for boys and girls aged 4 to 13 years. We are committed to an education both in and beyond the classroom, thereby enabling the academic, artistic and physical potential of each child to flourish. Coupled with their purpose and determination to succeed, this broad programme enables our children to acquire a strong sense of achievement, a quiet confidence and an awareness of both themselves and each other.

Chairman of Governors: Mr J W Sharman

Headmaster: **Mr W S D Austen**, BSc Hons, PGCE

Age Range. 4–13.
Number of Pupils. 251: Prep (age 8–13): 140 Boys (71 boarders, 18 day pupils); 111 Girls (48 boarders, 31 day pupils); Pre-Prep (age 4–8): 83 pupils.
Fees per term (2021–2022). Boarders £6,550–£7,995, Day pupils £5,925, Pre-Prep £3,515–£3,910.

The School is situated in a superb country house setting in the village of Witham on the Hill, close to the Lincolnshire-Rutland border. Boarding is very popular (weekly and flexi are available from Year 4) and benefits from first-class provision within the original Queen Anne house at the heart of the School.

There is a teaching staff of 45, and additional visiting teachers for instrumental music. The maximum class size is 18 and pupils benefit from outstanding pastoral care across the school. The majority of pupils join at the Pre-Prep stage, and then continue through to Common Entrance. Pupils progress to their first-choice senior school both locally (Oundle, Oakham, Uppingham and Stamford) and further afield (Eton, Rugby, Repton, Shrewsbury and Stowe). The School has a proud and enviable scholarship record across a range of disciplines, including academic, art, drama, music and sport.

Facilities are outstanding with modern, purpose-built Prep and Pre-Prep teaching areas. Significant developments have taken place in the last three years, the most recent being a superb Sports Centre (that includes a Dance/Drama Studio and Fitness Suite) and new ICT suites. The Stimson Hall, serving as a Concert Hall and Theatre, underpins a strong commitment to both Creative and Performing Arts. Most of the children learn one instrument or more and there are three bands and four choirs. Inclusivity is strong; within sport all Prep pupils represent the school on a regular basis each term. The standard is high, with teams regularly reaching National Finals in Rugby, Hockey, Netball, Cricket and Rounders (IAPS U11 National Champions 2016 and 2018). An Olympic-size all-weather AstroTurf complements magnificently maintained grass surfaces, including county-standard cricket facilities and a 9-hole golf course. The school has seen considerable growth in numbers in recent years and in almost every year group early registration is recommended.

Charitable status. Witham Hall School Trust is a Registered Charity, number 507070. It exists for the purpose of educating children.

Woodcote House

Windlesham, Surrey GU20 6PF

Tel: 01276 472115
email: info@woodcotehouseschool.co.uk
website: www.woodcotehouseschool.co.uk
Twitter: @woodcotehouse
Facebook: @woodcotehouseschool
Instagram: @woodcotehouse.school

Headmaster: **David Paterson**

Deputy Headmasters: Andrew Monk and Oliver Paterson

Age Range. 7–13.

Number of Boys. 98 (18 full boarders, 38 part boarders, 42 day).

Fees per term (2021–2022). £8,450 (Boarding), £6,300 (Day). No compulsory extras. Scholarship offered at the Headmaster's discretion.

Location. Originally a Coaching Inn on the old London to Portsmouth Road, Woodcote enjoys a beautiful, rural setting in 30 acres of grounds. The school is easily accessible from London and runs 2 daily bus services from SW & W London, 25 miles from Fulham via the M3 (Junction 3), 25 minutes from Heathrow and 40 minutes from Gatwick.

Pastoral care. Woodcote House has been owned and run by the Paterson family for over 75 years. With a settled and committed staff, most of whom live on site with their own families, Woodcote provides an exceptionally caring and supportive environment for both Boarders and Day Boys. Our unique, graduated approach to boarding has helped solve the modern boarding conundrum faced by parents torn between Full and Weekly options. A strong emphasis is placed on manners, consideration and respect for others. The school has its own Chapel in the woods and parents are welcome to Saturday services, as well as to school matches on Wednesdays and Saturdays (after which legendary Match Teas are served), so there is plenty of opportunity to see their boys and talk to staff and fellow parents.

Academic. There are two forms in each year group, with an average of 10 boys in each class, enabling the staff to offer all boys an enormous degree of individual attention. With SEN and EFL teaching also available, academic standards are high and the school is proud of its 100% Common Entrance and excellent Scholarship record. Woodcote boys go on to a wide variety of independent senior schools and the Headmaster takes particular care in assisting parents to choose the right school for their son.

Music and Drama. 80% of boys learn at least one musical instrument, and the young and innovative Director of Music has ensured that it is considered 'cool' to be in the excellent choir. There is an orchestra and a jazz band and the school holds regular concerts so that the boys are comfortable with public performance, both individually and as part of a group. The school produces a Junior and a Senior Play each year, in which all boys are involved one way or another.

Sports. Rugby, football, cricket and hockey are coached to a high standard and there are teams at all levels of age and ability, with a high success rate for a small school. Individual sports include tennis (the school has five courts), swimming, athletics, golf, judo, fencing, and rifle-shooting.

Hobbies and free time. With 'prep' done first thing in the morning, there are numerous opportunities for the boys to pursue hobbies after lessons and games, and each member of staff offers a 'club' during Hobbies Hour on Wednesday afternoons. These activities are also available at weekends, along with the traditional activities of 'hutting' (camp building in the woods), 'cooking' (frying potatoes on camp fires), and overnight camping in the grounds. Boys are also offered the opportunity to be involved in the CCF. Boys are encouraged to read and have a quiet time after lunch each day for this as well as before lights out in the evening.

Ethos. The school motto, "Vive ut Discas et Disce ut Vivas" (Live to Learn and Learn to Live), embodies the school's aim to give all boys a love of learning and to discover and nurture their individual talents in a happy and positive atmosphere.

Woodford Green Preparatory School

Glengall Road, Woodford Green, Essex IG8 0BZ

Tel: 020 8504 5045
email: bursar@wgprep.co.uk
website: www.wgprep.co.uk
Twitter: @wgprep
Facebook: @wgprep1

The School is an Educational Charity and registered company, controlled by a Board of Governors who are also its Directors and Trustees.

Chairman of Governors: Mrs G Haddon

Head: Mr Jonathan Wadge, BA Hons Dunelm, PGCE, NPQH

Age Range. 3–11.
Number of Pupils. 400 (Boys and Girls).
Fees per term (2021–2022). £3,725

Established in 1932 as a Christian, co-educational school, we are proud to have been entrusted with delivering a first class education for generations of pupils. We are a forward-thinking, diverse and inclusive community, welcoming children of all faiths and none; our approach is to enable children to learn with enthusiasm and flair. We aim to equip children with the skills and knowledge to get the best out of themselves and those around them.

A great education is where children are given the skills and knowledge to see how things connect. Our curriculum is broad, exciting, and designed to adapt to the ever-changing world. We encourage all our girls and boys to have a 'can-do' attitude and place great emphasis on our pupils being active investigators, whether in the classroom, using the latest technologies, or exploring outdoors in our adventure playground, nature trail or in Epping Forest nearby.

To complement the broad curriculum, there are a wide selection of clubs on offer. Similarly, there are a wealth of sports fixtures, musical events, and curriculum competitions, both inside and outside of school. These are carefully planned to give an enjoyment of friendly competition.

The school provides an exceptional learning environment in which children achieve their best, feeling valued and secure. We have an outstanding record of success in 11+ examinations to Senior Independent and Grammar Schools, and demand for places at Nursery (3+) and Reception far outstrips availability. We value, with pride, the offers that our pupils gain through their 11+ assessments, recent offers include City of London School, City of London School for Girls and Westminster School, as well as numerous offers for local independent schools.

We have purpose-built areas for science, sport, art, music, computing and MFL, complemented by specialist teachers. There are modern facilities throughout the school, including a fabulous library which is regularly used by the whole school to foster a love of reading. In the Early Years, highly qualified staff ensure that children have an outstanding foundation for the rest of their education both here at WGPS and beyond.

Parents are advised to make a very early application to the school via the website, and are encouraged to attend Open Events which are advertised also on the website. Means-tested Assisted Places, of up to 100% of the full fees, are available for 7+ entry or above.

We want to ensure that each child's curiosity and love of learning is harnessed, nurtured and developed, so that they are inspired and prepared for their life-long journey of discovery. We promote politeness, hard work, curiosity, creativity and independence. We want every child to do their very best and we are dedicated to ensuring all are given the necessary support and challenge. Our school crest reminds us that we are here to ignite a passion for learning and to '*let each flame burn brighter.*'

Charitable status. Woodford Green Preparatory School is a Registered Charity, number 310930.

Yarlet School

Yarlet, Nr Stafford, Staffordshire ST18 9SU

Tel: 01785 286568
email: julia.bryan@yarletschool.org
website: www.yarletschool.uk

Chairman of the Governors: Mr Antony Morris

Headmaster: Mr Ian Raybould, BEd Hons, ALCM, NPQH

Age Range. Co-educational 2–13.
Number of Pupils. 165 pupils: 107 Girls and Boys in the Preparatory and Senior School (aged 7 to 13) and 58 Girls and Boys in the Early Years, Pre-Prep School (aged 2 to 7).
Fees per term (2021–2022). £2,755–£4,580. Flexi boarding available (Wednesday and Thursday nights) at £32 per night.

Established in 1873, Yarlet stands in 33 acres of grounds in unspoilt open countryside 3 miles north of Stafford. The school offers small classes, enthusiastic, qualified teachers, excellent facilities and a warm, friendly environment conducive to learning. All teachers keep fully abreast of senior school entry requirements and ensure that pupils are prepared for the next stage of their education.

Pupils have access to a wide range of facilities which include a new, state-of-the-art Science Laboratory, an Information Technology Centre, a CDT Centre, a purpose-built Art Studio, an indoor Sports Hall; and extensive outdoor facilities which include a nature walk, a large wildlife pool, a heated swimming pool, four playing fields (for football, rugby, hockey, cricket and athletics), three tennis courts, a netball court, an all-weather Astroturf pitch (for football, hockey and netball) and a cross-country running course. These facilities support an extensive sports curriculum, which features a daily games lesson run by a team of qualified sports coaches.

Music and Drama complete the picture of a Yarlet education, with termly performances from the Music Department. The arts are brought to life at Yarlet, instilling self-belief and creative confidence in all our pupils. Whatever their talent, Yarlet pupils have the chance to shine. Clubs and extra-curricular activities are a further feature of Yarlet and include Music, Drama, Computing, Poetry, Golf,

Tennis, Cricket, STEM, Dance, Gymnastics, Fitness and Animal Kingdom.

Yarlet has high expectations of all its children. Children are prepared for entry to a wide variety of senior schools and their achievements in Common Entrance and Scholarship examinations are a source of great pride. In 2021 82% of children left with one or more award/s to their Senior School.

Charitable status. Yarlet is a Registered Charity, number 528618. It exists to provide education for boys and girls from 2 to 13.

Yateley Manor Preparatory School

51 Reading Road, Yateley, Hampshire GU46 7UQ

Tel: 01252 405500
email: office@yateleymanor.com
           registrar@yateleymanor.com
website: www.yateleymanor.com
Twitter: @YateleyManorSch
Facebook: @YateleyManorSchool
Instagram: @yateleymanorschool

The School is an Educational Trust controlled by a Board of Governors.

Chairman of Governors: John Ashworth

Headmaster: **Robert Upton**, BSc Hons, PGCE, MA Ed, NPQH

Age Range. 2–13.

Number of Pupils. Pre-Prep and Nursery: 60 Girls, 60 Boys; Prep: 100 Girls, 140 Boys.

Fees per term (2021–2022). £3,974–£5,449. Fees are fully inclusive of all normal activities, extended supervision from 8.00am until 6.30pm, meals, educational visits and residential field trips for Years 5, 6, 7 and 8.

Yateley Manor has a long and successful history of educating children from the age of 2 to 13.

The development of the Pre-Senior Baccalaureate (PSB), with its focus on rigorous academic standards, coupled with a broad and balanced curriculum, delivers an education for the twenty-first century. The PSB focuses on the vital skills of independence, collaboration, leadership and communication. It runs alongside the curriculum and encourages children to reflect on these additional skills. Its ethos is embedded throughout the school.

The School's emphasis on educating the whole child is supported by a broad enrichment programme. Activities include chess, dance, horse riding, drama and modern pentathlon and the school is always keen to find new opportunities for children to find their talents and strengths.

Nurtured in a warm, friendly and safe environment with excellent facilities and limited class sizes, children are given new experiences to explore, building confidence and stimulating a desire to learn.

Innovative, enthusiastic and committed teachers embrace the different learning styles of children and incorporate varied approaches into lessons. The result is that children may spend a day being Vikings, visiting the Houses of Parliament, creating maths games to bolster understanding of probability or fractions or cooking during science to reinforce the difference between physical and chemical changes.

There is a strong culture of continuing professional development with staff attending external courses, as well as weekly after-school workshops and sharing best practice. This ensures the School's innovative and committed staff are constantly challenging their own practice.

A building housing a state-of-the-art Music School, spacious and light rooms for Art and DT, a Modern Foreign Languages Department and a drama venue provides children with opportunities in performing and creative arts. The School's superb teaching facilities are complemented by excellent sports amenities including a heated indoor swimming pool, a large sports hall with indoor cricket nets and provision for football, netball and basketball, a gymnasium, a climbing wall, Aeroball and several pitches.

The Woodland Learning Area is an inspirational educational environment which gives children the freedom to explore nature in a hands-on and child-led approach. This helps build confidence, independence and self-esteem as well as giving children new life skills.

The school welcomes children of all ages at any point during the school year. The speed at which children new to the school settle demonstrates the strength of pastoral care. Means-tested bursaries are available.

A network of school coaches serves the surrounding areas including Camberley, Church Crookham, Farnborough, Fleet, Frimley, Hartley Wintney, Hook and Odiham.

Charitable status. Yateley Manor is a Registered Charity, number 307374. It is dedicated to providing the highest quality education for children of the local community.

York House School

Sarratt Road, Croxley Green, Rickmansworth, Herts WD3 4LW

Tel: 01923 772395
email: yhsoffice@york-house.com
website: www.york-house.com
Twitter: @SchoolYorkHouse
           @YHheadmaster

Founded in 1910, York House School is a non-profit making Educational Trust with a Board of Governors.

Chairman of the Governors: Mrs L Keating

Headmaster: **Mr Jon Gray**, BA Ed Hons, PGCE

Age Range. 3–13 Co-educational.

Number of Children. All are day pupils: 387 children – 156 Pre-Prep, 231 Prep.

Fees per term (2021–2022). Nursery £3,509 (if attending 5 full days a week); Reception £3,876; Year 1 £4,272; Year 2 £4,550; Years 3–8 £5,164.

York House School is a well-established, innovative and forward-looking school located in a Queen Anne country house standing in fifty acres of Hertfordshire countryside. The Headmaster is assisted by a fully-qualified and caring staff. Our extended day arrangements enable pupils to attend early-morning clubs and after-school clubs between 7.30am and 6.00pm.

The school's aim is to encourage children to achieve the highest academic results in a happy atmosphere while promoting self-discipline and caring for others.

The school has excellent facilities which include a multi-purpose hall, library, computer suite, a science laboratory, art room and music centre.

Sporting facilities are excellent with all-weather multi-purpose pitches for netball, tennis and hockey, 15 acres of playing fields for cricket, rugby, soccer, rounders and athletics as well as a 25-metre indoor heated swimming pool.

Our smallholding includes goats, chickens, pigs, sheep and ponies that provide the children with an invaluable opportunity to experience nature first hand. This approach to Outdoor Learning is further enhanced by our outdoor classroom, use of local Woodland Trust forest, activity equipment and orienteering trails, mountain biking track, nature pond and fruit orchard.

Pupils are prepared for Common Entrance and Independent School Scholarship. There is a Pre-Preparatory Department for children from age 4 to 7 and a Nursery for children from rising 3.

Charitable status. York House School is a Registered Charity, number 311076. It exists to provide high-quality education to boys and girls.

IAPS Overseas

ALPHABETICAL LIST OF SCHOOLS

GEOGRAPHICAL LIST OF SCHOOLS

Individual School Entries

The Banda School

PO Box 24722, Nairobi 00502, Kenya

Tel:	Office: 00 254 20 5131100
	School Mobile: 00 254 709 951000
email:	admissions@bandaschool.com
website:	www.bandaschool.com

Chairman of Governors: Mr D G M Hutchison

Headmistress: **Mrs A Francombe**, BEd Hons

Age Range. 12 months–13 years.

Number of Children. 435 (Day & Weekly/Flexi-Boarding).

Fees per term (2021–2022). Tuition: Kshs 645,000 (Years 3–8 including lunches). Sliding fee scale Year 2 and below.

The School was founded in 1966 by Mr and Mrs J A L Chitty. It is 9 miles from Nairobi and stands in its own grounds of 30 acres adjacent to the Nairobi Game Park. Boys and girls are admitted in equal numbers and are prepared for Independent Senior School Scholarship and Common Entrance Examinations to leading secondary schools in the UK, Kenya and South Africa. The Staff consists of 50+ teachers.

Facilities include a purpose-built Boarding House to accommodate up to 34 boarders on a weekly and flexi-boarding basis. The school campus also comprises Early Years section, Science laboratories, ICT rooms, Art rooms, Music rooms, well-equipped hall for Performing Arts, three Libraries, specialist subject rooms for Mathematics, English, MFL, Humanities, Design Technology, AstroTurf, two Squash courts and a six-lane 25-metre heated Swimming Pool. High-quality interactive multi-touch screens are available from Reception Classes through our Upper School. Banks of iPads enhance learning for use from Reception to Year 5 inclusive. From Year 6, pupils will require their own iPad as we run an e-learning programme which runs alongside our traditional written language practices.

Sports include Rugby, Football, Hockey, Cricket, Tennis, Swimming, Netball, Rounders, Athletics, Sailing, Squash and Cross-Country. A wide range of extra-curricular activities is available including instrumental and voice lessons, Modern Dance, Ballet, LAMDA, extra tennis, squash, swimming and cross-country, to name just a few.

The British School Al Khubairat, Abu Dhabi

PO Box 4001, Abu Dhabi, United Arab Emirates

Tel:	00 971 2 446 2280
email:	registrar@britishschool.sch.ae
website:	www.britishschool.sch.ae
Twitter:	@BSAKAbuDhabi
Facebook:	@BSAKAbuDhabi
Instagram:	@BSAK_AbuDhabi
LinkedIn:	/bsakabudhabi

Abu Dhabi's leading British, not-for-profit, co-educational day school. A member of HMC, IAPS and BSME and BSO Inspected.

Chair of Governors: Sean Magee

Headmaster: **Mark Leppard**, MBE

Head of Secondary School: Teresa Woulfe

Head of Primary School: Elaine Rawlings

Age Range. 3–18.

Number of Pupils. 975 Boys, 975 Girls (all day).

Fees per term (2021–2022). Nursery: AED14,384; Reception: AED16,234; Years 1–6: AED17,532; Years 7–9: AED22,627; Years 10–13: AED23,544.

The British School Al Khubairat (BSAK) is Abu Dhabi's leading British, not-for-profit, co-educational day school.

From Nursery to Sixth Form, their award-winning dynamic school culture offers students an enriching experience and outstanding results. Founded in 1968 on donated land, they are the British Embassy School of the UAE, and under the ongoing patronage of the British Ambassador and the current President of the United Arab Emirates.

The School's mission is to deliver excellence in teaching and learning, bringing everything that is outstanding about the British curriculum to the UAE. They are a member of IAPS, HMC and BSME.

They are rated outstanding across all performance standards, by both the local Government Agency inspection (ADEK) and the British Schools Overseas (BSO). In 2019 BSAK was awarded Best British School in the UAE and Best Post-16 Education in the Schools Compared, Top Schools Award.

BSAK provides a full and broad education. In addition to offering a wide range of GCSEs and A Levels, it also offers the BTEC Level 3 Diploma in Engineering, Business and Sport, and subsidiary BTECs in Creative Media, Music and Science.

The School fosters a welcoming environment for its BSAK families, that is genuinely friendly and happy. It engenders an inclusive community spirit, in which everyone is valued; reinforcing cultural diversity and empathy. It is a caring school, with the safety and well-being of its students always at the forefront.

It is through their academic excellence, outstanding sport and music programmes, and wide co-curricular activities, that BSAK supports its students to exceed expectations, ensuring their education becomes the foundation for happiness and success.

All of these exciting elements are set in a stunning campus and superbly housed in its purpose-built facility, which includes:

- Large, creative classrooms
- A 25m swimming pool
- Learner pool
- Grass pitch
- Two synthetic turf pitches
- Auditorium
- Theatre
- Gym
- Multimedia suites equipped with Apple Macs

The British School of Paris – Junior School

2 rue Hans List, 78290 Croissy sur Seine, France

Tel:	00 33 1 30 15 88 30
email:	junior@britishschool.fr
website:	www.britishschool.fr
Twitter:	@BritishSchParis
Facebook:	@BritishSchParis
Instagram:	@britishschparis

Chairman of Governors: Mr E Coutts

Headmaster: Mr N Hammond

Head of the Junior School: Mr M Potter

Age Range. 3–11 Co-educational.

Number of Pupils. 400.

Fees per annum (2021–2022). €17,753–€24,616.

The Junior School educates pupils aged 3–11 and is located very close to the Senior School along the leafy banks of the river Seine. This campus opened in September 2010; there are 35 classrooms accommodating up to 480 pupils, as well as 4 bespoke classrooms and 2 activity areas that are dedicated to our foundation stage/nursery section. The school was specifically designed to meet the educational and social welfare needs of junior school pupils. It is bristling with new technology and up-to-the-minute IT facilities to assist the pupils' learning and development.

The British School of Paris' philosophy of education permeates throughout the Junior School and has at its core the goal of unlocking the potential of all students, by identifying strengths and supporting areas of development, while having fun and enjoying happy and strong social relationships. Studies are based on the British National Curriculum with emphasis on English, Maths and Science, and of course, the French language. Various sports, music, drama and many other extracurricular activities are also provided.

For further details and applications, please contact the Registrar, email: registrar@britishschool.fr.

The English School
Kuwait

PO Box 379, 13004 Salmiya, Kuwait

Tel:	00 965 22271385
email:	registrar@tes.edu.kw
website:	www.tes.edu.kw

Owner: Mr Emad Mohamed Al-Bahar

Chair of the Governing Committee: Brigadier Huw Lloyd-Jones

Head: Alison Peterson

Age Range. 2½–13.

Number of Pupils. 650.

Fees per annum (2021–2022). Kindergarten KD1,741; Pre-Preparatory (Rec, Year 1 and Year 2) KD2,735; Lower Preparatory (Years 3–6) KD3,135; Upper Preparatory (Years 7 and 8) KD3,435.

The English School, founded in 1953 under the auspices of the British Embassy, is the longest established school in Kuwait catering for the expatriate community. The school operates as a not-for-profit, private co-educational establishment providing the highest standards in education for children of Pre-Kindergarten to Preparatory school age. The school is registered with the United Kingdom Department for Education (DfE No 703 6052) and the Head is a Member of the Independent Association of Prep Schools. TES is an Accredited Member of BSME, of COBIS, and is also accredited as a British School Overseas with the DfE and listed as a "world class British school". Uniquely in Kuwait, the language of the playground is English. The roll is predominantly British, as are the resources and texts. With the exception of foreign language teachers, the teaching staff are also predominantly British and qualified in the United Kingdom. The number of pupils in the school continues to increase although the average class size remains around 22. The school is housed in well-resourced and spacious, fully air-conditioned premises in a pleasant residential suburb of Kuwait City.

The curriculum is British, contemporary and delivers the best of traditional standards within a broad-based structure. Class teachers are supported by specialist coordinators in Art, Science, Design and Technology, Information Technology, Music, Library and PE and Games. Music is taught to all ages and French is introduced from Year 4. The National Curriculum for England is used as the core for the curriculum, although the most able are challenged and those in need of support benefit from individual tuition. Formal end of key stage assessment takes place in Years 2 and 6. In addition the pupils are prepared for entrance tests to other schools including, where appropriate, Common Entrance Examinations at 11+, 12+ and 13+, and scholarship examinations. Pupils in Years 3–8 use iPads as an integral tool and part of their teaching and learning. Pupils in Year 2 and below have access to banks of school iPads. The school's VLE (Virtual Learning Environment) is also at the heart of the pupils' studies and the development of skills for learning drive the school's innovative approach to teaching and learning.

Responsibility for the school is vested in the Governing Committee whose members serve in a voluntary capacity. The school provides a learning environment within which children develop their individual capacity for achievement to its fullest potential. The school's core values of Confidence, Empathy, Integrity, Positivity and Respect are at the heart of all that it does. Strong emphasis is placed on academic study, together with a wide range of non-academic activities to provide breadth and balance. The school aims to ensure that, by achieving standards at least equivalent and often better than those of competitive private and state schools in Britain, pupils are well prepared for the subsequent stages of their academic development whether in Britain, Kuwait or elsewhere in the world.

In the first instance application for enrolment should be made online via the website – please see drop-down menu: Admissions, Application Form.

The Registrar will confirm receipt of the Online Application Form. If there are places in the year requested, the Registrar will ask for copies of current academic reports and arrange a date for the child/children to be assessed. Where possible for children entering Year 4 and above, part of this assessment will be an online test. Pupils and parents will then be invited to attend one of the school's 'Welcome and Assessment Days' prior to the start of the academic year.

The Grange Preparatory School Chile

Av Principe de Gales 6154, La Reina, 687067, Santiago, Chile

Tel: 00 562 598 1500
email: rectoria@grange.cl
website: www.grange.cl

Co-educational Day School.

Headmaster of The Grange School: Mr Nicholas Eatough

Vice-Rector of The Grange School and Head of Senior: Mr Carlos Packer-Comyn

Head of the Upper Preparatory School: Ms Kate Ingamels

Head of the Lower Preparatory School: Mrs Carmen Gloria Gómez

Age Range. 4–12.
Number of Pupils. 1,300.
Fees per annum (2021–2022). Approximately £7,200 payable in one annual sum or 11 monthly instalments. There is a one-off incorporation fee payable on entry.

The Grange Preparatory School is the junior section of The Grange, founded in 1928 by John Jackson and based upon the British independent school which he had attended.

The Prep School is divided into the Lower Prep, which takes children from the age of 4 to the age of 8, and the Upper Prep, taking children from 8 to 12. Almost all pupils will transfer into The Grange senior school.

The ethos of the school is strongly based on giving a broad, all-round educational experience to find strengths for each child. The school may be very large but each child is valued as an individual within the team.

Entry to the school is usually at the age of 4, though entry at ages over 4 may be possible as vacancies occur in the course of the year. All teaching is in English except in those areas where the Chilean National Curriculum requires that they be taught in Spanish. The majority of the pupils are Chilean and begin an immersion course in English upon entry.

International assessment criteria are used at various stages of each pupil's career. The core curriculum is based largely upon the National Curriculum of England and Wales, fully encompassing and surpassing the local National Curriculum. Teaching is mainly by class teachers, though older children will find themselves being taught by specialists in many subjects. All heads of department are specialists. Approximately 20 of the teachers are expatriates.

Over the last few years strong progress has been made in the areas of Science, Music, Drama and Art and Design Technology, with new rooms having been dedicated to these subjects. There is a comprehensive after-school extracurricular programme in which children from the age of 7 upwards are strongly encouraged to take part.

Hillcrest International Schools

PO Box 24819, Karen 00502, Nairobi, Kenya

Tel: +254 20 883914/16/17
             or 254 20 806 7783/4
             +254 724 256 173
             or +254 717 969 450
email: admin@hillcrest.ac.ke
website: www.hillcrest.ac.ke
Twitter: @HillcrestKE
Facebook: @HillcrestKE

Chairman of Governors: Mr Bob Kikuyu

Head of Early Years: Mrs Miranda McGovern

Head of Prep School: Mrs Surbhi Vashisht

Head of Secondary School: Mr Andrew Boulle

Age Range. 18 months to 18 years Co-educational.
Number of Pupils. 610 in total across all 3 sections of the school.
Fees per term (2021–2022). Tuition in Hillcrest Early Years from Play Group to Year 1 ranges from Ksh 94,450 to Ksh 330,450 including lunch. Tuition in the Preparatory School from Year 2 to Year 8 ranges from Ksh 475,900 to Ksh 645,900. Tuition in Secondary School from Year 9 to Year 13 ranges from Ksh 667,300 to Ksh 761,500. Boarding (in addition to to tuition fees): Ksh 275,750 (full boarding); Ksh 175,000 (weekly boarding).

Hillcrest International Schools is a group of schools committed to inspiring each and every child to achieve their own individual personal excellence and to grow to become a valuable member of the global community in which we live. The schools are located on an attractive, purpose-built, 33-acre campus.

Guided by the British Curriculum, we cater for children aged 18 months to young adults aged 18 years. By stimulating each individual's abilities and talents within an atmosphere of mutual respect, we aim to ensure *Semper Prospice* (always looking forward) is a lifelong quest. A valuable boarding resource is offered to children in Prep and Secondary to complement our learning environment and cater for those families who live further afield or juggle work travel with family life.

Early Years: Offering young children a stimulating and creative play-based learning environment in a caring, family-style atmosphere, we foster and nurture a lifelong love of learning and sense of curiosity that lays strong foundations.

Prep: Recognising the uniqueness of each child, we place an emphasis on the development of the whole child and provide pupils of every level with an individualised approach to learning as they develop towards the Common Entrance Exam.

Secondary: Providing a diverse and stimulating environment, we motivate and guide each student to identify their strengths, achieve their individual academic potential at IGCSE, A Level or BTEC and grow into emotionally intelligent independent thinkers.

With over 30 different nationalities represented within the school community, it has a very multinational feel with its pupils drawn from the diplomatic community including the UN, expatriate families on contract, and Kenyan residents. The friendly family spirit and strong communication network that exists between staff, pupils and parents are of particular note.

Extensive information can be found at www.hillcrest.ac.ke.

Pembroke House School

P.O. Box 31, Gilgil 20116, Kenya

Tel:	+254 708143600
	+254 202312323
email:	registrar@pembrokehouse.sc.ke
website:	www.pembrokehouse.sc.ke

Chairman of Council: Mr Richard Vigne

Headmistress: Mrs Deborah Boyd-Moss

Age Range. 1–13.

Number of Pupils. 80 boy boarders, 100 girl boarders plus 33 Pre-Prep who are day pupils

Fees per term (2021–2022). Nursery Kshs 87,500, Pre-School Kshs 163,300, Year 1 Kshs 392,400, Year 2 Kshs 627,800, Year 3 to 8 Kshs 784,800 (approx. £580–£5,200).

The school was founded in 1927 and is presently owned and administered by the Kenya Educational Trust Limited. It is situated in over 40 hectares of well-maintained grounds in the Rift Valley at 2,000 metres elevation and is 120 km from Nairobi. The climate is sunny throughout the year, affording many opportunities for an extensive education.

Facilities include a Science Lab, Chapel, Theatre, Swimming Pool, Music School, Library, Art and Design Technology Centre, Computer Room, two Squash Courts and Tennis Courts, access to a neighbouring Golf Course,

and a multi-purpose Sports Hall, Stables, Meeting Room and Café. The school has a well-equipped Surgery on site.

The main sports are Cricket, Hockey, Rugby, Rounders and Netball, with Tennis, Swimming, Athletics, Squash, Golf, Horse Riding, Sailing, Football and Taekwondo on offer as well.

A full range of clubs and various extras, including individual music instruction, are also offered. Drama is strong with several productions put on each year. The school also has a vibrant and varied weekend programme to support the full boarding ethos of the school. This involves camping and other outdoor pursuits as well as many team building and leadership activities.

Children are admitted from five years as full boarders and are prepared, through the British Curriculum, for the ISEB Common Entrance Examinations which qualifies them for entry to Independent Senior Schools in the UK and South Africa as well as Kenyan schools. The school usually gains numerous academic scholarships and awards each year in addition to music and sports awards. The Learning Support facilities at Pembroke House have been developed over many years and now provide essential help for those who require such assistance. The school currently has children from seven different countries, including the United Kingdom.

The average number of pupils in each form is approximately 14, and there is a pupil-teacher ratio of six students per teacher. There are also three qualified Nurses, a Cateress, an Estate Manager, Registrar and a Bursar. Pembroke has a reputation for producing outstanding pupils. The Headmistress and the staff work together to produce kind, well-mannered, balanced children with integrity and courage who try their best at all times. This is the best preparation a child can have.

Peponi House

PO Box 23203, Lower Kabete, Nairobi 00604, Kenya

Tel:	+254 20 2585710–712, 734881255, 722202947
email:	registrar@peponihouse.sc.ke
website:	www.peponischool.org/house
Facebook:	@peponihouseschool

Headmaster: **Mr Neil A Price**, BA Hons, PGCE

Age Range. 6–13.

Number of Pupils. 373 boys and girls, all day.

Fees per term (2021–2022). Year 1: Kshs 316,000; Year 2: Kshs 582,000; Years 3 to 8: Kshs 632,285.

Founded in 1986, Peponi House has grown to become one of the leading preparatory schools in East Africa. The attractive and spacious site in Lower Kabete houses all that a thriving prep school requires to get the very best out of the children, both in and out of the classroom. The school was rated as 'Outstanding' in all respects in an inspection carried out in February 2018.

An ambitious building programme has started that will provide the finest school accommodation and that will reflect the school's forward-thinking curriculum. Phase One is nearing completion, comprising a new school hall, library, drama studio, spacious and bright classrooms and office accommodation, as well as spaces for computing, design, learning support and extended learning. A variety of landscaped outdoor learning areas are also integral to the project.

The Peponi curriculum is also undergoing change, with self-directed learning being allocated its own time in the week, alongside the traditional subjects. Children are encouraged to enquire and all children have access to either iPads or LearnPads. A virtual learning environment allows for clarity of communication between home and school.

Whilst always striving for academic excellence, it is central to Peponi's philosophy that education is not limited to the classroom. In addition to the numerous scholarships to senior schools that our pupils have won in the last three years, we have had notable successes in sport, music, art and drama. Peponi teams have won competitions at a national level, with many individuals going on to represent their country.

We follow the British National Curriculum but this is seen very much as a framework on which we build, adapt and extend. In addition to the core subjects of Literacy, Numeracy, Science and Computing, pupils in the Junior School (Years 2 to 4) also have lessons in Music, PE and Games, Swimming, Kiswahili, Art and DT, Tennis and, from Year 3, Spanish. Junior children are taught these subjects by specialist teachers while the class teachers deliver the core subjects and humanities. All children are taught in a way that best suits their individual needs and some children do require additional support. This is carried out by our learning support teachers who will help children either individually or in small groups, but mainly through integrated support in the classroom. Our learning support teachers also play a vital role in advising colleagues as to the strengths and weaknesses of particular children so that teaching can be differentiated to suit everyone.

In Year 5, children are taught Humanities and English by their form teachers, who also play a vital pastoral role in preparing the children for life in the senior school. In Year 6, all subjects are delivered by subject specialists. The sciences are taught separately and there is an option for children to study Kiswahili or Latin, or they can return to Spanish. French is taught from Year 5, with a busy French club that is open to all.

We also have a wide and varied range of extra-curricular activities. The whole school joins in the Activity Programme on Friday afternoons, with children from all year groups taking part in activities together. On Mondays, children in Years 5 to 8 take part in HOTS: higher order thinking skills activities.

Our music department flourishes in its own purpose-built accommodation. In addition to weekly class music lessons, the children have the opportunity to play in the orchestra or in one of the ensembles, or sing in either the Junior or Senior Choir. As well as the two major school concerts during the year, all children have the opportunity to perform in front of their peers and parents at our termly "Tea-Time Concerts". The Carol Service and Peponi Schools Concert offer other chances for our choirs to perform and all the children are encouraged to take part in the plays that are staged in December, March and June.

We have children from many different cultures and ethnic backgrounds and we encourage understanding and above all respect for each other. We are a Christian school and the ethos of "Love one another" is a recurring theme in our Monday Assemblies, but we are proud of our multi-faith

society where children learn to appreciate and value their differences as well as their similarities.

The school's motto, "A School of Many Nations, a Family of One" encapsulates all that we hold most dear. First and foremost, we are a school and the academic side of things lies at the heart of all that we do. However, we are also a family and that makes itself very clear in the day to day life of the school. We have an open door policy with our parents and encourage them to be very active in their support of what we do, either through our energetic PTA or through close consultation with the staff.

At Peponi House, we believe that our role as educators is to give our children the best possible foundation for what lies ahead. We are, after all, a preparatory school and excellent preparation is what we set out to achieve. By the time they leave us, our pupils will be confident young adults who are ready to face the future with poise and self-belief.

The Roman Ridge School

No. 8 Onyasia Crescent, Roman Ridge, Accra, Ghana

Tel: 00 233 302 780456 / 780457
email: enquiries@theromanridgeschool.com
website: www.theromanridgeschool.com

**Postal Address:
PO Box GP 21057, Accra, Ghana**

Co-educational Day School.

Governors:

Chairman: Dr Frank B Adu Jnr, BA Hons, MBA

Chair, Academic Board: Revd Dr Joyce Aryee, BA Hons, PG Cert Public Administration

Principal: Mrs Valerie Mainoo, BSc Psych, MA Ed

Head of Middle School: Mr Bruno Ted Waze

Head of Junior School: Ms Gloria Dakwa

Age Range. 4–18.

Numbers of Pupils. 352 Boys, 370 Girls.

Fees per term (2021–2022). Junior School (Reception–Class 6): US$1,840; Senior School (Forms 1–5) US$2,185; Sixth Form US$2,300.

Established in September 2002, The Roman Ridge School aims to provide the very best of British Education whilst being firmly rooted in Ghanaian life and culture. The school is a unique facility in Ghana as it offers small class sizes (20), individual pupil attention, a family atmosphere, firm discipline, emphasis on good manners, a sound Christian foundation, a caring environment and a full programme of Sports and extra-curricular activities.

The school is noted for its Individual Learning Programmes and its dedication to all pupils including the high and low ability learners and scholars. Pupils are carefully monitored and assessed regularly in order to achieve academic success and parents are encouraged to help in this process.

All teaching is initially based on the English National Curriculum for the Foundation Course and Key Stage One, after which the pupils progress to the 11+ examination, then take the full range of academic subjects at the 13+ Common Entrance and the IGCSE Courses (Cambridge Assessment International Education). The school runs a thriving AS & A Level programme and offers a comprehensive range of courses.

There are forty-two classrooms at present, three ICT suites, two Multimedia Centres, two up-to-date Libraries with full audio-visual facilities, E-Learning facilities, Primary & Secondary Science Labs, a Dance Studio, a Drama Studio, two Art Rooms and sporting facilities. Two clinics are on site staffed by two qualified SRNs.

Pupils play Football, Basketball, Volleyball, Netball, Hockey and Rounders and also enjoy a very successful Swimming programme. Pupils also benefit from an extensive extra-curricular programme which includes Karate, Ballet, Tennis, Drama Club and a highly successful Choir programme, which includes a Parent Choir. School productions and concerts take place at the end of each term.

The school also runs an excellent internal and external Community Literacy Programme, with Senior Pupils spearheading reading programmes for all age groups.

The school is open on Saturdays for extra work and pupil support programmes, swimming, games, music lessons, art and computer clubs, and special events.

Pupils thrive in The Roman Ridge School and are reluctant to go home at the end of the day.

St Andrew's Preparatory School

Private Bag, Molo 20106, Kenya

Tel:	+254 722 209750
	+254 735 2025709
email:	officeprep@turimail.co.ke
website:	www.standrewsturi.com
Twitter:	@st_andrewsturi
Facebook:	@Standrewsschoolturi
LinkedIn:	/company/st-andrew%27s-school-turi

Chair of Governors: Mr Ngunze Mbuvi

Headmaster: **Mr Ian Wright**

Age Range. 3–13.

Number of Pupils. 250: 126 Boys, 124 Girls.

Fees per term (2021–2022). Boarding: Kshs 650,000–822,000. Day: Kshs 342,000–534,000.

St Andrew's Preparatory School, Turi, is an international, multicultural, Christian boarding school offering British Curriculum education of the highest standard. The School aims to provide a happy, stimulating, well-rounded educational experience for children. Pupils are encouraged to grow into well-educated, confident, self-disciplined young adults with the potential to be future leaders.

The School (Prep School, Senior School and Sixth Form College) is situated 200 km north west of Nairobi on a beautiful 300-acre estate at an altitude of over 2,000 metres, where the climate is both healthy and invigorating. The School has its own private airstrip within the grounds.

Boarding pupils are accepted from the age of 5 and follow the British National Curriculum which prepares them for entry to St Andrew's Senior School and to other independent senior schools in the UK or elsewhere.

The original School, founded in 1931, was destroyed by fire in 1944. It was completely rebuilt and is uniquely designed and equipped as a modern purpose-built preparatory school. There are subject rooms for English, Mathematics, French, History, Geography and Science laboratories. Information Technology is an integral part of the curriculum throughout the School with two ICT suites and most classrooms are equipped with interactive whiteboards and data projectors. An exceptionally large Hall is used for plays, concerts and large functions. The average size of classes is 16.

Sport forms a key part of school life at St Andrew's School. The grounds and playing fields are extensive. Boys play cricket and rugby; girls play rounders and netball; all play football, hockey, tennis and take part in athletics and cross country. In the newly-opened Sports Centre, there are excellent facilities for a wide range of indoor sports including two glass-backed squash courts and a fitness suite. There are seven school tennis courts and a heated swimming pool, as well as a riding school on site where pupils of all abilities are taught by qualified instructors.

The School has a strong musical tradition. In addition to the many and varied opportunities for music within the curriculum over 80 pupils opt for specialist instrumental tuition in a wide range of instruments. Many of these pupils work towards ABRSM examinations. There are also several specialist music groups who practice and perform together and the Junior and Senior choirs.

A large and well-equipped Art Studio as well as Design Technology and Food Technology rooms allow pupils to express themselves creatively. A wealth of arts and crafts, hobbies and outdoor pursuits are actively encouraged. The School has its own Chapel and aims to give a practical Christian education in a community with high standards and in a supportive family atmosphere.

All staff live within the estate. The teaching staff are all qualified and are committed to the Christian ethos of the School.

On completing year 8, pupils move to St Andrew's Senior School which offers a three-year course to IGCSE examinations where excellent academic results are typically obtained and thereafter students can opt for A Levels at the incorporated St Andrew's College.

St. Paul's School

Rua Juquiá 166, Jardim Paulistano, São Paulo, Brazil/ São Paulo SP 01440–903, Brazil

Tel:	00 55 11 3087 3399
email:	contact@stpauls.br
website:	www.stpauls.br
Twitter:	@stpaulsschoolsp
Facebook:	@StPaulsschoolSP
Instagram:	@stpaulsschoolsp
LinkedIn:	/school/stpaulsschool

Chairman of the Board of Governors: Mr Edward Weaver

Headmaster: **Mr Titus Edge**

Deputy Head: Mrs Zeba Clarke

Senior Master: Dr Barry Hallinan

Head of Junior School (*Pre-Preparatory & Preparatory Schools*): Miss Amy Clifford

Head of Senior School: Mrs Martina Oparaocha

Age Range. 3–18.

Number of Pupils. 1,183: Pre-Preparatory 241, Preparatory 407, Senior 535.

Fees per annum (2021–2022). R$95,520–R$120,684.

St. Paul's School was the first British School to be established in São Paulo (Brazil) and continues to offer an Anglo-Brazilian curriculum, embracing the best of both cultures. As an all-through (ages 3–18) co-educational school, offering the IGCSE and IB courses to pupils, we are affiliated to a global network of top UK Schools through our membership of HMC (Headmaster's Conference) and COBIS (Council of British International Schools). Almost 100 years old, we draw on our proud heritage as the first British school in Latin America to be recognised as a British School Overseas (BSO) by the UK government. Yet, we look forward with creativity and confidence.

At St. Paul's we always strive to be our better selves. We have the courage of our convictions, essential values, freedom to imagine and create. This is achieved through our high quality British and Brazilian holistic education which drives the personal and academic development of pupils, within a framework of a caring, inclusive and united community.

It is our aim to discover the passion and talents of every pupil, and create the right environment to develop these. The school prides itself on an excellent enrichment programme ranging from MUN to Duke of Edinburgh, from knitting classes to a robotics programme, from mathematical Olympiads to outstanding drama and music. We have been awarded Microsoft Showcase School and Apple Distinguished School status in recognition of our excellence in transforming and enhancing our physical and online learning environment to deliver more personalised education to our pupils.

The school is a positive agent of change, helping its pupils to be caring individuals ready to inspire and mobilise those around them to impact the world for the best. Our commitment to broad educational experiences opens many opportunities for pupils who go on to leading universities in the United Kingdom, America and Brazil.

We believe in helping our pupils achieve their full intellectual, emotional, social, physical, artistic, creative and spiritual potential. An innovative, structured curriculum, combined with excellent teaching, state-of-the-art facilities, and the best in pastoral care, equip pupils to flourish.

St Saviour's School, Ikoyi
Lagos, Nigeria

54 Alexander Avenue, Ikoyi, Lagos, Nigeria

Tel: 00 234 1 8990153
email: info@stsavioursschikoyi.org
website: www.stsavioursschikoyi.org

St Saviour's is an Associate Member of COBIS.

Head Teacher: Mr Craig Heaton, BA Hons

Age Range. 4–11 Co-educational.

Number of Pupils. 320.

Fees per term (2021–2022). Naira 1,462,618.

A truly rounded education is a preparation for life. Grounded on our core values, St Saviour's seeks to provide an education that is challenging, relevant, exciting and delivered in a caring and thoroughly professional manner. We look, unashamedly, for academic achievement in each pupil alongside equal progress in spiritual growth, friendship, independence, confidence and some appreciation of their place in the world and their responsibilities towards others.

Christian principles are integrated into the daily life of the school which is an Anglican foundation. Children of a number of denominations and faiths attend the school and are warmly welcomed. Parents are welcomed as part of the learning cycle; communication with them is regular and their support of the school is exceptional.

The development of the whole child is at the heart of education at St Saviour's. Learning is about developing personal, emotional and social skills as well as being an intellectual and academic process. We aim to help children find their voice – their own unique, personal significance. We encourage them to think about what their contribution will be in the world – how they will try to make a difference as responsible and engaged members of the School community as well as citizens of the world.

St Saviour's has high expectations for all its learners. We pride ourselves on knowing each child as an individual in order to help them make progress. Teachers plan to scaffold success for all learners from their point of entry. This means that learning opportunities are planned so that all students are challenged appropriately, sometimes by providing work that is a little too hard and then providing support systems to enable students to work through their difficulties to achieve success.

Above all, we are interested in the learning process – learning how to learn and how to apply skills and knowledge across an ever-increasing spectrum of experience. From the earliest age we ensure that children have an enjoyable experience of school and are motivated to learn and improve. This positive attitude is supported by a team of highly professional teachers who are themselves engaged in lifelong learning and model effective habits of mind. The curriculum is based on that of the National Curriculum for England and Wales and the International Primary Curriculum adapted to reflect the needs of an increasingly international and multicultural student body We aim to build on the children's background knowledge and experience to equip them with the skills, strategies and a love of learning that will inspire them to succeed whatever the next step on their educational journey.

The school has developed and renewed its own sports facilities over the past few years and now has its own 25m swimming pool and extensive sports field, including football pitch and running track as well as informal play areas. Routinely, about 30 extracurricular Clubs operate after school each week and they are very well supported. Events such as Assemblies, Independence Day, Foundation, KS1 and KS2 Productions, Sports Day, International Week,

Flower Show, Fun Day and Harvest Festival add greatly to the school's character. Our support of local orphanages flows from monies raised at some of these events.

Pupils leave the school from Y6 to attend leading Secondary schools in Nigeria and approximately 40% move on to outstanding independent schools in the UK, where they prove to be excellent ambassadors of the holistic education they have received at St Saviour's.

Tanglin Trust School

95 Portsdown Road, Singapore 139299

Tel: +65 6778 0771
email: admissions@tts.edu.sg
website: www.tts.edu.sg
Twitter: @TanglinTrust
Facebook: @TanglinTrustSchool
LinkedIn: /tanglin-trust-school

Chair of Governors: Mr Dominic Nixon (Acting Chair)

Chief Executive Officer: **Mr Craig Considine [HMC]**

Head of Infant School: Mrs Paula Craigie [IAPS]

Head of Junior School: Mrs Clair Harrington-Wilcox [IAPS]

Head of Senior School: Mr Allan Forbes

Age Range. Nursery through Senior School (3–18 years).

Number of Pupils. 2,800 across Infant, Junior, Senior Schools.

Fees per annum (2021–2022). Nursery to Reception: S$28,794–S$35,295; Year 1 to 6: S$35,850–S$37,575; Year 7 to 13: S$43,095–S$46,965.

Established in 1925, Tanglin Trust School is the oldest British international school in Southeast Asia. It provides the English National Curriculum with an international perspective to children from three to 18 years.

Tanglin is a vibrant co-educational school of 2,800 students representing over 50 nationalities and provides a unique learning environment for children from Nursery right through to Sixth Form. As a not-for-profit school, tuition fees are devoted to the provision of an outstanding education.

As the only school in Singapore to offer A Levels or the IB Diploma in Sixth Form, all Sixth Formers study a programme that is tailored both to the subjects they are passionate about and to the style of learning that most suits them, ensuring they thrive and flourish.

The school has an excellent academic reputation. Students' examination results consistently surpass Singapore and global averages, with around 97% of graduates typically receiving their first or second choice university, which are among the best in the world.

Tanglin is inspected every year within the British Schools Overseas (BSO) framework, recognised by Ofsted. All three schools have been awarded 'Outstanding', the highest possible grade in their latest inspections (2017, 2018 and 2019).

Drawing on professional and dynamic staff, the school aims to nurture students to achieve their intellectual, spiritual, cultural, social and physical goals. Tanglin strives to make every individual feel valued, happy and successful. Responsibility, enthusiasm and participation are actively encouraged, and integrity is prized. Working together in a safe, caring yet stimulating environment, the School sets high expectations whilst offering strong support, resulting in a community of lifelong learners who can contribute with confidence to the world.

Tanglin encourages both broad participation and the achievement of excellence in the arts, sport, outdoor education and co-curricular activities.

Over 140 teams compete in 17 different sports each year, both in Singapore and the wider region. Exceptional sporting facilities enable students to participate in a wide range of competitive and non-competitive events. Tanglin looks forward to the opening of its new world class facilities, which include a 50m pool, gymnastics centre, climbing wall, physiotherapy clinic, music spaces and sport science centre.

Tanglin has a thriving and energetic Arts programme which plays an important part in school life. Students develop their skills in art, design, drama, music, and film-making; facilitating creative, social and intellectual development. Nearly 25% of students participate in a music co-curricular activity. Throughout the year, there are many opportunities for students to participate in high-quality ensembles, recitals, performances and exhibitions.

Students are also encouraged to contribute actively to the local community, support service projects and participate in a wide variety of extra-curricular pursuits that stimulate and broaden student experience. These include 80 outdoor education trips, the International Duke of Edinburgh's (DofE) Award, and the Creativity, Activity, Service (CAS) programme.

"Reflecting on eleven incredible years of education at Tanglin, it's safe to say I would never have wanted to grow up anywhere else. Tanglin has given me the best foundation and motivation for my next chapter, whilst giving me incredible friends, and unimaginable sports and academic experiences." **Grace, Head Team 2019/20**

"I am grateful to Tanglin for its nurturing culture. The team of staff at Tanglin goes above and beyond, ensuring we are equipped with knowledge and skills we can use for the rest of our lives. In addition, Tanglin's environment has given me the opportunity to thrive and become the best version of myself – from being a mentor to younger students to being mentored by my teachers. This kind of collaborative culture is what makes Tanglin invaluable." **Maia, Head Girl 2021–2022, Tanglin Trust School**

What the inspectors say:

"Tanglin pupils talk with passion about their school because it is special. They say it makes them feel happy and valued, not just for what they can do, but for who they are." **Junior School Inspection 2019**

"A rich and diverse curriculum provides outstanding learning across the school. Leaders are relentless in their ambition to offer pupils not only breadth but also depth in their learning. As a result, stimulating opportunities are built into everyday lessons for all pupils." **Infant School Inspection 2018**

"The teachers' enthusiasm for learning is often infectious, leading to students seeing learning as a highly worthwhile and enjoyable process; students are highly motivated to succeed." **Senior School Inspection 2017**

PART V
Schools whose Heads are members of the Independent Schools Association

ALPHABETICAL LIST OF SCHOOLS

896

The following schools, whose Heads are members of both ISA and HMC, can be found in the HMC section:

The Grange School

Leighton Park School

Lingfield College

New Hall School

Princethorpe College

The following schools, whose Heads are members of both ISA and GSA, can be found in the GSA section:

Alderley Edge School for Girls

Farnborough Hill

The Kingsley School

St Catherine's School, Twickenham

St James Senior Girls' School

St Mary's School, Colchester

St Mary's School, Gerrards Cross

The following schools, whose Heads are members of both ISA and The Society of Heads, can be found in The Society of Heads section:

Abbey Gate College

Bedstone College

Bournemouth Collegiate School

Bredon School

Highclare School

Kingsley School, Bideford

LVS Ascot

Mount House School, Barnet

Pitsford School

Portland Place School

St Edward's School, Cheltenham

St James Senior Boys' School

Shebbear College

Stonar

Tettenhall College

Tring Park School for the Performing Arts

Trinity School, Teignmouth

The following schools, whose Heads are members of both ISA and IAPS, can be found in the IAPS section:

Abercorn School

Birchfield School

Boundary Oak School

Crackley Hall School

Cranmore

Crescent School

Crosfields School

Downsend School

Eaton Square Belgravia

Gatehouse School

The Hampshire School, Chelsea

Holme Grange School

Knightsbridge School

Langley Prep School

Leehurst Swan School

Littlegarth School

Newbridge Preparatory School

Norfolk House School

The Old School Henstead

Orchard School

Reddiford School

Rosemead Preparatory School and Nursery

Ruckleigh School

Russell House

S. Anselm's

St James Prep School

St Mary's School, Hampstead

St Michael's Preparatory School

St Olave's Prep School

The Study Preparatory School

Wilmslow Preparatory School

ISA
GEOGRAPHICAL LIST OF SCHOOLS

Individual School Entries

Abbey College Manchester
Alpha Plus Group Limited

5–7 Cheapside, King Street, Manchester M2 4WG

Tel: 0161 817 2700
email: admin@abbeymanchester.co.uk
website: www.abbeymanchester.co.uk
Twitter: @AbbeyManchester
Facebook: @AbbeyCollegeManchester

Principal: **Mr Chris Randell**

Age Range. 15–19.
Number of Pupils. 215.
One Year GCSE, Two Year A Level, One Year A Level Retake, Combined Studies Programme, International Foundation Programme; plus Academic Studies with Football Training and Academic Studies with Basketball Training.

An independent day school with a college environment

- Year 11, Lower Sixth and Upper Sixth entry
- Very small classes (a maximum of 12 students in each) ensure excellent progress
- Unique one year GCSEs and A Levels for those sitting for the first time or retaking
- A Combined Studies Programme, which is an alternative to A Level and is now accepted by several universities
- High levels of personal support and individual responsibility gives good preparation for university life
- Expert advice is delivered for entry onto all university courses leading to strong relationships with the top universities in Britain
- City centre location means students will benefit from the unlimited arts, business, science, sports and music resources on offer

Flexible learning programmes mean that students can join at any time during the academic year, not just September.

Fees per annum (2022–2023): Year 12 (A Level or Combined Studies) £14,070; Year 13 (A Level or Combined Studies) £14,070; One Year A Level (1 subject) £7,330; One Year A Level (2 or 3 subjects) £14,070; Year 11 (GCSE – up to 6 subjects) £12,500.

Fees are inclusive of exam charges.

Abingdon House School and College
Cavendish Education Group

Broadley Terrace, London NW1 6LG

Tel: 020 3750 5526
email: office@abingdonhouseschool.co.uk
website: www.abingdonhouseschool.co.uk
Twitter: @AbingdonHouseSC

Headteacher: **Ms Tanya Moran**

Senior Deputy Headteacher: Mr Rory Vokes-Dudgeon

Deputy Headteacher: Mr James Gilbert-Farrell

Head of SEN: Ms Susannah Harris

Bursar: Ms Jenny Fromer

Senior Administrator, Marketing and Admissions: Mrs Claire Essien

Senior Administrator, Office Manager and H&S: Mrs Karen Franklin

Age Range. 5–19 Co-educational.
Number of Pupils. 90.
Fees per term (2021–2022). £12,190.
Abingdon House School is located in a refurbished Victorian building in London NW1 on four levels with facilities to educate up to 90 pupils aged between 5–19 years of age (Years 1–13). The school has specific expertise in the education of children who have Specific Learning Difficulties. This includes children with Dyslexia, Dyspraxia, Dyscalculia, Social Communication difficulties and associated learning needs.

The school provides a warm, nurturing environment in which the specific individual learning needs of our pupils are addressed through a multi-disciplinary approach. We provide an integrated, whole-school approach to meeting the needs of pupils who are diagnosed with a specific learning difficulty. When diagnosed early in their education, children generally respond well to intense intervention for a period of time, after which it is anticipated they would be able to return to the mainstream.

Effective learning and teaching is based on understanding a child's individual needs, nurturing a child's academic and social development and caring for a child's well-being. The environment is therefore warm and friendly and we are committed to each child's holistic development.

We aim to prepare the children for a return to mainstream schooling through:

- The provision of a holistic and individually tailored education programme.
- A whole-school teaching regime of small classes with teaching assistants, therapists and trained staff using a range of teaching strategies and therapeutic interventions. There is an appropriately low pupil to teacher ratio. Many

pupils have integrated successfully into various London day schools.

- Developing, monitoring and implementing an IEP (Individual Education Plan) for each pupil, which details SMART (Specific, Measurable, Achievable, Realistic and Timely) targets and describes the strategies and supports required to achieve those targets.

- Monitoring pupil progress through a rigorous system of assessment and tracking.

- Implementing a consistent system of positive behaviour support.

- Facilitating pupil-centred active learning.

- Placing special emphasis on the development of literacy and numeracy, social skills, language and communication and coordination, sequencing and movement.

Effort and achievement are praised and rewarded to build self-esteem. Merits and stickers are awarded daily. Certificates and rosettes are awarded each week. Pupils are given the opportunity for their efforts and achievements to be recognised and celebrated on a regular basis culminating in an end-of-term Musical Performance and Prize Giving.

We offer a full curriculum. PE/Games take place on a weekly basis at school and in local community facilities. Reading, Literacy and Maths lessons are ability grouped to enable pupils to progress as soon as they are ready. After-school clubs are offered several times a week, for example, ICT, Music, Games and Swimming.

We value teamwork and the partnership between parents and staff. Parent/Teacher meetings are held several times a term.

ACS International School Cobham

Heywood House, Portsmouth Road, Cobham, Surrey KT11 1BL

Tel: 01932 867251
email: cobadmissions@acs-schools.com
website: www.acs-schools.com/cobham
Twitter: @ACSintschools
Facebook: @ACSCobham
Instagram: @acscobhamschool
LinkedIn: /acs-international-schools-ltd-

Head of School: **Barnaby Sandow**

Age Range. 2–18.

Number in School. Day: 691 Boys, 627 Girls; 152 Boarders.

Fees per annum (2021–2022). Tuition: £8,230–£28,760. Boarding (including tuition fees): £46,880–£49,790 (full), £41,200–£44,110 (5-day).

ACS Cobham is a co-educational school for 1,400 students aged 2–18 and 300 expert faculty and staff, representing over 70 nationalities.

Far more than just a school, ACS Cobham is a friendly, vibrant international community with a global outlook that guides our world-renowned curriculum. Based on US educational best practice, we offer a new kind of learning for a new kind of world citizen. Our goal is as simple as it is inspiring: to make our students ready for the challenges of tomorrow, so they thrive at every stage of their lives.

Our teaching and academic credentials are second to none. Our students are encouraged to tailor their studies to suit their talents and ambitions, while a wealth of outstanding support amenities help deliver a well-rounded educational experience. Equally important is our beautiful, leafy campus, just 30 minutes from central London. Our location offers students the best of both worlds – the stimulation of one of the world's great cities, combined with the charms of the English countryside.

Unique amongst our four schools, ACS Cobham offer boarding as an option for students aged 12 to 18, who enjoy state-of-the-art facilities in our recently opened boarding house.

Academic Programme. At ACS Cobham, your child has access to an independent and flexible curriculum, underpinned by the International Baccalaureate (IB) Diploma, Advanced Placement (AP) courses and the ACS High School Diploma (US). These opportunities develop your child's learning and life skills. ACS graduates have established a tradition of attaining excellent exam results, enabling them to continue their studies at top universities around the world, including the US and UK.

Facilities. Situated on 128 acres approximately 30 minutes by train from Central London, ACS Cobham enrols over 1,400 students. Exceptional facilities include an Early Childhood village; purpose-built Lower, Middle, and High School buildings; gymnasium and cafeteria complex and two world-class boarding houses. All Lower, Middle and High School buildings have separate classrooms, science labs, libraries, computer labs, art and music studios and access to the school's state-of-the-art Interactive Learning Centre.

Enrichment Activities. ACS Cobham offers extensive and varied extracurricular clubs and community service activities both locally and internationally, which encourage students to participate in the richness of school life. Students also participate in international theatre arts programmes, maths, literature and music competitions in the UK and across Europe.

Sports. Our 128-acre campus is home to the best range of quality sports facilities of any international school in Europe, with soccer and rugby fields, softball and baseball diamonds, an all-weather Olympic-sized track, tennis courts, and a six-hole golf course. Our Sports Centre comprises a 25-metre competition indoor swimming pool, basketball/volleyball show courts, dance and fitness studios, and a café.

Boarding at ACS Cobham. As part of an increasingly mobile world, the ACS Cobham Boarding House has established itself as a genuine champion of internationalism, with students representing more than 30 countries. We are proud of our multicultural identity, and celebrate the things that make us different as an integral part of boarding life.

Expert residential house parents and nurse ensure our students have the constant support, guidance, and care to be happy, inspired, and ready to make their mark on the world.

A multi-million pound refurbishment of the existing boarding house Fields is now complete and features a new walk-in medical centre with a fully-trained medical team. All study bedrooms are either single or twin, and all have a private bathroom. Furnishings are to a very high standard and include wall-to-wall carpeting, built-in wardrobes (closets), desks, lamps, bookcases, beds and bedside units. There is WiFi throughout. There are spacious lounges with large screen television and DVD players, laundry facilities, and kitchenettes. Main meals are taken in the school's stunning dining hall located next to the Boarding House.

Boarders are allocated bedrooms on their own or with other boarders of the same age. Boys and girls are accommodated in separate areas, with some shared common rooms.

Accreditation. ACS Cobham is accredited by the New England Association of Schools and Colleges (NEASC) and is authorised by the International Baccalaureate (IB) to offer the International Baccalaureate Diploma Programme (IBDP). The school holds memberships in the US College Board Advanced Placement (AP) Program, the European Council of International Schools (ECIS), the Council of International Schools (CIS) and the Independent Schools Association (ISA).

Four Schools, One World-class Education. ACS Cobham is part of ACS International Schools. Founded in 1967 to serve the needs of international and local families, ACS International Schools now educates 3,500 students up to age 18, from more than 70 countries, at three London area campuses in England and one in Doha, Qatar.

Contact the Admissions team. The admissions team is available throughout the year to answer questions, book campus visits, and assist families through the enrolment process. Students are accepted in all grades throughout the year, on non-selective criteria.

ACS International School Egham

Woodlee, London Road (A30), Egham, Surrey TW20 0HS

Tel: 01784 430800

email: eghamadmissions@acs-schools.com

website: www.acs-schools.com/egham

Twitter: @ACSEgham

Facebook: @ACSEgham

Instagram: @acseghamschool

LinkedIn: /acs-international-schools-ltd-

Head of School: **Mr Jeremy Lewis**

Age Range. 4–18.

Number in School. Day only: 323 Boys, 268 Girls.

Fees per annum (2021–2022). Tuition: £11,540–£26,920.

At ACS Egham, the old blends seamlessly with the new. Our beautiful grounds and buildings in 20 acres of countryside give the school a village feel, while our cutting-edge dedicated International Baccalaureate (IB) centre allows for a truly modern learning experience. Just 25 miles from London, we are home to 600 students, aged 4 to 18, and 160 expert faculty and staff, from around the world. The school's global outlook informs our curriculum, building on the very best of international education standards, and providing our students with a world-class education that is fit for the 21st century.

Academic programmes. ACS Egham is the first and only school in the UK fully authorised to offer all four International Baccalaureate (IB) programmes, providing all our students with a globally recognised, reassuringly independent, and seamless route to success – both in and out of the classroom. These programmes are the IB Primary Years (IBPYP), the Middle Years (IBMYP) and IB Diploma (IBDP) Programmes, as well as the IB Career-related Programme (IBCP).

These programmes share a common philosophy and characteristics: they develop the whole student, helping them to grow socially, physically, aesthetically, and culturally; and provide a broad and balanced education that includes science and the humanities, languages and mathematics, technology, physical education, and the arts.

This academic programme challenges students to fulfil their potential, and offers a broad-based selection of courses and levels to meet individual needs and interests. An important characteristic of ACS Egham is individual attention to students' needs facilitated by an exceptionally well-qualified, experienced, and empathetic faculty; many of whom are IB examiners, moderators, and teacher trainers. The success of our programme is reflected in our IB Diploma pass rate over the last ten years, which has enabled our graduates to continue their studies at top universities around the world, including the UK and Europe as well as the US.

ACS Egham runs small class sizes which afford a greater opportunity for individual attention and support for various learning styles. Child Study Teams meet with individual students' teachers, administrators and parents, to ensure that every child is appropriately challenged and encouraged. A Language Coordinator assists families in organising native language lessons.

Facilities. Providing a great all-round education requires an amazing range of facilities. That is why we have spent £11m over the past seven years ensuring ACS Egham remains an outstanding educational environment. Our beautifully landscaped campus features: 21-acre site with Mansion House and playing fields; a 700 square-foot design technology and art annexe with 3D printer and laser cutter plus interactive modular classrooms; a science wing with five labs and a prep room; two IT labs; a student centre with performing arts centre; a dedicated IB centre for Grades 11 and 12; and two libraries. We also offer three music practice rooms as well as dedicated music classrooms and a forest school with pond and chickens with coop.

Sport and extracurricular activities. Our Woodlee Sports Centre comprises a dance studio, fitness suite, indoor climbing wall, two FIBA-sized basketball courts that can also convert to eight badminton courts and an outdoor traversing wall. ACS Egham offers an extensive range of extracurricular clubs and community service activities both locally and internationally. Students also participate in international theatre arts programmes, as well as maths, literature and music competitions in the UK and across Europe. The campus sports programme runs three seasons fielding teams in football, volleyball, cross-country, basketball, rugby, swimming, dance, tennis, athletics, baseball, softball and golf. We also offer tournament sports competitions across the UK and Europe.

Accreditation. ACS Egham is accredited by the New England Association of Schools and Colleges (NEASC) and is authorised by the International Baccalaureate (IB) to offer the IBPYP, IBMYP, IBDP and IBCP. The School holds memberships in the European Council of International Schools (ECIS), the Council of International Schools (COIS) and the Independent Schools Association (ISA).

Four schools, one world-class education. Founded in 1967 to serve the needs of global and local families, ACS International Schools educate over 3,700 students, aged 2 to 18, day and boarding, from more than 100 countries. Our schools – 3 in Greater London and 1 in Doha, Qatar – are all non-sectarian and co-educational.

Contact the Admissions Team. The admissions team is available throughout the year to answer questions, book campus visits, and assist families through the enrolment process. Students are accepted in all grades throughout the year. Partial and full bursaries in Grades 6/Year 7, Grade 8/Year 9 and Grade 11/Year 12 are now available.

ACS International School Hillingdon

Hillingdon Court, 108 Vine Lane, Hillingdon, Middlesex UB10 0BE

Tel: 01895 259771
email: hillingdonadmissions@acs-schools.com
website: www.acs-schools.com/acs-hillingdon
Twitter: @ACSintschools
Facebook: @ACSHillingdon
Instagram: @acshillingdonschool
LinkedIn: /acs-international-schools-ltd-

Head of School: **Martin Hall**

Age Range. 4–18.

Number in School. Day only: 306 Boys, 264 Girls.

Fees per annum (2021–2022). Tuition: £11,290–£25,900.

ACS Hillingdon is a beautifully green and welcoming campus close to central London, bursting with innovation and enterprise.

We're home to around 570 students, aged 4 to 18, from over 50 countries, taught and supported by 150 teachers and staff members. Our global perspective reflects our world-renowned curriculum that builds on the very best of leading education standards, giving our students the flexibility to tailor their studies from a wide range of options.

Academic programme. The broad and flexible curriculum at ACS Hillingdon is designed to help students excel, ensuring they're ready for the next stage of their academic career. Underpinned by the International Baccalaureate, Advanced Placement courses, AP Capstone Diploma and the US High School Diploma, our curriculum emphasises life skills as much as academic excellence, with a focus on experiential learning and leadership that ensures we nurture confident, caring, well-rounded individuals. ACS Hillingdon also has a new Film Programme working with Pinewood studios and working with film industry mentors.

Facilities. ACS Hillingdon campus boasts a stunning mansion house and modern wing extension with libraries, science and IT labs, art studios, cafeteria, gym, auditorium, and a dedicated music centre. Our grounds are home to an all-weather playing field, tennis and basketball courts, and adventure play areas, with off-site facilities for soccer, rugby, swimming, track and field. We have 13 acres of grounds including a G4 all-weather pitch and tennis courts, 14 acres of offsite playing fields, including a clubhouse, changing rooms and four sports fields for football, rugby, hockey and baseball.

Our new science wing has seven labs and a prep room. We also have a range of facilities including an auditorium with tiered theatre-style seating, an art gallery space, Think Tank/Maker space classrooms for STEAM, dedicated indoor gym for basketball/volleyball and other sports and Harmony House, with music practice rooms and recording studio. Our three divisional libraries are equipped with computers and our IT labs have film/media capability.

Enrichment. ACS Hillingdon also offers extensive and varied extracurricular clubs and community service activities both locally and internationally, which encourage students to participate in the richness of school life. Students also participate in international theatre arts programmes, maths, literature and music competitions in the UK and across Europe.

Four schools, one world-class education. Founded in 1967 to serve the needs of global and local families, ACS International Schools educate over 3,700 students, aged 2 to 18, day and boarding, from more than 100 countries. Our schools – 3 in Greater London and 1 in Doha, Qatar – are all non-sectarian and co-educational.

Contact the Admissions Team. The admissions team is available throughout the year to answer questions, book campus visits, and assist families through the enrolment process. Students are accepted in all grades throughout the year. Partial and full bursaries in Grades 6/year 7, Grade 8/year 9 and Grade 11/year 12 are now available.

Alton School

Anstey Lane, Alton, Hampshire GU34 2NG

Tel: 01420 82070
email: enquiries@altonschool.co.uk
website: www.altonschool.co.uk
Twitter: @AltonSchool1938
Facebook: @altonschool1938
LinkedIn: @altonschool1938

Motto: Be the best that you can be

Chairman of Governors: Mr Clive Hexton

Headmaster: **Mr Karl Guest**, MA, PGCE

Deputy Head: Mrs Susie Brooks, BA Hons, PGCE

Age Range. 6 months to 18 years.

Number in School. 450.

Fees per term (2021–2022). Lower School £3,629–£4,394, Senior £5,148.

Entrance. Nursery and Lower School – non-selective; Senior School – entrance assessment (Cat 4) and interview; Sixth Form – GCSE results and interview.

Details of Awards programme (scholarships) on website.

Alton School is an independent co-educational Catholic school located on the north Hampshire/Surrey border, on the outskirts of the market town of Alton. It is an all through School with a clear educational and pastoral pathway for boys and girls, from Nursery through to Sixth Form. Formerly known as Alton Convent, Alton School prides itself on its pastoral care and outstanding progress that it achieves for every child.

The minute you step foot in Alton School you feel the sense of family, care and community. We are a happy and friendly school, but we are also bold and ambitious in our approach and in our aspirations for our pupils. We guide our pupils in finding their moral compass, in understanding themselves and what they can contribute to the world.

Achieving and Caring. We know each of our pupils individually and understand how best to balance the challenge, support and encouragement that every student needs to succeed. Our A Level and GCSE results are consistently strong and our pupils regularly outperform expectations at every stage of their education.

At Alton School results matter but it is the progress that each individual makes that is of the greatest value. Progress is developed and monitored as pupils move through the School all the way from Nursery, through Prep and Senior school and often into Sixth Form. The effect of this is seen in the excellent Value-Added scores students obtain – this is the measure of progress that students achieve based on where a student started from and the progress they make relative to other similar students.

Extra-Curricular. Alton School students are invited to develop their talents and interests through a fantastic range of stimulating and inspiring learning experiences. There really is something for everyone including award-winning Science, thought-provoking field trips, and reflection time on spiritual retreats. There are a wide range of sports for boys and girls, music for all age groups, drama and art as well as CCF and Duke of Edinburgh.

International Opportunity. We are fortunate to be part of a vibrant international community. Our students have the opportunity to go to India to support the work of our sister school in Varanasi, join the annual pilgrimage to Lourdes and experience a fully immersive language programme in Columbia. Students regularly tell us that these trips are life changing.

Remote Learning. We are committed to preparing our students for the future and this need has never been more real than it is today. Our interactive Alton@Home Remote Learning Programme offers a full and structured timetable of remote, interactive lessons using Microsoft Teams.

Charitable status. The Alton Convent School Charity is a Registered Charity, number 1071684.

Argyle House School

19/20 Thornhill Park, Tunstall Road, Sunderland, Tyne & Wear SR2 7LA

Tel:	0191 510 0726
email:	office@argylehouseschool.co.uk
website:	www.argylehouseschool.co.uk

Head: Mr C Johnson

Age Range. 2½–16.

Number in School. 250 Boys and Girls.

Fees per term (2021–2022). £2,470–£2,950

Argyle House School was established in 1884 as a small independent day school for boys and girls, situated in the centre of Sunderland. Students travel from all parts of the region, by our buses, or local forms of transport. The school has maintained its high standards of academic achievement, whilst catering for a wide variety of abilities.

At Argyle House, we believe in the individual, and work with him or her to enable the achievement of each student's potential. This is due to attention to detail by fully qualified and dedicated staff, who help to mould the individual into a well-mannered and accomplished young individual, who will be able to meet future challenges.

Small class sizes and a friendly environment facilitate learning, but not all work is academic, as the school takes an active part in many sporting leagues, both within the school, and locally with other schools. We aim to offer all the facilities of a much larger school, whilst remaining at present student levels to keep the intimacy and friendliness of a smaller school, for both parents and students.

ArtsEd Day School & Sixth Form

Cone Ripman House, 14 Bath Road, Chiswick, London W4 1LY

Tel:	020 8987 6600
email:	pupils@artsed.co.uk
website:	www.artsed.co.uk
Twitter:	@ArtsEdLondon
Facebook:	@ArtsEdLondon

Headteacher: **Mr Matthew Bulmer**

Deputy Headteacher: Mrs Claire Parker-Wood

Director of Performing Arts: Ms Natalie Bareham

Director of Curriculum and Data Management: Mr Thamir Elzubaidi

Director of Sixth Form: Mr Mark Ferrington

Director of Engagement & Professional Development: Mr Christopher Reynolds

Head of BTEC: Ms Elizabeth Bellamy

Age Range. 11–18

Number in School. Day School: 141 Sixth Form: 171

Fees per term (2021–2022). £5,686–£6,276

ArtsEd Day School and Sixth Form offers pupils an outstanding education and training in a truly unique environment. Highly skilled staff create exciting opportunities for pupils to explore and develop their creativity, at the same time as enabling excellent academic achievement. Every member of the school community is committed to our supportive and welcoming ethos, demonstrated in the warm and friendly atmosphere that is evident from the moment you walk into our lively foyer.

ArtsEd is consistently the most academically successful performing arts school in the country. Pupils achieve excellent exam results at all levels and value-added scores place ArtsEd in the top 1% of all schools in the UK. With 100% of Year 13 BTEC students achieving Triple Distinction or better in Acting, Musical Theatre, and Dance in the last three years, ArtsEd is the UK's leading centre for Level 3 BTEC Performing Arts.

Autumn 2020 saw the completion of a £10 million capital project and the opening of a new wing on the Chiswick site. This new space adds dance studios and cutting edge classrooms to ArtsEd's training facilities, which include the industry standard Andrew Lloyd Webber Foundation Theatre.

Judged as Excellent in all areas in the ISI Educational Quality Inspection in 2019, ArtsEd continues to go from strength to strength and in 2020 was awarded the Best Contemporary Performing Arts Provider in the National Education and Training Awards. These accolades join many others over recent years including the ISA Excellence Award, The Stage's School of the Year and BE OPEN Foundation's recognition of the ArtsEd as one of the top five schools and colleges in the UK.

For over 100 years, ArtsEd alumni have significantly influenced the creative industries and beyond. They include doctors, lawyers and high-flying executives, as well as leading choreographers, directors and producers. The enthusiasm and expertise of our teachers fuels pupils' passion for performance and cultivates a zest for learning right across the curriculum. Outstanding pastoral care and the support and encouragement that pupils give one another makes enjoyment, as much as excellence, part of everyone's day.

"I wanted my daughter to be somewhere where she could continue her academic successes, but in a warm and happy environment that's fun and supportive, and ArtsEd was the answer." ArtsEd parent

"My daughter's maths grade has really shot up because of the brilliant teaching and small class sizes here." ArtsEd parent

"I am delighted with my son's progress since he's been at ArtsEd. The small class sizes and the creative environment have really helped him thrive." ArtsEd parent

Ashton House School

50–52 Eversley Crescent, Isleworth, Middlesex TW7 4LW

Tel: 020 8560 3902
email: school@ashtonhouse.com
website: www.ashtonhouse.com

Proprietor: Mr S J Turner, BSc

Head Teacher: Mrs Angela Stewart

Age Range. 3–11.
Number in School. 95 Day Pupils: 50 Boys, 45 Girls.
Fees per term (2021–2022). £2,865–£4,158.

Founded 1930. Proprietor: S J Turner. Entry by interview and assessment. Prospectus on request.

Choosing a school for your child is one of the most important decisions you will be making on their behalf and we fully understand that you want to get it right. At Ashton

House we do our very best to deliver a first-class education in a calm and happy atmosphere, where children learn and develop while still enjoying their childhood. Our results at 11 indicate that we are succeeding while our pupils have grown into confident, caring young people ready for the next phase in their education. Our most recent inspection judged the personal development of our pupils to be "outstanding".

Ayscoughfee Hall School

Welland Hall, London Road, Spalding, Lincolnshire PE11 2TE

Tel: 01775 724733
email: admin@ahs.me.uk
website: www.ahs.me.uk
Facebook: @Ayscoughfee-Hall-School-Life

Head: **Mrs Theresa Wright**

Bursar/Company Secretary: Mrs Emma Gibson

Age Range. 3–11 Co-educational.
Number of Pupils. Maximum capacity 160 Day Pupils.
Fees per term (2021–2022). £1,730–£2,560.

Ayscoughfee Hall School celebrated 100 years in 2020.

Founded in 1920, Ayscoughfee Hall School is centred around a beautiful Georgian family home. A purpose-built extension complements the already spacious accommodation. The School houses Kindergarten, Infant and Junior Departments and has further developed its facilities to include enlarged classrooms, a dedicated Science/Art Room, Music Department, Cookery Room, Library, a large Sports Hall and a Foreign Languages Room.

Following a full inspection in September 2021, Ayscoughfee Hall School was judged to be 'Excellent' in all areas. A very thorough inspection was carried out by the Independent Schools Inspectorate in which the school was awarded the highest possible grade.

The guidelines and principles of the National Curriculum are followed in all subjects but go far beyond the basic requirements in order to give each child a broader, more varied understanding. Academic standards are high and progress is well monitored throughout the school. The vast majority of pupils are successful in the Lincolnshire County Council 11+ selection examination (100% pass rate in 2021) and progress to secondary selective school education very well equipped to tackle all subjects. The curriculum is continually reviewed and class teachers are supported by specialist teachers for PE, ICT, languages, music and Forest School. French and Spanish are taught from Reception class.

iPads support learning in the classrooms and pupils receive weekly, dedicated ICT tuition in our up-to-date ICT suite.

The School excels with its music and drama productions over the academic year, in which all children perform in front of their parents and guests.

The school competes successfully in local and regional sports activities, including football, rugby, hockey, netball, cross-country and athletics.

There is a thriving programme of extracurricular activities, including sport, drama, cookery, chess, poetry, textiles, choir, instrumental groups, blogging, code club and Forest School. A wide variety of educational visits is offered, with the older children having the opportunity to participate in alternate cultural and activity residential trips, accompanied by the staff. Furthermore, regular visits by professional groups and individuals take place in school.

As a small school with small class sizes, we aim to provide a happy and caring environment where the individual child may flourish. We are proud of our academic standards but we also strive to give a broad and balanced education. Above all, we want our boys and girls to use and develop their different abilities and to enjoy the success this brings.

Charitable status. Ayscoughfee Hall School Limited is a Registered Charity, number 527294. It exists to provide education for boys and girls.

Babington House School

Grange Drive, Chislehurst, Kent BR7 5ES

Tel: 020 8467 5537
email: enquiries@babingtonhouse.com
website: www.babingtonhouse.com
Twitter: @babingtonbr7
Facebook: @BabingtonBR7
LinkedIn: /Babington-House-School

Chair of Governors: Mr C Turner

Headmaster: **Mr T W A Lello**, MA, FRSA, NPQH, PGCE

Head of Seniors: Mr P Showell, BMus Hons, QTS, FRSA

Head of Preparatory: Mrs B McDonald-Smith, BA Hons, PGCE, QTS

Age Range. Co-educational 3–18.

Number in School. 421 Day pupils: 151 Boys, 270 Girls.

Fees per term (2021–2022). £3,950–£5,725

Babington House School is an independent day school for pupils aged 3 to 18 years, situated in a beautiful group of buildings on Grange Drive in Chislehurst, near Bromley and close to Elmstead Woods station.

Our commitment is to provide an academic and well-rounded education with small class sizes which is tailored to the needs of our pupils, believing that bright children benefit from carefully monitored and well-directed learning, where self-discipline is highly prized and where each pupil is known as an individual. This helps Babington House pupils grow into confident, accomplished, creative young people with emotional intelligence and high standards.

Babington is an academic school. Our academic, social and sporting endeavours are underpinned by core Christian values which include a respect for others and an awareness of a purpose greater than ourselves. There is a strong sense of community at Babington House.

Top of the Bromley League tables for Early Years provision three years running. Top small independent school in England for A Level results 2018. Over the past four years, Babington has achieved 85% A* to B grades at A Level.

In its last inspection Babington House was praised by the ISI for achieving outstanding academic success at all key stages and providing exemplary pastoral care. The boys and girls receive a first-class education in a nurturing and supportive environment, set in pleasant suburban surroundings. Full range of courses for examinations at all levels. "Excellent" in all areas of the school and across every age group from 3–18 (ISI report November 2016).

Specialist facilities for Science, Music, Drama, Art, Sport, ICT, Languages, Maths & English.

Small classes: Maximum size 20 pupils. Careers guidance by a specialist.

Wide range of sports (Athletics, Swimming, Tennis, Netball, Gymnastics, Hockey, Football, Rugby, Cross Country) and extracurricular activities (Drama, Gym Club, Horse Riding, Cookery, Rock Climbing, Taekwondo, Archaeology Club, Choir, Ballet, Tap, Elocution and Instrumental Tuition).

Charitable status. Babington House School is a Registered Charity, number 307914. It exists to provide exemplary education.

Ballard School

Fernhill Lane, New Milton, Hampshire BH25 5SU

Tel: 01425 626900
email: registrar@ballardschool.co.uk
website: www.ballardschool.co.uk
Twitter: @BallardSchool
Facebook: @BallardSchoolNewMilton
LinkedIn: /BallardSchool

Chairman of the Board of Governors: Mr P Goodfellow

Headmaster: **Mr Andrew McCleave**

Age Range. 2 to 16 Co-educational.

Number of Children. 450 day children.

Fees per term (2021–2022). Autumn Term: Years 9–11 £5,550, Years 6–8 £5,275, Year 5 £5,130, Year 4 £4,970, Year 3 £4,320. Reception–Year 2 £2,875. Spring & Summer Terms: Years 9–11 £5,415, Years 6–8 £5,150, Year 5 £5,005, Year 4 £4,970, Year 3 £4,535. Reception–Year 2 £3,015. Fees include the cost of school lunches and most extra-curricular clubs. Sibling discounts available.

'Pupils are reflective and have high levels of self-esteem and empathy. They are highly successful in displaying these characteristics through academic study as well as the wealth of sporting performing arts and extra-curricular opportunities in which they participate.' ISI Inspection November 2017.

Ballard is an award-winning, independent, co-educational day school for children from Nursery to GCSE. Rated 'excellent & outstanding' by ISI, we believe in a bespoke education for your child within a nurturing and engaging environment. Set in 34 acres of beautiful grounds located between the New Forest National Park and the Solent, we serve Hampshire and Dorset.

Ballard pupils achieve excellent examination results: this year 100% of pupils achieved at least five GCSE passes graded 9–4 (including English and Maths), with 75% of pupils securing at least nine GCSE passes in total and a considerable number of pupils achieved the top grades of 9–7.

Subject specialist teaching staff, alongside small class sizes and a diverse and inspiring range of activities and trips, nurture self-confidence, aspiration and help develop each child's personality.

A family school with Christian values, Ballard offers inspiring teaching and excellent pastoral care; children are encouraged to take on responsibilities from an early age including a mentoring programme whereby older children help younger children.

There is a wealth of information on our website – www.ballardschool.co.uk – including our Open Morning dates. So come along and see for yourself why more parents are choosing a Ballard education for their children.

"Quite simply a remarkable school."

"Ballard should not be overlooked by parents wanting a thorough and bespoke education for their children. There is nowhere that offers each individual pupil the opportunity to fulfil their own potential in a lively, sincere environment, rich in the consistent achievement of outstanding results. The school community runs very deep and the children across all year groups are encouraged to 'mix and mentor' which clearly delivers a loyalty within the school community."

"My son's predicted grade for Maths GCSE has gone from a D/C to an A* because of the way he has been taught."

"The attitude at Ballard is very much 'You can do it' not 'Can you do it?'."

"It's been the making of both of our boys."

"You are not just a number."

"Ballard has given me everything I need so that I can go forward and achieve anything I want."

Charitable status. Ballard School Ltd is a Registered Charity, number 307328. It exists for the education of children.

Bedford Greenacre Independent School & Nursery

58–60 Shakespeare Road, Bedford MK40 2DL

Tel: 01234 352031
email: admissions@bedfordgreenacre.co.uk
website: www.bedfordgreenacre.co.uk

Chair of Governors: G M Bates, OBE, JP

Principal: **I M Daniel**, BA, NPQH

Age Range. 6 weeks to 18 co-educational
Number in School. 653 Day Pupils.
Fees per term (2021–2022). £2,329–£3,898.

Bedford Greenacre Independent School was formed on 1st May 2021 by the merger of Rushmoor School and St Andrew's School and Nursery.

Rushmoor School moved to Bedford in 1918 and had grown and improved over 102 years by investing greatly to provide excellent facilities. Rushmoor formed an alliance in 2013 with St Andrew's School and the formal merger and rebranding was the next step in this process. St Andrew's School had an equally strong reputation in Bedford, initially opening in 1896.

We appreciate the importance of selecting the right school for your son or daughter; childhood is something which can be experienced only once. With this in mind, and the belief that children learn best when they feel happy and secure, we aim to develop in our pupils a lifelong interest in learning – one which encompasses the full range of intellectual, cultural, artistic and sporting achievements of our society.

We believe in individual care and attention. Visitors to the school are impressed by the friendly, positive attitude of the pupils and their energetic sense of purpose. The staff are caring and understanding, yet know the importance of effort and personal discipline in enabling pupils to achieve the highest academic standards.

At the school we ensure that all children have opportunities to develop their intellectual, physical and creative gifts, across a broad and balanced curriculum. Children in Reception and Junior classes benefit greatly from a wide range of specialist teachers.

We emphasise the individual, recognising that all children are different and value each child in their own right. Encouraging children to develop their strengths improves their self-esteem, enabling them to find their role in the community. We promote children's personal development, encouraging lively and enquiring minds, respect for others and a high regard for truth. The stability of continuous education, spanning the school age ranges, is a major factor in helping us achieve this.

We pride ourselves on our ability to integrate children with Specific Learning Differences within mainstream school life, whilst still providing extended challenges for our gifted and talented pupils. We believe that every child should be allowed to embrace any aspect of the curriculum. Enabling children to receive support without undermining their confidence amongst their peers is of primary importance.

In 2019, under our former names, we won the *ISA Award for Outstanding Provision for Learning Support*. We have also won the *ISA Award for Excellence and Innovation in Early Years*. We boast successful sporting records, with many pupils gaining county and national honours. Under our former name, we won the *ISA Award for Outstanding Provision in Sport* in 2016. Children have also gained much success in national and local drama competitions and festivals, together with art and photography competitions. In 2014, under our former name, we were a finalist in the *ISA Award for Excellence* and winner of the 'Financial Innovation' category.

We are excited about the future where we will be on one site with new, purpose-built facilities. To find out more, please visit our website www.bedfordgreenacre.co.uk.

Prospective parents and children can tour the school at any time with the Principal and 'taster days' can be arranged. Come and experience our caring ethos which enables our children to develop the confidence and flexibility which allows them to face the demands of modern life. To view our excellent inspection reports please visit our website. Contact us on hello@bedfordgreenacre.co.uk.

Charitable status. Bedford Greenacre Independent School Limited is a Registered Charity, number 1194080. It exists to provide education.

Beech Hall School

Beech Hall Drive, Tytherington, Macclesfield, Cheshire SK10 2EG

Tel: 01625 422192
email: secretary@beechhallschool.org
website: www.beechhallschool.org
Twitter: @beechhall_macc
Facebook: @beechhallschool

Headmaster: **Mr J D Allen**, BA Ed Hons, MA, NPQH, FCoT

Deputy Headmistress: Mrs G Yandell, BA Hons, PGCE, L2 Elklan

Director of Teaching & Learning: Mrs K Griffin, BSc Hons, MBA, PGCE

Director of Finance & Operations: Mrs V Parkes, BA Hons, MSc, PGCE

Registrar: Mrs N Lindsay, BA Hons

Age Range. 6 months–16 years.

Number of Pupils. 180.

Fees per term (2021–2022). Infants £3,500 Junior School £4,315, Senior School £4,695. The fees are inclusive of lunches and snacks.

Nursery, Infant, Junior and Senior departments offer education between 8.30am and 4.00pm with further supervised sporting and leisure activities available until 5.00pm. If required, there is supervised care up until 6.00pm for all children.

Beech Hall is a co-educational Day school situated in spacious and attractive grounds with extensive playing fields, a heated outdoor swimming pool, new food technology lab and many other facilities.

Boys and girls are prepared for entry to a wide variety of Independent Schools and Sixth Form Colleges. Classes are kept small, making individual attention possible in every lesson.

There is a very popular Nursery, Pre-School and Reception department, consisting of children between the ages of 6 months and 5 years under the care of their own specialist teachers. These classes were started with the objective of giving boys and girls a good grounding in reading, writing and arithmetic.

Beech Hall aims to provide a sound all-round education. Rugby, football, hockey and netball are played in the winter terms and in summer, cricket, athletics, and rounders are taught. There is an extensive sporting fixture list covering all sports with children playing representative sport from Year 3 upwards. Swimming is taught throughout the year and other activities include badminton and fives.

The school is situated off the main Stockport–Macclesfield road, within easy reach of Manchester International Airport and the M6 and M62 motorways.

Further details and illustrated prospectus are obtainable from the school or via the school's website.

Beech House School

184 Manchester Road, Rochdale, Greater Manchester OL11 4JQ

Tel: 01706 646309
email: info@beechhouseschool.co.uk
website: www.beechhouseschool.co.uk

Principal: **Mr Kevin Sartain**, BSc Hons, PGCE, Dip Spo Psy, CBiol, FIBiol

Age Range. 2–16 Co-educational.

Number of Pupils. 180.

Fees per term (2021–2022). £1,947–£2,383.

Founded in 1850, Beech House School is an independent co-educational school for students aged two to sixteen years. An Upper Preparatory department for children aged eight to eleven years and a Senior department for those aged eleven to sixteen years have been based on the Manchester Road site in Rochdale for its entire history. The Lower Preparatory department for children aged two to seven has been based at Broadfield Style.

There is a real family atmosphere in the School, and this was reflected on during our recent independent school inspectorate report. I think that continuity plays a large role in nurturing such an environment and the fact that a number of students will spend 14 years of their lives with us mean the bonds we create are lasting. Staff and students have a different relationship than in many schools that is both closer and more personal. Parents are more invested in the school and our activities, with many families having sent children to the school for generations. Sadly, the state sector can no longer guarantee that children can attend the same school as their siblings, but the importance of family is not lost on us.

We put a limit on our class sizes of 16 because we know the importance of providing personal assistance to all our students, whatever their ability level. You cannot offer the service we do with larger numbers and our small size ensures that our students never miss out on opportunities. Our school trips and excursions always have sufficient space for everyone who is interested and students are able to build a closer bond with teachers because of the more dedicated contact time they receive.

In 2021, 30% of Year 11 GCSE entries achieved a grade 9/8. In Science this figure rose to 50%.

Beech House School are pleased to be recognised as leaders in Private Primary and Secondary Education in North West England 2019. Beech House School has also been recognised in the Parliamentary Review 2019. The School has been awarded *Independent School of the Year* and achieved the *Northern Enterprise Award*. In 2021 the School the school was recognised as the *The Most Outstanding Independent School – Greater Manchester*. We also achieved the *Excellence Award for Holistic Education and Development*.

Belmont School

Feldemore, Holmbury St Mary, Dorking, Surrey RH5 6LQ

Tel: 01306 730852
email: admissions@belmont-school.org
website: www.belmont-school.org
Twitter: @BelmontDorking
Facebook: @BelmontDorking
LinkedIn: /BelmontSchool

Chairman of the Governors: Mr A Baker

Headmistress: **Mrs H Skrine**, BA Hons Exeter, PGCE London, NPQH, FRSA

Age Range. 3–16.

Number of Pupils. 221 Boys and Girls: Day, Weekly and Flexible Boarding.

Fees per term (from January 2022). Day Pupils: Pre-Reception (based on 5 mornings a week) £1,790, Reception £3,580, Years 1–2 £4,200, Years 3–4 £5,550, Years 5–6 £5,820, Years 7–8 £6,020 and Years 9–10 £6,420. Boarding Pupils: day boarding £10/£21 per day (until 6.30pm/8.30pm), flexi-boarding from £5,755 (up to 5 nights per term), part-time boarding from £6,320 (2 nights per week), and weekly boarding from £7,150 (for 4/5 nights per week, Sunday/Monday to Friday).

Founded in London in 1880, the School is now established in 65 acres of woodland overlooking the picturesque village of Holmbury St Mary, between Guildford and Dorking. The school boasts an historic building with a purpose-built interior. Outstanding facilities include an impressive sports hall, well-equipped theatre, state-of-the-art IT capability, extensive sports pitches, mountain bike tracks, music school, new Science laboratory and Design Technology suite, heated outdoor swimming pool and woodland adventure courses. Our friendly, well-qualified and talented staff focus upon developing confident, happy and capable pupils, which makes Belmont a place that most boys and girls would only dream about. In addition we seek to smooth the logistics of family life by delivering flexible arrangements for parents and by providing a minibus service.

We offer co-educational day education for pupils aged 3 to 16, and optional weekly, flexible and day boarding arrangements for pupils from 7 years old. Breakfast club is available from 3 years old and extended day arrangements in the evening for pupils from Reception upwards.

Children qualify for 15 hours of Early Years funding from the term following their third birthday until the term following their fifth birthday.

At Belmont, we seek to discover and to develop what is best in each pupil, seeking to inspire and to unfurl the hidden strengths of every boy and girl. There is a happy, industrious atmosphere and high expectations pervade throughout all aspects of school life. We have a challenging curriculum and an extensive array of extra-curricular opportunities that together are designed to captivate the imagination, to nurture independence and to harness academic ambition for every pupil. Creativity is a particular strength of the school and healthy pupil: staff ratios have enabled us to develop a flexible setting system within a relatively small school.

The curriculum covers all the requirements leading from Early Years education to GCSE including Drama, Art, DT, Music, PSHE, Computing, PE and Games. Sports include Netball, Rugby, Football, Cross-Country, Hockey, Tennis, Swimming, Cricket and Athletics. Pupils have a busy life at Belmont; they are passionate and proud of their school and talk enthusiastically about how the educational experience shapes itself according to the age of the pupils, and the needs of the individual.

Children in Year 1 and above attend for a half day or full day visit prior to entry. Further details can be obtained from the Registrar, Charlotte Smith on 01306 730852 or admissions@belmont-school.org.

Charitable status. Belmont School (Feldemore) Educational Trust Limited is a Registered Charity, number 312077.

Bishop Challoner School

228 Bromley Road, Shortlands, Bromley, Kent BR2 0BS

Tel: 020 8460 3546
email: admissions@bishopchallonerschool.com
website: www.bishopchallonerschool.com
Twitter: @challoner_head

Headteacher: **Mr Mark Wallace**, BA Hons, MBA

Age Range. 3–18.

Number in School. 280 Day Pupils.

Fees per term (2021–2022). Seniors £4,725, Juniors £3,675, Infants £3,308, Nursery £948 (min 3 sessions), £3,024 (full time).

This is a Roman Catholic Independent Co-educational School for pupils aged 3–18 years.

Happiness, self-fulfilment and personal success are all embraced at Bishop Challoner.

The School welcomes all Faiths and none.

Admissions to the School follows the successful completion of an entrance examination/assessment and an interview with the Headteacher.

Scholarships and Bursaries are available.

Charitable status. Bishop Challoner School is a Registered Charity, number 1153948. It exists to provide an excellent education for boys and girls.

Bowbrook House School

Peopleton, Nr Pershore, Worcs WR10 2EE

Tel: 01905 841242/841843
email: enquiries@bowbrookhouseschool.co.uk
website: www.bowbrookhouseschool.co.uk
Twitter: @bowbrookhouse
Facebook: @Bowbrook-House-School
Instagram: @bowbrookhouse

Headmaster: **Mr C D Allen**, BSc Hons, CertEd, DipSoc

Age Range. 3½–16.

Number in School. Day 212: 111 Boys, 101 Girls.

Fees per term (2021–2022). £2,000–£4,100

Bowbrook House is set in 14 acres of picturesque Worcestershire countryside yet within easy reach of Worcester, Pershore and Evesham. The school caters for the academic child and also those of average ability, who can benefit from the small classes. All pupils are able to take full advantage of the opportunities offered and are encouraged to participate in all activities. As well as the academic subjects, the school has a flourishing art department, a computer room, hard tennis courts and an open air swimming pool in addition to extensive games fields.

The Pre-Prep department of 3½–8 year olds is a self-contained unit but enjoys the use of the main school facilities.

Whilst stressing academic achievement, the school aims to provide a structured and disciplined environment in which children of all abilities can flourish, gain confidence and achieve their true potential. The small school size enables the head and staff to know all pupils well, to be able to accurately assess their strengths and weaknesses it enables each pupil to be an important part of the school and to feel that their individual attitudes, behaviour, efforts and achievements are important.

There is an extended school day from 8.15am to 5.30pm, with supervised prep sessions. There is also an extensive and varied extracurricular programme run by specialist coaches from basketball, gym and dance to kickboxing and fencing.

Bridgewater School

Drywood Hall, Worsley Road, Worsley, Salford, Greater Manchester M28 2WQ

Tel: 0161 794 1463
email: admin@bwslive.co.uk
website: www.bridgewater-school.co.uk
Twitter: @BridgewaterScho
Facebook: @BridgewaterConnected
Instagram: @bridgewater_school
LinkedIn: /bridgewater-school-worsley

Chair of Governors: Mr C Haighton, BSc Hons

Headmistress: **Mrs J A T Nairn**, Cert Ed Distinction

Age Range. 3–18 Co-educational.

Number of Pupils. 433: 231 Boys, 202 Girls.

Fees per term (2021–2022). £2,060–£4,081.

In 1950, a group of parents wanted to find an alternative to schools in the area, believing that every child deserved access to the best education possible. Out of this shared vision, Bridgewater School was born.

Today, seventy years later, this aspiration remains at the heart of everything we do. Bridgewater School provides independent education for boys and girls aged 3–18 years in an inspirational setting that is inclusive, stimulating,

supportive and totally focused on achieving every pupil's individual goals.

Ever since the school's inception, our family ethos has ensured that each young person is treated very much as an individual and, although the scale and academic stature of the school have grown alongside our new buildings and facilities, we are still small enough to know each young person by name and develop a true understanding of their specific needs and abilities.

Whether your child joins us at the very start of their learning journey, as a Prep pupil, Senior School student or at Sixth Form level, they will enjoy consistently high teaching standards and a wonderfully varied extra-curricular programme. A programme designed to enrich their experiences, enhance their personal development and give them the opportunity to develop their individuality their way. The result is a vibrant community where children can flourish and thrive, learning together and achieving together.

The exceptional focus we can bring to all students through the intimacy and support of small classes can make all the difference. A difference which manifests itself in exceptional A Level and GCSE exam results, year after year. However, we believe that exam results are an end product of an outstanding, fully rounded education rather than an end in themselves. Our students are successful and achieve their personal best because they study a broad and challenging curriculum in a stable, happy and reassuring environment. They are given the opportunity to discover previously undiscovered talents both within and beyond the classroom, which explains why so many of our young people go on to make so much of their lives.

Our unique, outwardly focused approach to education engenders high standards of behaviour and self-discipline amongst pupils, as well as building a mature awareness of their personal and social responsibilities. This approach, together with the importance we place on the relationship between family and school, produces articulate, well-rounded individuals who take pride in their achievements and who are fully prepared to meet the exciting challenges yet to come.

We are committed to a programme of continuous development and improvement and the school governors, staff and pupils all share a real sense of excitement about both our recent accomplishments and Bridgewater's future.

If you have not yet visited us then may we recommend that you do so soon. We would be delighted to meet you and show you the uniquely individual features which set our school apart.

Charitable status. Bridgewater School is a Registered Charity, number 1105547.

Bronte School

Mayfield, 7 Pelham Road, Gravesend, Kent DA11 0HN

Tel: 01474 533805
email: enquiry@bronteschool.co.uk
website: www.bronteschool.co.uk

Headmistress: **Mrs Emma Wood**, BA Hons

Age Range. 3–11.

Number in School. 147 Day Pupils: 77 Boys, 70 Girls.

Fees per term (2021–2022). £3,345.

Bronte is a small, friendly, family-orientated, co-educational day school serving Gravesend and surrounding villages. The children are taught in small classes and are prepared for all types of secondary education. In 1999 the school moved to its present building which has since been expanded to accommodate specialist teaching rooms. A broadly-based curriculum and an extensive number of activity clubs provide the children with every opportunity to develop their individual interests and abilities. We achieve excellent 11+ results every year.

Entry is preferred at Kindergarten (age 3) following a parental visit to the school and an interview with the Head. Children joining at a later stage are assessed informally prior to entry.

Buxlow Preparatory School

5/6 Castleton Gardens, East Lane, Wembley, Middlesex HA9 7QJ

Tel: 020 8904 3615

email: admin@buxlowschool.org.uk

website: www.buxlowschool.org.uk

Headteacher: **Mr D May**

Deputy Headteacher: Mrs N Zaman

Head of EYFS: Mrs M Jobe

Sendco: Mrs P Kelly

School Secretary and Headteacher's PA: Mrs D Hutchinson

Age Range. 2–11 Co-educational, Nursery to Year 6.

Number of Pupils. 75.

Fees per term (2021–2022). Reception £3,170, Years 1–6 £3,300.

Founded in 1927, as an independent preparatory school for boys, Buxlow Preparatory School is now fully co-educational and offers quality education to children between 2 and 11 years of age. Buxlow is a calm, nurturing, stimulating, education based setting. We ensure the children are engaged in their learning and are provided with appropriate resources and opportunities to become active, independent learners

Our nursery provision is available for 51 weeks of the year, with a variety of different sessions. The children enjoy a range of activities to support them in reaching their potential through curriculum based learning that promotes independence from a young age. Children can join our Nursery when they are 2 years old and age appropriate children are given first consideration for our sought after Reception places.

The curriculum has a thematic approach and where possible, cross curricular links are made to motivate the children and promote creativity. We also ensure that children gain experiences of the curriculum outside the classroom through off site visits or workshops. We promote high levels of achievement and effort and encourage pupils to take pride and a greater responsibility in their work. As the year

progresses the children's sense of pleasure in their self-motivated achievements grows, laying a solid foundation for future study habits.

We also focus on independent thinking skills through verbal and non-verbal reasoning. We take the learning beyond school through educational visits. Through motivational teaching and attention to every child's needs our pupils experience an inspiring learning journey.

During the Spring Term in Year 5, the children are introduced to 11+ preparation in the form of weekly preparation sessions, involving practice papers and guidance to improve examination technique. The children become familiar with the style and expectations of the papers and these are embedded into their weekly learning, with any marks and general feedback going home to parents. Interview preparations also begin, with the children seen by the Headteacher and Year 6 teacher. LAMDA lessons also support this practice. As a result of this gradual yet thorough preparation, our pupils go into their exams confident and self-assured and our senior school successes speak for themselves.

Our aim is to establish a nurturing environment and an atmosphere where children feel valued and can thrive both emotionally and academically.

Cambridge Tutors College

Water Tower Hill, Croydon, Surrey CR0 5SX

Tel: 020 8688 5284

email: info@ctc.ac.uk

website: www.ctc.ac.uk

Principal: **Dr Chris Drew**, BSc Sussex, MA Bath, EdD Bath, PGCE, Dip RSA, FCCT

Age Range. 14–23.

Number of Pupils. 60.

Fees per annum (2021–2022). From £15,900 excluding accommodation; up to £31,920 including homestay accommodation or up to £39,990 for boarding accommodation.

2021 A Level results: 65% A*/A and 75% of students entering their first choice universities, mostly Russell Group.

Since 1958 Cambridge Tutors College (CTC) has been offering a very high quality academically focused education to young people from the United Kingdom and from across the world. Fundamental to the College's ethos is small group teaching – our average class size is just over 5 students – and regular testing: students sit weekly tests in every subject, under examination conditions. This combination of small classes, regular testing and expert teaching has proved to be highly successful in giving students the motivation and confidence to succeed.

CTC offers: A Level courses (two-year and 18-month), NCUK International Foundation Year and an accelerated 6 month course, one-year GCSE course and a one-year pre-GCSE course. CTC also offers one and two-term pre-sessional courses linked to the two-year A Level programme.

The College's most recent ISI Inspection reports in 2017 and 2020 were outstanding.

The college enjoys a particularly strong reputation for helping students to gain entry to the UK's most prestigious universities.

Situated in a pleasant parkside location in South Croydon, CTC is just a few minutes' walk from the town centre, East Croydon station and bus and tram routes. It is close to Central London, just 15 minutes away by train, but surrounded by parkland and quiet residential streets.

Facilities and resources are modern and well-appointed. The College has excellent technological infrastructure with fast Wi-Fi, and there is an ambitious development programme in place.

The College's welfare provision includes a team of trained professionals and all students have a personal tutor. A varied weekly programme of sporting and other activities is offered, as well as weekend excursions.

Charitable status. Cambridge Tutors Educational Trust Limited is a Registered Charity, number 312878.

Cameron Vale School

4 The Vale, Chelsea, London SW3 6AH

Tel: 020 7352 4040
email: admissions@cameronvaleschool.com
website: www.cameronvaleschool.com
Twitter: @CameronHouseSW3
Facebook: @cameronhouseschool
Instagram: @cameronvaleschool
LinkedIn: /company/cameron-house-school-limited

Chairman: Mr John Forsyth

Headteacher: **Miss Bridget Saul**, BA, MA Ed, PGCE

Deputy Head: Miss Chloe Dorrington, BSc, MA Ed, PGCE

Age Range. 2–11 Co-educational.
Number of Pupils. 60
Fees per term (2021–2022) £7,095

Based in a beautifully designed Edwardian building, just steps from London King's Road, Cameron Vale School prides itself on sending pupils to some of the most sought-after schools in the country.

What sets us apart from other schools is our distinctive family atmosphere and nurturing ethos which celebrates the individual and strives to unlock each child's true potential. Driven by the belief that a 'one size fits all' approach is limiting and supported by our small class sizes, which allow each child to shine, we are able to ensure children are known for who they are and develop their own gifts and talents; whether it be excelling in the classroom, on the sports field or the stage.

Whilst recognising that outcomes matter, we also know that the memories of a child's time with us will last a lifetime. Our aim is to ensure that, at the end of each child's time with us, they feel that Cameron Vale has made a positive difference to their character, thinking and outlook; that the school has shaped who they will become.

Whilst emphasis is placed on acquiring firm foundations in English and Maths, we aim to foster a life-long love of learning, through adopting a cross-curricular, enquiry-led curriculum. Our enquiry-led curriculum aims to deliver a twenty-first century education that will equip our children with the skills required to be independent learners, well-prepared for their next stage in learning.

We encourage learning outdoors and out of the school classroom and believe in offering the children a wealth of experiences to stimulate their questioning and learning. We aim to create memorable learning experiences with planned and spontaneous adventures within and beyond the classroom which often include work with experts. Our Forest School programme plays a major part in this.

We believe that children learn best when effective partnerships exist; a triangular approach with the child in the middle and the school and parents on either side. It is this view that lies behind our engagement and communication with parents and the premise upon which our open-door policy exists.

The relationship between home and school is of fundamental importance in ensuring every child is surrounded by the love, care and guidance which they require as they make their way through their educational journey.

Canbury School

Kingston Hill, Kingston-upon-Thames, Surrey KT2 7LN

Tel: 020 8549 8622
email: reception@canburyschool.co.uk
website: www.canburyschool.co.uk

Headmistress: **Ms C Yates**, BEd, MA

Academic Deputy Head: Mrs G Branney, BSc Hons

Pastoral Deputy Head: Mrs P Rich, BA, PGCE

Bursar & Clerk to the Governors: Mrs Lusia Anindita-Beckman, BA Hons, MSc, LLB, PG Dip Law

Head's PA and Registrar: Ms Louise Boggi

Age Range. 11–18.
Number in School. 75 boys and girls.

Founded in 1982, Canbury School is a unique and happy co-educational independent day school for students from the ages of 11 to 18 on the outskirts of London beside Richmond Park. With excellent transport links to the school, students come from various nearby areas such as Barnes, Putney, Wandsworth, New Malden, Richmond, Teddington, Twickenham, Hampton, Epsom, Central London, Surrey and other areas in the South East such as Esher and Effingham. We also welcome overseas students. Located on the top of Kingston Hill, the school affords our students the opportunity to experience the vast resources London has to offer such as museums, parks, galleries, and theatres literally via a bus ride. With class sizes of fifteen students or less, enthusiastic teaching, excellent pastoral care and a determination to target the needs of individual students, Canbury School gets the best out of students with a wide range of abilities.

Entry requirements. We don't look for students to fit a Canbury mould; we look for students whom we can help to grow. All applicants undertake a baseline assessment. For 11+ entry, we consider reports from Junior/ Primary schools and other documentation and then invite those selected to spend a day with us. If all goes well, we may make an offer. For occasional places in other year groups, the candidate would be invited to spend three days with us in order to secure a place. Any educational reports need to be submitted prior to interview with the Headmistress.

Curriculum. Broad range of GCSE subjects. Functional Skills. BTEC subjects up to Level 3 at KS5. Students are expected to take up to nine GCSEs and/or BTEC level 2 equivalent.

In Years 7–9, the students' timetable includes the following subjects Art, Drama, English, Geography, Graphics, History, ICT, Mathematics, Music, Science, Spanish, Physical Education and Well Being.

Games are taught throughout Key Stage 3. In Games, students are set into groups of equal ability for each sport. Winter sports are cross country, kayaking, football and netball. Summer sports are: athletics, cricket, tennis and rounders. Teams turn out throughout the year on weekends and midweek in inter-school matches. In PE lessons, classes are mixed ability and activities such as basketball, badminton, gymnastics and health-related fitness are taught in order to provide a wider diversity of opportunities for students. Students have weekly swimming lessons throughout the year

In addition to their studies, students have a structured PHSE programme throughout the year.

At KS4 students study a number of GCSEs suitable to their academic ability and personal inclination. They are encouraged to keep their choices as balanced and broad as possible. The school offers the facility to study for eight subjects. The compulsory subjects are Mathematics, English and Science.

Students also choose from a range of subjects: GCSE Art & Design, Business Studies, Geography, Graphics, History, Photography, Spanish, as well as BTEC Performing Arts and Travel & Tourism, and/or an ITQ (information Technology Qualification).

All students continue to have lessons in Physical Education and Games, and PHSE which includes a Careers programme and a work experience week.

Where appropriate, Functional Skills Maths and/or English can be taught as an alternative to a GCSE programme. Functional Skills are taught across all levels (Entry 1–Level 2). Level 2 Functional Skills are universally recognised as an 'alternative qualification to GCSE' enabling pupils to progress to college or on to an apprenticeship.

The final programme for each student is determined by the curriculum structure (distributed on Options Evening) and will be confirmed in consultation with students, parents, subject teachers, the student's tutor and the Senior Leadership Team.

We run a wide range of extracurricular activities and clubs including drama, art, karate, sports and table-tennis.

Canbury School is different in placing emphasis on small classes. No class has more than 15 students. Our aim is to embrace the differences and harness the talents of each student.

Students participate in the school council which is led by our Head Boy and Head Girl. The Prefect Team is responsible for Charity, Sport, and House activities. Students are all members of our very active House system led by Heads of Houses from the Prefect team.

Facilities. We are a small, friendly school with well-equipped classrooms. We have a dedicated science laboratory, classrooms, Art/DT Studio with pottery area and kiln, playground and a separate Sixth Form building. We access local facilities for a wide range of seasonal sporting activities including athletics, cricket, netball, softball, swimming, watersports, badminton, soccer, hockey, basketball, netball, dance, tennis and rock climbing.

Fees per term (2021–2022). £5,800 (£6,315 Sixth Form). Bursaries are means tested and are available at the discretion of the School subject to satisfactory completion of the School's Bursary Form.

Charitable status. Canbury School is a Registered Charity, number 803766. It exists to provide education to a broad range of children including some of various nationalities who stand to benefit from being in a small school.

Cardiff Sixth Form College

1–3 Trinity Court, 21–27 Newport Road, Cardiff CF24 0AA

Tel:	02920 493121
email:	marketing@ccoex.com
website:	www.ccoex.com
Twitter:	@csfcofficial
Facebook:	@csfcofficial
Instagram:	@csfcofficial

Motto: Ignite Your Future, Ignite Your Passion, Ignite Your Interest

Principal: **Mr Gareth Collier**

Head: Thomas Arrand

Director of Studies: Mrs Rebecca Clyde

Director of Marketing and Admissions: Mrs Henrietta Lightwood

Financial Director: Mr Rob Humphreys

Age Range. 14–18 Co-educational.
Number of Students. 350.

Cardiff Sixth Form College's results are outstanding. In 2021 98% of students received A*–A grades, with 100% of students achieving A*–B grades. Excellent teaching, one-to-one support, superb academic materials, nearly double the amount of teaching hours of any other school and developing academic students with programmes designed to enhance their careers is what really makes the difference. The staff offer outstanding one-to-one support, tutorials and academic enrichment on top of their extensive teaching programme.

Cardiff now runs not only a one year GCSE course but is offering two year GCSE from September 2022. GCSE results have also been outstanding with the College topping the small league tables for GCSE results in 2019 (league tables not available for 2020 and 2021 due to Covid-19). 95% of students got A*–B grades and 90% A*–A in 2020. This course provides a unique opportunity for younger students, many of whom aspire to progress on to the award-winning Sixth Form, to be able to take advantage of the inspirational teaching, excellent career development and modern boarding environment at the top school in the UK. Designed as a four-way career path into top universities, this new course gives students the opportunity to study up to 11 key academic subjects as well as improve their English proficiency in small class sizes with intensive teaching.

Cardiff Sixth Form College has an enviable careers department with five full-time careers advisors, personal tutors and a full-time work experience coordinator. In addition, the College is part of Dukes Education with expertise in medical applications, Oxbridge and Russell Group university placements, giving its students access to top industry specialists from across the professions. A two-year super programme of UCAS support, assistance with university entrance exams, lectures and work experience programmes, interview technique and one-to-one tutoring for personal statements ensures that Cardiff students are expertly prepared for the competitive courses they are applying to.

The College also offers a wide range of super-curricular activities. Internationally, students undertake voluntary and work placement programmes in Malaysia and India, join medical, architectural or finance societies and enter national academic competitions such as science Olympiads, Model United Nations and Maths challenges. The Debating Team's performance this year has been outstanding, coming first in the South Wales round of the Oxford Union Schools Debating Competition and for five years in a row Cardiff students have won NASA's International Space Settlement Design Competition in Florida.

From an extra-curricular perspective, students have plenty of opportunities to get involved with sports, performing and creative arts with highlights including an annual Sports Day, the Cultural Event, Talent Show and annual Glee production. Many are talented musicians and gold awards have been won this year in the Duke of Edinburgh's Award scheme.

Pastoral care is very strong with boarding staff and progress tutors constantly monitoring each student. Boarding accommodation is outstanding with every student having a university-style, single bedroom or studio apartment.

For more information or to find out about upcoming Open Days and the application process, please go to www.ccoex.com.

Fees per annum (2021–2022). Day £19,600; Boarding £46,900–£51,000.

Carleton House Preparatory School

145 Menlove Avenue, Liverpool L18 3EE

Tel: 0151 722 0756

email: schooloffice@carletonhouse.co.uk

website: www.carletonhouse.co.uk

Twitter: @carletonhouse

Chair of Governors: Mr Gareth Beck

Head Teacher: **Mrs S Coleman**, BEd Hons SLE

Age Range. 3+–11 Co-educational.

Number in School. 185

Fees per academic year (2021–2022). £8,500 inclusive of lunch, day trips, Spanish lessons and personal insurance cover.

Located in the leafy suburbs of south Liverpool, Carleton House is Merseyside's leading co-ed Preparatory School (13th in the Sunday Times Parent Power 2019). We are a Catholic school that welcomes children of all denominations.

They can because they think they can truly embodies the spirit of Carleton House. Our school is a lively, vibrant community that gives its pupils a first-class education for the 21st century.

Small class sizes (maximum of 23) and a high ratio of teaching staff to pupils enable the well-qualified and experienced staff to provide individual attention in a friendly, caring atmosphere. We nurture the development of the whole child – academically, spiritually and in the sporting and cultural aspects of their lives. Through excellent teaching and the close relationship that exists between school and home, our pupils are challenged, encouraged and supported to achieve their very best.

The implementation of all National Curriculum subjects ensures a broad, well-balanced curriculum is followed, but great importance is given to Maths and English as success in these subjects is central to development in other areas. Additional specialist teaching is provided for children requiring support in the basic subjects.

The children are taught Spanish throughout the school from Nursery to Year 6.

All children receive curriculum music lessons from our specialist teacher. Children in Year 3 to 6 benefit from instrumental music lessons through our external music tuition partner Pulse. Individual piano and guitar lessons are also available.

Children in Years 3 to 6 take part in weekly swimming and gym lessons at a local pool.

Emphasis is placed on high academic standards with our children being prepared for a variety of Entrance examinations at 11. A high percentage of our pupils successfully gain places at selective schools of their choice.

Our children are prepared for and take part in the English Speaking Board (ESB) examinations in year 5 and 6, supporting their public speaking skills.

We place a high importance on the development of computing skills for all pupils, with children from Year 1 to

Year 6 benefiting from specialist computing teaching in our newly refurbished computing suite. This is complemented through the use of iPads in class based lessons.

A wide range of sports and extracurricular activities are offered to both boys and girls, including football, netball, cricket, rounders, chess, debate club, first aid, orchestra, cookery, singing and speech choir. The children compete in local sporting events as well as choral festivals and national quiz competitions.

Theatre and educational visits to enhance our curriculum are provided in all year groups. Our residential trips start in Year 3 with an overnight stay in Barnstondale, followed by a weekend in Shropshire in Year 4, a weekend in Lockerbie in Year 5 and culminating in a week in France for our Year 6 pupils. These residentials provide field and adventure activities that help build confidence and self-esteem outside of the usual classroom environment.

Our open door policy encourages positive engagement with our parents, with regular parent/teacher meetings and biannual written reports on pupils progress.

A thriving Parent Teacher Association provides social functions for parents while raising funds for extra equipment for school and our chosen school charity.

After-school provision is provided by the 'Kids Club'. This operates daily from 3.30pm until 6.00pm and school is open from 8.00am for early drop-offs.

Parents are welcome to visit the school by appointment.

Charitable status. Carleton House Preparatory School is a Registered Charity, number 505310. It exists to provide education for boys and girls.

Claires Court

1 College Avenue, Maidenhead, Berkshire SL6 6AW

Tel: 01628 327710
email: registrar@clairescourt.com
website: www.clairescourt.com
Twitter: @clairescourt
Facebook: @clairescourt
Instagram: @clairescourtschool

Principals:

Mr H Wilding, BA, MCIM, FRSA

Mr J Wilding, BSc, FRSA

Head of Senior Boys: Mr J Wilding, BSc, FRSA

Head of Junior Boys: Mrs L Kirby, BA, QTS, MA

Head of Senior Girls: Mr S Richards, BA, PGCE, QTS

Head of Junior Girls & Nursery: Mrs L Kirby, BA, QTS, MA

Head of Sixth Form: Mrs S Rogers, BEd, Cert HE, Adv Dip Ex&HS

Age Range. 2–18.

Number of Pupils. 500 Boys, 260 Girls. Sixth Form: Co-educational 134.

Fees per term (2021–2022). £3,330–£6,030.

Claires Court is a school for families, run by a family, providing education for young people aged 2 to 18 years. Based on three sites across Maidenhead, we are a broad ability 'diamond model' day school where boys and girls are educated separately during their main school years, but come together for trips and visits, whilst the Nursery School and Sixth Form pupils benefit from a co-educational learning environment.

It is the feeling of belonging and the school's ethos that helps young people thrive and flourish in our school community. At Claires Court, we treat everyone as an individual, evaluating each child's ability to ensure we can enable them to reach their full potential, helping them achieve great results, whether that is in the classroom, on the sports field or in the creative arena. By offering the best education, strong pastoral care and a wealth of opportunities, our pupils achieve academically, feel valued and have a strong sense of self-belief and self-worth.

Pupils have access to excellent facilities across the sites, with indoor swimming pools, drama studios, extensive playing fields and music suites. Senior pupils have access to top-class facilities for training and playing rugby, football, cricket and hockey through our partnership agreements with local sports clubs. Sailing and rowing are also part of our sport offering with much success in regional and national competitions.

At the core of our learning philosophy are the Claires Court Essentials. Right from Nursery we make learning fun but challenging and from that springboard we focus on developing a variety of skills and behaviours that young people need to be a successful learner and individual in our fast-paced world. As they mature, pupils are expected to stretch themselves, push their own boundaries and limitations; we believe it is good to be wrong as long as we learn from that experience and bounce back. We develop boys and girls who are confident and resilient, learners who are critical thinkers and risk-takers, who can solve problems and communicate, as well as be creative and work collaboratively with others.

In the junior years, the creative, topic-based curriculum inspires a passion for learning and children quickly develop a taste for success. There is a focus on mastering the fundamental skills as well as academic attainment. Further up the school, the breadth and balance of the curriculum allows senior pupils to develop new interests and talents before focusing on their GCSEs.

The Sixth Form offers just as much variety with more than 24 A Level subjects as well BTECs in ICT and Sport. In recent years students have achieved an overall pass rate of 100% and our value added surpasses that of most other Sixth Forms, meaning our students achieve over and above their predicted grades. Alongside this, the team also offers development and training for the personal, social and work skills that are desired by universities and employers.

Collingwood School

3 Springfield Road, Wallington, Surrey SM6 0BD

Tel: 020 8647 4607
email: schooloffice@collingwoodschool.org.uk
website: www.collingwoodschool.org.uk
Twitter: @Collingwood_Sch
Facebook: @Collingwood-School

Headmaster: **Mr Leigh Hardie**

Age Range. 2–11 Co-educational.

Number in School. Day: 100.

Fees per term (2021–2022). £2,995 (Reception)–£3,170 (reduction for siblings).

Collingwood was founded in 1928

It is a school that has deliberately remained small in order to foster a very friendly and caring environment.

Our aim is to give children a first-class academic and sporting education while at the same time instilling the virtues of courtesy, respect and consideration for others. These traditional values, coupled with a modern, relevant education, make Collingwood the happy, purposeful and unique place that it is.

We offer an exciting range of subjects including ICT, DT, Music, French and Spanish. Currently we have over twelve extracurricular activities taking place each week including, drama, football, judo, gymnastics, robotics, construction, debating and Mandarin. Children are also able to learn to play a musical instrument such as piano, keyboard, drums, violin, cello, guitar or recorder. We also offer a breakfast and after-school club.

Although we are a non-selective school, many of our children over the years have gained entry into the local Grammar or Independent Selective Schools.

For a prospectus or to arrange a visit, call Mrs Goff, Head of Admissions, on 020 8647 4607.

Copthill School

Barnack Road, Uffington, Stamford, Lincolnshire PE9 3AD

Tel: 01780 757506
email: mail@copthill.com
website: www.copthill.com
Twitter: @copthill
Facebook: @copthill
Instagram: @copthillschool

Principal: **Mr J A Teesdale**, BA Hons, PGCE

Headteacher: Mrs Helen Schofield, BA Hons, PGCE

Lower School Leader, Pastoral: Mrs Anne Teesdale, BEd Hons

Lower School Leader, Academic: Mrs Judy Dimbleby

Age Range. Co-educational 2–11 years.

Number of Pupils. 300 total: Main School (age 4+ to 11) 240 and Nursery/Pre-School (age 2 to 4) 60.

Fees per term (2021–2022). £3,255–£3,655

Educational Aims.

- Put the child at the heart of their education, making the education fit the child rather than trying to make the child fit into a one-size-fits-all system.
- Care for our children as individuals within a supportive family community, learning and growing together; happy pupils learn.
- Have the highest expectations of our children across all areas of their education and development, with flexibility in our approach.
- Challenge and support our children to be confident in recognising their own and each other's strengths and talents across the broad Copthill curriculum.
- Acknowledge that learning can be difficult and aim to reassure our children that making mistakes is part of the process of learning.
- Work to instil in our children the curiosity, excitement, desire and drive to be lifelong learners, seizing every opportunity to pursue their dreams and to write their own success stories at each stage of their journey.
- Grow pupils as Copthill Learners (responsible citizens, independent explorers, team players, problem solvers, creative thinkers and reflective learners), respecting each other, our environment and ourselves and preparing for the next stage in life, whatever that might be.

Location. Purpose-built, modern facilities set within 350 acres of farmland, including river and woodland. 2 miles from Stamford and the A1 and 15 miles from Peterborough.

School Day. Monday to Friday from 8.35am to 4.40pm. After and before school care from 7.45am to 6.00pm. Breakfast and Tea available.

Facilities. Creative Suite, Music Suite, Library, Languages Suite, Sports Hall and playing fields including AstroTurf and a well-established on-site Forest School. High-quality catering facilities offering delicious, nutritionally balanced meals.

Pastoral Care. In addition to their forms, pupils from Year 5 upwards are also placed in small tutor groups in which their progress is closely monitored in preparation for senior school entrance. There is a genuine 'open door policy' throughout the School. Parents' Evenings are hosted twice a year and written reports are distributed at least 3 times a year.

Curriculum. A modern curriculum based on the National Curriculum. Combines traditional and innovative teaching methods. Learning support offered throughout the school where a specific need has been assessed.

Music, Speech & Drama. Music and Drama are taught as part of the curriculum. Regular drama productions encourage all pupils to participate. Pupils can also receive expert individual tuition and perform at school concerts, assemblies and in local music and drama festivals.

Sport. Rugby, Hockey (boy and girls), Netball, Cross-Country, Athletics, Cricket, Rounders, Swimming, Tennis plus many extracurricular sports including Sailing and Archery.

Future Schools. Pupils leave Copthill at 11 years old with great confidence and the ability to think for themselves.

Copthill is a truly independent school, offering thorough preparation to a wide variety of independent and state senior schools, both local and national, achieving a large number of scholarships and awards.

Cranford House

Moulsford, Wallingford, Oxfordshire OX10 9HT

Tel:	01491 651218
email:	admissions@cranfordhouse.net
website:	www.cranfordhouse.net
Twitter:	@CHSMoulsford
Facebook:	@CranfordHouse

Chair of Governors: Mr Stuart Wallis

Head: **Dr James Raymond**, PhD, BA Hons, PGCE, NPQH

Deputy Head (Academic & SENCo): Mr C Ellis, MA, MEd, BA Hons, PGCE

Deputy Head (Staff Development): Mrs M Carter, BA, PGCE

Deputy Head (Junior School): Mrs A Stewart, BA Hons, PGCE

Director Finance & Operations: Mrs E Taylor, MA

Assistant Head: Mr K McIntyre, BSc Hons QTS

Head of Pastoral Care (Senior): Mrs K Heard, BA Hons, PGCE

Director of Music: Mrs J Powell, BA Hons, Dip Adv Studies RAM

Director of Communications: Mr B Monet, BFA

Fees per term (2021–2022). £3,650–£6,175.

Cranford House is a leading co-educational independent day school for boys and girls aged 3–18 years. It has an excellent reputation for providing its 500 pupils with a balanced, all-round education within a warmly nurturing environment. Set in over 14 acres of rural South Oxfordshire, the small class sizes, close community and committed staff ensure each pupil is ably supported and challenged to achieve their full potential. The school was rated as 'Excellent' in all categories in its ISI Inspection of November 2014. The Early Years Foundation Stage was rated as 'Outstanding'. In September 2020, the school opened a new co-ed Sixth Form, with more than 20 A Level option choices and an extensive co-curricular programme.

At Cranford House, the aim is to encourage pupils to achieve their full potential, becoming motivated, confident and happy individuals, recognising the importance of respect and support for others, but ready to seize life's opportunities.

The Early Years Foundation Stage (EYFS) encompasses Nursery and Reception, catering for boys and girls aged 3–5 years. Pupils benefit from a large, Nursery School in a beautiful setting with plenty of green space for free-flow activities and outdoor learning. There are many links to the main school site for integration with Reception, swimming lessons and whole-school productions and activities.

The Junior School comprises Years 1 to 6. Juniors benefit from Senior School facilities and specialist subject teachers are used in a variety of disciplines. The school's all-inclusive approach sees all pupils taking part in competitive sports matches from Year 3 upwards. Lesson content is based on the National Curriculum, but supplemented to ensure pupils develop their own collaborative, reflective and reasoning skills and abilities. Results are excellent. Responsibility is offered at a young age through posts such as Junior Head Girl/Boy and team captains.

In the Senior School, pupils follow a common core curriculum, as well as an extensive range of extra-curricular opportunities. Academic ambition for each pupil is high and every child is supported in achieving to the very best of their ability. With 76.9% of all grades 9–7 (A*–A) the 2021 GCSE results demonstrate consistent academic excellence for which the school is renowned.

Pupils benefit from an excellent pastoral offering, key to which is a vibrant House system which encourages both a sense of community and leadership. On reaching Year 11, pupils enjoy further positions of responsibility. The school has extensive recreational and games fields. In winter, hockey, football and netball are played, and in summer, tennis, rounders, cricket and athletics. Swimming takes place on site. Dramatic, musical and dance productions are an important aspect of school life and all are encouraged to take part.

In addition to the extensive range of enrichment activities offered throughout the school, all pupils have the opportunity to join educational trips and excursions. For Senior pupils, Bronze and Silver levels of The Duke of Edinburgh's Award scheme are offered, in addition to far-flung expeditions with World Challenge. Opportunities for overseas travel are also offered through exchanges, ski and sports trips and choir tours. School transport operates over a wide area throughout both Berkshire and Oxfordshire.

Scholarships, bursaries and awards are offered for Year 7 and Year 12 entry points.

Charitable status. Cranford House School Trust Limited is a Registered Charity, number 280883.

Cransley School

Belmont Hall, Great Budworth, Nr Northwich, Cheshire CW9 6HN

Tel:	01606 891747
email:	admin@cransleyschool.org.uk
website:	www.cransleyschool.com
Twitter:	@CransleySchool
Facebook:	@CransleySchool

Headmaster: **Mr Richard Pollock**

Deputy Head: Mrs Clare Lancaster

Deputy Head and Head of Juniors: Mr Rob Morris

Assistant Head: Mrs Jill Cosgrove

Assistant Head: Mrs Jill Pargeter

Operations Manager: Mrs Clare Holt

Director of Finance: Mrs Suzanne Parrott

Age Range. Co-educational 4–16.

Number in School. 230; 115 girls and 115 boys.

Fees per term (2021–2022). £2,370–£4,022.

Set in the midst of beautiful Cheshire countryside, Cransley School really is a very special place to be educated. At Cransley we offer all our children the individual support that allows them to grow in confidence and to discover what makes them unique. Our pupils are given the attention and nurturing they need to excel academically and to reach their full potential. A Cransley education is more than just the excellent academic achievements we produce; we offer our pupils a wide range of extracurricular activities and encourage them to challenge themselves to learn outside of the classroom as well as within. Once again we were thrilled with the GCSE results this year as one of the top performing schools in Cheshire, enabling us to create firm foundations for bright and successful futures for all of our pupils.

Life is never dull at Cransley. There is a wide variety of extracurricular activities available throughout the School – sports, Performing Arts, and LAMDA groups, Duke of Edinburgh's Award expeditions and regular drama performances. Students have a choice of clubs – gymnastics, gardening, languages, rowing, fencing, cricket, football and rugby to name but a few. There are many sporting opportunities and Cransley teams regularly compete against other schools in the area.

Cransley students enjoy many visits to enrich the curriculum. We offer residential opportunities – groups have stayed overnight in London for theatre and museum visits; GCSE Geography students visit Llandudno and the Lake District; activity weekends are particular favourites for both Senior and Junior Department pupils; foreign travel is also on the menu, and has included skiing trips to Italy and musical performances in Barcelona and Lake Garda, with the most recent Geography trip to Iceland.

Cransley also has a thriving parent body who regularly organise events throughout the year which raise valuable funds to support staff and students and also offer a fantastic opportunity for parents to get to know each other.

Cundall Manor School

Cundall, North Yorkshire YO61 2RW

Tel:	01423 360200
email:	head@cundallmanor.org.uk
website:	www.cundallmanorschool.com
Twitter:	@CundallManor
Facebook:	@Cundall-Manor-School
Instagram:	@cundallmanor
LinkedIn:	/cundall-manor-school

Headmistress: **Mrs Amanda Kirby**, BA Hons, PGCE, NPQH

Age Range. 2–16 Co-educational.

Number of Pupils. 360.

Cundall Manor School is a thriving independent co-educational boarding school, catering for nearly 400 boys and girls from two to sixteen years of age. Set in 28 acres of

beautiful grounds between Harrogate, Ripon and York, it is easily accessed from the A1(M) and A19.

Cundall Manor School blends the best traditions of honour, integrity and courtesy with up-to-the-minute teaching facilities and approaches. The school has developed a reputation for ensuring that each and every child feels happy, safe, supported and celebrated. Within this environment, children engage fully with the educational challenges and risks that maximise learning and achievement. The rural setting allows pupils to embrace their childhoods while the innovative and unique curriculum provides opportunity for all to develop the confidence, judgement and personal skills that will benefit their futures.

Children are encouraged to participate in a number of sports and events outside of the curriculum including outward bound courses, travel, charity/community work and extracurricular sports. Whilst many children do achieve top standards and awards across academia, sports and music, competing and succeeding at area, county and national level, our aim is to ensure every child has the opportunity to participate in the full range of activities, whatever their level of ability and experience. We do this by cultivating a 'yes' mentality amongst our pupils, encouraging them to engage with the wider world and to think and act independently and without inhibition.

Fees per term (2021–2022). Nursery: £430 (1 full day per term); Reception–Year 2: Day £3,460; Years 3 & 4: Day £5,500, Weekly Boarding £7,255; Years 5–11: Day £5,600, Weekly Boarding £7,370.

Charitable status. Cundall Manor Limited is a Registered Charity, number 529540.

Daiglen Preparatory School

68 Palmerston Road, Buckhurst Hill, Essex IG9 5LG

Tel:	020 8504 7108
email:	admin@daiglenschool.co.uk
website:	www.daiglenschool.co.uk
Twitter:	@DaiglenSchool

Perstare et Praestare – Persevere and Excel

Head Teacher: **Mrs P Dear**, BEd

Age Range. 3–11.

Number in School. 150.

Fees per term (2021–2022). £3,500–£3,750 sibling discount available. Extras: music tuition, trips.

Daiglen Preparatory School is a small preparatory school which provides a happy and secure environment for all pupils. Kindness to others is valued above all, and pupils are polite and considerate with each other as well as with adults. We have a strong sense of family and community, underpinned by warm supportive relationships and mutual respect, which ensures that all pupils are valued and given the chance to shine.

Confident children relish challenge and the school promotes a culture of excellence. We celebrate individual and group successes as children learn the importance of pursuing their ambitions with determination and perseverance. They are inspired to do well both by the infectious enthusiasm of their excellent teachers and by the example of older children who become their role models. Our pupils flourish in this environment and leave as caring, confident, articulate and well-mannered young people, fully prepared for the next stage in their journey through life. We are justifiably proud of our pupils' academic achievements, as well as those on the sports field and other areas, and a good proportion leave with scholarships to selective independent and state secondary schools.

Founded in 1916, Daiglen Preparatory School is rich in history and tradition. The school is built around an elegant Victorian house with much of its stained glass and cornices intact. Modern features include a purpose-built gymnasium/hall and art room. It is pleasantly situated on the borders of Epping Forest and is well served by public transport.

Inspection: Daiglen School was inspected in September 2018. The full report is available to read on our website.

Choosing a school is arguably the most difficult decision you will make for your child, and one which will have the greatest consequences in his or her life. Most of our pupils come to Daiglen on personal recommendation from parents of past or present pupils. We encourage a close and mutually supportive partnership with parents. To find out more about us, you can visit our website or make arrangements to visit the school; you will receive a warm welcome.

Charitable status. The Daiglen School Trust Limited is a Registered Charity, number 273015.

Ditcham Park School

Ditcham Park, Petersfield, Hampshire GU31 5RN

Tel:	01730 825659
email:	admissions@ditchampark.com
website:	www.ditchampark.com
Twitter:	@DitchamJuniors
	@DitchamSeniors
Facebook:	@DitchamParkSchool

Headmaster: **Mr G D Spawforth**, MA, MEd

Age Range. 2½–16.
Number in School. Day: 220 Boys, 166 Girls.
Fees per term (from January 2022) £3,004.50 (Reception)–£5,037.50 (Senior 5), excluding lunch.

Situated high on the South Downs, the School achieves excellent results in a happy, purposeful atmosphere.

Charitable status. Ditcham Park School is a Registered Charity, number 285244R. It exists for educational purposes.

The Dixie Grammar School

Market Bosworth, Leicestershire CV13 0LE

Tel:	01455 292244
email:	info@dixie.org.uk
website:	www.dixie.org.uk
Twitter:	@DixieGrammar
Facebook:	@the.dixie.grammar
Instagram:	@dixie_grammar

Headmaster: **Mr Richard J Lynn**, BA Cardiff

Age Range. 3–18.
Number in School. 475.
Fees per term (2021–2022). Nursery: Daily Rate (inc lunch) £55; Reception, Years 1 and 2 £3,210, Years 3 to 5 £3,645, Year 6 to Sixth Form £4,365. Scholarships, Bursaries, Vouchers/Government Funding, Monthly Payment Scheme available.

The earliest records we have of the School's existence date from 1320, but the School gained its present name when it was re-founded in 1601 under the will of an Elizabethan merchant and Lord Mayor of London, Sir Wolstan Dixie.

The most distinguished of the School's former pupils is Thomas Hooker, founder of Hartford, Connecticut, and Father of American Democracy. The best known of its teachers is undoubtedly Dr Johnson, moralist, poet and author of the famous dictionary, who taught at the School in the mid-eighteenth century.

The main building of today's School was built in 1828 and faces the historic market square of Market Bosworth, making a distinctive landmark. However, in 1969 the School was closed, as new, much larger comprehensive schools found favour.

It was to revive the best aspects of the grammar school tradition that the Leicestershire Independent Educational Trust was formed in 1983, and four years later the School was reopened as a selective, independent, day school for boys and girls of all backgrounds between the ages of 10 and 18. Three years later our Junior School opened, moving to its present premises, Temple Hall in Wellsborough, in 2001, where we have The Pippins Nursery.

The emphasis remains the same as it ever was: to provide an excellent academic education that will be of lasting value to our children as they face the challenges of the future.

Both schools are selective and have academic achievement as their central aim. Music, drama, sport and service are also an integral part of the education offered. Both schools have an interdenominational Christian basis. The relative smallness of the schools ensures that they combine great friendliness with excellent discipline, providing a secure and well-ordered framework in which children can confidently achieve their full potential. We are ambitious for each of them.

The Grammar School offers academic, music, art, sports and sixth form scholarships.

Charitable status. The Leicestershire Independent Educational Trust is a Registered Charity, number 514407.

DLD College London
Alpha Plus Group

199 Westminster Bridge Road, London SE1 7FX

Tel: 020 7935 8411
email: dld@dld.org
website: www.dldcollege.co.uk
Twitter: @DLDcollege
Facebook: @DLDcollege
Instagram: @dldcollege
LinkedIn: /company/dldcollegelondon

Principal: **Mr Irfan Latif**, BSc Hons, PGCE, FRSA, FRSC

Age Range. 14+ Co-educational.
Number of Pupils. 350 Day and Boarding.
Fees per annum (2021–2022). £24,670.

Part of the Alpha Plus Group, DLD College London was established in 1931. After 10 years located in Marylebone, the college merged with its younger sister, Abbey College, and moved in 2015 to brand new, purpose-built facilities in the heart of London, looking over the River Thames to the Houses of Parliament. With bright, state-of-the-art teaching facilities and secure, on-site student accommodation, all in the centre of the amazing, historic and vibrant city of London, DLD College London is a truly unique college campus, with outstanding facilities including:

- 180 secure, ensuite student bedrooms within the College
- A dedicated wellbeing centre
- Restaurant facilities on site, including a Grumpy Mule Coffee franchise
- 6 high specification laboratories
- A creative arts and media faculty featuring art rooms, photography, drama, music and media suites, including a 100+ seat theatre
- Over 40 teaching rooms
- Learning hub, digital hub, study and ICT facilities
- Garden space and third floor roof garden
- Fully air-conditioned classrooms
- Access to shared swimming pool and gymnasium facilities

DLD College London is a co-educational London day and boarding school accepting pupils from the ages of 14+. There are over 300 students in the Sixth Form, most studying A Levels from a choice of over 20 subjects with no restrictions, and some studying BTEC programmes in Business and Creative Digital Media Production. A cohort join at the start of Upper Sixth to study a one year International Foundation Programme. GCSE courses are taught over either a two or one year period so pupils are able to join at the beginning of Year 11. The average class size is between 8 and 12 students.

An extensive range of co-curricular activities are offered including the prestigious Duke of Edinburgh's Award, as well as many traditional options such as Sport, Music, Drama and Art. Our wide enrichment programme supports our academic curriculum and forms an integral part of the wider education and college experience we offer our students. Our vision is to create all-rounded students, who excel academically and develop further their emotional, inter-personal and social skills. All students are encouraged to participate in one or more of our range of extra-curricular activities. This participation is important for students both as an opportunity for recreation and as an effective way to improve the quality of their UCAS personal statement and CV in the future.

While the atmosphere at the college is more informal than in mainstream independent schools, rules regarding academic performance are strictly enforced with an emphasis on attendance and punctuality. There are fortnightly tests in each subject and half-termly reports. Parents receive five reports each year and there are two parents' evenings and a parents' social evening.

The teaching staff are highly qualified and chosen not just for their expertise but also for their ability to relate positively to young people. The college aims to make learning interesting, active and rigorous. While clear guidelines are very important to ensure pupils establish a good working routine, the college believes strongly that students respond best when there is a culture of encouragement. Effort, progress, achievement and courtesy are regularly acknowledged and formally rewarded.

Duke of Kent School

Peaslake Road, Ewhurst, Surrey GU6 7NS

Tel: 01483 277313
email: office@dokschool.org
website: www.dukeofkentschool.org.uk
Twitter: @DoKSchool

Chairman of the Governing Body: Mr Richard Brocksom

Head: **Mrs Sue Knox**, BA Hons UCNW, MBA Cranfield, Grad DipEd & MEdLead Macquarie University Sydney

Age Range. 3–16.
Number of Pupils. 312.

Set in inspirational grounds high in the Surrey Hills, surrounded by forest land, Duke of Kent School provides an excellent co-educational option for pupils from 3 to 16 years. Coming from Guildford, Horsham, Dorking and surrounding local villages, many pupils use the School minibus service.

Extended day arrangements for those pupils who wish to arrive before or stay beyond the end of lessons (7.30 am to 7.30 pm) provide families with exceptional flexibility. At the end of the School day, pupils can choose to complete their Prep at school under supervision or at home, and can also choose from a varied programme of sport, academic and social activities.

The small size of the School enables us to know our pupils very well and to ensure that all pupils can reach their potential. All pupils receive the appropriate combination of academic challenge and support to enable them to achieve. A Duke of Kent School pupil is expected to contribute and participate to the very best of his or her ability, take an active role in community life and take responsibility for his or her learning. Our able and committed teaching and support staff work in partnership with pupils and their families. The expectation is that each pupil will strive to achieve a string of 'personal bests': in the classroom, on the sports field, in personal development, in exploring the arts and in a wide range of activities. We focus on each child's attitude to learning in order to ensure that they are fully equipped to make maximum progress. Teaching and learning is supported by a well established 1–1 iPad programme in the Prep School and all Senior School pupils use Chromebooks and are supported by our dedicated fibre optic line.

Pupils are prepared for GCSE/IGCSE examinations in the context of a curriculum which aims to take pupils above and beyond exam preparation. There is a focus throughout the School of encouraging pupils to adopt a growth mindset in order to become successful learners. Building on the work of our Prep School in which Creative Curriculum provides excellent stretch and challenge for pupils, our rigorous GCSE programme prepares pupils for A Level and university study and sparks what may be lifelong intellectual passions. Learning beyond the classroom, whether on educational visits or through outdoor learning on site, is a crucial aspect of our pupils' experience. Personal development receives close attention. Our pupils develop confidence and self-esteem from opportunities to lead and to serve. Kindness is expected and encouraged from pupils of all ages.

The School maintains a busy fixtures calendar at all ages. We have extensive playing fields, an all-weather turf pitch, all-weather tennis courts, a swimming pool and a full-sized sports hall. More than half of our pupils are learning a musical instrument. Music and Drama activities take place in a purpose-built Performing Arts Hall with facilities for Music Technology. The quality of Art on display and in production is a particular strength of the School.

In 2021 our Year 11 cohort achieved an overall pass rate of 99.7% with a commendable 85% of our pupils gaining a grade 7 or above. In recent years our pupils have gone on to successful courses of further study at day schools, boarding schools and colleges, both locally and further afield.

Prospective pupils are invited to attend a visit day during which they will be interviewed by the Head or another senior member of staff, and will take a range of cognitive tests (CAT4). No preparation is required for our admissions testing. We are looking for evidence of enthusiasm and willingness to get fully involved in our lively community.

Fees per term (2021–2022). £2,485–£6,540.

Charitable status. The Duke of Kent School is a Registered Charity, number 1064183.

Dwight School London

6 Friern Barnet Lane, London N11 3LX

Tel: 020 8920 0600
email: admissions@dwightlondon.org
website: www.dwightlondon.org
Twitter: @DwightSchoolUK
Facebook: @Dwight-School-London
Instagram: @Dwight-School-London
LinkedIn: /dwight-school-london

Head of School: **Mrs Alison Cobbin**, BA, Dip Ed, MBA

Lower School Principal: Matt Parkin

Upper School Principal: Chris Beddows

Age Range. 2–18.

Number in School. 284 Boys and Girls.

Fees per term (2021–2022). Nursery fees can be viewed on our website. Reception, Year 1 and Year 2 £6,009, Year 3 to Year 6 £6,290, M1–M5 (ages 11–15) £6,970, D1–D2 (Ages 16–18) £8,500

Dwight School London is part of a network of international schools in New York, Seoul, Shanghai, and Dubai, as well as Dwight Global Online School. Each Dwight School shares the same commitment to igniting the spark of genius in every child. No matter where in the world students attend Dwight, they are inspired to find their passions and receive the same high-quality IB education.

Being part of a global network affords students numerous benefits and countless opportunities. Travel and exchange programs, cross-campus curricular and creative collaborations, online learning programs, international athletic competitions, and global leadership conferences all foster the development of global citizens.

We are truly international with more than 50 nationalities represented at Dwight!

Our learners are proud to come from diverse backgrounds; they celebrate and learn from each others' perspectives, and they take pride in taking action to make a better world.

Our open-minded approach that values diversity and innovation is underpinned by the academically rigorous International Baccalaureate programmes that open pathways to the top universities across the globe. Our students are critical and creative thinkers, empowered by inquiry-led learning and an expectation that they will be independent learners who create meaning from their experiences.

IB Programmes

We offer the following programmes:

The Primary Years Programme (IBPYP) – ages 2 to 11
The Middle Years Programme (IBMYP) – ages 11 to 16
The Diploma Programme (IBDP) – ages 16 to 18

To learn about the benefits of the IB Curriculum visit www.dwightlondon.org/theib

Mission and Pillars

Through the academic breadth and depth of the International Baccalaureate programmes, Dwight London nurtures confident, compassionate young people who influence the future.

Our students thrive in a curriculum rooted in our three educational pillars:

Personalised learning: an education just for the student

Dwight School London prides itself on really getting to know each of our students and their families. We shape students' education around them: how they best learn, where their skills lie, what sparks their interest, and where we can best help them.

Community: earn your place in the wider world

Our students are best placed to make a positive difference: to their school, to their neighbours and the world beyond. For this, they need more than academic learning. We develop the aptitudes our students will need, through local and global projects, as well as joint ventures with the world-wide family of Dwight schools.

Global vision: for the future global citizen

With students representing the UK and more than 50 other nations, Dwight London is a culturally and socially rich and diverse school. We are committed to developing confident, compassionate, intellectually mature young people who will be a force for good across the world.

Our vision is to produce students who are inquiring, knowledgeable and caring, while fostering their academic growth. Dwight School London prepares students to move on to further education, to be active, and be desirable citizens and learners gaining places at top universities around the world.

Egerton Rothesay School

Durrants Lane, Berkhamsted, Herts HP4 3UJ

Tel: 01442 865275
email: admin.dl@eger-roth.co.uk
website: www.eger-roth.co.uk

A School with a Difference

Headteacher: **Mr Colin Parker**, BSc Hons, Dip Ed, PGCE, CMath

Age Range. 6–19 years: Poplar 6–11 years; Senior School 11–16 years; Sixth Form 16–19 years.

Number in School. 128 boys, 40 girls.

Fees per term (2021–2022). £5,720–£8,140 (lunches included).

ERS aims to provide an exciting and relevant educational experience for pupils who need that little bit more support from their school, whilst studying a mainstream curriculum.

It focuses especially on students who have found, or would find, it difficult to make progress and succeed within another school – perhaps because of an earlier, negative, educational experience or perhaps because of a specific learning difficulty, such as dyslexia or dyspraxia, a speech and language difficulty or an autistic spectrum condition. If your child has other educational difficulties the school may also be able to help with these.

Children come with a variety of learning styles and use is made of a wide range of teaching strategies in order to match these. The school provides additional levels of support both in the classroom and on an individual basis, varying to suit the need of the child. Throughout the school children are taught in small classes to match their need for support, to the level of teaching and support staff provided. The team of therapists includes Speech and Language, Occupational Therapy, Social Emotional Development and visiting physiotherapists. Our specialist teaching team provide individual lessons in literacy and numeracy.

The Sixth Form provides for students who continue to mature beyond the age of 16 and require an additional amount of support and time in order to enable them to transfer successfully into a further education establishment or employment. The school has developed both one and two year educational programmes within a high-quality, secure

and supportive environment, in which students are able to continue to mature, develop and learn whilst studying for additional examinations including GCSE, BTEC, Foundation and ASDAN awards. Examination results enable pupils to enter colleges and sixth forms in both state and independent schools to continue their education before university entrance, if appropriate.

Every child at Egerton Rothesay is seen as a unique person and an individual student. The school aims to make an excellent contribution into the life of each one ensuring that they can be supported in the way that they personally need to maximise their individual learning potential.

The school wants more than just to deliver a curriculum and has a learning skills approach throughout the school – aiming to prepare students not just for school and exams but for life in today's complex society and an ever changing world of work.

A child can often be able and talented in one aspect of the curriculum, yet find it difficult to make good progress in another. Some students will need support for the duration of their time in school, whilst others may only need a short amount of support to address a specific problem or to build confidence.

All activities takes place within an environment offering exceptional pastoral care and spiritual development that is driven and informed by the school's Christian foundation and its Chaplaincy team.

Transport: Egerton Rothesay is also more than just a local school – students travel to the school from all directions, many using the comprehensive bus service that the school runs over a 35-mile radius.

If you think this may be the right type of school for your child you can obtain more information from the Registrar on 01442 877060 or visit the website at www.eger-roth.co.uk.

Fairfield School

Fairfield Way, Backwell, Bristol BS48 3PD

Tel: 01275 462743
email: bursar@fairfieldschool.org.uk
website: fairfield.school
Twitter: @fairfieldpneu
Facebook: @fairfieldschoolbackwell
Instagram: @fairfieldpneu

Headteacher: **Mrs Lesley Barton**, BA Hons, PGCE

Age Range. 2–11.

Number in School. 64 Boys, 50 Girls.

Fees per term (2021–2022). Lambs Nursery from £58 per day, Upper Nursery from £39 per day; Reception, Years 1–2 £2,889; Years 3–6 £3,188.

Fairfield is an independent day school for boys and girls aged 2–11. The school was founded in 1935 and aims to provide a broad, traditional education. We encourage each child to maximise his or her potential through creating a family ethos in which children feel happy, secure and valued. A fundamental aspect of our ethos is our commitment to small classes, usually of 18–20. Fairfield offers a broad and balanced curriculum, informed by the

National Curriculum. Teachers and visiting coaches provide a wide range of extracurricular lessons including music, dance, sport, drama and creative activities. Pupils are prepared for entry into all local independent senior schools as well as for the local maintained sector schools.

For further details please apply to the Facilities Bursar.

Charitable status. Fairfield PNEU School (Backwell) Limited is a Registered Charity, number 310215.

Fairley House School

Junior Department:
218–220 Lambeth Road, London SE1 7JY

Tel: 020 7976 5456
email: junior@fairleyhouse.org.uk

Senior Department:
30 Causton Street, London SW1P 4AU

Tel: 020 7976 5456
email: senior@fairleyhouse.org.uk

website: www.fairleyhouse.org.uk

Headmaster: **Michael Taylor**, BA Hons, PGCE, FRGS

Age Range. 6–16.
Number of Pupils. 180 (117 Boys, 63 Girls).
Fees per term (2021–2022). £11,368

Fairley House School is a school for children with Specific Learning Difficulties, Dyslexia and Dyspraxia. The aim of the school is to provide intensive support to help children to overcome difficulties, coupled with a full, rich curriculum designed to bring out children's strengths and talents. Most children return to mainstream schooling after two to three years. Children's learning styles have often not been catered for in their previous school, leading to failure and loss of confidence, but Fairley House offers them a 'level playing field' where everyone has similar difficulties. Children receive a stimulating educational experience integrated with therapy and specialist teaching. Teaching is multi-sensory and children learn Science, Spelling, Geography and History through interesting, hands-on activities. There is a staff to pupil ratio of 1:3.5. This integration is one of the many things that sets us apart as a specialist day school for children with Specific Learning Difficulties.

We emphasise the development of the whole child, helping him or her to gain confidence and self-esteem through an encouraging and nurturing ethos. The children have plenty of opportunities to develop sound academic and social skills and to become independent. At Fairley House, everyone succeeds.

Falkner House

Girls' School:
19 Brechin Place, London SW7 4QB

Tel: 020 7373 4501
email: office@falknerhouse.co.uk

Boys' School:
20 Penywern Road, London SW5 9SU

Tel: 020 7373 2340
email: office20pr@falknerhouse.co.uk

website: www.falknerhouse.co.uk

Principal: **Mrs Anita Griggs**, BA Hons, PGCE

Headmistress, Girls' School: Mrs Flavia Rogers, BA Hons, PGCE

Headmistress, Boys' School: Mrs Eleanor Dixon, MA Cantab

Age Range. Girls 4–11, Boys 4–11, Co-educational Nursery (ages 3–4).
Number of Pupils. Girls: 188. Boys: 138.
Fees per term (2021–2022) Girls' School: £6,970; Boys' School: £7,155; Nursery: £3,485.

Girls' School. Falkner House is unashamedly academically ambitious and pupils achieve notable success at 11+ to the very top day and boarding schools. This is all within a naturally self-policing, civilised atmosphere where the development of self-confidence and happiness are seen as key goals. There is a busy yet friendly environment and as a result pupils have an engaging openness, intellectual curiosity and courtesy beyond their years. "We like them to have ability and oomph" says Mrs Rogers "but not to be sassy or precocious."

Excellent facilities include a science laboratory, art room, library and playground. State-of-the-art IT facilities now include individual iPads integrated into the curriculum. A strong musical tradition lies alongside an excellent sporting record. Pre/post school care is offered, as well as a wide range of after-school activities.

Entrance at 4+ by assessment.

Boys' School. The Boys' School started on a separate site nearby in September 2017, with the same ethos and values as the Girls' School.

Falkner House Boys provides an outstanding academic education in a family atmosphere. They offer a unique environment in which children can flourish and are given the opportunity and confidence to excel. Londoners through and through, they embrace the best of British values in the most dynamic and diverse of cities.

One of the most important spaces at Falkner House is the playground – a hardworking space that the school is particularly proud of given its central London location. It helps the boys learn, both directly and indirectly.

Falkner House embraces academic success at any stage of a boy's time at school, whether at 7, 8 or 11+. If they believe that a boy is ready for the 7 or 8+ exam process, and after discussions with the family, they will have a completely tailor-made programme for them to prepare, for success without strain. The years children spend at school are few and precious. The process of teaching and learning is at the heart of the school, and the very reason for its existence. The best teaching, the teaching that Falkner House offers, sets boys off on a lifelong path of satisfying, pleasurable and empowering learning.

Entrance is at 4+ by assessment.

Falkner House Nursery caters for boys and girls aged 3–4 years. Children thrive in a stimulating atmosphere under the care of professional and thoughtful teachers. Children are encouraged to be curious, to experiment and to learn through play. Specialist staff teach subjects such as music and PE to enrich the nursery curriculum.

Entrance at rising 3 is by date of registration.

Faraday Prep School

Old Gate House, 7 Trinity Buoy Wharf, London E14 0FH

Tel: 020 7719 9342
 020 8965 7374 (Admissions)
email: admissions@faradayschool.co.uk
 head@faradayschool.co.uk
website: www.faradayschool.co.uk

Head Teacher: **Lucas Motion**

Age Range. 4–11 Co-educational.
Number of Pupils. 111
Fees per term (2021–2022). £3,981.

Founded in 2009, Faraday Prep School offers inspirational learning in an inspirational setting. A happy, vibrant and diverse independent primary school in East London, the school's historic and artistic riverside location, provides a magical environment and access to a stimulating, creative community that offers exciting learning opportunities.

We give every child a first-class education rooted in a creative curriculum, with small classes, quality teaching and a personal approach in a caring and kind environment.

In these formative years our aim is to inspire a love of learning and that the desire to explore, grow and create will stay with our pupils for life. We place a strong focus on literacy and numeracy, with a targeted approach that enables each child to progress at their own level.

Our lessons stretch, challenge and engage pupils of all abilities and interests. We present children with the great literature, music and works of art to help them acquire an increased understanding of the world in which they live and build a thorough understanding of knowledge in each subject. As such, our curriculum is broad and stimulating, and includes specialist teaching in French, Music, Drama and Physical Education.

Children join our Reception class in their fifth year and leave for senior school at the age of eleven. The school day runs from 8.45am until 3.30pm, with our private buses running before and after school from a range of East London locations. We support busy parents by welcoming children from 8.15am and by offering after-school care until 5.30pm each day, with a wide range of extra-curricular activities on offer from gardening to robotics.

Entry into Reception is non-selective and based on the date the completed registration form is returned to our Registrar, with siblings given priority. Entry higher up the school is by interview and informal assessment in the classroom. We offer regular open days and welcome private tours.

Forest Park Preparatory School
Bellevue Education

Lauriston House, 27 Oakfield, Sale, Cheshire M33 6NB

Tel: 0161 973 4835
email: post@forestparkprep.co.uk
website: www.forestparkprep.co.uk
Twitter: @ForestParkPrep
Facebook: @forestpark
Instagram: @forestparkprepschool

Headteacher: **Mr Nick Tucker**, BEd Hons Prim Ed, MA Ed Leadership & Mgt

Age Range. 3–11.
Number in School. 85 Day Boys, 72 Day Girls.
Fees per term (2021–2022). £2,366–£2,580.

Forest Park occupies a pleasant site in a quiet road surprisingly close to the centre of Sale, easily accessible from motorways and surrounding areas.

The school aims to discover and develop each child's particular abilities by offering a varied curriculum in a stimulating and happy atmosphere. Forest Park has a good pupil to teacher ratio and offers a wide range of subjects with priority given to the traditional disciplines of English, mathematics and science. Pupils from three years of age are taught information technology by specialist staff. Swimming is taught from the age of five and games offered are football, cricket, netball, tennis and hockey. Pupils are taught Spanish from Pre-Prep. Older children have the opportunity to enjoy residential and activity trips to broaden their knowledge and develop self-confidence.

The confidence and social ease one expects of a private education is a product of the school. Our aim is to develop skills and knowledge through a habit of hard work in a secure and happy environment within a disciplined framework. The school prepares pupils for all independent grammar school examinations and has an excellent record in this respect.

The school prides itself on strong links and communication with a most supportive Parents' Association.

Gad's Hill School

Higham, Rochester, Kent ME3 7PA

Tel: 01474 822366
email: information@gadshillschool.org
website: www.gadshill.org
Twitter: @GadsHillSchool
Facebook: @GadsHillSchoolOfficial

Headmaster: **Mr Paul Savage**, BA Hons, PGCE

Age Range. Co-educational 3–16.

Number in School. 329.

Fees per term (2021–2022). £2,559–£4,748.

Entry requirements. Interview and assessment.

Aim. To provide a good all-round education, to build confidence, establish friendships, to reward success (however small) and to ensure our students leave as mature, self-reliant young people who depart Gad's for the career or University placement of their choice.

Kindergarten (3–6 years). From the very early years in Kindergarten the children are encouraged to learn through play, music and drama. Basic letter and number work is introduced within the nursery and reception class as the children concentrate on the Early Learning Goals. In Year 1 and Year 2 they largely follow Key Stage One of the National Curriculum although in addition; from Reception upwards, all of our children are taught French and also Information and Communications Technology.

Junior School (7–11 years). Our Junior School curriculum seeks to build upon the children's undaunted love of adventure. Literacy, Numeracy and Humanities continue to be taught by Form Tutors however, the children begin to benefit from more lessons delivered by specialist tutors particularly in French, Information Technology, Design & Technology, RE, Games and Drama.

Senior School (11–16 years). Senior School concentrates very much on the preparation for GCSE success and our classes are kept to a maximum of 20 children per class. This way the children benefit from smaller class sizes and consequently our tutors get to know each child as an individual and this enables them to provide the right level of support and assistance. This goes a long way to helping them achieve their goals for GCSEs and A Levels.

Location. Gad's Hill School is centred on the former home of Charles Dickens and is surrounded by beautiful grounds, playing fields and countryside. It is a few minutes' drive from the A2 and M2, with good access to the Medway Towns, Dartford and Gravesend.

Curriculum. At Gad's we largely follow the National Curriculum although we place a strong emphasis on "communication" with all of our children benefiting from lessons in French, Information and Communications Technology and Drama as well as English. Senior School children progress to take GCSEs in English, English Literature, Maths, French, Design & Technology, Combined Science (Double Award), Geography and GNVQ ICT (4 GCSEs).

Sports and Activities. We concentrate very much on team games (rugby, hockey, soccer, netball, cricket, athletics and rounders) to ensure that our children learn the values of team work and communication. In the Kindergarten and Junior Schools all students take part in weekly swimming lessons. Because of our small class sizes almost all of our children have the opportunity to represent the school in competitive fixtures against other schools. Gad's Hill also has a thriving Combined Cadet Force. Students join the CCF in Year 8 and take part in weekly training sessions as well as termly field days and an annual camp. The CCF allows children to experience fantastic outdoor pursuits, adventurous training and leadership courses and is essentially about doing something different and challenging. Gad's Hill pupils are also able to take part in a variety of after-school activities. These range from academic pursuits to a variety of other sports and Performing Arts.

Charitable status. Gad's Hill School is a Registered Charity, number 803153. It exists for the purpose of educating children aged 3–16.

Gidea Park Preparatory School and Nursery

2 Balgores Lane, Gidea Park, Romford, Essex RM2 5JR

Tel: 01708 740381
email: office@gideaparkprep.co.uk
website: www.gideaparkprep.co.uk
Facebook: @gideaparkcollege

Headmaster: **Mr Callum Douglas**, BA Hons, PGCE

Age Range. 2–11 Co-educational.

Number in School. 110 Day Pupils.

Fees per term (2021–2022). £3,585.

Gidea Park Preparatory School and Nursery is a very special school. Founded in 1917 we have been educating, nurturing and challenging children for over 100 years. Children are at the heart of everything we do; our small classes and school environment truly allow us to know our pupils as individuals and tailor our teaching and curriculum accordingly. We have high expectations of our pupils' academic progress and personal development and work closely with our parents to ensure that all our pupils get the very most from their time with us.

The school has an enviable academic record and a long tradition of sending pupils to grammar and selective independent schools. But there is a great deal more to Gidea Park Prep than that. We believe that happy children make better progress and to achieve this children need to be understood, listened to and valued.

The School has been part of the Inspired Learning Group since 2020 and has seen significant investment since then. All pupils from Reception to Year 6 have the use of 1:1 iPad devices and a new nursery was opened in January 2022, which now accepts pupils from age 2, and is a 51-week-a-year setting.

Grantham Preparatory International School

An IES School

Gorse Lane, Grantham, Lincolnshire NG31 7UF

Tel: 01476 593293
email: contact.grantham@iesmail.com
website: www.tgps.co.uk
Twitter: @tgps_school
Facebook: @GranthamPrep

Head: Mrs Kathryn Korcz, BSc Hons, CertEd

Age Range. 3–11 Co-educational.
Number of Pupils. 119
Fees per term (2021–2022). £2,755–£3,333.

The Grantham Preparatory International School is a non-denominational independent day school for boys and girls between the ages of three and eleven. The school was established in 1981 and moved to a modern purpose-built building in 1987. It is set in nearly four acres of grounds and playing fields and, being close to the A1, it is easily accessible.

The school is owned by International Education Systems. IES is a network of ten schools (three in South Africa, two in the UK, one in Hungary, one in the United States, one in Panama, one in Slovenia and one in Italy). IES's mission is to provide excellence in education provision within an international perspective. Here at The Grantham Preparatory International School we are committed to excellence in all areas of the curriculum, and we aim to provide the best for all our children in a happy family environment. We are now delighted to be a member of the ISA family after being accredited in November 2011.

Our children are prepared for entrance examinations to Independent senior schools and for Grammar school selection examinations. Children benefit from many specialist teachers who bring their own enthusiasm and knowledge to a particular subject. This ensures high academic standards and our broad and balanced curriculum enables our children to experience sport, art, music and drama and have the opportunity to pursue and develop their strengths, achieving their full potential. Specialist music teachers provide individual tuition in a wide variety of instruments.

The school wind band, choir and recital groups continue to delight audiences with their stunning performances. The school has been awarded the Platinum Award for Sport for four years in succession as well as other awards for Sport.

Learning is fun in our Early Years Foundation Unit. In our care, children thrive and make excellent progress in all areas of learning and development. Our last full ISI inspection report (2014) said that in EYFS there was a rich breadth of planned, purposeful activities, both indoors and outside, that enabled the children to develop and learn extremely effectively.

We believe that every child is an important unique individual that should be valued and nurtured during their time with us. We expect our children to leave us at age 11 as independent, confident individuals, tolerant of others and well prepared for the next stage of their education.

Greenbank Preparatory School and Day Nursery

Heathbank Road, Cheadle Hulme, Cheshire SK8 6HU

Tel: 0161 485 3724
email: office@greenbankschool.co.uk
website: www.greenbankschool.co.uk
Facebook: @Greenbank-Preparatory-School

Headteacher: Mr Malcolm Johnson

Age Range. 6 months–11 years.
Number in School. Day: 72 Boys, 54 Girls. Daycare: 89.
Fees per term (2021–2022). £3,160 including lunches from Reception to Year Six.

Greenbank is an independent co-educational school for pupils aged three to eleven years. A separate Nursery, open fifty weeks of the year, cares for babies and children from six months to four years old.

Greenbank School was founded in 1951 by Karl and Linda Orsborn. Since 1971 the School has been administered by an Educational Trust and is registered with the Department for Education.

Greenbank is situated within extensive grounds, comprises a mixture of traditional and modern buildings including an IT Suite and Library, separate play areas for Foundation, Infant and Junior children, playing fields with a cricket pavilion, an Astroturf area and netball court. 2009 saw the opening of state-of-the-art Science, Art and Music classrooms within a new administration building. Further developments in 2012 included a new Pre-school offering greater flexibility to parents.

The school day begins at 8.40am and ends at 3.30pm, however we provide wrap-around care from 7.30am until 6.00pm. The school also runs activity and sports clubs in the holidays.

Through its varied curricular and extracurricular activities the School provides pupils with the opportunity of expanding their natural abilities to the full. Music, drama, sport, computing and educational visits are some of the activities which play their part in providing a well-rounded programme of education. We strive to meet the social, emotional and intellectual needs of all pupils and the success of this philosophy is proven by the consistently outstanding examination results throughout the school, particularly at age eleven.

Charitable status. Greenbank School Limited is a Registered Charity, number 525930.

Greenfields Independent Day & Boarding School

Priory Road, Forest Row, East Sussex RH18 5JD

Tel: 01342 822189
email: admissions@greenfieldsschool.com
website: www.greenfieldsschool.com

Executive Head: **Mr Jeff Smith**, BSc Eng, AMIMechEng

Age Range. 3–18.

Number in School. Day: 87 Boys, 59 Girls. Boarding: 24 Boys, 9 Girls.

Tuition Fees per term (2021–2022). Day: £1,200–£4,180, Boarding: (Full) £3,860, (5 Nights) £2,980. Fees are reviewed annually.

Greenfields Independent Day and Boarding School is an Independent Schools Association school with a Nursery and a Reception class (forming the Early Years Foundation Stage), an Infant and Junior School, and a Senior School including Sixth Form and long and short-term (6 Month) English as a Foreign Language courses.

Students aged 3 to 18 receive an all-round education for life, using the Cambridge Curriculum from Infants upwards. Greenfields utilises a unique study method which ensures children can apply what they learn for use in life – not just to pass examinations. It has a strong moral code and zero tolerance on bullying, drugs and alcohol. Maximum to a class in Infants and Juniors, 16 and in Seniors, 20.

Situated in beautiful grounds, with its adventure playground backing onto the Ashdown Forest itself, the school is a safe and inspirational place to learn.

The main difference between Greenfields and other schools is the unique teaching method it uses. This method isolates the barriers preventing or hindering a child from learning and then provides precise tools to deal with them. Its use allows any child of any ability to learn anything.

There is a high level of open communication between students and staff that helps to prevent failure, bullying or drugs.

Every student is individually programmed and targeted to ensure each one achieves the success they are capable of.

The classes are small and an excellent curriculum using the Cambridge framework, providing core subjects and peripheral studies, is available up to GCSE and Advanced Levels.

A "qualifications" department exists for checking that students have fully understood each step of their studies, and also provides extra help for any student having any trouble in class. There is also a Student Consultant that helps to resolve any personal problems the student may have.

Entry is by assessments (not entry tests – Greenfields is non-selective) for literacy, science and numeracy. There is a pre-entry section for those who need a short programme to catch up and be ready to join their correct class.

Trains take under an hour from London to East Grinstead, which is a ten-minute car ride from the school. Gatwick Airport is a twenty-minute car ride away.

Charitable status. Greenfields Educational Trust is a Registered Charity, number 287037. The object for which the trust is established is the advancement of education.

The Gregg Preparatory School

17–19 Winn Road, Portswood, Southampton SO17 1EJ

Tel: 023 8055 7352
email: office@thegreggprep.org
website: www.thegreggprep.org
Facebook: @thegreggprep

Chairman of Board of Trustees: Mr J Watts (acting)

Head Teacher: **Mr Matt Pascoe**, BA Hons, PGCE

Age Range. 4–11 Co-educational.

Number of Pupils. 100.

Fees per term (2021–2022). £2,975 (Lunch £180).

The Gregg Preparatory School is a small school, on a pleasant, urban road in central Southampton, close to the university. It exists to make *the most of Individual Talent – nurturing every child*. The school caters for children aged 4–11; The school provides before and after care from 8.00 am until 6.00 pm.

The School aims to provide for the whole child through a varied curriculum, with a wide programme of study and opportunities to develop all aspects of every pupil's talents. The core subjects, English, Maths and Science, as well as the development of ICT skills, are at the centre of learning throughout the school. Pupils are encouraged and helped to develop a disciplined approach to personal study skills at all ages. Group and class activities help everyone to experience cooperative work and gain useful understanding of others skills and feelings.

Details of the curriculum can be found on our website. A structured academic program is covered by all age groups. This is delivered by specialist staff that enable every pupil to achieve their potential. Continuous assessment and tests prepare the upper school pupils for their entrance exams and for further achievement at secondary school.

The School provides regular feedback about pupils' progress at Parents' Evenings and through reports. Weekly newsletters are emailed to parents informing them of events pupils are involved in as well as activities happening within the school. Parents are encouraged to be involved in their children's education where ever possible.

The School is proud of its achievements in music, drama, games, swimming and dance. As well as our own two indoor hall spaces and playground, the school takes advantage of The Gregg School's sporting facilities. Weekly games, swimming and gym/dance sessions with qualified staff are provided, as well as a variety of after-school activities.

Upper school pupils gain valuable experience whilst preparing for Communication examinations. Each year many pupils achieve distinctions and merits but, most importantly, all gain much personal satisfaction and confidence that will help them in later life.

Further opportunities are provided, through extracurricular activities, to develop pupils' individual talents and personal strengths and interests. Monthly

Achievement Assemblies celebrate individual and group interests in and out of school as well as focusing on pupils Endeavour and Courtesy within school. These are an opportunity for every individual to learn their own self-worth.

For taster days and further information, please contact the school secretary or visit our website.

Charitable status. The Gregg Schools Trust is a Registered Charity, number 1089055.

The Gregg School

Townhill Park House, Cutbush Lane, Southampton SO18 3RR

Tel: 023 8047 2133
email: office@thegreggschool.org
website: www.thegreggschool.org
Twitter: @TheGreggSchool
Facebook: @TheGreggSchool
Instagram: @thegreggschool

Acting Chairman of Board of Trustees: Mr J Watts

Headteacher: **Mrs S Sellers**, MSc, BSc Hons, NPQH, PGCE

Age Range. 11–16 years.
Number in School. 350.
Fees per term (2021–2022). £4,600.

The Gregg School is situated to the east of Southampton and set in 23 acres of beautifully landscaped grounds. The School has a unique family atmosphere and an excellent reputation for its outstanding pastoral care. A high value is placed on identifying and developing each child's individual talents and abilities, and small classes, taught by experienced and dedicated staff, ensure that every student has the opportunity to achieve their very best.

A broad and balanced curriculum is supplemented by a wide range of extracurricular clubs and activities, ranging from orienteering to yoga, bouldering, first aid and the Duke of Edinburgh award.

The School's music and drama departments provide a host of opportunities for students to perform to a range of audiences, and the School regularly achieves success in sporting disciplines at both city and county level.

A comprehensive transport service is provided for students living within a 15 mile radius of the School.

Our Trust Partner, The Gregg Preparatory School, offers a high-quality educational experience for children aged 4–11.

Hale Preparatory School

Broomfield Lane, Hale, Cheshire WA15 9AS

Tel: 0161 928 2386
email: mail@haleprepschool.com
website: www.haleprepschool.com

Headmaster: **J Connor**, JP, BSc, FCP

Age Range. 4–11.
Number in School. Day: 110 Boys, 82 Girls.
Fees per term (2021–2022). £2,750.

Hale Preparatory School is a completely independent, co-educational school for children from the age of 4 to 11.

The school's most recent ISI inspection was in the summer of 2014. The overall summary of the report reads, "*Hale Prep is a very successful school. Throughout, the teaching is excellent and the pupils' industrious approach to their studies is reflected in their rapid progress and substantial academic achievement at all levels. Indeed, in some cases, levels of progress and achievement are exceptional. The pupils reach high standards of personal fulfilment and participate enthusiastically in a wide range of extra-curricular activities. The quality of the pupils' personal development is excellent, reflecting the school's highly effective emphasis on their welfare, safeguarding and well-being.*"

In recent years, the school was considered the Prep School of the Year by the Sunday Times and was referred to in two studies presented to the Department of Education: firstly, on "Best Practice in the Independent Sector" and secondly, as one of five examples of successful private schools.

One of the aims of the school is to develop each child to his or her fullest potential. This can only be achieved in a situation that emphasises a disciplined approach to school work. Teaching is carried out in a formal, traditional manner but one which also incorporates modern teaching aids. Homework is set every night.

The curriculum of the school is designed to create well-rounded children. Thus, whilst 50% of the curriculum is devoted to the core subjects of maths, English and science, all children have weekly lessons in drama, music, dance, art and design, information technology, history, geography, French, Spanish, ethics, physical education/games and Latin in year 6. Additionally, the school offers a range of extra-curricular activities including a dance club, theatre club, fencing, chess, sewing, gardening, choir, orchestra, a range of sports and outdoor pursuit holidays.

Harvington Prep School

20 Castlebar Road, Ealing, London W5 2DS

Tel: 020 8997 1583
email: admin@harvingtonschool.com
website: www.harvingtonschool.com
Facebook: @Harvingtonprepschool

Headmistress: **Mrs Anna Evans**, BA Hons, PGCE

Age Range. Girls 3–11, Boys 3–7.

Number in School. 90 Girls, 10 Boys.

Fees per term (2021–2022). Early Years £2,505–£4,610; Years 1–6 £4,920.

The School was founded in 1890 and made into an Educational Trust in 1970. Harvington is known for its high standards and happy atmosphere. Classes are small so that individual attention can be given by qualified and experienced staff. An academic education is offered preparing girls for senior school entrance examinations. The school continues to improve specialist facilities and also to provide a mixed nursery class for 3–4 year olds.

It is close to Ealing Broadway station and a number of bus routes.

Prospectus available from the Secretary.

Charitable status. Harvington School Education Trust Ltd is a Registered Charity, number 312621. It aims to subscribe to traditional values in behaviour and academic standards in a happy environment; to encourage a high standard of academic achievement for girls across a broad range of abilities; to encourage girls to develop their potential to the full, both in personal and academic terms; and to create an environment in which pupils will want to learn.

Heathcote School

Eves Corner, Danbury, Essex CM3 4QB

Tel: 01245 223131
email: enquiries@heathcoteschool.co.uk
website: www.heathcoteschool.co.uk

Headteacher: **Mrs Samantha Scott**

Age Range. 2–11+.

Number in School. 100.

Fees per term (2021–2022). £3,150

Founded in 1935, Heathcote School has achieved a high reputation and won many accolades. The school has been nominated as one of three finalists in the *Junior School of the Year Awards 2021*. One of our newly qualified teachers is also a silver award winner in the *2021 TES National Awards*.

Heathcote is a small, village school that encourages excellence in all areas.

Children may start in our Nursery from 2 years old. We offer wrap-around care from 7.30am to 6.00pm and have many extra-curricular activities.

Specialist subject teachers ensure the success of the high teaching standards expected at this school. Children are prepared for scholarships, entrance examinations and the Essex Selective Schools Examination at 11+. A very high pass rate is attained in these examinations.

The School participates in many sporting fixtures including netball, football and swimming and is particularly successful in horse jumping, cross country and triathlon.

Pupils are expected to show courtesy and consideration at all times and encouraged to develop self-discipline and pride in themselves and their environment. Regular consultations with parents are held and the Head Teacher is always available for any discussions that parents consider necessary. We have an active and dedicated "Friends of Heathcote School" who regularly hold social events and raise funds for charity and for the school.

For more information please contact us or visit our website.

Heathfield Knoll School and Day Nursery

Wolverley, Kidderminster, Worcestershire DY10 3QE

Tel: 01562 850204
email: info@hkschool.org.uk
website: www.hkschool.org.uk
Twitter: @heathfieldknoll
Facebook: @HeathfieldKnollSchool
LinkedIn: /Heathfield-School-and-Day-Nursery

Headmaster: **Mr Lawrence Collins**, MA, PGCE

Age Range. 0–16. Baby Unit for children 3 months plus.

Number in School. 200 Day pupils.

Fees per term (2021–2022). £3,015–£4,761. Pre School: £34 (afternoon), £38 (half day), £50 (full day). Nursery from £29 (afternoon & tea) to £62 (full day).

Heathfield Knoll School is a co-educational day school with nursery provision, governed by KSI Education. The School is situated in spacious grounds in a green belt area north of Kidderminster, within easy reach of Worcestershire, West Midlands and Shropshire.

The curriculum is broadly based and pupils are prepared for GCSE. Classes are small. Careers guidance is available to senior pupils.

The school is strong in Drama, Music, Art and Sport. A wide variety of team and individual sports is offered with some pupils achieving regional and national standards.

Prospectus available from the Admissions Administrator.

Herne Hill School

The Old Vicarage, 127 Herne Hill, London SE24 9LY

Tel: 020 7274 6336
email: enquiries@hernehillschool.co.uk
website: www.hernehillschool.co.uk

Headteacher: **Mrs Ngaire Telford**

Age Range. 2–7.

Number in School. 293 boys and girls.

Fees per term (2021–2022). £2,375–£5,415.

Herne Hill School is the largest independent Pre-School and Pre-Prep in the UK focusing exclusively on 2–7 year olds, i.e. the period research has shown to be the most important educational years in a person's life. Children join Kindergarten in the academic year they become 3 years old. Kindergarten is by far the greatest entry point, followed by

Pre-Reception and Reception. There are usually only chance vacancies for Years 1 and 2.

The school is well known as an oasis of happy learning and as the ideal setting for young children to acquire the key values and cognitive, physical, social and emotional skills they will require to lead happy, successful and balanced lives. At 7+, the children graduate to move on to a number of local independent and state schools, 'ready to shine with that special Herne Hill sparkle', as one of the heads of the receiving schools has described his Herne Hill School intake.

The school's grounds and facilities lie tucked away behind St Paul's Church on Herne Hill and combine to provide a 'homely', safe and nurturing feel while at the same time being open, green and deceptively large – the perfect environment for young children to blossom and enjoy discovering how to learn. The buildings consist of an Old Vicarage, recent purpose-built classrooms and a new building which provides a number of additional benefits. These include a large, state-of-the-art Kindergarten room; a modern, multi-functional hall; and a kitchen which produces healthy hot lunches freshly cooked on site daily.

By focusing on Early Years education, Herne Hill School has developed strong expertise in making the critical transition from Nursery to School seamless. Children joining the Kindergarten can avoid the disruption of a 4+ change and enjoy continuity of care for up to five years in what are arguably their most important educationally-formative years. Children joining in Reception benefit from the smooth progression from a play-based learning approach to more structured lessons.

"*Love • Care • Excellence*" encapsulates the school philosophy that love, nurture and a caring environment foster the children's self-confidence, sense of achievement and happiness, thereby stimulating their curiosity and desire to learn. The school's atmosphere lives this philosophy. It is a caring, friendly and stimulating place, and at the same time there is an air of achievement, respect and discipline.

The curriculum is finely balanced to develop all skills and interests of 'the whole child' and take account of each child's individual needs as well as the requirements of the 7+ entry tests – and to make learning fun! It is also designed to develop the skills of independent learning and to sustain the children's innate joy of learning. Music, drama, gym, dancing and French are emphasised and taught by specialists.

The most recent ISI inspection in March 2020 delivered a strong endorsement of the school's ethos, staff, curriculum, *modus operandi* and infrastructure by giving the highest possible rating of 'excellent' on the two overarching domains of quality of education, the pupils' academic and other achievements and the pupils' personal development. The full report can be found on the school's website.

The school holds two open mornings a year, typically on a Saturday in March and September. Prospective parents may also see the school 'in action' by joining one of the regular tours held during school hours. The school's website contains relevant information about life at the school, its curriculum, the destination of its leavers and some useful links.

Herries Preparatory School

Dean Lane, Cookham Dean, Berks SL6 9BD

Tel: 01628 483350
email: office@herries.org.uk
website: www.herries.org.uk
Twitter: @Herries_School
Facebook: @herriesschool

Chair of Governors: Christine Weaving

Headmaster: **Mr Robert Grosse**, MEd, BA Ed Hons

Age Range. 3–11 Co-educational.
Number of Pupils. 110 Day Boys and Girls.
Fees per term (2021–2022). £3,281–£3,847.

Herries has a delightful location alongside National Trust land and is close to Maidenhead and Marlow; all children can make use of the neighbouring Quarry woods. Small class sizes enable each child to receive individual attention and to flourish in a secure environment. The curriculum is broad and balanced and there is a wide range of extra curricular clubs including football, street dance, judo, cookery, archery and horse riding. Instrumental music lessons are available. Wrap-around care is available to all pupils from 8am until 5.30pm Monday to Friday. Herries has a distinctive family atmosphere and happy pupils who progress to the grammar, state and independent secondary schools of their choice.

Curriculum. The National Curriculum is covered and we teach beyond the levels expected of children in each age group. Class teachers deliver the core and foundation subjects in Key Stage 1 while there is subject specialist teaching in all subjects in KS2. Herries offer enrichment and study skills as part of the fees from Y3 upwards.

Examinations. Children are assessed through the NFER testing scheme and a variety of standardised tests. Emphasis is placed on preparing pupils for their next school of choice and the timetable includes 'Thinking Skills' which helps pupils learn to cope with a variety of different tests and exams.

Facilities. Set in a beautiful building which was the house in which Kenneth Grahame wrote 'The Wind in the Willows', the nursery occupies a purpose-built and spacious suite of rooms. ICT, coding and many lessons are taught on the school chrome books, all homework is set through Google classrooms. Class rooms are equipped with interactive Smart Boards and there is an excellent library. Games are played at the National Sports Centre at Bisham Abbey, only a few minutes away by coach; swimming at Wycombe Leisure Centre; cricket at Cookham Dean Cricket Club; athletics events at a local Sports Centre. There are weekly fixtures against other schools from Y3 upwards. Herries is a warm, friendly school where happy children achieve great things.

Highfield Priory School

Fulwood Row, Fulwood, Preston, Lancashire PR2 5RW

Tel: 01772 709624
email: schooloffice@highfieldpriory.co.uk
website: www.highfieldpriory.co.uk

Headmaster: **Mr J Duke**

    Age Range. 2–11 years.
    Number in School. Day: 109 Boys, 106 Girls.
    Fees per term (2021–2022). £2,835.
    Highfield is set in 8 acres of landscaped gardens, woodlands and playing fields and is a co-educational preparatory school for children aged 18 months to 11+ years. It is fully equipped with its own established Nursery and prepares children for all Independent, Grammar and Senior Schools in Lancashire, for which it has an excellent academic record.
    Class numbers average 20 and children are taught by fully-qualified and experienced staff. Specialist facilities and teachers ensure that children are challenged and fulfilled across the curriculum, most notably in Art and CDT with a new studio in 2005, an ICT suite (since 1994), a Science Laboratory (2006) and, most recently, a Performing Arts Studio in 2013. Children from Nursery through to Year Six are also able to enjoy the school Library, Sports Hall and the school's own nature reserve, Highfield Haven.
    The school has strong musical, dramatic and sporting traditions. Every child in the Junior School is given the opportunity to take part in competitive sporting fixtures and to perform in a full-scale dramatic production each year. In addition, Highfield examines the Junior children in the disciplines of Public Speaking, Elocution and Drama twice a year thereby greatly improving the children's eloquence and confidence.
    Highfield holds a Step into Quality Award for its Early Years and Foundation Stage and Potential Plus UK's Three Star Gold Membership for its work with Gifted and Talented children. Highfield encourages its pupils to 'Aim High' and gives them every opportunity to achieve this.
    Highfield offers an extended day from 7.15am until 6.00pm. Extra-curricular activities include Ballet, Gardening, Choir, Design, Dance, Judo, Public Speaking, Chess, Spanish, Homework Club and Instrument Tuition. The school is well supported by an enthusiastic Parents' Association. Prospective parents, and children, are encouraged to visit the school, have a tour with the Headmaster and to experience a school day.
    Charitable status. Highfield Priory School is a Registered Charity, number 532262. It exists to provide independent education to all children between the ages of 2 and 11 years within Preston and surrounding areas for all who wish to participate and to provide access to the community at large to all sporting, musical and artistic provision within the school.

Highfields School

London Road, Newark, Nottinghamshire NG24 3AL

Tel: 01636 704103
email: office@highfieldsschool.co.uk
website: www.highfieldsschool.co.uk
Twitter: @HighfieldsNG24
Facebook: @highfields.newark
Instagram: @highfields_school_

Head: **Mrs Sarah H Lyons**, BEd Hons Primary Early Years

    Age Range. 2–11 Co-educational.
    Number in School. 125.
    Fees per term (2021–2022). Reception £3,440, Pre-Prep £3,540, Prep £3,580 including lunch. Day Nursery from £17.40 per three-hour session to £40.30 per school day (8.30am – 3.30pm), £52.60 per full day (7.30am – 6.00pm).
    Highfields School is situated in fourteen acres of mature parkland and sports fields, an enviable setting for children to enjoy their education. It provides a happy, lively, caring community which allows the children to experience a sense of pride and fulfilment that comes from working to their full potential. Personal responsibility, initiative, good manners and smart appearance are encouraged and developed, in keeping with the School's pledge to combine modern methods with traditional values.
    Children enter a structured course of Nursery Education in the term in which they reach the age of three. Children enter the Reception Class before their fifth birthday and proceed through the School in year groups. Each class is taught by its own teacher in the basic subjects. The maximum class size is 24. All members of staff are fully qualified and specialist teachers assist with Art, ICT, Music, PE and Games throughout the School.
    Highfields has recently adopted the Cambridge Curriculum which is an education programme designed and administered by Cambridge University for young learners that combines a world-class curriculum, high-quality support for teachers and integrated assessment. By moving the curriculum away from the National Curriculum and SATs examinations, the school has greater flexibility when making decisions about what is important when equipping the children with the skills and knowledge required for them to succeed in a global community.
    Highfields has a fully deserved reputation for the quality of its pastoral care.
    All children are encouraged to be creative and exhibit a delight in learning. There is the optional opportunity for speech and drama tuition and music lessons including piano, woodwind, brass and strings ensembles, choir, advanced choir, orchestra and band. Peripatetic staff offer individual or joint music tuition in a wide variety of instruments including trumpet, saxophone, violin, cello, flute, clarinet, harp and guitar.
    The School offers a wide range of extracurricular activities and sports teams compete against other independent schools as well as local schools. Highfields has fully-qualified staff who teach tennis, hockey, cricket, football, rugby and netball. The School holds an Activemark Gold Award. All Pre-Prep children have a swimming lesson

each week; Prep children enjoy an enhanced PE programme which includes sailing, golf, table tennis and fitness.

Highfields pursues a non-selective admissions policy. The school has a very strong academic record and has been judged "excellent" in its recent ISI inspection (June 2019) which found "Academic achievement is excellent" and "Pupils' attitude to learning is exceptional". At the end of Form 6 most pupils go on to local selective independent senior schools or to grammar schools in Lincolnshire through 11+ entry.

The School is administered by a Board of Governors, including parent governors.

Charitable status. Newark Preparatory School Company Limited is a Registered Charity, number 528261. It exists to provide and further the education of children.

Hopelands Preparatory School

38/40 Regent Street, Stonehouse, Gloucestershire GL10 2AD

Tel: 01453 822164
email: admissions@hopelands.org.uk
website: www.hopelands.org.uk

Chairman of Governors: Mr R D James

Head: **Mrs Sheila Bradburn**, BA Hons, PGCE

Age Range. 4–11 Co-educational.
Number of Pupils. 75.
Fees per term (2021–2022). £2,332–£3,385.
Charitable status. Hopelands Preparatory School is a Registered Charity, number 1007707.

Howe Green House School

Great Hallingbury, Bishop's Stortford, Herts CM22 7UF

Tel: 01279 657706
email: schooloffice@howegreenhouse.essex.sch.uk
website: www.howegreenhouseschool.co.uk

Headmistress: **Mrs Deborah Mills**, BA Hons, QTS

Age Range. 2–11 years.
Number in School. 170.
Fees per term (2021–2022). Little Oaks up to £3,005; Pre-Prep up to £3,470; Prep £4,313.

Howe Green House offers an education of the highest quality in the widest sense. Facilities are excellent being sited in 15 acres of countryside adjacent to Hatfield Forest. It is a single-stream school which works broadly to the National Curriculum, offering additional French, Latin, Music, Drama and Sport. There is a strong parental involvement within the school whereby parents are actively encouraged to be part of their children's education. The school is seen as a community which fosters an understanding of children's development within both school and home. Children sit external examinations to senior

schools both boarding and day and have been highly successful.

Entry to the school is mainly via Little Oaks Nursery but children are considered for entry to the rest of the School if places are available. Please contact the school office for further information.

Charitable status. The Howe Green Educational Trust Ltd is a Registered Charity, number 297106. It exists to promote and provide for the advancement of education for the public benefit and in connection therewith to conduct a day school for the education of boys and girls.

Hulme Hall Grammar School

Beech Avenue, Stockport, Cheshire SK3 8HA

Tel: 0161 485 3524
email: secretary@hulmehallschool.org
website: www.hulmehallschool.org
Twitter: @HulmeHallGS
Facebook: @Hulme-Hall-Grammar-School
Instagram: @hulmehall

Headmaster: **Mr D Grierson**, BA Econ Hons, MEcon, PGCE

Business Manager: Mr M Lynch, BA Hons, ACMA, CGMA

Assistant Headteacher (*Curriculum*): Mr P Bradford, BSc, PGCE

Assistant Headteacher (*Pupil Progress*): Mrs J Smith, BEd Hons

Head of Pre-School: Mrs H Khinda, BEd Hons, QTS

Age Range. 2–4 and 11–16 Co-educational.
Number in School. 160.
Fees per term (2021–2022). £3,600.

Hulme Hall Grammar School is a non-selective school with an excellent reputation for providing a friendly, warm and positive atmosphere in which all pupils thrive and succeed. Its small class sizes, high quality teaching and superb enrichment programmes ensure that it provides the best possible educational journey for every pupil.

Situated in a beautiful conservation area in Stockport, Hulme Hall is split into two schools – the Pre-School and Senior School.

The **Pre-School** (2–4 years) builds relationships with families and has one shared goal: to create a place of awe and wonder where children can explore, create and grow. The setting has both indoor and outdoor learning environments where children are encouraged to become curious, confident and happy learners.

The **Senior School** (11–16 years) aims to provide every pupil with a challenging, dynamic and relevant education that enables them to attain their academic and personal potential and to prepare them fully and effectively for the next stage of their educational journey.

It delivers a curriculum covering a wide range of academic, creative and practical subjects. An extensive choice of GCSE and other external examinations enables pupils at KS4 to choose learning programmes tailored to the individual. This allows them to fulfil, if not exceed, expectations and achieve academic success.

Achievement out of the classroom is important too. Hulme Hall offers a wide and varied co-curricular programme including opportunities for trips abroad and the Duke of Edinburgh's Award Scheme.

There are numerous clubs available at lunchtime and after school and termly enrichment days that take the children outside the classroom.

Caring for the individual has always been at the heart of Hulme Hall's philosophy and an outstanding pastoral provision ensures that each child can thrive within the school and wider community. Pupils are nurtured through a vital phase in their growth and development focusing on all aspects of education – academic, personal, social and moral – to create confident and respectful individuals. All of Hulme Hall's pupils will continue their education at local colleges studying A Levels and other equivalent courses or an apprenticeship.

Charitable status. Hulme Hall Educational Trust is a Registered Charity, number 525931. The school aims to promote the personal, moral, social and academic development of all pupils.

Hurtwood House School

Holmbury St Mary, Dorking, Surrey RH5 6NU

Tel:	01483 279000
email:	info@hurtwood.net
website:	www.hurtwoodhouse.com
Twitter:	@hurtwoodhouse
Facebook:	@hurtwoodhouse

Headmaster: **C M Jackson**, BEd

Age Range. 16–18.

Number in School. 345 (225 girls, 120 boys).

Fees per term (2021–2022). Boarding £15,171, Day £10,113.

Hurtwood House is the only independent boarding school specialising exclusively in the Sixth Form. It concentrates on the 16–18 age range and offers students a caring, residential structure and a commitment to a complete education where culture, sport, friendship and a full range of extracurricular activities all play an important part. Hugely successful across the whole range of academic subjects, Hurtwood House is also widely recognised as having the best Creative and Performing Arts and Media departments in the country and is therefore especially attractive to aspiring actors, directors, film directors, dancers, singers, artists and fashion designers.

Many students now want to leave the traditional school system at 16. They are seeking an environment which is structured and safe, but which is less institutional and better equipped to provide the challenge and stimulation which they are now ready for, and which is therefore better placed to develop their potential. They also require teaching methods which will prepare them for an increasingly competitive world by developing their initiative and encouraging them to think for themselves.

Hurtwood House has 345 boys and girls. It is a small and personal school, but it is a large and powerful sixth form which benefits from having specialised A Level teachers. The examination results put Hurtwood House in the top independent school league tables, but it is equally important to the school that the students develop energy, motivation and self-confidence.

In short, Hurtwood House is a stepping-stone between school and university for students who are all in the same age group and who share the same maturity and the same ambitions.

The school is situated in its own grounds high up in the Surrey Hills and offers excellent facilities in outstandingly beautiful surroundings.

Ipswich High School

Woolverstone, Ipswich, Suffolk 1P9 1AZ

Tel:	01473 780201
email:	admissions@ipswichhighschool.co.uk
website:	www.ipswichhighschool.co.uk
Twitter:	@IpswichHigh
Facebook:	@ipswichhighschool
Instagram:	@ipswichhighschool
LinkedIn:	/school/ipswich-high-school

Head: **Mr Mark Howe**

Head of Prep School: Mrs Lisa Finch

Head of Senior School: Ms Kaye Extance

Head of Sixth Form & Boarding: Mr Rob Hastings

Registrar: Mrs Sue Burden

Ipswich High School is a vibrant day and boarding school for boys and girls aged 3–18, set in an idyllic 87-acre campus in Woolverstone on the banks of the River Orwell. With approximately 450 pupils, everyone at Ipswich High School is well known as an individual. We have small classes of hard-working pupils and inspirational teachers who help to instil a love of learning; the results of which are exceptional academic outcomes year-on-year.

We are just as ambitious outside of the classroom and pride ourselves on the huge breadth of our co-curricular programme as well as offering a home-away-from-home boarding environment in our stunning refurbished boarding houses, The Dairy House and The Barns, which have recently been awarded 'Best Boarding House Extension or Refurbishment'.

Above all, our ambition is not to make our pupils fit a pre-defined view of what they should be. We believe in getting to know every pupil and using our school to inspire them to achieve more than they previously thought possible and to leave us believing there are no limits to what they can achieve, for themselves and others.

The school was founded in 1878 and since 1992 has been situated in the Grade I listed Palladian mansion, Woolverstone Hall. The school occupies 87 acres of beautiful parkland in a rural location just four miles outside the county town of Ipswich. The spacious site has been adapted well to the needs of a forward-looking school with superb facilities, including a theatre, ICT suites, 25m indoor swimming pool, Sixth Form Centre, cookery rooms and AstroTurf pitch. The school capitalises on its outstanding natural surroundings: the woodland provides an outdoor learning area for the Prep School and the pond and parkland are often used for scientific research.

Pupils follow a broad and balanced curriculum from which they enjoy great academic success. In 2021, 71% of GCSE grades awarded were Levels 9–7. In total, over 31% of GCSE students achieved a Level 9 grade and more than 51% of GCSE pupils achieved grades 9–8. At A Level, 25% of the Year 13 students achieved three or more A* grades. Teachers and students alike were thrilled with the 100% A Level pass rate. Across the cohort, 40% of A Level grades were marked at A*, 66% gained A*–A and 89% achieved A*–B.

Admissions. Admission to Nursery is after the child's 3rd birthday. Admission into Reception is based on an informal assessment in a play situation. Entry to the rest of the Prep School is based on an assessment including written and numerical testing. Entry to the Senior School involves interviews, written tests, and a school report. Sixth Form entry is based on interviews, written assessments, GCSE results and a school report. International Boarding entry is based on written assessments and a school report.

Fees per term (2021–2022). Day: Reception £3,433, Years 1–2 £3,615, Years 3–6 £3,992, Year 7–8 £5,103, Year 9–13 £5,428.

Boarding per annum including school fees (from Year 7): Full £36,380, Weekly £28,500. Flexi Boarding options are available.

Woolverstone Scholarship Programme. Our Woolverstone Scholarship Programme is for our scholars from Years 7–13, with scholarships being awarded in Year 7, Year 9, and Year 12. This programme ensures that our scholars continue to develop their considerable talents by providing them with additional support and unique opportunities. Academic Scholars are supported to complete independent school projects, whilst Sport Scholars, Music Scholars, Art Scholars, Dance Scholars and Drama Scholars will enjoy scholarship programmes designed by the relevant Head of Department. These scholars are also able to access the academic scholar projects should they wish to do so.

Academic Scholarships. Upon receipt of a completed application form, all students will be invited into school to sit our Entrance Examination. The results of this assessment are combined with the information provided from recent school reports to decide who is eligible to receive an Academic Scholarship offer. These are then awarded by the Head, and you do not apply.

Year 7 Arthur Ransome Scholarships. All students entering Year 7, including those from our Prep School, may apply for one or more of the following Arthur Ransome Scholarships: Academic, Art, Dance, Drama, Music and Sport. These Scholarships, which may attract a tuition fee award, are awarded from Years 7 through to 11, provided the Scholar continues to demonstrate commitment to their chosen area.

Year 9 George Orwell Scholarships. George Orwell Scholarships are for pupils joining Ipswich High School for our GCSE programme in Year 9. Students can apply for one or more of the following: Academic, Art, Dance, Drama, Music and Sport. These Scholarships, which may attract a tuition fee award, are awarded for Years 9 through to 11,

provided the Scholar continues to demonstrate commitment to their chosen area.

Year 12 Woolverstone Scholarships. All students entering our Sixth Form, including those progressing from our GCSE programme, may apply for a Woolverstone Scholarship. These are our most prestigious Academic Scholarships and are awarded for Years 12 and 13 to pupils who demonstrate strength in any academic discipline, as well as being predicted a strong set of GCSE grades.

Those applying to Ipswich High School from state-funded schools are also eligible to apply for our Elliston Award.

Year 12 Sophie Youngman Scholarships. Named after the founder of Ipswich High School, this Scholarship exists to recognise any Sixth Form student who is currently excelling in an area outside of the formal curriculum, for example in charity or fundraising work. Like Woolverstone Scholarships, these are awarded for both Years 12 and 13.

King Alfred School

Manor Wood, 149 North End Road, London NW11 7HY

Tel:	020 8457 5200
email:	kas@kingalfred.org.uk
website:	www.kingalfred.org.uk
Twitter:	@kingalfredsch
Facebook:	@TheKingAlfredSchool
Instagram:	@the_king_alfred_school
LinkedIn:	/school/king-alfred-school

Head: **Robert Lobatto**, MA Oxon, NPQH London

Deputy Head Upper School: Alistair McConville, MA Cantab, PGCE Gloucestershire

Deputy Head, Head of Lower School: Karen Thomas, BEd Goldsmiths

Age Range. 4–18.

Number in School. Primary: approximately 300; Secondary: approximately 360.

Fees per term (2021–2022). Reception, Years 1–2: £5,657, Years 3–6: £6,518, Upper School (Years 7–13): £6,820.

The King Alfred School is unique among independent schools in North London. Apart from being all-age (4–18), co-ed and secular, it takes in a range of ability as opposed to its academically selective neighbours in the private sector.

The school's beginnings are unusual: it was founded in 1898 by a group of Hampstead parents and its governing body comprises mainly current and ex-parents. Visitors tend to comment on the pretty site (on the edge of Hampstead Garden Suburb), the "village" layout (carefully preserved by a succession of architects), and the friendly atmosphere – this is a no-uniform establishment and all are on first-name terms. The purchase of property across the road a few years ago enabled the school to extend its facilities.

Academic results are consistently impressive and constantly improving and almost 100% of the KAS Sixth Form go on to universities and some go to Art Foundation courses, music colleges and conservatoires; last year 100% students went on to their first choice. The school prides itself on its reputation as a relaxed, informal and vibrant community that focuses on the development of the whole child and achieves academic success within a non-pressured environment.

Bursaries for Year 7 and the Sixth Form are available.

Charitable status. King Alfred School is a Registered Charity, number 312590. It exists to provide quality education for boys and girls.

Kings Monkton School

6 West Grove, Cardiff CF24 3XL

Tel: 029 2048 2854
email: mail@kingsmonkton.org.uk
website: www.kingsmonkton.org.uk
Twitter: @kings_monkton
Facebook: @kings-monkton-school

Principal: **Mr Paul Norton**

Vice Principal and Head of Primary: Mrs Karen Norton

Age Range. 3–18.

Number in School. 297.

Fees per term (2021–2022). £3,495.00–£5,106.67.

Kings Monkton School is a co-educational day school for children from age 3–18. The school is owned by the Principal and Vice Principal, a husband and wife team, and it is renowned for its caring and inclusive ethos. The school motto is 'be the best you can be'.

Kings Monkton is one of South Wales's oldest and most innovative independent schools, having educated generations of local pupils since its foundation in 1870. The school prides itself on its excellent record of academic success, its system of pastoral care with its small classes of 18 or under, and its relations with parents. Pupils are drawn from a wide catchment area including Cardiff, the Vale of Glamorgan, the Valleys and Monmouth, as well as having a number of Tier 4-sponsored international pupils on educational visas. The school is housed in purpose-built accommodation in the centre of Cardiff, close to Queen Street station and to all amenities.

Kings Monkton's primary school has small classes in which young children can receive individual care and guidance. Pupils follow a well-balanced curriculum, designed to develop and stimulate young minds to the full. Children are taught both French and Mandarin and have extensive access to sports.

In the secondary school, pupils pursue a wide curriculum with their progress being carefully monitored and receive strong pastoral support throughout their adolescent years. All pupils are encouraged to strive for high standards in their work and to contribute to the well-being of the community to which they belong. Entry to the school is non-selective, with a maximum of 18 pupils per class to ensure that all achieve their highest potential.

In the sixth form, students follow a unique Level 3 offering incorporating their learning pathway and co-curriculum. Students are taught in small tutorial groups and in addition to their academic studies participate in a number of other activities including Young Enterprise, Public

Speaking and the Extended Project Qualification as part of the school's philosophy of giving its pupils thorough preparation for life. The minimum entry requirements to the Sixth Form are five GCSE passes at grades A–C. Links with industry and excellent work experience means that pupils are well prepared for university and have the necessary skills to make them stand out in the UCAS application process.

The school works in partnership with many different organisations including Oxford Royale Academy, HSA, Shelley Norton Drama and Wonderland Studios, as well as having close links with China, The Netherlands, Thailand and Spain.

Lime House School

Holm Hill, Dalston, Nr Carlisle, Cumbria CA5 7BX

Tel: 01228 710225
email: office@limehouseschool.co.uk
 admissions@limehouseschool.co.uk
website: www.limehouseschool.co.uk
Twitter: @limehouseschool
Facebook: @limehouseschooloffice

Headteacher: **Mrs M Robertson-Barnett**, MA Oxon

Age Range. 7–18. Boarders from age 9.

Number in School. Day: 25 Boys, 26 Girls; Boarding: 78 Boys, 49 Girls.

Fees per term (2021–2022). Boarding £9,250–£10,750; Day £3,600–£4,600.

Compulsory extras: Activities, Laundry.

Lime House School is a fully independent co-educational boarding and day school for pupils aged 7 to 18. Our aim is to ensure that each pupil achieves his or her potential both academically and socially, with each child treated individually. Our pupils are cared for in a safe rural environment and every possible attempt is made to ensure that they develop confidence and self-esteem. Boarding is available to all pupils, with the majority being full boarders.

Foreign students whose first language is not English add to the cosmopolitan atmosphere of the school. They are prepared for Cambridge English examinations (KET, PET & IELTS) and follow the same curriculum as all other students.

Games and sport form an important part of school life. All students participate and a wide range of team and individual sports is offered. Most pupils take games to GCSE level, with many continuing to A Level. In 2019 the GCSE pass rate was 100% and at A Level 64.3% of grades were A* or A.

We would welcome a visit to our school to see it in action. Simply contact the school and we will arrange a time convenient for you.

Loreto Preparatory School

Dunham Road, Altrincham, Cheshire WA14 4GZ

Tel: 0161 928 8310
email: info@loretoprep.org.uk
website: www.loretoprep.org.uk

Headteacher: **Mrs Anne Roberts**, BEd Hons Cantab

Age Range. Girls 3–11.
Number in School. 130 Day Girls.
Fees per term (2021–2022). £2,620

Loreto Preparatory School, founded in 1909, is a Catholic independent school and is one of many Loreto schools built on the foundations laid by Mary Ward, foundress of the Institute of the Blessed Virgin Mary, according to the vision of St Ignatius of Loyola. It is a modern, purpose-built school standing in pleasant grounds and offering an all-round education by well-qualified staff. The school's primary aim is to provide an environment that enables children to live by the principles of the gospel and in the tradition of the Catholic faith, upholding the values of Mary Ward. The school also seeks to help pupils reach their full potential in all aspects of the curriculum and thus to become happy and confident with an enduring love of learning.

Our latest ISI Inspection was excellent in all areas. The pupils' academic and personal development and other achievements were highly praised. "Pupils view the school as a family and show great respect for each other's culture, opinions and beliefs".

Music, PE, ICT and French are all taught by specialist teachers.

Music plays an important part in the life of the school. We have a school orchestra, and private individual lessons are available in most instruments. The children's dramatic ability and interest are developed through class lessons, theatre visits and regular productions.

Gymnastics, swimming, netball, cross country and athletics are important elements of our physical education programme and the school participates fully in local and national competitions.

Our ICT facilities are excellent and include a computer suite.

We offer a wide range of extracurricular activities including Spanish, Art Club, Zumbatomic, Street Dance, Chess, Football, Cricket, Tennis, Judo, Fencing, Archery and Mad Science.

Visits to the school are welcome by appointment. Admission at 3+ is usually by interview and for those wishing to join at 7+ by interview and Entrance Examination. Open Day is held in March each year.

Charitable status. Loreto Preparatory School is a Registered Charity, number 250607.

Loughborough Amherst School

Gray Street, Loughborough, Leicestershire LE11 2DZ

Tel: 01509 263901
email: Amherst.office@lsf.org
website: www.lsf.org/amherst
Twitter: @LboroAmherst
Facebook: @LboroAmherst
Instagram: @LboroAmherst
LinkedIn: /loughborough-schools-foundation

Chairman of Governors: Admiral Sir Trevor Soar, KCB, OBE, DEng Hon, FCMI

Headmaster: **Dr Julian Murphy**, DPhil Oxon

Age Range. Co-educational 4–18.
Number of Pupils. Approximately 200+.

Fees per term (2021–2022). Pre-Prep £3,545, Prep £3,630, Senior: Years 7–9 £4,420; Years 10–11 £4,473, Sixth Form £4,515. (Please email amherst.admissions@lsf.org for boarding fees.)

Loughborough Amherst School is a Catholic co-educational day and boarding school. Welcoming children of all faiths and non, the School is part of the Loughborough Schools Foundation, a foundation of four schools comprising: Fairfield Prep School (boys and girls 3–11), Loughborough Grammar School (boys 10–18), Loughborough Amherst School (boys and girls 4–18) and Loughborough High School (girls 11–18). The schools operate under one governing body and are situated on two neighbouring campuses in the town. The Foundation also includes The Loughborough Nursery for children from 6 weeks to 4 years.

We hold an open day each term, but encourage all prospective parents to see our Senior and Preparatory School departments in action on a normal working day, view our facilities and meet our Headmaster. Visitors continually note the happy classroom environment and the mutual respect between pupils, staff and visitors. Some of our children are with us from 4 to 18, but we welcome new pupils at all stages of their education.

Our focus is very much on the individual child and his/her personal progress and character growth. At all stages of their education, our pupils receive individual attention in small classes. The emphasis is on giving 'added value' through the patient nurturing of confidence and 'growth mindset' in our pupils. Our progressive approach to learning and character growth is embodied in the School philosophy we call 'Minerva'.

For a school with a very broad ability intake our public examination results are truly excellent, with 68% A*–A and 87% A*–B at A Level and 22% 9–8 and 42% 9–7 at GCSE. Our 'added value' scores are significantly above national average in almost all subjects. Our Learning Support department is very well staffed for a school of our size.

Our membership of the Loughborough Schools Foundation places us in a wonderful position, where we can combine all that is best in a small school community with the benefits of the human and physical resources of a campus of over two thousand students. This provides numerous enrichment possibilities for our pupils, whatever their personal interests. To give just four examples:

- Our budding musicians have access to one of the finest music provisions in the country
- Our Sixth Formers can choose from a very large range of A Level courses
- Our youngest pupils can enjoy outdoor learning in a Forest School and a year of free string instrument lessons
- Applicants for Oxford, Cambridge or the leading US universities will be able to access subject specialist mentoring from a large body of teaching staff stretching across three schools

In addition to the traditional sporting teams we offer morning fitness sessions for all, swimming, basketball, trampoline and football practices with the aim to enter local and ISA competitions. We also run a popular triathlon club. We have a new AstroTurf and sports hall, fitness suite and dance studio.

The School successfully participates in the Combined Cadet Force (CCF), The Duke of Edinburgh's Award and the Young Enterprise scheme.

The Nursery at the Loughborough Schools Foundation is based on our campus and offers childcare 51 weeks a year from age 6 weeks to 4 years.

For further information visit our website: www.lsf.org/amherst.

Charitable status. Loughborough Amherst School is part of the Loughborough Schools Foundation, which is a Registered Charity, number 1081765, and a Company Limited by Guarantee, registered in England, number 4038033. Registered Office: 3 Burton Walks, Loughborough, Leics LE11 2DU.

Lucton School

Lucton, Leominster, Herefordshire HR6 9PN

Tel: 01568 782000
email: admissions@luctonschool.org
website: www.luctonschool.org
Twitter: @LuctonSchool
Facebook: @Lucton-School
Instagram: @luctonschool
LinkedIn: /lucton-school

Headmaster: **Mr J Tyler**

Head of Prep School: Mr David Bicker-Caarten

Head of Sixth Form: Mr M Wolstenholme

Age Range. 6 months–19 years.

Number in School. 360

Fees per term (2021–2022). Day £2,500–£4,840, Weekly Boarding £8,115–£9,565, Full Boarding £9,565–£11,710.

UK Registration £75, Overseas Registration £150

About Lucton School. Founded in 1708, Lucton provides pupils with an excellent all-round education which aims to bring out their full potential. Pupils benefit from small classes, a friendly atmosphere and an idyllic rural location. There are extensive sports facilities and a good mix of day pupils, weekly boarders and full boarders.

Studying at Lucton School. Lucton has a strong academic record and an established tradition of getting the best possible results from each pupil. Subjects taught to GCSE include English language and literature, mathematics, biology, chemistry, physics, information technology, French, Spanish, German, history, geography, business studies, religious education, design & technology, art, music, drama and PE/games.

All the above GCSE subjects and more are available at AS and A2 Levels. The Sixth Form is housed in a new sixth form centre, including a new senior library and well-equipped IT suite.

School Facilities. The school is set in 55 acres of beautiful Herefordshire countryside. Facilities on-site include:

- Junior and senior libraries
- Science laboratories
- ICT rooms
- Design and technology workshop
- Tennis courts
- Indoor swimming pool
- Indoor sports hall
- Games fields
- Equestrian centre.

Boarding pupils are housed in modern buildings and senior pupils have individual rooms.

Admissions. Admission can take place at any time of the year by interview and assessment. Prospective pupils are always invited to spend a taster day in the school without obligation. Examinations for academic scholarships are held in January each year.

Affiliations. Lucton School is a member of the Independent Schools Association (ISA); the Head of Lucton Prep School is a member of The Independent Association of Prep Schools (IAPS); and Lucton School is in membership of the Boarding Schools' Association (BSA).

Charitable status. Lucton School is a Registered Charity, number 518076.

Lyonsdown School

3 Richmond Road, New Barnet, Hertfordshire EN5 1SA

Tel: 020 8449 0225
email: enquiries@lyonsdownschool.co.uk
website: www.lyonsdownschool.co.uk
Twitter: @LyonsdownSchool
Facebook: @LyonsdownSchool

Head: **Mrs Rittu Hall**, BSc Hons, PGCE

Age Range. Girls 3–11

Number of Pupils. 180.

Fees per term (2021–2022). Pre-Reception: £1,515–£4,049; Reception–Year 2 £3,589; Years 3–6 £3,922.

Lyonsdown School is a small, friendly school for girls aged three to eleven which, since September 2020, has fully embraced all-girls education. Situated in the leafy suburb of

New Barnet, within easy access to the North Circular and both Northern Line and mainline rail services.

Lyonsdown nurtures both potential and ability, allowing all pupils to thrive and achieve personal excellence. The school is non-selective at entry. Year 6 girls gain entry and scholarships to top senior schools, both independent (day and boarding) and selective maintained schools.

Class sizes are small with high teacher to pupil ratios, ensuring that both teaching and pastoral care are of the highest standard. A broad and balanced curriculum provides personalised learning and a great deal of specialist teaching. This allows pupils to flourish and discover their passions and abilities, whatever they might be.

Lyonsdown has significant strengths in Music, Drama and Art with recent successes coming in the North London Music Festival and the ISA Art competition and being shortlisted for the National ISA awards. The school runs two lively and popular choirs and individual instrumental lessons are taught by visiting specialists.

"Lyonsdown learning" is at the heart of the school and the pupils develop those skills that will prepare them for their senior school and a life of learning beyond. They are critical thinkers, exploring their lessons and activities with independence, responsibility and imagination.

The school is housed in a beautiful Edwardian building with modern facilities including a Science Laboratory, Library and Dining Room, a discovery garden, Art Studio, Computing Room and Music Room. Sport is both popular and important at Lyonsdown and the school makes good use of its own purpose-built hall and local facilities for PE and Games.

An extensive extra-curricular programme, including breakfast and after-school clubs, maypole dancing, homework club and fencing runs throughout the year. Visiting speakers, theatre groups and workshops are very popular with pupils and parents alike. The school makes excellent use of its location with visits into London a regular feature of the calendar and Year 5 and 6 pupils enjoying an annual residential trip.

Specialist learning support is also provided to those pupils who need additional focus, be it a specific need such as dyslexia, or for those who need a temporary boost. More able girls have their learning extended in lessons and in a variety of additional activities, and pupils of all abilities are challenged.

Lyonsdown is an inclusive community with a Christian ethos, welcoming a diverse mix of pupils of all faiths. The school is a community of learning and the partnership between home and school is of central importance. Regular communication ensures parents are well-informed and celebrates the pupils' many successes.

The school is a member of the Independent School's Association

Charitable status. Lyonsdown School Trust Ltd is a Registered Charity, number 312591.

Maldon Court Preparatory School

Silver Street, Maldon, Essex CM9 4QE

Tel: 01621 853529
email: enquiries@maldoncourtschool.org
website: www.maldoncourtschool.org

Principal: **Mrs L F Guest**, BEd Hons

Headteacher: Mrs E Mason

Age Range. 1–11 co-educational.
Number of Pupils. 144 Day pupils.
Fees per term (2021–2022). Reception £3,217; Years 1–6 £3,264.

Welcome to Maldon Court Preparatory School, a small, happy and caring school community where young children can flourish in a positive and supportive environment. Originally established in 1956, the school has maintained its vision of being run as a family-owned, friendly school with high expectations and standards.

Children here are encouraged to develop in all aspects of the broad and balanced curriculum. Each pupil is valued as an individual and allowed to develop at their own pace. Strengths and weaknesses are identified at an early age and our dedicated staff ensure that every child is challenged and supported to achieve their full potential through exploring the huge range of possibilities open to them.

Within this framework of close care and encouragement, Maldon Court delivers a first-class education, laying down strong foundations for the future. At the same time, great emphasis is placed on pastoral care, which is strengthened by a close partnership with parents and a strong family atmosphere that is evident throughout the school. The success of this ethos is reflected in the school's achievement of 'excellent' (the highest inspection rating) in every area in 2013. We are also delighted to have been graded 'Outstanding' in our Ofsted Nursery inspection in May 2017 and 'Outstanding' in our Nursery ISI Inspection in May 2017.

There is a love of sport at Maldon Court which has been nurtured and developed by the dedicated members of our PE Department. We aim for high levels of physical fitness and coordination, in turn fostering confidence and encouraging participation from children at all levels. The school enters teams both locally and nationally in a wealth of sporting events and competitions.

At the end of their time at Maldon Court, we are proud to see our boys and girls emerge as articulate, well-informed and interesting young people, comfortable in their abilities, buoyed by their achievements, ambitious and well equipped for the challenges that lie ahead.

Mander Portman Woodward (MPW)
London

90–92 Queen's Gate, London SW7 5AB

Tel: 020 7835 1355
email: london@mpw.ac.uk
website: www.mpw.ac.uk

Principal: **John Southworth**, BSc, MSc

Vice Principals:

Dee Robins

Rachel Shaw

Rachel Sherman

Age Range. 14–19+
Number in School. 600
Fees per term (2021–2022). From £10,252
Tailored, not uniform

Founded in 1973, MPW London is one of the UK's leading Sixth Form colleges. Situated in the heart of one of the capital's most exclusive and vibrant locations, the college offers small classes in a socially relaxed yet highly academically disciplined environment.

A unique teaching method

We have a distinct approach to education with small classes of no more than nine students and a strong emphasis on exam techniques which have been proven over decades. Our Director of Studies system offers a high level of personal care, supporting welfare and academic progress.

Unrivalled range of courses

We offer a highly flexible curriculum of unrivalled depth and breadth, comprising A level, GCSE, retakes and university foundation programmes. We also run an acclaimed programme of Easter Revision courses each year.

Strong results and progression

Despite having a non-selective admissions policy and a wide variety of courses targeted at students of different academic abilities, our students achieve outstanding overall results year after year, with more than one in three results at both A level and GCSE at MPW resulting in grades A* or A. These results unlock the doors to some of the UK's best universities – in 2020, 70% of our students progressed to top-tier destinations (Russell Group, University of London and specialist institutions), with 25% securing places at the UK's top 10 universities (Times Higher Education UK University Rankings). In 2021, there was a 100% pass rate across all A Level subjects with 62% graded A*/A.

Stunning location

MPW London is located in South Kensington (Zone 1), one of the most exclusive and affluent parts of the capital. MPW London is just a few minutes' walk from Hyde Park, Imperial College and many world-famous museums, including the Science Museum, the Natural History Museum and the Victoria & Albert Museum.

Rating 'Excellent' by ISI

In our last Independent School Inspectorate (ISI) report, we received the highest rating of 'Excellent', prompting the inspectors to report: 'The quality of the students' spiritual, moral, social and cultural development is excellent. In line with the aims of the college, students are encouraged to develop confidence, self-belief and self-discipline.'

Maple Hayes Hall
Specialist School for Dyslexics

Abnalls Lane, Lichfield, Staffordshire WS13 8BL

Tel: 01543 264387
email: office@dyslexia.school
website: www.dyslexia.school
Facebook: @Maple-Hayes-Hall-School

Principal: **Dr E N Brown**, PhD, MSc, BA, MSCME, MINS, AFBPsS, CPsychol

Headmaster: Dr D J Brown, DPhil, MEd Psychology of SpLD, MA Oxon, PGCE

Age Range. 7–17.
Number in School. 120 Day Boys and Girls.
Fees per term (2021–2022). £5,470–£7,308

Maple Hayes is a specialist independent day school approved under the 1996 Education Act as a co-educational school for children of average to very high intelligence who are not achieving their intellectual potential by normal teaching methods.

This school is under the direction of Dr E Neville Brown whose work in the field of learning strategies has achieved international recognition and includes a major breakthrough in the teaching of dyslexic children. Attention is paid to the individual child by teaching the basic literacy and numeracy skills required for the child to benefit from a full curriculum (with the exception of a foreign language). The school had an outstanding Ofsted report in November 2017.

The very favourable teacher to pupil ratio of 1:10 or better ensures a high standard of educational and pastoral care. The children's learning is under the supervision and guidance of a qualified educational psychologist.

Maple Walk Prep School

62A Crownhill Road, London NW10 4EB

Tel: 020 8963 3890
         020 8965 7374 (Admissions)
email: admissions@maplewalkschool.co.uk
website: www.maplewalkschool.co.uk

Head Teacher: **Claire Murdoch**

Age Range. 4–11 Co-educational.
Number of Pupils. 165
Fees per term (2021–2022). £3,866.

Maple Walk, judged excellent in all areas (ISI Inspection, March 2020), is a happy, vibrant, exceptional value prep school for boys and girls aged 4–11 in north west London, nurturing children's wellbeing and academic best through fun, kindness and respect for one another.

We provide a safe, supportive and stimulating environment with small class sizes for outstanding learning and personal development where children flourish, developing self-confidence, self-esteem and social awareness.

Cultivating a growth mindset, Maple Walk's innovative, creative curriculum underpinned by academic rigour instils a love of learning and resilience ensuring each child is well prepared for whatever the future holds.

The numerous opportunities outside the classroom are fundamental to the school day. Through sporting activities, first class music, art and drama, we encourage every child to find their own particular strength with many gaining scholarships at top independent secondary schools.

Our enriching selection of after school clubs allows pupils to explore a diverse range of activities beyond the school day including skateboarding, gymnastics, animation, robotics and plenty more.

This educational journey is housed in purpose-built accommodation and comes with a host of eco credentials, including a ground source heat pump for our heating and hot water, solar PV panels for electricity and a growing sedum roof to attract local wildlife.

Entry into Reception is non-selective and based on the date the completed registration form is returned to our Registrar, with siblings given priority. Entry higher up the school is by interview and informal assessment in the classroom. We offer regular open days and welcome private tours.

The Mead School

16 Frant Road, Tunbridge Wells, Kent TN2 5SN

Tel: 01892 525837
email: office@themeadschool.co.uk
website: www.themeadschool.co.uk
Twitter: @TheMeadSchoolTW
Facebook: @themeadschoolTW

Headmistress: **Mrs C E Openshaw**

Age Range. 3–11.

Number in School. 242.

Fees per term (2021–2022). Infants £3,655; Juniors £4,090 (nursery fees depending on sessions)

The Mead School is a thriving, co-educational prep school situated in the heart of Tunbridge Wells. The school, which was rated 'excellent' in all areas in its most recent ISI Inspection Report, is a true community and run as a large family living under one roof.

The Mead's ethos is that a child who is happy and secure in school is one who is going to learn, thrive and aspire. School must be an exciting, fulfilling and safe place where every day, whether you are aged three or eleven, is a new adventure and positively anticipated.

The Mead enjoys a reputation of high academic standards within a caring, happy environment. Children are prepared for the highly-selective Tunbridge Wells and Tonbridge Grammar Schools as well as a wide range of Independent and maintained secondary schools.

The Mead has exceptional music, drama and sport provision and over 30 extra-curricular clubs to choose from. Fully catered provision is offered from 7.45am to 5.30pm.

Mill Hill International

Milespit Hill, Mill Hill Village, London NW7 2RX

Tel: +44 (0)20 3826 3333
           +44 (0)20 3826 3366 (Admissions)
email: office@millhillinternational.org.uk
           registrar@millhillinternational.org.uk
website: www.millhill.org.uk/international

Motto: Instilling values, inspiring minds

Chair of the Court of Governors: Mr Elliot Lipton, BSc Hons, MBA, FRSA, FRICS

Head: **Ms Sarah Bellotti**, BEd

Registrar: Mrs Maria De Aveiro Fernandez, BSc

Age Range. 13–17 Co-educational.

Number of Pupils. 94

Fees per term (2021–2022). Day £9,000 including lunch, Weekly Boarding £12,500 (including meals), Full Boarding: £14,750 (Including all meals).

Mill Hill International is a co-educational boarding and day school for international pupils aged 13–17. It is situated in a Green Belt on the borders of Hertfordshire and Middlesex, just ten miles from Central London, and forms part of the Mill Hill School Foundation which is set in 150 acres of beautiful grounds. Day, weekly and full boarding places are available for entry at Year 9, Year 10 and Year 11. Pupils from all over the world come together in an inspiring school to gain internationally recognised qualifications, a transformational educational and cultural experience.

At Mill Hill International your child will develop habits of mind that will equip them for their educational journey in the UK and prepare them to face the challenges of life in the 21st century with confidence, resilience and creativity. We guide our pupils to seek courage and curiosity within themselves and apply them in all their endeavours. We offer a traditional British educational experience and an academic curriculum up to GCSE/IGCSE and specialist EAL teaching. Pupils for whom English is not their first language receive English language tuition while at the same time studying an appropriate range of other subjects in order to equip them for further study whether at Mill Hill School or elsewhere. Suitable also for British pupils returning to the UK after a period abroad, Mill Hill International offers a Fast Track course which is an Intensive English Language Programme, a year nine course to help pupils prepare for GCSE, an intensive one year GCSE course for pupils entering Year 11 and a two year GCSE programme where students will study between 8 and 12 subjects. In addition, there is a Spring and Summer School which offer courses to ages 12–17, combining English learning with academic subjects, including mathematics and science or sport. These core elements are complemented by a varied programme of creative activity classes including music, dance, drama and art.

Our teaching is rigorous, challenging and exciting and we have high expectations of every pupil. Class sizes are small and all our teachers are qualified or trained in teaching English as an additional language so every pupil can progress quickly. In addition to the impressive resources of the Mill Hill International campus, we use Mill Hill School's sports facilities, including the indoor heated swimming pool, sports hall, theatre and music school. Our pupils are fully integrated with those from Mill Hill School throughout.

Charitable status. The Mill Hill School Foundation is a Registered Charity, number 1064758. It exists for the education of boys and girls.

The Moat School

Bishop's Avenue, Fulham, London SW6 6EG

Tel: 020 7610 9018
email: office@moatschool.org.uk
website: www.moatschool.org.uk
Twitter: @TheMoatSchool
Facebook: @TheMoatSchool
LinkedIn: /company/the-moat-school

Headmaster: **Koen Claeys**, BA, GLSE Belgium

Head of Sixth Form: Steve Proctor, BA Hons, PGCE, QTLS, BOA, SENCo

Co-educational Day School.

Age Range. 9–18

Number of Pupils. 85 Boys, 44 Girls.

Fees per term (2021–2022). £11,975–£12,728.

Set within the historic conservation area of Fulham Palace, The Moat School is a specialist school for secondary-age SpLD pupils. Mainstream in structure and specialist in nature, The Moat caters successfully for the needs of pupils with specific learning difficulties. Alongside the curriculum, the school also offers expertise in speech and language therapy, occupational therapy and a school counsellor.

The Moat Sixth Form was established in September 2020. This will provide pupils post-16 from The Moat and other schools a chance to take A Level and BTEC options. Also offering a full range of GCSE resit options and therapeutic benefits for KS5 pupils with SpLDs and others with additional needs.

All teachers complete a postgraduate BDA approved course in teaching students with SpLD within their first 2 years of appointment. Qualified Learning Support Assistants accompany pupils throughout their lessons at Key Stage 3, where class sizes are a maximum of 10. Class sizes are even smaller at Key Stage 4.

Multi-sensory teaching is combined with advanced IT provision, each pupil being provided with a laptop computer for use in school and at home. Touch-typing is taught in Year 7 and there is a state-of-the-art wireless network which enables staff and pupils to access the school intranet with its wide range of learning resources and data, as well as the internet.

At Key Stage 3, pupils follow a mainstream curriculum (with the exception of foreign languages) before selecting their GCSE options alongside the core subjects of English, Mathematics and Single or Dual Award Science. The Moat offers excellent facilities for learning, with a suite of Design Technology workshops offering state-of-the-art facilities for Food Technology, Resistant Materials and Graphics. Art, Music, Drama, ICT and Business Studies each have dedicated studios or specialist classrooms.

The Moat has an extensive enrichment programme of extracurricular activities designed to widen experience and develop self-confidence. In Drama, all Year 9 pupils take part in an annual Shakespeare play and there are several productions and workshop performances each year. The Moat's proximity to the River Thames enables pupils to experience rowing as a sport, swimming is popular and 2012 saw the introduction of Martial Arts and boxing. The Duke of Edinburgh's Award encourages pupils to test their own limits and since 2020 we have also offered the Duke of Edinburgh Gold award with a full set of dedicated DofE accredited staff across both the school and Sixth Form.

The Moat School and Moat Sixth Form are a part of the Cavendish Education Group.

Moon Hall School
Specialist School for Dyslexic Children

Flanchford Road, Leigh, Reigate, Surrey RH2 8RE

Tel: 01306 611372
email: schooloffice@moonhall.co.uk
website: www.moonhallschoolreigate.co.uk
Twitter: @MoonHallReigate
Facebook: @moonhallschoolreigate
LinkedIn: /company/moon-hall-school-reigate

Chair of Governors: Mr Chris Goostrey

Headmistress: **Mrs Michelle Catterson**, BSc, PGCE

Age Range. 7–16.

Number of Children. 175

Fees per term (2021–2022). £6,630–£7,900

Moon Hall School is a thriving Mainstream specialist school for Dyslexic children. We are *hugely* ambitious for our pupils in all aspects of their school life, we all champion them to be the very best version of themselves.

We tailor our curriculum to meet the needs of our pupils; our pupils will be challenged to push on and aim higher whatever their ability may be. Challenge and being able to push themselves is of great importance, in order to achieve the very best in their studies, whether this be on the sports field, the stage or in their academic lessons. Our curriculum includes a wide range of creative subjects in which our pupils can excel. We want our pupils to enjoy learning and the excitement to be gained from having an enquiring mind, to appreciate the wonder and complexity of the world and to have opportunities to be innovative.

GCSE results 2021: 93% of GCSEs passed, 22% above national average. 83% pass GCSE English and 70% pass

GCSE Maths, both above national figures, a phenomenal achievement for all staff and pupils. Given our pupils have dyslexia, to achieve these wonderful results, demonstrates the value added that being a pupil at Moon Hall can bring.

Admission is based on a review of specialist reports relating to the child's educational needs or developmental progress and attendance at taster days. As a small school with a limited number of places, currently at full capacity, we have to carefully assess the suitability of each pupil before making a decision as to whether we can offer a place.

With high adult:pupil ratios our staff know our pupils individually and help them to develop independent learning strategies. Our pastoral support is exemplary, we know each pupil as an individual and we work with our families to create a supportive and enriching learning opportunity for them all. We work closely in partnership with our parents in all aspects of their child's development and wellbeing.

We provide our pupils with opportunities for teamwork and leadership, in which their personalities can develop and flourish. We encourage them to be positive, compassionate and know the value of making a contribution to their community. Our aim is for all our pupils to leave us with the qualifications they need for the next stage of their education and their adult life. Above all, we expect them to leave as confident, independent individuals, with integrity and enthusiasm for the future.

Charitable status. Moon Hall School is a Registered Charity, number 803481.

Moorland School

Ribblesdale Avenue, Clitheroe, Lancashire BB7 2JA

Tel:	01200 423833
email:	enquiries@moorlandschool.co.uk
website:	www.moorlandschool.co.uk
Twitter:	@MoorlandSchool1
Facebook:	@MoorlandPrivateSchool

Headteacher: **Mrs Deborah Frost**

Head of Juniors: Ms Rachel Peachey

Age Range. 3 months – 18 years.

Number of Pupils. 190 including 74 boarders.

Fees per term (2021–2022). Day (Reception–Year 13): £1,545–£3,940; Full Boarding: £6,930–£9,270; Weekly Boarding: £6,100–£8,160.

Moorland School is a thriving co-educational day and boarding school located in the historic town of Clitheroe within the picturesque Ribble Valley, in the North-West of England. The school enjoys excellent transport links to Manchester. We have an outstandingly beautiful site with more than 15 acres of grounds. Nearly half of the children at Moorland are boarders and we find it makes for a good social mix with our day pupils from the surrounding area. The opening of our purpose-built new building means our boarders can enjoy modern and spacious facilities, fully equipped with satellite television and Wi-Fi. Moorland can now offer the seamless transition from GCSE to A Level or BTEC study, through our thriving new Sixth Form Centre, which provides our students with the opportunity to settle in one place rather than having to move from school to school.

Furthermore, the School boasts an outstanding elite football and elite ballet, unique to any British boarding school. These courses are led by field professionals in their respective areas.

Admission to Moorland. Parents and children are encouraged to visit the school to meet the Headteacher and see the school in action. Boarding or Day children are also welcome to attend Moorland for a one or two day 'taster visit'.

Kindergarten & Nursery. As well as having its own indoor soft-play area, the nursery also has a large outdoor play area within its extensive grounds, with unbroken views over Waddington Fell. The Nursery's superb layout of colourful rooms and equipment make it an ideal and exceptional learning environment.

Junior School. The Preparatory Department takes children between the ages of 4 and 11. The children have their own play area and IT suite and benefit from using the facilities of the Senior School such as science laboratories and sports hall.

The children follow Key Stages 1 and 2 of the National Curriculum with particular emphasis on numeracy and literacy. Our small class sizes allow every child to read to the Teacher on a daily basis. French is also included in the Junior curriculum.

The Senior School follows the criteria set down in the National Curriculum. We enter our pupils for the Standard Attainment Tests and for GCSE at the end of Key stage 4.

Football at Moorland. Our FA approved coach, Charles Jackson, is one of the UK's most innovative and well-respected football coaches. He teaches to a Premier League standard. He has worked at Moorland since November 2002. He also worked at the Manchester United Advanced Coaching Centre up to July 2005 and is now the Under 14 academy technical skills Development Coach at Manchester City FC. Mr Jackson is a full-time teacher at Moorland School, teaching children from age 4–18.

Pastoral Care. At Moorland children benefit from continuous pastoral support within a friendly family environment. By day, teaching staff provide continual support within small classes. Evening and weekend care is undertaken by the House Parent team.

More House School

Frensham, Farnham, Surrey GU10 3AP

Tel:	01252 792303
	Admissions: 01252 797600
email:	schooloffice@morehouseschool.co.uk
website:	www.morehouseschool.co.uk
Twitter:	@MHSFrensham
Facebook:	@morehouseschoolfrensham
Instagram:	@morehouseschoolfrensham
LinkedIn:	/more-house-school-frensham

Headmaster: **Mr Jonathan Hetherington**, BA Hons, MSc Ed QTS

Age Range. 8 to 18.

Number in School. 493: 80 Boarders, 413 Day Boys.

Fees per term (2021–2022). Full Boarding £8,460–£10,369; Weekly Boarding £8,460–£9,573; Day £4,753–£6,662.

The largest school in the country for intelligent pupils with Dyslexia, Developmental Language Disorders and associated special educational needs.

More House School in Frensham, a registered charity, is rated 'Outstanding' by the government's schools inspectorate, Ofsted, in all aspects of its provision, including School, Sixth Form and Boarding, following an integrated inspection in March 2019 and Boarding and Welfare inspection in March 2020.

The school, for 488 boys aged eight to 18, is nationally recognised as a centre for excellence in supporting pupils with specific learning and language difficulties, and is a training centre in special educational needs for teachers across the region and nationally.

Founded 81 years ago, the school prides itself in using the best modern practice to increase confidence and make children feel valued, happy and to fulfil their potential at GCSE, AS, A Level and other public examinations.

Boarding is run by caring staff and is situated in beautiful grounds with ample opportunities for outdoor pursuits. Our activities programme, which offers 18 options each day, encourages all day boys and boarders to make good use of their leisure time. There is a strong sense of community.

There is an ongoing building programme and the facilities are very good in all departments.

We have a comprehensive information pack, hold 'Discover More House' open days biannually and welcome new enquiries.

Charitable status. More House School is a Registered Charity, number 311872. A Catholic foundation, open to all denominations, helping boys to succeed.

Moyles Court School

Moyles Court, Ringwood, Hampshire BH24 3NF

Tel: 01425 472856
email: sally.spark@moylescourt.co.uk
website: www.moylescourt.co.uk
Facebook: @moylescourt

Headmaster: **Mr Richard Milner-Smith**

Please see school website for full Staff list.

Age Range. 2½–16

Number in School. Boarders: 22 boys, 16 girls. Day: 74 boys, 82 girls.

Fees per term (2021–2022). Senior Day £4,798–£4,885; Senior Boarding £9,240; Junior Day £2,410–£4,368; Junior Boarding £7,420; Nursery: please contact the school for session rates.

Moyles Court School is a non-selective day and boarding co-ed school taking pupils from 3 to 16 years and is housed in a 16th Century Manor house close to Ringwood, set within the beautiful New Forest National Park. It offers individualised learning, affordable fees and traditional core values. The boarding environment at Moyles Court School aims to provide a welcoming and supportive setting where boarders can flourish and develop within a safe and beautiful campus environment. It is an environment in which children grow, where confidence and self-belief are heightened and where values and skills are learnt that will stay with them for the rest of their lives.

In 2021 100% of pupils gained 5 or more GCSE's at Grade 4 and above (including Maths, English and Science), with 99% of all grades being above Grade 4. Over half the grades awarded (51%) were at Grade 7 or above (A and A*), with 32% of all grades reaching either 9 or 8.

We are proud of our academic results, with all our pupils showing that with great effort and determination, from both teacher and pupil alike, they can secure GCSE results way above their national predictions. However, we are also committed to educating the whole child, on the understanding that academic results will only take you so far in life. Sport, music and drama all flourish here and a vast range of extra-curricular activities ensure children are exposed to an exciting range of opportunities that will help shape and develop them as individuals.

In 2016, Moyles Court partnered with Broadway Education, owned by Lymington family Mark and Jo Broadway, in order to further capitalise on Moyles Court's success. The new strategic relationship complements Broadway Education's portfolio of schools.

Small class sizes, individualised learning, great teaching, extensive after-school provision, tailored transport and excellent pastoral care provide your children with the best possible start in life. Parents are welcome to book an appointment at any time to see the school and find out why everyone is talking about Moyles Court School. For further details visit the website at www.moylescourt.co.uk or contact Mrs Sally Spark, Admissions Registrar.

Mylnhurst Preparatory School & Nursery

Button Hill, Woodholm Road, Ecclesall, Sheffield S11 9HJ

Tel: 0114 236 1411
email: enquiries@mylnhurst.co.uk
website: www.mylnhurst.co.uk

A Catholic Foundation Welcoming Families of All Faiths – maximising the potential of your children through partnership within a challenging and supportive Catholic Christian Community.

Headmistress: **Mrs Hannah Cunningham**

Age Range. 3–11 Co-educational.

Number of Pupils. 164.

Fees per term (2021–2022). £3,586.

Situated in extensive private grounds, Mylnhurst provides a state-of-the-art teaching environment supported by our outstanding school facilities, which include a 25m pool, dance studio, sports hall and Apple Mac suite.

With a strong emphasis on school-parent partnership, Mylnhurst embraces your high expectations and ensures each child benefits from an exciting and stimulating curriculum.

Top performing Sheffield School in the Times Top 100.

Be assured of a very warm welcome and the opportunity to work closely with our committed and talented staff. So, whether it be an informal chat or a school open day, we look forward to sharing our vision with you and discussing the exciting future of your children.

Charitable status. Mylnhurst Limited is a Registered Charity, number 1056683.

Northease Manor School

Rodmell, Lewes, East Sussex BN7 3EY

Tel: 01273 472915
email: office@northease.co.uk
          pa2headteacher@northease.co.uk
website: www.northease.co.uk
Twitter: @NortheaseManor
Facebook: @NortheaseManor

Chair of Governors: Julie Toben

Head: **Martyn Ward**

Type of School. Co-educational school.

Age Range. 10–18.

Number of Pupils. 71: 15 Girls, 56 Boys.

Fees per term (2021–2022). Day £7,786

Northease is a special school, but not necessarily the way you would think of one. We're special because our students are really happy, well cared for, known as individuals and nurtured to become more confident and successful than they thought possible.

The education we offer is special too, not just because of our highly qualified and experienced staff that truly understand your child, but because we combine academic study with a wide range of extra-curricular opportunities that bring out the best in everyone.

We are located in the beautiful Sussex countryside in a spacious 18th-century manor house that gives everyone space to grow and develop.

What do we offer? We're a co-educational Independent school for students primarily with autism and/or dyslexia. With specialist staff and resources, we offer high quality teaching, fully integrated occupational and speech and language therapy supported by our high quality pastoral support.

We are a registered charity, which means we do not have commercial owners We are DfE approved to accept students with local authority funding, if available, and because of our charitable status we are able to offer affordable fees for those who are self-funding.

Charitable status. Northease Manor School Trust Ltd is a Registered Charity, number 307005. It exists for the provision of high-quality education for pupils with Specific Learning Difficulties.

Notre Dame Preparatory School

147 Dereham Road, Norwich, Norfolk NR2 3TA

Tel: 01603 625593
email: headspa@notredameprepschool.co.uk
website: www.notredameprepschool.co.uk
Facebook: @notredameprepnorwich

Chairman of Governors: Mr Richard Bailey

Headmaster: **Mr Rob Thornton**, MA Ed

Age Range. 2–11 Co-educational.

Number of Pupils. 170 Day.

Fees per term (2021–2022). £2,140–£2,310.

Notre Dame Prep School was originally founded by the Sisters of Notre Dame de Namur in 1864. The school transferred to its present site in 1971 and is now a Company with charitable status. The school maintains the traditions and the spirit of the Sisters of Notre Dame and the former name and ethos.

As a Catholic school we endeavour to nurture a love of God through Jesus Christ in all the children. The school has an ethos of love and care and embraces children of all faiths or none.

Children are treated as individuals, respected, nurtured and encouraged to embrace and fulfil their potential in all areas of school life. We have excellent links with High Schools in both the maintained and independent sectors.

The school achieves well above-average results in external tests and has a strong academic reputation. Children are prepared for entry to selective independent schools on request. Subjects include English, Maths, Science, Computing, Design and Technology, Art, Geography, PE, History, Music, RE, French and Personal, Social and Health Education.

The school has a very strong musical tradition and has a wide range of extra-curricular musical activities on offer including Choir, Chamber Choir, Recorder, Piano, Guitar, Flute, Violin, Saxophone, Clarinet lessons, Drums and Singing.

Sports include Football, Cricket, Rugby, Netball, Rounders, Hockey, Tennis and Swimming.

The school offers a wide range of extra-curricular activities including Speech and Drama, Chess, Cookery, Debating, Photography, Arts and Crafts, Science, Sewing, Young Explorers, Creative Writing, Badminton and other sports and activities.

Catering is provided in house and lunches and dinners are excellent. We have an After-School Activities Club which runs until 6.00pm incorporating homework club (Prep) and games activities for younger children. Holiday clubs are available in school holidays at agreed times.

Charitable status. Notre Dame Preparatory School (Norwich) Limited is a Registered Charity, number 269003.

Oakfield Preparatory School

125–128 Thurlow Park Road, West Dulwich, London SE21 8HP

Tel: 020 8670 4206
email: admissions@oakfield.dulwich.sch.uk
website: www.oakfield.dulwich.sch.uk
Twitter: @oakfieldprep
Facebook: @OakfieldPrep
Instagram: @oakfieldprep

Head: **Mrs Moyra Thompson**, MA Cantab, PGCE, NPQH

Age Range. 2–11
Number in School. 163 Boys, 149 Girls.
Fees per term (2021–2022). Years 1–6: £4,778 including lunch. Fees for Early Years Foundation Stage fees based on chosen sessions and Early Years funding where applicable.

Oakfield is a nurturing, diverse co-educational prep school, founded in 1887 in the heart of Dulwich, which blends a modern curriculum with strong pastoral values. It is committed to supporting every child to be the absolute best that they can be and helping them find the right senior school for them at 11+.

The school site of nearly three acres allows plenty of space for play and games and we enjoy strong regional and national success in both sport and drama. We offer specialist teaching in Spanish, music and art and have taught philosophy for children for many years.

We offer full wraparound care and there are more than 40 after-school clubs available to children in Upper Foundation and above. These include Mandarin, Karate, Music Tech and Fencing among many others.

We are a non-selective school but we conduct observations to ensure Oakfield will be the best environment for your child. Entry to the 2+ Nursery is by observation. Once accepted, the child will progress automatically into the Foundation Years (subject to the admissions policy) and Main School. Entry at 3+ and 4+ is also by observation. Entry at 7+ follows an assessment and observation in a class setting.

Prospective parents – and children – would be very welcome to join one of our Open Mornings or arrange a private tour with our registrar.

Oakhyrst Grange School

160 Stanstead Road, Caterham, Surrey CR3 6AF

Tel: 01883 343344
email: office@oakhyrstgrangeschool.co.uk
website: www.oakhyrstgrangeschool.co.uk

Chairman of Board of Management: Mrs Brenda Davis

Headmaster: **Mr Alex Gear**, BEd

Age Range. 4–11.
Number in School. 152 Day Boys and Girls.
Fees per term (2021–2022). £1,472–£3,414

Oakhyrst Grange School is an independent, co-educational preparatory day school for boys and girls between 4 and 11 years.

The School was established in 1950 and moved to its present premises in Stanstead Road in 1957. Since September 1973 the School has been administered by a non-profit making trust.

Standing in five acres of open country and woodland and surrounded by the Green Belt, the School enjoys a fine position amongst the Surrey Hills.

The school has a wide and imaginative curriculum, which includes traditional teaching combined with innovative ideas. Small class sizes, with a maximum of 20 pupils, and an excellent teacher to pupil ratio enable pupils to work at their own rate and capabilities whilst being encouraged to meet new challenges.

Our pupils secure the offer of places at prominent senior schools, including scholarships and awards across the range of academic, all-rounder, music, sports and art.

There are many sporting opportunities offered and particularly high standards have been reached in cross-country, swimming, football, judo and athletics where ISA National level has been achieved. The pupils compete in many inter house, inter school and area competitions. The school also has its own heated indoor swimming pool, all-weather floodlit multi-use games area, tennis, netball, hockey and 5-a-side court, sports pitch, cross-country course and gymnasium.

Extra-curricular music lessons are offered and much music making also takes place as part of the normal school timetable. The school has an orchestra in addition to clarinet, flute, guitar, saxophone, violin and trumpet ensembles and a choir, all of whom perform regularly.

In addition to the curriculum the pupils can enjoy an extensive range of clubs and activities throughout the week. At Oakhyrst Grange School we are very proud of our Forest School status. A senior leader is fully trained in Forest School Activities and it is an integral part of our Year 3 curriculum and whole school extra-curricular activities.

Academic excellence is encouraged, every child is expected to attain his or her individual potential. The School helps children to develop into caring, thoughtful and confident adults.

Charitable status. Oakhyrst Grange School Educational Trust is a Registered Charity, number 325043. It exists to provide an all-round education, to give the children success and the best possible start.

Park School

Queens Park South Drive, Bournemouth BH8 9BJ

Tel: 01202 396640
email: office@parkschool.co.uk
website: www.parkschool.co.uk
Facebook: @ParkSchoolIndependant

Headteacher: **Mrs Melanie Dowler**, BSc Hons, PGCE

Age Range. 6 months to 11 years.
Number in School. Day: 204 Boys, 179 Girls.

Fees per term (2021–2022). £2,690–£3,275.

Park School is a thriving co-educational junior day school in a pleasant residential area near Bournemouth town centre. Our last full ISI inspection in June 2015 awarded us 'Excellent' across all areas of the School and EYFS and we passed the ISI Compliance Inspection in May 2018 with flying colours.

Pupils are taught in small classes in a caring, happy environment. The school is geared principally towards academic achievement, with an emphasis on nurturing individual progress. At the heart of all we do is the belief that children will achieve their best when they are happy. We foster a positive ethos and the development of the all-round child. This covers not only work in the classroom, but all other aspects of school life: games, music, the arts and other activities. Sport is an important part of Park School life and we use our stunning facility at Dean Park for games lessons and sports fixtures.

Pupils are prepared for entry to Senior Independent Schools and Bournemouth and Poole Grammar Schools through tests at 11+ years. Many children gain scholarships to Senior Independent Schools.

Most pupils join us in the Nursery and Reception years but there are occasionally vacancies further up the School. An offer of a place is made only after prospective pupils have been assessed.

Park School Nursery is open between 8.00am and 6.00pm Monday to Friday all year round with the exception of Christmas week and Bank Holidays.

Park School for Girls (Seniors) & Park School Prep (Co-Ed)

20–22 Park Avenue, Ilford, Essex IG1 4RS

Tel: Office: 020 8554 2466
email: admin@parkschool.org.uk
website: www.parkschool.org.uk
Facebook: @ParkSchoolWay

Head Teacher: **Mrs Catherine Redfern**, BA Hons, MA Ed

Age Range. 4–16.

Number in School. 150 Day Girls & Boys.

Fees per term (2021–2022). Reception £2,618; Pre-Prep £2,883 (Years 1/2); Prep School £3,032 (Years 3/4), £3,114 (Years 5/6). Senior School: Years 7–9 £3,914; Years 10–11 £3,946.

Our basic aim is to provide a full educational programme leading to recognised external examinations at the age of 16. We are consistently one of the top performing schools for GCSE in the London Borough of Redbridge. Our Prep School provides a broad and balanced education and pupils are well prepared to sit entrance exams at Year 6, including those for Independent and Grammar Schools.

We create a caring, well-ordered atmosphere and our pupils are encouraged to achieve their full academic and social potential. The well-qualified staff and the policy of small classes produce well above the national average GCSE results. Whilst we do not offer a Sixth Form, our pupils generally secure a place at their first-choice school, in either Independent, Grammar or State Schools.

Much emphasis is also placed on the development of each child as a whole person. We expect every pupil to strive for self-confidence in their ability to use his or her talents to the full and to respect individuality. Pupils are encouraged to make decisions and to accept responsibility for their own actions. The poise that comes from good manners and correct speech, we consider to be highly important. Honesty, reliability, courtesy, kindness and consideration for others are prime factors that we value highly.

We welcome visits from prospective parents at any time, in addition to our scheduled Open Days. Our Admissions Officer can be contacted on admin@parkschool.org.uk to arrange appointments. The Head Teacher will always be available to meet with prospective parents on any pre-arranged tours.

Charitable status. Park School for Girls is a Registered Charity, number 269936. It exists to provide a caring environment in which we develop our pupils' potential to the full.

Prenton Preparatory School

Mount Pleasant, Oxton, Wirral CH43 5SY

Tel: 0151 652 3182
email: enquiry@prentonprep.co.uk
website: www.prentonprep.co.uk
Twitter: @prentonprep
Facebook: @prenton.prep

Directors: Mr M J and Mrs N M Aloé

Headteacher: **Mr M T R Jones**

Deputy Headteacher: Miss J Orme

SENCo: Ms P Suchdev

Age Range. 2½–11.

Number in School. Day: 70 Boys, 56 Girls.

Fees per term (2021–2022). From £890 part-time in Foundation Stage (with free places available for up to 30 hours) to £3,220 (Juniors)

Founded in 1935.

Prenton Preparatory School is co-educational day school for children aged 2½–11 years, situated about a mile from Junction 3 of the M53.

The building is a large Victorian house which has been carefully converted into the uses of a school. There is a large playground and gardens. Facilities include an ICT/Science block and an Art block. The Foundation Stage outdoor play area is also a valuable addition to the school.

The children benefit from small classes and individual attention in a holistic approach to their education within a disciplined environment which enables them to realise their full potential.

The school offers a wide range of academic subjects with emphasis on the three main National Curriculum core subjects: English, Mathematics and Science. French is taught from an early age and swimming forms a regular part of the curriculum from Year 1 upwards.

Children are prepared for entrance examinations to county, independent and grant-maintained grammar schools, gaining well above-average pass rates.

Child care facilities are available from 8.00am to 6.00pm. Clubs are provided at lunchtime and after school. They include football, cricket, computers and technology, karate, swimming, dance, netball, music group, speech & drama and musical instruments.

The school has a wide range of sporting teams that compete in local and regional fixtures and competitions. These include: swimming, water polo, cross-country, football, netball, cricket, rounders and athletics. Several of these teams have been successful enough to qualify for National tournaments in recent years.

Art, drama, dance and music also play an important part in school life and parents and members of the wider school community enjoy the regular performances that are part of the annual calendar.

Priory School

Sir Harry's Road, Edgbaston, Birmingham B15 2UR

Tel: 0121 440 4103
email: enquiries@prioryschool.net
website: www.prioryschool.net
Twitter: @PrioryEdgbaston
Facebook: @prioryschooledgbaston

Chair of Governors: Ms Heather Somerfield

Headmaster: **Mr Jonathan Cramb**, BA Hons, PGCE, MEd

Age Range. 6 months to 18 years.
Number in School. 388.
Fees per term (2021–2022). £1,737–£5,285.

The school, founded on its present site in 1936 by the Sisters of the Society of the Holy Child Jesus, stands in 17 acres of parkland in the pleasant suburb of Edgbaston, only 2 miles from the centre of Birmingham. The school has extensive playing fields, excellent AstroTurf tennis courts, a multi-gym, athletics facilities and football and cricket pitches. There are minibuses running to and from school and frequent bus services to all parts of the city.

The school has an excellent Early Years Department on site which offers care for 51 weeks per annum and accepts children from the age of 6 months. All pupils are able to remain in After Care until 6.00pm if preferred.

The school has a diverse, inclusive pupil community and instils core Catholic values and attitudes into everyday school life, but welcomes children of all faiths and none. Pupils are taught by specialist teachers from the age of 9 and in the Senior School the curriculum is broad and balanced with pupils benefiting from small class sizes and individual attention, enabling them to make excellent progress in their academic development.

The school, whilst remaining proudly multi-ability, is justly proud of the academic achievements of the pupils. A wide range of subjects is available for GCSE and A Level, with good facilities, including well-equipped science laboratories, language resources rooms, Information

Technology facilities, sports centre, multi-gym and performing arts Suite. The new Mayfield building opened in 2019, housing six new Preparatory classrooms, it marks the initial stage of a five-year development programme.

Priory School aims to develop the whole child, so that as well as achieving academic excellence, its pupil grow into confident, articulate, well-rounded individuals.

Entry to the school is by interview, assessment and day visit. Scholarships are awarded at 11+. Means tested bursaries may be awarded in cases of financial need.

Parents are warmly welcomed into the school to discuss individual needs. Full details prior to the visit may be obtained from the Admissions Registrar.

Charitable status. Priory School is a Registered Charity, number 518009.

Queen Ethelburga's Collegiate

Thorpe Underwood, York YO26 9SS

Tel: 01423 333330
email: admissions@qe.org
website: www.qe.org
Twitter: @qethelburgas
Facebook: @queenethelburgas
LinkedIn: /queen-ethelburga's-college

Motto: *To be the best that I can with the gifts that I have.*

Co-educational Day and Boarding School.

Principal: **Dan Machin**

Age Range. 3 months–19 years.
Number of Pupils. 1,400.
Fees per term (2021–2022). Day: £1,454–£6,169; Boarding: £11,214–£14,012 (UK students), £13,850–£17,456 (International students).

Set in more than 220 acres of beautiful North Yorkshire countryside, Queen Ethelburga's has provided students with a vibrant and supportive school community since 1912.

Queen Ethelburga's is an Excellent rated Collegiate (ISI 2019). We are known locally, nationally, and internationally as a group of four schools that promotes the highest standards in all that it does. The Collegiate welcomes girls and boys from 3 months and supports them through four schools – Chapter House (3 months to Year 5), King's Magna (Year 6 to 9), The College and The Faculty (both Year 10 to 13).

This unique make up of four smaller schools is designed to maintain a nurturing family atmosphere and some individuality, each having their own Heads and Staff teams. This allows the staff to know students thoroughly and form outstanding student teacher relationships based on mutual respect and unwavering support. QE's Hill Standard is 'To be the best that I can with the gifts that I have' providing every child with a springboard to their individual successes, whichever pathway they choose. We place great emphasis on our children growing into resilient, caring, compassionate and confident adults, who develop independence and initiative, and who can take responsibility for their own learning and futures.

Our exam results speak for themselves, consistently ranking us amongst the top day and boarding schools in the UK, with students benefiting from incredible study, boarding and leisure facilities as part of campus life.

In 2021, students in The College achieved 85% A*/A at A Level (96% A*/B), with students in The Faculty achieving 77% A*/A (92% A*/B). The percentage of D*/D grades in The Faculty was 75%.

Alongside academic success, at Queen Ethelburga's Collegiate (QE) we aim to provide a holistic education which supports students to develop their knowledge, skills, and experience beyond the classroom. We provide a broad enrichment curriculum to ensure students become well-rounded individuals, gaining skills in leadership and teamwork, as well as developing self-confidence and self-awareness, respect for others, and their environment.

Care is the most important element within the QE community; every member of the Collegiate, staff and student, is responsible for the pastoral care and happiness of the site. QE offers support and guidance to all students and parents to ensure that we are all working to support individual student needs and equipping them with the right skills, not only to be successful in education, but to excel in their chosen career and life in general. Our dedicated THRIVE@QR programme offers all students a huge range of activities to support their positive mental health and wellbeing.

Our reputation has grown considerably over recent years, and we believe this is due to our drive to ensure that our outcomes for QE students, across all areas of their endeavour and aspiration, match those of the world's best schools.

Radnor House Sevenoaks School

Combe Bank Drive, Sundridge, Kent TN14 6AE

Tel:	Senior School 01959 563720
	Preparatory School 01959 564320
email:	admissions@radnor-sevenoaks.org
website:	www.radnor-sevenoaks.org
Twitter:	@radnorsevenoaks
Facebook:	@radnorsevenoaks

Chairman of Board of Directors: Mr Colin Diggory, BSc Hons, PGCE, MA, EdD, CMath, FIMA, FRSA

Head: **Mr Fraser Halliwell**, BSc Hons, PGCE, MEd, FRSA

Head of Senior School: Mr George Penlington, BA, DipT

Head of Prep School: Dr Emma Margrett, BA Hons, MA, EdD, CCRS, FCCT

Radnor House Sevenoaks is an independent school with entry from the term that pupils are aged 2 up to the age of 18. (*See also Preparatory School entry in IAPS section.*) In September 2014 the school became co-educational and in 2016 the school name was changed from Combe Bank to Radnor House Sevenoaks.

Aims and Ethos. As the world becomes more complex, diverse and fast paced, the school's mission is to future proof their pupils to give them the very best start in life.

Academic qualifications are an important aspect of this but so too are interpersonal skills such as emotional intelligence and leadership. Underpinning their approach to education is a set of core values – excellence, respect, courage and perseverance – which form the bedrock of the school and provide a moral compass for children from school through to adulthood. Pupil happiness is their first priority, as a happy child is one who will thrive, grasp opportunities to learn and develop and will become a confident and well-balanced young person. A focus of Radnor House is to be a pioneer in preparing the children for the digital age by working with Microsoft to become one of their flagship schools as they aim to build adults who can thrive in the world of tomorrow by using technology to propel their learning forward.

Location. Situated in a Palladian Mansion and set in superb grounds with 28 acres of parkland just outside Sevenoaks, the school has excellent facilities. The Nursery, Prep School, Senior School and Sixth Form are on the same site and there are many positive links between them, so that all pupils have guaranteed access through the school until they leave at 18.

Curriculum. A modern and broad range of subjects is taught at all age levels. English, Mathematics, Sciences and an MFL are compulsory at GCSE. Pupils can then choose from Art, Computer Science, Drama, Economics, English Literature, RE, Geography, History, Mathematics, iMedia, Business, Modern Languages, Music, PE, Politics, Psychology and Science Sociology and Photography subjects at A Level. The school boasts a strong Art department with an innovative graphic design suite, alongside a popular Music Department with regular exhibitions and musical performances in which wide participation is achieved. Radnor House Sevenoaks has a well-earned reputation for competitive success in a wide range of sports. Swimming in the 25-metre indoor pool is a particularly popular activity from Nursery through to Sixth Form. Outdoor Adventurous Education has taken a firm place on the curriculum in the form of Forest School and Bush Craft for the Prep school, with adventure weekends and DofE expeditions in the senior school.

Admission. Children enter the Prep school in Nursery and Reception. For the Senior School, pupils take the School's entrance examination at 11+ and 13+ Good passes at GCSE are also expected for the A Level subjects of choice in order to join the Sixth Form for external candidates.

Transport. Coach transport is organized for 5 significant routes, to be paid for on a termly basis.

Fees per term (2021–2022). Senior School £6,350–£6,850 (Lunch £320); Preparatory School £3,990–£5,150 (Lunch £265); Nursery: £1,140 for 3 sessions per week and Transition: £1,900 with an additional session being £380 (includes lunch).

Scholarships. Radnor House Sevenoaks offers a range of Academic, Art, Drama, Music, Sport and All-Rounder scholarships for entry into Year 7, Year 9 and the Sixth Form.

Scholarships are typically worth 10% of the annual tuition fee but may, in exceptional circumstances, be increased through the award of an Outstanding Scholarship which is entirely at the Head's discretion. In addition, means-tested bursaries worth up to 50% of the tuition fee, are also available but only after a scholarship has been awarded.

Rochester Independent College

254 St Margaret's Banks, Rochester, Kent ME1 1HY

Tel:　　　01634 828115
email:　　admissions@rochester-college.org
website:　www.rochester-college.org
Twitter:　@rochesterindcol
Facebook:　@RochesterIndependentCollege
Instagram:　@rochesterindcollege
LinkedIn:　/school/rochester-college

Principal: **Alistair Brownlow**, MA Hons St Andrews, MPhil Glasgow, MEd Buckingham

Vice Principals:

Kelly Flatman, BA Hons Leeds (Graphic Design)

Ian Pay, BA Hons, MA Lancaster (History, Politics)

Age Range. 11–19 Co-educational.

Number of Pupils. 345 (including 100 single room boarding places).

Fees per annum (2021–2022). Tuition: £13.900–£21,750. Weekly Boarding £13,500; Full Boarding: £13,500–£15,500.

Rochester Independent College is an alternative to conventional secondary education with a happily distinctive ethos. Accepting day students from the age of 11 and boarders from 15, the focus is on examination success in a lively, supportive and informal atmosphere. Students are encouraged to be themselves and achieve exam results that often exceed their expectations. There is no uniform, no bells ring and everybody is on first-name terms. The average class size is 8.

Students enjoy being here and are treated as young adults. We encourage them to search for their own answers, to voice their opinions, to think critically, creatively and independently. They leave not only with excellent examination results but with enthusiasm for the future and new confidence about themselves and their education.

Personal Tutors work closely with students on all courses to give advice about course combinations and help students to ensure that their courses are designed to meet the requirements of university entrance. With such small class sizes individual attention is not only available, it's practically inescapable.

The College has particular academic strengths in the Sciences, Mathematics, English Literature, Social Sciences and the Creative and Visual Arts including Film, Photography and Media.

The College's reputation for academic excellence is founded on over 35 years' experience of rigorous teaching. Students come to us for a variety of reasons and from many different backgrounds. We are not academically selective; our only entrance qualification is an honest determination to work hard. Our results however are always ranked among the best of the academically selective and students secure places at top universities. Direct entry into any year group is possible and the College also offers intensive one year GCSE and A Level courses as well as retake programmes. International students benefit from specialised English Language teaching support.

Rochester Independent College is the winner of the Independent Schools Association 2021 award for Excellence and Innovation in Fine Arts. The judges were impressed with the huge range of ways in which the College values, promotes and gives profile to the arts and considered the College an inspiration to the whole sector. The link between an aesthetic appreciation of the visual arts and personal development runs through all aspects of school life and is highly valued by the whole school community.

The College Halls combine the informality of a university residence with the supervision and pastoral support appropriate for young adults. The College offers students the opportunity to thrive in an atmosphere of managed independence and acts as a stepping stone between school and university. All accommodation is on campus and in single rooms.

Rochester Independent College is part of the Dukes Education Group.

Rookwood School

Weyhill Road, Andover, Hampshire SP10 3AL

Tel:　　　01264 325900
email:　　office@rookwoodschool.org
website:　www.rookwoodschool.org
Twitter:　@rookwood_school
Facebook:　@rookwoodschool

Headmaster: **Mr A Kirk-Burgess**, BSc, PGCE, MSc Oxon

Deputy Head: Mr R Hick, MA QTS

Head of Senior School: Mrs E Hacker, BA Hons

Head of Lower School: Mrs L Wowk, BA, PGCE

Age Range. Co-educational 2–18 with boarders from age 7.

Number in School. 283: 145 girls, 138 boys (EYFS 50).

Fees per term (2021–2022). Boarding: £7,180–£9,880. Day: £3,420–£5,725. Nursery: £5.60 per hour (Early Years Education Funding accepted). Flexi and occasional boarding also available.

Hailed by the ISI as an "outstandingly happy and successful school", Rookwood is an independent non-selective day and boarding school for girls and boys aged 2–18 years in Andover, Hampshire.

Described as "warm, welcoming and nurturing", Rookwood is known for its family atmosphere and strong pastoral care which encourages each and every child to achieve their very best with excellent results. In 2021 53% of all GCSEs were awarded at Grade 7 or above and 100% of our students achieved GCSEs in both English and Maths at Grade 4 or above.

Set in almost ten acres of private grounds Rookwood has an impressive range of amenities including a state-of-the-art sports hall, outdoor swimming pool, excellent art and science facilities. Rookwood's Private Sixth Form opened in September 2021.

Both Music and Drama thrive at Rookwood, with every child encouraged to take part, whilst the Physical Education department is equally busy with several pupils advancing to represent their favourite sports at national level in recent years.

In addition to its many tangible achievements Rookwood is committed to delivering excellent pastoral care and takes great pride in seeing its pupils develop into confident, resilient and principled young adults. The School also offers a rich and varied programme of extra-curricular activities for all ages and interests giving pupils the opportunity to develop new skills, discover new passions, grow socially and emotionally and to simply enjoy themselves.

Rookwood's boarding provision was recently rated as 'excellent' in all areas by the ISI with boarders receiving a unique 'home-from-home' experience. Family-style meal times, experienced and supportive boarding staff and busy weekends all combine to ensure that Rookwood's boarders receive the best possible care.

Prospective pupils and their parents are warmly invited to visit the school (please see website for latest information). Alternatively, if you require any further information or would like to make an individual appointment, please do not hesitate to contact the Registrar directly on 01264 325910.

Admission is by school reports and individual visits. Scholarships are available at 11+, 13+ and 16+. Means-tested bursaries are available throughout the school.

Rookwood is conveniently situated close to Andover town centre and less than 10 minutes' walk to Andover railway station, with good services to Salisbury, Basingstoke and London Waterloo. By road, there is easy access from the A303 and A343, with the journey from Andover to London taking about one and a half hours. School bus services are also available from Newbury and North West Hampshire.

Charitable status. Rookwood School is a Registered Charity, number 307322. It exists to provide education for children.

Sacred Heart School

Mayfield Lane, Durgates, Wadhurst, East Sussex TN5 6DQ

Tel: 01892 783414
email: admin@sacredheartwadhurst.org.uk
website: www.sacredheartwadhurst.org.uk

Chair of Governors: Mr Geoff Hughes

Head Teacher: **Mrs Johanna Collyer**, MA, NPQSL, PGCE

Age Range. 2–11 Co-educational.

Number of Pupils. 120.

Fees per term (2021–2022). £2,940

Sacred Heart School is a small independent Catholic primary school and Nursery, nestling in the heart of the Sussex countryside.

We welcome boys and girls from 2–11 and with pupil numbers around 140 we have the opportunity to know each child individually, to recognise and encourage their strengths and support them in overcoming areas of difficulty.

Our pupils enjoy a high degree of academic success, regularly obtaining places at their first choice of school, including passes at 11+ and Scholarships.

Courtesy and care for each other are important values nurtured at Sacred Heart School where children play and work well together.

Charitable status. Sacred Heart School, as part of the Arundel and Brighton Diocesan Trust, is a Registered Charity, number 252878.

St Anne's Preparatory School

154 New London Road, Chelmsford, Essex CM2 0AW

Tel: 01245 353488
email: admin@stannesprep.essex.sch.uk
website: stannesprep.co.uk
Twitter: @StAnnesPrep1925
Facebook: @stannespreparatory1925

Head Teacher: **Mrs V Eveleigh**

Proprietor: Mrs S Robson

DSL & Pastoral Lead: Miss L Emmerson

Age Range. 3–11.

Number of Children. 124.

Fees per term (2021–2022). £2,900–£3,050.

Recently ranked 12th nationally in *The Sunday Times* Parent Power Survey, St Anne's is a co-educational day school, with its own excellent nursery facility. Established in 1925, the school is conveniently situated in the centre of Chelmsford. The building is a large Victorian house, which has been carefully converted into the uses of a school. Extensive lawned areas, AstroTurf, playground and Nursery play area provide ample space for both recreation and games lessons. In addition, older pupils benefit from the use of the excellent sports facilities at the nearby Essex County Cricket Club.

The children benefit from small classes and individual attention in a disciplined but happy environment, which enables them to realise their full potential. Provision is made in the school for the gifted as well as those pupils less educationally able. Classrooms are bright and well equipped and the teachers are chosen for their qualifications, experience and understanding of the needs of their pupils.

St Anne's combines modern teaching with the best of traditional values. The school maintains a high standard of academic education giving great emphasis to a secure foundation in the basic subjects whilst offering a wide curriculum with specialist teaching in many areas.

Examination results at both KS1 and KS2 levels are excellent and many pupils gain places at the prestigious Grammar and Independent schools in the county.

The school offers a wide range of extra-curricular activities and an excellent after-care facility is available for all age groups. St Anne's is rightly recognised for its friendly and supportive ethos. Parents are particularly supportive of all aspects of school life. Visitors are always welcome.

St Christopher's School

6 Downs Road, Epsom, Surrey KT18 5HE

Tel: 01372 721807
email: office@st-christophers.surrey.sch.uk
website: www.st-christophers.surrey.sch.uk
Twitter: @StChrisEpsom
Facebook: @StChrisEpsom

Headteacher: **Mrs A C Thackray**, MA, BA, Dip Mus

Age Range. 3–7.

Number in School. 190.

Fees per term (2021–2022). £3,730 (Full time including lunch), £1,890 (5 mornings).

St Christopher's School (founded in 1938) is a co-educational, non-denominational, Nursery and Pre-Prep for children from 2¾ to 7 years of age. Set half way between Epsom Town and Downs in a quiet residential area it has attractive, secure grounds and a generous Nursery setting. As confirmed in a recent ISI inspection, St Christopher's is successful in their aim to offer the best possible start to their pupils who are subsequently well-prepared for a variety of Surrey and London schools enjoying a significant first choice pass rate for 7+ assessments.

St Christopher's has an award winning website and was shortlisted twice for two further awards in 2020. The school enjoys the support of an active parents association, that organises a wide variety of social and fundraising events.

Breakfast Club opens at 7.45 am and After School Care is available until 6 pm. There are also a rich range of after school clubs available.

For further information please visit the Website www.st-christophers.surrey.sch.uk or Twitter @StChrisEpsom. Parents are welcome to visit the school by appointment with the Headteacher.

Charitable Status. St Christopher's School Trust (Epsom) Limited is a Registered Charity, number 312045. It aims to provide a Nursery and Pre-Preparatory education in Epsom and district.

St Christopher's School

71 Wembley Park Drive, Wembley Park, Middlesex HA9 8HE

Tel: 020 8902 5069
email: admin@stchristophersschool.org.uk
website: www.stchristophersschool.org.uk
Twitter: @StChrisPrep
Facebook: @St-Christopher-School-104683814794567
Instagram: @stchristophersprepschool
LinkedIn: /company/stchristophersschool

Head: **Mr Jonathan Coke**

Age Range. 2–11.

Number in School. 36 Boys, 47 Girls.

Fees per term (2021–2022). £3,170–£3,485. Advance payment and Sibling discounts available.

Entry requirements: Interview and Assessment.

St Christopher's School, a large Victorian building on Wembley Park Drive, offers a caring family atmosphere coupled with an equal emphasis on good manners, enthusiastic endeavour and academic excellence. The School, originally a Christian foundation dating from 1928, welcomes children of all faiths and cultures.

Caring and supportive staff provide a well-structured, disciplined and stimulating environment in which children are nurtured and encouraged to develop the necessary skills – academic, social and cultural – so that when they leave us at the age of 11 they can be certain of future success. All children at St Christopher's are equal and we emphasise the qualities of equality, justice and compassion. Children benefit from a curriculum that offers both breadth and depth, an activity programme that teaches skills and develops talents, and a pastoral programme that develops social responsibility.

The full range of academic subjects is taught based on an enriched National Curriculum. Sports and Music are seen as central elements in school life with sports matches, regular concerts and an annual carol service. In addition there is a variety of clubs and activities both at lunchtime and after school; these include Arts & Crafts Club, Book Club, Booster Club, Choir, STEM, Football, Multi Sports, French Club, Supervised Study, Latin Club and Recorders.

Children are prepared for the full range of examinations at 11 years. Historically leavers have gained entry to a wide range of excellent schools including Haberdashers' Aske's Boys' and Girls' Schools, Merchant Taylors', Northwood College, St Helen's, North London Collegiate, Henrietta Barnett, Queen Elizabeth's Boys' School, City of London Boys and Girls, UCS, Aldenham, John Lyon, St Paul's Girls' School and South Hampstead High.

St Christopher's offers both Morning and After School Care, from 8.00am until 6.00pm.

Please phone for an appointment to view the school. We look forward to welcoming you.

St Clare's, Oxford

139 Banbury Road, Oxford OX2 7AL

Tel: 01865 552031
email: admissions@stclares.ac.uk
   reception139@stclares.ac.uk
website: https://stclares.ac.uk
Twitter: @StClaresOxford
Facebook: @stclaresoxford
Instagram: @stclaresoxford

Principal: **Mr Andrew Rattue**, MA Oxon, MA London, PGCE London

Vice Principal Pastoral: Elena Hesse, MSc, PaedDr, ACIPD, CELTA

Vice Principal Academic: Alastair Summers, BSc, PGCE Edinburgh

Age Range. 14–19 Co-educational.

Number of Students. 280

Fees per annum (2021–2022). Boarding £42,626, Day £20,480.

Established in 1953, St Clare's is an Oxford-based international school with the mission "to advance international education and understanding". We embrace internationalism and academic excellence as core values. St Clare's is a co-educational day and boarding school which has been offering the International Baccalaureate Diploma for over 40 years, longer than any other school or college in England.

Students regularly achieve the maximum 45 points, achieved by only 0.2% of candidates worldwide and a quarter achieve scores high than 40 points, placing them in the elite top 5% globally.

Students from over 40 countries study at St Clare's with a core group of British students. The caring atmosphere is informal, positive and friendly with an equal emphasis on hard work, tolerance and developing personal responsibility. Each student is paired with a personal tutor who oversees their welfare and progress and is the first point of contact for parents.

St Clare's has an especially wide range of IB Diploma subjects on offer at Higher and Standard level and, in addition, currently teaches 25 different languages.

For students not yet ready to begin the IB Diploma, the college also offers a one-year Pre-IB course which includes 2 iGCSE's in Maths and English, and a two-year Middle School Programme for students ages 14–16 years old which contains elements of the IB Middle Years Programme (MYP), with the opportunity to gain 5 iGCSE's in Maths, English and the Sciences.

As part of the Creativity, Activity, Service requirements of the Diploma there is an extensive programme of social, cultural and sporting activities and students are encouraged to take full advantage of the opportunities that Oxford provides.

In July each year, we run a 3-week introduction to the IB Diploma.

St Clare's is also authorised by the IBO to run IB workshops for teachers.

St Clare's is located in an elegant residential area that is part of the North Oxford Conservation Area. It occupies 25 large Victorian and Edwardian houses to which purpose-built facilities have been added. The campus is made up of classrooms, a dining room, a popular café, music department and activities department plus library (over 35,000 resources), an IT suite and a Careers and Higher Education Information Centre. Stunning buildings in college grounds and gardens provide science laboratories, prep rooms and a mathematics department, plus two modern boarding houses arranged around a quad with a beautiful art studio. There is Wi-Fi throughout both the academic facilities and student houses which are no more than five minutes' walk from the central campus.

We welcome applications from UK and international students. Entry is based on academic results, an interview and a placement test. There is a competitive scholarship and bursary programme awarded by interview and group exercises.

Charitable status. St Clare's, Oxford is a Registered Charity, number 294085.

St David's School

23–25 Woodcote Valley Road, Purley, Surrey CR8 3AL

Tel: 020 8660 0723

email: office@stdavidsschool.co.uk

website: www.stdavidsschool.co.uk

Head Teacher: **Miss Cressida Mardell**

Age Range. 3–11.

Number in School. 146 Day: 70 boys, 76 girls.

Fees per term (2021–2022). £2,415–£3,940 (including lunch).

We look forward to welcoming you to our happy and creative school, where we aim to achieve the highest academic standards. At St David's we offer a rich and stimulating curriculum, delivered by a talented and caring staff, giving your child the best possible start. The School has undergone many changes and developments since its foundation in 1912 and celebrated its 100th birthday in 2012. Please visit our website to find out more about all the exciting things that have been going on.

The small school atmosphere is, we believe, a strength and reassuring to parents and children alike. We aim to balance nurture with independence to equip your child to succeed academically and we are extremely proud of our results. Please do contact us to experience the warm inspiring environment that is the "St David's Family". Please telephone the School Office to arrange an appointment and we look forward to showing you round our school.

St David's participates in the 15 Hour Government Funding and accepts Childcare Vouchers.

Charitable status. St David's (Purley) Educational Trust is a Registered Charity, number 312613. It aims to provide a quality education for boys and girls from 3+ to 11 years old.

St Dominic's Grammar School

Bargate Street, Brewood, Staffordshire ST19 9BA

Tel: 01902 850248

email: secretary@stdominicsgrammarschool.co.uk

website: www.stdominicsgrammarschool.co.uk

Twitter: @StDomsBrewood

Facebook: @StDominicsGrammar

Headmaster: **Mr Peter McNabb**, BSc Hons, PGCE

Bursar: Mr Paul Tudor

Head of Preparatory School: Miss Louise Hovland, BEd Hons

Head of Senior School & Sixth Form (*Safeguarding*): Mrs Nicola Hastings Smith, BA Hons, PGCE, NPQH

Admissions & Marketing: Mrs Samantha Emery

Heads of Faculty:

Mathematics: Mr Richard Brocklehurst, BSc Hons, PGCE

Science & Technology: Mr Ian Henderson, BSc Hons, MRSC, PGCE, QTS

Expressive Arts: Mrs Carol Molin, BA Hons, PGCE, LGSM

Communications: Mrs Nicola Hastings Smith, BA Hons, PGCE, NPQH

Humanities: Mr Gareth Saul, BA Hons, PGCE

St Dominic's Grammar School Brewood provides education for over 210 girls and boys from the ages of 4 to 18.

Development of the 'whole person' is at the heart of our school. We believe each child has special talents and we work to enable them to achieve their full potential within a caring environment. We nurture the pupils academically, socially, creatively and spiritually.

Teaching & Learning. Small class sizes facilitates individual attention so strengths and weaknesses are diagnosed and all work is tailored to match individual's needs. We believe in a close partnership with parents, keeping you informed about your child's progress.

Curriculum. We offer a broad and balanced curriculum with enhancement and enrichment. The National Curriculum is taught throughout the school. This is enhanced with additional subjects including performing arts, dance, drama and singing which are integrated into the weekly timetable. We offer a comprehensive range of subjects at AS and A Level.

Sports. We offer a broad curriculum including netball, hockey, dance, gymnastics, aerobics, football, volleyball, basketball, badminton, rounders, tennis, athletics and cross-country. Our all-inclusive extra-curricular programmes provide further sporting variety including Zumba, gymnastics, trampolining, modern dance and ballet, with all abilities encouraged to attend.

There is a comprehensive fixtures programme incorporating inter-house events and annual Preparatory and Senior Sports Days. We take part in ISA sporting events at local, regional and national level.

The facilities include brand new outdoor cricket nets, newly-resurfaced netball and tennis courts, hockey, football and rounders pitches and an athletics track. We also have an excellent fully-equipped sports hall with cricket nets and electronic basketball hoops.

Expressive Arts. We are renowned for our musical and dramatic excellence. Our contemporary Performing Arts Centre houses a Drama and Dance Studio, a Music Suite and a Recording Studio. Pupils are encouraged to join the choirs, play an instrument, take up dance, singing or tread the boards. Throughout the year there are a variety of performances ranging from the Pre-Preparatory Christmas play, to productions such as *Thoroughly Modern Millie* and *High School Musical*. The pupils participate in many local and regional competitions, take part in local festivals and public speaking events. Many do LAMDA examinations and all Year 7s take English Speaking Board examinations.

Extra-Curricular Activities. Four days a week there is an all-inclusive after-school programme where pupils can undertake a variety of activities ranging from The Duke of Edinburgh's Award scheme to debating, cooking, bushcraft, Young Enterprise and STEM Club.

Throughout the year, pupils are encouraged to become involved in fundraising for local and national charities. These activities help each child develop a good community spirit with respect and consideration for others.

Pastoral Care. Our outstanding pastoral care system and Christian ethos create an atmosphere which fosters trust and mutual respect between pupils and teachers. Pupils feel relaxed and secure and develop their self-respect, self-confidence, personal discipline and consideration for others.

Examination Results. Our pupils achieve outstanding exam results year on year outperforming the national averages of both comprehensive and independent schools at Key Stage 2, GCSE and A Level. In 2021 we achieved a 100% pass rate in all subjects at both GCSE and A Level; English Baccalaureate was 94%.

Facilities. We have a purpose-built Preparatory building, which encompasses a brand new state of the art Science Laboratory, a Preparatory Hall, IT room, Home Economics room and library. The Senior building has fully-equipped science laboratories, IT room and library. All classrooms have networked computers and interactive whiteboards. The Sixth Form and Performing Arts Centre is a modern, state-of-the-art facility housing the latest technology in music, IT and the Performing Arts. It has a common room with terraces and a well-equipped Library with Wi-Fi technology.

Admissions. Although selective, we draw our pupils from a wide ability range, which makes our record of results outstanding. Assessment is made during trial days at school. Entry into Year 7 is dependent on the entrance examination held in October. Applications for all other year groups are considered, depending on availability. A place in the Sixth Form is conditional upon GCSE results.

Fees per term (2021–2022). Reception including lunch £1,833, Year 1 including lunch £1,955, Year 2 including lunch £2,059, Years 3–6 Please enquire, Year 7 £2,667, Year 8 £2,805, Year 9 £2,917, Year 10 £3,222, Year 11 Please enquire, Year 12 £2,667, Year 13 £2,635.

Scholarships and Bursaries. Scholarships may be available for Senior School applicants. Academic, Sport, Art and Performing Arts non-financial scholarships may be awarded for entry into Years 7 and 12. Means-tested Bursaries are also available.

St Dominic's Priory School, Stone

37 Station Road, Stone, Staffordshire ST15 8ER

Tel: 01785 814181
email: info@stdominicspriory.co.uk
website: www.stdominicspriory.co.uk
Twitter: @StDominicsStone
Facebook: @stdominicspriorystone
LinkedIn: /st-dominic's-priory-school-stone

Chair of Governors: Mrs Karen Champ

Headteacher: Mrs Rebecca Harrison

St Dominic's Priory School, Stone is an independent Catholic school, educating boys and girls from Pre-school to 16 years.

We are proud of our strong academic tradition alongside our reputation for nurturing individuals. Our high-quality teaching and small classes creates an environment in which true potential can be maximised at all times.

Not only are we ranked as one of the top performing schools in Staffordshire, we are non-selective, accepting children of all abilities. Our teachers are engaging and our low teacher to child ratio ensures that each child receives a high quality education with the individual support that they need.

The redevelopment of our school site has seen us benefit from brand new, state-of-the-art teaching facilities and landscaped recreational areas. The teaching block accommodates 10 new classrooms, all with interactive walls, state-of-the-art science laboratories and specialist art, music, performing arts and drama studios. We even have a roof-top classroom for vegetable growing, a bee hive, weather projects, outdoor performances and much more.

Location. Centrally located within North Staffordshire, the school is situated in the picturesque canal town of Stone, Staffordshire, within easy reach of Newcastle-under-Lyme, Stoke-on-Trent, Stafford, Uttoxeter, Cheadle and the surrounding villages. We provide school transport from a number of locations and Stone Railway Station is only a 5 minute walk from school.

Aims and Ethos. Our school mission statement is: Living and Learning with Christ as our Guide. We aim to create a love of learning in a friendly and happy environment, nurture individuality and instil in our students a sense of community spirit rooted in Dominican values. We wish to provide each child with tools that will equip them to not only succeed academically, but contribute positively to a society in which values of justice and compassion are paramount.

St Dominic's welcomes children of all faiths and within our school community diversity is embraced and respected.

Once again our students achieved fantastic examination results in their end-of-year GCSEs in 2021, which only highlights the school's strong academic tradition and reputation for giving an excellent all-round education. Students leave St Dominic's with superb academic grades, self-confidence and friends for life.

Religion. St Dominic's Priory is a Catholic school where children of all faiths are welcomed.

The Arts. The school excels in the creative and performing arts and our busy programme of cultural events, visits and activities ensures that there is something for everyone at St Dominic's. Students regularly take part in productions, festivals, concerts, recitals and exhibitions, both within and outside the school.

Sport. The school has a strong sporting tradition. Sports include badminton, hockey, netball, volleyball, gymnastics, athletics, cricket, football, table tennis, tennis, cross-country running, climbing, trampoline and tri-golf.

Extra-Curricular Activities. Numerous clubs and activities are held after school and during lunchtimes for both the Prep and Senior Schools. These include the Duke of Edinburgh's Award, sports, LAMDA, choir, and percussion ensemble.

Admission. Please contact Charlotte Brindley, our admissions secretary on 01785 814181 ext 1 or email admissions@stdominicspriory.co.uk or visit the website.

Scholarships and Bursaries. Scholarships are awarded irrespective of financial means in the senior school.

All students entering Year 7 the following academic year, are automatically entered for the academic scholarships. They also have the opportunity to apply for our performing arts, music, art and sport scholarships.

Bursaries will be considered if bursary funds are available and depending on the financial, compassionate or other circumstances of applicants.

Fees per term (2021–2022). Pre-School: £27 per session, £42 per day; £2,520 per term; Reception £3,035; Primary 1 £3,374; Primary 2–6 £3,475; Year 7 £3,702; Year 8–11 £3,813.

Further Information. The school welcomes visits from prospective parents and students. For more information please telephone the school office on 01785 814181.

Charitable status. St Dominic's Priory is a Registered Charity, number 1141147, providing quality education for boys and girls aged 3 to 16 years.

St Edward's Preparatory School

252 London Road, Charlton Kings, Cheltenham, Gloucestershire GL52 6NR

Tel:	01242 388550
email:	prepschool@stedwards.co.uk
website:	www.stedwards.co.uk
Twitter:	@StEdwards_Prep
Facebook:	@StEdwardsSchoolCheltenham
Instagram:	@stedwardsprepcheltenham

Co-educational day school for pupils aged 1–11.

Chair of Trustees: Dr Susan Honeywill

Principal: **Mr M Burke**, BA Hons, PGCE, Ad Dip Ed, NPQH

A wealth of opportunity exists for students at St Edward's Preparatory School. We teach that there is no ceiling to potential, focussing on the individual needs of each and every pupil, and valuing their unique gifts and talents.

Located in the heart of Cheltenham, the School is set in over 40 acres of grounds, with a range of creative and sporting facilities to enrich our academic provision. The School offers a strong and vibrant school community, based on Christian values, in which all children can thrive.

We provide a supportive family atmosphere in which pupils from Kindergarten right through to Year 6 are encouraged to develop their individual potential – academic, social, physical, creative and spiritual – in preparation for their secondary education.

Excellent teaching and pastoral care in our nurturing and encouraging environment allows our pupils to flourish. Our small class sizes mean that our teachers really know pupils as individuals and can provide tailored support to maximise achievement. Our School motto means to strive for the best and that is exactly what we want for all our students.

We encourage our pupils to become fully involved in all aspects of school life, offering an extensive range of extra-curricular clubs, sporting and cultural activities. It is important to us that our pupils are challenged to step outside of their 'comfort zone' and realise that they can achieve beyond their perceived potential.

Most importantly, our aim is to provide an education that will last a lifetime and enable our pupils to develop into happy, confident, resilient, compassionate, and aspirational individuals who are ready to become positive and life-long contributors to society.

Admission: The main entry points are at Kindergarten, Pre-School, Reception and Year 3. However, pupils are welcome to join at any point, providing there are spaces in the year group.

Fees per term (2021–2022): £2,660–£4,595.

Further information is available on the School's website, www.stedwards.co.uk. To request a prospectus or to arrange an appointment to visit the School, please contact our Admissions Manager at prepadmissions@stedwards.co.uk or on 01242 388006.

Charitable status: St Edward's is a Registered Charity, number 293360.

St Gerard's School
Bangor

Ffriddoedd Road, Bangor, Gwynedd LL57 2EL

Tel: 01248 351656
email: sgadmin@st-gerards.org
website: www.st-gerards.org
Twitter: @stgerardsbangor
Facebook: @St-Gerards-School-Trust

Chairman of the Governing Body: Dr P Thomas

Headteacher: **Mr C Harrison**

Age Range. 4–18.
Number in School. Day: 78 Boys, 77 Girls.
Fees per term (2021–2022). £2,565–£3,885.

Founded in 1915 by the Congregation of the Sisters of Mercy and relocated to Ffriddoedd Road in 1917, this co-educational school is now a lay trust and has just celebrated its centenary year at this site. The school welcomes pupils of all denominations and traditions and has an excellent reputation locally. It has consistently attracted a high profile in national league tables also.

Class sizes in both junior and senior schools ensure close support and individual attention in order to enable all pupils to achieve their full academic potential, within an environment which promotes their development as well-rounded individuals with a keen social conscience.

The curriculum is comprehensive – pupils in the senior section usually achieve 9/10 good GCSE grades, going on to A Level and to university.

Charitable status. St Gerard's School Trust is a Registered Charity, number 1001211.

St Hilda's School

28 Douglas Road, Harpenden, Hertfordshire AL5 2ES

Tel: 01582 712307
email: office@sthildasharpenden.co.uk
website: www.sthildasharpenden.co.uk
Facebook: @sthildasharpenden

Headteacher: **Mr D Sayers**, BA Hons, QTS

Deputy Head: Mrs N Comer, BA Hons, QTS

Business Manager: Mrs D Taylor, ACMA

Age Range. 3–11.
Number in School. 180 approximately.
Co-educational Nursery, all other year groups for female pupils.
Fees per term (2021–2022). £4,260 (Forms IV to VI*); £4,215 (Forms II & III*), £4,175 (Reception & Form I*), Nursery: flexible options with variable pricing. (* including lunch and free wraparound care from reception classes).

St Hilda's School was founded in 1891, it is privately owned and situated in a residential site of 1¼ acres in the beautiful village of Harpenden. The premises include an outdoor swimming pool, a hard tennis/netball court, an adjacent playing field used for outdoor learning, sport and break times, together with attractive play areas for all age ranges. The original building has been substantially improved with two extensions and includes a fully-equipped stage in the modern hall, a sound-proofed Performing Arts Studio, a suite of music rooms, a dedicated computer suite, a science lab, a purpose-built EYFS unit, an art room, and a lovely library in the old building.

Caring, Curious & Confident At St Hilda's School, we welcome all children irrespective of race, religion, culture, disability or ability. Christian values and an appreciation of British values are essential to the life of the school and our core values are those of tolerance, respect for others, integrity, industry, and achievement.

Our aim is to achieve the highest standard of education in a happy, safe and purposeful working environment, instilling in all pupils a love of learning, independent thinking and good manners.

We strive to nurture each child's individuality, developing talent and ability to the full.

St Hilda's has a mixed ability intake but enjoys a reputation for high academic standards. For example, pupils in our Nursery access a full phonics programme and access reading as soon as they are ready, prior to joining the Reception class. Throughout, the foundations for success are carefully laid. Careful consideration is given to ensure each child enters the secondary school best suited to their needs. Preparation for the exams starts in Form IV and progresses further from Form V, where additional setting and specialist teaching in Maths, English and Reasoning enables our pupils to achieve highly; including an impressive range of scholarships each year.

The school is well known for its high musical standards with almost all pupils learning an instrument, many two or three. The standards in drama, art and sport are also consistently high.

St Hilda's is a member of the Independent Schools Association and the Independent Schools Council. The School received an '*excellent in all areas*' rating in October 2019, and previously in November 2016 a Focused Compliance Inspection was successfully passed in all areas.

The School website has a wealth of information and links to our virtual tour, a prospectus is also available on application to the School Secretary.

Please call us if you would like to arrange a visit to our beautiful School.

St James' School

22 Bargate, Grimsby, North East Lincolnshire DN34 4SY

Tel: 01472 503260
email: enquiries@saintjamesschool.co.uk
website: www.saintjamesschool.co.uk
Twitter: @StJamesSchoolGY
Facebook: @stjamesschoolgrimsby

Headmaster: **Mr S Thompson**

Deputy Head: Ms T Harris

Assistant Head: Mr D Rose

Bursar: Mr A Major

Age Range. 11–18.

Fees per term (2021–2022). Tuition: Reception £2,105 to Year 6 £3,145, Senior School £4,140, Sixth Form £3,250. Weekly boarding: £2,150 (Prep), £2,285 (Senior).

St. James' School is built upon the tenet of family; caring, encouraging, supporting, and inspiring. Deliberately small, we passionately believe an extraordinary education is built upon strong, trusting relationships. At St. James', these are immediately obvious.

St. James' pupils are allowed time to follow their own passions within an environment that creates opportunities both in the 'here and now', but also for the future.

Outwardly facing and globally aware, we welcome pupils from across the globe into our school. Boarding remains central to the St. James' ethos, where the benefits of 'living your education' are available to all pupils.

Blending together a love of learning with the development of 'character', at St. James' our goal is not only to educate, but to 'Future Proof'; securing the qualifications to stand out, building the character to endear, and instilling the core values to succeed.

The School offers academic, musical, sporting and all-round scholarships as well as means-tested bursaries.

The School operates a morning and evening bus services calling in at villages from the Louth and Brigg areas and an evening service back to Brigg.

St John's School

47–49 Stock Road, Billericay, Essex CM12 0AR

Tel: 01277 623070
email: registrar@stjohnsschool.net
website: www.stjohnsschool.net
Facebook: @StJBillericay

Headteacher: **Mr A Angeli**, BA Hons

Age Range. 2–16.
Number in School. Day: 154 Boys, 156 Girls.
Fees per term (Lent term 2022). £762.80–£4,916.

From the moment a child enters St John's, whatever their age, they are treated as an individual. Our aim is to ensure that learning, creativity and success is enjoyed by everyone and that when a child leaves our school they have fully achieved their potential. Set on eight acres of land overlooking Lake Meadows Park in Billericay, St John's is ideally located for public transport links and is only a five minute walk from Billericay train station.

Pupils benefit greatly from lessons with specialist teachers. In the Kindergarten, children have weekly lessons in Music, Singing, IT, PE and visit our own Forest School. In the Junior School, pupils study verbal and non-verbal reasoning and have additional specialist teachers for PE, Art, Music, IT and French and Spanish in Year 6. Senior School pupils follow a broad curriculum, which leads to GCSE courses commencing in Year 10. Subjects include English Language, English Literature, Maths, Statistics, Double Science, Triple Science, Art, Drama, French, Spanish, Geography, History, Music, PE, Food Technology, Business and Computer Science. Pupils make excellent progress throughout the school and GCSE pass rates are consistently high.

Sport is not only an integral part of our curriculum but also part of our extracurricular programme. Our Sport England standard Sports Hall hosts a wide range of activities including trampolining, table tennis, badminton, and basketball to name but a few. The school participates in ISA Regional and National sporting events.

A wide range of extracurricular clubs and activities are offered including, karate, cookery, dance, Mandarin and homework club. Pupils have the opportunity to participate in instrumental lessons, perform in the school orchestra and join the choir. In addition, the performing arts, are a pivotal part of our school, with fantastic success rates for our LAMDA examination entrants. A number of day and residential trips are offered each year.

A child's education is one of the most important factors in their well-being and success. We instil all the virtues of politeness, integrity and consideration of others into our pupils.

Although our academic success over the years has been exceptional, we are equally proud that we have educated thousands of children who are confident, successful and who genuinely make a positive contribution to society when they leave.

Means-tested scholarships are available for Year 7 places in the Senior School. For more information and to arrange a tour of the school, please contact our Registrar on 01277 623070 or by email to registrar@stjohnsschool.net.

St Joseph's Park Hill School

Padiham Road, Burnley, Lancashire BB12 6TG

Tel: 01282 455622
email: office@parkhillschool.co.uk
website: www.parkhillschool.co.uk
Facebook: @stjosephsparkhill

Chair of Governors: Mrs Catherine McDermott

Headteacher: **Mrs Maria Whitehead**

Age Range. 3–11 Co-educational.
Number of Pupils. 82.
Fees per term (2021–2022). £2,346

St Joseph's was founded by the Sisters of Mercy in 1913 and has operated from its present site since 1957.

It is a small school with a warm, friendly atmosphere where the children are known personally by all the staff. We have a broad, enriched curriculum which provides many activities and opportunities, both sporting and musical. The children enjoy their learning experience and are encouraged to do their best, achieving excellent results.

The Catholic ethos permeates all areas of the school. Pupils learn to care for each other, and respect different cultures. We welcome children from all faiths.

The school has the benefit of extensive grounds and offers a morning and after-school service as well as a 2-week summer school.

Charitable status. St Joseph's School is owned by The Institute of our Lady of Mercy which is a Registered Charity, number 290544.

St Joseph's School

St Stephen's Hill, Launceston, Cornwall PL15 8HN

Tel: 01566 772580
email: registrar@stjosephscornwall.co.uk
website: www.stjosephscornwall.co.uk
Twitter: @StJosephsSch
Facebook: @StJosephsSchoolLaunceston
Instagram: @stjosephscornwall

Head Teacher: **Mr Oliver Scott**

Deputy Headteacher: Mr Sam Matthews

Junior School Headteacher: Mrs Caroline Skerry

Bursar: Mr Ian Barton

Registrar: Miss Rebecca Walker

Age Range. 4–16 Co-educational.
Number in School. 240.
Fees per term (2021–2022). £1,925–£4,880.

St Joseph's School, Launceston, is an award-winning independent day school for boys and girls between the ages of 4 and 16.

St Joseph's has a truly unique family atmosphere that is apparent from the moment you enter the school. The school's small size means that it is possible both to keep sight of strong family values, giving children the confidence necessary to succeed, and to allow staff and pupils to work happily together. Due to the high teacher to pupil ratio, St Joseph's is able to encourage each pupil to reach his or her full potential through positive encouragement and commendation. The ethos of care, compassion and community is integral to the daily life of the school.

In both the Junior and the Senior school, St Joseph's provides an excellent academic education for all, regardless of ability and background. Our individualised academic curriculum runs alongside a wide variety of extra-curricular activities that challenge, stimulate and inspire all pupils to unlock their potential in a safe and supportive environment. St Joseph's offers equal prospects to every individual child and it is the positive response to the school's ethos that sees pupils rising to challenges both within the classroom and as highly valued members of the wider school community.

St Joseph's GCSE pupils achieve superb results. An exceptional 90% of pupils gained the required 5 passes at grades 4–9 or A*–C including Maths and English in 2017, 85% in 2018, 89% in 2019 and 100% in 2020. This is a remarkable achievement as St Joseph's is a non-selective school, meaning there is no entrance exam and admission is possible at any point during a child's education. Fees are set at levels which offer tremendous value for money, particularly in light of what is available to all pupils at the school, coupled with excellent academic results.

During the Covid-19 pandemic full online timetables were followed by all in the Senior School, with an engaging mix of live lessons and teacher interaction, while live teacher time and individualised work across the Junior School ensured high-quality learning continued throughout lockdown.

Academic and Sports Scholarships are offered from age 7+ and Music and Art Scholarships from 11+. Bursaries are available and considered on an individual basis.

An extensive daily bus service (9 bus routes) allows pupils from a wide area across Devon and Cornwall to attend St Joseph's.

St Joseph's School offers a number of open events throughout the year for prospective parents. To arrange an individual visit please contact the Registrar. Further information can be found at www.stjosephscornwall.co.uk or by contacting the Registrar on 01566 772580, registrar@stjosephscornwall.co.uk.

Charitable status. St Joseph's School is a Registered Charity, number 289048.

St Joseph's School

33 Derby Road, Nottingham NG1 5AW

Tel: 0115 941 8356
email: office@st-josephs.nottingham.sch.uk
website: st-josephs.nottingham.sch.uk
Twitter: @StJosephsNG1
Facebook: @St-Josephs-Independent-School-and-Nursery

Head Teacher: **Mr A E Crawshaw**

Age Range. 1–11 years.

Number in School. 67 Boys, 47 Girls.

Fees per term (2021–2022). £2,703 (Main School Reception to Year 6). Nursery fees on application.

A co-educational day school providing the very highest standards to children of all abilities. Children receive individual attention in small classes. The curriculum is planned to encourage children to develop lively, enquiring minds with emphasis on literacy and numeracy.

Sports include Football, Netball, Cricket, Rounders, Tag Rugby and Squash.

Extra-curricular activities include Archery, Dance, Ballet, Piano, Recorder and Football.

It provides a happy and caring environment in which children can develop their full potential both socially and academically. The school is Roman Catholic but welcomes children of all faiths.

Charitable status. St Joseph's School Nottingham is a Registered Charity, number 1003916.

St Joseph's Preparatory School

Rookery Lane, Trent Vale, Stoke-on-Trent, Staffordshire ST4 5RF

Tel: 01782 417533
email: enquiries@stjosephsprepschool.co.uk
website: www.stjosephsprepschool.co.uk
Facebook: @St-Josephs-Preparatory-School-
           1197329703618731
Instagram: @st.josephsprep

Chair of Governors: Mrs L Atherton

Head: **Mr D Hood**

Age Range. 3–11 Co-educational.

Number of Pupils. 160 Day Pupils.

Fees per term (2021–2022). £2,930–£3,095.

Charitable status. The Congregation of Christian Brothers is a Registered Charity, number 254312.

St Michael's School

Bryn, Llanelli, Carmarthenshire SA14 9TU

Tel: 01554 820325
email: admissions@stmikes.co.uk
           office@stmikes.co.uk
website: www.stmikes.co.uk
Twitter: @StMikes
Facebook: @St-Michaels-School
Instagram: @stmikeswales

Headmaster: **Benson Ferrari**, MA, PG Cert, BA Hons, FRSA, FCIEA

Deputy Head: Kay Francis, BSc Hons, PGCE

Interim Head of Prep School: Melony Rees-Davies, BA Hons, PGCE, PGradDip

Age Range. 3–18.

Number in School. 423: 218 Female, 205 Male

Fees per term (UK resident students 2021–2022). Tuition: Preparatory School £1,796–£2,914; Senior School £4,081–£4,472. Full Boarding: Years 7–10: £9,300 (twin), £9,300 (single); Years 11–13: £9,800 (twin), £10,800 (single). Weekly Boarding: Years 7–10: £7,525 (twin), £7,525 (single); Years 11–13: £7,875 (twin), £8,925 (single). Sibling allowances available.

International Students per annum (2021–2022): Years 7–8 £24,500 (twin & single rooms), Year 9 £26,200 (twin and single rooms), Year 10 (GCSE) £26,200 (twin and single rooms), year 11 (GCSE) £27,700 (single en-suite room), Sixth Form (A Level) £29,900 (single en-suite room).

St Michael's combines great learning and excellent pastoral care as part of a well-rounded education. The school has a traditional approach to learning, which does not mean it lives in the past, but places emphasis on the importance of hard work and homework in the school curriculum. The high academic standards of the school are reflected in the National League Tables. In 2021 St Michael's was the recipient of the *Sunday Times Wales Independent Secondary School of the Decade* award. Previous accolades have included the 2019 *Sunday Times Welsh Independent Secondary School* award and in 2017, the school was ranked a Top 20 school in *The Times Top 100 Co-Educational Schools in the UK*. In the same year we were also the top school in Wales for GCSE results. In 2021, 80.2% of our pupils received an A* or A grade at A Level and 85.4% of our pupils received at least five A* or A grades at GCSE.

No school can build up such a strong reputation without a competitive, but well-disciplined atmosphere and a highly-qualified and dedicated staff. This is where we feel St Michael's is particularly fortunate.

Our boarding houses are excellent: Parc House for Years 7 to 10 is a handsome and historic mansion set in an acre of grounds in the village of Llangennech nearby and Tenby House is a purpose-built, on-site, state-of-the-art, 31-bedroom boarding house for those in Years 11 to 13. Both houses offer a high standard of comfort where every pupil feels safe, happy and protected. Pupils are accommodated in well-furnished and equipped, single en-suite or shared study-bedrooms. The houses provide spacious recreation rooms and pleasant grounds in which pupils may relax, play or watch TV.

We have well-equipped computer laboratories where pupils have access to a computer each from 3 years of age. Languages taught in the school are French, Spanish, Welsh and Chinese (Mandarin).

The school has an envied reputation for its academic achievement but is also proud of the wide range of traditional games and activities it offers. Pupils from Year 10 onwards pupils can also take part in The Duke of Edinburgh's Award scheme to Gold Award standard. We have a large choir and school orchestra and pupils may take music examinations at GCSE and A Level.

One of the main reasons behind the school's success is the thorough grounding that pupils receive in the 'basics' – English, Mathematics, IT/Computing and Science in the

Prep and Pre-Prep Schools, continuing into the Senior School.

We have enjoyed outstanding sporting success over the last few years in netball, rugby, football, tennis, cricket and athletics.

Every pupil is encouraged to develop their full potential whether in academic work or in all the extracurricular activities on offer.

Saint Nicholas School

Hillingdon House, Hobbs Cross Road, Old Harlow, Essex CM17 0NJ

Tel: 01279 429910
email: office@saintnicholasschool.net
               admissions@saintnicholasschool.net
website: www.saintnicholasschool.net
Twitter: @SaintNicksSch
Facebook: @saintnicholasschoolharlow
Instagram: @saintnicholasschoolharlow

Headmaster: **Mr Paul Wilson**, BA Hons, PGCE

Age Range. 2½–16.
Number in School. 440 Day Pupils: 235 Boys, 205 Girls.
Fees per term (2021–2022). Reception, Years 1 & 2 £3,515. Years 3, 4 & 5 £3,645. Years 6, 7 & 8 £4,040 and Years 9, 10 & 11 £4,405. Pre-school fees £24 per session.

Saint Nicholas is situated in a delightful rural location and combines a fresh and enthusiastic approach to learning with a firm belief in traditional values.

The academic record of the school is excellent, reflected in high pupil success rates in all competitive examinations. The dedicated team of staff involves itself closely with all aspects of pupils' educational progress and general development. High standards of formal teaching are coupled with positive encouragement for pupils to reason for themselves and develop a high degree of responsibility.

As part of the school's commitment to providing affordable, quality care to children in the community, Little Saints Pre-School opened its doors in September 2014 to children from 2½ years old. Recent building developments include magnificent junior and infant department buildings, theatre, science and technology centre, swimming pool and sports hall, and new on-site catering facilities opened in January 2015.

Main sports include netball, rugby, tennis, football, cricket, swimming, athletics and gymnastics. There are many optional extra-curricular activities available including ballet, individual instrumental lessons, karate, performing arts and yoga.

Charitable status. Saint Nicholas School (Harlow) Limited is a Registered Charity, number 310876. It exists to provide and promote educational enterprise by charitable means.

St Peter's School

52 Headlands, Kettering, Northamptonshire NN15 6DJ

Tel: 01536 512066
email: stpsoffice@st-peters.org.uk
website: www.st-peters.org.uk
Facebook: @stpetersschoolkettering

Headteacher: **Mark Thomas**, BEng Hons, PGDE

Age Range. 3–11.
Number in School. Day: 29 Boys, 41 Girls.
Fees per term (2021–2022). £2,999–£3,676.

Established in 1946, St Peter's is a small day school set in secure and beautifully green grounds in a quiet residential area of Kettering. It offers an enriched education based upon Christian values for boys and girls from the term of their third birthday to age 11. Pupils are thoroughly prepared for entry to a secondary school of their choice and have a high rate of success in entrance and scholarship examinations.

The School is situated in a leafy part of Kettering, which has excellent transport links via road and rail. Housed in the former family home of William Timpson, the school occupies a beautiful and secure campus. The School has grown from its 1946 beginnings, and now houses Sunnylands Nursery, Reception and KS1 within the gardens of the Victorian house. The latest addition in the development plan is a new eco teaching space housing Art and the wraparound care facility in the Cedar Hub building.

With academic excellence at our core, in addition to fulfilling the requirements of the National Curriculum the School emphasises the importance of Music, Art, Sport and Information Technology in its curriculum, providing children with a wide and rich spectrum of opportunities in which to thrive. Many of our children take part in additional instrumental lessons ranging from violin to saxophone, and all children from Year 2 upwards swim every Friday.

St Peter's School is a lively, friendly school with a strong family atmosphere and our highest pastoral care is noted at inspection. The School encourages all children to develop their individual strengths and talents It aims to promote a respect for traditional values, a sense of responsibility and a concern for the needs of others. Each child is encouraged and nurtured to fulfil their own potential. Inspection reports detail the excellent progress made together with a strong extra-curricular activity timetable.

Charitable status. St Peter's School is a Registered Charity, number 309914. It was originally incorporated in 1946 with an intention to maintain and manage a school for boys and girls in the town of Kettering. In addition to this it provides local employment and seeks to source from the local community wherever economically viable.

St Piran's School, Hayle

14 Trelissick Road, Hayle, Cornwall TR27 4HY

Tel: 01736 752612
email: admin@stpirans.net
website: www.stpiranshayle.net

Headteacher: **Mrs Lucy Draycott**, BEd Hons with English

Age Range. 4–16.
Number of Pupils. 70.
Fees per term (2021–2022) £1,980–£2,550

Established in 1988, St Piran's School is set in attractive and well-maintained premises which, at present, accommodates around seventy children, aged from four to sixteen. It is a friendly, well-ordered community with a positive ethos where pupils make good friendships with each other and relate well to staff. Pupils are treated with respect and valued equally. They have a clear sense of right and wrong. There is a good sense of community within the school and new pupils are quickly made to feel welcome. The school places a strong emphasis on good manners and politeness. Visitors often comment about the warm friendly atmosphere and how happy the pupils are.

The curriculum is broad and balanced and helps to prepare the children for the next stage in their education. A wide variety of after school and lunchtime clubs provide additional activities and experiences for pupils of all ages. Educational visits to local places of interest and annual residential visits (for Year 5 and up) further enrich the curriculum.

From Years 5 and 6 there is a greater emphasis on subjects being taught by specialists. Class size remains low, with the maximum class size being twelve. Well-qualified, conscientious and hard-working staff teach children in a supportive learning environment. Children are given the opportunity to explain their ideas and be involved in activities. There is a very well-equipped and effectively-organised computer suite, which ensures that the children are at the cutting edge of technology.

We offer our senior pupils all of the opportunities offered by larger secondary schools. Every pupil is encouraged to find their own strengths and build on that feeling of confidence in every subject and area of their lives.

St Winefride's RC Independent School
Shrewsbury

Belmont, Shrewsbury, Shropshire SY1 1TE

Tel: 01743 369883
email: admin@stwinefrides.com
website: www.stwinefrides.com

Headmistress: **Mrs Elizabeth Devey**, BSc Psychology, BA Hons, PGCE, NASENCO, NPQSL

Age Range. 4+–11. Nursery: 3+–4.
Number in School. Day: 51 Boys, 55 Girls.
Fees per term (2021–2022). £1,662–£1,742.

St Wystan's School

High Street, Repton, Derbyshire DE65 6GE

Tel: 01283 703258
email: head@stwystans.org.uk
website: www.stwystans.org.uk
Twitter: @StWystans
Facebook: @stwystansschool

Head teacher: **Ms K Lebihan**, BA Hons, PGCE

Age Range. 2½–11.
Number of Pupils. Day: Boys 42, Girls 47.
Fees per term (2021–2022). £2,770–£3,152 (plus compulsory extras), lunches £317.

Founded in 1926, St Wystan's is an independent preparatory day school and nursery for pupils aged 2½ to 11 years of age. The School is situated in the heart of Repton and is only a short distance from Burton-on-Trent and the city of Derby. St Wystan's benefits from being part of the Repton family of schools and pupils are fortunate to be able to share world-class facilities such as the newly redeveloped Sports Centre with 25m swimming pool. Their most recent ISI report stated that "pupils of all abilities make good progress during their time at the School and are prepared well for the next stage of education."

St Wystan's is a thriving non-selective school that prides itself on its reputation for producing happy, confident and successful children. Every child is recognised and cherished for their individual strengths and characteristics in an inspiring and nurturing learning environment. Dedicated staff encourage a love for learning and warm, respectful relationships are nurtured between the pupils, their peers and the staff. The children enjoy going to school and the staff relish having the opportunity to share laughter, adventures and interests.

St Wystan's continually strives to create a varied and stimulating curriculum so that pupils can develop, be happy and flourish. Specialist teaching in Music, Physical Education, French and Woodland School is introduced from Nursery through to Year 6, with Drama introduced into the curriculum for Years 3 to 6.

St Wystan's provides a comprehensive level of pastoral care through both the very popular wrap-around care, where children can arrive at school from 7.30am and are cared for after school until 6.30pm, and the preferential class sizes, which ensures each child receives a tailored learning experience to prepare pupils to face the wider world with confidence. There is a range of extra-curricular clubs to suit every individual, with many pupils having individual instrumental, music and LAMDA tuition.

The School enjoys an excellent reputation in music, sport and drama with pupils progressing to regional and national championships in swimming, tennis, athletics and music competitions. There is a thriving choir and orchestra, and pupils are actively encouraged to participate in clubs and groups in the wider community.

The benefits of a holistic education are valued and implemented to equip pupils with strong academic standards and behaviour, but also the essential qualities and skills required beyond their time at our school. We are proud of our strong links with many local secondary independent and state schools and pupils at St Wystan's have an excellent reputation for securing scholarship offers and first-choice destinations.

Beyond St Wystans. The School has a real gift for unlocking potential. Pupils achieve outstanding results with all July 2021 leavers achieving their first choice of senior school and 80% achieving scholarships. There are a number who move to Repton Prep for two years before going on to Repton School.

Charitable status. St Wystan's School Limited is a Registered Charity, number 527181. It exists to provide a quality education for both boys and girls.

Salesian College

119 Reading Road, Farnborough, Hampshire GU14 6PA

Tel: 01252 893000
email: office@salesiancollege.com
website: www.salesiancollege.com
Twitter: @SalesianFboro
Facebook: @Salesiancollegefarnborough

Headmaster: **Mr Gerard T Owens**, MA Hons, PGCE

Age Range. Boys 11–18 years, Girls 16–18. Co-educational Sixth Form.

Number in School. 630

Fees per term (2021–2022). £4,322.

As a Catholic school in the Salesian tradition, the College provides a Home that welcomes; a Church where Gospel values are shared and lived out on a daily basis; a School which educates for Life and prepares for future success and realisation of individual potential; and a Playground where personal, social, moral, sporting and cultural enrichment, beyond the academic curriculum, takes place and where lasting friendships are formed. Therefore, the formation of character and the development of social conscience are at the heart of our mission. Students of other Christian denominations and religious faiths are warmly welcomed.

Salesian College forms well-educated, happy and well-rounded, confident young men and women; good Christians; honest citizens who are comfortable with themselves and those around them. Students are decent, courteous, selfless people; well equipped to take their place in and make a significant contribution to society.

Staff are caring and provide an excellent all round education. Salesian has outstanding levels of academic, cultural, spiritual and physical achievement, exemplary student behaviour and a caring ethos. We are a happy and highly successful school.

Although selective, we admit students of a wide range and believe in the pursuit of excellence for all. As such it caters excellently for all levels of ability, providing stretch for the most able and support for those with additional learning needs.

Excellent relationships between staff and students, and the students themselves, are a key feature of the College which seeks at all times to provide a holistic approach to the education and formation of those entrusted to our care.

The recent ISI Inspection report rated Salesian College as excellent in all areas, stating that "*The excellence of academic achievement owes much to the excellence of the curriculum and the teaching. Pupils find the collaborative approach of the teaching staff very helpful and supportive. Teachers know their pupils extremely well; they plan their lessons carefully to include a variety of approaches which succeed in engaging pupils' interest and, in almost all cases, in enabling them to maintain strong progress*".

The school has its own chapel, chaplaincy and resident chaplain.

Prospective parents are always welcome to make an appointment to visit the College while in session. Please see our website for up-to-date details.

Charitable status. Salesian College Farnborough Limited is a Registered Charity, number 1130166. It exists to provide education in North East Hampshire and neighbouring counties.

Sancton Wood School

Nursery:
17 Station Road, Cambridge CB1 2JB

Tel: 01223 471703 (whole school)
email: office.Nurseries@sanctonwood.co.uk

Pre-Prep & Prep:
2 St Paul's Road, Cambridge CB1 2EZ

email: office.Prep@sanctonwood.co.uk

Senior:
57 Bateman Street, Cambridge CB2 1LR

email: office.Seniors@sanctonwood.co.uk
website: www.sanctonwood.co.uk
Twitter: @SanctonWood
Facebook: @SanctonWood
Instagram: @sancton_wood_school
LinkedIn: /company/sancton-wood-school-cambridge

Principal: **Mr Richard Settle**, BA Hons, PGCE

Age Range. 1–16

Number of Pupils. 365

Fees per term (2021–2022). Nursery £1,734 (2 days)–£4,335 (5 days); Reception–Year 2: £4,000; Years 3–6: £4,335; Years 7–11: £5,250. Baby Unicorns Nursery: minimum attendance of 2 days per week. Rising 3s and Unicorns Nursery: minimum attendance of 3 days a week.

Sancton Wood is a small independent, co-educational Nursery, Pre-Prep, Prep and Senior School for pupils aged from 1 to 16. The main aim of the school is to make each and every pupil aware of his or her innate qualities and skills, and to develop these to full capacity. Recently announced as a finalist for the Co-Educational Independent School of the Year 2021, we are extremely proud to be selected based on our co-educational provision; one that promotes the benefits of boys and girls working and learning together.

Despite our growing numbers we work hard to maintain small class-sizes of an average of 18, in order that students and teachers can foster strong relationships. We get to know the students as individuals and understand when they need help, and the best approach to take to engage with and support them.

We want our students to have a positive approach to life, to broaden their horizons, and to value the opportunity to think and study independently. We believe a happy child is a learning child and are recognised for our excellent pastoral care, building a memorable pupil journey around the core values of inclusivity, kindness, intellectual curiosity, pride, dignity, fun and energy.

This foundation of outstanding pastoral care leads to incredible academic success, as has been proven with our most recent GCSE results. Overall 97% of students achieved five or more GCSEs graded 4–9; 96% of students achieved these results including English, Maths and Science and 68% of these results were in the top 7, 8 and 9 grades. We regularly feature in the *Sunday Times Top 100* list; an impressive achievement for a non-selective, mixed ability school.

Sancton Wood is part of the Dukes Education. This extraordinary family of schools all share the same drive to "inspire, educate and support young people so they can be the very best versions of themselves". Being part of Dukes gives us strength, stability, and access to a wide network of expertise whilst celebrating our own unique character as a school.

Dukes Education have recently invested close to £10 million in the move of our Senior School to Bateman St. This has not only increased the quality of the provision we can offer for our senior students but has allowed us to answer the demand in admissions by increasing our capacity by 45%.

Seaton House School

67 Banstead Road South, Sutton, Surrey SM2 5LH

Tel: 020 8642 2332
email: office@seatonhouse.sutton.sch.uk
website: www.seatonhouse.sutton.sch.uk
Facebook: @SeatonHouseSchool

Chair of Governors: Mrs J Evans

Headteacher: **Mr Carl Bates**

Age Range. Girls 2½–11 years, Boys 2½–4 years (Nursery only).

Number of Pupils. Main School 140; Nursery 36

Fees per term (2021–2022). £2,134–£3,700.

Seaton House School was founded in 1930 by Miss Violet Henry and continues to have a strong family feel to this day. The school provides all children with an excellent start to their learning journey and girls consistently gain both academic and scholarship success at both grammar and local independent schools. Seaton House has consistently been ranked in the top 5 Prep Schools in the *Sunday Times* list and was 'Prep School of the Year in 2018–19'. ISI in its

Educational Quality report judged the school to be 'Excellent in All Areas'.

Small class sizes ensure that every pupil is known as an individual and supported to ensure that they make the most of their gifts and talents. Alongside excellent academic teaching, the girls have opportunities to develop artistic, musical, dramatic and sporting talents. There are specialist teachers for almost all subjects to ensure that the girls receive the very best education in every area of the curriculum. The girls also compete in a range of events ranging from ISA young musician of the Year, musical concerts, full-scale productions to regular sports fixtures. We have a school choir, orchestra, drama groups and sports teams as well as a range of lunchtime and after school clubs which include: fencing, rock choir, ballet, musical theatre and various sports clubs.

Outside speakers and educational visits are an integral part of the School's curriculum as first hand experiences are so important to both inspire and give context to the girls' learning. Alongside regular workshops and termly external day visits, the girls in Key Stage Two also have the opportunity to engage in an annual residential course. These are carefully planned and provide a wealth of outdoor learning and adventurous activities to aid the development of leadership skills, teamwork and resilience.

Pastoral care is of the highest calibre with all staff taking a keen interest in the personal development of all the pupils. Courtesy, good manners and kindness are expected as the norm and pupils are encouraged to develop initiative, independence and confidence. The School has a strong house system and the pupils are encouraged to engage in community and fund raising events.

By the end of Year Six we would hope that every girl will leave us as a confident, curious, creative individual who is fully prepared for the next step in her education and has made lasting memories and friendships. Please do come and see what makes Seaton House such a special place where you will always be assured of a warm welcome.

Charitable Status. Seaton House School is a Registered Charity, number 800673.

Sherfield School
Bellevue Education Group

Sherfield-on-Loddon, Hook, Hampshire RG27 0HT

Tel: 01256 884800
email: info@sherfieldschool.co.uk
website: www.sherfieldschool.co.uk
Twitter: @SchoolSherfield
Facebook: @SherfieldSchoolHampshire
Instagram: @sherfieldschool
LinkedIn: /school/sherfield-school

Executive Head: **Mr Nick Brain**

Age Range. 3 months – 18 years Co-educational.

Number in School. 460.

Fees per term (2021–2022). Day: £3,520–£5,870; Boarding: £6,510–£10,470.

Are you ready for an adventure?

You can start your Sherfield journey at any age, from 3 months to 18 years! We combine excitement and curiosity with new ventures and learning. Based in Hook, Hampshire, we offer plenty of boarding options as well as a day school.

The school has an inclusive family feel to it and most parents will tell you how much their children have grown in confidence and progressed because of this.

From the moment your child enters our outstanding nursery, they will start to develop their social and learning skills within our warm and nurturing school environment.

As they progress through the Prep and Senior schools, the children start to develop rigorous academic skills and enjoy world-class sports, arts and music programmes. With our small class sizes and bespoke learning, we regularly achieve outstanding results in academic league tables. Sixth Formers are exceptionally well-prepared by our dedicated staff for further education and gain entry into some of the best colleges and universities in the world. Regular fieldwork, sports exchanges and cultural trips round out their development and this integrated education instils a lifelong love of learning and culture.

We immerse our pupils in school life from day one of their journey here. Sherfield School is always a hive of activity. Our gifted and talented student body includes many musicians, artists, county players in tennis and rugby, plus national and international cycling, judo, equestrian and swimming stars. The school also plays host to many music and arts events throughout the school year.

Alongside academic learning and sports, we tailor pastoral care to meet your child's individual needs and aim to foster their unique talents and character, building confidence and respect.

Having a diverse demographic of pupils in the School is a fantastic opportunity for collaboration through peer-to-peer learning and is one of the reasons why our pupils enter the world well-rounded and prepared.

And with our Grade II listed manor house set in many acres of beautiful grounds, woods and gardens, there are plenty of opportunities for all ages to get outside in the fresh country air.

So, what makes us unique?

We have an extraordinary, thriving enrichment programme. We believe enrichment promotes employability, academic attainment and teaches pupils the skills they need to make good, informed choices. A successful enrichment programme can promote the life-skills needed for everyday life, develop "soft skills" that employers and universities look for, while also giving pupils the opportunity to find out more about their interests and passions.

Come and visit us to get a feel for our dynamic community and see how your child could benefit from The Sherfield Experience.

Sherrardswood School

Lockleys, Welwyn, Hertfordshire AL6 0BJ

Tel: 01438 714282
email: headmistress@sherrardswood.co.uk
website: www.sherrardswood.co.uk
Facebook: @sherrardswoodschool.co.uk

Headmistress: Mrs Anna Wright

Head of Prep: Mr Matt Capuano

Assistant Head – Academic: Mrs Koulla Theodoulou

Assistant Head – Pastoral: Mrs Nicci Venn

Age Range. 2–18.
Number in School. Day: 474.
Fees per term (2021–2022). £3,564–£5,750

Sherrardswood, founded in 1928, is a co-educational day school for pupils aged 2–18. The School is set in 40 acres of attractive parkland two miles north of Welwyn Garden City. The Prep Department is housed in a beautiful 18th century building whilst the Senior Department occupies a purpose-built facility. Games fields, tennis courts and woodlands trail are available on the Lockleys site for both departments.

Entry to the school is by interview and individual assessment. A broad curriculum is offered to GCSE level and a wide range of A Level subjects is available. We are the highest performing independent school in Hertfordshire for the measure: Value Added (gov.uk). A range of sport and extracurricular opportunities is available, both within the school day and out of school hours.

The recent ISI inspection confirmed that Sherrardswood is achieving its aims and that the quality of education and pastoral care is outstanding.

Shoreham College

St Julian's Lane, Shoreham-by-Sea, West Sussex BN43 6YW

Tel: 01273 592681
email: info@shorehamcollege.co.uk
website: www.shorehamcollege.co.uk
Twitter: @ShorehamCollege
Facebook: @shorehamcollege

Principal: Mrs Sarah Bakhtiari, BA, MA Brighton, QTS

Age Range. 3–16.
Number in School. 220 Day Boys, 128 Day Girls.
Fees per term (2021–2022). £3,400–£5,400.

Shoreham College is a school that cares – it values its children as individuals, knows them well, and ensures that they feel safe, secure and happy. Within a warm friendly environment, it instils traditional values of good manners and courtesy and teaches the children to respect themselves, their peers and their community.

Teachers encourage pupils to enjoy being children, which allows them to grow. They nurture, guide, support and inspire them to develop academically, emotionally, and spiritually and are rewarded by seeing them grow into confident young adults, ready to take on the challenges of life.

Adopting a broadly non-selective approach means that the College is committed to providing a first-class all-round education to children of varied ability, ensuring that every child can achieve their potential. Ambitious for them, we ensure that they are appropriately challenged: the gifted and talented extended and children with learning differences given what they need to thrive.

We look forward to welcoming you.

Charitable status. Shoreham College (The Kennedy Independent School Trust Limited) is a Registered Charity, number 307045. It exists to provide high-quality education for boys and girls.

Slindon College

Slindon House, Top Road, Arundel, West Sussex BN18 0RH

Tel: 01243 814320
email: registrar@slindoncollege.co.uk
website: www.slindoncollege.co.uk
Twitter: @SlindonCollege
Facebook: @SlindonCollege
LinkedIn: /slindon-college

Headmaster: **Mr Mark Birkbeck**, BEd Hons, NPQH

Age Range. 8–18.

Number in School. 10 Boarders, 65 Day Boys.

Fees per term (2021–2022). Termly Boarders £10,760, Weekly Boarders £9,305, Day Boys £7,265.

Slindon College is an independent day and boarding school for boys aged 8–18, set in the historic Slindon House, located in the South Downs National Park.

With unrivalled views of the south coast, the 14-acre setting provides the backdrop to a stimulating, broad and balanced educational experience for students of all academic abilities, taking into account their strengths and talents.

Slindon College's social and intelligent pupils have had setbacks in mainstream settings and the College provides outstanding transformative education and pastoral care for those who will thrive in a specialist learning environment. The College offers a well-developed pathway to success suited to boys with Specific Learning Difficulties, Developmental Language Disorders and associated conditions. We work with each boy on a rounded social and educational development foundation, offering both nationally recognised examinations and social advancement targets.

Learning Support. Slindon College is a centre of excellence for moderate learning difficulties. The College adopts a holistic approach to learning support so that class teachers and specialist staff work together for the benefit of pupils who require individual support. The Learning Support department aims for every pupil to be fully

included, enabled, valued and encouraged to be the best version of themselves by offering:

• Specialist dyslexia teachers
• Speech and language therapists
• Occupational therapists
• Learning support assistants

Slindon College has experience in supporting pupils with a range of difficulties such as Dyslexia, Dyspraxia, Autism, Attention Deficit Hyperactivity Disorder and Social Anxiety. The Learning Support department plays a key role in promoting the social and emotional skills that underpin effective learning, positive behaviour and the well-being of all pupils. Learning support also extends to helping pupils who have English as an Additional language (EAL). Multilingual pupils can take advantage of our intensive English tuition, which can be offered on an individual or small group basis.

Our Curriculum and Teaching. The optimisation of multi-sensory and augmentative teaching approaches for all pupils enables our staff to determine the most appropriate learning methods for each one. Our classrooms are all equipped with assisted technology: smartboards, tablets, reader pens and speech recognition tools, to better promote enjoyable, engaging learning. The high teacher-to-pupil ratio means that learning can be consistently monitored and evaluated. Small teaching groups allow for more pupil-teacher interaction, greater opportunities for 1:1 teaching, a wider variety of instructional approaches, increased social and academic engagement.

The College provides a curriculum that promotes personal development and a breadth of experience that encourages success and life-long engagement with learning. Our enrichment programme offers opportunities for self-exploration and a safe environment for calculated risk-taking. These activities enhance physical and emotional wellbeing, stamina, coordination, team building, initiative, creativity, self-expression, focus and curiosity are among many facets of the pupils' development to be improved or sparked by this programme. We cater for outdoor enthusiasts with mountain biking, orienteering, Greenpower electric car racing (national competition), Forest School, our school farm and horticulture.

Our range of sporting facilities includes sports halls, a swimming pool, multi-use games area and playing fields where pupils can enjoy rugby, football, cricket and softball among other activities. For the creatives, we offer a Trinity Arts programme, textile studies, graphics, photography, creative writing, drama and cookery. We have access to key links in the South Downs National Park and Chichester Festival Theatre.

Boarding. Our warm and welcoming boarding team offer the comfort and stability of family life whilst developing independent living skills and a thirst for new experiences. An outstanding pastoral support system enables every pupil to be listened to in a calm and caring environment. As well as full-time and weekly boarding, we offer flexi-boarding which can be adapted to the individual pupil's or family's needs. This includes occasional or one-off 'stay-overs' in the familiar and secure surroundings of the College. This provides respite for families and refuge for pupils from sometimes stressful social situations outside school.

Enrichment and House Activities The House system is central to the spirit of the school; it brings the boys together with a sense of belonging, competitiveness and creates opportunities for everyone to take part in the activities. There are many House competitions including drama, music, maths, athletics, basketball and badminton; giving all pupils an opportunity to represent their Houses. Each House raises money for a charity chosen by the boys. The Regular House assemblies encourage greater participation within the local community, while inviting external speakers to share their wealth of diverse experience enhances the pupils' understanding of the wider world

Pupils are encouraged to develop self-confidence and self-esteem, to be determined and motivated in both academic and personal development. The staff are dedicated to keeping the pupils healthy, happy and safe, encouraging each to feel that they are a valued member of society. We encourage pupils to accept, tolerate and celebrate diversity and differences in each other, in themselves and the wider community, showing care, concern and respect for themselves, for others and their environment.

Our pupils leave the College prepared and eager to meet the challenges ahead. Through work experience placements, life skills courses and building links with local colleges and universities, we give our boys the experience necessary to make this transition a positive one.

Snaresbrook Preparatory School

75 Woodford Road, South Woodford, London E18 2EA

Tel:	020 8989 2394
email:	office@snaresbrookprep.org
website:	www.snaresbrookprep.org
Twitter:	@SnaresbrookPrep
Facebook:	@SnaresbrookPrep
LinkedIn:	/snaresbrook-prep-school-ltd

Head: **Mr Ralph Dalton**

Age Range. 3½–11.

Number in School. 165.

Fees per term (Autumn 2021). £3,342–£4,471.

Snaresbrook Preparatory School is a vibrant independent day school for boys and girls aged from 3½ to 11 years. Founded in the 1930s, the school occupies a substantial Victorian building, once a large private family home – something that contributes to the strong community spirit within the school. We aim to cultivate an intimate, caring family atmosphere in which children feel secure and valued. Snaresbrook Values have been introduced and embedded by the current Head – they include Respect, Enjoyment and Excellence. The values are posted all around the School and even on the hopscotch in the playground!

The Lower Foundation Stage is extremely popular and is our main point of entry. Most children join the school at age 3½ and stay with us until they reach 11 when they leave for their senior schools.

We provide a rounded education covering every aspect of your child's early development. The curriculum has broadened in the last few years and is designed to prepare pupils for life as well as entrance and scholarship examinations to senior independent and grammar schools. The curriculum includes Mathematics, English, Science, Current Affairs, ICT, Art, DT, Music, Drama, French, PE/

Games, RE, Wellbeing and PSHEE. Latin and Swimming are introduced in the Juniors.

Areas such as Music, Drama, Sport, Computing and Languages are very strong and are led by passionate specialists. Ambitious School Development Plans have moved the School forward. At age 11, we find that Snaresbrook children are confident, cheerful and courteous, with a good sense of community and a readiness to care for each other and the world around them. They have learned how to work in the ways that suit them best, are receptive to teaching and are well prepared for the next stage of their education and development. We see ourselves as joint trustees, with parents, of the young lives in our care, bearing equal responsibility for their happiness, wellbeing and development.

In 2017 Snaresbrook came through its Regulatory Compliance Inspection fully compliant and without any action needed. The school feeds many of the top independent schools in the area including the City of London Schools, Forest, Chigwell and Bancroft's.

Anyone interested in the School is encouraged to contact the office to book a personal tour.

Steephill School

off Castle Hill, Fawkham, Longfield, Kent DA3 7BG

Tel:	01474 702107
email:	secretary@steephill.co.uk
website:	www.steephill.co.uk
Twitter:	@steephillonline
Facebook:	@Steephill-School

Head Teacher: **Mr John Abbott**, BA Hons, PGCE

Age Range. 3–11 co-educational.

Number of Pupils. 124.

Fees per term (2021–2022). £3,350. Pre-School Fees are pro rata.

Steephill School is a very successful School based on its academic, sporting and musical achievements. In 2017, 100% of Year 6 pupils gained entry to a selective school, many children won awards at music festivals and there were numerous successes at inter-school sports. In its 2013 ISI inspection report the school was given an "excellent" rating in Pastoral Care, Curriculum, Extra-Curriculum and the Spiritual, Moral, Social and Cultural Development of pupils. In 2016, the School was 100% compliant with Independent School Standards.

The School believes in high-quality teaching within a disciplined but relaxed atmosphere. The School holds traditional values and beliefs; working with and supporting each other is an important part of the ethos. There are close links with the church opposite the School. Four services per year are held there and the Rector takes a fortnightly assembly. The setting is very rural despite being only a few minutes' drive from the M2 and 5 miles from the M20 and M25. The School enjoys beautiful views of the countryside with very little traffic nearby.

The classes are a maximum of 16 and with only 124 pupils in the School, there is a close liaison between all members of the school community: children, staff, family members and governors. Parents are welcomed into the School and work closely with the teachers. There is regular feedback to parents on children's progress. Parents are also active in Friends of Steephill School, the Parents Association, to provide social and fundraising activities.

The children join the School aged 3 in the Pre-School and they leave at age 11. The curriculum is designed to support all abilities to achieve academically and in all the broader aspects of education such as drama, the arts and sports. Information Technology has been developed well over the last few years and is being continually updated.

There is a large selection of extracurricular activities at lunchtime and after school. Our Gardening Club is one of the more popular together with the choir, instruction on musical instruments, dance and football. We are very fortunate to have large grounds with a superb sports field, despite being a small school.

There is a care facility both before and after school so we are open from 7.00am to 5.30pm. The School is also very proud of the lunches. All the food is sourced from local shops: butcher, baker and greengrocer. The meals are carefully balanced and freshly made.

Charitable status. Steephill School is a Registered Charity, number 803152.

Stratford Preparatory School

Church House, Old Town, Stratford-upon-Avon, Warwickshire CV37 6BG

Tel:	01789 297993
email:	secretary@stratfordprep.co.uk
website:	www.stratfordprep.co.uk
Facebook:	@stratfordprep

Motto: Lux et Scientia

Principal: Mrs Catherine Quinn, MBA, BEd Hons

Headteacher: **Ms Tracey Woodcock**, BEd Hons

Age Range. Preparatory School 4–11 years. Montessori Nursery School 2–4 years.

Number in School. 70; 39 Boys, 31 Girls.

Fees per term (2021–2022). Juniors £3,920–£3,990; Infants £3,560; Reception £3,560 (non-funded); Lunch £170. Nursery School: according to sessions attended.

Stratford Preparatory School is situated in the heart of the historic town of Stratford-upon-Avon. The Preparatory school opened in September 1989 and has developed around a large town house. An additional detached house within the school's grounds provides accommodation for the Reception and Nursery children, a gymnasium, a science room and design and technology room.

The Nursery implements the Montessori philosophy of learning which encourages a structured learning environment. French and ballet are taught from the age of 2 years.

The main school offers a broad balanced learning plan adapted to the individual needs of the children using traditional teaching methods and with specific reference to the National Curriculum. All children are entered for the 11+ and independent school entrance examinations.

The school offers a high level of pastoral care and attention to personal development.

Physical education activities include: sailing, swimming, football, cricket, tennis, netball, rounders, ballet and athletics.

There are opportunities for the children to learn a variety of musical instruments. The school has two choirs and an orchestra.

Reduction in fees is offered for families with two or more children in the School.

The Headmistress is pleased to provide further details and meet prospective parents.

Study School

57 Thetford Road, New Malden, Surrey KT3 5DP

Tel:	020 8942 0754
email:	info@thestudyschool.co.uk
website:	www.thestudyschool.co.uk
Twitter:	@studyschooluk
Facebook:	@Thestudyschool
Instagram:	@thestudyschooluk

Headmaster: **Mr Alistair Bond**, BA Ed Hons, FRSA

Age Range. 2–11 Co-educational.

Number in School. Day: 61 Boys, 52 Girls.

Fees per term (2021–2022). Nursery from £1,770 (term-time mornings), Reception £3,500, Year 1 £3,641, Year 2 £4,002, Years 3–6 £4,161.
Additional Nursery afternoon sessions available each day of the week: from £285 per term for one afternoon/week until 3.00pm. Full-year Nursery also now available (8am–6pm). All fees include a cooked school lunch. The school belongs to the Early Years Funding Scheme for 3 and 4 year olds; we also offer the extended funding.

Since 1923 we have successfully given our children a firm foundation in reading, writing and number skills, whilst also teaching French, Spanish, Music, Art and Games. Science, Geography, History, Design and Technology and ICT play an important part in the curriculum, with interactive whiteboards in every classroom and a full set of iPads and laptops which augment the curriculum. All children also attend Forest School every week (Nursery children every fortnight).

Small classes allow us to stretch the most able pupils, whilst giving all our children individual attention.

Popular After-School Clubs include Football, Chess, Art, Computer Coding, Drama, Zumba, Winter and Summer Sports, Choir, Modern Foreign Languages and Cookery. Individual instrumental music tuition is also available. We have Before School Care from 7:30am and After School Care until 6:15pm. All classes go on a school trip once a term and Years Three, Four, Five and Six attend residential activity and field study courses and language trips abroad.

We provide a caring and stimulating atmosphere in which our children thrive. After Year Six they leave us to enter such schools at Kingston Grammar School, Wallington

Boys' School, Nonsuch Girls' School, Hampton School, the High Schools at Wimbledon, Sutton, Putney and Surbiton and both Tiffin Schools.

Please visit our website: www.thestudyschool.co.uk.

Sylvia Young Theatre School

1 Nutford Place, London W1H 5YZ

Tel:	020 7258 2330
email:	info@syts.co.uk
website:	www.syts.co.uk

Principal: Mrs Sylvia Young, OBE

Headteacher: **Ms Frances Chave**, BSc, PGCE, NPQH

Age Range. 10–16.

Number in School. Day: 58 Boys, 161 Girls.

Fees per term (2021–2022). Key Stage 2 & 3 (Years 6, 7, 8 & 9): £4,890; Key Stage 4 (Years 10 & 11): £4,890.

The School has a junior department (Year 6 only) and a secondary department (Years 7–11). We aim to provide an appropriately balanced academic and vocational experience for our students. We are proud of the caring and well disciplined environment that prevails and promotes a very positive climate of individual success.

Academic subjects are delivered by highly qualified staff to the end of Key Stage 4.

GCSE Examination subjects include English, English Literature, Mathematics, Combined or Triple Science, Art, Drama, Music, Media Studies, Spanish and History.

Theatrical training is given by experienced professional teachers. Pupils are prepared for examinations in Speech and Drama – LAMDA (London Academy of Music and Dramatic Art). Entry is by audition with academic ability assessed.

Thames Christian School

12 Grant Road, London SW11 2FR

Tel:	020 7228 3933
email:	admissions@thameschristianschool.org.uk
website:	www.thameschristianschool.org.uk
Twitter:	@ThamesCSchool
Facebook:	@Thameschristianschool
Instagram:	@thameschristianschool

Head: **Dr Stephen Holsgrove**, PhD

Age Range. 11–18 Co-educational.

Number of Pupils. 165.

These are exciting times for Thames. As we begin our third decade, there is increased awareness that young people require an education that prepares them to navigate life successfully. Faced with a fluid, and at times uncertain, world, they increasingly need to develop exceptional soft skills, resilience and deep-rooted values.

Academic rigour is foundational for us at Thames. However we are passionate about far more than this. We enjoy seeing young people understand their value, learn to honour and encourage others and contribute to the wider school community.

Small classes and excellent pastoral care enable us to challenge and support each individual in their learning and in building good interpersonal skills. Our ethos of compassion, respect and humility enables young people to grow in confidence and their appreciation of each other.

We look forward to moving into our new building adjacent to Clapham Junction station in January 2022. The new space will include multiple science laboratories, DT workshops, food technology room, library, theatre and dance/drama studio. As well as A levels, our new sixth form will offer a co-curricular and pastoral programme that will see our pupils further develop their leadership skills and understanding of the world so that they are prepared for a successful future.

This year 70% of our GCSE grades were 9–7 and 99% were 9–4. Whether your child enjoys science, humanities, languages, the arts, sport or technology, we offer choices to suit them. Pupils have opportunities to participate in a vibrant programme of co-curricular activities, external competitions and local and international trips, including our award-winning trip to Africa.

ISI Inspection Report, March 2015:

"Behaviour is excellent and pupils feel safe, secure, valued and well supported."

"Performance across the subject range at GCSE is markedly higher than that predicted from their prior attainment."

We are able to offer individual tours of the school, by appointment, to Year 6 parents. To make an appointment, please phone 020 7228 3933.

For further information please visit: www.thameschristianschool.org.uk

Fees per term (2021–2022). £6,280.

Charitable status. Thames Christian School is a Registered Charity, number 1081666.

Thorpe Hall School

Wakering Road, Thorpe Bay, Essex SS1 3RD

Tel:	01702 582340
email:	sec@thorpehallschool.co.uk
website:	www.thorpehallschool.co.uk
Twitter:	@ThorpeHall
Facebook:	@ThorpeHallSchool
Instagram:	@thorpehallschool

Headteacher: **Mr Stephen Duckitt**

Age Range. 2–16 years.

Number in School. Approximately 400 girls and boys.

Fees per term (2021–2022). £3,000–£4,452. Nursery: £25.22 per session (excluding EY funding).

Thorpe Hall School is a co-educational independent day school, pleasantly situated on green belt land on the outskirts of Southend-on-Sea, Essex. The buildings are modern and purpose-built.

Communications to London are good via the A13 and A127 and the Liverpool/Fenchurch Street railway lines. The nearest station is approximately 10 minutes' walk.

Founded in 1925, the school has been educating children for nearly 100 years years and consistently achieves excellent academic results with special emphasis being placed on the traditional values of good manners, behaviour, dress and speech.

The school has won many awards for its excellence and innovation across a number of different aspects. Best Senior School – ISA 2017; Best Early Years – ISA 2017, Best Pupil Wellbeing – ISA 2019. Top 100 Prep School in the Sunday Times every year since 2015. Nominated by the TES for Wellbeing initiative of the Year 2019 and 2020.

The school runs Forest School sessions and Beach School sessions in the Early Years along with French, yoga and dance. In the Prep school, pupils learn to read and write super-fast and are supported by the Read Write Inc and Accelerated Reader programmes. In the Senior School, pupils can choose what they do on a Wednesday afternoon from a list that includes drone flyer, radio-controlled car racing, archery, diving, Stage Make-up, Film Making, Kung Fu and many other activities. GCSE results are consistently good and outstrip national norms every year. Around 80% of leavers go to university 2 years after leaving.

The Charitable Trust status enables fees, which are very competitive, to be kept to a minimum. Nursery vouchers are accepted and some bursaries are available. The School is regularly inspected by the Independent Schools Inspectorate.

Charitable status. Thorpe Hall School Trust is a Registered Charity, number 298155. It exists to provide good quality education for boys and girls in South East Essex.

Tower College

Mill Lane, Rainhill, Merseyside L35 6NE

Tel: 0151 426 4333
email: msbingley@towercollege.com
           office@towercollege.com
website: towercollege.com
Facebook: @towercollege

Principal: **Ms A Bingley**

Vice-Principal: Mrs R Wright

Registrar: Ms C McNamara

Bursar: Mr M Taylor

Age Range. 3 months–16 years.
Number in School. Day: 155 Boys, 127 Girls.
Fees per term (2021–2022). £2,464–£2,867.

Tower College is a non-denominational Christian Day School housed in a beautiful Victorian mansion set in 11 acres.

We believe children thrive in our safe and secure environment where they do not have to conform to a peer group. They are free to become their best selves, to achieve the best possible academic results and are given every opportunity to excel in Sport, Art and Music.

Charitable status. Tower College is a Registered Charity, number 526611.

Trevor-Roberts School

55–57 Eton Avenue, London NW3 3ET

Tel: 020 7586 1444
email: trsenior@trevor-robertsschool.co.uk
website: www.trevor-robertsschool.co.uk

Headteacher: **Mr Simon Trevor-Roberts**, BA

Age Range. 5–13 Co-educational.
Number in School. 180 Day Pupils: 100 boys, 80 girls.
Fees per term (2021–2022). £5,500–£6,050.

Trevor-Roberts School was founded in Hampstead in 1955 by the headmaster's late father and moved to its present site in 1981. The school is made up of two departments but operates as one school and occupies two adjacent much-adapted late Victorian houses in Belsize Park. In addition to on-site facilities, the school makes use of nearby playing fields and a local leisure centre swimming pool.

Central to the education provided is the school's aim for all pupils to become happy and confident individuals who fulfil their potential. Strong emphasis is placed on personal organisation and pupils are encouraged to develop a love of learning for its own sake. In a happy, non-competitive atmosphere, pupils are well cared for and teachers' responses are tailored to the individual needs of pupils. It is the School's strong belief that much can be expected of a child if he or she is given self-confidence and a sense of personal worth and does not feel judged too early in life against the attainment of others.

High success rates throughout the school are achieved through small classes, individual attention and specialist teachers. The standards achieved enable almost all pupils to gain places in their first choice of school at either 11+ or 13+ into the main London day schools and academically selective independent boarding schools. In recent years a number of pupils have been awarded academic, art and music scholarships to these schools. The school aims to make pupils prepared for this process and give them the confidence to enjoy the academic challenges they will be offered.

The school provides a broad range of curricular and extra-curricular activities, contributing to pupils' linguistic, mathematical, scientific, technological, social and physical development in a balanced way. Aesthetic and creative development is strongly encouraged through art, drama and music. In the Senior Department the syllabus is extended to include Classical History, Latin and Greek. The curriculum is enriched at all stages by a variety of one-day educational visits as well as by residential trips for Years 5–8 on activity trips, a sailing weekend, geography field trips and visits to Belgium.

A range of extra-curricular activities and sporting opportunities appropriate for boys and girls of all ages is offered two afternoons a week and after school. The school's founder believed passionately in music and drama as a means of developing pupils' confidence and self-esteem and both subjects are a strong feature of the school today. All classes prepare and perform two drama performances each year in which every pupil has a speaking and/or singing part.

Pupils thrive in a caring family atmosphere where the emphasis is on individual progress and expectation, and where improvement is rewarded as highly as success. It has a broadly Christian tradition, but welcomes pupils of all faiths and of none.

Ursuline Preparatory School

Great Ropers Lane, Warley, Brentwood, Essex CM13 3HR

Tel: 01277 227152
email: headmistress@ursulineprepwarley.co.uk
website: www.ursulineprepwarley.co.uk

Awarded Independent Preparatory School of the Year 2021.

Headmistress: **Mrs Pauline Wilson**, MBE, MSc

Age Range. 3–11.
Number in School. Day 180.
Fees per term (2021–2022). £2,225–£4,145.

Founded in the early 1930s, the Ursuline Preparatory School enjoys a reputation as a happy family school, where pupils strive to give of their best in all areas of school life. Consequently, much emphasis is placed on encouraging the children to develop to the full their individual talents and interests, as well as fostering in each pupil a strong sense of well-being, self-reliance and team spirit.

This is achieved by the frequent use of praise, by adherence to an agreed policy of consistent and fair discipline and by the high standards, moral code and caring attitudes deriving from the strongly Catholic ethos which underpins the life of the whole school.

The Ursuline Preparatory School has well qualified and very experienced teachers and support staff.

It is committed to offering to all its pupils the distinct advantages of a broad and balanced curriculum. This includes a rigorous academic curriculum supplemented by the provision of an excellent PE, Drama, Music, ICT and Language programme.

A comprehensive range of extracurricular activities are offered to the pupils. These are often taught by specialist staff and include subjects such as Theatre Club, Art Appreciation, Computing, Photography, Sewing, Chess, Ballet and Speech and Drama. As well as many Instrumental Classes and Sporting Activities, with which the School has considerable success in gaining individual and team awards at competition level.

The School successfully prepares children for entry to local and national independent schools, Grammar Schools or local Secondary Schools.

The relatively small size of the School allows for very close contact between staff, pupils and parents and provides each child with the opportunity to fulfil his or her academic potential. The pupils are encouraged to follow their own interests and to develop a sense of self-confidence and self-worth which will hopefully remain with them throughout their lives, allowing them to reflect the school motto: *A Caring School that strives for excellence.*

Charitable status. The Ursuline Preparatory School is a Registered Charity, number 1058282, which is a non-profit making and managed by an independent board of voluntary trustees. It exists to provide Roman Catholic children and those of other denominations with the opportunity to reach the highest individual standards possible in every area of School life.

Waverley Preparatory School and Nursery

Waverley Way, Finchampstead, Wokingham, Berkshire RG40 4YD

Tel: 0118 973 1121
email: admissions@waverleyschool.co.uk
website: www.waverleyschool.co.uk
Twitter: @waverleyschool
Facebook: @waverleyschool
Instagram: @waverleyprepschool
LinkedIn: /waverley-preparatory-school-&-nursery

Chair of Governors: Mr Blair Jenkins

Head Teacher: **Mr Guy Shore**, BA Hons QTS

Assistant Head: Mr Henry Mitchell

Age Range. 3 months–11 years.
Number of Pupils. 240.
Fees per term (2021–2022). Reception–Year 6 Core day: £3,170–£3,790. Extended day package (Breakfast Club and After School Clubs) also available. Nursery according to the broad range of flexible sessions attended. Wrap-around care available for all children from 7.30am to 6.00pm.

Ethos. Waverley is ranked 'Best in Berkshire' and also no. 1 primary and Prep School in the Wokingham and Reading area based on our academic results. At the same time, Waverley provides a warm, family environment with small class sizes and an excellent pupil/teacher ratio. Despite being non-academically selective, last year all our Year 6 pupils were offered a place at their chosen secondary school, including to some of the most reputable senior schools in the country. We are a purpose-built Preparatory school which combines a traditional ethos towards a rewarding and thorough education, with a modern feel and the latest teaching technology. Located on the edge of the Berkshire countryside, we enjoy a rural setting and spacious playing fields as well as a large woodland area for our Forest School.

Our priority at Waverley is to challenge every pupil to achieve academic excellence. We recognise however that only happy children, who feel supported and confident, learn to the best of their ability. Waverley's unique cheerful, nurturing environment enables every child to succeed and reach his or her full potential.

Academic Excellence. We are very proud that we have been ranked in the *Top 100 Prep Schools in the UK* (The Sunday Times) consistently for the past 10 years – this is based purely on our academic success. Our educational prowess is also reflected in the exceptional exam results of our Year 6 students and the secondary schools they move on to – most of our students attain scholarships, or places at selective secondary schools.

We operate small class sizes, giving each child individual attention and enabling us to closely monitor every child's progress. Our purpose-built school enables daily school life to flow and function easily in a modern, welcoming and spacious learning environment. Our family atmosphere means that our teachers not only know every child by name – they also know what makes a child tick. This warm ethos is also visible amongst our children who play with each other freely across the year groups in the playground.

In addition to academic success, we aim to encourage self-discipline, respect, tolerance and kindness and to provide a broad, rich curriculum going far beyond national expectations. Our school motto is 'We Are Kind, We Are Honest, We Do Our Best' which we believe should apply to everything a child undertakes whether academic work, sporting performance or relationships with friends, teachers and family.

Curriculum. Waverley's curriculum provides children with a solid foundation, particularly in the areas of literacy and numeracy. Pre-prep and Preparatory children engage in a full curriculum of subjects including English, Mathematics, ICT, French, History, Geography, Latin, Science and Art. We enjoy a high number of specialist teachers across many of our core curriculum and supporting subjects.

Gifted and Talented. We have development programmes for gifted and talented children.

Sports. Waverley School's physical education curriculum includes football, rugby, hockey, tennis, netball, cricket, athletics and rounders. Swimming also takes place weekly throughout the year as part of our ethos that every child needs to learn this life skill. The children regularly take part in sports matches and swimming galas against other local independent schools.

The Arts. We have extremely strong Speech and Drama, and Music (both choral and instrumental) departments. As well as termly productions, the School regularly takes part in local concerts both in the local community and with other schools to build children's self-confidence.

Wrap-Around Care. Our After-School Clubs include Cookery, Fencing, Tennis, Chess, Cheerleading, Prep Club, Lego, ICT, Yoga and Cross Country. We offer over 75 different after-school activities each academic year which change every term.

Moving On. The majority of our students attain scholarships, or places at selective secondary schools. All our year 6 students last year were offered places at their first choice.

West Lodge School

36 Station Road, Sidcup, Kent DA15 7DU

Tel: 020 8300 2489
email: info@westlodge.org.uk
website: www.westlodge.org.uk

Chair of Governors: Mrs Chris Head-Rapson

Head Teacher: **Mr Robert Francis**, BEd Hons

Age Range. 3–11.
Number of Pupils. 170 Day Boys and Girls.
Fees per term (2021–2022). £1,974–£3,303.

West Lodge was founded in 1940 and is now an educational trust. The main building is an extended Victorian house, well adapted to use as a school, whilst still retaining its homely atmosphere. Facilities include a new extension, incorporating a science/cookery room and art room/crèche, which can also be used together as an additional hall facility, a fully-equipped gymnasium, Astroturf surface, music rooms and a computer suite. There are eight classes of up to 22 pupils, one class in each year group from Nursery through to Year 6. The staff to pupil ratio is extremely high and the children are taught in smaller groups by specialist teachers for many subjects. The school is open from 8.15am and an after-school crèche and homework club operate until 6.00pm.

The school has a strong academic tradition and a purposeful atmosphere permeates each class. The National Curriculum is at the core of our teaching but it is enhanced and enriched by the inclusion of a wider range of subjects. These include: English, mathematics, science, French, information technology, design technology, history, geography, religious education, music, art and craft, physical education and games, swimming and drama.

Great emphasis is placed on a thorough grounding in basic learning skills, with literacy and numeracy seen as key elements in the foundation, upon which future learning will be built. Particular care is taken to extend the most gifted children and support the less able. West Lodge has a consistent record of a high level of entry to local authority selective schools and independent schools.

Music has a particularly high profile within the school and all of the children are encouraged to develop their talents. Well-qualified peripatetic staff teach both group and individual lessons and children of all ages are encouraged to join the school orchestras and choir. Concerts and dramatic performances are staged regularly and parents are warmly invited to attend.

Sports of all sorts are taught and we are keen to get involved in both competitive and friendly sporting fixtures with other schools.

The school promotes a caring attitude between all its members and aims to help each child towards the achievement of self-control and self-discipline. The Head Teacher and the class teachers know each of the children well and the excellent pastoral care and family atmosphere are major features of the school.

Home-school links are strong and the open door policy gives parents immediate access to members of staff should worries occur. The school also has strong contacts with the local community.

Extracurricular activities are given the highest priority and clubs run each afternoon after school. Regular school outings form part of the curriculum for all children, the older pupils enjoying residential visits.

Charitable status. West Lodge School Educational Trust is a Registered Charity, number 283627. It exists for the provision of high quality education for boys and girls between 3 and 11 years.

Westbourne School

Hickman Road, Penarth, Vale of Glamorgan CF64 2AJ

Tel: 029 2070 5705
email: admissions@westbourneschool.com
website: www.westbourneschool.com
Twitter: @WestbourneS
Facebook: @WestbourneSchool
Instagram: westbourne.school

Principal: **Dr Gerard Griffiths**

IB Coordinator: Ms Lisa Phillips

GCSE Coordinator: Mrs Jodi Barber

Middle Years Coordinator: Mrs Jan Allen

Head of Prep School and Nursery: Mrs Joanne Chinnock

Director of Research, Development & Online Learning: Mr Stuart Ayres

Age Range. 2–18.

Number in School. 173 Boys, 170 Girls.

Boarding. From Senior School upwards.

Day fees per term (2021–2022). £2,840–£4,990.

Boarding fees per annum (2021–2022). £37,950 (Boarding House accommodation), £35,850 (local home stay accommodation); both fully inclusive of guardianship costs and annual airport transfers.

Westbourne Nursery accepts children from 2 years and is open for 51 weeks a year at a cost of £63 per day from 7.30am until 6.00pm.

Westbourne develops globally-minded, well-rounded, articulate young scholars who progress to the best universities in the world (90% Russell Group entry). 2021 saw record Sixth Form and GCSE results, with 50% of IB Diploma students achieving over 40 points (the equivalent of 4 A*s at A Level), 85% attaining 7/6 (A*/A equivalent), 96.8% 7–5 (A*–B). At GCSE, 100% attained A*–C (9–4 under the reformed grading system), with 86% achieving the highest grades, A*/A (9–7). Westbourne graduates possess the skills, knowledge, confidence and character to become leaders of the future, and they go on to secure top careers in fields including medicine, law, engineering and business.

Founded in 1896, Westbourne's reputation for academic excellence has been established for 125 years. Ranked 1st in the UK in smaller school league tables for five years in a row, and named *IB School of the Year 2019*, Westbourne is one of the UK's most academically elite schools. As referenced in the *Sunday Times Best School Guide 2021*: 'Westbourne is one of the most consistently high-achieving independent schools in Britain.'

Westbourne offers boarding from Senior School upwards, either in the school's Boarding House or via homestay with friendly local families. Westbourne's Boarding House accommodation is safe, secure and comfortable, with options for single or shared rooms, as well as dining, quiet study and socialising spaces. The boarding community is small, supportive, family-like and multicultural, providing the opportunity to meet and make friends with students from all over the world. Westbourne prides itself on being a distinctly British school complemented by a student body representing over 25 different nationalities.

Students benefit from smaller class sizes than at other schools, allowing personalised attention and one-to-one support. Offering a small, friendly community where every student is known by name by every teacher, Westbourne is described as having a family feel, blending traditional values with outstanding teaching. The school is committed to innovation in education, and combines traditional classroom teaching with the latest technology, including being one of the first schools in Wales to implement artificial intelligence-assisted learning.

Westbourne offers the International Baccalaureate (IB) Diploma Programme in Sixth Form, and GCSEs from Year 9, which allows students opportunity to study a wider range of subjects as excellent preparation for the IB.

Prep School pupils also benefit from a diverse curriculum, including early exposure to foreign languages, the arts, mathematics and science, as well as a range of excellent sporting opportunities. All children participate in a weekly STEM afternoon and attend Westbourne's FaB (Forest and Beach) School half termly – an immersive outdoors learning and wellbeing initiative set in local coastal and countryside settings, including the school's private forest site on a 20-acre farm.

Westbourne is located in Penarth, an affluent seaside suburb voted one of the best places to live in 2021 for health and wellbeing (The Times) and one of the Top 10 best places to live in the UK (Sunday Times). Ten minutes from vibrant, historic Cardiff (ranked by the EU Quality of Life Survey as the 3rd best European capital city) Westbourne offers the perfect blend of modern metropolis, suburban safety, seaside and countryside.

The school enjoys excellent transport links, with easy access to the M4. There is a convenient train service from Penarth to Cardiff Central, which offers direct trains to London and across the UK. The school has minibuses running each day across the Vale of Glamorgan and Cardiff.

Westville House School

Carter's Lane, Middleton, Ilkley, West Yorkshire LS29 0DQ

Tel: 01943 608053
email: hub@westvillehouseschool.co.uk
website: www.westvillehouseschool.co.uk
Twitter: @WestvilleHouseS

Chair of Governors: Mr Adam Holdsworth

Head: **Mrs Nikki Hammond**, BA Hons, PGCE

Age Range. 2–11.

Number of Pupils. 100.

Fees per term (2021–2022). £3,495 (Reception–Year 6).

Perched on the top of a stunning hillside location, with views across to The Cow and Calf, lies Westville House School, Ilkley's foremost provider of independent education. The gleaming white school building stands proud in acres of grounds and exudes fun, strong values, pride in tradition and a strong belief in the Westville family.

Originally based down in the town centre, the school relocated to its current site over 20 years ago and has gone from strength to strength, developing fantastic education facilities. Inspirational classrooms are to be seen throughout the school; specialist science, art and music classrooms along with a sophisticated IT suite, a state-of-the-art sports hall with attached playing fields and most recently a forest classroom stimulate learning and encourage fun.

From the minute a child begins their journey at Westville house they are valued for who they are. The Early Years Unit, which takes children from 2 years, devotes masses of energy to building foundations that will set the children up for life. Each child has education tailored to their needs – for those who are very able there is masses to challenge, whilst for those who need a little bit of extra help there is huge encouragement and a clear development of an excitement about learning.

Children progress through the Pre-Prep department (ages 2–7) and then on through the Prep department (ages 7–11). They emerge as well-rounded, confident, and above all very happy children whose memories of their time at Westville prompt them to return year after year.

Academics are brilliant here and the school is consistently ranked in the Sunday Times Top 100 Prep Schools in the UK – a fantastic achievement for a small non-selective school. Children regularly achieve scholarships to many independent senior schools and gain entrance to the local selective grammar schools.

Academics aside, there is a whole host of extracurricular activities designed to have something to suit every child. The school is particularly strong in swimming and cross country; drama and dance produce some excellent school productions. Music, in the form of choirs and instrumental lessons, is encouraged and the school ensemble is always seen as great fun. As the children progress through the school new activities and experiences are opened up to them – canoeing, fencing, first aid, street dancing – all geared to ensure that Westville children are totally prepared for their journey on to the senior school of their choice.

Having undergone a £1million development and refurbishment programme, Westville House now has a state-of-the-art Early Years facility situated in beautiful woodlands, new media suite, new library, new ICT suite and a brilliant new Hub entrance hall which has become the heart of the school.

The school's motto '*Quotidie Opus Novum – something new every day*' really does sum up the excitement of coming to Westville House – the beginning of a lifelong education where an appetite for learning is something to be nurtured and enjoyed.

Charitable status. Westville House School is a Registered Charity, number 1086711.

Westward School

47 Hersham Road, Walton-on-Thames, Surrey KT12 1LE

Tel: 01932 220911
email: admin@westwardschool.co.uk
website: www.westwardschool.co.uk
Facebook: @westwardschool47

Proprietor: Mrs Patricia Townley

Headmistress: **Mrs Shelley Stevenson**, BEd Hons

Age Range. 4–11 Co-educational.
Number of Pupils. 110.
Fees per term (2021–2022). £2,560–£2,845.

Whitehall School

117 High Street, Somersham, Cambs PE28 3EH

Tel: 01487 840966
email: office@whitehallschool.com
website: www.whitehallschool.com
Facebook: @Whitehall-School

Head of School: **Mr Chris Holmes**, BSc Hons, MA, PGCE

Age Range. 6 months to 11 years.
Number in School. 94 Day children: 46 boys, 48 girls.
Fees per term (2021–2022). £2,575–£2,980

'*A Unique School in Rural Cambridgeshire: A Dynamic, Forward-Thinking environment.*'

Set in extensive grounds with excellent facilities, Whitehall School provides a small, family environment where children are supported to achieve their best academically whilst also developing personality, creativity and social consciousness.

The school consists of an Edwardian house and 18th Century coach house and is set within approximately 1.5 acres of stunning grounds. Facilities include a covered heated swimming pool, playground, sensory garden, games field, library and iPad suite.

Small class sizes allow us to support children to access the curriculum at their own pace, catering for the specific needs of each child so that they excel. Our Individual Performance Programme allows us to work in partnership with parents to encourage children to become active, independent learners.

Windrush Valley School

The Green, Ascott-under-Wychwood, Chipping Norton, Oxfordshire OX7 6AN

Tel: 01993 831793
email: info@windrushvalleyschool.co.uk
website: www.windrushvalleyschool.co.uk
Facebook: @Windrush-Valley-School

Headteacher: **Mrs A Douglas**, BA Hons, QTS

Age range. 3–11 Co-educational.

Number of pupils. 96

Fees per term (2021–2022). £2,429–£2,514.

We believe that every child deserves the best possible start. With class sizes currently averaging 12, our pupils receive one-to-one attention, and the highest standards of education. We build self-esteem, self-confidence and independence; preparing boys and girls aged 3–11 for a successful future in either the independent or state senior school sectors. Over the last 21 years all pupils have passed their senior school entrance examination and attended their first-choice secondary school.

The school is ranked in the top 100 independent preparatory schools in England by the Sunday Times and has received an Award for Excellence by the Independent Schools Association.

Our inspiring and stimulating curriculum is delivered within a nurturing, supportive and positive environment, and includes; literacy, language, mathematics, science, technology, human & social, sports, art and music. In addition, adventure trips and foreign residential weeks away, further enrich the curriculum and the children's life-experience.

All children regularly play in the school band, perform in musicals on stage, compete in public speaking competitions and sing in the choir. Our sporting pedigree has resulted in children competing at the highest level in swimming, athletics and cross country. For the last 10 years, our pupils have competed at a national level at the Independent Schools Association championship.

We also provide a comprehensive after-school programme in which children enjoy a wide range of additional activities, including cooking, first aid, forest school, horse whispering and cycling proficiency.

To support the needs of working parents we provide supervised wraparound care daily, from 8.00am to 6.00pm.

Our affordable fees underpin our commitment to make educational excellence accessible to as many children as possible.

If you want to give your child the best possible start – *excellence starts here.*

Woodlands School – Great Warley

Warley Street, Great Warley, Brentwood, Essex CM13 3LA

Tel: 01277 233288
email: deborah.oram@woodlandsschools.co.uk
website: www.woodlandsschools.co.uk

Headmaster: **Mr David Bell**

Age Range. 2–11 years.

Number in School. 100

Fees per term (2021–2022). £2,608–£5,157

Woodlands School at Great Warley is set in attractive, spacious grounds, with excellent facilities for outdoor activities. The school also uses the extensive facilities of our sister school at Hutton Manor.

It is the School's principal aim to ensure that all the children are happy and secure and are as successful as possible. They are encouraged to work hard and to show kindness and consideration to their peers. The resulting ethos of the School is one of warmth, support and mutual respect.

The School provides an exciting learning experience that enables the pupils to achieve full academic potential and to develop qualities of curiosity, independence and fortitude. Classes are small. The school aims to develop high levels of self-esteem and a good attitude to learning. The School has an excellent record in public examinations. Pupils are highly successful in gaining places at the schools of their choice. Examination results in Music and LAMDA are also excellent.

A varied programme of team and individual sports aims to offer something for everyone.

There is a strong music tradition and a variety of dramatic and musical concerts and productions are staged throughout the year for children of each age group.

Modern languages are taught to a very high standard, with French introduced at the age of 3 and Spanish in the Upper School.

Pastoral care is a major feature. An 'Open House' policy is in place for parents, which results in any concern being dealt with promptly and effectively.

It is the School's view that the education of the whole child is the most important priority and is confident that the learning experience it provides is fun, truly stimulating and memorable.

The school offers places for children from 2 years in Lower Kindergarten who will then progress automatically into Upper Kindergarten at age 3.

Woodlands School – Hutton Manor

428 Rayleigh Road, Hutton, Brentwood, Essex CM13 1SD

Tel: 01277 245585
email: info@woodlandsschools.co.uk
website: www.woodlandsschools.co.uk

Head Teacher: **Mrs Paula Hobbs**, BEd Hons

Age Range. 3–11 Co-educational.
Number of Pupils. 215.
Fees per term (2021–2022). £2,608–£5,714.

Woodlands School at Hutton Manor is set in attractive, spacious grounds, with excellent facilities for outdoor activities. The school also uses the extensive facilities of our sister school at Great Warley.

It is the School's principal aim to ensure that all the children are happy and secure and are as successful as possible. They are encouraged to work hard and to show kindness and consideration to their peers. The resulting ethos of the School is one of warmth, support and mutual respect.

The School provides an exciting learning experience that enables the pupils to achieve full academic potential and to develop qualities of curiosity, independence and fortitude. Classes are small. The school aims to develop high levels of self-esteem and a good attitude to learning. The School has an excellent record in public examinations. Pupils are highly successful in gaining places at the schools of their choice. Examination results in Music and LAMDA are also excellent.

A varied programme of team and individual sports aims to offer something for everyone.

There is a strong music tradition and a variety of dramatic and musical concerts and productions are staged throughout the year for children of each age group.

Modern languages are taught to a very high standard, with French introduced at the age of 3 and Spanish in the Upper School.

Pastoral care is a major feature. An 'Open House' policy is in place for parents, which results in any concern being dealt with promptly and effectively.

It is the School's view that the education of the whole child is the most important priority and is confident that the learning experience it provides is fun, truly stimulating and memorable.

The school has an onsite day-care nursery, Little Acorns, which operates for 51 weeks of the year from 7:30–18:00 offering places for children from the age of 3 months.

INDEX OF ENTRANCE SCHOLARSHIPS

PAGE

PAGE

Academic Scholarships

Academic Scholarships ... /cont'd

Academic Scholarships .../cont'd

All-Rounder Scholarships

PAGE   PAGE

Art Scholarships .../cont'd

Art Scholarships .../cont'd

Design Technology Scholarships

PAGE

PAGE

Drama Scholarships

Drama Scholarships .../cont'd

Music Scholarships

PAGE

PAGE

Music Scholarships .../cont'd

Sport Scholarships

Sport Scholarships .../cont'd

INDEX OF BURSARIES AND DISCOUNTS

PAGE

PAGE

New entrant bursary

PAGE

New entrant bursary .../cont'd

PAGE

Existing pupil bursary/hardship award

Local resident bursary

Clergy discount

HM forces discount

Former pupil discount

INDEX OF EXAMINATIONS OFFERED

A Level

BTEC

GCSE

PAGE PAGE

IGCSE

GEOGRAPHICAL INDEX OF SCHOOLS

PAGE

PAGE

ENGLAND

OVERSEAS SCHOOLS

ALPHABETICAL LIST OF SCHOOLS